HERBERT BUCKSCH

Dictionary of Architecture Building Construction and Materials

English–German

Englisch–Deutsch

2

Wörterbuch für Architektur Hochbau und Baustoffe

BAUVERLAG GMBH · WIESBADEN UND BERLIN

CIP-Kurztitelaufnahme der Deutschen Bibliothek

Bucksch, Herbert:

Dictionary of architecture, building construction, and materials = Wörterbuch für Architektur, Hochbau und Baustoffe / Herbert Bucksch. – Wiesbaden ; Berlin : Bauverlag
   1 u.d.T.: Bucksch, Herbert: Wörterbuch für Architektur, Hochbau und Baustoffe

NE: HST

2. English German. – 2. Aufl., 1. Nachdr. – 1987

   ISBN 3-7625-2575-7

1. Auflage 1976
2. Auflage 1983
1. Nachdruck 1987

Das Werk ist urheberrechtlich geschützt.
Die dadurch begründeten Rechte, insbesondere die der Übersetzung,
des Nachdruckes, der Entnahme von Abbildungen, der Funksendung,
der Wiedergabe auf fotomechanischem oder ähnlichem Wege
(Fotokopie, Mikrokopie) und der Speicherung in Datenverarbeitungsanlagen,
bleiben, auch bei nur auszugsweiser Verwertung, vorbehalten.

© 1983 Bauverlag GmbH, Wiesbaden und Berlin
Druck: Druck- und Verlagshaus Hans Meister KG, Kassel
Einband: C. Fikentscher, Darmstadt

ISBN 3-7625-2575-7

PREFACE

Architecture, building and civil engineering are encountered everywhere; in monuments or ruins from the past, in the engineering feats of the industrial age or the modern buildings crowding our city centres. The English and German technical terms for civil engineering and construction machinery and equipment have already been compiled in a dictionary published like this one by the Bauverlag GmbH, Wiesbaden und Berlin. This dictionary rounds matters off.

Technical terms abound in architecture just as they do in any other branch of art or engineering. Anyone interested in architecture, whether as a specialist, art lover, student or layman, cannot hope to understand it without first mastering its concepts and the technical terms with which they are clothed. The same applies to building and building materials. A concept must be named in order to be understood. This principle is as fundamental to-day as ever it was and is one we share with our earliest ancestors.

This dictionary lists terms for many concepts from the aforementioned fields. Its aim is to help breach the language barrier and facilitate the perusal of architectural publications and trade journals in English and German.

The publisher and author hope the dictionary will fill a lexicographic gap.

Mr. Michael Fuad, Cologne, compiled the table of chemical formulas.

Herbert Bucksch

VORWORT

Baukunst und Bautechnik sind überall anzutreffen; seien es die Bauwerke oder deren Reste der Vergangenheit, die modernen Zweckbauten der Großstädte oder die Ingenieurbauwerke des Industriezeitalters. Die Fachsprachen der Bautechnik und der Baumaschinen sind bereits in einem im gleichen Verlag erschienenen Übersetzungsfachwörterbuch in englischer und deutscher Sprache lexikographisch erfaßt. Das hier vorliegende Übersetzungsfachwörterbuch ist somit eine Ergänzung zum vorgenannten.

Wie alle Zweige der Technik und der Kunst haben auch Architektur, Hochbau und Baustoffe ihre Fachsprachen. Jeder, der sich für die Architektur interessiert, sei es als Fachmann, Kunstinteressierter, Studierender oder interessierter Laie, muß die Fachbegriffe und Fachbenennungen der Architektur beherrschen, sonst wird er sie nicht begreifen. Das gleiche gilt für Hochbau und Baustoffe. Erst wenn ein Begriff mit einer Benennung belegt ist kann man diesen Begriff auch beherrschen. Diesen Glauben hatten die frühesten Naturvölker und heute ist dieser Glaube zur notwendigen Erkenntnis geworden.

Dieses Übersetzungsfachwörterbuch gibt Benennungen für viele Begriffe aus den genannten Gebieten. Es dient damit zur Überwindung der Sprachgrenze und zur Erschließung der Fachliteratur in den genannten Sprachen.

Verlag und Verfasser hoffen mit diesem Werk eine lexikographische Lücke geschlossen zu haben.

Herr Michael Fuad, Köln, stellte die Tabelle der chemischen Formeln zusammen.

Herbert Bucksch

INTRODUCTION

The words are compiled in alphabetical order. Certain words, however, forming subject titles from a technical point of view are accompanied by a subsection giving other words relevant to the subject. Example:

sink unit [*Combined sink and drainer*]   **Spültisch** *m*, **Abwaschtisch**
    waste connection   Ablaufverbindung *f*
    draining board, drain-board, absolution   Abtropfbrett *n*, Ablaufbrett, Abstell-
    board   brett
                                           etc.

Brackets are used:

a) *square brackets:*

    (1) *to explain or define a term or giving*   **dolerite** [*A basic hyperbyssal rock of*
         other information about it, e.g.   *medium-grained texture consisting of*
                                                     plagioclase feldspar, augite, iron ores,
                                                     and frequently olivine]

    (2) *To denote the particular field, e.g.*   **electric(al) floor** [*e.g. the Robertson Q-floor*]

b) *Round brackets:*

    (3) *for terms or part of terms which can*   **electric(al) heating system** = electric
         be omitted, e.g.   heating system

    (4) *for abbreviations, e.g.*   (Geol.) = Geology
                                                    (Min.) = Mineralogy
                                                    (Brit.) = Great Britain
                                                    (US)   = USA

The Tilde ~ *substitutes the word to be repeated, e.g. earth(ing) clamp, ground(ing)*
~ = *ground(ing) clamp*

The Tilde ~ *substitutes the preceding word printed above, e.g.*

earthenware

~ **cable cover** = earthenware cable cover

The comma separates equivalent words.

The semicolon separates equivalent words, but alternatively used either in the USA or Great Britain.

The gender of the German words is indicated by:

  m = *masculine*
  f = *feminine*
  n = *neutre*

mpl = *the word is given in its plural form, with the singular being masculine, fpl and npl apply accordingly*

Abbreviations: B.S.   = *British Standard*
                 A.S.T.M. = *American Society for Testing Materials*
                     DIN   = *DIN Deutsches Institut für Normung e.V.*
The appendix contains chemical formulas.

EINFÜHRUNG

Die Wörter sind alphabetisch geordnet. Zum Zwecke einer Darstellung nach technischen Gesichtspunkten sind bei manchen Wörtern weitere außerhalb der alphabetischen Reihenfolge aufgeführt. Beispiel:

sink unit [*Combined sink and drainer*] waste connection draining board, drain-board, absolution board	**Spültisch** *m*, **Abwaschtisch** Ablaufverbindung *f* Abtropfbrett *n*, Ablaufbrett, Abstellbrett

usw.

Anwendung der Klammern:

a) *Eckige Klammern:*

    1. *Erläuterung eines Wortes und sonstige Hinweise zu einem Wort, z.B.*   **dolerite** [*A basic hyperbyssal rock o medium-grained texture consisting of plagioclase feldspar, augite, iron ores, and frequently olivine*]

    2. *Bestimmung eines Sachgebietes, z.B.*   **electric(al) floor** [*e.g. the Robertson Q-floor*]

b) *Runde Klammern:*

    3. *Auslassungen, z.B.*   **electric(al) heating system** = electric heating system

    4. *Abkürzungen, z.B.*

        (Geol.) = Geologie
        (Min.) = Mineralogie
        (Brit.) = Großbritannien
        (US) = USA

Die Tilde ∼ tritt an die Stelle des zu wiederholenden Wortes, z.B. earth(ing) clamp, ground(ing) ∼ = ground(ing) clamp.

Die Tilde ∼ im Fettdruck tritt an die Stelle des darüber befindlichen Wortes, z.B.

earthenware

∼ cable cover = earthenware cable cover

Synonyma sind durch Komma getrennt.

Das Semikolon trennt einerseits in Großbritannien und andererseits in den USA gebräuchliche Wörter.

Die Artikel sind wie folgt angegeben:

m = männlich
f = weiblich
n = sächlich

mpl = Mehrzahlform für die männliche Einzahl. Dementsprechend sind fpl und npl zu verstehen.

Abkürzungen: B.S.   = *British Standard*
                    A.S.T.M. = *American Society for Testing Materials*
                         DIN   = *DIN Deutsches Institut für Normung e.V.*
Der Anhang enthält chemische Formeln.

IN MEMORIAM

MEINER FRAU ELLA BUCKSCH GEWIDMET

DEDICATED TO MY LATE, BELOVED WIFE

VOLUME 2

BAND 2

*

ENGLISH — GERMAN
ENGLISCH — DEUTSCH

A

Aaron's(-)rod [*A long, straight mo(u)lding with scroll and leaf ornament*] · Aaronstab *m*

A. A. tower, anti-aircraft ~ · Flakturm *m*

abacá, Manil(l)a hemp · Abakahanf *m*, Musahanf, Bananenhanf, Manil(l)ahanf

abacus, raised table, padstone [*The slab between the lintel and the supporting column, designed to concentrate the load. In the Greek Doric order the abacus is a simple square block; in the Roman orders it is thinner and mo(u)lded*] · (Säulen)Deckplatte *f*, Abakus *m*, Kapitellplatte, Kapitälplatte

~ **column** · Abakussäule *f*

~ **flower** · Abakusblume *f* [*In der Mitte jeder der vier konkav eingezogenen Seiten des Abakus am korinthischen Kapitell*]

abattoir, slaughterhouse, slaughter establishment · Schlachthof *m*

abbey [*A monastery headed by an abbot or a nunnery headed by an abbess*] · Abtei *f*

~ **block**, ~ building · Abtei(gebäude) *f*, (*n*) [*Das mit dem Kloster verbundene Haus des Abtes oder der Äbtissin*]

~ **building**, ~ block · Abtei(gebäude) *f*, (*n*) [*Das mit dem Kloster verbundene Haus des Abtes oder der Äbtissin*]

~ **church** · Abteikirche *f*

~ **court** · Abtshof *m*

abbot block, ~ building · Abtshaus *n*, Abtsgebäude *n*

~ **building**, ~ block · Abtshaus *n*, Abtsgebäude *n*

Abel c.c. testing apparatus, ~ flash point ~ · Flammpunktprüfer *m* Abel geschlossener Tiegel, Abel-Flammpunktprüfer [*Das Öl wird unter Deckelverschluß erhitzt und ein Ausschnitt im Deckel zum Hereingeben der Zündflamme kurzfristig geöffnet*]

abietic acid · Abietinsäure *f*, $C_{20}H_{30}O_2$

ablution board, drainboard, draining board · Abtropfbrett *n*, Ablaufbrett, Abstellbrett

~ **fountain**, wash ~ [*It is a circular bowl of fireclay or terrazzo standing on a pedestal of the same material and is designed to allow up to six persons to wash at the same time*] · Waschbrunnen *m*, Waschfontäne *f*

abnormal loading · ungewöhnliche Belastung *f*

~ **wear** · ungewöhnlicher Verschleiß *m*

above-grade → above-ground

~ **hydrant**, above-ground ~, pillar ~, surface ~ · Überflurhydrant *m*, Oberflächenhydrant, oberirdischer Hydrant, obererdiger Hydrant

~ **masonry wall**, above-ground ~ ~, surface ~ ~ · aufgehende Mauer *f*

~ ~ **(work)**, above-ground ~ (~), surface ~ (~) · Mauerwerk *n* über Geländeoberkante, aufgehendes ~ ~ ~

~ **(pipe)line** → above-ground ~

~ **wall**, above-ground ~, surface ~ · aufgehende Wand *f*

above-ground, above-grade, surface..., · obererdig, oberirdisch, Überflur...., Oberflächen......

~ **hydrant**, above-grade ~, pillar ~, surface ~ · Überflurhydrant *m*, Oberflächenhydrant, oberirdischer Hydrant, obererdiger Hydrant

~ **masonry wall**, above-grade ~ ~, surface ~ ~ · aufgehende Mauer *f*

~ ~ **(work)** → above-grade ~ (~)

~ **(pipe)line**, above-grade ~, AG ~, surface ~ · obererdige (Rohr)Leitung *f*, oberirdische ~, Überflur(rohr)leitung

~ **wall**, above-grade ~, surface ~ · aufgehende Wand *f*

abradability — absolute value

abradability, abrasiveness [*e.g. of sand*] · Abriebwirkung *f*, (Ab)Schleifwirkung

abradant, abrasive · Schleifmittel *n*

to abrade · (ab)schleifen

Abrams' fineness modulus, F.M. · Abramsscher (Feinheits)Modul *m*, ~ Feinmodul. F_m

~ law [*A rule stating that with given concrete materials and conditions of test the ratio of the amount of water to the amount of the cement in the mix determines the strength of the concrete provided the mix is of a workable consistency*] · Abramssches Gesetz *n*

~ method [*proportioning cement*] · Abramssches Verfahren *n*

~ test, extraction with caustic soda, calorimetric test (for organic impurities), organic test for fine aggregate, test for organic matter · Ätznatronprobe *f*, Ätznatronversuch *m*, Ätznatronprüfung *f* [*(Beton)Zuschlag(stoff)*]

abrasion, attrition · Abreiben *n*, Abrieb *m*

~ hardness, attrition ~· Schleifhärte *f*, Abriebhärte [*Gestein*]

~ loss, attrition ~ · Abreibeverlust *m*, Abriebverlust

abrasion-proof, abrasion(-)resistant · abreibefest, abriebfest

abrasion resistance, attrition ~, resistance to abrasion, resistance to attrition · Abriebfestigkeit *f*, Abreibefestigkeit, Abnutzbarkeit durch Schleifen, Verschleißfestigkeit, Abriebbeständigkeit [*DIN 52108. Die Abnutzbarkeit von Natursteinen und Beton wird an würfel- oder plattenförmigen Probekörpern mit 50 cm² Schleiffläche mit Hilfe einer Schleifscheibe ermittelt. Zuvor werden die Rohwichten bestimmt und die Gesamtgewichtsverluste auf Raummaß umgerechnet*].

abrasion(-)resistant, abrasion-proof · abreibefest, abriebfest

abrasion surface · Schleiffläche *f* [*Prüfung von Naturstein und Beton auf Abriebfestigkeit*]

~ test, attrition ~ · Abnutz(ungs)probe *f* durch Abschleifen, Abnutz(ungs)prüfung *f*, ~ ~, Abnutz(ungs)versuch *m* ~ ~, Abriebprobe, Abriebversuch, Abriebprüfung, Abreibeprobe, Abreibeversuch, Abreibeprüfung

~ tester, attrition ~ · Abriebprüfmaschine *f*

~ value, attrition ~ · Abnutz(ungs)wert *m* [*Gestein*]

abrasive, abradant · Schleifmittel *n*

~ blasting · Abstrahlen *n* mit Schleifmittel

~ cloth · Schleifleinen *n*

~ disk (US); ~ disc · Schleifscheibe *f*

~ grain, ~ particle · Schleifkorn *n*

(~) grinding wheel · Schleifstein *m*

~ paper · Schleifpapier *n*

~ particle, ~ grain · Schleifkorn *n*

~ powder · Schleifpulver *n*

~ resistance · Schleifwiderstand *m*

~ sand · Schleifsand *m*

~ steel shot · Strahlstahlschrot *m*, *n*

~ wear(ing) · Abriebverschleiß *m*, Abreibeverschleiß

abrasiveness, abradability [*e.g. of sand*] · Abriebwirkung *f*, (Ab)Schleifwirkung

abreuvoir, mortar joint [*In masonry, the joint to be filled with mortar*] · Mörtelfuge *f*

absence of cracks and crazes, freedom from cracking (and crazing) · Rissefreiheit *f*, Rißfreiheit

~ ~ defects · Beschaffenheit *f* [*Im Text einer Norm*]

~ ~ load · Lastfreiheit *f*

~ ~ loading · Belastungsfreiheit *f*

~ ~ moments · Momentenfreiheit *f*

~ ~ solvent(s) · Lösemittelfreiheit *f*, Lösungsmittelfreiheit

~ ~ streaks · Strichfreiheit *f* [*Mischen von Zement und Wirkstoff*]

~ ~ style, lack ~ ~ · Stillosigkeit *f*

~ ~ wear(ing) · Verschleißfreiheit *f*

absolute coefficient of expansion, ~ expansion coefficient · absoluter (Aus-) Dehn(ungs)beiwert *m*

~ deformation · Absolutformänderung *f*, absolute Formänderung, Absolutverformung, absolute Verformung

~ demineralization, practically ~ ~ Vollentsalzung *f* [*Wasser*]

~ determination · Absolutbestimmung *f*, absolute Bestimmung

~ displacement · Absolutverrückung *f*, absolute Verrückung

~ expansion coefficient, ~ coefficient of expansion · absoluter (Aus)Dehn-(ungs)beiwert *m*

~ humidity [*The mass of water vapo(u)r per unit volume of air*] · absolute Feuchtigkeit *f*, ~ Feuchte *f* [*Sie wird in g/m³ Luft angegeben*]

~ maximum · absolutes Maximum *n*, oberster Grenzwert *m*

~ measurement · Absolutmessung *f*, absolute Messung

~ minimum · absolutes Minimum *n*, unterster Grenzwert *m*, Absolutminimum

~ pressure · Absolutdruck *m*, absoluter Druck

~ specific gravity [*Ratio of the mass of a given volume of a solid or liquid, referred to a vacuum, at a stated temperature to the mass, referred to a vacuum, of an equal volume of gas-free distilled water at a stated temperature*] · Reinwichte *f*, echtes spezifisches Gewicht *n* [*DIN 1306*]

~ strength · absolute Festigkeit *f*, Absolutfestigkeit

~ value · Absolutwert *m*, absoluter Wert

absolute viscosity — absorbing fibre board

~ **viscosity** · dynamische Viskosität *f*, ~ Zähflüssigkeit *f*

~ ~ **coefficient** · dynamische Viskositätszahl *f*, dynamischer Viskositätsbeiwert *m*

~ **volume** · Absolutvolumen *n*, absolutes Volumen

absolutely dry · absolut trocken, atro

Abson recovery method · Extraktionsmethode *f* nach Abson

to absorb, to minimize · abbauen [*Kraft; Last; Spannung*]

absorbency → absorptive capacity

absorbent, absorbing, absorptive · absorbierend, aufsaugend, einsaugend

~ · Absorptionsmittel *n*, Absorptionsstoff *m*, Aufsaugmittel, Aufsaugstoff, Einsaugmittel, Einsaugstoff

~ **backing** → acoustic(al) ~
~ **blanket** → acoustic(al) ~
~ **board** → acoustic(al) ~
~ **brick** → (ceramic) acoustic(al) ~
~ **(building) unit** → acoustic(al) (~) ~
~ **capacity** → absorptive ~
~ **cassette** → (sound) absorbent pan(el)
~ **ceiling** → sound ~ ~
~ ~ **board** → acoustic(al) ceiling tile
~ ~ **paint** → acoustic(al) ~ ~
~ ~ **sheet** → acoustic(al) ceiling tile
~ ~ **system** → sound ~ ~ ~
~ ~ **tile** → acoustic(al) ~ ~
~ **chamber** → sound ~ ~
~ **coffer** → (sound) absorbent pan(el)
~ **construction material** → sound ~ ~ ~
~ ~ **(method)** → acoustic(al) ~ (~)
~ **(control) glass** → acoustic(al) (~) ~
~ **cover(ing)** → acoustic(al) lining
~ **facing** → acoustic(al) lining
~ **felt(ed fabric)** → acoustic(al) ~ (~)
~ **felt(ed fabric) ceiling** → acoustic(al) ~ (~) ~
~ **fibre board** → acoustic(al) ~ ~
~ **foil** → acoustic(al) ~
~ **glass** → acoustic(al) (control) ~
~ **hung ceiling** → (sound) absorbent suspended ~
~ **lining** → acoustic(al) ~
~ **masonry wall** → acoustic(al) ~ ~
~ **material** → (sound) ~ ~
~ ~, absorptive ~, absorbing ~ · Absorptionsstoff *m*, Absorptionsmaterial *n*, Absorptionsmittel *n*, Aufsaugstoff, Aufsaugmittel, Einsaugstoff, Einsaugmittel
~ **metal ceiling** → acoustic(al) ~ ~
~ **pad** → acoustic(al) blanket
~ **paint** → acoustic(al) ~
~ **panel** → acoustic(al) ~
~ **pan(el)** → sound ~ ~

~ **plaster** → anti-condensation ~
~ ~ **aggregate** → acoustic(al) ~ ~
~ ~ **ceiling** → acoustic(al) ~ ~
~ **powder,** absorbing ~, absorptive ~ · Absorptionspulver *n*, Einsaugpulver, Aufsaugpulver
~ **sheet** → acoustic(al) board
~ **sprayed-on plaster** → acoustic(al) ~ ~
~ **(sur)facing** → acoustic(al) lining
~ **suspended ceiling** → sound ~ ~ ~
~ **system** → (sound) absorptive ~
~ **tile** → acoustic(al) tile
~ ~ **ceiling** → acoustic(al) ~ ~
~ **unit** → (sound) absorptive system
~ ~ ~ → acoustic(al) (building) ~
~ **waffle** → (sound) absorbent pan(el)
~ **wall** → acoustic(al) ~
~ ~ **block** → acoustic(al) wall tile
~ ~ **brick** → acoustic(al) ~ ~
~ **wallpaper** → acoustic(al) ~
~ **wall tile** → acoustic(al) ~ ~
~ ~ ~ → sound-control ~ ~
~ **wood fibre board** (Brit.) → acoustic(al) ~ ~ ~

absorber → (sound) absorptive system

~ · Absorber *m* [*Jedes Gerät, das einen Stoff enthält, der Gase, Dämpfe oder Flüssigkeiten zu absorbieren vermag*]

~ · Absorptionsmittel *n*, Aufsaugmittel, Einsaugmittel

absorbing, absorbent, absorptive · absorbierend, einsaugend, aufsaugend

~ **backing** → acoustic(al) ~
~ **board** → acoustic(al) ~
~ **brick** → (ceramic) acoustic(al) ~
~ **(building) unit** → acoustic(al) (~) ~
~ **cassette** → (sound) absorbent pan(el)
~ **ceiling** → sound ~ ~
~ ~ **board** → accoustic(al) ceiling tile
~ ~ **paint** → acoustic(al) ~ ~
~ ~ **sheet** → acoustic(al) ceiling tile
~ ~ **system** → (sound) absorbent ~ ~
~ ~ **tile** → acoustic(al) ~ ~
~ **chamber** → sound ~ ~
~ **coffer** → (sound) absorbent pan(el)
~ **construction material** → sound ~ ~ ~
~ ~ **(method)** → acoustic(al) ~ (~)
~ **(control) glass** → acoustic(al) (~) ~
~ **cover(ing)** → acoustic(al) lining
~ **facing** → acoustic(al) lining
~ **felt(ed fabric)** → acoustic(al) ~ (~)
~ **felt(ed fabric) ceiling** → acoustic(al) ~ (~) ~
~ **fibre board** → acoustic(al) ~ ~

absorbing foil — absorptive construction material

~ **foil** → acoustic(al) ~
~ **glass** → acoustic(al) (control) ~
~ **hung ceiling** → (sound) absorbent suspended ~
~ **lining** → acoustic(al) ~
~ **masonry wall** → acoustic(al) ~ ~
~ **material,** absorptive ~, absorbent ~ · Absorptionsstoff *m*, Absorptionsmaterial *n*, Absorptionsmittel *n*, Aufsaugstoff, Aufsaugmaterial, Einsaugstoff, Einsaugmaterial, Aufsaugmittel, Einsaugmittel
~ ~ → (sound) ~ ~
~ **metal ceiling** → acoustic(al) ~ ~
~ **pad** → acoustic(al) blanket
~ **paint** → acoustic(al) ~
~ **pan(el)** → (sound) absorbent ~
~ **panel** → acoustic(al) ~
~ **plaster** → acoustic(al) ~
~ ~ **aggregate** → acoustic(al) ~ ~
~ ~ **ceiling** → acoustic(al) ~ ~
~ **powder,** absorptive ~, absorbent ~ · Absorptionspulver *n*, Einsaugpulver, Aufsaugpulver
~ **power** → absorptive capacity
~ **sheet** → acoustic(al) board
~ **sprayed-on plaster** → acoustic(al) ~ ~
~ **(sur)facing** → acoustic(al) lining
~ **suspended ceiling** → (sound) absorbent ~ ~
~ **system** → (sound) absorptive ~
~ **tile** → acoustic(al) ~
~ ~ **ceiling** → acoustic(al) ~ ~
~ **unit** → (sound) absorptive system
~ ~ → acoustic(al) (building) ~
~ **waffle** → (sound) absorbent pan(el)
~ **wall** → acoustic(al) ~
~ ~ **block** → acoustic(al) wall tile
~ ~ **brick** → acoustic(al) ~ ~
~ ~ **wallpaper** → acoustic(al) ~
~ **wall tile** → acoustic(al) ~ ~
~ ~ ~ → sound-control ~ ~
~ **wood fibre board** (Brit.) → acoustic(al) ~ ~ ~
absorption · Absorption *f*, Aufzehrung *f* [*Einsaugen eines Stoffes in das Innere eines anderen ohne chemische Vereinigung*]
~ **capacity** → absorptive ~
~ ~ → (sound) absorption property
~ **coefficient** · Absorptionsbeiwert *m*, Aufsaugbeiwert, Einsaugbeiwert
~ ~ → sound ~ ~
~ **colouring** (Brit.); ~ **coloring** (US) · Absorptionsfärbung *f*, Einsaugfärbung, Aufsaugfärbung
~ **field,** disposal ~, absorbing ~ [*A system of trenches containing coarse aggregate and distribution pipe through which effluent may seep or leach into surrounding soil*] · Beries(e)lungsfeld *n*, Rieselfeld

~ **(~) trench,** disposal ~ · Beries(e)lungsgraben *m*
~ **hygrometer** · Absorptionshygrometer *n*
~ **loss** · Absorptionsverlust *m*
~ **of sound,** sound absorption · (Schall-) Absorption *f*, (Schall)Schluckung *f* [*Abschwächung der Luftschallreflektion in geschlossenen Räumen durch schallschluckende Wand- oder Deckenverkleidungen, die in halligen Räumen die Nachhallzeit verkürzen und eine Senkung des Schallpegels bewirken*]
~ **power** → (sound) absorption property
~ **property** → sound ~ ~
~ ~ → absorptive capacity
~ **quality** → (sound) absorption property
~ **refrigerating compressor** · Absorptions-Kältemaschine *f*
~ **system** [*This system conditions air by bringing it into contact with a hygroscopic solution in a contactor*] · Absorptionsanlage *f*
~ **test** · Wasseraufnahmeprobe *f*, Wasseraufnahmeprüfung *f*, Wasseraufnahmeversuch *m*
~ **tower** · Absorptionsturm *m*
~ **unit** [*Is absorption equal to that of a square foot of an open window which is considered as 100 per cent efficient in absorbing sound, although it really transmits the sound outward instead of absorbing it*] · (Schall)Schluckeinheit *f*, (Schall)Absorptionseinheit
absorptive, absorbent, absorbing · absorbierend, aufsaugend, einsaugend
~ **backing** → acoustic(al) ~
~ **blanket** → acoustic(al) ~
~ **board** → acoustic(al) ~
~ **brick** → (ceramic) acoustic(al) ~
~ **(building) unit** → acoustic(al) (~) ~
~ **capacity,** absorbency, absorptivity, absortiveness, absorbent capacity, absorption capacity, absorption property, absorptive property, absorbing power · Absorptionsvermögen *n*, Absorptionsfähigkeit *f*, Einsaugvermögen, Einsaugfähigkeit, Aufsaugvermögen, Aufsaugfähigkeit, Absorbiervermögen, Absorbierfähigkeit
~ ~ **for water,** water-absorptive capacity · Wasseraufnahmefähigkeit *f*, Wasseraufnahmevermögen *n*
~ **cassette** → (sound) absorbent pan(el)
~ **ceiling** → sound ~ ~
~ ~ **board** → acoustic(al) ceiling tile
~ ~ **paint** → acoustic(al) ~ ~
~ ~ **sheet** → acoustic(al) ceiling tile
~ ~ **system** → (sound) absorbent ~ ~
~ ~ **tile** → acoustic(al) ~ ~
~ **chamber** → sound ~ ~
~ **coffer** → (sound) absorbent pan(el)
~ **construction material** → sound ~ ~ ~

absorptive construction (method) — accelerated ag(e)ing

~ ~ **(method)** → acoustic(al) ~ (~)
~ **(control) glass** → acoustic(al) (~) ~
~ **cover(ing)** → acoustic(al) lining
~ **facing** → acoustic(al) lining
~ **felt(ed fabric)** → acoustic(al) ~ (~)
~ **felt(ed fabric) ceiling** → acoustic(al) ~ (~) ~
~ **fibre board** → acoustic(al) ~ ~
~ **foil** → acoustic(al) ~
~ **glass** → acoustic(al) (control) ~
~ **hung ceiling** → (sound) absorbent suspended ~
~ **lining** → accoustic(al) ~
~ **masonry wall** → acoustic(al) ~
~ **material,** absorbing ~, absorbent ~, · Absorptionsstoff *m*, Absorptionsmaterial *n*, Absorptionsmittel *n*, Aufsaugstoff, Aufsaugmittel, Einsaugstoff, Einsaufmittel, Aufsaugmaterial *n*, Einsaugmaterial
~ ~ → (sound) ~ ~
~ **metal ceiling** → acoustic(al) ~ ~
~ **pad** → acoustic(al) blanket
~ **paint** → acoustic(al) ~
~ **pan(el)** → (sound) absorbent ~
~ **panel** → acoustic(al) ~
~ **plaster** → acoustic(al) ~
~ ~ **aggregate** → acoustic(al) ~ ~
~ ~ **ceiling** → acoustic(al) ~ ~
~ **powder,** absorbent ~, absorbing ~ · Absorptionspulver *n*, Einsaugpulver, Aufsaugpulver
~ **property** → ~ capacity
~ **sheet** → acoustic(al) board
~ **sprayed-on plaster** → acoustic(al) ~
~ **(sur)facing** → acoustic(al) lining
~ **suspended ceiling** → (sound) absorbent ~ ~
~ **system** → (sound) ~ ~
~ **tile** → acoustic(al ~
~ ~ **ceiling** → acoustic(al) ~ ~
~ **unit** → (sound) absorptive system
~ ~ → acoustic(al) (building) ~
~ **waffle** → (sound) absorbent pan(el)
~ **wall** → acoustic(al) ~
~ ~ **block** → acoustic(al) wall tile
~ ~ **brick** → acoustic(al) ~ ~
~ **wallpaper** → acoustic(al) ~
~ **wall tile** → acoustic(al) ~ ~
~ ~ ~ → sound-control ~ ~
~ **wood fibre board** (Brit.) → acoustic(al) ~ ~ ~

absorptiveness → absorptive capacity
absorptivity → absorptive capacity
abstract → divorced from reality
~, non functional · zweckfrei

abundance of carving · Reichtum *m* an plastischem Schmuck
to abut [*To join end to end; to touch at one end*] · stoßen
(a)butment [*Any solid structure which resists the lateral thrust of an arch, arcade or vault*] · Widerlager
~ **masonry** · Widerlagermauerwerk *n*
~ **piece,** solepiece (US); sill, sole plate (Brit.); cill [*deprecated*] (Brit.) [*The lowest horizontal member of a framed partition, or frame construction*] · (Holz-) Schwelle *f* [*Beim Holzfachwerk der untere waag(e)rechte Balken der Riegelwand*]
~ **pier,** buttressing ~ [*deprecated*]; buttress [*A projecting construction built against a wall to resist a lateral thrust*] · Strebepfeiler *m*, Stützpfeiler, Bogenpfeiler
~ **system,** system of buttresses and flying buttresses · Strebeapparat *m*, Strebewerk *n*, Strebesystem *n* [*Die Gesamtheit von Strebebögen und Strebepfeilern, wie sie vor allem die Gotik ausgebildet hat*]
~ **(wall)** · Strebemauer *f*
abutting · aneinanderstoßend
~ **property** · anliegender Grundbesitz *m*
abysmal rock, abyssal ~, intrusive ~, (igneous) plutonic ~ · plutonisches Gestein *n*, subkrustales ~, abyssisches ~, Tiefengestein, Plutonit *m*, älteres Eruptivgestein, Intrusivgestein
abyssal rock, abysmal ~, intrusive ~, (igneous) plutonic ~ · plutonisches Gestein *n*, abyssisches ~, subkrustales ~, Tiefengestein, Plutonit *m*, älteres Eruptivgestein, Intrusivgestein
A. C., paving (grade) asphalt, asphalt cement (US); (asphaltic-)bitumen for road purposes [*B.S. 3690*] · Straßenbaubitumen *n* [*DIN 1995*]
~ ~ **with road tar addition** → paving asphalt ~ ~ ~ ~
academic style of building · akademische Architektur *f*, ~ Baukunst
academicism · Akademismus *m*
Academy of Fine Arts · Akademie *f* der bildenden Künste
acanthus; bear's breech (Brit.) · Akanthus *m*, Bärenklau *m*
~ **frieze** · Akanthusfries *m*, Bärenklaufries
~ **leaf** · Akanthusblatt *n*, Bärenklaublatt
~ **scroll** · Akanthusranke *f*, Bärenklauranke
acaroid gum, ~ resin · Akaroid(harz) *n*, Erdschellack *m*
~ **resin,** ~ gum · Akaroid(harz) *n*, Erdschellack *m*
to accelerate, to advance · beschleunigen [*Das Abbinden bzw. das Erhärten eines Gemisches mit einem hydraulischen Binder*]
accelerated ag(e)ing · abgekürzte Alterung *f*, Kurzalterung, Schnellalterung

accelerated binder ... — acceptance certificate

~ **binder content determination,** ~ ~ portion ~ · Bindemittel-Schnellbestimmung f

~ **consistency test,** ~ consistence ~ · Schnell-Konsistenzprüfung f, Schnell-Konsistenzprobe f, Schnell-Konsistenzversuch m, Schnell-Steifeprüfung, Schnell-Steifeprobe, Schnell-Steifeversuch

~ **corrosion test** · Schnellkorrosionsprobe f, Schnellkorrosionsprüfung f, Schnellkorrosionsversuch m

~ **curing of concrete test cubes** · Schnellnachbehandlung f von Betonprobewürfeln

~ **durability test** · Schnellprobe f auf Haltbarkeit, Schnellprüfung f ~ ~, Schnellversuch m ~ ~

~ **hydration** · beschleunigte Hydra(ta)tion f

~ **lab(oratory) test** · Labor(atoriums)schnellprobe f Labor(atoriums)schnellversuch m Labor(atoriums)schnellprüfung f

~ **method** · abgekürzte Methode f, Kurzmethode, Schnellmethode, abgekürztes Verfahren n, Schnellverfahren, Kurzverfahren

~ **test** · abgekürzte Probe f, ~ Prüfung f, abgekürzter Versuch m, Schnellprobe, Schnellprüfung, Schnellversuch, Kurzprobe, Kurzprüfung, Kurzversuch

~ **weathering,** artificial ~ [*Laboratory tests designed to simulate but at the same time to intensify and accelerate the destructive action of natural outdoor weathering on paint films. The tests involve exposure to artificially produced components of natural weather, e.g. light, heat, cold, water vapour, rain, etc., which are arranged and repeated in a given cycle. There is no universally accepted test and different investigators use different cycles*] · (künstliche) Bewitterung f

~ ~ **test** · abgekürzte Wetterbeständigkeitsprobe f, ~ Wetterbeständigkeitsprüfung f, abgekürzter Wetterbeständigkeitsversuch m, Bewitterungskurzprüfung, Bewitterungsschnellprüfung, Bewitterungsschnellversuch, Bewitterungskurzversuch, Bewitterungskurzprobe, Bewitterungsschnellprobe

accelerating additive · Beschleuniger m für hydraulische Bindemittel, BE ~ ~ ~

~ ~ **for hardening** · (Er)Härtungs(zeit)-beschleuniger m für hydraulische Bindemittel, Schnell(er)härter ~ ~ ~

~ ~ ~ **set(ting),** set(ting) accelerator additive · (Ab)Binde(zeit)beschleuniger m für hydraulische Bindemittel, Erstarrungs(zeit)beschleuniger ~ ~ ~, Schnellbindemittel, Schnellbinder

~ **admix(ture)** · Beschleuniger m für hydraulische Gemische, ~ ~ ~ Mischungen, BE ~ ~ ~

~ ~ **for hardening** · Schnell(er)härter m für hydraulische Gemische, (Er)Härtungs(zeit)beschleuniger ~ ~ ~, ~ ~ ~ Mischungen

~ ~ ~ **set(ting),** set(ting) accelerator admix(ture) · (Ab)Binde(zeit)beschleuniger m für hydraulische Gemische, ~ ~ ~ Mischungen, Erstarrungs(zeit)beschleuniger ~ ~ ~, Schnellbindemittel ~ ~ ~, Schnellbinder ~ ~ ~

~ **agent,** accelerator [*An additive or admix(ture) which, when present in small quantities, increase the rate of setting and/or hardening of a cementitious material in a controllable manner*] · BE m, Beschleuniger m [*für hydraulische Bindemittel und hydraulische Gemische*]

~ ~, accelerator, catalyst, hardener · Härtemittel n, Katalysator m, Härter m, (Reaktions)Beschleuniger

~ **salt** [*Such salts as potassium sulphate or alum are added in small amounts to anhydrous gypsum-plasters so as to speed up the rate of reaction with water*] · Beschleunigersalz n

acceleration direction, direction of acceleration · Beschleunigungsrichtung f

~ **force,** force of acceleration · Beschleunigungskraft f

~ **method** · Beschleunigungsverfahren n

~ **of hardening by heat** · (Er)Härtungsbeschleunigung f durch Hitze

~ ~ **set(ting)** · (Ab)Binde(zeit)beschleunigung f, Erstarrungs(zeit)beschleunigung

accelerator, accelerating agent [*An additive or admix(ture) which, when present in small quantities, increase the rate of setting and/or hardening of a cementitious material in a controllable manner*] · BE m, Beschleuniger m [*für hydraulische Bindemittel und hydraulische Gemische*]

~, catalyst, promoter [*Strictly speaking a substance which increases the rate of a chemical reaction, but which remains itself chemically unchanged at the end of the reaction*] · Katalysator m, (Reaktions)Beschleuniger

~ **admix(ture) for hardening** · (Er-)Härtungs(zeit)beschleunigung m für hydraulische Gemische, ~ ~ ~ Mischungen, Schnell(er)härter ~ ~ ~

~ **for hardening,** rapid hardener, hardening accelerator, hardening accelerating agent, hardening acceleration promoter · Schnell(er)härter m, (Er)Härtungs(zeit)beschleuniger

to accept, to carry, to sustain · aufnehmen [*Last*]

acceptability · Abnehmbarkeit f

~ **criterion** → acceptance ~

acceptance · Aufnahme f [*Last*]

~, ~ **of (the) work** · (Bau)Abnahme f; Kollaudierung f [*Schweiz*] [*Die Übernahme des Bauwerkes oder Gebäudes nach Fertigstellung*]

~ **certificate,** certificate of acceptance · Abnahmebescheid m, Abnahmebescheinigung f, Abnahmeschein m, Abnahmeniederschrift f, Abnahmeprotokoll n, Abnahmezeugnis n

~ **committee** · Abnahmekommission f, Abnahmeausschuß m
~ **condition** · Abnahmebedingung f
~ **criterion**, acceptability ~ · Abnahmebewertungsmaßstab m, Abnahmemerkmal n
~ **deviation** → ~ tolerance
~ **documents** · Abnahmeunterlagen fpl
~ **drawing** · Abnahme-Zeichnung f, Revisions-Zeichnung [*Zeichnung mit Kennzeichnung der für die Revision (Abnahme) wichtigen Maße*]
~ **inspection** · (Bau)Abnahme f durch Augenschein
~ **margin** → ~ tolerance
~ **of the carcass**, ~ ~ ~ fabric; ~ ~ ~ shell [*Canada*] · Rohbauabnahme f
~ **(of (the) work)** · (Bau)Abnahme f; Kollaudierung f [*Schweiz*] [*Die Übernahme des Bauwerkes oder Gebäudes nach Fertigstellung*]
~ **off-size** → ~ tolerance
~ **permissible deviation** → ~ tolerance
~ **test** · Abnahmeprobe f, Abnahmeprüfung f, Abnahmeversuch m
~ **tolerance**, ~ margin, ~ deviation, ~ permissible variation, ~ off-size · Abnahmetoleranz f, Abnahmemaßabweichung f, Abnahmeabmaß n
accepted load · aufgenommene Last f
access · Einstieg m
~ · Zugang m
~ **balcony**, ~ gallery, exterior corridor, outside corridor, outdoor corridor, external corridor [*A balcony intended to give access to a number of separate dwellings above the first stor(e)y*] · offener Gang m, Laubengang
~ **chamber** → cleaning ~
~ **cover**, ~ plate, cleanout ~, cleaning ~, rodding ~, inspection ~ · Reinigungsdeckel m, Putzdeckel
~ **dimension** · Schlupfweite f [*Mannloch*]
~ **door** · Reinigungsklappe f [*Lüftung*]
~ **eye**, ~ opening, cleanout (~), cleaning ~, rodding ~, inspection ~ · Putzöffnung f, Reinigungsöffnung
~ **floor** · Doppel(fuß)boden m
~ **front**, entrance ~ · Eingangsfront f
~ **gallery**, ~ balcony, exterior corridor, outside corridor, outdoor corridor, external corridor [*A balcony intended to give access to a number of separate dwellings above the first stor(e)y*] · offener Gang m, Laubengang
~ **hatch** · Einsteigluke f, Einstiegluke
~ **hook**, step iron, hand iron, foot iron · Steigeisen n, Klettereisen [*DIN 1211 (kurz), DIN 1212 (lang)*]
~ ~ **for chimneys** [*B.S. 3678*] · Schornsteinklettereisen n, Schornsteinsteigeisen
~ **ladder** · Einsteigleiter f, Einstiegleiter [*Schwimmbecken*]

~ **opening** · Zugangsöffnung f
~ ~, ~ eye, cleanout ~, cleaning ~, rodding ~, inspection ~ · Putzöffnung f, Reinigungsöffnung
~ **pit** → cleaning chamber
~ **plate**, ~ cover, cleanout ~, cleaning ~, rodding ~, inspection ~ · Reinigungsdeckel m, Putzdeckel
~ **plug**, ~ screw, cleanout ~, cleaning ~, rodding ~, inspection ~ · Putzstopfen m, Reinigungsstopfen, Putzschraube f, Reinigungsschraube
~ **point** · Zugangspunkt m
~ **ramp** · Auffahrt(rampe) f
~ ~ · Zufahrtsrampe f
~ **screw**, ~ plug, cleanout ~, cleaning ~, rodding ~, inspection ~ · Putzstopfen m, Reinigungsstopfen, Putzschraube f, Reinigungsschraube
~ **shaft** · Zugangsschacht m
~ **side**, entrance ~ · Eingangsseite f, Zugangsseite
~ **tower** · Zugangsturm m
~ **tube** → inspection ~
~ **way**, entryway · Einfahrt f
accessories, ~ of a building · Beiwerk n
~, equipment · Zubehör n
~ **of style** [*e. g. columns, pillars, pilasters, cornices, etc.*] · Formenapparat m des Stils
accessory · Armatur f
~ **block** → ~ building
~ **building**, ancillary ~, subordinate ~, dependent ~, ~ block · Nebengebäude n
accident ambulance station · Unfallambulanzstation f
~ **hospital** · Unfallkrankenhaus n; Unfallspital n [*Schweiz*]
~ **prevention regulations** · Unfallverhütungsvorschriften fpl
accidental air → entrapped ~
accommodation, portion, block, unit · (Bau)Trakt m, Gebäudetrakt
~ · Unterkunft f
~ **area** · Unterkunftsgelände n
according to modular coordination · modulgerecht, maßordnungsgerecht
~ ~ **scale** · maßstäblich
accordion door, concertina ~, bellow-framed ~ · Akkordeontür f, (Zieh-)Harmonikatür
~ ~ **fitting** → concertina door furniture
~ ~ **furniture** → concertina ~ ~
accumulator metal · Sammlerhartblei n [*DIN 1728*]
accuracy · Genauigkeit f
~ **of level(s)**, flatness, evenness; surface smoothness (US) · (Plan)Ebenheit f, Ebenflächigkeit
~ ~ **shape** · Form(en)genauigkeit f

**acetate of lead, **lead acetate · Bleiazetat *n*
acetic acid · C₂H₄O₂, Essigsäure *f*
acetone, dimethyl ketone · Azeton *n*, CH₃COCH₃
acetylene, ~ gas · Azetylen(gas) *n*, C₂H₂ [*Es wurde früher zur Herstellung von Gasbeton verwendet. Wegen seiner Feuergefährlichkeit verwendet man heute andere Blähmittel*]
~ **black** · Azetylenruß *m*, Azetylenschwarz *n*
~ **removal of stress,** ~ stress relieving · mechanisches Entspannen *n* durch Wärmedehnung, autogenes Entspannen [*Baustahl*]
Achamenian Persian architecture · Achämenidenarchitektur *f*, Achämenidenbaukunst *f* [*6. bis 4. Jh. v.Chr.*]
acid, acidic · sauer, silikareich, reich an Silika [*Gestein*]
~ · Säure *f*
~ **attack** · Säureangriff *m*
~ **bath** [*electrogalvanizing*] · Säurebad *n*, saures Bad
~ **brittleness** [*The brittleness induced in steel when pickled in dilute acid for the purpose of removing scale or upon electroplating. This brittleness is commonly attributed to the absorption of hydrogen*] · Beizsprödigkeit *f*, Beizsprödheit
~ **dye** · saurer Küpenfarbstoff *m*
~ **dyestuff** · saurer Farbstoff *m*
(~) **embossing,** (~) **etching** [*It is a highly decorative process of obscuring the surface of glass by means of hydrofluoric acid. The amout of obscuration can be controlled and varying degrees obtained*] · Säuremattieren *n*, Mattätzen, (Säure)Ätzen
~ **emulsion,** cationic ~ · kationische Emulsion *f*, saure ~
acid-etched plaster → acid-washed ~
acid(-etch)ing → acid washing
(acid) etching [*A chemical process in which the surfaces of various plates are eaten away by an acid*] · (Säure)Ätzung *f*
(~) ~ → (~) embossing
~ ~, stamp ~, stamping · Stempelätzung *f* [*Glasbehandlung*]
acid-fast → acid-resisting
~ **asphalt(ic) tile** → acid-resisting ~ ~
~ **chimney** → acid-resisting ~
~ **joint** → acid-resisting ~
~ **mastic** → acid-resisting ~
~ **masonry (work)** → acid-resisting ~ (~)
~ **paint** → acid-resisting ~
~ **refractory concrete** → acid-resisting ~ ~
~ **sheet(ing)** → acid-resisting ~
~ **varnish** → acid-resisting ~
acid-fastness, acid-resistance · Säurefestigkeit *f*, Säurebeständigkeit, Säureechtheit, Säurewiderstand *m*

~ **test,** acid-resistance ~ · Säurebeständigkeitsprüfung *f*, Säurebeständigkeitsversuch *m*, Säurebeständigkeitsprobe *f*, Säurefestigkeitsprüfung, Säurefestigkeitsversuch, Säurefestigkeitsprobe
acid firebrick → gannister brick
~ **former,** acidifier · Säurebildner *m*
~ **fumes** · Säuredämpfe *mpl*
~ **heat** · Bildungswärme *f* bei der Säurereaktion
acid(ic) · sauer, silikareich, reich an Silika [*Gestein*]
acidifier, acid former · Säurebildner *m*
acidimeter · Säuremesser *m*
acidimetry · Säuremessung *f*
aciding → acid washing
acid polishing · Säurepolieren *n* [*Glas*]
acidproof → acid-resisting
~ **asphalt(ic) tile,** acid-resisting ~ ~, acid-resistant ~ ~ · Asphalthartstein(belag)platte *f*, Asphalthartsteinfliese *f*
~ **chimney,** acid-resistant ~, acid-resisting ~ · Säureschornstein *m*
~ **joint,** acid-resisting ~, acid-resistant ~ · Säurefuge *f*
~ **masonry (work),** acid-resisting ~ (~), acid-resistant ~ (~) · Säuremauerwerk *n*
~ **mastic,** acid-resisting ~, acid-resistant ~ · säurefester Kitt *m*, Säurekitt [*Fehlname: Säurezement m*]
~ **paint,** acid-resisting ~, acid-resistant ~ · Säureschutzfarbe *f*
~ **refractory concrete,** acid-resisting ~ ~, acid-resistant ~ ~ · säurebeständiger ff. Beton *m*, ~ feuerfester ~, säurefester ~ ~
~ **sheet(ing),** acid-resisting ~, acid-resistant ~ · Säureschutzbahn *f*
~ **varnish,** acid-resisting ~, acid-resistant ~ · Säureschutzlack *m*, säurefester Lack
acid-proofing agent · Säurebeständigkeitsmittel *n*, Säurefestigkeitsmittel
acid protection, protection against acids · Säureschutz *m*
~ **refractory product,** ~ ~ article · kieselsäurereiches Erzeugnis *n*, kieselsäurereicher Artikel *m*
acid-repelling · säureabweisend
acid residue · Säurerest *m*, Säurerückstand *m*
acid-resistance, acid-fastness · Säurefestigkeit *f*, Säurebeständigkeit, Säureechtheit, Säurewiderstand *m*
acid resistance test, acid-fastness ~ · Säurebeständigkeitsprüfung *f*, Säurebeständigkeitsversuch *m*, Säurebeständigkeitsprobe *f*, Säurefestigkeitsprüfung, Säurefestigkeitsversuch, Säurefestigkeitsprobe
acid-resistant → acid-resisting
~ **asphalt(ic) tile,** acid-resisting ~ ~, acidproof ~ ~, acid-fast ~ ~ · Asphalthartstein(belag)platte *f*, Asphalthartsteinfliese *f*

acid-resistant chimney — acoustic(al) brick

~ **chimney**, acid-resisting ~, acidproof ~, acid-fast ~ · Säureschornstein *m*

~ **joint**, acid-resisting ~, acidproof ~, acid-fast ~ · Säurefuge *f*

~ **mastic**, acid-resisting ~, acidproof ~, acid-fast ~ · säurefester Kitt *m*, Säurekitt [*Fehlname: Säurezement m*]

~ **masonry (work)**, acid-resisting ~ (~), acidproof ~ (~), acid-fast ~ (~) · Säuremauerwerk *n*

~ **paint**, acid-resisting ~, acidproof ~, acid-fast ~ · Säureschutzfarbe *f*

~ **refractory concrete**, acid-resisting ~ ~, acidproof ~ ~, acid-fast ~ ~ · säurebeständiger ff. Beton *m*, ~ feuerfester ~, säurefester ~ ~, säureechter ~ ~

~ **sheet(ing)**, acid-resisting ~, acidproof ~, acid-fast ~ · Säureschutzbahn *f*

~ **varnish**, acid-resisting ~, acidproof ~, acid-fast ~ · Säureschutzlack *m*, säurefester Lack

acid-resisting, acid-resistant, acidproof, AP, AR, fast to acid, acid-fast · säurefest, säurebeständig, säureecht

~ **asphalt(ic) tile**, acid-resistant ~ ~, acidproof ~ ~, acid-fast ~ ~ · Asphalthartstein(belag)platte *f*, Asphalthartsteinfliese *f*

~ **chimney**, acid-resistant ~, acidproof ~, acid-fast ~ · Säureschornstein *m*

~ **joint**, acid-resistant ~, acidproof ~, acid-fast ~ · Säurefuge *f*

~ **masonry (work)**, acid-resistant ~ (~), acidproof ~ (~), acid-fast ~ (~) · Säuremauerwerk *n*

~ **mastic**, acid-resistant ~, acidproof ~, acid-fast ~ · säurefester Kitt *m*, säurebeständiger ~, säureechter ~, Säurekitt [*Fehlname: Säurezement m*]

~ **paint**, acid-resistant ~, acidproof ~, acid-fast ~ · Säureschutzfarbe *f*

~ **refractory concrete**, acid-resistant ~ ~, acidproof ~ ~, acid-fast ~ ~ · säurebeständiger ff. Beton *m*, ~ feuerfester ~, säurefester ~ ~, säureechter ~ ~

~ **sheet(ing)**, acid-resistant ~, acidproof ~, acid-fast ~ · Säureschutzbahn *f*

~ **varnish**, acid-resistant ~, acidproof ~, acid-fast ~ · Säureschutzlack *m*, säurefester Lack

acid slurry, cationic ~ · kationische Schlämme *f*, saure ~

acid-soluble · säurelöslich

acid solution · Säurelösung *f*

~ **stain** [*The acid stains include many materials which are not acids*] · chemische (Holz)Beize *f*, Metallsalzbeize

~ **storage tank** · Säure-Lagerbehälter *m*

~ **streaking** · Schlierenbildung *f* durch Säureeinwirkung

acid-treated plaster → acid-washed ~

acid treatment · Säurebehandlung *f*, Säuern *n*

~ ~ → ~ washing

to acidulate · ansäuern

acidum hydrofluoricum, hydrofluoric acid · Fluorwasserstoffsäure *f*, Flußsäure

acid-washed plaster, acid-treated ~, acid-etched ~ · Waschputz *m* [*Dieser Putz wird 2 bis 3 Tage nach Fertigstellung mit verdünnter Salzsäure (etwa 1:1) abgewaschen, so daß die Zuschläge in Form und Farbe vollständig zum Vorschein kommen*]

acid washing, ~ treatment, acid(-etch)ing, etching [*The application of an acid solution to the inner surfaces of mo(u)lds so as to prevent setting at the surface of the concrete. The loose aggregate is brushed off after stripping thus producing slight exposure of the aggregate*] · Abbeizen *n* [*Betonwerkstein*]

~ ~, ~ treatment, acid(-etch)ing, etching · Absäuern *n*

Ackermann rib(bed) floor · Ackermanndecke *f* [*Rippendecke mit Tonhohlsteinen. Steinmaße 10 × 30 × 25 cm*]

acoustic impedance [*Of a specified configuration or medium. The complex ratio of the sound pressure to the volume velocity through a chosen surface. Symbol Z_a*] · akustische Impedanz *f*, Flußimpedanz [*Quotient aus Schalldruck und Schallfluß*]

~ **resistance** [*The real component of an acoustic impedance. Symbol R_a*] · Resistanz *f*, Widerstand *m* [*Akustik. Der Realteil der Impedanz*]

acoustical, sound absorbing, sound absorptive, sound absorbent [*The capability of a material to absorb noise to make a room quieter and more comfortable*] · schallschluckend

acoustic(al) alarm unit, audible ~ ~, sound ~ ~ · akustisches Alarmgerät *n*

~ **backing**, sound-control ~, (sound) absorbent ~, (sound) absorbing ~, (sound) absorptive ~ · Schallschluck-Hinterfüllung *f*, Akustik-Hinterfüllung, Schallabsorptions-Hinterfüllung [*Gips-Akustikplatte*]

~ **blanket**, ~ pad, sound-control ~, (sound) absorbent ~, (sound) absorbing ~, (sound) absorptive ~ · Schallschluckmatte *f*, Akustikmatte, Schallabsorptionsmatte

~ **board**, ~ sheet, sound-control ~, (sound) absorbent ~, (sound) absorbing ~, (sound) absorptive ~ · Akustikplatte *f*, Schallschluckplatte [*DIN 4109*]

~ **brick**, sound-control ~, (sound) absorbent ~, (sound) absorbing ~, (sound) absorptive ~ · Schallschluckziegel *m*, Akustikziegel, Schallabsorptionsziegel [*Hochkantvermauerter unverputzter Hochlochziegel*]

acoustic(al) (building) unit — acoustic(al) signal 24

~ **(building) unit**, sound-control (~) ~, (sound) absorbent (~) ~, (sound) absorbing (~) ~, (sound) absorptive (~) ~ · Schallschluckelement *n*, Akustikelement, Schallabsorptionsele-

~ **cassette** → ~ (sound) absorbent pan(el)

~ **ceiling**, sound-control ~, (sound) absorbent ~, (sound) absorbing ~, (sound) absorptive ~, · Schallschluckdecke *f*, Akustikdecke, Schallabsorptionsdecke

~ ~ **paint**, sound-control ~ ~, (sound) absorbent ~ ~, (sound) absorbing ~ ~, (sound) absorptive ~ ~ · Schallschluckdecken(anstrich)farbe *f*, Akustikdecken(anstrich)farbe, Schallabsorptionsdecken(anstrich)farbe

~ ~ **system** → ~ (sound) absorbent ~ ~

~ ~ **tile**, ~ ~ board, ~ ~ sheet, (sound) absorbing ~ ~, (sound) absorptive ~ ~, sound-control ~ ~ · Akustikdeckenplatte *f*, Deckenschallschluckplatte, Deckenakustikplatte, Schallschluckdeckenplatte

~ **coffer** → ~ (sound) absorbent pan(el)

~ **construction** · baulicher Schallschutz *m*

~ ~ **material**, (sound) absorbent ~ ~, (sound) absorbing ~ ~, (sound) absorptive ~ ~, sound-control ~ ~ · Schallschluckbaustoff *m*, Akustikbaustoff, Schallabsorptionsbaustoff

~ ~ **(method)**, (sound) absorbent ~ (~), (sound) absorbing ~ (~), (sound) absorptive ~ (~), sound-control ~ (~) · Schallschluckbauweise *f*, Akustikbauweise, Schallabsorptionsbauweise

~ **(control) glass**, (sound) absorbent ~, (sound) absorbing ~, (sound) absorptive ~, sound-control ~ · Schallschluckglas *n*, Akustikglas, Schallabsorptionsglas

~ **cover(ing)** → ~ lining

~ **facing** → ~ lining

~ **felt(ed fabric)**, sound-control ~ (~), (sound) absorbent ~ (~), (sound) absorbing ~ (~), (sound) absorptive ~ (~) · Schallschluckfilz *m*, Akustikfilz, Schallabsorptionsfilz

~ **felt(ed fabric) ceiling**, sound-control ~ (~) ~, (sound) absorbent ~ (~) ~, (sound) absorbing ~ (~) ~, (sound) absorptive ~ (~) ~ · Schallschluckfilzdecke *f*, Akustikfilzdecke, Schallabsorptionsfilzdecke

~ **fibre board** (Brit.); ~ fiber ~ (US); sound-control ~ ~, (sound) absorbent ~ ~, (sound) absorbing ~ ~, (sound) absorptive ~ ~ · Schallschluckfaserplatte *f*, Akustikfaserplatte, Faserschallschluckplatte, Faserakustikplatte, Schallabsorptionsfaserplatte

~ **foil**, sound-control ~, (sound) absorbing ~, (sound) absorbent ~, (sound) absorptive ~ · Schallschluckfolie *f*, Akustikfolie, Schallabsorptionsfolie

~ **glass** → ~ control ~

~ **insulation** → sound ~

~ **lining**, ~ (sur)facing, ~ cover(ing), sound-control ~, (sound) absorbent ~, (sound) absorbing ~, (sound) absorptive ~ · Schallschluckauskleidung *f*, Akustikverkleidung, Akustikauskleidung, Schallschluckbekleidung, Akustikbekleidung, Schallschluckverkleidung, Akustikbelag *m*, Schallabsorptionsauskleidung, Schallabsorptionsverkleidung, Schallabsorptionsbekleidung, Schallabsorptionsbelag

~ **masonry wall**, sound-control ~ ~, (sound) absorbent ~ ~, (sound) absorbing ~ ~, (sound) absorptive ~ ~ · Schallschluckmauer *f*, Akustikmauer, Schallabsorptionsmauer

~ **material**, sound-control ~, (sound) absorbent ~, (sound) absorbing ~, (sound) absorptive ~ · Schallschluckmaterial *n*, Akustikmaterial, Schallschluckstoff *m*, Akustikstoff, Schallabsorptionsmaterial, Schallabsorptionsstoff

~ **metal ceiling**, sound-control ~ ~, (sound) absorbent ~ ~, (sound) absorbing ~ ~, (sound) absorptive ~ ~ · Schallschluckmetalldecke *f*, Metallschallschluckdecke, Akustikmetalldecke, Metallakustikdecke, Schallabsorptionsmetalldecke, Metallschallabsorptionsdecke

~ **pad** → ~ blanket

~ **paint**, sound-control ~, (sound) absorbent ~, (sound) absorbing ~, (sound) absorptive ~ · Akustikfarbe *f*, Schallschluckfarbe, Schallabsorptionsfarbe

~ **panel**, sound-control ~, (sound) absorbent ~, (sound) absorbing ~, (sound) absorptive ~ · Schallschlucktafel *f*, Akustiktafel, Schallabsorptionstafel

~ **performance** · akustisches Verhalten *n*

~ **plaster**, sound-control ~, (sound) absorbent ~, (sound) absorbing ~, (sound) absorptive ~ · Schallschluckputz *m*, Akustikputz, Schallabsorptionsputz

~ ~ **aggregate**, sound-control ~ ~, (sound) absorbent ~ ~, (sound) absorbing ~ ~, (sound) absorptive ~ ~ · Schallschluckputzzuschlag(stoff) *m*, Akustikputzzuschlag(stoff), Schallabsorptionsputzzuschlag(stoff)

~ ~ **ceiling**, sound-control ~ ~, (sound) absorbent ~ ~, (sound) absorbing ~ ~, (sound) absorptive ~ ~, APC · Schallschluckputzdecke *f*, Akustikputzdecke, Schallabsorptionsputzdecke

~ **property** · akustische Eigenschaft *f*

~ **sheet** → ~ board

~ **signal**, sound ~, audible ~ · Hörsignal *n*, akustisches Signal, Akustiksignal, Schallsignal

acoustic(al) sprayed-on plaster — acrylate

~ **sprayed-on plaster,** sound-control ~ ~, (sound) absorbent ~ ~, (sound) absorbing ~ ~, (sound) absorptive ~ ~ · Schallschluckspritzputz *m*, Akustikspritzputz, Schallabsorptionsspritzputz

~ **(sur)facing** → ~ lining

~ **test** · akustische Probe *f*, ~ Prüfung *f*, akustischer Versuch *m* [*DIN 4109*]

~ **tile,** sound-control ~, (sound) absorbent ~, (sound) absorbing ~, (sound) absorptive ~, AT · Schallschluckfliese *f*, Akustikfliese, Schallschluckplatte *f*, Akustikplatte, Schallabsorptionsfliese, Schallabsorptionsplatte

~ ~ **(bonding) adhesive,** ~ ~ ~ medium, ~ ~ ~ agent, ~ ~ cement(ing agent) · Akustikplattenkleber *m*, Akustikplattenkleb(e)stoff *m*, Schallschluckplattenkleber, Schallschluckplattenkleb(e)stoff, Akustikfliesenkleber, Akustikfliesenkleb(e)stoff, Schallschluckfliesenkleber, Schallschluckfliesenkleb(e)stoff, Akustikplattenkleb(e)mittel, Schallschluckplattenkleb(e)mittel, Akustikfliesenkleb(e)mittel *n*, Schallschluckfliesenkleb(e)mittel

~ ~ **ceiling,** sound-control ~ ~, (sound) absorbent ~ ~, (sound) absorbing ~ ~, (sound) absorptive ~ ~, ATC · Schallschluckfliesendecke *f*, Schallschluckplattendecke, Akustikfliesendecke, Akustikplattendecke, Schallabsorptionsfliesendecke, Schallabsorptionsplattendecke

~ **ventilating ceiling,** ~ ventilation ~, vent(ilation) acoustical ~, ventilating acoustical ~ · Schallschucklüftungsdecke *f*, Lüftungsschallschluckdecke, Akustiklüftungsdecke, Lüftungsakustikdecke, Schallabsorptionslüftungsdecke, Lüftungsschallabsorptionsdecke

~ **ventilation ceiling,** ~ ventilating ~, ventilating acoustical ~, vent(ilation) acoustical ~ · Schallschucklüftungsdecke *f*, Lüftungsschallschluckdecke, Akustiklüftungsdecke, Lüftungsakustikdecke, Schallabsorptionslüftungsdecke, Lüftungsschallabsorptionsdecke

~ **waffle** → (sound) absorbent pan(el)

~ **wall,** sound-control ~, (sound) absorbent ~, (sound) absorbing ~, (sound) absorptive ~ · Schallschluckwand *f*, Akustikwand, Schallabsorptionswand

~ ~ **block** → ~ ~ tile

~ ~ **brick,** sound-control ~ ~, (sound) absorbent ~ ~, (sound) absorbing ~ ~, (sound) absorptive ~ ~ · Akustikwandziegel *m*, Schallschluckwandziegel, Schallabsorptionswandziegel

~ **wallpaper,** sound-control ~, (sound) absorbent ~, (sound) absorptive ~, (sound) absorbing ~ · Schallschlucktapete *f*, Akustiktapete, Schallabsorptionstapete

~ **wall tile** → sound-control ~ ~

~ ~ ~, ~ ~ block, sound-control ~ ~ (sound) absorbent ~ ~, (sound) absorbing ~ ~, (sound) absorptive ~ ~ [*See remark under 'Block'*] · Akustikwandblock(stein) *m*, Akustikwandstein, Schallschluckwandblock(stein), Schallschluckwandstein, Schallabsorptionswandblock(stein), Schallabsorptionswandstein

~ **wood fibre board** (Brit.); ~ ~ fiber ~ (US); (sound) absorbent ~ ~ ~, (sound) absorbing ~ ~ ~, soundcontrol ~ ~ ~, (sound) absorptive ~ ~ ~ · Akustik-Holzfaserplatte *f*, Schallschluck-Holzfaserplatte, Holzfaser-Schallschluckplatte, Holzfaser-Akustikplatte

acoustician, acoustics expert · Akustikfachmann *m*

acoustics [*The science relating to sounds, their production, transmission, and their effects on the organs of hearing. For the builder, it usually means controlling the transmission of noises, prevention of sounds passing through barriers of various types, assurance that speech sounds will be heard intelligibly, and assurance that music will be heard satisfactorily*] · Akustik *f*, Schallehre *f*

~ [*The totality of those physical characteristics of an auditorium or room which affect an individual's perception, and his judgement, of the quality of speech or music produced in the room*] · Akustik *f*

~ **consultant** · Akustikberater *m*

~ **engineer** · Akustikingenieur *m*

~ **expert,** acoustician · Akustikfachmann *m*

~ **insulation,** acoustic(al) ~, soundproofing · Schalldämmung *f*

~ **of churches** · Kirchenakustik *f*

A.C.P. Alocrom process (Brit.); Alodine ~ (US) [*U.S.Pat. 2,438,877, Can.Pat. 452,254. F. Spruance, Jr.*] · Alodine-Verfahren *n* [*Ein chemisches Oxydationsverfahren für die Oberflächenbehandlung von Aluminium auf Chromsäurebasis*]

acquisition of land, purchase ~ ~, land purchase, land acquisition · Grunderwerb *m*, Baulandbeschaffung *f* [*Österreich: Grundeinlösung*]

acropolis · Akropolis *f* [*Hochgelegene, befestigte Sied(e)lung oder Burg der griechischen Antike in der Nähe einer manchmal erst später entstandenen Stadt*]

acroter(ion), acroterium, corner ornament · Akroterion *n*, Giebel-~, (Giebel-) Akroterium, Bild(er)stuhl *m*, Giebelzinne *f* [*Bekrönendes Element, meist aufrechtstehende Giebelverzierung an Tempeln, Stelen usw., und zwar sowohl der Spitze als auch der seitlichen Ecken eines Giebeldreiecks*]

acroterium → acroter(ion)

acrylate, acrylic ester [*The word 'acrylic' is improperly used as a noun*] · Acrylsäureester *m* [*Fehlname: Acrylat n*]

**acrylate-based, **acrylic ester-based · acrylatgebunden

acrylic acid, $CH_2:CH\cdot COOH$·Acrylsäure f

~ **base,** ~ resin ~ · Acrylharzbasis f, Acrylharzgrundlage f

~ **(building) mastic,** ~ mastic joint sealer · Acryl(fugen)mastix m, Acryl(fugen)kitt m, Acryl(ver)füllkitt, Acryl-Fugen(ab)dicht(ungs)kitt

~ **(bulk) compound** → ~ (resin) seal(ing) ~

~ **caulking (compound)** (Brit.) → ~ (resin) seal(ing) ~

~ **coating** · Acrylharzlack m

~ **composition,** ~ compound, ~ material, ~ mass · Acrylmasse f

~ **compound,** ~ composition, ~ material, ~ mass · Acrylmasse f

~ ~ → ~ (resin) seal(ing) ~

~ **concrete,** ~ resin ~ · Acrylharzbeton m

~ **dispersion,** ~ resin ~ · Acrylharzdispersion f

~ **emulsion** → ~ resin ~

~ **ester,** acrylate [*The word 'acrylic' is improperly used as a noun*] · Acrylsäureester n [*Fehlname: Acrylat n*]

~ **ester-based,** acrylate-based · acrylatgebunden

~ **fibre** (Brit.); ~ fiber (US) · Acrylfaser f

~ **latex** · Acryllatex m

~ **mass,** ~ compound, ~ composition, ~ material · Acrylmasse f

~ **mastic,** ~ building ~, ~ mastic joint sealer · Acryl(fugen)mastix m, Acryl(fugen)kitt m, Acryl(ver)füllkitt, Acryl-Fugen(ab)dicht(ungs)kitt

~ ~ **joint sealer,** ~ (building) mastic · Acryl(fugen)mastix m, Acryl(fugen)kitt m, Acryl(ver)füllkitt, Acryl-Fugen(ab)dicht(ungs)kitt

~ **material,** ~ compound, ~ composition, ~ mass · Acrylmasse f

~ **plastic** · Acrylglas n

~ ~ **(bath) tub,** ~ ~ bath · Acrylglas(bade)wanne f

~ ~ **board** · Acrylglasplatte f

~ ~ **corrugated board** · Acrylglaswellplatte f

~ ~ **domed rooflight,** ~ ~ light cupola, ~ ~ saucer dome, ~ ~ dome(-light) · Acrylglaslichtkuppel f

~ ~ **dome(light),** ~ ~ saucer dome, ~ ~ light cupola, ~ ~ domed rooflight · Acrylglaslichtkuppel f

~ ~ **light cupola,** ~ ~ domed rooflight, ~ ~ saucer dome, ~ ~ dome(-light) · Acrylglaslichtkuppel f

~ ~ **saucer dome,** ~ ~ light cupola, ~ ~ domed rooflight, ~ ~ dome(-light) · Acrylglaslichtkuppel f

~ **polymer** · Acrylpolymer n

~ **polyurethane** · Acryl-Polyurethan n

~ **resin** [*A synthetic resin of the thermoplastic type made by the polymerization of an acrylic compound, e.g. methyl acrylate, methyl methacrylate*] · Acrylharz n

~ **(~) base** · Acrylharzbasis f, Acrylharzgrundlage f

~ **(~) (bulk) compound** → ~ (~) seal(ing) ~

~ **(~) caulking (compound)** → ~ (~) seal(ing) ~

~ **(~) concrete** · Acrylharzbeton m

~ **(~) dispersion** · Acrylharzdispersion f

~ **(~) emulsion** · Acrylharzemulsion f

~ **(~) ~ paint** · Acrylharz-Emulsionsfarbe f

~ **(~) seal(ing) compound,** ~ (~) (bulk) ~; ~ (~) caulking (~) (Brit.); ~ (~) calking (~) (US) · Acrylharz(fugen)kitt m, Acrylharz(fugen)masse f, Acrylharzabsieg(e)lungsmasse, Acrylharzversieg(e)lungsmasse

~ **rubber paste** · Acrylgummipaste f

~ **sealant** → ~ seal(ing) compound

~ **seal(er)** · Acrylsiegel m, Acrylabsperrmittel n [*Anstrichtechnik*]

~ **sealer** → ~ seal(ing) compound

~ **seal(ing) compound** → ~ resin ~ ~

acrylo nitrite · Acrylnitrit n

to act · (ein)wirken

~ ~ · beanspruchen, angreifen

acting force · beanspruchende Kraft f, angreifende ~

action · (Ein)Wirkung f

~ · Beanspruchung f

~ **of frost,** frost action · Frosteinwirkung f

~ ~ **magnesia,** expansion tendency due to ~ · Magnesiatreiben n

~ ~ **water,** water action · Wasser(ein)-wirkung f

to activate · aktivieren, anregen

activating · Aktivieren n, Anregen

activator, dope · Aktivator m, Erreger(-stoff) m, Anreger(stoff) [*z.B. Kalkhydrat*]

~, anti-stripping agent, adhesion (promoting) agent, non-stripping agent, anti-stripping additive, dope · Adhäsionsverbesserer m, Haftmittel n, Haftfestigkeitsverbesserer, Netz(haft)-mittel, Haftanreger, adhäsionsfördernder Zusatz(stoff) m, adhäsionsförderndes Zusatzmittel

active earth, bleaching ~, bleaching clay · Bleicherde f, Bleichton m

~ ~ **pressure,** ~ soil ~ · (aktiver) Erddruck m

~ ~ **(~) load,** ~ soil (~) ~ · Erddrucklast f, Last aus Erddruck

~ **fire defense;** ~ ~ defence (Brit.) [*It includes the installation of alarm and detector systems to give warnings of an outbreak. (2) The installation of*

active fire defense — additional round bars

equipment for automatic fire extinction (sprinklers, CO_2 flooding systems). (3) The provision of first-aid fire fighting appliances. (4) The provision of facilities to assist the fire services] · mechanisierter Brandschutz *m*, ~ Feuerschutz

~ **soil pressure**, ~ **earth** ~ · (aktiver) Erddruck *m*

~ ~ **(pressure) load**, ~ **earth** (~) ~ · Erddrucklast *f*, Last aus Erddruck

activity index, index of activity · Aktivitätsindex *m* [*Zement*]

actual allowance, real ~ · Istabmaß *n*, tatsächliches Abmaß

~ **construction time**, real ~ ~ · Istbauzeit *f*, tatsächliche Bauzeit

~ **cross-section**, real ~ · Istquerschnitt *m*, tatsächlicher Querschnitt

~ **dimension**, real ~ · Istabmessung *f*, Istmaß *n*, tatsächliche Abmessung, tatsächliches Maß

~ **fire of severe intensity** · Feuersbrunst *f*

~ **grading curve** · Istlinie *f*, Sieblinie des Rohmaterials

~ **moment** · tatsächliches Moment *n*

~ **order** · endgültiger Auftrag *m*

~ **personnel**, real ~, ~ **staff** · Istpersonalbestand *m*, tatsächlicher Personalbestand

~ **size**, real ~ · Istgröße *f*, tatsächliche Größe

~ **staff**, real ~, ~ **personnel** · Istpersonalbestand *m*, tatsächlicher Personalbestand

~ **strength** · erreichte Festigkeit *f*, vorhandene ~, tatsächliche ~

~ **time**, real ~ · Istzeit *f*, tatsächliche Zeit

~ **value**, real ~ · Istwert *m*, tatsächlicher Wert

acute arch, lancet ~ · überhöhter Spitzbogen *m*, lanzet(t)förmiger ~, Lanzet(t)bogen [*veraltete Benennung: überspitzter Bogen*]

~ **zed** · geneigtes Z-Profil *n*

acylation · Acylierung *f*

a.d., air-dried, sun-dried, sun-baked · luftgetrocknet [*Lehmstein*]

adaptability to natural surroundings · landschaftliches Anpassungsvermögen *n*

adapter (US) → diminishing piece

adaptor → diminishing piece

to add · beigeben, zusetzen, zugeben

~ ~ [*force*] · hinzufügen [*Kraft*]

adding, addition · Beigabe *f*, Zusatz *m*, Beigeben *n*, Zusetzen, Zugabe, Zugeben

~ **of cement**, addition ~ ~ · Zementzugabe *f*, Zementbeigabe, Zementzusatz *m*, Zementzugeben *n*, Zementzusetzen, Zementbeigeben

~ ~ **water**, addition ~ ~ · Wasserbeigabe *f*, Wasserzusatz *m*, Wasserbeigeben *n*, Wasserzusetzen, Wasserzugabe, Wasserzugeben

~ **rate**, addition, ~, rate of addition, rate of adding · Zusatzdosis *f*, Beigabedosis

addition [*Any construction which increases the size of a building or adds to the building such as a porch or an attached garage or carport*] · Erweiterung *f*

~ · Erweiterungsbau *m* [*Bauliche Anlage, durch welche die Nutzfläche bereits bestehender baulicher Anlagen im Wege des Anbaues oder der Aufstockung vergrößert wird*]

~, adding · Beigabe *f*, Zusatz *m*, Beigeben *n*, Zusetzen, Zugabe, Zugeben

~ [*A material that is interground or blended in limited amounts into a hydraulic cement during manufacture either as a 'processing addition' to aid in manufacturing and handling the cement or as a 'functional addition' to modify the use properties of the finished products*] · Beigabe(mittel) *f*, (*n*) zum Zement, Zusatz(mittel) *m*, (*n*) ~ ~

~ · Zuschlag *m* [*Baustatik*]

~ · Zutat *f* [*Architektur*]

~ **of alcohol** · Alkoholbeigabe *f*, Alkoholzugabe [*Zur Gefrierpunkterniedrigung des Anmach(e)wassers*]

~ ~ **cement**, adding ~ ~ · Zementsatz *m*, Zementbeigabe *f*, Zementsetzen *n*, Zementbeigeben, Zementzugabe, Zementzugeben

~ ~ **forces** · Hinzufügung *f* von Kräften

~ ~ **lime**, lime addition · Kalkbeigabe *f*, Kalkzugabe, Kalkzusatz *m*, Kalkbeigeben *n*, Kalkzusetzen, Kalkzugeben

~ ~ **plastic** · Kunststoffbeigabe *f*, Kunststoffzusatz *m*

~ ~ **sand**, sand addition · Sandbeigabe *f*, Sandzusatz *m*, Sandzugabe *f*

~ ~ **water**, adding ~ ~ · Wasserbeigabe *f*, Wasserzusatz *m*, Wasserbeigeben *n*, Wasserzusetzen

~ **rate**, adding ~, ~ rate of addition, rate of adding · Beigabedosis *f*, Zusatzdosis

additional halfspan loading · einseitige Zusatzbelastung *f* [*Bogensystem*]

~ **heating** · Zusatz(be)heizung *f*

~ **insulation** · Zusatzisolierung *f*

~ **load**, complementary ~ · Zusatzlast *f* [*Zusatzlasten sind Windlasten, Bremskräfte, thermische Belastungen, Reibungswiderstände, Erddruckkräfte, Schneelasten usw., d. h. Kräfte, die nicht als Hauptlasten in der statischen Berechnung aufgeführt sind und welche nur selten gleichzeitig mit den Hauptlasten zusammen ihre Größtwerte erreichen*]

~ **loading** · Mehrbelastung *f*, Zusatzbelastung

~ **round bars**, secondary ~ ~ · Zulagerundstäbe *mpl*, Zulagerundstähle *mpl*

additive — adhesive suspension

additive, agent [*A material, other than aggregate, cementitious material or water, added in small quantities to the binder to produce some desired modification of the properties of the mix(ture) or of the hardened product*] · Zusatz(mittel) *m*, (*n*), Zusatzstoff *m*, Wirkstoff, Bindemittel~

~ **colour mixing**, ~ mixing of primary colours (Brit.); ~ color mixing, ~ mixing of primary colors (US) · additive Farbmischung *f*

~ **mixing of primary colors** (US) → ~ colour mixing

addle, tartar · Weinstein *m*

ad(d)orsed [*An adjective applied to two figures, usually animals, placed symmetrically back to back; often found on capitals*] · Rücken an Rücken, abgekehrt

adduct · Addukt *n* [*Anstrichtechnik*]

adhesion → ~ property

~ **agent** → activator

~ **capacity** → ~ (property)

~ **coefficient**, specific ~ ~ · Adhäsionsbeiwert *m*, Adhäsionszahl *f*

~ **limit**, specific ~ ~ · Adhäsionsgrenze *f*

~ **loss**, loss of adhesion · Haft(ungs)verlust *m*

~ **of granules**, bonding ~ ~ · Streumittelhaftung *f* [*Dachpappe*]

~ **power** → ~ (property)

adhesion-preventing film · Trennfilm *m*

adhesion (promoting) agent → activator

~ **(property)**, ~ power, ~ quality, ~ capacity, adhesiveness, bond (strength), interface strength, bonding property, bonding quality, bonding power, bonding capacity, adhesion(al) strength · Haftfähigkeit *f*, Abreißwiderstand *m*, (An)Haften *n*, (An)Haftung *f*, Adhäsion *f*, (scheinbare) Haftfestigkeit, Grenzflächenkraft *f*, Flächenanziehung, Verbund(wirkung) *m*, (*f*), Haftvermögen *n*, Hafteigenschaft, Adhäsionseigenschaft, Adhäsionsvermögen, Adhäsionsfähigkeit

~ **quality** → ~ (property)

~ **strength** → ~ (property)

adhesion(al) strength → adhesion (property)

adhesive, glue [*Although no distinction can be made, the term 'glue' is sometimes understood to refer only to organic substances such as animal glue, fish glue, casein, blood albumin, and the synthetic plastics being termed 'adhesives'. Actually, the two terms are synonymous*] · Leim *m*

~, bonding ~, bonding agent, bonding medium, cement(ing agent) · Kleb(e)mittel *n*, Kleb(e)stoff *m*, Kleber *m*

~ **anchor**, ~ tie, bonding ~ · Kleb(e)anker *m*

adhesive(-backed) tape, bonding ~ · Kleb(e)band *n*, Kleb(e)streifen *m*

adhesive based on coal tar → bonding ~ ~ ~ ~ ~

~ **bond** · Kleb(e)haftung *f*

~ **bonded** · angeklebt, verklebt

~ **capacity** → ~ property

~ **cement**, bonding ~ · Kleb(e)kitt *m*

~ **coat**, bonding ~ · Kleb(e)anstrich *m*, Kleb(e)aufstrich

~ **composition**, ~ compound, bonding ~, cement(ing ~) · Kleb(e)masse *f*

~ **compound** → (chemical) bonding system

~ ~ → ~ composition

~ **dispersion**, bonding ~ · Kleb(e)dispersion *f*

~ **emulsion**, bonding ~ · Kleb(e)emulsion *f*

~ **for cold pressing**, glue ~ ~ ~ · Kaltpreßleim *m*

~ ~ **concrete** → bonding agent ~ ~

~ ~ **laying** → bonding agent ~ ~

~ ~ **structural timber elements**, glue ~ ~ ~ ~ · Holzleim *m* für (last)tragende Bauteile, Leim für (last)tragende Holzbauteile

~ **force** · Kleb(e)kraft *f*

~ **in film form** → sheet glue

~ **joint**, glue(d) ~, ~ line · Kleb(e)verbindung *f*, Leimverbindung, Kleb(e)fuge *f*, Leimfuge

~ **layer** → cementing ~

~ **line**, glue(d) ~, ~ joint · Kleb(e)verbindung *f*, Leimverbindung, Kleb(e)fuge *f*, Leimfuge

(~) **masking tape** · (Ab)Deckband *n* [*Anstrichtechnik*]

~ **mortar**, cementing ~, bond(ing) ~ · Kleb(e)mörtel *m*, Haftmörtel

~ **paper**, bonding ~, cementing ~ · Kleb(e)papier *n*

~ **paste**, bonding ~, cementing ~ · Kleb(e)paste *f*

~ **powder**, glue ~, powder(ed) glue, powder(ed) adhesive · Leimpulver *n*, Trockenleim *m*, Pulverleim [*Leim in Pulverform, meist Pflanzenleim oder Zelluloseleim*]

~ **power** → ~ property

~ **property**, ~ capacity, ~ power, ~ quality, bonding ~, cementing ~ · Kleb(e)eigenschaft *f*, Kleb(e)fähigkeit *f*, Kleb(e)vermögen *n*

~ **quality** → ~ property

~ **rubber**, bonding ~, cementing ~ · Kleb(e)gummi *m*, *n*

~ **strength**, bonding ~, cementing ~ · Kleb(e)festigkeit *f*

~ **suspension**, bonding ~ · Kleb(e)suspension *f*

adhesive system — adsorption quality

~ **system** → (chemical) bonding ~
~ ~, bonding ~, cementing ~ · Kleb(e)konstruktion f
~ **tape**, adhesive-backed ~, bonding ~ · Kleb(e)band n, Kleb(e)streifen m
~ **tar composition**, ~ ~ compound, cementing ~ ~ · Teerkleb(e)masse f
~ ~ **compound**, ~ ~ composition, cementing ~ ~ · Teerkleb(e)masse f
~ **tie** → ~ anchor
adhesiveness → adhesion (property)
adiabatic [*A condition in which heat neither enters nor leaves a system*] · adiabatisch
~ **calorimeter**, calorimeter without heat transmission · adiabatisches Kalorimeter n, Kalorimeter ohne Wärmeabfluß
~ **curing** [*The maintenance of adiabatic conditions in concrete or mortar during the curing period*] · adiabatische Nachbehandlung f
~ **saturation** · adiabatische Sättigung f
adjacent blocks, ~ buildings, adjoining ~; neighboring ~ (US); neighbouring ~ (Brit.) · Nachbarbebauung f
~ **buildings**, ~ blocks, adjoining ~; neighboring ~ (US); neighbouring ~ (Brit.) · Nachbarbebauung f
~ **opening**, ~ span, adjoining ~; neighboring ~ (US); neighbouring ~ (Brit.) · Nachbarfeld n, Nachbaröffnung f
~ **owner**, adjoining ~; neighbouring ~ (Brit.); neighboring ~ (US) · Angrenzer m
~ **premises** → neighbouring property
~ **property** → neighbouring ~
~ **room** → neighbouring ~
~ **span**, ~ opening, adjoining ~; neighboring ~ (US); neighbouring ~ (Brit.) · Nachbarfeld n, Nachbaröffnung f
~ **wall** → neighbouring ~
adjoining blocks, ~ buildings, adjacent ~; neighboring ~ (US); neighbouring ~ (Brit.) · Nachbarbebauung f
~ **buildings**, ~ blocks, adjacent ~; neighboring ~ (US); neighbouring ~ (Brit.) · Nachbarbebauung f
~ **opening**, ~ span, adjacent ~; neighboring ~ (US); neighbouring ~ (Brit.) · Nachbarfeld n, Nachbaröffnung f
~ **owner**, adjacent ~; neighbouring ~ (Brit.); neighboring ~ (US) · Angrenzer m
~ **premises** → neighbouring property
~ **property** → neighbouring ~
~ **room** → neighbouring ~
~ **span**, ~ opening, adjacent ~; neighboring ~ (US); neighbouring ~ (Brit.) · Nachbarfeld n, Nachbaröffnung f
~ **wall** → neighbouring ~
adjudicating panel, panel of judges · Preisgericht n
adjustable bar [*It is often desirable to make tension bars adjustable so that they may be tightened. The turnbuckle and the sleeve are used for this purpose*] · anziehbarer Stab m
adjusting · Justieren n [*Fertigteile*]
administration block, ~ unit, ~ building · Verwaltungsgebäude n, Verwaltungstrakt m
~ **building**, ~ block, ~ unit · Verwaltungsgebäude n, Verwaltungstrakt m
~ **complex** · Verwaltungskomplex m
~ **tower** · Verwaltungshochhaus n
~ **unit**, ~ block, ~ building · Verwaltungsgebäude n, Verwaltungstrakt m
Admiralty visco(si)meter · Redwood-Viskosimeter II n
admissible, permissible, safe, allowable · zulässig
~ **load** → allowable ~
~ **stress** → allowable ~
admission of heat · Wärmezutritt m
~ ~ **light** · Lichtzutritt m
admitted for use by the local government(s) · bauaufsichtlich zugelassen
adobe (clay) [*A colloidal clay found in many relative small areas, called playas, in the southwestern part of the U.S.A.*] · Adobe(ton) f, (m)
~ (~) **block** · Adobe(ton)stein m, Adobe(ton)block(stein) m
~ (~) **brick** [*A burned building element of adobe (clay)*] · Adobe(ton)ziegel m
~ (~) **construction** · Adobe(ton)bau m
~ (~) **mud** · Adobe(ton)schlamm m
adorned, enriched, ornamented, decorated · geziert, verziert, geschmückt
adornment · Ausschmückung f, Verzierung, Schmuck m
adrema · Anschriftendruckerei f
to adsorb [*To condense and hold a gas on the surface of a solid, particularly metals. Also to hold a mineral particle within a liquid interface*] · adsorbieren
adsorbed substance · angelagerte Substanz f, adsorbierte ~
adsorbent · Adsorptionsmittel n
adsorption · Adsorption f, Anlagerung f
~ **capacity**, ~ property, ~ quality, ~ power · Adsorptionsfähigkeit f, Adsorptionsvermögen n, Anlagerungsfähigkeit, Anlagerungsvermögen
~ **equilibrium** · Adsorptionsgleichgewicht n
~ **power**, ~ capacity, ~ property, ~ quality · Adsorptionsfähigkeit f, Adsorptionsvermögen n, Anlagerungsfähigkeit, Anlagerungsvermögen
~ **pressure** · Adsorptionsdruck m
~ **property**, ~ quality, ~ capacity, ~ power · Adsorptionsfähigkeit f, Adsorptionsvermögen n, Anlagerungsfähigkeit, Anlagerungsvermögen
~ **quality**, ~ property, ~ capacity, ~ power · Adsorptionsfähigkeit f, Adsorptionsvermögen n, Anlagerungsfähigkeit, Anlagerungsvermögen

adsorption rate — aerated structure

~ **rate**, rate of adsorption · Adsorptionsgeschwindigkeit *f*

~ **system** [*This system dries air by bringing it into contact with a solid desiccant*] · Adsorptionsanlage *f* [*Klimatisierung*]

adsorptive force · Adsorptionskraft *f*

~ **hull** · Adsorptionshülle *f*

adularia, moonstone [*A colourless and translucent variety of orthoclase usually in pseudoorthorhombic crystals*] · Adular *m*

adult suite, master ~ [*These rooms are separated from the children's bedrooms and the family rooms*] · Erwachsenenräume *mpl*

to advance, to accelerate · beschleunigen [*Das Abbinden bzw. das Erhärten eines Gemisches mit einem hydraulischen Binder*]

advanced, forward-looking · zukunftsweisend

~ **architecture** · höhere Architektur *f*, ~ Baukunst *f*

adventure playground · Abenteuerspielplatz *m*

advertising kiosk · Anschlagsäulenkiosk *m*, Litfaßsäulenkiosk

~ **sign** · Reklameschild *n*, Werbeschild

~ **wall** · Reklamewand *f*, Werbewand

adyton, adytum, abaton · Abaton *n*, Adyton *n* [*In griechischen Tempeln der Raum in dem das Kultbild stand und der als Allerheiligstes nur vom Priester betreten werden durfte*]

~, adytum · Abaton *n* [*Der von einer Ikonostasis abgeschlossene Chor als Allerheiligstes in orthodoxen Kirchen*]

adytum, adyton, abaton · Abaton *n*, Adyton *n* [*In griechischen Tempeln der Raum in dem das Kultbild stand und der als Allerheiligstes nur vom Priester betreten werden durfte*]

adz(e)-hewn · bebeilt

adzed work [*The treatment or smoothing of wood surfaces with an adz(e) instead of a plane*] · bebeiltes Holz *n*

aedicula · Grabkapelle *f*; Ädikula *f* [*im frühen Mittelalter*]

~ · Privatkapelle *f*; Ädikula *f* [*im frühen Mittelalter*]

aedicular architecture · Ädikulararchitektur *f*, Ädikularbaukunst *f*

aedicule, aedicula, sacellum · Ädikula *f*, Aedicula [*Jede aus Stützgliedern (Säulen, Pfeilern, Pilastern) und einem Giebel in Dreieck- oder Segmentbogenform bestehende Umrahmung einer Statuennische*]

~ **altar**, aedicula ~ · Ädikulaaltar *m*, Aediculaaltar

Aeolic capital [*misnomer*] → palm ~

aerated cement screed · Porenestrich *m* [*Zementestrich, der durch porenbildende Zusätze ein poriges Gefüge erhält*]

~ **concrete** [*Strictly the term 'aerated concrete' should be applied only to autoclaved precast aerated concrete, air cured mixes are most accurately described as cellular concrete, or air entrained lightweight concrete*] · Porenbeton *m*, poriger Beton, Pb [*DIN 4164*]

~ ~ **block masonry (work)**, ~ ~ blockwork · Poren(beton)steinmauerwerk *n*, Poren(beton)block(stein)mauerwerk [*Fehlname: Porenbetonmauerwerk*]

~ ~ **blockwork**, ~ ~ block masonry (work) · Poren(beton)steinmauerwerk *n*, Poren(beton)block(stein)mauerwerk [*Fehlname: Porenbetonmauerwerk*]

~ (~) **(building) block**, ~ (~) (~) tile [*B.S. 1364 See. remark under 'Block(stein)'*] · Poren(beton)block(stein) *m*, Poren(beton)stein

~ ~ (~) **slab** · Porenbeton(bau)platte *f*

~ (~) (~) **tile**, ~ (~) (~) block [*B.S. 1364. See remark under 'Block(stein)'*] · Poren(beton)block(stein) *m*, Poren(beton)stein

~ ~ **(floor) screed** · Porenbetonestrich(fuß)boden(belag) *m*

~ ~ **panel** · Porenbetontafel *f*

~ ~ **rib(bed) slab** · Porenbetonrippenplatte *f*

~ ~ **roof(ing) slab** · Porenbetondachplatte *f*

~ ~ **slab** · Porenbetonplatte *f*

~ ~ **(type) screed material** · Porenbetonestrich *m* [*Baustoff zur Herstellung von Porenbeton-Estrich(fuß)böden*]

~ ~ **wall panel** · Porenbetonwand(bau)tafel *f*

~ ~ **window panel** · Porenbeton-Fenstertafel *f*

~ **gypsum** · Porengips *m*, Leichtgips [*Er entsteht durch Zusätze von Treibmitteln, z.B. Wasserstoffsuperoxid oder Kalkpulver mit verdünnter Salzsäure*]

~ ~ **board**, ~ ~ sheet · Leichtgipsplatte *f*, Porengipsplatte

~ ~ **core** · Porengipskern *m*, Leichtgipskern

~ ~ **sheet**, ~ ~ board · Porengipsplatte *f*, Leichtgipsplatte

~ **mortar** · Porenmörtel *m*

~ **prestressed concrete**, prestressed aerated ~ · Porenspannbeton *m*

~ **R.C.**, ~ reinforced concrete, reinforced aerated concrete · Porenstahlbeton *m*, Stahlporenbeton

~ **reinforced concrete**, ~ R. C., reinforced aerated concrete · Porenstahlbeton *m*, Stahlporenbeton

~ **sintered (concrete) aggregate**, sintered aerated (~) ~ · Porensinter *m* [*Aufgeblähter Leichtbetonzuschlag(stoff) über Sintergrenze gewonnen*]

~ **structure** · Porengefüge *n*

aerating agent — agglomerated cork brick

aerating agent → gas-forming ~
~ chemical → gas-forming agent
aeration, air input · Luftzufuhr *f*, Luftzuführung *f*, Belüften *n*, Belüftung
~ of cement · Durchlüften *n* von Zement
aerial conductor · Freileitung *f*
~ gallery, antenna ~ · Antennengang *m* [*Rundfunkturm*]
~ installation, antenna ~ · Antennenanlage *f*
~ mast, antenna ~ · Antennenmast *m*
(~) plug-in point · Antennenanschluß *m* [*In einer Wohnung an eine Gemeinschaftsantenne*]
~ socket, antenna ~ · Antennensteckdose *f*
aerograph → (paint) spray gun
aeroplane hangar (Brit.); airplane ~ (US); aircraft ~ [*R.A.F. term*] · Flugzeughalle *f*
(a)esthetic appeal, ~ charm · ästhetischer Reiz *m*
~ aspect · Ästhetikfrage *f*
~ charm, ~ appeal · ästhetischer Reiz *m*
~ concept, ~ idea · ästhetische Vorstellung *f*
~ effect · ästhetische Wirkung *f*
~ feeling, ~ sense · ästhetisches Gefühl *n*
~ idea, ~ concept · ästhetische Vorstellung *f*
~ sense, ~ feeling · ästhetisches Gefühl *n*
(a)esthetically pleasing · formschön
affronted [*An adjective applied to two figures, usually animals, placed symmetrically facing each other; often found on capitals*] · zueinander gekehrt
aftercooler · Nachkühler *m*
afterexpansion · Nachwachsen *n* [*Steinzeugindustrie*]
after-flush [*The small quantity of water remaining in the cistern after a w.c. pan is flushed. It trickles slowly down and remakes the seal*] · Spülwasserrest *m*
aftertack, residual tack · Nachkleben *n* [*Bleibende Klebrigkeit eines abgebundenen Lack- oder Farbfilms*]
after-treatment · Nachbehandlung *f*
after-yellowing · Nach(ver)gilben *n*
AG (pipe)line → above-ground ~
agar-agar · Agar-Agar *m* [*Gelatine aus Seealgen*]
agate mortar · Achatmörser *m*, Achatreibschale *f*
agave fibre (Brit.); ~ fiber (US) · Agavefaser *f*
to age · altern
~ ~, to store · altern, verwittern, „wettern" [*Steinzeugindustrie*]

~ ~ artificially · künstlich altern
age at test · Prüf(ungs)alter *n*
~ ~ (the time of) loading · Belastungsalter *n*
~ of hardening, hardening age · (Er)Härtungsalter *n*
~ strength relation · Alter-Festigkeits-Beziehung *f*
aged peoples' apartment (unit) → ~ persons' ~ (~)
~ ~ community centre (Brit.); ~ ~ ~ center (US); old ~ ~ ~, ~ persons' ~ ~ · Altenstätte *f*
~ ~ dwelling → ~ persons' dwelling unit
~ ~ flat → ~ persons' apartment (unit)
~ ~ home → old persons' ~
~ persons' apartment (unit), old ~ ~ (~), ~ peoples' ~ (~), ~ ~ flat · Alten-Etagenwohnung *f*, Alten-Geschoßwohnung, Alten-Stockwerkwohnung
~ ~ community centre (Brit.); ~ ~ ~ center (US); old ~ ~ ~, ~ peoples' ~ ~ · Altenstätte *f*
~ ~ dwelling unit, old ~ ~ ~, ~ peoples' ~ ~ (US); ~ ~ dwelling (Brit.) · Altenwohnung *f*
~ ~ flat → ~ ~ apartment (unit)
~ ~ home → old ~ ~
age-fast, age-proof, age-resistant, age-resisting · alterungsbeständig, alterungsfest, echt gegen Alterung
ag(e)ing · Alterung *f*
agent, contract manager [*The contractor's representative on site*] · (Firmen-)Bauleiter *m*
~, matter, substance · Mittel *n*, Stoff *m*, Substanz *f* [*z.B. für Sperranstriche*]
~, additive [*A material, other than aggregate, cementitious material or water, added in small quantities to the binder to produce some desired modification to the properties of the mix(ture) or of the hardened product*] · Zusatz(mittel) *m*, (*n*), Zusatzstoff *m*, Wirkstoff, Bindemittel~
age-proof, age-fast, age-resistant, age-resisting · alterungsbeständig, alterungsfest, echt gegen Alterung
age-resistant, age-proof, age-fast, age-resisting · alterungsbeständig, alterungsfest, echt gegen Alterung
age-resisting, age-proof, age-fast, age-resistant · alterungsbeständig, alterungsfest, echt gegen Alterung
agglomerate · Agglomerat *n* [*Zusammenlagerung trockener Pigmente*]
agglomerated cork, baked ~, rock ~, cork worked by agglomeration [*Agglomerated cork made by the agglutination of granulated cork*] · Backkork *m*
~ ~ brick, baked ~ ~, rock ~ ~ · Backkorkstein *m*

agglomeration — air bar

agglomeration, community · menschliche Sied(e)lung *f*

~ (of primary particles) · Agglomeration *f* (von Pigmentteilchen)

agloporite · Aggloporit *m* [*Name für Sinterbims in den Normen der UdSSR*]

aggregate · Agglomeration *f* [*Raumordnung*]

~, construction ~ · Zuschlag(stoff) *m*, Zuschlagmaterial *n*

aggregate/cement ratio → construction ~ ~

aggregate composition → construction ~ ~

~ cost, overall ~, total ~ · Gesamtkosten *f*

~ crushing value · Druckprüfungswert *m* [*Straßenbaugestein*]

~ depth, overall ~, total ~ · Gesamthöhe *f* [*Balken(träger)*]

~ dimension, total ~, overall ~ · Gesamtabmessung *f*, Gesamtmaß *n*

~ exposure [*To obtain decorative effects*] · Freilegen *n* der Zuschläge, ~ Zuschlagstoffe, Bloßlegen ~ ~

~ filling · strukturgebender Füllstoff *m* [*Putz*]

~ floor depth, total ~ ~, overall ~ ~ · Gesamtdeckendicke *f*

~ ~ space → total ~ ~

(~) grading curve, particle-size distribution ~, grain-size distribution ~, sieve ~ · Siebkurve *f*, Sieblinie *f*, Körnungskurve, Körnungslinie, Kornverteilungskurve, Kornverteilungslinie

~ grain → construction ~ ~

~ heating → construction ~ ~

~ height, total ~, overall ~ · Gesamthöhe *f*, Höhe über alles

~ impact value · Schlagprüfungswert *m* [*Straßenbaugestein*]

~ length, total ~, overall ~ · Gesamtlänge *f*, Länge über alles

~ mix(ture) → mixed grains

~ number, overall ~, total ~ · Gesamtanzahl *f*

(~ of) broken concrete, concrete hardcore, crushed concrete · Betonpacklage *f*, Betonschotter *m*, Kleinschlag *m* aus Beton(brocken), Betonsteinschlag

~ particle → construction ~ ~

~ producer → construction ~ ~

~ reinforcement area → total steel ~

~ reinforcing area → total steel ~

~ steel area → total ~ ~

~ test, rock ~ · Gesteinsprobe *f*, Gesteinsprüfung *f*, Gesteinsversuch *m*

~ thickness, total ~, overall ~ · Gesamtdicke *f*

~ volume of construction, total ~ ~ ~, overall ~ ~ ~ · Gesamtbauvolumen *n*

~ width, overall ~, total ~ · Gesamtbreite *f*, Breite über alles

aggregates → construction ~

aggressive · aggressiv, angreifend

~ matter, ~ substance, deleterious ~ · Schadstoff *m*, angreifender Stoff, schädlicher Stoff

~ power → attacking ~

~ salt, deleterious ~ · angreifendes Salz *n*, aggressives ~, schädliches ~, Schadsalz

~ substance, deleterious ~, ~ matter Schadstoff *m*, angreifender Stoff, schädlicher Stoff

~ to(ward) building material(s), ~ ~ structural ~, ~ ~ construction(al) ~ · baustoffschädlich, baustoffaggressiv, baustoffangreifend

~ ~ concrete · betonaggressiv, betonschädlich, betonangreifend [*DIN 4030*]

~ ~ construction(al) material(s), ~ ~ building ~, ~ ~ structural ~ baustoffschädlich, baustoffaggressiv, baustoffangreifend

~ ~ groundwater · grundwasserangreifend, grundwasserschädlich, grundwasseraggressiv

~ ~ metal(s) · metallschädlich, metallaggressiv, metallangreifend

~ ~ steel · stahlangreifend, stahlschädlich, stahlaggressiv

~ ~ structural material(s), ~ ~ building ~, ~ ~ construction(al) ~ · baustoffschädlich, baustoffaggressiv, baustoffangreifend

~ water, deleterious ~ · aggressives Wasser *n*, angreifendes ~, schädliches ~, Schadwasser

aging, ageing · Alterung *f*

agitating, agitation, stirring · Auflockern *n* [*Masse durch Rühren*]

~, agitation, stirring · Rühren *n*, Nachmischen [*Transportbeton*]

agitation, agitating, stirring · Auflockern *n* [*Masse durch Rühren*]

~, agitating, stirring · Nachmischen *n*, Rühren [*Transportbeton*]

agitator, stirrer · Rührwerk *n*

agora, market place, town square · Agora *f*, Markt(platz) *m* [*Platz einer griechischen Stadt im Altertum, auf dem Versammlungen und Märkte abgehalten wurden*]

agrément certificate · amtliches Prüfzeugnis *n*

agricultural building, farm ~ · Landwirtschaftsgebäude *n*

~ service building, farm ~ ~ · (landwirtschaftliches) Wirtschaftsgebäude *n*

aid · Hilfe *f*, Hilfsmittel *n*

~ · Hilfsstoff *m*

air and air-conditioning equipment → vent(ilation) ~ ~ ~

~ bar → ~ distribution ~

~ **bell** · Luftblase f [*Fehler im optischen Glas*]

(air-)blowing, air-rectification, oxidizing · Blasen n [*(Erdöl)Bitumen*]

air blowing, ~ refining, converting (with air), purifying (with air) · Windfrischen n [*Stahlerzeugung*]

air-blowing installation → blowing ~

air-blown (asphaltic) bitumen, air-rectified (~) ~, oxidized (~) ~ (Brit.); ~ asphalt (US) · oxidiertes Bitumen n, geblasenes ~, Industriebitumen [*Geblasene Bitumen sind die durch Einblasen von Luft in geschmolzene, weiche Bitumen hergestellten hochschmelzenden Bitumen mit ausgeprägten plastischen und elastischen Eigenschaften*]

~ **mortar**, sprayed ~, shotcrete, pneumatically applied mortar [*Mortar conveyed through a hose and projected at high velocity onto a surface*] · Spritzmörtel m, Gebläsemörtel

~ **steel**, air refined ~ · Windfrischstahl m

airborne dust · Flugstaub m, Schwebestaub

~ **noise** · Luftlärm m

~ **sound** · Luftschall m [*Sich in der Luft ausbreitender Schall*]

~ ~ **insulation** · Luftschall(ab)dämmung f

~ ~ ~ · Luftschallschutz m

~ ~ ~ **material** · Luftschall(ab)dämmstoff m

~ ~ **intensity** · Luftschallstärke f

~ ~ **level** · Luftschallpegel m

~ ~ **reduction index** (Brit.); ~ ~ transmission loss (US); ~ ~ reduction factor [*deprecated*] [*See remark under 'Schalldämmaß'*] · Luftschalldämmaß n, Luftschalldämmzahl f, Luftschallschutzmaß, LSM

~ ~ **transmission** · Luftschallübertragung f

~ ~ **wave** · Luftschallwelle f

air-break contactor · Luftschütz m

air brick → vent(ilat)ing ~

~ **brush** → (paint) spray gun

~ **capacity**, air-handling ~ · Luftleistung f

~ **capping** → vent(ilat)ing ~

~ **carbon dioxide** (Brit.); ~ ~ dioxid(e) (US) · Luftkohlensäure f

~ **cavity** · Lufthohlraum m

~ ~ → ~-handling ~

~ **ceiling** → ~-handling ~

~ ~ **board** → vent(ilat)ing ~ ~

~ ~ **sheet** → vent(ilat)ing ceiling board

~ ~ **system** → vent(ilat)ing ~ ~

~ **change**, change of air · Luftwechsel m

~ **circulation** · Luftführung f

~ ~ · Luftumschichtung f, Luftumwälzung

~ **cleaner**, ~ purifier, ~ cleaning unit, ~ purifying unit · Luftreiniger m

~ **cleaning unit**, ~ purifying ~, ~ purifier, ~ cleaner · Luftreiniger m

~ **cleanliness**, ~ purity · Luftreinheit f

to (air-)condition · klimaregeln, klimatisieren

(air-)conditioned · klimageregelt, klimatisiert

~ **ceiling** · Klimadecke f

~ **duct** · Klimakanal m

~ **space** · klimageregelter Raum m, klimatisierter ~

air conditioner, room ~ ~, unit (~) ~, (~) conditioning unit, terminal unit · Klima(tisierungs)gerät n

(~) conditioning [*The simultaneous control of all, or at least the first three, of those factors affecting both the physical and chemical conditions of the atmosphere within any structure. These factors include temperature, humidity, motion, distribution, dust, bacteria, odo(u)r, and toxic gases*] · Klimaregelung f, Klimatisierung

(~) conditioning duct · Klima(tisierungs)kanal m

(~) ~ ~ shaft · Klima(tisierungs)kanalschacht m

air-conditioning engineering · Klimatechnik f

air conditioning equipment room · Klimaanlagenraum m

(~) ~ installation → central (air) conditioning plant

(~) ~ plant → central (~) ~ ~

(~) ~ station → central (air) conditioning plant

(~) ~ sub-station · Klimastation f

(~) ~ system, (~) ~ plant, (~) ~ installation · Klima(tisierungs)anlage f [*DIN 1946*]

(~) ~ pipe · Klimaanlagenrohr n

(~) ~ tower · Klimaanlagenturm m

(~) ~ unit → ~ conditioner

(~) ~ zone · Klimatisierungszone f

~ **connection** → ~-handling ~

~ **content** · Luftanteil m, Luftgehalt m

air-cooled slag → crushed ~

air cooler · Luftkühler m

~ **cooling** · Luftkühlung f

aircraft hangar [*R.A.F. term*]; aeroplane ~ (Brit.); airplane ~ (US) · Flugzeughalle f

~ ~ **door** · Flugzeughallentor n

~ **maintenance hangar**, technical (aircraft) ~ · (Flugzeug)Wartungshalle f, (Flugzeug)Werfthalle

~ **parking hangar** · Flugzeugabstellhalle f

air-cured · luftgehärtet [*Betonstein*]

air current · Luftstrom m

~ **curtain** → warm-~ ~

air curtain (door(way)) — air flue 34

~ ~ (door(way)) · (Warm)Lufttür f

~ ~ (~) installation → warm-~ ~ (~) ~

~ ~ (~) unit → (warm-)air curtain (door(way)) installation

~ cushion · Luftpolster n [*Österreich: m*]

~ deflector · Luftlenkeinrichtung f [*Diffusor*]

~ demand, ~ requirement · Luftbedarf m

air-detraining agent, air-reducing ~ · Luftporenminderer m

air diffusing ceiling suspension system · Luftverteilungsdeckensystem n

~ diffusor (Brit.); ~ diffuser (US) · Luftdiffusor m

~ discharge · Einblasen n der Luft [*Diffusor*]

~ distribution · Luftverteilung f

~ (~) bar, air-handling ~ ~, vent(-ilation) ~ ~, vent(ilat)ing ~ ~ · (Be- und Ent)Lüftungsschiene f

air-distribution line · Luftverteilungsleitung f

~ system · Luftverteilungsanlage f, Luftverteilungssystem n

air ditch, light ~ · Lichtgraben m

(~) draft (US) → (~) draught (Brit.)

~ drain, ~ supply duct · Zuluftkanal m [*Zur Zuführung frischer Luft für Fundamentmauerwerk, für Holzbauteile oder zu einer Feuerstelle*]

(~) draught (Brit.); (~) draft (US) · Luftzug m

air-dried, sun-dried, sunbaked, a.d. · luftgetrocknet [*Lehmstein*]

~ brick → mud ~

air-dry · lufttrocken

~ density · Betonrohdichte f lufttrocken

~ sand casting · Naßguß m [*Sandguß von Stahlguß oder Gußeisen. Die Form wird in nur lufttrockenem Zustand verwendet*]

air drying [*The drying process takes place during exposure to air at normal temperatures*] · Lufttrocknen n, Lufttrocknung f

air-drying · lufttrocknend

~ (clear) varnish · Luft(klar)lack m

~ varnish · Luftlack m

air duct → vent(ilation) ~

(~) ~ design · (Luft)Kanalbemessung f

~ ~ riser → warm-~ ~ ~

~ ducting → vent(ilation) ~

air-entrained concrete, air-entraining ~, air entrainment ~ · AEA-Beton m, belüfteter Beton, Luftporenbeton, Bläschenbeton

~ light(weight) concrete, air-entraining ~ ~, air-entrainment ~ ~ · Luftporenleichtbeton m, AEA-Leichtbeton, belüfteter Leichtbeton, Bläschenleichtbeton

~ mortar → air-entraining ~

air entrainer, air-entraining agent · Luftporenbildner m, Lufteinschlußmittel n, LP-(Zusatz)Stoff m, LP-Wirkstoff, Belüfter, Belüftungsmittel

~ ~ for concrete → air-entraining agent ~ ~

~ entraining [*The capability of a material or process to develop a system of minute bubbles of air in cement paste, mortar, or concrete*] · Lufteinführungsvermögen n

air-entraining · lufteinführend, luftporenbildend

~ agent, air entrainer · Luftporenbildner m, Lufteinschlußmittel n, LP-(Zusatz-)Stoff m, LP-Wirkstoff, Belüfter, Belüftungsmittel

~ ~ for concrete, air entrainer ~ ~ · Betonbelüfter m, Betonbelüftungsmittel n, luftporenbildender Betonwirkstoff m, Beton-Luftporenbildner, Beton-Lufteinschlußmittel, Beton-LP-(Zusatz)Stoff, Beton-LP-Wirkstoff

~ ~ ~ mortar, air entrainer ~ ~ · Mörtelbelüfter m, Mörtelbelüftungsmittel n

~ concrete → air-entrained ~

~ (hydraulic) cement · Luftporenzement m, L.P.-Zement

~ light(weight) concrete → air-entrained ~ ~

~ mortar, air-entrained ~, air entrainment ~ · AEA-Mörtel m, belüfteter Mörtel, Luftporenmörtel, Bläschenmörtel

~ solution · Luftporenbildnerlösung f

~ workability agent · luftporenbildender (Beton)Verflüssiger m, lufteinführender ~, LBV-(Zusatz)Stoff m, LBV-Wirkstoff, LBV-Zusatz(mittel) m, (n), LPV

air entrainment · entrainment of air

~ ~ concrete → air-entrained ~

~ ~ light(weight) concrete → air-entrained ~ ~

(~) (~) meter → concrete (~) (~) ~

~ ~ mortar → air-entraining ~

~ equipment → vent(ilation) ~

air-filled cell · Luftzelle f

air fixture → air(-handling) (luminaire) (~)

~ floor heating, floor heating by air · Luft(fuß)boden(be)heizung f [*Die Warmluft wird durch einen Hohlraum unter den (Fuß)Boden geleitet. Im (Fuß)Boden befindet sich keine Wärmespeicherung*]

~ flue [*A small duct, built to withdraw bad air from a room*] · Raum-Luftkanal m

~ **for combustion** [*The amount of air required for safe and proper combustion at the altitude of (name of municipality)*] · erforderliche Luftmenge *f* für vollkommene Verbrennung

~ **freight building** · Luftfrachthalle *f*

~ **furnace**, warm-~ ~ · (Warm)Luftofen *m*, Luftheizofen

~ **gap**, ~ **space** · Luftspalt *m*

~ **glass block** → vent(ilat)ing ~ ~

~ ~ **brick** → vent(ilat)ing glass block

~ **grating** · (Warm)Luftgitter *n* [*Lufttür*]

~ **grille** → ~-handling ~

~ **gun**, compressed-~ ~, pneumatic ~ · Druckluft(spritz)pistole *f*, Preßluft(spritz)pistole, Druckluftspritze *f*, Preßluftspritze

air-handling → ventilation

air(-handling) and air-conditioning equipment → vent(ilation) ~ ~ ~

air-handling area, vent(ilation) ~, vent(ilat)ing ~ · (Be- und Ent)Lüftungsfläche *f*

air(-handling) bar → air (distribution) ~

~ **block** → vent(ilat)ing ~

~ **brick** → vent(ilat)ing ~

~ **capacity** · Luftleistung *f*

~ **capping** → vent(ilat)ing ~

~ **cavity**, vent(ilation) ~, vent(ilat)ing ~ · (Be- und Ent)Lüftungsschlitz *m*, Luftschlitz

~ **ceiling** → vent(ilat)ing ~

~ ~ **board** → vent(ilat)ing ~ ~

~ ~ **sheet** → vent(ilat)ing ceiling board

~ ~ **system** → vent(ilat)ing ~ ~

~ **connection**, vent(ilation) ~, vent(ilat)ing ~ · (Be- und Ent)Lüftungsanschluß *m*, Luftanschluß

~ **duct** → vent(ilation) ~

~ **ducting** → vent(ilation) ~

~ **equipment** → vent(ilation) ~

~ **fixture** → ~ luminaire (~)

~ **glass block** → vent(ilat)ing ~ ~

~ ~ **brick** → vent(ilat)ing glass block

~ **grille**, vent(ilat)ing ~, vent(ilation) ~ [*Sometimes spelled 'grill'*] · (Be- und Ent)Lüftungsgitter *n*

~ **installation** → vent(ilation) system

~ **lay-in ceiling** → vent(ilat)ing ~ ~

~ **light fitting** (Brit.) → ~ luminaire (fixture)

~ **(light(ing)) fixture** → ~ luminaire (~)

~ **line**, vent(ilat)ing ~, vent(ilation) ~ · (Be- und Ent)Lüftungsleitung *f*

~ **luminaire (fixture)**, vent(ilat)ing ~ (~), vent(ilation) ~ (~) (US); light fitting (Brit.); ~ (light(ing)) fixture · (Be- und Ent)Lüftungsleuchte *f*

~ **opening**, vent(ilat)ing ~, vent(ilation) ~, ventilator · (Be- und Ent)Lüftungsöffnung *f*, Luftöffnung

~ **panel**, vent(ilat)ing ~, vent(ilation) ~ · (Be- und Ent)Lüftungstafel *f*

~ **piece**, vent(ilat)ing ~, vent(ilation) ~ · (Be- und Ent)Lüftungsstück *n*

~ **pipe**, vent(ilation) ~, vent(ilat)ing ~ · (Be- und Ent)Lüftungsrohr *n*, Luftrohr

~ **(~) tray** → vent(ilat)ing (~) ~

~ **plant** → vent(ilation) system

~ ~ **room**, vent(ilation) ~ ~, vent(ilat)ing ~ ~ · (Be- und Ent)Lüftungsanlagenraum *m*

air-handling position, vent(ilation) ~, vent(ilat)ing ~ · (Be- und Ent)Lüftungsstellung *f*

air(-handling) ridge, vent(ilat)ing ~, vent(ilation) ~ · (Be- und Ent)Lüftungsfirst *m*

~ **shaft** → vent(ilating) ~

~ **sliding window**, vent(ilation) ~ ~, vent(ilat)ing ~ ~ · (Be- und Ent-)Lüftungsschiebefenster *n*

~ **stack** → vent(ilation) ~

~ **station** → vent(ilat)ing ~

~ **stave**, vent(ilation) ~, vent(ilat)ing ~ · (Be- und Ent)Lüftungsdaube *f*, Luftdaube [*Betonsilo*]

~ **system** → vent(ilation) ~

~ **tray** → vent(ilat)ing (pipe) ~

~ **window**, vent(ilat)ing ~, vent(ilation) ~ · (Be- und Ent)Lüftungsfenster *n*

air-hardenable · lufthärtbar [*Legierung*]

air hardened block, ~ **tile** [*See remark under 'Block'*] · Mörtelblock(stein) *m*, Mörtelstein [*Lufterhärteter Mauerstein, gebunden mit Kalk, Gips oder Magnesit. Er hat geringe Festigkeit und Tragfähigkeit*]

air-hardening · luft(er)härtend

air heat · Luftwärme *f*

~ **heater**, ~ **heating unit**, **unit heater**, **plenum heater**, **plenum heating unit** · (Warm)Lufterhitzer *m*, (Warm)Luftheizgerät *n*, (Warm)Luftheizer, Warmlufterzeuger

~ **heating**, **plenum** ~ · Luft(be)heizung *f* [*Warmluft wird mit oder ohne Ventilator in die zu beheizenden Räume geführt*]

~ ~ · Lufterwärmung *f*

~ ~ **installation** → warm-~ ~ ~

~ ~ **plant** → warm-~ ~ ~

~ ~ **system** → warm-~ ~ ~

~ ~ **unit** → ~ heater

~ **hole**, ~ **vent**, **port** · Luftloch *n*, Zugloch

~ **humidification** · Luftanfeuchtung *f*, Luftbefeuchtung

(~) humidifier · (Luft)Anfeuchter *m*, (Luft)Befeuchter

air humidity — air right

~ **humidity,** ~ moisture · Luftfeuchte *f,* Luftfeuchtigkeit *f*

~ ~ **comfort curve,** ~ moisture ~ ~ · Luftfeuchte-Behaglichkeitskurve *f*

~ **infiltration** · Luftinfiltration *f*

air-inflated building, ~ structure, inflatable ~, air-supported ~ · Pneusystem *n,* luftgetragene Halle *f,* luftgestützte Halle, Traglufthalle, luftgestütztes System

~ **structure,** ~ building, inflatable ~, air-supported ~ · Pneusystem *n,* luftgetragene Halle *f,* luftgestützte Halle, Traglufthalle, luftgestütztes System

air inlet · Lufteinlaß *m*

~ ~ **chimney,** ~ intake ~ · Belüftungsschornstein *m*

~ ~ **pipe,** ~ intake ~ · Belüftungsrohr *n*

~ ~ **shaft,** ~ intake ~ · Belüftungsschacht *m*

~ ~ **stack** → (natural) (fresh-)air ~ ~

~ ~ **tower** → (natural) (fresh-)air ~ ~

~ **input,** aeration · Luftzufuhr *f,* Luftzuführung *f,* Belüften *n,* Belüftung

~ **installation** → vent(ilation) system

~ **insulation** · Luftisolierung *f*

~ **intake chimney,** ~ inlet ~ · Belüftungsschornstein *m*

~ ~ **pipe,** ~ inlet ~ · Belüftungsrohr *n*

~ ~ **shaft,** ~ inlet ~ · Belüftungsschacht *m*

~ ~ **stack** → (natural) (fresh-)air inlet ~

~ ~ **tower** → (natural) (fresh-)air inlet ~

~ **lay-in ceiling** → vent(ilat)ing ~ ~

airless paint spraying · (druck)luftloses Farbspritzen *n*

air light fitting (Brit.) → air(-handling) luminaire (fixture)

~ **line,** ~-handling ~, vent(ilation) ~, vent(ilat)ing ~ · (Be- und Ent)Lüftungsleitung *f*

~ ~, compressed-~ ~ · Druckluftleitung *f,* Preßluftleitung

~ **lock** · Luftschleuse *f*

~ **luminaire (fixture)** → ~-handling ~ (~)

~ **moisture,** ~ humidity · Luftfeuchte *f,* Luftfeuchtigkeit *f*

~ ~ **comfort curve,** ~ humidity ~ ~ · Luftfeuchte-Behaglichkeitskurve *f*

~ **motion,** ~ movement · Luftbewegung *f*

~ **opening** → vent(ilation) ~

~ **outlet** · Luftauslaß *m*

~ ~ → warm-~ ~

~ **output,** warm-~ ~, heated air ~ · Warmluftleistung *f*

~ **panel** → ~-handling ~

~ **passage** · Luftkanal *m* [*Pyramide*]

~ **patenting,** O.P. ~, old process ~ · Luftpatentieren *n*

~ **permeability test** [*A method for measuring the fineness of powdered materials such as portland cement*] · Luftdurchlässigkeitsverfahren *n*

~ **piece** → ~-handling ~

~ **pipe** → ~-handling ~

~ **(~) tray** → ~-handling (~) ~

air-placed concrete, pneumatically placed ~ · druckluftgeförderter Beton *m,* preßluftgeförderter ~

airplane hangar (US); aeroplane ~ (Brit.); aircraft ~ [*R.A.F. term*] · Flugzeughalle *f*

air plant → vent(ilation) system

~ ~ **room** → ~-handling ~ ~

~ **pocket** [*An air space which accidentally occurs in concrete work*] · Luftnest *n*

~ **pollution** · Luftverunreinigung *f,* Luftverschmutzung

~ **preheater** · Luftvorwärmer *m,* Luvo

~ **purification** · Luftreinigung *f*

~ **purifier,** ~ cleaner, ~ purifying unit, ~ cleaning unit · Luftreiniger *m*

~ **purifying unit,** ~ cleaning ~, ~ purifier, ~ cleaner · Luftreiniger *m*

~ **purity,** ~ cleanliness · Luftreinheit *f*

~ **quantity,** ~ volume · Luftmenge *f*

air-raid shelter, bomb ~ · Bombenschutzraum *m,* LS-Raum, (Luft)Schutzraum, LSR

~ ~ **door,** bomb ~ ~ · (Luft)Schutztür *f*

~ **shelter-garage,** bomb ~ · Schutzraum *m* mit Garage, Luft-~ ~ ~, Bomben-~ ~ ~, LS-Raum ~ ~

~ **sheltering bunker,** bomb shelter · (Luft)Schutzbunker *m,* Bombenschutzbunker

~ **siren** · Luftschutzsirene *f*

air-rectification, oxidizing, (air-)blowing · Blasen *n* [*(Erdöl)Bitumen*]

~ **installation** → blowing ~

air-rectified (asphaltic) bitumen, air-blown (~) ~, oxidized (~) ~ (Brit.); ~ asphalt (US) · oxidiertes Bitumen *n,* geblasenes ~, Industriebitumen [*Geblasene Bitumen sind die durch Einblasen von Luft in geschmolzene, weiche Bitumen hergestellten hochschmelzenden Bitumen mit ausgeprägten plastischen und elastischen Eigenschaften*]

air-reducing agent, air-detraining ~ · Luftporenminderer *m*

air refined steel, ~ blown ~ · Windfrischstahl *m*

~ **refining,** ~ blowing, converting (with air), purifying (with air) · Windfrischen *n* [*Stahlerzeugung*]

~ **requirement,** ~ demand · Luftbedarf *m*

~ **ridge** → ~-handling ~

~ **right** · Luftrecht *n* [*Es regelt die Überbauung von Eisenbahnen, Straßen, Strömen, usw.*]

air rising duct — aisle roof

~ **rising duct** → warm-~ ~ ~
air-separated cement · Windsichterzement *m*
air-setting · luftabbindend
~ **mortar,** non-hydraulic ~ · Luftmörtel *m*
~ ~ **cementing agent,** nonhydraulic ~ ~ ~ · mechanischer Mörtelstoff *m*
air shaft → vent(ilating) ~
~ ~, light well · Lichtschacht *m*
airship hangar · Luftschiffhalle *f*
air shutter [*An adjustable device for varying the effective opening of the air inlet(s)*] · Luftklappe *f*
~ **siltometer** [*An appliance in which an air current separates the particles of a sample of sediment into different sizes and measures the weight or volume of the different grades so separated*] · Kornverteilungsmesser *m*
air-slaked · luftgelöscht [*Kalk*]
~ **(quick)lime;** pulverized ~ (US); pulverised ~ (Brit.) · Staubkalk *m*, luftgelöschter Kalk, Pulverkalk
air slaking · Luftlöschen *n*
~ **sliding door drive,** compressed-~ ~ ~ ~, pneumatic ~ ~ ~ · Druckluft-Schiebetürantrieb *m*, Preßluft-Schiebetürantrieb, pneumatischer Schiebetürantrieb
~ ~ **window** → ~-handling ~ ~
~ **space,** cavity [*A cavity or space in walls or between various structural elements*] · Luft(zwischen)raum *m*, Luftschicht *f*
~ ~, ~ gap · Luftspalt *m*
~ **spectrography** [*Spectrographic identification of elements in a sample of material, heated to volatilization in an electric arc or spark*] · spektralanalytisches Verfahren *n*, spektralanalytische Methode *f*
~ **stack** → vent(ilation) ~
~ **stagnation** · Luftstille *f*
~ **station** → vent(ilat)ing ~
~ **stave** → ~-handling ~
~ **sterilization** · Luftsterilisation *f*
~ **storage** · Luftlagerung *f* [*Probe(-körper)*]
~ **supply duct,** ~ drain · Zuluftkanal *m* [*Zur Zuführung frischer Luft für Fundamentmauerwerk, für Holzbauteile oder zu einer Feuerstelle*]
~ ~ **panel,** perforated (floor) ~ · Lochtafel *f* [*Doppel(fuß)boden*]
~ ~ **system** · Zuluftanlage *f*
air-supported building, inflatable ~, air-inflated ~, ~ structure, pneumatic ~ · Pneusystem *n*, luftgetragene Halle *f*, luftgestützte Halle, Traglufthalle, luftgestütztes System
air system → vent(ilation) ~

~ **temperature gradient** · Lufttemperaturgefälle *n*
~ ~ **rise** · Lufttemperaturanstieg *m*
~ **termination network** · Dachleitungen *fpl* [*Blitzschutzanlage*]
airtight · luftdicht, luftundurchlässig
~ **seal** · luftdichter Abschluß *m*, luftundurchlässiger ~
air tightness · Luftundurchlässigkeit *f*
~ **tray** → ~-handling ~
~ **treatment** · Luftbehandlung *f*
~ ~ **plant** · Luftbehandlungsanlage *f*
~ **tube installation** → pneumatic ~ ~
~ ~ **system** → pneumatic tube installation
~ **tubes** → pneumatic tube installation
~ **velocity** · Luftgeschwindigkeit *f*
~ **vent,** ~ hole, port · Zugloch *n*, Luftloch
~ **vitiation** · Luftverschlechterung *f*
~ **void** · Luftpore *f*
air-void spacing · Luftporenverteilung *f*
~ **system,** system of air voids · Luftporensystem *n*
air volume, ~ quantity · Luftmenge *f*
~ **washer** · Luftwäscher *m*
airway → vent(ilation) duct
~ [*A space between roof insulation and roof boards for movement of air*] · Luftzirkulationsraum *m*
airways → vent(ilation) ducting
air window → ~ -handling ~
Airy's stress function · Airysche Spannungsfunktion *f* [*Eine nach dem Mathematiker Sir George Bidel Airy (1801–1892) benannte skalare Ortsfunktion*]
aisle, side ~, nave ~ [*A lateral division parallel with the nave in a basilica or church*] · Abseite *f*, (Seiten)Schiff *n*
~, lane, traffic ~ · Fahrgasse *f* [*Parkhaus; Tiefgarage*]
~ [*A passage in an auditorium sometimes between or beside seats and sometimes separated from the auditorium proper by a row of columns*] · (Zuschauerraum)Gang *m*
~ **bay,** side ~ ~, nave ~ ~ · (Seiten-)Schiffjoch(feld) *n*, Abseitenjoch(feld), (Seiten)Schiffeld, Abseitenfeld
aisled · mit (Seiten)Schiff(en) (versehen), ~ Abseite(n) (~)
~ **church** · Abseitenkirche *f*, (Seiten-)Schiffkirche
~ **hall,** principal building, main building · Langhaus *n*
aisle gallery → side ~ ~
aisleless → side ~
~ **church** → side ~ ~
aisle passage → side ~ ~
~ **pier,** side ~ ~, nave ~ ~ · (Seiten-)Schiffpfeiler *m*, Abseitenpfeiler
~ **roof** → side ~ ~

aisle-vault — alkali content

aisle-vault, side ~, nave ~ · (Seiten-) Schiffgewölbe n, Abseitengewölbe
aisle wall → side ~ ~
~ (~) window → side ~ (~) ~
Aix-la-Chapelle cathedral · Palastkapelle f zu Aachen, Kaiserkapelle ~ ~, Pfalzkapelle ~ ~
alabaster [*A fine(-grain(ed)) compact white or pale-colo(u)red variety of gypsum (hydrated calcium sulphate)*] · Alabaster(gips) m
~, calcareous ~, Mexican onyx, onyx marble [*A carbonate of lime*] · Kalkonyx m, Onyx(marmor) m, Kalkalabaster m
~ glass [*Translucent glass resembling the mineral alabaster*] · Alabasterglas n
alarm bell, call ~ · Alarmklingel f
~ light, warning ~, WL · Warnleuchte f, Warnlampe f, Warnlicht n, optisches Warnsignal n
~ siren · Alarmsirene f
~ system · Alarmanlage f, Raumschutzanlage
alarm-wire luminated safety glass · Alarmdraht-Verbund(-Sicherheits)glas n, Alarmdraht-Mehrscheiben(sicherheits)glas, Alarmdraht-Mehrschichten-(sicherheits)glas, Alarmdraht-Mehrfachglas, luminiertes Alarmdraht-Sicherheitsglas
Alberca court, Court of Alberca · Hof m der Alberca, ~ ~ Bäder, Myrthenhof [*Alhambra*]
albino asphalt (US); ~ asphaltic bitumen (Brit.) · Albinobitumen n, helles Bitumen, Weißbitumen
albite · Albit-Chloritschiefer m
albumen → serum albumin
albumin adhesive → (blood) albumin glue
~ glue → blood ~ ~
alcazar · Alkazar m
alcohol fastness, ~ resistance, resistance to alcohol, fastness to alcohol · Alkoholbeständigkeit f, Alkoholfestigkeit, Alkoholechtheit, Alkoholwiderstand m
~ resistance, ~ fastness, resistance to alcohol, fastness to alcohol · Alkoholbeständigkeit f, Alkoholfestigkeit, Alkoholechtheit, Alkoholwiderstand m
~ solution · Alkohollösung f
~ with four alcoholic groups · vierwertiger Alkohol m
~ ~ three alcoholic groups · dreiwertiger Alkohol m
alcosol · Alkosol n [*kolloidale Lösung in Alkohol*]
alcove [*A large recess in a room (extending to the floor as distinct from a niche), usually vaulted, and originally the place for the bed. Alcoves were also formed in garden walls, pavilions, etc., and even in hedges in many of the gardens of eighteenth-century houses in Great Britain*] · Alkoven m; Nebengemach n

aldehyde resin · Aldehydharz n
Alexandrinum work, opus Alexandrinum · Opus Alexandrinum n [*Ornamentales Fußbodenmosaik aus farbigen, zu geometrischen Mustern geordneten Marmorsteinen, besonders in Verbindung von Mosaik und Opus sectile*]
alfa fiber (US) → halfa ~
alga · Alge f
algae control · Algenbekämpfung f, Algenvernichtung
~ growth · Algenwachstum n, Algenwuchs m
algaecide, algicide · Algenbekämpfungsmittel n, Algenvernichtungsmittel, Algengift n
algicide, algaecide · Algenbekämpfungsmittel n, Algenvernichtungsmittel, Algengift n
alien structure · störendes Bauwerk n
alignment (Brit.); alinement (US); stone row [*A megalithic monument*] · Steinreihe f
~ chart (Brit.) → nomograph
A-line, influence line of reactions · Einflußlinie f der Auflagerkraft, A-Linie
alinement (US); alignment (Brit.); stone row [*A megalithic monument*] · Steinreihe f
~ chart (US) → nomograph
aliphatic · aliphatisch
~ compound · aliphatische Verbindung f
~ hydrocarbon · aliphatischer Kohlenwasserstoff m
alite [*A term given by Tornebohm in 1897 to the principal constituent of portland cement, later identified as* C_3S] · Alit m
~ cement · Alitzement m
alive · stromdurchflossen [*Leitung*]
alizarin(e) dyestuff · Alizarin(farbstoff) n, (m), Krappfarbstoff
~ lake · Alizarin(farblack) n, (m)
~ pigment · Alizarinpigment n
alkali · Alkali n
~ ag(e)ing · Alkalialterung f
alkali-aggregate expansion inhibitor, ~ reaction ~ · Schutzmittel n gegen alkaliempfindliche (Beton)Zuschlagstoffe, ~ ~ ~ (Beton)Zuschläge
~ reaction, ~ expansion · alkalische Reaktion f der (Beton)Zuschläge mit dem Zement [*Umsetzung zwischen reaktionsfähiger Kieselsäure der Zuschlagstoffe und dem Alkali des Zementes*]
alkali basalt · Alkalibasalt m
~ blue · Alkaliblau n
~ cellulose · Alkalizellulose f [*Vorprodukt bei der Herstellung von Regeneratfaserstoffen nach dem Viskoseverfahren. Sie entsteht durch Einwirkung von Natronlauge auf den Holzzellstoff*]
~ cleanser → alkali(ne) ~
~ content · Alkalianteil m, Alkaligehalt m

alkali detergent — (all) clay visible under-face

~ **detergent** → alkali(ne) cleanser
~ **elimination** · Alkalibeseitigung f
~ **expansion** · Alkalitreiben n
~ **fastness,** ~ resistance, resistance to alkali(s), fastness to alkali(s) · Alkali(en)festigkeit f, Alkali(en)widerstand m, Alkali(en)beständigkeit, Alkali(en)echtheit
~ **fel(d)spar** · Alkalifeldspat m
~ **fluorid(e)** (US); ~ fluoride (Brit.) · Alkalifluorid n
alkali-granite · Alkaligranit m
(alkali) reactive material in concrete, (~) ~ aggregate · alkaliempfindlicher (Beton)Zuschlag(stoff) m
~ **reactivity** · Alkaliempfindlichkeit f
~ **resistance,** ~ fastness, resistance to alkali(s), fastness to alkali(s) · Alkali(en)festigkeit f, Alkali(en)widerstand m, Alkali(en)beständigkeit, Alkali(en)echtheit
~ **resistant,** resistant to alkali(s), alkali-resisting · alkali(en)beständig, alkali(en)fest, alkali(en)widerstandsfähig, alkali(en)echt
~ **resisting varnish** · alkalibeständiger Lack m
~ **rock** · Alkaligestein n
alkali-soluble · alkalilöslich
alkali syenite · Alkalisyenit m
alkaline · alkalisch, laugensalzig
~ **action** · alkalische Wirkung f
~ **activation** · alkalische Anregung f
~ **bath** [*electro-galvanizing*] · alkalisches Bad n
~ **casein** · Alkali-Kasein n
alkali(ne) cleanser, ~ detergent · alkalisches Reinigungsmittel n, alkalischer Reiniger m
alkaline deposit · aklalische Ablagerung f
alkali(ne) detergent, ~ cleanser · alkalisches Reinigungsmittel n, alkalischer Reiniger m
alkaline earth [*Alkali(ne) earths are a group of chemical elements comprising calcium, strontium, barium and sometimes, beryllium, magnesium and radium*] · Alkalierde f, alkalische Erde, Erdalkalle f, Erdalkalimetall n
alkali(ne) metal · Alkalimetall n, alkalisches Metall
~ **(paint) remover,** ~ (~) stripper · alkalisches Abbeizmittel n, ablaugendes ~, Ablaugmittel
~ **(~) stripper,** ~ (~) remover · alkalisches Abbeizmittel n, ablaugendes ~, Ablaugmittel
~ **phase** · Alkaliphase f
~ **remover,** ~ stripper, ~ paint ~ · alkalisches Abbeizmittel n, ablaugendes ~, Ablaugmittel
~ **salt** · Alkalisalz n, alkalisches Salz

~ **solution** · Alkalilösung f alkalische Lösung
~ **solvent** · alkalisches Lösungsmittel n
~ **stripper,** ~ remover, ~ paint ~ · alkalisches Abbeizmittel n, ablaugendes ~, Ablaugmittel
alkalinity · Alkali(ni)tät f
to alkoxylate · veräthern
alkyd-modified · alkydmodifiziert
alkyd oil, very long ~ · Alkydöl n, abgewandeltes Standöl
~ **resin** · Alkydharz n
alkyd(-resin) base · Alkydharzgrundlage f, Alkydharzbasis f
~ **(clear) varnish** · Kunstharzlack m auf Alkydharzbasis, schlagfester (Emaille-) Lack, Schlagfestlack, Alkydharzlack
~ **exterior paint,** ~ external ~, ~ outside ~, ~ outer ~ · Außen-Alkydharz-(anstrich)farbe f
~ **gloss paint** · Alkydharzglanz(anstrich)-farbe f
~ **lacquer,** ~ pigmented varnish · Alkydharzlackfarbe f, pigmentierter Alkydharzklarlack m
~ **medium,** ~ vehicle · Alkydharz-Bindemittellösung f [*Anstrichfarbe*]
~ **paint** · Alkydharz(anstrich)farbe f
~ **pigmented varnish,** ~ lacquer · Alkydharzlackfarbe f, pigmentierter Alkydharzklarlack m
~ **primer** · Alkydharzgrundiermittel n
~ **priming** · Alkydharzgrundierung f
~ **solution** · Alkydharzlösung f
~ **undercoat(er)** · Alkydharzvorlack m
~ **varnish,** ~ clear ~ · Kunstharzlack m auf Alkydharzbasis, schlagfester (Emaille)Lack, Schlagfestlack, Alkydharzlack
~ **vehicle,** ~ medium · Alkydharz-Bindemittellösung f [*Anstrichfarbe*]
alkyl [*A univalent radical of the aliphatic hydrocarbons, obtained by removing one hydrocarbon atom*] · Alkyl n
~ **group** · Alkylgruppe f
all-aluminium building (Brit.); all-aluminum ~ (US) · Ganzalu(minium)gebäude n
~ **door** (Brit.); all-aluminum ~ (US) · Ganzalu(minium)tür f, Vollalu(minium)-tür
~ **wall element** (Brit.); all-aluminum ~ ~ (US) · Ganzalu(minium)-Wandelement n, Vollalu(minium)-Wandelement
all-brick block, ~ building · Ganzziegelgebäude n
~ **building,** ~ block · Ganzziegelgebäude n
(all) clay visible under-face, (~) ~ ~ underside · Ziegeluntersicht f

(all-)concrete soffit — all-purpose girder

(all-)concrete soffit → ~ visible underface

~ visible under-face, ~ ~ underside ~ soffit · Betonuntersicht *f*

all-dry cement mill, ~ ~ plant · Zementfabrik *f* nach dem Trockenverfahren, Zementwerk *n* ~ ~ ~

all-glass (building) unit, ~ (~) member, ~ (~) component · Ganzglas(bau)element *n*, Ganzglas(bau)körper *m*, Ganzglasbauteil *m, n* [*Fehlname: Ganzglasbaueinheit f*]

~ ceiling(-mounted) luminaire (fixture) (US); ~ light fitting (Brit.); ~ (light(ing)) fixture · Nurglas-Deckenleuchte *f*

~ component → ~ (building) unit

~ construction, ~ (structural) system · Ganzglasbausystem *n*, Ganzglas(konstruktions)system, Ganzglaskonstruktion *f*

~ door · Ganzglastür *f*

~ façade · Ganzglasfassade *f*

~ fixture → ~ ceiling(-mounted) luminaire (~)

~ light fitting (Brit.) → ~ ceiling(-mounted) luminaire (fixture)

~ (light(ing)) fixture → ~ ceiling(-mounted) luminaire (~)

~ member → ~ (building) unit

~ skyscraper · Ganzglas-Wolkenkratzer *m*

~ sliding sash · Ganzglas-Schiebe(fenster)flügel *m*

~ (structural) system → ~ construction

~ system → ~ construction

~ thermal insulation, cellular ~ ~ · Zellglasdämmung *f*

~ unit → ~ building ~

~ wall · Ganzglaswand *f*

allied substance · verwandter Stoff *m*

alligatoring, crocodiling · Reißlackierung *f* [*Eine Lackierungsart, bei der bewußt die Rißbildung herbeigeführt wird*]

~, crocodiling · Krakelierung *f*

~ lacquer, crackle ~ · Reißlack *m*, Krakelierlack

all-in-ballast · natürliches ungesiebtes Material *n*, ungesiebtes natürliches ~

all-insulated sheathed cable · berührungssicheres Mantelkabel *n*

~ wiring · berührungssichere Verdrahtung *f*

all-metal block, ~ building · Ganzmetallgebäude *n*

~ building, ~ block · Ganzmetallgebäude *n*

~ façade · Ganzmetallfassade *f*

~ panel · Ganzmetalltafel *f*

~ window · Ganzmetallfenster *n*

allotment(garden) · Laubengarten *m*, Kleingarten, Schrebergarten

allowable, safe, admissible, permissible · zulässig

~ load, admissible ~, permissible ~, safe ~, working ~ · zulässige Last *f*

~ stress, working ~, design ~, safe ~, admissible ~, permissible ~ · Bemessungsspannung *f*, zulässige Spannung

allowance for awkward work → bonus paid for extra-heavy ~

~ ~ extra-heavy work → bonus paid ~ ~ ~

~ ~ impact, impact allowance · Stoßzuschlag *m*

~ ~ length of moment · Überdeckungslänge *f*

~ ~ for moments at support · Deckung *i*der Stützenmomente

alloy layer · Legierungslage *f*, Legierungsschicht *f*

~ reinforcing steel, special ~ ~ · Legierungsbetonstahl *m*, legierter Betonstahl

~ steel, special ~ ~ · legierter Stahl *m*, Legierungsstahl

~ structural steel, special ~ ~ · legierter Baustahl *m*, Legierungsbaustahl

alloying · Legieren *n*

~ addition · Legierungszusatz *m*

~ technique, ~ technic · Legierungstechnik *f*

all-paper laminate, (paper) ~ · (Kunst-)Schichtstoffplatte *f*

all-plastic bearing structure → ~ load-~ ~

~ cold-glaze(d wall coat(ing)) · Kunststoff-Kaltglasur(überzug) *f, (m)*, Kunststoff-Wandkaltglasur(überzug)

~ door · Ganzkunststofftür *f*, Vollkunststofftür

~ (load)bearing structure, ~ (weight-carrying) ~, ~ supporting ~, ~ load-carrying ~, ~ loaded ~ · Ganzkunststofftragwerk *n*, Vollkunststofftragwerk [*Ein materielles System von Kunststoffbauelementen*]

~ sandwich panel · Ganzkunststoff-Dreilagentafel *f*, Ganzkunststoff-Dreischichtentafel, Vollkunststoff-Dreilagentafel, Vollkunststoff-Dreischichtentafel

~ structure → ~ (load)bearing ~

~ supporting structure → ~ (load-)bearing ~

~ (weight-carrying) structure → ~ (load)bearing ~

~ window · Ganzkunststoffenster *n*, Vollkunststoffenster

all-purpose aggregate → ~ concrete ~

~ (concrete) aggregate, ~ construction ~ · Allzweck(beton)zuschlag(stoff) *m*, Allzweck(beton)zuschlagmaterial *n*

~ (construction) aggregate → ~ concrete ~

~ door · Allzwecktür *f*

~ girder · Allzweckträger *m*

all-purpose primer — alternate immersion test

~ **primer** · Universalgrund(ierung) m, (f), Universalgrundiermittel n, Universalgrundanstrichmittel

~ **protective coating (material)** · Universalschutzanstrichmittel n, Universalschutzanstrich(stoff) m

~ **room**, family ~ · Mehrzweckraum m, Vielzweckraum

all-round anchorage · umlaufender Ringanker m [*Hochtief-Estiot-Großtafelbauweise*]

all-steel curtain wall · Ganzstahlvorhangwand f

~ **stair(case)** · Ganzstahltreppe f

all-timber door, all-wood ~ · Ganzholztür f

all-weather coat · Allwetteranstrich m, Allwetteraufstrich

~ **plywood** · Allwettersperrholz n

~ **slatted blind** · Allwetter-Jalousie f

~ **strip** · Allwetterstreifen m

all-welded steel structure · Ganzschweißstahlbauwerk n

all-wet cement plant, ~ ~ mill · Zementfabrik f nach dem Naßverfahren, Zementwerk n ~ ~ ~

all-wood door, all-timber ~ · Ganzholztür f

almery, alms-box, a(u)mbry · Opferkasten m

~ → ambry

almonry (house), elemosinaria, almshouse [*A house were alms were distributed*] · Almosenhaus n

~ **(place)** · Almosenplatz m

~ **(room)** [*In any medieval monastic or other church; a room where alms were distributed*] · Almosenkammer f, Almosenzimmer n

alms-box, almery, a(u)mbry · Opferkasten m

almshouse, poor(s)house [*A house built and endowed for the poor and aged*] · Armenhaus n

Alodine process (US); A.C.P. Alocrom ~ (Brit.) [*U.S.Pat. 2,438,877, Can. Pat. 452,254. F. Spruance, Jr.*] · Alodine-Verfahren n [*Ein chemisches Oxydationsverfahren für die Oberflächenbehandlung von Aluminium auf Chromsäurebasis*]

aloe fibre (Brit.); ~ **fiber** (US) · Aloefaser f

~ **hemp** · Aloehanf m

α-alumina, corundum [*The form of alumina stable at temperatures above about 1,000° C*] · Alpha-Tonerde f, Korund m, α-Tonerde, Al_2O_3

(alpha-)beta brass [*It contains between 36% and 45% zinc*] · Betamessing n, β-Messing

alpha brass [*It is ductile and can be both cold worked without annealing and hot worked*] · Alpha-Messing n, α-Messing

altar baldachino · Altarbaldachin m

~ **ciborium** [*A canopy supported by columns placed over an altar*] · Altarziborium n, Altarciborium

~ **facing** → altar-front(al)

~ **fresco** · Altarfreske f

~ **front(al)**, altar-facing, antependium [*The covering which can be either an ornamental cloth or a painted or carved panel, on the front of an altar*] · (Altar)Antependium n, Frontale f, Altarvorsatz m

Altar of Zeus · Zeusaltar m

~ ~ ~ **at Pergamon** · (Großer) Altar m von Pergamon, Pergamonaltar

altar over sarcophagus · Sarkophagaltar m

~ **piece**, ~ screen, retable, reredos · Retabel n, Altar~, Altaraufsatz m [*Im Deutschen oft nur "Altar" genannt. Eine entweder auf die Mensa des katholischen Altars aufgesetzte, auf einem Zwischenstück (Predella) oder hinter diesem auf einem Unterbau stehende Schauwand, die im Mittelalter aufkam*]

~ **rails** [*Those separating the sacrarium*] · Altarschranken fpl

~ **screen**, ~ piece, retable reredos · Altaraufsatz m, (Altar)Retabel n [*Im Deutschen oft nur "Altar" genannt. Eine entweder auf die Mensa des katholischen Altars aufgesetzte, auf einem Zwischenstück (Predella) oder hinter diesem auf einem Unterbau stehende Schauwand, die im Mittelalter aufkam*]

~ **shrine** · Altarschrein m

~ **slab**, altar-table, superaltar, mensa [*The slab forming the top of an altar*] · Altarplatte f, Mensa f

~ **stair** [*A flight of steps ascending to an altar*] · Altarstufen fpl

~ **step** [*A step ascending to an altar*] · Altarstufe f

~ **stone** · Altarsteinplatte f

~ **table** → altar-slab

~ **tomb** [*A tomb resembling a stone altar*] · Altargrab n

altarlet [*A small altar*] · Altärchen n

to alter · umbauen

alteration, conversion, structural ~ · bauliche Veränderung f, Bauveränderung, Umbau m

~ **work**, conversion ~, structural ~ ~ · Umbauarbeiten fpl

alternate bending strength · Biegewechselfestigkeit f, Wechselbiegefestigkeit

~ **climate** · Wechselklima n

~ **course** · Wechsellage f, Wechselschicht f

~ **folding** · Wechselfaltung f

~ **immersion test** · Wechseltauchversuch m, Wechseltauchprüfung f, Wechseltauchprobe f

alternate loading — aluminium bronze paint　　　　　　　　　　42

~ **loading,** changing ~ · Wechselbelastung f

~ **strength** · Wechselfestigkeit f [DIN 50100]

~ **system** → system with alternating columns and piers

alternating bending test, ~ flexure ~, test by bending in opposite directions, to-and fro bending test, to-and fro flexure test · Hin- und Her-Biegeprüfung f, Hin- und Her-Biegeversuch m, Hin- und Her-Biegeprobe f

~ **component of pressure** · Wechseldruck m [Akustik]

~ **flexure test** → ~ bending ~

~ **interpenetration of space and buildings** · wechselseitige Durchdringung f von Freiraum und Architektur

~ **load,** changing ~ · Wechsellast f

~ **notch bending test,** ~ ~ flexure ~ · Einkerbhin- und -herbiegeprüfung f, Einkerbhin- und -herbiegeversuch m, Einkerbhin- und -herbiegeprobe f

~ ~ **flexure test,** ~ ~ bending ~ · Einkerbhin- und -herbiegeprüfung f, Einkerbhin- und -herbiegeversuch m, Einkerbhin- und -herbiegeprobe f

~ **pressure,** changing ~ · Wechseldruck m

~ **rows of pillars and piers** → system with alternating columns and piers

~ **stress,** changing ~ · Wechselspannung f

alum · Alaun m

alum-saturated class D (gypsum-)plaster, ~ (gypsum-)plaster of Class D (Brit.); ~ hard-finish plaster [B.S. 1191] · Alaungips m, alaunisierter Gips, deutscher Marmorzement n

alum-shale · Alaunschiefer m, Vitriolschiefer

~ **concrete** · Vitriolschieferbeton m, Alaunschieferbeton

alum solution · Alaunlösung f

alum-stone, alunite · Alunit m [tonerdereicher Alaunschiefer]

alum treatment · Alaunisieren n

alumina; aluminium oxide (Brit.); aluminum oxid(e) (US) · Tonerde f, Alaunerde [Aluminiumsesquioxid, das in mehreren Modifikationen auftritt. Die wichtigsten sind γ- und α-Tonerde (Korund). Die β-Tonerde enthält geringe Mengen an Alkalioxiden]

~ **brick** → aluminous (fire)brick

~ **cement** → aluminous ~

~ **ceramics,** ~ keramics · Tonerdekeramik f

~ **(fire)brick** → aluminous ~

~ **fireclay brick** → aluminous (fire)brick

~ **mortar** · Tonerdemörtel m

~ **plant** · Tonerdefabrik f, Tonerdewerk n

~ **refractory (product)** → high-~ ~ (~)

aluminate · Aluminat n, Tonerdeverbindung f

aluminium (Brit.); aluminum (US); alum. · Alu(minium) n

~ **absorbent ceiling,** ~ acoustic(al) ~, ~ sound-control ~ (Brit.); aluminum ~ ~, aluminum acoustic tiled ~ (US); aluminium acoustic tiled ~ (Brit.) · Alu(minium)-Akustikdecke f, Alu(minium)-Schallschluckdecke

~ **acoustic tiled ceiling** → ~ absorbent ~

~ **acoustic(al) ceiling** → ~ absorbent ~

~ **alloy** (Brit.); aluminum ~ (US) · Alu(minium)legierung f

~ ~ **(blind) slat** (Brit.); aluminum ~ (~) ~ (US) · Alu(minium)-Legierungs-Lamelle f, Alu(minium)-Legierungs-Stäbchen n [Jalousie]

~ ~ **casting** (Brit.); aluminum ~ ~ (US) · Alu(minium)legierungsgußteil m, n

~ ~ **hinge** (Brit.); aluminum ~ ~ (US) · Alu(minium)legierungsband n [Baubeschlag]

~ ~ **section** → ~ ~ structural ~

~ ~ **shape** → ~ ~ (structural) section

~ **(~) sink (unit)** (Brit.); aluminum (~) ~ (~) (US) · Alu(minium)abwaschtisch m, Alu(minium)Spülausguß m, Alu(minium)spültisch

~ ~ **slat** → ~ ~ blind ~

~ ~ **(structural) section,** ~ ~ (~) shape, ~ ~ (~) unit, ~ ~ (~) trim [B.S. 1161]; aluminum ~ (~) ~ (US) · Alu(minium)legierungsprofil n

~ **architecture** (Brit.); aluminum ~ (US) · Alu(minium)architektur f, Alu(minium)baukunst f

~ **beam** (Brit.); aluminum ~ (US) · Alu(minium)balken(träger) m

~ **bearing structure** → ~ load~ ~

~ **bonded roof cover(ing),** ~ ~ ~ sheathing (Brit.); aluminum ~ ~ ~ (US); ~ ~ roofing · Metall-Klebe(dach)(ein)deckung f

~ **brass** (Brit.); aluminum ~ (US) · Alu(minium)messing n

~ **bronze** (Brit.); aluminum ~ flakes (Brit.), albronze (US) · Alu(minium)bronze f, Sparbronze [DIN 1714. Sn ist ganz oder fast ganz durch Al ersetzt]

~ ~ **cast(ing)** (Brit.); aluminum ~ ~ (US) · Sparbronzeguß m, Alu(minium)bronzeguß

~ ~ **paint** (Brit.); aluminum ~ (US) · Alu(minium)bronzefarbe f

aluminium (builders') hardware — aluminium flake pigment

~ **(builders') hardware** (Brit.); aluminum (~) ~ (US); ~ (~) fittings · Alu(minium)(bau)beschläge *mpl*

~ **(building) component** → ~ (~) unit

~ ~ **entrance door** (Brit.); aluminum ~ ~ ~ (US) · Alu(minium)-Gebäudetür *f*, Alu(minium)-Haustür

~ (~) **member** → ~ (~) unit

~ ~ **product** (Brit.); aluminum ~ ~ (US) · Alu(minium)(bau)artikel *m*

~ (~) **sheet** (Brit.); aluminum (~) ~ (US) · Alu(minium)(bau)blech *n*

~ (~) **unit** (Brit.); aluminum (~) ~ (US); ~ (~) member, ~ (~) component · Alu(minium)-(Bau)körper *m*, Alu(minium)-(Bau)Element *n*, Alu(minium)-(Bau)Teil *m*, *n* [*Fehlnamen: Alu(minium)-(Bau)Einheit f; Alu(minium)-Montageeinheit*

~ **cable,** ~ conductor (Brit.); aluminum ~ (US) · Alu(minium)leitung *f* [*Elektrotechnik*]

~ ~ **sheath** (Brit.); aluminum ~ ~ (US) · Alu(minium)kabelmantel *m*

~ **casette** → ~ waffle

~ **casting** (Brit.); aluminum ~ (US) · Alu(minium)gußstück *n*, Alu(minium)gußteil *m, n*

~ **ceiling** (Brit.); aluminum ~ (US) · Alu(minium)decke *f*

~ **channel** (Brit.); aluminum ~ (US) · Alu(minium)-U-Profil *n*

~ **channelled foil** (Brit.); aluminum chaneled ~ (US); ~ checker(ed) ~ · Alu(minium)riffelfolie *f*

~ **checker(ed) foil** → ~ channelled ~

~ **chloride** (Brit.); aluminum chlorid(e) (US) · Alu(minium)chlorid *n*, Al Cl₃

~ **coffer** → ~ waffle

~ **component** → ~ (building) unit

~ **compound** (Brit.); aluminum ~ (US) · Alu(minium)verbindung *f*

~ **conductor,** ~ cable (Brit.); aluminum ~ (US) · Alu(minium)leitung *f* [*Elektrotechnik*]

~ **corrugated (building) sheet** (Brit.); aluminum ~ (~) ~ (US) · Alu(minium)-Wellblech *n*

~ ~ **profile,** ~ ~ section, ~ ~ unit, ~ ~ shape, ~ ~ trim (Brit.); aluminum ~ ~ (US) · Wellalu(minium)profil *n*, Alu(minium)wellprofil

~ ~ **section,** ~ ~ profile, ~ ~ unit, ~ ~ shape, ~ ~ trim (Brit.); aluminum ~ ~ (US) · Wellalu(minium)profil *n*, Alu(minium)wellprofil

~ ~ **shape,** ~ ~ section, ~ ~ profile, ~ ~ unit, ~ ~ trim (Brit.); aluminum ~ ~ (US) · Wellalu(minium)profil *n*, Alu(minium)wellprofil

~ ~ **sheet** → ~ ~ building ~

~ ~ **trim,** ~ ~ section, ~ ~ profile, ~ ~ shape, ~ ~ unit (Brit.); aluminum ~ ~ (US) · Wellalu(minium)profil *n*, Alu(minium)wellprofil

~ ~ **unit,** ~ ~ section, ~ ~ profile, ~ ~ shape, ~ ~ trim (Brit.); aluminum ~ ~ (US) · Wellalu(minium)profil *n*, Alu(minium)wellprofil

~ **curtain wall** (Brit.); aluminum ~ ~ (US) · Alu(minium)vorhangwand *f*

~ **decorative section** → ~ ~ shape

~ ~ **shape,** ~ ~ section, ~ ~ unit, ~ ~ trim, ~ ornamental ~ (Brit.); aluminum ~ ~ (US) · Alu(minium)-Dekor(ations)profil *n*, Alu(minium)-Ornamentprofil, Alu(minium)-Zierprofil

~ ~ **trim** → ~ ~ ~ shape

~ ~ **unit** → ~ ~ ~ shape

~ **die casting** (Brit.); aluminum ~ ~ (US) · Alu(minium)-Druckgußteil *m, n*

~ **die-casting alloy** (Brit.); aluminum ~ ~ (US) · Alu(minium)-Druckguß-Legierung *f*

~ **door** (Brit.); aluminum ~ (US) · Alu(minium)tür *f*

~ **(~) pull (handle)** (Brit.); aluminum (~) ~ (~) (US) · Alu(minium)-(tür)griff *m*

~ **double window** (Brit.); aluminum ~ ~ (US) · Alu(minium)doppelfenster *n*

~ **eave(s) gutter** (Brit.); aluminum ~ ~ (US); ~ ~ trough [*A shallow channel or conduit set below and along the eave(s) of a house to catch and carry off rainwater from the roof*] · Alu(minium)traufrinne *f*

~ ~ **trough** → ~ ~ ~ gutter

~ **extrusion** (Brit.); aluminum ~ (US) · Alu(minium)-Strangpreßerzeugnis *n*

~ **façade,** ~ front, ~ face (Brit.); aluminum ~ (US) · Alu(minium)fassade *f*

~ **face,** façade ~ front (Brit.); aluminum ~ (US) · Alu(minium)fassade *f*

~ **facing,** ~ sur~, ~ lining (Brit.); aluminum ~ (US) · Alu(minium)auskleidung *f*, Alu(minium)verkleidung, Alu(minium)bekleidung

~ **fence** (Brit.); aluminum ~ (US) · Alu(minium)zaun *m*

~ **finger plate** (Brit.); aluminum ~ ~ (US) · Alu(minium)schonschild *n* [*Baubeschlag*]

~ **finish** (Brit.); aluminum ~ (US) · Alu(minium)-Oberflächengestaltung *f*

~ **fittings** → ~ (builders') hardware

~ **flake** (Brit.); aluminum ~ (US) Alu(minium)blättchen *n*

~ ~ (Brit.); aluminum ~ (US) · Alu(minium)schuppe *f*

~ ~ **pigment** (Brit.); aluminum ~ ~ (US); flake aluminium ~ (Brit.); flake aluminum ~ (US) · blättchenförmiges Alu(minium)pigment *n*

aluminium flakes — aluminium permanent moulding alloy 44

~ **flakes**, ~ bronze (Brit.); aluminum ~, albronze (US) · Sparbronze f, Alu(minium)bronze [DIN 1714. Sn ist ganz oder fast ganz durch Al ersetzt]

~ **flashing** (Brit.); aluminum ~ (US) · Alu(minium)abweis(e)blech n

~ ~ **(piece)** (Brit.); aluminum ~ (~) (US) [See remark under 'Anschluß'] · Alu(minium)(blech)anschluß(streifen) m

~ **floor cover(ing)**, ~ floor(ing) (finish) (Brit.); aluminum ~ (~) (US) · Alu(minium)(fuß)boden(belag) m

~ **floor(ing) (finish)**, ~ floor cover(ing) (Brit.); aluminum ~ (~) (US) · Alu(minium)(fuß)boden(belag) m

~ **floorplate** (Brit.); aluminum ~ (US) · Alu(minium)(fuß)bodenblech n

~ **foil** (Brit.); aluminum ~ (US) · Alu(minium)folie f

~ ~ **backing** (Brit.); aluminum ~ ~ (US) · Alu(minium)folienträger m

~ ~ **insert(ion)** (Brit.); aluminum ~ ~ (US) · Alu(minium)-Folien-Einlage f

~ ~ **insulation** (Brit.); aluminum ~ ~ (US) · Alu(minium)-Folien-Dämmung f

~ **folded plate roof**, ~ ~ slab ~ (Brit.); aluminum ~ ~ ~, aluminum hipped-plate ~ (US) · Alu(minium)-Dachfaltwerk n, Alu(minium)-Falt-(werk)dach n

~ ~ **slab roof** → ~ ~ plate ~

~ **forms** → ~ form(work)

~ **form(work)**, ~ forms, ~ shuttering (Brit.); aluminum ~ (US) · Alu(minium)schalung f

~ **frame** (Brit.); aluminum ~ (US) · Alu(minium)rahmen m

~ **front**, ~ façade, ~ face (Brit.); aluminum ~ (US) · Alu(minium)fassade f

~ **girder** (Brit.); aluminum ~ (US) · Alu(minium)träger m

~ **grid** (Brit.); aluminum ~ (US) · Alu(minium)raster m

~ ~ **ceiling** (Brit.); aluminum ~ ~ (US) · Alu(minium)rasterdecke f

~ ~ **(~) system** (Brit.); aluminum ~ (~) ~ (US) · Alu(minium)rasterdeckensystem n

~ **grille** (Brit.); aluminum ~ (US) [Sometimes spelled 'grill'] · Alu(minium)(zier)gitter n

~ **(hand) railing** (Brit.); aluminum (~) ~ (US) · Alu(minium)geländer n

~ **hardware** → ~ builders' ~

~ **hinge** (Brit.); aluminum ~ (US) · Alu(minium)band n [Baubeschlag]

~ **hollow section**, ~ ~ shape, ~ ~ unit, ~ ~ trim (Brit.); aluminum ~ ~ (US) · Alu(minium)hohlprofil n

~ **hydroxide** (Brit.); aluminum hydroxid(e) (US) · Tonerdehydrat n, Alu(minium)hydroxid n, Al(OH)$_3$

~ **jacket** (Brit.); aluminum ~ (US) · Alu(minium)mantel m

~ **leaves** (Brit.); aluminum ~ (US) · Blattaluminium n [Bezeichnung für besonders dünne Aluminiumblätter, im Gegensatz zur Aluminiumfolie]

~ **lining**, ~ (sur)facing (Brit.); aluminium ~ (US) · Alu(minium)auskleidung f, Alu(minium)verkleidung, Alu(minium)bekleidung

~ **lintel** (Brit.); aluminum ~ (US); ~ lintol [deprecated] · Alu(minium)sturz m

~ **(load)bearing structure**, ~ supporting ~, ~ load-carrying ~, ~ loaded ~, ~ (weight-carrying) ~ (Brit.); aluminum (~) ~ (US) · Alu(minium)-tragwerk n [Ein materielles System von Alu(minium)bauelementen bzw. Alu(minium)trägern]

~ **load-carrying structure** → ~ (load-) bearing ~

~ **loaded structure** → ~ (load)bearing ~

aluminium-manganese alloy (Brit.); aluminum-manganese ~ (US) · Mangan-Alu(minium)-Legierung f

aluminium member → ~ (building) unit

~ **mesh** (Brit.); aluminum ~ (US) · Alu(minium)maschenmatte f

~ **multi-compound bronze** (Brit.); aluminum ~ ~ (US) · Alu(minium)-Mehrstoffbronze f

~ **nail** [B.S. 1202]; aluminum ~ (US) · Alu(minium)nagel m

~ **ornamental section** → ~ decorative shape

~ **oxide** (Brit.) → alumina

~ **paint** (Brit.); aluminum ~ (US) · Alu(minium)(anstrich)farbe f

~ ~ **coat(ing)** (Brit.); aluminum ~ ~ (US) · Alu(minium)anstrich m, Alu(minium)aufstrich

~ **pan(el)** → ~ waffle

~ **panel** (Brit.); aluminum ~ (US) · Alu(minium)tafel f

~ ~ **ceiling** (Brit.); aluminum ~ ~ (US) · Alu(minium)tafeldecke f

~ **partition (wall)** (Brit.); aluminum ~ (~) (US) · Alu(minium)-Trennwand f

~ **paste** (Brit.); aluminum ~ (US) · Alu(minium)paste f

~ **patent glazing bar**, puttyless aluminium ~ ~ (Brit.); aluminum patent ~ ~, puttyless aluminum ~ ~ (US) · Alu(minium)sprosse f [Für kittlose Oberlichter und Glasdächer]

~ **perforated ceiling** (Brit.); aluminum ~ ~ (US) · Alu(minium)lochdecke f

~ **permanent mould casting alloy** → ~ ~ moulding alloy

~ ~ **moulding alloy**, ~ ~ mould casting alloy (Brit.); aluminum permanent molding alloy, aluminum permanent mold casting alloy (US) · Alu(minium)-Kokillenguß-Legierung f

aluminium pigment — aluminium soap

~ **pigment** (Brit.); aluminum ~ (US) · Alu(minium)pigment *n*

~ **pipe** (Brit.); aluminum ~ (US) · Alu(minium)rohr *n*

~ **plate** (Brit.); aluminum ~ (US) · Alu(minium)platte *f*

~ ~ **element** (Brit.); aluminum ~ ~ (US) · ebener Alu(minium)profilteil *m*, ebenes ~ *n*

~ **post** (Brit.); aluminum ~ (US) · Alu(minium)pfosten *m*

~ **powder** (Brit.); aluminum ~ (US) · Alu(minium)pulver *n*, Al-Pulver

~ **primer** (Brit.); aluminum ~ (US) · Alu(minium)-Grundiermittel *n*

~ **profile(d) panel,** profile(d) aluminium ~ (Brit.); aluminum profile(d) ~, profile(d) aluminum ~ (US) · Alu(minium)-Profiltafel *f*

~ ~ **sheet** (Brit.); aluminum ~ ~ (US) · Alu(minium)profilblech *n*

~ **pull (handle)** → ~ door ~ (~)

~ **purlin(e)** (Brit.); aluminum ~ (US) · Alu(minium)pfette *f*

~ **railing** → ~ hand ~

~ **residential sliding door** (Brit.); aluminum ~ ~ ~ (US) · Alu(minium)-Wohnungsschiebetür *f*

~ ~ ~ **window** (Brit.); aluminum ~ ~ ~ (US) · Alu(minium)-Wohnungsschiebefenster *n*

~ **rivet** (Brit.); aluminum ~ (US) · Alu(minium)niet *m*

~ ~ **head** (Brit.); aluminum ~ ~ (US) · Alu(minium)nietkopf *m*

~ **rolling grille** (Brit.); aluminum ~ ~ (US) [*See remark under 'Gitter'*] · Alu(minium)-Rollgitter *n*

~ ~ **shutter,** ~ roller ~ (Brit.); aluminum ~ ~ ~ (US) · Alu(minium)-rollabschluß *m*

~ **roof cladding** (Brit.); aluminum ~ ~ (US), ~ ~ cover(ing), ~ ~ sheathing, ~ roofing · Alu(minium)bedachung *f*, Alu(minium)(dach)(ein)deckung

~ **roof(ing) sheet** (Brit.); aluminum ~ ~ (US) · Alu(minium)dachblech *n*

~ ~ ~ (Brit.); aluminum ~ ~ (US) · Alu(minium)dachplatte *f*

~ ~ **sheet(ing)** (Brit.); aluminum ~ ~ (US) · Alu(minium)-Dachdeck(ungs)bahn *f*, Alu(minium)-Dacheindeck(ungs)bahn, Alu(minium)-Dachbahn, Alu(minium)-Bedachungsbahn

~ **sand-casting alloy** (Brit.); aluminum ~ ~ (US) · Alu(minium)-Sandguß-Legierung *f*

~ **sandwich panel** (Brit.); aluminum ~ ~ (US) · Alu(minium)-Dreilagentafel *f*, Alu(minium)-Dreischichtentafel

~ **sash** (Brit.); aluminum ~ (US) · Alu(minium)(fenster)flügel *m*

~ **screw** (Brit.); aluminum ~ (US) · Alu(minium)schraube *f*

~ **seal(ing) sheet(ing)** (Brit.); aluminum ~ ~ (US) · Alu(minium)-(blech)-(Ab)Dicht(ungs)bahn *f*

~ **section** → ~ structural ~

~ **shape** → ~ (structural) section

~ **sheathed cable** [*B.S. 480*]; aluminum ~ ~ (US) · Alu(minium)(mantel)-kabel *n*

~ **sheet** → ~ building ~

~ ~ (Brit.); aluminum ~ (US) · Alu(minium)blech *n*

~ ~ **facing,** ~ ~ sur~, ~ ~ lining (Brit.); aluminum ~ ~ (US) · Alu(minium)(blech)auskleidung *f*, Alu(minium)(blech)verkleidung, Alu(minium)(blech)bekleidung

~ ~ **lining,** ~ ~ (sur)facing (Brit.); aluminum ~ ~ (US) · Alu(minium)-(blech)auskleidung *f*, Alu(minium)-(blech)verkleidung, Alu(minium)-(blech)bekleidung

~ ~ **(sur)facing,** ~ ~ lining (Brit.); aluminum ~ ~ (US) · Alu(minium)-(blech)auskleidung *f*, Alu(minium)-(blech)verkleidung, Alu(minium)-(blech)bekleidung

~ **shutter** (Brit.); aluminum ~ (US) · Alu(minium)abschluß *m*

~ **shuttering** → ~ form(work)

~ **siding** (Brit.); aluminum ~ (US) · Alu(minium)-Wandschirm *m*, Alu(minium)-Wandbeschlag *m*, Alu(minium)-Wetterschirm

~ **silicate** (Brit.); aluminum ~ (US) · Alu(minium)silikat *n*

~ ~ **pigment** (Brit.); aluminum ~ ~ (US) · Alu(minium)silikatpigment *n*

~ **silo** (Brit.); aluminum ~ (US) · Alu(minium)silo *m*

~ **sink (unit)** (Brit.) → ~ alloy ~ (~)

~ **skin** (Brit.); aluminum ~ (US) · Alu(minium)haut *f*

~ **skyscraper** (Brit.); aluminum ~ (US) · Alu(minium)wolkenkratzer *m*

~ **slatted blind** (Brit.); aluminum ~ ~ (US) · Alu(minium)jalousie *f*

~ ~ **roller blind** (Brit.); aluminum ~ ~ ~ (US) · Alu(minium)-Rolladen *m*, Alu(minium)-Rolljalousie *f*

~ **sliding door** (Brit.); aluminum ~ ~ (US) · Alu(minium)-Schiebetür *f*

~ ~ **folded shutterdoor** (Brit.); aluminum ~ ~ ~ (US); ~ ~ ~ ~ shutter door · Alu(minium)-Faltschiebetor *n*, Alu(minium)-Schiebefalttor

~ ~ **window** (Brit.); aluminum ~ ~ (US) · Alu(minium)-Schiebefenster *n*

~ **smelting plant** (Brit.); aluminum ~ ~ (US) · Alu(minium)schmelze *f*, Aluminiumschmelzwerk *n*

~ **soap** (Brit.); aluminum ~ (US) · Alu(minium)seife *f*

aluminium soft wool — aluminous silicate

~ **soft wool** (Brit.); aluminum ~ ~ (US) · Alu(minium)-Weichwolle *f*

~ **solder** (Brit.); aluminum ~ (US) · Alu(minium)lot *n* [*DIN 1732*]

~ **sound-control ceiling** → ~ absorbent ~

~ **stearate** (Brit.); aluminum ~ (US) · Alu(minium)stearat *n*

~ **street lighting column** [*B.S. 3989*] · Alu(minium)-Straßenleuchtenmast *m*

~ **strip** (Brit.); aluminum ~ (US) · Alu(minium)-Paneel *n*

~ ~ (Brit.); aluminum ~ (US) · Alu(minium)streifen *m*

~ **(structural) section**, ~ (~) shape, ~ (~) unit, ~ (~) trim, ~ (~) profile (Brit.); aluminum (~) ~ (~) · Alu(minium)(bau)profil *n*

~ **structure** → ~ (load)bearing ~

~ **sunblind**, ~ sunbreaker (Brit.); aluminum ~ (US) · Alu(minium)-Sonnen(schutz)blende *f*

~ **sunbreaker** → ~ sunblind

~ **supporting structure** → ~ (load-)bearing ~

~ **surfacing** (Brit.); aluminum ~ (US) · Alu(minium)abstreuung *f*, Alu(minium)bestreuung [*Sonder-Bitumendachpappe*]

~ **(sur)facing**, ~ lining (Brit.); aluminum ~ (US) · Alu(minium)auskleidung *f*, Alu(minium)verkleidung, Alu(minium)bekleidung

~ **swing door** (Brit.); aluminum ~ ~ (US) · Alu(minium)-Pendeltür *f*, Pendeltür aus Alu(minium)

~ **T(ee)-bar** (Brit.); aluminum ~ (US) · Alu(minium)-T-Tragschiene *f* [*Hängedecke*]

~ **track** (Brit.); aluminum ~ (US) · Alu(minium)-Führungsschiene *f*

~ **trapezoidal section**, ~ ~ unit, ~ ~ shape, ~ ~ trim, ~ ~ profile (Brit.); aluminum ~ ~ (US) · Alu(minium)trapezprofil *n*

~ ~ **sheet** (Brit.); aluminum ~ ~ (US) · Alu(minium)-Trapezblech *n*

~ **trim** → ~ (structural) section

~ **tube** (Brit.); aluminum ~ (US) · Alu(minium)röhre *f*

~ **unit** → ~ building ~

~ **vapour barrier (membrane)**, ~ ~ proof ~ (Brit.); aluminum vapor barrier (~), aluminum vapor proof ~ (US) · Alu(minium)-Dampfsperre *f*

~ **waffle**, ~ casette, ~ coffer, ~ pan(el) (Brit.); aluminum ~ (US) · Alu(minium)kassette *f*

~ **wall** (Brit.); aluminum ~ (US) · Alu(minium)wand *f*

~ **wallpaper** (Brit.); aluminum ~ (US) · Alu(minium)tapete *f*

~ **(weight-carrying) structure** → ~ (load)bearing ~

~ **window** (Brit.); aluminum ~ (US) · Alu(minium)fenster *n*

~ ~ **fitting**, ~ ~ furniture (Brit.); aluminum ~ ~ (US) · Alu(minium)-fensterbeschlag *m*

~ ~ **fittings**, ~ ~ hardware (Brit.); aluminum ~ ~ (US) · Alu(minium)-fensterbeschläge *mpl*

~ ~ **furniture**, ~ ~ fitting (Brit.); aluminum ~ ~ (US) · Alu(minium)-fensterbeschlag *m*

~ ~ **hardware**, ~ ~ fittings (Brit.); aluminum ~ ~ (US) · Alu(minium)-fensterbeschläge *mpl*

~ **wire** (Brit.); aluminum ~ (US) · Alu(minium)draht *m*

~ ~ **cloth** (Brit.); aluminum ~ ~ (US) · Alu(minium)drahtgewebe *n*

~ **wood composite system** (Brit.); aluminum ~ ~ ~ (US) · Alu(minium)-Holz-Verbundkonstruktion *f*

~ **wool** (Brit.); aluminum ~ (US) · Alu(minium)wolle *f*

~ **wrought alloy** (Brit.); aluminum ~ ~ (US) · Alu(minium)-Knetlegierung *f* [*DIN 1725*]

~ **zinc** (Brit.); aluminum ~ (US) [*An alloy of aluminium and zinc. It frequently contains 88% aluminium and 12% zinc*] · Alu(minium)zink *n*

aluminosilicate, aluminous silicate · Alumosilikat *n*

alumino-thermic reaction · aluminothermische Reaktion *f*

~ **welding** · aluminothermisches Schweißen *n*

aluminous aggregate of the clinker type · Tonerdeklinkerzuschlag(stoff) *m*, Tonerdeklinkerzuschlagmaterial *n*

~ **brick** → ~ fire~

~ **cement**, calcium-aluminate ~, bauxitic ~, alumina ~ · Tonerdezement *m*, Aluminozement, (Kalzium-)Aluminatzement, TZ [*Fehlname: Elektrozement. Dieser Zement wird aus Bauxit in Öfen bis zur Sinterung gebrannt. Er kann aber auch in elektrischen Öfen erschmolzen werden*]

~ **clinker** · Tonerdeklinker *m*

~ **(fire)brick**, (high-)alumina ~, ~ fireclay brick · tonerdereicher Schamottestein *m*, tonerdehaltiger ~

~ **fireclay brick** → ~ (fire)brick

~ **refractory (product)**, high-alumina ~ (~) · hochtonerdehaltiges feuerfestes Erzeugnis *n*, tonerdereiches ~, ~ ff. ~

~ **silicate**, aluminosilicate · Alumosilikat *n*

alunite, alum-stone · Alunit *m* [*tonerdereicher Alaunschiefer*]

alunization · Alaunbildung *f*

alure [*An alley, walk or passage. A gallery behind a parapet*] · Weg *m*, Galerie *f*, Gang *m*

alveolina limestone · Alveolinenkalkstein *m*

amalgam fluorescent lamp · Amalgam-L-Lampe *f*

amber · Bernstein *m*

~ **glass** [*Glass varying in colour between light yellowish brown and deep reddish brown*] · Amberglas *n*, Bernsteinglas, Braunglas

~ **tar** · Bernsteinteer *m*

~ **varnish** · Bernsteinlack *m*

ambient noise, internal ~, **inside** ~, **interior** ~, **indoor** ~, **inner** ~ · Innenlärm *m*

~ **temperature** · Umwelttemperatur *f*

ambo(n) [*A stand raised on two or more steps, for the reading of the Epistle and the Gospel; a prominent feature in medieval Italian churches. Sometimes two were built, one for the Epistle and one for the Gospel, on the south and north sides respectively*] · Ambo *m*, Bema *n*

~ **ciborium** · Ambociborium *n*, Amboziborium

ambry, aumbry, almery, almary [*A cupboard in the wall of the sanctuary of a church, near the altar, where the sacred vessels could be locked up*] · Kirchenschrank *m*

ambulatory → de~

~ **aisle** → deambulatory

~ **church,** cross-domed ~, cruciform-domed ~, domed-cruciform ~ · Kreuzkuppelkirche *f*, Kuppelkreuzkirche

~ **vault,** de~ ~ · Umgangsgewölbe *n*, Deambulatoriumsgewölbe

American bond, common ~ (US); English garden-wall ~, Scotch ~ (Brit.) · amerikanischer (Mauerwerk)Verband *m*

~ **pitch pine strip floor(ing) (finish),** ~ ~ ~ **floor cover(ing)** · Fhp *m*, Pitchpineriemen(fuß)boden(belag) *m*

amine formaldehyde resin · Amin-Formaldehyd-Harz *n*

amino plastic · Aminoplast *n*

~ **resin** · Aminoharz *n*

ammonia · Ammoniak *n*, NH_3

~ **compressor set** · Ammoniakkältemaschine *f*

~ **solution, solution of ammonia** · Ammoniaklösung *f*

ammonium chloride (Brit.); ~ **chlorid(e)** (US) · Salmiak *m*, Ammoniumchlorid *n*, Chlorammonium *n*, NH_4Cl

~ **salt** · Ammoniumsalz *n*

~ **sulphate** (Brit.); ~ **sulfate** (US) · Ammoniumsulfat *n*

Amosite [*This name embodies the initials of the company exploiting this material in the Transvaal, viz. the 'Asbestos Mines of South Africa'*] · Amosit(asbest) *m*, gelber Hornblendeasbest

amount of bend(ing), bend(ing) amount · Biegebetrag *m*, Biegegröße *f*, Biegungsgröße, Biegungsbetrag

~ ~ **movement** · Bewegungsgröße *f*

~ ~ **prestress** · (Vor)Spannbetrag *m*

~ ~ **strength** · Festigkeitsgröße *f*

amphi-antis temple [*These temples have from one to four columns between antae at front and rear. Two is the usual number*] · Doppelantentempel *m*

amphibole asbestos · Amphibolasbest *m*, Hornblendeasbest

amphibolic gneiss, hornblende-gneiss · Hornblendegneis *m*

amphiprostyle [*The adjective applied to a temple with porticos at each end, but without columns along the sides*] · amphiprostyl

~ **temple** · Amphiprostylos *m* [*Antiker Tempel mit an den beiden Schmalseiten und nicht zwischen den Anten stehenden Säulen*]

~ **tetrastyle temple** · viersäuliger Amphiprostylostempel *m*

amphoteric · amphoter

Amsler abrasion test · Amsler-Versuch *m*, Amsler-Prüfung *f*, Amsler-Probe *f* [*Prüfung von Hartbetonbelägen*]

~ ~ **tester** · Amsler-Gerät *n*

Amsterdam exchange · Amsterdamer Börse *f*

~ **School** [*Group of architects who provided a parallel movement in the nineteen twenties and thirties to German Expressionism*] · Amsterdamer Schule *f*

amusement hall; ~ **centre** (Brit.); ~ **center** (US) · Vergnügungshalle *f*

~ **park, fun fair** · Vergnügungspark *m*

amygdaloidal diabase · Diabas-Mandelstein *m*

~ **Zechstein dolomite,** blasenschiefer · Blasenschiefer *m*

amyl acetate, banana oil · Amylacetat *n*

anachronistic feature · anachronistischer Zug *m*

anactoron [*A sacred building or part thereof, used in connection with the Mysteries, e.g. at Eleusis*] · Götterwohnung *f*, Anaktoron *n*

an(a)esthetic room · Betäubungsraum *m* [*Krankenhaus*]

to analyse · statisch berechnen

analysis, structural ~, **stress** ~ · (Bau-)Statik *f*

~, **calculation, structural** ~ · (statische) Berechnung *f*

~ **of continuous girders by successive approximations** · schrittweise Berechnung *f* durchlaufender Träger, ~ ~ von Durchlaufträgern

analyst — angle chapel

analyst, operator · Versuchslaborant *m*

analytical scale · Analysenwaage *f*

anatase [*An isomeric form of rutile titanium dioxid(e)*] · Anatas *m*

to anchor · verankern

anchor, (masonry) wall ~, (masonry) (wall) tie · (Mauer)Anker *m*, Mauer-(werk)haken *m*, Mauerwerkanker

~, tie, wall ~ · (Wand)Anker *m*

~ angle · Verankerungswinkel *m*

~ block (US); fixing ~, nailable ~ · nagelbarer Block *m*, nagelfester ~, Dübelblock

~ bolt · Ankerschraube *f*, Verankerungsschraube

~ brick (US) → fixing ~

~ channel · Ankerschiene *f*, Dübelschiene

~ hinge · Ankergelenk *n*

~ hole, tie ~ · Ankerloch *n*

~ plate · Ankerplatte *f*

~ point · Abspannpunkt *m* [*Zeltsystem*]

anchorage, tying · Verankerung *f* [*Zugfeste Verbindung zweier Bauteile mit Ankern*]

~ [*The securing of bars in cast-in-place concrete either by hooks, bends or embedment length*] · Verankerung *f* [*Bewehrung*]

~ · Einsiedelei *f*

~ beam · Ankerbalken(träger) *m*, Verankerungsbalken(träger)

~ by friction, anchoring ~ ~, friction-type anchorage, friction-type anchoring · Reib(ungs)verankerung *f*

~ deformation, ~ slip, ~ loss · Ankerschlupf *m*, Verankerungsschlupf, Rutschung *f* der Verankerung

~ force · Ankerkraft *f*

~ ~ · Verankerungskraft *f*

~ slip, ~ deformation, ~ loss · Rutschung *f* der Verankerung, Ankerschlupf *m*, Verankerungsschlupf

anchored to ground, tied ~ ~ · bodenverankert

~ wall, tied ~ · verankerte Wand *f*

anchoring, tying · Verankern *n*

~ by friction, anchorage ~ ~, friction-type anchorage, friction-type anchoring · Reib(ungs)verankerung *f*

~ method, ~ system, method of anchoring, system of anchoring · Verankerungssystem *n*, Verankerungsverfahren *n*

anchor(ing) rail · Verankerungsschiene *f*, Ankerschiene

anchoring system, ~ method, method of anchoring, system of anchoring · Verankerungssystem *n*, Verankerungsverfahren *n*

ancient character, antique ~ · altertümlicher Charakter *m*

~ monument, historic landmark · historisches Wahrzeichen *n*, Kulturdenkmal *n*

~ Roman · römisch-antik

ancillary block → ~ building

~ building, ~ block, dependent ~, subordinate ~, accessory ~ · Nebengebäude *n* [*Ein Gebäude von geringer Größe und Höhe, das Nebenzwecken dient, z.B. Garage*]

ancon(e), truss, console [*A scrolled bracket*] · Konsole *f*

~ [*A projection left on a block of stone, such as the drum of a column, to hoist it into position*] · Vorsprung *m*

andalusite · Al_2SiO_5, Andalusit *m*, Hartspat *m*

andalusite-gneiss · Andalusitgneis *m*

andesine · Andesin *m*

andesite · Andesit *m*

~ ash · Andesitasche *f*

~ (paving) sett · Andesit(pflaster)stein *m*

~ sett, ~ paving ~ · Andesit(pflaster)stein *m*

andesitic tuff · Andesittuff *m*

andiron, (iron) firedog [*It is used for supporting logs on the hearth of an open fireplace*] · Kaminbock *m*, Feuerbock

andradite garnet · Kalkeisengranat *m*

anechoic, nonreverberant · nachhallfrei, echowidrig

~ room, nonreverberant ~, ~ chamber, free-field ~ · echowidriger Raum *m*, nachhallfreier ~

Angel Choir [*Lincoln Cathedral*] · Engelschor *m*

angel triforium · Engeltriforium *n*

angle · Auflagerwinkel *m* [*Stahlbau*]

~ · Gradstellung *f* [*Rohrabzweig*]

~-balancing method · Drehwinkel(-Iterations)verfahren *n*

angle bar, ~ (section), L-section · Winkel(profil) *m*, (*n*)

~ bead, corner ~, corner guard; corner moulding (Brit.); corner molding (US) · Eck(schutz)leiste *f*, Kantenschützer *m*

~ ~ tile fitting · Winkel(belag)platte *f* mit Wulst, Winkelfliese *f* ~ ~

~ block, ~ tile [*See remark under 'Block'*] · Eckstein *m*, Winkelstein, Winkelblock(stein) *m*, Eckblock(stein)

~ board · Schrägbrett *n* [*Holzwand*]

~ ~ [*A board used as a gauge so as to plane a timber face to a definite angle*] · Schrägbrett *n*

(~) brace, ~ tie, strut, dragon tie · Bandholz *n*, Kopfband *n*, Kopfstrebe *f*, (Kopf)Bug(holz) *m*, (*n*), Kopfbiege *f*, Strebenband(holz) *n*, Winkelband, Tragband

~ bracket · Absetzwinkel *m*, Stützwinkel, Aufsetzwinkel

~ brick · Eckwinkel *m*

~ chapel · Winkelkapelle *f*

(angle) cleat — angular restraint

(~) cleat [*A small bracket of angle section fixed in a horizontal position, normally to a wall or stanchion, to support or to locate a structural member*] · (Auflage)Knagge *f*

~ column, corner ~ · Eckstütze *f*

~ ~, corner ~ · Ecksäule *f*

~ dunting, batting, broad tooling, droving · Schlaganarbeiten *n* [*Werksteinbearbeitung*]

~ fire place, corner ~ · Eckkamin *m*

~ guard · Winkelschutz *m*

~ hinge · Winkelband *n* [*Dieser Baubeschlag besteht aus einem kräftigen Stahlblechwinkel, an dessen senkrechtem Schenkel eine Hülse sitzt, die auf einem Kloben läuft*]

~ iron of the booms → boom plate

~ ~ ~ ~ chords → boom plate

~ ~ ~ ~ flanges → boom plate

~ ~ purlin(e), ~ steel ~ · Winkelstahlpfette *f*

~ lintel; ~ lintol [*deprecated*] · Winkeloberschwelle *f*, Winkelsturz *m*

~ loads method, ~ weights ~, elastic weights ~, elastic loads ~ · Winkelgewichtsverfahren *n*

~ of contact, contact angle · Berührungswinkel *m*

~ ~ deformation, deformation angle · Formänderungswinkel *m*, Verformungswinkel

~ ~ incidence → light angle

~ ~ light → light angle

~ ~ load distribution · Lastverteilungswinkel *m*

~ ~ obstruction · Verbauungswinkel *m* [*Tageslichtberechnung*]

~ ~ roof pitch, ~ ~ ~ slope · Dachneigungswinkel *m*

~ ~ ~ slope, ~ ~ ~ pitch · Dachneigungswinkel *m*

~ ~ rotation · Drehwinkel *m*

~ pavilion, wing ~ · Eckpavillon *m*, Winkelpavillon

(angle-)quoin, coi(g)n, coillon, corner stone [*One of the stones forming an external angle of a building*] · Winkelstein *m*, Eckstein

~, coi(g)n, coillon [*An external angle of a (masonry) wall*] · Maueraußenecke *f*; Wandaußenecke

~, coi(g)n, coillon, corner brick, angle stone [*One of the bricks forming an external angle of a building*] · Winkelziegel *m*, Eckziegel

angle rafter → ~ ridge

~ ~, hip ~, angle ridge · Dachschifter *m*, Anfallsparren *m*

~ ridge, ~ rafter, hip rafter · Gratsparren *m*, Gratbalken

~ ~ → ~ rafter

~ (section), ~ bar, L-section · Winkel(profil) *m*, (*n*)

~ separator [*For steel beams*] · Winkel-Stegverbindungsstück *n*

~ (shut-off) valve → right-angled ~

~ staff, staff angle, staff bead, plaster bead, plaster staff · Putzkantenschützer *m*, Putzschutzleiste *f*

~ steel purlin(e), ~ iron ~ · Winkelstahlpfette *f*

~ stiffening · Winkelaussteifung *f*, Winkelversteifung, Winkelverstärkung

~ threshold, L ~ · Winkel(tür)schwelle *f*

~ tie, (~) brace, strut, dragon tie · Bandholz *n*, Kopfband *n*, Kopfstrebe *f*, (Kopf-) Bug(holz) *m*, (*n*), Kopfbiege *f*, Strebenband(holz) *n*, Winkelband, Tragband

~ tile, ~ block [*See remark under 'Block'*] · Eckstein *m*, Winkelstein, Winkelblock(stein) *m*, Eckblock(stein)

~ tower · Wachtturm *m* [*Palast von Persepolis*]

~ turret, corner ~ · Recktürmchen *n*

angle(-type) step · Winkelstufe *f*

~ ~ with nosing · Winkelstufe *f* mit Bartprofil

angle valve → right-angled ~

~ weights method, ~ loads ~, elastic weights ~, elastic loads ~ · Winkelgewichtsverfahren *n*

~ with sharp corners · scharfkantiges Winkelprofil *n*, scharfkantiger Winkel *m*

Anglo-Saxon architecture [*The period from A.D. 449 to 1066. From the seventh century characterised by the use of rough fundamental forms, long and short work, pilaster strips or lesenes and baluster mullions. Because timber has perished, the style is represented only in churches*] · angelsächsische Architektur *f*, ~ Baukunst *f*

(Anglo-)Saxon façade · (angel)sächsische Fassade *f*

~ masonry (work) · (angel)sächsisches Mauerwerk *n*

~ tower · (angel)sächsischer Turm *m*

Angola copal · Angolakopal *m*

angular acceleration · Winkelbeschleunigung *f*

~ aggregate → ~ concrete ~

~ capital · mittelalterliches ionisches Kapitell *n*, ~ ~ Kapitäl

~ change · Winkeländerung *f*

~ (concrete) aggregate [*Aggregate, the particles of which possess well-defined edges formed at the intersection of roughly planar faces*] · kantiger (Beton)Zuschlag(stoff) *m*

~ displacement [*It is the change in angular position of a given line as measured from a convenient reference line*] · Winkelverrückung *f*

~ grain, ~ particle · kantiges Korn *n*

~ measure · Winkelmaß *n*

~ motion · Winkelbewegung *f*

~ particle, ~ grain · kantiges Korn *n*

~ restraint · wink(e)lige Einspannung *f*

angular velocity — animal symbolism

~ **velocity** · Winkelgeschwindigkeit *f*
angularity · Winkeligkeit *f*
anhydride · Anhydrid *n*
anhydrite [*This occurs as a natural mineral as well as being an industrial by-product. Its chemical name is anhydrous calcium sulphate, with the formula $CaSO_4$*] · Anhydrit *m*, wasserfreier Gips(stein) *m*, wasserfreies Kalziumsulfat *n*

~ **band** · Anhydritschnur *f*
~ **binder** · Anhydritbinder *m*, AB [*DIN 4208. Fabrikmäßige Herstellung durch gemeinsames Vermahlen von Anhydrit und Anreger oder durch Vermischen von gemahlenem Anhydrit und Anreger*]
~ **block,** ~ tile [*A building block manufactured from anhydrite plaster. See remark under 'Block'*] · Anhydritblock(stein) *m*, Anhydritstein
~ ~ **partition (wall),** ~ tile ~ (~) · Anhydrit(block)steintrennwand *f*, Anhydritblocktrennwand
~ **board,** ~ sheet · Anhydritplatte *f*
~ **cement** · Anhydritzement *m*
~ **jointless floor(ing),** ~ screed · Anhydritestrich *m* [*DIN 4109. Es dürfen nur Anhydritbinder nach DIN 4208 der Güteklasse AB 200 verwendet werden. Die Zuschläge sollen keine größeren Körner als 7 mm haben, die Mörtelsteife soll erdfeucht bis weich sein*]
~ **lime mortar** · Anhydritkalkmörtel *m*
~ **mortar** · Anhydritmörtel *m*
~ **rock** · Anhydrit(ge)stein *m*, (*n*)
~ **screed** → ~ jointless floor(ing)
~ **sheet,** ~ board · Anhydritplatte *f*
~ **tile** → ~ block
~ ~ **partition (wall),** ~ block ~ (~) · Anhydrit(block)steintrennwand *f*, Anhydritblocktrennwand

anhydrous · anhydrisch, wasserfrei, ohne Kristallisationswasser

(~) **calcium sulphate plaster** (Brit.) → ~ (gypsum-)plaster

~ **(gypsum-)plaster,** flooring ~; (anhydrous) calcium sulphate plaster, class C (gypsum-)plaster, (gypsum-)plaster of Class C (Brit.); anhydrous calcium sulfate plaster (US) · Estrichgips *m*, Anhydrit I *m, n*, Hochtemperaturanhydrit, $CaSO_4$ [*DIN 1060*]

~ (~); Class C ~, (gypsum-)plaster of Class C (Brit.) [*B.S. 1191*] · Putzgips *m* [*DIN 1168*]

~ **lime** [*substance*] → calcium oxid(e)
~ **phosphoric acid** · Phosphorpentoxid *n*, Phosphorsäureanhydrid *n*, wasserfreie Phosphorsäure *f*, P_2O_5
~ **plaster** → ~ gypsum-~

anileine, tyraline, aniline red · Anilinrot *n*
anilic sulphate, aniline ~ (Brit.); ~ sulfate (US) · schwefelsaures Anilin *n*, Anilinsulfat *n*

aniline · Anilin *n*, $C_6H_5NH_2$ [*Ein bei 182°C siedendes neutral reagierendes Öl*]
~ **black** · Anilinschwarz *n*, Pigmentschwarz
~ **dye** [*Any synthetic organic dyestuff may popularly be known as an aniline dye, though strictly speaking, the term may be incorrect*] · Anilinfarbe *f*
~ **point** · Anilinpunkt *m* [*DIN 51775*]
~ **-pyridine-insoluble matter** · Anilin-Pyridin-Unlösliche *n*

aniline red, anileine, tyraline · Anilinrot *n*

~ **resin** · Anilinharz *n*
~ **sulphate,** anilic ~ (Brit.); ~ sulfate (US) · Anilinsulfat *n*, schwefelsaures Anilin *n*
~ **violett,** regina purple · Anilinviolett *n*

animal adhesive, ~ glue, Scotch glue [*B.S. 745*] · Glutinleim *m*, tierischer Leim, Tierleim [*DIN 53260*]
~ ~ **in cake form,** ~ glue ~ ~ ~ · Tafelleim *m*
~ **black (pigment)** · schwarzes Pigment *n* tierischen Ursprungs, Schwarzpigment ~ ~, Schwarzfarbe *f* ~ ~, schwarze Farbe ~ ~ [*Siehe Anmerkung unter „Schwarzpigment"*]
~ **distemper** → ~ (glue(-bound))
~ **drying oil** · trocknendes Öl *n* tierischen Ursprungs (für Anstrichzwecke)
~ **fat** · Tierfett *n*
~ **fibre** (Brit.); ~ fiber (US) [*e.g. silk*] · tierische Faser *f*
~ **glue,** ~ adhesive, Scotch glue [*B.S. 745*] · Glutinleim *m*, tierischer Leim, Tierleim [*DIN 53260*]
~ ~ **in cake form,** ~ adhesive ~ ~ ~ · Tafelleim *m*
~ **(glue(-bound)) distemper;** ~ ~ water paint [*Australia*] · Leimfarbe *f* auf Tierleimgrundlage
~ **motif** · Tiermotiv *n*
~ **ornament** · Tierornament *n*
~ **pigment** · Pigment *n* tierischen Ursprungs
~ **quarter,** ~ shelter · Tierunterkunft *f*, Stall(ung) *m*, (*f*)
~ **quarters,** ~ shelters · Ställe *mpl*, Stallungen *fpl*, Tierunterkünfte *fpl*
~ **quarter's annex** (US); ~ ~ annexe (Brit.) · Stallanbau *m*
~ **relief** · Tierrelief *n*
~ **sculpture** · Tierplastik *f*
~ **shelter,** ~ quarter · Tierunterkunft *f*, Stall(ung) *m*, (*f*)
~ ~ **window,** window for animal shelter · Stallfenster *n*
~ **shelters,** ~ quarters · Tierunterkünfte *fpl*, Ställe *mpl*, Stallungen *fpl*
~ **symbolism** · Tiersymbolik *f*

animal wax — antefix (tile)

~ **wax** · Tierwachs *n*
anion exchanger · Anionenaustauscher *m*
anionic · anionaktiv [*Netzmittel*]
anisic aldehyde · Anisaldehyd *n*
anisotropic · anisotrop [*Ein Körper ist anisotrop, wenn seine physikalischen Eigenschaften richtungsabhängig sind*]
~ **elastic body** · anisotroper elastischer Körper *m*
~ **hardening** · anisotrope Stoffverfestigung *f*, ~ (Werkstoff)Verfestigung
~ **material** · anisotroper (Werk)Stoff *m*
~ **shell** · anisotrope Schale *f*
annealed wire, lashing ~, binding ~, iron ~, tying ~ [*Soft steel wire used for binding reinforcement*] · Rödeldraht *m*, Bindedraht
~ ~ · geglühter Draht *m* [*Zur Beseitigung der durch das Ziehen verursachten Härte und Sprödigkeit wird der Draht je nach dem Verwendungszweck schwarz (dunkel) oder unter Verhinderung von Luftzutritt blank geglüht*]
annealing · Glühen *n* [*Stahl*]
~ **oil**, hardening ~ · Härteöl *n*, Vergüteöl
annex (US) → ancillary building
annexe (Brit.) → ancillary building
~ (Brit.); annex (US) · (Gebäude)Anbau *m*, Erweiterungsbau
anniversary exhibition, jubilee ~ · Jubiläumsausstellung *f*
annual target · Jahresplansoll *n* [*Bausektor*]
annular arch · Kranzbogen *m*
~ **cell construction method** · Ringzellenbauweise *f*
~ **cross-section** · Ringquerschnitt *m*
~ **fin** · Rohr-Kreisrippe *f*
~ **girder** · Kreisringträger *m*
~ **longitudinal force** · Ringlängskraft *f*
~ **membrane** · Ringmembran(e) *f*
~ **plate**, ~ slab, circular ring(-shaped) ~ · Kreisringplatte *f*, kreisringförmige Platte
~ **slab**, ~ plate, circular ring(-shaped) ~ · Kreisringplatte *f*, kreisringförmige Platte
~ **space** · Ringraum *m*
~ **strain** · Ringdehnung *f*
~ **vault** · Ringgewölbe *n*
~ **zone** · Ringzone *f*
annularity · Ringförmigkeit *f*
annulet, shaft-ring, band, collar · Schaftring *m*, Bund *m*, Wirtel *m* [*Ringförmige Verstärkung am Säulenschaft. Der Schaftring ist technisch gesehen ein Binder = Zungenstein, der Wandsäulen mit dem Mauerwerk verbindet. Es gibt aber auch Schaftringe an freistehenden Säulen*]
~, gradetto, shaft ring [*In the Doric order of architecture one of the fillets beneath the capital*] · Riemchen *n*
anode metal · Anodenhartblei *n* [*DIN 1728*]

anodic coating, ~ finish, ~ film · Oxidhaut *f*, Oxidschicht *f*
~ **film**, ~ coating, ~ finish · Oxidhaut *f*, Oxidschicht *f*
~ **finish**, ~ coating, ~ film · Oxidhaut *f*, Oxidschicht *f*
~ **oxidation**; anodising (Brit.); anodizing (US) · anodische Oxydation *f*, Anodisieren *n*
~ **treatment method** · Anodisierverfahren *n*
to anodise (Brit.); to anodize (US) · anodisieren, elektrisch oxidieren
anodised (Brit.); anodized (US) · elektrisch oxidiert, anodisiert
~ **aluminium** (Brit.); anodized aluminum (US) · eloxiertes Aluminium *n*, elektrisch oxidiertes ~, anodisiertes ~
anodising (Brit.); anodizing (US); anodic oxidation · anodische Oxydation *f*, Anodisieren
~ **installation** (Brit.); anodizing ~ (US) · Anodisieranlage *f*
~ **plant** (Brit.); anodizing ~ (US) · Anodisierwerk *n*
anorthite, lime-fel(d)spar · Anorthit *m*, Kalkfeldspat *m*, $CaAl_2Si_2O_8$
~ **diorite** · Anorthitdiorit *m*
anse de panier → more-centered arch
ant attack · Ameisenfraß *m*
~ **salt of copper** · ameisensaures Kupfer *n*, Kupfer-Ameisensalz *n*
anta [*A type of projecting pier similar to a pilaster placed behind a column at the end of a side-wall of a Greek temple. The base and capital differ from those of the column; also used in Egyptian architecture*] · Antenpfeiler *m*
~ · Ante *f* [*Eine vorgezogene Seitenwand der Cella*]
~ **capital** · Antenkapitell *n*, Antenkapitäl [*Oberer Abschluß eines Antenpfeilers, meist aus Kymatien und Perlstäben bestehend*]
antechamber, anteroom, vestibule, vest. · Vestibül *n*, Vorraum *m*, Vorzimmer *n*
~ **with built-in wardrobe** · Garderobenvorraum *m* [*Hotelzimmer*]
antechapel [*A covered vestibule or transept forming a narthex to a collegiate chapel*] · Vorhalle *f* einer Stiftskapelle, ~ ~ Kollegiatkapelle, ~ ~ Kollegienkapelle
antechoir, antequire · Vorchor(bereich) *m*, (*m*, *n*)
antechurch, forechurch · Vorkirche *f*
antefix (tile) [*Antefixes or antefixa are ornamental blocks, fixed vertically at regular intervals along the lower edge of a roof, to cover the ends of tiles*] · Antefix *m*, Zierstirnziegel *m*, (ornamentaler) Stirnziegel, dekorativer Stirnziegel

antenave — anti-flux

antenave · (Kirchen)Vorschiff *n*
antenna gallery, aerial ~ · Antennengang *m* [*Rundfunkturm*]
~ installation, aerial ~ · Antennenanlage *f*
~ mast, aerial ~ · Antennenmast *m*
~ socket, aerial ~ · Antennensteckdose *f*
antependium → altar front(al)
antequire, antechoir · Vorchor(bereich) *m*, (*m*, *n*)
anteroom, vestibule, vest., antechamber · Vestibül *n*, Vorraum *m*, Vorzimmer *n*
antetemple · Antetemplum *n* [*Vorhalle eines antiken Tempels*]
anthemion (ornament) [*A favourite classical motif of alternating lotus and palmette connected by scrolls and forming a continuous pattern. The term, however, has now come to be used synonymously with palmette or honeysuckle to describe a single floral motif based on the palmette*] · Anthemion *n*
~ (~) → palmette
anthracene · Anthrazen *n*, Anthracen, $C_{14}H_{10}$
~ oil, green ~ · Anthrazenöl *n*, Anthracenöl [*Die bei 300° C bis 350° C übergehenden Anteile des Steinkohlenteeres, die für Ölfeuerungen verwendet werden*]
~ ~ tar, green ~ ~ · Anthrazenölteer *m*, Anthracenölteer
Anthracene II/Anthracene I ratio · Verhältnis *n* Anthrazenöl II : Anthrazenöl I, ~ Anthracenöl II : Anthracenöl I
anthracite stove · Anthrazitofen *m*
antiager · Alterungsschutzmittel *n*, Alterungsschutzstoff *m*
anti-aircraft tower, A.A. ~ · Flakturm *m*
anti-bacterial paint → bactericidal ~
anti-capillary · kapillarbrechend
anticlastic shell system · gegensinnig gekrümmtes Schalensystem *n*
anti-condensation ceiling · Kondenswasserdecke *f*, Tauwasserdecke, Schwitzwasserdecke, Schutzdecke
~ lining, ~ (sur)facing · Auskleidung *f* gegen Schwitzwasserbildung, Verkleidung ~ ~, Bekleidung ~ ~, ~ ~ Tauwasserbildung, ~ ~ Kondens(ations)wasserbildung
~ paint [*A paint designed to minimize the effects of condensation of moisture under intermittently dry and humid conditions. Such a material normally has a matt textured finish and frequently contains cork or some other heat-insulating material as a filler*] · Schwitzwasserfarbe *f*, Tauwasserfarbe, Kondenswasserfarbe, Kondensatfarbe
~ plaster, absorbent ~ · Kondensatverhütungsputz *m*, Kondenswasserverhütungsputz, Schwitzwasserverhütungsputz, Tauwasserverhütungsputz
~ protective measures · Schutzmaßnahmen *fpl* bei Tauwasserbildung

anticorrosion, corrosion prevention · Korrosionsverhütung *f*
anticorrosive (agent), anticorrosion ~, corrosion protection ~, corrosion protective ~ · Korrosionsschutzmittel *n*, Korrosionsschutzstoff *m*
~ coat, corrosion protection ~, anticorrosion ~ · Korrosionsschutzanstrich *m*, Korrosionsschutzaufstrich
~ coat(ing), anticorrosion ~, corrosion protection ~ · Korrosionsschutzschicht *f*
~ composition → ~ paint
~ foil, anticorrosion ~, corrosion protection ~ · Korrosionsschutzfolie *f*
~ grout → ~ slurry
~ mortar, anticorrosion ~, corrosion protection ~ · Korrosionsschutzmörtel *m*
~ paint, ~ composition, anticorrosion ~, corrosion protection ~ · Korrosionsschutzfarbe *f*
~ pigment, anticorrosion ~, corrosion protection ~ · Korrosionsschutzpigment *n*
~ prime coat, anticorrosion ~ ~, corrosion protection ~ ~ · Korrosionsschutzgrundierung *f*, Korrosionsschutzgrund(ier)anstrich *m*, Korrosionsschutzgrund(ier)aufstrich
~ primer, anticorrosion ~, corrosion protection ~ · Korrosionsschutzgrundier(ierung) *m*, (*f*), Korrosionsschutzgrundiermittel *n*, Korrosionsschutzgrundanstrichstoff *m*, Korrosionsschutzgrundanstrichmittel, Korrosionsschutzgrundierstoff
~ slurry, anticorrosion ~, corrosion protection ~, ~ grout · Korrosionsschutzschlämme *f*
anti-crack coating · Antirißbeschichtung *f*
~ reinforcement, ~ steel · Rißarmierung *f*, Rißbewehrung, Riß(stahl)einlagen *fpl*
~ steel, ~ reinforcement · Rißarmierung *f*, Rißbewehrung, Riß(stahl)einlagen *fpl*
anti-dazzle, dazzle-free, glare-free, glare-reducing; non-glare (US) · abblendend, blend(ungs)frei
~ glass, dazzle-free ~, glare-free ~, glare-reducing ~; non-glare ~ (US) · abblendendes Glas *n*, Blendschutzglas
anti-drumming agent, sound-deadening ~ · Antidröhnmittel *n*, Entdröhnungsmittel
~ coat(ing), sound-deadening ~ · Antidröhnbelag *m*
~ composition, ~ compound, sound-deadening ~ · Antidröhnmasse *f*
~ compound, ~ composition, sound-deadening ~ · Antidröhnmasse *f*
~ treatment, sound-deadening (~) · Entdröhnung *f*
anti-flux · flußhemmendes Mittel *n*

antifoaming agent — anti-siphonage device

antifoaming agent, antifoam (~), ~ aid, defoamant · Antischaummittel *n*, Schaumdämpfer *m*, Schaumverhütungsmittel, Schaumverhinderungsmittel, Entschäumungsmittel

anti-fouling · anwuchsverhindernder Schiffsbodenaufstrich *m*, ~ Schiffsbodenanstrich, vergifteter Anstrich, vergifteter Aufstrich

~ composition → ~ paint

~ paint, ~ composition, ship-bottom ~ [*A paint-like composition used to prevent the growth of barnacles and other organisms on ships' bottoms*] · Schiffsbodenfarbe *f*

antifreeze agent, antifreezer, frost protective, frost-proofer, frost-protection agent, antifreeze (mix(ture)) · Frostschutzmittel *n*, Gefrierschutzmittel

~ aid → anti-freezing ~

~ liquid, antifreezing ~, frost protective ~, frost protection ~ · Gefrierschutzflüssigkeit *f*, Frostschutzflüssigkeit

~ (mix(ture)) → ~ agent

~ powder, frost protective ~, frost-protection ~, antifreezing ~ · Frostschutzpulver *n*, Gefrierschutzpulver

~ solution, frost protective ~, frost-protection ~, antifreezing ~ · Frostschutzlösung *f*, Gefrierschutzlösung

antifreezer → antifreeze agent

antifreezing aid, antifreeze ~, frost-protection ~, frost protective ~ · Frosthilfe *f* [*Ein chloridfreies, hellgraues Pulver, das in der Betonmischung Reaktionswärme freisetzt und den (Ab)Bindeprozeß bei Frost in Gang hält*]

~ brick → frost(-)resistant (clay) ~

~ (clay) brick → frost(-)resistant (~) ~

~ liquid, antifreeze ~, frost protective ~, frost protection ~ · Gefrierschutzflüssigkeit *f*, Frostschutzflüssigkeit

~ powder → antifreeze ~

~ solution → antifreeze ~

anti-frost additive · Gefrierschutzzusatz(mittel) *m*, (*n*)

anti-glare shading · Blendschutz *m*

antileak ring, seal(ing) ~ · (Ab)Dicht(ungs)ring *m*, (Ab)Dicht(ungs)scheibe *f*

antimetric spanning system · antimetrisches Spannsystem *n* [*System der Lastenübertragung*]

~ wind loading · antimetrische Windbelastung *f*

antimonial lead, hard ~, regulus metal · Antimonblei *n*, Hartblei

~ ~ pipe, hard ~ ~ · Antimonbleirohr *n*, Hartbleirohr, Bleisparrohr

~ ~ pressure pipe, hard ~ ~ ~ · Antimonbleidruckrohr *n*, Hartbleidruckrohr

~ ~ sheet, hard ~ ~, roofing ~ ~ · Dachdeckerblei *n*, Hartbleiblech *n*, Antimonbleiblech

antimoniate of lead, lead antimoniate · antimonsaures Blei *n*, Bleiantimoniat *n*

antimony · Antimon *n*, Sb

~ metal · Antimonmetall *n*

~ oxide (Brit.); ~ oxid(e) (US); ~ tetroxide [*B.S. 338*] · Antimonweiß *n*, Antimontrioxid *n* [*Weißpigment*]

~ percentage · Antimongehalt *m*

~ tetroxide; ~ oxide (Brit.); ~ oxid(e) (US) [*B.S. 338*] · Antimonweiß *n*, Antimontrioxid *n* [*Weißpigment*]

anti-oscillation mounting, anti-vibration ~ · schwingungsfreie Montage *f*, erschütterungsfreie ~, vibrationsfreie ~

anti-oxidant · Antioxydans *n*, Antioxygen *n*, Oxidationsbremse *f* [*die Oxidation hemmender Stoff*]

anti-period style · nichthistorischer Stil *m*

antique building · antikes Gebäude *n*

~ character, ancient ~ · altertümliche Charakter *m*

~ drawn glass · gezogenes Antikglas *n*

~ effect · Antikeffekt *m*

~ glass · Antikglas *n*

~ marble · antike Marmorfigur *f*

~ motif · antikes Motiv *n*

~ structure · antikes Bauwerk *n*

~ temple · antiker Tempel *m*

anti-rot, rotproof, imputrescible · fäulnisfest, unfaulbar, fäulnisbeständig, unverrottbar, fäulniswidrig, verrottungsfest, verrottungswidrig, verrottungsbeständig

antirust action → rust preventive ~

~ agent → rust preventive ~

~ coat → rust preventive ~

~ compound → rust preventing ~

~ enamel → rust preventive ~

~ grease → rust preventing ~

~ hard gloss paint → rust preventive enamel

(~) metal coat(ing), (~) ~ finish · Metallbeschichtung *f*, Metallüberzug *m*, metallische Beschichtung, metallischer Überzug [*als Rostschutzschicht*]

~ oil → rust preventing ~

~ paint → rust preventive ~

~ pigment → rust preventive ~

~ solution → rust preventive ~

~ treatment → rust preventive ~

antiscald device · Verbrühungsschutz *m* [*Badebatterie*]

antisetting property · bodensatzverhindernde Eigenschaft *f* [*z.B. von Talk*]

anti-settling agent, suspending ~ · Antiabsetzmittel *n*, Schwebemittel

anti-siphonage → back-siphonage

~ device, ~ pipe, anti-siphoning ~, backsiphonage preventer, puff pipe · Rohrbelüfter *m* [*Fehlname: Rohrunterbrecher. DIN 3266*]

anti-siphonage device with leakage water ... — apex joint

~ **device with leakage water fitting,** ~ pipe ~ ~ ~ ~ ~, anti-siphoning ~ ~ ~ ~ ~, backsiphonage preventer ~ ~ ~ ~ ~ · Rohrbe- und -entlüfter *m*

~ **pipe,** ~ device, anti-siphoning ~, backsiphonage preventer, puff pipe · Rohrbelüfter *m* [*Fehlname: Rohrunterbrecher. DIN 3266*]

~ ~ **with leakage water fitting,** ~ device ~ ~ ~ ~, anti-siphonage ~ ~ ~ ~ ~, backsiphonage preventer ~ ~ ~ ~ · Rohrbe- und -entlüfter *m*

anti-siphoning device, ~ pipe, anti-siphonage ~, backsiphonage preventer, puff pipe · Rohrbelüfter *m* [*Fehlname: Rohrunterbrecher. DIN 3266*]

~ **pipe,** ~ device, anti-siphonage ~, backsiphonage preventer, puff pipe · Rohrbelüfter *m* [*Fehlname: Rohrunterbrecher. DIN 3266*]

anti-skid, non-skid, skidproof, anti-slip, non-slip(ping), non-slippery · gleitsicher, rutschfest, trittsicher, rutschsicher, griffig

~ **paint,** anti-slip ~, skidproof ~, non-slip(ping) ~, non-skid ~ non-slippery ~ · rutschfeste (Anstrich)Farbe *f*, trittsichere ~, gleitsichere ~, Gleitschutz(anstrich)farbe

~ **rib(bed) tile** → (anti-slip) ~ ~

anti-skinning agent · Hautverhinderungsmittel *n*, Hautverhütungsmittel

anti-slip → anti-skid

~ **aggregate,** non-slip ~, slip-resistant ~ · gehsicherer Zuschlag(stoff) *m*

~ **paint,** non-slip(ping) ~, anti-skid ~, nonskid ~, skidproof ~, non-slippery ~ · Gleitschutz(anstrich)farbe *f*, gleitsichere (Anstrich)Farbe, trittsichere (Anstrich)Farbe, rutschfeste (Anstrich)Farbe

(~) **rib(bed) tile,** nonskid ~ ~, skidproof ~ ~, non-slip(ping) ~ ~, antiskid ~ ~, non-slippery ~ ~ · (gleitsichere) gekörnte Platte *f*, (~) ~ Belagplatte, (~) ~ Fliese, trittsichere ~, ruschfeste ~

anti-spalling agent [*e.g. linseed oil*] · Anti-Abschuppungsmittel *n*, Anti-Abblätterungsmittel [*Beton*]

antistatic agent · Antistatikmittel *n*

anti-stripping additive → activator

~ **agent** → activator

antisun cantilever roof · Sonnenschutzkragdach *n*, Sonnenschutzauslegerdach

~ **glass,** solar ~ · Sonnenschutzglas *n*

anti-vibration mounting, anti-oscillation ~ · schwingungsfreie Montage *f*, erschütterungsfreie ~, vibrationsfreie ~

Antwerp blue [*Prussian blue made pale by reducing with large quantities of inert pigment. Sometimes applied to zinc ferrocyanide*] · Antwerpenerblau *n*

anywhere carpet, indoor-outdoor ~ · Allzweck-Teppichboden *m*, Allzweck-Textilboden(belag) *m*

AP → acid-resisting

apartment, suite (of rooms) · (Zimmer)Flucht *f*, Raumflucht

~ → ~ unit

~ **block** (US) → block (of flats)

~ **building** (US) → block (of flats)

(~) **dweller,** resident, (room) occupant, user · Raumbenutzer *m*, (Wohnungs)Benutzer, (Raum)Insasse *m*, Wohnungsinsasse, Bewohner

~ **entrance,** ~ unit ~, flat ~; living unit ~ (US) · (Geschoß)Wohnungseingang *m*, Etagenwohnungseingang, Stockwerkwohnungseingang

~ **floor,** residential ~; ~ storey (Brit.); ~ story (US) · Wohnetage *f*, Wohnstockwerk *n*, Wohngeschoß *n*

~ **hotel,** residential ~ · Hotel garni *n*

~ **house** (US) → block (of flats)

~ **housing,** multifamily ~ · Mehrfamilien(wohn)bauten *f*

~ **kitchen** → ~ unit ~

~ **skyscraper;** skyscraper block (of flats) skyscraper flats (Brit.) · Wohn(ungs)wolkenkratzer *m*

~ **storey,** residential ~ (Brit.); ~ story (US); ~ floor · Wohnetage *f*, Wohnstockwerk *n*, Wohngeschoß *n*

~ **tower** (US) → residence ~

~ **(unit),** APT., flat; living unit (US) [*A self-contained dwelling on one stor(e)y in a multi-stor(e)y building*] · Stockwerkwohnung *f*, Etagenwohnung, (Geschoß)Wohnung

~ (~) **entrance,** flat ~; living unit ~ (US) · (Geschoß)Wohnungseingang *m*, Etagenwohnungseingang, Stockwerkwohnungseingang

~ (~) ~ **door,** flat ~ ~; living unit ~ ~ (US) · (Geschoß)Wohnungseingangstür *f*, Etagenwohnungseingangstür, Stockwerkwohnungseingangstür

~ (~) **floor space,** flat ~ ~; living unit ~ ~ (US) · Stockwerkwohn(ungs)fläche *f*, Etagenwohn(ungs)fläche, (Geschoß)Wohn(ungs)fläche

~ (~) ~ **kitchen,** flat ~; living unit ~ (US) · Stockwerkwohnungsküche *f*, Etagenwohnungsküche, (Geschoß)Wohnungsküche

APC → acoustic(al) plaster ceiling

aperture → beam box

apex, vertex, key, top, crown · Scheitel(-punkt) *m*

~ · Anfallpunkt *m* [*Dachkonstruktion*]

~ **block,** vertex ~, crown ~, top ~, key ~, closer · (Bogen)Schlußstein *m*, (Bogen)Scheitelstein [*veraltet: König m, Kolophon m*]

~ **hinge,** vertex ~, top ~, key ~, crown ~ · Scheitelgelenk *n*

~ **hog,** vertex ~, key ~, crown ~, top ~ · Scheitelüberhöhung *f*

~ **joint,** vertex ~, key ~, top ~, crown ~ · Scheitelfuge *f*, Schlußfuge [*Fuge am höchsten Gewölbepunkt oder Bogenpunkt, wenn kein Scheitelstein vorhanden ist*]

apex mould — appliqué

~ **mould** (Brit.); ~ mold (US) · Scheitelform f [Betonsteinindustrie]

~ **sag**, crown ~, vertex ~, top ~, key ~ · Scheitelsenkung f

~ **stone**, saddle ~ [The top stone in a gable end] · Giebelschlußstein m

~ ~, top ~, vertex ~, crown ~, keystone [The central stone of an arch or a vault; sometimes carved] · Scheitelstein m aus Naturstein, Schlußstein ~ ~

aplite · Aplit m [Fehlname: Granitmarmor m]

apodyterium, discrobing room · Apodyterium n, Auskleideraum m, Auskleidezimmer n [römische Therme; Palästra]

apophyge, congé, scape [A slight concave sweep or extension at the top or bottom of a column shaft where it joins the capital or base] · Apophyge f

apparatus floor; ~ **story** (US); ~ **storey** (Brit.) · Betriebsetage f, Betriebsgeschoß n, Betriebsstockwerk n, Techniketage, Technikgeschoß, Technikstockwerk [Fernmeldeturm; Hochhaus; Stadion]

---

apparatus for the water retention test | **Absaug(e)gerät n nach ATSM C 91-51**
filter paper | Filterpapier n
flow after suction | Ausbreitmaß n nach Absaugen
flow determination | Bestimmung f des Ausbreitmaßes
flow table | Ausbreittisch m
funnel | (Setz)Trichter m
mercury manometer | Quecksilbermanometer n
mixing | Anrühren n
mixing bowl | Rührschüssel f
perforated dish | Nutsche f, Lochplatte f
pressure control device | Druckregler m
rubber gasket | Gummidicht(ungs)ring n
spatula | Spachtel m, f
straightedge | Lineal n
three-way stop cock | Dreiwegehahn m
water aspirator | Wasserstrahlpumpe f
water retention test | Absaug(e)prüfung f, Absaug(e)probe f, Absaug(e)versuch m
water retention value | Wasserhaltewert m, Wasserhaltevermögen n

---

apparatus storey (Brit.) → ~ **floor**

apparent porosity · scheinbare Porigkeit f, ~ Porosität f

~ **specific gravity** [The ratio of the mass in air of a unit volume of a material at a stated temperature to the mass in air at equal density of an equal volume of gas-free distilled water at a stated temperature. If the material is a solid, the volume is that of the impermeable portion] · (Roh)Dichte f, Raumgewicht n der Volumeneinheit, Rohwichte f

~ ~ ~ **of the (clay) body,** ~ ~ ~ ~ ~ **stone** [See remark under '(Roh-) Dichte'] · Scherben(roh)dichte f, Scherbenrohwichte

~ ~ ~ ~ ~ (~) **brick** [See remark under '(Roh)Dichte'] · Ziegel(roh)dichte f, Ziegelrohwichte

appearance · Aussehen n

appliance ventilation duct · Gerätelüftungskanal m

applicant proposing to build, person ~ ~ ~ · Bauantragsteller m

application · Angriff m [Baustatik]

~, distribution, spreading · Aufbringen n, Auftrag(en) m, (n)

~ **by brush(ing)**, brush application · Aufstreichen n [Aufstrichmittel]

~ ~ ~, brush application · Streichen n [Eine Fläche mit Aufstrichmittel]

~ **consistency** · Verarbeitungskonsistenz f, Verarbeitungssteife f

~ **method**, method of application · Auftragverfahren n [Anstrichtechnik]

~ **of a flame,** ~ ~ **flames** · Beflammen n

~ ~ **load**, loading, load application · Belasten n, Lastaufbringung f, Belastung, Lastangriff m

~ ~ **mortar;** rendering (US) · Mörtelauftrag m

~ ~ **wax resist** · Abdecken n [Wenn bei der Oberflächenbehandlung von Glas nicht alle Teile der Einwirkung des Sandstrahles oder der Ätzsäure ausgesetzt werden sollen, werden sie mit einem Schutzlack überzogen]

~ **thickness** → distribution ~

applied column, attached ~ [A column attached to a wall or pier] · Wandsäule f

~ **moment** · Momentenlast f

~ **thread**, laid-on ~ · Fadenauflage f [Plastische Verzierung der Oberfläche von Hohlgläsern]

appliqué [An ornament that is applied to another surface] · Auflegeornament n, Auflegeverzierung f

appliqué — apt for use in high-rise buildings 56

~ [*An ornamental wall bracket to hold candles or electric bulbs*] · Zierwandlampenkonsole f, Wandzierlampenkonsole

to apply, to lay on [*plaster*] · antragen [*Putz*]

~ ~, to distribute, to spread · aufbringen, auftragen

~ ~ **a header coat** · köpfen [*Anstrichtechnik*]

~ ~ ~ **mist coat** [*For instance, to blend with background when spotting in*] · ausnebeln [*Anstrichtechnik*]

~ ~ **by brushing** · aufstreichen

approach · (Lösungs)Ansatz m

approved combustible plastic · zugelassener brennbarer Kunststoff m

~ **(deposited) plans**, ~ (~) **drawings** · genehmigte Pläne mpl, ~ Zeichnungen fpl

~ **method** · zugelassenes Verfahren n, zugelassene Methode f

~ **plastic** · zugelassener Kunststoff m

~ **rule** [*Any legally adopted rule of the building official or of a recognized authoritative agency*] · anerkannte Regel f

to approximate · (an)nähern

approximate height · Ungefährhöhe f

~ **length** · Ungefährlänge f

~ **quantity** · Ungefährmenge f

~ **solution** · angenäherte (Auf)Lösung f, (An)Näherungs(auf)lösung f

~ **value** · Richtwert m, Richtzahl f

~ **value** · (An)Näherungswert m, Rundwert

~ **width** · Ungefährbreite f

approximation · (An)Näherung f

~ · (An)Näherungsrechnung f, Berechnung der (An)Näherungswerte, (an)näherungsweise Berechnung

~ **equation**, ~ **formula** · (An)Näherungsformel f, (An)Näherungsgleichung f

~ **hypothesis** · (An)Näherungsannahme f

~ **theory** · (An)Näherungstheorie f

appurtenance [*Any built-in, non-structural portion of a building, such as doors, windows, ventilators, heating equipment, partitions, etc.*] · (Innen-)Ausbauteil m, n

appurtenant structure [*A structure attached to the exterior or erected on the roof of a building designed to support service equipment or used in connection therewith, or for advertising or display purposes, or other similar uses*] · Nebenbau(werk) m, n

apron → (under-)window spandrel

~, **cap flashing (piece), counter flashing (piece), cover flashing (piece)** [*See remark under 'Anschluß'*] · Kappleiste f, Kappstreifen m, Überhangleiste, Überhangstreifen

~, **hangar** ~ · (Hallen)Vorfeld n [*Luftfahrtgelände*]

~ → ~ **flashing**

~ **area** · Vorfeldfläche f [*Flughafen*]

~ **facing** → spandrel (wall) (sur)facing

~ **(flashing)**, chimney apron [*A one-piece flashing, such as is used at the lower side of a chimney penetrating a sloping roof*] · (Front)Schürze f, vordere Schürze

~ **lining** → spandrel (wall) (sur)facing

~ **panel** → (under-)window spandrel ~

~ **wall** (US) → (under-)window spandrel

~ ~ **facing** (US) → spandrel (wall) (sur)facing

~ ~ **lining** (US) → spandrel (wall) (sur-)facing

~ ~ **panel** (US) → (under-)window spandrel ~

apse → apsis

~ **arch**, apsis ~, exedra ~ · Apsisbogen m, Apsidenbogen, Absidenbogen, Exedrabogen, Abseitenbogen

~ ~ **impost**, apsis ~ ~, exedra ~ ~ · Apsisbogenkämpfer m, Apsidenbogenkämpfer, Absidenbogenkämpfer, Exedrabogenkämpfer, Abseitenbogenkämpfer

~ **window**, exedra ~, apsis ~ · Apsisfenster n, Apsidenfenster, Absidenfenster, Exedrafenster, Abseitenfenster

apses in echelon, staggered apses [*A series of parallel chapels, aisles, c(h)ancels, etc., arranged stepwise and designed to produce an arrow-head or chevron formation*] · gestaffelte Apsiden fpl, ~ Absiden fpl

apsidal chapel → choir ~

~ **choir**, ~ **quire** · Absidenchor m, Apsischor, Apsidialchor, Apsidenchor

~ **entrance hall** · apsidiale Eingangshalle f, absidiale ~

apsidiole, absidiole [*Small apse, generally serving as chapel*] · Apsidiola f, Apsidiole

apsis, apse, exedra · (Chor)Apsis f, (Chor)Apside f, (Chor)Abside, (Chor-)Abseite f, Chorhaupt n, Chornische f, Konche f, Exedra f, Tribuna f; Altarnische, Altartribuna [*Halbrunder oder vieleckiger Abschluß einer romanischen Basilika, im weiteren Sinne jeder Chorschluß einer Kirche*]

~ **arch**, apse ~, exedra ~ · Apsisbogen m, Apsidenbogen, Absidenbogen, Exedrabogen, Abseitenbogen

~ ~ **impost**, apse ~ ~, exedra ~ ~ · Apsisbogenkämpfer m, Apsidenbogenkämpfer, Absidenbogenkämpfer, Exedrabogenkämpfer, Abseitenbogenkämpfer

~ **window**, apse ~ exedra ~ · Apsisfenster n, Apsidenfenster, Absidenfenster Exedrafenster, Abseitenfenster

apt for use in high-rise buildings · hochhaustauglich [*z.B. Fenster*]

apteral — arch bracing

apteral [*An adjective describing a classical-style building with columns at the end, but not along the sides*] · apteral

~ **temple** · Apteraltempel *m* [*Griechischer Tempel ohne Säulengang an den Längsseiten*]

aquatic building · Bäderbauwerk *n*

~ **buildings** · Bäderbauten *f*

aqueous corrosion · Feuchtigkeitskorrosion *f*, Feuchtekorrosion

~ **liquid** · wässerige Flüssigkeit *f*, wäßrige ~

~ **phase** · wässerige Phase *f*, wäßrige ~

~ **resin emulsion** · wässerige Harzemulsion *f*, wäßrige ~

~ **solution** · wäßrige Lösung *f*, wässerige ~

~ **wood preservative** · wäßriges Holzschutzmittel *n*, wässeriges ~

AR → acid-resisting

arabesque decoration, ~ ornamentation · Arabeskendekor(ation) *n*, (*f*)

~ **(ornament)** [*Intricate and fanciful surface decoration generally based on geometrical patterns and using combinations of flowing lines, tendrils, etc., and classical vases, sphinxes, etc.*] · Arabeske *f*

~ **ornamentation,** ~ decoration · Arabeskendekor(ation) *n*, (*f*)

Arab(ian) architecture → Muslim ~

Arabian capital · arabisches Kapitäl *n*, ~ Kapitell

Arabic arch → (round) horseshoe ~

ar(a)eostyle, wide-spaced [*Columns spaced at more than 3 diameters apart*] · lichtsäulig

~ **temple,** wide-spaced ~ . lichtsäuliger Tempel *m*, Aräostylostempel [*Ein Tempel, bei dessen Säulenstellung das Interkolumnium 3½ untere Säulendurchmesser beträgt. Der Ausdruck stammt von Vitruv*]

aragonite · Aragonit *m*, $CaCO_3$ [*Seltene, rhombische Form des kristallisierten Kalziumkarbonats*]

aragonitic lime(stone) · Schaumkalk(stein) *m*, Wellenkalk(stein)

arbitrary · beliebig, willkürlich

~ **assumption,** ~ hypothesis · willkürliche Annahme *f*, beliebige ~

~ **constant** · willkürliche Konstante *f*, beliebige ~

~ **moment diagram** · willkürliches Momentendiagramm *n*, beliebiges ~

arc welded · lichtbogengeschweißt

arcade → shopping ~

~ [*A covered walk with a line of such arches along one or both long sides*] · Arkadengang *m*, Bogengang

~ · Arkade *f* [*Ein Bogen mit seinen beiden Stützen; im weiteren Sinne eine Folge solcher Bogenstellungen*]

~ **apex** → ~ crown

~ **cornice** · Arkaden(ge)sims *m*, (*n*)

~ **crown,** ~ apex, ~ top, ~ key, ~ vertex · Arkadenscheitel *m*

~ **impost** · Arkadenkämpfer *m*

~ **key** → ~ crown

~ **pier** · Arkadenpfeiler *m*

~ **rib** · Arkadenrippe *f*

~ **top** → ~ crown

~ **vertex** → ~ apex

arcaded court · Arkadenhof *m*

~ **façade** · Arkadenfassade *f*

~ **gallery,** ~ tribune · Arkadenempore *f*

~ ~ · Säulengalerie *f*

~ **ground floor** · Arkadenerdgeschoß *n*

~ **tribune,** ~ gallery · Arkadenempore *f*

~ **window** · Arkadenfenster *n*

arcading · Bogenstellung *f*

~, arcature · Arkatur *f*, Arkaden *fpl* [*veraltet: Bogenwerk n, Arkadenwerk. Die Gesamtheit der Arkaden eines Gebäudes*]

arcature, miniature arcade · Zwergarkade *f*

~, arcading · Arkatur *f*, Arkaden *fpl* [*veraltet: Bogenwerk n, Arkadenwerk. Die Gesamtheit der Arkaden eines Gebäudes*]

arch, structural ~ [*A series of voussoirs spanning an opening*] · Bogen *m*

~ → arched girder

~ **action** · Bogenwirkung *f*

~ **analysis,** structural ~ ~, arch structural ~ · Bogenstatik *f*

~ **apex** → ~ key

~ **axis;** ~ center line (US); ~ centre line (Brit.) · Bogenachse *f*, Bogenmittellinie *f*

(~) back, (~) extrados, upper surface of arch, extrados of arch, back of arch [*The outer line or surface of the convex side of an arch*] · Rücken *m*, Bogen~, äußere Bogenfläche *f*

~ **band,** transverse arch, transversal arch · Doppelbogen *m*, (Quer)Gurt(bogen) *m*, Transversalgurt(bogen), Querbogen, Transversalbogen [*Quer zur Längsachse eines Raumes gespannter Entlastungsbogen*]

~ **barrel** → skewed ~ ~

~ **bay** · Bogenfeld *n* [*Das von einem Bogen und seiner Kämpferlinie umgrenzte Feld*]

~ **beam** [*It is an eccentrically curved beam in which the section depth shortens as the central section is approached*] · Bogenbalken(träger) *m*

~ **bearing** · Bogen(auf)lager *n* [*Für Hoch- und Tiefbauten*]

~ **bond** · Bogenverband *m*

~ **bracing** → ~ stiffening

arch brick — arch stone

~ **brick,** wedge-shaped ~, voussoir (~), featheredge ~; gauged (clay) ~ (Brit.); gaged (clay) ~ (US) [*One of a series of wedge-shaped bricks used to form an arch*] · Keilziegel *m*, Wölbziegel *m*, Bogenziegel, gebrannter Keilstein *m*

~ ~ **for manholes,** ~ ~ ~ manways · Mannlochklinker *m* für runde Schächte, Schachtklinker ~ ~ ~

~**-butment,** arch(ed) buttress, flying buttress, flying arch, flier (arch); bow [*old English term*] · (einfacher) Strebebogen *m*, Hochschiffstrebe *f* [*veraltet: fliegende Strebe, Fluchtstrebe*]; Schwibbogen [*Fehlname*]

arch buttress, arched ~, flying ~ · Strebebogen *m*, Schwibbogen

~ **casting,** ~ concreting, ~ pour(ing) · Bogenbetonieren *n*

~ **centre** (Brit.); ~center (US) · Bogenlehrgerüst *n*

~ ~ **line** (Brit.); ~ center ~ (US); ~ axis · Bogenachse *f*, Bogenmittellinie *f*

~ **chord** · Bogensehne *f*

~ **compression** · Bogenzusammendrückung *f*

~ **concreting,** ~ pour(ing), ~ casting · Bogenbetonieren *n*

~ **construction** → arched ~

~ **cornice** · Bogen(ge)sims *m*, (*n*)

~ **crown** → ~ key

~ **curvature** · Bogenkrümmung *f*

~ **depth** · Bogenkonstruktionshöhe *f*

~ **element** · Bogenelement *n*

(~) **extrados,** (~) back, upper surface of arch, extrados of arch, back of arch [*The outer line or surface of the convex side of an arch*] · äußere Bogenfläche *f*, (Bogen)Rücken *m*

~ **fixed at both ends** → fixed arch

~ **force** · Bogenkraft *f*

~ **girder without horizontal thrust,** arch(ed girder) ~ ~ ~ · Bogen(träger) *m* mit durch Zugband aufgehobenem Horizontalschub

~ **impost** · Bogenkämpfer *m*

(~) **intrados,** inner surface of arch, soffit of arch, underside of arch [*The inner line or surface of the concave side of an arch*] · (Bogen)Leibung *f*, innere Bogenfläche *f*

~ **key,** ~ vertex, ~ apex, ~ top, ~ crown · Bogenscheitel(punkt) *m*

~ **length** · Bogenlänge *f*

~ **line,** ~ outline, (out)line of arch · Bogenlinie *f*, Bogenprofil *n*, Wölbung *f*

~ **load** · Bogenlast *f*

~ **material** · Bogenbaumaterial *n* [*Schweiz*]; Bogenbaustoff *m*

~ **mechanism** · Bogen-Mechanismus *m*

Arch of Augustus · Augustusbogen *m*

~ ~ ~ **at Perugia** · Augustusbogen *m* zu Perugia

arch of brickwork, brick(work) arch · Ziegelbogen *m*

Arch of Constantine at Rome · Konstantinsbogen *m* in Rom

~ ~ **Janus Quadrifrones** · Janusbogen *m*

~ ~ **Septimus Severus at Rome** · (Triumph)Bogen *m* des Septimus Severus in Rom

~ ~ **Tiberius at Orange** · Tiberiusbogen *m* zu Orange

~ ~ **Titus at Rome** · Titusbogen *m* zu Rom

~ ~ **Trajan at Ancona** · Trajansbogen *m* zu Ancona

arch of triumph, triumphal arch, monumental ~ · Triumphbogen *m*, Monumentalbogen

~ **(out)line,** (out)line of arch · Bogenlinie *f*, Bogenprofil *n*, Wölbung *f*

~ **parabola** · Bogenparabel *f*

~ **plane** · Bogenebene *f*

~ **pour(ing),** ~ casting, ~ concreting · Bogenbetonieren *n*

~ **radius** · Bogenhalbmesser *m*

~ **reinforcing,** ~ stiffening, ~ bracing · Bogenabsteifung *f*, Bogenversteifung, Bogenaussteifung, Bogenverstärkung

~ **rib** · Bogenrippe *f*

(~) ~ **footing** · (Bogen)Rippenfundament *n*

~ **ring** · Bogenring *m*

~ **rise** · Bogenpfeil(höhe) *m*, (*f*), Bogenstich(höhe) *m*, (*f*), Bogenhöhe [*Höhe eines Bogens, gemessen als senkrechter Abstand zwischen Kämpferebene und Schlußstein*]

~ **section** · Bogenabschnitt *m*

arch(-shap)ed, arcuate(d), arcual; arquated [*obsolete*] · bogig, bogenförmig

arch soffit [*The surface underneath the curve of the arch*] · Bogenuntersicht *f*

(~) **spandrel** · (Bogen)Zwickel *m* [*Die dreieckige auf einer Spitze stehende Fläche zwischen zwei Bogenlinien*]

~ **springer** · Bogenanfänger *m*, Bogenanwölber, Bogenanfangsstein *m*, Bogenkämpferstein

~ **stay,** ~ stiffener · Bogenaussteif(ungs)element *n*, Bogenversteifungselement, Bogenverstärkungselement

~ **stiffener,** ~ stay · Bogenaussteif(ungs)element *n*, Bogenversteifungselement, Bogenverstärkungselement

~ **stiffening,** ~ bracing, ~ reinforcing · Bogenabsteifung *f*, Bogenversteifung, Bogenaussteifung, Bogenverstärkung

~ **stone,** wedge-shaped ~, voussoir [*One of a series of wedge-shaped stones used to form an arch*] · Bogen(-Natur)stein *m*, Keil(-Natur)stein, Wölb(-Natur)stein, Bogenkeilstein

arch stress — arched style (of architecture)

~ **stress** · Bogenspannung *f*

~ **structural analysis, (structural) arch** ~ · Bogenstatik *f*

~ **structure** → arched ~

~ **style (of architecture)** → arched ~ (~ ~)

~ **system** · Bogensystem *n*

~ ~ **for absorption of thrust** · Bogensystem *n* für Horizontalschubaufnahme

~ **template** · Bogenlehre *f*

~ **thrust** · Bogenschub *m*

~ **tie** · Zuganker *m*, Bogenanker [*Anker zur Sicherung gegen die Schubwirkung eines Bogens*]

~ **top** → ~ key

~ **vertex** → ~ key

~ **with apex hinge,** ~ ~ vertex ~, ~ ~ crown ~, ~ ~ top ~, ~ ~ key ~ · Scheitelgelenkbogen *m*, Bogen mit Scheitelgelenk

~ ~ **crown hinge,** ~ ~ apex ~, ~ ~ vertex ~, ~ ~ key ~, ~ ~ top ~ · Scheitelgelenkbogen *m*, Bogen mit Scheitelgelenk

~ ~ **joggled joints** · Hakensteinbogen *m*

~ ~ **key hinge,** ~ ~ top ~, ~ ~ apex ~, ~ ~ vertex ~, ~ ~ crown ~ · Scheitelgelenkbogen *m*, Bogen mit Scheitelgelenk

~ ~ **tie** → arched girder ~ ~

~ ~ **top hinge,** ~ ~ key ~, ~ ~ crown ~, ~ ~ apex ~, ~ ~ vertex ~ · Scheitelgelenkbogen *m*, Bogen mit Scheitelgelenk

~ ~ **vertex hinge,** ~ ~ apex ~, ~ ~ crown ~, ~ ~ top ~, ~ ~ key ~ · Scheitelgelenkbogen *m*, Bogen mit Scheitelgelenk

arch(a)eological discovery · archäologischer Fund *m*

archaic architecture · archaische Architektur *f*, ~ Baukunst *f*

~ **sepulchre** · archaische Grabanlage *f*

Archaic temple at Ephesus · Älterer Tempel *m* zu Ephesus

Archangel tar, Stockholm ~, wood ~ · Holzteer *m*

arched → arcual

arch(ed) boom, ~ chord, ~ flange · Bogenflansch *m*, Bogengurt(ung) *m*, (*f*), gekrümmter Gurt, gekrümmter Flansch, gekrümmte Gurtung

~ **building,** arcuated ~ · Bogengebäude *n*

~ **buttress,** flying ~, flying arch, flier (arch), arch-butment; bow [*old English term*] · (einfacher) Strebebogen *m*, Hochschiffstrebe *f* [*veraltet: fliegende Strebe, Fluchtstrebe*]; Schwibbogen [*Fehlname*]

~ **ceiling,** Schürmann's ~ · Gewölbeträgerdecke *f*, Schürmannsche Decke

~ **chord** → ~ boom

~ **concrete roof** · Betonbogendach *n*

~ **construction,** arcuate(d) ~, arcual ~, arcuation ~, arched work · Bogenbau *m*

(arched) corbel-table · Bogenfries *m* [*Eine Reihe von mindestens zwei kleinen Bögen nebeneinander. Verwendung im Mittelalter hauptsächlich unter Dachgesimsen. Ein der Giebellinie folgender Bogenfries wird „steigender Bogenfries" genannt*]

arch(ed) (culvert) pipe · Bogendurchlaßrohr *n*

~ **diagonal** · Bogendiagonale *f*

~ **door** · Bogentür *f*

~ **entrance** · Bogeneingang *m*

~ **flange** → ~ boom

~ **frame** · Bogenrahmen *m*

arch(ed girder), curved ~ · Bogen(träger) *m*, gekrümmter Träger [*Träger, der bei senkrechten Lasten nach außen gerichtete Stützkräfte (inclined reactions) auf die Auflager überträgt*]

~ ~ **chord** · Bogen(träger)sehne *f*

~ ~ **length** · Bogen(träger)länge *f*

~ ~ **load** · Bogen(träger)last *f*

~ ~ **of constant cross section** · Bogen(träger) *m* mit gleichbleibendem Querschnitt

~ ~ **parabola** · Bogen(träger)parabel *f*

~ ~ **plane** · Bogen(träger)ebene *f*

~ ~ **with tie, tied arch(ed girder), bowstring girder** · Bogen(träger) *m* mit Zugband, gekrümmter Träger ~ ~, Zugband-Bogen(träger), Stabbogen(träger)

~ ~ **without horizontal thrust,** arch girder ~ ~ ~ · Bogen(träger) *m* mit durch Zugband aufgehobenem Horizontalschub

arched opening · Bogenöffnung *f*

arch(ed) pipe, ~ culvert ~ · Bogendurchlaßrohr *n*

arched plate · Tonnenblech *n* [*Tonnenbleche werden aus glatten Grobblechen in warmem Zustand durch hydraulische Pressen in ihre gebogene Form gebracht*]

arch(ed) portal · Bogenportal *n*

~ **recess** · Bogennische *f*

~ **rib** · Bogenrippe *f*

~ **roof** · Bogendach *n*

~ **(~) truss** · Bogen(träger)(dach)binder *m*, (Dach)Binderbogen(träger) *m*

~ **stair(case)** · Bogentreppe *f*

~ **structure,** arcuate(d) ~, arcual ~ · Bogenbauwerk *n*

~ **style (of architecture),** arcual ~ (~ ~), arcuate(d) ~ (~ ~) [*A style of architecture in which the structure is supported on arches; in contrast to*

arch(ed) style... — architectural hardware

'trabeated' architecture where vertical posts and horizontal beams are used structurally throughout] · Bogenstil *m*

~ **system**, arcual ~, arcuate(d) ~ · Bogensystem *n*

~ ~ **for absorption of thrust**, arcual ~ ~ ~ ~ ~ ~, arcuate(d) ~ ~ ~ ~ ~ ~ · Bogensystem *n* für Horizontalschubaufnahme

~ **truss(ed girder)** · Bogenfachwerk(-träger) *n*, (*m*), gekrümmter Fachwerkträger, gekrümmtes Fachwerk

arched vault · Bogengewölbe *n*

arch(ed) window, round-headed ~, round-arched ~, camber ~ [*A window arched at the top*] · (Rund)Bogenfenster *n*, Halbkreisbogenfenster, rundbogiges Fenster

arched work, arch(ed) construction, arcual construction, arcuation construction, arcuate(d) construction · Bogenbau *m*

archer frieze · Bogenschützenfries *m*

architect and designer · entwerfender Architekt *m*

~ **errant** · Wanderarchitekt *m*

architect-in-charge · ausführender Architekt *m*, (bau)leitender ~

architect in private practice · Privatarchitekt *m*

~ **partnership** · Architektengemeinschaft *f*

architectonic [*A term implying that a structure shows a knowledge of architectural principles on the part of its designer*] · architektonisch

architectonics [*The science of architecture*] · Architektonik *f*

architect's fee · Architektengebühr *f*

~ **office** · Architektenbüro *n*

~ ~ · Architektenatelier *n*

architectural acoustics · Bauakustik *f*

~ **aggregate** → ~ concrete ~

~ **alloy** · Architekturlegierung *f*

~ **aluminium** (Brit.); ~ aluminum (US) · Architekturalu(minium) *n*

~ **assistant** → ~ draughtsman

~ **award**, prize for architecture · Architekturpreis *m*

~ **bronze** · Sondermessing *n*, Profilmessing, MS 56, Ms 56, Messing 56 [*Fehlnamen: Baubronze f, Bronzeprofile npl*]

~ **(builders') fitting** → ~ (~) furniture

~ **(~) fittings** → ~ (~) hardware

~ **(~) furniture**, ~ (~) fitting · Architekturbeschlag *m*

~ **(~) hardware**, ~ (~) fittings · Architekturbeschläge *mpl*

~ **building material**, ~ construction(al) ~, ~ structural ~ · Architekturbaustoff *m*; Architekturbaumaterial *n* [*Schweiz*]

~ **career** · Architekturlaufbahn *f*

~ **cast concrete product** → (pre)cast architectural (concrete) ~

~ **cast(ing)** → (pre)cast architectural (concrete) member

~ **competition** · Architekturwettbewerb *m*, Architektenwettbewerb

~ **concept** · Baugedanke *m*

~ **concrete** · Architekturbeton *m*

~ **(~) aggregate** · Architektur(beton)-zuschlag(stoff) *m*

~ **(~) cast(ing)** → (pre)cast architectural (concrete) member

~ ~ **product** → (pre)cast ~ (~) ~

~ **construction(al) material**, ~ building ~, ~ structural ~ · Architekturbaustoff *m*; Architekturbaumaterial *n* [*Schweiz*]

~ **course**, ~ seminar · Architekturseminar *n*

~ **critic** · Architekturkritiker *m*

~ **critics** · Architekturkritik *f*

(~) detail → (~) feature

(~) device → (~) feature

~ **division** · architektonische Gliederung *f*

~ **draughtsman** (Brit.); ~ draftsman (US); ~ assistant [*A man or woman working for an architect, normally in the drawing office but sometimes on a site*] · Architekturzeichner *m*

~ **drawing** · Architekturzeichnung *f*

~ **education**, ~ training · Architekturausbildung *f*

(~) element → (~) feature

~ **extruded section**, ~ ~ profile, ~ ~ shape, ~ ~ unit, ~ ~ product, ~ extrusion · gestaltendes Strangpreßprofil *n*, ~ Strangpreßerzeugnis *n*

~ **fashion** · Architekturmode *f*

(~) feature, (~) device, (~) detail, (~) element, style ~, feature (of style) · Gestaltungsfaktor *m*, Gestaltungselement *n*, Zug *m*, Stilelement, Stilfaktor, Form *f*, Stilzug

(~) finish(ing) · Oberflächengestaltung *f*

~ **firm** · Architekturfirma *f*

~ **fitting** → ~ (builders') furniture

~ **fittings** → ~ (builders') hardware

(~) flute · Riefe *f*, Kannelur(e) *f* [*Lotrechte Vertiefung am Säulenschaft*]

~ **form**, ~ shape · Architekturform *f*

~ **furniture** → ~ builders' ~

~ **glass article**, ~ ~ product · Architekturglasgegenstand *m*, Architekturglaserzeugnis *n*, Architekturglasartikel *m*

~ ~ **plant** · Architekturglaswerk *n*

~ ~ **product**, ~ ~ article · Architekturglaserzeugnis *n*, Architekturglasgegenstand *m*, Architekturglasartikel *m*

~ **granite** · Architekturgranit *m*

~ **grillework** · Architekturgitterwerk *n*

~ **hardware** → ~ builders' ~

architectural historian — arcuate(d)

~ **historian** · Architekturhistoriker *m*

~ **history,** history of architecture · Architekturgeschichte *f*

~ **hygiene,** sanitary science as applied to buildings · Bauhygiene *f*

~ **instruction** · Architekturunterricht *m*

~ **ironmongery** · Architektur-Eisenwaren *fpl*

~ **journal** · Architekturzeitschrift *f*

~ **laminated glass** · Mehrscheiben-Architekturglas *n*

~ **masonry (work)** · Architekturmauerwerk *n*

~ **metal** · Architekturmetall *n*

~ **modelling** (Brit.); ~ modeling (US) · Fertigung *f* von architektonischen Fertigteilen, Herstellung ~ ~ ~

~ **motif** · Formmotiv *n*

~ **movement** · Architekturbewegung *f*

~ **open-mindedness** · weltoffene Baugesinnung *f*

~ **order,** order (of architecture) [*A column together with its entablature, which is the beam and other horizontal members resting upon it*] · (Säulen)Ordnung *f*, Bauordnung

~ **organism** · Bauorganismus *m*

~ **ornament** · Architekturornament *n*

~ **panel** · Architekturtafel *f*

~ **planning** · Architekturplanung *f*

~ **porcelain** · Architekturporzellan *n*

~ **(pre)cast concrete product** → (pre-)cast architectural (~) ~

~ **safety glass,** ~ shatterproof ~ · Architektursicherheitsglas *n*

~ **sculpture** · Architekturplastik *f*

~ **section,** ~ shape, ~ unit, ~ trim, ~ profile · Architekturprofil *n*

~ **seminar,** ~ course · Architekturseminar *n*

~ **shape,** ~ form · Architekturform *f*

~ ~, ~ unit, ~ section, ~ trim, ~ profile · Architekturprofil *n*

~ **shatterproof glass,** ~ safety ~ · Architektursicherheitsglas *n*

~ **sketch** · Architekturskizze *f*

~ **slate** · Architekturschiefer *m*

~ **structural material,** ~ construction(al) ~, ~ building ~ · Architekturbaustoff *m*; Architekturbaumaterial *n* [*Schweiz*]

~ **style,** building ~ · Baustil *m* [*Die bauliche Ausdrucksform einer Kulturperiode*]

~ **team** · Architektengruppe *f*

~ **terra-cotta,** ATC [*It is used primarily for decorative purposes and for facing walls*] · Architekturterrakotta *f*

~ **theorist** · Architekturtheoretiker *m*

~ **theory** · Architekturtheorie *f*

~ **tradition,** tradition of building · Bautradition *f*

~ **training,** ~ education · Architekturausbildung *f*

~ **trend** · Architekturrichtung *f*

~ **trim,** ~ section, ~ unit, ~ shape, ~ profile · Architekturprofil *n*

~ **unit,** ~ shape, ~ section, ~ trim, ~ profile · Architekturprofil *n*

~ **writer,** writer on architecture · Architekturschriftsteller *m*

~ **work** · Architektenleistung *f*

architecturally beautiful square, place of outstanding architectural merit · Architekturalplatz *m*

architecturally-enframed window · architektonisch-(ein)gerahmtes Fenster *n*

architecture · Architektur *f*

~ **adaptable to conversions** · Umbauarchitektur *f*

~ ~ ~ **extension** · Anbauarchitektur *f*

architrave, epistyle · Architrav *m*, Epistyl(ion) *n* [*Von einer Säulenachse zur anderen reichender Steinbalken*]

~ **-cornice** [*An entablature from which the frieze is elided*] · Gebälk *n* ohne Fries, friesloses Gebälk

archives · Archiv *n*

~ **building** · Archivgebäude *n*

archivolt · Archivolte *f* [*Ein durch sich absetzende, der Gewändegliederung entsprechende Bogenläufe gegliedertes Portal; oft mit einem Tympanon versehen*]

~ · Archivolte *f* [*Veraltet: Schaubogen m, Schurbogen. Ursprünglich der Faszienbogen (Vignola); später ein künstlerisch behandelter Bogen mit seinen Stützen*]

archway, main ~ · Durchgang *m*, Durchfahrt *f* [*Stadttor*]

arch(way), four-sided (town) gateway · Straßenbogen *m* [*Ein freistehendes Bauwerk mit vier Ansichtsseiten*]

arcosic grit, arkose (sandstone), feldspathic sandstone · Arkose *f*, Arkosesandstein *m*, feldspatreicher Sandstein

arcual, arch(-shap)ed, arcuate(d); arquated [*obsolete*] · bogig, bogenförmig

~ **construction,** arch(ed) ~, arcuate(d) ~, arcuation ~, arched work · Bogenbau *m*

~ **structure,** arcuate(d) ~, arch(ed) ~ · Bogenbauwerk *n*

~ **style (of architecture)** → arcuate ~ (~ ~)

~ **system,** arcuate(d) ~, arch(ed) ~, arching · Bogensystem *n*

~ ~ **for absorption of thrust,** arcuate(d) ~ ~ ~ ~ ~, arch(ed) ~ ~ ~ ~ ~ · Bogensystem *n* für Horizontalschubaufnahme

arcuate(d), arch(-shap)ed, arcual; arquated [*obsolete*] · bogig, bogenförmig

arcuate(d) building — armoured cable

~ **building**, arch(ed) ~ · Bogengebäude *n*

~ **construction**, arch(ed) ~, arcual ~, arcuation ~, arched work · Bogenbau *m*

~ **structure**, arch(ed) ~, arcual ~ · Bogenbauwerk *n*

~ **style (of architecture)**, arcual ~ (~ ~), arch(ed) ~ (~ ~) [*A style of architecture in which the structure is supported on arches; in contrast to 'trabeated' architecture where vertical posts and horizontal beams are used structurally throughout*] · Bogenstil *m*

~ **system**, arch(ed) ~, arcual ~, arching · Bogensystem *n*

arcuation construction, arcuate(d) ~, arcual ~, arch(ed) ~, arched work · Bogenbau *m*

Ardand type polygonal roof, hammerbeam ~ [*A late Gothic form of roof without a direct tie, the finest example being in Westminster Hall*] · Vieleckdach *n*, Polygonaldach, Ardandsches Dach

area, surface ~, surface content, superficial content · (Ober)Flächeninhalt *m*, Flächenraum *m*

~ **cleared of buildings** → site ~ ~ ~

area-covering structural element · Flächentragwerk *n*

~ **structure** · Flächentragwerkbauwerk *n*

area curve · Flächenkurve *f*

~ **grating** · (Fuß)Bodengitter *n*, Gitterrost *m*

~ ~ **cover(ing)** · Gitterrostabdeckung *f*

~ **load** · Flächenlast *f*

~ **moment**, moment of area · Flächenmoment *n*

~ **of (a) building** [*The area of a horizontal section of a building taken at the level of its greatest area inclusive of external walls and such portions of party walls as belong to the building*] · (Gebäude)Grundrißfläche *f*

~ ~ **activity** [*In an apartment building*] · Wohnzone *f*

~ ~ **glazing** · Verglasungsfläche *f*

~ ~ **load distribution** · Lastverteilungsfläche *f*

~ ~ **loading**, loaded area, field of load · Lastfeld *n*, Lastfläche *f*, belastetes Feld, belastete Fläche

~ ~ **steel** [*The cross-sectional area of bars required for a given concrete section*] · Bewehrungsquerschnitt *m*, Armierungsquerschnitt

~ **requirement** · Flächenbedarf *m*

areaway (US), passage(way) · Durchgang *m*, Passage *f*

~ [*An open subsurface space adjacent to a building used to admit light and air or as a means of access to a basement or crawl space*] · Kellergraben *m*, Kellervorhof *m*

area with main services · kanalisiertes Gebiet *n*

arena · Arena *f*

Arena Chapel at Padua · Arenakapelle *f* in Padua

arena theatre, ~ theater, amphitheater, amphitheatre, coliseum, colosseum · Amphitheater *n*

arenaceous deposit, psammite · Psammit *m*

~ **shale**, schistous sandstone, foliated grit(-stone) · Sandschiefer *m*

arena(-type) stage · Arenabühne *f*

argentiferous lead, workable raw ~ · silberhaltiges Blei *n*, Werkblei [*Es wird durch Niederschlagsarbeit, Röstreaktionsarbeit oder Röstreduktionsarbeit gewonnen*]

argillaceous, clayey · ton(halt)ig

~ **gypsum**, clayey ~ · Tongips *m*

~ **limestone**, clayey ~, argillocalcite · ton(halt)iger Kalk(stein) *m*, Tonkalk(stein)

~ **rock**, clay ~ · Tongestein *n*

~ **sand**, clayey ~ · ton(halt)iger Sand *m*, Tonsand

~ **sandstone**, clayey ~ · Tonsandstein *m*

~ **slate** → (clay) ~

argillite · Argillit *m* [*natürlich entwässerter Tonschiefer*]

argillocalcite, clayey limestone, argillaceous limestone · ton(halt)iger Kalk(stein) *m*, Tonkalk(stein)

(Argyris) force method, flexibility matrix ~ · Kraft(größen)verfahren *n*, Kraft(größen)methode *f*

arisings, salvage · Altmaterial *n*

arkose (sandstone), arcosic grit, feldspathic sandstone · Arkose *f*, Arkosesandstein *m*, feldspatreicher Sandstein

armor door (US) → fire(-)resisting ~

~ **plate** (US); armour ~ (Brit.) · Panzerblech *n*

armored cable (US); armoured ~ (Brit) · Panzerkabel *n*, bewehrtes Kabel, armiertes Kabel

~ **concrete** (US); armoured ~ (Brit). · Panzer(hart)beton *m* [*Beim Panzerhartbeton als Platten oder Estrich sind auf die Gehschicht ausgestanzte, gelochte oder gewarzte Stahlplatten aufbetoniert*]

~ ~ **flag**, (US); armoured ~ ~ (Brit.); ~ paving ~, ~ ~ tile · Panzer(-Hart)beton(belag)platte *f*, Panzer-Hartbetonfliese *f* [*Mit metallischer Deckschicht für Industrie(fuß)böden*]

~ ~ **screed** (US); armoured ~ ~ (Brit). · Panzer(-Hart)betonestrich *m*

armorply (US) → armourply

armory (US); armoury (Brit.) · Waffenkammer *f*

armour door (Brit.) → fire(-resisting) ~

~ **plate** (Brit.); armor ~ (US) · Panzerblech *n*

~ **plating** (Brit.); armor ~ (US) · Blechfutter *n*

armoured cable (Brit.); armored ~ (US) · armiertes Kabel *n*, bewehrtes ~, Panzerkabel

armoured concrete — artificial aggregate

~ concrete (Brit.); armored ~ (US) · Panzer(hart)beton m [Beim Panzerhartbeton als Platten oder Estrich sind auf die Gehschicht ausgestanzte, gelochte oder gewarzte Stahlplatten aufbetoniert]

~ ~ flag (Brit.); armored ~ ~ (US); ~ ~ tile · Panzer(-Hart)beton(belag)-platte f, Panzer-Hartbetonfliese f [Mit metallischer Deckschicht für Industrie-(fuß)böden]

~ ~ screed (Brit.); armored ~ ~ (US) · Panzer(-Hart)betonestrich m

~ corner (Brit.); armored ~ (US) · gepanzerte Ecke f, ~ Kante f

~ door → armor ~

~ (fire(proof)) door (Brit.); armored (~) ~ (US) · Panzertür f

~ paving flag, ~ ~ tile, ~ concrete flag (Brit.); armored ~ ~ (US) · Panzer(-Hart)beton(belag)platte f, Panzer-Hartbetonfliese f [Mit metallischer Deckschicht für Industrie(fuß)böden]

~ ~ tile, ~ ~ flag, ~ concrete ~ (Brit.); armored ~ ~ (US) · Panzer(-Hart)beton(belag)platte f, Panzer-Hartbetonfliese f [Mit metallischer Deckschicht für Industrie(fuß)böden]

armourply, armoured plywood (Brit.); armorply, armored plywood (US); plymetal, metalclad plywood · Panzersperrholz n, Metall(schicht)sperrholz

armoury (Brit.); armory (US) · Waffenkammer f

aromatic compound · aromatische Verbindung f

~ hydrocarbon, aromatic · Aromat m, aromatischer Kohlenwasserstoff m, Benzolkohlenwasserstoff

~ solvent · aromatisches Lösungsmittel n, ~ Lösemittel

aromatics, aromatic hydrocarbons · Aromaten f, aromatische Kohlenwasserstoffe mpl, Benzolkohlenwasserstoffe

around(-the)-corner sliding shutter door, ~ ~ shutterdoor · Rundlauftor n

arquated [obsolete]; arcuate(d), arcual, arch(-shap)ed · bogig, bogenförmig

arrangement, layout · Anordnung f

~ · Bildungsweise f [z.B. eines Fachwerkes]

~ of beams, spacing ~ ~ · Balken(träger)anordnung f

~ ~ framework · Fachwerkbildungsweise f

array test for asbestos spinning fibre (Brit.)/fiber (US) · Stapelprüfung f für Asbestspinnfaser

ar(r)is [A sharp edge produced by the meeting of two surfaces] · scharfe Kante f

~ [The line at the intersection of two planes as distinct from an edge which is a measurable area] · Kante f

~ · Grat(linie) m, (f)

~ fillet → eave(s) board

~ protection · Kantenschutz m [als Maßnahme]

arrival level · Ankunftsebene f

~ lounge · Ankunftshalle f [Flughafen]

~ platform · Ankunftsbahnsteig m

arrow loop, loophole · Schießscharte f

~ slit · Bogenscharte f

ARS, asbestos roof shingle · Asbest-Dachschindel f

arsenal · Arsenal n, Zeughaus n

arsenic pigment · arsenhaltiges Pigment n

~ sulphide (Brit.); ~ sulfid(e) (US) · Arsensulfid n

arsenical copper [It contains between 0,30% and 0,50% of arsenic in solid solution] · Arsenkupfer n

art collection · Kunstsammlung f

~ college, ~ school · Kunstschule f

(~) connoisseur, art-lover · Kunstfreund m, Kunstliebhaber m

~ form · Kunstform f

(~) gallery [A building used for the display of works of art] · Kunstgalerie f

art-lover, (art) connoisseur · Kunstfreund m, Kunstliebhaber m

art museum · Kunstmuseum n

Art Nouveau, Modern Style · Jugendstil m

~ ~ faience, Modern Style ~ · Jugendstilfayence f

art of fortification · Festungsbau m

~ ~ sculpture · Plastik f

~ ~ the individual, individual form of art · Individualistenkunst f

~ ~ vaulting · Wölbekunst f

~ school, ~ college · Kunstschule f

~ treasure · Kunstschatz m

article, product · Artikel m, Gegenstand m, Erzeugnis n

articles, products, ware, goods · Artikel mpl, Ware(n) f, Gegenstände mpl, Erzeugnisse npl

articulated → hinged

~ arch(ed girder) → pin(ned) ~ (~)

~ bar → hinged ~

~ connection → hinge(d) joint

~ frame → hinged ~

~ joint → hinge(d) ~

~ purlin(e) → hinged ~

~ system, hinged ~, linked ~, pin(ned) ~, pin-jointed ~ · Gelenksystem n, Gelenkwerk n

articulation · Silbenreinheit f

artificial abradant, ~ abrasive · künstliches Schleifmittel n

~ abrasive, ~ abradant · künstliches Schleifmittel n

~ adhesive → synthetic (resin(-based)) (bonding) ~

~ aggregate → ~ concrete ~

artificial ag(e)ing — artificial weathering

~ ag(e)ing · künstliche Alterung *f*, künstliches Altern *n*

~ asbestos, man-made ~ · künstlicher Asbest *m*

(~) asphalt (Brit.); (~) asphalt-aggregate mix(ture) (US) · Asphalt *m*, künstliches Bitumen-Mineral-Gemisch *n*, künstliche Bitumen-Mineralmischung *f*

(~) asphalt-aggregate mix(ture) (US); (~) asphalt (Brit.) · Asphalt *m*, künstliches Bitumen-Mineral-Gemisch *n*, künstliche Bitumen-Mineralmischung *f*

~ (bonding) adhesive → synthetic (resin(-based)) (~) ~

~ ~ agent → synthetic (resin(-based)) (bonding) adhesive

~ ~ medium → synthetic (resin(-based)) (bonding) adhesive

~ carbonation, carbonation treatment · Karbonatisieren *n* [*Fehlname: Karbonisieren*]

~ cement(ing agent) → synthetic (resin(-based)) (bonding) adhesive

~ coarse aggregate, man-made ~ ~ · künstlicher (Beton)Grobzuschlag(stoff) *m*

~ ~ (concrete) aggregate, man-made ~ (~) ~ · künstlicher (Beton-)Grobzuschlag(stoff) *m*

~ (concrete) aggregate, man-made (~) ~ · künstlicher (Beton)Zuschlag(-stoff) *m*

~ draught (Brit.); ~ draft (US); forced ~ · künstlicher Zug *m*

~ fine aggregate, man-made ~ ~ · künstlicher Feinzuschlag(stoff) *m*

~ ~ (concrete) aggregate, man-made ~ (~) ~ · künstlicher (Beton) Feinzuschlag(stoff) *m*

~ ~ grain, finely ground ~ · Kunstfeinkorn *n* [*Siebtechnik*]

~ glue → synthetic (resin(-based)) (bonding) adhesive

~ grindstone [*It is made of artificial abrasives bound together with ceramic bonds*] · künstlicher Bimsstein *m*, ~ Schleifstein [*Nicht verwechseln mit „Kunstbims"*]

~ ice rink, ~ skating ~ · Kunsteis(lauf)- bahn *f*, Spritzeis(lauf)bahn

~ illumination, ~ lighting · künstliche Beleuchtung *f*

~ indoor illumination, ~ ~ lighting · Innen(raum)beleuchtung *f* mit künstlichem Licht [*DIN 5035*]

~ ~ lighting, ~ ~ illumination · Innen(raum)beleuchtung *f* mit künstlichem Licht [*DIN 5035*]

~ leather · Kunstleder *n*

~ ~ hanging · Kunstledertapete *f*

~ lighting, ~ illumination · künstliche Beleuchtung *f*

~ marble [*An imitation marble, usually colo(u)red, made with Keene's plaster*] · Alaungipsmarmor *m*

~ ~, manufactured ~, man-made ~, imitation ~ · Kunstmarmor *m* [*Fehlnamen: künstlicher Marmor, Glanzstein m*]

~ masonry unit, man-made ~ ~ · künstlicher Mauer(bau)stein *m*, ~ Wand(bau)stein [*Betonbaustein; Mauerziegel; Kalksandstein*]

~ pozzolan(ic material), man-made ~ (~), ~ pozz(u)olana [*See remark under „hydraulischer Zuschlag"*] · künstliche Puzzolane *f*, künstlicher hydraulischer Zuschlag *m*

~ radiation · künstliche Strahlung *f*

~ resin, manufactured ~, man-made ~, synthetic ~ · Kunstharz *n*, synthetisches Harz

~ (resin(-based)) (bonding) adhesive → synthetic (~) (~) ~

~ (~) ~ agent → synthetic (resin(-based)) (bonding) adhesive

~ (~) ~ medium → synthetic (resin(-based)) (bonding) adhesive

~ (~) cement(ing agent) → synthetic (resin(-based)) (bonding) adhesive

~ (~) glue → synthetic (resin(-based)) (bonding) adhesive

~ sand, manufactured ~, stone ~, crushed stone ~, (stone) screening(s), crushed screening(s) · Steinsand *m*, Brechsand [*Er umfaßt in den USA den Kornstufenbereich 0—4,76 mm*]

~ skating rink, ~ ice ~ · Kunsteis(lauf)bahn *f*, Spritzeis(lauf)bahn

~ stone [*deprecated*] → cast ~

~ ~ floor cover(ing) [*deprecated*] → cast stone floor(ing) (finish)

~ ~ floor(ing) (finish) [*deprecated*] → cast ~ ~ (~)

~ ~ shop [*deprecated*] → reconstituted ~ ~

~ ~ skin [*deprecated*] → cast ~ ~

~ ~ stair(case) [*deprecated*] → cast ~ ~

~ ~ tile [*deprecated*] → reconstituted ~ ~

~ ~ ~ floor cover(ing) [*deprecated*] → cast stone tile floor(ing) (finish)

~ ~ ~ floor(ing) (finish) [*deprecated*] → cast ~ ~ ~ (~)

~ ~ waterproofer [*deprecated*] → cast ~ ~

~ ~ work [*deprecated*] → cast ~ ~

~ travertine, man-made ~, manufactured ~, imitation ~ · Kunsttravertin *m*

~ ventilation, ~ venting · künstliche (Be- und Ent)Lüftung *f*

~ venting, ~ ventilation · künstliche (Be- und Ent)Lüftung *f*

~ weathering, accelerated ~ [*Laboratory tests designed to simulate but at the same time to intensify and accelerate the destructive action of natural*

outdoor weathering on paint films. The tests involve exposure to artificially produced components of natural weather, e.g. light, heat, cold, water vapour, rain, etc., which are arranged and repeated in a given cycle. There is no universally accepted test and different investigators use different cycles] · (künstliche) Bewitterung f

artificially precipitated calcite · künstlich (aus)gefällter Kalzit m

artisan's centre (Brit.); ~ center (US) · Handwerkerhof m

artist-craftsman · Kunsthandwerker m

artistic adviser · künstlerischer Berater m

~ circle, cultural ~ · Künstlerkreis m

~ design · künstlerische Gestaltung f

~ effect · künstlerische Wirkung f

~ expression, ~ form of ~ · künstlerische Ausdrucksweise f

~ (form of) expression · künstlerische Ausdrucksweise f

~ formation · Gestaltung f

~ maturity · künstlerische Reife f

~ monument · Kunstdenkmal n

~ use of materials · Materialkunst f

Artists' Plan of 1797 · „Plan m der Künstler" von 1797 [*Pariser Stadtbild. Lange, gerade Boulevards, die in runden Plätzen sternartig zusammentreffen, sind das Leitmotiv*]

artist's studio · Künstleratelier n

arts centre (Brit.); ~ center (US) · Kunsthalle f

ASB → asbestos

asbestine · Asbestine f [*Antiabsetzmittel in Lackfarben*]

asbestos, ASB · Asbest m [*Asbest ist ein Mineral, ein in feinsten Fasern kristallisierter Naturstein. Die einzelne Faser ist dünner als jede tierische, pflanzliche oder künstliche Faser, weil es sich bei Asbest um ein Fadenmolekül handelt.
Der Asbest kommt in der Natur im Gestein wie die Kohle in Flözen vor, nur daß die Asbestflöze gegenüber den Kohlenflözen sehr viel weniger mächtig sind und nur eine Höhe von wenigen Millimetern bis zu einigen Zentimetern besitzen. Die Faserflöze werden in Brechanlagen vom umgebenden Gestein getrennt, in Mühlen in Faserbündel aufgelöst und dann in Sichteranlagen entsprechend der Faserlänge sortiert.
Chemisch besteht Asbest aus kompliziert aufgebauten Silikathydraten. Technisch von Bedeutung sind die reinen Magnesiumsilikathydrate (der Serpentin- oder Chrysotil-Asbest) und die Natriummagnesiumeisensilikathydrate (Blau-Asbest). Alle Asbeste sind feuerfest, von hoher chemischer Beständigkeit, beständig gegenüber Angriffen von Bakterien und Pilzen und praktisch absolut witterungsbeständig, weil sie nur im Verlauf von Jahrtausenden einer geringen Erosion und Korrosion unterliegen. Die Reißfestigkeit ist abhängig von der Asbestsorte und kann zwischen wenigen kg pro mm^2 und der Festigkeit von Stahl liegen. Für die Eternit-Herstellung kommen nur Asbeste höchster Festigkeit zur Verwendung, insbesondere hochwertige Chrysotil- und Blau-Asbestsorten*]

~ article, ~ product · Asbestartikel m, Asbestgegenstand m, Asbesterzeugnis n

~ based · asbesthaltig

~ base(d) asphalt felt(ed fabric) → ~ ~ (asphaltic-)bitumen paper

~ ~ ~ paper (US) → ~ ~ (asphaltic-)bitumen ~ (Brit.)

~ ~ (asphaltic-)bitumen felt(ed fabric) → ~ ~ ~ paper

~ ~ ~ paper (Brit.); ~ ~ asphalt ~ (US); ~ ~ ~ felt(ed fabric) [*The base consists of a sheet of asbestos fibre (Brit.)/fiber (US) containing not less than 80 per cent of asbestos and is saturated with a suitable (asphaltic-) bitumen (Brit.)/asphalt (US)*] · Asbest-Bitumenpappe f, Bitumen-Asbestpappe

~ ~ asphalt paper → ~ ~ ~ (asphaltic-) bitumen ~

~ ~ bitumen felt(ed fabric) → ~ ~ ~ (asphaltic-)bitumen paper

~ ~ bitumen paper → ~ ~ ~ (asphaltic-) bitumen ~

~ blanket [*A small blanket wrapped round pipes being welded or annealed or brazed, to keep the heat in*] · Asbestdämmschicht f

~ board, ~ sheet · Asbestplatte f

~ building board, ~ ~ sheet · Asbestbauplatte f

~ ~ sheet, ~ ~ board · Asbestbauplatte f

~ card liner · Asbestpappenabklebung f [*(Preß-)Stroh(dämm)platte*]

~ cement; cement asbestos (US) · Asbestzement m [*Fehlname: Kunstschiefer m. DIN 274*]

asbestos-cement article → ~ product

~ board → ~ sheet

~ ~ 625 mm long → ~ ~ sheet ~ ~ ~

~ box (roof) gutter, ~ ~ rainwater ~; cement asbestos ~ (~) ~ (US) · Asbestzement-Kasten(dach)rinne f

~ (building) component → ~ (~) unit

~ (~) member → ~ (~) unit

~ (~) unit, ~ (~) member, ~ (~) component; cement asbestos ~ (~) (US) · Asbestzement(bau)element n, Asbestzement(bau)körper m, Asbestzementbauteil m, n [*Fehlname: Asbestzementbaueinheit f*]

~ cistern [*B.S. 2777*]; cement asbestos ~ (US) · Asbestzementzisterne f

asbestos-cement component — asbestos-cement (lining) sheet 66

~ **component** → ~ (building) unit
~ **conductor** (US) → ~ downpipe (Brit.)
~ **corrugated board** → ~ ~ sheet
~ ~ **boards** → ~ ~ ~ sheeting
~ ~ **panel**, corrugated asbestos-cement ~; cement asbestos corrugated ~, corrugated cement asbestos ~ (US) · Asbestzement-Welltafel f, Wellasbestzementtafel, gewellte Asbestzementtafel [*DIN 274*]
~ ~ **roof cladding**, corrugated asbestos-cement ~ ~, ~ ~ ~ covering, ~ ~ ~ sheathing, ~ ~ roof(ing) · Wellasbestzementdach(belag) n, (m), Asbestzementwelldach(belag), Wellasbestzement(ein)deckung f, Asbestzementwell(ein)deckung, Wellasbestzementdach(ein)deckung, Asbestzementwelldach(ein)deckung, Wellasbestzementbedachung, Asbestzementwellbedachung
~ ~ **roof(ing) board** → ~ ~ ~ sheet
~ ~ ~ **sheet**, ~ ~ ~ board; cement asbestos ~ ~ ~ (US) · Asbestzementdachwellplatte f, Asbestzementwelldachplatte, Wellasbestzementdachplatte
~ ~ **sheet**, corrugated asbestos-cement ~, ~ ~ board; corrugated cement asbestos ~, cement asbestos corrugated ~ (US) · Asbestzementwellplatte f, Wellasbestzementplatte
~ ~ **sheeting**, ~ ~ sheets, ~ ~ boards, corrugated asbestos-cement ~ [*B.S. 690*]; corrugated cement asbestos ~, cement asbestos corrugated ~ (US) · Asbestzementwellplatten fpl, Wellasbestzementplatten
~ ~ **sheets** → ~ ~ ~ sheeting
~ **discharge pipe** → ~ ~ drain(age) ~
~ **distance piece** → ~ ~ spacer
~ **downcomer** → ~ ~ downpipe
~ **downpipe**, ~ downcomer, ~ fall pipe, ~ rainwater pipe (Brit.) [*B.S. 569*]; ~ (rain) leader, ~ (rain) conductor, ~ downspout, cement asbestos (rain) leader, cement asbestos (rain) conductor, cement asbestos downspout (US) · Asbestzement-Abfallrohr n, Asbestzement-(Regen)Ablaufrohr, Asbestzement-(Regen)Fallrohr [*DIN 18471*]
~ **downspout** (US) → ~ ~ downpipe (Brit.)
~ **drain(age) pipe**, ~ draining ~, ~ discharge ~, ~ waste ~; cement asbestos ~ ~ (US) · Asbestzement-Abflußrohr n, Asbestzement-Entwässerungsrohr, Asbestzement-Ablaufrohr, Asbestzement-Dränrohr [*Fehlnamen: Asbestzementablauf m, Asbestzementabfluß m. DIN 19830, 19831 und 19841*]
~ **draining pipe** → ~ ~ drain(age) ~
~ **duct** [*B.S. 3954*]; cement asbestos ~ (US) · Asbestzementkanal m
~ **eave(s) gutter**, ~ ~ trough; cement asbestos ~ ~ (US) · Asbestzementtraufrinne f

~ ~ **trough**, ~ ~ gutter; cement asbestos ~ ~ (US) · Asbestzementtraufrinne f
~ **extract ventilation unit** → ~ ventilator
~ **extraction unit** → ~ ventilator
~ **extractor** → ~ ventilator
~ **façade**, ~ face, ~ front; cement asbestos ~ (US) · Asbestzementfassade f
~ ~ **slab**; cement asbestos ~ ~ (US) · Asbestzement-Fassadenplatte f, Fassaden-Asbestzementplatte
~ **face** → ~ façade
~ **facing** → ~ lining
~ ~ **sheet** → ~ (lining) ~
~ **fall pipe** → ~ downpipe
~ **fascia board (for flat roof(s))**; cement asbestos ~ ~ (~ ~ ~) (US) · Asbestzement(-Flachdach)blende f
~ **fence**; cement asbestos ~ (US) · Asbestzementzaun m
~ **fitting**; cement asbestos ~ (US) · Asbestzementformstück n, Asbestzementfitting m [*DIN 19830, 19831 und 19841*]
~ **flat board** → ~ ~ ~ sheet
~ ~ **(run) panel**; cement asbestos ~ (~) ~ (US) · Asbestzement-Flachtafel f, Asbestzement-Plantafel, ebene Asbestzementtafel
~ ~ **sheet**, ~ ~ board; cement asbestos ~ ~ (US) · Asbestzementflachplatte f, Flachasbestzementplatte
~ ~ ~ **siding**; cement asbestos ~ ~ ~ (US) · ebener Asbestzementplattenschirm m [*Wetterschutz für Außenwände*]
~ **floor(ing)**, ~ floor cover(ing), ~ floor finish; cement asbestos floor(-ing), cement asbestos floor cover(ing), cement asbestos floor finish (US) · Asbestzement(fuß)boden(belag) m
~ **flower container**; cement asbestos ~ ~ (US) · Asbestzement-Blumengefäß n
~ **flue**; cement asbestos ~ (US) · Asbestzementzug m
~ **fluted board**, ~ ~ sheet · gerieftе Asbestzementplatte f
~ **foul water pipe** → ~ ~ sewer ~
~ **fountain basin**; cement asbestos ~ ~ (US) · Asbestzement-(Spring-)Brunnenbecken n
~ **front** → ~ façade
~ **gutter** → ~ roof ~
~ **leader** (US) → ~ ~ downpipe (Brit.)
~ **lining**, ~ (sur)facing; cement asbestos ~ (US) · Asbestzementauskleidung f, Asbestzementverkleidung, Asbestzementbekleidung
~ **(~) sheet**, ~ (sur)facing ~ [*B.S. 690*]; cement asbestos (~) ~ (US) · Asbestzement-Auskleidungsplatte f, Asbestzement-Verkleidungsplatte, As-

asbestos-cement (lining) sheet — asbestos-cement shingle

bestzement-Bekleidungsplatte, Verkleidungs-Asbestzementplatte, Auskleidungs-Asbestzementplatte, Bekleidungs-Asbestzementplatte

~ **member** → ~ (building) unit

~ **mortar**; cement asbestos ~ (US) · Asbestzementmörtel *m*

~ **panel**; cement asbestos ~ (US) · Asbestzementtafel *f* [*DIN 274*]

~ **partition (wall)**; cement asbestos ~ (~) (US) · Asbestzementtrennwand *f*

~ **pipe**; cement asbestos ~ (US) · Asbestzementrohr *n*

~ **pressure pipe** [*B.S. 486*]; cement asbestos ~ ~ (US) · Asbestzement-Druckrohr *n* [*DIN 19800, DIN 19801, DIN 19630*]

~ **product**, ~ article; cement asbestos ~ (US) · Asbestzementartikel *m*, Asbestzementgegenstand *m*, Asbestzementerzeugnis *n*

~ **profile(d) board**, ~ ~ sheet; cement asbestos ~ ~ (US) · Asbestzementprofilplatte *f*, Profil-Asbestzementplatte

~ ~ **sheet**, ~ ~ board; cement asbestos ~ ~ (US) · Asbestzementprofilplatte *f*, Profil-Asbestzementplatte

~ **(rain) conductor** (US) → ~ downpipe (Brit.)

~ **(~) leader** (US) → ~ downpipe (Brit.)

~ **rainwater article**, ~ ~ product [*B.S. 569*]; cement asbestos ~ ~ (US) · Asbestzement-Dachzubehörteil *m, n*

~ ~ **goods**, ~ ~ products, ~ ~ articles [*B.S. 569*]; cement asbestos ~ ~ (US) · Asbestzement-Dachzubehör(-teile) *m, (mpl, npl)*

~ ~ **gutter**, ~ (roof) ~; cement-asbestos (roof) ~ (US) · Regen-Asbestzementrinne *f*, Dach-Asbestzementrinne, Asbestzementregenrinne, Asbestzement(dach)rinne

~ ~ **pipe** → ~ downpipe

~ ~ **product**, ~ ~ article [*B.S. 569*]; cement asbestos ~ ~ (US) · Asbestzement-Dachzubehörteil *m, n*

~ **refuse water pipe** → ~ sewer ~

~ **ridge capping tile**, ~ ~ cover(ing) ~, ~ ridging ~; cement asbestos ridge capping ~, cement asbestos ridge cover(ing) ~, cement asbestos ridging ~ (US) · Asbestzementfirsthaube *f*, Asbestzementfirstkappe *f*

~ ~ **cover(ing) tile** → ~ ~ ~ capping ~

~ **ridging tile** → ~ ridge capping ~

~ **roof cladding** → ~ ~ ~ covering

~ ~ **covering**, ~ ~ cladding, ~ ~ sheathing, ~ roof(ing); cement asbestos roof covering, cement asbestos roof cladding, cement asbestos roof sheathing, cement asbestos roof(ing) (US) · Asbestzement(dach)eindeckung *f*, Asbestzement(dach)deckung, Asbestzementdach(belag) *n, (m)*

~ **(~) gutter**, ~ rainwater ~; cement asbestos (~) ~ (US) · Dach-Asbestzementrinne *f*, Regen-Asbestzementrinne, Asbestzementregenrinne, Asbestzement(dach)rinne

~ ~ **sheathing** → ~ ~ covering

~ ~ **shingle**; cement asbestos ~ ~ (US) · Asbestzementdachschindel *f*

~ **roof(ing)** → ~ roof covering

~ ~ **board** → ~ ~ sheet

~ ~ **panel**; cement asbestos ~ ~ (US) · Asbestzementdachtafel *f*

~ ~ **sheet**, ~ ~ board; cement asbestos ~ ~ (US) · Asbestzementdachplatte *f*, Dach-Asbestzementplatte [*DIN 274*]

~ ~ **shingle**; cement asbestos ~ ~ (US) · Asbestzementdachschindel *f*

~ **(~) slate** [*B.S. 690*]; cement asbestos (~) ~ (US) [*A small plain sheet laid to overlap in the same manner as a roofing slate*] · Asbestzementbiber-(schwanz)stein *m*

~ **(~) tile**; cement asbestos (~) ~ (US) [*A usually large profiled sheet but so profiled as to interlock (in similar manner to single lap clay roofing tiles)*] · Asbestzement(dach)falzplatte *f*, Asbestzementfalzdachplatte, Falz-Asbestzement(dach)platte

~ **(~) ~**; cement asbestos ~ ~ (US) · Asbestzementdachstein *m*

~ **rubber tile**; cement asbestos ~ ~ (US) [*An asbestos-cement tile surfaced with rubber*] · Asbestzement-Gummi-(Belag)Platte *f*, Asbestzement-Gummi-Fliese *f*

~ **separator** → ~ spacer

~ **septic tank**; cement asbestos ~ ~ (US) · Asbestzement-Faulgrube *f*

~ **sewage pipe** → ~ sewer ~

~ **sewer pipe**, ~ sewage ~, ~ foul water ~, ~ refuse water ~; cement asbestos sewer ~, cement asbestos sewage ~, cement asbestos foul water ~, cement asbestos refuse water ~ (US) · Asbestzementabwasserrohr *n*, Asbestzementkanal(isations)rohr, Abwasser-Asbestzementrohr

~ **shake** [*misnomer*] → ~ shingle

~ **sheet** → ~ lining ~

~ ~, ~ board; cement asbestos ~, CEM AB, cem ab, CAB (US) [*A large unit, flat or profiled, laid to overlap*] · Asbestzementplatte *f*

~ ~ **625 mm long**, ~ ~ board ~ ~ ~; cement asbestos ~ ~ ~ ~ (US) · Kurzwellplatte *f*, Berliner-Welle *f*, KW-Platte [*Eine Asbestzementplatte von 625 mm Länge für die Eindeckung von Wohnhäusern*].

~ **sheeting**; cement asbestos ~ (US) [*Corrugated, reeded, or otherwise patterned or plain sheets for roofing and wall cladding, made of asbestos cement*] · Asbestzementplatten *fpl*

~ **shingle**; cement asbestos ~ (US) [*misnomer: asbestos-cement shake*] · Asbestzementschindel *f*

asbestos-cement siding — asbestos-pvc floor(ing) tile

~ **siding;** cement asbestos ~ (US) · Asbestzement-Wandschirm m, Asbestzement-Wandbeschlag m, Asbestzement-Wetterschirm

~ ~ **shake** [*misnomer*] → ~ ~ shingle

~ ~ **shingle;** cement asbestos ~ ~ (US) [*misnomer: asbestos-cement siding shake*] · Asbestzementwandschindel f, Wand-Asbestzementschindel

~ **slate** → ~ roofing ~

~ **solid board,** ~ ~ sheet; cement asbestos ~ ~ (US) · Asbestzementvollplatte f [*DIN 274*]

~ ~ **sheet,** ~ ~ board; cement asbestos ~ ~ (US) · Asbestzementvollplatte f [*DIN 274*]

~ **spacer,** ~ separator, ~ distance piece; cement asbestos spacer, cement asbestos distance piece, cement asbestos separator (US) · Abstandhalter m aus Asbestzement, Asbestzement-Abstandhalter

~ **(sur)facing** → ~ lining

~ ~ **sheet** → ~ ~ (lining) ~

~ **tile** → ~ ~ roofing ~

~ **unit** → ~ building ~

~ **valley gutter;** cement asbestos ~ ~ (US) · Asbestzementkehlrinne f

~ **vent(ilating) pipe** [*B.S. 582*]; cement asbestos ~ ~ (US) · Asbestzementlüftungsrohr n, Lüftungs-Asbestzementrohr

~ **ventilator,** ~ extractor, ~ extract ventilation unit, ~ extraction unit; cement asbestos ventilator, cement asbestos extractor, cement asbestos extract ventilation unit, cement asbestos extraction unit (US) · Asbestzemententlüfter m

~ **wall board,** ~ ~ sheet; cement asbestos ~ ~ (US) · Asbestzementwandplatte f

~ ~ **panel;** cement asbestos ~ ~ (US) · Asbestzementwandtafel f

~ ~ **sheet,** ~ ~ board; cement asbestos ~ ~ (US) · Asbestzementwandplatte f

~ ~ **shingle;** cement asbestos ~ ~ (US) · Asbestzementwandschindel f

~ **ware** → ~ mass-produced ~ ~

~ **waste pipe** → ~ drain(age) ~

~ **window sill;** ~ ~ cill (Brit.); cement asbestos window sill (US) · Asbestzementfenster(sohl)bank f, Asbestzementsohlbank

asbestos cloth, ~ woven fabric; ~ fabric [*misnomer*] · Asbestgewebe n

~ **cord covering** · Asbestschnur f [*für Dämm- und Isolierzwecke*]

~ **core** · Asbestkern m

~ **corrugated board,** ~ ~ sheet, corrugated asbestos ~ ~ · Asbestwellplatte f, Wellasbestplatte

~ ~ **panel,** corrugated asbestos ~ ~ · Asbestwelltafel f, Wellasbesttafel

~ **dust** · Asbeststaub m

~ **fabric** [*misnomer*]; ~ cloth, ~ woven fabric · Asbestgewebe n

~ **felt** · getränkter Asbestfilz m

~ **fibre** (Brit.); ~ fiber (US) · Asbestfaser f

~ ~ **board,** ~ ~ sheet (Brit.); asbestos fiber ~ (US) · Asbestfaserplatte f

~ ~ **insulation** (Brit.); ~ fiber ~ (US) · Asbestfaserisolierung f

~ **fibre-reinforced** (Brit.); ~ fiber-reinforced (US) · asbestfaserarmiert, asbestfaserverstärkt

~ ~ **sheet,** ~ ~ board (Brit.); asbestos fiber ~ (US) · Asbestfaserplatte f

~ ~ **sheet(ing)** (Brit.); ~ fiber ~ (US) · Asbestfaserbahn f

~ **filler** · Asbestfüller m

~ **flat board** → ~ ~ building ~

~ ~ **(building) board,** ~ ~ (~) sheet · Flachasbestplatte f

~ ~ **(~) sheet,** ~ ~ (~) board · Flachasbestplatte f

~ ~ **sheet** → ~ ~ building ~

~ **flour,** ~ powder, powder(ed) asbestos · Asbestmehl n, Asbestpulver n

~ **foamed concrete** · Asbestschaumbeton m

~ **glove** · Asbesthandschuh m

~ **gutter,** ~ roof ~, ~ rainwater ~ · Asbest(dach)rinne f, Asbestregenrinne

~ **insert(ion)** · Asbesteinlage f

~ **insulating board,** ~ ~ sheet, ~ insulation(-grade) ~ [*B.S. 3536*] · Asbestdämmplatte f

~ ~ **sheet** → ~ ~ board

~ **insulation** · Asbestisolierung f

~ **insulation(-grade) board** → ~ insulating ~

~ ~ **sheet** → ~ ~ insulating board

~ **(joint;** runner, ~ rope · Asbeststrick m [*Strick-Blei-Dichtung*]

~ **layer** · Asbestlage f, Asbestschicht f

~ **mortar** · Asbestmörtel m

~ **panel** · Asbesttafel f

~ **pipe** · Asbestrohr n

asbestos-plastic floor(ing) tile · Asbest-Kunststoff-(Fuß)Bodenplatte f, Asbest-Kunststoff-(Fuß)Bodenfliese f

asbestos powder, ~ flour, powder(ed) asbestos · Asbestmehl n, Asbestpulver n

~ **product,** ~ article · Asbestartikel m, Asbestgegenstand m, Asbesterzeugnis n

asbestos-protected · asbestgeschützt

asbestos-pvc floor(ing) tile, PVC asbestos ~ ~ [*A flooring tile composed of asbestos bonded with polyvinyl chloride. B.S. 3260*] · Asbest-PVC-(Fuß)Bodenplatte f

asbestos rainwater gutter — ash-lime tile

asbestos rainwater gutter, ~ (roof) ~ · Asbest(dach)rinne f, Asbestregenrinne

~ ring · Asbestring m

~ rock · Asbestgestein n

~ (roof) gutter, ~ rainwater ~ · Asbest(dach)rinne f, Asbestregenrinne

~ ~ shingle, ARS · Asbest-Dachschindel f

~ roofing sheet · Asbestdachplatte f

~ rope, ~ (joint) runner · Asbeststrick m [*Strick-Blei-Dichtung*]

~ roving, ~ rove · Asbestgrobgespinst n, Asbestgrobgarn n

~ sheet, ~ board · Asbestplatte f

~ shingle · Asbestschindel f

~ slate · Asbestschiefer m

~ tester, ~ testing machine · Asbestprüfmaschine f

~ tile · Asbest(belag)platte f, Asbestfliese f

asbestos-vinyl composition, ~ compound, ~ mass, ~ material, vinyl-asbestos ~ · Asbest-Vinyl-Masse f, Vinyl-Asbest-Masse

~ compound → ~ composition

~ floor cover(ing), vinyl-asbestos ~ ~, ~ floor(ing) (finish) · Flex-(Fuß-)Boden(belag) m

~ floor(ing) (finish), vinyl-asbestos ~ (~), ~ floor cover(ing) · Flex-(Fuß-)Boden(belag) m

~ mass → ~ composition

~ material → ~ composition

~ tile, vinyl-asbestos ~, VAT · Pastellplatte f, Flexfliese f, Vinylasbestfliese, Flex(belag)platte, Vinylasbest(belag)platte [*DIN 16950*]

asbestos wallboard, ~ wall sheet [*B.S. 3536*] · Asbestwandplatte f

~ wall sheet, ~ wallboard [*B.S. 3536*] · Asbestwandplatte f

~ wool · Asbestwolle f

~ woven fabric, ~ cloth; ~ fabric [*misnomer*] · Asbestgewebe n

~ yarn · Asbestgarn n

asbolan, → asbolite

asbolite, asbolan, earth cobalt; black oxide of cobalt (Brit.); black oxid(e) of cobalt (US) · Erdkobalt m, Asbolan m, Kobaltschwärze f

as-built drawing → as-completed ~

~ ~ for settling the accounts, as-constructed ~ ~ ~ ~ ~, as-completed ~ ~ ~ ~ ~ · Abrechnungsplan m, Abrechnungszeichnung f

as-completed drawing, as-built ~, as-constructed ~, 'work as executed' ~ · (Bau)Bestandsplan m, (Bau)Bestandszeichnung f

~ ~ for settling the accounts, as-constructed ~ ~ ~ ~ ~ ~, as-built ~ ~ ~ ~ ~ · Abrechnungsplan m, Abrechnungszeichnung f

as-constructed drawing → as-completed ~

~ ~ for settling the accounts, as-built ~ ~ ~ ~ ~, as-completed ~ ~ ~ ~ · Abrechnungsplan m, Abrechnungszeichnung f

as regards strength, strength-wise · festigkeitsmäßig

aseismic → (earth)quake-resistant

ash content · Asche(n)gehalt m

~ door, ~ pit ~ · Aschentür f, Entaschungstür

~ dump · Aschenschlucker m

ashlar → stone ~

~ bond → stone ~ ~

~ bonder → stone ~ ~

~ bonding header → (stone) ashlar bonder

~ bondstone → (stone) ashlar bonder

~ masonry (work) → stone ~ ~ (~)

~ piece [*A short upright timber fixed between the inner wall plate and the rafters*] · Dachverschalungsstütze f

~ slab → stone ~ ~

~ structure, stone ~ ~, (stone) ashler ~; hewn stone ~, cut stone ~ (US) · (Natur)Werksteinbau(werk) m, (n), Hausteinbau(werk)

~ vault → stone ~ ~

~ window → stone ~ ~

ashlaring, ashlering [*An arrangement of short vertical timbers cutting off the angle formed at the intersection of a sloping wood(en) roof with a floor, and forming a support for lath and plaster. This term, used in carpentry, is confusing because it has no connection with 'ashlar' in masonry*] · Dachverschalungsstützen fpl

ashler → (stone) ashlar

~ bond → (stone) ashlar ~

~ bonder → (stone) ashlar ~

~ bonding header → (stone) ashlar bonder

~ bondstone → (stone) ashlar bonder

~ masonry (work) → (stone) ashlar ~ (~)

~ slab → (stone) ashlar ~

~ structure → ashlar ~

~ vault, ashlar ~, stone ~ ~; hewn stone ~, cut stone ~ (US) · (Natur-)Werksteingewölbe n, Hausteingewölbe

~ window → (stone) ashlar ~

ashlering → ashlaring

ash lift · Aschenaufzug m

ash-lime block, ~ tile [*See remark under 'Block'*] · Kalkaschen(block)stein m, Kalkaschenblock m [*Dampfgehärteter Leicht(block)stein (1,8 kg/cbdm) aus Asche mit 10% Kalk als Binder*]

~ tile, ~ block [*See remark under 'Block'*] · Kalkaschen(block)stein m, Kalkaschenblock m [*Dampfgehärteter Leicht(block)stein (1,8 kg/cbdm) aus Asche mit 10% Kalk als Binder*]

ashpit — asphalt content

ashpit · Aschenraum *m*, Aschenfall *m*, Aschengrube *f*

ash(pit) door, cleanout ~, COD (US); soot door [*B.S. 1294*] · Kamintür *f*, Reinigungstür, Putztür, Schornsteinreinigungsverschluß *m*, Aschentür, Entaschungstür, Rußtür

ash slate · Aschentonschiefer *m*

~ tray · Asch(enbech)er *m*

ashy shale · Aschenschieferton *m*

Asiatic W. C. pan → squatting ~ ~ ~

asphalt, artificial ~ (Brit.); (artificial) asphalt-aggregate mix(ture) (US) · Asphalt *m*, künstliches Bitumen-Mineral-Gemisch *n*, künstliche Bitumen-Mineralmischung *f*

~, natural ~ (Brit.); rock ~ (US) · (Natur)Asphalt *m*, natürliches Bitumen-Mineralgemisch *n*, natürliche Bitumen-Mineralmischung *f* [*Das natürlich vorkommende Bitumen mit seinem Begleitgestein*]

~ (US); (asphaltic-)bitumen (Brit.) · Bitumen *n* [*Fehlname: Asphaltbitumen*]

~ addition (US) → (asphaltic-)bitumen ~

~ adhesion-preventing agent (US); (asphaltic-)bitumen ~ ~ (Brit.) · Bitumen-Trennmittel *n* [*Zur Ausbildung von wirksamen Trennfilmen für LKW-Ladeflächen, Aufzugkübel und Gußasphalteimer*]

~ adhesive (US) → (asphaltic-)bitumen bonding ~

asphalt-aggregate mix(ture), artificial ~ ~ (US); (artificial) asphalt (Brit.) · Asphalt *m*, künstliches Bitumen-Mineral-Gemisch *n*, künstliche Bitumen-Mineralmischung *f*

~ ~ (US); (asphaltic-)bitumen-aggregate ~ (Brit.) · Bitumen-Mineralgemisch *n*, Bitumen-Mineralmischung *f*

asphalt/asbestos composition → (asphaltic-)bitumen/asbestos compound

~ compound → (asphaltic-)bitumen/asbestos ~

~ fiber cement → (asphaltic-)bitumen/asbestos fibre ~

~ mass → (asphaltic-)bitumen/asbestos compound

~ material → (asphaltic-)bitumen/asbestos compound

asphalt base → (asphaltic-)bitumen ~

~ based, asphaltic (US); (asphaltic-)bitumen based, containing (asphaltic-)bitumen (Brit.) · bitumenhaltig

asphalt-based building mastic (US) → ~ ~ mastic joint sealer

~ mastic joint sealer (US); building mastic, (asphaltic-)bitumen-based building mastic, (asphaltic-)bitumen-based mastic joint sealer (Brit.) · plastische Bitumenfugen(ab)dicht(ungs)masse *f*, Bitumenfugenmasse, Bitumen(fugen)(ver)füllmasse, plastischer Bitumen(fugen)(ver)füller *m*, Bitumenfugen(ab)dicht(ungs)kitt *m*, Bitumen(ver)füllkitt, Bitumen(fugen)kitt, Bitumen(fugen)mastix

~ paste (US); (asphaltic-)bitumen-based ~ (Brit.) · Bitumenpaste *f* [*Bitumenpasten bestehen aus Bitumen und mineralischen Zusätzen – vielfach Faserstoff und Asbest – und werden entweder heiß verarbeitet oder können durch Lösungsmittelzusatz oder Emulgation des Bitumens, auch kalt verarbeitbar hergestellt werden*]

~ rust protective paint, ~ ~ protection ~ (US); (asphaltic-)bitumen-based ~ ~ ~ (Brit.) · Bitumenrostschutzfarbe *f*

asphalt binder → (asphaltic-)bitumen ~

asphalt-bonded (US); (asphaltic-)bitumen-bonded (Brit.) · bitumengebunden

asphalt bonding adhesive (US) → (asphaltic-)bitumen ~ ~

~ ~ agent (US) → (asphaltic-)bitumen bonding adhesive

~ ~ medium (US) → (asphaltic-)bitumen bonding adhesive

~ building paper, general-use ~ ~ (US); (asphaltic-)bitumen ~ ~ (Brit.). [*See remark under 'Pappe'*] · Asphaltbaupappe *f*, Bitumenbaupappe

~ cement, A.C., paving (grade) asphalt (US); (asphaltic-)bitumen for road purposes (Brit.) [*B.S. 3690*] · Straßenbaubitumen *n* [*DIN 1995*]

~ ~ with road tar addition (US) → paving asphalt ~ ~ ~ ~

~ cement(ing agent) (US) → (asphaltic-)bitumen bonding adhesive

~ coated → (asphaltic-)bitumen ~

asphalt-coated chip(ping)s (US); (asphaltic-)bitumen-coated ~ (Brit.) · Bitumensplitt *m*

~ crushed stone (US); (asphaltic-)bitumen-coated (road) metal (Brit.) · Bitumenschotter *m*

~ gravel (US) → gravel asphalt

~ sand (US); (asphaltic-)bitumen-coated ~ (Brit.) · Asphaltsand *m*, Bitu-(men)sand

asphalt coat(ing) (US) → ~ surface ~

~ ~ compound (US) → (asphaltic-)bitumen ~ ~

~ ~ (material) (US) → (asphaltic-)bitumen ~ (~)

~ composition (US) → (asphaltic-)bitumen ~

~ ~ roofing (US) → ~ ready ~

~ compound (US) → (asphaltic-)bitumen composition

~ concrete (mineral) skeleton, asphaltic ~ (~) ~ (US); (asphaltic-)bitumen ~ (~) ~ (Brit.) · Asphaltbetonmineralgerüst *n*

~ content → (asphaltic-)bitumen ~

~ **curb,** ~ kerb (Brit.); ~ ~ above ground · Asphalt-Bordschwelle f, Asphalt-Hochbordstein m, Asphalt-Bordstein

~ **dry penetration surfacing,** ~ ~ process penetration macadam · Asphalteinstreudecke f, Bitumeneinstreudecke, Bitumenstreumakadam m, Asphaltstreumakadam [*Eine Schotterdecke, bei der anstatt des Schlemmsandes ein mit Verschnittbitumen umhülltes Splittgemisch in die Zwischenräume des Schotters eingebaut und eingewalzt wird. Zum Abschluß erhält der Belag meist noch eine dünne Auflage von Bitumensplitt*]

~ ~ **process penetration macadam** → ~ ~ penetration surfacing

asphalter, asphalt layer · Asphaltleger m

asphalt-felt roof cladding, ~ ~ covering, ~ ~ sheathing, ~ roof(ing) (US); (asphaltic-)bitumen roof cladding, (asphaltic-)bitumen roof covering, (asphaltic-)bitumen roof sheathing, (asphaltic-)bitumen roofing (Brit.) · Asphalt-Kleb(e)dach(belag) n, (m), Asphalt-Kleb(e)(dach)(ein)deckung f, Asphalt-Kleb(e)bedachung, Asphalt-Spachteldach(belag), Asphalt-Spachtel(dach)(ein)deckung, Asphalt-Spachtelbedachung

~ ~ **covering,** ~ ~ cladding, ~ ~ sheathing, ~ roof(ing) (US); (asphaltic-)bitumen roof cladding, (asphaltic-)bitumen roof covering, (asphaltic-)bitumen roof sheathing, (asphaltic-)bitumen roofing (Brit.) · Asphalt-Kleb(e)dach(belag) n, (m), Asphalt-Kleb(e)d(ach)(ein)deckung f, Asphalt-Kleb(e)bedachung, Asphalt-Spachteldach(belag), Asphalt-Spachtel(dach)(ein)deckung, Asphalt-Spachtelbedachung

~ ~ **sheathing,** ~ ~ covering, ~ ~ cladding, ~ roof(ing) (US); (asphaltic-)bitumen roof cladding, (asphaltic-)bitumen roof covering, (asphaltic-)bitumen roof sheathing, (asphaltic-)bitumen roofing (Brit.) · Asphalt-Kleb(e)dach(belag) n, (m), Asphalt-Kleb(e)(dach)(ein)deckung f, Asphalt-Kleb(e)bedachung, Asphalt-Spachteldach(belag), Asphalt-Spachtel(dach)(ein)deckung, Asphalt-Spachtelbedachung

~ **roofing,** ~ roof cladding, ~ roof covering, ~ roof sheathing (US); (asphaltic-)bitumen roof cladding, (asphaltic-)bitumen roof sheathing, (asphaltic-)bitumen roof covering, (asphaltic-)bitumen roofing (Brit.) · Asphalt-Kleb(e)dach(belag) n, (m), Asphalt-Kleb(e)(dach)(ein)deckung f, Asphalt-Kleb(e)bedachung, Asphalt-Spachteldach(belag), Asphalt-Spachtel(dach)(ein)deckung, Asphalt-Spachtelbedachung

asphalt-filler mix(ture) → (asphaltic-)bitumen filler ~

asphalt film → (asphaltic-)bitumen ~

~ **floor cover(ing),** ~ ~ (finish), ~ flooring · Asphalt(fuß)boden(belag) m

~ ~ ~ **tile,** ~ flooring ~, ~ floor (finish) ~ · Asphalt(fuß)boden(belag)-platte f, Asphalt(fuß)bodenfliese f

~ ~ **(finish),** ~ ~ cover(ing), ~ flooring · Asphalt(fuß)boden(belag) m

~ ~ **(~) tile,** ~ flooring ~, ~ floor cover(ing) ~ · Asphalt(fuß)boden(belag)platte f, Asphalt(fuß)bodenfliese f

~ **flooring,** ~ floor cover(ing), ~ floor (finish) · Asphalt(fuß)boden(belag) m

~ ~ **tile,** ~ floor cover(ing) ~, ~ floor (finish) ~ · Asphalt(fuß)boden(belag)platte f, Asphalt(fuß)bodenfliese f

~ **for dampproof coatings** (US); (asphaltic-)bitumen ~ ~ ~ (Brit.) · Mauerbitumen n

~ **globule** (US); (asphaltic-)bitumen ~ (Brit.) · Bitumenkügelchen n

~ **grade** → (asphaltic-)bitumen ~

~ **gunite** (US); (asphaltic-)bitumen ~ (Brit.) · Bitumen-Torkret m

~ **hardness degree** (US); (asphaltic-)bitumen ~ ~ (Brit.) · Bitumen-Härtegrad m

asphalt-impregnated, asphalt-saturated (US); (asphaltic-)bitumen-impregnated, (asphaltic-)bitumen-saturated (Brit.) · bitumengetränkt

asphalt(-impregnated) calcium silicate brick (US) → ~ sand-lime ~

~ **joint runner** (US) → (asphaltic-)bitumen(-impregnated) seal(ing) rope (Brit.)

~ **lime-sand brick** (US) → ~ sand-lime ~

~ **pouring rope** (US) → (asphaltic-)bitumen(-impregnated) seal(ing) ~ (Brit.)

~ **protective felt** (US); (asphaltic-)bitumen ~ ~ (Brit.) · Asphaltschutzpappe f, Bitumenschutzpappe

~ **sand-lime brick,** ~ lime-sand ~, ~ calcium silicate ~ (US); (asphaltic-)bitumen (impregnated) sand-lime ~, (asphaltic-)bitumen (impregnated) lime-sand ~, (asphaltic-)bitumen (impregnated) calcium silicate ~ (Brit.) · Bitukasadstein m, Asphaltstein, Bitumen-Kalksandstein, bitumengetränkter Kalksandstein

~ **seal(ing) rope** (US) → (asphaltic-)bitumen(-impregnated) ~ ~ (Brit.)

~ **strip** (US) → (asphaltic-)bitumen(-impregnated) ~

asphalt impregnating → ~ saturating

~ **impregnation,** ~ saturation (US); (asphaltic-)bitumen ~ (Brit.) · Bitumenimprägnierung f, Bitumentränkung

~ **individual coat** → (asphaltic-)bitumen ~ ~

~ **insulating coat** → (asphaltic-)bitumen insulation(-grade) ~

asphalt insulating paste — asphalt saturation

~~ paste (US) → (asphaltic-)bitumen ~ ~ (Brit.)

~~ slab (US) → (asphaltic-)bitumen insulation(-grade) ~ (Brit.)

asphalt (joint) pouring compound → (asphaltic-)bitumen (~) ~ ~

~~ runner (US) → (asphaltic-)bitumen(-impregnated) seal(ing) rope

~ kerb, ~ curb (Brit.); ~ ~ above ground · Asphalt-Bordschwelle f, Asphalt-Hochbordstein m, Asphalt-Bordstein

asphalt-laminated (US); (asphaltic-)bitumen-laminated (Brit.) · bitumenkaschiert

asphalt/latex emulsion (US) → (asphaltic-)bitumen/latex ~

asphalt layer, asphalter · Asphaltleger m

~~ (US); (asphaltic-)bitumen ~ (Brit.) · Bitumenlage f, Bitumenschicht f

~ liner → (asphaltic-)bitumen ~

~ mastic, asphaltic ~ (US); mastic asphalt [B.S. 1446] · Bitumenmastix m, Asphaltmastix

asphalt perforated sheet(ing) → (asphaltic-)bitumen ~ ~

asphalt pipe · Asphaltrohr n [*Asphaltrohre sind aus nackten Pappen oder Dachpappen gerollt und mit heißem Bitumen verklebt*]

~ pouring compound → (asphaltic-)bitumen (joint) ~ ~

~~ rope, asphaltic ~ ~ (US); (asphaltic-)bitumen ~ ~ (Brit.); ~ joint runner · Bitumenstrick m [*Strick-Blei-Dichtung*]

~ pre-impregnation, ~ pre-saturation (US); (asphaltic-)bitumen ~ (Brit.) · Bitumenvorimprägnierung f, Bitumenvortränkung

(~) prepared roofing → ~ ready ~

~ pre-saturating, ~ pre-impregnating (US); (asphaltic-)bitumen ~ (Brit.) · Bitumenvorimprägnieren n, Bitumenvortränken

~ primer → (asphaltic-)bitumen ~

~ product → asphaltic ~

~ protection coat (US) → (asphaltic-)bitumen ~ ~

~ protective coat (US) → (asphaltic-)bitumen protection ~

~~ coating (material) (US) → (asphaltic-)bitumen ~ ~ (~)

~ ready roofing, (~) prepared ~, ~ composition ~, (~) roof(ing) felt, ~ rag felt, ~ wool felt (US); (asphaltic-)bitumen ~ ~, asphaltic felt, cold-process roofing, rolled (strip) roofing, sanded bituminous felt, saturated felt, self-finished roofing felt, bituminous roof(ing) felt [*B.S. 747*] · Bitumen(dach)pappe f, Asphalt(dach)pappe [*Fehlname: teerfreie Dachpappe*]

~ (~) ~ with asphalt coat(ing) on both sides (US); (asphaltic-)bitumen ready roofing with (asphaltic-)bitumen coat(ing) on both sides (Brit.) · Bitumendachpappe f mit beid(er)seitiger Bitumendeckschicht, ~ ~ beid(er)seitigem Bitumenüberzug m [*DIN 5218*]

~ roll(ed-strip) roofing (US); (asphaltic-)bitumen ~ ~ (Brit.) · Rollen-Bitumendachpappe f, Bitumendachpappe in Rollenform

~ roofing → ~ ready ~

~ roofing → mastic ~ ~

~~, ~ roof cover(ing), ~ roof sheathing, ~ roof cladding [*A waterproof roofing laid with bituminous felt*] · (Dach)(Ein)Deckung f mit Bitumendachpappe, Bedachung ~ ~

~~ cement → (asphaltic-)bitumen ~ ~

(~) ~ felt → ~ ready roofing

~~ sheet(ing) → (asphaltic-)bitumen ~ ~

asphalt-rubber mass, ~ composition, ~ material, ~ compound (US); (asphaltic-)bitumen-rubber ~ (Brit.) · Asphalt-Kautschuk-Masse f, Asphalt-Gummi-Masse

~ material → ~ mass

asphalt/rubber strip (US); (asphaltic-)bitumen/rubber ~ (Brit.) · Bitumen-Gummi-Streifen m

asphalt-saturated, asphalt-impregnated(US);(asphaltic-)bitumen-impregnated, (asphaltic-)bitumen-saturated (Brit.) · bitumengetränkt

~ felt(ed fabric) → (asphaltic-)bitumen-saturated ~ ~

~ ~ (~) mat, ~ ~ (~) pad (US); (asphaltic-)bitumen-saturated ~ (~) ~ (Brit.) · Bitumenfilzmatte f

~ ~ (~) ~ with cork, ~ ~ (~) pad ~ ~ (US); (asphaltic-)bitumen-saturated ~ (~) ~ ~ ~ (Brit.) · Bitumenkorkfilzmatte f

~ ~ (~) with cork (US); (asphaltic-)bitumen-saturated ~ (~) ~ ~ (Brit.) · Bitumenkorkfilz m [*Ein gröberer Filz als der Bitumenfilz, in dem Korkteilchen und expandierte Korkstückchen eingearbeitet sind*]

~ paper (US); (asphaltic-)bitumen-saturated ~ (Brit.) · getränktes Bitumenpapier n

asphalt saturating, ~ impregnating (US); (asphaltic-)bitumen ~ (Brit.) · Bitumenimprägnieren n, Bitumentränken

~ saturation → ~ impregnation

asphalt seal(ing) — (asphaltic-)bitumen bonding adhesive

~ seal(ing) → (asphaltic-)bitumen ~

~ ~ compound (US); (asphaltic-)bitumen ~ ~ (Brit.) · kaltstreichbare Bitumenkleb(e)masse f

~ seal(ing) rope (US) → (asphaltic-)bitumen(-impregnated) ~ ~

~ ~ sheet(ing) → (asphaltic-)bitumen ~ ~

~ sheet roofing → (asphaltic-)bitumen ~ ~

~ sheet(ing) → (asphaltic-)bitumen ~

~ shingle (US); (asphaltic-)bitumen ~ (Brit.); composition (roofing) ~, prepared-roofing ~, ready-roofing ~, strip slate · (Dach)Pappschindel f, (Dach)Schindel aus Dachpappe, Bitumen(dach)schindel, Asphalt(dach)-schindel

~ slurry (US) → (asphaltic-)bitumen ~

~ strip (US) → (asphaltic-)bitumen(-impregnated) ~

~ (surface) coat(ing) (US); (asphaltic-)bitumen (~) ~ (Brit.) · Bitumendeckschicht f, Bitumenüberzug m [*Dachpappe*]

~ tape → (asphaltic-)bitumen ~

~ test (US) → (asphaltic-)bitumen ~

~ tile → thermoplastic ~

~ top dressing → (asphaltic-)bitumen ~ ~

asphalt-type wood fiber board (US) → (asphaltic-)bitumen-type wood fibre ~

asphalt with rock flour (US); asphaltic-bitumen ~ ~ (Brit.) · Neobitumen n [*Bitumen mit Steinmehl; tauglich für Betonrohrauskleidungen*]

~ wood fiberboard (US); (asphaltic-)bitumen wood fibreboard (Brit.) · Bitumen-Holzfaserplatte f [*DIN 68752*]

~ wool felt → ~ ready roofing

asphaltene · Asphalten n, Hartasphalt m [*Dieser Ausdruck für den unlöslichen Rückstand im Bitumen stammt aus der Zeit, in der Bitumen mit Asphalt bezeichnet wurde*]

asphaltic, asphalt based (US); (asphaltic-)bitumen based, containing (asphaltic-)bitumen (Brit.) · bitumenhaltig

asphalt(ic) adhesive (composition) → (asphaltic-)bitumen ~ (~)

~ ~ compound → (asphaltic-)bitumen adhesive (composition)

asphalt(-base) crude, ~ (~) petroleum · asphaltbasisches Erdöl n, bitumenbasisches ~

~ (~) petroleum, ~ crude · asphaltbasisches Erdöl n, bitumenbasisches ~

~ petroleum → ~ crude

asphaltic binder → (asphaltic-)bitumen ~

(asphaltic-)bitumen (Brit.); asphalt (US) · Bitumen n [*Fehlname: Asphaltbitumen*]

~ addition (Brit.); asphalt ~ (US)· Bitumenbeigabe f, Bitumenzusatz m

~ adhesion-preventing agent (Brit.) → asphalt ~ ~

~ adhesive (composition), ~ ~ compound, ~ bonding ~, ~ cementing ~ (Brit.); asphalt(ic) ~ (~), asphalt(ic) adhesive (US) [*Asphaltic adhesives may be either emulsions in water or solutions in oils or other solvents*] · Bitumenkleb(e)masse f

~ ~ compound → ~ ~ (composition)

(asphaltic-)bitumen-aggregate mix(-ture) (Brit.) → asphalt-aggregate ~

(asphaltic-)bitumen/asbestos composition → ~ compound

~ compound (Brit.); asphalt/asbestos ~ (US); ~ mass, ~ composition, ~ material · Bitumen-Asbest-Masse f

~ fibre cement (Brit.); asphalt/asbestos fiber ~ (US) · Bitumenasbestfaser-Spachtel(masse) m, (f)

~ mass → ~ compound

~ material → ~ compound

(asphaltic-)bitumen base (Brit.); asphalt ~ (US) · Bitumenbasis f, Bitumengrundlage f

~ based, containing (asphaltic-)bitumen (Brit.); asphalt based, asphaltic (US) · asphalthaltig

(asphaltic-)bitumen-based building mastic, ~ mastic joint sealer (Brit.); asphalt-based building mastic, asphalt-based mastic joint sealer (US) · plastische Bitumenfugen(ab)dicht(ungs)-masse f, ~ Bitumenfugenmasse, ~ Bitumen(fugen)(ver)füllmasse, plastischer Bitumen(fugen)(ver)füller m, Bitumenfugen(ab)dicht(ungs)kitt m, Bitumen(ver)füllkitt, Bitumen(fugen)kitt, Bitumen(fugen)mastix m

~ mastic joint sealer, ~ building mastic (Brit.); asphalt-based building mastic, asphalt-based mastic joint sealer (US) · plastische Bitumenfugen(ab)dicht(ungs)masse f, Bitumenfugenmasse, Bitumen(fugen)(ver)füllmasse, plastischer Bitumen(fugen)(ver)füller m, Bitumenfugen(ab)dicht(ungs)kitt m, Bitumen(ver)füllkitt, Bitumen(fugen)kitt, Bitumen(fugen)mastix

~ paste (Brit.) → asphalt-based ~

~ rust protection paint (Brit.) → asphalt-based rust protective ~

~ ~ protective paint (Brit.) → asphalt-based ~ ~ ~

(asphaltic-)bitumen binder, asphaltic ~ (Brit.); asphalt ~ (US) · Bitumenbindemittel n, Bitumenbinder m

(asphaltic-)bitumen-bonded (Brit.); asphalt-bonded (US) · bitumengebunden

(asphaltic-)bitumen bonding adhesive, ~ cement(ing agent), ~ bonding agent, ~ bonding medium (Brit.) [*B.S. 3940*]; asphalt ~ ~ (US); (asphaltic-)bitumen adhesive (Brit.); asphalt adhesive (US) · Bitumenkleber m, Bitumenkleb(e)stoff m, Bitumenkleb(e)mittel n

(asphaltic-)bitumen bonding ... — (asphaltic-)bitumen ... 74

~ ~ **agent** → ~ ~ adhesive
~ **bonding composition** → ~ adhesive (~)
~ ~ **compound** → ~ adhesive (composition)
~ ~ **medium** → ~ ~ ~ adhesive
~ **briquette** (Brit.); asphalt(ic) ~ (US) · Bitumenformling *m*
~ **building paper** (Brit.); asphalt ~ ~, general-use ~ ~ (US) [*See remark under 'Pappe'*] · Asphaltbaupappe *f*, Bitumenbaupappe
~ **calcium silicate brick** (Brit.) → asphalt(-impregnated) sand-lime ~
~ **cement(ing agent)** → ~ bonding adhesive
~ **cementing composition** → ~ adhesive (~)
~ ~ **compound** → ~ adhesive (composition)
~ **coat** (Brit.) → asphalt (surface) coat(ing)
~ **coated** (Brit.); asphalt ~ (US) · bitumenbeschichtet, bitumenüberzogen
(asphaltic-)bitumen-coated chip(ping)s (Brit.) → asphalt-coated ~
~ **gravel** (Brit.) → gravel asphalt
~ **metal, ~ road ~** (Brit.); asphalt-coated crushed stone (US) · Bitumenschotter *m*
~ **(road) metal** (Brit.); asphalt-coated crushed stone (US) · Bitumenschotter *m*
~ **sand** (Brit.); asphalt-coated ~ (US) · Asphaltsand *m*, Bitu(men)sand
(asphaltic-)bitumen coat(ing) (Brit.) → asphalt (surface) ~
~ **coating compound** (Brit.); asphalt ~ ~ (US) · Bitumenanstrichmasse *f*, Bitumenaufstrichmasse
~ ~ **(material)** (Brit.); asphalt ~ (~) (US) · Bitumenanstrich(mittel) *m*, (*n*), Bitumenanstrichstoff *m*, Bitumenaufstrich(mittel), Bitumenaufstrichstoff
~ **composition, ~ compound** (Brit.); asphalt ~ (US) · Bitumenmasse *f*
~ ~ **roofing** → asphalt ready ~
~ **compound** → ~ composition
~ **concrete** (Brit.); asphalt(ic) ~ (US) · Asphaltbeton *m* [*Gemisch von Splitt, Natursand (oder Brechsand) und Füller mit Bitumen als Bindemittel*]
~ ~ **(mineral) skeleton** (Brit.) → asphalt ~ (~) ~ (US)
~ ~ **skeleton** (Brit.) → asphalt concrete (mineral) ~ (US)
~ **content** (Brit.); asphalt ~ (US) · Bitumenanteil *m*, Bitumengehalt *m*
~ **dispersion** (Brit.); asphalt(ic) ~ (US) · Bitumendispersion *f*
~ **emulsion with colloidal emulsifier** (Brit.); asphalt(ic) ~ ~ ~ ~ (US) · Bitumenemulsion *f* mit festem Emulgator, ~ ~ unlöslichem ~ [*Fehlname: Bitumensuspension*]

(asphaltic-)bitumen-filler mix(ture) (Brit.); asphalt-filler ~ (US) · Bitumen-Füller-Gemisch *n*, Bitumen-Füller-Mischung *f*
(asphaltic-)bitumen film (Brit.); asphalt ~ (US) · Bitumenfilm *m*
~ **for dampproof coating** (Brit.); asphalt ~ ~ ~ (US) · Mauerbitumen *n*
~ ~ **road purposes** (Brit.) [*B.S. 3690*]; paving (grade) asphalt, A.C., asphalt cement (US) · Straßenbaubitumen *n* [*DIN 1995*]
~ ~ ~ ~ **with road tar addition** (Brit.) → paving asphalt ~ ~ ~ ~
~ **globule** (Brit.); asphalt ~ (US) · Bitumenkügelchen *n*
~ **grade** (Brit.); asphalt ~ (US) · Bitumensorte *f*
~ **gunite** (Brit.) → asphalt ~
~ **hardness degree** (Brit.); asphalt ~ ~ (US) · Bitumen-Härtegrad *m*
(asphaltic-)bitumen-impregnated, (asphaltic-)bitumen-saturated (Brit.); asphalt-saturated, asphalt-impregnated (US) · bitumengetränkt
(asphaltic-)bitumen(-impregnated) calcium silicate brick (Brit.) → asphalt(-impregnated) sand-lime ~
~ **lime-sand brick** (Brit.) → asphalt(-impregnated) sand-lime ~
~ **sand-lime brick** (Brit.) → asphalt(-impregnated) ~ ~
~ **strip** (Brit.); asphalt-impregnated ~ (US) · Bitumenstreifen *m*
(asphaltic-)bitumen impregnating → asphalt saturating
~ **impregnation** → asphalt ~
~ **individual coat** (Brit.); asphalt ~ ~ (US) · Bitumenanstrichschicht *f*, Bitumenaufstrichschicht
~ **insulating coat** → ~ insulation(-grade) ~
~ ~ **paste, ~ insulation(-grade)** ~ (Brit.); asphalt ~ ~ (US) · Asphaltisolierpaste *f*, Bitumenisolierpaste
~ ~ **slab** → ~ insulation(-grade) ~
~ **insulation(-grade) coat, ~ insulating** ~ (Brit.); asphalt ~ ~ (US) · Bitumenisolieranstrich *m*, Bitumenisolieraufstrich
~ ~ **paste** → ~ insulating ~
~ ~ **slab, ~ insulating** ~ (Brit.); asphalt ~ ~ (US) · Asphaltisolierplatte *f*, Bitumenisolierplatte
~ **(joint) pouring compound** (Brit.); asphalt (~) ~ ~, asphalt(ic) (joint) filler (US) · Bitumen-Fugen(ver)gußmasse *f*, Bitumen-(Fugen)Ausgußmasse, Bitumen-Vergußmasse, Bitumen-(Fugen)Gießmasse
~ ~ **runner** → ~ ~ ? ouring rope

(asphaltic-)bitumen-laminated (Brit.); asphalt-laminated · bitumenkaschiert

(asphaltic-)bitumen/latex emulsion (Brit.); asphalt/latex ~ (US) · Bitumen-Latex-Emulsion *f*

(asphaltic-)bitumen layer (Brit.); asphalt ~ ~ (US) · Bitumenlage *f*, Bitumenschicht *f*

~ **lime-sand brick** (Brit.) → asphalt(-impregnated) sand-lime ~

~ **liner** (Brit.); asphalt ~ (US) · Bitumenabklebung *f* [*(Preß)Stroh-(dämm)platte*]

~ **lining,** ~ **(sur)facing** (Brit.); asphalt(-ic) ~ (US) · Bitumenauskleidung *f*, Bitumenverkleidung, Bitumenbekleidung, Asphaltauskleidung, Asphaltverkleidung, Asphaltbekleidung

~ **macadam** (Brit.); asphalt(ic) ~ (US) · Asphaltmakadam *m*, Bitumenmakadam

~ **mortar** (Brit.); asphalt(ic) ~ (US) · Asphaltmörtel *m*, Bitumenmörtel

~ **penetration macadam** (Brit.); asphalt(ic) ~ ~ (US) · Asphalttränkmakadam *m*, Bitumentränkmakadam

~ **perforated sheet(ing)** (Brit.); asphalt ~ ~ (US) · Bitumenlochbahn *f*

~ **pouring compound** → ~ **(joint)** ~

~ ~ **rope** (Brit.); asphalt(ic) ~ ~ (US); ~ joint runner · Bitumenstrick *m* [*Strick-Blei-Dichtung*]

~ **pre-impregnating** (Brit.) → asphalt pre-saturating

~ **pre-impregnation** (Brit.) → asphalt ~

~ **prepared roofing** → asphalt ready ~

~ **pre-saturating** (Brit.) → asphalt ~

~ **pre-saturation** (Brit.) → asphalt pre-impregnation

~ **primer** (Brit.); asphalt ~ (US) · Bitumengrund(ierung) *m*, (*f*), Bitumengrundiermittel *n*, Bitumen-Grundanstrichmittel, Bitumen-Grundierstoff *m*, Bitumen-Grundanstrichstoff

~ **product** (Brit.); asphalt ~ (US) · Bitumenerzeugnis *n*

~ **protection coat,** ~ **protective** (Brit.); asphalt ~ ~ (US) · Bitumenschutzanstrich *m*, Bitumenschutzaufstrich

~ **protective coat** → ~ **protection** ~

~ ~ **coating (material)** (Brit.); asphalt ~ ~ (~) (US) · Bitumenschutzanstrich(mittel) *m*, (*n*), Bitumenschutzaufstrich(mittel), Bitumenschutzanstrichstoff *m*, Bitumenschutzaufstrichstoff

~ ~ **felt** (Brit.); asphalt(-impregnated) ~ ~ (US) · Asphaltschutzpappe *f*, Bitumenschutzpappe

~ **rag felt** (Brit.) → asphalt ready roofing

~ **ready roofing** → asphalt ~ ~

~ ~ ~ **with (asphaltic-)bitumen coat(ing) on both sides** (Brit.) → asphalt ready roofing with asphalt ~ ~ ~ ~

~ **roll(ed-strip) roofing** (Brit.); asphalt ~ ~ (US) · Bitumendachpappe *f* in Rollenform, Rollen-Bitumendachpappe

~ **roof cladding ,** ~ ~ **covering,** ~ ~ **sheathing,** ~ **roofing** (Brit.) ;. asphaltfelt roof cladding, asphalt-felt roof covering, asphalt-felt roof sheathing, asphalt-felt roof(ing) (US) · Asphalt-Kleb(e)dach(belag) *n*, (*m*), Asphalt-Kleb(e)(dach)(ein)deckung *f*, Asphalt-Kleb(e)bedachung, Asphalt-Spacheldach(belag), Asphalt-Spachtel(dach)(ein)deckung, Asphalt-Spachtelbedachung

~ ~ **covering,** ~ ~ **cladding,** ~ ~ **sheathing,** ~ **roofing** (Brit.); asphalt-felt roof cladding, asphalt-felt roof covering, asphalt-felt roof sheathing, asphalt-felt roof(ing) (US) · Asphalt-Kleb(e)dach(belag) *n*, (*m*), Asphalt-Kleb(e)(dach)(ein)deckung *f*, Asphalt-Kleb(e)bedachung, Asphalt-Spachteldach(belag), Asphalt-Spachtel(dach)-(ein)deckung, Asphalt-Spachtelbedachung

~ ~ **sheathing,** ~ ~ **cladding,** ~ ~ **covering,** ~ **roofing** (Brit.); asphalt-felt roof cladding, asphalt-felt roof covering, asphalt-felt roof sheathing, asphalt-felt roof(ing) (US) · Asphalt-Kleb(e)dach(belag) *n*, (*m*), Asphalt-Kleb(e)(dach)(ein)deckung *f*, Asphalt-Kleb(e)bedachung, Asphalt-Spachteldach(belag), Asphalt-Spachtel(dach)-(ein)deckung, Asphalt-Spachtelbedachung

~ **roofing,** ~ **roof sheathing,** ~ **roof covering,** ~ **roof cladding** (Brit.); asphalt-felt roof cladding, asphalt-felt roof covering, asphalt-felt roof sheathing, asphalt-felt roof(ing) (US) · Asphalt-Kleb(e)dach(belag) *m*, (*m*), Asphalt-Kleb(e)(dach)(ein)deckung *f*, Asphalt-Kleb(e)bedachung, Asphalt-Spachteldach(belag), Asphalt-Spachtel(dach)(ein)deckung, Asphalt-Spachtelbedachung

~ ~ **cement** (Brit.); asphalt(ic) ~ ~ (US) · Bitumendachanstrichmittel *n*, Bitumendachaufstrichmittel *m*, Bitumendachaufstrichstoff, Bitumendeckenanstrichmittel, Bitumendeckenanstrichstoff, Bitumendeckenaufstrichmittel, Bitumendeckenaufstrichstoff

~ ~ ~ (Brit.); asphalt ~ ~ (US) · Bitumen(dach)spachtel(masse) *m*, (*f*), Bitumendachaufstrichmittel *n*, Bitumendeckmasse, Bitumendeckanstrichmittel, Bitumendachkitt *m*

~ ~ **felt** → asphalt ready roofing

~ **roof(ing) sheet(ing)** (Brit.); asphalt ~ ~ (US) · Bitumendachbahn *f*, Bitumendach(ein)deck(ungs)bahn

(asphaltic-)bitumen-rubber composition (Brit.) → asphalt-rubber mass

~ **compound** (Brit.) → asphalt-rubber mass

(asphaltic-)bitumen-rubber ... — asphalt(ic) limestone ...   76

~ **mass** (Brit.) → asphalt-rubber ~

~ **material** (Brit.) → asphalt-rubber mass

(asphaltic-)bitumen/rubber strip (Brit.); asphalt/rubber ~ (US) · Bitumen-Gummi-Streifen *m*

(asphaltic-)bitumen sand-lime brick (Brit.) → asphalt(-impregnated) ~ ~

(asphaltic-)bitumen-saturated, (asphaltic-)bitumen-impregnated (Brit.); asphalt-saturated, asphalt-impregnated (US) · bitumengetränkt

~ **felt(ed fabric)** (Brit.); asphalt-saturated ~ ~ (US) · Bitumenfilz *m* [*Ein mit Bitumen imprägnierter Filz aus Pflanzenfasern; er ist also keine Wollfilzpappe*]

~ ~ (~) **mat** → asphalt-saturated ~ (~) ~

~ ~ (~) ~ **with cork** (Brit.) → asphalt-saturated ~ (~) ~ ~ ~

~ ~ (~) **pad** → asphalt-saturated felt(ed fabric) mat

~ ~ (~) ~ **with cork** (Brit.) → asphaltic-saturated felt(ed fabric) mat ~ ~

~ ~ (~) **with cork** (Brit.) → asphalt-saturated ~ (~) ~ ~

~ **paper** (Brit.) → asphalt-saturated ~

(asphaltic-)bitumen saturating → asphalt ~

~ **saturation** → asphalt impregnation

~ **seal(ing)** (Brit.); asphalt(ic) ~ (US) · Asphalt-Absieg(e)lung *f*, Asphalt-Versieg(e)lung

~ ~ (Brit.); asphalt(ic) ~ (US) · Asphalt(ab)dichtung *f*

~ ~ (Brit.); asphalt ~ (US) · Bitumen(ab)dichtung *f*

~ **sealing compound** (Brit.) → asphalt ~ ~

~ **seal(ing) paste** (Brit.); asphalt(ic) ~ ~ (US) · Bitumen(ab)dicht(ungs)paste *f*

~ ~ **sheet(ing)** (Brit.); asphalt ~ ~ (US) · Bitumen(ab)dicht(ungs)bahn *f*

~ ~ **sheet roofing** (Brit.); asphalt ~ ~ (US) · Bitumendachpappe *f* in Bahnenform, Bahnen-Bitumendachpappe

~ **sheet(ing)** (Brit.); asphalt ~ (US) · Bitumenbahn *f*

~ **shingle** (Brit.) → asphalt ~

~ **slurry** (Brit.); asphalt ~ (US) · Bitumenschlämme *f*

~ **(surface) coat(ing)** (Brit.) → asphalt (~) ~

~ **(sur)facing,** ~ **lining** (Brit.); asphalt(ic) ~ (US) · Asphaltbekleidung *f*, Asphaltauskleidung, Asphaltverkleidung, Bitumenverkleidung, Bitumenauskleidung, Bitumenbekleidung

~ **tape** (Brit.); asphalt ~ (US); · Bitumenband *n* [*als Rohrdichtung*]

~ **test** (Brit.); asphalt ~ (US) · Bitumenprobe *f*, Bitumenversuch *m*, Bitumenprüfung *f*

~ **top dressing** (Brit.); asphalt ~ ~ (US) · Bitumendachanstrich *m*, Bitumendachaufstrich

(asphaltic-)bitumen-type wood fibre board (Brit.); asphalt-type wood fiber ~ (US) · Bitumenplatte *f*, Holzfaser~ [*Dem Faserbrei werden bis zu 25% Bitumen beigemischt*]

(asphaltic-)bitumen waterproofer coat (Brit.) → asphalt(ic) ~ ~

~ **with rock flour** (Brit.); asphalt ~ ~ ~ (US) · Neobitumen *n* [*Bitumen mit Steinmehl; tauglich für Betonrohrauskleidungen*]

~ **wood fibreboard** (Brit.); asphalt wood fiberboard (US) · Bitumen-Holzfaserplatte *f* [*DIN 68752*]

~ **wool felt** → asphalt ready roofing

asphalt(ic) bonding composition → (asphaltic-)bitumen adhesive (~)

~ ~ **compound** → (asphaltic-)bitumen adhesive (composition)

~ **briquette** (US); (asphaltic-)bitumen ~ (Brit.) · Bitumenformling *m*

~ **cementing composition** → (asphaltic-)bitumen adhesive (~)

~ **cementing compound** → (asphaltic-)bitumen adhesive (composition)

~ **composition,** ~ compound · Asphaltmasse *f*

~ **compound,** ~ composition · Asphaltmasse *f*

~ **concrete** (US); (asphaltic-)bitumen ~ (Brit.) · Asphaltbeton *m* [*Gemisch von Splitt, Natursand (oder Brechsand) und Füller mit Bitumen als Bindemittel*]

~ ~ **(mineral) skeleton** (US) → asphalt ~ (~) ~

~ ~ **skeleton** (US) → asphalt concrete (mineral) ~

~ **cutback,** cutback (asphalt) (US); cutback (asphaltic-)bitumen, cutback (Brit.) · Verschnittbitumen *n*

~ **dispersion** → (asphaltic-)bitumen ~

~ **emulsion with colloidal emulsifier** → (asphaltic-)bitumen ~ ~ ~ ~

~ **façade slab** · Asphaltfassadenplatte *f*

~ **facing,** ~ lining (US); (asphaltic-)bitumen ~ (Brit.) · Asphaltauskleidung *f*, Asphaltverkleidung, Asphaltbekleidung, Bitumenauskleidung, Bitumenverkleidung, Bitumenbekleidung

asphaltic felt → asphalt ready roofing

asphalt(ic) filler (US) → (asphaltic-)bitumen (joint) pouring compound

~ **limestone,** bituminous ~ · Stinkkalkstein *m*, Asphaltkalkstein, bituminöser Kalkstein [*Naturasphalt mit hohem Gehalt an Mineralstoffen*]

~ ~ **powder,** bituminous ~ ~ · Asphaltpulver *n* [*gemahlener Asphaltkalkstein*]

asphalt(ic) lining — assembly stage

~ **lining**, ~ (sur)facing (US); (asphalt-ic-)bitumen ~ (Brit.) · Asphaltauskleidung f, Asphaltverkleidung, Asphaltbekleidung, Bitumenbekleidung, Bitumenauskleidung, Bitumenverkleidung

~ **macadam** (US); (asphaltic-)bitumen ~ (Brit.) · Asphaltmakadam m, Bitumenmakadam

~ **mortar** (US); (asphaltic-)bitumen ~ (Brit.) · Asphaltmörtel m, Bitumenmörtel

~ ~ **masonry (work)** · Asphaltmauerwerk n [Mauerwerk mit Asphaltmörtel]

~ **penetration macadam** (US); (asphaltic-)bitumen ~ ~ (Brit.) · Asphalttränkmakadam m, Bitumentränkmadam

asphaltic petroleum · asphaltisches Erdöl n

asphalt(ic) pouring rope (US); (asphaltic-)bitumen ~ ~ (Brit.); ~ joint runner · Bitumenstrick. [Strick-Blei-Dichtung]

~ **product** · Asphalterzeugnis n, Asphaltgegenstand m, Asphaltartikel m

(asphaltic) pyrobituminous shale, bituminous oil ~ · bituminöser Ölschiefer m

asphalt(ic) residual oil · Asphaltöl n

asphaltic resin · Asphaltharz n

~ **rock**, bituminous ~ [A rock in which the impregnation is relatively low] · Asphaltgestein n, Bergasphalt m [Naturasphalt mit hohem Gehalt an Mineralstoffen, z.B. Asphaltkalkstein und Asphaltsand]

asphalt(ic) roof(ing) cement → (asphaltic-)bitumen ~ ~

asphaltic sand, bituminous ~ · Asphaltsand m, Bitumensand [Naturasphalt mit hohem Gehalt an Mineralstoffen]

~ **sand(stone)**, bituminous sandstone; sand asphalt (US) · Asphaltsand(stein) m, bituminöser Sandstein

asphalt(ic) seal(ing) (US); (asphaltic-)bitumen ~ (Brit.) · Asphalt-Absieg(e)lung f, Asphalt-Versieg(e)lung

~ ~ (US); (asphaltic-)bitumen ~ (Brit.) · Asphalt(ab)dichtung f

~ ~ **paste** → (asphaltic-)bitumen ~ ~

~ **(sur)facing**, ~ lining (US); (asphaltic-)bitumen ~ (Brit.) · Asphaltbekleidung f, Asphaltauskleidung, Asphaltverkleidung, Bitumenverkleidung, Bitumenbekleidung

asphaltic surfacing work · Asphaltbelagarbeiten fpl [DIN 18354]

asphalt(ic) terrazzo tile · Terrazzo-(Asphaltbelag)platte f, Terrazzo-Asphaltfliese f [Verbundplatte, deren Unterschicht aus Asphaltmaterial und deren Oberschicht aus Terrazzo besteht. Die beiden Schichten sind gleich dick]

~ **tile** [B.S. 1324] · Asphalt(belag)platte f, Asphaltfliese f [Asphaltplatten sind unter Druck in der Wärme gepreßte Platten aus Naturasphaltrohmehl oder gemahlenem oder gebrochenem Naturgestein und bituminösen Stoffen als Bindemittel]

~ ~ **floor cover(ing)**, ~ ~ ~ (finish), ~ ~ flooring · Asphaltfliesen(fuß)boden(belag) m, Asphaltplatten(fuß)boden(belag)

~ ~ ~ **(finish)**, ~ ~ ~ cover(ing), ~ ~ flooring · Asphaltfliesen(fuß)boden(belag) m, Asphaltplatten(fuß)boden(belag)

~ ~ **flooring**, ~ ~ floor cover(ing), ~ ~ floor (finish) · Asphaltfliesen(fuß)-boden(belag) m, Asphaltplatten(fuß)-boden(belag)

~ **varnish**, black ~ · Bitumenlack m, Bitumenlösung f [Fehlnamen: Asphaltlack, Asphaltlösung]

~ **wall tile** · Asphaltwand(belag)platte f, Asphaltwandfliese f

~ **waterproofer coat** (US); (asphaltic-)bitumen ~ ~, bituminous ~ ~ (Brit.) · Bitumensperranstrich m

asphaltic work · Asphaltarbeiten fpl

asphaltite · Asphaltit m [Naturasphalt von großer Härte mit sehr niedrigem Gehalt an Mineralstoffen, z.B. Gilsonit]

asphaltous acid anhydride · asphaltisches Säureanhydrid n

as-raised gravel · ungesiebter und ungewaschener Kies m

to assemble, to erect · montieren, zusammenbauen

assembler, assembling machine · Montiermaschine f für Scharniere

assembling, erecting · Zusammenbauen n, Montieren

~ **machine**, assembler · Montiermaschine f für Scharniere

~ **method** → method of erection

~ **rate** → ~ speed

~ **site**, erection ~ · Montagebaustelle f

~ **speed**, assembly ~, erection ~, ~ rate, rate of erection, rate of assembly, rate of assembling · Montagefortschritt m, Zusammenbaufortschritt, Montagegeschwindigkeit f, Zusammenbaugeschwindigkeit, Montagetempo n, Zusammenbautempo

~ **work** → erection ~

assembly, erection · Zusammenbau m, Montage f

~, set-up [for tests] · Prüf(ungs)anordnung f

~ **hall**, meeting ~ · Versammlungshalle f, Versammlungssaal m

~ **place**, meeting ~ · Versammlungsstätte f

~ **rate** → assembling speed

~ **room**, meeting ~ · Versammlungsraum m

~ **schedule**, erection ~ · Zusammenbauplan m, Montageplan

~ **speed** → assembling ~

~ **stage**, erection ~ · Zusammenbauphase f, Zusammenbaustadium n, Montagephase, Montagestadium

assembly stress — atomization glazing

~ **stress**, erection ~ · Montagespannung f, Anfangsspannung [*Die Spannung je Flächeneinheit eines Baugliedes bei der Montage eines Bauwerkes*]

~ **yard** · Montagehof m, Zusammenbauhof

association headquarters · Verbandshaus n

~ **of architects** · Architektenkammer f, Architektenverband m, Architektenvereinigung f

assumed load, designed ~, design ~ · Lastannahme f, Bemessungslast f, Entwurfslast, angenommene Last, rechnerisch vorgesehene Last

~ **loading**, designed ~, design ~ · Entwurfsbelastung f, rechnerisch vorgesehene Belastung, angenommene Belastung, Belastungsannahme f, Bemessungsbelastung

~ **stress approach** · Schnittkraftansatz m

assumption, hypothesis [*engineering structural analysis*] · Annahme f

Assyrian architecture · assyrische Architektur f

astatic buckling load · untere Grenze f der dynamischen Knicklast

Ast-Molin rib(bed) floor · Ast-Molin-Decke f

astragal [*A small convex mo(u)lding, often decorated with a bead and reel. There is a form of this mo(u)lding, sometimes called a 'bagnette' or 'baguette'*] · Astragal m

~ → (window) glazing bar

~ **cornice** · Astragal(ge)sims m, (n)

~ **frieze** · Astragalfries m

~ **window**, sash bar ~, glazing bar ~, division ~ ~; muntin ~ (US) · Sprossenfenster n

astylar [*A term applied to classical façades which have no pilasters*] · (wand-)pfeilerfrei, (wand)pfeilerlos

~ [*A term applied to classical façades which have no columns*] · säulenlos, säulenfrei

~ **back** · säulenfreie Rückfront f, säulenlose ~

asymmetrically-placed · unsymmetrisch angeordnet

AT → acoustic(al) tile

at ground level · ebenerdig

ATC → acoustic(al) tile ceiling

~, architectural terra-cotta [*It s used primarily for decorative purposes and for facing walls*] · Architekturterrakotta f

Athens Charter [*A manifesto published by the international architectural organization CIAM in 1933, setting out data and requirements connected with the problem of the modern city under five main headings (Dwellings, Recreation, Work, Transportation, Historic Buildings)*] · Charta f von Athen [*Von der internationalen Architektenorganisation CIAM 1933 herausgegebene Erklärung, die in fünf Hauptgruppen (Wohnung, Erholung; Arbeit, Verkehr, historisches Erbe) Feststellungen und Forderungen zum Problem der modernen Stadt formuliert*]

atlante, male caryatid, telamon, Persian [*Carved male figure used instead of columns to support an entablature in classical architecture*] · Atlant m, (Ge-)Simsträger m, Telamon m, Gebälkträger, Gigant m

atmospheric air, outdoor ~, external ~, exterior ~ · Außenluft f

~ **pollution** · Außenluftverunreinigung f

atmospheric-pressure boiler, ~ steam ~, low-pressure (steam) ~ · Niederdruck(dampf)kessel m

~ **equipment**, low-pressure ~ · Niederdruckgerät n

~ **gas**, low-pressure ~ · Niederdruckgas n

~ ~ **system**, low-pressure ~ ~ · Niederdruckgasanlage f

~ **saturated steam**, ~ wet ~, low-pressure ~ ~ · niedergespannter Naßdampf m

~ **spraying**, low-pressure ~ · Niederdruckspritzen n

~ **(steam) boiler**, low-pressure (~) ~ · Niederdruck(dampf)kessel m

~ **steam-cured**, low-pressure ~, cured by atmospheric-pressure steam, cured by low-pressure steam · dampfbehandelt, wärmebehandelt [*Beton*]

~ **steam curing**, low-pressure ~ ~, atmospheric ~ ~, steam curing at atmospheric pressure [*concrete*] · (Niederdruck)Dampfbehandlung f, Wärmebehandlung [*Es wird niedergespannter Naßdampf mit Temperaturen unter 100° C dem Beton zugeführt*]

~ ~ **heating**, low-pressure ~ ~ · Niederdruck-Dampfheizung f

~ ~ **pipe**, low-pressure ~ ~ · Niederdruckdampfrohr n

~ **system**, ~ installation, low-pressure ~ · Niederdruckanlage f [*Heizung*]

~ **wet steam**, ~ saturated ~, low-pressure ~ ~ · niedergespannter Naßdampf m

atmospheric steam curing → atmospheric-pressure ~ ~

~ **(water) vapour** (Brit.); ~ (~) vapor (US) · Wasserdampf m der Luft

atomic bunker · Atom(schutz)bunker m

~ **number** · Ordnungszahl f

atomization, atomizing, mist spraying, fog spray(ing), diffusion, diffusing · (Ver)Sprühen n, Versprühung f, Zerstäubung, Zerstäuben

~ **glazing**, glazing by atomization · Glasieren n durch Versprühen, Beglasen ~ ~, Sprühglasieren, Sprühbeglasen

atomization pattern — attrition test

~ pattern, diffusing ~, diffusion ~ · Zerstäubungsbild *n*

atomized air · Sprühluft *f*

atomizing, atomization, mist spraying, fog spray(ing), diffusion, diffusing · (Ver)Sprühen *n*, Versprühung *f*, Zerstäubung, Zerstäuben

~ application · Aufdüsen *n*, Aufsprühen

atrium, central (open) court(yard) · Atrium *n*, Mittelhof *m*

~ → ceremonial forecourt

~ house · Atriumhaus *n*, Gartenhofhaus

attached column, blind ~, engaged ~ [*A column partly sunk into a wall or pier*] · eingebundene Säule *f*, engagierte ~

~ decoration · (Mauer)Blende *f* [*Der Mauerfläche aufgelegtes, ,,vorgeblendetes" architektonisches Motiv, z.B. eine Reihe von Bögen*]

~ gable · Ziergiebel *m*, Blendgiebel [*Zur Gliederung der Traufseite eines Daches vorgeblendeter Giebel*]

~ garage [*A garage having all or part of one or more walls common to the dwelling or to a covered porch attached to the dwelling*] · Anbaugarage *f*

~ pier → engaged ~

~ ~ capital → engaged ~ ~

attachment, projection · Vorlage *f* [*Ein einer Wand oder Mauer vorgelegtes Bauglied wie Dienst, Lisene oder Pilaster*]

~ to a masonry wall, projection of ~ ~ ~, projection from ~ ~ ~ · Mauervorlage *f*, Mauervorsprung *m* [*Ein einer Mauer vorgelegtes Bauglied wie Dienst, Lisene oder Pilaster*]

~ ~ ~ wall, projection from ~ ~ · Wandvorlage *f* [*Ein einer Wand vorgelegtes Bauglied wie Dienst, Lisene oder Pilaster*]

attack · Angriff *m* [*durch einen Schadstoff*]

~, infestation [*The presence, within or contiguous to, a structure or premises of insects, rodents, vermin or other pests*] · Befall *m*

attacking power, aggresive ~ · Angriffsfähigkeit *f*, Angriffsvermögen *n* [*Schadstoff*]

attendant-controlled lift (Brit.); attendant-controled elevator (US) · Führeraufzug *m*

attendant-operated control · Führerbedienung *f* [*Fahrstuhl*]

~ goods lift (Brit.); ~ ~ elevator, ~ trunk lift, ~ freight lift (US) · Lastenaufzug *m* mit Personalbegleitung, Materialaufzug ~ ~

attendant parking · Parken *n* mit Bedienungspersonal

attenuation, sound ~ [*The reduction of the intensity of sounds*] · Schalldämpfung *f*

~ duct, sound ~ ~ · Schalldämpfungskanal *m*

attic, roof void, roof space [*Accessible space between top of uppermost ceiling and underside of roof. Inaccessible spaces are considered structural cavities*] · Dachraum *m*, Dachboden *m* [*volkstümlich ,,Bühne" f genannt*]

~ → ~ storey (Brit.)

~ · Attika *f* [*Oberer Abschluß von Säulenordnungen an Wandflächen*]

Attic base; moulded ~ (Brit.); molded ~ (US) · attischer Säulenfuß *m*, attische Basis *f*

attic order [*An order of pilasters applied to an attic stor(e)y*] · Wandpfeilerordnung *f* eines Dachstockwerkes, Halbpfeilerordnung ~ ~, Pilasterordnung ~ ~, ~ ~ Dachgeschosses

~ room, habitable attic, finished attic, garret; sky parlor, loft room (US) [*Attic space which is finished as living accommodations but which does not qualify as a half-stor(e)y*] · Dachkammer *f*, Dach(etagen)zimmer *n*, Dachgeschoßzimmer, Dachstockwerkzimmer, DG-Zimmer, Dachstube *f* [*Fehlname: Dachraum m*]

~ stair(case) · Bodentreppe *f*

~ (storey) (Brit.); loft (US) · Dachetage *f*, Dachgeschoß *n*, Dachstockwerk *n*, DG *n*, (Dach)Boden *m*

~ vent block → roof vent(ilating) ~

~ ~ opening, ~ ventilating ~, ~ ventilation ~, ~ ventilator · Dachlüftungsöffnung *f*

~ ~ tile → roof vent(ilating) block

~ vent(ilating) block → roof ~ ~

~ ~ opening, ~ ventilation ~, ~ ventilator · Dachlüftungsöffnung *f*

~ ~ tile → roof vent(ilating) block

~ ventilation opening, ~ vent(ilating) ~, ~ ventilator · Dachlüftungsöffnung *f*

~ ventilator, roof ~ [*A mechanical device to force ventilation by the use of a power-driven fan*] · Dachlüfter *m*

~ ~, ~ vent(ilating) opening, ~ ventilation opening · Dachlüftungsöffnung *f*

~ ~ (block) → roof vent(ilating) ~

~ ~ tile → roof vent(ilating) block

~ window, garret ~ · Mansard(en)dachfenster *n* [*Bei einem nicht halbschrägen Dachraum*]

attrition, abrasion · Abrieb *m*, Abreiben *n*

~ hardness, abrasion ~ · Abriebhärte *f*, Schleifhärte [*Gestein*]

~ loss, abrasion ~ · Abreibeverlust *m*, Abriebverlust

~ resistance → abrasion ~

~ test, abrasion ~ · Abnutz(ungs)probe *f* durch Abschleifen, Abnutz(ungs)prüfung *f* ~ ~, Abnutz(ungs)versuch *m* ~ ~, Abriebprobe, Abriebversuch, Abriebprüfung, Abreibeprobe, Abreibeversuch, Abreibeprüfung

attrition tester — autoclaving

~ **tester,** abrasion ~ · Abriebprüfmaschine f

~ **value,** abrasion ~ · Abnutz(ungs)wert m [*Gestein*]

attritor mill · Attritor m [*Mahlen in der Lackindustrie*]

auction hall · Auktionshalle f, Versteigerungshalle

audibility · Hörbarkeit f, Hörsamkeit

~ **range,** audible ~ range of audibility · Hör(barkeits)bereich m, n, Hörsamkeitsbereich

audible · hörbar

~ **alarm unit,** sound ~ ~, acoustic(al) ~ ~ · akustisches Alarmgerät n

~ **range,** audibility ~, range of audibility · Hör(barkeits)bereich m, n, Hörsamkeitsbereich

~ **signal,** sound ~, acoustic(al) ~ · akustisches Signal n, Hörsignal

audience-hall, hall for audience · Audienzhalle f, Audienzsaal m

audiometry · Audiometrie f [*Die Lehre von der Auswirkung von Geräuschen auf die Hörsamkeit*]

aud(itorium), lecture theatre, lecture hall · Vortragssaal m, Hörsaal, Vorlesungssaal

~ **(space)** · Zuschauerraum m, Zuschauersaal m

auditory impression, ~ sensation, aural ~ · Wahrnehmung f, Hörempfindung [*Akustik*]

~ **sensation,** ~ impression, aural ~ · Wahrnehmung f, Hörempfindung [*Akustik*]

~ ~ **area** [*The region enclosed by the curves defining the threshold of pain and the threshold of hearing as a function of frequency*] · Hörempfindungsbereich m, n

auger-type extrusion unit, extrusion auger, auger-type machine, extruder-screw, screw-extruder · Schneckenpresse f, Extruder-Schnecke f

~ **machine,** extruder-screw, screw-extruder, auger-type extrusion unit, extrusion auger · Schneckenpresse f, Extruder-Schnecke f

augite · Augit m

~ **diorite,** augitic ~ · Augitdiorit m

~ **granite,** augitic ~ · Augitgranit m

~ **granophyre,** augitic ~ · Augitgranophyr m

~ **melaphyre,** augitic ~ · Augitmelaphyr m

~ **porphyry,** augitic ~ · Augitporphyr m, schwarzer Porphyr

~ **rock,** augitic ~ · Augitfels m

~ **syenite,** augitic ~ · Augitsyenit m

augitite [*A limburgite without olivine*] · Augitit m

aula [*The assembly hall of a university or other scholastic building*] · Aula f

a(u)mbry [*A cupboard or recess in a church to contain sacred vessels*] · Kirchenschrank m

~, almery, alms-box · Opferkasten m

aural conditions · Hörverhältnisse f

~ **impression,** ~ sensation, auditory ~ · Wahrnehmung f, Hörempfindung [*Akustik*]

~ **sensation,** ~ impression, auditory ~ · Wahrnehmung f, Hörempfindung [*Akustik*]

aureole, vesica piscis, mandorla · Heiligenschein m, Mandorla f, Mandelglorie f

aurum foliatum, gold-leaf, gold leaves · Blattgold n [*Etwa 16½–23½ karätiges Gold, welches in hauchdünnen Blättchen meist in quadratischer Form in verschiedenen Sorten in den Handel kommt*]

austenitic manganese steel · Manganhartstahl m

~ **phase** · Austenitphase f

~ **region** · Austenitgebiet n

~ **stainless steel** · austenitischer (rostfreier) Edelstahl m

~ **steel** · austenitischer Stahl m, Austenitstahl

austenitizing · austenitisierend

austerity, precision, severity (of style) · Strenge f [*Stil*]

authority engineer · Behördeningenieur m

to autoclave, to steam cure at high pressure · autoklavi(si)eren, autoklavbehandeln, autoklavhärten, dampfdruckhärten

autoclave, pressure vessel · Autoklav m, (Druck)Härtekessel m, Druckkessel, (Dampf)Härtekessel, Dampfdruckerhitzer m

~ **curing** → autoclaving

~ **test** · Autoklavversuch m, Autoklavprüfung f, Autoklavprobe f

autoclaved, high-pressure steam cured · autoklavbehandelt, autoklavi(si)ert, autoklavgehärtet, dampfdruckgehärtet

autoclave(d) aerated concrete · Autoklav-Porenbeton m

~ **concrete** · Autoklavbeton m [*Unter hochgespanntem Dampf gehärteter Beton*]

~ ~ **article,** ~ ~ product · Autoklavbetonerzeugnis n, Autoklavbetongegenstand m, Autoklavbetonartikel m, Autoklavbetonware f

~ ~ **product,** ~ ~ article · Autoklavbetonerzeugnis n, Autoklavbetongegenstand m, Autoklavbetonartikel m, Autoklavbetonware f

~ **gypsum** · Autoklavgips m

autoclaving, steam curing at high pressure, autoclave curing, high pressure steam curing · Härten n im Druck(härte)kessel, Behandlung f mit Hochdruckdampf, Dampf(druck)härtung f, Autoklavhärtung, Behandlung mit hochgespanntem Dampf, Autoklav(is)ierung, Autoklavbehandlung

autogenous healing — available from stock

autogenous healing · Selbstdichtung f, Nachsintern n [Wie an Stahlbetondruckrohren nachgewiesen wurde, können durch Nachsintern (Selbstdichtung) sogar durchgehende Risse geschlossen werden, wenn die Rohre gefüllt und unter Druck gehalten werden]

autogenous-welded steel pipe · autogengeschweißtes Stahlrohr n

autogenous welding · Autogenschweißung f, Gasschmelzschweißung

auto-ignition, self-ignition · Selbst(ent)zündung f

~ **temperature,** self-ignition ~ · Selbst(ent)zündungstemperatur f

auto junkyard · Autofriedhof m

automated door · automatische Tür f

~ **sliding door** · automatische Schiebetür f

auto(matic) air heater, ~ ~ heating appliance, ~ ~ warming appliance, ~ ~ heating device, ~ ~ warming device, ~ ~ heating unit, ~ ~ warming unit, ~ ~ warmer, ~ ~ fire · Luft(heiz)automat m

~ **boiler** · Automatikkessel m

~ **burning appliance,** ~ furnace, ~ fire · automatische Feuerung f, ~ Feuerstätte f

~ **closing** · automatisches Schließen n

~ **depot** (Brit.); ~ ready(-)mix(ed) works · automatisches Transportbetonwerk n, ~ Lieferbetonwerk, ~ Betonlieferwerk,

~ **door closer,** ~ closing device, ~ ~ closing mechanism · automatischer Türschließer m, Türschließautomat m

~ **(~) operator** · automatische (Tür-)Öffnungsanlage f

~ **electric water heater,** ~ ~ ~ heating appliance · automatischer Elektro-Wasserheizer m, Elektro-Wasserheizautomat m

~ **fire,** ~ furnace, ~ burning appliance · automatische Feuerstätte f, ~ Feuerung f

~ ~ **door** · automatische Brand(schutz)tür f, ~ Feuer(schutz)tür

~ ~ **shutter** · automatischer Brandabschluß m

~ ~ **warning device** · automatischer Brandmelder m, ~ Feuermelder, automatische Brandmeldeeinrichtung f, automatische Feuermeldeeinrichtung f, Brandmeldeautomat m, Feuermeldeautomat

~ **furnace,** ~ fire, ~ burning appliance · automatische Feuerung f, ~ Feuerstätte f

(~) heat detector · Hitzemelder m, Hitzemeldeautomat m [Brandschutz]

~ **heating** · Automatikheizung f

~ **hinge assembling and double-sided hinge pin spinning machine** · Montier- und doppelseitige Scharnierstift-Nietwalzmaschine f

~ **parking ticket issuing machine** · automatischer Parkscheinspender m, Parkscheinautomat m

~ **rate-and-price indicator** · automatischer Börsenkursanzeiger m

~ **ready(-)mix(ed) concrete fabrication** · automatische Transportbetonherstellung f

~ **ready(-)mix(ed) works;** ~ depot (Brit.) · automatisches Transportbetonwerk n, ~ Lieferbetonwerk, ~ Betonlieferwerk

~ **return of water** · Dampfschleife f, Wasserkreislauf m

~ ~ **trap** · automatischer Rückspeiser m [Dampfheizung]

~ **shaft kiln** · automatischer Schachtofen m

~ **shutter door operator,** ~ shutterdoor ~ · automatische Torantriebvorrichtung f, automatischer Torantrieb m

~ **slab and tile grinder** · Plattenschleifautomat m

(~) smoke detector · Rauchmelder m, Rauchmeldeautomat m [Brandschutz]

~ **sprinkler** · Sprinklerautomat m

~ **system** · Automatik f

~ ~ **for boiler operation** · Kessel-Automatik f

~ **(tele)phone exchange** · Selbstwählzentrale f

~ **timing device** · Zeitschaltautomat m, Zeitschalter m

autonomy of functions · Autonomie f der Funktionen

autostacker, parking tower, pidgeonhole (parking structure) · Autosilo m, Parkturm m

autunite, lime uranite · Autunit m, Kalkuranglimmer m

Auvergne(-type) transept · (auvergnatischer) Querriegel m [Besonders betont ausgebildetes Querschiff romanischer Kirchen in der Auvergne]

auxiliary boiler house · Hilfskesselhaus

~ **civil defense** (US); ~ ~ defence (Brit.) · Behelfsschutz m

~ **cut,** breaking out ~ · Hilfsschnitt m [Schneiden von Flachglas]

~ **force** · Hilfskraft f [Statik]

~ **(pre)stressing,** ~ tensioning, ~ stretching · Hilfsvorspannung f

~ **reinforcement,** ~ steel [In a prestressed member, any reinforcement in addition to that participating in the prestressing function] · Hilfsarmierung f, Hilfsbewehrung, Hilfs(stahl)einlagen fpl

~ **steel** → ~ reinforcement

~ **stressing,** pre~, ~ tensioning, ~ stretching · Hilfsvorspannung f

~ **stretching,** ~ tensioning, ~ (pre-)stressing · Hilfsvorspannung f

~ **tensioning,** ~ stretching, ~ (pre-)stressing · Hilfsvorspannung f

available · lieferbar

~ **for prompt delivery** · kurzfristig lieferbar

~ **from stock** · lieferbar ab Lager

~ office space · Büronutzfläche f
avant-garde (style of) architecture · avantgardistische Architektur f, ~ Baukunst f
aventurine · Avanturin m, Aventurin
~ fel(d)spar, sunstone · Sonnenstein m
~ glass [*Glass made so that it contains specks of bright reflecting metallic or other crystalline material*] · Aventuringlas n, Avanturinglas, Goldfluß m
avenue of sphinxes, processional way ~ ~ · Sphinxallee f
average, mean · Mittel n
~, mean · durchschnittlich
~ **compressive strength**, ~ compression ~ · mittlere Druckfestigkeit f
~ **grain diameter**, mean ~ ~, ~ particle ~ · mittlerer Korndurchmesser m, durchschnittlicher ~
~ **particle diameter**, mean ~ ~, ~ grain ~ · mittlerer Korndurchmesser m, durchschnittlicher ~
~ **reflectance** · mittlerer Rückstrahlungsgrad m [*Tageslichtberechnung*]
~ **strength**, mean ~ · mittlere Festigkeit f, durchschnittliche ~
~ **temperature**, mean ~ · Mitteltemperatur f
~ **tensile strength**, mean ~ ~ · mittlere Zugfestigkeit f, durchschnittliche ~
~ **thickness**, mean ~ · mittlere Dicke f, durchschnittliche ~ [*Fehlnamen: mittlere Stärke, durchschnittliche ~*]
~ **volume of grain**, mean ~ ~ ~, ~ ~ ~ particle · mittleres Kornvolumen n, durchschnittliches ~
~ ~ ~ **particle**, mean ~ ~ ~, ~ ~ ~ grain · mittleres Kornvolumen n, durchschnittliches ~
aviary · Vogelhaus n [*Zoo*]
avoidance of cracking · Rißverhütung f
award-winning, prize-winning · preisgekrönt
awning · Sonnensegel n
~ sash, top-hinged ~ · Klapp(fenster)flügel m
~ (~) window, top-hinged ~ ~ · Klapp(flügel)fenster n
ax(hammer) (US); bricklayer's hammer, brick axe (Brit.) · Maurerhammer m [*DIN 5108*]
axial deformation · axiale Formänderung f, ~ Verformung
~ fixity, ~ restraint · axiale Einspannung f, mittige ~
~ flow fan · Axialventilator m
~ force · Axialkraft f
~ load · Axiallast f, Achslast
~ loading · axiale Belastung f
~ moment of inertia · axiales Trägheitsmoment n
~ porosity, central ~, coky centre · Fadenlunker m
~ pressure · Axialdruck m, mittiger Druck
~ (pre)stressing, ~ tensioning, ~ stretching · axiale Vorspannung f, mittige ~
~ restraint, ~ fixity · axiale Einspannung f, mittige ~
~ rib, ridge ~ · Scheitelrippe f [*Sie verläuft entlang der Scheitellinie eines Gewölbes. Die Scheitelrippe kommt meistens beim Fächergewölbe, Strahlengewölbe und Palmengewölbe der englischen Baukunst vor*]
~ stretching, ~ tensioning, ~ (pre-)stressing · axiale Vorspannung f, mittige ~
~ tensile strength, ~ tension ~ · Axialzugfestigkeit f, mittige Zugfestigkeit
~ tension · Axialzug m, mittiger Zug
~ tensioning, ~ stretching, ~ (pre-)stressing · axiale Vorspannung f, mittige ~
~ thrust, side ~, lateral ~ · (Seiten-)Schub m, Axialschub, achsrechter Schub [*Die waag(e)rechte Resultierende einer Gewölbekraft*]
axially loaded · axial belastet, mittig ~
~ symmetric, axisymmetric(al) · achs(en)symmetrisch, zentralsymmetrisch
axis of affinity · Affinitätsachse f
~ ~ inertia → center line ~ ~
~ ~ revolution · Drehachse f
axisymmetric(al), axially symmetric · achs(en)symmetrisch, zentralsymmetrisch
axle steel reinforcing bar, ~ ~ ~ rod [*A deformed reinforcing bar rolled from a carbon-steel axle for railroad cars*] · Bewehrungsstab m aus Achsenstahl
axonometric projection, parallel ~ · Parallelriß m, Parallelprojektion f, Axonometrie f, Parallelperspektive f, parallele Projektion
azide of lead, lead azide · Bleiazid n
azo dyestuff · Azofarbstoff m
azo-humic acid · Azohumussäure f
Aztec architecture · Azteken-Architektur f, Azteken-Baukunst f
azurite, chessylite, blue carbonate of copper · Azurit m

B

B → bathroom
B, BM, beam · Balken(träger) m
B → basement (level)
BA → burglar alarm (system)
B & S concrete pipe (US) → bell(-)and(-)spigot ~ ~
~ stoneware pipe, bell(-)and(-)spigot ~ (US); spigot(-)and(-)socket ~ (Brit.) · Steinzeug-Glockenmuffenrohr n, Glockenmuffen-Steinzeugrohr

Baader copper test · Baaderprobe f, Baaderprüfung f, Baaderversuch m
baby-care unit, ~ block, ~ accommodation · Säuglingsflügel m, Säuglingstrakt m, Säuglingsheim n
Babylonian architecture · babylonische Architektur f, ~ Baukunst f
bachelor's dwelling unit, bachelors' ~ ~ (US); ~ dwelling (Brit.) · Ledigenwohnung f, Junggesellenwohnung

~ **hostel,** bachelors' ~ · Ledigen(wohn)heim n, Junggesellen(wohn)heim
~ **kitchen,** bachelors' ~ · Junggesellenküche f, Ledigenküche
back · Rückfront f
~ → arch ~
~ → ~ of vault
~, reverse side · Rückseite f
~ [*The side of a panel etc. that is not finished*] · unbearbeitete Rückseite f
~ **door bell** · Hintertürklingel f
~ **dwelling-building** → ~ residential building
~ **dwelling-house** → ~ residential building
backed-up masonry (work) · hintermauertes Mauerwerk n
back elevation, elevation facing yard · Hinterfront f, Hinterseite f, Hoffront, Hofseite
backfill concrete · (Hinter)Füll(ungs)beton m
backflow [*Flow in a direction contrary to the natural or intended direction of flow*] · Rückstau m
~ **preventer** · Rückstauverhinderer m
back garden · Hausgarten m, Hintergarten
(back)ground · Fond m [*(Papier-) Tapete*]
~, base (surface), backing (material) · (Unter)Grund m
~ **(wall)paper** · Fondtapete f
backing [*Is the material between the facing and the back*] · Hintermauer(ungs)material n
~, ~ material, base (surface), (back-)ground · (Unter)Grund m
~, underlay, substrate, base, substratum, backup; underlayment (US) · Hinterlegung f, Unterlage f, Rücklage, Träger(schicht) m, (f), Rücken m
~ → ~ coat
~ **(brick),** back-up ~, common (stock) ~; building ~ (US) · Hintermauer(ungs)ziegel m, Hintermaurer m
~ **calcium silicate brick,** ~ sand-lime ~, ~ lime-sand ~ · Hintermauerkalksandstein m, Kalksandhintermauerstein

~ **(coat),** undercoat, basecoat, scratch coat [*A plastering or rendering coat other than the final coat*] · Grobputzlage f, Grobputzschicht f, Unterputzlage, Unterputzschicht, Rauhwerk n, Grundputzschicht, Grundputzlage
~ **(~) (mixed) plaster,** undercoat (~) ~, basecoat (~) ~ · Grundputz m, Unterputz, Grobputz
~ **(~) mix(ture),** ~ (~) stuff, ~ (~) plaster, undercoat ~, basecoat ~ · Unterputzmörtel m, Grobputzmörtel, Rauhwerkmörtel, Unterputzmasse f, Grobputzmasse, Rauhwerkmasse
~ **concrete,** core ~, hearting ~ · (Hinter)Füll(ungs)beton m, Kernbeton, Unterbeton [*Im Gegensatz zum Vorsatzbeton*]
~ **lime-sand brick,** ~ sand-lime ~, ~ calcium silicate ~ · Hintermauerkalksandstein m, Kalksandhintermauerstein
~ **(masonry),** back-up (~), masonry back-up · Hintermauerung f, Hintermauerwerk n
~ **material** [*A gypsum board used as the base layer for multi-layer gypsum board applications or for other finishing materials*] · Trägerplatte f
~ **(~),** (back)ground, base (surface) · (Unter)Grund m
~ **metal** · Unterlagsmetall n, Trägermetall
~ **(mixed) plaster** → ~ (coat) (~) ~
~ **mixture** → ~ coat ~
~ **paper** · Trägerpapier n
~ **plaster** → ~ (coat) mix(ture)
~ ~ → ~ (coat) (mixed) ~
~ **sand-lime brick,** ~ lime-sand ~, ~ calcium silicate ~ · Hintermauerkalksandstein m, Kalksandhintermauerstein
~ **sheet(ing),** underlay ~, base ~ · Trägerbahn f
~ **stuff** → ~ (coat) mix(ture)
back ledge · Rückleiste f, Stehbord n
~ **masonry wall,** ~ ~ work ~ · Rückmauer f, rückwärtige Mauer
~ ~ **(work) wall** · Rückmauer f, rückwärtige Mauer
~ **(mixed) plaster** [*This material is applied as a scratch coat to the back of laths fastened to the boarding between the studs*] · Hinter(innen)(ver)putz m
~ **of arch,** extrados ~ ~, upper surface ~ ~, (arch) extrados, (arch) back [*The outer line or surface of the convex side of an arch*] · Rücken m, Bogen~, äußere Bogenfläche f
~ ~ **vault,** extrados ~ ~, upper surface ~ ~, (vault) back, (vault) extrados · Rücken m, Gewölbe~, äußere Gewölbefläche f
~ ~ **wall** · Wandrückseite f
~ **patio,** ~ terrace · Hinterterrasse f

back plaster — bagged lime

~ plaster → ~ mixed ~
~ plate · Anschraubplatte f, Unterplatte [*Türbeschlag*]
backplate · Langschild n [*Türbeschlag*]
back pressure · Rückstaudruck m
~ residence block → ~ residential building
~ ~ building → ~ residential ~
~ residential block → ~ ~ ~ building
~ ~ building, ~ residence ~, ~ ~ block, ~ dwelling-house, ~ dwelling-building · Hinterwohngebäude n, Hinterwohnhaus n

back-siphonage, anti-siphonage [*The flowing back of used, contained, or polluted water from a plumbing fixture or vessel to other sources into a potable water supply pipe due to a negative pressure in such pipe*] · rückläufige Heberwirkung f

~ preventer, puff pipe, anti-siphonage device, anti-siphoning device, anti-siphonage pipe, anti-siphoning pipe · Rohrbelüfter m [*Fehlname: Rohrunterbrecher. DIN 3266*]

~ ~ with leakage water fitting, anti-siphonage device ~ ~ ~ ~, anti-siphonage pipe ~ ~ ~ ~, anti-siphoning device ~ ~ ~ ~, anti-siphoning pipe ~ ~ ~ ~ · Rohrbe- und -Entlüfter m

back stair(case) · Hintertreppe f

backstein Gothic [*A term used to denote the distinctive kind of Gothic architecture developed in North Germany particularly during the 14th c.*] · Backsteingotik f

back terrace, ~ patio · Hinterterrasse f

backup, underlay, substrate, base, backing, substratum; underlayment (US) · Rücklage f, Hinterlegung f, Unterlage, Rücken n, Träger(schicht) m, (f)

~ · Hintermauerung f

to back-up · hintermauern

back-up block, ~ tile [*See remark under 'Block'*] · Hintermauer(ungs)-block(stein) m, Hintermauer(ungs)-stein, Hintermauer m

~ brick, backing ~, common (stock) ~; building ~ (US) · Hintermauer-(ungs)ziel m, Hintermauer m

~ (masonry), backing (~), masonry back-up · Hintermauerung f, Hintermauerwerk n

~ tile, ~ block [*See remark under 'Block'*] · Hintermauer(ungs)block(-stein) m, Hintermauer(ungs)stein, Hintermauer m

back wall, rear ~ · Rückwand f, rückwärtige Wand

backyard → rear yard

bacteria resistance · Bakterienfestigkeit f

bactericidal · bakterienwidrig

~ paint, anti-bacterial ~ [*A bactericidal paint discourages the multiplication of bacteria on its dry applied film. The bactericidal properties are normally conferred by the use of special additives*] · bakterienwidrige (Anstrich)Farbe f

baddeleyite · Baddeleyit m [*Im wesentlichen aus ZrO_2 = Zirkondioxid bestehendes Gestein*]

baffled mixer · Mischer m für farbige Streumittel [*Dachpappenanlage*]

to bag · absacken, einsacken

bagasse, cane trash · Bagasse f, ausgepreßtes Zuckerrohr n

~ board, ~ sheet, cane trash ~ · Bagasseplatte f, Platte aus ausgepreßtem Zuckerrohr

~ sheet, ~ board, cane trash ~ · Platte f aus ausgepreßtem Zuckerrohr, Bagasseplatte

~ tar, cane trash ~ · Bagasseteer m

baggage cellar · Gepäckkeller m [*Hotel*]

~ claim area · Gepäckausgaberaum m

baggage-conveyance system · Gepäckförderanlage f

baggage corridor · Gepäckflur m, Gepäckgang m, Gepäckkorridor m

~ elevator (US); ~ lift (Brit.) · Gepäckaufzug m

~ entrance · Gepäckeingang m

~ flow · Gepäckdurchlauf m

~ ~ route · Gepäckdurchlaufroute f, Gepäckweg m

~ handling · Gepäckabfertigung f

baggage-handling counter · Gepäckschalter m

~ facility · Gepäckabfertigungsanlage f

baggage lift (Brit.); ~ elevator (US) · Gepäckaufzug m

~ platform · Gepäckbahnsteig m

~ rack · Kofferbock m [*im Hotelzimmer*]

~ room · Gepäckraum m

~ roundabout [*Colloquially: magic roundabout*] · Gepäckkarussell n

~ shed · Gepäckschuppen m

bag(gage) shelf [*In a counter for small handbags and so on*] · Gepäckablage f

baggage way · Gepäcktunnel m

bagged aggregate, ~ concrete ~ · eingesackter (Beton)Zuschlag(stoff) m

~ cement, sacked ~ · (ab)gesackter Zement m, eingesackter ~, Sackzement

~ concrete · Sackbeton m

~ (~) aggregate · eingesackter (Beton)Zuschlag(stoff) m

~ gypsum · Sackgips m

~ (hydrated) lime, hydrated lime powder supplied in bags · pulverförmig angelieferter Baukalk m [*Fehlnamen: Sackkalk(hydrat) m, (n)*]

~ lime → ~ hydrated ~

bagging · Absacken *n*, Einsacken
~ department, bag-packing ~ · Packerei *f* [*Zementfabrik*]
~ off by gravity · Schwergewichtsabsackung *f*, Schwergewichtseinsakkung
bagnette, baguet(te) [*A small mo(u)lding of semicircular section*] · Halbrundstab *m*
bag-packing department, bagging ~ · Packerei *f* [*Zementfabrik*]
baguet(te), bagnette [*A small mo(u)lding of semicircular section*] · Halbrundstab *m*
bailey, ward, ballium · Burghof *m*
baked aluminium paint, stoved ~ ~ (Brit.); ~ aluminum ~ (US) · Einbrennaluminiumfarbe *f*
~ cork → agglomerated ~
~ ~ brick, agglomerated ~ ~, rock ~ ~ · Backkorkstein *m*
~ enamel → baking (industrial) ~
~ (industrial) enamel → baking (~) ~
~ resin, stoved ~ · Einbrennharz *n*
baked-on · aufgeschmolzen
bakelite adhesive, ~ glue · Bakelitleim *m*
~ glue, ~ adhesive · Bakelitleim *m*
bakelite-impregnated wood, bakelitesaturated ~ · bakelisiertes Holz *n*
bakelite paint · Bakelit(anstrich)farbe *f*
~ resin [*Bakelite resins are oil-soluble and spirit-soluble synthetic resins used, among other purposes, also for paints and varnishes*] · Bakelitharz *m*
~ varnish · Bakelitlack *m*
to bake-on · aufschmelzen
baking, stoving [*The process of drying and hardening a paint or varnish coating by heating, usually at a temperature above 150° F*] · Einbrennen *n*, Ofentrocknung *f*
~ enamel → ~ industrial ~
~ filler, stoving ~, ~ filling composition · Einbrennfüller *m*
~ filling composition, stoving ~ ~, ~ filler · Einbrennfüller *m*
~ (industrial) enamel, stoving (~) ~, baked (~) ~ · Einbrennemaille *f*, Ofenemaille
~ oven, stoving ~ · Einbrennofen *m*
~ paint, stoving ~ · Einbrennfarbe *f*
~ quality, stoving ~ · Einbrenngüte *f*
~ stopper, stoving ~ · Einbrennspachtel(masse) *m*, (*f*) [*Anstrichtechnik*]
~ temperature, stoving ~ · Einbrenntemperatur *f*
~ varnish, stoving ~ · Einbrennlack *m*, ofentrocknender Lack
to balance · ausgleichen [*Baustatik*]
balance · Ausgleich *m* [*Baustatik*]

~ calculation, ~ method, balancing ~ · Ausgleichverfahren *n*, Ausgleichmethode *f*, Ausgleichrechnung *f* [*Baustatik*]
~ method, ~ calculation, balancing ~ · Ausgleichverfahren *n*, Ausgleichmethode *f*, Ausgleichrechnung *f* [*Baustatik*]
balanced (percentage of) reinforcement · spiegelgleich verteilte Armierung *f*, ~ ~ Bewehrung, ~ ~ (Stahl)Einlagen *fpl*
balanced rotary kiln · ausgewogener Drehofen *m*
balancing calculation → balance method
~ method → balance ~
~ of construction volume · Ausbalancieren *n* der Baumasse
~ ~ stresses · Spannungsausgleich *m*
balata · Balata *f* [*Die Balata wird aus Milchsaft der Pflanzenfamilie der Sapotazeen gewonnen und ist nicht vulkanisierfähig*]
balcony, BALC · Balkon *m*
balcony-access apartment (unit), ~ flat; ~ living unit (US) · Laubengangwohnung *f*
~ flat, ~ apartment (unit); ~ living unit (US) · Laubengangwohnung *f*
~ living unit (US); ~ flat, ~ apartment (unit) · Laubengangwohnung *f*
~ type of block, external-~ ~ ~ ~, block with external access galleries · Außenganghaus *n*
balcony balustrade · Balkonbalustrade *f*
~ beam · Balkonbalken(träger) *m*
~ door · Balkontür *f*
~ ~ fittings, ~ ~ hardware · Balkontürbeschläge *mpl*
~ ~ hardware, ~ ~ fittings · Balkontürbeschläge *mpl*
~ drainage · Balkonentwässerung *f*
~ facing → ~ lining
~ girder · Balkonträger *m*
~ lifting door · Balkonhebetür *f*
~ lining, ~ (sur)facing · Balkonauskleidung *f*, Balkonverkleidung, Balkonbekleidung
~ outlet [*A fitting intended to be interposed in a vertical rainwater pipe passing through a balcony, and providing an inlet for the drainage of rainwater from the balcony*] · Balkonablauf *m*
~ parapet · Balkonbrüstung *f*
~ partition (wall) · Balkontrennwand *f*
~ plate, ~ slab · Balkonplatte *f*
~ slab, ~ plate · Balkonplatte *f*
~ (sur)facing → ~ lining
baldachin → canopy
~ → ciborium
~ altar · Baldachinaltar *m*

baldachin tomb — banjo bolt

~ tomb · Baldachingrab n
balection moulding, bolection ~ (Brit.); bilection (molding), balection (molding), bolection (molding), belection (molding), bellexion (molding), bolexion (molding) (US) [*A mo(u)lding fixed round the edge of a panel and projecting beyond the surface of the framing in which the panel is held*] · Kehlstoß m
balistraria [*In medieval military architecture, the cross-shaped opening in battlements and elsewhere for the use of the crossbow*] · Armbrustschießscharte f
ball · Luppe f
ballast → railway ~
~ (Brit.) [*It contains nothing larger than 1½ inches*] · Zuschlag(stoff) m nicht größer als 37 mm
~ · Vorschaltgerät n
~ concrete · Schotterbeton m, Steinschlagbeton
~ lamp · Widerstandslampe f
ball clay, potter's ~, plastic ~ · hochplastischer Ton m, Letten m, Ballton, Töpferton
~ cock · Kugelhahn m
~ (door) knob · Kugel(tür)knopf m
ball-flower [*A characteristic ornament of English Decorated architecture and western Europe Gothic architecture generally. It resembles a ball half enclosed by three rounded petals and is spaced regularly in concave mouldings*] · Ballenblume f
ball-games hall · Ballspielhalle f
ball hardness test · Kugelhärteprüfung f, Kugelhärteversuch m, Kugelhärteprobe f
~ hinge · Kugelgelenk n
~ house, spherical ~ · Kugelhaus n [*Haus in Kugelform; der erste Idealentwurf stammt von Claude Nicolas Ledoux für ein Flurwächterhaus aus dem Jahre 1806*]
~ impact, sphere ~ · Kugelschlag m
ball(-impact) tester, dynamic ~ ~ · Kugelschlaggerät n, Kugelschlaghärteprüfer m
balling [*Gathering the pasty iron, produced by pudding, into a ball*] · Zusammenballung f
ball knob, ~ door ~ · Kugel(tür)knopf m
~ mill · Kugelmühle f
balloon hangar · Holzhalle f in Nagelbauweise
ballroom · Ballraum m, Ballsaal m
~ foyer · Ballraumfoyer n, Ballsaalfoyer
ball test, dynamic ball-impact ~ · Kugelschlagprobe f, Kugelschlagversuch m, Kugelschlagprüfung f [*Nach DIN 4240 (für Beton mit dichtem Gefüge) und DIN 4241 (für Gas- und Schaumbeton) genormte Verfahren zur Prüfung der Elastizität von Beton, um daraus auf dessen Festigkeit zu schließen*]
~ tester, (dynamic) ball-impact ~ · Kugelschlaggerät n, Kugelschlaghärteprüfer m
ball valve, floating globe ~ · (Schwimm-) Kugelventil n
~ ~ copper float [*B.S. 1968*] · Kugelventil-Kupferschwimmer m
balsam · Balsam m
~ turpentine · Balsamterpentinöl n
Baltic (linseed) oil · baltisches Leinöl n
baluster, ban(n)ister [*One of a row of vertical members supporting a handrail (if on a staircase) or a coping (if forming an external parapet)*] · Baluster m
balustrade, balustrading · Balustrade f, Brüstungsgeländer n, durchbrochene Brüstungswand f, Geländer aus Balustern; Trallwerk n [*mundartlich*]
banana oil, amyl acetate · Amylacetat n
band, ~ course [*Any horizontal flat member or mo(u)lding or group of mo(u)ldings projecting slightly from a wall plane and usually marking a division in the wall*] · Band n
~ → shaft ring
~ course → string (~)
~ decoration, ~ decorative feature, ~ enrichment, ~ ornament(al feature), ~ ornamental finish, ~ ornamental pattern, ~ (decorative) finish, ~ (decorative) pattern, continuous ornament, decorative band, (ornamental) band · Banddekor(ation) n, (f), Bandmuster(-ung) n, (f), Bandornament(ierung) n (f), Bandschmuck m, Bandverzierung f, Dekor(ations)band n, Zierband, Ornamentband, Schmuckband, (architektonisches) Band
~ hinge, hinge(d) strap · Schippenband n
~ iron, strip ~, hoop ~ · Bandeisen n
~ of statues of the Kings of France · Königsgalerie f
banded column, ringed ~, rusticated ~ · Ringsäule f, Bundsäule [*Säule mit durch ringförmige Zwischenglieder unterteiltem Schaft*]
~ gneiss, ribbon ~ · Bändergneis m, Lagengneis
~ pattern · Streifenmuster n
~ porphyry · Bandporphyr m
banderol(e), streamer, label scroll, bannerol · Spruchband n, Schriftband, Banderole f
bandshell [*It is a shell of tapering ribbed concrete*] · Bandschale f
bandstand · Musikpavillon m, Konzertpavillon
bandwidth, frequency ~ · (Frequenz-) Bandbreite f [*Akustik*]
banister → baluster
banjo bolt · Hohlschraube f
bank block, ~ building · Bankgebäude n

bank building, ~ block · Bankgebäude n

banker [*A platform on which concrete is mixed by hand*] · Mischunterlage f

bank gravel, bank-run ~, pit-run ~, run-of-bank ~ · ungesiebter Grubenkies m, ~ Wandkies

~ gravel-sand mix(ture), natural ~ ~ · Naturkiessand m

~ hall → banking ~

~ ~ floor → banking ~ ~

bank(ing) hall · Kassenhalle f, Schalterhalle, Kassensaal m, Schaltersaal, Bankhalle, Banksaal

~ ~ floor · Bankhallendecke f, Banksaaldecke, Kassenhallendecke, Schalterhallendecke, Kassensaaldecke, Schaltersaaldecke

~ room · Schalterraum m, Kassenraum

bank of bedroom closets, ~ ~ wardrobe(-type) ~, bedroom closet bank, wardrobe(-type) closet bank · Schlafzimmer-Schrankwand f

~ ~ closets, closet bank, cupboard-wall · Schrankwand f

~ ~ wardrobe(-type) closets, ~ ~ bedroom ~, bedroom closet bank, wardrobe(-type) closet bank · Schlafzimmer-Schrankwand f

bank-run aggregate · ungesiebter Grubenzuschlag(stoff) m

bank-slag · Bettschlacke f

(bank) strongroom, strongroom for valuables · Silberkammer f, Tresorraum m

~ with drive-in teller(s), drive-in bank · Bank f mit Autoschalter(n)

ban(n)ister → baluster

banquet(ing) hall, festival ~, grand ~, civic auditorium · Festhalle f, Bankett-halle

~ kitchen · Bankettküche f [*Hotel*]

~ room, festival ~, grand chamber · Festsaal m, Bankettsaal

baptismal room · Taufraum m

baptistery [*A building for baptismal rites containing the font; often separate from the church*] · Baptisterium n, Taufkirche f

~ [*A building for baptismal rites containing the font; incorporated into the church*] · Taufkapelle f, Baptisterium n

bar, rod, element, member · Füll(ungs)-stab m, Gitterstab, Glied n, (Träger-)Stab

~ · Schanktheke f

~ → (rolled) (steel) ~

~ bender, rod ~, steel ~ [*colloquially: iron fighter*] · Eisenbieger m

~ buckling, member ~, rod ~, element ~ · Gliedknickung f, Gliedknicken n, Stabknickung, Stabknicken

~ centre line (Brit.); ~ center ~ (US); rod ~ ~, member ~ ~, element ~ ~ · Stabachse f, Stabmittellinie f, Gliedachse, Gliedmittellinie

~ connection, rod ~, member ~, element ~ · Stabanschluß m, Gliedanschluß [*Stabwerkkonstruktion*]

~ cross-section, member ~, rod ~, element ~ · Gliedquerschnitt m, Stabquerschnitt [*Stabwerkkonstruktion*]

~ diameter, rod ~, diameter of rod, diameter of bar · Stabdurchmesser m, Stahldurchmesser, Eisendurchmesser [*Bewehrung*]

~ distance piece → ~ spacer

~ field, member ~, element ~, rod ~ · Gliedfeld n, Stabfeld [*Stabwerkkonstruktion*]

~ force, rod ~, member ~, element ~ · Stabkraft f, Gliedkraft [*Stabwerkkonstruktion*]

~ length, rod ~, member ~, element ~ · Gliedlänge f, Stablänge

~ ~, rod ~ · Stablänge f [*Bewehrung*]

~ list → ~ schedule

~ loading, rod ~, member ~, element ~ · Gliedbelastung f, Stabbelastung

~ mark · Eisen-Position f, Stahl-Position [*Stahlliste*]

~ mat, ~ sheet [*An assembly of steel reinforcement composed of two or more layers of bars placed at angles to each other and secured together by welding or ties*] · Baustahlmatte f aus Rundstäben, Bewehrungsmatte ~ ~, Armierungsmatte ~ ~, Rundstabbaustahlmatte, Rundstabbewehrungsmatte, Rundstabarmierungsmatte

~ moment, rod ~, member ~, element ~ · Stabmoment n, Gliedmoment

~ number, rod ~, number of bar, number of rod [*A number, approximately the bar diameter in eighths of inches, used to designate the bar size*] · Eisennummer f, Stabnummer, Stahlnummer [*Bewehrung*]

to bar off [*To unload bars from a truck bed by levering individual bundles over the side with pinch bars*] · abladen von Bewehrungsstäben, ~ ~ Armierungsstäben

(bar) placer → (reinforcing) iron worker

~ schedule, rod ~, ~ list [*Bill of materials, where all quantities, sizes, lengths and bending dimensions are shown*] · (Rund)Stahlliste f, Armierungsliste, Bewehrungsliste

~ separator → ~ spacer

bar-setter → (reinforcing) iron worker

bar shape, rod ~, member ~, element ~ · Stabform f, Gliedform

~ ~, rod ~ · Armierungsform f, Bewehrungsform, Eisenform, Stahl(einlagen)-form

(~) ~ code, rod ~ ~ · Armierungsformnummer f, Bewehrungsformnummer, Eisenformnummer, Eisenform-Nr., Bewehrungsform-Nr., Armierungsform-Nr. [*Stahlliste*]

~ sheet → ~ mat

bar size — baroque cathedral

~ **size**, member ~, rod ~, element ~ · Gliedgröße f, Stabgröße [*Stabwerkkonstruktion*]

~ ~, rod ~, size of bar, size of rod · Eisenabmessung f, Stababmessung, Stahlabmessung [*Bewehrung*]

~ **slope**, rod ~, member ~, element ~ · Gliedablenkung f, Stabablenkung [*Rahmenträger*]

~ **spacer**, ~ separator, ~ distance piece, reinforcing rod spacer, reinforcing rod separator, reinforcing rod distance piece · (Betonstahl)Abstandhalter m

~ **spacing**, rod ~ [*Distance between parallel reinforcing bars measured from centre-to-centre of the bars perpendicular to their longitudinal axes*] · Eisenabstand m, Stababstand, Stahlabstand [*Bewehrung*]

bar-steel, rod-steel, merchant steel · Stabeisen n [*Fehlname*]; Stabstahl m [*DIN 59051*]

bar stress, member ~, rod ~, element ~ · Stabspannung f, Gliedspannung [*Stabwerkkonstruktion*]

~ **subject to buckling**, rod ~ ~ ~, member ~ ~ ~ · Knickstab m

~ **support**, ~ chair [*A device, usually of formed wire, to support, hold, and space a reinforcing bar*] · Stabhalterung f

~ **system**, rod ~, member ~ · Stabsystem n, Stabwerk n

~ **tin** · Stangenzinn n

~ **transformation**, ~ transposition, rod ~, member ~, element ~ · Stabvertauschung f, Gliedvertauschung [*Stabwerkkonstruktion*]

~ **transposition**, ~ transformation, rod ~, member ~, element ~· Stabvertauschung f, Gliedvertauschung [*Stabwerkkonstruktion*]

~ **type**, type of bar · Eisenart f, Stahlart, Stabart [*Bewehrung*]

barbed wire; bobwire, barbwire (US) · Stacheldraht m

~ ~ **fence**; bobwire ~, barbwire ~ (US) · Stacheldrahtzaun m

barber's shop · Herrensalon m

barbican, barbacan · Barbakane f, Bastille f, Torzwinger m [*Dem Tor vorgelagerte, halbrunde oder (mehr)eckige Anlage aus Balken oder Mauerwerk zur Sicherung des (Burg- oder Stadt-)Tores*]

bare filler rod · nackter Schweißdraht m

bareness · Schmucklosigkeit f

barge board → gable ~

barite, natural barium sulfate (US); barytes, natural barium sulphate (Brit.) [*A mineral used in pure or impure form as concrete aggregate primarily for the construction of high-density radiation shielding concrete*] · BaO, Baryt m, Schwerspat m

~ **aggregate** (US); barytes ~ (Brit.) · Schwerspatzuschlag(stoff) m, Barytzuschlag(stoff)

~ (~) **concrete** (US); barytes (~) ~ (Brit.) · Barytbeton m, Schwerspatbeton

~ **breccia** (US); barytes ~ (Brit.) · Schwerspatbrekzie f

~ **concrete** → ~ aggregate ~

~ **grain mix(ture)**, mixed barite grains, mix(ture) of barite grains (US); barytes grain mix(ture), mixed barytes grains, mix(ture) of barytes grains (Brit.) · Barytkörnung f, Barytkörnergemisch n, Barytkorngemisch, Schwerspatkörnung, Schwerspatkörnergemisch, Schwerspatkorngemisch

~ **ore** (US); barytes ~ (Brit.) · Bariumsulfaterz n, Naturbaryt m

~ ~ (**concrete**) **aggregate** (US); barytes ~ (~) ~ (Brit.) ·· Naturbaryt(beton)zuschlag(stoff) m

~ **yellow** → barytes ~ (Brit.)

~ **slab** (US); barytes ~ (Brit.) · Barytplatte f

~ **wall slab** (US); barytes ~ ~ (Brit.) · Baryt-Wandplatte f

baritic cement · Bariumzement m, Edelzement, Barytzement [*Mit Ba(rium) anstelle von Ca. Wegen hohen Gewichtes für Schwerst-, Strahlenschutz- und Reaktorbeton verwendet*]

barium(-based) (mixed) plaster [*See remark under 'Putz'*] · Bariumputz m

barium carbonate, witherite · Bariumkarbonat n, Bariumcarbonat, $BaCO_3$

~ **chlorid(e)** (US); ~ chloride (Brit.) · $BaCl_2$, Bariumchlorid n

~ **compound** · Bariumverbindung f

~ **fluosilicate** · Bariumfluat n

~ **hydroxid(e)** (US); ~ hydroxide (Brit.) · Ätzbaryt m, Bariumhydroxid n, $Ba(OH)_2$ $8 H_2O$

~ (**mixed**) **plaster** [*It contains barytes aggregate with gypsum plaster or Portland cement as a binder*] · Baryt(ver)putz m

~ **oxid(e)** (US); ~ oxide (Brit.) · Bariumoxid n

~ **plaster** → ~ mixed ~

~ **salt** · Bariumsalz n

~ **sulfate pigment** (US); ~ sulphate ~ (Brit.) · Bariumsulfatpigment n

~ **sulphate** (Brit.); ~ sulfate (US) · schwefelsaures Barium n, $BaSO_4$, Bariumsulfat n

~ **sulphide** (Brit.); ~ sulfide (US) · Bariumsulfid n

barn · Scheune f

barometric damper, draft regulator (US); draught regulator (Brit.) · Zugregler m

~ **pressure**, atmospheric ~ · (Erd)Atmosphärendruck m

baroque architect · Barockarchitekt m

~ **architecture** · Barockarchitektur f, Barockbaukunst f

~ **building** · Barockgebäude n

~ **cathedral** · Barockkathedrale f

baroque church — basalt(ic) powder

~ **church** · Barockkirche *f*
~ **fountain** · Barockbrunnen *m*
~ **fresco painting** · Barockfreskenmalerei *f*
~ **master** · Barockbaumeister *m*
~ **palace** · Barockpalast *m*
~ **sanctuary** · Barockheiligtum *n*
~ **sculpture** · Barockplastik *f*
~ **square** · Barockplatz *m*
~ **statue** · Barockstatue *f*
barracks · Kaserne *f*
~ **block**, ~ building · Kasernengebäude *n*
~ **building**, ~ construction, construction of barracks, building of barracks · Kasernenbau *m*
~ ~, ~ block · Kasernengebäude *n*
~ **construction**, ~ building, construction of barracks, building of barracks · Kasernenbau *m*
~ **room** · Kasernenstube *f*
barred door → ledged ~
barrel, pipe ~ [*That portion of a pipe throughout which the internal diameter and thickness of wall remain uniform*] · (Rohr)Schaft *m*, Durchgangsrohr *n*
~ **arch** → skewed ~ ~
~ **frame**, tubing ~, tube ~, pipe ~, tubular ~ · Rohrrahmen *m*
~ **handrail**, tube ~, tubing ~, tubular ~, pipe ~ · Rohrhandlauf *m*
~ **mast**, tube ~, tubing ~, tubular ~, pipe ~ · Rohrmast *m*
~ **newel**, tubular ~, pipe ~, tubing ~, tube ~ · (Treppen)Rohrspindel *f*
~ **nipple**, shoulder ~ · Doppelnippel *m*
~ **purlin(e)**, tubing ~, tubular ~, tube ~, pipe ~ · (Dach)Rohrpfette *f*
~ **railing**, tube ~, tubing ~, pipe ~, tubular ~ · Rohrgeländer *n*
~ ~ **fitting**, tube ~ ~, tubing ~ ~, tubular ~ ~, pipe ~ ~ · (Rohr)Geländerfitting *m*, (Rohr)Geländerformstück *n*
~ **shell**, cylinder segment, segment of cylinder · Tonnenschale *f*
~ **(~) roof**, cylinder segment ~, arched barrel ~ · Tonnen(schalen)dach *n*
~ **skeleton**, tubular ~, tubing ~, tube ~, pipe ~ · Rohrskelett *n*, Rohrgerippe *n*
~ **theory**, theory of barrels · Tonnentheorie *f*
~ **vault**, tunnel ~, wagon(head) ~ · Tonne(ngewölbe) *f*, (*n*) [*Gewölbeform mit längs einer Achse gleichbleibendem viertelkreis-, halbkreis-, segmentbogen- oder spitzbogenförmigem Querschnitt*]
barrel-vaulted, wagon-vaulted, tunnel-vaulted, wagon-headed · tonnengewölbt
barrel(-vault(ed)) roof, tunnel(-vault(ed)) ~, wagon(-vault(ed)) ~ · Tonnen(gewölbe)dach *n*
barrel vaulting · Einwölbung *f* auf Kuf
barreled asphalt (US); barrelled (asphaltic-)bitumen (Brit.) · Faßbitumen *n*

barrier material, impervious ~, impermeable ~ · Sperrstoff *m*, Sperrmittel *n* [*Sperrstoffe schützen Bauwerke gegen Witterungseinflüsse, Feuchtigkeit, chemische Angriffe und Feuer. Sie werden in Sperrzusätze, Sperranstrichmittel, Frostschutzmittel, Feuerschutzmittel und Holzschutzmittel unterteilt. Nach der Sprachregelung der DIN 4117 allerdings werden als Sperrstoffe nur Sperrbeton und Sperrmörtel, allenfalls mit diesen hergestellter Sperrputz und Sperrestrich bezeichnet*]
~ **(membrane)** → impervious course
~ **sheet(ing)** · Sperrbahn *f*
barrow, grave-mound · Hügelgrab *n*
(~) run · Schubkarrensteg *m*
bartisan (Brit.); bartizan (US); watch turret · Erkertürmchen *n*
barytes, natural barium sulphate (Brit.); barite, natural barium sulfate (US); heavy spar [*A mineral used in pure or impure form as concrete aggregate primarily for the construction of high-density radiation shielding concrete*] · Schwerspat *m*, Baryt *m*, BaO
~ **aggregate** (Brit.); barite ~ (US) · Barytzuschlag(stoff) *m*, Schwerspatzuschlag(stoff)
~ **(~) concrete** (Brit.); barite (~) ~ (US) · Schwerspatbeton *m*, Barytbeton
~ **breccia** (Brit.); barite ~ (US) · Schwerspatbrekzie *f*
~ **concrete** (Brit.) → barite (aggregate) ~ (US)
~ **grain mix(ture)** (Brit.) → barite ~ ~
~ **ore** (Brit.); barite ~ (US) · Bariumsulfaterz *n*, Naturbaryt *m*
~ ~ **(concrete) aggregate** (Brit.); barite ~ (~) ~ (US) · Naturbaryt(beton)zuschlag(stoff) *m*
~ **slab** (Brit.) → barite ~ (US)
~ **wall slab** (Brit.) → barite ~ ~ (US)
~ **yellow** (Brit.); barite ~ ~ (US) · Bariumchromat *n*, Barytgelb *n*, BaCrO₄
basalt · Basalt *m*
~ **concrete slab**, basaltic ~ ~ · Basaltbetonplatte *f*
~ **fibre** (Brit.); ~ fiber (US) · Basaltfaser *f*
basalt-gabbro rock · Basaltgabbrogestein *n*
basalt(ic) chip(ing)s · Basaltsplitt *m*
~ ~ **concrete** · Basaltsplittbeton *m*
~ ~ **slab** · Basaltbetonplatte *f*
~ **floor tile** · Basalt-(Fuß)Bodenplatte *f*, Basalt-(Fuß)Bodenfliese *f*, Basalt-Belagplatte
~ **meal**, ~ powder, powder(ed) basalt · Basaltmehl *n*
~ **(paving) sett** · Basaltpflasterstein *m* [*DIN 18502*]
~ **pea gravel** · Basalterbskies *m*, Basaltperlkies
~ **powder** → ~ meal

basalt(ic) sand — basement boiler room

~ **sand** · Basaltsand *m*

~ **sandstone** · Basaltsandstein *m*

~ **sett,** ~ **paving** ~ · Basaltpflasterstein *m* [*DIN 18502*]

~ **slab** · Basaltplatte *f*

~ **stamp sand** · Basaltpochsand *m*, Basaltsplittsand, Basaltquetschsand

~ **tuff,** trapp ~ · Basalttuff *m*, Trapptuff

~ **wacke** · Basaltwacke *f*

~ **wool** · Basaltwolle *f*

base, pipe ~ · (Rohr)Fuß *m*

~ → (roof(ing)) substructure (system)

~ → sanitary cove

~, backing, underlay, substrate, backup, substratum; underlayment (US) · Rücklage *f*, Hinterlegung *f*, Unterlage *f*, Träger(schicht) *m*, (*f*), Rücken *m*

~ · Basis *f*, Grundlage *f*

~ → ~ plate

~ (Brit.) → substratum

~ [*The lowest course of masonry in a stone building*] · unterste Steinschicht *f*, ~ Steinlage *f*

~ [*The lowest stage of panel(l)ing in a panel(l)ed room*] · unterste (Ver)Täfelung *f*

~, circular base-line · Fußkreis *m* [*Kuppel*]

~ · tragende Unterlage *f* [*für einen Hartbetonbelag oder Zementestrich*]

~, **column** ~ [*The projecting member between the shaft of a column and its plinth*] · (Säulen)Fuß *m*

~ **asphalt** (US); ~ (asphaltic) bitumen (Brit.) · Ausgangsbitumen *n*, Grundbitumen

~ **(asphaltic) bitumen** (Brit.); ~ asphalt (US) · Grundbitumen *n*, Ausgangsbitumen

~ **(board)** → sanitary cove

~ **(~) component** → ~ (~) unit

~ ~ **for plaster,** plaster baseboard · Putzträgerplatte *f*

~ **(~) heater,** scrub ~ ~, mopboard ~, washboard ~, sanitary cove ~ (US); skirting board ~ (Brit.); base plate ~ [*Scotland*] · Fußleistenheizer *m*, Sockelleistenheizer, Scheuerleistenheizer

~ **(~) heating,** scrub ~ ~, mopboard ~, washboard ~, sanitary cove ~ (US); skirting (board) ~ (Brit.); base plate ~ [*Scotland*] · Fußleistenheizung *f*, Scheuerleistenheizung, Sockelleistenheizung

~ **(~) member** → ~ (~) unit

~ **(~) radiator,** scrub ~ ~, washboard ~, mopboard ~, sanitary cove ~ (US); skirting (board) ~ (Brit.); base plate ~ [*Scotland*] · Fußleisten-Radiator *m*, Sockelleisten-Radiator, Scheuerleisten-Radiator

~ **(~) unit,** ~ (~) member, ~ (~) component, scrub ~ ~, mopboard ~, washboard ~, sanitary cove ~ (US); skirting (board) ~ (Brit.); base plate ~ [*Scotland*] · Scheuerleisten-Wand-(bau)stein *m*, Scheuerleisten-Wand-(bau)block(stein) *m*

~ **bullion** · unreines (Werk)Blei *n*

basecoat, undercoat, backing (coat), scratch coat [*A plastering or rendering coat other than the final coat*] · Rauhwerk *n*, Unterputzschicht *f*, Unterputzlage *f*, Grobputzschicht, Grobputzlage, Grundputzschicht, Grundputzlage

~, prime coat(ing), priming coat(ing) · Grundierschicht *f*, Grundierlage *f*

~ **(mixed) plaster,** undercoat (~) ~, backing (coat) (~) ~ · Grundputz *m*, Unterputz, Grobputz

~ **mix(ture)** → backing (coat) ~

~ **plaster** → backing (coat) mix(ture)

~ ~, undercoat ~, ~ mixed ~, backing (coat) (mixed) ~ · Grundputz *m*, Unterputz, Grobputz

~ **stuff** → backing (coat) mix(ture)

base component → ~ (board) unit

~ **concrete** · Tragbeton *m* [*Der Beton, dessen Oberfläche durch den Hartbelag verschleißfest gemacht wird. Nicht verwechseln mit ,,Grundbeton" einer Hartbetonplatte*]

~ **course** → plinth

base-court [*The outer court of a medieval castle or, later, of a country manison, containing the servants' quarters*] · Außenhof *m*

base fabric · Trägergewebe *n*

~ **felt** · Unterlagsfilz *m*

~ **flashing** · unterer Anschluß *m* [*Siehe Anmerkung unter ,,Anschluß"*]

~ **foil** · Trägerfolie *f*

~ **glass,** parent ~ · Grundglas *n*, Stammglas, Mutterglas, Trägerglas

~ **heater** → ~ board ~

~ **heating** → ~ board ~

~ **hinge** · Fußgelenk *n*

~ **line** · Grundlinie *f*

~ **material,** basic ~ · Ausgangs(werk)stoff *m*, Grundwerkstoff

~ **member** → ~ (board) unit

basement · Sockelgeschoß *n*

~ → ~ level

~ **air shaft,** ~ **light well** · Kellergeschoßlichtschacht *m*

~ **area,** casemate · Kasematte *f*, Wallgewölbe *n*

~ **boiler room** · Heiz(ungs)keller *m*

basement car park — basic carbonate lead

~ **car park** · Kellergeschoßgarage f

~ **concourse** · Kellergeschoßhalle f *Beim Satellitsystem.* [*Flughafen*]

~ **door** · Kellergeschoßtür f

~ **drainage** · Kellergeschoßentwässerung f

~ **dwelling unit** (US); basement dwelling (Brit.) · Souterrainwohnung f, Keller(geschoß)wohnung

~ **entrance,** entrance to a basement · Kellergeschoßeingang m

~ **floor** · Kellergeschoßdecke f

~ **garage,** ~ level ~ · Kellergarage f, Tiefgarage

~ **kitchen** · Kellergeschoßküche f

~ **(level);** ~ story, B(SMT) (US); basement storey (Brit.) [*A stor(e)y wholly or mainly below ground level*] · Kellergeschoß n, Kelleretage f, Kellerstockwerk n, Untergeschoß, Unteretage, Unterstockwerk

~ **(~) garage** · Kellergarage f, Tiefgarage

~ **light well,** ~ air shaft · Kellergeschoßlichtschacht m

~ **masonry (work)** · Kellergeschoßmauerwerk n

~ **pit,** ~ hole · Kellergeschoßgrube f

~ **room** · Kellergeschoßraum m

~ **shelter** · Schutzkellergeschoß n [*baulicher Luftschutz*]

~ **slab** · Kellergeschoßplatte f

~ **stair(case)** · Kellergeschoßtreppe f

~ **storey** (Brit.) → ~ (level)

~ **vault** · Kellergeschoßgewölbe n

~ **wall** · Kellergeschoßwand f

~ **window** · Kellergeschoßfenster n

basementless · ohne Kellergeschoß

~ **space** (US); crawl ~, crawlway [*An underfloor space providing access to ducts, pipes, and other services hung or laid therein and of a height sufficient for crawling*] · Kriechkeller m, Bekriechungsraum m, Kriechraum

base metal [*Any metal as iron, lead, etc., which is altered by exposure to the air, etc., in contrast with the noble or precious metals*] · Grundmetall n, unedles Metall

~ **moment,** foot ~, moment at foot, moment at base · Fußmoment n

~ **moulding** (Brit.); ~ molding (US) [*The mo(u)lding immediately above the plinth of a wall, column, etc.*] · Fuß(ge)sims m, (n)

~ ~ (Brit.); ~ molding (US); ~ cap · Sockel(ge)sims m, (n)

~ **plastic film,** ~ ~ sheeting · Kunststoff-Trägerfolie f

baseplate, bedplate · Grundplatte f

base (plate) · Basis f, Fuß m [*Grundplatte, auf die eine Säule, ein Pilaster, eine Stütze oder ein Pfeiler ruht*]

~ **(~),** column ~ (~) [*The projecting member between the shaft of a column and its plinth*] · (Säulen)Fuß m, (Säulen)Basis f

~ **(~),** column ~ (~), support ~ (~) · (Stützen)Fuß m, (Stützen)Basis f

~ ~ · Unterlagsplatte f [*Aus Stahl oder Gußeisen als Druckverteiler beim Verlegen von Trägern und Stahlbetonstürzen*]

~ ~ [*Scotland*] → sanitary cove

~ ~ **component** [*Scotland*] → ~ (board) unit

~ ~ **heater** [*Scotland*]; skirting (board) ~ (Brit.); sanitary cove ~, base (board) ~, scrub board ~, mopboard ~, washboard ~ (US) · Scheuerleistenheizer m, Fußleistenheizer, Sockelleistenheizer

~ ~ **heating** [*Scotland*]; skirting (board) ~ (Brit.); sanitary cove ~, base (board) ~, scrub board ~, mopboard ~, washboard ~ (US) · Scheuerleistenheizung f, Fußleistenheizung, Sockelleistenheizung

~ ~ **member** [*Scotland*] → ~ (board) unit

~ ~ **radiator** [*Scotland*]; skirting (board) ~ (Brit.); sanitary cove ~, base (board) ~, scrub board ~, mopboard ~, washboard ~ (US) · Scheuerleisten-Radiator m, Sockelleisten-Radiator, Fußleisten-Radiator

~ ~ **unit** [*Scotland*] → ~ (board) ~

~ **point** · Fußpunkt m

~ **quadrilateral** · Basis-Viereck n

~ **radiator** → ~ board ~

~ **ring** · Fußring m

~ **sheet(ing),** backing ~, underlay ~ · Trägerbahn f

~ **square** · Grundquadrat n

~ **standard** · Grundnorm f

~ **(surface),** (back)ground, backing (material) · (Unter)Grund m

~ **(system)** → (roof(ing)) substructure (~)

~ **unit** · Unterbau m, Unterschrank m

~ ~ ~ → ~ board ~

basic · basisch [*Gestein*]

~ **assumption** · Grundannahme f

~ **Bessemer pig iron,** Thomas ~ · Thomasroheisen n

~ **blastfurnace slag** · basische Hochofenschlacke f

~ **brick** · basischer feuerfester Stein m, ~ ff. ~

~ **building material,** ~ construction(al) ~ · Grund-Baustoff m; Grund-Baumaterial n [*Schweiz*]

~ **carbonate lead** · basisches Bleikarbonat n, ~ Bleicarbonat

basic carbonate white lead — bastard amber

~ ~ **white lead** · Bleiweiß n aus basischem Bleikarbonat, basisches ~ [*Im Gegensatz zum Sulfo-Bleiweiß, welches durch Verbrennen von natürlichem Bleierz gewonnen wird*]

~ ~ ~ ~ **manufactured by the old Dutch process**, $Pb_3(CO_3)_2OH_2$ · Kammerbleiweiß n

~ **component** · Grundkomponente f, Stammkomponente

~ **condition** · Grundzustand m [*Baustatik*]

~ **construction(al) material**, ~ **building** · Grund-Baustoff m; Grund-Baumaterial n [*Schweiz*]

~ **converter steel, Thomas** ~ · Thomasstahl m, T ST [*DIN 17006*]

~ **copper acetate**, verdigris, aerugo [*It is the colo(u)ring ingredient of one type of patina on copper*] · Grünspan m, Kupfergrün n, basisches Kupferazetat n, basisches Kupferkarbonat n

~ **course** · Vorkursus m

~ **dimension**, standard ~ · Grundmaß n, Grundabmessung f, Typenmaß, Typenabmessung

~ **diorite** · basischer Diorit m

~ **dyestuff** · basischer Farbstoff m

~ ~ · Grundfarbstoff m

~ **equation**, fundamental ~ · Grundgleichung f

~ **façade unit** · Standard-Fassadenfertigteil m, n

~ **form** · Grundform f

~ **grade** · Grundsorte f

~ **lead acetate** · basisch-essigsaures Blei

~ **length** · Grundlänge f

~ **load** · Grundlast f

~ **material**, base ~ · Ausgangs(werk)stoff m, Grundwerkstoff

~ **module**, standard ~ [*It means a module with the dimension of 4 inches*] · Grundmodul M m, Modul von 10 cm, Modul von 4 Zoll

~ **pigment** · basisches Pigment n

~ **principles of concrete technology** · betontechnologische Grundsätze mpl

~ **rock** · basisches Gestein n

~ **slag**, Thomas ~ · Thomasschlacke f

~ **square** · Grundquadrat n

~ **stress** · Grundspannung f

~ ~ **state** · Grundspannungszustand m

~ **tolerance** · Grundtoleranz f

~ ~ **table** · Grundtoleranztabelle f

~ **type** · Grundtype f

~ **velocity** · Grundgeschwindigkeit f

basicity · Basizität f

~ **factor** · Basengrad m, Basizitätsgrad, Schlackenzahl f, Schlackenziffer f
$$\frac{CaO + MgO}{SiO_2}$$

basilica → civic ~

~ → ~ church

Basilica AEmilia · Basilika f Aemilia

~ **at Paestum** · Basilika f zu Paestum

basilica (church), Christian basilica, ecclesiastical basilica · (christliche) Basilika f, Basilikakirche f

~ **for public administration** · forensische Basilika f

Basilica Nova at Rome → ~ of Constantine (~ ~)

~ **of Constantine (at Rome)**, ~ ~ Maxentius (~ ~), ~ Nova ~ · Basilika f des Konstantin (in Rom), ~ ~ Maxentius (~ ~), Maxentiusbasilika (~ ~), Konstantinbasilika (~ ~), Friedenstempel m [*Diese Basilika wird auch als "Friedenstempel" bezeichnet, weil sie an der Stelle des abgebrannten, von Vespasian erbauten Tempels des Friedens erbaut war*]

~ ~ **Maxentius (at Rome)** → ~ ~ Constantine (~ ~)

basilica with columns and piers · Stützenwechselbasilika f

~ ~ **nave and aisles of different height** · Staffelbasilika f

basilica(l cathedral) of St. Mark at Venice · S. Marco zu Venedig

basilican · basilikal

Basilican church St Agnes without the walls of Rome · Basilika f S. Agnese vor den Mauern der Stadt Rom

basilican cross section · basilikaler Querschnitt m, basilikales Schema n

~ **(ground))plan** · basilikaler Grundriß m

basins in range, (lavatory basin) range · Reihenwaschanlage f, Waschreihe f

basis of calculation, calculating basis, calculation basis · Berechnungsgrundlage f, Rechengrundlage

~ ~ **design**, design fundamental · Entwurfsgrundlage f

~ ~ ~, design fundamental · Bemessungsgrundlage f

~ **sulfate white lead** (US); ~ **sulphate** ~ ~ (Brit.) · Sulfat-Bleiweiß n, Sulfo-Bleiweiß

basket arch → more-centered ~

~ **capital** · Korbkapitell n, Korbkapitäl

~ **guard** · Schutzkorb m [*Leuchte*]

~ **strainer waste (unit)** · Siebeinsatz m

bas-relief, low relief [*It is very shallow, like the relief of a coin*] · Flachrelief n

~ **frieze**, low relief · Flachrelieffries m

bast fiber (US); ~ **fibre** (Brit.) · Bastfaser f

~ **mat** · Bastmatte f

bastard amber, imperfect ~, impure ~ · Kunstbernstein m

bastard-grain shingle; flat-grain ~ (US) · Schindel *f* mit liegenden Jahr(es)ringen

bastide [*One of the small fortified towns, laid out during the Middle Ages on a rectilinear or chess-board plan, by the English in the parts of France occupied by them*] · Bastide *f*, Vorwerk *n*

bastion [*Solid tower to carry military engines*] · Bastei *f*, Bastion *f*

bastite, schillerspar · Bastit *m*, Schillerspat *m*

bat → bat(t)

~, batten, bato(o)n, strip · Leiste *f*

to batch, to proportion, to measure; to gauge; to gage (US) · abmessen, zumessen, zuteilen, dosieren

batch, parcel · Bündel *n* [*z.B. aus Parkettstäben*]

~ · Gemenge *n*, Massenversatz *m* [*Steinzeugindustrie*]

~ · Charge *f* [*Menge einer Mischung, die in einem bestimmten Herstellungsabschnitt auf einmal verarbeitet wird*]

~ → (~) mix(ture)

(~) mix(ture), (glass) batch, (glass) charge · Schmelzsatz *m*, Glasgemenge *n*, Glasmischung *f*

batched aggregate → dry-~ ~

~ materials → (dry-)batched aggregate

bath, ~room, B · Bad(ezimmer) *n*, Baderaum *m*

~ → (bath)tub

~ accessory · Badarmatur *f*

~ ~, indoor swimming pool, covered swimming pool, indoor swimming bath(s), covered swimming bath(s) · Hallenbadeanstalt *f*, Hallen(schwimm)bad *n*

~ filtration and chlorination plant · Bad-Filter- und Chlorierungsanlage *f*

~ grip → ((bath)tub) (hand)grip

~ (hand)grip → ((bath)tub) ~

bath-mixer · Mischbatterie *f*

bath of molten solder · Lötbad *n*

bath(room), B · Bad(ezimmer) *n*, Baderaum *m*

bathroom accessories · Badzubehör *n*

~ (and lavatory) unit, unitized ~ (~ ~) ~, bathroom building block module · Bade(zimmer)zelle *f*, Bade(zimmer)block *m*, Naß(installations)zelle *f*, Naß(installations)block

~ article → ~ product

~ building block module, (unitized) bathroom (and lavatory) unit · Bade(zimmer)zelle *f*, Bade(zimmer)block *m*, Naß(installations)zelle, Naß(installations)block

~ casting · Beton-Bade(zimmer)zelle *f*, Beton-Bade(zimmer)block *m*, Beton-Naß(installations)zelle, Beton-Naß(installations)block

~ closet · Badezimmer-Einbauschrank *m*, Badezimmer-Wandschrank

~ curtain · Badvorhang *m*

~ door · Badezimmer(abschluß)tür *f*

~ equipment · Badeinrichtung *f*, Badausstattung

~ fixtures · Badezimmerausrüstungen *fpl*

~ gull(e)y → trapped ~ ~

~ heater → ~ heating appliance

~ heating, ~ warming · Bad(ezimmer)beheizung *f*

~ ~ appliance, ~ ~ unit, ~ heater · Badezimmer-Heiz(ungs)gerät *n*, Badezimmer-Heizer *m*, Badezimmer-Erhitzer

~ installation · Badezimmeranlage *f*, Badezimmereinrichtung *f*

~ (light(ing)) fixture; ~ light fitting (Brit.); ~ luminaire (fixture) (US) · Badezimmerleuchte *f*, Badezimmer-Beleuchtungskörper *m*

~ product, ~ article · Badezimmerartikel *m*, Badezimmergegenstand *m*, Badezimmererzeugnis *n*

~ warming, ~ heating · Bad(ezimmer)beheizung *f*

(bath)tub, bath, BT [*A sanitary appliance in which the human body may be immersed in water*] · (Bade)Wanne *f*

(~) (hand)grip, bath ~ · (Bade)Wannengriff *m*, Griff

~ height, bath ~ · (Bade)Wannentiefe *f*

~ lead trap, tub ~ ~ · Blei-(Bade)Wannen-Geruchverschluß *m*

~ ledge, bath ~ · (Bade)Wannenrand *m*

~ rim, bath ~ · (Bade)Wannenwulst *m*, *f*

(bath)tub/shower installation · (Bade)Wannenfüll- und Duschbatterie *f*

bath waste · Badabwasser *n*, Badschmutzwasser

~ water · Badewasser *n*

~ ~ treatment · Badewasserpflege *f*

bato(o)n, bat(ten), strip · Leiste *f*

bat(t) · Wärmedämmatte *f*

~ insulation · Wärmemattendämmung *f*

bat(ten), bato(o)n, strip · Leiste *f*

batten; cover moulding (Brit.); cover molding (US) [*A mo(u)lding planted to cover a joint on a flush surface*] · (Ab)Deckleiste *f*, Fugen(deck)leiste, Fugenabdeckleiste

~ → roof ~

~ → ~ plate

~, raft ~ · Lagerholz *n* [*schwimmender Holz(fuß)boden(belag)*]

~, firring strip, furring strip · Unterkonstruktionsleiste *f* [*Putztechnik*]

~ door → ledged ~

~ floor(ing), floor boarding · Dielen(fuß)boden *m*, Dielung *f*, Bretter(fuß)boden

~ (light(ing)) fixture; ~ luminaire (~) (US); ~ light fitting (Brit.) · Lichtleiste *f*, Leuchtenleiste

~ luminaire (fixture) (US); ~ light fitting (Brit.); ~ (light(ing)) fixture · Lichtleiste *f*, Leuchtenleiste

batten (plate) — bd.

~ **(plate)**, cover ~, brace ~, stay ~, tie ~ · Bindeblech *n*, Schnalle *f* [*Bei zwei- und mehrteiligen Querschnitten werden die einzelnen Teile durch Bindebleche in ihrem gegenseitigen Abstand gehalten*]

~ **roof** · Bohlendach *n*

~ ~ **cladding** → ~ (seam) roofing

~ ~ **covering** → ~ (seam) roofing

~ ~ **sheathing** → ~ (seam) roofing

~ **roofing** → ~ (seam) ~

~ **seam**, rib(bed) ~ · Leistenfalz *m* [*Metallbedachung*]

~ **(~) roof cladding** → ~ (~) roofing

~ **(~) roofing**, rib(bed) (~) ~, ~ (~) roof cladding, ~ (~) roof covering, ~ (~) roof sheathing · Leisten(falz)bedachung *f*, Leisten(falz)-(dach)(ein)deckung, Leistensystem *n*

~ **wall**, battened ~, strapped ~ · gelattete Wand *f*

battens → roof ~

~ **in the filling**, raft ~ ~ ~ ~ · Lagerhölzer *npl* in der Auffüllung

~ **on resilient (quilt) strips and beams** raft ~ ~ ~ (~) ~ ~ · Lagerhölzer *npl* auf Dämmstreifen(unterlagen) und Balken

batter · Anlauf *m*, Anzug *m*, Dossierung *f*

battered masonry wall, battering ~ ~ · Mauer *f* mit Anzug, ~ ~ Anlauf, ~ ~ Dossierung, Schrägmauer

~ **wall**, battering ~, tal(l)us ~ · Wand mit einseitigem Anzug, ~ ~ ~ Anlauf, ~ ~ einseitiger Dossierung

battery-fed clock · Batterieuhr *f*

battery garages · Reihengaragen *fpl*

~ **mould** (Brit.); ~ **mold** (US) · Batterieform *f*

~ **moulding** (Brit.); ~ **molding** (US) · Batteriefertigung *f* [*Betonstein*]

~ **of boilers** · Kesselbatterie *f*, zusammenarbeitende Kesselreihe *f*

~ ~ **silos** · Silobatterie *f*

batting, angle dunting, droving, broad tooling · Schlaganarbeiten *n* [*Werksteinbearbeitung*]

~ **tool**, broad ~ [*A mason's chisel 3 to 4½ in. wide for surfacing sandstones*] · Schlageisen *n* für Sandsteinbearbeitung

to battlement → to embattle

battlement, em~, crenellation [*An indented parapet at the top of a wall, originally used for purposes of defence, subsequently for architectural decoration. The raised parts are 'cops' or 'merlons', the indentations 'embrasures' or 'crenel(le)s'*] · Zinnenkranz *m*, Zinnenbesatz *m*, Zinnenkrönung *f*

~ **tower** · Zinnenturm *m*

~ **turret** · Zinnentürmchen *n*

battlemented, with raised portions, with merlons, castellated, decorated with battlements, embattled, crenellated, brexted, decorated with battlements · mit Zinnen (versehen), ~ ~ gekrönt, gezinn(el)t bezinnt, krenelliert

~ **bridge parapet** → embattled ~ ~

~ **(masonry) wall**, defensive (~) ~ · Befestigungsmauer *f*, Verteidigungsmauer

~ **tower**, defensive ~ · Verteidigungsturm *m*, Befestigungsturm

~ **wall**, ~ masonry ~, defensive (masonry) ~ · Befestigungsmauer *f*, Verteidigungsmauer

battleship gray, ~ grey · schlachtschiffgrau

bauxite · Bauxit *m* [*Sedimentgestein, das im wesentlichen aus einem oder mehreren Aluminiumhydraten (Diaspor, Gibbsit, Boehmit) besteht und außerdem Tonminerale und Eisenhydroxide enthalten kann*]

~ **refractory (product)**, ~ ~ material · [*A high-alumina refractory material made from bauxite*] · Bauxiterzeugnis *n*

bauxitic cement → aluminious ~

Bavarian trass · bayerischer Traß *m*

bay, severy, compartment, vault ~ · Jochfeld *n*, (Gewölbe)Feld, (Gewölbe)Joch *n*, Gewölbeabteilung *f*, Gewölbebeschlag *m*, Gitterfeld [*Joche werden in Längsachse gezählt, Schiffe in Querachse*]

~, span · (Hallen)Schiff *n* [*Industriebau*]

~ · Feld *n*

~ **and cantilever system** · Raster- und Kragsystem *n*

~ **leaf** · Lorbeerblatt *n*

~ ~ **swag**, ~ ~ festoon, ~ ~ encarpa, ~ ~ garland, laurel ~ ~ · Lorbeerblattgehänge *n*, Lorbeerblattgewinde *n*, Lorbeerblattgirlande *f*, Lorbeerblattfeston *n*, Lorbeerblätterstrang *m*

~ **quoin (of masonry) wall)** · gebrochene rechtwinkelige Mauerecke *f*, kupierte ~

~ **span** · Joch *n* [*In der Antike bezeichnet „Joch" den Säulenabstand von Achse zu Achse*]

~ **system** · Rastersystem *n* [*Senkrechtes Tragsystem. Punkte der Lastenbündelung gleichmäßig verteilt*]

bay-type collection · Raster-Bündelung *f* [*Lastübertragungssystem*]

bay unit · Flächenraster *m*

~ **window** · Auslurchtfenster *n*

~ ~ [*misnomer*]; window(ed) bay, protruded bay · Auslucht *f*

Bayer process · Bayer-Verfahren *n* [*Gewinnung reiner Tonerde durch Aufschluß mit Natronlauge*]

Bayeux tapestry · Teppich *m* von Bayeux, Bayeuxteppich

bayonet lampholder [*B.S. 52*] · Bajonettfassung *f*

BC(L), broom closet, broom cupboard · Besenschrank *m*

bd., board, natural ~ · Brett

to be walked on · begehen [*(Fuß)Boden(belag)*]
beach gravel, shore ~ · Strandkies *m*
~ hut · Strandkorb *m*
~ rock, shell(y) sandstone · Muschelsandstein *m*
~ sand, shore ~ · Strandsand *m*
bead → round(ed) moulding
~ · Wulst *m, f*
~ and reel (enrichment), reel and bead (~), beadroll, beadstring [*In classical architecture, a mo(u)lding enriched with alternating 'beads' and 'reels'*] · Perl(en)stab *m*, Perl(en)schnur *f*
~ bend test · Aufschweißbiegeversuch *m*, Aufschweißbiegeprobe *f*, Aufschweißbiegeprüfung *f*
~ glue → Scotch glue in pearl form
~ (moulding) → round(ed) ~
~ seat band · Wulstband *n*
~ tile · Wulst(belag)platte *f*, Wulstfliese *f*
bead(ed) flat · Flachwulst(profil) *m, (n)* [*DIN 80291*]
~ ~ steel · Flachwulst(profil)stahl *m*, Wulstflachstahl [*DIN 1019*]
~ stripe · Glasperlen-Markierungsstreifen *m*
beading, fillet · Riemen *m*, schmales (Fuß)Bodenbrett *n*
beadroll → bead and reel (enrichment)
beaker · Becherglas *n*
beakhead (ornament) [*A Norman enrichment over doorways*] · Schnabelkopfverzierung *f*
beam, B, BM · Balken(träger) *m*
~ action [*The modulus of elasticity of a concrete slab is much greater than that of the foundation material, so that a major portion of the load-carrying capacity is derived from the slab itself. This is often referred to as beam action*] · Balkenwirkung *f*
~ anchor, ~ tie · Balken(träger)anker *m*, Kopfanker, Schlauder *f*, Stichanker, Zuganker
~ anchorage · Balken(träger)verankerung *f*
beam-and-colum work · Anschlußarbeiten *fpl* [*Schweißarbeiten zur Herstellung von Trägeranschlüssen bei Stahlskeletten*]
beam and filler floor → precast ~ ~ ~ ~
~ axis · Balken(träger)achse *f*
~ bending · Balken(träger)biegung *f*
~ bottom, ~ soffit · Balken(träger)unterseite *f*, Balken(träger)untersicht *f*
~ box, wall ~, wall frame, (wall) pocket, (wall) aperture [*A frame or box which is set into a brick, masonry, or stone wall to receive a timber beam or joist*] · Balken(träger)tasche *f*, Tasche, Balken(träger)kammer *f*, Kammer
~ butt joint · Balken(träger)stoß *m*

~ calculation · Balken(träger)berechnung *f*
~ casing → concrete ~ ~
~ casting · Betonbalkenherstellung *f*
~ centre line (Brit.); ~ center ~ (US) Balken(träger)mittellinie *f*
~ column · quer belasteter Druckstab *m*
~ connection → beam-to-column ~
~ ~ · Balken(träger)verbindung *f*, Balken(träger)anschluß *m*
~ construction → ~ (structural) system
~ cross section · Balken(träger)querschnitt *m*
~ crossing · Balken(träger)kreuzung *f*
~ curvature · Balken(träger)krümmung *f*
~ deflection, ~ deflexion · Balken(träger)durchbiegung *f*, Balken(träger)durchsenkung
~ deflexion, ~ deflection · Balken(träger)durchbiegung *f*, Balken(träger)durchsenkung
~ depth · Balken(träger)höhe *f*
~ design, design of beams · Balken(träger)bemessung *f*
~ ~ formula · Balken(träger)bemessungsformel *f*
~ distance · Balken(träger)abstand *m*
~ encasement → (concrete) beam casing
~ encasure → (concrete) beam casing
~ end · Balken(träger)kopf *m*
~ ~ face · Balken(träger)stirnfläche *f*
~ equation · Balken(träger)gleichung *f*
~ fixed at both ends → fixed beam
~ flexure theory · Balken(träger)biegetheorie *f*
~ floor, single ~, joist(ed) ~ · Balken(träger)decke *f*, Unterzugdecke
~ forms, ~ form(work), ~ shuttering · Balken(träger)schalung *f*
~ grid, ~ grill(ag)e · (Balken)Rost *m*, Balkenträgerrost, Balken(träger)kreuzwerk *n*
~ grill(ag)e, ~ grid · (Balken)Rost *m*, Balkenträgerrost, Balken(träger)kreuzwerk *n*
~ grille, ~ grillage, ~ grid · (Balken-)Rost *m*, Balkenträgerrost, Balken(träger)kreuzwerk *n*
~ hanger [*A stirrup hanging from a main beam to carry a secondary beam*] · Balken(träger)hänger *m*
~ haunching → (concrete) beam casing
~ hinge · Balken(träger)gelenk *n*
~ in prestressed clay → Stahlton (prestressed) beam
~ length · Balken(träger)länge *f*
beamless · balken(träger)los, balken(träger)frei
beam loading · Balken(träger)belastung *f*
~ mechanism · Balken(träger)mechanismus *m*

beam moment — bearing rib

~ moment · Balken(träger)moment *n*
~ of one bay → single-span beam
~ ~ ~ span → single-span beam
~ ~ three spans, three-span beam · Dreifeldbalken(träger)*m*
~ oscillation → ~ vibration
~ problem · Balken(träger)aufgabe *f*
~ profile · Balken(träger)profil *n*
~ redundant · Balken(träger)überzählige *f*
~ reinforcement · Balken(träger)bewehrung *f*, Balken(träger)armierung, Balken(träger)(stahl)einlagen *fpl*
~ rib · Balken(träger)rippe *f*
~ roof · Balken(träger)dach *n*
~ seat [*A steel bracket to a continuous column to carry a beam, in framed timber construction*] · Balken(träger)auflage *f*
~ sheat coat → (concrete) beam casing
~ shuttering → ~ forms
~ side · Balken(träger)seite *f*
~ ~ · Balken(träger)seitenschal(ungs)tafel *f*
~ simply supported at one end and fixed at the other; propped cantilever beam (US) · einseitig eingespannter und einseitig freiaufliegender Balken(träger) *m*
~ slab · Balken(träger)platte *f*
~ soffit → ~ bottom
~ strength · Balken(träger)festigkeit *f*
~ (structural) system, ~ construction · Balken(träger)konstruktion(ssystem) *f*, (*n*)
~ support · Balken(träger)auflager *n*
~ ~ · Balken(träger)unterstützung *f*
~ surface · Balken(träger)oberfläche *f*
~ system → ~ structural ~
~ test · Balken(träger)probe *f*, Balken(träger)prüfung *f*, Balken(träger)versuch *m* [*Zur Bestimmung der Biegezugfestigkeit nach DIN 1048 an einem Balken(träger) von 70 cm Länge, 15 cm Breite und 10 cm Höhe, der bei einer Stützweite von 60 cm durch eine Einzellast (Momentenlinie ein Dreieck) in Balken(träger)mitte bis zum Bruch belastet wird*]
~ ~ (to failure), ~ ~ ~ rupture · Balken(träger)bruchprüfung *f*, Balken(träger)bruchversuch *m*, Balken(träger)bruchprobe *f*
~ theory · Balken(träger)theorie *f*
~ tie · Balken(träger)anker *m*, Kopfanker, Schlauder *f*, Stichanker, Zuganker
~ timber, ~ wood · Balken(träger)holz *n*
beam(-to-column) connection · Balken(träger)anschluß *m*, Balken(träger)verbindung *f*
beam-to-girder connection · Balken-Träger-Anschluß *m*
beam type, type of beam · Balken(träger)art *f*

~ vibration, ~ oscillation · Balken(träger)schwingung *f*
~ web · Balken(träger)steg *m*
~ width · Balken(träger)breite *f*
~ wood, ~ timber · Balken(träger)holz *n*
bearer [*A joist supporting a winder or a landing*] · Treppenunterzug *m*
bearing, load~, load-carrying, weight-carrying, supporting, loaded · belastet, (last)tragend
~ [*The resistance of a rivet against crushing*] · Nietfestigkeit *f*
~ [*The support of a beam, or the length or the area of the beam which rests on its support*] · Auflagerung *f*
~ allowing freedom of rotation on rigid support · freidrehbare Lagerung *f* auf starrer Auflage
~ brick, load~ ~, weight-carrying ~, load-carrying ~, supporting ~ · (last-)tragender Ziegel *m*, statisch mitwirkender ~
~ capability → load-carrying capacity
~ capacity → load-carrying ~
~ ~ of beam(s) without cast-in-situ concrete → load~ ~ ~ ~ ~ ~ ~
~ construction → load~ ~
~ floor block → (load)bearing floor (clay) brick
~ ~ brick → (load)bearing floor (clay)~
~ ~ (clay) block → (load)bearing floor (clay) brick
~ ~ (~) brick → load~ ~ (~) ~
~ frame, load~ ~, supporting ~, (structural) ~, weight-carrying ~, load-carrying ~ · (Trag)Rahmen *m*
~ in longitudinal direction, load~ ~ ~ ~, weight-carrying ~ ~ ~, load-carrying ~ ~ ~, supporting ~ ~ ~ · längstragend
~ ~ transverse direction, load~ ~ ~ ~, weight-carrying ~ ~ ~, load-carrying ~ ~ ~, supporting ~ ~ ~ · quertragend
~ masonry (wall) → load~ ~ (~)
~ (work) → load~ ~ (~)
~ mechanism, load~ ~, weight-carrying ~, load-carrying ~, supporting ~, loaded ~ · Tragmechanismus *m*
~ pad · Lagerkissen *n*
~ partition (wall) → load~ ~ (~)
~ plane, load~ ~, weight-carrying ~, load-carrying ~, supporting ~, loaded ~ · Tragebene *f*
~ plate · Tragplatte *f*
~ ~ · Stützplatte *f* [*Spannbeton*]
~ power → load-carrying capacity
~ property → load-carrying capacity
~ quality → load-carrying capacity
~ rib, load~ ~, structural ~, supporting ~, weight-carrying ~, load-carrying ~ · Tragrippe *f*, Konstruktionsrippe, (last-)tragende Rippe, Auflagerrippe

bearing skeleton — beech(wood) shingle

~ **skeleton**, load~ ~, weight-carrying ~, (structural) ~ · (Trag)Skelett *n*, (Trag)Gerippe *n*

~ ~ **construction** → (structural) ~ ~

~ ~ **member** → (structural) ~ ~

~ ~ **structure** → (structural) ~ ~

~ **structure** → load~ ~

~ ~ **of plain web girders** → load~ ~ ~ ~ ~ ~

~ ~ ~ **solid web girders** → (load-) bearing structure of plain ~ ~

~ **system** → load~ ~

~ **wall**, load~ ~, weight-carrying ~, supporting ~, load-carrying ~, structural ~ · (last)tragende Wand *f*, Tragwand, Auflagerwand, Konstruktionswand

~ ~ **construction** → (load)bearing wall structure

~ ~ **structure** → load~ ~ ~ ~

bear's breech (Brit.); acanthus · Akanthus *m*, Bärenklau *m*

beast column · Bestiensäule *f*

beating hair [*Preparing hair for plastering by beating it with laths to remove dust and to open out the hair*] · Haarschlagen *n*

beauty parlor, ~ shop · Schönheitssalon *m*

to become brittle · verspröden

~ ~ **reemulsified** · reemulgieren

becoming mat(t), turning ~ · Vermatten *n* [*Anstrich*]

bed · Unterfütterung *f* [*Rohr in einem Graben*]

~ · Lager *n*, ~ fläche *f* [*Die untere oder obere Fläche eines Werksteines*]

bedded rock, sedimentary ~ · neptunisches Gestein *n*, Absetzgestein, Sedimentgestein, Ablagerungsgestein, Absatzgestein, Bodensatzgestein, Schichtgestein

bedding · Einbettung *f*

~ [*A layer on which something rests continuously*] · Bettung *f*

~ [*The act of placing a layer on which something rests continuously*] · Betten *n*

~ [*Setting bricks and stones on mortar beds*] · Vermauern *n* mit Mörtel

~ **compostion**, ~ compound · Verlegemasse *f*

~ **compound**, ~ composition · Verlegemasse *f*

~ **concrete** · Bettungsbeton *m*

bed(ing course) mortar, bedding ~ · Bettungsmörtel *m*, Ansetzmörtel, Verlegemörtel

bedding gravel · Bettungskies *m*

~ **material** · Bettungsmaterial *n*, Bettungsstoff *m*

~ **mortar** → bed(ding course) ~

bed elevator (US); ~ lift (Brit.)· Bettenaufzug *m*

bed-holding · Bettenkapazität *f* [*Krankenhaus*]

bed joint, horizontal ~, course ~ · Lagerfuge *f* [*Mauerwerk*]

~ **(~) mortar**, horizontal ~ ~, course ~ ~ · Lagerfugenmörtel *m* [*Mauerwerk*]

~ **lift** (Brit.); ~ elevator (US) · Bettenaufzug *m*

~ **mortar** → bedding course ~

~ **~**, ~ joint ~, horizontal joint ~, course joint ~ · Lagerfugenmörtel *m* [*Mauerwerk*]

~ **nook**, ~ recess · Bettnische *f*

bedplate · Grundplatte *f* [*Rollenlager für Hoch- und Tiefbauten*]

bed recess, ~ nook · Bettnische *f*

bedroom · Schlafzimmer *n*

~ → hotel ~

~ → guest ~

~ **basin** · Schlafzimmerwaschbecken *n*

~ **block** → dormitory ~

~ ~ ~ guest ~ ~

~ **building** → dormitory block

~ ~ ~ → guest ~ ~

~ **closet**, wardrobe ~ · Schlafzimmer-Einbauschrank *m*, Schlafzimmer-Wandschrank

~ ~ **bank**, wardrobe(-type) ~ ~, bank of wardrobe(-type) closets, bank of bedroom closets · Schlafzimmer-Schrankwand *f*

~ ~ **for children**, wardrobe ~ ~ ~ · Schlafzimmer-Einbauschrank *m* für Kinder, Schlafzimmer-Wandschrank ~ ~

~ ~ ~ **men**, wardrobe ~ ~ ~ ~ · Schlafzimmer-Einbauschrank *m* für Männer, Schlafzimmer-Wandschrank ~ ~

~ ~ ~ **women**, wardrobe ~ ~ ~ ~ · Schlafzimmer-Einbauschrank *m* für Frauen, Schlafzimmer-Wandschrank ~ ~

~ **door** · Schlafzimmertür *f*

~ **floor**; ~ story (US); ~ storey (Brit.)· Schlafzimmeretage *f*, Schlafzimmergeschoß *n*, Schlafzimmerstockwerk *n*

~ **house** → dormitory block

~ **story** (US); ~ storey (Brit.); ~ floor · Schlafzimmeretage *f*, Schlafzimmergeschoß *n*, Schlafzimmerstockwerk *n*

~ **unit** → dormitory block

~ **window** · Schlafzimmerfenster *n*

bedside table · Nachttisch *m*

bed-sitting room · Schlafzimmer-Wohnzimmer-Kombination *f*, Wohnschlafzimmer *n*, Wohnschlafraum *m*

bed-sitting-room dwelling unit (US); ~ dwelling (Brit.) · Wohnschlafzimmerwohnung *f*

bed surround, garden ~ · Beeteinfassung *f*

beech(wood) parquet(ry) · Buchenparkett *n*, Fhbp

~ **shingle** · Buchen(holz)schindel *f*

beech(wood) strip floor cover(ing) — bellow-framed door

~ strip floor cover(ing), ~~ floor(ing) (finish) · Buchenriemen(fuß)boden(belag) *m*, Fbh

~~ floor(ing) (finish), ~ ~ floor cover(ing) · Buchenriemen(fuß)boden(belag) *m*, Fbh

~ tar · Buchen(holz)teer *m*

~ tread · Buchen(holz)tritt(stufe) *m*, (*f*)

beehive house · Bienenkorbhütte *f*

~ tomb, tholus ~, thole ~, tholos ~ [*A subterranean stone-vaulted tomb shaped like an old-fashioned beehive*] · Tholosgrab *n*, unterirdisches kuppelförmiges Rundgrab

beer cellar · Bierkeller *m*

~ garden · Biergarten *m*

~ shop · Bierrestaurant *n*, Schwemme *f*

beerbachite, gabbro aplite · Gabbroaplit *m*

beeswax · Bienenwachs *n*

~ tar · Bienenwachsteer *m*

beetle (cement) [*Great Britain*]; urac [*USA*] · Kauritleim *m* [*Deutschland*]; Melocol *m* [*Schweiz*] [*Genormtes Kurzzeichen in Deutschland: K*]

behaviour on storage (Brit.); behavior ~~ (US) · Lagerungsverhalten *n*

~ under fire (Brit.); behavior ~ ~ (US) · Brandverhalten *n*, Feuerverhalten [*DIN 4102*]

~~ heat (Brit.); behavior ~ ~ (US) · Wärmeverhalten *n*

Belfast roof, bowstring ~ · Holz-Bogenbinderdach *n*

~ (~) truss → bowstring (~) ~

belfry · Belfried *m* [*Hoher, schlanker Rathaus- oder freistehender Turm in spätmittelalterlichen Städten Flanderns und Nordwestfrankreichs*]

~, campanile, isolated bell-tower, freestanding bell-tower · Campanile *m*, Kampanile, freistehender Glockenturm *m*

~, bell chamber, bell room [*The upper room in a tower or steeple of a church containing the bells and framing*] · Glockenstube *f*, Glockenkammer *f*

~, bell-tower [*A tower in which bells are hung, whether it is attached to or stands separate from the main building*] · Glockenturm *m*

Belgian black, Tournai marble · Tournai-Marmor *m*

~ method → ~ sandwich cable ~

~ (roof) truss · belgischer (Dach)Binder *m*

~ (sandwich cable) method, sandwich-plate ~ · Spannbetonverfahren *n* Magnel, (Vor)Spann(ungs)verfahren ~

~ zinc distilling furnace · belgischer Zinkdestillations-(Doppel)Ofen *m*

belite cement · Belitzement *m*

bell (US) → socket

~ · Klingel *f*

bell(-)and(-)spigot concrete pipe B&S ~ ~ (US); spigot(-)and(-)socke ~ ~ (Brit.) · Beton-Glockenmuffenrohr *n*, Zement-Glockenmuffenrohr, Glockenmuffen-Betonrohr, Glockenmuffen-Zementrohr, Betonrohr mit Glockenmuffenverbindung, Zementrohr mit Glockenmuffenverbindung

~ joint, B&S ~ (US); spigot(-)and(-)socket ~ (Brit.) · Glockenmuffenverbindung *f*

~ pipe, B&S ~ (US); spigot(-)and(-)socket ~ (Brit.) · Glockenmuffenrohr *n*

~ stoneware pipe, B&S ~ ~ (US); spigot(-)and(-)socket ~ (Brit.) · Steinzeug-Glockenmuffenrohr *n*, Glockenmuffen-Steinzeugrohr

bell button · Klingelknopf *m*

~ cage, ~ frame(work) · Glockenstuhl *m*

~ chamber, ~ room, belfry [*The upper room in a tower or steeple of a church containing the bells and framing*] · Glockenstube *f*, Glockenkammer *f*

~ cord · Klingelschnur *f*

~ gable, gable wall belfry, ringing-loft · Glockengiebel *m*

~ hanging · Klingelmontage *f*

~ installation, ~ system · Klingelanlage *f*

~ joint → bell(-)and(-)spigot ~

~ metal · Glockenbronze *f*

~ press (US); socket ~ (Brit.) · Glockenmuffenpresse *f*

~ push · Klingelplatte *f*

~ roof · Glockendach *n*

~ room → ~ chamber

bell-shaped dome, ~ cupola, ~ roof, campaniform ~ · Glockenkuppel *f*, Glockendach *n*

~ stupa(-mound), ~ tope(-mound) · glockenförmiger Stupa *m*

bell system, ~ installation · Klingelanlage *f*

bell-tower, belfry [*A tower in which bells are hung, whether it is attached to or stands separate from the main building*] · Glockenturm *m*

bell transformer · Klingeltrafo *m*, Klingeltransformator *m*

~ trap → -type ~

bell-turret · Glockentürmchen *n*

bell (type) flush(ing) cistern · Spülkastenglocke *f*

bell(-type) trap · Glocken(-Wasser)geruchverschluß *m*, Glockenverschluß ~

bellied [*e.g. panels that have buckled through swelling*] · ausgebeult

bellow-framed door, accordion ~, concertina ~ · Akkordeontür *f*, (Zieh)Harmonikatür

bellow-framed door fitting — bending moment

~ ~ fitting → concertina door furniture

~ ~ furniture → concertina ~ ~

Bellrock hollow plaster slab [*It consists of two gypsum plaster sheets bonded to a honeycomb core of gypsum plaster. One form is plain plaster on both faces, for conventional interior decoration. An alternative form has a waterproof bitumen emulsion treated face for external use*] · (Knauf-)Bellrockplatte *f*

belly-rod truss, inverted king (post) ~, trussed beam · umgekehrtes Hängewerk *n*, umgekehrter Hängebock *m*

below-grade masonry (work), belowground ~ (~) · Mauerwerk *n* im Erdreich, ~ unter Geländeoberkante

below-ground masonry (work), below-grade ~ (~) · Mauerwerk *n* im Erdreich, ~ unter Geländeoberkante

belt course → string (~)

~ **of fortresses** · Festungsgürtel *m*

~ **polishing** · Bandpolieren *n*

~ **stress** · waag(e)rechte Spannung *f* in einer Kuppel

belvedere, gazebo, lookout tower, standing tower [*A turret or lantern on a house to afford a view*] · Belvedere *n*, Aussichtsturm *m*

~, gazebo [*A summerhouse with view*] · Belvedere *n*

Belvedere at Prague, Queen Anna's summer house · Belvedere *n* zu Prag

bema [*Originally a low platform used by Athenian orators; later the raised sanctuary or chancel of an early Christian church, between the apse and the chancel steps; also in a synagogue*] · Bema *n*

bench · Werkbank *f*

~ · (Sitz)Bank *f*

~, berm · Berme *f*

~ **table** [*A (natural) stone seat fixed to a wall or round a pillar*] · (Natur-)Steinauflage *f*

~ **tomb** · Bermengrab *n*

benched footing, step(ped) ~ [*A stepped construction to spread the load at the foot of a wall or column*] · abgetrepptes Fundament *n*, treppenförmiges ~

benching [*Rounding the corners of manholes, etc. with cement*] · Ausrunden *n*

~, stepping · Abtreppen *n* [*Fundament*]

bend, pipe ~ · (Rohr)Krümmer *m*

~ **point** · Biegestelle *f* [*Bewehrung*]

~ **test** → bending ~

to bend up, to raise, to deflect · ablenken, anheben [*Litze in der Spannbetontechnik*]

bendability → bending capacity

bending · Biegen *n*

~ · Biegung *f*

~ **action** · Biegebeanspruchung *f*, Biegungsbeanspruchung

bend(ing) allowance · Biegetoleranz *f* [*Bewehrung*]

~ **amount,** amount of bend(ing) · Biegebetrag *m*, Biegegröße *f*, Biegungsbetrag, Biegungsgröße

bending analysis · Biegelehre *f* [*Teilgebiet der Statik zur Berechnung der Randspannungen bei Biegung beanspruchter Konstruktionsteile*]

~ **angle** · Biegewinkel *m*

~ **bond failure,** flexural ~ ~ · Haftungsbiegebruch *m*, Verbundbiegebruch

~ **capability** → ~ capacity

~ **capacity,** ~ property, ~ quality, ~ power, ~ capability, bendability, pliability, flexibility · Biegbarkeit *f*, Biegsamkeit, Biegefähigkeit, Biegeeigenschaft *f*, Biegevermögen *n*

~ **coefficient** · Biegebeiwert *m*, Biegezahl *f*

~ **connection,** ~ joint · Biegeverbindung *f*

~ **crack,** flexural ~ · Biegeriß *m*

~ **curve** → flexure ~

~ **cycles,** cycles of bending · Biegewechselanzahl *f*

~ **deformation** · Biegeformänderung *f*, Biegeverformung

~ **dimension** [*B.S. 1478*] · Biegeabmessung *f*, Biegemaß *n*, Biegungsmaß, Biegungsabmessung

~ **displacement** · Biegeverrückung *f*

~ **distribution,** distribution of bending · Biegevertailung *f*

~ **disturbance** · Biegestörung *f*

~ **elasticity,** flexional ~ · Biegeelastizität *f*, Biegungselastizität

~ **endurance** → fatigue in bending

~ **energy** · Biegeenergie *f*

~ **failure,** ~ rupture · Biegebruch *m*, Biegungsbruch

~ ~ **curve,** ~ rupture ~ · Biegebruchkurve *f*, Biegungsbruchkurve

~ ~ **stress,** ~ rupture ~ · Biegebruchspannung *f*, Biegungsbruchspannung

~ **fatigue** → fatigue in bending

~ **force,** ~ power · Biegekraft *f*, Biegungskraft

~ **formula,** flexure ~ · Biegeformel *f*

~ **joint,** ~ connection · Biegeverbindung *f*

~ **limit** → flexure ~

~ **list** · Biegeliste *f* [*Bewehrung*]

~ **load** → flexure ~

~ **loading** · Biegebelastung *f*, Biegungsbelastung

~ **mold** (US); ~ **mould** (Brit.) · Biegeform *f* [*Biegen von Hand*]

~ **moment,** B.M. · Biegemoment *n*, Biegungsmoment [*Die Summe der Wirkungen aller angreifenden Kräfte an ihrem Hebelarm bezogen auf einen bestimmten Querschnitt*]

bending moment at a corner — Benedictine quire

~ ~ **at a corner** · Eckbiegemoment *n*, Eckbiegungsmoment

~ ~ ~ **mid-span** · Biegemoment *n* in Feldmitte, Biegungsmoment ~ ~

bending(-)moment diagram, B.M.D. [*The B.M.D. is a diagram with the centre line of the member as base line and ordinates representing the bending moment at successive right sections, positive bending moment being plotted upwards and negative downwards*] · Biegemomentenlinie *f*, Biegungsmomentendiagramm *n*

~ **distribution** · Biegemomentenverteilung *f*, Biegungsmomentenverteilung

bending moment-less · biegemomentenfrei, biegungsmomentenfrei, biegemomentenlos, biegungsmomentenlos

bending(-)moment problem · Biegemomentenaufgabe *f*, Biegungsmomentenaufgabe

~ **ratio** · Biegemomentenverhältnis *n*, Biegungsmomentenverhältnis

~ **theory** · Biegemomententheorie *f*, Biegungsmomententheorie

bending oscillation → flexural ~

~ ~ **failure** → flexural ~ ~

~ ~ **strength** → flexural ~ ~

~ ~ **test** → flexural ~ ~

~ **plane**, plane of bending · Biegeebene *f*, Biegungsebene

~ **power** → ~ capacity

~ **property** → ~ capacity

~ **quality** → ~ capacity

~ **radius** · Biegehalbmesser *m*, Biegungshalbmesser

~ **resistance**, flexural ~, ~ stiffness, ~ rigidity, resistance to bending · Biegesteifigkeit *f*, Biegewiderstand *m*, Biegungswiderstand, Biegungssteifigkeit, Biegesteife *f*, Biegestarrheit *f*

bending-resistant → flexurally rigid

bending rigidity, flexural ~, ~ stiffness, ~ resistance, resistance to bending · Biegesteifigkeit *f*, Biegewiderstand *m*, Biegungswiderstand, Biegungssteifigkeit, Biegesteife *f*, Biegestarrheit *f*

~ **rupture**, ~ failure · Biegebruch *m*, Biegungsbruch

~ ~ **curve** → ~ failure ~

~ **schedule** · Bewehrungsplan *m*, Armierungsplan, (Stahl)Einlagenplan, (Stahl)Einlagenzeichnung *f*, Bewehrungszeichnung, (Eisen)Biegeplan, (Eisen)Biegezeichnung, Armierungszeichnung [*Auf diesem Plan werden die (Stahl)Einlagen herausgezeichnet*]

~ **stiffness**, flexural ~, ~ rigidity, ~ resistance, resistance to bending · Biegesteifigkeit *f*, Biegewiderstand *m*, Biegungswiderstand, Biegungssteifigkeit, Biegesteife *f*, Biegestarrheit *f*

~ **strain energy**, flexural ~ ~ · Biegedehnungsenergie *f*, Biegungsdehnungsenergie

~ **strength** · Biegefestigkeit *f*, Biegungsfestigkeit

~ **stress**, flexural ~ · Biegespannung *f*, Biegungsspannung

~ ~ **distribution**, flexural ~ ~ · Biegespannungsverteilung *f*, Biegungsspannungsverteilung

~ ~ **formula**, flexural ~ ~ · Biegespannungsformel *f*, Biegungsspannungsformel

~ **tension** · Biegezug *m*

~ ~ **failure**, flexural tensile ~ · Biegezugbruch *m*

bend(ing) test · Biegeprobe *f*, Biegeversuch *m*, Biegeprüfung *f*, Biegungsprobe, Biegungsversuch, Biegungsprüfung

~ ~, **mandrel** ~ ~ · Dornbiegeprobe *f*, Dornbiegeprüfung *f*, Dornbiegeversuch *m* [*DIN 53152*]

bending test beam, flexure ~ ~ · Probebalken *m*, Biegebalken, Prüfbalken, (Biege)Versuchsbalken

bend(ing) test in tempered (or quenched) state, flexure ~ ~ ~ (~ ~) ~ · Abschreck-Biegeversuch *m*, Härtungs-Biegeversuch, Abschreck-Biegeprobe *f*, Härtungs-Biegeprobe, Abschreck-Biegeprüfung *f*, Härtungs-Biegeprüfung

bending test specimen · Biegekörper *m*, Prisma *n* zur Ermitt(e)lung der Biegefestigkeit

~ ~ **specimen strength** · Biegekörperfestigkeit *f*, Prismenfestigkeit

~ **theory** · Biegetheorie *f* [*Schalen und Faltwerke erhalten außer Schub- und Normalspannungen auch Biegespannungen, die nach der Biegetheorie berechnet werden*]

~ **time**, ~ period · Biegedauer *f*, Biegefrist *f*, Biegezeit *f*

~ **up** · Aufbiegung *f* [*Tragstab einer Bewehrung*]

~ ~, draping, deflecting, raising · Anheben *n*, Ablenken [*Litzen in der Spannbetontechnik*]

~ ~ **technique** → deflected-strand ~

~ **value** · Biegewert *m*

~ **vibration** → flexural oscillation

~ ~ **failure** → flexural oscillation ~

~ ~ **strength** → flexural oscillation ~

~ ~ **test** → flexural oscillation ~

~ **wave** · Biegewelle *f* [*Schalltechnik*]

~ **width** · Biegebreite *f*

bendproof → flexurally rigid

Benedictine abbey · Benediktinerabtei *f*

~ ~ **church** · Benediktinerabteikirche *f*

~ **choir**, ~ quire · Staffelchor *m*

~ **church** · Benediktinerkirche *f*

~ **monastery** · Benediktinerkloster *n*

~ **quire**, ~ choir · Staffelchor *m*

benefication [*Improvement of the chemical and/or physical properties of a raw material or intermediate product by the removal of undesirable and/or impurities*] · Veredelung *f*

~ **of low-grade gypsum** · Gipsanreicherung *f*

benefit building society, cooperative ~ ~ · Baugenossenschaft *f*

benjamin, benzoin, gum ~ · Benzoeharz *n*

bent [*A structural frame which is self-supporting in two dimensions. It has at least two legs and is generally at right angles to the length of the structure which it supports*] · Querrahmen *m*

~ · gebogen

~ **bar** → curved rod

~ **element** → curved rod

~ **form** · gebogene Form *f* [*z.B. von Glas*]

~ **glass** · gebogenes Glas *n*

~ **member** → curved rod

~ **pyramide** [*There is a change of angle in the sloping sides*] · Knickpyramide *f*

~ **rod** → curved ~

~ **surface** · Biegefläche *f* [*Verformung der Mittelfläche einer Platte nach der Belastung*]

bentonite (clay), bentonitic ~ · Bentonit *m* [*Hochplastischer, montmorillonitischer Ton, der zumeist aus vulkanischen Aschen entstanden ist, 0,001 mm*]

~ **mud,** bentonitic ~ · Bentonitschlamm *m*

~ **suspension,** bentonitic ~ · Bentonitaufschwemmung *f*, Bentonitsuspension *f*

bentonitic mud, bentonite ~ · Bentonitschlamm *m*

bent(-up) bar, web ~, ~ rod · Schrägeisen *n*, Schräg(armierungs)stab *m*, Schrägbewehrungsstab, Schubeisen, Schub(armierungs)stab, Schubbewehrungsstab

~ **point,** ~ portion, point of bending up, portion of bending up · Abbiegestelle *f* [*Bewehrungsstab*]

~ **portion,** ~ point, point of bending up, portion of bending up · Abbiegestelle *f* [*Bewehrungsstab*]

~ **rod** → ~ bar

bentwood · Formvollholz *n*, Biegeholz

benzene, benzole · Benzol *n* [C_6H_6. *Klopffester Vergaserbrennstoff, durch Destillation des Steinkohlenteeres oder durch Auswaschen von Kokereigas gewonnen*]

~ **insolubles** → extrinsic ~

Benzinger metal lath(ing) · Baustahlputzmatte *f*, Benzinger-Matte

benzoic acid · Benzoesäure *f*

benzoin, benjamin, gum ~ · Benzoeharz *n*

benzole → benzene

benzyl cellulose · Benzylcellulose *f*, Benzylzellulose

Berlin black · Berlinerschwarz *n*

~ **blue (pigment)** · Berlinerblau *n*

~ **white** · Berlinerweiß *n*

berm, bench · Berme *f*

Bermudez asphalt · Bermudas-Asphalt *m*

Bernoulli assumption, ~ hypothesis · Bernoullische Annahme *f*

~ **equation** · Bernoullische Gleichung *f*, Bernoulli-Gleichung, Bernoulli-Satz *m*, Bernoullischer Satz

Bernoulli-Euler differential equation · Bernoulli-Euler-Differentialgleichung *f*

beryllia, BeO; beryllium oxide (Brit.); beryllium oxid(e) (US) · Berylliumoxid *n*

~ **refractory (product),** BeO ~ (~); beryllium oxide ~ (~) Brit.); beryllium oxid(e) ~ (~) (US) · Berylliumoxidartikel *m*, Berylliumoxidgegenstand *m*, Berylliumoxiderzeugnis *n*

beryllium copper · Berylliumbronze *f*, Berylliumkupfer *n*

~ **oxide** (Brit.) → beryllia

besant, bezant, byzant, pellet ornament; disc frieze (Brit.); disk frieze (US) · Scheibenfries *m*, Scheibenverzierung *f*, Scheibenornament *n*

Bessemer matte · Konverterstein *m*

~ **steel** · Bessemerstahl *m*

best hand-picked (quick)lime [*(Quick)Lime in lump form selected by hand for a particular purpose*] · handsortierter Stück(en)kalk *m*

~ **quality,** prime [*The standard of first-quality ware*] · erste Wahl *f*

beta alumina, β-alumina [*It contains a small amount of alkali metal oxide*] · Betatonerde *f*, β-Tonerde

~ **brass,** alpha-~ ~ [*It contains between 36% and 45% zinc*] · Betamessing *n*, β-Messing

~ **iron** · Betaeisen *n*, β-Eisen

betterment · Bodenwertsteigerung *f*

~ **levy,** increment value tax · Wertzuwachssteuer *f* [*im Grundstückswesen*]

betterments · Melioration *f* des Grundbesitzes

betting hall · Wetthalle *f*

Betti('s) law, ~ theorem [*In an elastic structure with unyielding supports and at constant temperature the external work done by a system of forces P during a distortion caused by a system of forces Q is equal to the external work done by the Q system during a distortion caused by the P system*] · Bettischer Satz *m*

between-season heating period · Übergangsheizperiode *f*

to bevel, to cant, to slope, to splay · abschrägen, abkragen, ausschrägen, verschrägen

bevel — billet rod

bevel [*A surface meeting another surface at an angle which is not a right angle. A 'chamfer' is a bevel cut off at 45°*] · Fase *f*
~, splay, cant, slope · Druckschlag *m* [*Gewölbe*]
~, splay, slope, cant · Ausschrägung *f*, Schräge *f*, Abschrägung, Abkragung, Verschrägung
~ **bonder** → splay ~
~ **bondstone** → splay bonder
~ **brick** → splay ~
~ **(corner) halving**; beveled (~) ~ (US); bevelled (~) ~ (Brit.) · Ecküberblattung *f* mit schrägem Schnitt
~ **header** → splay bonder
~ **moulding** → splay ~
~ **of a masonry wall** → splay ~ ~ ~ ~
~ ~ ~ **wall** → splay ~ ~ ~
~ **stretcher** → splay ~
beveled (corner) halving (US); bevelled (~) ~ (Brit.); bevel (~) ~ · Ecküberblattung *f* mit schrägem Schnitt
beveling (US); **bevelling** (Brit.) · Abschrägen *n*, Ausschrägen, Abkragen
bevelled (Brit.); beveled (US); splayed, sloped, canted · abgeschrägt, ausgeschrägt, abgekragt
~ **cocking**, ~ cogging, ~ corking (Brit.); beveled ~ (US); oblique ~ · schräger Kamm *m* [*Holzverbindung*]
~ **cogging**, ~ cocking, ~ corking (Brit.); beveled ~ (US); oblique ~ · schräger Kamm *m* [*Holzverbindung*]
~ **(corner) halving** (Brit.); beveled (~) ~ (US); bevel (~) ~ · Ecküberblattung *f* mit schrägem Schnitt
~ **end cocking** → ~ ~ cogging
~ ~ **cogging**, ~ ~ cocking, ~ ~ corking (Brit.); beveled ~ ~ (US); oblique ~ ~ · schräge Endverkämmung *f* [*Holzverbindung*]
~ ~ **corking** → ~ ~ cogging
~ **folding** (Brit.) → splayed ~
~ **glass** (Brit.); beveled ~ (US) · Facettenglas *n*
~ **halving** (Brit.) → ~ ~ corner ~
~ **joint** (Brit.); beveled ~ (US); oblique ~ · schräger Stoß *m* [*Holzverbindung*]
bevelling (Brit.); beveling (US); splaying, canting, sloping · Ausschrägen *n*, Abschrägen, Verschrägen, Abkragen
~ **cut of jack rafter** (Brit.); beveling ~ ~ ~ ~ (US) · Backenschmiege *f*, Wangenschmiege, Kleb(e)schmiege
beverage store · Getränkelager *n*
bezant, byzant, besant, pellet ornament; disc frieze (Brit.); disk frieze (US) · Scheibenfries *m*, Scheibenverzierung *f*, Scheibenornament *n*
B.F.B. → broad-flange(d) beam
BFP, boiler feed pump · Kesselspeisewasserpumpe *f*
BFW, boiler feed water · Kesselspeisewasser *n*

BH, boiler house · Kesselhaus *n*
~, Brinell hardness · Brinellhärte *f*, Metalldruckhärte, Druckhärte von Metallen, HB
B.H.N., Brinell hardness number · Brinell-Härtezahl *f*
biaxial · zweiachsig
bib(cock) → (sink) bib
bib nozzle (US) → (sink) bib (Brit.)
~ **tap** → (sink) bib
(bi)cycle park, ~ stand · Fahrradstand *m*
~ **room** · Fahrradraum *m*
~ **stand**, ~ park · Fahrradstand *m*
bidding period (US); tendering ~ (Brit.) · Ausschreibungsdauer *f*
bidet [*A vessel on a low narrow stand, which can be bestridden for bathing purposes*] · Bidet *n*, Sitzwaschbecken *n*
bifolding door · Doppelfalttür *f*
big brick chimney, ~ ~ ~ stack, radial brick industrial ~ · freistehender Ziegelschornstein *m*, Industrie-Ziegelschornstein, Ziegel-Industrieschornstein, Ziegelesse *f*, Ziegelschlot *m*
~ ~ **stack**, ~ ~ chimney, radial brick industrial ~ · freistehender Ziegelschornstein *m*, Industrie-Ziegelschornstein, Ziegel-Industrieschornstein, Ziegelesse *f*, Ziegelschlot *m*
~ **chimney**, industrial ~, (industrial) stack · Industrieschornstein *m*, Esse *f*, Schlot *m*, freistehender Schornstein [*DIN 1056*]
biga, two-horse(d) chariot [*A sculpture, often surmounting a monument*] · Biga *f*, Zweigespann *n*
bilection (molding) (US) → balection (moulding)
bill of material(s), ML, material list [*A list of the various portions of material for a construction, either proposed or completed, giving dimensions and weights or other quantitative measurements*] · Stoffliste *f*, Materialliste
~ ~ **quantities** · Leistungsverzeichnis *n*, L.V., LV
billet [*A semi-finished rolled or forge product intended for re-rolling or forging, usually square with chamfered or radiused corners and with a cross-sectional area generally not more than 25 sq. in.*] · Barren *m*, Knüppel *m*, Walzblock *m*
~ **bar**, natural ~, ~ rod, billet steel reinforcing ~ [*A reinforcing bar rolled from a steel billet in contrast to rail or axle steel*] · Armierungsstab *m* aus einem Knüppel hergestellt, Bewehrungsstab ~ ~ ~ ~
~ **(frieze)** [*It consists of several bands of raised square pieces placed at regular intervals*] · Würfelfries *m*, Schachbrettfries [*Fries mit vor- und zurückspringenden Elementen*]
~ **rod** → ~ bar

billet steel — (biological) shield(ing) concrete

~ steel · Knüppelstahl *m*
~ ~ reinforcing bar → ~ bar
~ ~ ~ rod → ~ bar
billing [*Totalling the separate trades when preparing a bill of quantities*] · Gesamtpreiserrechnung *f*
Billner method · Billner-Verfahren *n*, Vakuum-Behandlung *f* nach Billner [*Vakuumbeton*]
bi-metal strip · Bimetallstreifen *m*
binary · binär, aus zwei Elementen bestehend, zweiglied(e)rig, Zweistoff......
to bind the pigment particles together, ~ cement ~ ~ ~ ~ · untereinander verbinden [*Pigmentteilchen durch Bindemittel*]
binder, roof joist, binding beam, binding joist · Bundbalken *m*, Binderbalken
~, bond · Bindemittel *n* [*Feuerfestindustrie*]
~, binding joist · Zwischendeckenbalken *m* [*zwischen den Streichbalken liegend*]
~ → cementing material
~, hydrocarbon ~, bituminous ~, bitumen (~) (US) [*Strictly the portion of bituminous matter completely soluble in carbon disulphide; used loosely as a term for tar and asphalt (US)/(asphaltic-)bitumen (Brit.).*] · (Schwarz-)Bindemittel *n*, (Schwarz)Binder *m*, bituminöses Bindemittel, bituminöser Binder
~, link · Bügel *m* [*Bewehrung*]
~ → (paint) (binding) medium
binder-aggregate mix(ture) · Bindemittel-Mineral-Masse *f*, Bindemittel-Mineral-Gemisch *n*
binder content, ~ portion · Bindemittelanteil *m*, Binderanteil, Bindemittelgehalt *m*, Bindergehalt
~ ~ determination, ~ portion ~ · Bindemittel(anteil)bestimmung *f*, Binder(anteil)bestimmung, Bindemittelgehaltbestimmung, Bindergehaltbestimmung
~ derived from cork · korkeigenes Bindemittel *n*
~ dispersion, (binding) medium ~ · (Farben)Bindemitteldispersion *f*, Anstrichdispersion
~ emulsion, (binding) medium ~ · (Farben)Bindemittelemulsion *f*, Anstrichemulsion
binder-filler mix(ture) · Bindemittel-Füller-Gemisch *n*, Bindemittel-Füller-Mischung *f*
binder for construction(al) materials, ~ ~ building ~, ~ ~ structural ~ · Baustoff-Bindemittel *n*, Baustoff-Binder *m*
~ mix(ture) · Bindemittelmischung *f*, Bindemittelgemisch *n*
~ particle · Bindemittelteilchen *n*, Binderteilchen
~ portion → ~ content
~ ~ determination → ~ content ~

~ recovery · Bindemittelwiedergewinnung *f*, Bindemittelrückgewinnung
~ suspension, (binding) medium ~ · (Farben)Bindemittelsuspension *f*, Dispersionsbinder *m*
~ technology · Bindemitteltechnologie *f*
binders → lateral reinforcement
binding → ~ reinforcement
~ beam, ~ joist, binder, roof joist · Binderbalken *m*, Bundbalken
~ concrete course, ~ ~ layer, ~ (course) · Ausgleichbetonschicht *f*, Ausgleichbetonlage *f*
~ ~ layer, ~ ~ course, ~ (course) · Ausgleichbetonschicht *f*, Ausgleichbetonlage *f*
~ (course), ~ concrete ~, ~ concrete layer · Ausgleichbetonschicht *f*, Ausgleichbetonlage *f*
~ gravel → path ~
~ joist, ~ beam, binder, roof joist · Bundbalken *m*, Binderbalken
~ ~, binder · Zwischendeckenbalken *m* [*zwischen den Streichbalken liegend*]
(~) matrix (material) → cementing ~
~ medium → cementing material
(~) ~ → paint (~) ~
(~) ~ dispersion, binder ~ · (Farben-)Bindemitteldispersion *f*, Anstrichdispersion
(~) ~ emulsion, binder ~ · (Farben-)Bindemittelemulsion *f*, Anstrichemulsion
(~) ~ suspension, binder ~ · (Farben-)Bindemittelsuspension *f*, Dispersionsbinder *m*
~ piece → horizontal timber
~ plate → corner ~
~ rafter, purlin(e) · (Dach)Pfette *f*
~ (reinforcement), tying (~), reinforcement binding, reinforcement tying · Rodeln *n* (von Bewehrung(en)), Rödelung *f* (~ ~), Flechten (~ ~), Bewehrungsflechten
~ value under the action of water [*bituminous binder*] · Bindewert *m* unter Wassereinwirkung, BWW
~ wire, lashing ~, annealed ~, iron ~, tying ~ [*Soft steel wire used for binding reinforcement*] · Rödeldraht *m*, Bindedraht
bing brick, blaes ~, cliff ~, shale (clay) ~ [*B.S. 3921*] · Schiefertonziegel *m*

(biological) shielding, radiation ~ · (Strahlungs)Abschirmung *f*, Strahlenschutz *m*
(~) shield(ing) block, radiation ~ ~, (~) ~ tile [*See remark under 'Block'*] · Abschirm(ungs)stein *m*, Strahlenschutzstein, Abschirm(ungs)block(stein) *m*, Strahlenschutzblock(stein)
(~) ~ concrete, radiation ~ ~ · Abschirm(ungs)beton *m*, Strahlenschutzbeton [*Zur Abschirmung von Gamma- und Neutronenstrahlen*]

(biological) shield(ing) design — bitumen bonding agent

(~) ~ **design**, radiation ~ ~ · Abschirm(ungs)berechnung f [*Strahlenschutz*]

(~) ~ **door**, radiation ~ ~ · Abschirm(ungs)tür f, Strahlenschutztür

(~) ~ **glass**, radiation ~ ~ · Strahlenschutzglas n

~ ~ **material**, (radiation) ~ ~ · Abschirm(ungs)(bau)stoff m, Strahlenschutz(bau)stoff; Abschirm(ungs)-(bau)material n, Strahlenschutz(bau)material [*Schweiz*]

(~) ~ **tile**, radiation ~ ~, (~) ~ block [*See remark under 'Block'*] · Abschirm(ungs)stein m, Strahlenschutzstein, Abschirm(ungs)block(stein) m, Strahlenschutzblock(stein)

(~) ~ **wall**, radiation ~ ~ · Abschirm(ungs)wand f [*Zur Abschirmung von Gamma- und Neutronenstrahlen werden Wände aus Beton, Gußeisen, Stahl, Blei, Kunststoff oder Paraffin errichtet*]

~ **style** [*Style incorporating decorative motifs taken from nature*] · biologischer Stil m

biotite-gneiss · Biotitgneis m

biotite-granite, granitite · Biotitgranit m [*früher: Granitit m*]

biotite-schist · Biotitschiefer m, Dunkelglimmerschiefer

bipartite church · zweiteilige Kirche f [*Sie besteht aus Saal und Chor*]

birch-bark tar · Birkenrindenteer m

birch wood tar · Birkenholzteer m

birdsmouth, B.M. · Gabel(schmiege) f, Geißfuß m [*Holzverbindung*]

~ **joint** → toe-jointing

~ **quoin** (of (masonry) wall), obtuse ~ (~ (~) ~) · stumpfwink(e)lige Mauerecke f

birdsmouthed jointing → toe-jointing

birdsmouthing → toe-jointing

Birth House, Mammisi temple [*Such a structure often stood in the outer enclosure of a large Egyptian temple and was subsidiary to it*] · Mammisi m, heilige Geburtsstätte f, Geburtshaus n

biscuit firing, biscuiting [*The second burning of glazed bricks or tiles after the slip or glaze is applied*] · Schrühbrand m

~ **oven** · Schrühbrandofen m

~ **tile** · Schrüh(belag)platte f, Schrühfliese

biscuiting, biscuit firing [*The second burning of glazed bricks or tiles after the slip or glaze is applied*] · Schrühbrand m

bishop's palace · Bischofspalast m

Bismarck brown · Bismarckbraun n

bismite; bismuth ocher (Brit.); bismuth ocher (US) · Bismit m, Wismutocker m, Bi_2O_3 (Min.)

bismuth blende, eulytite · Wismutblende f

~ **glance**, bismuthinite · Bismuthin n, Wismutglanz m, Bi_2S_3 (Min.)

~ **ocher** (US) → bismite

~ **ochre** (Brit.) → bismite

bismuthinite, bismuth glance · Bi_2S_3, Wismutglanz m, Bismuthin n (Min.)

Bison floor [*A patent hollow beam fire-resisting floor*] · Bisondecke f

bi-stable · bistabil

bisulfite of lime (US); bisulphite ~ ~ (Brit.) · doppeltschwefligsaures Kalzium n, Kalziumhydrogensulfit n, saurer schwefligsaurer Kalk m, Kalziumbisulfit

bit, key ~ · (Schlüssel)Bart m

~ **key** · Bartschlüssel m

bitter spar → magnesite

bittiness · Stippigkeit f [*Anstrichtechnik*]

bitumen, asphaltic-~ (Brit.); asphalt (US) · Bitumen n [*Fehlname: Asphaltbitumen*]

~ · Bitumen n im weiteren Sinne

~ (US) → (bituminous) binder

~ **addition** → asphaltic-~ ~

~ **adhesion-preventing agent** (Brit.) → asphalt ~ ~

~ **adhesive** → (asphaltic-)bitumen bonding ~

~ ~ **(composition)** → asphaltic-~ ~ (~)

~ ~ **compound** → (asphaltic-)bitumen adhesive (composition)

bitumen-aggregate mix(ture) (Brit.) → asphalt-aggregate ~

bitumen/asbestos composition → (asphaltic-)bitumen/asbestos compound

~ **compound** → asphaltic-~ ~

~ **fibre cement** → asphaltic-~ ~ ~

~ **mass** → (asphaltic-)bitumen/asbestos compound

~ **material** → (asphaltic-)bitumen/asbestos compound

bitumen base → asphaltic-~ ~

~ **based**, asphaltic-~ ~, containing (asphaltic-)bitumen (Brit.); asphalt based, asphaltic (US) · asphalthaltig

bitumen-based building mastic → asphaltic-~ ~ ~

~ **mastic joint sealer** → asphaltic-~ ~ ~ ~

~ **paste** (Brit.) → asphalt-based ~

~ **rust protection paint** (Brit.) → asphalt-based rust protective ~

~ ~ **protective paint** (Brit.) → asphalt-based ~ ~ ~

bitumen binder → asphaltic-~ ~

~ (~) (US) → bituminous ~

~ **bonding adhesive** → asphaltic-~ ~ ~

~ ~ **agent** → (asphaltic-)bitumen bonding adhesive

104

bitumen bonding composition — bitumen lining

~ ~ **composition** → (asphaltic-)bitumen adhesive (~)

~ ~ **compound** → (asphaltic-)bitumen adhesive (composition)

~ ~ **medium** → (asphaltic-)bitumen bonding adhesive

~ **briquette,** asphaltic-~ ~ (Brit.); asphalt(ic) ~ (US) · Bitumenformling *m*

~ **building paper,** asphaltic-~ ~ ~, asphalt ~ ~, general-use ~ ~ (US) [*See remark under 'Pappe'*] · Asphaltbaupappe *f*, Bitumenbaupappe

~ **calcium silicate brick** (Brit.) → asphalt(-impregnated) sand-lime ~

~ **cement(ing agent)** → (asphaltic-)bitumen bonding adhesive

~ **cementing composition** → (asphaltic-)bitumen adhesive (~)

~ ~ **compound** → (asphaltic-)bitumen adhesive (composition)

~ **coat** (Brit.) → asphalt (surface) coat(ing)

~ **coated** → asphaltic-~ ~

bitumen-coated chip(ping)s (Brit.) → asphalt-coated ~

~ **gravel** → gravel asphalt

~ **(road) metal** → asphaltic-~ (~) ~

~ **sand,** asphaltic-~ ~ (Brit.); asphalt-coated ~ (US) · Asphaltsand *m*, Bitu(men)sand

bitumen coat(ing) (Brit.) → asphalt (surface) ~

~ **coating compound** → asphaltic-~ ~ ~

~ ~ **(material)** → asphaltic-~ ~ (~)

~ ~ **composition** → asphaltic-~ ~

~ ~ **roofing** → asphalt ready ~

~ **compound** → (asphaltic-)bitumen composition

~ **concrete,** asphaltic-~ ~ (Brit.); asphalt(ic) ~ (US) · Asphaltbeton *m* [*Gemisch von Splitt, Natursand (oder Brechsand) und Füller mit Bitumen als Bindemittel*]

~ ~ **(mineral) skeleton** (Brit.) → asphalt ~ (~) ~ (US)

~ ~ **skeleton** (Brit.) → asphalt concrete (mineral) ~

~ **content** → asphaltic-~ ~

~ **dispersion** → asphaltic-~ ~

~ **emulsion with colloidal emulsifier** → asphaltic-~ ~ ~ ~ ~

~ **facing** → (asphaltic-)bitumen (sur-)facing

bitumen-filler mix(ture) → asphaltic-~ ~

~ ~ (US) · (Schwarz)Bindemittel-Füller-Gemisch *n*, (Schwarz)Bindemittel-Füller-Mischung *f*

bitumen film → asphaltic-~ ~

~ ~ (US); hydrocarbon binder ~ (Brit.) · (Schwarz)Bindemittelfilm *m*

~ **for dampproof coatings,** asphaltic-~ ~ ~ ~ (Brit.); asphalt ~ ~ ~ (US) · Mauerbitumen *n*

~ ~ **road purposes** → asphaltic-~ ~ ~ ~

~ ~ ~ ~ **with road tar addition** (Brit.) → paving asphalt ~ ~ ~ ~

~ **globule,** asphaltic-~ ~ (Brit.); asphalt ~ (US) · Bitumenkügelchen *n*

~ **grade** → asphaltic-~ ~

~ **gunite** (Brit.) → asphalt ~

~ **hardness degree,** asphaltic-bitumen ~ ~ (Brit.); asphalt ~ ~ (US) · Bitumen-Härtegrad *m*

bitumen-impregnated, bitumen-saturated, asphaltic-~ (Brit.); asphalt-saturated, asphalt-impregnated (US) · bitumengeträngt

bitumen(-impregnated) calcium silicate brick (Brit.) → asphalt(-impregnated) sand-lime ~

~ **lime-sand brick** (Brit.) → asphalt(-impregnated) sand-lime ~

~ **sand-lime brick** (Brit.) → asphalt(-impregnated) ~ ~

~ **seal(ing) rope** → asphaltic-~ ~ ~

~ **strip** → asphaltic-~ ~

bitumen impregnating → asphalt saturating

~ **impregnation** → asphalt ~

~ **individual coat** → asphaltic-~ ~ ~

~ **insulating coat** → (asphaltic-)bitumen insulation (grade) ~

~ ~ **paste** → asphaltic-~ ~ ~ ~

~ ~ **slab** → (asphaltic-)bitumen insulation(-grade) ~

~ **insulation(-grade) coat** → asphaltic-~ ~ ~

~ ~ **paste** → (asphaltic-)bitumen insulating ~

~ ~ **slab** → asphaltic-~ ~ ~

~ **(joint) pouring compound** → asphaltic-~ (~) ~ ~

~ ~ **runner** → ~ pouring rope

~ **judaicum,** Jew's pitch, Dead Sea asphalt · Judenpech *n*

bitumen-laminated, asphaltic-~ (Brit.); asphalt-laminated (US) · bitumenkaschiert

bitumen/latex emulsion → asphaltic-~ ~

bitumen layer, asphaltic-~ ~ (Brit.); asphalt ~ (US) · Bitumenlage *f*, Bitumenschicht *f*

~ **lime-sand brick** (Brit.) → asphalt(-impregnated) sand-lime ~

~ **liner** → asphaltic-~ ~

~ **lining** → asphaltic-~ ~

bitumen macadam — bituminized floor covering material

~ **macadam,** asphaltic-~ ~ (Brit.); asphalt(ic) ~ (US) · Asphaltmakadam *m*, Bitumenmakadam

~ ~ **with gravel aggregate** → gravel asphalt

~ **mortar,** asphaltic-~ ~ (Brit.); asphalt(ic) ~ (US) · Asphaltmörtel *m*, Bitumenmörtel

~ **paint** (Brit.) → bituminous ~

~ **penetration macadam,** asphaltic-~ ~ ~ (Brit.); asphalt(ic) ~ ~ (US) · Asphalttränkmakadam *m*, Bitumentränkmakadam

~ **perforated sheet(ing)** → asphaltic-~ ~ ~

~ **pouring compound** → (asphaltic-)bitumen (joint) ~ ~

~ ~ **rope,** asphaltic-~ ~ ~ (Brit.); asphalt(ic) ~ ~ (US); ~ joint runner · Bitumenstrick *m* [*Strick-Blei-Dichtung*]

~ **pre-impregnating** (Brit.) → asphalt pre-saturating

~ **pre-impregnation** (Brit.) → asphalt ~

~ **prepared roofing** → asphalt ready ~

~ **pre-saturating** (Brit.) → asphalt ~

~ **pre-saturation** (Brit.) → asphalt pre-impregnation

~ **primer** → asphaltic-~ ~

~ **product** → asphaltic-~ ~

~ **protection coat** → asphaltic-~ ~ ~

~ **protective coat** → (asphaltic-)bitumen protection ~

~ ~ **coating (material)** → asphaltic-~ ~ (~)

~ ~ **felt,** asphaltic-~ ~ ~ (Brit.); asphalt(-impregnated) ~ ~ (US), Asphaltschutzpappe *f*, Bitumenschutzpappe

~ **rag felt** → asphalt ready roofing

~ **ready roofing** → asphalt ~ ~

~ ~ ~ **with (asphaltic-)bitumen coat(ing) on both sides** (Brit.) → asphalt ready roofing with asphalt ~ ~ ~ ~

~ **roll(ed-strip) roofing** → asphaltic-~ ~ ~

~ **roof cladding** → asphaltic-~ ~ ~

~ ~ **covering** → asphaltic-~ ~ ~

~ ~ **sheathing** → asphaltic-~ ~ ~

~ **roof(ing)** → asphaltic-~ ~ ~

~ ~ **cement** → asphaltic-~ ~ ~

~ ~ **felt** → asphalt ready roofing

~ ~ **sheet(ing)** → asphaltic-~ ~ ~

bitumen-rubber composition (Brit.) → asphalt-rubber mass

~ **compound** (Brit.) → asphalt-rubber mass

~ **mass** (Brit.) → asphalt-rubber ~

~ **material** (Brit.) → asphalt-rubber mass

bitumen/rubber strip, asphaltic-bitumen/rubber ~ (Brit.); asphalt/rubber ~ (US) · Bitumen-Gummi-Streifen *m*

bitumen sand-lime brick (Brit.) → asphalt(-impregnated) ~ ~

bitumen-saturated, bitumen-impregnated, asphaltic-~, (Brit.); asphalt-saturated, asphalt-impregnated (US) · bitumengetränkt

~ **felt(ed fabric)** → asphaltic-~ ~ ~

~ **felt(ed fabric) mat** → asphalt-saturated ~ (~)

~ ~ ~ ~ **with cork** (Brit.) → asphalt-saturated ~ (~) ~ ~ ~

~ ~ ~ **pad** → asphalt-saturated felt(ed fabric) mat

~ ~ ~ ~ **with cork** (Brit.) → asphalt-saturated felt(ed fabric) mat ~ ~

~ ~ ~ **with cork** (Brit.) → asphalt-saturated ~ (~) ~ ~

~ **paper** (Brit.) → asphalt-saturated ~

bitumen saturating → asphalt saturating ~

~ **saturation** → asphalt impregnation

~ **seal(ing),** asphaltic-~ ~ (Brit.); asphalt(ic) ~ (US) · Asphalt-Absieg(e)lung *f*, Asphalt-Versieg(e)lung

~ ~ → asphaltic-~ ~

~ **sealing compound** (Brit.) → asphalt ~ ~

~ **seal(ing) paste** → asphaltic -~ ~ ~

~ ~ **sheet(ing)** → asphaltic-~ ~ ~

~ **sheet roofing,** asphaltic-~ ~ ~ (Brit.); asphalt ~ ~ (US) · Bahnen-Bitumendachpappe *f*, Bitumendachpappe in Bahnenform

~ **sheet(ing)** → asphaltic-~ ~ ~

~ **shingle** (Brit.) → asphalt ~

~ **slurry** → asphaltic-~ ~

~ **strip** → asphaltic-bitumen-impregnated ~

~ **(surface) coat(ing)** (Brit.) → asphalt (~) ~

~ **(sur)facing** → (asphaltic-)bitumen ~

~ **tape** → asphaltic-~ ~

~ **test** → asphaltic-~ ~

~ **top dressing** → asphaltic-~ ~ ~

bitumen-type wood fibre board → asphaltic-~ ~ ~ ~

bitumen waterproofer coat (Brit.) → asphaltic(ic) ~ ~

~ **wood fibreboard,** asphaltic-bitumen ~ ~ (Brit.); asphalt wood fiberboard (US) · Bitumen-Holzfaserplatte *f* [*DIN 68752*]

~ **wool felt** → asphalt ready roofing

to bituminize · bituminieren

bituminized · bituminiert

~ **cement** · bituminierter Zement *m*

~ **concrete** · bituminierter Beton *m* [*Ein Beton mit einem Zusatz von stabiler Bitumenemulsion. Der Zusatz verringert die Schwindneigung*]

~ **cord** · bituminierte Schnur *f*

~ **floor covering material** · bituminierter (Fuß)Bodenbelagstoff *m*

bituminized paper — bituminous filler

~ **paper** · bituminiertes Papier *n*

~ **rope** · bituminierter Strick *m*

bituminizing · Bituminieren *n*, Bituminierung *f*

bituminous [*Containing bitumen, or pitch or tar or a mixture of some or all of them. The word 'bituminous' is, however, also used in such terms as 'bituminous mixing plant' although such a plant does naturally not contain bitumen, or pitch, or tar or a mixture of some or all of than*] · bituminös [*Nach der von Mallison vorgeschlagenen und nach DIN 55946 festgelegten Definition ist „bituminös" die Bezeichnung für Stoffe, die Bitumen, Teer und/oder Pech in irgendeinem Prozentsatz enthalten. Bituminöse Stoffe kommen entweder in der Natur vor oder werden technisch hergestellt. „Bituminös" ist daher nicht ein dem Hauptwort „Bitumen" ausschließlich zugeordnetes Eigenschaftswort. Das Wort „bituminös" wird aber auch im weiteren Sinne in Zusammensetzungen wie „bituminöse Mischanlage" usw. verwendet obgleich natürlich diese Mischanlage kein Bitumen, Teer und/oder Pech in irgendeinem Prozentsatz enthält*]

~ **adhesive composition**, ~ ~ compound, ~ cement(ing ~) · bituminöse Kleb(e)masse *f*

~ ~ **compound**, ~ ~ composition, ~ cementing ~ · bituminöse Kleb(e)masse *f*

~ **agent** → ~ substance

(~) **binder**, hydrocarbon ~; bitumen (~) (US) [*Strictly the portion of bituminous matter completely soluble in carbon disulphide; used closely as a term for tar and asphalt (US)/(asphaltic-)bitumen (Brit.)*] · (Schwarz)Bindemittel *n*, (Schwarz)Binder *m*, bituminöses Bindemittel, bituminöser Binder

~ **bound** [*Bonded with the aid of bituminous substances*] · bituminös gebunden

~ **brush(able) compound**, ~ ~ composition · bituminöse Streichmasse *f*

~ **(building) mastic**, ~ mastic joint sealer · bituminöser (Fugen)Mastix *m*, ~ (Fugen)Kitt *m*, ~ (Ver)Füllkitt, ~ Fugen(ab)dicht(ungs)kitt, bituminöse plastische Fugen(ab)dicht(ungs)masse *f*, bituminöse plastische Fugenmasse, bituminöse plastische (Fugen)(Ver)Füllmasse, bituminöser plastischer (Fugen-)(Ver)Füller *m*

~ ~ **material** → ~ (construction(al)) ~

~ ~ **paper** · bituminöses Baupapier *n*

~ **built-up roof(ing)** · bituminöse Spachtel(dach)(ein)deckung *f*, bituminöser Spachteldachbelag *m*

~ **cement**, ~ putty [*This material is of plastic, trowelling consistency and adapted for repairing metal or composition roofing, damp-proofing the inside of masonry walls above ground, and to a limited extent for waterproofing the outside of foundation walls below ground*] · bituminöser Kitt *m*

~ **cement(ing) composition)**, ~ ~ compound, ~ adhesive ~ · bituminöse Kleb(e)masse *f*

~ ~ **compound**, ~ ~ composition, ~ adhesive ~ · bituminöse Kleb(e)masse *f*

~ **coating composition**, ~ ~ compound, ~ ~ material, ~ ~ mass, ~ finish ~, ~ (sur)facing ~ · bituminöse Beschichtungsmasse *f*, ~ Überzugmasse, bituminöser Beschichtungsstoff *m*, bituminöser Überzugstoff

~ ~ **compound**, ~ ~ composition, ~ ~ material, ~ ~ mass, ~ finish ~, ~ (sur)facing ~ · bituminöse Beschichtungsmasse *f*, ~ Überzugmasse, bituminöser Beschichtungsstoff *m*, bituminöser Überzugstoff

~ ~ **mass**, ~ ~ material, ~ ~ composition, ~ ~ compound, ~ finish ~, ~ (sur)facing ~ · bituminöse Beschichtungsmasse *f*, ~ Überzugmasse, bituminöser Beschichtungsstoff *m*, bituminöser Überzugstoff

~ ~ **material**, ~ ~ composition, ~ ~ compound, ~ ~ mass, ~ finish ~, ~ (sur)facing ~ · bituminöse Beschichtungsmasse *f*, ~ Überzugmasse, bituminöser Beschichtungsstoff *m*, bituminöser Überzugstoff

~ **composition** → ~ compound

~ ~ · bituminöse Deckmasse *f*, ~ Überzugmasse [*Zur Beschichtung von (Dach)Pappe*]

~ **compound**, ~ composition, ~ mass ~ material · bituminöse Masse *f*

~ **concrete** · bituminöser Beton *m*, Schwarzbeton, Kohlenwasserstoffbindemittelbeton

~ **(construction(al)) material**, ~ building ~, ~ structural ~ · bituminöser Baustoff *m*; bituminöses Baumaterial *n* [*Schweiz*] [*Sammelbegriff für die im Bautenschutz, der Abdichtung (Sperrung) und der Dacheindeckung verwendeten bituminösen Stoffe sowie der bituminösen Straßenbaustoffe*]

~ **dampproofing agent** · bituminöses Sperrmittel *n* [*gegen Bodenfeuchtigkeit*]

~ ~ **and waterproofing** · bituminöse (Ab)Dichtung(en) *f(pl)* für Bauwerke, Bauwerk(ab)dichtung(en) [*DIN 4031*]

~ **dispersion** · bituminöse Dispersion *f*

~ **emulsion** · bituminöse Emulsion *f*

~ **facing composition** → ~ finish ~

~ ~ **compound** → ~ finish composition

~ **felt** · Bitumenfilzpappe *f*

~ **filler** · bituminöser Füller *m*, ~ Füllstoff *m*

bituminous finish composition — bituminous protective coat 108

~ **finish composition,** ~ ~ compound, ~ ~ material, ~ ~ mass, ~ coating ~, ~ (sur)facing ~ · bituminöse Beschichtungsmasse f, ~ Überzugmasse, bituminöser Beschichtungsstoff m, bituminöser Überzugstoff

~ ~ **compound,** ~ ~ composition, ~ material, ~ ~ mass, ~ coating ~, ~ (sur)facing ~ · bituminöse Beschichtungsmasse f, ~ Überzugsmasse, bituminöser Beschichtungsstoff m, bituminöser Überzugstoff

~ ~ **mass,** ~ ~ compound, ~ ~ composition, ~ ~ material, ~ coating ~, ~ (sur)facing ~ · bituminöse Beschichtungsmasse f, ~ Überzugmasse, bituminöser Beschichtungsstoff m, bituminöser Überzugstoff

~ ~ **material,** ~ ~ composition, ~ ~ compound, ~ ~ mass, ~ coating ~, ~ (sur)facing ~ · bituminöse Beschichtungsmasse f, ~ Überzugmasse, bituminöser Beschichtungsstoff m, bituminöser Überzugstoff

~ **floor cover(ing),** ~ floor(ing) (finish) · bituminöser (Fuß)Boden(belag) m

~ **floor(ing) (finish),** ~ floor cover(ing) · bituminöser (Fuß)Boden(belag) m

~ **grout** [*A mixture of bituminous material and sand finer than 1/4 in. which, when heated, will flow into place without mechanical manipulation*] · bituminöse Schlämme f

~ **highway emulsion,** ~ road ~ · bituminöse Straßenbauemulsion f

~ ~ **material,** ~ road ~ · bituminöser Straßenbaustoff m

~ **impregnating composition** → ~ saturating ~

~ ~ **mix(ture),** ~ saturating ~ · bituminöse Imprägnier(ungs)mischung f, ~ Tränkmischung, bituminöses Tränkgemisch n, bituminöses Imprägnier-(ungs)gemisch

~ **impregnation,** ~ saturation · bituminöse Imprägnierung f, ~ Tränkung

~ **insulating board,** ~ insulation (-grade) ~ · bituminöse Isolierplatte f

~ **insulation(-grade) board,** ~ insulating ~ · bituminöse Isolierplatte f

~ **lacquer,** solvent paint [*Bituminous lacquers are composed of a bituminous base, a volatile solvent, with or without the addition of vegetable drying oils, resins, mineral fillers and pigments, and are intended to dry or set by the spontaneous evaporation of the solvent*] · gefüllterer und pigmentierter bituminöser Lack m, pigmentierter und gefüllterter ~ ~, gefüllerte und pigmentierte bituminöse Lösung f, pigmentierte und gefüllerte bituminöse Lösung

~ **limestone,** asphaltic ~ · Asphaltkalkstein m, Stinkkalkstein, bituminöser Kalkstein [*Naturasphalt mit hohem Gehalt an Mineralstoffen*]

~ ~ **powder,** asphalt(ic) ~ ~ · Asphaltpulver n [*gemahlener Asphaltkalkstein*]

~ **macadam** [*A type of highway construction in which a broken stone aggregate of relatively coarse and uniform size fragments is first spread and interlocked by compaction after which the individual stones are coated and bound together with hot bituminous cement which is applied at the surface but penetrates the layer of stone before it cools. A bituminous macadam surface course is finished off with a surface treatment of bituminous cement and cover of stone chips to seal the surface. In the construction of a bituminous macadam base the seal coat is omitted*] · bituminöser (Tränk)Makadam m

~ **marl** · Stinkmergel m

~ **mass** → ~ compound

~ **mastic** → ~ building ~

~ ~ **concrete** (US); gußasphalt · Gußasphalt m [*Ein korngestuftes Mineralgemisch, das in heißem Zustand mit Straßenbaubitumen vermischt wird*]

~ ~ ~ **surfacing** (US); gußasphalt ~ · Gußasphaltbelag m, Gußasphaltdecke f

~ ~ **joint sealer** → ~ (building) mastic

~ **material,** ~ (plant) mix(ture) [*A combination of asphalt or tar, inert materials, and impurities, distillates, or emulsifiers*] · bituminöses Gemisch n, ~ Mischgut, bituminöse Mischung f, Schwarzdeckengemisch, Schwarzdeckenmischung

~ ~ → ~ construction(al) ~

~ ~ → ~ substance

~ ~ → ~ compound

~ **matter** → ~ substance

~ **mix(ture)** → ~ material

~ **mortar** · bituminöser Mörtel m

~ **oil shale** → (asphaltic) pyrobituminous ~

~ **paint;** bitumen ~ (Brit.) [*Bituminous paints are based on (asphaltic-) bitumen (Brit.)/asphalt (US), tar or pitch*] · bituminöse (Anstrich)Farbe f

~ **(plant) mix(ture),** ~ material [*A combination of asphalt or tar, inert materials, and impurities, distillates, or emulsifiers*] · Schwarzdeckengemisch n, Schwarzdeckenmischung f, bituminöses Gemisch, bituminöse Mischung, bituminöses Mischgut n

~ **preservative for structures and buildings** · bituminöser Bautenschutzstoff m, bituminöses Bautenschutzmittel n

~ **primer** [*A liquid bituminous road material of low viscosity which upon application to a nonbituminous surface is completely absorbed. Its purpose is to waterproof the existing surface and prepare it to serve as a base for the construction of a bituminous carpet or surface course*] · bituminöses Grundiermittel n

~ **product** · bituminöses Erzeugnis n

~ **protective coat** · bituminöser Schutzanstrich m, ~ Schutzaufstrich

bituminous putty — black japan

~ **putty** → ~ cement
~ **road emulsion,** ~ highway ~ · bituminöse Straßenbauemulsion *f*
~ ~ **material,** ~ highway ~ · bituminöser Straßenbaustoff *m*
~ **rock,** asphaltic ~ [*A rock in which the impregnation is relatively low*] · Asphaltgestein *n* [*Naturasphalt mit hohem Gehalt an Mineralstoffen, z.B.* Asphaltkalkstein *und* Asphaltsand]
~ **roof(ing) felt** → asphalt ready roofing
~ ~ **sheet(ing)** · bituminöse Dachbahn *f*
~ **sand,** asphalt ~ · Asphaltsand *m*, Bitumensand [*Naturasphalt mit hohem Gehalt an Mineralstoffen*]
~ **sandstone,** asphaltic sand(stone); sand asphalt (US) · Asphaltsand(stein) *m*, bituminöser Sandstein
~ **saturant** → ~ saturating composition
~ **saturating composition,** ~ impregnating ~, ~ saturant · bituminöse Imprägnier(ungs)masse *f*, ~ Tränkmasse, bituminöses Imprägnier(ungs)mittel *n*, bituminöses Tränkmittel
~ ~ **mix(ture),** ~ impregnating ~ · bituminöse Imprägnier(ungs)mischung *f*, ~ Tränkmischung, bituminöses Tränkgemisch *n*, bituminöses Imprägnier(ungs)gemisch
~ **saturation,** ~ impregnation · bituminöse Imprägnierung *f*, ~ Tränkung
~ **sheet(ing)** · bituminöse Bahn *f*
~ **solution** · bituminöse Lösung *f*
~ **structural material** → ~ (construction(al)) ~
~ **substance,** ~ matter, ~ agent, ~ material · bituminöse Substanz *f*, bituminöser Stoff *m*, bituminöses Mittel *n*, bituminöses Material *n*
~ ~ · Bitumen *n* und verwandte Stoffe *mpl*
~ **(sur)facing composition,** ~ ~ compound, ~ ~ material, ~ ~ mass, ~ coating ~, ~ finish ~ · bituminöse Beschichtungsmasse *f*, bituminöse Überzugmasse, bituminöser Beschichtungsstoff *m*, bituminöser Überzugstoff
~ ~ **compound,** ~ ~ composition, ~ ~ material, ~ ~ mass, ~ coating ~, ~ finish ~ · bituminöse Beschichtungsmasse *f*, ~ Überzugmasse, bituminöser Beschichtungsstoff *m*, bituminöser Überzugstoff
~ ~ **mass,** ~ ~ compound, ~ ~ composition, ~ ~ material, ~ coating ~, ~ finish ~ · bituminöse Beschichtungsmasse *f*, ~ Überzugmasse, bituminöser Beschichtungsstoff *m*, bituminöser Überzugstoff
~ ~ **material,** ~ ~ composition, ~ ~ compound, ~ ~ mass, ~ coating ~, ~ finish ~ · bituminöse Beschichtungsmasse *f*, ~ Überzugmasse, bituminöser Beschichtungsstoff *m*, bituminöser Überzugstoff

~ **varnish** [*It consists of a bituminous base, a volatile solvent and animal or vegetable 'drying oil' with or without the presence of resin. It has no filler and no pigment as the bituminous lacquer*] · bituminöser Lack *m*
~ **waterproofer coat** · bituminöser Sperranstrich *m*, ~ Sperraufstrich
~ ~ ~ (Brit.) → asphalt(ic) ~ ~
~ **work** · bituminöse Arbeiten *fpl*
birane → tower ~
bi-vault, double vault · Doppelgewölbe *n*
bizarre effect · Bizarrerie *f*
blabbing, blebbing (Brit.); bubbling, blistering · Blasigwerden *n*, Blasenbildung *f*
black → ~ pigment
~ **annealed wire** · dunkel geglühter Draht *m*
~ **bar(s),** merchant ~, commercial grade steel · Handelsstahl *m*
~ **blind** → blackout ~
~ **bolt** · schwarze Schraube *f*, rohe ~
~ **copper** · Schwarzkupfer *n*
~ **core,** ~ heart [*Dark central part of a fired product resulting from inadequate oxidation*] · schwarzer Kern *m* [*Feuerfestindustrie*]
black(en)ing, blackwash, founder's blackfacing · Gießer(ei)schwärze *f*
black-figure style · schwarzfiguriger Stil *m* [*Vasenmalerei*]
~ **vase** · schwarzfigurige Vase *f*
Black Gate · Porta Nigra *f* [*Trier*]
black heart → ~ core
blacking → blackening
black iron ore, psilomelane · Psilomelan *m*, schwarzer Glaskopf *m*, Hartmanganerz *n*
~ **(~) oxid(e) (pigment),** ~ oxid(e) of iron (~), iron (oxid(e)) black (~) (US); black (iron) oxide (~), black oxide of iron (~), iron (oxide) black (~) (Brit.) [*B.S. 284*] · (Eisen)Oxidschwarz(pigment) *n*, Eisenschwarz(pigment)
blackish · schwärzlich
blackjack · bituminöse Dachreparaturmasse *f*
black jack, (zinc) blende, sphalerite; zinc sulphide (Brit.); zinc sulfide (US) · Zinkblende *f*, Sphalerit *m*, ZnS
~ **japan** [*A black material, akin to normal oil varnish, containing a drying oil and gilsonite or other asphaltic material. It dries by oxidation to a hard-glossy film in which the gilsonite may be regarded as replacing the copal resin in a normal varnish. A good black japan can be varnished over without bleeding of the gilsonite*] · Japanlack *m* [*Bezeichnung für fette Holzöl-Kombinations-Harzlacke. Hat mit japanischen Lacken nichts zu tun*]

black malleable casting — blank wall 110

~ **malleable casting** · amerikanischer Temperguß *m*, schwarzer ~, Schwarzguß

(~) **manganese** [*A black mineral, now recognized as an oxide of a metal, used in glass-making and other processes*] · Mangan *n*

blackout · Verdunkelung *f*

black(out) blind, lighttight ~, dark ~ · (Verdunkelungs)Rollo *n*, Verdunkelung(sblende) *f*

blackout building, windowless ~ · fensterloses Gebäude *n*, fensterfreies ~

~ **door**, lighttight ~, dark ~, BOD · Verdunkelungstür *f*

~ **installation**, ~ **system**, lighttight ~, dark ~ · Verdunkelung(sanlage) *f*, Verdunkelungseinrichtung *f*

~ **jalousie**, dark ~, lighttight ~, ~ louvres, ~ louvers, ~ slatted blind · Verdunkelungsjalousie *f*

~ **louvres**, dark ~, lighttight ~, ~ louvers, ~ jalousie, ~ slatted blind · Verdunkelungsjalousie *f*

~ **slatted blind**, dark ~ ~, lighttight ~ ~, ~ jalousie, ~ louvres, ~ louvers · Verdunkelungsjalousie *f*

~ **system** → ~ installation

~ **window**, lighttight ~, dark ~, BOW · Verdunkelungsfenster *n*

black oxide of cobalt (Brit.) → asbolite

~ **oxid(e) of iron (pigment)** → ~ (iron) oxid(e) (~)

~ ~ **(pigment)** → ~ iron ~ (~)

~ **paste** · Schwarzpaste *f*

~ **(pigment)** · Schwarzpigment *n*, Schwarzfarbe *f*, schwarzes Pigment, schwarze Farbe

~ **plate** · Schwarzblech *n* [*Fehlname: Eisenblech. Feinblech ohne Nachbehandlung durch Beizen, Kaltwalzen usw.*]

~ **porphyry**, melaphyre · Melaphyr *m*, schwarzer Porphyr [*DIN 52100*]

~ **sheeting felt** [*B.S. 747*] · Zwischenlage *f* [*Sie hält den Asphalt von der vollflächigen Verklebung auf waag(e)rechten Flächen frei*]

~ **speck** [*A black inclusion in glass due to chrome iron ore*] · schwarzes Steinchen *n*

~ **tin**, cassiterite, tinstone · Kassiterit *m*, Zinnstein *m*, SnO_2

~ **varnish**, asphalt(ic) ~ · Asphaltlack *m*, Asphaltlösung *f* [*Fehlnamen: Bitumenlack, Bitumenlösung*]

blackwash, black(en)ing, facing, founder's black · Gießer(ei)schwärze *f*

blade, principal (rafter), main rafter · Hauptsparren *m*, Bundsparren, Bindesparren

blades, principals, principal rafters, main rafters [*The main rafters, those in the roof truss which carry the purlin(e)s on which the common rafters are laid*] · Bindersparren *mpl*, Hauptsparren, Bundsparren, Bundgespärre *n*, Bindergespärre

blaes brick, bing ~, cliff ~, shale (clay) ~ [*B.S. 3921*] · Schiefertonziegel *m*

Blaine apparatus [*Air-permeability apparatus for measuring the surface area of a finely ground cement, raw material or other product*] · Blaine-Gerät *n*

~ **fineness** [*The fineness of powdered materials such as cement and pozzolanas, expressed as surface area usually in square centimeters per gram, determined by the Blaine apparatus*] · Blaine-(Mahl)Feinheit *f*, Blaine-Wert *m*

~ **surface area** · Oberfläche *f* nach Blaine

~ **test** [*A method for determining the fineness of cement or other fine material on the basis of the permeability to air of a sample prepared under specifed conditions*] · Blaine-Verfahren *n*

blanc fixe → precipitated barium sulphate

blank, parison [*A preliminary shape or blank from which a glass article is to be formed*] · Külbel *m*

~ · Hüttenglas *n*, Rohglas [*In der Masse gefärbte Glastafeln werden in der Glasmalerei im Gegensatz zu den bemalten und gebrannten Tafeln als Hüttenglas oder Rohglas bezeichnet*]

~ **arcade**, blind ~, wall ~, dead ~, surface ~ [*An arcade applied to a wall face for ornamental purposes*] · Blendarkade *f*, Wandarkade

(~) **cap** [*A pipe fitting fixed over the spigot end of a pipe or fitting to close it*] · Kappe *f*

~ **ceiling mounting channel** · Decken-Montageschiene *f* als Leerprofil [*Deckenleuchte*]

~ **door**, blind ~, false ~ dead ~ · Blendtür *f*, Scheintür

~ **fenestration**, blind ~, false ~ · Blindbefensterung *f*

~ **flange** [*A solid disk with bolt holes for bolting to a flange to close the outlet of a pipe, fitting or vessel*] · Blindflansch *m*, Deckelflansch, Flanschendeckel *m*

~ **masonry wall**, dead ~ ~ [*A masonry wall without openings*] · vollflächige Mauer *f*, geschlossene ~

~ **rosette**, blind ~ · Blendrosette *f*

~ **tracery** → blind ~

~ **triforium** Blendtriforium *n* [*Zwischen den vorgelegten Arkaden und der rückwärtigen Wand ist kein Raum ausgespart*]

~ **wall**, dead ~, blind ~ [*A wall without openings*] · geschlossene Wand *f*, vollflächige ~

~ **window,** blind ~, false ~ · Blendfenster *n*, blindes Fenster, Blindfenster, Scheinfenster

blanket of dry air, hermetically sealed dehydrated captive air space · Zwischenraum *m* [*Beim Thermopane-Mehrscheibenisolierglas der hermetisch abgeschlossene Zwischenraum mit getrockneter Luft mit Taupunkt −70° C gefüllt*]

blasenschiefer, amygdaloidal Zechstein dolomite · Blasenschiefer *m*

blast, sand~ · (Sand)Strahl *m*

blast-cleaned · strahlgereinigt

blast cleaning [*The cleaning and roughening of a surface by the use of natural grit or artificial (-grit) or fine metal shot – usually steel – which is projected on to a surface by compressed air or mechanical means*] · Abstrahlen *n*, Strahlreinigen, Strahlreinigung *f*

~ **fence** · Abweiserwand *f* für Turbinenabgase [*Flugplatz*]

blastfurnace coal tar · Hochofenteer *m*

~ **coal-tar pitch** · Hochofenteerpech *n*

~ **coke** · Hochofenkoks *m*

~ **flue dust** · Gichtstaub *m*

~ **lump slag** (Brit.); lump cinder (US) [*See remark under '(Hochofen-) Schlacke*'] · Hochofenstück(en)schlacke *f*

(~) **slag** → iron (~) ~

(~) ~ **aggregate** → (iron) (~) ~ ~

(~) ~ **built-up roof(ing)** → (iron) (~) ~ ~ ~

(~) ~ **chip(ping)s** → iron (~) ~ ~

(~) ~ **coarse aggregate** → (iron) (~) ~ ~ ~

(~) ~ **concrete,** iron (~) ·~ ~ (Brit.); cinder ~ (US), · (Hochofen)Schlackenbeton *m*

(~) ~ **dust** → (iron) (blastfurnace) slag filler

(~) ~ **fibre** → (iron) (~) ~'~

(~) ~ **filler** → (iron) (~) ~ ~

(~) ~ **fill(ing)** → (iron) (~) ~ ~

~ ~ **(paving) sett** → (iron) (~) ~ (~) ~

(~) ~ **sand** → (iron) (~) ~ ~ ~

(~) ~ ~ **concrete,** iron (~) ~ ~ ~, granulated (blastfurnace) slag ~ (Brit.) cinder sand ~, granulated cinder ~ (US) · Schlackensandbeton *m*, Hochofen~, Hüttensandbeton

~ ~ **sett** → (iron) (blastfurnace) slag (paving) ~

~ **trass cement,** ~ terras ~ · Traßhochofenzement *m* [*DIN 1167; DIN 1164*]

blast pressure · Explosionsdruck *m*

blast-resistant civil defense structures (US); ~ ~ defence ~ (Brit.) · Luftstoßschutzbauten *f*

blast sand, sand ~ ~ · Gebläsesand *m*

~ **wall** · Bombenschutzmauer *f*

bleached lac → ~ shellac

~ **oil** · gebleichtes Öl *n*

~ **(shel)lac,** white ~ · gebleichter Schellack *m*

bleaching · Bleichen *n*

~ **agent** · Bleichstoff *m*

~ **clay,** ~ earth, active earth · Bleicherde *f*, Bleichton *m*

~ **earth,** active ~, bleaching clay · Bleicherde *f*, Bleichton *m*

~ **powder,** chloride of lime, chlorinated lime · Chlorkalk *m*, Bleichpulver *n*, Bleichkalk, Kalziumoxychlorid *n*, CaOCl$_2$

bleb, blister · (Luft)Blase *f*

blebbing, blabbing (Brit.); bubbling, blistering · Blasigwerden *n*, Blasenbildung *f*

bleeding, bleed-through [*The process of diffusion of a 'soluble' coloured substance from, into, and through a paint or varnish coating from beneath, thus producing an undesirable staining or discoloration. Examples of 'soluble' materials which may give rise to this defect are certain types of the following classes of materials: bituminous paints, wood preservatives, pigment dyestuffs and stains*] · Durchschlag(en) *m*, (*n*), (Aus-) Bluten

~, sweating, water gain [*The separation of water from an unhardened mix(ture)*] · Abscheiden *n* von Wasser, Abscheidung *f* ~ ~, ungenügende Anmach(e)-wasserhaltung, Wasserabstoßen, Wasserabsonderung, Bluten

~ **cement** · blutender Zement *m* [*stößt Wasser ab*]

~ **rate,** sweating ~, water gain ~ [*The rate at which water is released from an unhardened mix(ture)*] · Wasserabstoßgeschwindigkeit *f*, Waserabscheidungsgeschwindigkeit, Wasserabsonderungsgeschwindigkeit

bleed-through → bleeding

blemish · Schönheitsfehler *m*

to blend, to intermix · vermischen

blendable, intermixable · vermischbar

blende → zinc ~

blended cement [*A product consisting of a mixture of portland cement and other material such as granulated blastfurnace slag, pozzolan, hydrated lime, etc., combined either during the finish grinding of the cement at the mill or by the blending of the materials after grinding*] · Mischzement *m*

blender, blending mixer, showermixer, mixer (valve), mixing valve, blending valve, bath-mixer [*B.S. 1415*] · Badbatterie *f*, Mischbatterie

blending, grading · Korngattierung *f* [*Die Mischung von Kornklassen, um ein gewünschtes Korngefüge zu erhalten*]

~, intermixing · Vermischung *f* [*als Ergebnis der Tätigkeit*]

~, intermixing · Vermischen *n* [*als Tätigkeit*]

blending — bloating clay concrete 112

~ [*Combining the contents of two or more bins, tanks or silos of raw materials or cement to adjust the analysis of the final product*] · Vergleichmäßigung *f*

~ **mixer**, showermixer, blender, mixer (valve), mixing valve, blending valve, bath-mixer [*B.S. 1415*] · Badbatterie *f*

blind · Blende *f* [*An einem Fenster gegen Sonneneinstrahlung, gegen Einblick, zur Verdunkelung und/oder als Einbruchsicherung*]

~ **alley**, cul-de-sac · Sackgasse *f*

~ **arcade**, wall ~, blank ~, dead ~, surface ~ [*An arcade applied to a wallface for ornamental purposes*] · Blendarkade *f*, Wandarkade

~ **arch** · Blendbogen *m*, Bogenblende *f*, Nischenbogen [*Mauerbogen, der flache Nischen, die nicht durch die ganze Mauerdicke hindurchgehen, überdeckt*]

~ **column**, attached ~, engaged ~ [*A column partly sunk into a wall or pier*] · eingebundene Säule *f*, engagierte ~

~ **column** → engaged ~

~ **door**, blank ~, false ~ · Blendtür *f*, Scheintür

~ **dovetail**, secret ~ · verdeckter Schwalbenschwanz *m*

blind-nailed, secret-nailed, toe-nailed · verdeckt genagelt, ~ vernagelt

blind nailing → secret-~

blind pier → engaged ~

~ ~ **capital** → engaged ~ ~

~ **rosette**, blank ~ · Blendrosette *f*

(~) **slat** · (Jalousie)Lamelle *f*, (Jalousie-)Stäbchen *n*

~ **tracery**, blank ~ [*An imitation of window tracery on a flat solid surface, e.g. on chancel screens, vaulting, wall surfaces, etc. Used in Gothic architecture*] · Blendmaßwerk *n*

~ **triforium (gallery)**, unlit ~ (~) · Blendtriforium *n*, nicht durchfenstertes Triforium, blindes Triforium, Blindtriforium

~ **vault** · Scheingewölbe *n*

~ **wall**, dead ~, blank ~ [*A wall without openings*] · geschlossene Wand *f*, vollflächige ~

~ **window**, false ~, blank ~ · Blendfenster *n*, blindes Fenster

blinding [*The filling or plugging of the openings in a screen by the material being separated*] · Verstopfen *n* [*Sieb*]

~ **concrete** · Ausgleichbeton *m*

~ ~ **course**, ~ ~ layer · Ausgleichbetonschicht *f*, Ausgleichbetonlage *f*

~ ~ **layer**, ~ ~ course · Ausgleichbetonschicht *f*, Augsleichbetonlage *f*

blister, bleb · (Luft)Blase *f*

~ [*Local separation of a layer of iron causing a protuberance on the surface, underneath which is a cavity*] · Blase *f*, Naht *f*

~ [*A large bubble within glass*] · große Blase *f*

~ **copper** · Blasenkupfer *n*

blistering, bubbling; blebbing, blabbing (Brit.) · Blasigwerden *n*, Blasenbildung *f*

bloated (Brit.); expanded · (auf)gebläht, blasig aufgetrieben

~ **clay**, bloating ~ (Brit.); expanded ~ · (auf)geblähter Ton *m*, Blähton

~ ~ **aggregate**, bloating ~ ~ (Brit.); expanded ~ ~ · Blähtonzuschlag(stoff) *m*

~ ~ **concrete** → bloating ~ ~

~ ~ ~ **solid block** → bloating ~ ~ ~ ~

~ ~ ~ ~ **tile** → bloating clay concrete solid block

~ ~ (~) **wall slab** → bloating ~ (~) ~ ~

~ ~ **wall slab** → bloating clay (concrete) ~ ~

~ **concrete aggregate**, bloating ~ ~ (Brit.); expanded ~ ~ · Bläh-(Beton)Zuschlag(stoff) *m*

~ **pe(a)rlite**, bloating ~ (Brit.); expanded ~ · Blähperlite *n*, (auf)geblähtes Perlite

~ **shale (clay)**, bloating ~ (~) (Brit.); expanded ~ (~) · (auf)geblähter Schieferton *m*, Blähschieferton

~ ~ (~) **concrete** → expanded ~ (~) ~

~ **slate**, bloating ~ (Brit.); expanded ~ · (auf)geblähter (Ton)Schiefer *m*, Bläh-(ton)schiefer

~ ~ **concrete**; bloating ~ ~ (Brit.); expanded ~ ~ · Bläh(ton)schieferbeton *m*

~ ~ **factory**, bloating ~ ~ (Brit.); expanded ~ ~ · Bläh(ton)schieferwerk *n*

bloating (Brit.); expanding, expansion · (Auf)Blähen *n*, (Auf)Blähung *f* [*Herstellung von Leichtzuschlägen*]

~ **agent** (Brit.) → expanding chemical

~ **chemical** (Brit.) → expanding ~

~ **clay**, bloated ~ (Brit.); expanded ~ · (auf)geblähter Ton *m*, Blähton

~ ~ **aggregate**, bloated ~ ~ (Brit.); expanded ~ ~ · Blähtonzuschlag(stoff) *m*

~ ~ **concrete**, bloated ~ ~ (Brit.); expanded ~ ~ · Blähtonbeton *m* [*Im Schacht oder Drehofen hergestellter Blähbeton erlangt bimsähnliche Struktur. Der Drehofenblähton erlangt durch die Art des Herstellungsverfahrens rundliche Kornformen in der bei der Betonbereitung erforderlichen Korngrößen. Die Blähbetonpatzen aus dem Schacht- oder Ringofen werden im Steinbrecher zerkleinert und durch Sieben in die erforderlichen Körnungen zerlegt. Das Maß der Aufblähung und damit die Eigenfestigkeit des Blähtons ist bis zu einem gewissen Grade regelbar*]

113 bloating clay concrete solid ... — block (of) staggered design

~ ~ ~ **solid block**, ~ ~ ~ ~ **tile**, bloated ~ ~ ~ ~ (Brit.); expanded ~ ~ ~ ~ (US) [*See remark under 'Block'*] · Blähbeton-Vollstein *m*, Blähbeton-Vollblock(stein) *m*

~ ~ ~ ~ **tile** → ~ ~ ~ ~ **block**

~ ~ **(~) wall slab**, bloated ~ (~) ~ ~ (Brit.); expanded ~ (~) ~ ~ · Blähton(beton)-Wand(bau)platte *f*

~ ~ **wall slab** → ~ ~ ~ **concrete** ~ ~

~ **concrete aggregate**, bloated ~ ~ (Brit.); expanded ~ ~ · Bläh-(Beton)Zuschlag(stoff) *m*

~ **(of the stone)**, ~ ~ ~ (clay) **body** · Blasigwerden *n* des Scherbens

~ **pe(a)rlite**, bloated ~ (Brit.); expanded ~ · Blähperlite *n*, (auf)geblähtes Perlite

~ **plant** (Brit.); expanding ~ · Blähanlage *f*

~ **shale (clay)**, bloated ~ (~) (Brit.); expanded ~ (~) · Blähschieferton *m*, (auf)geblähter Schieferton

~ ~ **(clay) concrete** → expanded ~ (~) ~

~ **slate**, bloated ~ (Brit.); expanded ~ · (auf)geblähter (Ton)Schiefer *m*, Bläh(ton)schiefer

~ ~ **concrete**, bloated ~ ~ (Brit.); expanded ~ ~ · Bläh(ton)schieferbeton *m*

~ ~ **factory**, bloated ~ ~ (Brit.); expanded ~ ~ · Bläh(ton)schieferwerk *n*

block → **building (structure)**

~ [*An area of land bounded by streets*] · Block *m* [*Städtebau*]

~ → **building** ~

~, **unit, accommodation, portion** · (Bau-)Trakt *m*, Gebäudetrakt

~ (Brit.) → ~ **of flats**

~ **adaptable to extension(s), building** ~ ~ ~ ~ · Anbaugebäude *n*, anbaubares Gebäude

~ **arch**, tile ~ [*See remark under 'Block'*] · Block(stein)bogen *m*, Steinbogen

~ **beam**, tile ~ [*A flexural member composed of blocks which are joined together by prestressing*] · Block(stein)balken(träger) *m*, Steinbalken(träger)

~ **capital**, cubic ~, bowl ~ · Würfelkapitell *n*, Würfelkapitäl

~ **chimney**, ~ **stack**, tile ~ · Steinschornstein *m*, Block(stein)schornstein

~ **chopper, squarer, scabbler, stone dresser, stone cutter** · Steinmetz *m* [*Handwerker, der Werksteine zurichtet*]

~ **column, building** ~, **house** ~ · Hausstütze *f*, Gebäudestütze

~ **complex, building** ~ · Gebäudekomplex *m*

~ **construction method**, tile ~ ~ · Blockbau(weise) *m*, (*f*), (Block)Steinbau(weise)

block-cork insulation · Korksteindämmung *f*

blocked doorway, niche containing the cult statue · Kultnische *f*

~ ~, **niche** [*A small recess in a wall, not extending to the floor*] · Nische *f*

block entrance, building ~ · Gebäudeeingang *m*

~ ~ **door, building** ~ ~ · Gebäude(eingangs)tür *f*

~ **equipment** → **building** ~

~ **extension, building** ~ · Gebäudeerweiterung *f*

~ **factory** → **(building) block plant**

~ **fire** → **building** ~

~ **format**, tile ~ [*See remark under 'Block'*] · Blockformat *n*, (Block)Steinformat

~ **frame, building** ~ · Gebäuderahmen *m*

block-in-course masonry (work) → **hammer-dressed (stone) ashlar** (~)

blocking · Aneinanderkleben *n* [*Von Leimen in Filmform wird gefordert, daß benachbarte Lagen gleichen oder verschiedenen Stoffes während der Lagerung kein unerwünschtes Aneinanderkleben unter dem Einfluß von Wärmeplastizität oder Hygroskopizität erfahren*]

block-layer · Betonsteinmaurer *m*

block laying, tile ~, **laying blocks, laying tiles** [*See remark under 'Block'*] · Vermauern *n* [*Blocksteine*]

~ **leaf**, tile ~, **leaf of blocks, leaf of tiles** · Block(stein)schale *f*, Steinschale [*Hohlwand*]

~ **line, building** ~ · Gebäudeleitung *f*

~ **lintel** → **building** ~ ~

~ **load, building** ~ · Gebäudelast *f*

~ **making**, tile ~, **forming of blocks, forming of tiles** [*See remark under 'Block'*] · Steinfertigung *f*, Steinherstellung, Block(stein)herstellung, Block(stein)fertigung

~ **masonry** → **building block masonry work**

~ ~ **wall** → **(building)** ~ ~ ~,

~ ~ ~ [*deprecated*]; **building** ~ ~ · Gebäudemauer *f*

~ ~ **(work)** → **building** ~ ~ (~)

~ **(of flats), flats, building with dwellings, multiple dwelling building** (Brit.); **apartment building, apartment house, apartment block, multifamily house, multi-family building, multi-family block, multi-family dwelling, multiple dwelling (unit building)** (US) [*A building containing more than two dwelling units (US)/dwellings (Brit.)*] · Mehrfamilien(wohn)haus *n*, Mehrfamilien(wohn)gebäude *n*

~ ~ **grouped shops** → **shopping centre**

~ ~ **large blocks**, ~ ~ ~ **tiles, building** ~ ~ ~ · Großblock(stein)gebäude *n*, Großsteingebäude

~ ~ ~ **slabs, building** ~ ~ ~ · Großplattengebäude *n*

~ ~ ~ **tiles**, ~ ~ ~ **blocks, building** ~ ~ ~ · Großblockgebäude *n*

~ ~ **staggered design, building** ~ ~ ~ · gestaffeltes Gebäude *n*

block orientation — blue carbonate of copper 114

~ **orientation,** building ~ · Gebäudelage *f*

~ **oscillation,** building ~, ~ vibration · Gebäudeschwingung *f*

blockout, recess, embrasure, cavity, pocket · Aussparung *f*

~ **box** · Aussparungskasten *m*

block parquetry floor covering → wood ~ ~ ~ ~

~ **partition (wall),** tile ~ (~) · Block(stein)trennwand *f*, Steintrennwand

~ **plant** → (building) ~ ~

~ **roof,** (building) ~ · (Gebäude)Dach *n*

~ **stack,** ~ chimney, tile ~ · Steinschornstein *m*, Block(stein)schornstein

blockstone, pitcher, hand-placed stone, hand-packed stone, hand-pitched stone, pitching stone · Setzpacklagestein *m*, Vorlagestein, Stückstein

(block) storage heater → electric (~) ~ ~

~ **strength,** tile ~ · Block(stein)festigkeit *f*, Steinfestigkeit

~ **type,** building ~ · Gebäudeart *f*

~ **vibration,** building ~, ~ oscillation · Gebäudeschwingung *f*

~ **wall** → (building) block masonry ~

block-walling → (building) block masonry (work)

block with external access galleries, (external-)balcony-access type of block · Außenganghaus *n*

~ ~ ~ ~ ~ **of the conventional type,** conventional (external-)balcony-access type of block · Außenganghaus *n* konventioneller Form, Laubenganghaus [*An einer Längsseite, meist der Nordseite des Hauses, zieht sich ein offener Gang entlang, auf dem sich die Wohnungseingangstüren öffnen und der seinerseits den Verkehrsschacht oder die beiden Verkehrsschächte erreicht*]

~ ~ **four apartments per floor** → building ~ ~ ~ ~ ~

~ ~ **one apartment per floor,** building ~ ~ ~ ~ ~ · Einspänner *m*

~ ~ ~ **wing** → single-wing(ed) building

~ ~ **two apartments per floor,** building ~ ~ ~ ~ ~ · Zweispänner *m* [*Von jedem Stockwerkpodest aus sind zwei Wohnungen zugänglich*]

blockwork, (building) block masonry (work), (building) tile masonry (work) · Steinmauerwerk *n*, Block~, Blockmauerwerk

(blood) albumen → serum albumin

(~) albumin → serum ~

(~) adhesive → (~) ~ glue

(~) glue, (~) albumen ~, serum ~ ~, dried blood ~, ~ ~ adhesive, blood glue · Blutalbuminleim *m*

~ **glue** → (~) albumin glue

bloom → sulphate ~

~ · **Vorblock** *m*, vorgewalzter Block [*Halbzeug aus Stahl, mit etwa quadratischem Querschnitt, jedoch nicht unter 115×130 mm, Längen im allgemeinen 700–4000 mm. Vorblöcke werden mit schweren Walzenstraßen zu Flachknüppeln, Breitstahl, Platinen, Knüppeln, größerem Stabstahl, Formstahl und schwerem Eisenbahn-Oberbaumaterial ausgewalzt*]

bloom(ing) · Anlaufen *n* [*Anstrichmangel*]

to blow away · hinausblasen [*z.B. eine Wand durch eine Explosion*]

blowing, air-~, air-rectification, oxidizing · Blasen *n* [*(Erdöl)Bitumen*]

~ **installation,** (air-)~ ~, air-rectification ~, oxidizing ~ · (Erdöl)Bitumenblasanlage *f*

blowlamp → soldering lamp

blown Baltic oil · geblasenes baltisches Leinöl *n*, baltisches Blasleinöl

~ **Calcutta oil** · geblasenes indisches Leinöl *n*, indisches Blasleinöl

~ **cylinder glass;** ~ sheet (US) · geblasenes Walzenglas *n*, ~ Zylinderglas

~ **linseed oil** · geblasenes Leinöl *n*, Blasleinöl

~ ~ ~ **stand oil** · Bisöl *n*, geblasenes Leinölstandöl

~ **oil** [*Vegetable oil which has been partially oxidized by blowing with a current of air whilst at an elevated temperature. The characteristics of the oil such as its increased viscosity and degree of oxidation can be controlled by the time, the temperature and the amount of air*] · geblasenes Öl *n*, Blasöl

~ **pitch** · Blaspech *n*, geblasenes Pech

~ **plate oil** · geblasenes argentinisches Leinöl *n*, argentinisches Blasleinöl

~ **sheet** (US); ~ cylinder glass · geblasenes Walzenglas *n*, ~ Zylinderglas

~ **warm air hand dryer** (Brit.); ~ ~ ~ ~ drier (US) · Händetrockner *m*

blowpipe → soldering lamp

blowtorch (US) → soldering lamp

BLT, built, constructed · gebaut

BLT-IN → built-in

blue alizarin(e) lake · Alizarinblau *n*

~ **asbestos,** Cape ~, crocidolite ~ · Blauasbest *m*, Kapasbest

~ **brick,** iron ~ · Schlackenstein *m*, Eisenklinker *m*, (künstlicher) Baustein, gebundener Baustein, Eisen-Schmelz-Verblender [*Aus kalkarmen, eisenhaltigen Tonen hergestellter Ziegel mit völlig dichtem Scherben*]

~ ~ **paving,** iron ~ ~ · Eisenklinkerpflaster *n*, Schlackensteinpflaster, Fps

~ **brittleness,** ~ shortness · Blaubrüchigkeit *f*, Blausprödigkeit

~ **carbonate of copper,** chessylite, azurite · Azurit *m*

blue gas — boasted surface

~ **gas**, water ~ [*It is manufactured gas made by passing steam over a bed of incandescent coke, forming a mix(ture) of gases consisting of hydrogen and carbon monoxide*] · Blaugas *n*, Wassergas

~ ~ **tar**, water ~ ~ · Blaugasteer *m*, Wassergasteer

blu(e)ing · Bläuung *f* [*Anstrichtechnik*]

blue-iron earth, vivianite ~ · Blaueisenerz *n*, Blauerde *f*, Vivianit *m*

blue lead, lead glance, galena · Bleiglanz *m*, Galenit *m*, PbS

~ ~ (US) · Bleigrau *n*, schwefelhaltiges Bleiweiß *n*

~ ~ **pulp**, lead glance ~, galena ~ · Bleiglanztrübe *f*, Galenittrübe *f*, PbS-Trübe

~ **lias lime** [*A hydraulic lime burnt from blue lias limestone*] · Blaukalk *m*

~ **metal** [*Australia*] · blaufarbiges gebrochenes Material *n*

Blue Mosque at Istanbul · Blaue Moschee *f* in Istanbul

blue oil, pressed distillate · blaues Öl *n*

~ **organic pigment** · blaues organisches Pigment *n*

~ **pigment** · blaues Pigment *n*, Blaupigment

~ ~ **dyestuff** · blauer Pigmentfarbstoff *m*

blueprint, BP · Blaupause *f*

blueprinting · Blaupausen *n*

blue seal · Blausiegel *m* [*flüssiges Mörtel(ab)dicht(ungs)mittel*]

~ **shortness**, ~ **brittleness** · Blaubrüchigkeit *f*, Blausprödigkeit

bluestone · Blaustein *m* [*Sandstein mit kalkigem und eisenkarbolhaltigem Bindemittel*]

blue ultramarine, ultramarine blue [*B.S. 314*] · Ultramarinblau *n*, blaues Ultramarin *n*

~ **vitriol** · $CuSO_4 \cdot 5H_2O$, Kupfervitriol *n*, Kupfer(-II)-Sulfat-Pentahydrat *n*

bluntness · Direktheit *f*

blurring · Tonverwischung *f* [*Raumakustik*]

BM, B, beam · Balken(träger) *m*

B.M., birdsmouth · Gabel(schmiege) *f*, Geißfuß *m* [*Holzverbindung*]

~, bending moment · Biegemoment *n*, Biegungsmoment [*Die Summe der Wirkungen aller angreifenden Kräfte an ihrem Hebelarm bezogen auf einen bestimmten Querschnitt*]

B.M.D. → bending(-)moment diagram

BMKR, boilermaker · Kesselhersteller *m*

board, bd., natural ~ · Brett *n*

~, sheet · Platte *f*

~ **adhesive** → ~ bonding ~

~ **(bonding) adhesive**, sheet (~) ~, ~ ~ medium, ~ cement(ing agent) · Plattenkleber *m*, Plattenkleb(e)stoff *m*, Plattenkleb(e)mittel *n*

~ ~ **agent**, ~ ~ medium, ~ (~) adhesive, sheet (~) ~, ~ cement(ing agent) · Plattenkleber *m*, Plattenkleb(e)stoff *m*, Plattenkleb(e)mittel *n*

~ ~ **medium**, ~ ~ agent, ~ (~) adhesive, sheet (~) ~, ~ cement(ing agent) · Plattenkleber *m*, Plattenkleb(e)stoff *m*, Plattenkleb(e)mittel *n*

~ **cement(ing agent)** → ~ bonding ~

~ **core**, slab ~ · Plattenkern *m*

~ **finish plaster**, gypsum ~ ~ ~ · Gipsplatten(ver)putz *m*

~ **forms**, ~ form(work), ~ shuttering · Brett(er)schalung *f*

~ **form(work)**, ~ forms, ~ shuttering · Brett(er)schalung *f*

~ **insulation**, ~ thermal ~ · Platten(wärme)dämmung *f*

~ **lath** (US) → gypsum plank

~ **of felt(ed fabric)** → felt(ed fabric) board

~ ~ **paper**, sheet ~ ~, paper sheet, paper board · Pappenplatte *f*

~ **shuttering**, ~ forms, ~ form(work) · Brett(er)schalung *f*

~ **with tubular holes**, tubular particle board, tubular chipboard [*Particle board, usually extruded, having a series of holes running lengthwise through it*] · Röhren(span)platte *f*

boarded false ceiling · hölzerne Fehldecke *f*, ~ Zwischendecke, Holzzwischendecke Zwischendecke aus Brettern, Fehldecke aus Brettern

board(ed) fence, boarding, fence of boards · Brett(er)zaun *m*, Planke *f*

~ **partition** · Brett(er)wand *f*

~ **web** · Brett(er)steg *m* [*Vollwandbinder*]

boarding, fence of boards, board(ed) fence · Brett(er)zaun *m*, Planke *f*

~ **house**, lodging ~, tourist ~, rooming ~ [*A building arranged or used for the lodging with or without meals, for compensation, of more than five and not more than twenty individuals*] · Pension *f*, Logierhaus *n*

~ **joist**, common ~, wood(en) ~, timber ~, bridging ~ [*A wood beam directly supporting a floor*] · Holzdeckenbalken *m*

board-marked, rough-shuttered, natural · schalungsrauh

~ **(concrete) finish** · Schalbrettermuster *n*

~ **finish concrete** · Schalbrettermusterbeton *m*

boards, sheets, sheeting · Platten *fpl*

to boast; to drove [*Scotland; USA*] [*To finish stone with a drove chisel*] · scharrieren

boasted surface; drove work [*Scotland; USA*] [*The grooved surface of finished (natural) stone*] · Scharrierung *f* [*Furchung der Oberfläche eines Steines*]

boaster — bolt(ed) joint 116

boaster; drove (chisel) [*Scotland; USA*] · Scharriereisen *n*

boasting; droving [*Scotland; USA*] · Scharrieren *n*

boat house · Bootshaus *n*

~ **varnish** · Bootslack *m*

bobsleigh run · Bobbahn *f*

bobwire, barbwire (US); barbed wire · Stacheldraht *m*

~ **fence,** barbwire ~ (US); barbed wire ~· Stacheldrahtzaun *m*

BOD, blackout door, lighttight door, dark door · Verdunkelungstür *f*

bodied linsed oil · eingedicktes Leinöl *n*

~ **oil** · Dicköl *n*, eingedicktes Öl [*Oberbegriff für alle Öle von künstlich erhöhter Viskosität. Dicköl umfaßt Standöle, geblasene Öle und alle nach anderen Verfahren eingedickte Öle*]

body · (Fertig)Masse *f* [*Feuerfestindustrie. Angefeuchtete verformungsbereite Rohstoffmischung*]

~, clay ~, stone · (Ton)Scherben *m*, gebrannter Scherben

~, tile ~ · Rohfliese *f*

~ → spreading rate

~ **crushing strength** → clay ~ ~ ~

bodying, thermal polymerization · Eindicken *n*

boehmite [*One of the monohydrates of alumina, $Al_2O_3 \cdot H_2O$*] · Boehmit *m*

bog water · Moorwasser *n*

Bohemian crystal (glass), potash-lime ~, potassium carbonate-lime ~ · Kalikalkglas *n*, böhmisches Kristallglas [*mit Kalk erschmolzen*]

~ **vault** · böhmische Kappe *f*

boiled linseed oil → kettle ~ ~ ~

~ **oil** · gekochtes Öl *n*

boiler, heating ~ · Heiz(ungs)kessel *m*, Kessel

~ **cock** · Kesselhahn *m*

~ **control** [*1. Input control valve; 2. 'On' and 'off' type control valve; 3. Safety shut-off valve; 4. Throttling type control*] · Kesselregelungsorgan *n*, Kesselsteuerungsorgan

~ **equipment** · Kesselausrüstung *f*

~ **feed pump,** BFP · Kesselspeisewasserpumpe *f*

~ ~ **water,** BFW · Kesselspeisewasser *n*

~ **flue** · Kesselzug *m*

~ **for domestic use,** domestic boiler · Haushalt(heiz)kessel *m*

~ **foundation** · Kesselfundament *n*

~ **fuel** · Kesselbrennstoff *m*

~ **house,** BH · Kesselhaus *n*

boilerhouse stack, heating plant ~ · Kesselhausschornstein *m*, Heizwerkschornstein

boilermaker, BMKR · Kesselhersteller *m*

boiler making · Kesselbau *m*

~ **masonry (work)** · Kesselmauerwerk *n*, Kesseleinmauerung *f*

~ **plant** · Kesselanlage *f*

~ **plate** · Kesselblech *n*

~ **pressure,** BP · Kesseldruck *m*

~ **return** · Kesselrücklauf *m*

~ **room,** BR · Kesselraum *m*

~ **sequence control** · Kesselfolgeschaltung *f*

~ **steel** · Kesselstahl *m*

~ **thermostat** · Kesselthermostat *m*

~ **tower** · Kesselturm *m*, Kesselhaus *n* in Turmform

~ **tube** · Kesselrohr *n*, Kesselröhre *f*

~ **with single steam space** · Einfachdampfraumkessel *m*, Kessel mit einem Dampfraum

boiling point · Siedepunkt *m*

~ **range** · Siedebereich *m, n*

~ **test,** soundness test by immersion in boiling water · Kochprobe *f*, Kochprüfung *f*, Kochversuch *m* [*Prüfung von Zement auf Raumbeständigkeit. DIN 1048*]

~ **water preparation** · Kochendwasserbereitung *f*

boilings [*The cinder which overflows from the puddling furnace during the boil*] · Abzugsschlacke *f*, übergeflossene Schlacke

boilproof · koch(endwasser)fest

~ **-glued** · kochfest verleimt

bole, bolus · Boluserde *f*, Bol(us) *m*

bolection (moulding) (Brit.) → balection (~)

bolster, saddle, head tree, crown plate, corbel piece [*A short timber cap over a post to increase the bearing area under a beam*] · Sattelholz *n*

bolt, screwed ~ · (Schrauben)Bolzen *m*, Gewindebolzen

~ **with handle** · Stangenverschluß *m* [*Stangenverschlüsse nennt man Baubeschläge welche das Fenster oder die Tür (z.B. Verandatüren) mit Hilfe durchgehender oder geteilter Stangen oben und unten verschließen. Meist erfolgt auch noch ein dritter Verschluß, und zwar an der Stelle wo die Bewegung ausgeführt wird*]

bolted bridle joint · Stirnversatz *m* mit Schraube [*Dach*]

bolt(ed) connection, ~ joint · Bolzenverbindung *f*

bolted connector, ~ timber ~ · Einpreßdübel *m* [*Holzdübel*]

bolt(ed) joint, ~ connection · Bolzenverbindung *f*

boltel → three-quarter (attached) column

bolting (timber) connector · Einpreßdübel *m* [*Holzdübel*]

bolus, bole · Boluserde *f*, Bol(us) *m*

bomb-damaged site · Trümmergrundstück *n*

bomb shelter, air-raid sheltering bunker · (Luft)Schutzbunker *m*, Bombenschutzbunker

~ ~, air-raid ~ · Schutzraum *m*, Luft~, Bomben~, LS-Raum

~ ~ **door,** air-raid ~ ~ · (Luft)Schutztür *f*

~ **shelter-garage,** air-raid ~ ~ · Schutzraum *m* mit Garage, Luft~ ~ ~, Bomben~ ~ ~, LS-Raum ~ ~

Bommer type helical hinge · Bommer-Band *n* [*Eigenname*]

to bond · klammern [*zwei Mauerschalen*]

~ ~ · binden [*Mauerwerk*]

~ ~ · vorblenden

~ ~, to glue · verleimen

bond, binder · Bindemittel *n* [*Feuerfestindustrie*]

~, masonry ~ · (Mauerwerk)Gefüge *n*, (Mauerwerk)Verband *m*, Mauerverband, Mauergefüge

~ → adhesion (property)

~ **area** → bond(ing) ~

~ **beam block** → (precast) (concrete) ~ ~ ~

~ ~ **tile** → (precast) (concrete) bond beam block

~ **behavior** (US) → bond(ing) ~

~ **between binder and aggregate** · Bindemittelhaftung *f*, Bindemittelverbund *m*

~ **breaker,** ~ breaking agent · Antihaftmittel *n*, Haftverhinderungsmittel

~ **breaking agent** → ~ breaker

~ **clay** · Bindeton *m*

~ **coat** → bond(ing) ~

~ **concrete** → bond(ing) ~

~ **course** → bond(ing) ~

to bond down, to cement ~, to glue ~, ~ ~ to · (ver)kleben (mit)

bonded, glued · verleimt

~ **brick arch** → gauged (clay) ~ ~

~ **(clay) brick arch** → gauged (~) ~ ~

bonded-on · aufgeklebt

~, glued-on · aufgeleimt

bonded store · Wertlager *n*

~ **with synthetic resinous material,** synthetic resin-bonded · kunstharzgeleimt

~ **wood construction,** glued ~ ~ · (Holz)Leimbau *m*

bonder, (bonding) header, bondstone [*A masonry unit which ties two or more wythes of a wall together by overlapping*] · Binder(stein) *m*, Strecker(stein), Kopfstein

~ **brick,** header ~ [*A brick which ties two or more wythes of a wall together by overlapping*] · Binder(ziegel) *m*, Strecker(ziegel)

~ **course** → (bonding) header ~

bonder(ized) steel · gebonder(isier)ter Stahl *m*

bonderizing · Bonder(isiere)n *n*

bond external plaster → bond(ing) (external) rendering

~ **(~) rendering** (Brit.) → bond(ing) (~) ~

~ **failure** → detachment

~ **finish** → bond(ing) ~

bond-improving · haftverbessernd, verbundverbessernd

bonding, cementing · (Ver)Klebung *f*

~, gripping · Haftfestigkeit *f*, Haftvermögen *n*, Haftverbund *m* [*Bewehrung an Beton*]

~, cementing · (Ver)Kleben *n*

~, gluing · (Ver)Leimen *n*

(~) **adhesive** → ~ agent

(~) ~ **based on coal tar,** ~ medium ~ ~ ~ ~, ~ agent ~ ~ ~ ~, cement(ing agent) ~ ~ ~ ~ [*B.S. 3940*] · Kleb(e)stoff *m* auf (Stein)Kohlenteerbasis, Kleber *m* ~ ~, Kleb(e)mittel *n* ~ ~

(~) ~ **for concrete** → ~ agent ~ ~

(~) ~ **for laying** → ~ agent ~ ~

~ **agent,** ~ medium, (~) adhesive, cement(ing agent) · Kleb(e)mittel *n*, Kleb(e)stoff *m*, Kleber *m*

~ ~ [*A substance applied to a suitable substrate to create a bond between a subsurface and a terrazzo topping or a succeeding plaster application*] · Haftbrückenstoff *m*

~ ~ **for concrete,** ~ medium ~ ~, (~) adhesive ~ ~ · Betonkleb(e)mittel *n*, Betonkleber *m*, Betonkleb(e)stoff *m* [*Zur Verbindung abgebundener vorgefertigter Bauteile oder Formstücke*]

~ ~ **laying,** ~ medium ~ ~, (~) adhesive ~ ~, cement(ing agent) ~ ~ · Verlegekleber *m*, Verlegekleb(e)mittel *n*, Verlegekleb(e)stoff *m*

~ **anchor,** ~ tie, adhesive ~ · Kleb(e)anker *m*

bond(ing) area · Verbundfläche *f*, Haftfläche

~ **behavior** (US) → ~ performance

bonding capacity → adhesive property

~ **cement,** adhesive ~ · Kleb(e)kitt *m*

bond(ing) coat · Haftlage *f*, Haftschicht *f* [*allgemein*]

~ ~, adhesive ~ · Kleb(e)anstrich *m*, Kleb(e)aufstrich

bonding composition → adhesive ~

bonding compound — bone oil

~ compound → (chemical) bonding system
~ ~ → adhesive composition
bond(ing) concrete · Haftbeton *m*
~ course → ~ layer
~ ~ → (~) header ~
bonding dispersion, adhesive ~ · Kleb(e)dispersion *f*
~ emulsion, adhesive ~ · Kleb(e)emulsion *f*
~ exterior plaster → ~ (external) rendering (Brit.)
bond(ing) external plaster → ~ (~) rendering (Brit.)
~ (~) rendering (Brit.); ~ stucco (US); ~ exterior plaster, ~ external plaster · (Außen)Haft(ver)putz *m*
~ failure → (film) detachment
~ finish · Haft(ver)putz *m* [*Oberbegriff für Innen- und Außenhaft(ver)putz*]
(bonding) header → bonder
(~) course, heading ~, bonder ~, bondstone ~, bonding ~, course of (bonding) headers, course of bonders, course of bondstones · Binderschicht *f*, Streckerschicht, Binderlage *f*, Streckerlage, Kopfsteinlage, Kopfsteinschicht
bond(ing) layer, ~ course [*A layer of cement mortar, usually 1/8 to 1/2 in. (3 to 13 mm) thick, which is spread on a moist and prepared, hardened concrete surface prior to placing fresh concrete*] · Haftbrücke *f*, Haftlage *f*, Haftschicht *f*
~ ~ → cementing ~
bonding medium → ~ agent
~ ~ for concrete → ~ agent ~ ~
~ ~ ~ laying → ~ agent ~ ~
bond(ing) mortar, cementing ~, adhesive ~ · Kleb(e)mörtel *m*, Haftmörtel
bonding of granules, adhesion ~ · Streumittelhaftung *f* [*Dachpappe*]
~ ~ metal(s), metal bonding · Metall(ver)klebung *f*
~ paper, cementing ~, adhesive ~ · Kleb(e)papier *n*
~ paste, adhesive ~, cementing ~ · Kleb(e)paste *f*
bond(ing) performance; ~ behavior (US); ~ behaviour (Brit.) · Haftverhalten *n*, Verbundverhalten
~ plaster [*A gypsum plaster specially formulated for application over rough concrete as a bonding coat for a subsequent gypsum plaster layer*] · Haftgipsputz *m*
bonding power → adhesive property
~ property → adhesive ~
~ quality → adhesive property
bond(ing) rendering → ~ external ~
bonding resin, adhesive ~, Kleb(e)harz *n*, Harzkleber *m*
~ rubber, adhesive ~, cementing ~ · Kleb(e)gummi *m, n*

bond(ing) strength, adhesive ~, cementing ~ · Kleb(e)festigkeit *f*
bond(ing) strength · Verbundfestigkeit *f*, Haftfestigkeit
~ stress · Haftspannung *f*, Verbundspannung
~ stucco (US) → ~ (external) rendering (Brit.)
bonding suspension, adhesive ~ · Kleb(e)suspension *f*
~ system, adhesive ~, cementing · Kleb(e)konstruktion *f*
~ ~ → chemical ~ ~
~ tape, adhesive(-backed) ~ · Klebband *n*, Kleb(e)streifen *m*
~ technique, ~ technic · Kleb(e)technik *f*
bond(ing) test · Verbundprobe *f*, Verbundprüfung *f*, Verbundversuch *m*, Haftprobe, Haftprüfung, Haftversuch
~ test · Kleb(e)prüfung *f*, Kleb(e)probe *f*, Kleb(e)versuch *m*
bonding tie → ~ anchor
bond layer → bond(ing) ~
~ length → transmission ~
~ mortar → bond(ing) ~
~ performance → bond(ing) ~
~ plaster → bond(ing) ~
~ prevention · Haftverhinderung *f*, Haftverhütung
~ principles, masonry ~ ~ · Verbandsregeln *fpl*
~ rendering (Brit.) → bond(ing) (external) ~
bondstone → bonder
~ course → (bonding) header ~
bond strength → bond(ing) ~
~ ~ · Gleitwiderstand *m* [*Der Widerstand eines in Beton eingebetteten Bewehrungsstabes gegen Herausziehen*]
~ stress, bonding ~ · Haftspannung *f*, Verbundspannung
~ stucco (US) → bond(ing) ~
~ test → bond(ing) ~
~ type, masonry ~ ~, type of (masonry) bond · (Mauer)Verbandsart *f*
to bond to, to cement ~, to glue ~, ~ ~ down · (ver)kleben (mit)
bond transfer · Haftübertragung *f*
~ type, masonry ~ ~, type of (masonry) bond · (Mauer)Verbandsart *f*
bone black (pigment) · Knochenschwarz(pigment) *n*, Beinschwarz(pigment) [*Es wird durch Verkohlen von Knochen, Klauen, Häuten und ähnlichen tierischen Abfällen unter Luftabschluß hergestellt. Nach der Trokkendestillation erfolgt die Weiterbehandlung mit Säuren, durch Auswaschen, Trocknen und nochmaliges Erhitzen*]
~ glue · Knochenleim *m*, KN
~ oil, Dippels ~ · Knochenöl *n*

bone-shaped column · knochenförmige Säule f

bone tar [*It is produced by the destructive distillation of bones*] · Knochenteer m

bone-tar pitch · Knochenteerpech n

bonnet hip (tile), ~ tile, cone(-hip) ~ · gewölbter Gratstein m, ~ Walmstein

bonus paid for extra-heavy work, ~ ~ ~ awkward ~, allowance for extra-heavy ~, allowance for awkward ~ · Erschwerniszulage f

~ **target date** · Prämientermin m

book closet · Bücher-Einbauschrank m, Bücher-Wandschrank

booking hall · Schalterhalle f [*Bahnhof*]

booklift · Bücheraufzug m

book mica, sheet ~, mica in sheets · Spaltglimmer m, Plattenglimmer [*Er wird aus Blockglimmer durch Spalten in dünne Lagen hergestellt*]

~ **repository** [*Section of library where books are stored – in contrast to the reading room*] · Büchermagazin n

~ **tower;** multi-storey library (Brit.); multi-story library (US); multi-floor library · Bücherturm m

boom, flange, chord · Flansch m, Gurt(-ung) m, (f)

~ **area** → flange ~

~ **bar** → flange member

~ **bracing** → ~ stiffening

~ **element** → flange member

~ **member** → flange ~

~ **plane** → chord ~

~ **plate,** chord ~, flange ~ · Gurt(ungs)-blech n

~ **rod** → flange member

~ **stiffening,** ~ bracing, chord ~, flange ~ · Flanschaussteifung f, Flanschversteifung, Flanschverstärkung, Gurt(ungs)aussteifung, Gurt(ungs)versteifung, Gurt(ungs)verstärkung

~ **width,** chord ~, flange ~ · Flanschbreite f, Gurt(ungs)breite

boosted water supply · Wasserversorgung f mit Druckverstärkerpumpe(n)

booster installation, ~ station · Druckerhöhungsanlage f, Druckerhöhungsstation f

~ **pump** · Druckverstärkerpumpe f, Rohrpumpe

~ **station,** ~ installation · Druckerhöhungsanlage f, Druckerhöhungsstation f

~ **transformer** · Zusatztransformator m, Saugtransformator

boot money, dirty ~ [*Additional pay to a building worker for working in difficult or unusual conditions*] · Schmutzzulage f, Schmutzgeld n

bor(ac)ic acid · Borsäure f

borate of lime · borsaurer Kalk m

borax · Borax m, Natriumborat n, borsaures Natron n, $Na_2B_4O_7$ [*Salz der Tetraborsäure*]

border · Lagerfries m [*deutscher Fußboden*]

~ [*An edging used for strength or ornamentation*] · Randeinfassung f

~ **tile** · Randfliese f, Rand(belag)platte

bore · Nennweite f, NW, (Rohr)Innendurchmesser m, lichter Durchmesser

bore-hole method (Brit.); boring hole ~ (US) [*Introducing a chemical through holes bored in the bole*] · Bohrlochimpfung f, Bohrlochverfahren n, Bohrlochmethode f [*Holz*]

borehole water supply, well ~ ~ · Brunnenwasserversorgung f

boring hole method (US) → bore-hole ~ (Brit.)

~ **work,** drilling ~ · Bohrarbeiten fpl [*DIN 18301*]

boron-loaded concrete · Boronbeton m

boron steel · Bohrstahl m

borosilicate glass · Borsilikatglas n

borrowed light, blt [*A window in an internal wall or partition*] · Innenfenster n

bosket → bosquet

bosquet, bosket · Boskett n [*An das Broderieparterre anschließender Gartenteil, der aus streng beschnittenen geometrischen oder ornamental angelegten Buchshecken besteht, in Sonderfällen auch als Irrgarten*]

boss, roof ~ [*An ornamental knob or projection covering the intersection of ribs in a vault or ceiling; often carved with foliage*] · Bosse f, Buckel m, Knauf m [*An Decken oder Gewölben, um den Schnittpunkt der Rippen zu verdecken, meist geschmückt mit plastisch gestalteten Blättern*]

~ · Buckelquader m

bossage · Boss(ag)e f, Bossierung f [*Die roh zugerichtete, daher buck(e)lige Vorderseite bzw. Ansichtsfläche eines Werksteines oder Quader(steine)s*]

bossed (on) both sides · beidseitig bossiert

~ (~) **one side (only)** · einseitig bossiert

bossing, dressing · (Blech)Bossieren n

~, rough-hewing · (Stein)Bossieren n, Bosseln n

bottle cellar · Flaschenkeller m

~ **store** · Flaschenlager n

~ **trap** [*A compact form of trap in which the division between the inlet and outlet legs is formed by a dip tube or vane within the body of the trap. The lower part of the trap is removable for access*] · Flaschen(geruch)verschluß m

bottle-washing plant · Flaschenspülanlage f, Flaschenwaschanlage

bottle(d) beer store · Flaschenbierlager n

~ **cement** [*Steel bottles contain cement under pressure. The cement is shot from the bottles through an air line to a cement bin*] · Druckflaschenzement m

bottle(d) gas — bow girder

~ gas · Flaschengas *n*
bottling · Flaschenabfüllung *f*
~ hall · Flaschenabfüllhalle *f*
~ installation, ~ plant · Flaschenabfüllanlage *f*
~ plant, ~ installation · Flaschenabfüllanlage *f*
bottom, invert [*e.g. of a sewer*] · Sohle *f*
~ bed, lower **~** · untere Lagerfläche *f*, harte **~**, unteres Lager *n*, hartes **~** [*Werkstein*]
~ boom, ~ flange, ~ chord, lower **~** · Untergurt(ung) *m*, (*f*)
~ ~ bar → lower chord **~**
~ ~ junction plate, ~ flange ~ ~, ~ chord ~ ~, lower **~ ~ ~** · Untergurtknotenblech *n*
~ ~ longitudinal bar → lower chord **~ ~**
~ chord, ~ flange, ~ boom, lower **~** · Untergurt(ung) *m*, (*f*)
~ ~ bar → lower **~ ~**
~ ~ junction plate → **~ boom ~ ~**
~ ~ longitudinal bar → lower **~ ~ ~**
~ cupola → cupola bottom
~ dome → dome(-shape)d bottom
~ (door) rail, lower (**~**) **~** · unterer Querfries *m*, unteres Querrahmenstück *n* [*Holzfüllungstür*]
~ edge · Unterkante *f*
~ fitting, ~ furniture · Nur-Kippbeschlag *m* [*Drehkippfenster*]
~ flange, ~ chord, ~ boom, lower **~** · Untergurt(ung) *m*, (*f*)
~ ~ bar → lower chord **~**
~ ~ junction plate → **~ boom ~ ~**
~ ~ longitudinal bar → lower chord **~ ~**
~ guide, lower **~** · untere Führung *f*
~ ~ track, lower **~ ~** · untere Führungsschiene *f* [*Tor*]
~ hung opening window · Kippflügelfenster *n*
~ ~ (window) casement, ~ ~ hinge(d) ~, ~ ~ pivoted sash, ~ ~ opening sash, ~ ~ opening light, ~ ~ ventilator · Kipp(fenster)flügel *m*
~ leaf · unterer Flügel *m* [*Tor*]
~ rail, lower **~ ~, ~ door ~** · unterer Querfries *m*, unteres Querrahmenstück *n* [*Holzfüllungstür*]
~ ~ ~ · Sockel *m* [*Balustrade*]
~ socket · Untermuffe *f* [*Betonrohr*]
~ stone [*Of an arch or vault resting on an impost*] · erster Stein *m* [*Über dem Kämpfer eines Bogens oder Gewölbes*]
boucharde, bush hammer, granulating hammer · Stockhammer *m*
boulder clay, stony **~** · Geschiebeton *m*

bouleuterion, council house, Greek Senate building · B(o)uleuterion *n* [*Das Rathaus einer griechischen Stadt im Altertum*]
boulevard · Prachtstraße *f*
~ restaurant · Straßen-Terrassenrestaurant *n*
boultine → three-quarter (attached) column
bound reinforcement · geflochtene Bewehrung *f*, **~** Armierung, **~** (Stahl-)Einlagen *fpl*
~ with resinous material, resin-bound · harzgebunden
~ ~ synthetic resinous material, synthetic resin-bound · kunstharzgebunden
boundary action · Randwirkung *f*
~ arch, extreme **~** · Randbogen *m*
~ beam, edge **~** · Randbalken(träger) *m*
~ concrete block · Grenzstein *m* aus Beton, Beton-Grenzstein [*DIN 487*]
~ condition, marginal **~,** fringe **~,** edge **~** · Randbedingung *f*
~ disturbance · Biegespannungszustand *m*, Randstörung *f* [*Membran(e)theorie*]
~ element, ~ member, edge **~** · Randglied *n*, Randelement *n* [*Baustatik*]
~ fence · Grundstückszaun *m*
~ force, edge **~** · Randkraft *f*
~ gable · freistehender Grenzgiebel *m*
~ integral · Randintegral *n*
~ member, ~ element, edge **~** · Randglied *n*, Randelement *n* [*Baustatik*]
~ moment · Randmoment *n*
~ separating property from the neighbouring property · Nachbargrenze *f*
~ stone · Grenzstein *m* aus Naturstein, Naturstein-Grenzstein [*DIN 284*]
~ torque moment, fringe **~ ~,** edge **~ ~,** marginal **~ ~, ~ twist(ing) ~, ~ torsion(al) ~ ~** · Randrillmoment *n*, Randverdrehungsmoment, Randverwindungsmoment
~ value · Randwert *m*
~ ~ diagram · Randwertdiagramm *n*
~ ~ problem · Randwertproblem *n*, Randwertaufgabe *f*
~ wall · Grundstücksmauer *f*
~ zone, edge **~** · Randzone *f*
Bourdon tube pressure ga(u)ge · Röhrenfedermanometer *n*
bourg [*An early medieval 'new town'*] · (Burg)Flecken *m*
bourrette · Bourrette *f* [*versponnene Seidenabfälle*]
boutel(l) → three-quarter (attached) column
BOW, blackout window, dark window, lighttight window · Verdunkelungsfenster *n*
bower · Frauengemach *n*, Kemenate *f*
bow girder · gebogener Träger *m*

bowing in the length dimension, winding ~ ~ ~ ~ · Verkrümmung f in der Länge [*Tonhohlplatte*]

bowl, pan, (water) closet ~, lavatory ~, toilet ~, WC ~, wc ~ · (Spül)Abortbecken n, Klosettbecken, (Spül)Bekken, Sitzbecken, Toilettenbecken

bowl arrangement · Beckenanordnung f

~ capital, cubic ~, block ~ · Würfelkapitell n, Würfelkapitäl

bowl-fire · Heizsonne f

bowling alley · Bowlingbahn f

~ centre (Brit.); ~ center (US); ~ hall · Bowlinghalle f

~ green · Bowling-Rasenfläche f

~ hall; ~ center (US); ~ centre (Brit.) · Bowlinghalle f

Bow's polygon, reciprocal force ~ · reziproker Kräfteplan m, Bowscher ~ [*ebenes Fachwerk*]

bowstring girder, arch(ed girder) with tie, tied arch(ed girder) · Zugband-Bogen(träger) m, Bogen(träger) mit Zugband, gekrümmter Träger mit Zugband, Stabbogen (träger)

~ roof, Belfast ~ · Holz-Bogenbinderdach n

~ (~) truss, Belfast (~) ~ [*A segmentally shaped timber roof-truss, having a curved principal rafter and a horizontal tie-beam forming the board. These two members are connected by a diagonal lattice of light wooden ties*] · gebogener Binder m, Bogenbinder aus Holz, Holz-Bogenbinder

bowtel(l) → three-quarter (attached) column

bow window, compass ~ [*A curved bay window*] · gekrümmtes Auslüchtfenster n

~ ~ [*A window of which the frame encloses a projecting curve-sided bay*] · gekrümmtes Erkerfenster n

box beam, ~ section ~, hollow(-web) ~ · Balken(träger) m mit zwei Stegen, Hohlbalken(träger), Kastenbalken(träger)

~ ~ floor, ~ section ~ ~, hollow(-web) ~ ~ · Hohlbalken(träger)decke f, Kastenbalken(träger)decke

~ construction type, box-type of construction · Kastenbauart f [*Überträgt man bei Hochhäusern den Umfangs- und Innenwänden die Ableitung aller lotrechten und waag(e)rechten Lasten, so entsteht die Kastenbauart*]

~ footing · Kastenfundament n

~ frame → cross-wall type of construction

~ girder, ~ section ~, hollow(-web) ~ · Kasten(träger) m, Hohlträger

~ gutter → box(ed) roof ~

~ lattice(d) girder · Kastengitterträger m

~ mould (Brit.); ~ mold (US) · Kastenform f

to box out [*To form an opening or pocket in concrete by a box-like form*] · aussparen

box plate girder · Blechkastenträger m, Kastenblechträger

box-ply(wood) portal (frame) · Sperrholzportalrahmen m in Kastenquerschnitt

box profile · Kastenprofil n

~ rainwater gutter → box(ed) (roof) ~

~ rib profile · Kastenrippenprofil n

~ (roof) gutter → box(ed) (~) ~

~ section · Kastenquerschnitt m

~ (~) girder, hollow(-web) ~ · Kasten(träger) m, Hohlträger

~ (~) string (Brit.); ~ (~) stringer (US) · Kasten(treppen)wange f

box-shaped column · Kastenstütze f

~ pipe, rectangular ~ · Flachrohr n, Viereckrohr, Vierkantrohr, Rechteckrohr, viereckiges Rohr, flaches Rohr, rechteckiges Rohr

~ prestressed concrete structure · kastenförmiges Spannbetonbauwerk n

box-type of construction, box construction type · Kastenbauart f [*Überträgt man bei Hochhäusern den Umfangs- und Innenwänden die Ableitung aller lotrechten und waag(e)rechten Lasten, so entsteht die Kastenbauart*[

box weight [*deprecated*] → density

box(ed) (roof) gutter, trough (~) ~, parallel (~) ~, rectangular (~) ~, ~ rainwater ~, ~ R.W. ~ [*Such a gutter is of box section with parallel sides. It may be used as a parallel parapet gutter or as a valley gutter between identical slopes of two adjacent roofs*] · Kasten(dach)rinne f, Kastenregenrinne

boxed steel column · Stahlkastenstütze f

'boxes on stilts' [*Frank Lloyd Wright's scornful description of the new architecture in the late 1920s*] · „Kästen mpl auf Stelzen"

boxing-in, pocket setting · Einbauen n, Einschachteln [*Feuerfestindustrie. Das Anordnen von Schutzsteinen, um Verdrückungen zu vermeiden*]

boxing shutter, folding ~ · Klapp(fenster)laden m, Falt(fenster)laden

boys gym(nasium) · Knabenturnhalle f

BP, boiler pressure · Kesseldruck m

~, blueprint · Blaupause f

BR, boiler room · Kesselraum m

to brace (US); to strut (Brit.) · abstreben

brace → stiffener

~, angle ~, angle tie, strut, dragon tie · Bandholz n, Kopfband n, Kopfstrebe f, (Kopf)Bug(holz) m, (n) Kopfbiege f, Strebenband(holz) n, Winkelband, Tragband

~, tie-beam · Bandbalken m

brace plate — brass strip

~ **plate**, cover ~, tie ~, stay ~, batten (~) · Schnalle f, Bindeblech n [*Bei zwei- und mehrteiligen Querschnitten werden die einzelnen Teile durch Bindebleche in ihrem gegenseitigen Abstand gehalten*]

braced, stiffened · ausgesteift, versteift, verstärkt

~ **chimney** · abgesteifter Schornstein m

bracing, stiffening, reinforcing [*The act of inserting braces into a structure*] · Absteifen n, Aussteifen, Versteifen, Verstärken

~ → stiffening

~, stiffener, brace, bracing member, stiffening member · Steife f, Versteifungsglied n, Verstärkungsglied, Aussteif-(ungs)glied

~ **angle**, stiffening ~, reinforcing ~, stiffener ~ · Aussteif(ungs)winkel m, Versteifungswinkel, Verstärkungswinkel

~ **beam** → reinforcing ~

~ **diaphragm** → reinforcing ~

~ **frame** → stiffening ~

~ **girder** → reinforcing ~

~ **iron** → stiffening ~

~ **member** → stiffener

~ **of sloping members and without verticals forming part of the system** · Strebenfachwerk n [*Fachwerk mit nur geneigten Füllungsstäben, also ohne zum System gehörige Lotrechten außer gegebenenfalls den beiden Endpfosten. Als nicht zum System gehörig zählen Lotrechte zur Halbierung der Knicklänge von Gurtstäben oder zur Ermöglichung des Anschlusses von Querträgern*]

~ **plate** → stiffening ~

~ **purlin(e)**, stiffening ~, reinforcing ~ · aussteifende Pfette f, versteifende ~, verstärkende ~

~ **rib** → reinforcing ~

~ **ring** → reinforcing ~

~ **system**, system of bracing · (Aus)Füll-(ungs)system n [*Träger*]

~ **wall** → stiffening ~

bracket, corbel, shoulder [*A flat-topped underprop which projects from a wall or pier and forms a support for a beam or architectural member above it*] · Konsole f

~ → (masonry) corbel

bracket-mounted grinder · Wandarm-Schleifmaschine f

bracket scaffold · Konsolgerüst n

brad, wire nail [*A small headless nail. B.S. 1202*] · Drahtnagel m, (Draht)Stift m

~, glazing sprig, glazier's point · Fensterstift m

braided asbestos cord covering · geklöppelte Asbestschnur f [*für Dämm- und Isolierzwecke*]

Bramah lock · Brahmaschloß n

branch → ~ line (to a building)

~, inlet, junction, pipe ~ · (Rohr)Abzweig m, (Rohr)Zulauf m

~ **box**, sealing ~ · Hausanschlußkasten m, Gebäudeanschlußkasten

~ **flue** · Zweigzug m

~ **library** · Zweigbücherei f

~ **(line) (to a building)**, ~ (~) (~ ~ house) · Gebäudeanschluß(leitung) m, (f), Hausanschluß(leitung)

~ **pipe** [*hydrant system*] · Anschlußrohr n

~ ~, take-off ~ · Verzweigungsrohr n, Abgangsrohr, Abzweigrohr [*In Rohrleitung eingebautes Formstück um Durchflußmenge selbsttätig auf zwei Stränge unter verschiedenen Winkeln zu verteilen oder Seitenzufluß aufzunehmen*]

~ **steam line** · Dampfzweigleitung f

~ **switch** → wiring ~

~ **to a building**, ~ ~ ~ house · Gebäudeanschluß m, Hausanschluß

branching point · Verzweigungspunkt m

brand name, proprietary ~ · Markenbezeichnung f, Markenname m

~ **of cement**, cement brand · Zementmarke f

Brandenburg Gate · Brandenburger Tor n

to brass, ~ coat with ~, to brass plate · vermessingen

brass · Messing n [*DIN 17660*]

~ **and bronze** · Buntmetall n

~ **bar** · Messingstab m

~ **channel (section)** · Messing-U-Profil n

(~) **dish**, cup · Schale f [*Fließgrenzengerät nach A. Casagrande*]

~ **divider strip** · Messing-Terrazzostreifen m, Messing-Terrazzo(trenn)schiene f

~ **dowel** · Messingdübel m

~ **drift** · Messingdorn m

~ **extrusion** → extruded brass section

~ **fitting**, ~ furniture · Messing(bau)beschlag m

~ **fittings**, ~ hardware · Messing(bau)-beschläge mpl

~ **furniture**, ~ fitting · Messing(bau)beschlag m

~ **glazing** · Messingverglasung f, Messingeinglasung

~ **hardware**, ~ fittings · Messing(bau)-beschläge mpl

~ **hinge** · Messingband n [*Baubeschlag*]

~ **pipe** · Messingrohr n

to brass plate, to (coat with) brass · vermessingen

brass right-angled valve · Messing-Eckventil n

~ **sheet** · Messingblech n

~ **solder** · Messinglot n

~ **strip** · Messingband n

~ ~ · Messingstreifen m

brass tube — breast

~ **tube** · Messingröhre *f*
brass-ware · Gelbguß *m*
~ **wire** · Messingdraht *m*
~ **(~) rod** · Messingwalzdraht *m*
~ **with 72% to 90% copper content** · Tombak *m* [*Hochkupferhaltiges Messing mit 72% bis 90% Cu*]
~ ~ **67% copper content** · Halbtombak *m*, MS 67, Ms 67, Lötmessing *n*, Messing 67
~ ~ **63% copper content** · Druckmessing *n*, MS 63, Ms 63, Messing 63
brattice [*A projecting wood(en) gallery*] · vorkragender Holzgang *m* [*historischer Festungsbau*]
~, **timber tower, wood(en) tower** · Holzturm *m* [*historischer Festungsbau*]
brazed, hard soldered · hartgelötet
~ **joint, hard soldered** ~ [*A gas-tight joint obtained by the joining of metal parts and metallic alloys which melt at temperatures higher than 1,000 degrees Fahrenheit as determined in an approved manner*] · Hartlötverbindung *f*
Brazilian test, indirect tensile ~, splitting tensile ~, diametral compression ~ · Spaltzugversuch *m*, Spaltzugprobe *f*, Spaltzugprüfung *f*
brazing, hard soldering · Hartlötung *f*
~, **hard soldering** · Hartlöten *n*
~ **alloy, brazing solder, hard solder** · Schlaglot *n*, Strenglot, Hartlot [*Es wird verwendet, wenn neben Abdichtung noch Festigkeit verlangt wird. Die Schmelzpunkte der Hartlote liegen mindestens 50 grd. unterhalb des niedrigsten Schmelzpunktes der Metallteile und oberhalb von rund 600° C*]
~ **flap** · Lötlappen *m*
~ **socket** · Lötstutzen *m*
~ **solder, alloy, brazing solder, hard solder** · Schlaglot *n*, Strenglot, Hartlot [*Es wird verwendet, wenn neben Abdichtung noch Festigkeit verlangt wird. Die Schmelzpunkte der Hartlote liegen mindestens 50 grd. unterhalb des niedrigsten Schmelzpunktes der Metallteile und oberhalb von rund 600° C*]
~ **tongs** → soldering ~
to break · brechen, zerfallen [*Emulsion*]
~ ~ **down**, to carve up [*surface*] auflösen, zerklüften [*Fläche*]
~ ~ ~ **by grinding** · zermahlen
breakdown, carving-up [*surface*] · Auflösung *f*, Zerklüftung [*Fläche*]
~, **breaking** · Brechen *n*, Zerfall *m* [*Emulsion*]
~, **chemical** ~ · Zersetzung *f*
~ **of paint system** · Seuche *f*
to break open · aufbrechen [*Straße*]
~ ~ **through** · durchbrechen
breakage · Bruchverlust *m*
breaker dust, crushed ~ · Brechmehl *n*
breakfast kitchen · Frühstücksküche *f*

~ **nook** · Frühstücksnische *f*
~ **room** · Frühstücksstube *f*
~ ~ · Frühstücksraum *m* [*Hotel*]
breaking, breakdown · Brechen *n*, Zerfall *m* [*Emulsion*]
~, **rupture, failure** · Bruch *m*
~ **bending moment**, ultimate ~ ~, rupture ~ ~ · Bruchbiegemoment *n*, Bruchbiegungsmoment
~ **condition**, ultimate ~, rupture ~ · Bruchbedingung *f*
~ **cross-section**, failure ~, rupture ~ · Bruchquerschnitt *m*
~ **elongation**, rupturing ~, elongation at fracture, elongation at rupture · Bruchdehnung *f*
~ **in buckling** → failure ~ ~
~ **joints** [*The arrangement of masonry units so as to prevent continuous vertical joints in adjacent courses*] · Fugenversatz *m*
~ **load**, ultimate ~, rupture ~ · Bruchlast *f*
~ **loading**, ultimate ~, rupture ~, limit ~ · Bruchbelastung *f*, Grenzbelastung
~ **out cut**, auxiliary ~ · Hilfsschnitt *m* [*Schneiden von Flachglas*]
~ **point**, brittle ~, shatter ~ · Starrpunkt *m*, Brechpunkt [*Temperatur bituminöser Stoffe, bei der die Plastizität verschwindet und die Probe bei Biegebeanspruchung bricht. DIN 1995 – U 6*]
~ **strength**, ultimate ~, final ~, rupture ~ · Bruchfestigkeit *f*, Endfestigkeit, Endwiderstand *m*, Bruchwiderstand
~ **stress**, ultimate ~, rupture ~ · Bruchspannung *f*
~ ~ **condition**, ultimate ~ ~, rupture ~ ~ · Bruchspannungsbedingung *f*
~ **test**, crushing ~ · Brechprobe *f*, Brechprüfung *f*, Brechversuch *m*
~ ~, failure ~, rupture ~ · Bruchprüfung *f*, Bruchversuch *m*, Bruchprobe *f*
~ **time test of Caroselli** [*asphalt emulsion (US)*] · Brechbarkeitsprüfung *f* nach Caroselli
~ ~ ~ ~ **Weber and Bechler** [*bitumen emulsion (Brit.)*] · Zerfallswert-Bestimmung *f* nach Weber und Bechler
~ ~ ~ **with chip(ping)s** [*asphalt emulsion (US)*] · Brechbarkeitsprüfung *f* mit Splitt
breaking-up of light into facets · Facettierung *f* des Lichtes
breaking zone, failure ~, rupture ~ · Bruchzone *f*
breakproof, fracture-proof, rupture-proof · bruchsicher
breakthrough pitting · Lochfraß *m*
break-up · Zerfall *m* [*Farbanstrich*]
breast → (under-)window spandrel
~, **chimney** ~ [*A part of a chimney which projects from the surface of an adjoining wall*] · Kaminvorsprung *m*

breastboard — brick coursing module 124

breastboard · Verzugsbrett *n*
breast facing → spandrel (wall) (sur)facing
~ **high** · brusthoch
~ **lining** → spandrel (wall) (sur)facing
~ **panel** → (under-)window spandrel ~
~ **rail** → (window) sill ~
~-**summer** → summer beam
breast (sur)facing → spandrel (wall)

breathability · Atmungsaktivität *f*
'**breather-type**' **asphalt emulsion** (US); ~ (asphaltic-)bitumen — (Brit.) · atmungsaktive Bitumenemulsion *f*, atmungsfähige ~
breather type building paper [*B. S. 4016*] · atmendes Baupapier *n*
breathing · Atmen *n*
~ **capability**, ~ property, ~ power, ~ quality · Atmungsfähigkeit *f*, Atmungseigenschaft *f*, Atmungsvermögen *n*
~ **power** → ~ capability
~ **property** → ~ capability
~ **quality** → ~ capability
~ **(type) film**, ~ (~) membrane, ~ (~) skin · atmungsaktive Membran(e) *f*, ~ Haut *f*, atmungsfähige ~, atmungsfähiger Film *m*, atmungsaktiver Film

breech, double junction · Gabel *f* [*Rohrformstück*]
~ **fitting** → breeches
breech(es) fitting, breeching ~ [*A symmetrical pipe fitting in which two parallel pipes unite into one pipe. The flow may be in either direction according to the purpose for which the fitting is used*] · Hosenstück *n*
breeching · (Kessel)Abzugskrümmer *m* ~, main flue, up-take (US); flue connection to stack, flue connection to chimney · (Schornstein)Fuchs(kanal) *m* [*Waag(e)rechter oder mit leichter Steigung von der Heizanlage zum Schornstein führender Rauchkanal*]
~ **fitting** → breech(es)
breeze [*misnomer*] → (furnace) clinker
breeze → coke ~
~ **aggregate for concrete** [*misnomer*] → (furnace) clinker ~ ~ ~
Bremen blue [*Copper hydroxid(e) with copper carbonate*] · Bremerblau *n*
bressumer → summer beam
bretexed → battlemented
brick → (burnt) (clay) ~
~, masonry ~ · (gebrannter) Mauer(werk)stein *m*, Mauer(werk)ziegel *m* [*DIN 105. „Backstein" ist eine historische und volkstümliche Bezeichnung*]
~ **aggregate** → clay ~ ~
~ **aggregate concrete**, clay ~ ~ ~ · Ziegelbeton *m* [*Leichtbeton aus Ziegelbruch und Zement*]

~ ~ ~ **block**, ~ ~ ~ tile, clay ~ ~ ~ ~ [*See remark under 'Block'*] · Ziegelbetonblock(stein) *m*, Ziegelbetonstein [*DIN 4161*]
~ ~ ~ **tile**, ~ ~ ~ block, clay ~ ~ ~ ~ [*See remark under 'Block'*] · Ziegelbetonblock(stein) *m*, Ziegelbetonstein [*DIN 4161*]
brick-and-block cavity wall, brick-and-tile ~ ~ ~ · Ziegel-(Block)Stein-Hohlmauer *f*, Ziegel-Block-Hohlmauer
brick arch, brickwork ~, arch of brickwork · Ziegelbogen *m*
~ **architecture**, clay ~ ~ · Backsteinarchitektur *f*, Backsteinbaukunst *f*, Ziegelarchitektur, Ziegelbaukunst
~ **axe** → bricklayer's hammer
~ **backing** · Ziegelhintermauerung *f*
~ **barrel vault** → clay ~ ~ ~
~ **base** → brickwork single ~
~ **beam**, clay ~ ~ · Ziegelbalken(träger) *m* [*Lochziegel, zu Balken werkmäßig mit Mörtel verbunden*]
~ **bed joint**, ~ horizontal ~, ~ course ~ · Ziegellagerfuge *f*
brickblock, clay ~ [*A brickblock has a patterned face to simulate bonded brickwork*] · Ziegelblock *m*
brick bond → (clay) brick (masonry) ~
~ **bonder** → (clay) brick header
~ **bonding header** → (clay) brick ~
~ **bondstone** → (clay) brick header
~ **boundary wall** → clay ~ ~ ~
~ **bridge** · Ziegelmauerwerkfeuerbrücke *f* [*Teil einer Feuerung*]
brick-builder · Ziegelbauer *m*
brick building → clay ~ ~
brick-built, bricky [*built of brick*] · ziegelgemauert
~ **castle**, brickwork ~ · Ziegelschloß *n*
~ **garage** → clay ~ ~
brick burning, clay ~ ~ · Ziegelbrennen *n*, Ziegelbrand *m*
~ **carcase** [*deprecated*] → clay ~ ~ [*deprecated*]
~ **cathedral** → (clay) brick dome
~ **cavity wall** → clay ~ ~ ~
~ **chimney**, clay ~ ~ · Ziegelschornstein *m*
~ **church**, clay ~ ~ · Backsteinkirche *f*, Ziegelkirche
~ **cill** (Brit.) → brick window ~
~ **clay** → building-brick ~
~ **construction**, clay ~ ~ · Backsteinbau *m*, Ziegelbau
~ **corbel**, clay ~ ~ · Ziegel(ge)sims *m*, (*n*)
~ **course** → clay ~ ~ ~
~ ~ **joint**, ~ bed ~, ~ horizontal ~ · Ziegellagerfuge *f*
~ **coursing module**, clay ~ ~ ~ · Ziegelschichtmodul *m*

brick cradle vault — brick mound

~ **cradle vault** → clay ~ ~ ~

~ **cross-wall** → clay brick ~

~ **cube for compression test** · Probewürfel *m* für Druckprobe, ~ ~ Druckprüfung, ~ ~ Druckversuch [*Mauerziegel. DIN 105*]

~ **cupola**, ~ dome, clay ~ ~ · Ziegelkuppel *f*

~ **cut across** · Teilstein *m* des NF, ~ ~ Normalformats, Teilziegel *m* [*1/4-Stein; 1/2-Stein; 3/4-Stein*]

(~) **cutting wire** · (Ziegel)Abschneide(r)draht *m*

~ **dimension**, clay ~ ~ · Ziegelabmessung *f*, Ziegelmaß *n*

~ **dome**, ~ cupola, clay ~ ~ · Ziegelkuppel *f*

~ **dust** → clay ~ ~

~ **dwelling** (US) → clay ~ ~

~ **engineering** → clay ~ ~

~ **exterior wall**, ~ external ~, clay ~ ~ ~ · Ziegelumfassungsmauer *f*, Ziegelaußenmauer

~ **external wall**, ~ exterior ~, clay ~ ~ · Ziegelumfassungsmauer *f*, Ziegelaußenmauer

~ **fabric** → clay ~ ~

~ **façade**, clay ~ ~ · Ziegelfassade *f*

~ ~ **panel** → clay ~ ~ ~

brick-faced concrete window panel · ziegelverkleidete Fenstertafel *f* aus Beton

brick facing, ~ sur~, ~ lining, clay ~ · Ziegelauskleidung *f*, Ziegelverkleidung, Ziegelbekleidung

~ ~ **skin**, (clay) brick veneer [*A facing of brick laid against frame or tile wall construction*] · Ziegelverblendmauerwerk *n*, Ziegelverblendung *f*, Ziegelvorhangwand *f*

brick-field, brickwork, brick work, brickyard · Ziegelei *f*, Ziegelfabrik *f*, Ziegelwerk *n*

brick fireplace → clay brickwork ~

~ **floor** → clay ~ ~

~ ~ **cover(ing)**, clay ~ ~ ~, (clay) brick floor(ing) (finish) · Ziegel(fuß)-boden(belag) *m*

~ **floor(ing) (finish)**, clay ~ ~ (~), (clay) brick floor cover(ing) · Ziegel(fuß)boden(belag) *m*

~ **flour** → clay ~ ~

~ **footing** → clay ~ ~

~ **for chimney shafts** → masonry ~ ~ ~ ~

~ ~ **foundations** · Fundament(ierungs)-ziegel *m*, Gründungsziegel

~ **format**, clay ~ ~ · Ziegelformat *n*

~ **fortress church** · Backstein-Festungskirche *f*

~ **foundation** → clay ~ ~

brick gable → brickwork ~

brick grille → clay ~ ~

~ **hardcore**, clay ~ ~ · Kleinschlag *m* aus Ziegelbrocken, Ziegelschotter *m*, Ziegelbruch *m*

~ ~ **concrete**, clay ~ ~ ~ · Ziegelbruchbeton *m*, Ziegelschotterbeton

~ **header** → clay ~ ~

~ **hollow wall** → clay ~ ~ ~

~ **horizontal joint**, ~ bed ~, ~ course ~ · Ziegellagerfuge *f*

~ **individual base** → brickwork ~ ~

~ **infill masonry (work)**, clay ~ ~ ~ (~) · Ziegelausmauerung *f*

bricking, (clay) brick laying, laying (clay) bricks · Ziegelmauern *n*, Mauern mit Ziegeln, Vermauern von Ziegeln

brick insert → brickwork ~

~ **joint** → clay ~ ~

~ **kiln**, clay ~ ~ · Ziegel(brenn)ofen *m*

bricklayer; (brick) mason (US) · Maurer *m*, Ziegel~

~ **charge hand** · Maurerpolier *m*

bricklayer's hammer, brick axe (Brit.); ax(hammer) (US) · Maurerhammer *m* [*DIN 5108*]

~ **line** · Fluchtschnur *f*, Maurerschnur

~ **scaffold(ing)** · Maurergerüst *n*, Maurerrüstung *f*

~ **tool** · Maurerwerkzeug *n*

brick laying → bricking

bricklaying craft, handicraft of the bricklayer · Maurerhandwerk *n*

brick lightweight vault → clay ~ ~

brick-lined concrete slab, clay ~ ~ ~ · Ziegelbetonplatte *f* [*mit Ziegeln verblendete Betonplatte*]

brick lining, ~ (sur)facing, clay ~ ~ · Ziegelauskleidung *f*, Ziegelverkleidung, Ziegelbekleidung

~ ~ · Ziegelfutter *n* [*Schornstein*]

~ **lintel** → clay ~ ~

~ **lintol** [*deprecated*] → clay ~ ~ [*deprecated*]

brickmaker · Ziegelhersteller *m*

brickmaking, manufacture of bricks · Ziegelherstellung *f*

brick manhole, ~ manway · Ziegel-Einsteigschacht *m*, Ziegel-Mannloch *n*, Ziegel-(Einstieg)Schacht

~ **manway**, ~ manhole · Ziegel-Einsteigschacht *m*, Ziegel-Mannloch *n*, Ziegel-(Einstieg)Schacht

(~) **mason** (US); bricklayer · Maurer *m*

~ **(masonry) bond** → clay ~ (~) ~

~ ~ **(work)** → clay ~ ~ (~)

~ **mastaba** → clay ~ ~

~ **mortar** → clay brickwork ~

~ **mould** (Brit.); ~ mold (US) · Ziegelform *f*

~ **mound** → brickwork ~

brick nogging — to bridge

~ nogging, bricknogging [*Brickwork infilling between the studs of a wooden framed partition or building frame*] · Ziegelausfachung *f*, Ziegelausfüllung

brick-on-edge course → clay ~ ~

~ invert(ed) arch · Grundbogen *m* aus Ziegelrollschicht

brick (ornamental) string (course) · Ziegelgurt(ge)sims *m*, (*n*)

~ pack → clay ~ ~

~ panel · Ziegeltafel *f*

~ ~ (building) unit → clay ~ ~ (~) ~

~ partition (wall) → clay ~ ~ (~)

~ pattern, clay ~ ~ · Ziegelmauer(werk)muster *n*

~-paved road · Ziegelpflasterstraße *f*

~ paving, clay ~ ~ · Fpz *n*, Ziegelpflaster *n*

~ pier → brickwork ~

~ plinth → clay ~ ~

~ pointed arch → brickwork ~ ~

~ red [*A yellowish or brownish red*] · Ziegelrot *n*

~-red, bricky · ziegelrot

brick reinforcement fabric → clay ~ ~ ~

~ relieving arch · Ziegelentlastungsbogen *m*

~ rib, clay ~ ~ · Backsteinrippe *f*, Ziegelrippe

~ rubble → clay ~ ~

~ sewer · Ziegel(mauerwerk)-Abwasserkanal *m*

~ shaft → clay ~ ~

~ shape, clay ~ ~ · Ziegelform *f*, Ziegelgestalt *f*

~ shell [*Canada*] → clay ~ ~

~ sill → ~ window ~

~ size · Ziegelgröße *f*

~ skin → clay ~ ~

~ stair(case) → clay ~ ~

~ step → clay ~ ~

~ strength, clay ~ ~ · Ziegelfestigkeit *f*

~ string (course) → ~ ornamental ~ (~)

~ structure, clay ~ ~ · Ziegelbau(werk) *m*, (*n*)

~ structures, clay ~ ~ · Ziegelbauten *f*

~ (sur)facing, ~ lining, clay ~ ~ · Ziegelauskleidung *f*, Ziegelverkleidung, Ziegelbekleidung

~ system building → (clay) brick(work) ~ ~

~ tester → clay ~ ~

~ testing machine → clay ~ ~ ~

~ tracery → clay ~ ~

~ trowel · Maurerkelle *f*

~ tunnel vault → clay ~ ~ ~

~ type, clay ~ ~, type of (clay) brick · Ziegelart *f*

to brick up · (auf)mauern [*mit Ziegeln*]

brick vault, clay ~ ~ · gekurvte Ziegeldecke *f*, Ziegelgewölbe *n*, Gewölbe aus Ziegelmauerwerk

~ veneer → clay ~ ~

~ wagon vault → clay ~ ~ ~

~ wall, clay ~ ~ · Ziegelmauer *f* [*Fehlnamen: (gemauerte) Ziegelwand f*]

~ ~ arch → clay ~ ~ ~

~ weight → clay ~ ~

~ wheel window → clay ~ ~ ~

~ (window) cill (Brit.); ~ (~) sill · Ziegelsohlbank *f*, Ziegelfenstersohlbank, Ziegelfensterbank

~ with vertical coring type A, clay ~ ~ ~ ~ ~ ~ ~ · HLzA *m*, Hochlochziegel *m* (mit der Lochung) A

~ ~ ~ ~ ~ B, clay ~ ~ ~ ~ ~ ~ ~ · HLzB *m*, Hochlochziegel *m* (mit der Lochung) B

brickwork, brick work, brickyard, brickfield · Ziegelei *f*, Ziegelfabrik *f*, Ziegelwerk *n*

~ → clay ~

brick(work) arch, arch of brickwork · Ziegelbogen *m*

~ base → ~ single ~

~ bond → (clay) brick (masonry) ~

~ castle, brick-built ~ · Ziegelschloß *n*

~ fireplace, clay ~ ~ · Ziegel(mauerwerk)kamin *m*

~ gable · Ziegelgiebel *m*, Backsteingiebel

~ individual base, ~ (single) ~ · Sockelgründung *f* in Ziegelmauerwerk

~ insert · Ziegelmauerwerkdübel *m*

~ mortar → clay ~ ~

~ mound · Ziegelhügel *m*

~ pier, pier of brickwork · Ziegelpfeiler *m*

~ pointed arch, pointed arch of brickwork · Ziegelspitzbogen *m*

~ reinforcement → clay ~ ~

~ system building → prefab(ricated) (clay) brickwork construction

~ (single) base, ~ individual ~ · Sockelgründung *f* in Ziegelmauerwerk

bricky [*like a brick, especially in colo(u)r*] · ziegelähnlich

~, brick-built [*built of brick*] · ziegelgemauert

~ [*made of brick*] · ziegelgefertigt

~, brick-red · ziegelrot

brickyard, brick-field, brickwork, brick work · Ziegelei *f*, Ziegelfabrik *f*, Ziegelwerk *n*

bride-door · Brauttür *f* [*Seitenportal an der Nordseite einiger gotischer Kirchen; vor ihr wurde die Trauung vollzogen. Die Brauttür ist oft mit den biblischen Figuren der Klugen und Törichten Jungfrauen geschmückt, die den Bräutigam erwarten*]

to bridge · überbrücken

bridge art · Brückenbaukunst f
~ board · Holzsattelwange f
~ ~ stair(case) → cut-string ~
bridge-chapel · Brückenkapelle f
Bridge of Sighs · Seufzerbrücke f [Venedig]
bridge (paving) sett · Brückenstein m [Besonders niedriger Großpflasterstein]
~ sett, ~ paving · Brückenstein m [Besonders niedriger Großpflasterstein]
~ statue · Brückenstatue f
~ steel · Brücken(bau)stahl m
~ tower · Brückenturm m
bridging, crack ~ · (Riß)Überbrückung f
bright, light · hell
~ annealed wire · blank geglühter Draht m, Blankdraht
~ annealing · Blankglühen n
bright-annealing furnace · Blankglühofen m
bright etching, clear ~ · Hellätzen n, Klarätzen, Blankätzen [Ein Glasätzverfahren, bei dem mit verhältnismäßig schwacher Flußsäure und Grobkorn mattiert wird]
~ ~ bath, clear ~ ~ · Hellbad n [Glasätzen]
~ gold · Glanzgold n
~ ochre (Brit.); **~ ocher** (US) · Hellocker m
~ pickling · Auffrischung f
~ silver · Glanzsilber n
~ soft wire · blankweicher Draht m
~ steel, cold drawn ~ · kaltgezogener Stahl m, Blankstahl
brightly lighted · hell erleuchtet
brightness · Helligkeit f
~ degree, degree of brightness · Helligkeitsgrad m
~ of daylight · Tageslichthelligkeit f
~ ~ sky · Himmelshelligkeit f
brimstone, burning stone, sulfur (US); **sulphur** (Brit.) · Schwefel m
brindled brick [A brick which has a striped surface and is therefore unsuitable for facing but is otherwise perfect] · gestreifter Ziegel m, scheckiger ~, gescheckter ~
Brinell hardness, BH · Brinellhärte f, Metalldruckhärte, Druckhärte von Metallen, HB
~ ~ number, B. H. N. · Brinell-Härtezahl f
~ (~) test · Brinell(härte)prüfung f, Brinell(härte)versuch m, Brinell(härte)probe f, Kugeldruckprüfung nach Brinell, Kugeldruckversuch nach Brinell, Kugeldruckprobe nach Brinell [DIN 50351]
~ (~) testing machine, ~ (~) tester · Brinellpresse f, Brinellsche Kugeldruckpresse

~ test, ~ hardness ~ · Brinell(härte)prüfung f, Brinell(härte)versuch m, Brinell(härte)probe f, Kugeldruckprüfung nach Brinell, Kugeldruckversuch nach Brinell, Kugeldruckprobe nach Brinell [DIN 50351]
bringing up, carrying ~ [The erection of brick or stone walls to a specified level] · (Auf)Mauern n
briquette [Normally understood to mean a tensile test specimen as referred to in, e. g., B. S. 12] · Zugprobekörper m
Britannia metal · Britanniametall n
British gum → starch
~ ~ glue → starch ~ ~
~ Standard Section [There are joist, channel, angle and tee sections] · britisches Normal(walz)profil n
brittle film · spröder Film m
~ fracture · Sprödbruch m
~ material · spröder Werkstoff m
~ point, breaking ~, shatter ~ · Starrpunkt m, Brechpunkt [Temperatur bituminöser Stoffe, bei der die Plastizität verschwindet und die Probe bei Biegebeanspruchung bricht. DIN 1995 – U 6]
~ rock · spröder Fels m, sprödes Gestein n
brittleness · Sprödigkeit f, Sprödheit
broach, steeple, spire · Spitz(kirch)turm m
~ post · Hahnebaum m, Helmstange f, Kaiserstiel m [Mittlere Stuhlsäule eines Zelt- oder Helmdaches]
~ ~, king ~, crown ~; joggle ~ (US) [of a king post truss] · Hängesäule f
broad aisle (US) · Mittelgang m [Kirche]
broadcasting room, ~ studio · (Rundfunk)Senderaum m, Rundfunkstudio n
broad-flange(d), wide-flange(d) · breitflanschig
~ beam, ~ girder, B. F. B. [B. S. 2566]; **wide-flange(d) beam, wide-flange(d) girder** (US); **girder beam** · breitflanschiger Doppel-T-Stahl m, Breitflanschprofil n, Breitflanschträger m [DIN 1025]
broad tool, batting ~ [A mason's chisel 3 to 4½ in. wide for surfacing sandstones] · Schlageisen n für Sandsteinbearbeitung
~ tooling, droving, batting, angle dunting · Schlaganarbeiten n [Werksteinbearbeitung]
~ veining · netzartige Äderung f, netzartiges Geäder n [Marmor]
broken, crushed · gebrochen
~ · ungeschichtet [Mauerwerk]
~ aggregate, crushed ~ · gebrochener Zuschlag(stoff) m
~ (blastfurnace) slag sand, crushed (~) ~ ~, granulated (blastfurnace) slag (Brit.); **~ cinder sand, ~ granulated cinder** (US) · Schlackenbrechsand m, Hüttenbrechsand
~ (~) ~ 30/70 mm → crushed (iron) (~) ~ ~ ~

broken brick concrete — bronze curtain wall

~ **brick concrete,** crushed ~ ~ · Ziegelsplittbeton *m*, Trümmerbeton [*DIN 4163. Trotz des Namens ,,Ziegelsplittbeton'' enthält dieser Beton die Körnungen 0/3, (0/7), 3/7 mm = Ziegelsand; 7/15, 15/30 = Ziegelsplitt und 30/70 = Ziegelschotter*]

~ ~ ~ **filler block,** ~ ~ ~ ~ **tile,** crushed ~ ~ ~ ~ ~ · Trümmerbeton-Deckenblock(stein) *m*, Trümmerbeton-Deckenstein, Ziegelsplittbeton-Deckenblock(stein), Ziegelsplittbeton-Deckenstein

~ ~ ~ **wall slab,** crushed ~ ~ ~ ~ · Trümmerbeton-Wand(bau)platte *f*, Ziegelsplittbeton-Wand(bau)platte

~ **bricks,** crushed ~, ~ clay ~ · Ziegelbrechgut *n*

~ **chip(ping)s,** crushed ~ · Brechsplitt *m*

~ **cinder sand** (US) → crushed (blastfurnace) slag ~

~ ~ **slag 30/70 mm** crushed ~ ~ ~ ~ (US); ~ (iron) (blastfurnace) ~ ~ ~ (Brit.) · (Hochofen)Schlackenschotter *m*

~ **(clay) bricks,** crushed (~) ~ · Ziegelbrechgut *n*

~ **concrete, aggregate of** ~ ~, concrete hardcore, crushed concrete · Betonpackage *f*, Betonschotter *m*, Kleinschlag *m* aus Beton(brocken), Betonsteinschlag

~ **(concreting) sand** → crushed (~) ~

~ **expanded cinder** (US) → crushed foamed (blastfurnace) slag

~ **fine aggregate** → crushed (concreting) sand

~ **foamed (blastfurnace) slag** → crushed ~ (~) ~

~ ~ **slag** → crushed foamed (blastfurnace) ~

~ **glass,** cullet · Glasbrocken *m*, (Glas-)Scherben *m*

~ **granite,** crushed ~ · Granitschotter *m*

~ **granulated (blastfurnace) slag** → crushed (blastfurnace) slag sand

~ ~ **cinder** (US) → crushed (blastfurnace) slag sand

~ ~ **slag** → crushed (blastfurnace) slag sand

~ **gravel,** crushed ~ · Brechkies *m*

~ **hard rock,** crushed ~ ~ · Hartschotter *m* [*Schotter aus Hart(ge)stein*]

~ **(iron) (blastfurnace) slag 30/70 mm,** crushed (~) (~) ~ ~ ~ (Brit.); ~ cinder ~ ~ (US) · (Hochofen)Schlakkenschotter *m*

~ **lava,** crushed ~ · Brechlava *f*

~ **limestone,** crushed ~ · gebrochener Kalkstein *m*

~ ~, crushed ~ · Kalksteinschotter *m*

~ ~ **sand,** crushed ~ ~ · Kalkstein-Brechsand *m*

~ **lump slag,** crushed ~ ~ · gebrochene Stückschlacke *f*, Betonschlacke

~ **marble,** crushed ~ · Brechmarmor *m*

~ **material,** crushed ~, ~ product · Brech(er-Fertig)gut *n*, gebrochenes Material *n*

~ **pediment** · gesprengter Giebel *m*

~ **product,** crushed ~, ~ material · Brech(er-Fertig)gut *n*, gebrochenes Material *n*

~ **range masonry (work)** [*The stones are laid in courses but the courses are continuous for short distances only*] · unregelmäßiges Schichtenmauerwerk *n*

~ **rock,** ~ stone, crushed ~; (road-)metal (Brit.) · (Brech)Schotter *m*, Steinschlag *m*, Straßen(bau)schotter

~ ~, ~ stone, crushed ~, crusher-run ~ · gebrochenes ungesiebtes Gestein *n*, ungesiebtes gebrochenes ~, Brechgut *n*

~ **sand** → crushed (concreting) ~

~ **slag** → crushed ~

~ ~ **sand** → crushed (blastfurnace) ~ ~

~ ~ **30/70 mm** → crushed (iron) (blastfurnace) ~

~ **slate,** crushed ~ · Schiefersplitt *m* [*Zur Bestreuung von Dachpappe*]

~ **sticks,** zig-zag ~ · gebrochene Stäbe *mpl* [*Verzierung*]

~ **stone,** crushed ~, ~ rock [*The product resulting from the artificial crushing of rocks, boulders or large cobblestones, substantially all faces of which have resulted from the crushing operation*] · gebrochenes Material *n*, ~ Gestein *n*

~ ~, ~ rock, crushed ~; (road-)metal (Brit.) · (Brech)Schotter *m*, Steinschlag *m*, Straßen(bau)schotter

~ ~, crushed ~ · Betonsteinschlag *m* [*als Zuschlag(stoff). 30/70 mm*]

bronze [*Essentially bronze is an alloy of copper and tin, other elements such as zinc, phosphorus, nickel and lead being added to produce alloys with specific properties. When they contain about 2 per cent zinc they are known as gunmetals*] · Bronze *f*

bronze-age building · Bronzezeitgebäude *n*

~ **palace** · Bronzezeitpalast *m*

bronze anchor, ~ tie · Bronzeanker *m*

~ **annulet,** ~ shaft-ring · Bronzebund *m*, Bronzeschaftring *m*, Bronzewirtel *m*

~ **blue (pigment)** · bronzierendes Blau(pigment) *n*

~ **(builders') fitting** → ~ (~) furniture

~ **(~) fittings** → ~ (~) hardware

~ **(~) furniture,** ~ (~) fitting · Bronze(bau)beschlag *m*

~ **(~) hardware,** ~ (~) fittings · Bronze(bau)beschläge *mpl*

~ **cast(ing)** · Bronzegußstück *n*

~ **clamp** · Bronzekrampe *f*, Bronzekramme

~ **connector** · Bronzedübel *m*

~ **curtain wall** · Bronzevorhangwand *f*

bronze door — brownstone

~ door · Bronzetü *f*
~ fitting → ~ (builders') furniture
~ fittings → ~ (builders') hardware
~ flagpole, ~ flagstaff · Bronze-Fahnenmast *m*, Bronze-Flaggenmast
~ flakes, ~ pigment, ~ powder, powder(ed) bronze · Bronzepulver *n* [*Metalleffektpigment*]
~ foil · Bronzefolie *f*
~ furniture → ~ builders' ~
~ glass · Bronzeglas *n*
~ grille [*Sometimes spelled 'grill'*] · Bronzegitter *n*
~ hardware → ~ builders' ~
~ hinge · Bronzeband *n* [*Baubeschlag*]
~ mould (Brit.); ~ mold (US) · Bronzeform *f*
bronze-on pipe fitting · Löt(rohr)fitting *m*, Löt(rohr)formstück *n*
bronze paint, metallic ~ [*A paint which on application gives a film with a metallic appearance. This effect is normally produced by the incorporation of fine flakes of such metals as copper, alloys of copper or aluminium. The aluminium used may be leafing or non-leafing, the former giving a far more brilliant metallic effect. These metals can be used in tinted or coloured media to give polychromatic finishes*] · Bronzefarbe *f*
~ paste [*A paste consisting of fine metallic flakes in a volatile medium, usually white spirit. It is used in combination with media to make metallic and polychromate paints. The metal may be alumin(i)um, copper or alloys of copper*] · Bronzepaste *f*
~ pigment, ~ flakes, ~ powder, powder(ed) bronze · Bronzepulver *n* [*Metalleffektpigment*]
~ powder, ~ pigment, ~ flakes, powder(ed) bronze · Bronzepulver *n* [*Metalleffektpigment*]
~ profile → ~ unit
~ relief · Bronzerelief *n*
~ (roof) tile · Bronze(dach)platte *f*
~ section → ~ unit
~ shaft-ring, ~ annulet · Bronzebund *m*, Bronzeschaftring *m*, Bronzewirtel *m*
~ shape → ~ unit
~ sheet · Bronze(fein)blech *n*
~ ~ panel · Bronze(fein)blechtafel *f*
~ skyscraper · Bronze-Wolkenkratzer *m*
~ surround · Bronzeeinfassung *f*
~ swing door · Bronze-Pendeltür *f*, Pendeltür aus Bronze
~ tie, ~ anchor · Bronzeanker *m*
~ tile, ~ roof ~ · Bronze(dach)platte *f*
~ trim → ~ unit
~ unit, ~ section, ~ shape, ~ trim, ~ profile · Bronzeprofil *n*
~ window · Bronzefenster *n*
~ wire · Bronzedraht *m*
bronze-working · Bronzearbeit *f*
bronzing [*A characteristic metallic lustre shown by certain highly coloured pigments in full strength, e. g. certain Prussian and phthalocyanine blues*] · Bronzeglanz *m*
~ fluid, ~ liquid [*A common vehicle for bronze paints is nitrocellulose lacquer called 'bronzing liquid' made by dissolving nitrated cotton (nitrocellulose) in amylacetate. This bronzing liquid is sometimes called 'banana oil' but this name applies only to amylacetate and not to the solution of nitrated cotton in amylacetate*] · Bronzetinktur *f*
~ lacquer · Bronzelack *m*
~ liquid → ~ fluid
broom closet, ~ cupboard, BC(L) · Besenschrank *m*
~ finish · Besenabzug *m*
to broom into a surface · einfegen
brown-coal tar, lignite · Braunkohlenteer *m*
~ ~ pitch · Braunkohlenteerpech *n*
brown coat, second ~ · zweite Unterputzschicht *f*, ~ Unterputzlage *f*, ~ Grobputzschicht, ~ Grobputzlage, zweites Rauhwerk *n*, Zwischenputzschicht, Mittelputzschicht [*dreilagiger Putz*]
browning · Braunfärben *n*, Brünieren [*Stahl*]
~ agent · Brüniermittel *n*
~ paste · Brüniersalbe *f*
~ plaster [*A retarded hemihydrate undercoat plaster for use with sand with or without fibre or hair*] · zweiter Grobputz *m*, ~ Unterputz [*Beim dreilagigen Putz*]
~ salt · Brüniersalz *n*
~ solution · Brünierlösung *f*
brown (iron) oxid(e) (pigment), ~ oxid(e) of iron (~), iron (oxid(e)) brown (~) (US); brown (iron) oxide (~), brown oxide of iron (~), iron (oxide) brown (~) (Brit.) [*B.S. 851*] · Eisenbraun(pigment) *n*, (Eisen)Oxidbraun(pigment)
brownmillerite [*A ternary compound originally regarded as* $4CaO \cdot Al_2O_3 \cdot Fe_2O_3$ *(C_4AF) occurring in portland cement and high alumina cement; now used to refer to a series of solid solutions between* $2CaO \cdot Fe_2O_3$ *(C_2F) and* $2CaO \cdot Al_2O_3$ *(C_2A)*] · Brownmillerit *m*
brown oxide of iron (pigment) (Brit.) → ~ (iron) oxid(e) (~)
~ ~ (pigment) (Brit.) → ~ (iron) oxid(e) (~)
~ pigment · braunes Pigment *n*, Braunpigment
~ staining · Braunfleckigkeit *f* [*Mörtelfuge*]
brownstone · Braunstein *m* [*Sandsteinart*]

Brunswick black — buckling stress

Brunswick black [*A solution normally consisting of gilsonite, petroleum pitch, or similar material, in white spirit or aromatic hydrocarbons. It dries to a glossy, often brittle film, by simple evaporation of the solvents*] · Braunschweigerschwarz *n*

~ **blue**, celestial ~ · Braunschweigerblau *n*

~ **green** [*Mixture of Prussian blue, chrome yellow and barytes. B. S. 303*] · Braunschweigergrün *n*

brush application, application by brush(ing) · Streichen *n* [*Eine Fläche mit Aufstrichmittel*]

~ ~, application by brush(ing) · Aufstreichen *n* [*Aufstrichmittel*]

~ ~ **method** · Streichverfahren *n*

~ **applied**, brushed · aufgestrichen

~ ~ **roof(ing) membrane** → brushed ~ ~

~ **mark** · Pinselstrich *m*

to brush off · wegbürsten

brush painting · Pinselauftrag *m*

~ **polishing** · Bürsten *n*

brushability · (Auf)Streichfähigkeit *f*, (Auf)Streichbarkeit [*Anstrichmittel; Fläche*]

brushable · (auf)streichbar, (auf)streichfähig [*Anstrichmittel; Fläche*]

~ **consistence**, brushing ~, ~ consistency · Streichkonsistenz *f*

~ **consistency**, brushing ~, ~ consistence · Streichkonsistenz *f*

~ **filler**, ~ stopping, ~ stopper · Pinselspachtel(masse) *m*, (*f*), Pinselfüllspachtel(masse), Streich(füll)spachtel(masse), Streichausfüller *m*, Pinselausfüller

~ **in cold condition**, ~ ~ ~ **state** · kaltstreichbar

~ **stopping**, ~ stopper, ~ filler · Pinselspachtel(masse) *m*, (*f*), Pinselfüllspachtel(masse), Streich(füll)spachtel(masse), Streichausfüller *m*, Pinselausfüller

brushed, brush applied · aufgestrichen

~ **on strippable coating** · aufgestrichener Abziehlack *m*

~ **roof(ing) membrane**, brush applied ~ ~ · aufgestrichener Kunststoffdachbelag *m*, aufgestrichenes Kunststoffdach *n*

brushing consistence, brushable ~, ~ consistency · Streichkonsistenz *f*

~ **consistency**, brushable ~, ~ consistence · Streichkonsistenz *f*

~ **(down)** · (Ab)Bürsten *n*

~ **quality** · Streichgüte *f*

Brutalism [*In architecture, a style characterised by ruthlessness, clarity and the straightforward presentation of structures and materials*] · Brutalismus *m*

Brutalist architecture · brutalistische Architektur *f*, ~ Baukunst *f*

B & S joint → bell(-)and(-)spigot ~

~ **pipe** → bell(-)and(-)spigot ~

BSB4 cup [*Viscosity. Paint manufacture*] · AK4 *m*

B(SMT) → basement (level)

BT → (bath)tub

bubble [*A gas filled cavity within glass*] · Blase *f*

bubbling, blistering; blebbing, blabbing (Brit.) · Blasigwerden *n*, Blasenbildung *f*

Buchner funnel · Buchnertrichter *m*

to buckle · (aus)knicken, einknicken

buckled region · Knickzone *f*

buckle(d) (steel) plate, dished (~) ~ · Buckelblech *n*, geknickte Platte *f*.

buckling · Ausknicken *n*, (Ein)Knicken

~ **action** · Knick(ungs)beanspruchung *f*, Beanspruchung auf Knickung, Beanspruchung auf Knicken

~ **analysis** · Knickberechnung *f*

~ **behaviour** (Brit.); ~ behavior (US) · Knickverhalten *n*

~ **breaking** → failure in buckling

~ **case** · Knickfall *m*

~ **coefficient** · Knickbeiwert *m*, Knickzahl *f*

~ **condition** · Knickbedingung *f*

~ **configuration** · Knickfigur *f*

~ **criterion** · Knickmerkmal *n*

~ **failure** → failure in buckling

~ **fatigue** · Knickermüdung *f*

~ **force** · Knickkraft *f*

~ **formula** · Knickformel *f*

~ **height**, effective ~, ~ length · Knicklänge *f*

~ **instability** · Knicklabilität *f*

~ **investigation** · Knickuntersuchung *f*

~ **length**, effective ~, ~ height · Knicklänge *f*

~ **limit** · Knickgrenze *f*

~ **load** · Knicklast *f*

~ **loading** · Knickbelastung *f*

~ **modulus** · Knickmodul *m*

~ **point** · Knick(ungs)stelle *f*, Knick(ungs)punkt *m*

~ **problem** · Knickaufgabe *f*, Knickproblem *n*

~ **resistance**, ~ stability, ~ strength, ultimate column ~ · Knickfestigkeit *f*, Knickwiderstand *m*, Knickstabilität *f*

~ **risk**, risk of buckling · Knickgefahr *f*

~ **rupture** → failure in buckling

~ **safety** · Knicksicherheit *f*

~ **stability**, ~ resistance, ~ strength, ultimate column ~ · Knickfestigkeit *f* Knickwiderstand *m*, Knickstabilität *f*

~ **stiffness** · Knicksteifigkeit *f*

~ **strength**, ~ resistance, ~ stability, ultimate column ~ · Knickfestigkeit *f* Knickwiderstand *m*, Knickstabilität *f*

~ **stress** · Knickspannung *f*

buckling test — (building) block masonry (work)

~ **test** · Knickprobe *f*, Knickprüfung *f*, Knickversuch *m*

~ **value** · Knickwert *m*

bucrane, bucranium, ox-head · Bukranion *n*, Aaskopf *m*, Rindschädel *m* [*Dem Schädelskelett der Opfertiere nachgebildetes Schmuckmotiv an hellenistischen und römischen Altären, Grabmälern und Metopen dorischer Friese, meist mit Blumen und Bändern verziert*]

~ **frieze,** bucranium ~, ox-head ~ · Bukranienfries *m*

bucranium → bucrane

~ **frieze,** bucrane ~ · Bukranienfries *m*

bud · Knospe *f*, Knolle *f* [*Kapitell*]

~ **capital** · Knollenkapitell *n*, Knollenkapital, Knospenkapitell, Knospenkapitäl

Buddhist architecture · buddhistische Architektur *f*, ~ Baukunst *f*

to buff · bohnern

buffability · Bohnerbarkeit *f*

buffable · bohnerbar

buffet bar · Eßbar *f*

buffing · Bohnern *n* [*(Fuß)Boden(belag)*]

to buggy away [*concrete*] · verfahren mit Japanern

buggying · Verfahren *n* mit Japanern, Japanertransport *m* [*Beton*]

to build, to construct, to erect · errichten, bauen [*im Hochbau*]

build [*The thickness (either real or apparent) of a dry paint or varnish film*] · Dicke *f*

~ · Füllkraft *f* [*Die Eigenschaft eines Anstrichmittels, Rauhigkeiten des Untergrundes — besonders bei Putzuntergründen — durch stärkere Filmbildung auszugleichen*]

~, (head) joint (US); cross joint (Brit.); perpendicular ~ joint, side joint, vertical joint · Stoßfuge *f*

builder · Erbauer *m*

(builders') fitting, (~) furniture · (Bau)Beschlag *m*

(~) fittings, (~) hardware [*B.S. 1331*] · (Bau)Beschläge *mpl*

(~) ~ factory, (~) hardware ~ · Beschlagfabrik *f*, Bau~

(~) furniture, (~) fitting · (Bau)Beschlag *m*

(~) glass fittings, (~) ~ hardware · Glas(bau)beschläge *mpl*

builder's handyman, jobber [*A semi-skilled man who can do any sort of repair to small houses*] · Reparaturhochbauarbeiter *m*

(builder's) hardware, (~) fittings [*B.S. 1331*] · (Bau)Beschläge *mpl*

(~) factory, (~) fittings ~ · Beschlagfabrik *f*, Bau~

~ **iron supplies,** ~ ironmongery [*Also loosely called 'hardware'*] · Baueisenware *f*, Kleineisenwaren *fpl*, Kleineisen(zeug) *n*

~ **merchant** · Baustoffhändler *m*

~ **rough planks** · Vorhalteholz *n*

~ **rubbish** · Bauschutt *m*

~ **treat,** topping-out ceremony · Richtfest *n*

~ **yard** · Bauhof *m*

building → ~ structure

~, erection, construction · Errichtung *f*, Bau *m* [*im Hochbau*]

~, ~ construction, ~ design and ~ · Hochbau *m* [*als Bauweise*]

~ **activity,** construction ~ · Bautätigkeit *f*

~ ~, ~ construction ~ · Hochbautätigkeit *f*

~ **adaptable to extension(s),** block ~ ~ ~ · Anbaugebäude *n*, anbaubares Gebäude

~ **adhesive** → ~ bonding ~

~ **administration,** ~ construction ~ · Hochbauverwaltung *f*

~ **alteration** · Gebäudeumbau *m*

~ **and construction industry** · Hoch- und Tiefbauindustrie *f*

~ ~ **loan association** (US); ~ society (Brit.) · Bausparkasse *f*

~ **application,** ~ use · Verwendung *f* im Hochbau

~ **area** [*The total ground area of each building and accessory building but not including uncovered entrance platforms, terraces, and steps*] · überbaute Fläche *f*, bebaute ~

~ **article,** ~ product · Bauartikel *m*, Bauerzeugnis *n*, Baugegenstand *m*, Bauware *f*

~ **articles,** ~ ware, ~ products, ~ goods · Bauwaren *fpl*, Bauerzeugnisse *npl*, Bauartikel *mpl*, Baugegenstände *mpl*

~ **authority,** construction ~ · Baubehörde *f*

(~) block, (~) tile [*The terms 'tile' and 'block' as used in the construction of walls, partitions and floors are synonymous, but the clay and gypsum products are commonly called 'tile' and the concrete and glass products are usually called 'block'*] · Block *m,* (Block)Stein *m*

(~) ~ factory, (~) tile ~, (~) ~ plant · Steinwerk *n*, Block~, Blockwerk

(~) ~ lintel; (~) tile ~ [*deprecated: lintol*] · (Block)Steinsturz *m*, (Block-) Steinoberschwelle *f*, Blocksturz, Blockoberschwelle

(~) ~ (masonry) wall, (~) tile (~) ~ · (Block)Steinmauer *f*, Blockmauer

(~) ~ ~ (work), (~) tile ~ (~), blockwork, block-walling · (Block-) Steinmauerwerk *n*, Blockmauerwerk

building block module — building construction site 132

~ ~ **module**, unitized unit · Installationsblock *m*, Installationszelle *f*, (Raum)Zelle

(~ ~) ~ **method**; unitized unit ~; modular housing (US) · (Raum)Zellenbauweise *f*, Installationszellenbauweise, Installationsblockbauweise, Bauen *n* mit Raumzellen [*Die Bauten sind mit dem Grundstück dauerhaft verbunden. Gegensatz: bewegliche Raumzellen = mobile homes*]

(~) ~ **plant**, (~) tile ~, (~) ~ factory · (Block)Steinwerk *n*, Blockwerk

(~) ~ **wall** → (~) ~ masonry ~

~ **bloom** · Mauersalpeter *m*, Mauerschweiß *m*, Mauerbeschlag *m*

~ **board**, ~ sheet · Bauplatte *f*

~ ~ **facing** → ~ ~ lining

~ ~ **for industrial construction**, ~ sheet ~ ~ ~ · Bauplatte *f* für den Industriebau, Industrie(-Bau)platte

~ ~ **lining**, ~ ~ (sur)facing, ~ sheet ~, ~ slab ~, sheeting board ~ · (Bau)Plattenauskleidung *f*, (Bau)Plattenverkleidung, (Bau)Plattenbekleidung

~ (**bonding**) **adhesive**, ~ ~ agent, ~ ~ medium, ~ cement(ing agent) · Bauklebe(stoff) *m*, Baukleber *m*, Baukleb(e)mittel *n*

~ **boom** · Bauhochkonjunktur *f*

~ **brick** (US); backing (~), back-up ~, common (stock) ~ · Hintermauer(ungs)ziegel *m*, Hintermauerer *m*

(**building-**)**brick clay** · Ziegelton *m*

building campaign · Baukampagne *f*

~ **carcass**, ~ fabric; ~ shell [*Canada*]; ~ carcase [*deprecated*] · Gebäuderohbau *m*

~ **chimney**, domestic ~ · Gebäudeschornstein *m*, Hausschornstein [*DIN 18160. Jeder Bauteil in oder an einem Gebäude, der dazu geeignet oder bestimmt ist, Rauch oder Abgase von Feuerstätten über Dach abzuführen*]

~ **climatology**, construction ~ · Bauklimatologie *f*

~ **clock** · Gebäudeuhr *f*

~ **club** · aufhörende Bausparkasse *f* [*in England*]

~ **code** · Baugesetz *n*

~ ~ **requirements for reinforced concrete** · Stahlbetonbestimmungen *fpl*

~ **column**, house ~, block ~ · Gebäudestütze *f*

~ **combined drain** · Grundmischleitung *f*

~ ~ **sewer** · Grundstücksanschlußmischleitung *f*

~ **complex**, block ~, complex of buildings, complex of blocks · Gebäudekomplex *m*

(~) **component** → (prefab(ricated)) (building) unit

~ **concrete**, ~ construction ~ · Hochbaubeton *m*

~ **construction**, ~ (structural) system · Gebäudekonstruktion(ssystem) *f*, (*n*)

~ (~), ~ design and ~ · Hochbau *m* [*als Bauweise*]

~ (~) **activity** · Hochbautätigkeit *f*

~ (~) **administration** · Hochbauverwaltung *f*

~ ~ **component** → (prefab(ricated)) building construction unit

~ (~) **concrete** · Hochbaubeton *m*

~ (~) **contract** · Hochbauvertrag *m*

~ (~) **control**, ~ (~) supervision · Hochbauüberwachung *f*

~ (~) ~, ~ (~) regulation · Hochbaubestimmung *f*, Hochbauvorschrift *f*

~ (~) **cost(s)**, cost(s) of building (construction) work · Hochbaukosten *f*

~ (~) **department** · Hochbauabteilung *f*

~ (~) **drawing** · Hochbauzeichnen *n*

~ (~) **engineer** · Hochbauingenieur *m*

~ (~) **engineering** · Hochbautechnik *f*

~ (~) **expert** · Hochbaufachmann *m*, Hochbausachverständiger *m*

~ (~) **field** · Hochbausektor *m*

~ (~) **firm** · Hochbaubetrieb *m*, Hochbaufirma *f*, Hochbauunternehmung *f*

~ (~) **ground** · Hochbaugelände *n*

~ (~ **industry** · Hochbauindustrie *f*

~ (~) **labour** (Brit.); ~ (~) labor (US) · Hochbau-Arbeitskräfte *fpl*

~ (~) **legislation** · Hochbaugesetzgebung *f*

~ ~ **lot** (US); ~ ~ site [*Land which is used or to be used for building construction*] · Hochbau-Bauplatz *m*, Hochbaugrundstück *n*

~ (~) **material** · Hochbaustoff *m*; Hochbaumaterial *n* [*Schweiz*]

~ ~ **member** → (prefab(ricated)) building construction unit

~ (~) **method** · Hochbauweise *f*, Hochbauverfahren *n*

~ (~) **office** · Hochbaubüro *n*

~ (~) **operation** · Hochbauvorgang *m*

~ (~) **operations** · Hochbaubetrieb *m*

~ (~) **panel** · Hochbautafel *f*

~ (~) **phase** · Hochbaustadium *n*

~ (~) **plan** · Hochbauplan *m*, Hochbauzeichnung *f*

~ (~) **plastic** · Hochbaukunststoff *m*

~ (~) **price** · Hochbaupreis *m*

~ (~) ~ **index** · Hochbaupreisindex *m*

~ (~) **programme** (Brit.); ~ (~) program (US) · Hochbauprogramm *n*

~ (~) **regulation**, ~ (~) control · Hochbaubestimmung *f*, Hochbauvorschrift *f*

~ (~) **research** · Hochbauforschung *f*

~ ~ **site** [*Land which is used or to be used for building construction*] · Hochbau-Bauplatz *m*, Hochbaugrundstück *n*

building (construction) site — building insulating slab

~ (~) ~ · Hochbau-Baustelle f
~ (~) ~ installation · Hochbau-Baustelleneinrichtung f
~ (~) speed · Hochbautempo n
~ (~) standard (spec(ification)) Hochbaunorm f
~ (~) supervision, ~ (~) control · Hochbauüberwachung f
~ (~) system, ~ structural ~ · Hochbaukonstruktion(ssystem) f, (n), Hochbausystem
~ (~) technician · Hochbautechniker m
~ (~) type, type of building (construction) · Hochbauart f
~ ~ unit → ~ prefab(ricated) ~ ~ ~
~ (~) work · Hochbauarbeiten fpl
~ (~) worker · Hochbauarbeiter m
~ contract, ~ construction ~ · Hochbauvertrag m
~ control, ~ regulation, ~ construction ~ · Hochbaubestimmung f, Hochbauvorschrift f
~ ~, ~ regulation, construction ~ · Baubestimmung f, Bauvorschrift f
~ ~, ~ supervision, ~ construction ~ · Hochbauüberwachung f
~ core, mechanical ~, service ~, utility ~, (reinforced) concrete ~, R. C. ~ · (Hoch)Hauskern m, (Stahl)Betonkern, Betriebskern, (Gebäude)Kern
~ cost(s), ~ construction ~, cost(s) of building (construction) work · Hochbaukosten f
~ ~ ~ · Baukosten f
building-cost(s) index · Baukostenindex m
building department, ~ construction ~ · Hochbauabteilung f
~ (design and) (construction) · Hochbau m [als Bauweise]
(~) dimension · (Bau)Abmessung f, (Bau)Maß n
~ documents → ~ particulars and plans
~ drain · Grundleitung f
~ ~ system · Grundstücksentwässerungsanlage f, Gebäudeentwässerungsanlage
~ drainage · Grundstücksentwässerung f, Einzelentwässerung [DIN 1986 und 4251]
~ drawing, ~ construction ~ · Hochbauzeichnen n
~ engineer, ~ construction ~ · Hochbauingenieur m
~ engineering, ~ construction ~ · Hochbautechnik f
~ entrance, block ~ · Gebäudeeingang m
~ ~ door, block ~ ~ · Gebäude(eingangs)tür f
~ ~ plastic door · Kunststoff-Gebäudetür f
~ equipment, block ~ · Gebäudeausrüstung f
~ erection system · Bau-Montageverfahren n

~ expert, ~ construction ~ · Hochbaufachmann m, Hochbausachverständiger m
~ extension, block ~ · Gebäudeerweiterung f
~ fabric → ~ carcass
~ failure · Hochbauschaden m
~ field, ~ construction ~ · Hochbausektor m
~ fire, block ~ · Gebäudebrand m, Gebäudefeuer n
~ firm, ~ construction ~ · Hochbaubetrieb m, Hochbaufirma f, Hochbauunternehmung f
~ fit · Hochbaupassung f
~ foundation · Gebäudegründung f
~ frame, block ~ · Gebäuderahmen m
~ glass, construction ~ · Bauglas n
~ goods, ~ articles, ~ ware, ~ products · Bauwaren fpl, Bauerzeugnisse npl, Bauartikel mpl, Baugegenstände mpl
~ ground, ~ construction ~ · Hochbaugelände n
~ heating · Gebäude(be)heizung f
~ ~ installation · Gebäudeheiz(ungs)anlage f
~ industry, ~ construction ~ · Hochbauindustrie f
~ information centre (Brit.); ~ ~ center (US) · bautechnische Auskunftstelle f, Bauzentrum n
~ insulant → ~ insulation(-grade) material
~ insulating article → ~ ~ product
~ ~ board, ~ ~ slab, ~ ~ sheet, ~ insulation(-grade) ~ · Bauisolierplatte f
~ ~ ~, ~ ~ slab, ~ ~ sheet, ~ insulation(-grade) ~ · Baudämmplatte f [Gegen Wärme, Kälte oder Schall]
~ ~ brick, ~ insulation(-grade) ~ · Baudämmziegel m
~ ~ compound, ~ insulation(-grade) ~ · Baudämmasse f
~ ~ felt, ~ insulation(-grade) ~ · Baudämmfilz m
~ ~ foil, ~ insulation(-grade) ~ · Bauisolierfolie f
~ ~ ~, ~ insulation(-grade) ~ · Baudämmfolie f
~ ~ material → ~ insulation(-grade) ~
~ ~ panel, ~ insulation(-grade) ~ · Baudämmtafel f
~ ~ paper, ~ insulation(-grade) ~ [See remark under 'Pappe'] · Baudämmpapier n
~ ~ ~, ~ insulation(-grade) ~ [See remark under 'Pappe'] · Baudämmpappe f
~ ~ product, ~ insulation(-grade) ~, ~ ~ article · Bauisoliererzeugnis n, Bauisolierartikel m, Bauisoliergegenstand m
~ ~ sheet → ~ ~ board
~ ~ slab → ~ ~ board

building insulating unit — building materials testing machine 134

~ ~ **unit**, ~ insulation(-grade) ~ · Baudämmelement *n*

~ ~ **wool**, ~ insulation(-grade) ~ · Baudämmwolle *f*

~ **insulation** · Hausisolierung *f*, Gebäudeisolierung

~ ~ · Gebäudedämmung *f*, Hausdämmung

~ **insulation(-grade) article** → ~ insulating product

~ ~ **board** → ~ insulating ~

~ ~ **brick**, ~ insulating ~ · Baudämmziegel *m*

~ ~ **compound**, ~ insulating ~ · Baudämmasse *f*

~ ~ **felt**, ~ insulating ~ · Baudämmfilz *m*

~ ~ **foil** → ~ insulating ~

~ ~ **material**, construction ~ ~, insulating ~, ~ insulator, ~ insulant · Baudämmstoff *m*, Dämmbaustoff, Dämmbaumaterial *n*, Baudämmaterial

~ ~ **panel**, ~ insulating ~ · Baudämmtafel *f*

~ ~ **paper** → ~ insulating ~

~ ~ **product** → ~ insulating ~

~ ~ **sheet** → ~ insulating board

~ ~ **slab** → ~ insulating board

~ ~ **unit**, ~ insulating ~ · Baudämmelement *n*

~ ~ **wool**, ~ insulating ~ · Baudämmwolle *f*

~ **insulator** → ~ insulation(-grade) material

~ **interior** · Gebäudeinneres *n*

~ **labour** → ~ construction ~

~ **legislation**, ~ construction ~ · Hochbaugesetzgebung *f*

~ **lime**, construction ~, structural ~, trowel trades ~, mason's ~, finish ~ [*B.S. 890*] · Baukalk *m* [*DIN 1060*]

~ **line**, block ~ · Gebäudeleitung *f*

~ ~ · Baulinie *f* [*Die im Bebauungsplan festgesetzte Grenzlinie einer überbaubaren Fläche*]

~ **load**, block ~ · Gebäudelast *f*

~ **maintenance** · Gebäudeunterhaltung *f*

~ **masonry wall**; block ~ ~ [*deprecated*] · Gebäudemauer *f*

~ **mass** · Gebäudemasse *f*

~ ~, structural ~, volume, massing · Baumasse *f*

(~) **mastic**, mastic joint sealer · plastische Fugen(ab)dicht(ungs)masse *f*, ~ Fugenmasse, ~ (Fugen)(Ver)Füllmasse, plastischer (Fugen)(Ver)Füller *m*, Fugen(ab)dicht(ungs)kitt *m*, (Ver)Füllkitt, (Fugen)Kitt, (Fugen)Mastix *m*, (Ab)Dicht(ungs)mastix

(~) **mat** [*It has a low density*] · (Bau-)Matte *f* Dämmatte

~ **material**, ~ construction ~ · Hochbaustoff *m*; Hochbaumaterial *n* [*Schweiz*]

~ ~, construction(al) ~, structural ~ · Baustoff *m*; Baumaterial *n* [*Schweiz*]

~ ~ **dealer**, construction(al) ~ ~, structural ~ ~ · Baustoffeinzelhändler *m*

~ ~ **distributor**, construction(al) ~ ~, structural ~ ~ · Baustoffgroßhändler *m*

~ ~ **engineer** → construction(al) ~ ~

~ ~ **failure**, construction(al) ~ ~, structural ~ ~ · Baustoffschaden *m*

~ ~ **machine**, construction(al) ~ ~, structural ~ ~ · Baustoff(-Herstellungs)maschine *f*

~ ~ **manufacturer** → ~ ~ producer

~ ~ **producer**, construction(al) ~ ~, structural ~ ~, ~ ~ manufacturer · Baustoffhersteller *m*, Baustofferzeuger Baustoffabrikant *m*

~ ~ **production**, construction(al) ~ ~, structural ~ ~ · Baustofferzeugung *f*, Baustoffherstellung

~ ~ **standards**, structural ~ ~, construction(al) ~ ~ · Baustoff(prüf)normen *fpl*

~ **materials delivery**, structural ~ ~, construction(al) ~ ~ · Baustoffanfuhr *f*

~ ~ **deposit**, construction(al) ~ ~, structural ~ ~ · Baustoffvorkommen *n*

~ ~ **industry** → construction(al) ~ ~

~ ~ **market**, construction(al) ~ ~, structural ~ ~ · Baustoffmarkt *m*

~ ~ **practice**, construction(al) ~ ~, structural ~ ~ · Baustofftechnik *f*

~ ~ **processing**, construction(al) ~ ~, structural ~ ~ · Baustoffaufbereitung *f*

~ ~ **quality**, construction(al) ~ ~, structural ~ ~ · Baustoffgüte *f*

~ ~ ~ **control**, structural ~ ~, construction(al) ~ ~ ~ · Baustoff-(güte)überwachung *f*

~ ~ **requirement**, construction(al) ~ ~, structural ~ ~ · Baustoffbedarf *m*

~ ~ **saving**, construction(al) ~ ~, structural ~ ~ · Baustoffersparnis *f*

~ ~ **scale**, construction(al) ~ ~, structural ~ ~ · Baustoffwaage *f*

~ ~ **show**, construction(al) ~ ~, structural ~ ~ · Baustoffausstellung *f*

~ ~ **storage** → construction(al) ~ ~

~ ~ **store** → construction(al) ~ ~

~ ~ **test**, construction(al) ~ ~, structural ~ ~ · Baustoffprobe *f*, Baustoffprüfung *f*, Baustoffversuch *m*

~ ~ **testing device**, construction(al) ~ ~ ~, structural ~ ~ ~ · Baustoffprüfgerät *n*

~ ~ ~ **institute**, construction(al) ~ ~ ~, structural ~ ~ ~ · Baustoffprüf(ungs)anstalt *f*

~ ~ ~ **machine**, construction(al) ~ ~ ~, structural ~ ~ ~ · Baustoffprüfmaschine *f*

(building) member — building sand

(~) member → (prefab(ricated)) (building) unit

~ metal, construction(al) ~ · Baumetall *n*

~ method, ~ construction ~ · Hochbauweise *f*, Hochbauverfahren *n*

~ mortar, construction ~ · Baumörtel *m*

~ number, street ~ · Hausnummer *f*, Gebäudenummer

~ of barracks, construction ~ ~, barracks construction, barracks building · Kasernenbau *m*

~ ~ historic interest, historic building · historisches Gebäude *n*

~ ~ large blocks, ~ ~ ~ ~ tiles, block ~ ~ ~ · Großblock(stein)gebäude *n*, Großsteingebäude

~ ~ ~ slabs, block ~ ~ ~ · Großplattengebäude *n*

~ ~ ~ tiles → ~ ~ ~ blocks

~ ~ staggered design, block ~ ~ ~ · gestaffeltes Gebäude *n*

~ office, ~ construction ~ · Hochbaubüro *n*

~ operation, ~ construction ~ · Hochbauvorgang *m*

~ operations, ~ construction ~ · Hochbaubetrieb *m*

~ orientation, block ~ · Gebäudelage *f*

~ oscillation, block ~, ~ vibration · Gebäudeschwingung *f*

~ paint · Hochbau(anstrich)farbe *f*

~ panel, ~ construction ~ · Hochbautafel *f*

~ paper → (waterproof) sheathing ~

~ ~, sheathing ~, general-use ~, waterproof ~ [*B.S. 1521. See remark under 'Pappe'*] · Baupapier *n*

~ part, part of a building · Gebäudeteil *m, n* [*Räumlich und/oder funktionell abgegrenzter Teil eines Gebäudes. Beispiele: Treppenhaus; Aufzugschacht; Geschoß usw.*]

~ particulars and plans, ~ ~ ~ drawings, ~ documents · Bauvorlagen *fpl* [*Die vom Bauherrn für die Beurteilung eines Bauvorhabens und die Bearbeitung des Bauantrages der Baugenehmigungsbehörde einzureichenden Unterlagen*]

~ phase, ~ construction ~ · Hochbaustadium *n*

~ pipe · Hochbaurohr *n*

~ pit sheeting work · Baugrubenverkleidungsarbeiten *fpl* [*DIN 18303*]

~ plan, ~ construction ~ · Hochbauplan *m*, Hochbauzeichnung *f*

~ planning · Hochbauplanung *f*

~ plaster, gypsum ~ ~ [*B.S. 1191*] · Baugips *m* [*DIN 1168*]

~ plastic, construction ~, plastic building material, plastic construction material · Bau-Kunststoff *m*

~ ~, ~ construction ~ · Hochbaukunststoff *m*

~ ~ film, ~ ~ sheeting, construction ~ ~ · Baukunststoffolie *f*

~ ~ for external use, construction ~ ~ ~, ~ ~ outdoor ~, ~ ~ ~ exterior ~, ~ ~ ~ outer ~ · Außenbaukunststoff *m*

~ ~ ~ indoor use → construction plastic for internal ~

~ ~ ~ inside use → construction plastic for internal ~

~ ~ ~ internal use → construction ~ ~ ~ ~

~ ~ sheeting, ~ ~ film, construction ~ ~ · Baukunststoffolie *f*

~ population · Bewohneranzahl *f*

~ preservative · Gebäudeschutzmittel *n*

~ price, ~ construction ~ · Hochbaupreis *m*

~ ~ index, ~ construction ~ ~ · Hochbaupreisindex *m*

~ principles · Baugrundsätze *mpl*

~ product, ~ article · Bauartikel *m*, Bauerzeugnis *n*, Baugegenstand *m*, Bauware *f*

~ products, ~ goods, ~ articles, ~ ware · Bauwaren *fpl*, Bauerzeugnisse *npl*, Bauartikel *mpl*, Baugegenstände *mpl*

~ programme → ~ construction ~

~ proposal · Bauantrag *m*, Baugesuch *n*

~ quicklime, construction ~, quicklime for structural purposes, quicklime for building purposes · Baubranntkalk *m*, Baubrennkalk

(~) quilt [*It has a high density*] · (Bau-)Matte *f*, Isoliermatte

~ regulation, ~ control, ~ construction ~ · Hochbaubestimmung *f*, Hochbauvorschrift *f*

~ ~, ~ control, construction ~ · Baubestimmung *f*, Bauvorschrift *f*

~ regulations · Bau(polizei)ordnung *f*, Bau-O, Ortsbausatzung [*Die für das Bauen maßgeblichen gesetzlichen Vorschriften*]

~ repair · Gebäudereparatur *f*

~ research · Bauforschung *f*

~ ~, ~ construction ~ · Hochbauforschung *f*

~ ~ institute, ~ ~ station · Bauforschungszentrum *n*, Institut *n* für Bauforschung, Bauforschungsanstalt *f*

~ restriction line · Baugrenze *f*

(~) roof, block ~ · (Gebäude)Dach *n*

(~) roofer, roof tiler · Dachdecker *m*

~ rubbish (Brit.) → demolition ~

~ ruins · Gebäudetrümmer *f*, Haustrümmer, Häusertrümmer

~ sand, construction(al) ~ · Bausand *m*

building sand from ... — building with service core 136

~ ~ **from natural sources,** construction(al) ~ ~ ~ ~, natural building sand, natural construction(al) sand, soft sand [*B.S. 1198–1200*] · Natur-Bausand *m*

~ **sanitary drain** · Grundtrennleitung *f*

~ ~ **sewer** · Grundstücksanschlußtrennleitung *f*, Gebäudeanschlußtrennleitung

(~) **services** (US); mechanical equipment (of a building) [*Lifts, escalators or similar mechanical equipment*] · (Haus)Betriebsanlagen *fpl*, Gebäudebetriebsanlagen, (Haus)Betriebseinrichtungen *fpl*, Gebäudebetriebseinrichtungen, technische Anlagen, technische Einrichtungen

~ **sewer** · Grundstücksanschlußleitung *f*, Gebäudeanschlußleitung

~ **shape** · Gebäudegestalt *f*

~ **sheet,** ~ board · Bauplatte *f*

~ ~ **facing** → ~ board lining

~ ~ **for industrial construction,** ~ board ~ ~ ~ · Bauplatte *f* für den Industriebau, Industrie(-Bau)platte

~ ~ **lining** → ~ board ~

~ ~ **(sur)facing** → ~ board lining

~ **shell** [*Canada*] → ~ carcass

~ **silhouette** · Gebäudesilhouette *f*

~ **site,** ~ construction ~ · Hochbau-Baustelle *f*

~ ~ **installation,** ~ construction ~ ~ · Hochbau-Baustelleneinrichtung *f*

~ **skeleton** · Gebäudeskelett *n*, Gebäudegerippe *n*

~ **slab facing** → ~ board lining

~ ~ **lining** → ~ board ~

~ ~ **(sur)facing** → ~ board lining

~ **society** (Brit.); ~ and loan association (US) · Bausparkasse *f*

~ **speed,** ~ construction ~ · Hochbautempo *n*

~ **stair(case)** · Gebäudetreppe *f*

~ **standard (spec(ification)),** ~ construction ~ (~) · Hochbaunorm *f*

~ **stone,** structural ~ · (Natur)Baustein *m*, natürlicher Baustein

(~) ~, structural ~ · (Bau)Stein *m*, Baugestein *n*, bautechnisches Gestein, Naturbaustein, natürlicher Baustein

~ **structural system,** ~ (construction) ~ · Hochbaukonstruktion(ssystem) *f*, (*n*), Hochbausystem

~ (~) ~, ~ construction · Gebäudekonstruktion(ssystem) *f*, (*n*)

~ **(structure),** block [*A structure or combination of structures erected where it is to stand and having as one of its main purposes the provision of shelter from the weather*] · Bau *m*, Gebäude *n* [*Manchmal fälschlicherweise „Bauwerk" genannt*]

~ **style,** architectural ~ · Baustil *m* [*Die bauliche Ausdrucksform einer Kulturperiode*]

~ **supervision,** ~ control, ~ construction ~ · Hochbauüberwachung *f*

~ ~, ~ control · Bauüberwachung *f*, Bauaufsicht *f* [*Hochbau*]

~ **system,** ~ structural ~, ~ construction · Gebäudekonstruktion(ssystem) *f*, (*n*)

~ ~, ~ construction ~, ~ structural ~ · Hochbaukonstruktion(ssystem) *f*, (*n*), Hochbausystem

~ **technician,** ~ construction ~ · Hochbautechniker *m*

(~) **tile,** (~) block [*The terms 'tile' and 'block' as used in the construction of walls, partitions and floors are synonymous, but the clay and gypsum products are commonly called 'tile' and the concrete and glass products are usually called 'block'*] · Stein *m*, Block~, Block *m*

(~) ~ **factory,** (~) block ~, (~) ~ plant · Steinwerk *n*, Block~, Blockwerk

(~) ~ **lintel** → (~) block ~

(~) ~ **(masonry) wall,** (~) block (~) ~ · Steinmauer *f*, Block~, Blockmauer

(~) ~ **(work),** (~) block ~ (~), blockwork · Steinmauerwerk *n*, Block~, Blockmauerwerk

(~) ~ **plant,** (~) block ~, (~) ~ factory · Steinwerk *n*, Block~, Blockwerk

~ ~ **wall** → ~ ~ masonry ~

~ **timber** → structural ~

~ ~ **grade** → structural ~ ~

~ **tower** → service ~

~ **type,** block ~ · Gebäudeart *f*

~ ~, ~ construction ~, type of building (construction) · Hochbauart *f*

(~) **unit** → prefab(ricated) (~) ~

~ **use,** ~ application · Verwendung *f* im Hochbau

~ **vibration,** block ~, ~ oscillation · Gebäudeschwingung *f*

~ **wall** · Gebäudewand *f*, Hauswand

~ **ware,** ~ products, ~ goods, ~ articles · Bauwaren *fpl*, Bauerzeugnisse *npl*, Bauartikel *mpl*, Baugegenstände *mpl*

~ **with cantilevered access galleries** · Kanzelhaus *n* [*Wohnhaus mit vorgekragten Laubengängen, den Kanzeln, in den oberen Geschossen*]

~ ~ **central space** → centralized building

~ ~ **dwellings** → block (of flats)

~ ~ **four apartments per floor,** block ~ ~ ~ ~ ~ [*Four apartments per floor results in a generally square plan, approximately 60 to 75 ft on a side, with a minimum of service space and perimeter wall*] · Vierspänner *m* [*Von jedem Stockwerkspodest aus sind vier Wohnungen zugänglich*]

~ ~ **mechanical core,** ~ ~ ~ tower, ~ ~ service ~ · Kernbauwerk *n*

~ ~ **one apartment per floor,** block ~ ~ ~ ~ ~ · Einspänner *m*

~ ~ ~ **wing** → single-wing(ed) building

~ ~ **service core,** ~ ~ ~ tower, ~ ~ mechanical ~ · Kernbauwerk *n*

building with three staircase-...—bulk gypsum

~ ~ **three staircase-access dwellings** (Brit.) /**dwelling units** (US) **per floor** · Dreispänner m [*Miethaus, bei dem in jedem Geschoß drei Wohnungen am Treppenhaus angeordnet sind*]

~ ~ **two apartments per floor**, block ~ ~ ~ ~ ~ ~ · Zweispänner m [*Von jedem Stockwerkspodest aus sind zwei Wohnungen zugänglich*]

~ **work**, ~ construction ~ · Hochbauarbeiten *fpl*

~ **worker**, ~ construction ~ · Hochbauarbeiter m

~ **yard** · Bauhütte f

build-up of pressure, pressure build-up · Druckaufbau m

built, constructed, BLT · gebaut

~ **by the Owner**, constructed ~ ~ ~ · bauseits hergestellt

built-in, in-built, BLT-IN · eingebaut

~ **antisplash**, in built ~ · Wasserstrahlregler m [*Hahn*]

~ **arch** → fixed ~

~ **ashtray**, in-built ~ · Einbauaschenbecher m

~ **(bath)tub**, encased ~, in-built ~, ~ bath · Einbau(bade)wanne f, eingebaute (Bade)Wanne [*Solche Wannen stehen vor der Wand, in einer Ecke oder Nische*]

~ **beam** → fixed ~

~ **furniture** → fitment

~ **garage**, in-built ~ [*A garage located within the exterior walls of a dwelling*] · Einbaugarage f

~ **girder**, no-hinged ~, constrained ~, fixed(-end(ed)) ~ (US); girder fixed at both ends · beidseitig eingespannter Träger m, zweiseitig ~, ~ doppelseitig ~ ~, gelenkloser ~

~ **kitchen**, in-built ~ · Einbauküche f

~ ~ **cabinet**, in-built ~ ~ · Einbauküchenschrank m

~ **shower stall**, in-built ~ ~ · Einbau-Duschstand m

~ **tub** → ~ bath~

~ **unit** → fixture

~ **units**, in-built ~, fixtures, trim · Einbauten f im Bauwesen, Einbauteile *mpl, npl*

~ **wardrobe**, in-built ~ · Einbau-Kleiderschrank m, Wand-Kleiderschrank

built-up area · bebautes Gebiet n, bebaute Zone f

~ **asphalt roof cover(ing)**, ~ ~ ~ cladding, ~ ~ ~ sheathing (US); ~ (asphaltic-)bitumen ~ (Brit.); ~ asphalt roofing (US); ~ (asphaltic-)bitumen roofing (Brit.) · Bitumen-Kleb(e)dach(belag) n, (m), Bitumen-Kleb(e)(dach)(ein)deckung f, Bitumen-Kleb(e)bedachung, Bitumen-Spachteldach(belag), Bitumen-Spachtel(dach)-(ein)deckung, Bitumen-Spachtelbedachung

~ **beam**, compound ~, keyed ~ · zusammengesetzter Holzbalken(träger) m

~ **(cross) section** · zusammengesetzter Querschnitt m [*Zusammengesetzte Querschnitte bestehen aus mehreren durch Schweißung, Nietung, Schraubung oder Verklebung zusammengesetzten Querschnittsteilen zwecks Anpassung an die statischen Gegebenheiten bzw. zur wirtschaftlichsten Ausnutzung*]

~ **(~) ~**, composite (~) ~ · Verbundquerschnitt m [*z.B. bei einer Stütze aus Stahlkern und Betonummantelung*]

~ **roof(ing)**, ~ roof sheathing, ~ roof covering, ~ roof cladding · Spachteldach(belag) n, (m), Spachtel(dach)-(ein)deckung f, Spachtelbedachlung, Kleb(e)dach(belag), Kleb(e)dach)(ein)-deckung, Kleb(e)bedachung

~ ~ **with wall coping** · Attika f [*Traufpunktausbildung. Der Kleb(e)dachbelag wird über die Stirnfläche eines Wandelements auf die Vorderseite geführt und ein Haltewinkel und eine Attikakappe decken den Belag ab, wobei Blechtreibschrauben die Befestigung erzielen*]

~ **section** → ~ cross ~

bulb, web · Steg m, Wulst m, f [*Fugenband*]

bulb-angle · Bulbwinkel(profil) m, (n), Wulstwinkel, Winkelwulstprofil [*DIN 8093*]

bulb iron · Bulbeisen n, Wulsteisen

~ **pile**, pedestal ~ · Aufstandpfahl m [*Betonbohrpfahl mit keulenförmigem Fuß*]

~ **section** · Wulstprofil n

~ **t(ee) patent glazing bar**, ~ ~ puttyless ~ ~ · Einstegsprosse f [*kittlose Verglasung*]

~ ~ **puttyless glazing bar**, ~ ~ patent ~ ~ · Einstegsprosse f [*kittlose Verglasung*]

bulbous dome, ~ cupola, Moorish ~, imperial ~ · Zwiebelkuppel f

bulk-active (load)bearing system, ~ weight-carrying ~, ~ supporting ~, ~ structure ~, ~ load-carrying ~ · massenaktives Tragsystem n, ~ (last-)tragendes System

bulk cement · Behälterzement m, Silozement, loser Zement, unverpackter Zement, ungesackter Zement

~ **concrete** → mass(ive) ~

~ **structure**, mass(ive) ~ ~, concrete-in-mass ~ · Massenbetonbauwerk n

~ **density**, ~ specific gravity · Rohwichte f; Schüttgewicht n [*Dieser Begriff ist insofern ungenau, als es sich nicht um ein Gewicht (gemessen in kg) handelt, sondern um eine Art Raumgewicht (gemessen in kg/Ltr.)*]

~ **gypsum** · Behältergips m

bulk (hydrated) lime — burlap

~ **(hydrated) lime** · loser Feinkalk *m*, (Lösch)Kalk, loses Kalkhydrat *n*

~ **loading of cement** · sacklose Zementverladung *f*, ~ Verladung von Zement

~ **oxygen system** · Sauerstoffversorgungsanlage *f*

(~) shield · Abschirm(ungs)wand *f* eines Reaktors, Reaktorabschirm(ungs)wand, (biologischer) Schirm *m*

~ **shipping of cement** · sackloser Zementversand *m*, ~ Versand von Zement

~ **specific gravity**, ~ density · Rohwichte *f*; Schüttgewicht *n* [*Dieser Begriff ist insofern ungenau, als es sich nicht um ein Gewicht (gemessen in kg) handelt, sondern um eine Art Raumgewicht (gemessen in kg/Ltr.)*]

~ **zoning** · Baubeschränkung *f*

bulkhead, end plate, diaphragm (plate · Binderscheibe *f* [*Faltwerk*]

bulkiness · Sperrigkeit *f*

bull capital · Stierkapitell *n*, Stierkapitäl

bulldog connecter, claw ~ (US); ~ plate, ~ connector · einseitiger Krallendübel *m*, Krallenplatte *f*, Bulldogdübel

~ **plate** → ~ connector

bulletin board · Anschlagtafel *f*, ,,schwarzes Brett" *n*

bulletproof, bullet-resisting, bullet-resistant · kugelsicher, schußsicher

~ **glass,** bullet-resisting ~, bullet-resistant ~ · kugelsicheres Glas *n*, schußsicheres ~, Panzerglas

bullet-resistant, bullet-resisting, bulletproof · kugelsicher, schußsicher

~ **glass,** bullet-resisting ~, bulletproof ~ · kugelsicheres Glas *n*, schußsicheres ~, Panzerglas

bullet-resisting, bullet-resistant, bulletproof · kugelsicher, schußsicher

~ **glass,** bullet-resistant ~, bulletproof ~ · kugelsicheres Glas *n*, schußsicheres ~, Panzerglas

bull-fighting arena · Stierkampfarena *f*

bullion [*A disk of spun handmade flat glass, or the central portion of it, to which the glass maker's iron has been attached*] · Butze *f*

bull's-eye · Ochsenauge *n*

~ **window,** oxeye ~ [*A round or oval window, usually with glazing bars radiating from a circular centre*] · Ochsenauge *n*

bulwark · Bollwerk *n* [*Eine mit Bohlen befestigte Erdaufschüttung, die als behelfsmäßiges Verteidigungswerk diente*]

bumper rail [*It is used for protecting walls from damage by trucks or room contents*] · Stoßschiene *f*

Buna N, nitrile (rubber) adhesive, nitrile (rubber) glue · Nitrilkleber *m*

bundle, cluster · Bündel *n*

~ **of columns,** cluster ~ ~, clustered column, bundle column · Bündelsäule *f*, Säulenbündel *n*

~ ~ **piers,** cluster ~ ~, clustered pier bundle pier, membered pier · Bündelpfeiler *m*, Pfeilerbündel *n*

~ ~ **pillars** → clustered pillar

~ **pier,** clustered ~, membered ~, cluster of piers, bundle of piers · Bündelpfeiler *m*, Pfeilerbündel *n*

~ **pillar** → clustered ~

bung-hole (boiled linseed) oil [*Practically none of the linseed oil now marketed as boiled has actually been heated. The same effect is now obtained by using certain additives or driers. Since the driers were presumably added while the barrelled oil laid in storage, it was thought probably that the driers were introduced through the bungholes of the barrels, and the term 'bunghole boiled' was used, in disparagement, for this practice. Although the oil now treated is accepted as fully equal (and in some cases superior) to oil that has actually been boiled, the term 'bunghole boiled' has persisted and is still often heard*] · kaltbereiteter Leinölfirnis *m*

bungled (piece of) work · Pfuscharbeit *f*

bunter sandstone, mottled ~, Lower-Triassic ~; variegated ~ (Brit.) · Buntsandstein *m*

buoyancy, uplift · Auftrieb *m*

~ **pressure,** uplift ~ · Auftriebsdruck *m*

burglar alarm (system), ~ ~ installation, BA · Einbruchalarmanlage *f*, Einbruchmeldeanlage

burglar-proof, vandal-proof · einbruchsicher

burglar(y) protection · Einbruchschutz *m*, Einbruchsicherung *f*

Burgundian church · burgundische Kirche *f*

~ **Gothic (style)** · burgundische Gotik *f*

~ **portal** · burgundisches Portal *n*

~ **style of sculpture** · burgundische Plastik *f*

~ **vault** · burgundisches Gewölbe *n*

Burgundy pitch · Burgunderpech *n*

burial chamber, tomb ~, sepulchral ~, chamber tomb, hypogeum tomb · Grabkammer *f*, Kammergrab *n*

burial-chamber hypogeum, sepulchral pit · unterirdische Grabkammer *f*

burial mound, funerary ~, tumulus · Grabhügel *m*

~ **place** · Begräbnisplatz *m*, Grabstätte *f*

~ **vault** · Gruftgewölbe *n*

buried tubular conduits, secret installation, hidden installation, concealed installation · Unterputzinstallation *f*

burlap (US); hessian (canvas) (Brit.) · Sackleinen *n*

burlap (canvas) mat — (burnt) clay article

~ **(canvas) mat** (Brit.); hessian (~)
~ (US) · Sackleinenbahn f

burn → burning

to burn, to fire · brennen [*Feuerfest- und Zementindustrie*]

~ ~ **off (paint)** · abbrennen, flammstrahlreinigen

burnability · Brennbarkeit f [*Feuerfest- und Zementindustrie*]

burnable · brennbar [*Feuerfest- und Zementindustrie*]

burned → kiln-~

~ **brick** → (burnt) (clay) ~

~ **clay article** → (burnt) clay product

~ **(~) brick** → (burnt) (~) ~

~ ~ **curved roof(ing) tile** → (burnt) ~ ~ ~ ~

~ ~ ~ **tile roof** → (burnt) ~ ~ ~ ~

~ ~ **hip tile** → (burnt) ~ ~ ~

~ ~ **light(weight) aggregate** → fired ~ ~ ~

~ ~ **product** → (burnt) ~ ~

~ ~ **ridge tile** → (burnt) ~ ~ ~

~ **down** → burnt ~

~ **dust** → ~ filler

~ **filler,** ~ dust, burnt ~ · gebrannter Füller m, ~ Füllstoff m [*Ziegelmehl; Schamottemehl*]

~ **lime** [*substance*] → calcium oxid(e)

~ **ocher,** burnt ~ (US); ~ ochre (Brit.) · gebrannter Ocker m

~ **pipe** → burnt ~

~ **product,** fired ~, burnt ~ · Brenngut n, gebranntes Gut

~ **shale,** burnt ~, fired ~ · gebrannter Schieferton m

~ ~ **product, fired** ~ ~, burnt ~ ~ · gebranntes Schieferton-Erzeugnis n

~ **sienna** burnt ~, orange-red ~ · gebrannte (Terra f di) Siena f, (Terra di) Siena gebrannt

~ **state,** burnt ~, fired ~ · gebrannter Zustand m

~ **umber,** burnt ~ · Umbra f gebrannt, gebrannte Umbra

~ **ware** → burnt ~

~ **wood** burnt ~, charcoal · Holzkohle f

burner capacity · Brennerleistung f

burn(ing), firing · Brand m, Brennen n [*Feuerfest- und Zementindustrie*]

burning → ~ effect

~ **action** → ~ ~ (effect)

~ **appliance,** fire, furnace · Feuerung f, Feuerstätte f [*Jede Einrichtung, in der feste, flüssige oder gasförmige Brennstoffe in solcher Menge verbrannt werden, daß die dabei entstehenden Verbrennungserzeugnisse Feuergefahr und/oder Gesundheitsschädigungen hervorrufen können. Feuerstätten beheizen entweder die Räume in denen sie aufgestellt sind unmittelbar oder von einer Zentrale aus durch Wärmeträger*]

~ ~ **installation,** fire ~, furnace ~ · Feuerungsanlage f, Feuerstättenanlage [*Sie besteht aus Feuerstätte, Verbindungsstück und Schornstein*]

~ ~ **room,** fire ~, furnace ~ [*A room primarily used for the installation of fuel-fired heating equipment other than boilers*] · Feuerungsraum m, Feuerstättenraum

burn(ing) crack, crazing ~, firing ~ · Brandriß m, Brennriß [*Feuerfestindustrie*]

~ **defect,** firing ~ · Brennfehler m

burning (effect), ~ action [*As of a catalyst on the skin*] · ätzende Wirkung f

burn(ing) expansion, firing ~ [*Increase in size from the dry to the fired state of refractory material*] · Brennwachsen n [*Feuerfestindustrie*]

burning installation, ~ plant, firing ~ · Brennanlage f [*Feuerfest- und Zementindustrie*]

(~) **kiln** · (Brenn)Ofen m [*Keramische Industrie und Zementindustrie*]

~ **off (paint),** paint burning [*The removal of paint by a process in which the paint is softened by heat, e.g. from a flame, and then scraped off while still soft*] · Abbrennen n, Flammstrahlreinigen

~ **plant,** ~ installation, firing ~ · Brennanlage f [*Feuerfest- und Zementindustrie*]

burn(ing) process, firing ~ · Brennprozeß m, Brennvorgang m [*Feuerfest- und Zementindustrie*]

~ **range,** firing ~ · Brennbereich m, n [*Feuerfest- und Zementindustrie*]

~ **rate,** firing ~, rate of burning, rate of firing · Brenngeschwindigkeit f [*Feuerfest- und Zementindustrie*]

burning reinforcement [*Cutting reinforcing bars with an oxyacetylene torch*] · Brennschneiden n von Bewehrung, ~ ~ Armierung, ~ ~ (Stahl-)Einlagen

burn(ing) shrinkage → firing ~

burning stone, brimstone; sulfur (US); sulphur (Brit.) · Schwefel m

~ **to (cement) clinker,** firing ~ (~) ~ · (Zement)Klinkerbrennen n

burnish(ing) gold · Mattgold n, Glättgold, Poliergold

~ **silver** · Poliersilber n, Mattsilber, Glättsilber

burn-out · Ausbrennen n [*Gebäude*]

burnt → kiln-~

~ **brick** → ~ clay ~

~ **clay,** burned ~, fired ~ · gebrannter Ton m

(~) ~ **article** → (~) ~ product

(~) (~) **brick**, burned (~) ~, fired (~) ~, clay building ~ [*B.S. 3921*] · (künstlicher) Baustein *m*, gebrannter ~, (Ton)Ziegel *m*, (gebrannter) Stein [*In den USA dürfen auf Grund einer Regierungsentscheidung nur solche Baustoffe als Ziegel (brick) bezeichnet werden, die aus Ton gebrannt sind. Die Bezeichnung anderer Baustoffe als „brick" ist nur in Verbindung mit näherer Charakterisierung gestattet, z.B. concrete brick = Betonblock*]

(~) ~ **curved roof(ing) tile**, burned ~ ~ ~ ~, fired ~ ~ ~ ~ · Dach-Hohlziegel *m*, Hohl(-Dach)ziegel, S-Ziegel [*Dachziegel mit stark gekrümmten Flächen im Gegensatz zu Flachziegeln mit ebenen Flächen. Hohlziegel sind: 1. Firstziegel, 2. Gratziegel, 3. Mönch(ziegel), 4. Nonne(nziegel), 5. Hohlpfanne und 6. Krempziegel*]

(~) ~ ~ **tile roof**, burned ~ ~ ~ ~, fired ~ ~ ~ ~ · Hohlziegeldach *n*, S-Ziegeldach [*Es besteht aus einer Doppelreihe von übereinandergreifenden, gewölbten Dachziegeln, welche Mönch und Nonne genannt werden*]

(~) ~ **hip tile**, burned ~ ~ ~, fired ~ ~ · Gratziegel *m*, Walmziegel [*Der Ausdruck „Walmziegel" wird auch für den Firstziegel verwendet*]

~ ~ **light(weight) aggregate** → fired ~ ~ ~

(~) ~ **masonry (work)**, burned ~ ~ (~) · Mauerwerk *n* aus gebrannten Steinen

(~) ~ **product**, burned ~ ~, fired ~ ~, (~) ~ ~ article · (gebranntes) Tonerzeugnis *n*, (gebrannter) Tongegenstand *m*, (gebrannter) Tonartikel *m*

(~) ~ **ridge tile**, burned ~ ~ ~, fired ~ ~ ~ · Dachkenner *m*, Kammziegel *m*, Walmziegel, Firstziegel [*Der Ausdruck „Walmziegel" wird auch für den Gratziegel verwendet*]

~ **down**, burned ~, destroyed by fire, (fire-)gutted, ruined by fire · abgebrannt, ausgebrannt, niedergebrannt

~ **dust** → burned filler

~ **filler** → burned ~

~ **lime** [*substance*] → calcium oxid(e)

~ **ocher** → burned ~

~ **pipe**, burned ~, fired ~ · gebranntes Rohr *n*

~ **product**, burned ~, fired ~ · Brenngut *n*, gebranntes Gut

~ **shale**, burned ~, fired ~ · gebrannter Schieferton *m*

~ ~ **product**, fired ~ ~, burned ~ ~ · gebranntes Schieferton-Erzeugnis *n*

~ **sienna**, burned ~ orange-red ~ [*B.S. 312*] · gebrannte (Terra *f* di) Siena *f*, (Terra di) Siena gebrannt

~ **state**, burned ~, fired ~ · gebrannter Zustand *m*

~ **umber**, burned ~ [*B.S. 313*] · Umbra *f* gebrannt, gebrannte Umbra

~ **ware**, burned ~, fired ~ · gebrannte Ware *f*

~ **wood**, burned ~, charcoal · Holzkohle *f*

bursting strength · Berstfestigkeit *f*

bus (bar) [*B.S. 159*] · Sammelschiene *f*, Stromschiene

~ **station**, ~ **terminal** · (Auto)Busbahnhof *m*

bush hammer, granulating ~, boucharde · Stockhammer *m*

~ ~ **finish**, bush-hammered ~ · gestockte Oberflächenbehandlung *f*

~ ~ **plaster**, bush-hammered ~ · aufgespitzter (Ver)Putz *m*, gestockter ~

bush-hammered, granulated · gestockt

bush hammering, granulating · Stokken *n*

business area, central ~, ~ district, nucleus, heart of the town, city (area); centre of the town (Brit.) · Geschäftsgebiet *n*, Innenstadt *f*, Stadtkern *m*, Kerngebiet, Stadtzentrum *n*, Kernzone *f*

~ **block**, ~ building · gewerbliches Gebäude *n*

~ **centre** (Brit.); ~ **center** (US) · Geschäftsviertel *n*, Geschäftszentrum *n*

~ **complex** → (retail) shopping ~

~ **district** → ~ area

~ **(local) street** · Geschäftsstraße *f*

~ **parade** → ~ street

~ **premises**, commercial ~, ~ property · bebautes Geschäftsgrundstück *n*

~ **property**, commercial ~, ~ premises · bebautes Geschäftsgrundstück *n*

~ **street**, shopping ~, ~ parade, retail ~ ~, shops street, shops parade · Geschäftsstraße *f*, Ladenstraße, (Ein)Kaufstraße

~ ~, ~ local ~ · Geschäftsstraße *f*

bust pier · Büstenpfeiler *m*

butadiene, $CH_2:CH \cdot CH:CH_2$ · Butadien *n*

~ **styrene synthetic rubber** · Styrol-Butadien-Mischpolymerisat *n*

butanol, butyl alcohol · Butanol *n*, Butylalkohol *m*, C_4H_9OH

Butchers' Hall at Haarlem · Haus *n* der Schlächtergilde zu Harlem

butment → abutment

~ **masonry** → abutment ~

~ **pier** → buttress

~ **wall**, abutment ~ · Strebemauer *f*

buton asphalt · Boetonasphalt *m*

butt (hinge) · Einstemmband *n*, Fi(t)schband, Fitsche *f* [*DIN 401 und DIN 402*]

~ (~) **pin** · Fi(t)schbandstift *m*

to butt joint (stumpf) stoßen

butt joint [*The junction where the ends of two members meet in a square joint*] · stumpfer Stoß *m*, Stumpfstoß

~ ~, heading ~, end-to-end ~ · Stumpffuge f

~ ~ with cover, joint with butt strap · Überlaschung f, Stoß m mit Lasche

~ jointed, butted · (stumpf) gestoßen

~ pin, ~ hinge ~ · Fi(t)schbandstift m

~ strap · Lasche f

~ strap(ped) joint · Laschensicherung f, Laschenverbindung, Laschenstoß m

~ welded · stumpf geschweißt

butted, butt jointed · (stumpf) gestoßen

to butter with mastic · auskitten

butterfly gate · Drosselklappe f

buttery concrete, high-slump ~, plastic(ised) ~ (Brit.); plastic(ized) ~ (US) · Weichbeton m, weicher Beton [Fehlname: plastischer Beton]

button plate · Warzenblech n

buttress; buttressing pier, (a)butment pier [deprecated] [A projecting construction built against a wall to resist a lateral thrust] · Strebepfeiler m, Stützpfeiler, Bogenpfeiler

~ thread · Sägezahngewinde n

~ wall [It is a relatively short wall placed at right angle to the outside of another wall to provide stability] · Stützwand f, Strebewand

buttressed arch · abgestrebter Bogen m

buttressing pier, (a)butment ~ [deprecated]; buttress [A projecting construction built against a wall to resist a lateral thrust] · Strebepfeiler m, Stützpfeiler, Bogenpfeiler

butyl acetate · Butylacetat n

~ alcohol, butanol · Butanol n, Butylalkohol m, C₄H₉OH

~ (preformed) gasket, ~ sealing ~, ~ structural ~ · Butyl(ab)dicht(ungs)profil n, Butylselbstdichtung f

~ rubber · Butylkautschuk m

~ ~ base · Butylkautschukbasis f, Butylkautschukgrundlage f

~ ~ (building) mastic, ~ ~ mastic joint sealer · Butylkautschuk(fugen)mastix m, Butylkautschuk(fugen)kitt m, Butylkautschuk(ver)füllkitt, Butylkautschuk-Fugen(ab)dicht(ungs)kitt, plastische Butylkautschuk-Fugen(ab)dicht(ungs)masse f, plastische Butylkautschuk-Fugenmasse, plastische Butylkautschuk-(Fugen)(Ver)Füllmasse, plastischer Butylkautschuk-(Fugen-)(Ver)Füller m

~ ~ foam · Butylkautschukschaum m

~ sealing gasket → ~ (preformed) ~

~ structural gasket → ~ (preformed) ~

butyric acid · Buttersäure f [Sie entsteht im Grünfuttersilo bei falschgeleiteter Gärung und Ranzigwerden von Fetten und ist ein Betonschädling]

buyers' entrance · Käufereingang m

~ exit · Käuferausgang m

buying department · Einkauf(abteilung) m, (f)

bylaw · Gemeindeordnung f

by-pass [An alternative path for diverting the flow of liquid past instead of through a fitting or appliance] · Umführung f

by-pass(ing) door · Teleskoptür f

by-product · Nebenerzeugnis n

~ anhydrite, chemical ~, synthetic ~ · künstlicher Anhydrit m

~ ~ screed (material), synthetic ~ ~ (~), chemical ~ ~ (~) · Estrich m aus künstlichem Anhydrit [als Baustoff]

~ ~ ~ (topping), chemical ~ ~ (~), synthetic ~ ~ (~) · Estrich m aus künstlichem Anhydrit [als verlegter Baustoff]

~ coke-oven gas · Verkokungsgas n

~ lime, carbide ~ [It is formed as a by-product in the manufacture of acetylene gas by treating calcium carbide with water. This by-product may be in the form of a putty or a dry hydrate] · Karbidkalk m [DIN 1060]

~ ~ putty, carbide ~ ~ · Karbidkalkteig m, Karbildkalkbrei m

byzant, bezant, besant, pellet ornament; disc frieze (Brit.); disk frieze (US) · Scheibenfries m, Scheibenornament n, Scheibenverzierung f

Byzantine architecture · byzantinische Architektur f, ~ Baukunst f

~ building · byzantinisches Bauen n

~ capital · Trapezkapitell n, Trapezkapitäl

~ church · byzantinische Kirche f, orthodoxe ~

~ column · byzantinische Säule f

~ house · byzantinisches Haus n

C

CAB → cement asbestos board

cabinet for drying washing, enclosed ~ ~ ~ ~, (clothes-)drying cabinet · (Wäsche)Trocknungsschrank m [in einer Wohnung]

~ (type) (air) conditioner, ~ (~) (~) conditioning unit · Schrankklimagerät n

cable → prestressing ~

~ action, rope ~ · Kabelwirkung f, Seilwirkung

~ branch, ~ branching · Kabelverzweigung f

~ cantilevering roof → ~-suspended ~ ~

cable CD — cadmium sulphide 142

~ **CD**, ~ conduit, ~ subway, ~ duct; conduit tile (US) · Kabel(kanal)formstein m, Kabel(Kanal)formstück n [DIN 457 und DIN 1049]

~ **clip** · Kabelschelle f

~ **conduit**, ~ duct, ~ subway, ~ CD; conduit tile (US) · Kabel(kanal)formstein m, Kabel(Kanal)formstück n [DIN 457 und DIN 1049]

~ **cover** [B.S. 2484] · Kabelabdeckstein m

~ **distribution box** · Kabel(verteiler)kasten m, Kabelschrank m

~ **duct**, ~ conduit, ~ subway, CD; conduit tile (US) · Kabel(kanal)formstein m, Kabel(Kanal)formstück n [DIN 457 und DIN 1049]

~ ~ · Kabelkanal m

~ **elliptic(al) roof** → ~-suspended ~ ~

~ **entry** · Kabeleinführung f

~ **filling compound**, electrical compound for cable isolations · Kabelausgußmasse f, Kabelvergußmasse

~ **flat roof** → ~-suspended ~ ~

~ **for lighting(s)**, ~ ~ illumination(s) · Lichtkabel n

~ **geometry**, geometry of cables · Seilstatik f

~ **laying**, ~ placing, placing of cables, laying of cables · Kabeleinbau m, Kabelverlegung f

~ **marker** · Kabelmerkstein m

~ **moulding** (Brit.); ~ molding (US); rope ~ · Taustab m [Tauartig gedrehter Stab als Schmuckglied der normannischen Baukunst]

~ **net with opposite curvature**, reversely curved cable net · gegensinnig gekrümmtes Seilnetz n

~ **network** · Kabelnetz n

~ **pipe**, electric ~ ~ · Kabelschutzrohr n

~ **piping** · Kabel-Rohrleitung f

~ **placing**, ~ laying, laying of cables, placing of cables · Kabeleinbau m, Kabelverlegung f

~ **roof** → ~-suspended ~

~ ~ **with saddle shape**, ~ saddle(-shaped) roof · Hängesatteldach n, Sattelhängedach

~ **run** [The general layout of the cables in a building] · Kabelführung f

~ **saddle(-shaped) roof**, ~ roof with saddle shape · Hängesatteldach n, Sattelhängedach

~ **sag**, rope ~, sag of rope, sag of cable · Kabeldurchhang m, Seildurchhang

~ **shaft** · Kabelschacht m

~ **steel** · Kabelstahl m

~ **subway**, ~ conduit, ~ duct, ~ CD; conduit tile (US) · Kabel(kanal)Formstein m, Kabel(Kanal)Formstück n [DIN 457 und DIN 1049]

~ **system**, rope ~ · Seilsystem n, Kabelsystem

~ **tile** · Kabelschutzhaube f [DIN 279]

~ **trench** · Kabelgraben m

~ **trough** · Kabelschale f

~ **wire**, rope ~ · Kabeldraht m, Seildraht

cabled · tauartig gedreht [Taustab]

~ **fluting**, cabling [Slender cylindrical mo(u)ldings in the flutes of columns, for about one-third of the height] · verstäbte Kannelierung f

cable(-suspended) cantilevering roof, rope(-suspended) ~ ~, ~ cantilever(-ed) ~ · Seilkragdach n, Seilauslegerdach, Kabelkragdach, Kabelauslegerdach

~ **elliptic(al) roof**, rope(-suspended) ~ ~ · elliptisches Kabelhängedach n, ~ Seilhängedach

~ **flat roof**, rope(-suspended) ~ ~ · Seilhängeflachdach n, Kabelhängeflachdach

~ **roof**, rope(-suspended) ~, suspension ~ · Seil(hänge)dach n, Kabel(hänge)dach, Hängedach

cabling, cabled fluting [Slender cylindrical mo(u)ldings in the flutes of columns, for about one-third of the height] · verstäbte Kannelierung f

~; cable moulding, rope moulding (Brit.); cable molding, rope molding (US) · Taustab m, Schiffstauverzierung f [Tauartig gedrehter Stab als Schmuckglied der normannischen Baukunst]

cadastral map · Katasterkarte f

~ **survey** · Katastervermessung f

cadmium · Cd, Kadmium n

~ **coat**, ~ coating, ~ finish [B.S. 1706] · Kadmiumbeschichtung f, Kadmiumüberzug m [als Schicht]

~ **coating** · Kadmiumbeschichten n, Kadmiumüberziehen, Kadmiumbeschichtung f, Kadmiumüberzug m [als Tätigkeit]

~ **coat(ing)**, ~ finish [B.S. 1706] · Kadmiumbeschichtung f, Kadmiumüberzug m [als Schicht]

~ **colour** (Brit.); ~ color (US); ~ (pigment) · Kadmiumfarbe f, Kadmium(-pigment) n

~ **finish**, ~ coat(ing) [B.S. 1706] · Kadmiumbeschichtung f, Kadmiumüberzug m [als Schicht]

~ **orange (pigment)** · Kadmiumorange(-pigment) f, (n)

~ **(pigment)**; ~ colour (Brit.); ~ color (US) · Kadmiumfarbe f, Kadmium(-pigment) n

~ **red (pigment)** [It is precipitated cadmium sulphoselenide; manufactured since 1910; not permanent in thin washes and sunlight, not compatible with malachite green] · Kadmiumrot(pigment) n

~ **sulphide**, sulphide of cadmium; cadmium sulfide, sulfide of cadmium (US) · Kadmiumsulfid n, Schwefelkadmium n

~ **yellow (pigment)** [*Cadmium sulphide, manufactured since 1846. Pale varieties prone to fading; susceptible to damp as water-colour, neither compatible with Prussian blue nor, according to some authorities, with several other pigments*] · Kadmiumgelb(-pigment) *n*

cafeteria [*A restaurant in which customers serve themselves from the counter*] · Selbstbedienungsrestaurant *n*

cage, reinforcing ~ · Bewehrungskorb *m*, Armierungskorb

~ → enclosing safety ~

cairn · Steinhaufengrab *n*

caisson → pan

~ **ceiling**, waffle ~, pan(el) ~, cassette ~, coffer(ed) ~, rectangular grid ~, cored ~ · Kassettendecke *f*, kassettierte Decke

~ **design** → waffle pattern

~ **(floor) plate** → rectangular grid (floor) slab

~ **(~) slab** → rectangular grid (~) ~

~ **(panel) floor** → waffle (slab) ~

~ **pattern** → waffle ~

~ **plate** → rectangular grid (floor) slab

~ ~ **floor** → waffle (slab) ~

~ **slab** → rectangular grid (floor) ~

~ **(~) floor** → waffle (~) ~

~ **soffit**, waffle ~, cassette ~, coffer(ed) ~, pan(el) ~, rectangular grid ~, cored ~ · Kassettenuntersicht *f*, kassettierte Untersicht

calathus · Kalathos *m* [*Der geflochtene, offene Korb des korinthischen Kapitäls*]

calc-alkali basalt · Alkalikalkbasalt *m*

~ **granite** · Kalkalkaligranit *m*

~ **rock** · Alkalikalkgestein *n*, Kalkalkaligestein

~ **syenite** · gewöhnlicher Syenit *m*, Kalkalkalisyenit

calcareous, limy [*Of, like, or containing calcium carbonate, calcium, or lime*] · kalk(halt)ig

~ **alabaster** · Kalkalabaster *m*

~ **clay**, lime ~ · Kalkton *m*

~ **concretion**, concretion of lime · Kalkkonkretion *f*

~ **gravel**, limy ~ · Kalkkies *m*

~ **iron-stone**, ferruginous limestone · Kalkeisenstein *m*

~ **marl**, lime ~ · Kalkmergel *m* [*In Deutschland 75%–90% CaCO₃*]

~ **sand**, lime ~ · Kalksand *m*

~ **sandstone**, lime(-cemented) ~ · kalk(halt)iger Sandstein *m*, Kalksandstein

~ **sinter**, calc-sinter · Kalksinter *m*

~ **slate**, limestone ~ · Kalktonschiefer *m*

(calc(areous)) tufa → tufaceous limestone

calcilutyte, lime mud rock · Kalktonstein *m*

calcination, calcining · Kalzinieren *n* [*Austreiben des Kristallwassers durch Erhitzen*]

~ **plant** → calcining ~

to calcine [*To alter composition or physical state by heating below the temperature of fusion*] · kalzinieren

calcined alumina · kalzinierte Tonerde *f*

~ **calcium carbonate** [*substance*] → calcium oxid(e)

~ **gypsum** · Branntgips *m*, gebrannter Gips

~ **magnesite** · gebrannter Magnesit *m*

calcining, calcination · Kalzinieren *n* [*Austreiben des Kristallwassers durch Erhitzen*]

~ **installation**, ~ plant, calcination ~ · Kalzinieranlage *f*

~ **plant**, calcination ~, ~ installation · Kalzinieranlage *f*

calcite, calcspar · Kalkspat *m*, Kalzit *m*, Kanonenspat, CaCO₃ [*Fehlname: Weiß Carrara m*] [*Rhomboedrisch kristallisierte Form des Kalziumkarbonates, gesteinsbildend*]

calcitic limestone · Kalkspat-Kalkstein *m*

~ **marble**, limestone ~, crystalline limestone · Kalkmarmor *m*, kristalliner Kalkstein *m*

calcium · Kalzium *n*, Ca [*Erdalkalimetall*]

~ **aluminate** · Kalziumaluminat *n*

calcium-aluminate cement → high-alumina ~

calcium aluminate hydrate · Kalziumaluminathydrat *n*

~ **aluminoferrite** · Kalziumaluminatferrit *n*

~ **borate** · Boraxkalk *m*

~ **carbide**, carbide of calcium · Kalziumkarbid *n*, CaC₂ [*Durch Zusammenschmelzen von Branntkalk und Kohle gewonnenes Ausgangserzeugnis für Azetylen*]

~ ~ **powder**, powder(ed) calcium carbide · Kalziumkarbidpulver *n*

~ **carbonate** [*chemical name*], carbonate of lime [*substance*] · CaCO₃, Kalziumkarbonat *n* [*Hauptbestandteil des Kalksteins und der Kreide*]

~ **chlorid(e)** (US); ~ chloride (Brit.) · CaCl₂, Chlorkalzium *n*, Kalziumchlorid *n* [*Ein Abbinde(zeit)beschleuniger. Die Abbindezeit läßt sich je nach dem Kalziumchloridanteil im Anmach(e)wasser auf Minuten oder sogar Sekunden verkürzen*]

~ **compound** · Kalziumverbindung *f*

~ **dialuminate** · Kalziumdialuminat *n*

~ **fluoride** (Brit.); ~ fluorid(e) (US) · Kalziumfluorid *n*, CaF₂

~ **grease**, lime base ~ · Kalk(seifen)fett *n*, kalkverseiftes Fett

calcium hydroxid(e) — calculation of wall thickness(es)

~ hydroxid(e) (US); ~ hydroxide (Brit.) · Ca(OH)₂, Kalziumhydroxid *n* [*Molekulargewicht 74,10; es besteht aus 75,7% Kalziumoxid und 24,3% Wasser*]

~ iron silicate · Kalkeisensilikat *n*

calciumlignosulphonate · Kalziumligninsulfonat *n*

calcium lime → commercial (quick-)lime

~ oleate · Kalziumölseife *f*

~ oxid(e) (US); ~ oxide (Brit.) [*chemical names*]; common lime, anhydrous lime, (quick)lime, calcined calcium carbonate, burnt lime, burned lime [*substance*] · Branntkalk *m*, gedeihender Kalk, Brennkalk, gebrannter Kalk, CaO

~ ~ (US); ~ oxide (Brit.) · CaO, Kalziumoxid *n*

~ phosphate · Kalziumphosphat *n*

~ plumbate · Kalziumplumbat *n*

~ (quick)lime → commercial ~

~ rosinate · Kalzium-Harzseife *f*

~ salt · Kalziumsalz *n*

~ silicate, lime ~ · Kalksilikat *n*, Kalziumsilikat, KS, CaSiO₃

~ ~ brick → sand-lime ~

~ ~ ~ lintel → sand-lime brick ~

~ ~ facing brick, sand-lime ~ ~, lime-sand ~ ~ · Kalksandverblender *m*, Kalksandverblendstein *m*

~ ~ hydrate, hydrous calcium silicate [*Any of the various reaction products of calcium silicate and water, often produced by autoclave curing*] · Kalziumsilikathydrat *n*

~ ~ insulation [*Hydrated calcium silicate with organic fiber reinforcement mo(u)lded into rigid shapes*] · Kalziumsilikatdämmung *f*

~ soap · Kalziumseife *f*

~ stearate · Kalziumstearat *n*

~ sulfate hydrate, hydrous calcium sulfate (US); calcium sulphate hydrate, hydrous calcium sulphate (Brit.) · Kalziumsulfathydrat *n*

~ sulphate (Brit.) [*chemical name*]; ~ sulfate (US) [*chemical name*]; sulphate of lime, lime sulphate (Brit.) [*substance*]; sulfate of lime, lime sulfate (US) [*substance*] · Kalziumsulfat *n*, schwefelsaurer Kalk *m*, CaSO₄

~ sulphoaluminate hydrate · Kalziumaluminatsulfathydrat *n*

~ sulphate plaster (Brit.) → anhydrous (gypsum-)plaster

~ ~ ~ screed (Brit.); ~ sulfate ~ ~ (US) · Gipsestrich *m*

calc-sinter, calcareous sinter · Kalksinter *m*

calcspar, calcite · Kalkspat *m*, Kalzit *m*, Kanonenspat, CaCO₃ [*Fehlname: Weiß Carrara m*] [*Rhomboedrisch kristallisierte Form des Kalziumkarbonats, gesteinsbildend*]

calc tufa → tufaceous limestone

calculable value, computable ~ · Rechengröße *f*

calculated · rechnerisch ermittelt, errechnet

~ point of origin for moment allowance · rechnerischer Anfangspunkt *m* der Momentendeckung

calculating, calculation · Berechnung

~ assumption → ~ hypothesis

~ basis, calculation ~, basis of calculation · Rechengrundlage *f*, Berechnungsgrundlage

~ error, calculation ~ · Rechenfehler *m*, Berechnungsfehler

~ formula, calculation ~ · Rechenformel *f*, Berechnungsformel

~ hypothesis, calculation ~, ~ assumption · Rechenannahme *f*, Berechnungsannahme

~ method, calculation ~, method of calculation · Rechenverfahren *n*, Berechnungsverfahren, rechnerisches Verfahren

~ operation, calculation ~ · Berechnungsgang *m*, Rechengang [*Baustatik*]

~ table, calculation ~ · Berechnungstabelle *f*, Berechnungstafel *f*, Rechentabelle, Rechentafel

~ weight, calculation ~ · Berechnungsgewicht *n*

calculation, calculating · Berechnung *f*

~, analysis, structural ~ · (statische) Berechnung *f*

~ aid · Rechenhilfsmittel *n*

~ assumption, ~ hypothesis, calculating ~ · Rechenannahme *f*, Berechnungsannahme

~ basis, calculating ~, basis of calculation · Berechnungsgrundlage *f*, Rechengrundlage

~ error, calculating ~ · Berechnungsfehler *m*, Rechenfehler

~ formula, calculating ~ · Berechnungsformel *f*, Rechenformel

~ hypothesis, ~ assumption, calculating ~ · Rechenannahme *f*, Berechnungsannahme

~ method, calculating ~, method of calculation · Berechnungsverfahren *n* rechnerisches Verfahren, Rechenverfahren

~ of daylight, daylight calculation · Tageslichtberechnung *f*

~ ~ diffusion · Diffusionsberechnung *f*

~ ~ heat insulation · Wärmedämmberechnung *f*

~ ~ ~ loss(es), computation ~ ~ ~, heat loss calculation, heat loss computation · Wärmeverlustberechnung *f*

~ ~ loading, loading calculation · Belastungsberechnung *f*

~ ~ wall thickness(es) · Wanddickenberechnung *f* [*Fehlname: Wandstärkenberechnung*]

calculation operation — candle lighting

~ **operation**, calculating ~, · Berechnungsgang *m*, Rechengang [*Baustatik*]

~ **table**, calculating ~ · Rechentabelle *f*, Rechentafel *f*, Berechnungstabelle, Berechnungstafel

~ **value** · Rechenwert *m*

~ **weight**, calculating ~ · Berechnungsgewicht *n*

(~) **work sheet** · Kalkulationsvordruck *m*

Calcutta (linseed) oil · indisches Leinöl *n*

caldarium, hot room · Caldarium *n*, römisches Schwitzbad *n* [*Heißbaderaum römischer Thermen*]

calefactory, warming-house · Calefactorium *n*, Wärmestube *f*

calibre (Brit.); caliber (US) [*The bore of a pipe*] · Kaliber *n*

calked, caulked, fullered · verstemmt, kalfatert

~ **joint**, caulked ~, fullered ~ · Stemmdichtung *f*

~ ~, caulked ~, fullered ~ · Stemmuffe *f*

calking, fullering, caulking, CLKG · Kalfatern *n*, Verstemmen

~, caulking, CLKG · Verkitten *n*

~, caulking, cogging, cocking, corking, cogged joint · Verkämmung *f* [*Holzverband im Fachwerkbau*]

~ **(compound)**, caulking (~) · Stemmmasse *f*

call and signalling system (Brit.); ~ ~ signaling ~ (US) · Ruf- und Signalanlage *f*

~ **bell**, alarm ~ · Alarmklingel *f*

~ **box** → public (tele)phone coin ~

~ **lamp** · Ruflampe *f*

~ **system** · Rufanlage *f*

callow, place brick [*Underburned soft brick, used only for walls that are to be plastered*] · Schwachbrandziegel *m*, Schwachbrandstein *m*

calorific value, heating ~ · Heizwert *m*, Brennwert, Verbrennungswärme *f* [*Anzahl der Kalorien der bei völliger Verbrennung von Brennstoff je Mengeneinheit (1 kg fest oder flüssig, 1 m³ gasförmig) des Brennstoffes freiwerdenden Wärme*]

calorifier · Gegenstromapparat *m* [*Er überträgt Dampfwärme oder Wasserwärme an Wasser*]

calorimeter [*An instrument for measuring heat exchange during a chemical reaction such as the quantities of heat liberated by the combustion of a fuel or hydration of a cement*] · Kalorimeter *n*

~, solution ~ [*The materials are allowed to react in the dissolved state inside an insulated vessel*] · Lösungskalorimeter *n*, Lösungswärmemesser *m*

~ **without heat transmission**, adiabatic calorimeter · adiabatisches Kalorimeter *n*, Kalorimeter ohne Wärmeabfluß

calorimetric measurement(s), measurement(s) of heat (capacities), calorimetry · Kalorimetrie *f*, Wärmemengenmessung(en) *f(pl)*

~ **test (for organic impurities)** → Abrams' test

calorimetry, calorimetric measurement(s), measurement(s) of heat (capacities) · Kalorimetrie *f*, Wärmemengenmessung(en) *f(pl)*

calorised (Brit.); calorized · kalorisiert, alitiert [*Stahl*]

calorising (heat treatment) (Brit.); calorizing (~ ~) [*steel*] · Alitierung *f*, Kalorisierung

calorized; calorised (Brit.) · kalorisiert, alitiert [*Stahl*]

calorizing (heat treatment); calorising (~ ~) (Brit.) [*steel*] · Alitierung *f*, Kalorisierung

calotte, spherical segment, (spherical) cap · (Kugel)Kalotte *f*, Kugelsegment *n*, Kugelabschnitt *m*, Kugelhaube *f*, Kugelhelm *m*, Kugelmütze *f*

Calvary · Kalvarienberg *m*

camber, hog(ging) [*Girders and trusses may be built with hog to counteract their sag*] · Aufwölbung *f*, Stich *m*, Überhöhung

came [*An H-section strip of lead or of soft copper, shaped to fix each piece of glass to the next one, in leaded lights or stained-glass windows*] · Rute *f*, Steg *m* [*Verglasung*]

camouflage coat · Tarnanstrich *m*, Tarnaufstrich

~ **lacquer** · Tarnlack *m*

~ **paint** · Tarn(anstrich)farbe *f*

campanile, belfry, isolated bell-tower, free-standing bell-tower · freistehender Glockenturm *m*, Campanile *m*, Kampanile

campus, university ground · Hochschulgelände *n*

Camus system · Montagebauweise *f* Camus, Fertig(teil)bauweise

Canadian asbestos, chrysotile ~ · Chrysotilasbest *m*, Kanadaasbest

~ **latch** → thumb ~

~ **(oil of) turpentine**, ~ spirit ~ ~ · kanadisches Terpentinöl *n*

canal(is), channel · Kanalis *m* [*Der seit klassischer Zeit konkave Teil zwischen den Voluten am ionischen Kapitäl*]

canary yellow · Kanariengelb *n*

cancel → chancel

~ **arch** → chancel ~

cancelli · Cancelli *f* [*In der altchristlichen Basilika meist steinerne Chorschranken, die den Raum für den Chor gegen den Gemeinderaum abgrenzen*]

candelabra, candelabrum [*A branched stand to carry lights. A chandelier*] · Kandelaber *m*

candidate material · Konkurrenzwerkstoff *m*

candle lighting, ~ illumination · Kerzenbeleuchtung *f*

candle pitch — cantilever(ed) folded (flat) slab roof

~ **pitch,** fat(ty-acid) ~ · Fettpech *n*

~ **works** · Kerzenfabrik *f*

Candlot's salt, Michaelis' ~ · Zementbazillus *m*

cane fibre insulation (Brit.); ~ fiber ~ (US) · Zuckerrohrfaserdämmung *f*

~ **trash,** bagasse · ausgepreßtes Zuckerrohr *n,* Bagasse *f*

~ ~ **board,** ~ ~ sheet, bagasse ~ · Bagasseplatte *f,* Platte aus ausgepreßtem Zuckerrohr

~ ~ **sheet,** ~ ~ board, bagasse ~ · Platte *f* aus ausgepreßten Zuckerrohr, Bagasseplatte

~ ~ **tar,** bagasse ~ · Bagasseteer *m*

canephora [*A sculptured female figure carrying a basket on her head*] · Kanephore *f,* Korbträgerin *f*

canon · Kanon *m* [*Zur Bestimmung von Reihenfolge und Größenordnung*]

~ · Domherr *m*

canaopy, baldachin, baldaauin [*A projection or hood over a tomb, altar, or niche*] · Baldachin *m*

~ · Schutzdach *n,* Vordach

~ → ciborium

~ **lip** · Schutzdachkante *f,* Vordachkante

to cant, to bevel, to slope, to splay · ausschrägen, abschrägen, abkragen, verschrägen

cant, bevel, splay, slope · Ausschrägung *f,* Abschrägung, Verschrägung, Abkragung, Schräge *f*

~, slope, bevel, splay · Druckschlag *m* [*Gewölbe*]

cant(-bay) window [*A window in which the sides are not at right angles to the wall*] · polygonales Erkerfenster *n*

cant bonder → splay ~

~ **bondstone** → splay bonder

~ **brick** → splay ~

~ **column** [*A column with a polygonal section*] · polygonale Säule *f*

~ **header** → splay bonder

~ **moulding** → splay ~

~ **of a masonry wall** → splay ~ ~ ~ ~

~ ~ ~ **wall** → splay ~ ~ ~

~ **stretcher** → splay ~

~ **strip** (US) → eave(s) board

canted, sloped, splayed; bevelled (Brit.); beveled (US) · abgeschrägt, ausgeschrägt, abgekragt

~ **folding** → splayed ~

canteen · Kantine *f*

~ **block,** ~ building · Kantinengebäude *n*

~ **building,** ~ block · Kantinengebäude *n*

~ **counter** · Kantinentresen *m*

~ **store** · Kantinenlager *n*

cantharus · Kantharus *m*

to cantilever · auskragen, vorkragen

cantilever [*A self-supporting projection without external bracing*] · Auskragung *f,* Vorkragung

~ [*A beam, girder or slab fixed at one extremity and unsupported at the other*] · Auslegerarm *m,* Kragarm, vorkragender Arm, auskragender Arm

~ **conoid,** cantilevered ~, cantilevering ~, oversailing ~ · Kragkonoid *n,* Auslegerkonoid

~ **course** → cantilevering ~

~ **diaphragm** · Kragscheibe *f*

~ **effect** · Kragwirkung *f*

~ **floor** → cantilevering ~

~ **girder** → cantilevering ~

~ **length** → cantilever(ed) ~

~ **load** · Kragarmlast *f*

~ **method** · Freiträger-Methode *f* [*Baustatik*]

~ **moment** · Kragmoment *n*

~ **segment** → cantilever(ed) ~

~ **storey** (Brit.) → cantilever(ing) floor

~ **vault** → corbel ~

cantilever(ed) arch(ed girder), cantilevering ~ (~), corbel ~ (~), false ~ (~), ~ curved ~ · vorkragender Bogen(träger) *m,* auskragender ~, ~ gekrümmter Träger, Auslegerbogen(-träger), Kragbogen(träger)

~ **beam,** cantilevering ~; outrigger (US) · Freibalken(träger) *m* Krag(arm)balken(träger), vorkragender Balken(träger), Auslegerbalken(träger), auskragender Balken(träger)

~ **brick** → corbel ~

~ **component,** ~ unit, ~ member, cantilevering ~ · Auslegerelement *n,* Kragelement, vorkragendes Element, auskragendes Element

~ **conoid,** cantilevering ~, oversailing ~ · Kragkonoid *n,* Auslegerkonoid

~ **course** → cantilever(ing) ~

~ **crane (runway) girder,** cantilevering ~ (~) · Kran(bahn)kragträger *m*

~ **cupola** → corbel dome

~ **curved girder** → ~ arch(ed girder)

~ **disc** → ~ sheet

~ **dome** → corbel ~

~ **end,** cantilevering ~ · Auslegerende *n,* Kragende

~ **floor,** cantilevering ~, oversailing ~ · Auslegerdecke *f,* Kragdecke, auskragende Decke, vorkragende Decke

~ ~ **slab,** cantilevering ~, ~ auskragende Deckenplatte *f,* vorkragende ~, Kragdeckenplatte, Auslegerdeckenplatte

~ **folded (flat) slab roof** → ~ ~ plate ~

cantilever(ed) folded plate roof — cantilevering plate

~ ~ **plate roof**, ~ ~ slab ~, ~ prismatic shell ~, cantilevering ~ ~ ~; ~ hipped-plate ~, ~ tilted-slab ~ (US) · Auslegerfaltwerkdach n, Kragfaltwerkdach, auskragendes Faltwerkdach, vorkragendes Faltwerkdach

~ ~ **slab roof** → ~ ~ plate ~

~ **frame** · Kragrahmen m

~ **girder**, cantilevering ~ [It is supported at one end only but is rigidly held in position at that end] · vorkragender Träger m, auskragender ~, frei ausladender ~, Freiträger, Konsolträger, Kragträger, Auslegerträger, einseitig eingespannter Träger

~ **hipped-plate roof** (US) → ~ folded plate ~

~ **landing**, cantilevering ~ · Krag(treppen)podest n

~ **length**, cantilevering ~ · Auslegerlänge f, Kraglänge, Freilänge

~ **load**, cantilevering ~ · Auslegerlast f, Kraglast

~ **masonry (work)**, corbel ~ (~), cantilevering ~ (~), false ~ (~) · vorkragendes Mauerwerk n, auskragendes ~, Auslegermauerwerk, Kragmauerwerk

~ **member** → ~ component

~ **patio** → ~ terrace

~ **plate** → ~ slab

~ **prismatic shell roof** → ~ folded plate ~

~ **roof**, cantilevering ~ · Kragdach n, Auslegerdach, vorkragendes Dach, auskragendes Dach, Konsoldach

~ ~ **slab**, cantilevering ~ ~ · Auslegerdachplatte f, Kragdachplatte, vorkragende Dachplatte, auskragende Dachplatte

~ **segment**, cantilevering ~ · auskragendes Segment n, vorkragendes ~, Kragsegment, Auslegersegment

~ **sheet**, cantilevering ~, ~ disc; ~ disk (US) · auskragende Scheibe f, vorkragende ~, Kragscheibe, Auslegerscheibe

~ **shell**, cantilevering ~ · auskragende Schale f, vorkragende ~, Auslegerschale, Kragschale

~ **slab**, cantilevering ~, ~ plate · auskragende Platte f, vorkragende ~, Kragplatte, Auslegerplatte

~ **stair(case)**, cantilevering ~ · auskragende Treppe f, vorkragende ~, Auslegertreppe, Kragtreppe

~ **step**, cantilevering ~, hanging ~ · auskragende Stufe f, vorkragende ~, Auslegerstufe, Kragstufe, Freiträger m

~ **storey** (Brit.) → cantilever(ing) floor

~ **system**, cantilevering ~ · Kragsystem n [Senkrechtes Tragsystem. Punkte der Lastenbündelung in der Mitte]

~ **terrace**, ~ patio, cantilevering ~ · auskragende Terrasse f, vorkragende ~, Auslegerterrasse, Kragterrasse

~ **tilted-slab roof** (US) → ~ folded plate ~

~ **unit** → ~ component

cantilevering, projecting · Auskragen n, Vorkragen, Überstehen, Ausladen

~, projecting · Ausladung f, Überstand m, Vorkragung, Auskragung

~ **arch(ed girder)** → cantilever(ed) ~ (~)

~ **beam**, cantilever(ed) ~; outrigger (US) · Freibalken(träger) m, Krag(arm)balken(träger), vorkragender Balken(träger), Auslegerbalken(träger), auskragender Balken(träger)

~ **brick** → corbel ~

~ **component** → cantilever(ed) ~

~ **conoid**, oversailing ~, cantilever(ed) ~ · Kragkonoid n, Auslegerkonoid

cantilever(ing) course, cantilevered ~, oversailing ~ [A course of bricks or stones that projects over the face of a masonry wall] · Kragschicht f, Auslegerschicht

cantilevering crane (runway) girder → cantilever(ed) ~ (~) ~

~ **cupola** → corbel dome

~ **curved girder** → cantilever(ed) arch(ed girder)

~ **disk** → cantilever(ed) sheet

~ **dome** → corbel ~

~ **end**, cantilever(ed) ~ · Kragende n, Auslegerende

cantilever(ing) floor, cantilevered ~; ~ storey (Brit.); ~ story (US) · Kranzgeschoß n, Kranzstockwerk n, Kranzetage f, Kraggeschoß, Kragstockwerk, Kragetage

cantilevering floor, cantilever(ed) ~, oversailing ~ · Auslegerdecke f, Kragdecke, auskragende Decke, vorkragende Decke

~ ~ **slab** → cantilever(ed) ~ ~

~ **folded (flat) slab roof** → cantilever(ed) folded plate ~

~ ~ **plate roof** → cantilever(ed) ~ ~ ~

~ ~ **slab roof** → cantilever(ed) folded plate ~

~ **girder**, cantilevering ~ · Konsolträger m, Kragträger, Auslegerträger

~ **hipped-plate roof** (US) → cantilever(ed) folded plate ~

~ **landing**, cantilevering ~ · Krag(treppen)podest n

~ **length**, cantilever(ed) ~ · Auslegerlänge f, Kraglänge, Freilänge

~ **load**, cantilever(ed) ~ · Auslegerlast f, Kraglast

~ **masonry (work)** → corbel ~ (~)

~ **member** → cantilever(ed) component

~ **patio** → cantilever(ed) terrace

~ **plate** → cantilever(ed) slab

cantilevering prismatic shell roof — capillary motion 148

~ prismatic shell roof → cantilever(ed) folded plate ~

~ roof, cantilever(ed) ~ · Kragdach n, Auslegerdach, vorkragendes Dach, auskragendes Dach, Konsoldach

~ ~ slab → cantilever(ed) ~ ~

~ segment → cantilever(ed) ~

~ sheet → cantilever(ed) ~

~ shell, cantilever(ed) ~ · auskragende Schale f, vorkragende ~, Auslegerschale, Kragschale

~ slab → cantilever(ed) ~

~ stair(case) → cantilever(ed) ~

~ step, cantilever(ed) ~, hanging ~ · auskragende Stufe f, vorkragende ~, Auslegerstufe, Kragstufe, Freiträger m

~ stone step, cantilever(ed) ~ ~ · Krag-Steinstufe f

cantilever(ing) storey (Brit.) → ~ floor

cantilevering system, cantilever(ed) ~ · Kragsystem n [*Senkrechtes Tragsystem. Punkte der Lastenbündelung in der Mitte*]

~ terrace → cantilever(ed) ~

~ tilted-slab roof → cantilever(ed) folded plate ~

~ unit → cantilever(ed) component

canting, sloping, splaying; bevelling, (Brit.); beveling (US) · Ausschrägen n, Abschrägen, Verschrägen, Abkragen

contoned pier · kantonierter Pfeiler m

canvas, jute ~ · Baumwolljute f

~ painting · Leinwandmalerei f

canyon effect (of high buildings) · Schluchtwirkung f

~ street · Schluchtstraße f

cap, blank ~ [*A pipe fitting fixed over the spigot end of a pipe or fitting to close it*] · Kappe f

~ · Glocke f [*Sonderform des First- oder Gratziegels für Zeltdächer zur Abdeckung der am Firstpunkt zusammentreffenden Grate.*]

~, pipe ~ · (Rohr)Deckel m, (Rohr)Kappe f

~ → (slab) cap(ping)

~ · Kappe f [*Metallbedachung*]

~ concrete · Kappenbeton m

to cap-flash · mit Kappleiste (versehen), ~ Kappstreifen (~), ~ Überhangleiste (~), ~ Überhangstreifen (~)

cap flashing, counter ~ · oberer Anschluß [*Siehe Anmerkung unter „Anschluß"*]

~ ~ (piece), counter ~ (~), cover ~ (~), apron [*See remark under 'Anschluß'*] · Kappleiste f, Kappstreifen m, Überhangleiste, Überhangstreifen

~ sheet [*The top layer of mineral surfaced bitumen felt when employed in built-up roof(ing)*] · oberste Dachhautlage f

~ ~ · Decklage f [*Dachpappe*]

~ (vault) · gewölbte Kappe f, Kappengewölbe n

capability, property, capacity, power, quality · Eigenschaft f, Vermögen n, Fähigkeit f

capable of bearing wheel loads, traversable · befahrbar

~ ~ taking a high luster polish, ~ ~ ~ ~ ~ lustre ~ · hochglanzpolierbar

capacity, quality, power, capability, property · Eigenschaft f, Vermögen n, Fähigkeit f

~ moment · Tragmoment n

~ of initial set(ting) → power ~ ~ ~

~ ~ set(ting) → set(ting) power

Cape asbestos, blue ~, crocidolite ~ · Blauasbest m, Kapasbest

capilla mayor · Hauptkapelle f [*In spanischen Kirchen der Altarraum im mittleren Teil des Chors, vom Chorumgang und dem Gemeinderaum durch hohe steinerne Schranken getrennt, die meist mit reichem plastischen Schmuck ausgestattet sind*]

capillarimeter, capillary apparatus · Kapillarimeter n

capillarity → capillary action

~ → capillary movement

~ of concrete · Betonkapillarität f

capillary · Kapillare f

~ → ~ tube

~ absorption · kapillare Aufsaugung f

~ action, capillarity · Kapillarfähigkeit f, Kapillarwirkung f, Haarröhrchenwirkung

~ apparatus, capillarimeter · Kapillarimeter n

~ attraction · Porensaugwirkung f, Rohrsaugkraft f, Kapillarattraktion f [*Folge des Unterdruckes, welcher durch die molekularen Anziehungskräfte in der Grenzfläche der Bodenteilchen gegen Wasser entsteht*]

~ break, ~ groove · Kapillarsperre f

~ condensation · Kapillarkondensation f

~ equilibrium · kapillares Gleichgewicht n

~ flow → ~ rise

~ force · Haarröhrchenkraft f, Kapillarkraft

~ fringe · Kapillarsaum m, Saugsaum, Kapillarzone f, Saugraum m [*Der Grundwasseroberfläche aufliegender Raum, in welchem der Wasserdruck von unten nach oben noch abnimmt*]

~ groove, ~ break · Kapillarsperre f

~ head · kapillare Druckhöhe f

~ moisture, ~ water, water of capillarity, fringe water · Porensaugwasser n, Haarröhrchenwasser, Kapillarwasser [*Wasser, welches der Porensaugwirkung gefolgt ist*]

~ motion → ~ movement

capillary movement — carbolic acid

~ **movement,** ~ **motion, capillarity** [*The movement of a liquid in the interstices of soil or other porous material due to surface tension*] · Kapillarbewegung *f*, Kapillarität *f*

~ **path** · Kapillarweg *m*

~ **pore** · Kapillarpore *f*

~ **potential** · Kapillarpotential *n*

~ **pressure** · Kapillardruck *m*, Krümmungsdruck [*Formelzeichen: P_k. Resultierende der Kapillarspannungen in Richtung der Normalen zur Oberfläche, bezogen auf die Flächeneinheit*]

capillaryproof · kapillardicht

capillary pyrite, millerite · Haarkies *m*, Millerit *m*, NiS (Min.)

~ **radius** · Kapillarhalbmesser *m*

~ **rise,** ~ **flow** · Kapillaranstieg *m*, kapillarer Anstieg [*Anstieg einer Flüssigkeit unter dem Einfluß der Kapillarspannung*]

~ **saturation** · kapillare Sättigung *f*

~ **siphoning** · kapillare Heberwirkung *f*

~ **(tube)** · Haarrohr *n*, Kapillarrohr, Kapillarröhrchen *n*, Haarröhrchen

~ **visco(si)meter** · Kapillar-Viskosimeter *n*

~ **water,** ~ **moisture, water of capillarity, fringe water** · Porensaugwasser *n*, Haarröhrchenwasser, Kapillarwasser [*Wasser, welches der Porensaugwirkung gefolgt ist*]

capital · Kapitell *n*, Kapitäl

~ **carving** · Kapitellplastik *f*, Kapitälplastik

capok cloth; ~ **fabric** [*misnomer*] · Kapokgewebe *n*

capped pipe [*A drain pipe with coverplate for cleaning purposes*] · Reinigungsdeckelrohr *n*, Putzdeckelrohr

capping, coping, cope · Abdeckung *f*, Abwässerung [*Freistehende Bauteile wie Einfried(ig)ungsmauern, Pfeiler usw. müssen mit einer wetterfesten, wasserundurchlässigen Schicht abgedeckt werden, um das Eindringen von Wasser in das Innere des Mauerwerks zu verhindern*]

~ [*A separate metal section fixed externally to certain types of patent glazing bar to secure the glass, afford protection to the stem of the bar and check weather penetration*] · Deckkappe *f* [*kittlose Verglasung*]

~ · Kappe *f*

cap(ping) → slab ~

capping block → (concrete) coping ~

~ **slab, coping** ~ · (Ab)Deckplatte *f* [*DIN 455*]

~ ~ → (concrete) coping ~

~ **stone** → coping ~

~ **tile** → (concrete) coping block

capstone · Deckstein *m*, Überlieger *m* [*Megalithgrab*]

caption · Bildunterschrift *f*

car park, parking garage · Großgarage *f*

~ ~ **basement** · Kellergroßgarage *f*

(~) **parking roof** · Parkdach *n*

~ **place** · (PKW-)Einstellplatz *m*, (PKW-)Standplatz, (PKW-)Parkstand *m*, (PKW-)Abstellplatz [*Die zum Aufstellen eines PKW bestimmte Fläche; sie setzt sich zusammen aus der Stellfläche, den Zwischenräumen, dem Abstand sowie gegebenenfalls einem Schutzstreifen*]

~ **port** · Wagenunterstand *m*

~ **ramp** · PKW-Rampe *f*

~ **stall** · PKW-Boxe *f*

car-wash booth · Wagenwaschkabine *f*

car wash(down) (yard) · PKW-Waschplatz *m*, Waschplatz für PKW

caracole, vis, helical stair(case), spiral stair(case), cockle stair(case), corcscrew stair(case), circular stair(case) · Wendeltreppe *f*, Schnecke(ntreppe) *f*, Schneckenstiege *f*

caravan city · Karawanenstadt *f*

caravansary, khān, caravanserai · Karawanserei *f*, Konak *m*, (C)Han *m*, karawan serail *m*

carbamide resin, urethane ~ · Karbamidharz *n*, Urethanharz

carbide lime → by-product ~

~ ~ **putty, by-product** ~ ~ · Karbidkalkteig *m*, Karbidkalkbrei *m*

~ **of calcium, calcium carbide** · Kalziumkarbid *n*, CaC_2 [*Durch Zusammenschmelzen von Branntkalk und Kohle gewonnenes Ausgangserzeugnis für Azetylen*]

~ ~ **silicon, carbon silicide, silicon carbide** · Karborund *n*, Siliziumkarbid *n*, Siliziumkohlenstoff *m* [*Synthetisches Erzeugnis mit der Formel SiC. Das industriell hergestellte Produkt kann Verunreinigungen enthalten*]

~ ~ ~ **brick, carbon silicide** ~**, silicon carbide** ~ · Siliziumkarbidstein *m*, Karborundstein, Siliziumkohlenstoffstein, SiC-Stein

~ ~ ~ **mortar, silicon carbide** ~**, carbon silicide** ~ · Siliziumkarbidmörtel *m*, Karborundmörtel, Siliziumkohlenstoffmörtel, SiC-Mörtel

~ ~ ~ **slab, carbon silicide** ~**, silicon carbide** ~ · Siliziumkarbidplatte *f*, Karborundplatte, Siliziumkohlenstoffplatte, SiC-Platte

~ **refractory (product)** · Karbiderzeugnis *n*

carbolic acid, coal tar creosote, phenol [*BS 144*] · Phenol *n*, Karbolsäure *f*, Steinkohlenteerkreosot *n*, Phenylalkohol *m*, C_6H_5OH

carbolineum — cargo (handling) block

carbolineum, peterlineum · Karbolineum n [*Der Begriff Karbolineum, den heute die Mehrheit auch der Bau- und Holzfachwelt für alle möglichen Mittel verwendet, wurde von Avenarius geschaffen, womit er eine ganz bestimmte Qualität eines hochwertigen Teeröls festlegte*]

carbon · Kohlenstoff m

~ **bisulphide,** ~ disulphide (Brit.); ~ bisulfide, ~ disulfid(e) (US) · Schwefelkohlenstoff m

~ **black (pigment)** · Ruß m, Schwarzpigment m aus Kohlenstoff, Kohlenstoffpigment, Rußpigment

~ **brick** · Kohlenstoffstein m

~ **construction(al) (grade) steel,** ~ structural (~) ~ · Kohlenstoffbaustahl m

~ **content,** percentage of carbon · Kohlenstoffanteil m, Kohlenstoffgehalt m

~ **dioxid(e)** (US); ~ dioxide (Brit.) · Kohlendioxid n, CO_2 [*Fehlname: Kohlensäure f*]

~ **disulphide,** ~ bisulphide (Brit.); ~ disulfide, ~ bisulfide (US) · Schwefelkohlenstoff m

~ **rivet steel** · Kohlenstoffnietstahl m

~ **rock** · karbonisches Gestein n

~ **silicide,** carbide of silicon, silicon carbide · SiC n, Karborund n, Siliziumkarbid n, Siliziumkohlenstoff m [*Synthetisches Erzeugnis mit der Formel SiC. Das industriell hergestellte Produkt kann Verunreinigungen enthalten*]

~ ~ **brick,** carbide of silicon ~, silicon carbide ~ · Siliziumkarbidstein m, Karborundstein, Siliziumkohlenstoffstein, SiC-Stein

~ ~ **mortar,** silicon carbide ~, carbide of silicon ~ · Siliziumkarbidmörtel m, Karborundmörtel, Siliziumkohlenstoffmörtel, SiC-Mörtel

~ ~ **refractory material** → silicon carbide refractory (product)

~ ~ **slab,** carbide of silicon ~, silicon carbide ~ · Siliziumkarbidplatte f, Karborundplatte, Siliziumkohlenstoffplatte, SiC-Platte

~ **steel** · (einfacher) Kohlenstoffstahl m (unlegierter) ~

~ ~ **curtain wall** · Kohlenstoffstahl-Vorhangwand f

~ **structural (grade) steel,** ~ construction(al) (~) ~ · Kohlenstoffbaustahl m

~ **tetrachloride,** tetrachloromethane, CCl_4 · Tetrachlorkohlenstoff m, Tetrachlormethan n

carbonaceous shale, combustible ~ · Brandschiefer m, Brennschiefer, Kohlenschiefer

to carbonate · karbonatisieren

carbonate hardness, temporary ~ · Karbonathärte f, vorübergehende Härte, KH

~ **of lead,** lead carbonate · Bleikarbonat n, $PbCO_3$

~ ~ **lime** [*substance*], calcium carbonate [*chemical name*] · $CaCO_3$, Kalziumkarbonat n [*Hauptbestandteil des Kalksteins und der Kreide*]

~ (~) **potash,** potassium carbonate · Kaliumkarbonat n, Pottasche f, kohlensaures Kalium n, K_2CO_3

~ **rock** · Karbonatgestein n, karbonatisches Gestein

carbonation [*Reaction between carbon dioxid(e) and calcium compounds, especially in cement paste, mortar, or concrete, to produce calcium carbonate*] · Karbonatisierung f [*Fehlname: Karbonisierung*]

~ **treatment,** artificial carbonation · Karbonatisieren n [*Fehlname: Karbonisieren*]

carbonator, vat · Fällbottich m [*Niederschlagsverfahren zur Bleiweißherstellung*]

carboniferous limestone · Kohlenkalk-(stein) m, Kulmkalk [*Fehlname: belgischer Granit m. Ein dunkelfarbiger Kalkstein, der zu Platten verarbeitet und als Werkstein verwendet wird*]

~ **sandstone** → ganister

carbonitrided steel · gasnitrierter Stahl m, karbonitrierter ~

carbonitriding · Karbonitrierung f, Gasnitrierung

carbonized bones, charred ~ · Knochenkohle f

carcass, fabric; shell [*Canada*]; carcase [*deprecated*] [*A building or structure that is structurally complete but otherwise unfinished*] · Rohbau m

~ **work,** fabric ~, carcassing; shell work [*Canada*] [*Constructing the carcass of a building*] · (Gebäude)Rohbauarbeiten fpl

carcassing, carcass work, fabric work; shell work [*Canada*] [*Constructing the carcass of a building*] · Rohbauarbeiten fpl, Gebäude~

~ **timber,** framing ~ [*Timber in a building or structure that performs a structural function*] · Bauholz n für den Hochbau, Rohbauholz, Zimmereiholz, Konstruktionsholz, Bau(nutz)holz

card-holder · Namenschildausschnitt m

card(paper) liner · Papierabklebung f [*Preßstroh-Dämmplatte*]

cardinal point · Himmelsrichtung f

care · Pflege f

caretaker, porter · Hausmeister m, Hauswart m

caretaker's flat, porter's ~, ~ apartment (unit) · Hausmeister-(Geschoß-) Wohnung f, Hausmeister-Etagenwohnung, Hausmeister-Stockwerkwohnung

cargo block, ~ handling ~, ~ (handling) building · Frachtgebäude n

~ **building,** ~ handling ~, ~ (handling) block · Frachtgebäude n

~ **(handling) block,** ~ (~) building · Frachtgebäude n

cargo (handling) building — cartridge

~ (~) building, ~ (~) block · Frachtgebäude n

Carmelite church · Karmeliterkirche f

carmine (pigment) · Karmin(pigment) n

carnary, charnel-house, skullhouse, bone house, ossuary, ossarium · Karner m, Beinhaus n, Karcher, Kerner, Kärner [Eine meist zweigeschossige Friedhofskapelle. Der Karner ist meist ein Zentralbau mit kleiner Ostapsis. Im Untergeschoß wurden ausgegrabene Gebeine aufbewahrt, im Obergeschoß ist ein Altarraum für Totenmessen]

carnauba (wax) · Karnaubawachs n

carol → carrel

Carolingian architecture · karolingische Architektur f, ~ Baukunst f

~ basilica(n church) · karolingische Basilika(kirche) f

carotid, heart-shaped · herzförmig

to carpenter [To make by carpentry; to work with wood] · zimmern

~ · Zimmerer m, Zimmermann m

carpentering, carpentership, carpentry · Zimmerei(wesen) f, (n)

carpenters · Zimmerleute f

carpenter's apprentice · Zimmerlehrling m

~ art · Zimmermannskunst f

~ shop · Zimmerwerkstatt f

~ tool · Zimmerwerkzeug n

~ trade, carpentership, carpentry · Zimmerhandwerk n

~ undertaking · Zimmerei(betrieb) f, (m)

~ work · Zimmerarbeit(en) f(pl) [DIN 18334]

~ yard · Zimmerplatz m

carpentership, carpentry, carpentering · Zimmerei(wesen) f, (n)

~, carpenter's trade, carpentry · Zimmerhandwerk n

carpentry [Permanent or temporary carcassing timber] · Holzrohbau m

~, carpentership, carpenter's trade · Zimmerhandwerk n

~ [Timberwork constructed by the carpenter] · Zimmerung f

~, carpentership, carpentering · Zimmerei(wesen) f, (n)

carpet adhesive → ~ bonding agent

~ base · Teppichunterlage f

~ (bonding) agent, ~ ~ medium, ~ (~) adhesive, ~ cement(ing agent) · Teppichkleb(e)stoff m, Teppichkleb(e)mittel n, Teppichkleber m

~ cement(ing agent) → ~ bonding ~

carpetless · teppichlos

carport [A roofed space having at least one side open to the weather, primarily designed or used for motor vehicles] · (Ein)Stellplatz m mit Schutzdach

carragheen, Irish moss [A seaweed of the Atlantic found on the coasts of Ireland and America. It varies from purple to green in colour, is used as a food and a jelly and by painters to make size] · irländisches Moos n, Perlmoos, Knorpeltang m

Carrara marble, Sicilian ~ [It was called 'marmor lunense' in ancient Rome] · Carraramarmor m

carrel, carol, cubicle [A niche in a cloister where a monk might sit and work or read; sometimes applied to a bay window] · Lesenische f, Lesezelle f

carriage-entrance, porte-cochère, carriage porch [A gateway for carriages, leading into a court-yard] · Wageneinfahrt f, Wagentor n, Torweg m, Toreinfahrt

carriage gate, gateway [The way through a gate] · Torweg m

carriageway cover · befahrbare Schachtabdeckung f

~ slab · Fahrbahnplatte f

(carrier) air tube installation → pneumatic ~ ~

(~) ~ ~ system → pneumatic tube installation

(~) ~ tubes → pneumatic tube installation

to carry, to sustain, to accept · aufnehmen [Last]

~ ~ off [rainwater] · abführen [Regenwasser]

carrying channel · Trag(e)-U-Profil n, U-Trag(e)profil

~ cupola, ~ dome · Tragkuppel f, Außenkuppel [Im Gegensatz zur Sichtkuppel, die an einer Tragkuppel hängt]

~ no floor load · deckenunbelastet

~ rail · Trag(e)schiene f

~ up, bringing ~ [The erection of brick or stone walls to a specified level] · (Auf)Mauern n

carry-over moment · Übertragungsmoment n [Momentenausgleichverfahren]

cart grease · Wagenfett n, Wagenschmiere f

cartage · Verkarrung f [Aushubmaterial]

Carthusian monastery · Kartause f, Kartäuserkloster n

carton-pierre [A mix(ture) of paperpulp, whiting and size used for casting from reverse mo(u)lds] · Papierstuck m, Steinpappe f, Papiermaché n

~ and gravel roofing · Kiespapp(e)dach n, ~ (ein)deckung f

cartouche [A shaped tablet enclosed in an ornamental frame or scroll and often bearing an inscription or heraldic device] · Kartusche f, Rolle f

~ · Zierrahmen m

cartridge · Kartusche f

cartridge brass — casern

~ **brass** · Messing 70 n, MS 70, Ms 70
~(**-type**) **fuse** · Sicherungspatrone f
to carve · schnitzen
~ ~, to hew, to cut, to sculpture [*out of stone, in ivory, etc.*] · skulptieren, skulpturieren
~ ~ **up**, to break down [*surface*] · auflösen, zerklüften [*Fläche*]
carved altar · Schnitzaltar m
~ **capital** · Plastikkapitell n, Plastikkapitäl, Skulpturkapitell, Skulpturkapitäl
~ **decoration** → ~ pattern
~ **decorative feature** → ~ pattern
~ ~ **finish** → ~ pattern
~ **enrichment** → ~ pattern
~ **foliage**, hewn ~, cut ~, sculptured ~ · skulpt(ur)iertes Blattwerk n, ~ Laubwerk, plastisch gestaltete Blätter npl
~ **motif** · geschnitztes Motiv n
~ **ornament** · Schnitzornament n
~ **ornament(al feature)** → ~ pattern
~ **ornamental finish** → ~ pattern
~ **pattern**, ~ enrichment, ~ decoration, sculptural ~, ~ decorative finish, ~ ornamental finish, ~ decorative feature, ~ ornament(al feature) · plastische Dekoration f, ~ Ornamentierung f, ~ Musterung f, ~ Verzierung, plastisches Dekor n, plastisches Ornament n, plastisches Muster n, plastischer Schmuck m
~ **pulpit** · geschnitzte Kanzel f
~ **relief** · Schnitzrelief n
~ **style**, sculptural ~ · plastischer Stil m
(~) **waterspout**, gargoyle [*A projecting stone spout, usually carved with a grotesque figure*] · (figürlicher) Wasserspeier m
~ **wood(en) wall panelling** (Brit.); ~ ~ ~ **paneling** (US) · Boiserie f [*hölzerne geschnitzte Wandverkleidung*]
carver · Holzschnitzer m
carving, hewing, cutting, sculpturing [*out of stone, in ivory, etc.*] · Skulptieren n, Skulpturieren
caryatid [*A sculptured female figure used as a column. The term is also applied loosely to various other columns and pillars carved wholly or partly in the form of human figures*] · Karyatide f, Kore f
~ **porch**, southern ~ · Karyatidenhalle f vom Erechtheion, Korenhalle ~ ~
cascade, water ramp · Kaskade f [*künstlich abgetreppter Wasserfall*]
case, lock ~ · (Schloß)Kasten m
~ · Zarge f
~ **front** → lock ~ ~
~ **hardening** · Einsatzhärtung f, Zementierung [*als technisches Verfahren*]

~ ~ · Einsatzhärten n, Zementieren, Einsatzhärtung f, Zementieren [*als technischer Vorgang*]
~ **history** · Fallbeschreibung f
~ **of bending** · Biegefall m
~ ~ **stability**, stability case · Stabilitätsfall m, Standsicherheitsfall, Standfestigkeitsfall
cased column · feuerschutzumhüllte Stütze f
casein · Kasein n, Käsestoff m, Käseeiweiß n der Milch, CS
~**-bonded**, casein-glued · kaseinverleimt
~(**-bound**) **distemper**, washable ~, casein (glue-)bound water paint · Kasein(anstrich)farbe f, Käse(anstrich)-farbe
~ **bound water paint**→ casein(-bound) distemper
~ **distemper** → casein-bound ~
~ **emulsion** · Kaseinemulsion f
~**-formaldehyde resin**, casein plastic · Kaseinformaldehydharz n
casein glue · Kaseinleim m, Käseleim [*Eiweißleim aus Milchkasein, der durch chemische Umsetzung wasserunlöslich wird. Im Handel meistens als „Kaltleim" bezeichnet*]
~ (**glue-**)**bound water paint** → casein(-bound) distemper
~**-glued**, casein-bonded · kaseinverleimt
casein medium, ~ binding ~, ~ binder · Kaseinbindemittel n [*Anstrichtechnik*]
~ **mixed with slaked lime and borax** · Kalkkasein n
~ **plastic**, casein-formaldehyde resin · Kaseinformaldehydharz n
~ **powder**, powder(ed) casein · Kaseinpulver n
~ **size**, ~ sizing material · Kaseinlösung f, Kaseinwasser n
~ **sizing material**, ~ size · Kaseinlösung f, Kaseinwasser n
casemate, basement area · Kasematte f, Wallgewölbe n
casement, window ~, hinged ~, pivoted sash, (casement) ventilator, opening sash, opening light · (Fenster)Flügel m
~ [*A deep concave mo(u)lding, used chiefly in cornices*] · Hohlkehle f, Sims~, Gesims~
~ **fastener**, window ~ ~ · Vorreiber m
~ **frame**, window ~ ~, hinged ~ ~, pivoted sash ~, opening sash ~, opening light ~, ventilator ~ · (Fenster-)Flügelrahmen m
~ **stay**, window ~ ~ · (Fenster)Feststeller m, (Fenster)Feststellhaken m, (Fenster)Sperrhaken, (Fenster)Sperre
~ **window** · Flügelfenster n
casern [*A small building for military purposes*] · kleines Kasernengebäude n

cashew nut resin — cast (building) member

cashew nut resin [*This resin is produced from the brown liquid which occurs between the shell and the kernel of the cashew nut. This resin, when mixed with a filler and a catalyst, sets to form a flexible cement which resists all acids except concentrated nitric and sulphuric acid and fairly concentrated alkali*] · Acajounußharz *n*, Marknußharz

casing → (concrete) encasement

~ **nail**, ~ wire ~ · runder Drahtnagel *m* mit Senkkopf, ~ Drahtstift *m* ~ ~

~ **pipe** · Schalrohr *n* [*Als Baurohr für Betonstützen, Fundamentschalungen und Schalgründungen*]

~ **(wire) nail** · runder Drahtnagel *m* mit Senkkopf, ~ Drahtstift *m* ~ ~

casino · Kasino *n* [*Tanz-, Konzert- und Spielhaus in Kurorten*]

~ · Kasino *n* [*Landhaus inmitten eines Gartens in der italienischen Renaissance*]

~, gambling ~ · (Spiel)Kasino *n*, Spielhaus *n*

~, ornamental pavilion · Zierpavillon *m*

cask beer store · Faßbierlager *n*

Cassel brown, ~ earth · Kasselerbraun *n*

~ **earth**, ~ brown · Kasselerbraun *n*

~ **yellow** · Kasselergelb *n*

cassette → pan

~ **ceiling**, coffer(ed) ~, waffle ~, caisson ~, pan(el) ~, rectangular grid ~, cored ~ · Kassettendecke *f*, kassettierte Decke

~ **design** → waffle pattern

~ **floor** → waffle (slab) ~

~ **(~) panel** → rectangular grid (floor) slab

~ **(~) plate** → rectangular grid (floor) slab

~ **(~) slab** → rectangular grid (~) ~

~ **panel** → rectangular grid (floor) slab

~ **(~) floor** → waffle (slab) ~

~ **pattern** → waffle ~

~ **plate** → rectangular grid (floor) slab

~ **(~) floor** → waffle (slab) ~

~ **slab** → rectangular grid (floor) ~

~ **(~) floor** → waffle (~) ~

~ **soffit**, coffer(ed) ~, caisson ~, waffle ~, pan(el) ~, rectangular grid ~, cored ~ · Kassettenuntersicht *f*, kassettierte Untersicht

cassiterite, tinstone, black tin · Zinnstein *m*, Kassiterit *m*, SnO₂

to cast, to pour, to concrete · betonieren

cast → (pre)cast (concrete) (building) unit

~, casting [*The finished product from the mo(u)ld*] · Formen-(Fertig)Bauteil *m*, *n*, Formen-Fertigteil, Formen-Montageteil

~ · Gießen *n*, Guß *m*

~, pre~ · vorgefertigt [*aus Beton*]

~ **aerated concrete**, pre~ ~ ~, prefab(ricated) ~ ~ ~ · Fertigteil-Porenbeton *m*, Poren-Fertigteilbeton

~ ~ ~ **wall panel**, pre~ ~ ~ ~ ~, prefab(ricated) ~ ~ ~ ~ · Porenbetonwand(bau)tafel *f*

~ ~ ~ **slab**, pre~ ~ ~ ~ ~ prefab(ricated) ~ ~ ~ ~ · Porenbetonwand(bau)platte *f*

~ ~ ~ **works**, pre~ ~ ~ ~, prefab(ricated) ~ ~ ~ ~ · Porenbetonwerk *n*

~ **air-raid sheltering bunker** → (pre-)cast (concrete) ~ ~ ~

~ **alloy** · Gußlegierung *f* [*DIN 1725*]

~ **aluminium alloy** (Brit.); ~ aluminum ~ (US) · Alu(minium)gußlegierung *f* [*DIN 1725*]

~ **architectural component** → (pre)cast architectural (concrete) member

~ ~ **concrete**, pre~ ~ ~ ~ · Architektur-Betonerzeugnis *n*, Architektur-Betonstein *m*

~ ~ (~) **component** → (pre)cast architectural (concrete) member

~ ~ (~) **member** → (pre)~ ~ (~) ~

~ ~ (~) **product** → (pre)~ ~ (~) ~

~ ~ **member** → (pre)cast architectural (concrete) ~

~ ~ **product** → (pre)cast architectural (concrete) ~

~ **articles** → (mass-produced) (pre)cast (concrete) ware

~ **balcony** → (pre)cast (concrete) ~

~ **bay**, ~ house, casting ~ · Gießhalle *f*, Gießerei *f*

~ **beam**, (pre)cast (concrete) ~, prefab(ricated) concrete ~ · Montage-(Beton)balken(träger) *m*, Fertig(teil)-Betonbalken(träger), (Beton-)Fertig(teil)balken(träger)

~ ~ **and filler floor** → (precast) ~ ~ ~ ~

~ ~ **floor** → (pre)cast (concrete) ~ ~

~ **(~) lintel block** → ((pre)cast) (concrete) (~) ~ ~

~ **block** → (pre)cast (concrete) building ~

~ ~ **flue** → (pre)cast (concrete) ~ ~

~ **bomb shelter** → (pre)cast (concrete) air-raid sheltering bunker

~ **boundary beam** → (pre)cast (concrete) edge ~

~ **brass**, CB · Gußmessing *n* [*Eine Legierung, die mindestens 50% Kupfer und den Hauptlegierungszusatz Zink enthält. DIN 1709*]

~ **bronze** · Gußbronze *f*

~ **building** → (pre)cast (concrete) ~

~ **(~) component** → (pre)cast (concrete) (building) unit

~ **(~) ~** → ~ (~) unit

~ **(~) member** → (pre)cast (concrete) (building) unit

cast (building) member — cast (concrete) frame 154

~ (~) ~ → ~ (~) unit
~ (~) unit, ~ (~) member, ~ (~) component · Guß(bau)körper m, Guß(bau)element n [Fehlname: Gußbaueinheit f]
~ (~) unit → (pre)cast (concrete) (~) ~
~ chimney → (pre)cast (concrete) ~
~ cladding panel → (pre)cast (concrete) (in)filler ~
~ ~ slab → (pre)cast (concrete) (in-)filler ~
~ column → (pre)cast (concrete) (lighting) ~
~ ~ → (pre)cast (concrete) ~
~ component → (pre)cast (concrete) (building) unit
~ ~ → (building) unit
~ compound unit → (pre)cast (concrete) ~ ~
~ ~ for building construction → (pre)cast (concrete) ~ ~ ~ ~ ~
~ concrete → (pre)cast (concrete) product
~ ~, pre~ ~, prefab(ricated) ~ [Concrete cast elsewhere than its final position in the structure] · Fertigteilbeton m
~ ~ admix(ture) → (pre)~ ~ ~ ~
~ (~) air-raid sheltering bunker → (pre)~ (~) ~ ~ ~
~ (~) articles → (mass-produced) (pre)cast (concrete) ware
~ (~) balcony → (pre)~ (~) ~
~ (~) beam, pre~ (~) ~, prefab(ricated) ~ ~ · Montage(-Beton)balken(träger) m, Fertig(teil)-Betonbalken(träger), (Beton-)Fertig(teil)balken(träger)
~ (~) ~ floor → (pre)~ (~) ~ ~
~ (~) (~) lintel block → ((pre)cast) (~) (~) ~ ~
~ (~) block → (pre)cast (concrete) building ~
~ (~) ~ flue → (pre)~ (~) ~ ~ ~
~ (~) bomb shelter → (pre)cast concrete) air-raid sheltering bunker
(~) (~) bond beam block → (pre)~ (~) ~ ~ ~
~ (~) boundary beam → (pre)cast (concrete) edge ~
~ (~) building → (pre)~ (~) ~
~ ~ (~) block → (pre)~ ~ (~) ~
~ (~) (~) component → (pre)cast (concrete) (building) unit
~ (~) (~) member → (pre)cast (concrete) (building) unit
~ (~) (~) unit → pre~ (~) (~) ~
~ (~) chimney → (pre)~ (~) ~
~ (~) cill (Brit.) → (pre)cast concrete sill
~ (~) cladding → (pre)~ (~) ~
~ (~) ~ slab → (pre)cast (concrete) (in)filler ~

~ (~) column → (pre)~ (~) ~
~ (~) ~ → ~ (~) (lighting) ~
~ (~) component → (pre)cast (concrete) (building) unit
~ (~) compound unit → pre~ (~) ~ ~
~ (~) ~ ~ for building construction → pre~ (~) ~ ~ ~ ~ ~
~ (~) construction → pre~ (~) ~
~ (~) ~ division → (pre)~ (~) ~ ~
~ (~) ~ method → (pre)~ (~) ~ ~
~ (~) cupola → (pre)cast (concrete) dome
~ (~) curb of white granite aggregate → (pre)~ (~) ~ ~ ~ ~ ~
~ (~) dome → (pre)~ (~) ~
~ (~) door frame → (pre)~ (~) ~ ~
~ (~) eave(s) gutter → (pre)~ (~) ~ ~
~ (~) ~ trough → (pre)cast (concrete) eave(s) gutter
~ (~) edge beam → (pre)~ (~) ~ ~
~ (~) end-block → (pre)~ (~) ~
~ (~) exposed aggregate panel → (pre)~ (~) ~ ~ ~
~ (~) ~ slab → (pre)~ (~) ~ ~
~ (~) façade → (pre)~ (~) ~
~ ~ factory, ~ ~ plant, pre~ ~ ~, (concrete) (pre)casting ~, ((pre-)cast) concrete ware ~ · Beton(stein)werk n, (Beton)Fertigteilwerk, Betonwarenwerk; Zementwarenwerk [Schweiz]
~ (~) filler (block) → (pre)~ (~) ~ (~)
~ (~) ~ panel → (pre)cast (concrete) (in)filler ~
~ (~) ~ slab → (pre)cast (concrete) (in)filler ~
~ (~) ~ tile → (pre)cast (concrete) filler (block)
~ (~) flag [B.S. 368] → sidewalk concrete flag(stone)
~ (~) flight (of stairs) → (pre)~ (~) ~ (~ ~)
~ (~) floor → (pre)~ (~) ~
~ (~) ~ member → (pre)~ (~) ~ ~
~ (~) ~ rib → (pre)~ (~) ~ ~
~ (~) ~ slab → (pre)~ (~) ~
~ (~) floor(ing) construction → (pre)cast (concrete) floor(ing) system
~ (~) ~ system → (pre)cast (~) ~ ~
~ (~) flue → (pre)~ (~) ~
~ (~) ~ block, pre~ (~) ~ ~ · Beton-Rauch(gas)kanalstein m, Rauch(gas)kanalbetonstein
~ (~) ~ tile → (pre)cast (~) ~ ~
~ (~) frame, pre~ (~) ~, prefab(ricated) ~ ~ · (Beton-)Montagerahmen m, (Beton-)Elementrahmen, (Beton-)Fertig(teil)rahmen

cast (concrete) gable — cast (concrete) storey height ...

~ (~) gable → (pre)~ (~) ~
~ (~) ~ beam → (pre)~ (~) ~ ~
~ (~) garage → (pre)~ (~) ~
~ (~) garden (building) unit → (pre-)~ (~) ~ (~) ~
~ (~) girder → (pre)~ (~) ~
~ (~) goods → (mass-produced) (pre-)cast (concrete) ware
~ (~) grandstand → (pre)~ (~) ~
~ (~) green tile → (pre)cast (concrete) green block
~ (~) gutter → (pre)~ (~) ~
~ (~) hollow block → pre~ (~) ~ ~
~ (~) ~ tile → ((pre(cast) (concrete) hollow block
~ (~) home → (pre)~ (~) ~
~ (~) ~ construction, pre~ (~) ~ ~, prefab(ricated) ~ ~ ~ · (Beton-)Fertighausbau *m*
~ (~) housing (construction) → (pre)~ (~) ~ (~)
~ (~) industry → (pre)cast (~) ~
~ (~) (in)filler slab → (pre)~ (~) ~ ~
~ (~) infill(ing) slab → (pre)cast (concrete) (in)filler ~
~ (~) inspection chamber → (pre)~ (~) ~ ~
~ (~) kerb of white granite aggregate (Brit.) → (pre)cast (concrete) curb ~ ~ ~ ~
~ (~) landing → (pre)~ (~) ~
~ (~) (lighting) column → (pre)~ (~) (~) ~
~ (~) (~) mast (US) → (pre)cast (concrete) (lighting) column (Brit.)
~ (~) lintel → (pre)~ (~) ~
~ (~) (load)bearing skeleton → (pre-)cast (concrete) (structural) ~
~ ~ maker → (pre)cast (concrete) product manufacturer
~ ~ manufacturer → (pre)cast (concrete) product ~
~ (~) manhole → (pre)~ (~) ~
~ (~) manway → (pre)cast (concrete) manhole
~ (~) member → (pre)cast (concrete) (building) unit
~ (~) non-housing construction, pre~ (~) ~ ~, prefab(ricated) ~ ~ ~ · (Beton-)Fertignichtwohn(ungs)bau *m*, Fertig-Betonnichtwohnungsbau
~ (~) non-residential building → (pre)~ (~) ~ ~
~ (~) panel → prefab(ricated) ~ ~
~ (~) ~ wall, pre~ (~) ~ ~, prefab(ricated) ~ ~ ~ · Betontafelwand *f*
~ (~) parachute, ~ (~) umbrella, pre~ (~) ~ · vorgefertigter Betonschirm *m*
~ (~) parapet → (pre)~ (~) ~

~ (~) partition (wall) block → (pre)~ (~) ~ (~) ~
~ (~) perimeter frame → (pre)~ (~) ~ ~
~ (~) pilaster block → (pre)~ (~) ~ ~
~ (~) ~ tile → (pre)cast (concrete) pilaster block
~ (~) pile → (pre)~ (~) ~
~ (~) pipe → (pre)~ (~) ~
~ (~) pointed arch → (pre)~ (~) ~ ~
~ (~) portal (frame) → (pre)~ (~) ~ (~) ~
~ ~ producer → (pre)cast (concrete) product manufacturer
~ (~) product → (pre)~ (~) ~
~ (~) ~ maker → (pre)cast (concrete) product manufacturer
~ (~) ~ manufacturer → (pre)~ (~) ~ ~
~ (~) ~ producer → (pre)cast (concrete) product manufacturer
~ (~) products → (mass-produced) (pre)cast (concrete) ware
~ (~) profile(d) panel → (pre)~ (~) ~ ~
~ (~) purlin(e) → (pre)~ (~) ~
~ (~) (raking) strut → (pre)~ (~) (~) ~
~ (~) rib → (pre)~ (~) ~
~ (~) ~ slab → (pre)~ (~) ~ ~
~ (~) rib(bed) floor → (pre)~ (~) ~ ~
~ (~) roof → (pre)~ (~) ~
~ ~ septic tank, pre~ ~ ~ ~ · vorgefertigte Beton-Hauskläranlage *f*, ~ Beton-Grundstückskläranlage, ~ Beton-Kleinkläranlage
~ (~) shell → (pre)~ (~) ~
~ (~) shop → (pre)~ (~) ~
~ (~) sill → (pre)cast (concrete) threshold
~ (~) silo → (pre)~ (~) ~
~ (~) skeleton → (pre)cast (concrete) (structural) ~
~ (~) slab → (pre)~ (~) ~
~ (~) ~ floor → (pre)~ (~) ~ ~
~ (~) solid block → ((pre)cast) (~) ~ ~
~ (~) ~ tile → ((pre)cast) (concrete) solid block
~ (~) stair(case), pre~ (~) ~, prefab(ricated) ~ · (Beton-)Fertigtreppe *f*, Fertig-Betontreppe, Montage-Betontreppe, Beton-Montagetreppe
~ (~) ~ flight → (pre)~ (~) ~ ~
~ (~) stave → (pre)~ (~) ~
~ (~) ~ silo → (pre)~ (~) ~ ~
~ (~) step → (pre)~ (~) ~
~ (~) storey height wall panel → (pre)~ (~) ~ ~ ~ ~

~ (~) string (Brit.) → (pre)~ (~) ~
~ (~) (structural) frame(work) → (pre)~ (~) (~) ~
~ (~) (~) skeleton → (pre)~ (~) (~) ~
~ (~) (~) system → (pre)~ (~) (~) ~
~ (~) (~) wall → (pre)~ (~) (~) ~
~ (~) structure, pre~ (~) ~, prefab(ricated) ~ ~ · (Beton)Montagebauwerk n, (Beton)Fertigbauwerk, Fertig(teil)(-Beton)Bauwerk
~ (~) strut → (pre)cast (concrete) (raking) ~
~ (~) support → (pre)cast (concrete) column
~ ~ symposium, pre~ ~ ~, congress on (pre)cast concrete · Betonsteinkongreß m
~ (~) system → (pre)cast (concrete) (structural) ~
~ (~) ~ construction → (pre)cast (concrete) ~
~ (~) threshold → (pre)cast concrete sill
~ (~) tile flue → (pre)cast (concrete) block ~
~ (~) tower block → (pre)~ (~) ~ ~
~ (~) ~ building → (pre)cast (concrete) tower block
~ (~) tread → (pre)~ (~) ~
~ (~) umbrella, ~ (~) parachute, pre~ (~) ~ · vorgefertigter Betonschirm m
~ (~) unit → (pre)cast (concrete) (building) ~
~ (~) valley beam → (pre)~ (~) ~ ~
~ (~) ~ girder → (pre)cast (concrete) valley beam
~ (~) gutter → (pre)~ (~) ~ ~
~ (~) vault → (pre)~ (~) ~
~ (~) vent(ilation) duct → (pre)~ (~) ~ ~
~ (~) wall → (pre)cast (concrete) (structural) ~
~ (~) ~ slab → ((pre)cast) (~) ~
~ (~) ~ with pre-installed services → (pre)~ (~) ~ ~ ~ ~
~ (~) ware → (mass-produced) pre~ (~) ~
(~) ~ ~ factory → ~ concrete ~
~ (~) weight-carrying skeleton → (pre)cast (concrete) (structural) ~
~ (~) window frame → (pre)~ (~) ~ ~
~ ~ worker, pre~ ~ ~ · Betonsteinarbeiter m
~ construction → (pre)cast (concrete) ~
~ ~ division → (pre)cast (concrete) ~
~ ~ method → (pre)cast (concrete) ~
~ cupola → (pre)cast (concrete) dome

~ curb of white granite aggregate → (pre)cast (concrete) ~ ~ ~ ~ ~
~ dome → (pre)cast (concrete) ~
~ door frame → (pre)cast (concrete) ~
~ dwelling tower → (pre)cast residence ~
~ eave(s) gutter → (pre)cast (concrete) ~ ~
~ ~ through → (pre)cast (concrete) eave(s) gutter
~ edge beam → (pre)cast (concrete) ~
~ end-block → (pre)cast (concrete) ~
~ expanded concrete (building) component → (pre)cast gas concrete (building) unit
~ ~ ~ (~) member → (pre)cast gas concrete (building) unit
~ ~ ~ (~) unit → (pre)cast gas ~ (~) ~
~ exposed aggregate panel → (pre-)cast (concrete) ~ ~ ~
~ ~ ~ slab → (pre)cast (concrete) ~ ~ ~
~ façade → (pre)cast concrete ~
~ factory manufacture, pre~ ~ ~ · fabrikmäßige Vorfertigung f
~ filler (block) → (pre)cast (concrete) ~ (~)
~ ~ panel → (pre)cast (concrete) (in-)filler ~
~ ~ slab → (pre)cast (concrete) (in-)filler ~
~ ~ tile → (pre)cast (concrete) filler (block)
~ flag [B.S. 368] → sidewalk concrete flag(stone)
~ flange · Gußflansch m [Für Gußrohre, Formstücke, Armaturen und Gehäuse aus Grauguß nach DIN 2532 bis 2535, aus Stahlguß nach DIN 2543 bis 2545 und aus Rotguß nach DIN 86021 und 86022]
~ flight (of stairs) → (pre)cast (concrete) ~ (~ ~)
~ floor → (pre)cast (concrete) ~
~ ~ member → (pre)cast concrete ~ ~
~ ~ rib → (pre)cast (concrete) ~ ~
~ ~ slab → (pre)cast (concrete) ~ ~
~ ~ with in-situ structural topping of concrete, pre~ ~ ~ ~ ~ ~ ~ ~, prefab(ricated) concrete ~ ~ ~ ~ ~ ~ ~ · Teilmontagedecke f [Die Decke erhält erst mit einer Ortbeton-Druckplatte das volle Tragvermögen]
~ floor(ing) construction → (pre)cast (concrete) floor(ing) system
~ ~ system → (pre)cast (concrete) ~ ~
~ flue → (pre)cast (concrete) ~
~ frame → ~ (concrete) ~
~ gable → (pre)cast (concrete) ~
~ ~ beam → (pre)cast (concrete) ~ ~

cast garage — cast non-housing construction

~ **garage** → (pre)cast (concrete) ~
~ **garden (building) unit** → (pre)cast (concrete) ~ (~) ~
~ **gas concrete (building) component** → (pre)cast gas concrete (building) unit
~ ~ ~ (~) **member** → (pre)cast gas concrete (building)unit
~ ~ ~ (~) **unit** → pre~ ~ ~ (~) ~
~ ~ ~ ~ **compound unit** → pre~ ~ ~ ~ ~ ~
~ **girder** → (pre)cast (concrete) ~
~ **glass** → rolled ~
~ ~ **balcony parapet**, rolled ~ ~ ~ · Gußglasbalkonbrüstung f
~ ~ **Calorex** · Sonnenreflexionsglas Calorex n
~ ~ **canopy**, rolled ~ ~, ~ ~ roof overhang · Gußglasvordach n, Gußglasabdach, Gußglaswetter(schutz)dach
~ ~ **door**, rolled ~ ~ · Gußglastür f, Tür aus gegossenem (Flach)Glas
~ ~ **partition (wall)**, rolled ~ ~ (~) · Gußglastrennwand f
~ ~ **roof overhang**, rolled ~ ~ ~, ~ ~ canopy · Gußglasvordach n, Gußglasabdach, Gußglaswetter(schutz)dach
~ **goods** → (mass-produced) (pre-)cast (concrete) ware
~ **grandstand**, pre~ (concrete) ~, prefab(ricated) concrete ~ · (Beton)Fertig(teil)tribüne f
~ **green block** → (pre)cast (concrete) ~ ~
~ ~ **tile** → (pre)cast (concrete) green block
~ **gutter** → (pre)cast (concrete) ~
~ **gypsum product** → (pre)~ ~ ~
~ **high (rise) block (of flats)** (Brit.) → (pre)cast residence tower
(~) **hollow block** → ((pre)cast) (concrete) ~ ~
~ ~ **(concrete) floor** → (pre)~ ~ ~ (~) ~
~ ~ **floor** → (pre)cast hollow (concrete) ~
~ ~ **tile** → ((pre)cast) (concrete) hollow block
~ **home** → (pre)cast (concrete) ~
~ ~ **construction** → ~ concrete ~ ~
~ **house**, ~ bay, casting ~ · Gießhalle f, Gießerei f
~ **housing (construction)** → (pre)cast (concrete) ~ (~)
to **cast in contact with each other** · gegeneinander betonieren [*Fertigteile*]
cast industry → (pre)cast (concrete) ~
~ **(in)filler panel** → (pre)cast (concrete) ~ ~
~ ~ **slab** → (pre)cast (concrete) ~ ~
~ **infill(ing) panel** → (pre)cast (concrete) (in)filler ~

~ ~ **slab** → (pre)cast (concrete) (in-)filler ~
~ **inspection chamber** → (pre)cast (concrete) ~ ~
cast kerb of white granite aggregate (Brit.) → (pre)cast (concrete) curb ~ ~ ~ ~ ~
~ **landing** → (pre)cast (concrete) ~
~ **lead trap** · gegossener Blei-(Wasser-)(Geruch)Verschluß m
~ **light concrete box construction type** → (pre)cast light(weight) ~ ~ ~ ~
~ **(lighting) column** → (pre)cast (concrete) (~) ~
~ **(~) mast** (US) → (pre)cast (concrete) (lighting) column
~ **light(weight) (building) component** → (pre)cast light(weight) (concrete) (building) unit
~ ~ **(~) member** → (pre)cast light(weight) (concrete) (building) unit
~ ~ **(~) unit** → (pre)cast light(weight) (concrete) (~) ~
~ ~ **component** → (pre)cast light(weight) (concrete) (building) unit
~ ~ **concrete box construction type** → (pre)~ ~ ~ ~ ~ ~
~ ~ **(~) (building) component** → (pre)cast light(weight) (concrete) (building) unit
~ ~ **(~) (~) member** → (pre)cast light(weight) (concrete) (building) unit
~ ~ **(~) (~) unit** → pre~ ~ (~) (~) ~
~ ~ **(~) component** → (pre)cast light(weight) (concrete) (building) unit
~ ~ ~ **factory**, pre~ ~ ~ ~, prefab(ricated) ~ ~ ~ ~ · Leichtbeton-(stein)werk n
~ ~ **(~) member** → (pre)cast light(weight) (concrete) (building) unit
~ ~ **(~) unit** → (pre)cast light(weight) (concrete) (building) ~
~ ~ **member** → (pre)cast light(weight) (concrete) (building) unit
~ ~ **unit** → (pre)cast light(weight) (concrete) (building) ~
~ **lintel** → (pre)cast (concrete) ~
~ ~ **block** → (pre)cast (concrete) (beam) ~ ~
~ **(load)bearing skeleton** → (pre-)cast (concrete) (structural) ~
~ **manhole** → (pre)cast (concrete) ~
~ **manway** → (pre)cast (concrete) manhole
~ **marble tile** → (pre)~ ~ ~
~ **mast** (US) → (pre)cast (concrete) (lighting) column (Brit.)
~ **member** → (pre)cast (concrete) (building) unit
~ **non-housing construction** → ~ (concrete) ~ ~

cast nonresidential building — cast (pre)stressed lintel

~ **nonresidential building** → (pre-)cast (concrete) ~ ~

~ **normal(-weight) (building) component** → (pre)cast normal(-weight) (concrete) (building) unit

~ ~ (~) **member** → (pre)cast normal(-weight) (concrete) (building) unit

~ ~ (~) **unit** → (pre)cast normal(-weight) (concrete) (~) ~

~ ~ **(concrete) component** → (pre-)cast normal(-weight) concrete) (building) unit

~ ~ (~) **compound unit** → pre~ ~ (~) ~ ~

~ ~ (~) **member** → (pre)cast normal(-weight) (concrete) (building) unit

~ ~ (~) **unit** → (pre)cast normal(-weight) (concrete) (building) ~

~ ~ **member** → (pre)cast normal(-weight) (concrete) (building) unit

~ ~ **unit** → (pre)cast normal(-weight) (concrete) (building) ~

~ **panel** → prefab(ricated) concrete ~

~ ~ **fence** → ((pre)cast) concrete ~ ~

~ ~ **wall,** (pre)cast concrete ~ ~, prefab(ricated) concrete ~ ~ · Betontafelwand *f*

~ ~ **with window opening** → ((pre)cast) (concrete) ~ ~ ~ ~

~ **parachute,** (pre)cast (concrete) ~, (pre)cast (concrete) umbrella · vorgefertigter Betonschirm *m*

~ **parapet** → (pre)cast (concrete) ~

~ **partition block** → (pre)cast (concrete) partition (wall) ~

~ ~ **(wall) (concrete) block** → (pre)cast (concrete) partition (wall) ~

~ **perimeter frame** → (pre)cast (concrete) ~ ~

~ **permanent light(weight) concrete form(s)** → (pre)cast permanent light(-weight) concrete formwork

~ ~ ~ ~ **formwork** → (pre)~ ~ ~ ~ ~

~ ~ ~ ~ **shuttering** → (pre)cast permanent light(weight) concrete formwork

~ **pilaster block** → (pre)cast (concrete) ~ ~

~ ~ **tile** → (pre)cast (concrete) pilaster block

~ **pile** → (pre)cast (concrete) ~

~ **pipe** → (pre)cast (concrete) ~

~ ~ **fitting** · Guß(rohr)fitting *m*, Guß(rohr)formstück *n*

~ **plank** → (pre)cast (concrete) ~

~ **pointed arch** → (pre)cast (concrete) ~ ~

~ **portal (frame)** → (pre)cast (concrete) ~ (~)

~ **(pre)stressed (building) component** → (pre)cast prestressed (concrete) (building) unit

~ ~ (~) **member** → (pre)cast prestressed (concrete) (building) unit

~ ~ (~) **unit** → (pre)cast prestressed (concrete) (~) ~

~ ~ **component** → (pre)cast prestressed (concrete) (building) unit

~ ~ **compound unit** → prefab(ricated) prestressed (concrete) ~ ~

~ ~ **(concrete) beam** → (pre)~ ~ (~) ~

~ ~ (~) **(building) component** → (pre)cast prestressed (concrete) (building) unit

~ ~ (~) (~) **member** → (pre)cast prestressed (concrete) (building) unit

~ ~ (~) (~) **unit** → pre~ ~ (~) (~) ~

~ ~ (~) **component** → (pre)cast prestressed (concrete) (building) ~

~ ~ (~) **compound unit** → prefab(ricated) ~ (~) ~ ~

~ ~ (~) **construction** → pre~ ~ (~) ~

~ ~ (~) **floor** → (pre)~ ~ (~) ~

~ ~ (~) ~ **component** → (pre)cast prestressed (concrete) floor unit

~ ~ (~) ~ **member** → (pre)cast prestressed (concrete) floor unit

~ ~ (~) ~ **unit** → pre~ ~ (~) ~ ~

~ ~ (~) **lintel** → (pre)~ ~ (~) ~

~ ~ (~) **member** → (pre)cast prestressed (concrete) (building) unit

~ ~ (~) **panel** → (pre)~ ~ (~) ~

~ ~ (~) **slab** → (pre)~ ~ (~) ~

~ ~ (~) **string** → (pre)~ ~ (~) ~

~ ~ (~) **(structural) system** → (pre)~ ~ (~) (~) ~

~ ~ (~) **construction** → (pre)cast prestressed (concrete) construction

~ ~ (~) **tee-section** → (pre)~ ~ (~) ~

~ ~ (~) **unit** → (pre)cast prestressed (concrete) (building) ~

~ ~ (~) **wall** → (pre)~ ~ (~) ~

~ ~ (~) ~ **slab** → (pre)~ ~ (~) ~

~ ~ **construction** → (pre)cast prestressed (concrete) ~

~ ~ **floor** → (pre)cast prestressed (concrete) ~

~ ~ ~ **component** → (pre)cast prestressed (concrete) floor unit

~ ~ ~ **member** → (pre)cast prestressed (concrete) floor unit

~ ~ ~ **unit** → (pre)cast prestressed (concrete) ~ ~

~ ~ **light(weight) aggregate concrete,** prefab(ricated) ~ ~ ~ ~, precast ~ ~ ~ ~ · Fertigteil-Leichtzuschlag(stoff)-Spannbeton *m*

~ ~ **lintel** → (pre)cast prestressed (concrete) ~

cast (pre)stressed member — cast reinforced (concrete) ...

~~ **member** → (pre)cast prestressed (concrete) (building) unit
~~ **panel** → (pre)cast prestressed (concrete) ~
~~ **slab** → (pre)cast prestressed (concrete) ~
~~ **string** → (pre)cast prestressed concrete ~
~~ **(structural) system** → (pre)cast prestressed (concrete) (~) ~
~~ **system construction** → (pre)cast prestressed (concrete) ~
~~ **tee-section** → (pre)cast prestressed (concrete) ~
~~ **unit** → (pre)cast prestressed (concrete) (building) ~
~~ **wall** → (pre)cast prestressed (concrete) ~
~~~ **slab** → (pre)cast prestressed (concrete) ~ ~
~ **product** → (pre)cast (concrete) ~
~~ **maker** → (pre)cast (concrete) product manufacturer
~~ **manufacturer** → (pre)cast (concrete) ~ ~
~~ **producer** → (pre)cast (concrete) product manufacturer
~ **products** → (mass-produced) (pre-)cast (concrete) ware
~~ **for roads and streets** → (pre)cast concrete ~ ~ ~ ~ ~
~ **profile(d) panel** → (pre)cast (concrete) ~ ~
~ **pumice (building) component** → (pre)cast pumice (concrete) (building) member
~~ **(~) member** → (pre)cast pumice (concrete) (~) ~
~~ **(~) unit** → (pre)cast pumice (concrete) (building) member
~~ **component** → (pre)cast pumice (concrete) (building) member
~~ **concrete** → (pre)~ ~ ~
~~ **(~) (building) component** → (pre)cast pumice (concrete) (building) member
~~ **(~) (~) member** → pre~ ~ (~) (~) ~
~~ **(~) (~) unit** → (pre)cast pumice (concrete) (building) member
~~ **(~) component** → (pre)cast pumice (concrete) (building) member
~~ **(~) member** → (pre)cast pumice (concrete) (building) ~
~~ **(~) unit** → (pre)cast pumice (concrete) (building) member
~~ **member** → (pre)cast pumice (concrete) (building) ~
~~ **unit** → (pre)cast pumice (concrete) (building) member
~ **purlin(e)** → (pre)cast (concrete) ~
~ **(raking) strut** → (pre)cast (concrete) (~) ~

~ **R.C. beam** → (pre)cast reinforced (concrete) ~
~ **R.C. beam floor** → (pre)cast reinforced (concrete) ~ ~
~ **R.C. (building) component** → (pre)cast reinforced (concrete) (building) unit
~ **R.C. (building) member** → (pre-)cast reinforced (concrete) (building) unit
~ **R.C. (building) unit** → (pre)cast reinforced (concrete) (~) ~
~ **R.C. component** → (pre)cast reinforced (concrete) (building) unit
~ **R.C. compound unit** → (pre)cast reinforced (concrete) ~ ~
~ **R.C. construction** → (pre)cast reinforced (concrete) ~
~ **R.C. floor** → reinforced (concrete) (pre)cast ~
~ **R.C. frame** → (pre)~ ~ ~ ~
~ **R.C. girder** → reinforced (pre)cast (concrete) ~
~ **R.C. member** → (pre)cast reinforced (concrete) (building) unit
~ **R.C. panel** → (pre)cast reinforced (concrete) ~
~ **R.C. pile** → prefab(ricated) reinforced (concrete) ~
~ **R.C. rib** → (pre)cast reinforced (concrete) ~
~ **R.C. slab,** pre~ ~ ~ ~, ~ reinforced (concrete) ~ · Stahlbeton-Fertigplatte *f*
~ **R.C. system construction** → (pre-)cast reinforced (concrete) ~
~ **R.C. unit** → (pre)cast reinforced (concrete) (building) ~
~ **R.C. wall** → prefab(ricated) reinforced (concrete) ~
~ **R.C. wall slab** → (pre)cast reinforced (concrete) ~ ~
~ **reinforced beam** → (pre)cast reinforced (concrete) ~
~~~ **floor** → (pre)cast reinforced (concrete) ~ ~
~~ **(building) component** → (pre-)cast reinforced (concrete) (building) unit
~~ **(~) member** → (pre)cast reinforced (concrete) (building) unit
~~ **(~) unit** → (pre)cast reinforced (concrete) (~) ~
~~ **component** → (pre)cast reinforced (concrete) (building) unit
~~ **compound unit** → (pre)cast reinforced (concrete) ~ ~
~~ **(concrete) beam** → (pre)~ ~ (~) ~
~~ **(~) ~ floor** → (pre)~ ~ (~) ~ ~
~~ **(~) (building) component** → (pre)cast reinforced (concrete) (building) unit

cast reinforced (concrete) (building) member — cast stone

~ ~ (~) (~) member → (pre)cast reinforced (concrete) (building) unit

~ ~ (~) (~) unit → pre~ ~ (~) (~) ~

~ ~ (~) component → (pre)cast reinforced (concrete) (building) unit

~ ~ (~) compound unit → pre~ ~ (~) ~ ~

~ ~ (~) construction → pre~ ~ (~) ~

~ ~ (~) floor → reinforced (concrete) (pre)cast ~

~ ~ (~) frame → (pre)cast R.C. ~

~ ~ (~) member → (pre)cast reinforced (concrete) (building) unit

~ ~ (~) pile → prefab(ricated) ~ (~) ~

~ ~ (~) rib → (pre)~ ~ (~) ~

~ ~ (~) step → pre~ ~ (~) ~

~ ~ (~) wall → prefab(ricated) ~ (~) ~

~ ~ fair-faced concrete member → (pre)~ ~ ~ ~ ~

~ ~ ~ manufacturing yard → (pre)~ ~ ~ ~ ~

~ ~ (~) member → (pre)~ ~ (~) ~

~ ~ (~) panel → (pre)~ ~ (~) ~

~ ~ (~) pile, pre~ ~ ~ ~, prefab(ricated) ~ ~ ~, ~ R.C. ~ · Stahlbeton-Fertigpfahl *m*

~ ~ (~) slab, pre~ ~ (~) ~, ~ R.C. ~ · Stahlbeton-Fertigplatte *f*

~ ~ (~) system construction → (pre)cast reinforced (concrete) ~

~ ~ (~) unit → (pre)cast reinforced (concrete) (building) ~

~ ~ (~) wall slab → (pre)~ ~ (~) ~ ~

~ ~ construction → (pre)cast reinforced (concrete) ~

~ ~ fair-faced concrete compound unit → pre~ ~ ~ ~ ~ ~

~ ~ floor → reinforced (concrete) (pre)cast ~

~ ~ frame → (pre)cast R.C. ~

~ ~ member → (pre)cast reinforced (concrete) (building) unit

~ ~ panel → (pre)cast reinforced (concrete) ~

~ ~ rib → (pre)cast reinforced (concrete) ~

~ ~ slab, (pre)cast reinforced (concrete) ~, ~ R.C. ~ · Stahlbeton-Fertigplatte *f*

~ ~ step → (pre)cast reinforced concrete step

~ ~ system construction → (pre)cast reinforced (concrete) ~

~ ~ unit → (pre)cast reinforced (concrete) (building) ~

~ ~ wall → prefab(ricated) reinforced (concrete) ~

~ ~ ~ slab → (pre)cast reinforced (concrete) ~ ~

~ residence tower → (pre)cast ~ ~

~ residential tower → (pre)cast residence ~

~ resin, casting ~ · Gießharz *n*, Schmelzharz

~ rib → (pre)cast (concrete) ~

(~) ~ and filler (block) floor → (pre)~ ~ ~ (~) ~

(~) ~ ~ ~ floor → ((pre)cast) rib and filler (block) ~

(~) ~ ~ ~ tile floor → ((pre)cast) rib and filler (block) ~

~ ~ slab → (pre)cast (concrete) ~ ~

~ rib(bed) floor → (pre)cast (concrete) ~ ~

~ roof → (pre)cast (concrete) ~

~ shadow · Schlagschatten *m*

~ sheet glass, ~ window ~, rolled ~ · Fensterglas *n*, Gußfensterglas

~ shell → (pre)cast (concrete) ~

~ shop → (pre)cast (concrete) ~

~ sill → (pre)cast (concrete) threshold

~ silo → (pre)cast (concrete) ~

~ skeleton → (pre)cast (concrete) (structural) ~

~ slab → (pre)cast (concrete) ~

~ ~ floor → (pre)cast (concrete) ~ ~

~ slag copper ~ · Kupferschlacke *f*

~ ~ block → copper ~ ~

~ ~ sett → copper ~ ~

~ ~ tile → copper slag block

~ solid block → ((pre)cast) (concrete) ~ ~

~ ~ tile → ((pre)cast) (concrete) solid block

~ stair(case) → (pre)cast (concrete) ~

~ ~ flight → (pre)cast (concrete) ~ ~

~ stave → (pre)cast (concrete) ~

~ ~ silo → (pre)cast (concrete) ~ ~

~ steel · Stahlguß *m*, Stg [*Fehlname: Stahlformguß. Der Werkstoff von Stahlstücken, die ihre endgültige Gebrauchsform durch Gießen von Stahl in feuerfeste Formen unter Vermeidung von Schmieden, Hämmern, Walzen usw. erhalten*]

~ ~ grade · Stahlgußsorte *f*

~ ~ pipe · Stahlgußrohr *n*

~ ~ ~ flange · Stahlguß(rohr)flansch *m* [*DIN 2543–2553*]

~ step → (pre)cast (concrete) ~

~ stone, pre~ ~, reconstituted ~, synthetic ~, reconstructed ~, patent ~; artificial ~ [*deprecated*] [*Cast stones consist of mo(u)lded blocks of concrete with special surface treatment. They may be formed in any of the shapes obtained by cutting the natural stone and may have surface finishes which resemble the rubbed*

cast stone — castable refractory concrete

finish commonly used on limestone and other stones, or any of the tooled finishes. B.S. 1217] · Betonwerkstein *m [DIN 18500]*; Kunststein, (künstlicher) Baustein, gebundener Baustein, Edelbeton *[Fehlnamen]*

~ ~ **floor cover(ing)** → ~ ~ floor(-ing) (finish)

~ ~ **floor(ing) (finish)**, reconstituted ~ (~), reconstructed ~ ~ (~), patent ~ ~ (~) ~ ~ floor cover(ing); artificial stone floor(ing) (finish), artificial stone floor cover(ing) *[deprecated]* · Betonwerkstein-(Fuß-)Bodenbelag) *m*

~ ~ **shop** → reconstituted ~ ~

~ ~ **skin**, reconstituted ~ ~, reconstituted ~ ~, patent ~ ~; artificial ~ ~ *[deprecated]* · Betonwerksteinverblendung *f [Fehlname: Kunststeinverblendung]*

~ ~ **stair(case)**, reconstituted ~ ~, reconstructed ~ ~, patent ~ ~; artificial ~ ~ *[deprecated]* · Betonwerksteintreppe *f [Fehlname: Kunststeintreppe]*

~ ~ **tile** → reconstituted ~ ~

~ ~ ~ **floor cover(ing)** → ~ ~ ~ floor(ing) (finish)

~ ~ ~ **floor(ing) (finish)**, reconstituted ~ ~ ~ (~), reconstructed ~ ~ (~), patent ~ ~ ~ (~), ~ ~ ~ floor cover(ing); artificial stone tile floor(ing) (finish), artificial stone tile floor cover(ing) *[deprecated]* · Betonwerksteinplatten(fuß)boden(belag) *m*, Fbku *[Fehlnamen: Kunststeinplatten-(fuß)boden(belag)]*

~ ~ **waterproofer**, reconstructed ~ ~, reconstituted ~ ~, patent ~ ~; artificial ~ ~ *[deprecated]* · Betonwerksteinveredler *m*; Kunststeinveredler *[Fehlname] [Zur Herstellung von wasserdichten Betonwerksteinen]*

~ ~ **work**, reconstructed ~ ~, reconstituted ~ ~, patent ~ ~; artificial ~ ~ *[deprecated]* · Betonwerksteinarbeiten *fpl [DIN 18333. Fehlname: Kunststeinarbeiten]*

~ **storey height wall panel** → (pre-)cast (concrete) ~ ~ ~ ~

~ **string** (Brit.) → (pre)cast (concrete) ~

~ **structural concrete** → (pre)~ ~ ~

~ ~ **(~) compound unit** → pre~ ~ (~) ~ ~

~ **(~) skeleton** → (pre)cast (concrete) (~) ~

~ **(~) system** → (pre)cast (concrete) (~) ~

~ **(~) wall** → (pre)cast (concrete) (~) ~

~ **structure**, (pre)cast (concrete) ~, prefab(ricated) concrete ~ · (Beton-)Montagebauwerk *n*, (Beton)Fertigbauwerk, Fertig(teil)(-Beton)bauwerk

~ **strut** → (pre)cast (concrete) (raking) ~

~ **support** → (pre)cast (concrete) column

~ **system** → (pre)cast (concrete) (structural) ~

~ ~ **construction** → (pre)cast (concrete) ~

~ **tall block (of flats)** (Brit.) → (pre-)cast residence tower

~ ~ **flats** (Brit.) → (pre)cast residence tower

~ **terrazzo**, pre~ ~, terrazzo tile *[B.S. 4131]* · Terrazzo(belag)platte *f*, Terrazzofliese *f*

~ **threshold** → (pre)cast (concrete) ~

~ **tile flue** → (pre)cast (concrete) block ~

~ **tower block** → (pre)cast (concrete) ~ ~

~ ~ **building** → (pre)cast (concrete) tower block

~ **tread** → (pre)cast (concrete) ~

~ **umbrella**, (pre)cast (concrete) ~, (pre)cast (concrete) parachute · vorgefertigter Betonschirm *m*

~ **unit** → (pre)cast (concrete) (building) ~

~ **valley beam** → (pre)cast (concrete) ~ ~

~ ~ **girder** → (pre)cast (concrete) valley beam

~ ~ **gutter** → (pre)cast (concrete) ~ ~

~ **vault** → (pre)cast (concrete) ~

~ **vent(ilation) duct** → (pre)cast (concrete) ~ ~

~ **wall** → (pre)cast (concrete) (structural) ~

~ ~ → (pre)cast (concrete) ~

~ ~ **panel** → ((pre)cast) (concrete) ~ ~

~ ~ **slab** → ((pre)cast) (concrete) ~ ~

~ ~ **with pre-installed services** → (pre)cast concrete ~ ~ ~ ~

~ **ware** → (mass-produced) (pre)cast (concrete) ~

~ **weight-carrying skeleton** → (pre-)cast (concrete) (structural) ~

~ **window frame** → (pre)cast (concrete) ~ ~

~ ~ **glass**, ~ sheet ~, rolled ~ ~ · Fenstergußglas *n*, Gußfensterglas

~ **wood concrete block** → (pre)~ ~ ~ ~

~ ~ ~ **tile** → (pre)~ ~ ~ ~

castable · hydraulisch abbindende Masse *f [Schamotteindustrie]*

~ **refractories**, plastic ~ · feuerfeste Stampf-, Flick- und Spritzmassen *fpl* auf der Basis von Schamotte (fireclay), Sillimanit, Korund, Magnesit, Chrommagnesit, Chromerz und Siliziumkarbid

~ **refractory concrete** · Feuerbeton *m*, Feuerfestbeton, ff. Beton, feuerfester Beton *[Masse aus einem feuerfesten Gemenge und einem hitzebeständigen hydraulischen Zement]*

to castellate — cast(-)in(-)place reinforced concrete floor

to castellate → to embattle

castellated → battlemented

~ bridge parapet → embattled ~ ~

castellation, castle-building [*The building of castles. A castle is a fortress or fortified building*] · Burgenbau *m*

~ [*The furnishing of a building with battlements*] · Bezinnung *f*

caster, pre**~** · (Beton-)Fertigteilhersteller *m*

Castigliano's theorem, ~ law, ~ method, ~ principle, minimizing principle of Castigliano, strain energy method · Castiglianoscher Satz *m*, Prinzip *n* von Castigliano, Castiglianosches Prinzip, Castigliano-Prinzip, Castigliano-Satz [*Von allen möglichen Gleichgewichtszuständen tritt derjenige ein, für den die Formänderungsarbeit ein Minimum wird*]

cast(ing) → (pre)cast (concrete) (building) unit

~ [*The finished product from the mo(u)ld*] · Formen-(Fertig)Bauteil *m, n*, Formen-Fertigteil, Formen-Montageteil

casting · Gußstück *n*

~, pre~ · Vorfertigung *f* aus Beton

cast(ing) bay, ~ house · Gießerei *f*, Gießhalle *f*

casting composition, ~ compound, ~ mass, ~ material · Gießmasse *f* [*allgemein*]

~ compound → ~ composition

~ concrete ware, pre~ ~ ~ · Betonwarenfertigung *f*

~ factory → (concrete) pre~ ~

~ house, ~ bay · Gießhalle *f*, Gießerei *f*

casting mass → ~ composition

~ material → ~ composition

~ mortar · Gießmörtel *m*

~ of commerce · Handelsguß(teil) *m*, (*m, n*)

~ plant → (concrete) (pre)casting factory

~ plaster · Form(en)gips *m* [*Zur Herstellung von Formen verwendet*]

~ process [*A process of shaping glass by pouring it into a mould or on to a table or passing it between rollers*] · Gießverfahren *n*

cast(ing) resin · Gießharz *n*, Schmelzharz

casting ring · Gießring *m*

casting-slip · Gießschlicker *m*

casting system → pre~ ~

~ table · Fertigungstisch *m*, Arbeitstisch [*zur Herstellung von großformatigen Fertigteilen*]

~ yard, pre~ ~ · (Beton-)Fertigteilplatz *m*

cast(-)in(-)place, cast(-)in(-)situ, in(-)situ(-)cast, poured(-)in(-)place · ortbetoniert, Ortbeton ....

~ aerated concrete → cast(-)in(-)situ ~ ~

~ architectural concrete, in(-)situ (cast) ~ ~, cast(-)in(-)situ ~ ~, poured (-in-place) ~ ~, site-placed ~ ~, field ~ ~ · Architektur-Ortbeton *m*

~ concrete, cast(-)in(-)situ ~, in(-)situ (cast) ~, site-placed ~, poured(-in-place) ~, field ~ · Ortbeton *m* [*DIN 1045*]

~ (~) balcony, in(-)situ (cast) (~) ~, cast(-)in(-)situ (~) ~, site-placed (~) ~, field ~ ~, poured(-in-place) (~) ~ · Ortbetonbalkon *m*

~ (~) cable duct, cast(-)in(-)situ (~) ~ ~, in(-)situ (cast) (~) ~ ~, site-placed (~) ~ ~, field ~ ~ ~, poured(-in-place) (~) ~ ~ · Ortbetonkanal *m*

~ (~) eave(s) unit, cast(-)in(-)situ (~) ~ ~, in(-)situ (cast) (~) ~ ~, site-placed (~) ~ ~, field ~ ~ ~, poured(-in-place) (~) ~ ~ · Ortbeton-Traufenteil *m, n*

~ (~) filling, site-placed (~) ~, field ~ ~, cast(-)in(-)situ (~) ~, in(-)situ (cast) (~) ~, poured(-in-place) (~) ~ · Ortbetonfüllung *f*

~ (~) floor, site-placed (~) ~, field ~ ~, cast(-)in(-)situ (~) ~, in(-)situ (cast) (~) ~, poured(-in-place) (~) ~ · Ortbetondecke *f*

~ (~) frame, ~ (~) framing, site-placed (~) ~, field ~ ~, cast(-)in(-)situ (~) ~, in(-)situ (cast) (~) ~, poured(-in-place) (~) ~ · Ortbetonrahmen *m*

~ (~) rib(bed) floor, site-placed (~) ~ ~, cast(-)in(-)situ (~) ~ ~, in(-)situ (cast) (~) ~, field ~ ~ ~, poured(-in-place) (~) ~ ~ · Ortbeton-Rippendecke *f*

~ (~) shell, site-placed (~) ~, field ~ ~, cast(-)in(-)situ (~) ~, in(-)situ (cast) (~) ~, poured(-in-place) (~) ~ · Ortbetonschale *f*

~ (~) stair(case), site-placed (~) ~, field ~ ~, cast(-)in(-)situ (~) ~, in(-)situ (cast) (~) ~, poured(-in-place) (~) ~ · Ortbetontreppe *f*

~ (~) structure, cast(-)in(-)situ (~) ~, in(-)situ (cast) (~) ~, site-placed (~) ~, field ~ ~, poured(-in-place) (~) ~ · Ortbetonbauwerk *n*

~ light(weight) concrete, site-placed ~ ~, field ~ ~, cast(-)in(-)situ ~ ~, in(-)situ (cast) ~ ~, poured(-in-place) ~ ~ · Ortleichtbeton *m*, Leicht-Ortbeton

~ mortar, site-placed ~, cast(-)in(-)situ ~, in(-)situ (cast) ~, field ~, poured(-in-place) ~ · Ortmörtel *m*

~ reinforced concrete, ~ R.C., site-placed ~ ~, field ~ ~, cast(-)in(-)situ ~ ~, in(-)situ (cast) ~ ~, poured(-in-place) ~ ~ · Ort-Stahlbeton *m*, Stahlortbeton

~ ~ ~ floor, ~ R.C. ~, cast(-)in(-)situ ~ ~ ~, in(-)situ (cast) ~ ~, site-placed ~ ~ ~, field ~ ~ ~, poured(-in-place) ~ ~ ~ · Ortstahlbetondecke *f*, Stahlortbetondecke

cast(-)in(-)place terrazzo — cast-iron (door) pull (handle)

~ **terrazzo** → cast(-)in(-)situ ~

cast(-)in(-)situ, in(-)situ(-)cast, cast(-)in(-)place, poured(-)in(-)place · ortbetoniert, Ortbeton.......

~ **aerated concrete**, in(-)situ (cast) ~, cast-in-place ~ ~, site-placed ~ ~, field ~ ~, poured(-in-place) ~ ~ · Ort-Porenbeton *m*

~ **architectural concrete** → cast-in-place ~ ~

~ **concrete**, in(-)situ (cast) ~, cast-in place ~, site-placed ~, poured(-in-placed) ~, field ~ ~ · Ortbeton *m* [*DIN 1045*]

~ **(~) balcony**, in(-)situ (cast) (~) ~, cast-in-place (~) ~, site-placed (~) ~, field ~ ~, poured(-in-place) (~) ~ · Ortbetonbalkon *m*

~ **(~) cable duct**, in(-)situ (cast) (~) ~ ~, cast-in-place (~) ~ ~, site-placed (~) ~ ~, field ~ ~ ~, poured(-in-place) (~) ~ ~ · Ortbetonkanal *m*

~ **(~) eave(s) unit**, in(-)situ (cast) (~) ~ ~, cast-in-place (~) ~ ~, site-placed (~) ~ ~, field ~ ~ ~, poured(-in-place) (~) ~ ~ · Ortbeton-Traufenteil *m, n*

~ **(~) filling**, in(-)situ (cast) (~) ~, cast-in-place (~) ~, site-placed (~) ~, field ~ ~, poured(-in-place) (~) ~ · Ortbetonfüllung *f*

~ **(~) floor**, in(-)situ (cast) (~) ~, cast-in-place (~) ~, site-placed (~) ~, field ~ ~, poured(-in-place) (~) ~ · Ortbetondecke *f*

~ **(~) frame**, ~ (~) framing, in(-)situ (cast) (~) ~, cast-in-place (~) ~, site-placed (~) ~, field ~ ~, poured(-in-place) (~) ~ · Ortbetonrahmen *m*

~ **(~) rib(bed) floor**, in(-)situ (cast) (~) ~, cast-in-place (~) ~ ~, site-placed (~) ~ ~, field ~ ~ ~, poured(-in-place) (~) ~ ~ · Ortbeton-Rippendecke *f*

~ **(~) shell**, in(-)situ (cast) (~) ~, cast-in-place (~) ~, site-placed (~) ~, field ~ ~, poured(-in-place) (~) ~ · Ortbetonschale *f*

~ **(~) stair(case)**, in(-)situ (cast) (~) ~, cast-in-place (~) ~, site-placed (~) ~, field ~ ~, poured(-in-place) (~) ~ · Ortbetontreppe *f*

~ **(~) structure**, in(-)situ (cast) (~) ~, cast-in-place (~) ~, site-placed (~) ~, field ~ ~, poured(-in-place) (~) ~ · Ortbetonbauwerk *n*

~ **light(weight) concrete**, (in-)situ (cast) ~ ~, cast-in-place ~ ~, site-placed ~ ~, field ~ ~, poured(-in-place) ~ ~ · Ortleichtbeton *m*, Leicht-Ortbeton

~ **mortar**, in(-)situ (cast) ~, cast-in-place ~, site-placed ~ field ~, poured(-in-place) ~ · Ortmörtel *m*

~ **reinforced concrete**, ~ R.C., in(-)situ (cast) ~ ~, cast-in-place ~ ~, site-placed ~ ~, field ~ ~, poured(-in-place) ~ ~ · Ort-Stahlbeton *m*, Stahlortbeton

~ ~ ~ **floor**, ~ R.C. ~, in(-)situ (cast) ~ ~ ~, cast-in-place ~ ~ ~, site-placed ~ ~ ~, field ~ ~ ~, poured(-in-placed) ~ ~ ~ · Ortstahlbetondecke *f*, Stahlortbetondecke

~ **terrazzo**, cast in place ~, terrazzo laid in situ, terrazzo cast in place ~, terrazzo placed in situ · Terrazzo *m* an Ort und Stelle ausgeführt

cast iron, C.I. ~ · Gußeisen *n*, Ge

cast-iron area grating, C.I. ~ ~ · Gußeisengitterrost *m*

~ **B & S discharge pipe** (US) → ~ spigot and socket draining ~

~ ~ **draining pipe** (US) → ~ spigot and socket ~ ~

~ ~ **waste (pipe)** (US) → ~ spigot and socket draining ~

~ **(bath)tub**, ~ bath, C.I. ~ · Gußeisen(bade)wanne *f*, gußeiserne (Bade)Wanne [*DIN 4470 bis 4477*]

~ **bedplate**, C.I. ~ ~ · Gußeisen-Grundplatte *f*, gußeiserne Grundplatte

~ **bell(-)and(-)spigot discharge pipe** (US) → ~ spigot and socket draining ~

~ ~ **draining pipe** (US) → ~ spigot and socket ~ ~

~ ~ **waste (pipe)** (US) → ~ spigot and socket draining ~

~ **(biological) shielding wall**, ~ radiation ~, C.I. ~ ~ ~ · Gußeisen-Abschirmwand *f*, gußeiserne Abschirmwand

~ **boiler**, C.I. ~ [*B.S. 779*] · Gußeisen(-Heiz)kessel *m*, gußeiserner (Heiz)Kessel

~ **box gutter** → ~ ~ roof ~

~ ~ **rainwater gutter** → ~ ~ (roof) ~

~ ~ **(roof) gutter**, ~ ~ rainwater ~, C.I. ~ ~ ~ · Gußeisen-Kastenregenrinne *f*, Gußeisen-Kasten(dach)rinne, gußeiserne Kasten(dach)rinne, gußeiserne Kastenregenrinne

~ **column**, C.I. ~ · Gußeisenstütze *f*, gußeiserne Stütze

~ ~ **for street lighting**, C.I. ~ ~ ~ ~ [*B.S. 1249*] · Gußeisen-Beleuchtungsmast *m*, gußeiserner Beleuchtungsmast, Gußeisen-Lichtmast, gußeiserner Lichtmast

~ **connector**, ~ timber ~ · Gußeisendübel *m*, gußeiserner Dübel [*Holzverbinder*]

~ **cover**, C.I. ~ · Gußeisendeckel *m*, gußeiserner Deckel

~ **cover(ing) plate**, C.I. ~ ~ · Gußeisen-(Ab)Deckplatte *f*, gußeiserne (Ab)Deckplatte

~ **discharge pipe** → ~ drain(age) ~

~ **(door) pull (handle)**, C.I. (~) ~ (~) · Gußeisen(tür)griff *m*, gußeiserner (Tür)Griff

cast-iron drain(age) pipe — castle-like town

~ drain(age) pipe, ~ draining ~, ~ discharge ~, ~ waste (~), C.I. ~ (~) · Gußeisenabflußrohr n, Gußeisendränrohr, Gußeisenentwässerungsrohr, gußeisernes Abflußrohr, gußeisernes Ablaufrohr, gußeisernes Dränrohr, gußeisernes Entwässerungsrohr, GA [*DIN 19500. Fehlnamen: gußeiserner Abfluß m, gußeiserner Ablauf, Gußeisenabfluß, Gußeisenablauf*]

~ façade, C.I. ~ · Gußeisenfassade f, gußeiserne Fassade

~ fish-bellied girder, C.I. ~ ~ · Gußeisen-Fischbauchträger m, gußeiserner Fischbauchträger

~ fitting → ~ pipe ~

~ flange, C.I. ~ · Gußeisenflansch m, gußeiserner Flansch [*DIN 2530–2535*]

~ flange(d) pipe, C.I. ~ ~ · [*B.S. 2035*] · Gußeisenflansch(en)rohr n, gußeisernes Flansch(en)rohr [*DIN 2422*]

~ ~ (~) fitting, C.I. ~ (~) ~ [*B.S. 2035*] · Gußeisenflansch(en)(form)stück n, gußeisernes Flansch(en)-(form)stück

~ floor plate, C.I. ~ ~ · Gußeisen-(fuß)bodenplatte f, gußeiserne (Fuß-)Bodenplatte

~ flushing cistern → ~ ~ tank

~ ~ tank, ~ ~ cistern, ~ water waste preventer, C.I. flushing tank, C.I. flushing cistern, C.I. water waste preventer · Gußeisenspülkasten m, gußeiserner Spülkasten [*Abort*]

~ girder, C.I. ~ · Gußeisenträger m, gußeiserner Träger

~ mast, C.I. ~ · Gußeisenmast m, gußeiserner Mast

(cast-)iron paving, C.I. ~ [*A non-skid paving of studded cast-iron blocks*] · Gußeisenplattenbelag m, (Fuß)Boden m aus Gußeisenplatten

cast-iron pipe, C.I. ~, CIP · Guß(eisen)rohr n, gußeisernes Rohr

~ (~) fitting, C.I. (~) ~ · Gußeisen(-Form)stück n, gußeisernes (Form-)Stück

~ pipeline, C.I. ~ · Gußeisen(rohr)leitung f, gußeiserne (Rohr)Leitung

~ plate, C.I. ~ · Gußeisenplatte f, gußeiserne Platte

~ pressure pipe, C.I. ~ ~ · Gußeisen-Druckrohr n, gußeisernes Druckrohr

~ products for sewerage (systems), C.I. ~ ~ ~ (~) · Kanalguß m

~ pull (handle) → ~ door ~ (~)

~ radiation shielding wall → ~ (biological) ~ ~

~ radiator, C.I. ~ · gußeiserner (Glieder)Heizkörper m, ~ Radiator, Gußeisen-(Glieder)Heizkörper, Guß(eisen)-Radiator

~ rail, C.I. ~ · Gußeisenschiene f, gußeiserne Schiene

~ rainwater goods, ~ ~ products, ~ ~ articles, C.I. ~ ~ [*B.S. 460*] · Gußeisen-Dachzubehör(teile) m, (mpl, npl)

~ ~ product, ~ ~ article, C.I. ~ ~ [*B.S. 460*] · Gußeisen-Dachzubehörteil m, n

~ sectional boiler, C.I. ~ ~ · Gußeisen-Gliederkessel m, gußeiserner Gliederkessel

~ ~ tank, C.I. ~ ~ ~ [*B.S. 1563*] · Gußeisen-Gliederbehälter m, gußeiserner Gliederbehälter

~ shielding wall → ~ biological ~ ~

~ spigot and socket discharge pipe → ~ ~ ~ ~ draining ~

~ ~ ~ ~ draining pipe, ~ ~ ~ ~ drain(age) ~, ~ ~ ~ ~ discharge ~, ~ ~ ~ ~ waste (~) [*B.S. 437*]; ~ bell(-)and(-)spigot ~ ~, B&S ~ ~, ~ B&S waste (~) (US) · Gußeisen-Glockenmuffen-Abflußrohr n, Gußeisen-Glockenmuffen-Entwässerungsrohr, Gußeisen-Glockenmuffen-Ablaufrohr [*Fehlnamen: Gußeisen-Glockenmuffenabfluß, Gußeisen-Glockenmuffenablauf*]

~ ~ ~ ~ waste (pipe) → ~ ~ ~ ~ draining ~

~ structural pipe, ~ ~ tube, C.I. ~ ~ · Gußeisen-Konstruktionsrohr n, gußeisernes Konstruktionsrohr

~ ~ tube, ~ ~ pipe C.I. ~ ~ · Gußeisen-Konstruktionsrohr n, gußeisernes Konstruktionsrohr

~ (timber) connector · Gußeisendübel m, gußeiserner Dübel [*Holzverbinder*]

~ tracery, C.I. ~ · Gußeisenmaßwerk n

~ tub → ~ bathtub

~ tubular column, C.I. ~ ~ · Gußeisen-Rohrstütze f, gußeiserne Rohrstütze

~ waste (pipe) → ~ drain(age) ~

~ water waste preventer → ~ flushing tank

~ window, C.I. ~ · Gußeisenfenster n, gußeisernes Fenster

castle · Schloß n, ~bau(werk) m, (n) [*Ursprünglich ein in sich abgeschlossener Verteidigungsbezirk. Die Benennungen „Schloß" und „Burg" überschneiden sich, wobei häufig Grenzfälle auftreten. Eine Burg ist immer befestigt, ein Schloß kann auch unbefestigt sein*]

~ architecture · Schloßarchitektur f, Schloßbaukunst f

castle-building → castellation

~ · Schloßbau m

castle church · Schloßkirche f

castle-court · Schloßhof m

castle-gate · Schloßtor n

castle-like town, fortified ~, walled ~, fortress-town · befestigte Stadt f

castle set in artificial lake · Wasserburg f
~ **sited on high-lying ground** · Höhenburg f
~ ~ ~ **low-lying ground** · Niederburg f
castle-tower · Schloßturm m
castle-wall · Schloßmauer f
castor oil [*B.S. 650*] [*A nondrying oil obtained from the castor bean. It may be converted to a drying oil by chemical treatment, and is then known as dehydrated castor oil*] · Rizinusöl n
~ ~ **alkyd** · Rizinusölalkyd m
castrum · Kastell n
casual ward · Obdachlosenasyl n
casualty station · Unfallstation f
cat ladder, roof ~, duck board · Dachleiter f
catacomb, underground cemetery, hypogeum · Katakombe f, unterirdischer Friedhof m, Hypogäum n
~ **grave** · Katakombengrab n
catafalque, catafolco · Katafalk m
catalyst, promoter, accelerator [*Strictly speaking a substance which increases the rate of a chemical reaction, but which remains itself chemically unchanged at the end of the reaction*] · Katalysator m, (Reaktions)Beschleuniger
cat-and-clay chimney, catted ~ (US) · Lehmschornstein m, Schornstein aus Lehm
catechu mordant · Katechubeize f
cathedra · Kathedra f [*Bischofsstuhl in der frühchristlichen Basilika*]
cathedral → dome
~ **architecture** · Kathedralenarchitektur f, Kathedralenbaukunst f
~ **builder** · Dombauer m
~ **choir,** ~ **quire** · Domchor m
~ **(church)** → dome
~ **cupola,** ~ **dome** · Domkuppel f
~ **dome,** ~ **cupola** · Domkuppel f
~ **glass,** ~ **sheet** · Kathedralglas n
~ **Gothic, Gothic cathedral style** · Kathedral(en)gotik f
~ **library** · Kathedralbücherei f, Kathedralbibliothek f
~ **mason-architect,** ~ **master-mason,** ~ **master builder** · Kathedralenbaumeister m, Dombaumeister
Cathedral of the Assumption at Vladimir [*It dates from 1158 and is probably the finest ecclesiastical building in Russia*] · Himmelfahrtsdom m zu Vladimir
cathedral quire, ~ **choir** · Domchor m
~ **sculpture** · Kathedralplastik f, Kathedralskulptur f
~ **sheet,** ~ **glass** · Kathedralglas n
~ **tower** · Domturm m

(Catherine) wheel window · Katharinenrad n, Radfenster n [*Rundfenster mit speichenartiger Unterteilung*]
cathole · Katzenloch n
cation exchanger · Kationenaustauscher m
cationic · kationaktiv [*Netzmittel*]
~ **dye** · kationischer Küpenfarbstoff m
~ **dyestuff** · kationischer Farbstoff m
~ **emulsion, acid ~** · kationische Emulsion f, saure ~
~ **slurry, acid ~** · kationische Schlämme f, saure ~
~ **wetting agent** · kationisches Benetzungsmittel n, saures ~
catted chimney (US); cat-and-clay ~ · Schornstein m aus Lehm, Lehmschornstein
cauk, cawk [*Scotland*]; **chalk** · Kreide f [*DIN 1280*]
~ [*Scotland*] → limestone
caulicole · Helix m [*Der zwischen Akanthusblättern des korinthischen Kapitells aus gerieften Blatthülsen herauswachsende und in einer Volute endende Stengel*]
caulicoli capital · klassisches korinthisches Kapitell n, ~ ~ Kapitäl
ca(u)lked, fullered · verstemmt, kalfater
~ **joint** · Stemmuffe f
~ ~ · Stemmdichtung f
ca(u)lking, fullering, CLKG · Kalfatern n, Verstemmen
~, **CLKG** · Verkitten n
~, **cogging, corking, cocking, cogged joint** · Verkämmung f [*Holzverband im Fachwerkbau*]
~ **(compound)** · Stemmasse f
~ **gun** · Kitt(spritz)pistole f, Kittspritze f
caustic alkalinity · Ätz-Alkalität f
~ **magnesia** · kaustische Magnesia f [*DIN 273 Bl. 1*]
~ **magnesite** · kaustisch gebrannter Magnesit m
~ **potash, potassium hydrate; potassium hydroxide (Brit.); potassium hydroxid(e) (US)** · Ätzkali n, Kaliumhydrat n, KOH, Kaliumhydroxid n
~ **soda, sodium hydroxide** · Natriumhydroxid n, Ätznatron n, kaustische Soda f, kaustisches Soda n, Natronhydrat n, NaOH
caustification · Kaustifizierung f
cave · Höhle f
~ **architecture** → rock(-cut) ~
~ **chaitya hall** → (rock(-cut)) ~ ~
~ **church** → rock(-cut) ~
~ **dwelling** · Höhlenwohnung f
~ **hall, rock-hewn ~, rock(-cut) ~** · Felsenhalle f
~ **in rock, rock(-cut) chamber, rock-hewn chamber** · Felsenkammer f

cave monastery — cavity-wall tie

~ **monastery**, rock(-cut) ~, rock-hewn ~, vihara · (buddhistisches) Felsenkloster *n*, (~) Höhlenkloster, (Felsen)Vihara *m*

~ **sanctuary**, rock(-cut) ~, rock-hewn ~ · Felsheiligtum *n*, Höhlenheiligtum

~ **sepulchre** → rock-hewn ~

~ **temple** → rock-hewn ~

~ **tomb**, rock(-cut) ~, rock-hewn ~ · Felsen(kammer)grab *n*, Felsgrab

cavetto, throat · Ablauf *m* [*Konkave kurvierte Vermittlung zwischen einem vorspringenden oberen und einem zurücktretenden unteren Bauglied*]

~ **(moulding)**, cove (~) (Brit.); ~ (molding), cove (molding) (US); scotia, conge, gorge [*These are the names universally given by carpenters and millwork men to simple hollowed mo(u)ldings of all types. It is a stock pattern in wood (mou)ldings, available in various sizes and patterns*] · (einfache) Hohlkehle *f*, (Einfach-Hohl-) Kehle

~ ~ (Brit.); ~ molding (US) [*A hollow mo(u)lding, about a quarter of a circle in section*] · Viertelkehle *f*

~ **vault** · Spiegelgewölbe *n* [*Auseinandergezogenes Muldengewölbe mit waag(e)rechter Deckenfläche*]

caving, lime ~ · (Kalk)Nachlöschen *n*

~ **bin**, lime ~ ~ · (Kalk)Nachlöschbunker *m*

cavity, core hole, cell; core (US) · Loch *n*, Kammer *f*, Hohlraum *m* [*Ziegel; Block(stein)*]

~, pocket, embrasure, blockout, recess · Aussparung *f*

~, void · Hohlraum *m* [*z.B. über einer Hängedecke*]

~, air space [*A cavity or space in walls or between various structural elements*] · Luftschicht *f*, Luft(zwischen)raum *m*

~ **block** → hollow ~

~ ~ **floor** → hollow ~ ~

~ ~ **for walls** → hollow ~ ~ ~

~ ~ **making machine** → hollow-block ~ ~

~ ~ **masonry wall** → hollow ~ ~ ~

~ ~ ~ **(work)** → hollow ~ ~ (~)

~ ~ **mold** (US) → hollow-block mould

~ ~ **roof** → hollow tile ~

~ ~ **step**, hollow ~ ~, ~ tile ~, pot ~ · Block(stein)-Hohlstufe *f*, Stein-Hohlstufe

~ ~ **wall** → hollow ~ ~

~ **brick**, hollow ~ · Hohlziegel *m*

~ ~ **masonry (work)** → hollow (clay) ~ ~ (~)

~ **brickwork** → hollow (clay) brick masonry (work)

~ **brick(work) wall** → ~ clay ~ ~

~ **(clay) brick masonry (work)** → hollow (~) ~ ~ (~)

~ (~) **brickwork** → hollow (clay) brick masonry (work)

~ (~) **brick(work) wall**; hollow (~) ~ ~ [*See remark under 'Hohlmauer'*] · Hohlziegelmauer *f*

~ **concrete block for walls** → hollow ~ ~ ~

~ ~ **tile for walls** → hollow concrete block ~ ~

~ **concrete wall**; hollow ~ ~ [*See remark under 'Hohlwand'*] · Betonhohlwand *f*, Beton-(Zwei)Schalenwand

~ **construction** [*This type of construction is now almost a universal feature of external walling. Besides being, in certain circumstances, the surest form of protection against damp penetration it offers other advantages, such as enhanced thermal insulation*] · Hohlmauerbau *m*

~ **cross-wall** · Hohlquerwand *f*

~ **external masonry wall**, external masonry wall of double-leaf cavity construction · zweischalige Außenmauer *f*, Außenhohlmauer

~ **filling** · Hohlraumauffüllung *f*

~ **in the concrete** · Betonnest *n* [*Hohlraum im Beton infolge ungenügender Verdichtung oder falscher Kornzusammensetzung*]

~ **(masonry) wall** → hollow (~) ~

~ ~ **(work)**, hollow ~ (~) · (Zwei-) Schalenmauerwerk *n*, Hohlmauerwerk, Luftschichtmauerwerk

~ **panel**, hollow ~ · Hohltafel *f*

~ ~ **wall**, hollow ~ ~ · Hohltafelwand *f*

~ **partition (wall) block** → hollow ~ (~) ~

~ ~ (~) **tile** → hollow partition (wall) block

~ **party (masonry) wall**, hollow ~ (~) ~ · Brandhohlmauer *f*, Hohl-Feuermauer, Feuer-Hohlmauer, gemeinschaftliche Giebelhohlmauer, Hohlbrandmauer

~ ~ **wall** → ~ ~ masonry ~

~ **ring**, hollow ~ · Hohlring *m*

~ **tile** → hollow block

~ ~ **floor** → hollow block ~

~ ~ **for walls** → hollow block ~ ~

cavity-tile making machine → hollow-block ~ ~

cavity tile masonry wall → hollow block ~ ~

~ ~ ~ **(work)** → hollow block ~ (~)

cavity-tile mold (US) → hollow-block mould

~ **mould** (Brit.) → hollow-block ~

cavity tile roof → hollow ~ ~

~ ~ **wall** → hollow block ~

~ **wall** → hollow (masonry) ~

~ ~ **insulation**, hollow ~ ~ · Hohlwanddämmung *f*

cavity-wall tie, ~ anchor · Luftschichtanker *m*

cavity with rarefied air · Hohlraum *m* mit verdünnter Luft [*Glasbaustein*]

cawk [*Scotland*] → limestone

~, cauk [*Scotland*]; **chalk** · Kreide *f* [*DIN 1280*]

CB, cast brass · Gußmessing *n* [*Eine Legierung, die mindestens 50% Kupfer und den Hauptlegierungszusatz Zink enthält. DIN 1709*]

CCS → colour-coated steel

CD → (multiple way) cable duct

cedar shingle · Zeder(n)schindel *f*

~ slatted ceiling · Zeder(n)lattendecke *f*

ceiling, CLG, soffit of structural slab, floor soffit [*A construction covering the underside of a floor or roof to provide the overhead surface of a room or other enclosed space*] · (sichtbare) Decke *f*, Deckenuntersicht *f*, Raumdecke

~ accessory · Decken(ausbau)zubehör *n*

~ adhesive, ~ cement((ing) agent), ~ bonding agent, ~ bonding medium [*It is used for fixing sheets to ceilings*] · Deckenkleb(e)stoff *m*, Deckenkleber *m*, Deckenkleb(e)mittel *n*

~ board, ~ sheet, ~ tile · Decken(belag)platte *f*, Deckenfliese *f* [*Für Deckenuntersichten*]

~ boarding · Deckenschalung *f*

~ bonding agent → ~ adhesive

~ ~ medium → ~ adhesive

~ cement((ing) agent) → ~ adhesive

~ coat · Deckenanstrich *m*, Deckenaufstrich

~ conduit, ~ wiring ~ · Elektro-Deckenleerrohr *n*, (Elt-)Deckenleerrohr

~ construction, ~ structure, ~ system · Deckenkonstruktion *f*, Deckensystem *n*

~ cooling · Deckenkühlung *f*

~ cover(ing) · Deckenbelag *m*

~ diffuser · ~ diffusor (Brit.); ~ outlet · Deckendiffusor *m*

~ dome(light), ~ saucer dome, ~ light cupola · Deckenlichtkuppel *f*

~ enrichment · Deckenverzierung *f*

~ facing → ~ lining

~ ~ work → ~ lining ~

~ fan, ceiling-type ~ [*B.S. 367*] · Deckenventilator *m*

~ framing, ~ trimming · Deckenauswechs(e)lung *f*, Deckenwechsel *m*

~ fresco · Deckenfreske *f*

~ grille, CG [*Sometimes spelled 'grill'*] · Deckengitter *n*

~ grinder · Deckenschleifmaschine *f*

~ gypsum baseboard → gypsum ceiling ~

~ hanger, ~ strap · Deckenhänger *m*

~ heating → (radiant) ceiling (panel) ~

~ panel · Deckenheiz(ungs)platte *f*

~ height · Deckenuntersichthöhe *f*

~ hook · Deckenhaken *m*

ceiling-hung chandelier · Deckenkronleuchter *m*

ceiling illumination, ~ lighting · Deckenbeleuchtung *f*

~ incorporating services → service(d) ceiling

~ joint · Deckenfuge *f*

~ joist, (intermediate) (floor) ~ · Deckenunterzug *m*, Trenn~, Etagen~, Stockwerk~, Geschoß~

~ lath · Deckenlatte *f*

~ lathes · Deckenlattung *f*

~ light, lay ~ [*A glazed opening in a ceiling, designed to admit light to the space below*] · Deckenoberlicht *n*

~ ~ cupola, ~ saucer dome, ~ dome(-light) · Deckenlichtkuppel *f*

~ ~ fitting (Brit.) → ceiling(-mounted) luminaire (fixture)

~ lighting, ~ illumination · Deckenbeleuchtung *f*

~ lining, ~ (sur)facing · Deckenauskleidung *f*, Deckenverkleidung, Deckenbekleidung

~ ~ work, ~ (sur)facing · Deckenauskleidungsarbeiten *fpl*, Deckenbekleidungsarbeiten, Deckenverkleidungsarbeiten

~ luminaire (fixture) (US) → ceiling-mounted ~ (~)

~ (mixed) plaster · Decken(ver)putz *m*

ceiling(-mounted) fixture → ~ luminaire (~)

~ luminaire (fixture), surface(-mounted) ~ (~) (US); ~ (light) fitting (Brit.); ~ (light(ing)) fixture · Deckenleuchte *f*

~ luminaire (fixture) with louver and frame (US); ~ light fitting ~ ~ ~ (Brit.); ~ (lighting)) fixture ~ ~ ~ ~ · Deckenleuchte *f* mit Großraster und Rahmen

ceiling mounting channel · Decken-Montageschiene *f* [*Deckenleuchte*]

~ night light · Deckennachtlampe *f*

~ ornament · (Raum)Deckenverzierung *f*, (Raum)Deckenschmuck *m*, (Raum-)Deckenornament *n*

~ paint · Decken(anstrich)farbe *f*

~ painting · Deckenmalerei *f*

~ panel · Deckentafel *f*

~ (~) heating → radiant ~ (~) ~

~ paper · Deckentapete *f*

~ picture · Deckengemälde *n*

~ plaster, ~ mixed ~ · Decken(ver)putz *m*

~ ~ lath(ing) · Deckenputzträger *m*

~ ~ on reed lath(ing) · Rohrdeckenputz *m*

~ plate [*Scotland*]; **gypsum ceiling board** · Gipsdeckenplatte *f*, Deckenplatte aus Gips [*DIN 18169*]

ceiling plenum — cellar room

~ plenum · Zwischendeckenraum *m*
~ profile → ~ shape
~ reflection factor · Deckenrückstrahlgrad *m*
~ rose [*B.S.* 67] · Deckenkappe *f*
~ rosette · Deckenrosette *f*
~ saucer dome, ~ dome(light), ~ light cupola · Deckenlichtkuppel *f*
~ section → ~ shape
~ shape, ~ section, ~ unit, ~ trim, ~ profile · Deckenprofil *n*
~ sheet, ~ tile, ~ board · Decken(belag)platte *f*, Deckenfliese *f* [*Für Deckenuntersichten*]
~ slot diffuser (US); ~ ~ diffusor (Brit.); ~ ~ outlet · Decken-Schlitzdiffusor *m*, Schlitz-Deckendiffusor
~ strength · Grenzfestigkeit *f* [*(Beton-) Leichtzuschlag(stoff)*]
~ strip · Deckenleiste *f*
~ structure, ~ construction, ~ system · Deckenkonstruktion *f*, Deckensystem *n*
~ (sur)facing, ~ lining · Deckenauskleidung *f*, Deckenverkleidung, Deckenbekleidung
~ ~ work → ~ lining ~
~ suspension · Deckenabhängung *f*
~ ~ system, ~ ~ construction · Decken(ab)hängebausystem *n*, Decken(ab)hängekonstruktion(ssystem) *f*, (*n*), Decken(ab)hängesystem
~ switch · Deckenschalter *m*
~ system, ~ construction, ~ structure · Deckenkonstruktion *f*, Deckensystem *n*
~ tile, ~ board, ~ sheet · Decken(belag)platte *f*, Deckenfliese *f* [*Für Deckenuntersichten*]
~ ~ adhesive → ~ ~ bonding ~
~ ~ (bonding) adhesive, ~ ~ ~ agent, ~ ~ ~ medium, ~ ~ ~ cement(ing) agent · Deckenfliesenkleber *m*, Deckenfliesenkleb(e)mittel *n*, Deckenfliesenkleb(e)stoff *m*, Decken(belag)plattenkleber, Decken(belag)plattenkleb(e)mittel, Decken(belag)plattenkleb(e)stoff
~ trim → ~ shape
~ trimming, ~ framing · Deckenauswechs(e)lung *f*, Deckenwechsel *m*
~(-type) fan [*B.S.* 367] · Deckenventilator *m*
~ unit → ~ shape
~ ventilator · (Raum)Deckenlüfter *m*
~ void · Deckenzwischenraum *m*
~ (wiring) conduit · (Elt-)Deckenleerrohr *n*, Elektro-Deckenleerrohr
celestial blue, Brunswick ~ · Braunschweigerblau *n*
celite [*A name used by Tornebohm (1897) to identify the calcium alumino ferrite constituent of portland cement*] · Zelit *m*
cell, web [*One of the compartments of a groin(ed) vault*] · Gewölbekappe *f*, Tonnen(gewölbe)kappe [*Eines der vier Teilstücke des Kreuz(grat)gewölbes, das aus zwei sich rechtwinklig schneidenden Tonnengewölben gleichen Querschnittes entsteht*]
~, web [*One of the compartments of a rib(bed) vault*] · (Rippen)Gewölbekappe *f*
~, cavity, core hole; core (US) · Loch *n*, Kammer *f*, Hohlraum *m* [*Ziegel; Block-(stein)*]
~ → monastic ~
~ block, ~ building · Zellengebäude *n* [*Straf(vollzugs)anstalt*]
~ building, ~ block · Zellengebäude *n* [*Straf(vollzugs)anstalt*]
~ enamel, cloisonné (work) · Zellenschmelz *m*
(~) rubber (joint) filler · Gummi(fugen)einlage *f*
~ vault, diamond ~ [*A vault consisting of concave troughs or hollows separated by groins*] · Zellengewölbe *n*
cella [*The main body of a temple as distinct from the portico and the naos*] · Cella *f*
~ door · Cellatür *f*
~ façade · Cellafassade *f*
~ masonry wall · Cellamauer *f*
~ structure · Cellabau *m*
~ wall · Cellawand *f*
~ window · Cellafenster *n*
cellar [*A space within a building or structure and below ground level, designed for storage, boiler room etc.*] · Keller *m*
~ covering half of the area of a building · Halbkeller *m*
~ ~ part of the area of a building · Teilkeller *m*
~ ~ the whole area of a building · Vollkeller *m*
~ door · Kellertür *f*
~ drainage · Kellerentwässerung *f*
~ dwelling (Brit.); ~ ~ unit (US) · Kellerwohnung *f*, Souterrainwohnung
~ entrance, entrance to a cellar · Kellereingang *m*
~ ~ door · Kellereingangstür *f*
~ floor · Kellerdecke *f*
~ ~ cover(ing), ~ floor(ing) (finish) · Keller(fuß)boden(belag) *m*
~ floor(ing) (finish), ~ floor cover(ing) · Keller(fuß)boden(belag) *m*
~ for branches · Gebäudeanschlußkeller *m*, Hausanschlußkeller [*DIN 18012*]
~ grating · Kellergitter *n*
cellarless · kellerlos, nichtunterkellert
cellar masonry wall · Kellermauer *f*
~ ~ (work) · Kellermauerwerk *n*
~ niche, ~ recess · Kellernische *f*
~ recess, ~ niche · Kellernische *f*
~ room · Kellerraum *m*

cellar shelter — cellulose ester

~ **shelter** · Schutzkeller m [*baulicher Luftschutz*]

~ **sink** · Kellerausguß m

~ **slab** · Kellerplatte f

~ **stair(case)** · Kellertreppe f

~ **under a street** · Straßenkeller m

~ **vault** · Kellergewölbe n

~ **wall** · Kellerwand f

~ **window** · Kellerfenster n

cellophane [*A regenerated cellulose obtained from viscose solution*] · Cellophan n, Zellophan

cellular block [*Holes closed at one end exceed 20 per cent of the volume of the block. B.S. 3921*] · Hohlgroßblockziegel m

~ ~, ~ **tile** [*It is a block in which cavities (holes closed at one end) exceed 20% of the volume of the block. See remark under 'Block'*] · Zellenblock(stein) m, Zellenstein

~ ~ **for walls**, ~ **tile** ~ ~ [*See remark under 'Block'*] · Zellenwandblock(stein) m, Zellenwandstein

~ **brick** [*It is a brick, in which cavities (holes closed at one end) exceed 20% of the volume of the brick. B.S. 3921*] · Zellenziegel m [*Fehlname: Zellenstein m*]

~ **concrete**, cellular-expanded ~ · Zellenbeton m [*manchmal "Seifenbeton" genannt*]

~ ~ **block**, ~ ~ **tile** [*See remark under 'Block'*] · Zellenbetonblock(stein) m, Zellenbetonstein

~ ~ **factory**, ~ ~ works, cellular-expanded ~ ~ · Zellenbetonwerk n

~ ~ **screed**, (lightweight) cellular-expanded ~ ~ · Zellenbetonestrich m

~ ~ **slab**, cellular-expanded ~ ~ · Zellenbeton(bau)platte f

~ ~ **tile**, ~ ~ block [*See remark under 'Block'*] · Zellenbetonblock(stein) m, Zellenbetonstein

~ ~ **works**, ~ ~ factory, cellular-expanded ~ ~ · Zellenbetonwerk n

~ **core**, hollow ~ · Zellenkern m, Hohlkern

~ **design** · Zellenentwurf m

cellular(-expanded) concrete · Zellenbeton m [*Manchmal „Seifenbeton" genannt*]

~ ~ **factory**, ~ ~ works · Zellenbetonwerk n

~ ~ **screed**, lightweight ~ ~ ~ · Zellenbetonestrich m

~ ~ **slab** · Zellenbeton(bau)platte f

~ ~ **works**, ~ ~ factory · Zellenbetonwerk n

cellular floor · Zellendecke f

~ **frame**, multiple ~, multi(ple)-bay ~ · Mehrfeldrahmen m

~ **framing** → cross-wall type of construction

~ **glass** → multi~ ~

~ ~ **block** → multi~ ~ ~

~ ~ **tile** → multi~ ~ ~

~ **gypsum** · Zellengips m

~ (~) **plasterboard** · Zellengips(bau)platte f

~ **limestone** · Zellenkalkstein m

~ **mortar** · Zellenmörtel m

~ **pier** · Zellenpfeiler m

~ **plasterboard**, ~ gypsum ~ · Zellengips(bau)platte f

~ **raft** [*A raft in which the intersecting beams form a number of cells*] · Zellenfundamentplatte f

~ **section**, (~ steel) Q-floor unit · Zellenprofil n, Profiltafel f [*Robertson-Stahlzellendecke*]

~ ~, ~ **shape**, ~ unit · Zellenprofil n

~ **shape**, ~ section, ~ unit · Zellenprofil n

~ **steel floor** → ~ ~ ~ sub-floor

(~ ~) **Q-floor unit**, ~ section · Profiltafel f, Zellenprofil n [*Robertson-Stahlzellendecke*]

~ ~ **(sub-)floor** · Stahlzellendecke f

~ ~ **unit**, steel cellular ~ · Abkantprofil n [*Stahldecke*]

~ **structure** · Zellenstruktur f

~ **thermal insulation**, all glass ~ · Zellglasdämmung f

~ **tile**, ~ **block** [*It is a block in which cavities (holes closed at one end) exceed 20% of the volume of the block. See remark under 'Block'*] · Zellenblock(stein) m, Zellenstein

~ ~ **for walls**, ~ block ~ ~ [*See remark under 'Block'*] · Zellenwandblock(stein) m, Zellenwandstein

cellular-type block, ~ building · Zellengebäude n

cellular unit, ~ section, ~ shape · Zellenprofil n

cellulated ceramics · keramische Erzeugnisse npl mit Zellenbildung, ~ Leichterzeugnisse

celluloid · Zelluloid n, Zellhorn n

~ **scrap**, scrap celluloid · Zelluloidabfall m, Zellhornabfall

cellulose · Cellulose f, Zellulose, $C_6H_{10}O_5$

~ **acetate** · Celluloseacetat n, Celluloseazetat, Acetylcellulose f

~ ~ **butyrate** · Mischester m aus Essig- und Buttersäure, Cellulose-Acetobutyrat n, Zellulose-Acetobutyrat

~ **acetate/butyrate lacquer** · Zelluloseacetobutyratlack m, Zelluloseazetatbutyratlack

~ **acetate propionate** · Cellulose-Acetopropionat n, Zellulose-Acetopropionat

~ **adhesive**, ~ glue [*It is used as a household adhesive, but not as a structural glue*] · Zelluloseleim m, Celluloseleim, Zelleim, Zellulosekleber m, Cellulosekleber

~ **enamel** → ~ (nitrate) lacquer

~ **ester** · Celluloseester m, Zelluloseester

cellulose ether — cement asbestos duct 170

~ ether · Celluloseäther *m*, Zelluloseäther

~ foil · Cellulosefolie *f*, Zellulosefolie

~ glue → ~ adhesive

~ lacquer → ~ nitrate ~

~ medium, ~ vehicle · Zellulosebindemittellösung *f*, Cellulosebindemittellösung [*Anstrichmittel*]

~ nitrate, pyroxylin; nitrocellulose [*misnomer*] · Cellulosenitrat *n*, Zellulosenitrat [*Fehlnamen: Nitrozellulose f, Nitrocellulose, N.C. Diese Bezeichnungen sind falsch, weil es sich nicht um einen Nitrokörper, sondern um einen Salpetersäureester handelt*]

~ (~) lacquer, nitrocellulose ~, pyroxylin ~, cellulose enamel · Celluloselack *m*, (Nitro)Zelluloselack, Nitro(cellulose)-lack

~ ~ paint → nitrocellulose ~

~ ~ stopper → nitrocellulose ~

~ paste · Cellulosekleister *m*, Zellkleister, Zellulosekleister [*Er wird zum Kleben von Tapeten verwendet*]

~ solvent · Celluloselösungsmittel *n*, Zellulosölösungsmittel

~ stopper, ~ stopping, ~ filler · Nitroausfüller *m* [*Anstrichtechnik*]

~ thinner · Celluloseverdünnungsmittel *n*, Zelluloseverdünnungsmittel

~ vehicle, ~ medium · Zellulosebindemittellösung *f*, Cellulosebindemittellösung [*Anstrichmittel*]

~ wool · Chemiespinnfasern *fpl* [*Die alte Bezeichnung „Zellwolle" findet nur noch für die nach dem Viskoseverfahren hergestellten Chemiespinnfasern Anwendung*]

cellulosic plastic · Zellulosekunststoff *m*, Cellulosekunststoff

Celtic architecture · keltische Architektur *f*, ~ Baukunst *f*

~ cross, Runic ~ · keltisches Kreuz *n*

~ ornamentation · keltische Ornamentik *f*

CEM, cement matrix, water cement, (hydraulic) cement · Zement *m* [*hydraulisches Bindemittel*]

~ AB (US) → asbestos-cement sheet

~ MORT, (hydraulic-)cement mortar · Zementmörtel *m*

CEM PLAS, CPL, cement plaster, patent plaster · Zementputz *m* [*DIN 18550*]

cement, putty · Kitt *m*

~ → cementing material

~, dressing composition, dressing compound · Dachkleb(e)masse *f*, (Dach-)Spachtel(masse) *m*, (*f*)

~ → bonding agent

~ → adhesive composition

~, hydraulic ~, water ~, ~ matrix, CEM · Zement *m* [*hydraulisches Bindemittel*]

cement-aggregate ratio [*The ratio, by weight or volume, of cement to aggregate*] · Zement-Zuschlag(stoff)-Verhältnis *n*, Trockenbeton-Mischungsverhältnis

~ reaction · Zement-Zuschlag(stoff)-Reaktion *f*

cement article, ~ product · Zementartikel *m*, Zementerzeugnis *n*, Zementgegenstand *m*

~ artificial marble → (Portland) cement imitation ~

~ asbestos (US); asbestos cement · Asbestzement *m* [*Fehlname: Kunstschiefer m. DIN 274*]

~ ~ article (US) → asbestos-cement product

~ ~ board, ~ ~ sheet, CEM AB, cem ab, CAB (US); asbestos cement board, asbestos cement sheet [*A large unit, flat or profiled, laid to overlap*] · Asbestzementplatte *f*

~ ~ ~ 625 mm long → ~ ~ sheet ~ ~ ~

~ ~ box (roof) gutter, ~ ~ ~ rainwater ~ (US); asbestos-cement ~ (~) ~ · Asbestzement-Kasten(dach)rinne *f*

~ ~ (building) component (US) → asbestos-cement (building) unit

~ ~ (~) member (US) → asbestos-cement (building) unit

~ ~ (~) unit (US) → asbestos-cement (~) ~

~ ~ cistern (US) → asbestos-cement ~

~ ~ component (US) → asbestos-cement (building) unit

~ ~ conductor (US) → asbestos-cement downpipe

~ ~ corrugated board (US) → asbestos-cement corrugated sheet

~ ~ ~ boards (US) → asbestos-cement corrugated sheeting

~ ~ ~ panel (US) → asbestos-cement ~ ~

~ ~ ~ roof(ing) board (US) → asbestos corrugated roof(ing) sheet

~ ~ ~ sheet (US) → asbestos-cement ~ ~

~ ~ ~ sheeting (US) → asbestos-cement ~ ~

~ ~ discharge pipe (US) → asbestos-cement drain(age) ~

~ ~ distance piece (US) → asbestos-cement spacer

~ ~ downspout (US) → asbestos-cement downpipe

~ ~ drain(age) pipe (US) → asbestos-cement ~ ~

~ ~ duct (US); asbestos-cement ~ [*B.S. 3954*] · Asbestzementkanal *m*

171 cement asbestos eave(s)... — cement asbestos ((roofing))...

~ ~ **eave(s) gutter** (US) → asbestos-cement ~ ~

~ ~ ~ **trough** (US) → asbestos-cement ~ ~

~ ~ **extract ventilation unit** (US) → asbestos-cement ventilator

~ ~ **extraction unit** (US) → asbestos-cement ventilator

~ ~ **extractor** (US) → asbestos-cement ventilator

~ ~ **façade** (US) → asbestos-cement ~

~ ~ ~ **slab** (US); asbestos-cement ~ ~ · Asbestzement-Fassadenplatte f, Fassaden-Asbestzementplatte

~ ~ **face** (US) → asbestos-cement façade

~ ~ **facing** (US) → asbestos-cement lining

~ ~ ~ **sheet** (US) → asbestos-cement (lining) ~

~ ~ **fascia board (for flat roof(s))** (US); asbestos-cement ~ ~ (~ ~ ~ ~) · Asbestzement(-Flachdach)blende f

~ ~ **fence** (US) → asbestos-cement ~

~ ~ **fitting** (US); asbestos-cement ~ ~ · Asbestzementformstück n, Asbestzementfitting m [DIN 19830, 19831 und 19841]

~ ~ **flat board** (US) → asbestos-cement flat sheet

~ ~ ~ **(run) panel** (US); asbestos-cement ~ (~) ~ · Asbestzement-Flachtafel f, Asbestzement-Plantafel, ebene Asbestzementtafel

~ ~ ~ **sheet** (US) → asbestos-cement ~

~ ~ ~ ~ **siding** (US); asbestos-cement ~ ~ ~ · ebener Asbestzementplattenschirm m [*Wetterschutz für Außenwände*]

~ ~ **floor(ing)** (US) → asbestos-cement ~

~ ~ **flower container** (US); asbestos-cement ~ ~ · Asbestzement-Blumengefäß n

~ ~ **flue** (US); asbestos-cement ~ · Asbestzementzug m

~ ~ **foul water pipe** (US) → asbestos-cement sewer ~

~ ~ **fountain basin** (US); asbestos-cement ~ ~ · Asbestzement-(Spring-)Brunnenbecken n

~ ~ **front** (US) → asbestos-cement façade

~ ~ **gutter** → ~ ~ roof ~

~ ~ **leader** (US) → asbestos-cement-downpipe (Brit.)

~ ~ **lining** (US) → asbestos-cement ~

~ ~ **(~) sheet** (US) → asbestos-cement (~) ~

~ ~ **member** (US) → asbestos-cement (building) unit

~ ~ **mortar** (US); asbestos-cement ~ · Asbestzementmörtel m

~ ~ **panel** (US) → asbestos-cement ~

~ ~ **partition (wall)** (US) → asbestos-cement ~ (~)

~ ~ **pipe** (US) → asbestos-cement ~

~ ~ **pressure pipe** (US); asbestos-cement ~ ~ [*B.S. 486*] · Asbestzement-Druckrohr n [*DIN 19800, DIN 19801, DIN 19630*]

~ ~ **product** (US) → asbestos-cement ~

~ ~ **profile(d) board** (US) → asbestos-cement ~ ~

~ ~ ~ **sheet** (US) → asbestos-cement ~ ~

~ ~ **(rain) conductor** (US) → asbestos-cement downpipe (Brit.)

~ ~ **(~) leader** (US) → asbestos-cement downpipe

~ ~ **rainwater article**, ~ ~ ~ product (US); asbestos-cement ~ ~ [*B.S. 569*] · Asbestzement-Dachzubehörteil m, n

~ ~ ~ **articles** (US) → asbestos-cement rainwater goods

~ ~ ~ **goods** (US) → asbestos-cement ~ ~

~ ~ ~ **product,** ~ ~ ~ ~ **article** (US); asbestos-cement ~ ~ [*B.S. 569*] · Asbestzement-Dachzubehörteil m, n

~ ~ ~ **products** (US) → asbestos-cement rainwater goods

~ ~ **refuse water pipe** (US) → asbestos-cement sewer ~

~ ~ **ridge capping tile** (US) → asbestos-cement ~ ~ ~

~ ~ ~ **cover(ing) tile** (US) → asbestos-cement ridge capping ~

~ ~ ~ **ridging tile** (US) → asbestos-cement ridge capping ~

~ ~ **roof cladding** (US) → asbestos-cement roof covering

~ ~ ~ **covering** (US) → asbestos-cement ~ ~

~ ~ **(~) gutter,** ~ ~ **rainwater** ~ (US); asbestos-cement (~) ~ · Dach-Asbestzementrinne f, Regen-Asbestzementrinne, Asbestzementregenrinne, Asbestzement(dach)rinne

~ ~ ~ **sheathing** (US) → asbestos-cement roof covering

~ ~ ~ **shingle** (US); asbestos-cement ~ ~ · Asbestzementdachschindel f

~ ~ **roof(ing)** (US) → asbestos-cement roof covering

~ ~ ~ **board** (US) → asbestos-cement roof(ing) sheet

~ ~ ~ **panel** (US); asbestos-cement ~ ~ · Asbestzementdachtafel f

~ ~ ~ **sheet** (US) → asbestos-cement ~ ~

~ ~ ~ **shingle** (US) → asbestos-cement ~ ~

~ ~ **(~) slate** (US) → asbestos-cement (~) ~

cement asbestos (roof(ing)) tile — cement-bound mineral ... 172

~~ (~) tile (US) → asbestos-cement ~ ~

~~ rubber tile (US); asbestos-cement ~ ~ [*An asbestos-cement tile surfaced with rubber*] · Asbestzement-Gummi-(Belag)Platte *f*, Asbestzement-Gummi-Fliese *f*

~~ separator (US) → asbestos-cement spacer

~~ septic tank (US); asbestos-cement ~ ~ · Asbestzement-Faulgrube *f*

~~ sewage pipe (US) → asbestos-cement sewer ~

~~ sewer pipe (US) → asbestos-cement ~ ~

~~ sheet → ~ ~ board

~~~ (US) → asbestos-cement (lining) ~

~~~ 625 mm long, ~ ~ board ~ ~ ~ (US); asbestos-cement ~ ~ ~ · Kurzwellplatte *f*, Berliner-Welle *f*, KW-Platte [*Eine Asbestzementplatte von 625 mm Länge für die Eindeckung von Wohnhäusern*]

~~ sheeting (US) → asbestos-cement ~

~~ shingle (US) → asbestos-cement ~

~~ siding (US); asbestos-cement ~ · Asbestzement-Wandschirm *m*, Asbestzement-Wandbeschlag *m*, Asbestzement-Wetterschirm

~~~ shingle (US) → asbestos-cement ~ ~

~~ slate (US) → asbestos-cement (roofing) ~

~~ solid board (US) → asbestos-cement ~ ~

~~~ sheet (US) → asbestos-cement ~ ~

~~ spacer (US) → asbestos-cement ~

~~ (sur)facing (US) → asbestos-cement lining

~~~ sheet (US) → asbestos-cement (lining) ~

~~ tile (US) → asbestos-cement (roofing) ~

~~ unit (US) → asbestos-cement (building) ~

~~ valley gutter (US); asbestos-cement ~ ~ · Asbestzementkehlrinne *f*

~~ vent(ilating) pipe (US); asbestos-cement ~ ~ [*B.S. 582*] · Asbestzementlüftungsrohr *n*, Lüftungs-Asbestzementrohr

~~ ventilator (US) → asbestos-cement ~

~~ wall board (US) → asbestos-cement ~ ~

~~~ panel (US) → asbestos-cement ~ ~

~~~ sheet (US) → asbestos-cement ~ ~

~~~ shingle (US); asbestos-cement ~ ~ · Asbestzementwandschindel *f*

~~ ware (US) → (mass-produced) asbestos-cement ~

~~ waste pipe (US) → asbestos-cement drain(age) ~

~~ window sill (US); asbestos-cement ~ ~; asbestos-cement window cill (Brit.) · Asbestzementfenster(sohl)bank *f*, Asbestzementsohlbank

cement-asphalt (US) → cement-bitumen

~ composition floor(ing) (US) → cement-bitumen (jointless) ~

~ floor(ing) (US) → cement-bitumen (jointless) ~

~ (jointless) floor(ing) (US) → cement-bitumen (~) ~

cement bacillus → Michaelis' salt

~ base · Zementbasis *f*, Zementgrundlage *f* [*z.B. Mauermörtel auf Zementbasis*]

cement(-)based · zementhaltig

~ adhesive, thin-bed ~ [*A material in which the principal bonding component is a hydraulic cement, e.g. Portland cement, modified by the inclusion of such other additives as may be necessary in order to achieve satisfactory fixing of ceramic tiles*] · Dünnbettkleber *m*

cement((-)based) glaze(d finish), ~ glazing, ~ glazed coat(ing) · Zementglasur *f*, Zementbeglasung *f*

cement based on coal tar → (bonding) adhesive ~ ~ ~ ~

cement(-)based product · zementhaltiges Erzeugnis *n*

cement((-)based) waterproof coating · wasserdichter Überzug *m* auf Zementbasis, Sperrschicht *f* ~ ~, Sperrlage *f* ~ ~, Zementsperrlage, Zementsperrschicht

cement bed, test bed of cement · Zementbett *n* [*Blaine-Gerät*]

cement-bitumen (Brit.); cement-asphalt (US) [*Portland-cement mortar gauged with bitumen emulsion is commonly used as a patching compound for factory floors, and to a lesser but growing extent as a floor finish. Only dark colours are available, and the floor finish is laid 5/8 in. thick*] · Zement-Bitumen-Masse *f*

~ (jointless) floor(ing), ~ composition ~ (Brit.); cement-asphalt (~) ~ (US) · Bitumenzementestrich *m*

cement board roof cladding, ~ sheet ~ ~, ~ ~ ~ covering, ~ ~ ~ sheathing, ~ ~ ~ roofing · Zementbedachung *f*, Zementdach(ein)deckung, Zement(ein)deckung

~~~ covering → ~ ~ ~ cladding

~~~ sheathing → ~ ~ ~ cladding

~~ roofing → ~ ~ ~ roof cladding

cement-bound, cemented · zementgebunden

~ mineral fibre light(weight) building slab (Brit.); ~ ~ ~ fiber ~ ~ ~ (US) · Mineralfaser-Zement-Leichtbauplatte *f*

cement brand, brand of cement · Zementmarke f

~ chemist · Zementchemiker m

~ chemistry, chemistry of cement · Zementchemie f

(~) clinker · (Zement)Klinker m [Der Name „Klinker" stammt noch aus der Zeit, als man das Rohmehl in ziegelartigen Rohlingen formte und diese wie Mauerklinker brannte]

(~) ~ chemistry · (Zement)Klinkerchemie f

(~) ~ composition · (Zement)Klinkerzusammensetzung f

(~) ~ grain · (Zement)Klinkerkorn n, (Zement)Klinkerteilchen n

(~) ~ grinding · (Zement)Klinkermahlung f

(~) ~ mineral · (Zement)Klinkermineral n

(~) ~ phase · (Zement)Klinkerphase f

~ coat · Zementanstrich m, Zementaufstrich

cement-coated · zementumhüllt

cement coating · Zementumhüllung f

~ colour → **~ pigment**

~ compressive strength · Zementdruckfestigkeit f

(~) concrete, CONC · (Zement)Beton m [Im Gegensatz zum Teer- und Asphaltbeton]

~ ~ aerated with foam, foam(ed) cement concrete · Zement-Schaumbeton m [Die Herstellung von Zement-Schaumbeton beruht auf der Durchmischung eines Zementbreis mit wäßrigen schaumfähigen Lösungen in schaumschlagenden Misch- oder Peitsch-Maschinen]

(~ ~) gunite machine, ~ gun · (Torkret)Beton-Spritzmaschine f, (Torkret-)Zement(mörtel)kanone f, Zementmörtel-Spritzapparat m nach dem Torkretverfahren, Tektor m, Torkretkanone

~ consumer, ~ user · Zementverbraucher m

~ consumption · Zementverbrauch m

~ content, ~ factor [The quantity of cement contained in a unit volume of concrete or mortar, preferably expressed as weight] · Zementanteil m, Zementfaktor m, Zementgehalt m

~ cooler · Zementkühler m

to cement down, to glue ~, to bond ~, ~ ~ to · (ver)kleben (mit)

cement dust · Zementstaub m

~ economiser · zementsparendes Mittel n

~ (exterior) plaster → **~ (external) rendering**

~ external plaster → **~ (~) rendering**

~ (~) rendering (Brit.); **~ stucco** (US); ~ (exterior) plaster, ~ external plaster, ~ finish, CEM PLAS, CPL · Zement(ver)putz m [DIN 18550]

~ factor, ~ content [The quantity of cement contained in a unit volume of concrete or mortar, preferably expressed as weight] · Zementanteil m, Zementfaktor m, Zementgehalt m

cementfast, fast to cement · zementecht, zementbeständig, zementfest

cement fastness, fastness to cement · Zementechtheit f

~ filler · Zementfüller m

cement-filler grout, ~ slurry · Zement-Füller-Schlämme f, Zement-Füller-Schlempe

~ slurry, ~ grout · Zement-Füller-Schlämme f, Zement-Füller-Schlempe

cement film, ~ skin · Zementhaut f

~ fineness · Zementfeinheit f

~ finish → **~ (external) rendering**

~ fixing method, tile ~ ~ ~, thin-bed ~, glue fixing ~, thin-bed fixing technique · Dünnbettverfahren n, Kleb(e)verfahren [Ansetzen von Fliesen]

~ flat (roof(ing)) tile → **plain concrete (~) ~**

~ foam · Zementschaum m

~ for road and street construction · Straßenbauzement m

~ gel [The colloidal material which makes up the major portion of the porous mass of which mature hydrated cement paste is composed] · Zementgel n

~ glazed coat(ing) → **cement((-)based) glaze(d finish)**

~ glaze(d finish) → **cement((-)based) ~ (~)**

~ glazing → **cement((-)based) glaze(d finish)**

~ grade, grade of cement · Zementgüteklasse f

~ grain, ~ particle · Zementkorn n, Zementteilchen n

~ gray, ~ grey · zementgrau

~ grey, ~ gray · zementgrau

~ grinding · Zementvermahlung f

~ (~) mill · Zementmühle f

~ grout · Zementschlämme f

~ gun → **(~ concrete) gunite machine**

~ ~ work → **guniting**

~ hangar · Zementlagerhalle f

~ imitation marble → **Portland ~ ~ ~**

~ injection · Zementschlämmeauspressung f, Zementschlämmeeinpressung, Zementschlämmeverpressung, Zementschlämmeinjektion f

~ jointless floor(ing) · Zement(fuß)bodenestrich m

~ kiln · Zementofen m

~ lab(oratory) · Zementlabor(atorium) n

~ latex [It is used both for jointless floor(ing)s and as a bed and jointing for clay tiles] · Zement-Latex-Masse f

cement-less concrete — cement rock

cement-less concrete [*A polyester 'concrete' containing no cement at all — simple aggregate is bound with a greatly extended polyester*] · zementloser „Beton" *m*, zementfreier „~"

cement-like · zementartig

cement-lime mortar, gauged ~, cement/lime/sand ~, compo (~) · Kalkzementmörtel *m*, Zementkalkmörtel, verlängerter Zementmörtel, Magermörtel

cement-lime-sand mix(ture) · Zement-Kalk-Sand-Gemisch *n*, Zement-Kalk-Sand-Mischung *f*

cement/lime/sand mortar, cement-lime ~, gauged ~, compo (~) · Zementkalkmörtel *m*, Kalkzementmörtel, verlängerter Zementmörtel, Magermörtel

cement-lined · zementausgekleidet, zementverkleidet, zementbekleidet [*gegen Korrosion*]

cement lining · Zementauskleidung *f*, Zementverkleidung, Zementbekleidung

~ **man-made marble** → (Portland) cement imitation ~

~ **manufactured marble** → (Portland) cement imitation ~

~ **matrix,** (hydraulic) cement, water cement, CEM · Zement *m* [*hydraulisches Bindemittel*]

~ **mill,** ~ plant · Zementfabrik *f*, Zementwerk *n*

~ ~, ~ grinding ~ · Zementmühle *f*

~ **mineral** · Zementmineral *n*

~ **mixing test** · Zementmischprobe *f*, Zementmischversuch *m*, Zementmischprüfung *f* [*Bitumenemulsion*]

~ **mortar,** hydraulic-~, CEM MORT · Zementmörtel *m*

~ ~ **grouting,** ~ ~ injection · Zementmörtelauspressung *f*, Zementmörtelverpressung, Zementmörteleinpressung, Zementmörtelinjektion *f*

~ ~ **injection,** ~ ~ grouting · Zementmörtelauspressung *f*, Zementmörtelverpressung, Zementmörteleinpressung, Zementmörtelinjektion *f*

~ ~ **joint** · Zementmörtelfuge *f*

~ **of rapid initial set(ting),** rapid-setting cement · Schnellbinder *m* [*Fehlname*]; Schnellerstarrer [*Zement DIN 1164*]

~ **paint** [*A mix(ture) of cement and water which applied to concrete, masonry, or brickwork makes it waterproof*] · Zement-Wasser-Anstrich *n* für (Ab-) Dicht(ungs)anstriche

~ ~, concrete ~ [*A paint having a cement base. It is eminently satisfactory for painting on concrete and contains waterproofer and hardener*] · Betonfarbe *f*

cement-painted · zementgestrichen

cement particle, ~ grain · Zementkorn *n*, Zementteilchen *n*

~ **paste,** wet (~) ~ · Bindemittelleim *m*, Zementpaste *f*, Zementleim, (frischer) Zementbrei *m*, flüssiger Zement *m*, Schlämpe *f*, Schlempe [*Zement plus Wasser*]

~ **pat,** pat of cement-water paste, circular-domed pat of cement, soundness test pat · (Probe)Kuchen *m* (aus Zement), Zementkuchen

Cement Pavilion [*Designed by Robert Maillart for the Swiss Provinces Exhibition, Zürich 1939*] · Zementhalle *f*

cement phase · Zementphase *f*

~ **physics,** physics of cement · Zementphysik *f*

~ **pigment;** ~ colour, colour for incorporating in cement, pigment for colouring cement [*B.S. 1014*] · zementechte Farbe *f*, Zement(echt)farbe, zementechtes Farbpigment *n* [*Pigment zum Durchfärben von Zement*]

~ **plain (roof(ing)) tile** → plain concrete (~) ~

~ **plant,** ~ mill · Zementfabrik *f*, Zementwerk *n*

~ **plaster** → ~ (external) rendering

~ ~ → hard (gypsum) ~

cement-plaster ceiling, CPC · Zement(ver)putzdecke *f*

cement-plastic cold glaze, plastic-cement ~ ~, ~ vitreous surfacing · Kaltglasur *f* aus Zement und Kunststoff, Kaltkeramik *f* ~ ~ ~ ~

~ **cold-glaze(d wall coat(ing)),** plastic-cement ~ (~ ~) · (Wand)Kaltglasur(überzug) *f*, (*m*) aus Zement und Kunststoff, Kalt-Wandglasur(überzug) ~ ~ ~ ~, Kaltglasur-Wandverkleidung *f* ~ ~ ~ ~

~ **vitreous surfacing,** plastic-cement ~ ~, ~ cold glaze · Kaltglasur *f* aus Zement und Kunststoff, Kaltkeramik *f* ~ ~ ~ ~

cement-polyvinyl acetate emulsion concrete · Polyvinylacetat-Plastbeton *m*, PVA(C)-Plastbeton [*Siehe Anmerkung unter „Plastbeton"*]

~ ~ ~ **mortar** · Polyvinylacetat-Plastmörtel *m*, PVA(C)-Plastmörtel

cement product, ~ article · Zementartikel *m*, Zementerzeugnis *n*, Zementgegenstand *m*

~ **raw meal** · Zementrohmehl *n*

~ **rendering** → ~ external ~

~ **replacement material,** ~ substitute [*e.g. fly ash*] · Zementersatz *m*

~ **requirement** · Zementbedarf *m*, Zementanspruch *m*

(cement-)rich concrete, fat ~ · fetter Beton *m*, zementreicher ~

cement rock, ~ stone · Kalktonerdegestein *n*

cement (roof(ing)) tile — cement(ing) capacity

~ (roof(ing)) tile → concrete (~) ~

~ (~) ~ machine, concrete (~) ~ ~ · (Zement)Dachsteinmaschine f, Betondachsteinmaschine

~ (~) ~ tester → concrete (~) ~ ~

~ sample · Zementprobe f

cement-sand grout, sand-cement ~ · Sand-Zement-Schlämme f, Sand-Zement-Schlämpe f, Sand-Zement-Schlempe

~ mix(ture) · Zement-Sand-Gemisch n, Zement-Sand-Mischung f

cement:sand mortar · Zementsandmörtel m

cement(/sand) screed · Fez m, Zementestrich m

cement screed, cement/sand ~ · Fez m, Zementestrich m

~ shed, shed for cement · Zement(lager)schuppen m

~ sheet roof cladding → ~ board ~ ~

~ ~ ~ covering → ~ board roof cladding

~ ~ ~ sheathing → ~ board roof cladding

~ ~ roofing → ~ board roof cladding

cement-silica mix(ture) · Zement-Quarz-Mischung f, Zement-Quarz-Gemisch n

cement silo · Bindemittelsilo m, Zementsilo

~ skin, surface laitance · Zementschleier m

~ ~, ~ film · Zementhaut f

~ slurry · Zement-Rohschlamm m

~ soundness [Freedom from excessive increase in volume after setting] · Zementraumbeständigkeit f

~ standard spec(ification) · Zementnorm f

~ storage · Zement(ein)lagerung f

~ store · Zementlager n

~ strength · Zementfestigkeit f [DIN 1164]

(~) stucco (US); smooth external plastering · (Außen)Glatt(ver)putz m

~ substitute, ~ replacement material [e.g. fly ash] · Zementersatz m

~ surface · Zementoberfläche f

~ technology · Zementtechnologie f

~ tending to increase its volume · Treiber m [Ein zum Treiben neigender Zement]

~ test · Zementprobe f, Zementprüfung f, Zementversuch m [DIN 1164]

~ testing sand, standard ~ · Norm(en)sand m [DIN 1164]

to cement the pigment particles together, ~ bind ~ ~ ~ · untereinander verbinden [Pigmentteilchen durch Bindemittel]

cement tile · Zement(belag)platte f, Zementfliese f

~ ~ roof cladding, ~ ~ ~ cover(ing), ~ ~ ~ sheathing, concrete ~ ~ ~, ~ ~ roofing · Betonstein(dach)(ein)deckung f, Betonsteinbedachung, (Beton)Dachsteindeckung, Zementdachsteindeckung

to cement to, to bond ~, to glue ~, ~ ~ down · (ver)kleben (mit)

cement transport in bulk transporters · Silotransport m von Zement

cement-trass mortar · Zement-Traßmörtel m

cement type, type of cement · Zementart f

~ ~ IV (US) → low heat cement

cement(-type) cold glaze(d wall coat(ing)) · Zementkaltglasur(überzug) f, (m)

cement user, ~ consumer · Zementverbraucher m

~ waterprof coating → cement(-)based ~ ~

~ water ~ ratio · Zement-Wasser-Verhältnis n

~ waterproofer, ~ waterproofing powder [It is added to the cement] · Zementdichter m, Zementsperrpulver n

~ waterproofing powder, ~ waterproofer [It is added to the cement] · Zementdichter m, Zementsperrpulver n

~ weighing · Zement(ver)wiegung f

~ with excessive gypsum content · Gipstreiber m [Zement mit einem zu hohen Gipsanteil]

~ ~ more than 65% of lime · Kalktreiber m

cement-wood floor(ing) (finish), ~ floor cover(ing) [A jointless floor(ing) consisting of 1 part cement, 1½ parts aggregate, and 1½ parts specially treated sawdust, and required pigments] · Sägemehlbeton(fuß)boden(belag) m

cementation [Impregnating wrought-iron bars with carbon by packing them with charcoal and heating them for several days] · Aufkohlen n

cemented, cement-bound · zementgebunden

~ carbide, sintered ~ · Sinterkarbid n

cementing, bonding · (Ver)Kleben n

~, bonding · (Ver)Klebung f

~, cementitious · kleb(e)fähig, bindefähig

~ agent → ~ material

cement(ing agent) → bonding ~

~ (~) based on coal tar → (bonding) adhesive ~ ~ ~ ~

~ (~) for laying → bonding ~ ~ ~

~ capacity → adhesive property

cement(ing composition) — central conditioning plant 176

cement(ing composition) → adhesive ~

cement(ing compound) → adhesive composition

cementing layer, adhesive ~, bond(ing) ~ · Kleb(e)lage f, Kleb(e)schicht f

~ material, cementitious ~, ~ agent, binder, binding medium, (binding) matrix (material), cement · Bindemittel n, Binder m

~ ~ for masonry, masonry cement, mortar cement · (Putz- und) Mauer(werk)binder m, Fugenmörtelzement m, Mauerwerkbinder, Mauermörtelzement, Mauerwerkzement, PM-Binder

~ mortar, adhesive ~, bond(ing) ~ · Kleb(e)mörtel m, Haftmörtel

~ paper, adhesive ~, bonding ~ · Kleb(e)papier n

~ paste, adhesive ~, bonding ~ · Kleb(e)paste f

~ power → adhesive property

~ property → adhesive ~

~ quality → adhesive property

~ rubber, bonding ~, adhesive ~ · Kleb(e)gummi m, n

~ strength, adhesive ~, bonding ~ · Kleb(e)festigkeit f

~ system, adhesive ~, bonding ~ · Kleb(e)konstruktion f

~ tar composition, ~ ~ compound, adhesive ~ ~ · Teerkleb(e)masse f

~ ~ compound, ~ ~ composition, adhesive ~ ~ · Teerkleb(e)masse f

cementitious agent → cementing material

~ material · kleb(e)fähiger Stoff m

~ ~ → cementing ~

~ ~ · Kittstoff m

cemetery, graveyard · Friedhof m

~ basilica, graveyard ~, mortuary ~, funeral ~ [As distinct from a basilica in the city used for ordinary services] · Friedhofsbasilika f

~ chapel, graveyard ~, mortuary ~, funeral ~ · Friedhofskapelle f, Totenkapelle

~ church, graveyard ~, mortuary ~, funeral ~ · Friedhofskirche f

cenotaph [A monument to a person or persons buried elsewhere] · Kenotaph m, Zenotaph, Scheingrab n, (leeres) Ehrengrabmal n, Leergrab

Centenary Hall at Breslau, Centennial ~ ~ ~ · Jahrhunderthalle f in Breslau

center (US) → centre

~ bay (US); centre ~ (Brit.); central ~ · Mitteljoch n

~ gutter (US); valley ~ [A gutter formed at a valley, having sloping sides and exposed to view] · Kehlrinne f

~ light (US); centre ~ (Brit.); window ~ ~ · (Fenster) Mittelteil m, n

center line of inertia (US); centre ~ ~ ~ (Brit.); axis ~ ~ · Trägheitsachse f, Trägheitsmittellinie f

~ of cult (US) → place of worship

~ ~ curvature (US); centre ~ ~ (Brit.) · Krümmungsmittelpunkt m

~ ~ pressure (Brit.); center ~ ~ (US) · Druckmittelpunkt m

~ span (US); centre ~ (Brit.); central ~ · Mittelfeld n

~ split pipe (US) → half ~ ~

~ ~ ~ duct (US) → half split pipe (gutter)

~ ~ ~ gutter (US) → half ~ ~ (~)

center-to-center distance between columns (US) → centre-to-centre ~ ~ ~

~ ~ ~ supports (US) → centre-to-centre distance between columns

~ window (US) → central ~

centimetre-gramme-second system · absolutes Maßsystem n, CGS-System

centipoise · Centipoise f, cps

central (air) conditioning installation → ~ (~) ~ plant

~ (~) ~ plant, ~ (~) ~ installation, ~ (~) ~ station, air ~ ~ ~ · Klima(tisierungs)station f, Klima(tisierungs)zentrale f

~ (~) ~ station → ~ (~) ~ plant

~ ~ heating · zentrale Lufterwärmung f, Feuerluftheizung

~ altar · Mittelaltar m

~ arch · Mittelbogen m

~ archway, ~ main ~ · Mitteldurchgang m, Mitteldurchfahrt f [Stadttor]

~ area → business ~

~ atmospheric-pressure boiler station, ~ low-pressure ~ ~ · Niederdruckkesselzentrale f

~ avenue · Mittelallee f

~ axis; centre line (Brit.); center line (US) · Mittelachse f, Symmetrieachse

~ baths · Zentralbad n

~ bay; center ~ (US); centre ~ (Brit.) · Mitteljoch n

~ block · Zentralbau m

~ boiler installation, ~ ~ plant · Kesselzentrale f

~ burning appliance, ~ fire, ~ furnace [A self-contained furnace intended primarily to supply heated air through ducts] · Feuerluftofen m

~ chapel · Mittelkapelle f, Zentralkapelle

~ city, nucleus · Kernstadt f

~ column; center ~ (US); centre ~ (Brit.) · Mittelsäule f

~ conditioning installation → ~ (air) conditioning plant

~ ~ plant → ~ air ~ ~

~~ **station** → ~ **(air) conditioning plant**
~ **core** · Mittelkern m, Zentralkern
~~ **of strength** · Stabilisierungskern m
~ **corridor; centre** ~ **(Brit.); center** ~ **(US)** · Mittelflur m, Mittelkorridor m, Mittelgang m
central-corridor residential building, ~ ~ **block,** ~ **domestic** ~, ~ **residence** ~, ~ **multiple dwelling** ~, · Mittelgang(wohn)haus n, Mittelgang(wohn)gebäude n
central court · Zentralhof m
~~ → inner ~
~ **court(yard),** ~ **open** ~, **atrium** · Mittelhof m, Atrium n [*Der offene Mittelraum des römischen Hauses*]
~ **crawlway** · Mittel(kriech)gang m
~ **cupola,** ~ **dome** · Zentralkuppel f, Mittelkuppel
~ **district** → business area
~ **dome,** ~ **cupola** · Zentralkuppel f, Mittelkuppel
~ **door** · Mitteltür f
~ **entrance** · Mitteleingang m
~ **feature** · zentrale Raumform f [*z.B. ein Bogen*]
~ **fire,** ~ **burning appliance,** ~ **furnace** [*A self-contained furnace intended primarily to supply heated air through ducts*] · Feuerluftofen m
~ **frame,** ~ **framing** · Mittelrahmen m
~ **furnace,** ~ **fire,** ~ **burning appliance** [*A self-contained furnace intended primarily to supply heated air through ducts*] · Feuerluftofen m
~ **gable** · Mittelgiebel m
~ **hall(-way)** · Mittelhalle f, Zentralhalle
~ **heating** · Sammelheizung f [*Fehlname*]; Zentralheizung
~~ **appliance** · Zentralheizungsgerät n
~~ **boiler** · Zentralheiz(ungs)kessel m
~~ **chimney** · Zentralheizungsschornstein m [*DIN 4705*]
~~ **installation,** ~ ~ **system,** ~ ~ **plant, centrally fired** ~ ~ ~ · Sammelheizung(sanlage) f [*Fehlname*]; Zentralheizung(sanlage) [*DIN 18380*]
~ **hot water preparation plant** · zentrale Warmwasserbereitungsanlage f, ~ WW-Bereitungsanlage [*DIN 18380*]
~ **kitchen** · Zentralküche f
~~ **heating** · Küchenzentralheizung f
~ **laundry** · Zentralwäscherei f
~ **library** · Zentralbücherei f
~ **loading** · mittige Belastung f
~ **low-pressure boiler station,** ~ **atmospheric-pressure** ~ ~ · Niederdruckkesselzentrale f
~ **(main) archway** · Mitteldurchgang m, Mitteldurchfahrt f [*Stadttor*]

~ **master key** · Zentralhauptschlüsse m
~ **master-keyed lock** · Zentralschloß n
~~ **locks, series of** ~ ~ ~ · Zentralschloß-Anlage f
central-mixed concrete · stationär aufbereiteter Beton m
central moment of inertia, ~ **second moment (of area)** [*of a section*] · zentrales Trägheitsmoment n
~ **motif** · Zentralmotiv n
~ **(open) court(yard), atrium** · Mittelhof m, Atrium n [*Der offene Mittelraum des römischen Hauses*]
~ **opening** · Mittelöffnung f
~ **part** → ~ section
~ **pillar** · Mittelpfeiler m [*In der Mitte eines Raumes stehender Freipfeiler*]
~ **place** · Zentralort m [*Raumordnung*]
central-plan building, centrally-planned ~ · Zentralanlage f
central point load · mittige Punktlast f
~ **pool (of water),** ~ **water pool** · zentrales Wasserbecken n [*Als Verzierung eines Platzes*]
~ **porosity, axial** ~; **coky centre (Brit.); coky center (US)** · Fadenlunker
~ **portal** · Mittelportal n
~ **portion** → ~ section
~ **position** · Mittellage f
~ **post** · (Dach)Stuhlsäule f [*Kehlbalkendach*]
~ **purlin(e), middle** ~; **centre** ~ **(Brit.); center** ~ **(US)** · Zwischenpfette f, Mittelpfette
~~ **connection, middle** ~ ~; **centre** ~ ~ **(Brit.); center** ~ ~ **(US)** · Zwischenpfettenanschluß m, Mittelpfettenanschluß
~ **(railway) station, main (**~**)** ~, **principal (**~**)** ~ **(Brit.);** ~ **(railroad)** ~ **(US)** · Hauptbahnhof m, Zentralbahnhof
~ **receiving aerial** · Gemeinschaftsantenne f
~~ **radio aerial, master radio antenna** · Gemeinschaftsrundfunkantenne f
~~ **T.V. aerial, master television antenna** · Gemeinschaftsfernsehantenne f
~ **roof** · Zentraldach n
~ **row of columns** · Mittel-Säulenreihe f
~ **second moment (of area),** ~ **moment of inertia** [*of a section*] · zentrales Trägheitsmoment n
~ **section,** ~ **portion,** ~ **part; centrepiece (Brit.); center-piece (US)** · Mittelteil m, n [*Bauwerk*]
~ **shell** · Mittelschale f
~ **shrine** · Zentralschrein m
~ **space** · Zentralraum m [*Raum mit gleich oder annähernd gleich langen Hauptachsen, z.B. der Innenraum eines Zentralbaues*]

central span — centre vault 178

~ span; center ~ (US); centre ~ (Brit.) · Mittelfeld *n*

(~) station · Zentrale *f*

~ ~ → ~ railway ~

~ steam heating · Zentraldampfheizung *f*

~ store · Zentrallager *n*

~ structure · Mittelbau(werk) *m,* (*n*)

~ support; center ~ (US); centre ~ (Brit.) · Mittelstütze *f*

~ ~ · Hausbaum *m* [*Stralsunder Bürgerhaus*]

~ tapered · beidseitig konisch

~ tower · Mittelturm *m,* Zentralturm

~ transept(al) portal · Querhausmittelportal *n*

~ tube · Kernstab *m* [*Spannbeton*]

~ vault; centre ~ (Brit.); center ~ (US) · Mittelgewölbe *n*

~ water pool, ~ pool (of water) · zentrales Wasserbecken *n* [*Als Verzierung eines Platzes*]

~ ~ supply · Sammelwasserversorgung *f,* zentrale Wasserversorgung [*Die öffentliche Wasserversorgung eines Ortes, Ortsteiles oder mehrerer Orte im Gegensatz zur Eigenwasserversorgung*]

~ window; centre ~ (Brit.); center ~ (US) · Mittelfenster *n*

centralization; centralisation (Brit.) · Ballung *f*

centralized building; centralised ~ (Brit.); centrally-planned ~, building with central space · Zentralbau *m,* zentrale Anlage *f*

~ ~ architecture; centralised ~ ~ (Brit.) · Zentralbau-Architektur *f*

~ church; centralised ~ (Brit.); centrally-planned ~, church with central space · sakraler Zentralbau *m,* Zentralkirche *f*

~ factory; centralised ~ (Brit.) · stationäre Fabrik *f,* ortsfeste ~

~ (ground(-)plan; centralised ~ (Brit.) · Zentral(bau)grundriß *m*

~ plan, ~ ground(-)~; centralised ~ (Brit.) · Zentral(bau)grundriß *m*

centrally-heated · zentralgeheizt, zentralbeheizt

centrally hung swing shutterdoor · mittig gelagertes Drehtor *n*

centrally-planned building, centralplan ~ · Zentralanlage *f*

~ church, centralized ~, church with central space; centralised church (Brit.) · sakraler Zentralbau *m,* Zentralkirche *f*

centre (Brit.); center (US) · Heim *n* [*Eine Gemeinschaftseinrichtung. Es gibt Wohnheime, Freizeit- und Bildungsheime und Heime mit fürsorgerischer Zwecksetzung, meist im Bereich der allgemeinen Wohlfahrt*]

~ (Brit.); center (US) · Stätte *f*

~ bulb (Brit.); center ~ (US) · Mittelsteg *m* Mittelwulst *m, f* [*Fugenband*]

~ column (Brit.); center ~ (US); central ~ · Mittelsäule *f*

~ corridor (Brit.); center ~ (US); central ~ · Mittelflur *m,* Mittelkorridor *m,* Mittelgang *m*

~ hose (Brit.); center ~ (US) · Mittelschlauch *m* [*Fugenband*]

~ light (Brit.); center ~ (US); window ~ ~ · (Fenster)Mittelteil *m, n*

~ line (Brit.); center ~ (US); central axis ~ · Mittelachse *f,* Symmetrieachse

~ ~ of inertia (Brit.); → center ~ ~

~ of apex, ~ ~ vertex, ~ ~ crown, ~ ~ top, ~ ~ key (Brit.); center ~ ~ (US) · Scheitelmitte *f*

~ ~ crown, ~ ~ top, ~ ~ key, ~ ~ apex, ~ ~ vertex (Brit.); center ~ ~ (US) · Scheitelmitte *f*

~ ~ cult (Brit.) → place of worship

~ ~ moment (Brit.); center ~ ~ (US); fulcrum ~ ~ · Momentendrehpunkt *m*

~ ~ rotation (Brit.) → moment pole

~ ~ the Ionic volute (Brit.); center ~ ~ ~ (US) · Schneckenauge *n*

~ ~ ~ town (Brit.) → business area

~ ~ top, ~ ~ key, ~ ~ crown, ~ ~ apex, ~ ~ vertex (Brit.); center ~ ~ (US) · Scheitelmitte *f*

~ ~ vertex, ~ ~ apex, ~ ~ crown, ~ ~ top, ~ ~ key (Brit.); center ~ ~ (US) · Scheitelmitte *f*

centre-piece (Brit.) → central section

centre purlin(e) (Brit.); center ~ (US); central ~, middle ~ · Zwischenpfette *f,* Mittelpfette

~ ~ connection (Brit.); center ~ ~ (US); central ~ ~, middle ~ ~ · Zwischenpfettenanschluß *m,* Mittelpfettenanschluß

~ spacing (Brit.); center ~ (US) · Mittenabstand *m*

~ span (Brit.); center ~ (US); central ~ · Mittelschiff *n* [*Halle*]

~ split pipe (Brit.) → half ~ ~

~ ~ ~ duct (Brit.) → half split pipe (gutter)

~ ~ ~ gutter (Brit.) → half ~ ~ (~)

~ support (Brit.); center ~ (US); central ~ · Mittelstiel *m* [*Zweifeldrahmen*]

~ ~ (Brit.); center ~ (US); central ~ · Mittelstütze *f*

centre-to-centre distance between columns (Brit.); center-to-center ~ ~ ~ (US); ~ ~ ~ supports · Stützenmittenabstand *m*

~ ~ of columns (Brit.); center-to-center ~ ~ ~ (US) · Säulenweite *f* [*Abstand von Säulenachse zu Säulenachse*]

centre vault (Brit.); center ~ (US); central ~ · Mittelgewölbe *n*

centre wall — ceramic component

~ **wall** (Brit.); center ~ (US) · Mittelwand f

~ **window** (Brit.) → central ~

centrifugability · Schleuderverhalten n [*Material beim Schleuderverfahren*]

centrifugal action, spinning · Schleudern n, Schleuderung f [*Herstellung von Rohren, Masten und Pfählen*]

~ **atomizer** · Zentrifugal-Zerstäuber m

~ **cast-iron pipe,** spun ~ ~, spun-iron ~, centrifugal C.I. ~ · Gußeisenschleuderrohr n, gußeisernes Schleuderrohr, Schleudergußrohr

~ **casting** · Schleuderguß m

~ ~ **of concrete, spinning** ~ ~, (concrete) spinning · (Beton)Schleuderung f

~ **C.I. pipe,** spun C.I. ~, spun-iron ~, spun cast-iron ~, centrifugal cast-iron ~ · Gußeisenschleuderrohr n, gußeisernes Schleuderrohr, Schleudergußrohr

~ **extractor** · Durchlaufzentrifuge f [*Zur exakten Trennung des Füllers vom Bindemittel eines Straßenbaugemisches*]

~ **fan** · Schleuderventilator m, Fliehkraftventilator, Zentrifugalventilator, Radialventilator

~ **grease interceptor** · Zentrifugal-Fettabscheider m, Zentrifugal-Fettfänger, Zentrifugal-Fettfang m [*DIN 4040 für Baugrundsätze, DIN 4041 für Einbau, Größe und Betrieb, DIN 4042 für Prüfverfahren*]

~ **interceptor,** ~ **intercepter** · Zentrifugalabscheider m, Zentrifugalfang m, Zentrifugalfänger

~ **method** · Zentrifugalverfahren n

centrifugally cast, spun · geschleudert [*Betonrohr; Betonmast*]

~ ~ **C.I. pressure pipe,** ~ ~ cast-iron ~ ~, spun C.I. ~ ~, spun cast-iron ~ ~ [*B.S. 1211*] · Gußeisen-Schleuderdruckrohr n

~ ~ **column** (Brit.); ~ ~ mast (US); spun ~ · Schleudermast m

~ ~ **concrete,** spun ~ · Schleuderbeton m

~ ~ ~ **column,** spun ~ ~ · Betonschleuderstütze f, Schleuderbetonstütze

~ ~ ~ **drain pipe,** spun ~ ~ ~ · Betonschleuderdränrohr n, Schleuderbetondränrohr

~ ~ ~ **mast,** spun ~ ~ · Betonschleudermast m, Schleuderbetonmast [*DIN 4234*]

~ ~ ~ **pipe,** spun ~ ~ · Betonschleuderrohr n, Schleuderbetonrohr

~ ~ ~ **pressure pipe,** spun ~ ~ ~ · Betonschleuderdruckrohr n, Schleuderbetondruckrohr

~ ~ **mast** (US); ~ ~ column (Brit.); spun ~ · Schleudermast m

~ ~ **pipe,** spun ~ · Schleuderrohr n

~ ~ **R.C. pressure pipe,** ~ ~ reinforced concrete ~ ~, spun ~ ~ ~ ~ ~ · Stahlbetonschleuderdruckrohr n, Schleuderstahlbetondruckrohr

~ ~ **reinforced concrete pressure pipe,** ~ ~ R.C. ~ ~, spun ~ ~ ~ ~ ~ · Stahlbetonschleuderdruckrohr n, Schleuderstahlbetondruckrohr

cephalophorous · Hauptträger m

ceramic · keramisch

(~) **acoustic(al) brick,** (~) sound-control ~, (~) (sound) absorbent ~, (~) (sound) absorbing ~, (~) (sound) absorptive ~ · (keramischer) Schallschluckstein m, (~) Akustikstein, Keramik-Schallschluckstein, Keramik-Akustikstein, Akustikziegel m, Schallschluckziegel, Schallabsorptionsziegel [*Hochkantvermauerter unverputzter Hochlochziegel*]

~ **adhesive** [*An inorganic adhesive which has been developed for bonding metals which have to be subjected to high temperatures (1,000° F and more). This adhesive is a glass-like material such as occurs in porcelain enamels and ceramic coatings. It is applied as a frit to clean metal surfaces and fired to produce the bond*] · metallkeramischer Kleber m, ~ Kleb(e)stoff m, metallkeramisches Kleb(e)mittel n

~ **aggregate** · keramischer Zuschlag(-stoff) m

~ **article,** ~ **product** · Keramikartikel m, Keramikerzeugnis n, Keramikgegenstand m, keramisches Erzeugnis, keramischer Artikel, keramischer Gegenstand

~ **bond** · keramische Bindung f

~ **(building) component** → ~ (~) unit

~ ~ **material** → ~ ~ construction(al) ~

~ (~) **member** → ~ (~) unit

~ (~) **unit,** ~ (~) component, ~ (~) member, clay (~) ~, ~ · keramisches (Bau)Element n, ~ Montageelement, ~ Fertig(bau)element, keramischer (Bau)Körper m, keramischer Montagekörper, keramischer Fertig(bau)körper, Keramik(bau)element, Keramikmontageelement, Keramikfertig(bau)element, Keramik(bau)körper, Keramikmontagekörper, Keramikfertig(bau)körper [*Fehlnamen: keramische (Bau)Einheit f, keramische Montageeinheit, Keramik(bau)einheit, Keramikmontageeinheit*]

~ **ceiling tile,** clay ~ ~ · Keramikdecken(belag)platte f, Keramikdeckenfliese, Tondecken(belag)platte, Tondeckenfliese, keramische Decken(belag)platte, keramische Deckenfliese

~ **cellular block for walls,** ~ ~ tile ~ · [*See remark under 'Block'*] · keramischer Zellenwandblock(stein) m, ~ Zellenwandstein

~ **component** → ~ (building) unit

ceramic composition — ceramic structural material 180

~ composition · keramische Masse *f*

~ constituent · keramischer Bestandteil *m*

~ construction(al) material, ~ building ~, ~ structural ~, clay ~ ~ · keramischer Baustoff *m*; keramisches Baumaterial *n* [*Schweiz*]

~ discharge pipe → ~ draining ~

~ (door) knob · Keramik(tür)knopf *m*, keramischer (Tür)Knopf

~ drain(age) pipe → ~ draining ~

~ draining pipe, ~ drain(age) ~, ~ discharge ~, ~ waste (~) · Keramikabflußrohr *n*, Keramikablaufrohr, Keramikdränrohr, Keramikentwässerungsrohr [*Fehlnamen: Keramikablauf m, Keramikabfluß*]

~ extrusion machine · keramische Strangpresse *f*

~ facing, ~ sur~, ~ lining · Keramikbekleidung *f*, Keramikverkleidung, Keramikauskleidung

~ floor (cover(ing)) → ~ (tile) floor(-ing) (finish)

~ ~ (finish) → ~ (tile) floor(ing) (~)

~ floor(ing) (finish) → ~ tile ~ (~)

~ flooring tile, clay ~ ~; (flooring) quarry (tile) [*A (flooring) quarry has a minimum thickness of ⅝″, while a ceramic flooring tile can be as little as 3/8″ in thickness. B.S. 1286*] · (Fuß-)Boden-Keramik(belag)platte *f*, (Fuß-)Boden-Keramikfliese *f*, Keramik-(Fuß-)Bodenfliese, Keramik-(Fuß)Boden(belag)platte, keramische (Fuß)Bodenfliese, keramische (Fuß)Boden(belag)-platte [*DIN 18155. Frühere Bezeichnungen: Steinzeugplatte, Bodenplatte, Mosaikplatte*]

~ ~ ~ for animal shelters → (flooring) quarry (~) ~ ~ ~

~ glazed coat(ing), ~ glaze(d finish), ~ glazing · keramische Beglasung *f*, ~ Glasur *f*

~ glaze(d finish), ~ glazing, ~ glazed coat(ing) · keramische Beglasung *f*, ~ Glasur *f*

~ glazing, ~ glaze(d finish), ~ glazed coat(ing) · keramische Beglasung *f*, ~ Glasur *f*

~ granular cover material, ~ ~ (sur)facing ~, ~ ~ wearing surface ~, ~ granules [*Roofing granules where colo(u)r is fused to rock under extreme heat to provide a long-lasting finish*] · keramisches Bestreu(ungs)material *n*, ~ Abstreu(ungs)material, ~ Bestreu(ungs)gut *n*, ~ Abstreu(ungs)gut [*für Dachpappen und (bituminöse) Spachteldachbeläge*]

~ ~ facing material → ~ ~ cover ~

~ ~ (sur)facing material → ~ ~ cover ~

~ ~ wearing surface material → ~ ~ cover ~

~ granules → ~ granular cover material

~ isolating material, ~ isolation ~ · keramischer Isolierstoff *m*, Keramikisolierstoff, KER

~ isolation material, ~ isolating ~ · keramischer Isolierstoff *m*, Keramikisolierstoff, KER

~ knob, ~ door ~ · Keramik(tür)knopf *m*, keramischer (Tür)Knopf

~ lavatory (basin), ~ wash ~, ~ washbowl, ~ wash-hand basin [*B.S. 1188*] · Keramik-(Hand)Waschbecken *n*, Keramik-Waschtisch *m*, keramisches (Hand)Waschbecken, keramischer Waschtisch

~ lay-in panel, clay ~ ~ · Keramikeinlegetafel *f*, keramische Einlegetafel

~ lining, ~ (sur)facing · Keramikbekleidung *f*, Keramikverkleidung, Keramikauskleidung

~ masonry (work) · keramisches Mauerwerk *n*, Keramikmauerwerk

~ material · Keramik-Werkstoff *m*, keramischer Werkstoff

~ member → ~ (building) unit

~ mosaic · keramisches Mosaik *n*, Keramikmosaik

~ ~ floor(ing) (finish), ~ ~ floor cover(ing) · Keramik-Mosaik(fuß)boden(belag) *m*, keramischer Mosaik-(fuß)boden(belag)

~ (~) tessera · keramisches (Mosaik-)Steinchen *n*

~ ~ tile, mosaic clay ~ · Keramikmosaik(belag)platte *f*, Keramikmosaikfliese, keramische Mosaik(belag)platte, keramische Mosaikfliese

~ panel · Keramik(bau)tafel *f*, keramische (Bau)Tafel

~ partition (wall) tile, ~ ~ (~) block · keramischer Trennwandblock(stein) *m*, ~ Trennwandstein [*DIN 18167*]

~ product, ~ article · Keramikartikel *m*, Keramikerzeugnis *n*, Keramikgegenstand *m*, keramisches Erzeugnis, keramischer Artikel, keramischer Gegenstand

~ raw material · Keramik-Rohstoff *m*, keramischer Rohstoff

~ seal(ing) · Keramik(ab)dichtung *f*, keramische (Ab)Dichtung

~ shower tray, clay ~ ~ · Keramik-Duschtasse *f*, Keramik-Duschwanne [*DIN 4486*]

(~) (sound) absorbent brick → (~) acoustic(al) ~

(~) (~) absorbing brick → (~) acoustic(al) ~

(~) (~) absorptive brick → (~) acoustic(al) ~

(~) sound-control brick → (~) acoustic(al) ~

~ spray shower tray, clay ~ ~ ~ · Keramik-Brausetasse *f*, Keramik-Brausewanne [*DIN 4486*]

~ structural material → ~ construction(al) ~

ceramic (sur)facing — cesspit

~ **(sur)facing**, ~ lining · Keramikbekleidung f, Keramikverkleidung, Keramikauskleidung, Keramikbelagen

~ **technology** · Keramiktechnologie f

~ **tessera** → ~ mosaic ~

~ **tile**, clay ~ · Keramik(belag)platte f, Keramikfliese, keramische Fliese, keramische (Belag)Platte, Ton(belag)platte, Tonfliese [*DIN 18155/56*]

~ ~ **adhesive** → ~ ~ bonding ~

~ ~ **(bonding) adhesive**, clay ~ (~) ~, ~ ~ ~ agent, ~ ~ ~ medium, ~ ~ cement(ing) agent) · Keramikfliesenkleber m, Keramikfliesenkleb(e)mittel n, Keramikfliesenkleb(e)stoff m, Tonfliesenkleber, Tonfliesenkleb(e)mittel, Tonfliesenkleb(e)stoff, Keramik(belag)plattenkleber, Keramik(belag)plattenkleb(e)stoff, Keramik(belag)plattenkleb(e)mittel, Ton(belag)plattenkleber, Ton(belag)plattenkleb(e)mittel, Ton(belag)plattenkleb(e)stoff

~ ~ ~ **agent** → ~ ~ ~ (~) adhesive

~ ~ ~ **medium** → ~ ~ ~ (~) adhesive

~ ~ **cement(ing) agent)** → ~ ~ ~ (bonding) adhesive

~ (~) **floor(ing) (finish)**, ~ (~) floor cover(ing) · Keramik-(Fuß)Boden(belag) m, keramischer (Fuß)Boden(belag)

~ ~ **panel**, prefabricated ceramic tiling · Keramik(belag)plattentafel f, Keramikfliesenplattentafel, Tafel aus keramischen Fliesen, Tafel aus keramischen (Belag)Platten, Tafel aus Keramikfliesen, Tafel aus Keramik(belag)platten [*Zu einer Verlegeeinheit zusammengefaßte Keramikfliesen*]

~ **unit** → ~ building ~

~ **vertical tilework** → ~ wall tiling

~ ~ **tiling** → ~ wall ~

~ **wall tile**, clay ~ ~ · Keramik-Wand-(belag)platte f, Keramik-Wandfliese f, Wand-Keramikfliese, Wand-Keramik(belag)platte, keramische Wandfliese, keramische Wand(belag)platte, Ton-Wandfliese, Ton-Wand(belag)platte, Wand(belag)-Tonplatte, Wand(belag)-Tonfliese

~ ~ **tilework** → ~ ~ ~ tiling

~ ~ **tiling**, ~ vertical ~, ~ ~ tilework · Keramikwandfliesenbelag m, Keramikwandplattenbelag

~ **wash basin**, ~ lavatory (~), ~ washhandbasin, washbowl [*B.S. 1188*] · Keramik-(Hand)Waschtisch n, Keramik-Waschtisch m, keramisches (Hand)Waschbecken, keramischer Waschtisch

~ **washbowl**, ~ lavatory (basin), ~ wash basin, ~ wash-handbasin [*B.S. 1188*] · Keramik-(Hand)Waschbecken n, Keramik-Waschtisch m, keramisches (Hand)Waschbecken, keramischer Waschtisch

~ **waste (pipe)** → ~ ~ draining ~

~ **window cill**, clay ~ ~ (Brit.); ~ ~ sill · Keramikfensterbank f, keramische Fensterbank

~ ~ **sill**, clay ~ ~; ~ ~ cill (Brit.) · Keramikfensterbank f, keramische Fensterbank

ceramics · Keramik f

~ **factory**, ~ plant, ~ works · Keramikfabrik f, Keramikwerk n, keramischer Betrieb m

~ **plant**, ~ works, ~ factory · Keramikfabrik f, Keramikwerk n, keramischer Betrieb m

~ **works**, ~ factory, ~ plant · Keramikfabrik f, Keramikwerk n, keramischer Betrieb m

cereal starch paste · Getreidestärkekleister m

ceremonial courtyard · Feierhof m

~ **forecourt**, atrium, paradise, parvis(e), galilee [*An open court surrounded by portico(e)s in front of a church (some medieval writers gave this name to the atrium of Old St. Peter's)*] · Atrium n, Galiläa f, Paradies n, Vorhof m (vor dem Narthex einer Basilika)

cermet · Cermet n [*Erzeugnis aus keramischen und metallischen Bestandteilen*]

~ **coat(ing)**, ~ finish · Cermetüberzug m, Cermetbeschichtung f [*als Schicht*]

~ **coating**, ~ (sur)facing · Cermetbeschichten n, Cermetbeschichtung f, Cermetüberziehen, Cermetüberzug m [*als Tätigkeit*]

~ **facing**, ~ sur~, ~ coating · Cermetbeschichten n, Cermetbeschichtung f, Cermetüberziehen, Cermetüberzug m [*als Tätigkeit*]

~ **finish**, ~ coat(ing) · Cermetüberzug m, Cermetbeschichtung f [*als Schicht*]

~ **(sur)facing**, ~ coating · Cermetbeschichten n, Cermetbeschichtung f, Cermetüberziehen, Cermetüberzug m [*als Tätigkeit*]

certificate of acceptance, acceptance certificate · Abnahmebescheid m, Abnahmebescheinigung f, Abnahmeschein m, Abnahmeniederschrift f, Abnahmeprotokoll n, Abnahmezeugnis n

certification, registered ~, registered (trade-)mark, (trade-)mark · Güteschutzzeichen n, Güteschutzmarke f, eingetragenes Warenzeichen

~ **(trade-)mark scheme** → registered ~ ~ ~

cerulean blue (pigment) · Coelinblau n

cesspit, (leaching) cesspool, pervious cesspool · Senkgrube f

CF — champlevé enamel

CF, colling fan · Kühlventilator *m*
chain barrier · Kettenabsperrung *f*
~ **hanger** · Kettenaufhänger *m*
~ **of hinges** · Gelenkkette *f*
~ **riveting** · Parallelnietung *f*, Kettennietung
~ **stopped alkyd** · Kettenabbruch-Alkyd *n*
~ **traverse** · geknickter Polygonzug *m*, ~ Standlinienzug, geknicktes Polygon *n*
chair [*Support, usually of metal, for reinforcement*] · Bewehrungshalter *m*
~ **of architecture** · Lehrstuhl *m* für Architektur
~ **rail,** surbase, dado capping, dado rail; dado molding (US); dado moulding (Brit.) [*A mo(u)lding round a room to prevent chairs, when pushed back against the walls, from damaging their surface*] · obere Wandsockelleiste *f*, Schutzleiste
~ **storage** · Stuhllagerung *f*
~ **store** · Stuhllager(raum) *n*, (*m*)
chaitya hall → rock(-cut) ~ ~
chalcedony · Chalzedon *m*, Chalcedon [*Faserige, kryptokristalline Modifikation des Quarzes*]
chalcography [*The art of engraving copper*] · Kupferstechkunst *f*
chalet, Swiss cottage [*A house built in the Swiss style*] · Schweizerhaus *n*
to chalk · (ab)kreiden, auskreiden, abfärben [*Farbanstrich*]
chalk; cauk, cawk [*Scotland*] · Kreide *f* [*DIN 1280*]
~ **containing clay** · Tonkreide *f*
~ **drawing** · Kreidezeichnung *f*
~ **lime** → high-calcium ~
~ **line** · Kreideschnur *f*
~ ~ **marking** · Abschnüren *n*, Abkreiden
~ **marl** · Kreidemergel *m*
chalking [*The breakup of pigmented films on exposure. The binder is so much decomposed by the weather that the pigment can be removed by lightly rubbing it. The term is used for all colours, not only for near-white colours, although it originates from those. Chalking looks like a fading, but the colour can be restored by a coat of varnish*] · (Ab)Kreiden *n*, Abfärben, Auskreiden [*Farbanstrich*]
~ **tester** · Abkreideprüfer *m*, Auskreideprüfer, Abfärbprüfer
chalkproof, chalk-resistant · abfärbbeständig, (ab)kreidungsbeständig, auskreidungsbeständig
chalk-resistance · (Ab)Kreidungsbeständigkeit *f*, Abfärbbeständigkeit, Auskreidungsbeständigkeit
chalk-resistant, chalkproof · abfärbbeständig, (ab)kreidungsbeständig, auskreidungsbeständig

chalky, chalked · ausgekreidet, abgekreidet
chamber, room · Zimmer *n*, Raum *m*
~ · Nebenraum *m* [*Sakralbau*]
~ **door,** room ~ · Zimmertür *f*, Raumtür
chamber-door lock, room-door ~ · Zimmertürschloß *n*, Raumtürschloß
chamber interceptor [*A trap to a manhole to prevent the gases from the sewer entering the drains*] · Schachtverschluß *m*
~ **music room** · Kammermusikraum *m*
~ **tomb,** hypogeum ~, burial chamber, sepulchral chamber, tomb chamber · Grabkammer *f*, Kammergrab *n*
to chamfer · abfasen mit 45°, abkanten ~ ~, abschrägen ~ ~
chamfer [*A right-angle corner cut off symmetrically, that is, at 45°. When cut off unsymmetrically, the surface is called a bevel*] · Fase *f* mit 45°, Schmiege *f* ~ ~
~ **shape** → chamfering ~
chamfered, chfd. · abgefast mit 45°
~ **edge** · Kantenschlag *m* mit 45°
~ **square bar(s)** · mit 45° abgefaster Quadratstahl *m*, ~ ~ abgekänteter ~
chamfering · Abfasen *n* mit 45°, Abkanten ~ ~, Abschrägen ~ ~
chamfer(ing) shape · Abfasungsprofil *n* [*Die beim Abfasen am meisten verwendeten Profile sind Schrägen, Wulste, Viertelstäbe und Hohlkehlen*]
chamotte · Schamotte *f* [*Die Schamotte wird durch Brennen von reinen flußmittelarmen Tonen, Schiefertonen oder Kaolinen und durch anschließendes Mahlen auf bestimmte Korngrößen gewonnen. Bei feinerer Mahlung erhält man Schamottemehl*]
~ **burning** · Schamottebrennen *n*
~ **concrete** · Schamottebeton *m*
~ **facing** → ~ surfacing
~ **flour** · Schamottemehl *n*
~ **lining,** ~ (sur)facing · Schamotteauskleidung *f*, Schamotteverkleidung, Schamottebekleidung, Schamottefutter *n*
~ **mortar** · Schamottemörtel *m* [*Er wird aus feuerfestem Ton, Schamottemehl und Wasser angemacht*]
~ **pipe** · Schamotterohr *n*
~ **product** · Schamotteerzeugnis *n*, Schamottekörper *m*
~ **rotary kiln** · Schamottedrehofen *m*, Schamotterotierofen
~ **(sur)facing** · ~ lining · Schamotteauskleidung *f*, Schamotteverkleidung, Schamottebekleidung, Schamottefutter *n*
~ **vent pipe** · Schamotte-Entlüftungsrohr *n*
~ **wall tile** · Schamottewand(belag)platte *f*, Schamottewandfliese *f*
~ **ware** · Schamotteware *f*
champlevé enamel, ~ work, entaille d'épargne, hollowed out enamel · Grubenschmelz *m*, Kupferschmelz [*Emailmalerei*]

c(h)ancel — characteristic feature

c(h)ancel, choir rail, quire rail · Chorschranke *f*

~ **arch** · Triumphbogen *m* [*In der christlichen Basilika der Bogen, der Chor und Querhaus gegen das Mittelschiff des Langhauses abgrenzt*]

chandelier · Kronleuchter *m*

change, chemical ~ · (chemische) Umsetzung *f*

~ **in length** · Längenänderung *f*

~ ~ **shear(ing) force** · Schubkraftwechsel *m*

~ **of air**, air change · Luftwechsel *m*

~ ~ **condition** · Zustandsänderung *f*

~ ~ **direction** · Richtungswechsel *m*

~ ~ **equilibrium**, equilibrium change · Gleichgewichtswechsel *m*

~ ~ **levels** · Höhenwechsel *m*

~ ~ **stability** · Stabilitätswechsel *m*, Standfestigkeitswechsel, Standsicherheitswechsel

~ ~ **style** · Stilwandel(ung) *m*, (*f*)

change-over spray head · Umstellbrausekopf *m*

'changeover town' [*Term coined by Le Corbusier to describe a metropolis with diverse functions*] · ,,Austausch-Stadt" *f*

change-point · Umwandlungspunkt *m* [*Anlassen von Eisen oder Stahl*]

changing cab(in) → (un)dressing ~

~ **cubicle** → (un)dressing cab(in)

~ **load**, alternating ~ · Wechsellast *f*

~ **loading**, alternate ~ · Wechselbelastung *f*

~ **pressure**, alternating ~ · Wechseldruck *m*

~ **room**, (un)dressing ~ · Aus- und Ankleide(raum) *f*, (*m*), Umkleide(raum)

~ **stress**, alternating ~ · Wechselspannung *f*

channel · U-Profil *n*

~ → ~ stone

~, canal(is) · Kanalis *m* [*Der seit klassischer Zeit konkave Teil zwischen den Voluten am ionischen Kapitäl*]

~ → half split pipe

~ → (concrete) channel (unit)

~ **black**, ~ carbon ~ · Farbruß *m*

~ **block**, ~ tile [*A hollow unit with portions depressed less than 1¼ in. (2.6 cm) to form a continuous channel for reinforcing steel and grout*] · Rillenblock(stein) *m*, Rillenstein

~ ~, ~ tile [*See remark under 'Block'*] · Trogblock(stein) *m*, Trogstein, U-Block(stein), U-Stein

~ **(carbon) black** · Farbruß *m*

~ **frame shutter door** · U-Rahmentor *n*

~ **(iron)**, iron channel · U-Eisen *n*

~ ~ **frame**, CIF · U-Eisen-Rahmen *m*

~ ~ **purlin(e)**, steel channel ~ · U-Eisen-Pfette *f*

~ **profile**, ~ (section) · U-Profil *n*

~ **purlin(e)** · U-Pfette *f*

~ **slab** · ,,U"-Element *n*

~ **reinforced** · verstärkt durch U-Profil

~ ~ · mit U-Eisen verstärkt

~ **ring** · U-Profil-Ring *m*

~ **(section)**, ~ profile · U-Profil *n*

~ **(stone)**, split duct, split pipe · (Rohr-)Schale *f*, (auf)gespaltenes Rohr *n*, Rinne *f*

~ **string** (Brit.); ~ stringer (US) · U-Profil-Wange *f*

~ **tile**, ~ block [*A hollow unit with portions depressed less than 1¹/₄ in. (2.6 cm) to form a continuous channel for reinforcing steel and grout*] · Rillenblock(stein) *m*, Rillenstein

~ ~, ~ block [*See remark under 'Block'*] · Trogblock(stein) *m*, Trogstein, U-Block(stein), U-Stein

~ **(unit)** → concrete ~ (~)

channeled plate (US); channelled ~ (Brit.); checker(ed) · Riffelblech *n*, geriffeltes Blech

chanelled (Brit.); chaneled (US); checkered · geriffelt

~ **block** (Brit.) → triglyph

~ **foil** (Brit.); chaneled ~ (US); checker(ed) ~ · geriffelte Folie *f*, Riffelfolie

~ **plate** (Brit.); channeled ~ (US); checker(ed) ~ · Riffelblech *n*, geriffeltes Blech

chantlate, eave(s) lath · Saumlade *f*, Saumlatte *f*

chantry-altar · Meßaltar *m*

chantry (chapel) [*A chapel within or attached to a church, endowed for the saying of masses for the soul of the testator or others*] · Votivkapelle *f*

chapel · Kapelle *f*

~ **arcade** · Kapellenarkade *f*

chapel-builder · Kapellenbauer *m*

chapel-in-the-round, round chapel, circular chapel · Rundkapelle *f*

Chapel of Charlemagne at Aachen,
~ ~ ~ ~ Aix-la-Chapelle · Palastkapelle *f* in Aachen

~ ~ **the Resurrection** · Auferstehungskapelle *f*

chapel vault · Kapellengewölbe *n*

~ **window** · Kapellenfenster *n*

chapterhall, chapter-room · Kapitelsaal *m*

chapterhouse · Domkapitel *n*, Kapitelhaus *n*, Stift(shaus) *n*

chapter-room, chapterhall · Kapitelsaal *m*

chaptrel · Dienstkapitell *n*, Dienstkapitäl

characteristic diagram · Kenndiagramm *n*

~ **feature** · Merkmal *n*

characteristic impedance — chemical anhydrite screed ... 184

~ impedance · Kennimpedanz f, Schall~ [*Impedanz in einer eben fortschreitenden Welle. Anmerkung: Die Kennimpedanz dient in erster Linie zur Kennzeichnung der Übertragungseigenschaften eines Schallmediums. Ist das Medium verlustfrei, so wird die Kennimpedanz reell, sie wird dann auch als Wellenwiderstand bezeichnet. Bei der Feldimpedanz ist diese Impedanz eine spezifische Größe im Sinne von DIN 5490*]

~ quality, property · Güteeigenschaft f

charcoal, burned wood, burnt wood · Holzkohle f

charge → (glass) batch

~ hand · Schachtmeister m

~ ~ · Polier m [*Ursprünglich der ,,Sprecher" in den mittelalterlichen Bauhütten. Heute der Vorarbeiter bei den Zimmerleuten und Maurern*]

charged paint particle, ~ particle of paint [*electrostatic coating*] · geladenes Farbteilchen n

~ particle of paint, ~ paint particle [*electrostatic paint*] · geladenes Farbteilchen n

charging period (at night) · Aufladezeit f [*Nachtstrom-Speicherofen*]

Charles Bridge at Prague, Gothic ~ ~ ~ ~ · Karlsbrücke f zu Prag

~ University at Prague · Karlsuniversität f zu Prag

charnel-house → carnary

charred bones, carbonized ~ · Knochenkohle f

chart → graphic representation

charterhouse · Kartäuserhaus n, Kartause f

Charterhouse at Granada, sacristy of la Cartuja · Kartause f von Granada

chase, chasing [*A channel or groove formed or cut in a material*] · Nut f, Rille f

chastity · Schlichtheit f

chatri · Tschatri m

chauffeur's room, driver's ~ · Kraftfahrerraum m

Chauvel safety glass · Chauvel-Sicherheitsglas n, Chauveldrahtglas [*A s Guß-, Roh- oder Kristallspiegelglas hergestelltes Drahtglas, dessen Drahteinlage nicht aus einem Netz oder Gewebe, sondern aus einzelnen parallel gespannten Drähten von 0,5 mm ⌀ in rund 5 cm Abstand besteht*]

to check · nachprüfen, kontrollieren

~ ~ · nachweisen

check [*Scotland*] → (window) rebate

~, surface crack · Kaltsprung m, Riß m, Peture f [*Flachglasfehler*]

~ · Kontrolle f

~ ·Längsriß m [*Holz*]

~ · Wange f

~ action · Hemmwirkung f [*Tür*]

~ calculation · Nachweis m, Nachrechnung f, Nachrechnen n, Rechenkontrolle f

~ design (for comparison), ~ version (~ ~) · Vergleichskonstruktion f

~ measurement · Kontrollmessung f

~ test · Prüf(ungs)probe f, Prüf(ungs)versuch m

~ valve, flap ~ · Rückstauklappe f

~ version (for comparison), ~ design (~ ~) · Vergleichskonstruktion f

checker board (masonry) bond · Schachbrett(mauerwerk)verband m

checkered, chequered · geschacht, schachbrettartig, kariert

checker(ed) foil; channelled ~ (Brit.); channeled ~ (US) · Riffelfolie f, geriffelte Folie

~ plate; channeled ~ (US); channelled ~ (Brit.) · Riffelblech n, geriffeltes Blech

checker-work, chequer-work [*A method of decorating walls or pavements with alternating squares of contrasting materials (e.g. stone, brick, flint) to produce a chessboard effect*] · Schachbrettmuster n

~, chequer work · Gitterwerk n [*Auf Papier für Skizzen*]

checking [*Defect in a coat of paint*] · Netzadern fpl

check(ing), confirmatory ~ · Nachweis m

checking of structural strength for given loads · statischer Nachweis m

~ (up) of the safety against cracking · Nachweisen n der Rißsicherung

~ ~ ~ ~ stresses, stress check (calculation) · Spannungsnachweis m

checkroom (US); cloakroom, left-luggage office · Handgepäckaufbewahrung f

checkweigher · Nachwaage f

chemical · Chemikal n

~ adhesive, ~ glue · chemischer Leim m

(~) ~ compound → (~) bonding system

(~) ~ system → (~) bonding ~

~ analysis · chemische Analyse f

~ anhydrite, by-product ~, synthetic ~ · künstlicher Anhydrit m

~ ~ screed (material), by-product ~ ~ (~), synthetic ~ ~ (~) · Estrich m aus künstlichem Anhydrit [*als Baustoff*]

~ ~ ~ (topping), by-product ~ ~ (~), synthetic ~ ~ (~) · Estrich m aus künstlichem Anhydrit [*als verlegter Baustoff*]

chemical atmosphere — cherry-red

~ **atmosphere** · chemische Atmosphäre *f*
~ **attack** · Chemikalienangriff *m*, chemischer Angriff
~ **bond** [*Bond between materials that is the result of cohesion and adhesion developed by chemical reaction*] · chemische Haftung *f*
(~) **bonding system**, (~) adhesive ~, (~) ~ compound · (chemische) Verbindung *f* mit Kleb(e)eigenschaft
(~) **breakdown** · Zersetzung *f*
~ **building** [*water filtration plant*] · Chemikaliengebäude *n*
~ ~ **material**, ~ structural ~, ~ construction(al) ~ · Chemiewerkstoff *m* für das Bauwesen, chemischer Baustoff; chemisches Baumaterial *n* [*Schweiz*]
~ **capacity** → ~ property
(~) **change** · (chemische) Umsetzung *f*
~ **composition** · chemische Zusammensetzung *f*
(~) **compound**, (~) system · (chemische) Verbindung *f*
~ **constitution** · Aufbau *m* [*Teer; Bitumen; Pech*]
~ **construction** · Chemiebau *m*
~ **construction(al) material**, ~ building ~, ~ structural ~ · Chemiewerkstoff *m* für das Bauwesen, chemischer Baustoff; chemisches Baumaterial *n* [*Schweiz*]
~ **dampcourse** → ~ dampproof(ing) course
~ **dampproofing** · chemische (Ab-)Dichtung *f*, ~ Sperrung [*gegen Feuchtigkeit*]
~ **dampproof(ing) course**, ~ dampcourse, ~ d.p.c., ~ dpc · chemische Feuchtesperrschicht *f*
~ **d.p.c.** → ~ dampproof(ing) course
~ **durability** [*The resistance of a material to chemical attack*] · chemische Beständigkeit *f*, ~ Widerstandsfähigkeit
~ **energy** · chemische Energie *f*
~ **environment(s)** · chemische Umweltverhältnisse *npl*
~ **fastness**, ~ resistance · Chemikalienbeständigkeit *f*, Chemikalienechtheit, Chemikalienfestigkeit, Chemikalienwiderstand *m*
~ **foam** · Gasschaum *m*
~ **glue**, ~ adhesive · chemischer Leim *m*
~ **grout**, ~ slurry · Chemikalienschlämme *f*
~ **hardening** · chemische (Er)Härtung *f*
~ **inertness** · chemische Trägheit *f*
~ **investigation** · chemische Untersuchung *f*
~ **lab(oratory)** · chemisches Labor(atorium) *n*
~ **oxidation process** · chemisches Oxidationsverfahren *n*
~ **plant** · chemische Fabrik *f*, chemisches Werk *n*, Chemiewerk

~ **polishing** · chemisches Polieren *n*
~ **power** → ~ property
~ **preservative for structures and buildings** · chemischer Bautenschutzstoff *m*, chemisches Bautenschutzmittel *n*
~ **property**, ~ capacity, ~ quality, ~ power · chemische Eigenschaft *f*, chemisches Vermögen *n*, chemische Fähigkeit *f*
~ **quality** → ~ property
~ **reaction** · chemische Reaktion *f*
~ **resistance**, ~ fastness · Chemikalienbeständigkeit *f*, Chemikalienechtheit, Chemikalienfestigkeit, Chemikalienwiderstand *m*
chemical(-)resistant, chemical resisting · chemikalienbeständig, chemikalienfest
chemical slurry, ~ grout · Chemikalienschlämme *f*
~ **stoneware** · chemisches Steinzeug *n*
~ **stress relaxation** · chemische Spannungsrelaxation *f*
~ **structural material**, ~ building ~, ~ construction(al) ~ · Chemiewerkstoff *m* für das Bauwesen, chemischer Baustoff; chemisches Baumaterial *n* [*Schweiz*]
~ **surface treatment** · chemische Oberflächenbehandlung *f*
(~) **system**, (~) compound · (chemische) Verbindung *f*
chemically acting · chemisch wirkend
~ **bonded brick** · chemisch gebundener Stein *m* [*Stein, dessen Festigkeit durch chemische Bindemittel und nicht durch Brennen erreicht wird*]
~ **combined water**, fixed ~ · chemisch gebundenes Wasser *n*
~ **inert** · chemisch träge
chemically-prepared inorganic pigment · Metallpigment *n* [*nicht verwechseln mit Metalleffektpigment*]
~ **iron oxid(e) (pigment)** (US); ~ ~ oxide (~) (Brit.) · künstliches (Eisen-)Oxidpigment *n*
chemically pure chrome yellow · reines Chromgelb *n*
~ ~ **zinc** · chemisch reines Zink *n*
chemistry of cement, cement chemistry · Zementchemie *f*
chequered, checkered · geschacht, schachbrettartig, kariert
chequer-work, checker-work [*A method of decorating walls or pavements with alternating squares of contrasting materials (e.g. stone, brick, flint) to produce a chessboard effect*] · Schachbrettmuster *n*
~, checker-work · Gitterwerk *n* [*Auf Papier für Skizzen*]
cherry-red · kirschrot
~ · hellrotwarm

cherry-red heat — chimney fan 186

~ **heat** · hellrotwarmer Zustand *m*
chessylite, azurite, blue carbonate of copper · Azurit *m*
chestnut (wood) shingle · Kastanienschindel *f*
cheval glass [*A mirror usually standing on the floor. It is swung on a frame and large enough to reflect the whole figure*] · Drehspiegel *m*
chevet [*The apsidal east end of a medieval church, including the aisle or ambulatory round the apse, girdled with chapels*] · Chorhaupt *n*,
chevron (moulding) (Brit.); ~ (molding) (US); zigzag ~, dancette, zigzag ornament · Zickzackband *n*, Kallenschnitt *m*, Zickzackverzierung *f*
chfd., chamfered · abgefast mit 45°
Chicago School · Schule *f* von Chicago [*Diese Bezeichnung wird im allgemeinen auf eine Gruppe von Geschäfts- und Bürobauten angewandt, die im letzten Viertel des 19. Jahrhunderts im amerikanischen mittleren Westen und vor allem in Chicago entstanden*]
~ **window** [*Rectangular in shape, runs horizontally and features several lights with a large central pane*] · Chicagoer Fenster *n*
children's bath, infant's ~ · Kinderbad *n*
~ **(bath)tub**, infant's ~, ~ bath · Kinder(bade)wanne *f*
~ **bedroom** · Kinderschlafzimmer *n*
~ **hostel** · Kinderwohnheim *n*
~ **library** · Kinderbücherei *f*, Kinderbibliothek *f*
~ **maze** · Kinderlabyrinth *n*
(~) play area · Spielfläche *f*
~ **playground**, games area · (Kinder-) Spielplatz *m*
(~) play(ground) equipment item · Spielplatzgerät *n*, Kinder~
~ **pool**, paddling ~, wading ~ · Planschbecken *n*, Kinderbecken
to chill · härten [*Grauguß*]
chill block, ~ building, chilling ~ · Kühlhaus *n*
~ **cast(ing)** · Hartguß *m* [*Erzeugnis*]
chilled C.I., ~ (cast) iron · Hartguß *m*, weißes Gußeisen *n* [*Das weiße Bruchgefüge ist nicht nur in der Außenschicht wie beim Schalenguß vorhanden, sondern über den Querschnitt des Gußstückes verteilt*]
~ **(cast) iron**, ~ C.I. · Hartguß *m*, weißes Gußeisen *n* [*Das weiße Bruchgefüge ist nicht nur in der Außenschicht, sondern über den Querschnitt des Gußstückes verteilt*]
(~) ~ shot, ~ C.I. ~ · Hartgußeisenschrot *m, n*
(~) ~ (~) concrete · Hartgußeisenschrotbeton *m*
~ **C.I. shot** → ~ (cast) iron ~
~ **iron** → ~ cast ~

~ ~ **shot** → ~ **cast** ~ ~
chilling · Härten *n* [*Abkühlen von Grauguß von Temperaturen oberhalb Umwandlungstemperaturen mit solcher Geschwindigkeit, daß eine beträchtliche Steigerung der Härte eintritt. Abschrecken mit Wasser, Öl oder Luft*]
chill(ing) block, ~ building · Kühlhaus *n*
chime of bells · Glockenspiel *n*
~ **unit** · Läutewerk *n*
chimney [*A construction containing one or more flues*] · Kamin *m*, Schornstein *m*
~, cooling tower ~ · (Kühlturm)Steigschacht *m*, Zuflußsteigschacht
~ **apron**, apron (flashing) [*A one-piece flashing, such as is used at the lower side of a chimney penetrating a sloping roof*] · Schürze *f*, Front~, vordere ~
~ **base** · Schornsteinfuß *m*
~ **block** (US); round concrete flue [*Precast circular concrete pipe used as flue lining*] · Kamin(form)stein *m*, Formstück *n* für Hausschornstein(e), Schornsteinformstück, Kaminformstück, Schornsteinformstein, rundes Beton-Kaminformstück
~ **bond** → (conventional) running (masonry) ~
(~) breast [*A part of a chimney which projects from the surface of an adjoining wall*] · Kaminvorsprung *m*
~ **brick** · Schornstein(mauer)ziegel *m*
~ **brickwork** · Schornstein-Ziegelmauerwerk *n*
~ **builder** · Schornsteinbauer *m*
~ **cap**, ~ terminal, ~ hood, ~ pot, bonnet [*It increases the height of a chimney to prevent down-draught*] · Schornsteinhaube *f*, Schornsteinaufsatz *m*
(~) clay pot, clay chimney ~ · gebranntes Schornsteinformstück *n*
~ **component**, ~ unit, ~ member · Schornsteinbauteil *m, n*, Schornsteinelement *n*
~ **concrete** · Schornsteinbeton *m*
~ **connector** → smoke pipe
~ **construction** · Schornsteinbau *m*
~ ~ **material** · Schornsteinbaumaterial *n* [*Schweiz*]; Schornsteinbaustoff *m*
~ ~ **scaffold(ing)** · Schornsteinbaugerüst *n*
~ **-corner**; ingle-nook [*Scotland*] · Kamin(sitz)ecke *f*
chimney cross-section · Schornsteinquerschnitt *m*
~ **design** · Schornsteinbemessung *f*
~ **draft** (US); ~ draught (Brit.) · Schornsteinzug *m*, Ziehen *m* der Schornsteine
~ **draught** (Brit.); ~ draft (US) · Schornsteinzug *m*, Ziehen *m* der Schornsteine
~ ~ **regulator** (Brit.); ~ draft ~ (US) · Schornsteinzugregler *m*
~ **effect** · Steigwirkung *f* [*Gas*]
~ **fan** · Schornsteinventilator *m*

chimney fire — chipping

~ **fire** · Schornsteinbrand *m*

~ **flue** [*The space or passage in a chimney through which smoke, gas, or fumes ascend*] · Schornsteinzug *m*

~ **for outgoing air,** ~ ~ **exit** ~ · Fortluftschornstein *m*

~ **foundation** · Schornsteingründung *f*

~ **gas** · Schornsteingas *n*

~ **group,** group of chimneys · Schornsteingruppe *f*

~ **gutter** · Schornsteinrinne *f*

~ **junction** · Schornsteinanschluß *m*

~ **ladder,** stack ~ · Schornsteinleiter *f*

~ **liner,** ~ lining · Schornsteinfutter *n*

~ **(masonry) bond** → (conventional) running (~) ~

~ ~ **(work)** · Schornsteinmauerwerk *n*

~ **member,** ~ unit, ~ component · Schornsteinbauteil *m, n,* Schornsteinelement *n*

~ **outlet** · Kaminmündung *f,* Schornsteinmündung, Kaminöffnung, Schornsteinöffnung

~ **piece,** (~) breast [*A part of a chimney which projects from the surface of an adjoining wall*] · Kaminvorsprung *m*

~ **pipe** · Kaminrohr *n,* Schornsteinrohr

~ **pot,** ~ terminal, ~ hood, ~ cap, bonnet [*It increases the height of a chimney to prevent down-draught*] · Schornsteinhaube *f,* Schornsteinaufsatz *m*

~ **shaft,** free-standing ~ [*It is a free-standing structure enclosing a flue which, by virtue of the size of heating apparatus it serves, is generally larger than a normal domestic flue*] · einzügiger freistehender Schornstein *m,* freistehender einzügiger ~

~ ~, structural shell, structural chimney, chimney shell [*It is protected by the lining*] · Schornsteinschaft *m*

~ ~, roof chimney [*That part of a chimney that is external to a building*] · Dachschornstein *m*

~ **shell,** structural chimney, structural shell, chimney shaft [*It is protected by the lining*] · Schornsteinschaft *m*

~ ~ ~ · Schornsteinmantel *m*

(~) **stack,** ~ stalk, ~ fun, factory chimney, factory stack, industrial chimney, industrial stack, big chimney · Fabrikschornstein *m,* (Fabrik)Kamin *m,* (Fabrik)Esse *f,* (Fabrik)Schlot *m,* Industrieschornstein *m,* freistehender Schornstein

~ **taper** · Schornsteinanzug *m,* Schornsteindossierung *f*

~ **terminal,** ~ pot [*It increases the height of a chimney to prevent down-draught*] · Schornsteinaufsatz *m*

~ ~, ~ cap [*An ornamental finish to the top of a chimney*] · Schornsteinzieraufsatz *m*

~ **tray** · Schornsteineinfassung *f*

~ **unit,** ~ member, ~ component · Schornsteinbauteil *m, n,* Schornsteinelement *n*

~ **wall** · Schornsteinwange *f*

china clay → kaolin

~ **painting** · Porzellanmalerei *f*

(~) **sanitary ware** [*Wash tubs, sinks, tanks, and ordinary bathroom equipment formed of clay, baked and glazed*] · Sanitärkeramik *f,* sanitäre Keramik

(China) wood oil → raw (~) ~ ~

(~) ~ ~ **stand oil,** tung ~ ~ ~ · Holzöl-Standöl *n,* Tungöl-Standöl

(~) ~ ~ **varnish,** tung ~ ~ · Tungöllack *m*

(~) ~ **stand oil,** tung ~ ~ · Holzstandöl *n,* Tungstandöl

Chinese architecture · chinesische Architektur *f,* ~ Baukunst *f*

~ **blue** · Chinesischblau *n*

~ **lacquer** [*A natural product made from the sap of a genus of the sumac*] · chinesischer Lack *m*

~ **red** · Chinesischrot *n*

~ **white,** zinc ~ . Zinkweiß *n,* Schneeweiß, ZnO *n* [*Pigment. Ein aus metallischem Zink hergestelltes reinweißes oder ganz schwach gelb- oder blaustichiges technisch reines Zinkoxid (ZnO). Mit absteigendem Feinheitsgrad unterscheidet man die Marken Weißsiegel, Grünsiegel und Rotsiegel; ZnO-Gehalt mindestens 99%*]

~ ~ **stand oil enamel** → stand oil zinc white ~

chinoiserie · Chinoiserie *f* [*Bezeichnung für die Übernahme bzw. Nachahmung chines. oder überhaupt ostasiatischer Formen durch die europäische Baukunst und Innenarchitektur des 17. und 18. Jh. Chinesische Zimmer gibt es in den meisten Residenzen des Barocks und des Rokokos, auch in den Gärten und Parks wurden Pavillons und Pagoden in chinesischem Stil errichtet (Potsdam, Sanssouci; Nymphenburg; Kassel)*]

chintz · Chintz *m* [*Bedrucktes Baumwollgewebe mit sehr dünnem Wachsüberzug für Wandbespannungen*]

to chip, to spall · abplatzen, zerspringen [*Keramikindustrie*]

chipped wood · Holzspäne *mpl,* zerspantes Holz *n*

(~) ~ **concrete** · Holzspanbeton *m,* Holzspänebeton

~ ~ **material,** wood particle ~ · Holzspanwerkstoff *m,* HSW

chipping, chip(ping)s, stone ~ [*deprecated: screening(s)*] · Splitt *m*

~, spalling · Abplatzen *n,* Zerspringen [*Keramikindustrie*]

~ [*Removing surface defects by manual or pneumatic chisel*] · Abklopfen *n* [*Stahl; Eisen*]

~ [*The detachment of flakes of a paint coat due to penetration of water behind the paint coat or greasiness of the surface or, in distempers, by too much size*] · Abplatzen, Abspringen, Absplittern

chip(ping)s — choir loft

chip(ping)s, chipping stone ~ [*deprecated: screening(s)*] · Splitt *m*

~ **aggregate**, ~ concrete ~ · Betonsplitt *m*

~ **compound** [*For bonding stone chip(ping)s to built-up flat roofs*] · Dachsplitt-Kleb(e)masse *f*

~ **concrete**, concrete made from natural and broken aggregates · Splittbeton *m*

~ **(~) aggregate** · Betonsplitt *m*

~ **for roughening treatment** · Aufrauhsplitt *m*

~ **precoated with tar**, tarcoated chip(ping)s, tar(red) chip(pings) · Teersplitt *m*, teerumhüllter Splitt

~ **skeleton framework**, ~ ~ structure · Splittgerüst *n*

~ ~ **structure**, ~ ~ framework · Splittgerüst *n*

~ **surfacing** · Splittabstreuung *f*, Splittbestreuung, Besplittung

chloride (Brit.); chlorid(e) (US) · Chlorid *n*

~ **migration** (Brit.); chlorid(e) ~ (US) · Chloridwanderung *f*

~ **of lime**, chlorinated ~, bleaching powder · Chlorkalk *m*, Bleichpulver *n*, Bleichkalk, Kalziumoxychlorid *n*, CaOCl₂

~ **stress corrosion cracking** (Brit.); chlorid(e) ~ ~ ~ (US) · Chloridspannungsrißkorrosion *f*

to chlorinate · chloren

chlorinated lime, chloride of ~, bleaching powder · Chlorkalk *m*, Bleichpulver *n*, Bleichkalk, Kalziumoxychlorid *n*, CaOCl₂

~ **polyvinyl chloride**, ~ PVC · PVC-C *n*, chloriertes Polyvinylchlorid *n*

~ ~ **pipe**, ~ PVC ~ · PVC-C-Rohr *n*, Rohr aus chloriertem Polyvinylchlorid [*DIN 8079 Maße; DIN 8080 allgemeine Güteanforderungen und Prüfung*]

~ **PVC**, ~ polyvinyl chloride · PVC-C *n*, chloriertes Polyvinylchlorid *n*

~ ~ **pipe**, ~ polyvinyl chloride ~ · PVC-C-Rohr *n*, Rohr aus chloriertem Polyvinylchlorid [*DIN 8079 Maße; DIN 8080 allgemeine Güteanforderungen und Prüfung*]

~ **resin** · Chlorharz *n*

~ **rubber** · Chlorkautschuk *m*, chlorierter Kautschuk

~ ~ **adhesive**, ~ ~ glue · Chlorkautschukleim *m*

~ ~ **base** · Chlorkautschukbasis *f*, Chlorkautschukgrundlage *f*

~ ~ **(bonding) adhesive**, ~ ~ ~ agent, ~ ~ ~ medium, ~ ~ cement(ing agent) · Chlorkautschukkleb(e)stoff *m*, Chlorkautschukkleb(e)mittel *n*, Chlorkautschukkleber *m*

~ ~ **coat** · Chlorkautschukanstrich *m*, Chlorkautschukaufstrich

~ ~ **curing compound** · Chlorkautschuk-Nachbehandlungsmittel *n*

~ ~ **glue**, ~ ~ adhesive · Chlorkautschukleim *m*

~ ~ **lacquer**, ~ ~ pigmented varnish · Chlorkautschuklackfarbe *f*, Chlorkautschuklackemaille *f*, pigmentierter Chlorkautschuk(klar)lack *m*

~ ~ **paint** · Chlorkautschukfarbe *f*

~ ~ **pigmented varnish**, ~ ~ lacquer · Chlorkautschuklackfarbe *f*, Chlorkautschuklackemaille *f*, pigmentierter Chlorkautschuk(klar)lack *m*

~ ~ **polymer** · Chlorkautschukpolymer *n*

~ ~ **priming paint** · Chlorkautschukgrundier(anstrich)farbe *f*

~ **solvent** · Chlorlösemittel *n*, Chlorlösungsmittel

chlorination · Chlorung *f*

chlorine · Chlor *n*

~ **recorder** · Chlorregistriergerät *n*, Chlorschreiber *m*

chlorite, green earth · Chlorit *m* (Min.)

chlorite-schist · Chloritschiefer *m*

chlorite slate · Tonschiefer *m* mit viel Chlorit

chloritic mineral · chloritisches Tonmineral *n*

chloritization · Chloritbildung *f*

chloritoid schist · Chloritoidschiefer *m*

chloroform-insoluble matter · Chloroform-Unlösliche *n*

choice of mix(ture), selection ~ ~ · Gemischwahl *f*, Mischungswahl

~ ~ **site** · Baustellenwahl *f*

choir, quire [*The part of a church where divine service is sung*] · Chor *m*

~ **aisle**, quire ~, ~ side ~ · Chorseitenschiff *n*

~ **arcade**, quire ~ · Chorarkade *f*

~ **arch**, quire ~ · Chorbogen *m* [*Bogen, der einen Chor vom Langhaus bzw. der Vierung trennt*]

~ **architecture**, quire ~ · Chorarchitektur *f*, Chorbaukunst *f*

~ **bay**, quire ~ · Chorjoch(feld) *n*, Chorfeld

~ ~ **wall**, quire ~ ~ · Chorjochwand *f*, Chorfeldwand

~ **buttress**, quire ~ · Chorstrebepfeiler *m*

~ **chapel**, apsidal ~, quire ~, apse ~ · Chorkapelle *f*, Apsidialkapelle, Absidenkapelle, Apsidenkapelle, Apsiskapelle, Abseitenkapelle

~ **fresco**, quire ~ · Chorfreske *f*

~ **gallery**, ~ loft, quire ~ · Sängerempore *f*, Sängergalerie *f*, Chorempore, Chorgalerie, Sängerbühne *f*, Chorbühne

~ **grille**, quire ~, ~ (lattice(d)) screen · Chorgitter *n*

~ **(lattice(d)) screen**, quire (~) ~, ~ grille · Chorgitter *n*

~ **limb**, quire ~ · Chorflügel *m*

~ **loft**, ~ gallery, quire ~ · Sängerempore *f*, Sängergalerie *f*, Chorempore, Chorgalerie, Sängerbühne *f*, Chorbühne

choir pier — chuff

~ **pier**, quire ~ · Chorpfeiler *m*

~ **school**, quire ~ · Chorschule *f*

~ **screen**, quire ~, ~ lattice(d) ~, ~ grille · Chorgitter *n*

~ **(side) aisle**, quire (~) ~ · Chorseitenschiff *n*

~ **stall**, quire ~ · Chorgestühl *n*, Chorstühle *mpl*

~ **termination**, quire ~ · Chor(ab)schluß *m*

~ **tower**, quire ~ · Chorturm *m*

~ **vault**, quire ~ · Chorgewölbe *n*

~ **wall**, quire ~ · Chorwand *f*

chopped strands · Glasstapelseide *f*, Stapelglasseide

choragic monument · choragisches Monument *n*

chord, boom, flange · Flansch *m*, Gurt(ung) *m*, (*f*)

~ **area** → flange ~

~ **bar** → flange member

~ **bracing** → boom stiffening

~ **element** → flange member

~ **member** → flange ~

~ **plane**, flange ~, boom ~ · Gurt(ungs)ebene *f*

~ **plate**, flange ~, boom ~ · Gurt(ungs)blech *n*

~ **rod** → flange member

~ **stiffening** → boom ~

~ **width**, boom ~, flange ~ · Flanschbreite *f*, Gurt(ungs)breite

chrismon · konstantinisches Kreuz *n* [*Christusmonogramm aus den griechischen Buchstaben χ (= Chi) und P (= Rho), den Anfangsbuchstaben des Wortes Christus*]

Christian basilica, ecclesiastical ~, basilica (church) · (christliche) Basilika *f*, Basilikakirche *f*

~ **bema** · Bema *n* [*In einer christlichen Kirche*]

~ **church architecture** · christliche Kirchenarchitektur *f*, ~ Kirchenbaukunst *f*

chromate · Chromat *n*

chrom(at)e of lead, lead chrom(at)e · Bleichromat *n*

chrome brick, ~ refractory ~ · Chromerzstein *m*

chrome-dolomite refractory (product), chromite-dolomite ~ (~) · Chrom(it)-Dolomit-Erzeugnis *n*

chrome green paint · Chromgrün(anstrich)farbe *f*

~ ~ **(pigment)** [*A mix(ture) of Prussian blue and chrome yellow*] · Chromgrün(pigment) *n*

~ **magnesite** · Chrommagnesit *m*

~ **mortar** · Chrommörtel *m*

~ **ochre** (Brit.); ~ ocher (US) · Chromocker *m*

~ **ore** [*A rock containing a major proportion of chrome spinels*] · Chrom(eisen)erz *n*, Chromeisenstein *m*

~ **pigment** · Chrompigment *n* [*Fehlname: Chromfarbe f*]

~ **red (pigment)**, red chrome (~) · Chromrot(pigment) *n*

~ **(refractory) brick** · Chromerzstein *m*

~ **yellow (pigment)** · Chromgelb(pigment) *n*, chromsaures Pb *n*

chromic oxide (pigment) [*B.S. 318*]; ~ oxid(e) (~) (US); chromium ~ (~) · Chromoxid(pigment) *n*

chromite [*The ferrous chrome spinel*] · Chromit *m*, FeO·Cr$_2$O$_3$

chromium · Chrom *n*, Cr

~ **coating** · Chrombeschichten *n*, Chromüberziehen, Chromüberzug *m*, Chrombeschichtung *f* [*als Tätigkeit*]

~ **coat(ing)**, ~ finish · Chrombeschichtung *f*, Chromüberzug *m* [*als Schicht*]

~ **finish**, ~ coat(ing) · Chrombeschichtung *f*, Chromüberzug *m* [*als Schicht*]

~ **molybdenum stainless steel** · Chrom-Molybdän-Stahl *m*

chromium-nickel · Chromnickel *n*

~ **stainless steel** · Chrom-Nickel-Stahl *m*, rostsicherer Stahl, nichtrostender Stahl, rostbeständiger Stahl, säurebeständiger Stahl [*Im Bauwesen sind Chrom-Nickel-Stähle hauptsächlich als rostsichere Stähle bekannt; sie enthalten meistens etwa 18% Chrom und etwa 8% Nickel*]

chromium oxide green (pigment) (Brit.); ~ oxid(e) (~) (US); green (anhydrous) oxide chromium (~) [*B.S. 318*] · Chromoxidgrün(pigment) *n*

~ ~ **(pigment)** (Brit.); ~ oxid(e) (~) (US); chromic ~ (~) [*B.S. 318*] · Chromoxid(pigment) *n*

~ **plating** · Verchromung *f*

~ ~ **for decorative purposes**, ~ ~ ornamental ~ · dekorative Verchromung *f*, Glanzverchromung, Ornamentverchromung, Zierverchromung, Schmuckverchromung

~ **slag** · Chromschlacke *f* [*Sie fällt bei der Verhüttung von Chromeisenstein als Nebenerzeugnis an*]

~ **stainless steel**, plain chromium ~ · Chromstahl *m*

chrysotile asbestos, Canadian ~ · Chrysotilasbest *m*, Kanadaasbest

Chubb (lever-tumbler) lock · Chubbschloß *n*

chuff [*A brick full of cracks through exposure during burning, and unsuitable for use*] · Ausschußziegel *m*

church architect, ecclesiastical ~ · Kirchenarchitekt *m*

~ architecture, religious ~, ecclesiastical ~ · kirchliche Architektur *f*, ~ Baukunst, Kirchenbaukunst, Kirchenarchitektur, Sakralbaukunst, Sakralarchitektur

Church at Qalb Louzeh · Kirche *f* von Qualb-Luzeh

church bell · Kirchenglocke *f*

~ builder · Kirchenbauer *m*

~ building, ecclesiastical ~ · Kirchengebäude *n*

~ ~, ecclesiastical ~ · Kirchenbau *m*

~ ~ style, ecclesiastical ~ ~ · Kirchenbaustil *m*

~ buildings, ecclesiastical ~ · Kirchenbauten *f*

~ built on the axial principle, long church · Longitudinalhauskirche *f*, Langhauskirche [*Kirchenbaukunst. Gegensatz „Zentralbaukirche"*]

~ ceiling · Kirchendecke *f*

~ cross · Kirchenkreuz *n*

~ façade · Kirchenfassade *f*

~ fittings · Kircheneinbauten *f*

~ form · Kirchenform *f*

~ fresco · Kirchenfreske *f*

~ (ground(-))plan · Kirchengrundriß *m*

~ heating · Kirchen(be)heizung *f*

~ illumination, ~ lighting · Kirchenbeleuchtung *f*

~ interior · Kirchen(innen)raum *m*, Kircheninnere *n*

church-in-the-round, circular church, round church · Rundkirche *f*

church lighting, ~ illumination · Kirchenbeleuchtung *f*

~ monument · Kirchendenkmal *n*, Kirchenmonument *n*

(~) nave, middle vessel · Hauptschiff *n*, Mittelschiff, Lang(haus)schiff, Mittelhaus *n*

(~) ~ arcade, middle vessel ~ · Mittelschiffarkade *f*, Hauptschiffarkade, Lang(haus)schiffarkade, Mittelhausarkade

(~) ~ bay → (~) ~ vault

(~) ~ ceiling, middle vessel ~ · Mittelschiffdecke *f*, Hauptschiffdecke, Lang(haus)schiffdecke, Mittelhausdecke

(~) ~ pier, middle vessel ~ · Hauptschiffpfeiler *m*, Mittelschiffpfeiler, Lang(haus)schiffpfeiler, Mittelhauspfeiler

(~) ~ range of columns, (~) ~ row ~ ~, middle vessel ~ ~ ~ · Mittelschiffsäulenreihe *f*, Hauptschiffsäulenreihe, Lang(haus)schiffsäulenreihe

(~) ~ vault, middle vessel ~ · Hauptschiffgewölbe *n*, Mittelschiffgewölbe, Lang(haus)schiffgewölbe, Mittelhausgewölbe

(~) ~ (~) bay, middle vessel (~) ~ · Mittelschiffjoch(feld) *n*, Hauptschiffjoch(feld), Langschiffjoch(feld), Mittelschiffeld, Hauptschiffeld, Lang(haus)schiffeld

(~) ~ window, middle vessel ~ · Hauptschiffenster *n*, Mittelschiffenster, Lang(haus)schiffenster, Mittelhausfenster

church of Corpus Christi · Fronleichnamskirche *f*

~ ~ Holy Trinity, ~ ~ the ~ · Dreifaltigkeitskirche *f* [*Solche Kirchen sind meistens auf ein Dreieck oder einen Dreipaß aufgebaute Zentralbauten, besonders in der Barockzeit vorkommend*]

~ ~ St. Charles · Karlskirche *f*

~ ~ ~ Elisabeth · Elisabethkirche *f*

~ ~ ~ George · Georgskirche *f*

~ ~ ~ John · Johanniskirche *f*

Church of St. Mary at Halle · Marktkirche *f* U. L. Fr. in Halle

~ ~ the Apostles at Cologne · S. Apostolen zu Köln

~ ~ ~ ~ Constantinople · Apostelkirche *f* von Konstantinopel

church of the Holy Cross · Kirche *f* zum Heiligen Kreuz, (Heilig)Kreuzkirche

Church of the Holy Sepulchre at Jerusalem · Kirche *f* des Heiligen Grabes zu Jerusalem ~ vom Heiligen Grab ~ ~

church of the Holy Spirit, ~ ~ ~ ~ Ghost · Heiliggeistkirche *f*

~ ~ ~ Trinity · Dreifaltigkeitskirche *f*

~ ~ ~ Magdalen · Magdalenenkirche *f*

Church of the Miraculous Virgin [*in Mexico City*] · Kirche *f* der Wundertätigen Jungfrau

~ ~ ~ Nativity at Bethlehem · Geburtskirche *f* zu Bethlehem, Muttergotteskirche ~ ~

church of the Resurrection · Auferstehungskirche *f*

~ ~ ~ Trinity → ~ ~ Holy ~

~ plan, ~ ground-plan · Kirchengrundriß *m*

~ porch · Kirchenvorhalle *f*

~ portal · Kirchenportal *n*

~ roof · Kirchendach *n*

~ room, parish hall, parish room · (kirchlicher) Gemeinderaum *m*

Church S. Paolo fuori le Mura, Rome · Paulskirche *f* vor den Mauern Roms

~ S. Sophia at Constantinople, Hágia Sophia ~ ~ · Sophienkirche *f* zu Konstantinopel

church termination · Kirchen(ab)schluß *m*

~ tower · Kirchturm *m*

~ window · Kirchenfenster *n*

~ with central space, centrally-planned church, centralized church; centralised church (Brit.) · sakraler Zentralbau *m*, Zentralkirche *f*

~~~~ encircled by columns · sakraler Zentralbau *m* mit innerem Säulenkranz, Zentralkirche *f* ~~~~

churchwarden's pew · Kirchenratsbank *f*

churchyard · Kirchhof *m*

~ **cross** · Kirchhofskreuz *n*

~ **path** · Kirchhofsweg *m*

Churrigueresque style [*This style was developed in the late seventeenth Century and continued to mid-eighteenth; due to a family of architects led by José de Churriguera (1665–1725), though he was not himself the most extreme of the exponents of the style*] · Churriguerismus *m*

chute, shaft, disposal ~, disposer · Abwurfanlage *f*, Abwurfschacht *m* [*Es gibt Abwurfanlagen für Müll, Papier und Wäsche*]

~ · Rutsche *f*

chuted concrete · Gußbeton *m*, Rinnenbeton, gießfähiger Beton, flüssiger Beton [*Dieser Beton ist so weich, daß er ohne Entmischung in Rinnen von etwa 25° Gefälle fließt. Der große Wasserzusatz zur Erzielung einer solchen Fähigkeit ergibt eine geringe Güte. Dieser Beton wird daher heute kaum noch verwendet*]

CI, coolant inlet · Kühlmitteleinlaß *m*

C.I., cast iron · Gußeisen *n*, Ge

~~ **area grating**, cast-iron ~ ~ · Gußeisengitterrost *m*

~~ **bath** → cast-iron (bath)tub

~~ **(bath)tub** → cast-iron ~

~~ **bedplate**, cast-iron ~ · Gußeisen-Grundplatte *f*, gußeiserne Grundplatte

~~ **(biological) shielding wall** → cast-iron (~) ~ ~

~~ **boiler**, cast-iron ~ [*B.S. 779*] · Gußeisen(-Heiz)kessel *m*, gußeiserner (Heiz)Kessel

~~ **box gutter** → cast-iron box (roof) ~

~~~ **rainwater gutter** → cast-iron box (roof) ~

~~~ **(roof) gutter** → cast-iron ~ (~) ~

~~ **column**, cast-iron ~ · Gußeisenstütze *f*, gußeiserne Stütze

~~~ **for street lighting**, cast-iron ~ ~ ~ ~ [*B.S. 1249*] · Gußeisen-Beleuchtungsmast *m*, gußeiserner Beleuchtungsmast, Gußeisen-Lichtmast, gußeiserner Lichtmast

~~ **cover**, cast-iron ~ · Gußeisendeckel *m*, gußeiserner Deckel

~~~ **plate** → cast-iron cover(ing) ~

~~ **cover(ing) plate** → cast-iron ~ ~ ~

~~ **discharge pipe** → cast-iron drain(-age) ~

~~ **(door) pull (handle)** → cast-iron (~) ~ (~)

~~ **drain(age) pipe** → cast-iron ~ ~

~~ **draining pipe** → cast-iron drain(-age) ~

~~ **façade**, cast-iron ~ · Gußeisen-Fassade *f*, gußeiserne Fassade

~~ **fish-bellied girder**, cast-iron ~ ~ · Gußeisen-Fischbauchträger *m*, gußeiserner Fischbauchträger

~~ **fitting** → cast-iron (pipe) ~

~~ **flange**, cast-iron ~ · Gußeisenflansch *m*, gußeiserner Flansch [*DIN 2530–2535*]

~~ **flange(d) pipe**, cast-iron ~ ~ · Gußeisenflansch(en)rohr *n*, gußeisernes Flansch(en)rohr

~~~ **(~) fitting** → cast iron ~ (~) ~

~~ **floor plate**, cast-iron ~ ~ · Gußeisen(fuß)bodenplatte *f*, gußeiserne (Fuß)Bodenplatte

~~ **flushing cistern** → cast-iron flushing tank

~~~ **tank** → cast-iron ~ ~

~~ **girder**, cast-iron ~ · Gußeisenträger *m*, gußeiserner Träger

~~ **mast**, cast-iron ~ · Gußeisenmast *m*, gußeiserner Mast

~~ **paving** → (cast-)iron ~

~ ~ **pipe**, cast-iron ~, CIP · Guß(eisen)rohr *n*, gußeisernes Rohr

~~ **(~) fitting** → cast-iron (~) ~

~~ **pipeline**, cast-iron ~ · Gußeisen(rohr)leitung *f*, gußeiserne (Rohr-)Leitung

~~ **plate**, cast-iron ~ · Gußeisenplatte *f*, gußeiserne Platte

~~ **pressure pipe**, cast-iron ~ ~ · Gußeisen-Druckrohr *n*, gußeisernes Druckrohr

~~ **products for sewerage (systems)**, cast-iron ~ ~ ~ (~) · Kanalguß *m*

~~ **pull (handle)** → cast-iron (door) ~ (~)

~~ **radiation shielding wall** → cast-iron (biological) ~ ~ ~

~~ **radiator**, cast-iron ~ · gußeiserner (Glieder)Heizkörper *m*, ~ Radiator, Gußeisen-(Glieder)Heizkörper, Guß(-eisen)-Radiator

~~ **rail**, cast-iron ~ · Gußeisenschiene *f*, gußeiserne Schiene

~~ **rainwater article** → cast-iron rainwater product

~~~ **articles** → cast-iron rainwater goods

~~~ **goods** → cast-iron ~ ~

~~~ **product** → cast-iron ~ ~

~~~ **products** → cast-iron rainwater goods

~~ **sectional boiler**, cast-iron ~ ~ · Gußeisen-Gliederkessel *m*, gußeiserner Gliederkessel

C. I. sectional tank — cinder sett

~ ~ ~ **tank**, cast-iron ~ ~ [*B.S. 1563*] · Gußeisen-Gliederbehälter *m*, gußeiserner Gliederbehälter

~ ~ **shielding wall** → cast-iron (biological) ~ ~

~ ~ **structural pipe**, ~ ~ tube, cast-iron ~ ~ · Gußeisen-Konstruktionsrohr *n*, gußeisernes Konstruktionsrohr

~ ~ ~ **tube**, ~ ~ pipe, cast-iron ~ ~ · Gußeisen-Konstruktionsrohr *n*, gußeisernes Konstruktionsrohr

~ ~ **tracery**, cast-iron ~ · Gußeisenmaßwerk *n*

~ ~ **tub** → cast-iron (bath)tub

~ ~ **tubular column**, cast-iron ~ ~ · Gußeisen-Rohrstütze *f*, gußeiserne Rohrstütze

~ ~ **waste (pipe)** → cast-iron drain(-age) ~

~ ~ **water waste preventer** → cast-iron flushing tank

~ ~ **window**, cast-iron ~ · Gußeisenfenster *n*, gußeisernes Fenster

ciborium [*A receptable for the preservation of the Eucharist*] · Ciborium *n*, Ziborium, Tabernakel *n*

~ [*A canopy supported by columns, generally placed over an altar or tomb*] · Ciborium *n*, Ziborium

~ **altar** · Ciboriumaltar *m*, Ziboriumaltar

cicoil · Cicöl *n* [*Veredelungsprodukt des schnelltrocknenden Oiticicaöles*]

CIE diagram · Normfarbtafel *f* [*Das international übliche x–y Diagramm. CIE = Commission Internationale de l'Eclairage = Internationale Beleuchtungskommission*]

CIF, channel iron frame · U-Eisen-Rahmen *m*

cill (Brit.) → (window) sill

~ [*deprecated*] (Brit.); sole plate, sill (Brit.); (a)butment piece, solepiece (US) [*The lowest horizontal member of a framed partition, or frame construction*] · Schwelle *f*, Holz~ [*Beim Holzfachwerk der untere waag(e)rechte Balken der Riegelwand*]

~ **block** (Brit.) → (window) sill ~

~ **cover** (Brit.) → (window) sill ~

~ **(head) height** (Brit.) → (window) sill (~) ~

~ **height** (Brit.) → (window) sill (head) ~

~ **rail** (Brit.) → (window) sill ~

~ **tile** (Brit.) → (window) sill block

cima-inversa → sima-inversa

cima-recta → sima-recta

cimborio, lantern tower · Cimborio *m*, Laterne *f*

cincfoil, cinquefoil · Fünfblatt *n*

cinder (US) → (iron) (blastfurnace) slag

~ ~ → (furnace) clinker

~ **aggregate** (US); (iron) (blastfurnace) slag ~ (Brit.) · (Hochofen-)Schlackenzuschlag(stoff) *m*, (Hochofen)Schlackenzuschlagmaterial *n*

~ ~ **for concrete** (US) → (furnace) clinker ~ ~ ~

~ **block** (US); clinker ~ (Brit.); ~ tile [*See remark under 'Block'*] · Schlacken(beton)stein *m*, Schlacken(beton)block(stein) *m*

~ **chip(ping)s** (US); (iron) (blastfurnace) slag ~ (Brit.) · Schlackensplitt *m*, Hochofen~

~ **coarse aggregate** (US); (iron) (blastfurnace) slag ~ ~ (Brit.) [*B.S. 1047*] · (Hochofen)Schlacken-Grobzuschlag(stoff) *m*

~ **concrete** (US); (iron)· (blastfurnace) slag ~ (Brit.) · (Hochofen)Schlackenbeton *m*

~ ~, **furnace** ~ ~ (US); (furnace) clinker ~ (Brit.) · Kesselschlackenbeton *m*, (Stein)Kohlenschlackenbeton, Feuerungsschlackenbeton, (Verbrennungs)Schlackenbeton

~ ~ **roof(ing) slab** (US); clinker ~ ~ ~ (Brit.) · Schlacken(beton)dachplatte *f*

~ ~ **wall slab** (US); clinker ~ ~ (Brit.) · Schlacken(beton)-Wand-(bau)platte *f*

~ **dust**, ~ filler (US); (iron) (blastfurnace) slag filler, (iron) (blastfurnace) slag dust (Brit.) · (Hochofen)Schlackenfüller *m*, (Hochofen)Schlackenfüllstoff *m*

~ **fiber** (US); (iron) (blastfurnace) slag fibre (Brit.) · (Hochofen)Schlackenfaser *f*

~ **filler**, ~ dust (US); (iron) (blastfurnace) slag filler, (iron) (blastfurnace) slag dust (Brit.) · (Hochofen)Schlackenfüller *m*, (Hochofen)Schlackenfüllstoff *m*

~ **fill(ing)** (US); (iron) (blastfurnace) slag~ (Brit.) · (Hochofen)Schlacken(auf)füllung *f*, (Hochofen)Schlackenschüttung

~ **(paving) sett** (US); (iron) (blastfurnace) slag (~) ~ (Brit.) · (Hochofen)Schlackenpflasterstein *m*

~ **pot** (US) → hollow clinker block

~ **sand**, granulated cinder (US); (iron) (blastfurnace) slag sand (Brit.); granulated (blastfurnace) slag · Schlakkensand *m*, künstlicher ~, Hüttensand, granulierte Hochofenschlacke *f*, gekörnte Hochofenschlacke, Hochofenschlackensand

~ ~ **block** (US) → slag ~ ~

~ ~ **concrete**, granulated cinder ~ (US); granulated (blastfurnace) slag ~, (iron) (blastfurnace) slag sand (Brit.) · Schlackensandbeton *m*, Hochofen~, Hüttensandbeton

~ ~ **cored block**, granulated cinder ~ ~ (US); slag sand ~ ~, granulated slag ~ ~ (Brit.) · Hütten-Lochstein *m*, HSL [*DIN 398*]

~ ~ **tile** (US) → slag sand block

~ **sett** → ~ paving ~

~ **slab** (US); clinker ~ (Brit.) · Schlacken(beton)diele f, Schlacken(beton)-platte f [*Mit Zement oder Gips gebunden*]

~ **tile;** ~ block (US); clinker ~ (Brit.) [*See remark under 'Block'*] · Schlacken(beton)stein m, Schlacken(beton)-block(stein)

~ **track** · Aschenbahn f

cinema, motion picture theatre · Kino n, Lichtspielhaus n, Lichtspieltheater n

~ **auditorium** · Lichtspielsaal m

~ **building** · Kinogebäude n

~ **equipment** · Kinoausrüstung f

~ **heating** · Kino(be)heizung f

(cinerary) urn, cremation ~ · (Aschen-) Urne f

(~) ~ pit, cremation ~ ~ · (Aschen-) Urnengrab n, Brandgrab

cinnabar · Zinnober m

cinquefoil, cincfoil · Fünfblatt n

CIP, cast-iron pipe, C.I. pipe · Guß-(eisen)rohr n, gußeisernes Rohr

circle of hues · Farb(en)kreis m, Farbtonkreis

~ ~ **inertia** · Trägheitskreis m

~ ~ **wall plates** · Mauerlattenkranz m

circuit · Ringleitung f

~ · Stromkreis m

circular abacus, ~ raised table · Rundabakus m, Rundkapitellplatte f, Rundkapitälplatte, Rund(säulen)deckplatte

~ **arch** · Kreisbogen m, Ringbogen

~ **arch(ed girder)** · Kreisbogen(träger) m

~ **balcony** · Rundbalkon m

~ **bar** → round (reinforcing) ~

~ **barrel vault,** ~ tunnel ~, ~ wagon ~ · ringförmiges Tonnengewölbe n

~ **base-line,** base · Fußkreis m [*Kuppel*]

~ **beam,** ring(-shaped) ~ · Ringbalken(träger) m

~ **bowl** · Rundschale f [*Blumenschale; Pflanzenschale*]

~ **box beam** · kreisförmiger Kastenbalken(träger) m

~ **brick window** → ~ clay ~ ~

~ **building,** cylindric(al) ~ [*When the inside is also circular, the building is called a rotunda*] · Rundbau m, Rundgebäude n

~ ~ **with niches,** cylindric(al) ~ ~ ~ · Nischenrundbau m

~ **campanile,** round ~, cylindrical ~ · runder freistehender Glockenturm m

~ **capital,** round ~ · Rundkapitell n, Rundkapitäl

~ **cella,** round ~ · Rundcella f

~ **chamber** · Kreisraum m [*Nebenraum im Sakralbau*]

~ **chapel,** round ~, chapel-in-the-round · Rundkapelle f

~ **chimney,** cylindrical ~, round ~ · Rundschornstein m

~ **church,** round ~, church-in-the-round · Rundkirche f

~ **(clay) brick window,** round (~) ~ ~ · Ziegelkreisfenster n, Ziegelrundfenster

~ **column,** cylindrical ~, round ~ · Rundsäule f

~ ~, cylindrical ~, round ~ · Rundstütze f

~ **concrete column,** cylindrical ~ ~ · Betonrundstütze f

~ ~ **manhole,** cylindrical ~ ~, ~ ~ manway · Betonrundschacht m

~ **conoid** · Rundkonoid n

~ **core,** cylindrical ~, round ~ · Rundkern m [*Hochhaus*]

~ **corridor** · Rundgang m

~ **cross-section,** round ~ · Rundquerschnitt m, Kreisquerschnitt

~ **curved beam** · kreisförmig gekrümmter Balken m

~ **cylinder** · Kreiszylinder m

~ **cylindrical northlight roof shell** · Kreiszylinder-Shedschale f

~ **cylindrical shell** · Kreiszylinderschale f

~ **diminutive tower,** round ~ ~, small ~, ~ turret · Rundtürmchen n, kleiner Rundturm m

~ **dome,** ~ cupola · Kreiskuppel f

~ **domed building** · Kuppelrundbau m

circular-domed pat of cement, cement pat, pat of cement-water paste, soundness test pat · (Probe)Kuchen m (aus Zement), Zementkuchen

~ ~ ~ **gypsum,** gypsum pat · Gipskuchen m, Probekuchen aus Gips

~ ~ ~ **lime,** lime pat · Kalkkuchen m, Probekuchen aus Kalk

circular donjon → ~ keep

~ **dungeon** → ~ keep

~ **enclosure** · Plattenring m [*in Mykene*]

~ **floor,** round ~; ~ story (US); ~ storey (Brit.) · Rundetage f, Kreisetage, Rundstockwerk n, Kreisstockwerk, Rundgeschoß n, Kreisgeschoß

~ **folded plate roof,** round ~ ~ ~, ~ ~ slab ~; ~ hipped-plate ~, ~ tilted-slab ~ (US) · Rundfalt(werk)-dach n, Runddachfaltwerk n, Kreisfalt-(werk)dach, Kreisdachfaltwerk

~ ~ **slab roof** → ~ ~ ~ plate ~

~ **foundation,** round ~ · Kreisgründung f, Rundgründung

~ **function,** trigonometric ~ · trigonometrische Funktion f

~ **girder,** ring(-shaped) ~ · Ringträger m

~ **glass tower,** round ~ ~, cylindrical ~ ~ · Rundglasturm m, Glasrundturm

circular (ground(-))plan — circulation 194

~ **(ground(-))plan**, round ~ · runder Grundriß m, kreisförmiger ~

~ **hipped-plate roof** (US) → ~ folded plate ~

~ **hole**, round ~ · Rundloch n, Kreisloch

~ **house**, round ~ · Rundhaus n

~ **hut**, tholus, tholos, thole · Säulenrundbau m, Tholos m [*Tempelform. Runde Cella mit rundem Säulenumgang*]

~ **interlocking pipe**, cylindrical ~ ~, round ~ ~ · rundes Falzrohr n

~ **keep**, round ~, ~ donjon, ~ dungeon, cylindrical ~ · Rundbergfried m, Rundbelfried, Rundberchfrit, Runddonjon m

~ **kiln** · Ringofen m

~ **linear load** · Kreislinienlast f

~ **load** · Kreislast f

~ **manhole**, cylindrical ~, round ~, ~ manway · Kreisschacht m, Rundschacht

~ **manway**, cylindrical ~, round ~, ~ manhole · Kreisschacht m, Rundschacht

~ **membrane** · Kreismembran(e) f

~ **moulding** → round(ed) ~

~ **peripteral temple**, round ~ ~ · Ringhallentempel m, Peripteralrundtempel

~ **pipe**, cylindrical ~, round ~ · Zylinderrohr n, Kreisrohr, Rundrohr, rundes Rohr, kreisförmiges Rohr

~ **plan**, ~ ground(-)~, round ~ · runder Grundriß m, kreisförmiger ~

circular-plan building · Rundbau m

circular plate, round ~, ~ slab · kreisförmige Platte f, ~ Scheibe, runde ~, Kreisplatte, Kreisscheibe, Rundplatte, Rundscheibe

~ **profile**, round ~ · Rundprofil n, Kreisprofil

(~) **protractor** · Winkelmesser m für Linienwinkel

~ **raised table**, ~ abacus · Rundabakus m, Rundkapitellplatte f, Rundkapitälplatte, Rund(säulen)deckplatte

~ **ramp**, helic(oid)al ~, spiral ~, helicline, ramp tower · Schraubenrampe f, Wendelrampe, Spiralrampe

~ **reinforcement bar** → round (reinforcing) ~

~ ~ **rod** → round (reinforcing) bar

~ **(~) bar** → round (~) ~

~ **(~) rod** → round (reinforcing) bar

~ **ring(-shaped) plate**, ~ ~ slab, annular ~ · Kreisringplatte f, kreisringförmige Platte

~ ~ **slab**, ~ ~ plate, annular ~ · Kreisringplatte f, kreisringförmige Platte

~ **rod** → round (reinforcing) bar

~ ~ **web**, cylindrical ~ ~, round ~ ~, ~ bar ~ · Rundstabsteg m

~ **roll with knife** · Rundmesser n zur Aufteilung in Längsrichtung [*Dachpappenanlage*]

~ **roof**, round ~ · Runddach n, Kreisdach

~ **roof-light**, round ~ · Kreis(decken)-oberlicht n, Rund(decken)oberlicht

~ **shaft**, round ~ · Kreisschaft m, Rundschaft

~ **shed**, round ~ · Rundschuppen m, Kreisschuppen

~ **shell** [*A shell with a constant radius of curvature*] · Kreisschale f, Rundschale

~ **silo**, round ~, cylindrical ~ · Rundsilo m, Kreissilo

~ **slab**, round ~, ~ plate · kreisförmige Platte f, ~ Scheibe, runde ~, Kreisplatte, Kreisscheibe, Rundplatte, Rundscheibe

~ **small tower**, round ~ ~, ~ diminutive ~, ~ turret · Rundtürmchen n, kleiner Rundturm m

~ **spike plate** · Krallenringdübel m

~ **steel column**, cylindrical ~ ~, round ~ · Rundstahlstütze f, Stahlrundstütze

~ **story** (US) → ~ floor

~ **temple**, round ~ · Rundtempel m

~ **tilted-slab roof** (US) → ~ folded plate ~

~ **tower**, round ~ · Rundturm m

~ **traceried window**, round ~ ~ · Rundmaßwerkfenster n

~ **transept(al) window**, transept(al) circular ~ · Querhausrundfenster n

~ **tube**, cylindrical ~, round ~ · Zylinderröhre f, Kreisröhre, Rundröhre, runde Röhre, kreisförmige Röhre

~ **tunnel vault**, ~ barrel ~, ~ wagon ~ · ringförmiges Tonnengewölbe n

~ **turret** → ~ small tower

~ **vault** · Kreisgewölbe n

(~) **vestibule**, tambour · Drehtürgehäuse n

~ **wagon vault**, ~ barrel ~, ~ tunnel ~ · ringförmiges Tonnengewölbe n

~ **window**, round ~ · Rundfenster n, Kreisfenster

to circulate · umwälzen

circulating equipment · Umlaufanlage f, Umwälzanlage

~ **heating system**, ~ ~ installation · Umlauf-Heiz(ungs)anlage f, Umwälz-Heiz(ungs)anlage

~ **pipe for cooling water** · Kühlwasserumwälzrohr n

~ **tank** · Umlaufbehälter m, Umwälzbehälter

~ **water** · Umlaufwasser n, Umwälzwasser

~ ~ **pump**, CWP · Umlaufwasserpumpe f, Umwälzwasserpumpe, Wasserumwälzpumpe, Wasserumlaufpumpe

circulation · Umlauf m, Umwälzung f

circulation area — civil engineering material

~ **area,** ~ **space** · Personenverkehrsfläche *f* [*Gebäude*]
~ **heating** · Umlaufheizung *f*, Umwälzheizung
~ ~ **installation,** ~ ~ **system** · Umlauf-Heiz(ungs)anlage *f*, Umwälz-Heiz(ungs)anlage
~ **line, pipe** ~ ~ · Umlauf(rohr)leitung *f*, Umwälz(rohr)leitung
~ **loss** · Umwälzverlust *m*
~ **pipework, pipe circulation system, pipe circulating system** · Umlaufrohrnetz *n*, Umwälzrohrnetz
~ **space,** ~ **area** · Personenverkehrsfläche *f* [*Gebäude*]
~ **tower** · Personenverkehrsschacht *m* [*Gebäude*]
circulator → gas (water) ~
circumferential stress, hoop ~ · Umfangsspannung *f*
circus 'big top', ~ **tent** · Zirkuszelt *n*
cire-perdue method · Wachsausschmelzverfahren *n*, Guß *m* mit verlorener Form
cissing, sissing [*See remark under 'crawling'*] · leichtes Abrollen *n*, ~ Kriechen *n* [*Anstrichtechnik*]
Cistercian abbey · Zisterzienserabtei *f*
~ **architecture** · Zisterzienserarchitektur *f*, Zisterzienserbaukunst *f*
~ **chapter-house** · Zisterzienserstift *n*
~ **choir,** ~ **quire** · Zisterzienserchor *m*
~ **church** · Zisterzienserkirche *f*
~ **edifice** · Zisterzienserbau(werk) *m*, (*n*)
~ **Gothic (style)** · Zisterziensergotik *f*
~ **monastery** · Zisterzienserkloster *n*
cistern → water ~
~ **head** (US); **rainwater** ~, **leader** ~, **conductor** ~ [*The enlarged entrance at the head of a downpipe. It collects the water from the gutters*] · Regenrinnenkasten *m*, Regenrinnenkessel *m*, (Dach)Rinnenkasten, (Dach)Rinnenkessel
citadel · Feste *f*, Zitadelle *f*
~, **upper city** · Stadtkrone *f* [*Kernzelle einer Stadt mit den wichtigsten Monumentalbauten und in stark hervortretender Lage, z.B. Akropolis, Kapitol usw.*]
cité industrielle, manufacturing town, industrial quarter [*Planned by Tony Garnier*] · Industriestadt *f*
citizen's hall · Bürgerhaus *n*
citrated copper salt · zitronengesäuertes Kupfer *n*
city · Stadtkreis *m*
~ → business area
~ **(area)** → business ~
city-centre hotel (Brit.); **city-center** ~ (US) · Hotel *n* in Stadtmitte
City church · Pfarrkirche *f* [*in London*]
city hall (US); **town** ~ (Brit.) · Rathaus *n*

~ ~ **complex** (US); **town** ~ ~ (Brit.) · Rathauskomplex *m*
~ **road** → urban ~
(~) **street** → urban road
civic architecture, profane ~, **secular** ~, **nonecclesiastical** ~ · Profanbaukunst *f*, Profanarchitektur *f*, weltliche Architektur, weltliche Baukunst
~ **auditorium, festival hall, grand hall, banquet(ing) hall** · Festhalle *f*, Bananketthalle
~ **axis** · Stadtachse *f*
(~) **basilica, imperial** ~, **Roman** ~, **pagan** ~, **secular** ~ · (römische) (Zivil)Basilika *f*
~ **centre** (Brit.); ~ **center** (US); **social** ~ · Gemeinschaftszentrum *n*
~ **Gothic (style), profane** ~ (~), **secular** ~ (~), **nonecclesiastical** ~ (~) · Profangotik *f*, weltliche Gotik
~ **monument, profane** ~, **secular** ~, **nonecclesiastical** ~ · Profanmonument *n*
~ **structure, profane** ~, **secular** ~, **nonecclesiastical** ~, ~ **building** · Profanbau(werk) *m*, (*n*), Profangebäude *n*
~ **structures, profane** ~, **secular** ~, **nonecclesiastical** ~ · Profanbauten *f*, Profangebäude *npl*
civil defense (US); ~ **defence** (Brit.) · (ziviler) Bevölkerungsschutz *m*, Zivilschutz
~ ~ **against air raids** (US); ~ **defence** ~ ~ ~ (Brit.) · Luftschutz *m*
~ ~ **construction** (US); ~ **defence** ~ (Brit.) · baulicher Luftschutz *m*, bautechnischer Luftschutz, Schutzbau *m*
~ ~ **shelter** (US); ~ **defence** ~ (Brit.) · Schutzraumbau(werk) *m*, (*n*)
~ ~ ~ (US); ~ **defence** ~ (Brit.) · Zivilschutzraum *m*
~ ~ ~ **door** (US); ~ **defence** ~ ~ (Brit.) · Schutzraumtür *f*
~ ~ ~ **extract ventilation** (US); ~ **defence** ~ ~ ~ (Brit.) · Schutzraumentlüftung *f*
~ ~ ~ **inlet ventilation** (US); ~ **defence** ~ ~ ~ (Brit.) · Schutzraumbelüftung *f*
~ ~ ~ **ventilation** (US); ~ **defence** ~ (Brit.) · Schutzraumlüftung *f*, Schutzraumbe- und -entlüftung
~ ~ ~ **wall** (US); ~ **defence** ~ ~ (Brit.) · Schutzraumwand *f*
~ ~ ~ **window** (US); ~ **defence** ~ ~ (Brit.) · Schutzraumfenster *n*
~ ~ **structure** (US); ~ **defence** ~ (Brit.) · Schutzbau(werk) *m*, (*n*) [*baulicher Luftschutz*]
~ ~ **structures for radiation protection** (US); ~ **defence** ~ ~ ~ (Brit.) · Strahlungsschutzbauten *f*
~ **engineering material** · Ingenieurbaustoff *m*; Ingenieurbaumaterial *n* [*Schweiz*]

CJ, cooling jacket · Kühlmantel *m*
CL, cross-linked · kreuzgittervernetzt
cladded plate · plattiertes Blech *n* [*durch Aufwalzen hergestellt*]
~ steel plate · plattiertes Stahlblech *n* [*durch Aufwalzen hergestellt*]
~ strip · plattiertes Band *n* [*durch Aufwalzen hergestellt*]
cladding · Plattieren *n* durch Aufwalzen
~, lining, skin · (Außenwand)Versteifung *f*
~ element · (Außenwand)Versteifungselement *n*
~ material → lining ~
~ panel, lining ~ · (Außenwand)Versteifungstafel *f*
~ slab, lining ~ · (Außenwand)Versteifungsplatte *f*
clamp, cramp [*A strip steel fixed to a door frame or lining and built into a wall to fix the frame or lining*] · Bandstahlanker *m* für Zargen
~ → cramp (iron)
~ (Brit.); scove kiln (US) · Feld(brand)ofen *m*, Meiler *m* [*Ziegelherstellung*]
clamp-burnt brick, clamp-burned ~ (Brit.); scove kiln-burnt ~, scove kiln-burned ~ (US) · Feld(brand)ofenziegel *m*, Meilerziegel
clamp (iron), cramp (~) · Schlauder *f*, Bankeisen *n* [*Zur Verbindung der Futterrahmen von Türen oder Fenstern mit dem Mauerwerk*]
clamping · Verankerung *f* [*Mauerwerk*]
~ plate · Krallenband *n*
clapboard (US); weather-board · (waag(e)rechtes) Stülpschalungsbrett *n*
clare-obscure · Helldunkel *n*, Hellschatten *m*
clarity, definition · Klangreinheit *f*
CLASP school [*School built from prefabricated components under the Consortium of Local Authorities Special Programme set in up Britain in 1957*] · CLASP-Schule *f*
class A plaster (Brit.) → plaster of Paris
~ B (gypsum-)plaster → retarded hemihydrate ~
~ C (gypsum-)plaster, (gypsum-)plaster of Class C (Brit.); anhydrous (gypsum-)plaster [*B.S. 1191*] · Putzgips *m* [*DIN 1168*]
~ D (gypsum-)plasrer m Keene's cement
~ of girder · Trägergruppe *f*
~ ~ hardness, hardness class · Härteklasse *f*
~ ~ mortar · Mörtelgruppe *f*
classic [*A term applying to a work of art of the first class or rank, or an established standard and acknowledged excellence*] · klassig

~ construction method, conventional ~ ~, orthodox ~ ~ · herkömmliche Bauweise *f*
~ restraint, ~ severity · klassizistische Strenge *f*
Classic Revival · Klassizismus *m* der Goethezeit, Neuklassizismus, Neoklassizismus [*etwa 1770–1830*]
~ ~ form of decoration · klassizistische Dekorationsform *f*
classic severity, ~ restraint · klassizistische Strenge *f*
classical · klassisch
classical architecture · klassische Architektur *f*, ~ Baukunst *f*
~ Baroque · klassischer Barock *m*
classical building · klassisches Gebäude *n*
~ conception · klassische Konzeption *f*
~ form · klassische Form *f*
~ motif · klassisches Motiv *n*
~ order (of architecture) · klassische (Säulen)Ordnung *f*
~ purity · klassische Klarheit *f*
~ structure · klassisches Bauwerk *n*
~ temple · klassischer Tempel *m*
~ theory of architecture · klassische Baugesinnung *f*
classically symmetrical · klassizistisch-symmetrisch
classicism [*A style imitating, or inspired by, ancient Greece or Rome or by the classical trend in C16 Italy*] · Klassizismus *m*
classicizing · klassizistisch
classification · (Klassen)Einteilung *f*, Klassifizierung
~ characteristic · Klassifizierungseigenschaft *f*
~ of bricks · Ziegeleinteilung *f*
~ ~ flat roofs · Flachdacheinteilung
classified road network, ~ highway ~ · klassifiziertes Straßennetz *n*
classroom · Klassenraum *m*, Klassenzimmer *n*
~ block → ~ building
~ building, ~ block · Klassen(zimmer)gebäude *n*, Klassenraumgebäude
~ door · Klassen(zimmer)tür *f*, Klassenraumtür
~ hut · Klassen(raum)baracke *f*, Klassenzimmerbaracke
~ unit · Klassenraumtrakt *m*, Klassen(zimmer)trakt
clastic eruptive rock · klastisches Eruptivgestein *n*
~ (lime) tuff, detrital (~) ~ · klastischer Kalktuff *m*
~ rock · klastisches Gestein *n*
~ (sedimentary) rock, mechanically deposited (~) ~ · Bruchstückgestein *n*, Trümmergestein, mechanisches Sediment(gestein) *n*, klastisches Sediment(gestein), Trümmersediment(gestein)

clastic tuff — (clay) brick footing

~ **tuff** → ~ lime ~

clauster, (monastic) cell · Klausur f, Klause f, (Mönchs)Zelle f

claw plate, bulldog ~, ~ connector; ~ connecter (US) · Bulldogplatte f, Bulldogdübel m, Bulldog(-Holz)verbinder m [*Markenbezeichnungen für Einpreßdübel*]; Krallenplatte f, einseitiger Krallendübel m

clay, raw ~ · (Roh)Ton m [< 0,002 mm]

~ **aggregate concrete** · Tonsplittbeton m [*Leichtbeton aus ungeformtem Ton oder Ziegelbruch und Zement*]

~ **article** → (burnt) clay product

~ **ball** · Tonkügelchen n

~ **block** → quarry (tile)

(~) **body**, stone ~ · (Ton)Scherben m, gebrannter Scherben

(~) ~ **crushing strength**, stone ~ ~ · Scherbendruckfestigkeit f

clay-bound · tongebunden

(**clay**) **brick** → burnt (~) ~

(~) ~ **aggregate** · Ziegelzuschlag(stoff) m

(~) ~ ~ **concrete** · Ziegelbeton m [*Leichtbeton aus Ziegelbruch und Zement*]

(~) ~ ~ ~ **block**, (~) ~ ~ ~ tile [*See remark under 'Block'*] · Ziegelbetonblock(stein) m, Ziegelbetonstein [*DIN 4161*]

(~) ~ ~ ~ **tile**, (~) ~ ~ ~ block [*See remark* [*under 'Block'*] · Ziegelbetonblock(stein) m, Ziegelbetonstein [*DIN 4161*]

(~) ~ **architecture** · Backsteinarchitektur f, Backsteinbaukunst f, Ziegelarchitektur, Ziegelbaukunst

(~) ~ **barrel vault**, (~) ~ tunnel ~, (~) ~ wagon ~ · Ziegeltonne(ngewölbe) f, (n)

(~) ~ **beam** · Ziegelbalken(träger) m [*Lochziegel, zu Balken werkmäßig mit Mörtel verbunden*]

(~) ~ **block**, (~) ~ building · Ziegelgebäude n, Ziegelhaus n

(~) **brickblock** [*A brickblock has a patterned face to simulate bonded brickwork*] · Ziegelblock m

(~) **brick bond** → (~) ~ masonry ~

(~) ~ **bonder** → (~) ~ header

(~) ~ **bonding header** → (~) ~ header

(~) ~ **bondstone** → (~) ~ header

(~) ~ **boundary wall** · Ziegel-Grundstücksmauer f

(~) ~ **building**, (~) ~ block · Ziegelgebäude n, Ziegelhaus n

(~) ~ **-built garage** · Ziegelgarage f

(~) **brick burning** · Ziegelbrennen n, Ziegelbrand m

(~) ~ **carcase** [*deprecated*]; (~) ~ shell [*Canada*]; (~) ~ carcass, (~) ~ fabric [*A (clay) brick building or structure that is structurally complete but otherwise unfinished*] · Ziegelrohbau m

(~) ~ **cathedral**, (~) ~ dome · Ziegelkathedrale f, Ziegeldom m, Backsteindom, Backsteinkathedrale

(~) ~ **cavity wall**, (~) ~ hollow ~ · Ziegelhohlmauer f

(~) ~ **church** · Backsteinkirche f, Ziegelkirche

(~) ~ **construction** · Backsteinbau m, Ziegelbau

(~) ~ **corbel** · Ziegel(ge)sims m, (n)

(~) ~ **course** · Ziegellage f, Ziegelschicht f

(~) ~ **cradle vault** · zylindrisches Ziegelgewölbe n, walzenförmiges ~

(~) ~ **cross-wall** · Ziegelquerwand f

(~) ~ **cupola**, (~) ~ dome · Ziegelkuppel f

(~) ~ **dimension** · Ziegelabmessung f, Ziegelmaß n

(~) ~ **dome**, (~) ~ cathedral · Backsteindom m, Backsteinkathedrale f, Ziegeldom, Ziegelkathedrale

(~) ~ ~, (~) ~ cupola · Ziegelkuppel f

(~) ~ **dwelling** (US); residential (clay) brick building, domestic (clay) brick building, residence (clay) brick building, residential (clay) brick block, domestic (clay) brick block, residence (clay) brick block · Ziegel-Wohnhaus n, Ziegel-Wohngebäude n

(~) ~ **dust**, (~) ~ flour, ground (clay) brick(s) · Ziegelmehl n, Ziegelstaub m

(~) ~ **engineering** · Ziegeltechnik f

(~) ~ **exterior wall**, (~) ~ external ~ · Ziegelumfassungsmauer f, Ziegelaußenmauer

(~) ~ **external wall**, (~) ~ exterior ~ · Ziegelumfassungsmauer f, Ziegelaußenmauer

(~) ~ **fabric**, (~) ~ carcass; (~) ~ shell [*Canada*]; (~) ~ carcase [*deprecated*] [*A (clay) brick building or structure that is structurally complete but otherwise unfinished*] · Ziegelrohbau m

(~) ~ **façade** · Ziegelfassade f

(~) ~ ~ **panel**, façade (clay) brick ~ · Fassadentafel f aus Ziegeln, Ziegelfassadentafel [*Fehlnamen: (vorgefertigte) Ziegelfassadenplatte f*]

(~) ~ **facing**, (~) ~ sur~, (~) ~ lining · Ziegelauskleidung f, Ziegelverkleidung, Ziegelbekleidung

~ ~ **fireplace** → ~ brickwork ~

(~) ~ **floor** · Decke f aus (gebrannten) Steinen, Ziegeldecke

~ ~ ~ → ~ ~ flooring finish

(~) ~ ~ **cover(ing)**, (~) ~ floor(ing) (finish) · Ziegel(fuß)boden(belag) m

(~) ~ **floor(ing)** (**finish**), (~) ~ floor cover(ing) · Ziegel(fuß)boden(belag) m

(~) ~ **flour**, (~) ~ dust, ground (clay) brick(s) · Ziegelmehl n, Ziegelstaub m

(~) ~ **footing** · Ziegelfundament n

(~) ~ format · Ziegelformat n

(~) ~ foundation · Ziegelgründung f

(~) ~ grille [*sometimes spelled 'grill'*] · Ziegelgitter n

(~) ~ hardcore · Ziegelschotter m, Ziegelbruch m, Kleinschlag m aus Ziegelbrocken

(~) ~ ~ concrete · Ziegelbruchbeton m, Ziegelschotterbeton

(~) ~ header, (~) ~ bonder, (~) ~ bondstone, (~) ~ bonding header, header (clay) brick · Ziegelbinder(stein) m, Ziegelstrecker

(~) ~ hollow wall, (~) ~ cavity ~ · Ziegelhohlmauer f

(~) ~ infill masonry (work) · Ziegelausmauerung f

(~) ~ joint · Ziegelmauerwerkfuge f

(~) ~ kiln · Ziegelofen m, Ziegelbrennofen

(~) ~ laying, laying (clay) bricks, bricking · Mauern n mit Ziegeln, Vermauern von ~, Ziegelmauern

(~) ~ laying, (~) ~ setting, laying (clay) bricks, setting (clay) bricks, bricking · Mauern n mit Ziegeln, Vermauern von ~, Ziegelmauern

(~) ~ light(weight) vault · Ziegelleichtgewölbe n

(~) brick-lined concrete slab · Ziegelbetonplatte f [*mit Ziegeln verblendete Betonplatte*]

(~) brick lining, (~) ~ (sur)facing · Ziegelauskleidung f, Ziegelverkleidung, Ziegelbekleidung

(~) ~ lintel; (~) ~ lintol [*deprecated*] · Ziegeloberschwelle f, Ziegelsturz m

(~) ~ (masonry) bond, (~) brickwork ~ · Ziegel(mauer)verband m, Ziegelmauerverband, Ziegel(mauerwerk)gefüge n, Ziegelmauergefüge

(~) ~ ~ (work), (~) brickwork · Ziegelmauerwerk n

(~) ~ mastaba · Ziegelmastaba f

~ ~ mortar → ~ brickwork ~

(~) brick-on-edge course, ro(w)lock, (Ziegel)Rollschar f, (Ziegel)Rollschicht f

(~) brick pack, pre-packed (clay) bricks, pack of (clay) bricks · Ziegelpaket n

(~) ~ panel (building) unit · Ziegelwandbaueinheit f [*Fehlname*]; Ziegelwand(bau)element n, Ziegelwand(bau)körper m

(~) ~ partition (wall) · Ziegelwand f [*Leichte Trennwand. DIN 4103*]

(~) ~ pattern · Ziegelmauermuster n, Ziegelmauerwerkmuster

(~) ~ paving · Ziegelpflaster n, Fpz f

(~) ~ pier · Ziegelmauerwerkpfeiler m

(~) ~ plinth · Ziegelplinthe f

(~) ~ reinforcement fabric · Ziegelmauerwerk-Bewehrungsmatte f

(~) ~ rib · Backsteinrippe f, Ziegelrippe

(~) ~ rubble · Ziegelschutt m, Ziegeltrümmer f

(~) ~ setting, (~) ~ laying, setting (clay) bricks, laying (~) bricks, bricking · Ziegelmauern n, Mauern mit Ziegeln, Vermauern von Ziegeln

(~) ~ shaft [*chimney*] · Ziegelschaft m [*Schornstein*]

(~) ~ shape · Ziegelform f, Ziegelgestalt f

(~) ~ shell [*Canada*]; (~) ~ carcase [*deprecated*]; (~) ~ carcass, (~) ~ fabric · [*A (clay) brick building or structure that is structurally complete but otherwise unfinished*] · Ziegelrohbau m

(~) ~ skin · Ziegelvorsatzschicht f

(~) ~ stair(case) · Ziegeltreppe f

(~) ~ step · Ziegelstufe f

(~) ~ strength · Ziegelfestigkeit f

(~) ~ structure · Ziegelbau(werk) m, (n)

(~) ~ structures · Ziegelbauten f

(~) ~ (sur)facing, (~) ~ lining · Ziegelverkleidung f, Ziegelauskleidung, Ziegelbekleidung

(~) ~ tester, (~) ~ testing machine · Ziegel-Prüfmaschine f

(~) ~ testing machine, (~) ~ tester · Ziegel-Prüfmaschine f

(~) ~ tracery · Ziegelmaßwerk n

(~) ~ tunnel vault, (~) ~ barrel ~, (~) ~ wagon ~ · Ziegeltonne(nge)wölbe f, (n)

(~) ~ type, type of (clay) brick · Ziegelart f

(~) ~ vault · gekurvte Ziegeldecke f, Ziegelgewölbe n, Gewölbe aus Ziegelmauerwerk

(~) ~ veneer, brick facing skin [*A facing of brick laid against frame or tile wall construction*] · Ziegelverblendmauerwerk n, Ziegelverblendung f, Ziegelvorhangwand f

(~) ~ wagon vault, (~) ~ barrel ~, (~) ~ tunnel ~ · Ziegeltonne(nge)wölbe f, (n)

(~) ~ wall · Ziegelmauer f [*Fehlnamen: (gemauerte) Ziegelwand f*]

(~) ~ ~ arch · Ziegelmauerbogen m

(~) ~ weight · Ziegelgewicht n

(~) ~ wheel window · Ziegelradfenster n [*Ziegelrundfenster mit speichenartiger Unterteilung*]

(~) ~ with vertical coring type A · HLzA m, Hochlochziegel m (mit der Lochung) A

(~) ~ ~ ~ ~ ~ B · HLzB m, Hochlochziegel m (mit der Lochung) B

(~) brickwork, (~) brick masonry (work) · Ziegelmauerwerk n

(~) ~ bond, (~) brick (masonry) ~ · Ziegel(mauerwerk)verband m, Ziegelmauerverband, Ziegel(mauerwerk)gefüge n, Ziegelmauergefüge

(clay) brickwork fireplace — clay member

(~) ~ fireplace · Ziegel(mauerwerk)kamin *m*

(~) ~ mortar, mortar for (clay) brickwork · Ziegel(mauerwerk)mörtel *m*

(~) ~ reinforcement · Ziegel(mauerwerk)armierung *f*, Ziegelmauerwerkbewehrung, Ziegelmauerwerk(stahl)einlagen *fpl*

(~) ~ system building, prefab(ricated) (clay) brickwork construction · Ziegelmontagebau *m*, Ziegelfertigteilbau, Bauen *n* mit Ziegelfertigteilen

~ bubble · Tonhohlkügelchen *n*, Tonhohlkugel *f*

~ building brick [As opposed to a clay engineering brick] → (burnt) (clay) ~

~ (~) component → ceramic (building) unit

~ ~ material → ceramic construction(al) ~

~ (~) member → ceramic (building) unit

~ (~) unit → ceramic (~) ~

~ burning · Tonbrennen *n*

~ ~ curve · Tonbrennkurve *f*

~ ceiling tile, ceramic ~ ~ · Keramikdecken(belag)platte *f*, Keramikdeckenfliese, Tondecken(belag)platte, Tondeckenfliese, keramische Decken(belag)platte, keramische Deckenfliese

clay-cement · Tonzement *m*

~ grout · Ton-Zement-Schlämme *f*, Zement-Ton-Schlämme

clay chimney pot, (chimney) clay ~ · gebranntes Schornsteinformstück *n*

~ chip(ping)s · Tonsplitt *m*

~ coat, ~ coating, ~ film · Tonhäutchen *n*, Tonüberzug *m*

clay-coated finish · Beguß *m* [Weißer oder farbiger Überzug zur Verschönerung keramischer Erzeugnisse; er wird durch Gießen auf den lederharten oder formfeuchten Rohling aufgebracht]

clay coat(ing), ~ film · Tonhäutchen *n*, Tonüberzug *m*

~ component → ceramic (building) unit

~ concrete, clay-stabilized sand · Tonbeton *m* [Straßenbau]

~ construction(al) material → ceramic ~ ~

~ content, ~ fraction · Tonanteil *m*, Tonfraktion *f*, Tongehalt *m*, Tonkomponente *f*

~ cross → ~ pellet

~ cupola, ~ dome · Tonkuppel *f*

~ curved roof(ing) tile → burnt ~ ~ ~

~ ~ tile roof → burnt ~ ~ ~, ~

~ dome, ~ cupola · Tonkuppel *f*

~ dormer-ventilator · Lüftergaube *f*, Lüftergaupe, Lüftungsgaube, Lüftungsgaupe, (Dach)Gaupe, (Dach)Gaube, (Dach)Lüfter *m*, (Dach)Lüftungsziegel *m*, Gaupenziegel, Gaubenziegel, Kaffziegel, Lukenziegel, Haubenziegel, Kappziegel [Dachziegel, zu Flach-, Hohl- oder Falzziegeln passend, mit einem meist halbkegelförmigen Aufbau zum Einlaß von Licht und Luft in einen Dachraum]

~ ~ opening · Kaffenster *n*, Kappfenster [Dachluke, die von einem Kaffziegel mit halbkreisförmiger Öffnung überdeckt wird]

~ emulsion · Tonemulsion *f*

(~) ~ engineering brick [B.S. 1301] → clinker

~ filler · gebrannter (Decken)Füllkörper *m*

(~) ~ brick, ~ ~ tile · (Decken)Füllziegel *m*, Füll-Deckenziegel

~ ~ tile, (~) ~ brick · Füll-Deckenziegel *m*, (Decken)Füllziegel

~ film, ~ coat(ing) · Tonhäutchen *n*, Tonüberzug *m*

~ flap tile · Blattziegel *m*, Breitziegel, Krampziegel, Krempziegel, Kremper *m* [Auf Stempelpresse hergestellter Dachziegel. Er besteht aus einer Platte, an deren linker Seite eine konische Krempe ist]

~ ~ ~ roof cladding, ~ ~ ~ covering, ~ ~ ~ sheathing, ~ ~ ~ roofing · Krempziegel(dach)(ein)deckung *f*, Blattziegel(dach)(ein)deckung, Breitziegel(dach)(ein)deckung, Krampziegel(dach)(ein)deckung, Kremper(dach)(ein)deckung, Krempziegeldach(belag) *n*, (*m*), Blattziegeldach(belag), Breitziegeldach(belag), Krampziegeldach(belag), Kremperdach(belag), Krempziegelbedachung, Blattziegelbedachung, Breitziegelbedachung, Krampziegelbedachung, Kremperbedachung

~ floor cover(ing) tile, ~ floor(ing) (finish) ~ · Ton-(Fuß)Boden(belag)platte *f*, Ton-(Fuß)Bodenfliese *f*

~ floor(ing) (finish) tile, ~ floor cover(ing) ~ · Ton-(Fuß)Boden(belag)platte *f*, Ton-(Fuß)Bodenfliese *f*

~ ~ tile → ceramic ~ ~

~ ~ ~ for animal shelters → (floor-ing) quarry (~) ~ ~ ~

~ fraction, ~ content · Tonanteil *m*, Tonfraktion *f*, Tongehalt *m*, Tonkomponente *f*

~ grain · Tonkorn *n*

~ hip tile → burnt ~ ~ ~

~ key → ~ pellet

~ lath(ing) → ~ pellet ~

~ lay-in panel, ceramic ~ ~ · Keramikeinlegetafel *f*, keramische Einlegetafel

~ lump · Tonklumpen *m*

~ marl · Tonmergel *m*

~ masonry (work), burnt ~ ~ (~), burned ~ ~ (~) · Mauerwerk *n* aus gebrannten Steinen

~ member → ceramic (building) unit

clay mineral — clay tile line

~ **mineral**, layer silicate · Tonmineral *n*, Schichtsilikat *n* [*Dieses Mineral – charakteristischer Bestandteil des Tones – ist hydratisiertes Alumosilikat, das geringe Mengen an Mg, Fe, K etc. eingebaut hat. Durch Mischen mit Wasser entsteht eine mehr oder minder plastische Masse, die beim Trocknen oder Brennen erhärtet*]

~ **mortar** · Tonmörtel *m*

~ **pantile** · Pfannenziegel *m*, S-~, Hohl~, Dach~, holländischer ~ [*DIN 52250*]

~ ~ **roof cladding**, ~ ~ ~ covering, ~ ~ ~ sheathing, ~ ~ roof(ing) · (Hohl)Pfannenziegel(dach)(ein)deckung *f*, (Hohl)Pfannenziegeldach(belag) *n*, (*m*), (Hohl)Pfannenziegelbedachung

~ **pellet** · Tonpellet *n*

~ ~, ~ cross, ~ key · Lehmkörperchen *n*, Lehmstückchen, Lehmkreuzchen [*Fehlnamen*]; Tonkörperchen, Tonstückchen, Tonkreuzchen [*Staußziegelgewebe*]

~ (~) **lath(ing)** [*B.S. 2705*] · Rollengewebe *n*, Drahtziegelgewebe, Ziegel(draht)gewebe, Tondrahtgewebe, Ziegelputzträger *m* [*Auf jeden Kreuzungspunkt des Gewebes ist ein Tonkörperchen gepreßt. Die Saugfähigkeit der Tonkörperchen gewährleistet ein gutes Haften des Putzmörtels*]

~ **pipe**, CP; (drain) tile, DT (US) · Tonrohr *n*

~ ~ **drainage**; tile ~ (US) · Tonrohrdränage *f*

~ ~ **line** (Brit.) → (drain) tile ~

~ **pit** · Tongrube *f*

~ **plain roof(ing) tile**, ~ plane ~ ~ [*B.S. 402*] · Biber(schwanz)ziegel *m* [*DIN 454*]

~ **plane roof(ing) tile**, ~ plain ~ ~ [*B.S. 402*] · Biber(schwanz)ziegel *m*

~ **plant** · Blähtonwerk *n*

~ **pot**, chimney ~ ~, clay chimney · gebrannter Schornsteinformstück *n*

~ ~ **floor**, hollow clay (building) block ~ · Tonhohl(stein)plattendecke *f*, Ziegelhohlplattendecke, Hohlnutensteindecke, H(o)urdidecke

~ ~ **for tiled roofs** → hollow clay (building) block ~ ~ ~

~ ~ **with keyed underside** → hollow clay (building) block ~ ~ ~

~ **powder**, powder(ed) clay, finely ground fire clay · Tonmehl *n*

~ **product** → burnt ~ ~

(~) **puddle** · Lehmschlag *m*, Tonschlag, Puddle *m*

~ **ridge tile** → burnt ~ ~ ~

~ **rock**, argillaceous ~ · Tongestein *n*

~ **roof(ing) tile**, roof(ing) clay ~ · Dachziegel *m*, Tondachstein *m* [*DIN 456*]

~ ~ ~ **factory**, roof(ing) clay ~ ~ · Dachziegelei *f*, Dachziegelfabrik *f*, Dachziegelwerk *n*

clay-sand-gravel mix(ture) · Ton-Sand-Kies-Gemisch *n*, Ton-Sand-Kies-Mischung *f*

clay **shower tray**, ceramic ~ ~ · Keramik-Duschtasse *f*, Keramik-Duschwanne *f* [*DIN 4486*]

~ **single-lap (roof(ing)) tile** · Einfalz(dach)ziegel *m*

~ **sintering process** · Tonsinterverfahren *n*

(~) **slate**, argillaceous ~ [*A rock derived from argillaceous sediments or fine-grained volcanic ashes by metamorphism and characterized by cleavage along planes independent of the original bedding*] · Tonschiefer *m*

~ **slip** · Tonbrei *m* [*Keramik*]

(~) ~ **tile** [*(Clay) slip tiles, grooved like the blocks, can be laid between the blocks to cover the soffit of the ribs and give a uniform key for plaster. They also increase the fire resistance of the floor*] · Rippendeckplättchen *n*, Rippenhohlkörper *m*, Rippendeckplatte *f*

~ **slurry** · Tonschlämme *f*

~ **spray shower tray**, ceramic ~ ~ ~ · Keramik-Brausetasse *f*, Keramik-Brausewanne *f* [*DIN 4486*]

clay-stabilized sand, clay concrete · Tonbeton *m* [*Straßenbau*]

clay **structural material** → ceramic construction(al) ~

~ **surface** · Tonoberfläche *f*

~ **suspension** · Tonsuspension *f*

~ **tablet** · Tontafel *f*

~ **tempering** · Tonanfeuchtung *f*, Tonbefeuchtung [*Ziegelindustrie*]

~ **tile**, ceramic ~ · Keramik(belag)platte *f*, Keramikfliese, keramische Fliese, keramische (Belag)Platte, Ton(belag)platte, Tonfliese

~ ~, quarry (~), clay block [*Burnt clay, flooring or wall-facing tile of black, buff, or red colour. They are from 9 × 9 to 4 × 4 in. in size, unglazed, but not porous*] · gebrannter Block(stein) *m*, ~ Stein

~ ~ [*Roof tile made from clay*] · Tondachstein *m*

~ ~ **adhesive** → ceramic tile (bonding) ~

~ ~ **(bonding) adhesive** → ceramic ~ (~) ~

~ ~ ~ **agent** → ceramic tile (bonding) adhesive

~ ~ ~ **medium** → ceramic tile (bonding) adhesive

~ ~ **cement(ing agent)** → ceramic tile (bonding) adhesive

~ ~ **floor cover(ing)**, ~ ~ floor(ing) (finish) · Fbt, Tonplatten(fuß)boden(belag) *m*

~ ~ **floor(ing) (finish)**, ~ ~ floor cover(ing) · Fbt, Tonplatten(fuß)boden(belag) *m*

~ ~ **line** → (drain) ~ ~

clay tile valley — cleanout plate

~ **tile valley** · Ziegelkehle f [*Dach*]

~ **tile(d) roof cladding,** ~~~~ sheathing, ~ ~ ~ cover(ing), ~ ~ roofing · Ziegel(dach)(ein)deckung f, Ziegelbedachung, Dachziegel(ein)deckung [*Fehlname: Ziegeldach n*]

~ **unit** → ceramic (building) ~

~ **vent pipe** · Ton-Entlüftungsrohr n

~ **visible under-face** → all ~ ~ ~

~ **wall tile,** ceramic ~ ~ · Keramik-Wand(belag)platte f, Keramik-Wandfliese f, Wand-Keramikfliese, Wand-Keramik(belag)platte, keramische Wandfliese, keramische Wand(belag)platte, Ton-Wandfliese, Ton-Wand(belag)platte, Wand(belag)-Tonplatte, Wand(belag)-Tonfliese

clay-water relationship · Ton-Wasser-Beziehung f

clay window cill, ceramic ~ ~ (Brit.); ~ ~ ~ sill · Keramikfensterbank f, keramische Fensterbank

~ ~ **sill,** ceramic ~ ~ ~; ~ ~ ~ cill (Brit.) · Keramikfensterbank f, keramische Fensterbank

clayey, argillaceous · ton(halt)ig

~ **gypsum,** argillaceous ~ · Tongips m

~ **limestone,** argillaceous ~, argillo-calcite · ton(halt)iger Kalk(stein) m, Tonkalk(stein)

~ **sand,** argillaceous ~ · ton(halt)iger Sand m, Tonsand

~ **sandstone,** argillaceous ~ · Tonsandstein m

clayware · Tonwaren f

clean air, purified ~ · Gutluft f, Reinluft

~ **bright drawn wire** · hellblank gezogener Draht m

cleaner, clean(s)ing agent · Reiniger m, Reinigungsmittel n, Reinigungsstoff m

~ **for cast and natural stone,** cleaning agent ~ ~ ~ ~ ~ · Steinreinigungsmittel n, Steinreiniger m [*Zur Reinigung von Natur- und Betonwerkstein*]

cleaning → cleansing

~, **window,** window washing · (Fenster)Putzen n, (Fenster)Reinigung f

~ **agent** → cleansing ~

~ ~ **for cast and natural stone,** cleaner ~ ~ ~ ~ ~ ~ · Steinreinigungsmittel n, Steinreiniger m [*Zur Reinigung von Natur- und Betonwerkstein*]

~ **and care** · Reinigung f und Pflege f

~ **balcony,** window ~ ~ ~ · (Fenster-)Reinigungsbalkon m

~ **chamber,** cleanout ~, rodding ~, inspection ~, access ~, ~ pit [*A chamber constructed over a subsidiary sewer or drain of not more than 9 in. diameter to permit inspection and access for rodding*] · (Reinigungs- und) Revisionsschacht m, Reinigungsschacht, Putzschacht

~ **cover,** ~ plate, cleanout ~, rodding ~, access ~, inspection ~ · Reinigungsdeckel m, Putzdeckel

~ **cradle,** cradle machine, window ~ ~, wall lift, roof cradle [*Motorized carriage running vertically on rails let into the window frames*] · (Fenster)Putzwagen m, (Fenster)Reinigungswagen

~ **emulsion** → cleansing ~

~ **equipment,** window-~ ~, window-washing ~ · (Fenster)Reinigungsgerät n, (Fenster)Putzgerät

~ **(~) closet,** closet for cleaning equipment · Reinigungsgeräte-Einbauschrank m, Reinigungsgeräte-Wandschrank

~ ~ **room,** household ~ ~ ~, (household) store ~ · Abstellraum m, Putzraum, (Haus)Geräteraum

~ **eye,** ~ opening, cleanout ~, rodding ~, access ~, inspection ~ · Putzöffnung f, Reinigungsöffnung

~ **machine for bottom sockets** · Untermuffen-Reinigungsmaschine f

~ **opening,** ~ eye, cleanout ~, rodding ~, access ~, inspection ~ · Putzöffnung f, Reinigungsöffnung

~ **paste** → cleansing ~

~ **pit** → ~ chamber

~ **plate,** ~ cover, cleanout ~, rodding ~, access ~, inspection ~ · Reinigungsdeckel m, Putzdeckel

~ **plug,** ~ screw, rodding ~, cleanout ~, access ~, inspection ~ · Putzstopfen m, Reinigungsstopfen, Putzschraube f, Reinigungsschraube

~ **powder** → cleansing ~

~ **screw,** ~ plug, rodding ~, cleanout ~, access ~, inspection ~ · Putzstopfen m, Reinigungsstopfen, Putzschraube f Reinigungsschraube

~ **solution** → cleansing ~

~ **tube** → inspection ~

cleanout chamber → cleaning ~

~ **cover,** ~ plate, cleaning ~, rodding ~, access ~, inspection ~ · Reinigungsdeckel m, Putzdeckel

~ **door,** ash(pit), COD (US); soot door [*B.S. 1294*] · Kamintür f, Reinigungstür, Putztür, Schornsteinreinigungsverschluß m, Aschentür, Entaschungstür, Rußtür

~ **eye,** ~ opening, cleaning ~, rodding ~, access ~, inspection ~ · Putzöffnung f, Reinigungsöffnung

~ **fitting,** rodding ~, inspection ~ · Putzformstück n, Reinigungsformstück

~ **opening,** ~ eye, cleaning ~, rodding ~, access ~, inspection ~ · Putzöffnung f, Reinigungsöffnung

~ **pit** → cleaning chamber

~ **plate,** ~ cover, cleaning ~, rodding ~, access ~, inspection ~ · Reinigungsdeckel m, Putzdeckel

cleanout plug — clearcole

~ **plug**, ~ screw, rodding ~, cleaning ~, access ~, inspection ~ · Putzstopfen m Reinigungsstopfen, Putzschraube f, Reinigungsschraube

~ **screw,** ~ plug, rodding ~, cleaning ~, access ~, inspection ~ · Putzstopfen m, Reinigungsstopfen, Putzschraube f, Reinigungsschraube

~ **tube** → inspection ~

clean(s)er for masonry, masonry clean(s)er · Mauerwerkreinigungsmittel n, Mauerwerkreiniger m, Mauerwerkreinigungsstoff m

clean(s)ing · Reinigung f

~ **agent,** cleaner · Reiniger m, Reinigungsmittel n, Reinigungsstoff m

~ **emulsion** · Reinigungsemulsion f

~ **paste** · Reinigungspaste f

~ **powder,** powder(ed) clean(s)ing agent, powder(ed) cleaner · Pulverreiniger m, Reinigungspulver n

~ **solution** · Reinigungslösung f

clean-up, equipment ~ · Reinigen n (der Arbeitsgeräte)

clear; colourless (Brit.); colorless (US) · farblos, klar (durchsichtig) [*Glas*]

~, transparent; colorless, uncolored (US); colourless, uncoloured (Brit.) · farblos

~, column-free, column-less, support-free, support-less · stützenfrei, stützenlos

~ **amber** · Klarbernstein m

~ **arch span,** ~ span of arch · Bogenlichtweite f, Bogen(spann)weite, lichte Bogenweite

~ **coat** · Klaranstrich m, Klaraufstrich

~ **cross section** · lichter Querschnitt m

clear-cut rectilinear architecture · kristallisch geschnittene Architektur f des rechten Winkels

clear dimension, inner ~, inside ~, internal ~, interior ~ · Innenabmessung f, Innenmaß n, lichte Abmessung, lichtes Maß, Lichtmaß

to clear down · abtragen [*Bauwerk*]

clear etching, bright ~ · Hellätzen n, Klarätzen, Blankätzen [*Ein Glasätzverfahren, bei dem mit verhältnismäßig schwacher Flußsäure und Grobkorn mattiert wird*]

~ ~ **bath,** bright ~ ~ · Hellbad n [*Glasätzen*]

~ **glass,** transparent ~ · durchsichtiges Glas n, Klarglas

~ **plate glass of selected glazing quality 8 to 40 mm thick** · Dickkristall n für mittlere Ansprüche [*Kristallspiegelglas von 8 bis 40 mm Dicke*]

~ ~ ~ ~ **silvering quality 8 to 40 mm thick** · Dickkristall n für hohe Ansprüche [*Kristallspiegelglas von 8 bis 40 mm Dicke*]

~ **rib interval,** ~ ~ spacing · lichter Rippenabstand m

~ ~ **spacing,** ~ ~ interval · lichter Rippenabstand m

~ **sheet glass,** ~ window ~ · Fensterklarglas n, Klarfensterglas

~ **span of arch,** ~ arch span · Bogenlichtweite f, Bogen(spann)weite, lichte Bogenweite

~ **(through-)vision,** unobstructed ~ · ungehinderte Durchsicht f, vollständige ~ [*Glas*]

(~) varnish, natural finish [*A liquid coating material, containing no pigment, which flows out to a smooth coat when applied and dries to a smooth, glossy, relatively hard, permanent solid when exposed in a thin film to the air. Some materials possessing the other characteristics dry without the usual gloss and are termed 'flat varnish'. B.S. 256*] · (fabloser) Lack m, Klarlack [*Lacktechniker verstehen unter der Bezeichnung „Lack" nur den Klarlack. Ein pigmentierter Klarlack wird als Lackfarbe, verschiedentlich auch als Lackemaille, bezeichnet*]

(~) ~ for building construction purposes · Bautenlack m [*Fehlname: Malerlack*]

(~) ~ medium, (~) ~ vehicle · (Klar-)Lack-Bindemittellösung f

(~) ~ system · (Klar)Lacksystem n

(~) ~ vehicle, (~) ~ medium · (Klar-)Lack-Bindemittellösung f

~ **vision,** through-~, unobstructed (through-)vision · ungehinderte Durchsicht f, vollständige ~ [*Glas*]

clear-water basin · Reinwasserbehälter m

clear window glass, ~ sheet ~ · Fensterklarglas n, Klarfensterglas

~ **wire glass,** CL W GL · Drahtklarglas n, Klardrahtglas

clearance · Abbruch m, Abreißen n, Abriß m [*Stadtgebiet*]

~ · Abräumung f, Baureifmachung [*Sie gehört nach DIN 276 A 1. 32 zum Herrichten eines Baugrundstücks. Der Begriff der Abräumung eines Grundstücks muß nach dem Sprachgebrauch bestimmt werden. Es ist die Beseitigung aller lose oder leicht abräumbarer mit dem Grundstück verbundenen Teile im Sinne einer Baureifmachung desselben*]

~, clearage · Lichtraum m, lichter Raum

~ **area,** ~ zone, ~ site · Abbruchgebiet n, Abreißgebiet, Abrißgebiet

~ **order** · Abrißerlaß m, Abbrucherlaß [*Stadtgebiet*]

~ **site,** ~ area, ~ zone · Abbruchgebiet n, Abreißgebiet, Abrißgebiet

~ **slum area** → slum clearance ~

~ ~ **site** → slum clearance area

~ ~ **zone** → slum clearance area

~ **zone,** ~ site, ~ area · Abbruchgebiet n, Abreißgebiet, Abrißgebiet

clearcole, clairecolle [*Glue size in appropriate dilution with the addition of a small quantity of whiting. It is used to reduce the porosity of ceilings and other surfaces prior to the application of size-bound distemper*] · (Ab)Decklack m

cleared area — clinkstone

cleared area, ~ zone, ~ site, site cleared of buildings, zone cleared of buildings, area cleared of buildings · abgebrochenes (Stadt)Gebiet *n*, abgerissenes ~

~ site → ~ area

~ slum area, ~ ~ site, ~ ~ zone, slumcleared ~ · abgebrochenes Elendsviertel *n*, abgerissenes ~

~ zone → ~ area

clearing · Freilegung *f* [*Bauwerk*]

clearly defined massing · klar begrenzter Baukörper *m*, ~ ~ Raumkörper

clearstor(e)y → clerestor(e)y

~ window, clerestor(e)y ~, overstory ~, high-light ~ · Ober(gaden)fenster *n*, (Licht)Gadenfenster, Hochschiffenster

to cleat · haften, mit Haftern befestigen [*Metallbedachung*]

cleat → angle ~

~, soldered (metal) ~ · (Löt)Hafter *m* [*Metallbedachung*]

~, metal ~ · Hafter *m*

~ locked into the seam, metal ~ ~ ~ ~ ~ · Falzhafter *m* [*Metallbedachung*]

cleaved glass · gespaltenes Glas *n*

clench nail, clinch ~ · Stauchnagel *m*

clepsydra [*Water clock used by the ancient Greeks, which measures time by the discharge of water*] · Wasseruhr *f*

clerestor(e)y → over-story

~ window → clerestor(e)y ~

clevis [*The forked end of a rod used in steel connections*] · Gabelkopf *m*

CLG → ceiling

cliff brick, bing ~, blaes ~, shale (clay) ~ [*B.S. 3921*] · Schiefertonziegel *m*

cliffstone Paris white · Dover-Schlämmkreide *f*

climatic fluctuation, ~ variation · Klimaänderung *f*

~ variation, ~ fluctuation · Klimaänderung *f*

climbing aperture · Deckenausschnitt *m* [*Kletterkran*]

~ forms, ~ form(work), ~ shuttering · Kletterschalung *f*

~ form(work), ~ forms, ~ shuttering · Kletterschalung *f*

~ shuttering, ~ forms, ~ form(work) · Kletterschalung *f*

clinch nail, clench ~ · Stauchnagel *m*

clincher-built (wood(en)) ceiling, ~ timber ~ · gestülpte Holzdecke *f*, Stülpdecke

clinic · Klinik *f*

clinker, cement ~ · (Zement)Klinker *m* [*Der Name „Klinker" stammt noch aus der Zeit, als man das Rohmehl in ziegelartigen Rohlingen formte und diese wie Mauerklinker brannte*]

~ → furnace ~

~ [*(Clay) engineering brick (for civil engineering work). B.S. 1301. Clinkers are over-burnt bricks, usually those near to the fire-holes of the kiln. They are hard, but their bad shape makes them useless for general building purposes*] · (Tiefbau)Klinker *m*, Ingenieurbauklinker [*Sammelbezeichnungen für Kanal-, Wasserbau-, Tunnel- und Straßenbauklinker*]

~ · totgebranntes Erzeugnis *n* [*Feuerfestindustrie. In Großbritannien bezeichnet dieser Ausdruck „clinker" oft totgebrannten Dolomit*]

~ aggregate for concrete → furnace ~ ~ ~ ~

~ block (Brit.); cinder ~ (US); ~ tile [*See remark under 'Block'*] · Schlacken(beton)stein *m*, Schlacken(beton)-block(stein) *m*

~ brick → clinker

~ chemistry, cement ~ ~ · (Zement-)Klinkerchemie *f*

~ composition, cement ~ ~ · (Zement-)Klinkerzusammensetzung *f*

~ concrete, furnace ~ ~ (Brit.); (furnace) cinder ~ (US) · Kesselschlackenbeton *m*, (Stein)Kohlenschlackenbeton, Feuerungsschlackenbeton, (Verbrennungs)Schlackenbeton

~ ~ roof(ing) slab (Brit.); cinder ~ ~ ~ (US) · Schlacken(beton)dachplatte *f*

~ ~ wall slab (Brit.); cinder ~ ~ ~ (US) · Schlacken(beton)-Wand-(bau)platte *f*

~ for dampproof courses, ~ ~ hydraulic structures · Wasserbauklinker *m* [*DIN 105*]

~ ~ hydraulic structures, ~ ~ dampproof courses · Wasserbauklinker *m* [*DIN 105*]

~ ~ road construction purposes · Pflasterklinker *m*, Straßen(bau)klinker

~ formation · Klinkerbildung *f*, Klinkerisierung

~ grain, cement ~ ~ · (Zement)Klinkerkorn *n*, (Zement)Klinkerteilchen *n*

~ grinding, cement ~ ~ · (Zement-)Klinkermahlung *f*

~ mineral, cement ~ ~ · (Zement-)Klinkermineral *n*

~ phase, cement ~ ~ · (Zement)Klinkerphase *f*

~ pot → hollow clinker block

~ slab (Brit.); cinder ~ (US) · Schlacken(beton)diele *f*, Schlacken(beton)platte *f* [*Mit Zement oder Gips gebunden*]

~ tile, ~ block (Brit.); cinder ~ (US) [*See remark under 'Block'*] · Schlacken(beton)stein *m*, Schlacken(beton)-block(stein) *m*

clinkstone, phonolite · Klingstein *m*, Phonolith *m* [*Fehlname: Porphyrschiefer m*]

cloak hook — closet flush(ing) 204

cloak hook, robe ~, coat ~ · Kleiderhaken *m*

cloakroom, vestiary, wardrobe, garderobe · Garderobe *f*, Kleiderablage *f*

~, left-luggage office; checkroom (US) · Handgepäckaufbewahrung *f*

(~) locker · Garderobenschrank *m*, Spind *m*

clock chamber · Uhrenraum *m* [*Kirchturm*]

~ control · Uhr(en)steuerung *f* [*Steuerung durch Uhr(en)*]

~ installation, ~ system · Uhrenanlage *f*

~ system, ~ installation · Uhrenanlage *f*

~ tower · Uhr(en)turm *m*

~ turret · Uhrentürmchen *n*

clockwise · uhrzeigersinnmäßig, im Uhrzeigersinn

~ polygon · Polygon *n* im Uhrzeigersinn, Vieleck *n* ~ ~

clockwork · Uhrwerk *n*

clogged · verstopft [*Leitung*]

cloisonné (work), cell enamel · Zellenschmelz *m*

cloister → ~ walk

~ cemetery, paradise · Ambitusfriedhof *m*, Kreuzgangfriedhof

cloister-garth · Ambitushofrasen *m*, Rechteckhofrasen, Kreuzganghofrasen

cloister (walk) · Ambitus *m*, Kreuzgang *m* [*Um den Rechteckhof einer Klausur angelegter Gang, in welchem Prozessionen mit einem Kreuz abgehalten werden. Der Kreuzgang bildet mit der Kirche das Kernstück eines Klosters*]

cloister(ed) vault, domical ~, covered ~ [*A vault rising direct on a square or polygonal base, the curved surfaces separated by groins*] · Domikalgewölbe *n*, gebustes Gewölbe, busiges Gewölbe

closable, lockable, lockfast, lock fitted · verschließbar

close-boarded (battened) roofing, close-sheeted ~, double ~ · Doppel-(dach)(ein)deckung *f*, Doppelbedachung

(~) hoarding, close-sheeted ~ [*Any person intending to erect a building abutting on a street must erect a hoarding for the protection of the passers-by, unless the local authority signifies in writing that they do not consider any hoarding is necessary*] · Bauzaun *m* (aus Brettern), Bretterbauzaun

close-contact adhesive, ~ glue [*B.S. 1204*] · Flächenleim *m*

~ glue, ~ adhesive [*B.S. 1204*] · Flächenleim *m*

close-coupled closet, ~ suite · Tiefspülabort *m*, Tiefspülklosett *n*

~ suite, ~ closet · Tiefspülabort *m*, Tiefspülklosett *n*

close-graded, dense(-graded) · dicht, hohlraumarm, geschlossen (abgestuft)

~ aggregate → ~ mineral ~

~ ~ asphalt(ic) concrete · geschlossen abgestufter Asphaltbeton *m*, ~ ~ Bitumenbeton

~ (mineral) aggregate, dense(-graded) (~) ~, DGA · dichte Mineralmasse *f*, hohlraumarme ~, geschlossen (abgestufte) ~, dichtes Mineralgemisch *n*, hohlraumarmes Mineralgemisch, geschlossen (abgestuftes) Mineralgemisch

close mesh grating · feinmaschiger Rost *m*

close-sheeted roofing, double ~, close-boarded (battened) ~ · Doppel(dach)-(ein)deckung *f*, Doppelbedachung

closed building block module · geschlossene Baumzelle *f*

~ cell · geschlossene Zelle *f*

closed-end driveway · Sackzufahrt *f*

closed eye bolt · Augenschraube *f* [*Fehlname: Klappschraube. DIN 444*]

~ newel · gemauerte (Treppen)Spindel *f*

~ position · Schließstellung *f*

~ space · geschlossener Raum *m*

close(d) string, housed ~, curb ~ (Brit.); ~ stringer (US) · (Treppen-)Wange *f* mit eingestemmten Stufen

closely-spaced · engstehend [*z.B. Säulen*]

closely windowed Doric column · dorische Säule *f* von eng gesetzten Fensterreihen gegliedert

closer, device for closing, closing device, closing mechanism · Schließer *m*, Verschluß *m*, (Ver)Schließvorrichtung *f*

closet · Einbauschrank *m*, Wandschrank, eingebauter Schrank

~, toilet [*The term 'lavatory' is also used as a euphemism for 'toilet' or 'closet'*] · Abort *m*, Toilette *f*, Klosett *n*, Abtritt

~ bank, bank of closets, cupboard wall · Schrankwand *f*

~ bowl → bowl

~ cubicle, toilet ~ · Abortkabine *f*, Toilettenkabine, Klosettkabine, Abtrittkabine, Abortzelle *f*, Toilettenzelle, Klosettzelle, Abtrittzelle

~ door · Einbauschranktür *f*, Wandschranktür

~ facility, toilet ~ · Abortanlage *f*, Toilettenanlage, Klosettanlage

~ fan, lavatory ~, toilet ~ · Abortventilator *m*, Klosettventilator, Toilettenventilator

~ flush(ing), toilet ~, lavatory ~, flush(-ing) · Spülung *f*, Abort~, Klosett~, Toiletten~

closet flush(ing) pipe — clothes-locker room

~ ~ **pipe**, toilet ~ ~, (lavatory) ~ ~ [*B.S. 1125*] · Spülrohr *n*, Klosett~, Abort~, Toiletten~

~ ~ **water**, toilet ~ ~, (lavatory) ~ ~ · Spülwasser *n*, Abort~, Klosett~, Toiletten~

~ **for cleaning equipment**, cleaning (equipment) closet · Reinigungsgeräte-Einbauschrank *m*, Reinigungsgeräte-Wandschrank

~ ~ **infants** · Kleinkinder-Einbauschrank *m*, Kleinkinder-Wandschrank

~ **pan** → bowl

~ **room**, toilet ~ · Abortraum *m*, Toilettenraum, Klosettraum, Abtrittraum

~ **seat**, toilet ~, W.C. ~, (lavatory) ~ [*B.S. 1254*] · Sitz *m*, Abort~, Klosett~, Toiletten~

~ ~ **lid**, lavatory ~ ~, (toilet) ~ ~ · (Abort)Deckel *m*, Toilettendeckel, Klosettdeckel

~ **waste water**, toilet ~ ~; soil (Brit.) [*The discharge from water closets and urinals*] · Abort(ab)wasser *n*, Klosettabwasser, Toilettenabwasser

~ ~ ~ **pipe**, toilet ~ ~ ~; soil ~ (Brit.) [*A pipe collecting from W.C.s and urinals*] · Abortrohr *n*, Klosett(abwasser)rohr, Toiletten(abwasser)rohr, Abortfallrohr, Abfallrohr für Aborte

close-up (view) · Nahansicht *f*

closing action · Schließwirkung *f*

~ **and check action** → combined ~ ~ ~ ~

~ **device**, device for closing, closing mechanism, closer · Schließer *m*, Verschluß *m*, (Ver)Schließvorrichtung *f*

~ **force** · Schließkraft *f* [*automatisches Schließen von Türen*]

~ **line** · Schlußlinie *f*

~ **mechanism**, ~ device, device for closing, closer · Schließer *m*, Verschluß *m*, (Ver)Schließvorrichtung *f*

~ **noise** · Schließgeräusch *n*

~ **order** · Räumungserlaß *m* [*Haus*]

~ **pressure** · Schließdruck *m*

~ **range** · Schließbereich *n, m*

~ **section of vaulting** · Wölbungsschluß *m*

~ **speed** · Schließgeschwindigkeit *f*

~ **system** · Schließanlage *f*

closure → closer

~ · Abschluß *m* [*einer Öffnung*]

~ **position** · Verschlußstellung *f*

~ **system** · Verschlußsystem *n*

clot · Batzen *m*, Rohling *m* [*Feuerfestindustrie. Zur endgültigen Formgebung oder zum Brennen der Rohstoffe aufbereitete vorgeformte Masse*]

cloth, woven fabric; fabric [*misnomer*] [*A woven fabric of wool, cotton, rayon, wire, etc. The word 'fabric' has many meanings and there is no all-embracing equivalent in German for it. The word 'fabric' may mean 1. A woven, felted, or knitted material, as cloth felt, hosiery, or lace; also, the material used in its making. 2. Something that has been fabricated, constructed, or put together; any complex construction. 3. An edifice: St. Paul's, that noble fabric. 4. The manner of construction: workmanship; texture: cloth of a very intricate fabric. 5. The texture or structure of igneous rock. (Geol.)*] · Gewebe *n*

~ **backing** → ~ base

~ **base**, ~ backing, ~ underlay; fabric ~ [*misnomer*] · Gewebehinterlegung *f*, Gewebeunterlage *f*, Geweberücken *m*, Geweberücklage, Gewebeträger(-schicht) *m, (f)*

~ **flashing**, membrane ~; fabric ~ [*misnomer*] [*See remark under 'Anschluß'*] · Gewebeanschluß *m*

~ ~ **(piece)**, membrane ~ (~); fabric ~ (~) [*misnomer*] · Gewebeanschluß(-streifen) *m*

~ **hall** · Gewandhaus *n*, Tuchhalle *f*, Halle der Tuchmacher

~ **insert(ion)**; fabric ~ [*misnomer*] · Gewebeeinlage *f*

~ **lath(ing)**, woven fabric ~; fabric ~ [*misnomer*] · Putz(träger)gewebe *n*

~ **ply**; fabric ~ [*misnomer*] · Gewebelage *f*

cloth-reinforced, woven fabric-reinforced; fabric-reinforced [*misnomer*] · gewebeverstärkt

~ **sheet(ing)**; fabric ~ [*misnomer*] · Gewebebahn *f*

~ **underlay** → ~ base

~ **wire**; fabric ~ [*misnomer*] [*See remark under 'cloth'*] · Gewebedraht *m*

clothes chute, laundry ~, (soiled) linen ~ · (Schmutz)Wäscheabwurfanlage *f*, (Schmutz)Wäscherutsche *f*

~ **closet** · Kleider-Einbauschrank *m*, Kleider-Wandschrank

~ **drier** · Wäschetrockner *m*

(clothes-)drying cabinet, (enclosed) cabinet for drying washing · (Wäsche-)Trocknungsschrank *m* [*in einer Wohnung*]

~ **ground**, ~ area, laundry-drying ~ · Bleiche *f*, Wäschetrocknungsplatz *m*

clothes line concrete pole, ~ ~ ~ post [*B.S. 1373*] · Beton-Wäscheleinepfosten *m*, Beton-Wäscheleinestange *f*

~ ~ **pole**, ~ ~ post · Wäscheleinepfosten *m*, Wäscheleinestange *f*

~ ~ **post**, ~ ~ pole · Wäscheleinepfosten *m*, Wäscheleinestange *f*

~ **locker**, dressing ~ · Kleiderspind *m*

clothes-locker room, dressing-locker ~ · Kleiderspindraum *m*

'Cloud Props' project [*Scheme by El Lissitzky and Mart Stam in 1924 for office blocks erected on huge supports straddling a city thoroughfare*] · Wolkenbügel-Projekt *n*

clouding, cloudiness · Wolkenbildung *f* [*Anstrichtechnik*]

club block, ~ building · Klubhaus *n*, Klubgebäude *n*

~ building, ~ block · Klubhaus *n*, Klubgebäude *n*

~ changing room · Umkleide(raum) *f*, (*m*) für Vereine

~ room · Klubraum *m*, Klubzimmer *n*

clump of buildings (US) → group ~ ~

~ ~ houses (US); group ~ ~, complex ~ ~, house complex · Häusergruppe *f*, Häuserkomplex *m*

clunch, hard chalk · Hartkreide *f*

cluster, bundle · Bündel *n*

~ of columns, bundle ~ ~, clustered column, bundle column · Bündelsäule *f*, Säulenbündel *n*

~ ~ piers, bundle ~ ~, clustered pier, bundle pier, membered pier · Bündelpfeiler *m*, Pfeilerbündel *n*

~ ~ pillars → clustered pillar

clustered chimneys · Schornsteinbündel *n* [*Dicht nebeneinander stehende Schornsteine*]

~ column, bundle ~, cluster of columns, bundle of columns · Bündelsäule *f*, Säulenbündel *n*

~ pier, bundle ~, membered ~, cluster of piers, bundle of piers · Bündelpfeiler *m*, Pfeilerbündel *n*

~ pillar, bundle ~, compound ~, multiple rib ~, cluster of pillars, bundle of pillars · Bündelfreipfeiler *m*, gegliederter Freipfeiler, gegliederter freistehender Pfeiler

CLV board; coreboard (Brit.) · Tischlerplatte *f* [*DIN 68705*]

~ ~ door (US); coreboard ~ (Brit.) · Tischlerplattentür *f*

~ ~ for building purposes → coreboard ~ ~ ~

CL W GL → clear wire glass

C/M → concrete masonry

CMP, corrugated metal pipe · Blech-Wellrohr *n*, Wellblechrohr

CO, coolant outlet · Kühlmittelauslaß *m*

coach bolt, carriage ~ · Wagenbauschraube *f*

~ varnish · Kutschenlack *m*

coal-ash slag · Kohlenascheschlacke *f*

coal cellar · Kohlenkeller *m*

coal-fired boiler · Kohlenkessel *m*

~ range · Kohlenherd *m*

~ stove · Kohleofen *m*

coal-mining town · Kohlenbergbaustadt *f*

coal powder → powder(ed) coal

~ ~ fuel, powder(ed) coal ~; pulverized coal ~ (US); pulverised coal ~ (Brit.) · Kohle(n)staub *m* als Brennstoff, Kohle(n)pulver *n* ~ ~

~ ~ line marking · Abschnüren *n*, Abkohlen [*Anbringen von Hilfslinien an Flächen mit Hilfe einer Schlagschnur, welche mit Kohlepulver eingefärbt wurde*]

coal-shed · Kohlenschuppen *m*

coal stor(ag)e, ~ yard · Kohlenlager(platz) *n*, (*m*)

~ storage tower · Kohlenturm *m*

~ (~) yard · Kohlenlager(platz) *n*, (*m*)

~ store, ~ storage, ~ yard · Kohlenlager(platz) *n*, (*m*)

~ tar · Steinkohlenteer *m* [*DIN 52136*]

~ ~ coat(ing), ~ ~ finish · Steinkohlenteerbeschichtung *f*, Steinkohlenteerüberzug *m*

~ ~ creosote, carbolic acid, phenol [*B.S. 144*] · Phenol *n*, Karbolsäure *f*, Steinkohlenteerkreosot *n*, Phenylalkohol *m*, C₆H₅OH

~ ~ finish, ~ ~ coat(ing) · Steinkohlenteerbeschichtung *f*, Steinkohlenteerüberzug *m*

(coal-)tar-impregnated · teergetränkt, teerimprägniert

coal tar oil · Steinkohlenteeröl *n*

~ ~ pitch, straight run coal tar [*B.S. 1210*] · Steinkohlenteerpech *n* [*DIN 55946*]

~ ~ ~ cement · Steinkohlenteerpechkitt *m*

~ ~ ~ dispersion, straight run coal tar ~ · Steinkohlenteerpechdispersion *f*

~ ~ ~ emulsion, straight run coal tar ~ · Steinkohlenteerpechemulsion *f* [*Sie besteht aus feinstverteiltem Steinkohlenteerweichpech und Wasser*]

~ ~ ~ solution, straight run coal tar ~ · Steinkohlenteerpechlösung *f*

(coal-)tar-saturated · vollteergetränkt, vollteerimprägniert

coal tar scale · Barretskala *f*

~ ~ solution · Steinkohlenteerlösung *f*

~ yard, ~ stor(ag)e · Kohlenlager(platz) *n*, (*m*)

coalescence · Einformen *n* [*Metallurgie. Übergang zu kugeligem Gefügebestandteil*]

coarse, ~-grain(ed) · grob(körnig)

~ aggregate → coarse(-grain(ed)) (concrete) ~

~ asphalt (Brit.); coarse(-graded) asphaltic concrete (US) · Asphaltgrobbeton *m*, Grobasphaltbeton

~ blast, ~ sand~ · (Sand)Grobstrahl *m*

~ blend(ed) aggregate · Grobzuschlag(stoff)gemenge *n*, Grobzuschlagmaterialgemenge

~ broken stone, ~ crushed ~ · Grobschotter *m*

~ chip(ping)s, coarse-grained ~ · Grobsplitt *m*

~ concrete, coarse-grained ~ · Grob(korn)beton *m*, grob(körnig)er Beton

~ (~) aggregate → coarse(-grain(ed)) (~) ~

~ crushed stone, ~ broken ~ · Grobschotter *m*

coarse-fibrous · grobfas(e)rig

coarse filler → ~ stopper

~ ~, coarse-grained ~ · Grobfüller *m*

~ flour, coarse-grained ~ · Grobmehl *n*

~ fraction · Grobfraktion *f*, Grobkörnung *f*, Grobkorn *n*

coarse(-graded) asphaltic concrete (US); coarse asphalt (Brit.) · Asphaltgrobbeton *m*, Grobasphaltbeton

coarse grading, ~ size ~ · Grob(korn)abstufung *f*

~ grain · Grob(gut)korn *n*

coarse(-grain(ed)) · grob(körnig)

~ aggregate → ~ concrete ~

~ chip(ping)s · Grobsplitt *m*

~ concrete · Grob(korn)beton *m*, grob(körnig)er Beton

~ (~) aggregate · Grobzuschlag(stoff) *m*, Grobzuschlagmaterial *n*

~ filler · Grobfüller *m*

~ flour · Grobmehl *n*

~ gravel · Grobkies *m*, Steine *mpl*

~ ~ (concrete) aggregate · Betongrobkies *m*

~ light(weight) (concrete) aggregate · Grob-Leicht(beton)zuschlag(-stoff) *m*, Leicht(beton)-Grobzuschlag(-stoff)

~ mortar, ~ sand ~ · Grobmörtel *m*

~ ~ with synthetic resin dispersion, coarse sand ~ ~ ~ ~ ~ · Kunstharz-Grobmörtel *m*, Plast-Grobmörtel

~ Portland cement mortar, ~ portland ~ ~ · Portlandzement-Grobmörtel *m*

~ powder · Grobpulver *n*

~ sand · Grobsand *m*, Schottersand

~ ~ (concrete) aggregate · Betongrobsand *m*

~ sandstone, gritstone · grob(körnig)er Sandstein *m*, Kristallsandstein

~ silt · Grobschluff *m*

~ steel, open(-)grained ~ · Grobkornstahl *m*

coarse gravel → coarse(-grain(ed)) ~

~ ~ aggregate → coarse(-grain(ed)) gravel (concrete) ~

~ ~ (concrete) aggregate → coarse(-grain(ed)) ~ (~) ~

~ gravel-surfaced · grobbekiest

coarse-ground · grobgemahlen

~ cement · grobgemahlener Zement *m*

coarse levelling (Brit.); ~ leveling (US) · Grobegalisieren *n*

~ limestone, coarse-grain(ed) ~ · Grobkalk(stein) *m*, Massenkalk(stein), körniger Kalk(stein)

~ ~ chip(ping)s · Kalk(stein)grobsplitt *m*

~ manufactured sand, manufactured coarse ~ · Brechgrobsand *m*, Grobbrechsand

~ material · Grobmaterial *n*

~ mineral granules, ~ ~ surfacing · grobmineralische Abstreuung *f*, ~ Bestreuung, Grobmineralbestreuung, Grobmineralabstreuung [*Dachpappe*]

~ mortar, coarse-grain(ed) ~, ~ sand ~ · Grobmörtel *m*

~ ~ with synthetic resin dispersion → coarse(-grain(ed)) ~ ~ ~ ~ ~

coarse-pored · grobporig

coarse porosity · Grobporigkeit *f*

~ powder, coarse-grain(ed) ~ · Grobpulver *n*

~ sand, coarse-grain(ed) ~ · Grobsand *m*, Schottersand

~ ~ (concrete) aggregate → coarsegrain(ed) ~ (~) ~

~ (~) mortar, coarse-grain(ed) (~) ~ · Grobmörtel *m*

~ ~ ~ with synthetic resin dispersion, coarse(-grain(ed)) ~ ~ ~ ~ ~ ~ · Kunstharz-Grobmörtel *m*, Plast-Grobmörtel

~ sandstone, coarse-grain(ed) ~, gritstone · grob(körnig)er Sandstein *m*, Kristallsandstein

~ scrubbed (concrete) finish → ~ ~ (~) surface

~ ~ (~) surface, ~ ~ (~) finish · grobe Bürstenwaschbetonoberfläche *f*

~ ~ finish → ~ ~ (concrete) surface

~ silt, coarse-grain(ed) ~ · Grobschluff *m*

~ (size) grading · Grob(korn)abstufung *f*

~ steel, coarse-grain(ed) ~, open(-)grain(ed) ~ · Grobkornstahl *m*

~ stopper, ~ stopping, ~ filler · Grobausfüller *m*, Grob(füll)spachtel(masse) *m*, (*f*) [*Siehe Anmerkung unter „Spachtel(masse)"*]

~ stopping → ~ stopper

~ stuff, lime-sand mortar, lime:sand mortar · Kalksandmörtel *m*

~ tar concrete · Teergrobbeton *m*

~ vibrated concrete · Rüttelgrobbeton *m*

coarsely dressed, roughly ~, ~ shaped · grob zugerichtet [*(Natur)Stein*]

~ ground cork · gemahlener Kork *m*

~ ~ talc · Grobspeckstein *m*, Grobtalk *m*

~ ~ ~ (sur)facing, ~ ~ ~ dusting finish · Grobspecksteinabstreuung *f*, Grobspecksteinbestreuung, Grobtalkabstreuung, Grobtalkbestreuung

coarsely shaped — coating (medium)

~ **shaped**, roughly ~, ~ dressed · grob zugerichtet [*(Natur)Stein*]

to coat, to (sur)face · beschichten, überziehen

~ ~, to wet · benetzen, umhüllen [*mit Bindemittel*]

~ ~ [*pipe*] · anstreichen, bestreichen

~ ~, to paint · (an)streichen [*Fehlname: malen*]

coat · Anstrich *m*, Aufstrich [*Eine aus Anstrichstoff oder aus Anstrichstoffen hergestellte Beschichtung auf einem Untergrund. Der Anstrich kann mehr oder weniger in den Untergrund eingedrungen sein. Er kann aus einer oder mehreren Schichten bestehen. Ein mehrschichtiger Anstrich wird als „Anstrichaufbau" und „Anstrichsystem" bezeichnet*]

~, coating, finish · Beschichtung *f*, Überzug *m* [*als Schicht*]

~, layer · Schicht *f*, Lage *f*

to coat and wrap, to dope · beschichten, isolieren [*Rohr*]

coat closet [*It is located near an entrance door*] · Garderoben-Einbauschrank *m*, Garderoben-Wandschrank

~ **defect** · Anstrichfehler *m*, Aufstrichfehler, Anstrichmangel *m*, Aufstrichmangel

~ **on concrete** · Betonüberzug *m*, Betonbeschichtung *f*

~ **film**, ~ membrane, ~ skin · Anstrichfilm *m*, Anstrichhaut *f*, Anstrichmembran(e) *f* [*Die nach physikalischer und/oder chemischer Trocknung zusammenhängende Schicht eines Anstriches*]

~ **hook**, cloak ~, robe ~ · Kleiderhaken *m*

~ **membrane** → ~ film

~ **of glue(-bound) water paint** [*Australia*] → (glue(-bound)) distemper coat

~ ~ **paint**, paint coat · Farbanstrich *m*, Farbaufstrich

~ ~ **wax**, wax coat · Wachsschicht *f*

~ ~ **on concrete** · Betonbeschichtung *f*, Betonüberzug *m*

~ ~ **light(weight) concrete** · Leichtbetonbeschichtung *f*, Leichtbetonüberzug *m*

~ ~ **metal**, protective ~ ~ ~ · Metall(schutz)anstrich *m*, Metall(schutz)aufstrich

~ **room** · Garderobenraum *m*

coat-room equipment · Garderobenraumeinrichtung *f*

coat skin → ~ film

~ **surface** · Anstrichoberfläche *f*, Aufstrichoberfläche

~ **thickness**, layer ~ · Schichtdicke *f*, Lagendicke

to (coat with) brass, to brass plate · vermessingen

~ (~ ~) **copper**, to copper plate · verkupfern

coatability, wettability · Benetzbarkeit *f*

coatable, wettable · benetzbar

coated, (sur)faced · überzogen, beschichtet

~ **both sides** → ~ on ~ ~

~ **chip(ping)s** · Mischsplitt *m*, umhüllter Splitt

~ **cloth**, leathercloth; coated fabric, leatherfabric [*misnomers*] · Gewebe-Kunstleder *n*, Wachstuch *n*, Ledertuch

~ **fabric** [*misnomer*] → ~ cloth

~ **gravel** · Mischkies *m*, umhüllter Kies

~ **(on) both sides**, (sur)faced (~) ~ ~ · beidseitig beschichtet

~ **paper** · beschichtetes Papier *n*

~ **steel** · überzogener Stahl *m*

~ **wire** · überzogener Draht *m*

~ **with baked enamel** · einbrennlackiert

~ ~ **oxidized asphalt on each side** (US); ~ ~ ~ (asphaltic) bitumen ~ ~ ~ (Brit.) · mit beiderseitiger Bitumendeckschicht (versehen) [*Bitumenpappe*]

~ ~ **stucco** · geputzt mit Stuck, verputzt ~ ~

coat(ing), finish · Beschichtung *f*, Überzug *m* [*als Schicht*]

~, surface ~ · Deckschicht *f*, Überzug *m* [*(Dach)Pappe*]

coating, (sur)facing · Beschichten *n*, Beschichtung *f*, Überziehen, Überzug *m* [*als Tätigkeit*]

~ → ~ work

~ [*pipe*] · Anstreichen *n*, Bestreichen

~, wetting; wet mixing (US) · Benetzen *n*, (Bindemittel)Umhüllung *f*, Umhüllen, Benetzung

~ · Deckanstrich *m*, Deckaufstrich [*(bituminöser) Spachteldachbelag*]

~ · flüssiger Kunststoff *m* für Beschichtung und Isolierung, Flüssigkunststoff ~ ~ ~ ~

~ **action**, wetting ~ · Benetzungswirkung *f*

~ **angle**, wetting ~ · Benetzungswinkel *m*

~ **capacity** → ~ power

~ **clay** · Engobeton *m*

~ **composition** → ~ material

~ **compound** → ~ material

~ ~ · Deck(schicht)masse *f*, Aufstrichmasse [*(Dach)Pappe*]

~ **heat**, wetting ~ · Benetzungswärme *f*

~ **mass** → ~ material

~ **material**, ~ composition, ~ compound, ~ mass, finish ~, (sur)facing ~ · Beschichtungsmasse *f*, Beschichtungsstoff *m*, Überzugsmasse, Überzugstoff

~ **(medium)**, surface ~ (~), liquid coating (material) · Anstrich(stoff) *m*, Anstrichmittel *n*, Aufstrich(stoff), Aufstrich(stoff), flüssiger Beschichtungsstoff, Anstrichmaterial *n*, Aufstrichmaterial

coating metal — coffer pattern

∼ metal · Überzugmetall *n*
∼ plastic · Beschichtungskunststoff *m*
∼ power, wetting ∼, ∼ capacity, ∼ property, ∼ quality · Benetzungseigenschaft *f*, Benetzungsvermögen *n*, Benetzungsfähigkeit *f*
∼ practice, painting ∼ · Anstrichtechnik *f*, Anstrichwesen *n*
∼ property → ∼ power
∼ quality → ∼ power
∼ resin · Beschichtungsharz *n*
∼ roll · Belagwalze *f* [*Dachpappenanlage*]
∼ rolls · Deckmassen-Belags-Apparatur *f* [*Dachpappenmaschine*]
∼ storage · Belagmasse-Vorrat *m* [*Dachpappenanlage*]
∼ with grease · einfetten
∼ ∼ zapon lacquer · Zaponieren *n*
∼ (work) · Anstrich *m*, Aufstrich, Anstreicherarbeiten *fpl*, Anstreichen *n*, Anstricharbeiten, Aufstricharbeiten

cob, pisé (de terre) [*A mix(ture) of stiff clay and chopped straw, well kneaded, used for building the walls of cottages, etc.*] · Pisee *m*, Pisé, Stampflehm *m*
∼ construction, pisé (de terre) ∼, rammed-loam ∼, rammed-earth ∼ · Lehmstampfbau *m*, Piseebau, Kastenwerk *n*
∼ wall · Piseewand *f*, Lehmstampfwand

cobalt · Kobalt *n*, Co
∼ aluminate · Kobaltaluminat *n*
∼ arsenate · Kobaltarsenat *n*
∼ blue (pigment), Thenards' ∼ (∼) [*A blue pigment composed of the oxides of alumin(i)um and cobalt*] Kobaltblau(pigment) *n*
∼ chloride (Brit.); ∼ chlorid(e) (US) · Kobaltchlorid *n*
∼ drier · Kobalttrockenstoff *m*
∼ green (pigment) · Kobaltgrün(pigment) *n*
∼ naphthenate · Kobaltnaphthenat *n*
∼ phosphate · Kobaltphosphat *n*
∼ salt · Kobaltsalz *n*
∼ siccative, soluble cobalt drier · Kobaltsikkativ *n*, Kobalttrockenstoff *m* in gelöster Form
∼ soap · Kobaltseife *f*
∼ violet (pigment) · Kobaltviolett(-pigment) *n*

cobaltous stannate · Kobaltstannat *n*

cobble (stone), nigger head · Katzenkopf *m*, Kopfstein *m* [*Pflasterstein*]

cobweb pattern · Spinnwebenmuster *n*
∼ (random rubble) masonry (work) → polygonal (∼ ∼) ∼ (∼)

cochineal · Kermesfarbstoff *m*, Cochenille *f*

cochleoid · Schraubenkurve *f*

to cock [*To set anything out of the horizontal*] · aufrichten

cock · Hahn *m*
∼, vane, weather ∼ · Windfahne *f*, Wetterhahn *m*

cocking piece, sprocket (∼) · Strebeschwarte *f*, Schwibbe *f*, Sturmlatte *f*, Windrispe *f*, Windlatte

coconut oil · Kokosfett *n*, Kokosöl *n* [*DIN 55963*]

COD, ash(pit) door, cleanout door (US); soot door [*B.S. 1294*] · Kamintür *f*, Reinigungstür, Putztür, Schornsteinreinigungsverschluß *m*, Aschentür, Entaschungstür, Rußtür

code of practice · Merkblatt *n*

(coding) legend, key · Legende *f*, Zeichenerklärung *f*, Zeichenschlüssel *m*

coefficient · Beiwert *m*, (Bei)Zahl *f*, Koeffizient *m*
∼ of consistency, ∼ ∼ consistence, consistence coefficient, consistency coefficient · Steifebeiwert *m*, Konsistenzbeiwert
∼ ∼ creep, creep coefficient · Kriechbeiwert *m*, Kriechzahl *f*
∼ ∼ friction · Reibungsbeiwert *m*
∼ ∼ linear expansion · linearer Ausdehnungsbeiwert *m*
∼ ∼ reduction, reduction coefficient · Herabsetzungsbeiwert *m*, Herabsetzungszahl *f*, Minderungsbeiwert, Minderungszahl
∼ ∼ safety against cracking · Rißsicherheitsbeiwert *m*
∼ ∼ ∼ ∼ rupture · Bruchsicherheitsbeiwert *m*
∼ ∼ (thermal) expansion, ∼ ∼ ∼ movement, ∼ ∼ heat ∼ · Wärme(aus)dehnungskoeffizient *m*
∼ ∼ turbidity, turbidity coefficient · Trübungsbeiwert *m*
∼ ∼ viscosity · Viskositätsbeiwert *m*
∼ value · Beiwertgröße *f*

coffee shop · Kaffeestube *f*, Kafferestaurant *n*

coffer → pan
∼ ceiling → waffle soffit
∼ design → waffle pattern
∼ floor → waffle (slab) ∼
∼ (∼) panel → rectangular grid (floor) slab
∼ (∼) plate → rectangular grid (floor) slab
∼ (∼) slab → rectangular grid (∼) ∼
∼ grid → waffle pattern
panel → rectangular grid (floor) slab
∼ (∼) floor → waffle (slab) ∼
∼ pattern → waffle ∼

coffer soffit — cold asphalt mortar

~ **soffit** → waffle ~
coffered, cored · kassettiert
coffering, coring · Kassettierung f
cog, nib · (Aufhänge)Nase f [*Dachziegel*]
coi(g)n → (angle-)quoin
coil coating · Walzlackieren n
coi(llo)n → (angle-)quoin
coin-box (tele)phone → public (tele-) phone coin box
coin-operated (automatic) washer, ~ (~) washing machine · Münzwaschmaschine f
~ **dryer** (Brit.); ~ drier (US) · Münzwäschetrockner m
coin-scratch test · Spanprüfung f von Anstrichen mit einer Münze
coir [*The prepared fibre of the husks of coconuts, used to make rope, etc.*] Kokosfaser f
~ **board lath** (US); ~ gypsum plank · Kokos(faser)diele f [*Gipsdiele, bei der zur Erhöhung der Bruchfestigkeit Kokosfasern dem Stuckgips beigemengt sind*]
~ **(building) mat** [*It has a low density*] Kokosfaserdämmatte f, Kokosfaser(bau)matte
~ **door mat** [*B.S. 4037*] · Kokos(faser)matte f
~ **(insulating) material,** ~ insulation (-grade) ~ · Kokosfaserdämmstoff m
~ ~ **sheet(ing),** ~ insulation(-grade) ~ · Kokosfaserdämmbahn f
~ ~ **strip,** ~ insulation(-grade) ~ · Kokosfaserdämmstreifen m
~ **insulation material,** ~ insulation-grade ~, ~ (insulating) ~ · Kokosfaserdämmstoff m
~ ~ **strip,** ~ insulation-grade ~, ~ insulating ~ · Kokosfaserdämmstreifen m
~ **insulation(-grade) material,** ~ (insulating) ~ · Kokosfaserdämmstoff m
~ ~ **strip,** ~ insulating ~ · Kokosfaserdämmstreifen m
~ **mat,** ~ building ~ [*It has a low density*] · Kokosfaserdämmatte f, Kokosfaser(bau)matte
~ **material,** ~ insulating ~, ~ insulation(-grade) ~ · Kokosfaserdämmstoff m
~ **rope** [*B.S. 2052*] · Kokos(faser)strick m
coir-type gypsum plank; ~ board lath (US) · Kokos(faser)diele f [*Gipsdiele, bei der zur Erhöhung der Bruchfestigkeit Kokosfasern dem Stuckgips beigemengt sind*]
coir wallboard · Kokos(faser)wandplatte f [*DIN 4105*]
(coke) breeze [*It is produced by screening coke at both the coke plant and blast furnaces, is utilized as fuel in steel-plant boiler houses to generate steam and in ore agglomerating plants. When used as boiler fuel, coke breeze is burned on chain-grate stokers*] · Koksgrus m
~ **dust** · Kokslösche f

coke-fired · koksgefeuert
~ **boiler** · Kokskessel m
~ **stove** · Koksofen m [*Raumheizung*]
coke furnace · Koksfeuerung f
~ **oven** · Koksofen m
coke-oven acid firebrick → ~ silica brick
~ **coal-tar** · Koksofenteer m
~ ~ **pitch** · Koksofenteerpech n
~ **gannister brick** (Brit.) → ~ silica ~
~ **silica brick,** ~ acid firebrick. ~ gannister brick (Brit.); ~ ganister brick (US) · Koksofenstein m
~ **tar** · Kokereiteer m
coky centre (Brit.); ~ center (US); axial porosity, central porosity · Fadenlunker m
Colcrete concrete · Colcret(e)beton m, Ausgußbeton [*Prepaktbeton und Colcretebeton unterscheiden sich im wesentlichen dadurch, daß beim Prepaktbeton dem Ausgußmörtel zur Verringerung des Wasserzusatzes und zur Erhöhung der Geschmeidigkeit ein Zusatzmittel beigegeben wird, während beim Colcretebeton ein bestimmtes Misch- und Herstellungsverfahren vorliegt*]
cold · Kälte f
~ **adhesive** → ~ bonding agent
~ ~ **composition,** ~ ~ compound, ~ bonding ~, ~ cement(ing ~) · Kaltkleb(e)masse f
~ ~ **compound** → ~ ~ composition
~ **air, cool** ~ · Kaltluft f
~ ~ **blower, cool** ~ ~ · Kaltluftgebläse n
~ ~ **curtain door, cool** ~ ~ ~ · Kalttür f
~ ~ **damper, cool** ~ ~ · Kaltluftschieber m
~ ~ **duct, cool** ~ ~ · Kaltluftkanal m
~ **application** · Kaltaufbringung f
~ ~ **sealer,** ~ ~ sealing composition, ~ ~ sealing compound · Kalt-(Ab-)Dicht(ungs)masse f
~ ~ **sealing composition,** ~ ~ ~ compound, ~ ~ sealer · Kalt-(Ab)Dicht(ungs)masse f
~ ~ ~ **compound,** ~ ~ ~ composition, ~ ~ sealer · Kalt-(Ab)Dicht(ungs)masse f
~ **asphalt** (US); ~ (asphaltic-)bitumen (Brit.) · Kaltbitumen n [*Es besteht aus Straßenbaubitumen B 200 oder B 80, das durch Zusatz leicht flüchtiger Lösungsmittel in seiner Zähigkeit erniedrigt wird, was eine Verarbeitung in unerwärmten Zustand gestattet*]
~ **asphalt-based adhesive** (US); ~ bitumen-based ~ (Brit.) · bituminöser Kaltkleber m
~ **asphalt emulsion** (US); ~ (asphaltic-)bitumen ~ (Brit.) · Kaltbitumenemulsion f
~ ~ **mortar** (US) → ~ asphaltic ~

cold (asphaltic-)bitumen — cold insulation

~ **(asphaltic-)bitumen** (Brit.) → ~ asphalt

~ ~ **emulsion** (Brit.); ~ asphalt ~ (US) · Kaltbitumenemulsion *f*

~ ~ **mortar** (Brit.); ~ asphalt(ic) ~ (US) · Kaltbitumenmörtel *m* [*Aus Bitumen, Sand und Lösungsmittel*]

~ **asphalt(ic) mortar** (US); ~ (asphaltic-)bitumen ~ (Brit.) · Kaltbitumenmörtel *m* [*Aus Bitumen, Sand und Lösungsmittel*]

to cold bend · kaltbiegen

cold bending · Kaltbiegen *n*

~ **bitumen** (Brit.) → ~ asphalt

~ **bitumen-based adhesive** (Brit.); ~ asphalt-based ~ (US) · bituminöser Kaltkleber *m*

~ **bitumen emulsion**, ~ asphaltic-~ ~ (Brit.); ~ asphalt ~ (US) · Kaltbitumenemulsion *f*

~ ~ **mortar** → ~ asphaltic-~ ~

cold bonding · Kalt(ver)kleben *n*

~ ~ · Kalt(ver)klebung *f*

~ (~) **adhesive** → ~ ~ agent

~ ~ **agent**, ~ ~ medium ~ (~) adhesive, ~ cement(ing agent), cold(-setting) glue, cold-setting adhesive, no-heat glue, no-heat adhesive · Kaltkleber *m*, Kaltkleb(e)stoff *m*, Kaltkleb(e)mittel *n*, Kaltleim *m*

~ ~ **composition** → ~ adhesive ~

~ ~ **compound** → ~ adhesive composition

~ ~ **medium** → ~ ~ agent

~ **bridge** · Kältebrücke *f*

cold-cathode-lamp · Leuchtstofflampe *f*

cold cellar · Kaltkeller *m*

cold cement(ing agent) → ~ bonding ~

~ **cement(ing composition)** → ~ adhesive ~

~ **cement(ing compound)** → ~ adhesive composition

~ **coat** · Kaltanstrich *m*, Kaltaufstrich [*Siehe Anmerkung unter „Anstrich"*]

~ **coating (work)** · Kaltanstrich *m*, Kaltaufstrich, Kaltanstreicherarbeiten *fpl*, Kaltanstreichen *n*, Kaltanstricharbeiten, Kaltaufstricharbeiten

cold-cured material, ~ paint [*The cold-curing is induced by adding chemical agents, known as activators or catalysts, the most widely used coatings of this type are based on epoxy and polyurethane resins*] · kalthärtender Lack *m*, Additionslack, Komponentenlack, Reaktionslack

~ **paint**, ~ material [*The cold-curing is induced by adding chemical agents, known as activators or catalysts, the most widely used coatings of this type are based on epoxy and polyurethane resins*] · kalthärtender Lack *m*, Additionslack, Komponentenlack, Reaktionslack

~ **resin**, cold-curing ~ · Reaktionsharz *n*

cold-curing · Kalthärtung *f* [*Lack*]

~ **material** → ~ ~ paint

~ **paint**, ~ material [*The cold-curing is induced by adding chemical agents, known as activators or catalysts; the most widely used coatings of this type are based on epoxy and polyurethane resins*] · Reaktionslack *m*, Additionslack, kalthärtender Lack

~ **resin**, cold-cured ~ · Reaktionsharz *n*

cold-deformed, cold-worked · kaltverformt [*Betonstahl*]

cold-drawn steel, bright ~, CDS · kaltgezogener Stahl *m*, Blankstahl

~ **wire** [*Wire made from the rods hot rolled from billets and then cold-drawn through dies*] · kaltgezogener Draht *m*

cold-driven rivet · Kaltniet *m*

cold expanding · Kaltaufweiten *n* [*Rohr*]

~ **extraction** · Kaltextraktion *f*

~ ~ **method** · Differenzverfahren *n* mittels Kaltextraktion

~ **extrusion of steel** · Fließpressen *n* von Stahl

~ **fine asphalt**, Damman cold ~, fine cold ~ (Brit.); Damman cold asphaltic concrete (US) · Asphaltkaltbeton *m*

~ **gagging**, ~ bending · Kaltbiegen *n* [*Metall*]

~ **galvanising paint**, zinc-rich ~, zinc dust shop primer, zinc-rich primer [*A paint, the pigment of which is zinc powder. It is used as a primer and as a special protection for steel*] · Zinkstaubgrund(ier)farbe *f*, Kaltzinkfarbe, zinkstaubreiche (Anstrich)Farbe, (Zinkstaub-)Werkstattgrund(ierung) *m*, (*f*), Zinkstaubfarbe

~ **glaze**, vitreous surfacing · Kaltglasur *f*, Kaltkeramik *f*

~ **glazed** · kaltglasiert

cold-glazed concrete wall tile · Kaltglasur(belag)platte *f*, Kaltglasurfliese *f* [*Betonwand(belag)platte mit Kaltglasur(überzug)*]

cold-glaze(d wall coat(ing)), vitreous surfacing · (Wand)Kaltglasur(überzug) *f*, (*m*), Kalt-Wandglasur(überzug) *m*, Kaltglasur-Wandverkleidung *f*, Kaltkeramik *f*

cold glue, no-heat ~ · Kaltleim *m*

~ **gluing** · Kalt(ver)leimen *n*

~ ~ · Kalt(ver)leimung *f*

cold-hardening · kalthärtend

cold insulant, ~ insulator, ~ insulating material, ~ insulation(-grade) material · Kältedämmstoff *m*, Kältedämmaterial *n*

~ **insulating material**, ~ insulation(-grade) ~, ~ insulator, ~ insulant · Kältedämmstoff *m*, Kältedämmaterial *n*

~ **insulation** [*The property that opposes the transmission of cold from one side to the other*] · Kälte(ab)dämmung *f*

cold insulation — (cold-)water paint

~ ~ [*Means taken to reduce the transmission of cold*] · Kälteschutz *m*

~ **insulation(-grade) material,** ~ insulating ~, ~ insulator, ~ insulant · Kältedämmstoff *m*, Kältedämmaterial *n*

~ **insulation material,** ~ insulationgrade ~, ~ insulating ~, ~ insulator, ~ insulant · Kältedämmstoff *m*, Kältedämmaterial *n*

~ **insulator,** ~ insulant, ~ insulating material, ~ insulation(-grade) material · Kältedämmstoff *m*, Kältedämmaterial *n*

cold-laid · kaltverlegt

~ **asphalt(ic) concrete** · kalteinbaufähiger Asphaltbeton *m*

~ **coarse asphalt(ic) concrete** · kalteinbaufähiger Asphaltgrobbeton *m*, ~ Grobasphaltbeton

~ ~ **tar concrete** · kalteinbaufähiger Teergrobbeton *m*, ~ Grobteerbeton

~ **fine asphalt(ic) concrete** · kalteinbaufähiger Asphaltfeinbeton *m*, ~ Feinasphaltbeton

~ ~ **tar concrete** · kalteinbaufähiger Teerfeinbeton *m*, ~ Feinteerbeton

~ **laying** · Kaltverlegung *f*

~ **liquid coating (material)** · Kaltanstrichmittel *n*, Kaltaufstrichmittel, Kaltanstrich(stoff) *m*, Kaltaufstrich(stoff), kalter flüssiger Beschichtungsstoff, flüssiger kalter Beschichtungsstoff

~ **mastic** · Kaltmastix *m*

~ **mix(ture)** · Kaltgemisch *n*, Kaltmischung *f*, Kaltmischgut *n* [*Straßenbau*]

~ **moist bending** · Kaltfeuchtbiegen *n*

~ **pilgered pipe, rocked** ~ · kaltgepilgertes Rohr *n*

to cold-pour · kaltvergießen

cold pourable · kaltvergießbar

~ **poured** · kaltvergossen

cold-pressed process · Kaltpressung *f*, Kaltpreßverfahren *n* [*Leinöl*]

cold requirement · Kältebedarf *m*

~ **riveting** · Kaltnieten *n*

~ **rolled,** c.r., CR · kaltgewalzt

cold-rolled beam, c.r. ~, CR ~ · kaltgewalzter Balken(träger) *m*

~ **channel,** c.r. ~, CR ~ · kaltgewalztes U-Eisen *n*

~ **section,** c.r. ~, CR ~, ~ structural ~ · kaltgewalztes Profil *n*

~ **steel,** c.r. ~, CRS · kaltgewalzter Stahl *m*, Kaltwalzstahl

~ ~ **section,** c.r. ~ ~, CR ~ ~ [*B.S. 2994*] · kaltgewalztes Stahlprofil *n*

~ **strip,** c.r. ~, CR ~ · Kaltband *n* [*kaltgewalzter Bandstahl, bis 5 mm dick und 630 mm breit*]

~ ~ **steel,** c.r. ~ ~, CR ~ · kaltgewalzter Bandstahl *m*

~ **(structural) section,** c.r. (~) ~, CR (~) ~ · kaltgewalztes Profil *n*

~ **thread,** c.r. ~, CR ~ · kaltgewalztes Gewinde *n*

cold rolling · Kaltwalzen *n*

cold-setting · kalthärtend [*Leim; Kunstharz*]

cold(-setting) adhesive → cold bonding agent

~ **glue** → cold bonding agent

cold short · kaltbrüchig, kaltspröde [*Stahl mit hohem Phosphorgehalt*]

~ **shortness** · Kaltbrüchigkeit *f*, Kaltsprödigkeit [*Stahl mit hohem Phosphorgehalt*]

~ **shower** · Kaltdusche *f*

~ **spray** · Kaltbrause *f*

cold-storage door, cold-store ~ · Kühlraumtür *f*

~ **wall,** cold-store ~ · Kühlraumwand *f*

cold store · Kühlraum *m*

cold-store door, cold-storage ~ · Kühlraumtür *f*

~ **wall,** cold-storage ~ · Kühlraumwand *f*

cold-strained · kaltgereckt [*Betonstahl*]

cold straining · Kaltrecken *n* [*Betonstahl*]

~ **surface treating (road) tar** · (Straßen)Teer *m* für kalte Oberflächenteerung

~ **tar,** TC · Kaltteer *m* [*Steinkohlenteer mit flüchtigen organischen Lösungsmitteln, im allgemeinen Benzol*]

cold-twisted special reinforcing bars grade III of grade IIIb DIN 1045 · kaltverwundener Sonderbetonstahl III *m* der Gruppe IIIb DIN 1045

cold water · Kaltwasser *n*, KW

~ ~ **apartment (unit);** ~ ~ flat (Brit.); ~ ~ living unit (US) · Stockwerkwohnung *f* ohne Komfort, Etagenwohnung ~ ~, (Geschoß)Wohnung ~ ~

~ ~ **circuit** · Kaltwasserringleitung *f*, KW-Ringleitung

~ ~ **cistern,** ~ ~ storage ~ · Kaltwasserzisterne *f*, KW-Zisterne

~ ~ **consumption** · Kaltwasserverbrauch *m*, KW-Verbrauch

~ ~ **feed** · Kaltwasserzufluß *m*, KW-Zufluß

~ ~ **tank** · Kaltwasserspeisebehälter *m*, KW-Speisebehälter

~ ~ **flat (Brit.);** ~ ~ apartment (unit); ~ ~ living unit (US) · Stockwerkwohnung *f* ohne Komfort, Etagenwohnung ~ ~, (Geschoß)Wohnung ~ ~

~ ~ **line** · Kaltwasserleitung *f*, KW-Leitung

~ ~ **living unit (US);** ~ ~ apartment (~); ~ ~ flat (Brit.) · Stockwerkwohnung *f* ohne Komfort, Etagenwohnung ~ ~, (Geschoß)Wohnung ~ ~

~ ~ **meter** · Kaltwasseruhr *f*, KW-Uhr [*Fehlnamen*]; Kaltwasserzähler *m*, KW-Zähler

(cold)water paint, water-carried ~, water-base(d) ~ · Binderfarbe *f*, Dispersionsfarbe [*Ein aus Binder und Pigmenten hergestellter Anstrichstoff*]

cold water pressure pipe — colloidal

cold water pressure pipe · Kaltwasser-Druckrohr *n*, KW-Druckrohr

~ ~ **service** [*The piped cold-water supply into a building*] · Kaltwasserzuführung *f*, KW-Zuführung

~ ~ **(storage) cistern** · Kaltwasserzisterne *f*, KW-Zisterne

~ ~ ~ **tank** · Kaltwasser(lager)behälter *m*, KW-(Lager)Behälter

~ ~ **supply** · Kaltwasserversorgung *f*, KW-Versorgung

~ ~ **system** · Kaltwassernetz *n*, KW-Netz

~ ~ **tap** · Kaltwasserhahn *m*, KW-Hahn

~ ~ **test, soundness test by immersion in cold water** · Kaltwasserprobe *f*, Kaltwasserprüfung *f*, Kaltwasserversuch *m* [*Prüfung von Zement auf Raumbeständigkeit; DIN 1164*]

~ **weather protection** · Kaltwetterschutz *m*

~ **work drawing, (wire)** ~ · (Draht)Ziehen *n*

cold-worked, cold-deformed · kaltverformt [*Betonstahl*]

cold working · Kaltverformen *n* [*Betonstahl*]

to collapse, to fail · versagen, einstürzen [*Konstruktion*]

collapse, failure · Versagen *n*, Einsturz *m* [*Konstruktion*]

~ **condition, failure** ~ · Einsturzbedingung *f*

~ **due to instability,** ~ ~ ~ **lability, failure** ~ ~ ~ · Labilitätseinsturz *m*

~ **load, failure** ~ · Einsturzlast *f*

~ **mechanism, failure** ~ · Einsturzmechanismus *m*

~ **rubbish** · Einsturzschutt *m*

~ **strength, failure** ~ · Einsturzfestigkeit *f*, Einsturzwiderstand *m*

collar → neck(ing)

~ · Wulst *m*, *f*

~ **beam,** ~ **tie, spanpiece, wind beam, top beam, sparpiece** · Kehlbalken *m*, Querriegel *m* [*Der beim Kehlbalkendach in die Sparren eingezapfte Balken. Darüber hinaus alle oberhalb des Dachgebälks im Dachraum liegenden Balken (= Kehlgebälk) in Quer- und Längsrichtung des Daches*]

~ (~) **roof,** ~ **tie** ~ [*Common rafters, jointed halfway up their length by a horizontal tie-beam. This roof gives more headroom in the centre of the room than a close-couple roof*] · Kehlbalkendach *n*

~ (~) ~ **with jamb walls,** ~ **tie** ~ ~ ~ ~ · Drempel-Kehlbalkendach *n*

~ **roof** → ~ **tie** ~

~ **stud, shoulder** ~ · Rundbolzen *m*

~ **tie** → ~ **beam**

~ ~ **roof,** ~ **(beam)** ~ [*Common rafters, jointed halfway up their length by a horizontal tie-beam. This roof gives more headroom in the centre of the room than a close-couple roof*] · Kehlbalkendach *n*

~ ~ ~ **with jamb walls,** ~ **(beam)** ~ ~ ~ ~ · Drempel-Kehlbalkendach *n*

collar(ino) → neck(ing)

collecting chamber → refuse ~

~ **line** · Sammelleitung *f*

collective (body of) grains · Körnerkollektiv *n*

~ **control** [*This is an improved form of automatic control in which calls from the liftcar and lift-landings are registered and are answered by the lift car stopping in floor sequence at each lift-landing for which a call has been registered, until all calls have had attention*] · Sammelsteuerung *f* [*Aufzug*]

~ **dwellings** · Kollektivwohnbau *m*

~ **grains,** ~ **body of** ~ · Körnerkollektiv *n*

college of applied art, school ~ ~ ~ · Kunstgewerbeschule *f*

~ ~ **architecture, school** ~ ~ · Architekturhochschule *f*

~ ~ **Design** · Hochschule *f* für Gestaltung

~ ~ **Fine Arts** · Hochschule *f* für Bildende Kunst

collegiate chapel · Kollegiatkapelle *f*, Kollegienkapelle, Stiftskapelle

~ **church** · Kollegiatkirche *f*, Kollegienkirche, Stiftskirche

~ **mosque** → madrasah

(col)linear load, line ~, **strip** ~, **knife edge** ~ [*Forces on a long narrow member, e.g. a beam*] · Linienlast *f*, Streckenlast, Schneidenlast

(col)linear loading → line ~

collodion cotton · Kollodiumwolle *f*, Collodiumwolle, lösliche Schießbaumwolle, Lackwolle, Nitrowolle

colloid [*1. The finely divided suspended matter which will not settle and the apparently dissolved matter which may be transformed into suspended matter by contact with solid surfaces or precipitated by chemical treatment. 2. Substance which is soluble as judged by ordinary physical tests but will not pass through a parchment membrane*] · Kolloid *n*

colloidal · fest, unlöslich [*Emulgator*]

colloidal albumin ... — color(ed) pigment for concrete

~ **albumin solution**; ~ albumen ~ [*misnomer*] · kolloid(al)e Eiweißlösung f

~ **chemistry** · Kolloidchemie f, Kolloidik f, Kolloidlehre f

~ **clay** · kolloid(al)er Ton m, Kolloidton

~ **compound** · kolloid(al)e Masse f

~ **concrete, grouted** ~ [*e.g. Colcrete*] · Kolloid(al)beton m, kolloid(al)er Beton

~ **dispersion** · kolloid(al)e Lösung f, Kolloid(al)lösung, kolloiddisperses System n

~ **emulsifier,** ~ emulsifying agent, ~ emulsion stabilizing agent, ~ emulsion stabilizer · fester Emulgator m, unlöslicher ~, ~ Stabilisator, festes Schutzkolloid n, festes Emulgiermittel n, unlösliches Schutzkolloid, unlösliches Emulgiermittel

~ **emulsifying agent** → ~ emulsifier

~ **emulsion** · Kolloid(al)emulsion f, kolloid(al)e Emulsion

~ ~ **stabilizer** → ~ emulsifier

~ ~ **stabilizing agent** → ~ emulsifier

~ **gel** · Kolloid(al)gel n, kolloid(al)es Gel

~ **grout** · Kolloid(al)schlämme f, kolloid(al)e Schlämme

~ **matter** · kolloid(al)er Stoff m, Kolloid(al)stoff

~ **mortar** · Kolloid(al)mörtel m, kolloid(al)er Mörtel

~ ~ **visco(si)meter** · Fließfähigkeitsmesser m für kolloidalen Mörtel

~ **solid substance,** solid colloidal ~ · kolloid(al)e Festsubstanz f

~ **state** · Kolloid(al)zustand m, kolloid(al)er Zustand

~ **suspension** · kolloid(al)e Aufschwemmung f, ~ Aufschlämmung, ~ Suspension f

~ **system** · kolloid(al)es System n, Kolloid(al)system

colonial house · Kolonialstilhaus n

colonnade [*Arcade with arches supported on columns*] · Kolonnade f, Säulenarkade f

colonnaded avenue [*Palace of Diocletian at Spalato*] · Arkadenstraße f

~ **court** · Säulenhof m

~ **street** · Hallenstraße f, Säulenstraße [*römische Baukunst im Osten*]

colonnade-encircled piazza · Kolonnadenplatz m

colon(n)ette, small column, columella · Säulchen n, kleine Säule f

colony unit → housing ~ ~

Colophonian (resin), colophony, resin, rosin · Kolophonium n, Spiegelharz n, griechisches Pech n, Geigenharz [*DIN 55935*]

colophony, Colophonian (resin), resin, rosin · Kolophonium n, Spiegelharz n, griechisches Pech n, Geigenharz [*DIN 55935*]

color (US) → colour

~ **coated (concrete) aggregate** (US) → colour ~ (~) ~

color-corrected mercury lamp (US); colour-corrected ~ ~ (Brit.) · Quecksilberdampf-Niederdruck-Leuchtstofflampe f

to color integrally (US); ~ colour ~ (Brit.) · einfärben

color marking (US) → colour ~

(~) matching (US) → (colour) ~

color-matching unit (US); colour-matching ~ (Brit.) · Farbprüfleuchte f

color measurement (US) → measuring of colours

~ **selection** (US) → colour ~

~ **system** (US) → colour ~

~ **television studio** (US); colour ~ ~ (Brit.) · Farbfernsehstudio n

coloration · Färbung f

colored (US); coloured (Brit.) · farbig

color(ed) aluminum (US) → colour(ed) aluminium

~ **cement** (US); colour(ed) ~ (Brit.); pigmented ~ · Farbzement m, Buntzement

~ **concrete** (US); colour(ed) ~ (Brit.); pigmented ~ · Buntbeton m, farbiger Beton, Farbbeton

~ **finish** (US); colour(ed) ~ (Brit.) Farb(ver)putz m, Bunt(ver)putz

~ **garden tile** (US) → colour(ed) ~ ~

~ **glass** (US) → colour(ed) ~

~ ~ **block** (US) → colour(ed) ~ ~

~ ~ **brick** (US) → colour(ed) ~ ~

~ **glazed coat(ing)** (US) → colour(ed) glaze(d finish)

~ **glaze(d finish)** (US) → colour(ed) ~

~ **glazing** (US) → colour(ed) glaze(d finish)

~ **laminated glass** (US); colour(ed) ~ ~ (Brit.); tinted ~ ~ · Farbverbundglas n, Verbundfarbglas

~ **marble** (US); colour(ed) ~ (Brit.) Buntmarmor m

~ **mastic asphalt** (US); colour(ed) ~ ~ (Brit.); pigmented ~ ~ · Buntgußasphalt m, Farbgußasphalt, farbiger Gußasphalt

~ **(mixed) plaster** (US) → colour(ed) (~) ~

~ **mortar** (US); colour(ed) ~ (Brit.); pigmented ~ · Buntmörtel m, farbiger Mörtel, Farbmörtel

~ **pigment** (US); colour(ed) ~ (Brit.) · Buntpigment n, Farbpigment

~ ~ **for concrete** (US) → colour(ed) ~ ~ ~

color(ed) plaster — colour(ed) concrete

~ **plaster** (US) → coloured (mixed) ~

~ **tile** (US); colour(ed) ~ (Brit.); pigmented ~ · Bunt(belag)platte f, Buntfliese f, Farb(belag)platte f, Farbfliese

colorfast (US); colourfast (Brit.) · farbbeständig, farbecht

colorimeter · Farbmesser m

colorimetry → measuring of colours

coloring agent (US) → (organic) colouring substance

~ **matter** (US) → colouring ~

~ ~ (US) → (organic) colouring substance

~ **of aluminum** (US); colouring of aluminium (Brit.) · Alu(minium)färbung f

~ **substance** (US) → (organic) colouring ~

~ ~ (US) → (organic) colouring ~

colorless (US) → colourless

~ **glass** (US) → colourless ~

colossal order (of architecture), grand ~ (~ ~), giant ~ (~ ~) · große Ordnung f, Riesenordnung, Kolossalordnung [*Eine Ordnung bei der die Pilaster oder Säulen über mehrere Geschosse reichen und sie somit zusammenfassen*]

~ **pilaster** · Kolossalpilaster m [*Wandpfeiler einer Kolossalordnung*]

~ **statue**, colossus · Kolossalstatue f, Riesenstatue, Kolossalfigur f, Riesenfigur

~ ~ **of Ramses** · Ramseskoloß m

~ **temple** · Riesentempel m

Colosseum at Rome, Flavian Amphitheatre [*sometimes spelt, 'Coliseum'*] · flavisches Amphitheater n zu Rom, Kolosseum n

Colossi of Memnon · Memnonkolosse mpl [*Theben*]

colossus → colossal statue

Colossus of Rhodes · Koloß m von Rhodos

colour (Brit.); color (US) · Farbe f [*Farbe ist (im Sinne von DIN 5033 Blatt 1) ein durch das Auge vermittelter Sinneseindruck, der durch die auf das menschliche Auge auftretenden Strahlen ausgelöst wird. Eine Farbe ist durch Farbton, Sättigungsstufe und Dunkelstufe gekennzeichnet. Anmerkung: Das Wort „Farbe" wird im täglichen Sprachgebrauch auch für Pigmente, Farbstoffe und farbige Anstrichstoffe gebraucht. In wissenschaftlichen und fachlichen Abhandlungen soll das Wort „Farbe" für sich allein nicht als Benennung für Stoffe benutzt werden. Für Stoffe, mit deren Hilfe man Gegenständen eine andere Farbe geben kann, sind gegebenenfalls Wortzusammensetzungen mit „Farbe" zu wählen, z.B. Anstrichfarbe, Leimfarbe, Künstlerfarbe*]

~ **chart** (Brit.); color ~ (US) · Farb(ton)karte f

~ **coated aggregate** → ~ ~ concrete ~

~ ~ **(concrete) aggregate** (Brit.); color ~ (~) ~ (US) [*It has been found practicable to coat natural aggregates with resin in which suitable inorganic or organic pigments may be incorporated to produce an almost unlimited range of colour*] · gefärbte (Beton)Zuschlagstoffe mpl, ~ (Beton)Zuschläge mpl

colour-coated steel (Brit.); color-coated ~ (US); CCS · Stahl m in Farbe [*Mehrschichteinbrennlackiertes Stahlband und Stahlblech*]

colour conditioning (Brit.); color ~ (US) · Schaffen n von farblichen Umweltbedingungen

~ **contrast** (Brit.); color ~ (US) · Farbgegensatz m

~ **development**, development of colour (Brit.); development of color, color development (US) · Farbentwick(e)lung f

~ **fastness** (Brit.); color ~ (US) · Farbbeständigkeit f, Farbechtheit

~ **for incorporating in cement** → cement pigment

to colour integrally (Brit.); to color ~ (US) · einfärben

colour marking (Brit.); color ~ (US); pipe ~ · Farbkennzeichnung f von Rohrleitungen, Rohrkennzeichnung [*DIN 2403*]

(~) **matching** (Brit.); (color) ~ (US) · (Farb)Angleichung f

colour-matching unit (Brit.); color-matching ~ (US) · Farbprüfleuchte f

colour measurement → measuring of colours

~ **measurements** (Brit.); color ~ (US) · messende Farbenlehre f

~ **measuring instrument** (Brit.); color ~ ~ (US) · Farbmeßgerät n

~ **mixing** (Brit.); color ~ (US) · Farbmischung f

~ **retention** (Brit.); color ~ (US) · Farbhaltung f

~ **selection** (Brit.); color ~ (US) · Farb(en)wahl f

~ **system** (Brit.); color ~ (US) · Farbsystem n

~ **television studio** (Brit.); color ~ ~ Fernsehstudio n

~ **temperature** (Brit.); color ~ (US) · Farbtemperatur f

~ **undertone** (Brit.); color ~ (US) · Unterton m [*Farbe*]

coloured (Brit.); colored (US) · farbig

colour(ed) aluminium (Brit.); color(ed) aluminum (US) · Buntalu(minium) n, Farbalu(minium)

~ **cement** (Brit.); color(ed) ~ (US); pigmented ~ · Farbzement m, Buntzement

~ **concrete** (Brit.); color(ed) ~ (US); pigmented ~ · Buntbeton m, farbiger Beton, Farbbeton

colour(ed) finish — (column) drum

~ **finish** (Brit.); color(ed) ~ (US) · Farb(ver)putz *m*, Bunt(ver)putz

~ **garden tile** (Brit.); color(ed) ~ ~ (US); pigmented ~ ~ · farbige Gartenplatte *f*, Gartenbuntplatte

~ **glass** (Brit.); color(ed) ~ (US); tinted ~, stained ~ · Farbglas *n*, farbiges Glas, Buntglas, gefärbtes Glas

~ ~ **block** (Brit.) → tinted ~ ~

~ ~ **brick** (Brit.) → tinted glass block

~ **glazed coat(ing)** → ~ glaze(d finish)

~ **glaze(d finish),** ~ glazed coat(ing), ~ glazing (Brit.); color(ed) glaze(d finish), colored glazed coat(ing), colored glazing · gefärbte Glasur *f*, ~ Beglasung *f*, Farbglasur, Farbbeglasung

~ **glazing** → ~ glaze(d finish)

~ **laminated glass** (Brit.); color(ed) ~ ~ (US); tinted ~ ~ · Farbverbundglas *n*, Verbundfarbglas

~ **marble** (Brit.); color(ed) ~ (US) · Buntmarmor *m*

~ **mastic asphalt** (Brit.); color(ed) ~ ~ (US); pigmented ~ ~ · Buntgußasphalt *m*, Farbgußasphalt, farbiger Gußasphalt

~ **(mixed) plaster** (Brit.); color(ed) (~) ~ (US) · gefärbter (Innen)(Ver)Putz *m*

~ **mortar** (Brit.); color(ed) ~ (US); pigmented ~ · Buntmörtel *m*, farbiger Mörtel, Farbmörtel

~ **pigment,** colouring ~ (Brit.); color(ed) ~, coloring ~ (US) · Buntpigment *n*, Farbpigment

~ ~ **for concrete** (Brit.); color(ed) ~ ~ ~ (US) · Betonfarbstoff *m*

~ **plaster** → ~ mixed ~

~ **tile** (Brit.); color(ed) ~ (US); pigmented ~ · Bunt(belag)platte *f*, Buntfliese *f*, Farb(belag)platte, Farbfliese

colourfast (Brit.); colorfast (US) · farbbeständig, farbecht

colouring agent (Brit.) → ~ matter

~ **matter,** ~ agent, ~ substance (Brit.); coloring ~ (US) · Farbmittel *n*, Farbsubstanz *f*, färbende Substanz, färbendes Mittel [*Sammelname für alle farbgebenden Stoffe, wie Farblack, Farbstoff, Pigment und Pigmentfarbstoff. DIN 55944*]

~ **of aluminium** (Brit.); coloring of aluminum (US) · Alu(minium)färbung *f*

~ **pigment,** coloured ~ (Brit.); coloring ~, colored ~ (US) · Buntpigment *n*, Farbpigment

~ **substance** → ~ matter

colourless, uncoloured (Brit.); colorless, uncolored (US); clear, transparent · farblos

~ (Brit.); colorless (US); clear · farblos, klar (durchsichtig) [*Glas*]

columbarium [*A building with tiers or niches for holding cinerary urns*] · Urnenhaus *n*

~, dove-cote, pigeon-cote, pigeon-house, culverhouse [*A number of historical examples still exist in England, some with nests for over a thousand birds each*] · Taubenhaus *n*, Kolumbarium *n*

column [*Round upright member, including the base and capital. The proportions vary according to the style or order*] · Säule *f*

~, post, leg, frame ~, framing ~, supporting member, vertical (member) · (Rahmen)Pfosten *m*, (Rahmen)Stiel *m*, (Rahmen)Stütze *f*

~ [*Standing isolated as a monument, e.g. Nelson's Column in London*] · Säule *f*

~, support · Stütze *f*

~, support, floor ~ · (Decken)Stütze *f*

~, lighting ~ (Brit.); mast (US) · Beleuchtungsmast *m*, (Straßen)Leuchtenmast, (Licht)Mast

~ **analogy,** support ~ · Stützenanalogie *f*

~ **anchorage,** support ~ · Stützenverankerung *f*

~ **architecture** · Säulenarchitektur *f*, Säulenbaukunst *f*

~ **bar,** support ~ · Stützenstab *m* [*Bewehrung*]

(~) **base (plate),** support ~ (~) · (Stützen)Fuß *m*, (Stützen)Basis *f*

~ **basilica,** ~-type ~ · Säulenbasilika *f*

~ **bearing,** support ~ · Stützenauflagerung *f*

~ **bent,** support ~ [*A bent composed of columns and bracing in contradistinction to 'pile bent'*] · Stützen-Querrahmen *m*

~ **bracket,** support ~ · Stützenkonsole *f*

~ ~ **(Brit.);** mast arm (US) · Mastausleger *m*

~ **cap,** support ~ · Stützenkopfplatte *f*

~ **capital** · Säulenkapitell *n*, Säulenkapitäl

~ **casing,** support ~ · Stützenummantelung *f* (mit Beton)

~ **clamp,** support ~ · Stützenzwinge *f*

~ **concrete,** support ~ · Stützenbeton *m*

~ **condition,** support ~ · Stützenbedingung *f*

~ **connection,** support ~ · Stützenanschluß *m*

~ **core,** support ~ · Stützenkern *m*

~ **cross section** · Säulenquerschnitt *m*

~ **creep,** support ~ · Stützenkriechen *n*

~ **design,** support ~ · Stützenbemessung *f*

~ **dimension,** support ~ · Stützenabmessung *f*, Stützenmaß *n*

(~) **drum** · (Säulen)Trommel *f*

column end moment — column with services

~ **end moment,** support ~ ~ · Stützenendmoment *n*

~ **facing** → ~ lining

column-figure · Säulenfigur *f*

~ **portal** · Säulenfigurportal *n*

column flange, support ~ · Stützenflansch *m*

~ **foot,** ~ base, support ~ · Stützenfuß *m*

~ **footing,** support ~ · Stützenfundament *n*

~ **forming,** support ~ · Stützeneinschalen *n*

~ **forms,** ~ form(work), ~ shuttering, support ~ · Stützenschalung *f*

~ **formula,** support ~ · Stützenformel *f*

~ **form(work),** ~ forms, ~ shuttering, support ~ · Stützenschalung *f*

column-free, column-less, clear, support-free, support-less · stützenfrei, stützenlos

column grid pattern, support ~ ~ · Stützenraster *m* [*Anordnung der Stützen im Rastersystem*]

~ **guard,** pier ~ · Kantenschutz *m* [*für Betonstützen und Betonpfeiler*]

~ **head,** support ~ · Stützenkopf *m*

~ ~ · Säulenkopf *m*

~ ~, support ~, flared ~, flaring ~, mushroom ~, flared haunch [*In flat slab construction. An enlargement at the top of a column supporting a flat slab, designed and constructed to act monolithically with the column and with the flat slab*] · Pilzkopf *m*, Stützenkopf

~ **height,** support ~ · Stützenhöhe *f*

~ **hinge,** support ~ · Stützengelenk *n*

~ **instability,** support ~ · Stützenlabilität *f*

~ **interval** → ~ spacing

~ **layout,** support ~ · Stützenanordnung *f*

~ **length,** support ~ · Stützenlänge *f*

column-less, column-free, clear, support-free, support-less · stützenfrei, stützenlos

column-like pier · säulenähnlicher Pfeiler *m*

column lining, ~ (sur)facing, support ~ · Stützenauskleidung *f*, Stützenverkleidung, Stützenbekleidung

~ **load,** support ~ · Stützenlast *f*

~ **movement,** support ~ · Stützenbewegung *f*

~ **of air** · Luftsäule *f*

~ ~ **clay** · Tonstrang *m* [*Ziegelherstellung*]

Column of Jupiter · Jupitersäule *f*

~ ~ **Marcus Aurelius at Rome** · Marc-Aurelsäule *f* zu Rom

column of tapered sheet construction → lantern ~ ~ ~ ~ ~

~ **of Trajan,** Trajan's column · Trajansäule *f*

~ ~ **triumph,** triumphal column · Triumphsäule *f*

~ ~ **welded sheet construction** → lantern ~ ~ ~ ~ ~

~ **opening,** support ~ · Stützenöffnung *f*

~ **pair,** support ~ · Stützenpaar *n*

~ **pedestal** · (Säulen)Sockel *m*, (Säulen-)Unterbau *m*

~ **problem** · Stützenaufgabe *f*

~ **radiator** · Röhrenradiator *m*

~ **radius,** support ~ · Stützenhalbmesser *m*

~ **reaction,** support ~ · Stützenreaktion *f*

~ **reinforcement,** support ~ · Stützenarmierung *f*, Stützenbewehrung, Stützen(stahl)einlagen *fpl*

~ **rib,** rib of column · Säulenrippe *f*

~ **rigidity,** ~ stiffness, support ~ · Stützensteifigkeit *f*

~ **section** · Stützenschuß *m*, Stützenabschnitt *m*

~ ~, support ~ · Stützenprofil *n*, Stützenquerschnitt *m*

~ **shaft,** support ~ · Stützenschaft *m*

(~) ~, fust · (Säulen)Schaft *m*, (Säulen-)Rumpf *m*

~ **shape** · Säulenform *f*

~ **shuttering,** ~ form(work), ~ forms, support ~ · Stützenschalung *f*

~ **side,** support ~ · Stützenschalungstafel *f*

~ **size,** support ~ · Stützengröße *f*

~ **spacing,** support ~, ~ interval, spacing of columns, spacing of supports, interval of columns, interval of supports · Stützenabstand *m*, Stützenentfernung *f*

~ **stiffness,** ~ rigidity, support ~ · Stützensteifigkeit *f*

~ **strength,** support ~ · Stützenfestigkeit *f*

~ **stress,** support ~ · Stützenspannung *f*

~ **(sur)facing** → ~ lining

column-to-column joint, support-to-support ~ · Stützen-Stützen-Verbindung *f*

column-to-floor connection → column-to-slab ~

column-to-footing connection, support-to-footing ~ · Stützen-Fundament-Verbindung *f*

column-to-slab connection, column-to-floor ~, support-to-slab ~, support-to-floor ~ · Stützen-Platten-Verbindung *f*, Stützen-Decken-Verbindung, Stützen-Platten-Anschluß *m*, Stützen-Decken-Anschluß

column(-type) basilica · Säulenbasilika *f*

column vector, support ~ · Stützenvektor *m*

~ **web,** support ~ · Stützensteg *m*

~ **width,** support ~ · Stützenbreite *f*

~ **with bracket** → lighting ~ ~ ~

~ ~ **cosmati work** · Kosmatensäule *f*

~ ~ **services** · Installationsstütze *f*

column with two brackets — combustible material 218

~ ~ **two brackets**, lighting ~ ~ ~ ~ (Brit.); mast with two arms (US) · Doppelausleger-(Licht)Mast m

~ **zone**, support ~ · Stützenbereich m, n

columnar · säulenförmig

~ **basalt** · säuliger Basalt m, Säulenbasalt

~ **basilica** · Säulenbasilika f

~ **building** · Säulengebäude n

~ **decoration** · Säulenausstattung f, Ausstattung mit Säulen

~ **interior**, columned hall, hall of columns · Säulenraum m, Säulensaal m, Säulenhalle f

~ **ornament** · Säulenornament n

~ **portal** · Säulenportal n [*In der abgetreppten Portalleibung sind Säulen eingesetzt*]

~ **style** · Säulenstil m

columned Greek temple · Säulenhaus n [*Das Wesen des griechischen Tempels wird durch den Begriff „Säulenhaus" ausgedrückt*]

~ **hall**, hall of columns, columnar interior · Säulenraum m, Säulensaal m, Säulenhalle f

comb · Kamm m [*Putztechnik*]

~ **plaster**; ~ rendering (Brit.) · Kamm(ver)putz m

~ **rendering** (Brit.); ~ plaster · Kamm(ver)putz m

combination concrete curing and sealing compound · (Beton)Nachbehandlungs- und -absieg(e)lungsmittel n

~ **lock**, dial ~, puzzle ~ · Kombi(nations)schloß n, Vexierschloß, Ringschloß

~ **padlock**, dial ~ · Ring-Vorhängeschloß n, Kombi(nations)-Vorhängeschloß, Vexier-Vorhängeschloß

~ **range** · Kombi(nations)herd m

~ **sink cabinet and cooker unit** · Herd-Spültisch-Kombination f, Herd-Abwaschtisch-Kombination

~ **stopper** · Kombi(nations)spachtel(-masse) m, (f) [*Anstrichtechnik*]

combinatorial analysis · Kombinatorik f, kombinatorische Analyse f, Kombinationslehre f

combined aggregate → ~ construction ~

~ **bending and axial loading** · zusammengesetzte Biegung f, Biegung mit Längskraft [*Zug- oder Druckkräfte greifen außerhalb der Schwerlinie eines Balkens an*]

~ **building materials**, ~ construction(al) ~ · Baustoffkombination f; Baumaterialkombination [*Schweiz*]

(~) **closing and check action** · Schließ- und Hemmwirkung f [*Tür*]

~ **concrete aggregate**, total ~ ~ · Betonzuschlag(stoff)gemenge n, Betonzuschlag(stoff)gemisch n, Beton-Gesamtzuschlag(stoff) m

~ **(construction) aggregate**, total (~) ~ · Zuschlag(stoff)gemenge n, Zuschlag(stoff)gemisch n, Gesamtzuschlag(stoff) m

~ **construction(al) materials**, ~ building ~ · Baustoffkombination f; Baumaterialkombination [*Schweiz*]

~ **drainage** → ~ system (of sewers)

~ **flat bending and compression**, ~ plane ~ ~ ~, ~ planar ~ ~ ~ · ebene zusammengesetzte Biegung f

~ **materials**, mix(ture) · Mischung f, Gemisch n

~ **planar bending and compression**, ~ plane ~ ~ ~, ~ flat ~ ~ ~ · ebene zusammengesetzte Biegung f

~ **plane bending and compression**, ~ planar ~ ~ ~, ~ flat ~ ~ ~ · ebene zusammengesetzte Biegung f

~ **Rabitz (type) wire cloth and reed lath(ing)**, ~ ~ (~) woven wire fabric ~ ~ ~; ~ ~ (~) wire fabric ~ ~ ~ [*misnomer*] · Rabitzmatte f, Rabitzrohrmatte, Rabitzrohrgewebe n [*Putzträger aus Rabitzgewebe und Rohrgewebe. Gewicht etwa 1 kg/m²*]

~ **service(d) ceiling** · Decke f mit unterschiedlichen Leitungen

~ **sewage** · Mischwasser n [*Schmutzwasser + Niederschlagswasser*]

~ **sewerage (system)** → ~ system (of sewers)

~ **sieve and sedimentation test**, mechanical analysis · kombinierte Sieb- und Schlämmanalyse f

~ **sponge and soap holder**, ~ ~ ~ ~ tray · Schwamm- und Seifenschale f

~ **stresses** · zusammengesetzte Spannungen fpl

~ **style**, composite ~ · Mischstil m

~ **system intercepting sewer** · Misch(wasser)sammler m

~ ~ **(of sewerage)**, ~ ~ ~ sewers, ~ sewerage (system), ~ drainage [*A system of sewers, in which sewage and storm water are carried*] · Mischentwässerung f, Mischsystem n, Mischkanalisation f

~ **use of field concrete and (pre-)cast elements** · Gemischtanwendung f von Ortbeton und Fertigteilen

~ **water**, water of crystallization · Kristallwasser n [*Wasser, das in Kristallen chemisch gebunden ist*]

combing · Kämmen n [*Außenputz*]

combustibility · Brennbarkeit f [*Baustoff. DIN 4102*]

~ **grading period** · Brennbarkeitsklasse f [*Baustoff*]

~ **test** · Brennbarkeitsprobe f, Brennbarkeitsprüfung f, Brennbarkeitsversuch m [*Baustoff*]

combustible [*Capable of undergoing combustion*] · brennbar [*DIN 4102*]

~ **material** · brennbarer Stoff m

combustible shale — commercial tower (block)

~ **shale,** carbonaceous ~ · Brandschiefer *m*, Brennschiefer, Kohlenschiefer

combustion air · Verbrennungsluft *f*

~ **chamber** [*The space in a heating appliance provided for the combustion of fuel*] · Brennkammer *f*

~ **gas** · Verbrennungsgas *n*

~ **rate,** rate of combustion · Brenngeschwindigkeit *f* [*Baustoff*]

come-along · Seilzug *m*

comfort condition · Behaglichkeitsbedingung *f*

~ **curve** · Behaglichkeitskurve *f*

~ **index** · Behaglichkeitsindex *m*

~ **zone** [*The range of temperatures, humidities and air velocities at which the greatest percentage of people feel comfortable*] · Behaglichkeitszone *f*

comfortable feeling, feeling of comfort · Behaglichkeitsgefühl *n*

commemorative arch, memorial ~ · Denkbogen *m*, Ehrenbogen

~ **basilica,** memorial ~, martyrium ~ · Memorienbasilika *f*, Gedächtnisbasilika, Memorialbasilika *f*, Märtyrerbasilika, Coemetrialbasilika, Martyria *f*, Denkmalbasilika

~ **chapel,** memorial ~ · Gedächtniskapelle *f*, Totenkapelle, Memorienkapelle , Memorialkapelle

~ **church,** memorial ~, martyrium ~ · Coemetrialkirche *f*, Martyria *f*, Memoria(lkirche), Denkmalkirche, Gedächtniskirche, Memorienkirche [*Kirche auf oder in einem Coemeterium, meist nahe oder über einem Märtyrergrab*]

~ **figure,** memorial ~ · Gedenkfigur *f*

~ **hall,** memorial ~ · Memorienhalle *f*, Gedächtnishalle, Memorialhalle , Totenhalle

~ **monument,** memorial ~ · Gedenkmonument *n*

~ **stone,** memorial ~ · Gedenkstein *m*

~ **structure,** memorial ~ · Memorialbau *m*, Gedächtnisbau

~ **tablet,** memorial ~, plaque · Gedenktafel *f*

commencement of initial set(ting) · Erstarrungsanfang *m*, Erstarrungsbeginn *m* [*Beton; Mörtel*]

~ ~ **set(ting)** · (Ab)Bindeanfang *m*, (Ab)Bindebeginn *m* [*hydraulisches Bindemittel*]

~ ~ **work** · Baubeginn *m*

commercial aggregates plant → ~ construction ~ ~

~ **alloy** · Handelslegierung *f*

~ **architecture** · kommerzielle Architektur *f*, ~ Baukunst *f*

~ **asbestos** [*A term which includes many fibrous heat-resisting minerals*] · Handelsasbest *m*

~ **block,** ~ building, utilitarian ~ [*A building used principally for business or professional practice*] · Geschäftsgebäude *n*, Geschäftshaus *n*

~ **bronze** · Rottombak *m*, Ms 90 *n*, MS 90, Messing 90

~ **building,** ~ block, utilitarian ~ [*A building used principally for business or professional practice*] · Geschäftsgebäude *n*, Geschäftshaus *n*

~ **(concrete) aggregate plant,** stationary (~) ~ ~ · (Beton)Zuschlag(stoff)werk *n*

~ **(construction) aggregates plant,** stationary (~) ~ ~ · Zuschlag(stoff)werk *n*

~ **copper** · Handelskupfer *n*

~ **cork** · Handelskork *m*

~ **distemper** · Handelsleimfarbe *f*

~ **fiber** (US); ~ fibre (Brit.) · Handelsfaser *f*

~ **flat glass** · Handelsflachglas *n*

~ **form** · Handelsform *f* [*Erzeugnis*]

~ **grade,** ~ quality · Handelsgüte *f*

~ ~ **steel,** merchant bar(s), black bar(s) · Handelsstahl *m*

~ **high-rise block** → ~ tower (~)

~ ~ **building** → ~ tower (block)

~ **iron** · Handelseisen *n*, gewalztes Grobeisen

~ **length** · Handelslänge *f*

~ **lime** → ~ quick~

~ ~ · Handelskalk *m*

~ **name** · handelsübliche Bezeichnung *f*

~ **pipe** · Handelsrohr *n*

~ **premises,** business ~, ~ property · bebautes Geschäftsgrundstück *n*

~ **prestressing** · Fertigung *f* im Spannbetonwerk, Herstellung ~ ~

~ **property,** business ~, ~ premises · bebautes Geschäftsgrundstück *n*

~ **quality,** ~ grade · Handelsgüte *f*

~ **(quick)lime,** calcium ~ [*It contains 75 to 90 per cent of calcium oxid(e)*] · Handelsbranntkalk *m*

~ **rolled section** · Handels(walz)profil *n*

~ **rustless steel,** ~ stainless ~ · (rostfreier) Handelsstahl *m*

~ **shellack** · Handelsschellack *m*

~ **silver** · Handelssilber *n*

~ **size** · Handelsgröße *f*

~ **sort** · Handelssorte *f*

~ **stainless steel,** ~ rustless ~ · (rostfreier) Handelsstahl *m*

~ **stone-crushing plant** · Schotterwerk *n*

~ **structural steel** · Handelsbaustahl *m* [„St.H.W.", DIN 1050 für Stahlhochbau. Nicht geschweißt. Zugfestigkeit 34 bis 50 kp/mm²]

~ **tall block** → ~ tower (~)

~ ~ **building** → ~ tower (block)

~ **tower (block),** ~ ~ building, ~ tall ~, ~ high-rise ~ · Geschäftshochhaus *n*

commercial value — compacting concrete by vibration

~ value · Ertragswert m [Gebäude]
to comminute, to reduce · zerkleinern
commissioning · Inbetriebnahme f
commode-type toilet, ~ closet [The term 'lavatory' is also used as a euphemism for 'toilet' or 'closet'] · Sitzabort m, Sitzklosett n, Sitztoilette f, Sitzabtritt m
common bond (US) → American ~
~ brick, ~ stock, backing (~), back-up ~; building ~ (US) · Hintermauer-(ungs)ziegel m, Hintermaurer m
~ ~, standard ~ · Normalziegel m
~ carport, communal ~ · Gemeinschafts(ein)stellplatz m mit Schutzdach
~ chamotte brick, standard ~ ~ · Schamotte-Normalstein m
~ consumer system, communal ~ ~ · Gemeinschaftsanlage f
~ drying room, communal ~ ~ · Gemeinschaftstrocknungsraum m
~ flue · Sammelzug m
~ garage, communal ~ · Gemeinschaftsgarage f
~ illumination, ~ lighting, communal ~ · Allgemeinbeleuchtung f
~ joist, boarding ~, wood(en) ~, timber ~ [A wood beam directly supporting a floor] · Holzdeckenbalken m
~ kitchen, communal ~ · Gemeinschaftsküche f
~ laundry, communal ~, laundry club · Gemeinschaftswäscherei f
~ lighting, ~ illumination, communal ~ · Allgemeinbeleuchtung f
~ lime [substance] → calcium oxid(e)
~ lock seam, hook ~ · Hakenfalz m [Metallbedachung]
~ lounge → ~ room
~ mica, potash ~, muscovy glass, muscovite · heller Glimmer m, Kaliglimmer, Muskovit m
~ nail → ~ wire ~
~ normal · gemeinsame Normale f
~ rafter, intermediate ~, spar · Leersparren m, Zwischensparren
~ rafters, intermediate ~, spars · Leergebinde n, Leergespärre, Leersparren mpl, Zwischensparren
~ room, dayroom · Tagesraum m
~ ~, communal ~, ~ lounge · Gemeinschaftsraum m
~ salt, rock ~, halite · Salzgestein n, Steinsalz n
~ services, communal ~ · Gemeinschaftseinrichtungen fpl
~ (stock) brick, backing (~), back-up ~; building ~ (US) · Hintermauer(ungs)ziegel m, Hintermaurer m
common-type of curved beam, concentric ~ · konzentrischer Balken(träger) m
common washroom, communal ~ · Gemeinschaftswaschraum m

~ (wire) nail · runder Drahtstift m mit glattem Flachkopf, ~ Drahtnagel m ~ ~ ~
commons, hall · Mensa f
communal building · Kommunalgebäude n
~ carport, common ~ · Gemeinschafts(ein)stellplatz m mit Schutzdach
~ consumer system, common ~ ~ · Gemeinschaftsanlage f
~ drying room, common ~ ~ · Gemeinschaftstrocknungsraum m
~ garage, common.~ · Gemeinschaftsgarage f
~ illumination, ~ lighting, common ~ · Allgemeinbeleuchtung f
~ kitchen, common ~ · Gemeinschaftsküche f
~ laundry, common ~, laundry club · Gemeinschaftswäscherei f
~ lighting, ~ illumination, common ~ · Allgemeinbeleuchtung f
~ lounge → common room
~ room → common ~
~ services, common ~ · Gemeinschaftseinrichtungen fpl
~ washroom, common ~ · Gemeinschaftswaschraum m
commune · Gemeinde f
Communication pipe [The portion of the service pipe from the main to the boundary of consumers' premises] · Endstrang m
~ system · Übermittelungsanlage f
communion table · Abendmahltisch m
community, agglomeration · menschliche Sied(e)lung f [Dieser Ausdruck wird im nichttechnischen Sinne verwendet]
~ administration building · Gemeindeverwaltungsgebäude n
~ centre (Brit.); ~ center (US); cultural ~ · Kulturhaus n, Kulturzentrum n, Gemeindezentrum
~ ground · Gemeindegrund m, Gemeindegelände n
~ gymnasium · Gemeinde-Turnhalle f
~ living · Wohnen n in Gemeinschaft
~ planning · Gemeindeplanung f
compact edge · geschlossene Kante f
~ gypsum, gypseous solid rock · kompakter (Roh)Gipsstein m, dichter ~, fest(gelagert)er ~, Gipsfels m
~ limestone · dichter Kalkstein m
~ polishable limestone · polierbarer dichter Kalkstein m, technischer Marmor m, Marmorkalkstein
compacting by hand · Handverdichtung f
compacting concrete by surface vibrator(s) · Rüttel-Auflastverfahren n [Beton]
~ ~ ~ vibration · (Ein)Rütteln n [Beton]

221 compacting concrete by vibration ... — compass stretcher

~ ~ ~ ~ **and compression,** compaction of ~ ~ ~ ~ ~ · (Ein) Rütteldruckverdichtung f [*Beton*]

~ **factor** · Verdichtungsquotient m, Verdichtungsfaktor m [*Beton*]

~ ~ **test** · Verdichtungsquotientenprüfung f, Verdichtungsquotientenversuch m, Verdichtungsquotientenprobe f [*Beton*]

compaction of concrete by vibration and compression, compacting ~ ~ ~ ~ ~ · (Ein) Rütteldruckverdichtung f [*Beton*]

compactness (of proportion) · Gedrungenheit f

compactor · Stampfgerät n zur Herstellung von Probewürfeln [*DIN 1996*]

company office · Schreibstube f

company's administration building, ~ ~ unit, ~ ~ block · Verwaltungsgebäude n, Verwaltungstrakt m [*einer Firma*]

~ ~ **tower** · Verwaltungshochhaus n [*einer Firma*]

~ **fuse,** principal ~, main ~ · Hauptsicherung f

comparative concrete, comparison ~ · Vergleichsbeton m [*Normal erhärtende Probekörper bei warmbehandeltem Beton*]

~ **size,** comparison ~ · Vergleichsgröße f

~ **strength,** comparison ~ · Vergleichsfestigkeit f

~ **test,** comparison ~ · Vergleichsversuch m

~ ~ **series,** comparison ~ ~ · Reihen-Vergleichsversuche mpl, Vergleichsversuchsreihe f

comparing of colours (Brit.); ~ ~ colors (US) · Farbvergleich m

comparison concrete, comparative ~ · Vergleichsbeton m [*Normal erhärtende Probekörper bei warmbehandeltem Beton*]

~ **size,** comparative ~ · Vergleichsgröße f

~ **slenderness** · Vergleichsschlankheit f

~ **strength,** comparative ~ · Vergleichsfestigkeit f

~ **stress** · Vergleichsspannung f

~ **test,** comparative ~ · Vergleichsversuch m

~ ~ **series,** comparative ~ ~ · Reihen-Vergleichsversuche mpl, Vergleichsversuchsreihe f

compartment · Zelle f [*Hohlkasten(-träger)*]

~, **fire lobby** [*A space within a building designed to delay the passage or facilitate the control of fire*] · Brandabschnitt m [*DIN 14011*]

~ → (vault) bay

~ · Gefach n [*Fachwerkbau*]

~ **box** [*A box for joining pipes in different directions. It may be 3-way, 4-way, 5-way, etc.*] · Rohrverzweigungskasten m

~ **division masonry wall** (Brit.); fire ~ ~ ~ (US) [*A fire-resisting masonry wall from the lowest floor up to the roof used in dividing a building into separate compartments*] · durchgehende Brand(schutz)mauer f, ~ Feuer(schutz)mauer

~ ~ **wall** (Brit.); fire ~ ~ (US) [*A fire-resisting wall from the lowest floor up to the roof used in dividing a building into separate compartments*] · durchgehende Brand(schutz)wand f, ~ Feuer(schutz)wand

~ **floor** → fire(-)resisting ~

~ **(masonry) wall** (Brit.) → fire (~) ~

~ **wall** (Brit.) → fire ~

compartmentation · Aufteilung f eines Gebäudes durch Feuer(schutz)mauern, ~ ~ ~ ~ Brand(schutz)mauern

~ **(by fire-resistant materials)** [*Dividing a building up into 'fire cells' by means of internal walls of concrete block or other fire-resistant material which restrict or prevent the lateral spread of fire to other parts of the building*] · Zellenbrandschutz m, Zellenfeuerschutz

compass block, ~ tile, radial ~, radiating ~ [*See remark under 'Block'*] · Radialstein m, Radialblock(stein) m, Ringstein, Ringblock(stein) [*DIN 1057*]

~ **(bonding) header,** radial (~) ~, radiating (~) ~, ~ bonder, ~ bondstone · Radialstrecker m, Radialbinder(-stein) m

~ **brick,** radial ~, radiating ~, radius ~ [*A brick the two end faces of which are parts of concentric cylinders*] · Ringziegel m, Radialziegel, Schachtziegel, Brunnenziegel, Rz

~ **engineering brick,** radial ~ ~, radiating ~ ~ [*It tapers in at least one direction*] · Radialklinker m, Ringklinker, R 350 [*DIN 1057*]

~ **format,** radial ~, radiating ~ · Radialformat m

~ **hard brick,** ~ well-burned ~, ~ well-burnt ~, radial ~ ~, radiating ~ · Radialhart(brand)ziegel m, Ringhart(brand)ziegel, Rz 250 [*DIN 1057*]

~ **header** → ~ bonding ~

~ **rafter,** curved ~ · gebogener Sparren m

~ **solid block,** radial ~ ~, radiating ~, ~ ~ tile [*See remark under 'Block'*] · Radialvollblock(stein) m, Radialvollstein, Ringvollblock(stein), Ringvollstein, Rs 150

~ ~ **brick,** radial ~ ~, radiating ~ ~ · Radialmauerziegel m, Ringmauerziegel, Radialvollziegel, Rz 150

~ ~ **tile** → ~ ~ block

~ **stretcher,** radial ~, radiating ~ · Radialläufer m

compass tile — composite capital

~ **tile**, ~ block, radial ~, radiating ~ [*See remark under 'Block'*] · Radialstein *m*, Radialblock(stein) *m*, Ringstein, Ringblock(stein) [*DIN 1057*]

~ **well-burned brick**, ~ well-burnt ~, ~ hard ~, radial ~ ~, radiating ~ ~ · Radialhart(brand)ziegel *m*, Ringhart(brand)ziegel, Rz 250 [*DIN 1057*]

~ **window** [*An oriel window circular in plan*] · rundes (Obergeschoß)Erkerfenster *n*

~ ~, bow ~ [*A curved bay window*] · gekrümmtes Ausluchtfenster *n*

compatibility · Verträglichkeit *f*

~ **approach** · Verträglichkeitsansatz *m*

~ **condition** · Verträglichkeitsbedingung *f*

~ **equation**, equation of compatibility · Verträglichkeitsgleichung *f*

~ **law** → law of compatibility

~ **requirement** · Verträglichkeitsforderung *f*

compatible · verträglich

~ **with Chinese white**, ~ ~ zinc ~ schneeweißverträglich, zinkweißverträglich, ZnO-verträglich

~ ~ **zinc white**, ~ ~ Chinese ~ · schneeweißverträglich, zinkweißverträglich, ZnO-verträglich

compensation device, expansion loop [*A loop in a pipeline which, by flexing, can accommodate expansion and contraction movements*] · (Dehnungs)Ausgleicher *m*, Kompensator *m*, (Aus-)Dehn(ungs)schleife *f*, Ausgleichsrohr *n*, Ausgleichsschleife, Schleifenkompensator

competition design · Wettbewerbsarbeit *f*

~ **entry** · Wettbewerbsbeitrag *m*

competitive design · Wettbewerbsentwurf *m*

COMPF → jointless floor(ing)

complementary colour (Brit.); ~ color (US) · Ergänzungsfarbe *f*, Komplementärfarbe [*Eine sich auf dem Wege der optischen Farbenmischung zu Weiß ergänzende Farbe*]

~ **energy** · Zusatzkraft *f* [*Baustatik*]

~ **hydration** · komplementäre Hydra(ta)tion *f*

~ **load**, additional ~ · Zusatzlast *f* [*Zusatzlasten sind Windlasten, Bremskräfte, thermische Belastungen, Reibungswiderstände, Erddruckkräfte, Schneelasten usw., d.h. Kräfte, die nicht als Hauptlasten in der statischen Berechnung aufgeführt sind und welche nur selten gleichzeitig mit den Hauptlasten zusammen ihre Größtwerte erreichen*]

~ **work** · Ergänzungsarbeit *f*

complete (end-)restraint · vollständige Einspannung *f* [*Baustatik*]

~ **separation** · vollständiges Trennen *n*

completion · Fertigstellung *f*

~ **cycle** · Takt *m*

complex · vielgestaltig

~ · Anlage *f*, Komplex *m*

~ **frame** · komplexer Rahmen *m*

~ **of blocks**, ~ ~ buildings, building complex, block complex · Gebäudekomplex *m*

~ ~ **houses**, house complex · Hauskomplex *m*

~ **ratio** · komplexes Verhältnis *n*

complicated (cross) section, intricate (~) ~ · komplizierter Querschnitt *m*

~ **section**, ~ cross ~, intricate (cross) ~ · komplizierter Querschnitt *m*

compluvium · Compluvium *n* [*Öffnung im Dach des römischen Atriums*]

compo (mortar), cement/lime/sand ~, cement-lime ~; gauged ~ (Brit.); gauged ~ (US) · Zementkalkmörtel *m*, Kalkzementmörtel, verlängerter Zementmörtel, Magermörtel

component → (prefab(ricated)) (building) unit

~ **of deflection**, ~ ~ deflexion · Durchbiegungskomponente *f*, Durchsenkungskomponente

~ **square** · Grundquadrat *n* [*Einheit aus Mosaikparkettstäben, die Kante an Kante zu einem Quadrat zusammengesetzt sind, dessen Seiten der Stablänge entsprechen*]

composite → ~ material

~ **beam (in steel and concrete)** · Stahl-Beton-Verbundbalken(träger) *m*, Verbundbalken(träger) Stahl/Beton

~ **bearing structure**, ~ load~ ~, ~ (weight-carrying) ~, ~ supporting ~ · Verbundtragwerk *n*

~ **board**, ~ sheet · Verbundplatte *f*

~ **building block module method** · gemischte Raumzellenbauweise *f*

~ ~ **board**, ~ ~ sheet, ~ ~ slab, ~ sheeting board · Verbundbauplatte *f*

~ (~) **component** → ~ (~) unit

~ ~ **(in steel and concrete)** · Verbundgebäude *n* Stahl/Beton

~ (~) **member** → ~ (~) unit

~ ~ **sheet**, ~ ~ slab, ~ ~ board, ~ sheeting board · Verbundbauplatte *f*

~ ~ **slab**, ~ ~ board, ~ ~ sheet, ~ sheeting board · Verbundbauplatte *f*

~ (~) **unit**, ~ (~) member, ~ (~) component · Verbund(bau)element *n*, Verbund(bau)körper *m*, Verbundmontageelement, Verbundmontagekörper, Verbundfertig(bau)element, Verbundfertig(bau)körper [*Fehlnamen: Verbund(bau)einheit [!]; Verbundmontageeinheit*]

~ **capital** · Composit-Kapitell *n*, Komposit-Kapitell, Komposit-Kapitäl, Composit-Kapitäl, römisches Kapitell, römisches Kapitäl

composite column — composite unit

~ **column** · Kompositsäule f, komposite Säule

~ **component** → ~ (building) unit

~ **compound unit** · Verbundbauteil m, n [z.B. Stütze; Wand; Binder; Deckenplatte usw.]

~ **compressive member,** ~ compression ~ · mehrteiliger Druckstab m

~ **construction** · Verbundbau m

~ **(cross-)section** · mehrteiliger Querschnitt m, gegliederter ~

~ **(cross) section,** built-up (~) ~ · Verbundquerschnitt m [z.B. bei einer Stütze aus Stahlkern und Betonummantelung]

~ **design in steel and concrete** · Bemessung f von Verbundbauwerken Stahl/Beton

~ **divider strip** · Verbund-Terrazzo-(trenn)schiene f, Verbund-Terrazzostreifen m

~ **floor,** ~ intermediate ~ · Verbund-Stockwerkdecke f, Verbund-Etagendecke, Verbund(-Geschoß)decke, Verbund-Gebäudedecke, Verbundtrenndecke, Verbundhochbaudecke

~ ~ **cover(ing) tile,** ~ floor(ing) (finish) ~ · (Fuß)Boden(belag)-Verbundfliese f, (Fuß)Boden(belag)-Verbundplatte f [Asphalt und Beton]

~ ~ **panel,** ~ ~ slab · Verbunddeckenplatte f

~ ~ **slab,** ~ ~ panel · Verbunddeckenplatte f

~ ~ **system** · Verbunddeckensystem n

~ **floor(ing) (finish) tile,** ~ floor cover(ing) ~ · (Fuß)Boden(belag)-Verbundfliese f, (Fuß)Boden(belag)-Verbundplatte f [Asphalt und Beton]

~ ~ **tile,** ~ ~ finish ~, ~ floor cover(ing) ~ · (Fuß)Boden(belag)-Verbundfliese f, (Fuß)Boden(belag)-Verbundplatte f [Asphalt und Beton]

~ **folded slab** · Verbundfaltwerk n Fertigteile/Ortbeton

~ **framed structure** · Verbund-Rahmentragwerk n

~ **girder (in steel and concrete)** · Stahl-Beton-Verbundträger m, Verbundträger Stahl/Beton

~ **(intermediate) floor** · Verbund-Stockwerkdecke f, Verbund-Etagendecke, Verbund(-Geschoß)decke, Verbund-Gebäudedecke, Verbundtrenndecke, Verbundhochbaudecke

~ **(load)bearing structure,** ~ (weight-carrying) ~, ~ supporting ~ · Verbundtragwerk n

~ **masonry wall** · Verbundmauer f

~ **(material)** [The several constituents of a composite (material) are combined to provide synergistic behaviour unattainable by the constituents acting alone] · Verbund(werk)stoff m

~ **member** → ~ (building) unit

~ **order** · Komposit(säulen)ordnung f

~ **panel** · Verbundtafel f

~ **pigment,** mixed ~ · Mischpigment n, Kompositionspigment

~ **pile** [A pile made up of different materials, usually concrete and wood, or steel fastened together end to end, to form a single pile] · Verbundpfahl m

~ **plasterboard** → gypsum ~ ~

~ **plate** [Scotland] → (gypsum) composite plasterboard

~ **profile,** ~ shape, ~ trim, ~ section, ~ unit · Verbundprofil n [z.B. aus PVC und Holz]

~ **reed board,** ~ ~ sheet · Rohrverbundplatte f, Schilf~

~ ~ **sheet,** ~ ~ board · Rohrverbundplatte f, Schilf~

~ **(roof) truss** · Verbund(-Dach)binder m

~ **roof(ing) slab** · Verbunddachplatte f

~ **sample** [A sample obtained by blending two or more individual samples of a material] · zusammengesetzte Probe f

~ **section** → ~ profile

~ ~, ~ cross-~ · mehrteiliger Querschnitt m, gegliederter ~

~ ~, ~ cross ~, built-up (cross) ~ · Verbundquerschnitt m [z.B. bei einer Stütze aus Stahlkern und Betonummantelung]

~ **shape** → ~ profile

~ **sheet,** ~ board · Verbundplatte f

~ **sheeting board,** ~ building ~, ~ building sheet, ~ building slab · Verbundbauplatte f

~ **solid structure** · Verbund-Massivtragwerk n

~ **state** · Verbundzustand m [Verbundträger]

(~) **steel-and-concrete floor** [This floor occurs in two common forms: the beam-and-slab floor, in which steel beams support concrete slabs, and the filler-joist-floor, in which the steel beams are embedded in concrete] · Stahl/Beton-Verbunddecke f

~ **structure,** ~ weight-carrying ~, ~ (load)bearing ~, ~ supporting ~ · Verbundtragwerk n

~ ~ **in steel and concrete** · Verbundbauwerk n Stahl/Beton

~ **style,** combined ~ · Mischstil m

~ **supporting structure,** ~ (load)bearing ~, ~ (weight-carrying) ~ · Verbundtragwerk n

~ **trim** → ~ profile

~ **truss,** composite roof ~ · Verbund(-Dach)binder m

~ ~ **frame** · zusammengesetztes Hängewerk n, Hängesprengwerk, vereinigtes Hänge- und Sprengwerk

~ **unit** → ~ building ~

composite (weight-carrying) structure — compressed peat 224

~ **(weight-carrying) structure,** ~ (load)bearing ~, ~ supporting ~ · Verbundtragwerk *n*

composition, compound, mass, material · Masse *f* [*Erzeugnis*]

~ · Komposition *f*

~ · Gemenge *n* [*Gesamtheit der in einem bestimmten Verhältnis gemischten Rohstoffe für die Herstellung eines Erzeugnisses*]

~ · Aufbau *m*, Zusammensetzung *f* [*Mischung*]

~ **cork** [*Agglomerated cork made with the addition of a binder not derived from cork*] · Backkork *m* mit nicht korkeigenem Bindemittel

~ **floor cover(ing)** → jointless floor(ing)

~ **floor(ing)** → jointless ~

~ ~ **finish** → jointless floor(ing)

compo(sition material) · Verbundbaustoff *m*

composition of forces acting at any given points · Zusammensetzung *f* von Kräften mit beliebigen Angriffspunkten

~ **roofing** → ready ~

~ ~ **manufacture** → ready ~ ~

composition (roofing) shingle → asphalt ~

~ **sheet roofing (paper)** → ready ~ ~ (~)

compound, composition, mass, material · Masse *f* [*Erzeugnis*]

~, system, chemical ~ · (chemische) Verbindung *f*

~ [*An enclosure containing house and grounds*] · eingefriedetes bebautes Grundstück *n*, bebautes eingefriedetes ~

~ **arch** → more-centered ~

~ **beam,** built-up ~, keyed ~ · zusammengesetzter Holzbalken(träger) *m*

~ **bending** · Biegung *f* mit Normalkraft

~ **chimney** → Schofer's ~ ~

~ **for building purposes,** ~ ~ construction(al) ~ [*See remark under 'Kleb(e)masse'*] · Baukleb(e)masse *f*

~ **girder,** built-up ~, keyed ~ · zusammengesetzter Holzträger *m*

~ **mastaba(h)** → terraced ~

~ **pillar** → clustered ~

~ **steel beam structure** · Stahlträger-Verbundkonstruktion *f*

~ **unit** · Bauteil *m, n* [*z.B. Stütze; Wand; Binder; Deckenplatte usw.*]

~ ~ **under compression** · gedrückter Bauteil *m*, gedrücktes ~ *n* [*unter Druck stehend*]

~ ~ ~ **tension** · gezogener Bauteil *m*, gezogenes ~ *n* [*unter Zug stehend*]

comprehensive school · Gesamtschule *f*

compressed, under compression · gedrückt

(compressed-)air gun, pneumatic ~ · Druckluft(spritz)pistole *f*, Preßluft-(spritz)pistole, Druckluftspritze *f*, Preßluftspritze

~ **sliding door drive,** pneumatic ~ ~ ~ · Druckluft-Schiebetürantrieb *m*, Preßluft-Schiebetürantrieb, pneumatischer Schiebetürantrieb

compressed asbestos-cement panel; ~ cement-asbestos ~ (US) · gepreßte Asbestzementtafel *f* [*DIN 274*]

~ **bar** → ~ element

~ **boom** → compression ~

~ **cement-asbestos panel** (US); ~ asbestos-cement ~ · gepreßte Asbestzementtafel *f* [*DIN 274*]

~ **chord** → compression boom

~ **column,** compression ~ · Druckstütze *f*, gedrückte Stütze

~ **concrete,** compression ~ · Druckbeton *m*, gedrückter Beton

~ **cork** · Preßkork *m*

~ **corkboard,** ~ cork slab · Preßkorkplatte *f* [*Korkmehl stark zu Blöcken gepreßt, von denen verschiedene Dicken, ab 4 mm, abgesägt werden*]

~ **cork factory** · Preßkorkwerk *n*, Preßkorkfabrik *f*

~ ~ **slab,** ~ corkboard · Preßkorkplatte *f* [*Korkmehl stark zu Blöcken gepreßt, von denen verschiedene Dicken, ab 4 mm, abgesägt werden*]

~ **diagonal,** compression ~, diagonal in compression · Druckdiagonale *f*, Druckschräge *f*, gedrückte Schräge, gedrückte Diagonale

~ **edge,** compression ~ · Druckrand *m*, gedrückter Rand

~ **element,** ~ rod, ~ member, ~ bar, compression ~ · Druckglied *n*, gedrücktes Glied, Druckstab *m*, gedrückter Stab

(com)pressed felt → ready roofing

~ ~ **manufacture** → ready roofing ~

compressed flange → compression boom

~ **member** → ~ element

~ **(natural) rock asphalt** [*B.S. 348*] · Stampfasphalt *m* [*Er besteht aus erhitztem Naturasphalt(roh)mehl und Bitumen*]

~ (~) ~ **with coarse surface** · Rauhstampfasphalt *m*

~ (~) ~ **asphalt(ic) tile with terrazzo wearing course** *f*, Asphalt-Terrazzo(belag)platte *f*, Asphalt-Terrazzofliese *f*, Verbund(belag)platte, Verbundfliese [*Sie besteht aus einer Stampfasphaltplatte als dämmende Unterschicht und einer zementgebundenen geschliffenen Terrazzooberschicht*]

~ **peat** · Preßtorf *m*

~ **reinforcement**, compression ~, reinforcement in compression · gedrückte Armierung f, ~ Bewehrung, ~ (Stahl-)Einlagen fpl

~ **reinforcing** → compression reinforcement

~ **ring**, compression ~ · Druckring m, gedrückter Ring

~ ~ **beam**, compression ~ ~ · Druckringbalken(träger) m, gedrückter Ringbalken(träger)

~ **rock asphalt** → ~ natural ~ ~

~ ~ ~ **with coarse surface**, ~ natural ~ ~ ~ ~ ~ · Rauhstampfasphalt m

~ ~ **asphalt(ic) tile with terrazzo wearing course** → ~ natural ~ ~ ~ ~ ~ ~

~ **rod** → ~ element

~ **straw** · Preßstroh n

~ ~ **slab**, strawboard ~ · (Preß)Strohplatte f [*Strohplatten werden aus Getreidestroh hergestellt und sind je nach Herstellung entweder Preßstroh-Bauplatten oder Strohfaser-Platten*]

~ ~ ~ **partition (wall)**, strawboard ~ (~) · (Preß)Strohplattentrennwand f

~ **vegetable fibres** (Brit.); ~ ~ **fibers** (US) · pflanzliche Fasern fpl in Matten

~ **width** → compression ~

~ **zone**, compression ~ · Druckzone f, gedrückte Zone

compressibility · Zusammendrückbarkeit f

compression bar → compressed element

compression-bending stress · Druckbiegespannung f

compression boom, ~ chord, ~ flange, compressed ~ · Druckflansch m, Druckgurt(ung) m, (f), gedrückter Flansch, gedrückter Gurt, gedrückte Gurtung

~ **chord** → ~ boom

~ **column**, compressed ~ · Druckstütze f, gedrückte Stütze

~ **component** · Druckkomponente f, gedrückte Komponente

~ **concrete** → compressed ~

~ **cross-section**, compressive ~ · Druckquerschnitt m, gedrückter Querschnitt

~ **cube** → concrete (test) ~

~ **cylinder** → concrete (test) ~

~ **diagonal**, compressed ~, diagonal in compression · Druckdiagonale f, Druckschräge f, gedrückte Schräge, gedrückte Diagonale

~ **edge**, compressed ~ · Druckrand m, gedrückter Rand

~ **element** → compressed ~

~ **failure**, ~ rupture · Druckbruch m

~ **flange** → ~ boom

~ **force**, compressive ~ · Druckkraft f

~ **joint** [*It has an elastic sealing enclosing the joint*] · weiche Fuge f

~ **load** → compressive ~

~ **machine**, ~tester · Baustoff(prüf)presse f

~ **member** → compressed element

~ **resistance**, resistance to compression · Druckwiderstand m [*Er wird im wesentlichen von der Festigkeit der Betondruckzone geleistet und hängt von der Querschnittsgröße und der Betongüte ab. Stahleinlagen steigern den Druckwiderstand*]

compression-resistant, compression-resisting · druckfest

compression-resisting → compression resistant

compression ring, compressed ~ · Druckring m, gedrückter Ring

~ ~ **beam**, compressed ~ ~ · Druckringbalken(träger) m, gedrückter Ringbalken(träger)

~ **rod** → compressed element

~ **rupture**, ~ failure · Druckbruch m,

~ **stalk breaking** → compressive web rupture

~ ~ **rupture** → compressive web ~

~ **strength**, crushing ~, compressive ~ · Druckfestigkeit f

~ ~ **class**, crushing ~ ~, compressive ~ ~ · Druckfestigkeitsgruppe f

~ ~ **range**, crushing ~ ~, compressive ~ ~, range of compression strength, range of crushing strength, range of compressive strength · Druckfestigkeitsbereich m, f

~ ~ **test**, crushing (~) ~, compressive ~ ~ · Druck(festigkeits)versuch m, Druck(festigkeits)prüfung f, Druck(festigkeits)probe f

~ **stress**, compressive ~ · Druckspannung f, negative Normalspannung

~ ~ **field**, compressive ~ ~ · Druckspannungsfeld n

~ ~ **of concrete** → compressive ~ ~ ~

~ **tester**, ~ machine · Baustoff(prüf)presse f

~ **web breaking** → compressive web rupture

~ ~ **rupture** → compressive ~ ~

~ **width**, compressed ~ · Druckbreite f [*Balken(träger) mit Druckflansch*]

~ **yield point**, compressive ~ · Quetschgrenze f [*Baustahl*]

~ **zone**, compressed ~ · Druckzone f, gedrückte Zone

~ **with bending** · Biegedruck m, Biegungsdruck

compressional wave, longitudinal ~ · Longitudinalwelle f, Längswelle

compressive cross-section → compression ~

(~) **cube strength at 28 days** · Würfel(druck)festigkeit f W_{28}

compressive force — concentrated load

~ force, compression ~ · Druckkraft *f*
~ load, compression ~ · Drucklast *f*
~ stalk breaking → ~ web rupture
~ ~ rupture → ~ web
~ strength → compression ~
~ ~ class → compression ~ ~
~ ~ (of concrete) at 28 days · 28-Tage-Festigkeit *f*
~ ~ range → compression ~ ~
~ ~ test → compression ~ ~
~ stress, compression ~ · Druckspannung *f*, negative Normalspannung
~ ~ field, compression ~ ~ · Druckspannungsfeld *n*
~ ~ of concrete, compression ~ ~ ~ · Betonpressung *f* [*Spannung eines auf Druck beanspruchten Betonteiles in kg/cm²*]
~ web breaking → ~ ~ ~ rupture
~ ~ rupture, ~ stalk ~, compression ~ ~, ~ ~ ~ breaking · Stegdruckbruch *m*
~ yield point, compression ~ ~ · Quetschgrenze *f* [*Baustahl*]
compromise (form of) architecture · Kompromißarchitektur *f*, Kompromißbaukunst *f*
compulsory purchase · Zwangskauf *m*
computable value, calculable ~ · Rechengröße *f*
computation of area(s), calculation ~ ~ · Flächenberechnung *f*
~ ~ **heat loss(es),** calculation ~ ~ ~, heat loss calculation, heat loss computation · Wärmeverlustberechnung *f*
computational labour (Brit.); ~ labor (US) · Berechnungsarbeit *f*, Rechenarbeit
computed bending stress · rechnerische Biegespannung *f*
~ **maximum load** · rechnerische Höchstlast *f*, ~ Größtlast
~ **tensile stress** · rechnerische Zugspannung *f*
computer architecture · Rechner-Baukunst *f*, Rechner-Architektur *f*
~ **centre** (Brit.); ~ **center** (US) · Rechenzentrum *n*, Rechenzentrale *f*
~ **check** · Rechnernachweis *m*
computing elevations · Höhenberechnung *f*
con spec, construction spec(ification)s · Baudaten *f*
CONC, (cement) concrete · (Zement-)Beton *m* [*Im Gegensatz zum Teer- und Asphaltbeton*]
conc blk → ((pre)cast) concrete (building) block
CONC C, concrete ceiling · Betondecke *f*
~ **F** → concrete (suspended) floor
to concamerate, to vault · einwölben, überwölben
~ ~, to arch over · überspannen mit Bogen

concave · hohlrund, konkav
~ **ceiling,** vault(ed) ~ · Deckengewölbe *n*, Gewölbedecke *f*
~ **corner** · konkave Ecke *f*
~ **curve** · konkave Rundung *f*
~ **joint** · konkave Fuge *f*
~ **shell** · konkave Schale *f*
~ **tile,** under-tile; mission tile (US) Rinnenziegel *m*, Nonne(nziegel) *f*, (*m*), Haken *m*
concealed, hidden, secret · verdeckt(liegend)
~ **cable,** hidden ~, secret ~ · Unterputzkabel *n*
~ **closing mechanism,** ~ ~ device, ~ closer · verdeckte Türschließvorrichtung *f*, verdeckter Türschließer *m*
~ **conduit,** conduit embedded in plaster · Unterputzleitung *f*, Unterputzleerrohr *n* [*Elektrotechnik*]
~ **door,** secret ~, jib ~, gib ~ [*A door whose face is flush with the wall and decorated so as to be as little seen as possible*] · Geheimtür *f*, Tapetentür
~ ~ **closer,** ~ ~ closing device, ~ ~ closing mechanism · verdeckte Türschließvorrichtung *f*, verdeckter Türschließer *m*
~ ~ **closing device,** ~ ~ ~ mechanism, ~ ~ closer · verdeckte Türschließvorrichtung *f*, verdeckter Türschließer *m*
~ **flashing (piece)** [*See remark under 'Anschluß'*] · verdeckter Anschluß(streifen) *m*
~ **heating** · verdeckte Heizung *f*
~ **illumination,** indirect ~, ~ lighting · indirekte Beleuchtung *f*
~ **installation,** secret ~, hidden ~, buried tubular conduits · Unterputzinstallation *f*
~ **light,** indirect ~ · indirektes Licht *n*
~ **lighting,** indirect ~, ~ illumination · indirekte Beleuchtung *f*
~ **nailing** → secret ~
~ **pipe,** hidden ~, secret ~ · Unterputzrohr *n*
~ **suspension system** · verdecktes Hängesystem *n*
~ **symmetry** · verborgene Symmetrie *f*
~ **system of axes** · verborgenes Achsensystem *n*
~ **tack,** hidden ~, secret ~ · verdeckter Hafter *m*
~ **valley,** secret ~, hidden ~, closed ~ · verdeckte Kehle *f*
~ **valve,** hidden ~, secret ~ · Unterputzventil *n*
~ **wiring,** hidden ~, secret ~ · Unterputzverdrahtung *f*
concentrate · Konzentrat *n*
concentrated force, point ~ · Punktkraft *f*
~ **load,** point ~ · Punktlast *f*

~ ~ at the crown, point ~ ~ ~ ~ · Kronenpunktlast *f*

concentrated-load stress, point-load-~ · Punktlastspannung *f*

~ system, point-load ~ · Punktlastsystem *n*

concentrated loading, point ~ · Punktbelastung *f*

~ reaction · Einzelstützkraft *f*

~ support · Punktstütze *f*

concentration of pigment-vehicle system, pigment concentration · Pigmentvolumenkonzentration *f*, PVK

concentric beam, common-type of curved ~ · konzentrischer Balken(träger) *m*

~ reducer, ~ taper fitting · konzentrisches Übergangsstück *n*, konzentrischer Übergang *m*

~ taper fitting, ~ reducer · konzentrisches Übergangsstück *n*, konzentrischer Übergang *m*

~ ~ pipe · konzentrisches Übergangsrohr *n*, konzentrischer Übergang *m*

concept of expressive form · expressiver Formwille *m*

~ ~ form, ~ ~ shape, form concept, shape concept · Formvorstellung *f*

~ ~ ~ and space, ~ ~ shape ~ ~, formal and spatial concept · Formen- und Raumsprache *f*, Raum- und Formensprache

~ ~ shape → ~ ~ form

~ ~ style, idea ~ ~, notion ~ ~ · Stilbegriff *m*, Stilkonzeption *f*

conception of space · Raumbegriff *m*, Raumanschauung *f*

concert hall, music ~ · Konzerthalle *f*, Konzerthaus *n*, Tonhalle

concertina door, accordion ~, bellow-framed ~ · Akkordeontür *f*, (Zieh)Harmonikatür

~ ~ fitting → ~ ~ furniture

~ ~ furniture, accordion ~ ~, ~ ~ fitting · Akkordeontürbeschlag *m*, (Zieh)Harmonikatürbeschlag

concha → semi-dome

concordant tendon [*A tendon in statically indeterminate prestressed concrete structures which does not produce secondary moments*] · zwängungsfreies Spannglied *n*

to concrete, to cast, to pour · betonieren

concrete, cement ~, CONC · (Zement-)Beton *m* [*Im Gegensatz zum Teer- und Asphaltbeton*]

~ additive powder, powder(ed) additive for concrete · Betonwirkstoffpulver *n*, Betonzusatzpulver

~ adhesive → ~ bonding ~

~ admix(ture), ~ agent [*A material, other than aggregate, cementitious material or water, added in small quantities to the concrete mix(ture) to produce some desired modifications to the properties of the mix(ture) or of the hardened product*] · Betonwirkstoff *m*, Betonzusatzstoff, Betonzusatz(mittel) *m*, (*n*)

~ advisory service · Betonberatungsdienst *m*

~ aerated with foam → foam(ed) (plastic) (light(weight)) concrete

~ agent → ~ admix(ture)

~ aggregate [*B.S. 882*] · Betonzuschlag(stoff) *m* [*DIN 1045*]

~ aggregate/cement ratio · Betonzuschlag(stoff)-Zement-Verhältnis *n*

~ aggregate composition · Betonzuschlag(stoff)zusammensetzung *f*

~ ~ from natural sources → natural (concrete) aggregate

~ ~ grain → ~ ~ particle

~ ~ heating · Betonzuschlag(stoff)-Erwärmung *f*

~ ~ particle, ~ ~ grain · Betonzuschlag(stoff)korn *n*, Betonzuschlag(stoff)teilchen *n*

~ ~ producer · Betonzuschlag(stoff)hersteller *m*

~ aggregates · Betonzuschläge *mpl*, Betonzuschlagstoffe *mpl*, Betonzuschlagmaterial *n*

~ aid · Betonhilfe *f*, Betonhilfsmittel *n*, Betonhilfsstoff *m*

(~) (air) (entrainment) meter, entrained air indicator · (Beton)Luftmengenmesser *m*, (Beton)Belüftungsmesser, (Beton)Luftmeßgerät *n*, (Beton)Luftporenmesser, (Beton)Luftporenprüfer, (Beton)Luftporenprüfgerät, (Beton-)Luftgehaltprüfer, LP-Messer

(~) (~) meter → (~) (~) entrainment ~

~ anchor block · Ankerblock *m* aus Beton, Verankerungsblock ~ ~

~ anchorage → ~ deadman

~ and reinforced concrete work, ~ ~ R. C. ~ · Beton- und Stahlbetonarbeiten *fpl* [*DIN 18331*]

~ antifreezer, ~ antifreezing agent · Betonfrostschutzmittel *n*

~ appearance · Betonaussehen *n*

~ arch · Betonbogen *m*

~ ~ rib · Betonbogenrippe *f*

~ arch(ed girder) · Betonbogen(träger) *m*

~ architecture · Betonarchitektur *f*, Beton-Baukunst *f*

~ area · Betonfläche *f*

~ articles → (mass-produced) (pre)cast (concrete) ware

~ astragal, ~ glazing bar; ~ muntin (US) · Betonsprosse *f* [*Oberlichtverglasung*]

~ back filling · Betonhinterfüllung *f*

concrete ballast — concrete circular (flat) slab

~ **ballast** (Brit.) · Betonzuschlag(stoff) *m* nicht größer als 37 mm, Betonzuschlagmaterial *n* ~ ~ ~ ~ ~

~ **barrel shell** · Beton-Tonnenschale *f*

~ ~ **vault,** ~ **tunnel** ~, ~ **wagon** ~ · Betontonne(ngewölbe) *f*, (*n*)

~ **base,** ~ **supporting medium** · Betonunterlage *f*

~ ~, ~ **(slab) sub-floor** · Betonunterboden *m* [*Fehlname: Betonboden*]

~ ~ **laid at ground level,** ~ **(slab) sub-floor** ~ ~ ~ ~ · Betonunterboden *m* ohne Blindboden [*Fehlname: Betonboden* ~ ~]

~ **bay** · Betonfeld *n* [*in einem Rahmen*]

~ **beam** · Betonbalken(träger) *m*

(~) ~ **casing,** (~) ~ **encasure,** (~) ~ **encasement,** (~) ~ **haunching,** (~) ~ **sheathcoat** · Balken(träger)umhüllung *f*, Balken(träger)ummantelung

(~) ~ **encasement** → (~) ~ casing

(~) ~ **encasure** → (~) ~ casing

(~) ~ **haunching** → (~) ~ casing

~ ~ **making machine** · Betonbalkenformmaschine *f*

(~) ~ **sheath coat** → (~) ~ casing

~ **bearing system,** ~ **load** ~ · Betontragwerk *n*

~ **bed(ding)** · Betonbett(ung) *n*, (*f*)

~ **belfry,** ~ **bell tower** · Beton-Glockenturm *m*

~ **bell tower,** ~ **belfry** · Beton-Glockenturm *m*

~ **bend** → ~ pipe ~

~ **bending stress** · Betonbiegespannung *f*

~ **binder** · Betonbindemittel *n*, Betonbinder *m*

~ **biological shield(ing)** · biologische Betonabschirmung *f*

~ (~) **shielding wall,** ~ **radiation** ~ · Beton-Abschirmwand *f*

~ **block** → ((pre)cast) concrete (building) ~

~ ~, ~ **building** · Betongebäude *n*

~ ~ · Beton-Versetzblock *m*

~ ~ **bar support** [*A precast concrete block, with or without tie wire, used to support a bar above the subgrade or to space a bar of a vertical form and sometimes above a horizontal form*] · Beton-Stabhalterung *f* [*Bewehrung*]

~ **(block) masonry wall,** ~ **tile** (~) ~, ~ **block** ~ · Betonblock(stein)mauer *f*, Beton(werk)steinmauer, Betonmauer

~ (~) ~ **(work),** ~ **tile** ~ (~), ~ **blockwork,** ~ **block-walling** · Betonblock(stein)mauerwerk *n*, Beton(werk)steinmauerwerk, Betonmauerwerk

~ ~ **wall** → ~ (~) masonry ~

~ **block-walling** → ~ (block) masonry (work)

~ **blockwork** → ~ (block) masonry (work)

(~) **bond beam block** → (pre)cast (~) ~ ~ ~

~ **(bonding) adhesive,** ~ ~ **agent,** ~ ~ **medium,** ~ **cement(ing agent)** · Betonhaftmittel *n*

~ ~ **agent** → ~ (~) adhesive

~ ~ **medium** → ~ (~) adhesive

~ **bottom** · Betonsohle *f*

~ **boom** → ~ ~ chord

~ ~ **chord,** ~ **lower** ~, ~ ~ **boom** · Betonuntergurt *m*

~ **boundary beam,** ~ **edge** ~ · Beton-Randbalken(träger) *m*

~ ~ **wall** · Beton-Grundstücksmauer *f*

~ **bracket,** ~ **corbel** · Betonkonsole *f*

~ **brick** [*B. S. 1180*] [*A solid unit having a rectangular prismatic shape usually not larger than 4 × 4 × 12 in. made from Portland cement and suitable aggregates, with or without the inclusion of other materials*] · Betonblock(stein) *m*, Betonstein [*im allgemeinen nicht größer als 10 × 10 × 30 cm*]

~ **building,** ~ **block** · Betongebäude *n*

~ (~) **block** → ((pre)cast) ~ (~) ~

~ ~ ~ **module,** ~ **unitized unit** · Beton(raum)zelle *f*

~ ~ **(construction),** ~ ~ **design and** ~ · Betonhochbau *m*

~ (~) **tile** → ((pre)cast) concrete (building) block

~ ~ **unit floor** · Betonsteindecke *f*, Betonblock(stein)decke

~ **cable cover** [*B. S. 2484*] · Beton-Kabelabdeckstein *m*

~ **cantilever** · Betonkragarm *m*

(~) **capping block** → (~) coping ~

(~) ~ **slab** → (~) coping ~

(~) ~ **tile** → (~) coping block

(~) ~ **casing** → (~) encasement

(~) **cast for building construction** → (pre)cast (concrete) member ~ ~ ~

(~) **cast(ing)** → (pre)cast (concrete) (building) unit

~ **casting system** → ~ precasting ~

~ **ceiling,** CONC C, conc clg · Betondecke *f*

~ **cellar window** · Betonkellerfenster *n*

~ **cement(ing agent)** → ~ (bonding) adhesive

(~) **channel (unit),** (~) **trough slab** · (Beton-)Trogplatte *f*, (Beton-)U-Platte

~ **chimney** · Betonkamin *m*, Betonschornstein *m*

~ ~ **door** · Betonkamintür, Betonschornsteintür

~ **church** · Betonkirche *f*

~ **cill** (Brit.) ~ **sill,** ~ **threshold** · Beton(tür)schwelle *f*

~ **circular (flat) slab,** ~ ~ **plate** · Betonkreisplatte *f*, Betonrundplatte

concrete circular plate — (concrete) cylinder ...

~~ plate, ~ ~ (flat) slab · Betonkreisplatte f, Betonrundplatte

~ cladding → (pre)cast ~ ~

~~ slab → ~ (in)filler ~

~~ unit → ~ infill(ing) ~

~ class · Betongruppe f

~ code · Betonbestimmungen fpl

~ column · Betonstütze f

~~ · Betonsäule f

~~ , ~ lighting ~ (Brit.); ~ mast (US) [B. S. 1308] · Beton-Beleuchtungsmast m, Beton-Lichtmast

~ compacted by jolting · Schockbeton m, Stoßbeton

~ composition · Betonaufbau m, Betonzusammensetzung f

~ compression boom → ~ ~ chord

~~ chord, ~ ~ boom, ~ ~ flange · Betondruckgurt m

~~ flange → ~ ~ chord

~~ ring · Betondruckring m

~~ strength → ~ compressive ~

~ compressive strength, ~ crushing ~, ~ compression ~ · Betondruckfestigkeit f

~~ stress · Betondruckspannung f

~~ test · Betondruckprüfung f, Betondruckprobe f, Betondruckversuch m

~~ zone · Betondruckbereich m, n, Betondruckzone f

~ consistency, ~ consistence · Betonkonsistenz f, Betonsteife f

~ construction type, ~ type of construction · Betonbauart f

~ constructional industry · Betonbauindustrie f

~ construction(al work) · Betonbau m

~ cooling · Betonkühlung f

(~) cope block → (~) coping ~

(~) ~ tile → (~) coping block

(~) coping block, (~) ~ tile, (~) cope ~, (~) capping ~ [See remark under 'Block'] · (Ab)Deckblock(stein) m, (Ab)Deckstein, Beton~

(~) ~ slab, (~) capping ~, (~) cover(ing) ~ · (Beton)(Ab)Deckplatte f [Betonplatte zum Abdecken für Kaminköpfe, freistehende Mauern und Einfried(ig)ungen. DIN 455]

(~) ~ tile → (~) ~ block

~ corbel · bracket · Betonkonsole f

~ core, reinforced ~ ~, R. C. ~, service ~, utility ~, building ~, mechanical ~ · (Hoch)Hauskern m, (Stahl)Betonkern, Betriebskern, (Gebäude)Kern

~~ · Betonkern m

~ corner · Betonecke f, Betonkante f

~ cornice · Beton(ge)sims m, (n)

~ corrosion · Betonkorrosion f

~ counterweight · Betongegengewicht n

~ covering foil, concreting ~ · Betonierfolie f

(~) ~ cover(ing) slab → (~) coping ~

~ creep, creep of concrete · Betonkriechen n

~ cross · Betonkreuz n

~ (cross-)section · Betonquerschnitt m

~ crushing strength → ~ compressive ~

~ cubage, ~ cubic yardage · Betonkubatur f

~ cube → ~ test ~

(~) ~ crushing strength after 28 days · W_{28}

(~) ~ test · (Beton)Würfelprobe f, (Beton)Würfelprüfung f, (Beton)Würfelversuch m [DIN 1048]

~ cubic yardage, ~ cubage · Betonkubatur f

~ cupola, ~ dome · Betonkuppel f

~ curb; ~ kerb [B. S. 340] · Betonbordstein m [DIN 483]

(~) ~ mold (US); (~) kerb mould (Brit.) · (Beton)Bordsteinform f

(~) curing · (Beton)Nachbehandlung f

(~) ~ agent → (~) ~ compound

(concrete-)curing blanket · Abdeckmatte f [Nachbehandlung von Beton]

(concrete) curing chamber, (~) ~ room · Behandlungskammer f, Dampfkammer [Betonsteinfertigung]

(~) ~ compound, (~) ~ agent, (liquid) membrane (~) ~ ~ · (Beton)Nachbehandlungsmittel n, (Ab)Dicht(ungs)mittel

(~) ~ fixture · (Beton)Nachbehandlungsvorrichtung f

(~) ~ membrane · (Beton)Nachbehandlungsfilm m

(concrete-)curing paper, overlay ~ · (Beton)Nachbehandlungspapier n, Abdeckungspapier

(concrete) curing room, (~) ~ chamber · Behandlungskammer f, Dampfkammer [Betonsteinfertigung]

(~) ~ solution · (Beton)Nachbehandlungslösung f

(~) ~ water · (Beton)Nachbehandlungswasser n

(~) ~ yard · (Beton)Nachbehandlungsplatz m

~ curtain wall · Betonvorhangwand f

~~~ panel · Beton-Vorhangwandtafel f

~ (cycle) stand [B. S. 1716] · Beton-Fahrradstand m

~ cylinder → ~ test ~

(~) ~ compressive strength, (~) ~ crushing ~ · Zylinderdruckfestigkeit f, Beton~

~~~ test, ~ ~ crushing ~ ~ · (Beton)Zylinderdruckprobe f, (Beton-)Zylinderdruckversuch m, (Beton)Zylinderdruckprüfung f

(concrete) cylinder crushing ... — concrete fence post 230

(~) ~ **crushing strength**, (~) ~ compressive ~ · (Beton)Zylinderdruckfestigkeit f

~ ~ ~ ~ **test**, ~ ~ compressive ~ ~ · Zylinderdruckprobe f, Zylinderdruckversuch m, Zylinderdruckprüfung f, Beton~

(~) ~ **strength** · Zylinderfestigkeit f, Beton~

(~) ~ **tester**, (~) ~ testing machine · Zylinder-Druck(prüf)presse f, Beton~

(~) ~ **testing machine**, (~) ~ tester · Zylinder-Druck(prüf)presse f, Beton ~

~ **cylindrical pipe** [B. S. 556] · Betonrohr n mit kreisförmigem Abflußquerschnitt, Zementrohr ~ ~ ~, ~ ~ rundem ~, rundes Betonrohr, kreisförmiges Betonrohr, Betonrundrohr, Betonkreisrohr, rundes Zementrohr, kreisförmiges Zementrohr, Zementrundrohr, Zementkreisrohr

~ **deadman**, ~ anchorage [*A buried plate, wall, or block of concrete, some distance from a sheet pile wall, retaining wall and the like which serves to anchor back the wall through a tie between the two*] · Betonverankerung f

~ **deck**, ~ roof ~ · Betondachdecke f, Betonunterkonstruktion f

~ **densifier** → ~ densifying agent

~ **densifying admix(ture)** → ~ ~ agent

~ ~ **agent**, ~ ~ admix(ture), ~ densifier, ~ integral waterproofer, ~ integral waterproof(ing) agent, ~ integral waterrepeller, ~ integral water repellent admix(ture), ~ integral water repelling agent · BD m, Betondichter m, Beton(ab)dicht(ungs)mittel n, Beton(ab)dicht(ungs)stoff m, Beton-DM

~ **density** · Betonrohdichte f

~ ~ · Betonrohwichte BR f; Betonraumgewicht BR n [*Fehlname*]

~ **design criteria** · Betonbemessungsgrundlagen fpl

~ **destruction**, destruction of concrete · Betonzerstörung f

~ **diagonal (rod)** · Betondiagonale f, Betonschräge f, Betondiagonalstab m

~ **discharge channel**, ~ draining ~, ~ drain(age) ~, ~ ~ gutter · Betonabflußrinne f, Betonentwässerungsrinne, Betonablaufrinne, Betonwasserrinne

~ ~ **gutter**, ~ draining ~, ~ drain(age) ~, ~ ~ channel · Betonabflußrinne f, Betonentwässerungsrinne, Betonablaufrinne, Betonwasserrinne

~ ~ **pipe** → ~ waste ~

~ **disintegration**, disintegration of concrete · Betonzersetzung f

~ **distance piece** → ~ spacer

~ **dome**, ~ cupola · Betonkuppel f

~ **door frame** · Beton-Türrahmen m

~ **drain pipe** · Dränbetonrohr n, Betondränrohr

(~) ~ **drain(age) article**, (~) ~ product · (Beton-)Entwässerungsgegenstand m, (Beton-)Entwässerungsartikel m, (Beton-)Entwässerungserzeugnis n

~ ~ **channel**, ~ discharge ~, ~ draining ~, ~ ~ gutter · Betonabflußrinne f, Betonentwässerungsrinne, Betonablaufrinne, Betonwasserrinne

(~) ~ **goods**, (~) ~ articles, (~) ~ products, (~) ~ ware · (Beton-)Entwässerungsgegenstände mpl, (Beton-)Entwässerungsware(n) f, (Beton-)Entwässerungserzeugnisse npl, (Beton-)Entwässerungsartikel mpl [*DIN 4281*]

~ ~ **gutter**, ~ draining ~, ~ discharge ~, ~ ~ channel · Betonabflußrinne f, Betonentwässerungsrinne, Betonablaufrinne, Betonwasserrinne

~ ~ **pipe** → ~ waste ~

(~) ~ **product** → (~) ~ article

~ **draining channel**, ~ discharge ~, ~ drain(age) ~, ~ ~ gutter · Betonabflußrinne f, Betonentwässerungsrinne, Betonablaufrinne, Betonwasserrinne

~ ~ **gutter**, ~ discharge ~, ~ drain(age) ~, ~ ~ channel · Betonabflußrinne f, Betonentwässerungsrinne, Betonablaufrinne, Betonwasserrinne

~ ~ **pipe** → ~ waste ~

~ **droppings** · Betonkruste f

~ **durability** · Betonhaltbarkeit f

~ **edge beam**, ~ boundary ~ · Beton-Randbalken(träger) m

~ ~ **stress** · Betonrandspannung f

(~) ~ **edging** · (Beton)Einfassungsstein m

~ **emulsion** · Betonemulsion f, wäßrige Kunstharzemulsion

(concrete-)**encased**, (concrete-)haunched · (beton)umhüllt, (beton)ummantelt

(concrete) **encasement**, (~) encasure, (~) haunching, (~) sheath coat, (~) casing · (Beton)Umhüllung f, (Beton-)Mantel m, (Beton)Ummantelung f

(~) **encasure** → (~) encasement

~ **engineering** · Betontechnik f

(~) (**entrainment**) **meter** → (~) air (~) ~

~ **fabrication**, ~ production · Beton-(auf)bereitung f, Betonherstellung, Betonerzeugung

~ **façade** · Betonfassade f

~ ~ **panel** · Betonfassadentafel f

~ ~ **slab** · Betonfassadenplatte f

~ **faced iron pipe** → ~ surfaced ~ ~

~ **facing** · Betonverblendung f

~ ~ → ~ lining

~ **failure**, ~ rupture · Betonbruch m

~ **farm building** · landwirtschaftliches Betongebäude n

~ **fence** · Betonzaun m

~ ~ **picket** → ~ ~ ~ stake

~ ~ **post** → ~ ~ ~ stake

~ ~ **stake,** ~ ~ **picket,** ~ ~ **post,** ~ **fencing** · Betonzaunpfahl m, Betonzaunpfosten m

~ **fencing** · Betoneinzäunung f, Betonumzäunung

~ ~ **picket** → ~ fence stake

~ ~ **post** → ~ fence stake

~ ~ **stake** → ~ fence ~

~ **filled** · betongefüllt

~ **filler (block)** → (pre)cast (~) ~ (~)

~ ~ **slab** → ~ in~ ~

~ ~ **tile** → (pre)cast (concrete) filler (block)

~ ~ **unit** → ~ infill(ing) ~

~ **fill(ing)** · Betonfüllung f, Betonverguß m

~ **filter pipe** · Betonbrunnenrohr n, Betonfilterrohr

~ **finish,** ~ **surface** ~ · Betonoberflächengestaltung f

~ **finishing** · Betonfertigbehandlung f

~ **fireproofing** · Betonfeuerschutzummantelung f

~ **fitting** · Beton(rohr)formstück n, Beton(rohr)fitting m, Zementrohrformstück, Zementrohrfitting

~ **flag** → ~ paving ~

~ **flat (roof(ing)) tile** → plain concrete (~) ~

~ ~ **tile** → plain concrete (roof(ing)) ~

~ **floor** → ~ suspended ~

~ ~ **beam** · Betondeckenbalken(träger) m

(~) ~ **cast(ing)** → (pre)cast (concrete) floor member

~ ~ **cover(ing),** ~ **floor(ing) (finish)** · Beton(fuß)boden(belag) m

~ ~ **dust** · Beton(fuß)bodenstaub m

~ ~ **finish** → ~ flooring ~

(~) ~ **member** → (pre)cast (~) ~ ~

(~) ~ **panel** → (~) ~ slab

~ ~ **rib** · Betondeckenrippe f

~ ~ **screed (material)** → (monolithic) fine ~ ~ (~)

~ ~ ~ **(topping),** (monolithic) (fine) ~ ~ ~ (~) · (Fein)Beton(fuß)bodenestrich m [als verlegter Baustoff]

~ ~ **seal(er)** · Beton(fuß)bodensiegel n

(~) ~ **slab,** (~) ~ **panel** [A slab forming the continuous loadbearing structure of a floor] · (Beton)Deckenplatte f, (Beton)Deckentafel f

(~) ~ ~ → (pre)cast (~) ~ ~

~ ~ **system** · Betondecken(bau)system n

~ ~ **tile** → ~ flooring ~

~ **floor(ing) (finish),** ~ **floor cover(ing)** · Beton(fuß)boden(belag) m

~ ~ **tile** [B. S. 1197] · Beton(fuß)bodenplatte f, Beton(fuß)bodenfliese f

~ **flower container** · Beton-Blumengefäß n

~ ~ **trough** · Beton-Blumentrog m

~ **flue** · Betonzug m

~ ~ **block** → precast ~ ~ ~

~ ~ **tile** → precast ~ ~ ~

~ **foam** · Bauschaum m [Für die Herstellung von Schaumbeton]

~ **for carriageway markings** · Markierungsbeton m

~ ~ **civil defence structures** (Brit.); ~ ~ ~ **defense** ~ (US) · Luftschutzbeton m

~ ~ **X-ray rooms,** X-ray protective concrete, X-ray shielding concrete · Röntgen(strahlen)schutzbeton m

(~) **forms,** (~) **form(work),** (~) **shuttering** · Schalung f, Beton~

~ **formulation** · Betonrezept n

(~) **form(work),** (~) **forms,** (~) **shuttering** · Schalung f, Beton~

~ **foul water pipe,** ~ **refuse** ~ ~, ~ **sewer** ~, ~ **sewage** ~ · Abwasser-Betonrohr n, Beton-Abwasserrohr

~ **foundation** · Betongründung f

~ ~ **wall** · Betongründungswand f

~ **frame** · Betonrahmen m

~ **gable beam** · Beton-Giebelbalken(träger) m

~ **gasholder** · Beton-Gasbehälter m

~ **girder** · Betonträger m

~ **glazing bar,** ~ **astragal;** ~ **muntin** (US) · Betonsprosse f [Oberlichtverglasung]

~ **goods** → (mass-produced) (pre)cast (concrete) ware

~ **grade,** ~ **quality** ~, **(quality) grade of concrete** · Betongüteklasse f

~ **gray,** ~ **grey** · betongrau

~ **ground floor slab** · EG-Betonplatte f, Erdgeschoß-Betonplatte

~ **guard fence** → ~ safety ~

~ ~ **rail** → ~ safety fence

~ **gutter** → ~ roof ~

~ ~ · Betonsohlschale f

~ **hardcore** → broken concrete

~ **hardener,** ~ **hardening agent** · Betonhärtemittel n, Betonhärtungsmittel, Betonhärtungsstoff m, Betonhärter m

~ **hardening agent** → ~ hardener

(concrete-)haunched, (concrete-)encased · (beton)umhüllt, (beton)ummantelt

(concrete) haunching → (~) encasement

~ **hearth** [The concrete floor of a fireplace] · Beton-Kaminboden m

~ **hinge** · Betongelenk n

~ **hip tile** · Beton-Gratstein m, Beton-Walmstein [Der Ausdruck „Walmstein" wird auch für den Firststein verwendet. DIN 1119]

~ **hollow block making** → hollow (concrete) ~ ~

concrete hollow(-core) plank — concrete lining

~ **hollow(-core) plank**, reinforced ~ ~ ~, R. C. ~ ~ · Stahlbeton(hohl)diele f, Steg(zement)diele [*DIN 4028*]

~ **hollow filler (block)**, ~ ~ ~ tile [*See remark under 'Block'*] · Beton-(decken)hohlkörper m, Beton-Hohl-(Decken)Füllstein m, Beton-Hohl-(Decken)Füllblock(stein) m, Beton-Hohldeckenblock(stein), Beton-Hohldeckenstein, Beton-Deckenhohl(block)stein, Beton-Deckenhohlblock, Beton-Hohldeckenblock

~ ~ **floor**, hollow (concrete) ~ · Hohl(beton)decke f, Betonhohldecke

~ ~ ~ **slab** → hollow (concrete) ~ ~

(~) ~ **mast**, (~) ~ pole, hollow concrete ~ · (Beton)Hohlmast m, Hohl-Betonmast

~ ~ **panel**, hollow (concrete) ~ · Betonhohltafel f, Hohl(-Beton)tafel

~ ~ **plank** → (reinforced) concrete hollow(-core) ~

(~) ~ **pole**, (~) ~ mast, hollow concrete ~ · (Beton)Hohlmast m, Hohl-Betonmast

~ ~ **slab**, hollow (concrete) ~ · (Beton-)Hohlplatte f, Hohl-Betonplatte

~ ~ ~ **floor**, hollow (concrete) ~ ~ · (Beton)Hohlplattendecke f, Hohl-Betonplattendecke

(~) ~ ~ ~ → reinforced (~) ~ ~ ~

(~) ~ ~ **floor(ing) construction** → (reinforced (concrete)) hollow slab floor(ing) system

(~) ~ ~ ~ **system** → reinforced (~) ~ ~ ~ ~ ~

~ ~ **tile making** → hollow (concrete) block ~

(~) ~ **ware**, hollow (~) ~ · (Beton-)Hohlware f

~ **impregnation agent** · Beton-Imprägnier(ungs)mittel n

~ **improvement**, ~ modification · Betonvergütung f

~ **improver**, ~ modifier, ~ improving agent, ~ modifying agent · Betonvergüter m, Betonvergütungsmittel n

~ **in aggressive water and soils** · Beton m in betonschädlichen Wässern und Böden [*DIN 4030*]

~ **(in)filler slab**, ~ infill(ing) ~, ~ cladding ~ · Betonausfüll(ungs)platte f, Betonausfachungsplatte

~ **infill(ing) unit**, ~ (in)filler ~, ~ cladding ~ · Betonausfachungselement n, Betonausfüll(ungs)element

~ **ingredient** · Betonbestandteil m, Betonkomponente f

concrete-in-mass, mass(ive) concrete, bulk concrete · Massenbeton m

~ **structure**, mass(ive) concrete ~, bulk concrete ~ · Massenbetonbauwerk n

concrete insert · Betondübel m [*Eine Hülse aus Blech oder einem anderen Stoff, die beim Betonieren an der entsprechenden Stelle einbetoniert wird und später ein Befestigungsmittel aufnimmt*]

~ **inspection chamber** [*B. S. 556*] Beton-Revisionsschacht m

~ **integral waterproofer** → ~ densifying agent

~ ~ **waterproof(ing) agent** → ~ densifying agent

~ ~ **water repellent admix(ture)** → ~ densifying agent

~ ~ **water-repeller** → ~ densifying agent

~ ~ **water repelling agent** → ~ densifying agent

~ **interlocking pipe** → interlocking concrete ~

~ ~ **(roof(ing)) tile** [*B. S. 550*] · Beton-Dachfalzstein m, Betonfalz(dach)stein [*DIN 1117*]

~ **intermediate floor** → ~ (suspended) ~

~ **irrigation pipe** · Beton-Bewässerungsrohr n, Bewässerungsbetonrohr

~ **jamb** [*The vertical concrete face inside an opening, to the full thickness of a wall*] · Betongewände n

~ **joint** · Betonfuge f

~ ~ **sealing compound** · Betonfugenvergußmasse f

~ **joist** · Betonunterzug m

~ **kerb** [*B. S. 340*]; ~ curb · Betonbordstein m [*DIN 483*]

(~) ~ **mould** (Brit.); (~) curb mold (US) · (Beton)Bordsteinform f

~ **lab(oratory)** · Betonlabor(atorium) n

~ **lath(ing)** · Betondrahtgewebe n [*Putzträger aus Draht und Beton. Das Gewebe besteht aus einem starken verzinktem, in sich festgewebtem Drahtnetz. Nur die Querdrähte sind rippenförmig durch Hartbeton ummantelt*]

~ **lattice beam** → ~ truss(ed girder)

~ ~ **girder** → ~ truss(ed ~)

~ **levelling layer** (Brit.); ~ leveling ~ (US); ~ ~ course · Betonausgleichschicht f, Betonnivellierschicht, Betonausgleichlage f, Betonnivellierlage

(~) **lift** [*The concrete placed between two consecutive horizontal construction joints; usually contains several layers or courses*] · Betonierlage f, Betonierschicht f

~ **lighthouse** · Betonleuchtturm m

~ **(lighting) column** (Brit.); ~ mast (US) [*B. S. 1308*] · Beton-Beleuchtungsmast m, Beton-Lichtmast

~ **line** · Betonleitung f,

~ **lined iron pipe**, ~ (sur)faced ~ ~ · betonausgekleidetes Eisenrohr n, betonverkleidetes ~, betonbekleidetes ~

~ **lining**, ~ (sur)facing · Betonauskleidung f, Betonbekleidung, Betonverkleidung

concrete lintel — concrete (paving) sett

~ **lintel;** ~ lintol [*deprecated*] · Betonoberschwelle *f*, Betonsturz *m*

~ **(load)bearing system** · Betontragwerk *n*

~ **lower boom** → ~ bottom chord

~ ~ **chord** → ~ bottom ~

~ **made from natural and broken aggregates,** chip(ping)s concrete · Splittbeton *m*

~ ~ **of cement and clay powder** · Tonbeton *m* [*Verbindung von Zement mit Tonpulver*]

~ **manhole,** ~ manway [*B.S. 556*] · Beton(einstieg)schacht *m*, Betonmannloch *n*, Betonmanneinsteigloch, Betoneinsteigschacht, Betonmanneinstieg(loch) *m*, (*n*)

~ ~ **ring,** ~ manway ~ · Beton(einstieg)schachtring *m*, Betonmannlochring, Betoneinsteigschachtring

~ **manway,** ~ manhole [*B. S. 556*] · Beton(einstieg)schacht *m*, Betonmannloch *n*, Betonmanneinsteigloch, Betoneinsteigschacht, Betonmanneinstieg(loch) *m*, (*n*)

~ ~ **ring** → ~ manhole ~

~ **masonry,** CIM · Betonblock(stein)mauerwerk *n*, Beton(werk)steinmauerwerk

~ ~ **block,** ~ ~ tile, ~ ~ unit [*See remark under 'Block(stein)'*] · Betonmauerwerkblock(stein) *m*, Betonmauerwerkstein

~ ~ **chimney** · Betonmauerwerksschornstein *m*

~ ~ **home** · Betonmauerwerk-Einfamilienhaus *n*

~ ~ **partition wall** · Betonmauerwerk-Trennwand *f*

~ ~ **wall** → ~ block ~ ~ ·

~ ~ **window opening** · Betonmauerwerk-Fensteröffnung *f*

~ ~ **(work)** → ~ block ~ (~)

~ ~ **(~) wall** · Betonmauer *f*

~ **mast** (US); ~ (lighting) column (Brit.) [*B. S. 1308*] · Beton-Beleuchtungsmast *m*, Beton-Lichtmast

~ ~ · Betonmast *m*

~ **material** · Betonstoff *m*

(~) **meter** → ~ (~) (air) (entrainment) ~

~ ~ **box** · Beton-Zählerkasten *m*

~ **mix** → ~ mixture

~ ~ **electric testing apparatus,** ratiometer · Gerät *n* zur Bestimmung des W/Z-Faktors

~ ~ **proportions** · Betonmisch(ungs)formel *f*, Betonmisch(ungs)verhältnis *n*

~ **mixing** · Betonmischen *n*, Betonmischung *f*

~ ~ **temperature** · Beton(auf)bereitungstemperatur *f*, Betonmischtemperatur

~ **mix(ture)** · Betongemenge *n*, Betongemisch *n*, Betonmischung *f*

~ **modification,** ~ improvement · Betonvergütung *f*

~ **modifier** → ~ improver

~ **modulus of elasticity** · Betonelastizitätsmodul *m*

~ **monolithic construction** · Beton-Monolithbau *m*

~ **mould** (Brit.); ~ mold (US) · Betonform *f*

(~) ~ **(release) oil** (Brit.); (~) mold (~) ~ (US) · (Beton)Form(en)öl *n*

~ **moulding equipment factory** (Brit.); ~ molding ~ ~ (US) · Betonformenfabrik *f*, Betonformenwerk *n*

~ **muntin** (US); ~ glazing bar, ~ astragal · Betonsprosse *f* [*Oberlichtverglasung*]

~ **northlight (roof) shell,** ~ sawtooth (~) ~ · Betonshed(dach)schale *f*

~ **oil sump** · betonierte Ölauffangwanne *f*

~ **(ornamental) string (course)** · Betongurt(ge)sims *m*, (*n*)

~ **overlay,** ~ topping · Betonüberzug *m*

~ **palisade fence** · Betonpalisadenzaun *m*

(~) **panel,** (pre)cast (~) ~, prefab(ricated) ~ ~ · Betontafel *f*

(~) ~ **fence,** (pre)cast (~) ~ ~, prefab(ricated) ~ ~ ~ · Betontafelzaun *m*

(~) ~ **with window opening,** (pre-)cast (~) ~ ~ ~ ~, prefab(ricated) ~ ~ ~ ~ ~ · Betontafel *f* mit Fensteröffnung

~ **pantile** · Beton-Dachpfanne *f*, Beton-Hohlpfanne, Beton-(S-)Pfanne, holländische Betonpfanne [*DIN 1118*]

~ **parachute,** ~ umbrella · Betonschirm *m*

~ **parapet element** · Beton-Brüstungselement *n*

~ **pat** · Betonkuchen *m*

~ **patch** · Betonflickstelle *f*

~ **patching,** ~ reintegration, ~ repair · Betonausbesserung *f*, Betonreparatur *f*

~ ~ **material,** ~ repair ~, ~ reintegration ~ · Betonausbesserungsstoff *m*, Betonausbesserungsmittel *n*, Betonreparaturstoff, Betonreparaturmittel

~ ~ **medium** · Betonflickmasse *f*, Betonflickstoff *m*

~ **pavement,** ~ paving · Betondecke *f*

~ ~ **joint sealing compound,** ~ surfacing ~ ~ ~ · Betondeckenfugenvergußmasse *f*

~ **(paving) flag** · Beton-Belagplatte *f*, Beton-Gehbahnplatte, Beton-Gehwegplatte, Beton-Fußwegplatte, Beton-Gehsteigplatte, Beton-Pflasterplatte, Beton-Bürgersteigplatte

~ (~) **sett** · Betonpflasterstein *m* [*DIN 18501*]

concrete pergola — concrete reintegration

~ **pergola** · Betonpergola f
~ **pile** · Betonpfahl m
~ ~ **foundation** · Betonpfahlgründung f
~ **pipe** [*B. S. 556*] · Betonrohr n, Zementrohr [*DIN 4032*]
~ (~) **bend** · Beton(rohr)krümmer m, Zementrohrkrümmer
~ ~ **compression tester** · Betonrohrprüfpresse f, Zementrohrprüfpresse
(~) ~ **mould** (Brit.); (~) ~ **mold** (US) · (Beton)Rohrform f, Zementrohrform
~ ~ **press** · Betonrohrpresse f, Zementrohrpresse
~ ~ ~ **head** · Preßkopf m [*Betonrohrpresse*]
~ ~ **producer**, ~ ~ maker, ~ ~ manufacturer · Betonrohrhersteller m, Zementrohrhersteller, Betonrohrfabrikant m, Zementrohrfabrikant
~ ~ **spinning machine** · Betonrohrschleudermaschine f, Schleuderbetonrohrmaschine, Zementrohrschleudermaschine, Schleuderzementrohrmaschine
~ ~ **works** · Betonrohrfabrik f, Betonrohrwerk n
~ **pipeline** · Betonrohrleitung f, Zementrohrleitung
~ **placing** → pouring
~ **placing sequence** · Betonierfolge f, Betoniereinbaufolge
~ **plain (roof(ing)) tile** → plain concrete (~) ~
~ ~ **tile** → plain concrete (roof(ing)) ~
~ **plane (roof(ing)) tile** → plain concrete (~) ~
~ ~ **tile** → plain concrete (roof(ing)) ~
~ **plank** · Betondiele f, Zementdiele
(~) ~ → (pre)cast (~) ~
~ ~ **silo** · Beton-Fahrsilo m, Beton-Flachsilo
(~) **plasticising agent** (Brit.) → (~) workability ~
~ **plate** → ~ structural ~
~ **platform** · Betonplattform f
~ **pole** [*For electrical transmission and traction systems. B.S. 607*] · Betonleitungsmast m
~ /**polymer composition** · Polymerbeton m
~ **pool**, ~ swimming ~ · Beton(schwimm)becken n
~ **porous pipe**, porous concrete ~ [*B. S. 1194*] · wasserdurchlässiges Betonrohr n, Sickerbetonrohr, Betonsickerrohr
~ **portal frame** · Betonportalrahmen m
~ **post** · Betonpfosten m
~ **pot for walls** → hollow concrete block ~ ~
(~) **(pre)casting factory**, (pre)cast concrete ~ · Beton(stein)werk n, (Beton)Fertigteilwerk
~ **preservative** · Betonschutzmittel n

~ **pressure pipe** · Betondruck(leitungs)rohr n
~ **primer** · Betonfibel f
~ **prism** · Betonprisma n
~ **product** → (pre)cast (~) ~
~ ~ **maker** → (pre)cast (concrete) product manufacturer
~ ~ **maker** → (pre)cast (concrete) product manufacturer
~ ~ **manufacturer** → (pre)cast (~) ~ ~
~ ~ **producer** → (pre)cast (concrete) product manufacturer
~ **production** → ~ fabriaction
~ **products** → (mass-produced) (pre-)cast (concrete) ware
~ **promenade roof** · begehbares Betondach n
~ **property** · Betoneigenschaft f
~ **protection** · Betonschutz m
~ ~ **fence** → ~ safety ~
~ **pumping**, pumping of concrete · Betonverpumpen n, Pumpbetoneinbringung f
~ **purlin(e)** · Betonpfette f
~ **quality**, quality of concrete · Betongüte f, Betonqualität f
~ ~ **control** · Betongüteüberwachung f
~ (~) **grade**, (quality) grade of concrete · Betongüteklasse f
~ **radiation shielding wall**, ~ (biological) ~ ~ · Beton-Abschirmwand f
~ **raft** [*A precision made reinforced concrete floor slab of the highest quality. It consists on a dense concrete base topped by a fully integrated wearing surface*] · Großflächenplatte f [*Stelcon*]
~ **railroad tie** (US); ~ railway sleeper (Brit.) [*B.S. 986*] · Beton(schienen)schwelle f, Betongleisschwelle
~ **railway sleeper** (Brit.); ~ railroad tie (US) [*B.S. 986*] · Betongleisschwelle f, Beton(schienen)schwelle
~ **(rainwater) gutter**, ~ roof ~ · Beton(dach)rinne f, Betonregenrinne
~ **refuse water pipe**, ~ foul ~ ~, ~ sewer ~, ~ sewage ~ · Abwasser-Betonrohr n, Beton-Abwasserrohr
~ **re-handling** · Betonumschlag m
(~) **reinforcement**, ~ steel, reinforcing steel · (Beton)Bewehrung f, (Beton-)Armierung, (Beton)Stahleinlagen fpl
(~) ~ **distance piece**, (~) ~ spacer · (Stahl)Betonabstandhalter m aus Beton
(~) ~ **loop** · (Beton)Stahlschlaufe f
(~) ~ **spacer**, (~) ~ distance piece (Stahl)Betonabstandhalter m aus Beton
~ **reintegration**, ~ patching, ~ repair · Betonausbesserung f, Betonreparatur f

concrete reintegration material — concrete shear wall

~ ~ **material**, ~ patching ~, ~ repair ~ · Betonausbesserungsstoff *m*, Betonreparaturstoff, Betonausbesserungsmittel *n*, Betonreparaturmittel

~ **remover** → ~ solvent

~ **repair**, ~ reintegration, ~ patching · Betonausbesserung *f*, Betonreparatur *f*

~ ~ **material**, ~ reintegration ~, ~ patching ~ · Betonausbesserungsstoff *m*, Betonreparaturstoff, Betonausbesserungsmittel *n*, Betonreparaturmittel

~ **reservoir**, ~ tank · Betonbehälter *m*

~ **retarder**, ~ retarding agent · Beton-(Ab)Binde(zeit)verzögerer *m*, Beton-Erstarrungs(zeit)verzögerer, Beton-(Er-)Härtungs(zeit)verzögerer, Beton-VZ

~ **retarding agent** → ~ retarder

~ **rib** · Betonrippe *f*

~ **rib** → (pre)cast (~) ~

~ **rib(bed) floor** · Betonrippendecke *f*

~ ~ **slab** · Betonrippenplatte *f*

~ **ridge tile** · Beton-Dachkenner *m*, Beton-Walmstein *m*, Beton-Firststein, Beton-Kammstein [*DIN 1119*]

~ **ring** · Betonring *m*

~ ~, ~ **well** ~ · Betonbrunnenring *m*, Brunnenring aus Beton [*DIN 4034*]

~ ~ **beam** · Betonringbalken(träger) *m*

~ **road (inlet) gull(e)y**, ~ street (~) ~, ~ ~ outlet ~ · Beton-Straßenablauf *m*, Beton-Straßeneinlauf [*DIN 4052*]

~ ~ **outlet** → ~ ~ (inlet) gull(e)y

~ **roof** · Betondach *n*

~ (~) **deck** · Betondachdecke *f*, Betonunterkonstruktion *f*

~ (~) **gutter**, ~ rainwater ~ · Beton-(dach)rinne *f*, Betonregenrinne

~ ~ **shell** · Betondachschale *f*

~ **roof(ing) slab** · Beton-Bedachungselement *n*, Betondachplatte *f*, Betondachelement, Beton-Bedachungsplatte

~ ~ **tile**, cement ~ ~ [*B.S. 473, 550*] · (Beton)Dachstein *m*, zementgebundener Dachstein, Zementdachstein [*DIN 1115. Aus Zementmörtel oder Feinbeton*]

~ ~ ~ **machine**, cement ~ ~ ~ · (Zement)Dachsteinmaschine *f*, Betondachsteinmaschine

~ ~ ~ **tester**, cement ~ ~ ~ · (Beton-)Dachsteinprüfgerät *n*, (Beton)Dachsteinprüfgerät, Zementdachsteinprüfgerät, Zementdachsteinprüfmaschine

~ **rupture**, ~ failure · Betonbruch *m*

~ **safety fence**, ~ guard ~, ~ protection ~, ~ guard rail · Beton-(Sicherheits-)Leitplanke *f*

~ **sample** · Betonprobe(stück) *f*, (*n*), Betonprobekörper *m*

~ **sandwich panel**, ~ ~ unit [*It is composed of two layers of concrete enclosing a layer of rigid insulation material such as cellular glass, fibrous glass or foamed polystyrene*] · Betonsandwichtafel *f*, Beton-Dreischichtentafel, Beton-Dreilagentafel

~ **sanitary building block module**, ~ ~ unitized unit · Beton-Sanitärinstallationsblock *m*, Beton-Sanitärinstallationszelle *f*, Beton-Sanitär(raum)zelle, Beton-Sanitär(raum)block

~ ~ **unitized unit** → ~ ~ ~ building block module

~ **saw-tooth (roof) shell**, ~ northlight (~) ~ · Betonshed(dach)schale *f*

~ **scrap** [*It is used as ballast*] · Betonschutt *m*

~ **screed** [*A band of concrete carefully laid to the correct surface as a guide for the screed rail when concreting*] · Betonleiste *f*

concrete-screed floating floor covering, ~ ~ floor(ing) (finish), floating concrete screed · schwimmender (Zement-)Estrich(fuß)boden(belag) *m*, ~ (Zement)Estrich *m*

~ ~ **floor(ing) (finish)**, ~ ~ floor cover(ing), floating concrete screed · schwimmender (Zement)Estrich(fuß)boden(belag) *m*, (Zement-)Estrich *m*

concrete screed (material) → (monolithic) (fine) ~ ~ (~)

~ ~ **(topping)** → (monolithic) fine ~ ~ (~)

~ ~ **with hard aggregate sprinkled on the surface** · Aufstreubetonbelag *m*

~ **sculpture** · Betonskulptur *f*

~ **seal(ant)** → ~ seal(ing) material

~ **sealer** → ~ seal(ing) material

~ **sealing** · Betonabsieg(e)lung *f*, Betonversieg(e)lung

~ **seal(ing) agent** → ~ ~ material

~ ~ **material**, ~ ~ agent, ~ ~ seal(ant), ~ sealer · Betonversiegeler *m*, Betonsiegel *n*, Betonabsieg(e)lungsmittel *n*, Betonversieg(e)lungsmittel [*Fehlname: Betonüberzug m*]

~ **seat** · Betonsitz *m*

~ **section**, ~ cross-~ · Betonquerschnitt *m*

~ ~ · Betonprofil *n*

~ **separator** → ~ spacer

~ **sett**, ~ paving ~ · Betonpflasterstein *m* [*DIN 18501*]

~ **setting below 0° Centigrade** · Kaltbeton *m* [*Bei Temperaturen unter 0° C abbindender Beton*]

~ **sewage pipe**, ~ sewer ~, ~ refuse water ~, ~ foul water ~ · Abwasser-Betonrohr *n*, Beton-Abwasserrohr

~ **sewer** · Abwasser-Betonleitung *f*, Betonabwasserleitung

~ ~ **pipe**, ~ sewage ~, ~ refuse water ~, ~ foul water ~ · Abwasser-Betonrohr *n*, Beton-Abwasserrohr

~ **shaft** · Betonschacht *m*

~ **shear wall** · Beton-Windscheibe *f*

(~) sheath coat → (~) encasement
~ shell · Betonschale f
~~ cupola, ~~ dome · Betonschalenkuppel f
~~ design · Betonschalenentwurf m
~~ dome, ~~ cupola · Betonschalenkuppel f
~~ roof, shell concrete ~ · Schalenbetondach n, Betonschalendach
~~~ construction, shell concrete ~ ~ · Betonschalendachbau m
~~ structure · Betonschalenbauwerk n
~ shelter · Beton(schutz)bunker m
~ shield · Betonschirm m [Strahlenschutz]
~ shielding wall → ~ biological ~ ~
(~) shuttering, (~) formwork, (~) form(s) · (Beton)Schalung f
~ sill, ~ threshold; ~ cill (Brit.) · Beton(tür)schwelle f
~ silo · Betonsilo m, n
~ skeleton construction · Betonskelettkonstruktion f
~ skyscraper · Betonwolkenkratzer m
~ slab · (Beton)Bauplatte f
~~ → ~ (structural) plate ~
(~) ~ compressive strength, (~) ~ crushing ~ · (Beton)Plattendruckfestigkeit f
~~ construction · Betonplattenbau m
(~) ~ crushing strength, (~) ~ compressive ~ · Plattendruckfestigkeit f, Beton~
~~ edge · Betonplattenrand m
~~ end · Betonplattenende n
~~ façade · Betonplattenfassade f
~~ facing → ~ ~ lining
~~ lining, ~ ~ (sur)facing · Betonplattenauskleidung f, Betonplattenverkleidung, Betonplattenbekleidung
~ (~) sub-floor, ~ base · Betonunterboden m [Fehlname: Betonboden]
~ (~) ~ laid at ground level, ~ base ~ ~ ~ ~ · Betonunterboden m ohne Blindboden [Fehlname: Betonboden ~ ~]
~~ (sur)facing → ~ ~ lining
~ slatted floor · Betonrostboden m, Betonspaltenboden
~ soffit → (all-)concrete visible underface
(~) solid block → (pre)cast (~) ~ ~
(~) ~ tile → ((pre)cast) (concrete) solid block
~ solvent, ~ remover [It is used to soften and remove built-up concrete on mixers, moulds, barrows, etc.] · Betonlösungsmittel n, Betonlöser m, Betonlösemittel
~ spacer, ~ distance piece, ~ separator · Abstandhalter m aus Beton, Betonabstandhalter

(~) spinning, centrifugal casting of concrete, spinning of concrete · (Beton)Schleuderung f
(~) ~ method · (Beton)Schleuderverfahren n
~ spiral stair(case) · Betonwendeltreppe f
~ splashing · Betonspritzer m
~ split duct · Beton(rohr)schale f, Zementrohrschale
~-spraying → guniting
~ stair(case) · Betontreppe f
~~ builder · Betontreppenbauer m
~ (~) step · Beton(treppen)stufe f
~~ tower · Beton-Treppenturm m
~ stand → ~ cycle ~
~ steel, reinforcing ~, (concrete) reinforcement · (Beton)Bewehrung f, (Beton)Armierung, (Beton)Stahleinlagen fpl
~ step → ~ (stair(case)) ~
~ strain · Betondehnung f
~ street (inlet) gull(e)y → ~ road (~) ~
~ strength · Betonfestigkeit f
~ stress · Betonspannung f
~ string (course), ~ ornamental ~ (~) · Betongurt(ge)sims m, (n)
~ structural panel → (~) floor slab
~ (structural) plate, ~ (~) slab, structural concrete ~ · (Konstruktions-)Betonplatte f, Betonkonstruktionsplatte
~~ slab → (~) floor ~
~ (~) ~ → ~ (~) plate
~ structure · Betonbau(werk) m, (n) [DIN 1047]
~ sub-floor, ~ slab ~, ~ base · Betonunterboden m [Fehlname: Betonboden]
~~ laid at ground level, ~ slab ~ ~ ~ ~ ~, ~ base ~ ~ ~ ~ · Betonunterboden m ohne Blindboden [Fehlname: Betonboden ~ ~]
~ subgrade paper, concreting ~, underlay ~, subsoil ~, road lining (~) · (Autobahn-)Unterlagspapier n, Straßenbaupapier, Papierunterlage f
~ supporting medium, ~ base · Betonunterlage f [für einen Belag]
~ surcharge · Betonauflast f
~ surface [Of a sound insulating floor] · Betonüberdeckung f
~~ · Betonoberfläche f
~ (~) finish · Betonoberflächengestaltung f
~~ hardener, ~ ~ hardening agent · (Beton)Oberflächenhärter m
~~ hardening agent, ~ ~ hardener · (Beton)Oberflächenhärter m
~~ improving agent · Betonkosmetikerzeugnis n

(~) ~ retardant [*The retarded surface is usually washed off when the base concrete reaches 1,000–1,500 psi*] · Oberflächenverzögerer *m* zur Herstellung von Waschbeton, Waschbetonhilfe *f*, Waschbetonverzögerer

(~) ~ ~ in liquid form · Waschbetonflüssigkeit *f*

(~) ~ ~ ~ paste form · Waschbetonpaste *f*

~ (sur)faced iron pipe, ~ lined ~ ~ · betonausgekleidetes Eisenrohr *n*, betonverkleidetes ~, betonbekleidetes ~

~ (sur)facing, ~ lining · Betonauskleidung *f*, Betonbekleidung, Betonverkleidung

~ ~ joint sealing compound, ~ pavement ~ ~ ~ · Betondeckenfugenvergußmasse *f*

~ (suspended) floor, ~ intermediate ~, CONC F, conc fl [*B. S. 1207*] · Beton(trenn)decke *f*, Beton-Etagendecke, Beton-Geschoßdecke, Beton-Stockwerkdecke, Betonhochbaudecke

~ (swimming) pool · Beton(schwimm)becken *n*

~ table · Betontabelle *f*

~ tank, ~ reservoir · Betonbehälter *m*

~ technician · Betontechniker *m*

~ technologist · Betontechnologe *m*

~ technology · Betontechnologie *f*

~ television tower, ~ ~ torch, ~ TV ~ · Beton-Fernsehturm *m*

~ temperature · Betontemperatur *f*

~ tensile strength, ~ tension ~ · Betonzugfestigkeit *f*

~ ~ stress, ~ tension ~ · Betonzugspannung *f*

~ ~ zone, ~ tension ~, tension zone of the concrete · Betonzugzone *f*

~ tension · Betonzug *m* ,

~ ~ crack · Betonzugriß *m*

~ ~ strength, ~ tensile ~ · Betonzugfestigkeit *f*

~ ~ stress, ~ tensile ~ · Betonzugspannung *f*

(~) terrazzo, terrazzo concrete · Terrazzo *m* [*Gemisch aus Zement und farbigen schleiffähigen Zuschlägen aus Natursteinen. DIN 1965*]

(~) ~ aggregate, (~) ~ chip (ping)s · Steinkörnungen *fpl*, Terrazzokörnungen, Terrazzomaterial *n*

(~) ~ capping → (~) ~ (wall) coping

(~) ~ chip(ping)s → (~) ~ aggregate

(~) ~ coping → (~) ~ wall ~

(~) ~ cove, (~) ~ coving [*A quadrant terrazzo moulding joining a wall to a ceiling*] · Terrazzoviertelstab *m* [*Wand-Decke*]

(~) ~ coving → (~) ~ cove

(~) ~ dado · Terrazzosockel *m*

(~) ~ floor cover(ing), (~) ~ floor(ing) (finish) · Terrazzo(fuß)boden(belag) *m*

(~) ~ floor(ing) (finish), (~) ~ floor cover(ing) · Terrazzo(fuß)boden(belag) *m*

(~) ~ ~ tile · Terrazzo(fuß)boden(belag)platte *f*, Terrazzo(fuß)bodenfliese *f*

(~) ~ grain · Terrazzokorn *n*

(~) ~ mix(ture) · Terrazzogemisch *n*, Terrazzomischung *f*

(~) ~ plant · Terrazzobetrieb *m*, Terrazzowerk *n*

(~) ~ sink drop · Terrazzospültisch *m*

(~) ~ skirting · Terrazzofußleiste *f*, Terrazzoscheuerleiste

(~) ~ stair tread · Terrazzotritt(stufe) *m*, (*f*)

(~) ~ (wall) coping, (~) ~ (~) cope, (~) ~ (~) capping · Terrazzo-(Mauer-)Abdeckung *f*

(~) ~ ~ tile, (pre)cast ~ ~ ~ · Terrazzowand(belag)platte *f*, Terrazzowandfliese *f*

(~) ~ ware · Terrazzoware(n) *f*

(~) ~ window cill; (~) ~ ~ sill (Brit.) · Terrazzofensterbank *f*

(~) ~ work · Terrazzoarbeiten *fpl*

~ test · Betonprobe *f*, Betonversuch *m*, Betonprüfung *f*

~ ~ beam · Betonprobebalken *m*, Betonprüfbalken, Betonversuchsbalken

~ (~) cube, compression ~ · (Beton-)(Probe)Würfel *m*, (Beton)Prüfwürfel, (Beton)Versuchswürfel, (Beton)Druckwürfel

~ (~) cylinder, compression ~ · (Beton)(Probe)Zylinder *m*, (Beton)Versuchszylinder, (Beton)Druckzylinder, (Beton)Prüfzylinder

~ ~ hammer, rebound tester, scleroscope [*A tester indexing the compressive strength of concrete by the height of the elastic rebound*] · Betonprüfhammer *m*, Betonschlaghammer, Rückprall-Härteprüfer, Rückprallhammer

~ tester, ~ test(ing) apparatus · Betonprüfgerät *n*

~ testing lab(oratory) · Betonprüflabor(atorium) *n*

~ ~ machine · Betonprüfmaschine *f*

~ ~ method [*B.S. 1881*] · Betonprüfverfahren *n*

~ texture · Betongefüge *n*, Betonstruktur *f*

~ thickness · Betondicke *f* [*Fehlname: Betonstärke f*]

~ threshold, ~ sill; ~ cill (Brit.) · Beton(tür)schwelle *f*

~ tile · Beton(belag)platte *f*, Betonfliese *f*

~ ~ → ((pre)cast) concrete (building) block

~ ~ factory → ~ ~ works

~ ~ floor(ing) (finish), ~ ~ floor cover(ing) · Betonfliesen(fuß)boden(-belag) *m*, Betonplatten(fuß)boden(belag)

concrete tile masonry wall — concrete workability agent

~ ~ masonry wall → ~ (block) ~ ~
~ ~ ~ (work) → ~ (block) ~ (~)
~ ~ plant → ~ ~ works
~ ~ press · Beton(belag)plattenpresse *f*, Betonfliesenpresse
~ ~ roof cover(ing), ~ ~ ~ cladding, ~ ~ ~ sheathing, cement ~ ~ ~, ~ ~ roofing · Betonstein(dach)(ein)deckung *f*, Betonsteinbedachung, (Beton-)Dachstein(ein)deckung, Zementdachstein(ein)deckung
~ ~ works, ~ ~ factory, ~ ~ plant · Beton(belag)plattenfabrik *f*, Beton(belag)plattenwerk *n*, Betonfliesenwerk, Betonfliesenfabrik
~ topping, ~ overlay · Betonüberzug *m*
~ ~ ~ → topping (slab)
~ tower → service ~
~ ~ · Betonturm *m*
~ treated with SiF₄, ocrated concrete · Ocratbeton *m*, Okratbeton
~ trimmer plank (unit) · Betonstreichdiele *f* [*Auswechs(e)lung*]
~ trough · Betontrog *m*
(~) ~ slab (~) channel (unit) · (Beton-)Trogplatte *f*, (Beton-)U-Platte
~ trussed beam → ~ truss(ed girder)
~ truss(ed girder), ~ lattice ~, ~ ~ beam · Betonfachwerk(träger) *n*, (*m*)
~ tunnel vault → ~ barrel ~
~ TV torch → ~ television tower
~ type, type of concrete · Betonart *f*
~ ~ of construction, ~ construction type · Betonbauart *f*
~ umbrella, ~ parachute · Betonschirm *m*
~ unitized unit, ~ building block module · Beton(raum)zelle *f*
~ vault · Betongewölbe *n*
~ visible under-face → all-~ ~ ~
~ wagon vault → ~ barrel ~
~ wall · Betonwand *f*
~ ~ block, ~ ~ tile [*See remark under 'Block'*] · Betonwand(bau)block(stein) *m*, Betonwand(bau)stein
(~) ~ panel → (pre)cast (~) ~ ~
~ ~ pot → hollow concrete block for walls
(~) ~ slab → (pre)cast (~) ~ ~
~ ~ tile → ~ ~ block
~ ~ ~ · Betonwand(belag)platte *f*, Betonwandfliese *f*
~ ware → (mass-produced) (pre)cast (~) ~
~ ~ factory → (pre)cast concrete ~
~ waste pipe, ~ draining ~, ~ drain(age) ~, ~ discharge ~ · Betondränrohr *n*, Dränbetonrohr, Betonentwässerungsrohr, Betonabflußrohr, Abflußbetonrohr, Betonablaufrohr, Ablaufbetonrohr, Entwässerungsbetonrohr [*Fehlnamen: Betonablauf m, Betonabfluß m*]
~ water waste preventer, ~ flushing tank, ~ flushing cistern · Betonspülkasten *m* [*Abort*]
~ ~ waterproofer, ~ waterproofing powder [*It is incorporated in the dry mix*] · Betondichter *m*, Betonsperrpulver *n*
~ waterproofing · Betondichtung *f*
~ ~ powder → ~ waterproofer
~ water-reducing agent → ~ workability ~
~ water tank · Beton-Wasserbehälter *m*
~ wearing surface · Betonverschleißoberfläche *f*
~ web · Betonsteg *m* [*Zug- und Druckflansch eines Betonbalkens sind durch den Betonsteg miteinander verbunden, der die Schubspannungen aufnimmt*]
~ wedge · Betonkeil *m*
~ (well) ring · Betonbrunnenring *m*, Brunnenring aus Beton [*DIN 4034*]
~ wet density · Beton-Feuchtraumgewicht BR$_F$ *n* [*Fehlname*]; Beton-Feuchtrohwichte BR$_F$ *f*
~ window sill; ~ ~ cill (Brit.) · Beton-Fensterbank *f*, Beton-(Fenster-)Sohlbank
~ with cork aggregate · Korkbeton *m*
~ ~ high early stability · frühstandfester Beton *m*
~ ~ ~ strength, high-early-strength concrete · frühtragfester Beton *m*
~ ~ large aggregate · Großkornbeton *m*
~ ~ oil addition · Petroleum-Beton *m* [*Durch Zusatz von Petroleum oder Ölrückständen zum angemachten Zement soll die Dichte gesteigert werden. Erfolg ist zweifelhaft*]
~ ~ synthetic resin dispersion · Kunstharzbeton *m*, Plastbeton, kunststofflegierter Beton [*Er besteht aus Zement, Zuschlagstoffen und Wasser, dem eine wäßrige Kunststoffdispersion zugesetzt wird*]
~ ~ washed pumice gravel · Edelbimsbeton *m* [*Sand als Zuschlagstoff wird nur für Mauerwerkbeton beigegeben*]
~ work · Betonarbeiten *fpl* [*DIN 1967*]
~ workability, workability of concrete · (Beton)Verarbeitbarkeit *f*
~ ~ agent, ~ water-reducing ~, ~ workability aid; ~ wetting agent, ~ plasticising agent, ~ plasticiser (Brit.); ~ plasticizing agent, ~ plasticizer (US) · (Beton)Verflüssiger *m*, Betonweichmacher, (Beton)Plastifizierungsmittel *n*, BV, Betonverarbeitungshilfe *f*, Plastifizierer, plastifizierendes (Betonzusatz-)Mittel, wassereinsparendes Betonzusatzmittel, betonverflüssigender Wirk-

concrete workability agent — conditioned space

stoff, BV-(Zusatz)Stoff *m*, betonverflüssigender Zusatz *m*, BV-Wirkstoff, BV-Zusatz(mittel)

~ **yard (inlet) gull(e)y** · Beton-Hofeinlauf *m*, Beton-Hofablauf

concreting → pouring

~ **aid** · Betonierhilfe *f*

~ **foil**, concrete covering ~ · Betonierfolie *f*

~ **paper**, underlay ~, sub-soil ~, road lining (~), concrete subgrade ~ · Papierunterlage *f*, (Autobahn-)Unterlagspapier *n*, Straßenbaupapier

concretion of lime, calcareous concretion · Kalkkonkretion *f*

concretor · Betonbauer *m*, Beton(fach)arbeiter

concussion, water hammer, reverberation [*A hammering sound caused by violent surges of pressure in water pipes*] · Wasserstoß *m*, Wasserschlag *m*, Druckstoß

condemned, demolishable, fit for demolition, fit for wrecking · abbruchreif, abreißreif

condensate → condens(at)ing water

~ **drainage** · Kondensatentwässerung *f*, Kondenswasserentwässerung, Schwitzwasserentwässerung, Tauwasserentwässerung

condensate-less, condensate-free · schwitzwasserfrei, schwitzwasserlos, kondenswasserfrei, kondenswasserlos, kondensatfrei, kondensatlos, tauwasserfrei, tauwasserlos

condensate pipework · Kondensatleitung *f*

~ **return pipework** · Kondensatrücklaufleitung *f*

condens(at)ing water, condensed ~, dripping moisture, condensate, condensation moisture, condensation water · Kondenswasser *n*; Schwitzwasser, Tauwasser, Kondensat *n*

condensation [*The cure of a synthetic resin*] · Kondensation *f*

~ → surface ~

~ **channel**, ~ gutter, ~ sinking, ~ groove, ~ trough, water channel · Schwitzwasserrinne *f*, Kondenswasserrinne, Kondensatrinne, Tauwasserrinne, Schwitzwasserrille *f*, Kondenswasserrille, Kondensatrille, Tauwasserrille

~ **control** · Kondenswasserregelung *f*, Schwitzwasserregelung, Kondensatregelung, Tauwasserregelung

~ **dampproofing** · Kondensatisolierung *f*, Kondenswasserisolierung, Schwitzwasserisolierung, Tauwasserisolierung

~ **groove** → ~ gutter

~ **gutter**, ~ sinking, ~ channel, ~ groove, ~ trough, water channel · Kondensatrinne *f*, Kondenswasserrinne, Schwitzwasserrinne, Tauwasserrinne, Schwitzwasserrille *f*, Kondenswasserrille, Kondensatrille, Tauwasserrille

~ **heat**, heat of condensation · Kondensationswärme *f*

~ **moisture** → condens(at)ing water

~ **product** · Kondensationserzeugnis *n*

~ **resin** · Kondensationsharz *n*

~ **sinking**, ~ gutter, ~ channel, ~ groove, ~ trough, water channel · Schwitzwasserrinne *f*, Kondenswasserrinne, Kondensatrinne, Tauwasserrinne, Schwitzwasserrille *f*, Kondenswasserrille, Kondensatrille, Tauwasserrille

~ **temperature**, dew point, saturation point, 100% relative humidity · Kondensationstemperatur *f*, Taupunkt *m*

~ ~ **diagram**, dew point ~, saturation point ~, diagram of 100% relative humidity · Taupunktdiagramm *n*, Kondensationstemperaturdiagramm

~ **tendency**, sweating ~ · Schwitzneigung *f* [*Beeinträchtigung der Atmungs- und Wasserdampfaufnahmefähigkeit*]

~ **tray** · Schwitzwasserschale *f*, Kondenswasserschale, Kondensatschale, Tauwasserschale

~ **water** → condens(at)ing ~

condensed water → condens(at)ing ~

condenser [*An apparatus for condensing vapo(u)rs, e.g. in a steam engine, or in the refrigeration plant of an air conditioning unit*] · Kondensator *m*

condensery · Kondensmilchfabrik *f*

condensing coil · Kondenserschlange *f*

~ **water** → condensating ~

to condition, to air-condition · klimaregeln, klimatisieren

condition · Bedingung *f*

~, state · Zustand *m*

~ **of equilibrium**, equilibrium condition · Gleichgewichtsbedingung *f*

~ ~ **plasticity** · Plastizitätsbedingung *f*

~ ~ **rigidity**, ~ ~ stiffness, rigidity condition, stiffness condition · Starrheitsbedingung *f*, Steifigkeitsbedingung [*Statik*]

~ ~ **similitude**, ~ ~ similarity, similitude condition, similarity condition · Ähnlichkeitsbedingung *f*

~ ~ **stability** → stability condition

~ ~ **static equilibrium**, static equilibrium condition · statische Gleichgewichtsbedingung *f*

~ ~ **stiffness**, ~ ~ rigidity, rigidity condition, stiffness condition · Starrheitsbedingung *f*, Steifigkeitsbedingung *f* [*Statik*]

condition(al) equation, equation of condition · Bestimmungsgleichung *f*, Bedingungsgleichung

conditioned, air-~ · klimageregelt, klimatisiert

~ **air** · klimageregelte Luft *f*, klimatisierte ~

~ **ceiling**, air-~ ~ · Klimadecke *f*

~ **space**, air-~ ~ · klimageregelter Raum *m*, klimatisierter ~

conditioner, air ~, (air) conditioning unit · Klimagerät *n*

conditioning → air ~

~ duct, air ~ ~ · Klima(tisierungs)kanal *m*

~ ~ shaft, air ~ ~ ~ · Klima(tisierungs)-kanalschacht *m*

~ equipment room, air ~ ~ ~ · Klimaanlagenraum *m*

~ installation → (air) conditioning system

~ plant → (air) conditioning system

~ station → central (air) conditioning plant

~ sub-station, air ~ ~ · Klimastation *f*

~ system → air ~ ~

~ ~ pipe, air ~ ~ ~ · Klimaanlagenrohr *n*

~ tower, air ~ ~ · Klimaanlagenturm *m*

~ unit, air ~ ~, terminal ~, (room) air conditioner, unit (air) conditioner · Klima(tisierungs)gerät *n*

~ zone, air ~ ~ · Klimatisierungszone *f*

conditions of statics · statische Bedingungen *fpl,* ~ Gegebenheiten

condominium (US); freehold flat, freehold apartment (unit) · Etageneigentum *n*, Geschoßeigentum, Stockwerkeigentum, Eigentumswohnung *f*, EW

conducive to cleaner surrounding(s) · umweltfreundlich

conductance → heat ~

conduction · Ableitung *f [Blitzschutz]*

~, heat ~ *[The process of transferring heat along the elements of a substance, as from a tube to a fin]* · (Wärme)Übertragung *f,* (Wärme)Leitung

~, sound ~ · Schalleitung *f*

conductive · ableitfähig, elektrisch leitend

~ floor cover(ing), ~ ~ finish, ~ floor(ing) · ableitfähiger (Fuß)Boden(belag) *m,* elektrisch leitender ~

~ ~ finish, ~ ~ cover(ing), ~ floor(ing) · ableitfähiger (Fuß)Boden(belag) *m*

~ (floor) tile · elektrisch leitende (Fuß-)Bodenfliese *f,* ~ ~ (Fuß)Boden(belag)-platte *f,* ableitfähige ~

~ floor(ing), ~ floor finish, ~ floor cover(ing) · ableitfähiger (Fuß)Boden(belag) *m*

conductor, heat ~ · (Wärme)Leiter *m*

~ (US) → downpipe

~, lightning ~, lightning rod · (Blitz)Ableiterstab *m*

~ head, leader ~, cistern ~ (US); rainwater ~ (Brit.) *[The enlarged entrance at the head of a downpipe. It colletcs the water from the gutters]* · Regenrinnenkasten *m,* Regenrinnenkessel *m,* (Dach)Rinnenkasten, (Dach)-Rinnenkessel

~ of sound, sound conductor · Schalleiter *m*

conduit, wiring ~, electrical ~ · Elektroleerrohr *n,* (Elt)Leerrohr

~ *[A channel or pipe to convey liquids]* · Leitung *f*

~ box, distribution ~, junction ~ · Anschlußkasten *m,* Verteilerkasten, Anschlußschrank *m,* Verteilerschrank, Abzweigkasten, Abzweigschrank, Verteilungskasten, Verteilungsschrank

~ clay pot, ~ hollow clay (building) block · Tonhohlplatte *f* für Installationsleitungen, Tonhohlsteinplatte ~ ~, H(o)urdi *m* ~ ~, Ziegelhohlplatte ~ ~, Hohlnutenstein *m* ~ ~

~ embedded in plaster, concealed conduit · Unterputzleitung *f,* Unterputzleerrohr *n [Elektrotechnik]*

~ groove · Leitungsfalz *m [Hourdi für Installationsleitungen]*

~ hollow clay (building) block, ~ clay pot · Tonhohlplatte *f* für Installationsleitungen, Tonhohlsteinplatte ~ ~, H(o)urdi *m* ~ ~, Ziegelhohlplatte ~ ~, Hohlnutenstein *m* ~ ~

~ line, wiring ~ ~, electrical ~ ~ · Elektroleerrohrleitung *f,* (Elt)Leerrohrleitung

~ network, wiring ~ ~, electrical ~ ~ · Elektroleerrohrnetz *n,* (Elt)Leerrohrnetz

~ pipe, line ~ · Leitungsrohr *n*

~ tile (US); cable duct, cable conduit, cable subway, cable CD · Kabel(kanal)formstein *m,* Kabelformstück *n [DIN 457 und DIN 1049]*

conduit-type concrete sewer · Abwasser-Betonkanal *m,* Beton(abwasser)kanal, Betonleitungskanal

~ sewer · Abwasserkanal *m,* Abflußkanal für Abwasser, Ablaufkanal für Abwasser, Entwässerungskanal für Abwasser *[DIN 19540]*

~ ~ work · Abwasserkanalarbeiten *fpl [DIN 18306]*

cone, pyrometric ~ · (Brenn)Kegel *m [Pyrometer aus Tonerdesilikaten zur Bestimmung der Wärmegrade in keramischen Brennöfen]*

~ · Kegel *m,* Konus *m*

~ anchorage · Kegelverankerung *f,* Konusverankerung

~ cable net, cone-shaped ~ ~, conical ~ ~ · kegelförmiges Seilnetz *n*

cone-cut veneer · Radialfurnier *n*

cone dome, conical ~ · Kegelkuppel *f*

~ equivalent, pyrometric ~ ~ · Feuerfestigkeit *f,* (Brenn)Kegelfallpunkt *m [Bestimmung des Wärmegrades in einem keramischen Brennofen]*

~ foundation, conical ~, taper(ed) ~ · kegelförmige Gründung *f,* konische ~

cone(-hip) tile, bonnet hip (~), bonnet ~ · gewölbter Gratstein *m,* ~Walmstein

cone hip(ped end), conical ~ (~) · Kegelwalm *m*
~ penetration test, deep ~ ~ · Kegeleindring(ungs)probe *f*, Kegeleindring(ungs)versuch *m*, Kegeleindring(ungs)prüfung *f*
cone(-shaped) cable net, conical ~ ~ · kegelförmiges Seilnetz *n*
cone shell, conical ~ · Kegelschale *f*, Kegelstumpf-Mantelfläche *f*
~ ~ foundation, conical ~ ~ · Kegelschalengründung *f*
~ slip(ping) · Keilschlupf *m*
~ tile, cone-hip ~, bonnet hip (~), bonnet ~ · gewölbter Gratstein *m*, ~ Walmstein
~(-type) vault, conical ~ · Kegelgewölbe *n* [*Bei dieser Gewölbeart verringert sich die Spannweite der Zylinder-Erzeugenden in der Achsenrichtung*]
cone visco(si)meter · Kegelviskosimeter *n*
conference block, ~ unit · Konferenztrakt *m*, Sitzungstrakt
~ building · Tagungsgebäude *n*
~ hall, ~ theatre · Konferenzsaal *m*, Sitzungssaal
~ room · Konferenzzimmer *n*, Konferenzraum *m*, Sitzungsraum, Sitzungszimmer
~ ~ · Besprechungsraum *m*
~ theatre, ~ hall · Konferenzsaal *m*, Sitzungssaal
~ unit, ~ block · Sitzungstrakt *m*, Konferenztrakt
confessio · Konfessio *f*, Confessio, Heiligengrab-Raum *m* unter dem Altar
confessional · Beichtstuhl *m*
configuration · Figur *f*
(confirmatory) check(ing) · Nachweis *m*
conformity to shaped surfaces · Formenanpassungseigenschaft *f*, Formenanpassungsvermögen *n*, Formenanpassungsfähigkeit *f*
congé → cavetto (moulding)
~ → apophyge
~; sanitary shoe (US) [*A small concave mo(u)lding joining the base of a wall to the floor*] · (Fuß)Bodenkehle *f*
conglomerate [*A rock consisting of round pebbles held together by a natural cement*] · Konglomerat *n*, „Naturbeton" *m*
conglomeratic sandstone · konglomeratischer Sandstein *m*
Congo copal · Kongokopal *m*
congregational mosque → Friday ~
~ ~ with antique columns [*e.g. the Great Mosque at Cordova*] · Säulensaalmoschee *f* [*Ihr Hauptraum ist durch Säulen unterteilt*]
congress on (pre)cast concrete, (pre-)cast concrete symposium · Betonsteinkongreß *m*

conic section · Kegelschnitt *m*
conical bolt · Bolzen *m* mit Anzug, konischer Bolzen
~ cable net, cone(-type) ~ ~ · kegelförmiges Seilnetz *n*
~ dome, cone ~ · Kegelkuppel *f*
~ folding · konische Faltung *f*
~ foundation, taper(ed) ~, cone ~ · kegelförmige Gründung *f*, konische ~
~ groin · Kegelgewölbegrat *m*
~ hip(ped end), cone ~ (~) · Kegelwalm *m*
~ roof · Kegeldach *n*
~ shell, slump cone; mold (US); mould (Brit.) · Setzbecher *m*, Trichter *m* [*Zur Ermittlung des Setzmaßes von Beton*]
~ ~, cone ~ · Kegelschale *f*, konische Schale, Kegelstumpf-Mantelfläche *f*
~ ~ foundation, cone ~ ~ · Kegelschalengründung *f*
~ spire · Kegeldach *n*, Kegelhelm *m* [*Turmdach mit kreisförmigem Grundriß und rundum aufsteigender Dachfläche*]
~ suspension roof · Hängekegeldach *n*
~ vault, cone(-type) ~ · Kegelgewölbe *n* [*Bei dieser Gewölbeart verringert sich die Spannweite der Zylinder-Erzeugenden in der Achsenrichtung*]
~ wedge · Kegelkeil *m*, Konuskeil
conifer balsam · Koniferenbalsam *m*
coning · Konstruieren *n* in Kegelform
~ and quartering · Kegelverfahren *n*, Viertelung *f*, Quadrantenverfahren [*DIN 51701*]
conjugate diameter · konjugierter Durchmesser *m*, zugeordneter ~
~ direction · zugeordnete Richtung *f*, konjugierte ~
~ line · konjugierte Gerade *f*, zugeordnete ~
~ matrix · konjugierte Matrix *f*, zugeordnete ~
~ plane · konjugierte Ebene *f*, zugeordnete ~
~ pressure · konjugierter Druck *m*, zugeordneter ~
conjugated oil · konjugiertes Öl *n*, Konjuenöl
to connect, to join [*bar; girder*] · verbinden, anschließen [*Stab; Träger*]
connecter (US); connector · Dübel *m*
~ joint (US); connector ~ · Dübelverbindung *f*
connecting angle, joint ~ · Anschlußwinkel *m*, Beiwinkel
~ bar → starter ~
~ corridor, connection ~, enterclose, linkway · Verbindungsgang *m*
~ joint, connection ~ · Anschlußfuge *f*, Verbindungsfuge
~ line, connection ~ · Anschlußleitung *f*, Verbindungsleitung

connecting loop — console

~ **loop**, connection ~ · Verbindungsschlaufe f

~ **means**, fastening · Verbindungsmittel n

~ **piece**, connection ~, jointing ~ · Anschlußstück n, Verbindungsstück

~ **plate**, connection ~, binding ~, fish ~, joint ~, gusset ~, corner ~, knee gusset ~ · Knoten(punkt)verbindung f

~ **rivet**, connection ~, jointing ~ · Anschlußniet m, Verbindungsniet

~ **structure**, connection ~ · Verbindungsbauwerk n

~ **surface**, connection ~ · Anschlußfläche f, Verbindungsfläche

connection · Anschluß m, Verbindung f

~, joint · Verbindung f, Anschluß m [bei Fachwerkstäben]

~ **bar** → starter ~

~ **box** · Anschluß(steck)dose f

~ **corridor**, connecting ~, enterclose, linkway · Verbindungsgang m

~ **dimension** · Anschlußmaß n, Anschlußabmessung f [Maß eines Bauteiles zum Anschluß an einen anderen]

~ **for protective earth wire to VDE 0100** · Anschlußstelle f für Schutzleitung nach VDE 0100

~ **joint**, connecting ~ · Anschlußfuge f, Verbindungsfuge

~ **line**, connecting ~ · Anschlußleitung f, Verbindungsleitung

~ **loop**, connecting ~ · Verbindungsschlaufe f

~ **piece**, connecting ~, jointing ~ · Anschlußstück n, Verbindungsstück

~ **plate**, connecting ~, binding ~, fish ~, joint ~, gusset ~, corner ~, knee bracket ~ · Knoten(punkt)verbindung f

~ **rivet**, connecting ~, jointing ~ · Anschlußniet m, Verbindungsniet

~ **structure**, connecting ~ · Verbindungsbauwerk n

~ **surface**, connecting ~ · Anschlußfläche f, Verbindungsfläche

~ **to a public sewer** · Anschluß m an die öffentliche Kanalisation

~ ~ **water supply system** · Wasserversorgungsanschluß m

connector; connecter (US) · Dübel m

~ → timber ~

~ **joint**; connecter ~ (US) · Dübelverbindung f

connoisseur, art ~, art-lover · Kunstfreund m, Kunstliebhaber m

conoid · Konoid n

conoidal form, ~ shape · Konoidform f

~ **roof** · Konoiddach n

~ **shape**, ~ form · Konoidform f

~ **shell** · Konoidschale f, konoidische Schale

~ **surface** · Konoidfläche f

~ **vault**, fan ~ [All the ribs have an identical curvature, resembling a fan. This type is peculiar to England, and occurs only in late Gothic work] · Fächergewölbe n, Trichtergewölbe, normannisches Gewölbe, (angel)sächsisches Gewölbe

~ **vaulted**, fan ~ · fächerüberwölbt,

consent to build, building permit · Bauerlaubnis f, Baugenehmigung f

conservation · Erhaltung f

~ **of energy** · Energieerhaltung f

conservatory · Schauhaus n [Ein dem öffentlichen Verkehr zugängliches Gewächshaus. DIN 11535 Bl. 1]

consistence, consistency · Konsistenz f, Steife f

~ **coefficient**, consistency ~, coefficient of consistence, coefficient of consistency · Steifebeiwert m, Konsistenzbeiwert

~ **degree**, consistency ~ · Steifegrad m, Konsistenzgrad

~ **measurement method**, consistency ~ ~ · Konsistenzmeßverfahren n, Steifemeßverfahren

~ **meter**, consistency ~ · Konsistenzmesser m, Steifemesser

~ **range**, consistency ~ · Konsistenzbereich m, n, Steifebereich

consistency, consistence · Konsistenz f, Steife f

~ **coefficient**, consistence ~, coefficient of consistency, coefficient of consistence · Konsistenzbeiwert m, Steifebeiwert

~ **degree**, consistence ~ · Konsistenzgrad m, Steifegrad

~ **factor** [A measure of grout fluidity roughly analogous to viscosity, which describes the ease with which grout may be pumped into pores or fissures; usually a laboratory measurement in which consistency is reported in degrees of rotation of torque viscosimeter in a specimen of grout] · Konsistenzfaktor m

~ **measurement method**, consistence ~ ~ · Konsistenzmeßverfahren n, Steifemeßverfahren

~ **meter**, consistometer · Konsistenzmesser m, Steifemesser, Konsistenzprüfer, Steifeprüfer

~ **range**, consistence ~ · Konsistenzbereich m, n, Steifebereich

~ **test**, slump test (for consistency) · Setzprüfung f, Setzprobe f, Setzversuch m, Konsistenzprüfung, Konsistenzprobe, Konsistenzversuch, Ausbreit(ungs)versuch, Ausbreit(ungs)prüfung, Ausbreit(ungs)probe [Betonprüfung. DIN 1048]

consistometer, consistency meter · Konsistenzmesser m, Steifemesser, Konsistenzprüfer, Steifeprüfer

console, ancon(e), truss [A scrolled bracket] · Konsole f

console — construction lumber

~, corbel, (natural) stone corbel, (natural) stone bracket, (natural) stone shoulder [*A small supporting piece of stone, often formed of scrolls or volutes, to carry a projecting weight*] · Kragstein *m*, Konsole *f*, steinerner Konsolträger *m*, Tragstein, (Natur)Steinkonsole, Notstein, Kraftstein, Balkenstein

~ cornice · Konsol(ge)sims *m*, (*n*) [*Dieses Gesims ist wegen seiner großen Auskragung von Konsolen gestützt*]

constancy of volume, stability ~ ~, volume stability, volume constancy · Raumbeständigkeit *f*, Raumkonstanz *f*

constant · konstant, unveränderlich, gleichbleibend, gleichmäßig

~ · Konstante *f*

~ **of integration**, integration constant · Integrationskonstante *f*

~ ~ **linearity** · Linearitätskonstante *f*

constant-section beam · Balken(träger) *m* mit unveränderlichem Querschnitt

constant weight · Gewichtskonstanz *f*

constituent · Bestandteil *m*

constitutive law · Formänderungsgesetz *n*

constrained arch → built-in ~

~ **beam** → built-in ~

~ **damping layer**, ~ ~ **course** · Mitteldämpfungslage *f*, Mitteldämpfungsschicht *f*

~ **girder** → built-in ~

(con)striction, reduction in area, necking down · Einschnürung *f*

to construct, to erect, to build · errichten, bauen [*im Hochbau*]

constructed, built, BLT · gebaut

~ **by the Owner**, built ~ ~ ~ · bauseits hergestellt

constructing, construction · Bauen *n*

construction, building, erection · Errichtung *f*, Bau *m* [*im Hochbau*]

~ · Aufbau *m*

~ → construction(al) system

~, constructing · Bauen *n*

~, structure · Bau(werk) *m*, (*n*), bauliche Anlage *f*

~ **activity**, building ~ · Bautätigkeit *f*

~ **administration** · Bauverwaltung *f*

~ **advisory service** · Bauberatung *f*

(~) **aggregate** · Zuschlag(stoff) *m*, Zuschlagmaterial *n*

(~) ~/**cement ratio** · Zuschlag(stoff)-Zement-Verhältnis *n*

(~) **aggregate composition** · Zuschlag(stoff)zusammensetzung *f*

(~) ~ **grain**, (~) ~ **particle** · Zuschlag-(stoff)korn *n*, Zuschlag(stoff)teilchen *n*

(~) ~ **heating** · Zuschlag(stoff)-Erwärmung *f*

(~) ~ **particle**, (~) ~ **grain** · Zuschlag-(stoff)korn *n*, Zuschlag(stoff)teilchen *n*

(~) ~ **producer** · Zuschlag(stoff)hersteller *m*

(~) **aggregates** · Zuschläge *mpl*, Zuschlagstoffe *mpl*, Zuschlagmaterial *n*

~ **and erection method** · Bau- und Montageverfahren *n*

~ **authority**, building ~ · Baubehörde *f*

~ **boom** · Bauhochkonjunktur *f*

~ **chemical** · Bauchemikal *n*

~ **chemistry** · Bauchemie *f*

~ **climatology**, building ~ · Bauklimatologie *f*

~ **control**, ~ **regulation** · Bauvorschrift *f*, Baubestimmung *f*

~ ~, ~ **supervision** · Bauüberwachung *f*, Bauaufsicht *f*, Bauführung *f*

~ **copper** · Baukupfer *n*

~ **department** · Bauabteilung *f*

~ **diary** · Bau(tage)buch *n*

~ **dirt** · Bauschmutz *m*

~ **document phase** · Detailplanungsstadium *n* für den Bau

~ **engineering** · Bautechnik *f*

~ **expert** · Bausachverständiger *m*, Baufachmann *m*

~ **field** · Bausektor *m*

~ **firm** · Bauunternehmung *f*, Baubetrieb *m*, Baufirma *f*, Bauunternehmen *n*

~ **fit** · Baupassung *f*

~ **flexibility** · bauliche Anpassungsfähigkeit *f*

~ **foil** · Bau(dichtungs)folie *f*, Baudichtfolie

~ **glass**, building ~ · Bauglas *n*

~ **gravel** · Baukies *m*

~ **ground** · Baugelände *n*, Bauland *n*

~ **in freezing weather**, winter construction · Winterbau *m*

'**Construction in Space**' [*Immense structure by Naum Gabo, located in Rotterdam*] · „Konstruktion *f* im Raum"

construction insulant → building insulation(-grade) material

~ **insulating material** → building insulation(-grade) ~

~ **insulation(-grade) material** → building ~ ~

~ **insulator** → building insulation(-grade) material

~ **iron**, structural ~ · Baueisen *n*

~ **joint** · Arbeits(beton)fuge *f*

~ **lead** · Baublei *n*, Konstruktionsblei

~ **lime**, structural ~, trowel trades ~, building ~ [*B.S. 890*] · Baukalk *m* [*DIN 1060*]

~ **load** · Last *f* aus Bauzuständen, Baulast

~ **lumber** (US); wood in building sizes, sawn engineered timber, sawed engineered timber, cut engineered timber · Schnittholz *n* für Ingenieurholzbau, Bauschnittholz

construction management ... — construction(al) ... 244

~ **management in building (construction)** · Betriebsführung f im Hochbau

~ **metal plate** → ~ plate metal

~ ~ **sheet** → ~ sheet metal

~ **method** · Bauweise f, Bauverfahren n

~ **mortar**, building ~ · Baumörtel m

~ **nail** · Baunagel m

~ **nickel** · Baunickel m

~ **noise** · Baulärm m

~ **of barracks**, building ~ ~, barracks building, barracks construction · Kasernenbau m

~ ~ **stair(case)s**, stair(case) construction · Treppenbau m

~ ~ **windows** · Fensterbau m

~ ~ **worker's dwellings**, ~ ~ ~ dwelling units, ~ ~ working-class dwellings, ~ ~ working-class dwelling units · Arbeiterwohn(ungs)bau m

~ ~ **working-class dwellings** → ~ ~ ~ worker's dwellings

~ **office** · Baubüro n

~ **operations** · Baubetrieb m

~ **phase** · Baustadium n, Bauphase f, Ausführungsstadium, Ausführungsphase

~ **plastic**, building ~, plastic building material, plastic construction material · Bau-Kunststoff m

~ ~ **film**, ~ ~ sheeting, building ~ ~ · Baukunststoffolie f

~ ~ **for external use**, building ~ ~ ~ ~, ~ ~ ~ outdoor ~, ~ ~ ~ exterior ~, ~ ~ ~ outer ~ · Außenbaukunststoff m

~ ~ ~ **internal use**, building ~ ~ ~ ~, ~ ~ ~ inside ~, ~ ~ ~ ~ interior ~, ~ ~ ~ indoor ~ · Innenbaukunststoff m

~ ~ **sheeting**, ~ ~ film, building ~ ~ · Baukunststoffolie f

~ **plate metal**, ~ metal plate · Bau(grob)blech n, Konstruktions(grob)blech

~ **price** · Baupreis m

~ ~ **index** · Baupreisindex m

~ **quicklime**, building ~, quicklime for structural purposes, quicklime for building purposes · Baubranntkalk m, Baubrennkalk

~ **regulation**, ~ control · Bauvorschrift f, Baubestimmung f

(~) **roundwood** → timber in the round (for construction purposes)

~ **sand**, building ~ [B.S. 1198–1200] · Bausand m

~ **sheet metal**, ~ metal sheet · Bau(fein)blech n, Konstruktions(fein)blech

~ **spec(ification)s**, con spec · Baudaten f

~ **speed** · Bautempo n

~ **standardization** · Baunormung f

Construction Standards Committee · Fachkommission f Baunormung

construction supervising authority, ~ supervision ~ · Bauaufsichtsbehörde f, Bauaufsichtsorgan n, Baupolizei f

~ **supervision**, ~ control · Bauüberwachung f, Bauaufsicht f, Bauführung

~ **system** → constructional ~

~ **type**, type of construction · Bauart f [Die Art, in der Baustoffe und Bauteile für sich allein oder gemeinsam zu Bauwerken zusammengefügt werden; nicht zu verwechseln mit Bauweise]

~ **waterbar** → ~ waterstop

~ **waterstop**, ~ waterbar, stop-end ~ · Arbeits(beton)fugenband n, Betonbeitsfugenband, Betonier(ungs)fugenband

~ **with concrete slabs used as formwork**, ~ ~ ~ ~ ~ ~ forms, ~ ~ ~ ~ ~ shuttering · Betonschalplattenbauweise f

~ ~ **logs** · Blockbau m [Besonders in Skandinavien, Rußland und den Alpenländern verbreitete Art des Holzbaus, bei der die Wände aus waagerecht aufeinander geschichteten Balken (Blockhölzern) oder Stämmen (Rundhölzern) gebildet und die dabei entstehenden Fugen meist mit Moos, Lehm und dergl. abgedichtet sind. An den Ecken sind die Querschnitte der Blockhölzer um die Hälfte in der Höhe versetzt und stehen über. Meist ruht die unterste Lage auf hölzernen oder steinernen Stützen oder auf einer Untermauerung, die vielfach Erdgeschoßhöhe erreichen kann]

~ **work** · Baumaßnahmen fpl

~ **zone** · Aufbaugebiet n

constructional activities · Baugeschehen n

construction(al) aluminium (Brit.); ~ aluminum (US); structural ~ · Baualu(minium) n

constructional detail, constructive ~ · Konstruktionselement n, Konstruktionseinzelheit f, bauliche Einzelheit

construction(al) drawing · Bauzeichnung f

~ ~ · Bauzeichnen n

constructional engineer [A fabricator or contractor working on steel frames] · Stahlbauer m

~ **fitter and erector**, steel erector · Stahlbaumonteur m

~ **form** · Bauform f

construction(al) grade steel → construction(al) ~

~ **material**, building ~, structural ~ · Baustoff m; Baumaterial n [Schweiz]

~ ~ **dealer**, building ~ ~, structural ~ ~ · Baustoffeinzelhändler m

~ ~ **distributor**, building ~ ~, structural ~ ~ · Baustoffgroßhändler m

~ ~ **engineer**, building ~ ~, structural ~ ~ · Baustoffingenieur m

~ ~ **failure**, building ~ ~, structural ~ ~ · Baustoffschaden m

~ ~ **machine** → building ~ ~
~ ~ **manufacturer** → building material producer
~ ~ **producer** → building ~ ~
~ ~ **production** → building ~ ~
~ ~ **standards**, building ~ ~, structural ~ ~ · Baustoff(prüf)normen *fpl*
~ ~ **delivery**, building ~ ~, structural ~ ~ · Baustoffanfuhr *f*
~ ~ **deposit**, building ~ ~, structural ~ ~ · Baustoffvorkommen *n*
~ ~ **industry**, building ~ ~, structural ~ ~ · Baustoffindustrie *f*
~ ~ **market** → building ~ ~
~ ~ **practice** → building ~ ~
~ ~ **processing** → building ~ ~
~ ~ **quality control**, building ~ ~ ~, structural ~ ~ ~ · Baustoff(güte)überwachung *f*
~ ~ **requirement**, building ~ ~, structural ~ ~ · Baustoffbedarf *m*
~ ~ **saving** → building ~ ~
~ ~ **scale** → building ~ ~
~ ~ **show** → building ~ ~
~ ~ **storage**, building ~ ~, structural ~ ~ · Baustoffbevorratung *f*, Baustoffeinlagerung
~ ~ **store**, building ~ ~, structural ~ ~ · Baustofflager *n*
~ ~ **test** → building ~ ~
~ ~ **testing device**, building ~ ~ ~, structural ~ ~ ~ · Baustoffprüfgerät *n*
~ ~ ~ **institute**, building ~ ~ ~, structural ~ ~ ~ · Baustoffprüf(ungs)anstalt *f*
~ ~ ~ **machine**, structural ~ ~ ~, building ~ ~ ~ ~ · Baustoffprüfmaschine *f*
~ **member** · Bauglied *n*
~ **metal**, building ~ · Baumetall *n*
~ **plastic profile** → (~) ~ shape
(~) ~ **section** → (~) ~ shape
(~) ~ **shape**, (~) ~ section, (~) ~ profile, (~) ~ trim, (~) ~ unit, structural ~ ~ · Kunststoff(bau)profil *n*
(~) ~ **trim** → (~) ~ shape
(~) ~ **unit** → (~) ~ shape
~ **principle** · konstruktiver Grundsatz *m*
~ **profile** → ~ shape
~ **rubber profile** → ~ ~ shape
~ ~ **section** → ~ ~ shape
~ ~ **shape**, ~ ~ section, ~ ~ profile, ~ ~ trim, ~ ~ unit, structural ~ ~ · Gummi(-Bau)profil *n*
~ ~ **trim** → ~ ~ shape
~ ~ **unit** → ~ ~ shape
~ **sand**, building ~ · Bausand *m*
~ ~ **from natural sources**, building ~ ~ ~ ~, natural building sand, natural construction(al) sand [*B.S. 1198–1200*] · Natur-Bausand *m*
~ **section** → ~ shape

~ **shape**, ~ profile, ~ section, ~ trim, ~ unit, (structural) ~ · Bauprofil *n*, (Konstruktions)Profil
~ **standard (specification)** · Baunorm *f*
~ **steel**, structural ~, ~ grade ~ [*B.S. 15*] · Baustahl *m*, Konstruktionsstahl [*DIN 17100*]
~ ~ **profile** → (structural) steel section
~ ~ **section** → (structural) ~ ~
~ ~ **shape** → (structural) steel section
~ ~ **trim** → (structural) steel section
~ ~ **unit** → (structural) steel section
~ **system**, (structural) ~, construction · Bausystem *n*, Konstruktion *f*, (Konstruktions)System *n* [*Abgegrenzte Anordnung von montierten Bauteilen, die nach bestimmten Regeln untereinander in Wechselwirkung stehen*]
~ **timber** → structural ~
~ ~ **grade** → structural ~ ~
~ **tin**, structural ~ · Bauzinn *n*
~ **trim** → ~ shape
~ **unit** → ~ shape
~ **zinc**, structural ~ · Bauzink *n*
constructive art · gestaltende Kunst *f*
~ **detail**, constructional ~ · Konstruktionselement *n*, Konstruktionseinzelheit *f*, bauliche Einzelheit
Constructivism [*Principally a Russian movement, covering hanging and relief constructions, abstract in conception, and made of a variety of materials*] · Konstruktivismus *m*
Constructivist movement · konstruktivistische Bewegung *f*
consult room · Sprechzimmer *n* [*Arztpraxis*]
consultant · Berater *m*
consultation, consulting · Beratung *f*
consulting, consultation · Beratung *f*
~ **centre** (Brit.); ~ center (US); consultation ~ · Beratungsstelle *f*
consumption point, demand ~, point of consumption, point of demand · Abnehmer *m*, Verbrauchsstelle *f* [*Wasser; Strom; Gas; Dampf; Druckluft*]
contact adhesive, ~ cement(ing agent), ~ bonding agent, ~ bonding medium · Kontaktkleb(e)stoff *m*, Kontaktkleb(e)mittel *n*, Kontaktkleber *m*
~ **angle**, angle of contact · Berührungswinkel *m*
~ **area** · Berührungsfläche *f*, Kontaktfläche
~ **bonding agent** → ~ adhesive
~ ~ **medium** → ~ adhesive
~ **cement(ing agent)** → ~ adhesive
~ **form area** · eingeschalte Fläche *f*, Schalfläche
'**contact noise**', impact sound, structure-borne sound · Körperschall *m* [*Schall, der sich in festen Stoffen fortpflanzt (Erschütterungen sind Körperschall)*]

contact paste — continuous in one direction

contact paste · Kontaktpaste f
~ polyester → unsaturated polyester (resin)
~ solution · Kontaktlösung f
contact(ing) area, ~ surface · Berührungsfläche f, Kontaktfläche
~ surface, ~ area · Berührungsfläche f, Kontaktfläche
container · Innenbehälter m [*Heißwasserspeicher*]
~ for refuse → waste container
~ ~ rubbish (US) → refuse container
~ ~ waste(s) → waste container
containing asbestos fibre (Brit.); ~ ~ fiber (US) · asbestfaserhaltig
~ (asphaltic-)bitumen, (asphaltic-)bitumen based (Brit.); asphalt based, asphaltic (US) · asphalthaltig
~ bitumen, ~ asphaltic-~, (asphaltic-)bitumen based (Brit.); asphalt based, asphaltig (US) · asphalthaltig
~ too little lime · kalkarm
~ ~ ~ superfine sand, ~ ~ ~ ultrafine ~ · feinstsandarm
containment · Reaktorschale f
contemporary · Zeitgenosse m
~ · zeitgenössisch
~ architecture · zeitgenössische Architektur f, ~ Baukunst f
content, percentage, fraction · Gehalt m, Prozentsatz m, Anteil m
~ → enclosed space
~ expressed in percentage · prozentmäßiger Anteil m, ~ Gehalt
~ of voids → porosity
contingency sum, ~ allowance · Summe f für Unvorhergesehenes, ~ ~ unvorhergesehene Arbeiten
continuity · Kontinuität f, Stetigkeit f
~ → effect of ~
~ bar → ~ rod
~ bars → ~ reinforcement
~ condition · Kontinuitätsbedingung f, Stetigkeitsbedingung
~ equation · Kontinuitätsgleichung f, Stetigkeitsgleichung
~ of space · Raumkontinuität f, Raumstetigkeit f
~ reinforcement → continuous ~
~ rod, ~ bar · durchlaufender Armierungsstab m, ~ (Bewehrungs)Stab, durchgehender ~, durchlaufendes Eisen n, durchgehendes Eisen, Durchlaufeisen
~ rods → ~ reinforcement
~ stirrup · Durchlaufbügel m
~ stress · Durchlaufspannung f
continuous · durchgehend, durchlaufend
~ apron walls (US); ~ spandrel ~, ~ (under-)window spandrels, ~ spandrels, ~ breasts, ~ aprons · (Fenster-)Brüstungsband n

~ aprons, ~ breasts, ~ spandrels, ~ spandrel walls, ~ (under-)window spandrels; ~ apron walls (US) · (Fenster-)Brüstungsband n
~ arch · Durchlaufbogen m, Mehrfeldbogen
~ arch(ed girder) · Durchlauf-Bogen(träger) m, durchlaufender Bogen(träger), durchgehender Bogen(träger), kontinuierlicher Bogen(träger)
~ bar reinforcement → ~ rod ~
~ ~ reinforcing → ~ rod reinforcement
~ bars, ~ rods · nichtabgestufte Bewehrung f, ~ Armierung, ~ (Stahl)Einlagen fpl
~ beam [*Continuous beams are beams on more than two supports, in which the successive spans are rigidly connected to one another over the supports*] · Durchlaufbalken(träger) m, durchlaufender Balken(träger), durchgehender Balken(träger)
~ box girder · Durchlauf-Hohlkastenträger m, durchlaufender Hohlkastenträger, durchgehender Hohlkastenträger
~ breasts, ~ spandrels, ~ (under-)window spandrels, ~ spandrel walls, ~ aprons; ~ apron walls (US) · (Fenster)Brüstungsband n
~ ceiling → ~ suspended ~
~ columns, ~ supports · ungestoßene Stützen fpl
~ cylindrical shell · Zylinderdurchlaufschale f, Durchlaufzylinderschale
~ effect → (effect of) continuity
~ extract ventilation unit → streamline ventilator
~ extraction unit → streamline ventilator
~ extractor → streamline ventilator
~ (filament) yarn · Glasseidengarn n
~ floor · Durchlaufdecke f, durchlaufende Decke, durchgehende Decke
~ footing, strip ~, strap ~ · Bankett n, Fundamentstreifen m, Streifenfundament n
~ foundation, strip ~ · Gründungsstreifen m, Streifengründung f
~ frame · durchgehender Rahmen m, durchlaufender ~, Durchlaufrahmen
~ girder · durchgehender Träger m, durchlaufender ~, Durchlaufträger
~ glass surface · durchgehende verglaste Fläche f, durchlaufende ~ ~
~ grading · stetige Kornabstufung f, kontinuierliche ~, Kornzusammensetzung ohne Ausfallkörnung
~ handrail · Durchlaufhandleiste f
~ heating, permanent ~ · Dauerheizung f
~ hinge · Stangenscharnier n
~ in both directions · in beiden Richtungen durchlaufend
~ ~ one direction · in einer Richtung durchlaufend

continuous (lavatory basin) range — continuum mechanics

~ **(lavatory basin) range** [*The basins have overlaps to form a continuous range, as opposed to basins 50 mm or more apart*] · durchgehende Waschreihe *f*

~ **light**, window band, ribbon window · Bandfenster *n*, Langfenster, Fensterband *n*

~ **line of forces** · stetiger Kräftezug *m*

~ **ornament** → band ornament(al feature)

~ **pilot**, pilot light [*A small gas flame which on some gas water heaters is left always burning so as to ignite the main gas burners immediately the tap is opened*] · Sparflamme *f*

~ **plate** → ~ slab

~ **prestressed beam** → ~ ~ concrete ~

~ ~ **(concrete) beam**, prestressed (concrete) continuous ~ · durchlaufender Spannbetonbalken(träger) *m*, Durchlauf-Spannbetonbalken(träger), Spannbeton-Durchlaufbalken(träger)

~ ~ **(~) frame**, prestressed (concrete) continuous ~ · durchlaufender Spannbetonrahmen *m*, Durchlauf-Spannbetonrahmen, Spannbeton-Durchlaufrahmen

~ ~ **(~) girder** · durchlaufender Spannbetonträger *m*, Spannbeton-Durchlaufträger, Durchlauf-Spannbetonträger

~ ~ **frame** → ~ ~ concrete ~

~ ~ **girder** → ~ ~ concrete ~

~ **purlin(e)** · Durchlaufpfette *f*, durchlaufende Pfette, durchgehende Pfette

~ **range** → ~ lavatory basin ~

~ **R. C. beam** → ~ reinforced concrete ~

~ **R. C. girder** → ~ reinforced concrete ~

~ **reinforced concrete beam**, ~ R. C. ~ · Durchlauf-Stahlbetonbalken(träger) *m*, Stahlbeton-Durchlaufbalken(träger), durchlaufender Stahlbetonbalken(träger), durchgehender Stahlbetonbalken(träger)

~ ~ ~ **girder**, ~ R. C. ~ · Durchlauf-Stahlbetonträger *m*, Stahlbeton-Durchlaufträger, durchlaufender Stahlbetonträger, durchgehender Stahlbetonträger

~ **reinforcement**, continuity ~ · durchlaufende Bewehrung *f*, ~ Armierung, ~ (Stahl)Einlagen *fpl*, durchgehende ~, kontinuierliche ~, Durchlaufbewehrung, Durchlaufarmierung, Durchlaufstahleinlagen

~ **rod reinforcement**, ~ bar ~, ~ ~ reinforcing · Durchlaufstab(stahl)einlagen *fpl*, Durchlaufstabbewehrung *f*, Durchlaufstabarmierung

~ ~ **reinforcing** → ~ ~ reinforcement

~ **rods**, ~ bars · nichtabgestufte Bewehrung *f*, ~ Armierung, ~ (Stahl-)Einlagen *fpl*

~ **roll (type) filter**, roller curtain (~) ~ · Rollbandfilter *m, n* [*Lüftungszentrale*]

~ **roof-light** · (Dach)Oberlichtstreifen *m*

~ **row (light(ing)) fixtures** → stripline (~) ~

~ **sense of direction** · stetiger Umfahrungssinn *m* [*Baustatik*]

~ **shell** · Durchlaufschale *f*, durchlaufende Schale, durchgehende Schale

~ **slab**, ~ plate · durchgehende Platte *f*, durchlaufhende ~, Durchlaufplatte, Mehrfeldplatte

~ **spandrel walls**, ~ (under-)window spandrels, ~ spandrels, ~ breasts, ~ aprons; ~ apron walls (US) · (Fenster)Brüstungsband *n*

~ **spandrels**, ~ (under-)window ~, ~ spandrel walls, ~ breasts, ~ aprons; ~ apron walls (US) · (Fenster)Brüstungsband *n*

~ **stave-pipe** → machine-banded pipe

~ **strand** → strand

~ **stress** · nichtperiodische Spannung *f*

continuous-stringer (US); continuous-string (Brit.) · Durchlauf(treppen)-wange *f*

(continuous) strip windows · Bandfenster *n*, Fensterband *n* [*Eine Reihe nebeneinanderliegender Fenster*]

~ **supports**, ~ columns · ungestoßene Stützen *fpl*

~ **(suspended) ceiling** · Durchlaufhängedecke *f*, durchlaufende Hängedecke, durchgehende Hängedecke

~ **suspension system** · Durchlauf-(Ab-)Hängekonstruktion *f*, durchlaufende (Ab)Hängekonstruktion, durchgehende (Ab)Hängekonstruktion

~ **traffic wear** · Dauerverkehrsverschleiß *m*, Dauerverschleiß durch Verkehr

~ **truss(ed girder)** · Durchlauf-Fachwerk(träger) *n, (m)*, durchlaufender Fachwerkträger, durchlaufendes Fachwerk, durchgehender Fachwerkträger, durchgehendes Fachwerk

~ **two-way slab** · mehrfeld(e)rige kreuzweise bewehrte Platte *f*, ~ ~ armierte ~

~ **(under-)window spandrels**, ~ spandrels, ~ spandrel walls, ~ breasts, ~ aprons; ~ apron walls (US) · (Fenster)Brüstungsband *n*

~ **ventilator** → streamline ~

~ **wear** · Dauerverschleiß *m*

~ **window spandrels** → ~ under-~ ~

~ **yarn**, ~ filament ~ · Glasseidengarn *n*

continuously moving hearth, sinter ~ · Sinterband *n*

continuum · Kontinuum *n* [*Die idealisierte (fiktive) Vorstellung von einem materiellen Körper (Baustoff), der in Gestalt unendlich vieler, kleiner Massenelemente, zusammenhängend (kontinuierlich) über das Körpervolumen verteilt, angenommen wird. Das Kontinuum ist das Gegenteil des starren Körpers*]

~ **mechanics**, mechanics of continua · Kontinuumsmechanik *f*

contract control — convector/radiant heating appliance

contract control · Baubetriebssteuerung f

~ **drawing** · Vertragszeichnung f

~ **letting**, order ~, letting of the contract, letting of the order · Auftragerteilung f, Vergabe f

~ **manager**, (contractor's) agent [*The contractor's representative on site*] · (Firmen)Bauleiter m

~ **particulars** [*Drawings, specification and form of contract, also the quantities where they form part of the contract*] · Vertragsunterlagen fpl

contractor · Unternehmer m

(contractor's) agent, contract manager [*The contractor's representative on site*] · (Firmen)Bauleiter m

~ **site office** · (Firmen)Bauleitung f, Unternehmer-Bauleitung

~ **supervisor** · Bauführer m [*Er leitet die Bauarbeiten unternehmerseitig*]

contributary population, population served · angeschlossene Bevölkerung f

to control [*set(ting)*] · regeln [*Abbinden*]

control · Bekämpfung f

~ → quality audit

~ **building** · Schaltgebäude n, Schalthaus n [*Kraftwerk*]

~ **cement** · Vergleichszement m

~ **chart**, quality ~ ~ · Güteüberwachungstabelle f

~ **room** · Schaltwarte f

~ ~ **block**, ~ ~ building · Wartengebäude n

~ ~ **building**, ~ ~ block · Wartengebäude n

~ **specimen** · Vergleichsprobekörper m

~ **valve manifold** · Regelventilverteiler m, Steuerventilverteiler

controlled thermal severity test · CTS-Prüfung f, CTS-Probe f, CTS-Versuch m [*Zur Erforschung der Rißbildung unter der Schweißnaht*]

controlling agent · Bekämpfungsmittel n

~ **dimension** [*The controlling dimensions are a dimensional framework within which buildings are designed and to which buildings, assemblies and components are related*] · Baurichtmaß n [*DIN 4172*]

~ **wood protection** · bekämpfender Holzschutz m

conurbation (Brit.); urbanized area (US) · verstädterte Zone f

convalescent centre (Brit.); ~ center (US); ~ home · Sanatorium m, Genesungsheim n

~ ~ **for children** (Brit.); ~ center ~ ~ (US); ~ home ~ ~ · Kindergenesungsheim n, Kindersanatorium n

~ **home**; ~ centre (Brit.); ~ center (US) · Sanatorium n, Genesungsheim n

~ ~ **for children**; ~ centre ~ ~ (Brit.); ~ center ~ ~ (US) · Kindergenesungsheim n, Kindersanatorium n

convected air, convective ~, convection ~ · Konvektionsluft f

~ **heat**, convective ~, convection ~ · Konvektionswärme f

~ ~ **loss**, convective ~ ~, convection ~ ~ · Konvektionswärmeverlust m

~ ~ **transfer** → convective ~ ~

convection air, convective ~, convected ~ · Konvektionsluft f

~ **current** · Konvektionsstrom m

~ **heat**, convective ~, convected ~ · Konvektionswärme f

~ ~ **loss**, convective ~ ~, convected ~ ~ · Konvektionswärmeverlust m

~ ~ **transfer** → convective ~ ~

~ **heating**, convective ~, indirect ~ Konvektionsheizung f

~ **(~) surface** · Nachschaltheizfläche f [*Kessel*]

~ ~ **system**, convective ~ ~ · konvektives Heiz(ungs)system n [*Dampf-, Warmwasser- und Warmluftheizung*]

~ **(of heat)** → convective heat transfer

~ **oven stoving** [*A stoving treatment in which heat is transferred to the paint surface largely, although not entirely, by convection*] · Konvektionstrocknung f

convective air, convection ~, convected ~ · Konvektionsluft f

~ **heat**, convection ~, convected ~ · Konvektionswärme f

~ ~ **loss**, convection ~ ~, convected ~ ~ · Konvektionswärmeverlust m

~ ~ **transfer**, convection ~ ~, convected ~ ~, convection (of heat) [*Transfer of heat in or by a liquid or a gas by the movement of the medium*] · Konvektion f, Wärmemitführung f

~ **heating**, convection ~, indirect ~ · Konvektionsheizung f

~ ~ **system**, convection ~ ~ · konvektives Heiz(ungs)system n [*Dampf-, Warmwasser- und Warmluftheizung*]

convector fire, ~ (heater), heating convector, convector radiator · Konvektionsheiz(ungs)gerät n, Konvektionsheizer m, Konvektionserhitzer, Konvektor m [*Direktheizgerät*]

~ **(heater)**, ~ fire, heating convector, convector radiator · Konvektionsheiz(ungs)gerät n, Konvektionsheizer m, Konvektionserhitzer, Konvektor m [*Direktheizgerät*]

~ **panel** · Konvektorplatte f

convector/radiant heater, ~ heating appliance, ~ heating unit · kombinierter Direktheizer m, Direkterhitzer, kombiniertes Direktheiz(ungs)gerät n

~ **heating appliance**, ~ ~ unit, ~ heater · kombinierter Direktheizer m, ~ Direkterhitzer, kombiniertes Direktheiz(ungs)gerät n

convector/radiant heating unit — cooling-off curve

~ ~ unit, ~ ~ appliance, ~ heater · kombinierter Direktheizer m, ~ Direkterhitzer, kombiniertes Direktheiz(ungs)gerät n

convector radiator, ~ (heater), ~ fire, heating convector · Konvektionsheiz(ungs)gerät n, Konvektionsheizer m, Konvektionserhitzer, Konvektor m [*Direktheizgerät*]

convent, religious house [*A religious house of monks is called a 'monastery', and one of nuns a 'nunnery', and both monasteries and nunneries may have the title of 'abbey' or 'priory'. The distinction here is one of status, an abbey being presided over by an abbot in the case of monks, or an abbes in the case of nuns, whilst a priory has no resident abbot or abbess, is presided over by a prior or prioress, and is usually an offshoot from, and dependent upon an abbey*] · Kloster n

~ **limb** · Konventflügel m

~ **parlour,** parlatory · Parlatorium n, Sprechsaal m

conventional church, conventual ~, monastic ~ · Klosterkirche f, Konventualkirche

~ **construction method,** classic ~ ~, orthodox ~ ~ · herkömmliche Bauweise f

~ **(external-)balcony-access type of block** → block with external access galleries of the conventional type

(~) **mortar-bed method,** thick-bed ~ · Dickbettverfahren n [*Ansetzen von Fliesen*]

~ **paint** · Unifarbe f [*Im Gegensatz zur Metalleffektfarbe*]

(~) **running (masonry) bond,** stretching (~) ~, stretcher (~) ~, chimney (~) ~ [*The vertical joints are centered on the stretchers above and below*] · Läuferverband m, Schornsteinverband, mittiger (Mauerwerk)Verband, mittiger Mauerverband, mittiges (Mauerwerk-)Gefüge n, mittiges Mauergefüge, Längsverband [*DIN 18151. Die Stoßfugen sind um ½ Steinlänge gegeneinander versetzt*]

conventional(ized) → divorced from reality

conventual building, monastic ~ · Klostergebäude n

~ **church,** monastic ~, conventional ~ · Klosterkirche f, Konventualkirche

~ **community,** monastic ~ · Wohngemeinschaft f eines Klosters

~ **kitchen,** monastic ~ · Klosterküche f

conversion, alteration, structural ~ · bauliche Veränderung f, Bauveränderung, Umbau m

~ · langsame Umwandlung f [*Langsame und nicht unmittelbar reversible Kristallumwandlung durch Temperaturänderung*]

~ **burner** · kombinierter (Gas-Öl-)Brenner m [*Er gestattet ein Umschalten vom einen auf den anderen Brennstoff*]

~ **gas(-fired) burner** · kombinierter Gasbrenner m

~ **oil(-fired) burner** · kombinierter Ölbrenner m

~ **work,** alteration ~, structural ~ ~ · Umbauarbeiten fpl

converted timber → sawn wood

converting (with air) purifying (~ ~), air blowing, air refining · Windfrischen n [*Stahlerzeugung*]

convex moulding → round(ed) ~

~ **part** · konvexes Element n, Stab m [*Karnies*]

~ **tile,** over-tile; mission tile (US) · Deckziegel m, Mönch(ziegel) m, Preiße m

cooked mix(ture) · Verkochung f [*Öllack*]

cooker cock · Kocherhahn m

(~) **hood,** range ~ · Dunstabzug(-haube) m, (f), Dunsthaube [*über einem Küchenherd*]

cooking, heating · (Ver)Kochen n

~ **place** · Kochstelle f

~ **temperature** · Kochtemperatur f [*Mastix*]

cool air, cold ~ · Kaltluft f

~ ~ **blower,** cold ~ ~ · Kaltluftgebläse n

~ ~ **curtain door,** cold ~ ~ ~ · Kaltlufttür f

~ ~ **damper,** cold ~ ~ · Kaltluftschieber m

~ ~ **duct,** cold ~ ~ · Kaltluftkanal m

to cool down · abkühlen

coolant, cooling medium · Kühlmittel n

~ **inlet,** CI · Kühlmitteleinlaß m

~ **outlet,** CO · Kühlmittelauslaß m

cooling · Kühlung f

~ **air** · Kühlluft f

~ **bath** · Kühlbad n

~ **coil** · Kühlschlange f

~ **-down period,** taking-down ~, standing-off ~ · Abstehen n, Kaltschüren [*Glasschmelze*]

~ **effect** · Kühlwirkung f

~ **fan,** CF · Kühlventilator m

~ **grid** · Kühlregister n

~ **jacket,** CJ · Kühlmantel m

~ **load** · (trockene) Kühllast f [*Die abzuführende fühlbare Wärmemenge, um in zu kühlenden Räumen die gewünschte Lufttemperatur aufrecht zu erhalten. Die (trockene) Kühllast ist gleich der Wärmeabgabe aller Wärmequellen, die diese Temperatur zu erhöhen trachten*]

~ **looper** · Kühlhänge f [*Dachpappenanlage*]

~ **medium,** coolant · Kühlmittel n

~ **off** · Abkühlen n, Auskühlen

cooling-off · Abkühlung f

~ **curve** · Abkühl(ungs)kurve f

cooling-off period — coping

~ **period** · Abkühl(ungs)dauer f, Abkühl(ungs)frist f, Abkühl(ungs)zeit f
~ **rate** · Abkühl(ungs)geschwindigkeit f
~ **surface** · Abkühl(ungs)fläche f
cooling panel · Kühltafel f
~ **pipe** · Kühlrohr n
~ **pond**, spray ~ · Kühlbecken n, Kühlteich m
~ **shaft** · Kühlschacht m [*Abkühlen von Trink- und Brauchwasser*]
~ **tonnage** · Kühltonnage f
~ **tower** · Kühlturm m, Kühlwerk n
(~ ~) **chimney** · Zuflußsteigschacht m, (Kühlturm)Steigschacht
~ ~ **saucer** · Kühlturmtasse f
~ **water** · Kühlwasser n
~ ~ **circuit**, ~ ~ cycle · Kühlwasserkreislauf m
~ ~ **circulation** · Kühlwasserumlauf m
~ ~ **cycle**, ~ ~ circuit · Kühlwasserkreislauf m
~ ~ **inlet duct** · Kühlwassereinlaufkanal m
~ ~ **installation**, ~ ~ plant · Kühlwasseranlage f
~ ~ **intake (structure)** · Kühlwassereinlauf(bauwerk) m, (n)
~ ~ **outfall**, ~ ~ outlet · Kühlwasserauslaß m
~ ~ **outlet**, ~ ~ outfall · Kühlwasserauslaß m
~ ~ **plant**, ~ ~ installation · Kühlwasseranlage f
~ ~ **pump(ing) plant**, ~ ~ ~ station · Kühlwasserpumpenhaus n
~ ~ ~ **station**, ~ ~ ~ plant · Kühlwasserpumpenhaus n
~ ~ **return pump(ing) plant**, ~ ~ ~ ~ station · Kühlwasserrücklaufpumpwerk n
~ ~ ~ ~ **station**, ~ ~ ~ ~ plant · Kühlwasserrücklaufpumpwerk n
cooperative apartment house · Genossenschaftshaus n
~ **building society**, benefit ~ ~, ~ housing ~ · Baugenossenschaft f
~ **housing society** → ~ building ~
coordinate axis · Koordinatenachse f
~ **origin** · Koordinatenursprung m
~ **paper**, quadrille ~ · Koordinatenpapier n
~ **system (of axes)** · Achsenkreuz n, Achsensystem n, Koordinatensystem, Koordinatenkreuz
coordination → dimensional ~
cop, merlon · Zinne f, Mauerzacke f, Windberg m, Zinnenzahn m [*Zur Deckung der Verteidiger schildartige Erhöhung der Brustwehr am Wehrgang und an der Wehrplatte eines Turmes*]
copaiba balsam, copaiva ~, copaivic ~ · Kopaivabalsam m

copal · Kopal m
~ **adhesive** → ~ (resin) bonding agent
~ **(bonding) adhesive** → ~ (resin) bonding agent
~ ~ **agent** → ~ resin ~ ~
~ ~ **medium** → ~ (resin) bonding agent
~ **(bulk) compound** → ~ (resin) seal(ing) ~
~ **caulking (compound)** → ~ (resin) seal(ing) ~
~ **cement(ing) agent)** → ~ (resin) bonding ~
~ **compound** → ~ (resin) seal(ing) ~
~ **ester** · Kopalester m
~ **mastic** → ~ (resin) seal(ing) compound
~ **(oil type) varnish** · Kopallack m
~ **(resin)** · Kopal(harz) m, (n) [*Sammelbenennung für die in tropischen Böden liegenden Naturharze, die erhärtete Ausflüsse von ausgestorbenen oder noch existierenden Baumarten darstellen*]
~ **(~) adhesive** → ~ (~) bonding agent
~ **(~) (bonding) adhesive** → ~ (~) ~ agent
~ **(~) ~ agent**, ~ (~) ~ medium, ~ (~) (~) adhesive, ~ (~) cement(ing agent) · Kopal(harz)kleber m, Kopal(harz)kleb(e)mittel n, Kopal(harz)kleb(e)stoff m
~ **(~) ~ medium** → ~ (~) ~ agent
~ **(~) (bulk) compound** → ~ ~ seal(-ing)
~ **(~) caulking (compound)** → ~ (~) seal(ing) ~
~ **(~) cement(ing) agent)** → ~ (~) bonding ~
~ **(~) compound** → ~ (~) seal(ing) ~
~ **(~) mastic** → ~ (~) seal(ing) compound
~ **(~) seal(ing) compound**, ~ (~) (bulk) ~, ~ (~) caulking (~), ~ (~) mastic · Kopal(harz)kitt m
~ **seal(ing) compound** → ~ resin ~ ~
~ **stopper** · Kopalspachtel(masse) m, (f) [*Anstrichtechnik*]
~ **varnish**, ~ oil type ~ · Kopallack m
cope → coping
~ **block** → (concrete) coping ~
~ **stone** → coping ~
~ **tile** → (concrete) coping block
coping [*Splitting stones by drilling them and driving in steel wedges along a line*] · Steinespalten n
~, **hood** · Mauerhut m, Schweifkappe f, Mauerkappe, Abdachung f [*Die schräge oder konvexe Abdeckung einer Mauer*]

coping — copper one-pipe

~, capping, cope · Abdeckung f, Abwässerung [*Freistehende Bauteile wie Einfried(ig)ungsmauern, Pfeiler usw. müssen mit einer wetterfesten, wasserundurchlässigen Schicht abgedeckt werden, um das Eindringen von Wasser in das Innere des Mauerwerks zu verhindern*]

~ block → concrete ~ ~

~ brick, capping ~ · (Ab)Deckziegel m

~ slab → concrete ~ ~

~ ~, capping ~ · (Ab)Deckplatte f [*DIN 455*]

~ stone, cope ~, capping ~ [*A top stone, generally slightly projecting, to shelter the masonry from the weather, or distribute the pressure from exterior loading. A projecting covering stone of a wall*] · (Natur)(Ab)Deckstein m

~ tile → (concrete) coping block

copolymer · Mischpolymerisat n, MP

~ emulsion paint · Mischpolymerisat-Emulsionsfarbe f

to copper, to coat with copper, to copper plate · verkupfern

copper alloy · Kupferlegierung f

~ ~ trap [*B.S. 1184*] · (Wasser)(Geruch)Verschluß m aus Kupferlegierung

~ anchor, ~ tie · Kupferanker m

~ angle (section) · Kupferwinkel m

~ bend, ~ pipe ~ · Kupfer(rohr)krümmer m

~ billet · Kupferbarren m

~ bit, coppering ~, soldering iron · Lötkolben m

~ block · Kupferstück n [*Lötkolben*]

~ box (roof) gutter, ~ ~ rainwater ~, ~ ~ R.W. ~ · Kupfer-Kasten(dach)rinne f

~ bronze, ~ flakes · Kupferbronze f

copper-bronze paint · Kupferbronzefarbe f

copper casting · Kupferguß m

~ chloride (Brit.); ~ chlorid(e) (US) · Kupferchlorid n

~ cistern · Kupferzisterne f

~ -clad pitched roof · Kupfergiebeldach n

copper cleat, soldered ~ ~ · Kupfer(löt)hafter m [*Metallbedachung*]

~ -coated paper [*See remark under 'Pappe'*] · kupferbeschichtete Pappe f

copper compound · Kupferverbindung f

~ core · Kupferkern m

~ coupling, ~ pipe ~ · Kupfer(rohr)kupp(e)lung f

~ cramp · Kupferkrampe f, Kupferkramme

~ cross → ~ pipe ~

~ dampproof(ing) course, ~ dampcourse, ~ DPC, ~ d.p.c., ~ dpc · Kupfersperrschicht f [*gegen Feuchtigkeit*]

~ discharge pipe, ~ drain(age) ~, ~ draining ~, ~ waste (~) · Kupferabflußrohr n, Kupferablaufrohr, Kupferentwässerungsrohr, Kupferdränrohr [*Fehlnamen: Kupferablauf m, Kupferabfluß*]

~ dish test · Kupferschalenprüfung f, Kupferschalenprobe f, Kupferschalenversuch m

~ dowel · Kupferdübel m

~ DPC → ~ dampproof(ing) course

~ drain(age) pipe → ~ discharge ~

~ draining pipe → ~ discharge ~

~ elbow, ~ pipe ~ · Kupfer(rohr)bogen m

copper-engraving · Kupferstich m

~ · Kupferstechen n

copper facing → ~ lining

~ filter pipe · Kupferbrunnenrohr n, Kupferfilterrohr

~ fin · Kupferlamelle f

~ fin(ned) pipe · Kupferlamellenrohr n

~ fitting [*Bends, couplings, crosses, elbows, unions, etc.*] · Kupferfitting m, Kupferformstück n, Kupferverbindungsstück

~ flakes, ~ bronze · Kupferbronze f

~ flashing (piece) [*See remark under 'Anschluß'*] · Kupfer(blech)anschluß(-streifen) m

~ fluosilicate · Kupferfluat n

~ foil · Kupferfolie f

~ ~ insert(ion) · Kupferfolieneinlage

~ glazing → copper(light) ~

~ gutter → ~ roof ~

~ hydroxid(e) (US); ~ hydroxide (Brit.) · Kupferhydroxid n

~ ingot · Kupferblock m

copper-lined cistern · kupferverkleidete Zisterne f

copper lining, ~ (sur)facing · Kupferauskleidung f, Kupferverkleidung, Kupferbekleidung

copper-manganese alloy · Manganbronze f

copper nail · Kupfernagel m

copper-nailed · kupfergenagelt

copper-nailing · Kupfer(ver)nagelung f

copper(-)nickel (alloy) · Kupfernickel n, Kupfer-Nickel-Legierung f

copper one-pipe · Kupfereinrohr n [*Zentralheizung*]

copper one-pipe ring system — coppered

~ ~ **ring system** · Kupfer-Ring-Einrohrsystem *n*, waag(e)rechte Kupfereinrohrheizung *f*
~ **panel** · Kupfertafel *f*
~ **pipe** · Kupferrohr *n*
~ (~) **bend** · Kupfer(rohr)krümmer *m*
~ (~) **coupling** · Kupfer(rohr)kupp(e)lung *f*
~ (~) **cross** · Kupfer(rohr)kreuz(stück) *n*
~ (~) **elbow** · Kupfer(rohr)bogen *m*
~ ~ **for central heating (systems)** · Kupferrohr *n* für Zentralheiz(ungs)anlagen
~ ~ ~ **cold water lines** · Kupferrohr *n* für Kaltwasserleitungen
~ ~ ~ **gas lines** · Kupferrohr *n* für Gasleitungen
~ ~ ~ **hot water lines** · Kupferrohr *n* für Warmwasserleitung
~ ~ ~ **radiant heating (systems)** · Kupferrohr *n* für Strahlungsheizung
~ ~ ~ **radiator heating** · Kupferrohr *n* für Radiatorenheizung
~ ~ ~ **sewage disposal** · Kupferrohr *n* für Abwasserleitungen
~ ~ ~ **water lines** · Kupferrohr *n* für Wasserleitungen
~ ~ **union** · Kupferrohrverbinder *m*
to copper plate, to coat with copper, to copper · verkupfern
copper plating · Kupferüberzug *m*
~ ~, **coppering** · Kupferplattierung *f*, Verkupferung
~ ~ **liquid**, coppering ~ · Verkupferungsflüssigkeit *f*
~ **profile** → ~ shape
~ **rainwater articles**, ~ ~ products, ~ ~ goods · Kupfer-Dachzubehör(-teile) *n*, (*mpl, npl*)
~ ~ **goods**, ~ ~ articles, ~ ~ products · Kupfer-Dachzubehör(teile) *n*, (*mpl, npl*)
~ ~ **gutter** → ~ (roof) ~
~ ~ **products**, ~ ~ articles, ~ ~ goods · Kupfer-Dachzubehör(teile) *n*, (*mpl, npl*)
copper-rich alloy · kupferreiche Legierung *f*
copper rivet · Kupferniet *m*
~ **roof cladding** → ~ roofing
~ ~ **cover(ing)** → ~ roofing
~ (~) **gutter**, ~ rainwater ~, ~ R.W. ~ · Kupfer(dach)rinne *f*, Kupferregenrinne
~ ~ **sheathing** → ~ roofing
~ **roofing**, ~ roof cover(ing), ~ roof cladding, ~ roof sheathing · Kupfer(dach)(ein)deckung *f*, Kupferbedachung
~ ~ **practice** · Kupfer(dach)(ein)deckungstechnik *f*
~ **R.W. gutter** → ~ (roof) ~
~ **salt** · Kupfersalz *n*

~ **sealing strip**, ~ water stop · Kupfer(ab)dicht(ungs)streifen *m*
~ **section** → ~ shape
~ **shape**, ~ section, ~ unit, ~ trim, ~ profile · Kupferprofil *n*
~ **sheathed cable** [*B.S. 3207*] · Kupfer(mantel)kabel *n*
~ **sheet**, sheet copper [*B.S. 1569*] · Kupfer(fein)blech *n*
~ **shingle** · Kupferschindel *f*
~ **shot**, Cu ~ · Kupferschrot *m, n*
~ **slab** · Kupferplatte *f*
~ **slag**, cast ~ · Kupferschlacke *f*
~ ~ **block**, cast ~ ~, ~ ~ tile [*See remark under 'Block'*] · Kupferschlakkenblock(stein) *m*, Kupferschlackenstein
~ ~ **sett**, cast ~ ~ · Kupferschlacken(pflaster)stein *m*
~ ~ **tile** → ~ ~ block
~ **soap** · Kupferseife *f*
~ **solid section**, ~ ~ unit, ~ ~ shape, ~ ~ trim, ~ ~ profile · Kupfervollprofil *n*
~ **solubility** · Kupferlöslichkeit *f*
~ **stain** · Kupferfleck *m*
~ **strip** [*B.S. 1569*] · Kupferstreifen *m*
~ ~, strip copper · Kupferband *n*
~ ~ · Kupfersteg *m* [*Elektroglas*]
~ ~ **corrosion** · Kupferstreifenkorrosion *f*
~ **sulfate** (US); ~ **sulphate** (Brit.) · Kupfersulfat *n*
~ **(sur)facing** → ~ lining
~ **tack** · Kupferhafter *m*
~ **tie**, ~ anchor · Kupferanker *m*
~ **tile** · Kupferdach(ein)(deckungs)element *n*, Kupferbedachungselement
~ **-tin alloy** · Kupfer-Zinn-Legierung *f*
~ **trap** · Kupfer-(Wasser)(Geruch)Verschluß *m* [*Fehlnamen: Kupfersiphon m, Kupfersyphon, Kupfertraps m*]
~ **trim** → ~ shape
~ **tube ceiling radiant heating panel** · Decken(strahlungs)heizplatte *f* aus Kupferrohr
~ ~ **for general purposes** [*B.S. 2017*] · Kupferröhre *f* für allgemeine Zwecke
~ **unit** → ~ shape
~ **valley gutter** · Kupferkehlrinne *f*
~ **washer** · Kupfer(unterleg)scheibe *f*
~ **waste (pipe)** → ~ discharge ~
~ **water stop**, ~ sealing strip · Kupfer(ab)dicht(ungs)streifen *m*
~ **wedge** · Kupferkeil *m*
~ **wire** · Kupferdraht *m*
~ **wrought alloy**, wrought copper ~ · Kupfer-Knetlegierung *f* [*DIN 17666*]
copperas, melanterite, green vitriol · Melanterit *m*
coppered · verkupfert

coppered wire — corebord door

~ wire · verkupferter Draht *m* [*Stahldraht, der vor dem letzten Zug in ungesäuerter Kupfersulfatlösung verkupfert wird*]

coppering, copper plating · Verkupferung *f*, Kupferplattierung

~ liquid, copper plating **~** · Verkupferungsflüssigkeit *f*

copper(light) glazing, electro-copper **~**, fire-retarding **~**; electro-copper glass method (Brit.); copper(lite) glass method (US) · Elektroglas *n* [*Elektroglas ist keine Glassorte, sondern der Name bezeichnet das Verfahren kleine Glasscheiben beliebiger Glasart und bis zu 100 cm² Fläche zu feuerhemmenden Scheiben zusammenzufassen*]

Coptic architecture · koptische Architektur *f*, **~** Baukunst *f*

~ church · koptische Kirche *f*

~ monastery · koptisches Kloster *n*

copy machine, photo**~ ~** · (Photo-)Kopiergerät *n*

copying of natural forms · Nachahmung *f* von Naturformen

coquina → shell(y) limestone

coral (concrete) aggregate · Korallen(beton)zuschlag(stoff) *m*, Korallen(beton)zuschlagmaterial *n*

~ sand · Korallensand *m*

corbel, console, (natural) stone corbel, (natural) stone shoulder, (natural) stone bracket [*A small supporting piece of stone, often formed of scrolls or volutes, to carry a projecting weight*] · Kragstein *m*, Konsole *f*, steinerner Konsolträger *m*, Tragstein, (Natur)Steinkonsole, Kraftstein, Notstein, Balkenstein

~ → bracket

~ → masonry **~**

~ arch(ed girder) → cantilever(ed) **~** (**~**)

~ brick, false **~**, cantilever(ed) **~**, cantilevering **~** · auskragender Ziegel *m*, vorkragender **~**, Auslegerziegel, Kragziegel

~ course [*A course of bricks or stones projecting from a wall as a continuous corbel, to carry a superincumbent weight*] · Kragsteinschicht *f*

~ cupola → **~** dome

~ curved girder → cantilever(ed) arch(ed **~**)

~ dome, ~ cupola, false **~** · Kragkuppel *f*

~ masonry (work), cantilever(ed) **~** (**~**), cantilevering **~** (**~**), false **~** (**~**) · vorkragendes Mauerwerk *n*, auskragendes **~**, Auslegermauerwerk, Kragmauerwerk

~ piece, bolster, saddle, head tree, crown plate [*A short timber cap over a post to increase the bearing area under a beam*] · Sattelholz *n*

corbel table [*A projecting course of stones or bricks, resting upon a series of corbels*] · Mauervorsprung *m* auf Kragsteinen

corbel-table frieze → arched **~ ~**

corbel vault, false **~** · Kraggewölbe *n*

corbelling [*Setting successive courses outward in a brick wall*] · Vorkragung *f*, Auskragung [*Mauerwerk*]

corbie gable, crow **~**, step **~**; corbel **~** [*misnomer*] · Stufengiebel *m*, Staffelgiebel, Treppengiebel, abgetreppter Giebel

corbie(step), crowstep, catstep; corbelstep [*misnomer*] [*One of a series of steps forming the roofs of certain gable(d) houses*] · Giebelstufe *f*

corbie(-step)s · Katzensteige *f*, Katzentreppe *f*, Giebelstufen *fpl*

cord · Schnur *f*

~, heavy **~** · Rampe [*Glasschmelzfehler*]

~ cloth, ~ woven fabric; **~** fabric [*misnomer*] · Kordgewebe *n*

~ content · Kordgehalt *m*

~ control · Schnurzug *m* [*Jalousie*]

~ covering · Schnur *f* [*für Dämm- und Isolierzwecke*]

~ fabric [*misnomer*]; **~** woven fabric, **~** cloth · Kordgewebe *n*

~ grip [*It is screwed on top of a lampholder*] · Schnurklemme *f*

~ operated · schnurzugbedient [*Jalousie*]

~ seal(ing) · Kordel(ab)dichtung *f* [*Sprosse für kittlose Verglasung*]

~ strength · Kordfestigkeit *f*

~ woven fabric, ~ cloth; **~** fabric [*misnomer*] · Kordgewebe *n*

cordierite · Cordierit *m* [*Synthetisches oder natürliches Magnesium-Aluminium-Silikat. Es gibt mangan- oder eisenhaltigen Cordierit. In Erweiterung dient dieser Ausdruck auch zur Bezeichnung des Gesteins (Rohstoffs)*]

cordon → string (course)

corduroy cloth, ~ woven fabric; **~** fabric [*misnomer*] · Tressengewebe *n*

~ fabric [*misnomer*]; **~** woven fabric, **~** cloth · Tressengewebe *n*

~ woven fabric, ~ cloth; **~** fabric [*misnomer*] · Tressengewebe *n*

core (US); cell, cavity, core hole · Loch *n*, Kammer *f*, Hohlraum *m* [*Ziegel; Block(stein)*]

~, unburned lime, unburnt lime · Fehlbrand *m*, Kalkkern *m*, (Kalk)Krebs *m*

~ · Einlage *f*, Kern *m*, Seele *f* [*Drahtseil*]

~ · Kern(schicht) *m*, (f)

~ area · Hohlräume *mpl* [*Blockstein*]

corebord (Brit.); CLV board · Tischlerplatte *f* [*DIN 68705*]

~ door (Brit.); CLV board **~** (US) · Tischlerplattentür *f*

corebord for building purposes — cork block board

~ for building purposes, ~ ~ construction ~ (Brit.); CLV board ~ ~ ~, cross-banded lumber veneered board ~ ~ ~ (US) · Bau-Konstruktionsplatte f, Bau-Mittellagenplatte, Bau-Sperrplatte mit Einlage, Bau-Tischlerplatte, Bau-Paneelplatte

core concrete, backing ~, hearting ~ · (Hinter)Füll(ungs)beton m, Kernbeton, Unterbeton [*Im Gegensatz zum Vorsatzbeton*]

~ foundation · kernförmige Gründung f

~ hole, cell, cavity; core (US) · Loch n, Kammer f, Hohlraum m [*Ziegel; Block(-stein)*]

~ material · Kernwerkstoff m, Kernmaterial n

~ of gypsum, gypsum core · Gipskern m

~ pipe, pipe core · Kernrohr n, Rohrkern m [*Teil eines Betonrohres*]

~ strength, kern ~ · Kernfestigkeit f [*umschnürte Betonstütze*]

~ wall · Kernwand f

~ zone · Kernzone f [*Spannbeton*]

cored, coffered · kassettiert

~ block → ~ tile

~ ~ masonry (work), ~ tile ~ (~) [*See remark under 'Block'*] · Lochblock(stein)mauerwerk n, Lochsteinmauerwerk

~ brick, perforated ~ · Lochziegel m [*DIN 105*]

~ ~ masonry (work) → perforated ~ ~ (~)

~ calcium silicate brick ~ sand-lime ~, ~ lime-sand ~ · Kalksandlochstein m, Lochkalksandstein, KSL [*DIN 106*]

~ ~ ~ slab, ~ sand-lime ~ ~, ~ lime-sand ~ ~ · Kalksandlochplatte f, Lochkalksandplatte

~ ceiling, rectangular grid ~, waffle ~, caisson ~, pan(el) ~, cassette ~, coffer(ed) ~ · Kassettendecke f, kassettierte Decke

~ expanded cinder concrete block (US) → ~ foamed slag ~ ~

~ floor → waffle (slab) ~

~ (~) slab, pan(el) (~) ~, waffle (~) ~, cassette (~) ~, caisson (~) ~, coffer(ed) (~) ~, (~) plate, rectangular grid (~) ~ · Kassetten(decken)-platte f, kassettierte (Decken)Platte

~ foamed slag concrete block, ~ ~ ~ ~ brick (Brit.); ~ expanded cinder ~ ~ (US) · Lochhüttenbimsstein m, Lochhüttenbimsblock(stein) m [*Fehlname: Lochschwemmblock(stein)*]

~ lime-sand brick, ~ sand-lime ~, ~ calcium silicate ~ · Kalksandlochstein m, Lochkalksandstein, KSL [*DIN 106*]

~ ~ slab, ~ sand-lime ~, ~ calcium silicate ~ · Kalksandlochplatte f, Lochkalksandplatte

cored-out floor unit · Kassetten-Deckenkörper m, Kassetten-Deckenelement n

cored panel · Kerntafel f

~ ~ ~ → rectangular grid (floor) slab

~ (~) floor → waffle (slab) ~

~ paper, perforated ~ [*See remark under 'Pappe'*] · durchlochte Pappe f, gelochte ~, Lochpappe

~ pattern → waffle ~

~ plate → rectangular grid (floor) slab

~ (~) floor → waffle (slab) ~

~ sand-lime brick, ~ lime-sand ~, ~ calcium silicate ~ · Kalksandlochstein m, Lochkalksandstein, KSL [*DIN 106*]

~ ~ slab, ~ lime-sand ~, ~ calcium silicate ~ · Kalksandlochplatte f, Lochkalksandplatte

~ slab → rectangular grid (floor) ~

~ (~) floor → waffle (~) ~

~ soffit → cassette ~

~ tile, ~ block [*See remark under 'Block'*] · Lochblock(stein) m, Lochstein

~ ~ · Loch(belag)platte f, Lochfliese f

~ ~ masonry (work) → ~ block ~ (~)

~ wall panel · Kernwandtafel f

coring · Lochung f [*Ziegel; Block(stein)*]

~, coffering · Kassettierung f

~ · Kernherstellung f [*Bauplatte; Bautafel*]

~ row, row of coring · Lochreihe f [*Mauerziegel*]

Corinthian(esque) base → ~ column ~

~ capital · korinthisches Kapitell n, ~ Kapitäl

~ column · korinthische Säule f

~ (~) base · korinthischer (Säulen)Fuß m

~ order (of architecture) · korinthische (Säulen)Ordnung f

~ peripteral octastyle temple with fifteen columns on the flanks · korinthischer Peripterostempel m von 8:15 Säulen

~ ~ temple · korinthischer Peripteraltempel m

~ portico · korinthischer Portikus m

Coriolis component · Corioliskraft f [*ablenkende Kraft der Erddrehung*]

cork · Kork m

~ article, ~ product · Korkartikel m, Korkgegenstand m, Korkerzeugnis n

~ backing, ~ underlay, ~ base · Korkhinterlegung f, Korkunterlage f, Korkrücklage, Korkträger(schicht) m, (f)

~ base, backing, ~ underlay · Korkhinterlegung f, Korkunterlage f, Korkrücklage, Korkträger(schicht) m, (f)

~ based · korkhaltig

~ block · Korkstein m

~ ~ board, ~ ~ slab, ~ ~ sheet · Korksteinplatte f

cork (block) for cold insulation — cork tar

~ (~) for cold insulation, ~ (~) ~ ~ lagging · Kältekork(stein) m, Kälteschutzkork(stein)

~ (~) ~ ~ lagging, ~ (~) ~ ~ insulation · Kältekork(stein) m, Kälteschutzkork(stein)

~ (~) ~ heat insulation, ~ (~) ~ ~ lagging · Korkstein m für den Wärmeschutz, Wärme(schutz)kork(stein) m

~ (~) ~ ~ lagging, ~ (~) ~ ~ insulation · Korkstein m für den Wärmeschutz, Wärme(schutz)kork(stein) m

~ (~) ~ sound insulation · Schallschutz-Kork(stein) m

~ ~ sheet, ~ ~ board, ~ ~ slab · Korksteinplatte f

~ ~ slab, ~ ~ sheet, ~ ~ board · Korksteinplatte f

~ (~) wall · Kork(stein)wand f

corkboard, cork slab · Korkplatte f

~ for ceilings, cork slab ~ ~ · Decken-Korkplatte f, Korkdeckenplatte

~ ~ cold lagging, ~ ~ ~ insulation, cork slab ~ ~ ~ · hartpechgebundene Platte f, Kältekorkplatte [*Der geblähte Korkschrot wird mit Hartpech gebunden. Die Platten sind wasser- und fäulnisfest sowie geruchlos*]

~ ~ heat insulation, ~ ~ ~ ~ lagging, cork slab ~ ~ ~ · tongebundene Korkplatte f, Wärmekorkplatte [*Der geblähte Korkschrot wird mit Tonmilch oder Tonpech gebunden*]

~ ~ ~ lagging, ~ ~ ~ ~ insulation, cork slab ~ ~ ~ · tongebundene Korkplatte f, Wärmekorkplatte [*Der geblähte Korkschrot wird mit Tonmilch oder Tonpech gebunden*]

~ ~ roof(ing)s, cork slab ~ ~ · Dach-Korkplatte f, Korkdachplatte

~ ~ walls. cork slab ~ ~ · Korkwandplatte f, Wandkorkplatte

cork carpet [*B.S. 810*] · Korklinoleum n [*DIN 18172*]

~ cell · Korkzelle f

~ cover(ing) · Korkbelag m [*Preßkorkplatten aus Korkschrot mit Kunstharzbindemitteln werden vorwiegend als Wärme- und schalldämmende Korkment-Unterlagen für Linoleum- und PVC-Beläge gebraucht. Korkparkett mit hellen und dunklen 4 bis 10 mm dicken Fliesen ist wenig strapazierfähig*]

~ covering cord · Korkschnur f [*für Dämm- und Isolierzwecke*]

~ filler, ~ joint ~ · Kork(fugen)einlage f

~ fill(ing) · Korkschüttung f [*unter Fußböden*]

~ floor cover(ing), ~ ~ finish, ~ floor(ing) · Kork(fuß)boden(belag) m

~ ~ ~ tile → ~ floor(ing) (finish) ~

~ ~ finish, ~ ~ cover(ing), ~ floor(-ing) · Kork(fuß)boden(belag) m

~ floor(ing), ~ floor finish, ~ floor cover(ing) · Kork(fuß)boden(belag) m

~ ~ (finish) tile, ~ floor cover(ing) ~ · (Fuß)Bodenkorkfliese f, (Fuß)Bodenkorkplatte f, Kork(-Fuß)bodenplatte, Kork(-Fuß)bodenfliese

~ flour, ~ powder, ground cork, powder(ed) cork · Korkmehl n

~ for cold insulation, ~ block ~ ~ ~, ~ (block) for cold lagging · Kältekork(stein) m, Kälteschutzkork(stein)

~ ~ ~ lagging, ~ block ~ ~ ~, ~ (block) for cold insulation · Kältekork(-stein) m, Kälteschutzkork(stein)

~ ~ heat insulation, ~ ~ ~ ~ lagging, ~ block ~ ~ ~ · Korkstein m für den Wärmeschutz, Wärme(schutz)kork(-stein) m

~ ~ ~ lagging, ~ ~ ~ ~ insulation, ~ block ~ ~ ~ · Korkstein m für den Wärmeschutz, Wärme(schutz)kork(stein) m

~ ~ sound insulation → ~ block ~ ~ ~

~ granules · grobes Korkmehl n

~ insulation, ~ lagging · Korkdämmung f

~ (joint) filler · Kork(fugen)einlage f

cork-lagged · korkgedämmt

cork lagging, ~ insulation · Korkdämmung f

~ (paving) sett · Korkpflasterstein m

~ pipe section, preformed cork (pipe insulating) ~ · Korkschale f

~ powder, ~ flour, ground cork, powder(ed) cork · Korkmehl n

~ product, ~ article · Korkartikel m, Korkgegenstand m, Korkerzeugnis n

corkscrew rule · Korkenzieherregel f

cork sett, ~ paving ~ · Korkpflasterstein m

~ sheet(ing) · Korkbahn f

~ slab, corkboard · Korkplatte f

~ ~ for ceilings, corkboard ~ ~ · Decken-Korkplatte f, Korkdeckenplatte

~ ~ ~ cold insulation → corkboard for cold lagging

~ ~ ~ ~ lagging → corkboard ~ ~ ~

~ ~ ~ heat insulation, ~ ~ ~ ~ ~ lagging, cork board ~ ~ ~ · tongebundene Korkplatte f, Wärmekorkplatte [*Der geblähte Korkschrot wird mit Tonmilch oder Tonpech gebunden*]

~ ~ ~ ~ lagging, ~ ~ ~ ~ ~ insulation, cork board ~ ~ ~ · tongebundene Korkplatte f, Wärmekorkplatte [*Der geblähte Korkschrot wird mit Tonmilch oder Tonpech gebunden*]

~ ~ ~ roof(ing)s, corkboard ~ ~ · Dach-Korkplatte f, Korkdachplatte

~ ~ ~ walls, corkboard ~ ~ · Korkwandplatte f, Wand-Korkplatte

~ (stair) tread · Korktritt(stufe) m, (f)

~ subfloor · Korkunterboden m

~ tar · Korkteer m

cork tile — corps de logis

~ tile [*Cork tiles are made from pure cork shavings compressed in mo(u)lds to a thickness of about ½ in., and baked. Cork tiles are used for wall coverings as well as for flooring*] · Kork(belag)platte *f*, Korkfliese *f*

~ tread, ~ stair ~ · Korktritt(stufe) *m*, (*f*)

~ underlay, ~ base, ~ backing · Korkhinterlegung *f*, Korkunterlage *f*, Korkrücklage, Korkträger(schicht) *m*, (*f*)

~ wall, ~ block ~ · Kork(stein)wand *f*

~ ~ tile · Kork-Wand(belag)platte *f*, Kork-Wandfliese *f*, Wand-Kork(belag)platte, Wand-Korkfliese

~ wool [*Very thin cork ribbons used principally in packaging and to fill mattresses*] · Korkwolle *f*

~ worked by agglomeration → agglomerated cork

corn starch · Maisstärke *f*

corner · Ecke *f*

~ angle · Eckwinkel *m*, Saumwinkel

~ apartment (unit) ~ flat; ~ living unit (US) · Eck-Etagenwohnung *f*, Eck-Stockwerkwohnung, Eck(-Geschoß)wohnung

~ balcony · Eckbalkon *m*

~ (bath)tub, ~ bath · Eck(bade)wanne *f*

~ bead, ~ guard; ~ moulding (Brit.); ~ molding (US); angle bead · Eck(schutz)leiste *f*, Kantenschützer *m*

~ bench · Eckbank *f*

~ block, ~ building · Eckgebäude *n*

~ bond · Eckverband *m* [*Mauerwerk*]

~ bonder → quoin header

~ bondstone → quoin header

~ brace · Ecksteife *f* [*Holzrahmen*]

~ bracing · Eckversteifung *f* [*Holzrahmen*]

~ brick → (angle-)quoin

~ building, ~ block · Eckgebäude *n*

~ buttress · Eckstützpfeiler *m*

~ chapel · Eckkapelle *f*

~ column, angle ~ · Eckstütze *f*

~ ~, angle ~ · Ecksäule *f* [*Eine in einer Mauer- oder Wandecke angeordnete Säule*]

~ fibre (Brit.); ~ fiber (US) · Eckfaser *f*

~ fireplace, angle ~ · Eckkamin *m*

~ flat, ~ apartment (unit); ~ living unit (US) · Eck-Etagenwohnung *f*, Eck-Stockwerkwohnung, Eck(-Geschoß)wohnung

~ force · Eckkraft *f*

~ garden edging · Beetwinkel *m*

~ guard → ~ bead

~ header → quoin ~

~ hinge · Eckgelenk *n*

~ house · Eckhaus *n*

~ illumination, ~ lighting · Eckbeleuchtung *f*

~ lighting, ~ illumination · Eckbeleuchtung *f*

~ living unit (US); ~ apartment (~), ~ flat · Eck-Etagenwohnung *f*, Eck-Stockwerkwohnung, Eck(-Geschoß)wohnung

~ oriel · Auslugerker *m*, Eckerker

~ ornament → acroter(ion)

~ panel · Ecktafel *f*

~ piece · Eckstück *n*

~ pin · Winkelstift *m*

~ plate, connecting ~, connection ~, binding ~, joint ~, fish ~, gusset ~, knee bracket ~ · Knoten(punkt)verbindung *f*

~ post, ~ vertical, principal ~, angle ~ · Eckpfosten *m*, Eckständer *m*, Eckstiel *m*, Ecksäule *f* [*Fachwerkbau*]

~ rib · Eckrippe *f*

~ shower stall · Eckduschstand *m*

~ stone → (angle-)quoin

corner-supported rectangular slab · eckgestützte Rechteckplatte *f*

corner tower · Eckturm *m*

~ tub, ~ bath~, ~ bath · Eck(bade)wanne *f*

~ turret, angle ~ · Ecktürmchen *n*

~ vertical, ~ post, principal ~, angle ~, main ~ · Eckpfosten *m*, Eckständer *m*, Eckstiel *m*, Ecksäule *f* [*Fachwerkbau*]

~ window · Eckfenster *n*

cornice [*Any mo(u)lded projection which crowns or finishes the part to which it is fixed, e.g. a wall, door or window*] · (Ge)Sims *m*, (*n*)

~ [*Any projecting ornamental mo(u)lding along the top of a building, wall, arch, etc., finishing or crowning it. Also loosely called 'mo(u)lding'*] · (Haupt-)Gesims *n*, Dachgesims, Kranzgesims Hauptsims *m*, Dachsims, Kranzsims

~ · (Gebälk)Kranz *m*, Kornies *n*, Karnies [*Der dritte Oberteil des Haupt(ge)simses, oder der oberste Teil dessen gleich über dem Fries, welcher mit seiner Breite die ganze Ordnung bedeckt*]

~ boarding · (Ge)Sims(ver)schalung *f*

~ stone · (Ge)Simsstein *m*

coro alto, raised choir, upper choir, raised quire, upper quire · Oberchor *m*, Hochchor

corona · Hängeplatte *f* [*Teil eines Geison*]

coronation cathedral · Krönungskathedrale *f*

~ chamber · Krönungskammer *f*

~ church · Krönungskirche *f*

corps de logis · Wohnhaus *n* der Herrschaft [*Bei Schlössern des 17. und 18. Jahrhunderts, z.B. in Ludwigsburg oder Bruchsal*]

corpse gate, lych ~, lich ~ · überdachtes Friedhofstor *n*
Corpus Christi chapel, chapel of Corpus Christi · (Fron)Leichnamskapelle *f*
~ ~ **church**, church of Corpus Christi · (Fron)Leichnamskirche *f*
correct → correctly sized
correction coefficient · Berichtigungsbeiwert *m*
~ **of the (ground(-))plan** · Grundrißkorrektur *f*
correct(ly sized), of standard particle size distribution, exactly conform to the nominal size · korngerecht
correct(ly sized) product · Normalkorn *n* [*In die richtige Kornklasse gelangter Kornanteil*]
corridor [*A comparatively narrow enclosed thoroughfare within a building*] · Flur *m*, Gang *m*, Korridor *m*
~ **duct** · Flurkanal *m*, Gangkanal, Korridorkanal
~ **floor;** ~ story (US); ~ storey (Brit.) Korridoretage *f*, Korridorstockwerk *n*, Korridorgeschoß *n*
~ ~ · Korridor(geschoß)decke *f*, Korridoretagendecke, Korridorstockwerkdecke
~ **illumination,** ~ lighting · Flurbeleuchtung *f*, Gangbeleuchtung, Korridorbeleuchtung
~ **lighting,** ~ illumination · Flurbeleuchtung *f*, Gangbeleuchtung, Korridorbeleuchtung
~ **locker** · Gangspind *m*
~ **storey** (Brit.); ~ story (US); ~ floor · Korridoretage *f*, Korridorgeschoß *n*, Korridorstockwerk *n*
~ **wall** · Korridorwand *f*, Flurwand
to corrode · anfressen, korrodieren, angreifen
corrosion · Anfressen *n*, Anfressung *f*, Angriff *m*, Angreifen, Korrosion *f*
~ **control** · Korrosionsbekämpfung *f*
~ **fatigue** · Korrosionsermüdung *f*
~ **inhibiting** · korrosionshemmend
(~) ~ **pigment** · korrosionshemmendes Pigment *n*
~ **inhibitor** · Korrosionshemmstoff *m*
~ **loss** · Korrosionsverlust *m*
~ **mechanism** · Korrosionsmechanismus *m*
~ **prevention,** anti-corrosion · Korrosionsverhütung *f*
corrosion-promoting · korrosionsfördernd
corrosion-proof → corrosion-resistant
corrosion protection · Korrosionsschutz *m*
~ ~ **(agent),** ~ protective ~, anticorrosion ~, anticorrosive ~ · Korrosionsschutzmittel *n*, Korrosionsschutzstoff *m*
~ ~ **coat(ing),** anti-corrosion ~, anticorrosive ~ · Korrosionsschutzanstrich *m*, Korrosionsschutzaufstrich, Korrosionsschutzschicht *f*, Korrosionsschutzüberzug *m*
~ ~ **composition** → anti-corrosive paint
~ ~ **foil,** anti-corrosive ~, anti-corrosion ~ · Korrosionsschutzfolie *f*
~ ~ **grout** → anti-corrosive slurry
~ ~ **mortar,** anti-corrosion ~, anti-corrosive ~ · Korrosionsschutzmörtel *m*
~ ~ **paint** → anti-corrosive ~
~ ~ **pigment,** anti-corrosive ~, anticorrosion ~ · Korrosionsschutzpigment *n*
~ ~ **prime coat** → anti-corrosive ~ ~
~ ~ **primer** → anti-corrosive ~
~ ~ **slurry** → anti-corrosive ~
~ **protective (agent),** corrosion protection ~, anticorrosion ~, anticorrosive ~ · Korrosionsschutzmittel *n*, Korrosionsschutzstoff *m*
~ **rate** · Korrosionsgeschwindigkeit *f*
~ **resistance,** stainlessness · Korrosionsbeständigkeit *f*, Korrosionswiderstand *m*, Korrosionsfestigkeit, KF
corrosion-resistant, corrosion-resisting, corrosion-proof · korrosionsbeständig, korrosionsfest, korrosionssicher
~ **anodic coating,** corrosion-resisting ~ ~ · korrosionsbeständige Schutzschicht *f* [*Aluminiumveredelung*]
corrosion-resisting → corrosion-resistant
~ **anodic coating** → corrosion-resistant ~ ~
corrosion sensitivity · Korrosionsempfindlichkeit *f*
~ **tendency** · Korrosionsneigung *f*
~ **test** · Korrosionsprobe *f*, Korrosionsversuch *m*, Korrosionsprüfung *f*
~ ~ **in boiling liquids** · Kochprobe *f*, Kochprüfung *f*, Kochversuch *m*
~ **under mechanical stress** · Korrosion *f* unter gleichzeitiger Beanspruchung
corrosive · korrodierend, korrosiv
~ **action,** ~ effect · Korrosions(ein)wirkung *f*
~ **agent** · Korrosionsschadstoff *m*
~ **attack chamber** · Korrosionsprüfkammer *f*
~ **effect,** ~ action · Korrosions(ein)wirkung *f*
~ **sublimate;** mercuric chlorid(e) (US); mercuric chloride (Brit.) [*It is a white crystalline solid, sparingly soluble in cold, more easily in hot, water*] · Quecksilberchlorid *n*, Sublimat *n*, Hg Cl₂
corrugated absorbent panel → ~ acoustic(al) ~
~ **absorbing panel** → ~ acoustic(al) ~
~ **acoustic(al) panel,** ~ sound-control ~, ~ (sound) absorbent ~, ~ (sound) absorbing ~ · gewellte Akustiktafel *f*, ~ Schallschlucktafel, Wellakustiktafel, Wellschallschlucktafel

corrugated aluminium — corrugated metal lath(ing) 258

~ **aluminium** (Brit.); ~ aluminum (US) · Wellalu(minium) *n*

~ ~ **roof cover(ing),** ~ ~ sheathing (Brit.); ~ aluminum ~ ~ (US); ~ ~ roof(ing) · Wellalu(minium)dach(belag) *n*, (*m*), Wellalu(minium)(dach)(ein)-deckung *f*

~ **anchor,** ~ tie · Wellanker *m*

~ **arch** · Wellbogen *m*

~ **asbestos** · Wellasbest *m*

~ ~ **board,** ~ ~ sheet, asbestos corrugated ~ · Asbestwellplatte *f*, Wellasbestplatte

~ **asbestos-cement board** → asbestos-cement corrugated sheet

~ ~ **boards** → asbestos-cement corrugated sheeting

~ ~ **panel** → asbestos-cement corrugated ~

~ ~ **roof sheathing** → asbestos-cement corrugated roof cladding

~ ~ **sheet** → asbestos-cement corrugated ~

~ ~ **sheeting** → asbestos-cement corrugated ~

~ ~ **sheets** → asbestos-cement corrugated sheeting

~ ~ **siding;** ~ cement asbestos ~ (US) · (Asbestzement)Well(platten)schirm *m* [*Wetterschutz für Außenwände*]

~ **asbestos panel,** asbestos corrugated ~ · Asbestwelltafel *f*, Wellasbesttafel

~ ~ **roof** · Wellasbestdach *n*, Asbestwelldach

~ ~ **wall** · Wellasbestwand *f*, Asbestwellwand

~ **asphalt board** (US); ~ bituminous ~ (Brit.) · Bitumenwellplatte *f* [*Sie besteht aus Faserstoffen mit bindefähigen Materialien verbunden und mit Bitumen getränkt*]

~ ~ **paper** (US); ~ (asphaltic-)bitumen ~ (Brit.) · Bitumenwellpappe *f*, Wellbitumenpappe

~ **barrel vault,** ~ tunnel ~, ~ wagon(-head) ~ · gewellte Tonne *f*, gewelltes Tonnengewölbe *n*

~ **bituminous board** (Brit.); ~ asphalt ~ (US) · Bitumenwellplatte *f* [*Sie besteht aus Faserstoffen mit bindefähigen Materialien verbunden und mit Bitumen getränkt*]

~ **board,** ~ sheet · Wellplatte *f*

~ **boards,** ~ sheets, ~ sheeting · Wellplatten *fpl*

~ **building paper,** ~ general-use ~ [*See remark under 'Pappe'*] · Bauwellpappe *f*, Well-Baupappe

~ **cement asbestos board** (US) → asbestos-cement corrugated sheet

~ ~ ~ **boards** (US) → asbestos-cement corrugated sheeting

~ ~ ~ **panel** (US) → asbestos-cement corrugated ~

~ ~ ~ **sheet** (US) → asbestos-cement corrugated ~

~ ~ ~ **sheeting** (US) → asbestos-cement corrugated ~

~ ~ ~ **sheets** (US) → asbestos-cement corrugated sheeting

~ ~ ~ **siding** (US); ~ asbestos-cement ~ · (Asbestzement)Well(platten)schirm *m* [*Wetterschutz für Außenwände*]

~ ~ **board roof cladding,** ~ ~ sheet ~ ~, ~ ~ ~ ~ cover(ing), ~ ~ ~ ~ ~ sheathing, ~ ~ ~ ~ roofing · gewellte Zementbedachung *f*, ~ Zement(dach)-(ein)deckung *f*

~ ~ **sheet roof cladding** → ~ ~ ~ board ~ ~

~ **clay roof(ing) tile** · Wellen(dach)ziegel *m*

~ ~ **tile roof sheathing,** ~ ~ ~ ~ cladding, ~ ~ ~ ~ cover(ing), ~ ~ ~ roofing · Wellenziegel(dach)(ein)-deckung *f*, Wellenziegelbedachung

~ **copper sheet** · Kupferwellblech *n*, Wellkupferblech

~ **expansion pipe** · Wellrohrkompensator *m*, Ausgleichswellrohr *n*

~ **fastener,** joint ~, wiggle nail, dog; mitre brad (Brit.); miter brad (US) · Wellennagel *m*, gewellter Nagel

~ **foil** · Wellfolie *f*

~ **general-use paper,** ~ building ~ [*See remark under 'Pappe'*] · Bauwellpappe *f*, Well-Baupappe

~ **glass,** ~ rolled ~ · gewelltes Glas *n*, Wellglas

~ ~ **partition (wall),** ~ rolled ~ ~ (~) · Wellglastrennwand *f*, Glas-Welltrennwand

~ **iron sheet,** ~ steel ~, ~ sheet steel, ~ sheet iron · Stahlwellfeinblech *n*

~ **lath(ing)** · Rillenputzgeflecht *n* [*In das Geflecht sind Rillen eingepreßt, welche auf dem Putzgrund aufliegen, sodaß der Putzträger in der Mitte der Putzschicht liegt*]

~ **light-admitting board,** ~ ~ sheet · Lichtwellplatte *f*

~ ~ ~ **roofing,** ~ ~ sheet ~ · Lichtwellplattendach(belag) *n*, (*m*), Lichtwellplattenbedachung *f*, Lichtwellplatten(dach)(ein)deckung

~ ~ **sheet roofing,** ~ ~ ~ board ~ · Lichtwellplattendach(belag) *n*, (*m*), Lichtwellplattenbedachung *f*, Lichtwellplatten(dach)(ein)deckung

~ **metal** · Wellblech *n* [*DIN 59231*]

~ ~ **arch(ed) (culvert) pipe** · Wellblech-Bogendurchlaßrohr *n*

~ ~ **building sheet** · Bauwellfeinblech *n*

~ ~ **lath(ing),** ~ ~ sheet ~, ~ sheet metal ~ · Wellputzblech *n*, Putzwellblech

corrugated metal pipe — corrugated sheet metal ...

~ ~ **pipe,** CMP · Blech-Wellrohr *n*, Wellblechrohr

~ ~ **plate** · Wellgrobblech *n*

~ ~ **roof cover(ing),** ~ ~ ~ sheathing, ~ ~ ~ cladding, ~ ~ (sheet) roofing, ~ ~ sheet roof cover(ing) · Wellblech(dach)(ein)deckung *f*, Wellblechbedachung

~ ~ **sheath** → ~ sheath(ing)

~ ~ **sheet,** ~ sheet (metal) · Wellfeinblech *n*

~ ~ ~ **curved in two planes,** ~ sheet (metal) ~ ~ ~ ~ · bombiertes Wellfeinblech *n*, gewölbtes ~

~ ~ (~) **lath(ing),** ~ sheet metal ~ · Wellputzblech *n*, Putzwellblech

~ ~ **silo** · Wellblechsilo *m*

~ ~ **structures** · Wellblechbauten *f*

~ **panel** · gewellte Tafel *f*, Welltafel

~ **paper** [See remark under 'Pappe'] · Wellpappe *f*

~ **perspex** (Brit.); ~ plexiglass (US) · Wellplexiglas *n* [Siehe Anmerkung unter „Plexiglas"]

~ **plastic** · Wellkunststoff *m*

~ ~ **board,** ~ ~ sheet, plastic corrugated ~ · gewellte Kunststoffplatte *f*, Kunststoffwellplatte, Well-Kunststoffplatte

~ ~ **film,** ~ ~ sheeting, plastic corrugated ~ · Kunststoffwellfolie *f*

~ ~ **sheet,** ~ ~ board, plastic corrugated ~ · gewellte Kunststoffplatte *f*, Kunststoffwellplatte, Well-Kunststoffplatte

~ ~ **sheeting,** plastic corrugated ~ · Kunststoffwellbahn *f*, Well-Kunststoffbahn, gewellte Kunststoffbahn

~ ~ ~ ~ → ~ ~ ~ film

~ **plexiglass** (US); ~ perspex (Brit.) · Wellplexiglas *n* [Siehe Anmerkung unter „Plexiglas"]

~ **polyester (resin) board,** ~ ~ (~) sheet · Polyester(harz)wellplatte *f*

~ ~ (~) **sheet,** ~ ~ (~) board · Polyester(harz)wellplatte *f*

~ ~ (~) **sheet(ing),** polyester (resin) corrugated ~ · Polyester(harz)-Wellbahn *f*

~ **polyvinyl chloride film,** ~ ~ ~ sheeting, ~ PVC ~ · Polyvinylchlorid-Wellfolie *f*, PVC-Wellfolie

~ ~ ~ **sheeting,** ~ ~ ~ film, ~ PVC ~ · Polyvinylchlorid-Wellfolie *f*, PVC-Wellfolie

~ **profile,** ~ trim, ~ unit, ~ section, ~ shape · Wellprofil *n*

~ **PVC film** ~ ~ sheeting, ~ polyvinyl chloride ~ · Polyvinylchlorid-Wellfolie *f*, PVC-Wellfolie

~ ~ **sheeting** ~ ~ film, ~ polyvinyl chloride ~ · Polyvinylchlorid-Wellfolie *f*, PVC-Wellfolie

~ **rib** · Wellrippe *f*

~ **ridge capping** · Wellfirsthaube *f*

~ **(rolled) glass** · gewelltes Glas *n*, Wellglas

~ (~) ~ **partition (wall)** · Wellglastrennwand *f*, Glas-Welltrennwand

~ (~) **wire(d) glass** CWG · Drahtwellglas *n*, Welldrahtglas

~ (~) ~ ~ **roof cover(ing)** ~ (~) ~ ~ ~ sheathing, ~ (~) ~ ~ roofing · Welldrahtglas(dach)(ein)deckung *f*, Drahtwellglas(dach)(ein)deckung, Welldrahtglasbedachung, Drahtwellglasbedachung

~ **roof cladding,** ~ ~ cover(ing), ~ ~ sheathing, ~ roofing · Wellbedachung *f*, Well(dach)(ein)deckung

~ ~ **cover(ing),** ~ ~ sheathing, ~ ~ cladding, ~ roofing · Wellbedachung *f*, Well(dach)(ein)deckung

~ ~ **insulation** · Welldachisolierung *f*

~ ~ ~ **board** → ~ ~ ~ sheet

~ ~ ~ **material,** ~ ~ insulating ~ · Welldachisoliermaterial *n*

~ ~ ~ **sheet,** ~ ~ ~ board, ~ ~ insulating ~ · Welldachisolierplatte *f*

~ ~ **sheathing,** ~ ~ cladding, ~ ~ cover(ing), ~ roofing · Wellbedachung *f*, Well(dach)(ein)deckung

~ **roofing,** ~ roof cover(ing), ~ roof cladding, ~ roof sheathing · Wellbedachung *f*, Well(dach)(ein)deckung

~ **roof(ing) sheet** · Dachwellpappe *f*, Welldachpappe

~ ~ **sheet(ing)** · Well-Bedachungsbahn *f*, Well-Dachbahn, Well-Dach-(ein)deck(ungs)bahn

~ **rubber strip** · Wellgummistreifen *m*, Gummiwellstreifen

~ **section,** ~ unit, ~ shape, ~ trim, ~ profile · Wellprofil *n*

~ **shape,** ~ unit, ~ trim, ~ section, ~ profile · Wellprofil *n*

~ **sheath(ing),** ~ (sheet-)metal sheath [*prestressed concrete*] · Well(hüll)rohr *n*, Wellröhre *f*, Wellhülle *f*, Well-Gleitkanal *m*, Well-Spannkanal

~ **sheet,** ~ board · Wellplatte *f*

~ ~ **curved in two planes,** ~ ~ metal ~ ~ ~ ~, ~ metal sheet ~ ~ ~ ~ · bombiertes Wellfeinblech *n*, gewölbtes ~

~ ~ **iron,** ~ ~ steel, ~ steel sheet, ~ iron sheet · Stahlwellfeinblech *n*

~ ~ **(metal),** ~ metal sheet · Wellfeinblech *n*

~ ~ (~) **curved in two planes,** ~ metal sheet ~ ~ ~ ~ · bombiertes Wellfeinblech *n*, gewölbtes ~

~ ~ ~ **lath(ing),** ~ metal (sheet) ~ · Wellputzblech *n*, Putzwellblech

corrugated (sheet-)metal sheath — cottage hospital

~ **(sheet-)metal sheath** → ~ sheath(-ing)

~ **sheet roofing,** ~ ~ roof cladding, ~ ~ roof cover(ing), ~ ~ roof sheathing · Wellplattendach(belag) *n*, (*m*), Wellplattenbedachung *f*, Wellplatten(dach)(ein)deckung

~ ~ **steel,** ~ ~ iron, ~ steel sheet, ~ iron sheet · Stahlwellfeinblech *n*

~ ~ **zinc,** ~ zinc sheet · Zinkwellblech *n*, Wellzinkblech

~ **sheet(ing)** · Wellbahn *f*

~ **sheeting,** ~ sheets, ~ boards · Wellplatten *fpl*

~ **sheets,** ~ sheeting, ~ boards · Wellplatten *fpl*

~ **shell** · Well(en)schale *f*

~ ~ **roof,** waved ~ ~ · Well(en)schalendach *n*

~ **(sound) absorbent panel** → ~ acoustic(al) ~

~ **(~) absorbing panel** → ~ acoustic(al) ~

~ **sound-control panel** → ~ acoustic(al) ~

~ **stalk girder,** ~ web ~ · Wellstegträger *m*

~ **steel sheet,** ~ iron ~, ~ sheet steel, ~ sheet iron · Stahlwellfeinblech *n*

~ **tapered sheet,** tapered corrugated ~ · konische Wellplatte *f*

~ **tie,** ~ anchor · Wellanker *m*

~ **trim,** ~ unit, ~ shape, ~ section, ~ profile · Wellprofil *n*

~ **tunnel vault,** ~ barrel ~, ~ wagon(head) ~ · gewellte Tonne *f*, gewelltes Tonnengewölbe *n*

~ **unit,** ~ trim, ~ shape, ~ section, ~ profile · Wellprofil *n*

~ **wagon(head) vault,** ~ tunnel ~, ~ barrel ~ · gewellte Tonne *f*, gewelltes Tonnengewölbe *n*

~ **waterbar,** ~ waterstop · Wellfugenband *n*

~ **waterstop,** ~ waterbar · Wellfugenband *n*

~ **web girder,** ~ stalk ~ · Wellstegträger *m*

~ **wire(d) glass,** ~ rolled ~ ~, CWG · Drahtwellglas *n*, Welldrahtglas

~ **zinc panel** · Zinkwellblechtafel *f*, Wellzinkblechtafel

~ ~ **roof cover(ing),** ~ ~ ~ sheathing, ~ ~ ~ cladding, ~ ~ ~ roofing · Zinkwellblechbedachung *f*, Zinkwellblech(dach)(ein)deckung

~ ~ **sheet,** ~ sheet zinc · Zinkwellblech *n*, Wellzinkblech

corrugation · Welle *f* [*Wellplatte; Welltafel*]

~ · Wellenbildung *f*

corrugation(s) · Wellung(en) *f(pl)*

corundum, α-alumina [*The form of alumina stable at temperatures above about 1,000° C*] · Alpha-Tonerde *f*, Korund *m*, α-Tonerde, Al₂O₃

~ **powder,** powder(ed) corundum · Korundmehl *n*, Korundpulver *n*

~ **refractory brick** · Korundstein *m*

~ ~ **(product)** · Korundartikel *m*, Korunderzeugnis *n*, Korundgegenstand *m*

Coslettized · coslettiert

Coslettizing · Coslettieren *n*

Cosmati · Cos(i)maten *mpl* [*Eine vom 12. bis 14. Jahrhundert in Rom tätige Gruppe von Bau- und Dekorationskünstlern, in deren Inschriften der Name Cosmas häufig vorkommt. Da sie eine besondere Fertigkeit in der Dekoration von Säulen, Fußböden, Wänden usw. mit feiner Einlegearbeit aus buntem Marmor besaßen, wird diese Technik „Cosmatenarbeit" genannt*]

~ **work** · Cos(i)matenarbeit *f* [*Mosaikarbeit aus Marmor, so genannt nach Cosmas, dem bedeutendsten römischen „Marmorarius" um 1100 n.Chr.*]

cost breakdown · Kostenaufschlüsselung *f*, Kostengliederung

~ **comparison** · Kostenvergleich *m*

~ **investigation** · Kostenuntersuchung *f*

~ **limit** · Kostengrenze *f*

~ **per person served** · Kosten *f* je EG [*Wasserversorgung*]

~ **planning** · Kostenplanung *f*

~ **rent** · unkostendeckende Miete *f*

costing, pricing · (Kosten)Kalkulation *f*

~ **department,** pricing ~ · Kalkulationsbüro *n*, Kalkulationsabteilung *f*

(cost(s)) estimate · (Kosten)(Vor)Anschlag *m* [*DIN 276*]

~ **of building (construction) work,** building (construction) cost(s) · Hochbaukosten *f*

~ ~ ~ **work,** ~ ~ ~ construction ~, building (construction) cost(s) · Hochbaukosten *f*

cosy, homely, snug · wohnlich

cot [*A protection for the hand when handling bricks*] · Handschutz *m* [*beim Ziegelumschlag*]

cot(e) · Kate *f*

cottage [*A small dwelling-house; generally applied to one having four rooms only, living room, kitchen-scullery, and bedrooms*] · kleines Landhaus *n*

~ · Hütte *f*

~ **community,** nesting (US); (housing) estate, housing colony · Wohnkolonie *f*, (Wohn)Sied(e)lung *f*

~ ~ **unit,** nesting ~ (US); (housing) estate ~, (housing) colony ~ · Sied(e)lungshaus *n*

~ **hospital** · Kleinstkrankenhaus *n*; Kleinstspital *n* [*Schweiz*]

cottage orné — course(d) paving

~ orné · Kleinvilla f mit Park
~ suburb (US); suburban (housing) estate · Vorstadtsied(e)lung f, Vorortsied(e)lung
cotter(ed) joint · Splintverbindung f
cotton cloth, woven cotton fabric; cotton fabric [*misnomer*] · Baumwollgewebe n
~ fabric [*misnomer*]; woven cotton fabric, cotton cloth · Baumwollgewebe n
~ fibre (Brit.); ~ fiber (US) · Baumwollfaser f
~ rag · Baumwollumpen m
~ (seed) oil [*B.S. 655*] · Baumwollsamenöl n
couloir · Wandelgang m [*Theater*]
coumarone resin · Kumaronharz n
Council chamber · Großer Remter m [*Marienburg*]
council house, Greek Senate building, bouleuterion · B(o)uleuterion n [*Das Rathaus einer griechischen Stadt im Altertum*]
counter · Ladentisch m
~, teller · (Kunden)Schalter m
counterbalance weight · Ausgleichgewicht n, Gegengewicht
counter-balanced shutter door, ~ shutterdoor · Gegengewichtstor n
counter brace · Gegenstrebe f
~ cable · Gegenseil n
~ ceiling [*A ceiling fixed independently on its own framework below a structural floor or flat roof*] · Unterdecke f
counter-current boiler · Gegenstrom-(Heiz)Kessel m
~ method, ~ system · Gegenstrommethode f, Gegenstromverfahren n
~ system, ~ method · Gegenstrommethode f, Gegenstromverfahren n
counter diagonal · Gegendiagonale f, Gegenschräge f, Wechselstab m
counter-flap hinge · Nußband n
counter flashing, cap ~ · oberer Anschluß m [*Siehe Anmerkung unter „Anschluß"*]
~ ~ (piece), cap ~ (~), cover ~ (~), apron [*See remark under 'Anschluß'*] · Kappleiste f, Kappstreifen m, Überhangleiste, Überhangstreifen
~ floor, dead ~ · Blindboden m, Blendboden
counter-pressure · Gegendruck m
counterscarp [*The face of the ditch of a fortress sloping towards the defender*] · Gegenböschung f
countersinking of rivet(s) · Nietversenkung f
counterweight vertical sliding shutterdoor, ~ vertically opening ~, ~ ~ ~ shutter door · Gegengewichts-Dekkentor n
country builder · Provinzbaumeister m

~ church, village ~, rural ~ · Dorfkirche f, Landkirche
~ house 'castle' · burghafter Landsitz m
(~) manison, manor house, manor-castle · Landsitz m
couple · Kräftepaar n
~ [*A pair of rafters*] · (Dach)Sparrenpaar n
coupled colonnettes · gekoppelte Säulchen npl, gekuppelte ~
~ columns [*Columns placed close together in pairs, under the same entablature*] · gekuppelte Säulen fpl, gekoppelte ~
~ pilasters · gekoppelte Pilaster mpl, gekuppelte ~
couple(d) roof [*A simple roof formed of pairs of rafters (or couples) joined at the apex without tie beams or collar beams*] · Satteldach n ohne Kehlbalken oder Querriegel
coupled windows · gekoppelte Fenster npl, gekuppelte ~
coupler → socket
coupling, pipe ~ [*A (pipe) fitting used for connecting together pipes or fittings*] · Rohrkupplung f
~ of pipes, (pipe) joint assembly, pipe coupling · Rohrkuppeln n, Kuppeln von Rohren
course, masonry (work) ~ [*A horizontal layer of masonry units such as brick, tile, stone, or other materials, as they are laid in a wall*] · (Mauerwerk)Schar f, (Mauerwerk)Schicht f, (Mauerwerk) Lage f
~ (US); shell ring, shell belt · Kesselschuß m, Mantelschuß
~ depth · Lagenhöhe f, Schichthöhe [*Mauerwerk*]
~ joint, bed ~, horizontal ~ · Lagerfuge f [*Mauerwerk*]
~ ~ mortar, bed (~) ~, horizontal ~ ~ · Lagerfugenmörtel m [*Mauerwerk*]
~ of bonders → (bonding) header course
~ ~ (bonding) headers → (bonding) header course
~ ~ bondstones → (bonding) header course
~ with bricks laid on bed · Lagerschicht f [*Lage flach gelegter Mauerziegel im Gegensatz zur Rollschicht*]
~ ~ diagonally laid component units · Schrägschar f, Schrägschicht f [*Eine Reihe schrägliegender Steine bei gewissen Mauer- oder Gewölbeverbänden*]
coursed · geschichtet [*Mauerwerk*]
course(d) block masonry (work), ~ blockwork · Schicht(en)-Blockmauerwerk n, geschichtetes Blockmauerwerk
~ masonry (work), ~ work · Schicht(en)mauerwerk n, geschichtetes Mauerwerk
~ paving, paving in rows · Großpflaster(decke) n, (f) in Reihenform Reihen(stein)pflaster(decke)

course(d) rubble masonry (work) — covering-over 262

~ **rubble masonry (work)**, ~ ~ (work) [*Masonry (work) composed of roughly shaped stones fitting approximately on level beds and well bonded*] · geschichtetes Bruchsteinmauerwerk *n*, gleichmäßiges ~, lagerhaftes ~

~ ~ (work) → ~ ~ masonry (~)

coursing · Schicht(en)anordnung *f* [*Mauerwerk*]

court, yard [*An unroofed space with access wholly or mainly enclosed by a building or buildings*] · Hof *m*

~ · Zentralhof *m* [*in der Palastanlage von Khorsabad*]

~ **architect** · Hofarchitekt *m*

~ **chapel** · Hofkapelle *f*

~ **entrance**, yard ~ · Hofeingang *m*

~ **garden**, garden court · Gartenhof *m*, Zierhof, Hofgarten *m*

courthouse · Gerichtsgebäude *n*

Court Library at Vienna · Nationalbibliothek *f* in Wien

~ **of Alberca**, Alberca court · Hof *m* der Alberca, ~ ~ Bäder, Myrthenhof [*Alhambra*]

court of honour · Ehrenhof *m*

Court of (the) Lions · Löwenhof *m* [*Alhambra*]

court pavement, yard ~ · Hofbefestigung *f*

~ **stables** · Marstall *m*

~ **theatre** · Hoftheater *n*

curtain-wall · Mittelwall *m* [*Der zwischen je zwei Bollwerken gelegene Teil eines Walles oder einer Festungsmauer*]

(court)yard · befestigter Hof *m*

courtyard garden, garden court · Zierhof *m*, Gartenhof

(court)yard mosque · Hofmoschee *f*

cove, coving, hollow cornice [*A concave quadrant moulding joining a wall to a ceiling*] · Viertelstab *m* [*An der Berührungslinie von Wand und Decke*]

~ **(molding) (US)** → cavetto (moulding)

to cover · überdecken

cover · (Ab)Deckung *f*

~, covering · Belag *m*

~, lid · Deckel *m*

~ **board** · (Ab)Deckbrett *n*

~ **fillet** → ~ moulding

~ **grate**, covering ~ · (Ab)Deckrost *m*

~ **moulding (Brit.)**; ~ molding (US); ~ fillet, batten [*A mo(u)lded strip used to cover a joint on a flush surface, as, for instance, in panel(l)ing*] · Fugen(deck)leiste *f*, Fugenabdeckleiste, (Ab-)Deckleiste

~ **paper** → cover(ing) ~

~ **plate**, brace ~, stay ~, tie ~, batten (~) · Schnalle *f*, Bindeblech *n* [*Bei zwei- und mehrteiligen Querschnitten werden die einzelnen Teile durch Bindebleche in ihrem gegenseitigen Abstand gehalten*]

~ ~, covering ~ · (Ab)Deckblech *n*

~ ~ · Decklasche *f*

~ **price**, total (~) · Gesamtpreis *m*

~ **ring** · Deckelring *m*

~ **slab** → (concrete) coping ~

to cover with lining paper · makulieren

cover woven fabric → cover(ing) cloth

covered, roofed · (ein)gedeckt, bedacht, abgedeckt

~ **market**, roofed ~, indoor ~, market hall · (Markt)Halle *f*

~ ~ **(place)**, roofed ~ (~) · überdachter Markt(platz) *m*, gedeckter ~

~ **passage**, roofed ~, ~ way, ~ walk · überdachter Gang *m*, gedeckter ~

~ **railway station (Brit.)**; ~ railroad ~ (US); roofed ~ ~ · Hallenbahnhof *m*

~ **shrine**, roofed ~ · überdachtes Heiligtum *n*, gedecktes ~

~ **skating rink**, indoor ice ~, ice palace · Halleneis(lauf)bahn *f*, Eispalast *m*, Eisstadion *n*, Eis(lauf)halle *f*

~ **spectator's stand**, roofed ~ ~ · Dachtribüne *f*

~ **swimming bath(s)**, roofed ~ ~, indoor ~ ~, ~ ~ pool, bath building · Hallenbadeanstalt *f*, Hallen(schwimm)bad *n*

~ ~ **pool** → ~ ~ bath(s)

~ **timber bridge**, ~ wood(en) ~, roofed ~ ~ · Dachbrücke *f*

~ **walk**, roofed ~ · Laube *f* [*Offener, meist gewölbter Bogengang als Teil des Erdgeschosses, besonders von Wohn- und Rathäusern der deutschen Renaissance, auch dem Erdgeschoß vorgelagert*]

~ ~, roofed ~, ~ way, ~ passage · überdachter Gang *m*, gedeckter ~

~ **way**, roofed ~, ~ walk, ~ passage · überdachter Gang *m*, gedeckter ~

~ **with granulated cork** · korkbestreut

~ **wood(en) bridge**, ~ timber ~, roofed ~ ~ · Dachbrücke *f*

covering · Abdecken *n*; Abdeckung *f*

cover(ing) · Belag *m*

~ **cloth**, ~ woven fabric; ~ fabric [*misnomer*] · (Ab)Deckgewebe *n* [*Im Bauwesen verwendete Textilerzeugnisse, z.B. Jutegewebe, Nesselgewebe usw*]

~ **fabric** [*misnomer*] → ~ cloth

~ **foil**, protecting ~ · (Ab)Deckfolie *f*

~ **grate** · (Ab)Deckrost *m*

covering material → lining ~

covering-over · Überdecken *n*, Überdeckung *f*

cover(ing) paper — crane beam

cover(ing) paper · (Ab)Deckpapier *n* [*Als Baustoff erfüllt das Abdeckpapier gleiche oder ähnliche Aufgaben wie das (Ab)Deckgewebe*]

~ **plate** · (Ab)Deckblech *n*

~ **slab** → (concrete) coping ~

covering tape, pipe ~ ~ · (Rohr)Isolierband *n*

cover(ing) woven fabric → ~ cloth

coving → cove

~ [*The metal or tiled top to a range*] · Herdplatte *f*

CO-warning system for garage · CO-Warnanlage *f* für Garage

cow hair · Kuhhaar *n*

cowl → vent(ilat)ing capping

CP, clay pipe; (drain(age)) tile, DT (US) · Tonrohr *n*

CPC, cement-plaster ceiling · Zement(ver)putzdecke *f*

CPL · Zementputz *m*

c.r., cold-rolled, CR · kaltgewalzt

~ ~ **beam,** cold-rolled ~ · kaltgewalzter Balken(träger) *m*

~ ~ **channel,** cold-rolled ~ · kaltgewalztes U-Eisen *n*

~ ~ **steel,** cold-rolled ~ · kaltgewalzter Stahl *m*, Kaltwalzstahl

~ ~ ~ **section,** cold-rolled ~ ~ [*B.S. 2994*] · kaltgewalztes Stahlprofil *n*

~ ~ **strip** → cold-rolled ~

~ ~ **steel,** cold-rolled ~ ~ · kaltgewalzter Bandstahl *m*

crack · Riß *m*

(~) **bridging** · (Riß)Überbrückung *f*

~ **control** · Rißbeherrschung *f*

(crack-control) (metal) joint strip · Fugenbewehrungsstreifen *m*, Fugenbewehrungsstoff *m* [*Fugenbewehrungsstoffe sind Metallnetzstreifen, Lochmetallstreifen, Streckmetallstreifen oder ähnliche P-tzträger, die auf die Fugen von Leichtbauplatten gebracht werden, um Rissebildung zu vermeiden*]

crack due to expansion, ~ ~ ~ volume increase · Treibriß *m*

~ ~ ~ **volume increase,** ~ ~ ~ expansion · Treibriß *m*

~ **edge** · Rißkante *f*

~ **extension force** · Rißausbreitungskraft *f*

~ **filler,** plastic wood · flüssiges Holz *n*, plastisches ~, künstliches ~, Holzkitt *m*, Kunstholz, Holzzement *m*, Lignozement [*Eine pastenartige Masse zum Ausbessern von Rissen im Holz, Ausfüllen von Astlöchern usw.*]

~ **formula** · Rißformel *f*

crack-free, free of cracks · rißfrei, rissefrei, rißlos, risselos

crack geometry · Rißgeometrie *f*

~ **injection** · Rißauspressung *f*, Rißeinpressung, Rißverpressung

~ **interval,** ~ spacing · Rißabstand *m*

crack-measuring ga(u)ge · Rißbreitenmesser *m*

crack-proof · rißsicher

crack-resistant · rißfest

~ **concrete** · rissefester Beton *m*, rißfester ~

crack seal(ing) · Rißabsieg(e)lung *f*, Rißversieg(e)lung

~ **sharpness** · Rißschärfe *f*

~ **spacing,** ~ interval · Rißabstand *m*

~ **starter** · Rißursprung *m*, Rißanfang *m*

~ **wall** · Rißflanke *f*, Rißwand(ung) *f*

~ **width** · Rißbreite *f*, Rißweite

cracked · gerissen

cracking · Rißbildung *f*

~ **limit state,** limit state of cracking Rißbildungs-Grenzzustand *m*

~ **load** · Rißlast *f*

~ **loading** · Rißbelastung *f*

~ **moment** · Rißmoment *n*

~ **risk** · Rißgefahr *f*

~ **strength,** extensibility, resistance to cracking · Rißfestigkeit *f*

crack(ing) stress · Rißspannung *f*

crackle lacquer, alligatoring ~ · Reißlack *m*, Krakelierlack

crackle(d) glassware [*Glassware, the surface of which has been intentionally cracked by water immersion and partially heated by reheating before final shaping*] · krakeliertes Glas *n*, Krokodilglas

cradle machine, cleaning cradle, window ~ ~, wall lift, roof cradle [*Motorized carriage running vertically on rails let into the window frames*] · (Fenster)Putzwagen *m*, (Fenster)Reinigungswagen

~ **vault,** cylindrical ~ · zylindrisches Gewölbe *n*, walzenförmiges ~

craftsman, journeyman, tradesman · Geselle *m*

cramp, clamp [*A strip steel fixed to a door frame or lining and built into a wall to fix the frame or lining*] · Bandstahlanker *m* für Zargen

~ [*misnomer: cramp iron*] · Kramme *f*, Krampe

~ **(iron),** clamp (~) · Bankeisen *n*, Schlauder *f* [*Zur Verbindung der Futterrahmen von Türen oder Fenstern mit dem Mauerwerk*]

~ ~ [*misnomer*]; cramp · Kramme *f*, Krampe

~ **joint** · Krampenverbindung *f*

cramped flue · verengter Rauch(gas)-kanal *m*

crane aisle · Krangang *m*

~ **bay** · Kranschiff *n* [*Industriehalle*]

~ ~ · Kranhalle *f*

~ **beam** · Kranbalken(träger) *m*

crane girder — crenellated

~ **girder,** ~ runway ~ · Kran(bahn)träger *m*

~ **runway,** craneway · Kranbahn *f*

~ **(~) girder** · Kran(bahn)träger *m*

craneway, crane runway · Kranbahn *f*

cranked flat iron · gekröpftes Flacheisen *n*

cranking, offsetting · Verkröpfen *n*, Verkröpfung *f*

crape cotton → crepe(d) ~

~ **paper** → crepe(d) ~

~ **rubber** → crepe(d) ~

~ **wool** → crepe(d) ~

crash program (US); ~ **programme** (Brit.) · Sofortprogramm *n*

crashing through a floor · Durchschlagen *n* durch eine Decke

cratch, fodder rack · Futterraufe *f*

crater bloom [*on paint and varnishes*] Krater *m*

cratering [*The formation of small bowl-shaped depressions in a paint or varnish film*] · Kraterbildung *f* [*Anstrich*]

crawl space, crawlway; basementless space (US) [*An underfloor space providing access to ducts, pipes, and other services hung or laid therein and of a height sufficient for crawling*] · Kriechraum *m*, Bekriechungsraum, Kriechkeller *m*

crawling [*A cracking in glass-finish topcoats containing drying oils which shrink and reveal a ground. It may be caused by grease on the ground. Cissing is mild crawling*] · Abrollen *n*, Kriechen

crawlway, crawl space; basementless space (US) [*An underfloor space providing access to ducts, pipes, and other services hung or laid therein and of a height sufficient for crawling*] · Kriechraum *m*, Bekriechungsraum, Kriechkeller *m*

crazing · Brandrisse *mpl*, Brennrisse [*Feuerfestindustrie*]. Netzwerk von Oberflächenrissen]

~ **crack,** firing ~, burn(ing) ~, craze ~ · Brandriß *m*, Brennriß [*Feuerfestindustrie*]

creation of airborne sound · Luftschallanregung *f*

~ ~ **footstep sound** · Trittschallanregung *f*

~ ~ **impact sound,** ~ ~ structureborne ~ · Körperschallanregung *f*

~ ~ **structure-borne sound,** ~ ~ impact ~ · Körperschallanregung *f*

creative design material · gestalterischer Baustoff *m*

~ **thought,** ~ thinking · bildnerisches Denken *n*

credence [*A small table at the side of an altar*] · Kredenz(tisch) *f*, (*m*)

creep, plastic flow · plastischer Fluß *m*, Kriechen *n*

~ **behaviour** (Brit.); ~ behavior (US) Kriechverhalten *n*

~ **coefficient,** coefficient of creep · Kriechbeiwert *m*, Kriechzahl *f*

~ **crack** · Kriechriß *m*

~ **deflection,** ~ deflexion, inelastic ~ Kriechdurchbiegung *f*, Kriechdurchsenkung

~ **deflexion,** ~ deflection, inelastic ~ · Kriechdurchbiegung *f*, Kriechdurchsenkung

~ **deformation,** inelastic ~ · Kriechverformung *f*, Kriechformänderung

~ **growth,** ~ increase · Kriecherhöhung *f*, Kriechzunahme *f*, Kriechsteigerung

~ **increase,** ~ growth · Kriecherhöhung *f*, Kriechzunahme *f*, Kriechsteigerung

~ **limit** · Kriechgrenze *f*

~ **mechanism,** mechanism of creep · Kriechmechanismus *m*

~ **modulus,** modulus of creep · Kriechmodul *m* [*Baustoffkonstante, die zur Berechnung der Kriechverformung von Beton dient*]

~ **of concrete,** concrete creep · Betonkriechen *n*

~ ~ **mortar,** mortar creep · Mörtelkriechen *n*

~ **process** · Kriechvorgang *m*

~ **rate,** rate of creep [*The slope of the creep-time curve at a given time*] · Kriechgeschwindigkeit *f*

creep(-)resistant, creep-resisting · kriechfest

creep-resisting, creep(-)resistant · kriechfest

creep strain, inelastic ~ · Kriechdehnung *f*

~ **stress** · Kriechspannung *f*

~ **test** · Kriechprobe *f*, Kriechprüfung *f*, Kriechversuch *m*

~ ~ **machine** · Kriechprüfmaschine *f*

~ **theory,** theory of creep · Kriechtheorie *f*

~ **trench** [*A small subway, containing a drain, and large enough to allow a man to crawl along to inspect the drain*] · Kriech(drän)kanal *m*

~ **value** · Kriechwert *m*

~ **variation** · Kriechschwankung *f*

creeping rafter, jack (~), cripple ~ [*A short rafter between hip rafter and eave(s) or between valley and ridge*] · Gratstichbalken *m*, Schiftsparren *m*, Schifter *m*

cremation urn, (cinerary) ~ · (Aschen-)Urne *f*

~ ~ **pit,** (cinerary) ~ ~ · (Aschen-)Urnengrab *n*, Brandgrab

crematorium, crematory · Krematorium *n*

crematory, crematorium · Krematorium *n*

Cremona's polygon of forces · Cremonascher Kräfteplan *m*, Kräfteplan nach Cremona, Cremonaplan [*Zeichnerisches Verfahren zur Ermitt(e)lung der Stabkräfte eines Fachwerkträgers*]

to crenellate → to embattle

crenellated → battlemented

crenellated bridge parapet — crocket capital

~ **bridge parapet** → embattled ~ ~

crenellation, battlement [*An indented parapet at the top of a wall, originally used for purposes of defence, subsequently for architectural decoration. The raised parts are 'cops' or 'merlons' the indentations 'embrasures' or 'crenel(le)s'*] · Zinnenkranz *m*, Zinnenbesatz *m*, Zinnenkrönung *f*

crenel(le), embrasure [*A gap in a battlemented parapet*] · Zinnenfenster *n*

creosol pitch · Kreosolharz *n*, Karbolpech *n*, Phenolpech

to creosote [*To treat (wood, etc.) with creosote*] · kreosotieren

creosote (oil), dead ~, pitch ~ · Imprägnier(ungs)öl *n*, Kreosot(öl) *n*, Tränk(ungs)öl

creosoted · kreosotiert

to crepe · kreppen

creped · gekreppt

crepe(d) cotton, crêpe ~, crape ~ · Kreppbaumwolle *f*

~ **paper,** crêpe ~, crape ~ [*A thin paper crinkled like crepe*] · Kreppapier *n*

~ **rubber,** crêpe ~, crape ~ · Kreppgummi *m*

~ **wool,** crêpe ~, crape ~ · Kreppwolle *f*

crepidoma [*The stepped base of a classic structure, especially of a Doric temple*] · Krepidoma *n*, Krepsis *m*, (Stufen)Unterbau *m*

creping (treatment) · Kreppen *n*

crescent, sickle-shaped · sichelförmig

~ **oblique rib,** sickle-shaped ~ ~ · sichelförmige Schrägrippe *f*

~ **roof,** sickle-shaped ~ · sichelförmiges Dach *n*

cresol pitch · Phenolpech *n*, Karbolpech, Kresolharz *n*

cress tile, crease ~, crest ~, crested ridge ~ · (Zier)Firstziegel *m*, Dekor(ations)firstziegel, Ornamentfirstziegel, Schmuckfirstziegel

crest, roof ~ · Dachkamm *m*, (Dach-)Firstverzierung *f*

~ **tile,** crease ~, cress ~, crested ridge ~ · (Zier)Firstziegel *m*, Dekor(ations)firstziegel, Ornamentfirstziegel, Schmuckfirstziegel

crest(ing) crowning, end ornament [*An ornamental finish along the top of a screen, wall, or roof*] · (Be)Krönung *f*, Krone *f* [*Ornamentik*]

~ → roof ~

Cretan architecture · kretische Architektur *f*, ~ Baukunst *f*

~ **column** · kretische Säule *f*

crevice corrosion · Spaltkorrosion *f*

~ ~ **at a contact with non-metallic material** · Berührungskorrosion *f*

cricket, saddle · Schornsteinsattel *m*

~ **cap flashing** saddle ~ ~, ~ counter ~ [*See remark under 'Anschluß'*] · sattelförmiger Kappanschluß *m*, ~ Überhanganschluß

~ ~ ~ **(piece),** ~ cap ~ (~), ~ counter ~ (~) [*See remark under 'Anschluß'*] · sattelförmige Kappleiste *f*, ~ Überhangleiste, sattelförmiger Kappstreifen *m*, sattelförmiger Überhangstreifen

~ **counter flashing,** ~ cap ~, saddle ~ ~ [*See remark under 'Anschluß'*] · sattelförmiger Kappanschluß *m*, ~ Überhanganschluß

~ ~ ~ **(piece),** ~ cap ~ (~), saddle ~ ~ (~) [*See remark under 'Anschluß'*] · sattelförmige Kappleiste *f*, ~ Überhangleiste, sattelförmiger Kappstreifen *m*, sattelförmiger Überhangstreifen

crimped (web) stiffener · gekröpfter Aussteif(ungs)winkel *m*

crinkling, wrinkling, (sh)rivelling · Kräuseln *n*, Runzeln, Faltenbildung *f* [*Anstrich*]

crinoidal limestone [*It contains fragments of crinoids, or sea-lilies*] · Seelilienkalkstein *m*

critical amplitude · kritische Schwingungsweite *f*

~ **cooling-off rate** · kritische Abkühl(ungs)geschwindigkeit *f* [*Die Geschwindigkeit, mit der ein Werkstück auf Härtetemperatur abgekühlt werden muß, damit Martensitbildung eintritt*]

~ **cross section** · gefährdeter Querschnitt *m*

~ **frequency** · kritische Frequenz *f*

~ **load** · kritische Last *f*

~**-load design,** ~ method [*This method is based on a critical load at which large deformations and the formation of wide, open cracks render the structure unserviceable*] · Verfahren *n* der kritischen Last

critical plane · kritische Ebene *f*

~ **range** · kritischer Bereich *m*, kritisches ~ *n*

~ **wind velocity** · kritische Windgeschwindigkeit *f*

crocidolite asbestos, Cape ~, blue ~ · Blauasbest *m*, Kapasbest

crocket [*plural: crocketing*] [*A decorative feature carved in various leaf shapes and projecting at regular intervals from the angles of spires, pinnacles, canopies, gables, etc., in Gothic architecture*] · Krabbe *f*, Steinblume *f*, Knolle *f*, Kriechblume, Kantenblume, Krappe, Käpfer *m*, Häkchen *n*

~ **capital** [*An Early Gothic form, consisting of stylized leaves with endings rolled over similar to small volutes*] · Kriechblumenkapitell *n*, Steinblumenkapitell, Krabbenkapitell, Kriechblumen-

crocket capital — cross member

kapitäl, Steinblumenkapitäl, Krabbenkapitäl

crocketed · kantenblumenverziert, kriechblumenverziert, steinblumenverziert, krabbenverziert, knollenverziert

crocodiling, alligatoring · Rißlackierung *f* [*Eine Lackierungsart, bei der bewußt die Rißbildung herbeigeführt wird*]

~, alligatoring · Krakelierung *f*

cromlech · Cromlech *m*, Kromlech, Steinkreis *m* [*Vorgeschichtliches Grabdenkmal aus kreisförmig gestellten unbehauenen oder nur roh bearbeiteten Steinblöcken. In der Mitte steht ein hoher Stein*]

crope [*deprecated*] → flower shaped ornament

cross, pipe ~ · (Rohr)Kreuz(stück) *n*

~, rood · Kreuz *n* [*Kirche*]

~ aisle, transverse ~ · Quer(haus)schiff *n*, Kreuzschiff

~ arm, transverse ~ · Kreuzarm *m*, Kreuzflügel *m*, Querhausarm, Querhausflügel, Kreuzvorlage *f* [*Der über das Langhaus vorspringende Teil des Querhauses*]

crossband, under-veneer · Blindfurnier *n*

cross-banded lumber veneered board for building purposes (US) → coreboard ~ ~ ~ (Brit.)

cross-beam, transverse beam · Querbalken(träger) *m*

~ · Holm *m*, Geländer~

cross beam · Traverse *f*

~ block, ~ building · Quergebäude *n*

~ bond, ~ masonry ~ · Kreuz(mauer)verband *m*

~ brace, X-brace, diagonal strut · Kreuzstrebe *f*

cross-braced end frame · Endquerrahmen *m*

cross bracing, X-bracing · Kreuzverband *m*

cross bracing · Kreuzverband *m*

~ building, ~ block · Quergebäude *n*

~ cocking, ~ corking, ~ cogging · Kreuzkamm *m* [*Holzverbindung*]

~ cogging, ~ corking, ~ cocking · Kreuzkamm *m* [*Holzverbindung*]

~ column → cross-shaped ~

~ core, cross-shaped ~, cruciform ~ · kreuzförmiger Kern *m*

~ corking, ~ cocking, ~ cogging · Kreuzkamm *m* [*Holzverbindung*]

cross-domed church, ambulatory ~, cruciform-domed ~, domed-cruciform ~ · Kreuzkuppelkirche *f*, Kuppelkreuzkirche

cross-folded · kreuzgefaltet

cross garnet, T(ee) hinge [*It is intended for hinging components of ledged construction, such as ledged, braced and battened doors, or where weight must be distributed over a large area*] · Zungenband *n*, gerades Band, Kegelband [*Baubeschlag*]

cross-grooved flag(stone), ~ paving flag · gekuppte Bürgersteigplatte *f*

~ floor(ing) (finish) tile, ~ floor cover(ing) ~ · gekuppte (Fuß)Bodenplatte *f* [*Eine (Fuß)Bodenplatte deren Oberfläche zur besseren Trockenhaltung und zur sicheren Begehbarkeit kreuzweise mit Rillen durchzogen ist. Dadurch werden auf der Oberfläche Kuppen gebildet*]

cross (ground(-))plan → cross-shaped ~

~ head · Querhaupt *n* [*Prüfmaschine*]

crossing · Kreuzung *f*

~ · Vierung *f*, Kreuzbau *m*, Kreuzwerk *n*, Kreuzung, Kreuzfeld *n*, Kreuzmittel *n*

~ arch · Vierungsbogen *m*

~ bay · Vierungsjoch(feld) *n*, Vierungsfeld

~-cupola, crossing-dome · Vierungskuppel *f*

~-dome, crosing-cupola · Vierungskuppel *f*

~ impost · Vierungskämpfer *m*

~ of masonry walls, masonry wall crossing · Mauerkreuzung *f*

~ ~ purlin(e)s and rafters · Überkreuzung *f* der Pfetten und Sparren

~ ~ two cross arches · Kreuzung *f* von zwei Kreuzbogen, ~ ~ ~ Kreuzgurten

~ ~ walls, wall crossing · Wandkreuzung *f*

~ over a footway · Bürgersteigüberfahrt *f*

~ pier · Eckpfeiler *m*, Vierungspfeiler

~ square, transept ~, square of crossing · Vierungsquadrat *n* [*Es ergibt sich aus der Durchdringung von Langhaus und Querhaus bei gleichen Breiten*]

~-tower · Vierungsturm *m*

~ vault · Vierungsgewölbe *n*

~ width · Vierungsbreite *f*

cross iron, ~ section bar · Kreuzeisen *n*

~ joint (Brit.); vertical ~, side ~, perpendicular ~; (head) ~, build (US) · Stoßfuge *f* [*Mauerwerk*]

~ limb, limb of cross · Kreuzarm *m*

cross-linked, CL · kreuzgittervernetzt

cross-linking (of polymers) · Kreuzgittervernetzung *f*

cross louver shielding, ~ louvre ~ · Lamellenraster *m* [*Leuchte*]

~ member, horizontal ~, rail [*A horizontal bar of wood or metal extending from one post or support to another as a guard or barrier in a fence, balustrade, staircase, etc.*] · Querstück *n*, Riegel *m*

Cross (moment distribution) method — crosswise ...

Cross (moment distribution) method, moment-balance ~, moment-distribution ~ · Cross-Methode f, Cross-Verfahren n, Momentenausgleichsverfahren, Näherungsrechnung f nach Cross [*Rechnungsverfahren zur Ermitt(e)lung der Momente von Rahmen und Durchlaufträgern. Ein Iterationsverfahren mit schrittweiser Verbesserung der Ergebnisse*]

cross nailing · Überkreuznagelung f [*Waagerecht und senkrecht eingeschlagene Nägel kreuzen sich im Holz aneinander vorbei*]

~ of Jerusalem · Jerusalemskreuz n, Krückenkreuz

~ ~ St. James · Jakobskreuz n

~ partition (wall) · Quertrennwand f

~ patance · Schlüsselringkreuz n

~ pattee · Tatzenkreuz n

~ pier, cross-shaped ~, cruciform ~ · Kreuzpfeiler m

~ plan → cross(-shaped) (ground(-)) plan

~ product, vector ~, outer ~ · äußeres Produkt n, Vektorprodukt

~ reinforcement, transverse ~ [*Reinforcement at right angles to the main reinforcement*] · Querarmierung f, Querbewehrung, Quer(stahl)einlagen fpl

~ rib, diagonal ~ · Kreuzrippe f, Diagonalrippe

~-ribbed · kreuzgerippt, gekreuzt gerippt

cross ribs · Kreuzrippen fpl [*Rippendecke*]

~ seam, ~ welt(ed seam) [*A seam between adjacent sheets of roofing, usually parallel to the ridge or gutter*] · Querfalz m [*Metallbedachung*]

~ section · Querschnitt m

~ ~ bar, ~ iron · Kreuzeisen n

cross-section(al) area · Querschnittfläche f

~ ~ of compressive reinforcement · Querschnitt m der Druckarmierung, ~ ~ Druckbewehrung, ~ ~ Druck(stahl)einlagen

~ ~ ~ tensile reinforcement · Querschnitt m der Zugarmierung, ~ ~ Zugbewehrung, ~ ~ Zug(stahl)einlagen

~ capacity, ~ power, ~ property, ~ quality · Querschnitteigenschaft f, Querschnittfähigkeit f, Querschnittvermögen n

~ power, ~ property, ~ capacity, ~ quality · Querschnitteigenschaft f, Querschnittfähigkeit f, Querschnittvermögen n

~ property, ~ power, ~ capacity, ~ quality · Querschnitteigenschaft f, Querschnittfähigkeit f, Querschnittvermögen n

~ quality, ~ power, ~ property, ~ capacity · Querschnitteigenschaft f, Querschnittfähigkeit f, Querschnittvermögen n

~ shape · Querschnittform f

~ value · Querschnittgröße f

~ view · Querschnittansicht f

cross(-shaped) column, cruciform ~, ~ support · Kreuzstütze f

~ core, cruciform ~ · kreuzförmiger Kern m

~ (ground(-))plan, cruciform ~ · kreuzförmiger Grundriß m, Kreuzgrundriß

~ pier, cruciform ~ · Kreuzpfeiler m

~ plan → ~ (ground(-))~

~ support, cruciform ~, ~ column · Kreuzstütze f

cross support → cross-shaped ~

~ timber, intertie [*framed partition*] · Sturzriegel m

cross-ventilated · quergelüftet

cross ventilation · Querlüftung f [*An den gegenüberliegenden Wänden sind Zu- und Ablufföffnungen angeordnet*]

cross-vista, through view · Durchblick m

cross wall, shear ~ [*A wall which in its own plane carries shear resulting from wind, blast, or earthquake forces. It relieves the floors and columns of the necessity of resisting lateral loads and, in addition, it is useful architecturally*] · Scheibe f, Wand~, Wind~

crosswall [*A wall that gives lateral support to another and which runs across a building*] · Querwand f, Schott(e) m, (f)

~ type of construction, ~ construction type, cellular framing, box frame · Schottenbauart f [*Eine Sonderheit der Kastenbauart ist die Schottenbauart. Bei ihr tragen die rechtwinklig zur Frontwand stehenden Querwände und die inneren Längswände, aber nicht die leichten Trennwände und die Außenwände der Gebäudelängsseiten*]

crosswelded (flat) wire(d) (clear) (polished) plate (glass), ~ polished wire(d) ~ · Spiegeldrahtglas n mit punktgeschweißtem Netz, Drahtspiegelglas ~ ~ ~

~ polished wire(d) plate, ~ (flat) wire(d) (clear) (polished) plate (glass) · Spiegeldrahtglas n mit punktgeschweißtem Netz, Drahtspiegelglas ~ ~ ~

~ wire(d) glass · Drahtglas n mit punktgeschweißtem Netz

cross welt(ed seam), ~ seam [*A seam between adjacent sheets of roofing, usually parallel to the ridge or gutter*] · Querfalz m [*Metallbedachung*]

~ window, mullion(ed) [*A window with one mullion and one transom*] · Kreuzfenster n, Pfostenfenster

crosswise trussing of diagonal prism sections · kreuzweise Aussteifung f der diagonalen Prismenschnitte

crow gable, step ~, corbie ~; corbel ~ [*misnomer*] · abgetreppter Giebel *m*, Stufengiebel, Treppengiebel, Staffelgiebel

~ step, catstep, corbie(step); corbelstep [*misnomer*] [*One of a series of steps forming the roofs of certain gable(d) houses*] · Giebelstufe *f*

~ stepping · Abtreppen *n*, Staffeln [*Giebel*]

~ stone · Scheitelstein *m* [*Staffelgiebel*]

crowde, crypt · Krypta *f*, Gruft *f*

crown, top key, vertex, apex · Scheitel(punkt) *m*

~ block, apex ~, vertex ~, top ~, key ~, closer · Scheitelstein *m*, Schlußstein

~ glass · Schleuderglas *n*, Butzenglas, Kronglas, Mondglas

~ hinge, top ~, key ~, apex ~, vertex ~ · Scheitelgelenk *n*

~ hog, apex ~, vertex ~, top ~, key ~ · Scheitelüberhöhung *f*

~ joint, top ~, key ~, apex ~, vertex ~ · Scheitelfuge *f*, Schlußfuge [*Fuge am höchsten Gewölbepunkt oder Bogenpunkt, wenn kein Scheitelstein vorhanden ist*]

crown-like top · Gebäudekrone *f* [*z.B. beim Torre Velasca in Mailand*]

crown of corrugation · Wellenberg *m* [*Wellplatte; Welltafel*]

~ plate, head tree, saddle, bolster, corbel piece [*A short timber cap over a post to increase the bearing area under a beam*] · Sattelholz *n*

~ post → king ~

~ process · Kronglasverfahren *n*, Butzenglasverfahren, Mondglasverfahren, Schleuderglasverfahren

~ sag, apex ~, vertex ~, top ~, key ~ · Scheitelsenkung *f*

~ stone, apex ~, vertex ~, top ~, keystone [*The central stone of an arch or a vault; sometimes carved*] · Scheitelstein *m* aus Naturstein, Schlußstein ~ ~

crowning, crest(ing), end ornament [*An ornamental finish along the top of a screen wall, or roof*] · (Be)Krönung *f*, Krone *f* [*Ornamentik*]

~ feature, terminal ~, ~ member · (be)krönendes Element *n*

~ member, terminal ~, ~ feature · (be)krönendes Element *n*

CRS → cold-rolled steel

crucible steel · Tiegelstahl *m*

crucifix, rood · Kruzifix *n*

cruciform building · Kreuzbau *m*

~ centralized church (US); ~ centralised ~ (Brit.); ~ centrally-planned ~, ~ church with central space · kreuzförmige zentrale Anlage *f*, kreuzförmiger Zentralbau *m*

~ centrally-planned church, ~ church with central space; ~ centralized church (US); ~ centralised church (Brit.) · kreuzförmige zentrale Anlage *f*, kreuzförmiger Zentralbau *m*

~ church · Kreuzkirche *f* [*Kirche mit kreuzförmigem Grundriß*]

~ ~ with central space, ~ centrally-planned church; ~ centralized church (US); ~ centralised church (Brit.) · kreuzförmige zentrale Anlage *f*, kreuzförmiger Zentralbau *m*

~ column · Kreuzsäule *f*

~ ~, cross(-shaped) ~, ~ support · Kreuzstütze *f*

~ core, cross(-shaped) ~ · kreuzförmiger Kern *m*

~ cross-section · kreuzförmiger Querschnitt *m*

~ crypt · Kreuzkrypta *f*, Kreuzgruft *f*

cruciform-domed church, domed-cruciform ~, cross-domed ~, ambulatory ~ · Kreuzkuppelkirche *f*, Kuppelkreuzkirche

cruciform effect · kreuzförmige Wirkung *f*

~ (ground(-))plan → cross(-shaped) ~

~ in (ground(-))plan · kreuzgrundrißförmig

~ mass (of a building) · kreuzförmige Baumasse *f*, Baumasse mit kreuzförmigem Grundriß

~ network · kreuzförmig gespanntes Netzsystem *n*

~ pier, cross(-shaped) ~ · Kreuzpfeiler *m*

~ plan → cross(-shaped) (ground(-))plan

~ skyscraper [*Form chosen by Le Corbusier for his 'City of Three Million'*] · Wolkenkratzer *m* auf kreuzförmigem Grundriß

~ support, cross(-shaped) ~, ~ column · Kreuzstütze *f*

~ symmetry · Kreuzsymmetrie *f*

crude alabaster · Rohalabaster *m*

~ foul water, ~ refuse ~, ~ sewage · Rohabwasser *n*

~ masonry (work) · Rohmauerwerk *n*

~ oil, petroleum · Erdöl *n*, Roh(erd)öl, (Roh)Petroleum *n*, Öl [*Man nennt die hellen Öle „Naphtha", die gelblichen „Petroleum" und die bräunlichen, zähen „Bergteere"*]

(~) pe(a)rlite (rock), pe(a)rlite ore [*The petrographic terms for a naturally occurring siliceous volcanic rock*] · (Roh)Perlite *m*

~ refuse water, ~ foul ~, ~ sewage · Rohabwasser *n*

~ rock · Rohgestein *n*

~ sewage, ~ foul water, ~ refuse water · Rohabwasser *n*

(~) shale oil · Schieferöl *n*

~ sugar solution · Rohzuckerlösung *f*

~ tall oil · rohes Tallöl *n*

(~) Trinidad Lake asphalt · Trinidad-(Roh)Asphalt *m*

~ tar [*deprecated: green tar*] · Rohteer *m*

crumpled aluminium foil (Brit.); ~ **aluminum ~** (US) · Alu(minium)dicht-(ungs)stoff *m*

crusader architecture · Kreuzfahrerarchitektur *f*, Kreuzfahrerbaukunst *f*

~ castle · Kreuzritterburg *f*

Crusader(-type) church · Kreuzfahrerkirche *f*

crush-room [*A small hall to relieve the pressure of the crowd at the exit of a public building*] · Pufferraum *m*

~ (Brit.); foyer · Foyer *n*

crushed, broken · gebrochen

~ aggregate, broken ~ · gebrochener Zuschlag(stoff) *m*

~ basalt(ic) stone · Basaltschotter *m*

~ (blast-furnace) slag sand, broken (~) ~ ~, ~ granulated (blast-furnace) slag (Brit.); ~ cinder sand, ~ granulated cinder (US) · Hüttenbrechsand *m*, Schlackenbrechsand

~ (~) ~ 30/70 mm → ~ iron (~) ~ ~ ~

~ brick concrete, broken ~ ~ · Trümmerbeton *m*, Ziegelsplittbeton [*DIN 4163. Trotz des Namens ,,Ziegelsplittbeton" enthält dieser Beton die Körnungen 0/3, (0/7), 3/7 mm = Ziegelsand; 7/15, 15/30. = Ziegelsplitt und 30/70 mm = Ziegelschotter*]

~ ~ ~ filler block, ~ ~ ~ ~ tile, broken ~ ~ ~ ~ ~ · Trümmerbeton-Deckenblock(stein) *m* Trümmerbeton-Deckenstein, Ziegelsplittbeton-Deckenblock(stein), Ziegelsplittbeton-Deckenstein

~ ~ ~ wall slab, broken ~ ~ ~ ~ · Trümmerbeton-Wand(bau)platte *f*, Ziegelsplittbeton-Wand(bau)platte

~ bricks, broken ~, ~ clay ~ · Ziegelbrechgut *n*

~ chip(ping)s, broken ~ · Brechsplitt *m*

~ cinder sand (US) → ~ (blastfurnace) slag ~

~ ~ slag 30/70 mm, broken ~ ~ ~ ~ (US); ~ (iron) (blastfurnace) ~ ~ ~ (Brit.) · (Hochofen)Schlackenschotter *m*

~ (clay) bricks, broken (~) ~ · Ziegelbrechgut *n*

~ concrete → broken ~

~ (concreting) sand, broken (~) ~, ~ concrete ~, ~ fine aggregate · Betonbrechsand *m*, zerkleinerter (Beton)Feinzuschlag(stoff) *m*

~ dust, breaker ~ · Brechmehl *n*

~ expanded cinder (US) → ~ foamed (blastfurnace) slag

~ fine aggregate → ~ (concreting) sand

~ foamed (blastfurnace) slag, broken ~ (~) ~ (Brit.); ~ expanded cinder (US) · Hüttenbims *m*, Kunstbims [*Gebrochene geschäumte Hochofen-*schlacke. *Die Struktur dieses Baustoffes ähnelt der des Naturbimses und beim technischen Schäumvorgang laufen ab wie beim Naturbims*]

~ ~ slag → ~ ~ blastfurnace ~

~ glass, finely ~ ~, granulated glass · Glasgrieß *m*, Krösel *m*

~ granite, broken ~ · Granitschotter *m*

~ granulated (blastfurnace) slag → ~ (blastfurnace) slag sand

~ ~ cinder (US) → ~ (blastfurnace) slag sand

~ ~ slag → ~ (blastfurnace) slag sand

~ gravel, broken ~ · Brechkies *m*

~ hard rock, broken ~ ~ · Hartschotter *m* [*Schotter aus Hart(ge)stein*]

~ (iron) (blastfurnace) slag 30/70 mm, broken (~) (~) ~ ~ ~ (Brit.); ~ cinder ~ ~ (US) · (Hochofen-)Schlackenschotter *m*

~ (~) slag 30/70 mm → ~ (~) blastfurnace ~ ~ ~

~ lava, broken ~ · Brechlava *f*

~ limestone, broken ~ · Kalksteinschotter *m*

~ ~, broken ~ · gebrochener Kalkstein *m*

~ ~ sand, broken ~ ~ · Kalkstein-Brechsand *m*

~ lump slag, broken ~ ~ · Betonschlacke *f*, gebrochene Stuckschlacke

~ marble, broken ~ · Brechmarmor *m*

~ material, broken ~, ~ product · Brech(er-Fertig)gut *n*, gebrochenes Material *n*

~ product, broken ~, ~ material · Brech(er-Fertig)gut *n*, gebrochenes Material *n*

~ rock, broken ~, ~ stone; (road-)metal (Brit.) · Schotter *m*, Brech~, Steinschlag *m*, Straßen(bau)schotter

~ sand → ~ concreting ~

~ slag, broken ~, air-cooled ~ [*This slag is prepared by pouring the molten slag onto a slag bank or into a pit. After solidifying and cooling, the slag is excavated, crushed and screened*] · Brech(er)schlacke *f*

~ ~ sand → ~ blastfurnace ~ ~

~ ~ 30/70 mm → ~ (iron) (blastfurnace) ~ ~ ~

~ slate, broken ~ · Schiefersplitt *m* [*Zur Bestreuung von Dachpappe*]

~ stone, broken ~, ~ rock; road-metal (Brit.) · (Brech)Schotter *m*, Steinschlag *m*, Straßen(bau)schotter

~ ~, broken ~, ~ rock [*The product resulting from the artificial crushing of rocks, boulders or large cobblestones, substantially all faces of which have resulted from the crushing operation*] · gebrochenes Material *n*, ~ Gestein

~ ~, broken ~ · Betonsteinschlag *m* [*als Betonzuschlag(stoff). 30/70 mm*]

crushed stone sand — cubing

~ ~ **sand**, artificial ~, stone ~, manufactured ~, (stone) screening(s), crusher screening(s) · Steinsand m, Brechsand [*Er umfaßt in den USA den Kornstufenbereich 0–4,76 mm*]

crusher-run aggregate [*Aggregate that has been broken in a crusher and has not been subjected to any subsequent screening proces*] · gebrochener ungesiebter Zuschlag(stoff) m, ungesiebter gebrochener ~

~ **material** → broken ~

~ **product** → broken material

~ **rock** → broken ~

~ **stone** → broken rock

crusher screening(s), (stone) ~, artificial sand, manufactured sand, stone sand, crushed stone sand · Steinsand m, Brechsand [*Er umfaßt in den USA den Kornstufenbereich 0–4,76 mm*]

crushing load · Scheitelbruchlast f [*Rohr*]

~ **operation**, ~ process · Brechvorgang m [*Hartzerkleinerung*]

~ **process**, ~ operation · Brechvorgang m [*Hartzerkleinerung*]

~ **(proof) test** · Scheiteldruckprüfung f, Scheiteldruckprobe f, Scheiteldruckversuch m [*Rohr*]

~ **strength** → compression ~

~ ~ · Scheiteldruckfestigkeit f, Widerstandsfähigkeit f gegen Scheiteldruck [*Rohr. DIN 52150*]

~ ~ **class**, compression ~ ~ · Druckfestigkeitsgruppe f

~ ~ **range** → compression ~ ~

~ **(~) test**, compression ~ ~ · Druck(festigkeits)versuch m, Druck(festigkeits)prüfung f, Druck(festigkeits)probe f

~ **test**, ~ strength ~, compression strength ~ · Druck(festigkeits)versuch m, Druck(festigkeits)prüfung f, Druck(festigkeits)probe f

~ ~, breaking ~ · Brechprobe f, Brechprüfung f, Brechversuch m

~ ~ [*pipe*] → ~ proof ~

crux commissa, Tau cross · Antoniuskreuz n, Taukreuz, ägyptisches Kreuz

~ **decussata**, St. Andrew's cross, Saltire cross · Andreaskreuz n

~ **immissa**, Latin cross · lateinisches Kreuz n

cry room · schalldichter Raum m für Mutter und Kind

cryolite · Eisstein m, Kryolith m

crypt, crowde · Krypta f, Gruft f

crypto-crystalline [*Having a crystalline structure, however, of crystals too small to be seen even with a microscope*] · kryptokristallin

cryptoporticus [*In Roman architecture, an enclosed gallery having walls with openings instead of columns; also a covered or subterranean passage*] · Kryptoportikus m

crystal chandelier · Kristall-Kronleuchter m

~ **glass** [*A colourless, highly transparent glass of high refractive index, frequently used for tableware*] · Kristallglas n

Crystal Palace · Kristallpalast m

crystal sheet glass, heavy ~ (~) (US); thick ~ ~ · Dickglas n

crystalator, glass-balustrade escalator · Glas-Rolltreppe f

crystalline gypsum · kristalliner Gips m

~ **limestone**, calcitic marble, limestone marble · Kalkmarmor m, kristalliner Kalkstein m

~ **plutonic rock** · kristallines Tiefengestein n

~ **rock** · kristallines Gestein n

(~) **schist** · kristalliner Schiefer m

~ **shape** · Kristallform f

crystallizable · kristallisierbar

crystallization · Kristallisation f

~ · Alterung f, Rekristallisation f [*Schraube; Niet*]

~ **pressure** · Kristallisationsdruck m

Cu shot, copper ~ · Kupferschrot m, n

cubage · Rauminhalt m

cube → enclosed space

~ **mould** → test ~ ~

~ **(paving) sett** · Pflasterwürfel m, Würfel(pflaster)stein m

~ **sett** → ~ paving ~

~ **size** · Würfelgröße f

~ **strength at 28 days**, compressive ~ ~ ~ ~ ~ · Würfel(druck)festigkeit f W_{28}

~ **test** → concrete ~ ~

cubic capacity → enclosed space

~ **capital**, block ~, bowl ~ · Würfelkapitell n, Würfelkapital

~ **content** · Kubikinhalt m

~ **conversion** · Kubikumrechnung f

~ **form** · kubisches Formbild n

~ **measure** · Kubikmaßeinheit f

~ **parabola** · kubische Parabel f

cubical · kubisch

~ **aggregate** [*Angular aggregate most of whose particles have length, breadth, and thickness approximately equal*] · kubischer Zuschlag(stoff) m, kubisches Zuschlagmaterial n

~ **chip(ping)s** · kubischer Splitt m

(cubic(al)) content → enclosed space

cubical element · Kubuselement n [*Betonfertigteil*]

~ **mass (of a building)** · kubische Baumasse f

~ **product** · kubisches Endkorn n, ~ Endprodukt n [*Hartzerkleinerung*]

cubicle · Kabine f, Zelle f [*Sehr kleiner Raum*]

cubing · Steinpaketieren n

~ · Kubieren *n*
Cubism · Kubismus *m*
Cubist architecture · kubische Architektur *f*, ~ Baukunst *f*
cubist style · kubische Formsprache *f*
cuboctahedron · Kubooktaeder *n*
cuboid house · Würfelhaus *n*
cul-de-sac, blind alley · Sackgasse *f*
cull [*Brick rejected in culling*] · aussortierter Ziegel *m*
cullet, broken glass · Glasbrocken *m*, (Glas)Scherben
culling [*Picking out something, especially something rejected as not up to standard*] · Aussortieren *n*
~ [*Sorting brick for size, colour and quality*] · Ziegelsortieren *n*
Culmann('s) method · Culmannsches Verfahren *n*, Culmannverfahren [*Ein Schnittverfahren zur Ermitt(e)lung der Stabkräfte eines statisch bestimmten ebenen Fachwerkes*]
~ **moment area** · Culmannsche Momentenfläche *f*
cult image · Kultbild *n*
~ **room** · Kultraum *m*
~ **statue** · Kultstandbild *n*, Kultbildnis *n*, Kultstatue *f*, Kultbildsäule *f*
~ **temple**, processional ~ · Kulttempel *m*, Göttertempel
cultural and commercial zone · Kultur- und Geschäftsbereich *m, n*
~ **centre** (Brit.); ~ center (US); community ~ · Kulturzentrum *n*, Kulturzentrum *n*, Gemeindezentrum.
~ **circle**, artistic ~ · Künstlerkreis *m*
~ **hall** · Unterhaltungshalle *f* [*Mit Bühne und Zuschauerraum, die aber auch als Sporthalle dienen kann*]
~ **movement** · Kulturbewegung *f*
culverhouse → columbarium
culvert pipe · Abzugskanalrohr *n*, Durchlaßrohr
culvertail, dovetail, DVTL · Schwalbenschwanz *m*
cumulative consumption, total ~ · Gesamtverbrauch *m*
cuneate, cuneiform, wedge-shaped · keilförmig
cuneiform, cuneate, wedge-shaped · keilförmig
~ **tablet** · Keilschrifttafel *f*
cup, (brass) dish · Schale *f* [*Fließgrenzengerät nach A. Casagrande*]
cupboard-wall, bank of closets, closet bank · Schrankwand *f*
cupola, dome · Kuppel *f*
~ **above a square** → dome ~ ~ ~
~ **apex** → ~ vertex
~ **bar**, dome ~ · Kuppelstab *m*
~ **bottom**, dome ~, domic(al) ~, dome(-shape)d ~, ~ floor, bottom dome, bottom cupola · Kuppelboden *m*, Domboden [*Behälter*]

~ **cornice**, dome ~ · Kuppel(ge)sims *m*, (*n*)
~ **edge**, dome ~ · Kuppelrand *m*
~ **floor**, dome ~, domic(al) ~, dome(-shape)d ~, ~ bottom, bottom dome, bottom cupola · Kuppelboden *m*, Domboden [*Behälter*]
~ **form** → dome(-shape)d ~
~ **impost**, dome ~ · Kuppelkämpfer *m*
~ **key** → ~ vertex
~ **of multiangular plan** → multiangular dome
~ ~ **polygonal plan** → multiangular dome
~ ~ **revolution (subjected to loads of rotational symmetry)**, dome ~ ~ (~ ~ ~ ~ ~ ~), ~ ~ rotational symmetry · Drehkuppel *f*, Rotationskuppel, drehsymmetrische Kuppel
~ ~ **rotational symmetry** → ~ ~ ~ revolution (subjected to loads of rotational symmetry)
~ **on drum** → dome on tambour
~ ~ **tambour** → dome ~ ~
~ **ring**, dome ~ · Kuppelring *m*
~ **roof** → dome(-shape)d ~
~ **segment**, dome ~ · Kuppelscheibe *f*, Kuppelsegment *n*
~ **shell** → dome(-shape)d ~
~ **slab** → dome(-shape)d ~
~ **slag** · Kupolofenschlacke *f*
~ **stress**, dome ~ · Kuppelbeanspruchung *f*
~ ~, dome ~ · Kuppelspannung *f*
~ **surface**, dome ~ · Kuppeloberfläche *f*
~ **top** → ~ vertex
~ **vertex**, ~ apex, ~ key, ~ top, ~ crown, dome ~ · Kuppelscheitel *m*
cuprammonium rayon · Cupra(faser) *f*; Kupferseide *f* [*Dieser Begriff ist veraltet*]
curb · Aufsatzkranz *m*, Aufsetzkranz [*Lichtkuppel*]
~; kerb (Brit.) · Bordstein *m* [*DIN 483 Betonbordsteine; DIN 482 Natursteinbordsteine*]
~, roof ~ · Dachbruch *m*, (Dach)Knick *m* [*Jene Linie des Daches, an der die steilere Neigung der Hauptdachfläche in weichem Übergang in die sanfter geneigte Dachfläche an der Traufe durch den Aufschiebling übergeleitet wird*]
~, ~ **plate** [*A circular wall plate*] · Kranz *m*
~ **below ground**, inverted curb, flush curb; kerb below ground, inverted kerb, flush kerb (Brit.) · (Tief)Bordstein *m*, Tiefbord *m*
~ **clay tile**, roof ~ ~ ~ · Dachbruchziegel *m*
~ **mold**, concrete ~ ~ (US); (concrete) kerb mould (Brit.) · (Beton)Bordsteinform *f*

curb (plate) — curtain wall

~ **(plate)** [*A circular wall plate*] · Kranz *m*

~ **rafter** · oberer Mansardendachsparren *m*

~ **roof**, double-pitched ~ (US); hip(ped) mansard ~ (Brit.) [*It slopes in four directions, but there is a break on each slope*] · abgewalmtes Mansard(en)dach *n*, Mansard(en)-walmdach, Walmmansard(en)dach

~ **tile**, roof ~ ~ · Dachbruchstein *m*

curbed footway; kerbed ~ (Brit.) · Fußweg *m* mit Bordstein

curdling · Gerinnen *n* [*Anstrichschaden*]

to cure, to set · abbinden [*Kleber*]

~ ~ · nachbehandeln [*Beton*]

cured by atmospheric-pressure steam, ~ ~ low-pressure ~, low-pressure steam-cured, atmospheric-pressure steam-cured · dampfbehandelt, wärmebehandelt [*Beton*]

~ ~ **low-pressure steam**, ~ ~ atmospheric-pressure ~, low-pressure steam-cured, atmospheric-pressure steam-cured · dampfbehandelt, wärmebehandelt [*Beton*]

curing, concrete ~ · (Beton)Nachbehandlung *f*

~ **agent**, setting ~ [*e.g. as part of an epoxy resin adhesive*] · Abbindemittel *n* [*Kleber*]

~ ~ → (concrete) curing compound

~ **area** · Trockenplatz *m* [*Betonwerk*]

~ **at maximum temperature** · Warmbehandlung *f* [*Beton*]

~ **blanket**, concrete-~ ~ · Abdeckmatte *f* [*Nachbehandlung von Beton*]

~ **capacity**, ~ quality, ~ property, ~ power · (Ab)Bindeeigenschaft *f*, (Ab-)Bindefähigkeit *f*, (Ab)Bindevermögen *n* [*Verschnittbitumen*]

~ **chamber**, ~ room, concrete ~ ~ · Behandlungskammer *f*, Dampfkammer [*Betonsteinfertigung*]

~ **compound** → concrete ~ ~

~ **fixture**, concrete ~ ~ · (Beton)Nachbehandlungsvorrichtung *f*

~ **membrane**, concrete ~ ~ · (Beton-)Nachbehandlungsfilm *m*

~ **overlay** · Abdeckung *f* [*Nachbehandlung von Beton*]

~ **paper**, concrete-~ ~, overlay ~ · (Beton)Nachbehandlungspapier *n*, Abdeckungspapier

~ **period**, ~ time, time of curing, period of curing · (Ab)Bindedauer *f*, (Ab)Bindezeit *f*, (Ab)Bindefrist *f* [*Verschnittbitumen*]

~ ~ **at maximum temperature**, ~ time ~ ~ ~ · Warmbehandlungsdauer *f*, Warmbehandlungszeit *f* [*Beton*]

~ **power**, ~ capacity, ~ quality, ~ property · (Ab)Bindeeigenschaft *f*, (Ab)Bindefähigkeit *f*, (Ab)Bindevermögen *n* [*Verschnittbitumen*]

~ **process**, process of curing · (Ab)Bindeprozeß *m*, (Ab)Bindevorgang *m*, (Ab)Bindeverlauf *m* [*Verschnittbitumen*]

~ **property**, ~ capacity, ~ quality, ~ power · (Ab)Bindeeigenschaft *f*, (Ab-)Bindefähigkeit *f*, (Ab)Bindevermögen *n* [*Verschnittbitumen*]

~ **quality**, ~ property, ~ capacity, ~ power · (Ab)Bindeeigenschaft *f*, (Ab-)Bindefähigkeit *f*, (Ab)Bindevermögen *n* [*Verschnittbitumen*]

~ **rack**, rack for curing concrete blocks · Hordengestell *n* [*Betonsteinherstellung*]

~ **rate**, rate of curing · (Ab)Bindegeschwindigkeit *f* [*Verschnittbitumen*]

~ **room**, ~ chamber, concrete ~ ~ · Behandlungskammer *f*, Dampfkammer [*Betonsteinfertigung*]

~ **solution**, concrete ~ ~ · (Beton-)Nachbehandlungslösung *f*

~ **time**, ~ period, time of curing, period of curing · (Ab)Bindedauer *f*, (Ab)Bindezeit *f*, (Ab)Bindefrist *f* [*Verschnittbitumen*]

~ ~ **at maximum temperature**, ~ period ~ ~ ~ · Warmbehandlungsdauer *f*, Warmbehandlungszeit *f* [*Beton*]

~ **water**, concrete ~ ~ · (Beton)Nachbehandlungswasser *n*

~ **yard**, concrete ~ ~ · (Beton)Nachbehandlungsplatz *m*

curled clouds; nebule moulding (Brit.); nebule molding (US) · Wolkenverzierung *f*, rundliches Zickzack *n*

current from irregular source(s), stray current, leak(age) current · Streustrom *m*, vagabundierender (Erd-)Strom, Irrstrom, Erdstrom, Schleichstrom

current-impulse switch · Stromstoßschalter *m*

current-using apparatus · elektrische Verbrauchsvorrichtung *f*

curtain → run

~ → ~ wall

~ **arch** · (einfacher) Vorhangbogen, (~) Gardinenbogen, konkaver Spitzbogen, gebrochener Spitzbogen, umgekehrter Spitzbogen, Sternbogen

~ **coating (method)** · Gießen *n*, Gießverfahren

(~) **lath** → (~) slat

~ **(masonry) wall** [*In medieval architecture the outer wall of a castle, surrounding it and usually punctuated by towers or bastions*] · Umfassungsmauer *f*

~ **rail**, ~ track · Vorhangschiene *f*

(~) **slat**, (~) lath, shutter ~ · (Abschluß-)Lamelle *f*

~ **track**, ~ rail · Vorhangschiene *f*

~ **wall** → ~ masonry ~

curtain wall — curvilinear ornament

~ ~, skin, cladding [*It is a non-bearing wall between columns or piers and is not supported by girders or beams. Many building codes apply the term 'curtain' wall to a panel wall*] · Vorhangwand f, vorgehängte Wand, vorgeblendete Fertigwand, Außenhaut f, Vorhangfassade f, vorgehängte Fassade

~ (~), enceinte (~) [*The outer wall of a castle, connecting towers and gatehouse*] · Kurtine f [*historischer Festungsbau*]

~ ~, filler ~, panel ~ [*It is a non-bearing wall in skeleton construction, built between columns, posts or piers and wholly supported at each stor(e)y*] · Tafelwand f

curtain-wall block, ~ building, panelwall ~ · Vorhangwandgebäude n

~ **building**, ~ block, panel-wall ~ · Vorhangwandgebäude n

curtain wall frame · Vorhangwandrahmen m

~ ~ **panel** · Vorhangfassadentafel f, Vorhangwandtafel

~ ~ **sealing material** · Vorhangwand-(Ab)Dicht(ungs)stoff m

curtaining, running, sagging · Nasenbildung f, Läuferbildung, Gardinenbildung [*Fehler beim Verarbeiten von Lack oder Lackfarbe*]

curvature in (ground(-))plan · Grundrißkrümmung f

~ **line**, line of curvature · Krümmungslinie f

curve in space, three-dimensional curve, spatial curve, space curve · räumliche Kurve f, dreidimensionale ~, Raumkurve

~ **of final set(ting)**, final set(ting) curve · (Ab)Bindeendekurve f [*hydraulisches Bindemittel*]

~ ~ **hardening**, hardening curve · (Er-)Härtungskurve f [*Mörtel; Beton; Zementpaste; Gips. Siehe Anmerkung unter „Abbinden"*]

~ ~ **initial set(ting)**, initial set(ting) curve · Erstarrungskurve f [*Siehe Anmerkung unter „Abbinden"*]

~ ~ **set(ting)**, set(ting) curve · (Ab-)Binde(zeit)kurve f, Verfestigungskurve

~ **plate**, shell ~ · Schale f

curved · kurviert, gekrümmt

~ **area** · gekrümmte Fläche f

~ **bar** → ~ rod

~ **beam** · gekrümmter Balken(träger) m

~ ~ **with eccentric boundaries**, eccentrically curved beam [*Such a beam is bounded by areas having different centres of curvature. In addition it is possible for either radius to be the larger one*] · ausmittig gekrümmter Balken(träger) m, exzentrisch ~ ~

~ **block**, ~ building · Gebäude n mit gekrümmtem Grundriß

~ **building** → ~ block

~ **(concrete) roof**, non-planar (~) ~ [*shell; dome*] · gekrümmtes (Beton-)Dach n

~ **corrugated aluminum** (US); ~ ~ aluminium (Brit.) · gekrümmtes Wellalu(minium) n

~ **curb**; ~ kerb (Brit.) · Bogen(bord)stein m

~ **element** → ~ rod

~ **gable** · geschweifter Giebel m, kurvenförmiger ~, Rundgiebel [*Er ist halbkreisförmig im Umriß*]

~ **girder**, arch(ed girder) · gekrümmter Träger m, Bogen(träger) m [*Träger, der bei senkrechten Lasten nach außen gerichtete Stützkräfte (inclined reactions) auf die Auflager überträgt*]

~ **(ground(-))plan** · gekrümmter Grundriß m

~ **kerb** (Brit.); ~ curb · Bogen(bord)stein m

~ **member** → ~ rod

~ **pediment**, round ~ · runder Ziergiebel m

~ **plan**, ~ ground(-)~ · gekrümmter Grundriß m

~ **plank roof** · Bohlensparrendach n, geschweiftes Dach

~ **plate**, ~ slab · gekrümmte Platte f

~ **projection**, projecting curvature · Verwölbung f

~ **pyramidal roof** · geschweiftes Pyramidendach n

~ **rafter**, compass ~ · gebogener Sparren m

~ **ramp** · Bogenrampe f

~ **rod**, ~ bar, ~ member, ~ element, bent ~ · gekrümmter Stab m, gebogener ~, gekrümmtes Glied n, gebogenes Glied

~ **roof**, ~ concrete ~, non-planar (concrete) ~ [*shell; dome*] · gekrümmtes (Beton)Dach n

curve(d ruler) · Kurvenlineal n

curved shell [*As opposed to a prismatic shell*] · gekrümmte Schale f

~ **slab**, ~ plate · gekrümmte Platte f

~ **slat** · gebogene Lamelle f

~ **sliding door** · Über-Eck-Schiebetür f

~ **surface of a liquid** · gekrümmte Flüssigkeitsoberfläche f

~ **track** · gebogene Deckenschiene f [*Türanlage*]

~-**trough flow-device** · Kurvenkonsistenzmesser m

curved work, (natural) stone curving · nichtgerad(linig)e (Natur)Steinbearbeitung f

curvilinear · krummlinig, kurvenförmig

~ **ornament** · kurvig gewelltes Ornament n

Curvilinear Style — cutting down 274

Curvilinear Style, Middle Pointed ~, Decorated ~, Middle Gothic ~, Geometrical ~, flowing ~ [*It was the phase of Gothic prevailing in England during the fourteenth Century, when the lancet windows of the so-called 'Early English' style were replaced by tracery — at first geometrical, afterwards flowing*] · englische Hochgotik *f*

curvilinear tracery, flowing ~ · fließendes Maßwerk *n* [*Die im Decorated Style der englischen Gotik angewandte Form des Maßwerks*]

curving metal plate in two planes · Bombieren *n* [*Wölben von Blech durch entsprechend profilierte Walzen*]

cushion capital, cubiform ~, cubic ~, block ~, bowl ~ · Würfelkapitell *n*, Würfelkapität

cushioned frieze, pulvinated ~, swell(ed) ~ [*A frieze with a convex face*] · Pulvinusfries *m*, konvexer Fries

cusp · Nase *f* [*gotisches Maßwerk*]

cusped arch, foiled ~ · Nasenbogen *m* [*veraltet: nasiger Bogen, vielgenaster Bogen*]

cuspidated · genast [*gotisches Maßwerk*]

cuspidation, cusping · Nasenbildung *f*, Nasenverzierung [*gotisches Maßwerk*]

cusping, cuspidation · Nasenbildung *f*, Nasenverzierung [*gotisches Maßwerk*]

custom-house, guild-hall · Kaufhaus *n*, Kaufhalle *f* [*Im Mittelalter ein städtisches Gebäude mit großen Sälen zum Auslegen und Aufspeichern von Waren*]

customer circulation · Kundenverkehr *m*

~ parking, driver ~ · Selbstparken *n* [*In einem Parkhaus. Gegenteil: Parken mit Bedienungspersonal*]

~ ~ building, driver ~ ~ · Parkhaus *n* mit Selbstparkbetrieb, Parkgebäude *n* ~ ~, Parkbau *m* ~ ~, Parkgarage *f* ~ ~, Selbstparkhaus, Selbstparkgebäude, Selbstparkbau, Selbstparkgarage

customs clearance area, ~ control ~ · Zollabfertigungsbereich *m*, *n* [*Flughafen*]

~ control · Zollbüro *n*

~ ~ area, ~ clearance ~ · Zollabfertigungsbereich *m*, *n* [*Flughafen*]

to cut, to hew, to carve, to sculpture [*out of stone, in ivory, etc.*] · skulpt(ur)ieren

cut · Schliff *m* [*Hohlglas*]

~, scratch, graze · Schramme *f*, Kratzer *m* [*Fehler im optischen Glas*]

~ away view · Schnittbild *n*

cutback · verschnittenes bituminöses Bindemittel *n*, bituminöses verschnittenes ~ [*Verschnittbitumen und Kaltteer*]

~ (Brit.) → asphalt(ic) ~

~ (asphalt) → asphalt(ic) cutback

~ ~ emulsion (US); ~ (asphaltic) bitumen-emulsion (Brit.) · Verschnittbitumenemulsion *f*

~ (asphaltic-)bitumen (Brit.) → asphalt(ic) cutback

~ ~ distillation apparatus (Brit.); ~ asphalt ~ ~ (US) · Prüfgerät *n* für die Siedeanalyse von Verschnittbitumen

~ (asphaltic) bitumen-emulsion (Brit.); ~ asphalt emulsion (US) · Verschnittbitumenemulsion *f*

~ bitumen (Brit.) → asphalt(ic) cutback

~ road tar · Verschnittstraßenteer *m*

~ (~) ~ for cold repairs · Kaltausbesserungs(straßen)teer *m*

cut edge · geschnittene Kante *f*, Schnittkante

~ engineered timber, sawed ~ ~, sawn ~ ~, wood in building sizes; construction lumber (US) · Schnittholz *n* für Ingenieurholzbau, Bauschnittholz

~ foliage, hewn ~, carved ~, sculptured ~ · skulpt(ur)iertes Blattwerk *n*, ~ Laubwerk, plastisch gestaltete Blätter *npl*, skulpt(ur)ierte Blätter, plastisch gestaltetes Blattwerk, plastisch gestaltetes Laubwerk

~ glass; deep cut [*This term should preferably not be used. Glass decorated by grinding figures or patterns on its surface over an abrasive wheel, followed by polishing*] · geschliffenes Hohlglas *n*

~ joint · Schnittfuge *f*

~ nail, ~ steel ~ [*B.S. 1202*] · geschnittener Nagel *m*, Schnittnagel

cut-off · Abschnitt *m* [*Beim Zuschnitt abfallender Glasstreifen*]

~ angle · abgeschnittene Ecke *f*

cut-out · Ausschalter *m*

~ valve · Abschaltventil *n*, Ausschaltventil

cut roof, terrace ~, truncated ~ [*A pitched roof terminated by a flat roof, thus having no ridge*] · abgestumpftes Dach *n*

~ (steel) nail [*B.S. 1202*] · geschnittener Nagel *m*, Schnittnagel

cut-string stair(case), open-string ~, bridge board ~; open-stringer ~, cut-stringer ~ (US) · aufgesattelte Treppe *f*

cut stringer, open ~ (US); ~ string (Brit.) [*An outer string(er) which is cut to the profile of the steps*] · Sattelwange *f*

cutting, hewing, carving, sculpturing [*out of stone, in ivory, etc.*] · Skulpt(ur)ieren *n*

~ · Schleifen *n* [*Hohlglas*]

~ back, thinning · Verschneiden *n*

~ diamond, glazier's ~ · Diamantschneider *m*, Glaserdiamant *m* [*Werkzeug*]

~ down [*Cleaning of a polished or painted surface with an abrasive preparatory to re-polishing or painting*] · Abreiben *n*

cutting list — cylindrical concrete manway

~ **list,** summary of reinforcement [*A list of steel bars showing diameters and length only, from which the reinforcement is ordered. This list is prepared by the contractor from the bending schedules issued by the reinforced concrete designer with his detail drawings*] · Stahlauszug *m*

~ ~ · Schnittliste *f* [*Bauholz*]

cutting-list structural timber, ~ building ~, ~ construction(al) ~ · Bauholz *n* nach Liste, Listenbauholz

cutting of glass · Glasschneiden *n*

~ **plane** · Schnittebene *f*

~ **speed** · Schnittgeschwindigkeit *f* [*z.B. bei der spanabhebenden Bearbeitung von Automatenstahl*]

~ **to length** · Ablängen *n*, Abschneiden auf Länge

~ ~ **size** · Zuschneiden *n*

~ **tolerance** · Schneidtoleranz *f* [*Bewehrung*]

~ **wire,** brick ~ ~ · (Ziegel)Abschneide(r)draht *m*

CWG, corrugated (rolled) wire(d) glass · Drahtwellglas *n*, Welldrahtglas

CWP, circulating water pump · Umlaufwasserpumpe *f*, Umwälzwasserpumpe, Wasserumwälzpumpe, Wasserumlaufpumpe

cycle of load(ing), load(ing) cycle, repeated loading · Lastspiel *n*, Belastungsspiel

~ **park,** ~ stand, bi~ ~ · Fahrradstand *m*

~ **path,** cycleway · Rad(fahr)weg *m*

~ ~ **edging,** cycleway ~ · Rad(fahr)wegkante *f* [*Erzeugnis der Betonsteinindustrie*]

~ **room,** bi~ ~ · Fahrradraum *m*

~ **stand,** ~ park, bi~ ~ · Fahrradstand *m*

cycles of bending, bending cycles · Biegewechselanzahl *f*

~ **to failure,** load ~ ~ ~, loading ~ ~ ~, repeated loadings ~ ~ · Lastspiele *npl* bis zum Bruch, Belastungsspiele ~ ~ ~

cycleway, cycle path · Rad(fahr)weg *m*

~ **edging,** cycle path ~ · Rad(fahr)wegkante *f* [*Erzeugnis der Betonsteinindustrie*]

cyclic deformation · Wechselverformung *f*

~ **loading,** repeated loadings · Lastspiele *npl*

cyclic(al) permutation · zyklische Vertauschung *f*

cyclized rubber · Cyclokautschuk *m*

cyclone cellar, storm ~ ~ · Wirbelsturm-Schutzkeller *m*

cyclopean block · Zyklopenstein *m*

~ **concrete** · Bruchsteinbeton *m*, Zyklopenbeton

~ **(masonry) work,** ~ masonry · zyklopisches (Mauer)Werk *n*, pelasgisches ~, Zyklopen(mauer)werk, Polygon(mauer)werk

~ **(~) ~** → rock-faced (~) ~

~ **rustication** → rock-faced (masonry) work

~ **work,** ~ masonry ~, ~ masonry · zyklopisches (Mauer)Werk *n*, pelasgisches ~, Zyklopen(mauer)werk, Polygon(mauer)werk

~ ~ → rock-faced (masonry) ~

cylinder · Farbroller *m*, Rolle *f*, Walze *f* [*Farbrollgerät*]

~, **storage** ~ · (Innen)Kessel *m* [*Heißwasserspeicher*]

~, **round pier** · Rundpfeiler *m*, Kreispfeiler [*Er hat kreisrunden Grundriß, jedoch keine Verjüngung und keine Entasis wie die Säule*]

~, **storage water heater,** storage calorifier · Speicher-Warmwasserbereiter *m*

~ **compressive strength** → concrete ~ ~ ~

~ **crushing strength** → concrete ~ ~ ~

~ **glass** [*blown or drawn*] · Walzenglas *n*, Zylinderglas

~ **key** · Zylinderschlüssel *m*

~ **segment,** barrel shell, segment of cylinder · Tonnenschale *f*

~ ~ · Zylindersegment *n*

~ ~ **roof,** barrel (shell) ~, arched barrel ~ · Tonnen(schalen)dach *n*

~ **strength,** concrete ~ ~ · (Beton-)Zylinderfestigkeit *f*

~ **test,** concrete ~ ~, (Beton)Zylinderdruckprüfung *f*, (Beton)Zylinderdruckprobe *f*, (Beton)Zylinderdruckversuch *m*

~ **tester** → concrete ~ ~

~ **testing machine** → concrete ~ ~ ~

~ **twist** · Zylinderverwindung *f*

cylindrical bar → round (reinforcing) ~

~ **bending** · zylindrische Biegung *f*

~ **building,** circular ~, cylindric ~ [*When the inside is also circular, the building is called a rotunda*] · Rundbau *m*, Rundgebäude *n*

~ **campanile,** circular ~, round ~ · runder freistehender Glockenturm *m*

~ **chimney,** circular ~, round ~ · Rundschornstein *m*

~ **column,** circular ~, round ~ · Rundstütze *f*

~ ~, circular ~, round ~ · Rundsäule *f*

~ **concrete column,** circular ~ ~, round ~ ~ · Betonrundstütze *f*

~ ~ **manway** → circular concrete manhole

cylindrical concrete pipe — dado frame

~ ~ pipe · Rundbetonrohr *n*

~ **coordinate system** · Zylinder-Koordinatensystem *n*

~ **core**, circular ~, round ~ · Rundkern *m* [*Hochhaus*]

~ **donjon** → ~ dungeon

~ **dungeon**, circular ~, ~ donjon, ~ keep, round ~ · Rundbergfried *m*, Rundbelfried, Rundberchfrit, Runddonjon *m*

~ **function**, cylindric ~ · Zylinderfunktion *f*, Besselsche Funktion

~ **glass tower**, circular ~ ~, round ~ ~ · Rundglasturm *m*, Glasrundturm

~ **hinge** · Zylindergelenk *n*

~ **hip**; ~ piend [*Scotland*] · Zylinderwalm *m*

~ **interlocking pipe**, circular ~, round ~ ~ · rundes Falzrohr *n*

~ **keep** → ~ dungeon

~ **manhole**, circular ~, round ~, ~ manway · Kreisschacht *m*, Rundschacht

~ **manway**, circular ~, round ~, ~ manhole · Kreisschacht *m*, Rundschacht

~ **minaret** · Zylinderminarett *n*

~ **mould** (Brit.); ~ mold (US) · Zylinderform *f*

~ **piend** [*Scotland*]; ~ hip · Zylinderwalm *m*

~ **pipe**, circular ~, round ~ · Zylinderrohr *n*, Kreisrohr, Rundrohr, rundes Rohr, kreisförmiges Rohr

~ **prestressed (concrete) shell**, prestressed (concrete) cylindrical ~ · Spannbetonzylinderschale *f*

~ **projection** · Zylinderprojektion *f*

~ **R.C. shell** → reinforced (concrete) cylindrical ~

~ **reinforced (concrete) shell** → reinforced (concrete) cylindrical ~

~ ~ **shell** → reinforced (concrete) cylindrical ~

~ **reinforcement bar** → round (reinforcing) ~

~ ~ **rod** → round (reinforcing) bar

~ **(reinforcing) bar** → round (~) ~

~ **(~) rod** → round (reinforcing) bar

~ **rod** → round (reinforcing) bar

~ ~ **web**, circular ~ ~, round ~ ~, ~ bar ~ · Rundstabsteg *m*

~ **shell** · Zylinderschale *f*

~ ~ **roof** · Zylinderschalendach *n*

~ ~ **sandwich panel**, ~ three-layer(ed) ~ · Zylinderschalen-Dreischichtentafel *f*, Zylinderschalen-Dreilagentafel

~ **silo**, round ~, circular ~ · Rundsilo *m*, Kreissilo

~ **steel column**, circular ~ ~, round ~ ~ · Rundstahlstütze *f*, Stahlrundstütze

~ **surface** · Zylinderfläche *f*

~ **tank** · Zylinderbehälter *m*

~ **three-layer(ed) panel**, ~ shell sandwich ~ · Zylinderschalen-Dreischichtentafel *f*, Zylinderschalen-Dreilagentafel

~ **tube**, circular ~, round ~ · Zylinderröhre *f*, Kreisröhre, Rundröhre, runde Röhre, kreisförmige Röhre

~ **vault**, cradle ~ · walzenförmiges Gewölbe *n*, zylindrisches ~

~ **wire**, round ~ · Runddraht *m*

cyma (Brit.); sima, cima (US) · Sima *f*, Wasserrinne *f*, Rinnleiste *f*, Traufleiste [*antike Ordnung*]

cyma(tium); ogee moulding (Brit.); ogee molding (US) [*If the concave part is uppermost, it is called 'cyma recta'. If the convex part is uppermost, it is called 'cyma reversa'*] · Kyma(tion) *n*, Blattwelle *f* [*Schmuckleiste aus stilisierten Blattformen, besonders am Gesims griechischer Tempel*]

~ **recta**, Doric cyma(tium) · dorisches Kyma(tion) *n*, dorische Blattwelle *f*

~ **reversa**, Ionic cyma(tium); egg and tongue moulding, egg and dart moulding (Brit.); egg and tongue molding, egg and dart molding (US) · ionisches Kyma(tion) *n*, Eierstab *m*

cypress-wood column · Zypressenholzsäule *f*

cyrtostyle [*A circular portico projecting from a building*] · Rundportikus *m*

Cyrus' tomb · Kyrosgrab *n*

D

D ST → door stop

dab, mortar ~ · (Mörtel)Punkt *m*

~, plaster ~ · (Gips)Punkt *m*

dacite · Dazit *m*

~ **tuff** · Dazittuff *m*

dado, die [*Properly the portion of a pedestal between its base and its cornice; thus the lower part of a wall when divided in the classical ratios. Often simply the lower part of a wall, differentiated by panel(l)ing or colo(u)r, etc.*] · Sockel *m*

~ [*The clearly marked off lower portion of a wall*] · Wandsockel *m*

~, die · Sockelschaft *m*

~ **base** · Sockelfuß *m*

~ **capping**, ~ rail, ~ molding (US); ~ moulding (Brit.); chair rail, surbase [*A mo(u)lding round a room to prevent chairs, when pushed back against the walls, from damaging their surface*] · obere Wandsockelleiste *f*, Schutzleiste

~ **frame**, ~ framing · Sockelrahmen *m*

dado moulding — dampproof(ing) product

~ **moulding** (Brit.); ~ molding (US); ~ capping, ~ rail, chair rail, surbase [*A mo(u)lding round a room to prevent chairs, when pushed back against the walls, from damaging their surface*] · obere Wandsockelleiste *f*, Schutzleiste

~ **rail**, ~ capping, ~ molding (US); ~ moulding (Brit.); chair rail, surbase [*A mo(u)lding round a room to prevent chairs, when pushed back against the walls, from damaging their surface*] · obere Wandsockelleiste *f*, Schutzleiste

~ **tile** · Sockel(belag)platte *f*, Sockelfliese

dagoba, domic(al) mound, stupa (-mound), tope(-mound) [*A mound forming a Buddhist sacred monument*] · Reliquienhügel *m*, Stupa *m*, Tope *m*, Dagob *m*

dairy building, ~ block · Molkereigebäude *n*

dais [*A platform or place of honour, raised at the end of a room. Originally found in the halls of large medi(a)eval and Tudor houses*] · Podium *n*

~, speaker's platform · Rednertribüne *f*, Rednerpodium *n*

damage due to humidity, ~ ~ ~ moisture · Feuchtigkeitsschaden *m*, Feuchteschaden

~ **fastness**, ~ resistance, resistance against damage, fastness against damage · Beständigkeit *f* gegen Beschädigungen, Festigkeit ~ ~, Widerstand *m* ~ ~

~ **of a structure**, ~ ~ structures · Bauschaden *m*

~ **resistance**, ~ fastness, resistance against damage, fastness against damage · Beständigkeit *f* gegen Beschädigungen, Festigkeit ~ ~, Widerstand *m* ~ ~

damascened · damasziert [*Stahl*]

damascening · Damaszierung *f* [*Stahl*]

damask-hung · damastausgeschlagen, damastbehangen, damastbespannt

damask steel · Damaststahl *m*

Damman cold asphaltic concrete (US); ~ ~ asphalt, cold fine asphalt, fine cold asphalt (Brit.) · Asphaltkaltbeton *m*

dam(m)ar (resin), dammer (~) · (ostindisches) Dammarharz *n*, Dammar *m*, Steinharz [*Rezentes, weiches und helles Harz von lebenden Laubbäumen auf den Sundainseln und in Malaya*]

~ **(~) varnish**, dammer (~) ~ · Dammar(harz)lack *m*

damp, humid, moist · feucht

to damp, to dull, to deaden · dämpfen [*Schall; Schwingung*]

~ ~, to moisten, to humidify · anfeuchten, befeuchten

damp → damps

dampcourse → dampproof(ing) course

to damp-cure · feucht nachbehandeln

damp diffusion; (water) vapour ~ (Brit.); (water) vapor ~ (US) · Wasserdampfdiffusion *f*

damper [*A valve, usually made of steel plates or sheet metal, and used to control the flow of air or gas in a duct*] · Gasströmungsregler *m*

damping, dulling, deadening [*sound; oscillations*] · 1.) Dämpfung *f*; 2.) Dämpfen *n*

~ **capacity**, ~ property, ~ quality, ~ power · Dämpfungseigenschaft *f*, Dämpfungsvermögen *n*, Dämpfungsfähigkeit *f*

~ **course**, ~ layer · Dämpfungslage *f*, Dämpfungsschicht *f*

~ **degree**, degree of damping · Dämpfungsgrad *m*

~ **layer**, ~ course · Dämpfungslage *f*, Dämpfungsschicht *f*

~ **material** · Erschütterungsdämmstoff *m*

~ **power** → ~ capacity

~ **property** → ~ capacity

~ **quality** → ~ capacity

dampness, humidity, moisture · Feuchtigkeit *f*, Feuchte *f*

dampproof · dicht gegen Feuchtigkeit, feuchtigkeitsisolierend

~ **concrete** → dampproof(ing) ~

dampproofing [*The prevention of moisture penetration by capillary action, in contrast to 'waterproofing' which prevents the actual flow of water through a wall, etc.*] · (Ab)Dichtung(en) *f(pl)* gegen aufsteigende und seitlich eindringende Bodenfeuchtigkeit, ~ ~ nichtdrückendes Wasser, Feuchteisolierung, Feuchtigkeitsisolierung [*DIN 18337*]

~ **and waterproofing of aboveground rising structures** · (Ab)Dichtung(en) *f(pl)* von Hochbauten gegen Erdfeuchtigkeit [*DIN 4117*]

dampproof(ing) concrete · Dichtbeton *m* [*Gegen betonschädliche atmosphärische Nässe und für wasserdichte Betonwaren*]

~ **course**, dampcourse, DPC, dpc, d.p.c. [*A layer or sheet of material placed within a wall, column, chimney stack or chimney shaft or similar construction to prevent passage of moisture*] · Feuchtigkeitssperrschicht *f*, Feuchtesperrschicht, Feuchtigkeitsisolierschicht, Feuchte(ab)dicht(ungs)schicht

~ **material** → ~ product

~ **membrane**, d.p.m. [*A dampproof course within a floor or flat roof*] · Feuchtigkeitsisolierhaut *f*, Feuchteisolierhaut, Feuchtigkeitssperrhaut, Feuchtesperrhaut, Feuchte(ab)dicht(ungs)-, haut, Haut(ab)dichtung *f*

~ **product**, ~ material · Feuchte(ab)dicht(ungs)mittel *n*

damp-resistant compound, damp-resisting ~ · Isoliermasse f [*Zum Isolieren von Restfeuchtigkeit in Estrichen und Wandflächen sowie kapillarer Feuchtigkeit in nicht unterkellerten Räumen*]

damp room, humid ~ · Feuchtraum m

~ ~ **dampproofing,** humid ~ ~ · Feuchtraum(ab)dichtung f

~ ~ **light fitting** (Brit.) → humid room luminaire (fixture)

~ ~ **(light(ing)) fixture** → humid room luminaire (~)

~ ~ **luminaire (fixture)** → humid ~ ~ (~)

~ ~ **partition (wall),** humid ~ ~ (~) · Feuchtraumtrennwand f

~ ~ **service(s),** humid ~ ~ · Feuchtrauminstallation(en) f(pl)

damp(s) [*Some kind of noxious gas or fumes*] · Schadgas n, Schadschwaden m

dancette → chevron (moulding)

dancing step, ~ winder, balanced step [*A winder not radiating from one common centre*] · verzogene Stufe f

danger of fire, fire risk, fire hazard · Brandrisiko n, Feuerrisiko, Brandgefährlichkeit f, Feuergefährlichkeit

dangerous drug cupbourd, poison · Giftschrank m

~ **structure** [*A structure certified by a local authority to be in a dangerous condition. The owner must repair or pull down the structure, according to instructions*] · einsturzgefährdetes Bauwerk n

dappled, variegated, speckled [*Marked with spots of a different colo(u)r or shade*] · (bunt)gefleckt

darby · Abziehlatte f

dark blind, lighttight ~, black(out) ~ · (Verdunkelungs)Rollo n, Verdunkelung(sblende) f

dark-coloured (Brit.); dark-colored (US) · dunkelfarbig

dark door, lighttight ~, blackout ~, BOD · Verdunkelungstür f

~ **installation** → blackout ~

~ **jalousie,** lighttight ~, blackout ~, ~ louvres, ~ louvers, ~ slatted blind · Verdunkelungsjalousie f

~ **room,** photographic ~ ~ · Dunkelarbeitsraum m, Dunkelkammer f

~ **slatted blind,** blackout ~ ~, lighttight ~ ~, ~ jalousie, ~ louvres, ~ louvers · Verdunkelungsjalousie f

~ **system** → blackout installation

~ **window,** lighttight ~, blackout ~, BOW · Verdunkelungsfenster n

date · Datum n, Termin m

~ **of sampling,** sampling date · Probenahmetermin m, Probenahmedatum n

~ ~ **shipment,** shipping date · Liefertermin m, Lieferdatum n

datum-line, reference line · Bezugslinie f

datum(-plane), reference plane [*An assumed horizontal plane used as a basis for computing elevations*] · Bezugshöhe f, Bezugsebene f

daughter-house · Tochterabtei f

day, light, aperture · Fensterlicht n, Fensteröffnung f

day-care centre (Brit.); ~ center (US); ~ facility · Tagesstätte f

daylight, natural light · Tageslicht n [*DIN 5034*]

~ **calculation,** calculation of daylight, calculation of natural light · Tageslichtberechnung f

~ **hour** · Hellstunde f, Tageslichtstunde

~ **illumination,** daylighting, natural lighting · Innen(raum)beleuchtung f mit Tageslicht, Tages(licht)beleuchtung [*Fehlnamen: (Tages)Belichtung*] [*DIN 5034*]

~ **photometry** · Tageslichtphotometrie f

~ **source** · Tageslichtquelle f

daylighted, naturally lighted · tagesbelichtet [*Fehlname: belichtet*]

~ **from both sides** · zweiseitig tagesbelichtet

~ ~ **one side,** naturally lighted ~ ~ ~ · einseitig tagesbelichtet [*Fehlname: einseitig belichtet*]

daylighting, daylight illumination, natural lighting · Innen(raum)beleuchtung f mit Tageslicht, Tages(licht)beleuchtung [*Fehlnamen: (Tages)Belichtung*] [*DIN 5034*]

daylightproof · tageslichtbeständig, tageslichtfest

day nursery · Kindertagesstätte f

~ **of shipment,** ~ ~ shipping · Liefertag m

~ ~ **test(ing)** · Prüftag m

dayroom, common room · Tagesraum m

day safe · Tagtresor m

day-time area and night-time area [*Division of living space featured in houses designed by Marcel Breuer*] · Tages- und Nachtbereich m, n

~ **home** · Tagesheim n

~ **zone** · Tagesbereich m, n

day-to-day fabrication → mass production

~ **production** → mass ~

day visibility · Tagessichtbarkeit f

daywork · Tagelohnarbeit f

~ **joint** · Tagesarbeitsfuge f

dazzle-free, glare-free, glare-reducing, anti-dazzle; non-glare (US) · abblendend, blend(ungs)frei

~ **glass,** anti-dazzle ~, glare-free ~, glare-reducing ~, non-gare ~ (US) · abblendendes Glas n, Blendschutzglas

dB, decibel · db, Dezibel n, dB

~ **scale,** decibel ~ · Dezibelskala f

DC → door closer

D. C. O., dehydrated castor oil · dehydratisiertes Ricinusöl n, entwässertes ~, Ricinenöl

D. C. O. alkyd, dehydrated castor oil ~ · dehydratisiertes Ricinusölalkyd n, entwässertes ~, Ricinenölalkyd

DD, deep-drawn · tiefgezogen

~, deep drawing · Tiefziehen n

~ quality, deep-drawing ~ · Tiefziehgüte f

de-luxe shower · Luxusdusche f

de luxe type hotel, international ~ ~ ~ ~, luxury ~ · Luxushotel n

(de) Saint Venant('s) principle (of elasticity), (~) St. ~ ~ (~ ~) · Saint-Venantsches Prinzip n

(de) St. Venant's torsion, (de) Saint ~ ~ · freie Torsion f, Saint-Venantsche ~

dead air, (en)trapped ~ [Air trapped in cells, which is the basis of most insulating materials] · eingeschlossene Luft f

~ ~ void → (en)trapped ~ ~

~ alloy, stabilized ~, (fully) killed ~, quiet ~ · stabilisierte Legierung f, beruhigte ~

~ arcade → blind ~

dead(-)burned, dead(-)burnt · totgebrannt [Ein Stoff ist totgebrannt, wenn er durch eine bestimmte Wärmebehandlung möglichst reaktionsträge und raumbeständig geworden ist]

~ gypsum, dead-burnt ~; anhydrous calcium sulfate (US); anhydrous calcium sulphate (Brit.) · totgebrannter Gips m

~ magnesia, dead(-)burnt ~, heavy ~ · geglühte Magnesia f

~ magnesite, dead(-)burnt ~, sintered ~ · Sintermagnesit m, Schmelzmagnesit, geglühter Magnesit [Hochfeuerfester bis zur beginnenden Schmelzung bei rund 1500° C gebrannter Magnesit]

dead burning · Totbrennen n

dead(-)burnt → dead(-)burned

dead door, blind ~, blank ~, false ~ · Blendtür f, Scheintür

dead-drawn wire · biegungsfreier gezogener Draht m

to deaden, to deafen [To make impervious to sound by means of pugging] · auffüllen

~ ~, to damp, to dull · dämpfen [Schall; Schwingung]

dead-end(ed) corridor · Sackkorridor m, Kopfkorridor

~ hangar, ~ shed · Kopfhalle f, Halle in Kopfform

~ (railroad) station (US); ~ (railway) ~ (Brit.) · Kopfbahnhof m, Sackbahnhof

~ shed, ~ hangar · Kopfhalle f, Halle in Kopfform

deadening, deafening · Auffüllung f [Strohlehm, Bimskies usw. zur Wärme- und Schalldämmung beim Einschub von Holzbalkendecken]

~, damping, dulling [sound; oscillations] · Dämpfen n

dead floor, counter ~ · Blindboden m, Blendboden

dead-house, mortuary (block) · Totenhaus n, Leichenhaus

dead level, flush (with), level (to), flush to · bündig (mit), niveaueben

dead-level roof · Flachdach n ohne Neigung zur Entwässerung

dead light → fixed sash

~ load, DL · Totlast f, Eigenlast

dead-load deflection, ~ deflexion · Totlastdurchbiegung f, Eigenlastdurchbiegung, Totlastdurchsenkung, Eigenlastdurchsenkung

dead(-)lock [An ordinary lock which opens and shuts only with a key] · Schloß n ohne Klinke, klinkenloses Schloß

deadlocking latch bolt, auxiliary ~ ~, trigger ~, auxiliary dead latch · riegelartige (Feder)Falle f

deadman, fixed mooring · Ankerstein m, Ankerholz n [Hafen]

dead masonry wall, blank ~ ~ [A masonry wall without openings] · vollflächige Mauer f, geschlossene ~

~ oil, heavy ~ · Schweröl n

~ ~, pitch, creosote (~) · Imprägnier(ungs)öl n, Kreosot(öl) n, Tränk(ungs)öl

Dead Sea asphalt, Jew's pitch, bitumen judaicum · Judenpech n

dead steel, (fully) killed ~, quiet ~, stabilized ~ · beruhigter Stahl m, stabilisierter ~

~ true · haargenau

~ wall, blank ~ [A wall without openings] · geschlossene Wand f, vollflächige ~

~ weight, self ~, own ~ · Eigengewicht n, EG, Totgewicht

~ ~ moment, self ~ ~, own ~ ~ · Eigengewichtsmoment n, EG-Moment, Totgewichtsmoment

~ wire · tote Leitung f [Elektrotechnik]

de-aerating layer → pressure equalizing ~

to deafen, to deaden [To make impervious to sound by means of pugging] · auffüllen

deafening, deadening · Auffüllung f [Strohlehm, Bimskies usw. zur Wärme- und Schalldämmung beim Einschub von Holzbalkendecken]

deairing · Entlüften n [Entfernung der in einer Masse eingeschlossenen Luft durch Evakuieren]

dealer — Decorated Style

dealer · Einzelhändler m

(de)ambulatory, ambulatory aisle [*In large aisled churches, the processional aisle or walk round the east end, behind the high altar*] · Chor(um)gang m, Deambulatorium n, Umgang

~ vault · Umgangsgewölbe n, Deambulatoriumsgewölbe

death mask · Totenmaske f

debiteuse bubble, ~ seed · Düsenblase f, Düsengispe f [*Flachglasfehler*]

deburring · Abgraten n [*Vollständiges (Ab)Trennen überflüssigen Werkstoffes bei Preß- und Gußteilen*]

decagon · Dekagon n, Zehneck n

decagonal, ten-sided · zehnseitig, zehneckig

decahedron · Dekaeder m, Zehnflach n, Zehnflächner m

decal(comania) (decoration) (US); transfer (~) (Brit.) · Übertragungsbild n, Abziehbild

~ process, ~ method (US); transfer ~ (Brit.) [*A decorative process in which a colo(u)red design is applied to unglazed or glazed ceramic ware or glass by means of a transfer*] · Abziehverfahren n

decantation, decanting · Schlämmen n [*Das Abscheiden von Sand aus Ton, der dadurch fetter wird*]

~ test (US); sedimentation ~ · Absetzversuch m, Absetzprobe f, Absetzprüfung f, Sedimentationsprobe, Sedimentationsversuch, Sedimentierprobe, Sedimentierversuch, Sedimentierprüfung, Schlämmanalyse

decanting, decantation · Schlämmen n [*Das Abscheiden von Sand aus Ton, der dadurch fetter wird*]

decarburisation (Brit.); decarburization (US) · Entkohlung f

~ slag (Brit.); decarburization ~ (US) · Entkohlungsschlacke f

to decarburise (Brit.); to decarburize (US) · entkohlen

decastyle [*Having ten columns in front*] · dekastyl, zehnsäulig

~ [*A portico or colonnade having a row of ten front columns*] · Dekastylos m

~ temple · Dekastylostempel m, Tempel mit zehnsäuliger Giebelfront

to decay · abklingen [*Spannung*]

decay · Abklingen n

~ [*Disintergration of wood or other substance through the action of fungi*] · Pilzzerfall m

~ constant · Abklingkennwert m

~ factor · Abklingfaktor m

~ of sound · Schallabnahme f

~ period, ~ time · Abklingzeit f

~ time, ~ period · Abklingzeit f

decentralization · Entballung f

to decentralize · entballen

dechlorination · Entchlorung f

decibel, dB · db, Dezibel n, dB, 1/10 Bel

~ scale, dB ~ · Dezibelskala f

deck → (roof(ing)) substructure (system)

~ · Flachteil m, n [*Mansard(en)flachdach*]

~ dormer, ~ roof ~ · (Dach)Gaube f in Mansard(en)flachdachform, (Dach-)Gaupe f ~ ~

~ enamel, ~ paint, porch enamel [*It is used for boat decks, porch floors, and such*] · Überwasser(anstrich)farbe f

~ paint, ~ enamel, porch enamel [*It is used for boat decks, porch floors, and such*] · Überwasser(anstrich)farbe f

~ roof (US); mansard flat ~ (Brit.) [*It slopes in four directions, but has a deck at the top*] · Mansard(en)flachdach n

~ (~) dormer · (Dach)Gaube f in Mansard(en)flachdachform, (Dach)Gaupe f ~ ~

deck(ing) (system) → (roof(ing)) substructure (~)

decline, decrease, drop · Abfall m, Abnahme f, Rückgang m

~ in pressure, drop ~ ~, decrease ~ ~, pressure decline, pressure drop, pressure decrease · Druckrückgang m, Druckabfall m, Druckabnahme f

~ of stress → decrease ~ ~

decolourization (Brit.); decolorization (US) · Entfärbung f

to decolourize (Brit.); to decolorize (US) · entfärben

decolourizer (Brit.); decolorizer (US) · Entfärbungsmittel n, Entfärbemittel

decomposed · zersetzt

~ · zerlegt

decomposition · (Komponenten)Zerlegung f

~ · Zersetzung f

~ of a vector · Vektorzerlegung f

~ ~ forces · Kräftezerlegung f

to decontaminate · entseuchen

decontaminating installation, decontamination ~ · Entseuchungsanlage f

decontamination shower, decontaminating ~ · Giftdusche f

decorated, enriched, ornamented, adorned · geschmückt, geziert, verziert

~ arch · gezierter Bogen m, verzierter ~, besetzter ~

~ archivolt, ornamental ~, decorative ~ · ornamentierte Archivolte f, dekorierte ~, Schmuck-Archivolte, Zier-Archivolte, Dekor(ations)-Archivolte

~ area, decorative ~, ornamental ~ · Ornamentfläche f, Schmuckfläche, Zierfläche, Dekor(ations)fläche

~ ceiling, decorative ~, ornamental ~ · Dekor(ations)decke f, Zierdecke, Ornamentdecke, Schmuckdecke

~ door, decorative ~, ornamental ~ · Dekor(ations)tür f, Ziertür, Ornamenttür, Schmucktür

Decorated Style → Curvilinear ~

decorated surface — decorative element

decorated surface, ornamental ~, decorative ~ · Ornamentfläche f, Zierfläche, Schmuckfläche, Dekor(ations)fläche

~ **tile** → decorative ~

~ **with battlements** → battlemented

~ ~ **statues** · statuengeschmückt, statuenverziert

decorating, decoration · Dekorieren n, Verzieren, Ornamentieren

~ **art,** decorative ~, decoration ~, ornamental ~ · Ornamentik f, Zierkunst f, Ornamentkunst, dekorative Kunst

decoration, ornamentation · Dekor(ation) n, (f) [*Die Gesamtheit der „Ausschmückung" von Bauwerken, besonders von Innenräumen, im Gegensatz zum Ornament, das als einzelnes Schmuckmotiv nur ein Teil der Dekoration ist*]

~ → (decorative) pattern

~, decorating · Dekorieren n, Verzieren, Ornamentieren

~ **art,** decorating ~, decorative ~, ornamental ~ · Ornamentik f, Zierkunst f, Ornamentkunst, dekorative Kunst

decorative [*Pertaining to, or of the nature of, decoration*] · dekorativ

~ **acoustical gypsum pan(el) slab** → ornamental acoustical gypsum waffle ~

~ **aggregate,** ornamental ~ · Dekor(ations)zuschlag(stoff) m, Zierzuschlag(stoff), Dekor(ations)zuschlagmaterial n, Zierzuschlagmaterial

~ **aluminium,** ornamental ~ (Brit.); ~ aluminum (US) · Dekor(ations)aluminium n, Ornamentaluminium, Zieraluminium, Schmuckaluminium

~ **appearance** · dekoratives Aussehen n

~ **arch,** ornamental ~, decorated ~ · Dekor(ations)bogen m, Zierbogen, Ornamentbogen, Schmuckbogen

~ **architecture,** ornamental ~, florid ~ · Dekor(ations)architektur f, Ornamentarchitektur, Zierarchitektur, Schmuckarchitektur, Dekor(ations)baukunst f, Ornamentbaukunst, Zierbaukunst, Schmuckbaukunst

~ **archivolt,** ornamental ~, decorated ~ · ornamentierte Archivolte f, dekorierte ~, Schmuckarchivolte, Dekor(ations)archivolte, Zierarchivolte

~ **area,** ornamental ~, decorated ~ · Ornamentfläche f, Zierfläche, Schmuckfläche, Dekor(ations)fläche

~ **art,** decoration ~, decorating ~, ornamental ~ · Ornamentik f, Zierkunst f, Ornamentkunst, dekorative Kunst

~ **artificial stone** → ~ reconstructed ~

~ **band** → band ornament(al feature)

~ **barrel vault** → ornamental tunnel ~

~ **board,** ~ sheet, ornamental ~ · Dekor(ations)platte f, Zierplatte, Ornamentplatte, (dekorative) Sichtplatte, Schmuckplatte

~ **bond** → ~ masonry ~

~ **bracket** → ~ wall ~

~ **brick,** ornamental ~ · Dekor(ations)ziegel m, Zierziegel, Ornamentziegel, Schmuckziegel

~ ~ **masonry (work)** (US) → ~ (pattern) brickwork

~ **brickwork** → ~ (pattern) ~

~ **(building) unit** → ornamental (~) ~

~ **capacity** → ~ property

~ **cast block** → ~ (pre)cast (concrete) ~

~ ~ **(concrete) block** → ~ pre~ (~)

~ ~ **(~) product** → ~ precast (~) ~

~ ~ **(~) tile** → ~ (pre)cast (concrete) block

~ ~ **product** → ~ (pre)cast (concrete) ~

~ ~ **stone** → ~ reconstructed ~

~ ~ **tile** → ~ (pre)cast (concrete) block

~ **ceiling,** ornamental ~, decorated ~ · Dekor(ations)decke f, Zierdecke, Ornamentdecke, Schmuckdecke

~ ~ **board** → ~ sheet

~ ~ **sheet,** ornamental ~ ~, ~ ~ board · Deckenzierplatte f, Dekor(ations)deckenplatte, Dekorativdeckenplatte, Ornamentdeckenplatte, Zierdeckenplatte, Schmuckdeckenplatte, Deckenschmuckplatte, Deckenornamentplatte

~ **coat(ing),** ~ finish, ornamental ~ · Dekor(ations)beschichtung f, Dekor(ations)überzug m, Schmucküberzug, Zierbeschichtung, Zierüberzug, Ornamentbeschichtung, Ornamentüberzug, Schmuckbeschichtung [*als Schicht*]

~ **(cold-)water paint,** ~ water-carried ~, ornamental ~ ~ · Schmuck-Binderfarbe f, Schmuck-Dispersionsfarbe

~ **column,** ornamental ~ · Dekor(ations)stütze f, Zierstütze, Ornamentstütze, Schmuckstütze

~ **composition floor(ing),** ~ jointless ~, ~ in-situ ~, ~ seamless ~, ~ ~ floor cover(ing), ~ ~ floor finish · Ornament-Spachtel(fuß)boden(belag) m, Zier-Spachtel(fuß)boden(belag), Dekor(ations)-Spachtel(fuß)boden(belag)

~ **concrete,** ornamental ~ · Dekor(ations)beton m, Zierbeton, Ornamentbeton, Schmuckbeton

~ ~ **product** → ~ (pre)cast (~) ~

~ ~ **tile,** ornamental ~ ~ · Zier-Beton(belag)platte f, Zier-Betonfliese f, Dekor(ations)beton(belag)platte, Dekor(ations)betonfliese, Ornament-Beton(belag)platte, Ornament-Betonfliese, Schmuck-Beton(belag)platte, Schmuck-Betonfliese

~ **door,** ornamental ~, decorated ~ · Dekor(ations)tür f, Ziertür, Ornamenttür, Schmucktür

~ **element,** ornamental ~ · Ornamentglied n, Zierglied, Dekor(ations)glied, Schmuckglied, (architektonisches) Glied [*Fries, Stab, Karnies usw.*]

decorative embossment — decorative paint

~ **embossment,** ornamental ~ · Ornamentprägung f, Dekor(ations)prägung, Zierprägung, Schmuckprägung

~ **feature,** ornamental ~ · Ornamentelement n, Zierelement, Dekor(ations)element, Schmuckelement

~ **felt(ed fabric),** ornamental ~ (~) · Dekor(ations)filz m, Zierfilz, Ornamentfilz, Schmuckfilz

~ **finish,** ~ coat(ing), ornamental ~ · Ornamentbeschichtung f, Schmucküberzug m, Ornamentüberzug, Schmuckbeschichtung, Dekor(ations)beschichtung, Dekor(ations)überzug, Zierbeschichtung, Zierüberzug [*als Schicht*]

~ ~, ornamental ~ · Effekt(ver)putz m, Ornament(ver)putz, Dekor(ations)(ver)putz, Zier(ver)putz, Schmuck(ver)putz [*Oberbegriff für Innen- und Außen(ver)putz*]

(~) ~ → pattern

~ **fittings,** ~ hardware, ornamental ~ · Ornamentbeschläge mpl, Zierbeschläge, Dekor(ations)beschläge, Schmuckbeschläge

~ **fixture,** enrichment, ornament · Ornament n, Zierelement n, Zierglied n, Dekor(ations)element, Dekor(ations)glied, Schmuckglied, Schmuckelement, Verzierung f

~ ~ → ~ luminaire (~)

~ **floor cover(ing)** → ornamental floor(-ing)

~ ~ **finish** → ornamental floor(ing)

~ **floor(ing)** → ornamental ~

~ **foil,** ornamental ~ · Dekor(ations)folie f, Zierfolie, Ornamentfolie, Schmuckfolie

~ **form,** ornamental ~ · Ornamentform f, Schmuckform, Zierform, Dekor(ations)form, Verzierungsform

~ **gable,** ornamental ~ · Dekor(ations)giebel m, Ornamentgiebel, Schmuckgiebel, Ziergiebel

~ **glass** → pattern(ed) ~

~ ~ **block,** ~ ~ brick, ornamental ~ ~ · Dekor(ations)-Glas(bau)stein m, Schmuck-Glas(bau)stein, Zier-Glas(bau)stein, Ornament-Glas(bau)stein

~ ~ **brick** → ~ ~ block

~ **grille,** ornamental ~ [*A decorative openwork screen within an opening. Sometimes spelled 'grill'*] · Dekor(ations)gitter n, Ziergitter, Ornamentgitter, (Schmuck)Gitter

~ **hardware,** ornamental ~, ~ fittings · Ornamentbeschläge mpl, Zierbeschläge, Dekor(ations)beschläge, Schmuckbeschläge

~ **heavy ceramics,** ~ structural ~, ornamental ~ ~ · dekorative Baukeramik f, Zier-Baukeramik, Schmuck-Baukeramik, Dekor(ations)-Baukeramik

~ **hung ceiling** → ~ suspended ~

~ **in-situ floor(ing),** ~ jointless ~, ~ composition ~, ~ seamless ~, ~ floor cover(ing), ~ ~ floor finish · Ornament-Spachtel(fuß)boden(belag) m, Zier-Spachtel(fuß)boden(belag), Dekor(ations)-Spachtel(fuß)boden(belag)

~ **iron,** ornamental ~ · Dekor(ations)eisen n, Ziereisen, Ornamenteisen, Schmuckeisen

~ **ironwork,** ornamental ~ · Kunstschmiedearbeit(en) f(pl)

~ ~ **technique,** ~ ~ technic, ornamental ~ ~ · Kunstschmiedetechnik f

~ **joint,** ornamental ~ · Dekor(ations)fuge f, Zierfuge, Ornamentfuge, Schmuckfuge

~ **jointless floor(ing),** ~ in-situ ~, ~ composition ~, ~ seamless ~, ~ floor cover(ing), ~ ~ floor finish · Dekor(ations)-Spachtel(fuß)boden-(belag) m, Ornament-Spachtel(fuß)boden(belag), Zier-Spachtel(fuß)boden(belag)

~ **laminate(d) board,** ~ ~ sheet, ornamental ~ ~ · Ornament-Schichtpreßstoffplatte f, Dekor(ations)-Schichtpreßstorfplatte, Zier-Schichtpreßstoffplatte, Schmuck-Schichtpreßstoffplatte

~ **light fitting** (Brit.) → ~ luminaire (fixture)

~ **(light(ing)) fixture** → ~ luminaire (~)

~ **link,** ornamental ~ · Dekor(ations)zwischenglied n, Ornamentzwischenglied, Schmuckzwischenglied, Zierzwischenglied

~ **lock,** ornamental ~ · Dekor(ations)schloß n, Zierschloß, Ornamentschloß, Schmuckschloß

~ **luminaire (fixture),** ornamental ~ (~) (US); ~ light fitting (Brit.); ~ (light(ing)) fixture · Dekor(ations)leuchte f, Zierleuchte, Ornamentleuchte, Schmuckleuchte

~ **(masonry) bond,** ornamental (~) ~ · Dekor(ations)verband m, Zierverband, Ornamentverband, Schmuckverband [*Mauerwerk*]

~ **metal,** ornamental ~ · Dekor(ations)metall n, Ornamentmetall, Schmuckmetall

~ **modelled coat** (Brit.) → ornamental ~ ~

~ ~ **stuccowork** (Brit.) → ornamental ~ ~

~ **motif,** ornamental ~ · Ornamentmotiv n, Schmuckmotiv, Dekor(ations)motiv, Ziermotiv

~ ~ **taken from nature,** ornamental ~ ~ ~ ~ · Ornamentmotiv n aus der Natur, Schmuckmotiv ~ ~ ~, Ziermotiv ~ ~ ~, Dekor(ations)motiv ~ ~ ~

~ **nail,** ornamental ~ · Schmucknagel m, Ziernagel, Ornamentnagel, Dekor(ations)nagel

~ **niche,** ornamental ~ · Ziernische f, Schmucknische, Dekor(ations)nische, Ornamentnische

~ **paint,** ornamental ~ · Schmuck(an-strich)farbe f, Verzierungs(anstrich)farbe

decorative painting — decorative tablet

~ **painting**, ornamental ~ · Schmuckmalerei *f*

~ **panel**, ornamental ~ · Ornamenttafel *f*, Ziertafel, Dekor(ations)tafel, Schmucktafel

~ **patent stone** → ~ reconstructed ~

(~) **pattern**, (~) finish, ornamental ~, decoration, decorative feature, ornament(al feature), enrichment · Dekor(ation) *n, m, (f)*, Ornament(ierung) *n, (f)*, Schmuck *m*, Verzierung, Muster(ung) *n, (f)*

~ ~, ornamental ~ · Ornamentmuster *n*, Schmuckmuster, Ziermuster, Dekor(ations)muster

~ (~) **brickwork**, (ornamental) ~ ~, ornamental ~; decorative (pattern) brick masonry (work), ornamental brick masonry (work), (ornamental) pattern brick masonry (work) (US) Ornamentziegelmauerwerk *n*, Zierziegelmauerwerk, Dekor(ations)ziegelmauerwerk, Schmuckziegelmauerwerk

~ **pavilion**, ornamental ~, casino Zierpavillon *m*, Schmuckpavillon

~ **paving** → ~ sett ~

~ **perforation**, ornamental ~ · Dekor(ations)lochung *f*, Zierlochung, Ornamentlochung, Schmucklochung

~ **plastic board** → ornamental ~ ~

~ **plastic-faced board**, ~ ~ sheet · Platte *f* mit kunstharzgetränkter Dekorpapierbeschichtung

~ **plastic-faced wall board**, ~ ~ ~ sheet · Wandplatte *f* mit kunstharzgetränkter Dekorpapierbeschichtung

~ **plastic film**, ~ ~ sheeting, ornamental ~ ~ · Dekor(ations)folie *f* aus Kunststoff, Zierfolie ~ ~, Ornamentfolie ~ ~, Schmuckfolie ~ ~

~ ~ **sheet** → ornamental plastic board

~ ~ **sheeting**, ~ ~ film, ornamental ~ ~ · Ornamentfolie *f* aus Kunststoff, Zierfolie ~ ~, Dekor(ations)folie ~ ~, Schmuckfolie ~ ~

~ **pool**, ornamental ~ · Dekor(ations)becken *n*, Zierbecken, Ornamentbecken, Schmuckbecken

~ **portal**, ornamental ~ · Schmuckportal *n*, Zierportal

~ **power** → ~ property

~ **(pre)cast (concrete) block**, ornamental ~ (~) ~, ~ ~ (~) tile [*See remark under 'Block'*] · Beton-Dekor(ations)block(stein) *m*, Beton-Ornamentblock(stein), Beton-Zierblock(stein), Beton-Schmuckblock(stein)

~ ~ (~) **product**, ornamental ~ (~) ~, ~ concrete ~ · dekorativer Betonstein *m*, dekoratives Betonerzeugnis *n*, Ornament-Betonerzeugnis, Ornament-Betonstein, Zier-Betonerzeugnis, Zier-Betonstein, Schmuck-Betonerzeugnis, Schmuck-Betonstein

~ ~ (~) **tile** → ~ ~ (~) block

~ ~ **product** → ~ ~ (concrete) ~

~ ~ **tile** → ~ ~ (concrete) block

~ **property**, ~ capacity, ~ quality, ~ power, ornamental ~ · Dekor(ations)-eigenschaft *f*, Dekor(ations)fähigkeit, Dekor(ations)vermögen *n*

~ **quality** → ~ property

~ **railing**, ornamental ~ · Dekor(ations)geländer *n*, Ziergeländer, Ornamentgeländer, Schmuckgeländer

~ **reconstituted stone** → ~ reconstructed ~

~ **reconstructed stone**, ~ cast ~, ~ patent ~, ~ artificial ~, ornamental ~ ~, ~ reconstituted ~ · Ornament-Betonwerkstein *m*, dekorativer Betonwerkstein, Zier-Betonwerkstein, Schmuck-Betonwerkstein [*Fehlnamen: Ornament-Kunststein, dekorativer Kunststein, Zier-Kunststein, Schmuck-Kunststein*]

~ **rib**, ornamental ~ · Dekor(ations)rippe *f*, Zierrippe, Schmuckrippe, Ornamentrippe

~ ~, ornamental ~ · Gurtrippe *f* [*Bei einem Kranzstein oder einer Konsole*]

~ **ro(w)lock paving**, ornamental ~ ~ · zierendes Rollschichtpflaster *n*, ~ Rollscharfpflaster, dekoratives ~

~ **SC** → ~ suspended ceiling

~ **screen**, ornamental ~ · Schauwand *f* [*z.B. ein Retabel*]

~ **seamless floor(ing)**, ~ in-situ ~, ~ jointless ~, ~ composition ~, ~ floor cover(ing), ~ floor finish · Ornament-Spachtel(fuß)boden(belag) *m*, Zier-Spachtel(fuß)boden(belag), Dekor(ations)-Spachtel(fuß)boden(belag)

~ **(sett) paving**, ornamental (~) ~ · Dekor(ations)pflaster(decke) *n, (f)*, Zierpflaster(decke), Ornamentpflaster(-decke), Schmuckpflaster(decke)

~ **sheet**, ~ board, ornamental ~ · Ornamentplatte *f*, Zierplatte, Dekor(ations)platte, (dekorative) Sichtplatte, Schmuckplatte

~ **sintered glass**, ornamental ~ ~ · Glaspaste *f*

~ **steel**, ornamental ~ · Dekor(ations)stahl *m*, Zierstahl, Ornamentstahl, Schmuckstahl

~ **structural ceramics**, ~ heavy ~, ornamental ~ ~ · dekorative Baukeramik *f*, Zier-Baukeramik, Schmuck-Baukeramik, Dekor(ations)-Baukeramik

~ **structure**, ornamental ~ · Zierbau(-werk) *m, (n)*

~ **style**, ornamental ~ · Ornamentstil *m*, Schmuckstil, Dekor(ations)stil, Zierstil

~ **surface**, ornamental ~ · Dekor(ations)oberfläche *f*, Zieroberfläche, Ornamentoberfläche, Schmuckoberfläche

~ **suspended ceiling**, ornamental ~ ~, ~ hung ~, ~ SC · Dekor(ations)-hängedecke *f*, Zierhängedecke, Schmuckhängedecke, Ornamenthängedecke

~ **tablet** → ornamental ~

decorative tile — deficiency of water

~ tile, ornamental ~, decorated ~ · Dekor(ations)fliese *f*, Dekor(ations)(belag)platte *f*, Zierfliese, Zier(belag)platte, Ornamentfliese, Ornament(belag)platte, Schmuckfliese, Schmuck(belag)platte, dekorierte (Belag)Platte, dekorierte Fliese, ornamentierte (Belag-)Platte, ornamentierte Fliese

~ touch, ornamental ~ · dekorativer Anklang *m*

~ tower, ornamental ~ · Zierturm *m*, Schmuckturm

~ town gateway → ornamental ~ ~

~ trim, ornamental ~ · Ziereinfassung *f*, Schmuckeinfassung, Dekor(ations)einfassung, Ornamenteinfassung, Simswerk *n*

~ tunnel vault → ornamental ~ ~

(~) turret, ornamental ~, diminutive tower, small tower · kleiner (Zier)Turm *m*, (Zier)Türmchen *n*

~ unit → ornamental (building) ~

~ vault, ornamental ~ · dekoratives Gewölbe *n*, Ziergewölbe, Schmuckgewölbe, Ornamentgewölbe, Dekor(ations)gewölbe

~ wagon vault → ornamental tunnel ~

~ wall, ornamental ~ · Dekor(ations)wand *f*, Ornamentwand, Zierwand, Schmuckwand

~ (~) bracket, ornamental (~) ~ · Dekor(ations)(wand)konsole *f*, Schmuck(wand)konsole, Zier(wand)konsole, Ornament(wand)konsole

~ water-carried paint, ~ (cold-)water ~, ornamental ~ ~ · Schmuck-Binderfarbe *f*, Schmuck-Dispersionsfarbe

~ water paint, ~ cold-~ ~, watercarried ~, ornamental ~ ~ · Schmuck-Binderfarbe *f*, Schmuck-Dispersionsfarbe

~ window, ornamental ~ · Dekor(ations)fenster *n*, Zierfenster, Ornamentfenster, Schmuckfenster

~ wire(d) glass → figure(d) ~ ~

~ work, ornamental ~ · Schmuckarbeit *f*, Ornamentarbeit, Zierarbeit, Dekor(ations)arbeit

decrease, drop, decline · Abnahme *f*, Abfall *m*, Rückgang *m*

~ · Verringerung *f*

~ in pressure, decline ~ ~, drop ~ ~, pressure decline, pressure drop, pressure decrease · Druckrückgang *m*, Druckabfall *m*, Druckabnahme *f*

~ ~ volume, volume decrease · Volumenverringerung *f*, Raumverringerung

~ of stress, drop ~ ~, decline ~ ~, stress decrease, stress decline, stress drop · Spannungsrückgang *m*, Spannungsabfall *m*, Spannungsabnahme *f*

dedicatory inscription · Widmung(sinschrift) *f*

deep beam · hoher Balken(träger) *m*

~ channel (section) · hohes U-Profil *n*

~ cleaning · Tiefenreinigung *f*

~ cut → cut glass

~ drawing, DD · Tiefziehen *n*

deep-drawing quality, DD ~ · Tiefziehgüte *f*

deep-drawn, DD · tiefgezogen

deep etching [*deprecated: rotting*] · Tiefätze *f* [*Säurebehandlung von Glas*]

deep-etching paste · Streichtief *n* [*Säurebehandlung von Glas*]

deep girder · hoher Träger *m*

~ green pigment · Tiefgrün(pigment) *n*

~ Indian red pigment · Tiefindischrot(-pigment) *n*

~ lattice(d) girder · hoher Gitterträger *m*

~ penetration test, cone ~ ~ · Kegeleindring(ungs)probe *f*, Kegeleindring(ungs)versuch *m*, Kegeleindring(ungs)prüfung *f*

deep-ribbed slab, T(ee)-beam slab with deep ribs · Rippenplatte *f* mit hohen Rippen

deep seal trap [*A trap having a water seal 3 in. or more deep*] · (Wasser-)(Geruch)Verschluß *m* mit großer (Wasser)Verschlußhöhe

~ webbed · hochstegig [*Träger*]

deeply model(l)ed concrete [*for the façades of buildings*] · tief gegliederter Beton *m*

defacement · Beschädigung *f*

defect, fault · Fehler *m*, Mangel *m*

defective, faulty, unsound · fehlerhaft, mangelhaft, schadhaft

defence (Brit.); **defense** · Einfriedigung *f*, Befriedung, Einfriedung

~ parapet (Brit.); defense ~ · Brustwehr *f*

~ wall (Brit.); defense ~ · Einfriedigungsmauer *f*, Einfriedungsmauer

defense; defence (Brit.) · Einfried(ig)ung *f*, Befriedung

~ parapet; defence ~ (Brit.) · Brustwehr *f*

~ wall; defence ~ (Brit.) · Einfriedigungsmauer *f*, Einfriedungsmauer

defensive gateway, fortified town gate · Befestigungsstadttor *n*, Verteidigungsstadttor, befestigtes Stadttor

~ (masonry) wall, battlemented (~) ~, fortification (~) ~ · Befestigungsmauer *f*, Verteidigungsmauer

~ tower, battlemented ~ · Verteidigungsturm *m*, Befestigungsturm

~ wall → ~ masonry ~

~ work → fortification

deferrization, iron elimination, iron removal · (Wasser)Enteisenung *f*

deficiency, shortage · Mangel *m*, Fehlbedarf *m*, Klemme *f*

~ of water, shortage ~ ~, water shortage, water deficiency · Wassermangel *m*, Wasserfehlbedarf *m*, Wasserklemme *f*

defining space with one spherical surface · Raumbildung *f* mit einer Kugelfläche
definite integral · bestimmtes Integral *n*
definition, clarity · Klangreinheit *f*
deflatable rubber tube, inflatable ~ ~, ~ ~ core · Gummischlauchschalung *f*
to deflect, to raise, to bend up, to drape · ablenken, anheben [*Litze in der Spannbetontechnik*]
deflected area, deflective ~ · Durchbiegungsfläche *f*, Durchsenkungsfläche
~-cable technique → deflected-strand ~
deflected-strand technique, draped-strand ~, raised-strand ~, deflected-cable ~, raised-cable ~, ~ technic, bending-up ~ · (Litzen)Anhebenverfahren *n*, (Litzen)Ablenkverfahren [*Spannbeton*]
deflecting force · Ablenkungskraft *f*
deflection, deflection, downward ~ · Durchbiegung *f*, Durchsenkung
~ curve, deflexion ~, elastic ~ · Biegelinie *f*, Biegungslinie [*Elastische Linie eines Balkens oder Trägers*]
~ formula, deflexion ~ · Durchbiegungsformel *f*, Durchsenkungsformel
~ theory, deflexion ~ · Durchbiegungstheorie *f*, Durchsenkungstheorie
deflective area, deflected ~ · Durchbiegungsfläche *f*, Durchsenkungsfläche
deflectometer · Durchbiegungsmesser *m*
deflexion, deflection, downward ~ · Durchsenkung *f*, Durchbiegung
~ curve, deflection ~, elastic ~ · Biegelinie *f*, Biegungslinie [*Elastische Linie eines Balkens oder Trägers*]
~ formula, deflection ~ · Durchsenkungsformel *f*, Durchbiegungsformel
~ theory, deflection ~ · Durchbiegungstheorie *f*, Durchsenkungstheorie
deflocculant, deflocculating agent · Aufschlußmittel *n*, Verflüssigungsmittel [*Steinzeugindustrie*]
~, deflocculating agent · Ausfäll(ungs)-mittel *n* [*Anstrichtechnik*]
to deflocculate, to dissolve, to disintegrate · aufschließen, verflüssigen [*Steinzeugindustrie*]
deflocculating agent → deflocculant
deflocculation, disintegration, dissolving · Aufschließung *f*, Verflüssigung, Aufschluß *m* [*Steinzeugindustrie*]
~ · Ausfällen *n* [*Anstrichtechnik*]
defoamant, antifoam (agent), antifoam aid, antifoaming agent, antifoaming aid · Antischaummittel *n*, Schaumdämpfer *m*, Schaumverhütungsmittel, Schaumverhinderungsmittel, Entschäumungsmittel
to deform · verformen
deformability due to axial force(s) · Axialkraftverformbarkeit *f*
~ ~ ~ bending · Biegeverformbarkeit *f*

~ ~ ~ shear(ing) force(s) · Schubkraftverformbarkeit *f*
deformable · verformbar
deformation · Formänderung *f*, Verformung, Gestaltänderung
~, deforming · Verformen *n*
~ action, deforming ~ · Formänderungswirkung *f*, Verformungswirkung, Gestaltänderungswirkung
~ angle, angle of deformation · Formänderungswinkel *m*, Verformungswinkel
~ condition, deforming ~ · Deformationsbedingung *f*, Verformungsbedingung, Formänderungsbedingung, Gestaltänderungsbedingung
~ direction, direction of deformation · Formänderungsrichtung *f*, Verformungsrichtung
~ during burning · Brandverzug *m*, Verziehen *n* im Feuer [*Keramik*]
~ effect, deforming ~ · Formänderungsauswirkung *f*, Gestaltänderungsauswirkung, Verformungsauswirkung, Deformationsauswirkung
~ energy · Gestaltänderungsenergie *f*, Formänderungsenergie, Verformungsenergie
~ limit state, limit state of deformation · Verformungs-Grenzzustand *m*
~ modulus, modulus of deformation · Formänderungsmodul *m*, Verformungsmodul, Gestaltänderungsmodul
~ state, state of deformation · Formänderungszustand *m*, Verformungszustand, Gestaltänderungszustand
~ ~, second-order ~ [*Initial deformations are taken into account*] · (Spannungs-)Theorie *f* 2. Ordnung, linearisierte Verformungstheorie
~ under heat · Wärmeformänderung *f*, Wärmeverformung
~ ~ load · Lastformänderung *f*, Lastverformung
~ work, work of deformation · Formänderungsarbeit *f*, Verformungsarbeit, Gestaltänderungsarbeit
deformed · verformt
~ (concrete) bars grade III b → (twisted-type) deformed (concrete) reinforcing ~ ~, ~
~ (~) (reinforcing) bars, twisted-type (~) (~) ~, high-bond (~) (~), ~ (~) (~) rods · (Beton)Formstahl *m*
~ (~)(~) ~ grade III b with oblique sickleshaped ribs, twisted-type ~ (~) (~) ~ ~ ~ ~ ~ ~ ~ ~ · (Beton)Formstahl *m* der Betonstahlgüte III b mit schrägen sichelförmigen Rippen
~ Tor-Steel, twisted(-type) ~ ~ · Rippen-Torstahl *m*
deforming, deformation · Verformen *n*
~ action, deformation ~ · Formänderungswirkung *f*, Verformungswirkung, Gestaltänderungswirkung
~ condition, deformation ~ · Deformationsbedingung *f*, Verformungsbedingung, Formänderungsbedingung, Gestaltänderungsbedingung

deforming effect — to deionize

~ effect, deformation ~ · Formänderungsauswirkung f, Gestaltänderungsauswirkung, Verformungsauswirkung, Deformationsauswirkung

de-frosting · Abtauen n

degenerated · entartet, verkümmert

dégras-oil, distilled-grease olein, dégras-oil · Wollfett-Olein n

to degrease · entfetten

degreasing · Entfetten n, Entfettung f

~ installation · Entfettungsanlage f

degree-day · (Heiz)Gradtag m [*Eine Zahl, die sich aus der Multiplikation des Temperaturunterschiedes zwischen Innen- und mittlerer Außentemperatur mit der Zahl der Heiztage ergibt*]

degree of angle of obstruction · Verbauungswinkelgrad m [*Tageslichtberechnung*]

~ ~ brick burning, ~ ~ clay ~ ~ · Ziegelbrenngrad m

~ ~ brightness, brightness degree · Helligkeitsgrad m

~ ~ (clay) brick burning · Ziegelbrenngrad m

~ ~ damping, damping degree · Dämpfungsgrad m

~ ~ dissociation, dissociation degree · Dissoziationsgrad m

~ ~ dullness, ~ ~ mattness · Vermattungsgrad m

~ ~ fastness, ~ ~ resistance, resistance degree, fastness degree · Widerstandsgrad m, Festigkeitsgrad, Beständigkeitsgrad

~ ~ fineness, fineness degree · Feinheitsgrad m

~ ~ freedom, freedom degree, DF · Freiheitsgrad m

~ ~ glossiness, glossiness degree · Glanzgrad m

~ ~ hardening, hardening degree · (Er)Härtungsgrad m

~ ~ hardness, hardness degree · Härtegrad m

~ ~ hydration, hydration degree · Hydra(ta)tionsgrad m

~ ~ impregnation, impregnation degree · Tränk(ungs)grad m, Imprägnier(ungs)-grad

~ ~ indeterminacy · Unbestimmtheitsgrad m

~ ~ lime saturation, lime saturation degree · Kalksättigungsgrad m

~ ~ mattness, ~ ~ dullness · Vermattungsgrad m

~ ~ nitration · Nitrierungsstufe f

~ ~ purity · Reinheitsgrad m

~ ~ redundancy · Überzähligkeitsgrad m

~ ~ resistance, ~ ~ fastness, resistance degree, fastness degree · Widerstandsgrad m, Festigkeitsgrad, Beständigkeitsgrad

~ ~ rusting, rusting degree · Rostgrad m

~ ~ saturation, saturation degree · Volltränk(ungs)grad m, Vollimprägnier(ungs)grad

~ ~ settling of traffic paint · Absetzgrad m von Markierungsfarbe

~ ~ slenderness, slenderness degree · Schlankheitsgrad m

~ ~ stability, stability degree · Stabilitätsgrad m, Beständigkeitsgrad [*Emulsion*]

~ ~ temperature, temperature degree · Temperaturgrad m

~ ~ tightness, tightness degree · Dichtigkeitsgrad m, Dichtheitsgrad

~ ~ torsion, ~ ~ twist(ing), torsion degree, twist(ing) degree · Verdrehungsgrad m, Torsionsgrad, Verwindungsgrad, Drill(ungs)grad

~ ~ twist(ing) → ~ ~ torsion

dehumidification, dehumidifying · Entfeuchten n, Entfeuchtung f, Feuchtigkeitsentzug m, Feuchteentzug

dehumidifier · Entfeuchter m, Entfeuchtungsgerät n

to dehumidify · entfeuchten

dehumidifying, dehumidification · Entfeuchten n, Entfeuchtung f, Feuchtigkeitsentzug m, Feuchteentzug

to dehydrate [*To remove water, or its constituents, in a chemical combination*] · entwässern, dehydratisieren

dehydrated · entwässert, dehydratisiert

~ castor oil, D.C.O. · dehydratisiertes Ricinusöl n, entwässertes ~, Ricinenöl

~ ~ ~ alkyd, D.C.O. · dehydratisiertes Ricinusölalkyd n, entwässertes ~, Ricinenölalkyd

~ oil · dehydratisiertes Öl n, entwässertes ~

~ water-gas tar · Kohlenwassergasteer m

dehydrating → dehydration

~ agent, dehydrator · Anhydrisierungsmittel n

dehydration, dehydrating [*The removal of water, or of its constituents, in a chemical combination*] · Dehydration f, Wasserentzug m, Entwässerung f, Dehydratisierung

~ of air, dehydrating ~ ~ · Luftentfeuchtung f

~ test · Entwässerungsprobe f, Entwässerungsversuch m, Entwässerungsprüfung f [*Bitumenemulsion*]

dehydrator, dehydrating agent · Anhydrisierungsmittel n

de-icing salt, ice-melting ~ · (Auf-)Tausalz n

~ ~ solution, ice-melting ~ ~ · (Auf-)Tausalzlösung f

deionization · Entionisierung f

to deionize · entionisieren

delamination · Klaffer m [*Verbundglas*]
~ [*The separation of layers in a laminated assembly*] · Schicht(en)ablösung f

delay, holding · Vorlagerung f, VL [*Dampfbehandlung von Beton*]

~ **period** → presteaming ~

delayed closing · gebremstes Schließen n [*Tür*]

deleterious matter → ~ substance

~ **salt, aggressive** ~ · angreifendes Salz n, aggressives ~, schädliches ~, Schadsalz

~ **substance, aggressive** ~, ~ matter · Schadstoff m, angreifender Stoff, schädlicher Stoff

~ **water, aggressive** ~ · aggressives Wasser n, angreifendes ~, schädliches ~, Schadwasser

delft pottery, Delft, delftware · Delfter Kacheln fpl und Delfter Wandplatten fpl, ~ Fayence f, ~ Ware f

delineator · Leitpflock m, Leitpfosten m [*Straße*]

deliquescence, liquefying · Zerfließen n, Flüssigwerden n

delivered site, free ~ · frei Baustelle

delivery, supply · (An)Lieferung f

~ **floor** → supply ~

~ **ramp, supply** ~ · Liefer(anten)rampe f, (An)Lieferungsrampe

~ **stall** · Ausfahrtstand m [*Parkhaus*]

~ **story** (US) → supply floor

Delta metal · Delta-Metall n [*Bezeichnung für hochfeste Sondermessinge mit warmem Bronzeton und guter Witterungsbeständigkeit*]

demand point, consumption ~, point of consumption, point of demand · Abnehmer m, Verbrauchsstelle f [*Wasser; Strom; Gas; Dampf; Druckluft*]

demanganization, manganese removal, manganese elimination · (Wasser-)Entmanganung f

demanganize · entmanganieren [*Wasser*]

dematerialized multiformity · entmaterialisierte Vielglei(ch)rigkeit f

demi-bastion [*A work with one face and one flank*] · Halbbastion f

demi-bath(tub), hip bath(tub) · Sitzbad(ewanne) n, (f)

demi-column [*A column half sunk into a wall*] · Halbsäule f

demi-double thickness; ~ **strength** (US) · MD, mittlere Dicke f [*Tafelglas*]

demi-metope, semi-metope · Halbmetope f, Halbzwischenfeld n

demineralization, desalting, desalination, water ~ · (Wasser)Entsalzung f

demineralizer · (Wasser)Entsalzungsgerät n

demirelief · Halbrelief n

D(E)ML, demolition, wrecking, demolishing; demolishment [*now rare*] · Abreißen n, Abbruch m, Einreißen, Niederreißen, Abbrechen [*Bauwerk*]

to demolish, to wreck · abbrechen, abreißen, einreißen, niederreißen [*Bauwerk*]

demolishable, condemned, fit for demolition, fit for wrecking · abbruchreif, abreißreif

demolisher, wrecker, mattock man, topman · (Gebäude)Abbrucharbeiter m, Hausabbrucharbeiter

demolishing → demolition

demolishment → demolition

demolition, wrecking, demolishing, D(E)ML; demolishment [*now rare*] · Abbruch m, Abreißen n, Abbrechen, Einreißen, Niederreißen [*Bauwerk*]

~ **contract,** wrecking ~ · Abbruchvertrag m, Abreißvertrag

~ **contractor,** wrecking ~ · Abbruchunternehmer m

~ **permission,** wrecking ~ · Abbruchgenehmigung f, Abreißgenehmigung

~ **permit,** wrecking ~ · Abbrucherlaubnis f, Abbruchschein m

~ **project,** wrecking ~, ~ scheme · Abbruchvorhaben n, Abreißvorhaben

~ **rubble** (Brit.), ~ rubbish (US) · Abbruchschutt m, Abbruchtrümmer f, Abbruchmaterial n, Abreißschutt, Abreißtrümmer, Abreißmaterial

~ **scheme** → ~ project

~ **site,** wrecking ~ · Abbruchstelle f, Abreißstelle

~ **spoil** (Brit.) → ~ rubbish

(~) **waste** → ~ rubbish

~ **work,** wrecking ~ · Abbrucharbeit(en) f(pl), Abreißarbeit(en) [*DIN 4420*]

demonstration building, ~ block · Demonstrationsgebäude n, Demonstrativgebäude

~ **kitchen** · Vorführungsküche f

demoulding (Brit.); demolding (US) · Ausformen n, Entformen [*Betonsteinindustrie*]

~ **agent** (Brit.); demolding ~ (US) · Ausformungsmittel n, Entformungsmittel [*Betonsteinindustrie*]

to demount [*obsolete*]; to dismount · demontieren

demountability [*obsolete*]; dismountability · Demontierbarkeit f

demountable [*obsolete*]; dismountable · demontierbar

~ **connection,** ~ joint [*obsolete*]; dismountable ~ · lösbare Verbindung f

~ **partition** [*obsolete*]; dismountable ~, movable ~ · versetzbare (Montage)Trennwand f

~ **partitioning** [*obsolete*]; dismountable ~ · versetzbare Trennwände fpl

~ **division wall** [*obsolete*] → dismountable partition ~

demountable joint — depth of a room

~ **joint,** ~ connection [*obsolete*]; dismountable ~ · lösbare Verbindung *f*

~ **partition (wall)** [*obsolete*] → dismountable ~ (~)

demulsibility · Entemulgierbarkeit *f*

denaturated alcohol · denaturierter Alkohol *m*, vergällter ~

dense, ~-graded, close-graded · dicht, hohlraumarm, geschlossen (abgestuft)

~ **aggregate** → ~-graded mineral ~

~ **(~) concrete** [*Concrete containing a minimum of voids*] · Beton *m* mit geschlossenem Gefüge

dense(-graded), close-graded · dicht, hohlraumarm, geschlossen (abgestuft)

~ **(mineral) aggregate,** close-graded (~) ~, DGA · dichte Mineralmasse *f*, hohlraumarme ~, geschlossene ~, geschlossene abgestufte ~, dichtes Mineralgemisch *n*, hohlraumarmes Mineralgemisch, geschlossenes (abgestuftes) Mineralgemisch

densified plywood, superpressed ~, high density ~ · Preßsperrholz *n*, PSP *n*, verdichtetes Sperrholz [*Es entsteht durch Warmpressen dünner Furniere mit dazwischenliegenden härtbaren Kunstharzen*]

~ **wood,** superpressed ~, high density ~ · Preßvollholz *n*, PVH, verdichtetes Vollholz

~ ~ **door,** superpressed ~ ~, high density ~ ~ · Preßvollholztür *f*, Vollholzpreßtür, PVH-Tür

densifier → (integral) waterproof(ing) agent

densifying admix(ture) → (integral) waterproof(ing) agent

~ **agent** → (integral) waterproof(ing) ~

density, specific gravity, volume weight [*deprecated: box weight. The weight of a body per unit of volume*] · Wichte *f*, spezifisches Gewicht *n*, Gewicht je Raumeinheit [*früher: Raumgewicht g/cm₃; t/m₃*]

~ **bottle,** weighing ~, (fruit jar) pycnometer · (Flaschen)Pyknometer *n*

~ **of buildings** · Bebauungsdichte *f*

dental clinic · Zahnklinik *f*

denticle, dentil [*A small square block used in series in Ionic, Corinthian, composite, and more rarely Doric cornices*] · Zahn *m*

~ **frieze** → zigzag ~

denticular, finely toothed, denticulate(d), having dentils · (fein)gezahnt

~ **cornice** · Zahn(ge)sims *m*, (*n*) [*dorische Säule*]

denticulate(d), denticular, finely toothed, having dentils · (fein)gezahnt

denticulation, dentil band, dentil course · Zahnschnitt *m*, Zahnreihe *f*

~ · [*Gezahnte Anschlußstelle für eine später hochzuführende Mauer*] Verzahnung *f*

~ **corona** · Zahnschnittcorona *f*, Zahnschnittkorona

dentil, denticle [*A small square block used in series in Ionic, Corinthian, composite, and more rarely Doric cornices*] · Zahn *m*

~ **band,** ~ course, denticulation · Zahnschnitt *m*, Zahnreihe *f*

~ **course,** ~ band, denticulation · Zahnschnitt *m*, Zahnreihe *f*

~ **frieze,** dentils · (Zahn)Schnittfries *m*, deutsches Band *n* [*Dieser speziell im Backsteinbau vorkommende Fries besteht aus einer Schicht über Eck gelegter Steine, wobei ihre Vorderkanten nicht über die Mauerfläche vorstehen*]

dentils → dentil frieze

deodorization, deodorizing · Geruchbeseitigung *f*

deodorizing, deodorization · Geruchbeseitigung *f*

~ **material** · Geruchbeseitigungsmaterial *n*

department · Abteilung *f*

~ **block,** faculty ~, ~ building · Fakultätsbau *m*, Fakultätsgebäude *n* [*Hochschule*]

~ **building,** faculty ~, ~ block · Fakultätsbau *m*, Fakultätsgebäude *n* [*Hochschule*]

~ **of architecture** · Architekturabteilung *f*

Department of Architecture, Civil Engineering and Building Construction · Fakultät *f* für Architektur und Bauwesen

~ ~ **Building and Housing** · Fakultät *f* für Hochbau und Wohnungswesen

department(al) store · Kaufhaus *n*, Warenhaus

~ ~ **passenger elevator** (US); ~ ~ ~ lift (Brit.) · Kaufhaus-Fahrstuhl *m*, Warenhaus-Fahrstuhl, Warenhaus-Personenaufzug *m*, Kaufhaus-Personenaufzug

departure lounge · Abflughalle *f* [*Flughafen*]

~ **platform** · Abfahrtbahnsteig *m*

dependent block → ~ building

~ **building,** subordinate ~, ancillary ~, accessory ~, ~ block · Nebengebäude *n*

deposited drawings, ~ plans · eingereichte Pläne *mpl*, vorgelegte ~ [*Der Baugenehmigungsbehörde vorgelegte Pläne*]

depressed arch → four-centred ~

depth · Tiefe *f*

~, thickness · Dicke *f*, (Konstruktions-)Höhe *f*, Bauhöhe; Stärke *f* [*Fehlname*] [*Träger; Decke; Platte*]

~ **effect** · Tiefenwirkung *f*

~ **measurement** · Höhenmessung *f* [*Ziegel; Block*]

~ **of a room** · Raumtiefe *f*

depth of arch — design load

~ ~ **arch**, thickness ~ ~ · Bogendicke *f*, Bogen(konstruktions)höhe *f*, Bogenbauhöhe; Bogenstärke *f* [*Fehlname*] [*Höhe der Vorderfläche eines Bogens*]

~ ~ **foundation**, foundation depth · Gründungstiefe *f*

~ ~ **penetration**, penetration depth · Eindring(ungs)tiefe *f*

~ ~ **seal**, ~ ~ water ~, ~ ~ trap ~ · (Wasser)Verschlußhöhe *f* [*Geruchverschluß*]

~ (~ **the corrugation(s)**), pitch (~ ~ ~) · Wellenhöhe *f* [*Wellplatte; Welltafel*]

~ ~ **trap seal**, ~ ~ (water) ~ · (Wasser)Verschlußhöhe *f* [*Geruchverschluß*]

~ ~ **(water) seal**, ~ ~ trap ~ · (Wasser)Verschlußhöhe *f* [*Geruchverschluß*]

depth-to-span ratio · Konstruktionshöhen-Spannweiten-Verhältnis *n*

derivation · Ableitung *f* [*eines Gesetzes in der Baustatik*]

derivative form · abgeleitete Form *f*

derived function, differential quotient · Differentialquotient *m*

~ **product** · Abkömmling *m*, Derivat *n*

derusting agent, rust remover · Rostentfernungsmittel *n*, Entrostungsmittel, Abrostungsmittel, Rostbeseitigungsmittel

desalination, demineralisation, desalting, water ~ · (Wasser)Entsalzung *f*

desalting, desalination, demineralization, water ~ · (Wasser)Entsalzung *f*

to descale, to remove scale · abzundern, entzundern

descaling, scale removal, removal of scale [*Removal of surface scale from a hot worked or heat treated product by pickling, shot-blasting, oxy-gas flame etc. Also removal of scale during hot working by the application of water, coal-dust, brushwood, oil etc.*] · Abzundern *n*, Abzunderung *f*, Entzundern, Entzunderung

description of work content · Baubeschreibung *f*

descriptive geometry, three-dimensional ~, solid ~ · darstellende Geometrie *f*

desecrated church · profanierte Kirche *f*

'desert concrete' [*Compound of large rough blocks of local stone with a minimum of cement binding. Used by Frank Lloyd Wright*] · „Wüstenbeton" *m*

~ **residence** · Wüstenschloß *n*

to design · durchformen

~ ~ · auslegen, bemessen, dimensionieren

~ ~ · entwerfen, konstruieren

design, DSGN · Dimensionierung *f*, Bemessung, Auslegung [*Rechnerische Ermittl(e)lung der Querschnittsabmessungen aus zuvor ermittelten Biegemomenten, Längskräften, Querkräften und Drillmomenten*]

~, DSGN · Durchformung *f*, Form(geb)ung, Gestaltung

~, structural ~, DSGN · (Bau)Entwurf *m*, baulicher Entwurf

~ **action** · Rechenwert *m* der Beanspruchung

~ **and construct firm** · Konstruktions- und Baufirma *f*

~ **assumption** → ~ hypothesis

~ **bending moment** · Bemessungsbiegemoment *n*, Bemessungsbiegungsmoment

~ **chart**, ~ **table** · Bemessungstabelle *f*, Bemessungstafel *f*

~ **constant** · Bemessungskonstante *f*

~ **criterium** · Bemessungskriterium *n*

~ ~ · Entwurfskriterium *n*

~ **curve** · Bemessungskurve *f*

~ **data** · Entwurfsangaben *fpl*, Entwurfsdaten *f*

~ ~ · Bemessungsangaben *fpl*, Bemessungsdaten *f*

~ ~ **sheet** · Bemessungsblatt *n*

~ **department**, ~ **office** · Konstruktionsabteilung *f*, Konstruktionsbüro *n*

~ **development** · Entwurfsbearbeitung *f*

~ ~ **phase** · Ausführungsentwurfstadium *n*

~ **diagram** · Rechendiagramm *n*

~ **drawing** · Entwurfszeichnung *f*

~ **engineer** · Bemessungsingenieur *m*

~ **equation** · Bemessungsgleichung *f*

~ **error** · Bemessungsfehler *m*

~ **example** · Bemessungsbeispiel *n*

~ **factor** · Bemessungsfaktor *m*

~ **feature** · Entwurfsmerkmal *n*

~ ~ · Bemessungsmerkmal *n*

~ **formula** · Bemessungsformel *f*

~ **fundamental**, basis of design · Entwurfsgrundlage *f*

~ ~, basis of design · Bemessungsgrundlage *f*

~ **heat loss** · Bemessungswärmeverlust *m*

~ **hypothesis**, structural ~ ~, (structural) design assumption · Bemessungsannahme *f*

~ **in reinforced concrete**, reinforced-concrete design, R. C. design · Bemessung *f* im Stahlbetonbau, Stahlbetonbemessung

~ **latitude** · Bemessungsspielraum *m* [*Im Sinne von vielen Bemessungsmöglichkeiten*]

~ ~ · Entwurfsspielraum *m* [*Im Sinne von vielen Entwurfsmöglichkeiten*]

~ **load**, assumed ~, designed ~ · Lastannahme *f*, Bemessungslast *f*, Entwurfslast, angenommene Last, rechnerisch vorgesehene Last

design loading — detachment

~ **loading**, assumed ~, designed ~ · Entwurfsbelastung f, rechnerisch vorgesehene Belastung, angenommene Belastung, Belastungsannahme f, Bemessungsbelastung

~ **method**, method of design · Bemessungsverfahren n

~ ~, method of design · Entwurfsverfahren n

~ **mix(ture)** · Ausgangsgemisch n, Ausgangsmischung f

~ **moment** · Bemessungsmoment n

~ **of a floor system**, ~ ~ ~ ~ structure, ~ ~ ~ ~ construction, floor design · Deckenbemessung f

~ ~ **beams**, beam design · Balken(träger)bemessung f

~ ~ **window(s)**, window design · Fensterform(geb)ung f, Fensterdurchformung

~ **office**, ~ department · Konstruktionsabteilung f, Konstruktionsbüro n

~ **parameter**, ~ value · Bemessungswert m

~ **pressure** · Bemessungsdruck m

~ **principles** · Bemessungsgrundsätze mpl

~ ~ · Entwurfsgrundsätze mpl

~ **problem**, ~ task · Entwurfsaufgabe f, Entwurfsproblem n

~ ~, ~ task · Bemessungsaufgabe f, Bemessungsproblem n

~ ~ · Gestaltungsfrage f

~ **rule** · Entwurfsregel f

~ ~ · Bemessungsregel m

~ **seismic force** · Bemessungserdbebenkraft f

~ **specifications**, ~ spec(s) · Entwurfsrichtlinien fpl

~ ~, ~ spec(s) · Bemessungsrichtlinien fpl

~ **strength** · Bemessungsfestigkeit f

~ **stress**, working ~, allowable ~, safe ~, permissible ~, admissible ~ · zulässige Spannung f, Bemessungsspannung

~ **system** · Bemessungssystem n

~ **table**, ~ chart · Bemessungstabelle f, Bemessungstafel f

~ **task**, ~ problem · Bemessungsaufgabe f, Bemessungsproblem n

~ ~, ~ problem · Entwurfsaufgabe f, Entwurfsproblem n

~ **temperature** · Bemessungstemperatur f

~ ~ **map** · Klimakarte f [Zur Bemessung von Heizungs- und Klimaanlagen]

~ **theory** · Entwurfstheorie f

~ ~ · Bemessungstheorie f

~ **thickness** · Bemessungsdicke f

~ **value**, ~ parameter · Bemessungswert m

~ **weight** · Bemessungsgewicht n

~ **wind pressure** · Bemessungswinddruck m

~ ~ **velocity**, ~ ~ speed · Bemessungswindgeschwindigkeit f

designation · Bezeichnung f

designed load, assumed ~, design ~ · Lastannahme f, Bemessungslast f, Entwurfslast, angenommene Last, rechnerisch vorgesehene Last

~ **loading**, assumed ~, design ~ · Entwurfsbelastung f, rechnerisch vorgesehene Belastung, angenommene Belastung, Belastungsannahme f, Bemessungsbelastung

designer · Entwerfer m, Entwurfsverfasser, Konstrukteur m

~, structural ~ · Statiker m

~ · Formgestalter m

~ **of formal gardens and parks**, garden architect · Garten(bau)architekt m, Gartengestalter m

desintegrating slag, slaking ~ · Zerfallschlacke f

desk calculator · Tischrechner m

destroyed, ruined · zerstört

~ **by fire**, ruined ~ ~, (fire-)gutted, burnt down, burned down · abgebrannt, ausgebrannt, niedergebrannt

destroying substance, killing ~ · Vernichtungsmittel n [z.B. gegen Schimmel, Bakterien, Insekten, Algen usw.]

destruction of concrete, concrete destruction · Betonzerstörung f

destructive concrete test · zerstörende Betonprobe f, ~ Betonprüfung f, zerstörender Betonversuch m

~ **distillation**, dry ~ [Sometimes referred to as 'pyrolysis'] · Entgasung f, trockene Destillation f, Zersetzungsdestillation

~ **movement** · zerstörende Bewegung f

destructively distilled wood turpentine · Holzterpentinöl n durch trockene Destillation gewonnen, Wurzelterpentinöl ~ ~ ~ ~

destructor, incinerator, waste ~, refuse ~; rubbish ~ (US) · Abfall(stoff)verbrenner m, (Müll)Verbrenner

desulfurizing (US); desulphur(iz)ation (Brit.) · Entschwef(e)lung f

detachable specular reflector · Einsatzspiegel m [Deckenleuchte]

detached, free-standing, isolated [Said of a structure which is completely surrounded by permanent open spaces] · freistehend

~ **building**, isolated ~, free-standing ~ · freistehendes Gebäude n, Einzelgebäude

~ **house**, free-standing ~, isolated ~ · freistehendes Haus n, Einzelhaus

~ **shaft**, engaged ~ · vorgelegter Schaft m

~ **statuary** · Rundwerk n, Rundplastik f

detachment → film ~

detail — dextrin(e)

detail → (architectural) feature

~ of façade · Fassadenausschnitt *m*

detail(ed) drawing · Detailplan *m*, Detailzeichnung *f*

detailing · Detailbehandlung *f*

to detension · entspannen, ablassen der Pressenkraft [*Spannbeton*]

detensioning · Ablassen *n* der Pressenkraft, Entspannen [*Spannbeton*]

determinacy → statical ~

determinant, determiner · Determinante *f*

determinate, determined · bestimmt

determinateness → statical ~

determination · Bestimmung *f*, Ermitt(e)lung

~, determining · Bestimmen *n*, Ermitteln

~ of fineness, fineness determination · Feinheitsbestimmung *f*, Feinheitsermitt(e)lung

~ ~ hardness, hardness determination · Härtebestimmung *f*, Härteermitt(e)lung

~ ~ the roof shape · Dachgestaltung *f*

determinator · Determinator *m*

determined, determinate · bestimmt

determiner, determinant · Determinante *f*

determining, determination · Bestimmen *n*, Ermitteln

detrital (lime) tuff, clastic (~) ~ · klastischer Kalktuff *m*

Deval test, ~ attrition ~ · Deval-Prüfung *f*, Deval-Versuch *m*, Deval-Probe *f*

~ testing machine, ~ attrition ~ · Deval(-Abnutzungs)trommel *f*, Deval-Trommelmühle *f*

to develop · abwickeln [*z.B. eine Wölbungsleibung*]

~ ~ · erschließen [*Bauland*]

developed area, ~ land, improved ~ · erschlossenes Bauland *n*, baufertiges Land, erschlossene Fläche *f*, baufertige Fläche

~ length [*The length of a pipe line measured along the centre line of the pipe and fittings*] · abgewickelte Länge *f*

~ quarter, ~ sites · Bauland *n*, baufertige Grundstücke *npl*

~ site, improved · baufertiges Grundstück *n*, erschlossenes ~

developer · Bauträger *m*

developing area · Neubaugebiet *n*, Stadterweiterungsgebiet

development, site ~ · Erschließung *f*, Bodenaufschließung [*Maßnahmen, um aus dem rohen Land „baufertige" Grundstücke (= Bauland) herzustellen*]

~, expansion · Ausbau *m*, Erweiterung *f*, Vergrößerung [*einer bestehenden Anlage*]

~ · Bebauung *f*

~ · Abwicklung *f* [*Aneinanderreihung von Ansichten eines Baukörpers oder Raumes in Normalprojektion*]

~ area, site ~ ~ · Erschließungsgebiet *n*, Bodenaufschließungsgebiet

~ district · Vorranggebiet *n* [*Regionalplanung*]

~ of colour, colour development (Brit.); development of color, color development (US) · Farbentwick(e)lung *f*

~ ~ rigidity, rigidity development [*In a freshly mixed cement paste, mortar or concrete without the evolution of much heat*] · Ansteifen *n*

~ ~ soffit, soffit development · Abwicklung *f* der Wölbungsleibung

~ ~ strength, strength development · Festigkeitsentwick(e)lung *f*

~ ~ style, stylistic development · Stilentwick(e)lung *f*

~ with block-dwellings (US); ~ ~ block residential buildings · Blockbebauung *f*

deviation · Abweichung *f*

~, margin, off-size · Abmaß *n*, Maßabweichung *f*, Genauigkeitsgrad *m* [*DIN 18201. Der Unterschied zwischen Grenz- und Nennmaß*]

~ moment · Deviationsmoment *n*

device → (architectural) feature

~ for closing, closing device, closing mechanism, closer · Schließer *m*, Verschluß *m*, (Ver)Schließvorrichtung *f*

devitrification, devitrifying · Entglasen *n*, Entglasung *f*

to devitrify [*To deprive of vitreous qualities; to cause glass, etc. to become opaque, hard, and crystalline in structure*] · entglasen

devitrifying, devitrification · Entglasen *n*, Entglasung *f*

devoid of directionality, nondirectional · richtungslos

dew point, condensation temperature, saturation point, 100% relative humidity · Kondensationstemperatur *f*, Taupunkt *m*

~ ~ diagram, saturation ~ ~, condensation temperature ~, diagram of 100% relative humidity · Taupunktdiagramm *n*, Kondensationstemperaturdiagramm

Dewar flask, ~ vessel, vacuum bottle [*A silvered glass flask with double walls, the space between them being evacuated. It is used for the storage of liquid air*] · Dewargefäß *n*, Weinholdgefäß

dewdrop glass, waterdrop ~ · Ornamentglas Nr. 521 *n*, Regentropfenglas, Tautropfenglas

dextrin(e) → starch gum

dextrin(e) glue — diagonal-wise placed

~ glue → starch gum ~

dextrose, glucose, grape sugar · Glukose f

dezincation [*The removal of zinc from an alloy or composition*] · Entzinken n

to dezincify, to dezinkify · entzinken

DF, drinking fountain · Trinkbrunnen m

~, freedom degree, degree of freedom · Freiheitsgrad m

DFTSMN, drawer; draughtsman (Brit.); draftsman (US) [*A man employed or skilled in making drawings*] · Zeichner m

DGA → dense(-graded) (mineral) aggregate

diabase · Diabas m

~ **chip(ping)s** · Diabassplitt m

diabasic tuff, greenstone ~ · Diabastuff m, Grünsteintuff

diaconicum, diaconicon [*In ecclesiastical architecture, a sacristy or vestry adjoining a church, and used for the storage of vestments and sacred vessels*] · Diakonikon n

diacoustics · Diakustik f [*Die Lehre von der Schallfortpflanzung*]

diagonal · Diagonale f, Schräge f [*diagonaler (Fachwerk)Füllstab*]

~ **(a)butment pier** [*deprecated*] → ~ buttress

~ **bar**, ~ rod, ~ member · Diagonale f, Diagonalglied n, Diagonalstab m

~ ~ **head**, ~ rod ~, ~ member ~ · Diagonalenkopf m, Diagonalstabkopf, Diagonalgliedkopf

~ **beam floor** · Diagonalbalken(träger)-decke f

~ **bond** → ~ masonry ~

~ **brace** · Diagonalsteife f, Diagonalstrebe f

~ **butment pier** [*deprecated*] → ~ buttress

~ **buttress**; ~ buttressing pier, ~ (a)butment pier [*deprecated*] · Diagonalstützpfeiler m, Diagonalstrebepfeiler

~ **buttressing pier** [*deprecated*] → ~ buttress

~ **cassette (slab) floor** → ~ waffle (~) ~

~ **coffer (slab) floor** → ~ waffle (~) ~

~ **coffered soffit** → ~ waffle (slab) floor

~ **compression** · Diagonaldruck m

~ ~ **stress**, ~ compressive ~ · Diagonaldruckspannung f

~ **compressive stress**, ~ compression ~ · Diagonaldruckspannung f

~ **cored (slab) floor** → ~ waffle (~) ~

~ **frame** · Diagonalrahmen m

~ **hole pattern** · Diagonallochbild n

~ **in compression**, compression diagonal, compressed diagonal · Druckdiagonale f, Druckschräge f, gedrückte Diagonale, gedrückte Schräge

~ ~ **tension**, ~ tie, tension diagonal · Zugdiagonale f, Zugschräge f, gezogene Diagonale, gezogene Schräge

~ **junction of flat bars**, ~ ~ ~ flats Flacheisenkreuzung f

~ **laying** · Diagonalverlegung f

~ **(masonry) bond** (Brit.); ~ (~) pattern (US); oblique (~) ~, raking (~) ~ · Diagonalverband m

~ **(~) pattern** (US) → ~ (~) bond

~ **member**, ~ bar, ~ rod · Diagonale f, Diagonalglied n, Diagonalstab m

~ ~, sloping ~ · Strebe f [*Fachwerk(-träger)*]

~ ~ **head**, ~ rod ~, ~ bar ~ · Diagonalenkopf m, Diagonalstabkopf, Diagonalgliedkopf

~ ~ **truss**, sloping ~ ~ · Strebenfachwerk(träger) n, (m)

~ **pan(el) (slab) floor** → ~ waffle (~) ~

~ **pattern** (US) → ~ (masonry) bond

~ **rectangular grid floor** → ~ waffle (slab) ~

~ **rib**, cross ~ · Kreuzrippe f, Diagonalrippe

~ **rod**, ~ bar, ~ member · Diagonale f, Diagonalglied n, Diagonalstab m

~ ~ **head**, ~ bar ~, ~ member ~ · Diagonalenkopf m, Diagonalstabkopf, Diagonalgliedkopf

~ **siding** · Diagonal-Wandschirm m, Diagonal-Wandbeschlag m, Diagonal-Wetterschirm

~ **square grid** · Diagonal-Quadratraster m

~ **strut** · Kreuzstrebe f

~ **struts**, St. Andrew's cross, Saltire cross · Andreaskreuz n, Kreuzgebälk n, Kreuzstreben fpl, Abkreuzung f, Kreuzverband m

~ **tensile stress** → ~ tension ~

~ **tension** · Diagonalzug m

~ ~ **stress**, ~ tensile ~ · Diagonalzugspannung f

~ **tie**, ~ in tension, tension diagonal · Zugdiagonale f, Zugschräge f, gezogene Diagonale, gezogene Schräge

~ **tile** · Schablone f

~ **tube** · Rohrdiagonale f

~ **waffle (slab) floor**, ~ cassette (~) ~, ~ coffer (~) ~, ~ pan(el) (~) ~, ~ cored (~) ~, ~ rectangular grid (~) ~, ~ coffered soffit · Diagonalkassettendecke f

diagonality · Diagonalität f

diagonally placed, diagonal-wise ~ · diagonal angeordnet

diagonal-wise placed, diagonally ~ · diagonal angeordnet

diagram — diazo compound

diagram → graphic representation

~ of 100% relative humidity, dew point diagram, saturation point diagram, condensation temperature diagram · Taupunktdiagramm *n*, Kondensationstemperaturdiagramm

~ ~ stresses, stress diagram [*A skeleton drawing of a truss, upon which are written the stresses in the different members*] · Spannungsdiagramm *n*

~ ~ velocities, velocity diagram · Geschwindigkeitsplan *m* [*Alle Punkte einer kinematischen Kette erfahren bei Verschiebung eines Punktes eine zwangsläufige Richtung und Geschwindigkeit. Diese werden zeichnerisch mit dem Geschwindigkeitsplan bestimmt*]

diagrammatic representation → graphic ~

~ sketch · Schaubild *n*

diagrid · Diagonalraster *m*

dial lock, combination ~, puzzle ~ · Kombi(nations)schloß *n*, Vexierschloß, Ringschloß

~ padlock, combination ~ · Ring-Vorhängeschloß *n*, Kombi(nations)-Vorhängeschloß, Vexier-Vorhängeschloß

diallage · Diallag *m*

diamantini, flake glass, frost · Flitterglas *n*, Schuppenglas

diameter of bar, ~ ~ rod, rod diameter, bar diameter · Stabdurchmesser *m*, Stahldurchmesser, Eisendurchmesser [*Bewehrung*]

~ ~ rod, ~ ~ bar, bar diameter, rod diameter · Stabdurchmesser *m*, Stahldurchmesser, Eisendurchmesser [*Bewehrung*]

diamond → ~ shape

~ cloth, lozenge ~, ~ woven fabric; ~ fabric [*misnomer*] [*See remark under 'Gewebe'*] · Rauten(maschen)gewebe *n*

~ drawn wire · Draht *m* mit Diamantenziehdüse hergestellt

~ expanded metal, lozenge ~ ~ · Rautenstreckmetall *n*

~ fabric [*misnomer*] → ~ cloth

~ frieze, lozenge ~ · Rautenfries *m*

~ girder · Rautenfachwerk(träger) *n*, (*m*), Rhombenfachwerk(träger), Rautenträger [*Träger mit doppeltem Diagonalenzug ohne Vertikalen, also Träger aus einer Aufeinanderfolge von zwischen den beiden Gurten auf der Spitze stehenden Vierecken*]

~ mesh, lozenge ~ · Rautenmasche *f*

~ motif → diamond-shaped ~

~ moulding (Brit.); ~ molding (US); ~ ornament, nail-head ~ · Nagelkopfverzierung *f*, Diamantverzierung

~ ornament; ~ moulding (Brit.); ~ molding (US); nail-head ~ · Diamantverzierung *f*, Nagelkopfverzierung

~ pattern, lozenge ~ · Rautenmuster *n*

diamond-patterned, lozenge-patterned, with diamond pattern, with lozenge pattern · gerautet

~ glass; lozenge(-patterned) ~ (US) · gerautetes Glas *n*, Rautenglas, rautenförmig gemustertes Glas

diamond plate, lozenge ~ · Rauten-(grob)blech *n*

~ point engraving [*Incising glass surfaces, usually for decoration, with a diamond point or hard steel stylus*] · Diamantgravieren *n* [*Glas*]

diamond-pointed cut stone · Diamantquader(stein) *m*

~ rustication · Diamantrustikal(werk) *f*, (*n*), Diamantrustikamauerwerk

diamond pyramid hardness test · Oberflächenhärteprüfung *f* mit einer Diamant-Pyramide, Oberflächenhärteprobe *f* ~ ~ ~, Oberflächenhärteversuch *m* ~ ~ ~

~ (shape), lozenge · Raute *f*

diamond-shaped, lozenge-shaped · rautenförmig

~ core, lozenge(-shaped) ~ · rautenförmiger Kern *m*

~ (ground(-))plan, lozenge(-shaped) ~ · rautenförmiger Grundriß *m*

~ motif, lozenge ~ · Rautenmotiv *n*

diamond tool · Diamantwerkzeug *n*

~ vault, cell-vault [*A vault consisting of concave troughs or hollows separated by groins*] · Zellengewölbe *n*

~ woven fabric → ~ cloth

diaper [*A pattern or design with a diamond-shaped basis formed on a flat surface*] · Diamantierung *f*

diaphragm · Abschlußmauer *f*

~, ~ plate, end plate, bulkhead · Binderscheibe *f* [*Faltwerk*]

~ · lotrechte Scheibe *f*

~ arch · Schwibbogen *m*, Schwebebogen

~ wall · Schlitzwand *f*

diaspore [*1. One of the monohydrates of alumina. 2. A rock containing a major proportion of this mineral*] · Diaspor *m*

~ refractory (product), ~ ~ material · Diasporerzeugnis *n* [*Hochtonerdehaltiges feuerfestes Erzeugnis, das hauptsächlich aus Diaspor hergestellt wird*]

diastyle [*The spacing of columns 2¾ to 4 diameters apart*]

diatomaceous earth → kieselguhr

~ ooze · Diatomeenschlamm *m*

diatomite [*A rock formed essentially from the siliceous skeletons of vegetable organisms (diatoms)*] · Diatomit *m*

~ brick · Diatomitstein *m* [*Poröser, wärmehaltender, gegen schwache Säure beständiger gebrannter feuerfester Stein für Back- und Härteöfen, Winderhitzer usw.*]

diazo compound · Diazo(nium)verbindung *f*

diazo reaction — digestion tower

~ **reaction** · Diazotierung *f*

diazoma · Diazoma *n* [*Im Halbkreis angeordneter Umgang zwischen den Sitzstufen im griechischen Theaterbau*]

to diazotize · diazotieren

dibutyl phthalate (plasticizer) · Dibutylphthalat *n*, DBP [*Weichmacher*]

dicalcium ferrite · Dikalziumferrit *n*, Bikalziumferrit

~ **silicate** · Bikalziumsilikat *n*, Dikalziumsilikat, 2CaO × SiO₂ [*abgekürzt C₂S*]

~ ~ **hydrate** · Dikalziumsilikathydrat *n*, Bikalziumsilikathydrat

dichroic glass · Changeantglas *n*

die → dado

~ → (wire-)drawing ~

die-casting material, ~ **metal** · Druckgußmetall *n*, Druckgußwerkstoff *m*

~ **metal,** ~ **material** · Druckgußmetall *n*, Druckgußwerkstoff *m*

die orifice, (wire-)drawing ~ ~ · (Draht)Zieh(eisen)düse *f*, (Draht)Ziehsteindüse

Diels-Alder reaction · Diels-Alder-Reaktion *f*

Differdinge beam · Differdinger Träger *m*, Grey-Träger

difference in colour (Brit.); ~ ~ **color** (US) · Farbabweichung *f*

~ **method** [*The difference between the original weight of the asphaltic mix(ture) and the weight of the dry aggregate after extraction is used as the basis for determining the proportions of asphalt (US)/(asphaltic-)bitumen (Brit.) and aggregate in a mix(ture)*] · Differenzmethode *f* [*Bindemittelgehaltbestimmung*]

differential calculus · Differentialrechnung *f*

~ **equation** · Differentialgleichung *f*

~ **force** · Differentialkraft *f*

~ **movement,** ~ **motion** [*e.g. between the two leaves of a cavity wall*] · Bewegungsunterschied *m*

~ **pressure** · Differenzdruck *m*

~ **quotient, derived function** · Differentialquotient *m*

~ **settlement, uneven ~** · Setzungsunterschied *m*

~ **shrinkage,** shrinkage difference · Schwindunterschied *m*

~ **thermal analysis,** DTA · Differential-Thermoanalyse *f*

difficultly soluble · schwerlöslich

difficult-to-screen material, hard-to-screen ~ · schwer siebbares Gut *n*, siebschwieriges ~

diffuse-porous · zerstreutporig [*Laubhölzer sind zerstreutporig, wenn die Tracheen über die Jahresringe verteilt sind*]

diffuse (sound) field [*A sound field of uniform energy density for which the directions of propagation of waves are random from point to point*] · diffuses Schallfeld *n*

diffused illumination, ~ **lighting** · gestreute Beleuchtung *f*

~ **light** · gestreutes Licht *n*

~ **lighting,** ~ **illumination** · gestreute Beleuchtung *f*

diffuser · Wanne *f* [*Leuchte*]

~, **air** ~ · (Luft)Diffusor *m*

diffusibility → diffusivity

diffusing → mist-spraying

~ **ceiling, light-~ ~, luminous ~, illuminated ~, luminescent ~** · Leuchtdecke *f*, Lichtdecke

~ ~ **system** → light-~ ~ ~

~ **glass, light-~ ~, lighting ~** · Lichtstreuglas *n*, lichtstreuendes Glas

~ **panel, light-~ ~, lighting ~** · Lichtstreutafel *f*, lichtstreuende Tafel

~ **pattern, diffusion ~, atomization ~** · Zerstäubungsbild *n*

~ **unit, light-~ ~, lighting diffuser** · Lichtstreuelement *n*, lichtstreuendes Element

~ **wall** → light-~ ~

diffusion, diffusivity, diffusibility [*Of a reverberant sound field. The degree to which the directions of propagation of waves are random from point to point*] · Schallzerstreuung *f*

~ → mist-spraying

~ **barrier** · Diffusionsdampfsperre *f*

~ **coefficient** · Diffusionszahl *f*, Diffusionsbeiwert *m*

~ **fastness,** ~ **resistance** · Diffusionswiderstand *m*, Diffusionsbeständigkeit *f*

~ **humidity,** ~ **moisture** · Diffusionsfeuchte *f*, Diffusionsfeuchtigkeit *f*

~ **moisture,** ~ **humidity** · Diffusionsfeuchte *f*, Diffusionsfeuchtigkeit *f*

~ **pattern, atomization ~, diffusing ~** · Zerstäubungsbild *n*

~ **process** · Diffusionsvorgang *m*

~ **resistance,** ~ **fastness** · Diffusionswiderstand *m*, Diffusionsbeständigkeit *f*

diffusion(-)tight · diffusionsdicht

diffusivity, diffusion, diffusibility [*Of a reverberant sound field. The degree to which the directions of propagation of waves are random from point to point*] · Schallzerstreuung *f*

dig, pit · Grübchen *n* [*Fehler im optischen Glas*]

digestion (of sewage), sewage digestion · (Abwasser)Faulung *f*

~ **tower, sewage ~ ~** · (Abwasser-)Faulturm *m*

diglyph [*A projecting face or tablet with two vertical grooves or channels*] · Diglyph *m*, Zweischlitz *m*

dihydrate · Dihydrat *n*, Doppelhydrat

to dilapidate · verfallen [*Bauwerk*]

dilapidated · baufällig

dilapidating, dilapidation · Verfallen *n* [*Bauwerk*]

dilapidation · Baufälligkeit *f*

~, dilapidating · Verfallen *n* [*Bauwerk*]

dilatancy · Dilatanz *f* [*Eigenschaft kolloider oder grobdisperser Systeme bei starker Beanspruchung zu erstarren und beim Stehen wieder flüssig zu werden*]

diluent · Verschnittmittel *n* für Lösungsmittel

~ → inactive solvent

diluted mineral acid · verdünnte Mineralsäure *f*

dimension, building ~ · (Bau)Abmessung *f*, (Bau)Maß *n*

dimensional accuracy · Maßgenauigkeit *f*

~ change · Maßänderung *f*

(~) coordination [*The application of a range of related dimensions to the sizing of building components and assemblies and the buildings incorporating them*] · Maßordnung *f*

~ data · Abmessungsangaben *fpl*, Maßangaben

~ discrepancy · Nichtmaßhaltigkeit *f*

~ framework, modular (measure) system · Maßsystem *n* (gegenseitig zusammenhängender Maße)

~ limit · Maßgrenze *f*, Abmessungsgrenze

~ limitation · Maßbegrenzung *f*

~ line · Maßlinie *f*

~ range · Maßbereich *m, n*

(~) reference system [*A system of points, lines and planes to which sizes and positions of a building component or assembly may be related*] · (Maß)Bezugssystem *n*

~ relationship · Maßbeziehung *f*

~ stability · Maßbeständigkeit *f*, Maßhaltigkeit

~ standard (specification), ~ ~ spec · Maßnorm *f*

~ tolerance · Maßtoleranz *f* [*DIN 18201*]

~ unit · Maßeinheit *f*

~ variation · Maßschwankung *f*

dimensionally accurate · maßgenau, maßgerecht

~ co-ordinated · maßgeordnet

~ stable · maßbeständig, maßhaltig

dimension(-cut) shingle · Dimensionsschindel *f*

dimensioning · Bemessung *f*, Dimensionierung

~ of joint(s) · Fugenbemessung *f*, Fugendimensionierung

~ ~ locks [*The method of measuring and describing the length, height, thickness and size of locks and latches*] · Schloßbemessung *f*, Schloßdimensionierung

~ rules · Regeln *fpl* für die Bemessung, ~ ~ ~ Dimensionierung, Bemessungsregeln, Dimensionierungsregeln

dimethyl ketone, acetone · Azeton *n*

~ sulfate test (US); ~ sulphate ~ (Brit.) · Dimethylsulfatprüfung *f*, Dimethylsulfatversuch *m*, Dimethylsulfatprobe *f*

diminishing piece, reducing ~, reducing fitting, (pipe) reducer, adaptor; adapter (US) [*A pipe fitting for connecting together two or more pipes where one or more of the pipes differ in diameter from the others*] · Reduktionsstück *n*, Reduktionsmuffe *f*, Reduzierstück, Reduziermuffe, Paßstück, Übergangsstück

diminutive tower, small ~, (decorative) turret, ornamental turret · kleiner (Zier-) Turm *m*, (Zier)Türmchen *n*

dimmer, lamp ~ · Lichtregler *m*

~ [*Adjustable shutter, or louvre, to regulate the passage of sound*] · Schallregler *m*

~ switch · Abblendschalter *m*

~ unit · Lichtstreugerät *n*

dimpled plate · kalottenförmig geriffeltes Blech *n*

dimpling · kalottenförmige Riffelung *f*

dinanderie · Dinanderie *f*, Gelbguß *m* [*Getriebene Messing- und Kupferware aus Dinant. Hauptblütezeit 13.–14. Jahrh.*]

dinas brick → gannister ~

dinette, dining recess, dining nook · Eßnische *f*

dining area with terrace · Eßplatz *m* mit Terrasse

~ corner, ~ place · Eßplatz *m*, Eßecke *f*

~ hall · Eßsaal *m*, Speisesaal [*Hotel*]

~ ~ for lay brethren → frater ~ ~ ~

~ kitchen, dwelling ~, kitchen/dining room · Wohnküche *f*, Eßküche

~ nook, ~ recess, dinette · Eßnische *f*

~ place, ~ corner · Eßplatz *m*, Eßecke *f*

~ recess, ~ nook, dinette · Eßnische *f*

~ room · Eßraum *m*, Eßzimmer *n*, Speisezimmer, Speiseraum

~ space · Eßplatz *m*

~ terrace · Eßterrasse *f*

~ zone · Eßbereich *m, n*

Diocletian window → therm(al) ~

Diocletian's palace at Split, ~ ~ ~ Spalato, Palace of Diocletian at Split, Palace at Diocletian at Spalato · Diokletianspalast *m* zu Split, ~ ~ Spalato, Palast des Diokletian zu Split, Palast des Diokletian zu Spalato

diorite — direct sun rays

diorite · Diorit *m* [*Fehlnamen: (schwedischer) schwarzer Granit m, schwarzer schwedischer Granit*]
~ **porphyrite** · Dioritporphyr *m*
dioritic · dioritisch
dip coated with baked enamel · einbrenntauchlackiert
~ **coating** · Tauchbeschichtung *f*
~ ~ · Tauchlackierung *f*
~ **colouring** (Brit.); ~ coloring (US) · Tauchfärbung *f*
~ **galvanising** (Brit.); ~ galvanizing (US) · Tauchverzinken *n*
dip-primed · tauchgrundiert
dip soldering · Tauchlötung *f*
diplomat enclave · Diplomatenviertel *n*
Dippels oil, bone ~ · Knochenöl *n*
dipping [*The process of applying paints, etc., by immersing therein an object to be coated and allowing it to drain during and after removal*] · Tauchen *n*
~ **consistence**, ~ consistency · Tauchkonsistenz *f*, Tauchsteife *f* [*(Anstrich-) Farbe*]
~ **engobe** · Tauchengobe *f*
~ **glazing**, glazing by dipping · (Ein-)Tauchglasieren *n*, (Ein)Tauchbeglasen, Glasieren durch Eintauchen, Beglasen durch Eintauchen
~ **lacquer** · Tauchlackfarbe *f*
~ **method**, ~ process · Tauchverfahren *n*
~ **varnish** · Tauchlack *m*
~ **viscosity** · Tauchviskosität *f*
dipteral [*A term applied to a building with a double row of columns on each side*] · dipteral
~ **building**, double-wing(ed) ~, two-wing(ed) ~ · zweiflügeliges Gebäude *n*, doppelflügeliges ~
~ **temple**, dipteros · Dipteraltempel *m*, Dipeteros(tempel) *m*, doppellaubiger Tempel [*Ein Tempel mit doppelter Säulenstellung an den Langseiten, besonders im ionischen Kleinasien verbreitet*]
dipteros → dipteral temple
diptych · Diptychon *n*
direct action · direkte Beanspruchung *f*
~ **compression**, pure ~ · reiner Druck *m*
~ **compressive stress**, normal ~ ~ · Normaldruckspannung *f*
~ **costing** · Teilkostenberechnung *f* bei der zwischen variablen und festen Kosten unterschieden wird
~ **diffused light** · direktes diffuses Licht *n*
~ ~ **lighting**, ~ ~ illumination · direkte diffuse Beleuchtung *f*
~ **electric heating** · elektrische Direktheizung *f*
~ **field** → ~ sound ~

~ **fire** → ~ heating unit
~ **flexure**, pure ~, ~ bending · reine Biegung *f*
~ **gas heating** · Direkt-Gas(be)heizung *f*, Gas-Direkt(be)heizung
~ **glare** · direkte Blendung *f*
direct-heat drying · Kontakttrocknung *f*
direct heater → ~ heating unit
~ **heating** · Direkt(be)heizung *f*
~ ~ **appliance** → ~ ~ unit
~ ~ **device** → ~ ~ unit
~ (~) **system** · Direkt(be)heizung *f*
~ ~ **unit**, ~ ~ device, ~ ~ appliance, ~ warming ~, ~ heater, ~ fire, ~ warmer · Direktheiz(ungs)gerät *n*, Direktheizer *m*, Direkterhitzer
~ **hot water system** · direkte Warmwasseranlage *f*
~ **illumination**, ~ lighting · direkte Beleuchtung *f*
~ **labour** (Brit.); ~ labor (US) [*Productive labo(u)r as distinct from administration and supervision*] · Produktions(arbeits)kräfte *fpl*
~ **light** · direktes Licht *n*
~ **lighting**, ~ illuminations · direkte Beleuchtung *f*
~ **load**, pure ~ · reine Last *f*
~ **material** [*A material which is physically incorporated in the work(s)*] · (Bau)Hauptstoff *m*, Hauptbaustoff; (Bau)Hauptmaterial *n*, Hauptbaumaterial [*Schweiz*]
~ **moment distribution**, moment distribution without successive approximations · direkter Momentenausgleich *m*
~ **nailing**, face ~ [*Neiling perpendicular to the initial surface or to the junction of the pieces joined*] · direkte (Ver-)Nagelung *f*
~ **radiant heater**, ~ ~ heating appliance, ~ ~ ~ heating unit · Direktstrahlungsheizer *m*, Direktstrahlunserhitzer, Direktstrahl(ungs)heiz(ungs)gerät *n*
~ ~ **heating appliance**, ~ ~ ~ unit, ~ ~ heater · Direktstrahlungsheizer *m*, Direktstrahlungserhitzer, Direktstrahl(ungs)heiz(ungs)gerät *n*
~ ~ ~ **unit**, ~ ~ ~ appliance, ~ ~ heater · Direktstrahlungsheizer *m*, Direktstrahlungserhitzer, Direktstrahl(ungs)heiz(ungs)gerät *n*
~ **sound** · Direktschall *m*
~ (~) **filed** [*Of a source. That part of the sound field of a source wherein the effects of the boundaries of the medium can be neglected*] · Direktschallfeld *n*
~ (~) **transmission** · unmittelbare (Schall)Übertragung *f*
~ **stress**, normal ~ [*A stress which is entirely tensile or entirely compressive, without any bending or shear*] · Normalspannung *f*
~ **sun rays** · pralle Sonne

~ suspension from central pylon · Direktaufhängung f von Mittelpylone

~ system, ~ heating ~ · Direkt(be)heizung f

~ tensile stress, normal ~ ~ · Normalzugspannung f

~ tension, pure ~ · reiner Zug m

~ transmission, ~ sound ~ · unmittelbare (Schall)Übertragung f

~ ~ · Direktübertragung f

~ warmer → ~ heating unit

~ warming appliance → ~ heating unit

~ ~ device → ~ heating unit

~ ~ unit → ~ heating ~

direction of acceleration, acceleration direction · Beschleunigungsrichtung f

~ ~ deformation, deformation direction · Formänderungsrichtung f, Verformungsrichtung, Gestaltänderungsrichtung

~ ~ (floor) span · (Decken)Spannrichtung f

~ ~ forces, force direction · Kraftrichtung f

~ ~ load application, ~ ~ the applied load · Lastangriffsrichtung f

~ ~ loading · Belastungsrichtung f

~ ~ main stress, ~ ~ principal ~ · Hauptspannungsrichtung f

~ ~ movement · Bewegungsrichtung f

~ ~ principal stress, ~ ~ main ~ · Hauptspannungsrichtung f

~ ~ sound, sound direction · Schallrichtung f

~ ~ span, ~ ~ floor ~ · (Decken-)Spannrichtung f

~ ~ the applied force, ~ ~ force application · (Kraft)Angriffsrichtung f

~ ~ ~ ~ load, ~ ~ load application · Lastangriffsrichtung f

directions for laying, spec(ification)s ~ ~ · Verlegeanleitung f

~ of use · Verarbeitungsrichtlinien fpl

directivity factor · Richtungsfaktor m [*Schalltechnik*]

directly proportional · direkt proportional

directors' block, ~ building · Direktionsgebäude n

~ building, ~ block · Direktionsgebäude n

directory · Bezugsquellennachweis m

directrix · Direktrix f, Leitkurve f, Leitlinie f

dirt; feather [*B.S. 3447; B.S. 952*]; feathers [*ASTM C 162–56*] · Blasenschleier m [*Glas*]

~ filter · Schmutzfilter m, n

~ penetration · Staubeindringung f, Staubeintritt m

dirt-repellent, dirt-repelling · schmutzabweisend

dirt-repelling, dirt-repellent · schmutzabweisend

dirt retention · Staubrückhaltung f

~ screed, loam ~ · Lehmestrich m

dirty money, boot ~ [*Additional pay to a building worker for working in difficult or unusual conditions*] · Schmutzzulage f, Schmutzgeld n

disappearing ladder, ~ stair, folding ~, loft ~ · Schiebetreppe f, Einschiebtreppe, hochschiebbare Treppe; Aufzugtreppe [*Schweiz*]

~ stair, ~ ladder, folding ~, loft ~ · Schiebetreppe f, Einschiebtreppe, hochschiebbare Treppe; Aufzugtreppe [*Schweiz*]

to disassemble · demontieren

disc, sheet; disk (US) · Scheibe f [*Ein Flächentragwerk, das nur durch Kräfte belastet ist, die in seiner Ebene wirken*]

~ action, sheet ~; disk ~ (US) · Scheibenwirkung f

~ frieze (Brit.); disk ~ (US); bezant, pellet ornament · Scheibenfries m

discharge → refuse water

~ channel, drain(age) ~, draining ~, ~ gutter · Abflußrinne f, Ablaufrinne, Entwässerungsrinne, Wasserrinne

~ grate → inlet ~

~ grating → inlet grate

~ grid → inlet grate

~ gutter, drain(age) ~, draining ~, ~ channel · Abflußrinne f, Ablaufrinne, Entwässerungsrinne, Wasserrinne

~ lamp [*B.S. 1270*] · Entladungslampe f

~ line, draining ~, drain(age) ~ · Abflußleitung f, Entwässerungsleitung, Ablaufleitung

~ pipe, draining ~, drain(age) ~, waste (~) · Abflußrohr n, Ablaufrohr, Dränrohr, Entwässerungsrohr [*Fehlnamen: Ablauf m, Abfluß m*]

~ ~ elbow → draining ~ ~

~ ~ system → draining pipework

~ pipeline, draining ~, drain(age) ~, ~ piping · Abflußrohrleitung f, Entwässerungsrohrleitung, Ablaufrohrleitung

~ pipework → draining ~

~ point, draining ~ · Abflußstelle f, Ablaufstelle

discharging arch, relieving ~, rough ~, safety ~ · Entlastungsbogen m, Ablastebogen, Überfangbogen

~ vault, relieving ~ · Entlastungsgewölbe n

discoloration (US); discolouration (Brit.) · falsche Farbe f, verschießende ~, abschießende ~, Mißfarbe

disconnecting chamber [*A manhole separating a drainage system from the sewer. The separate drains for a building are usually collected in this chamber and the sewage conveyed by one pipe to the sewer*] · Sammelschacht m

discontinuous beam — display cabinet

discontinuous beam · Einzelbalken(-träger) *m*, unterbrochener Balken(träger)

~ grading → gap ~

~ granulometry → gap grading

discontinuously-graded aggregate, gap-graded ~ · diskontinuierlich abgestufte Mineralmasse *f*, unstetig ~ ~

~ concrete, gap-graded ~ · diskontinuierlich abgestufter Beton *m*, unstetig ~ ~

discotheque · Schallplattenbar *f*

dish → brass ~

dished (steel) plate, buckle(d) (~) · Buckelblech *n*, geknickte Platte *f*

dish spray · Geschirrbrause *f*

dishwasher · Geschirrspülmaschine *f*

dishwashing basket · Geschirrspülkorb *m*

~ sink (unit) → wash-up ~ (~)

dishwater → slop water

to disintegrate, to dissolve, to deflocculate · aufschließen, verflüssigen [*Steinzeugindustrie*]

disintegration, deflocculation, dissolving · Aufschließung *f*, Verflüssigung, Aufschluß *m* [*Steinzeugindustrie*]

~ of concrete, concrete disintegration · Betonzersetzung *f*

disk (US); disc, sheet · Scheibe *f* [*Ein Flächentragwerk, das nur durch Kräfte belastet ist, die in seiner Ebene wirken*]

~ action (US); disc ~, sheet ~ · Scheibenwirkung *f*

disc-type (load)bearing system with three areas, sheet-type ~ ~ ~ ~ ~; disk-type ~ ~ ~ ~ ~ (US) · dreiflächiges Scheibentragwerk *n*

dislodg(e)ment → (film) detachment

to dismount; to demount [*obsolete*] · demontieren

dismountability; demountability [*obsolete*] · Demontierbarkeit *f*

dismountable; demountable [*obsolete*] · demontierbar

~ connection, ~ joint; demountable ~ [*obsolete*] · lösbare Verbindung *f*

~ division wall → ~ partition (~)

~ joint, ~ connection; demountable ~ [*obsolete*] · lösbare Verbindung *f*

~ partition, movable ~; demountable ~ [*obsolete*] · versetzbare (Montage-) Trennwand *f*

~ partitioning; demountable ~ [*obsolete*] · versetzbare (Montage)Trennwände *fpl*

dispersal, sprawl, suburban ~ · Zersied(e)lung *f* [*Stadt*]

to disperse · dispergieren, feinverteilen

disperse phase · disperse Phase *f*

dispersed resin · dispergiertes Harz *n*, feinverteiltes ~

~ town · aufgelockerte Stadt *f*

dispersing agent, ~ medium · Dispergier(ungs)mittel *n*, Dispersionsmittel, Dispersionsstoff, Dispergier(ungs)stoff *m*, Dispergens *n*

~ medium, ~ agent · Dispergier(ungs)mittel *n*, Dispersionsmittel, Dispersionsstoff, Dispergier(ungs)stoff *m*, Dispergens *n*

dispersion · Dispersion *f* [*Unter „Dispersionen" versteht man Systeme, bei denen eine Flüssigkeit, ein fester Stoff oder auch ein Gas außerordentlich fein in einem „Dispersionsmittel" verteilt ist. Das Dispersionsmittel kann wiederum flüssig, fest oder gasförmig sein. Anstrichtechnisch von Bedeutung sind nur Dispersionen, in denen das Dispersionsmittel eine Flüssigkeit, z.B. Wasser, und die disperse Phase flüssig oder fest ist. Erstere nennt man „Emulsionen", letztere „Suspensionen". Eine scharfe Grenze zwischen beiden Systemen besteht nicht. Bei dispergierten Teilchen sehr hoher Viskosität kann es zweifelhaft sein, ob eine Emulsion oder eine Suspension vorliegt. Vielfach wird der Begriff „Dispersion" auf diese Systeme angewendet, z.B. bei den „Kunststoffdispersionen". In einigen Fällen nennt man sie auch in Anlehnung an den Kautschuklatex „Latex". Einer typischen Suspension begegnen wir im „Glassival"*]

dispersion-based plastic (bonding) adhesive, ~ ~ ~ medium, ~ ~ ~ agent, ~ ~ cement(ing agent) · Kunststoffdispersionskleb(e)stoff *m*, Kunststoffdispersionskleb(e)mittel *n*, Kunststoffdispersionskleber *m*

dispersion in quality, scattering of qualities · Gütestreuung *f*

~ ~ strength, scattering of strengths · Festigkeitsstreuung *f*

~ property · Dispersionseigenschaft *f*

displacement · Verrückung *f*

~ → (film) detachment

~ compatibility · Verrückungsverträglichkeit *f*

~ indicator, stripping ~ · Ablösungsanzeiger *m* [*Haftfestigkeit zwischen bit. Bindemittel und Mineralmasse*]

~ method, stiffness (matrix) ~ · Steifheitsmatrizenverfahren *n*, Verrückungsverfahren

~ of coordinate axis · Parallelverrückung *f* der Koordinatenachsen, Koordinatenachsenverrückung *f*

~ test (in the presence of water), stripping ~ (~ ~ ~ ~ ~ ~) · Ablösungsprobe *f*, Ablösungsversuch *m*, Ablösungsprüfung *f*, Wasserlagerungsversuch *m*, Wasserlagerungsprüfung, Wasserlagerungsprobe [*Zur Bestimmung der Haftung bituminösen Bindemittels am Gestein*]

displacer, plum · Stein *m* beim Prepaktbeton, Zyklopenbeton-Stein

display cabinet, show ~, ~ case, silent salesman · Schaukasten *m*, Vitrine *f*

display case — distribution assembly

~ **case** → ~ cabinet

~ **window**, show ~, shop ~ · Schaufenster n, Ladenfenster

disposable bag, throw-away-type ~ · Einwegsack m, Wegwerfsack

~ **filter**, throw-away-type ~ · Wegwerffilter m, n

~ **house**, throw-away-type ~ · Wegwerfhaus n [*Es besteht aus Pappschaumstoff und ist für 35 Jahre Lebensdauer konstruiert*]

(disposal) chute, (~) shaft, disposer · Abwurfanlage f, Abwurfschacht m [*Es gibt Abwurfanlagen für Müll, Papier und Wäsche*]

~ **field**, absorption ~ [*A system of trenches containing coarse aggregate and distribution pipe through which effluent may seep or leach into surrounding soil*] · Beries(e)lungsfeld n, Rieselfeld

~ **of refuse**, ~ ~ waste(s), refuse disposal, waste disposal; rubbish disposal, disposal of rubbish (US) · Abfall(stoff)-beseitigung f, Müllbeseitigung

~ ~ **rubbish**, rubbish disposal (US); disposal of refuse, disposal of waste(s), refuse disposal, waste disposal · Abfall(stoff)beseitigung f, Müllbeseitigung

~ ~ **waste(s)**, ~ ~ refuse, refuse disposal, waste disposal; rubbish disposal, disposal of rubbish (US) · Abfall-(stoff)beseitigung f, Müllbeseitigung

~ ~ ~, waste disposal · Abfall(stoff)beseitigung f [*Die flüssigen Abfallstoffe werden durch die Kanalisation und die festen durch die Straßenreinigung und die Müllabfuhr beseitigt*]

(~) shaft → (~) chute

~ **trench**, absorption ~, ~ field ~, drain (field) ~ · Beries(e)lungs(feld)-graben m, Riesel(feld)graben

dispose-all (US); garbage disposer, waste disposer, garbage disposal shaft, waste disposal shaft, garbage disposal chute, waste disposal chute (Brit.); refuse chute, refuse shaft, rubbish chute [*B.S. 1703*] · Müllschlucker m, Müll-(abwurf)schacht m, Abwurfschacht für Müll, Müllabwurfanlage f, Abfallschlukker, Abfallschacht, Schüttkammer f

disposer → (disposal) shaft

dissociation degree, degree of dissociation · Dissoziationsgrad m

dissolution of the masonry wall, masonry wall dissolution · Auflösung f der Mauer, Mauerauflösung

~ ~ ~ **wall**, wall dissolution · Wandauflösung f, Auflösung der Wand

to dissolve, to disintegrate, to defloc- culate · aufschließen, verflüssigen [*Steinzeugindustrie*]

dissolver · Lösebehälter m [*Niederschlagsverfahren zur Bleiweißherstellung*]

dissolving, disintegration, deflocculation · Aufschließung f, Verflüssigung, Aufschluß m [*Steinzeugindustrie*]

distance · Entfernung f

~ **between buildings** · Bauwich m, seitlicher Grenzabstand m

~ ~ **girders**, girder interval · Trägerabstand m

~ ~ **nails** · Nagelabstand m

~ ~ **rafters**, rafter spacing, rafter interval · (Dach)Sparrenabstand m

~ ~ **ribs**, rib spacing, rib interval · Rippenabstand m

~ ~ **rivets**, rivet interval · Nietabstand m

~ ~ **screws**, screw interval · Schraubenabstand m

~ ~ **stair(case) wells** · Treppenhausabstand m

~ **piece**, spacer, separator · Abstandhalter m

distemper coat → (glue(-bound)) ~ ~

~ **(paint)** → (glue(-bound)) ~ (~)

distillate fraction, oil ~ ~, tar distillation ~, tar-oil ~ · Ölfraktion f [*Herstellung präparierten Teeres*]

distillation coal · Schwelkohle f

~ **residue**, residue by distillation · Destillationsrückstand m

distilled coconut fatty acid · destillierte Fettsäure f des Kokosfettes, ~ ~ ~ Kokosöles, Kokos-Fettsäure [*DIN 55963*]

distilled-grease olein, dégras oil · Wollfett-Olein n

distilled linseed fatty acid · Leinöl-Fettsäure f, destillierte Fettsäure des Leinöles [*DIN 55960*]

~ **tar** · destillierter Teer m

distinction [*e.g. an architect of distinction*] · Rang m [*z.B. ein Architekt von Rang*]

distinguished antique (style), noble ~ (~) · repräsentative Antike f

distortion · Verzerrung f

distressed area · Notstandsgebiet n

to distribute, to spread, to apply · aufbringen, auftragen

distributed load · verteilte Last f

~ **moment** · Verschiebungsmoment n [*Momentenausgleichverfahren*]

distributing line, distribution ~ · Verteilungsleitung f

~ **pipe**, distribution ~ [*A pipe conveying water from a cistern, and under pressure from that cistern*] · Versorgungsrohr n, Verteilungsrohr [*von einem Wasserbehälter aus*]

~ **storey** (Brit.); ~ **story** (US); ~ **floor** · Verteileretage f, Verteilergeschoß n, Verteilerstockwerk n

distribution · Verteilung f

~ **assembly** · Verteilungseinsatz m [*in einem Verteilungsschrank*]

distribution bar — dog

~ **bar**, ~ rod · Verteilerstab *m*, Verteilungsstab [*Fehlnamen: Verteilereisen n, Verteilungseisen*]

~ **board** · Verteiler *m*, Verteilung(stafel) *f* [*Elektroinstallation*]

~ **box**, conduit ~, junction ~ · Anschlußkasten *m*, Verteilerkasten, Anschlußschrank *m*, Verteilerschrank, Abzweigkasten, Abzweigschrank, Verteilungskasten, Verteilungsschrank

~ **duct** · Verteilungskanal *m*

~ **factor** · Verteilungsfaktor *m*

~ **factor** · Verteilungszahl *f* [*Momentenausgleichverfahren*]

~ **floor** → ~ storey

~ **line**, distributing ~ · Verteilungsleitung *f*

~ **network** · Verteil(ungs)netz *n*

~ **of bending**, bending distribution · Biegeverteilung *f*

~ ~ **forces**, flow ~ ~ · Kräftefluß *m*

~ ~ **gas** · Gasverteilung *f*

~ ~ **heat**, heat distribution · Wärmeverteilung *f*

~ ~ **load**, spreading ~ ~, load distribution · Lastverteilung *f*

~ ~ **pores**, pore distribution · Porenverteilung *f*

~ ~ **pressure**, pressure distribution · Druckverteilung *f*

~ ~ **slip** · Schlupfverteilung *f*

~ **panel**, panelboard · Verteilertafel *f*

~ **pattern** · Verteilungsfigur *f*

~ **pipe**, distributing ~ [*A pipe conveying water from a cistern, and under pressure from that cistern*] · Versorgungsrohr *n*, Verteilungsrohr [*von einem Wasserbehälter aus*]

~ **reinforcement** → ~ steel

~ **rod**, ~ bar · Verteilerstab *m*, Verteilungsstab [*Fehlnamen: Verteilereisen n, Verteilungseisen*]

~ **steel**, ~ rods, ~ bars, ~ reinforcement, temperature ~ · Verteilerbewehrung *f*, Verteilerarmierung, Verteiler(stahl)einlagen *fpl*, Verteilerstähle *mpl*, Verteilerstäbe *mpl*, Verteilungsstäbe [*Fehlnamen: Verteilereisen npl, Verteilungseisen*]

~ **system** · Verteilungssystem *n*

~ **thickness**, spreading ~, application ~ · Aufbringungsdicke *f*, Auftragdicke [*Fehlnamen: Aufbringungsstärke f, Auftragstärke*]

distributor · Großhändler *m*

district · Landkreis *m*

~ **chilled water plant** · Wasserkühlzentrale *f*, zentrale Kühlwasseranlage *f*

~ **cooling** · Fernkühlung *f*

~ **heating** · Fernheizung *f*

~ ~ **cable** · Fernheiz(ungs)kabel *n*

~ ~ **duct** · Fernheiz(ungs)kanal *m*

~ ~ **line** · Fernheiz(ungs)leitung *f*

~ ~ **plant** · Fernheizwerk *n*

~ **school** · Quartierschule *f*

disturbance of set(ting), set(ting) disturbance · (Ab)Bindestörung *f* [*hydraulisches Bindemittel*]

distyle [*Having two styles or columns*] · distyl, zweisäulig

~ [*A porch having two styles or columns*] · Distylos *m*

~ **in antis** [*There are only two columns between pilasters or antae*] · Distylos *m* in Antis

divergence of style · stilistische Divergenz *f*

divide → division element

divider strip, dividing ~ [*Divider strips are used to control and localize any shrinkage or flexure cracks. The strips also fulfill an important decorative purpose by creating scale and pattern and permitting changes of colour to be made with ease and accuracy*] · Terrazzostreifen *m*, Terrazzo(trenn)schiene *f*

dividing strip → divider ~

diving pool · Sprungbecken *n*

division · Gliederung *f*

~ **bar** → (window) glazing ~

~ **element**, (room) divide · Raumteiler *m*

~ **for occupational purposes** · Gliederung *f* für Belegungszwecke

~ **into (vault) bays** · (Gewölbe)Joch(ein)teilung *f*, (Gewölbe)Jochgliederung

~ **masonry wall** (Brit.); fire ~ ~ (US) [*A fire-resisting wall from the lowest floor up to the roof*] · durchgehende Brandmauer *f*, durchlaufende ~

~ **wall** [*Any wall in the interior of a building*] · Scheidewand *f*

divorced from reality, abstract, conventional(ized), formalized, stylized · entnaturalisiert, (um)stilisiert [*z.B. Arabeske*]

DL, dead load · Totlast *f*, Eigenlast

DML, DEML, demolition, wrecking · Abbruch *m*, Abreißen *n* [*Bauwerk*]

doctors' library · Ärztebibliothek *f*

document glass [*ultraviolet-absorbing glass*] · Dokumentenglas *n* [*UV-absorbierendes Glas*]

documents for settling the accounts · Abrechnungsunterlagen *fpl*

dodecastyle [*A portico or colonnade having a row of twelve front columns*] · Dodekastylos *m*

~ · zwölfsäulig

~ **temple** · Dodekastylostempel *m*, Tempel mit zwölfsäuliger Giebelfront

dog, ~ anchor, ~ iron · Bauklammer *f*

~, wiggle nail, corrugated fastener, joint fastener; mitre brad (Brit.); miter brad (US) · Wellennagel *m*, gewellter Nagel

Doges' Palace — domed basilica (church)

Doges' Palace, Ducal ~ · Dogenpalast m [Venedig]

dog-leg(ged) stair(case) · gerade zweiläufige Treppe f mit Richtungswechsel, ~ doppelläufige ~ ~ ~, gegenläufige Treppe

dog-tooth (ornament), tooth ~; ~ moulding (Brit.); ~ molding (US) [Stonework decoration typical of late Norman and Early English architecture, i.e. about the end of the 12th and beginning of the 13th century. Generally found round door openings and in the archivolts of the arches] · Hundezahnornament n, Hundezahn m, Hundezahnverzierung f, Hundszahn

do-it-yourself garage · Selbstbaugarage f

dolerite [A basic hypabyssal rock of medium-grained texture, consisting of plagioclase feldspar, augite, iron ores, and frequently olivine] · Dolerit m

dolmen · Dolmen(grab) m, (n), Teufelsstein m, Feenstein [Vorgeschichtlicher Grabbau aus meist vier bis sechs aufrecht stehenden unbehauenen Felsblöcken mit einem ebensolchen als Deckstein darüber (Megalithbau), ursprünglich mit Erde überdeckt]

dolomite · Dolomit m [Kalzium-Magnesiumkarbonat. Wesentlicher Bestandteil des Dolomitgesteins. Anmerkung: Der Ausdruck „dolomite" wird im englischen Sprachgebrauch auch anstelle von „dead burned dolomite" verwendet und bezeichnet dann sowohl das totgebrannte Erzeugnis als auch die daraus hergestellten Steine]

~ **brick** · Dolomitstein m

~ ~ **press** · Dolomitsteinpresse f

~ **marble** [A crystalline variety of limestone, containing more than 40% of magnesium carbonate as the dolomite molecule] · Dolomitmarmor m

~ **(processing) plant,** ~ (~) installation · Dolomitwerk n

~ **refractory (product),** ~ ~ material [A refractory material made from calcined dolomite] · Dolomiterzeugnis n

dolomitic · dolomitisch

~ **hydrate,** hydrated dolomitic lime, hydrated magnesian lime · Dolomitkalkhydrat n [DIN 1060]

~ **lime,** magnesian ~, lean ~, poor ~ · Magerkalk m, Graukalk m, Dolomitkalk [90% Kalksubstanz und mehr als 5% Magnesiumoxid]

~ ~ **putty,** ~ ~ paste, magnesian ~ ~ · Dolomitkalkteig m [DIN 1060]

~ **limestone** → dolomite (rock)

~ **marble,** magnesian ~ · Dolomitmarmor m mit zwischen 5–40% Magnesiumkarbonat

~ **marl** · Dolomitmergel m

~ **sand** · Dolomitsand m

to dome · überkuppeln

dome, cathedral (church), minster · Dom m, Kathedrale f, Hochstiftskirche f; Münster m [Süddeutschland] [Die Hauptkirche einer Stadt, in der es keine Bischofskirche gibt, wird häufig auch „Dom" genannt]

~, cupola · Kuppel f

~ → ~light

~ **above a square,** cupola ~ ~ · Kuppel f über einem Viereck

~ **apex** → ~ vertex

~ **bar,** cupola ~ · Kuppelstab m

~ **bottom** → dome(-shape)d ~

~ **cornice,** cupola ~ · Kuppel(ge)sims m, (n)

~ **crown** → ~ vertex

~ **edge,** cupola ~ · Kuppelrand m

~ **floor** → dome(-shape)d ~

~ **form** → dome(-shape)d ~

~ **impost,** cupola ~ · Kuppelkämpfer m

~ **key** → ~ vertex

~ **of multiangular plan** → multiangular dome

~ ~ **polygonal plan** → multiangular dome

~ ~ **revolution (subjected to loads of rotational symmetry),** cupola ~ ~ (~ ~ ~ ~ ~ ~), ~ ~ rotational symmetry · Drehkuppel f, Rotationskuppel, drehsymmetrische Kuppel

~ ~ **rotational symmetry,** ~ ~ revolution (subjected to loads of rotational symmetry), cupola of revolution (subjected to loads of rotational symmetry) · Drehkuppel f, Rotationskuppel, drehsymmetrische Kuppel

Dome of the Invalides · Invalidendom m [Paris]

~ ~ ~ **Rock** · Felsendom m, Omarmoschee f, Kubbet-es-Sachra [in Jerusalem]

dome on tambour, cupola ~ ~, ~ ~ drum · Kuppel auf Tambour, ~ ~ Trommel, Tambourkuppel, Trommelkuppel

~ **ring,** cupola ~ · Kuppelring m

~ **roof** → dome(-shape)d ~

~ **rooflight** → domed ~

~ **segment,** cupola ~ · Kuppelscheibe f, Kuppelsegment n

~ **shell** → dome(-shape)d ~

~ **slab** → dome(-shape)d ~

~ **stress,** cupola ~ · Kuppelspannung f

~ **surface,** cupola ~ · Kuppeloberfläche f

~ **top** → ~ vertex

~ **vertex,** ~ apex, ~ key, ~ top, ~ crown, cupola ~ · Kuppelscheitel(punkt) m

domed, dome-shaped, domic(al) · kuppelförmig, kuppelartig

~ · kuppelgekrönt, überkuppelt, kuppeüberdacht

~ **basilica (church)** · Kuppelbasilika f

domed central-plan church — domestic heating

~ **central-plan church** · Kuppel-Zentralanlage f
~ **chapel** · Kuppelkapelle f
~ **church** · Kuppelkirche f
domed-cruciform church, cruciform-domed ~, cross-domed ~, ambulatory ~ · Kreuzkuppelkirche f, Kuppelkreuzkirche
domed diminutive tower, ~ turret · Kuppeltürmchen n
~ **floor** → dome-shaped ~
~ **form** → dome- haped ~
~ **hall** · Kuppelsaal m
~ ~ · Kuppelhalle f
~ ~ **church** · Kuppelhalle(nkirche) f
~ **mosque** · Kuppelmoschee f
~ **pavilion** · Kuppelpavillon m
~ **roof** → dome-shaped ~
~ **roof-light,** light cupola, saucer dome, dome(light) · (Dach)Lichtkuppel f, Oberlichtkuppel
~ **shell** → dome-shaped ~
~ **slab** → dome-shaped ~
~ **square** · Kuppelquadrat n
~ **stadium** · Kuppelsporthalle f
~ **structure** · Kuppelbau(werk) m, (n)
~ **turret,** ~ diminitive tower · Kuppeltürmchen n
~ **style** · Kuppelstil m
~ **temple** · Kuppeltempel m
dome(light), saucer dome, light cupola, domed roof-light · (Dach)Lichtkuppel f, Oberlichtkuppel
domelike shell · Kappenschale f [*Eine durch senkrechte Bandträger, z.B. Bögen mit Zugband, gestützte, doppelt gekrümmte kuppelartige Schale*]
dome(-shape)d, domic(al) ~ · kuppelförmig, kuppelartig
~ **bottom,** dome ~, domic(al) ~, cupola ~, ~ floor, bottom dome, bottom cupola · Kuppelboden m, Domboden [*Behälter*]
~ **floor,** dome ~, domic(al) ~, cupola ~, ~ bottom, bottom dome, bottom cupola · Kuppelboden m, Domboden [*Behälter*]
~ **form,** domic(al) ~, dome ~, cupola ~ · Kuppelform f
~ **roof,** domic(al) ~, cupola ~, dome ~ · Dachhaube f, Haubendach n, Kuppeldach [*Dach mit geschweifter Kontur*]
~ **shell,** domic(al) ~, cupola ~, dome ~ · Kuppelschale f
~ **slab,** domic(al) ~, cupola ~, dome ~ · Kuppelplatte f
domestic altar · Hausaltar m
~ **appliance** · Haushaltgerät n
~ ~ **burning town gas** [*B.S. 1250*] · Stadtgas-Haushaltgerät n
~ ~ **circuit** · Haushaltgerätestromkreis m
~ **bathroom** · Wohnungs-Badezimmer n

~ **block** → residential building
~ ~ **type,** residential ~ ~, residence ~ ~, ~ building ~; multiple dwelling ~ (US) · Wohngebäudeart f, Wohnhausart, Wohngebäudetyp m, Wohnhaustyp
~ **boiler,** boiler for domestic use · Haushalt(heiz)kessel m
~ **brick block** → ~ clay ~ ~
~ ~ **building** → ~ clay ~ ~
~ **building** → residential ~
~ ~ **roof** · Wohnhausdach n
~ ~ **type,** residential ~ ~, residence ~, ~ block ~; multiple dwelling ~ (US) · Wohngebäudeart f, Wohnhausart, Wohngebäudetyp n, Wohnhaustyp
~ **burning appliance,** ~ fire, ~ furnace · häusliche Feuerstätte f, ~ Feuerung f
~ **ceramics** · Wohnkeramik f
~ **chapel,** private ~ · Hauskapelle f, Privatkapelle, private Kapelle
~ **chimney** → building ~
~ **(clay) brick block,** residential (~) ~ ~, residence (~) ~ ~, ~ (~) ~ building; (clay) brick dwelling (US) · Ziegel-Wohngebäude n
~ **(~) ~ building,** residential (~) ~ ~, residence (~) ~ ~, ~ (~) ~ block; (clay) brick dwelling (US) · Ziegel-Wohngebäude n
~ **consumption** · Haus(halt)verbrauch m, Hausverbrauch [*Wasser*]
~ **construction,** housing (~) · WBau m, Wohnhausbau, Wohn(ungs)bau
~ **cullet,** factory ~ · Eigenbrocken m, Eigenscherben [*Glasgemenge*]
~ **electric water heater,** ~ ~ ~ heating appliance · Haushalt-Elektro-Wassererhitzer m, Haushalt-Elektro-Wasserheizer, Haushalt-Elektro-Wasserheizgerät n, Haushalt-Elektro-Wassererwärmer
~ **electric(al) appliance** · Elektrohaushaltgerät n
~ **electrical installation,** electrical domestic ~ · elektrische Hausanlage f
~ **filter** · Hausfilter m, n, Kleinfilter
~ **fire,** ~ furnace, ~ burning appliance · häusliche Feuerstätte f, ~ Feuerung f
~ **floor,** ~ intermediate ~ · Wohnungstrenndecke f [*Es gibt Holzbalkendecken und Massivdecken*]
~ **flue** · Hausschornsteinzug m, Gebäudeschornsteinzug
~ **furnace,** ~ fire, ~ burning appliance · häusliche Feuerstätte f, ~ Feuerung f
~ **garage,** residential ~ · Hausgarage f
~ **gas (burning) appliance,** residential ~ (~) ~ · Haushalt-Gasgerät n
~ ~ **meter** · Hausgaszähler m
~ **grade block,** ~ parquet(ry) ~ · Parkettstab m für Wohnräume und Räume mit nur Fußgängerverkehr [*DIN 280*]
~ **heating** · Hausheizung f

domestic heating installation — domus

~ ~ installation, residential ~ ~, ~ ~ system, ~ ~ plant · Wohnungs(be)heizungsanlage f

~ ~ plant → ~ ~ installation

~ ~ system → ~ ~ installation

~ hot water · Haushalt-Heißwasser n

~ ~ ~ heating · Haushalt-Heißwasserbereitung f

~ (intermediate) floor · Wohnungstrenndecke f [Es gibt Holzbalkendecken und Massivdecken]

~ kitchen · Haushaltküche f, häusliche Küche, Wohnungsküche

~ marble · einheimischer Marmor m, Inlandmarmor

~ meter · Haushaltzähler m

~ noise · Wohnlärm m

~ parquet(ry) block, ~ grade ~ · Parkettstab m für Wohnräume und Räume mit nur Fußgängerverkehr [DIN 280]

~ passenger · Inlandpassagier m

~ (~) terminal building · Abfertigungsgebäude n für Inlandverkehr, Empfangsgebäude ~ ~

~ pump · Haushaltpumpe f

~ quarter, residential ~ · Wohnviertel n

~ range · Haushaltherd m

~ refuse, house(hold) ~ · Hausmüll m, (Haushalt)Müll, Kehricht m

~ ~ disposal, house(hold) ~ ~ · Haus(halt)müllbeseitigung f, Müllbeseitigung, Kehrichtbeseitigung

~ room door · Stubentür f

~ sauna bath · Familiensauna f

~ sewage → house(hold) ~

~ softener, ~ water ~ · Hausenthärter m

~ solid fuel boiler, solid fuel domestic ~ · Haushalt(heiz)kessel m für feste Brennstoffe

~ stair(case) · Wohnhaustreppe f [DIN 18065]

(~) stove, solid fuel room heater [The second designation is now universally accepted to emphasize the development away from the traditional conception of the stove to sophisticated heating units which may incorporate boilers for the provision of hot water or for room heating via a radiator system or both] · (Haushalt)Ofen m, Heizofen

(~) ~ connection · (Haushalt)Ofenanschluß m, Heizofenanschluß

(~) ~ pipe · (Haushalt)Ofenrohr n, Heizofenrohr

(~) ~ ~ casing · (Haushalt)Ofenrohrfutter n, Heizofenrohrfutter

(~) ~ size · (Haushalt)Ofengröße f, Heizofengröße

~ tariff · Haushalttarif m

~ terminal building, ~ passenger ~ ~ · Abfertigungsgebäude n für Inlandverkehr, Empfangsgebäude ~ ~

~ timber, ~ wood, home-grown ~ · einheimisches Holz n

~ utility corridor · Wirtschaftsflur m, Wirtschaftsgang m, Wirtschaftskorridor m

~ ~ patio · Wirtschaftshof m

~ ~ room, ~ workroom · Hauswirtschaftsraum m

~ waiting room · Inlandwarteraum m [Flughafen]

~ waste → (liquid) ~

~ water, house(hold) ~ · Haushaltwasser n

~ ~ heating · Hauswasserheizung f

~ ~ meter · Hauswasserzähler m [DIN 3260]

~ ~ pipe, household ~ ~ · Haushaltwasserrohr n

~ ~ piping system, household ~ ~ ~ · Haushaltwasserleitungssystem n

~ (~) softener · Hausenthärter m

~ window, residential ~ · Wohn(gebäude)fenster n, Wohnhausfenster, Wohnungsfenster

~ wood, ~ timber, home-grown ~ · einheimisches Holz n

~ workroom, ~ utility room · Hauswirtschaftsraum m

domic(al), dome(-shape)d · kuppelförmig, kuppelartig

~ bottom → dome(-shape)d ~

~ floor → dome(-shape)d ~

~ mound, stupa(-mound), tope(mound), dagoba [A mound forming a Buddhist sacred monument] · Reliquienhügel m, Stupa m, Tope m, Dagoba m, Dagaba m, Dagop m

~ roof, dome(-shape)d ~, cupola ~, dome ~ · Dachhaube f, Haubendach n, Kuppeldach [Dach mit geschweifter Kontur]

~ shell, dome(-shape)d ~, dome ~, cupola ~ · Kuppelschale f

~ slab, dome(-shape)d ~, dome ~, cupola ~ · Kuppelplatte f

domical vault, cloister(ed) ~, coved ~ [A vault rising direct on a square or polygonal base, the curved surfaces separated by groins] · gebustes Gewölbe n, busiges ~, Domikalgewölbe

dominant harmony → monochrome painting

Dominican architecture · Dominikanerarchitektur f, Dominikanerbaukunst f

~ church · Dominikanerkirche f, Predigerkirche

~ monastery · Dominikanerkloster n

~ novitiate monastery · DominikanerStudienkloster n

~ nunnery · Dominikanerinnenkloster n

domus, family mansion · römisches Privathaus n

donjon — door plate

donjon, dungeon, keep · Donjon *m*, Bergfried *m*, Belfried, Berchfrit *m*

door [*B.S. 459*] · Tür *f*

~ **accessories,** ~ equipment · Türzubehör *n*

~ **aperture,** ~ opening · lichter Durchgang *m*, Türloch *n*, Türöffnung *f*

~ **arch** · Türbogen *m*

~ **axis;** ~ centre line (Brit.); ~ center line (US) · Türachse *f*

~ **bell** · Türklingel *f*

~ **bumper,** ~ stop · Türpuffer *m*

~ **case,** ~ casing · Türzarge *f*

~ **centre line** (Brit.); ~ center ~ (US); ~ axis · Türachse *f*

~ **chain** · Türkette *f*

~ **check** → ~ closer

~ **closer,** ~ check, ~ closing device, ~ closing mechanism, DC · Türschließer *m*, Türzuwerfer, Türschließvorrichtung *f*

~ **cornice** · Tür(ge)sims *m*, (*n*)

~ **dimension** · Türabmessung *f*, Türmaß *n*

~ **draught excluder,** ~ ~ seal (Brit.); ~ draft ~ (US) · Tür-Zugluftschützer *m*

~ **drive operator,** ~ ~ (system) · Tür(en)antrieb(vorrichtung) *m*, (*f*)

~ **equipment,** ~ accessories · Türzubehör *n*

~ **factory** · Türenfabrik *f*, Türenwerk *n*

~ **finishing** [*The ornamental door feature about a door such as lining, architrave, plinth blocks, moulded ground, pediment, etc.*] · Türverzierung *f*

~ **fitting** → ~ furniture

~ **fittings,** ~ hardware · Türbeschläge *mpl*

~ **frame,** ~ framing · Türumrahmung *f*, Türrahmen *m*, Türstock *m*

~ ~ **fixing,** ~ framing ~ · Türrahmenbefestigung *f*

~ **furniture,** ~ fitting [*Any functional or decorative fitting, excluding the lock and hinges, for a door*] · Türbeschlag *m*

~ **gasket** · Tür(ab)dichtung *f*, Tür(ab)dicht(ungs)profil *n*

~ **gear,** ~ mechanism · Türmechanismus *m*

~ **glass** · Tür(en)glas *n*

(~) ~ **knob** · (Tür)Glasknopf *m*

~ **grille** [*sometimes spelled 'grill'*] · Türgitter *n* [*Ein Baubeschlag, der vorzugsweise an Haus- und Korridortüren angebracht wird, wenn diese Glasscheiben enthalten*]

~ **handle,** lever (~) · (Tür)Drücker *m*, (Tür)Klinke *f* [*DIN 18255*]

~ ~ **fittings,** ~ ~ hardware, lever (~) ~ · (Tür-)Drückerbeschläge *mpl*, (Tür-)Klinkenbeschläge

~ **hardware,** ~ fittings · Türbeschläge *mpl*

~ **hinge** · Türscharnier *n*, Türband *n*

~ **holder** · Türhalter *m*

~ **hood** · Tür-Wetter(schutz)dach *n*

~ **installation,** ~ system · Türanlage *f*

~ **jamb,** ~ post, ~ tree, ~ ingoing, ~ cheek · Türpfosten *m*, Türständer *m*, Türsäule *f*

~ **joinery** · Türentischlereiwesen *n*

doorkeeper, gatekeeper, porter · Pförtner *m*

doorkeeper's house → porter's lodge

~ **lodge** → porter's ~

~ **room,** gatekeeper's ~, porter's ~ · Pförtnerraum *m*

(door) knob · (Tür)Knopf *m*

(~) ~ **fitting** → knob (door) ~

(~) ~ **fittings,** (~) ~ hardware, knob (door) ~ · Knopf(tür)beschläge *mpl*, Türknopfbeschläge

(~) ~ **furniture** → knob (door) fitting

(~) ~ **hardware** → (~) ~ fittings

(~) **knocker** · (Tür)Klopfer *m*

~ **leaf,** garage ~ ~ · (Garagen)Torblatt *n*

(~) ~ · (Tür)Blatt *n*, (Tür)Flügel *m* [*Beweglicher Verschluß der Öffnung einer Tür*]

(~) **ledge** · Querleiste *f*, Tür~ [*Brettertür*]

~ **lintel;** ~ lintol [*deprecated*] · Türoberschwelle *f*, Türsturz *m*

~ ~ **in prestressed clay** → Stahlton (prestressed) door lintel

~ ~ ~ **Stahlton** → Stahlton (prestressed) door lintel

(~) **lock** · (Tür)Schloß *n* [*DIN 18251*]

doorman · Portier *m*

door manufacturer · Türenhersteller *m*

~ **mat** · Türmatte *f*, Abtretmatte

~ **mechanism,** ~ gear · Türmechanismus *m*

~ **niche arch** · Türnischenbogen *m*

(~) **opener** · (Tür)Öffner *m*

~ **opening,** ~ aperture · lichter Durchgang *m*, Türloch *n*, Türöffnung *f*

(~) ~ **handle** · (Tür)Öffnungsgriff *m*

(~) ~ **operator,** door-opening system · (Tür)Öffnungsanlage *f*, (Tür)Öffneranlage

(~) **panel** · (Tür)Füllung *f*

(~) ~ **arrangement** · (Tür)Füllungsausbildung *f*

~ **pier** · Türpfeiler *m*

~ **plate** [*A metal plate on the door of a house or apartment carrying the name of the occupant*] · Türschild *m*

door plate — dormitory unit

~ ~ · Türblech *n*

~ **pocket** [*sliding door*] · Türschlitz *m*

~ **post,** ~ tree, ~ ingoing, ~ cheek, ~ jamb · Türpfosten *m*, Türständer *m*, Türsäule *f*

~ **profile,** ~ section, ~ trim, ~ shape, ~ unit · Tür(en)profil *n*

(~) **pull (handle)** · (Tür)Griff *m*

(~) **rail** · Querrahmenstück *n*, (Tür)Riegel *m* [*Holzfüllungstür*]

~ **reveal** · Türleibung *f*

~ **scraper** · Abtretrost *m*

~ **seal(ing) fillet** · Tür(ab)dicht(ungs)leiste *f*

~ **section,** ~ trim ~ unit, ~ shape, ~ profile · Tür(en)profil *n*

~ **shape,** ~ profile, ~ section, ~ trim, ~ unit · Tür(en)profil *n*

~ **size** · Türgröße *f*

~ **spring** · Türfeder *f*

~ **stay** · Türfeststeller *m*

~ ~ · Türkettelhaken *m*, Türsturmhaken

~ **step** · Türstufe *f*

~ **stop,** doorstop, D ST · Türanschlag *m* [*Eine Fläche gegen welche die Tür schlägt*]

~ ~, ~ bumper · Türpuffer *m*

~ **stud,** ~ post, principal ~, door check · Türpfosten *m*, Türständer *m*, Türsäule *f* [*Fach(werk)wand*]

~ **switch,** DSW · Türschalter *m*

~ **system,** ~ installation · Türanlage *f*

(~) **threshold** · (Tür)Schwelle *f*

~ **trim,** ~ section, ~ unit, ~ shape, ~ profile · Tür(en)profil *n*

~ **unit,** ~ trim, ~ section, ~ shape, ~ profile · Tür(en)profil *n*

(~) **viewer,** judas · (Tür)Gucker *m*, (Tür)Spion *m*

doorway [*An opening provided with a door for access through a wall*] · Türdurchgang *m*

door window · Fenstertür *f*

to dope, to coat and wrap · beschichten, isolieren [*Rohr*]

dope → activator

doped · gedopt

~ **binder** · gedoptes Bindemittel *n*, gedopter Binder *m*

~ **cutback,** ~ ~ (asphaltic-)bitumen (Brit.); ~ asphalt(ic) cutback, ~ cutback (asphalt) (US) · Verschnittbitumen *n* mit Haftanreger, gedoptes Verschnittbitumen

~ **emulsion** · Emulsion *f* mit Haftanreger, gedopte Emulsion

doping of binders, promotion of binder adhesion · Haft(fähigkeits)verbesserung *f*, Haftanregung [*Von plastischen Bindemitteln am Gestein*]

Dora reinforced block floor · Dora-Decke *f*

Doric architrave, ~ epistyle · dorischer Architrav *m*, dorisches Epistyl(ion) *n*

~ **base,** ~ column ~ · dorischer (Säulen)Fuß *m*, dorische Basis *f*

~ **capitel** · dorisches Kapitell *n*, ~ Kapitäl

~ **colonnade** · dorische Kolonnade *f*

~ **column** · dorische Säule *f*

~ (~) **base** · dorischer (Säulen)Fuß *m*, dorische Basis *f*

Doric-columned · mit dorischen Säulen (versehen)

Doric cornice · dorischer Sims *m*, dorisches Gesims *n*

~ **cyma(tium),** cyma(tium) recta · dorisches Kyma(tion) *n*, dorische Blattwelle *f*

~ **echinus** · dorischer Echinus *m*

~ **entablature** · dorisches Gebälk *n*

~ **epistyle,** ~ architrave · dorischer Architrav *m*, dorisches Epistyl(ion) *n*

~ **frieze** · dorischer Fries *m*

~ **order (of architecture)** · dorische (Säulen)Ordnung *f*, D.O.

~ **portico** · dorischer Portikus *m*

~ **structure** · dorisches Bauwerk *n*

~ **style** · dorischer Stil *m*

~ **temple** · dorischer Tempel *m*

dormer, roof ~ [*The structure containing a dormer window*] · (Dach)Gaube *f*, (Dach)Gaupe

~ **cheek** → roof ~ ~

~ **covering** roof ~ ~ · (Dach)Gaubendeckung *f*, (Dach)Gaupendeckung

~ **rafter** · Reitersparren *m*, Klauensparren

~ **roof,** dormered ~ · Gaubendach *n*, Gaupendach

dormer-ventilator · Lüftergaube *f*, Lüftergaube, Lüftungsgaube, Lüftungsgaupe, (Dach)Gaube, (Dach)Gaube, (Dach)Lüfter *m*, (Dach)Lüftungsstein *m*, Gaupenstein, Gaubenstein, Lukenstein, Haubenstein, Kaffstein, Kappstein [*Dachstein, zu Flach-, Hohl- oder Falzsteinen passend mit einem meist halbkegelförmigen Aufbau zum Einlaß von Licht und Luft in einen Dachraum*]

dormer (window), roof ~ (~) · (Dach)Gaubenfenster *n*, (Dach)Gaupenfenster

dormer(ed) roof · Gaubendach *n*, Gaupendach

dormitory, dorter, dortour · Dormitorium *n*, Schlafsaal *m*

~ **block,** ~ unit, ~ building, ~ house, bedroom ~ · Schlaftrakt *m*, Schlafgebäude *n*, Schlafflügel *m* [*Krankenhaus; Hotel*]

~ **building** → ~ block

~ **house** → ~ block

~ **suburb,** ~ sub. · Schlafstadt *f*

~ **unit** → ~ block

Dorr Fluo-Solide Reactor [*Trademark*]
· Kalk(brenn)ofen *m* für das Fließverfahren

dorter, dormitory, dortour · Dormitorium *n*, Schlafsaal *m*

dosage pump set · Dosierpumpenaggregat *n*

dosseret, pulvin(us), superabacus, supercapital, impost block · Pulvinus *m*

dot · Lehrkopf *m*

double-acting door, double-action ~, double-swinging ~ [*This type of swing door can easily be pushed open in either direction*] · zweiseitig aufschlagende Pendeltür *f*, Durchgangstür

double-action door, double-acting ~, double-swinging ~ [*This type of swing door can easily be pushed open in either direction*] · zweiseitig aufschlagende Pendeltür *f*, Durchschlagtür

double ambulatory, ~ de~ · doppelter (Chor)Umgang *m*, doppeltes Deambulatorium *n*

~ angle · Winkelpaar *n* [*für Ober- und Untergurt*]

~ ~ bar, ~ ~ (section) · Doppelwinkel *m* [*Ein kaltgewalztes Profil in Form zweier zusammengesetzter stumpfer Winkel*]

~ ~ (section), ~ ~ bar · Doppelwinkel *m* [*Ein kaltgewalztes Profil in Form zweier zusammengesetzter stumpfer Winkel*]

~ ~ tie · Winkelpaar-Zugglied *n* [*Fachwerk(dach)binder*]

~ arched corbel-table · Rund- und Kreuzbogenfries *m* [*Jeder für sich an einer Schräge desselben Giebels, z.B. an der Kirche von Brusasco*]

~ archway · Doppeldurchfahrt *f*, Doppeldurchgang *m* [*Stadttor*]

double-articulated arch(ed) frame, double-pin(ned) ~ ~, double-hinge(d) ~ ~, double-linked ~ ~, two-pin(ned) ~ ~, two-hinged ~ ~, two-linked ~ ~, two-articulated ~ ~ · Zweigelenk-Bogenrahmen *m*

~ flat arch(ed girder), double pin(ned) ~ ~ (~), double-hinge(d) ~ ~ (~), double-linked ~ ~ (~), two-pin(ned) ~ ~ (~), two hinge(d) ~ ~ (~), two-articulated ~ ~ (~), two-linked ~ ~ (~), ~ segmental ~ (~) · Zweigelenk-Flachbogen(träger) *m*, Zweigelenk-Stichbogen(träger), Zweigelenk-Segmentbogen(träger)

~ ~ parabolic arch(ed girder), double-pin(ned) ~ ~ ~ (~), double-hinge(d) ~ ~ ~ (~), double-linked ~ ~ ~ (~), two-hinge(d) ~ ~ ~ (~), two-pin(ned) ~ ~ ~ (~), two-linked ~ ~ ~ (~), two-articulated ~ ~ ~ (~) · Zweigelenkflachparabelbogen(träger) *m*

~ frame, double-pin(ned) ~, double-hinge(d) ~, double-linked ~, two-pin(ned) ~, two-hinge(d) ~, two-linked ~, two-articulated ~ · Zweigelenkrahmen *m*

~ gable(d) frame, double-pin(ned) ~ ~, double-hinge(d) ~ ~, double-linked ~ ~, two-pin(ned) ~ ~, two-hinge(d) ~ ~, two-linked ~ ~, two-articulated ~ ~ · Zweigelenk-Giebelrahmen *m*

~ parabolic arch(ed girder), double-linked ~ ~ (~), double-pin(ned) ~ ~ (~), double-hinge(d) ~ ~ (~), two-pin(ned) ~ ~ (~), two-hinge(d) ~ ~ (~), two-linked ~ ~ (~), two-articulated ~ ~ (~) · Zweigelenkparabelbogen(träger) *m*

~ rectangular frame, double-pin(ned) ~ ~, double-hinge(d) ~ ~, double-linked ~ ~, two-pin(ned) ~ ~, two-hinge(d) ~ ~, two-linked ~ ~, two-articulated ~ ~ · Zweigelenk-Rechteckrahmen *m*

~ segmental arch(ed girder), double-linked ~ ~ (~), double-pin(ned) ~ ~ (~), double-hinge(d) ~ ~ (~), two-pin(ned) ~ ~ (~), two-hinge(d) ~ ~ (~), two-linked ~ ~ (~), two-articulated ~ ~ (~), ~ flat ~ (~) · Zweigelenk-Flachbogen(träger) *m*, Zweigelenk-Stichbogen(träger), Zweigelenk-Segmentbogen(träger)

double-axis symmetry · doppelachsige Symmetrie *f*

double batten, ~ lath · Doppellatte *f* [*Dach(ein)deckung*]

~ bay · Doppeljoch(feld) *n*, Doppelfeld

~ bed room, ~ (guest) ~ · Doppelschlafraum *m*, Zweibettenraum, Zweibettenzimmer *n*, Doppel(bett)zimmer [*Hotel*]

~ bond · Doppelbindung *f* [*ungesättigte Säure*]

double-box girder, twin-box ~ · Doppelkastenträger *m*

double bracing, ~ triangulated system · zweiteiliges Netzwerk *n* [*Träger*]

~ branch pipe, ~ Y · Doppelabzweig(-er) [*Rohrformstück*]

~ brick · Doppelziegel *m*

~ broken and double screened chip(ping)s, twice crushed and ~ ~ · Edelsplitt *m*

double-broken chip(ping)s, double-crushed ~ · doppelt gebrochener Splitt *m*

double bull (type) column · Doppelstiersäule *f*

double-burnt gypsum, double-burned ~ · Doppelbrandgips *m*

double-cage reinforcement, ~ reinforcing · Armierungsdoppelkorb *m*, Bewehrungsdoppelkorb

~ reinforcing, ~ reinforcement · Armierungsdoppelkorb *m*, Bewehrungsdoppelkorb

double-cantilever (roof) truss · Doppelausleger(-Dach)binder *m*, Doppelkrag(-Dach)binder

~ shell · Doppelauslegerschale *f*, Doppelkragschale

double casement fastener · doppelter Vorreiber *m*, ganzer ~

~ **channel section** · Doppel-U-Profil *n*

~ **chime unit, twin** ~ ~, **dual** ~ ~ · Doppel(ton)-Läutewerk *n*

~ **choir,** ~ **quire** · Doppelchor *m*

double-choir church, double-quire ~ · doppelchörige Anlage *f* [*Kirche mit einem Ost- und einem Westchor*]

double clay pot → hollow clay (building) block

~ **colonade** · doppelte Kolonnade *f*

~ **compartment septic tank, dual** ~ ~ ~, **two-**~ ~ ~ · Zweikammer-Grundstückskläranlage *f*, Doppelkammer-Grundstückskläranlage, Zweikammer-Hauskläranlage, Doppelkammer-Hauskläranlage, Zweikammer-Kleinkläranlage, Doppelkammer-Kleinkläranlage, Doppelkammer-Kleinkläranlage [*DIN 4261*]

double-cone moulding (Brit.); ~ **molding** (US) · Doppelkegelverzierung *f*

double corrugated sheet · Doppelwellblech *n*

~ **cross, patriarchal** ~ · Patriarchenkreuz *n*, Doppelkreuz, Patriarchalkreuz, Kardinalskreuz

~ **cross-section, dual** ~, **twin** ~ · zweiteiliger Querschnitt *m*, doppelter ~

~ **cross timber,** ~ **intertie** · Doppelsturzriegel *m* [*Fachwerkwand*]

double-crushed chip(ping)s, double-broken ~ · doppelt gebrochener Splitt *m*

double crypt · Doppelkrypta *f*, Doppelgruft *f*

~ **cube** · Doppelwürfel *m*

double-cube room · Doppelwürfelsaal *m*

double curvature shell → shell of double curvature

~ ~ **translation(al) shell** → translational shell of double curvature

~ **curved, doubly** ~ · doppelt gekrümmt, zweifach ~

double-curved rib, sweeping ~ · (kurvig) geschwungene Rippe *f*

double curved spike grid · doppelt gekrümmter (zweiseitiger) Krallendübel *m*, gekrümmtes Krallenplattenpaar *n*

~ **cylinder** · Doppelspindel *f* [*Wendeltreppe*]

~ ~ **(staircase), staircase with two cylinders** · Doppelspindel(treppe) *f*, doppelspindlige Treppe [*Eine Wendeltreppe mit zwei Achsen, deren Stufen in ihrer Aufeinanderfolge eine Schleife bilden*]

~ **(de)ambulatory** · doppelter (Chor-)Umgang *m*, doppeltes Deambulatorium *n*

~-**deck elevator** → tandem ~

~-**deck lift** (Brit.) → tandem elevator

double deformation · doppelte Formänderung *f*, ~ Verformung

~ **door** · Doppeltür *f*

~ ~, **folding** ~ · Falttür *f*

~ ~ **fitting, ** ~ ~ **furniture, folding** ~ · Falttürbeschlag *m*

~ ~ **fittings,** ~ ~ **hardware, folding** ~ ~ · Falttürbeschläge *mpl*

~ ~ **furniture,** ~ ~ **fitting, folding** ~ ~ · Falttürbeschlag *m*

~ ~ **hardware,** ~ ~ **fittings, folding** ~ ~ · Falttürbeschläge *mpl*

~ **doored** · doppeltürig, zweitürig

~ **false ceiling** · doppelte Einschubdecke *f*, ~ Zwischendecke

~ **flanged zed** · (doppelt) abgekantetes Z-Profil *n*

~ **flap clay pantile** · Doppelkrempziegel *m*, Doppelkrampziegel, Doppelblattziegel, Doppelkremper *m*, Doppelbreitziegel [*Hohlpfanne mit einer Höhlung und zwei Wülsten, nur an einer Ecke abgeschrägt, und zwar links als rechter Ortziegel oder rechts als linker Ortziegel*]

~ ~ **pantile** · Doppelkrampstein *m*, Doppelkrampstein, Doppelblattstein, Doppelkremper *m*, Doppelbreitstein

~ **Flemish bond** · polnischer (Mauerwerk)Verband *m*, gotischer ~

double-flight stair(case), dual-flight ~, **two-flight** ~ · zweiläufige Treppe *f*, doppelläufige ~

double floor cover(ing) → ~ floor(-ing) (finish)

~ ~ **(finish)** → ~ flooring (~)

~ **floor(ing) (finish),** ~ **floor cover(-ing)** [*Flooring laid in two layers on joists, the lower layer providing strength and the upper a wearing surface*] · Doppel(fuß)boden(belag) *m*

~ **frame** · Doppelrahmen *m*

double-frame(d) window · Doppelrahmenfenster *n*

double-frogged brick · Ziegel *m* mit zwei Aushöhlungen, ~ ~ ~ Austiefungen, ~ ~ ~ Vertiefungen, ~ ~ ~ ~ Mulden

double gateway · Doppel(stadt)tor *n*

~ **girder, dual** ~, **twin** ~ · Zwillingsträger *m*

~ **glass** → insulating ~

double-glazed unit · doppelt verglastes Element *n*

~ **window** · Panzerfenster *n*, Doppelfenster

double glazing, dual ~ [*Two layers of glass are separated by an air space for thermal or acoustic insulation*] · Doppelverglasung *f*, Doppeleinglasung

~ ~ **unit,** ~ **pane** ~ · Doppel(glas)scheibe *f*

double (guest) room — double-linked flat parabolic... 308

~ **(guest) room,** ~ bed ~ · Doppelschlafraum *m*, Zweibettenraum, Zweibettenzimmer *n*, Doppel(bett)zimmer [*Hotel*]

~ **H steel column** · Doppel-H-Stahlstütze *f*

~ **hanging (roof) truss** → queen post (~) ~

double-headed nail, duplex-headed ~, scaffold ~, form ~, dual-head ~ · Duplexnagel *m*, Doppelkopfnagel

double header · Doppelwechsel(balken) *m*

double-hinge(d) arch(ed) frame, double-linked ~ ~, double-pin(ned) ~ ~, double-articulated ~ ~, two-pin(ned) ~ ~, two-linked ~ ~, two-hinged ~ ~, two-articulated ~ ~ · Zweigelenk-Bogenrahmen *m*

~ **flat arch(ed girder),** double-pin(ned) ~ ~ (~), double-linked ~ ~ (~), double-articulated ~ ~ (~), two-pin(ned) ~ ~ (~), two-hinge(d) ~ ~ (~), two-linked ~ ~ (~), two-articulated ~ ~ (~), ~ segmental ~ (~) · Zweigelenk-Flachbogen(träger)*m*, Zweigelenk-Stichbogen(träger), Zweigelenk-Segmentbogen(träger)

~ ~ **parabolic arch(ed girder),** double-pin(ned) ~ ~ ~ (~), double-linked ~ ~ ~ (~), double-articulated ~ ~ ~ (~), two-hindge(d) ~ ~ ~ (~), two-pin(ned) ~ ~ ~ (~), two-linked ~ ~ (~), two-articulated ~ ~ ~ (~) · Zweigelenkflachparabelbogen(träger) *m*

~ **frame,** double-pin(ned) ~, double-linked ~, double-articulated ~, two-pin(ned) ~, two-hinge(d) ~, two-linked ~, two-articulated ~ · Zweigelenkrahmen *m*

~ **gable(d) frame,** double-pin(ned) ~ ~, double-linked ~ ~, double articulated ~ ~, two-pin(ned) ~ ~, two-hinge(d) ~ ~, two-linked ~ ~, two-articulated ~ ~ · Zweigelenk-Giebelrahmen *m*

~ **parabolic arch(ed girder),** double-pin(ned) ~ ~ (~), double-linked ~ ~ (~), double-articulated ~ ~ (~), two-hinge(d) ~ ~ (~), two-pin(ned) ~ ~ (~), two-linked ~ ~ (~), two-articulated ~ ~ (~) · Zweigelenkparabelbogen(träger) *m*

~ **rectangular frame,** double-pin(ned) ~ ~, double-linked ~ ~, double-articulated ~ ~, two-pin(ned) ~ ~, two-hinge(d) ~ ~, two-linked ~ ~, two-articulated ~ ~ · Zweigelenk-Rechteckrahmen *m*

~ **segmental arch(ed girder),** double-pin(ned) ~ ~ (~), double-linked ~ ~ (~), double-articulated ~ ~ (~), two-pin(ned) ~ ~ (~), two-hinge(d) ~ ~ (~), two-linked ~ ~ (~), two-articulated ~ ~ (~), ~ flat ~ (~) · Zweigelenk-Flachbogen(träger) *m*, Zweigelenk-Stichbogen(träger), Zweigelenk-Segmentbogen(träger)

double hollow clay (building) block, ~ clay pot · Doppelhourdi *m*, Doppel-Tonhohl(stein)platte *f*, Doppel-Ziegelhohlplatte, Doppel-Hohlnutenstein *m* [*Er hat zwei Hohlräume übereinander*]

~ **house (US); twin** ~ [*A pair of semidetached houses*] · Doppelhaus *n*

double-hung (sash) window · Doppel-Vertikal-Schiebe(flügel)fenster *n*, Doppel-Senkrecht-Schiebe(flügel)fenster, zweiteiliges Senkrecht-Schieba(flügel)fenster, zweiteiliges Vertikal-Schiebe-(flügel)fenster

double (insulating) reed mat, ~ insulation(-grade) ~ · Doppel(schilf)rohrgewebe *n*; Doppel(schilf)rohrmatte *f*, Doppel(isolier)rohrung *f* [*Fehlname: Doppelrohrgeflecht n. Die Rohrstengel sind durch Drähte verwebt, nicht verflochten*]

~ **intertie,** ~ cross timber · Doppelsturzriegel *m* [*Fachwerkwand*]

~ **jack rafter** · Doppelschifter *m*

~ **junction,** breech · Gabel *f* [*Rohrformstück*]

~ **lap tile** → plain (roof(ing)) ~

~ **lath,** ~ batten · Doppellatte *f* [*Dach-(ein)deckung*]

double-layer(ed), two-layer(ed) · doppellagig, zweilagig, zweischichtig, doppelschichtig

~ **space frame shell, two-layer(ed)** ~ ~ · zweischaliges Raumfachwerk *n*, doppelschaliges ~

double-lead process · Tauchpatentieren *n*

double-leaf (clay) brick veneer · zweischalige Ziegelverblendung *f*, zweischaliges Ziegelverblendmauerwerk *m*

~ **door,** two-leaf ~ · zweiflügelige Tür *f*, Zweiflügeltür

double leg stirrup · zweischnittiger Bügel *m*

double-linked arch(ed) frame, double-hinge(d) ~ ~, double-pin(ned) ~ ~, double-articulated ~ ~, two-pin(ned) ~ ~, two-linked ~ ~, two-hinged ~ ~, two-articulated ~ ~ · Zweigelenk-Bogenrahmen *m*

~ **flat arch(ed girder),** double-pin(ned) ~ ~ (~), double-hinge(d) ~ ~ (~), double-articulated ~ ~ (~), two-pin(ned) ~ ~ (~), two-hinge(d) ~ ~ (~), two-linked ~ ~ (~), two-articulated ~ ~ (~), ~ segmental ~ (~) · Zweigelenk-Flachbogen(träger) *m*, Zweigelenk-Stichbogen(träger), Zweigelenk-Segmentbogen(träger)

~ ~ **parabolic arch(ed girder),** double-pin(ned) ~ ~ ~ (~), double-hinge(d) ~ ~ ~ (~), double-articulated ~ ~ ~ (~), two-pin(ned) ~ ~ ~ (~), two-hinge(d) ~ ~ ~ (~), two-linked ~ ~ ~ (~), two-articulated ~ ~ ~ (~) · Zweigelenkflachparabelbogen(träger) *m*

double-linked frame — double quarter-turn ...

~ **frame,** double-hinge(d) ~, double-pin(ned) ~, double-articulated ~, two-pin(ned) ~, two-hinge(d) ~, two-linked ~, two-articulated ~ · Zweigelenkrahmen *m*

~ **gable(d) frame,** double-pin(ned) ~ ~, double-hinge(d) ~ ~, double-articulated ~ ~, two-pin(ned) ~ ~, two-hinge(d) ~ ~, two-linked ~ ~, two-articulated ~ ~, ~ ~ framing · Zweigelenk-Giebelrahmen *m*

~ **parabolic arch(ed girder),** double-pin(ned) ~ ~ (~), double-hinge(d) ~ ~ (~), double-articulated ~ ~ (~), two-hinge(d) ~ ~ (~), two-pin(ned) ~ ~ (~), two-linked ~ ~ (~), two-articulated ~ ~ (~) · Zweigelenkparabelbogen(träger) *m*

~ **rectangular frame,** double-hinge(d) ~ ~, double-pin(ned) ~ ~, double-articulated ~ ~, two-pin(ned) ~ ~, two-hinge(d) ~ ~, two-linked ~ ~, two-articulated ~ ~, ~ ~ framing · Zweigelenk-Rechteckrahmen *m*

~ **segmental arch(ed girder),** double-hinge(d) ~ ~ (~), double-pin(ned) ~ ~ (~), double-articulated ~ ~ (~), two-pin(ned) ~ ~ (~), two-hinge(d) ~ ~ (~), two-linked ~ ~ (~), two-articulated ~ ~ (~), flat ~ (~) · Zweigelenk-Flachbogen(träger) *m*, Zweigelenk-Stichbogen(träger), Zweigelenk-Segmentbogen(träger)

double linking · Doppelbindung *f* [*Bitumenchemie*]

double-lock seam, double welt(ed ~) · liegender Doppelfalz *m*, Liegedoppelfalz [*Metallbedachung*]

double loop for girders, ~ stirrup ~ ~ · doppelter Trägerbügel *m*, Doppel-Trägerbügel

~ **membrane pneumatic system** · Kissensystem *n*, Doppelmembran(e)-Pneusystem

~ **mould** (Brit.); ~ mold (US); dual ~, twin ~ · Doppelform *f*, Zwillingsform

double-naved church · zweischiffige Kirche *f*, doppelschiffige ~

double oblique junction · Doppelabzweig(er) *m* [*Rohrformstück*]

~ **pack,** twin ~ · Doppelpaket *n*

double-pane sash, dual-pane ~, two-pane ~ · Doppelflügel *m* [*Der doppelt verglaste Flügel eines Verbundfensters*]

double pane unit, ~ glazing ~ · Doppel(glas)scheibe *f*

~ **parabolic girder** · Zweiparabelträger *m*

~ **partition (wall)** → hollow ~ (~)

double-pin(ned) arch(ed) frame, double-hinged ~ ~, double-linked ~, double-articulated ~ ~, two-linked ~ ~, two-pin(ned) ~ ~, two-hinged ~ ~, two-articulated ~ ~ · Zweigelenk-Bogenrahmen *m*

~ **flat arch(ed girder),** double-hinge(d) ~ ~ (~), double-linked ~ ~ (~), double-articulated ~ ~ (~), two-pin(ned) ~ ~ (~), two-hinge(d) ~ ~ ~ (~), two-linked ~ ~ ~ (~), two-articulated ~ ~ ~ (~), ~ segmental ~ (~) · Zweigelenk-Flachbogen(träger) *m*, Zweigelenk-Stichbogen(träger), Zweigelenk-Segmentbogen(träger)

~ ~ **parabolic arch(ed girder),** double-hinge(d) ~ ~ ~ (~), double-linked ~ ~ ~ (~), double-articulated ~ ~ ~ (~), two-pin(ned) ~ ~ ~ (~), two-hinge(d) ~ ~ ~ (~), two-linked ~ ~ ~ (~), two-articulated ~ ~ ~ (~) · Zweigelenkflachparabelbogen(träger) *m*

~ **frame,** double-hinge(d) ~, double-linked ~, double-articulated ~, two-pin(ned) ~, two-hinge(d) ~, two-linked ~, two-articulated ~ · Zweigelenkrahmen *m*

~ **gable(d) frame,** double-hinge(d) ~ ~, double-linked ~ ~, double-articulated ~ ~, two-pin(ned) ~ ~, two-hinge(d) ~ ~, two-linked ~ ~, two-articulated ~ ~ · Zweigelenk-Giebelrahmen *m*

~ **parabolic arch(ed girder),** double-hinge(d) ~ ~ (~), double-linked ~ ~ (~), double-articulated ~ ~ (~), two-hinge(d) ~ ~ (~), two-pin(ned) ~ ~ (~), two-linked ~ ~ (~), two-articulated ~ ~ (~) · Zweigelenkparabelbogen(träger) *m*

~ **rectangular frame,** double-hinge(d) ~ ~, double-linked ~ ~, double-articulated ~ ~, two-pin(ned) ~ ~, two-hinge(d) ~ ~, two-linked ~ ~, two-articulated ~ ~ · Zweigelenk-Rechteckrahmen *m*

~ **segmental arch(ed girder),** double-hinge(d) ~ ~ (~), double-linked ~ ~ (~), double-articulated ~ ~ (~), two-pin(ned) ~ ~ (~), two-hinge(d) ~ ~ (~), two-linked ~ ~ (~), two-articulated ~ ~ (~), ~ flat ~ (~) · Zweigelenk-Flachbogen(träger) *m*, Zweigelenk-Stichbogen(träger), Zweigelenk-Segmentbogen(träger)

double-pipe meter, two-pipe ~ · Zweirohrzähler *m*

double pitch sodium paper · Natron-Doppelpechpapier *n*

double-pitched roof, curb ~ (US); hip(ped) mansard ~, hip(ped) French ~ [*It slopes in four directions, but there is a break on each slope*] · abgewalmtes Mansard(en)dach *n*, Mansard(en)walmdach

double-pole on-off switch · zweipoliger Ausschalter *m*

~ **pull(cord) (type) switch** · zweipoliger Zugschnurschalter *m*, doppelpoliger ~

double portico · Doppelportikus *m*

~ **pressed brick,** twice-pressed ~ · Doppelpreßziegel *m*

~ **projected window** · Doppel-Lüftungsflügelfenster *n*

~ **quarter-turn stair(case) with winders** · zweiviertelgewendelte Treppe *f*

double quire — double tee roof slab

~ **quire,** ~ **choir** · Doppelchor *m*
double-quire church, double-choir ~ · doppelchörige Anlage *f* [*Kirche mit einem Ost- und einem Westchor*]
double reed mat → ~ **insulating** ~ ~
~ **rib** · Doppelrippe *f*
~ **roll** · Doppelrolle *f* [*Tapete*]
~ **Roman (clay tile),** ~ ~ **tile** · Doppelfalz(dach)ziegel *m*
~ ~ **(tile)** · Doppelfalz(dach)stein *m*
~ **roof** · Pfettendach *n*
~ **roofing,** close-boarded (battened) ~, close-sheeted ~ · Doppel(dach)- (ein)deckung *f*, Doppelbedachung
~ **(roofing) skin (construction)** [*It has an air space between the skins*] · Doppeldachhaut *f*
~ **room,** ~ **guest** ~, ~ **bed** ~ · Doppelschlafraum *m*, Zweibettenraum, Zweibettenzimmer *n*, Doppel(bett)zimmer [*Hotel*]
double-sash window (US) · zweiflügeliges Fenster *n*, Zweiflügelfenster [*Siehe Anmerkung unter „Flügel"*]
double shear rivet joint · zweischnittige Nietung *f*
~ **shell** · Doppelschale *f*
~ **shutter curtain** · Doppelpanzer *m* [*Rolltor*]
double-side shuttering, ~ **formwork,** ~ **forms** · zweihäuptige Schalung *f* [*Beiderseitig eingeschalt im Gegensatz zur einhäuptigen Schalung bei der das stehende Erdreich eine Seitenschalung der Wand ersetzt*]
double-sided partition (wall) · Duplextrennwand *f*
~ **(toothed) plate** · Zahndübel *m* mit nach beiden Seiten aufgebogenen Zähnen
double-sized brick, twin ~ · Doppelformatziegel *m*
double skew notch · doppelter Versatz *m* [*Holzkonstruktion*]
~ **skin (construction)** → ~ **roofing** ~ (~)
double-skin partition (wall) [*It comprises two outside layers and an interior material*] · Dreilagen-Trennwand *f*, Dreischichten-Trennwand
double slab-type block, ~ ~ **building,** ~ **straight-line** ~ · Zweischeibenhaus *n*
~ ~ **building,** ~ ~ **block,** ~ **straight-line** ~ · Zweischeibenhaus *n*
~ **sliding door** · doppelflügelige Schiebetür *f*, zweiflügelige ~, Doppel-Schiebetür, Schiebetür mit zwei Flügeln
~ ~ ~ **installation** · doppelflügelige Schiebetüranlage *f*, zweiflügelige ~, Schiebetüranlage mit zwei Flügeln, Doppelschiebetüranlage

310

~ ~ **table press** · Doppelschiebetischpresse *f*
~ **sound-boarded floor** · doppelte Einschubdecke *f*
double-spiral ramp · Doppelwendelrampe *f*
double square junction, tee ~, T(ee) ~ · Doppelabzweig(er) *m* 90°, T-Stück *n* [*Rohrformstück*]
~ **standing seam** → ~ **welted** ~ ~
~ ~, ~-**type zinc roof,** ~ ~ welt-type ~ ~ · Zink-Doppelstehfalzdach *m*
~ ~ **welt,** ~ **(welted) standing seam** · Doppelstehfalz *m*, stehender Doppelfalz [*Metallbedachung*]
~ ~ ~-**type zinc roof,** ~ ~ seam-type ~ ~ · Zink-Doppelstehfalzdach *n*
~ **stirrup for girders,** ~ **loop** ~ ~ · doppelter Trägerbügel *m*, Doppel-Trägerbügel
~ **straight-line block,** ~ ~ **building,** ~ **slab-type** ~ · Zweischeibenhaus *n*
~ ~ **building,** ~ ~ **block,** ~ **slab-type** ~ · Zweischeibenhaus *n*
double-strap web joint · doppelte Stegverlaschung *f*
double strength window glass (US) → ~ **thickness sheet** ~
~ **stretcher** · Doppelläufer *m*
double-strut trussed beam · umgekehrter zweisäuliger Hängebock *m*, umgekehrtes zweisäuliges Hängewerk *n*
double strutted frame · doppeltes Sprengwerk *n*
double-swinging door, double-acting ~, double-action ~ [*This type of swing door can easily be pushed open in either direction*] · zweiseitig aufschlagende Pendeltür *f*, Durchschlagtür
double symmetrical cross-section · doppelt symmetrischer Querschnitt *m*
~ **T bed,** double-tee ~ · Spannbett *n* für Doppel-T-Träger
~ **T(ee) (floor slab)** · Doppel-T-Deckenelement *n*, Doppel-T-Deckenplatte *f*, T-T-Deckenelement, T-T-Deckenplatte
~ ~ **floor(ing) system,** ~ ~ ~ construction, ~ tee ~ ~ · Doppel-T-Decken(bau)system *n*, Doppel-T-Deckenkonstruktion (ssystem) *f*, (*n*)
~ ~ **frame,** ~ tee ~ · Doppel-T-Rahmen *m*, T-T-Rahmen
~ ~ **plate,** ~ ~ **slab,** ~ tee ~ · Doppel-T-Platte *f*, T-T-Platte
~ ~ **prefab(ricated) girder,** ~ tee ~ · Doppel-T-Fertigträger *m*, Fertigträger I, Montageträger I, Doppel-T-Montageträger
~ **tee roof slab,** ~ T(ee) ~ ~ · Doppel-T-Dachplatte *f*

double T(ee) slab — down draft

~ T(ee) slab, ~ ~ plate, ~ tee ~ · Doppel-T-Platte *f*, T-T-Platte

~ thickness sheet glass; ~ ~ window ~, ~ strength window ~, DS ~ (US) · doppeltdickes Glas *n*, DD

~ ~ window glass (US) → ~ ~ sheet ~

~ timber lintel; ~ ~ lintol [*deprecated*] · Doppelsturzholz *n*

double-tower façade, dual-tower ~, two-tower ~, twin-tower ~ · Doppelturmfassade *f*, Zweiturmfassade

double towered, twin-towered · doppeltürmig, zweitürmig

~ ~ gatehouse, twin-towered ~ · doppeltürmige Vorburg *f*, zweitürmige ~

~ transept · Doppelquerhaus *n*

~ triangulated system, ~ bracing · zweiteiliges Netzwerk *n* [*Träger*]

~ trimmer · Doppelstreichbalken *m*

~ T-roof(ing) slab, ~ tee-roof ~ · Bedachungselement *n* in Form von Doppel-T-Trägern, Bedachungsplatte *f* ~ ~ ~ ~, Dachelement ~ ~ ~ ~, Dachplatte ~ ~ ~ ~

~ turn lock · zweitouriges Schloß *n*

~-unit · zweilängig, 2-längig [*Schienenleuchte*]

double vault, bi-vault · Doppelgewölbe *n*

~ v(ee) gutter · W-Rinne *f*

~ wall · Doppelwand *f*

double-walled, two-walled · zweiwandig, doppelwandig

double wash(ing) stand · Doppelwaschtisch *n*

double-webbed, twin-webbed, two-webbed · zweistegig, doppelstegig

~ plate girder, two-webbed ~ ~, twin-webbed ~ ~ · Zweigstegblechträger *m*, Doppelstegblechträger

~ T-beam, twin-webbed ~, two-webbed ~ · zweistegiger Plattenbalken *m*, doppelstegiger ~

double welt(ed seam), double-lock ~ · liegender Doppelfalz *m*, Liegedoppelfalz [*Metallbedachung*]

~ (welted) standing seam, ~ standing welt · Doppelstehfalz *m*, stehender Doppelfalz [*Metallbedachung*]

~ window · Doppelfenster *n*

double-wing(ed) building, two-wing(ed) ~ · zweiflügeliges Gebäude *n*, doppelflügeliges ~

double Y, ~ branch pipe · Doppelabzweig(er) *m* [*Rohrformstück*]

~ ~ branch(es), ~ ~ junction, ~ ~ inlet · doppelt schräger (Rohr)Zulauf *m*, ~ ~ (Rohr)Abzweig *m*

doubled form · Doppelform *f* [*Zweigelenkrahmen*]

doubled-up column · aufgedoppelte Stütze *f*

~ door · aufgedoppelte Tür *f*

doubling piece → eave(s) board

doubly curved, double ~ · doppelt gekrümmt, zweifach ~

~ ~ shell, shell of double curvature · doppelt gekrümmte Schale *f*

~ ~ translation(al) shell → translational shell of double curvature

~ reinforced · doppelt armiert, ~ bewehrt, mit doppelten (Stahl)Einlagen

dove-cote → columbarium

dove hole · Taubenloch *n*

dovetail, DVTL, culvertail · Schwalbenschwanz *m*

~ anchor, ~ tie · Schwalbenschwanz(-Mauer)anker *m*

~ rib · Schwalbenschwanzrippe *f*

~ slot · Langloch *n* für Schwalbenschwanz

~ tie, ~ anchor · Schwalbenschwanz(-Mauer)anker *m*

~ vaulting · Einwölbung *f* auf Schwalbenschwanz, (Über)Wölbung ~ ~

dovetail(ed) joint · Schwalbenschwanzverbindung *f*

~ merlon · Kerbzinne *f*, Schwalbenschwanzzinne

dowel · (Stab)Dübel *m*, Döbel *m*, Dolle *f*, Dollen *m*; Dippel *m* [*Österreich*]

~ joint, dowelled ~ · Verdübelung *f*

~ lubricant [*Lubricating material applied to bars in expansion joints to reduce bond with the concrete and promote unrestrained longitudinal movement*] · (Stab)Dübelschmiere *f*

~ pin [*A short wire nail pointed at both ends*] · Verbandstift *m* [*DIN 1156*]

~ sleeve [*A cap of light metal or cardboard on one end of a dowel bar to allow free movement of an expansion joint*] · Dübelhülse *f*

~ spacer, spacing dowel · Abstanddübel *m*

dowelled (Brit.); doweled (US) · verdübelt

dowel(led) beam, ~ wood(en) ~, ~ timber ~ · Dübelbaum *m*, Dübelbalken *m*; Dippelbaum, Dippelbalken [*Österreich*]

~ connection · (Stab)Dübelverbindung *f*

~ joint · Verdübelung *f*

~ timber beam, ~ (wood(en)) ~ · Dübelbaum *m*, Dübelbalken *m*; Dippelbaum, Dippelbalken [*Österreich*]

~ (wood(en)) beam, ~ timber ~ · Dübelbaum *m*, Dübelbalken *m*; Dippelbaum, Dippelbalken [*Österreich*]

dowelling (Brit.); doweling (US) · Verdübeln *n*

downcomer → downpipe

~ [*A pipe leading water from a cistern to a point of consumption*] · Zuleitungsrohr *n*

down draft (US); ~ draught (Brit.) · fallende Luftströmung *f*, Fallzug *m* [*Schornstein*]

down draught — drainage of a building

~ **draught** (Brit.); ~ draft (US) · fallende Luftströmung *f*, Fallzug *m* [*Schornstein*]

downpipe, downcomer, downspout, fall pipe, rainwater pipe, (rain) leader, (rain) conductor, drainpipe, drain spout · (Ab)Fallrohr *n*, (Regen)Ablaufrohr, Regenfallrohr [*An der Hauswand befestigtes, senkrechtes Rohr zum Ableiten des Wassers von Dachrinnen*]

downspout → downpipe

downtown parking · Parken *n* im Geschäftsviertel

(downward) deflection (~) deflexion · Durchbiegung *f*, Durchsenkung

dpc → dampproof(ing) course

d.p.m. → dampproof(ing) membrane

draft (US); draught (Brit.); air ~ · Luftzug *m*

~ **air** (US); draught ~ (Brit.) · Zugluft *f*

drafted masonry (work) → rustic(ated) ashlar

draft excluder (US) → draught preventer

~ **excluding threshold** (US); draught ~ ~ (Brit.) · zugdichte Türschwelle *f*

~ **exclusion,** exclusion of draft, draftproofing (US); draught exclusion, exclusion of draught, draughtproofing (Brit.) · Zug(ab)dichten *n*, Dichtschließen

~ ~ (US); draught ~ (Brit.) · Zugfreiheit *f*, Zugluftfreiheit

~ **-free** (US); draught-free (Brit.) · zugluftfrei

~ **less** (US); draughtless (Brit.) · zugfrei

~ **lobby** (US) → draught preventer

~ **loss** (US); draught ~ · Zug(luft)verlust *m*

~ **preventer** (US) → draught ~

draftproof (US); draughtproof · zugdicht

~ **barrier** (US); draughtproof ~ (Brit.) · Zug(ab)dichtung *f*, Dichtschluß *m*

~ **door** (US); draughtproof ~ (Brit.) · Windfangtür *f*

~ **lobby** (US); draughtproof ~ (Brit.) · Windfanggehäuse *n* [*Drehtür*]

draftproofing (US); draughtproofing (Brit.) · Zug(ab)dichtung *f*, Dichtschluß *m*

~, exclusion of draft, draft exclusion (US); exclusion of draught, draughtproofing, draught exclusion (Brit.) · Zug(ab)dichten *n*, Dichtschließen

draft regulator, barometric damper (US); draught regulator (Brit.) · Zugregler *m*

draftsman (US) → draughtsman

draftsmanship (US); draughtsmanship (Brit.) · Zeichenwesen *n*

drafty (US); draughty (Brit.) · zugig

dragladled cullet → quenched ~

dragon beam, ~ piece [*A horizontal timber into which the end of the hip rafter is framed. The outer end of it is carried on the corner of the building where the wall plates meet the inner end at the angle tie*] · Stichbalken *m*

~ **piece,** ~ beam [*A horizontal timber into which the end of the hip rafter is framed. The outer end of it is carried on the corner of the building where the wall plates meet the inner end at the angle tie*] · Stichbalken *m*

~ **tie** → angle ~

drain → drain(age) pipe

~ **hole,** weep ~ · Entwässerungsloch *n*, Sickerloch

to drain into · entwässern in

(drain) tile, DT (US); clay pipe, CP · Tonrohr *n*

(~) ~ **line,** clay ~ ~, DT ~ (US); clay pipe ~ (Brit.) · Tonrohrleitung *f*

~ **trench,** disposal ~, absorption ~, ~ field ~ · Beries(e)lungs(feld)graben *m*, Riesel(feld)graben

drainage · Entwässerung *f*, Wasserableitung

drain(age) article → concrete ~ ~

~ ~, ~ product · Entwässerungsartikel *m*, Entwässerungsgegenstand *m*, Entwässerungserzeugnis *n* [*DIN 4281*]

~ **articles** → (concrete) drain(age) goods

~ ~ → ~ goods

drainage board · Entwässerungsverband *m*

~ **by gravity,** gravity drainage · Schwerkraftentwässerung *f*

drain(age) channel, draining ~, discharge ~, ~ gutter · Abflußrinne *f*, Ablaufrinne, Entwässerungsrinne, Wasserrinne

drainage excavation · Entwässerungsaushub *m*

drain(age) fitting, ~ pipe ~ · Entwässerungsfitting *m*, Entwässerungs(rohr)formstück *n*

~ **goods,** ~ articles, ~ products, ~ ware · Entwässerungsartikel *mpl*, Entwässerungsgegenstände *mpl*, Entwässerungserzeugnisse *npl*, Entwässerungsware(n) *f* [*DIN 4281*]

~ ~ → concrete ~ ~

~ **grate** → inlet ~

~ **grating** → inlet grate

~ **grid** → inlet grate

~ **gutter,** draining ~, discharge ~, ~ channel · Abflußrinne *f*, Ablaufrinne, Entwässerungsrinne, Wasserrinne

~ **line** → draining ~

drainage network · Entwässerungsnetz *n*

~ **of a building,** building drainage · Gebäudeentwässerung *f*

drain(age) pipe — draught regulator

drain(age) pipe, drain(ing ~), discharge ~, waste (~) · [*Any pipe which carries waste water or water-borne wastes in a building drainage system*] · Abflußrohr *n*, Ablaufrohr, Dränrohr, Entwässerungsrohr [*Fehlnamen: Ablauf m, Abfluß m*]

~ ~ elbow → draining ~ ~

~ (~) fitting · Entwässerungsfitting *m*, Entwässerungs(rohr)formstück *n*

~ ~ system → draining pipework

~ pipeline, discharge ~, draining ~, ~ piping · Abflußrohrleitung *f*, Ablaufrohrleitung, Entwässerungsrohrleitung

~ pipework → draining ~

~ product → (concrete) drainage article

~ ~, ~ article · Entwässerungsartikel *m*, Entwässerungsgegenstand *m*, Entwässerungserzeugnis *n* [*DIN 4281*]

~ products → (concrete) drain(age) goods

~ ~ → ~ goods

drainage slope · Entwässerungsgefälle *n*

~ system · Entwässerungsanlage *f*

(drain(age)) tile, DT (US); clay pipe, CP · Tonrohr *n*

drain(age) trench · Drängraben *m*

~ ware → (concrete) drainage goods

~ ~ → ~ goods

drainage work · Dränarbeiten *fpl* [*DIN 18308*]

drainboard, draining board, ablution board · Abtropfbrett *n*, Ablaufbrett, Abstellbrett

drained joint · entwässerte Fuge *f*

drainer · Abtropffläche *f*, Ablauffläche, Abstellfläche, Abtropfplatte *f*, Ablaufplatte, Abstellplatte

draining board → drainboard

~ channel, drain(age) ~, discharge ~, ~ gutter · Abflußrinne *f*, Ablaufrinne, Entwässerungsrinne, Wasserrinne

~ ~, drain(age) ~, discharge ~ · Entwässerungskanal *m*

~ grate → inlet ~

~ grating → inlet grate

~ grid → inlet grate

~ gutter, drain(age) ~, discharge ~, ~ channel · Abflußrinne *f*, Ablaufrinne, Entwässerungsrinne, Wasserrinne

~ line, drain(age) ~, discharge ~ · Abflußleitung *f*, Entwässerungsleitung, Ablaufleitung

~ pipe, drain(age) ~, discharge ~, waste (~) · Abflußrohr *n*, Ablaufrohr, Dränrohr, Entwässerungsrohr [*Fehlnamen: Ablauf m, Abfluß m*]

~ ~ elbow, drain(age) ~ ~, discharge ~ ~, waste (~) ~ · Abflußrohrbogen *m*, Ablaufrohrbogen, Dränrohrbogen, Entwässerungsrohrbogen, Fallrohrbogen [*DIN 540*]

~ ~ system → ~ pipework

~ pipeline, discharge ~, drain(age) ~, ~ piping · Abflußrohrleitung *f*, Entwässerungsrohrleitung, Ablaufrohrleitung

~ pipework, drain(age) ~, discharge ~, ~ pipe system · Abflußrohr(leitungs)system *n*, Entwässerungsrohr(leitungs)system, Ablaufrohr(leitungs)system, Dränrohr(leitungs)system

~ point, discharge ~ · Abflußstelle *f*, Ablaufstelle

to drape, to deflect, to raise, to bend up · ablenken, anheben [*Litze in der Spannbetontechnik*]

draped-strand technique → deflected-strand ~

draping, raising, bending up, deflecting · Anheben *n*, Ablenken [*Litzen in der Spannbetontechnik*]

draught (Brit.); draft (US); air ~ · Luftzug *m*

~ air (Brit.); draft ~ (US) · Zugluft *f*

~ excluder (Brit.) → ~ preventer

~ excluding threshold (Brit.); draft ~ ~ (US) · zugdichte Türschwelle *f*

~ exclusion, exclusion of draught, draughtproofing (Brit.); draft exclusion, exclusion of draft, draftproofing (US) · Zug(ab)dichten *n*, Dichtschließen *n*

~ ~ (Brit.); draft ~ (US) · Zug(luft)freiheit *f*

~ fillet (Brit.); draft ~ (US); windguard · (Ab)Dicht(ungs)latte *f* [*kittlose Verglasung*]

~-free (Brit.); draft-free (US) · zugluftfrei

draughtless (Brit.); draftless (US) · zugfrei

draught lobby (Brit.) → ~ preventer

~ loss (Brit.); draft ~ (US) · Zug(luft)verlust *m*

~ preventer, ~ excluder, ~ lobby (Brit.); draft ~ (US) · Windfang *m*

draughtproof (Brit.); draftproof (US) · zugdicht

~ barrier (Brit.); draftproof ~ (US) · Zug(ab)dichtung *f*, Dichtschluß *m*

~ door (Brit.); draftproof ~ (US) · Windfangtür *f*

draughtproofing, exclusion of draught, draught exclusion (Brit.); draftproofing, exclusion of draft, draft exclusion (US) · Zug(ab)dichtung *f*, Dichtschluß *m*

~, draught exclusion, exclusion of draught (Brit.); draftproofing, exclusion of draft, draft exclusion (US) · Zug(ab)dichten *n*, Dichtschließen *n*

draught regulator (Brit.); draft ~, barometric damper (US) · Zugregler *m*

draughtsman — dressed stone

draughtsman (Brit.); draftsman (US); drawer, DFTSMN [*A man employed or skilled in making drawings*] · Zeichner *m*

draughtsmanship (Brit.); draftsmanship (US) · Zeichenwesen *n*

draughty (Brit.); drafty (US) · zugig

Dravidian style, South Indian ~ [*A.D. 625–1750*] · Dravidastil *m*

to draw · zeichnen

~ ~ **out**, to stretch, to expand · strecken [*Streckmetall*]

drawbridge · Zugbrücke *f*

drawer → draughtsman

draw-in system [*A wiring system in conduits. The cables can be pulled in and replaced when required*] · Verlegung *f* in Isolierrohr

drawing · Plan *m*, Zeichnung *f* [*Im Sinne als Zeichnungsarbeit eine Darstellung, die angibt, wie Gegenstände in ihrer Lage oder Funktion zusammengehören*]

~, wire ~, cold work ~ · (Draht)Ziehen *n*

~ · Zeichnen *n*

~ · Zug *m* [*Drahtherstellung*]

~ [*The mechanical method of manufacturing ordinary window glass*] · Ziehen *n*

~ **appliances and instruments** · Zeichenzubehör *n*

~ **block**, wire ~ ~ · (Draht)Ziehtrommel *f*

~ **board** · Reißbrett *n*

~ **die** → wire-~

~ ~ **orifice**, wire-~ ~ ~, die ~ · (Draht)Zieh(eisen)düse *f*, (Draht)Ziehsteindüse *f*

~ **grease** · Ziehfett *n*

~ **'issued for construction'** · baureifer Plan *m*, baureife Zeichnung *f*

~ **lines**, piano ~, line · Kämmung *f* [*Flachglasfehler*]

~ **machine**, wire-~ ~ · (Draht)Ziehbank *f*

~ **number** · Zeichnungsnummer *f*, Plannummer

~ **office** · Zeichenbüro *n*

~ **paper** · Zeichenpapier *n*

~ **pencil** · Zeichenbleistift *m*

~ **room** [*A room where guests are received or entertained. Originally so called because it was the room into which guests withdrew after dinner*] · Empfangszimmer *n*, Empfangsraum *m*, Salon *m*

~ ~ · Zeichenraum *m*, Zeichensaal *m*

~ **standard spe(ification)s** · Zeichnungsnorm *f*

~ **table** · Zeichentisch *m*

drawn · gezogen

~ **cylinder glass** · gezogenes Walzenglas *n*, ~ Zylinderglas

~ **glass** · Ziehglas *n*

~ **lead** · gezogenes Blei *n*

~ ~ **trap** [*B.S. 504*] · gezogener Blei-(Wasser)(Geruch)Verschluß *m*, (Wasser)(Geruch)Verschluß aus gezogenem Blei

~ **profile**, ~ unit, ~ trim, ~ section, ~ shape · gezogenes Profil *n*

~ ~ **in stainless steel**, ~ section ~ ~ ~, ~ unit ~ ~ ~, ~ shape ~ ~ ~, ~ trim ~ ~ ~ · gezogenes Edelstahlprofil *n*

~ **section**, ~ shape, ~ unit, ~ profile, ~ trim · gezogenes Profil *n*

~ ~ **in stainless steel**, ~ shape ~ ~ ~, ~ unit ~ ~ ~, ~ profile ~ ~ ~, ~ trim ~ ~ ~ · gezogenes Edelstahlprofil *n*

~ **shape**, ~ section, ~ unit, ~ profile, ~ trim · gezogenes Profil *n*

~ ~ **in stainless steel**, ~ section ~ ~, ~ profile ~ ~ ~, ~ unit ~ ~ ~, ~ trim ~ ~ ~ · gezogenes Edelstahlprofil *n*

~ **trim**, ~ profile, ~ unit, ~ section, ~ shape · gezogenes Profil *n*

~ ~ **in stainless steel**, ~ unit ~ ~ ~, ~ shape ~ ~ ~, ~ section ~ ~ ~, ~ profile ~ ~ ~ · gezogenes Edelstahlprofil *n*

~ **unit**, ~ section, ~ shape, ~ profile, ~ trim · gezogenes Profil *n*

~ ~ **in stainless steel**, ~ shape ~ ~ ~, ~ section ~ ~ ~, ~ profile ~ ~ ~, ~ trim ~ ~ · gezogenes Edelstahlprofil *n*

~ **wire** · gezogener Draht *m*

draw-off · Entnahme *f* [*z.B. von Warmwasser*]

~ **pipe** · Entnahmerohr *n*

~ **tap** · Entnahmehahn *m*

draw plate [*A steel plate pierced with small holes through which a wire is drawn during its manufacture*] · Ziehplatte *f*

draw roll · Zugwalze *f* [*Dachpappenanlage*]

dream hole [*An opening in the wall of a tower to admit light*] · Lichtöffnung *f*

drencher system, sprinkler ~ · Sprinkleranlage *f* [*Brandbekämpfung*]

Dresden china · Meißner Porzellan *n*

to dress, to hew, to mill, to shape · (steinmetzmäßig) bearbeiten, (~) behauen, (~) zurichten

~ ~ **coarsely**, ~ ~ **roughly**, ~ shape ~, ~ mill ~, ~ hew ~ · grob zurichten, ~ behauen, ~ bearbeiten [*(Natur-)Stein*]

~ ~ **roughly** → ~ ~ coarsely

dressed, hewn, milled, shaped · (steinmetzmäßig) bearbeitet, (~) behauen, (~) zugerichtet

~ **fair face** → (natural) stone finish

~ **(natural) stone**, shaped (~) ~, milled (~) ~, (hewn) (~) ~ · steinmetzmäßig bearbeiteter (Natur)Stein *m*

~ **stone** → ~ natural ~

(~) stonework, hewn ~, milled ~, shaped ~ · zugerichtete Werksteine *mpl*, bearbeitete ~, behauene ~

~ with (natural) stone · (natur)steinverkleidet

dresser · Steinausmesser *m*

dressing, milling, shaping · (Natur)Steinbearbeitung *f*, Bearbeitung, Behauen *n*, Zurichten

~ → materials ~

~ → dressed stone

~ cab(in) → un~ ~

~ composition, ~ compound, cement Dachkleb(e)masse *f*, (Dach)Spachtel(masse) *m*, (*f*)

~ compound, ~ composition, cement Dachkleb(e)masse *f*, (Dach)Spachtel(masse) *m*, (*f*)

~ ~ for Häusler (type) roof(ing) · Holzzement *m* [*für Holzzementdach*]

~ cubicle → (un)dressing cab(in)

~ locker, clothes ~ · Kleiderspind *m*

dressing-locker room, clothes-locker ~ · Kleiderspindraum *m*

dressing paint · Dachfarbe *f* [*Dachfarben sind Anstrichmittel – streichfertige Farben oder Farbbindemittel – welche sich zum Anstrich von Dachpappen oder geteerten Mauerflächen eignen. Meist auf Kunstharzbasis oder Bitumenbasis hergestellt*]

~ room, un~ ~, changing ~ · Aus- und Ankleide(raum) *f*, (*m*), Umkleide(raum)

~ ~ · Ankleidezimmer *n*, Ankleideraum *m* [*Teil einer Wohnung*]

~ ~ · Künstlergarderobe *f*, Künstlerumkleide(raum) *f*, (*m*)

dressings [*The mo(u)ldings and embellishments to a façade in the Renaissance and derivative styles, especially where they are of a colo(u)r or material contrasting with the main walling*] · Fassadenschmuck *m*

dried blood adhesive → (blood) albumin glue

~ ~ glue → (blood) albumin ~

~ out · ausgetrocknet, vertrocknet

~ to (the) touch, touch-dry · griffest [*Anstrichfarbe*]

drier (US); dryer (Brit.); drying agent [*A dessicating substance*] · Trockenstoff *m*

driftbolt, driftpin · Keiltreiber *m*, Splintentreiber, Runddorn *m*

drifting snow · Flugschnee *m*

driftwood peat · Driftholztorf *m*

drilling work, boring ~ · Bohrarbeiten *fpl* [*DIN 18301*]

drinking fountain, DF · Trinkbrunnen *m*

~ water, potable ~ · Gebrauchswasser *n*, Trinkwasser

~ ~ network, potable ~ ~ · Trinkwassernetz *n*

~ ~ pressure pipe, potable ~ ~ ~ · Trinkwasser-Druckrohr *n*

~ ~ reservoir, potable ~ ~, ~ ~ tank · Trinkwasserbehälter *m*

~ ~ supply, potable ~ ~ · Trinkwasserversorgung *f*

~ ~ ~ pipe, potable ~ ~ ~ · Trinkwasserrohr *n*

~ ~ tank, potable ~ ~, ~ ~ reservoir · Trinkwasserbehälter *m*

drip [*The container placed at a low point in a piping system to collect condensate and from which it may be removed*] · Wasserabscheider *m*, Kondensatabscheider

~, water~, throat(ing), weather groove · (Wasser)Nase *f*, Unterschneidung *f*

~ · Abkantung *f* [*Dachrinne*]

dripping moisture → condens(at)ing water

drip(stone) → hood-mould(ing)

drive · (Auto)Vorfahrt *f*

~ (Brit.); driveway (US); private access · Privatzufahrt *f*

~ → entrance driveway

drive-in bank, bank with drive-in teller(s) · Bank *f* mit Autoschalter(n)

~ cinema, ~ (motion picture) theatre; ~ movie (US) · Autokino *n*

~ teller · Auto(bank)schalter *m*

to drive off · austreiben [*Kohlensäure*]

~ ~ ~ · austreiben [*Kristallwasser aus Gipsstein*]

driver parking, customer ~ · Selbstparken *n* [*In einem Parkhaus. Gegenteil: Parken mit Bedienungspersonal*]

~ ~ building, customer ~ ~ · Parkhaus *n* mit Selbstparkbetrieb, Parkgebäude *n* ~ ~, Parkbau *m* ~ ~, Parkgarage *f* ~ ~, Selbstparkhaus, Selbstparkgebäude, Selbstparkbau, Selbstparkgarage

driver's room, chauffeur's ~ · Kraftfahrerraum *m*

driver-training field, ~ ground · Verkehrsübungsplatz *m*

driveway (US); drive (Brit.); private access · Privatzufahrt *f*

drive(way), entrance ~, vehicular access · (Gebäude)Zufahrt *f*, Hausrzufahrt

driving rain, wind-driven ~, pelting ~ · Schlagregen *m* [*Mit Regen verbundener Wind von mindestens Beaufortstärke 5*]

~ work → pile and sheetpile ~ ~

dromos, walled passage · Dromos *m*

drop · Fall(rohr)strang *m* [*Zentralheizung*]

~ → ~ panel

~, decline, decrease · Abnahme *f*, Abfall *m*, Rückgang *m*

~ · Tropfen *m*

~ arch; four-centred ~ (Brit.); four-centered ~ (US) · flacher Spitzbogen *m*, gedrückter ~, stumpfer ~ [*Er ist aus vier Kreisbögen zusammengesetzt*]

drop-ball (penetration) test, dropping-ball (~) ~, drop ~ · Kugelfallprüfung *f*, Kugelfallprobe *f*, Kugelfallversuch *m*

drop black (pigment) → bone ~ (~)

~ in pressure, decrease ~ ~, decline ~ ~, pressure decline, pressure drop, pressure decrease · Druckrückgang *m*, Druckabfall *m*, Druckabnahme *f*

~ manhole, wellhole [*A vertical shaft in which sewage is allowed to fall from one sewer to another at a lower level*] · Absturz(schacht) *m*

~ of stress → decrease ~ ~

~ ~ viscosity, fall ~ ~, lowering ~ ~ · Viskositätsrückgang *m*, Zähigkeitsrückgang, Viskositätsabfall *m*, Zähigkeitsabfall

~ (panel), thickened portion of the slab [*These drop panels are formed at columns to provide increased cross-sectional area and depth to resist negative moments and shears*] · Deckplatte *f*, Pilzkopfverstärkung *f*, Pilzkopfplatte, Verstärkung(splatte) [*Zwischen Pilzkopf und Pilzdecke*]

~ point → · drop(ping) ~

~ siding, rustic ~, novelty ~ · Wandschirm *m*, Wandbeschlag *m*, Wetterschirm, Verschalung *f*

~ test, drop(ping)-ball (penetration) ~ · Kugelfallprüfung *f*, Kugelfallprobe *f*, Kugelfallversuch *m*

~ window · Versenkfenster *n*

~ wire [*A cable from the nearest pole of an overhead supply line, connecting a building with the grid*] · Einführungsleitung *f*

drop(ped) ceiling → suspended ~

drop(ping)-ball (penetration) test, drop ~, falling ball ~ · Kugelfallprüfung *f*, Kugelfallprobe *f*, Kugelfallversuch *m*

drop(ping) point · Tropfpunkt *m*

dropproof · tropf(en)sicher

drops, guttae · Guttae *fpl*, Tropfen *mpl* [*Tropfenartige Gebilde der dorischen Ordnung, die in drei Gruppen zu sechs Tropfen an den Mutuli (= Dielenköpfen) und außerdem sechs Guttae in einer Reihe unter den Regulae angebracht sind*]

to drove [*Scotland; USA*]; [*To finish stone with a drove chisel*] · scharrieren

drove (chisel) [*Scotland; USA*]; boaster · Scharriereisen *n*

~ work, ~ surface [*Scotland; USA*]; boasted ~ [*The grooved surface of finished (natural) stone*] · Scharrierung *f* [*Furchung der Oberfläche eines Steines*]

droving [*Scotland; USA*]; boasting · Scharrieren *n*

~, angle dunting, batting, broad tooling · Schlaganarbeiten *n* [*Werksteinbearbeitung*]

drum, column ~ · (Säulen)Trommel *f*, (Säulen)Tambour *m*

~ → tambour

drum-built column · Tamboursäule *f*, Trommelsäule [*Der Schaft ist aus Trommeln zusammengesetzt*]

~ pillar · freistehender Tambourpfeiler *m*, ~ Trommelpfeiler [*Der Schaft ist aus Trommeln zusammengesetzt*]

drumminess · Dröhnneigung *f*

drumming · Dröhnen *n*

~ · Dröhnung *f*

drum(-type) gas meter [*B.S. 4161*] · nasser Gaszähler *m*, ~ Gasmesser [*Nasse Gasuhr ist eine veraltete Bezeichnung und sollte nicht mehr verwendet werden*]

Drusian foot, northern ~ [*13.12 in., 333.25 mm*] · drusianischer Fuß *m*

dry, uncoated · roh [*Straßenbaugestein ohne Bindemittelumhüllung*]

~, mortarless · mörtelfrei, mörtellos, trokken

~ after-treatment → ~ curing

~ air · entfeuchtete Luft *f*, trockene ~

~ batch · Trockencharge *f* [*Beton*]

(dry-)batched aggregate, ~ materials, dry-batch ~, matched ~, recombined ~ · Trockenbeton *m* [*Korngemisch ohne Wasser*]

dry bonding strength · Trockenhaftfestigkeit *f*

dry-bound macadam, dry-process penetration ~ · (Ein)Streumakadam *m*

dry bright polish · Selbstglanzwachs *n*

~ brushing · Trocken(ab)bürsten *n*

~ (bulk) density → ~ volume weight

~ ~ specific gravity → ~ volume weight

~ cast method, ~ ~ process · Trockenverfahren *n* [*Betonrohrherstellung*]

~ ~ pipe · Betonrohr *n* nach dem Trockenverfahren hergestellt, Zementrohr ~ ~ ~ ~

~ ~ process, ~ ~ method · Trockenverfahren *n* [*Betonrohrherstellung*]

~ ceiling, (gypsum) plasterboard (sheet) ~, gypsum board ~; plate ~ [*Scotland*] · Gipskartonplattendecke *f*

~ chip(ping)s, uncoated ~ · Rohsplitt *m*

~ cleaning shop · Reinigungsanstalt *f* [*für Bekleidung*]

~ closet, ~ conservancy, earth ~ · Trockenabort *m*

~ ~ receptacle, ~ conservancy ~, earth ~ ~ · Trockenabortgefäß *n*

~ cold bending · Trockenkaltbiegen *n*

~ concrete → earth-moist ~

~ conservancy, ~ closet, earth ~ · Trockenabort *m*

~ ~ receptacle, ~ closet ~, earth ~ ~ · Trockenabortgefäß *n*

~ construction, ~ technique of ~, ~ system of ~, ~ wall ~ · Trockenbautechnik *f*, Trockenbauweise *f* [*Verlegung von Platten anstelle von Verputzen*]

dry construction — dry rolled concrete

~ ~ · mörtelloses Bauen *n*

~ ~ **partition (wall)** · (Trocken)Putztrennwand *f*

dry-cup method · Diffusionsmeßverfahren *n* im Feuchtigkeitsbereich 0–50% r.F.

dry curing, ~ **after-treatment** · Nachbehandlung *f* ohne Feuchthaltung [*Beton*]

~ **density** → ~ **volume weight**

~ **distillation, destructive** ~ [*Sometimes referred to as 'pyrolysis'*] · Entgasung *f*, trockene Destillation *f*, Zersetzungsdestillation

dry-feed chlorination · direkte Chlorung *f*

dry felt, (~) **felt(ed fabric) for roofing** · Rohfilz(pappe) *m*, (*f*) [*Oberbegriff für "Roh(dach)pappe" und "Wollzfilzpappe". DIN 52117*]

~ ~ **jumbo roll, unwinder** · Abwickelbock *m* für Rohfilzpappe, Rohpappenbock [*Dachpappenanlage*]

~ ~ **manufacture** · Rohfilz(pappen)herstellung *f*

~ ~ **web,** web of dry felt · Rohfilz(pappen)bahn *f*

(~) **felt(ed fabric) for roofing,** ~ **felt** · Rohfilz(pappe) *m*, (*f*) [*Oberbegriff für "Roh(dach)pappe" und "Wollfilzpappe". DIN 52117*]

~ **film** · Trockenfilm *m*

dry-film build, ~ **thickness** · Trockenfilmdicke *f* [*Anstrichtechnik*]

~ **thickness,** ~ **build** · Trockenfilmdicke *f* [*Anstrichtechnik*]

dry-fixed · trockenverlegt [*Bauplatte*]

to dry flat, ~ ~ **mat(t)** · matt auftrocknen

dry formed, formed in dry state · trocken verformt [*Schamottestein*]

~ **glazing, patent** ~**, puttyless** ~ · kittlose Verglasung *f*, ~ Einglasung, kittloses Verglasen *n*, kittloses Einglasen

~ ~ **roof, patent** ~ ~**, puttyless** ~ ~ · kittloses Glasdach *n*

~ **hydrate(d lime)** · Löschkalk *m*, Kalkhydrat *n*, Ca(OH)$_2$; (Ver)Putzkalk, Pulverkalk, Mauerkalk, (Bau)Ätzkalk, Sackkalk, (Bau)Sichtkalk, gemahlener Stück(en)kalk [*Fehlnamen*]

dry-hydrate(-type) by-product lime, ~ **carbide** ~ · Karbildkalkhydrat *n*, Karbidtrockenkalk *m*

~ **carbide lime,** ~ **by-product** ~ · Karbidkalkhydrat *n*, Karbidtrockenkalk *m*

dry installation · Trockeneinbau *m*

~ **joint, non-bonded** ~ · Knirschfuge *f*, Trockenfuge

~ **lining** [*The technique of applying plasterboard sheets direct to the wall. A level surface is first obtained by fixing impregnated fibreboard dots on the uneven wall surface. The plasterboard sheets are then fixed on plaster dabs set in the spaces between the dots*] · Trokken(gips)(ver)putzen *n*

~ **looper** · Rohpappenvorrateinrichtung *f* [*Dachpappenanlage*]

~ **loose bulk density** · Schüttdichte *f* des Zuschlag(stoffes)

~ **manufacture** · Trockenaufbereitung *f* [*Zement*]

~ **masonry** · mörtelloses Mauerwerk *n*

~ ~ **wall,** ~ **(stone)** ~**, dike, dyke** [*Wall built without mortar*] · Trocken(stein)mauer *f*, mörtellose Steinmauer, Steinsatz(mauer) *m*, (*f*)

~ ~ **(work),** ~ **stone** ~ **(~)** · Trocken(stein)mauerwerk *n*

to dry mat(t), ~ ~ **flat** · matt auftrocknen

dry-mix shotcrete, gunite [*Pneumatically conveyed shotcrete in which most of the mixing water is added at the nozzle*] · Trockenspritzbeton *m*, Torkretbeton

dry mixing · Trockenmischen *n*

~ **mix(ture), earth-moist** ~ · erdfeuchte Mischung *f*, erdfeuchtes Gemisch *n*

~ ~ **(concrete)** → **earth-moist** ~

dry-out, drying(-out) · (Aus)Trocknen *n*

~ **period** → **drying(-out) time**

~ **time** → **drying(-out)** ~

dry partition (wall), ~ **wall partition** [*This term infers that the construction is ready for decoration without the application of a wet plaster skin coat*] · Trennwand *f* in Trockenbauweise

~ **penetration surfacing** · (Ein)Streudecke *f*

~ **polishing** · Trockenpolieren *n*

~ **powder** · trockenes Pulver *n*, Trockenpulver

~ **pre-mixing** · trockenes Vormischen *n* [*Betonbereitung*]

~ **press method** · Trockenpreßverfahren *n*

dry-press(ed) brick · Trockenpreßziegel *m*

~ **engineering brick** · Preßklinker *m* [*Nach einem patentierten Trockenpreßverfahren, dem Laun-Spengler-Verfahren, hergestellt und meist in Tunnelöfen gebrannt*]

dry pressing → **semi-dry** ~

~ **process** · Trockenverfahren *n* [*Zementherstellung*]

~ ~ **penetration macadam, dry-bound** ~ · (Ein)Streumakadam *m*

~ **rolled concrete, lean(-mixed)** ~ ~ · Magerwalzbeton *m*, Walzmagerbeton

dry roof glazing — drying shrinkage 318

~ **roof glazing**, puttyless ~ ~, patent ~ ~ · kittlose Dachverglasung *f*, ~ Dacheinglasung

~ **room** · trockener Raum *m*

~ **rubble construction**, ~ ~ masonry · mörtelloses Bruchsteinmauerwerk *n*

dry-sand casting · Trockenguß *m* [*Sandguß von Gußeisen oder Stahlguß. Die Form wird vor dem Guß im Ofen bei 200°–400° C getrocknet*]

dry (saturated) steam · trockener Dampf *m*, getrockneter ~, Trockendampf

to dry slake · trockenlöschen

dry-slaked · trockengelöscht [*Kalk*]

~ **quicklime** · gedämpfter (Brannt)Kalk *m*, trockengelöschter ~ [*Fehlname: nichttreibender Kalk*]

dry (stone) wall, ~ masonry ~, dike, dyke · mörtellose Steinmauer *f*, Trokken(stein)mauer, Steinsatz(mauer) *m*, (*f*)

~ ~ ~ **with moss-filled joints**, ~ masonry ~ ~ ~ ~ · Moosmauer *f*

~ **storage** · Trockenlagerung *f*

~ **strength**, green ~ · Grünfestigkeit *f*, Trockenfestigkeit [*Die mechanische Festigkeit von getrockneten, aber nicht gebrannten Formlingen*]

(~) **sweating room** · Schwitzraum *m*

(~) ~ ~, sudatorium, laconicum [*The (dry) sweating room in a Roman bath building*] · römischer Schwitzraum *m*, Sudatorium *n*, Schwitzraum einer römischen Therme

~ **system of construction**, ~ (technique ~), ~ wall ~ · Trockenbautechnik *f*, Trockenbauweise *f* [*Verlegung von Platten anstelle von Verputzen*]

~ **(technique of) construction**, ~ system ~ ~, ~ wall ~ · Trocken autechnik *f*, Trocken auweise *f* [*Verlegung von Platten anstelle von Verputzen*]

to dry through well, to through-dry [*The opposite of to skin dry*] · durchtrocknen

dry to recoat by brushing · überstreichbar [*Anstrich*]

~ ~ ~ ~ **spraying** · überspritzbar [*Anstrich*]

~ **unit weight** → ~ volume ~

~ **volume weight**, ~ unit ~, ~ (bulk) density, ~ bulk specific gravity [deprecated: dry box weight] · Trockenraumgewicht *n* der Volumeneinheit, Trockenrohdichte *f*, Trockenrohwichte

~ **wall partition**, ~ partition (wall) [*This term infers that the construction is ready for decoration without the application of a wet plaster skim coat*] · Trennwand *f* in Trockenbauweise

~ **wedging** [*Wedging-up temporarily, without paint or glue*] · Verkeilen *n* ohne Anstrich

~ **weight** · Trockengewicht *n*

~ **white lead** · Pulverbleiweiß *n*

to dry without (a) gloss · glanzlos (auf)trocknen

dryer (Brit.); **drier** (US); **drying agent** [*A dessiccating substance*] · Trockenstoff *m*

drying action · Trocknungswirkung

~ **area** → (clothes-)drying ground

~ **balcony** · Wäschebalkon *m*

~ **behaviour** (Brit.); ~ **behavior** (US) · Trocknungsverhalten *n*

~ **by evaporation** · physikalische Trocknung *f*, physikalisches Trocknen *n* [*Trocknung durch Verdunsten der Lösungsmittel*]

~ ~ **oxidation** · oxidative Trocknung *f*, oxidatives Trocknen *n* [*Trocknung durch Aufnahme von Luftsauerstoff*]

~ ~ **waste heat**, waste-heat drying · Abwärmetrocknung *f*, Trocknung mit Abwärme

~ **cabinet**, clothes-~ ~, (enclosed) cabinet for drying washing · (Wäsche-) Trocknungsschrank *m* [*In einer Wohnung*]

~ **crack** · Trocknungsriß *m*

~ **fault** · Trocknungsfehler *m*

~ **frame** · Trocknungsgerüst *n* [*Ziegelherstellung*]

~ **gradually to an insoluble film** · unlöslich auftrocknen [*Kaseinfarbe*]

~ **ground** → clothes-~ ~

~ **mechanism** · Trocknungsmechanismus *m*

~ **oil**, fixed ~, paint ~ · trocknendes Öl *n*

drying(-out), **dry-out** · (Aus)Trocknen *n*

~ **period** → ~ time

~ **time**, dry-out ~, ~ period · (Aus-)Trocknungsfrist *f*, (Aus)Trocknungsdauer *f*, (Aus)Trocknungszeit *f*

drying power · Trocknungskraft *f*

~ **process** · Trocknungsvorgang *m*

~ ~ · Trocknungsverlauf *m*

~ **property** [*The property of a coat of paint or varnish to dry by evaporation of the vehicle or chemical change (usually oxidation) or the two together*] · Trocknungsfähigkeit *f* [*Fehlname: Trockenfähigkeit*]

~ **rack** · Trocknungsgestell *n*

~ **rate**, rate of drying · Trocknungsgeschwindigkeit *f*

~ **room** · Trocknungsraum *m* [*Fehlname: Trockenraum*]

~ **shed**, open air corridors, permanent hack · Freiluftschuppen *m* [*Ziegelindustrie*]

~ **shrinkage**, water-loss ~ [*Contraction caused by moisture loss*] · Schrumpfung *f*

drying shrinkage — ductility

~ ~, water-loss ~ [*Contracting caused by moisture loss*] · Schrumpfen *n*

~ ~ **behaviour**, water-loss ~ ~ (Brit.); ~ ~ behavior (US) · Schrumpfverhalten *n*

~ ~ **crack**, water-loss ~ ~ · Schrumpfriß *m*

~ ~ **curve**, water-loss ~ ~ · Schrumpfkurve *f*, Schrumpflinie *f*

~ ~ **limit**, water-loss ~ ~ · Schrumpfgrenze *f*

~ ~ **stress**, water-loss ~ ~ · Schrumpfspannung *f*

~ ~ **value**, water-loss ~ ~ · Schrumpfmaß *n*, Schrumpfwert *m*

~ **stress** · Trocknungsspannung *f*

~ **temperature** · Trocknungstemperatur *f*

~ **through** · Durchtrocknen *n*, Durchtrocknung *f*

~ **time** → drying-out ~

drying-up · Auftrocknen *n*, Auftrocknung *f*

drywall [*A type of interior wall where the finish is applied in a dry condition (in sheets or panels) rather than as a wet plaster. Plasterboard and plywood are usually preferred drywall materials. Hardboard and fibreboard are all classed as drywall finishes*] · Trockenwand *f*

~ **construction** · Trockenwandbau *m*

~ **finish** [*Interior covering material, such as gypsum board or plywood, applied in large sheets or panels*] · Trockenwandabschluß *m* [*Fehlname: Trockenputz m*]

~ **material** · Trockenwandbaustoff *m*

dry waste · trockner Abfall(stoff) *m* [*Kehricht; Küchenabfall; Asche usw.*]

DS (US) → double thickness sheet glass

DSGN, design · Durchformung *f*, Form(geb)ung, Gestaltung

~, **design** · Bemessung *f*, Auslegung, Dimensionierung [*Rechnerische Ermitt(e)lung der Querschnittsabmessungen aus zuvor ermittelten Biegemomenten, Längskräften, Querkräften und Drillmomenten*]

~, **design** · (Bau)Entwurf *m*

D-shaped tower, half-round ~, semicircular ~ · Schalenturm *m*, Halb(kreis-)turm [*Nach außen aus der Mauer vorspringender, nach innen jedoch offener Turm einer mittelalterlichen Burg*]

DSW, door switch · Türschalter *m*

DT, (drain(age)) tile (US); clay pipe, CP · Tonrohr *n*

~ **line** → (drain) tile ~

dual chime unit, double ~ ~, twin ~ ~ · Doppel(ton)-Läutewerk *n*

~ **compartment septic tank**, double ~ ~ ~, two-~ ~ ~ · Zweikammer-Grundstückskläranlage *f*, Doppelkammer-Grundstückskläranlage, Zweikammer-Hauskläranlage, Doppelkammer-Hauskläranlage, Zweikammer-Kleinkläranlage, Doppelkammer-Kleinkläranlage [*DIN 4261*]

~ **cross-section**, twin ~, double ~ · doppelter Querschnitt *m*, zweiteiliger ~

dual-duct system · Zwei-Kanal-System *n* [*Luftverteilung*]

dual-flight stair(case), two-flight ~, double-flight ~ · zweiläufige Treppe *f*, doppelläufige ~

dual girder, double ~, twin ~ · Zwillingsträger *m*

~ **mould** (Brit.); ~ mold (US); double ~, twin ~ · Zwillingsform *f*, Doppelform

~ **offset** · zweimalige Abknickung *f* [*Fassade*]

dual-pane sash, double-pane ~, two-pane ~ · Doppelflügel *m* [*Der doppelt verglaste Flügel eines Verbundfensters*]

dual portal · Doppelportal *n*

dual-purpose room · Doppelzweckraum *m*

~ **tinter;** ~ tinting color (US) · Zweizweck-Mischfarbe *f*, Zweizweck-Abtönfarbe

~ **tinting color** (US); ~ tinter · Zweizweck-Mischfarbe *f*, Zweizweck-Abtönfarbe

dual-tower façade, double-tower ~, two-tower ~, twin-tower ~ · Doppelturmfassade *f*, Zweiturmfassade

Ducal Palace, Doges' ~ · Dogenpalast *m* [*Venedig*]

duck board, roof ladder, cat ladder · Dachleiter *f*

duckfoot (pipe) bend, rest ~ · Fuß(rohr)krümmer *m*

duct [*A tube or other provision for the passage of air, gas or services*] · (geschlossener) Kanal *m*

~ **construction** · Kanalbau *m* [*für öffentliche Versorgungsleitungen*]

~ **cover** · Kanaldeckel *m*

~ **design**, air ~ ~ · (Luft)Kanalbemessung *f*

ducted warm air · Kanalwarmluft *f*, kanalisierte Warmluft

duct for electric wiring · Verdrahtungskanal *m*

~ ~ **services**, service duct, mains subway · Betriebskanal *m*, Leitungskanal

duct-generated noise · kanalerzeugtes Geräusch *n*, Kanalgeräusch [*Klimaanlage*]

ductile, extensible · streckbar, dehnbar

~ **cast iron** → nodular (graphite) ~ ~

~ **iron** → nodular (graphite) cast ~

~ **joint ring** · Dichtung *f* [*Flanschenrohr*]

ductility, extensibility, yield [*That property of a material by virtue of which it may undergo large permanent deformation without rupture*] · Streckbarkeit *f*, Duktilität *f*, Dehnbarkeit, Fadenziehvermögen *n*

ductility test — dust protection agent

~ **test** · Streckbarkeitsversuch *m*, Streckbarkeitsprüfung *f*, Streckbarkeitsprobe *f*

ductility-test mould (Brit.); ~ **mold** (US) · (Messing)Form *f* [*Streckbarkeitsmessung von Bitumen*]

ductilometer · Streckbarkeitsmesser *m*, Duktilometer *n* [*Bitumenmessung*]

ducting · Kanäle *mpl*

~ **for electric wiring** · Verdrahtungskanäle *mpl*

duct opening · Kanalöffnung *f*

~ **riser, rising duct** [*A duct which extends vertically one full stor(e)y or more*] · Steig(e)kanal *m*

~ **trench** · Kanalgraben *m*

ductube · Gummischlauchschalung *f* mit schmiegsamen Diagonalgewebeeinlagen

ductwork · Kanalleitung *f*

~ · Kanalsystem *n*

dug peat · Stichtorf *m*

to dull, to deaden, to damp · dämpfen [*Schall; Schwingung*]

dull polishing · Mattpolieren *n*

dulling, loss of gloss · Glanzverlust *m*, Blindwerden *n*, Mattwerden [*Anstrichtechnik*]

~, deadening, damping [*sound; oscillations*] · Dämpfen *n*

dullness, mattness · Vermattung *f*

dumping angle · Schüttwinkel *m*

dumpling [*Unexcavated ground surrounded by an excavation*] · Kern *m*

dungeon, donjon, keep · Donjon *m*, Bergfried *m*, Belfried, Berchfrit *m*

~ · Verließ *n*

dunite, olivine-rock · Dunit *m*, Olivinfels *m*, Olivinstein *m*

dunting · Klangfehlerhaftigkeit *f* [*Ziegel*]

duplex cable, twin ~ · doppeladriges Kabel *n*, paarverseiltes ~, Duplexkabel

duplex-headed nail, double-headed ~, scaffold ~, form ~, dual-head ~ · Doppelkopfnagel *m*, Duplexnagel

duplex paper, laminated ~ · Hartpapier *n*, HP, kaschiertes Papier, Mehrschichtenpapier

duplicate · Abguß *m* [*von Modellen*]

~ **test** · Gegenprobe *f*, Gegenprüfung *f*, Gegenversuch *m*

duplicating, tracing · Pausen *n*

~ **room,** tracing ~ · Paus(en)raum *m*

durability · Dauerhaftigkeit *f*, Haltbarkeit

dural(umin) · Duraluminium *n* [*Alu-(minium)legierung in der Regel als Al-Cu-Mg-Knetlegierung*]

duration of load · Lastdauer *f*

~ ~ **test(ing)** → test(ing) time

to dust · abstauben

dust and noise abatement · Staub- und Lärmfreiheit *f*

dustbin · Abfall(stoff)kübel *m*, Müllkübel

~ **chamber** · Abfall(stoff)kübelschrank *m*, Müllkübelschrank

dustcoat · staubbindende Lage *f*, ~ Schicht *f*

dust content, percentage of dust · Staubgehalt *m*, Staubanteil *m*

~ **dry,** dust-free · staubtrocken [*Anstrich*]

~ **explosion** · Staubexplosion *f*

~ **formation,** dustiness · Abstauben *n*, Staubbildung *f*

dustfree, dustless · staubfrei, staublos

~, dust dry · staubtrocken [*Anstrich*]

dust impurity · Staubunreinheit *f*

dustiness, dust formation · Staubbildung *f*, Abstauben *n*

dusting · abstaubend, staubbildend

~ Stauben *n*

~ · Zerrieseln *n* [*Feuerfestindustrie. Spontanes Zerfallen eines Stoffes, hervorgerufen durch eine physikalisch-chemische Umwandlung. Anmerkung: In Großbritannien wird der Ausdruck "dusting" nur für das Zerrieseln von Calcium-O-Silikat beim Abkühlen verwendet*]

~ **finish,** granular (sur)facing, mineral (sur)facing, mineral granules · Mineralbestreuung *f*, Mineralabstreuung, (mineralische) Bestreuung, (mineralische) Abstreuung, Streuschicht *f* [*Dachpappe und Spachteldachbelag*]

~ **with cement** · Einpudern *n* mit Zement

dust-laying · Staubbindung *f*

~ **agent** · Staubbindemittel *n*

~ **oil,** road ~ · Straßenöl *n* [*Ein hochsiedendes Steinkohlenteeröl zur Wiederbelebung alter bituminöser Straßendecken als Behelfsmaßnahme*]

~ ~ · staubbindendes Öl *n*, Reißöl

dustless, dustfree · staubfrei, staublos

dust-like · staubähnlich

dust-pan dormer · Schlepp(dach)gaupe *f*, Schlepp(dach)gaube

dust-pressed process · hydraulische Pressung *f* von Tonpulver mit 5–6% Feuchtigkeit [*Herstellung von (Fuß)Bodenplatten*]

dust preventer [*for concrete*] · Staubschutzmittel *n*

dust-preventing seal(er) · Staubsiegel *m*

dust-prevention · Staubverhütung *f*

dust-producing, dusty · staubend

to dustproof · staubfrei machen

dustproof ceiling · Staubdecke *f*

dustproofer, dust protection agent, dust protective agent · Anti-Abstaubmittel *n*, Abstaubverhütungsmittel

dustproofing · Staubfreimachung *f*

dust protection agent, ~ protective ~, dustproofer · Anti-Abstaubmittel *n*, Abstaubverhütungsmittel

~ **protective agent,** ~ protection ~, dustproofer · Anti-Abstaubmittel *n*, Abstaubverhütungsmittel

dust-repelling · staubabweisend

dusty, dust-producing · staubend

~ · staubig

~ **chalk** · Kalkerde *f*, Kalkstaub *m*

Dutch Baroque Cathedral of St Peter and St Paul · holländisch-barocke Peter-Pauls-Kathedrale *f* zu Petersburg

~ **bond** [*misnomer*] → Flemish ~

~ **brick,** ~ clinker · holländischer Klinke *m*

~ **door** [*Such a door is made so that the upper half may be opened without opening the lower half*] · Stalltür *f*

~ **Renaissance** · holländischer Renaissancestil *m*

~ **stove,** tiled ~ · Kachelofen *m* [*DIN 1294*]

~ **tile** · Kachel *f*

DVTL, dovetail, culvertail · Schwalbenschwanz *m*

dwarf door · Kleintür *f*

~ **gallery** · Zwerggalerie *f*

~ **partition (wall)** [*A low partition (wall) with capping, often used as an enclosure in offices*] · Kleintrennwand *f*, Zwergtrennwand

~ **wall** → sleeper ~

~ ~ [*A wall less than a stor(e)y in height*] · Kleinwand *f*, Zwergwand

dweller → apartment ~

dwelling (Brit.) → dwelling unit

~ **(US)** → residential building

~ · Behausung *f*

~ **kitchen,** dining ~, kitchen/dining room · Wohnküche *f*, Eßküche

~ **tower** → residence ~

~ **unit (US);** dwelling (Brit.) [*One or more rooms arranged for the use of one or more individuals living together as a single house-keeping unit, with cooking, living, sanitary and sleeping facilities*] · Wohnung *f*

~ **units for low-income families** (US); dwellings ~ ~ ~ (Brit.) · Sozialwohnungen *fpl*

dwellings for low-income families (Brit.) → dwelling units ~ ~ ~

to dye [*concrete during casting*] · einfärben, durchfärben

dye → vat ~

dyeing [*concrete during casting*] · Einfärben *n*, Durchfärben

dyestuff · Farbstoff *m*

~ **lake** → lake (pigment)

~ **solution,** solution of dyestuff · Farbstofflösung *f*

~ **suspension** · Farbstoffsuspension *f*

dying away · Abklingen *n* [*Schwingung*]

dyke, dike, dry (stone) wall, dry masonry wall · mörtellose Steinmauer *f*, Trocken-(stein)mauer, Steinsatz(mauer) *m*, (*f*)

Dymaxion House [*A 'machine for living in' designed by Richard Buckminster Fuller. The name signifies dynamic plus maximum efficiency. The house is a combination of mechanical services and living areas*] · Dymaxion-Haus *n*

dynamic ball impact test → ball ~

(~) **ball(-impact) tester** · Kugelschlaggerät *n*, Kugelschlaghärteprüfer *m*

(~) **ball tester,** (~) ball-impact ~ · Kugelschlaggerät *n*, Kugelschlaghärteprüfer *m*

~ **buckling** · dynamische Knickung *f*

~ ~ · dynamisches Knicken *n*

~ **elastic behaviour** (Brit.); ~ ~ behavior (US) · dynamisches elastisches Verhalten *n*

~ **force** · dynamische Kraft *f*

~ **indentation ball test** · Kugeldruckhärteprobe *f*, Kugeldruckhärteprüfung *f*, Kugeldruckhärteversuch *m*

~ **load** · dynamische Last *f*

~ **loading** · dynamische Belastung *f*

~ **modulus of elasticity** · dynamischer E-Modul *m*, ~ Elastizitätsmodul

~ **rigidity,** ~ stiffness · dynamische Steifigkeit *f*, ~ Starrheit

~ **similarity,** ~ similitude · dynamische Ähnlichkeit *f*

~ **similitude,** ~ similarity · dynamische Ähnlichkeit *f*

~ **stiffness,** ~ rigidity · dynamische Steifigkeit *f*, ~ Starrheit

~ **strength** · dynamische Festigkeit *f*

~ **thoughness** · dynamische Zähigkeit *f*

dynamically loaded beam · dynamisch belasteter Balken(träger) *m*

E

E, efficiency · Wirkungsgrad *m*

eagle capital · Adlerkapitell *n*, Adlerkapitäl

ear, nose and throat clinic · Hals-, Nasen- und Ohrenklinik *f*

early baroque · Frühbarock *m*

~ **Christian church** · altchristliche Kirche *f*, frühchristliche ~

~ ~ (~) **architecture** · frühchristliche (Kirchen)Architektur *f*, ~ (Kirchen-)Baukunst *f*, altchristliche ~

~ ~ **structures** · frühchristliche Bauter. *f*, altchristliche ~, ~ Bauwerke *npl*

~ **curing period** · Frühnachbehandlungszeit *f*

Early English cathedral style, E. E. ~ ~ · hochgotischer englischer Kathedralstil *m*, bischöflicher Stil

~ ~ **church,** E. E. ~ ~ · hochgotische englische Kirche *f*

Early English (style) — earth-leakage (current) circuit ...

~ ~ (style), E. E. ~, early English ~, Early Pointed [*C. 1200–C. 1300*] · frühenglischer Stil *m*, frühgotischer englischer ~, englische Frühgotik *f*

~ **Florentine Renaissance (style)**, early ~ ~ ~ · florentinische Frührenaissance *f*

~ **French Gothic (style)**, early ~ ~ ~ · französische Frühgotik *f*

~ **Gothic (style)**, early Gothic ~ · Frühgotik *f*

early hardening → initial ~

~ **loading**, initial ~ · Erstbelastung *f*, Anfangsbelastung, Frühbelastung

Early Pointed → ~ English (style)

early Renaissance cupola, ~ ~ dome · Frührenaissancekuppel *f*

~ ~ **dome**, ~ ~ cupola · Frührenaissancekuppel *f*

~ ~ **(style)**, early Renaissance ~ · Frührenaissance *f*

~ **Romanesque (style)** · Frühromanik *f*, frühe Romanik, frühromanische Architektur *f*, frühromanische Baukunst

~ **stability** · Frühstandfestigkeit *f*, Frühstandsicherheit, Frühstabilität *f*

early-stage cracking · frühzeitige Rißbildung *f*

early stiffening → false set(ting)

~ **strength** · Frühfestigkeit *f*

early-strength cement · frühfester Zement *m*, hochwertiger ~

~ **concrete**, high-grade ~ · frühfester Beton *m*, hochwertiger ~

early work · Frühwerk *n*

to earth · erden [*Elektrotechnik*]

earth (Brit.); **ground** (US) · Erde *f* [*Elektrotechnik*]

~ **balsam** [*A variety of asphalt from Pechelbronn, Alsace*] · Erdbalsam *m*

~ **clamp** → earth(ing) ~

~ **closet**, ~ conservancy, dry ~ · Trockenabort *m*

~ ~ **receptacle**, ~ conservancy ~, dry ~ ~ · Trockenabortgefäß *n*

~ **colour** (Brit.) → natural earth

~ **connection**, earthing, grounding · Erden *n*, (Schutz)Erdung *f*, Erdverbindung [*Elektrotechnik*]

~ **conservancy**, ~ closet, dry ~ · Trockenabort *m*

~ ~ **receptacle**, ~ closet ~, dry ~ ~ · Trockenabortgefäß *n*

~ **contact** → earth(ing) ~

earth-continuity conductor, earth(ing) lead, ground(ing) lead · Erddraht *m*, Erd(zu)leitung *f*, Erdungsleitung

earth cover(ing), fill · Überdeckung *f*, Überschüttung [*erdverlegte Leitung*]

earth-damp concrete → earth-moist ~

(earth-)dry concrete → earth-moist ~

earth electrode · Erdelektrode *f*, Erder *m*

~ **embankment stadium** · Erdwallstadion *n*

earthen mound, mound of earth · Erdhügel *m*

earthenware · Irdengut *n*, Steingut [*Glasur über weißer, dichtender Porzellanengobe auf hellem, porösen, nicht durchscheinenden Scherben. Wasseraufnahme über 15%. Mit Quarzmehl und Kreide gemagert (Kalksteingut). Steingut neigt zu Glasurrissen*]

~ **cable cover** [*B.S. 2484*] · Irdengut-Kabelabdeckstein *m*, Steingut-Kabelabdeckstein

~ **filter pipe** · Irdengutbrunnenrohr *n*, Irdengutfilterrohr, Steingutfilterrohr, Steingutbrunnenrohr

~ **glaze(d finish)**, ~ glazing, ~ glazed coat(ing) · Irdengutglasur *f*, Steingutglasur, Irdengutbeglasung *f* Steingutbeglasung

~ **mosaic** · Irdengutmosaik *n*, Steingutmosaik

~ **pipe** · Steingutrohr *n*, Irdengutrohr

~ **small(-sized) mosaic** · Irdengut-Kleinmosaik *n*, Steingut-Kleinmosaik

~ **tile** · Irdengut(belag)platte *f*, Irdengutfliese *f*, Steingutfliese, Steingut(belag)platte

~ **wall tile** · Irdengut-Wand(belag)platte *f*, Irdengut-Wandfliese *f*, Steingut-Wand(belag)platte, Steingut-Wandfliese

earth fault · Erdschluß *m*

earthing, earth connection, grounding · Erden *n*, (Schutz)Erdung *f*, Erdverbindung [*Elektrotechnik*]

earth(ing) clamp, ground(ing) ~ · Erdungsschelle *f*

~ **contact**, ground(ing) ~ · Erdungskontakt *m*

~ **lead**, ground(ing) ~, earth-continuity conductor · Erddraht *m*, Erd(zu)leitung *f*, Erdungsleitung

~ **material**, ground(ing) ~ · Erdungsmaterial *n* [*Elektrotechnik*]

~ **metal sheet**, ground(ing) ~ · Erdungsblech *n*

~ **network**, ground(ing) ~ · Erdungsnetz *n*

~ **plate**, ground(ing) ~ · Erdungsplatte *f*, Plattenerder *m*

~ **rod**, ground(ing) ~ · Erdungsstab *m*, Staberder *m*

~ **switch**, ground(ing) ~ · Erdungsschalter *m*

earthing system · Erdungsanlage *f* [*Sie besteht aus Erdungsleitungen und Erdern*]

earth(ing) washer, ground(ing) ~ · Erdungsscheibe *f*

earth lead → earth-continuity conductor

earth-leakage current, fault ~ · Fehlerstrom *m*, Erdschlußstrom

~ (~) **circuit breaker**, fault ~ ~ ~ · Fehlerstrom-Schutzschalter *m*, Erdschlußstrom-Schutzschalter

earth material — eave(s) fa(s)cia

earth material → earth(ing) ~
~ metal sheet → earth(ing) ~ ~
earth-moist concrete, earth-damp ~, (earth-)dry ~, no-slump ~, dry mix(ture) (~) [*A concrete with just the correct water/cement ratio, to distinguish from a wet mix(ture)*] · erdfeuchter Beton *m*
earth network → earth(ing) ~
~ pigment → natural earth
~ plate → earth(ing) ~
earthquake · Erdbeben *n*
~ activity, seismic ~ · Erdbebentätigkeit *f*
~ area → ~ region
~ ~ map → ~ zone ~
~ bracing · erdbebensichere Aussteifung *f*, ~ Versteifung
~ construction, seismic ~ · erdbebensicheres Bauen *n*
~ design, seismic ~ · Erdbebenbemessung *f*, erdbebensichere Bemessung
~ engineering, seismic ~ · Erdbebentechnik *f*
~ force, seismic ~ · Erdbebenkraft *f*
~ load, seismic ~ · Erdbebenlast *f*
~ observatory · Erdbebenwarte *f*
~ oscillation, ~ vibration, seismic ~ · Erdbebenerschütterung *f*
(earth)quake-proof → (earth)quake-resistant
earthquake propagation · Erdbebenfortpflanzung *f*
~ region, ~ area, ~ zone, seismic ~ · Erdbebengebiet *n*, Erdbebenzone *f*
~ ~ map → ~ zone ~
~ resistance · Erdbebensicherheit *f*
(earth)quake-resistant, (earth)quake-proof, (earth)quake-resisting, aseismic · erdbebensicher [*Gestaltung der Bauwerke gegen plötzliche und rasch vorübergehende Erschütterungen durch tektonische und vulkanische Beben*]
earthquake response, seismic ~ · Erdbebenreaktion *f* eines Bauwerkes oder Gebäudes
~ scale · Erdbebenskala *f*
~ shock, seismic ~ · Erdbebenstoß *m*
~ vibration, ~ oscillation, seismic ~ · Erdbebenerschütterung *f*
~ wave, seismic ~ · Erdbebenwelle *f*
~ zone → ~ region
~ ~ map, ~ region ~, ~ area ~, seismic ~ ~ · Karte *f* der Erdbebengebiete, Erdbeben(zonen)karte
earth resin, ~ type ~ · Erdharz *n*
~ rod → earth(ing) ~
~ switch → earth(ing) ~
~ table → plinth

~ (type) resin · Erdharz *n*
earthwork · Erdarbeiten *fpl*, Erdbau *m* [*DIN 18300*]
earthy arseniate of lead · erdiges Flockenerz *n*, erdige Bleiblüte *f*
~ cobalt → asbolite
~ gypsum → gypsite
~ lime · steiniartiger Kalk *m*, erdiger ~
easel-picture · Staffeleigemälde *n*
easily workable glass, sweet ~ · leicht bearbeitbares Glas *n*
easing wedge · Entlastungskeil *m*
East African copal · ostafrikanischer Kopal *m*
east orientation · Ostorientierung *f*
Easter sepulchre (Brit.); ~ sepulcher (US) · Ostergrab *n*
east(ern) apsis, ~ apse, ~ exedra · Ostapside *f*, Ostapsis *f*, Ostabside, Ostexedra *f*
~ bay · Ostjoch *n*
~ chapel · Ostkapelle *f*
~ choir, ~ quire · Ostchor *m*
~ ~ tower, ~ quire ~ · Ostchorturm *m*
~ crossing tower · Ostvierungsturm *m*
~ exedra, ~ apsis, ~ apse · Ostapside *f*, Ostapsis *f*, Ostabside, Ostexedra *f*
~ pediment · Ostgiebel *m* [*griechischer Tempel*]
~ quire, ~ choir · Ostchor *m*
~ ~ tower, ~ choir ~ · Ostchorturm *m*
Eastern W. C. pan → squa.ting ~ ~ ~
east(ern) window · Ostfenster *n*
easy-machining steel → free-cutting ~
eaves [*This is the plural of 'eave', but the singular is seldom used. The overhanging part of a roof*] · Dachfuß *m*, (Dach-)Traufe *f*
eave(s) board, ~ catch, tilting fillet, tilting piece, doubling piece, arris fillet, eave(s) pole (Brit.); cant strip (US) [*A board of triangular cross-section nailed to the rafters or roof boarding under the double eave(s) course to tilt it slightly less steeply than the rest of the roof and to ensure that the tails of the lowest tiles bed tightly on each other*] · Aufschiebling *m*
~ catch → ~ board
~ course [*A first course of plain tiles, slates, or shingles on a roof, including the course of plain tiles at eave(s) on which the first course of single-lap tiles is bedded*] · (Dach)Trauflage *f*, (Dach)Traufschicht *f*
~ fa(s)cia, fa(s)cia, fa(s)cia (board) [*A board on edge nailed along the feet of the rafters. It often carries the eave(s) gutter and may also act as a tilting fillet*] · Traufbrett *n*, Stirnbrett, Windbrett

eave(s) flashing (piece) — economy sink unit 324

~ **flashing (piece)** [*A drop apron from an asphalt roof dressed into an eave(s) gutter*] · Traufanschluß(streifen) *m*

eave(s)-fronted house · Traufenhaus *n* [*Ein Haus mit der Traufe zur Straße hin*]

(eaves) gutter, ~ trough, roof ~, rain-water ~, R.W. ~ · (Dach)Rinne *f*, Abflußrinne, Regenrinne [*DIN 18460*]

~ **height** · (Dach)Trauf(en)höhe *f*

~ **lath**, chantlate · Saumlade *f*, Saumlatte *f*

~ **moulding** (Brit.); ~ molding (US) · (Dach)Traufkante *f*

~ **plate** [*A wall plate spanning between posts or pieces at eave(s). It carries the feet of the rafters when no wall is there to carry them*] · Fußpfette *f*, Sparrenschwelle *f*

~ **pole** → ~ board

~ **projection** · Traufenüberhang *m*

~ **soffit** · Traufenuntersicht *f*

~ **tile** [*A short tile about 7 in. long used in the eave(s) course, or under-eaves course, in plain tiling*] · Traufziegel *m*; Traufstein *m* [*Fehlname*]

~ **trough** → ~ gutter

~ **trow** → ~ gutter

~ **unit** · (Dach)Traufenteil *m, n*

ebonite, hard rubber · Hartgummi *m* [*Ein Isolierstoff aus Natur- oder Kunstkautschuk, Schwefel, organischen und anorganischen Zusätzen, durch Heißvulkanisation gehärtet. DIN 7711*]

eccentric; off-center (US); off-centre (Brit.) · ausmittig, exzentrisch

~ **application of force**, off-centre ~ ~ (Brit.); off-center ~ ~ (US) · ausmittiger Kraftangriff *m*, exzentrischer ~

~ **compression**; off-centre ~ (Brit.); off-center ~ (US) · ausmittiger Druck *m*, exzentrischer ~

~ **load**; off-centre ~ (Brit.); off-center ~ (US) · ausmittige Last *f*, exzentrische ~

~ **loading**; off-centre ~ (Brit.); off-center ~ (US) · ausmittige Belastung *f*, exzentrische ~

eccentrically braced, ~ stiffened · exzentrisch ausgesteift, ~ versteift, ausmittig ~

~ **curved beam**, curved beam with eccentric boundaries [*Such a beam is bounded by areas having different centres of curvature. In addition it is possible for either radius to be the larger one*] · ausmittig gekrümmter Balken(träger) *m*, exzentrisch ~ ~

~ **loaded column** · ausmittig belastete Stütze *f*, exzentrisch ~ ~

~ **stiffened**, ~ braced · exzentrisch ausgesteift, ~ versteift, ausmittig ~

eccentricity · Ausmitte *f*, Ausmittigkeit *f*, Exzentrizität *f*

~ **of load** · Lastausmittigkeit *f*, Lastausmitte *f*, Lastexzentrizität *f*

ecclesiastical architect, church ~ · Kirchenarchitekt *m*

~ **architecture**, church ~, religious ~ kirchliche Architektur *f*, ~ Baukunst *f*, Kirchenbaukunst, Kirchenarchitektur, Sakralbaukunst, Sakralarchitektur

~ **basilica**, Christian ~, basilica (church) · (christliche) Basilika *f*, Basilikakirche *f*

~ **building**, church ~ · Kirchengebäude *n*

~ ~, religious ~ · Sakralgebäude *n*

~ ~ **style**, church ~ · Kirchenbaustil *m*

~ **buildings**, church ~ · Kirchenbauten *f*

~ **Gothic (style)**, religious ~ (~) · Sakralbaugotik *f*

~ **monument**, religious ~ · Sakraldenkmal *n*, Sakralmonument *n*

~ **structure**, religious ~ · Sakralbau(werk) *m*, (*n*)

ecclesiologic(al) · kirchenbaulich

ecclesiology · Kirchenbauwesen *n*

echinus; (Greek) ovolo (moulding) (Brit.); (Greek) ovolo (molding) (US) [*The term applied to the convex or projecting mo(u)lding, resembling the shell of a sea-urchin, which supports the abacus of the Greek Doric capital; sometimes painted with the egg and dart ornament*] · Echinus *m*, Echinos

echo [*Sound which has been reflected and arrives with such a magnitude and time interval after the direct sound as to be distinguishable as a repetition of it. Note. In common usage the term is limited to reflection distinguishable by the ear*] · Echo *n*

Echo Portico · Echohalle *f* [*in Olympia*]

eclectic structure · eklektisches Bauwerk *n*

eclecticism [*Style which borrows freely from various sources*] · Eklektizismus *m*, Historismus

eclogite · Eklogit *m*

economic height · wirtschaftliche Höhe *f*

~ **planning board** · Amt *n* für Wirtschaftsplanung

~ ~ **council** · Rat *m* für Wirtschaftsplanung

~ **utilization** (US); ~ utilisation (Brit.) · wirtschaftliche Nutzung *f*

economical height · wirtschaftliche Höhe *f*

~ **of space**, space-saving · raumsparend

economically sound thermal design · wärmewirtschaftliches Bauen *n*

economiser · Rauchgas-Wasservorwärmer *m*, Eko(nomiser) *m*, Speisewasservorwärmer

economy of materials · Materialeinsparung *f*

~ **sink unit**, popular ~ ~ · Volksspültisch *m*, Volksabwaschtisch, Sied(e)lungsspültisch, Sied(e)lungsabwaschtisch

eddy trail, vortex ~, von Karman ~ ~ · (Karmansche) Wirbelstraße f

edge · Längskante f

~ **arch** · Randbogen m

~ **beam**, boundary ~ · Randbalken(träger) m

~ **column** → perimeter ~

~ **compression** · Randpressung f [*Fehlname: Kantenpressung*]

~ **condition**, fringe ~, boundary ~, marginal ~ · Randbedingung f

~ **cross member**, ~ horizontal ~, ~ rail · Randriegel m

~ **design** · Randausbildung f

~ **displacement** · Randverrückung f

~ **distance**, edge-to-edge ~ · Randabstand m

~ **element**, boundary ~, ~ member · Randglied n, Randelement n [*Baustatik*]

edge-fixed · randeingespannt

edge force, boundary ~ · Randkraft f

~ **girder** · Randträger m, Endträger

~ **grain shingle** [*deprecated*]; radial section ~, radial surface ~ · Spiegelschnittschindel f, Radialschnittschindel, Spaltschnittschindel

edge-holding power · Kantenfestigkeit f

edge horizontal member, ~ cross ~, ~ rail · Randriegel m

~ **joint** · Randfuge f

~ **length** · Kantenlänge f

~ **load** · Randlast f

~ **loaded** · randbelastet

~ **loading** · Randbelastung f

~ **member** → ~ element

~ **plate**, ~ slab · Randplatte f

~ **preparation** · Kantenbearbeitung f

~ **profile**, ~ section, ~ shape, ~ unit, ~ trim · Randprofil n, Einfassungsprofil, Abschlußprofil

~ **protection with rubber** · Vollgummikantenschutz m

~ **purlin(e)** · Randpfette f

~ **rail**, ~ cross member, ~ horizontal member · Randriegel m

~ **reinforcement** · Randarmierung f, Randbewehrung, Rand(stahl)einlagen fpl

~ **restraint** · Randeinspannung f

~ **roll** → round(ed) moulding

~ **rotation** · Randdrehung f

~ **seal(ing)** · Rand(ab)dichtung f

~ **section** → ~ profile

~ **shape** → ~ profile

~ **shear**, shear along edge · Randschubkraft f

~ **slab**, ~ plate · Randplatte f

edge-stiffened · randausgesteift, randversteift

edge stiffening · Randaussteifung f, Randversteifung

~ **stress** → (edge stress of) extreme fibre ~

~ ~ · Kantenspannung f

~ ~ · Kantenbeanspruchung f

(~ ~ of) ~ extreme fibre stress (Brit.); (~ ~ ~) ~ fiber ~ (US); edge ~ · Randspannung f

~ **thickening** · Randverstärkung f

edge(-to-edge) distance · Randabstand m

edge torque moment, fringe ~ ~, boundary ~ ~, marginal ~ ~, torsion(al) ~, ~ twist(ing) ~ · Randdrillmoment n, Randtorsionsmoment, Randverdrehungsmoment, Randverwindungsmoment

~ **trim**, ~ section, ~ unit, ~ profile, ~ shape · Randprofil n, Einfassungsprofil, Abschlußprofil

~ **unit**, ~ section, ~ trim, ~ profile, ~ shape · Randprofil n, Einfassungsprofil, Abschlußprofil

edgewise · hochkant

~ **(clay) brick paving** · hochkantiges Ziegelpflaster n, Hochkantziegelpflaster

~ **placing** · Hochkantstellen n

edge zone, boundary ~ · Randzone f

edging [*The finishing operation of rounding off the edge of a slab to prevent chipping or damage*] · Abrunden n

~ → ~ strip

~, concrete ~ · (Beton)Einfassungsstein m

~ **board** · Blendleiste f [*Dach*]

~ ~ · Blendbrett n [*Flachdach*]

~ **press** · Abkantpresse f [*Ziegelindustrie*]

~ **(strip)** · Randleiste f

~ **(~)** · Randstab m [*Gitterrost*]

edifice · Monumentalbau(werk) m, (n)

educational block, ~ building · Lehranstaltgebäude n

~ **building** · Bau m von Lehranstalten, Lehranstaltbau

~ ~, ~ block · Lehranstaltgebäude n

E.E. cathedral style, Early English ~ ~ · hochgotischer englischer Kathedralstil m, bischöflicher Stil

E.E. church, Early English ~ · hochgotische englische Kirche f

E.E. style → Early English (~)

eel grass [*A sea plant (Zostera marina) whose dried leaves when loosely packed are very sound absorbent*] · gemeines Seegras n

effect · Auswirkung f

(~ **of) continuity**, fixity, continuous effect [*The joining of floors to girders, of girders to other girders and columns so effectively that they bend together under load and so strengthen each other*] · Durchlaufwirkung f, durchlaufende Wirkung, durchgehende Wirkung

effect of restraint — eight-blade fan

~ ~ restraint · Einspann(ungs)wirkung f

effective · wirksam

~ · mittragend, mitwirkend [z.B. Plattenbreite bei Plattenbalken]

~ arch span · Bogenstützweite f

~ arch(ed girder) span · Bogen(träger)stützweite f

~ area · wirksame Fläche f

~ chimney height · wirksame Schornsteinhöhe f [Die Höhe von Rost oder Brenner der Strömungssicherung der Feuerstätte bis zur Schornsteinmündung]

~ cross-section · wirksamer Querschnitt m

~ depth of slab · wirksame Plattenhöhe f

~ height, buckling ~, ~ length · Knicklänge f

~ ~ · wirksame Höhe f

~ length, laying ~ · Baulänge f [Rohr]

~ ~ · wirksame Länge f

~ ~, buckling ~, ~ height · Knicklänge f

~ separating size · Trennkorngröße f

~ ~ ~ of a screen using the Heidenreich-Paul method · Trennkorngröße f HP, Ausgleichskorngröße nach Heidenreich-Paul

~ size (Hazen) (D_{10}) [The grain size on mechanical analysis curve corresponding to W% = 10] · wirksame Korngröße f

~ span [The distance between the centres of the supports of a beam or girder. This length, which is larger than the clear span, is used in calculating the bending moment of a beam or girder] · Stützweite f

~ ~/length ratio · Stützweitenverhältnis n

~ thickness · wirksame Dicke f [Fehlname: wirksame Stärke]

~ width · wirksame Breite f

~ ~ of slab [That part of the width of a slab taken into account when designing T- or L-beams] · mitwirkende Plattenbreite f, mittragende ~

efficiency, E · Wirkungsgrad m

~ of buildings, ~ ~ blocks · Nutzungswert m von Gebäuden

to effloresce · ausschlagen, ausblühen, auswittern, aussalzen, auskristallisieren

efflorescence of salt, flower of salt, (salt) efflorescence · (Salz)Ausblühen n, (Salz)Ausschlagen, Auswittern, Aussalzen, Auskristallisation f (von Salzen) [Äußerlich sichtbares Ausscheiden von Salzen auf Mauerwerk]

~ resistance, resistance to efflorescence · Ausblühungsbeständigkeit f, Aussalzungsbeständigkeit, Ausschlagbeständigkeit, Auswitterungsbeständigkeit, Auskristallisationsbeständigkeit

~ test · Ausblühversuch m, Ausblühprobe f, Ausblühprüfung f, Aussalzungsversuch, Aussalzungsprobe, Aussalzungsprüfung, Ausschlagversuch, Ausschlagprobe, Ausschlagprüfung, Auswitterungsprobe, Auswitterungsversuch, Auswitterungsprüfung, Auskristallisationsversuch, Auskristallisationsprobe, Auskristallisationsprüfung

efflorescent · ausblühfähig, ausschlagfähig, auswitterungsfähig, aussatzfähig, auskristallisationsfähig

efflorescent-proof · nichtausblühend, nichtausschlagend, nichtauswitternd, nichtauskristallisierend

efflorescent salt · Ausblüh(ungs)salz n [Ammoniumsalz im Erdreich und/oder im Grundwasser führt zu Ausblühungen wenn es in einen Bauteil gelangt]

egg and dart moulding (Brit.); ~ ~ ~ molding (US); ~ ~ tongue ~, cyma(tium) reversa, Ionic cyma(tium) · ionisches Kyma(tion) n, Eierstab m

egg-shaped · eiförmig

egg(-shaped) barrel with base · eiförmiges Durchgangrohr n mit Fuß

~ concrete pipe · eiförmiges Betonrohr n, Betonrohr mit eiförmigem Abflußquerschnitt, Betonrohr mit Eiprofil, Zementrohr mit Eiprofil, Ei(profil)-Betonrohr, Eiprofil-Zementrohr

~ cross-section · Eierquerschnitt m

~ interlocking pipe · Ei-Falzrohr n, eiförmiges Falzrohr

~ pipe · eiförmig gedrücktes Rohr n, Eiformrohr, Ei(profil)rohr, eiförmiges Rohr

~ profile · eiförmiges Profil n, Eiprofil

~ section · eiförmiger Querschnitt m

eggshell, eggshelling, chip cracks · Eierschalentextur f

~ flat varnish · Eierschalenmattlack m

~ gloss, ~ luster, ~ finish [A term referring to the gloss of a dried paint film, the glossiness of which is between flat and semi-gloss, and resembles the glossiness of an eggshell] · Eierschalenglanz m

~ paint · Eierschalen(anstrich)farbe f

egress of heat · Wärmeaustritt m

Egyptian architecture · ägyptische Baukunst f, ~ Architektur

~ capital · ägyptisches Kapitäl n, ~ Kapitell

~ Hall of Vitruvius · ägyptische Halle f des Vitruv

~ minaret, ~ prayer-tower · ägyptisches Minarett n, ägyptischer Gebetsturm m

~ prayer-tower, ~ minaret · ägyptisches Minarett n, ägyptischer Gebetsturm m

eight-bed ((pre)stressing) yard, ~ (~) plant, ~ (~) factory, ~ tensioning ~ · Spannbetonwerk n mit acht Spannbetten, Vorspannwerk ~ ~ ~

eight-blade fan · 8-flügeliger Ventilator m

eight columned — elastic design

eight columned, octastyle · achtsäulig
eight-leaf folding sliding shutterdoor, ~ sliding folding ~ · achtflügeliges Faltschiebetor n, ~ Schiebefalttor
eight-hole brick · Achtlochziegel m
eight-lobe tracery, octofoil · Achtpaß m [*gotisches Maßwerk*]
eight-pointed · achtzackig
eight-sided aisle, octagonal ~ · Achteckschiff n, Achtkantschiff
~ bar, ~ rod, octagonal ~ · Achteckstab m, Achtkantstab
~ base → octagonal (ground(-))plan
~ block, ~ building, octagonal ~ · Achteckgebäude n, Achtkantgebäude
~ building, ~ block, octagonal ~ · Achteckgebäude n, Achtkantgebäude
~ chapter-house, octagonal ~ · achteckiges Kapitellhaus n, achtseitiges ~
~ chimney, octagonal ~ · Achteckschornstein m, Achtkantschornstein
~ cupola, octagonal ~, ~ dome · Achteckkuppel f, Achtkantkuppel
~ dome, octagonal ~, ~ cupola · Achteckkuppel f, Achtkantkuppel
~ donjon → octagonal keep
~ dungeon → octagonal keep
~ footing, octagonal ~ · Achteckfundament n, Achtkantfundament
~ foundation, octagonal ~ · Achteckgründung f, Achtkantgründung
~ girder four columns space frame, octagonal ~ ~ ~ ~ ~ ~ · räumlicher Vier-Säulen-Rahmen m als Achteckträger
~ (ground(-))plan → octagonal ~
~ keep → octagonal ~
~ lantern, octagonal ~ · Achtecklaterne f, Achteck-Dachkappe f, Achtkantlaterne, Achtkant-Dachkappe
~ mosaic tile, octagonal ~ ~ · Achteckmosaikfliese f, Achteckmosaik(belag)platte f, Achtkantmosaik(belag)platte, Achtkantmosaikfliese
~ plan → octagonal (ground(-))plan
~ pyramid, octagonal ~ · achtseitige Pyramide f, achteckige ~
~ rod, ~ bar, octagonal ~ · Achteckstab m, Achtkantstab
~ spire, octagonal ~ · Achteck(turm)-helm m, Achtkant(turm)helm
~ steel, octagonal ~ · Achteckstahl m, Achtkantstahl
~ tile, octagonal ~ · Achteck(belag)-platte f, Achteckfliese f, Achtkant(belag)platte, Achtkantfliese
~ tower, octagonal ~ · Achteckturm m, Achtkantturm
~ turret, octagonal ~ · Achtecktürmchen n, Achtkanttürmchen
~ vault, octagonal ~ · Achteckgewölbe n, Achtkantgewölbe
~ wire, octagonal ~ · Achteckdraht m, Achtkantdraht

8-wheeled trolley · achtteilige Laufrolle f [*Schiebetor*]
eighth (pipe) bend → one-~ (~) ~
Einstein Tower [*At Potsdam; designed by Erich Mendelsohn*] · Einsteinturm m
ejector · Abwasserhebepumpe f, Abwasserhebeanlage f
~ chimney [*Induced draught is provided by means of a high-pressure blower discharging into a venturi and producing suction*] · Saugzugschornstein m
ekistics [*The science of human settlements*] · Sied(e)lungswesen n
elaeolite-syenite · Elaeolithsyenit m
elastic after-effect, ~ hysteresis, ~ lag · elastische Hysterese f, ~ Nachwirkung f, Elastizitätshysterese
~ arch, ~ structural ~ · elastischer Bogen m
~ bearing, ~ support · elastische Auflagerung f, federnde ~, elastisches Auflager n, federndes Auflager
~ bitumen → mineral caoutchouc
~ body · elastischer Körper m
~ buckling · elastisches Ausknicken n, ~ (Ein)Knicken
~ ~ load · elastische Knicklast f
~ centre method (Brit.); ~ center ~ (US) · elastisches Schwerpunktverfahren n
~ compatibility [*e.g. compatibility between stresses in the edge beams and stresses in the edge zone*] · Elastizitätsverträglichkeit f
~ composition, ~ compound, ~ mass, ~ material · elastische Masse f
~ compound, ~ composition, ~ mass, ~ material · elastische Masse f
~ condition → elasticity ~
~ constant · elastische Konstante f, Elastizitätskonstante
~ construction, ~ (structural) system · elastische Konstruktion f, elastisches (Konstruktions)System n, elastisches Bausystem
~ cracking strain · elastische Rißdehnung f
~ critical load · elastische kritische Last f
~ curve, deflection ~, deflexion ~ · Biegelinie f, Biegungslinie [*Elastische Linie eines Balkens oder Trägers*]
~ deflection, rebound ~, ~ deflexion · elastische Durchbiegung f, ~ Durchsenkung f
~ deformation · elastische Formänderung f, ~ Verformung, federnde ~
~ ~ energy, internal resilience · elastische Verformungsenergie f, ~ Formänderungsenergie, federnde ~
~ design, ~ method, permissible-stress ~, working load ~ [*It is based on service loads and on permissible stresses in concrete and steel*] · Verfahren n zur Ermitt(e)lung der Schnittkraftgrößen nach der Elastizitätstheorie

elastic end-restraint — elaterite

~ **end-restraint** · elastische Einspannung f
~ **equation** → elasticity ~
~ **equilibrium** · elastisches Gleichgewicht n
~ **frame** · elastischer Rahmen m
~ **hysteresis,** ~ after-effect, ~ lag · elastische Hysterese f, ~ Nachwirkung f, Elastizitätshysterese
~ **impact** · elastischer Stoß m, federnder ~
~ **joint seal(ing) compound,** ~ ~ sealant · elastische Fugen(ab)dicht(ungs)masse f, ~ Fugenmasse, ~ (Fugen)(Ver)Füllmasse, elastischer (Fugen)(Ver)Füller m
~ **lag,** ~ after-effect, ~ hysteresis · elastische Hysterese f, ~ Nachwirkung f, Elastizitätshysterese
~ **limit** → elasticity ~
~ **line method** · Biegelinienverfahren n, Biegungslinienverfahren
~ **loads method,** ~ weights ~, angle loads ~, angle weights ~ · Winkelgewichtsverfahren n
~ **mass,** ~ material, ~ compound, ~ composition · elastische Masse f
~ **material,** ~ compound, ~ composition, ~ mass · elastische Masse f
~ **medium** · elastisches Medium n
~ **method,** ~ design, permissible-stress ~, working load ~ [It is based on service loads and on permissible stresses in concrete and steel] · Verfahren n zur Ermitt(e)lung der Schnittkraftgrößen nach der Elastizitätstheorie
~ **modulus** → modulus of elasticity
~ **moment** · elastisches Moment n

elastic-plastic, elastoplastic · elastisch-plastisch, elastoplastisch
~ **bending,** elastoplastic ~ · elastisch-plastische Biegung f, elastoplastische ~
~ **deformation,** elastoplastic ~ · elastisch-plastische Verformung f, elastoplastische ~

elastic plate, ~ slab · elastische Platte f
~ **rebound** · elastischer Rückprall m
~ **seal(ing)** · elastische (Ab)Dichtung f
~ **section** · elastischer Querschnitt m
~ **sheet,** ~ board · elastische Platte f
~ **shortening** [In prestressed concrete, the shortening of a member which occurs immediately on the application of forces induced by prestressing] · elastische Verkürzung f
~ **slab,** ~ plate · elastische Platte f
~ **stability** · elastische Stabilität f, ~ Standfestigkeit f, ~ räumliche Steifigkeit, räumliche elastische Steifigkeit
~ **state** · elastischer Zustand m
~ **strain** · elastische Dehnung f
~ **stress distribution** · elastische Spannungsverteilung f

~ **(structural) arch** · elastischer Bogen m
~ **(~) system,** ~ construction · elastische Konstruktion f, elastisches (Konstruktions)System n, elastisches Bausystem
~ **support** · elastische Unterlage f
~ **~,** ~ bearing · elastische Auflagerung f, federnde ~, elastisches Auflager n, federndes Auflager
~ **system,** ~ structural ~, ~ construction · elastische Konstruktion f, elastisches (Konstruktions)System n, elastisches Bausystem
~ **tensile strain** · elastische Zugdehnung f
~ **theory,** elasticity ~, theory of elasticity · Elastizitätstheorie f
~ **translation** · elastische Verschiebung f
~ **weight** · elastisches Gewicht n
~ **weights method,** ~ loads ~, angle loads ~, angle weights ~ · Winkelgewichtsverfahren n
~ **zone** · elastischer Bereich m, elastisches ~ n

elastically bedded, ~ em~ · elastisch gebettet
~ ~ **plate,** ~ em~ ~ · Platte f auf elastischer Unterlage
~ **(em)bedded** · elastisch gebettet
~ ~ **plate** · Platte f auf elastischer Unterlage
~ **fixed,** ~ restrained · elastisch eingespannt [Baustatik]
~ **restrained,** ~ fixed · elastisch eingespannt [Baustatik]

elasticity, resilience · Elastizität f
elastic(ity) condition · Elastizitätsbedingung f
~ **equation** · Elastizitätsgleichung f [Zur Berechnung von statisch unbestimmten Größen in Fach- oder Stabwerken. Diese Gleichung ist eine Arbeitsgleichung eines Gleichgewichtssystems nach dem Prinzip der virtuellen Arbeit]
~ **limit** · Elastizitätsgrenze f
~ **problem** · Elastizitätsaufgabe f
~ **theory,** theory of elasticity · Elastizitätstheorie f

elastomer-based contact solution · Elastomer-Kontaktlösung f
elastomer disperion · Elastomerdispersion f
~ **paste** · Elastomerpaste f
elastoplastic, elastic-plastic · elastisch-plastisch, elastoplastisch
~ **bending,** elastic-plastic ~ · elastisch-plastische Biegung f, elastoplastische ~
~ **deformation,** elastic-plastic ~ · elastisch-plastische Verformung f, elastoplastische ~
elaterite → mineral caoutchouc

elbow [*A pipe fitting for providing a sharp change of direction in a pipeline*] · (Ronr)Bogen *m* [*DIN 19502*]

~ · Armstütze *f*, Armlehne *f* [*Chorgestühl*]

ele, eling, (side) aisle, nave aisle [*A lateral division parallel with the nave in a basilica or church*] · (Seiten)Schiff *n*, Abseite *f*

electoral castle · kurfürstliches Schloß *n*

electric alarm system · elektrische Alarmanlage *f*

~ **bell** · elektrische Klingel *f*, Elektroklingel

(~) (block) storage heater, (~) night ~ ~ · Nachtstrom-Speicherofen *m*, Elektrowärme-Speicherofen, Nacht-(strom)-Wärmespeicher *m*, Elektrowärmeofen, (Nacht)Speicherofen

~ **boiler,** electrical ~, electrically heated ~ · Elektroheizkessel *m*

(~) cable pipe · Kabelschutzrohr *n*

~ **ceiling heating** → (radiant) ~ ~

~ **clock** · Elektrouhr *f*

~ **convector** · Elektrokonvektor *m*

~ **curing,** electro-thermal ~ · elektrische (Beton)Nachbehandlung *f*

~ **current consumer,** (electrical) power ~, electricity ~ · Stromabnehmer *m*

~ ~ **failure,** electricity supply ~, (electrical) power ~ · Stromausfall *m*

~ ~ **meter,** electricity ~ [*B.S. 37*] · Energiezähler *m*, Stromzähler

~ ~ **supply,** (electric) power ~, electricity ~ · Stromversorgung *f*, Elektrizitätsversorgung

~ ~ **tariff,** (electrical) power ~, electricity ~ · Stromtarif *m*

~ **(disappearing) stairway** · Elektro-Schiebetreppe *f*; Elektro-Aufzugtreppe [*Schweiz*]

~ **discharge lamp,** gas ~ · Gasentladungslampe *f*

~ **elevator** (US); ~ lift [*B.S. 2655*] · Elektroaufzug *m*

~ **eye,** photoelectric cell · elektrisches Auge *n*, Photozelle *f*

~ **fan** → electrically driven ~

~ **fixture,** ~ light(ing) ~; ~ light fitting (Brit.); ~ luminaire (fixture) (US) · elektrische Leuchte *f*, Elektroleuchte

~ **floor services carried in conduit(s)** → electrical underfloor services ~ ~ ~

~ **(furnace) steel** · Elektrostahl *m*

~ **hardening,** electro-thermal ~ · elektrische (Er)Härtung *f*

~ **heating** · Elektro(be)heizung *f*

~ ~ **ceiling,** electrically heated ~ · Elektroheiz(ungs)decke *f*

~ ~ **element** · Elektroheizelement *n*

~ ~ **tube** · Elektroheizrohr *n*

~ **hospital elevator** (US); ~ ~ lift (Brit.) · Elektro-Krankenhausaufzug *m*, Krankenhaus-Elektroaufzug, Elektro-Krankenbahrenaufzug, Krankenbahren-Elektroaufzug

(~) ~ lift (Brit.); (~) ~ elevator (US) · Krankenhaus-Elektroaufzug *m*, Elektro-Krankenhausaufzug, Krankenbahren-Elektroaufzug, Elektro-Krankenbahrenaufzug

~ **(hot) water heater,** ~ thermal ~ ~, ~ (~) ~ heating appliance · Elektro-Wassererhitzer *m*, Elektro-Wassererwärmer, Elektro-Wasserheizgerät *n*, Elektro-Wasserheizer, elektrischer Heißwasserbereiter, Elektro-Heißwasserbereiter

~ **(~) ~ heating appliance** → ~ (~) ~ heater

~ **illumination,** ~ lighting · elektrische Beleuchtung *f*, Elektro-Beleuchtung

~ ~ **system,** ~ lighting ~ · elektrische Lichtanlage *f*, Elektrolichtanlage

~ **insulating (clear) varnish,** ~ insulation(-grade) (~) ~ · Elektroisolier(klar)lack *m*

~ **lift** [*B.S. 2655*]; ~ elevator (US) · Elektroaufzug *m*

~ **light fitting** (Brit.); ~ luminaire (fixture) (US); ~ (light(ing)) fixture · elektrische Leuchte *f*, Elektroleuchte

~ **lighting,** ~ illumination · elektrische Beleuchtung *f*, Elektro-Beleuchtung

~ **(light(ing)) fixture;** ~ light fitting (Brit.); ~ luminaire (fixture) (US) · elektrische Leuchte *f*, Elektroleuchte

~ **lighting system,** ~ illumination ~ · elektrische Lichtanlage *f*, Elektrolichtanlage

~ **luminaire (fixture)** (US); ~ light fitting (Brit.); ~ (light(ing)) fixture · elektrische Leuchte *f*, Elektroleuchte

~ **meter enclosure,** ~ ~ niche · Elektrozähler(ablese)nische *f*

~ ~ **niche,** ~ ~ enclosure · Elektrozähler(ablese)nische *f*

(~) night storage heater → (~) (block) ~ ~

(~) oil-filled radiator · ölgefüllter Radiator *m*

~ **operator,** ~ shutterdoor ~, ~ shutter door ~ · Elektro-Torantrieb(vorrichtung) *m*, (*f*)

(~) power requirement · Kraftbedarf *m*, Strombedarf, Elektrizitätsbedarf

(~) ~ supply, electricity ~, electric current ~ · Stromversorgung *f*, Elektrizitätsversorgung

~ **pressure type water heater,** ~ ~ ~ ~ heating appliance · elektrischer Druckspeicher *m*, Elektro-Druckspeicher

~ **radiant heater,** radiant electric ~ · Elektrostrahler *m*

~ ~ **heating,** radiant electric ~ · Elektrostrahlungsheizung *f*

~ **service elevator** (US); ~ ~ lift (Brit.) · Elektro-Speisenaufzug *m*

electric service lift — electric(al) heating unit

~~ **lift** (Brit.); ~ ~ elevator (US) · Elektro-Speisenaufzug *m*

~ **(shutterdoor) operator,** ~ shutter door ~ · Elektro-Torantrieb(vorrichtung) *m*, (*f*)

~ **space heating** · elektrische Raumheizung *f*, Elektro-Raumheizung

~ **stairway,** ~ disappearing ~ · Elektro-Schiebetreppe *f*; Elektro-Aufzugtreppe [*Schweiz*]

~ **steam curing** · Elektrobedampfung *f*, Elektro-Dampfhärtung, Elektro-Dampfbehandlung [*Dampfbehandlung von Beton durch elektrisch beheizte Dampferzeuger*]

~ **steel,** ~ furnace ~ · Elektrostahl *m*

(~) **storage heater** → (~) block ~ ~

~ ~ ~ → ~ (thermal) storage (water) ~

~ ~ **heating** · elektrische Speicherheizung *f*

~ ~ ~ **appliance** → ~ (thermal) storage (water) heater

~ ~ **(water) heating appliance** → ~ (thermal) storage (water) heater

~ **switch** · Elektroschalter *m*

~ **(thermal) storage (water) heater,** ~ (~) ~ (~) heating appliance · Elektro-Heißwasserspeicher *m*, elektrischer Heißwasserspeicher [*DIN 44901 und DIN 44902*]

~ ~ **water heater** → ~ (hot) ~ ~

~ ~ ~ **heating appliance** → ~ (hot) water heater

(~) **tubular heater** · (elektrischer) Rohrheizkörper *m*

(~) **(under)floor heating system** → (~) ~ warming installation

(~) ~ **warming installation,** (~) ~ heating ~, (~) ~ ~ system · Bodenheiz(ungs)anlage *f*, (Elektro-)Fußbodenheiz(ungs)anlage, FB-Heiz(ungs)anlage

(~) **water-filled radiator** · wassergefüllter Radiator *m*

~ **water heater** → ~ hot ~ ~

~ ~ **heating** · elektrische Wassererhitzung *f*, ~ Wassererwärmung

~ ~ ~ **appliance** → ~ (hot) water heater

(~) **wiring** · (Elektro)Verdrahtung *f*

electric(al) accessories · Elektrozubehör *n*

electrical analogy method · elektrisches Analogieverfahren *n*

~ **appliance** · Elektrogerät *n*

electric(al) blower · Elektrogebläse *n*

~ **boiler,** electrically heated ~ · Elektroheizkessel *m*

~ **cable** · elektrisches (Leitungs)Kabel *n*, Kabel, Elektrokabel, Elt-Kabel

~ **ceiling panel heating** → (radiant) ceiling ~

~ **central heating** · Elektrozentralheizung *f*

electrical ceramics, electroceramics · Elektrokeramik *f*

electric(al) clock · Elektrouhr *f*

electrical compound for cable isolations, cable filling compound · Kabelausgußmasse *f*, Kabelvergußmasse

~ **conductivity** · elektrische Leitfähigkeit *f*

~ **conduit,** (wiring) ~ · Elektroleerrohr *n*, (Elt)Leerrohr

~ ~ **line,** (wiring) ~ ~ · Elektroleerrohrleitung *f*, (Elt)Leerrohrleitung

~ ~ **network,** (wiring) ~ · Elektroleerrohrnetz *n*, (Elt)Leerrohrnetz

~ **control** · elektrische Bedienung *f* [*Raffjalousie*]

~ **domestic installation,** domestic electrical ~ · elektrische Hausanlage *f*

electric(al) duct · Elektrokanal *m*

electrical engineering · Elektrotechnik *f*, E(lt)-Technik

electric(al) fan, electrically driven ~ · Elektroventilator *m*

~ **finned strip heater,** (fin(ned)) strip electric ~ · Elektro-Lamellenheizkörper *m*

~ **fire** → ~ heating appliance

electrical fire alarm · Elektro-Feuermelder *m*, Elektro-Brandmelder

electric(al) fireplace · Elektrokamin *m*

~ **floor** [*e.g. the Robertson Q-floor*] · elektrotechnisch genutzte Decke *f*

~ ~ **heating** → ~ (under)floor (panel) ~

~ ~ **(panel) heating** → ~ underfloor (~) ~

~ ~ **(~) warming** → ~ (under)floor (panel) heating

~ ~ **warming** → ~ (under)floor (panel) heating

electrical garage door operator · Garagentor-Elektroantrieb(vorrichtung) *m*, (*f*)

electric(al) heater → ~ heating appliance

~ **heating** · Elektro(be)heizung *f*

~ ~ **appliance,** ~ ~ unit, ~ ~ device, ~ warming ~, ~ ~ heater, ~ ~ fire, ~ warmer · Elektroheizer *m*, Elektroheiz(ungs)gerät *n*, Elektroerhitzer

(~) ~ **ceiling panel** · (Elektro)Deckenheiz(ungs)platte *f*

~ ~ **device** → ~ ~ ~ appliance

~ ~ **installation,** ~ ~ system · Elektroheizung *f*

electrical heating of high-tensile bars, electro-thermal pre-tensioning, electrical prestressing · elektrothermisches Spannen *n* von Spannstahl, Vorspannung *f* auf elektrischem Wege

electric(al) heating system, ~ ~ installation · Elektroheizung *f*

~ ~ **unit** → ~ ~ ~ appliance

electric(al) immersion heater — electroacoustic transducer

~ **immersion heater** · Elektrotaucherhitzer m, Elektrotauchheizgerät n

~ **incinerator** · Elektro-Verbrenner m

electrical installation, ~ system, ~ services · Elektroanlage f, Elektroinstallation f, Elt-Anlage, Elt-Installation

~ **insulating putty** · Isolierkitt m

~ **insulation** · Elektroisolierung f

~ **layout** · Elektroanordnung f

~ **loading** · Anschlußwert m [*Bei elektrischen Lampen, Geräten, Motoren usw. Er wird entsprechend deren Leistungsaufnahme als Höchstwert in W oder KW ausgedrückt*]

electric(al) low-water alarm · Elektro-Wassermangelsicherung f

electrical network · elektrisches Netzwerk n [*Planungsrechnung*]

~ **oil**, insulating ~ · Isolieröl n

~ **paint** · elektroisolierende (Anstrich-) Farbe f

(~) **power consumer**, electric current ~, electricity ~ · Stromabnehmer m

(~) ~ **failure**, electric current ~, (electricity) supply ~ · Stromausfall m

(~) ~ **supply**, electric current ~, electricity ~ · Stromversorgung f

(~) ~ **tariff**, electric current ~, electricity ~ · Stromtarif m

~ **(pre)stressing**, ~ stretching, ~ heating of high-tensile bars, ~ tensioning, electro-thermal pré-tensioning · elektrothermisches Spannen n von Spannstahl, Vorspannung f auf elektrischem Wege

electric(al) range · Elektroherd m

electrical resistivity heating of concrete · Betonerwärmung f mit Elektroden, elektrische Widerstandserwärmung des Betons

~ **re-wiring** · (elektrische) Nachverdrahtung f, Elektro-Nachverdrahtung

electric(al) sanitary incinerator · Elektro-Sanitärverbrenner m

electrical services, ~ system, ~ installation · Elektroanlage f, Elektroinstallation f, Elt-Anlage, Elt-Installation

~ **shutter** · Elektro(raum)abschluß m

electric(al) storage heater, ~ ~ heating appliance · Elektrospeicherheizgerät n, Elektrospeicherheizer m, Elektrospeichererhitzer

~ ~ **heating appliance**, ~ ~ heater · Elektrospeicherheizgerät n, Elektrospeicherheizer m, Elektrospeichererhitzer

electrical stressing → ~ pre~

~ **stretching** → ~ (pre)stressing

~ **supply main** · Elektro-Hauptleitung f

~ ~ **shaft** · Energieschacht m

electric(al) switch · Elektroschalter m

electrical system, ~ services, ~ installation · Elektroanlage f, Elektroinstallation f, Elt-Anlage, Elt-Installation

~ **tensioning** → ~ (pre)stressing

electric(al) (under)floor heating → ~ ~ panel ~

~ ~ **(panel) heating**, ~ ~ (~) warming · Elektro-FB-Heizung f, Elektro- (Fuß)Bodenheizung

~ ~ **(~) warming**, ~ ~ (~) heating · Elektro-FB-Heizung f, Elektro-(Fuß)Bodenheizung

~ ~ **services carried in conduit(s)** · Elektroleitungen fpl unter der Decke

~ ~ **warming** → ~ ~ panel ~

(~) ~ ~ **cable**, (~) ~ heating ~ · (Elektro-)(Fuß)Bodenheiz(ungs)kabel n, FB-Heiz(ungs)kabel

~ **warmer** → ~ heating appliance

~ **warming appliance** → ~ heating ~

~ ~ **device** → ~ heating appliance

~ ~ **unit** → ~ heating appliance

(electric(al)) wiring · (Elektro)Verdrahtung f, elektrische Verdrahtung

~ **work** · Elektroarbeiten fpl

electrically conducting rubber floor(ing) (finish), ~ ~ ~ floor cover(ing) [*B.S. 3187*] · elektrisch leitender Gummi(fuß)boden(belag) m

~ **driven fan**, electric(al) ~ · Elektroventilator m

~ **heated boiler**, electric(al) ~ · Elektroheizkessel m

~ ~ **ceiling**, electric heating ~ · Elektroheiz(ungs)decke f

~ ~ **concrete** · Elektrobeton m [*Dieser Beton wird zwecks schnellerer Erhärtung elektrisch erwärmt*]

~ ~ **glass panel**, glass heating ~, radiant-heating ~ · strahlungsheizende Glastafel f

(~) ~ **hung ceiling**, (~) ~ suspended ~, (~) ~ SC · (Elektro)Heizhängedecke f

(~) ~ **metal suspended ceiling**, (~) ~ ~ hung ~, (~) ~ ~ SC · (Elektro-) Metallheizhängedecke f

~ ~ **sauna stove** · Elektro-Keramik-Saunaofen m

(~) ~ **suspended ceiling**, (~) ~ hung ~, (~) ~ SC · (Elektro)Heizhängedecke f

~ ~ **tape** → (pipe) heating ~

electrically-lit · elektrisch beleuchtet

electricity cable duct · Energiekanal m

~ **consumer**, electric current ~, (electrical) power ~ · Stromabnehmer m

~ **failure**, electric current ~, (electrical) power ~ · Stromausfall m

~ **meter**, electric current ~ [*B.S. 37*] · Energiezähler m, Stromzähler

~ **supply**, electric current ~, (electric) power ~ · Stromversorgung f, Elektrizitätsversorgung

~ **tariff**, electric current ~, (electrical) power ~ · Stromtarif m

electroacoustic transducer · elektroakustischer Wandler m

electroacoustics · Elektroakustik f

electro-cast refractory (product) · elektro-schmelzgegossenes Erzeugnis n [*Ein feuerfestes Erzeugnis, das aus einer im elektrischen Ofen geschmolzenen Charge gegossen wird*]

electroceramics, electrical ceramics · Elektrokeramik f

electrochemical corrosion · elektrochemische Korrosion f

~ **polishing** · elektrochemisches Polieren n

electro-coating, electrodeposition · Elektrophorese f, Elektrotauchverfahren n, Elektrotauchlackierung f, elektrophoretische Lackierung, elektrophoretische Beschichtung

~ **paint** · Elektrophoreselack m

electro-copper glass method (Brit.); copper(lite) ~ ~ (US) · Elektroglas n [*Elektroglas ist keine Glassorte, sondern der Name bezeichnet das Verfahren, kleine Glasscheiben beliebiger Glasart und bis zu 100 cm² Fläche zu feuerhemmenden Scheiben zusammenzufassen*]

electrode boiler [*B.S. 1894*] · Elektrodenkessel m

electrodeposition, electro-coating · Elektrophorese f, Elektrotauchverfahren n, Elektrotauchlackierung f, elektrophoretische Lackierung, elektrophoretische Beschichtung

electro-gilding · galvanische Vergoldung f

electro immersion hot water heating, ~ ~ (water) ~ · Elektro-Tauch-Wassererwärmung f

electroless plating · stromloses Verfahren n [*Zur Herstellung von Überzügen auf Metalloberflächen*]

electrolier · Elektrohängeleuchte f

~ **switch** · Hängeleuchtenschalter m

electrolysis · Elektrolyse f

electrolytic corrosion · elektrolytische Korrosion f

~ **method** · Elektrolyseverfahren n

~ **polishing** · elektrolytisches Polieren n

~ **process,** Sperry ~ · Fällungsverfahren n, Niederschlagsverfahren [*Bleiweißherstellung*]

~ **tinning** · elektrolytische Verzinnung f

~ **zinc** · elektrolytisches Zink n

electrolytical oxide layer (Brit.); ~ oxid(e) ~ (US) · elektrolytisch erzeugte Oxydschicht f

electromotive force, EMF · elektromotorische Kraft f, EMK

electronic door · elektronisch gesteuerte Tür f

electronically controlled shower · Elektronik-Dusche f

electroplated coating [*B.S. 1224*] · elektrolytischer Überzug m

~ ~ **of nickel plus chromium** · elektrolytisch erzeugter Nickel-Chrom-Überzug m

electroplating → galvanizing

electro-polishing · Elektropolieren n

electrostatic attraction · elektrostatische Anziehung f

~ **charge** · elektrostatische (Auf)Ladung f

~ **coating** → ~ spraying

~ **spraying,** ~ coating [*Method of spraying in which an electrostatic potential is created between the work to be coated and the atomized paint particles. The charged particles of paint are attracted to the article being painted and are there deposited and discharged. The electrostatic potential is used in some process to aid the atomization of the paint*] · elektrostatisches (Pulver)Spritzen n, EPS

electro-thermal curing, electric ~ · elektrische (Beton)Nachbehandlung f

~ **hardening,** electric ~ · elektrische (Er)Härtung f

~ **pre-tensioning,** electrical prestressing, electrical heating of high-tensile bars · elektrothermisches Spannen n von Spannstahl, Vorspannung f auf elektrischem Wege

element, member, bar, rod · Füll(ungs)stab m, Gitterstab, Glied n, (Träger)stab

~ → (architectural) feature

~ **buckling,** member ~, bar ~, rod ~ · Gliedknickung f, Gliedknicken n, Stabknickung, Stabknicken

~ **centre line** (Brit.); ~ center ~ (US); bar ~ ~, rod ~ ~, member ~ ~ · Stabachse f, Stabmittellinie f, Gliedachse, Gliedmittellinie

~ **connection,** member ~, rod ~, bar ~ · Stabanschluß m, Gliedanschluß [*Stabwerkkonstruktion*]

~ **cross-section,** rod ~, member ~, bar ~ · Stabquerschnitt m, Gliedquerschnitt [*Stabwerkkonstruktion*]

~ **field,** bar ~, rod ~, member ~ · Stabfeld n, Gliedfeld [*Stabwerkkonstruktion*]

~ **force,** bar ~, rod ~, member ~ · Stabkraft f, Gliedkraft [*Stabwerkkonstruktion*]

~ **length,** bar ~, rod ~, member ~ · Stablänge f, Gliedlänge

~ **loading,** bar ~, rod ~, member ~ · Stabbelastung f, Gliedbelastung

~ **moment,** member ~, rod ~, bar ~ · Gliedmoment n, Stabmoment

~ **of a loaded area** · Teil m, n einer belasteten Fläche

~ **shape,** member ~, bar ~, rod ~ · Gliedform f, Stabform

~ **size,** bar ~, rod ~, member ~ · Stabgröße f, Gliedgröße [*Stabwerkkonstruktion*]

~ **slope,** member ~, bar ~, rod ~ · Stabablenkung f, Gliedablenkung [*Rahmenträger*]

element stress — elevator-type car park

~ **stress,** rod ~, member ~, bar ~ · Stabspannung f, Gliedspannung [Stabwerkkonstruktion]

~ **transformation,** ~ transposition, member ~, bar ~, rod ~ · Stabvertauschung f, Gliedvertauschung [Stabwerkkonstruktion]

~ **transposition,** ~ transformation, member ~, bar ~, rod ~ · Stabvertauschung f, Gliedvertauschung [Stabwerkkonstruktion]

elemental carbon, uncombined ~ · elementarer Kohlenstoff m

Elementarism [Kind of 'philosophy' of the elements that form the structure of a building] · Elementarismus m

elementary bearing structure, ~ load~ ~, ~ (weight-carrying) ~ · Elementar-Tragwerk n

~ **(load)bearing structure,** ~ (weight-carrying) ~ · Elementar-Tragwerk n

~ **school,** primary ~ · Grundschule f

~ **statics of shells** · elementare Schalenstattik f

~ **structure,** ~ weight-carrying ~, ~ (load)bearing ~ · Elementar-Tragwerk n

~ **(weight-carrying) structure,** ~ (load)bearing ~ · Elementar-Tragwerk n

elemi balsam · Elemibalsam m

~ **resin** · Elemiharz n

elemosinaria → almonry (house)

elevated heliport, roof (top) ~, rooftop helicopter airport · Hubschrauber-Dachflugplatz m

~ **platform** · Hochplattform f

~ **pulpit** · erhöhte Kanzel f

~ **(storage) tank** · Hochbehälter m, Turmbehälter

~ **water storage tank** · Wasser-Hochbehälter m, Wasser-Turmbehälter

elevation · Aufriß m

~ **facing yard,** back elevation · Hinterfront f, Hinterseite f, Hoffront, Hofseite

elevational design · Aufrißentwurf m

~ **presentation** · Darstellung f im Aufriß

elevator (US); lift [B.S. 2655] [An enclosed platform for carrying goods or passengers from one stor(e)y to another in a tall building] · Aufzug m

~, **passenger** ~ (US); (passenger) lift (Brit.) · Fahrstuhl m, (Personen)Aufzug m [DIN 15301 und DIN 15302]

~ **apartment block** (US) → ~ residential building

~ ~ **building** (US) → ~ residential ~

~ ~ **house** (US) → ~ residential building

~ **attendant** (US); lift ~ (Brit.) · Aufzugführer m

~ **building,** ~ block (US); lift ~ (Brit.) · Fahrstuhlgebäude n, Fahrstuhlhaus n

(~) **cage** (US); (lift) car (Brit.) · (Aufzug)Korb m, (Aufzug)Kabine f, Fahrkorb, Fahrkabine

(~) ~ **door** (US); (lift) car ~ (Brit.) · Aufzugtür f, Fahrkorbtür

~ **control** (US); lift ~ (Brit.) · Aufzugsteuerung f

~ **door,** passenger ~ (US); (passenger) lift door (Brit.) · (Personen)Aufzugtür f, Fahrstuhltür

~ **dwelling block** (US) → ~ residential building

~ ~ **building** (US) → ~ residential ~

~ ~ **house** (US) → ~ residential building

~ **entrance** (US); lift ~ (Brit.) · Aufzugeingang m

~ ~ (US) → (passenger) lift (landing) ~

~ **guide rail** (US); lift ~ ~ (Brit.) · Aufzugführungsschiene f

~ **hall** (US); lift ~ (Brit.) · Aufzughalle f

(~) **hoistway,** (~) shaft(way) (US); lift well (Brit.) · Aufzugschacht m, Aufzugkern m, Fahrschacht, Fahrkern

(~) ~ **door,** (~) shaft(way) ~ (lift) ~ ~ (Brit.) · Aufzugschachttür f, Aufzugkerntür, Fahrschachttür, Fahrkerntür

~ **installation** (US) → (passenger) lift ~

~ **landing** (US) → lift ~ (Brit.)

~ (~) **entrance** (US) → (passenger) lift (~) ~

~ **machine room** (US); lift ~ ~ (Brit.) · Aufzug(maschinen)raum m

~ **maker** (US); lift ~ (Brit.) · Aufzughersteller m

~ **multiple dwelling** (US) → ~ residential building

~ **pit** (US); lift ~ (Brit.) · Aufzugkerngrube f, Fahrkerngrube, Aufzugschachtgrube, Fahrschachtgrube

~ **residence block** (US) → ~ residential building

~ **residence building** (US) → ~ residential ~

~ ~ **house** (US) → ~ residential building

~ **residential block** (US) → ~ ~ building

~ ~ **building** (US); lift ~ ~ (Brit.); ~ residence ~, ~ dwelling ~, ~ apartment ~, ~ block, ~ ~ house, ~ multiple dwelling · Fahrstuhlwohngebäude n, Fahrstuhlwohnhaus n

~ ~ **house** (US) → ~ ~ building

(~) **shaft** → (~) hoistway

(~) **shaft(way)** → (~) hoistway

(~) ~ **door** → ~ hoistway ~

elevator/stair(case) core (US) → lift/stair(case) ~

elevator-type car park (US); lift-type ~ ~ (Brit.) · Aufzuggarage f

elevator with automatic push-button ... — embossed panel 334

elevator with automatic push-button control (US); lift ~ ~ ~ ~ (Brit.) · Selbstfahrer(aufzug) *m*

elevatoring (US) · Fahrstuhlbetrieb *m*

~ equipment (US) · Fahrstuhlausrüstung *f*

Elgin gravel · Elginkies *m* [*Ein in den USA verwendeter Normalbetonzuschlag-(stoff) aus Quarz und Kalkgestein*]

~ sand · Elginsand *m* [*Ein in den USA verwendeter Normalbetonzuschlag-(stoff) aus Quarz und Kalkgestein*]

eliminating determinant · Eliminationsdeterminante *f*

eling, ele, (side) aisle, nave aisle [*A lateral division parallel with the nave in a basilica or church*] · (Seiten)Schiff *n*, Abseite *f*

(e)liquation, segregation · Seigerung *f*

ell [*A pipe shaped like an L*] · rechtwink(e)liger Fitting *m*

ell-beam · L-Balken(träger) *m*

ell girder · L-Träger *m*

ellipse of inertia · Trägheitsellipse *f*

~ ~ stress(es), stress ellipse · Spannungsellipse *f*

ellipsoid of inertia · Trägheitsellipsoid *n*

~ ~ revolution, spheroid · Rotationsellipsoid *n*, Drehellipsoid [*Ein durch die Umdrehung einer halben Ellipse und ihre (große oder kleine) Achse entstandener Körper, dessen ebene Schnitte Ellipsen oder Kreise sind*]

~ ~ stress(es), stress ellipsoid · Spannungsellipsoid *n*

ellipsoidal shell · Ellipsoidschale *f*

elliptic(al) arch [*A half-ellipse drawn from a centre on the springing line*] · Ellipsenbogen *m*, elliptischer Bogen

~ barrel vault · elliptisches Tonnengewölbe *n*, Ellipsentonnengewölbe

~ column · elliptische Säule *f*, Ellipsensäule

~ concrete pipe · Ellipsen-Betonrohr *n*, elliptisches Betonrohr

~ conoid · elliptisches Konoid *n*, Ellipsenkonoid

~ cross-section · Ellipsenquerschnitt *m*, elliptischer Querschnitt

~ cupola, ~ dome · Ellipsenkuppel *f*, elliptische Kuppel

~ curvature · elliptische Krümmung *f*, Ellipsenkrümmung

~ dome, ~ cupola · Ellipsenkuppel *f*, elliptische Kuppel

~ function · elliptische Funktion *f*, Ellipsenfunktion

~ integral · elliptisches Integral *n*, Ellipsenintegral

~ paraboloid · elliptisches Paraboloid *n*, Ellipsenparaboloid

~ ~ shell · elliptische Paraboloidschale *f*, Ellipsenparaboloidschale

~ plate, ~ slab · Ellipsenplatte *f*, elliptische Platte

~ ring · Ellipsenring *m*, elliptischer Ring

~ roof · Ellipsendach *n*, elliptisches Dach

~ shell cupola, ~ ~ dome · elliptische Schalenkuppel *f*, Ellipsenschalenkuppel

~ slab, ~ plate · Ellipsenplatte *f*, elliptische Platte

~ stair(case) · elliptische Wendeltreppe *f*, Ellipsenwendeltreppe

~ vault · Ellipsengewölbe *n*, elliptisches Gewölbe

elongation · Dehnung *f*, Längung [*positiv*]

~ at fracture → breaking elongation

~ ~ rupture → breaking elongation

EM → expanded (metal) mesh

to embattle, to crenellate, to battlement, to castellate [*To finish or decorate with battlements*] · bezinnen

embattled → battlemented

~ bridge parapet, (em)battlemented ~ ~, crenellated ~ ~, castellated ~ ~ · Brückenkopf *m* [*Schanze oder Befestigungsanlage am Ende einer Brücke oder in ihrer Nähe zur Verteidigung des Brückenüberganges*]

~ parapet (wall) · Zinnenbrüstung(smauer) *f*

(em)battlement, crenellation [*An indented parapet at the top of a wall, originally used for purposes of defence, subseqently for architectural decoration. The raised parts are 'cops' or 'merlons', the indentations 'embrasures' or 'crenel(le)s'*] · Zinnenkranz *m*, Zinnenbesatz *m*, Zinnenkrönung *f*

embattlemented → battlemented

embedded · eingebettet

~ electric heating cable · Heiz(ungs)-kabel *n* im (Fuß)Boden verlegt, ~ ~ ~ eingebettet

~ (in the coating) · eingedrückt [*Abstreumaterial beim Dachbelag*]

to embellish, to renovate, to redecorate · renovieren, verschönern

embellishment, redecoration · Verschönerung *f*

~ work, redecoration ~ · Verschönerungsarbeiten *fpl*

emblem · Emblem *n*

to emboss · prägen

embossed [*A surface design, impressed into the face of resilient tile or sheet goods*] · geprägt

~ aluminium foil (Brit.); **~ aluminum ~** (US) · geprägte Alu(minium)folie *f*

~ design, ~ pattern · Prägemuster *n*

~ (hard)board · (Holz)Faser-Hartplatte *f* mit eingepreßtem Muster, harte (Holz-) Faserplatte ~ ~ ~, HFH1 ~ ~ ~, Hart(faser)platte ~~~, Prägeplatte

~ panel · Prägetafel *f*

embossed paper — emulsifier

~ **paper**, ~ wallpaper · Prägetapete *f*
~ **pattern**, ~ design · Prägemuster *n*
~ **texture** · Prägestruktur *f*
~ **tile** · Präge(belag)platte *f*, Prägefliese
~ **(wall)paper** · Prägetapete *f*
embossing · Prägen *n*
~ → acid ~
embossment · Prägung *f*
embrasure, recess, blockout, cavity, pocket · Aussparung *f*
~, crenel(le) [*A gap in a battlemented parapet*] · Zinnenfenster *f*
embrittlement · Versprödung *f*
~ **temperature** · Versprödungstemperatur *f*
~ **tendency** · Versprödungsneigung *f*
embrittling · Verspröden *n*
emerald green · Smaragdgrün *n*
emergency accommodation · Notunterkunft *f*
~ **and accident department** · Notaufnahmestation *f* [*Krankenhaus*]
~ **call system** · Notrufanlage *f*
~ **church** · Notkirche *f*
~ **corridor**, (fire) escape ~ · Fluchtkorridor *m*, Feuerkorridor, Notkorridor, Brandkorridor
~ **door** · Nottür *f*, Fluchttür
~ **dwelling unit** (US); ~ dwelling (Brit.) · Notwohnung *f*
~ **exit** · Notausgang *m*
~ ~ **window** · Notausstiegfenster *n*
~ **housing scheme** · Wohn(ungs)hilfswerk *n*
~ **illumination**, ~ lighting · Notbeleuchtung *f*
~ **key** · Gefahrenschlüssel *m*
~ **ladder**, (fire) escape ~ · Feuerleiter *f*, Fluchtleiter, Brandleiter, Notleiter
~ **lighting**, ~ illumination · Notbeleuchtung *f*
~ **overflow pipe** · Not-Überlaufleitung *f*
~ **phone**, ~ tele~ · Notruffernsprecher *m*
~ ~ **cable**, ~ tele~ ~ · Notruf(fernsprecher)kabel *n*
~ ~ **system**, ~ tele~ ~ · Notfernsprechanlage *f*
~ **power installation** · Notstromanlage *f*
~ ~ **supply** · Notstromversorgung *f*
~ **repair** · Notreparatur *f*
~ **roof (walk)way**, (fire) escape ~ ~ · Fluchtweg-Dachlaufsteg *m*, Notweg-Dachlaufsteg, Rückzugsweg-Dachlaufsteg
~ **route**, (fire) escape ~ · Fluchtweg *m*, Notweg, Rückzugsweg
~ **service (line)** · Notversorgungsleitung *f*
~ **shower** · Branddusche *f*, Notdusche
~ **stair(case)**, (fire) escape ~ · Feuertreppe *f*, Fluchttreppe, Brandtreppe, Nottreppe
~ ~ **well**, (fire) escape ~ ~ · Feuertreppenhaus *n*, Brandtreppenhaus, Fluchttreppenhaus, Nottreppenhaus
~ **(tele)phone** · Notruffernsprecher *m*
~ ~ **cable** · Notruf(fernsprecher)kabel *n*
~ ~ **system** · Notfernsprechanlage *f*
~ **traffic** · Notverkehr *m* [*Arzt; Polizei usw*]
~ **window**, (fire) escape ~, fire ~ · Brand(schutz)fenster *n*, Notfenster, Feuer(schutz)fenster, Fluchtfenster
emery · Schmirgel *m*, Amarillstein *m*
~ **aggregate** → ~ construction ~
~ **cloth** · Schmirgelleinwand *f*
~ **(construction) aggregate** · Schmirgelzuschlag(stoff) *m*
~ **paper** · Schmirgelpapier *n*
EMF, electromotive force · elektromotorische Kraft *f*, EMK
eminently hydraulic lime · Edelkalk *m*, hochhydraulischer Kalk, HK 50 [*DIN 1060 Fehlnamen: Zementkalk, höchsthydraulischer Kalk*]
~ ~ ~ **mortar** · Edelkalkmörtel *m*, hochhydraulischer Kalkmörtel, HK 50-Mörtel
emission [*The discharge or escape into the atmosphere of one or more air polluants*] · Emission *f*, Abgabe *f*
~ **of smoke** · Rauchabgabe *f*, Rauchemission *f*
emissivity factor · Emissionsverhältnis *n*, Abgabeverhältnis
emotionalism · gefühlsbetontes Pathos *n*
to emphasize the grain · betonen der Maserung [*durch (Holz)Beizen*]
Empire Style [*The style of design, for French architecture and furniture, in vogue after Napoleon became emporor in 1804*] · Empirestil *m*
empirical formula · empirische Formel *f*
employee's canteen · Angestelltenkantine *f*
empty bottle store · Leerflaschenlager *n*
emptying cock · Entleerungshahn *m*
emulsifiability · Emulgierbarkeit *f*
emulsifiable (in water) · (wasser)emulgierbar
~ **oil** · wasserlösliches Öl *n*
emulsification, emulsifying process · Emulgation *f*, Emulgieren *n*, Emulgierung *f*
emulsi(ficati)on water · Emulsionswasser *n*
emulsified · emulgiert
~ **binder** · emulgiertes Bindemittel *n*, emulgierter Binder *m*
emulsifier, emulsifying agent, emulsion stabilizing agent, emulsion stabilizer · Emulgator *m*, Stabilisator, Emulgiermittel *n*

emulsifier layer — enamelized paint 336

~ **layer** · Emulgatorschicht f

~ **molecule** · Emulgatormolekül n

to emulsify · emulgieren

emulsifying agent, emulsion stabilizing ~, emulsion stabilizer, emulsifier · Emulgator m, Stabilisator, Emulgiermittel n

~ **process,** emulsification · Emulgation f, Emulgieren n, Emulgierung f

emulsion · Emulsion f [*Wäßrige Aufschlämmung eines flüssigen, sich nicht lösenden Stoffes*]

~ [*misnomer*]; emulsion-like dispersion · Emulsion f (für Anstrichfarbe); Binder m [*Fehlname*]

~ **adhesive** → ~ bonding ~

~ **base** · Emulsionsbasis f, Emulsionsgrundlage f

~ **binder,** emulsion-type ~, emulsion(-type) (binding) medium · Emulsions(farben)bindemittel n

~ **(binding) medium,** emulsion-type (~) ~, emulsion(-type) binder · Emulsions(farben)bindemittel n

~ **(bonding) adhesive,** ~ ~ medium, ~ ~ agent, ~ cement(ing agent) · Emulsionskleb(e)stoff m, Emulsionskleb(e)mittel n, Emulsionskleber m

~ ~ **agent** → ~ (~) adhesive

~ ~ **medium** → ~ (~) adhesive

~ **cement(ing agent)** → ~ (bonding) adhesive

~ **chemistry** · Emulsionschemie f

~ **for highway construction,** ~ ~ road ~, road emulsion, highway emulsion · Straßenbauemulsion f

~ ~ **road construction,** ~ ~ highway ~, road emulsion, highway emulsion · Straßenbauemulsion f

emulsion-like dispersion [*misnomer: emulsion*] · Emulsion f (für Anstrichfarbe) [*Fehlname: Binder m*]

emulsion medium, emulsion(-type) (binding) ~, emulsion(-type) binder · Emulsions(farben)bindemittel n

~ **of road tar,** road tar emulsion · Straßenteeremulsion f

~ ~ **tar/asphalt mix(ture)** (US); ~ ~ tar/(asphaltic-)bitumen ~ (Brit.) · Teerbitumenemulsion f

~ ~ **tar/(asphaltic-)bitumen mix(ture)** (Brit.); ~ ~ tar/asphalt ~ (US) · Teerbitumenemulsion f

~ ~ **water-gas tar,** water-gas tar emulsion · Wassergasteeremulsion f

~ **paint** [*Generally, a paint in which the medium is an 'emulsion' or emulsion-like dispersion of an organic binder in water. Industriallyy, the name is mainly restricted to those paints in which the medium is an 'emulsion' of a synthetic resin. The medium may also be called a latex by analogy with a natural rubber latex; polyvinyl acetate emulsion paint is a typical example*] · Emulsionsfarbe f

~ **polish,** polish emulsion · Wachsemulsion f

~ **polymerization,** ~ polymerizing · Emulsionspolymerisation f

~ **polymerizing,** ~ polymerization · Emulsionspolymerisation f

~ **product** · Emulsionserzeugnis n

~ **slurry** [*A mix(ture) of slow-setting asphalt emulsion, fine aggregate, mineral filler and water*] · Emulsionsschlämme f

~ **stabilizer,** ~ stabilizing agent, emulsifying agent, emulsifier · Emulgator m, Stabilisator, Emulgiermittel n

~ **stabilizing agent,** ~ stabilizer, emulsifier, emulsifying agent · Emulgator m, Stabilisator, Emulgiermittel n

emulsion(-type) binder, ~ (binding) medium · Emulsions(farben)bindemittel n

~ **(binding) medium,** ~ binder · Emulsions(farben)bindemittel n

~ **(cold-)water paint,** ~ ~ water-carried ~ · Emulsionsbinderfarbe f, Emulsionsdispersionsfarbe

~ **medium,** ~ binding ~, ~ binder · Emulsions(farben)bindemittel n

~ **water-carried paint,** ~ ~ (cold-)water ~ · Emulsionsbinderfarbe f, Emulsionsdispersionsfarbe

emulsion water, emulsification ~ · Emulsionswasser n

~ **wax,** self polishing ~ · Emulsionswachs n

enamel · Emaillelack m

~ **(glaze),** opaque ~, ~ glazed finish, ~ glazing, ~ glazed coat(ing) · Email(glasur) n, (f), Emaille f, opake Glasur, Emailbeglasung f, opake Beglasung

~ **glazed coat(ing),** ~ glazing, ~ glazed finish, ~ (glaze), opaque ~ · Email(glasur) n, (f), Emaille f, opake Glasur, Emailbeglasung f, opake Beglasung

~ **glazed finish,** ~ glazing, ~ glazed coat(ing), ~ (glaze), opaque ~ · Email(glasur) n, (f), Emaille f, opake Glasur, Emailbeglasung f, opake Beglasung

~ **glazing,** ~ glazed coat(ing), ~ glazed finish, ~ (glaze), opaque ~ · Email(glasur) n, (f), Emaille f, opake Glasur, Emailbeglasung f, opake Beglasung

~ **paint;** enamelized ~, enamelized finish [*Australia*] [*This term is now rather loosely used, but implies, as a rule, a superior quality paint, the outstanding characteristic of which is its hard gloss. When these very high-gloss paints were first made, the name 'enamel' was borrowed from the ceramic industry to describe the brillance of the gloss obtained by this process*] · Emaillefarbe f

~ **painter** · Schmelzmaler m

~ **stove** · Emaillierofen m

enamelized finish → ~ paint

~ **paint,** ~ finish [*Australia*]; enamel paint [*This term is now rather loosely used, but implies, as a rule, a superior quality paint, the outstanding characteristic of which is its hard gloss. When*

enamelized paint — end

these very high-gloss paints were first made, the name 'enamel' was borrowed from the ceramic industry to describe the brillance of the gloss obtained by this process] · Emaillefarbe *f*

enamelled brick (Brit.); enameled ~ (US); glazed ~ [*A brick faced with enamel, or opaque glaze*] · Glasurziegel *m*, glasierter Ziegel

~ **wire** (Brit.); enameled ~ (US) · Lackdraht *m*

enameller · Schmelzarbeiter *m*

enamelling (Brit.); enameling (US) · Emaillieren *n*

~ (Brit.); enameling (US) · Schmelzkunst *f*

~ **clay** (Brit.); enameling ~ (US) · Emaillierton *m*

encarpa, swag, garland, festoon [*A carved, modelled or painted garland of flowers, fruit or leaves, suspended in a curve between two points*] · Gehänge *n*, Gewinde *n*, Feston *n*, Girlande *f*

~ **leaf**, swag ~, festoon ~, garland ~ · Gehängeblatt *n*, Gewindeblatt, Festonblatt, Girlandenblatt

encased, haunched, concrete-~ · (beton)umhüllt, (beton)ummantelt

~ **(bath)tub** → built-in ~

~ **tub** → built-in (bath)tub

encasement, integral and monolithic concrete ~ · volle Betonummantelung *f* [*Rohr*]

~ → concrete ~

~ **concrete** · Hüllbeton *m*

~ **encasing of girder(s)** · Trägerummantelung *f*

encastered → hingeless

encastré → hingeless

~ **bending moment**, terminal ~ ~, (fixed-)end ~ ~ · Einspann(ungs)biegemoment *n*

~ **condition**, terminal ~, (fixed-)end ~ · Einspann(ungs)bedingung *f*

~ **length**, fixing ~ · Einspann(ungs)länge *f*

~ **moment** → (fixed-)end ~

encasure → (concrete) encasement

encaustic painting · Enkaustik *f*, Wachsmalerei *f*

~ **tile** · buntgemusterte Kachel *f*

enceinte (wall), curtain (~) · Kurtine *f*; Mittelwall *m*; Mittelmauer *f* [*Der zwischen je zwei Bollwerken gelegene Teil eines Festungswalles oder einer Festungsmauer*]

encircled by a palisade · palisadenbewehrt

encircling chapels → surrounding ~

to enclose · umgeben, umschließen

~ ~ **by masonry walls** · ummauern

enclosed block → ~ building

~ **building**, ~ block · Gebäude *n* mit Umfassungswänden

(~) **cabinet for drying washing**, (clothes-)drying cabinet · (Wäsche-)Trocknungsschrank *m* [*In einer Wohnung*]

~ **exit stairwell** · Sicherheitstreppenhaus *n*

~ **space**, maqsurah · Fürstenloge *f*, Maqsura [*Moschee*]

~ ~, space enclosed, cube, (cubic(al)) content, cubic capacity; architectural volume (US) [*The space contained within the external surfaces of the walls and roof and the upper surface of the lowest floor*] · umbauter Raum *m*

enclosing by masonry walls · Ummauern *n*

~ **cage** → ~ safety ~

~ **design function** · raumabschließende Wirkung *f*

~ **masonry wall** → exterior ~ ~

~ ~ ~ **column** → exterior ~ ~ ~

~ ~ ~ **facing** → exterior masonry wall lining

~ ~ ~ **lining** → exterior ~ ~ ~

~ ~ ~ **(sur)facing** → exterior masonry wall lining

~ ~ **(work)** → exterior ~ (~)

(~) **(safety) cage** · Rückenschutz *m* [*Schornstein; Turmdrehkran; Turm*]

~ **(structural) system** → external wall construction

~ **system** → external wall construction

~ **wall** → exterior ~

~ ~ **(building) component** → external wall (building) unit

~ ~ (~) **member** → external wall (building) unit

~ ~ (~) **unit** → external ~ (~) ~

~ ~ **component** → external wall (building) unit

~ ~ **construction** → external ~ ~

~ ~ **facing** → exterior wall lining

~ ~ **finish** → exterior ~ ~

~ ~ **lining** → exterior ~ ~

~ ~ **member** → external wall (building) unit

~ ~ **(sur)facing** → exterior wall lining

~ ~ **unit** → external wall (building) ~

enclosure, inclosure · Umschließung *f*

~ **of space**, inclosure ~ ~ · Raumhülle *f*

~ ~ ~, inclosure ~ ~ ~ · Raumabschluß *m*

~ **wall**, inclosure ~ [*An exterior non-bearing wall in skeleton construction, anchored to columns, piers, or floors, but not necessarily built between columns or piers*] · nicht(last)tragende Außenwand *f* [*Skelettbauweise*]

end · Stirn *f* [*Bei Zapfen oder Versatzungen die auf Druck beanspruchte Hirnholzfläche. Auch die sichtbare Hirnholzfläche am Ende von Balken, Sparren usw., im Traufgesims mit dem Stirnbrett verkleidet*]

end — endurance characteristic

~ [*As opposed to the side*] · Querseite f

~ [*The narrow surface of a parquet block where the grain is cut across more or less at right angles to the longitudinal axis of the block*] · Stirnseite f [*Die schmale Fläche eines Parkettstabes, wo die Faser mehr oder weniger rechtwinklig zur Achse des Parkettstabes durchtrennt ist*]

~ · Kopfseite f, Stirnseite, Giebelseite [*Gebäude*]

~ acroterion [*An acroterion placed at the end of a pediment*] · Eckakroterion n, Eckakroterium

~ anchorage · Endverankerung f

~ ~ failure · Endverankerungsbruch m

end-anchored · endverankert

end arch · Schlußbogen m

~ assemblage point, ~ joint · Endknoten m

~ bending moment, fixed-~ ~ ~, encastré ~, terminal ~ ~ · Einspann(ungs)biegemoment n

end-block · Abschlußblock m, Endblock [*Bei Balken aus Blöcken*]

end bulb, ~ web · Randsteg m, Randwulst m, f [*Fugenband*]

~ cap · Endkaschierung f [*Lichtleiste*]

~ ~ · Abdeckkappe f [*Wandleuchte*]

~ column · Endstütze f

~ condition, fixed-~ ~, encastré ~, terminal ~ · Einspann(ungs)bedingung f

end-construction tile [*The cells are placed vertically*] · Querlochblock(stein) m, Querlochstein

end degree, fixed-~ ~, fixing ~, terminal ~ · Einspann(ungs)grad m

~ diagonal · Enddiagonale f, Endschräge f

(~) diaphragm, bulkhead · Binderscheibe f [*Faltwerk*]

~ door · Stirntür f

~ façade · Stirnfassade f, Giebelfassade, Seitenfassade

(~) fixity, (~) restraint, immov(e)able (~) ~, fixed-end ~ · unverschiebliche Einspannung f, feste ~, Endeinspannung

~ frame, ~ framing · Endrahmen m, Portal(verband) n, (m), Stirnrahmen

~ framing, ~ frame · Endrahmen m, Portal(verband) n, (m), Stirnrahmen

~ girder · Endträger m

end-grain (wood) (paving) block · Hirnholz(pflaster)block m [*Schweiz: Stirnholz(pflaster)block*]

end hook, hook of rod · Endhaken m [*Das um 180° herumgebogene Ende eines Betonstahles*]

~ joint, ~ assemblage point · Endknoten m

~ lighting · Stirnbeleuchtung f

~ loop · Randschlaufe f [*Fugenband*]

~ masonry wall, side ~ ~, flank ~ ~, lateral ~ ~ · Seitenmauer f, Stirnmauer [*Fehlname: Giebelmauer*]

~ moment → fixed-~ ~

~ of a pipe, pipe end · Rohrstirnfläche f, Stirnfläche eines Rohres

~ ornament, crowning, crest(ing) [*An ornamental finish along the top of a screen, wall, or roof*] · (Be)Krönung f, Krone f [*Ornamentik*]

~ plate · Stirnwand f [*Zum Abschluß der Schienenenden je Lichtband*]

~ ~, diaphragm (~), bulkhead · Binderscheibe f [*Faltwerk*]

~ point, final boiling ~ · Endsiedepunkt m

~ pot · Bodenstück n [*Spannbetonverfahren Coff-Roebling, Wayss & Freytag und Dischinger*]

~ restraint → ~ fixity

~ rotation · Enddrehung f

end-row dwelling → semi-detached ~

~ house → semi-detached ~

end span, extreme ~ · Endfeld n

~ stair(case) · Stirn-Treppenhaus n

~ stiffener, ~ stiffening angle · Endsteife f [*Blechträger*]

~ stiffening angle, ~ stiffener · Endsteife f [*Blechträger*]

~ support [*pin-jointed*] · Endauflager n [*frei drehbar*]

~ tie-plate · Endbindeblech n [*Stütze*]

~ tile, flap ~ · Schluß(dach)ziegel m

end-to-end joint, butt ~, heading ~ · Stumpffuge f

end twist · Endverdrehung f

~ wall, lateral ~, flank ~, side ~ · Stirnwand f, Seitenwand [*Fehlname: Giebelwand*]

~ ~ balcony, flank ~ ~ · Stirnwandbalkon m [*Fehlname: Giebelwandbalkon*]

~ web, ~ bulb · Randsteg m, Randwulst m, f [*Fugenband*]

~ window · Stirnfenster n

endecagon, hendecagon · Elfeck n

endothermic [*Pertaining to a reaction which occurs with the absorption of heat*] · endotherm(isch)

ends, offcuts, trim [*Short pieces trimmed from round or rough-sawn timber when cutting them to length*] · kleines Bauholz n, Sparrholz, Ablängreste mpl

endurance, fatigue ~ · (Werk)Stoffermüdung f, (Material)Ermüdung

~ → fatigue resistance

~ action, fatigue ~ · Ermüdungsbeanspruchung f

~ behaviour (Brit.); ~ behavior (US); fatigue ~ · Ermüdungsverhalten n

~ bending failure, fatigue ~ ~ · Dauerbiegebruch m

~ bend(ing) test, fatigue ~ ~ · Dauerbiegeprobe f, Dauerbiegeprüfung f, Dauerbiegeversuch m

~ characteristic, fatigue ~ · Ermüdungsmerkmal n

~ **coefficient,** fatigue ~ · Ermüdungsbeiwert *m*

~ **crack,** fatigue ~ · Ermüdungsriß *m*

~ **degree,** fatigue ~ · Ermüdungsgrad *m*

~ **failure,** ~ rupture, ~ fracture, fatigue ~ · Dauerbruch *m*, Ermüdungsbruch

~ **fracture,** ~ rupture, ~ failure, fatigue ~ · Dauerbruch *m*, Ermüdungsbruch

~ **in bending** → fatigue ~ ~

~ ~ **compression,** fatigue ~ ~ · Druckermüdung *f*

~ ~ **flexure** → fatigue in bending

~ ~ **limit** → fatigue resistance

~ **load,** fatigue ~ · Ermüdungslast *f*

~ **of bond,** fatigue ~ ~ · Haftermüdung *f*, Verbundermüdung [*Beton*]

~ ~ **the concrete,** fatigue ~ ~ ~ · Betonermüdung *f*

~ **phenomenon,** fatigue ~ · Ermüdungserscheinung *f*

~ **rupture,** ~ fracture, ~ failure, fatigue ~ · Dauerbruch *m*, Ermüdungsbruch

~ **(strength)** → fatigue resistance

~ **test,** fatigue ~ · Ermüdungsversuch *m*, Ermüdungsprüfung *f*, Ermüdungsprobe *f*

energy approach · Energie(lösungs)ansatz *m*

~ **equation** · Energiegleichung *f*

~ **method** · Energiemethode *f*, Energieverfahren *n*

~ **of hardening,** hardening energy · (Er)Härtungsenergie *f*

~ ~ **initial set(ting),** initial set(ting) energy · Erstarrungsenergie *f* [*Beton; Mörtel*]

~ ~ **position,** geodetic head, potential energy, position energy [*It is the energy possessed by a body in virtue of its position relative to some zero position*] · Potential *n*, Energie *f* der Lage, potentielle Energie, latente Energie

~ ~ **set(ting),** set(ting) energy · (Ab-)Bindeenergie *f* [*hydraulisches Bindemittel*]

~ **theorem** · Energiesatz *m*

enframed · umrahmt

enframing arcades [*e.g. of the Porta Nigra at Reèves*] · Arkadensystem *n*

engaged column [*A column partly sunk into a wall or pier*] · eingebundene Säule *f*, engagierte ~

~ **Corinthian(esque) column** · eingebundene korinthische Säule *f*, engagierte ~ ~

~ **pier,** wall ~, attached ~, blind ~, pilaster [*A shallow pier or rectangular column projecting only slightly from a wall and, in classical architecture, conforming with one of the orders*] · Wandpfeiler *m*, eingebundener Pfeiler, Pilaster *m*, Halbpfeiler, Pfeilervorlage *f* [*Fehlname: Wandpilaster*]

~ ~ **capital,** wall ~ ~, attached ~ ~, blind ~ ~, pilaster ~ · Wandpfeilerkapitell *n*, Wandpfeilerkapitell, Pilasterkapitell, Pilasterkapitell, Halbpfeilerkapitell, Halbpfeilerkapitell

~ **shaft,** detached ~ · vorgelegter Schaft *m*

engine shed · Lok(omotiv)schuppen *m*

Engineer, resident engineer · Bauleitung *f* (der Bauherrschaft)

engineer for erection (work) · Montageingenieur *m*

engineering · Technik *f* [*Als Wissenschaft, nicht als Anwendung*]

~ **and construction of complete plants** · Anlagenbau *m*

~ **brick** [*B.S. 1301*] → clinker

~ ~ **face work,** ~ ~ facing · Klinkerverblendung *f*

~ ~ **facing,** ~ ~ face work · Klinkerverblendung *f*

~ ~ **floor cover(ing),** ~ ~ floor(ing) (finish) · Fbk, Klinker(ziegel)(fuß)boden(belag) *m*

~ ~ **floor(ing) (finish),** ~ ~ floor cover(ing) · Fbk, Klinker(ziegel)(fuß)boden(belag) *m*

~ ~ **for floor(ing)s** · (Fuß)Bodenklinker *m*

~ ~ ~ **manholes,** ~ ~ ~ manways · Schachtklinker *m*, Mannlochklinker

~ ~ ~ **paving (purposes)** · Klinkerpflasterstein *m*

~ ~ **masonry wall** · Klinkermauer *f* [*Fehlname: Klinkerwand f*]

~ ~ ~ **(work)** · Klinkermauerwerk *n*

~ ~ **paving,** paving of engineering bricks · Klinkerpflaster(decke) *n*, (*f*)

~ **consultation service,** ~ counsel ~ · technischer Beratungsdienst *m*

~ **data,** technical ~, spec(ification)s · technische Angaben *fpl*, ~ Daten *f*, ~ Aufzählung *f*

~ **diploma** · Ingenieurdiplom *n*

~ **foil** · technische Folie *f*

~ **of services and technical equipment of buildings** · Haustechnik *f* [*Sammelbegriff für alle fest eingebauten und beweglichen Einrichtungen, Geräte, Werkzeuge sowie Arbeitsverfahren, die dem technischen Betrieb von Gebäuden aller Art dienen*]

~ **property** · technische Eigenschaft *f*

English bond · Blockverband *m* [*Mauerwerkverband, bei dem über der Stoßfuge der Läuferschicht die Mittellinie eines Binders liegt*]

~ **cross bond,** St. Andrew's ~ ~; Dutch ~ [*misnomer*] · holländischer Verband *m*

~ **dinas** · kalkgebundener Dinasstein *m*

~ **garden-wall bond** (Brit.) → American ~

~ **Gothic architecture** · englische Gotik *f*

English landscape garden — (en)trapped air void

~ **landscape garden** · (englischer) Landschaftsgarten *m*
~ **Romanesque** · englische Romanik *f*, ~ romanische Baukunst *f*, ~ romanische Architektur *f*
~ **vermilion** · Englischrot *n*
~ **'Wrenaissance'** · Wren-Renaissance *f*
~ **yellow** · Englischgelb *n*
to engobe, to slip · engobieren
engobe · Engobe *f*, Anguẞfarbe *f* [*Engoben sind feine Tonmassen, die sich in bestimmten Farben brennen lassen und die vor allem auf Dachziegel und Verblender oberflächlich aufgetragen werden um ihnen eine andere Farbe als die des gebrannten Scherbens zu geben*]
engobing, slipping · Engobieren *n*
engrain lining paper, ingrain ~ ~ · Rauhfasermakulatur *f*
~ **wallpaper**, ingrain ~ · Rauhfaser(tapete) *f*
~ ~ **coat**, ingrain ~ ~ · Rauhfaseranstrich *m*, Rauhfaseraufstrich
engraving · Gravieren *n*
~ · Stich *m*
enneastyle · neunsäulig
enquiry desk, inquiry ~ · Auskunftsschalter *m*
enriched, ornamented, decorated, adorned · geziert, verziert, geschmückt
enrichment, ornament, decorative fixture · Ornament *n*, Zierelement *n*, Zierglied *n*, Dekor(ations)element *n*, Dekor(ations)glied, Schmuckglied, Schmuckelement, Verzierung *f*
~ → pattern
entablature · (Säulen)Gebälk *n*
to entail [*To ornament with carvings*] · schmücken mit Schnitzereien
entaille d'épargne → champlevé enamel
enterclose, linkway, connecting corridor, connection corridor · Verbindungsgang *m*
entering catch · Einreiber *m*
~ ~ **closer** · Einreiberverschluẞ *m*
enthalpy, heat content · Enthalpie *f*, Wärmeinhalt *m* [*Energieinhalt eines Gases; nicht verwechseln mit der inneren Energie*]
to entrain · einführen [*Luft in Beton, Mörtel oder Zementpaste*]
entrained air [*Microscopic air bubbles intentionally incorporated in mortar, concrete, or cement paste*] · eingeführte Luft *f*, eingetragene ~
~ ~ **indicator** → (concrete) (air) (entrainment) meter
~ ~ **void** [*t is typically between 10 and 1,000 microns in diameter and spherical or nearly so*] · eingeführte Luftpore *f*, eingetragene ~
~ **stone sand mortar** · AEA-Mörtel *m* aus Brechsand, Luftporenmörtel ~ ~, Bläschenmörtel ~ ~, belüfteter Mörtel ~ ~

(entrainment) meter → (concrete) air (~)
~ **of air**, entrapping ~ ~, air entrainment [*The occlusion of air in the form of minute bubbles (generally smaller than 1 mm) during the mixing of concrete or mortar*] · Belüftung *f*, Lufteinführung, Belüften *n*, Lufteinschluẞ *m*
entrance, pedestrian ~ [*A confined passageway immediately adjacent to the door through which people enter a building*] · Eingang *m*
~ **arch** · Eingangsbogen *m*
~ **area** · Eingangsbereich *m, n*
~ **canopy**, ~ roof overhang · Eingangs-Abdach *n*, Eingangs-Vordach, Eingangs-Wetter(schutz)dach
~ **corridor** · Eingangsflur *m*, Eingangskorridor *m*
~ **door** · Eingangstür *f*
(~) **drive(way)**, vehicular access · (Gebäude)Zufahrt *f*, Hauszufahrt
~ **façade** · Eingangsfassade *f*
~ **foyer**, lobby [*A circulation space into which one or more rooms open. A small vestibule*] · Diele *f*
~ **front**, access ~ · Eingangsfront *f*
~ **gate** · Eingangs(auẞen)tor *n*
(~) **hall**, reception ~ [*An entrance space, often containing a staircase*] · (Eingangs)Halle *f*, Empfangshalle
~ **heating** · Eingangs(be)heizung *f*
~ **installation** · Eingangsanlage *f*
~ **level** · Eingangsebene *f*
~ **lobby** · Eingangsflur *m* [*Hotelzimmer*]
~ **masonry wall** · Eingangsmauer *f*
~ **piazza** · Vorplatz *m*
~ **portal** · Eingangsportal *n*
~ **pylon** · Eingangspylon(e) *m*, (*f*)
~ **roof overhang**, ~ canopy · Eingangs-Abdach *n*, Eingangs-Vordach, Eingangs-Wetter(schutz)dach
~ **side**, access ~ · Zugangsseite *f*, Eingangsseite
~ **stair(case)** · Eingangstreppe *f*
~ **step** · Eingangsstufe *f*
~ **switch** · Eingangsschalter *m*
~ **terrace** · Eingangsterrasse *f*
~ **to a basement**, basement entrance · Kellergeschoẞeingang *m*
~ ~ ~ **cellar**, cellar entrance · Kellereingang *m*
(en)trapped air, dead ~ [*Air trapped in cells, which is the basis of most insulating materials*] · eingeschlossene Luft *f*
~ ~, accidental ~ [*Air voids in concrete, mortar, or cement paste which are not purposely entrained*] · Verdichtungsporen *fpl*
~ ~ **void**, dead ~ ~ [*It is characteristically 1 mm or more in size and irregular in shape*] · eingeschlosssene Luftpore *f*

entrapped humidity — epoxy (resin) (binding) medium

~ **humidity,** ~ moisture · eingeschlossene Feuchtigkeit f, ~ Feuchte f

~ **moisture,** ~ humidity · eingeschlossene Feuchtigkeit f, ~ Feuchte f

entrapping of air → entrainment ~ ~

entresol, mezzanine · Zwischengeschoß n, Mezzanin n, Halbstockwerk n, Halbetage f, Halbgeschoß, Beigeschoß

~ **floor,** mezzanine ~ · Zwischengeschoßdecke f, Beigeschoßdecke, Mezzanindecke, Halbetagendecke, Halbgeschoßdecke, Halbstockwerkdecke

entrochal limestone · Trochitenkalkstein m

entry [*A narrow passage between buildings*] · Durchgang m

~ **lock** · Eingangsschleuse f

~ **of direct sunshine** → insolation

entryway, access way · Einfahrt f

envelope · Umhüllende f

~ **of grading,** grading envelope · Siebbereich m, n

~ **wall** · Ummantelungswand f [*Atomkraftwerk*]

environmental conditions · Umweltbedingungen fpl

~ **design** · Umweltgestaltung f

environment(s) · Umweltverhältnisse f

epichlorohydrin · Epichlorhydrin n

epicycloid · Epizykloide f

epigraphy · Inschriftenkunde f

Epikote resin(-based) (bonding) adhesive, ~ ~ ~ agent, ~ ~ ~ medium, ~ ~ cement(ing agent) · Epikote-Kunstharzkleb(e)stoff m, Epikote-Kunstharzkleb(e)mittel n, Epikote-Kunstharzkleber m

episcopal church, bishop's ~ · Bischofskirche f, Episkopalkirche

~ **palace,** bishop's ~ · Bischofspalast m

epistle ambo(n) · Epistelambo(n) m, Epistelpult n [*auf der Südseite*]

epistle-side · Epistelseite f, Männerseite, Kelchseite, Südseite [*Die vom Westeingang aus rechte (= südliche) Seite der Kirche und des Altars, weil auf dieser Seite die Epistel verlesen wird*]

epistyle, architrave · Architrav m, Episty(lion) n [*Von einer Säulenachse zur anderen reichender Steinbalken*]

epitaph · Grab(in)schrift f, Epitaph(ium) n

epoch-making · epochemachend

epoch of style · Stilepoche f

epoxide resin → epoxy ~

epoxy adhesive → ~ (resin) (bonding) ~

~ **-asphalt material** (US); epoxy-(asphaltic-)bitumen ~ (Brit.) · Epoxidharz n mit Bitumen

epoxy-based (bonding) adhesive → epoxy (resin) (~) ~

~ ~ **agent** → epoxy (resin) (bonding) adhesive

~ ~ **medium** → epoxy (resin) (bonding) adhesive

~ **cement(ing agent)** → · epoxy (resin) (bonding) adhesive

~ **crack filler** → epoxy (resin) ~ ~

~ **enamel** → epoxy (resin) ~

~ **hard gloss paint** → epoxy (resin) enamel

~ **mortar** → epoxy (resin) ~

~ **paint** → epoxy (resin) ~

~ **paste** → epoxy (resin) ~

epoxy binder → ~ resin ~

~ **(binding) medium** → ~ (resin) binder

epoxy-bitumen material (Brit.) → epoxy-asphalt ~

~ ~ (US); epoxy-hydrocarbon binder ~ (Brit.) · Epoxidharz n mit Schwarzbindemittel

epoxy (bonding) adhesive → ~ resin (~) ~

~ ~ **agent** → ~ (resin) (bonding) adhesive

~ ~ **medium** → ~ (resin) (bonding) adhesive

~ **cement(ing agent)** → ~ (resin) (bonding) adhesive

~ **-coal tar material** · Epoxidharz n mit Kohlenteer

~ **coating resin** · Epoxidüberzugharz n [*Oberbegriff für 1. Epoxidharzbindemittel und 2. Epoxidharzkleber*]

~ **crack filler** → ~ resin ~ ~

~ **enamel** → ~ resin ~

~ **floor cover(ing),** ~ floor(ing) (finish) · Epoxidharz(fuß)boden(belag) m

~ **floor(ing) (finish)** ~ floor cover(ing) · Epoxidharz(fuß)boden(belag) m

~ **hard gloss paint** → ~ (resin) enamel

~ **-hydrocarbon binder material** (Brit.); epoxy-bitumen ~ (US) · Epoxidharz n mit Schwarzbindemittel

~ **medium** → ~ (resin) binder

~ **mortar** → ~ resin ~

~ **paint** → ~ resin ~

~ **paste** → ~ resin ~

~ **powder coating** · Epoxidharz-Pulverlack m

~ **resin,** epoxide ~ · Epoxidharz n, Epoxyharz, Äthoxilinharz, EP(-Harz) [*Epoxidharze sind Kondensationsprodukte, vorwiegend aus Epichlorhydrin und Phenolen, die durch Polyaddition mit Polyaminen und/oder Polyamiden härten*]

~ **(~) adhesive** → ~ (~) bonding ~

~ **(~) binder,** ~ (~) (binding) medium [*This term is used to describe a formulation used as a cementing agent to bind particles of aggregate into a mass that is originally plastic but later becomes rigid*] · Epoxidharzbindemittel n

~ **(~) (binding) medium** → ~ (~) binder

epoxy (resin) (bonding) adhesive — equilibrium polygon

~ (~) (bonding) adhesive, ~ (~) ~ agent, ~ (~) ~ medium, ~ (~) cement(ing agent), epoxy-based (~) ~ · Epoxidharzkleb(e)stoff m, Epoxidharzkleb(e)mittel n, Epoxidharzkleber m

~ (~) ~ agent → ~ (~) (~) adhesive

~ (~) ~ medium → ~ (~) (~) adhesive

~ (~) cement(ing agent) → ~ (~) (bonding) adhesive

~ (~) crack filler, epoxy-based ~ ~ · Epoxidharzrißfüller m

~ (~) enamel, ~ (~) hard gloss paint, epoxy-based enamel, epoxy-based hard gloss paint · Epoxidharzlackfarbe f [Fehlname: Epoxidharzlack m]

~ (~) hard gloss paint → ~ (~) enamel

~ (~) medium → ~ (~) binder

~ (~) mortar, epoxy-based ~ · Epoxidharzmörtel m

~ ~ of petrochemical origin · Epoxidharz n bei der Erdöldestillation als Nebenprodukt gewonnen

~ (~) paint, epoxy-based ~ [A paint based on an epoxy resin; the designation is frequently qualified to indicate the nature of the crosslinking agent used, e.g. 'epoxy/amine', 'epoxy/polyamide' or 'epoxy/isocyanate' where the crosslinking agents are polyamines, polyamides and isocyanates respectively] · Epoxidharz(anstrich)farbe f

~ (~) paste, epoxy-based ~ · Epoxidharzpaste f

Epsom salt [A colo(u)rless or white crystalline salt, chemically magnesium sulphate heptahydrate, $MgSO_4 \cdot 7H_2O$] · Bittersalz n

equal and opposite forces · entgegengesetzt gleiche Kräfte fpl

~ **angle iron**, equal(-leg) ~ ~ · gleichschenk(e)liges Winkeleisen n

~ ~ (section) → equal-leg ~ (~)

equal(-leg) angle iron · gleichschenk(e)liges Winkeleisen n

~ ~ (section), ~ ~ bar, ~ L-section · gleichschenk(e)liger Winkel m, gleichschenk(e)liges Winkelprofil n

~ ~ steel · gleichschenk(e)liger Winkelstahl m [DIN 1028]

~ **bulb-angle** · gleichschenk(e)liger Wulststahl m

equal planar unit · gleiches Flächenteil n, gleicher ~ m [Faltsystem]

equality of the rotation angles · Drehwinkelgleichheit f

equal-sized meshes · Maschengleichheit f

equating the moments · Momentengleichsetzen n

equation connecting the components · Komponentengleichung f, Seitenkraftgleichung, Zweigkraftgleichung, Teilkraftgleichung

~ **of compatibility** · Verträglichkeitsgleichung f

~ ~ **condition**, condition(al) equation · Bestimmungsgleichung f, Bedingungsgleichung

~ ~ **equilibrium**, equilibrium equation · Gleichgewichtsgleichung f

~ ~ **forces** · Kräftegleichung f

~ ~ **moments**, moment equation · Momentengleichung f

~ ~ **static equilibrium** · statische Gleichgewichtsgleichung f

~ ~ **three moments**, three-moment equation · Dreimomentengleichung f [Zur Ermitt(e)lung der Stützmomente bei durchlaufenden Trägern über drei benachbarte Auflagerpunkte. Die Clapeyronsche Gleichung ist eine Dreimomentengleichung für gleichmäßig verteilte Belastung]

~ ~ **work**, work equation · Arbeitsgleichung f

equestrian monument · Reiterdenkmal n

~ **picture** · Reiterbild n

~ **statue** · Reiterstatue f

equigranular, even-grained, uniform, like-grained, single-sized · einkörnig, gleichkörnig

~ **aerated concrete** → like-grained ~ ~

~ **concrete** → like-grained ~

~ **mortar** → like-grained ~

equilateral pointed arch · gleichseitiger Spitzbogen m

~ **roof** [A roof whose section is an equilateral triangle, pitch 60 degree] · Giebeldach n von 60°

equilibrium · Gleichgewicht n

~ **approach** · Gleichgewichts(lösungs)ansatz m

~ **change**, change of equilibrium · Gleichgewichtswechsel m

~ **condition**, condition of equilibrium · Gleichgewichtsbedingung f

~ **configuration** · Gleichgewichtsfigur f

~ **equation**, equation of equilibrium · Gleichgewichtsgleichung f

~ **humidity**, ~ moisture · Ausgleichfeuchtigkeit f, Ausgleichfeuchte f, Gleichgewichtsfeuchtigkeit, Gleichgewichtsfeuchte

~ **method** · Deformationsmethode f [Baustatik]

~ **moisture**, ~ humidity · Ausgleichfeuchtigkeit f, Ausgleichfeuchte f, Gleichgewichtsfeuchtigkeit, Gleichgewichtsfeuchte

~ **of angles of rotation** · Drehwinkelausgleich m

~ ~ **forces** · Kräftegleichgewicht n

~ ~ ~ **acting at one point** · Gleichgewicht n von Kräften mit gemeinsamem Angriffspunkt

~ **polygon** · Gleichgewichtspolygon n

equilibrium problem — erection speed

~ problem · Gleichgewichtsaufgabe *f*, Gleichgewichtsproblem *n*

~ requirement · Gleichgewichtsforderung *f*

~ state, state of equilibrium, balance · Gleichgewichtszustand *m*

~ temperature · Gleichgewichtstemperatur *f*

equipment, accessories · Zubehör *n*

(~) clean-up · Reinigen *n* (der Arbeitsgeräte)

~ cupboard · Geräteschrank *m*

~ floor; ~ storey (Brit.); ~ story (US) · Anlagengeschoß *n*, Anlagenetage *f*, Anlagenstockwerk *n*

~ room → machine(ry) ~

~ ~ · Apparateraum *m*, Geräteraum

~ station → machine(ry) ~

~ storey (Brit.); ~ story (US); ~ floor · Anlagengeschoß *n*, Anlagenetage *f*, Anlagenstockwerk *n*

equivalent absorption surface · äquivalente Absorptionsfläche *f* [*Akustik*]

~ beam method · Ersatzbalkenverfahren *n*

~ cube method [*Determination of compressive strength of concrete using portions of beams broken in flexure*] · äquivalentes Würfelverfahren *n* [*Bei diesem Verfahren werden Teile von Prüfbalken der Biegezugprüfung verwendet*]

~ grain diameter → ~ particle ~

~ ~ size, ~ particle ~ · äquivalente Korngröße *f*, gleichwertige ~

~ load · Vergleichslast *f*

~ loading · äquivalente Belastung *f*

~ particle diameter, ~ grain ~ · Äquivalentkorndurchmesser *m* [*Durchmesser von Kugeln, die die gleiche Fallgeschwindigkeit (in Gas oder Flüssigkeit) wie unregelmäßige Teilchen haben*]

~ ~ size → ~ grain ~

~ round hole diameter · äquivalente Rundlochweite *f*

(~ sound pressure) level difference, sound reduction · Schallpegeldifferenz D *f* [*Maß dB. Unterschied zwischen dem Schallpegel im Senderaum (L₁) und dem Schallpegel im Empfangsraum (L₂). D = L₁−L₂. Diese Differenz wird bei der Prüfung der Luftschalldämmung von Wänden und Decken bestimmt. Sie ist auch vom Schallschluckvermögen des Empfangsraumes abhängig*]

equi-viscous temperature [*abbrev. E.V.T.*] · äquiviskose Temperatur *f*, Äquiviskositätstemperatur [*Vergleichstemperatur, bei der Teer eine Viskosität von 50 Sekunden hat*]

Erechtheion · Erechtheion *n*, Tempel *m* der Pallas Polias

to erect, to assemble · montieren, zusammenbauen

~ ~, to set (up), to fit · aufbauen, aufstellen, montieren

~ ~, to build, to construct · errichten, bauen [*im Hochbau*]

erecting, assembling · Montieren *n*, Zusammenbauen

~ bill [*A bill for material for a bridge, etc., so arranged as to facilitate the finding and placing of members during erection*] · Montageliste *f*

~ deck → ~ platform

~ platform, ~ deck · Arbeitsbühne *f*, Montagebühne, Montageplattform *f*, Arbeitsplattform

~ shop, setting (up) ~, fitting ~ [*A large open workshop or yard where steel frames are joined up after fabrication to make sure that they fit before sent to the site*] · Aufbauwerkstatt *f*, Montagewerkstatt, Aufstell(ungs)werkstatt

erection, fitting, setting (up) · Aufbau(en) *m*, (*n*), Aufstellen, Aufstellung *f*, Montieren, Montage *f*

~, building, construction · Errichtung *f*, Bau *m* [*im Hochbau*]

~, assembly · Montage *f*, Zusammenbau *m*

~ aid · Montagehilfe *f*

~ bolt · Montagebolzen *m*

~ column, temporary ~ · Montagestütze *f*

~ contract · Montagevertrag *m*

~ crew, ~ gang, ~ party, ~ team · Montagekolonne *f*, Montagetrupp *m*, Montagemannschaft *f*

~ device · Montagevorrichtung *f*

~ diagram · Montagediagramm *n*

~ drawing · Montagezeichnung *f*

~ gang → ~ crew

~ hinge · Montagegelenk *n*

~ joint · Montagestoß *m*

~ load · Montagelast *f*

~ of steelwork, steel erection · Stahlbaumontage *f*

~ party → ~ crew

~ procedure, setting (up) ~, fitting ~ · Aufbauvorgang *m*, Montagevorgang, Aufstell(ungs)vorgang

~ rate → assembling speed

~ reinforcement, reinforcement for stress in erection · Montagebewehrung *f*, Montagearmierung, Montage(stahl)-einlagen *fpl*, Montageeisen *fpl*

~ scaffold(ing) · Montagegerüst *n*, Montagerüstung *f*

~ schedule, assembly ~ · Montageplan *m*, Zusammenbauplan

~ sequence, setting (up) ~, fitting ~ · Aufbaufolge *f*, Montagefolge, Aufstell-(ungs)folge

~ service · Montagedienst *m*

~ site, assembling ~ · Montagebaustelle *f*

~ speed → assembling ~

erection stage — etched

~ **stage**, assembly ~ · Montagephase f, Montagestadium n, Zusammenbauphase, Zusammenbaustadium

~ **state** · Montagezustand m

~ **strength** · Montagefestigkeit f

~ **stress**, assembly ~ · Montagespannung f, Anfangsspannung [*Die Spannung je Flächeneinheit eines Baugliedes bei der Montage eines Bauwerkes*]

~ **team** → ~ crew

~ **time** · Montagezeit f

~ **tolerance** · Montagetoleranz f

~ **weight** · Montagegewicht n

~ **with spacings** · Abstandmontage f

~ **work**, assembling ~ · Zusammenbauarbeiten fpl, Montagearbeiten

erector, steelwork erector [*One engaged in erecting steelwork*] · (Stahl)Montagebauarbeiter m

Erichsen indentation test · Tiefungsprobe f nach Erichsen, Tiefungsprüfung f ~ ~, Tiefungsversuch m ~ ~ [*DIN 53156*]

Erlenmeyer flask · Erlenmeyerkolben m

erosion, wearing away · Erosion f, Abbau m, Abtragung f [*Anstrichfilm*]

eruptive rock · Eruptivgestein n

escalade · Sturmleiter f

escalator, moving stair(case), motorstair [*B.S. 2655*] · Fahrtreppe f, Treppenaufzug m, Rolltreppe

~ **shutter**, motorstair ~, moving stair(case) ~ · Fahrtreppenabdeckung f, Rolltreppenabdeckung, Treppenaufzugabdeckung

escape corridor, fire ~ ~, emergency ~ · Fluchtkorridor m, Feuerkorridor, Notkorridor, Brandkorridor

~ **ladder**, fire ~ ~, emergency ~ · Feuerleiter f, Fluchtleiter, Notleiter, Brandleiter

~ **roof (walk)way**, fire ~ ~ ~, emergency ~ ~ · Fluchtweg-Dachlaufsteg m, Notweg-Dachlaufsteg

~ **route**, fire ~ ~, emergency ~ · Fluchtweg m, Notweg, Rückzugsweg

~ **stair(case)**, fire ~ ~, emergency ~ · Feuertreppe f, Fluchttreppe, Brandtreppe, Nottreppe

~ ~ **well**, fire ~ ~ ~, emergency ~ ~ · Feuertreppenhaus n, Brandtreppenhaus, Fluchttreppenhaus, Nottreppenhaus

~ **window**, fire ~ ~, emergency ~, fire ~ · Brand(schutz)fenster n, Notfenster, Feuer(schutz)fenster, Fluchtfenster

(e)scutcheon, key plate · Schild m, Schlüssel~, Schlüssellochdeckel m

espagnolette bolt, cremo(r)ne ~ · Espagnolettenverschluß m, Drehstangenverschluß

esparto grass fiber (US) → (h)alfa ~

esplanade [*A public drive or walk along the sea-side*] · Strandboulevard m

~ [*A terace along the sea-side*] · Strandterrasse f

estate, housing ~, housing colony; cottage community, nesting (US) · Wohnkolonie f, (Wohn)Sied(e)lung f

~ **area** · Sied(e)lungsgebiet n

~ **battery garage** · Reihengarage f für Sied(e)lungen

~ **development** → housing ~ ~

~ **road** → housing ~ ~

~ **unit** → housing ~ ~

ester · Ester m [*Ester sind chemische Verbindungen, die durch Einwirkung von Säuren auf Alkohole entstehen*]

~ **gum,** rosin ester, esterified natural resin · Esterharz n

~ ~ **varnish**, rosin ester ~, esterified natural resin ~ · Esterharz(klar)lack m

~ **plasticizer** · Esterweichmacher m

esterification · Esterbildung f, Veresterung, Verestern n

esterified · verestert

~ **natural resin**, ester gum, rosin ester · Esterharz n

~ ~ ~ **varnish**, rosin ester ~, ester gum ~ · Esterharz(klar)lack m

to esterify · verestern

esthetic appeal, ~ charm, aesthetic ~ · ästhetischer Reiz m

~ **aspect**, aesthetic ~ · Ästhetikfrage f

~ **charm**, ~ appeal, aesthetic ~ · ästhetischer Reiz m

~ **effect**, aesthetic ~ · ästhetische Wirkung f

~ **feeling**, ~ sense, aesthetic ~ · ästhetisches Gefühl n

~ **idea**, ~ concept, aesthetic ~ · ästhetische Vorstellung f

~ **sense**, ~ feeling, aesthetic ~ · ästhetisches Gefühl n

esthetically pleasing, aesthetically ~ · formschön

estimate, cost(s) ~ · (Kosten)(Vor)Anschlag m [*DIN 276*]

estimating, estimation · Veranschlagen n

~ **of cost** · Kostenschätzung f, Kostenüberschlag m

estimation, estimating · Veranschlagen n

~ · Veranschlagung f

esto-asphalt, esto-bitumen · Estobitumen n

esto-bitumen, esto-asphalt · Estobitumen n

Estonian shale oil · estnisches Schieferöl n

estrade · Estrade f [*Fußbodenerhöhung in einem Raum*]

to etch [*To roughen a surface by a chemical agent prior to painting in order to increase adhesion*] · chemisch aufrauhen

etched · abgesäuert [*Werkstein-Bearbeitung*]

~ · geätzt

etched glass — evaporation of the solvent

~ **glass** · Ätzglas n, geätztes Glas [*Mattglas, dessen Oberfläche auf chemischem Wege mit Flußsäure oder flußsauren Salzen behandelt wird*]

etching → acid washing

~ → (acid) embossing

~, **acid** ~ [*A chemical process in which the surfaces of various plates are eaten away by an acid*] · (Säure)Ätzung f

~ [*A term almost synonymous with 'acid treatment' but generally assumed to be a rather more severe treatment producing a greater aggregate exposure*] · starkes Absäuern n [*Betonwerkstein*]

~ **paste** · Ätzpaste f, Ätztinte f [*Eine aus Bariumsulfat, Ammoniumfluorid und Schwefelsäure bestehende Mischung, die zum Ätzen mit Gummistempeln auf Glas verwendet wird*]

~ **primer,** self etch ~, wash ~, pretreatment ~ [*A priming paint usually supplied as two separate components which require to be mixed immediately prior to use and thereafter is usable for a limited period only. The mixed paint contains carefully balanced proportions of an inhibiting chromate pigment, phosphoric acid, and a synthetic resin binder in a mixed alcohol solvent. On clean light alloy or ferrous surfaces and on many non-ferrous surfaces such paints give excellent adhesion, partly due to chemical reaction with the substrate (hence the term 'etching primer'), and give a corrosion inhibiting film which is a very good basis for the application of subsequent coats of paint. Although these materials are referred to as primers, the films which they give are so thin that it is better to consider them as etching solutions and to follow them with an ordinary primer if maximum protection is required. These materials are also known as 'pretreatment primers' 'wash primers' and 'self etch primers'*] · Haftgrund m, Aktivgrund, Haftgrundierung f, Haftgrund(ier)mittel n [*DIN 55945*]

~ **solution** [*See remark under 'Haftgrund'*] · Aktivgrundlösung f, Haftgrundlösung

~ **varnish** · Ätzgrund m

Eternit corrugated board, ~ ~ sheet · Eternit-Wellplatte f, Well-Eternitplatte, gewellte Eternitplatte

~ ~ **sheets,** ~ ~ boards, ~ ~ sheeting · Eternit-Wellplatten fpl, Well-Eternit(platten) n, (fpl), gewellte Eternitplatten

~ **pipe** · Eternitrohr n

~ **roof coveryering),** ~ ~ sheathing, ~ roofing · Eternit(dach)(ein)deckung f

~ ~ **sheathing,** ~ ~ cover(ing), ~ roofing · Eternit(dach)(ein)deckung f

~ **roofing,** ~ roof sheathing, ~ roof cover(ing) · Eternit(dach)(ein)deckung f

~ **slab** · Eternitplatte f

~ **slate** · Eternit-Schiefer m

ethyl alcohol · Äthylalkohol m

~ **cellulose** · Äthylcellulose f, Äthylzellulose

~ **silicate** · Äthylsilikat n

ethylene · Äth(yl)en n

~ **glycol** · Äthyl(en)glykol n, $HOCH_2CH_2OH$

Etruscan architecture · etruskische Baukunst f, ~ Architektur f

~ **column** · etruskische Säule f

~ **style** · etruskischer Stil m

~ **temple** · etruskischer Tempel m

Eulerian buckling stress, ~ crippling ~, Euler('s) ~ ~ · Eulersche Knickspannung f

~ **column formula** → Euler('s) (buckling) ~

~ **crippling stress,** ~ buckling ~, Euler('s) ~ ~ · Eulersche Knickspannung f

Euler('s) (buckling) formula, ~ column ~, Eulerian ~ ~ · Eulersche Knickformel f

~ ~ **length,** Eulerian ~ ~ · Eulersche Knicklänge f

~ ~ **load,** Eulerian ~ ~ · Eulersche Knicklast f [*Kritische Drucklast, unter der ein gerader Stab ausknickt*]

~ ~ **stress,** ~ crippling ~, Eulerian ~ ~ · Eulersche Knickspannung f

~ **crippling stress,** ~ buckling ~, Eulerian ~ ~ · Eulersche Knickspannung f

~ **solution,** Eulerian ~ · Eulersche Lösung f

~ **stress,** Eulerian ~ · Eulersche Spannung f

eulytite, bismuth blende · Wismutblende f

Euston process · Kammerverfahren n [*Bleiweißherstellung*]

eustyle [*Columns spaced 2¹/₄ diameter apart*] · schönsäulig

eutectic [*The quality of an alloy that causes it to melt more readily than any of its ingredients*] · eutektisch

~ **(alloy)** [*A metal alloy which has a definite melting point with no range. Eutectics with low melting points are used as fusible links in fire-sprinkler systems, to control firedoors and in fire alarms*] · eutektische Legierung f

~ **(~) system,** ~ (composition) · Eutektikum n

~ **(composition),** ~ (alloy) system · Eutektikum n

~ **system,** ~ alloy ~, ~ (composition) · Eutektikum n

euthynteria · Euthynterie f [*griechischer Tempelbau*]

evaporation burner, evaporative ~ · Verdampfungsbrenner m, Schalenbrenner

~ **cooler** → ~ room ~

~ **of the solvent** · Verdunsten n des Lösungsmittels; Verdunstung f ~ ~

evaporation rate — exclusion of draught

~ **rate,** rate of evaporation · Verdunstungsgeschwindigkeit f

~ **residue** · Abdampfrückstand m [*Für Trink- und Brauchwasser ist ein Abdampfrückstand, also ein nach Eindampfen durch Wägung festzustellender Gehalt an gelöster Substanz von weniger als 500 g/l erwünscht, weil größere Lösungsinhalte durch zu große Härte, Salzgehalt usw. die Verwendungsmöglichkeiten beeinträchtigen*]

~ **(room) cooler,** evaporative (~) ~ · Verdampfungskühler m

evaporative burner, evaporation ~ · Verdampfungsbrenner m, Schalenbrenner

~ **cooler** → ~ room ~

~ **cooling** · Verdampfungskühlung f

~ **(room) cooler,** evaporation (~) ~ · Verdampfungskühler m

evaporator coil · Verdampferschlange f

even-grained, equigranular, uniform, like-grained, single-sized · einkörnig, gleichkörnig

~ **aerated concrete** → like-grained ~ ~

~ **concrete** → like-grained ~

~ **mortar** → like-grained ~

evening peak · Abendspitze f [*Höchste Belastung der Elektrizitätswerke und Leitungsnetze in den frühen Abendstunden*]

evenness, accuracy of level(s), flatness; surface smoothness (US) · (Plan)Ebenheit f, Ebenflächigkeit

even-temperature conditions · gleichbleibende Temperaturverhältnisse f

every-day architecture [*Style more concerned with function than with form*] · Alltagsarchitektur f, Alltagsbaukunst f

evolute · Evolute f

ex voto church · Votivkirche f

exact · streng [*Theorie*]

~ **curve** · Genaukurve f

~ **height** · Genauhöhe f

~ **length** · Genaulänge f

~ **plastic theory** → nonlinear ~ ~

~ **value** · Genauwert m

~ ~ **table** · Genauwerttabelle f

~ **width** · Genaubreite f

exactly conform to the nominal size → correct(ly sized)

examination cubicle · Untersuchungskabine f, Untersuchungszelle f [*Krankenhaus*]

example derived from nature · Naturvorbild n

~ **of application,** ~ ~ use · Anwendungsbeispiel n

~ ~ **calculation,** worked example · Rechenbeispiel n, Berechnungsbeispiel

~ ~ **solution,** solution example · (Auf-)Lösungsbeispiel n

~ ~ **use,** ~ ~ application · Anwendungsbeispiel n

excavation · Ausgrabung f [*Archäologie*]

excelsior · oberster Abschnitt m [*Turm*]

~, **wood** ~ (US); wood wool (Brit.) · Holzwolle f [*DIN 4077*]

~ **absorbent board** (US) → wood wool acoustic(al) ~

~ ~ **sheet** (US) → wood wool acoustic(al) board

~ **acoustic(al) board** (US) → wood wool acoustic(al) ~

~ ~ **sheet** (US) → wood wool acoustic(al) board

~ **(building) slab**·(US) → wood wool (~) ~

~ **concrete,** wood ~ ~ (US); wood wool ~ (Brit.) · Holzwollebeton m

~ ~ **slab,** wood ~ ~ (US); wood wool cement ~ [*B.S. 1105*] · Holzwollebetonplatte f

~ **covering rope,** wood ~ ~ (US); wood wool ~ ~ (Brit.) · Holzwolleseil n [*für Dämm- und Isolierzwecke*]

~ **hollow filler,** wood ~ ~ (US); wood wool ~ ~ (Brit.) · Holzwolle-(Decken)Hohlkörper m

~ **insulation,** wood ~ ~ (US); wood wool ~ (Brit.) · Holzwolle(ab)dämmung f

~ **slab** (US) → wood wool (building) ~

~ ~ **partition (wall),** wood ~ ~ ~ (~) (US); wood wool ~ ~ ~ (Brit.) · Holzwolle-Leichtbauplatten-Trennwand f

~ **sound-control board** (US) → wood wool acoustic(al) ~

~ ~ **sheet** (US) → wood wool acoustic(al) board

excess air · Luftüberschuß m

~**-current protection,** overcurrent ~ · Überstromschutz m

~ **protective breaker,** overcurrent ~ ~ · Überstrom-Schutzschalter m

excess humidity, ~ moisture · Überschußfeuchtigkeit f, Überschußfeuchte f

~ **moisture,** ~ humidity · Überschußfeuchtigkeit f, Überschußfeuchte f

~ **of heat** · Wärmeüberschuß m

~ ~ **lime** · Kalküberschuß m

~ **pigment dispersion,** over-pigmentation · Überpigmentierung f

~ **water** · Über(schuß)wasser n [*Zur Bedarfsdeckung nicht benötigtes und auch nicht aufspeicherbares Wasser*]

~ ~ **in concrete** · Wasserüberschuß im Beton

exciter [*Lime, alkali, sulphates, etc., which, added to a crushed blastfurnace slag, cause it to set when mixed with water*] · Erreger m

exclusion of draught, draughtproofing, draught exclusion (Brit.); draftproofing, draft exclusion, exclusion of draft (US) · Zug(ab)dichten n, Dichtschließen

execution — to expand

execution · Ausführung f [Vertrag]
~ **of the order** · Auftragsabwicklung f, Auftragsdurchführung
~ ~ (~) **work** · Arbeitsausführung f
~ ~ **work** · Bauausführung f

exedra [In classical architecture, a semicircular or rectangular recess with raised seats; also, more loosely, any apse or niche or the apsidal end of a room] · Exedra f
~ → apsis
~ **arch**, apsis ~, apse ~ · Apsisbogen m, Apsidenbogen, Absidenbogen, Exedrabogen, Abseitenbogen
~ ~ **impost**, apsis ~ ~, apse ~ ~ · Apsisbogenkämpfer m, Apsidenbogenkämpfer, Absidenbogenkämpfer, Exedrabogenkämpfer, Abseitenbogenkämpfer
~ **window**, apsis ~, apse ~ · Apsisfenster n, Apsidenfenster, Absidenfenster, Exedrafenster, Abseitenfenster

(exfoliated) vermiculite · (auf)geblähter Glimmer m, Vermiculit m, Blähglimmer [Ein Wärme- und Schalldämmstoff aus durch Erhitzen auf ca. 1200° aufgeblähtem Glimmer]
(~) ~ **aggregate** [A light (weight) aggregate produced from vermiculite when exfoliated by heat] · Blähglimmerzuschlag(stoff) m, Vermiculitzuschlag(stoff)
(~) ~ **brick** · Blähglimmer(beton)stein m, Vermiculit(beton)stein
(~) ~ **concrete** · Blähglimmerbeton m, Vermiculitbeton
(~) ~ ~ **screed** · Blähglimmerestrich m, Vermiculitestrich
(~) ~-**gypsum plaster** · Blähglimmergipsputz m, Vermiculitgipsputz
(~) ~ **insulation in bags** · Blähglimmer-Sack(ab)dämmung f, Vermiculit-Sack(ab)dämmung
(~) ~ **plaster** · Blähglimmer(ver)putz m, Vermiculit(ver)putz
(~) ~ **slab** · Blähglimmerplatte f, Vermiculitplatte
(~) ~ **sound-control plaster**, (~) ~ acoustic(al) ~, (~) ~ (sound) absorbent ~, (~) ~ sound absorbing ~ · Blähglimmer-Akustikputz m, Blähglimmer-Schallschluckputz, Vermiculit-Schallschluckputz, Vermiculit-Akustikputz

exfoliation of vermiculite · Aufblättern n von Vermiculit

exhaust grille [Sometimes spelled 'grill'] · Luftaustrittrost m, Luftaustrittgitter n
~ **hood** · Abzugshaube f
~ **pipe** → vent ~
~ **shaft** · Abzugsschacht m

exhaust(ing) fan, extract ~; induced draught ~ (Brit.); ~ draft ~ (US) · Saugzugventilator m

exhibition, exposition · Ausstellung f

~ **architecture**, exposition ~ · Ausstellungsarchitektur f, Ausstellungsbaukunst f
~ **area**, exposition ~ · Ausstellungsfläche f
~ **block** → ~ building
~ **building**, exposition ~, ~ block · Ausstellungsgebäude n
~ **garden**, exposition ~ · Ausstellungsgarten m
~**ground**, exposition ~ · Ausstellungsgelände n
~ **hall**, exposition ~ · Ausstellungshalle f
~ **of applied art** · Kunstgewerbeausstellung f
~ **palace**, exposition ~ · Ausstellungspalast m
~ **pavilion**, exposition ~ · Ausstellungspavillon m
~ **stand**, exposition ~ · Ausstellungsstand m

exit · Ausgang m
~ **air**, outgoing ~ · Fortluft f
~ ~ **station**, outgoing ~ ~ · Fortluftstation f
~ **door** · Ausgangstür f
~ **gas** · Abgas n [Es entsteht bei der Verbrennung von gasförmigen Brennstoffen im Gegensatz z.B. zu Rauchgas, das bei der Verbrennung von festen Brennstoffen entsteht]
~ ~ **chimney** · Abgaskamin m, Abgasschornstein m [DIN 18160]
~ ~ **duct** · Abgaskanal m
~ ~ **installation**, ~ ~ system · Abgasanlage f
~ ~ **line** · Abgasleitung f
~ ~ **pipe** · Abgasrohr n
~ ~ **pipeline** · Abgasrohrleitung f
~ ~ **socket** · Abgasstutzen m [Gasfeuerstätte]
~ ~ **system**, ~ ~ installation · Abgasanlage f
~ ~ **temperature** · Abgastemperatur f
~ **illumination**, ~ lighting · Ausgangsbeleuchtung f
~ **lighting**, ~ illumination · Ausgangsbeleuchtung f
~ **opening**, trap door on roof · Dachausstieg m, Dachaussteigluke f
~ **ramp**, out ~ · Ausfahrtrampe f, Abfahrtrampe
~ **sign** [B.S. 2560] · Ausgangsschild n

exothermic reaction [Chemical reaction in which heat is given off after the action commences. Examples: hydration of cement, and clinkering in the burning zone in kilns] · exotherme Reaktion f

to expand · aufbördeln, (auf)weiten [Rohr]
~ ~ · ausdehnen
~ ~, to stretch, to draw out · strecken [Streckmetall]

expandable · erweiterungsfähig, ausbaubar

~ **polystyrene** · aufschäumbares Polystyrol *n*

expanded [*Expanded plastics are those produced from a solid material and are usually of closed cell construction*] · geschäumt [*Kunststoff*]

~; bloated (Brit.) · (auf)gebläht, blasig aufgetrieben

~ **cement** → expansive ~

~ **cinder** (US); foam(ed) (iron) (blastfurnace) slag [*B.S. 877*]; expanded slag, light(weight) slag · schaumige Hochofenschlacke *f*, geschäumte ~, aufgeblähte ~, (Hochofen)Schaumschlacke [*Die gebrochene, geschäumte Hochofenschlacke wird „Hüttenbims" oder „Kunstbims" genannt*]

~ ~ **aggregate**, light(weight) ~ ~ (US); ~ **slag** ~; foamed ~; foamed (iron) (blastfurnace) slag ~ [*B.S. 877*] · (Hochofen)Schaumschlackenzuschlag(stoff) *m*

~ ~ **block** → foamed (blastfurnace) slag (concrete) (building) ~

~ ~ **(building) block** → foamed (blastfurnace) slag (concrete) (building) (~) ~

~ ~ **(~) tile** → foamed (blastfurnace) slag (concrete) (building) block

~ ~ **concrete** (US); foamed (iron) (blastfurnace) slag ~ (Brit.); expanded slag ~, light(weight) slag ~ · (Hochofen)Schaumschlackenbeton *m*, (Kunst)Bimsbeton, Hüttenbimsbeton

~ ~ **(~) (building) block** (US) → foamed (iron) (blastfurnace) slag (~) (~) ~

~ ~ **(~) (~) tile** (US) → foamed (iron) (blastfurnace) slag (concrete) (building) block

~ ~ ~ **cavity block** (US) → foamed slag concrete hollow ~

~ ~ ~ ~ **brick** (US) · foamed slag concrete hollow block

~ ~ ~ ~ **tile** (US) → foamed slag concrete hollow block

~ ~ ~ **hollow block** (US) → foamed slag ~ ~ ~

~ ~ ~ ~ **brick** (US) · foamed slag concrete hollow block

~ ~ ~ ~ **tile** (US) → foamed slag concrete hollow block

~ ~ ~ **pot** (US) → foamed slag concrete hollow block

~ ~ **(~) slab** (US); foamed slag (~) ~ (Brit.) · Hüttenbims(beton)-Bauplatte *f*, Kunstbims(beton)-Bauplatte [*Fehlnamen: (Hütten)Schwemmsteinbauplatte, Hochofenschwemmstein-Bauplatte*]

~ ~ **(~) tile** → foamed slag concrete block

~ ~ **(~) wall slab** (US); foamed slag (~) ~ ~ (Brit.) · Hüttenbims(beton)-Wand(bau)platte *f*, Kunstbims(beton)-Wand(bau)platte

~ ~ **powder** (US); foamed (iron) (blastfurnace) slag ~ (Brit.); expanded slag ~, light(weight) slag ~ · Hüttenbimsmehl *n*, (Kunst)Bimsmehl

~ ~ **slab** → ~ ~ (concrete) ~

~ ~ **tile** → foamed (blastfurnace) slag (concrete) (building) block

~ ~ **wall slab** → ~ ~ concrete ~ ~

~ **clay**; bloating ~, bloated ~ (Brit.) · Blähton *m*, (auf)geblähter Ton

~ ~ **aggregate**; bloating ~ ~, bloated ~ ~ (Brit.) · Blähtonzuschlag(stoff) *m*

~ ~ **concrete** → bloating ~ ~

~ ~ ~ **solid block** (US) → bloating ~ ~ ~ ~

~ ~ ~ ~ **tile** (US) → bloating clay concrete solid block

~ ~ **(~) wall slab** → bloating ~ (~) ~ ~

~ ~ **wall slab** → bloating clay (concrete) ~ ~

~ **composition cork** [*Composition cork made by a process that appreciably alters the suberous tissue*] · geblähter Backkork *m* mit nicht korkeigenem Bindemittel

~ **concrete**, gas ~ · Blähton *m*, Gasbeton [*DIN 4164*]

~ ~ **aggregate**; bloating ~ ~, bloated ~ ~ (Brit.) · Bläh-(Beton)Zuschlag(stoff) *m*

~ ~ **article** → gas concrete product

~ ~ **block** → gas concrete (building) ~

~ ~ **(building) block** → gas ~ (~) ~

~ ~ **(~) tile** → gas concrete (building) block

~ ~ **cavity block** → gas concrete hollow ~

~ ~ ~ **tile** → gas concrete hollow block

~ ~ **hollow block** → gas ~ ~ ~

~ ~ ~ **tile** → gas concrete hollow block

~ ~ **insulating block** → gas ~ ~ ~

~ ~ ~ **brick** → gas concrete insulating block

~ ~ ~ **slab** → gas concrete insulation(-grade) ~

~ ~ **insulation(-grade) block** → gas concrete insulating ~

~ ~ ~ **brick** → gas concrete insulating block

~ ~ ~ **slab** → gas ~ ~ ~

~ ~ **plant**, gas ~ ~ · Blähbetonwerk *n*, Gasbetonwerk

~ ~ **pot** → gas concrete hollow block

~ ~ **product** → gas ~ ~

~ ~ **purpose-made block** → gas ~ ~ ~

~ ~ ~ **brick** → gas concrete purpose-made block

~ ~ ~ **tile** → gas concrete purpose-made block

~ ~ **slab**, gas ~ ~ · Blähbetonplatte *f*, Gasbetonplatte

expanded concrete special block — expanded pure ...

~ ~ **special block** → gas concrete purpose-made ~

~ ~ ~ **brick** → gas concrete purpose-made block

~ ~ ~ **(purpose) block** → gas concrete purpose-made ~

~ ~ ~ **(~) brick** → gas concrete purpose-made block

~ ~ ~ **(~) tile** → gas concrete purpose-made block

~ ~ **tile** → gas concrete (building) block

~ **cork,** ~ granulated ~ · Blähkork *m*, Exp.-Kork, expandierter Kork(schrot) *m*, expandiertes Korkschrot *n*, geblähter Kork(schrot), geblähtes Korkschrot

~ ~ **slab,** ~ granulated ~ ~ · Blähkorkplatte *f*, Exp.-Korkplatte

~ **(granulated) cork** · Blähkork *m'* Exp.-Kork, expandierter Kork(schrot) *m*, expandiertes Korkschrot *n*, geblähter Kork(schrot), geblähtes Korkschrot

~ **(~) ~ slab** · Blähkorkplatte *f*, Exp.-Korkplatte

~ **hard rubber** · expandierter Hartgummi *m*

~ **in-situ capability,** foamed in-situ ~ · Aufschäumbarkeit *f* an Ort und Stelle

~ **lime concrete,** gas ~ ~ · Gaskalkbeton *m*

~ ~ **block,** ~ ~ ~ tile, gas ~ ~ ~ [*See remark under 'Block'*] · Gaskalkbetonblock(stein) *m*, Gaskalkbetonstein

~ ~ ~ **tile,** ~ ~ ~ block, gas ~ ~ ~ [*See remark under 'Block'*] · Gaskalkbetonblock(stein) *m*, Gaskalkbetonstein

~ **mesh** → ~ metal ~

~ **metal** → ~ (~) mesh

~ ~ **fabric** → ~ (~) reinforcement

~ ~ **fence** · Streckmetallzaun *m*

~ ~ **grate,** ~ ~ grid · Streckmetallrost *m*

~ ~ **grid,** ~ ~ grate · Streckmetallrost *m*

~ ~ **integral lath(ing)** · Streckmetallputzblech *n*

~ ~ **lath(ing)** · Streckmetallputzträger *m*

~ **(~) mesh,** ~ metal, XPM, EM [*It is made by slitting sheet metal and stretching the strands so formed at right angles to the plane of the sheet thereby forming a diamond mesh. B.S. 405*] · Streckmetall *n*

~ **(~) reinforcement,** ~ (~) fabric · Streckmetallbewehrung *f*, Streckmetallarmierung, Streckmetalleinlagen *fpl*

~ ~ **strip** · Streckmetallstreifen *m*

~ **natural rubber,** foam(ed) ~ ~ · Kautschukschaum(stoff) *m*, Zellkautschuk *m*, Zellgummi *m, n*, Schaumgummi

~ **neoprene,** foamed ~, neoprene foam · Neoprenschaum(stoff) *m*

~ **pe(a)rlite;** bloating ~, bloated ~ (Brit.) · Blähperlite *n*, (auf)geblähtes Perlite

~ **plastic** → foam(ed) (~)

~ ~ **board** → foam(ed) (~) ~

~ ~ **concrete** → foam(ed) (plastic) (light(weight)) ~

~ ~ **cupola** → plastic foam ~

~ ~ **dome** → plastic foam cupola

~ ~ **insulation,** foam(ed) (~) ~, plastic foam ~ · Schaumdämmung *f*, Schaumstoffdämmung, Kunstschaum-(stoff)dämmung, Kunststoffschaumdämmung, Schaumkunststoffdämmung

~ ~ **(light(weight)) concrete** → foam(ed) (~) (~) ~

~ ~ **plaster baseboard,** foam(ed) ~ ~ ~, plastic foam ~ ~ · Putzträgerplatte *f* aus Kunststoffschaum, Kunststoffschaum-Putzträgerplatte, Schaum-(kunst)stoff-Putzträgerplatte

~ ~ **seal** → foam(ed) ~

~ ~ **seal(ing),** foam(ed) (~) ~, plastic foam ~ · Schaum(kunst)stoff(ab)dichtung *f*, Kunststoffschaum(ab)dichtung, Schaum(ab)dichtung, Kunstschaum-(stoff)(ab)dichtung

~ ~ **sheet,** ~ ~ board, plastic foam ~, foam(ed) plastic ~ · Schaum(kunst)-stoffplatte *f*, Kunststoffschaumplatte

~ **polystyrene,** foam(ed) ~, polystyrene foam · Polystyrolschaum(stoff) *m*, Schaum(stoff)polystyrol *n*, PS-Schaum(stoff)

~ ~ **board for thermal insulation purposes,** foam(ed) ~ ~ ~ ~ ~ ~, polystyrene foam ~ ~ ~ ~ ~ [*B.S. 3837*] · Polystyrolschaum(stoff)wärmedämmplatte *f*

~ ~ **tile,** foam(ed) ~ ~, polystyrene foam ~ · Polystyrolschaum(stoff)fliese

~ **polyurethane,** foamed ~, polyurethane foam · Polyurethanschaum(stoff) *m*, PUR-Schaum(stoff)

~ ~ **board,** ~ ~ sheet, polyurethane foam ~ · Polyurethanschaumplatte *f*, PUR-Schaumplatte

~ ~ **sheet,** ~ ~ board, polyurethane foam ~ · Polyurethanschaumplatte *f*, PUR-Schaumplatte

~ ~ **strip,** foamed ~ ~, polyurethane foam ~ · Polyurethanschaum(fugen)-band *n*, PUR-Schaum(fugen)band

~ **polyvinyl chloride** → PVC foam

~ **pumice concrete,** gas ~ ~, pumice gas ~, pumice expanded ~ · (Natur-)Bims-Gasbeton *m*, (Natur)Bims-Blähbeton

~ **pure agglomerated cork,** ~ ~ baked ~ · expandierter Backkork *m* mit korkeigenem Harz gebunden, geblähter ~ ~ ~ ~ ~

~ ~ **baked cork,** ~ ~ agglomerated ~ · expandierter Backkork *m* mit korkeigenem Harz, gebunden, geblähter ~ ~ ~ ~ ~

expanded PVC — expansion agent 350

~ **PVC** → PVC foam

~ **reinforcement,** ~ metal ~ · Streckmetallbewehrung f, Streckmetallarmierung, Streckmetalleinlagen fpl

~ **rigid polyurethane,** polyurethane rigid foam, rigid polyurethane foam · Polyurethanhartschaum(stoff) m, Hartpolyurethanschaum(stoff), PUR-Hartschaum(stoff)

~ ~ **polyvinyl chloride** → ~ ~ PVC

~ ~ **PVC,** foamed rigid ~, rigid expanded ~, rigid foamed ~, ~ ~ polyvinyl chloride, rigid PVC foam, rigid polyvinyl chloride foam, rigid expanded polyvinyl chloride · Hart-PVC-Schaum(stoff) m, PVC-Hartschaum(stoff)

~ **rubber,** ~ natural ~, foam(ed) (natural) ~, cellular ~, swelling ~, expansive ~, expanding ~, sponge ~ · Gummischaum(stoff) m, Quellgummi, Kautschukschaum(stoff), Zellkautschuk m, Zellgummi n, m, Schaumgummi

~ **shale (clay);** bloating ~ (~), bloated ~ (~) (Brit.) · Blähschieferton m, (auf)geblähter Schieferton

~ ~ **(~) concrete;** bloating ~ (~) ~, bloated ~ (~) ~ (Brit.) · Blähschieferfertonbeton m

~ **slag,** light(weight) ~; expanded cinder (US); foam(ed) (iron) (blastfurnace) slag [B.S. 877] · schaumige Hochofenschlacke f, geschäumte ~, aufgeblähte ~, (Hochofen)Schaumschlacke [*Die gebrochene, geschäumte Hochofenschlacke wird „Hüttenbims" oder „Kunstbims" genannt*]

~ ~ **aggregate,** light(weight) ~ ~ ~ cinder ~ (US); foamed (iron) (blastfurnace) slag ~ [B.S. 877] · (Hochofen)Schaumschlackenzuschlag(stoff) m

~ ~ **block** → foamed (blastfurnace) slag (concrete) (building) ~

~ ~ **(building) block** → foamed (blastfurnace) slag (concrete) (~) ~

~ ~ **(~) tile** → foamed (blastfurnace) slag (concrete) (building) block

~ ~ **concrete,** light(weight) ~ ~; expanded cinder ~ (US); foamed (iron) (blastfurnace) slag ~ (Brit.) · (Hochofen)Schaumschlackenbeton m, (Kunst)Bimsbeton, Hüttenbimsbeton

~ ~ **(~) block** → foamed (blastfurnace) slag (concrete) (building) ~

~ ~ **(~) (building) tile** → foamed (iron) (blastfurnace) ~ (~) (~) block

~ ~ ~ **plank** (US); foamed ~ ~ ~ (Brit.) · Kunstbims(beton)diele f, Hüttenbims(beton)diele

~ ~ **(~) tile** → foamed (blastfurnace) slag (concrete) (building) block

~ ~ **powder,** light(weight) ~ ~; expanded cinder ~ (US); foamed (iron) (blastfurnace) slag ~ (Brit.) · Hüttenbimsmehl n, (Kunst)Bimsmehl

~ ~ **tile** → foamed (blastfurnace) slag (concrete) (building) block

~ **slate;** bloating ~, bloated ~ (Brit.) · (auf)geblähter (Ton)Schiefer m, Bläh(ton)schiefer

~ ~ **concrete;** bloating ~ ~, bloated ~ ~ (Brit.) · Bläh(ton)schieferbeton m

~ ~ **factory;** bloating ~ ~, bloated ~ (Brit.) · Bläh(ton)schieferwerk n

~ **urea-formaldehyde** → foamed ~

~ **urethane,** urethane foam · Urethanschaum(stoff) m

expanding, expansion; bloating (Brit.) · (Auf)Blähen n, (Auf)Blähung f [*Herstellung von Leichtzuschlägen*]

~, froth formation, foaming, frothing · (Auf)Schäumen n, Schaumbildung f

~ **action,** frothing ~, foaming ~, froth formation ~ · schäumende Wirkung f, Schäumwirkung

~ **agent,** swelling ~, expansive ~ · Quellwirkstoff m, Quellzusatzstoff, Quellzusatz(mittel) m, (n)

~ **arm** · Scherenarm m

~ **bolt,** ~ anchor, ~ shield, expansion ~ · Spreizdübel m, Spreizhülsenanker m

~ **cement,** expansive ~, high-expansion ~ · Dehnzement m, Schwellzement, Quellzement, Expansivzement

~ ~ **concrete,** expansive ~ ~, high-expansion ~ ~ · Dehnzementbeton m, Quellzementbeton, Schwellzementbeton, Expansivzementbeton

~ ~ **mortar,** expansive ~ ~, high-expansion ~ ~ · Dehnzementmörtel m, Schwellzementmörtel, Quellzementmörtel, Expansivzementmörtel

~ **chemical,** foaming ~, expansion ~, ~ agent; bloating ~ (Brit.) · Schaumbildner m, Treibmittel n, Schaumstoff m, Schaummittel, schaumbildender Zusatz(stoff) m, (Auf)Blähmittel [*Betonherstellung*]

~ **in situ,** frothing ~ ~, foaming ~ ~, froth formation ~ ~ · Schaumbildung f an Ort und Stelle, (Auf)Schäumen n ~ ~ ~ ~

~ **plant;** bloating ~ (Brit.) · Blähanlage f

~ **plug,** expansion ~ · Blindschraube f

~ **shell,** expansion ~ · Spreizhülse f

expansibility · Schwellfähigkeit f, Schwellvermögen n, Schwelleigenschaft f

expansion, expanding; bloating (Brit.) · (Auf)Blähen n, (Auf)Blähung f [*Herstellung von Leicht(beton)zuschlägen*]

~, development · Ausbau m, Erweiterung f, Vergrößerung [*einer bestehenden Anlage*]

~, increase in volume · Treiben n

~ · Streckung f [*Streckmetall*]

~ · Volumenvergrößerung f [*z.B. von Perlite*]

~ **agent** → expanding chemical

expansion chemical — exposed aggregate finish

~ **chemical** → expanding ~
~ **coefficient** · (Aus)Dehn(ungs)beiwert *m*
~ **due to free lime** · Kalktreiben *n*
~ ~ ~ **gypsum** · Gipstreiben *n*
~ **joint** [*A separation between adjoining parts of a concrete structure which is provided to allow small relative movements such as those caused by thermal changes to occur independently*] · (Aus-)Dehn(ungs)fuge *f*, Raumfuge
~ ~ **filler** · Raumfugeneinlage *f*
~ ~ **mastic (sealer)** · Dehn(ungs)fugenkitt *m*, Raumfugenkitt
~ ~ **profile** → ~ ~ section
~ ~ **ridge capping** · Dehn(ungs)fugenkappe *f*
~ ~ **seal(ing)** · Dehn(ungs)fugendichtung *f*, Raumfugendichtung
(~) (~) **sealing filler** → (joint) sealing strip
~ ~ **section**, ~ ~ unit, ~ ~ shape, ~ ~ trim, ~ ~ profile · Dehn(ungs)-fugenprofil *n*, Raumfugenprofil
~ ~ **shape**, ~ ~ unit, ~ ~ section, ~ ~ trim, ~ ~ profile · Raumfugenprofil *n*, Dehn(ungs)fugenprofil
~ ~ **trim** → ~ ~ section
~ ~ **unit**, ~ ~ shape, ~ ~ section, ~ ~ trim, ~ ~ profile · Raumfugenprofil *n*, Dehn(ungs)fugenprofil
~ ~ **waterstop**, ~ ~ waterbar · Dehn-(ungs)fugenband *n*, Raumfugenband
(~) **joint(ing) strip** → (joint) sealing ~
~ **loop**, compensating device [*A loop in a pipeline which, by flexing, can accommodate expansion and contraction movements*] · (Dehnungs)Ausgleicher *m*, Kompensator *m*, (Aus)Dehn(ungs)schleife *f*, Ausgleichzrohr *n*, Ausgleichsschleife, Schleifenkompensator
~ **period** → ~ time
~ **pipe** → vent ~
~ **plug**, expanding ~ · Blindschraube *f*
(~) **sealing filler** → (joint) sealing strip
~ **shield** · Spreizdübel *m*
~ **tank**, ~ vessel · (Druck)Ausdehnungsgefäß *n*, Entspannungsgefäß, Expansionsgefäß [*Warmwasserheizung*]
~ **tendency due to magnesia**, action of ~ · Magnesiatreiben *n*
~ **time**, ~ period · (Aus)Dehn(ungs)zeit *f* [*Quellzement*]
~ **vessel**, ~ tank · (Druck)Ausdehnungsgefäß *n*, Entspannungsgefäß, Expansionsgefäß [*Warmwasserheizung*]

expansive agent, swelling ~, expanding ~ · Quellwirkstoff *m*, Quellzusatzstoff, Quellzusatz(mittel) *m*, (*n*)
~ **cement**, expanding ~, high-expansion ~, expanded ~ · Dehnzement *m*, Schwellzement, Quellzement, Expansivzement
~ ~ **concrete**, expanding ~ ~, high-expansion ~ ~, expanded ~ ~ · Dehnzementbeton *m*, Quellzementbeton, Schwellzementbeton, Expansivzementbeton
~ '~ **grout(ing compound)** → ~ ~ slurry
~ ~ **mortar**, expanding ~ ~, high-expansion ~ ~, expanded ~ ~ · Dehnzementmörtel *m*, Schwellzementmörtel, Quellzementmörtel, Expansivzementmörtel
~ **rubber**, expanding ~, swelling ~, cellular ~, sponge ~, expanded (natural) ~, foam(ed) (natural) ~ · Kautschukschaum(stoff) *m*, Quellgummi *m*, *n*, Gummischaum(stoff), Zellkautschuk *m*, Schaumgummi, Zellgummi

expansivity · (Aus)Dehn(ungs)verhalten *n*

experience record · Befähigungsnachweis *m*

experimental building [*of the Bauhaus*] · Versuchshaus *n* [*des Bauhauses*]
~ **estate** · Versuchssied(e)lung *f*
~ **finding**, ~ result, test ~ · Prüf(ungs)-ergebnis *n*, Versuchsergebnis
~ **result**, ~ finding, test ~ · Prüf(ungs)-ergebnis *n*, Versuchsergebnis
~ **wall**, test ~ · Versuchswand *f*

expert · Sachverständiger *m*, Fachmann *m*
~ **committee** · Sachverständigenausschuß *m*

to explain geometrically, ~ interpret ~ · geometrisch deuten

explanatory drawing · Erläuterungszeichnung *f*
~ **report** · Erläuterungsbericht *m*

exploded view · auseinandergezogene Ansicht *f*

explosion-proof, EP · explosionssicher

explosion(-proof) door, EP ~ · explosionssichere Tür *f*

explosive fixing · Einschießbefestigung *f*
~ **technique** [*In this type of fixing technique the fixing device is driven in by the immense instantaneous explosive thrust from a captive cartridge*] · Einschießtechnik *f*

exponential formula · Exponentialformel *f*
~ **function** · Exponentialfunktion *f*
~ **series** · Exponentialreihe *f*

exposed, unlined ~ unverkleidet
~ **aggregate** → architectural (concrete) ~
~ ~ **concrete** · Beton *m* mit bloßgelegten Zuschlägen, ~ ~ ~ Zuschlagstoffen, ~ ~ bloßgelegtem Zuschlagmaterial
~ ~ **finish** [*A decorative finish for concrete work achieved by removing, generally before the concrete has fully hardened, the outer skin of mortar and exposing the coarse aggregate*] · bloßgelegte Zuschläge *mpl*, bloßgelegter Zuschlag(stoff) *m*, bloßgelegtes Zuschlagmaterial *n*

exposed aggregate ((pre)cast) ... — exposition area

~ ~ ((pre)cast) (concrete) panel, ~ ~ prefab(ricated) ~ ~ · (Beton)Tafel f mit bloßgelegten Zuschlägen, ~ ~ ~ Zuschlagstoffen, ~ ~ freigelegten ~, ~ ~ bloßgelegtem Zuschlagmaterial n, ~ ~ freigelegtem Zuschlagmaterial

~ **block**, ~ tile, fair-faced ~ [*See remark under 'Block'*] · Sichtblock(stein) m, Sichtstein

~ **brickwork**, fair-faced ~ · Sichtziegelmauerwerk n

~ **cast component** → fair-faced (pre-)cast (concrete) ~

~ ~ **(concrete) component** → fair-faced (pre)cast (~) ~

~ ~ **(~) member** → fair-faced (pre-)cast (concrete) component

~ ~ **(~) unit** → fair-faced ~ precast ~ ~

~ **cast-in-place concrete** → fair-faced in(-)situ (cast) ~

~ **cast(-)in(-)situ concrete** → fair-faced in(-)situ (cast) ~

~ **cast member** → fair-faced (pre)cast (concrete) component

~ ~ **unit** → fair-faced cast-concrete component

~ **concrete**, fair-faced ~, architectural ~ · Architekturbeton m, Sichtbeton, Dekorativbeton, Dekor(ations)beton

~ **(~) aggregate** → architectural (~) ~

~ ~ **beam**, fair-faced ~ ~, architectural ~ ~ · Sichtbetonbalken(träger) m, Architekturbetonbalken(träger), Dekorativbetonbalken(träger), Dekor(ations)betonbalken(träger)

~ **(~) cast(ing)** → fair-faced (~) ~

~ ~ **column**, fair-faced (~) ~, architectural ~ ~ · Sichtbetonstütze f, Architekturbetonstütze, Dekorativbetonstütze, Dekor(ations)betonstütze

~ ~ **façade (building) component**, ~ ~ ~ (~) member, ~ ~ ~ (~) unit, fair-faced (~) ~ (~) ~ · Sichtbeton-Fassaden(bau)körper m, Sichtbeton-Fassaden(bau)element n [*Fehlname: Sichtbeton-Fassadenbaueinheit f*]

~ ~ ~ **(~) member**, ~ ~ ~ (~) component, ~ ~ ~ (~) unit, fair-faced (~) ~ (~) ~ · Sichtbeton-Fassaden-(bau)körper m, Sichtbeton-Fassaden-(bau)element n [*Fehlname: Sichtbeton-Fassadenbaueinheit f*]

~ ~ ~ **(~) unit**, ~ ~ ~ (~) compo-nent, ~ ~ ~ (~) member, fair-faced (~) ~ (~) ~ · Sichtbeton-Fassaden-(bau)körper m, Sichtbeton-Fassaden-(bau)element n [*Fehlname: Sichtbeton-Fassadenbaueinheit f*]

~ ~ **finish**, fair-faced (~) ~ · Betonsichtfläche f

~ ~ **forms** → fair-faced ~ ~

~ ~ **form(work)** → fair-faced (concrete) forms

~ ~ **panel**, fair-faced (~) ~, architectural ~ ~ · Sichtbetontafel f, Architekturbetontafel, Dekor(ations)betontafel, Dekorativbetontafel

~ ~ **shuttering** → fair-faced (concrete) forms

~ ~ **stair(case)**, fair-faced (~) ~, architectural ~ ~ · Sichtbetontreppe f, Architekturbetontreppe, Dekorativbetontreppe, Dekor(ations)betontreppe

~ ~ **texture**, fair-faced (~) ~, architectural ~ ~ · Sichtbetonstruktur f, Architekturbetonstruktur, Dekorativbetonstruktur, Dekor(ations)betonstruktur

~ ~ **wall**, fair-faced (~) ~, architectural ~ ~ · Sichtbetonwand f, Architekturbetonwand, Dekorativbetonwand, Dekor(ations)betonwand

~ **field concrete** → fair-faced in(-)situ (cast) ~

~ **finish**, fair-faced ~, ~ work · Sichtausführung f

~ **flashing (piece)** [*See remark under 'Anschluß'*] · sichtbarer Anschluß(streifen) m

~ **granite aggregate finish**, fair-faced ~ ~ · Granitsichtbetonoberfläche f

~ **in(-)situ (cast) concrete** → fair-faced ~ (~) ~

~ **light(weight) concrete** → fair-faced ~ ~

~ ~ ~ **block** → fair-faced ~ ~ ~

~ ~ ~ **tile** → fair-faced light(weight) concrete block

~ **masonry (work)**, fair-faced ~ (~) · Sichtmauerwerk n

~ **nailing** · sichtbare (Ver)Nagelung f

~ **position**, ~ situation · freie Lage f [*Gebäude*]

~ **poured(-in-place) concrete** → fair-faced in(-)situ (cast) ~

~ **(pre)cast (concrete) component** → fair-faced ~ (~) ~

~ ~ **(~) member** → fair-faced ~ (~) ~

~ ~ **(~) unit** → fair-faced ~ (~) ~

~ **reinforced concrete**, ~ R.C., fair-faced ~ ~, reinforced fair-faced concrete, reinforced exposed concrete · Sichtstahlbeton m, Stahlsichtbeton

~ **rib** · freiliegende Rippe f

~ **site-placed concrete** → fair-faced in(-)situ (cast) ~

~ **situation**, ~ position · freie Lage f [*Gebäude*]

~ **steel framing**, ~ ~ frame · Sichtstahlrahmen m, Stahlsichtrahmen

(~ sur)face, fair face · Sichtfläche f

~ **tile**, ~ block, fair-faced ~ [*See remark under 'Block'*] · Sichtblock(stein) m, Sichtstein

~ **work**, fair-faced ~ · Sichtarbeiten fpl

~ ~, fair-faced ~, ~ finish · Sichtausführung f

exposition, exhibition · Ausstellung f

~ **architecture**, exhibition ~ · Ausstellungsarchitektur f, Ausstellungsbaukunst f

~ **area**, exhibition ~ · Ausstellungsfläche f

exposition block — exterior lighting

~ **block** → exhibition building
~ **building** → exhibition ~
~ **garden**, exhibition ~ · Ausstellungsgarten *m*
~ **ground**, exhibition ~ · Ausstellungsgelände *n*
~ **hall**, exhibition ~ · Ausstellungshalle *f*
~ **palace**, exhibition ~ · Ausstellungspalast *m*
~ **pavilion**, exhibition ~ · Ausstellungspavillon *m*
~ **stand**, exhibition ~ · Ausstellungsstand *m*
express drive · Schnellvorfahrt *f*
~ **elevator** (US); ~ lift; high speed ~ · Schnellaufzug *m*
~ **exit ramp** · Schnellabfahrtsrampe *f*
~ **goods elevator** (US); ~ ~ lift (Brit.); high-speed ~ ~ · Schnellastenaufzug *m*
~ ~ **lift** (Brit.); ~ ~ elevator (US); high-speed ~ ~ · Schnellastenaufzug *m*
~ **lift** (Brit.); ~ elevator (US); high-speed ~ · Schnellaufzug *m*
~ **passenger elevator** (US); ~ ~ lift (Brit.); high-speed ~ ~ · Schnellfahrstuhl *m*
~ ~ **lift** (Brit.); ~ ~ elevator (US); high-speed ~ ~ · Schnellfahrstuhl *m*
expression of style · Stiläußerung *f*
Expressionism [*A deliberate turning away of the naturalism implicit in Impressionism*] · Expressionismus *m*
expressive content · Ausdrucksgehalt *m*
expressiveness, power of expression · Ausdruckskraft *f*, Aussagekraft
expressway · Schnellstraße *f*, Schnellverkehrsstraße, Schnellweg *m*
expropriation · Enteignung *f*; Expropriation *f* [*Schweiz*]
~ **law** · Enteignungsgesetz *n*
ex(-)stock, from stock · ab Lager
extended · gestreckt [*mit Streckmittelzusatz*]
extender → paint ~
~ [*A finely divided inert mineral added to provide economical bulk in paints, synthetic resins, adhesives, or other products*] · Streckzusatz *m*, Streckmittel *n*
extensibility → ductility
~, **resistance to cracking**, cracking strength · Rißfestigkeit *f*
extensible, ductile · streckbar, dehnbar
extension ladder · Ausziehleiter *f*
~ **of time** · Fristverlängerung *f*
~ **pipe** · Verlängerungsrohr *n*
exterior air → outdoor ~
~ **application**, outside ~, external ~, outer ~, ~ use · Außenverwendung *f*
~ **architecture** → outdoor ~
~ **bending moment**, external ~ ~, outside ~ ~, outer ~ ~ · äußeres Biegemoment *n*, ~ Biegungsmoment

~ **blind** → outside ~
~ **brick**, external ~, outer ~, outside ~ · Außenziegel *m*
~ **(building) panel** → external (~) ~
~ **chlorinated rubber paint**, external ~ ~, outer ~, outside ~ ~ · Außen-Chlorkautschukfarbe *f*, Chlorkautschuk-Außenfarbe
~ **coat**, external ~, outer ~, outside ~ · Außenanstrich *m*, Außenaufstrich
~ ~ **of paint** → external paint coat
~ **coating**, external ~, outside ~, outer ~ · Außenbeschichtung *f*, Außenüberzug *m* [*als Schicht*]
~ **column** → external ~
~ **core**, outer ~, outside ~, external ~ · Außenkern *m*
~ **corner** → outside ~
~ **corridor**, outside ~, outdoor ~, external ~, access gallery, access balcony [*A balcony intended to give access to a number of seperate dwellings above the first story*] · offener Gang *m*, Laubengang
~ **cupola**, external ~, outer ~, ~ dome · Schutzkuppel *f*
~ **dome**, external ~, outer ~, ~ cupola · Schutzkuppel *f*
~ **door** → external ~
~ **fibre** → external ~
~ **final rendering** → (external) ~ ~
~ ~ ~ **mix(ture)** → (external) final rendering stuff
~ ~ ~ **stuff** → (external) ~ ~ ~
~ **floor slab** → external ~ ~
~ **force**, external ~, outside ~, outer ~ · Außenkraft *f*, äußere Kraft
~ **gallery**, external ~, outside ~, outer ~ · Außen-Laubengang *m*
~ **girder**, outer ~ · Außenträger *m*
~ **glass wall** · Außenglaswand *f*
~ **gloss paint**, external ~ ~, outer ~ ~, outside ~ ~ · Außenglanz(anstrich)farbe *f*
~ **handrail**, external ~, outside ~, outer ~, ~ stairrail · Außenhandlauf *m*, Außenhandleiste *f* [*Treppe*]
~ **home decoration**, external ~ ~, outdoor ~ ~ · Außenwandgestaltung *f* von Einfamilienhäusern
~ **illumination** → outdoor ~
~ **insulation**, outer ~, outside ~, external ~ · Außen(ab)dämmung *f*
~ **latex paint**, external ~ ~, outside ~ ~, outer ~ ~ · Außenlatexfarbe *f*
~ **layer** → ~ leaf
~ **leaf**, external ~, outside ~, outer ~, ~ shell, ~ wythe, ~ withe, ~ tier, ~ layer, ~ skin · Außenschale *f*, Vorsatzschale, äußere Schale [*Hohlmauer*]
~ **lighting** → outdoor illumination

~ **loading** → external ~

~ **marble** → outside ~

~ **masonry,** external ~, outside ~, outer ~ · Außenmauerwerk n

~ ~ **wall,** external ~ ~, outside ~ ~, perimeter ~ ~, outer ~ ~, enclosing ~ ~ · Außenmauer f, Umfassungsmauer [*Mauer, die ein Gebäude nach außen abschließt. Sie kann eine Decke tragen oder deckenunbelastet sein*]

~ ~ ~ **column,** external ~ ~ ~, outside ~ ~ ~, perimeter ~ ~ ~, outer ~ ~ ~, enclosing ~ ~ ~ · Außenmauerstütze f, Umfassungsmauerstütze

~ ~ ~ **lining,** ~ ~ ~ (sur)facing, external ~ ~ ~, outside ~ ~ ~, enclosing ~ ~ ~, perimeter ~ ~ ~, outer ~ ~ ~ · Außen(mauer)bekleidung f, Außen(mauer)verkleidung, Außen(mauer)auskleidung, Umfassungsmauerverkleidung, Umfassungsmauerauskleidung, Umfassungsmauerbekleidung

~ ~ **(work),** external ~ (~), enclosing ~ (~), outside ~ (~), perimeter ~ (~), outer ~ (~) · Außenmauerwerk n

~ **mosaic finish** → external ~ ~

~ **oil paint,** external ~ ~, outside ~ ~, outer ~ ~ · Außenöl(anstrich)farbe f

~ **paint,** external ~, outside ~, outer ~ · Außen(anstrich)farbe f

~ ~ **coat** → external ~ ~

~ **painting (work)** → external ~ (~)

~ **panel** → external (building) ~

~ **plaster,** external ~; stucco (US); (external) rendering (Brit.) [*1. A mix based on cement and/or lime or organic binder with the addition of sand or other aggregates, which is applied while plastic to external building surfaces and which hardens after application. 2. This material in its hardened form*] · Putz m, (Außen)(Ver)~, Außenwand~ [*DIN 18550*]

~ ~ **aggregate** (Brit.) → stucco ~

~ ~ **base,** external ~; (~) rendering ~ (Brit.); stucco ~ (US) · Putz(unter)grund m, Außen~

~ ~ **mix(ture)** → (external) rendering stuff (Brit.)

~ ~ **practice** → (external) rendering ~ (Brit.)

~ ~ **scheme** → (external) rendering ~ (Brit.)

~ ~ **stuff** → (external) rendering ~ (Brit.)

~ ~ **system** → (external) rendering scheme (Brit.)

~ ~ **technique** → (external) rendering practice (Brit.)

~ **plastering,** external ~; (~) rendering (Brit.) · (Außen)(Ver)Putzen n, Außenputzarbeit f

~ **plaster(ing)** → (external) rendering

~ ~ **aggregate** → (external) rendering ~

~ ~ **base,** external ~ ~; (~) rendering ~ [*This product is used as a base for the application of stucco on the outer walls of buildings*] · (Außen)(Ver)Putzträgerplatte f

~ ~ ~, external ~ ~; (~) rendering ~ (Brit.) · (Außen)Putz(unter)grund m

~ ~ **coat,** external ~ ~; (~) rendering ~ (Brit.) · (Außen)Putzüberzug m, (Außen)Putzschicht f, (Außen)Putzhaut f, (Außen)Putzlage f

~ ~ **mix(ture)** → (external) rendering stuff

~ ~ **practice** → (external) rendering ~

~ ~ **scheme** → (external) rendering ~

~ ~ **stuff** → (external) rendering ~

~ ~ **system** → (external) rendering scheme

~ ~ **technique** → (external) rendering practice

~ **(pre)cast block,** ~ ~ brick, external ~ ~, outside ~ ~, outer ~ ~ · Außen-Betonblock(stein) m

~ ~ **brick** → ~ ~ block

~ **pressure,** external ~ · Außendruck m

~ **prestressed (concrete) column,** external ~ (~) ~, perimeter ~ (~) ~ · Spannbeton-Außenstütze f

~ **primer** → external ~

~ **pulpit,** external ~, outside ~, outer ~ · Außenkanzel f

~ **R.C. column** → ~ reinforced (concrete) ~

~ **reinforced column** → ~ concrete ~ ~

~ ~ **(concrete) column,** external ~ (~) ~, perimeter ~ (~) ~, ~ R.C. ~ · Stahlbeton-Außenstütze f

~ **rendering** → (external) ~

~ ~, (external) ~ (Brit.); ~ plastering · (Außen)(Ver)Putzen n, Außenputzarbeit f

~ ~ **aggregate** → (external) ~ ~

~ ~ **base,** (external) ~ ~ (Brit.); ~ plaster(ing) ~ [*This product is used as a base for the application of stucco on the outer walls of buildings*] · (Außen-)(Ver)Putzträgerplatte f

~ ~ ~, (external) ~ ~ (Brit.); ~ plaster(ing) ~ · (Außen)Putz(unter)grund m

~ ~ **coat,** (external) ~ ~ (Brit.); ~ plaster(ing) ~ · (Außen)Putzüberzug m, (Außen)Putzschicht f, (Außen)Putzhaut f, (Außen)Putzlage f

~ ~ **mix(ture)** → (external) rendering stuff

~ ~ **practice** → (external) ~ ~

~ ~ **scheme** → (external) ~ ~

~ ~ **stuff** → (external) ~ ~

~ ~ **system** → (external) rendering scheme

~ ~ **technique** → (external) rendering practice

exterior reveal — external coat of paint

~ **reveal,** external ~, outer ~, outside ~ · Außenleibung *f*

~ **sealing,** external ~, outer ~, outside ~ · Außen(ab)dichtung *f*

~ **shaft** → external ~

~ **sheet,** external ~, outer ~, outside ~ · Außenplatte *f* [*einer Sandwichplatte*]

~ **shell** → ~ leaf

~ ~ **component** → outer shell unit

~ ~ **member** → outer shell unit

~ ~ **unit** → outer ~ ~

~ **skin** → ~ leaf

~ **slatted blind,** external ~ ~, outer ~ ~, outside ~ ~ · Außenjalousie *f*

~ **stain** → ~ wood ~

~ **stairrail** → ~ ~ handrail

~ **stretched (concrete) column** → perimeter (pre)stressed (~) ~

~ **string** → outer ~

~ **(structural) system** → external wall construction

~ **stud** → outer ~

~ **system** → external wall construction

~ **tensioned (concrete) column** → perimeter (pre)stressed (~) ~

~ **tieback,** external ~ · freiliegendes Zugband *n*, außenliegendes ~

~ **tier** → ~ leaf

~ **tile,** external ~, outside ~, outer ~ · Außen(belag)platte *f*, Außenfliese

~ **torque** → external twist(ing) moment

~ **torsion(al) moment** → external twist(ing) ~

~ **twist(ing) moment** → external ~ ~

~ **undercoat plaster,** external ~ ~; (external) undercoat rendering (Brit.); undercoat stucco (US) · (Außen)Grund-(ver)putz *m*, (Außen)Unter(ver)putz, (Außen)Grob(ver)putz

~ **undercoat(er),** external ~, outside ~, outer ~, undercoat(er) for external use · Außenvorlack *m*

~ **use** → ~ ~ application

~ **varnishing,** external ~, outside ~, outer ~ · Außenlackierung *f*

~ **veneer** → face ~

~ **view,** external ~ · Außenansicht *f*

~ **vinyl paint,** outside ~ ~, outer ~ ~, external ~ ~ · Außenvinylfarbe *f*

~ **wall,** external ~, outside ~, perimeter ~, outer ~, enclosing ~ · Außenwand *f*, Umfassungswand [*Wand, die ein Gebäude nach außen abschließt. Sie kann eine Decke tragen oder deckenunbelastet sein*]

~ ~ **block** → external ~ ~ ~

~ ~ **(building) component** → external wall (building) unit

~ ~ **(~) member** → external wall (building) unit

~ ~ **(~) unit** → external ~ (~) ~

~ ~ **component** → external wall (building) unit

~ ~ **construction** → external ~ ~

~ ~ **facing** → ~ ~ lining

~ ~ **finish,** external ~ ~, outside ~ ~, enclosing ~ ~, perimeter ~ ~, outer ~ ~ · Außenwandbelag *m*, Umfassungswandbelag

~ ~ **lining,** ~ ~ (sur)facing, external ~ ~, outside ~ ~, enclosing ~ ~, perimeter ~ ~, outer ~ ~ · Außen-(wand)bekleidung *f*, Außen(wand)verkleidung, Außen(wand)auskleidung, Umfassungswandbekleidung, Umfassungswandverkleidung, Umfassungswandauskleidung

~ ~ **member** → external wall (building) unit

~ ~ **panel** → external ~ ~

~ ~ **slab** → external ~ ~

~ ~ **(sur)facing** → ~ ~ ~ lining

~ ~ **tile** → external wall block

~ ~ **unit** → external wall (building) ~

~ **window,** outer ~, external ~, outside ~ ~, storm ~ [*A window with an air space between it and the inner window*] · Außenfenster *n* [*bei einem Doppelfenster*]

~ ~, external ~, outside ~, outer ~ · Außenfenster *n* [*Im Gegensatz zu einem Fenster innerhalb eines Gebäudes*]

~ ~ **check** [*Scotland*] → external window rabbet

~ ~ **frame** → storm ~ ~

~ ~ **rabbet** → external ~ ~

~ ~ **sill** → external ~ ~

~ **withe** → ~ leaf

~ **(wood) stain** · (Holz)Beize *f* für Außenverwendung

~ **work** → external ~

~ **wythe** → ~ leaf

external air → outdoor ~

~ **application** → exterior ~

~ **architecture** → outdoor ~

(external-)balcony-access type of block, block with external access galleries · Außenganghaus *n*

external balcony slab · Laubengangplatte *f*

~ **bending moment,** exterior ~ ~, outside ~ ~, outer ~ ~ · äußeres Biegemoment *n*, ~ Biegungsmoment

~ **blind** → outside ~

~ **brick,** exterior ~, outside ~, outer ~ · Außenziegel *m*

~ **(building) panel,** exterior (~) ~, outside (~) ~, outer (~) ~ · Außen-(bau)tafel *f*

~ **cellar wall** · Kelleraußenwand *f*

~ **chlorinated rubber paint,** exterior ~ ~ ~, outside ~ ~ ~, outer ~ ~ ~ · Außen-Chlorkautschukfarbe *f*

~ **coat,** exterior ~, outer ~, outside ~ · Außenanstrich *m*, Außenaufstrich

~ ~ **of paint** → ~ paint coat

external coating — external plaster stuff 356

~ **coating,** exterior ~, outside ~, outer ~ · Außenbeschichtung f, Außenüberzug m [als Schicht]

~ **column,** exterior ~, perimeter ~, outside ~, outer ~, edge ~ · Außenstütze f, Randstütze, Perimeterstütze

~ ~ ~, exterior ~, outside ~, outer ~, perimeter ~, edge ~ · Randsäule f, Perimetersäule, Außensäule

~ **core,** outer ~, outside ~, exterior ~ · Außenkern m

~ **corner** → outside ~

~ **corridor,** exterior ~, outdoor ~, outside ~, access gallery, access balcony [*A balcony intended to give access to a number of seperate dwellings above the first story*] · offener Gang m, Laubengang

~ **cupola** → ~ dome

~ **decoration** → ~ decorative finish

~ **decorative feature** → ~ ~ ~ finish

~ ~ **finish,** ~ ~ feature, ~ ornamental ~, ~ decoration, ~ enrichment · Außenschmuck m, Außenverzierung f

~ **dome,** outer ~, exterior ~, ~ cupola · Schutzkuppel f

~ **door,** exterior ~, outside ~, outer ~ · Außentür f

~ **enrichment** → ~ decorative finish

~ **fibre** (Brit.); ~ fiber (US); exterior ~, outer ~ · Außenfaser f

(~) **final rendering,** exterior ~ ~ (Brit.); final coat exterior plaster, final coat external plaster · (Außen)Oberputz m, (Außen)Feinputz, (Außen)Deckputz

(~) ~ ~ **mix(ture)** → (~) ~ ~ stuff

(~) ~ ~ **stuff,** (~) ~ ~ mix(ture), exterior ~ ~ ~ (Brit.); final coat exterior plaster(ing), final coat external plaster(ing) · (Außen)Oberputzmasse f, (Außen)Oberputzmörtel m, (Außen)Deckputzmasse, (Außen)Deckputzmörtel, (Außen)Feinputzmasse, (Außen-)Feinputzmörtel

~ **(fire) hazard** [*This hazard arises outside the building as opposed to an internal hazard which arises from the structure of the contents of the building*] · Fremdgefahr f

~ **floor slab,** exterior ~ ~, outer ~ ~, outside ~ ~ [*äußere Bodenplatte*] · Unterkellerung f

~ **force,** exterior ~, outer ~, outside ~ · äußere Kraft f, Außenkraft

~ **gallery,** exterior ~, outside ~, outer ~ · Außen-Laubengang m

~ **glazing** [*Glazing, either side of which is exposed outside the building*] · Außenverglasung f, Außeneinglasung

~ **gloss paint** → exterior ~ ~

~ **handrail** → exterior ~

~ **hazard** → ~ fire ~

~ **home decoration** → exterior ~ ~

~ **illumination** → outdoor ~

~ **insulation,** outside ~, exterior ~ outer ~ · Außen(ab)dämmung f

~ **layer** → exterior leaf

~ **leaf** → exterior ~

~ **lighting** → outdoor illumination

~ **loading,** exterior ~, outside ~, outer ~ · Außenbelastung f, äußere Belastung

~ **marble** → outside ~

~ **masonry** → exterior ~

~ ~ **wall** → exterior ~ ~

~ ~ ~ **column** → exterior ~ ~ ,~

~ ~ ~ **facing** → exterior masonry wall lining

~ ~ ~ **lining** → exterior ~ ~ ~

~ ~ ~ **of double-leaf cavity construction,** cavity external masonry wall · Außenhohlmauer f, zweischalige Außenmauer

~ ~ ~ **(sur)facing** → exterior masonry wall lining

~ ~ **(work)** → exterior ~ (~)

~ **moment** · äußeres Moment n

~ **mosaic finish,** exterior ~ ~, outer ~ ~, outdoor ~ ~, mosaic external ~, mosaic exterior ~ ~, mosaic outdoor ~ · Mosaikaußenhaut f

~ **oil paint,** outside ~ ~, exterior ~ ~, outer ~ ~ · Außenöl(anstrich)farbe f

~ **ornamental feature** → ~ decorative finish

~ ~ **finish** → ~ decorative ~

~ **paint,** exterior ~, outside ~, outer ~ · Außen(anstrich)farbe f

~ ~ **coat,** exterior ~ ~, outside ~ ~, outer ~ ~, ~ coat of paint · Außenfarbanstrich m, Außenfarbaufstrich

~ **painting (work),** exterior ~ (~), outside ~ (~), outer ~ (~) · Außenanstreichen n, Außenanstrich m, Außen-Anstreicherarbeiten fpl; Außen-Malerarbeiten [Fehlname]

~ **panel** → ~ building ~

~ **pipe thread,** EPT · Rohraußengewinde n

~ **plaster,** exterior ~; stucco (US); (external) rendering (Brit.) [*1. A mix based on cement and/or lime or organic binder with the addition of sand or other aggregates, which is applied while plastic to external building surfaces and which hardens after application. 2. This material in its hardened form*] · Putz m, (Außen)(Ver)~, Außenwand~ [*DIN 18550*]

~ ~ **aggregate** (Brit.) → stucco ~

~ ~ **base,** exterior ~ ~; (~) rendering ~ (Brit.); stucco ~ (US) · Putz(unter)grund m, Außen~

~ ~ **façade,** exterior ~ ~; stucco ~ (US) · Putzfassade f

~ ~ **mix(ture)** → (~) rendering stuff

~ ~ **practice** → (~) rendering ~

~ ~ **scheme** → (~) rendering system

~ ~ **stuff** → (~) rendering ~

external plaster system — external tieback

~ ~ **system** → (~) rendering scheme
~ ~ **technique** → (~) rendering practice
~ **plastering**, exterior ~; (~) rendering (Brit.) · (Außen)(Ver)Putzen *n*, Außenputzarbeit *f*
~ **plaster(ing)** → (~) rendering
~ **plaster(ing) aggregate** → ~ rendering ~
~ ~ **base**, exterior ~ ~; (~) rendering ~ [*This product is used as a base for the application of stucco on the outer walls of buildings*] · (Außen)(Ver-)Putzträgerplatte *f*
~ ~ ~, exterior ~ ~; (~) rendering ~ (Brit.) · (Außen)Putz(unter)grund *m*
~ ~ **coat**, exterior ~ ~; (~) rendering ~ (Brit.) · (Außen)Putzüberzug *m*, (Außen)Putzschicht *f*, (Außen)Putzhaut *f*, (Außen)Putzlage *f*
~ ~ **mix(ture)** → (~) rendering stuff
~ ~ **practice** → (~) rendering ~
~ ~ **scheme** → (~) rendering ~
~ ~ **stuff** → (~) rendering ~
~ ~ **system** → (~) rendering scheme
~ ~ **technique** → (~) rendering practice
~ **precast block** → exterior ~ ~
~ ~ **brick** → exterior precast block
~ **pressure** · Scheiteldruck *m* [*Rohr*]
~ ~, exterior ~ · Außendruck *m*
~ **prestressed column** → ~ prestressed concrete ~
~ ~ **(concrete) column**, exterior ~ (~) ~, perimeter ~ (~) ~ · Spannbeton-Außenstütze *f*
~ **primer**, exterior ~, outer ~, outside ~ · Außen-Grundanstrichmittel *n*, Außen-Grundanstrichstoff *m*, Außen-Grundiermittel, Außen-Grundierstoff, Außen-Grund(ierung) *m*, (f)
~ **pulpit**, exterior ~, outside ~, outer ~ · Außenkanzel *f*
~ **R.C. column** → exterior reinforced (concrete) ~
~ **reading** · Zählerablesen *n* außerhalb der Räume
~ **reinforced column** → exterior reinforced (concrete) ~
~ ~ **(concrete) column** → exterior ~ (~) ~
(~) **rendering**, exterior ~ (Brit.); ~ plaster(ing) [*1. A mix based on cement and/or lime or organic binder with the addition of sand or other aggregates, which is applied while plastic to external building surfaces and which hardens after application. 2. This material in its hardened form*] · (Außen)(Ver)Putz *m* [*DIN 18550*]
(~) ~, exterior ~ (Brit.); ~ plastering · (Außen)(Ver)Putzen *n*, Außenputzarbeit *f*
(~) ~ **aggregate**, exterior ~ ~ (Brit.); ~ plaster(ing) ~ · (Außen)Putzzuschlag(stoff) *m*, (Außen)Putzzuschlagmaterial *n*
(~) ~ **base**, exterior ~ ~ (Brit.); ~ plaster(ing) ~ [*This product is used as a base for the application of stucco on the outer walls of buildings*] · (Außen)(Ver)Putzträgerplatte *f*
(~) ~ **base**, exterior ~ ~ (Brit.); ~ plaster(ing) ~ · (Außen)Putz(unter)grund *m*
(~) ~ **coat**, exterior ~ ~ (Brit.); ~ plaster(ing) ~ · (Außen)Putzüberzug *m*, (Außen)Putzschicht *f*, (Außen)Putzhaut *f*, (Außen)Putzlage *f*
(~) ~ **mix(ture)** → (~) ~ stuff
(~) ~ **practice**, (~) ~ technique, (~) ~ technic, exterior ~ ~ (Brit.); ~ plaster(ing) ~ · (Außen)(Ver)Putztechnik *f*
(~) ~ **scheme**, exterior ~ ~, (~) ~ system (Brit.); ~ plaster(ing) ~ · (Außen)Putzaufbau *m*, (Außen)Putzsystem *n*
(~) ~ **stuff**, (~) ~ mix(ture), exterior ~ ~ (Brit.); ~ plaster(ing) ~ · (Außen-(Ver)Putzmörtel *m*, (Außen)(Ver)Putzmasse *f*
(~) ~ **system** → ~ (~) scheme
(~) ~ **technique** → (~) ~ practice
~ **reveal**, exterior ~, outer ~, outside ~ · Außenleibung *f*
~ **sealing**, exterior ~, outer ~, outside ~ · Außen(ab)dichtung *f*
~ **shaft**, exterior ~, outside ~, outer ~ · Außenschaft *m* [*Schornstein. DIN 1058*]
~ **sheet**, exterior ~, outer ~, outside ~ · Außenplatte *f* [*einer Sandwichplatte*]
~ **shell** → exterior leaf
~ ~ **component** → outer shell unit
~ ~ **member** → outer shell unit
~ ~ **unit** → outer ~ ~
~ **skin** → exterior leaf
~ **slatted blind** → exterior ~ ~
(~) **stair(case) tower** · Treppen(haus)turm *m*, Treppen(haus)vorbau *m*, Außentreppenhaus *n*
~ **stairrail** → exterior handrail
~ **stretched (concrete) column** → perimeter (pre)stressed (~) ~
~ **string** → outer ~
~ **(structural) system** → ~ wall construction
~ **stud** → outer ~
~ **system** → ~ wall construction
~ **(tele)phone** · Auswärtsfernsprecher *m* [*Im Gegensatz zum Hausfernsprecher*]
~ **tensioned (concrete) column** → perimeter (pre)stressed (~) ~
~ **tieback**, exterior ~ · außenliegendes Zugband *n*, freiliegendes ~

external tier — extract ventilation concrete block

~ tier → exterior leaf

~ tile → exterior ~

~ torque → ~ twist(ing) moment

~ torsion(al) moment → ~ twist(ing) ~

~ twist(ing) moment, ~ torsion(al) ~, exterior ~ ~, outside ~ ~, outer ~ ~, ~ torque · äußeres Drill(ungs)moment n, ~ Torsionsmoment, ~ Verdrehungsmoment, ~ Verwindungsmoment

~ undercoat plaster → (~) ~ rendering

(~) ~ rendering (Brit.); undercoat stucco (US); exterior undercoat plaster, external undercoat plaster · (Außen-)Grob(ver)putz m, (Außen)Grund(ver)putz, (Außen)Unter(ver)putz

~ undercoat(er), exterior ~, outside ~, outer ~, undercoat(er) for external use · Außenvorlack m

~ use → exterior application

~ varnishing, exterior ~, outside ~, outer ~ · Außenlackierung f

~ veneer → face ~

~ view, exterior ~ · Außenansicht f

~ vinyl paint → exterior ~ ~

~ wall → exterior ~

~ ~ block, ~ ~ tile, exterior ~ ~, outer ~ ~, outside ~ ~ [See remark under 'Block'] · Außenwandblock m, Außenwand(block)stein m

~ ~ (building) component → ~ ~ (~) unit

~ ~ (~) member → ~ ~ (~) unit

~ ~ (~) unit, ~ ~ (~) member, ~ ~ (~) component, exterior ~ (~) ~, outer ~ (~) ~, outside ~ (~) ~, perimeter ~ (~) ~, enclosing ~ (~) ~ [See remark under '(Bau)Element'] · Außenwand(bau)körper m, Außenwand(bau)element n [Fehlnamen: Außenwand(bau)einheit f]

~ ~ component → ~ ~ (building) unit

~ ~ construction, outer ~ ~, exterior ~ ~, perimeter ~ ~, outside ~ ~, enclosing ~ ~, ~ (structural) system · Außenwand(konstruktions)system m, Außenwandkonstruktion f, Außenwandbausystem

~ ~ facing → exterior wall lining

~ ~ finish → exterior ~ ~

~ ~ lining → exterior ~ ~

~ ~ member → ~ ~ (building) unit

~ ~ panel, exterior ~ ~, outside ~ ~, outer ~ ~ · Außenwandtafel f

~ ~ slab, exterior ~ ~, outer ~ ~, outside ~ ~ · Außenwand(bau)platte f

~ ~ (sur)facing → exterior wall lining

~ ~ tile → ~ ~ block

~ ~ unit → ~ ~ building ~

~ window → exterior ~

~ ~ check [Scotland] → ~ ~ rabbet

~ ~ frame → storm ~ ~

~ ~ rabbet, exterior ~ ~, outer ~ ~, ~ ~ rebate; ~ ~ check [Scotland] · äußerer (Fenster)Anschlag m

~ ~ sill; ~ ~ cill (Brit.); exterior ~ ~, outside ~ ~, outer ~ ~ · Außenfensterbank f, Außen(fenster)sohlbank

~ withe → exterior leaf

~ wythe → exterior leaf

~ work, exterior ~, outdoor ~, outside ~, outer ~ · Außenarbeiten fpl [Beim Bau eines Hauses]

externally plastered; (~) rendered (Brit.) · (außen)verputzt

~ reflected component · Außen-Rückstrahlanteil m

(~) rendered (Brit.); ~ plastered · (außen)verputzt

extinguisher, fire ~ · (Feuer)Löscher m

~ bracket, fire ~ ~ · (Feuer)Löscher-Halterung f

~ cabinet, fire ~ ~ · (Feuer)Löscherschrank m

extinguishing, fire ~ · (Feuer)Löschen n

~ device, fire ~ ~ · (Feuer)Löschgerät n

~ engineering → fire ~ ~

~ foam → fire (~) ~

~ installation, fire ~ ~ · (Feuer-)Löscheinrichtung f

~ line, ~ run, fire ~ ~ · (Feuer)Löschleitung f

~ method → fire ~ ~

~ run, ~ line, fire ~ ~ · (Feuer)Löschleitung f

~ system fire ~ ~ · (Feuer)Löschanlage f

extra heavy fuel oil [3,500 seconds] · Heizöl S n, schwer(flüssig)es Heizöl [DIN 51603]

extra-heavy sheet (glass) (US); extra-thick ~ (~) · überdickes Glas n, extradickes ~

~ strength (concrete) pipe · hochfestes (Beton)Rohr n

~ ~ pipe, ~ ~ concrete ~ · hochfestes (Beton)Rohr n

extra-thick sheet (glass); extra-heavy ~ (~) (US) · überdickes Glas n, extradickes ~

extra-thin sheet glass · extradünnes Glas n

extra water · Zuschußwasser n

extract fan, exhaust(ing) ~; induced draught ~ (Brit.); ~ induced draft ~ (US) · Saugzugventilator m

~ ventilation, ~ venting · Entlüftung f

~ ~ block, ~ ~ tile, ~ ~ venting ~ [See remark under 'Block'] · Entlüftungsblock(stein) m, Entlüftungsstein

~ ~ chimney, ~ ~ venting ~ · Entlüftungsschornstein m

~ ~ concrete block, ~ ~ ~ tile, ~ ~ venting ~ ~ · Betonentlüftungsstein m

extract ventilation duct — extruded particle board

~ ~ duct, ~ venting ~ · Entlüftungskanal *m*

~ ~ line, ~ venting ~ · Entlüftungsleitung *f*

~ ~ pipe, ~ venting ~ · Entlüftungsrohr *n*

~ ~ shaft, ~ venting ~ · Entlüftungsschacht *m*

~ ~ tile, ~ ~ block, ~ venting ~ [*See remark under 'Block'*] · Entlüftungsblock(stein) *m*, Entlüftungsstein

~ ~ unit, extraction ~, extractor, ventilator · (Ent)Lüfter *m*

~ venting → ~ ventilation

~ ~ block, ~ ~ tile, ~ ventilation ~ [*See remark under 'Block'*] · Entlüftungsblock(stein) *m*, Entlüftungsstein

~ ~ chimney, ~ ventilation ~ · Entlüftungsschornstein *m*

~ ~ duct → ~ ventilation ~

~ ~ line → ~ ventilation ~

~ ~ pipe → ~ ventilation ~

~ ~ shaft → ~ ventilation ~

~ ~ tile, ~ ~ block, ~ ventilation ~ [*See remark under 'Block'*] · Entlüftungsblock(stein) *m*, Entlüftungsstein

extracted asphalt (US); ~ (asphaltic-) bitumen (Brit.) · Extraktbitumen *n*

~ (asphaltic-)bitumen (Brit.) → ~ asphalt

~ bitumen (Brit.) → ~ asphalt

extraction method, ~ procedure · Extraktionsverfahren *n* [*Zerlegung von Mischgut in seine Bestandteile*]

~ procedure, ~ method · Extraktionsverfahren *n* [*Zerlegung von Mischgut in seine Bestandteile*]

~ unit, extract ventilation ~, extractor, ventilator · (Ent)Lüfter *m*

~ with caustic soda → Abrams' test

extractor, ventilator, extract ventilation unit, extraction unit · (Ent)Lüfter *m*

extract(or) fan · Abluftventilator *m*

extrados → vault ~

~ of arch, back ~ ~, upper surface ~, (arch) extrados, (arch) back [*The outer line or surface of the convex side of an arch*] · Rücken *m*, Bogen~, äußere Bogenfläche *f*

extras required · Unvorhergesehene *n* [*Position in einem Angebot*]

extremal distribution of response · Extremverteilung *f* der Reaktion

extreme arch, boundary ~, edge ~ · Randbogen *m*

~ case · Extremfall *m*

~ cross girder · Endquerträger *m*

~ fibre(Brit.); **~ fiber** (US) · Randfaser *f*

~ ~ stress (Brit.); **~ fiber ~** (US); flexural tensile ~ · Biegezugspannung *f*

~ ~ ~ → edge stress of ~ ~ ~

~ part of beam · Balken(träger)endbereich *m, n*

~ span, end ~ · Endfeld *n*

extrinsic insolubles, insoluble in benzene, benzene insolubles · Benzol-Unlösliches *n*

extruded · stranggepreßt

~ aluminium (Brit.); **~ aluminum** (US) · Strangpreßalu(minium) *n*

~ asbestos cement · stranggepreßter Asbestzement *m*

~ brass section, ~ ~ shape, ~ ~ unit, ~ ~ product, ~ ~ trim, ~ ~ profile, brass extrusion · Messingstrangpreßprofil *n*, Messingstrangpreßerzeugnis *n*

~ chipboard, extrusion ~, ~ particle board [*Particle board made by extrusion through a die. The particles lie with their larger dimensions mainly perpendicular to the direction of extrusion*] · Spanplatte *f* nach dem Strangpreßverfahren erzeugt Strangpreßplatte, stranggepreßte Spanplatte

~ clay (roof(ing)) tile, extrusion ~ (~) ~, ~ roof(ing) clay ~ · Strang(dach)ziegel *m* [*DIN 456*]

~ concrete, extrusion ~ · Strangpreßbeton *m* [*International geschützte Markenbezeichnung: Pressolit m*]

~ ~ girder, extrusion ~ ~ · Strangpreßbetonträger *m*

~ ~ product → ~ ~ ~ section

~ ~ profile → ~ ~ ~ section

~ ~ section, extrusion ~ ~, ~ ~ profile, ~ ~ shape, ~ ~ product, ~ ~ trim, ~ ~ unit, concrete extrusion · Strangpreßbeton-Profil *n*, stranggepreßtes Betonprofil

~ ~ shape → ~ ~ ~ section

~ ~ trim → ~ ~ ~ section

~ ~ unit → ~ ~ ~ section

~ floor tile, extrusion ~ ~ · stranggepreßte (Fuß)Bodenfliese *f*, ~ (Fuß-)Bodenplatte *f*

~ interlocking clay roof(ing) tile, extrusion ~ ~ ~ ~, ~ ~ roof(ing) clay ~ · Strangfalz(dach)ziegel *m* [*Ebener oder leicht profilierter Strang(dach)ziegel mit Falzen an den Längsseiten*]

~ ~ ~ tile roof cover(ing), ~ ~ ~ ~ ~ ~ sheathing, ~ ~ ~ ~ ~ cladding, extrusion ~ ~ ~ ~, ~ ~ ~ ~ ~ roofing · Strangfalzziegel(dach)(ein)deckung *f*, Strangfalzziegelbedachung *f*

~ ~ roof(ing) clay tile, extrusion ~ ~ ~ ~, ~ ~ roof(ing) ~ · Strangfalz(dach)ziegel *m* [*Ebener oder leicht profilierter Strang(dach)ziegel mit Falzen an den Längsseiten*]

~ particle board, extrusion ~ ~, ~ chipboard [*Particle board made by extrusion through a die. The particles lie with their larger dimensions mainly perpendicular to the direction of extrusion*] · Spanplatte *f* nach dem Strangpreßverfahren erzeugt, Strangpreßplatte, stranggepreßte Spanplatte

extruded product — extrusion plant

~ **product**, ~ shape, ~ profile, ~ unit, ~ section, ~ trim, extrusion · Strangpreßartikel *m*, Strangpreßgegenstand *m*, Strangpreßerzeugnis *n*, Strangpreßprofil *n*

~ **profile**, ~ shape, ~ product, ~ unit, ~ section, ~ trim, extrusion · Strangpreßartikel *m*, Strangpreßgegenstand *m*, Strangpreßerzeugnis *n*, Strangpreßprofil *n*

~ **railing**, extrusion ~ · Strangpreßgeländer *n*

~ **rib section**, ~ ~ trim, ~ ~ unit, ~ ~ shape, rib(bed) extrusion · stranggepreßtes Rippenprofil *n*, Strangpreß-Rippenprofil

~ ~ **shape**, ~ ~ section, ~ ~ unit, ~ ~ trim, rib(bed) extrusion · stranggepreßtes Rippenprofil *n*, Strangpreß-Rippenprofil

~ ~ **trim**, ~ ~ shape, ~ ~ unit, ~ ~ section, rib(bed) extrusion · stranggepreßtes Rippenprofil *n*, Strangpreß-Rippenprofil

~ ~ **unit**, ~ ~ section, ~ ~ trim, ~ ~ shape, rib(bed) extrusion · stranggepreßtes Rippenprofil *n*, Strangpreß-Rippenprofil

~ **roof(ing) clay tile**, extrusion ~ ~ ~, ~ clay (roof(ing)) ~ · Strang(dach)ziegel *m* [*DIN 456*]

~ **section**, ~ shape, ~ profile, ~ unit, ~ product, ~ trim, extrusion · Strangpreßartikel *m*, Strangpreßgegenstand *m*, Strangpreßerzeugnis *n*, Strangpreßprofil *n*

~ **shape**, ~ section, ~ profile, ~ unit, ~ product, ~ trim, extrusion · Strangpreßartikel *m*, Strangpreßgegenstand *m*, Strangpreßerzeugnis *n*, Strangpreßprofil *n*

~ **terra-cotta** → machine-~ ~

~ **trim**, ~ profile, ~ unit, ~ product, ~ shape, ~ section, extrusion · Strangpreßartikel *m*, Strangpreßgegenstand *m*, Strangpreßerzeugnis *n*, Strangpreßprofil *n*

~ **unit**, ~ profile, ~ trim, ~ product, ~ shape, ~ section, extrusion · Strangpreßartikel *m*, Strangpreßgegenstand *m*, Strangpreßerzeugnis *n*, Strangpreßprofil *n*

~ **vinyl (builders') fitting**, extrusion ~ (~) ~, ~ ~ (~) furniture · Strangpreß-Vinyl(bau)beschlag *m*

~ ~ **(builders') furniture**, extrusion ~ (~) ~, ~ ~ (~) fitting · Strangpreß-Vinyl(bau)beschlag *m*

~ ~ **(~) hardware**, ~ ~ (~) fittings, extrusion ~ (~) ~ · Strangpreß-Vinyl(bau)beschläge *mpl*

~ ~ **section**, ~ ~ shape, ~ ~ unit, ~ ~ product, ~ ~ trim, vinyl extrusion · Vinylstrangpreßprofil *n*, Vinylstrangpreßerzeugnis *n*

extruder, extrusion press, extrusion machine, extruding machine, extruding press · Strangpresse *f*

~ **-screw**, screw-extruder, extrusion auger, auger-type extrusion unit, auger-type machine · Schneckenpresse *f*, Extruder-Schnecke *f*

extruding, extrusion · Strangpressen *n*

~ **machine**, extrusion press, extruder, extrusion machine, extruding press · Strangpresse *f*

~ **press**, extruding machine, extrusion press, extrusion machine, extruder · Strangpresse *f*

extrusion, extruded section, extruded shape, extruded profile, extruded product, extruded unit, extruded trim · Strangpreßartikel *m*, Strangpreßgegenstand *m*, Strangpreßerzeugnis *n*, Strangpreßprofil *n*

~, extruding · Strangpressen *n*

~ **auger**, auger-type extrusion unit, auger-type machine, extruder-screw, screw-extruder · Extruder-Schnecke *f*, Schneckenpresse *f*

~ **chipboard** → extruded ~

~ **clay (roof(ing)) tile**, extruded ~ (~), ~ roof(ing) clay ~ · Strang(dach)ziegel *m* [*DIN 456*]

~ **concrete**, extruded ~ · Strangpreßbeton *m* [*International geschützte Markenbezeichnung: Pressolit*]

~ ~ **girder**, extruded ~ ~ · Strangpreßbetonträger *m*

~ ~ **product** → extruded concrete section

~ ~ **profile** → extruded concrete section

~ ~ **section** → extruded ~ ~

~ ~ **shape** → extruded concrete section

~ ~ **trim** → extruded concrete section

~ ~ **unit** → extruded concrete section

~ **floor tile**, extruded ~ ~ · stranggepreßte (Fuß)Bodenfliese *f*, ~ (Fuß-)Bodenplatte *f*

~ **interlocking clay roof(ing) tile**, extruded ~ ~ ~ ~, ~ ~ roof(ing) clay ~ · Strangfalz(dach)ziegel *m* [*Ebener oder leicht profilierter Strang-(dach)ziegel mit Falzen an den Längsseiten*]

~ ~ ~ **tile roof cover(ing)**, ~ ~ ~ ~ ~ sheathing, ~ ~ ~ ~ ~ cladding, extruded ~ ~ ~ ~, ~ ~ ~ ~ ~ roofing · Strangfalzziegel(dach)(ein)deckung *f*, Strangfalzziegelbedachung

~ **machine**, extruding machine, extrusion press, extruding press, extruder · Strangpresse *f*

~ **method**, ~ system · Strangfertigungsverfahren *n*, Strangpreßverfahren

~ **particle board** → extruded ~ ~

~ **plant** · Strangpreßanlage *f*

extrusion press — fabricating method

~ press, extruding machine, extruder, extrusion machine, extruding press · Strangpresse *f*

~ railing, extruded ~ · Strangpreßgeländer *n*

~ roof(ing) clay tile, extruded ~ ~ ~, ~ clay (roof(ing)) ~ · Strang-(dach)ziegel *m* [*DIN 456*]

~ system, ~ method · Strangfertigungsverfahren *n*, Strangpreßverfahren

~ vinyl (builders') fitting, extruded ~ (~) ~, ~ ~ (~) furniture · Strangpreß-Vinyl(bau)beschlag *m*

~ ~ (~) fittings, ~ ~ (~) hardware, extruded ~ (~) ~ · Strangpreß-Vinyl-(bau)beschläge *mpl*

~ ~ (~) furniture, extruded ~ (~) ~, ~ ~ (~) fitting · Strangpreß-Vinyl-(bau)beschlag *m*

~ ~ (~) hardware, ~ ~ (~) fittings, extruded ~ (~) ~ · Strangpreß-Vinyl-(bau)beschläge *mpl*

eye [*In classical architecture, the small disk in the centre of the volute of an Ionic capital*] · Auge in einer Schneckenlinie

~ → opaion

~ bar · Augenstab *m* [*U-Stahl, Flachstahl oder am Ende flach ausgeschmiedeter Rundstahl mit einem Bolzenloch in Stabendnähe, Auge genannt, für einen gelenkigen Anschluß mit Gelenkbolzen*]

~ bolt · Aug(en)bolzen *m*, Schraubenbolzen mit Ring, Ringbolzen, Ösenbolzen, Schrauböse *f*, Ösenschraube *f*

eye-brow (dormer), ~ **window** [*A window over which the eaves are raised in the form of a flat segment*] · Fledermausgaube *f*, Fledermausgaupe, Froschmaul *n*

eye level · Augenhöhe *f*, Sichthöhe

~ of a volute · Auge *n* in einer Schneckenlinie, Schneckenlinienauge [*Die Zirkelfläche in einer Schnecke eines ionischen oder korinthischen Kapitäls von welcher aus die Schneckenzüge konstruiert werden*]

eye-pleasing · gefällig [*im Aussehen*]

eye washing bath, eyewash shower [*A sanitary appliance installed in work places where there is risk of injury to eyes by solid particles or dangerous liquids. The appliance consists of a small bowl with two jets of water controlled by a hand or foot operated valve in such a way that the user can bathe the eyes without touching them*] · Augenwaschanlage *f*

F

f cut, flame-cut · brenngeschnitten

fabric · Einlage *f* [*(Dach)Pappe*]

~ [*misnomer*] → cloth

~, carcass; shell [*Canada*]; carcase [*deprecated*] [*A building or structure that is structurally complete but otherwise unfinished*] · Rohbau *m*

~ → ~ for roofing

~ → ~ reinforcement

~ → (felt) layer

~ backing [*misnomer*] → cloth base

~ base [*misnomer*] → cloth ~

~ fiber (US) → roofing ~ ~

~ flashing [*misnomer*] → cloth ~

~ ~ (piece) [*misnomer*] → cloth ~ (~)

~ for roofing, (roofing) fabric · Roh-(dach)pappe *f*

~ insert(ion) [*misnomer*] → cloth ~

~ lath(ing) [*misnomer*]; cloth ~, woven fabric ~ · Putz(träger)gewebe *n*

~ ply [*misnomer*] → cloth ~

fabric-reinforced [*misnomer*] → cloth-reinforced

fabric (reinforcement), mesh ~, reinforcing fabric · Stahlgewebebewehrung *f*, Stahlgewebebeeinlagen *fpl*, Mattenbewehrung, Mattenarmierung, Netzarmierung, Netzbewehrung, Netz(stahl)einlagen [*Eigenname: Baustahlgewebe*]

~ sheet(ing) [*misnomer*] → cloth ~

~ underlay [*misnomer*] → cloth bas₃

~ web, web of fabric · Rohpappenbahn *f*

~ wire [*misnomer*] → cloth ~

~ work, carcass ~, carcassing: shell work [*Canada*] [*Constructing the carcass of a building*] · Rohbauarbeiten *fpl*, Gebäude-~

to fabricate, to make, to manufacture · fertigen, herstellen

~ ~, to prepare [*sometimes incorrectly called 'to mix'*] · aufbereiten, herstellen, erzeugen [*Beton; Mörtel; Schwarz-(decken)mischgut*]

fabricating, making, fabrication, manufacturing · Fertigen *n*, Herstellen

~ bay, manufacturing ~, fabrication ~ · Herstellungsabteilung *f*, Fabrikationsabteilung, Produktionsabteilung, Fertigungsabteilung

~ cost(s), fabrication ~, manufacturing ~ · Herstellungskosten *f*, Fabrikationskosten, Produktionskosten, Fertigungskosten

~ cycle, fabrication ~, manufacturing ~ · Herstellungszyklus *m*, Fabrikationszyklus, Produktionszyklus, Fertigungszyklus

~ defect, fabrication ~, manufacturing ~ · Fabrikationsfehler *m*, Herstellungsfehler, Produktionsfehler, Fertigungsfehler

~ dimension → manufacturing ~

~ drawing, fabrication ~, manufacturing ~ · Herstellungszeichnung *f*, Fabrikationszeichnung, Produktionszeichnung, Fertigungszeichnung

~ method, fabrication ~, manufacturing ~ · Herstellungsverfahren *n*, Fabrikationsverfahren, Produktionsverfahren, Fertigungsverfahren

fabricating plant — façade panel 362

~ **plant,** fabrication ~, manufacturing ~ · Herstellungsbetrieb *m*, Fabrikationsbetrieb, Produktionsbetrieb, Fertigungsbetrieb

~ **process** → manufacturing ~

~ **program** (US); ~ **programme** (Brit.); fabrication ~, manufacturing ~ · Fabrikationsprogramm *n*, Herstellungsprogramm, Fertigungsprogramm, Produktionsprogramm

~ **technique,** ~ technic, fabrication ~, manufacturing ~ · Fertigungstechnik *f*, Herstellungstechnik, Fabrikationstechnik, Produktionstechnik

~ **technology,** fabrication ~, manufacturing ~ · Herstellungstechnologie *f*, Fabrikationstechnologie, Produktionstechnologie, Fertigungstechnologie

fabrication, preparation [*sometimes incorrectly called 'mixing'*] · (Auf)Bereitung *f*, Herstellung, Erzeugung, Erzeugen *n*, Herstellen, (Auf)Bereiten [*Beton; Mörtel; Schwarz(decken)mischgut*]

~, manufacturing, fabricating, making · Fertigen *n*, Herstellen

~ · Zuschnitt *m* [*Sprosse für kittlose Verglasung*]

~ **bay,** fabricating ~, manufacturing ~ · Fabrikationsabteilung *f*, Herstellungsabteilung, Produktionsabteilung, Fertigungsabteilung

~ **cost(s),** fabricating ~, manufacturing ~ · Herstellungskosten *f*, Fabrikationskosten, Produktionskosten, Fertigungskosten

~ **cycle,** fabricating ~, manufacturing ~ · Herstellungszyklus *m*, Fabrikationszyklus, Produktionszyklus, Fertigungszyklus

~ **defect,** fabricating ~, manufacturing ~ · Fabrikationsfehler *m*, Herstellungsfehler, Produktionsfehler, Fretigungsfehler

~ **dimension** → manufacturing ~

~ **drawing,** fabricating ~, manufacturing ~ · Herstellungszeichnung *f*, Fabrikationszeichnung, Produktionszeichnung, Fertigungszeichnung

~ **method,** fabricating ~, manufacturing ~ · Herstellungsverfahren *n*, Fabrikationsverfahren, Produktionsverfahren, Fertigungsverfahren

~ **operation** · Verarbeitungsvorgang *m* [*Stahl*]

~ **plant,** fabricating ~, manufacturing ~ · Herstellungsbetrieb *m*, Fabrikationsbetrieb, Produktionsbetrieb, Fertigungsbetrieb

~ **process** → manufacturing ~

~ **program** (US); ~ **programme** (Brit.); fabricating ~, manufacturing ~ · Fabrikationsprogramm *n*, Herstellungsprogramm, Fertigungsprogramm, Produktionsprogramm

~ **technique,** ~ technic, fabricating ~, manufacturing ~ · Fertigungstechnik *f*, Herstellungstechnik, Fabrikationstechnik, Produktionstechnik

~ **technology,** fabricating ~, manufacturing ~ · Herstellungstechnologie *f*, Fabrikationstechnologie, Produktionstechnologie, Fertigungstechnologie

fabricator, producer, maker, manufacturer · Erzeuger *m*, Hersteller, Fabrikant *m*

~ · Verarbeiter *m* [*Werkstoff*]

fabricators' test, manufacturers' ~, makers' ~ · Werkprobe *f*, Werkprüfung *f*, Werkversuch *m*

fac [*abbreviated*]; façade · Fassade *f*

façade [*abbreviated: fac*] · Fassade *f*

~ **articulation,** ~ division · Fassadengliederung *f*

~ **brick panel** → (clay) brick façade ~

~ **(building) component** → ~ (~) unit

~ **(~) member** → ~ (~) unit

~ **(~) unit,** ~ (~) member, ~ (~) component · Fassaden(bau)körper *m*, Fassaden(bau)element *n*, Fassadenbauteil *m*, *n* [*Fehlname: Fassadenbaueinheit f*]

~ **(clay) brick panel** → (clay) brick façade ~

~ **clean(s)ing** · Fassadenreinigung *f*

~ ~ **agent,** ~ **cleaner** · Fassadenreiniger *m*, Fassadenreinigungsmittel *n*, Fassadenreinigungsstoff *m*

~ **coat** · Fassadenbeschichtung *f*

~ **column** · Fassadenstütze *f*

~ **component** → ~ (building) unit

~ **construction** · Fassadenbau *m*

~ **covering** · Fassadenbelag *m*

~ **design** · Fassadengestaltung *f*

~ **development** · Fassadenabwicklung *f* [*Abwicklung der Schauseiten eines Bauwerkes oder mehrerer nebeneinanderstehende Bauten*]

~ **division,** ~ articulation · Fassadengliederung *f*

~ **double T frame** · Doppel-T-Fassadenrahmen *m*

~ **facing** → ~ lining

~ **girder** · Fassadenträger *m*

~ **H frame** · H-Fassadenrahmen *m*, Fassaden-H-Rahmen

~ **joint** · Fassadenfuge *f*, Fassadenstoß *m*

~ **lining,** ~ (sur)facing · Fassadenauskleidung *f*, Fassadenbekleidung, Fassadenverkleidung

~ **masonry wall,** front ~ ~ · Fassadenmauer *f*, Frontmauer

~ **member** → ~ (building) unit

~ **painting** · Fassadenmalerei *f*

~ **panel** · Fassadentafel *f*

façade pavilion — faced quilt

~ **pavilion** · Pavillon *m* [*Als Vorbau eines Barockschlosses*]

~ **polyvinyl chloride coat,** ~ PVC ~ · Polyvinylchlorid-Fassadenbeschichtung *f*, PVC-Fassadenbeschichtung

~ **protection agent,** ~ protection ~, ~ protective ~ · Fassadenschutzmittel *n*

~ **protection** · Fassadenschutz *m*

~ ~ **agent** → ~ protecting ~

~ **protective agent** → ~ protecting ~

~ **PVC coat,** ~ polyvinyl chloride ~ · Polyvinylchlorid-Fassadenbeschichtung *f*, PVC-Fassadenbeschichtung

~ **rendering** (Brit.); ~ stucco (US) · Fassaden(ver)putz *m*

~ **slab** · Fassadenplatte *f*

~ **stucco** (US); ~ rendering (Brit.) · Fassaden(ver)putz *m*

~ **(sur)facing** → ~ lining

~ **system** · Fassadenkonstruktion *f*

~ **tower** · Fassadenturm *m*

~ **unit** → ~ building ~

~ **ventilation grating,** ~ vent(ilating) ~ · Fassaden-Lüftungsgitter *n*

~ **wall** · Fassadenwand *f*

~ **with air circulation,** ventilated facade · durchlüftete Fassade *f*, zweischalige ~, Kaltfassade

to face, to sur ~, to line · auskleiden, bekleiden, verkleiden

~ ~, to sur~, to coat · überziehen, beschichten

~ ~ · verblenden

face · Außenfläche *f*, Kopffläche, Haupt *n*, Kopfseite *f*, Stirn(fläche) *f* [*Die Sichtfläche der Steine beim Natursteinmauerwerk*]

~ [*The surface of a parquet block on which the grade is determined*] · Güteseite *f* [*Die Fläche eines Parkettstabes, welche die Güte desselben bestimmt*]

~ · Stirn *f*, Haupt *n* [*Die vordere Ansichtsfläche eines Bogens, eines offenen Gewölbes, eines Trägers, usw.*]

~ → fair ~

~, **front** · Vorderseite *f*

~ · Haupt *n*, Stirn *f* [*Die vordere Ansichtsfläche eines Bogens, eines offenen Gewölbes, eines Trägers, usw.*]

~ **bend test,** normal ~ · Biegeprobe *f*, Faltversuch *m*,, Normalversuch mit der Raupe im Zug [*Die Raupe liegt im Zug. "R.i.Z"*]

~ **brick,** ~ clay ~, facing (clay) ~ · Ziegelverblender *m*, Vorsatzziegel, (Ver)Blendziegel, Fassadenziegel

~ ~ **bond** → ~ clay ~ ~

~ **(building) component,** ~ (~) unit, ~ (~) member · Sicht(bau)körper *m*, Sicht(bau)element *n* [*Fehlname: Sichtbaueinheit f*]

~ **(~) member,** ~ (~) unit, ~ (~) component · Sicht(bau)körper *m*, Sicht(bau)element *n*, [*Fehlname: Sichtbaueinheit f*]

~ **(~) unit,** ~ (~) member, ~ (~) component · Sicht(bau)körper *m*, Sicht(bau)element *n*, [*Fehlname: Sichtbaueinheit f*]

~ **(clay) brick,** facing (~) ~ · Ziegelverblender *m*, Vorsatzziegel, (Ver)Blendziegel, Fassadenziegel

~ **(~)** ~ **bond,** facing (~) ~ ~ · Verblenderverband *m*

~ **coat (plaster)** → finish(ing) ~ (~)

~ **component** → ~ building ~

~ **masonry wall** · Schildmauer *f*, Stirnmauer [*Mauer unter einem Schildbogen*]

~ **member** → ~ building ~

~ **mix(ture),** facing ~ · Vorsatzmischung *f*, Vorsatzgemisch *n*, (Ver-)Blendmischung, (Ver)Blendgemisch

~ **nailing,** direct ~ [*Nailing perpendicular to the initial surface or to the junction of the pieces joined*] · direkte (Ver)Nagelung *f*

~ **of an arch** · Stirnseite *f* eines Bogens

~ **paper** · Ansichtsseitenkarton *m* [*Gipskartonplatte*]

~ **slab** (US); facing ~ (Brit.) · Sichtplatte *f*, Frontplatte, Vorsatzplatte, Verblendplatte

~ ~ (US) → (stone) facing ~

~ **stone** → natural ~ ~

~ **string** → outer ~

~ **surface** · Sichtoberfläche *f*

~ **unit** → ~ building ~

~ **veneer,** outer ~, external ~, exterior ~, outside ~ [*Either side of a plywood panel where the grading rules draw no distinction between face and back*] · Außenfurnier *n*, Deckfurnier, Außenlage *f*, Außenschicht *f*

~ **wall** · Schildwand *f*, Stirnwand [*Wand unter einem Schildbogen*]

~ ~, **front** ~ · Vorderwand *f*, Frontwand

~ ~, **retaining** ~ · Stützwand *f*

face-work → facing

faced, sur~, coated · überzogen, beschichtet

~ **(building) mat** [*It has either paper or scrim stuck on or stitched to the base*] · abgedeckte (Bau)Matte *f*, ~ Dämmmatte

~ **(~) quilt** [*It has either paper or scrim stuck on or stitched to the base*] · abgedeckte (Bau)Matte *f*, ~ Isoliermatte

~ **concrete panel** · verblendete Betontafel *f*

~ **façade** · (Ver)Blendfassade *f* mit tragendem (Ver)Blendmauerwerk

~ **mat** → ~ building ~

~ **(on) both sides,** sur~ (~) ~ ~, coated (~) ~ ~ · beidseitig beschichtet

~ **quilt,** ~ building ~ [*It has either paper or scrim stuck on or stitched to the base*] · abgedeckte (Bau)Matte *f*, ~ Isoliermatte

faced wall — factor for impact

~ wall [*If the facing and backing are securely bonded together so that they will act as a unit, the entire thickness of the wall may be considered in strength calculations and in satisfying the requirements for minimum thickness*] · Mauer f mit tragendem (Ver)Blendmauerwerk

~ with granular cork → sur~ ~ ~ ~

~ ~ ~ material, sur~ ~ ~ ~ · bestreut, abgestreut [*Dachpappe und (bituminöser) Spachteldachbelag*]

~ ~ granulated cork → (sur)faced with granular ~

facia → fascia

facing, founder's black, black(en)ing, blackwash · Gießer(ei)schwärze f

~, sur~, coating · Beschichten n, Beschichtung f, Überziehen, Überzug m [*als Tätigkeit*]

~, sur~, lining · Auskleidung f, Bekleidung, Verkleidung, Belag m

~ [*Is the material which forms the face*] · Sichtflächenmaterial n

~ · Verblenden n

~, face-work, facing masonry (work) [*A finishing which requires a continuous 'background' structure to give the necessary support and fixing facilities for the materials forming the external face of the building. In no case, except in ashlar work, will the facing materials take loads more than their own weight*] · (Ver)Blendmauerwerk n, Vorsatzmauerwerk, Verblendung f

~ aggregate, ~ concrete ~ · Vorsatzzuschlag(stoff) m, Vorsatzzuschlagmaterial n

~ block, ~ tile [*See remark under 'Block'*] · (Ver)Blendblock(stein) m, (Ver)Blendstein, Vorsatzstein Vorsatzblock(stein)

~ ~ partition (wall), ~ tile ~ (~) (Ver)Blendblock(stein)-Trennwand f, (Ver)Blendsteintrennwand, Vorsatzsteintrennwand, Vorsatzblock(stein)-trennwand

~ board, ~ sheet, sur~ ~, lining ~ · Auskleidungsplatte f, Verkleidungsplatte, Bekleidungsplatte

~ brick, ~ clay ~, face (clay) ~ · Ziegelverblender m, Vorsatzziegel, (Ver-)Blendziegel, Fassadenziegel

~ ~ bond → ~ clay ~ ~

~ (clay) brick, face (~) ~ ~ · Ziegelverblender m, Vorsatzziegel, (Ver)Blendziegel, Fassadenziegel

~ (~)~bond, face (~) ~ ~ · Verblenderverband m

~ component → ~ unit

~ composition → coating material

~ compound → coating material

~ concrete · Vorsatzbeton m, (Ver-)Blendbeton

~ (~) aggregate · Vorsatzzuschlag(stoff) m, Vorsatzzuschlagmaterial n

~ ~ slab → lining ~ ~

~ engineering brick · Fassadenklinker m, (Ver)Blendklinker, Hochbauklinker, KMz [*DIN 105*]

~ foil, sur~ ~, lining ~ · Auskleidungsfolie f, Verkleidungsfolie, Bekleidungsfolie

~ layer · Vorsatzlage f, Vorsatzschicht f, (Ver)Blendlage, (Ver)Blendschicht

~ masonry wall · (Ver) Blendmauer f, Vorsatzmauer

~ ~ (work) → facing

~ mass → coating material

~ material → coating ~

~ ~ → lining ~

~ ~ · (Ver)Blend(werk)stoff m, Vorsatzmaterial n

~ member → ~ unit

~ method, ~ system, method of facing, system of facing · (Ver)Blendsystem n. (Ver)Blendverfahren n, Vorsatzsystem, Vorsatzverfahren

~ mix(ture), face ~ · Vorsatzmischung f, Vorsatzgemisch n, (Ver)Blendmischung, (Ver)Blendgemisch

~ panel, sur~ ~, lining ~ · Bekleidungstafel f, Auskleidungstafel, Verkleidungstafel

~ ~ · (Ver)Blendtafel f, Vorsatztafel

~ sheet → ~ board

~ slab → stone ~ ~

~ ~ (Brit.); face ~ ~ (US) · Sichtplatte f, Frontplatte, Vorsatzplatte, Verblendplatte

~ (stone)ware, sur~ ~, lining ~ · Auskleidungssteinzeug n, Verkleidungssteinzeug, Bekleidungssteinzeug

~ system → ~ method

~ tile · Verkleidungsfliese f, Verkleidungsplatte f [*Für Wände und Decken, aber nicht für (Fuß)Böden*]

~ ~ · (Ver)Blend(belag)platte f, (Ver-)Blendfliese, Vorsatz(belag)platte, Vorsatzfliese

~ ~, ~ block [*See remark under 'Block'*] · (Ver)Blendblock(stein) m, (Ver)Blendstein, Vorsatzstein, Vorsatzblock-(stein)

~ ~ partition (wall), ~ block ~ (~) · (Ver)Blendblock(stein)-Trennwand f, (Ver)Blendsteintrennwand, Vorsatzsteintrennwand, Vorsatzblock(stein)-trennwand

~ unit, ~ member, ~ component, sur~ ~, lining ~ · Auskleidungselement n, Verkleidungselement, Bekleidungselement

~ wall · (Ver)Blendwand f, Vorsatzwand

~ ware, (sur)facing (stone)~, lining (stone)~ · Auskleidungssteinzeug n, Verkleidungssteinzeug, Bekleidungssteinzeug

~ work · (Ver)Blendarbeiten fpl

factor for impact, allowance ~ ~, impact allowance, impact factor · Stoßzuschlag m, Stoßfaktor m

factor of safety — to fail

~ **of safety**, safety factor, FOS [*Many authorities prefer to use the term 'reduction factor' as being more realistic than the term 'safety factor'*] · Sicherheitsbeiwert *m*, Sicherheitsgrad *m*, Sicherheitszahl *f*, Sicherheitsfaktor *m* [*Baustoff*]

factory block → ~ (frame(d)) building

~ **bonding** · Werkleimung *f*

~ **building** → ~ frame(d) ~

~ ~, ~ block, industrial ~ · Industriegebäude *n*, Werkgebäude, Fabrikgebäude

factory-built chimney, prefab(ricated) ~ · Fertigschornstein *m*

~ **door** → stock (machine-made) ~

~ ~ **element**, prefab(ricated) ~ ~, stock (machine-made) ~ ~ · Fertigtürelement *n*

~ **fireplace**, prefab(ricated) ~ · Fertigkamin *m*

~ **girder**, prefab(ricated) ~ · Fertigträger *m*, Montageträger

~ **house**, industrially manufactured ~ · industriell gefertigtes Haus *n*

~ **partition (wall)**, prefab(ricated) ~ (~) · Trennmontagewand *f*, Fertigtrennwand, Trennfertigwand, Montagetrennwand, vorgefertigte Trennwand

~ **stair(case)**, prefab(ricated) ~ · Montagetreppe *f*, Fertig(teil)treppe

factory casting, ~ pre~ · Vorfertigung *f* im Betonwerk

~ **chimney** → ~ stack

~ **construction** · Fabrikbau *m*

~ **content**, prefabrication ~, ~ percentage, ~ fraction · Anteil *m* der Vorfertigung, Prozentsatz *m* ~ ~, Gehalt *m* ~ ~

~ **control** · Eigenüberwachung *f* [*Güteüberwachung im Werk*]

~ **cullet**, domestic ~ · Eigenbrocken *m*, Eigenscherben *f* [*Glasgemenge*]

~ **entrance** · Fabrikeingang *m*

~ **for (pre)cast (concrete) buildings**, ~ ~ ~ (~) blocks, ~ ~ prefab(ricated) ~ ~ · (Beton)Gebäudefabrik *f*, (Beton)Häuserfabrik

~ **fraction**, ~ percentage, ~ content, prefabrication ~ · Prozentsatz *m* der Vorfertigung, Anteil *m* ~ ~, Gehalt *m* ~ ~

~ **(frame(d)) building**, ~ (~) block, industrial (~) ~, ~ hangar · Fabrikhalle *f*, (Fabrikrahmen)Halle, Industrie(rahmen)halle, Werkhalle, (Werk)Rahmenhalle

~ **hygiene**, industrial ~ · Arbeitshygiene *f*, Industriehygiene

~ **lab(oratory)** · Werklabor(atorium) *n*, Betriebslabor(atorium)

factory-made · werkgefertigt

~ **block** → ~ building

~ **building**, ~ block, unit-built ~, prefab(ricated) ~ · Elementgebäude *n*, Montagegebäude, Fertig(teil)gebäude

~ **house**, unit-built ~, prefab(ricated) ~ · Elementhaus *n*, Montagehaus, Fertig(teil)haus

factory-painted, mill-painted, shop-painted · werkgestrichen

factory percentage, ~ fraction, ~ content, prefabrication ~ · Prozentsatz *m* der Vorfertigung, Anteil *m* ~ ~, Gehalt *m* ~ ~

~ **(pre)casting** · Vorfertigung *f* im Betonwerk

~ **prefabrication** · Fabrikvorfertigung *f*, Vorfertigung in der Fabrik

~-**primed**, mill-primed, shop-primed · werkgrundiert

factory primer, shop ~, mill ~ · Fertigungs-Grundanstrichmittel *n*, Fertigungsgrundiermittel, Fertigungsgrund(ierung) *m*, (*f*), Werkgrund(ierung) *m*, Werkgrundiermittel, Werkgrundanstrichmittel

~ **priming**, shop ~, mill ~ · Fertigungsgrundierung *f*, Fertigungsgrundieren *n*, Werk(statt)grundierung, Werk(statt)-grundieren

~-**produced component**, ~ member, ~ unit · Serien(bau)element *n*, Serien(bau)körper *m* [*Fehlname: Serienbaueinheit f*]

factory stack, ~ chimney, (chimney) stack, chimney stalk, chimney fun, industrial chimney, industrial stack, big chimney · (Fabrik)Esse *f*, (Fabrik-) Schlot *m*, Fabrikschornstein *m*, (Fabrik)Kamin *m*, Industrieschornstein, freistehender Schornstein

~ **window** · Fabrikfenster *n*

~ **with workers' housing** · Wohn- und Produktionskomplex *m*

faculty block, department ~, ~ building · Fakultätsbau *m*, Fakultätsgebäude *n* [*Hochschule*]

to fade · verbleichen, ausbleichen, verblassen

faded · verblaßt, verblichen

fading [*Bleaching of a colo(u)r by ag(e)ing or weathering. Chalking looks like fading, but the colo(u)r can be restored by a coat of varnish*] · Ausbleichen *n*, Verblassen, Verbleichen

f(a)eces pit, privy ~ · Fäkaliengrube *f*, Abortgrube, Latrinengrube, Abtrittgrube

fag(g)ot steel · Bundstahl *m*

FAI → (natural) fresh-air intake

faïence, ~ pottery [*Faïence is twice fired terra cotta — first the body at high temperature, then the body and the glaze at low temperature*] · Fayence *f*

~ **grille** [*Sometimes spelled 'grill'*] · Fayencegitter *n*

~ **mosaic tile** · Fayencemosaik(belag)-platte *f*, Fayencemosaikfliese *f*

~ **tile** · Fayence(belag)platte *f*, Fayencefliese *f*

to fail, to collapse · versagen, einstürzen [*Konstruktion*]

failure — fair-faced light(weight) concrete tile 366

failure, rupture, breaking, fail. · Bruch *m*

~, collapse · Versagen *n*, Einsturz *m* [*Konstruktion*]

~ bending angle, ultimate ~ ~, collapse ~ ~, breaking ~ ~, rupture ~ ~ · Bruchbiegewinkel *m*, Bruchbiegungswinkel

~ ~ moment → ultimate ~ ~

~ condition, collapse ~ · Einsturzbedingung *f*

~ ~, rupture ~, ultimate ~, breaking ~ · Bruchbedingung *f*

~ cross-section, rupture ~, breaking ~ · Bruchquerschnitt *m*

~ due to instability, ~ ~ ~ lability, collapse ~ ~ ~ · Labilitätseinsturz *m*

~ in buckling, rupture ~ ~, breaking ~, buckling failure, buckling rupture, buckling breaking · Knickbruch *m*

~ limit, limit of the ultimate strength · Bruchgrenze *f* [*Druckspannung im Beton bzw. Zugspannung in Stahl, die den Bruch verursachen*]

~ load, collapse ~ · Einsturzlast *f*

~ ~, rupture ~, breaking ~, ultimate ~ · Bruchlast *f*

~ loading → ultimate ~

~ mechanism, collapse ~ · Einsturzmechanismus *m*

~ strength, collapse ~ · Einsturzwiderstand *m*, Einsturzfestigkeit *f*

~ test, rupture ~, breaking ~ · Bruchprüfung *f*, Bruchversuch *m*, Bruchprobe *f*

~ zone, rupture ~, breaking ~ · Bruchzone *f*

fair building · Messegebäude *n*, Messehaus *n*

~ face, (exposed sur)face · Sichtfläche *f*

fair-faced aggregate → architectural (concrete) ~

~ block, ~ tile, exposed ~ [*See remark under 'Block'*] · Sichtblock(stein) *m*, Sichtstein

~ brickwork → ~ clay ~

~ cast compound unit → ~ (pre)cast (concrete) ~ ~

~ cast-concrete component, exposed ~ ~, ~ (concrete) cast(ing), ~ precast (concrete) component, ~ (pre)cast (concrete) member, ~ (pre)cast (concrete) unit · Sichtbeton(bau)körper *m*, Sichtbeton(bau)element *n* [*Fehlname: Sichtbetonbaueinheit f*]

~ cast (concrete) compound unit → ~ precast (~) ~ ~

~ cast-in-place concrete → ~ in(-)situ (cast) ~

~ cast(-)in(-)situ concrete → ~ in(-)situ (cast) ~

~ (clay) brickwork · Ziegelsichtmauerwerk *n*

~ concrete, architectural ~, exposed ~ · Architekturbeton *m*, Sichtbeton, Dekorativbeton, Dekor(ations)beton, Schmuckbeton, Ornamentbeton

~ (~) aggregate → architectural (~) ~

~ (~) beam, exposed ~ ~, architectural ~ ~ · Sichtbetonbalken(träger) *m*, Architekturbetonbalken(träger), Dekorativbetonbalken(träger), Dekor(ations)-betonbalken(träger)

~ (~) cast(ing), exposed ~ ~, ~ (pre)cast (concrete) component, ~ (pre)cast (concrete) member, ~ (pre-)cast (concrete) unit · Sichtbeton(bau)körper *m*, Sichtbeton(bau)element *n* [*Fehlname: Sichtbetonbaueinheit f*]

~ (~) column, architectural ~ ~, exposed ~ ~ · Sichtbetonstütze *f*, Architekturbetonstütze, Dekorativbetonstütze, Dekor(ations)betonstütze

~ (~) façade (building) unit, exposed ~ ~ (~) ~, ~ ~ ~ (~) member, ~ ~ ~ (~) component · Sichtbeton-Fassaden(bau)körper *m*, Sichtbeton-Fassaden(bau)element *n* [*Fehlname: Sichtbeton-Fassadenbaueinheit f*]

~ (~) finish, exposed ~ ~ · Betonsichtfläche *f*

~ (~) forms, ~ ~ form(work), ~ ~ shuttering, exposed ~ ~, architectural ~ ~ · Sichtbetonschalung *f*, Architekturbetonschalung, Dekorativbetonschalung, Dekor(ations)betonschalung

~ (~) form(work) → ~ ~ ~ forms

~ (~) panel, architectural ~ ~, exposed ~ ~ · Sichtbetontafel *f*, Architekturbetontafel, Dekorativbetontafel, Dekor(ations)betontafel

~ (~) shuttering → ~ ~ ~ forms

~ (~) stair(case), exposed ~ ~, architectural ~ ~ · Sichtbetontreppe *f*, Architekturbetontreppe, Dekorativbetontreppe, Dekor(ations)betontreppe

~ (~) texture, exposed ~ ~, architectural ~ ~ · Sichtbetonstruktur *f*, Architekturbetonstruktur, Dekorativbetonstruktur, Dekor(ations)betonstruktur

~ (~) wall, exposed ~ ~, architectural ~ ~ · Sichtbetonwand *f*, Architekturbetonwand, Dekorativbetonwand, Dekor(ations)betonwand

~ field concrete → ~ in(-)situ (cast) ~

~ finish, exposed ~, ~ work · Sichtausführung *f*

~ granite aggregate finish, exposed ~ ~ ~ · Granitsichtbetonoberfläche *f*

~ in(-)situ (cast) concrete, exposed ~ (~) ~, ~ cast(-)in(-)situ ~, ~ cast-in-place ~, ~ site-placed ~, ~ field ~, ~ poured(-in-place) ~ · Ort-Sichtbeton *m*

~ light(weight) concrete, exposed ~ ~, light(weight) fair-faced ~, light-(weight) exposed ~ · Architekturleichtbeton *m*, Sichtleichtbeton, Leicht-Architekturbeton, Leicht-Sichtbeton

~ ~ ~ block, exposed ~ ~ ~, light-(weight) fair-faced ~ ~, light(weight) exposed ~ ~, ~ ~ ~ tile · Architekturleichtbetonblock(stein) *m*, Sichtleichtbetonblock(stein)

~ ~ ~ tile → ~ ~ ~ block

~ **masonry (work)**, exposed ~ (~) · Sichtmauerwerk n

~ **poured(-in-place) concrete** → ~ in(-)situ (cast) ~

~ **(pre)cast compound unit** → ~ ~ concrete ~ ~

~ ~ **(concrete) component**, exposed ~ (~) ~, ~ ~ (~) unit, ~ ~ (~) member, ~ (concrete) cast(ing) · Sichtbeton(bau)körper m, Sichtbeton(bau)element n [*Fehlname: Sichtbetonbaueinheit f*]

~ ~ **(~) compound unit**, ~ prefab(ricated) ~ ~ ~ · Sicht(beton)fertig(bau)teil m, n, Architekturbetonfertig(bau)teil, Sicht(beton)montage(bau)teil, Architekturbetonmontage(bau)teil, Sichtfertigbeton(bau)teil, Sichtmontagebeton(bau)teil, Architekturmontagebeton(bau)teil [*Fehlnamen: Sichtbetonbauteil, Architekturbetonbauteil*]

~ ~ **(~) member**, exposed ~ (~) ~, ~ ~ (~) component, ~ ~ (~) unit, ~ (concrete) cast(ing) · Sichtbeton(bau)körper m, Sichtbeton(bau)element n [*Fehlname: Sichtbetonbaueinheit f*]

~ ~ **(~) unit**, exposed ~ (~) ~, ~ ~ (~) member, ~ ~ (~) component, ~ (concrete) cast(ing) · Sichtbeton(bau)körper m, Sichtbeton(bau)element n [*Fehlname: Sichtbetonbaueinheit f*]

~ **prefab(ricated) · concrete compound unit** → ~ (pre)cast (~) ~ ~

~ **R. C.**, ~ reinforced concrete, exposed ~ ~, reinforced fair-faced concrete, reinforced exposed concrete · Sichtstahlbeton m, Stahlsichtbeton

~ **reinforced concrete**, ~ R. C., exposed ~ ~, reinforced fair-faced concrete, reinforced exposed concrete · Sichtstahlbeton m, Stahlsichtbeton

~ **site-placed concrete** → ~ in(-)situ (cast) ~

~ **tile**, ~ block, exposed ~ [*See remark under 'Block'*] · Sichtblock(stein) m, Sichtstein

~ **work**, exposed ~, ~ finish · Sichtausführung f

~ ~, exposed ~ · Sichtarbeiten fpl

fair ground · Messegelände n

~ **stand** · Messestand m

fairy-tale Gothic (style) · Märchengotik f

fall, drop, lowering, decrease, decline · Rückgang m, Abfall m, Abnahme f

~ · Gefälle n

~ **of roof** → roof pitch

~ ~ **viscosity**, drop ~ ~, lowering ~ ~ · Viskositätsrückgang m, Zähigkeitsrückgang, Viskositätsabfall m, Zähigkeitsabfall

~ **pipe** → downpipe

falling ball test · Kugelfallversuch m, Kugelfallprobe f, Kugelfallprüfung f

~ **off in strength**, strength reduction, strength decrease · Festigkeitsabfall m, Festigkeitsabnahme f, Festigkeitseinbuße f, Festigkeitsminderung f

~ **sphere visco(si)meter** · Kugelfallviskosimeter n

false air · Falschluft f [*Luftmengen, die durch Undichtigkeit oder Rauchkanal und Schornstein eindringen und die Gasströmung stören*]

~ **arch**, corbel(led) ~, cantilever(ed) ~ [*It is not really an arch but is called an arch because of its shape. There is no real arch action, each course being corbel(l)ed out over the course below until the two sides meet*] · falscher Bogen m, Pseudobogen, Kragbogen

~ **arch(ed girder)** → cantilever(ed) ~ (~)

~ **brick** → corbel ~

~ **ceiling**, counter ~ [*A ceiling fixed independently on its own framework below a structural floor or flat roof*] · Unterdecke f, Zwischendecke, Fehldecke

~ ~ **of light(weight) blocks**, ~ ~ ~ ~ tiles · Zwischendecke f aus Leichtsteinen, Fehldecke ~ ~

~ ~ ~ ~ **slabs** · Zwischendecke f aus Leicht(bau)platten, Fehldecke ~ ~

~ ~ **slab** · Zwischendeckenplatte f, Fehldeckenplatte

~ ~ **with slanting joints** · Zwischendecke f mit schrägen Fugen, Fehldecke ~ ~ ~

~ ~ ~ **straight joints** · Zwischendecke f mit geraden Fugen, Fehldecke ~ ~ ~

~ **cupola** → corbel dome

~ **curved girder** → cantilever(ed) arch(ed girder)

~ **dome** → corbel ~

~ **door**, blank ~, blind ~, dead ~ · Blendtür f, Scheintür, Blindtür

~ **double-winged temple**, pseudo-dipteral ~ · Pseudodipteros(tempel) m, falscher Dipteros(tempel) [*1. Tempel mit Wandsäulen und umgebendem Säulenkranz. 2. Tempel mit doppelt breitem Pteron, jedoch ohne die innere Stützenreihe eines Dipteros*]

~ **fenestration**, blind ~, blank ~ · Blindbefensterung f

~ **masonry (work)** → corbel ~ (~)

~ **peripteral**, pseudoperipteral · pseudoperipteral

~ ~ **temple** → falsely ~ ~

~ **selvedge** · falsch geschnittene Kante f [*Sieb*]

~ **set(ting)**, quick ~, hesitation ~, rubber ~, premature stiffening, early stiffening · falsches Abbinden n, ~ Erstarren [*Die Erscheinung, daß ein Zementbrei beim Erstarrungsversuch vorübergehend ansteift und dann wieder weicher wird. Bei der Verarbeitung eines solchen Zements zu Mörtel und Beton wird diese vorübergehende Ansteifung meist gar nicht bemerkt*]

false vault — farm stock fence

~ vault → corbel ~

~ **vaulting** · falsche Wölbung f [*Die Steine sind stufenweise vorgekragt, um eine Öffnung oder einen Raum zu überspannen und treffen sich im Scheitelpunkt*]

~ **window**, blank ~, blind ~, dead ~ · blindes Fenster n, Blindfenster, Blendfenster, Scheinfenster

false(ly) peripteral temple, pseudoperipteral ~, pseudoperipteros (~) [*A Greek temple with two porticos and engaged columns or pilasters on the sides*] · falscher Peripteros(tempel) m, Pseudoperipteros(tempel)

~ **prostyle temple**, pseudoprostyle ~ · Pseudoprostylos(tempel) m, falscher Prostylos(tempel) [*Ein griechischer Tempel mit Wandsäulen anstelle der Säulen an den Stirnseiten*]

family · Gruppe f [*Werkstoff*]

~ **dwelling unit** (US); ~ dwelling (Brit.) · Familienwohnung f

~ **mansion**, domus · römisches Privathaus n

~ **of cables**, ~ ~ ropes, rope family, cable family · Seilschar f

~ ~ **ropes**, ~ ~ cables, rope family, cable family · Seilschar f

~ **room**, all-purpose ~ · Mehrzweckraum m, Vielzweckraum

~ **unit** → house

fan · Ventilator m

~ **air heating** → fan(-assisted) (warm-)air (central) ~

~ **anchorage** · Fächerverankerung f

fan(-assisted) operation · Ventilatorbetrieb m [*Luft(be)heizung*]

~ **ventilation**, ~ venting · Ventilatorlüftung f, Drucklüftung [*Die Frischluft wird mit Ventilatoren in einen Raum gedrückt, wodurch im Raum ein Überdruck entsteht*]

~ **(warm-)air (central) heating**, (warm-)air (~) ~, (warm-)air heating system · (Warm)Luft-Zentralheizung f (mit Ventilatoren), (Warm)Luft-Mehrraumheizung (~ ~) [*Die Warmluft wird mit Ventilatoren in die zu beheizenden Räume gedrückt*]

fan beam, ~-shaped ~ · Fächer-Lichtstrahl m

~ **central heating** → fan(-assisted) (warm-)air (~) ~

~ **convector (heater)**, ~ ~ fire, ~ heating convector · Lüftungskonvektor m, Klimakonvektor, Düsenkonvektor

~-**cooled** · ventilatorgekühlt

~ **cooling** · Ventilatorkühlung f

fancy sheet metal, show ~ ~, textured ~ ~, ~ metal sheet · Dessinblech n, dessiniertes Blech

~ **veneer**, patterned ~, figured ~, rare ~ · Maserfurnier n

fan drive · Ventilatorantrieb m

~ **engineering** · Ventilatortechnik f

~ **guard** · Ventilatorschutzkorb m

~ **heater** · Ventilatorheizer m

~ **heating** → fan(-assisted) (warm-)air (central) ~

~ ~ **convector**, ~ convector (heater), ~ convector fire · Lüftungskonvektor m, Klimakonvektor, Düsenkonvektor

fanlight [*An area of glazing above a door*] · Oberlicht n, Tür~

~ **opener** · Oberlichtöffner m, Tür~

fanlike decorative fixture, ~ ornament, ~ enrichment · Fächerornament n, Fächerverzierung f

fan noise, ~ sound · Ventilatorgeräusch n

~ **operation** → fan(-assisted) ~

fan-palm vault [*A hybrid of the palm and fan types of vault*] · Fächerpalmengewölbe n, Palmenfächergewölbe

fan(-shaped) beam · Fächer-Lichtstrahl m

~ **tracery** [*The elaborate ribs and veins of a fan vault*] · Rippenwerk n [*Fächergewölbe*]

~ **window** · Fächerfenster n [*Fenster des romanischen Stils mit schmalem Unterteil und ausgebreitetem Oberteil aus kleinen Rundbogen gebildetem Rand*]

fan shroud · Schirmblech n, Ventilatorhaube f

~ **sound**, ~ noise · Ventilatorgeräusch n

~ **tracery**, fan-shaped ~ [*The elaborate ribs and veins of a fan vault*] · Rippenwerk n [*Fächergewölbe*]

~ **vault**, conoidal ~ [*All the ribs have an identical curvature, resembling a fan. This type is peculiar to England, and occurs only in late Gothic work*] · Fächergewölbe n, Trichtergewölbe, normannisches Gewölbe, (angel)sächsisches Gewölbe

~ **vaulted**, conoidal ~ · fächerüberwölbt

~ **ventilation** → fan(-assisted) ~

~ **venting** → fan(-assisted) ventilation

~ **(warm-)air (central) heating** → fan(-assisted) ~ (~) ~

~ **window**, fan-shaped ~ · Fächerfenster n [*Fenster des romanischen Stils mit schmalem Unterteil mit aus kleinen Rundbogen gebildetem Rand*]

far face [*e.g. of a wall. The face farthest from the viewer, may be the outside or inside face, depending on whether one is inside looking out or outside looking in*] · gegenüberliegende Seite f [*z.B. einer Wand*]

farm building, agricultural ~ · Landwirtschaftsgebäude n

~ ~ **construction** · Bau m landwirtschaftlicher Gebäude

~ **service building**, agricultural ~ ~ · (landwirtschaftliches) Wirtschaftsgebäude n

~ **stock fence** [*B.S. 3854*] · Viehzaun m

fa(s)cia — fatigue behaviour

fa(s)cia [*The long and relatively narrow upright name board over a shop front*] · Ladenschild *n*

~ · Faszie *f*, Gurt *m* [*Einer der drei, manchmal auch zwei, übereinanderliegenden, von unten nach oben leicht vorspringenden Streifen, die den Architrav der ionischen und korinthischen (Säulen)Ordnung waag(e)recht unterteilen*]

~, fasc. [*A strip of wood covering the ends of the rafters at the eaves of a roof*] · Sparrenabdeckung *f*, (Dach)Traufenstreifen *m*

~ (board), eave(s) fa(s)cia [*A board on edge nailed along the feet of the rafters. It often carries the eave(s) gutter and may also act as a tilting fillet*] · Stirnbrett *n*, Traufbrett, Windbrett

fashionable Louis XVI architect · Modearchitekt *m* des Louis-Seize

fast, proof, resistant, resisting · beständig, fest, echt gegen, sicher, widerstandsfähig

~ paint · echte Farbe *f*, feste **~**, dauerhafte **~**, beständige **~**

~-setting glass, short **~**, quick-setting **~** · kurzes Glas *n*

~ sheet, stand **~**, dead light, fixed sash [*A window or part of a window which does not open*] · Festfenster *n*

~ to acid → acid-resisting

~ ~ cement, cementfast · zementecht, zementbeständig, zementfest

~ ~ light, lightfast, proof to light, lightproof, resistant to light, light resistant · lichtbeständig, lichtecht

~ ~ lime, limefast · kalkecht, kalkbeständig, kalkfest [*Kalkecht, d.h. gegen Basen widerstandsfähig sind nur Farben, die sich, in Kalkmilch oder Kalkwasser erhitzt, nicht verändern*]

~ ~ soap(s), soapproof · seifenfest, seifenbeständig, seifenecht

to fasten, to fix · befestigen

fastener, retainer · Halter(ung) *m*, (*f*)

~, fastening, fixing device, fixing (acessory), fixing means · Befestigungsmittel *n*

fastening, fastener, fixing device, fixing (acessory), fixing means · Befestigungsmittel *n*

~ hardware [e.g. clips, angles, inserts, bolts, etc.] · Befestigungszeug *n*

~ point, fixing **~** · Befestigungsstelle *f*

~ with transverse cables anchored to ground · Verspannung *f* mit bodenverankerten Querseilen

fastness, resistance [*Ability to resist attacks*] · Beständigkeit *f*, Festigkeit, Widerstand *m*, Echtheit

~ against damage, resistance **~ ~**, damage resistance, damage fastness · Beständigkeit *f* gegen Beschädigungen, Festigkeit **~ ~**, Widerstand *m* **~ ~**

~ degree, resistance **~**, degree of resistance, degree of fastness · Widerstandsgrad *m*, Festigkeitsgrad, Beständigkeitsgrad

~ property, resistance **~** · Beständigkeitseigenschaft *f*, Echtheitseigenschaft

~ to alcohol, resistance **~ ~**, alcohol resistance, alcohol fastness · Alkoholbeständigkeit *f*, Alkoholfestigkeit, Alkoholechtheit, Alkoholwiderstand *m*

~ ~ alkali(s), resistance **~ ~**, alkali resistance, alkali fastness · Alkali(en)festigkeit *f*, Alkalie(n)widerstand *m*, Alkali(en)beständigkeit, Alkali(en)echtheit

~ ~ bleeding, resistance **~ ~** · Ausblutechtheit *f* [*Pigment*]

~ ~ cold, resistance **~ ~** · Kältebeständigkeit *f*, Kältewiderstand *m*, Kälteechtheit, Kältefestigkeit

~ ~ cement, cement fastness · Zementechtheit *f*

~ ~ heat, resistance **~ ~**, heat resistance, heat fastness, thermal resistance, thermal fastness · Hitzebeständigkeit *f*, Hitzeechtheit, Hitzefestigkeit, Hitzewiderstand *m*

~ ~ ~, resistance **~ ~**, stability **~ ~**, heat resistance, heat fastness, heat stability, thermal resistance, thermal fastness, thermal stability · Hitzebeständigkeit *f*, Hitzeechtheit, Hitzefestigkeit, Hitzewiderstand *m*

~ ~ light, proofness to light, lightfastness, lightproofness, light resistance, stability to light · Lichtechtheit *f*, Lichtbeständigkeit *f*

~ ~ lime, resistance **~ ~**, lime resistance, lime fastness · Kalkbeständigkeit *f*, Kalkechtheit, Kalkwiderstand *m*, Kalkfestigkeit

~ ~ oil → oil fastness

~ ~ soluble glass, **~ ~** water **~,** resistance **~ ~ ~** · Wasserglasechtheit *f*

~ ~ spirit → spirit resistance

~ ~ swelling, resistance **~ ~**, swelling fastness, swelling resistance · Quellfestigkeit *f*, Quellbeständigkeit

~ ~ washing, resistance **~ ~** · (Ab-)Waschfestigkeit *f*, (Ab)Waschwiderstand *m*, (Ab)Waschbeständigkeit

~ ~ water, resistance **~ ~**, water resistance, water fastness · Wasserbeständigkeit *f*, Wasserfestigkeit, Wasserwiderstand *m*

~ ~ ~ glass, **~ ~** soluble **~,** resistance **~ ~ ~** · Wasserglasechtheit *f*

fat concrete, (cement-)rich **~** · fetter Beton *m*, zementreicher **~**

~ lime → high-calcium **~**

~ mix(ture) → rich **~**

~ mortar, rich **~** · fetter Mörtel *m*, Fettmörtel

~ pitch, candle **~**, fatty-acid **~** · Fettpech *n*

fatigue, endurance · (Werk)Stoffermüdung *f*, (Material)Ermüdung

~ action, endurance **~** · Ermüdungsbeanspruchung *f*

~ behaviour (Brit.); **~** behavior (US); endurance **~** · Ermüdungsverhalten *n*

fatigue bending failure — felt

~ **bending failure**, endurance ~ ~ · Dauerbiegebruch *m*

~ **bend(ing) test**, endurance ~ ~ · Dauerbiegeprobe *f*, Dauerbiegeprüfung *f*, Dauerbiegeversuch *m*

~ **characteristic**, endurance ~ · Ermüdungsmerkmal *n*

~ **coefficient**, endurance ~ · Ermüdungsbeiwert *m*

~ **crack**, endurance ~ · Ermüdungsriß *m*

~ **degree**, endurance ~ · Ermüdungsgrad *m*

~ **failure**, ~ rupture, ~ fracture, endurance ~ · Dauerbruch *m*, Ermüdungsbruch

~ **fracture**, ~ rupture, ~ failure, endurance ~ · Dauerbruch *m*, Ermüdungsbruch

~ **in bending**, endurance ~ ~, ~ ~ flexure, flexural fatigue, flexural endurance, bending fatigue, bending endurance · Biegeermüdung *f*, Biegungsermüdung

~ ~ **compression**, endurance ~ ~ · Druckermüdung *f*

~ ~ **flexure** → ~ ~ bending

~ ~ **tension** · Zugermüdung *f*

~ **limit**, endurance ~, limit of endurance, limit of fatigue · Ermüdungsgrenze *f*

~ **load**, endurance ~ · Ermüdungslast *f*

~ **of bond**, endurance ~ ~ · Haftermüdung *f*, Verbundermüdung [*Beton*]

~ ~ **the concrete**, endurance ~ ~ ~ · Betonermüdung *f*

~ **phenomenon**, endurance ~ · Ermüdungserscheinung *f*

~ **resistance**, ~ strength, endurance (strength), endurance limit [*Is defined as the number of cycles of loading imposed before fracture terminates the test*] · Arbeitsfestigkeit *f*, Dauerfestigkeit, Ermüdungsfestigkeit

~ **rupture**, ~ fracture, ~ failure, endurance ~ · Dauerbruch *m*, Ermüdungsbruch

~ **strength** → ~ resistance

~ ~ **under pulsating tensile stresses** · Zugschwellfestigkeit *f*

~ **test**, endurance ~ · Ermüdungsversuch *m*, Ermüdungsprüfung *f*, Ermüdungsprobe *f*

fattening, thickening [*An increase in consistency of paint on storage, not necessarily to such an extent as to make it unusable*] · Nachdicken *n*, Eindicken

fatty acid · Fettsäure *f*

~ ~ **of linseed oil** · Leinöl-Fettsäure *f*, destillierte Fettsäure des Leinöls [*DIN 55960*]

fatty-acid pitch, candle ~, fat ~ · Fettpech *n*

fatty alcohol · Fettalkohol *m*

~ **oil** · fettes Öl *n*

fauces, passage · Gang *m* [*in einem römischen Privathaus*]

fault, defect · Fehler *m*, Mangel *m*

~ **current**, earth-leakage ~ · Fehlerstrom *m*, Erdschlußstrom

~ ~ **circuit breaker**, earth-leakage (~) ~ ~ · Fehlerstrom-Schutzschalter *m*, Erdschlußstrom-Schutzschalter

faulty, defective, unsound · fehlerhaft, mangelhaft, schadhaft

fayalite, ferrous orthosilicate · Fayalit *m*, eisenhaltiges Orthosilikat *n*, Eisenglas *n*, $2FeO \cdot SiO_2$

FBRK → firebrick

FD → fire department

FD → forced draught

FDW HTR, feedwater heater · Speisewassererwärmer *m*

to feather [*To blend the edge of a new material smoothly into the old surface*] · einbinden

feather [*B.S. 3447; B.S. 952*]; feathers [*ASTM C 162–56*]; dirt · Blasenschleier *m* [*Glas*]

featheredge brick → arch ~

feathers [*ASTM C 162–56*]; feather [*B.S. 3447; B.S. 952*]; dirt · Blasenschleier *m* [*Glas*]

feature (of style) → (architectural) feature

feces pit → faeces ~

fee system, scale of professional charges · Architektengebührenordnung *f*, Gebührenordnung für Architekten

feebly hydraulic lime · schwach hydraulischer Kalk *m*

feed, head, screen ~, material to be screened · Aufgabegut *n*, Haufwerk *n*, Siebgut, Einlaufgut [*Siebtechnik*]

~ **line**, flow ~ · Vorlaufheizung *f*, Zulaufheizung

~ **(~)** · Zu(bringer)leitung *f*

~ **pipe**, flow ~ · Vorlaufrohr *n*, Zulaufrohr

feedwater, FW · Speisewasser *n*

~ **heater**, FDW HTR · Speisewassererwärmer *m*

feed water preparation · Speisewasseraufbereitung *f*

~ ~ **tank** · Speisewassergefäß *n*

feeding passage · Futtergang *m* [*Stall*]

feeling of comfort, comfortable feeling · Behaglichkeitsgefühl *n*

feet run → foot ~

fel(d)spar · Feldspat *m*

~ **glaze(d finish)**, ~ glazing, ~ glazed coat(ing) · Feldspatbeglasung *f*, Feldspatglasur *f*

~ **meal** · Feldspatmehl *n*

feldspathic sandstone, arcosic grit, arkose (sandstone) · Arkose *f*, Arkosesandstein *m*, feldspatreicher Sandstein

to felt · verfilzen

felt · Filzpappe *f*

felt — Ferrari cement

~ → felt(ed fabric)

~-and-gravel roof · Kiespreßdach(belag) n, (m)

felt-backed lino(leum), lino(leum) calendered on to a bitumen impregnated paper felt [B.S. 1863] · Linoleum n auf Filzhinterlegung, ~ ~ Filzunterlage, ~ ~ Filzrücklage, ~ ~ Filzträger(schicht)

felt back(ing) → felt(ed fabric) backing

felt-base floor cover(ing), ~ floor (ing) (finish) · Feltbase(belag) f, (m) [Zu diesen Belägen gehören Stragula, Balatum und Bedola. Es sind mit Bitumen getränkte Wollfilzpappen mit beiderseitigem Isolieranstrich. Auf der Schauseite sind die Bahnen mit einer Schutzschicht gespachtelt, um sie für den Auftrag eines Lackfarben-Druckmusters vorzubereiten]

felt for roofing → dry felt

(~) layer, (~) ply, fabric · Einlage f, Träger m [Rohfilzpappe ist ein Erzeugnis, das als Einlage für die Herstellung von Dachpappen und nackten Pappen dient]

(~) ply → (~) layer

to felt-treat · abfilzen [Putz]

felt with cork, felted fabric ~ ~ · Korkfilz m

felt(ed fabric) · Filz m

~ (~) backing → ~ (~) base

~ (~) base, ~ (~) back(ing), ~ (~) underlay, underfelt, felting · Filzhinterlegung f, Filzrücklage f, Filzunterlage, Filzträger(schicht) m, (f)

~ (~) board, ~ (~) sheet, board of felt(ed fabric), sheet of felt(ed fabric) · Filzplatte f

~ (~) cylinder · Filzfarbroller m, Filzrolle f, Filzwalze f, Filz-Farbrollgerät]

~ (~) foil · Filzrolle f

~ (~) for roofing → dry felt

~ (~) insert · Filzeinlage f

~ (~) insulating strip, ~ (~) insulation(-grade) ~ ~ · Filz-Isolierstreifen m

~ (~) mat, ~ (~) pad · Filzmatte f

~ (~) ~ with cork, ~ (~) pad ~ ~ · Korkfilzmatte f

~ (~) pad, ~ (~) mat · Filzmatte f

~ (~) ~ with cork, ~ (~) mat ~ ~ · Korkfilzmatte f

~ (~) panel · Filztafel f

~ (~) roller · Filz-Farbrollgerät n

~ (~) seal · Filz(ab)dichtung f [Erzeugnis]

~ (~) seal(ing) · Filz(ab)dichtung f

~ (~) sheet → ~ (~) board

~ (~) strip · Filzband n

~ (~) underlay → ~ (~) base

~ (~) washer · Filzunterlegscheibe f

~ (~) web, web of felt(ed fabric) · Filzbahn f

~ (~) with cork · Korkfilz m

felted jute · Jutefilz m

felting → felt(ed fabric) base

~ material · Verfilzungsstoff m, Verfilzungsmaterial n [Asbestfasern, Pflanzenfasern und Tierhaare. Sie werden unter anderem für Wärmeschutzmassen verwendet]

~ property · Verfilzbarkeit f

F(E)M → (fixed-)end moment

female changing room, women's ~ ~, ladies' ~ ~ · Damenumkleide(raum) f, (m), Frauenumkleide(raum)

~ (drawing) room, ladies' (~) ~, women's (~) ~ [See remark under 'drawing room'] · Damenzimmer n, Damenraum m

~ hairdressing shop, ladies' ~ ~, women's ~ ~ · Damen(friseur)salon m

~ room → ~ drawing ~

~ toilet, women's ~, ladies' ~ · Damentoilette f

to fence · abzäunen, umzäunen, einzäunen

~ ~ · einfried(ig)en

fence · Zaun m

(~) hurdle, (wattle) ~ · (Zaun)Hürde f

~ material · Einzäunungsmaterial n, Zaunmaterial

~ of boards, board(ed) fence, boarding · Brett(er)zaun m, Planke f

(~) picket, (~) stake, (~) post, fencing ~ · Pfahl m, Pfosten m, Zaun~

(~) post, (~) stake, (~) picket, fencing ~ · Pfahl m, Pfosten m, Zaun~

(~) stake, (~) picket, (~) post, fencing ~ · Pfahl m, Pfosten m, Zaun~

~ wire netting · Zaundrahtgeflecht n

fencing [The action of putting up fences or enclosing with a fence] · Abzäunen n, Umzäunen, Einzäunen

~ [fences collectively] · Einzäunung f, Umzäunung

~ [The action of protecting, or of setting up a defence against] · Einfried(ig)en n

~ picket → fence ~

~ piste · Fechtbahn f

~ post → fence ~

~ stake → fence ~

fenes(tration) · Befensterung f

feretory [A chapel in which a shrine or shrines containing relics are kept] · Reliquienkapelle f

~ [A room in which a shrine or shrines containing relics are kept] · Reliquienraum m

~ [A shrine containing relics, placed behind the high altar] · Reliquienschrein m

~, tomb chapel · Grabkapelle f, Coemetrialkapelle

Ferrari cement iron-ore ~ · (Eisen-)Erzzement m, Ferrarizement

ferric oxid(e) — fiberglass reinforced plastic 372

ferric oxid(e) (US); ∼ oxide (Brit.) [*chemical names*]; hematite [*substance*] · Hämatit *m*, Roteisenstein *m*, Eisenglanz *m*, Eisenglimmer *m*, Glanzeisenerz *n*, Roteisenerz, Eisenrahm *m*, roter Glaskopf *m*, Blutstein, Fe_2O_3

∼ sulphate (Brit.); ∼ sulfate (US) · Eisen-III-Sulfat *n*

ferrite · Ferrit *m*

∼ grain · Ferritkorn *n*

∼ region · Ferritgebiet *n*

∼ stainless steel · ferritischer (rostfreier) Edelstahl *m*

ferritic steel · ferritischer Stahl *m*

ferritising (Brit.); ferritizing (US) · ferritisierend

ferritizing (US); ferritising (Brit.) · ferritisierend

ferro-clad brick metal-cased ∼ · blechummantelter Stein *m*

∼ refractory (product), metal-cased ∼ (∼) · blechummanteltes feuerfestes Erzeugnis *n*, ∼ ff. *n*

ferrocyanid(e) blue, iron ∼ · Zyaneisenblau *n*, Eisencyan(pigment) *n*, Zyaneisenfarbe *f*

∼ ferrous article, ∼ product, iron ∼ · Eisenartikel *m*, Eisengegenstand *m*, Eisenerzeugnis *n*

∼ chlorid(e) (US); ∼ chloride (Brit.) · Eisenchlorür *n*, Ferrochlorid *n*, $FeCl_2 + 4H_2O$

∼ connector → ∼ timber ∼

∼ floor hardener, ∼ ∼ hardening agent · Eisen-(Fuß)Bodenhärtemittel *n*, Eisen-(Fuß)Bodenhärter *m*, Eisen-(Fuß)Bodenhärtungsmittel, Eisen-(Fuß)Bodenhärtungsstoff *m*

∼ metal · Eisenmetall *n*

∼ orthosilicate, fayalite · Fayalit *m*, eisenhaltiges Orthosilikat *n*, Eisenglas *n* $2FeO \cdot SiO_2$

∼ pipe, iron ∼ · Eisenrohr *n*

∼ product, ∼ article, iron ∼ · Eisenartikel *m*, Eisengegenstand *m*, Eisenerzeugnis *n*

∼ sulphate (Brit.); ∼ sulfate (US) · Eisen-II-Sulfat *n*

∼ (timber) connector, iron (∼) ∼ (Brit.); ∼ connector (US) · Eisendübel *m* [*Holzverbinder*]

∼ titanate, ilmenite · Eisentitanat *n*, Ilmenit *m*, Titaneisen *n*, $FeO \cdot TiO_2$

∼ trap, iron ∼ [*A tubular ferrous device designed to prevent by means of a water seal the passage of foul gases from a waste pipe into a building*] · Eisen-(Wasser)(Geruch)Verschluß *m* [*Fehlnamen: Eisensiphon m, Eisensyphon, Eisentraps m*]

∼ wire, iron ∼ · Eisendraht *m*

ferruginous limestone, calcareous ironstone · Kalkeisenstein *m*

ferrule, sleeve, tailpiece · Muffenverbindung *f* (mit Stemmdichtung)

festival hall, grand ∼, banquet(ing) ∼, civic auditorium · Festhalle *f*, Bananketthalle

∼ room, banquet(ing) ∼, grand chamber · Festsaal *m*, Bankettsaal

∼ theatre · Festspielhaus *n*, Festspielbühne *f*

festoon, swag, encarpa, garland [*A carved, modelled or painted garland of flowers, fruit or leaves, suspended in a curve between two points*] · Gehänge *n*, Feston *n*, Gewinde *n*, Girlande *f*

∼ leaf, garland ∼, swag ∼, encarpa ∼ · Gehängeblatt *n*, Gewindeblatt, Festonblatt, Girlandenblatt

fettling, towing · Lederhartverputzen *n*, Verputzen in trockenem Zustand [*Steinzeugrohrindustrie*]

fftg → fire fighting

FH → fire-hose

FH → flat head

FHC, (fire-)hose cabinet · (Feuer-)Löschschlauchschrank *m*

FHR, (fire-)hose rack · (Feuer)Löschschlauchgestell *n*

FHY, fhy, fire hydrant, fire plug · (Feuer-)Löschwasserständer *m* [*DIN 14244*]

fiber backing (US) → fibre base

∼ base (US) → fibre ∼

fiberboard (US) → (wood) fibreboard

∼ board, ∼ sheet (US); fibreboard ∼ (Brit.) · Faserschliffplatte *f*

∼ ceiling (US) → (wood) fibreboard ∼

∼ finish (US); fibreboard ∼ (Brit.) · (Holz)Faserplattenbelag *m*

fiber(board) lath(ing) (US) → fibre(board) ∼

fiberboard nail (US); fibreboard ∼ (Brit.) · Faserplattennagel *m*

∼ sheathing (US) → fibreboard ∼

∼ sheet → ∼ board

∼ tile (US); fibreboard ∼ (Brit.) · Faserschliff(belag)platte *f*, Faserschliif-Fliese *f*

fiber (building) mat (US); fibre (∼) ∼ (Brit.) [*It has a low density*] · Faser(bau)matte *f*, Faserdämmatte

∼ conduit → ∼ wiring ∼

fibered glass (US) → glass wool

∼ plaster (US); fibrous ∼ · Faser(stoff)putz *m*

fiberglass (US); fibre glass (Brit.) [*Glass drawn into thin threads for spinning and weaving*] · Faserglas *n*

∼ insulation (material) (US); fibre glass ∼ (∼) (Brit.) · Glasfaserdämmstoff *m*, Glasfaserdämmaterial *n*

∼ reinforced plastic (US) → glass reinforced laminate

fiberglass staple fiber — fibre plug

~ staple fiber (US); fibreglass staple fibre (Brit.) · Glasstapelfaser f, Stapelglasfaser

fiber grease (US); fibre ~ (Brit.) · Faserfett n

~ insulation(-grade) material, ~ insulating ~ (US); fibre ~ ~, fibre lagging (Brit.); ~ insulator · Faserdämmstoff m [D N 18165]

fiber lath(ing) (US) → fibre(board) ~

~ mat (US) → ~ building ~

~ metallurgy (US); fibre ~ (Brit.) · Fasermetallurgie f

~ netting (US); fibre ~ (Brit.) · Fasergeflecht n

~ plug (US) → fibre ~

~-reinforced (US); fibre-reinforced (Brit.); fibrated · faserarmiert

~ reinforcement (US); fibre ~ (Brit.) · Faserverstärkung f, Faserarmierung [Werkstoff]

~ rope (US); fibre ~ (Brit.) · Faserstrick m

~ stress (US) → fibre ~

~ tube (US); fibre ~ (Brit.) · Faserröhre f

~ underlay (US) → fibre base

~ wallboard (US); fibre ~ (Brit.) · Faserwandplatte f, Wandfaserplatte

~ washer (US); fibre ~ (Brit.) · Faserunterlegscheibe f

~ (wiring) conduit (US); fibre (~) ~ (Brit.) [These conduits consist of solid tubes composed of fiber or other bibulous substance, impregnated and coated with asphalt or coal-tar pitch or wax] · Faser-(Elt)Leerrohr n [Leerrohr]

fibrated · faserhaltig, gefasert

~; fiber-reinforced (US); fibre-reinforced (Brit.) · faserarmiert

~ asphalt emulsion; ~ emulsified asphalt (US); ~ (asphaltic-)bitumen emulsion (Brit.) · Faser-Bitumenemulsion f

~ (asphaltic-)bitumen emulsion (Brit.) → ~ asphalt ~

~ bitumen emulsion (Brit.) → ~ asphalt ~

~ composition, ~ compound · Fasermasse f

~ compound, ~ composition · Fasermasse f

~ concrete · Faserbeton m, Faserzement m [Ein Gemenge aus Zement und Fasern, das unter großem Druck zu Platten oder Röhren gepreßt wird]

~ ~ product · Faserbetonerzeugnis n, Faserzementerzeugnis

~ ~ slab · Faserbetonplatte f, Faserzementplatte

~ ~ tube · Faserbetonröhre f, Faserzementröhre

~ dampproofing · Faserisoliermaterial n, Faserisolierstoff m [Feuchtigkeitsisolierung]

~ emulsified asphalt (US) → ~ asphalt emulsion

fibre backing → ~ base

~ base, ~ backing, ~ underlay (Brit.); fiber ~ (US) · Faserhinterlegung f, Faserunterlage f, Faserrücklage, Faserträger(schicht) m, (f)

fireboard → wood ~

~ board, ~ sheet (Brit.); fiberboard ~ (US) · Faserschliffplatte f

~ ceiling → wood ~ ~

~ finish (Brit.); fiberboard ~ (US) · (Holz)Faserplattenbelag m

fibre(board) lath(ing) (Brit.); fiber (board) ~ (US) [It is made of cane fibre or of other fibrous materials pressed into sheets] · Faser-Putz(mörtel)träger m, Faserplattenputzträger

fibreboard nail (Brit.); fiberboard ~ (US) · Faserplattennagel m

~ sheathing (Brit.); fiberboard ~ (US) · Faserplattenverschalung f

~ sheet → ~ board

~ tile (Brit.); fiberboard ~ (US) · Faserschliff(belag)platte f, Faserschliff-Fliese f

fibre building board, ~ ~ sheet (Brit.) [B.S. 1142]; fiber ~ ~ (US) · Faser(bau)platte f, Faserstoff(bau)platte

~ ~ sheet → ~ ~ board

~ core (Brit.); fiber ~ (US) · Fasereinlage f, Faserseele f, Faserkern m [Drahtseil]

~ glass (Brit.); fiber ~ (US) [Glass drawn into thin threads for spinning and weaving] · Faserglas n

~ ~ cored bituminous felt RUBEROID (Brit.); fiber ~ ~ ~ ~ ~ (US) · Glasgewebe-RUBEROID n

~ ~ insulation (material) (Brit.); fiber ~ ~ (~) (US) · Glasfaserdämmstoff m, Glasfaserdämmaterial n

fibreglass staple fibre (Brit.); fibreglass staple fiber (US) · Stapelglasfaser f, Glasstapelfaser

fibre grease (Brit.); fiber ~ (US) · Faserfett n

~ in compression (Brit.); fiber ~ ~ (US) · Druckfaser f

~ ~ tension (Brit.); fiber ~ ~ (US) · Zugfaser f

~ insulation layer (Brit.); fiber ~ ~ (US) · Faserdämmschicht f

~ insulator → fiber insulating(-grade) material

~ lath(ing) → fibre(board) ~

~ metallurgy (Brit.); fiber ~ (US) · Fasermetallurgie f

~ netting (Brit.); fiber ~ (US) · Fasergeflecht n

~ paper (Brit.); fiber ~ (US) · Vulkanfiber f

~ plug (Brit.); fiber ~ (US) · Hanfdübel m

fibre reinforced plastic — field concrete stair(case)

~ **reinforced plastic** (Brit.); fiber ~ ~ (US) · faserverstärkter Kunststoff *m*

~ **reinforcement** (Brit.); fiber ~ (US) · Faserverstärkung *f*, Faserarmierung [*Werkstoff*]

~ **rope** (Brit.); fiber ~ (US) · Faserstrick *m*

~ **stress** (Brit.); fiber ~ (US) [*in beams*] · Faserspannung *f* [*in Balken(trägern)*]

~ **tube** (Brit.); fiber ~ (US) · Faserröhre *f*

~ **underlay** → ~ base

~ **wallboard** (Brit.); fiber ~ (US) · Faserwandplatte *f*, Wandfaserplatte

~ **washer** (Brit.); fiber ~ (US) · Faserunterlegscheibe *f*

fibrous · faserig

~ **(asphaltic) compound,** ~ (~) composition [*For stopping leaks in roofs of all kinds and for general repair work*] · Faserpaste *f*

~ **bituminous composition** → ~ ~ compound

~ ~ **compound,** ~ ~ composition · bituminöse Fasermasse *f*

~ **composite (material)** · Faserverbund(werk)stoff *m*

~ **composition** → ~ (asphaltic) compound

~ ~ **seal(ing) ring,** ~ ~ packing ~, ~ ~ washer · Faserstoffdicht(ungs)ring *m*

~ ~ **washer** → ~ ~ ~ seal(ing) ring

~ **compound** → ~ asphaltic ~

~ **concrete** · Beton *m* mit faserigen Zuschlägen, ~ ~ ~ Zuschlagstoffen

~ **filler** · Faserfüllstoff *m* [*Fugenvergußmasse*]

~ **fracture** · faseriger Bruch *m*

~ **glass** → glass wool

~ ~ **insulation** → ~ ~ lagging

~ ~ **lagging,** ~ ~ insulation, glass wool ~ · Glaswolledämmung *f*

~ ~ **reinforced plastic** → glass reinforced laminate

~ ~ **strip,** glass wool ~ · Glaswollestreifen *m*

~ **gypsum,** satin spar · Fraueneis *n*, Marienglas *n*, Frauenglas, Fasergips *m*, spätiger Gips, Alabasterglas [*perlmutterglänzender Gipsspat*]

~ ~ ~ → haired ~

~ **jointing material** · faserige (Fugen-)Einlage *f*

~ **lime-mortar** → haired ~

~ **material** · Faserstoff *m*

~ **mortar** → haired ~

~ **paper** · Faserpapier *n*

fictitious (design) load (factor), imaginary (~) ~ (~) · fiktive Traglast *f*

~ **eccentricity,** imaginary ~ · fiktive Ausmittigkeit *f*, ~ Ausmitte

~ **(pre)stressing** → imaginary ~

~ **stressing** → imaginary (pre)stressing

~ **stretching** → imaginary (pre)stressing

~ **tensioning** → imaginary (pre)stressing

field · Sektor *m* [*Teil einer Industrie, z.B. Wohnungsbausektor*]

~, **site** · Baustelle *f*

~ **aerated concrete** → cast(-)in(-)situ ~ ~

~ **architectural concrete** → cast-in-place ~ ~

~ **assembly** → site ~

~ **beam test** · Baustellen-Balkenprüfung *f*, Baustellen-Balkenprobe *f*, Baustellen-Balkenversuch *m*

~ **bolt** · Montageschraube *f* [*Schraube, die in eine Stahlkonstruktion auf der Baustelle eingezogen wird und im Gegensatz zu der nur zum Heften dienenden Montierschraube darin verbleibt*]

~ **chapel** · Feldkapelle *f*

~ **church** · Feldkirche *f*

~ **concrete,** job-mix(ed) ~ · Baustellenbeton *m*

~ ~, in(-)situ (cast) ~, cast(-)in(-)situ ~, cast-in-place ~, site-placed ~, poured(-in-place) ~ · Ortbeton *m* [*DIN 1045*]

~ ~ **balcony,** in(-)situ (cast) (~) ~, cast(-)in(-)situ (~) ~, cast-in-place (~) ~, site-placed (~) ~, poured(-in-place) (~) ~ · Ortbetonbalkon *m*

~ ~ **cable duct,** site-placed (~) ~ ~, cast-in-place (~) ~ ~, cast(-)in(-)situ (~) ~ ~, in(-)situ (cast) (~) ~, poured(-in-place) (~) ~ ~ · Ortbetonkanal *m*

~ ~ **eave(s) unit,** site-placed (~) ~, cast(-)in(-)situ (~) ~ ~, in(-)situ (cast) (~) ~ ~, cast-in-place (~) ~, poured(-in-place) (~) ~ ~ · Ortbeton-Traufenteil *m, n*

~ ~ **filling,** site-placed (~) ~, cast-in-place (~) ~, cast(-)in(-)situ (~) ~, in(-)situ (cast) (~) ~, poured (in-place) (~) ~ · Ortbetonfüllung *f*

~ ~ **floor,** site-placed (~) ~, cast-in-place (~) ~, cast(-)in(-)situ (~) ~, in(-)situ (cast) (~) ~, poured(-in-place) (~) ~ · Ortbetondecke *f*

~ ~ **frame,** ~ ~ framing, cast-in-place (~) ~, site-placed (~) ~, cast(-)in(-)situ (~) ~, in(-)situ (cast) (~) ~, poured(-in-place) (~) ~ · Ortbetonrahmen *m*

~ ~ **rib(bed) floor,** cast-in-place (~) ~ ~, site-placed (~) ~ ~, cast(-)in(-)situ (~) ~ ~, in(-)situ (cast) (~) ~ ~, poured(-in-place) (~) ~ ~ · Ortbeton-Rippendecke *f*

~ ~ **shell,** cast-in-place (~) ~, site-placed (~) ~, cast(-)in(-)situ (~) ~, in(-)situ (cast) (~) ~, poured(-in-place) (~) ~ · Ortbetonschale *f*

~ ~ **stair(case),** site-placed (~) ~, cast-in-place (~) ~, cast(-)in(-)situ (~) ~, in(-)situ (cast) (~) ~, poured(-in-place) (~) ~ · Ortbetontreppe *f*

~ ~ **structure,** site-placed (~) ~, cast-in-place (~) ~, cast(-)in(-)situ (~) ~, in(-)situ (cast) (~) ~, poured(-in-place) (~) ~ · Ortbetonbauwerk *n*

~ **connection,** site ~ · Montageverbindung *f*

~ **cube test** · Baustellen-Würfelprüfung *f*, Baustellen-Würfelprobe *f*, Baustellen-Würfelversuch *m*

fielded panel, raised ~ · Tafel *f* mit überhobener Füllung

field hand · Baustellenarbeiter *m*

~ **light(weight) concrete,** site-placed ~ ~, cast-in-place ~ ~, cast(-)in(-)situ ~ ~, in(-)situ (cast) ~ ~, poured(-in-place) ~ ~ · Ortleichtbeton *m*, Leicht-Ortbeton

~ **maintenance** · Baustellen-Unterhaltung *f*

~ **mortar,** cast(-)in(-)situ ~, in(-)situ (cast) ~, cast-in-place ~, site-placed ~, poured(-in-place) ~ · Ortmörtel *m*

~ **of application,** ~ ~ use · Anwendungsgebiet *n*

~ ~ **forces,** force field · Kraftfeld *n*, Kräftefeld

~ ~ **load,** area of loading, loaded area · Lastfeld *n*, Lastfläche *f*, belastetes Feld, belastete Fläche

~ ~ **use,** ~ ~ application · Anwendungsgebiet *n*

~ ~ **view,** observer's ~ ~ ~ · Blickfeld *n* [*Tageslichtberechnung*]

~ **office,** site ~ · Baustellenbüro *n*

field-painted, site-painted · baustellengestrichen

field reinforced concrete, ~ R.C., site-placed ~ ~, cast-in-place ~ ~, cast(-)in(-)situ ~ ~, in(-)situ (cast) ~ ~, poured(-in-place) ~ ~ · Ort-Stahlbeton *m*, Stahlortbeton

~ ~ ~ **floor,** ~ R.C. ~, site-placed ~ ~ ~, cast-in-place ~ ~ ~, cast(-)in(-)situ ~ ~ ~, in(-)situ (cast) ~ ~ ~, poured(-in-place) ~ ~ ~ · Ortstahlbetondecke *f*, Stahlortbetondecke

~ **rivet** · Baustellenniet *m*

~ **staff,** site ~ · Baustellenpersonal *n*

fieldstone (US); rubble (Brit.) · Feldstein *m*, Findling *m*

~ **fireplace** (US); rubble ~ (Brit.) · Kamin *m* aus Feldsteinen, Feldsteinkamin

field test · Naturprobe *f*, Naturversuch *m*, Naturprüfung *f* [*Korrosionsversuch*]

~ **tile** [*A full-sized tile used in ceilings, walls or floor(ing)s in all areas except the borders*] · Ganzfliese *f*, Ganz(belag)-platte *f*

field-welded, site-welded · baustellengeschweißt

field welding, site ~ · Baustellenschweißen *n*

fighting gallery · Wehrgang *m*, Letze *f*, Vohr *m*, Rondengang *m*, Umlauf *m* [*Verteidigungsgang auf dem Bering einer Burg oder auf der Stadtmauer, geschützt durch Brustwehr mit oder ohne Zinnen, häufig auch überdacht. Eine Sonderform ist die Verbindung des Wehrganges mit der Hurde*]

figural · figürlich

figurative character, ~ element · Figuratives *n*

~ **element,** ~ character · Figuratives *n*

figure, geometric ~ · (geometrische) Figur *f*

~ **portal** · Figurenportal *n*

figure-sculpture · Figurenplastik *f*, Figurenskulptur *f*

figured veneer, rare ~, fancy ~, patterned ~ · Maserfurnier *n*

(figur(ed)) rolled glass → pattern(ed) ~

figure(d) wire(d) glass, ornamental ~ ~, pattern(ed) ~ ~, decorative ~ ~, wire(d) figure(d) ~, wire(d) decorative ~, wire(d) pattern(ed) ~, wire(d) ornamental ~ · Drahtornamentglas *n*, Ornamentdrahtglas, Drahtzierglas, Zierdrahtglas, Dekor(ations)drahtglas, Drahtdekor(ations)glas, ornamentiertes Drahtglas

filament [*A glass fibre as drawn*] · Elementarfaden *m*, Einzelfaser *f*

filigree decorative fixture, ~ ornament, ~ enrichment · Filigranornament *n*, Filigranverzierung *f*

~ **effect** [*Such an effect can be created by fabricating a grill(e) over all or part of a concrete panel surface*] · Filigranwirkung *f*

~ **enrichment,** ~ ornament, ~ decorative fixture · Filigranornament *n*, Filigranverzierung *f*

~ **floor** · Filigrandecke *f* [*Sie besteht aus dem Stahlgitterträger mit angerüttelter Ziegelsplittbetonleiste und den Hohlkörpern aus Ziegelsplitt- oder Bimsbeton*]

~ **girder** · Filigranträger *m*

~ **ornament,** ~ enrichment, ~ decorative fixture · Filigranornament *n*, Filigranverzierung *f*

~ **rib(bed) floor** · Filigranrippendecke *f*

filings, turnings · Feilspäne *mpl*

fill, filling · Füllung *f*

~, **earth cover(ing)** · Überdeckung *f*, Überschüttung *f* [*erdverlegte Leitung*]

~, **filling** · (Auf)Schüttung *f*

~ **boarding** → filling ~

to fill in · ausfachen, ausfüllen [*Süddeutschland: ausriegeln*]

fill insulation → loose-~ ~

~ **plate,** filler (~) · Futter(blech) *n*

to fill with concrete · ausbetonieren

~ ~ ~ **mortar,** to mortar in · ausmörteln, vermörteln [*Mauerwerkfuge*]

filled stiffener · Steifenwinkelanschluß *m* mit Futter

filler — filling

filler, stopper, stopping; Swedish putty, spactling compound (US) · Spachtel(-masse) *m*, (*f*), Füll~, Ausfüller *m* [*Spachtel(masse) ist ein stark pigmentierter und/oder gefüllter Anstrichstoff, vorwiegend zum Ausgleichen von Unebenheiten des Untergrundes. Der Spachtel kann zieh-, streich- oder spritzbar eingestellt werden. Die getrocknete Spachtelschicht muß schleifbar sein.
Nach der Zusammensetzung unterscheidet man z.B. Leimspachtel, Dispersionsspachtel, Ölspachtel, Lackspachtel, Nitrocellulosespachtel*]

~ · Füllstück *n*

~ → ~ plate

~ → inert ~

~, filling material · Füller *m*, Füllstoff *m*

~, filling composition [*A composition used for filling fine cracks and indentations to obtain a smooth, even surface preparatory to painting. It may vary in consistency from a paint to a paste*] · Füller *m*, Füllstoff *m*

~ → mineral ~

~ → (joint) sealing strip

~ → (paint) extender

~ → (floor) filler (block)

~ **adding,** ~ addition · Füllerzusatz *m*, Füllerzusetzen *n*, Füllerzugabe *f*, Füllerzugeben, Füllerbeigabe, Füllerbeigeben

~ **addition,** ~ adding · Füllerzugabe *f*, Füllerzusetzen *n*, Füllerbeigabe, Füllerbeigeben, Füllerzusatz *m*, Füllerzugeben

~ **bending tester** → stopper ~ ~

~ **block** → floor ~ (~)

~ ~ → in~ ~

~ **brick** → infill(ing) ~

~ ~, **clay** ~ ~, **clay filler tile** · (Decken-)Füllziegel *m*, Füll-Deckenziegel

~ **coat** → stopping ~

~ **concrete panel,** in~ ~ ~, infill(ing) ~ ~ · Ausfachungsbetontafel *f*,·(Aus-)Füll(ungs)betontafel

~ **for brush application,** stopper ~ ~ ~, stopping ~ ~ ~; Swedish putty ~ ~ ~, spactling compound ~ ~ ~ (US) · Streich(füll)spachtel(masse) *m*, (*f*), Pinsel(füll)spachtel(masse), Streichausfüller *m*, Pinselausfüller

~ **gypsum,** stopping ~, stopping ~ · Spachtelgips *m*

~ **masonry (work)** → infill(ing) ~ (~)

~ **material** → infill(ing) ~

~ **panel,** in~ ~, infill(ing) ~ · (Aus-)Füll(ungs)tafel *f*, Ausfachungstafel

~ **(plate),** fill ~ · Futter(blech) *n*

~ **powder,** stopper ~, stopping ~ · Spachtelpulver *n*, Füll~, Ausfüllerpulver

~ **rod,** welding ~, ~ wire · Schweißdraht *m* [*DIN 1913*]

~ **seal(ing)** → stopper ~

~ **slab** → in~ ~

~ ~, **floor** ~ ~ · (Decken)Füllplatte *f*, Füll-Deckenplatte, plattenförmiger Zwischenbauteil *m*, plattenförmiges Zwischenbauteil *n*

~ **strip** · Einlagestreifen *m*

~ **tile** → (in)filler block

~ ~ → (floor) filler (block)

~ **wall,** in~ ~, panel ~, infill(ing) ~ · Ausfachung *f*, Ausfüllung *f* [*Süddeutschland: Ausriegelung*]

~ ~, curtain ~, panel ~ [*It is a nonbearing wall in skeleton construction, built between columns, posts or piers and wholly supported at each stor(e)y*] · Tafelwand *f*

~ **wire** → ~ rod

to fillerise (Brit.); **to fillerize** (US) · füllern, anreichern mit Füller

fillerised (Brit.); **fillerized** (US) · gefüllert

~ **binder** (Brit.); fillerized ~ (US) · gefüllertes Bindemittel *n*, gefüllerter Binder *m*, Bindemittel mit Füller, Binder mit Füller

fillerising (Brit.); fillerizing (US) · Fülleranreicherung *f*, Füllern *n*, Anreicherung mit Füller

to fillerize (US); to fillerise (Brit.) · füllern, anreichern mit Füller

fillerized (US); fillerised (Brit.) · gefüllert

~ **binder** (US); fillerised ~ (Brit.) · gefüllertes Bindemittel *n*, gefüllerter Binder *m*, Bindemittel mit Füller, Binder mit Füller

fillerizing (US); fillerising (Brit.) · Fülleranreicherung *f*, Füllern *n*, Anreicherung mit Füller

fillet, listel · Band *n*, Riemen *m*, Plättchen *n* [*antike Säule*]

~, beading · Riemen *m*, schmales (Fuß-)Bodenbrett *n*

~, listel · Steg *m* [*zwischen zwei Einkehlungen einer kannelierten Säule*]

~ **of plaster of Paris** · Gipsbett *n* [*Prüfung der Scheiteldrucklast von Rohren*]

~ **profile,** ~ shape, ~ trim, ~ section, ~ unit · Wandanschlußprofil *n*

~ **section,** ~ trim, ~ shape, ~ profile, ~ unit · Wandanschlußprofil *n*

~ **shape,** ~ section, ~ trim, ~ profile, ~ unit · Wandanschlußprofil *n*

~ **trim,** ~ shape, ~ unit, ~ section, ~ profile · Wandanschlußprofil *n*

~ **unit,** ~ shape, ~ section, ~ profile, ~ trim · Wandanschlußprofil *n*

fill(ing) · (Auf)Schüttung *f*

~ · Füllung *f*

filling · Ausfüllen *n*

~, joint ~ · (Fugen)(Ab)Dichten *n*, (Fugen)Verfüllen, (Fugen)(Aus)Füllen, Ausfugen, (Ver)Fugen

filling — final coat exterior plaster stuff

~, joint ~, jointing · (Fugen)(Ab)Dichtung f, Ausfugung, (Fugen)(Aus)Füllung, Verfugung, (Fugen)Verfüllung

fill(ing) boarding · Schüttschalung f [*Holzbalkendecke*]

filling composition, filler [*A composition used for filling fine cracks and indentations to obtain a smooth, even surface preparatory to painting. It may vary in consistency from a paint to a paste*] · Füller m, Füllstoff m

~ compound, grouting ~ · Spachtel(-masse) m, (f) [*Zum Maschinenspachteln von Terrazzoplatten*]

~ ~ → joint ~ ~

~ knife · Spachtelmesser n [*DIN 7126*]

~ material, filler · Füllstoff m, Füller m

~ ~ → inert ~ ~

~ panel, filler ~, in~, cladding ~ · (Aus)Füll(ungs)tafel f, Ausfachungstafel, (Außenwand)Versteifungstafel

~ powder · Füllpulver n

~ up · Schiefergrau n, Auffüller m [*Gemahlener, grauer Schiefer. Er dient hauptsächlich zur Bereitung von Ölspachtelmasse. Er wird mit Bleiweiß, etwas Halböl und Harttrockenöl gemischt und ergibt eine Masse, die sich zum Spachteln von Maschinen und Fahrzeugen eignet. Als Pigment wird Schiefergrau nicht verwendet*]

~ with concrete · Ausbetonieren n

film, membrane, skin · Film m, Membran(e) f, Haut f, Häutchen n

~ adhesive → sheet glue

(~) bond(ing) failure → (~) detachment

~ build · Filmdicke f [*Anstrichtechnik*]

(~) detachment, (~) stripping, (~) dislodg(e)ment, (~) displacement, (~) bond(ing) failure · (Film)Loslösen n, (Film)Loslösung f, (Film)Ablösen, (Film)Ablösung

(~) dislodg(e)ment → (~) detachment

(~) displacement → (~) detachment

~ formation, ~ forming · Filmbildung f, Verfilmung

~-former → film-forming medium

~ forming, ~ formation · Filmbildung f, Verfilmung

film-forming · filmbildend

~ agent → ~ medium

~ component → ~ medium

~ medium, ~ agent, ~ component, film-former, filmogen · Filmbildner m, filmbildender Stoff m [*Filmbildner sind diejenigen Bestandteile des Bindemittels, die für das Zustandekommen des Anstrichfilms wesentlich sind. Man unterscheidet selbständige und nichtselbständige Filmbildner: Selbständige Filmbildner sind solche, die allein, d.h. ohne Zusatz von weiteren Substanzen, mit oder ohne Sauerstoffeinfluß einen Anstrichfilm zu bilden vermögen. Nichtselbständige Filmbildner sind solche, die nur in geeigneten Gemischen einen Anstrichfilm zu bilden vermögen. Anmerkung: Man muß zwischen Filmbildner und Filmbestandteil unterscheiden. Auch Pigmente sind z.B. Filmbestandteile*]

film glue → sheet ~

~ piece · Filmspanstück n [*DIN 53155*]

~-proof · filmbeständig

~ rust · Flugrost m

(~) stripping → (~) detachment

~ thickness · Filmdicke f [*Fehlname: Filmstärke f*]

filmogen → film-forming medium

FILON glazing pane · FILON-Scheibe f

filter aid, filtering ~ · Filtrierhilfe f

~ block · Filterstein m

~ gravel · Filterkies m

~ paper · Filtrierpapier n, Filterpapier

~ ~ disk (US); ~ ~ disc · Filtrierpapierscheibe f

~ pipe · Brunnenrohr n, Filterrohr

~ ~ of single-size material concrete · Einkornbeton-Filterrohr n

~ sand · Filtersand m

~ slag, slag filter material · Filterschlacke f

filterability · Filtrierbarkeit f

filt(e)rable · filtrierbar

filtering, filtration · Filtern n, Filtrieren

filter(ing) aid · Filtrierhilfe f

filtration, filtering · Filtern n, Filtrieren

~ · Filterung f

filtros · Filtrosplatte f

fin · Rohrrippe f

~ heating tube → finned ~ ~

(~) strip electric heater → fin(ned) ~ ~ ~

~ tube → fin(ned) ~

~ ~ heater → fin(ned) ~ ~

~ ~ radiator → fin(ned) tube heater

final acceptance · Schlußabnahme f

~ assembly · Endmontage f

~ boiling point, end ~ · Endsiedepunkt m

~ coat, finish(ing ~) [*painting system*] · Schlußanstrich m, Schlußaufstrich, Deckanstrich, Deckaufstrich

~ ~, face ~, skim(ming) ~, finish(ing) ~, setting ~ · Oberputz m, Feinputz, ~schicht f, ~lage f [*Oberschicht des zweilagigen oder dreilagigen Putzes, die im besonderen Maße die ästhetische Wirkung des Putzes bestimmt. Bei Außenputzen muß sie witterungsbeständig sein*]

~ ~ exterior plaster → (external) final rendering

~ ~ ~ ~ mix(ture) → (external) final rendering stuff

~ ~ ~ ~ stuff → (external) final rendering ~

final coat exterior plaster(ing) — fine flour

~ ~ ~ **plaster(ing)** → (external) final rendering stuff
~ ~ **external plaster** → (external) final rendering
~ ~ ~ ~ **mix(ture)** → (external) final rendering stuff
~ ~ ~ ~ **stuff** → (external) final rendering ~
~ ~ ~ ~ **plaster(ing)** → (external) final rendering stuff
~ ~ **(mixed) plaster** · Deckputz m, Feinputz, Oberputz
~ ~ **paint** · Schluß(anstrich)farbe f
~ ~ **(plaster)** → finish(ing) ~ (~)
~ ~ ~, ~ ~ mixed ~ · Deckputz m, Feinputz, Oberputz
~ **design** · Ausführungsentwurf m
~ **drawing**, working ~ · Ausführungszeichnung f, Arbeitszeichnung, Ausführungsplan m, Arbeitsplan, Musterriß m, Bauriß
~ **grinding**, fine ~, finish ~ · Feinmahlung f, Feinmahlen n [allgemein]
~ -**hardened and tempered steel wire** · schlußvergüteter Stahldraht m
final individual coat · Endanstrichschicht f, Endaufstrichschicht, Schlußanstrichschicht, Schlußaufstrichschicht [Die letzte (Anstrich)Schicht des Anstrichsystems]
~ **load** · endgültige Last f
~ **moment** · endgültiges Moment n
~ **planning** · Ausführungsplanung f
~ **(pre)stressing**, ~ tensioning, ~ stretching · endgültiges (Vor)Spannen n
~ **project**, ~ scheme · Ausführungsprojekt n
~ **rendering** → external ~ ~
~ ~ **mix(ture)** → (external) final rendering stuff
~ ~ **stuff** → external ~ ~ ~
~ **scheme**, ~ project · Ausführungsprojekt n
~ **set(ting)** · (Ab)Bindeende n [hydraulisches Bindemittel]
~ ~ **curve**, curve of final set(ting) · (Ab)Bindeendekurve f [hydraulisches Bindemittel]
~ **shape** · Endform f, Endgestalt f
~ **strength**, ultimate ~, rupture ~, breaking ~ · Endfestigkeit f, Endwiderstand m, Bruchfestigkeit, Bruchwiderstand
~ **stress** [In prestressed concrete, the stress which exists after substantially all losses have occurred] · Endvorspannung f
~ ~ · endgültige Spannung f
~ **stucco mix(ture)** (US) → (external) final rendering stuff
~ ~ **stuff** (US) → (external) final rendering ~
~ **treatment** · Endbehandlung f, Schlußbehandlung

~ **varnishing** · Schlußlackierung f
~ **welding** · Fertigschweißen n [im Gegensatz zum Heftschweißen]
financial heart · Bankenviertel n
financing of housing, housing financing · Wohn(ungs)baufinanzierung f
fine aggregate → ~ concrete ~
~ **asbestos** · Feinasbest m
~ **asphalt** (Brit.); fine(-graded) asphaltic concrete (US) · Asphaltfeinbeton m, Feinasphaltbeton
~ ~ **tile** (Brit.); fine(-graded) asphaltic concrete (US) · Asphaltfeinbeton-(belag)platte f, Asphaltfeinbetonfliese f, Feinasphaltbeton(belag)platte, Feinasphaltbetonfliese
~ **asphaltic concrete** → ~-graded ~
~ **blast**, ~ sand~ · (Sand)Feinstrahl m
~ **broken rock**, ~ ~ stone, ~ crushed ~; ~ (road-)metal (Brit.) · Feinschotter m, Feinsteinschlag m
~ ~ **stone**, ~ ~ rock, ~ crushed ~; ~ (road-)metal (Brit.) · Feinschotter m, Feinsteinschlag m
~ **bronze wire** · Bronzefeindraht m
~ ~ ~ **netting** · Bronze-Feindrahtgeflecht n
~ **chipboard**, ~ particle board · Feinspanplatte f
fine:coarse aggregate ratio, sand:coarse ~ ~ [Ratio of fine to coarse aggregate in a batch of concrete, by weight or volume] · (Beton)Feinzuschlag(stoff)-Grobzuschlag(stoff)-Verhältnis n
fine cold asphalt, cold fine ~, Damman cold ~ (Brit.); Damman cold asphaltic concrete (US) · Asphaltkaltbeton m
~ **concrete**, ~ sand ~, fine-grain(ed) ~ · Feinbeton m
~ **(~) aggregate** · (Beton)Feinzuschlag-(stoff) m
(~) ~ floor screed (material) → monolithic (~) ~ ~ ~ (~)
(~) ~ ~ ~ (topping) → monolithic (~) ~ ~ ~ (~)
(~) ~ screed (material) → (monolithic) (~) ~ ~ ~ (~)
(~) ~ ~ (topping) → monolithic (~) ~ ~ (~)
~ **crushed gravel** · Feinbrechkies m, Brechfeinkies
~ ~ **rock**, ~ ~ stone, ~ broken; ~; ~ (road-)metal (Brit.) · Feinschotter m, Feinsteinschlag m
~ ~ **stone**, ~ ~ rock, ~ broken ~; ~ (road-)metal (Brit.) · Feinschotter m, Feinsteinschlag m
fine-fibrous · feinfas(e)rig
fine filler, ~ stopping, ~ stopper · Feinausfüller m, Fein(füll)spachtel(masse) m, (f) [Siehe Anmerkung unter "Spachtel(masse)"]
~ **flour** · Feinmehl n

fine fraction — fine talc

~ **fraction** → ~ particles
~ ~ **curve,** ~ ~ **line** · Feinkornlinie f, Feinkornkurve f
~ ~ **range** · Feinkornbereich m, n
fine(-graded) asphaltic concrete (US); fine asphalt (Brit.) · Asphaltfeinbeton m, Feinasphaltbeton m
~ ~ ~ **tile** (US); fine asphalt ~ (Brit.) · Asphaltfeinbeton(belag)platte f, Asphaltfeinbetonfliese f, Feinasphaltbeton(belag)platte, Feinasphaltbetonfliese
fine grading, ~ **size** ~ · Feinkornabstufung f
~ **grain** · Feinkorn n [als Teilchen]
~ ~ **(size)** · Feinkorn(größe) n, (f)
fine(-grain(ed)) · feinkörnig
~ **artificial stone** [deprecated] → ~ cast ~
~ **cast stone,** ~ reconstituted ~, ~ reconstructed ~, ~ patent ~; ~ artificial ~ [deprecated] · Feinbetonwerkstein m
~ **chip(ping)s** · Feinsplitt m
~ **concrete,** fine (sand) ~ · Feinbeton m
~ **gravel (concrete) aggregate,** ~ ~ for concrete · Betonfeinkies m
~ ~ **from 7 to 30 mm grain size** · Feinkies m [DIN 1179. Korngröße zwischen 7 mm und 30 mm Maschensieb]
~ **light(weight) concrete aggregate** · Feinleicht(beton)zuschlag(stoff) m, Feinleicht(beton)zuschlagmaterial n
~ **reconstituted stone** → ~ cast ~
~ **mortar,** fine (sand) ~ · Feinmörtel m
~ ~ **with synthetic resin dispersion** · Kunstharz-Feinmörtel m, Plast-Feinmörtel
~ **patent stone** → ~ cast ~
~ **perlite** · feiner Perlit m, Feinperlit
~ **powder** · Feinpulver n
~ **reconstructed stone** → ~ cast ~
~ **sand** [Division of Soil Survey (US) 0.25–0.05 mm; A.S.E.E. fraction 0.25 to 0.074 mm; British Standard 0.2 bis 0.06 mm; fine sand and coarse silt (Brit.) 0.2–0.02 mm] · Staubsand m, Feinsand [Nach DIN 4022 0,2 bis 0,1 mm; nach DIN 1179 0,2–0,09 mm; nach Atterberg 0,2–0,02 mm; nach Fischer und Üdluft (Jahr 1936) 0,2–0,02 mm (man heißt hier "Silt")]
~ **steel** · Feinkornstahl m
fine grains → ~ particles
~ **gravel from 7 to 30 mm grain size,** fine-grain(ed) ~ ~ ~ ~ ~ ~ · Feinkies m [DIN 1179. Korngröße zwischen 7 mm und 30 mm Maschensieb]
~ **grinding,** final ~, finish ~ · Feinmahlung f, Feinmahlen n [allgemein]
~ **levelling** (Brit.); ~ leveling (US) · Feinegalisieren n, Feineinebnen, Feinausgleichen, Fein(aus)ebnen, Feinnivellieren
~ **light(weight) concrete aggregate** → fine-grain(ed) ~ ~ ~

~ **limestone chip(ping)s** · Kalk(stein)feinsplitt m
~ **-line compound veneer** · Feinstreifenfurnier n, Feinlinienfurnier
fine manufactured sand, manufactured fine ~ · Feinbrechsand m, Brechfeinsand
~ **material** → ~ particles
~ ~ · kostbarer Baustoff m; kostbares Baumaterial n [Schweiz]
~ **mesh silk,** silk gauze · Seidengaze f
~ ~ **wire netting** · feinmaschiges Drahtgeflecht n
~ **metal** → ~ road-~
~ **mortar,** ~ sand ~, fine-grain(ed) ~ · Feinmörtel m
~ ~ **with synthetic resin dispersion** → ~-grain(ed) ~ ~ ~ ~ ~
~ **particle** · Feinteilchen n
~ ~ **board,** chipboard · Feinspanplatte f
~ **particles,** ~ grains, ~ material, ~ fraction, fines · Feinstoffe mpl, Feinmaterial n, Feingut n, Feinkorn n
~ **perlite,** fine-grain(ed) ~ · feiner Perlit m, Feinperlit
~ **polishing** · Feinpolieren n, Fertigen, Fertigung f [Glas]
~ ~ · Feinpolieren n
~ **pore** · Feinpore f
fine-pored · feinporig
fine powder · feiner Staub m [Staub nicht im Sinne von "Schmutz"]
~ ~, fine-grain(ed) ~ · Feinpulver n
~ **(road-)metal** (Brit.); ~ broken stone, ~ broken rock, ~ crushed stone, ~ crushed rock · Feinschotter m, Feinsteinschlag m
~ **sand** → ~-grained ~
~ **(sand)blast** · (Sand)Feinstrahl m
~ **(sand) concrete,** fine-grain(ed) ~ · Feinbeton m
~ ~ **(concrete) aggregate** · Betonfeinsand m
~ **(~) mortar,** fine-grain(ed) ~ · Feinmörtel m
~ **scrubbed (concrete) surface,** ~ ~ (~) finish · feine Bürstenwaschbetonoberfläche f
~ **seed** → seed
~ **(size) grading** · Feinkornabstufung f
~ **stopper,** ~ stopping, ~ filler · Feinausfüller m, Fein(füll)spachtel(masse) m, (f) [Siehe Anmerkung unter "Spachtel(masse)"]
~ **stopping,** ~ stopper, ~ filler · Feinausfüller m, Fein(füll)spachtel(masse) m, (f) [Siehe Anmerkung unter "Spachtel(masse)"]
~ **stream sand** · Flußfeinsand m
~ **talc,** powder(ed) ~, talc(um) powder, talcum, French chalk · Talk(um) n, Federweiß n, Talkmehl n, Specksteinmehl, Glitschpulver n [Ein sehr feines und weiches mineralisches und sich fettig anfühlendes Pulver]

fine tar concrete — finish material

~ **tar concrete** · Teerfeinbeton m, Feinteerbeton

~ **texture** · Feinstruktur f [Putz]

~**-textured** · feinstrukturiert [Betonoberfläche]

fine wire netting · Feindrahtgeflecht n

(finely) crushed glass, granulated ~ · Glasgrieß m, Krösel m

~ **ground** · feingemahlen

~ ~ **barite** (US); ~ ~ barytes (Brit.) · Schwerspatmehl n, feingemahlener Baryt m

~ ~ **barytes** (Brit.); ~ ~ barite (US) · feingemahlener Baryt m, Schwerspatmehl n

~ ~ **fire clay**, clay powder, powder(ed) clay · Tonmehl n, Tonpulver n

~ ~ **grain**, artificial fine ~ · Kunstfeinkorn n [Siebtechnik]

~ **powdered** · feingepulvert

~ **toothed**, having dentils, denticulate(d), denticular · (fein)gezahnt

fineness [A measure of particle-size distribution] · Feinheit f

~ **degree**, degree of fineness · Feinheitsgrad m

~ **determination**, determination of fineness · Feinheitsbestimmung f, Feinheitsermitt(e)lung

~ **limit**, limit of fineness · Feinheitsgrenze f

~ **modulus**, modulus of fineness [An empirical factor obtained by adding the total percentages of an aggregate sample retained on each of a specified series of sieves, and dividing the sum by 100; in the United States the U.S. Standard sieve sizes are No. 100 (149 micron), No. 50 (297 micron), No. 30 (590 micron), No. 16 (1190 micron), No. 8 (2380 micron), No. 4 (4760 micron), and 3/8 in. (9.52 mm), 3/4 in. (19.05 mm), 1 1/2 in. (38.1 mm), 3 in. (76.2 mm), and 6 in. (152.4 mm)] · Feinheitsmodul m, Körnungsmodul

~ **of grinding**, grinding fineness · Mahlfeinheit f

~ ~ ~ **of cement**, grinding fineness ~ ~, cement grinding fineness · Zementfeinheit f

fines → fine particles

~ **content**, percentage of fines · Feinkornanteil m, Feinkorngehalt m

~ **output**, true undersize recovery · Fein(korn)ausbringen n, Unterkornausbringes [Siebdurchgang, Fehlkorn abgerechnet]

finest fraction → ultra-fine particles

~ **grains** → ultra-fine particles

~ **material** → ultra-fine particles

~ **particles** → ultra-fine ~

~ **sizes** · Allerfeinste n [Siebtechnik]

finger · Sparparkettstab m, Lamelle(nparkettstab) f, (m), Kleinparkettstab, Mosaikparkettstab, Dünnparkettstab

~ · Verbindungsgang m, Finger(flugsteig) m [Zwischen Flugsteigkopf und Empfangsgebäude]

~ **head** · Finger(flugsteig)kopf m

~ **layout** · Finger(flugsteig)form f

~**-nail indentation test** · Fingernagelprobe f, Fingernagelversuch m, Fingernagelprüfung f

~ **plate** · Schonschild m [Baubeschlag]

· **post** · Wegweiser m

~ **system** · Finger(flugsteig)system n

fingers, mosaic ~, mosaïc parquet(ry) · Dünnparkett n, Sparparkett, Lamellenparkett, Kleinparkett, Mosaikparkett

finial → flower shaped ornament

fining, re~, plaining · Läutern n, Läuterung f [Glasherstellung]

~ **agent**, re~ ~, plaining ~ · Läuterungsmittel n [Glasherstellung]

finish, coat(ing) · Überzug m, Beschichtung f [als Schicht]

~ → surface ~

~ → (architectural) finish(ing)

~, (mixed) plaster · Verputz m

~ → pattern

~, finishing coat, final coat [painting system] · Schlußanstrich m, Schlußaufstrich, Deckanstrich, Deckaufstrich

~ [A paint for use as finish(ing coat)] · Deckschicht(anstrich)farbe f

~ **and service** (US); finishings ~ ~ (Brit.) · Ausbau m [als Ergebnis der Tätigkeit]

~ ~ **services work** (US) → finishings ~ ~ ~

~ **(builders') fittings** → ~ (~) hardware

~ **(~) hardware**, ~ (~) fittings, architectural (~) ~, builders' finish ~ · Architekturbeschläge mpl

~ **coat**, ~ layer · Deckschicht f, Decklage f

~ ~ · Deckanstrich m, Deckaufstrich

~ ~ → finishing ~

~ ~ **(plaster)** → finishing ~ (~)

~ **composition** → coating material

~ **fittings** → ~ (builders') hardware

~ **grinding** [The final grinding of clinker into cement, with calcium sulphate in the form of gypsum or anhydrite generally being added] · Feinmahlen n, Feinmahlung f [Zement]

~ ~, fine ~, final ~ · Feinmahlung f, Feinmahlen n [allgemein]

~ **hardware** → ~ builders' ~

~ **layer**, ~ coat · Deckschicht f, Decklage f

~ **mass** → coating material

~ **material** → coating ~

~ **nail,** ~ wire ~ [*The head is sunk below the surface with a nail set and the hole thus formed is filled with putty to conceal the nail*] · runder Drahtnagel *m* mit Stauchkopf, ~ Drahtstift *m* ~ ~

~ **varnishing** · Fertiglackierung *f*

~ **(wire) nail** [*The head is sunk below the surface with a nail set and the hole thus formed is filled with putty to conceal the nail*] · runder Drahtnagel *m* mit Stauchkopf, ~ Drahtstift *m* ~ ~

finished attic → attic room

~ **bolt,** turned ~ · blanke Schraube *f*

~ **sand** · Fertigsand *m*

finishing · Blauen *n*, Glänzen, Feinmachen [*Hohlglas*]

~ · Fertigbehandlung *f*

~ · Nachbearbeitung *f*

~ · Innenbearbeitung *f*

finish(ing) → architectural ~

finish(ing coat), final ~ [*painting system*] · Schlußanstrich *m*, Schlußaufstrich, Deckanstrich, Deckaufstrich

finish(ing) coat (plaster), setting ~ (~), skimming ~ (~), final ~ (~), face ~ (~) · Feinputz *m*, Oberputz, ~schicht *f*, ~lage *f* [*Oberschicht des zweilagigen oder dreilagigen Putzes, die im besonderen Maße die ästhetische Wirkung des Putzes bestimmt. Bei Außenputzen muß sie witterungsbeständig sein*]

finishing lime [*It is used as base and finish coats*] · Putzkalk *m*

~ **machine** · Adjustagemaschine *f* [*Rohrherstellung*]

~ **material** · Deckwerkstoff *m*

finishing system · Decklackierung *f*

~ **trowel,** smoothing ~, float · Glättkelle *f*

finishings [*Fixture to and treatment of surfaces to convert the carcass into a complete building, excluding services*] · Ausstattung *f*

~ **and services** (Brit.); finish ~ ~ (US) · Ausbau *m* [*als Ergebnis der Tätigkeit*]

~ ~ ~ **work** (Brit.); finish ~ ~ ~ (US); interior ~, internal ~, inner ~, inside ~ · Ausbau(arbeiten) *m*, (*fpl*), Ausbauen *n*, Innen(ausbau)arbeiten, Innenausbau *m* [*Zum Ausbau gehören alle Lieferungen und Leistungen, die nach der Rohbauabnahme zur Fertigstellung des Gebäudes bis zur Schlußabnahme und zur schlüsselfertigen Übergabe üblicherweise erforderlich sind*]

finite · endlich

~ **bending** · endliche Biegung *f*

~ **deformation** · endliche Formänderung *f*, ~ Verformung

~ **displacement** · endliche Verschiebung *f*

~ **element** · endliches Element *n*

~ ~ **method** · Verfahren *n* der endlichen Elemente

~ ~ **solution** · abschnittsweise Lösung *f*

~ **length** · endliche Länge *f*

~ **number** · endliche Anzahl *f*

~-**size panel** · endliche Tafel *f*

finite strain · endliche Dehnung *f*

~ **twisting** · endliche Verwindung *f*

~ **width** · endliche Breite *f*

Fink truss, ~ gable roof ~, French ~ · Polonceau-(Dach)Binder *m*, französischer (Dach)Binder

finned · berippt [*Rohr*]

fin(ned) duplex tube, rib(bed) ~ ~, g(r)illed ~ ~ · Duplex-Rippenrohr *n*, Duplex-Lamellenrohr, beripptes Duplexrohr

~ **heater** → strip ~

~ **heating tube,** rib(bed) ~ ~, g(r)illed ~ ~ · Rippenheizrohr *n*, beripptes Heizrohr, Lamellenheizrohr

(fin(ned)) strip electric heater, electric(al) finned strip ~ · Elektro-Lamellenheizkörper *m*

(~) ~ heater, rib(bed) ~, g(r)illed ~ · Rippenheizkörper *m*, beripptes Heizkörper, Lamellenheizkörper

(~) ~ heating tube, rib(bed) ~ ~, g(r)illed ~ ~ · Rippenheizrohr *n*, beripptes Heizrohr, Lamellenheizrohr

(~) ~ tube, g(r)illed ~, rib(bed) ~, fin(ned) ~ · berippte Röhre *f*, Rippenröhre, Lamellenröhre, beripptes Rohr *n*, Rippenrohr, Lamellenrohr

to fire, to burn · brennen [*Feuerfest- und Zementindustrie*]

fire [*A process of combustion characterized by heat or smoke or flame or any combination of these*] · Brand *m*, Feuer *n*

~, **furnace, burning appliance** · Feuerung *f*, Feuerstätte *f* [*Jede Einrichtung, in der feste, flüssige oder gasförmige Brennstoffe in solcher Menge verbrannt werden, daß die dabei entstehenden Verbrennungserzeugnisse Feuergefahr und/oder Gesundheitsschädigungen hervorrufen können. Feuerstätten beheizen entweder die Räume in denen sie aufgestellt sind unmittelbar oder von einer Zentrale durch Wärmeträger*]

~ → heating appliance

~ **action** · Feuereinwirkung *f*

~ **alarm** · Brandmelder *m*, Feuermelder

~ ~ **system** · Brandmeldeanlage *f*, Feuermeldeanlage

~ **attack** · Feuerangriff *m*

fireback · Kaminrückwand *f*

fire bar · Feuerroststab *m*

~ **barrier,** ~ stop, ~ break, firestopping [*A physical barrier designed to resist the spread of fire in cavities within and between elements of building construction*] · Brand(schutz)sperre *f*, Feuer(schutz)sperre, Brandblende *f*, Feuerschutzabschluß *m*, Brandschutzabschluß

fire bat(t) — (fire) extinguisher bracket

~ **bat(t)** · Brandschutz(bau)platte f, Feuerschutz(bau)platte

~ **break** → ~ barrier

firebreak partition (wall) · Feuer(schutz)trennwand f, Brand(schutz)trennwand

firebrick → refractory brick

fire cement → refractory ~

fireclay · Feuerton m [*Durchsichtige Glasur über dichtender weißer Porzellanengobe oder farbiger Engobe auf gelbem, porösen, mit Schamotte␣magerten Scherben. Daher kein Verziehen beim Brand. Für große Stücke, z.B. Spültische, geeignet*]

~ **articles** → ~ ware

~ **(bath)tub**, ~ bath · Feuerton(bade)wanne f

~ **brick** → refractory ~

~ **goods** → ~ ware

~ **grog refractory** · zementgebundener feuerfester Schamottestein m

~ **products** → ~ ware

~ **refractory material** → refractory brick

~ **sink unit** [*Combined sink and drainer*] · Feuertonabwaschtisch m, Feuertonspültisch

~ **tub**, ~ bath(tub) · Feuerton(bade)wanne f

~ **ware**, ~ products, ~ goods, ~ articles · Feuertonartikel mpl, Feuertongegenstände mpl, Feuertonerzeugnisse npl, Feuertonware(n) f

fire coal · Feuerkohle f

fire-coat → fire-proof(ing) coat

~ **cement** → fire-proof(ing) mortar

~ **mortar** → fire-proof(ing) ~

~ **paint**, fire-proof(ing) ~ · Brandschutz(anstrich)farbe f, Feuerschutz(anstrich)farbe

fired → kiln-~

~ **brick** → (burnt) (clay) ~

~ **clay**, burnt ~, burned ~ · gebrannter Ton m

~ ~ **article** → (burnt) clay product

~ (~) **brick** → (burnt) (~) ~

~ ~ **curved roof(ing) tile** → (burnt) ~ ~ ~ ~

~ ~ ~ **tile roof** → (burnt) ~ ~ ~ ~

~ ~ **hip tile** → (burnt) ~ ~ ~

~ ~ **light(weight) aggregate**, burnt ~ ~ ~, burned ~ ~ ~ · (Beton)Leichtzuschlag(stoff) m aus gebranntem Ton, (Beton)Leichtzuschlagmaterial n ~ ~ ~, Leichtbetonzuschlag(stoff), Leichtbetonzuschlagmaterial

~ ~ **product** → (burnt) ~ ~

~ ~ **ridge tile** → (burnt) ~ ~ ~

fired-on [*Enamel(l)ed devices which are permanently fixed to the surface of glass by heat treatment*] · eingebrannt [*Glas*]

fired pipe, burnt ~, burned ~ · gebranntes Rohr n

~ **product**, burned ~, burnt ~ · Brenngut n, gebranntes Gut

~ **shale**, burned ~, burnt ~ · gebrannter Schieferton m

~ ~ **product**, burnt ~ ~, burned ~ ~ · gebranntes Schieferton-Erzeugnis n

~ **state**, burned ~, burnt ~ · gebrannter Zustand m

~ **ware**, burnt ~, burned ~ · gebrannte Ware f

fire department, FD · Feuerwehr f

~ **detection** · Brandentdeckung f

~ ~ **device** · Branddetektor m

~ ~ **system** · Branddetektoranlage f

~ **division (masonry) wall** (US); compartment (~) ~ (Brit.); party (~) ~, common (~) ~ [*A fire-resisting (masonry) wall from the lowest floor up to the roof used in dividing a building into separate compartments*] · Brand(schutz)mauer f, Feuer(schutz)mauer

firedog → andiron

fire durability · Brandhaltbarkeit f, Feuerhaltbarkeit

~ **duration** · Feuerdauer f, Branddauer

fire-duration test · Branddauerprüfung f, Branddauerprobe f, Branddauerversuch m, Feuerdauerprüfung, Feuerdauerprobe, Feuerdauerversuch

fire endurance → ~ resistance

fire-endurance period, fire(-resistance) ~ · Feuerwiderstandsdauer f, Feuerwiderstandszeit f

fire escape · Fluchtanlage f [*Eine Leiter, ein Gang und dergleichen zum Verlassen eines Bauwerks bei einem Brand*]

(~) ~ **corridor**, emergency ~ · Fluchtkorridor m, Feuerkorridor, Notkorridor, Brandkorridor

(~) ~ **ladder**, emergency ~, fire ~ · Feuerleiter f, Fluchtleiter, Brandleiter, Notleiter

(~) ~ **roof (walk)way**, emergency ~ ~ · Fluchtweg-Dachlaufsteg m, Notweg-Dachlaufsteg

(~) ~ **route**, emergency ~, fire ~ · Fluchtweg m, Notweg, Rückzugsweg

(~) ~ **stair(case)**, emergency ~ · Feuertreppe f, Fluchttreppe, Brandtreppe, Nottreppe

(~) ~ **stair(case) well**, emergency ~ ~ · Feuertreppenhaus n, Brandtreppenhaus, Fluchttreppenhaus, Nottreppenhaus

(~) ~ **window**, emergency ~, fire ~ · Brand(schutz)fenster n, Notfenster, Feuer(schutz)fenster, Fluchtfenster

~ **exit** · Notausgang m

(~) **extinguisher** · (Feuer)Löscher m

(~) ~ **bracket** · (Feuer)Löscher-Halterung f

(fire) extinguisher cabinet — fire polished

(~) ~ cabinet · (Feuer)Löscherschrank m

(~) extinguishing · (Feuer)Löschen n

(~) ~ device · (Feuer)Löschgerät n

(~) ~ engineering · (Feuer)Löschtechnik f [DIN 14011. Die Lehre über die zweckmäßige Anwendung der Löschverfahren und Bedienung der Löschgeräte]

~ (~) foam, extinguishing ~ · (Feuer-)Löschraum m

(~) ~ installation · (Feuer)Löscheinrichtung f

(~) ~ line, (~) ~ run · (Feuer)Löschleitung f

(~) ~ method · (Feuer)Löschverfahren n, Brandverfahren [DIN 14011]

(~) ~ run, (~) ~ line · (Feuer)Löschleitung f

(~) ~ system · (Feuer)Löschanlage f

~ fighting, fftg · Brandbekämpfung f, Feuerbekämpfung

~-fighting procedure · Brandbekämpfungssystem n, Feuerbekämpfungssystem

~ finish, ~ polish, glaze · Feuerblänke f, Feuerblankheit f [Fehlname: Feuerpolitur f. Die sich bei Abkühlung des Glases natürlich bildende blanke Oberfläche]

~ finished, ~ polished [Glass which has been surface polished by heating, for example in a flame] · feuerblank [Fehlbezeichnung: feuerpoliert]

~ foam, ~ extinguishing ~ · (Feuer-)Löschraum m

~ gable · Brand(schutz)giebel m, Feuer(schutz)giebel

~ grading → fire-resistance ~

~ ~ period → fire-resistance ~ ~

(fire-)gutted, ruined by fire, burnt down, burned down, destroyed by fire · abgebrannt, ausgebrannt, niedergebrannt

~ structure · Brandruine f

fire hazard, ~ risk, danger of fire · Brandrisiko n, Feuerrisiko, Brandgefährlichkeit f, Feuergefährlichkeit

~-hearth · Herd m [In einem griechischen Haus der Antike]

fire-hose, FH · (Feuer)Löschschlauch m

(fire-)hose cabinet, FHC · (Feuer-)Löschschlauchschrank m

fire-hose connection · (Feuer)Löschschlauchanschluß m

(fire-)hose rack, FHR · (Feuer)Löschschlauchgestell n

fire hydrant, ~ plug, FHY, fhy · (Feuer-)Löschwasserständer m [DIN 14244]

~ installation, furnace ~, burning appliance ~ · Feuerungsanlage f, Feuerstättenanlage [Sie besteht aus Feuerstätte, Verbindungsstück und Schornstein]

~ ladder, emergency ~, (fire) escape ~ · Feuerleiter f, Fluchtleiter, Brandleiter, Notleiter

~ legislation · Brandschutzgesetzgebung f, Feuerschutzgesetzgebung

~ line [A system of pipes and equipment used exclusively to supply water for extinguishing fires] · (Feuer)Löschleitung f

~ load [It is the amount of heat, expressed in British Thermal Units, which would be generated per square foot of floor area of a compartment of the building by the complete combustion of its contents and any combustible parts of the building] · Brandbelastung f [DIN 18230] [Fehlname: Brandlast f]

~ lobby, compartment [A space within a building designed to delay the passage or facilitate the control of fire] · Brandabschnitt m [DIN 14011]

~ loss · Brandschaden m, Feuerschaden

~ (masonry) wall (US); compartment (~) ~ (Brit.); party (~) ~ [A (masonry) wall which divides up a building to resist the spread of fire. Unlike a fire division wall it does not necessarily rise through more than one stor(e)y] · Brand(schutz)mauer f, Feuer(schutz)mauer

~ mortar → refractory cement

~ ordinance(s), ~ regulations · Brandschutzbestimmungen fpl, Feuerschutzbestimmungen, feuerpolizeiliche Bestimmungen

~ outbreak, outbreak of fire · Brandausbruch m, Feuerausbruch

~ penetration · Brandübergriff m, Feuerübergriff, Brandübertragung f, Feuerübertragung

~ period → fire-resistance ~

fireplace [An open place for a fire built in a wall, at the base of a chimney] · (offener) Kamin m

~ brick · Kaminziegel m

~ chimney · Kaminschornstein m

~ construction · Kaminbau m

~ flue · Kaminzug m

(~) grate · Feuerrost m

~ lounge, fireside ~ · Kaminplatz m

~ masonry (work) · Kaminmauerwerk n

~ material · Kaminbaustoff m

~ opening · Kaminöffnung f

~ recess · Kaminnische f

~ wall · Kaminwand f

fire plug, ~ hydrant, FHY, fhy · (Feuer-)Löschwasserständer m [DIN 14244]

~ point · Brennpunkt m

~ polish, ~ finish, glaze · Feuerblänke f, Feuerblankheit f [Fehlname: Feuerpolitur f. Die sich bei Abkühlung des Glases natürlich bildende blanke Oberfläche]

~ polished, ~ finished [Glass which has been surface polished by heating, for example in a flame] · feuerblank [Fehlbezeichnung: feuerpoliert]

fire prevention — fire(-resistance) grading

~ prevention · Brandverhütung f, Feuerverhütung

~ (~ and fire proofing) regulation · Brand(schutz)vorschrift f, Feuer(schutz)vorschrift, feuerpolizeiliche Vorschrift

~ preventive appliance, ~ ~ device · Brandverhütungsvorrichtung f, Feuerverhütungsvorrichtung

~ ~ device, ~ ~ appliance · Brandverhütungsvorrichtung f, Feuerverhütungsvorrichtung

fireproof, fire safe, fprf, FPRF [*The term 'fireproof' is a misnomer, when applied to buildings. No material and, hence, no structure is entirely fireproof, but practically all materials properly used and protected can be made reasonably fire safe*] · feuersicher, brandsicher

~ cement → fire-proofing mortar

~ construction, nonmetallic ~ ~, non-combustible ~ · Massivbau m

~ construction(al) material → non-metallic ~ ~ ~

~ floor, non-metallic ~ ~, non-combustible ~ · Massivdecke f

~ ~ with suspended ceiling → non-metallic ~ ~ ~ ~ ~

~ impregnation → fire-proofing ~

~ (intermediate) floor → non-metallic ~ (~) ~

~ mortar → fire-proofing ~

~ prefab(ricated) (building) element → non-metallic ~ ~ (~) ~

~ roof floor → non-metallic ~ ~ ~

~ slab floor → non-metallic ~ ~ ~

~ stair(case), non-metallic ~ ~, non-combustible ~ · Massivtreppe f

~ uncovered floor → non-combustible ~ ~

fireproofing · Brandschutz m, Feuerschutz [*Maßnahmen, um Bauteile feuerbeständig zu machen*]

~ · Brandschutzisolierung f, Feuerschutzisolierung

fire-proof(ing) agent · Brandschutzmittel n, Feuerschutzmittel

~ cement → ~ mortar

~ coat, fire-coat · Brandschutzüberzug m, Feuerschutzüberzug, Brandschutz-Beschichtung f, Feuerschutz-Beschichtung

~ ~, fire-coat · Brand(schutz)anstrich m, Brand(schutz)aufstrich, Feuer(schutz)anstrich, Feuer(schutz)aufstrich

~ hanging · Feuerschutztapete f, Brandschutztapete

~ mortar, fire-coat ~, ~ cement [*It is used as protection to steelwork*] · Brandschutzmörtel m, Feuerschutzmörtel

~ impregnation · Feuerschutztränkung f, Brandschutztränkung

~ paint, fire-coat ~ · Brandschutz(anstrich)farbe f, Feuerschutz(anstrich)farbe

~ plaster · Brandschutz(innen)(ver)putz m, Feuerschutz(innen)(ver)putz [*DIN 4102*]

fire propagation · Feuerfortpflanzung f, Brandfortpflanzung

~ property · Brandverhaltenseigenschaft f

~ protection, protection against fire · Brandschutz m, Feuerschutz

~ ~ drawing · Feuerschutzzeichnung f, Brandschutzzeichnung

~ ~ encasement, ~ ~ haunching, ~ ~ sheath coat · Brandschutzummantelung f, Brandschutzumhüllung, Feuerschutzummantelung, Feuerschutzumhüllung

~ ~ haunching → ~ ~ encasement

~ ~ installations · Brandschutzeinrichtungen fpl, Feuerschutzeinrichtungen

~ ~ of structural steelwork · Brandschutz m von Stahlkonstruktionen, Feuerschutz ~ ~, Brand(schutz)umhüllung f ~ ~, Feuer(schutz)umhüllung ~ ~

~ ~ sheath coat → ~ ~ ~ encasement

~ ~ system · Brandschutzanlage f, Feuerschutzanlage

fire-pump · (Feuer)Löschpumpe f

fire-rated · brandklassiert

fire rating, fire-resistive ~ · Brandklassenwert m

~ regulation, ~ prevention and fire proofing ~ · Brand(schutz)vorschrift f, Feuer(schutz)vorschrift, feuerpolizeiliche Vorschrift

~ regulations, ~ ordinance(s) · Brandschutzbestimmungen fpl, Feuerschutzbestimmungen, feuerpolizeiliche Bestimmungen

~ research · Brand(schutz)forschung f, Feuer(schutz)forschung

~ ~ station · Brandforschungsanstalt f, Brand(schutz)forschungsanstalt, Feuer(schutz)forschungsanstalt

~ resistance, ~ endurance [*It is defined as the ability of an element of building construction to fulfil(l) its assigned function in the event of a fire. It is not the property of an individual material but the behavio(u)r of a recognizable constructional element which may consist of a single material or may be fabricated from a number of different materials*] · Feuerwiderstand(sfähigkeit) m, (f), Feuerbeständigkeit

fire(-resistance) grading, ~ rating [*This term has two-fold application. (a) It is applied to the classification or grading of the elements of structure of buildings in terms of their degree of resistance to fire. (b) With a broader meaning, it is applied to the classification of buildings according to the* *purpose for which they are used, that is, according to occupancy, and according to the fire resistance of the elements of which they are constructed*] · Brandklasseneinteilung f

~ **grading period** · Feuerwiderstandsklasse f

~ **period,** fire-endurance ~ · Feuerwiderstandsdauer f, Feuerwiderstandszeit f

~ **test** [*B.S. 476*] · Brandprobe f, Brandversuch m, Brandprüfung f [*DIN 4102*]

fire(-)resistant, fire(-)resisting, fire(-)resistive · feuerbeständig, feuerwiderstandsfähig

~ **(building) component** → fire(-)resisting (building) member

~ **(~) member** → fire(-)resisting (~) ~

~ **(~) unit** → fire(-)resisting (building) member

~ **component** → fire(-)resisting (building) member

~ **constructing,** ~ construction, fire(-)resisting ~, fire(-)resistive ~ · feuerwiderstandsfähiges Bauen n, feuerbeständiges ~

~ **construction,** ~ constructing, fire(-)resisting ~, fire(-)resistive ~ · feuerwiderstandsfähiges Bauen m, feuerbeständiges ~

~ **construction,** ~ structure, fire(-)resisting ~, fire(-)resistive ~ · feuerwiderstandsfähiges Bauwerk n, feuerbeständiges ~

~ **door** → fire(-)resisting ~

~ **finish,** fire(-)resisting ~, fire(-)resistive ~ · feuerbeständige Deckschicht(anstrich)farbe f, feuerwiderstandsfähige ~

~ **floor** → fire(-)resisting ~

~ **member** → fire(-)resisting (building) ~

~ **paint,** fire(-)resisting ~, fire(-)resistive ~ · feuerbeständige (Anstrich)Farbe f, feuerwiderstandsfähige ~

~ **partition (wall)** → fire(-)resisting ~ (~)

~ **roof,** fire(-)resisting ~, fire(-)resistive ~ [*A roof construction which, when subjected to conditions of internal fire, is capable of satisfying for a stated period of time the criteria of fire resistance with respect to collapse and flame penetration*] · feuerwiderstandsfähiges Dach n, feuerbeständiges ~

~ **shutter,** fire(-)resisting ~, fire(-)resistive ~ [*A shutter which, together with its frame, is capable of satisfying for a stated period of time the criteria of fire resistance with respect to collapse and flame penetration*] · Brandabschluß m

~ **structure,** ~ construction, fire(-)resisting ~, fire(-)resistive ~ · feuerwiderstandsfähiges Bauwerk n, feuerbeständiges ~

~ **unit** → fire(-)resisting (building) member

~ **wall** → fire ~

fire(-)resisting → fire(-)resistant

~ **(building) component** → ~ (~) member

~ **(~) member,** ~ (~) unit, ~ (~) component, fire(-)resistant (~) ~, fire(-)resistive (~) ~ · feuerbeständiges (Bau)Element n, ~ Montageelement, Fertig(bau)element, feuerbeständiger (Bau)Körper m, feuerbeständiger Montagekörper, feuerbeständiger Fertig(bau)körper [*Fehlnamen: feuerbeständige (Bau)Einheit f, feuerbeständige Montageeinheit*]

~ **(~) unit** → ~ (~) member

~ **component** → ~ (building) member

~ **constructing,** ~ construction, fire(-)resistant ~, fire(-)resistive ~ · feuerbeständiges Bauen n, feuerwiderstandsfähiges ~

~ **construction,** ~ constructing, fire(-)resistant ~, fire(-)resistive ~ · feuerwiderstandsfähiges Bauen n, feuerbeständiges ~

~ **~,** ~ structure, fire(-)resistant ~, fire(-)resistive ~ · feuerwiderstandsfähiges Bauwerk n, feuerbeständiges ~

~ **door,** fire(-)resisting ~, fire(-)resistant ~; armor ~ (US); armour ~ (Brit.) [*A door which, together with its frame, is capable of satisfying for a stated period of time the criteria of fire resistance with respect to collapse, flame penetration and excessive temperature rise*] · Feuer(schutz)tür f, Brand(schutz)tür, feuerbeständige Tür [*DIN 18081*]

~ **finish** → fire(-)resistant ~

~ **floor,** fire(-)resistant ~, fire(-)resistive ~, compartment ~ [*A floor used in dividing a building into separate compartments*] · Feuer(schutz)decke f, Brand(schutz)decke

~ **member** → ~ building ~

~ **paint,** fire(-)resistive ~, fire(-)resistant ~ · feuerbeständige (Anstrich-)Farbe f, feuerwiderstandsfähige ~

~ **partition (wall),** fire(-)resistant ~ (~), fire(-)resistive ~ (~) [*A partition (wall), either load-bearing or non-loadbearing, capable of satisfying for a stated period of time the criteria of fire resistance with respect to collapse, flame penetration and excessive temperature rise*] · feuerbeständige Trennwand f, feuerwiderstandsfähige ~

~ **roof,** fire(-)resistant ~, fire(-)resistive ~ [*A roof construction which, when subjected to conditions of internal fire, is capable of satisfying for a stated period of time the criteria of fire resistance with respect to collapse and flame penetration*] · feuerwiderstandsfähiges Dach n, feuerbeständiges ~

fire(-resisting) shutter — fire(-)retarding chemical

~ **shutter,** fire(-)resistant ~, fire(-)resistive ~ [*A shutter which, together with its frame, is capable of satisfying for a stated period of time the criteria of fire resistance with respect to collapse and flame penetration*] · Brandabschluß *m*

~ **structure,** ~ construction, fire(-)resistant ~, fire(-)resistive ~ · feuerwiderstandsfähiges Bauwerk *n*, feuerbeständiges ~

~ **unit** → ~ (building) member

~ **wall** → fire ~

fire(-)resistive (building) component → fire(-)resisting (building) member

~ **(~) member** → fire(-)resisting (~) ~

~ **(~) unit** → fire(-)resisting (building) member

~ **ceiling,** fire(-)resisting ~, fire(-)resistant ~ · feuerwiderstandsfähige Decke *f*, feuerbeständige ~

~ **component** → fire(-)resisting (building) member

~ **constructing,** ~ construction, fire(-)resistant ~, fire(-)resisting ~ · feuerwiderstandsfähiges Bauen *n*, feuerbeständiges ~

~ **construction,** ~ constructing, fire(-)resistant ~, fire(-)resisting ~ · feuerwiderstandsfähiges Bauen *n*, feuerbeständiges ~

~ **~,** ~ structure, fire(-)resistant ~, fire(-)resisting ~ · feuerwiderstandsfähiges Bauwerk *n*, feuerbeständiges ~

~ **door** → fire(-)resisting ~

~ **finish,** fire(-)resistant ~, fire(-)resisting ~ · feuerbeständige Deckschicht(anstrich)farbe *f*, feuerwiderstandsfähige ~

~ **floor** → fire(-)resisting ~

~ **member** → fire(-)resisting (building) ~

~ **paint,** fire(-)resistant ~, fire(-)resisting ~ · feuerbeständige (Anstrich)Farbe *f*, feuerwiderstandsfähige ~

~ **partition (wall),** fire(-)resistant ~ (~), fire(-)resisting ~ (~) [*A partition (wall), either load-bearing or non-loadbearing, capable of satisfying for a stated period of time the criteria of fire resistance with respect to collapse, flame penetration and excessive temperature rise*] · feuerbeständige Trennwand *f*, feuerwiderstandsfähige ~

fire(-resistive) rating · Brandklassenwert *m*

fire(-)resistive roof, fire(-)resisting ~, fire(-)resistant ~ [*A roof construction which, when subjected to conditions of internal fire, is capable of satisfying for a stated period of time the criteria of fire resistance with respect to collapse and flame penetration*] · feuerwiderstandsfähiges Dach *n*, feuerbeständiges ~

~ **shutter,** fire(-)resisting ~, fire(-)resistant ~ [*A shutter which, together with its frame, is capable of satisfying for a stated period of time the criteria of fire resistance with respect to collapse and flame penetration*] · Brandabschluß *m*

~ **structure,** ~ construction, fire(-)resistant ~, fire(-)resisting ~ · feuerwiderstandsfähiges Bauwerk *n*, feuerbeständiges ~

~ **unit** → fire(-)resisting (building) member

~ **wall** → fire ~

fire retardant [*A substance applied to a material to increase its resistance to destruction by fire*] · Feuerhemmstoff *m*

fire(-)retardant, fire(-)retarding · feuerhemmend

~ **additive** → ~ chemical

~ **(building) component** → fire(-)retarding (building) member

~ **(~) member** → fire(-)retarding (~) ~

~ **(~) unit** → fire(-)retarding (building) member

~ **chemical,** fire(-)retarding ~, ~ additive · feuerhemmendes Chemikal *n*

~ **component** → fire(-)retarding (building) member

~ **construction,** fire(-)retarding ~, ~ (structural) system · feuerhemmendes (Konstruktions)System *n*, ~ Bausystem, feuerhemmende Konstruktion *f*

~ **door,** fire(-)retarding ~ · feuerhemmende Tür *f*, FT [*DIN 18082*]

~ **member** → fire(-)retarding (building) ~

~ **(mixed) plaster,** fire(-)retarding (~) ~ · feuerhemmender Putz *m*

~ **paint,** fire(-)retarding ~ · feuerhemmende (Anstrich)Farbe *f*

~ **plaster,** ~ mixed ~, fire(-)retarding (mixed) ~ · feuerhemmender Putz *m*

~ **(structural) system** → ~ construction

~ **system** → ~ construction

~ **treatment,** fire(-)retarding ~ [*A treatment applied to a material to increase its resistance to destruction by fire*] · feuerhemmende Behandlung *f*

~ **unit** → fire(-)retarding (building) member

fire(-)retarding, fire(-)retardant · feuerhemmend

~ **additive** → fire(-)retardant chemical

~ **(building) member,** fire(-)retardant (~) ~, ~ (~) unit, ~ (~) component · feuerhemmendes Bauelement *n*, feuerhemmer (Bau)Körper *m* [*DIN 4102. Fehlname: feuerhemmende Baueinheit f*]

~ **chemical** → fire(-)retardant ~

~ **component** → ~ (building) member
~ **construction** → fire(-)retardant ~
~ **door,** fire(-)retardant ~ · feuerhemmende Tür f, FT [DIN 18082]
~ **glazing,** electro-copper ~, copper(-light) ~; electro-copper glass method (Brit.); copper(lite) glass method (US) · Elektroglas n [*Elektroglas ist keine Glassorte, sondern der Name bezeichnet das Verfahren kleine Glasscheiben beliebiger Glasart und bis zu 100 cm^2 Fläche zu feuerhemmenden Scheiben zusammenzufassen*]
~ **liquid coating (material),** fire(-)retardant ~ ~ (~) · feuerhemmender Anstrich(stoff) m, ~ Aufstrich(stoff), ~ flüssiger Beschichtungsstoff, feuerhemmendes Anstrichmittel n, feuerhemmendes Aufstrichmittel
~ **member** → ~ building ~
~ **(mixed) plaster,** fire(-)retardant (~) ~ · feuerhemmender Putz m
~ **paint,** fire(-)retardant ~ · feuerhemmende (Anstrich)Farbe f
~ **system** → fire(-)retardant construction
~ **treatment** → fire(-)retardant ~
~ **unit** → ~ (building) member

fire risk, ~ **hazard,** danger of fire · Brandrisiko n, Feuerrisiko, Brandgefährlichkeit f, Feuergefährlichkeit
~ **room,** burning appliance ~, furnace ~ [*A room primarily used for the installation of fuel-fired heating equipment other than boilers*] · Feuerungsraum m, Feuerstättenraum
~ **route,** (~) escape ~, emergency ~ · Fluchtweg m, Notweg, Rückzugsweg
~ **safe** → fireproof
~ **safety** · Brandsicherheit f

fireside lounge, fireplace ~ · Kaminplatz m

fire spread, flame ~, spread of fire, spread of flame · Brandausbreitung f, Brandausweitung, Feuerausbreitung, Feuerausweitung, Flammenausbreitung
~ **stain** [*The stain left after a fire*] · Brandfleck m
~ **station** · Brandwache f, Feuerwache

firestone, quartz-schist · Quarzschiefer m [*Kieselsäurehaltiges Gestein, das nur gesägt wird und ohne weitere Verarbeitung zur Auskleidung von Öfen dient*]

to firestop · absperren gegen Brand, ~ Feuer

fire stop → ~ barrier

firestopping → fire barrier

fire-susceptible · feuerempfindlich, brandempfindlich

fire technology · Brandtechnologie f
~ **temperature** · Brandtemperatur f, Feuertemperatur
~ **temple** · (iranischer) Feuertempel m
~ **test** → fire-resistance ~

~ ~ **department** · Brandversuchsabteilung f [*Materialprüf(ungs)anstalt*]
~ ~ **testing lab(oratory)** · Brandversuchsanstalt f
~ **tower,** smokeproof ~ [*In tall buildings, a stair designed as a fire escape with entries at each floor, protected by fire doors so that smoke cannot enter the stair*] · Feuertreppenschacht m, Nottreppenschacht
~ **ventilation,** ~ venting · Brandlüftung f
~ **ventilator** [*It opens automatically at a pre-determined temperature, releasing smoke, heat and fumes, keeping the fire localized*] · Ventilator m zum Absaugen von Rauchgasen und Dämpfen
~ **wall** → ~ masonry ~
~ ~, FW (US); compartment ~ (Brit.); fire(-)resisting ~, fire(-)resistant ~, fire(-)resistive ~ [*A wall which divides up a building to resist the spread of fire. Unlike a division wall it does not necessarily rise through more than one stor(e)y*] · Feuer(schutz)wand f, Brand(schutz)wand
~ **warning** · Brandmeldung f, Feuermeldung
~ ~ **device** · Brandmelder m, Feuermelder, Brandmeldeeinrichtung f, Feuermeldeeinrichtung
~ ~ **point** · Feuermeldestelle f

firewater · (Feuer)Löschwasser n, (Brand)Löschwasser
~ **pond** · (Feuer)Löschteich m

fire welding, forge ~ · Feuerschweißen n [*DIN 1910*]
~ **window,** (~) escape ~, emergency ~ · Brand(schutz)fenster n, Notfenster, Feuer(schutz)fenster, Fluchtfenster

firing · (Kessel)Beheizung f
~, burn(ing) · Brand m, Brennen n [*Feuerfest- und Zementindustrie*]
~ **crack,** burn(ing) ~, crazing ~, craze ~ · Brandriß m, Brennriß [*Feuerfestindustrie*]
~ **defect,** burn(ing) ~ · Brennfehler m
~ **equipment** [*e.g. burner, stoker, etc.*] · Brennausrüstung f [*Heiz(ungs)kessel*]
~ **expansion,** burn(ing) ~ [*Increase in size from the dry to the fired state of refractory material*] · Brennwachsen n [*Feuerfestindustrie*]
~ **installation,** ~ plant, burning ~ · Brennanlage f [*Feuerfest- und Zementindustrie*]
~ **process,** burn(ing) ~ · Brennprozeß m, Brennvorgang m [*Feuerfest- und Zementindustrie*]
~ **range,** burn(ing) ~ · Brennbereich m, n [*Feuerfest- und Zementindustrie*]
~ **rate** → burning ~

firing shrinkage — fitment

~ **shrinkage**, burn(ing) ~ [*Decrease in size from the dry to the fired state of a refractory material*] · Brennschwindung f [*Feuerfestindustrie*]

~ **to (cement) clinker**, burning ~ (~) ~ · (Zement)Klinkerbrennen n

~ **up**, warming ~, heating ~ · (An-)Tempern n, Auftempern [*Glasherstellung*]

firm of specialists, specialist firm · Spezialunternehmen n, Spezialfirma f

~ **price**, fixed ~ · Festpreis m, Festsumme f

firm-price bid (US) → fixed-price tender

~ **contract**, fixed-price ~ · Festpreisvertrag m

~ **offer** → fixed-price tender

~ **proposal** (US) → fixed-price tender

~ **tender** → fixed-price ~

firmary, in~ · Infirmeria f, Krankenhaus n [*Teil eines Klosters*]

~ **for lay brethren**, in~ ~ ~ ~ · Laienkrankenhaus n, Laieninfirmeria f

firm's dwelling unit (US); ~ dwelling (Brit.) · Werkswohnung f

firring → furring

first aid room · Sanitätsdienstzimmer n, Verbandsraum m, Erste-Hilfe-Raum

~ **coat** · erste Lage f, ~ Schicht f

~ **floor**; ~ story (US); ~ storey (Brit.) · erste Etage f, erstes Stockwerk n, erstes Geschoß n [*über dem Erdgeschoß*]

~ ~ (US); ground ~ (Brit.) [*In buildings with a basement or cellar the first floor is the first above ground level called 'ground floor' in Great Britain*] · Erdgeschoß n

~ **glazing** · Neuverglasung f, Neueinglasung

~ **newel (post)**, starting ~ (~) · Antrittpfosten m

first-order equation · Gleichung f ersten Grades, lineare Gleichung

~ **theory**, simple plastic ~, linear plastic ~ · (Spannungs)Theorie f 1. Ordnung, einfache plastische Theorie, lineare plastische Theorie

first slab, starting ~ · Antrittplatte f

~ **step** → starting ~

~ **story** (US); ~ storey (Brit.); ~ floor · erste Etage f, erstes Stockwerk n, erstes Geschoß n [*über dem Erdgeschoß*]

~ **undercoat** · erste Unterputzschicht f, ~ Unterputzlage f, ~ Grobputzschicht, ~ Grobputzlage, erstes Rauhwerk n [*Beim dreilagigen Außenputz ohne Putzträger*]

Fischer's yellow (pigment) · Kobaltgelb(pigment) n

fish-bellied girder, fish-belly ~ · Paulitträger m, Linsenträger, Fischbauchträger [*Vollwand- oder Fachwerkträger mit geradem Ober- und nach unten gebogenem Untergurt*]

~ **purlin(e)**, fish-belly ~ · Fischbauchpfette f

fish-belly [*The form taken by some girders, trusses of purlin(e)s where the bottom flange is convex downward*] · Fischbauch m

~ **girder**, fish-bellied ~ · Fischbauchträger m, Linsenträger, Paulitträger [*Vollwand- oder Fachwerkträger mit geradem Ober- und nach unten gebogenem Untergurt*]

~ **purlin(e)**, fish-bellied ~ · Fischbauchpfette f

fished joint, fishplate ~ · Klammerlaschenverbindung f, Klammerlaschenstoß m

fish glue, isinglass · Fischleim m [*Aus Fischabfällen gewonnener saurer Leim. Er wird als Klebstoff für Papier und Gewebe und als Kitt für Porzellan und Glas benutzt*]

fishing [*Lengthening timbers with the assistance of fish plates*] · Anlaschen n, Verlaschen

fish oil · Fischöl n [*Meist schlecht trocknendes Öl, welches mit Trockenstoff versetzt wird und hauptsächlich als Streckmittel für Firnis- oder Lackherstellung Verwendung findet*]

~ **plate**, joint ~, gusset ~, corner ~ connecting ~, connection ~, binding ~, knee bracket ~ · Knoten(punkt)verbindung f

fishplate · Klammerlasche f

~ **joint**, fished ~ · Klammerlaschenverbindung f, Klammerlaschenstoß m

fish's bladder, vesica piscis [*A pointed oval form like a bladder of a fish*] · Schneuß m, Fischblase f, Schneuz m

fish-scale tiling · Fischschuppen-Fliesenbelag m, Fischschuppen-Plattenbelag

to fit, to erect, to set (up) · aufbauen, aufstellen, montieren

fit · Passung f [*Der Grad der Bewegungsfähigkeit zwischen zwei zusammengefügten Teilen. Die Passung wird vom Unterschied der Anschlußnahme der beiden Teile bestimmt*]

~ **for demolition**, ~ ~ wrecking, demolishable, condemned · abbruchreif, abreißreif

~ ~ **human habitation**, ~ to live in, habitable · (be)wohnbar

~ ~ **testing** · prüfgerecht

~ ~ **wrecking**, ~ ~ demolition, demolishable, condemned · abbruchreif, abreißreif

~ **to live in**, ~ for human habitation, habitable · (be)wohnbar

fitch · Fitscher m, Lampenputzer [*Anstreicherpinsel*]

fitment, fitting, built-in furniture, fitted furniture, inbuilt furniture [*Furniture fixed, often by the builder, as opposed to the loose furniture bought by the occupier*] · Einbaumöbel n

fitted assembly — fixed-price tender

fitted assembly · Einlegemontage f [*Leuchte*]

~ **carpet**, wall-to-wall carpeting · Teppich(fuß)boden(belag) m, Teppichbelag

~ **furniture** → fitment

fitter, installer · Installateur m, Monteur

~ **for heating installations**, installer ~ ~ ~ · Heizungsmonteur m, Heizungsinstallateur

fitting, erection, setting (up) · Aufbau(en) m, (n), Aufstellen, Aufstellung f, Montieren, Montage f

~, furniture, builders' ~ · (Bau)Beschlag m

~ · Bearbeitung f [*Parkettstab*]

~ → fitment

~, fitment [*A functional or decorative object fixed to, rather than built into, the carcase of a building but not forming part of it*] · Ausstattungselement n

~, ftg [*Either a pipe fitting or a water fitting*] · Fitting m, Formstück n

~ **procedure**, erection ~, setting (up) ~ · Montagevorgang m, Aufbauvorgang, Aufstell(ungs)vorgang

~ **sequence**, erection ~, setting (up) ~ · Aufbaufolge f, Montagefolge, Aufstell(ungs)folge

~ **shop** → erecting ~

fittings, hardware, builders' ~ [*B.S. 1331*] · (Bau)Beschläge mpl

~ **factory** → builders' ~ ~

five-bay · fünfjochig

five-bed · fünfbettig

five-centred arch (Brit.); five-centered ~ (US) · Fünfzentrenbogen m

five(-)coat system · Fünfschichtenaufbau m, Fünfschichtensystem n

five-foiled arch, cinquefoil ~ · Fünfpaßbogen m

five-leaf sliding folding shutterdoor, ~ ~ ~ shutter door · fünfflügeliges Faltschiebetor n, ~ Schiebefalttor

five-lobe tracery · Fünfpaß m

five(-)moment equation · Fünfmomentengleichung f

five-panel(led) door (Brit.); five-panel(ed) ~ (US) · Fünf-Füllungstür f

five-ply, 5-ply · fünflagig, fünfschichtig [*Klcb(e)dach(belag)*]

five-pointed star · fünfzackiger Stern m

five-room(ed) dwelling unit (US); ~ dwelling (Brit.) · Fünfraumwohnung f, Fünfzimmerwohnung

to fix, to restrain · (gelenklos) einspannen

~ ~, to fasten · befestigen

~ ~ **by nailing** · annageln

fixed, with fixed ends, encastré, without articulations, hingeless, rigid, no-hinged · eingespannt, gelenklos [*Bogen; Träger; Stütze; Balken(träger); Rahmen(-tragwerk)*]

~, immov(e)able · fest, unverschieblich

~ **arch**, fixed-end(ed) ~, built-in ~, no-hinged ~, hingeless ~, arch fixed at both ends · beidseitig eingespannter Bogen m, zweiseitig ~ ~, doppelseitig ~ ~, gelenklos(er) ~ ~

~ **beam**, fixed-end(ed) ~, built-in ~, no-hinged ~, hingeless ~, beam fixed at both ends · beidseitig eingespannter Balken(träger) m, zweiseitig ~ ~, doppelseitig ~ ~, gelenklos(er) ~

~ **column** → support

(fixed-)end bending moment, encastré ~ ~, terminal ~ ~ · Einspann(ungs)biegemoment n

~ **condition**, encastré ~, terminal ~ · Einspann(ungs)bedingung f

~ **fixity**, (~) restraint, (immov(e)able) (end) ~ · unverschiebliche Einspannung f, feste ~, Endeinspannung

~ **moment**, encastré ~, fixing ~, terminal ~, moment at point of fixation, moment at fixed end, F(E)M · Einspann(ungs)moment n, Grundmoment

~ **restraint**, (~) fixity, (immov(e)able) (end) ~ · unverschiebliche Einspannung f, feste ~, Endeinspannung

fixed(-end(ed)) arch → fixed ~

~ **beam** → fixed ~

~ **girder** → built-in ~

fixed equipment circuit [*This is a type of circuit in domestic installations. Apparatus with a rating of 3 kilowatts and above should be fused independently and requires separate circuits. This range includes immersion heaters, cookers and fixed electric fires*] · Starkstromleitung f, Kraftstromleitung [*DIN 18382*]

~ **form(work)**, ordinary ~, ~ forms, ~ shuttering · Standschalung f

~ **girder**, fixed-end(ed) ~, no-hinged ~, built-in ~ (US); girder fixed at both ends · beidseitig eingespannter Träger m, zweiseitig ~ ~, doppelseitig ~ ~, gelenklos(er) ~

~ **glass wall** · fest(stehend)e Glaswand f

~ **glazing** · Festverglasung f, Festeinglasung

~ **heater** · ortsfestes Raumheizgerät n, ortsfester Raumheizer m

~ **hinge** · festes Gelenk n

~ **light** → ~ sash

~ **mooring**, deadman · Ankerholz n, Ankerstein m [*Hafen*]

~ **oil**, drying ~, paint ~ · trocknendes Öl n

~ **pin** · fester Stift m [*Einstemmband*]

~ **point** · Festpunkt m [*Durchlaufträger*]

~ **price**, firm ~ · Festpreis m, Festsumme f

fixed-price contract, firm-price ~ · Festpreisvertrag m

~ **tender**, ~ offer (Brit.); ~ proposal, ~ bid (US); firm-price ~ · Festpreisangebot n

fixed sash — flag(stone)

fixed sash, ~ light, dead light, fast sheet, stand sheet [*A window or part of a window which does not open*] · Festfenster *n*, rahmenloses Fenster

~ shuttering, ordinary ~, ~ form(work), ~ forms · Standschalung *f*

~ simple frame, simple fixed ~ · einfach eingespannter Rahmen *m*

~ support, ~ column, no-hinged ~, hingeless ~ · feste Stütze *f*, starre ~ unbewegliche ~, eingespannte ~, gelenklose ~

~ water, chemically combined ~ · chemisch gebundenes Wasser *n*

fixer, tile ~, (floor-and-wall) tiler · Fliesenleger *m*, Plattenleger

fixing → ~ device

~ → ~ fillet

~ · Befestigen *n*

~ · Befestigung *f*

~ accessories · Befestigungszubehör *n*

~ (accessory), ~ device, ~ means, fastening, fastener · Befestigungsmittel *n*

~ angle · Befestigungswinkel *m*

~ base, nailable ~ · nagelbare Unterlage *f*, nagelfeste ~

~ block, nailable ~, nailing ~; anchor ~ (US) · nagelfester Block *m*, nagelbarer ~, Dübelblock

~ brick, nailable ~, nailing ~; anchor ~ (US) [*It is of a consistency to permit the easy driving of, and provide a good purchase for nails or screws. B.S. 1180*] · nagelbarer Stein *m*, nagelfester ~, Dübelstein

~ channel · Befestigungsschiene *f*

~ clip · Befestigungsklemme *f*

~ concrete, nailable ~ · nagelfester Beton *m*, nagelbarer ~

~ degree, (fixed-)end ~, terminal ~ · Einspann(ungs)grad *m*

~ device → ~ means

~ dimension · Befestigungsmaß *n*

~ (fillet), ~ slip, nailing strip, (common) ground, rough ground, pallet, pad, nailer [*A thin slip of wood, 9 in. × 4½ in., built in a joint of a wall to serve as a fixing for joinery work*] · Nagel(ungs)streifen *m*

~ flange · Befestigungsflansch *m*

~ foot · Befestigungsfuß *m*

~ frame · Befestigungsrahmen *m*

~ hole · Befestigungsloch *n*

~ hook · Befestigungshaken *m*

~ length, encastré ~ · Einspann(ungs)länge *f*

~ material · Befestigungsmaterial *n*

~ means, ~ (accessory), ~ device, fastening, fastener · Befestigungsmittel *n*

~ method, ~ technique, ~ technic · Befestigungsverfahren *n*, Befestigungsweise *f*

~ moment → (fixed-)end ~

~ piece · Befestigungsstück *n*

~ pin · Befestigungsstift *m*

~ plate · Befestigungsplatte *f*

~ point, fastening ~ · Befestigungsstelle *f*

~ (~) · Befestigungspunkt *m*

~ profile, ~ section, ~ shape, ~ unit, ~ trim · Halteprofil *n*, Befestigungsprofil

~ screw, retaining bolt · Befestigungsschraube *f* [*Sie dient zur festen, aber lösbaren Verbindung von Teilen*]

~ section, ~ profile, ~ shape, ~ unit, ~ trim · Halteprofil *n*, Befestigungsprofil

~ shape, ~ section, ~ proifle, ~ unit, ~ trim · Halteprofil *n*, Befestigungsprofil

~ stirrup · Befestigungsbügel *m*

~ strip · Befestigungsleiste *f*

~ system · Befestigungssystem *n*

~ technique → ~ method

~ trim, ~ unit, ~ section, ~ profile, ~ shape · Halteprofil *n*, Befestigungsprofil

~ unit, ~ trim, ~ section, ~ profile, ~ shape · Halteprofil *n*, Befestigungsprofil

~ wall · Befestigungswand *f*

~ web · Befestigungssteg *m*

~ wedge · Befestigungskeil *m*

~ work · Befestigungsarbeiten *fpl*

fixings [*Grounds, plugs, etc., to which joinery is fixed*] · Befestigungspunkte *mpl*

fixity → (effect of) continuity

~, restraint, (immov(e)able) end ~, (fixed-)end ~ · unverschiebliche Einspannung *f*, feste ~, Endeinspannung

~, immovability · Unverschieblichkeit *f*

~ at the connection, rigid joint, stiff joint · starre Verbindung *f*

fixture → luminaire ~

~, built-in unit, fix. [*A functional or decorative object built into, rather than fixed to, the carcass of a building but not forming part of it*] · Einbauteil *m*, *n* im Bauwesen

~ with integral mounting rail → (light(ing)) ~ ~ ~ ~ ~

fixtures, built-in units, in-built units, trim · Einbauten *fpl* im Bauwesen, Einbauteile *mpl*, *npl* ~ ~

Fl. → floor

fl → floor

~ → flashing (material)

flagging · Bürgersteigplattenbelag *m*, Gehbahnplattenbelag, Fußwegplattenbelag, Gehsteigplattenbelag, Gehwegplattenbelag

flagpole, flagstaff · Fahnenmast *m*, Flaggenmast

flagstaff, flagpole · Fahnenmast *m*, Flaggenmast

flagstone · dünnplattiges Gestein *n*

flag(stone) · Pflasterplatte *f*

flake — flange plane

flake · Blättchen *n*
~, ribbon · Filmspan *m* [*DIN 53155*]
~ aluminium pigment (Brit.); **~ aluminum ~** (US); aluminium flake **~** (Brit.); aluminum flake **~** (US) · blättchenförmiges Alu(minium)pigment *n*
~ glass, frost, diamantini · Flitterglas *n*, Schuppenglas
to flake off [*Said of the face of walling stone*] · abplatzen
flake(d) aluminium powder, leafed **~ ~** (Brit.); **~** aluminum **~** (US) · blättchenförmiges Alu(minium)pulver *n*
~ graphite · Lamellengraphit *m*, Flockengraphit, blättchenförmiger Graphit
~ iron oxide, leafed **~ ~** (Brit.); **~ ~** oxid(e) (US) · blättchenförmiges Eisenoxid *n*, Schuppeneisenoxid
~ mica · Schuppenglimmer *m*, blättchenförmiger Glimmer
~ pigment, leafed **~** · Schuppenpigment *n*, blättchenförmiges Pigment
~ powder, leafed **~** · Blättchenpulver *n*, blättchenförmiges Pulver
flakiness index · Scherbenindex *m* [*Kies*]
flaking · Schuppenbildung *f* [*Anstrichschaden*]
flaky · flach, scherbig, platt(ig) [*Korn*]
~ grain · flaches Korn *n*, plattes **~**, scherbiges **~** [*Zuschlag(stoff)*]
flamboyant arch · Flammenbogen *m*, geflammter Bogen
~ rose window · Flamboyantfensterrose *f*, Flamboyantrose(nfenster) *f*, (*n*)
Flamboyant style [*The last phase of French Gothic architecture, so called because the flowing lines of the tracery resemble flames in shape*] · Flamboyantstil *m*, Flammstil, Flamboyantgotik *f*
flamboyant tracery · Flamboyantmaßwerk *n*
flame cleaning · Flammstrahlreinigung *f*, Flammstrahlentrostung
~ cut, f cut · brenngeschnitten
~ cutting, burning · Brennschneiden *n*, Schneidbrennen
~ nozzle · Düse *f* [*Spritzpistole für das Drahtspritzverfahren*]
~ photometry · Flammenphotometrie *f*
flameproof, flame(-)resisting, flame(-)resistive, FP, flmprf · flammwidrig
~ glass, flame(-)resistant **~**, ovenproof **~**, ovenware · flammwidriges Glas *n*
flameproofing · Flammenschutz *m*
~ agent · Flammenschutzmittel *n*
~ wall · Flammenschutzwand *f*
flame resistance · Flammwidrigkeit *f*
flame(-)resistant glass, flameproof **~**, ovenproof **~**, ovenware · flammwidriges Glas *n*
flame(-)resisting, flame(-)resistive, flameproof, FP, flmprf. · flammwidrig

flame-retardant · flammenhemmend
~ chemical · flammenhemmende Chemikalie *f*, flammenhemmendes Chemikal *n*
flame safeguard · Flammenüberwachungsgerät *n*, Flammenwächter *m* [*DIN 4787*]
~ soldering, torch **~** · Flammenlötung *f*
~-sprayed · flammengespritzt
~ spread, fire **~**, spread of fire, spread of flame · Brandausbreitung *f*, Brandausweitung, Feuerausbreitung, Feuerausweitung, Flammenausbreitung, Flammenausweitung
~ travel · Flammenweg *m*
flammability, in**~** · Entzündlichkeit *f*, Entflammbarkeit
flammable, in**~** [*The term 'flammable' is sometimes preferred to 'inflammable' because of the possibility of confusion over the prefix in-, which in most words is a negative, meaning not, non, or un-*] · entflammbar, entzündlich
flanc [*local term*]; (roof) valley · (Dach-)Kehle *f*, (Dach)Kehlung *f*, Einkehle
flange, chord, boom, flg · Flansch *m*, Gurt(ung) *m*, (*f*)
~, flg [*A projecting flat rim cast, screwed or welded on a pipe, fitting or vessel*] · Flansch *m*
~ angle, boom **~**, chord **~**, cover **~**, **~ plate** · Gurt(ungs)winkel *m*, Gurt(ungs)blech *n*
~ area, boom **~**, chord **~** · Gurt(ungs)fläche *f*
~ bar → **~ member**
~ bend → **flange(d) ~**
~ bolt → **flange(d) ~**
~ bracing → **boom stiffening**
~ breech(es) fitting → **flange(d) ~ ~**
~ connection → **flange(d) ~**
~ cross → **flange(d) ~**
~ element → **~ member**
~ fitting → **flange(d) ~**
~ gasket → **flange(d) ~**
~ joint → **flange(d) connection**
~ member, boom **~**, chord **~**, **~ rod**, **~ bar**, **~ element** · Gurt(ungs)stab *m*
to flange-mount · anflanschen
flange mounted · angeflanscht
flange-mounting · Anflanschen *n*
flange nozzle → **flange(d) ~**
~ pipe → **flange(d) ~**
~ (~) fitting → **flange(d) ~ ~**
~ (~) joint → **flange(d) connection**
~ (~) socket → **flange(d) (~) ~**
~ (~) spigot → **flange(d) (~) ~**
~ plane → **chord ~**

flange plate — flaring head

~ **plate** → flange(d) ~

~ ~, boom ~, chord ~, cover ~, ~ angle · Gurt(ungs)blech *n*, Gurt(ungs)winkel *m*

~ **pressure pipe** → flange(d) ~ ~

~ **return bend** → flange(d) ~ ~

~ **rod** → ~ member

~ **section**, chord ~, boom ~ · Gurt(ungs)profil *n*

~ **slope** · Flansch(en)neigung *f*

~ **socket** → flange(d) ~

~ **spring (bend)** → flange(d) ~ (~)

~ **stiffening** → boom ~

~ **tee** → flange(d) ~

~ **union** → flange(d) connection

to flange up · zuflanschen

flange width, chord ~, boom ~ · Flanschbreite *f*, Gurt(ungs)breite

flange(d) bend · Flansch(en)krümmer *m*

~ **bolt** · Flansch(en)schraube *f*

~ **breech(es) fitting**, ~ breeching ~ · Flansch(en)hosenstück *n*

flanged clamping plate · geflanschtes Krallenband *n*

flange(d) connection, ~ union, ~ (pipe) joint · Flansch(en)rohrverbindung *f*, Flansch(en)verbindung, Verflanschung

~ **cross** · Flansch(en)-Kreuzstück *n*

~ **fitting**, ~ pipe ~ · Flansch(en)(form)stück *n*

~ **gasket** · Flansch(en)dichtung *f*

~ **joint** → ~ connection

~ **nozzle** (US); ~ socket; 90° (pipe) junction (piece) · Rohransatz *m*, (Rohr-)Stutzen *m*

~ **pipe** · Flansch(en)rohr *n*

~ **(~) fitting** · Flansch(en)(form)stück *n*

~ **(~) joint** → ~ connection

~ **(~) socket** · (Rohr)Flansch(en)muffe *f*, geflanschte (Rohr)Muffe

~ **(~) spigot** · Flansch(en)(rohr)einsteckende *n*, geflanschtes (Rohr)Einsteckende

~ **plate** · Bördelblech *n*, Krempblech, Kümpelblech

~ **pressure pipe** · Druckflansch(en)rohr *n*, Flansch(en)druckrohr

~ **return bend** · Flansch(en)doppelkrümmer *m*

~ **socket**, ~ pipe ~ · (Rohr)Flansch(en)muffe *f*, geflanschte (Rohr)Muffe

~ ~; ~ nozzle (US); 90° (pipe) junction (piece) · Rohransatz *m*, (Rohr)Stutzen *m*

~ **spigot**, ~ pipe ~ · Flansch(en)(rohr)einsteckende *n*, geflanschtes (Rohr)Einsteckende

~ **spring (bend)** · Flansch(en)knie(stück) *n*

~ **tee** · Flansch(en)-T-Stück *n*

~ **union** → ~ connection

flank · Gebäudeseite *f*

~ **masonry wall**, side ~ ~, lateral ~ ~, end ~ ~ ~ · Seitenmauer *f*, Stirnmauer [*Fehlname: Giebelmauer*]

~ **(of an arch)**; half-arch (Brit.); haunch (US) · Bogenhälfte *f*, Halbbogen *m*, (Bogen)Schenkel *m* [*Die Bogenhälfte zwischen Kämpfer und Scheitel*]

~ **transmission (of sound)** → flank(ing) ~ (~ ~)

~ **wall**, side ~, lateral ~, end ~ · Stirnwand *f*, Seitenwand [*Fehlname: Giebelwand*]

~ ~ **balcony**, end ~ ~ · Stirnwandbalkon *m* [*Fehlname: Giebelwandbalkon*]

flanked · flankiert

flanking of sound · Schallflankenübertragung *f*

~ **path**, sound ~ ~ · Schallflankenübertragungsweg *m*

~ **sound** · Flankenübertagungsschall *m*

~ **tower** · Flankierungsturm *m*, Flankenturm

flank(ing) transmission (of sound) [*The transmission of sound from one room to an adjacent room, via common walls, floors or ceilings, flanking a partition between the rooms, when airborne sound is generated in the first room. Note. The term may also be used to describe any indirect path of sound transmission*] · Flankenübertragung *f*, Schalllängsleitung

flap · Krempe *f* [*Dachziegel*]

~, hinge ~ · (Band)Lappen *m*

~ **hinge** · Scharnierband *n*

~ **tile** · Blattstein *m*, Krempstein, Breitstein, Krampstein, Kremper *m*

~ ~, end ~ · Schluß(dach)ziegel *m*

~ **valve** [*A sheet at a fresh air inlet, hinged to allow air to flow inwards only*] · Verschlußklappe *f*

~ ~, check ~ · Rückstauklappe *f*

flared haunch, flared head, flaring head, mushroom head, support head, column head [*In flat slab construction. An enlargement at the top of a column supporting a flat slab, designed and constructed to act monolithically with the column and with the flat slab*] · Pilzkopf *m*, Stützenkopf

~ **head**, support ~, column ~, flaring ~, mushroom ~, flared haunch [*In flat slab construction. An enlargement at the top of a column supporting a flat slab, designed and constructed to act monolithically with the column and with the flat slab*] · Pilzkopf *m*, Stützenkopf

~ ~ **column**, flaring ~ ~, mushroom (~) ~ · Pilz(decken)stütze *f* [*Fehlnamen: Tragsäule f, Pilzsäule*]

flaring head, mushroom ~, flared ~, support ~, column ~, flared haunch · [*In flat slab construction. An enlargement at the top of a column supporting a flat slab, designed and constructed to act monolithically with the column and with the flat slab*] · Pilzkopf *m*, Stützenkopf

flaring head column — flat concrete (roof(ing)) tile

~ ~ **column,** flared ~ ~, mushroom (~) ~ · Pilz(decken)stütze f [Fehlnamen: Tragsäule f, Pilzsäule]

flash → flashed glass

to flash · (ab)dichten, einfassen, mit Anschluß(streifen) versehen [Schornstein]

~ ~ **chrome plate** · hauchdünn verchromen

flash drying · Warmtrocknung f [Anstrich]

~ ~ **with hot air** · Warmlufttrocknung f [Anstrich]

to flash (off) · abdunsten, ablüften [Anstrichmittel]

flash (off) time [The time allowed to elapse between the spray application of successive wet-on-wet coats or the time allowed for the evaporation of the bulk of the solvent before entering into a stoving oven] · Abluftzeit f, Abdunstzeit [Anstrichmittel]

~ **point,** F.P. · Flammpunkt m

~ ~ **determination** · Flammpunktbestimmung f

~ ~ **(testing) apparatus** · Flammpunktprüfer m

~ **ruby** [struck by reheating] · Anlaufrubinglas n

flash-setting alumina cement · Stopfbinder m, Löffelbinder [Tonerdezement, mit Kalkhydrat oder mit Portlandzement gemischt und mit Wasser angemacht]

~ **cement** · Stopfbinder m, Löffelbinder [In ca. 3 Minuten abbindender Zement]

~ **gypsum** · Stopfbinder m, Löffelbinder [Besonders schnell abbindender Gips]

flash time → ~ off ~

flashed glass, case(d) ~, overlay ~ · Überfangglas n, plattiertes Glas

~ **opal (glass)** [blown sheet] · Opalüberfang(tafel)glas n

flashing → ~ piece

~ **block** · Anschlußstein m [Siehe Anmerkung unter "Anschluß"]

~ **board** [A board on which flashings are fixed] · Anschlußbrett n

~ **(material),** fl [Any impervious material used in roof and wall construction to protect a building from seepage of water] · Anschlußbaustoff m

~ **method** · Anschlußverfahren n [Siehe Anmerkung unter "Anschluß"]

~ **of a vent (pipe),** vent (pipe) flashing [See remark under 'Anschluß'] · Lüftungsrohranschluß m

~ **(piece)** · Anschluß(streifen) m

~ **strip** · Anschlußstreifen m [Siehe Anmerkung unter "Anschluß"]

flat, plane, planar · eben

~, apartment (unit), APT.; living unit (US) [A self-contained dwelling on one stor(e)y in a multi-stor(e)y building] · Stockwerkwohnung f, Etagenwohnung, (Geschoß)Wohnung

~ · Flachprofil n

~ → flats

~ → ~ roof

~ · plan [Platte. Im Gegensatz zu gewellt]

~, mat [The description of a painted surface, which scatters or absorbs the light falling on it, so as to be substantially free from gloss or sheen] · matt

~ **arch** → segmental ~

~ ~ **(lintel)** → straight ~ (~)

~ **arched girder,** segmental ~ ~ · Flachbogenträger m, Stichbogenträger, Segmentbogenträger, flacher Bogenträger

~ ~ ~ **roof,** segmental ~ ~ ~ · Flachbogenträgerdach n, Stichbogenträgerdach, Segmentbogenträgerdach

~ **bar** · Flachstab m

~ **bars** → ~ (rolled) steel

~ ~, ~ **iron** ~, ~ (rolled) iron, flat(s) · Flacheisen n

~ ~ **lacing** → ~ (rolled) iron ~

~ **bearing structure** → plane (load-) bearing ~

~ **block,** ~ building, low ~ · Flachgebäude n [Fehlnamen: Flachbau(werk) m, (n). Im Gegensatz zum Hochhaus]

~ **board** → ~ (run) sheet

~ **brass** · Flachmessing n

~ **brick paving** · Flachschicht f, flachseitige Ziegelpflasterung f

~ **brush,** ~ paint ~, ~ enamel ~ · Flachpinsel m

~ **building,** ~ block, low ~ · Flachgebäude n [Fehlnamen: Flachbau(werk) m, (n). Im Gegensatz zum Hochhaus]

~ **bulb iron** · Flachwulsteisen n

~ **ceiling** · Flachdecke f

~ **cement (roof(ing)) tile** → plain concrete (~) ~

~ **clamping plate** · flaches Krallenband n

~ **clay roof(ing) tile** · Flachziegel m, Zungenziegel, Dachblattziegel, Ochsenzungenziegel, Dachtaschenziegel, Dachplattenziegel, Flachwerkziegel, Plattenziegel, Brettziegel [Dachziegel in Form einer flachen Platte im Gegensatz zum Hohl- und Falzziegel, z.B. Biberschwanzziegel, Schwalbenschwanzziegel mit Regenrinne, Turmziegel]

~ **(~) tile roof** · Zungenziegeldach n, Ochsen~, Taschenziegeldach, Blattziegeldach, Brettziegeldach, Plattenziegeldach, Flach(werk)ziegeldach

~ **concrete roof** · Betonflachdach n, Flachbetondach

~ ~ **(roof(ing)) tile** → plain ~ (~) ~

flat copper — flat (paint) brush

~ **copper** · Flachkupfer n
~ **corbel-table (frieze)** · Flachbogenfries m
~ **cost,** prime ~ · Gestehungskosten f
~ **cradle vault,** ~ cylindrical ~ · flaches zylindrisches Gewölbe n, ~ walzenförmiges ~
~ **cupola** → ~ dome
flat-cut, knife cut, sliced · gemessert, vermessert [*Furnier*]
~ **veneer,** knife-cut ~, sliced ~ · Messerfurnier n [*DIN 68330*]
flat cylindrical vault, ~ cradle ~ · flaches zylindrisches Gewölbe n, ~ walzenförmiges ~
~ **dome,** ~ cupola, shallow(-rise) ~ · Flachkuppel f, Stichkugelgewölbe n, Kugelkappe(ngewölbe) f, (n) [*Der Pfeil ist geringer als der Halbmesser*]
~ **dormer (window)** · Flachgaube f, Flachgaupe
~ **enamel,** mat ~ · Mattemaillelack m
~ ~ **brush,** ~ (paint) ~ · Flachpinsel m
~ **entrance,** apartment (unit) ~; living unit ~ (US) · Stockwerkwohnungseingang m, Etagenwohnungseingang, (Geschoß)Wohnungseingang
~ ~ **door** → apartment (unit) ~ ~
~ **façade** · Flachfassade f
~ **finish,** mat ~ [*A term applied to surfaces free from gloss or polish*] · mattes Aussehen n
~ ~ **paint,** mat ~ ~ · Mattglanzdeckschicht(anstrich)farbe f
~ **fishplate** · Flachlasche f
~ **floor space,** apartment (unit) ~ ~; living unit ~ ~ (US) · Etagenwohn(ungs)fläche f, Stockwerkwohn(ungs)fläche, (Geschoß)Wohn(ungs)fläche
~ **frame,** plane ~, ~ framing · ebener Rahmen m
~ ~ **element,** plane ~ ~, planar ~ ~, ~ framing ~ · ebenes Rahmenelement n
~ ~ **structure,** planar ~ ~, plane ~ ~, ~ framing ~ · ebenes Rahmentragwerk n
~ **glass** · Flachglas n
~ **-glazed,** mat-glazed · mattglasiert, mattbeglast
~ **coat(ing)** → flat(-surface) ~ ~
flat glaze(d finish) → flat(-surface) glazed coat(ing)
~ **glazing** → flat(-surface) glazed coat(ing)
~ **gloss,** mat ~ [*Practically free from sheen even when viewed from oblique angles*] · Mattglanz m
~ ~ **oil paint,** mat ~ ~ ~ · Mattglanzölfarbe f
flat-grain shingle (US); bastard-grain ~ · Schindel f mit liegenden Jahr(es)ringen

flat guard rail section → ~ handrail ~
~ **gutter** → ~ roof ~
~ **handrail section,** ~ ~ shape, ~ ~ unit, ~ ~ trim, ~ ~ profile, ~ guard rail ~ · Flachprofilhandlauf m, Flachprofilhandleiste f
~ **hanger** · Flachhänger m, Flachhängeeisen n [*Hängedecke*]
~ **head,** FH · Flachkopf m
flat-head nail · Flachkopfnagel m
~ **rivet** · Flachkopfniet m
~ **screw** · Flachkopfschraube f
flat (heavy) plate · Flach(grob)blech n
~ **hinge** · Flachgelenk n
~ **interlocking (clay) tile** · Flachdachziegel m [*Tonziegel für flachgeneigte Dächer*]
~ **(iron) bars,** ~ (rolled) iron, flat(s) · Flacheisen n
~ **(~) ~ lacing** → ~ (rolled) iron ~
~ ~ **butt joint** · Flacheisenstoß m
~ ~ **lacing** → ~ (rolled) ~ ~
~ **joint,** flush(ed) ~ · bündige Fuge f, Vollfuge
~ **jointed,** flush ~, solidly filled · vollfugig, bündig verfugt
~ **key** · Flachkeil m, Keil mit flachem Anzug
~ **key** · Ausgleichkeil m [*Hubdeckenverfahren*]
~ **kitchen,** apartment (unit) ~; living unit ~ (US) · (Geschoß)Wohnungsküche f, Stockwerkwerkwohnungsküche, Etagenwohnungsküche
~ **lacquer** · Mattlackfarbe f
flatlet, one-room(ed) flat, one-room(-ed) apartment (unit) · Ein-Raum-Etagenwohnung f, Ein-Raum-Geschoßwohnung, Ein-Raum-Stockwerkwohnung, Ein-Zimmer-Stockwerkwohnung, Ein-Zimmer-Geschoßwohnung, Ein-Zimmer-Etagenwohnung
~; one-room dwelling unit (US); one-room dwelling (Brit.) · Ein-Raum-Wohnung f, Ein-Zimmer-Wohnung
flat (load)bearing structure → plane ~ ~
flat(-lock) seam · einfach(er) liegender Falz m [*Metallbedachung*]
~ ~ **roofing** · Metallbedachung f mit einfach liegenden Falzen
~ **soldered seam** · einfach(er) liegender Falz m mit (Löt)Hafter [*Metallbedachung*]
flatness, accuracy of level(s), evenness; surface smoothness (US) · (Plan)Ebenheit f, Ebenflächigkeit
flat oil paint · Mattöl(anstrich)farbe f
~ **ornament** · Flächenornament n [*In gleicher Fläche gehaltenes Zierwerk*]
~ **paint** · Matt(anstrich)farbe f
~ **(~) brush,** ~ enamel ~ · Flachpinsel m

flat panel — flat seam

~ **panel** → ~ run ~

~ **parabola** · Flachparabel f

~~ **arch(ed girder)** · Flachparabelbogen(träger) m

~ **parallel system,** planar ~ ~, plane ~ ~ · ebenes Parallelsystem n [Seilsystem]

~ **plate** · Flachdeckenplatte f

~ ~, ~ **heavy** ~ · Flach(grob)blech n

~ ~ **floor** [*The flat plate floor is a special type of flat slab construction in which column capitals and drop panels, as well as beams, are eliminated*] · Flachdecke f

~ **porcelain enamel,** ~ vitreous ~, mat ~ ~ · Mattschmelzemaille f, Schmelzmattemaille

~ **rail** · Flachschiene f

~ **rainwater gutter** → ~ (roof) ~

~ **raised band** → ta(e)nia

~ **recess** · (Mauer)Blende f [*Eine flache Mauervertiefung mit ebenem Hintergrund*]

~ **rib expanded metal,** ~ ~ lath(ing) · Flachrippen-Streckmetall n

~ **(rolled) iron,** ~ (iron) bars, flat(s) · Flacheisen n

~ **(~) ~ lacing,** ~ (iron) bars ~, flat(s) ~, lacing of flat bars · Flacheisengitterwerk n, Flacheisenvergitterung f

~ **(~) steel,** ~ (steel) bars, flat(s) ~ · Flachstahl m [*DIN 1017*]

~ **(roof);** platform · ~ [*Scotland*] [*A roof the pitch of which is 10° or less to the horizontal*] · Flachdach n

flat-roof basilica, flat-roofed ~, flat-topped ~ · flachgedeckte Basilika f

flat roof drainage · Flachdachentwässerung f

~ ~ **extract ventilation duct,** ~ ~ ~ venting ~ · Flachdachentlüftungskanal m

~ ~ **fan** · Flachdachventilator m

~ ~ **fascia board** · Flachdachblende f

~ ~ **form** · Flachdachform f, Flachdachgestaltung f, Flachdachausbildung

~ ~ **glazing** · Flachdachverglasung f, Flachdacheinglasung

~ **(~) gutter,** level (~) ~, ~ rainwater ~, ~ R.W. ~ · waag(e)rechte Dachrinne f, ~ (Regen)Rinne

~ ~ **hatch** · Flachdachaussteigluke f, Flachdachausstieg m

flat-roof house, flat-roofed ~, flat-top(ped) ~ · Flachdachhaus n

flat roof insulating compound, ~ ~ insulation(-grade) ~ · Flachdachdämmmasse f

~ ~ ~ **material,** ~ ~ insulation(-grade) ~ · Flachdachdämmstoff m

~ ~ ~ **slab,** ~ ~ insulation(-grade) ~ · Flachdachdämmplatte f

~ ~ ~ **unit,** ~ ~ ~ insulation(-grade) ~ · Flachdachdämmelement n

~ ~ **insulation** · Flachdachisolierung f

(~) ~ **outlet** · (Flach)Dachablauf m

~ ~ **slab** · Flachdachelement n, Flachdachplatte f

~ ~ **system** · Flachdachaufbau m, Flachdachsystem n

~ ~ **tile** → ~ roofing ~

~ ~ **ventilator** · Flachdachlüfter m

(~) ~ **with air circulation,** ventilated (flat) roof · zweischaliges Flachdach n, durchlüftetes ~, Kaltdach [*Es hat zwischen oberster Geschoßdecke und dem Dach einen durchlüfteten Raum*]

flat-roof(ed), flat-topped · mit flacher Decke (versehen)

~ **annexe** (Brit.); ~ annex (US); flat-top(ped) ~ · Flachdachanbau m

~ **basilica,** flat-topped ~ · flachgedeckte Basilika f

~ **block** → ~ building

~ **building,** ~ block, flat-top(ped) ~ · Flachdachgebäude n

~ **house,** flat-top(ped) ~ · Flachdachhaus n

~ **structure,** flat-top(ped) ~ · Flachdachbauwerk n

~ **unit,** flat-top(ped) ~ · Flachdachtrakt m

flat roof(ing) tile · Flachstein m, Zungenstein, Dachblatt n, Ochsenzunge f, Dachtasche f, Dachplatte f, Flachwerk n, Plattenstein, Brettstein [*Dachstein in Form einer flachen Platte im Gegensatz zum Hohl- und Falzstein, z.B. Biberschwanz, Schwalbenschwanz mit Regenrinne und Turmstein*]

~ **rotational system,** plane ~ ~, planar ~ ~ · ebenes Rotationssystem n [Seilsystem]

~ **(run) board** → ~ (~) sheet

~ **(~) panel** · ebene Tafel f, Plantafel f, Flachtafel [*Gegenteil: Welltafel*]

~ **(~) sheet,** ~ (~) board · ebene Platte f, Flachplatte, Planplatte [*Gegenteil: Wellplatte*]

~ **R.W. gutter** → ~ (roof) ~

flat(s), flat (rolled) steel, flat (steel) bars · Flachstahl m

~, flat (rolled) iron, flat (iron) bars · Flacheisen n

flats → block (of ~)

flats-and-offices block, ~ building, office-and-flat ~ · Büro- und Wohnhaus n, Wohn- und Bürohaus

flat seam, ~-lock ~ · einfach(er) liegender Falz m [*Metallbedachung*]

flat seam roofing — flat vault 396

~ ~ roofing, flat-lock ~ ~ · Metallbedachung f mit einfach liegenden Falzen

~ sheet → ~ run ~

~ ~ · Flach(fein)blech n

~ ~ metal lath(ing) · flaches Putzblech n

~ shell, low-rise ~, shallow ~ · krumme Platte f, ~ Schale f, schwach gekrümmte ~, Flachschale, flache Schale

~ skylight · Dachflächenoberlicht n

flat-slab · Pilzdeckenplatte f

~ construction, mushroom ~ · Pilzdeckenbau m

~ floor, mushroom ~ · Pilzdecke f

~ lavatory (basin), ~ washbowl, ~ wash-basin, ~ wash-handbasin [See remark under 'Waschbecken'] · (Hand-)Waschbecken n ohne Rückwand, Waschtisch m ~ ~

flat(s) lacing → flat (rolled) iron ~

flat slat · flache Lamelle f, Flachlamelle

~ soldered seam, ~-lock ~ ~ · einfach(er) liegender Falz m mit (Löt-)Hafter [Metallbedachung]

~ spherical shell, low-rise ~ ~, shallow ~ ~ · flache Kugelschale f, schwach gekrümmte ~

~ spike grid · flacher (zweiseitiger) Krallendübel m, flaches Krallenplattenpaar n

~ state of stress, two-dimensional ~ ~, plane ~ ~ ~, planar ~ ~ ~, state of plane ~ · zweidimensionaler Spannungszustand m, ebener ~

~ steel → ~ rolled ~

~ (~) bars → ~ (rolled) steel

flat-steel profile, ~ section · Flachstahlprofil n

~ section, ~ profile · Flachstahlprofil n

~ wire, steel flat ~ · Flachstahldraht m, Stahlflachdraht

flat stress problem, plane ~ ~, planar ~ ~ · ebene Spannungsaufgabe f, ebenes Spannungsproblem n

~ (supporting) structure → plane (load) bearing ~

~(-surface) glazed coat(ing), mat(-surface) ~ ~, ~ glaze(d finish), ~ glazing · Mattglasur f, Mattbeglasung f

~(-surface) glazing → ~ glazed coat(ing)

flat suspension rod · Hängeband n

~ tapered · einseitig konisch

flattened · abgeflacht

~ (door) knob · (Tür)Flachknopf m

~ expanded (metal) mesh, ~ ~ metal, ~ XPM, ~ EM · Flachstreckmetall n

~ half-round steel · abgeflachter Halbrundstahl m

~ knob, ~ door ~ · (Tür)Flachknopf m

~ rivet head · Flachnietkopf m

~ round bar, ~ ~ rod · abgeflachtes Rundeisen n

~ strand · Litze f mit dreieckigem Querschnitt, Dreikantlitze, Flach(draht)litze

~ ~ cable, ~ ~ rope · Dreikantlitzen(-Draht)seil n, Flachlitzen(-Draht)seil

~ XPM → ~ expanded (metal) mesh

flattening · Abflachung f

~ · Flachwerden n

~, smoothing · Strecken n, Bügeln [Tafelglasherstellung]

~ kiln, smoothing ~ · Streckofen m [Tafelglasherstellung]

flat test specimen · plattenförmiger Probekörper m

~ tile roof → ~ clay ~ ~

~ timber roof, ~ wood(en) ~, wood(-en) flat ~, timber flat ~ · Holzflachdach n, Flachholzdach

flatting · Planschliff m, Verkollerung f [Hohlglas]

~ agent, matting ~, gloss reducer [A material incorporated in a paint, varnish or other coating material to reduce the gloss of the dried film] · Matt(ierungs)mittel n, Matt(ierungs)stoff n

~ down, ~ operation, matting operation, rubbing [Sanding the surface of a paint or varnish with fine abrasives to produce a smooth dull surface] · Mattieren n

~ operation → ~ down

~ ~ · Verkollern n, Planschleifen [Hohlglas]

~ process · Verkollerungsverfahren n, Planschleifverfahren [Hohlglas]

~ ~, matting ~ · Mattierungsverfahren n

~ varnish, rubbing ~ [A hard-drying varnish which may be rubbed with an abrasive and water or oil to a uniform level(l)ed surface] · Schleiflack m, Präparationslack, Vorlack, Hartmattlack

flat-top(ped) flat-roofed · mit flacher Decke (versehen)

~ annexe (Brit.); ~ annex (US); flat-roof(ed) ~ · Flachdachanbau m

~ basilica, flat-roof(ed) ~ · flachgedeckte Basilika f

~ block → ~ building

~ building, ~ block, flat-roof(ed) ~ · Flachdachgebäude n

~ house, flat-roof(ed) ~ · Flachdachhaus n

~ structure, flat-roof(ed) ~ · Flachdachbauwerk n

~ unit, flat-roof(ed) ~ · Flachdachtrakt m

flat varnish, matt(e) ~, mat ~ [A varnish made to dry with a dull surface by incorporating metallic soaps or certain mineral fillers, e. g. diatomaceous earth] · Mattlack m

~ vault, straight ~, jack ~; floor ~ (US) · scheitrechtes Gewölbe n, g(e)rades ~, flaches ~, Geradgewölbe, Sturzgewölbe, Horizontalgewölbe, Flachgewölbe

flat vitreous enamel — flexible industrial door

~ **vitreous enamel,** ~ porcelain ~, mat ~ ~ · Mattschmelzemaille f, Schmelzmattemaille

~ **vitrifiable colour** (Brit.) → mat enamel

~ **wall paint,** mat ~ ~ · Mattwand(anstrich)farbe f

~ **(weight-carrying) structure** → plane (load)bearing ~

~ **window on pitched roof** · Dachflächenfenster n

~ **wire** · Flachdraht m

~ ~ **cloth,** ~ ~ woven fabric; ~ ~ fabric [*misnomer*] · Flachdrahtgewebe n

~ ~ **fabric** [*misnomer*]; ~ ~ cloth, ~ ~ woven fabric · Flachdrahtgewebe n

~ ~ **woven fabric,** ~ ~ clòth; ~ ~ fabric [*misnomer*] · Flachdrahtgewebe n

(~) wire(d) (clear) (polished) plate (glass), polished wire(d) ~ · Drahtspiegelglas n, Spiegeldrahtglas

~ ~ **glass,** wire(d) flat ~ · Drahtflachglas n, Flachdrahtglas

~ **wood(en) roof,** ~ timber ~, wood(en) flat ~, timber flat ~ · Holzflachdach n, Flachholzdach

Flavian Amphitheatre, Colosseum at Rome · Colosseum n, flavisches Amphitheater n zu Rom

~ **architecture** · flavische Architektur f, ~ Baukunst f

flaw, incipient crack, incipient tear · Anriß m [*Baustahl*]

flax · Flachs m, Leinpflanze f

flaxboard, flax shive board [*Particle board made from flax shives, the residue from the flax plant after removal of flax fibres*] · Flachsschäbenplatte f, Flachs(span)platte

flax burlap (US); ~ hessian (Brit.) · Flachssackleinen n

~ ~ **mat** (US); ~ hessian ~ (Brit.) · Flachssackleinenbahn f

~ **felt** · Flachs(dach)pappe f

~ **felt(ed fabric)** · Flachsfilz m

~ **hessian** (Brit.); ~ burlap (US) · Flachssackleinen n

~ ~ **mat** (Brit.); ~ burlap ~ · Flachssackleinenbahn f

~ **sacking** · Flachsgrobgewebe n

flax-seed, linseed · Flachssamen m, Leinsaat f

flax shive board, flaxboard [*Particle board made from flax shives, the residue from the flax plant after removal of flax fibres*] · Flachsschäbenplatte f, Flachs(span)platte

~ **shives** · Flachsschäben fpl

fleaking → (reed) thatch(ing)

flèche [*A ventilating turret or spire placed astride a roof and forming a dominant architectural feature*] · Luftürmchen n

fleckschiefer, maculose rock, mottled schist, spotted schist · Fleck(en)schiefer m

flection curve → flexure ~

~ **limit** → flexure ~

~ **load** → flexure ~

fleece-wool · Schurwolle f

Flemish bond, block ~; Dutch ~ [*misnomer*] [*Each course consists of alternate headers and stretchers, the alternate headers of each course being centered over the stretchers in the course below*] · flämischer Verband m

fleur-de-lis, lily-flower · (Bourbonische) Lilie f, Wappenlilie

fleuron [*A floral ornament on the centre of the abacus of the Corinthian capital. The term is sometimes loosely applied to medieval decoration as well*] · Fleuron m

flex, flexible cable; lamp cord (US) · (Geräte)Anschlußschnur f, Verbindungsschnur

flexibility, yield · Nachgiebigkeit f

~ → bending capacity

~ **in planning** · Vielgestaltigkeit f der Planung

~ **matrix** · Nachgiebigkeitsmatrix f

~ ~ **method,** (Argyris) force ~ · Kraft(größen)verfahren n, Kraft(größen)methode f

~ **number** · Biegsamkeitsziffer f, Biegsamkeitszahl f [*Maß für die Biegung eines Stabes; abhängig vom Elastizitätsmodul, dem Trägheitsmoment, der Stablänge und den Einspannverhältnissen des Stabes*]

flexible, nonrigid · nichtstarr, schmiegsam, unsteif, biegeweich

~ · biegsam

~, yielding · nachgiebig

~ **cable,** flex; lamp cord (US) · (Geräte-)Anschlußschnur f, Verbindungsschnur

~ **door,** ~ swing · flexible Pendeltür f

~ **expanded plastic** → ~ foam(ed) ~

~ **floor** [*A timber floor may be regarded as a flexible floor in comparison with a reinforced concrete floor which is stiffer*] · biegeweiche Decke f, nichtstarre ~

~ **foam** → ~ foam(ed) plastic

~ **foam(ed) plastic,** ~ expanded ~, ~ (plastic) foam · (Kunststoff)Weichschaum m, Weichkunststoffschaum, Weichschaum(kunst)stoff m

~ ~ **polyurethane** · Polyurethan-Weichschaum(stoff) m, PUR-Weichschaum(-stoff)

~ **foundation beam** · Zerrbalken m

~ ~ **slab** · Zerrplatte f

~ **handling of space** · Freiheit f der Raumgestaltung

~ **industrial door,** ~ ~ swing ~ · (flexible) Industrie-Pendeltür f

flexible industrial (swing) door — flexural buckling 398

~ ~ **(swing) door** · (flexible) Industrie-Pendeltür f
~ **insulation** · Mattenisolierung f
~-**metal conduit** [*Conduit made from spirally wound steel strip*] · biegsames Elektro-Metallrohr n
(flexible) metal cornice flashing (piece), sheet ~ ~ ~ (~) · (Ge-)Simsabdeckung f aus Blech, (Ge-)Simsblech n
(~) ~ **flashing (piece),** sheet ~ ~ (~) [*See remark under 'Anschluß'*] · Anschlußblech(streifen) n, (m), Blechanschluß(streifen) m
~ ~ **for roofing** [*Sheet metal, originally zinc, lead, copper, or painted tinplate, but now also aluminium. Unlike corrugated sheet, flexible metal cannot span a gap, and so, like roofing felt, it must be laid on close boarding or plywood, covered with an underlay*] · ebenes Bedachungsblech n, ~ Dach(ein)(deckungs)blech
(~) ~ **masonry wall flashing (piece),** sheet ~ ~ ~ ~ (~) [*See remark under 'Anschluß'*] · Mauerabdeckung f aus Blech, Mauerblech n
(~) ~ **sheet roof cladding** → (sheet-)metal ~ ~
(~) ~ ~ ~ **covering** → (sheet-)metal roof cladding
(~) ~ ~ ~ **sheathing** → (sheet-)metal roof cladding
(~) ~ ~ ~ **roofing** → (sheet-)metal roof cladding
~ **(metallic) tube,** metal (reinforced) hose · Metallschlauch m, Panzerschlauch
~ **neoprene door,** ~ ~ swing ~ · (flexible) Neopren-Pendeltür f
~ ~ **(swing) door** · (flexible) Neopren-Pendeltür f
~ **plastic door,** ~ ~ swing ~ · (flexible) Kunststoff-Pendeltür f
~ (~) **foam** → ~ foam(ed) plastic
~ ~ **(swing) door** · (flexible) Kunststoff-Pendeltür f
~ **polyethylene,** ~ polythene · PE weich n, Weichpolyäthylen n
~ ~ **pipe,** ~ polythene ~ · Weichpolyäthylenrohr n [*DIN 19533 für Trinkwasserversorgung*]
~ **polythene,** ~ polyethylene · PE weich n, Weichpolyäthylen n
~ ~ **pipe,** ~ polyethylene ~ · Weichpolyäthylenrohr n [*DIN 19533 für Trinkwasserversorgung*]
~ **polyurethane** · Weich-Polyurethan n, Weich-PUR
~ **polyvinyl chloride door** → ~ PVC (swing) ~
~ ~ ~ **film,** ~ ~ ~ sheeting, ~ PVC ~ · Polyvinylchloridweichfolie f, Weichpolyvinylchloridfolie, Weich-PVC-Folie, PVC-Weichfolie

~ ~ ~ **(resin),** ~ PVC (~) · Weich-Polyvinylchlorid n, Weich-PVC
~ ~ ~ **(swing) door,** ~ PVC (~) ~ · Polyvinylchlorid-Pendeltür f, PVC-Pendeltür, flexible ~
~ **PVC door** → ~ ~ swing ~
~ **PVC film,** ~ ~ sheeting, ~ polyvinyl chloride ~ · Polyvinylchloridweichfolie f, Weichpolyvinylchloridfolie, Weich-PVC-Folie, PVC-Weichfolie
~ ~ **floor cover(ing),** ~ ~ floor(ing), ~ ~ floor finish [*B.S. 3261*] · Polyvinylchlorid-Boden(belag) m auf Träger(schicht), Polyvinylchlorid-Fußboden(belag) ~ ~, PVC-(Fuß)Boden(belag) ~ ~
~ ~ ~ **finish,** ~ ~ floor(ing), ~ ~ floor cover(ing) [*B.S. 3261*] · Polyvinylchlorid-Boden(belag) m auf Träger(schicht), Polyvinylchlorid-Fußboden(belag) ~ ~, PVC-(Fuß)Boden(belag) ~ ~
~ ~ **floor(ing),** ~ ~ floor cover(ing), ~ ~ floor finish [*B.S. 3261*] · Polyvinylchlorid-Boden(belag) m auf Träger(schicht), Polyvinylchlorid-Fußboden(belag) ~ ~, PVC-(Fuß)Boden(belag) ~ ~
~ ~ ~ **(resin),** ~ polyvinyl chloride (~) · Weich-Polyvinylchlorid n, Weich-PVC
~ ~ **sheet(ing)** · Polyvinylchlorid-Bodenbahn f auf Träger(schicht), Polyvinylchlorid-Fußbodenbahn ~ ~, PVC-(Fuß)Bodenbahn ~ ~
~ ~ **sheeting** → ~ ~ film
~ ~ **(swing) door,** ~ polyvinyl chloride (~) ~ · (flexible) Polyvinylchlorid-Pendeltür f, (~) PVC-Pendeltür
~ **R.C. foundation beam** → reinforced (concrete) flexible ~ ~
~ **reinforced (concrete) foundation beam** → reinforced (concrete) flexible ~ ~
~ **rubber (swing) door** · (flexible) Gummi-Pendeltür f
~ **steel arch** · „biegeweicher" Stahlbogen m
~ **(swing) door** · flexible Pendeltür f
~ **tube** → ~ metallic ~
flexing curve → flexure ~
~ **limit** → flexure ~
~ **load** → flexure ~
flexion curve → flexure ~
~ **limit** → flexure ~
~ **load** → flexure ~
flexional elasticity → bending ~
flexural beam · Biegebalken(träger) m
~ **bond failure,** bending ~ ~ · Haftungsbiegebruch m, Verbundbiegebruch
~ ~ **test** · Biege-Haftfestigkeits-Versuch m, Biege-Haftfestigkeits-Probe f, Biege-Haftfestigkeits-Prüfung f
~ **buckling** · Biegeknicken n, Biegeknickung f

flexural compressive failure — flight (of stairs)

~ **compressive failure** · Biegedruckbruch *m*, Biegungsdruckbruch

~ **crack**, bending ~ · Biegeriß *m*

~ **endurance** → fatigue in bending

~ **equation** · Biegegleichung *f*

~ **fatigue** → fatigue in bending

~ ~ **limit** · Biegeermüdungsgrenze *f*, Biegungsermüdungsgrenze

~ ~ **resistance**, ~ ~ strength · Biege-Dauerfestigkeit *f*, Biege-Ermüdungsfestigkeit, Biege-Arbeitsfestigkeit

~ **limit** → flexure ~

~ **load** → flexure ~

~ **loop joint** [*It uses vertical loops*] · Biegeschlaufenstoß *m*

~ **member**, bending ~, ~ element · Biegestab *m* [*Rahmen*]

~ **oscillation**, bending ~, ~ vibration · Biegeschwingung *f*

~ ~ **failure**, bending ~ ~, ~ vibration ~ · Biegeschwingungsbruch *m*

~ ~ **strength**, bending ~ ~, ~ vibration ~ · Biegeschwingungsfestigkeit *f*

~ ~ **test**, bending ~ ~, ~ vibration ~ · Biegeschwingungsversuch *m*, Biegeschwingungsprobe *f*, Biegeschwingungsprüfung *f*

~ **resistance**, bending ~, ~ stiffness, ~ rigidity, resistance to bending · Biegesteifigkeit *f*, Biegewiderstand *m*, Biegungssteifigkeit, Biegungswiderstand, Biegesteife *f*, Biegestarrheit, Biegesteifheit

~ **rigidity**, bending ~, ~ stiffnes, ~ resistance, resistance to bending · Biegesteifigkeit *f*, Biegewiderstand *m*, Biegungswiderstand, Biegungssteifigkeit, Biegesteife, Biegestarrheit, Biegesteifheit

~ **shear crack** · Schubbiegeriß *m*

~ ~ **failure** · Schubbiegebruch *m*

~ **stiffness**, bending ~, ~ rigidity, ~ resistance, resistance to bending · Biegesteifigkeit *f*, Biegewiderstand *m*, Biegungswiderstand, Biegungssteifigkeit, Biegsteife *f*, Biegestarrheit, Biegesteifheit

~ **strain energy**, bending ~ ~ · Biegedehnungsenergie *f*, Biegungsdehnungsenergie

~ **strength**, lateral ~, transverse ~, modulus of rupture [*The strength of a specimen tested in transverse bending; normally synonymous with 'modulus of rupture' but also used to refer to breaking load (see B.S. 340, 368, 550 and 2028)*] · Querbiegefestigkeit *f*

~ **stress**, bending ~ · Biegespannung *f*, Biegungsspannung

~ ~ **distribution**, bending ~ ~ · Biegespannungsverteilung *f*, Biegungsspannungsverteilung

~ ~ **formula**, bending ~ ~ · Biegespannungsformel *f*, Biegungsspannungsformel

~ **tensile failure**, bending tension ~ · Biegezugbruch *m*

~ ~ **strength** · Biegezugfestigkeit *f*

~ ~ **stress**; extrem fibre ~ (Brit.); extreme fiber ~ (US) · Biegezugspannung *f*

~ ~ **test** · Biegezugversuch *n*, Biegezugprobe *f*, Biegezugprüfung *f*

~ **torsion** · Biegetorsion *f*, Biegungstorsion

flexural-torsional buckling · Biegedrillknicken *n* [*als Vorgang*]

~ ~ · Biegedrillknickung *f* [*als Ergebnis des Vorganges*]

flexural vibration → ~ oscillation

~ ~ **failure** → flexural oscillation ~

~ ~ **strength** → ~ oscillation ~

~ ~ **test** → ~ oscillation ~

flexurally rigid, resistant to bending, bending-resistant, rigid, stiff, bendproof · (biege)steif, starr, biegefest, biegungssteif, biegungsfest

flexure, bending · Biegen *n*

~, (downward) deflection, (downward) deflexion · (Durch)Biegung *f*, Durchsenkung

~ **curve**, bending ~, flexion ~, flexing ~, flection ~ · (Durch)Biegungskurve *f*

~ **formula**, bending ~ · Biegeformel *f*

~ **limit**, bending ~, flexion ~, flexing ~, flection ~, flexural ~ · Biegegrenze *f*, Biegungsgrenze

~ **load**, bending ~, flexion ~, flexing ~, flection ~, flexural ~ · Biegelast *f*, Biegungslast

~ **test beam**, bending ~ ~ · Biegebalken *m*, Probebalken, (Biege)Prüfbalken, (Biege)Versuchsbalken

~ ~ **in tempered (or quenched) state**, bend(ing) ~ ~ ~ (~ ~) ~ · Abschreck-Biegeversuch *m*, Härtungs-Biegeversuch, Abschreck-Biegeprobe *f*, Härtungs-Biegeprobe, Abschreck-Biegeprüfung *f*, Härtungs-Biegeprüfung

flg → flange

~ → floor(ing)

flier → flying shore

~ **(arch)**, flying ~, flying buttress, arch(ed) buttress, arch-butment; bow [*old English term*] · (einfacher) Strebebogen *m*, Hochschiffstrebe *f* [*veraltet: fliegende Strebe f, Fluchtstrebe*]; Schwibbogen *m* [*Fehlname*]

flight announcement center (US); ~ ~ **centre** (Brit.) · Flugansagezentrum *n*

~ **of front steps**, perron [*An outside stair(case), usually extending up the slope of a terrace, as to the front entrance of a building*] · Freitreppe *f*, Gebäudeeingangstreppe

~ **(~ stairs)**, stair flight, flight of steps, flt · (Treppen)Lauf *m*

flint — flooded

flint [*A chalcedonic variety of quartz, found as nodules and nodular bands in chalk and as residual pebbles*] · Feuerstein *m*, Flint(stein) *m*, Silex *m*, SiO_2

~, white ~, flint glass · weißes Hohlglas *n*, Weißglas

~ **clay** · Flint-Ton *m*

~ **glass**, (white) flint · weißes Hohlglas *n*, Weißglas

~ **paper** · Flintpapier *n* [*Schleifpapier mit Feuersteinpulverbelag, je nach Feinheit graduiert*]

~ **pebble** · Feuersteinknollen *m*, Flint-(stein)knollen, Silexknollen

~ **rubble** · Feuerstein-Bruchstein *m*, Flint(stein)-Bruchstein, Silex-Bruchstein

flitch beam, flitched ~, sandwich ~ · Sandwich-Balken(träger) *m*

~ **plate** [*The steel plate which reinforces a flitched beam*] · Sandwichplatte *f*

flmprf. → flameproof

to float · (auf)spachteln, verstreichen

float, smoothing trowel, finishing trowel · Glättkelle *f*

~, spreader · Glätter *m* [*Putztechnik*]

~ [*A body lighter than water riding on a water surface and actuating a mechanism by its response to rise or fall of the surface*] · Schwimmer *m*

~ **glass**, plate ~ [*Thick sheets of glass made by floating the molten glass on a surface of molten metal, which produces a smooth, polished surface*] · Schwimmglas *n*

~**(-operated) valve** [*A valve, for controlling the flow into a cistern or other vessel, which is operated by the movement of a float riding on the surface of the water in the vessel*] · Schwimmerventil *n*

float stone [*A stone for rubbing bricks, to clean or level them*] · Reib(e)stein *m*

~ **test** · Schwimmprobe *f*, Schwimmprüfung *f*, Schwimmversuch *m* [*Kohlenwasserstoffbindemittel*]

~ **valve** → ~-operated ~

floated coat [*A plaster coat smoothed by a float*] · Ziehschicht *f*, Glättschicht [*Putztechnik*]

~ **filler**, ~ **stopper**, ~ **stopping** · Ziehausfüller *m*, Glättausfüller, Glätt(füll)-spachtel(masse) *m*, (*f*), Zieh(füll)spachtel(masse)

~ **finish** · Reibeputz *m*

floating [*A defect which is sometimes apparent in coloured paints containing mixtures of different pigments. During drying or on storage one or more of the pigments separates, or floats apart from the others and concentrates in streaks or patches on the surface of the paint, producing a variegated effect*] · Streifenbildung *f*

~, flooding · Ausschwimmen *n* [*Pigment*]

~ [*A slab finishing operation which embeds aggregate, removes slight imperfections, humps and voids to produce a level surface, and consolidates mortar at the surface*] · Glattstreichen *n*

~ **ball** · Schwimm(er)kugel *f*

~ **calcium sulphate plaster screed** (Brit.); ~ ~ sulfate ~ ~ (US) · schwimmender Gipsestrich *m*

~ **ceiling** · Schwebedecke *f*

~ **coat**, straightening ~ · Unterputzschicht *f*, Unterputzlage *f*, Grobputzschicht, Grobputzlage, Rauhwerk *n* [*Beim zweilagigen Putz*]

~ ~, straightening ~, second ~, browning ~, topping ~ · zweite (Unter)Putzschicht *f*, ~ (Unter)Putzlage *f*, ~ Grobputzschicht, ~ Grobputzlage, zweites Rauhwerk *n* [*Beim dreilagigen Putz*]

~ **concrete screed**, concrete-screed floating floor cover(ing), concrete-screed floating floor(ing) (finish) · schwimmender (Zement)Estrich(fuß)-boden(belag) *m*, ~ (Zement)Estrich *m*

~ **floor(ing) (finish)**, ~ floor cover(ing) · schwimmender (Fuß)Boden(belag) *m*

~ **globe valve**, ball ~ · (Schwimm-)Kugelventil *n*

~ **hostel** · schwimmendes Wohnheim *n*

~ **parquet(ry)** · schwimmendes Parkett *n*

~ **pyrometer** · Schwimmerpyrometer *n*

~ **roof(ing) screed** · schwimmender Dachestrich *m*

~ **warehouse** [*Is used to increase docking facilities in crowded harbo(u)rs*] · Schwimm-Lagerhaus *n*

flocculant, flocculating agent · Flokkulierungsmittel *n*, Ausflockungsmittel

to flocculate · flokkulieren, ausflocken

flocculated latex crumb, rubber powder, powder(ed) rubber · Kautschukmehl *n*, Kautschukpulver *n*

flocculating agent, flocculant · Flokkulierungsmittel *n*, Ausflockungsmittel

flocculation [*The development of loosely coherent solid aggregates in a pigment-vehicle dispersion*] · Ausflocken *n*, Flokkulation *f*

flocculent gypsum, gypsum insulation · Flockengips *m* [*für Schüttisolierungen*]

flock paper, velvety ~ ~ · Samttapete *f*, Velourstapete

flood coat · Einbettmasse *f* [*Spachteldach(belag)*]

~ ~, flow ~ · Flutlackierschicht *f*

~ ~ **for chip(ping)s** · Splitteinbettmasse *f* [*Spachteldach(belag)*]

flooded [*The condition which results when the liquid in a container or receptacle rises to the flood-level rim*] · randvoll

flooding [*An extreme case of floating in which pigment particles float in such a manner as to produce a colour which, though uniform over the whole surface, is markedly different from that of the newly applied wet film*] · Schwimmen *n*, Aus~

flood level rim [*The edge of a receptacle or container from which water overflows*] · Überlaufrand *m*

flood-light · Flutlichtstrahler *m*

floodlighting · Anstrahlen *n* [*als Vorgang*]

~ · Anstrahlung *f* [*als Ergebnis des Vorganges*]

~ · Flutlichtbeleuchtung *f*

~ **system** · Flutlichtanlage *f*

floodlit · angestrahlt [*durch Scheinwerfer*]

~ · flutlichtbeleuchtet

floor; story (US); **storey** (Brit.), fl, fl., flr · Geschoß *n*, Etage *f*, Stock(werk) *m*, (*n*)

~ → (stair(case)) ~

~, **flooring** [*A construction that provides the surface on which one walks in a building or structure*] · (Fuß)Boden *m*

~, **intermediate** ~ · (Gebäude)Decke *f*, Trenndecke, Hochbaudecke, Etagendecke, Stockwerkdecke, Geschoßdecke

~ **adhesive** → floor(ing) (bonding) ~

(floor-and-wall) tiler, (tile) fixer · Fliesenleger *m*, Plattenleger

floor-and-wall tiling work, tile fixing ~ · Fliesen- und Plattenarbeiten *fpl* [*DIN 18352*]

floor arch (lintel) (US) → straight ~ (~)

~ **area,** ~ space · Deckenfläche *f*

~ ~, ~ space · Geschoßfläche *f*, Etagenfläche, Stockwerkfläche

~ **batten** → flooring ~

~ **beam** → suspended ~ ~

~ ~ → (stair(case)) landing ~

~ **bearer** → (stair(case)) landing ~

~ **binder** → (stair(case)) landing bearer

~ **(binding) joist** → (stair(case)) landing bearer

~ **board,** plancher, plancier, plance(e)r · (Fuß)Bodenbrett *n*, (Fuß)Bodendiele *f*, Dielenbrett

~ **boarding,** batten floor(ing), planching, plancher, plancier, plance(e)r · Dielung *f*, Dielen(fuß)boden *m*, Brett(er)(fuß)boden

~ **(bonding) adhesive** → flooring (~) ~

~ ~ **agent** → floor(ing) (bonding) adhesive

~ ~ **medium** → floor(ing) (bonding) adhesive

~ **branch ; story** ~ (US); **storey** ~ (Brit.) · Stockwerkleitung *f*, Etagenleitung, Geschoßleitung [*Die von einer Steigleitung innerhalb eines Stockwerkes abzweigende Verbrauchsleitung*]

~ **breakthrough** · Deckendurchbruch *m*

~ **brick,** ~ clay ~, ~ clay block · Deckenziegel *m*, gebrannter Deckenstein *m* [*DIN 4159 und DIN 4160. Fehlname: Deckenstein*]

~ ~ → floor(ing) (clay) ~

~ **(building) component** → (prefab(ricated)) floor (building) unit

~ **(~) member** → (prefab(ricated)) floor (building) unit

~ **(~) unit** → (prefab(ricated)) ~ (~) ~

~ **burning appliance** → ~ furnace

~ **care** → flooring ~

~ **cast(ing)** → (pre)cast (concrete) floor member

floor-ceiling glazing · raumhohe Verglasung *f*

floor ceiling joist → (stair(case)) landing bearer

floor-ceiling partition (wall) with (built-in) door · raumhohe Trennwand *f* mit (eingebauter) Tür

floor cement(ing agent) → floor(ing) (bonding) adhesive

~ **centre(s),** ~ **centreing** (Brit.); ~ **centers,** ~ **centering** (US) · Deckenrüstung *f*

~ **clay block,** ~ (~) **brick** · Deckenziegel *m*, gebrannter Deckenstein *m* [*DIN 4159 und DIN 4160. Fehlname: Deckenstein*]

~ **(~) brick,** ~ ~ **block** · Deckenziegel *m*, gebrannter Deckenstein *m* [*DIN 4159 und DIN 4160. Fehlname: Deckenstein*]

~ **(~) ~** → flooring (~) ~

~ **cleaner,** flooring ~ · (Fuß)Bodenreinigungsmittel *n*

~ **(clear) varnish** → flooring (~) ~

~ **closer** · (Fuß)Bodentürschließer *m*, (Fuß)Bodentürschließvorrichtung *f*

~ **coat** → floor(ing) ~

(~) column, (~) support · (Decken-)Stütze *f*

~ **component** → (prefab(ricated)) floor (building) unit

~ **composed of large units** · Großformatdecke *f*

~ **compound unit** → prefab(ricated) ~ ~ ~

~ **construction** · Deckenbau *m*

~ ~, ~ **(structural) system,** ~ **scheme,** ~ **structure** · Decken(bau)system *n*, Deckenkonstruktion(ssystem) *f*, (*n*)

~ **cover(ing),** floor(ing) (finish) [*The upper layer of a floor providing a finished surface*] · (Fuß)Boden(belag) *m*, Fb

~ ~ **coat,** floor(ing) (finish) ~ · (Fuß-) Bodenbeschichtung *f*

floor cover(ing) emulsion — floor height

~ ~ emulsion, floor(ing) (finish) ~ (Fuß)Bodenemulsion f
~ ~ felt, floor(ing) (finish) ~ · (Fuß-)Boden(belag)pappe f
~ ~ hardboard → floor(ing) ~
~ ~ lino(leum), floor(ing) (finish) ~ · (Fuß)Bodenlinoleum n
~ ~ material, floor(ing) (finish) ~ · (Fuß)Boden(belag)stoff m
~ ~ plastic, floor(ing) (finish) ~ · (Fuß)Boden(belag)kunststoff m
~ ~ screed (material), floor(ing) (finish) ~ (~) · (Fuß)Bodenestrich m [als Material]
~ ~ ~ (topping), floor(ing) (finish) ~ (~) · (Fuß)Bodenestrich m [als verlegter Baustoff]
~ ~ slate, floor(ing) ~ · (Fuß)Boden(belag)schiefer m
~ ~ tile, floor(ing) (finish) ~ · (Fuß-)Boden(belag)platte f, (Fuß)Bodenfliese f
~ ~ work → floor(ing) (finish) ~
~ cross-section · Deckenquerschnitt m
~ depth, ~ thickness · Deckendicke f
~ design → design of a floor system
~ disc, ~ sheet; ~ disk (US) · Deckenscheibe f
~ disk (US); ~ sheet, ~ disc · Deckenscheibe f
~ door catch → flooring ~ ~
~ ~ stop → floor(ing) door catch
~ drain · (Fuß)Bodendrän m
~ drainage · (Fuß)Bodenentwässerung f
~ duct · (Fuß)Bodenkanal m
~ emulsion → floor(ing) ~
~ felt → floor(ing) ~
(~) filler (block), (~) ~ tile, soffit (~ ~) ~ [See remark under 'Block'] · Füllblock(stein) m, Füllkörper m, Füllstein, (Rippen)Decken~, Deckenkörper, Deckenstein [Ein Zwischenbauteil, der sich über die volle Höhe der Rohdecke erstreckt]
(~) ~ slab · Füll-Deckenplatte f, (Decken)Füllplatte, plattenförmiger Zwischenbauteil m, plattenförmiges Zwischenbauteil n
(~) ~ tile → (~) ~ (block)
~ filling material · Deckenfüllstoff m [Zum Ausfüllen von Zwischendecken zur Verbesserung der Schall- und Wärmedämmung]
~ (finish) → flooring (~)
~ ~ coat → floor(ing) ~
~ ~ emulsion → floor(ing) ~
~ ~ felt → floor(ing) ~
~ ~ hardboard → floor(ing) ~
~ (~) lino(leum) → ~ cover(ing) ~
~ ~ material → floor(ing) ~
~ (~) screed (material) → floor(ing) (~) ~ (~)

~ (~) ~ (topping) → floor(ing) (~) ~ (~)
~ (~) work → flooring (~) ~
~ fire → ~ furnace
~ forms → ~ formwork
~ formwork, ~ forms, ~ shuttering · Decken(beton)schalung f
~ furnace, ~ fire, ~ burning appliance [A self-contained connected or vented furnace designed to be suspended from the floor of the space being heated, taking air for combustion outside this heated space and with a means for observing flame and lighting the appliance from the space being heated] · Deckenstrahler m
~ girder · Deckenträger m
~ ~ ~ → (stair(case)) landing beam
~ grating, flooring ~ · (Fuß)Bodenrost m
~ grid · Deckenraster m
~ ~ plane · Deckenrasterebene f
~ (ground(-))plan; story ~ (US); storey ~ (Brit.) · Stockwerkgrundriß m, Etagengrundriß, Geschoßgrundriß
~ guide → flooring ~
~ gull(e)y, ~ inlet, ~ outlet · Deckenablauf m, Deckeneinlauf [DIN 4282, 4283 und 4284]
~ gully → flooring ~
~ hardboard → flooring ~
~ hardener, ~ hardening agent · (Fuß-)Bodenhärtemittel n, (Fuß)Bodenhärter m, (Fuß)Bodenhärtungsmittel, (Fuß-)Bodenhärtungsstoff m
~ hardness tester · (Fuß)Boden-Härteprüfgerät n
~ hardwood (timber), ~ hdwd. · (Fuß-)Bodenlaubholz n
~ hdwd. ~ hardwood (timber) · (Fuß-)Bodenlaubholz n
~ header → (stair(case)) landing ~
floor-heated · (fuß)bodenbeheizt
floor heating, ~ warming, under~ · FB-Heizung f, (Fuß)Boden(strahlungs)heizung
~ ~ by air, air floor heating · Luft(fuß)boden(be)heizung f [Die Warmluft wird durch einen Hohlraum unter den (Fuß-)Boden geleitet. Im (Fuß)Boden befindet sich keine Wärmespeicherung]
~ ~ cable → (electric(al)) (under)floor warming ~
~ ~ installation → (electric) (under-)floor warming ~
~ ~ panel, ~ ~ plate · (Fuß)Bodenheiz(ungs)platte f
~ ~ plate, ~ ~ panel · (Fuß)Bodenheiz(ungs)platte f
~ ~ system → (electric) (under)floor warming installation
~ height; storey ~ (Brit.); story ~ (US) [The vertical distance from a finished floor level to the next finished floor level] · Stockwerkhöhe f, Etagenhöhe, Geschoßhöhe

floor in (pre)stressed clay — floor slab

~ **in (pre)stressed clay,** Stahlton ((pre)stressed) floor, (pre)stressed clay floor · Spanntondecke f, Stahltondecke, vorgespannte Ziegeldecke

~ **inlet,** ~ outlet, ~ gull(e)y · Deckenablauf m, Deckeneinlauf [DIN 4282, 4283 und 4284]

~ ~ → flooring ~

~ **insulation** · Deckenisolierung f

~ ~ · Deckendämmung f

~ ~ · (Fuß)Bodendämmung f

~ **joint** → flooring ~

~ ~ · Deckenfuge f

(~) **joist,** intermediate (~) ~, ceiling ~ · Deckenunterzug m, Trenn~, Etagen~, Stockwerk~, Geschoß~

~ ~ → (stair(case)) landing beam

~ **lacquer** → floor(ing) ~

~ **lamp** · Stehlampe f

~ **landing;** story ~ (US); storey ~ (Brit.) · Geschoßabsatz m, Etagenabsatz, Stockwerkabsatz, Stockwerkpodest n, m, Etagenpodest, Geschoßpodest

~ **layer** → flooring ~

~ **length** → (stair(case)) landing ~

~ **level** → (stair(case)) landing ~

~ ~; story ~ (US); storey ~ (Brit.) · Etagenebene f, Stockwerkebene, Geschoßebene

~ **light** · Deckenfenster n

~ **lino(leum)** → ~ cover(ing) ~

~ **live load,** imposed floor ~, variable floor ~ · veränderliche Deckenlast f, wechselnde ~, bewegliche ~, Decken-Verkehrslast, Verkehrs-Deckenlast

~ **load** · Deckenlast f

~ **loading** · Deckenbelastung f

~ **marble,** flooring ~ · (Fuß)Bodenmarmor m

~ **mastic** → flooring ~

~ **material** · Deckenbaumaterial n [Schweiz]; Deckenbaustoff m

~ ~ → flooring ~

~ **member** → (prefab(ricated)) floor (building) unit

~ **mosaic,** flooring ~ · (Fuß)Bodenmosaik n

floor-mounted drinking fountain, pedestal-type ~ ~ · Säulenbrunnen m

~ **fire warning device** · Standfeuermelder m, Standbrandmelder, Standfeuermeldeeinrichtung f, Standbrandmeldeeinrichtung

~ **(hot) water heater,** ~ (~) ~ heating appliance · Stand-Wassererhitzer m, Stand-Wassererwärmer, Stand-Wasserheizgerät n, Stand-Wasserheizer

~ **unit heater** · Stand-Luftheizgerät n

floor of dowelled (wood(en)) beams, ~ ~ ~ timber ~ · Dübel(balken)decke f, Dübelbaumdecke [Dippel(balken)decke, Dippelbaumdecke in Österreich] [Massivdecke aus dicht gereihten verdübelten ("verdippelten") Holzbalken]

~ **opening** · Deckenöffnung f

~ **outlet** → flooring ~

~ ~, ~ **inlet,** ~ gull(e)y · Deckenablauf m, Deckeneinlauf [DIN 4282, 4283 und 4284]

~ **pad** [For the actuation of a door mechanism] · Mattenunterlagekontakt m

~ **paint** → flooring ~

~ **panel** → (concrete) floor slab

~ ~ **heating** · FB-Strahlplattenheizung f, (Fuß)Bodenstrahlplattenheizung

~ **plan** → ~ ground(-) ~

~ **plastic** → floor(ing) (finish) ~

floorplate · (Fuß)Bodenblech n

floor (plug) socket → flooring (~) ~

~ **polish,** flooring ~ · (Fuß)Bodenpoliermittel n

~ **post** → (stair(case)) landing ~

~ **power point** → floor(ing) (plug) socket

~ **protection agent,** flooring ~ ~ · (Fuß)Bodenschutzstoff m, (Fuß)Bodenschutz(mittel) m, (n)

~ **recess,** flooring ~ · (Fuß)Bodenvertiefung f

~ **reflection factor** · (Fuß)Boden-Rückstrahlgrad m

~ **reinforced with twin-twisted round bars** · Istegdecke f

~ **reinforcement** · Deckenarmierung f, Deckenbewehrung, Decken(stahl)einlagen fpl

~ **rib** · Deckenrippe f

~ **sander,** ~ sanding machine · (Fuß-)Bodenschleifmaschine f

~ **scheme,** ~ structure, ~ (structural) system, ~ construction · Decken(bau)system n, Deckenkonstruktion(ssystem) f, (n)

~ **seal(ing)** → floor(ing) ~

~ **sheen** [It is a transparent seal(er) which can be used on wood, concrete, flagstone or metal surfaces] · farbloses (Fuß)Boden-Versieg(e)lungsmittel n, ~ (Fuß)Boden-Absieg(e)lungsmittel

~ **sheet,** ~ disc; ~ disk (US) · Deckenscheibe f

~ **shuttering** → ~ formwork

~ **skin** · Bodendichtung f [Unterkellerung]

~ **slab** → concrete ~ ~

~ ~ → (stair(case)) landing ~

~ ~ → (pre)cast concrete ~ ~

~ ~ · Bodenplatte f [Unterkellerung]

~ ~, ground floor [A floor slab designed to transmit the whole of the building load to the ground becomes a raft foundation] · Decke f auf Grund, Fußbodendecke [Erdgeschoß oder Keller eines Hauses]

floor slate — floor(ing) (finish) lino(leum) 404

~ **slate**, floor(ing) ~, floor cover(ing) ~ · (Fuß)Boden(belag)schiefer *m*

~ **socket** → floor(ing) (plug) ~

~ **soffit** → ceiling

~ **softwood (timber)**, flooring ~ (~) · (Fuß)Boden-Nadelholz *n*

~ **space** → ~ area

floor-space efficiency [*The relation of usable space to services and corridors*] · Flächennutzungsgrad *m*

~ **index** · Etagenflächenziffer *f*, Geschoßflächenziffer, Stockwerkflächenziffer, GFZ

floor span · Deckenweite *f*

~ **standard**, standard lamp · Standleuchte *f*, Stehleuchte

~ **stirrup** · Deckenbügel *m*

~ **stress during operation** · Deckenbelastung *f* bei der Arbeit [*Kletterkran*]

~ ~ **when climbing** · Deckenbelastung *f* beim Klettern [*Kletterkran*]

~ **(structural) system**, ~ construction, ~ scheme, ~ structure · Decken(bau)system *n*, Deckenkonstruktion(ssystem) *f*, (*n*)

~ **structure**, ~ scheme, ~ (structural) system, ~ construction · Decken(bau)system *n*, Deckenkonstruktion(ssystem) *f*, (*n*)

(~) **support**, (~) column · (Decken-)Stütze *f*

~ **system**, ~ structural ~, ~ scheme, ~ structure, ~ construction · Decken(bau)system *n*, Deckenkonstruktion-(ssystem) *f*, (*n*)

~ **thickness**, ~ depth · Deckendicke *f*

~ **tile** → floor(ing) (finish) ~

~ ~ [*Structural unit for floor construction*] · Deckenblock(stein) *m*, Decken(bau)stein

~ **tiling** → flooring ~

~ **timber**, ~ wood · (Fuß)Boden-Holz *n*

floor-(to-)ceiling glazing · raumhohe Einglasung *f*, ~ Verglasung, Ganzeinglasung, Ganzverglasung, Volleinglasung, Vollverglasung

~ **height** [*The height between the upper reference plane of a floor and the surface finish of the ceiling above*] · (lichte) Deckenhöhe *f*

~ **window**, full-height ~, room-high ~ · raumhohes Fenster *n*

floor-to-floor height [*B.S. 4176*] · Deckenhöhe *f*

floor-to-wall joint · Decken-Wand-Fuge *f*

floor track, flooring ~ · (Fuß)Bodenschiene *f* [*Türanlage*]

~ **unit** → ~ building ~

~ **varnish** → floor(ing) (clear) ~

~ **vault** (US) → flat ~

~ **warming** → ~ heating

~ ~ **cable** → (electric(al)) under~ ~ ~

~ ~ **installation** → (electric) (under-)floor ~ ~

~ ~ **system** → (electric) (under)floor warming installation

~ **wax**, flooring ~ · (Fuß)Bodenwachs *n*

~ **weight** · Deckengewicht *n*

~ **width** → (stair(case)) landing ~

~ **with (pre)cast beams placed close together** · Balkendecke *f* mit dicht verlegten Balken [*DIN 4225. Decke mit unmittelbar nebeneinander verlegten Stahlbeton-Fertigbalken*]

~ **wood**, ~ timber · (Fuß)Bodenholz *n*

~ **work** → floor(ing) (finish) ~

~ **zone** · Deckenbereich *m*, *n*

flooring, floor(ing) material · (Fuß)Bodenwerkstoff *m*, (Fuß)Bodenbaustoff, (Fuß)Boden(bau)material *n* [*Schweiz*]

floor(ing), flg [*A construction that provides the surface on which one walks in a building or structure*] · (Fuß)Boden *m*

~ → ~ (finish)

~ **adhesive** → ~ bonding ~

~ **batten** · (Fuß)Bodenleiste *f* [*Unter den (Fuß)Bodenbrettern*]

~ **(bonding) adhesive**, ~ ~ medium, ~ ~ agent, ~ cement(ing agent) · (Fuß)Bodenkleber *m*, (Fuß)Bodenkleb(e)stoff *m*, (Fuß)Bodenkleb(e)mittel *n*

~ ~ **agent** → ~ (~) adhesive

~ ~ **medium** → ~ (~) adhesive

~ **brick** → ~ clay ~

~ **care** · (Fuß)Bodenpflege *f*

flooring cement → Keene's ~

floor(ing) cement(ing agent) → ~ (bonding) adhesive

~ **(clay) brick** · (Fuß)Bodenziegel *m*

~ **cleaner** · (Fuß)Bodenreinigungsmittel *n*

~ **(clear) varnish** · (Fuß)Boden(klar)lack *m*

~ **coat** · (Fuß)Bodenanstrich *m*, (Fuß-)Bodenaufstrich

~ ~, ~ finish ~, floor cover(ing) ~ · (Fuß)Bodenbeschichtung *f*

~ **door catch**, ~ ~ stop · (Fuß)Bodentürpuffer *m*

~ **emulsion**, ~ finish ~, floor cover(ing) ~ · (Fuß)Bodenemulsion *f*

~ **felt**, ~ finish ~, floor cover(ing) ~ · (Fuß)Boden(belag)pappe *f*

~ **(finish)**, floor cover(ing) ~ [*The upper layer of a floor providing a finished surface*] · (Fuß)Boden(belag) *m*, Fb

~ **(~) coat**, floor cover(ing) ~ · (Fuß-)Bodenbeschichtung *f*

~ **(~) emulsion**, floor cover(ing) ~ · (Fuß)Bodenemulsion *f*

~ **(~) felt**, floor cover(ing) ~ · (Fuß)Boden(belag)pappe *f*

~ **(~) lino(leum)**, floor cover(ing) ~ · (Fuß)Bodenlinoleum *n*

floor(ing) (finish) material — floriated decoration

~ (~) **material,** floor cover(ing) ~ · (Fuß)Boden(belag)stoff *m*

~ (~) **plastic,** floor cover(ing) ~ · (Fuß)Boden(belag)kunststoff *m*

~ (~) **screed (material),** floor cover(ing) ~ (~) · (Fuß)Bodenestrich *m* [*als Material*]

~ (~) ~ **(topping),** floor cover(ing) ~ (~) · (Fuß)Bodenestrich *m* [*als verlegter Baustoff*]

~ (~) **tile,** floor cover(ing) ~ · (Fuß-)Boden(belag)platte *f*, (Fuß)Bodenfliese *f*

~ (~) **work,** floor cover(ing) ~ · (Fuß-)Boden(belag)arbeiten *fpl*, (Fuß)Bodenverlegearbeiten [*DIN 18365*]

~ **grating** · (Fuß)Bodenrost *m*

~ **guide** · (Fuß)Bodenführung *f*

~ **gull(e)y,** ~ inlet, ~ outlet · (Fuß-)Bodenablauf *m*, (Fuß)Bodeneinlauf

~ **(gypsum-)plaster** → anhydrous ~

~ **hardboard,** floor cover(ing) ~, floor finish ~ · Hartfaser(fuß)bodenplatte *f*

~ **inlet,** ~ outlet, ~ gull(e)y · (Fuß-)Bodenablauf *m*, (Fuß)Bodeneinlauf

~ **joint** · (Fuß)Bodenfuge *f*

~ **lacquer,** pigmented floor(ing) varnish · (Fuß)Bodenlackemaille *f*, (Fuß)Bodenlackfarbe *f*

~ **layer** · (Fuß)Bodenleger *m*

~ **lino(leum),** ~ finish ~, floor cover(ing) ~ · (Fuß)Bodenlinoleum *n*

~ **marble** · (Fuß)Bodenmarmor *m*

~ **mastic** · (Fuß)Bodenkitt *m* [*Im Farbton des (Fuß)Bodens meist von Anstreichern selbst hergestellter Kitt zum Auskitten der Nagellöcher und Fugen des (Fuß)Bodens*]

~ **material,** ~ finish ~, floor cover(ing) ~ · (Fuß)Boden(belag)stoff *m*

~ ~, **flooring** · (Fuß)Bodenwerkstoff *m*, (Fuß)Bodenbaustoff; (Fuß)Boden(bau)material *n* [*Schweiz*]

~ **mosaic** · (Fuß)Bodenmosaik *n*

flooring nail · (Fuß)Bodennagel *m*

floor(ing) outlet, ~ inlet, ~ gull(e)y · (Fuß)Bodenablauf *m*, (Fuß)Bodeneinlauf

~ **paint** · (Fuß)Boden(anstrich)farbe *f*

~ **plaster** → anhydrous (gypsum-)plaster

~ **plastic,** ~ finish ~, floor cover(ing) ~ · (Fuß)Boden(belag)kunststoff *m*

~ ~ **sealing** · (Fuß)Bodenkunststoffabsieg(e)lung *f*, (Fuß)Bodenkunststoffversieg(e)lung

~ **(plug) socket,** ~ power point · (Fuß-)Boden(steck)dose *f*

~ **polish** · (Fuß)Bodenpoliermittel *n*

~ **power point** → ~ (plug) socket

~ **protection agent** · (Fuß)Bodenschutzstoff *m*, (Fuß)Bodenschutz(mittel) *m*, (*n*)

(~) **quarry (tile)** → ceramic flooring ~

(~) ~ (~) **for animal shelters,** ceramic flooring ~ ~ ~ ~ ~, clay flooring ~ ~ ~ ~ · Stallbodenplatte *f*

~ **recess** · (Fuß)Bodenvertiefung *f*

~ **screed (material),** ~ finish ~ (~), floor cover(ing) ~ (~) · (Fuß)Bodenestrich *m* [*als. Material*]

~ ~ **(topping),** ~ finish ~ (~), floor cover(ing) ~ (~) · (Fuß)Bodenestrich *m* [*als verlegter Baustoff*]

~ **seal(er)** → penetrating ~ ~

~ **seal(ing)** · (Fuß)Bodenabsieg(e)lung *f*, (Fuß)Bodenversieg(e)lung

~ **slate,** floor cover(ing) ~ · (Fuß)Boden(belag)schiefer *m*

~ **socket** → ~ plug ~

~ **softwood (timber)** · (Fuß)Boden-Nadelholz *n*

~ **tile,** ~ finish ~, floor cover(ing) ~ · (Fuß)Boden(belag)platte *f*, (Fuß)Bodenfliese *f*

~ **tiling** · (Fuß)Bodenfliesenbelag *m*, (Fuß)Bodenplattenbelag

~ **track** · (Fuß)Bodenschiene *f* [*Türanlage*]

~ **varnish,** ~ clear ~, finishing ~ · (Fuß)Boden(klar)lack *m*

~ **wax** · (Fuß)Bodenwachs *n*

(~) **wear(ing) course** → (~) ~ surface

(~) ~ **layer** → (~) ~ surface

(~) ~ **surface,** (~) ~ layer, (~) ~ course · (Fuß)Bodennutzschicht *f*, (Fuß)Bodennutzbelag *m*, Nutzbelag, Gehschicht, Deckschicht, Laufschicht, Nutzschicht

~ **work** → ~ finish ~

floors · Nutzfläche *f* [*Gebäude*]

floral decoration → ~ ornament

~ **decorative fixture** → ~ ornament

~ **enrichment** → ~ ornament

~ **ornament,** floriated ~, ~ enrichment, ~ decoration, ~ decorative fixture · Blumenornament *n*, Blumenschmuck *m*, Blumenverzierung *f*

~ **pattern,** (foliage) scrolls, scrollwork · Ranken(werk) *fpl*, (*n*)

~ ~ **glass** → ice-patterned ~

~ **scroll** · Blumenranke *f*

floreated → floriated

Florence Cathedral · Dom *m* von Florenz, Florentiner Dom

Florentine arch, Tuscan ~ · Florentiner Bogen *m*, Sieneser ~, toskanischer ~ [*seit der Renaissance*]; Sichelbogen

~ **style** · florentinische Renaissance *f*

floriated, floreated [*Decorated with floral ornament: applied to tracery, etc.*] · blumengeschmückt, blumenverziert

~ **decoration** → floral ornament

floriated decorative fixture — fluate hardener for gypsum

~ **decorative fixture** → floral ornament
~ **enrichment** → floral ornament
~ **ornament** → floral ~
Floricin oil · Floricinöl n [*Durch Warmbehandlung öllöslich gemachtes Rizinusöl*]
florid architecture, decorative ~, ornamental ~ · Dekor(ations)architektur f, Ornamentarchitektur, Zierarchitektur, Schmuckarchitektur, Dekor(ations)baukunst f, Ornamentbaukunst, Zierbaukunst, Schmuckbaukunst
Flory cross · Wiederkreuz n
flour lime → pulverized limestone
~ **limestone** → powder(ed) ~
~ **mill** · Getreidemühle f, (Mehl)Mühle
~ **of emery** · Schmirgelmehl n
~ **paste** · Mehlkleister m
flous → fluosilicate
flow → plastic ~
~ · Vorlauf m [*Heizung*]
~ · Strömung f, Fluten n
~ **coat, flood** ~ · Flutlackierschicht f
~ **coating** · Flutlackierung f
~ ~ · Fluten n
~ **cone** [*For measuring the fluidity of the grout for prestressed concrete*] · Fließkegel m
~ **control valve** · Durchgangsabsperrventil n
~ **cup** · Auslaufbecher m [*DIN 53211*]
~ **line, feed** ~ · Vorlaufheizung f, Zulaufheizung
~ **model** · Strömungsmodell n
~ **of curves,** undulating flow · Kurvenfluß m
~ ~ **forces,** distribution ~ ~ · Kräftefluß m
~ ~ **pedestrians** · Fußgängerstrom m
~ ~ **stress(es)** · Spannungsfluß m
~ **pipe, feed** ~ · Vorlaufrohr n, Zulaufrohr
~ **pressure** [*The pressure in the water supply pipe near the faucet or water outlet while the faucet or water outlet is wide-open and flowing*] · (Wasser-)Leitungsdruck m
~ **production** · Fließfertigung f
~ **range** · Fließbereich m, n
~ **side** [*heat exchanger*] · Vorlaufseite f
~ **state** · Fließzustand m
~ **stress** · Fließspannung f
~ **table (with cone)** · Ausbreit(ungs)tisch m mit Trichter, Setztisch [*Betonprüfung. DIN 1048*]
~ **temperature** · Vorlauftemperatur f, Zulauftemperatur
flow-type calorifier, non-storage ~ · Durchflußerhitzer m, Durchlauferhitzer
~ **gas water heater,** non-storage ~ ~ ~, instantaneous ~ ~ ~ ~, ~ heating appliance · (Durchlauf-)Gaswasserheizer m, Geyser [*DIN 3368, 3369*]

~ **water heater** → instantaneous ~ ~
flowability, fluidity [*The ability of a material to flow*] · Fließfähigkeit f, Fließvermögen n, Fließeigenschaft f
flower basin · Blumenbecken n
~ **bed surround** · Blumenbeeteinfassung f
~ **bowl** · Blumenschale f
~ **box** · Blumenkasten m
~ **container** · Blumengefäß n
~ **-like design** · blütenähnliche Form f
flower market · Blumenmarkt m
~ **motif** · Blumenmotiv n
~ **of salt,** efflorescence of salt, (salt-)efflorescence · (Salz)Ausblühen n, (Salz)Ausschlagen, Auswittern, Aussalzen, Auskristallisation f (von Salzen) [*Äußerlich sichtbares Ausscheiden von Salzen auf Mauerwerk*]
~ **shaped ornament,** finial; crope [*deprecated*] · Kreuzblume f, Blätterknauf m, Firstblume, Giebelblume, Endblume [*In Grund- und Aufriß kreuzförmiges, stilisiertes Blattgebilde als Krönung von Fialen, Wimpergen, Turmpyramiden und dergleichen*]
~ **show** · Gartenschau f
~ **trough** · Blumentrog m
~ **tub** · Blumenkübel m
~ **window** · Blumenfenster n
~ **work** [*See remark under 'Gehänge'*] · Blumengehänge n, Blumengewinde n, Blumengirlande f, Blumenfeston n
flowers of sulphur (Brit.); ~ ~ sulfur (US) · Schwefelblüte f
flowing colour (Brit.); ~ color (US) · Flußfarbe f [*Sie wird durch Einwirkung von Chlordämpfen im Brande auf die in der Glasurmasse des Steingutes enthaltenen Metalloxide erzielt, wodurch schwache, zarte Farbtönungen von eigenartiger Wirkung hervorgerufen werden*]
~ **contours,** ~ lines · Linienspiel n, fließende Konturen fpl
~ **lines,** ~ contours · Linienspiel n, fließende Konturen fpl
~ **plan form** · fließende Raumdisposition f
~ **style** → Curvilinear ~
~ **tracery,** curvilinear ~ · fließendes Maßwerk n [*Die im Decorated Style der englischen Gotik angewandte Form des Maßwerks*]
flr → floor
flt → flight (of stairs)
fluate, fluosilicate · Silicofluorid n, Fluorsilikat n, Fluat n, Fluatierungsmittel n, Fluorsilizium n, Siliziumtetrafluorid
~ **coat,** fluosilicate ~ · Fluatanstrich m, Fluataufstrich
~ **hardener for gypsum,** fluosilicate ~ ~ ~ · Gipsfluat n [*Ein Silicofluorid als Gipshärtemittel*]

fluate treatment — flush handle

~ **treatment**, fluosilicate ~ · Fluatieren *n*, Fluatierung *f*

flue · Zug *m*

~ [*A duct designed to convey the products of combustion from a fire to the open air*] · Rauch(gas)kanal *m*

~ **area** · Zugfläche *f*

~ **block** · Rauch(gas)kanalstein *m*

~ ~, ~ **tile** · Zugblock(stein) *m*, Zugstein *m*

~ **brick** · Zugziegel *m*

~ **connection** · Zuganschluß *m*

~ ~ **to stack**, ~ ~ ~ **chimney**; **main flue**, **up-take**, **breeching** (US) · (Schornstein)Fuchs(kanal) *m* [*Waag(e)rechter oder mit leichter Steigung von der Heizanlage zum Schornstein führender Rauchkanal*]

~ **for gas appliance**, **gas flue** · Gasfeuerungszug *m*

~ **gas** · Feuergas *n*, Verbrennungsgas, Rauchgas

~ ~ **analysis** · Feuergasanalyse *f*, Verbrennungsgasanalyse, Rauchgasanalyse

~ ~ **condensate** · Feuergaskondensat *n*, Verbrennungsgaskondensat, Rauchgaskondensat

~ **liner**, ~ **lining** · Zugfutter *n*

~ **lining**, ~ **liner** · Rauch(gas)kanalfutter *n*

~ ~, ~ **liner** · Zugfutter *n*

~ **opening** · Zugöffnung *f*

~ **outlet** · Zugauslaß *m*

~ **pipe** · Zugrohr *n*

~ **tile**, ~ **block** · Zugblock(stein) *m*, Zugstein *m*

~ **wall** · Zugwand *f*

fluid · Strömungsmedium *n*

~ **concrete**, **wet** ~, **sloppy** ~ · flüssiger Beton *m*

~ **pressure** · Strömungsdruck *m*

fluidity, **flowability** [*The ability of a material to flow*] · Fließfähigkeit *f*, Fließvermögen *n*, Fließeigenschaft *f*

fluidizing calciner · Kalk(brenn)ofen *m* für das Fließverfahren

fluor spar, **fluorite** · Flußspat *m*, Fluorit *m*

fluorescence · Fluoreszenz *f*

fluorescent [*Able to emit visible light only when exposed to the activating radiation*] · fluoreszierend

~ **composition** → ~ **compound**

~ **compound**, **luminescent** ~, **phosphorescent** ~, ~ **composition** · Leuchtmasse *f*

~ **fixture** → ~ **light(ing)** ~

~ **glass**, **luminescent** ~ · leuchtendes Glas *n*, **luminiszierendes** ~, **phosphoreszierendes** ~

~ **indicator** · Fluoreszenz-Indikator *m*

~ **lamp**, **cold-cathode** ~ [*B. S. 1853*] · Leuchtstofflampe *f* [*DIN 49862*]

~ ~ **ballast** · Vorschaltgerät *n* für Leuchtstofflampe

~ **light fitting** (Brit.) → ~ **(light(ing)) fixture**

~ **lighting** · fluoreszierende Beleuchtung *f*

~ **(light(ing)) fixture**; ~ **luminaire** (~) (US); ~ **light fitting** (Brit.) · fluoreszierende Leuchte *f*

~ **luminaire (fixture)** (US) → ~ **(light(ing))** ~

~ **paint** · fluoreszierende Leuchtfarbe *f*

~ **pigment** · fluoreszierendes Pigment *n*

fluoride of alumin(i)um and sodium, Na_3AlF_6 · Natrium-Aluminiumfluorid *n*

fluorine · Fluor *n* [*Chemisches Element F, Atomgewicht 19*]

fluorite, **fluor spar** · Flußspat *m*, Fluorit *m*

~ ~ → **calcium fluoride**

fluorocarbon · Fluorkohlenstoff *m*

fluorous salt of copper · flußspatsaures Kupfer *n*, flußspatsäurehaltiges Kupfersalz *n*

fluorspat of baryte · Barytflußspat *m*, Flußschwerspat

fluosilicate, **fluate**, **flous** · Silicofluorid *n*, Fluorsilikat *n*, Fluat *n*, Fluatierungsmittel *n*, Fluorsilizium *n*, Siliziumtetrafluorid

~ **coat**, **fluate** ~ · Fluatanstrich *m*, Fluataufstrich

~ **hardener for gypsum**, **fluate** ~ ~ ~ · Gipsfluat *n* [*Ein Silicofluorid als Gipshärtemittel*]

~ **of lead**, **lead fluosilicate** · Bleifluat *n*, Bleisilicofluorid *n*

~ **treatment**, **fluate** ~ · Fluatieren *n*; Fluatierung *f*

fluosilicic acid · Flußkieselsäure *f*, Kieselflußsäure, Kiesel(fluor)wasserstoffsäure

to flush · (durch)spülen

~ ~ [*To flake off, said of the face of walling stone*] · abblättern, abschuppen

flush → ~ **with**

~ → **flushing**

~ **bolt** · Kantenriegel *m*

~ **cistern** → **flush(ing)** ~

~ **curb** → **curb below ground**

~ **door** · Flächentür *f*, abgesperrte (Platten)Tür, Sperrtür [*DIN 68706*]

flush-encased dead bolt lock · Blind-Riegelschloß *n*, Einlaß-Riegelschloß, eingelassenes Riegelschloß

~ **lock** · Blindschloß *n*, Einlaßschloß, eingelassenes Schloß

flush equipment → **flushing** ~

~ **fixing**, **letting-in flush** (on both meeting faces) · Einstemmen *n* [*Einstemmband*]

~ **handle** [*This term is also used for the Klappringmuschel*"] · Klappringschild *n* [*Türbeschlag*]

flush handle — fluxed pitch roll(ed-strip) roofing (felt) 408

~ ~ [*This term is also used for the 'Klappringschild'*] · Klappringmuschel f [*Türbeschlag*]

~ **joint**, flushed ~, flat ~ · bündige Fuge f, Vollfuge

~ **jointed**, flat ~, solidly filled · vollfugig, bündig verfugt

~ **kerb** → curb below ground

~ **masonry jointing** · Fugenglattstrich m

~ **mounting** · Unterputzeinbau m, Unterputzverlegung f [*Zähler-Verteilungsschrank; Zählertafelschrank*]

~-**mounting frame** · Mauereinputzrahmen m

flush panel [*A panel, the outer surface of which is completely flat, and flush with, i.e. in the same plane, as the face of the frame which surrounds it*] · Flächentafel f

~ **pipe** → (lavatory) flush(ing) ~

~ **side** · Bundseite f

~ **socket** · Unterputzsteckdose f

~ **soffit**, ~ visible under-face, ~ visible underside [*As opposed to the open soffit*] · ebene Untersicht f, geschlossene ~, bündige ~, ~ Unterdecke

~ **switch** · Unterputzschalter m

~ **tank** → flush(ing) ~

~ **to** → ~ (with)

~ **toilet**, water closet, W. C., wc [*A room in which one or more W. C. pans are installed*] · Spülabort m, Wasserabort, Spülklosett n, Wasserklosett

~ **valve** → flushing ~

~ **visible under-face** → ~ soffit

~ **water** → lavatory flushing ~

~ **(with)**, level (to), flush to, dead level · bündig (mit), niveaueben

~ ~ **(the) ceiling** · deckengleich, deckenbündig

flush(ed) joint, flat ~ · bündige Fuge f, Vollfuge

flushing · (Durch)Spülen n

~; **levelling off** (Brit.); **leveling off** (US) · (Aus)Ebnen n, Egalisieren, Einebnen, Nivellieren, Ausgleichen, Abgleichen

~ [*The fracturing, or spalling, of small pieces from the edges of stones*] · Abbrechen n

flush(ing), lavatory ~, toilet ~, closet ~ · Spülung f, Abort~, Klosett~, Toiletten~

flushing → pigment flushing method

flush(ing) cistern · (Abort)Spülkasten m, Klosettspülkasten, Toilettenspülkasten

~ **equipment** · WC-Spüler m

flushing method → pigment ~ ~

flush(ing) pan · Ausspülklosettkörper m

~ **pipe** → lavatory ~ ~

flushing process → pigment ~ ~

flush(ing) tank [*A tank from which water is discharged to flush a system of drains. Not to be confused with a 'flush(ing) cistern'*] · Spülkasten m

~ **valve** (Brit.); flushometer (US) · (Abort)Druckspüler m, Klosettdruckspüler, Toilettendruckspüler, Wasserdruckspüler, Spülhahn m [*DIN 3265*]

~ **water** → lavatory ~ ~

flushometer (US) → flush(ing) valve

to flute [*To make long, rounded grooves in a column, etc.*] · kannelieren, riefeln

flute, architectural ~ · Einkehlung f, Riefe f, Kannelur(e) f, Kehle f [*Lotrechte Vertiefung am Säulenschaft*]

fluted · kanneliert, gerieft

~ **brass tube** · kannelierte Messingröhre f, kanneliertes Messingrohr n [*Hauptsächlich für elektrische Leuchten und Treppengeländer verwendet*]

~ **column** · kannelierte Säule f, geriefelte ~

~ **copper tube** · kannelierte Kupferröhre f, kanneliertes Kupferrohr n [*Hauptsächlich für elektrische Leuchten und Treppengeländer verwendet*]

~ **drainer** · gerillter Ablauf m

~ **glass**, ~ sheet [*Blown sheet glass with rolled flutes for ray diffraction*] · geriffeltes Glas n, kanneliertes ~

~ **sheet** → ~ glass

fluting [*A decoration consisting of long rounded grooves, as in a column*] · Kannelierung f, Riefelung

~ [*The making of shallow and narrow concave grooves on columns, pilasters, etc.*] · Riefeln n, Kannelieren

to flux · fluxen

flux · Flußmittel n [*Vorhandene oder zugefügte Substanz, die selbst in geringen Mengen die Bildungstemperatur einer flüssigen Phase herabsetzt*]

~ · Fluxmittel n, Verschnittmittel [*Bitumenindustrie*]

~ · Schmelzmittel n

~-**cored solder wire** · Röhrenlötzinn n mit Flußmittel gefüllt

flux-oil · Fluxöl n

flux paste, paste flux · Flußmittel n [*für Lötpaste*]

~ **residue** · Flußmittelrückstand m

fluxed asphalt (US); ~ **bitumen** (Brit.) [*The flux used is a residual product*] · gefluxtes Bitumen n

~ **Lake Asphalt** · gefluxtes Trinidadbitumen n

~ **pitch/(asphaltic-)bitumen roof(ing) felt** (Brit.) → tar/asphalt ready roofing

~ **pitch paper** (Brit.); tar(red) ~ [*See remark under 'Pappe'*] · Teerpappe f

~ ~ **roll(ed-strip) roofing (felt)** (Brit.); tar(red) ~ ~ (~) (US) · Rollen-Teerdachpappe f, Teerdachpappe in Rollenform

~ ~ roof(ing) felt (Brit.) → tar(red) ready roofing

~ ~ sheet roof(ing) felt (Brit.) → tar(red) ready sheet roofing (paper)

fluxing · Fluxen *n*

fly ash, PFA; pulverized fuel ash (US); pulverised fuel ash (Brit.) · Filterasche *f*, Flugasche [*DIN E 4209*]

~ ~ aggregate, PFA ~, pulverized fuel ash ~ [*The basic raw material is a product of the combustion of coal at extremely high temperatures. In processing, the material is formed into accurately sized particles and again subjected to intense heat. Thus the material is transformed into a ceramic product, basically composed of silica and alumina. It is strong, inert, very light in weight. It can be shaped, sized and processed to meet specific needs*] · Flugaschen(beton)zuschlag(stoff) *m*

~ ~ cement → sintered ~ ~ ~

~ ~ collector pulverized ~ ~, PFA ~ [*An auxiliary equipment designed to remove fly ash in dry form from the products of combustion*] · Filteraschensammler *m*, Flugaschensammler

~ ash-lime block, ~ ~ tile, PFA-lime ~, pulverized fuel ash-lime ~ [*See remark under 'Block'*] · Kalkflugaschen-(block)stein *m*, Kalkflugaschenblock *m* [*Dampfgehärteter Leicht(block)stein (1 kg/cbdm) aus Flugasche mit 10% Kalk als Binder*]

flyer, solid rectangular step · Klotzstufe *f*, Blockstufe, Massivstufe [*Stufe mit rechteckigem Querschnitt*]

~ → flying shore

flying arch, flier (~), flying buttress, arch(ed) buttress, arch-butment; bow [*old English term*] · (einfacher) Strebebogen *m*, Hochschiffstrebe *f* [*veraltet: fliegende Strebe, Fluchtstrebe*]; Schwibbogen [*Fehlname*]

~ buttress, arch(ed) ~, flying arch, flier (arch), arch-butment; bow [*old English term*] · (einfacher) Strebebogen *m*, Hochschiffstrebe *f* [*veraltet: fliegende Strebe, Fluchtstrebe*]; Schwibbogen [*Fehlname*]

Flying Mercury · Geflügelter Merkur *m* [*von Giovanni da Bologna, Bronze, 1564*]

flying scaffold, suspended ~, hanging ~ · Hängegerüst *n*, Hängerüstung *f*

~ shore, flyer, flier [*A temporary timber support fixed high above ground level, between the external walls of two buildings to prevent their collapse*] · Hochsteife *f*, waag(e)rechte Steife

~ stair(case) · stützenfreie Treppe *f*, stützenlose ~

fly-proof screen · Fliegengitter *n*

fly-proofing · Fliegenschutz *m*

fly tower · Schnürbodenturm *m*

~ wire · Fliegendraht *m*

F. M., Abrams' fineness module · Abramsscher (Feinheits)Modul *m*, ~ Feinmodul, F_m

FM → (fixed-)end moment

fmg → foaming

FO → fuel oil

foam · Schaum *m*

~ → foam(ed) (plastic)

~ adhesive → ~ glue

~-ash-silicate concrete · Aschen-Silikat-Schaumbeton *m*, Silikat-Aschen-Schaumbeton, Schaum-Aschen-Silikat-Beton, Schaum-Silikat-Aschen-Beton

foam board → foam(ed) (plastic) ~

~ bubble · Schaumblase *f*

~ cell · Schaumzelle *f*

~ cement concrete → foamed ~ ~

~ ~ screed → foamed ~ ~

foamclay · Schaumbeton *m*

foam concrete → foam(ed) (plastic) (light(weight)) ~

~ ~ (building) block → foam(ed) ~ (~) ~

~ ~ (~) tile → foam(ed) ~ (~) ~

~ ~ filler → foam(ed) ~ ~

~ ~ screed → foam(ed) ~ ~

~ ~ slab → foam(ed) ~ ~

~ ~ tile → foam(ed) concrete building ~

~ control agent · Schaumregulierungsmittel *n*, Schaumregler *m*

~ cored wall panel · Schaumkernwandtafel *f*

~ cupola → plastic ~ ~

~ dome → plastic foam cupola

~ extinguisher, ~ fire ~ · Schaum(feuer)löscher *m*

~ (fire) extinguisher · Schaum(feuer)löscher *m*

~-forming fire retardant agent · schaumschichtbildendes Feuerschutzmittel *n*, ~ Brandschutzmittel

foam-gas concrete, gas foam ~ · Schaum-Gasbeton *m*, Gas-Schaumbeton [*Kombination von Gas- und Schaumbeton*]

foam glass → foam(ed) ~

~ glue, ~ adhesive [*A glue made into foam with a gas to increase the area covered by a given amount of glue*] · Schaumkleber *m*, Schaumkleb(e)stoff *m*, Schaumkleb(e)mittel *n*

~ insulation → foam(ed) (plastic) ~

to foam into place · einschäumen

foam latex → foam(ed) ~

~ layer, layer of foam · Schaumlage *f*, Schaumschicht *f*

~ (light(weight)) concrete → foam(ed) (plastic) (~) ~

~ mortar → foam(ed) ~

~ plastic → foam(ed) ~

~ (~) concrete → foam(ed) (plastic) (light(weight)) ~

~ ~ cupola → plastic foam ~

~ ~ cylinder → foam(ed) ~ ~

foam plastic dome — foamed lava

~ ~ dome → plastic foam cupola
~ (~) (light(weight)) concrete → foam(ed) (~) (~) ~
~ ~ plaster baseboard → foam(ed) ~ ~ ~
~ ~ sheet → foam(ed) ~ ~
~ polystyrene → foam(ed) ~
~ polyurethane → foam(ed) ~
~ polyvinyl chloride → PVC foam
~ rubber → foam(ed) (natural) ~
~ seal → foam(ed) (plastic) ~
foam-silicate · Schaumsilikat *n*
~ **concrete** · Schaum-Silikat-Beton *m*, Silikat-Schaum-Beton
~ ~ **slab** · Schaumsilikatbetonplatte *f*, Silikatschaumbetonplatte
foam slag [*B.S. 877*] → foam(ed) blastfurnace ~
foam-slag silicate concrete · Schaum-Schlacken-Silikat-Beton *m*, Schlacken-Silikat-Schaumbeton, Silikat-Schlacken-Schaumbeton
foam urea-formaldehyde → foam(ed) ~
foam waterbar → foam(ed) (plastic) ~
~ **waterstop** → foam(ed) (plastic) ~
~ **with interconnecting shells** · Lamellenschaum *m*
foamed [*Foamed plastics are those produced from a liquid mix*] · geschäumt [*Kunststoff*]
foam(ed) blastfurnace slag → ~ iron ~ ~ ~
~ ~ ~ **concrete** → ~ iron ~ ~ ~
~ ~ ~ ~ **building block** → ~ iron ~ ~ ~ ~ ~
~ ~ ~ **powder** → ~ iron ~ ~ ~
~ **board** → ~ (plastic) ~
~ **cement concrete,** cement concrete aerated with foam · Zement-Schaumbeton *m* [*Die Herstellung von Zement-Schaumbeton beruht auf der Durchmischung eines Zementbreis mit wäßrigen schaumfähigen Lösungen in schaumschlagenden Misch- oder Peitsch-Maschinen*]
~ ~ **screed** · Schaumstrich *m* [*Zementestrich, der durch schaumbildende Zusätze ein schaumiges Gefüge erhält*]
~ **concrete** → ~ (plastic) (light(weight)) ~
~ ~ **(building) block,** ~ ~ (~) **tile** [*See remark under 'Betonblock(stein)'*] · Schaumbetonblock(stein) *m*, Schaumbetonstein
~ ~ (~) **tile,** ~ ~ (~) **block** [*See remark under 'Betonblock(stein)'*] · Schaumbetonblock(stein) *m*, Schaumbetonstein
~ ~ **filler** · Schaumbeton(-Decken)füllkörper *m*, Schaumbeton-Deckenkörper
~ ~ **screed** · Schaumbetonestrich *m*
~ ~ **slab** · Schaumbetonplatte *f*

~ ~ **tile** → ~ ~ building ~
~ ~ ~ (~) **tile,** ~ ~ ~ (~) **block** [*See remark under 'Block'*] · Schaumbetonwand(bau)stein *m*, Schaumbetonwand(bau)block(stein) *m* [*DIN 4165*]
~ ~ ~ **slab** · Schaumbetonwand(bau)platte *f* [*DIN 4166*]
~ **cupola** → plastic foam ~
~ **dome** → plastic foam cupola
~ **glass,** (multi)cellular ~ · poriges Glas *n*, Schaumglas, Vielzellenglas [*Es besteht aus meist hermetisch geschlossenen Mikroglaszellen und hat deshalb keine kapillare Wirkung*]
~ ~ **block,** (multi)cellular ~ ~, ~ ~ **tile** [*See remark under 'Block'*] · Schaumglasblock(stein) *m*, Vielzellenglasblock(-stein), Schaumglasstein, Vielzellenglasstein
~ ~ **tile,** (multi)cellular ~ ~, ~ ~ **block** [*See remark under 'Block'*] · Schaumglasblock(stein) *m*, Vielzellenglasblock(stein), Schaumglasstein, Vielzellenglasstein
foamed-in situ capability, expanded-in ~ ~ · Aufschäumbarkeit *f* an Ort und Stelle
foam(ed) insulation → ~ plastic ~
~ **(iron) (blastfurnace) slag** [*B.S. 877*]; expanded cinder (US); expanded slag, light(weight) slag · schaumige Hochofenschlacke *f*, geschäumte ~, aufgeblähte ~, (Hochofen)Schaumschlacke [*Die gebrochene geschäumte Hochofenschlacke wird "Hüttenbims" oder "Kunstbims" genannt*]
~ (~) (~) ~ **concrete** (Brit.); expanded cinder ~ (US); expanded slag ~, light(weight) slag ~ · (Hochofen-) Schaumschlackenbeton *m*, (Kunst-) Bimsbeton, Hüttenbimsbeton
~ (~) (~) ~ (~) **(building) block,** ~ (~) (~) ~ (~) (~) **tile** (Brit.); expanded cinder (~) (~) ~ (US); expanded slag (~) (~) ~, light(weight) slag (~) (~) ~ [*See remark under '(Block)Stein'*] · (Hochofen)Schaumschlackenbetonblock(stein) *m*, (Hochofen)Schaumschlackenbetonstein, Hüttenbimsstein, Hüttenbimsblock(stein), Leichtbetonblock(stein) mit Hüttenbims als Zuschlag(stoff), Leichtbetonstein mit Hüttenbims als Zuschlag(stoff) [*Fehlnamen: (Hütten-)Schwemmstein, Hochofenschwemmstein*]
~ (~) (~) ~ **powder** (Brit.); expanded cinder ~ (US); expanded slag ~, light(weight) slag ~ · Hüttenbimsmehl *n*, (Kunst)Bimsmehl
~ **latex,** latex foam · Latexschaum(-stoff) *m*, Schaum(stoff)latex *m*
foamed lava, scoria(ceous ~) · Schaumlava *f*, vulkanische Schlacke *f*, poröse Lava, Lavaschlacke, Lungstein *m*, Lavakrotze *f*, Basaltlava, Basaltschlacke [*Basaltische feinporige bis blasige vulkanische Auswurfmasse. "Lavalit" ist ein geschützter Handelsname für gebrochene Lavaschlacke, die in verschiedenen Körnungen aufbereitet ist*]

foamed lava concrete — foamed slag (concrete) slab

~ ~ **concrete**, scoria(ceous ~) ~ · Lavaschlackenbeton *m*, (Schaum)Lavabeton, Basaltlavabeton, Basaltschlackenbeton, Lavakiesbeton

~ ~ **(~) wall** scoria(ceous ~) (~) ~ ~ · (Schaum)Lava(beton)-Wand(bau)platte *f*

~ **(light(weight)) concrete** → ~ plastic (~) ~

foam(ed) mortar, mortar aerated with foam · Schaummörtel *m*

~ **(natural) rubber**, expanded (~) ~ · Gummischaum(stoff) *m*, Kautschukschaum(stoff) *m*, Zellkautschuk *m*, Zellgummi *m, n,* Schaumgummi

foamed neoprene, expanded ~, neoprene foam · Neoprenschaum(stoff) *m*

foam(ed) (plastic), expanded ~, plastic foam · Schaum(kunst)stoff *m*, Schaum (stoff), Kunststoffschaum(stoff) *m,* Kunstschaum(stoff) [*Genau genommen ist „Schaum(kunst)stoff" der technisch richtige Ausdruck, denn Schäume, z.B. Seifenschaum, sind nicht beständig und vergehen, während Schaumstoffe beständig sind. Die Kurzform „Schaum" für „Schaum(kunst)stoff" ist allerdings üblich. Das gleiche gilt für den englischen Begriff*]

~ **(~) board**, ~ (~) sheet, expanded ~ ~, plastic foam ~ · (Kunststoff-) Schaumplatte *f,* Schaum(kunst)stoffplatte

~ **(~) concrete** → ~ (~) light(weight) ~

~ ~ **cupola** → plastic foam ~

~ ~ **cylinder** · Schaumstoffarbroller *m,* Schaumstoffwalze *f,* Schaumstoffrolle *f*

~ **(~) dome** → plastic foam cupola

~ **(~) insulation**, expanded ~ ~, plastic foam ~ · Schaumdämmung *f,* Schaumstoffdämmung, Kunstschaum (stoff)dämmung, Kunststoffschaumdämmung, Schaumkunststoffdämmung

~ **(~) (light(weight)) concrete**, expanded ~ (~) ~, plastic foam (~) ~, concrete aerated with foam [*Concrete made very light and cellular by the addition of a prepared foam*] · Kunststoff-Leichtbeton *m,* Leichtbeton auf Kunststoffbasis, Schaumbeton [*DIN 4164*]

~ ~ **plaster baseboard**, expanded ~ ~ ~, plastic foam ~ ~ · Putzträgerplatte *f* aus Kunststoffschaum, Kunststoffschaum-Putzträgerplatte, Schaum (kunst)stoff-Putzträgerplatte

~ ~ **roller** · Schaumstoffarbrollgerät *n*

~ **(~) seal**, expanded ~ ~, plastic foam ~ · Kunststoffschaum(ab)dichtung *f,* Schaumkunststoff(ab)dichtung, Schaum(stoff)(ab)dichtung, Kunstschaum(stoff)(ab)dichtung [*Erzeugnis*]

~ **(~) seal(ing)**, expanded ~ ~, plastic foam ~ · Kunststoffschaum(ab)dichtung *f,* Schaumkunststoff(ab)dichtung, Schaum(stoff)(ab)dichtung, Kunstschaum(stoff)(ab)dichtung

~ ~ ~ **strip** · Schaum(stoff)(ab)-dicht(ungs)streifen *m*

~ ~ **sheet**, ~ ~ board, expanded ~ ~, plastic foam ~ · Schaum(kunst)stoffplatte *f,* Kunststoffschaumplatte

~ **(~) waterbar**, ~ (~) waterstop · Schaumband *n,* Schaumstoffband [*Mit Bitumen getränktes Fugenband zur Abdichtung von Dehnungsfugen und Anschlüssen*]

~ **(~) waterstop**, ~ (~) waterbar · Schaumband *n,* Schaumstoffband [*Mit Bitumen getränktes Fugenband zur Abdichtung von Dehnungsfugen und Anschlüssen*]

~ **polystyrene**, expanded ~, polystyrene foam · Polystyrolschaum(stoff) *m,* Schaum(stoff)polystyrol *n,* PS-Schaum(stoff)

~ ~ **board for thermal insulation purposes**, expanded ~ ~ ~ ~ ~ ~, polystyrene foam ~ ~ ~ ~ ~ [*B.S. 3837*] · Polystyrolschaum(stoff)wärmedämmplatte *f*

~ ~ **tile**, expanded ~ ~, polystyrene foam ~ · Polystyrolschaum(stoff)(belag)platte *f,* Polystyrolschaum(stoff)-fliese *f*

~ **polyurethane**, expanded ~, polyurethane foam · Polyurethanschaum(-stoff) *m,* PUR-Schaum(stoff)

~ ~ **strip**, expanded ~ ~, polyurethane foam ~ · Polyurethanschaum(fugen)-band *n,* PUR-Schaum(fugen)band

~ **polyvinyl chloride** → PVC foam

~ **PVC** → PVC foam

~ **rigid polyvinyl chloride** → expanded rigid PVC

~ ~ **PVC** → expanded ~ ~

~ **rubber**, ~ natural ~, expanded (natural) ~ · Gummischaum(stoff) *m,* Kautschukschaum(stoff), Zellkautschuk *m,* Zellgummi *m, n,* Schaumgummi

~ ~ **latex** · Kautschukmilchschaum *m*

~ **seal** → ~ plastic ~

~ **seal(ing)** → ~ plastic ~

~ **sheet** → ~ plastic ~

~ **slag** → ~ iron blastfurnace ~

~ ~ **aggregate** → ~ (iron) (blastfurnace) ~ ~

~ ~ **concrete hollow block**, ~ ~ ~ cavity ~, ~ ~ ~ ~ ~ tile, ~ ~ ~ ~ brick (Brit.); expanded cinder ~ ~ ~ (US); ~ ~ ~ pot · Hüttenbims(beton)-Hohlblock(stein) *m,* Hüttenbims(beton)-Hohlblock(stein), Kunstbims(beton)-Hohlblock(stein), Kunstbims(beton)-Hohlstein [*DIN 18151*]

~ ~ ~ **plank** (Brit.); expanded ~ ~ ~ (US) · Kunstbims(beton)diele *f,* Hüttenbims(beton)diele

~ ~ ~ ~ ~ ~ **hollow block**

~ ~ **(~) slab** (Brit.); expanded cinder (~) ~ (US) · Hüttenbims(beton)-Bauplatte *f,* Kunstbims(beton)-Bauplatte [*Fehlnamen: (Hütten)Schwemmstein-Bauplatte, Hochofenschwemmstein-Bauplatte*]

foamed slag (concrete) wall slab — folding shutter door

~ ~ (~) **wall slab** (Brit.); expanded cinder (~) ~ ~ (US) · Hüttenbims(beton)-Wand(bau)platte f, Kunstbims(beton)-Wand(bau)platte

~ **urea-formaldehyde,** expanded ~, urea formaldehyde foam · Harnstoff-Formaldehyd(harz)schaum(stoff) m

~ **waterbar** → ~ plastic ~

~ **waterstop** → ~ plastic ~

foaming, froth formation, frothing, expanding, fmg · (Auf)Schäumen n, Schaumbildung f

~ **action,** frothing ~, expanding ~, froth formation ~ · schäumende Wirkung f, Schäumwirkung

~ **agent** → expanding chemical

~ **chemical** → expanding ~

~ **in situ,** expanding ~ ~, frothing ~ ~, froth formation ~ ~ · Schaumbildung f an Ort und Stelle, (Auf)Schäumen n ~ ~ ~ ~

foamy · schaumig

fodder rack, cratch · Futterraufe f

~ **silo** · Futtersilo m

~ **tower** · Futterhochsilo m

fog spray(ing) → mist-spraying

fogged, struck, tarnished · angelaufen, beschlagen, blind geworden, erblindet [Glas]

fogger, mist sprayer · Sprühgerät n

fogging, tarnishing · Erblinden n, Anlaufen, Blindwerden, Beschlagen [Glas]

foil, lobe [Foils are small arches inside Gothic (window) tracery and intersecting as cusps] · Paß m, Nasenschwung m, Zirkelschlag m [gotisches Maßwerk]

~ · Folie f

~ · Blatt n [Ornament]

~ **cover(ing)** · Folienabdeckung f

~ **insert(ion)** · Folieneinlage f

~ **insulation** · Folienisolierung f

~ ~ · Foliendämmung f

~ **jacket** · Folienmantel m

~ **paper,** ~ wallpaper · folienkaschierte Tapete f

~ **sheet(ing)** · Folienbahn f

~ **surface insulation** · Folienoberflächendämmung f, Oberflächenfoliendämmung

~ **(wall)paper** · folienkaschierte Tapete f

fold · Falte f

~ **angle** · Faltwinkel m

to fold down(wards), to tip ~, to turn ~ · umlegen nach unten, abkanten ~ ~

~ ~ **up(wards),** to tip ~ · abkanten nach oben, umlegen ~ ~, aufkanten, hochkanten

folded area · Faltenfläche f [Falt(werk)dach]

~ **base ring on end supports** · geknickter Ringträger m auf Endstützen

~ **concrete** · Faltwerkbeton m

~ **cylindrical surface** · gefaltete Zylinderfläche f

~ **plate** → ~ ~ structure

~ ~ **action** [It is a combination of transverse and longitudinal beam action] · Faltwerkwirkung f

~ ~ **cupola** → ~ ~ dome

~ ~ **dome,** ~ ~ cupola, ~ slab ~, prismatic shell ~; tilted-slab ~ (US) · Faltwerkkuppel f

~ ~ **roof,** ~ slab ~, prismatic shell ~; tilted-slab ~ (US) · Dachfaltwerk n, Falt(werk)dach n

~ ~ **segment,** ~ slab ~, prismatic shell ~; tilted-slab ~ (US) · Falt(werk)scheibe f, (Einzel)Scheibe

~ ~ **(structure),** ~ slab (~), prismatic shell (~); tilted-slab (~) (US) [It is an approximation to the curved shell made by panels] · (Platten)Faltwerk n

~ **slab** → ~ plate (structure)

~ ~ **cupola** → ~ plate dome

~ ~ **dome** → ~ plate ~

~ ~ **roof** → ~ plate ~

~ ~ **segment** → ~ plate ~

~ ~ **(structure),** ~ plate (~), prismatic shell (~); tilted-slab (~) (US) [It is an approximation to the curved shell made by panels] · (Platten)Faltwerk n

folding · Abkanten n [Abbiegen langer Kanten an Blechen mittels Prägestempel und dazu passendem Gesenk in einer Abkantmaschine]

~ · Faltung f

~ **altar,** altar with side wings · Flügelaltar m, Flügelschrein m

~ **door,** double ~ · Falttür f

~ ~ **fitting ,** ~ ~ furniture, double ~ ~ · Falttürbeschlag m

~ ~ **fittings,** ~ ~ hardware, double ~ ~ · Falttürbeschläge mpl

~ ~ **furniture** → ~ ~ fitting

~ ~ **hardware,** ~ ~ fittings, double ~ ~ · Falttürbeschläge mpl

~ **ladder,** ~ stair, loft ~, disappearing ~ · Schiebetreppe f, Einschiebtreppe, hochschiebbare Treppe; Aufzugtreppe [Schweiz]

~ **machine** (Brit.) → ~ press

~ **of drawings** · Falten n von Zeichnungen

~ **partition (wall),** sliding ~ (~), concertina ~ (~), accordion ~ (~) · (Zieh)Harmonikatrennwand f, Falt(trenn)wand, Akkordeontrennwand

~ **press,** ~ machine (Brit.); press brake (US) · Abkantmaschine f, Abkantpresse f

~ **shutter,** boxing ~ · Klapp(fenster)laden m, Falt(fenster)laden

~ ~ **door,** ~ shutterdoor · Falttor n

folding sliding door — footpath flag of basalt(ic) ...

~ **sliding door,** sliding folding ~ · Schiebefalttür *f*, Faltschiebetür

~ ~ **grille,** sliding folding ~ [*See remark under 'Gitter'*] · Schiebefaltgitter *n*, Faltschiebegitter

~ ~ **shutter,** sliding folding ~ · Schiebefaltabschluß *m*, Faltschiebeabschluß

~ ~ ~ **door,** sliding folding ~ ~ · Schiebefalttor *n*, Faltschiebetor

~ **stair,** ~ ladder, loft ~, disappearing ~ · Schiebetreppe *f*, Einschiebetreppe, hochschiebbare Treppe; Aufzugtreppe [*Schweiz*]

~ **system with equal planar units** · Faltsystem *n* mit gleichen Flächenteilen

~ **test** · Faltversuch *m*, Faltprüfung *f*, Faltprobe *f*, Kaltbiegeversuch, Kaltbiegeprüfung. Kaltbiegeprobe [*DIN 1605. Dieser Versuch dient zum Nachweis der Biegekraft eines metallischen Werkstoffes be Raumtemperatur im Zustand der Lieferung oder nach dem Glühen*]

(~) **triptych,** threefold altarpiece · Triptychon *n*, Flügelaltarschrein *m*, dreiteiliger Klappaltar *m*

~ **wall,** sliding ~, concertina ~, ~ partition (~) · Akkordeontrennwand *f*, (Zieh)Harmonikatrennwand, Falt(trenn)wand

~ **window** · Faltfenster *n*

foliage, leaves · Blattwerk *n*, Laubwerk

~ **capital** → foliated ~

~ **cusp** → foliated ~

~ **frieze,** foliated ~, leafy ~ · Blatt(werk)fries *m*, Laub(werk)fries, Blätterfries

(~) **scroll** · Ranke *f*

~, **leaves** · Laubwerk *n*, Blattwerk

foliate and strapwork, Régence ornament · Laub- und Bandelwerk *n*

foliated · blattgeschmückt, blattverziert, laubwerkgeschmückt, laubwerkverziert

~, **foiled** · paßverziert, paßgeschmückt

~ **capital,** foliage ~ · Blatt(werk)kapitell *n*, Blatt(werk)kapitäl, Blätterkapitell, Blätterkapitäl, Laubwerkkapitell, Laubwerkkapitäl

~ **cusp,** foliage ~ · Blattwerknase *f*, Laubwerknase [*Mit Blattwerk besetzte Nase*]

~ **frieze** → foliage ~

~ **grit(-stone),** arenaceous shale, schistous sandstone · Sandschiefer *m*

~ **gypsum** · Schiefergips *m*

~ **sandstone** · Blättersandstein *m*

foliation · Paßverzierung *f*, Paßschmuck *m*, Paßdekor(ation) *m*, (*f*)

~, **leaf-like decoration** · Blattverzierung *f*, Blattschmuck *m*, Blattdekor(ation) *m*, (*f*)

font [*A basin to hold the water used in baptismal services*] · Taufbecken *n*

food processing plant · Nahrungsmittelbetrieb *m*

~ **room** · Nahrungsmittellagerraum *m*

fool's gold, mundic, (iron) pyrite(s), yellow pyrite(s) · Eisenkies *m*, Schwefelkies, Schwefeleisen *n*

foot bath [*A bath for washing the feet, and generally of ceramic ware, fixed at a low level and provided with hot and cold water taps and a waste outlet*] · Fußbadewanne *f*, Fußwaschbecken *n* [*DIN 13214, 13215*]

footboard · Fußtritt *m* [*Chorgestühl*]

foot cut (US) → toe-jointing

footing [*The gradual deposition of 'foots' from an oil or varnish*] · Entschleimung *f*

~ **anchorage** · Fundamentverankerung *f*

~ [*for wall, masonry wall or column*] · Fundament *n* [*für Mauer, Wand oder Stütze*]

~ **beam,** principal ~, tie ~, main ~ · Hauptbalken *m*, Zugbalken, Spannbalken, Trambalken [*einsäuliges Hängewerk*]

~ **brick masonry (work),** ~ brickwork · Fundament-Ziegelmauerwerk *n*

~ **brickwork,** ~ brick masonry (work) · Fundament-Ziegelmauerwerk *n*

~ **clinker** · Fundamentklinker *m*

~ **concrete** · Fundamentbeton *m*

~ **depth,** depth of footing · Fundamenttiefe *f*

~ **drain** · Fundamentdrän *m*

~ **drawing** · Fundamentplan *m*, Fundamentzeichnung *f*

~ **grid plane** · Fundamentrasterebene *f*

~ **masonry wall,** masonry footing ~ · Fundamentmauer *f*

~ ~ **(work)** · Fundamentmauerwerk *n*

~ **piece,** solepiece, plate · Unterschiebling *m* [*Dach*]

~ **pier** · Fundamentpfeiler *m*

~ **pressure** · Fundamentdruck *m*

~ **shell** · Fundamentschale *f*

~ **vault** · Fundamentgewölbe *n*

~ **wall brick** · Fundamentmauerziegel *m*

foot iron, step ~, hand ~, access hook · Steigeisen *n*, Kletterreisen [*DIN 1211 (kurz), DIN 1212 (lang)*]

foot-measure · Fußmaß *n*

foot moment, base ~, moment at foot, moment at base · Fußmoment *n*

~ **pace** → (stair(case)) floor

footpath concrete flag(stone) (Brit.) → sidewalk ~ ~

~ ~ **paving flag** (Brit.) → sidewalk concrete flag(stone)

~ **flag** (Brit.) → sidewalk (paving) ~

~ ~ **of basalt(ic) chip(ping)s concrete** (Brit.); sidewalk ~ ~ ~ ~ ~ (US) · Basaltsplittplatte *f* [*Beton-Bürgersteigplatte aus Basaltsplitt und Portlandzement*]

footpath flagstone — forced (warm) air heating

~ flagstone (Brit.) → (natural) stone sidewalk (paving) flag
~ (paving) flag (Brit.) → sidewalk (~) ~
foot run, feet ~, lineal foot · laufender Fuß *m* [*Längenmaß*]
foots · Schleimstoffe *mpl* [*in Öl oder Lack*]
~ scraper · Fußabstreicher *m*, Schuhabstreicher, Fußreiniger, Fußkratzer
~ stall → plinth
footstep sound · Trittschall *m* [*Schall, der beim Begehen einer Decke entsteht, als Körperschall weitergeleitet und teilweise als Luftschall abgestrahlt wird*]
~ ~ insulation · Trittschall(ab)dämmung *f*
~ ~ ~ [*Means taken to reduce the transmission of footstep sound*] · Trittschallschutz *m*
~ ~ ~ board, ~ ~ ~ sheet · Trittschall(ab)dämmplatte *f*
~ ~ ~ felt(ed fabric) · Trittschall(ab)-dämmfilz *m*
~ ~ ~ material · Trittschall(ab)dämmstoff *m*
~ ~ ~ sheet, ~ ~ ~ board · Trittschall(ab)dämmplatte *f*
~ ~ intensity · Trittschallstärke *f*
~ ~ level · Trittschallpegel *m*
~ ~ measurement · Trittschallmessung *f*
~ ~ reduction index (Brit.); ~ ~ transmission loss (US); ~ ~ reduction factor [*deprecated*] · Trittschalldämmmaß *n*, Trittschalldämmzahl *f*, Trittschallschutzmaß, TSM
~ ~ transmission · Trittschallübertragung *f*
~ ~ ~ loss (US); ~ ~ reduction index (Brit.); ~ ~ reduction factor [*deprecated*] · Trittschalldämmaß *n*, Trittschalldämmzahl *f*, Trittschallschutzmaß, TSM
~ switch · Fußschalter *m*
~ traffic · Fußverkehr *m*, Trittverkehr
~ valve · Fußventil *n*
footway, side ~ · Fußgängerpforte *f*, Seitenpforte [*in einem Stadttor*]
~ · Fußweg *m*
Föppl network dome, ~ ~ cupola · Föpplsche Netzwerkkuppel *f*
force · Kraft *f*
~(-)account construction, ~ work · Regiearbeiten *fpl*
force acting in the direction of motion · antreibende Kraft *f* [*Schalltechnik*]
~ application · Anbringen *n* einer Kraft, Kraftanbringung *f*, (Kraft)Angriff *m*
~ component · Kraftkomponente *f*
~-deformation diagram · Kräfte-Verformungs-Diagramm *n*, Kräfte-Formänderungs-Diagramm
force developed at a re-entrant angle · Umlenkkraft *f* [*Treppe*]

~ diagram · Kräftediagramm *n*
~ direction, direction of force · Kraftrichtung *f*
~ distribution · Kraftverteilung *f*
~ field, field of forces · Kraftfeld *n*, Kräftefeld
force-free edge · kräftefreier Rand *m*
force method, Argyris ~ ~, flexibility matrix ~ · Kraft(größen)verfahren *n*, Kraft(größen)methode *f*
~ moment · Kraftmoment *n*
~-moment diagram · Kraft-Momenten-Diagramm *n*
force parallelogram, parallelogram of forces · Parallelogramm *n* der Kräfte, Kräfteparallelogramm
~ polygon, polygon of force vectors, polygon of forces [*A polygonal figure illustrating a theorem relating to a number of forces acting at one point, each of which is represented in magnitude and direction by one of the sides of the figure*] · Krafteck *n*, Kräftevieleck, Kräftezug *m*, Kräftepolygon *n*
~ scale · Kräftemaßstab *m*
~ triangle, triangle of forces · Krafteck *n*, Kräftedreieck
~ vector · Kraftvektor *m*, Kräftevektor
forced air furnace → ~ warm ~ ~
~ air heating, ~ warm ~ ~ [*The air circulation is by means of a fan*] · Umlauf-Luftheizung *f*, Umwäz-Luftheizung
~ circulation by pump · Pumpenumlauf *m*
~-circulation central heating · Pumpen-Umlaufheizung *f*
forced convection · erzwungene Konvektion *f*
~ draught (Brit.); ~ draft (US); artificial ~, FD · künstlicher Zug *m*
~ heating · Pumpenheizung *f*
~ ~ installation, ~ ~ system · Pumpenheiz(ungs)anlage *f*
~ ~ system, ~ ~ installation · Pumpenheiz(ungs)anlage *f*
~ hot water heating · Pumpen-Heißwasserheizung *f*
~ one-pipe heating, one-pipe forced ~ · Einrohr-Pumpenheizung *f*, Pumpen-Einrohrheizung
~ oscillation → ~ vibration
~ ventilation, venting · Zwangs-Be- und Entlüftung *f*, Kraft-Be- und -Entlüftung, Zwangslüftung, Kraftlüftung
~ vibration, ~ oscillation [*A vibration maintained solely by one or more periodic forces, and having frequencies related to the frequencies of those forces*] · erzwungene Schwingung *f*
~ (warm) air furnace [*A furnace equipped with a blower to provide the primary means for circulating air*] · Gebläse-(Warm)Luftofen *m*, Gebläse-Luftheizofen
~ (~) ~ heating [*The air circulation is by means of a fan*] · Umlauf-Luftheizung *f*, Umwälz-Luftheizung

forces acting in any direction — formation of lime silicate

forces acting in any direction · beliebig gerichtete Kräfte *fpl*, willkürlich ~ ~

~ **balanced in pairs** · sich paarweise aufhebende Kräfte *fpl*

~ **compensating one another,** ~ **counteracting** ~ ~ · zwei sich aufhebende Kräfte *fpl*

~ **counteracting one another,** ~ compensating ~ ~ · zwei sich aufhebende Kräfte *fpl*

~ **in plane** · Kräfte *fpl* in der Ebene

~ ~ **space** · Kräfte *fpl* im Raum

~ **intersecting at an acute angle** · sich unter einem spitzen Winkel schneidende Kräfte *fpl*

forcing · Vortreiben *n*, Vortrieb *m* [*Material in einer Strangpresse*]

~ **screw** · Preßschraube *f*, Treibschraube

ford cup [*A flow cup used for measuring the viscosity of paint, standardized in B.S. 1733*] · Fordbecher *m*

fore-arch · Vorbogen *m*

forebuilding, projection · Vorbau *m*, vorspringender Bau

forechurch, antechurch · Vorkirche *f*

forecourt · Vorhof *m*

~, front garden; front yard (US) · Vorgarten *m* [*Gelände zwischen der Baufluchtund der Straßenfluchtlinie, das nicht zur Straße sondern zum Anliegergrundstück gehört*]

foreign cullet · Fremdbrocken *m*, Fremdscherben *m* [*Glasgemenge*]

~ **labourer** (Brit.); ~ **laborer** (US) · Gastarbeiter *m*

~ **matter,** ~ **substance** · Fremdstoff *m*

~ **substance,** ~ **matter** · Fremdstoff *m*

foreman carpenter · Zimmerpolier *m*

~ **scaffolder** · Gerüstbaupolier *m*

~ **steel erector** · Stahlbaumontagemeister *m*

forend → keeper (plate)

forest cemetery · Waldfriedhof *m*

~ **crematorium** · Waldkrematorium *n*

~ **of columns** · "Säulenwald" *m*

forge welding, fire ~ · Feuerschweißen *n* [*DIN 1910*]

forged nail · geschmiedeter Nagel *m*

~ **steel,** FST, fst · geschmiedeter Stahl *m*

forging · Schmieden *n*

~ · Schmiedestück *n*

~ **brass** · Messing 60 Pb *n*, Schmiedemessing, Ms 60 Pb, MS 60 PB

~ **steel** · Schmiedestahl *m* [*Gegossener Flußstahl, der durch Schmieden oder Pressen weiterverarbeitet wird*]

forked mortice and tenon joint, ~ **mortise** ~ ~ ~ · Gabelzapfen *m*, Scher(en)zapfen [*Holzverbindung*]

~ **pipe** · Gabelrohr *n*

~ **strap,** two-way ~ · Gabelband *n*, gegabelte Kopfschiene *f* [*Holzbau*]

~ **tie** · Gabelanker *m*, Schließanker

~ **wood** · Band *n*, Gabelholz *n*

fork-test · Gabelprüfung *f*, Gabelversuch *m*, Gabelprobe *f* [*Korrosionsprüfung*]

form · Ausbildung *f*, Gestaltung, Form *f*

to form a paste, to make ~ ~, ~ ~ into ~ ~ · anpasten

form-active redirection of forces · formaktive Kraftumlenkung *f*

~ **structure system** · formatives Tragsystem *n* [*Die senkrechte Stütze und das senkrechte Hängeseil sind Prototypen der formativen Tragsysteme*]

form agent → forms ~

~ **aid** → forms ~

~ **board** → forms ~

~ **concept,** concept of form · Formvorstellung *f*

~ **lining** → forms ~

~ **lube** → formwork ~

~ **of arch** · Bogenform *f*

~ ~ **shell structure** · Schalenbauwerkform *f*

~ **oil** → form(work) lube

~ **panel** → forms ~

~ **paste** → forms ~

~ **plate** → formwork ~

~ **removal** → formwork ~

form-retentive, shape-retentive · formbeständig, formtreu

form-retentiveness, shape-retentiveness · Formbeständigkeit *f*, Formtreue *f*

form-set · Schalungssatz *m*

form tie → form(work) ~

~ **wax** → forms ~

forma [*A channel for water or an aqueduct*] · Wasser(ge)rinne *f*, (*n*)

formability · Verformbarkeit *f*, (Um)Formbarkeit

formal and spatial concept, concept of form and space, concept of shape and space · Formen- und Raumsprache *f*, Raum- und Formensprache

~ **garden,** French ~ ~ · französischer (Barock)Park *m*, ~ Garten *m*

~ **symmetrical elevation** · streng symmetrischer Aufriß *m*

formaldehyde resin · Formaldehydharz *n*

formalism · Formalismus *m*

to formalize, to stylize, to conventionalize · stilisieren

formalized → divorced from reality

format · Format *n*, Größe *f*

~ **symbol** · Formatkurzzeichen *n*

formation · Bildung *f*, Entstehung

~ **of calcium silicate,** ~ ~ lime · Kalksilikatbildung *f*

~ ~ **gas bubbles** → gas formation

~ ~ **lime silicate,** ~ ~ calcium · Kalksilikatbildung *f*

formation of lumps — (form(work)) tie 416

~ ~ **lumps,** lump formation · Klumpenbildung f [*Zement*]

~ ~ **pockets** · Nesterbildung f [*Beton*]

~ ~ **rust,** rust formation, rusting · Rostbildung f, Rosten n

formed in dry state, dry formed · trocken verformt [*Schamottestein*]

~ **plate,** profile(d) ~ · profiliertes Grobblech n, Profilgrobblech

~ **sheet** · profiliertes Feinblech n, Profilfeinblech

~ ~, profile(d) ~ · Profilblech n, profiliertes Blech

formeret · (Längs)Schildbogen m [*Ein Bogen, der sich im Anlauf eines Gewölbes auf eine Schildmauer ergibt; zu unterscheiden vom Wandbogen*]

formic acid · Formylsäure f, Ameisensäure f, H_2CO_2

forming · Form(geb)ung f

~ **crew,** ~ gang, ~ party, ~ team · Schal(ungs)kolonne f, Schal(ungs)mannschaft f, Schal(ungs)trupp m

~ **gang,** ~ crew, ~ party, ~ team · Schal(ungs)kolonne f, Schal(ungs)trupp m, Schal(ungs)mannschaft f

~ **of blocks,** ~ ~ tiles, block making, tile making [*See remark under 'Block'*] · Steinfertigung f, Steinherstellung, Block(stein)herstellung, Block(stein)fertigung

~ ~ **tiles,** ~ ~ blocks, block making, tile making [*See remark under 'Block'*] · Steinfertigung f, Steinherstellung, Block(stein)herstellung, Block(stein)fertigung

~ **party,** ~ crew, ~ gang, ~ team · Schal(ungs)kolonne f, Schal(ungs)trupp m, Schal(ungs)mannschaft f

~ **pressure** · Formdruck m, Form(geb)ungsdruck

~ **team,** ~ crew, ~ gang, ~ party · Schal(ungs)kolonne f, Schal(ungs)trupp m, Schal(ungs)mannschaft f

forms → concrete ~

~ **agent,** form(work) ~, release ~, shuttering ~, form(work) sealer, forms sealer, shuttering sealer · (Ent)Schal(ungs)mittel n, (Ent)Schal(ungs)hilfe f

~ **aid,** form(work) ~, shuttering ~ · Schal(ungs)hilfsmittel n

~ **board,** form(work) ~, shuttering ~, ~ sheet · Schal(ungs)platte f

~ ~, shuttering ~, form(work) ~ · Schal(ungs)brett n

~ **facing** → ~ surfacing

~ **lining,** ~ (sur)facing, shuttering lining, form(work) ~ [*The material forming the contact face of forms*] · Schal(ungs)auskleidung f, Schal(ungs)bekleidung, Schal(ungs)verkleidung

~ **lube** → form(work) ~

~ **oil** → form(work) lube

~ **paint,** form(work) ~, shuttering ~ · Schal(ungs)farbe f

~ **panel,** form(work) ~, shuttering ~ · Schal(ungs)tafel f

~ **paste,** release ~, form(work) ~, shuttering ~ · Schal(ungs)paste f, Ent~

~ **plate,** form(work) ~, shuttering ~ · Schal(ungs)blech n

~ **removal,** shuttering ~, form(work) ~, stripping, release · Ausschalen n, Entschalen, Ausschalung f, Entschalung

~ **sealer,** form(work) ~, shuttering ~, ~ agent, release agent · (Ent)Schal(ungs)mittel n, (Ent)Schal(ungs)hilfe f

~ **sheet(ing),** form(work) ~, shuttering ~ · Schal(ungs)folie f aus Kunststoff

~ **(sur)facing,** ~ lining, form(work) ~, shuttering ~ [*The material forming the contact face of forms*] · Schal(ungs)auskleidung f, Schal(ungs)bekleidung, Schal(ungs)verkleidung

~ **tie,** shuttering ~, (form(work)) ~, tie rod · Schal(ungs)anker m

~ **wax,** release ~, shuttering ~, form(work) ~ · Schal(ungs)wachs n, Ent~

to formulate · rezeptieren

formulation · Rezept(ur) n, (f), Mischungsformel f

~ [*e.g. adhesives are formulated of epoxy resin, a plasticizer, and a curing agent*] · Zusammensetzung f

form(work) → concrete ~

~ **agent,** release ~, forms ~, shuttering ~, form(work) sealer, forms sealer, shuttering sealer · (Ent)Schal(ungs)mittel n, (Ent)Schal(ungs)hilfe f

~ **aid,** shuttering ~, forms ~ · Schal(ungs)hilfsmittel n

~ **board,** shuttering ~, forms ~ · Schal(ungs)brett n

~ ~, forms ~, shuttering ~, ~ sheet · Schal(ungs)platte f

~ **lining,** shuttering ~, forms ~, ~ (sur)facing [*The material forming the contact face of forms*] · Schal(ungs)auskleidung f, Schal(ungs)bekleidung, Schal(ungs)verkleidung

~ **lube,** ~ oil, shuttering ~, forms ~ release ~ · (Ent)Schal(ungs)öl n

~ **oil** → ~ lube

~ **paint,** shuttering ~, forms ~ · Schal(ungs)farbe f

~ **panel,** shuttering ~, forms ~ · Schal(ungs)tafel f

~ **paste,** release ~, shuttering ~, forms ~ · Schal(ungs)paste f, Ent~

~ **plate,** forms ~, shuttering ~ · Schal(ungs)blech n

~ **removal,** shuttering ~, forms ~, stripping, release · Ausschalung f, Entschalung

~ **sealer,** forms ~, shuttering ~, ~ agent, release agent · (Ent)Schal(ungs)mittel n, (Ent)Schal(ungs)hilfe f

~ **sheet(ing),** shuttering ~, forms ~ · Schal(ungs)folie f aus Kunststoff

(~) tie, forms ~, shuttering ~, tie rod · Schal(ungs)anker m

~ **wax**, release ~, shuttering ~, forms ~ · Schal(ungs)wachs *n*, Ent~

formworkless, shutteringless · schalungsfrei, schalungslos

forsterite · Forsterit *m*, Magnesiumolivin *m*

~ **refractory brick** · Forsteritstein *m*

~ ~ **(product)**, ~ ~ **material** · Forsteriterzeugnis *n*

fort · Fort *n*

fortalice, fortilage, outwork; outer defence (Brit.); outer defense (US) · Vorwerk *n*, Außenwerk, Veste *f*

fortifiable [*That may be fortified*] · befestigungsfähig

fortification · Befestigung *f*

~, (fortified) stronghold, defensive work, military stronghold, fortified place · Befestigung(sanlage) *f*, befestigter Stützpunkt *m*, Wehrbau *m*, Festungsanlage

~ **(masonry) wall**, battlemented (~) ~, defensive (~) ~ · Befestigungsmauer *f*, Verteidigungsmauer

fortified, walled · befestigt

~ **church** · befestigte Kirche *f*

~ **monastery**, walled ~, fortress-monastery · befestigtes Mönchskloster *n*

~ **palace**, walled ~, fortress-palace · befestigter Palast *m*

~ **place** → fortification

~ **residence** · befestigte Wohnanlage *f*

(~) **stronghold** → fortification

~ **structure** · Wehrbau(werk) *m*, (*n*) [*Ein Bau, der durch Mauern, Bastionen usw. geschützt ist, z.B. Burg, Festung usw.*]

~ **town**, walled ~, caste-like ~, fortress-town · befestigte Stadt *f*

~ ~ **gate**, defensive gateway · Befestigungsstadttor *n*, Verteidigungsstadttor, befestigtes Stadttor

to fortify, to fortress [*To furnish with a fortress or fortification(s); to protect with or as with a fortress*] · befestigen

fortifying · Befestigen *n*

fortilage, fortalice, outwork; outer defence (Brit.); outer defense (US) · Vorwerk *n*, Außenwerk, Veste *f*

to fortress, to fortify [*To furnish with a fortress of fortification(s); to protect with or as with a fortress*] · befestigen

fortress · Festung *f*

~ **castle** · Burg *f*

~ ~ **architecture** · Burgarchitektur *f*, Burgbaukunst *f*

~ **castle-chapel** · Burgkapelle *f*

~ **castle-church** · Burgkirche *f*

~ **castle-ditch**, moat, foss(e) · Burggraben *m*, Halsgraben, Befestigungsgraben

~ **castle-gate** · Burgtor *n*

~ **castle-tower** · Burgturm *m*

~ **castle-wall** · Burgmauer *f*

fortress-chapel · Festungskapelle *f*

fortress-church · Festungskirche *f*

fortress-house tower · Geschlechterturm *m*, Wohnturm [*Wohnturm des Adels in einer Stadt. Der Eingang lag oft wie beim Bergfried hoch, als Abschluß findet man häufig Zinnen. Geschlechtertürme kommen hauptsächlich in Italien (Florenz, S. Gimignano, Bologna, Pavia) vor und sind im deutschen Mittelalter selten*]

fortress-like · festungshaft

fortress masonry · Festungsmauerwerk *n*

fortress-monastery, fortified monastery, walled monastery · befestigtes Mönchskloster *n*

fortress-palace, fortified palace, walled palace · befestigter Palast *m*

fortress-town, fortified town, walled town, castle-like town · befestigte Stadt *f*

fortress wall · Festungsmauer *f*

~ **well** · Festungsbrunnen *m*

forum · Forum *n* [*Ein meist viereckiger Platz einer römischen Stadt*]

Forum of Trajan · Trajansforum *n*

forward-looking, advanced · zukunftsweisend

FOS → factor of safety

foss(e), moat, fortress castle-ditch · Burggraben *m*, Halsgraben, Befestigungsgraben

fossil copal, hard ~, true ~ · Hartkopal(harz) *m*, (*n*), fossiler Kopal, fossiles Kopalharz

~ **fuel** · fossiler Brennstoff *m*

~ **resin** [*Any of the natural or earth type resins, which derive their characteristics through ag(e)ing in the ground*] · (rezent)fossiles Harz *n*

foul air · Kanalgas *n*

~ ~, vitiated ~ · Abluft *f*, Schlechtluft [*Ins Freie abströmende Abluft heißt „Fortluft" und ganz oder teilweise nach Filterung wieder der Lüftungszentrale zugeführte Abluft heißt „Umluft"*]

~ ~ **chimney**, vitiated ~ ~ · Abluftschornstein *m*, Schlechtluftschornstein

~ ~ **duct**, vitiated ~ ~, ~ ~ **flue** · Abluftkanal *m*, Schlechtluftkanal

~ ~ **floor duct**, vitiated ~ ~ ~, ~ ~ ~ **flue** · Abluft-(Fuß)Bodenkanal *m*, Schlechtluft-(Fuß)Bodenkanal

~ ~ ~ **flue**, vitiated ~ ~ ~, ~ ~ ~ **duct** · Abluft-(Fuß)Bodenkanal *m*, Schlechtluft-(Fuß)Bodenkanal

~ ~ **flue**, vitiated ~ ~, ~ ~ **duct** · Abluftkanal *m*, Schlechtluftkanal

~ ~ **grate**, vitiated ~ ~ · Schlechtluftrost *m*, Abluftrost

~ ~ **hole**, ~ ~ **opening**, vitiated ~ ~ · Schlechtluftdurchlaß *m*, Schlechtluftöffnung *f*, Abluftöffnung, Abluftdurchlaß; Lufteinlaß [*Fehlname*] [*Eine Öffnung in einer Raumbegrenzungsfläche*

foul air hole — four-cornered mesh wire netting

durch die Raumluft (Abluft) in den Abluftkanal oder als Fortluft ins Freie abgesaugt oder gedrückt wird]

~~ **opening**, vitiated ~ ~, ~ ~ hole · Schlechtluftdurchlaß, Schlechtluftöffnung, Abluftöffnung, Abluftdurchlaß; Lufteinlaß [*Fehlname*] [*Eine Öffnung in einer Raumbegrenzungsfläche, durch die Raumluft (Abluft) in den Abluftkanal oder als Fortluft ins Freie abgesaugt oder gedrückt wird*]

~~ **pipe**, vitiated ~ ~ · Abluftrohr *n*, Schlechtluftrohr

~~ **shaft**, vitiated ~ ~ · Abluftschacht *m*, Schlechtluftschacht [*DIN 18017*]

~ **drain**, ~ water ~, refuse water ~, sewage ~ [*It discharges into a sewer or other outfall*] · Abwasserdrän *m*

~ **water** → refuse ~

~~ **disposal facility**, refuse ~ ~ ~, sewage ~ ~ · Abwasserbeseitigungsanlage *f*

~~ **gallery** → ~ ~ tunnel

~~ **pipe** → sewer ~

~~ **(~) trench** → sewer (~) ~

~~ **purification** → refuse ~ ~

~~ **trench** → sewer (pipe) ~

~~ **tunnel**, ~ ~ gallery, refuse ~ ~, sewer ~, sewage ~ · Abwasserstollen *m*, Kanal(isations)stollen

foundation, fdn [*A construction to spread loads applied to the supporting soil or rock*] · Gründung *f*

~ [*The soil or rock upon which a structure rests*] · Gründungsuntergrund *m*

~ **anchorage** · Gründungsverankerung *f*

~ **bolt**, anchor ~, rag ~, stone ~, hold(ing)-down ~ · Ankerschraube *f*, Steinschraube, Verankerungsschraube, Klauenschraube, Fundamentschraube

~ **brick masonry (work)**, ~ brickwork · Gründungs-Ziegelmauerwerk

~ **ceremony** · Grundsteinlegung *f*

~ **clinker** · Gründungsklinker *m*

~ **concrete** · Gründungsbeton *m*

~ **depth**, depth of foundation · Gründungstiefe *f*

~ **drain** · Gründungsdrän *m*

~ **drainage** · Gründungsdränage *f*

~ **drawing** · Gründungsplan *m*, Gründungszeichnung *f*

~ **grid plan** · Gründungsrasterebene *f*

~ **masonry wall**, masonry foundation ~ · Grundmauer *f*, Gründungsmauer

~~ **(work)** · Gründungsmauerwerk *n*, Grundmauerwerk

~ **pier** · Gründungspfeiler *m*

~ **pressure** · Gründungsdruck *m*

~ **raft**, grade slab [*A reinforced concrete slab which forms the foundation for the superstructure; it is normally placed directly on the ground*] · Fundamentplatte *f*, Gründungsplatte, Grundplatte

~ **shell** · Gründungsschale *f*

~ **stone** · Grundstein *m*

~ **vault** · Gründungsgewölbe *n*

~ **wall**, ground ~ · Gründungswand *f*

~~ **brick** · Gründungsmauerziegel *m*, Grundmauerziegel

founder-member · Gründungsmitglied *n*

founder's black, facing, black(en)ing, blackwash · Gießer(ei)schwärze *f*

Foundling Hospital at Florence [*Ospedale degli Innocenti*] · Findelhaus *n* in Florenz, Florentiner Findelhaus

foundry building · Gießereigebäude *n*

~ **clay**, ladle ~ · Gießton *m*

~ **slag** · Gießereischlacke *f*

fountain, water ~ · Brunnen *m* [*als Oberflächenbauwerk*]

~ **basin** · Brunnenbecken *n*

~ **for ceremonial ablutions**, ~ ~ ritual ~ · Brunnen *m* für rituelle Waschungen [*Moschee*]

~~ **ritual ablutions**, ~ ~ ceremonial ~ · Brunnen *m* für rituelle Waschungen [*Moschee*]

~ **pipe** [*A pipe which supplies a fountain with water*] · Brunnenrohr *n*

~ **plaza**, ~ site · Brunnenplatz *m*

~ **site**, ~ plaza · Brunnenplatz *m*

~ **water** · Brunnenwasser *n*

fountainlet · Brünnlein *n*

four-bay · vierjochig

~, four-span · vierschiffig [*Rahmenhalle*]

four-bed · vierbettig

~ **ward** · Vierbettkrankenzimmer *n*

Fourcault glass · Fourcaultglas *n*

four-centred arch (Brit.); four-centered ~ (US); drop ~ · flacher Spitzbogen *m*, gedrückter ~, stumpfer ~ [*Er ist aus vier Kreisbögen zusammengesetzt*]

(~) Tudor arch (Brit.); (four-centered) ~ ~, four-centered pointed ~ (US) · Tudorbogen *m*, Vier-Zentren-Bogen

four-columned hall · Viersäulenhalle *f*

four-compartment revolving door · vierflügelige Drehtür *f*

four-cornered, four-sided · viereckig, vierkantig, vierseitig

~ **bar** → ~ rod

~ **brass**, four-sided ~ · Vierkantmessing *n*, Viereckmessing, vierkantiges Messing, viereckiges Messing, vierseitiges Messing

~ **column**, four-sided ~, box ~ · Vierkantstütze *f*, Viereckstütze, vierkantige Stütze, viereckige Stütze, vierseitige Stütze

~ **copper**, four-sided ~ · Vierkantkupfer *n*, Viereckkupfer, vierkantiges Kupfer, viereckiges Kupfer, vierseitiges Kupfer

~ **mesh wire netting**, four-sided ~ ~ · Viereckdrahtgeflecht *n*, Vierkantdrahtgeflecht, vierkantiges Drahtgeflecht, viereckiges Drahtgeflecht

four-cornered mosaic tile — four-sided slab

~ **mosaic tile,** four-sided ~ ~ · Viereckmosaik(belag)platte *f*, Viereckmosaikfliese *f*, viereckige Mosaik(belag)-platte, viereckige Mosaikfliese, vierseitige Mosaik(belag)platte, vierseitige Mosaikfliese, Vierkant-Mosaik(belag)platte, Vierkant-Mosaikfliese

~ **panel,** four-sided ~ · Vierkanttafel *f*, Viereicktafel, vierkantige Tafel, viereckige Tafel, vierseitige Tafel

~ **pier,** four-sided ~ · Viereckpfeiler *m*, viereckiger Pfeiler, Vierkantpfeiler, vierkantiger Pfeiler, vierseitiger Pfeiler [*Ein quadratischer oder rechteckiger Pfeiler*]

~ **plate,** ~ slab, four-sided ~ · Viereckplatte *f*, viereckige Platte, Vierkantplatte, vierkantige Platte, vierseitige Platte

~ **rod,** ~ bar, four-sided ~ · Vierkantstab *m*, Viereckstab, vierkantiger Stab, viereckiger Stab, vierseitiger Stab

~ **slab,** ~ plate, four-sided ~ · Viereckplatte *f*, viereckige Platte, Vierkantplatte, vierkantige Platte, vierseitige Platte

~ **steel,** four-sided ~ · Vierkantstahl *m*, Viereckstahl, vierkantiger Stahl, viereckiger Stahl, vierseitiger Stahl

~ **tower,** four-sided ~ · Vierkantturm *m*, Viereckturm, vierkantiger Turm, viereckiger Turm, vierseitiger Turm

~ **wire,** four-sided ~ · Viereckdraht *m*, Vierkantdraht, viereckiger Draht, vierkantiger Draht, vierseitiger Draht

four-edge support · Vierrandauflagerung *f*

four gable form [*hyperbolic paraboloid*] · Viergiebelform *f*

four-horse(d) chariot, quadriga [*A sculpture, often surmounting a monument*] · Quadriga *f*, Viergespann *n*

4 lamp (light(ing)) fixture; ~ ~ luminaire (~) (US); ~ ~ light fitting (Brit.) · Vierlampenleuchte *f*

four-leaf around(-the)-corner sliding shutter door, ~ ~ ~ shutterdoor · vierflügeliges Rundlauftor *n*

~ **sliding folding shutterdoor,** ~ ~ ~ shutter door · vierflügeliges Faltschiebetor *n*, ~ Schiebefalttor

four-leaved tracery, quatrefoil, tracery with four leaf-shaped curves · Vierblatt *n* [*gotisches Maßwerk*]

four-lobe tracery, quatrefoil · Vierpaß *m* [*gotisches Maßwerk*]

four-moment equation · Vier-Momente-Gleichung *f*, Viermomentengleichung

~ **theorem** · Vier-Momente-Lehrsatz *m*, Viermomentenlehrsatz

four-panel(led) door, framed and ~ ~ (Brit.); (framed and) four panel(ed) ~ (US) · Kreuztür *f*, Vierfüllungstür

four-part cross-rib(bed) vault, quadripartite ~ ~ · vierteiliges Kreuzrippengewölbe *n*

~ **narrow multi-storey block** (Brit.) → quadripartite ~ ~ ~

~ **shutter,** quadripartite ~ · vierteiliger (Raum)Abschluß *m*

~ **tracery,** quadripartite ~ · vierteiliges Maßwerk *n*

~ **vault,** quadripartite ~ · vierteiliges Gewölbe *n*

four-pipe system · Vier-Rohr-System *n*

four-ply built-up roof cover(ing), ~~ roofing · vierlagige Spachtel(dach)-deckung *f*, vierschichtige ~, vierlagiger Spachteldachbelag *m*, vierschichtiger Spachteldachbelag

~ **tar and gravel-type (built-up) roofing,** ~ ~ ~ ~ (~) roof cover(ing) · vierlagiger Teerspachteldachbelag *m* mit Kiesabstreuung, ~ ~ ~ Kiesbestreuung, vierschichtiger ~ ~ ~, vierlagige Teerspachtel(dach)deckung *f* ~ ~, vierschichtige Teerspachtel(dach)deckung

four-point suspension mounting · Vierpunktaufhängung *f*

four quarters, whole (clay) brick · Ganzziegel *m*

four-room(ed) dwelling unit (US); ~ dwelling (Brit.) · Vierraumwohnung *f*, Vierzimmerwohnung

four-sided, four-cornered · viereckig, vierkantig, vierseitig

~ **bar** → four-cornered rod

~ **brass,** four-cornered ~ · Vierkantmessing *n*, Viereckmessing, vierkantiges Messing, viereckiges Messing, vierseitiges Messing

~ **column,** four-cornered ~, box ~ · Vierkantstütze *f*, Viereckstütze, vierkantige Stütze; viereckige Stütze, vierseitige Stütze

~ **copper,** four-cornered ~ · Vierkantkupfer *n*, Viereckkupfer, vierkantiges Kupfer, viereckiges Kupfer, vierseitiges Kupfer

~ **gateway** → ~ town ~

~ **mesh wire netting,** four-cornered ~ ~ ~ · Viereckdrahtgeflecht *n*, Vierkantdrahtgeflecht, vierkantiges Drahtgeflecht, viereckiges Drahtgeflecht

~ **mosaic tile,** four-cornered ~ ~ · Viereckmosaik(belag)platte *f*, Viereckmosaikfliese *f*, viereckige Mosaik(belag)platte, viereckige Mosaikfliese, vierseitige Mosaik(belag)platte, vierseitige Mosaikfliese, Vierkant-Mosaik(belag)platte, Vierkant-Mosaikfliese

~ **panel,** four-cornered ~ · Vierkanttafel *f*, Viereicktafel, vierkantige Tafel, viereckige Tafel, vierseitige Tafel

~ **pier,** four-cornered ~ · Viereckpfeiler *m*, viereckiger Pfeiler, Vierkantpfeiler vierkantiger Pfeiler, vierseitiger Pfeiler [*Ein quadratischer oder rechteckiger Pfeiler*]

~ **plate,** ~ slab, four-cornered ~ · Viereckplatte *f*, viereckige Platte, Vierkantplatte, vierkantige Platte, vierseitige Platte

~ **rod** → four-cornered ~

~ **slab,** ~ plate, four-cornered ~ · Viereckplatte *f*, viereckige Platte, Vierkantplatte, vierkantige Platte, vierseitige Platte

four-sided steel — frame partition (wall)

~ **steel,** four-cornered ~ · Vierkantstahl *m*, Viereckstahl, vierkantiger Stahl, viereckiger Stahl, vierseitiger Stahl

~ **tower,** four-cornered ~ · Vierkantturm *m*, Viereckturm, vierkantiger Turm, viereckiger Turm, vierseitiger Turm

~ **(town) gateway,** arch(way) · Straßenbogen *m* [*Ein freistehendes Bauwerk mit vier Ansichtsseiten*]

~ **wire,** four-cornered ~ · Viereckdraht *m*, Vierkantdraht, viereckiger Draht, vierkantiger Draht, vierseitiger Draht

four-span, four-bay · vierschiffig [*Rahmenhalle*]

four-stepped pyramid · Vierstufenpyramide *f*

fourth-degree parabola · Parabel *f* vierten Grades

fourth order differential equation · Differentialgleichung *f* vierter Ordnung

fourth-order equation · Gleichung *f* vierten Grades

~ **theory** · (Spannungs)Theorie *f* 4. Ordnung

45° (pipe) bend, (one-)eighth (~) ~ · (Rohr)Krümmer *m* 45°, 45°-(Rohr-) Krümmer, Achtel(rohr)krümmer

four-way arch · Viertoranlage *f*, viertoriger (Straßen)Bogen *m*

4-wheeled trolley · vierteilige Laufrolle *f* [*Schiebetor*]

foyer; crush-room (Brit.) · Foyer *n*

~ **where smoking is permitted** · Raucherfoyer *n*

FP → flameproof

F.P. → flash point

fp → freezing point

f.p. → freezing point

fprf → fireproof

fr → frame

Fraas breaking point, ~ brittle ~, ~ brittle temperature · Brechpunkt *m* nach Fraas, Brechtemperatur *f* ~ ~

fraction, percentage, content · Anteil *m*, Prozentsatz *m*, Gehalt *m*

~ → size range

fracture appearance · Bruchgefüge *n*

~ **load,** breaking ~, rupture ~, ultimate ~ · Bruchlast *f*

~**-proof,** rupture-proof, breakproof · bruchsicher

fracture toughness · zähe Widerstandsfähigkeit *f* gegen die Sprödbruchbildung

~ **transition temperature for elastic and plastic loading** · Bruchumwandlungstemperatur *f* für elastische und plastische Beanspruchung

fragment · (Über)Rest *m* [*z.B. einer Mauer*]

fragmentation · Stückigkeit *f*, Stückung *f*

to frame → to trim

~ ~ · verrahmen

frame, fr · Rahmen *m*, Aufsatz *m* [*Für Straßen- und Hofabläufe. Prüfung DIN 1213. Mit seitlichem Abfluß DIN 1235*]

~, framing, fr · Rahmen *m*

~, structural ~, weight carrying ~, load-carrying ~, supporting ~, (load)bearing ~ · (Trag)Rahmen *m*

~ **action** · Rahmenwirkung *f*

~ **analysis** · Rahmenstatik *f*

~ **axis** · Rahmenachse *f*

~ **bar,** ~ rod, ~ member · Rahmenstab *m*, Rahmenglied *n*

~ **bay,** ~ span · Rahmenschiff *n*

~ **bearing structure** → frame(d) supporting ~

~ **board** · Friesbrett *n*

~ **building,** framed ~, (structural) skeleton ~ · Skelettgebäude *n*, Rahmengebäude, Gerippegebäude

~ **column,** (~) post, (~) leg, framing ~, supporting member, vertical (member) · (Rahmen)Pfosten *m*, (Rahmen-) Stiel *m* (Rahmen)Stütze *f*

~ **connection** · Rahmenverbindung *f*

~ **constant** · Rahmenkonstante *f*

~ **construction,** ~ system · Rahmenkonstruktion *f*, Rahmensystem *n*

~ ~ **type,** ~ type of construction · Fachwerkbauart *f*

~ **corner** · Rahmenecke *f*

~ **crippling,** crippling of frame · Rahmenverbiegung *f*

~ **diagram** · Rahmendiagramm *n*

~ **diaphragm** · Windausfachung *f*

~ **distortion** · Rahmenverzerrung *f*

~ **formula** · Rahmenformel *f*

~ **girder,** Vierendeel ~ · Rahmenträger *m*, Vierendeelträger

~ **hinge** · Rahmengelenk *n*

~ **instability** · Rahmenlabilität *f*

~ **leg** · Rahmenschenkel *m*

(~) ~ → ~ column

frameless · rahmenlos, rahmenfrei

frame-like (load)bearing structure, ~ (weight-carrying) ~, ~ supporting ~ · rahmenartiges Tragwerk *n*

~ **supporting structure,** ~ (weight-carrying) ~, ~ (load)bearing ~ · rahmenartiges Tragwerk *n*

~ **(weight-carrying) structure,** ~ (load)bearing ~, ~ supporting ~ · rahmenartiges Tragwerk *n*

frame (load)bearing structure → frame(d) supporting ~

~ **loading** · Rahmenbelastung *f*

~ **member,** ~ rod, ~ bar · Rahmenstab *m*, Rahmenglied *n*

~ **of one bay** → simple frame

~ ~ ~ **span** → simple frame

~ **partition (wall)** → framed ~ (~)

frame plane — framing timber

~ **plane** · Rahmenebene f
~ **post** → ~ column
~ **problem** · Rahmenaufgabe f
~ **rigidity** · Rahmensteifigkeit f
~ **rod,** ~ bar, ~ member · Rahmenstab m, Rahmenglied n
~ **section** · Rahmenprofil n
~ **shape** · Rahmenform f, Rahmengestalt f
~ **span,** ~ bay · Rahmenschiff n
~ ~ · Rahmenstützweite f
~ **statically indeterminate to the second degree** · zweifach statisch unbestimmter Rahmen m
~ ~ ~ ~ ~ **third degree** · dreifach statisch unbestimmter Rahmen m
~ **structure** → frame(d) supporting ~
~ **supporting structure** → frame(d) ~ ~
~ **system,** ~ construction · Rahmenkonstruktion f, Rahmensystem n
~ **thrust** · Rahmenschub m
~ **type of construction,** ~ construction type · Fachwerkbauart f
~ **wall** → framed ~
~ **(weight-carrying) structure** → frame(d) supporting ~
~ **with** *n*-**column** · *n*-stieliger Rahmen m
~ ~ **three hinges,** three-hinge(d) frame, three-pin(ned) frame · Dreigelenkrahmen m

(framed and) double-panel(led) door, (~ ~) two-panel(led) ~ (Brit.); (~ ~) two-panel(ed) ~, (~ ~) double-panel(ed) ~ (US) · Zwei-Füllungstür f

(~ ~) four-panel(led) door (Brit.); (~ ~) four-panel(ed) ~ (US) · Kreuztür f, Vierfüllungstür f

(~ ~) multiple-panel door · Mehrfüllungstür f

(~ ~) panel(led) door (Brit.); (~ ~) panel(ed) ~ (US) · Füllungstür f

(~ ~) two-panel(led) door, (~ ~) double-panel(led) ~ (Brit.); (~ ~) two-panel(ed) ~, (~ ~) double-panel(ed) ~ (US) · Zwei-Füllungstür f

frame(d) bearing structure → ~ supporting ~

~ **building,** (structural) skeleton ~ · Skelettgebäude n, Rahmengebäude, Gerippegebäude
~ **cellular floor** · Rahmenzellendecke f
~ **construction** · (Trag)Rahmenbau m
~ **dado** · Rahmensockel m
~ **door** [*Frame(d) doors consist of slides, rails, and muntins, which are framed together, the enclosed areas being filled with panels*] · Rahmendoppeltür f
~ **floor cover(ing),** ~ flooring · Fries(fuß)boden m
~ **flooring,** ~ floor cover(ing) · Fries(fuß)boden m

~ **(load)bearing structure** → ~ supporting ~
~ **partition (wall), truss**(ed) ~ (~) [*A partition (wall) built up on its own frame of timber or less commonly of other material such as reinforced concrete or metal*] · Fachwerktrennwand f, Riegeltrennwand
~ **roof** · Rahmendach n
~ **structure** · (Trag)Rahmenbauwerk n
~ ~ ~ → ~ supporting ~
~ **supporting structure,** ~ (load)bearing ~, ~ (weight-carrying) ~ · Rahmentragwerk n
~ **timber door,** ~ wood(en) ~ · Rahmen-Holztür f
~ **wall** · Fach(werk)wand f, Riegelwand
~ **(weight-carrying) structure** → ~ supporting ~
~ **wood(en) door,** ~ timber ~ · Rahmen-Holztür f

framework, frwk · Fachwerk n [*Das tragende Gerippe aus Holz, Stahl, Stahlbeton usw. von Wänden, deren übrige Teile aus nicht oder nicht ausreichend tragfähigen Stoffen bestehen, z.B. Holzwolleleichtbauplatten usw.*]

~ **analogy** · Fachwerkanalogie f
~ **bay** · Fachwerkfeld n
~ **calculation** · Fachwerkberechnung f
~ **construction** · Fachwerkbau m
~ ~ **method** · Fachwerkbauweise f

(~) timber rail, (~) wood(en) ~ · (Fachwerk)Holzriegel m
(~) wood(en) rail, (~) timber ~ · (Fachwerk)Holzriegel m

framing, trimming · (Balken(träger)-)(Aus)Wechseln n [*DIN 104*]
~, **trimming** · (Balken(träger)-)Wechsel m, (Balken(träger)-)Auswechs(e)lung f [*DIN 104*]
~ · Umrahmung f
~, **frame,** fr · Rahmen m
~ [*The act of constructing a frame*] · Rahmenbau m
~ **column,** (~) post, (~) leg, vertical (member), supporting member, frame leg, frame post, frame column · Pfosten m, Stiel m, Stütze f, Rahmen~
(~) leg, (~) post, ~ column, vertical (member), supporting member, frame leg, frame post, frame column · Pfosten m, Stiel m, Stütze f, Rahmen~
(~) post, (~) leg, ~ column, vertical (member), supporting member, frame leg, frame post, frame column · Pfosten m, Stiel m, Stütze f, Rahmen~
~ **structure,** ~ system · Rahmenkonstruktion f
~ **system,** ~ structure · Rahmenkonstruktion f
~ **timber,** carcassing ~ [*Timber in a building or structure that performs a structural function*] · Bauholz n für den Rohbau, Rohbauholz, Zimmereiholz, Konstruktionsholz, Bau(nutz)holz

Franciscan church — free-standing support

Franciscan church · Franziskanerkirche f, Minoritenkirche, Barfüßerkirche

Frankfort black (pigment), German ~ (~) [*A variety of bone black*] · Samtschwarz n, Frankfurterschwarz

frater, monastic hall, refectory [*The communal dining-hall in a convent*] · Klosterspeisesaal m, Refektorium n, Speisesaal im Kloster

~ · Brüdersaal m [*Tages- und Arbeitsraum der Mönche*]

~ **for lay brethren**, refectory ~ ~ ~, dining hall ~ ~ ~ · Laienrefektorium n [*Refektorium der Laienbrüder in einem Kloster des Zisterzienserordens*]

free bearing → ~ support

~ **bending moment diagram** · freies Biegemomentdiagramm n

~ **carbon** [*misnomer*]; insoluble matter · Unlösliche n; freier Kohlenstoff m [*Fehlname*]

~ **convection** · freie Konvektion f

free-cutting steel, easy-machining ~ · Automatenstahl m [*Dieser Stahl läßt bei spanabhebender Bearbeitung hohe Schnittgeschwindigkeiten zu. Die Fertigstücke haben saubere und blanke Oberfläche*]

free diffusion [*The spreading of one gas into another*] · freie Diffusion f

freedom degree, degree of freedom, DF · Freiheitsgrad m

~ **from corrosion** · Korrosionsfreiheit f

~ ~ **cracking (and crazing)**, absence of cracks and crazes · Rissefreiheit f, Rißfreiheit

~ ~ **ground connection** · Erdanschlußfreiheit f

~ ~ **odour** (Brit.); ~ ~ odor (US) · Geruchlosigkeit f

~ ~ **warpage** · Verwerfungsfreiheit f

~ **memorial**, monument of liberty · Freiheitsdenkmal n

~ **of creep** · Kriechfreiheit f

free edge · freier Rand m

~ **end** [*The end of a beam in a condition of hinge*] · nichteingespanntes Ende n

free-field chamber → anechoic room

~ **room** → anechoic ~

free form (ground(-))plan · unregelmäßiger Grundriß m

free-form roof structure · freigestaltete Dachkonstruktion f

free from chloride(s) · chloridfrei, chloridlos

~ ~ **volume increase** · treibfrei

freehand drawing · Freihandzeichnen n

~ ~ · Freihandzeichnung f

freehold flat, ~ apartment (unit); condominium (US) · Etageneigentum n, Geschoßeigentum, Stockwerkeigentum, Eigentumswohnung f, EW

free-lance architect, private ~, independent ~ · freischaffender Architekt m

free lime · Ca(OH)$_2$, freies Kalkhydrat n, freier Kalk m

freely adapted Gothic manner · freigotisierende Auffassung f

~ ~ **style** · freier Stil m

~ **articulated (ground(-))plan** · artikulierte Grundrißgliederung f

~ **supported** → simply ~

free massing · freie Gliederung f der Massen

~ **moment** · freies Moment n

~ **of cracks**, crack-free · rißfrei, rissefrei, rißlos, risselos

~ ~ **embrittlement** · sprödfrei

~ ~ **shrinkage crack(s)** · schwindrißfrei, schwindrissefrei

~ ~ **stress**, stress relieved, SR · spannungsfrei, entspannt

~ **outline** · freier Umriß m

~ **pattern** · freies Muster n

~ **school of architecture** · freie Architekturschule f

~ **site**, delivered ~ · frei Baustelle

free-span and cantilever system · Freispann- und Kragsystem n

~ **system** · Freispannsystem n [*Senkrechtes Tragsystem. Punkte der Lastenbündelung in der Außenhaut*]

~ ~ **with central support** · Freispannsystem n mit Mittelunterstützung

free-standing, isolated, detached [*Said of a structure which is completely surrounded by permanent open spaces*] · freistehend

~ **assembly hall** → ~ chaitya (~)

~ **(bath)tub**, isolated ~, ~ bath · freistehende (Bade)Wanne f, Freisteh(bade)wanne [*DIN 4470 bis 4477*]

~ **bell-tower**, isolated ~, campanile, belfry · Campanile m, Kampanile, freistehender Glockenturm m

~ **block** → ~ house

~ **building**, detached ~, isolated ~ · freistehendes Gebäude n, Einzelgebäude

~ **chaitya (hall)**, ~ assembly ~ · freistehende Gebetshalle f, ~ Tschaitya-Halle, freistehender Tschaitya m

~ **chapel**, isolated ~ · freistehende Kapelle f

~ **column**, isolated ~ · Vollsäule f, freistehende Säule, Freisäule

~ **house**, isolated ~, detached ~ · freistehendes Haus n, Einzelhaus

~ **masonry wall**, isolated ~ ~ · freistehende Mauer f

~ **shaft**, chimney ~ [*It is a free-standing structure enclosing a flue which, by virtue of the size of heating apparatus it serves, is generally larger than a normal domestic flue*] · einzügiger freistehender Schornstein m, freistehender einzügiger ~

~ **support**, isolated ~ · freistehende Stütze f, eingestellte ~

~ **surface silo** → horizontal (plank) free standing ~

~ **tub,** ~ bath(tub), isolated ~ · freistehende (Bade)Wanne f, Freisteh(bade)wanne [*DIN 4470 bis 4477*]

freestone · dickbandiges Gestein n

free support, ~ bearing [*See remark under 'Auflager(ung)'*] · freie Auflagerung f, freies Auflager n

~ **ventilation,** ~ venting · freie (Be- und Ent)Lüftung f

~ **venting** → ~ ventilation

freeze thaw durability · Gefrier-Auftau-Haltbarkeit f

freezer (case) · Gefriertruhe f, Tiefkühltruhe

~ **room,** ~ (space), refrigeration room, cold room, frozen store · Gefrierraum m

freeze-thaw-cycling · Frost-Tau-Wechsel m, Gefrier- und Auftau-Folge f

freezing agent · Gefriermittel n

~ **point,** fp, f.p. · Gefrierpunkt m

~ **resistance** → resistance to frost attack

Freiburg Cathedral · Freiburger Dom m

freight elevator, goods ~, trunk ~ (US); ~ lift (Brit.) · Lastenaufzug m, Materialaufzug

~ **lift,** trunk ~, goods ~ (Brit.); ~ elevator (US) · Lastenaufzug m, Materialaufzug

French chalk → fine talc

~ ~ **surfacing** → talcum (powder) ~

~ **classicism** · französischer Klassizismus m

~ **door,** ~ window, casement door, door window [*A window which opens in two vertical halves without a central post or mullion and extends to floor level, for use as a door*] · Fenstertür f

~ **embossing,** multi-tone etching · Tonätzung f [*Säurebehandlung von Glas*]

(~) formal garden · französischer (Barock)Park m, ~ Garten m

~ **Gothic (style)** · französische Gotik f

~ **ochre** (Brit.); ~ ocher (US) · französischer Ocker m

~ **(oil of) turpentine,** ~ spirit ~ ~ · französisches Terpentinöl n

~ **order** · französische Säulenordnung f

~ **Renaissance** · französische Renaissance f

~ **Romanesque (style)** · französische Romanik f, ~ romanische Baukunst f, ~ romanische Architektur f

~ **roof** → mansard (~)

~ **scarf (joint),** oblique ~ (~) · französisches Blatt n, schräges Hakenblatt [*Holzverbindung*]

~ ~ **(~) with wedge,** oblique ~ (~) ~ ~ · schräges Hakenblatt n mit Keil [*Holzverbindung*]

~ **spirit of turpentine,** ~ (oil ~) ~ · französisches Terpentinöl n

~ **tile** → Ludowici ~

~ **truss,** Fink (gable roof) ~ · Polonceau-(Dach)Binder m, französischer (Dach-) Binder

~ **window,** ~ door, door window, casement door [*A window which opens in two vertical halves without a central post or mullion and extends to floor level, for use as a door*] · Fenstertür f

(frequency) bandwidth · (Frequenz-)Bandbreite f [*Akustik*]

~ **curve** · Häufigkeitskurve f, Häufigkeitslinie f

~ **diagram** · Häufigkeitsdiagramm n

~ **equation** · Frequenzgleichung f

~ **of resonance,** resonance frequency · Resonanzfrequenz f

~ ~ **sound** · Schallfrequenz f

~ **range** · Frequenzbereich m, n

fresco · Fresko n

~ **of griffins,** griffin fresco · Greifenfresko n

~ **painter** · Freskenmaler m, Freskomaler

~ **painting** · Freskenmalerei f, Freskomalerei

~ **plaster** · Freskoputz m, Freskenputz

frescoed · freskobemalt, freskenbemalt

~ **decoration** · Freskenschmuck m, Freskenschmuck

fresh air · Frischluft f

fresh-air circulation · Frischluftumlauf m, Frischluftumwälzung f

~ **duct** · Frischluftkanal m

~ **heater,** ~ warmer, ~ heating appliance, ~ warming appliance · Frischluftheizgerät n, Frischluftheizer m, Frischlufterhitzer

~ **heating,** ~ warming · Frischluftheizung f

~ ~ **appliance** → ~ heater

~ **inlet** → (natural) (fresh-)air intake

(fresh-)air inlet stack → natural ~ ~ ~

~ ~ **tower** → natural ~ ~ ~

~ **intake** → natural ~ ~

~ ~ **stack** → (natural) (fresh-)air inlet ~

~ ~ **tower** → (natural) (fresh-)air inlet ~

fresh-air operation · Frischluftbetrieb m

~ **supply** · Frischluftzufuhr f

~ ~ **to roof(s)** · Dachbelüftung f

~ **warmer** → ~ heater

~ **warming,** ~ heating · Frischluftheizung f

~ ~ **appliance** → ~ heater

fresh concrete density, freshly-mixed ~ ~, green ~ ~ · Frischbeton-Raumgewicht n, Frischbeton-Wichte f

freshly-made product — front yard

freshly-made product → green ~

fresh(ly-made) slab, newly-made ~, green ~ · frischgeformte Platte f, Plattenformling m, Plattengrünling, Plattenfrischling

fresh(ly-mixed) concrete, green ~ [*Concrete which has set but not appreciably hardened*] · Frischbeton m

fresh(ly-mixed) concrete density, green ~ · Frischbeton-Raumgewicht n, Frischbeton-Wichte f

fresh(ly-mixed) mortar, green ~ · Frischmörtel m

fresh mortar, freshly-mixed ~, green ~ · Frischmörtel m

fresh product → green ~

~ slab, freshly-made ~, newly-made ~, green ~ · frischgeformte Platte f, Plattenformling m, Plattengrünling, Plattenfrischling

~ state, green ~ · frischer Zustand m, grüner ~

fresh-water line · Frischwasserleitung f

~ ~ pressure pipe · Frischwasserleitungsdruckrohr n

~ supply, ~ input · Frischwassereinspeisung f, Frischwasserzufuhr f

fret, Greek ~, Grecian ~, labyrinth ~, (Greek) key pattern, Greek key · rechtwink(e)lig gebrochener Mäander m, ~ gebrochenes Mäanderornament n, à la greque-Ornament

fretting corrosion [*Corrosion under mechanical stress*] · Reibkorrosion f, Reiboxydation [*Korrosion unter gleichzeitiger mechanischer Beanspruchung.* DIN 50900]

friable · abreibbar [*(Beton)Zuschlag-(stoff)*]

~ calcite · Bergmilch f

~ gypsum → gypsite

friction bond · Reib(ungs)verbund m ·

friction-caused wear · Reib(ungs)verschleiß m

friction constant · Reib(ungs)kennwert m

~ loss · Reib(ungs)verlust m

friction-sparking · Reibfunkenbildung f

friction-type anchorage, ~ anchoring, anchorage by friction, anchoring by friction · Reib(ungs)verankerung f

~ anchoring, ~ anchorage, anchorage by friction, anchoring by friction · Reib(ungs)verankerung f

~ connection · Reibverbindung f

frictional heat loss · Reib(ungs)wärmeverlust m

frictionless hinge · reibungsfreies Gelenk n

Friday mosque, congregational ~, Masjid-i-Juma, jami (masjid) [*As opposed to a tomb-mosque or mausoleum used only for private prayers*] · Freitagsmoschee f, Alltagsmoschee, Mesdschid il-Dschuma, Medschid

frieze [*In classical architecture, the middle member of the entablature in one of the Orders*] · Fries m

~-like · friesähnlich, friesartig

frieze of the Greek Doric Order, triglyph frieze · Dreischlitzfries m, Triglyphenfries

~ rail · Querfries m [*Holzfüllungstür*]

~ with animal reliefs · Bilderfries m

~ ~ inscription · Schriftfries m

frigidarium [*A cooling-room or a cold-water swimming-bath in one of the Roman public baths*] · Frigidarium n

fringe condition, edge ~, boundary ~, marginal ~ · Randbedingung f

~ torque moment, edge ~ ~, boundary ~ ~, marginal ~ ~, ~ torsion(al) ~, ~ twist(ing) ~ · Randdrillmoment n, Randtorsionsmoment, Randverdrehungsmoment, Randverwindungsmoment

~ water → capillary ~

frit · Fritte f

fritted glass, sintered ~ [*A porous glass made for filtration and other purposes by heating graded glass powder*] · Sinterglas n, gefrittetes Glas

fritting · Fritten n

frog · Aushöhlung f, Austiefung, Vertiefung, Mulde f [*in einer Ziegelfläche*]

from stock, ex(-)stock · ab Lager

front, face · Vorderseite f

~ balcony · Vorderbalkon m

~ building · Vordergebäude n

~ column → fronted ~

~ ~, frontal ~ · Frontsäule f

~ curtain wall · vorgehängte Wand f auf der Straßenseite, Vorhangwand ~ ~ ~

~ door bell · Vordertürklingel f

~ ~ canopy · Haustürüberdachung f

~ ~ fitting, ~ ~ furniture · Haustürbeschlag m

~ ~ furniture, ~ ~ fitting · Haustürbeschlag m

~ ~ telephone, intercom(munication system) [*The installation in houses to facilitate answering the door*] · Haustürtelefon n

~ entrance · Vordereingang m

~ garden → forecourt

~ grill(e) [*See remark under 'Gitter'*] · Frontgitter n

~ masonry wall, façade ~ ~ · Fassadenmauer f, Frontmauer

~ plot line, ~ property ~ · vordere Grundstücksgrenze f

~ property line, ~ plot ~ · vordere Grundstücksgrenze f

~ view, FV · Front(al)ansicht f, Vorderansicht

~ wall, face ~ · Frontwand f, Vorderwand

~ yard (US) → forecourt

frontage — frost(-)resistant solid sand-lime brick

frontage [*The length of a site in contact with a road*] · Straßenfront *f*

frontager · Anlieger *m*

~ traffic · Anliegerverkehr *m*

frontal column, prostyle ~, front(ed) ~ · Giebelseitensäule *f*, Frontsäule [*eines antiken Tempels*]

~ system · System *n* der Betriebsplätze unmittelbar vor dem Abfertigungsgebäude [*Flughafen*]

front(ed) column → frontal ~

frontispiece · Frontispiz *n*

~, main façade, principal façade · Hauptfassade *f*

to frost, to web · eisblumenartig auftrocknen [*Anstrich*]

~ ~ · mattieren [*Glas*]

frost, diamantini, flake glass · Flitterglas *n*, Schuppenglas

~ action, action of frost · Frosteinwirkung *f*, Frosteinfluß *m*

~ attack · Frostangriff *m*

~ blanket sand · Frostschutzsand *m*

~ damage · Frostschaden *m*

frosted dried film webbed ~ ~ · eisblumenartig aufgetrockneter Film *m*

~ glass, iced ~ · Eisglas *n*

~ ~ with muslin pattern · Gardinenglas *n*, M(o)usselinglas

frost-induced cracking · Abfrieren *n* [*Mauer*]

frosting · Eisätzen *n* [*Säurebehandlung von Glas*]

frost line [*The depth below finish grade where frost action on footings or foundations is improbable*] · Frostgrenze *f*

~ penetration · Frosteindringung *f*

~ precaution · Frostschutzmaßnahme *f*

frostproof, frost(-)resisting, frost(-)resistant, non-frost-active · frostbeständig, frostsicher, frostunempfindlich

~ brick → frost(-)resistant (clay) ~

~ calcium silicate brick → frost(-)resistant sand-lime ~

~ (clay) brick → frost(-)resistant (~) ~

~ engineering brick, frost(-)resistant ~ ~ · Vormauerklinker *m*

~ horizontal coring (clay) brick, frost(-)resistant ~ ~ (~) ~ · Vormauerlanglochziegel *m*, VLLz

~ lime-sand brick → frost(-)resistant sand-lime ~

~ porous brick, frost(-)resistant ~ ~ · Vormauerporenziegel *m*, VPMz

~ sand-lime brick → frost(-)resistant ~ ~

~ solid brick, ~ ~ clay ~, frost(-)resistant solid (clay) ~ · Vormauervollziegel *m*, VMz

~ ~ calcium silicate brick → frost(-)resistant solid sand-lime ~

~ ~ (clay) brick, frost(-)resistant ~ (~) ~ · Vormauervollziegel *m*, VMz

~ ~ lime-sand brick → frost(-)resistant solid sand-lime ~

~ vertical coring (clay) brick, frost(-)resistant ~ ~ (~) ~ · Vormauerhochlochziegel *m*, VHLz [*DIN 105*]

frost-proofer → antifreeze agent

frost-protection agent → antifreeze ~

~ aid → anti-freezing ~

frost protection liquid, ~ protective ~, antifreeze ~, antifreezing ~ · Gefrierschutzflüssigkeit *f*, Frostschutzflüssigkeit

frost-protection powder → antifreeze ~

~ solution → antifreeze ~

frost-protective → antifreeze agent

frost protective aid → anti-freezing ~

~ ~ liquid, ~ protection ~, antifreeze ~, antifreezing ~ · Gefrierschutzflüssigkeit *f*, Frostschutzflüssigkeit

~ ~ powder → antifreeze ~

~ ~ solution → antifreeze ~

~ resistance, freezing ~, resistance to frost attack, resistance to freezing · Frostbeständigkeit *f*, Frostwiderstand *m*

~ ~ test · Frostbeständigkeitsprobe *f*, Frostbeständigkeitsprüfung *f*, Frostbeständigkeitsversuch *m*

frost(-)resistant, frost(-)resisting, frostproof, non-frost-active · frostbeständig, frostsicher, frostunempfindlich

~ brick → ~ clay ~

~ calcium silicate brick → ~ sand-lime ~

~ (clay) brick, frostproof (~) ~, frost(-)resisting (~) ~, non-frost-active (~) ~, antifreezing (~) ~ · V, frostbeständiger Ziegel *m*, Vormauerziegel

~ engineering brick, frostproof ~ ~ · Vormauerklinker *m*

~ horizontal coring (clay) brick, frostproof ~ ~ (~) ~ · Vormauerlanglochziegel *m*, VLLz

~ masonry (work) · Vormauerung *f*

~ porous brick, frostproof ~ ~ · Vormauerporenziegel *m*, VPMz

~ sand-lime brick, frostproof ~ ~, ~ lime-sand ~, ~ calcium silicate ~ · Vormauerkalksandstein *m*, Kalksandvormauerstein, VKS

~ solid brick, ~ ~ clay ~, frostproof solid (clay) ~ · Vormauervollziegel *m*, VMz

~ ~ calcium silicate brick → ~ ~ sand-lime ~

~ ~ (clay) brick, frostproof ~ (~) ~ · Vormauervollziegel *m*, VMz

~ ~ lime-sand brick → ~ ~ sand-lime ~

~ ~ sand-lime brick, frostproof ~ ~ ~, ~ ~ lime-sand ~, ~ ~ calcium silicate ~ · Vormauerkalksandvollstein *m*, Kalksandvormauervollstein, VKSV

frost(-)resistant solid . . . — full development 426

[*Der Querschnitt darf durch Lochung senkrecht zur Lagerfläche bis zu 25% gemindert sein*]

~ **vertical coring (clay) brick,** frost-proof ~ ~ (~) ~ · Vormauerhochlochziegel *m*, VHLz [*DIN 105*]

frost(-)resisting, frost(-)resistant, frost-proof, non-frost-active · frostbeständig, frostsicher, frostunempfindlich

~ **brick** → frost(-)resistant (clay) ~

~ **(clay) brick** → frost(-)resistant (~) ~

~ **property** → resistance to frost attack

frost-susceptible · frostempfindlich

'**frosty' wrinkled appearance** · Eisblumenform *f* [*Holzöl*]

froth formation, foaming, frothing, expanding · (Auf)Schäumen *n*, Schaumbildung *f*

~ ~ **action,** foaming ~, frothing ~, expanding ~ · schäumende Wirkung *f*, Schäumwirkung

~ ~ **in situ,** foaming ~ ~, expanding ~ ~, frothing ~ ~ · Schaumbildung *f* an Ort und Stelle, (Auf)Schäumen *n* ~ ~ ~ ~

frothed glass · geblähtes Glas *n*

frothing, expanding, foaming, froth formation · (Auf)Schäumen *n*, Schaumbildung *f*

~ **action,** expanding ~, foaming ~, froth formation ~ · schäumende Wirkung *f*, Schäumwirkung

~ **in situ,** expanding ~ ~, foaming ~ ~, froth formation ~ ~ · Schaumbildung *f* an Ort und Stelle, (Auf)Schäumen *n* ~ ~ ~ ~

frozen fish store · Fischgefrierraum *m*

~ **food store** · Gefrierlagerhaus *n*

FRP → glass reinforced laminate

fruit festoon → ~ work

~ **garden** · Obstgarten *m*

(~ **jar**) **pycnometer,** weighing bottle, density bottle · (Flaschen)Pyknometer *n*

~ **work,** ~ **festoon** [*See remark under 'Gehänge'*] · Fruchtgirlande *f*, Fruchtfeston *n*, Fruchtgehänge *n*, Fruchtgewinde *n*

fruity odour (Brit.); ~ **odor** (US) · Früchtegeruch *m*

frustum · Stumpf *m*

~ **of a cone,** truncated ~ · Kegelstumpf *m*

~ ~ ~ **pyramid,** truncated ~ · Pyramidenstumpf *m*, Spitzsäulenstumpf *m*, abgestumpfte Pyramide *f*

frwk → framework

FST, forged steel, fst · geschmiedeter Stahl *m*

ftg → fitting

fuel · Brennstoff *m*

~ · Treibstoff *m*

~ **brown coal** [*Incorrectly termed 'nonbituminous brown coal'*] · Feuerbraunkohle *f*

~ **cellar** · Brennstoffkeller *m*

~ **consumption** · Brennstoffverbrauch *m*

fuel-fired heating equipment · brennstoffbetriebenes Heiz(ungs)gerät *n*

fuel for household use · Hausbrand *m*

~ **gas** · Brenngas *n* [*DIN 1340*]

~ **oil,** heating ~, FO · Heizöl *n* [*DIN 51603*]

~ ~ **barrier,** heating ~ ~ · Heizölsperre *f*

(~) **oil(-fired) central heating** · (Heiz-)Öl-Zentralheizung *f*

(~) **oil interceptor,** heating ~ ~ [*A device designed and installed so as to separate and retain (heating) oil from normal wastes while permitting normal sewage or liquid wastes to discharge into the drainage system by gravity*] · (Heiz)Ölabscheider *m*, (Heiz)Ölfang *m* [*DIN 4043*]

(~) ~ **pipe,** heating ~ ~ · (Heiz)Ölrohr *n*

(~) **oilproof,** (fuel) oil-resistant · (heiz-)ölfest, (heiz)ölbeständig

(~) **oil-resistant,** (~) oilproof · (heiz-)ölfest, (heiz)ölbeständig

(~) **oil storage,** heating ~ ~ · (Heiz-)Öllagerung *f*

(~) ~ **(storage) tank,** heating ~ (~) ~ · (Heiz)Ölbehälter *m*, (Heiz)Öl(lager)tank *m*

(~) ~ **store,** heating ~ ~ · (Heiz)Öllagerraum *m*

(~) **oiltight,** heating ~ · (heiz)öldicht, (heiz)ölundurchlässig

fuel-resistant · treibstoffbeständig

~ **joint sealing compound** · treibstoffbeständige Fugenvergußmasse *f*

fuel room · Brennstoffraum *m* [*Kesselhaus*]

~ **saving** · Brennstoffeinsparung *f*, Brennstoffersparnis *f*

~ **store** · Brennstofflager *n*

fulcrum, ful · Drehpunkt *m*

~ **of moment;** center ~ ~ (US); centre ~ ~ (Brit.) · Momentendrehpunkt *m*

full annealed sheet, true ~ ~ · Feinblech *n* [*über A₃ hinaus gebeizt*]

~ **bearing,** ~ **support** · satte Auflagerung *f*, sattes Auflager *n*

~**-bodied,** to have good build · festkörperreich, füllkräftig, füllstark [*Anstrichmittel*]

full bonding · vollflächiges (Ver)Kleben *n*, Vollverkleben

~ **brick,** ~ **clay** ~ · ganzer Ziegel *m*, Vierquartier *m* [*Fehlname: ganzer Stein m*]

~**-centred arch** (Brit.); **full-centered** ~ (US); semicircular ~, (half-)round ~, perfect ~ · Rundbogen *m*, Halbkreisbogen, römischer Bogen, halbzirkelförmiger Bogen [*veraltet: Vollbogen, voller Bogen*]

full (clay) brick · ganzer Ziegel *m*, Vierquartier *m* [*Fehlname: ganzer Stein m*]

~ **development** · Vollerschließung *f*

~ **exposure to weather** · ungeschützter Witterungseinfluß *m*

~ **fixity,** ~ **restraint** · Volleinspannung *f*

~ **floor;** ~ **story (US);** ~ **storey (Brit.)** · Vollgeschoß *n*, Vollstockwerk *n*, Volletage *f* [*Vollgeschosse sind Geschosse, die vollständig über der festgelegten Geländeoberfläche liegen und über mindestens zwei Drittel ihrer Grundfläche die für Aufenthaltsräume erforderliche lichte Höhe haben. Auf die Zahl der Vollgeschosse sind anzurechnen: 1. Geschosse mit einer lichten Höhe von mehr als 1,80 m unterhalb der Traufenoberkante, 2. Kellergeschosse, die im Mittel mehr als 1,40 m und 3. Garagengeschosse, die im Mittel mehr als 2 m über die festgelegte Geländeoberfläche hinausragen*]

~ **gloss,** high ~ [*Smooth and almost mirror-like surface when viewed from all angles*] · Vollglanz *m*, Hochglanz

full-gloss enamel · Vollglanzemaillelack *m*

~ **finish,** high gloss ~ · Vollglanzdeckschicht(anstrich)farbe *f*

~ **oil paint** · Vollglanzölfarbe *f*

~ **paint,** high gloss ~ · Vollglanz(anstrich)farbe *f*, Hochglanz(anstrich)farbe

~ **wall slab,** high gloss ~ ~ · Hochglanzwandplatte *f*, Vollglanzwandplatte [*aus Beton*]

full heat protection · Vollwärmeschutz *m*

~**-height window,** room-high ~, floor-to-ceiling ~ · raumhohes Fenster *n*

(full) lead crystal (glass) · englisches Kristallglas *n*, Bleikristall(glas) *n* [*unter Zusatz von Bleioxid hergestellt*]

~**-length** · ganzlängig

~ **mirror** · Spiegelband *n*

full line department store · Großwarenhaus *n*

~ **loading** · Vollbelastung *f*

~ **pickled sheet** · Feinblech *n* [*mehrmals gebeizt*]

~ **protection of wood** · Vollschutz *m* des Holzes

~ **relief,** high ~ [*It is cut more deeply than the low relief, with its figures standing out more fully from the stone*] · Hochrelief *n*

~ **restraint,** ~ fixity · Volleinspannung *f*

full-scale construction → ~ structure

~ **load(ing) test** · Belastungsversuch *m* im Maßstab 1:1, Belastungsprüfung *f* ~ ~ ~, Belastungsprobe *f* ~ ~ ~

~ **model** · Modell *n* in Ausführungsgröße

~ **pretensioned** · voll vorgespannt

~ **structure,** full-size ~, ~ construction · Bauwerk *n* in Originalgröße [*Im Gegensatz zum Modellbauwerk*]

full sewerage (system) → ~ system (cf sewerage)

~ **size,** whole ~ · Originalgröße *f*

full-size construction → full-scale structure

~ **structure** → full-scale ~

full storey (Brit.) → ~ floor

~ **story (US)** → ~ floor

~**-strength colour (Brit.);** ~ color (US) · Volltonfarbe *f*

full support, ~ bearing · satte Auflagerung *f*, sattes Auflager *n*

~ **vision cupola,** ~ ~ dome · Rundsichtkuppel *f*

~ ~ **dome,** ~ ~ cupola · Rundsichtkuppel *f*

~ **wind pressure** · voller Winddruck *m*

fullered, ca(u)lked · verstemmt, kalfatert

fullering, ca(u)lking, CLKG · Kalfatern *n*, Verstemmen

Fuller's (best mix) curve, Fuller-Thompson ideal grading ~ · Fullerkurve *f*, Fullerlinie *f* [*Die Sieblinie, aus der sich die Sieblinien A......F (DIN 1045) entwickelt haben. Sie hat den Nachteil, daß sie Zement und Zuschlagstoffe enthält und in Werte ohne Zement umgerechnet werden muß*]

fuller's earth · Fullererde *f*, Walkerde

Fuller's parabola · Fullerparabel *f* [*Bindemittel ausgenommen*]

~ **rule** [*This rule is used for estimating the quantities of the various ingredients required for a cubic yard of concrete. It is stated as follows:* $P = \dfrac{11}{c+s+g} =$ *the number of barrels of cement required per cubic yard of concrete where:*
c equals the number of parts of cement,
s equals the number of parts of sand,
g equals the number of parts of gravel or crushed stone,
$P \times s \times .14$ *equals the number of cubic yards of sand per cubic yard of cement,*
$P \times g \times .14$ *equals the number of cubic yards of gravel per cubic yard of concrete*] · Fullerregel *f*

fully air-conditioned · ganzklimatisiert, vollklimatisiert

~ **automatic sliding door installation** · vollautomatische Schiebetüranlage *f*

~ ~ **telecontrol** · vollautomatische Fernsteuerung *f*

~ **developed** · vollerschlossen, bebaubar [*Hochbaugrundstück*]

~ **fixed,** ~ restrained · volleingespannt

~ **glazed** · vollverglast, volleingeglast, ganzverglast, ganzeingeglast

(~) killed alloy, quiet ~, stabilized ~, dead ~ · stabilisierte Legierung *f*, beruhigte ~

(~) ~ steel, quiet ~, stabilized ~, dead ~ [*A steel in which the carbon-oxygen reaction is completely stopped by the addition of silicon and/or alumin(i)um*] · stabilisierter Stahl *m*, beruhigter ~

~ **restrained,** ~ fixed · volleingespannt

fully rigid framing — funicular tension line

~ **rigid framing**, ~ ~ frame · Vollsteifrahmen *m*, Vollstarrahmen [*Rahmen mit ausschließlich biegesteifen Knoten*]

~ **sprung floor** · Vollschwingboden *m*

~-**stable** · hochstabil [*Bitumenemulsion*]

fully system (of sewerage), ~ ~ ~ sewers, ~ sewerage (system) · Vollentwässerung *f*, Vollsystem *n*, Vollkanalisation *f* [*Die Vollkanalisation umfaßt zwei Arten: 1. Misch- oder Schwemmkanalisation und 2. Trennkanalisation*]

~ **tiled** · vollverfliest, vollgefliest

~ **vented** · vollentlüftet

fun fair, amusement park · Vergnügungspark *m*

function room · zweckbestimmter Raum *m* [*Hotel*]

functional · funktionsbestimmt

~ **addition** [*A material that is interground or blended in limited amounts into a hydraulic cement during manufacture to modify the use properties of the finished product*] · Vergütungsmittel *n*, Vergüter *m* [*Zement*]

~ **analysis** · Funktionsanalyse *f*

~ **beauty** · funktionelle Schönheit *f*

~ **city**, ~ town · funktionelle Stadt *f*

~ **concept of architecture** · funktionelle Baugesinnung *f*

~ **design** · funktioneller Entwurf *m*

~ **determination** · Eignungsbestimmung *f*

~ **differentiation** · funktionelle Differenzierung *f*, funktionsbedingte ~

~ **form**, ~ shape · Nutzform *f*

~ **grille** [*A functional openwork screen within an opening. Sometimes spelled 'grill'*] · funktionelles Gitter *n*

~ **sphere**, ~ zone, zone of function, sphere of function · Funktionsbereich *m*, *n*

~ **structure** · Zweckbau(werk) *m*, (*n*)

~ **town**, ~ city · funktionelle Stadt *f*

~ **wall** · Betriebswand *f*

~ **zone**, ~ sphere, zone of function, sphere of function · Funktionsbereich *m*, *n*

Functionalism [*Form follows function*] · Funktionalismus *m* [*Form folgt der Funktion*]

functionalist · Funktionalist *m*

functionalistic architecture · funktionelle Architektur *f*, ~ Baukunst *f*

functionality · Funktionalität *f*

functionally designated area · funktionsbedingte Zone *f*

fundamental · elementar

~ **equation**, basic ~ · Grundgleichung *f*

~ **formula** · Grundformel *f*

~ **frequency** · Grundfrequenz *f*

~ **strength (of concrete)** [*Is understood as a stage of concrete loading representing the limit the structure can withstand under given conditions and still perform its given function*] · Urfestigkeit *f*

~ **(tone)** → pure ~

funeral art · Grabmalskunst *f*, Sepulkralkunst

~ **basilica** → cemetery ~

~ **chapel**, mortuary ~, cemetery ~, graveyard ~ · Friedhofskapelle *f*, Totenkapelle

~ **church**, mortuary ~, cemetery ~, graveyard ~ · Friedhofskirche *f*

funerary monument, burial ~, sepulchral ~, headstone · Grabmonument *n*, Grabdenkmal *n*

~ **mound**, burial ~, tumulus · Grabhügel *m*

~ **slab**, sepulchral ~, tomb ~, grave ~ · Grabplatte *f*

~ **temple**, mortuary ~ · Gedächtnistempel *m*, Memnonium *n*, Totentempel, Memorialbau *m*, Memorie *f*

fungal resistance · Pilzwidrigkeit *f*

fungi growth, growth of fungi · Pilzwuchs *m*

fungicidal · pilzwidrig, fungizid

~ **paint** · pilzwidrige (Anstrich)Farbe *f*, fungizide ~ ,Antipilz(anstrich)farbe

~ **wall paint** · fungizide Wand(anstrich)farbe *f*

fungus attack, ~ infestation · Pilzbefall *m*

~ **infestation**, ~ attack · Pilzbefall *m*

funicular arch, linear ~ [*An arch which is purely in compression under a series of point loads. It is the reverse of a string carrying the same load system as a suspension cable*] · Stützbogen *m*

~ **curve** → ~ polygon

~ **diagram**, polar ~ · Seildiagramm *n*

~ **force** · Seilkraft *f*

~ **line**, polar ~ · Pollinie *f*, Polstrahl *m*, Seilstrahl, Seillinie, Seilkurve *f*

~ **polygon**, string ~, link ~, ~ curve · Seilzug *m*, Seilplan *m*, Seilpolygon *n*, Gelenkpolygon, Seil(viel)eck *n*

(~) **pressure line** · Drucklinie *f*, Stützlinie, Mittelkraftlinie [*Die „natürliche" Kräftelinie des formaktiven Drucksystems*]

(~) ~ ~ **arch** · Drucklinienbogen *m*, Stützlinienbogen, Mittelkraftlinienbogen

(~) ~ ~ **method** · Drucklinienverfahren *n*, Stützlinienverfahren, Mittelkraftlinienverfahren

(~) ~ ~ **vault** · Drucklinengewölbe *n*, Stützliniengewölbe, Mittelkraftliniengewölbe

~ **tension line** · Hängelinie *f* [*Die „natürliche" Kräftelinie des formaktiven Zugsystems*]

furane resin · Furanharz *n*

furnace · Brandraum *m* [*Prüfung des Brandverhaltens von Bauteilen*]

~, fire, burning appliance · Feuerung *f*, Feuerstätte *f* [*Jede Einrichtung, in der feste, flüssige oder gasförmige Brennstoffe in solcher Menge verbrannt werden, daß die dabei entstehenden Verbrennungserzeugnisse Feuergefahr und/oder Gesundheitsschädigungen hervorrufen können. Feuerstätten beheizen entweder die Räume in denen sie aufgestellt sind unmittelbar oder von einer Zentrale aus durch Wärmeträger*]

~ black, ~ carbon ~ · Flammruß *m*

~ brazing, ~ hard soldering · Ofenhartlötung *f*

~ (carbon) black · Flammruß *m*

(~) cinder (US) → **(~) clinker**

(~) ~ aggregate for concrete (US) → **(~) clinker ~ ~ ~**

(~) ~ concrete (US); **(~) clinker ~** (Brit.) · Kesselschlackenbeton *m*, (Stein)Kohlenschlackenbeton, Feuerungsschlackenbeton, (Verbrennungs-)Schlackenbeton

(~) clinker (Brit.); **(~) cinder** (US); **~ slag** [*misnomer: breeze*] · (verklinkerte) Feuerungsschlacke *f*, (Verbrennungs)Schlacke, (Stein)Kohlenschlacke, Kesselschlacke, Rostschlacke [*Teilweise geschmolzene Aschen fester Brennstoffe, die auch noch unverbrannte Anteile enthalten können*]

(~) ~ aggregate for concrete [*B.S. 1165*]; **(~) cinder ~ ~ ~** (US) [*misnomer: breeze aggregate*] · (Kessel)Schlackenzuschlag(stoff) *m*, (Stein)Kohlenschlackenzuschlag(-stoff), Verbrennungsschlackenzuschlag(stoff), (verklinkerter) Feuerungsschlackenzuschlag(stoff) ·

(~) ~ concrete (Brit.); **(~) cinder ~** (US) · Kesselschlackenbeton *m*, (Stein-)Kohlenschlackenbeton, Feuerungsschlackenbeton, (Verbrennungs-)Schlackenbeton

~ for conducting fire(-resistance) tests · Brandofen *m*

~ hard soldering, ~ brazing · Ofenhartlötung *f*

~ installation, fire ~, burning appliance ~ · Feuerungsanlage *f*, Feuerstättenanlage [*Sie besteht aus Feuerstätte, Verbindungsstück und Schornstein*]

~ patenting · Durchlaufpatentieren *n*

~ residue · Feuerungsrückstand *m*

~ room, fire ~, burning appliance ~ [*A room primarily used for the installation of fuel-fired heating equipment other than boilers*] · Feuerungsraum *m*, Feuerstättenraum

~ slag → **(~) clinker**

~ temperature · Brandraumtemperatur *f*

~ test · Brandofenprobe *f*, Brandofenprüfung *f*, Brandofenversuch *m* [*baulicher Brandschutz*]

furnish and install, F & I · liefern und ein(zu)bauen

furniture, fitting, builders' ~ · (Bau-)Beschlag *m*

~ varnish · Möbellack *m*

~ warehouse · Möbelspeicher *m*

furring, firring; strapping [*Scotland*] [*Light wooden battens or metal sections fixed to solid backgrounds, for subsequent attachment of lath(ing) or sheet materials*] · Unterkonstruktion *f* [*Putztechnik*]

~ (brick), soap (~), queen closer Meisterquartier *m*, Riemen(stein) *m*, Riem(en)stück *n*, Riemchen *n*, Längsquartier

fusain, motherham, mineral charcoal, mother of coal · mineralische Holzkohle *f*

fuseboard [*B.S. 214*] · Sicherungstafel *f*

fuse cabinet, ~ chamber · Sicherungskasten *m*

~ chamber, ~ cabinet · Sicherungskasten *m*

fused colophony → **~ resin**

~ ~ with lime hydrate, ~ rosin ~ ~ ~, ~ resin ~ ~ ~ · Kalkharz *n* [*Durch Zusammenschmelzen von Kolophonium mit Kalkhydrat gewonnen*]

~ copal, run ~ · ausgeschmolzener Kopal *m*

~ quartz, vitreous silica, fused silica, quartz glass, silica glass, vitrified silica [*A vitreous material consisting almost entirely of silica, made in translucent and transparent forms. The former has minute gas bubbles disseminated in it*] · Quarzglas *n* [*Fehlname*]; Kiesel(säure)glas

~ resin, ~ rosin, ~ colophony · Hartharz *n* [*Es wird durch Zusammenschmelzen von Kolophonium mit Kalkhydrat oder Zinkoxid bei hohen Temperaturen gewonnen*]

~ silica, vitreous ~, vitrified ~, quartz glass, silica glass, fused quartz [*A vitreous material consisting almost entirely of silica, made in translucent and transparent forms. The former has minute gas bubbles disseminated in it*] · Quarzglas *n* [*Fehlname*]; Kiesel(säure)glas

fusel oil · Fuselöl *n*

~-oil tar · Fuselölgasteer *m*

fusibility · Schmelzbarkeit *f*

fusible alloy · leichtschmelzende Legierung *f*

~ link · Schmelzkörper *m*, Temperaturkennkörper

~ ~ damper · Temperaturkennkörperschieber *m*, Schmelzkörperschieber

~ member · Schmelzelement *n*

~ plug [*A device having a predetermined temperature fusible member for the relief of pressure*] · Schmelzpfropfen *m*, Schmelzstöpsel *m*

fusing — gadroon

fusing, sealing, welding [*Joining a piece of glass to glass or another material by heating and pressing together; also applied to the fire finishing of ends of tubular glasses*] · Schweißen *n*, Verschmelzen [*Glas*]

~, **running** · Ausschmelzen *n* [*Kopal*]

~ **temperature** · Schmelztemperatur *f*

fusion-cast refractory (product) feuerfestes schmelzgegossenes Erzeugnis *n*, ff. ~ ~ [*schmelzflüssig gegossenes feuerfestes Erzeugnis*]

fusion casting · Schmelzgießen *n* [*Formgebungsverfahren, bei dem das geschmolzene Material in Formen gegossen wird*]

~ **process** · Schmelzverfahren *n* [*Alkydharzherstellung*]

~-**welded** · schmelzgeschweißt

fusion welding · Schmelzschweißen *n*

~ ~ **technic,** ~ ~ **technique** · Schmelzschweißtechnik *f*

fust, (column) shaft · (Säulen)Schaft *m*, (Säulen)Rumpf *m*

Futurism [*A short-lived movement founded in Italy in 1909. It represented an extreme reaction against the past and approval of the speed and mechanical powers of the 20th century*] · Futurismus *m*

Futurist architecture · futuristische Architektur *f*, ~ Baukunst *f*

~ **movement** · futuristische Bewegung *f*

FV, front view · Front(al)ansicht *f*, Vorderansicht

FW→ fire wall

FW, feedwater · Speisewasser *n*

G

gabbro · Gabbro *m* [*Fehlnamen: (schwedischer) schwarzer Granit m, schwarzer schwedischer Granit. Kristallines Tiefengestein mit den Hauptbestandteilen Kalknatronfeldspat und Diallag, dazu meist reichlich Eisenerz, öfters Olivin, auch wohl Augit oder Hornblende, selten Quarz*]

~ **aplite,** beerbachite · Gabbroaplit *m*

~ **diorite** · Gabbrodiorit *m*

~ **magma** · Gabbromagma *n*

~ **nelsonite** · Gabbronelsonit *m*

~ **porphyrite** [*A porphyritic igneous rock with phenocrysts of augite and plagioclase in a crystalline base of similar materials*] · Gabbroporphyrit *m*

gable, ~ end · Giebel *m*

~ **board,** verge ~, barge ~ [*Barge boards are placed at gable ends to conceal the projecting ends of the roof purlins or timbers, they are frequently carved into an ornamental feature*] · Windbrett *n*, Windfeder *f*

~ **brick** · Giebelziegel *m*

~ **cross** [*A decorative cross surmounting the gable of a church building*] · Giebelkreuz *n*

~ **(end)** · Giebel *m*

~ ~ [*An end wall having a gable*] · Giebelwand *f*

~ **frame,** gabled ~, ~ **framing** · Giebelrahmen *m*

gable-fronted house, gable(d) ~ · Giebelhaus *n* [*Haus mit einem Satteldach, dessen Giebel die Hauptfront bildet*]

gable inlet ventilation, ~ ~ **venting** · Giebelbelüftung *f*

~ **masonry wall** · Giebelmauer *f*

~ **painting** · Giebelmalerei *f*

~ **peak** · Giebelspitze *f*

~ **roof** · Giebeldach *n*

~ **shaped lintel** · giebelförmiger Sturz *m*, giebelförmige Oberschwelle *f*

~ **slab** · Giebelplatte *f*

~ **slate** · Giebelstein *m*, Ortstein

~ **tower** · Giebelturm *m*

~ **tracery** · Giebelmaßwerk *n*, Schleierwerk

~ **wall** [*A wall which is crowned by a gable*] · Giebelwand *f*

~ ~ **balcony** · Giebelwandbalkon *m*

~ ~ **belfry,** bell-gable, ringing-loft · Glockengiebel *m*

~ **window** · Giebelfenster *n*

gabled · gegiebelt

gable(d) dormer, ~ roof ~ · Dachhäuschen *n*, Giebelgaube *f*, Giebelgaupe

~ **frame,** ~ **framing** · Giebelrahmen *m*

~ ~ **of two bays,** two-bay gable(d) frame · Zweifeld-Giebelrahmen *m*

~ **house,** gable-fronted ~ · Giebelhaus *n* [*Haus mit einem Satteldach, dessen Giebel die Hauptfront bildet*]

gabled hip [*A hip with a small gable over it*] · Giebelwalm *m*

gable(d) (roof) dormer · Giebelgaube *f*, Giebelgaupe, Dachhäuschen *n*

gablet · Ziergiebel *m* [*Im gotischen Stil ein Wimperg zur Zier über einem Fenster, einer Tür usw.*]

gadroon, godroon [*A decorative pattern formed of a series of convex ridges*] · rundgeschweifte Randverzierung *f*

to gage (US); to gauge, to batch, to proportion, to measure · abmessen, zumessen, zuteilen, dosieren

gage (US); gauge, thickness of ~ · Dicke f [*Linoleum*]

gaged arch (US); gauged ~, bonded ~ · Keilziegelbogen m, Wölbziegelbogen

~ mortar (US); gauged ~ (Brit.); cement/lime/sand ~, compo (~), cement-lime ~, lime-and-cement ~, lean ~ · Kalkzementmörtel m, Zementkalkmörtel, verlängerter Zementmörtel, Magermörtel

~ stuff, gaging plaster (US); gauged stuff, gauging plaster · Kalkgipsputz m

gaging board (US); gauging ~ · Mischbrett n

~ box (US); gauging ~, batch ~ · Zumeßkiste f

~ plaster, gaged stuff (US); gauging plaster, gauged stuff · Kalkgipsputz m

gaging water (US) → mix(ing) ~

gain in space, space gain · Raumgewinn m

gaize · Gaize f, Pseudokieselgur m

~ cement · Gaizezement m, Pseudokieselgurzement

galena, lead glance, blue lead · PbS m, Galenit m, Bleiglanz m

~ pulp, blue lead ~, lead glance ~ · Bleiglanztrübe f, Galenittrübe, PbS-Trübe

galilee [*A term of various meanings and of dubious origin. At Durham Cathedral it is applied to a chapel at the west end, at Ely to the west porch, at Lincoln to a porch on the west side of the south transept*] · Galiläa f

~ → narthex

galleried upper storey (Brit.); ~ ~ story (US) · Emporengeschoß n, Emporenstockwerk n, Emporenetage f

gallery [*A room used for the display of works of art*] · Kunstgalerieraum m

~, art(s) ~, art(s) centre (Brit.); art(s) center (US) [*A building used for the display of works of art*] · Kunsthalle f, Kunstgalerie f

~ → tribune

~, walk [*A covered space for walking in, with one side open*] · Galerie f, Weg m, (Lauf)Gang m

~ arcade · Emporenarkade f

~ column, tribune ~ · Emporensäule f

~ crypt · Stollenkrypta f, Stollengruft f [*Krypta aus sich schneidenden Kammern, die meist tonnengewölbt sind*]

~ grave, passage ~ · Ganggrab n

~ niche, tribune ~ · Emporennische f

~ roof, tribune ~ · Emporendach n

~ vault, tribune ~ · Emporengewölbe n

~ window, tribune ~ · Emporenfenster n

galvanic corrosion, electrochemical ~ · elektrochemische Korrosion f

to galvanize; to galvanise (Brit.); to zinc coat · verzinken

galvanized, zinc coated; galvanised (Brit.) · verzinkt, zinkbeschichtet, zinküberzogen

~-steel tile; galvanised-steel ~ (Brit.); zinc coated steel ~ · verzinktes Stahldach(deckungs)element n

galvanized wire; galvanised ~ (Brit.); zinc coated ~ · verzinkter Draht m

galvanizing, zinc coating, electroplating; galvanising (Brit.) · Galvanisieren n, galvanische Metallabscheidung f, elektrolytische Metallabscheidung, elektrolytisches Überziehen, Galvanisierung f, Galvanisation f, Verzinken, Elektroplattierung, Galvanostegie f, Galvanoplattierung, Galvanoplattieren, galvanische (Metall)Veredelung, Verzinkung

(gambling) casino · Spielhaus n, (Spiel-)Kasino n

~ hall · Spielhalle f

gambrel roof, gambril ~ (Brit.) [*No US term*] · Schopfwalmdach n, Krüppelwalmdach, Fußwalmdach, Dach mit halben Walmen

~ ~ (US) → mansard (~)

gambril roof, gambrel ~ (Brit.); [*No US term*] · Schopfwalmdach n, Krüppelwalmdach, Fußwalmdach, Dach mit halben Walmen

~ ~ (US) → mansard (~)

game room · Spielzimmer n [*nicht für Kinder*]

games area, childrens' playground · (Kinder)Spielplatz m

gamma ray shielding · Gammastrahlenabschirmung f

gang, trade ~ · Kolonne f

~-board (Brit.); gangplank (US) · Laufplanke f

gang mould (Brit.); ~ mold (US) [*A mo(u)ld in which several similar concrete components may be cast at the same time*] · Reihenform f

ganger · Vorarbeiter m

gangplank (US); gang-board (Brit.) · Laufplanke f

gang showers · Reihendusche f

ganister, carboniferous sandstone · Ganister m, Kohlensandstein m [*Festes, sehr feines feinkörniges und hochkieselsäurehaltiges Gestein der Karbonformation. In den USA meist gleichbedeutend mit Quarzit.*
Anmerkung: Im englischen Sprachgebrauch werden mit „ganister" auch kieselsäurereiche Flick- und Stampfmassen bezeichnet]

gannister (Brit.); ganister (US) · englischer Quarzit m

~ brick, dinas ~ (Brit.); ganister ~ (US); acid firebrick, silica brick · Quarzitstein m, Quarzkalkziegel m, Silikastein, Quarzitziegel; Dinasstein [*veraltete Bezeichnung*]

gap, joint ~ · (Fugen)Spalt m

gap — garden (housing) estate

~, pigeonhole · Kästel *n*, Durchbruch *m* [*Mauer*]

~ **filled joint**, monolithic ~ [*It is made with in-situ concrete, grout or synthetic resin*] · harte Fuge *f*, Hartfuge

gap-filling adhesive, ~ glue, gap filler [*B.S. 1204*] · fugenfüllender Leim *m*, Fugenleim

~ **no-heat adhesive**, ~ ~ glue · Fugenkaltleim *m*, fugenfüllender Kaltleim

gap-graded aggregate, discontinuously-graded ~ · diskontinuierlich abgestufte Mineralmasse *f*, unstetig ~ ~

~ **concrete**, discontinuously-graded ~ · diskontinuierlich abgestufter Beton *m*, unstetig ~ ~

gap grading, discontinuous ~, discontinuous granulometry · unstetige Kornabstufung *f*, diskontinuierliche ~, Kornaufbau *m* der Zuschläge nach unstetigen Sieblinien [*Fehlen in den Zuschlagstoffen einzelne Korngruppen, so ergeben sich unstetige Sieblinien*]

~ **heating** · Fugenheizung *f* [*Direkte innere Erwärmung der Klebstoffschicht zum Zwecke des Abbindens (Härtens), z.B. durch elektrisch beheiztes Drahtgewebe oder Hochfrequenzheizung. DIN 16921*]

~ **site** · Baulücke *f* [*An einer anbaufähigen Straße zwischen bebauten Grundstücken unbebautes Grundstück*]

gaping of the joints of a vault · Klaffen *n* des Gewölbes

garage (building) [*A building to shelter a car. The term was first used about 1902*] · (Auto)Garage *f*

~ **compound** [*Of a rental row-house development*] · Sammelgarage *f*

~ **construction** · Garagenbau *m*

~ **court**, ~ fore~, ~ (court)yard · Garagenhof *m*

~ **(court)yard**, ~ (fore)court · Garagenhof *m*

~ **door** · Garagentor *n*

(~) ~ **leaf** · (Garagen)Torblatt *n*

~ ~ **operator** · Garagentorantrieb(vorrichtung) *m*, (*f*)

~ **drainage** · Garagenentwässerung *f*

~ **drive** · Garageneinfahrt *f*, Garagenzufahrt

~ ~ · Garagenweg *m*

~ **floor(ing) (finish)**, ~ floor cover(ing) · Garagen(fuß)boden(belag) *m*

~ **(fore)court**, ~ (court)yard · Garagenhof *m*

~ **heating**, ~ warming · Garagen(be)heizung *f*

~ **rolling door** · Garagenrolltor *n*

~ **roof** · Garagendach *n*

~ **steel door**, steel garage ~ · Stahl-Garagentor *n*, Garagen-Stahltor

~ **warming**, ~ heating · Garagen(be)heizung *f*

~ **yard**, ~ court~, ~ (fore)court · Garagenhof *m*

garaging facility · Garagenanlage *f*

garbage [*The animal and vegetable waste resulting from the handling, preparation, cooking and consumption of food*] · Küchenabfall *m*, Küchenabfälle *mpl*

~ **collection**, ~ disposal · Küchenabfallbeseitigung *f*, Küchenabfällebeseitigung

~ **container** · Küchenabfallbehälter *m*, Küchenabfällebehälter

~ **disposal**, ~ collection · Küchenabfallbeseitigung *f*, Küchenabfällebeseitigung

~ ~ **chute** (Brit.) → dispose-all

~ ~ **shaft** (Brit.) → dispose-all

~ **disposer** (Brit.) → dispose-all

~ **grinder** → (mechanical) refuse ~

garden architect, designer of formal gardens and parks · Gartengestalter *m*, Garten(bau)architekt *m*

~ **architecture** [*The architectural embellishments of gardens, e.g. garden-houses, pavilions, walls, piers, terraces, etc.*] · Gartenarchitektur *f*, Gartenbaukunst *f*

~ **bench** · Gartenbank *f*

~ **brick wall** → ~ clay ~ ~

~ **(building) unit** · Garten(-Bau)element *n*, Garten(-Bau)körper *m*

~ **ceramics** · Gartenkeramik *f*

Garden City latch → thumb ~

garden (clay) brick wall · Ziegelgartenmauer *f*, Gartenziegelmauer

~ **colony**, ~ (housing) estate; ~ cottage community, ~ nesting (US) · Garten(wohn)sied(e)lung *f*, Gartenwohnkolonie *f*

~ **cottage community**, ~ nesting (US); ~ colony, ~ (housing) estate · Garten(wohn)sied(e)lung *f*, Gartenwohnkolonie *f*

~ **court**, courtyard garden · Zierhof *m*, Gartenhof

~ ~, (open) peristyle ~ · Peristylhof *m* [*Von einem Peristyl umgebener Hof*]

~ **dwelling unit** (US); ~ dwelling (Brit.) · Gartenwohnung *f*

~ **estate**, ~ housing ~, ~ colony; ~ cottage community, ~ nesting (US) · Garten(wohn)sied(e)lung *f*, Gartenwohnkolonie *f*

~ **façade** · Gartenfassade *f*

~ **fence** · Gartenzaun *m*

~ **figure** · Gartenfigur *f*

~ **flag(stone)** → ~ (path) (paving) ~

~ **fountain** · Gartenspringbrunnen *m*

~ **front** · Gartenfront *f*

~ **ground** · Gartenland *n*

~ **house** · Gartenlaube *f*

~ **(housing) estate**, ~ colony; ~ cottage community, ~ nesting (US) · Garten(wohn)sied(e)lung *f*, Gartenwohnkolonie *f*

garden hydrant — gas concrete hollow block

~ **hydrant** · Gartenhydrant *m*

~ **making** · Gartenbau *m*, Ausführung *f* von Gartenanlagen

~ **masonry wall** · Gartenmauer *f*

~ **nesting,** ~ **cottage community** (US); ~ **(housing) estate,** ~ **colony** · Garten(wohn)sied(e)lung *f*, Gartenwohnkolonie *f*

~ **path** · Gartenweg *m*

~ **(~) (paving) flag(stone)** · Garten(bau)platte *f*, Garten(bau)stein *m*, Gartenwegplatte, Gartenwegstein

~ **restaurant** · Gartenrestaurant *n*

~ **shed,** ~ **tool** ~ · Gartenschuppen *m*

~ **stair(case)** · Gartentreppe *f*

~ **suburb** · Gartenvorstadt *f*

~ **surround, bed** ~ · Beeteinfassung *f*

~ **temple** · Gartentempel *m*

~ **(tool) shed** · Gartenschuppen *m*

~ **town** · Gartenstadt *f* [*Planmäßige Neugründung in sich geschlossener Sied(e)lung auf bodenreformerischer Grundlage*]

~ **unit** → ~ **building** ~

~ **wall** · Gartenwand *f*

~ **work** · gärtnerische Arbeiten *fpl*

gargoyle, (carved) waterspout [*A projecting stone spout, usually carved with a grotesque figure*] · (figürlicher) Wasserspeier *m*

garland, swag, encarpa, festoon [*A carved, modelled or painted garland of flowers, fruit or leaves, suspended in a curve between two points*] · Gehänge *n*, Gewinde *n*, Feston *n*, Girlande *f*

~ **leaf,** festoon ~, swag ~, encarpa ~ · Gehängeblatt *n*, Gewindeblatt, Festonblatt, Girlandenblatt

~ **ornament** · Blätterstrang *m*

garlanded circular window, ~ **round** ~ · umkränztes Kreisfenster *n*, ~ Rundfenster

garnet (shel)lac · Granatschellack *m*

garnison church · Garnisonkirche *f*

garret → **attic room**

~ · Mansarde *f* [*Dachraum im ausgebauten Teil eines Daches, der jedoch nicht die Form eines Mansard(en)daches haben muß*]

~ **window, attic** ~ · Mansard(en)dachfenster *n* [*Bei einem nicht halbschrägem Dachraum*]

gas adsorption · Gasadsorption *f*, Gasanlagerung *f*

~ **analysis** · Gasanalyse *f*

~ **appliance** → ~ **burning** ~

~ ~ **recess,** ~ burning ~ ~, ~ furnace ~, ~ fire ~ · Gasfeuerungsnische *f*, Gasgerätnische

gas-ash concrete · Gas-Aschen-Beton *m*, Aschen-Gas-Beton [*Gasbeton mit Mischbinder aus Zement und Asche*]

~ **silicate** · Gas-Aschen-Silikat *n*, Aschen-Gas-Silikat [*Gassilikat mit Mischbinder aus ungelöschtem Kalk und Asche*]

gas-ash-silicate concrete · Aschen-Silikat-Gasbeton *m*, Silikat-Aschen-Gasbeton, Gas-Aschen-Silikat-Beton

gas barrel handrail, ~ **tubing** ~, ~ **tube** ~ · Gasrohr-Handlauf *m* [*Geländer*]

~ **barrier** · Gassperre *f*

~ **black (pigment)** · Gasruß(pigment) *m*, (*n*)

~ **boiler** → **gas(-fired)** ~

~ ~ **flue, gas-fired** ~ ~ · Gaskesselzug *m*

~ **bottle,** ~ **cylinder** · Gasflasche *f*, Stahlflasche

~ ~ **room,** ~ **cylinder** ~ · Gasflaschenlagerraum *m*, Stahlflaschenlagerraum

~ **burner, gas-fired** ~ · Gasbrenner *m*

~ **(burning) appliance,** ~ **fire, gas(-fired) furnace, gas(-fired) appliance** · Gasfeuerung *f*, Gasfeuerstätte *f*, Feuerung für gasförmigen Brennstoff, Feuerstätte für gasförmigen Brennstoff, Gasgerät *n*

~ **(~)** ~ **recess,** ~ **furnace** ~, ~ **fire** ~ · Gasfeuerungsnische *f*, Gasgerätnische

~ **carbon black (pigment)** · Gasruß(pigment) *m*, (*n*)

~ **central heating, gas-fired** ~ ~ · Gaszentralheizung *f*, Zentralgasheizung

~ **chromatography** · Gaschromatographie *f*

~ **circulation heating,** ~ **water** ~ ~ · Umlauf-Gaswasserheizung *f*, Umwälz-Gaswasserheizung

(~) circulator → ~ **water** ~

~ **concrete, expanded** ~ · Blähbeton *m*, Gasbeton [*DIN 4164*]

~ ~ **article** → ~ ~ **product**

~ ~ **block** → ~ ~ ~ **building** ~

~ ~ **(building) block, expanded** ~ **(~)** ~, ~ ~ ~ **(~) tile** [*See remark under 'Block'*] · Gasbeton(werk)stein *m*, Gasbetonblock(stein) *m*, Blähbeton(werk)stein, Blähbetonblock(stein)

~ ~ **(~) tile** → ~ ~ ~ **(~) block**

~ ~ **cast(ing)** → **(pre)cast gas concrete (building) unit**

~ ~ **cavity block** → ~ ~ ~ **hollow** ~

~ ~ ~ **tile** → ~ ~ ~ **hollow block**

~ ~ **coating** · Blähbeton-Beschichtung *f*, Gasbeton-Beschichtung, Blähbeton-Überzug *m*, Gasbeton-Überzug, Überziehen *n* von Blähbeton, Überziehen von Gasbeton, Beschichten von Blähbeton, Beschichten von Gasbeton

~ ~ **hollow block,** ~ ~ **cavity** ~, ~ ~ ~ **tile, expanded** ~ ~ ~, ~ ~ **pot** ~ · Blähbetonhohlblock(stein) *m*, Gasbetonhohlblockstein(), Gasbetonhohlstein, Blähbetonhohlstein

gas concrete hollow tile — gas-forming

~ ~ ~ tile → ~ ~ ~ block
~ ~ indoor wall → ~ ~ ~ internal ~
~ ~ inside wall → ~ ~ ~ internal ~
~ ~ insulating block, expanded ~ ~ ~, ~ ~ ~ ~ brick, ~ ~ ~ insulation(-grade) ~ · Blähbeton-Isolierblock(stein) m, Blähbeton-Isolierstein, Gasbeton-Isolierblock(stein). Gasbeton-Isolierstein
~ ~ ~ slab, expanded ~ ~ ~, ~ ~ ~ insulation(-grade) ~ · Blähbeton-Isolierplatte f, Gasbeton-Isolierplatte
~ ~ internal wall, ~ ~ interior ~, ~ ~ indoor ~, ~ ~ inside ~ · Blähbeton-Innenwand f, Gasbeton-Innenwand
~ ~ plant, expanded ~ ~ ~ · Blähbetonwerk n, Gasbetonwerk
~ ~ pot → ~ ~ ~ hollow block
~ ~ product, ~ ~ article, expanded ~ ~ · Blähbetonerzeugnis n, Gasbetonerzeugnis, Gasbetongegenstand m, Gasbetonartikel m, Blähbetongegenstand, Blähbetonartikel
~ ~ purpose-made block, expanded ~ ~ ~ ~, ~ ~ ~ ~ tile, ~ ~ ~ ~ brick, ~ ~ special (purpose) ~ [See remark under 'Block'] · Blähbeton-Formstein m, Blähbeton-Profilstein, Blähbeton-Profilblock(stein) m, Blähbeton-Formblock(stein), Gasbeton-Formstein, Gasbeton-Profilblock(stein), Gasbeton-Formblock(stein)
~ ~ slab, expanded ~ ~ ~ · Blähbetonplatte f, Gasbetonplatte
~ ~ tile → ~ ~ ~ (building) block
~ ~ wall block ~ ~ ~ ~ tile [See remark under 'Block'] · Blähbetonwand(bau)block(stein) m, Blähbetonwand(bau)stein, Gasbetonwand(bau)block(stein), Gasbetonwand(bau)stein [DIN 4165]
~ ~ ~ slab · Blähbetonwand(bau)platte f, Gasbetonwand(bau)platte [DIN 4166]
~ ~ ~ tile ~ ~ ~ ~ block [See remark under 'Block'] · Blähbetonwand(bau)block(stein) m, Blähbetonwand(bau)stein, Gasbetonwand(bau)block(stein), Gasbetonwand(bau)stein [DIN 4165]
~ constant · Gaskonstante f
~ consumption · Gasverbrauch m
~ convector, gas-fired ~ · Gaskonvektor m
~ cooker · Gaskocher m
~ cylinder, ~ bottle · Gasflasche f, Stahlflasche
~ ~ room, ~ bottle ~ · Gasflaschenlagerraum m, Stahlflaschenlagerraum
~ detector system · Gasspüranlage f
~ development → ~ formation
~ discharge lamp, electric ~ ~ · Gasentladungslampe f
~ distribution installation · Gasverteilungsanlage f [DIN 19630]
~ fire → ~ (burning) appliance
~ ~ recess, ~ furnace ~, ~ (burning) appliance ~ · Gasfeuerungsnische f, Gasgerätnische

gas-fired · gasbefeuert
~ · gasgefeuert
gas(-fired) appliance → gas (burning) ~
~ boiler · Gaskessel m
~ ~ flue · Gaskesselzug m
~ burner · Gasbrenner m
~ central heating · Gaszentralheizung f, Zentralgasheizung
~ convector · Gaskonvector m
~ floor furnace [See remark under 'floor furnace'] · Gas-Deckenstrahler m
~ furnace → gas (burning) appliance
~ heating → ~ (space) ~
~ ~ installation · Gasheiz(ungs)anlage f
~ (hot) water heater, ~ (~) ~ heating appliance · Gas-Wassererhitzer m, Gas-Wasserheizgerät n, Gas-Wassererwärmer, Gas-Wasserheizer
~ (~) ~ system · Gas-Warmwasseranlage f
~ incinerator → ~ waste ~
~ range · Gasherd m
~ refuse incinerator, ~ (waste) ~; ~ rubbish ~ (US) · Gas-(müll)Verbrenner m, Gas-Abfall(stoff)verbrenner
~ rubbish incinerator (US); ~ (waste) ~, ~ refuse ~ · Gas-(Müll)Verbrenner m, Gas-Abfall(stoff)verbrenner
~ (space) heating, ~ (~) warming · Gasraumheizung f, Gas(be)heizung [1. Mit Gas beheizte Zentralheizungskessel. 2. In den Räumen aufgestellte Gasraumheizer mit Gaszuleitung]
~ warm air heating · Gasluft(be)heizung f
~ warming → ~ (space) heating
~ washing machine · Gaswaschmaschine f
~ (waste) incinerator, ~ refuse ~; ~ rubbish ~ (US) · Gas-(Müll)Verbrenner m, Gas-Abfall(stoff)verbrenner
~ water heating · Wassererhitzung f mit Gas, Wassererwärmung ~ ~
~ ~ ~ appliance → ~ (hot) ~ ~ ~
~ ~ system → ~ (hot) ~ ~
gasfitter · Gasinstallateur m
gas floor furnace, gas-fired ~ ~ [See remark under 'floor furnace'] · Gas-Deckenstrahler m
~ flue, flue for gas appliance · Gasfeuerungszug m
~-foam concrete, foam-gas ~ · Schaum-Gasbeton m, Gas-Schaumbeton [Kombination von Gas- und Schaumbeton]
gas formation, ~ generation, ~ development, formation of gas bubbles · Gasbildung f, Gasentwick(e)lung [Gasbeton]
gas-forming, generating bubbles of gas · gasbildend, gasentwickelnd [Gasbeton]

gas-forming agent — gas pumice concrete

~ **agent**, aerating ~, ~ chemical, metallic additive · gasbildender Zusatz m, (Metall)Treibmittel n, gaserzeugendes Mittel, Blähmittel, Gasentwickler m, Gasbildner, (gasbildender) Treiber [z.B. Alu-(minium)pulver]

~ **chemical** → ~ agent

gas furnace [For testing refractory bricks under load at high temperatures] · Gasofen m

~ **furnace** → ~ (burning) appliance

~ ~ **recess**, ~ fire ~, ~ (burning) appliance ~ · Gasfeuerungsnische f, Gasgerätnische

~ **generation** → ~ formation

(~) **generator ash** · (Gas)Generatorasche f

(~) ~ **cinder** (US); (~) ~ **clinker** (Brit.) · (Gas)Generatorschlacke f

~ **geyser** · Gasbadeofen m

~ **grid** · Gas(leitungs)netz n, Gasversorgungsnetz

~ ~ **line**, ~ transmission ~, grid gas ~ · Ferngasleitung f, Gasfernleitung

gas-heated · gasbeheizt, gasgeheizt, gaserwärmt

~ **air**, gas-warmed ~ · gaserwärmte Luft f

~ **panel** · (Infrarot-)Hochtemperaturstrahler m, (Infrarot-)Gasglühstrahler, Infrarotstrahler

gas heater → ~ heating appliance

~ **heating** → gas(-fired) (space) ~

~ ~ **appliance**, ~ ~ unit, ~ ~ device, ~ warming ~, ~ heater, ~ fire, ~ warmer · Gasheiz(ungs)gerät n, Gasheizer m, Gaserhitzer

~ ~ **boiler** · Gasheizkessel m

~ ~ **device** → ~ ~ appliance

~ ~ **installation**, gas-fired ~ ~ · Gasheiz(ungs)anlage f

~ ~ **unit** → ~ ~ ~ appliance

~ **hose** · Gasschlauch m

~ **(hot) water heater** → gas(-fired) (~) ~ ~

~ (~) ~ **system**, gas-fired (~) ~ ~ · Gas-Warmwasseranlage f

~ **hotplate** · Gaskochplatte f

~ **(hot) water heater** → gas-fired (~) ~ ~

~-**house coal-tar**, gas-works ~ · Gasanstaltsteer m, Gas(werks)teer

~ ~ **pitch**, gas-works ~ ~ · Gasanstaltspech r, Gas(werks)teerpech

gas illumination, ~ lighting · Gasbeleuchtung f

~ **impermeability** → imperviousness to gas

~ **imperviousness** → imperviousness to gas

~ **incinerator** → gas(-fired) (waste) ~

~ **installation** → (internal) ~

~ ~ **work**; (internal) ~ ~ (Brit.) · Gasinstallationsarbeiten fpl

~ **lantern** · Gaslaterne f

~ **lighting**, ~ illumination · Gasbeleuchtung f

~ **lime concrete**, expanded ~ ~ · Gaskalkbeton m

~ ~ ~ **block**, ~ ~ ~ ~ tile, expanded ~ ~ ~ ~ [See remark under 'Block'] · Gaskalkbetonblock(stein) m, Gaskalkbetonstein

~ ~ ~ **tile**, ~ ~ ~ ~ block, expanded ~ ~ ~ ~ [See remark under 'Block'] · Gaskalkbetonblock(stein) m, Gaskalkbetonstein

~ **line**, ~ piping · Gas(rohr)leitung f

~ ~ **material** · Gasleitungswerkstoff m

~ (~) **pipe** · Gas(leitungs)rohr n [Stumpf geschweißtes Stahlrohr, vorwiegend für Gasleitungen nach DIN 2440]

~ **luminaire (fixture)** (US); ~ light fitting (Brit.); ~ (light(ing)) fixture · Gasleuchte f

~ **main** · Gashauptleitung f

~ **meter** [B. S. 4161] · Gasmesser m, Gaszähler [Gasuhr ist eine veraltete Bezeichnung und sollte nicht mehr verwendet werden]

~ ~ **enclosure**, ~ ~ inclosure · Gasmessernische f, Gaszählernische

~ ~ **inclosure**, ~ ~ enclosure · Gasmessernische f, Gaszählernische

~ ~ **house** · Gasmesserhaus n, Gaszählerhaus

~ **oil** [35 seconds] · extraleichtflüssiges Heizöl n, Heizöl EL [DIN 51603]

~ **outlet** [A threaded connection in a house gas piping system to which a gas-burning appliance is or may be attached] · Gasanschluß m

~ ~ **point** · Gasverbrauchsstelle f

~ **permeability** · Gasdurchlässigkeit f

~ **pipe** → ~ line ~

~ ~ **network**, ~ ~ system · Gas(rohr)netz n

~ ~ **thread** · Gasrohrgewinde n

~ **piping**, ~ line · Gas(rohr)leitung f

~ **point** · Gasstelle f

~ **pressure** · Gasdruck m

~-**pressure cable** · Druckgaskabel n

~ **regulator** · Gasdruckregler m

gas-producer · Gasgenerator m

~ **coal tar**, producer-gas ~ ~ · Steinkohlen(heiz)generatorteer m

gas-proof, gasoline-proof, gasolene-proof, gpf (US); petrol-proof (Brit.) · benzinfest

gas pumice concrete, expanded ~ ~, pumice gas ~, pumice expanded ~ · (Natur)Bims-Gasbeton m, (Natur)Bims-Blähbeton

gas radiant heater — gate post

~ **radiant heater,** radiant gas ~ · Gasstrahler *m*, Gasstrahlungsheizgerät *n*, Gasstrahlungserhitzer
~ **radiator** · Gas(glieder)heizkörper *m*, Gasradiator *m*
~ **range,** ~-fired ~ · Gasherd *m*
~ **refuse incinerator** → gas-fired ~ ~
~ **re-heater** · Gas-Nachwärmer *m*
~ **room heating** → ~ (space) ~
~ **rubbish incinerator** → gas-fired ~ ~
~ **scrubber,** ~ washer · Gaswäscher *m*
~ **service pipe** · Gasinstallationsrohr *n*
~ **shut-off valve** · Gasabsperrschieber *m*
~ **silicate** · Gassilikat *n*
~**-silicate concrete** · Silikat-Gasbeton *m*, Gas-Silikat-Beton
gas-slag concrete · Schlackengasbeton *m*, Gasschlackenbeton [*Gasbeton mit Mischbinder aus Schlackenzement und Kalk*]
gas-silicate concrete · Gas-Schlacken-Silikat-Beton *m*, Silikat-Schlacken-Gasbeton, Schlacken-Silikat-Gasbeton
gas space heating → ~-fired ~ ~
~ ~ **warming** → ~-fired space heating
~ **stove** · Gasofen *m*
~ **supply** · Gasversorgung *f* [*DIN 2425*]
~ **thread** · Gasgewinde *n*
gastight · gasdicht, gassicher
gastightness → impervousness to gas
gas transmission line, ~ grid ~, grid gas ~ · Ferngasleitung *f*, Gasfernleitung
~ **tube** · Gasröhre *f*
~ ~ **handrail** → ~ barrel ~
~ **tubing handrail** → ~ barrel ~
~ **tungsten arc welding method** · WIG-(Schweiß)Verfahren *n*, Wolfram-Inert-(Schweiß)Verfahren, Wolfram-Inert-Gasschweißverfahren
~ **untertaking,** gas-works · Gaswerk *n*, Gasanstalt *f*
~ **vent** · Gasentlüfter *m*
~ **warm air heating,** gas-fired ~ ~ ~ · Gasluft(be)heizung *f*
gas-warmed, gas-heated · gasbeheizt, gasgeheizt, gaserwärmt
~ **air,** gas-heated ~ · gaserwärmte Luft *f*
gas warmer → ~ heating appliance
~ **warming** → gas(-fired) (space) heating
~ ~ **appliance** → ~ heating ~
~ ~ **device** → ~ heating appliance
~ ~ **unit** → ~ heating appliance
~ **washer,** ~ scrubber · Gaswäscher *m*
~ **washing machine** → ~-fired ~ ~
~ **(waste) incinerator** → gas-fired (~) ~
gas, water and sewage installation work · Gas-, Wasser- und Abwasser-Installationsarbeiten *fpl* [*DIN 18381*]
~ **(water) circulation heating** · Umlauf-Gaswasserheizung *f*, Umwälz-Gaswasserheizung

~ **(~) circulator,** circulator · (Gas)Heiztherme *f*, Umlauf-Gaswasserheizer *m*, Umwälz-Gaswasserheizer, Gas-Durchlauf-Wasserheizer [*Zum Erzeugen von Heizwasser für Umlauf-Gaswasserheizungen*]
~ ~ **heater** → gas(-fired) (hot) ~ ~
~ ~ **heating** → ~-fired ~ ~
~ ~ **system** → gas(-fired) (hot) ~ ~
gas-works, gas undertaking, gas-house · Gaswerk *n*, Gasanstalt *f*
~ **coal-tar,** gas-house ~ · Gasanstaltsteer *m*, Gas(werks)teer
~ ~ **pitch,** gas-house ~ ~ · Gasanstaltsteerpech *n*, Gas(werks)teerpech
gaseous · gasförmig
~ **chlorine** · Chlorgas *n*, gasförmiges Chlor *n*
~ **fuel** · gasförmiger Brennstoff *m* [*DIN 51850*]
~ **heating fuel** · gasförmiger Heiz(ungs)stoff *m* [*DIN 51850*]
gasket → preformed ~
~ **glazing** · Profilverglasung *f*, Verglasung mit (Ab)Dicht(ungs)profilen, Profileinglasung, Einglasung mit (Ab)Dicht(ungs)profilen
~ **joint** → preformed ~ ~
~ **seal,** static ~ · Flach(ab)dichtung *f*, Manschetten(ab)dichtung, starre (Ab-)Dichtung
gasketed pipe · Rohr *n* mit (Ab)Dicht(ungs)profil, ~ ~ Selbstdichtung
gasolene-proof, gas(oline)-proof, gpf (US); petrol-proof (Brit.) · benzinfest
gas(oline)-proof, gasolene-proof, gpf (US); petrol-proof (Brit.) · benzinfest
gate · (Außen)Tor *n*
~ · Flugsteig *m*
~, ~**way,** town ~ · Straßentor *n*
~, ~**way** · Pforte *f* [*antike Baukunst*]
gatehouse · Vorburg *f* [*Befestigte Anlage zur Sicherung des Tores einer Burg*]
gatekeeper, porter, doorkeeper · Pförtner *m*
gatekeeper's dwelling, porter's ~, doorkeeper's ~ (Brit.); ~ ~ unit (US) · Pförtnerwohnung *f*
~ **house** → porter's lodge
~ **lodge** → porter's ~
~ **room,** doorkeeper's ~, porter's ~ · Pförtnerraum *m*
gate occupancy time · Belegungsdauer *f* [*Flughafen*]
Gate of Herculaneum at Pompeii · Herculaner Tor *n* zu Pompeji
~ ~ **Lions,** Lion Gate [*Mycenae*] · Löwentor *n*
gate pier [*Stone, brick or reinforced concrete pier to which a gate is hung*] · Torpfeiler *m*
~ **post** [*Timber or metal post to which a gate is hung*] · Torpfosten *m*

gate(way) — General Post Office

gate(way), town ~ · Straßentor n
~ · Pforte f [antike Baukunst]

gateway [It is characteristic of Hindu architecture] · Torbau m

~, pylon [The mass of masonry with central opening, forming a monumental entrance to Egyptian temples] · Pylon(e) m, (f)

~, carriage gate [The way through a gate] · Torweg m

~ · Portalbau m

~ **arch** · Torbogen m

Gateway of the Sun at Tiahuanaco · Sonnentor n zur Tiahuanaco

gate(way) of triumph, triumphal gate(-way) · Triumphtor n

gate(way) tower · (Burg)Torturm m

gathering bubble · Schöpfblase f, Stichblase [Glas]

to gauge (Brit.); to gage (US); to batch, to proportion, to measure · abmessen, zumessen, zuteilen, dosieren

gauge; gage (US); thickness of ~ · Dicke f [Linoleum]

~ **(No.)**; gage (~) (US); ~ number, sheet ~ (~) · (Blech)Lehrennummer f

gauge system; gage ~ (US); sheet ~ ~ · (Blech)Lehre f

gauged arch, bonded ~; gaged ~ (US) · Keilziegelbogen m, Wölbziegelbogen

gauged brick arch (Brit.) → ~ clay ~ ~

~ **brickwork**; gaged ~ (US) [Brickwork with fine joints and in which the bricks are cut and rubbed to the required size and shape] · Maßmauerwerk n

~ **(clay) brick** (Brit.) → arch ~

~ **mortar** (Brit.); gaged ~ (US); cement/lime/sand ~, cement-lime ~, lime-and-cement ~, compo (~), lean ~ · Kalkzementmörtel m, Zementkalkmörtel, Magermörtel, verlängerter Zementmörtel

gauged stuff, gauging plaster; gaged stuff, gaging plaster (US) · Kalkgipsputz m

gauging, soaking · Einsumpfen n [Kalkteig]

~ **board**; gaging ~ (US) · Mischbrett n

~ **box**, batch ~; gaging ~ (US) · Zumeßkiste f

~ **period**, ~ time, soaking ~ · Einsumpfdauer f, Einsumpfzeit f [Kalkteig]

~ **plaster**, gauged stuff; gaging plaster, gaged stuff (US) · Kalkgipsputz m

~ **time**, ~ period, soaking ~ · Einsumpfdauer f, Einsumpfzeit f [Kalkteig]

~ **water** (Brit.) → mix(ing) ~

Gaussian curvature · Gaußsche Krümmung f

gauze · Gaze f

gazebo → belvedere

GB → glass block

GCI → gray cast iron

gel · Gel n [Gallertartig erstarrte kolloidale Lösung]

~ **condition**, ~ state · Gelzustand m

~ **formation** → gelling

~ **gel particle** · Gelteilchen n

~ **pore** · Gelpore f

~ **state**, ~ condition · Gelzustand m

~ **strength** · Gelfestigkeit f

~ **structure** · Gelstruktur f

~ **water** · Gelwasser n

gelatin(e) · Gelatine f

gelati(nitati)on → gelling

gelatinization → gelling

gelatinizing → gelling

gelation → gelling

gel-like · vergelt, gelartig

~ **compound** · gelartige Verbindung f, vergelte ~

gelling, gel formation, gelatinizing, gelati(nitati)on, livering, gelatinization [The congulation of a finishing material into a viscous rubber-like mass] · Gelieren n, Gelbildung f, Gelatinierung

gemel window, two-light ~ · Zwillingsfenster n, zweiteiliges Fenster

general acceptability criterion, ~ acceptance ~ · allgemeines Abnahmemerkmal n, allgemeiner Abnahmebewertungsmaßstab m

~ **acceptance criterion**, ~ acceptability ~ · allgemeines Abnahmemerkmal n, allgemeiner Abnahmebewertungsmaßstab m

~ **contractor** · Generalunternehmer m

~ **contractor's fixed price offer** (Brit.); ~ ~ ~ ~ bid (US) · Generalunternehmer-Festpreis-Angebot n

~ ~ **order** · Generalunternehmerauftrag m

~ **diffuse luminaire (fixture)** (US); ~ ~ light fitting (Brit.); ~ ~ (light(-ing)) fixture · freistrahlende Leuchte f, freistrahlender Beleuchtungskörper m

~ **drawing** · Einzelplan m, Einzelzeichnung f

~ **foreman** [He has control over all the workmen, or charge hands, who have control over groups of tradesmen] · Oberpolier m, Oberschachtmeister m

General Post Office · Hauptpostamt n

general public room — Georgian glass 438

general public room · Gesellschaftsraum m, Gesellschaftszimmer n [Hotel]
~ purpose adhesive → ~ ~ bonding ~
~ ~ (bonding) adhesive, ~ ~ ~ agent, ~ ~ ~ medium, ~ ~ cement(ing agent) · Allzweckkleber m, Allzweckkleb(e)stoff m, Allzweckkleb(e)mittel n
~ ~ ~ agent → ~ ~ (~) adhesive
~ ~ ~ medium → ~ ~ ~ (~) adhesive
~ ~ (burnt) (clay) brick, ~ ~ burned (~) ~, ~ ~ ~ fired (~) ~ [See remark under 'Ziegel'] · Allzweck(ton)ziegel m, gebrannter Allzweckstein m
~ ~ cement(ing agent) → ~ ~ ~ (bonding) adhesive
~ ~ (clay) brick → ~ ~ ~ burnt (~) ~
~ ~ fired (clay) brick → ~ ~ ~ (burnt) (~) ~
~ ~ varnish · Allzwecklack m
~ service paint · Gebrauchs(anstrich)farbe f
~ store · Hauptmagazin n
~ supply · Allgemeinversorgung f
general-use building paper, asphalt ~ ~ (US); (asphaltic-)bitumen ~ ~ (Brit.) [See remark under 'Pappe'] · Asphaltbaupappe f, Bitumenbaupappe
~ paper, sheathing ~, building ~ [See remark under 'Pappe'] · Baupappe f
~ ~ → (waterproof) sheathing ~
generalization · Verallgemeinerung f
generalizing · Verallgemeinern n
generating bubbles of gas, gasforming · gasbildend, gasentwickelnd [Gasbeton]
~ line, generatrix (Brit.); generator (US) · Erzeugende f, erzeugende Linie f
~ of steam → steam generation
generation of heat (during set(ting)) · Wärmeentwick(e)lung f [Zement]
~ ~ steam → steam generation
generator (US); generatrix, generating line (Brit.) · Erzeugende f, erzeugende Linie f
~ ash, gas ~ ~ · (Gas)Generatorasche f
~ building · Generatorgebäude n, Generatorhaus n
~ cinder → gas ~ ~
~ clinker (Brit.) → (gas) generator cinder
~ floor · Maschinenflur m [Krafthaus]
~ room · Generatorraum m
generatrix, generating line (Brit.); generator (US) · Erzeugende f, erzeugende Linie f
generous flowing lines · großzügig fließende Konturen fpl
gently modulated profile · elastische Linienführung f
geodesic cupola, geodetic ~, ~ dome · geodätische Kuppel f, halbsphärisches geodätisches Gewölbe n

~ dome, geodetic ~, ~ cupola · geodätische Kuppel f, halbsphärisches geodätisches Gewölbe n
~ structure, geodetic ~ · geodätisches Bauwerk n
geodetic cupola → geodesic ~
~ dome → geodesic ~
~ head, energy of position, potential energy, position energy [It is the energy possessed by a body in virtue of its position relative to some zero position] · Potential n, Energie f der Lage, potentielle Energie, latente Energie
~ structure → geodesic ~
geographic location · geographische Lage f
(geometric) figure · (geometrische) Figur f
geometrical canon · Teilungskanon m
Geometric(al) Decorated style [The first phase of the 'Middle Pointed' or 'Decorated' Period of English Gothic architecture, in which the tracery consists of strictly geometrical forms and has not yet become 'flowing'] · geometrischer Dekorationsstil m
geometric(al) drawing · geometrische Zeichnung f
~ funicular form · geometrische Seillinienform f
Geometric(al) Gothic (style) · geometrische Gotik f
geometric(al) grid system for bay-type horizontal load collection · Grundriß-Rastersystem n für horizontale Lastenbündelung
~ mean · geometrisches Mittel n
~ motif · geometrisches Motiv n
~ ornament · geometrische Verzierung f, geometrisches Ornament n
~ pattern · mathematische Figur f, geometrisches Muster n
~ shape · geometrische Form f
~ stair(case) [A stair(case) having a continuous handrail and string; usually planned around a semicircular or elliptical well] · gerundete Treppe f, gewundene ~
Geometric(al) Style → Curvilinear ~
geometric(al) tracery · geometrisches Maßwerk n
geometrically progressing series · geometrisch gestufte (Sieb)Reihe f, geometrische Abstufung f der Maschenweiten
~ shaped · geometrisch geformt
(~) true pyramid [As opposed to the step pyramid] · eigentliche Pyramide f [Im Gegensatz zur Stufenpyramide]
geometry of cables, cable geometry · Seilstatik f
~ ~ shells · Schalengeometrie f
Georgian glass · Drahtglas n mit quadratischen Maschen

Georgian style — girder grid

~ **style** [*A term applied to English Late Renaissance architecture of the period 1702–1830*] · georgianischer Stil *m*

Gerber girder, hinged ~; slung span continuous beam (Brit.) · Gelenkträger *m*, Gerberträger

~ **hinge** · Gerbergelenk *n*, Gerbersches Gelenk

~ **lattice(d) girder**, hinge(d) ~ ~; slung span continuous lattic(d) beam (Brit.) · Gerbergitterträger *m*, Gelenkgitterträger

~ **purlin(e)** · Gerberpfette *f*

Gerber's diagram of moments · Gerbersche Momentenfläche *f*

German Baroque · deutscher Barock *m*

~ **black (pigment)**, Frankfort ~ (~) [*A variety of bone black*] · Samtschwarz *n*, Frankfurterschwarz

~ **brick architecture** · deutsche Backsteinarchitektur *f*, ~ Backsteinbaukunst *f*

~ **Gothic** · deutsche Gotik *f*

~ **Late Gothic (style)**, particularistic Gothic · (deutsche) Sondergotik *f*

~ **(oil of) turpentine**, ~ spirit ~ ~ · deutsches Terpentinöl *n*

~ **Renaissance** · deutsche Renaissance *f*

~ **silver**, nickel ~ [*Not to be confused with nickel silver (US) = Nickelbronze*] · Neusilber *n*

~ **spirit of turpentine**, ~ (oil ~) ~ · deutsches Terpentinöl *n*

~ **turpentine**, ~ oil of ~, ~ spirit of ~ · deutsches Terpentinöl *n*

germ-free · keimfrei, steril

germicidal · keimtötend

geyser → instantaneous (gas) water heater

geyserite, (silicious) sinter, siliceous sinter · (Kiesel)Sinter *m*

GG, glass for glazing, glazing glass [*B.S. 952*] · Glas *n* für Verglasung, ~ ~ Einglasung, Verglasungsglas, Einlasungsglas

ghost marking · Schmutzfahne *f* [*An hellen Wand- und Deckenflächen infolge ungleichen Wärmeschutzes in den betreffenden Zonen*]

giant head · riesiger Kopf *m*

~ **order (of architecture)**, grand ~ (~ ~), colossal ~ (~ ~) · große Ordnung *f*, Riesenordnung, Kolossalordnung [*Eine Ordnung bei der die Pilaster oder Säulen über mehrere Geschosse reichen und sie somit zusammenfassen*]

gib door, jib ~, secret ~, concealed ~ [*A door whose face is flush with the wall and decorated so as to be as little seen as possible*] · Geheimtür *f*, Tapetentür

gibbsite, hydrargillite [*1. A trihydrate of alumina, $Al_2O_3 \cdot 3H_2O$. 2. A rock containing a major proportion of this mineral*] · Gibbsit *m*, Hydrargillit *m*

~ **refractory (product)**, ~ ~ material · Gibbsiterzeugnis *n* [*Vorwiegend aus Gibbsit hergestelltes feuerfestes Erzeugnis mit hohem Tonerdegehalt*]

gigantomachy [*of the Altar of Zeus at Pergamon*] · Gigantomachie *f*

gilded, gold plated · vergoldet

gilding, gold plating · Vergoldung *f*

~, gold plating · Vergolden *n*

gilled heater → grilled ~

~ **heating tube** → grilled ~ ~

~ **tube** → grilled ~

~ ~ **heater** → fin(ned) ~ ~

~ ~ **radiator** → fin(ned) tube heater

Gillmore apparatus, ~ needles · Nadelgerät *n* nach Gillmore

gilsonite, uintaite · Gilsonitasphalt *m*, Uintait *m*

girder · Träger *m* [*Jeder Balken ist ein Träger, aber jeder Träger ist nicht notwendigerweise ein Balken: denn es gibt Balken(träger) und Bogen(träger)*]

~ **action** · Trägerwirkung *f*

~ **beam** → broad-flange(d) ~

~ **bearing** · Trägerlager *n*

~ **boom**, ~ flange, ~ chord · Trägergurt(ung) *m*, (*f*), Trägerflansch *m*

~ **bottom boom**, ~ ~ flange, ~ ~ chord, ~ lower ~ · Trägeruntergurt(ung) *m*, (*f*), Trägerunterflansch *m*

~ ~ **chord**, ~ ~ flange, ~ ~ boom, ~ lower ~ · Trägeruntergurt(ung) *m*, (*f*), Trägerunterflansch *m*

~ ~ **flange**, ~ ~ chord, ~ ~ boom, ~ lower ~ · Trägeruntergurt(ung) *m*, (*f*), Trägerunterflansch *m*

~ **casing** · Trägerummantelung *f*

~ **chord**, ~ boom, ~ flange · Trägergurt(ung) *m*, (*f*), Trägerflansch *m*

~ **connection**, ~-to-column ~ · Trägeranschluß *m*, Trägerverbindung *f*

~ ~ **at an angle** · spitze Trägerverbindung *f*, spitzer Trägeranschluß *m*

~ **construction**, ~ (structural) system · Träger(bau)system *n*, Trägerkonstruktion(ssystem) *f*, (*n*)

~ **cross section** · Trägerquerschnitt *m*

~ **depth** · Trägerhöhe *f*

~ **design formula** · Trägerbemessungsformel *f*

~ **element** · Trägerelement *n*

~ **(en)casing block** · Anfängerstein *m*, Trägerummantelungstein [*Steineisendecke*]

~ **fixed at both ends** → built-in girder

~ **flange**, ~ chord, ~ boom · Trägergurt(ung) *m*, (*f*), Trägerflansch *m*

~ **floor** · Plattendecke *f* zwischen Trägern, Trägerdecke [*Geeignete Bauplatten für Trägerdecken sind Hourdiplatten, bewehrte Schwerbetonplatten und bewehrte Leichtbetonplatten*]

~ **grid** · Trägerraster *m*

girder grid — glass-block partition (wall)

~ ~, ~ grill(ag)e · (Träger)Kreuzwerk n, (Träger)Rost m

~ ~ system · Trägerrastersystem n

~ grill(ag)e, ~ grid · (Träger)Kreuzwerk n, (Träger)Rost m

~ grille, ~ grillage, ~ grid · (Träger-)Kreuzwerk n, (Träger)Rost m

~ interval, ~ spacing, distance between girders · Trägerabstand m

~ joint · Trägerstoß m

girderless · trägerfrei, trägerlos

~ floor · trägerfreie Decke f, trägerlose ~ [*Eine Pilzdecke mit oder ohne Stützenköpfe. Eine letztere heißt Flachdecke*]

girder load moment · Trägerlastmoment n

~ loading · Trägerbelastung f

~ lower boom → ~ bottom ~

~ ~ chord → ~ bottom ~

~ ~ flange → ~ bottom ~

~ manufacture · Trägerherstellung f

~ material · Trägerwerkstoff m

~ of one bay → single-span girder

~ ~ ~ span → single-span girder

~ restraint provided by walls with openings · Trägereinspannungen *fpl* durch Wände

~ roof · Trägerdach n

~ section · Trägerprofil n

~ simply supported at one end and fixed at the other; propped cantilever girder (US) · einseitig eingespannter und einseitig freiauffliegender Träger m

~ spacing, ~ interval, distance between girders · Trägerabstand m

~ span · Trägerfeld n, Trägeröffnung f

~ (structural) system, ~ construction · Träger(bau)system n, Trägerkonstruktion(ssystem) f, (n)

~ subjected to bending · Biegeträger m

~ support · Trägerauflager n

~ system, ~ structural ~, ~ construction · Träger(bau)system n, Trägerkonstruktion(ssystem) f, (n)

~(-to-column) connection ·Trägeranschluß m, Trägerverbindung f

girder top boom, ~ ~ flange, ~ ~ chord, ~ upper ~ · Trägerobergurt(ung), m, (f), Trägeroberflansch m

~ ~ chord, ~ ~ boom, ~ ~ flange, ~ upper ~ · Trägerobergurt(ung) m, (f), Trägeroberflansch m

~ ~ flange, ~ ~ chord, ~ ~ boom, ~ upper ~ · Trägerobergurt(ung) m, (f), Trägeroberflansch m

~ upper boom → ~ top ~

~ ~ chord → ~ top ~

~ ~ flange → ~ top ~

~ wall · Trägerwand f

girls' gymnasium · Mädchenturnhalle

girt, plate [*A rail or intermediate beam in wooden-framed buildings, often carrying floor joists*] · Brustschwelle f, Sattelschwelle, Saumschwelle, Setzschwelle

to give a decorative finish, to pattern · ornamentieren, mustern

~ ~ off, to throw ~ [*heat*] · abgeben [*Wärme*]

gl → gloss

~ → glass

~ → glaze(d finish)

glacial acetic acid · Eisessigsäure f

glance pitch · Glanzpech n, Maniak n

glare, glr · Blendung f

~ control · Abblenden n

~ ~ · Abblendung f

glare-free, glare-reducing, glareless, dazzle-free, anti-dazzle; non-glare (US) · abblendend, blend(ungs)frei

~ glass, anti-dazzle ~, dazzle-free ~, glare-reducing ~; non-glare ~ (US) · abblendendes Glas n, Blendschutzglas

glare-reducing, anti-dazzle, dazzle-free, glareless, glare-free; non-glare (US) · abblendend, blend(ungs)frei

~ glass, dazzle-free ~, glare-free ~, anti-dazzle ~; non-glare ~ (US) · abblendendes Glas n, Blendschutzglas

glass, gl [*An inorganic product of fusion which has cooled to a rigid condition without crystallizing*] · Glas n

~ abrasive paper → ~ (sand)paper

~ aggregate · Glaszuschlag(stoff) m

~-and-metal style · Glas- und Metallstil m

glass appliance · Glasgerät n

~ architecture · Glasarchitektur f, Glasbaukunst f

~ area, window ~ ~ · Glasfläche f, Lichtfläche, Scheibenfläche [*Fenster*]

~-balustrade escalator, crystalator · Glas-Rolltreppe f

glass bar, ~ rod · Glasstange f, Glasstab m [*Verwendung als Handtuchhalter, Haltestangen im Bad und Schutzstangen an Glastüren*]

(~) batch, (~) charge, (batch) mix(-ture) · Glasgemenge n, Glasmischung f, Schmelzsatz m

~ block, ~ brick, GB · Glas(bau)stein m; Glasziegel m [*Fehlname*] [*DIN 18175*]

glass-block floor, glass-brick ~ · Glas(bau)steindecke f [*Decke aus Glasprismen, zwischen denen Stahlbetonrippen angeordnet sind*]

~ masonry (work), glass-brick ~ (~) · Glas(bau)steinmauerwerk n

~ panel, glass-brick ~; structural glass ~ · Glas(bau)steintafel f

~ partition (wall), glass-brick ~ (~) · Glas(bau)steinwand f [*DIN 4242*]

glass-block roof-light — glass fibre formwork

~ **roof-light,** glass-brick ~ · Glas(bau)stein(dach)oberlicht *n*

~ ~ **panel,** glass-brick ~ ~ · Glas(bau)stein-(Dach)Oberlichttafel *f*

~ **skylight,** glass-brick ~ · Glas(bau)stein-(Dach)Raupe *f*

~ **window,** glass-brick ~ · Glas(bau)steinfenster *n*

glass blocks, ~ bricks; structural glass (US) · Glas(bau)steine *mpl*

~ **blowing** · Glasblasen *n*

~ **box** [*A frequent feature in houses designed by Mies van der Rohe*] · Glaskasten *m*

~ **brick** → ~ block

~ **bricks,** ~ blocks; structural glass (US) · Glas(bau)steine *mpl*

~ **(building) component** → ~ (~) unit

~ **(~) member** → ~ (~) unit

~ **(~) unit,** ~ (~) component, ~ (~) member · Glas(bau)körper *m*, Glas(bau)element *n* [*Fehlname: Glasbaueinheit f*]

~ **cassette** → ~ core

~ **cell** · Glaszelle *f*

(~) charge, (~) batch, (batch) mix(ture) · Schmelzsatz *m*, Glasgemenge *n*, Glasmischung *f*

~ **church** · Glaskirche *f*

~-**clad,** glass-enclosed · umglast, eingeglast, glasumgeben

glass clear · glasklar

~ **coffer** → ~ core

~ ~ · Steinhälfte *f* [*Glas(bau)stein*]

~ **component** → ~ (building) unit

~ **concrete,** reinforced ~ ~ · Glasstahlbeton *m* [*DIN 4229*]

~ ~ → translucent ~

~ ~ **bearing structure** → (reinforced) glass concrete (load)bearing ~

~ ~ **block,** ~ ~ brick · Glasbetonstein *m* [*Gepreßter Glaskörper für den Einbau in Tragwerke aus Glasstahlbeton oder verglaste Stahlbetongerippe*]

~ ~ **construction** → (reinforced) glass concrete (structural) system

~ ~ **floor,** translucent ~ ~ · Glasbetondecke *f*

~ ~ ~, reinforced ~ ~ ~ · Glasstahlbetondecke *f*

~ ~ **(load)bearing structure** → reinforced ~ ~ ~ ~

~ ~ **plank,** reinforced ~ ~ ~ · Glasstahlbetondiele *f*

~ ~ **rooflight,** reinforced ~ ~ ~ · Glasstahlbeton(-Dach)oberlicht *n*

~ ~ **(structural) system** → reinforced ~ ~ (~) ~

~ ~ **supporting structure** → (reinforced) glass concrete (load)bearing ~

~ ~ **system** → (reinforced) glass concrete (structural) ~

~ ~ **window,** translucent ~ · Glasbetonfenster *n*

~ **construction,** ~ system · Glaskonstruktion *f*

~ **core,** ~ waffle, ~ pan(el), ~ coffer, ~ cassette · Glaskassette *f*

~ **corridor,** glazed ~ · Glasflur *m*, Glasgang *m*, Glaskorridor *m*

~ **counter ceiling** · Glasunterdecke *f*

~ **cupola,** ~ dome · Glaskuppel *f*

~ **curtain wall** · Glasvorhangwand *f*

~ **curved in two planes** · bombiertes Glas *n*, gewölbtes ~

~ **cutter** · Glasschneider *m*

~ **dome,** ~ cupola · Glaskuppel *f*

~ **domed roof-light,** ~ dome(light), ~ light cupola, ~ saucer dome · Glas-(Dach)Lichtkuppel *f*, Glas-Oberlichtkuppel

~ **dome(light),** ~ saucer dome, ~ light-cupola, ~ domed roof-light · Glas-(Dach)Lichtkuppel *f*, Glas-Oberlichtkuppel

~ **door** · Glastür *f*

~ ~ **control** · Glastürsteuerung *f*

~ **dust** → ~ powder

~ **edge sealed glazing unit** [*The two sheets of glass fused together at their edges enclose an air space*] · Glasverbundrand-Verglasungseinheit *f*

~-**enclosed** · glasumgeben, umglast

glass façade · Glasfassade *f*

glass-façade block, ~ building · Glasfassadengebäude *n*

glass face work, ~ facing · Glasverblendung *f*

~ **facing,** ~ face work · Glasverblendung *f*

~ **fibered plaster** (US); ~ fibred ~ (Brit.) · Glasfaser(ver)putz *m*

~ **fibre** (Brit.); ~ fiber (US) · Glasfaser *f*

~ ~ **acoustic(al) ceiling** (Brit.); ~ fiber ~ ~ (US) · Glasfaser-Schallschluckdecke *f*, Glasfaser-Akustikdecke

~ ~ **bar** (Brit.) → ~ ~ rod

~ ~ **based strip** (Brit.); ~ fiber ~ ~ (US) · Glasfaserband *n*

~ ~ **beam mould** (Brit.); ~ fiber beam mold (US) · Glasfaser-Balkenform *f*

~ ~ **board,** ~ ~ slab, ~ ~ sheet (Brit.); ~ fiber ~ (US) · Glasfaserplatte *f*

~ ~ **covering cord** (Brit.); ~ fiber ~ (US) · Glasfaserschnur *f* [*für Dämm- und Isolierzwecke*]

~ ~ **facing unit** (Brit.) → ~ ~ ~ surfacing ~

~ ~ **formwork,** ~ ~ shuttering, ~ ~ forms (Brit.); ~ fiber ~ (US) · Glasfaserschalung *f*

glass fibre insulating slab — 'Glass House'

~ ~ **insulating slab** (Brit.); ~ fiber ~ ~ (US); ~ ~ insulation(-grade) ~ · Glasfaserdämmplatte f

~ ~ **insulation** (Brit.); ~ fiber ~ (US)· Glasfaserdämmung f

~ ~ **joint runner** (Brit.) → ~ ~ seal(-ing) rope

~ ~ **lining unit** (Brit.) → ~ ~ (sur-)facing ~

~ ~ **mould**, reinforced ~ ~ ~ (Brit.); (reinforced) glass fiber mold (US) · Glasfaserform f

~ ~ **pipe** (Brit.); ~ fiber ~ (US) · Glasfaserrohr n

~ ~ **plastic panel** (Brit.) → ~ fibre-reinforced ~ ~

~ ~ **polyester** (Brit.) → ~ fibre(-reinforced) ~

~ ~ **pouring rope** (Brit.) → ~ ~ ~ seal(-ing) ~

~ ~ **product** (Brit.); ~ fiber ~ (US) · Glasfasererzeugnis n

~ **fibre-reinforced** (Brit.); ~ fiberreinforced (US) · glasfaserverstärkt, glasfaserarmiert

~ **fibre(-reinforced) concrete pipe** (Brit.); ~ fiber(-reinforced) ~ ~ (US) · glasfaserverstärktes Betonrohr n

~ ~ **plastic** (Brit.) → ~ reinforced laminate

~ ~ ~ **panel** (Brit.); ~ fiber(-reinforced) ~ ~ (US); ~ resin ~ · glasfaserverstärkte Kunststofftafel f, ~ Kunstharztafel f, GFK-Tafel

~ ~ ~ **profile**, ~ ~ ~ shape, ~ ~ ~ trim, ~ ~ ~ section, ~ ~ ~ unit (Brit.); ~ glass-fiber (-reinforced) ~ ~ (US) · GFK-Profil n, glasfaserverstärktes Kunststoffprofil

~ ~ ~ **roof(ing) slab** (Brit.); ~ fiber(-reinforced) ~ ~ ~ (US) · GFK-Dachplatte f, glasfaserverstärkte Kunststoffdachplatte

~ ~ ~ **sheet**, ~ ~ ~ board (Brit.); ~ fiber(-reinforced) ~ ~ (US); grp ~, GRP ~ · glasfaserverstärkte Kunststoffplatte f, GFK-Platte

~ ~ **polyester** (Brit.); ~ fiber(-reinforced) ~ ~ (US); GRP · glasfaserverstärkter Polyester m, glasfaserverstärktes Polyesterharz n, GP

~ ~ **resin panel** (Brit.) → ~ ~ ~ plastic ~

~ ~ **(synthetic) resin** (Brit.); ~ fiber(-reinforced) (~) ~ (US) · glasfaserverstärktes Kunstharz n

~ ~ **unsaturated polyester** (Brit.); ~ fiber(-reinforced) ~ ~ (US) · glasfaserverstärkter ungesättigter Polyester m, glasfaserverstärktes ungesättigtes Polyesterharz n, GUP

~ **fibre reinforcement** (Brit.); ~ fiber ~ (US) · Glasfaserarmierung f, Glasfaserverstärkung

~ ~ **resin panel** (Brit.) → ~ ~ fibre(-reinforced) plastic ~

~ ~ **rod** (Brit.); ~ fiber ~ (US); ~ ~ bar · Glasfaserstab m, Glasfaserstange f

~ ~ **rope** (Brit.); ~ fiber ~ (US) · Glasfaserstrick m

~ ~ **seal(ing) rope**, ~ ~ pouring ~, ~ ~ joint runner (Brit.); glass-fiber ~ ~ (US) · Glasfaser-(Ab)Dicht(ungs)-strick m, Glasfaserstrick

~ ~ **sheet** (Brit.) → ~ ~ board

~ ~ **shuttering** (Brit.) → ~ ~ formwork

~ ~ **slab** (Brit.) → ~ ~ board

~ ~ **(sur)facing unit**, ~ ~ lining ~ (Brit.); ~ fiber ~ ~ (US) · Glasfaser-Auskleidungselement n, Glasfaser-Verkleidungselement, Glasfaser-Bekleidungselement

~ ~ **technique** (Brit.); ~ fiber ~ (US) · Glasfasertechnik f

~ **filaments** → long glass fibres

~ **fittings** → builders' ~ ~

~ **flake** · Glasplättchen n

~ **flask** · Glaskolben m

~ **floor cover(ing)**, ~ ~ finish, ~ flooring · Glas(fuß)boden(belag) m

~ ~ **finish**, ~ ~ cover(ing), ~ flooring · Glas(fuß)boden(belag) m

~ **flooring**, ~ floor cover(ing), ~ floor finish · Glas(fuß)boden(belag) m

~ ~ **tile** · Glas(fuß)boden(belag)platte f, Glas(fuß)bodenfliese f

~ **flour** → ~ powder

~ **flushing tank**, ~ ~ cistern, ~ water waste preventer · Glasspülkasten m [Abort]

~ **for glazing**, glazing glass, GG [B.S. 952] · Glas n für Verglasung, ~ ~ Einglasung, Verglasungsglas, Einglasungsglas

~ ~ **X-ray rooms**, X-ray protective glass, X-ray shielding glass [Glass which contains a high percentage of lead and sometimes also barium and which has a high degree of opacity to X-rays. The opacity is usually expressed in terms of the thickness of metallic lead which would give equal absorption of X-rays of stated wavelength] · Röntgen(strahlen)schutzglas n

~ **former** · Glasbildner m

~ **forming oxide** (Brit.); ~ ~ oxid(e) (US) · glasbildendes Oxid n

~ **fragment** · Glasbruchstück n

~ **gutter** → ~ roof ~

~ **hardware** → (builder's) glass fittings

(~) **heating pane**, heating glass ~ · Heizglasscheibe f, heizbare Glasscheibe

~ ~ **panel**, radiant-heating ~, electrically heated glass ~ · strahlungsheizende Glastafel f

'**Glass House**' [by Bruno Taut] · Glashaus n [von Bruno Taut]

'**Glass House**' [Designed by Philip Johnson for himself in 1949, it is composed of a glass 'box', a brick 'box' and a pool diagonally opposed to one another and set in a park-like landscape] · Glashaus n

glass-house — glass tinted by impurities

glass-house, greenhouse · Gewächshaus *n* [*DIN 11535 Bl. 1*]

to glass-in, to glaze · einglasen, verglasen

glass insert · Glaseinsatz *m*

~ **jalousie** (US); ~ **louvre,** ~ **louver** · Glasjalousie *f*

~ **knob,** door ~ ~ · (Tür)Glasknopf *m*

~ **letter** · Glasbuchstabe *m*

~ **light cupola,** ~ dome(light), ~ saucer dome, ~ domed roof-light · Glas(-Dach)Lichtkuppel *f*, Glas-Oberlichtkuppel

~-**lined pipe** · glasausgekleidetes Rohr *n*

glass lookout area, ~ **viewing** ~, ~ **observation** ~ · Glasaussichtsfläche *f*

~ **louver,** ~ louvre; ~ jalousie (US) · Glasjalousie *f*

~ **(-making) sand** · Glassand *m*, Schmelzsand

glass melt · Glasschmelze *f*

~ **melted from cullet** · Scherbenglas *n*

~ **member** → ~ (building) unit

~ **mosaic** · Glasmosaik *n*

~ **observation area,** ~ viewing ~, ~ lookout ~ · Glasaussichtsfläche *f*

~ **painter** · Glasmaler *m*

~ **painting** · Glasmalerei *f*

'Glass Palace' [*Department store in Helsinki designed by Revell and two associates*] · „Glaspalast" *m*

glass pane, square, pane (of glass) [*A piece of glass cut to size and shape ready for glazing*] · (Glas)Scheibe *f*

~ **pan(el)** → ~ core

~ **panel** · Glasfüllung *f* [*Tür*]

~ **paper** → ~ sand~

~ **parapet slab** · Glas-Brüstungsplatte *f*, Brüstungs-Glasplatte

~ **partition (wall),** glazed ~ (~) · verglaste Trennwand *f*, Glastrennwand

~ **patio** → ~ terrace

~ **pipe** · Glasrohr *n*

~ **pipeline** [*B.S. 2598*] · Glasrohrleitung *f*

~ **plate,** ~ slab · Glasplatte *f*

~ **powder,** ~ flour, ~ dust, ground glass, powder(ed) glass · Glaspulver *n*, Glasmehl *n*, Glaspuder *n*, Glasstaub *m*

~-**pumice concrete plank** · Glasstahlbimsbetondiele *f*

glass rainwater gutter, ~ (roof) ~ · Glas(dach)rinne *f*, Glasregenrinne

~ **reinforced laminate,** fibrous glass reinforced plastic; glass fiber reinforced plastic, fiberglass reinforced plastic (US); glass fibre reinforced plastic (Brit.); FRP, GRP, grp · Glasfaserkunststoff *m*, GFK, Glasfaserschichtstoff, glasfaserverstärkter Kunststoff

~ ~ **plastic** → ~ ~ laminate

~ **rest** [*A device upon which a piece of glass rests*] · Glasauflage *f*

~ **rod** → ~ bar

~ **roof cladding,** glazed ~ ~, ~ ~ cover(ing), ~ ~ sheathing, ~ roofing · Glasbedachung *f*, Glaseindeckung, Glasdachdeckung, Glasdach(belag) *n*, (*m*), Glas(dachein)deckung

~ **(~) gutter,** ~ rainwater ~ · Glas(dach)rinne *f*, Glasregenrinne

~ **(roof)) tile,** ~ slate · Glasdachstein *m* [*Fehlname: Glasdachziegel m*]

~ ~ **with patent glazing bars,** ~ ~ ~ puttyless ~ ~ · Sprossenglasdach *n*

~ **roundle** · Butzenscheibe *f*

~ **sand,** ~-making ~ · Glassand *m*, Schmelzsand

~ **(sand)paper,** ~ sanding paper, ~ abrasive paper · Glaspapier *n* [*Mit Glaspulver belegtes Schleifpapier in verschiedenen Graden von feinkörnig bis grobkörnig*]

~ **saucer dome,** ~ dome(light), ~ light cupola, ~ domed roof-light · Glas-(Dach)Lichtkuppel *f*, Glas-Oberlichtkuppel

~ **sheet** · Glastafel *f*

~ **side panel** · Glasseitenwand *f* [*Leuchte*]

(~) **silk** → long glass fibres

(~) ~ **wall lining,** (~) ~ ~ (sur-)facing, (~) ~ ~ cover(ing), spun glass ~ ~ · Glasgespinst-Wandauskleidung *f*, Glasgespinst-Wandverkleidung, Glasgespinst-Wandbelag *m*, Glasgespinst-Wandbekleidung

~ **skylight** · Glas(-Dach)raupe *f*

~ **skyscraper** · Glaswolkenkratzer *m*

~ **slab,** ~ plate · Glasplatte *f*

~ **slate,** ~ (roof(ing)) tile · Glasdachstein *m* [*Fehlname: Glasdachziegel m*]

~ ~ **roof,** ~ tile ~ · Glassteindach *n* [*Fehlname: Glasziegeldach*]

~ **sliding door,** sliding glass ~ · Glasschiebetür *f*, Schiebeglastür

~ **splinter** · Glassplitter *m*

~ **staple fibre yarn** (Brit.); ~ ~ fiber ~ (US) · Glasstapelfasergarn *n*

~ **strip for outlining patterns** · Glas-Terrazzoschiene *f*, Glas-Terrazzostreifen *m*

~ **substitute** · Glasersatz *m*

~ **swing door** · Glas-Pendeltür *f*, Pendeltür aus Glas, Glas-Schwingflügeltür, Schwingflügeltür aus Glas

~ **system,** ~ construction · Glaskonstruktion *f*

~ **technology** · Glastechnologie *f*

~ **terrace,** glazed ~, ~ patio · Glasterrasse *f*

~ **tile** · Glas(belag)platte *f*, Glasfliese *f* [*DIN 18170. Fehlname: Glasprisma n*]

~ ~ → ~ roof(ing) ~

~ ~ **roof,** ~ slate ~ · Glassteindach *n* [*Fehlname: Glasziegeldach*]

~ **tinted by impurities** · halbweißes Glas *n*

glass tissue — glazed look-out platform

~ **tissue** · Glasgewebe n [*Nicht verwechseln mit „Glasvlies"*]

~ ~ **sheet(ing)** · Glasgewebebahn f

glass-to-metal seal · dichte Verbindung f von Glas mit Metall

glass tower · Glasturm m

~ **-tube fenestration** · Fensterbänder npl aus Glasröhren

glass unit → ~ building ~

~ **vault** · Glasgewölbe n

~ **viewing area**, ~ observation ~, ~ lookout ~ · Glasaussichtsfläche f

~ **wadding** · Glaswatte f

~ **waffle** → ~ core

~ **wall** · (Bau)Glaswand f

~ ~ **panel** · Glaswandtafel f

~ ~ **system** · Glaswand(-Konstruktions)system n

~ ~ **tile** · Glaswand(belag)platte f, Glaswandfliese f

~ **wall(ing) (building) unit**, ~ ~ (~) member, ~ ~ (~) component · Wand-Glas(bau)element n, Wand-Glas(bau)körper m [*Fehlnamen: Wandglas(bau)einheit f, Glaswandmontageeinheit*]

~ **water waste preventer** → ~ flushing tank

~ **window** · Glasfenster n

~ **with applied threads** · Glas n mit Fadenauflage, umsponnenes Glas

~ ~ **cords**, ~ ~ heavy ~ · rampiges Glas n

~ ~ **grey blibe**, ~ ~ gray ~ · galliges Glas n [*Flachglasfehler*]

~ ~ **(heavy) cords** · rampiges Glas n

~ ~ **reams** · schlieriges Glas n

~ ~ **wavy cords** · windiges Glas n

~ **wool**, fibrous glass; fibered glass (US) [*The word 'Fiberglas' is a registered trade name, and it should not be used indiscriminately*] · Glaswolle f

~ ~ **insulation**, ~ ~ lagging, fibrous glass ~ · Glaswolledämmung f

~ ~ **lagging** → ~ ~ insulation

~ ~ **mat (for building purposes)**, ~ ~ (~ construction ~) · Glaswolle-(Bau)matte f

~ ~ **strip**, fibrous glass ~ · Glaswollestreifen m

glassed-in, glazed · eingeglast, verglast

~ **area**, glazed ~ · eingeglaste Fläche f, verglaste ~

~ **lookout deck** → ~ observation ~

~ ~ **platform** → ~ observation deck

~ **observation deck**, glazed ~ ~, viewing ~, ~ lookout ~, ~ ~ platform · verglaste Aussichtsplattform f, eingeglaste ~

~ ~ **platform** → ~ ~ deck

~ **opening**, glazed ~ · eingeglaste Öffnung f, verglaste ~

~ **timber door**, glazed ~ ~, ~ wood(en) ~ [*B.S. 459, Part I*] · verglaste Holztür f, eingeglaste ~

~ **veranda(h)**, glazed ~; sun parlor (US) · Glasveranda f

~ **viewing deck** → ~ observation ~

~ ~ **platform** → ~ observation deck

~ **wood(en) door**, glazed ~ ~, ~ timber ~ [*B.S. 459, Part I*] · verglaste Holztür f, eingeglaste ~

glassy · glasig

glauconite [*A greenish silicate of iron and potassium, found in greensand*] · Glaukonit m

glauconitic limestone · Glaukonitkalkstein m

~ **sandstone** · Glaukonitsandstein m

to glaze, to glass-in · einglasen, verglasen

glaze → glaze(d finish)

~, fire finish, fire polish · Feuerblänke f, Feuerblankheit f [*Fehlname: Feuerpolitur f. Die sich bei Abkühlung des Glases natürlich bildende blanke Oberfläche*]

~ **crazing** · Glasurrißbildung f

glazed · glasiert

~, glassed-in · eingeglast, verglast

~ **area**, glassed-in ~ · eingeglaste Fläche f, verglaste ~

~ **brick** · glasierter Ziegel m

~ **ceramic tile**, ~ (clay) ~, GT · glasierte Keramik(belag)platte f, ~ Keramikfliese f, ~ Ton(belag)platte, ~ Tonfliese

~ **(clay) tile**, ~ ceramic ~, GT · glasierte Keramik(belag)platte f, ~ Keramikfliese f, ~ Ton(belag)platte, ~ Tonfliese

~ **coat(ing)** → glaze(d finish)

~ **concrete** · Glasurbeton m, glasierter Beton

~ **corridor**, glass ~ · Glasflur m, Glasgang m, Glaskorridor m

~ **door**, half-glass ~, sash ~ [*A door of which the upper half is glazed*] · Glasfüllungstür f

~ **earthenware wall tile** [*B.S. 1281*] · glasierte Steingut-Wand(belag)platte f, ~ Steingut-Wandfliese, ~ Irdengut-Wand(belag)platte, ~ Irdengut-Wandfliese f, Glasur-Steingut-Wand(belag)platte, Glasur-Steingut-Wandfliese, Glasur-Irdengut-Wand(belag)platte, Glasur-Irdengut-Wandfliese

glaze(d finish), glazing, glazed coat(-ing), gl [*In the tiling trade the terms 'glaze' and 'enamel' have become practically synonymous, although, strictly speaking, glaze should only apply to a coating that is glassy, and presumably transparent, whilst enamel should apply to one that is opaque*] · Beglasung f, Glasur f

glazed lookout deck → glassed-in observation ~

~ ~ **platform** → glassed-in observation deck

~ **observation deck** → glassed-in ~ ~

~ ~ **platform** → glassed-in observation deck

~ **opening,** glassed-in ~ · eingeglaste Öffnung *f*, verglaste ~

~ **partition (wall),** glass ~ (~) · verglaste Trennwand *f*, Glastrennwand

~ **patio** → ~ terrace

~ **roof (cladding)** → glass ~ ~

~ ~ **covering** → glass roof cladding

~ ~ **sheathing** → glass roof cladding

~ **(stone)ware** · glasiertes Steinzeug *n*, Glasur-Steinzeug

~ ~ **pipe** · glasiertes Steinzeugrohr *n*, Glasur-Steinzeugrohr

~ **terrace,** glass ~, ~ patio · Glasterrasse *f*

~ **tile** → ~ clay ~

~ **timber door,** glassed-in ~ ~, ~ wood(en) ~ [*B.S. 459, Part I*] · verglaste Holztür *f*, eingeglaste ~

~ **veranda(h),** glassed-in ~; sun parlor (US) · Glasveranda *f*

~ **viewing deck** → glassed-in observation ~

~ ~ **platform** → glassed-in observation deck

~ **wall coat(ing)** · Wandglasur(überzug) *f*, (*m*)

~ **ware,** ~ stone~ · glasiertes Steinzeug *n*, Glasur-Steinzeug

~ ~ **pipe,** ~ stone~ ~ · glasiertes Steinzeugrohr *n*, Glasur-Steinzeugrohr

~ **wood(en) door,** glassed-in ~ ~, ~ timber ~ [*B.S. 459, Part I*] · verglaste Holztür *f*, eingeglaste ~

glazier · Glaser *m*

glazier's brad, glazing ~, ~ point, ~ sprig · Fenstereckenstift *m* [*DIN 1147*]

~ **diamond,** cutting ~ · Diamantschneider *m*, Glaserdiamant *m* [*Werkzeug*]

~ **lead** · Glaserblei *n*

~ **point,** glazing ~, ~ sprig, ~ brad · Fenstereckenstift *m* [*DIN 1147*]

~ **putty,** glazing ~, sash ~ · Fensterkitt *m*, Verglasungskitt, Glaserkitt [*DIN 1975*]

~ **work,** glazing ~ · Glaserarbeiten *fpl*, Verglasungsarbeiten [*DIN 18361*]

glazing · Beglasen *n*, Glasieren

~ → glaze(d finish)

~ [*Any glass secured in a prepared opening such as a window, door, panel, screen or partition*] · Verglasung *f*, Einglasung

~ [*The securing of glass in prepared openings such as windows, door panels, screens or partitions*] · Einglasen *n*, Verglasen

~ **bar** · Falzleiste *f*, Schiene *f* [*kittlose Verglasung*]

~ ~ · Kittleiste *f*, Scheibenleiste [*Glasfüllungstür*]

~ ~ → window ~ ~

~ ~ **window,** sash ~ ~, division ~ ~, astragal ~; muntin ~ (US) · Sprossenfenster *n*

~ **bedded in washleather,** washleather glazing · Putzlederverglasung *f*, Waschlederverglasung

~ **by atomization,** atomization glazing · Glasieren *n* durch Versprühen, Beglasen ~ ~, Sprühglasieren, Sprühbeglasen

~ ~ **dipping,** dipping glazing · (Ein-) Tauchglasieren *n*, (Ein)Tauchbeglasen, Glasieren durch Eintauchen, Beglasen durch Eintauchen

~ ~ **salting,** salt glazing · Beglasen *n* durch Salzen, Glasieren ~ ~, Salzglasieren, Salzbeglasen

~ ~ **spraying,** spraying glazing · Glasieren *n* durch Begießen, Beglasen ~ ~, Gießglasieren, Gießbeglasen

~ **compound** [*A setting or nonsetting material used in glazing applied by hand, knife, gun or as a preformed strip to provide a bedding for glass and surround. Linseed oil putty is an example of such a glazing compound*] · Verglasungsmasse *f*, Einglasungsmasse

~ **dimension** · Einglasungsmaß *n*, Verglasungsmaß

~ **gasket** · Verglasungsselbstdichtung *f*, Verglasungs(ab)dicht(ungs)profil *n*, Einglasungsselbstdichtung, Einglasungs(ab)dicht(ungs)profil

~ **glass,** GG, glass for glazing [*B. S. 952*] · Glas *n* für Verglasung, ~ ~ Einglasung, Verglasungsglas, Einglasungsglas

~ **instructions** · Verglasungsanleitung *f*, Einglasungsanleitung

~ **material** · Einglasungsmaterial *n*, Verglasungsmaterial

~ **method** · Glasurverfahren *n*, Beglasungsverfahren, Glasierungsverfahren

~ ~ · Einglasungsverfahren *n*, Verglasungsverfahren

~ **product** · Einglasungserzeugnis *n*, Verglasungserzeugnis

~ **profile** → ~ unit

~ **purlin(e)** · Verglasungspfette *f*, Einglasungspfette

~ **putty,** glazier's ~, sash ~ · Fensterkitt *m*, Verglasungskitt, Glaserkitt [*DIN 1975*]

~ **section** → ~ unit

~ **shape** → ~ unit

~ **size** · Einglasungsgröße *f*, Verglasungsgröße

~ **sprig,** glazier's ~, ~ point, ~ brad · Fenstereckenstift *m* [*DIN 1147*]

~ **technique** · Verglasungstechnik *f*

~ **trade** · Glaserhandwerk *n*

glazing trim — glue(d) joint of steel reinforcement

~ trim → ~ unit

~ **unit** · Verglasungselement n, Einglasungselement, Verglasungskörper m, Einglasungskörper [Fehlnamen: Verglasungseinheit f, Einglasungseinheit]

~ ~, ~ trim, ~ shape, ~ section, ~ profile · Verglasungsprofil n, Einglasungsprofil

~ **with light-admitting plastic (material)** · Kunststoffverglasung f, Kunststoffeinglasung [Siehe Anmerkung unter "Kunststoffglas"]

~ **work,** glazier's ~ · Glaserarbeiten fpl, Verglasungsarbeiten [DIN 18361]

globe housing, spherical ~ · Kugelgehäuse n

~ **retaining ring** · Glashaltering m [Leuchte]

gloss, gl [The degree to which a painted surface possesses the property of reflecting light in a mirrow-like manner (specular reflection). The extent to which this property is developed depends mainly on the composition of the paint, surface ranging from dead flat to full gloss being obtainable] · Glanz m

~ **(clear) varnish** · Glanz(klar)lack m

~ **coat** · Glanzanstrich m, Glanzaufstrich [Siehe Anmerkung unter "Anstrich"]

~ **enamel** · Glanzemaillelack m

~ **paint** · Glanz(anstrich)farbe f

glossproof · glanzbeständig, glanzecht

gloss reducer, matting agent, flatting agent [A material incorporated in a paint, varnish or other coating material to reduce the gloss of the dried film] · Matt(ierungs)mittel n, Matt(ierungs)stoff m

~ **retention** · Glanzhaltung f

glossiness degree, degree of glossiness · Glanzgrad m

glossy · glänzend

gloss(y) (clear) varnish · Glanz(klar)lack m

~ **glazed coat(ing),** ~ glaze(d finish), ~ glazing · Glanzglasur f, Glanzbeglasung f

~ **glaze(d finish),** ~ glazing, ~ glazed coat(ing) · Glanzglasur f, Glanzbeglasung f

~ **glazing,** ~ glazed coat(ing), ~ glaze(d finish) · Glanzglasur f, Glanzbeglasung f

glossy up [The undesirable development of gloss on a flat paint due to handling or polishing] · Glänzendwerden n

gloss(y) varnish, ~ clear ~ · Glanz(klar)lack m

glow lamp, incandescent ~ · Glühlampe f

glr, glare · Blendung f

glucose, grape sugar, dextrose · Glukose f, Traubenzucker m

to glue, to bond · verleimen

glue, adhesive [Although no distinction can be made, the term 'glue' is sometimes understood to refer only to organic substances such as animal glue, fish glue, casein, blood albumin, and the synthetic plastics being termed 'adhesives'. Actually, the two terms are synonymous] · Leim m

~ **(binding) medium,** ~ binder · Leimbindemittel n [Anstrichtechnik]

to glue down, to cement ~, to bond ~, ~ ~ to · (ver)kleben (mit), (ver-)leimen (~)

~ ~ **to,** ~ cement ~, ~ bond ~, ~ ~ down · (ver)kleben (mit), (ver)leimen (~)

(glue(-bound)) distemper (paint); glue(-bound) water ~ [Australia] · Leimfarbe f

(~) ~ coat; coat of glue(-bound) water paint [Australia] · Leimfarbenanstrich m, Leimfarbenaufstrich

glue-etched glass → ice-patterned ~

glue-etching · Eisblumieren n [Glas]

glue fixing method, thin-bed ~, (tile) cement fixing ~, thin-bed fixing technique · Dünnbettverfahren n, Kleb(e)verfahren [Ansetzen von Fliesen]

~ **for cold pressing,** adhesive ~ ~ ~ · Kaltpreßleim m

~ ~ **structural timber elements,** adhesive ~ ~ ~ ~ · Holzleim m für (last)tragende Bauteile, Leim für (last-)tragende Holzbauteile

~ **in film form** → sheet glue

~ **joint** → glued ~

glue(-jointe)d sectional panel, ~ two-piece ~, sectional glue(-jointe)d ~, two-piece glue(-jointe)d ~ · verleimte zweiteilige Tafel f, zweiteilige verleimte ~

~ **two-piece panel** → ~ sectional ~

glue line, adhesive ~ · Leimfuge f

~ **medium,** ~ binding ~, ~ binder · Leimbindemittel n [Anstrichtechnik]

~ **powder,** adhesive ~, powder(ed) glue, powder(ed) adhesive · Leimpulver n, Trockenleim m, Pulverleim [Leim in Pulverform, meist Pflanzenleim oder Zelluloseleim]

~ **resin** · Leimharz n

glue water paint [Australia] → (glue(-bound)) distemper

glueability · (Ver)Leimbarkeit f, (Ver-)Leimfähigkeit, (Ver)Leimvermögen n

glued, bonded · verleimt

~ **boarding,** ~ boards · verleimte Bretter npl

~ **boards,** ~ boarding · verleimte Breter npl

glue(d) joint, adhesive ~, ~ line · Kleb(e)verbindung f, Leimverbindung, Kleb(e)fuge f, Leimfuge

~ ~ **of steel reinforcement** · Verbindung f von Bewehrungsstählen mit Gießharz zur Kraftübertragung

glued laminate, laminated material, laminated plastic · Schichtstoff *m*
(glue(d)) laminated timber (Brit.) → glulam (wood)

(~) ~ (~) arch(ed girder), (~) ~ wood ~ (~); glulam (~) ~ (~) (US) · (Brett)Lamellenbogen(träger) *m*, Schichtholzbogen(träger), gekrümmter Schichtholzträger, gekrümmter (Brett-)Lamellenträger

(~) ~ (~) beam; glulam (~) ~ (US) · (Brett)Lamellenbalken(träger) *m*, Schichtholzbalken(träger)

(~) ~ (~) edge beam; glulam (~) ~ ~ (US) · Schichtholzrandbalken(träger) *m*, (Brett)Lamellenrandbalken(-träger)

(~) ~ (~) frame; glulam (~) ~ (US) · (Brett)Lamellenrahmen *m*, Schichtholzrahmen

(~) ~ (~) girder; glulam (~) ~ (US) · (Brett)Lamellenträger *m*, Schichtholzträger

(~) ~ (~) lattice girder; glulam (~) ~ ~ (US) · Schichtholzgitterträger *m*, verleimter geschichteter Gitterträger

(~) ~ (~) portal frame; glulam (~) ~ ~ (US) · Schichtholzportalrahmen *m*, (Brett)Lamellen-Portalrahmen

(~) ~ (~) rafter; glulam (~) ~ (US) · (Brett)Lamellensparren *m*, Schichtholzsparren

(~) ~ (~) (raking) strut; glulam (~) (~) ~ (US) · (Brett)Lamellenstrebe *f*, Schichtholzstrebe

(~) ~ (~) shell roof; glulam (~) ~ ~ (US) · (Brett)Lamellenschalendach *n*, Schichtholzschalendach

(~) ~ (~) truss(ed) girder); glulam (~) ~ ~ (~) (US) · Schichtholzfachwerk(träger) *n*, (*m*), verleimtes geschichtetes Fachwerk *n*, verleimter geschichteter Fachwerkträger *m*

(~) ~ wood, (glued) laminated timber (Brit.); glulam (wood) (US) · Schichtholz *n*, SCH, lamelliertes Holz

(~) ~ ~ arch(ed girder), (glued) laminated timber ~ (~) (Brit.); glulam (wood) ~ (~) (US) · gekrümmter Schichtholzträger, Schichtholzbogen(träger) *m*, (Brett)Lamellenbogen(träger), gekrümmter (Brett)Lamellenträger

~ line, adhesive ~, ~ joint · Kleb(e)verbindung *f*, Leimverbindung, Kleb(e)fuge *f*, Leimfuge

glued-on, bonded-on · aufgeleimt

glued plywood system · Schichtsperrholzkonstruktion *f*, geleimte Sperrholzkonstruktion

~ (roof) truss, nail-~ (~) ~ · Leim(dach)binder *m*

~ sectional panel → glue(-jointe)d ~ ~

~ together · zusammengeleimt

~ truss, (nail-)glued (roof) ~ · Leim(dach)binder *m*

~ two-piece panel → glue(-jointe)d sectional ~

~ wood construction, bonded ~ ~ · (Holz)Leimbau *m*

gluing, bonding · (Ver)Leimen *n*

glulam → ~ wood

~ arch(ed girder) → (glue(d)) laminated wood ~ (~)

~ (timber) arch(ed girder) (US); (glue(d)) laminated (~) ~ (~) · Schichtholzbogen(träger) *m*, (Brett)Lamellenbogen(träger), gekrümmter Schichtholzträger, gekrümmter (Brett-)Lamellenträger

~ beam (US); (glue(d)) laminated (~) ~ · Schichtholzbalken(träger) *m*, (Brett)Lamellenbalken(träger)

~|(~) edge beam (US); (glue(d)) laminated (~) ~ ~ · Schichtholzrandbalken(träger) *m*, (Brett)Lamellenrandbalken(träger)

~ (~) frame (US); (glue(d)) laminated (~) ~ · Schichtholzrahmen *m*, (Brett-)Lamellenrahmen

~ (~) girder (US); (glue(d)) laminated (~) ~ · Schichtholzträger *m*, (Brett-)Lamellenträger

~ (~) lattice girder (US); (glue(d)) laminated (~) ~ ~ · Schichtholzgitterträger *m*, verleimter geschichteter Gitterträger

~ (~) portal frame (US); (glue(d)) laminated (~) ~ ~ · Schichtholzportalrahmen *m*, (Brett)Lamellen-Portalrahmen

~ (timber) rafter (US); (glue(d)) laminated (~) ~ · Schichtholzsparren *m*, (Brett)Lamellensparren

~ (~) (raking) strut (US); (glue(d)) laminated (~) (~) ~ · Schichtholzstrebe *f*, (Brett)Lamellenstrebe

~ (~) shell roof (US); (glue(d)) laminated (~) ~ ~ · Schichtholzschalendach *n*, (Brett)Lamellenschalendach

~ (~) truss(ed girder) (US); (glue(d)) laminated (~) ~ (~) · Schichtholzfachwerk(träger) *n*, verleimtes geschichtetes Fachwerk *n*, verleimter geschichteter Fachwerkträger *m*

~ (wood) (US); (glue(d)) laminated ~, (glue(d)) laminated timber (Brit.) · Schichtholz *n*, lamelliertes Holz, SCH

~ (~) arch(ed girder) (US) → (glue(d)) laminated ~ (~)

glyceril stearate → stearin(e)

glycerin(e) (US); glycerine (Brit.) [*The name in chemistry is 'glycerol'*] · Glycerin *n*, Glyzerin [*veraltete Benennung: Ölsüß n*]

glycerol ester · Tallöl *n* mit Glycerin verestert, ~ ~ Glyzerin ~

~ esterification · Glycerinveresterung *f*, Glyzerinveresterung

glycol · zweiwertiger Alkohol *m*, Glykol *n*

glyph [*A carved vertical channel, e.g. a triglyph*] · Schlitz *m*, Zierrille *f*, Glyphe *f*

glyptal resin · Glyptal(harz) *n*
glyptotheca [*A building to contain sculpture*] · Glyptothek *f*
gneiss · Gneis *m*
gnomon · Sonnenzeiger *m*
to go slack · schlaff werden, erschlaffen
goffered plate · Waffelblech *n*
going → run
gold bromide (Brit.); ~ bromid(e) (US) · Bromgold *n*
~ bronze [*A copper or copper alloy powder for bronzing*] · Goldbronze *f*
gold-bronze paint · Goldbronze(anstrich)farbe *f*
~ powder, powder(ed) gold bronze · Goldbronzepulver *n*
gold chloride (Brit.); ~ chlorid(e) (US) · Goldchlorid *n*
gold-leaf, gold leaves, aurum foliatum · Blattgold *n* [*Etwa 16½–23½ karätiges Gold, welches in hauchdünnen Blättchen meist in quadratischer Form in verschiedenen Sorten in den Handel kommt*]
gold leaves, aurum foliatum, gold-leaf · Blattgold *n* [*Etwa 16½–23½ karätiges Gold, welches in hauchdünnen Blättchen meist in quadratischer Form in verschiedenen Sorten in den Handel kommt*]
~ mosaic · Goldmosaik *n*
~ plated, gilded · vergoldet
~ plating, gilding · Vergolden *n*
~ ~, gilding · Vergoldung *f*
~ powder, powder(ed) gold · Pudergold *n*, Staubgold, Goldpuder *n*, Goldstaub *m*
~ size [*B.S. 311*] · Anlegeöl *n*, Goldgrundöl, Mixtion *n*, Goldlack *m* [*Ein dicker Leinölfirnis, der mit Bleiglätte, Naturharzen oder Ocker gekocht wurde. Es dient zum Auflegen von echtem Blattgold oder -silber auf den Untergrund*]
gold-work · Goldarbeit *f*
Golden gateway · Goldene Pforte *f* [*Palast des Diocletian zu Spalato*]
~ House, Ca' d'Oro [*It was built between 1421 and 1440 and named for the gilding originally applied to its facade. It now contains an art collection*] · Cà doro [*Venedig*]
~ Mean, ~ Section, sectio aurea · Goldener Schnitt *m*, Goldenes Verhältnis *n*
~ Section, ~ Mean, sectio aurea · Goldener Schnitt *m*, Goldenes Verhältnis *n*
goldfish pond · Goldfischbecken *n*
goniometer · Winkelmesser *m* für Flächenwinkel
Gooch crucible · Goochtiegel *m*
Good King James's Gothic, Jacobean style · Stil *m* der Zeit Jakobs I

goods, products, articles, ware · Artikel *mpl*, Waren *fpl*, Erzeugnisse *npl*, Gegenstände *mpl*
~ elevator, freight ~, trunk ~ (US); ~ lift (Brit.) · Lastenaufzug *m*, Materialaufzug
~ entrance · Lieferanteneingang *m* [*Hotel*]
~ lift, freight ~, trunk ~ (Brit.); ~ elevator (US) · Lastenaufzug *m*, Materialaufzug
~ reception · Warenannahme *f*
good's traffic · Lastenverkehr *m*
gooseneck, swan's neck, swan-neck, offset [*A pipe fitting used to connect two pipes whose axes are parallel but not in line*] · Schwanenhals *m*, S-Stück *n*, Etagenbogen *m*, Sprungrohr *n* [*DIN 19506*]
gopura(m) [*The elaborate gateway tower to South Indian temples*] · Gopura(m) *m*
gorge → cavetto (moulding)
gospel ambo · Evangelienambo *m*, Evangelienpult *n* [*An der Nordseite einer Kirche*]
~ side · Evangelienseite *f*, Frauenseite, Nordseite, Brotseite [*Die vom Westeingang aus linke (= nördliche, in frühchristlicher Zeit also den Heiden zugewandte) Seite der Kirche und des Altars, von der aus das Evangelium verlesen wird*]
Gothic, ~ style, pointed style · Spitzbogenstil *m*, gotischer Stil, Gotik *f*
~ abacus, ~ raised table · gotische (Säulen)Deckplatte *f*, ~ Kapitellplatte, ~ Kapitälplatte, gotischer Abakus *m*
~ (a)butment [*deprecated*] → ~ buttress
~ altar · gotischer Altar *m*
~ arcade · gotische Arkade *f*
~ architecture, pointed ~, ~ (building) style, ~ architectural style · gotische Architektur *f*, ~ Baukunst *f*, Spitzbogenstil *m*, Spitzbogenarchitektur, Gotik *f*, Spitzbogenbaukunst, germanischer Baustil, gotischer (Bau)Stil
~ basilica · gotische Basilika *f*
~ bond, ~ masonry ~ · gotischer (Mauerwerk)Verband *m*
~ brick architecture → ~ clay ~ ~
~ (building) style → ~ architecture
~ buttress; ~ buttressing pier, ~ (a)butment [*deprecated*] · gotischer Strebepfeiler *m*
~ buttressing pier [*deprecated*] → ~ buttress
~ cathedral of St. Vitus · Dom *m* zu Prag
~ ~ style, cathedral Gothic · Kathedral(en)gotik *f*
(~) Charles Bridge at Prague · Karlsbrücke *f* zu Prag
~ choir, ~ quire · gotischer Chor *m*
~ church · gotische Kirche *f*

Gothic (church) nave — grading

~ (~) nave, ~ middle vessel · gotisches Hauptschiff n, ~ Mittelschiff, ~ Langschiff

~ (clay) brick architecture · Ziegelgotik f, Backsteingotik

~ crypt · gotische Krypta f, ~ Gruft f

~ decorating art, ~ decoration ~, ~ ornamental ~ · gotische Zierkunst f, ~ Ornamentik f

~ detail · gotisches Detail n

~ (masonry) bond · gotischer (Mauerwerk)Verband m

~ master · gotischer Baumeister m

~ middle vessel, ~ (church) nave · gotisches Hauptschiff n, ~ Mittelschiff, ~ Langschiff

~ nave, ~ church ~, ~ middle vessel · gotisches Hauptschiff n, ~ Mittelschiff, ~ Langschiff

~ ornamental art, ~ decorating ~, ~ decoration ~ · gotische Ornamentik f, ~ Zierkunst f

~ palace · gotischer Palast m

~ parish church · gotische Pfarrkirche f

~ pillar · freistehender gotischer Pfeiler m, gotischer freistehender ~

~ pulpit · gotische Kanzel f

~ quire, ~ choir · gotischer Chor m

~ raised table → ~ abacus

~ Revival, revived Gothic style, Neo-Gothic · posthume Gotik f, Neugotik, Neogotik

~ (style) → ~ architecture

~ tower · gotischer Turm m

~ tracery · gotisches Maßwerk n

~ vault · gotisches Gewölbe n

~ window · gotisches Fenster n

~ ~ tracery · gotisches Fenstermaßwerk n

Gothicist · gotisierend

Gothicized · gotisiert

gouache [*The pigment is first mixed with a white zinc powder to make it opaque. It is than thinned to the proper consistency with water and is applied to the paper or other background; but it is sufficiently opaque to completely cover the surface, so that only the pigment shows*] · Gouache(malerei) f, Guaschmalerei, deckende Wasserfarbenmalerei

goudron · Mauerteer m

government block, ~ building · Regierungsgebäude n

~ **building**, ~ block · Regierungsgebäude n

~ **commission** · staatlicher Bauauftrag m

~ **palace** · Regierungspalast m

gpf → gas-proof

GPO cable (Brit.); post office ~, telecommunication ~ · Fernmeldekabel n

~ **line** (Brit.); post office ~, telecommunication ~ · Fernmeldeleitung f

~ **tower** (Brit.); post office ~, telecommunication ~ · Fernmeldeturm m

grab bar · Griffstange f, Stangengriff m

~ **rail** [*A handrail along a wall*] · Wand-Handlauf m, Wand-Handleiste f

graceful sweep · zierliche Rundung f

gradation limit, grading ~, limiting (grading) curve, particle (distribution) limit · Siebgrenze f, Grenzsieblinie f

to grade · abstufen [*nach Körnungen*]

grade, quality ~ · Güteklasse f

~, level of ground, ground level · Geländehöhe f, Niveau n

~ · Sorte f

~ **description**, quality ~ ~ · Güteklassebeschreibung f

~ **beam** [*A reinforced concrete beam which forms the foundation for the superstructure; it is normally placed directly on the ground*] · Fundamentbalken m, Gründungsbalken

~ **of cement**, cement grade · Zementgüteklasse f

~ ~ **concrete**, quality ~ ~ ~, concrete (quality) grade · Betongüteklasse f

~ ~ **pipe** · Rohrsorte f

~ ~ **slab**, foundation raft [*A reinforced concrete slab which forms the foundation for the superstructure; it is normally placed directly on the ground*] · Fundamentplatte f, Gründungsplatte, Grundplatte

graded · güteklassiert

~, screened · (korn)abgestuft, gesiebt [*Mineralmasse*]

~ (concrete) aggregate, screened (~) ~ · (korn)abgestufter (Beton)Zuschlag-(stoff) m, gesiebter ~

~ **glass powder**, screened ~ ~, ~ powder(ed) glass · gesiebtes Glaspulver n, (korn)abgestuftes ~

~ **gravel**, screened ~ · gesiebter Kies m, (korn)abgestufter ~, Siebkies

~ ~ **mix(ture)**, screened ~ · Siebkiesgemenge n, Siebkiesmischung f, Siebkiesgemisch n

~ **powder(ed) glass**, screened ~ ~, ~ glass powder · gesiebtes Glaspulver n, (korn)abgestuftes ~

~ **sand**, screened ~ · (korn)abgestufter Sand m, gesiebter ~, Siebsand

~ ~ **mix(ture)** · Siebsandgemenge n, Siebsandmischung f, Siebsandgemisch n

gradetto, annulet [*In the Doric order of architecture one of the fillets beneath the capital*] · Riemchen n

grading, granulometric composition, texture, grain-size distribution, particle-size distribution · Kornaufbau m, Kornzusammensetzung f, Korn(größen)verteilung

~ · Körnungslehre f, Lehre vom Kornaufbau

grading — granite chip(ping)s

~, blending · Korngattierung f [*Die Mischung von Kornklassen, um ein gewünschtes Korngefüge zu erhalten*]

~ **analysis** → particle-size ~

~ **bracket** → size range

~ **curve** → aggregate ~ ~

~ ~ **representation in normal scale** · Siebliniendarstellung f im gewöhnlichen Maßstab [*In einem Liniennetz sind im Abstand der Sieblochdurchmesser (in mm) senkrechte Linien gezogen, auf denen die entsprechenden Siebdurchgänge in Gew.-% aufgetragen werden*]

~ **envelope**, envelope of grading · Siebbereich m, n

~ **fraction** → size range

~ **limit**, gradation ~, particle (distribution) ~, limiting (grading) curve · Siebgrenze f, Grenzsieblinie f

~ **period** · Brandklasse f

~ **range** → size ~

gradually applied load · allmählich aufgebrachte Last f

to graduate (in architecture) · erlangen, ein Architektendiplom ~

Graeco-Roman Corinthian column · griechisch-römisch korinthische Säule f

~ **façade** · griechisch-römische Fassade f

grain, particle, mineral ~ · (Einzel)Korn n, Gesteinskorn, Mineralkorn, Partikelchen n, (Einzel)Teilchen, Körnchen

~ **adhesive**, ~ glue · Körnerleim m

~ **diameter**, particle ~ · Korndurchmesser m

~ **fineness**, particle ~ · Kornfeinheit f

~ **glue**, ~ adhesive · Körnerleim m

~ **mix(ture)** → mixed grains

~ **porosity**, particle ~, porosity of grains, porosity of particles · Korneigenporigkeit f

~ **shape**, particle ~ · Kornform f, Korngestalt f

~ ~ **factor**, particle ~ ~ · Kornformfaktor m, Korngestaltfaktor

~ ~ **test**, particle ~ ~ · Kornformprobe f, Kornformversuch m, Kornformprüfung f

(grain-)size, particle size · Korngröße f [*Größenbezeichnung für ein Korn in mm oder cm. Das Meßverfahren ist anzugeben. Ist kein Meßverfahren angeführt, dann gilt die Loch- bzw. Maschenweite nach DIN 1170 bzw. 4188*]

~ **analysis** → particle-size ~

~ **determination**, particle-size ~ · Korngrößenbestimmung f

~ **distribution**, particle-size ~, grading, texture, granulometric composition · Kornaufbau m, Kornzusammensetzung f, Korn(größen)verteilung

~ ~ **curve**, particle-size ~ ~, (aggregate) grading ~, sieve ~ · Siebkurve f, Sieblinie f, Körnungskurve, Körnungslinie, Kornverteilungskurve, Kornverteilungslinie

~ **distribution diagram**, system of coordinates for representation of (grain) size distribution curves R.R.B. · Körnungsnetz n, RRB-Netz

~ **limit**, particle-size ~ · Korngrenze f

grain storage · Getreidelagerung f

~ **(~) silo** · Getreidesilo m

~ **strength**, particle ~ · Kornfestigkeit f

~ **surface**, particle ~ · Kornoberfläche f

graining · Maser(iere)n n [*In der Holzmalerei die Imitation des jeweiligen Holzmaserbildes mit Wasser- oder Öllasur auf deckend gestrichenen Flächen*]

grains, material, particles · Gekörn n, Körner npl, Korn n

~ **in bulk**, heap of granular material · Kornschüttung f

~ **of equal size**, uniformly sized grains · gleichkörniges Gut n, monodisperses ~, einkörniges ~, Einkorngut

granary · Getreideschuppen m, Getreidespeicher m

grand chamber, banquet(ting) room, festival room · Festsaal m, Bankettsaal

~ **entrance court** · Wirtschaftshof m [*in der Palastanlage von Khorsabad*]

~ **hall**, festival ~, banquet(ing) ~, civic auditorium · Festhalle f, Banketthalle

~ **order (of architecture)**, giant ~ (~ ~), colossal ~ (~ ~) · große Ordnung f, Riesenordnung, Kolossalordnung [*Eine Ordnung bei der die Pilaster oder Säulen über mehrere Geschosse reichen und sie somit zusammenfassen*]

~ **stair(case)**, ~ stairway, stately ~ · Prunktreppe f, Prachttreppe

~ **stairway**, ~ stair(case), stately ~ · Prunktreppe f, Prachttreppe

grandmaster key · Generalhauptschlüssel m

grandmaster-keyed lock · Generalhauptschlüssel, schloß n

~ **series**, series of grandmasterkeyed locks · Generalhauptschlüsselanlage f

grandstand, spectator's stand · Tribüne f

~-**type seat** · Tribünensitz m

granite arch · Granitbogen m

~ **ballast concrete** · Granitbeton m

~ **block** · Granitblock m

~ **broken sand**, ~ crushed ~ · Granit-Brechsand m

~ **chip(ping)s** · Granitsplitt m

~ **coarse aggregate** · Granitgrobzuschlag(stoff) *m*, Granitgrobzuschlagmaterial *n*

~ **column** · Granitsäule *f*

~ **crushed sand**, ~ broken ~ · Granit-Brechsand *m*

~ **cube** · Granitwürfel *m*

~ **curb**; ~ kerb [*B.S. 435*] · Granitbordstein *m*

~ **curtain (wall)**, ~ enceinte · Granitkurtine *f*

~ **dust**, ~ flour, ~ powder, powder(ed) granite · Granitmehl *n*, Granitpulver *n*, Granitstaub *m*, Granitpuder *n*

~ **enceinte**, ~ curtain (wall) · Granitkurtine *f*

~**-faced** → granite-surfaced

granite facing → ~ sur~

~ **finish** · Granit(ver)putz *m*

~ **flour**, ~ dust, ~ powder, powder(ed) granite · Granitmehl *n*, Granitpulver *n*, Granitstaub *m*, Granitpuder *n*

~ **gravel** · Granitkies *m*

~ **kerb** [*B.S. 435*]; ~ curb · Granitbordstein *m*

~**-lined** → granite-(sur)faced

granite lining → ~ (sur)facing

~ **lino(leum)** · granitiertes Linoleum *n*, Granit-Linoleum

~ **masonry (work)** · Granit(stein)-mauerwerk *n*

~ **(paving)** sett, pitcher [*B.S. 435*] · Granitpflasterstein *m* [*DIN 18502*]

~ **plaster** · Gipsestrichhartputz *m*

~**-porphyry**, porphyroid granite · Granitporphyr *m*

granite powder, ~ dust, ~ flour, powder(ed) granite · Granitmehl *n*, Granitpulver *n*, Granitstaub *m*, Granitpuder *n*

~ **sand** · Granitsand *m*

~ **sett** → ~ paving ~

~ ~ **paving** · Granitsteinpflaster *n*, Fpg

~ **setter** · Granitplattenleger *m*

~ **slab** · granitene Platte *f*, Granitplatte

~ ~ **floor(ing) (finish)**, ~ ~ floor cover(ing) · Granitplatten(fuß)boden(belag) *m*, Fbgr

~ **step** · Granitstufe *f*

~**-(sur)faced**, granite-lined · granitverkleidet, granitausgekleidet, granitbekleidet

granite (sur)facing, ~ lining · Granitverkleidung *f*, Granitauskleidung, Granitbekleidung

granitic finish [*A face mix(ture) resembling granite, on (pre)cast concrete*] · Betongranit *m*

granitite, biotite-granite · Biotitgranit *m* [*früher: Granitit m*]

grano(lithic) concrete · Hartbeton *m*

~ **(~) aggregate** · Hart(beton)zuschlag(stoff) *m*

~ **(~) course** → ~ (~) layer

~ **(~) floor(ing)**, ~ (~) floor cover(ing), ~ (~) floor finish, ~ (~) floor topping, ~ (~) floor overlay · Hartbeton(fuß)boden(belag) *m*

~ **(~) ~ tile**, ~ (~) floor cover(ing) ~, ~ (~) floor finish ~ · Hartbeton-(fuß)bodenplatte *f*, Hartbeton(fuß)-bodenfliese *f*

~ **(~) ~ tiling**, ~ (~) floor cover(ing) ~, ~ (~) floor finish ~ · Hartbeton-(fuß)bodenplattenbelag *m*, Hartbeton-(fuß)bodenfliesenbelag

~ **(~) layer**, ~ (~) course · Hartbetonschicht *f*, Hartbetonlage *f* [*Sie liegt über dem Grundbeton einer Hartbetonplatte*]

~ **(~) paving** · Hartbetonbefestigung *f* [*Von Wegen, Plätzen und anderen Verkehrsflächen*]

~ **(~) screed** · Hartbetonestrich *m*

~ **(~) tile** · Hartbeton(belag)platte *f*, Hartbetonfliese *f*

~ **(~) tiling** · Hartbetonplattenbelag *m*

~ **(~) topping**, ~ (~) overlay, granolithic · Hartbetonbelag *m*, Hartbetondecke *f*, Hartbetonverschleißschicht *f* [*Hartbetonbeläge werden auf den tragenden Unterlagen – Fußböden, Decken, Wege- und Platzbefestigungen, Treppenanlagen, Behälterauskleidungen aus Beton – zur Erhöhung des Verschleißwiderstandes der Oberfläche aufgebracht. Sie sind aus Beton, dessen Zuschlagstoffe in der Verschleißschicht aus Hartbetonstoffen bestehen. Hartbetonbeläge werden als Estriche oder als Platten verlegt. Fehlname: Hartbeton-Nutzschicht. DIN 1100*]

~ **(~) tread** · Hartbeton-Tritt(stufe) *m*, (*f*)

~ **sprinkle finish** · Einstreubelag *m* [*Die durch Einstreuen von Hartbetonstoffen in die Betonoberfläche hergestellten Beläge dürfen nicht als Hartbetonbeläge bezeichnet werden, sondern nur die Beläge bei denen die Hartbetonstoffe mit dem Bindemittel gemischt worden sind*]

~ ~ ~ **floor(ing)**, ~ ~ ~ floor cover(ing) · Einstreu(fuß)boden(belag) *m* [*Siehe Anmerkung unter „Einstreubelag"*]

granular · körnig

~ **cork**, granulated ~ · geschroteter Kork *m*, Korkschrot *m*, *n*

~ ~ **surfacing**, granulated ~ ~ · Korkschrotabstreuung *f*, Korkschrotbestreuung [*Dachpappe*]

~ **cover material**, ~ (sur)facing ~, ~ wearing surface ~, (roofing) granules · Bestreu(ungs)mineral *n*, Abstreu(ungs)-mineral, Bestreu(ungs)material *n*, Abstreu(ungs)material, Bestreu(ungs)gut *n*, Abstreu(ungs)gut [*Kies oder Splitt für Dachpappen und (bituminöse) Spachteldachbeläge*]

~ **crystalline gypsum** · körnig-kristalliner Gips *m*

~ **dust** → (mineral) filler

granular facing — graphic(al) construction

~ facing → ~ sur~
~ ~ material → ~ cover ~
~ filler → (mineral) ~
~ insulant → ~ insulating material
~ insulating material, ~ insulation(-grade) ~, ~ insulator, ~ insulant · körniger (Bau)Dämmstoff *m*, körniges (Bau)Dämmaterial *n* [*Gegen Kälte, Wärme oder Schall*]
~ insulation(-grade) material → ~ insulating ~
~ insulation material → ~ insulating ~
~ insulator → ~ insulating material
~ limestone · körniger Kalkstein *m*, Massenkalkstein
~ material, ~ product · körniges Gut *n*, ~ Material *n*
~ powder · körniges Pulver *n*, Kornpulver
~ product, ~ material · körniges Gut *n*, ~ Material *n*
~ skeleton · Korngerüst *n*
~ (sur)facing, mineral ~, mineral granules, dusting finish · Mineralbestreuung *f*, Mineralabstreuung, (mineralische) Bestreuung, (mineralische) Abstreuung, Streuschicht *f* [*Dachpappe und (bituminöser) Spachteldachbelag*]
~ ~ material → ~ cover ~
~ wearing surface material → ~ cover ~
to granulate · granulieren, zerkörnen
granulated, bush-hammered · gestockt
~ (blastfurnace) slag; cinder sand, granulated cinder (US); (iron) (blastfurnace) slag sand (Brit.) · Schlackensand *m*, künstlicher ~, Hüttensand, granulierte Hochofenschlacke *f*, gekörnte Hochofenschlacke, Hochofenschlackensand
~ (~) ~ concrete, (iron) (blastfurnace) slag sand ~ (Brit.), cinder sand ~, granulated cinder ~ (US) · Schlackensandbeton *m*, Hochofen~, Hüttensandbeton
~ (~) ~ sand, (iron) (~) ~ ~ (Brit.); (granulated) cinder ~ (US) · gekörnte Hochofenschlacke *f*, granulierte ~, Hochofenschlackensand *m*, (künstlicher) Schlackensand, Hüttensand
~ cinder, cinder sand (US); (iron) (blastfurnace) slag sand (Brit.); granulated (blastfurnace) slag · Schlackensand *m*, künstlicher ~, Hüttensand, granulierte Hochofenschlacke *f*, gekörnte Hochofenschlacke, Hochofenschlackensand
~ ~ block (US) → slag sand ~
~ ~ concrete, cinder sand ~ (US); (iron) (blastfurnace) slag sand ~, granulated (blastfurnace) slag ~ (Brit.) · Schlackensandbeton *m*, Hochofen~, Hüttensandbeton
~ ~ cored block, cinder sand ~ ~ (US); slag sand ~ ~, granulated slag ~ ~ (Brit.) · Hütten-Lochstein *m*, HSL [*DIN 398*]

(~) ~ sand (US); ~ (blastfurnace) slag ~, (iron) (blastfurnace) slag ~ (Brit.) · gekörnte Hochofenschlacke *f*, granulierte ~, Hochofenschlackensand *m*, (künstlicher) Schlackensand, Hüttensand
~ ~ tile (US) → slag sand block
~ cork, granular ~ · geschroteter Kork *m*, Korkschrot *m*, *n*
~ ~ surfacing, granular ~ ~ · Korkschrotabstreuung *f*, Korkschrotbestreuung [*Dachpappe*]
~ finish, bush hammer ~, bush-hammered ~ · gestockte Oberflächenbehandlung *f*
~ glass, (finely) crushed ~ · Glasgrieß *m*, Krösel *m*
~ plaster, bush hammer ~, bush hammered ~ · gestockter (Ver)Putz *m*
~ slag → ~ blastfurnace ~
~ ~ block → slag sand ~
~ ~ concrete → ~ blastfurnace ~ ~
~ ~ cored block, slag sand ~ ~ (Brit.); cinder sand ~ ~, granulated cinder ~ ~ (US) · Hütten-Lochstein *m*, HSL [*DIN 398*]
~ ~ sand → ~ (blastfurnace) ~ ~
~ ~ tile → slag sand block
~ slate surfacing · Schieferabstreuung *f*, Schieferbestreuung [*Dachpappe*]
granulating · Granulieren *n*, Zerkörnen
~, bush hammering · Stocken *n*
~ hammer, bush ~, boucharde · Stockhammer *m*
granulation (process) · Granulation *f*, Körnungsverfahren *n*, Granulierung *f*
granule hopper · Streuer *m* [*Dachpappenanlage*]
granules → granular cover material
granulometric composition, grading, texture, grain-size distribution, particle-size distribution · Kornaufbau *m*, Kornzusammensetzung *f*, Korn(größen)verteilung
granulometry, size gradation · (Korn-)Abstufung *f*, Granulometrie *f*, Korngrößenabstufung
grape sugar, dextrose, glucose · Glukose *f*, Traubenzucker *m*
graph → graphic representation
graphic granite · Schriftgranit *m*
graphic(al) analysis · bildliche Analyse *f*, graphische ~, zeichnerische ~
~ arch analysis · graphische Bogenstatik *f*, bildliche ~, zeichnerische ~
~ calculation · bildliche Berechnung *f*, graphische ~, zeichnerische ~, bildliches Rechnen *n*, graphisches Rechnen, zeichnerisches Rechnen
~ check · graphischer Nachweis *m*, zeichnerischer ~, bildlicher ~
~ construction, ~ method, ~ procedure · graphisches Verfahren *n*, zeichnerisches ~, bildliches ~

graphic(al) integration — gravel screening

~ **integration,** visual ~ · graphische Integration f, zeichnerische ~, bildliche ~

~ **investigation** · graphische Untersuchung f, zeichnerische ~, bildliche ~

~ **method** → ~ construction

~ **procedure** → ~ construction

~ **representation,** diagrammatic ~, graph, chart, diagram, plot · Diagramm n, bildliche Darstellung f, graphische Darstellung

~ **solution** · graphische Bestimmung f, ~ Ermitt(e)lung, ~ Lösung, zeichnerische ~, bildliche ~

~ **statics,** ~ structural analysis, graphostatics · graphische (Bau)Statik f, zeichnerische ~, bildliche ~, ~ Gleichgewichtslehre f, Graphostatik

~ **structural analysis,** ~ statics, graphostatics · graphische (Bau)Statik f, bildliche ~, zeichnerische ~, ~ Gleichgewichtslehre f, Graphostatik

graphite, pot-lead [*An allotropic crystalline form of carbon*] · Graphit m

~ **paint** · Graphitfarbe f [*Rostschutz-Deckfarbe*]

~ **refractory (product)** · Graphiterzeugnis n

~ **clay** · Schieferkreide f

graphostatics, graphic(al) statics, graphic(al) structural analysis · graphische (Bau)Statik f, bildliche ~, zeichnerische ~, ~ Gleichgewichtslehre f, Graphostatik

grappling of arch · Bogenverankerung f

grass-covered ground for sunbathing or resting · Liegewiese f

grass playground (for children), (outdoor) grass lay area · Spielwiese f, Kinder~

'**grass roots scheme',** '~ ~ project' · "Projekt n auf der grünen Wiese"

grass rope (US) → Manil(l)a hawser

~ **strip** · Grasstreifen m

~-**table** → plinth

grate, fireplace ~ · Feuerrost m

grave-mound, barrow · Hügelgrab n

grave slab, sepulchral ~, funerary ~, tomb ~ · Grabplatte f

~ **surround** · Grabeinfassung f

gravel · Kies m [*DIN 1179. Korngröße von 7 mm bis 70 mm Maschensieb; Feinkies 7–30 mm. Grobkies 30–70 mm*]

~ **aggregate,** ~ concrete ~ · Kies(beton)zuschlag(stoff) m, Betonkies m

~ (~) **concrete** · Kiesbeton m

~ (~) ~ **wall panel** · Kiesbetonwand-(bau)tafel f

~ **asphalt,** asphalt-coated gravel (US); bitumen macadam with gravel aggregate, (asphaltic-)bitumen-coated gravel [*B.S. 2040*] [*Dense hot-rolled asphalt with gravel as aggregate*] · Bitumenkies m, Bitukies Asphaltkies, Kies(walz)asphalt m

~ **bed** · Kiesbett n

~ **board,** ~ plank [*A horizontal board fixed to the underside of a close-boarded fence to prevent the vertical boards from reaching the ground. It is more easily replaced than a vertical board and is less easily rotted than is the end grain of the vertical boards*] · Sockelbrett n [*Bretterzaun*]

~ **built-up roof cladding,** ~ ~ ~ covering, ~ ~ ~ sheathing, ~ ~ roofing · Kieskleb(e)dach(belag) n, (m), Kieskleb(e)d(ach)(ein)deckung f, Kieskleb(e)bedachung, Kiesspachteldach(belag), Kiesspachtel(dach)(ein)-deckung, Kiesspachtelbedachung

~ **chip(ping)s** · Kiessplitt m

~ **concrete,** ~ aggregate ~ · Kiesbeton m

~ (~) **aggregate** · Kies(beton)zuschlag-(stoff) m, Betonkies m

~ ~ **wall panel** → ~ aggregate ~ ~ ~

~ **deposit** · Kiesvorkommen n, Kieslager(stätte) n, (f), Kiesfundstätte, Kiesvorkommnis n

~ **dressing,** ~ preparation · Kiesaufbereitung f

~ ~ **plant,** ~ preparation ~ · Kiesaufbereitungsanlage f, Kieswerk n

~ **extraction** · Kiesgewinnung f

~ ~ **and preparation,** ~ production · Kiesgewinnung f und -aufbereitung

~ ~ **plant,** ~ ~ installation · Kiesgewinnungsanlage f

~ **fillet** → ~ stop

~ **fill(ing)** · Kies(auf)schüttung f

~ **filter layer** · Sickerpackung f aus Grobkies

~ **flood coat** · Kies(dach)-Einbettmasse f [*Fehlname: Kiesdach-Kleb(e)-masse*]

~ **for garden paths** · Gartenkies m

~ ~ **sett paving(s)** · Pflasterkies m

~ **layer** · Kieslage f, Kiesschicht f

~ **packed well** · Kiesschüttungsbrunnen m

~ **pit** · Kiesgrube f

~ **plank,** ~ board [*A horizontal board fixed to the underside of a close-boarded fence to prevent the vertical boards from reaching the ground. It is more easily replaced than a vertical board and is less easily rotted than is the end grain of the vertical boards*] · Sockelbrett n [*Bretterzaun*]

~ **pocket** · Kiesnest n

~ **preparation,** ~ dressing · Kiesaufbereitung f

~ ~ **plant,** ~ dressing ~ · Kiesaufbereitungsanlage f, Kieswerk n

~ **production,** ~ extraction and preparation · Kiesgewinnung f und -aufbereitung

~ **roof(ing)** · Kiesschüttungs-Flachdach n

~ **screening** · Kiessiebung f

gravel stop — grease trap

~ **stop**, ~ fillet, ~ strip, slag ~ · Dachabschluß(blende) *m*, (*f*), Flachdach(rand)abschluß(blende), Dachrandprofil *n*, Flachdachrand *m*, Flachdach(rand)einfassung *f*, Blende, Dachkantprofil, Kiesleiste *f*

~ **surfaced** · bekiest

~ **surfacing** · Bekiesung *f*

~ **walk** · Kiesweg *m*

gravel(l)ed area, gravel(l)ing · Kiesfläche *f*

gravel(l)ing, gravel(l)ed area · Kiesfläche *f*

~ [*The action of laying down gravel*] · Kieseinbau *m*

gravelly · kiesig

~ **ground** · Kiesgrund *m*

~ **sand**, sandy gravel · Kiessand *m* [*Natürliches Gemisch aus Sand und Kies; Betonkiessand < 70 mm. Mittelkiessand < 30 mm*]

~ ~ **(concrete) aggregate**, sandy gravel (~) ~ · Betonkiessand *m*, Monierkies *m* [< 70 mm]

graveyard, cemetery · Friedhof *m*

~ **basilica** → cemetery ~

~ **chapel**, cemetery ~, mortuary ~, funeral ~ · Friedhofskapelle *f*, Totenkapelle

~ **church**, cemetery ~, mortuary ~, funeral ~ · Friedhofskirche *f*

gravity acceleration · Schwerebeschleunigung *f*

~ **action** · Schwerewirkung *f*

~ **air heating**, ~ plenum ~ · Schwerkraft-Luft(be)heizung *f* [*Warmluft wird ohne Ventilator in die zu beheizenden Räume geführt*]

~ **burning appliance** → ~ furnace

~ **circulation** · Schwerkraftumlauf *m*

~ ~ **heating installation**, ~ ~ ~ system · Schwerkraftheiz(ungs)anlage *f*

~ ~ ~ ~ **system**, ~ ~ ~ ~ installation · Schwerkraftheiz(ungs)anlage *f*

~ ~ **of hot water** · Warmwasser-Schwerkraftumlauf *m*, WW-Schwerkraftumlauf

~ **die foundry** · Dauerformgießerei *f*

~ **drainage**, drainage by gravity · Schwerkraftentwässerung *f*

~ **feed type boiler** · Natur-Umlaufkessel *m*

~ **fire** → ~ furnace

~ **flow installation** · Schwergewichtsflußanlage *f*

~ **furnace**, ~ fire, ~ burning appliance [*A furnace which depends on the difference of the density of warm and cool air for circulation*] · Feuerung *f* mit Schwerkraftwirkung, Feuerstätte *f* ~ ~

~ **heating** · Schwerkraftheizung *f*

~ **hot water (central) heating** → ~-type ~ ~ (~) ~

~ **interceptor** · Schwerkraftabscheider *m*, Schwerkraftfang *m*, Schwerkraftfänger

~ **load** · Schwergewichtslast *f*

~ **masonry wall** · Schwergewichtsmauer *f*

~ **plenum heating**, ~ air ~ · Schwerkraft-Luft(be)heizung *f* [*Warmluft wird ohne Ventilator in die zu beheizenden Räume geführt*]

~ **sewer** · Schwergewichtsfluß-Abwasserleitung *f*

~ **system** · Schwerkraftsystem *n*

~(-type) **hot water (central) heating** · Schwerkraft-Warmwasserheizung *f*

gravity(-type) one-pipe heating, one-pipe gravity(-type) ~ · Einrohr-Schwerkraftheizung *f*, Schwerkraft-Einrohrheizung

gravity ventilation, ~ venting · Schwerkraftlüftung *f*

gray board, grey ~, news ~, mill ~ · Graupappe *f*

~ **cast iron**, grey ~ ~, GCI · Gußeisen *n* mit Lamellengraphit, Grauguß *m* (~ ~), GGL [*DIN 1691*]

~ ~ ~ **(bath)tub**, ~ ~ ~ bath, grey ~ ~ ~, GCI ~ · Grauguß(bade)wanne *f* [*DIN 4470–4477*]

~ ~ ~ **fitting**, grey ~ ~ ~, GCI ~ · Grauguß-Formstück *n*, Grauguß-Fitting *m*

~ ~ ~ **pipe**, gray ~ ~ ~, GCI · Graugußrohr *n*

~ **concrete**, grey ~ · Graubeton *m*

~ **granite**, grey ~ · grauer Granit *m*

~ **marble**, grey ~ · Granitmarmor *m*

~-**stone**, grey-stone · Graustein *m*

graywacke, greywacke · Grauwacke *f*

~ **limestone**, greywacke ~, transition-lime · Grauwackenkalk *m*, Übergangskalk

~ **schist**, greywacke ~ · schieferige Grauwacke *f*

~ **slate**, greywacke ~ · Grauwackenschiefer *m*

graze, cut, scratch · Schramme *f*, Kratzer *m* [*Fehler im optischen Glas*]

grease bearing waste · fett(halt)iges Abwasser *n*

~ **free** · fettfrei, fettlos

~ **interceptor** [*A chamber, on the line of a drain or waste pipe, for preventing grease from passing into the drainage system. Grease collects and solidifies in the chamber and can be removed*] · Schwerkraftfettfänger *m*, Schwerkraftfettabscheider, Schwerkraftfettfang *m*

~ **polluted** · verfettet, fettverschmutzt

~ **remover**, ~ stripper · Entfettungsmittel *n*

~ **residue** · Fettrückstand *m*, Fettrest *m*

~ **seal** · Fettdichtung *f*

~ **stripper**, ~ remover · Entfettungsmittel *n*

~ **trap**, GT [*The function of a grease trap is to separate grease and oil from kitchen, laundry, and other specialized*

grease trap — green earth (pigment)

wastes, and thus prevent it from entering the sewage disposal system] · Fettfang m, Fettfänger m

~ **wastes** · Fettabwässer npl

greasiness · Fettigkeit f [einer Oberfläche]

~ [A greasy surface on a paint film caused by lack of compatibility] · Schmierigkeit f

greasy water · Fettwasser n

great altar · Altarbau m, großer Altar m, Riesenaltar [z.B. von Pergamon]

Great Palace of Minos at Knossos · Palast m (des Minos) in Knossos

~ **Pyramid of Cheops** · Cheopspyramide f

~ **Temple of Amon at Karnak, ~ ~ ~** Amen ~ ~ · Amontempel m zu Karnak

~ ~ ~ **the Sun at Palmyra** · Tempel m des Sonnengottes zu Palmyra

~ **Wall of China** · Chinesische Mauer f

Grecian acanthus leaf → ~ type ~ ~

~ **architectural style** → ~ building ~

~ **architecture,** Greek ~ · griechische Architektur f, ~ Baukunst f

~ **building style,** ~ architectural ~, Greek ~ ~ · griechischer Baustil m

~ **column,** Greek ~ · griechische Säule f

~ **cross,** St. George's ~, Greek ~ · griechisches Kreuz n

~ **decorating art** → Greek ornamental ~

~ **decoration art** → Greek ornamental ~

~ **Doric capital,** Greek ~ ~ · griechisch-dorisches Kapitell n, ~ Kapitäl

~ ~ **order,** Greek ~ ~ · griechisch-dorische (Säulen)Ordnung f

~ ~ **temple,** Greek ~ ~ · griechisch-dorischer Tempel m

~ **fret,** (Greek) ~, labyrinth ~, (Greek) key pattern, Greek key, Grecian Key pattern · rechtwink(e)lig gebrochener Mäander m, ~ gebrochenes Mäanderornament n, à la greque Ornament, Labyrinth n

~ **Ionic order,** Greek ~ ~ · griechisch-ionische (Säulen)Ordnung f

~ **key pattern** → ~ fret

~ **order,** Greek ~ · griechische (Säulen-)Ordnung f

~ **ornamental art** → Greek ~ ~

~ **temple,** Greek ~ · griechischer Tempel m

~ **(type) acanthus leaf,** Greek (~) ~ · griechisches Akanthusblatt n

Greek architectural style → ~ building ~

~ **architecture,** Grecian ~ · griechische Architektur f, ~ Baukunst f

~ **building style,** ~ architectural ~, Grecian ~ ~ · griechischer Baustil m

~ **column,** Grecian ~ · griechische Säule f

~ **cross,** St. George's ~, Grecian ~ griechisches Kreuz n

~ **decoration art** → ~ ornamental ~

~ **Doric capital,** Grecian ~ ~ · griechisch-dorisches Kapitell n, ~ Kapitäl

~ ~ **order,** Grecian ~ ~ · griechisch-dorische (Säulen)Ordnung f

~ ~ **temple,** Grecian ~ ~ · griechisch-dorischer Tempel m

(~) **fret** → Grecian ~

~ **Ionic order,** Grecian ~ ~ · griechisch-ionische (Säulen)Ordnung f

(~) **key pattern** → Grecian ~ ~

~ **order,** Grecian ~ · griechische (Säulen)Ordnung f

~ **ornamental art,** ~ decorating ~, ~ decoration ~, Grecian ~ ~ · griechische Ornamentik f, ~ Zierkunst f

~ **ovolo (moulding)** (Brit.) → echinus

~ **Revival** · griechischer Neuklassizismus m, ~ Neoklassizismus

~ **Senate building,** bouleuterion, council house · B(o)uleuterion n [Das Rathaus einer griechischen Stadt im Altertum]

~ **stela,** Grecian ~ · griechische Stele f

~ **temple,** Grecian ~ · griechischer Tempel m

~ **(type) acanthus leaf,** Grecian (~) ~ ~ · griechisches Akanthusblatt n

green · grün, ungebrannt [Zustand eines keramischen Erzeugnisses nach der Formgebung, aber vor dem Trocknen. In verschiedenen Ländern wird dieser Ausdruck auch für ein getrocknetes, nicht gebranntes Erzeugnis verwendet]

~ **(anhydrous) oxide chromium (pigment)** → chromium oxide green (~)

~ **area** · Grünfläche f

~ **basic copper carbonate,** mineral green · Berggrün n [Malachit]

~ **belt** · Grüngürtel m, Grünzug m, Grünring m

greenbelt town (US) · Wohnvorstadt f mit weiträumiger Einfamilienhausbebauung

green block, ~ tile [See remark under 'Block'] · Block(stein)frischling m, Steinfrischling, Grünling, Formling, Rohling

~ **(clay) brick** · (Ziegel)Formling m, (Ziegel)Rohling, Grünling, grüner Ziegel m

~ **concrete,** fresh(ly-mixed) ~ [Concrete which has set but not appreciably hardened] · Frischbeton m

~ ~ **density,** fresh(ly-mixed) ~ ~ · Frischbeton-Raumgewicht n, Frischbeton-Wichte f

~ **earth,** chlorite · Chlorit m (Min).

~ ~ **(pigment),** terre verte (~) · Grünerde f, grüne Erde [Eine natürliche Erdfarbe. Sie besteht aus einer komplizierten Tonerde-Eisen-Verbindung der Kieselsäure und etwas Kalzium]

green efflorescence — grid dimension

~ **efflorescence** · grüne Ausblühung f, Vanadiumausblühung

~ **glass** · Grünglas n

~ **ground** · Grüngelände n

greenhouse, glass-house · Gewächshaus n [DIN 11535 Bl. 1]

~ **cast glass**, horticultural ~ ~ · (genörpeltes) Gartenklarglas n [DIN 11526]

~ **glass**, horticultural sheet ~ · (Garten-)Blankglas n, Gartenglas, Gärtner(ei)glas [DIN 11525]

~ **with two equal sides** · Sattelhaus n, gleichseitiges Gewächshaus

(greenish) patina [The thin, stable film of oxid(e) or other metallic compounds which forms on metal surfaces on exposure to air] · Edelrost m, Patina f

green mortar, fresh(ly-mixed) ~ · Frischmörtel m

Green Mosque, Yesil Jami · Grüne Moschee f von Isnik [Nicaea]

green network [Formed by interconnected parks, rivers, lakes, etc.] · Grünnetz n

~ **oil** → anthracene ~

~ ~ **tar**, anthracene ~ ~ · Anthrazenölteer m, Anthracenölteer

~ **organic pigment** · grünes organisches Pigment n; grüne organische Farbe f [Fehlname]

~ **oxide chromium (pigment)** → chromium oxide green (~)

~ **panel**, fresh(ly-made) ~, newly-made ~ · Tafelformling m, Tafelgrünling, Tafelfrischling, frischgeformte Tafel f

~ **pigment** [B.S. 303 and 318] · grünes Pigment n, Grünpigment

~ **product**, fresh(ly-made) ~, newly-made ~ · Formling m, Grünling, Frischling, frischgeformtes Erzeugnis n, frischgeformtes Produkt n, frischgeformter Artikel m, frisches Formstück n, Rohling

~ **room** [A rest room for artists in a theatre or concert hall] · Künstlerraum m

greensand · Grünsand m

green schist · Grünschiefer m

~ **seal** · Grünsiegel n [Betondichtungsmittel]

~ ~ · Grünsiegel n [40% ZnS]

~ **slab**, fresh(ly-made) ~, newly-made ~ · frischgeformte Platte f, Plattenformling m, Plattengrünling, Plattenfrischling

~ **stability** · Grünstandfestigkeit f, Grünstandsicherheit, Grünstabilität f

~ **state**, fresh ~ · frischer Zustand m, grüner ~

greenstone [altered diabase] · Grünstein m

~ **chip(ping)s** · Grünsteinkörnungen fpl, Grünsteinsplitt m, Terrazzokörnungen aus Grünsteinvorkommen

~ **tuff**, diabasic ~ · Diabastuff m, Grünsteintuff

green strength → dry ~

~ ~, initial ~, early ~ · Anfangsfestigkeit f, Frühfestigkeit

~ **strip** · Grünzone f, Grünstreifen m [Städtebau]

~ **tar** [deprecated]; crude ~ · Rohteer m

~ **tile**, ~ block [See remark under 'Block'] · Block(stein)frischling m, Steinfrischling, Grünling, Formling, Rohling

~ **ultramarine** · Ultramaringrün n, grünes Ultramarin n

~ **vitriol**, copperas, melanterite · Melanterit m

grey board, news ~, mill ~, gray ~ · Graupappe f

~ **concrete**, gray ~ · Graubeton m

~ **granite**, gray ~ · grauer Granit m

~ **lime** → ~stone ~

~ ~ **mortar** → grey(stone) ~ ~

~ **marble**, gray ~ · Granitmarmor m

greyness · Apfelsinenschalenanschein m, Orangenschalenanschein [Fehler im optischen Glas]

grey-stone, gray-stone · Graustein m

grey(stone) lime, semi-hydraulic ~ [It contains a smaller proportion of silicates and aluminates than eminently hydraulic lime and is intermediate in properties between this and non-hydraulic lime] · Schwarzkalk m, Zementkalk [Fehlnamen]; gemischter Kalk, hydraulischer Kalk [DIN 1060]

~ ~ **mortar**, semi-hydraulic ~ ~ · Mörtel m aus hydraulischem Kalk, ~ ~ gemischtem ~

greywacke, graywacke · Grauwacke f

~ **limestone**, graywacke ~, transition-lime · Grauwackenkalk m, Übergangskalk

~ **schist**, graywacke ~ · schieferige Grauwacke f

~ **slate**, graywacke ~ · Grauwackenschiefer m

gribble · Bohrassel f [Limnoria lignorum Rathke]

grid → structural ~

~ → planning ~

~ · Raster n

~, **grillage** · Rost m

~ **action** · Rostwirkung f

~ **beam**, grillage ~ [A steel beam of I section, used in broad foundations on yielding soil, where the central load must be distributed] · Rostbalken(träger) m

~ **block** → grid-pattern building

~ **building** → ~-pattern ~

~ **cantilever footing**, grillage ~ ~ · Kragrostfundament n

~ **construction**, ~ (structural) system · Rostkonstruktion(ssystem) f, (n), Rost(bau)system

~ **dimension** · Rasterabmessung f, Rastermaß n

grid façade — grinding line

~ **façade,** grid(-pattern) ~ · Rasterfassade *f*

~ **floor cover(ing),** ~ floor(ing) (finish) · Rost(fuß)boden(belag) *m*

~ **footing,** grillage ~ · Rostfundament *n*

~ **formation** · Rasteranordnung *f*

~ **frame(work),** ~ structure, lattice plate, space frame(work), three-dimensional frame(work), spatial frame(work) [*Grid structures, apart from single layer flat grids, are three-dimensional structures. Unlike shells or folded slabs, however, they are constructed not with solid membranes but with lattice or grid frameworks. In some sytems, however, the grid is formed by the edge junctions of bent or folded sheet panels of suitable material in which the skin strength of the sheet element forms a very large proportion of the total strength of the structure*] · Raumfachwerk *n*, räumliches Fachwerk, dreidimensionales Fachwerk

~ **gas** · Ferngas *n* [*DIN 1340. Ein brennbares technisches Gas aus Großerzeugungsstätten, welches auf weite Entfernungen unter erhöhtem Druck den Stellen der Gasfernversorgung zugeleitet wird*]

~ ~ **line,** gas transmission ~, gas grid ~ · Ferngasleitung *f*, Gasfernleitung

~ **line,** setting-out ~ · Rasterlinie *f*

~ **location,** ~ position [*e.g. of walls, floors, openings, etc.*] · Rasterlage *f*

~ **opening** · Rasteröffnung *f*

grid(-pattern) building, ~ block · Rastergebäude *n*

~ **façade** · Rasterfassade *f* ·

~ **town** · Rasterstadt *f*

grid pipe · Registerrohr *n* [*Strahlungsheizung*]

~ **plan,** reference grid [*A plan in which setting-out lines called grid lines coincide with the most important wall and other building components. Prefabricated buildings are usually designed to fit a grid plan. A grid plan is not a planning grid = Raster*] · Rasternetz *n*

~ **plane** · Rasterebene *f*

~ **plate,** ~ slab · Rasterplatte *f*

~ **position,** ~ location [*e.g. of walls, floors, openings, etc.*] · Rasterlage *f*

~ **slab,** ~ plate · Rasterplatte *f*

~ **(structural) system,** ~ construction · Rostkonstruktion(ssystem) *f*, (*n*), Rost(bau)system

~ **structure,** ~ frame(work), lattice plate, space frame(work), three-dimensional frame(work), spatial frame(work) [*Grid structures apart from single layer flat grids, are three-dimensional structures. Unlike shells or folded slabs, however, they are constructetd not with solid membranes but with lattice or grid frameworks. In some systems, however, the grid is formed by the edge junctions of bent or folded sheet panels of suitable material in which the skin strength of the sheet element forms a very large proportion of the total strength of the structure*] · Raumfachwerk *n*, räumliches Fachwerk, dreidimensionales Fachwerk

~ **suspension system,** ~ ~ ceiling ~ · Rasterdeckensystem *n*

~ **system** · Rastersystem *n*

~ ~ → ~ structural ~

~ **town,** grid-pattern ~ · Rasterstadt *f*

griffe, spur [*An ornament, usually of foliage, on the corner of a square plinth surmounted by a circular pier*] · (Teufels)Klaue *f*

griffin fresco, fresco of griffins · Greifenfresko *n*

grill room · Grillraum *m*

grillage, grid · Rost *m*

~ **beam,** grid ~ [*A steel beam of I section, used in broad foundations on yielding soil, where the central load must be distributed*] · Rostbalken(träger) *m*

~ **cantilever footing,** grid ~ ~ · Kragrostfundament *n*

~ **footing,** grid ~ · Rostfundament *n*

grille [*A functional or decorative openwork screen within an opening. Sometimes spelled 'grill'*] · (Öffnungs)Gitter *n*

~, ventilator grate · Luftgitter *n*, Luftrost *m*

~ **block,** ~ tile · Gitterblock(stein) *m*, Gitterstein

~ **tile,** ~ block · Gitterblock(stein) *m*, Gitterstein

g(r)illed duplex tube, fin(ned) ~ ~, rib(bed) ~ ~ · Duplex-Rippenrohr *n*, Duplex-Lamellenrohr, beripptes Duplexrohr

~ **heater,** rib(bed) ~, (fin(ned)) strip ~ · Rippenheizkörper *m*, berippter Heizkörper, Lamellenheizkörper

~ **heating tube,** rib(bed) ~ ~, (fin(ned)) strip ~ ~ · Rippenheizrohr *n*, beripptes Heizrohr, Lamellenheizrohr

~ **tube,** fin(ned) ~, rib(bed) ~ · beripptes Rohr *n*, Rippenrohr, Lamellenrohr

~ ~ **heater** → fin(ned) ~ ~

~ ~ **radiator** → fin(ned) tube heater

griminess · Schmutzablage *f*

to grind · mahlen

grindability · Mahlbarkeit *f*

~ **curve** · Mahl(barkeits)kurve *f*

~ **tester** · Mahl(barkeits)prüfer *m*

grinding · Mahlen *n*, Mahlung *f*

~ [*smoothing by friction*] · Schleifen *n*

~ **department** · Schleiferei *f*

~ **fineness,** fineness of grinding · Mahlfeinheit *f*

~ ~ **of cement,** fineness of grinding ~ ~, cement grinding fineness · Zementmahlfeinheit *f*

~ **line** · Schleifstraße *f*

grinding mill block — ground contact

~ mill block, ~ ~ building · Mühlengebäude n [Zementwerk]
~ of base, puntying · Bodenschleifen n [Hohlglas]
~ wear · Schleifverschleiß m
~ wheel, abrasive ~ ~ · Schleifstein m
grinning (through) [The showing through plaster of lathing beneath, or the showing of a lower coat of paint through a top coat] · Durchscheinen n
grip → ((bath)tub) hand ~
~ [A small trench to convey water away from a foundation during erection] · Wasserhaltungsgraben m
~ groove → gripping ~
~ handle → swing door ~ ~
~ length → transmission ~
gripping, bonding · Haftung f, Haftfestigkeit f, Haftvermögen n, Haftverbund m [Bewehrung an Beton]
grip(ping) → (mechanical) key
~ groove, (mechanical) key ~ [e.g. on the back of an architectural panel] · Haftrille f, Verbundrille
grit · Körnung f [Schleifpapier]
~ [The heavy mineral matter contained in sewage, such as sand, gravel, cinders, etc.] · "Sand" m, (Trocken)Schlamm m [Straßenentwässerung]
~ box, mud ~, silt ~, ~ bucket [A loose iron box fitted in the bottom of a gulley for collecting deposited silt. It can be removed periodically for emptying and flushing] · (Naß)Schlammfang m, Schmutzfang, (Naß)Schlammfänger m, Schmutzfänger, (Naß)Schlamm(fang)eimer, Schmutzfangeimer
~ bucket → ~ box
~ collector, mud ~, silt ~ · Schlammfang m, Schmutzfang [Straßenentwässerung]
~ erosion, wearing away by wind-borne particles of grit · Sanderosion f, Sandabbau m, Sandabtragung f [Anstrichfilm]
~ trap, mud ~, gull(e)y (~) · Schlammfang m [Ein Straßen- oder Hofablauf mit Rostabdeckung und aushebbarem Schlammeimer]
gritstone, coarse(-grain(ed)) sandstone · grob(körnig)er Sandstein m, Kristallsandstein
gritting material · Streugut n [Abstreuen von Verkehrsflächen]
grog · Brocken m, Bruch m [Feuerfestindustrie. Hiermit werden fehlerhafte Steine und Stein aus dem Abbruch eines Mauerwerks bezeichnet, die gekörnt als Magermittel verwendet werden. Anmerkung: In England wird mit "grog" manchmal gemahlene Schamotte bezeichnet]
~ [Hard-burned and ground fireclays, sometimes used as an ingredient in firebricks. The grog used as an aggregate in refractory mortars and castables is sometimes ground firebrick] · gemahlene Schamotte f

groin, vault ~ [In vaulting, the line of intersection of two vaults] · (Gewölbe-)Grat m, Gierung f, Verschneidungslinie f
~ rib · Gratrippe f
groin(ed) vault · (Kreuz)Gratgewölbe n
groove · Nut f
grooved, keyed · gerillt, (lang)genutet
~ and tongued flooring · gespundete Dielung f
~ dowel, keyed ~ · gerillter (Stab)Dübel m, (lang)genuteter ~
groove(d) match ceiling boarding · genutete Deckenschalung f
grooved pipe · Endrillenrohr n
~ tile · Rillen(belag)platte f, Rillenfliese
gross area · Bruttofläche f
~ column area · Bruttostützenfläche
~ cross-sectional area · Bruttoquerschnittfläche f
~ floor area [The total area of all habitable space in a building] · Brutto-Geschoßwohnfläche f, Brutto-Etagenwohnfläche, Brutto-Stockwerkwohnfläche
~ load · Bruttolast f
~ moment of inertia · Bruttoträgheitsmoment n
~ sectional area · Gesamtquerschnittfläche f
~ weight · Bruttogewicht n, Rohgewicht
grotesque · Groteske f, Grillenwerk n [Ornament aus dünnem Rankenwerk, in das menschliche und tierische Wesen, Früchte, Blumen, Trophäen, Architekturteile und dergleichen eingefügt sind]
grotto · Grotte f
~ column · Grottensäule f
Grotto of Pythagoras in Cartone · Tomba di Pitagora zu Cartone
grotto work · Grottenarbeit f, Grottenwerk n
ground · gemahlen
~ · geschliffen
~ → fixing (fillet)
~, land · Gelände n
~ (US); earth (Brit.) · Erde f [Elektrotechnik]
~ (US) → substratum
~, back~ · Fond m [(Papier)Tapete]
~, back~, base (surface), backing (material) · (Unter)Grund m
~ asbestos · gemahlener Asbest m
~ basic slag, slag flour, Thomas meal · Schlackenmehl n, Thomasmehl, Thomasphosphat n
~ clamp → grounding ~
~ (clay) brick(s), (clay) brick dust, (clay) brick flour · Ziegelstaub m, Ziegelmehl n
~ connection · Erdanschluß m
~ contact → grounding ~

ground cork — ground(ing) lead

~ cork, powder(ed) ~, cork powder, cork flour · Korkmehl *n*

~ course → plinth

to ground dry · trockenmahlen

ground floor → floor slab

~ ~ (Brit.); first ~ (US) [*In buildings with a basement or cellar the first floor is the first above ground level called 'ground floor' in Great Britain*] · Erdgeschoß *n*, EG

ground(-)floor building · Erdgeschoßgebäude *n*, EG-Gebäude

~ column · Erdgeschoßstütze *f*, EG-Stütze

~ dwelling (Brit.) → ~ dwelling unit

~ dwelling unit (US); ~ dwelling (Brit.) · Erdgeschoßwohnung *f*, EG-Wohnung

~ entrance · Erdgeschoßeingang *m*, EG-Eingang

~ fireplace · Erdgeschoßkamin *m*, EG-Kamin

~ floor · EG-Decke *f*, Erdgeschoßdecke

~ ~ cover(ing), ~ floor(ing) (finish) · Erdgeschoß(fuß)boden(belag) *m*, EG-Fuß(Boden)belag

~ floor(ing) (finish), ~ floor cover(ing) · Erdgeschoß(fuß)boden(belag) *m*, EG-(Fuß)Boden(belag)

~ (ground(-))plan · Erdgeschoßgrundriß *m*, EG-Grundriß

~ height · Erdgeschoßhöhe *f*, EG-Höhe

~ masonry wall · Erdgeschoßmauer *f*, EG-Mauer

~ slab · Erdgeschoßplatte *f*, EG-Platte

~ window · Erdgeschoßfenster *n*, EG-Fenster

ground floor(ing) (finish) → ~ level ~ (~)

~ glass → glass powder

~ gypsum, powder(ed) ~, gypsum powder · gemahlener Gips *m*, Gipsmehl *n*, Gipspulver *n*

~ in oil · (in Öl) angerieben [*Kammerbleiweiß*]

~ lead → grounding ~

~ level, level of ground, grade · Geländehöhe *f*, Niveau *n*

~ ~ · Bodenebene *f*, Vorfeldebene [*Abfertigungsgebäude*]

~ ~ car park, ~ ~ parking place, ~ ~ parking lot · ebenerdige (Auto)Parkfläche *f*, ebenerdiger (Auto)Parkplatz *m*

~ ~ parking lot, ~ ~ ~ place, ~ ~ car park · ebenerdige (Auto)Parkfläche *f*, ebenerdiger (Auto)Parkplatz *m*

~ limestone → powder(ed) ~

~ mass, matrix · Grundmasse *f*, Matrix *f* [*Substanz, in die Körner oder Kristalle eingebettet sind*]

~ material → grounding ~

~ metal sheet → grounding ~ ~

~ moisture · Bodenfeuchte *f*, Bodenfeuchtigkeit *f*

~ ~ · Erdfeuchte *f*, Erdfeuchtigkeit *f*

~ mould (Brit.); ~ mold (US) [*A mo(u)ld for the invert of a gallery or drain*] · Sohlenform *f*

~ (natural) stone · gemahlener (Natur-)Stein *m*

~ network → grounding ~

groundnut oil [*B. S. 629*] · Erdnußöl *n*

ground paper, (back)ground wall~ · Fondtapete *f*

~ oscillation, ~ vibration · Bodenerschütterung *f*

(ground(-))plan · Grundriß *m*

~ area · Grundrißfläche *f*

~ dimension · Grundrißabmessung *f*, Grundrißmaß *n*

~ form → ~ shape

~ geometry · Grundrißgeometrie *f*

~ shape, ~ form · Grundrißform *f*

~ type · Grundrißart *f*

ground plate → grounding ~

~ powder · gemahlenes Pulver *n*

~ product · Mühlen-Fertiggut *n*

~ rock · gemahlenes (Natur)Gestein *n*

~ rod → grounding ~

~ set flagpole · Boden-Fahnenmast *m*, Boden-Flaggenmast

~ stone, ~ natural ~ · gemahlener (Natur)Stein *m*

~ storey (Brit.); ~ story (US) [*The space in a building between ground floor and first floor*] · Parterre *n*

~ switch → grounding ~

ground-table → plinth

ground Trinidad épuré with rock flour, ~ ~ ~ ~ ~ dust (US); ~ ~ ~ ~ stone ~ (Brit.) · Trinidadpulver *n* [*Wird der Trinidad Epuré unter Zusatz von Kalksteinmehl oder anderen Steinmehlen gemahlen, so bezeichnet man dieses Material als Trinidadpulver*]

~ vibration, ~ oscillation · Bodenerschütterung *f*

~ wall, foundation ~ · Gründungswand *f*

~ (wall)paper, back~ ~ · Fondtapete *f*

~ washer → grounding ~

~ white lead (in oil), white lead in oil paste · Ölbleiweiß *n*

grounding, earth connection, earthing · Erden *n*, (Schutz)Erdung *f*, Erdverbindung [*Elektrotechnik*]

ground(ing) clamp, earth(ing) ~ · Erdungsschelle *f*

~ contact, earth(ing) ~ · Erdungskontakt *m*

~ lead, earth(ing) ~, earth-continuity conductor, grounding connector · Erddraht *m*, Erd(zu)leitung *f*, Erdungsleitung

~ **material,** earth(ing) ~ · Erdungsmaterial *n* [*Elektrotechnik*]

~ **metal sheet,** earth(ing) ~ ~ · Erdungsblech *n*

~ **network,** earth(ing) ~ · Erdungsnetz *n*

~ **plate,** earth(ing) ~ · Erdungsplatte *f*, Plattenerder *m*

~ **rod,** earth(ing) ~ · Erdungsstab *m*, Staberder *m*

~ **switch,** earth(ing) ~ · Erdungsschalter *m*

~ **washer,** earth(ing) ~ · Erdungsscheibe *f*

groundwater · drückendes Wasser *n*, Druckwasser, Grundwasser

~ **lowering work** · Wasserhaltungsarbeiten *fpl* [*DIN 18305*]

(~) **waterproofing material** → (~) ~ product

(~) ~ **product,** (~) ~ material · druckwasserhaltender Stoff *m*, druckwasserhaltendes Mittel *n*, druckwasserhaltendes Erzeugnis *n*, Grundwasser(ab)-dicht(ungs)mittel, Grundwasser(ab)-dicht(ungs)stoff, Grundwasser(ab)-dicht(ungs)erzeugnis

group connection · Gruppenschaltung *f* [*Leuchten*]

~ **of blocks** → ~ ~ buildings

~ ~ **buildings,** ~ ~ blocks, complex ~ ~, building complex; clump of buildings (US) · Gebäudeblock *m*, Gebäudekomplex *m*

~ ~ **chimneys,** chimney group · Schornsteingruppe *f*

~ ~ **houses,** complex ~ ~, house complex; clump of houses (US) · Häuserblock *m*, Häuserkomplex *m*

~ ~ **loads** · Lastengruppe *f*

~ **stand** · Gemeinschaftsstand *m*, Gruppenstand [*Auf einer Messe oder Ausstellung*]

grouped meters, grouping of (tenants') ~ · zentrale Zähleranordnung *f*

grouping of rafter(s) according to lengths · Einteilung *f* der Sparrenlänge, Sparrenaufteilung

~ ~ **(tenants') meters,** grouped ~ · zentrale Zähleranordnung *f*

to grout [*terrazzo tiles*] · spachteln [*Terrazzoplatten*]

grout (US); quarry waste · Abfallsteine *mpl*, Steinbruchabfall *m*

~ → grouting compound

~ **box** [*A conical box formed of expanded metal, cast into concrete, and having an anchor plate at its foot to receive a foundation bolt*] · konisches Loch *n*

~ **hole** · Mörtelauspreßloch *n*, Mörteleinpreßloch, Mörtelverpreßloch, Mörtelinjektionsloch ·

~ **injection** · Mörtelauspressung *f*, Mörtelverpressung, Mörteleinpressung, Mörtelinjektion *f*

~ **seal,** grouting compound ~, slurry ~ · Schlämmeabsieg(e)lung *f*, Schlämmeversieg(e)lung

~ **void** [*Between adjacent floor units or roof units*] · Einpreßhohlraum *m*, Verpreßhohlraum, Auspreßhohlraum, Injektionshohlraum, Injizierhohlraum

grouted concrete, colloidal ~ [*e.g. Colcrete*] · Kolloid(al)beton *m*, kolloid(-al)er Beton

~ **macadam** · (Asphalt-)Mörtelmakadam *m*, Bitumen-Mörtelmakadam [*Die Hohlräume einer abgewalzten Schotterschicht werden durch Einbringen eines bituminösen Mörtels verfüllt*]

grouting → grout(ing compound)

~ **agent,** ~ aid, injection ~ · Auspreßhilfe *f*, Einpreßhilfe, Verpreßhilfe, Injektionshilfe, EH [*Verminderung des Absetzens des Zementmörtels im Spannkanal bzw. mäßiges Quellen. Verbesserung des Fließens des Mörtels beim Einpressen und Verminderung des Wasseranspruches des Mörtels*]

~ **aid** → ~ agent

~ **cement,** injection ~ · Auspreßzement *m*, Verpreßzement, Einpreßzement, Injizierzement, Injektionszement

~ **compound,** filling ~ · Spachtel(-masse) *m*, (*f*) [*Zum Maschinenspachteln von Terrazzoplatten*]

grout(ing compound), slurry, grouting [*A fluid mix(ture) of binder, sand and water or of binder and water*] · Schlämme *f*

~ ~ **seal,** slurry ~ · Schlämmeabsieg(e)lung *f*, Schlämmeversieg(e)lung

grouting cross-section [*between floor slabs*] · Vergußquerschnitt *m* [*zwischen Deckenplatten*]

grout(ing fluid) → intrusion mortar

grouting gun, injection ~ · Injektions-(spritz)pistole *f*, Einpreß(spritz)pistole, Injektionsspritze *f*, Einpreßspritze, Auspreß(spritz)pistole, Verpreß(spritz)-pistole, Auspreßspritze, Verpreßspritze, Injizier(spritz)pistole, Injizierspritze

grout(ing) hole · Eindringmörtelloch *n*, Injiziermörtelloch, Injektionsmörtelloch

grouting mortar → intrusion ~

~ **resin,** injection ~ · Injektionsharz *n*, Einpreßharz, Auspreßharz, Verpreßharz, Injizierharz [*Zum monolithischen Verbund von Rissen in Beton, Betonfertigteilen und Zementestrichen*]

~ **suspension** · Auspreßsuspension *f*, Einpreßsuspension, Verpreßsuspension, Injektionssuspension

~ **work** · Auspreßarbeiten *fpl*, Injektionsarbeiten, Einpreßarbeiten, Verpreßarbeiten [*DIN 18309*]

groutnick [*A special groove formed in a masonry joint for pouring in grout*] · Schlämmespalt *m*

'**growing house**' [*Designed by Hans Scharoun in 1932, based on the grid system to give the owner a precise*

'growing house' — gun(-grade) (clear) varnish

cost synopsis throughout erection, together with the necessary extensions] · „wachsendes Haus" *n*

growth defect, ~ fault · Wuchsfehler *m* [*Holz*]

~ fault, ~ defect · Wuchsfehler *m* [*Holz*]

~ of fungi, fungi growth · Pilzwuchs *m*

grp → glass reinforced laminate

GRP → glass reinforced laminate

~ → glass fibre(-reinforced) polyester

GT → grease trap

~ → glazed (clay) tile

guard · Schutz *m* [*z.B. Kantenschutz*]

guardhouse · Wache *f*

~ → porter's lodge

guard room · Wachlokal *n*, Wache *f*, Wachraum *m*

guest bathroom · Gästebad(ezimmer) *n*, Gästebaderaum *m*

(~) bedrom, hotel ~ · Bettenraum *m*, Bettenzimmer *n*, Schlafraum [*Hotel*]

(~) ~ block, (~) ~ building · Bettenzimmergebäude *n*, Bettenraumgebäude, Schlafraumgebäude [*Hotel*]

(~) ~ building, (~) ~ block · Schlafraumgebäude *n*, Bettenraumgebäude [*Hotel*]

~ cabin · Gästehütte *f*

~ drive · Gästevorfahrt *f* [*Hotel*]

guesthouse · Gästehaus *n*

guest-pavilion · Gästepavillon *m*

guest refrigerator · Gästekühlschrank *m*

~ room · Fremdenzimmer *n*, Gästezimmer, Gastzimmer

guide · Führung *f*

~ angle · Führungswinkel *m*

~ coat · Kontrollgrund *m* [*Anstrichtechnik*]

~ roller · Führungsrolle *f*, Leitrolle

guide(line spec(ification)) · Richtlinie *f*

guiding rafter · Lehrsparren *m*

~ rafters · Lehrgespärre *n*

guild-hall, custom-house · Gildenhalle *f*, Gildenhaus *n*, Kaufhalle, Kaufhaus [*Im Mittelalter ein städtisches Gebäude mit großen Sälen zum Auslegen und Aufspeichern von Waren*]

guilloche, plait-band, braid pattern [*A decorative border design in which two or more lines or bands are interwoven so as to make circular spaces between them. It is frequently used to ornament the 'torus' mo(u)lding*] · Guillochierung *f*, Schlangenverzierung

gull(e)y, inlet · (Regen)Wasserablauf *m*, Regen(wasser)einlauf, Sinkkasten *m*, Gully *m* [*DIN 4052*]

~ grate → inlet ~

~ grating → inlet grate

~ grid → inlet grate

~ opening, inlet ~ · Einlauföffnung *f*, Ablauföffnung

~ surround, inlet ~ · Einlaufeinfassung *f*, Ablaufeinfassung

~ (trap), gum ~, mud ~ · Schlammfang *m* [*Ein Straßen- oder Hofablauf mit Rostabdeckung und aushebbarem Schlammeimer*]

gum [*misnomer*]; gum resin · harziges Gummi *n*, harziger ~ *m*, Gummiharz *n*

~ arabic, (~) acacia · Gummiarabikum *n*, arabisches Gummi *n*, arabischer Gummi *m*

(~) benzoin, (~) benjamin · Benzoeharz *n*

~ resin [*misnomer: gum*] · harziges Gummi *n*, harziger ~ *m*, Gummiharz *n*

~ rosin · Balsamkolophonium *n*

~ turpentine · Terpentin *n* [*Fichtenharz. Ausgangsstoff für Terpentinöl*]

gummy, sticky · kleb(e)rig [*Anstrichmittel*]

gun · Pistole *f*, Spritz~, Spritze *f*

~ · (Spritz)Kanone *f*

~ application · (Spritz)Kanonenauftrag *m*

~ ~ · (Spritz)Pistolenauftrag *m*

gun-applied, gunned, sprayed(-on) · pistolengespritzt, pistolenaufgetragen

~, gunned, sprayed(-on) · pneumatisch aufgetragen, ~ gespritzt

~ exterior plaster(ing) → gun(-grade) (external) rendering

~ ~ rendering → gun(-grade) (external) ~

~ external plaster(ing) → gun(-grade) (external) rendering

~ (~) rendering → gun(-grade) (~) ~

~ mortar, pneumatic ~ · pneumatisch aufgetragener Mörtel *m*

~ rendering → gun(-grade) (external) ~

gun cement → gun-grade ~

~ consistence → ~-grade ~

~ exterior plaster(ing) → gun(-grade) (external) rendering

~ ~ rendering ~ gun(-grade) (external) ~

~ external plaster(ing) → gun(-grade) (external) rendering

~ (~) rendering → gun-grade (~) ~

gun-grade, spray-applied, sprayable · spritzbar, spritzfähig

gun(-grade) asphalt, gunned ~, spray(-ing) ~, sprayed(-on) ~, pressure-gun type ~, gun-applied ~ · Spritzasphalt *m*

~ cement, ~ putty, gunned ~, spray(-ing) ~, sprayed(-on) ~, pressure-gun type ~ [*It is generally a soft material which is forced by hand or air pressure through a variety of nozzles*] · (Spritz-)Pistolenkitt *m*

~ (clear) varnish, gunned (~) ~, spray(ing) (~) ~, sprayed(-on) (~) ~, pressure-gun type (~) ~, gun-applied (~) ~ · Spritz(klar)lack *m*

gun(-grade) composition — gunned paint coat

~ **composition**, ~ compound, ~ mass, ~ material, gunned ~, spray(ing) ~, sprayed(-on) ~, pressure-gun type ~, gun-applied ~ · Spritzmasse *f*

~ **compound**, ~ material, ~ mass, ~ composition, gunned ~, spray(ing) ~, sprayed(-on) ~, pressure-gun type ~, gun-applied ~ · Spritzmasse *f*

~ **consistence**, ~ consistency · Spritzkonsistenz *f*, Spritzsteife *f*

~ **cork**, gunned ~, spray(ing) ~, sprayed(-on) ~, pressure-gun type ~, gun-applied ~ · Spritzkork *m*

~ **exterior plaster(ing)** → sprayed(-on) (external) rendering

~ ~ **rendering** → sprayed(-on) (external) ~

~ **(external) rendering** → sprayed(-on) (~) ~

~ **foam**, gunned ~, spray(ing) ~, sprayed(-on) ~, pressure-gun type ~, gun-applied ~ · Spritzschaum *m*

~ **mass**, ~ material, ~ compound, ~ composition, gunned ~, spray(ing) ~, sprayed(-on) ~, pressure-gun type ~, gun-applied ~ · Spritzmasse *f*

~ **mastic**, spray(ing) ~, gunned ~, sprayed(-on) ~, pressure-gun type ~, gun-applied ~ · Spritzmastix *m*

~ **material**, ~ compound, ~ mass, ~ composition, gunned ~, spray(ing) ~, sprayed(-on) ~, pressure-gun type ~, gun-applied ~ · Spritzmasse *f*

~ **plastic**, gunned ~, spray(ing) ~, sprayed(-on) ~, pressure-gun type ~, gun-applied ~ · Spritzkunststoff *m*

~ **putty** → gunned ~

~ ~ → ~ cement

~ **rendering** → sprayed(-on) (external) ~

~ **varnish** → ~ clear ~

~ **vermiculite**, gunned ~, spray(ing) ~, sprayed(-on) ~, pressure-gun type ~, gun-applied ~ · Spritzvermiculite *m*

gunite, dry-mix shotcrete [*Pneumatically conveyed shotcrete in which most of the mixing water is added at the nozzle*] · Trockenspritzbeton *m*, Torkretbeton

~ **coating** · Torkretschicht *f*
~ **jacket** · Torkretmantel *m*
~ **-jacketed** · torkretummantelt

gunite machine → cement concrete ~ ~

~ **mortar** · Torkretmörtel *m*

guniting → shooting

~, concrete-spraying, cement gun work [*A special process for placing concrete or mortar employing compressed air to convey the dry ingredients to a spraying nozzle where the water is added. This process and plant must not be confused with the concrete gun*] · Torkretverfahren *n*, Betonspritzverfahren

~ **aid** · Torkret(ier)hilfe *f*

gunmetal [*It contains 90 per cent copper, 8 per cent tin and 2 per cent zinc*] · Geschützbronze *f*

gunnable · verspritzbar [*Masse*]

gunned, sprayed(-on), gun-applied · pistolengespritzt, pistolenaufgetragen

~, gun-applied, sprayed(-on) · pneumatisch aufgetragen, ~ gespritzt

~ **asphalt**, gun-grade ~, spray(ing) ~, sprayed(-on) ~, pressure-gun type ~, gun-applied ~ · Spritzasphalt *m*

~ **cement** → gun(-grade) ~

~ **(clear) varnish**, gun(-grade) (~) ~, spray(ing) (~) ~, sprayed(-on) (~) ~, pressure-gun type (~) ~, gun-applied (~) ~ · Spritz(klar)lack *m*

~ **coat**, spray(ing) ~, sprayed(-on) ~, gun-applied ~ · Spritzanstrich *m*, Spritzaufstrich

~ ~ **of paint**, gun-applied ~ ~ ~, spray(ing) ~ ~ ~, sprayed(-on) ~ ~ ~, ~ paint coat · Spritzfarbanstrich *m*, Spritzfarbaufstrich

~ **composition**, ~ compound, ~ mass, ~ material, gun(-grade) ~, spray(ing) ~, sprayed(-on) ~, pressure-gun type ~, gun-applied ~ · Spritzmasse *f*

~ **compound**, ~ material, ~ mass, ~ composition, gun(-grade) ~, spray(-ing) ~, sprayed(-on) ~, pressure-gun type ~, gun-applied ~ · Spritzmasse *f*

~ **concrete** → sprayed(-on) ~

~ **cork**, gun(-grade) ~, spray(ing) ~, sprayed(-on) ~, pressure-gun type ~, gun-applied ~ · Spritzkork *m*

~ **exterior plaster(ing)** → sprayed(-on) (external) rendering

~ ~ **rendering** → sprayed(-on) (external) ~

~ **external plaster(ing)** → sprayed(-on) (external) rendering

~ **(~) rendering** → sprayed(-on) (~) ~

~ **film**, gun-applied ~, spray(ing) ~, sprayed(-on) ~, ~ membrane · Spritzhaut *f*, Spritzfilm *m*

~ **foam**, gun(-grade) ~, spray(ing) ~, sprayed(-on) ~, pressure-gun type ~, gun-applied ~ · Spritzschaum *m*

~ **insulation**, spray(ing) ~, spayed(-on) ~, gun-applied ~ · Spritzisolierung *f*

~ **mass**, ~ material, ~ compound, ~ composition, gun(-grade) ~, spray(-ing) ~, sprayed(-on) ~, pressure-gun type ~, gun-applied ~ · Spritzmasse *f*

~ **mastic**, gun(-grade) ~, spray(ing) ~, sprayed(-on) ~, pressure-gun type ~, gun-applied ~ · Spritzmastix *m*

~ **material**, ~ compound, ~ mass, ~ composition, gun(-grade) ~, spray(-ing) ~, sprayed(-on) ~, pressure-gun type ~, gun-applied ~ · Spritzmasse *f*

~ **membrane**, gun-applied ~, spray(-ing) ~, sprayed(-on) ~, ~ film · Spritzfilm *m*, Spritzhaut *f*

~ **paint coat**, gun-applied ~ ~, sprayed(-on) ~ ~, spray(ing) ~ ~, ~ coat of paint · Spritzfarbanstrich *m*, Spritzfarbaufstrich

gunned plastic — Gypstele system

~ **plastic,** gun(-grade) ~, spray(ing) ~, sprayed(-on) ~, pressure-gun type ~, gun-applied ~ · Spritzkunststoff *m*

~ **putty,** gun(-grade) ~, spray(ing) ~, sprayed(-on) ~, pressure-gun type ~, gun-applied ~ · Verglasungs-Spritzkitt *m*, Einglasungs-Spritzkitt

~ ~ → gun(-grade) cement

~ **rendering** → sprayed(-on) (external) ~

~ **varnish** → ~ clear ~

~ **vermiculite,** gun(-grade) ~, spray(-ing) ~, sprayed(-on) ~, pressure-gun type ~, gun-applied ~ · Spritzvermiculite *m*

gunning → shooting

~ **technique,** ~ technic · Torkrettechnik *f*

gun putty → gun(-grade) cement

~ **rendering** → gun(-grade) (external) ~

(~) **spraying,** spray application [*A method of application in which the liquid coating material is broken up into a fine mist which is directed on to the surface to be coated. This atomization process is usually, but not necessarily, effected by a compressed air jet*] · (Auf)Spritzen *n*

gusset plate, binding ~, fish ~, corner ~, joint ~, connection ~, connecting ~, knee bracket ~ · Knoten(punkt)-verbindung *f*

gusseted connection, ~ joint · Knotenblechanschluß *m*, Knotenblechverbindung *f*

~ **joint,** ~ connection · Knotenblechanschluß *m*, Knotenblechverbindung *f*

gust, wind ~, gusty wind · böiger Wind *m*, Böe *f*

~ **loading factor** · Böigkeitsbeiwert *m*

~ **speed,** wind ~ ~, gusty wind ~ · Böengeschwindigkeit *f*

gustiness · Böigkeit *f*

gusty wind, (wind) gust · böiger Wind *m*, Böe *f*

~ ~ **speed,** (wind) gust ~ · Böengeschwindigkeit *f*

gußasphalt; bituminous mastic concrete (US) · Gußasphalt *m* [*Ein korngestuftes Mineralgemisch, das in heißem Zustand mit Straßenbaubitumen vermischt wird*]

~ **surfacing;** bituminous mastic concrete ~ (US) · Gußasphaltbelag *m*, Gußasphaltdecke *f*

gutta · Tropfen *m* [*dorischer Stil*]

gutta-percha · Gettaniagummi *m, n*, Gummi plasticum, (Gutta)Percha *f*, Tubangummi

gutted, fire-~, ruined by fire, burnt down, burned down, destroyed by fire · abgebrannt, ausgebrannt, niedergebrannt

~ **structure,** fire-~ ~ · Brandruine *f*

gutter, roof ~, rainwater ~, R.W. ~ · (Dach)Rinne *f*, Regenrinne, Abflußrinne [*DIN 18460*]

~ · Sohlschale *f*

~ **angle** · Rinnenwinkel *m*

~ **beam of U section** · Kasten(dach)-binder *m* [*Shedhalle*]

~ **block** · Schalenstein *m* [*Schweiz*]

~ **board,** roof ~ ~ · (Dach)Rinnenbrett *n*, Regenrinnenbrett

~ **bottom,** ~ sole · Rinnenboden *m*

~ **bracket,** ~ hanger · Rinnenhalter *m*

~ **-float** · halbrundes Kehlreibebrett *n* [*Asphaltarbeiterwerkzeug*]

gutter for chemical wastes · Chemieabwasserrinne *f*

~ **hanger,** ~ bracket · Rinnenhalter *m*

~ **heating,** roof ~ ~, rainwater ~ ~ · (Dach)Rinnenbeheizung *f*, Regenrinnenbeheizung

~ **hook,** roof ~ ~, rainwater ~ ~ · (Dach)Rinnenhaken *m*, Regenrinnenhaken

~ **(paving) sett** · Rinnenstein *m* [*Straßenbau*]

~ **sett,** ~ paving ~ · Rinnenstein *m* [*Straßenbau*]

~ **sheet,** roof ~ ~ · (Dach)Rinnenblech *n*, Regenrinnenblech

~ **sole,** ~ bottom · Rinnenboden *m*

~ **tile** · Rinnen(belag)platte *f*, Rinnenfliese *f*

guy anchor · Trossenanker *m*, Abspannseilanker

~ **(rope)** · Trosse *f*, Abspannseil *n*, Ankerseil

~ **wire** · Abspanndraht *m*

guyed chimney · abgespannter Schornstein *m*, Trossenschornstein

~ **tower** · abgespannter Turm *m*, Trossenturm

gym(nasium) · Turnhalle *f*

~ **equipment** [*B.S. 1892*] · Turnhallengeräte *npl*

~ **for boys and girls** · Doppelturnhalle *f*

~ **locker** · Turnhallenspind *m*

gyppo (US); piece work · Akkordarbeit *f*

gypseous marl, gypsum ~ · Gipsmergel *m*

~ **spar,** gypsum ~ · Gipsspat *m*

~ **sand,** gypsum ~ · Gipssand *m* (Geol.)

~ **solid rock,** compact gypsum · dichter (Roh)Gipsstein *m*, fest(gelagert)er ~, kompakter ~, Gipsfels *m*

gypsite, friable gypsum, earthy gypsum, gypsum earth [*A gypsum variety containing dirt and sand*] · erdiger Gips *m*, erdiges Gipsgestein *n*, feinporiges Gipsgestein, Gipserde *f*

Gypstele system (Brit.) · Alu(minium)-profile *npl* mit eingeschobenen Gipsbrettern

gypsum — gypsum earth

gypsum → massive ~

~ [*It is a naturally occurring mineral composed of hydrous calcium sulphate with two molecules of combined water and having the chemical formula $CaSO_4 \cdot 2H_2O$. It is also formed as by-product in the manufacture of phosphate fertilisers by the treatment of phosphate rock with sulphuric acid, and gypsum plasters are made from both the natural gypsum and this by-product*] · $CaSO_4 \cdot 2H_2O$, Gips *m*

~ **article**, ~ product · Gipsartikel *m*, Gipsgegenstand *m*, Gipserzeugnis *n*

~ **backing (coat) (mixed) plaster** → ~ basecoat (~) ~

~ ~ **(mixed) plaster** → ~ basecoat (~) ~

~ ~ **plaster** → ~ basecoat (mixed) ~

~ **(base)board**; plate [*Scotland*] · (Gipskarton-)Stuckplatte *f*

~ **basecoat (mixed) plaster**, ~ undercoat (~) ~, ~ backing (coat) (~) ~ · (Innen)Gipsgrob(ver)putz *m*, (Innen-)Gipsgrund(ver)putz, (Innen)Gipsunter(ver)putz

~ **based** · gipshaltig

~ ~ **mortar** · gipshaltiger Mörtel *m*

~ **block** → ~ building ~

~ ~ · Gips(stein)block *m* [*Naturstein*]

~ **board** → ~ building ~

~ ~ → (~) plasterboard (sheet)

~ ~, ~ base~, plate [*Scotland*] · (Gipskarton-)Stuckplatte *f*

~ ~ **ceiling** → ~ building ~ ~

~ ~ ~ → dry ~

(~) ~ **finish plaster** · Gipsplatten(ver)putz *m*

~ **(~) lath(ing)**, board ~, rock ~, sheet of gypsum plasterboard; gypsum plank (Brit.); plaster lath(ing) [*deprecated*] [*A gypsum plasterboard designed to receive gypsum plaster. It is produced in relatively small sheets and has a specially designed edge*] · Gipskarton-Putzträgerplatte *f*

~ ~ **panel** → (~) plasterboard ~

~ ~ ~ **partition (wall)** → (~) plasterboard ~ ~ (~)

~ ~ **partition** → ~ building ~ ~

~ ~ ~ **(wall)** → (~) plasterboard (sheet) ~ (~)

~ **(~) sheathing**, ~ plasterboard ~ · Gipskartonplattenverschalung *f*

~ ~ **wall** → (~) plasterboard (sheet) ~

~ **bond(ing) plaster** · Gips(innen)haft(ver)putz *m*

~-**bound** · gipsgebunden

gypsum breaker, ~ crusher · Gipsbrecher *m*

~ **(building) block**, ~ (~) tile [*See remark under 'Block'*] · Gipsbaustein *m*, Gipsblock *m*, Gips(block)stein

~ **(~) board**, ~ (~) sheet · Gips(bau)platte *f*, Bau-Gipsplatte

~ **(~) ~ ceiling**, ~ (~) sheet ~ · Bau-Gipsplattendecke *f*, Gips(bau)plattendecke

~ **(~) ~ partition**, ~ (~) sheet ~ · Gips(bau)plattentrennwand *f*, Bau-Gipsplattentrennwand

~ **(~) component** → ~ (~) unit

~ ~ **material** · Gipsbaumaterial *n* [*Schweiz*]; Gipsbaustoff *m*

~ **(~) member** → ~ (~) unit

(~) ~ plaster [*B.S. 1191*] · Baugips *m* [*DIN 1168*]

~ **(~) sheet** → ~ (~) board

~ **(~) ~ ceiling**, ~ (~) board ~ · Gips(bau)plattendecke *f*, Bau-Gipsplattendecke

~ **(~) ~ partition**, ~ (~) board ~ · Gips(bau)plattentrennwand *f*, Bau-Gipsplattentrennwand

~ **(~) tile** → ~ (~) block

~ **(~) unit**, ~ (~) member, ~ (~) component · Gips(bau)element *n*, Gips(bau)körper *m*, Gipsmontageelement, Gipsmontagekörper, Gipsfertig(bau)element, Gipsfertig(bau)körper [*Fehlnamen: Gips(bau)einheit f, Gipsmontageeinheit*]

~ **cassette slab**, ~ waffle ~, ~ pan(el) ~, ~ coffer ~ · Gipskassettenplatte *f*

~ **cast building unit** → ~ pre~ ~ ~

~ **ceiling baseboard**, ceiling gypsum ~ · (Gipskarton-)Deckenstuckplatte *f*, (Gipskarton-)Stuckdeckenplatte, (Gipskarton-)Deckenputzträgerplatte, (Gipskarton-)Putzträgerdeckenplatte

~ ~ **board**; ceiling plate [*Scotland*] · Gipsdeckenplatte *f*, Deckenplatte aus Gips [*DIN 18169*]

~ **coffer slab**, ~ pan(el) ~, ~ cassette ~, ~ waffle ~ · Gipskassettenplatte *f*

~ **component** → ~ (building) unit

~ **composite board** → (~) ~ plasterboard

(~) ~ plasterboard, ~ ~ board; composite plate [*Scotland*] · Gipskarton-Verbundplatte *f*

~ **concrete** · Gipsbeton *m* [*Estrichgips mit $^1/_1$ bis $^1/_3$ Rtl. Schlacken, Ziegelbruch u.a. (seltener mit Kiessand)*]

~ ~ **block**, ~ ~ tile [*See remark under 'Block'*] · Gipsbetonblock(stein) *m*, Gipsbetonstein

~ ~ **tile** → ~ ~ block

~ **content** · Gipsgehalt *m*

~ **core**, core of gypsum · Gipskern *m*

~ **crusher**, ~ breaker · Gipsbrecher *m*

~ **earth** → gypsite

gypsum filler (block) — gypsum retarder

~ **filler (block)**, ~ ~ tile [*See remark under 'Block(stein)'*] · Gipsdeckenstein *m*, Gipsdeckenblock(stein) *m*, Gips(decken)füllstein, Gips(decken)füllblock(stein)

~ **finish**, ~ plaster · Gipsverputz *m*

~ **floor pot** → hollow floor tile

~**-free**, gypsum-less · gipsfrei, gipslos

gypsum heated in pan(s) · Kesselgips *m*

~ ~ ~ **kettle(s)** · Kammerofengips *m*

~ **hollow floor tile**, ~ floor pot [*See remark under 'Block'*] · Gips-Deckenhohlblock *m*, Gips-Deckenhohl(block)stein *m*, Gips-Hohldecken(block)stein, Gips-Hohldeckenblock

~ **industry** · Gipsindustrie *f*

~ **insulation**, flocculent gypsum · Flockengips *m* [*für Schüttisolierungen*]

~ **job-mix(ed) basecoat plaster**, ~ ~ undercoat ~, ~ ~ backing (coat) ~ · Baustellen-(Innen)Gipsgrob(ver)putz *m*, Baustellen-(Innen)Gipsgrund(ver)putz, Baustellen-(Innen)Gipsunter(ver)putz

(~) **kettle** · (Gips)Kammerofen *m*

~ **lath(ing)** → ~ board ~

gypsum-less, gypsum-free · gipsfrei, gipslos

gypsum-lime mortar · Gipskalkmörtel *m*

~ **plaster** · Gipskalk(ver)putz *m*

~ **stuff**, ~ mix(ture) · Gipskalkputzmasse *f*, Gipskalkputzmörtel *m*

gypsum marl, gypseous ~ · Gipsmergel *m*

~ **meal** · Gips(ge)steinmehl *n*, Rohgipsmehl, Naturgipsmehl

~ **member** → ~ (building) unit

~ **mortar** · Gipsmörtel *m* [*Er hat nur Gips als Bindemittel und keine Zuschläge. Gips muß solange langsam in Wasser eingestreut werden, bis auf der Oberfläche trockene Flecken auftreten. Verzögerungsmittel müssen vorher im Wasser gelöst werden*]

~ **neat plaster** · reiner Gipsputz *m*

(~) **pan** · (Gips)Kessel *m*

~ **pan(el) slab**, ~ waffle ~, ~ cassette ~, ~ coffer ~ · Gipskassettenplatte *f*

~ **partition tile**, ~ ~ block [*See remark under '(building) block'*] · Gipstrennwandblock(stein) *m*, Gipstrennwandstein

~ **paste**, ~ putty · Gipsbrei *m*, Gipspaste *f*

~ **pat**, circular-domed pat of gypsum · Gipskuchen *m*, Probekuchen aus Gips

~ **plank** (Brit.) → ~ (board) lath(ing)

~ ~ · Gipsdiele *f*

~ ~ **with reed** · Gipsdiele *f* mit Schilfrohreinlage

~ **plant** · Gipswerk *n*

(~) **plaster** → ~ stuff

~ ~, ~ finish · Gipsverputz *m*

~ ~ **ceiling** · Gips(-Unter)decke *f*

~ ~ **crack** · Gipsputzriß *m*

(~) ~ **(mixture))** → ~ stuff

(gypsum-)plaster of Class A (Brit.) → plaster of Paris

~ ~ ~ **B** (Brit.) → retarded hemihydrate (gypsum-)plaster

~ ~ ~ **C** (Brit.) → anhydrous (gypsum-)plaster

~ ~ ~ **D** (Brit.) → Keene's cement

(gypsum) plasterboard panel, ~ board ~; plate ~ [*Scotland*] · Gipskartontafel *f*

(~) ~ ~ **partition (wall)**, ~ board ~ (~); plate ~ ~ (~) [*Scotland*] Gipskartontafeltrennwand *f*

~ ~ **sheathing**, ~ (board) ~ · Gipskartonplattenverschalung *f*

(~) ~ **(sheet)**, ~ board; plate ~ [*Scotland*] [*A building board composed of a core of set gypsum plaster or anhydrite plaster, enclosed between, and firmly bonded to, two sheets of heavy paper. The core may be solid or cellular gypsum or gypsum containing a small proportion of fibre. B.S. 1230*] · Gipskartonplatte *f* [*DIN 18180 und 18181*]

(~) ~ (~) **ceiling** → dry ~

(~) ~ (~) **partition (wall)**, ~ board ~ (~); plate ~ (~) [*Scotland*] · Gipskartonplattentrennwand *f*

(~) ~ (~) **wall**, gypsum board ~; plate ~ [*Scotland*] · Gipskartonplattenwand *f*

~ **plastering mortar** → ~ stuff

~ **powder**, ground gypsum, powder(ed) gypsum · gemahlener Gips *m*, Gipsmehl *n*, Gipspulver *n*

~ **(pre)cast building unit**, ~ prefab(ricated) ~ ~, (pre)cast gypsum product, prefab(ricated) gypsum product · Gipsformstück *n*

~ **prefab(ricated) building unit**, ~ (pre)cast ~ ~, (pre)cast gypsum product, prefab(ricated) gypsum product · Gipsformstück *n*

~ **product**, ~ article · Gipsartikel *m*, Gipsgegenstand *m*, Gipserzeugnis *n*

~ **putty**, ~ paste · Gipspaste *f*, Gipsbrei *m*

~ **quarry** · Gipsbruch *m*

~ **ready-mix(ed) plaster**, ~ ~ stuff, ready-mix(ed) gypsum ~, prepared gypsum ~, premix(ed) gypsum stuff, ready-mix(ed) light(weight) gypsum plaster, premix(ed) light(weight) gypsum plaster · Gipstrocken(putz)mörtel *m*, Gipstrockenputzmasse *f*, Gipsfertig(putz)mörtel, Gipstrockenputzmasse *f*, Gipsfertigputzmasse

~ ~ **stuff** → ~ ~ plaster

~ **retarder**, ~ retarding agent [*A substance which, when present in small quantities, delays the setting and hardening of gypsum in a controllable way*] · Gips(ab)binde(zeit)verzögerer *m*, Gipserstarrungs(zeit)verzögerer, Gips(er)härtungs(zeit)verzögerer

gypsum retarding agent — haired lime-mortar

~ **retarding agent** → ~ retarder

~ **rock,** plaster ~, plaster stone, potter's stone (Brit.); (massive) gypsum, natural gypsum, raw gypsum · Rohgips *m*, Naturgips, Gipsstein *m*, Gipsgestein *n*, $CaSO_4 \cdot 2H_2O$

~ **roof(ing) board,** ~ ~ slab · Gipsdachplatte *f*

~ ~ **tile** · Gipsdachstein *m*

~ **sand,** gypseous ~ · Gipssand *m* (Geol.)

~ **-sand mortar** · Gipssandmörtel *m*

gypsum-sand plaster, sand-gypsum ~, patent ~, sanded · Gipssandputz *m*

gypsum sheathing, ~ board ~, ~ plasterboard ~ · Gipskartonplattenverschalung *f*

(~) ~ **plasterboard,** (~) ~ **board;** sheathing plate [*Scotland*] [*A gypsum board usually tongued and grooved, covered with a weatherproof(ed) paper for use as exterior sheathing*] · Gipskartonplatte *f* für Außenverwendung, Gipskarton-Verschalungsplatte

~ **sheet** → ~ (building) board

~ ~ **ceiling** → ~ (building) board ~

~ ~ **partition** → ~ building ~ ~

~ **slag cement** (US); supersulphated (slag) ~ (Brit.) · SHZ *m*, Sulfathüttenzement *m*, Gipsschlackenzement

~ **spar,** gypseous ~ · Gipsspat *m*

~ **stuff,** ~ plastering mortar, (~) plaster (mix(ture)) [*A mix(ture) based on gypsum plaster, with or without the addition of aggregate, hair or other materials, which is applied while plastic to internal building surfaces and which hardens after application*] · Gipsputz(mörtel) *m*, Gipsputzmasse *f*

~ **tile** → ~ (building) block

~ **undercoat (mixed) plaster** → ~ basecoat (~) ~

~ **unit** → ~ building ~

~ **waffle slab,** ~ coffer ~, ~ pan(el) ~, ~ cassette ~ · Gipskassettenplatte *f*

~ **wall baseboard,** wall gypsum ~ · (Gipskarton-)Stuckwandplatte *f*, (Gipskarton-)Wandstuckplatte, (Gipskarton-)Putzträgerwandplatte, (Gipskarton-)Wandputzträgerplatte

~ **wallboard** · Gipswand(bau)platte *f*, Wand(bau)platte aus Gips [*DIN 18163. Wandbauplatten aus Gips sind leichte Bauplatten, die aus Baugips (DIN 1168) oder Anhydritbinder (DIN 4208) mit oder ohne organische oder anorganische Zuschlagstoffe oder Füllstoffe oder unter Verwendung porenbildender Zusätze hergestellt werden. Die Platten sind mikroporig oder makroporig und dürfen Hohlräume haben*]

~ ~; plate for walls [*Scotland*] [*A gypsum plasterboard having its faces either self-finished or designed to receive decoration direct without first applying a plaster coat or coats. The surface of the back of the board is designed to receive gypsum plaster. The edges may be square or specially shaped*] · Gipskarton-Wandplatte *f*

~ **wall plaster** · Gipswandputz *m*

~ **wood-fibred plaster** (Brit.); ~ wood-fibered ~ (US) [*It is a gypsum plaster in which wood fiber (US)/fibre (Brit.) is used as an aggregate*] · Holzfaser-Gipsputz *m*

H

HA → housing authority

habitability, habitableness · (Be)Wohnbarkeit *f*

habitable, fit to live in, fit for human habitation · (be)wohnbar

~ **attic** → attic room

~ **room** [*A space used for living, sleeping, eating or cooking, or combinations thereof, but not including bathrooms, toilet compartments, closets, halls, storage rooms, laundry and utility rooms, basement recreation rooms and similar spaces*] · (be)wohnbarer Raum *m*

habitacle · Statuennische *f*

habitation [*A place in which to live*] Behausung *f*

hacked, keyed · aufgerauht, rauh [*zum Verputzen*]

~ **soffit,** keyed ~ [*for plaster finish*] aufgerauhte Untersicht *f*, rauhe ~

hacking, keying · Aufrauhen *n* [*zum Verputzen*]

Hadrian's Villa at Tivoli · Hadrian-Villa *f* in Tivoli, Villa des Kaisers Hadrian in Tivoli

Hagia Sophia at Constantinople, Church S. Sophie ~ ~ · Sophienkirche *f* zu Konstantinopel

hagioscope, squint, speculatory [*An oblique opening in a mediaeval church wall to give a view of the altar*] · Hagioskop *n*

hair catcher · Haarfänger *m*, Haarfang *m*

~ **crack** · Haarriß *m*

~ **cracking** [*In painting. Fine cracks which do not penetrate the top coat; they occur erratically and at random*] · Haarrißbildung *f*

~ ~ **resistance,** resistance to hair cracking · Haarrißfestigkeit *f*

hairdressing saloon · Frisiersalon *m*

haired cement mortar (Brit.); hair-fibered ~ ~ (US) · Haarzementmörtel *m*, Zementhaarmörtel

~ **gypsum** (Brit.); hair-fibered ~ (US); fibrous ~ [*The term 'fibrous gypsum' is also used for 'satin spar' = Fasergips*] · Haargips *m*

~ **lime-mortar** (Brit.); hair-fibered ~ (US); fibrous ~ · Haarkalkmörtel *m* Kalkhaarmörtel

~ mortar (Brit.); hair-fibered ~ (US); fibrous ~ · Haarmörtel *m* [*Haarmörtel sind Mörtel denen Kälberhaare, Renntierhaare, Kuhhaare, Kaninchenhaare, Filzhaare, Kokosfasern, Flachsschäben oder ähnliche Stoffe beigemischt sind*]

hair felt(ed fabric) · Haarfilz *m*

hair-fibered cement mortar (US); haired ~ ~ (Brit.) · Haarzementmörtel *m*, Zementhaarmörtel

~ gypsum (US) → haired ~

~ gypsum-lime mortar (US); hair-fibered ~ ~ (Brit.) · Gipshaarkalkmörtel *m*

~ lime-mortar (US) → haired ~

~ mortar (US) → haired ~

hair net · Haarnetz *n*, Verbleiung *f* [*Kirchenfenster*]

half-arch (Brit.); haunch (US); flank (of an arch) · Bogenhälfte *f*, Halbbogen *m*, (Bogen)Schenkel *m*

half bat, ~ brick, snap header, two quarters, H.B. · halber Ziegel *m*, ~ Stein *m*, Halbstein, Halbziegel, Zweiquartier *m*, Kopf *m*

half-bat thick, half-brick ~ · halbsteinstark, halbziegelstark

~ wall, half-brick ~ · Halbsteinmauer *f*, Halbziegelmauer, halbsteinstarke Mauer, halbziegelstarke Mauer [*Fehlnamen: Halbsteinwand f, Halbziegelwand, halbsteinstarke Wand, halbziegelstarke Wand*]

half-bay · Halbjoch *n*

half-beam · Balken(träger)hälfte *f*, Halbbalken(träger) *m*

half block → ~ tile

~ brick → ~ bat

half-brick thick, half-bat ~ · halbsteinstark, halbziegelstark

~ wall, half-bat ~ · Halbsteinmauer *f*, Halbziegelmauer, halbsteinstarke Mauer, halbziegelstarke Mauer [*Fehlnamen: Halbsteinwand f, Halbziegelwand, halbsteinstarke Wand, halbziegelstarke Wand*]

half-broken, half-crushed · halbgebrochen [*Zuschläge*]

half-burnt (clay) brick, half-burned (~) ~, half-fired (~) ~ · Blöckchen *n*, halbgebrannter Stein *m*, halbgebrannter (Ton)Ziegel *m*

half chimney block, split ~ ~ · halber Kamin(form)stein *m*, halbes Schornsteinformstück *n*

half-column, demi-column [*A column half sunk into a wall*] · Halbsäule *f*

half cross section · Halbquerschnitt *m*

half-crushed, half-broken · halbgebrochen [*Zuschläge*]

half-crystal (glass), semi-crystal (~) · Halbkristall(glas) *n* [*Ein Bleiglas, in dem ein Teil des Bleioxids durch Kalk oder Baryt ersetzt ist*]

half-cupola → semi-dome

half deformation · halbe Formänderung *f*, ~ Verformung, ~ Gestaltänderung

half-dome → semi-dome

half-ellipse, semi-ellipse · Halbellipse *f*

half-fired (clay) brick → half-burnt (~) ~

half flat · halbflach

~ flight · Halblauf *m* [*Treppe*]

~ floor → half-landing

half-frame · einhüftiger Rahmen *m*, Halbrahmen

half-gas fired furnace, semi-producer type ~ · Halbgasfeuerung *f*

half-girder, half span of the girder · Halbträger *m*

half-glas door, sash ~, glazed ~ [*A door of which the upper half is glazed*] · Glasfüllungstür *f*

half-groove · Halbschlitz *m* [*Triglyphe*]

half hip, partial ~ · halber Walm *m*, Krüppelwalm, Schopfwalm, Kielende *n*, Kühlende

half-hipped roof; gambrel ~, gambril ~ (Brit.) [*A roof having a gablet near the ridge and the lower part hipped*] · Fußwalmdach *n*

~ ~, gambrel ~ [*A roof hipped for part of its height and terminated by a gablet*] · Krüppelwalmdach *n*, Schopfwalmdach

half life-size · Halbfigur *f*

half-load · Halblast *f*

half main rafter → half-principal (~)

~ module · Halbmodul *m*

half-oval wire · Halbovaldraht *m*

half parameter · Halbparameter *m*

half-pier · Halbpfeiler *m*

half-plane, semi-plane · Halbebene *f*

half-portal · Halbportal *n*

half-prestressed beam · Balken(träger) *m* mit halber Vorspannung

~ girder · Träger *m* mit halber Vorspannung

half-principal (rafter), half main ~ [*A rafter which does not reach the ridge*] · halber Bindesparren *m*, ~ Hauptsparren, ~ Bundsparren

half-rib · Halbrippe *f*

half (roof(ing)) tile · Schnittling *m* [*halber Dachziegel*]

~ round · Halbrundprofil *n*

half-round, semicircular, $^1/_2$rd · halbrund, halbkreisförmig

~ aspe → ~ exedra

~ apsis → ~ exedra

(half-)round arch, semicircular ~, perfect ~; full-centred ~ (Brit.); full-centered ~ (US) · Rundbogen *m*, Halbkreisbogen, römischer Bogen, halbzirkelförmiger ~ [*veraltet: Vollbogen, voller Bogen*]

half-round barrel vault → semicircular wagon(head) ~

~ bastion, semicircular ~ · Halbrundbastei *f*, Halbrundbastion *f*

~ ceiling, semicircular ~ · Halbkreisdecke *f*

half-round cross-vault — hall building

~ **cross-vault**, semicircular ~ · halbrundes Kreuzgewölbe *n*

~ **cylindrical roof**, semicircular ~ ~ · Zylinderdach *n*

~ **exedra**, ~ apsis, ~ apse, semicircular ~ · Halbkreisapsis *f*, Halbkreisapside *f*, Halbkreisabside, Halbkreisexedra *f*, Halbkreisabseite *f*, Halbkreischorhaupt *n*, Halbkreiskonche *f*

~ **gutter** → semicircular (roof) ~

~ **iron**, semicircular ~ · Halbrundeisen *n*

~ **moulding** (Brit.); ~ molding (US); half round · Halbrundprofil *n*

~ **niche**, semicircular ~ · Halbkreisnische *f*

~ **profile**, ~ section, semicircular ~ · Halbkreisprofil *n*, Halbkreisschnitt *m* [*Halbkreisförmige Umrißlinie eines durchschnittenen Körpers*]

~ **rainwater gutter** → semicircular (roof) ~

~ **rib**, semicircular ~ · Halbkreisrippe *f*

~ **rivet**, semicircular ~ · Halbrundniet *m* [*Der Setzkopf ist ein Halbrundkopf. DIN 123, 124, 660 und 663*]

~ **(roof) gutter** → semicircular (~) ~

half(-round) section → half split pipe

~ ~, ~ profile, semicircular ~ · Halbkreisprofil *n*, Halbkreisschnitt *m* [*Halbkreisförmige Umrißlinie eines durchschnittenen Körpers*]

~ ~ **duct** → half split pipe (gutter)

~ ~ **gutter** → half split pipe (~)

half-round steel, semicircular ~ · Halbrundstahl *m*

~ **stretcher**, semicircular ~ · Halbrundläufer *m*

~ **termination**, semicircular ~ · halbrunder (Ab)Schluß *m*

~ **tower**, D-shaped ~, semicircular ~ · Schalenturm *m*, Halb(kreis)turm [*Nach außen aus der Mauer vorspringender, nach innen jedoch offener Turm einer mittelalterlichen Burg*]

~ **transverse arch**, semicircular ~ ~ · Halbrundquerbogen *m*, Halbkreisquerbogen

~ **tunnel vault** → semicircular wagon ~

~ **wagon vault** → semicircular ~ ~

~ **window**, semicircular ~ · Halbrundfenster *n*, Halbkreisfenster

~ **wire**, semicircular ~ · Halbrunddraht *m*

~ **wood screw**, semicircular ~ ~ · Halbrund-Holzschraube *f*

half rounds · Halbeisen *n*

~ **section** → half split pipe

~ ~ **duct** → ~ ~ split pipe (gutter)

~ ~ **gutter** → ~ split pipe (~)

~ ~ **pipe duct** → ~ split pipe (gutter)

~ ~ ~ **(gutter)** → ~ split ~ (~)

~ **small column** · Halbsäulchen *n*, Halbdienst *m*

halfspace, semi-infinite mass, semi-infinite solid, semi-infinite space · Halbraum *m*

half span of the girder, half-girder · Halbträger *m*

~ **split pipe**, half(-round) section, channel (stone); center split pipe (US); centre split pipe (Brit.) · halbiertes Rohr *n*, Halb(rohr)schale *f*

~ ~ ~ **duct** → ~ ~ ~ (gutter)

~ ~ ~ **(gutter)**, ~ section ~ (~), ~ ~ ~ duct, half(-round) section ~; center split pipe (~) (US); centre split pipe (~) (Brit.) · Halb(rohr)schale(nrinne) *f*

~ **sunk** · halbversenkt [*Niet*]

~ ~ **rivet** · Halbversenkniet *m*

~ **tile**, ~ block [*See remark under 'Block'*] · Halbblock(stein) *m*, Halbstein

~ ~ → ~ **roofing** ~

half-timber construction · Fachwerkbauweise *f* [*Holzhausbau*]

~ **house** · Fachwerkhaus *n*

half tunnel vault · Halbtonne(ngewölbe) *f*, (*n*), Tonne(ngewölbe) mit viertelkreisförmigem Querschnitt

half-turn stair(case) with landing(s) · gerade dreiläufige Treppe *f* mit gleichsinnigem Richtungswechsel

~ ~ ~ **winders** · halbgewendelte Treppe *f*

half-window · Mezzaninfenster *n*, Bastardfenster

(h)alfa fiber (US); ~ fibre (Brit.); Spanish grass ~, esparto grass ~ · (H)Alfafaser *f*, Espartofaser [*Als Einlage für Gipsdielen, Faserbeton usw.*]

Halfen anchor channel · Halfen-Dübelschiene *f*, Halfen-Ankerschiene

~ **(concrete) insert** · Halfeneisen *n*

Halicarnassos Mausoleum, Mausoleum at Halicarnassos · Mausoleum *n* zu Halikarnass

halite, common salt, rock salt · Salzgestein *n*, Steinsalz *n*

hall [*Nave and aisles are of equal height, and thus there is no triforium or clearstor(e)y*] · Hallenraum *m* [*z.B. Elisabethkirche in Marburg*]

~ [*A large building devoted to public or semipublic business or entertainments. The term 'hall' is, however, also misused in such terms as 'machinery hall', etc.*] · Halle *f*

~ → **entrance** ~

~ → ~**way**

~ [*A large room devoted to public or semipublic business or entertainments*] · Saal *m*

~, **commons** · Mensa *f*

~ **building** · Saalbau *m* [*Ein Gebäude, das im Hauptgeschoß – außer kleinen Nebenräumen – nur einen Saal enthält*]

hall-choir, hall-quire · Hallenchor *m*
hall-church · Hallenkirche *f*
hall closet · Hallen-Einbauschrank *m*, Hallen-Wandschrank
~ construction · Hallenbau *m*
~ ~ system · Hallenbausystem *n*
~ cupola, ~ dome · Hallenkuppel *f*
~ dome, ~ cupola · Hallenkuppel *f*
~-donjon → hall-keep
hall-dungeon → hall-keep
hall for audience, audience-hall · Audienzhalle *f*, Audienzsaal *m*
hall-form · Hallenform *f*
hall ground area · Hallenfläche *f*
hall-keep, hall-donjon, hall-dungeon · Bergfried *m* mit Wohnräumen, Berchfrit *m* ~ ~, Belfried ~ ~, Donjon *m* ~ ~, Wohnturm *m* [*Ein für Wohnzwecke ausgestatteter Turm, der in seiner Funktion dem Belfried nahestand*]
hall-nave · Hallenschiff *n* [*Kirchenbau*]
Hall of Ambassadors · Saal *m* der Gesandten [*Alhambra*]
hall of columns, columnar interior, columned hall · Säulenraum *m*, Säulensaal *m*, Säulenhalle *f*
Hall of Fame, Valhalla · Ruhmeshalle *f*, Walhalla *f* [*bei Regensburg*]
~ ~ Judg(e)ment · Saal *m* des Gerichts [*Alhambra*]
~ ~ (the) Abencerrages · Halle *f* der Abencerrages [*Alhambra*]
~ ~ ~ Double Axes · Saal *m* der Doppeläxte [*Palast zu Knossos*]
~ ~ ~ Hundred Columns [*Persepolis*] · Hundertsäulenhalle *f*
~ ~ (~) Mysteries at Eleusis, Telesterion · Telesterion *n* zu Eleusis, Weihetempel *m* ~ ~, Mysterienhalle *f* ~ ~
~ ~ (~) Two Sisters · Halle *f* der zwei Schwestern [*Alhambra*]
hall-quire, hall-choir · Hallenchor *m*
hall roof · Hallendach *n*
hall-transept · Hallenquerhaus *n*
hall-type block, ~ house, ~ building · Gebäude *n* in Hallenbauweise
~ building, ~ block, ~ house · Gebäude *n* in Hallenbauweise
~ house, ~ building, ~ block · Gebäude *n* in Hallenbauweise
halloysite · Halloysit *m* [*Tonmineral der Kaolinit-Gruppe*]
hall(way) · Hausgang *m*, Hausflur *m* [*Zwischen Hauseingangstür und Treppenhaus*]
halogenated hydrocarbon · Halogenkohlenwasserstoff *m*
halved joint, halving [*Halving consists of cutting the ends of each piece to half the depth and securing with either bolts, nails, screws, or wooden pegs*] · Plattung *f*, Blattung, Über~, Blatt *n* [*Holzverbindung*]

halving · Einblatten *n*, Anblatten [*Verbindung zweier Kanthölzer durch ein Blatt*]
~, halved joint [*Halving consists of cutting the end of each piece to half the depth and securing with either bolts, nails, screws, or wooden pegs*] · Blatt *n*, (Über)Blattung *f*, (Über)Plattung [*Holzverbindung*]

hammer-beam roof, Ardand type polygonal ~ [*A late Gothic form of roof without a direct tie, the finest example being in Westminster Hall*] · Vieleckdach *n*, Polygonaldach, Ardandsches Dach
~ ~ truss · Vieleckdachbinder *m*, Polygonaldachbinder
hammer-blow type pulse-velocity measuring device · mechanisches Hammergerät *n* [*Zerstörungsfreie Prüfung von Beton*]
hammer-dressed (stone) ashlar masonry (work), ~ (~) ashler ~ (~), ~ hewn stone ~ (~), block-in-course ~ (~) [*Squared stone masonry (work) laid in regular courses with the stones roughly squared with a hammer*] · hammerrechtes Schicht(en)mauerwerk *n*, ~ geschichtetes Mauerwerk
hammered · gehämmert [*Oberflächenbehandlung*]
hammer finish → hammer(tone) ~
~ ~ enamel, hammertone ~ · Hammerschlaglack *m*
~-headed chisel [*Any mason's chisel with a flat conical steel head, which is struck by a hammer and not by a mallet*] · Schlageisen *n*
hammering away · Abhämmern *n*
hammertone, hammer finish · Hammerschlag *m*
~ enamel, hammer finish ~ · Hammerschlaglack *m*
hammer(tone) finish [*A finish like hammered metal, produced by colo(u)red enamels containing metal powder applied with a spray gun*] · Hammerschlaglackierung *f*
hammertone hardboard · Hammerschlagplatte *f*
hammer (type) roof, Ardand (type) polygonal ~ [*An open timber roof structure. This style was frequently used in churches and halls during the 15th and 16th centuries*] · Polygonaldach *n*, Ardandsches Dach, Vieleckdach
hammer-weld(ed) pipe · hammergeschweißtes Rohr *n*
hammer welding · Hammerschweißung *f*
hand → ~ of door
~ applied (mixed) plaster · Hand(innen)(ver)putz *m*, handaufgetragener (Innen)(Ver)Putz
~-blocked (wall)paper, hand-printed ~ · Handdrucktapete *f*, Holzmodeltapete

hand broken metal (Brit.); ~ ~ stone (US) · Handschotter *m*, Schlagsteine *mpl*, Krotzen *f* [*Handgeschlagener Schotter für den Straßenbau*]

~ cleft (wood) shingle, ~ ~ wooden ~, ~ split (~) ~, riven (~) ~, (wood) shake, wooden shake, hand-split shake · gerissene (Holz)Schindel *f*, (hand)gespaltene ~

~ ~ (~) siding shingle, ~ split (~) ~ ~, riven (~) ~ ~, siding (wood) shake, wood(en) siding shake · (hand-) gespaltene (Holz)Wandschindel *f*, gerissene ~

~-finish concrete · handabgezogener Beton *m*

hand-forged ironwork · handgeschmiedete Eisenarbeit *f*

hand-formed brick, hand-made ~, struck ~; hand-moulded ~ (Brit.); hand-molded ~ (US) · Handformstein *m*, Handformziegel *m*, Hand(strich)ziegel, Hand(strich)stein

hand-formed joint · handausgebildete Fuge *f*, Handfuge

(hand)grip → ((bath)tub) ~

hand gun · Hand(spritz)pistole *f*, Handspritze *f*

handicapped person's centre (Brit.); ~ ~ center (US) · Versehrtenstätte *f*

(handi)craft · Handwerk *n*

~ of the bricklayer, bricklaying craft · Maurerhandwerk *n*

~-type metal grille [*sometimes spelled 'grill'*] · kunstgewerbliches Metallgitter *n*

handing over, transfer, handover · Übergabe *f*

hand iron, step ~, foot ~, access hook · Steigeisen *n*, Klettereisen [*DIN 1211 (kurz), DIN 1212 (lang)*]

~-laid stone-filled asphalt, hard mastic ~ · Hart(guß)asphalt(estrich) *m*

handle-plate → lever ~

hand lead · Lot(blei) *n*, Bleigewicht *n*

handling device · Griffhilfe *f*, Grifföffnung *f*, Griffloch *n* [*Ziegel; Block(stein)*]

~ of all technical and structural and planning details · technische und konstruktive und planerische Ausführungsbearbeitung *f*

~ ~ passengers, processing ~ ~ · Fahrgastabfertigung *f*

~ ~ plane surfaces · geometrische Behandlung *f* der Fläche

~ reinforcement [*A material, such as mild steel rod, incorporated in cast stone solely for the purpose of permitting the unit to be handled without damage until it is built into position on the site*] · Transportarmierung *f*, Transportbewehrung, Transport(stahl)einlagen *fpl*

~ slot · Griffschlitz *m*

~ strength · Transportfestigkeit *f*

~ stress · Transportspannung *f* [*Betonfertigteil*]

handmade · handgefertigt

~ brick → hand-formed ~

~ shingle · handgefertigte Schindel *f*

hand method, shanty ~ [*Manufacture of roof(ing) slate*] · Spaltung *f* in Spalthütten

~ mix, ~ mixture · Handgemisch *n*, Handmischung *f*

~-mixed concrete · handgemischter Beton *m*

hand mixing · Handmischung *f*, Handmischen *n*

~ mix(ture) · Handgemisch *n*, Handmischung *f*

~ mould (Brit.); ~ mold (US) · Handform *f* [*Ziegelherstellung*]

~ moulded (Brit.); ~ molded (US) handgeformt

~-moulded brick (Brit.) → hand-formed ~

~ grey iron casting(s) (Brit.); hand-molded ~ ~ ~ (US); ~ gray ~ ~ · handgeformter Grauguß *m*

hand-moulding (Brit.); hand-molding (US) · Handform(geb)ung *f*

hand (of door) [*Facing a door that opens toward you, if the knob is on the right it is a right-hand door. Similarly, if the knob is on the left, it is a left-hand door*] · (Tür)Aufschlag *m*

~ operation, manual ~ · Handbedienung *f*, Handbetätigung, Handbetrieb *m*

handover, handing over, transfer · Übergabe *f*

hand-packed hardcore, hand-placed ~, ~ rubble · Handpacke *f*, Setzpacke

~ rubble, hand-placed ~, ~ hardcore · Handpacke *f*, Setzpacke

~ stone, hand-placed ~, hand-pitched ~, pitching ~, pitcher, blockstone · Setzpacklagestein *m*, Vorlagestein, Stückstein

hand-painted picture tile · freihändig bemalte Bildfliese *f*, ~ ~ Bild(belag)-platte

hand-pitched stone, hand-placed ~, hand-packed ~, pitching ~, pitcher, blockstone · Setzpacklagestein *m*, Vorlagestein, Stückstein

hand-placed hardcore, hand-packed ~, ~ rubble · Handpacke *f*, Setzpacke

~ rubble, hand-packed ~, ~ hardcore · Handpacke *f*, Setzpacke

~ stone, hand-packed ~, hand-pitched ~, pitching ~, pitcher, blockstone · Setzpacklagestein *m*, Vorlagestein Stückstein

hand placement, ~ placing · Handverlegung *f*, Handeinbau *m*

~ placing, ~ placement · Handverlegung *f*, Handeinbau *m*

~ plastering, manual ~ · Hand(ver)putzen *n*

~ power, manual ~ · Handkraft *f*

hand-printed (wall)paper — hardboard floor(ing)

~-printed (wall)paper, hand-blocked ~ · Handdrucktapete *f*, Holzmodeltapete

hand printing · Handdruck *m* [*(Papier-) Tapete*]

handrail, handrailing [*A rail forming the top of a balustrade on a balcony, bridge, stair, etc.*] · Handlauf *m*, Handleiste *f*

~ baluster, ~ ban(n)ister · Geländerbaluster *m*

~ ban(n)ister, ~ baluster · Geländerbaluster *m*

~ profile → ~ section

~ screw · Handlaufschraube *f*, Handleistenschraube

~ scroll [*A spiral ending to a handrail*] · Handlaufspirale *f*, Handleistenspirale

~ section, ~ unit, ~ trim, ~ shape, ~ profile · Handlaufprofil *n*, Handleistenprofil [*Fehlname: Handlaufeisen n*]

~ shape → ~ section

~ standard · Geländerpfosten *m*, Geländerstütze *f*, Geländerstab *m*

~ trim → ~ section

~ unit → ~ section

handrailing [*The art of constructing handrails to stairs, especially when entailing wreaths. Various methods are used, viz., tangent, normal sections, bevel cut, falling line, etc.*] · Handlaufbau *m*, Handleistenbau

~ → handrail

hand rendering, manual ~ · Hand(ver)putzen *n* [*Außenputz*]

~ riveting, manual ~, riveting by hand · Handnieten *n*, Handnietung *f* [*Von Hand geschlagene Nietung mit Handdöpper und Hammer*]

~ ~ machine, manual ~ ~ · Handnietmaschine *f*

~ sample, ~ specimen · Handstück *n* [*Gestein*]

~ shower, mov(e)able ~ · Schlauchdusche *f*, Handdusche

~ sieving · Hand(ab)siebung *f*

~ specimen, ~ sample · Handstück *n* [*Gestein*]

~ split (wood) shingle → ~ cleft (~)
~
~ ~ (~) siding shingle → ~ cleft (~)
~ ~

hand spray, mov(e)able ~ · Schlauchbrause *f*, Handbrause

~-tamped pipe · handgestampftes Rohr *n*

hand test sieving · Hand-Prüfsiebung *f*

~ testing sieve · Hand-Prüfsieb *n*

to hang ((wall)paper) · tapezieren mit (Wand)Papiertapete

hangar [*A shed for the shelter of aircraft or airship*] · Halle *f*

(~) apron · (Hallen)Vorfeld *n* [*Luftfahrtgelände*]

~ shutter door, ~ shutterdoor · Hallentor *n*

hanger [*Generally, a steel member from which other parts are hung*] · Aufhänger *m*, Aufhängeeisen *n*

~ · Hängeglied *n*, (Ab)Hänger *m* [*Drahtputzdecke*]

~, pipe ~ · (Rohr)Schelle *f*, (Rohr)Bügel *m*

~, sliding door gear · (Schiebetür)Gehänge *n*, (Schiebetür)Laufwerk *n*

~, paper~, (wall)paperhanger · Tapezierer *m*

~ rod, suspension ~, suspender · (Auf-)Hängestange *f*

~ wire · (Ab)Hängedraht *m*

hanging · Tapete *f*

~ bracket · Hängekonsole *f*

~ floor, suspension ~, hung ~; ~ story (US); ~ storey (Brit.) · Hängeetage *f*, Hängestockwerk *n*, Hängegeschoß *n*

Hanging Gardens · Hängende Gärten *mpl* [*in Babylon*]

hanging gutter → ~ roof ~

~ lamp · Moscheeampel *f*

~ paste → paper~ ~

~ rainwater gutter → ~ (roof) ~

~ R. W. gutter → ~ (roof) ~

~ (roof) gutter, ~ rainwater ~, ~ R.W. ~ · Vorhängerinne *f* [*DIN 18460. Sie hängt an Rinnenhaltern unter der (Dach)Traufe*]

~ scaffold, flying ~, suspended ~, hung ~ · Hängegerüst *n*, Hängerüstung *f*

~ shelf · Hängeregal *n*

~ socket · Hängesteckdose *f*, Kupp(e)lungssteckdose

~ step, cantilever(ed) ~, cantilevering ~ · auskragende Stufe *f*, vorkragende ~, Auslegerstufe, Kragstufe, Freiträger *m*

~ story (US) → ~ floor

~ truss · Hängewerk *n*, Angehänge *n*

~ ~ roof · Hängewerkdach *n*

haphazard building, sporadic ~ · regellose Bebauung *f*, sporadische ~, wilde ~

haram · Betsaal *m* [*Moschee*]

~ → harim

hard → ~ dry

~ aggregate sprinkled on the surface, ~ ~ for sprinkling ~ ~ ~ · Aufstreukörnung *f*

hardboard · harte (Holz)Faserplatte *f*, HFH 1, Hart(faser)platte, (Holz)Faserhartplatte [*DIN 68750*]

~ door · Hart(faser)plattentür *f*

~ finish · (Holz)Faserhartplattenbelag *m*, Hart(faser)plattenbelag

~ floor(ing), ~ floor cover(ing), ~ floor finish · Hart(faser)platten(fuß)boden(belag) *m*

hardboard siding — hardening time

~ siding · Hart(faser)platten-Wandschirm *m*, Hart(faser)platten-Wandbeschlag *m*, Hart(faser)platten-Wetterschirm, (Holz)Faserhartplatten-Wandschirm, (Holz)Faserhartplatten-Wandbeschlag, (Holz)Faserhartplatten-Wetterschirm

hard-burned, well-burned, hard-burnt, well-burnt, hard-fired, well-fired · hartgebrannt

~ brick, well-burned ~, hard-burnt ~, well-burnt ~, hard-fired ~, well-fired ~ · Hart(brand)ziegel *m*, Hart(brand)stein *m*, hartgebrannter (Ziegel)Stein, hartgebrannter Ziegel

~ plaster, hard-burnt ~ · entwässertes Halbhydrat *n*, löslicher Anhydrit *m*, lösliches Anhydrit *n*, β-Anhydrit III, β-CaSO₄ [*Ofengipsart*]

hard calcareous slate · Schiefermarmor *m*

~ chalk, clunch · Hartkreide *f*

~-chromed, hard chromium-plated · hartverchromt

hard chromium-plating · Hartverchromung *f*

~ copal, true ~, fossil ~ · Hartkopal-(harz) *m*, (*n*), fossiler Kopal. fossiles Kopalharz

hardcore · Kleinschlag *m*

~ · Schüttpack(lag)e *f*, verfestigte ~

hard-drawn copper wire · hartgezogener Kupferdraht *m*

hard (dry) · durchgetrocknet [*Anstrich*]

~-drying · hart auftrocknend [*Lack*]

to harden · (er)härten

~ ~ by polymerization (US); ~ ~ ~ polymerisation (Brit.) · polymerisieren

hardenable · härtbar [*Legierung*]

hardened cement paste, paste matrix · erhärteter Zementleim *m*, ~ Zementbrei *m*, erhärtete Zementpaste *f*, Zementstein *m*

~ concrete · erhärteter Beton *m*, Festbeton

~ dust → ~ filler

~ filler, ~ dust, hardener ~, hardening ~ · Härtestoffüller *m*, Härtestoffüllstoff *m*, Härtemittelfüllstoff, Härtungsmittelfüllstoff [*z.B. Korund, Siliziumkarbid*]

~ mortar · Festmörtel *m*, erhärteter Mörtel

~ steel · härtebehandelter Stahl *m*, gehärteter ~

hardener, accelerator, catalyst, hardening agent [*It promoetes setting of synthetic resins for gluing*] · Härtemittel *n*, Katalysator *m*, Härter *m*, (Reaktions)Beschleuniger

~, hardening agent · Härtemittel *n*, Härtungsmittel, Härtungsstoff *m*, Härter *m*, Härtestoff

~ dust → hardened filler

~ filler → hardened ~

~ for gypsum, hardening agent ~ ~ · Gipshärtemittel *n*, Gipshärter *m*, Gipshärtungsstoff *m*, Gipshärtungsmittel, Gipshärtestoff

hardening · (Er)Härten *n*

~ · (Er)Härtung *f*

~ · Materialverfestigung *f*, (Werk)Stoffverfestigung

~ accelerating agent, ~ acceleration promoter, ~ accelerator, accelerator for hardening, rapid hardener · Schnell(er)härter *m*, (Er)Härtungs(zeit)beschleuniger, Beschleuniger

~ admix(ture), ~ agent · Härtezusatz-(stoff) *m*, Härtezusatzmittel *n*, Härtewirkstoff

~ age, age of hardening · (Er)Härtungsalter *n*

~ agent, hardener · Härtemittel *n*, Härtungsmittel, Härtungsstoff *m*, Härter *m*, Härtestoff

~ ~, ~ admix(ture) · Härtezusatz(stoff) *m*, Härtezusatzmittel *n*, Härtewirkstoff

~ ~ for gypsum → hardener ~ ~

~ behaviour (Brit.); ~ behavior (US) · (Er)Härtungsverhalten *n*

~ by drying out and slowly combining with the carbon-dioxid(e) in the air · Karbonat(er)härtung *f* [*Luftkalk*]

~ chamber · Härtekammer *f*

~ coat · härtender Anstrich *m*, ~ Aufstrich

~ curve, curve of hardening · (Er)Härtungskurve *f* [*Mörtel; Beton; Zementpaste; Gips. Siehe Anmerkung unter "Abbinden"*]

~ degree, degree of hardening · (Er)Härtungsgrad *m*

~ dust → hardened filler

~ energy, energy of hardening · (Er)Härtungsenergie *f*

~ filler → hardened ~

~ oil, annealing ~ · Härteöl *n*, Vergüteöl

~ period → ~ time

~ process, process of hardening · (Er-)Härtungsvorgang *m*, (Er)Härtungsprozeß *m*, (Er)Härtungsverlauf *m*, (Er)Härtungsablauf, Härtevorgang, Härteverlauf, Härteprozeß, Härteablauf

~ rate, rate of hardening · (Er)Härtungsgeschwindigkeit *f*

~ rule, Materialverfestigungsregel *f*, (Werk)Stoffverfestigungsregel

~ seal(er) · Hartsiegel *m* [*Für nachträgliche Festigung einer Betonoberfläche*]

~ stress · (Er)Härtungsspannung *f*, Härtespannung

~ temperature · (Er)Härtungstemperatur *f*, Härtetemperatur

~ test · (Er)Härtungsprobe *f*, (Er)Härtungsprüfung *f*, (Er)Härtungsversuch *m*

~ time, ~ period, period of hardening, time of hardening · (Er)Härtungsdauer *f*, (Er)Härtungszeit *f*, (Er)Härtungsfrist *f*, Härtezeit, Härtedauer, Härtefrist

hardening treatment — hard stopping

~ **treatment** · Härtung f
hard fibre (Brit.); ~ **fiber** (US) · Hartfaser f
~**-finish plaster** → Keene's cement
hard-fired, well-fired, hard-burnt, hard-burned, well-burnt, well-burned · hartgebrannt
~ **brick** → hard(-burned) ~
hard floor cover(ing), ~ ~ finish, ~ floor(ing) · Hart(fuß)boden(belag) m
~ **glass** · Hartglas n, hartes Glas [*Eine Gruppe von Elektrogläsern, die auf das Einschmelzen von Molybdän- oder Wolframdrähten bezüglich ihres Wärmeausdehnungskoeffizienten abgestimmt sind*]
~ **glazed coat(ing), ~ glaze(d finish), ~ glazing** · Hartglasur f, Hartbeglasung f
~ **gloss** · Hartglanz m
~ ~ **paint** · Hartglanz(anstrich)farbe f
~ **glossy film** · Hartglanzfilm m
~ **(granular) abrasive (material) for grano(lithic) (concrete) toppings (or overlays)** · (fester) Hart(beton)-stoff m, (~) Betonhartstoff, Hartkornstoff, Härtezugschlagstoff, Härtemittel n [*DIN 1100*]
~ **(gypsum) plaster,** cement ~; hardwall ~ [*deprecated*] · Hartputzgips m [*Estrichputzgips in Südwestdeutschland. Ein Gips, der, verarbeitet, eine besonders hohe Widerstandsfähigkeit gegen Stoß und Schlag hat und eventuell wasserabweisend ist*]
~ **lead,** antimonial ~, regulus metal · Hartblei n, Antimonblei
~ ~ **pipe,** antimonial ~ ~ · Bleisparrohr n, Hartbleirohr, Antimonbleirohr [*DIN 8601*]
~ ~ **pressure pipe,** antimonial ~ ~ ~ · Antimonbleidruckrohr n, Hartbleidruckrohr
~ ~ **sheet,** roofing ~ ~ antimonial ~ ~ · Dachdeckerblei n, Hartbleiblech n, Antimonbleiblech
~ **limestone** · Hartkalkstein m
~ **mastic asphalt,** hand-laid stone-filled ~ · Hart(guß)asphalt(estrich) m
~ **mortar** · Hartmörtel m
hardness · Härte f
~ **class,** class of hardness · Härteklasse f
~ **crack** · Härteriß m
~ **degree,** degree of hardness · Härtegrad m
~ **determination,** determination of hardness · Härtebestimmung f, Härteermitt(e)lung
~ **given by the dynamic indentation test** · Kugeldruckhärte f
~ ~ ~ ~ **rebound height** · Rücksprunghärte f
~ **loss,** loss of hardness · Härteverlust m
~ **number** · Härtezahl f
~ **of water,** water hardness · Wasserhärte f
~ **range,** range of hardness · Härte(n)bereich m, n
~ **scale** · Härteskala f
~ **test** · Härteprobe f, Härteversuch m, Härteprüfung f
~ **testing machine,** ~ **tester,** durometer · Härteprüfer m, Härteprüfgerät n, Härteprüfmaschine f, Härtemesser
hard paste · Hartporzellan n
~ **(phenolic) resin** · Hartharz n
~ **plaster** → ~ gypsum ~
~ **resin,** ~ phenolic ~ · Hartharz n
~ **rock** · hartes Felsgestein n, Hartling m, Hart(ge)stein m, (n) [z.B. Basalt, Diorit, Gabbro, Granit, Diabas]
~ ~ **chip(ping)s** · Hartsplitt m [*Splitt aus Hart(ge)stein*]
~ ~ **flour** · Hart(ge)steinmehl n
~ ~ **product,** ~ ~ **article** · Hart(ge)-steinerzeugnis n, Hart(ge)steinartikel m, Hart(ge)steingegenstand m
~ ~ **quarry** · Hart(ge)steinbruch m
~ ~ **slab** · Hart(ge)steinplatte f
~ **rubber,** ebonite · Hartgummi m, n [*Ein Isolierstoff aus Natur- oder Kunstkautschuk, Schwefel, organischen und anorganischen Zusätzen, durch Heißvulkanisation gehärtet. DIN 7711*]
~ ~ **board,** ~ ~ **sheet** · Hartgummiplatte f [*DIN 7712*]
~ ~ **circular rod,** ~ ~ **round** ~ · Hartgummirundstange f [*DIN 7713*]
~ ~ **round rod,** ~ ~ **circular** ~ · Hartgummirundstange f [*DIN 7713*]
~ ~ **sheet,** ~ ~ **board** · Hartgummiplatte f [*DIN 7712*]
~ ~ **tube** · Hartgummirohr n [*DIN 7714*]
~ **sandstone** · Hartsandstein m
~ **schist** · Hartschiefer m
~ **solder,** brazing ~, brazing alloy · Hartlot n, Schlaglot, Strenglot [*Es wird verwendet, wenn neben Abdichtung noch Festigkeit verlangt wird. Die Schmelzpunkte der Hartlote liegen mindestens 50 grd. unterhalb des niedrigsten Schmelzpunktes der Metallteile und oberhalb von rund 600° C. DIN 1733*]
~ **soldered,** brazed · hartgelötet
~ ~ **joint,** brazed ~ [*A gas-tight joint obtained by the joining of metal parts and metallic alloys which melt at temperatures higher than 1,000 degrees Fahrenheit as determined in an approved manner*] · Hartlötverbindung f
~ **soldering,** brazing · Hartlöten f
~ ~, brazing · Hartlötung f
~ **stopper** → ~ stopping
~ **stopping,** ~ **stopper** [*A material in stiff paste form, which is usually applied by means of a knife, to fill deep indentations in a surface and which dries hard throughout. It should not be confused with glazing putty which is of a different consistency and which hardens more slowly*] · Hartspachtel(masse) m, (f), Expreßspachtel(masse)

hard surface — hazard bonus

~ surface · Hartoberfläche f

hard-textured chipped wood concrete · Hartholzspanbeton m, Hartholzspänebeton

~ wood · Hartholz n

~ ~ fibre concrete (Brit.); ~ ~ fiber ~ (US) · Hartholzfaserbeton m

hard-to-reach · schwer zugänglich

hard-to-screen material, difficult-to-screen ~ · schwer siebbares Gut n, siebschwieriges ~

hardwall plaster [deprecated] → hard (gypsum) ~

hardware → builder's iron supplies

~, fittings, builders' ~ [B.S. 1331] · (Bau)Beschläge mpl

~ factory → builders' ~ ~

~ mounting machine, machine for letting in mounts · Beschlag-Einlaßmaschine f

~ work · (Bau)Beschlagarbeiten fpl [DIN 18357]

hard water · hartes Wasser n

~ wax · Hartwachs n

hardwearing · strapazierfähig, strapazierbar, strapazierfest, verschleißfest, verschleißbeständig

~ coat · Strapazieranstrich m, Strapazieraufstrich

~ floor cover(ing). ~ floor finish, ~ floor(ing) · Strapazier(fuß)boden(belag) m

hardwood tar · Laubholzteer m

~-tar pitch · Laubholzteerpech n

hare(e)m → harim

harim, haram, hare(e)m, women's quarter · Harem m

harl(e) [Scotland] → rough cast

harling [Scotland] → rough cast

harm done to concrete · Betonschädigung f

harmonic → ~ tone

~ oscillation, ~ vibration · harmonische Schwingung f

~ proportion [A system of proportions relating architecture to music] · harmonische Proportion f

~ scale · Obertonskala f

~ (tone) · harmonischer Ton m, Oberton

~ vibration, ~ oscillation · harmonische Schwingung f

harmonical vase · Schallgefäß n

harp mesh · Harfenmasche f, Schlitzmasche

~ ~ cloth, ~ ~ woven fabric; ~ ~ fabric [misnomer] · Harfen(sieb)gewebe n

~(-type) screen · Harfensieb n

Harrison cone · Harrisonkegel m

hasp and staple · Haspen m und Krampe f, Überwurf m

hat and coat hook · Hut- und Kleiderhaken m

~ hook · Huthaken m

to hatch, to shade · schraffieren

hatch, service ~, serving ~ · Durchreiche f, Durchreichöffnung f, Durchgabe f

hatched area, shaded ~ · schraffierte Fläche f

hatching, shade · Schraffur f, Schraffierung f

~, shading · Schraffieren n

hatch(way) [A small opening in a ceiling, roof or wall] · (Aussteig)Luke f, Ausstieg m

Hathor column · Hathorsäule f, Sistrumsäule [Säule mit blockförmigem Aufsatz über einem Hathorkapitell]

~ head · Hathorkopf m

~(-headed) capital · Hathor(kopf)kapitell n, Hathor(kopf)kapital

~ mask · Hathormaske f

~ temple · Hathortempel m

haunch · (Bogen)Schenkel m [Die Bogenhälfte zwischen Kämpfer und Scheitel]

~ [An overstress occurring in nonuniform beams may be eliminated by increasing the cross-section area towards the supports through haunches] · Verstärkung f

~ (US); half-arch (Brit.); flank (of an arch) · Bogenhälfte f, Halbbogen m, (Bogen)Schenkel m

to haunch by masonry (work) · ummauern [Rohrstöße im Erdreich abdichten]

haunched, encased, concrete-~ · (beton)umhüllt, (beton)ummantelt

haunching → (concrete) encasement

~ (concrete) · Füllbeton m, Mantelbeton [Beton, der ein Rohr umschließt]

Häusler type roof cladding, ~ ~ ~ covering, ~ ~ ~ sheathing, ~ ~ roofing · Holzzementdach n [Der Erfinder des Holzzementdaches, Häusler, wählte für die Deckung 4 Lagen Holzzementpapier. Neuerdings wird für die unterste Lage Dachpappe und die übrigen drei Holzzementpapier verwendet. Der Holzzement als Klebemasse ist eine Mischung aus 60 Teilen wasserfreiem Steinkohlenteer, 15 Teilen Asphalt und 25 Teilen Schwefel oder 70% destilliertem Steinkohlenteer, 10% Schmieröl und 20% amerikanischem Harz]

to have a tendency to freeze · gefrieranfällig

~ ~ good build, full-bodied · festkörperreich, füllkräftig, füllstark [Anstrichmittel]

having dentils, finely toothed, denticulate(d), denticular · (fein)gezahnt

~ zero moment, momentless, moment-free · momentenfrei, momentenlos

hawk-bill (pliers) → soldering tongs

hay shed · Heuschuppen m

hazard bonus · Gefahrenzulage f

hazel (wattle) hurdle, ~ wattle · Haselnuß(zaun)hürde *f*

hazel(nut) sapling, sway · Haselnuß *f* [*Zum Binden beim Strohdach*]

hazing · Hauchbildung *f* [*Anstrichmangel*]

hazy light · dunstiges Licht *n*

H. B. → half bat

H-beam (section) → broad-flange(d) beam

HC → hollow core

H-column, H-shaped column · H-Stütze *f*

H.C.V., higher calorific value · H₀ *m*, oberer Heizwert *m*, Verbrennungswärme V *f*

HDW → hardware

HE → heat exchanger

~ tower, heat exchanger ~ · Wärmeübertragungsturm *m* [*Fehlnamen: Wärme(aus)tauscherturm*]

~ with internal heat source, heat exchanger ~ ~ ~ ~ · Wärmeübertrager *m* mit innerer Wärmequelle [*Fehlnamen: Wärme(aus)tauscher ~ ~ ~*]

head, screen ~, (screen) feed, material to be screened · Aufgabegut *n*, Haufwerk *n*, Siebgut, Einlaufgut [*Siebtechnik*]

~ · Binderkopf *m*, Streckerkopf

~ → ~ rail

~ attachment, ~ construction · Kopfausbildung *f* [*Säule; Stütze*]

~ construction, ~ attachment · Kopfausbildung *f* [*Säule; Stütze*]

~-end · Kopfende *n*

header → bonder

~ [*A beam which carries the ends of beams which are cut off in framing around an opening*] · Schlüsselbalken *m*, Trumpfbalken, Wechsel(balken) *m*

~, lintel; lintol [*deprecated*] [*The horizontal framing member over window or door openings*] · Oberschwelle *f*, Sturz(balken) *m*

~ bond → heading ~

~ brick → (clay) brick header

~ (clay) brick, (clay) brick header, (clay) brick bonder, (clay) brick bondstone, (clay) brick bonding header · Ziegelstrecker *m*, Ziegelbinder(stein) *m*

~ course → bonding ~ ~

~ (flue), horizontal ~ · waag(e)rechter Zug *m*

~ plank (unit) · Wechseldiele *f* [*Auswechs(e)lung*]

head groove · Kopffalz *m* [*(Dach)Falzstein*]

heading bond, header ~ · Binderverband *m*, Streckerverband, Kopfverband [*Die Steine liegen mit Längsseite senkrecht zur Mauerfläche; die Schichten sind zueinander um ¼ Stein verschoben*]

~ course → (bonding) header ~

~ joint, butt ~, end-to-end ~ · Stumpffuge *f*

(head) joint (US); cross ~ (Brit.); vertical ~, perpendicular ~, side ~; build (US) · Stoßfuge *f* [*Mauerwerk*]

headlap · Endüberlappung *f* [*Im Gegensatz zur Seitenüberlappung*]

headless nail · kopfloser Nagel *m*

~ rivet · kopfloser Niet *m*

head moment, moment at head · Kopfmoment *n*

~ of drain [*The highest point of a drainage system*] · Dränscheitel(punkt) *m*

~ ~ pressure, pressure head · Druckhöhe *f*

~ office block, ~ ~ building, headquarter ~ · Hauptverwaltungsgebäude *n*

~ plate · Kopfplatte *f*

headquarter(s) · Hauptsitz *m*

~ block, ~ building, head office ~ · Hauptverwaltungsgebäude *n*

head (rail) · Bundbalken *m*, Oberschwelle *f*, Rähm *m*, Rahmholz *n* [*Oberer Abschlußbalken, der auf den Ständern eines Fachwerkes ruht*]

~ slab · Kopfplatte *f* [*Säule*]

~stone, funerary monument, burial monument, sepulchral monument · Grabmonument *n*, Grabdenkmal *n*

~ to head · affrontiert

~ tree, crown plate, saddle, bolster, corbel piece [*A short timber cap over a post to increase the bearing area under a beam*] · Sattelholz *n*

healing (Brit.) → (placing the) roofing

health hazards in paint making · Gefahren *fpl* für die Gesundheit bei der (Anstrich)Farbenherstellung

~ resort, spa · Kurort *m*

~ ~ garden, ~ ~ park, spa ~ · Kurgarten *m*, Kurgarten *m*

~ ~ hotel, spa ~ · Kurhotel *n*

~ ~ park, ~ ~ garden, spa ~ · Kurpark *m*, Kurgarten *m*

~ ~ promenade, spa ~ · Kurpromenade *f*

heap → stock pile

~ of granular material, grains in bulk · Kornschüttung *f*

heart · Kern *m* [*Holz*]

~ cut · Herzschnitt *m* [*Destillatfraktion eines Erdölerzeugnisses mit engen Siedegrenzen*]

~-leaves · Herzlaub *n*

~ of the town → business area

~ plank · Herzbrett *n*, Kernbrett

~ rot · Kernfäule *f* [*Holz*]

~ shake · Kernriß m [*Holz*]

~-shaken wood, ~ timber · kernrissiges Holz n

heart-shaped, carotid · herzförmig

(~) leaf-and-dart moulding (Brit.); (~) ~ molding (US) · Herzblattstab m

hearth [*The floor of a fireplace*] · Kaminboden m

~ fire; ingle [*A medieval Scotch word for a fire upon a hearth against a wall*] · Kaminfeuer n

~ refining · Herdfrischen n

hearting [*Filling the interior of a wall between the facings*] · Ausfüllen n, Kernfüllung f [*Hohlwand*]

~ concrete, core ~, backing ~ · (Hinter)Füll(ungs)beton m, Kernbeton, Unterbeton [*Im Gegensatz zum Vorsatzbeton*]

to heat · anwärmen, erwärmen, aufwärmen [*Bindemittel; Wasser; Zuschläge und dgl.*]

heat · Schmelze f, Schmelzung f [*Stahl*]

~ · Wärme f

~-absorbing · wärmeabsorbierend

heat absorbing (plate) glass · Wärmeschutzglas n [*Gegossenes oder gewalztes Glas mit leicht blaugrüner Eigenfarbe; als Spiegelglas beidseitig geschliffen und poliert. Durch Zusatz von Eisenoxiden wird ein großer Teil der Ultrarot- oder Infrarotstrahlen im Glas zurückgehalten. Die Sonnenschutzwirkung beruht fast ausschließlich auf der Absorption eines Teiles der ultraroten Strahlen*]

~ absorption · Wärmeabsorption f, Wärmeaufnahme f, Wärmeentzug m

~ accumulation, ~ storage, ~ retention · Wärme(auf)speicherung f, Wärmehaltung f

~ ~ capacity → ~ storage ~

~ ~ power → ~ storage capacity

~ ~ property → ~ storage capacity

~ ~ quality → ~ storage capacity

~ action · Wärmewirkung f

~ balance [*A method of accounting for all the heat units supplied, transferred, utilized in, and lost from a kiln*] · Wärmebilanz f, Wärmehaushalt m

~ balancer · Wärmemengenmesser m

~ barrier · Wärmesperre f

~ bat(t) (US) → ~ insulation(-grade) mat

~ blanket → ~ insulation(-grade) mat

~ bridge, ~ build-up · Wärmebrücke f

~ build-up, ~ bridge · Wärmebrücke f

~ circulation · Wärmeumlauf m

(~) conductance [*The capacity or fitness for conducting or transmitting. This term is generally used in problems of heat transmission through walls. It always implies that a conductor, or material path of some kind, is present. Symbol: C*] · (Wärme)Leitvermögen n, (Wärme)Leitfähigkeit f

(~) conduction [*The process of transferring heat along the elements of a substance, as from a tube to a fin*] · (Wärme)Übertragung f, (Wärme)Leitung

(~) conductor · (Wärme)Leiter m

~ conservation shutter [*fan*] · wärmehaltende Lamelle f

~ consumption · Wärmeverbrauch m

~ content, enthalpy · Enthalpie f, Wärmeinhalt m [*Energieinhalt eines Gases; nicht verwechseln mit der inneren Energie*]

~ control · Wärmesteuerung f

~ crack · Wärmeriß m

to heat-cure · nachbehandeln mit Heißluft [*Beton*]

heat cycle (of a welding operation) · Wärmespiel n (eines Schweißvorganges)

~ detector, automatic ~ ~ · Hitzemelder m, Hitzemeldeautomat m [*Brandschutz*]

~ distribution, distribution of heat · Wärmeverteilung f

~ drying · wärmetrocknend

~ economising, heat-saving · wärmesparend

~ economy · Wärmewirtschaft f

heated · beheizt

~ air output, warm ~ ~ · Warmluftleistung f

~ ceiling · beheizte Decke f

~ concrete, warm ~ · Warmbeton m

~ glass · beheiztes Glas n

~ hung ceiling, ~ suspended ~, ~ SC, electrically ~ ~ ~ · (Elektro-)Heizhängedecke f

~ metal hung ceiling → (electrically) heated metal suspended ~

~ ~ SC → (electrically) heated metal suspended ceiling

~ ~ suspended ceiling → electrically ~ ~ ~ ~

~ mortar, warm ~ · Warmmörtel m

~ SC → ~ suspended ceiling

~ suspended ceiling, ~ hung ~, ~ SC, electrically ~ ~ ~ · (Elektro)Heizhängedecke f

~ towel rail · beheizte Handtuchschiene f

~ wire · beheizter Draht m

heat emissivity · Emissionsvermögen n, Wärmeausstrahlungsvermögen

~ emitting apparatus · Wärmeverbrauchsstelle f

~ energy · Wärmeenergie f

~ engineering · Wärmetechnik f

heater → heating appliance

heat evolution · Wärmeentwick(e)lung *f*
~ exchange · Wärmeübertragung *f* [*Fehlnamen: Wärme(aus)tausch m*]
~ exchanger, HE · Wärmeübertrager *m* [*Fehlnamen: Wärme(aus)tauscher*]
~ excluding glass · wärmeabweisendes Glas *n*
~ expansion · Wärme(aus)dehnung *f*
~ fastness, ~ resistance, resistance to heat, fastness to heat, thermal resistance, thermal fastness · Hitzebeständigkeit *f*, Hitzeechtheit, Hitzefestigkeit, Hitzewiderstand *m*
~ ~, ~ resistance, resistance to heat, fastness to heat · Wärmebeständigkeit *f*, Wärmefestigkeit, Wärmewiderstand *m*
~ flow, flow of heat · Wärmeströmung *f*, Wärmefluß *m*
~ gain · Wärmegewinn *m*
~-gain calculation · Wärmegewinnberechnung *f*
heat generated by equipment · Anlagenwärme *f*
~ ~ ~ lighting, ~ ~ ~ illumination · Beleuchtungswärme *f*
~ ~ ~ people · Personenwärme *f*
~ generating device · Wärmeerzeuger *m*
~ generation, ~ production · Wärmeerzeugung *f*
~ gradient · Wärmegefälle *n*, Wärmeunterschied *m*
~ influence, influence of heat · Wärmeeinfluß *m*
heating · Aufheizung *f*, Erhitzung
~ · Erwärmen *n*, Erwärmung *f*, Aufwärmen, Anwärmen, Anwärmung, Aufwärmung, Aufheizen, Aufheizung, Erhitzung, Erhitzen [*Bindemittel; Zuschlagstoffe; Anmach(e)wasser*]
~, cooking · (Ver)Kochen *n*
~, warming · (Be)Heizung *f*
~ accessories · Heiz(ungs)zubehör *n*
~ air · Heiz(ungs)luft *f*
~ and ventilating · (Be)Heizung *f* und Lüftung
~ ~ ~ consultants · beratende Ingenieure *mpl* der Heizungs- und Lüftungstechnik
~ appliance, ~ unit, ~ device, warming **~,** heater, fire, warmer · Heiz(ungs)gerät *n*, Heizer *m*, Erhitzer
~ area of boiler · Kesselheizfläche *f*
~ basement · Heiz(ungs)kellergeschoß *n*
~ battery [*The heating surface of a calorifier*] · Heizbatterie *f*
(~) boiler · Heiz(ungs)kessel *m*, Kessel
~ by town gas · Stadtgasheizung *f*
~ ~ waste heat · Abwärmeheizung *f*, Abhitzeheizung [*Durch Zwischenschaltung von Wärmespeichern wird der fast wertlose Abdampf von Fördermaschinen, Dampfhämmern usw. für Heizzwecke genutzt. Auch Auspuffgase sind verwendbar*]
~ cable · Heizkabel *n*
~ calculation · Heiz(ungs)berechnung *f*
~ ceiling, heated **~** · Heiz(ungs)decke *f*
~ ~ panel, electric(al) **~ ~ ~** · (Elektro)Deckenheiz(ungs)platte *f*
~ cellar, basement boiler room · Heiz(ungs)keller *m*
~ chamber · Heizkammer *f*
~ circuit · Heizkreis *m*
~ circulating pump · Heiz(ungs)umwälzpumpe *f*
~ coil · Erhitzerschlange *f*, Wärmeschlange, Heizschlange, (Heiz)Rohrschlange, (Heiz)Rohrregister *n*
~ contractor · Heizungsunternehmer *m*
~ convector, convector radiator, convector (heater), convector fire · Konvektionsheizer *m*, Konvektionsheiz(ungs)gerät *n*, Konvektionserhitzer, Konvektor *m* [*Direktheizgerät*]
~ curve · Aufheizkurve *f*
~ device → **~ appliance**
~ duct, ~ trough · Heiz(ungs)kanal *m*
~ element [*The part of an electric heater which consists of a wire which is heated by an electric current*] · Heizelement *n*
~ engineer · Heiz(ungs)ingenieur *m*
~ engineering · Heiz(ungs)technik *f*
~ ~ requirement · heiz(ungs)technische Forderung *f*
~ equipment · Heizausrüstung *f*
~ expert · Heiz(ungs)fachmann *m*
~ firm · Heizungsfirma *f*
~ for building operations · Bauheizung *f*
~ fuel · Heiz(ungs)stoff *m*
~ gas · Heizgas *n*, technisches Gas
~ glass pane, (glass) heating **~** · Heizglasscheibe *f*, heizbare Glasscheibe
~ grid · Heizgitter *n*
~ ~ · Heizregister *n* [*Strahlungsheizung*]
~ ground gypsum in pan(s) · Kochen *n* [*Austreiben des Kristallwassers aus dem Gipsstein in Kesseln*]
~ heat · Heiz(ungs)wärme *f*
~ ~ capacity · Heiz(ungs)wärmemenge *f*
~ ~ requirement · Heiz(ungs)wärmebedarf *m*
~ industry · Heizungsindustrie *f*
~ installation → **~ system**
~ jacket, ~ mantle · Heizmantel *m*
~ line · Heiz(ungs)leitung *f*
~ load · Heiz(ungs)last *f*
~ mantle, ~ jacket · Heizmantel *m*
~ medium · Heizmittel *n*

heating medium — heat insulating material

~ ~, heat transfer ~ [*Heating mediums in general are steam, hot water and air*] · Wärmeträger *m*
~ **oil,** fuel ~ · Heizöl *n* [*DIN 51603*]
~ ~ **barrier,** fuel ~ ~ · Heizölsperre *f*
~ **oil-fired central heating,** (fuel) ~ ~ ~ · (Heiz)Öl-Zentralheizung *f*
~ **oil interceptor** → (fuel) ~ ~
~ ~ **pipe,** (fuel) ~ ~ · (Heiz)Ölrohr *n*
~ **oil-resistant,** fuel ~ · heizölfest, heizölbeständig
~ **oil storage,** (fuel) ~ ~ · (Heiz)Öllagerung *f*
~ ~ **(~) tank,** (fuel) ~ (~) ~ · (Heiz-)Ölbehälter *m*, (Heiz)Öl(lager)tank *m*
(~) ~ store, fuel ~ ~ ~ · (Heiz)Öllagerraum *m*
~ **oil-tight,** (fuel) ~ · (heiz)öldicht, (heiz)ölundurchlässig
~ **output** · Heizleistung *f*
~ **pane,** glass ~ ~, heating glass ~ · Heizglasscheibe *f*, heizbare Glasscheibe
~ **panel,** ~ plate · Heiz(ungs)platte *f*
~ **period,** ~ time · Aufheizdauer *f*, Aufheizzeit *f*
~ **pipe** · Heiz(ungs)rohr *n*
~ **plant** → ~ system
~ ~ **room** · Heiz(ungs)raum *m*
~ ~ **stack,** boilerhouse ~ · Heizwerkschornstein *m*, Kesselhausschornstein
~ **pump** · Heizungspumpe *f*
~ **rate** [*The rate expressed in degrees per hour at which the temperature of the kiln or autoclave is raised to the desired maximum temperature*] · Aufheizgeschwindigkeit *f*
~ ~ · Erhitzungsgeschwindigkeit *f* [*Kalkbrennen*]
~ **season** · Heiz(ungs)saison *f*
~ **steam** · Heiz(ungs)dampf *m*
~ **strip,** room ~ ~ · (Raum)Heizleiste *f*
~ **surface** · Heiz(ungs)fläche *f*
~ ~ **in contact with the steam** · dampfberührte Heiz(ungs)fläche *f*, Dampfheiz(ungs)fläche
~ **system,** ~ installation, ~ plant · Heizanlage *f*, Heizung(sanlage) *f*, Heiz(ungs)installation *f*
~ ~ · Heiz(ungs)system *n*
~ **tape** → pipe ~ ~
~ **technician** · Heiz(ungs)techniker *m*
~ **time** → ~ period
~ **trough** → duct
~ **unit** → ~ appliance
~ ~, **(electric) heating element** [*The part of an electric heater which consists of a wire which is heated by an electric current*] · Heizelement *n*
~ **up,** warming ~, firing ~ · (An)Tempern *n*, Auftempern [*Glasherstellung*]
~ ~ **(from cold)** · Anfahren *n* einer Heiz(ungs)anlage, Anheizen
heating-up loss · Anheizverlust *m*

~ **period,** ~ time · Aufladezeit *f* [*Nachtstromspeicherheizung*]
~ ~ · Anheizzeit *f*
~ **time,** ~ period · Aufladezeit *f* [*Nachtstromspeicherheizung*]
heating value → calorific ~
~ **water** · Heiz(ungs)wasser *n*
~ ~ **pipe** · Heizwasserrohr *n*
~ **wire** · Heizdraht *m*
~ ~ **method,** ~ ~ system · Heizdrahtverfahren *n*, Heizdrahtmethode *f*
~ **with recirculated air** · Umluftheizung *f*
heat input, ~ supply, H.I. · Wärmeeinspeisung *f*, Wärmezufuhr *f*
~ **insulant** → ~ insulating material
heat-insulating · wärmedämmend
heat (insulating) bat(t) (US) → ~ insulation(-grade) mat
~ **(~) blanket** → ~ insulation(-grade) mat
~ ~ **block,** ~ ~ tile, ~ insulation(-grade) ~ [*See remark under 'Block'*] · Wärmedämmblock(stein) *m*, Wärmedämmstein, Wärmeschutz(block)stein, Wärmeschutzblock
~ ~ **board,** ~ ~ sheet · Wärmedämmplatte *f*
~ ~ **capacity,** ~ ~ power, ~ ~ quality, ~ ~ property · Wärmedämmfähigkeit *f*, Wärmedämmeigenschaft *f*, Wärmedämmvermögen *n*, Wärmeschutzvermögen, Wärmeschutzfähigkeit, Wärmeschutzeigenschaft
~ ~ **composition** → ~ insulation(-grade) compound
~ ~ **compound** → ~ insulation(-grade) ~
~ ~ **concrete** [*It is made with high alumina cement and light aggregate*] · Wärmedämmbeton *m*
~ ~ **course,** ~ ~ layer · Wärmedämmlage *f*, Wärmedämmschicht *f*, Wärmeschutzlage, Wärmeschutzschicht
~ ~ **efficiency,** ~ insulation ~ · Wärmedämmwirkung *f*
(~) ~ glass · wärmedämmendes Isolierglas *n* [*z.B. Thermopane*]
(heat-)insulating glazing unit · Glas-Isoliereinheit *f*, Isolier-Glaseinheit
heat insulating hanging, ~ insulation(-grade) ~ · Wärmedämmtapete *f*
~ ~ **layer,** ~ ~ course · Wärmedämmlage *f*, Wärmedämmschicht *f*, Wärmeschutzlage, Wärmeschutzschicht
~ ~ **mass** → ~ insulation(-grade) compound
~ ~ **material,** ~ insulation(-grade) ~, ~ insulator, ~ insulant [*B.S. 3958*] · Wärme(ab)dämmstoff *m*, Wärme(ab)dämmaterial *n* [*Feinporiger Baustoff mit geringer Wärmedurchlässigkeit, z.B. Kork, Schaumglas, Kunststoffschaum usw. Er verhindert die Wärmefortleitung*]

heat insulating material — heat of reaction

~ ~ ~ → ~ insulation(-grade) compound

~ ~ **(mixed) plaster,** ~ insulation(-grade) (~) ~ · Wärmedämmputz *m*, Wärmeschutzputz

~ ~ **paper** → ~ ~ wall~

~ ~ ~, ~ insulation(-grade) ~ [*See remark under 'Pappe'*] · Wärmedämmpappe *f*

~ ~ **plaster** → ~ ~ mixed ~

~ ~ **power,** ~ ~ quality, ~ ~ property, ~ ~ capacity · Wärmedämmfähigkeit *f*, Wärmedämmeigenschaft *f*, Wärmedämmvermögen *n*, Wärmeschutzvermögen, Wärmeschutzfähigkeit, Wärmeschutzeigenschaft

~ ~ **property,** ~ ~ capacity, ~ ~ power, ~ ~ quality · Wärmedämmfähigkeit *f*, Wärmedämmeigenschaft *f*, Wärmedämmvermögen *n*, Wärmeschutzvermögen, Wärmeschutzfähigkeit, Wärmeschutzeigenschaft

~ ~ **quality,** ~ ~ property, ~ ~ capacity, ~ ~ power · Wärmedämmfähigkeit *f*, Wärmedämmeigenschaft *f*, Wärmedämmvermögen *n*, Wärmeschutzvermögen, Wärmeschutzfähigkeit, Wärmeschutzeigenschaft

~ (~) **quilt** → ~ insulation(-grade) mat

~ ~ **sheet,** ~ ~ board · Wärmedämmplatte *f*

~ ~ **structural panel** · Wärmekonstruktionstafel *f*

~ ~ **tile** → ~ ~ block

~ ~ **(wall)paper,** ~ insulation(-grade) ~ · Wärmedämm-(Wand)Papiertapete *f*, Wärmedämmtapete

~ ~ **zone** · Wärmedämmgebiet *n*

~ **insulation,** thermal ~ [*The property that opposes the transmission of heat from one side to the other*] · Wärme(ab)dämmung *f*

~ ~ [*Means taken to reduce the transmission of heat*] · Wärmeschutz *m* [*DIN 4108*]

~ ~ **bat(t)** (US) → ~ insulation(-grade) mat

~ ~ **block** → ~ insulating ~

~ ~ **efficiency,** ~ insulating ~ · Wärmedämmwirkung *f*

~ ~ **hanging,** ~ ~-grade ~, ~ insulating ~ · Wärmedämmtapete *f*

~ ~ **material** → ~ insulating ~

~ **(mixed) plaster** → ~ insulating (~) ~

~ ~ **paper,** ~ ~-grade ~, ~ insulating ~ [*See remark under 'Pappe'*] · Wärmedämmpappe *f*

~ ~ ~ → ~ insulating (wall)paper

~ ~ **plaster** → ~ insulating (mixed) ~

~ ~ **requirement** · Wärmedämmforderung *f*

~ ~ **test** · Wärmeschutzversuch *m*, Wärmeschutzprobe *f*, Wärmeschutzprüfung *f*, Wärmedämmversuch, Wärmedämmprüfung, Wärmedämmprobe, wärmeschutztechnische Prüfung, wärmeschutztechnische Probe, wärmeschutztechnischer Versuch [*DIN 52612*]

~ ~ **tile** → ~ insulating block

~ ~ **value** · Wärmedämmwert *m*

~ ~ **(wall)paper** → ~ insulating ~

~ ~ **work** · Wärmedämmungsarbeiten *fpl* [*DIN 18421*]

~ **insulation(-grade) bat(t)** (US) → ~ ~ mat

~ ~ **block** → ~ insulating ~

~ ~ **composition** → ~ ~ compound

~ ~ **compound,** ~ ~ composition, ~ ~ mass, ~ ~ material, ~ insulating ~ · (plastische) Wärmeschutzmasse *f*, (~) Wärmedämmasse [*Alle plastischen Wärmeschutzmassen sind pulverförmig und werden mit Wasser angerührt*]

~ ~ **hanging,** ~ insulating ~ · Wärmedämmtapete *f*

~ ~ **mass** → ~ ~ compound

~ ~ **mat,** ~ ~ blanket, ~ ~ quilt, ~ (insulating) ~; ~ ~ bat(t) (US) · Wärmedämmatte *f*, Wärmeschutzmasse

~ ~ **material** → ~ ~ compound

~ ~ ~, heat-insulating ~ · Wärme(ab)dämmstoff *m*

~ ~ **(mixed) plaster** → ~ insulating (~) ~

~ ~ **paper,** ~ insulating ~ [*See remark under 'Pappe'*] · Wärmedämmpappe *f*

~ ~ ~ → ~ insulating (wall)~

~ ~ **plaster** → ~ insulating (mixed) ~

~ ~ **tile** → ~ insulating block

~ ~ **(wall)paper** → ~ insulating ~

~ **insulator** → ~ insulating material

~ **loss,** loss of heat · Wärmeverlust *m*

~ ~ **calculation,** ~ ~ computation, calculation of heat loss(es), computation of heat loss(es) · Wärmeverlust(be)rechnung

~ ~ **computation,** ~ ~ calculation, calculation of heat loss(es), computation of heat loss(es) · Wärmeverlust(be)rechnung *f*

~ **mat** → ~ insulation(-grade) ~

~ **meter** · Wärmezähler *m*

~ **movement** · Wärmebewegung *f*

~ **nuisance** · Hitzebelästigung *f*

~ **of condensation,** condensation heat · Kondensationswärme *f*

~ ~ **fusion,** melting heat · Schmelzwärme *f*

~ ~ **hydration,** hydration heat [*The heat given off by cement paste during the chemical combination of cement with water. An exothermic process*] · Hydra(ta)tionswärme *f*

~ ~ **initial set(ting),** initial set(ting) heat · Erstarrungswärme *f* [*Beton; Mörtel*]

~ ~ **reaction,** reaction heat · Reaktionswärme *f*

heat of set(ting) — heat-treatable steel

~~ set(ting), set(ting) heat · (Ab-) Bindewärme f

~~ solution [*Heat evolved by the solution of a material in a solvent*] · Lösungswärme f

~~~ method · Lösungswärmeverfahren n

~ output · Wärmeabgabe f

~~, thermal ~ · thermischer Wirkungsgrad m, Wärmeleistung f

~ pre-control · Wärmevorregelung f

~-producing appliance · wärmeerzeugendes Gerät n

heat production, ~ generation · Wärmeerzeugung f

heatproof, heat-resistant, heat-resisting, resistant to heat, resisting to heat · hitzebeständig, hitzefest, hitzesicher, hitzewiderstandsfähig

heat protection · Hitzeschutz m

~ pump · Wärmepumpe f

~ quilt → ~ insulation(-grade) mat

~ radiation → temperature ~

~ reclamation system, ~ recovery ~ · Wärmerückgewinnungsanlage f

~ recovery · Wärmerückgewinnung f, Wärmewiedergewinnung

~~ system, ~ reclamation ~ · Wärmerückgewinnungsanlage f

~-reflecting · wärmereflektierend, wärmerückstrahlend

heat reflectivity · Wärmerückstrahlung f

~-rejecting glass · hitzeabweisendes Glas n

heat release · Wärmeabgabe f

~~ of humans · Wärmeabgabe f durch den Menschen

~-repellent, heat-repelling · hitzeabwehrend

heat-repelling, heat-repellent · hitzeabwehrend

heat requirement · Wärmebedarf m [*DIN 4701*]

~~ calculation · Wärmebedarfsrechnung f

~ resistance, ~ fastness, resistance to heat, fastness to heat, thermal resistance, thermal fastness · 1.) Hitzebeständigkeit f, Hitzeechtheit, Hitzefestigkeit, Hitzewiderstand m; 2.) Wärmebeständigkeit, Wärmeechtheit, Wärmefestigkeit, Wärmewiderstand

~~, thermal ~ · Wärmeübergangswiderstand m

heat-resistant, heat-resisting, heatproof, resistant to heat, resisting to heat · hitzebeständig, hitzefest, hitzesicher, hitzewiderstandsfähig

heat-resisting glass [*A glass able to withstand high thermal shock, generally because of a low coefficient of thermal expansion*] · hitzebeständiges Glas n, Hitzeschutzglas

~ paint [*A paint with improved resistance to heat. The term is used in a comparative sense but is of little value unless it is referred to some standard of performance under specified conditions*] · hitzebeständige (Anstrich)Farbe f

heat retention, ~ storage, ~ accumulation · Wärmehaltung f, Wärme(auf)speicherung

~~ capacity → ~ storage ~

~-saving, heat-economising · wärmesparend

heat-setting · wärmeabbindend

heat shock · Wärmestoß m

~ source · Wärmequelle f

~ stability → stability to heat

~ storage, ~ accumulation, ~ retention · Wärme(auf)speicherung f, Wärmehaltung

~~ capacity, ~ storing ~, ~~ quality, ~~ power, ~~ property, ~ retention ~, ~ accumulation ~ · Wärmespeicher(ungs)fähigkeit f, Wärmespeicher(ungs)vermögen n, Wärmehaltungsfähigkeit, Wärmehaltungsvermögen

~~ material · Wärmespeicherstoff m, Wärmehaltungsstoff

~~ power → ~~ capacity

~~ property → ~~ capacity

~~ quality → ~~ capacity

~ storing capacity → ~ storage ~

~ supply, ~ input, H.I. · Wärmeeinspeisung f, Wärmezufuhr f

~~, provision of heat · Wärmeversorgung f

~ temperature · Wärmezustand m [*Er wird in °C, °R oder °F gemessen*]

~ transfer area · Austauschfläche f [*Wärme(aus)tauscher*]

heat-transfer element · Heizkörper m [*Zur Raumerwärmung dienende Heizfläche einer Heizungsanlage, z.B. Radiator, Konvektor usw.*]

~ medium, heating ~ [*Heating mediums in general use are steam, hot water and air*] · Wärmeträger m

(heat) transference, (~) transferral · (Wärme)Übertragung f

(~) transferral, (~) transference · (Wärme)Übertragung f

~ transmissibility · Wärmedurchlässigkeit f [*DIN 52611*]

~ transmission · Abfließen n der entwickelten Wärme, Wärmeabfluß m [*Kalorimetrie*]

~~ · Wärmedurchlaß m

~~ loss · Wärmedurchlaßverlust m

~-transmitting glass · wärmedurchlässiges Glas n

to heat treat · wärmebehandeln

heat-treatable · (warm) aushärtbar [*Alu(minium)legierung*]

~ steel, quenched and subsequently tempered ~ · Vergütungsstahl m

heat-treated — heavy(weight) aggregate

heat-treated, HT · wärmebehandelt

~, HT · warm ausgehärtet [*Alu(minium)-legierung*]

~ plate (glass) → ~ polished ~ (~)

~ (polished) plate (glass), toughened (~) ~ (~), tempered (~) ~ (~) [*For instance ARMOURCLAD*] · vorgespanntes (Kristall)Spiegelglas *n*

~ (safety) glass → toughened (~) ~

heat treatment · Wärmebehandlung *f*

~ unit · Wärmeeinheit *f*

~ utilization (US); ~ utilisation (Brit.) · Wärme(aus)nutzung *f*

~ variation · Wärmeschwankung *f*

heavily developed populated area · dichtes Wohngebiet *n*

heavy aggregate → ~weight ~

~ ceramics, structural ~ · Baukeramik *f*

~ ~ articles → structural ceramics products

~ ~ goods → structural ceramics products

~ ~ products → structural ~ ~

~ clay article, structural ~ ~, ~ ~ product · baukeramischer Artikel *m*, ~ Gegenstand *m*, baukeramisches Erzeugnis *n*

~ ~ flooring tile, structural ~ ~ ~ · Baukeramik(fuß)bodenplatte *f*, Baukeramik(fuß)bodenfliese *f*

~ ~ industry, structural ~ ~ · baukeramische Industrie *f*

~ ~ kiln · grobkeramischer Ofen *m*

~ ~ product, structural ~ ~, ~ ~ article · baukeramischer Artikel *m*, ~ Gegenstand *m*, baukeramisches Erzeugnis *n*

~ concrete → ~-weight ~

(~) cord · Rampe *f* [*Glasschmelzfehler*]

heavy-duty cable · Starkstromkabel *n*

~ flexible (swing) door · schwere flexible Pendeltür *f*

~ industrial floor cover(ing), ~ ~ floor finish, ~ ~ floor(ing) · schwerer Betriebs(fuß)boden(belag) *m*, ~ Industrie(fuß)boden(belag), ~ Fabrik(fuß)boden(belag), ~ Werk(fuß)boden(belag)

~ lock · schweres Schloß *n*

heavy element · Schwereelement *n*

~ fuel oil, medium ~ ~ [*950 seconds*] · Heizöl M *n*, mittelflüssiges Heizöl [*DIN 51603*]

heavy-gauge copper tube for general purposes [*B.S. 61*] · schwere Kupferröhre *f* für allgemeine Zwecke

heavy industrial landscape · Schwerindustrielandschaft *f*

~ load → ~-weight ~

~ magnesia, dead-burned ~, dead-burnt ~ · geglühte Magnesia *f*

~ metal · Schwermetall *n*

(~) (~) plate · (Grob)Blech *n*

(~) (~) ~ cover(ing) · (Grob)Blechabdeckung *f*

(~) (~) ~ girder, composite ~ [*It is built up from plates or from combinations of plates with shapes. Connection may be by riveting or welding*] · Blechträger *m*

(~) (~) ~ lining, (~) (~) ~ (sur)facing · (Grob)Blechauskleidung *f*, (Grob-)Blechverkleidung, (Grob)Blechbekleidung

(~) (~) ~ rigidity → (~) (~) ~ stiffness

(~) (~) ~ stiffness, (~) (~) ~ rigidity · (Grob)Blechstarrheit *f*, (Grob)Blechsteifigkeit

(~) (~) ~ (sur)facing → (~) (~) ~ lining

(~) (~) ~ suspension roof(ing) · Blechhängedach *n*, hängendes Blechdach

~ oil, dead ~ · Schweröl *n*

~ panel · Tafel *f* mit hohem Massenwiderstand [*Dieser Widerstand setzt sich der Erregung durch den Schalldruck entgegen*]

~ paper · Karton *m*

~ pelting rain · schwerer Schlagregen *m* [*Mit Regen verbundener Wind von mindestens Beaufortstärke 8*]

~ petroleum spirit · hochsiedendes Lösungsbenzin *n*

(~) plate facing → (~) ~ lining

(~) ~ girder → (~) metal ~ ~

(~) ~ lining, (~) ~ (sur)facing · Blechauskleidung *f*, Blechverkleidung, Blechbekleidung

(~) ~ (sur)facing → (~) ~ lining

~ precasting · schwere Vorfertigung *f*

~ profile, ~ section, ~ shape, ~ unit, ~ trim · Schwerprofil *n*

~ Romanesque (style) · schwere Romanik *f*

~ section, ~ shape, ~ unit, ~ trim, ~ profile · Schwerprofil *n*

~ seed · Gispennest *n*

~ shape, ~ section, ~ unit, ~ trim, ~ profile · Schwerprofil *n*

~ sheet (glass), crystal ~ ~ (US); thick ~ ~ · Dickglas *n*

~ spar → barytes

(~) steel plate · Stahl(grob)blech *n* [*DIN 1543*]

~ structural system · Schwerbausystem *n*

~ tar oil · schweres Teeröl *n*

~ trim, ~ unit, ~ shape, ~ section, ~ profile · Schwerprofil *n*

~ unit, ~ trim, ~ shape, ~ section, ~ profile · Schwerprofil *n*

~-wall(ed), thick-wall(ed) · dickwandig

heavy(weight) aggregate [*Aggregate of heigh specific gravity such as barite, magnetite, limonite, ilmenite, iron, or* *steel used to produce heavy concrete*] · Schwerstzuschlag(stoff) *m*, Schwerstzuschlagmaterial *n*

~ **concrete, high density** ~ [*Concrete of exceptionally high unit weight, usually obtained by use of heavyweight aggregates, used especially for radiation shielding*] · Schwerstbeton *m*

~ **load** · Schwerlast *f*

hecatonstylon · hundertsäuliges Gebäude *n*

hectastyle, (h)exastyle [*Having six front(ed) columns*] · sechssäulig

heel damage · Beschädigung *f* durch Schuhabsätze, Schaden *m* durch Eindrücke scharfkantiger Absätze [*(Fuß-) Boden(belag)*]

~ **mark** · Absatzeindruck *m*

height between stories · [Einspann-(ungs)höhe *f* [*Kletterkran*]

~ **dimension** · Höhenabmessung *f*

~ **money** [*Additional pay for working more than 40 ft above the ground or above a building*] · Höhenzulage *f*

~ **of building** [*The vertcial distance from the ground to the top of the external wall including any parapet. The term has special statutory definitions*] · Gebäudehöhe *f*

~ ~ **chimney** · Schornsteinhöhe *f*

~ ~ **door** · Türhöhe *f*

~ ~ **step** · Stufenhöhe *f*

~ **regulations** · Vorschriften *fpl* über die Bauhöhe

~ **restriction,** restricted height · Höhenbeschränkung *f*

height-to-width ratio · Höhen-Breiten-Verhältnis *n*, Höhe-zu-Breite-Verhältnis

heightened block, ~ **building,** raised ~ · aufgestocktes Gebäude *n*

heightening · Aufstocken *n*, Erhöhen [*Gebäude*]

helical barrel vault · Schneckengewölbe *n*, schraubenförmig steigendes Tonnengewölbe, Spindelgewölbe, Spiralgewölbe

~ **binding,** ~ reinforcement, lateral reinforcement, transverse reinforcement, helix; spiral reinforcement [*misnomer*] · Querbewehrung *f* nach der Schraubenlinie, Spiralbewehrung, Spiralarmierung, Spiral(stahl)einlagen *fpl*, Umschnürung

~ **hinge** [*A hinge for a swing door which is hung from its frame*] · Federband *n*, Pendeltürband

~ **ramp** → helicline

~ **reinforcement,** lateral ~, transverse ~, helical binding, helix; spiral reinforcement [*misnomer*] · Querbewehrung *f* nach der Schraubenlinie, Spiralbewehrung, Spiralarmierung, Spiral(stahl)einlagen *fpl*, Umschnürung

~ **shell,** helicoidal ~ · Schraubenflächenschale *f*

~ **spring** · Kernspirale *f*, Wendel *f* [*Verfahren Freyssinet*]

helically reinforced column, ~ ~ support · Stütze *f* mit Spiralbewehrung, ~ ~ Spiralarmierung, ~ ~ Spiral-(stahl)einlagen, (spiral)umschnürte Stütze, spiralbewehrte Stütze, spiralarmierte Stütze

~ **threaded nail** · Spiralgewindenagel *m*

helicline, ramp tower, spiral ramp, helic(oid)al ramp, circular ramp · Schraubenrampe *f*, Wendelrampe, Spiralrampe

helic(oid)al ramp, spiral ~, circular ~, helicline, ramp tower · Schraubenrampe *f*, Wendelrampe, Spiralrampe

~ **shell** · Schraubenflächenschale *f*

helicopter ground · Hubschrauberplatz *m*

helium luminous tube light · Helium-Leuchtröhre *f*

helix [*One of the small spirals or volutes under the abacus of the Corinthian capital*] · Schnörkel *m*

~ · Schraubenlinie *f*

~, helical binding, helical reinforcement, transverse reinforcement, lateral reinforcement; spiral reinforcement [*misnomer*] · Querbewehrung *f* nach der Schraubenlinie, Spiralbewehrung, Spiralarmierung, Spiral(stahl)einlagen *fpl*, Umschnürung

Hellenic architecture [*This principal phase of Greek architecture lasted from 650–323 B.C.*] · hellenische Architektur *f*

Hellenistic architecture [*This principal phase of Greek architecture lasted from 323–30 B.C.*] · hellenistische Architektur *f*

~ **Baroque** · hellenistischer Barock *m*

~ **basilica,** open-air (type) ~ · hellenistische Basilika *f*

~ **house** · hellenistisches Haus *n*

helm roof [*It has four inclined faces joined at the top, with a gable at the foot of each*] · Helmdach *n*, Rhombendach, Rautendach

helying (Brit.) → (placing the) roofing

hematite [*substance*] → ferric oxid(e)

hemicycle, semicircular niche, semicircular space · Halbkreisnische *f* [*Basilika*]

~ [*A half-circle; a semicircular structure, as an apse-like recess, etc.*] · Hemicyclium *n*

hemihydrate [*A compound containing one-half of a molecule of water to one molecule of another substance*] · Halbhydrat *n*

~ **(gypsum-)plaster** [*An intermediate phase in the dehydration of gypsum by heat wherein the amount of combined water corresponds approximately to the formula $2CaSO_4 \cdot H_2O$, calcium sulphate hemihydrate. The formula is often written $CaSO_4 \cdot 1/2 H_2O$, hence the designation hemihydrate*] · Halbhydrat(putzgips) *n*, (*m*)

hemisphere · Halbkugel *f*

~ **of sky of uniform brightness** · gleichmäßig helles Himmelsgewölbe *n* [*Tageslichtberechnung*]

hemispherical stupa(-mound), ~ **tope(-mound)** · halbkugelförmiger Stupa *m*

hemp · Hanf *m*

~ **burlap mat** (US); ~ **hessian** ~ (Brit.) · Hanfsackleinenbahn *f*

~ **cord** · Hanfkordel *f*

~ **core** · Hanfeinlage *f*, Hanfkern *m*, Hanfseele *f*

~ **fibre** (Brit.); ~ **fiber** (US) · Hanffaser *f*

~ **hessian mat** (Brit.); ~ **burlap** ~ (US) · Hanfsackleinenbahn *f*

~ **rope** [*B.S.* 2052] · Hanfseil *n*, Hanfstrick *m*

~ **sacking** · Hanfgrobgewebe *n*

~ **-seed oil** · Hanfsamenöl *n*

~ **shives** · Hanfschäben *fpl*

~ **washer** · Hanfunterlegscheibe *f*

~ **-wrapped** · hanfumwickelt

hench [*The narrow side of a chimney shaft*] · Schornstein-Schmalseite *f*

(h)endecagon · Elfeck *n*

Henneberg's method · Hennebergsche Methode *f*, Hennebergsches Verfahren *n*, (Henneberg-)Ersatzstabverfahren [*ebenes Fachwerk*]

henostyle · einsäulig

Hephaisteion, Theseion · Hephästostempel *m* [*Agora von Athen*]

heptagon · Siebeneck *n*

heptastyle [*Having seven columns in front*] · heptastyl, siebensäulig

~ [*A portico or colonnade of seven columns*] · Heptastylos *m*

~ **temple** [*A temple having a row of seven front(ed) columns*] · Heptastylostempel *m*, siebensäuliger Tempel, Tempel mit siebensäuliger Giebelfront

heraeum, Temple of Hera · Hera-Tempel *m*, Heraion *n*

Heraion at Olympia · olympisches Heraion *n*, Heraion zu Olympia

Heraklith magnesite-bound excelsior building slab (Brit.); ~ ~ **wood-wool** ~ ~ (Brit.) · Heraklitplatte *f* [*magnesitgebundene Holzwolle-Leichtbauplatte. DIN 1101*]

Hercules fountain at Augsburg · Herkulesbrunnen *m* zu Augsburg [*von Adrian de Vries, 1602*]

hercynite, iron spinel · Eisen-Tonerdespinell *m*, Hercynit *m*, $FeO.Al_2O_3$

herdman's hut · Schäferhütte *f*

herm, term(inal figure) [*A pedestal, pier, pilaster, etc., tapering towards the base and having a sculptured head or upper part of a human figure growing out of it*] · Herme *f*

hermetically sealed, HS · absolut dicht abgeschlossen

~ ~ **dehydrated captive air space, blanket of dry air** · Zwischenraum *m* [*Beim Thermopane-Mehrscheibenisolierglas der hermetisch abgeschlossene Zwischenraum mit getrockneter Luft mit Taupunkt $-70°$ C gefüllt*]

~ ~ **edge** · Verbundrand *m* [*wärmedämmendes Isolierglas*]

heroum [*Shrine or chapel dedicated to a deified or semideified dead person*] · Heroon *n*

herringbone (masonry) bond (Brit.); ~ (~) **pattern** (US); raking ~ · Festungsverband *m*, Kornährenverband, (Fisch)Grätenverband, Stromverband

~ **(~) course,** ~ **(~) layer** · Stromschicht *f*, Stromlage *f*, Kornährenschicht, Kornährenlage,(Fisch)Grätenschicht,(Fisch-)Grätenlage, Festungsverbandschicht, Festungsverbandlage, Schmiegelage *f*, Schmiegeschicht

~ **mesh** → ~ **pattern**

~ ~ **opening** · Grätenfeld *n* [*Streckmetall*]

~ **pattern** · (Fisch)Grätenmuster *n*, Kornährenmuster, Fischgrat *m*

~ ~ → ~ **(masonry) bond**

~ **(~) mesh** · Grätenstruktur *f* [*Streckmetall*]

~ **strut** · (Kreuz)Stake *f*, (Kreuz)Stakholz *n*

~ **strutting,** cross bridging, diagonal bridging · (Kreuz)Stakung *f* [*Abkreuzung von Balken durch kreuzweise angeordnete Stakhölzer*]

~ **work** · Ähren(mauer)werk *n*, Fischgräten(mauer)werk [*Mauerwerk, bei dem die Steine ein Ähren- oder Fischgrätmuster haben. Altrömisch: opus spicatum, spicatum opus*]

herse → **portcullis**

hesitation set(ting) → **false** ~

hessian (canvas) (Brit.); burlap (US) [*Strong coarse material woven from jute, hemp, or flax*] · Sackleinen *n*

~ **(~) mat** (Brit.); burlap ~ (US) · Sackleinenbahn *f*

to hew, to dress, to mill, to shape · (steinmetzmäßig) bearbeiten, (~) behauen, (~) zurichten

~ ~, to cut, to curve, to sculpture [*out of stone, in ivory, etc.*] · skulpt(ur)ieren

~ ~ **coarsely** → ~ **dress**

~ ~ **roughly** → ~ **dress coarsely**

hewing, cutting, carving, sculpturing [*out of stone, in ivory, etc.*] · Skulpt(ur)ieren *n*

~, dressing, milling, shaping · Bearbeitung *f*, Behauen *n*, Zurichten, (Natur)Steinbearbeitung

hewn, milled, shaped, dressed · (steinmetzmäßig) bearbeitet, (~) behauen, (~) zugerichtet

hewn foliage — H-girder

~ **foliage,** cut ~, carved ~, sculptured ~ · skulpt(ur)iertes Blattwerk *n*, ~ Laubwerk, plastisch gestaltete Blätter *npl*

~ **(natural) stone** → dressed (~) ~

~ **sandstone** (US); sandstone ashlar, sandstone ashler · Sandstein-Haustein *m*, Sandstein-Bruchsteine

~ **stone** → dressed (natural) ~

~ ~ (US) → (stone) ashlar

~ ~ **arch** (US); (stone) ashlar ~, (stone) ashler ~ · Hausteinbogen *m*, (Natur-) Werksteinbogen

~ ~ **bond** (US) → (stone) ashlar ~

~ ~ **bonder** → (stone) ashlar ~

~ ~ **(bonding) header** → (stone) ashlar bonder

~ ~ **bondstone** → (stone) ashlar bonder

~ ~ **header** → (stone) ashlar bonder

~ ~ **masonry (work)** (US) → (stone) ashlar ~ (~)

~ ~ **slab** (US) → (stone) ashlar ~

~ ~ **structure,** cut ~ ~ (US); (stone) ashlar ~, (stone) ashler ~ · (Natur-)Werksteinbau(werk) *m*, (*n*), Hausteinbau(werk)

~ ~ **vault** (US) → (stone) ashlar ~

~ ~ **window** (US) → (stone) ashlar ~

~ **stonework,** (dressed) ~, milled ~, shaped ~ · zugerichtete Werksteine *mpl*, bearbeitete ~, behauene ~

hexacalcium aluminate · Hexalkalziumaluminat *n*

hexagon · Sechseck *n*

hexagon(al) · sechseckig, sechskantig

~ **bar** · Sechseckstab *m*, Sechskantstab

~ **bastion** · Sechseckbastion *f*, Sechskantbastion *f*

~ **bolt** · Sechseckschraube *f*, Sechskantschraube

~ **brass** · Sechseckmessing *n*, Sechskantmessing

~ **chimney** · Sechseckschornstein *m*, Sechskantschornstein

~ **forecourt** · sechseckiger Vorhof *m*, sechskantiger ~

~ **(ground(-))plan** · sechskantiger Grundriß *m*, sechseckiger ~

~ **head** · Sechseckkopf *m*, Sechskantkopf

~ **mesh** · sechseckige Masche *f*, sechskantige ~

~ (~) **wire(d) glass** · Drahtglas *n* mit sechseckigen Maschen, ~ ~ sechskantigen ~

~ **mosaic tile** · Sechseckmosaikfliese *f*, Sechseckmosaikplatte, Sechkantmosaikfliese, Sechskantmosaikplatte

~ **netting** · sechseckiges Geflecht *n*, sechskantiges ~

~ **nut** · Sechseckmutter *f*, Sechskantmutter

~ **(paving) sett** · Sechseck(pflaster)stein *m*, Sechskantblock *m*

~ **plan** → ~ ground(-)~

~ **profile,** ~ section, ~ shape, ~ unit, ~ trim · Sechseckprofil *n*, Sechskantprofil

~ **pyramid** · Sechseckpyramide *f*, Sechseckspitzsäule *f*, Sechskantpyramide, Sechskantspitzsäule

~ **rib** · Sechseckrippe *f*, Sechskantrippe

~ **section,** ~ shape, ~ unit, ~ trim, ~ profile · Sechseckprofil *n*, Sechskantprofil

~ **shape,** ~ section, ~ unit, ~ trim, ~ profile · Sechseckprofil *n*, Sechskantprofil

~ **solid bar,** ~ ~ rod · Sechseck-Vollstab *m*, Sechskant-Vollstab

~ **tile** · Sechseck(belag)platte *f*, Sechseckfliese *f*, Sechskant(belag)platte, Sechskantfliese

~ **trim,** ~ unit, ~ shape, ~ section, ~ profile · Sechseckprofil *n*, Sechskantprofil

~ **turret** · Sechsecktürmchen *n*, Sechskanttürmchen

~ **unit,** ~ trim, ~ shape, ~ section, ~ profile · Sechseckprofil *n*, Sechskantprofil

~ **wire netting** · sechseckiges Drahtgeflecht *n*, sechskantiges ~

~ **wire(d) glass** → ~ (mesh) ~ ~

~ **wood screw** · Sechskant-Holzschraube *f* [*DIN 571*]

hexahedral · sechsflächig

hexahedron · Sechsflach *n*, Sechsflächner *m*

hexapartite vault, sexpartite ~, ploughshare ~ · sechsteiliges Gewölbe *n*

(h)exastyle, hectastyle [*Having six front(ed) columns*] · sechssäulig

~ → ~ structure

~ **peripteral temple with fourteen columns on the flanks,** peripteral (h)exastyle ~ ~ ~ ~ ~ ~ ~ · Peripteros(tempel) *m* von 6:14 Säulen, Periptertaltempel ~ ~ ~, einlaubiger Tempel ~ ~ ~

~ **porch** · sechssäulige Vorhalle *f*, Hexastylosvorhalle

~ **portico** · sechssäuliger Portikus *m*, Hexastylosportikus

~ **(structure)** [*A portico, temple or porch having a row of six front(ed) columns*] · Hexastylos *m*, sechssäuliges Bauwerk *n*

~ **temple** · Hexastylostempel *m*, sechssäuliger Tempel

h. f. induction soldering, high frequency ~ ~ · Induktionslötung *f*

H-frame · H-Rahmen *m*

H-girder → broad-flange(d) beam

H.I. → heat input

Hiberno-Romanesque style · irisch-romanischer Stil *m*

hibiscus root powder, powder(ed) hibiscus root · gepulverte Eibischwurzel *f*

hidden, secret, concealed · verdeckt(liegend)

~ **cable,** secret ~, concealed ~ · Unterputzkabel *n*

~ **gutter,** concealed ~, secret ~ · verdeckte Rinne *f*

~ **installation,** secret ~, concealed ~, buried tubular conduits · Unterputzinstallation *f*

~ **pipe,** secret ~, concealed ~ · Unterputzrohr *n*

~ **staircase** · Geheimtreppe *f*

~ **tack,** concealed ~, secret ~ · verdeckter Hafter *m*

~ **valley,** secret ~, concealed ~ · verdeckte Kehle *f*

~ **valve,** secret ~, concealed ~ · Unterputzventil *n*

~ **wiring,** secret ~, concealed ~ · Unterputzverdrahtung *f*

hiding power, obliterating ~, opacity [*1. Qualitatively. The ability of a coat of paint (or a paint system) to obliterate the colour of a surface to which it is applied. 2. Quantitatively. The extent to which a paint obliterates the colour of an underlying surface of a different colour when a film of it is applied by some standard method*] · Deckfähigkeit *f*, Deckvermögen *n*, Deckkraft *f*

High altar, high ~ · Hochaltar *m*, Hauptaltar, Fronaltar, Choraltar, Sakramentsaltar

high-alumina cement, calcium aluminate ~ [*B.S. 915*] · Tonerdeschmelzzement *m* [*Eine Art des Tonerdezements ist der Tonerdeschmelzzement, der aus fein gemahlener, praktisch vollständig kristallisierter Schlacke mit mehr als 30% Tonerde, die bei der Gewinnung eines Sonderroheisens im Hochofen anfällt, gewonnen wird*]

~ **clay** · hochtonerdehaltiger Ton *m*, tonerdreicher ~

(high-)alumina fireclay brick → aluminous (fire)brick

~ **refractory (product),** aluminous ~ (~) · hochtonerdehaltiges feuerfestes Erzeugnis *n*, tonerdereiches ~ ~, tonerdereiches ff. ~

high apartment (unit); ~ flat (Brit.); ~ living unit (US) · Hochhauswohnung *f*

~ **Baroque** · Hochbarock *m*

~ ~ **effect** · hochbarocke Wirkung *f*

~ ~ **Rome** · römischer Hochbarock *m*

high bay warehouse · Hochregallager *n*

~ **block (of flats)** (Brit.) → residence tower

~ **boiler** · Hochsieder *m* [*Lacktechnik. Siedpunkt über 150° C*]

high-bond (concrete) (reinforcing) bars, twisted-type (~) (~) ~, deformed (~) (~) ~, ~ (~) (~) rods · (Beton)Formstahl *m*

high-calcium lime, white (chalk) ~, rich ~, pure ~, fat ~, (lime)stone ~, chalk ~, mountain ~ [*A non-hydraulic lime having a high content of calcium oxide (when a quicklime) or of calcium hydroxide (when a hydrated lime). These limes are normally fat limes*] · Fettkalk *m*, Weißkalk [*Fehlname: Marmorkalk*]

~ ~ **mortar,** white ~ ~, rich ~ ~, pure ~ ~ · Weißkalkmörtel *m*

~ ~ **paste** → ~ ~ putty

~ ~ **putty,** ~ ~ paste, white ~ ~, rich ~ ~, pure ~ ~ · Weißkalkbrei *m*, Weißkalkteig *m*, Weißbreikalk *m*, Breiweißkalk [*DIN 1060. Mit Wasserüberschuß naß gelöschter, eingesumpfter Weißkalk*]

~ **lump lime,** white ~ ~, rich ~ ~, pure ~ ~ · Weißstück(en)kalk *m* [*DIN 1060*]

~ **quicklime,** white ~, rich ~, pure ~ · Weißbranntkalk *m*

high-carbon steel · (öl)schlußvergüteter Kohlenstoffstahl *m*, Hartstahl

~ ~ **plate** · Hartstahlgrobblech *n*

~ **wire** · Draht *m* mit hohem Kohlenstoffgehalt

high-class residential area · Villenzone *f*, Villengebiet *n*

high conductivity copper · Leitkupfer *n* für elektrotechnische Zwecke

High Cross · Hochkreuz *n*

high density concrete, heavy(-weight) ~ [*Concrete of exceptionally high unit weight, usually obtained by use of heavyweight aggregates, used especially for radiation shielding*] · Schwerstbeton *m*

~ ~ **plywood,** superpressed ~, densified ~ · Preßsperrholz *n*, PSP *n*, verdichtetes Sperrholz [*Es entsteht durch Warmpressen dünner Furniere mit dazwischenliegenden härtbaren Kunstharzen*]

~ ~ **wood,** superpressed ~, densified ~ · Preßvollholz *n*, PVH, verdichtetes Vollholz

~ ~ ~ **door,** superpressed ~ ~, densified ~ ~ · Preßvollholztür *f*, Vollholzpreßtür, PVH-Tür

high-early-strength · frühhochfest

high early strength · Frühhochfestigkeit *f*

high-early-strength concrete, concrete with high early strength · frühtragfester Beton *m*

high early (or initial) strength Portland cement; rapid hardening Portland cement type III (US) · Schnell(er)härter *m*, hochwertiger Portlandzement *m*, frühhochfester Portlandzement [*in Dtschld. Z 325 und Z 425*]

highest bid, ~ proposal (US); ~ offer ~ tender (Brit.) · Höchst(an)gebot *n*

high-expansion cement — highly ornamented

high-expansion cement, expanding ~, expansive ~ · Dehnzement *m*, Schwellzement, Quellzement, Expansivzement

~ ~ **concrete,** expansive ~ ~, expanding ~ ~ · Dehnzementbeton *m*, Quellzementbeton, Schwellzementbeton, Expansivzementbeton

~ ~ **mortar,** expanding ~ ~, expansive ~ ~ · Dehnzementmörtel *m*, Schwellzementmörtel, Quellzementmörtel, Expansivzementmörtel

high-fire-risk · hochfeuergefährlich

high flats (Brit.) → residence tower

~ **format** · HF *n*, Hochformat *n*

~ ~ **(clay) brick** · Hochformatziegel *m*

~ ~ **vertical coring block,** ~ ~ ~ ~ **tile** [*See remark under 'Block'*] · Hochformat-Hochlochstein *m*, Hochformat-Hochlochblock(stein) *m*

~ **frequency induction soldering,** h.f. ~ ~ · Induktionslötung *f*

high-frequency sound insulation, ~ ~ **protection** · Hochfrequenz-Schallschutz *m*

~ **vibrated concrete** · hochfrequenzgerüttelter Beton *m*

high gloss, full ~ [*Smooth and almost mirror-like surface when viewed from all angles*] · Vollglanz *m*, Hochglanz

high-gloss · hochglänzend

high gloss finish, full ~ ~ · Vollglanzdeckenschicht(anstrich)farbe *f*

~ ~ **paint,** full ~ ~ · Vollglanz(anstrich)farbe *f*, Hochglanz(anstrich)farbe

~ ~ **wall slab,** full ~ ~ ~ · Hochglanzwandplatte *f*, Vollglanzwandplatte [*aus Beton*]

High Gothic, high Gothic style · Hochgotik *f* [*Die Zeit vom 1194 begonnenen Wiederaufbau der Kathedrale von Chartres bis zum Ende des 13. Jahrhunderts (Kathedralen von Chartres, Soissons, Reims, Amiens, Beauvais, Köln)*]

~ ~ **tracery** · hochgotisches Maßwerk *n*

high-grade · hochwertig

high grade · Sondergüte *f*

high-grade concrete, early-strength ~ · frühfester Beton *m*, hochwertiger ~

~ ~, high-strength ~ · hochfester Beton *m*, Qualitätsbeton [*B 300–B 600*]

~ **construction(al) steel,** ~ **structural** ~ · hochwertiger Baustahl *m*

~ **reinforcement steel,** ~ **reinforcing** ~ · hochwertiger Armierungsstahl *m*, ~ Bewehrungsstahl, ~ Betonstahl

~ **steel** · hochwertiger Stahl *m*

~ **structural steel,** ~ **construction(al)** ~ · hochwertiger Baustahl *m*

~ **timber,** ~ **wood** · Edelholz *n*

~ ~ **board,** ~ **wood** ~ · Edelholzplatte *f*

high-heat coat(ing) · hochhitzebeständiger Anstrich *m*, ~ Aufstrich, hochhitzebeständige Anstrichschicht *f*, hochhitzebeständige Aufstrichschicht

high humidity and condensation test, ~ moisture ~ ~ ~ · Feuchtlagerversuch *m*, Feuchtlagerprobe *f*, Feuchtlagerprüfung *f* [*Korrosionsprüfung*]

~ **industrialized block (of flats)** (Brit.) → (pre)cast residence tower

~ **initial (or early) strength Portland cement,** rapid hardening Portland cement type III (US) · frühhochfester Portlandzement *m*, hochwertiger ~, Schnell(er)härter *m* [*in Deutschland Z 325 und Z 425*]

high-level cistern → ~ ~ (W.C.) (flushing) ~

~ **flush toilet,** ~ **water closet,** ~ **type of W.C.** [*A room in which one or more high-level water closet pans are installed*] · Spülabort mit Hochspülkasten, Wasserabort ~ ~, Spülklosett ~ ~, Wasserklosett ~ ~

~ **housing** · hohe Wohnbauten *f*

~ **suite** · Hochspülabort *m*

~ **water closet,** ~ **flush toilet,** ~ **type of W.C.** [*A room in which one or more high-level water closet pans are installed*] · Spülabort *m* mit Hochspülkasten, Wasserabort ~ ~, Spülklosett ~ ~, Wasserklosett *n* ~ ~

~ **(W.C.) (flushing) cistern,** ~ (~ ~) ~ **tank,** ~ (~ ~) water waste preventer · hochhängender Spülkasten *m*

high-light window, over-story ~, clearstor(e)y ~, clearestor(e)y ~ · Ober-(gaden)fenster *n*, (Licht)Gadenfenster, Hochschiffenster

high living unit (US); ~ **apartment** (~); ~ **flat** (Brit.) · Hochhauswohnung *f*

~ **luster polishing,** ~ **lustre** ~ ~ · Hochglanzpolieren *n*

highly abrasion-proof, ~ abrasion(-)resistant · hochabreibefest, hochabriebfest

highly-(com)pressed · hochverdichtet

~ · hochgepreßt

~ **asphalt(ic) tile** · Hochdruck-Asphalt-belag)platte *f*, Hochdruck-Asphaltfliese *f*, Stampfasphalt(belag)platte, Stampfasphaltfliese [*Hergestellt aus Naturasphaltrohmehl oder gemahlenem Naturgestein und Bitumen als Bindemittel*]

~ **special asphalt(ic) tile** · Hochdruck-Sonder-Asphalt(belag)platte *f*, Hochdruck-Sonder-Asphaltfliese *f*, Hochdruck-Spezial-Asphalt(belag)platte, Hochdruck-Spezial-Asphaltfliese, Spezial-Stampfasphalt(belag)platte, Spezial-Stampfasphaltfliese, Sonder-Stampfasphalt(belag)platte, Sonder-Stampfasphaltfliese

highly decorated → ~ ornamented

~ **effective** · hochwirksam

~ **elastic** · hochelastisch

~ **fire-resistant** · hochfeuerbeständig [*Bauteile*]

~ **insulating** · hochisolierend

~ **ornamented,** richly ~, ~ **decorated** · reich geziert, ~ geschmückt, ~ verziert

highly pigmented — high relief

~ pigmented · hochpigmentiert
~ plastic · hochbildsam, hochplastisch
~ polishable · hochpolierbar
~ porous · hochporös
highly-pressed, highly-compressed · hochverdichtet
~, highly-compressed · hochgepreßt
highly resistant calcium silicate brick, ~ ~ lime-sand ~, ~ ~ sand-lime ~ · Kalksandhartstein m, KSH [*Fehlname: Klinker m*]
~ ~ **compass engineering brick,** ~ ~ radial ~ ~, ~ ~ radiating ~ ~ · Radialhartklinker m, Ringhartklinker, R 450 [*DIN 1057*]
~ ~ ~ **sand-lime brick,** ~ ~ ~ lime-sand ~, ~ ~ ~ radiating ~ ~, ~ ~ ~ calcium silicate ~ · Radialkalksandhartstein m, Ringkalksandhartstein, Rs 250 [*DIN 1057*]
~ ~ **engineering brick** · Hartklinker m
~ ~ **lime-sand brick,** ~ ~ sand-lime ~, ~ ~ calcium silicate ~ · Kalksandhartstein m, KSH [*Fehlname: Klinker m*]
~ ~ **radial engineering brick,** ~ ~ radiating ~ ~, ~ ~ compass ~ ~ · R 450 m, Radialklinker m, Ringhartklinker
~ ~ ~ **lime-sand brick,** ~ ~ radiating ~ ~, ~ ~ compass ~ ~, ~ ~ ~ sand-lime ~, ~ ~ radiating calcium silicate ~ · Radialkalksandhartstein, Rs 250 [*DIN 1057*]
~ ~ **radiating engineering brick,** ~ ~ radial ~ ~, ~ ~ compass ~ ~ · R 450 m, Radialhartklinker m, Ringhartklinker
~ ~ ~ **lime-sand brick,** ~ ~ radial ~, ~ ~ compass ~ ~, ~ ~ ~ sand-lime ~, ~ ~ ~ calcium silicate ~ · Radialkalksandhartstein m, Ring-kalksandhartstein, Rs 250 [*DIN 1057*]
~ ~ **sand-lime brick,** ~ ~ lime-sand ~, ~ ~ calcium silicate ~ · Kalksandhartstein m, KSH [*Fehlname: Klinker m*]
~ ~ **to acid(s)** · hochsäurefest
~ **sensitive** · hochempfindlich
~ **shock resistant** · hochschlagfest
~ **stressed** · hochbeansprucht
~ **sulfate-resistant,** ~ sulfate-resisting (US); ~ sulphate-resistant, ~ sulphate-resisting (Brit.) · hochsulfatbeständig
~ **wear-resistant** · hochverschleißfest
~ **weather resistant** · hochwetterbeständig
high melting wax, solid ~ ~ · Hartparaffin n
~ **mirror finished sheet** · Hochglanzblech n
~ **moisture and condensation test,** ~ humidity ~ ~ ~ · Feuchtlagerversuch m, Feuchtlagerprobe f, Feuchtlagerprüfung f [*Korrosionsprüfung*]
~ **partition** · hohe Trennwand f [*Im Gegensatz zur halbhohen Trennwand*]

high-peaked roof, steep-pitched ~ · Steildach n
high pitch · Hochton m
high-pitched buzzer · Hochtonsummer m
~ **roof** · Ritterdach n, Kronendach, schwediches Dach [*Geringste Dachneigung 35°, am Aufschiebling ≥ 30°*]
high-placed window · hochsitzendes Fenster n
high point · Hochpunkt m
~ ~ **of the slope** · höchster Gefällepunkt m [*Dachrinne*]
high-pressure air-conditioning system · Hochdruckklimaanlage f
~ **boiler** · Hochdruckkessel m
~ **cold water** · Hochdruckkaltwasser n
~ **fan** · Hochdruckventilator m
~ **gas pipe line** · Hochdruck-Gas(rohr)-leitung f
~ **heating** · Hochdruckheizung f
~ **hot water heating** · Hochdruckwarmwasserheizung f
~ **installation,** ~ system · Hochdruckanlage f [*Heizung*]
~ **live steam** · gespannter Sattdampf m
~ **pipe,** solid ~ · Hochdruckrohr n, robustes Rohr
~ **steam** · hochgespannter Dampf m, Hochdruckdampf
~ ~ **boiler** · Hochdruckdampfkessel m
~ ~ **cured,** autoclaved · autoklavbehandelt, autoklavi(si)ert, autoklavgehärtet, dampfdruckgehärtet
~ ~ **curing** → autoclaving
~ ~ **heating** · Hochdruckdampfheizung f
~ ~ **installation,** ~ ~ plant · Hochdruckdampfanlage f
~ ~ **line** · Hochdruckdampfleitung f
~ ~ **plant,** ~ ~ installation · Hochdruckdampfanlage f
~ **superheated steam** · Hochdruck-Heißdampf m
~ **system,** ~ installation · Hochdruckanlage f [*Heizung*]
~ **water hose** · Hochdruckwasserschlauch m
~ ~ **main** · Hochdruckwasserleitung f
high-quality grade · hochwertige Sorte f
high-refractory · hochfeuerfest [*Keramische Rohstoffe, Massen und Werkstoffe werden als „Hochfeuerfest" bezeichnet, wenn ihr Segerkegelfallpunkt, bestimmt nach DIN 51063, mindestens dem des kleinen Segerkegels 37/150°/h (mittlerer Fallpunkt 1830° C) entspricht. Begriffsbestimmung nach DIN 51060 Blatt 1*]
high relief, full ~ [*It is cut more deeply than the low relief, with its figures standing out more fully from the stone*] · Hochrelief n

High Renaissance — high-tension porosity tester

High Renaissance, high Renaissance style · Hochrenaissance *f,* römische Renaissance

high-rise archives building · Archivhochhaus *n*

~ **block,** ~ building, tower (~), tall ~ · Hochhaus *n,* Turmgebäude *n,* Turmhaus

~ ~ **building** → ~ ~ construction

~ ~ **construction,** ~ ~ building, tower (~) ~, tall ~ ~, tower building construction, tall building construction, high-rise building construction · Hochhausbau *m*

~ ~ **façade** → tower (~) ~

high (rise) block (of flats) (Brit.) → residence tower

high-rise block rising line → tower (~) ~ ~

~ **building,** ~ block, tower (~), tall ~ · Hochhaus *n,* Turmgebäude *n,* Turmhaus

~ ~ **with Y (ground-)plan** · Y-Hochhaus *n*

~ ~ **construction** → ~ block ~

~ ~ **façade** → tower (block) ~

~ ~ **rising line** → tower (block) ~ ~

high (rise) flats (Brit.) → residence tower

high-rise luxury apartment (unit), ~ ~ flat; ~ ~ living unit (US) · Hochhausluxuswohnung *f*

~ **parking building** · Parkhochhaus *n*

~ **slums** · Elendswohnungen *fpl* in Wolkenkratzern

~ **structure,** tall ~ · hohes Bauwerk *n,* hochaufgehendes ~

High Romanesque, high Romanesque style · Hochromanik *f*

high-slump concrete, buttery ~; plastic(ised) ~ (Brit.); plastic(ized) ~ (US) · Weichbeton *m,* weicher Beton [*Fehlname: plastischer Beton*]

high-speed elevator → express ~

~ **goods elevator** (US); ~ ~ lift (Brit.); express ~ ~ · Schnellastenaufzug *m*

~ ~ **lift** (Brit.); ~ ~ elevator (US); express ~ ~ · Schnellastenaufzug *m*

~ **lift** → express ~

~ **passenger elevator** (US); ~ ~ lift (Brit.); express ~ ~ · Schnellfahrstuhl *m*

~ ~ **lift** (Brit.); ~ ~ elevator (US); express ~ ~ · Schnellfahrstuhl *m*

high strength · Hochfestigkeit *f*

high-strength · hochfest

~ **cement,** HSC · hochfester Zement *m*

~ **cinder sand block** (US) → ~ slag ~ ~

~ ~ ~ **tile** (US) → ~ slag sand block

~ **concrete,** high-grade ~ · hochfester Beton *m,* Qualitätsbeton [*B 300–B 600*]

~ **granulated cinder block** (US) → ~ slag sand ~

~ ~ ~ **tile** (US) → ~ slag sand block

~ ~ **slag block** → ~ slag sand ~

~ ~ ~ **tile** → ~ slag sand block

~ **mortar** · hochfester Mörtel *m*

~ **Portland cement** · Portlandzement 425 *m*

~ **rivet** · hochfester Niet *m*

~ **screw** · hochfeste Schraube *f*

~ **slag sand block,** ~ ~ ~ tile, ~ granulated slag ~ (Brit.); ~ cinder sand ~, ~ granulated cinder ~ (US) [*See remark under 'Block(stein)'*] · Hüttenhartstein *m,* HHS [*mittlere Druckfestigkeit 250 kp/cm², Mindestdruckfestigkeit 200 kp/cm². DIN 398*]

high-talc body · talkreiche keramische Masse *f*

high-temperature calcination of (raw) gypsum · Gipsbrennen *n* [*Erhitzen des Gipssteines über die Gluthöhe hinaus*]

~ **chimney** · Heißschornstein *m* [*Schornstein mit Abgasen über 300° C*]

~ **coal tar** · Hochtemperaturteer *m*

~ **embrittlement** · Hochtemperaturversprödung *f*

~ **(engineering) material** · Material *n* höchster Warmfestigkeit, (Werk)Stoff *m* ~ ~

~ **grease** · Hochtemperaturfett *n*

~ **insulant** · Hochtemperaturdämmstoff *m*

~ **material** → ~ engineering ~

~ **pitch** · Hochtemperaturpech *n*

~ **scaling** · Verzunderung *f*

high-tensile, HT · hochzugfest

~ **bolt,** high-tension ~ · hochzugfester Bolzen *m*

~ **brass;** manganese bronze [*deprecated*] · Manganbronze *f*

~ **cast iron,** HTCI · hochzugfestes Gußeisen *n*

~ **construction(al) (grade) steel,** ~ structural (~) ~ [*B.S. 548*] · hochzugfester Baustahl *m*

~ **quality,** HTQ · hochzugfeste Güte *f*

~ **strength,** HTS · Hochzugfestigkeit *f*

~ **structural (grade) steel,** ~ construction(al) (~) ~ [*B.S. 548*] · hochzugfester Baustahl *m*

high-tension cab(in), high-voltage ~ · Hochspannungskabine *f*

~ **(overhead) transmission line,** high-voltage (~) ~ ~ · Hochspannungs(frei)leitung *f*

~ **porosity tester,** high-voltage ~ ~ · Hochspannungs-Porenprüfgerät *n*

high-tension transmission line — hinge(d) (window) shutter

~ transmission line → ~ overhead ~ ~

~ ~ mast, high-voltage ~ ~ · Hochspannungs(-Überland)mast *m*

high tomb · Turmgrab *n*

high-torqued bolt · hochverdrillte Schraube *f*

high-vacuum asphalt (US); ~ (asphaltic) bitumen (Brit.) · Hartbitumen *n*, Hochvakuumbitumen, HVB

high vault · Hochgewölbe *n*

high-vaulted · hochgewölbt

high velocity air conditioning system · Hochgeschwindigkeits-Klimaanlage *f*

high-viscosity asphalt(ic) cutback, ~ cutback (asphalt) (US); ~ cutback (asphaltic-)bitumen, ~ cutback (Brit.) · hochviskoses Verschnittbitumen *n*, zähflüssiges ~, VB 500

high-voltage cab(in), high-tension ~ · Hochspannungskabine *f*

~ **(overhead) transmission line**, high-tension (~) ~ ~ · Hochspannungs-(frei)leitung *f*

~ **porosity tester**, high-tension ~ ~ · Hochspannungs-Porenprüfgerät *n*

~ **transmission mast**, high-tension ~ · Hochspannungs(-Überland)mast *m*

highway binder, road ~ · (Straßenbau)Bindemittel *n*, (Straßenbau)Binder *m*, Straßenbauhilfsstoff *m*

~ **chip(ping)s**, road ~, ~ chipping, ~ stone chips · Straßenbausplitt *m*

~ **concrete**, road ~ · Straßenbeton *m*

~ ~ **sand**, road ~ ~ · Straßenbetonsand *m*

~ **emulsion**, road ~, emulsion for highway construction, emulsion for road construction · Straßenbauemulsion *f*

~ **furniture**, road ~ · Straßenware(n) *f(pl)*

~ **gravel**, road ~ · Straßenbaukies *m*

~ **illumination** → ~ lighting

~ **lighting**, ~ illumination · Straßenbeleuchtung *f*

~ ~ **mast**, road ~ ~ · Straßen-Beleuchtungsmast *m*, Straßen-Leuchtenmast, Straßen-Lichtmast

~ **material**, road ~ · Straßenbaustoff *m*

~ **stone chips**, road ~ ~, ~ chipping, ~ chip(ping)s · Straßenbausplitt *m*

high window · Hochfenster *n*

higher calorific value, H.C.V. · H₀ *m*, oberer Heizwert *m*, Verbrennungswärme V *f*

hill-city · Hügelstadt *f*

hillside architecture · Hangarchitektur *f*, Hangbaukunst *f*

Hindoo architecture, Hindu ~ · hinduistische Architektur *f*

~ **temple**, Hindu ~ · Hindutempel *m*

hinge · Band *n* [*Baubeschlag*]

~ · Gelenk *n*

~ · Scharnier *n*

~ **pressure** · Gelenkdruck *m*

hinged, articulated, linked, pinned, pin(-)jointed · angelenkt, gelenkig (gelagert), gelenkig verbunden

hinge(d) action · Gelenk(ein)wirkung *f*

~ **arch(ed girder)** → pin(ned) ~ (~)

~ **bar**, linked ~, articulated ~, pin(-ned) ~, pin-jointed ~ · Gelenkstab *m*, gelenkig angeschlossener Stab

~ **bearing** · Gelenklager *n*

~ **casement**, (window) ~, pivoted sash, opening ~, opening light, (casement) ventilator · (Fenster)Flügel *m*

~ ~ **frame**, (window) ~ ~, pivoted sash ~, opening sash ~, opening light ~, ventilator ~ · (Fenster)Flügelrahmen *m*

~ **connection** → ~ joint

~ **cover** · Scharnierverkleidung *f*

~ **door** · Scharniertür *f*

~ **firedoor** · Scharnier-Brand(schutz)tür *f*

(~) **flap** · (Band)Lappen *m*

~ **frame**, linked ~, articulated ~, pin(-ned) ~, pin-jointed ~ · Gelenkrahmen *m*

~ **garage shutter door** · Garagendrehtor *n*

~ **girder**, Gerber ~; slung span continuous beam (Brit.) · Gelenkträger *m*, Gerberträger

~ **grid** · Klapprost *m*

~ **hatch** · Klappluke *f*

~ **joint**, articulated ~, linked ~, pin(-ned) ~, ~ connection, pin-connected joint · Gelenkverbindung *f*, gelenkige Verbindung, Gelenkknoten(punkt) *m*, gelenkiger Knoten(punkt), Gelenkstoß *m*

~ ~ **section** · Scharnierrollenlappen *m*

~ **knuckle** · Scharnierrolle *f*

~ **lattice(d) girder**, Gerber ~ ~; slung span continuous lattice(d) beam (Brit.) · Gerbergitterträger *m*, Gelenkgitterträger

~ **mechanism** · Gelenkmechanismus *m*

~ **pin**, pin of a hinge, pintle · Scharnierstift *m*

~ **point** · Gelenkpunkt *m*

~ **purlin(e)**, linked ~, articulated ~, pin(ned) ~, pin-jointed ~ · Gelenkpfette *f*

~ **seat** · Klappsitz *m*

~ **shutter** → ~ (window) ~

~ ~ **door** · Drehtor *n*

~ **steel rib** · Gelenkstahlrippe *f*

~ ~ **shutter door** · Stahldrehtor *n*

~ **support** · gelenkige Auflagerung *f*

~ **system** → articulated ~

~ **truss** [*A steel roof truss fixed at one end only, to allow for expansion and contraction with change of temperature*] · Gelenk(dach)binder *m*

~ **(window) shutter** · (An)Schlagladen *m* [*Fenster*]

hingeless — holding

hingeless, encastré, fixed, with fixed ends, without articulations, rigid, no-hinged, encastered · eingespannt, gelenklos [*Bogen; Träger; Stütze; Balken(träger) Rahmen(tragwerk)*]

~ **arch** → fixed ~

~ **beam** → fixed ~

~ **column** → fixed support

~ **support** → fixed ~

to hip · abwalmen

hip; piend [*Scotland*] [*The meeting line of two inclined roof surfaces which meet at a salient angle*] · Walm *m*

~ **bath(tub),** demi-bath(tub), sitting ~ · Sitzbad(ewanne) *n*, (*f*)

~ **capping** [*A protective covering at a hip*] · Walmschutz *m*

~ ~ · Gratkappe *f*

~ **dormer** → hip(ped) (roof) ~

~ **gable** → hip(ped) ~

~ **jack (rafter)** · Gratschifter *m*

~ **mansard (roof)** → hip(ped) ~ (~)

~ **plate roof** → hipped ~ ~

~ **purlin(e) roof** → hip(ped) ~ ~

~ **rafter,** angle ~, angle ridge · Gratsparren *m* [*Er liegt unter dem Grat des Daches diagonal zu den Wänden und nimmt beiderseits die Gratstichbalken auf*]

~ ~, angle ~, angle ridge · Anfallsparren *m*, Dachschifter *m*

~ **rafters,** angle ridges, angle rafters [*The rafters forming hips. The jack-rafters meet on them*] · Anfallgebinde *n*, Anfallgespärre *n* [*Walmdach*]

~ **roof** → hip(ped) ~

~ (~) **dormer** → hipped (~) ~

~ **sheet** · Gratblech *n*

~ **slab roof** → hipped ~ ~

~ **soaker** · Gratgebindewinkel *m*

~ **starting tile,** starting hip ~, hip starter · Grantanfänger *m*, Walmanfänger [*Der Ausdruck „Walmanfänger" wird auch für den Firstanfänger verwendet*]

~ **tile** · Gratstein *m*, Walmstein [*Der Ausdruck „Walmstein" wird auch für den Firststein verwendet*]

hipped · abgewalmt

hip(ped) dormer → ~ roof ~

~ **end** [*A roof surface usually triangular, bounded by the hips at the sides and the eaves at the base*] · Walmfläche *f*

~ **gable** [*A gable with the uppermost part sloped back*] · abgewalmter Giebel *m*, Walmgiebel

~ **mansard (roof),** ~ French ~; double-pitched ~, curb ~ (US) [*It slopes in four directions, but there is a break on each slope*] · abgewalmtes Mansard(en)dach *n*, Mansard(en)-walmdach, Walmmansard(en)dach

~ **plate roof,** ~ slab ~ [*A hip(ped) roof formed by folded plates*] · Faltwerk-Walmdach *n*, abgewalmtes Faltwerkdach

~ **purlin(e) roof** · Pfettenwalmdach *n*

~ **roof** · abgewalmtes Dach *n*, Walmdach

~ (~) **dormer** · Walmgaube *f*, Walmgaupe

~ **slab roof,** ~ plate ~ [*A hip(ped) roof formed by folded plates*] · Faltwerk-Walmdach *n*, abgewalmtes Faltwerkdach

hippodrome · Hippodrom *n*

Hispano-Moresque architecture · spanisch-maurische Architektur *f*, ~ Baukunst *f*

historiated capital · Kapitell *n* mit historischen Figuren, Kapitäl ~ ~ ~

historic building, building of historic interest · historisches Gebäude *n*

~ **heritage** · historisches Erbe *n*

~ **landmark,** ancient monument · historisches Wahrzeichen *n*, Kulturdenkmal *n*

~ **preservation,** preservation of monuments · Denkmalpflege *f*

historicising, non-revivalist · historisierend

historicism · Historismus *m*

history of architecture, architectural history · Architekturgeschichte *f*

hit and miss · Bearbeitungsfehler *m* [*Parkettstab*]

hoarding → close-boarded ~

hobby room, home workshop · Bastlerwerkstatt *f*, Bastelwerkstatt, Freizeitwerkstatt

Hoffmann kiln · Hoffmannscher Ringofen *m*

hog → hogging

~ **back(ed) girder,** semi-parabolic ~ · Halbparabelträger *m*

~ ~ ~ **with sloping end posts,** semi-parabolic ~ ~ ~ ~ ~ · Halbparabelträger *m* mit abgeschrägten Enden

~ **deformation,** hogging ~ · Aufwölbungsverformung *f*

hoggin (Brit.) → path gravel

hog(ging), camber [*Girders and trusses may be built with hog to counteract their sag*] · Stich *m*, Überhöhung *f*, Aufwölbung

~ **deformation** · Aufwölbungsverformung *f*

~ **moment** → negative ~

to hold · abfangen [*z.B. durch Zuganker*]

holder [*A device for holding something*] · Haltevorrichtung *f*

holding · Abfangung *f* [*Abfangungen sind bei der Umgestaltung tragender Baukonstruktionen, bei der nachträglichen Herstellung großer Maueröffnungen und bei Unterfangungen erforderlich*]

holding — hollow cast-iron column

~, delay · Vorlagerung f, VL [Dampfbehandlung von Beton]
~ force · Festhaltekraft f
~ girder · Abfangeträger m, Sturzträger [DIN 1053]
~ moment · Festhaltemoment n
~ period → presteaming ~
hole diameter · Lochdurchmesser m
~ footing · Köcherfundament n
~ pattern, perforation of screen, punching of screen · Sieblochung f
~ pitch · Lochteilung f [Siebtechnik]
~ screen, perforated ~ · Loch(blech)sieb n
holiday apartment (unit) → ~ dwelling (~)
~ ~ (~) → ~ flat
~ camp · Ferienkolonie f
~ dwelling (unit), ~ apartment (~) · Ferienwohnung f
~ flat, ~ apartment (unit) · Ferien-(-Etagen)wohnung f, Ferien-Stockwerkwohnung, Ferien-Geschoßwohnung
~ hostel, vacation ~ · Ferienwohnheim n
~ hotel, vacation ~ · Ferienhotel n
~ house, vacation ~ · Ferienhaus n
holing [Punching holes in slates by hand or machine before fixing them] · (Löcher)Einschlagen n
Hollocast floor [The cavity in this type of floor is created by using cages of expanded metal, which constitute the cavity and are allowed to remain in position as a reinforcement and as a means of securing the primary tensile reinforcement. Where a smooth undersurface is not required, the cavity can be allowed to remain open, which will not affect the strength of the floor] · Hollocast-Decke f
hollow · großes Loch n [Ziegel]
~ · Höhlung f
~ article, ~ product · Hohlartikel m, Hohlerzeugnis n, Hohlgegenstand m
~ beam, box ~ · Balken(träger) m mit zwei Stegen, Hohlbalken(träger), Kastenbalken(träger)
~ ~ floor, box ~ ~ · Hohlbalken(träger)decke f, (Hohl)Kasten(träger)decke
~ block, cavity ~, ~ tile, pot [See remark under 'Block'] · Hohl(block)stein m, Hohlblock m
~ ~ ~ ((pre)cast) (concrete) ~ ~
~ ~ [Holes passing through the block exceed 25 per cent of its volume, and the holes are not small. B.S. 3921] · Lochgroßblockziegel m mit großen Hohlräumen
~ ~ density, ~ tile ~ · Steinraumgewicht SR n [Fehlname]; Steinrohwichte SR f [Raumerfüllung von einem Hohlblockstein, Deckenstein oder ähnlichem Formkörper, welcher durch die Herstellungsmaschine ausgeformte Luftkammern besitzt]
~ ~ floor, cavity ~ ~, ~ tile ~, pot ~ [See remark under 'Block'] · Hohlblock(stein)decke f, Hohlsteindecke
~ ~ for walls, cavity ~ ~ ~, ~ tile ~ ~, pot ~ ~, wall pot [See remark under 'Block'] · Hohl-Wandblock m, Hohl-Wand(block)stein m, Wand-Hohlblock, Wand-Hohl(block)stein
~ ~ making → ~ concrete ~ ~
~ ~ ~ machine, hollow-tile ~ ~, cavity-block ~ ~, cavity-tile ~ ~, pot ~ ~ · Hohlblockfertiger m, Hohl(block)steinfertiger
~ ~ masonry wall, cavity ~ ~ ~, ~ tile ~ ~, pot ~ ~ [See remark under 'Block'] · Hohlblockmauer f, Hohl(block)steinmauer
~ ~ (work), cavity ~ ~ (~), ~ tile ~ (~), pot (~) ~ [See remark under 'Block'] · Hohlblockmauerwerk n, Hohl(block)steinmauerwerk
~ ~ mould (Brit.); ~ ~ mold (US); hollow-tile ~, cavity-block ~, cavity-tile ~, pot ~ · Hohlblockform f, Hohl(block)steinform
~ ~ roof → ~ tile ~
~ ~ step, ~ tile ~, cavity ~ ~, pot ~ · Block(stein)-Hohlstufe f, Stein-Hohlstufe
~ ~ wall, cavity ~ ~, ~ tile ~, pot ~ [See remark under 'Block'] · Hohlblockwand f, Hohl(block)steinwand
~ board, ~ sheet · Hohlplatte f
~ brick, cavity ~ · Hohlziegel m
~ ~ masonry (work) → ~ clay ~ ~ (~)
~ brickwork → ~ (clay) brick masonry (work)
~ brickwork wall → ~ clay ~ ~
~ (building) component → ~ (~) unit
~ (~) member → ~ (~) unit
~ (~) unit, ~ (~) member, ~ (~) component [Hollow building material which is formed as a single article complete in itself but which is intended to be part of a compound unit or building or structure. Examples are hollow bricks, hollow blocks, hollow piles etc.] · Hohl-Bauteil m, n, Hohl(-Bau)element n, Hohl(-Bau)körper m [Fehlname: Hohl-Baueinheit f]
~ calcium silicate brick, ~ sand-lime ~, ~ lime-sand ~ · Kalksandhohl-(block)stein m, KSHBl [Großformatiger Zweihandmauerstein mit fünfseitig geschlossenen Hohlräumen senkrecht zur Lagerfläche. DIN 106]
~ cassette plank, ~ coffer ~, ~ waffle ~, ~ pan(el) ~, ~ core ~ · Stegkassettenplatte f
~ cast-iron column, ~ C.I. ~ · Gußeisenhohlstütze f, gußeiserne Hohlstütze

hollow cast prestressed concrete floor slab — hollow cupola

~ **cast prestressed concrete floor slab** → ~ precast ~ ~ ~ ~

~ **chamfer** · gekehlte Fase *f* [*Die abgefaste Fläche ist konkav*]

~ **C.I. column**, ~ cast-iron ~ · Gußeisenhohlstütze *f*, gußeiserne Hohlstütze

~ **cinder block** (US) → ~ clinker ~

~ ~ **tile** (US) → ~ clinker block

~ **circular column**, ~ round ~, ~ cylindrical ~ · Hohlrundstütze *f*, Rundhohlstütze

~ **clay block**, ~ ~ building ~ · Hourdi *m*, Tonhohl(stein)platte *f*, Ziegelhohlplatte, Hohlnutenstein *m*

~ ~ ~ **for tiled roofs** → ~ ~ building ~ ~ ~ ~

~ (~) **brick masonry (work)**, ~ (~) brickwork; cavity (clay) brick masonry (work), cavity (clay) brickwork [*See remark under 'Hohlmauer'*] · Hohlziegelmauerwerk *n*

~ (~) **brickwork** → ~ (~) brick masonry (work)

~ (~) **brick(work) wall**; cavity (~) ~ ~ [*See remark under 'Hohlmauer'*] · Hohlziegelmauer *f*

~ ~ **(building) block** [*B.S. 1190*] · Hourdi *m*, Tonhohl(stein)platte *f*, Ziegelhohlplatte, Hohlnutenstein *m*

~ ~ (~) ~ **floor**, clay pot ~ · Tonhohl(stein)plattendecke *f*, Ziegelhohlplattendecke, Hohlnutensteindecke, Hourdidecke

~ ~ (~) ~ **for tiled roofs**, clay pot ~ ~ ~ ~ · Dachhourdi *m*, Dach-Tonhohl(stein)platte *f*, Dach-Ziegelhohlplatte, Dach-Hohlnutenstein *m* [*Mit nasenförmigem Aufsatz zum Aufhängen der Dachziegel*]

~ ~ (~) ~ **with keyed underside**, clay pot ~ ~ ~ [*The key provided for plaster or rendering is of dovetail form*] · Rippenhohlnutenstein *m*, Rippenhourdi *m*, Rippentonhohlplatte *f*, Tonhohlrippenplatte, Rippenziegelhohlplatte

~ **clinker block**, ~ ~ tile, clinker pot (Brit.); hollow cinder tile, hollow cinder block, cinder pot (US) [*See remark under 'Block'*] · Schlacken(beton)hohlblock(stein) *m*, Schlacken(beton)hohlstein

~ ~ **tile** → ~ ~ block

~ **coffer plank**, ~ waffle ~, ~ pan(el) ~, ~ cassette ~, ~ core ~ · Stegkassettenplatte *f*

~ **column** · Hohlstütze *f*

~ ~ · Hohlsäule *f*

~ **component** → ~ (building) unit

~ **composite slab** · Hohlverbundplatte *f*, Verbundhohlplatte

~ **concrete beam** · Betonhohlbalken(-träger) *m*

~ (~) **block** → ((pre)cast) (concrete) hollow ~

~ ~ **block for walls**, cavity ~ ~ ~ ~, ~ ~ tile ~ ~, concrete pot ~ ~, concrete wall pot [*See remark under 'Block'*] · Beton-Hohlwandblock *m*, Beton-Wandhohlblock, Beton-Wandhohl(block)stein *m*, Beton-Hohlwand-(block)stein [*DIN 18151*]

~ (~) ~ **making**, ~ (~) tile ~, concrete hollow ~ ~ [*See remark under 'Block'*] · (Beton)Hohlblock(stein)fertigung *f*, (Beton)Hohlblock(stein)herstellung, (Beton)Hohlsteinherstellung, (Beton)Hohlsteinfertigung

~ (~) **floor**, concrete hollow ~ · Hohl(beton)decke *f*, Betonhohldecke

~ (~) ~ **slab**, concrete hollow ~ ~ · (Beton)Hohl(decken)platte *f*, Hohl-Betondeckenplatte, Beton(decken)-hohlplatte

~ ~ **mast**, ~ ~ pole, (concrete) hollow ~ · (Beton)Hohlmast *m*, Hohl-Betonmast

~ ~ **method** · Betonhohlbauweise *f*

~ (~) **panel**, concrete hollow ~ · Betonhohltafel *f*, Hohl(-Beton)tafel

~ ~ **pole**, ~ ~ mast, (concrete) hollow ~ · (Beton)Hohlmast *m*, Hohl-Betonmast

~ (~) **slab**, concrete hollow ~ · (Beton)Hohlplatte *f*, Hohl-Betonplatte

~ (~) ~ **floor**, concrete hollow ~ ~ · (Beton)Hohlplattendecke *f*, Hohl-Betonplattendecke

~ ~ **tile for walls** → ~ ~ block ~ ~

~ (~) ~ **making** → ~ (~) block ~

~ ~ **wall**; cavity ~ ~ [*See remark under 'Hohlwand'*] · Betonhohlwand *f*, Beton-(Zwei)Schalenwand

~ (~) **ware**, (concrete) ~ ~ · (Beton)Hohlware *f*

~ **cone**, female ~ · Hohlkegel *m*

~ **core**, cellular ~, HC · Hohlkern *m*, Zellenkern

~ (~) **floor slab (unit)** · Deckenhohlplatte *f*, Hohldeckenplatte

hollow(-core) gypsum plank; ~ board lath (US) · Gipshohldiele *f*, Hohlgipsdiele

~ **plank** · Hohldiele *f*, Steg(zement)diele

hollow core plank, ~ cassette ~, waffle ~, ~ coffer ~, ~ pan(el) ~ · Stegkassettenplatte *f*

~ ~ **sandwich panel**, ~ ~ three-layer(-ed) ~ · Hohlkern-Dreischichtentafel *f*, Hohlkern-Dreilagentafel

~ ~ **slab** · Hohlkernplatte *f*

~ ~ **three-layer(ed) panel**, ~ ~ sandwich ~ · Hohlkern-Dreischichtentafel *f*, Hohlkern-Dreilagentafel

~ (~) **wall panel** · Wandhohltafel *f*

~ **cornice** → cove

~ (**cross**) **section** · Hohlprofil *n*, Hohlquerschnitt *m*

~ **cupola**, ~ dome · Hohlkuppel *f*

~ **cylindrical column,** ~ **circular** ~, ~ **round** ~ · Hohlrundstütze f, Rundhohlstütze

~ **dome,** ~ **cupola** · Hohlkuppel f

~ **expanded cinder concrete block,** ~ ~ ~ ~ **tile** (US); ~ **foamed slag** ~ ~ (Brit.) [*See remark under 'Block(stein)'*] · Hüttenbimshohlblock m, Hüttenbimshohl(block)stein m, Kunstbimshohlblock, Kunstbimshohl(block)stein

~ ~ ~ ~ **tile,** ~ ~ ~ ~ **block** (US); ~ **foamed slag** ~ ~ (Brit.) [*See remark under 'Block(stein)'*] · Hüttenbimshohlblock m,, Hüttenbimshohl(block)stein m, Kunstbimshohlblock, Kunstbimshohl(block)stein

~ **expanded slag concrete block** (US) → ~ **foamed (blastfurnace) slag** ~ ~

~ ~ ~ ~ **tile** (US) → ~ **foamed (blastfurnace) slag concrete block**

~ **filler,** ~ **floor** ~ · (Decken)Hohlkörper m

~ ~ **block floor,** ~ ~ (**tile**) ~, **rib and tile** ~, **rib and block** ~ [*See remark under 'Block'*] · Hohl(körper)decke f, Montagehohlkörperdecke, Hohlkörpermontagedecke [*Rippendecke, in welche zur Herstellung der Schalung meist zur Erzielung einer ebenen Deckenuntersicht Formsteine eingelegt werden*]

~ ~ ~ ~ **system** → **rib and tile floor(ing)** ~

~ ~ **brick** · Deckenhohlziegel m, Hohl(Decken)Füllziegel, Hohldeckenziegel, tongebrannter Hohlstein m für Leicht(dach)decken [*DIN 4159*]

~ ~ **floor** → ~ ~ **block** ~

~ ~ **system** → **rib and tile floor(ing)** ~

~ ~ (**tile**) **floor** → ~ ~ **block** ~

~ ~ (~) **system** → **rib and tile floor(ing)** ~

~ **fillet** · Hohlleiste f

~ **floor** → ~ **concrete** ~

~ ~ **beam** · Deckenhohlbalken(träger) m

~ (~) **filler** · (Decken)Hohlkörper m

~ ~ **girder** · Deckenhohlträger m

~ ~ **slab** → ~ **concrete** ~ ~

~ ~ ~ (**unit**), ~ **core** ~ ~ (~) · Dekkenhohlplatte f, Hohldeckenplatte

~ **foamed (blastfurnace) slag concrete block,** ~ ~ (~) ~ ~ **tile** (Brit.); ~ **expanded cinder** ~ ~, ~ **expanded slag** ~ ~, ~ **light(weight) slag** ~ ~ (US) [*See remark under 'Block'*] · Hohl-(Hochofen)Schaumschlackenbetonstein m, Hohl-(Hochofen)Schaumschlackenbeton(block)stein m, Hohl-(Kunst)Bimsbetonstein, Hohl-(Kunst)Bimsbetonblock(stein), Hohl-Hüttenbimsbetonstein, Hohl-Hüttenbimsbetonblock(stein)

~ ~ (~) ~ ~ **tile** → ~ ~ ~ (~) ~ ~ **block**

~ ~ **slag concrete block,** ~ ~ ~ ~ **tile** (Brit.); ~ **expanded cinder** ~ ~ (US) [*See remark under 'Block(stein)'*] · Hüttenbimshohlblock m, Hüttenbimshohl(block)stein m, Kunstbimshohlblock, Kunstbimshohl(block)stein

~ ~ ~ ~ **tile,** ~ ~ ~ ~ ~ **block** (Brit.); ~ **expanded cinder** ~ ~ (US) [*See remark under 'Block(stein)'*] · Hüttenbimshohlblock m, Hüttenbimshohl(block)stein m

~ **frame section** · Hohlrahmenprofil n

~ **girder** · Hohlträger m

~ **glass** · Hohlglas n

~ ~ **block,** ~ ~ **brick** [*B.S. 1207*] · Glashohl(bau)stein m, Vakuum-Glas(bau)stein, Hohl-Glas(bau)stein, Glasvakuumstein, Beton-Hohlglas(bau)stein [*DIN 18175*]

~ ~ ~ **floor,** ~ ~ **brick** ~ · Glashohl(bau)steindecke f, Glasvakuumsteindecke, Glas(bau-)steindecke, Glasvakuumsteindecke, Beton-Hohlglas(bau)steindecke

~ ~ ~ **panel,** ~ ~ **brick** ~ · Glashohl(bau)steintafel f, Glasvakuumsteintafel, Hohl-Glas(bau)steintafel. Vakuum-Glas(bau)steintafel

~ ~ ~ **wall,** ~ ~ **brick** ~ · Glashohl(bau)steinwand f, Vakuum-Glas(bau)-steinwand, Hohl-Glas(bau)steinwand, Glasvakuumsteinwand, Beton-Hohlglas(bau)steinwand

~ ~ **brick,** ~ ~ **block** [*B.S. 1207*] · Glashohl(bau)stein m, Vakuum-Glas(bau)stein, Hohl-Glas(bau)stein, Glasvakuumstein, Beton-Hohlglas(bau)stein [*DIN 18175*]

~ ~ ~ **floor,** ~ ~ **block** ~ · Glashohl(bau)steindecke f, Vakuum-Glas(bau)-steindecke, Hohl-Glas(bau)steindecke, Glasvakuumsteindecke, Beton-Hohlglas(bau)steindecke

~ ~ ~ **wall,** ~ ~ **block** ~ · Glashohl(bau)steinwand f, Vakuum-Glas(bau)-steinwand, Hohl-Glas(bau)steinwand, Glasvakuumsteinwand, Beton-Hohlglas(bau)steinwand

~ **gypsum (building) block,** ~ ~ (~) **tile** [*See remark under 'Block'*] · Gips-Hohlblock(stein) m, Gips-Hohlstein, Hohl-Gips(block)stein, Hohl-Gipsblock, Hohl-Gipsbaustein, Gips-Hohlbaustein

~ ~ **roof(ing) block,** ~ ~ ~ **tile** · Gipsdachhohlstein m

~ **light(weight) slag concrete block** (US) → ~ **foamed (blastfurnace)** ~ ~ ~

~ ~ ~ ~ **tile** (US) → ~ **foamed (blastfurnace) slag concrete block**

~ **lime-sand brick,** ~ **sand-lime** ~, ~ **calcium silicate** ~ · Kalksandhohl(block)stein m, KSHBI [*Großformatiger Zweihandmauerstein mit fünfseitig geschlossenen Hohlräumen senkrecht zur Lagerfläche. DIN 106*]

~ **lintel;** ~ **lintol** [*deprecated*] · Hohloberschwelle f, Hohlsturz m

hollow (masonry) wall — hollow slab

~ (masonry) wall; cavity (~) ~ [*Strictly speaking, the cavity (masonry) wall is a hollow (masonry) wall in which the headers used in the rolock wall and the bonded hollow wall are replaced with metal ties*] · Hohlmauer f, (Zwei)Schalenmauer, Luftschichtmauer; Hohlwand f, (Zwei)Schalenwand, Luftschichtwand [*Fehlnamen*]

~ ~ (work), cavity ~ (~) · Hohlmauerwerk n, Luftschichtmauerwerk, (Zwei-) Schalenmauerwerk

~ mast, ~ pole, concrete ~ ~, hollow concrete ~ · (Beton)Hohlmast m, Hohl-Betonmast

~ ~, ~ pole, ~ transmission line ~ · Hohl(leitungs)mast m, Hohlüberlandmast

~ member → ~ (building) unit

~ metal door · Hohl-Metalltür f, Metall-Hohltür

~ ~ window · Metallhohlfenster n, Hohlmetallfenster

~ mould (Brit.); ~ mold (US) · Hohlform f

~ moulding (Brit.); ~ molding (US) · Hohlstab m

~ pan plank → ~ panel ~

~ panel → ~ concrete ~

~ ~, cavity ~ · Hohltafel f

~ pan(el) plank, ~ coffer ~, ~ waffle ~, ~ cassette ~, ~ core · Stegkassettenplatte f

~ panel wall, cavity ~ ~ · Hohltafelwand f

~ partition block → ~ ~ wall ~

~ ~ slab → ~ ~ wall ~

~ ~ tile → ~ ~ (wall) block

~ ~ (wall), double ~ (~) [*Hollow partitions are those formed of clay, terracotta, or breeze hollow blocks for lightness or for sound insulation. They may also be formed by staggering the studs*] · Hohltrennwand f, Trennhohlwand

~ ~ (~) block, ~ ~ (~) tile, cavity ~ (~) ~, partition (wall) pot [*B.S. 728. See remark under 'Block'*] · Trennwand-Hohl(block)stein m, Trennwand-Hohlblock m, Hohl-Trennwandblock, Hohl-Trennwand(block)stein

~ ~ (~) slab · Trennwandhohlplatte f, Hohl-Trennwandplatte

~ ~ (~) tile → ~ ~ (~) block

~ party (masonry) wall, cavity ~ (~) ~ · Brandhohlmauer f, Hohl-Feuermauer, Feuer-Hohlmauer, gemeinschaftliche Giebelhohlmauer, Hohlbrandmauer

~ pile · Hohlpfahl m

~ pillar [*A free-standing hollow column which does not necessarily accord with the proportions of classic architecture*] · Hohl(-Frei)pfeiler m

~ plank, hollow-core ~ · Hohldiele f, Steg(zement)diele

~ plaster (building) component → ~ ~ (~) unit

~ ~ (~) member → ~ ~ (~) unit

~ ~ (~) unit, ~ ~ (~) member, ~ ~ (~) component · Gipshohl(bau)körper m, Gipshohl(bau)element n; Gipshohlbaueinheit f [*Fehlname*]

~ ~ component → ~ ~ (building) unit

~ ~ member → ~ ~ (building) unit

~ ~ panel · Gipshohltafel f, Hohlgipstafel

~ ~ unit → ~ ~ ~ building ~

~ plastic board, ~ ~ sheet · Hohl-Kunststoffplatte f, Kunststoff-Hohlplatte

~ ~ sheet, ~ ~ board · Hohl-Kunststoffplatte f, Kunststoff-Hohlplatte

~ pole, ~ mast · Hohlmast m

~ ~, ~ mast, concrete ~ ~, hollow concrete ~ · (Beton)Hohlmast m, Hohl-Betonmast

~ ~, ~ mast, ~ transmission line ~ · Hohl(leitungs)mast m, Hohlüberlandmast

~ (pre)cast prestressed (concrete) floor slab · Spannbeton-Fertig-Deckenhohlplatte f

~ prestressed beam floor → ~ ~ ~ concrete ~ ~

~ ~ (concrete) beam floor, prestressed (concrete) hollow ~ ~ · Spannbeton-Hohlbalkendecke f

~ ~ (~) slab · Spannbetonhohlplatte f

~ ~ (~) ~ floor, prestressed (concrete) hollow ~ ~ · Spannbetonhohl(platten)decke f

~ ~ slab → ~ ~ ~ concrete ~

~ ~ ~ floor → ~ ~ ~ concrete ~ ~

~ product, ~ article · Hohlartikel m, Hohlerzeugnis n, Hohlgegenstand m

~ profile → ~ section

~ purlin(e) · Hohlpfette f

~ pyramid · Hohlpyramide f

~ rib · Hohlrippe f

~ ring, cavity ~ · Hohlring m

~ round column, ~ circular ~, ~ cylindrical ~ · Hohlrundstütze f, Rundhohlstütze

~ sand-lime brick, ~ lime-sand ~, ~ calcium silicate ~ · Kalksandhohl(block)stein m, KSHBI [*Großformatiger Zweihandmauerstein mit fünfseitig geschlossenen Hohlräumen senkrecht zur Lagerfläche. DIN 106*]

~ section · Hohlprofil n [*als Form*]

~ ~, ~ shape, ~ unit, ~ trim ~ profile [*structural steel section. B.S. 4*] · Hohlprofil n

~ ~ → ~ cross ~

~ ~ girder · Hohlprofilträger m

~ shaft · Hohlschaft m, Schaftschale f

~ shape → ~ section

~ sheet, ~ board · Hohlplatte f

~ slab, reinforced concrete ~ ~, R. C. ~ ~ · (Stahlbeton-)Hohlplatte f

hollow slab — homogeneous unit

~ ~ → ~ concrete ~

~ ~ **floor** → reinforced (concrete) ~ ~ ~

~ ~ ~, ~ concrete ~ ~, concrete hollow ~ ~ · (Beton)Hohlplattendecke f, Hohl-Betonplattendecke

~ ~ **floor(ing) construction** → (reinforced (concrete)) hollow slab floor(ing) system

~ ~ ~ **system** → reinforced (concrete) ~ ~ ~ ~

~ **space in cupola**, ~ ~ ~ dome · Kuppelspore f

~ **steel frame** · Stahlhohlrahmen m

~ **step** · Hohlstufe f

~ **structural section**, structural hollow ~ · Konstruktionshohlprofil n, konstruktives Hohlprofil

~ **style** · Muldenstil m

~ **tile** → ~ block

~ ~ → ~ ((pre)cast) (concrete) hollow block

~ ~ **density**, ~ block ~ · Steinraumgewicht SR n [Fehlname]; Steinrohwichte SR f [*Raumerfüllung von einem Hohlblockstein, Deckenstein oder ähnlichem Formkörper, welcher durch die Herstellungsmaschine ausgeformte Luftkammern besitzt*]

~ ~ **floor** → ~ block ~

~ ~ **for walls** → ~ block ~ ~

~ ~ **making machine** → hollow-block ~ ~

~ ~ **masonry wall** → ~ block ~ ~

~ ~ ~ **(work)** → ~ block ~ (~)

~ ~ **mold (US)** → ~ block mould

~ ~ **roof**, ~ block ~, cavity ~ ~, pot ~ [*See remark under 'Block'*] · Hohlblock(stein)dach n, Hohlsteindach

~ ~ **wall** → ~ block ~

~ **(transmission line) mast**, ~ (~ ~) pole · Hohl(leitungs)mast m, Hohlüberlandmast

~ **trim** → ~ section

~ **unit** → ~ section

~ ~ → ~ building ~

~ **vault** · aufgelöstes Gewölbe n, Spargewölbe, Hohlgewölbe

~ **waffle plank**, ~ coffer ~, ~ pan(el) ~, ~ cassette ~, ~ core ~ · Stegkassettenplatte f

~ **wall** → ~ masonry ~

~ ~ **insulation**, cavity ~ ~ · Hohlwanddämmung f

~ **ware** → ~ concrete ~

~**(-web) girder**, box (section) ~ · Kasten(träger) m, Hohlträger

hollowed out enamel → champlevé ~

holocrystalline · ganzkristallin, holokristallin

Holy Cross church · Heiligkreuzkirche f

holy door · Jubiläumstür f [*Eine Kirchentür, die außer der Jubiläumszeit geschlossen ist*]

Holy Grail · Heiliger Graal m

~ **of the Holies** · Allerheiligste n

~ **Sepulchre at Jerusalem** · Heiliges Grab n in Jerusalem

holy water basin, stoup [*A vessel to contain holy water, sometimes freestanding, but usually fixed to, or carved out of, a wall placed near the door of a church*] · Weihwasserbecken n

home, owner-occupied house · Eigenheim n

~ → house

~ **elevator (US)**; ~ lift (Brit.) · Eigenheimaufzug m

~ **for the homeless** · Obdachlosenheim n

home-grown timber, ~ wood, domestic ~ · einheimisches Holz n

~ **wood**, ~ timber, domestic ~ · einheimisches Holz n

home heating oil · Haushaltheizöl n

~ **lift (Brit.)**; ~ elevator (US) · Eigenheimaufzug m

~ **roof(ing) slab** · Eigenheimdachplatte f, Eigenheimbedachungselement n, Eigenheimbedachungsplatte, Eigenheimdachelement, Eigenheimdach(ein)deck(ungs)element

~ **scrap**, revert ~ · Rücklaufschrott m, Umlaufschrott

~ **water softener** · Hauswasserenthärter m

~ **workshop**, hobby room · Bastlerwerkstatt f, Bastelwerkstatt, Freizeitwerkstatt

homely, snug, cosy · wohnlich

homestead · Heimstätte f, H

~ **exemption law** · Heimstättenrecht n

homogeneity · Einschichtigkeit f

homogeneous → single-coat

~ **cover(ing)** · Einschichtbelag m, homogener Belag

~ **fibre wallboard (Brit.)**; ~ fiber ~ (US) · Einschicht-Faserwandplatte f, Einschicht-Wandfaserplatte

~ **floor** · einschalige Decke f

~ **member**, ~ unit · einschaliger Bauteil m, einschaliges ~ n

~ **polyvinyl chloride cover(ing)**, ~ PVC ~ · Polyvinylchlorid-Einschichtbelag m, Einschicht-Polyvinylchlorid-Belag, homogener Polyvinylchloridbelag, PVC-Einschichtbelag, Einschicht-PVC-Belag, homogener PVC-Belag

~ **PVC cover(ing)**, ~ polyvinyl chloride ~ · Einschicht-Polyvinylchlorid-Belag m, Polyvinylchlorid-Einschichtbelag, homogener Polyvinylchloridbelag, PVC-Einschichtbelag, Einschicht-PVC-Belag, homogener PVC-Belag

~ **state of stress** · homogener Spannungszustand m

~ **tile** · Einschichtfliese f, Einschicht(belag)platte f

~ **unit**, ~ member · einschaliger Bauteil m, einschaliges ~ n

homologous — horizontal coring 496

homologous, specular · spiegelbildlich
honeycomb(ed) · wabenförmig
~ block, ~ tile [See remark under 'Block']
· Waben(block)stein m, Wabenblock m
~ bond, pigeonhole(d) ~, pierced ~, (open) trellis ~ · Kästelverband m
~ (clay) brick · Gitterziegel m, Wabenziegel [DIN 105. Langlochziegel mit gegeneinander versetzten sechseckigen bzw. rhombischen Löchern]
~ coffering, ~ coring · Kassettierung f in Wabenmuster, Wabenkassettierung
~ core · wabenförmige Mittellage f, Wabenkern m
~ coring, ~ coffering · Kassettierung f in Wabenmuster, Wabenkassettierung
~ element · Wabenelement n [Es besteht aus zwei Sperrplatten, auch Gipskartonplatten, die mit zwischengelegtem Wabenkörper aus Wellpapierschichten fest verleimt sind]
~ (masonry) wall, pigeonhole(d) (~) ~, (open) trellis (~) ~, pierced (~) ~ [A half-brick wall built of stretchers with gaps between, so that they are only held by bed joints at their ends, above and below] · Kästelmauer f, durchbrochene Mauer
~ masonry (work), pigeonhole(d) ~ (~), (open) trellis ~ (~), pierced ~ (~) · durchbrochenes Mauerwerk n, Kästelmauerwerk
~ paper [See remark under 'Pappe'] · Wabenpappe f
~ ~ core · Papp(en)wabenkern m
~ sandwich radome · Radialkuppel f aus Wabenkerntafeln
honeycomb(ed) slating · Waben(dach)(ein)deckung f
~ tile, ~ block [See remark under 'Block'] · Waben(block)stein m, Wabenblock m
~ wall → sleeper ~
~ ~ → ~ masonry ~
~ window · Wabenfenster n
honeycombing · Wabenbildung f
honeysuckle → palmette
hood, cooker ~, range ~ · Dunstabzug(haube) m, (f), Dunsthaube [Über einem Küchenherd]
~ [A canopy to throw rainwater off a window or door or other opening] · Wetter(schutz)dach n
~, coping · Mauerhut m, Schweifkappe f, Mauerkappe, Abdachung f [Die schräge oder konvexe Abdeckung einer Mauer]
~-mould(ing), weather moulding (Brit.); hood-mold(ing), weather molding, drip mold(ing), headmold (US); drip(stone), label, water table, throating [A projecting mo(u)lding to throw off the rain, on the face of a wall above an arch, doorway, or window] · Kranzleiste f, Kaff(ge)sims m, (n), Wasserschlag m, Kapp(ge)sims
hook allowance · Hakentoleranz f

~ and eye · Haken m und Öse f
~ bending · Hakenbiegen n
~ bolt · Hakenschraube f
~ for pipe fixing · Rohrhaken m
~ length · Hakenlänge f
~ of rod, end hook · Endhaken m [Das um 180° herumgebogene Ende eines Betonstahles]
~ seam, common lock ~ · Hakenfalz m [Metallbedachung]
hook(ed) bar, ~ rod · Hakenstab m
hooked lath(ing) nail · Rabitzhaken m [DIN 1158]
hook(ed) nail · Hakenstift m [DIN 1158. Drahtstift aus Flußstahl]
~ rod, ~ bar · Hakenstab m
Hooke's law, law of elasticity · Elastizitätsgesetz n, Hookesches Gesetz
hooklike halving · Hakenblatt n, hakenförmige Überblattung f
hoop deflection (US); ~ deflexion (Brit.) · Ringverformung f
~ deflexion (Brit.); ~ deflection (US) · Ringverformung f
~ force · Ringkraft f
~ iron, band ~, strip ~ · Bandeisen n
~ reinforcement → lateral ~
~ stress, ring ~ · Ringspannung f
~ tension, ring ~ · Ringzug m
hooped column · ringarmierte Säule f, ringbewehrte
hooping → lateral reinforcement
hoops → lateral reinforcement
hopper vent(ilator), ~ light · Kipp(fenster)flügel m nach innen
~ (~) window, hospital ~, bottom hung opening inwards ~ · Kippflügelfenster n nach innen
horizontal assembly, ~ erection · Horizontalmontage f, Horizontalzusammenbau m [Ein Geschoß wird auf der ganzen Grundrißfläche fertig montiert]
~ boom angle iron, ~ chord ~ ~, ~ flange ~ ~ · Streckflanschwinkeleisen n, Streckgurt(ungs)winkeleisen
~ bracing, ~ stiffening, ~ reinforcing · waag(e)rechte Absteifung f, ~ Aussteifung, ~ Versteifung, ~ Verstärkung
~ cavity → ~ core
~ cell → ~ core
~ chord angle iron, ~ flange ~ ~, ~ boom ~ ~ · Streckflanschwinkeleisen n, Streckgurt(ungs)winkeleisen
~ component · Horizontalkomponente f, waag(e)rechte Teilkraft f
~ core, ~ cavity, ~ cell · Langloch n [Mauerziegel]
~ coring · Lang(durch)lochung f [Mauerziegel]

horizontal coring block — (horizontal) tieback

~ ~ **block,** ~ ~ **tile** [*See remark under 'Block'*] · Langlochblock(stein) *m*, Langlochstein [*Er ist gleichlaufend zur Lagerfläche durchlocht*]

~ ~ **(clay) brick** · Langlochziegel *m*, LLz [*Mauerziegel nach DIN 105, der gleichlaufend zur Lagerfläche durchlocht ist*]

~ ~ **(~)light(weight) brick** · Langloch-Leichtziegel *m*, LLz [*DIN 18505*]

~ ~ **light(weight) prefab(ricated) brick panel (unit)** · Langloch-Leichtziegelplatte *f*, LLp [*DIN 18505*]

~ **cut (of jack rafter)** · Fußschmiege *f*

~ **cylindrical tank** · liegender Zylinderbehälter *m*

~ **d. p. c.,** ~ **dampproof course** · waag(e)rechte Absperrung *f*

~ **dampproof course,** ~ **d. p. c.** · waag(e)rechte Absperrung *f*

~ **displacement** · horizontale Verrückung *f*, waag(e)rechte ~

~ **division,** layer-cake form of elevation · Horizontalgliederung *f*

~ **erection,** ~ **assembly** · Horizontalmontage *f*, Horizontalzusammenbau *m* [*Ein Geschoß wird auf der ganzen Grundrißfläche fertig montiert*]

~ **flange angle iron,** ~ **chord** ~ ~, ~ **boom** ~ ~ · Streckflanschwinkeleisen *n*, Streckgurt(ungs)winkeleisen

~ **flue,** header (~) · waag(e)rechter Zug *m*

~ **force** · waag(e)rechte Kraft *f*, Horizontalkraft

~ **form(work) support,** ~ **shuttering** ~, ~ **forms** ~ · Schal(ungs)träger *m*

~ **frame** · Horizontalrahmen *m*

~ **girder** · Horizontalträger *m*

~ **glazing** · Horizontalverglasung *f*, Waag(e)rechtverglasung

~ **grid** · waag(e)rechter Raster *m*

~ **illumination,** ~ **lighting** · Horizontalbeleuchtung *f*, Waag(e)rechtbeleuchtung

~ **joint,** bed ~, course ~ · Lagerfuge *f* [*Mauerwerk*]

~ ~ · waag(e)rechte Fuge *f*, Horizontalfuge

~ ~ **mortar,** course ~ ~, bed (~) · Lagerfugenmörtel *m* [*Mauerwerk*]

~ **lighting,** ~ **illumination** · Horizontalbeleuchtung *f*, Waag(e)rechtbeleuchtung

~ **line** · liegende Leitung *f*

~ ~ · Waag(e)rechte *f*

~ **load** · Horizontallast *f*, waag(e)rechte Last

~ **loading** · Horizontalbelastung *f*

~ **member** · Rahmenriegel *m*

~ ~, cross ~, rail [*A horizontal bar of wood or metal extending from one post or support to another as a guard or barrier in a fence, balustrade, staircase, etc.*] · Querstück *n*, Riegel *m*

(~) **overhang** · Überstand *m* [*Sonnenschutz*]

~ **plane** · waag(e)rechte Ebene *f*

~ **(plank) free standing silo,** free standing surface ~ [*As opposed to a horizontal (plank) silo in a portal framed structure = Portalrahmen-Fahrsilo*] · freistehender Fahrsilo *m*, ~ Flachsilo, ~ Grünfutter~, ~ oberirdischer Grabensilo

~ **(~) silo** · (Grünfutter)Fahrsilo *m*, (Grünfutter)Flachsilo, oberirdischer Grabensilo

~ **(~)** ~ **in a portal framed structure** · Portalrahmen-Fahrsilo *m*, Portalrahmen-Flachsilo

~ **(~)** ~ **with erected slabs** · (Grünfutter)Fahrsilo *m* mit aufgerichteten Wandplatten, (Grünfutter)Flachsilo ~ ~ ~, oberirdischer Grabensilo ~ ~ ~.

~ **projection** · Horizontalprojektion *f*

~ **property** · Wohn(ungs)eigentum *n*, WE

~ **reinforcing,** ~ **bracing,** ~ **stiffening** · waag(e)rechte Absteifung *f*, ~ Aussteifung, ~ Versteifung, ~ Verstärkung

~ **-retort tar** · Horizontal-Retortenteer *m*

horizontal section, sectional plan · Horizontalschnitt *m*

~ **shuttering support** ~ **form(work)** ~, ~ **forms** ~ · Schal(ungs)träger *m*

~ **siding,** ~ **wood(en)** ~ · waag(e)rechte Verbretterung *f*, waag(e)rechter Holz-Wandschirm *m*

~ **silo,** plank ~ · (Grünfutter)Fahrsilo *m*, (Grünfutter)Flachsilo, oberirdischer Grabensilo

~ ~ **in a portal framed structure** → ~ plank ~ ~ ~ ~ ~ ~

~ ~ **with erected slabs,** ~ plank ~ ~ ~ ~ · (Grünfutter)Fahrsilo *m* mit aufgerichteten Wandplatten, (Grünfutter-)Flachsilo ~ ~ ~ ~, oberirdischer Grabensilo ~ ~ ~

~ **slide door,** ~ **sliding** ~ · Horizontalschiebetür *f*, Waag(e)rechtschiebetür

~ **sliding door,** ~ **slide** ~ · Horizontalschiebetür *f*, Waag(e)rechtschiebetür

~ ~ **sash,** horizontally ~ ~, ~ ~ **window** ~ · Horizontal-Schiebefensterrahmen *m*, Waag(e)recht-Schiebefensterrahmen

~ **stiffener** · Horizontalsteife *f*

~ **stiffening,** ~ **bracing,** ~ **reinforcing** · waag(e)rechte Absteifung *f*, ~ Aussteifung, ~ Versteifung, ~ Verstärkung

~ **thrust** · Horizontalschub *m*

(~) **tieback,** (~) **tie member** · Zugband *n* [*Ein Verbindungsstab zwischen den Fußgelenken von Bogenträgern oder Rahmen, der den Horizontalschub dieser Tragwerke auf die Auflager aufhebt, indem er ihn als Zugkraft aufnimmt*]

(**~**) **tie member,** (**~**) **tieback** · Zugband *n* [*Ein Verbindungsstab zwischen den Fußgelenken von Bogenträgern oder Rahmen, der den Horizontalschub dieser Tragwerke auf die Auflager aufhebt, indem er ihn als Zugkraft aufnimmt*]

~ timber, waling (Brit.); wale (piece) (US); w(h)aler, transverse plank, binding piece · Zange *f* [*Rechteckiges oder halbrundes Holz für Verstrebungen und zum Zusammenhalten von Holzkonstruktionen*]

~ translation, sidesway · Horizontalverschiebung *f*, Waag(e)rechtverschiebung

~ wall slab · horizontale Wand(bau-)platte *f*, waag(e)rechte ~

~ (wood(en)) siding · waag(e)rechte Verbretterung *f*, waag(e)rechter Holz-Wandschirm *m*

horizontal(ly) sliding (window) sash Waag(e)recht-Schiebefensterrahmen *m*, Horizontal-Schiebefensterrahmen

horn aerial · Hornantenne *f*

hornblende · Hornblende *f*

~-gneiss, amphibolic gneiss · Hornblendegneis *m*

~-granite · Hornblendegranit *m*

~-schist, schistous amphibolite [*A foliated metamorphic rock, consisting of hornblende, with various proportions of feldpar, biotite, etc.*] · Hornblendeschiefer *m*

hornfels [*A hard, compact and granular metamorphic rock, formed by the action of intense heat on clayey rocks as in contact metamorphism*] · Hornfels(gestein) *m*, (*n*)

hornwork [*An outwork, consisting of two demibastions connected by a curtain and joined to the main work by two parallel wings*] · Sternschanze *f*

Horologium of Andronikos Cyrrhestes, Tower of the Winds · Horologium *n* des Andronikos von Kyrrhe, Turm *m* der Winde [*in Athen*]

horse, carriage (piece), roughstring, sloping beam, inclined beam · (Trag-)Holm *m*, Treppenbaum *m*, Laufbaum, Quartierbaum, Stiegenbaum, Tragbalken *m*, Zarge *f*, Treppenbalken

horseman frieze · Reiterfries *m*

horseshoe apsis, ~ apse · Hufeisenabside *f*, Hufeisenapside, Hufeisenapsis *f* [*Manchmal auch "Hufeisenabseite" genannt*]

~ arch → round ~ ~

~ stair(case) · Hufeisentreppe *f*

horticultural building · Gärtnereigebäude *n*

~ cast glass, greenhouse ~ ~ · (genörpeltes) Gartenklarglas *n* [*DIN 11526*]

~ glass, plain rolled ~ · Gartenrohglas *n*

~ sheet glass, greenhouse ~ · (Garten-)Blankglas *n*, Gartenglas, Gärtner(ei)glas [*DIN 11525*]

hose building, ~ house · Schlauchhaus *n* [*Es dient zur Aufbewahrung von Feuerwehrschläuchen*]

~ cabinet, fire-~ ~, FHC · (Feuer-)Löschschlauchschrank *m*

~-drying tower · Schlauchturm *m*

hose house, ~ building · Schlauchhaus *n* [*Es dient zur Aufbewahrung von Feuerwehrschläuchen*]

~ rack, fire-~ ~, FHR · (Feuer)Löschschlauchgestell *n*

~ tap [*A draw-off tap with a screw or union on the outlet for the attachment of the coupling of a hose*] · Schlauchhahn *m*

hospital · Spital *n* [*Schweiz*]; Krankenhaus *n*, Krankenanstalt *f*, Hospital *n*

~ block, ~ building · Krankenhausgebäude *n*

~ building, ~ block · Krankenhausgebäude *n*

~ construction · Krankenhausbau *m*; Spitalbau [*Schweiz*]

~ elevator (US) → (electric) hospital lift

~ grounds · Krankenhausgelände *n*

~ lift → electric ~ ~

~ service system [*For instance an internal drainage pipework*] · Krankenhaus-Betriebsanlage *f*

~ structures · Krankenhausbauten *f*

(~) surgical suite · chirurgische Abteilung *f*

~ tile · Krankenhaus(belag)platte *f*, Krankenhausfliese *f*

~ window, hopper (ventilator) ~, bottom hung opening inwards ~ · Kippflügelfenster *n* nach innen

host bakery · Hostienbäckerei *f*

hostel, residential home · (Wohn-)Heim *n* [*Ein Heim, das nach baulicher Anlage und Ausstattung für die Dauer dazu bestimmt und geeignet ist, Wohnbedürfnisse zu befriedigen. Neben den einzelnen mehr oder weniger selbständigen Wohneinheiten sind in der Regel noch Gemeinschaftsräume, z.B. zur Einnahme einer Gemeinschaftsverpflegung, vorhanden*]

~ → hostel(ry)

~ building · (Wohn)Heimbau *m*

~ for seamen, seamen's hostel · Seemannsheim *n*

~ ~ the elderly · (Alten)Wohnheim *n* [*Gebäude, in dem eine Anzahl abgeschlossener Wohnungen für bejahrte Menschen, namentlich Ehepaare, zusammengefaßt sind und in denen den Bewohnern die Möglichkeit geboten wird, im Bedarfsfall wirtschaftliche und soziale Betreuung in Anspruch zu nehmen. Es besteht teils aus kleinen selbständigen Wohnungen, teils aus Einzelzimmern mit Kochnische*]

~ occupant, ~ user · (Wohn)Heimbewohner m, (Wohn)Heiminsasse m
~ residence · (Wohn)Heimunterkunft f
~ user, ~ occupant · (Wohn)Heimbewohner m, (Wohn)Heiminsasse m
hostel(ry), inn · Herberge f
hot adhesive composition, ~ ~ compound, ~ bonding ~, ~ cement(ing) ~ · Heißkleb(e)masse f
~ air · Heißluft f
hot-air duct · Heißluftkanal m
~ furnace · Heißluftheizer m, Heißluftgerät n
~ generator · Heißlufterzeuger m
~ heating · Heißluftheizung f
~ treatment · Heißluftbehandlung f [Beton]
hot applied (joint) pouring compound → hot (~) ~ ~
~ ~ (~) sealing compound → hot (joint) pouring ~
~ asphalt, penetration-grade ~, saturating ~, impregnating ~ (US); 'penetration-grade' (asphaltic) bitumen, refinery (asphaltic) bitumen of penetration-grade, hot (asphaltic-)bitumen (Brit.) · Heißbitumen n, Tränkbitumen, Imprägnierbitumen
~ ~ adhesive composition (US) → ~ (asphaltic-)bitumen ~ ~
~ ~ ~ compound (US) → ~ (asphaltic-)bitumen adhesive composition
~ ~ bonding composition (US) → ~ (asphaltic-)bitumen adhesive ~
~ ~ ~ compound (US) → ~ (asphaltic-)bitumen adhesive composition
~ ~ cement → ~ (asphaltic-)bitumen adhesive composition
~ ~ cementing composition (US) → ~ (asphaltic-)bitumen adhesive ~
~ ~ ~ compound (US) → ~ (asphaltic-)bitumen adhesive composition
hot asphalt-coated gravel (US); ~ (asphaltic-)bitumen-coated ~ (Brit.) · Heißasphaltkies m, Heißbitu(men)kies
~ ~ sand (US); ~ (asphaltic-)bitumen-coated ~ (Brit.) · Heißbitu(men)sand m, Heißasphaltsand
~ asphalt concrete → ~ asphalt(ic) ~
~ ~ impregnation (US); ~ (asphaltic-)bitumen ~ (Brit.) · Heißbitumentränkung f, Heißbitumenimprägnierung
~ asphalt(ic) adhesive composition (US) → ~ (asphaltic-)bitumen ~ ~
~ ~ ~ compound (US) → ~ (asphaltic-)bitumen adhesive composition
~ (asphaltic-)bitumen, refinery (asphaltic) bitumen of penetration-grade, 'penetration-grade' (asphaltic) bitumen (Brit.); penetration-grade asphalt, hot asphalt, saturating asphalt, impregnating asphalt (US) · Heißbitumen n, Tränkbitumen, Imprägnierbitumen

~ ~ adhesive composition, ~ ~ ~ compound, ~ ~ bonding ~, ~ ~ cementing ~ (Brit.); ~ asphalt(ic) ~ ~ (US); ~ ~ cement · Heiß-Bitumenkleb(e)masse f, Bitumen-Heißkleb(e)masse, heißflüssige Bitumenkleb(e)masse
~ ~ ~ compound → ~ ~ ~ composition
~ ~ bonding composition → ~ ~ ~ adhesive ~
~ ~ ~ compound → ~ ~ adhesive composition
~ ~ cement → ~ ~ adhesive composition
~ ~ cementing composition → ~ ~ adhesive ~
~ ~ ~ compound → ~ ~ adhesive composition
~ (asphaltic-)bitumen-coated gravel (Brit.) → ~ asphalt-coated ~
~ ~ sand (Brit.) → ~ asphalt-coated ~
~ (asphaltic-)bitumen concrete (Brit.); ~ asphalt(ic) ~ (US) · Heißasphaltbeton m, Asphaltheißbeton
~ ~ impregnation (Brit.) → ~ asphalt ~
~ ~ mortar (Brit.) → ~ asphalt(ic) ~
~ asphalt(ic) bonding composition (US) → ~ (asphaltic-)bitumen adhesive ~
~ ~ ~ compound (US) → ~ (asphaltic-)bitumen adhesive composition
~ ~ cement → ~ (asphaltic-)bitumen adhesive composition
~ ~ cementing composition (US) → ~ (asphaltic-)bitumen adhesive ~
~ ~ ~ compound (US) → ~ (asphaltic-)bitumen adhesive composition
~ ~ concrete (US); ~ (asphaltic-)bitumen ~ (Brit.) · Heißasphaltbeton m, Asphaltheißbeton
~ ~ mortar (US); ~ (asphaltic-)bitumen ~ (Brit.) · Heißbitumenmörtel m, Heißbitumenmörtel [Aus Bitumen und Sand]
~ bending · Heißbiegen n
~ binder · Heißbindemittel n, Heißbinder m
~ bitumen → 'penetration-grade' (asphaltic) ~
~ ~ adhesive composition → ~ asphaltic-~ ~ ~
~ ~ ~ compound → ~ (asphaltic-)bitumen adhesive composition
~ ~ bonding composition → ~ (asphaltic-)bitumen adhesive ~
~ ~ ~ compound → ~ (asphaltic-)bitumen adhesive composition
~ ~ cement → ~ (asphaltic-)bitumen adhesive composition
~ ~ cementing composition → ~ (asphaltic-)bitumen adhesive ~
~ ~ ~ compound → ~ (asphaltic-)bitumen adhesive composition

hot bitumen-coated gravel — hot-setting glue

~ **bitumen-coated gravel** (Brit.) → ~ asphalt-coated ~

~ ~ **sand** (Brit.) → ~ asphalt-coated ~

~ **bitumen concrete,** ~ asphaltic-~ ~ (Brit.); ~ asphalt(ic) ~ (US) · Heißasphaltbeton *m*, Asphaltheißbeton

~ ~ **impregnation** (Brit.) → ~ asphalt ~

~ **bonding** · Heiß(ver)klebung *f*

~ ~ · Heiß(ver)kleben *n*

~ ~ **composition** → ~ adhesive ~

~ ~ **compound** → ~ adhesive composition

~ ~ **roofing cement,** ~ gravel-~ ~ ~ · heißflüssige (Kies)Einbettmasse *f*

~ **cell lab(oratory)** · "heißes Labor(atorium)" *n* [*Atomanlage*]

~ **cement** · Schmelzkitt *m*

~ **cement(ing) composition** → ~ adhesive ~

~ **chip(ping)s-bonding roofing cement** · heißflüssige (Splitt)Einbettmasse *f*

~ **cupboard** · Wärmeschrank *m*

hot-dip coating · Warmtauchbeschichtung *f*

~ **galvanising** (Brit.); ~ galvanizing · Feuerverzinkung *f*

~ **galvanized mild steel window;** ~ galvanised ~ ~ ~ (Brit.) · feuerverzinktes Flußstahlfenster *n*

~ ~ ~ **steel;** ~ galvanised ~ (Brit.) · feuerverzinkter Stahl *m*

~ **tinning** · Feuerverzinnung *f*

hot dipping · Heißtauchen *n*

~ **dressing compound,** ~ ~ composition · Heißdachkleb(e)masse *f*, Heiß(dach)spachtel(masse) *m*, (*f*)

~ **embrittlement** · Warmversprödung *f*

~ **floor** · Darre *f*, Trockenboden *m*

~ **-floor drying** · Heißflurtrocknung *f* [*Ziegel*]

hot forming · Warmverformung *f*, Warmumformung *f* [*Edelstahl*]

~ **gas main** · Heißgasleitung *f*

~ ~ **plant** · Heißgasanlage *f*

~ **glue,** cooked ~, warm-setting ~, warm-setting adhesive, intermediate temperature setting adhesive, intermediate temperature setting glue · Warmleim *m*

~ **gluing** · Heiß(ver)leimung *f*

~ ~ · Heiß(ver)leimen *n*

~ **(gravel-)bonding roofing cement** · heißflüssige (Kies)Einbettmasse *f*

hothouse · beheiztes Gewächshaus *n*, Treibhaus [*DIN 11535 Bl. 1*]

hot (joint) pouring compound, ~ (~) sealing ~, ~ applied (~) ~ ~ [*B.S. 2499*] · Heiß(fugen)gießmasse *f*, Heißvergußmasse, Heiß(fugen)ausgußmasse Heißfugen(verguß)masse

hot-laid coarse tar concrete · Heißeinbau-Teergrobbeton *m*, Heißeinbau-Grobbeton

~ **fine tar concrete** · Heißeinbau-Teerfeinbeton *m*, Heißeinbau-Feinteerbeton

~ **mix(ture)** · Heißeinbaugemisch *n*, Heißeinbaumischung *f*, Heißeinbaumischgut *n*

~ **rolled asphalt** · Heißwalzasphalt *m*

hot laying · Heißeinbau *m* [*Straßenbau*]

~ **material** · Heißgut *n*

~ **melt** · Heißschmelze *f*

hot-mix(ed) macadam · Heiß(misch)makadam *m*

hot mix(ture) · Heißgemisch *n*, Heißmischgut *n*, Heißmischung *f*

~ **paste** · Heißpaste *f*

~ **plate** · Darre *f*, Röstplatte *f*

~ **pourable** · heißvergießbar

~ **poured** · heißvergossen

~ **-poured compound** → hot (joint) pouring ~

hot-pouring · Heißvergießen *n*, Heißverguß *m*

hot pouring compound → ~ joint ~ ~

~ **-pressed process** · Warmpressung *f*, Warmpreßverfahren *n* [*Leinöl*]

hot pressing · Warmpressen *n*

hot-riveted · warmgenietet

hot riveting · Warmnieten *n*

hot-rolled, HR [*Tubes produced hot by one of several processes employing rolls. NOTE: It is incorrect to use the term except in this sense and, generally speaking, the term is obsolescent*] · warmgewalzt

~ **asphalt** · Heißasphalt *m*

~ ~ · Sandasphalt *m* mit eingewalztem Grobsplitt

~ **section,** ~ structural ~ · warmgewalztes Profil *n*

~ **(structural) section** · warmgewalztes Profil *n*

hot rolling · Warmwalzen *n*

~ ~ **mill** · Warmwalzwerk *n*

~ **room,** (dry) sweating ~, caldarium, laconium, sudatorium [*The (dry) sweating room in a Roman bath building*] · römischer Schwitzraum *m*, Sudatorium *n*, Schwitzraum einer römischen Therme, römisches Schwitzbad *n*, Caldarium *n*, Sudatio *n*, Assun *n*

~ **-room** · Schwitzbad *n*

hot sawing [*Cutting hot iron to length during or immediately following hot rolling, by a circular saw*] · Warmsägen *n*

~ **sealing compound** → ~ (joint) pouring ~

hot-setting adhesive, ~ glue · Heißleim *m*

~ **glue,** ~ adhesive · Heißleim *m*

hot shortness — house column

hot shortness [*Brittleness resulting from working hot metal; in the case of steel it is caused by a low manganese and a high sulphur content*] · Warmbrüchigkeit *f*

~ **shower** · Warmdusche *f*

~ **spa** · Thermalquelle *f*

~ **spraying** · Heißspritzen *n* [*Arbeitstemperaturen von 60° C bis 80° C*]

~ **surface treating (road) tar** · (Straßen)Teer *m* für heiße Oberflächenteerung

~ **tar, TH** · Heißteer *m*

~ **tarring** · Heißteerung *f*

~ **water, HW** · Warmwasser *n*, WW [*Es hat Temperaturen bis zum Siedepunkt bei Atmosphärendruck*]

(~) ~ **apparatus** → (~) ~ heater

~ ~ **(central) heating** · Warmwasserheizung *f*, WW-Heizung [*Vorlauftemperatur bis 90° C*]

~ ~ (~) ~ **installation,** ~ ~ (~) ~ **system** · Warmwasserheiz(ungs)anlage *f*, WW-Heiz(ungs)anlage

~ ~ **circulating, HWC** · Warmwasserumlauf *m*

~ ~ **flow** · Warmwasservorlauf *m*, WW-Vorlauf

~ ~ **generator** · Warmwasserbereiter *m*, WW-Bereiter, Warmwassererzeuger, WW-Erzeuger

~ ~ **heat** · Warmwasserwärme *f*

(~) ~ **heater,** (~) ~ **apparatus,** (~) ~ **heating appliance, WH** · Wassererhitzer *m*, Wasserheizer, Wasserheizgerät *n*, Wassererwärmer, Warmwasserheizer, WW-Heizer, WW-Erhitzer, WW-Erwärmer, WW-Heizgerät

~ ~ **heating,** ~ ~ **central** ~ ~ · Warmwasserheizung *f*, WW-Heizung [*Vorlauftemperatur bis 90° C*]

(~) ~ ~ **appliance,** (~) ~ **heater,** (~) ~ **apparatus, WH** · Wassererhitzer *m*, Wasserheizer, Wasserheizgerät *n*, Wassererwärmer, Warmwasserheizer, WW-Heizer, WW-Erhitzer, WW-Erwärmer

(~) ~ ~ **coil** · warmwasserdurchströmte Rohrschlange *f*, warmwasserdurchströmtes Rohrregister *n*

~ ~ ~ **installation** → ~ ~ central ~ ~

~ ~ ~ **system** → ~ ~ central ~ ~

~ ~ **line,** ~ ~ (supply) pipe ~ · Warmwasserleitung *f*, WW-Leitung

~ ~ **meter** · Warmwasserzähler *m*, WW-Zähler [*Fehlnamen: Warmwasseruhr f, WW-Uhr*]

~ ~ **network** · Warmwassernetz *n*, WW-Netz

~ ~ **pipe,** ~ ~ supply ~ · Warmwasserrohr *n*, WW-Rohr

~ ~ **(pipe)line,** ~ ~ supply ~ · Warmwasserleitung *f*, WW-Leitung

~ ~ **preparation** · Warmwasserbereitung *f*, WW-Bereitung

~ ~ ~ **plant** · Warmwasserbereitungsanlage *f*, WW-Bereitungsanlage [*DIN 18380*]

~ ~ **return** · Warmwasserrücklauf *m*, WW-Rücklauf

~ ~ **supply** · Warmwasserversorgung *f*, WW-Versorgung

~ ~ (~) **pipe** · Warmwasserrohr *n*, WW-Rohr

~ ~ (~) **(pipe)line** · Warmwasserleitung *f* WW-Leitung

~ ~ **vessel** · Warmwassergefäß *n*, WW-Gefäß

~ **working** [*The shaping of metal components by extrusion forging, hot rolling or similar processes at temperatures which are high enough to prevent the hardness and brittleness caused by cold working*] · Warmform(geb)ung *f*

hotel bedroom, (guest) ~ · Schlafraum *m*, Bettenraum, Bettenzimmer *n* [*Hotel*]

~ **block,** ~ **building** · Hotelgebäude *n*

~ **building,** ~ **block** · Hotelgebäude *n*

~ **construction** · Hotelbau *m*

~ **dining room** · Hotelspeiseraum *m*

~ **entrance** · Hoteleingang *m*

~ **foyer** · Hotelfoyer *n*

~ **heating** · Hotelheizung *f*

~ **laundry** · Hotelwäscherei *f*

~ **lock** · Hotelschloß *n*

~ **restaurant** · Hotelrestaurant *n*

~ **swimming pool** · Hotelschwimmbad *n*

house [*British standard name. B.S. 3589: 1963. A building forming o n e self-contained dwelling. It would not be correct in Great Britain to describe a building containing more than one dwelling as a house. Such a building might be a pair of (semi-detached) houses, a row of (terrace) houses or a block of flats or of maisonettes*]; one-family dwelling, (one-)family unit, ((one-)family) home, single-family unit, single-family home [*abbreviated: hse*] · Einfamilienhaus *n*, Familienheim *n* [*Fehlname: Wohnhaus. Nach der Definition in § 7 des II. WoBauG sind Familienheime „Eigenheime, Kaufeigenheime und Kleinsiedlungen, die nach Größe und Grundriß ganz oder teilweise dazu bestimmt sind, dem Eigentümer und seiner Familie oder einem Angehörigen und dessen Familie als Heim zu dienen"*]

~ · Haus *n*

~ **adaptable to extension(s)** · Anbauhaus *n*, anbaubares Haus

~ **agent** (Brit.); **real estate** ~ (US) · Grundstücksmakler *m*, Häusermakler

~ **alteration, building** ~ · Hausumbau *m*, Gebäudeumbau

~ **clock, building** ~ · Hausuhr *f*, Gebäudeuhr

~ **column, building** ~, **block** ~ · Hausstütze *f*, Gebäudestütze

house complex — housing

~ **complex**, complex of houses, group of houses; clump of houses (US) · Häusergruppe f, Häuserkomplex m

~ **connection**, building sewer · Grundstücksanschlußleitung f, Gebäudeanschlußleitung

~ **construction** → building ~

~ **decorator**, interior ~, internal ~, ~ designer · Raumgestalter m, Innenarchitekt m

~ **designer** → ~ decorator

~ **drain**, building ~ · Grundleitung f

~ **drainage**, building ~, drainage of a building, drainage of a house · Gebäudeentwässerung f, Hausentwässerung

~ **dweller** · Einzelhausbewohner m, Einzelhausinsasse f

~ **entrance**, building ~, block ~ · Hauseingang m, Gebäudeeingang

~ ~ **door**, block ~ ~, building ~ ~ · Haus(eingangs)tür f, Gebäude(eingangs)tür

~ **equipment** → building ~

~ **fire** → building ~

~ **foundation (structure)** → building ~ (~)

~ **frame**, building ~, block ~ · Hausrahmen m, Gebäuderahmen

~ **gas piping** [*The system of piping within a structure or a building, either exposed or concealed, which conveys gas from the outlet of the service meter or line to appliances at various places throughout the building or structure. Any piping underground which contains measured gas is also house gas piping*] · Gas-Hausleitung f, Haus-Gasleitung

~ **hunter** · Wohnungssuchender m

~ **line**, block ~, building ~ · Hausleitung f, Gebäudeleitung

~ **load**, block ~, building ~ · Hauslast f, Gebäudelast

~ **masonry wall**, building ~ ~; block ~ ~ [*deprecated*] · Hausmauer f, Gebäudemauer

House of Pansa at Pompeii · Haus n des Pansa zu Pompeji

'House of the Future' [*Designed by Jacobsen and Larssen for an exhibition in 1929. Circular in shape, it had a helicopter landing place on the roof*] · „Haus n der Zukunft"

house of the provost · Rektorat n

~ **orientation**, building ~, block ~ · Hauslage f, Gebäudelage

~ **oscillation**, building ~, block ~, ~ vibration · Gebäudeschwingung f, Hausschwingung

(~) **painter** · Anstreicher m [*Fehlbezeichnung: Maler*]

(~) **painter's tool** · Malerwerkzeug n, Anstreicherwerkzeug

~ **preservative**, building ~ · Gebäudeschutzmittel n, Hausschutzmittel

~ **refuse**, household ~, domestic ~ · Hausmüll m, (Haushalt)Müll, Kehricht m

~ ~ **disposal**, household ~ ~, domestic ~ ~ · Haus(halt)müllbeseitigung f, Müllbeseitigung, Kehrichtbeseitigung

~ **roof**, block ~, (building) ~ · (Gebäude)Dach n, Hausdach

~ **sewage** → household ~

~ **silhouette**, building ~ · Gebäudesilhouette f, Haussilhouette

~ **(structural) system** → building construction

~ **substructure** → building foundation (structure)

~ **vibration**, block ~, building ~, ~ oscillation · Gebäudeschwingung f, Hausschwingung

~ **water**, household ~, domestic ~ · Haushaltwasser n

~ **with court(yard)** · Hofhaus n

housed string, close(d) ~, curb ~ (Brit.); ~ stringer (US) · (Treppen-)Wange f mit eingestemmten Stufen

household chemical · Haushaltchemikalie f

~ **cinder** (US); ~ clinker (Brit.) · Haushaltschlacke f

(~) **cleaning equipment room**, (~) store ~ · Abstellraum m, Putzraum, (Haus)Geräteraum

~ **clinker** (Brit.); ~ cinder (US) · Haushaltschlacke f

~ **detergent** · Haushalt-Reinigungsmittel n

~ **god** · Hausgott m

house(hold) refuse, domestic ~ · Hausmüll m, (Haushalt)Müll, Kehricht m

~ ~ **disposal**, domestic ~ ~ · Haus(halt)müllbeseitigung f, Müllbeseitigung, Kehrichtbeseitigung

~ **sewage**, sanitary ~, soil-sewage [*The sewage from water closets, slop sinks and urinals*] · Gebäudeabwasser n, Haus(halt)abwasser

(household) store room, (~) cleaning equipment ~ · Abstellraum m, Putzraum, (Haus)Geräteraum

house(hold) water, domestic ~ · Haushaltwasser n

~ ~ **pipe**, domestic ~ ~ · Haushaltwasserrohr n

~ ~ **piping system**, domestic ~ ~ ~ · Haushaltswasserleitungssystem n

housemaid's sink, slop [*A low sink, large enough to take a bucket under the tap, often installed in hospitals*] · tiefliegender Ausguß m

housing · Wohnungswesen n

housing — HTQ

~, residential ~, residences [*A collective term used to designate human shelter*] · Wohnbauten *f*

~ · Unterstellen *n* von Fahrzeugen

~ **act,** ~ law · Wohn(ungs)baugesetz *n*, WBauG

~ **area,** populated ~, residential (building) ~, living ~ · Wohn(bau)gebiet *n*, Wohn(bau)zone *f*, Wohnungsbaugebiet, Wohnungsbauzone

~ **authority,** HA · Wohn(ungs)(bau)behörde *f*

~ **betterment** · Verbesserung *f* der Wohnverhältnisse

~ **bill** · Wohn(ungs)baugesetzvorlage *f*

~ **colony,** (~) estate; cottage community, nesting (US) · Wohnkolonie *f*, (Wohn)Sied(e)lung *f*

(~) ~ **unit,** (~) estate ~; cottage community ~, nesting ~ (US) · Sied(e)lungshaus *n*

~ **complex,** ~ development · Wohnanlage *f*

~ **conditions,** living ~ · Wohnbedingungen *fpl*

~ **(construction),** domestic ~ · WBau *m*, Wohnhausbau, Wohn(ungs)bau

~ **demand** · Wohn(ungs)nachfrage *f*

~ **density** · Wohnraumdichte *f*

~ **development,** ~ complex · Wohnanlage *f*

~ ~, ~ project, ~ scheme, multi-building ~ · Wohn(ungs)(bau)projekt *n*, Wohn(ungs)(bau)vorhaben *n*

(~) **estate,** ~ colony; cottage community, nesting (US) · Wohnkolonie *f*, (Wohn-)Sied(e)lung *f*

(~) ~ **development** · Sied(e)lungsprojekt *n*

(~) ~ **road** · Sied(e)lungsstraße *f*

(~) ~ **unit,** (~) colony ~; cottage community ~, nesting ~ (US) · Sied(e)lungshaus *n*

~ **financing,** financing of housing · Wohn(ungs)baufinanzierung *f*

~ **funds** · Wohn(ungs)baumittel *f*

~ **law,** ~ act · WBauG *n*, Wohn(ungs)baugesetz

~ **legislation** · Wohn(ungs)baugesetzgebung *f*

~ **market** · Wohnungsmarkt *m*

~ **need,** ~ requirement · Wohn(ungs)bedarf *m*

~ **needs,** living requirements · Wohnbedürfnisse *npl*

~ **policy** · Wohn(ungs)(bau)politik *f*

~ **programme** (Brit.); ~ program (US) · Wohn(ungs)bauprogramm *n*

~ **project,** ~ development, ~ scheme, multi-building ~ · Wohn(ungs)(bau)projekt *n*, Wohn(ungs)(bau)vorhaben *n*

~ **requirement,** ~ need · Wohn(ungs)bedarf *m*

~ **scheme,** ~ development, ~ project, multi-building ~ · Wohn(ungs)(bau)projekt *n*, Wohn(ungs)(bau)vorhaben *n*

~ **shortage** · Wohnungsfehlbestand *m*, Wohnungsmangel *m*, Wohnungsknappheit *f*, Wohnraumfehlbestand, Wohnraummangel, Wohnraumknappheit

~ **system** · Wohn(ungs)bauverfahren *n*

~ ~ **producer** · Wohnungsbausystemhersteller *m*

~ **tower** → residence ~

~ **tradition** · Wohnkultur *f*

~ **undertaking** · Wohnungsunternehmen *n*, WU

Howe (roof) truss · englischer (Dach-)Binder *m*

Hoyer beam · Hoyer-Balken(träger) *m*, (Stahl)Saitenbeton-Balken(träger)

~ **effect** [*In prestressed concrete, frictional forces which result from the tendency of the tendons to regain the diameter which they had before they were stressed*] · Hoyerwirkung *f*

~ **girder** · Hoyer-Träger *m*, (Stahl)Saitenbetonträger

~ **hollow (floor) filler** · Hoyer(-Decken)hohlkörper *m*

~ **method,** prestressed concrete with thin wires · Saitenbeton *m*, Stahl~, Bauweise *f* Hoyer

~ **slab** · Hoyer-Platte *f*, (Stahl)Saitenbetonplatte

HR → hot-rolled

H.R. gutter → half-round (roof) ~

~ ~ **rainwater gutter** → half-round (roof) ~

~ ~ **(roof) gutter** → half-round (~) ~

HS, hermetically sealed · absolut dicht abgeschlossen

HSC, high-strength cement · hochfester Zement *m*

hse → house

H-section → broad-flange(d) beam

~ **sash** · H-Profil-Flügel *m*

H-shaped column, H-column · H-Stütze *f*

HT, high-tensile · hochzugfest

HT → heat-treated

HTCl, high-tensile cast iron · hochzugfestes Gußeisen *n*

HTQ, high-tensile quality · hochzugfeste Güte *f*

HTS — hung scaffold

HTS, high-tensile strength · Hochzugfestigkeit f

hue [*The attribute of a colo(u)r that determines whether is it red, yellow, green, blue, purple, etc.*] · Farbton m

human comfort · Behaglichkeit f

(~) occupation, (~) occupancy · Belegung f [*Haus*]

~ sensitivity of vibration · menschliche Erschütterungsempfindlichkeit f, ~ Schwingungsempfindlichkeit

humic acid · Humussäure f [*Allgemeine Bezeichnung für die verschiedenen meist noch wenig bekannten Huminsäuren*]

humid, moist, wet, damp · feucht, naß

~ air, moisture-laden ~ · Feuchtluft f

~ refuse → ~ waste

~ room, damp ~ · Feuchtraum m

~ ~ dampproofing, damp ~ ~ · Feuchtraum(ab)dichtung f

~ ~ luminaire (fixture), damp ~ ~ (~) (US); ~ ~ light fitting (Brit.); ~ ~ (light(ing)) fixture · Feuchtraumleuchte f

~ ~ partition (wall), damp ~ ~ (~) · Feuchtraumtrennwand f

~ ~ service(s), damp ~ ~ · Feuchtrauminstallation(en) f(pl)

~ rubbish (US) → ~ waste

~ waste, ~ refuse; ~ rubbish (US); damp ~ · Feuchtmüll m, Feuchtabfall(stoff) m

~ weight · Feuchtgewicht n

humidification, moistening, humidifying · Anfeuchten n, Befeuchten

~ [*The state of being humidified*] · Befeuchtung f, Anfeuchtung, Feuchthaltung

~ → air ~

~ agent, humidifying ~, moistening ~ · Anfeuchtungsstoff m, Befeuchtungsstoff

~ system → air ~ ~

humidifier, air ~ [*A device designed to discharge water vapo(u)r into a confined space for the purpose of increasing or maintaining the relative humidity in an enclosure*] · (Luft)Anfeuchter m, (Luft)Befeuchter

to humidify, to damp, to moisten · anfeuchten, befeuchten

humidifying, humidification, moistening · Anfeuchten n, Befeuchten

~ agent, moistening ~, humidification ~ · Anfeuchtungsstoff m, Befeuchtungsstoff

humidistat [*A device designed to regulate humidity input by reacting to changes in the moisture content of the air*] · Feuchtigkeitsfühler m, Feuchtefühler

humidity, moisture · Feuchtigkeit f, Feuchte f, Nässe f

~, moisture · nichtdrückendes Wasser n

~ absorption, moisture ~ · Feuchtigkeitsaufnahme f, Feuchteaufnahme

~ barrier, ~ seal, ~ stop, moisture ~ · Feuchtesperre f, Feuchtigkeitssperre, Feuchtigkeitssperrschicht f, Feuchtesperrschicht

~ content → moisture ~

~ control, moisture ~ · Feuchteregelung f, Feuchtigkeitsregelung

~(-)controlling → moisture(-)controlling

humidity cover, moisture ~ · Feuchtigkeitsbelag m, Feuchtebelag

~ entry → moisture ~

~ equilibrium → moisture ~

~-free, moisture-free · feuchtefrei

humidity increase, moisture ~ · Feuchtigkeitszuwachs m, Feuchtezuwachs

~ limit, moisture ~ · Feuchtegrenze f, Feuchtigkeitsgrenze

~ migration, moisture ~, ~ movement · Feuchtewanderung f, Feuchtigkeitswanderung

~ movement → ~ migration

~ passage → moisture ~

~ penetration, moisture ~ · Feuchtigkeitseindringung f, Feuchteeindringung

~ permeability → moisture ~

~ proof roof(ing) sheet(ing), moisture ~ ~ ~ · Dach(ab)dicht(ungs)bahn f

~ quantity, moisture ~ · Feuchtigkeitsmenge f, Feuchtemenge

~ removal from roof(s), moisture ~ ~ ~ · Dachentfeuchtung f

~ resistance → moisture ~

~ seal, ~ stop, ~ barrier, moisture ~ · Feuchtesperre f, Feuchtigkeitssperre, Feuchtigkeitssperrschicht f, Feuchtesperrschicht

~ stop, ~ seal, ~ barrier, moisture ~ · Feuchtesperre f, Feuchtigkeitssperre, Feuchtigkeitssperrschicht f, Feuchtesperrschicht

100 per cent phenolic resin · 100%iges Phenolharz n, Alkylphenolharz

hung acoustic(al) ceiling → (sound) absorbent suspended ~

~ ceiling → suspended ~

~ ~ incorporating services, suspended ~ ~ ~ · Hängedecke f mit Leitungen

~ floor → hanging ~

~ glazing, suspended ~, suspension ~ · hängende Verglasung f, ~ Einglasung, Hängeverglasung, Hängeeinglasung

~ partition (wall), suspended ~ (~) · Hänge(trenn)wand f

~ plaster(ed) ceiling, suspended ~ ~ · abgehängte Putzdecke f, untergehängte ~, Putzhängedecke, Hängeputzdecke

~ scaffold, hanging ~, flying ~, suspended ~ · Hängegerüst n, Hängerüstung f

∼ **shell**, suspended ∼ · Hängeschale *f*

∼ **story** (US) → hanging floor

∼ **tilework**, wall ∼, vertical ∼, ∼ tiling · Wand(fliesen)belag *m*, Wandplattenbelag

∼ **tiling**, wall ∼, vertical ∼, ∼ tilework · Wand(fliesen)belag *m*, Wandplattenbelag

Hungarian architecture · ungarische Architektur *f*, ∼ Baukunst *f*

hungry joint, starved ∼ · ausgehungerte Fuge *f*

hunting box [*A small country house generally only used during the hunting season*] · Jagdhaus *n*

∼**-lodge** · Jagdhütte *f*

hurdle, wattle ∼, fence ∼ · (Zaun)Hürde *f*

∼ **fence,** wattle ∼ · Hürdenzaun *m*, Flechtzaun

hurdles · Hürdengalerie *f*

hut · Baracke *f*

∼ · Bude *f*

hutments · Barackenlager *n*

HVAC (practice) · Heizung *f*, Lüftung und Klimatisierung

HW → hot water

HWC, hot-water circulating · Warmwasserumlauf *m*

hyalography · Hyalographie *f*, Glasdruck *m*

hydrant · Hydrant *m*

∼ **bend** · Hydrantenkrümmer *m*

∼ **inside a building** · Innenhydrant *m*

∼ **tee** · Hydranten-T-Stück *n*

hydrargillite, gibbsite [*1. A trihydrate of alumina, Al_2O_3 · $3H_2O$. 2. A rock containing a major proportion of this mineral*] · Gibbsit *m*, Hydrargillit

to hydrate → to slake

hydrate [*A chemical combination of water with another compound or an element*] · Hydrat *n*

∼ **conversion** · Hydratumwand(e)lung *f*

hydrated · hydratisiert

∼, slaked, run to putty · (ab)gelöscht, naßgelöscht [*Kalk*]

∼ **basic carbonate of copper** · Kupferlasur *f*

∼ **calcium silicate**, ∼ lime ∼ · Kalkhydrosilikat *n*, Kalksilikathydrat *n*, Kalziumhydrosilikat

∼ **chromium oxide green** (Brit.); ∼ ∼ oxid(e) ∼ (US) · Chromoxidhydratgrün *n*, Guignet(s)grün

∼ **dolomitic lime**, ∼ magnesian ∼, dolomitic hydrate · Dolomitkalkhydrat *n* [*DIN 1060*]

∼ **ferric oxide** (Brit.); ∼ ∼ oxid(e) (US); ∼ iron ∼ · Eisenoxidhydrat *n*

∼ **hydraulic lime** · Wasserkalkhydrat *n* [*DIN 1060*]

∼ **iron oxide** (Brit.); ∼ ∼ oxid(e) (US); ∼ ferric ∼ · Eisenoxidhydrat *n*

∼ **lime powder** · pulverförmiger Löschkalk *m*, pulv(e)riger ∼, Staubkalkhydrat *n*

∼ ∼ ∼ **supplied in bags**, bagged (hydrated) lime · pulverförmig angelieferter Baukalk *m* [*Fehlnamen: Sackkalk(hydrat) m, (n)*]

∼ ∼ **putty**, carbide ∼ ∼, by-product ∼ ∼ · Karbidkalkbrei *m*, Karbidkalkteig *m*

∼ ∼ **silicate**, ∼ calcium ∼ · Kalkhydrosilikat *n*, Kalksilikathydrat *n*, Kalziumhydrosilikat

∼ **magnesium lime**, ∼ dolomitic ∼, dolomitic hydrate · Dolomitkalkhydrat *n* [*DIN 1060*]

∼ **potash** · Hydratpottasche *f*, K_2CO_3 · $1½H_2O$

∼ **white lime** · Weißkalkhydrat *n* [*DIN 1060*]

hydrating, running to putty, (lime) slaking · (Ab)Löschen *n*, Naßlöschen [*Kalk*]

hydration [*Formation of a compound by the combining of water with some other substance; in concrete, the chemical reaction between cement and water*] · Hydra(ta)tion *f*

∼ **chemistry** · Hydra(ta)tionschemie *f*

∼ **degree**, degree of hydration · Hydra(ta)tionsgrad *m*

∼ **heat**, heat of hydration [*The heat given off by cement paste during the chemical combination of cement with water. An exothermic process*] · Hydra(ta)tionswärme *f*

∼ **process**, process of hydration [*The process of formation of a compound by the combining of water with some other substance; in concrete, the chemical reaction between cement and water*] · Hydra(ta)tionsvorgang *m*, Hydra(ta)tionsprozeß *m*, Hydra(ta)tionsablauf *m*, Hydra(ta)tionsverlauf

∼ **rate**, rate of hydration · Hydra(ta)tionsgeschwindigkeit *f*

∼ **temperature**, temperature of hydration · Hydra(ta)tionstemperatur *f*

∼ **water**, water of hydration · Hydra(ta)tionswasser *n*

hydrator, (lime) slaking machine, lime hydrating machine · (Kalk)Löschmaschine *f*

hydraulic · hydraulisch, wasserbindend [*Bindemittel, die nach Zugabe von Wasser in sich, also auch unter Wasser, erhärten, nennt man hydraulische Bindemittel*]

∼ **additive**, ∼ agent, ∼ admix(ture) · hydraulischer Zusatz(stoff) *m*, wasserbindender ∼, hydraulisches Zusatzmittel *n*, wasserbindendes Zusatzmittel, Hydraulit *m* [*Ein Stoff, der den Weißkalk befähigt, auch unter Wasser zu erhärten*]

∼ **admix(ture)** → ∼ additive

∼ **agent** → ∼ additive

∼ **binder** → ∼ cementing material

hydraulic binder manufactured ... — hydrogen halide

~ ~ manufactured according to DIN 4207 · Mischbinder *m*

~ binding medium → ~ cementing material

(~) cement, water ~, cement matrix, CEM · Zement *m* [*hydraulisches Bindemittel*]

(hydraulic-)cement mortar, CEM MORT · Zementmörtel *m*

hydraulic cementing agent → ~ ~ material

~ ~ material, ~ cementitious ~, ~ ~ agent, ~ binder, ~ binding medium, ~ matrix · hydraulisches Bindemittel *n*, Mörtelbildner *m*, Mörtel(binde)stoff *m* [*Pulverförmiger Stoff, der beim Anrühren mit Wasser einen Brei, den Mörtel, liefert, der nach mehr oder minder langer Zeit, in der Regel nach einigen Stunden, unter Bindung von Wasser erstarrt, und der sich dann unter fortschreitender Erhärtung in ein steinartiges, in Wasser unlösliches und damit gegen den Angriff des Wassers beständiges Gebilde verwandelt. Der Ausdruck „hydraulisches Bindemittel" ist sprachlich kaum zu rechtfertigen; denn das Wort hydraulisch wird hier etwa in der Bedeutung „wasserfest" gebraucht, also in einem ganz anderen Sinne wie in der Physik*]

~ cementitious agent → ~ cementing material

~ ~ material → ~ cementing ~

~ finish · hydraulischer (Ver)Putz *m*

~ glue [*An old term for glue which remains hard under water*] · wasserfester Leim *m*

~ hardening · hydraulische (Er)Härtung *f*

~ index · hydraulischer Index *m*

~ lime [*Lime containing silicates and aluminates, formed during burning, similar to those present in Portland cement. These constituents give the lime the property of hardening in water, whereas non-hydraulic lime hardens only by combining with carbon dioxide from the air. Semihydraulic lime contains a smaller proportion of silicates and aluminates than eminently hydraulic lime and is intermediate in properties between this and non-hydraulic lime*] · Wasserkalk *m* [*Aus mergeligem Kalkstein durch Brennen unterhalb der Sintergrenze hergestellter Baukalk. DIN 1060*]

~ ~ mortar · Wasserkalkmörtel *m*

~ matrix → ~ cementing material

~ mix(ture) · hydraulische Mischung *f*, hydraulisches Gemisch *n*

~ modulus · hydraulischer Modul *m* [*Zement. Das Verhältnis von Kalk zu den Hydraulefaktoren Kieselsäure, Tonerde und Eisenoxid. Dieser Modul sollte etwas über 2 liegen*]

~ mortar · hydraulischer Mörtel *m*, Wassermörtel [*Er hat die Fähigkeit, sowohl unter Wasser zu erhärten als auch dauernd dem Angriff des Wassers zu widerstehen*]

~ overhead door closer, ~ ~ closing device, ~ ~ device for closing, ~ ~ closing mechanism · hydraulische Obenschließvorrichtung *f*, ~ Oben-Türschließvorrichtung, hydraulischer Oben-(Tür)schließer *m*

~ quicklime · Wasserstückkalk *m* [*DIN 1060*]

~ refractory cement, ~ ~ mortar · hydraulisch erhärtender feuerfester Mörtel *m*, ~ ~ ~ ff. ~

~ shutter door operator · hydraulische Torantriebvorrichtung *f*, hydraulischer Torantrieb *m*

~ substance · hydraulischer Stoff *m*

~ test · Wasserdruckversuch *m*, Wasserdruckprüfung *f*, Wasserdruckprobe *f* [*Rohr*]

~ window opening device · hydraulischer Fensteröffner *m*

hydraulically pressed · hydraulisch gepreßt

hydraulicity · Hydraulizität *f*

hydrazin(e) · Hydrazin *n*, NH_2NH_2 [*Wasseranziehende alkalische Flüssigkeit; rauchend, giftig; als Treibmittel für Porengips und Porenbeton verwendet*]

hydrocarbon · Kohlenwasserstoff *m*, KW

(~) binder, bituminous ~; bitumen (binder) (US) [*Strictly the portion of bituminous matter completely soluble in carbon disulphide; used loosely as a term for tar and asphalt (US)/(asphaltic-)bitumen (Brit.)*] · bituminöses Bindemittel *n*, bituminöser Binder *m*, (Schwarz)Bindemittel, (Schwarz)Binder

(~) ~ film, bituminous ~ ~; bitumen (binder) ~ (US) · (Schwarz)Bindemittelfilm *m*, (Schwarz)Binderfilm, bituminöser Bindemittelfilm, bituminöser Binderfilm

~ compound · Kohlenwasserstoffverbindung *f*

~ soluble dyestuff · kohlenwasserstofflöslicher Farbstoff *m*

~ solvent · Kohlenwasserstofflösungsmittel *n*, Kohlenwasserstofflösemittel

hydrochloric solution of cupreous chloride (Brit.); ~ ~ ~ ~ chlorid(e) (US) · $Cu_2Cl_2 + HCl + aq$, salzsaure Kupferchlorürlösung *f*

hydrofluoric acid, acidum hydrofluoricum · Fluorwasserstoffsäure *f*, Flußsäure

hydrogen-embrittlement of copper · Wasserstoffkrankheit *f* des Kupfers

~ ~ metals · Versprödung *f* von Metallen durch Wasserstoffgas

hydrogen gas · Wasserstoffgas *n*

~ halide · Halogenwasserstoffsäure *f*

hydrogen peroxid(e) — hyperstatic to the first degree

~ **peroxid(e)** (US); ~ peroxide (Brit.) · Wasserstoffsuperoxid n, H_2O_2

~ ~ **and calcium chlorid(e)** (US); ~ peroxide and calcium chloride (Brit.) · Wasserstoffsuperoxid n plus Chlorkalk [*Gasbildner beim Gasbeton*]

Hydroment [*Trademark*] · Hydroment n [*Schutzmarke. Ein Bindemittel aus Steinkohlenflugasche, Schlemmkreide und Kalkstein 1:1:1 gemahlen, bis zur Sinterung gebrannt und nochmals gemahlen*]

hydrophibic, hydrophilic, hydrophile, water-loving, water-attracting · wasserliebend

hydrophile, water-loving, hydrophibic, hydrophilic, water-attracting · wasserliebend

hydrophilic, hydrophibic, hydrophile, water-loving, water-attracting · wasserliebend

hydrophobe, water-hating, water-fearing, hydrophobic, water-repellent, water-repelling, water-rejecting · wasserabstoßend, hydrophob, wasserabweisend, wassermeidend

hydrophobic, water-rejecting, water-repellent, water-repelling · wasserabweisend, wasserabstoßend, wasserfeindlich, hydrophob

~ **agent,** water-repellent ~ · Hydrophobierungsmittel n [*Pulverförmige Metallseife, die Beton, Mörtel und Putz wasserabweisend macht; in der Praxis zuweilen als Stearat bezeichnet*]

~ **cement** [*A Portland cement having a water-repellent agent added during the process of manufacture, with the intention of resisting the entry of water into the concrete, rendering or mortar*] · hydrophober Zement m, Sperrzement

~ **treatment of masonry (work),** water-repellent ~ ~ ~ (~) · Hydrophobierung f von Mauerwerk

hydrosol(e) · Hydrosol n [*Kolloidale Lösung mit Wasser als Dispersionsmittel*]

hydrous · wasserenthaltend

~ **calcium silicate,** calcium silicate hydrate [*Any of the various reaction products of calcium silicate and water, often produced by autoclave curing*] · Kalziumsilikathydrat n

~ ~ **sulfate,** calcium sulfate hydrate (US); calcium sulphate hydrate, hydrous calcium sulphate (Brit.) · Kalziumsulfathydrat n

~ **magnesium silicate** · wasserhaltiges Magnesiumsilikat n

hydroxyl group · Hydroxylgruppe f

hygiene research centre (Brit.); ~ ~ center (US) · Laboratorium n für Hygiene

hygroscopic [*A property of materials indicating their ability to absorb moisture from the air*] · hygroskopisch, wassersaugend

~ **humidity,** ~ moisture · hygroskopische Feuchtigkeit f, ~ Feuchte f

~ **moisture,** ~ humidity · hygroskopische Feuchtigkeit f, ~ Feuchte f

~ **substance** · hygroskopische Substanz f [*Verschiedene Salze haben das Bestreben, aus der Luft Wasser aufzunehmen und zu zerfließen. Solche Salze werden als hygroskopische Substanzen bezeichnet*]

~ **water** · Anlagerungswasser n, hygroskopisches Wasser [*Das an der Oberfläche von Bodenteilchen angelagerte verdichtete Wasser*]

hygroscopicity · Hygroskopizität f, Wasseranlagerung f

hypaethral · Hypät(h)ros m [*Ein Bau ohne Dach*]

~ **temple** · Hypät(h)raltempel m [*Tempel mit nicht überdeckter Cella*]

hypar shell, hyperbolic-paraboloid(al) ~ · HP-Schale f, hyperbolische Paraboloidschale, hyperbolisch-paraboloidische Schale

hyperbola · Hyperbel f

hyperbolic paraboloid · HP n, hyperbolisches Paraboloid n

~ ~ **concrete shell roof** · HP-(Schalen)Dach n, hyperbolisches Paraboloiddach

~ ~ **conoid** · hyperbolisches Paraboloidkonoid n

~ ~ **umbrella roof of folded shell,** ~ ~ ~ shell roof · hyperbolisches Paraboloid-Regenschirmschalendach n

~ ~ ~ **shell roof,** ~ ~ ~ roof of folded shell · hyperbolisches Paraboloid-Regenschirmschalendach n

~ **paraboloidal conoid** · hyperbolisches Paraboloidkonoid n

~ **-paraboloid(al) shell,** hypar ~ · HP-Schale f, hyperbolische Paraboloidschale, hyperbolisch-paraboloidische Schale

hyperbolic shell roof · hyperbolisches Schalendach n

hyperboloid of one sheet · einschaliges Hyperboloid n

~ ~ **revolution (subjected to loads of rotational symmetry),** ~ ~ rotational symmetry · Drehhyperboloid n, drehsymmetrisches Hyperboloid, Rotationshyperboloid

~ ~ **rotational symmetry,** ~ ~ revolution (subjected to loads of rotational symmetry) · Rotationshyperboloid n, Drehhyperboloid, drehsymmetrisches Hyperboloid

hyperboloid(al) shell · Hyperboloidschale f

hyperoon . Hyperoon m [*Das Obergeschoß eines altgriechischen Wohnhauses*]

hyperstatic, (statically) indetermined, (statically) indeterminate · (statisch) unbestimmt

~ **to the first degree,** (statically) indetermined ~ ~ ~ ~, (statically) indeterminate ~ ~ ~ ~ ~ · (statisch) unbestimmt ersten Grades

~ ~ ~ **n-th degree,** (statically) indetermined ~ ~ ~ ~, (statically) indeterminate ~ ~ ~ ~ ~ · (statisch- unbestimmt *n*-ten Grades

~ ~ ~ **second degree,** (statically) indeterminate ~ ~ ~ ~, (statically) indetermined ~ ~ ~ ~ ~ · (statisch) unbestimmt zweiten Grades

~ ~ ~ **third degree,** (statically) indetermined to the third degree, (statically) indeterminate to the third degree · (statisch) unbestimmt dritten Grades

hyperthyrum, overdoor, sopraporte, sopraporta, supraporte · Supraporte *f*, Sopraporte, Portalbekrönung *f*, Türbekrönung [*Ein Wandfeld (mit Relief oder Gemälde) über einer Tür oder einem Portal, besonders beim Rokoko*]

hypo, sodium thiosulfate · Fixiersalz *n*, Natriumthiosulfat *n*, $Na_2S_2O_3 \cdot 5H_2O$

hypocaust [*The underground chamber or duct of the Roman system of central heating by means of air flues*] · Hypocaustum *n*, Hypokaustum

~ **heating** · Hypocaustenheizung *f*, Hypokaustenheizung

hypocrystalline · halbkristallin, hypokristallin

hypocycloid · Hypozykloide *f*

hypogeum, underground cemetery, catacomb · Katakombe *f*, unterirdischer Friedhof *m*, Hypogäum *n*

~ **tomb,** chamber ~, burial chamber, sepulchral chamber, tomb chamber · Grabkammer *f*, Kammergrab *n*

hypostyle · hypostyl

~ **(hall)** · ägyptischer Saal *m*, Hypostyl *m*, Säulenhalle *f* mit belichtetem Mittelschiff, Säulensaal mit belichtetem Mittelschiff

hypothesis, assumption [*engineering structural analysis*] · Annahme *f*, Hypothese *f*

hypotrachelion, hypotrachelium, gorgerin, neck(ing) · (Säulen)Hals *m*, Hypotrachelion *n*, Epitrachelion, Unterhals, Epitrachelium *n* [*dorische Säule*]

I

IABSE, International Association for Bridge and Structural Engineering · Internationale Vereinigung *f* für Brücken- und Hochbau

I-beam (section) → (rolled-)steel joist

ice cellar · Eiskeller *m* [*Hotel*]

~ **concrete** [*A type of light(weight) cellular concrete in which the cells are formed by ice*] · Eisbeton *m*, Schmelzbeton

~**-flow glass** → ice-patterned ~

ice lens · Eislinse *f*

~**-melting salt,** de-icing ~ · (Auf)Tausalz *n*

~**-melting salt solution,** de-icing ~ ~ · (Auf)Tausalzlösung *f*

ice palace, covered skating rink, indoor ice rink · Halleneis(lauf)bahn *f*, Eispalast *m*, Eisstadion *n*, Eis(lauf)halle *f*

~**-patterned glass,** ice-flow ~, glue-etched ~, floral pattern ~ · Eisblumenglas *n*, eisblumiertes Glas [*Ein Tafelglas, das aus Mattglas durch Auftragen von warmem, flüssigen Leim hergestellt wird. Der Leim reißt beim Auftrocknen Teile der matten Oberfläche in dem Fensterfrost ähnelnden Mustern ab*]

ice water · Eiswasser *n*

~ ~ **pipe** · Eiswasserrohr *n*

iced glass, frosted ~ · Eisglas *n*

icing · Eisbildung *f*

icon · Ikone *f*

iconography [*The study of ancient mosaic work, fresco(e)s, statues, etc.*] · Ikonographie *f*

iconostasis [*A screen in Byzantine churches separating the sanctuary from the nave and pierced by three doors; originally a lattice of columns joined by a decorated parapet and coping. Since the C 14-15 it has become a wooden or stone wall covered with icons, hence the name*] · Ikonostas(e) *m*, (*f*), Bilderstand *m* [*Mehrzahl: Ikonostasen*]

icosahedron · Zwanzigflach *n*, Zwanzigflächner *m*, Ikosaeder *n*

ID, internal diameter · lichter Durchmesser *m*, Innendurchmesser

iddingsite · Iddingsit *m* [*Buntes Verwitterungsprodukt von Olivin*]

idea of style, notion ~ ~, concept ~ ~ · Stilbegriff *m*, Stilkonzeption *f*

ideal buckling load · ideale Knicklast *f*

~ **building** · Idealgebäude *n*

~ **cupola,** ~ **dome** · Idealkuppel *f*

~ **dome,** ~ **cupola** · Idealkuppel *f*

~ **framework** · ideales Fachwerk *n* [*Hierunter versteht man ein System von Stäben, das folgenden Bedingungen genügt: Die Stäbe sind reibungsfrei gelenkig miteinander verbunden und im Vergleich zu den Lasten so leicht, daß sie als gewichtslos gelten können; die äußeren Kräfte (Lasten und Reaktionen) greifen nur in den Knoten an. Diese Voraussetzungen idealisieren das wirkliche Fachwerk (bei dem insbesondere die Verbindung der Stäbe vielfach durch Vernieten oder Verschweißen erfolgt); die mit ihnen erhaltenen Resultate lassen sich aber nötigenfalls leicht verfeinern*]

~ **grading curve,** nominal ~ ~ · Sollkurve *f*, Sollsieblinie *f*, Idealkurve, Idealsieblinie [*Sieblinie des gewünschten Endproduktes*]

~ **grain size,** ~ **particle** ~, nominal ~ ~ · Sollkorngröße *f*, Idealkorngröße, nominelle Korngröße [*Korngröße des gewünschten Endproduktes*]

~ **(ground(-))plan** · Idealgrundriß *m*, Idealplan *m* [*Es werden nur die Räume aufgezählt, aber nicht in ihrem wirklichen Verhältnis zueinander dargestellt. In der Renaissance verwendet*]

ideal main stress — immersion heater

~ **main stress,** ~ principal ~ · ideale Hauptspannung *f*

~ **particle size,** ~ grain ~, nominal ~ ~ · Sollkorngröße *f*, Idealkorngröße, nominelle Korngröße [*Korngröße des gewünschten Endproduktes*]

~ **plan** → ~ ground(-)~

~ **plastic mechanism,** perfectly ~ ~ · ideal-plastischer Mechanismus *m*

~ ~ **theory,** perfectly ~ ~ · ideal-plastische Theorie *f*

~ **plasticity** · ideale Plastizität *f*

~ **principal stress,** ~ main ~ · ideale Hauptspannung *f*

~ **stress** · Idealspannung *f*

~ **town** · Idealstadt *f*

idealization · Idealisierung *f*

idealized · idealisiert

ideas competition · Ideenwettbewerb *m*, freier Wettbewerb

identification colour (Brit.); ~ color (US) · Kennfarbe *f*

idiom of form · Formenkanon *m*

Igel Monument near Trèves · Grabmonument *n* der Secundiner in Igel bei Trier

(igneous) plutonic rock, intrusive ~, abyssal ~, abysmal ~ · plutonisches Gestein *n*, subkrustales ~, abyssisches ~, Tiefengestein, Plutonit *m*, älteres Eruptivgestein, Intrusivgestein

~ **rock** → primary ~

illite · Hydroglimmer *m*, Illit *m* [*Dem Glimmer nahestehendes alkalihaltiges Tonmineral*]

ill-lit · schlecht beleuchtet

illuminant · Lichtquelle *f*

illuminated ceiling, luminous ~, luminescent ~, (light-)diffusing ~ · Leuchtdecke *f*, Lichtdecke

~ ~ **system** → (light-)diffusing ~ ~

(~) **indoor fountain** · Zimmerspringbrunnen *m*

~ **mirror** · beleuchteter Spiegel *m*

~ **system,** luminous ~ · Licht(bau)-system *n*

~ **wall,** luminous ~, luminescent ~, (light-)diffusing ~ · Lichtwand *f*, Leuchtwand

illuminating device, lighting ~ · Beleuchtungsgerät *n*

~ **gas** · Leuchtgas *n*

~ **glassware** · Beleuchtungsglas *n*, Lampenglas

illumination, lighting · Beleuchtung *f*

~ · Lichtdurchgang *m* [*Fenster*]

~ **cable,** lighting ~ · Lichtstromkabel *n*

~ **calculation,** lighting ~ · Beleuchtungsberechnung *f*

~ **circuit,** lighting ~ · Lichtstromkreis *m*

~ **component,** lighting ~ · Beleuchtungsanteil *m*

~ **current,** lighting ~ · Lichtstrom *m*

~ **device,** lighting ~ · Beleuchtungsvorrichtung *f*

~ **engineer,** lighting ~ · Beleuchtungsingenieur *m*

~ **engineering,** lighting ~ · Beleuchtungstechnik *f*

~ **from skylight(s)** · (Dach)Raupenbelichtung *f*

~ **installation,** lighting ~ · Beleuchtungsanlage *f*

~ **load,** light(ing) ~ · Beleuchtungslast *f*, Lichtlast

~ **system,** lighting ~ · Lichtinstallation *f*, Lichtsystem *n*, Beleuchtungsinstallation, Beleuchtungssystem

~ **tariff,** lighting ~ · Lichttarif *m*

ilmenite, ferrous titanate · Eisentitanat *n*, Ilmenit *m*, Titaneisen *n*, $FeO \cdot TiO_2$

~ **black** · Ilmenitschwarz *n*

image of a saint · Heiligenbild *n*

imaginary (design) load (factor), fictitious (~) ~ (~) · fiktive Traglast *f*

~ **eccentricity,** fictitious ~ · fiktive Ausmittigkeit *f*, ~ Ausmitte *f*

~ **hinge** · ideelles Gelenk *n*, imaginäres ~, gedachtes ~

~ **load factor** → ~ design ~ ~

~ **number,** ~ quantity · imaginäre Zahl *f*

~ **part** · Imaginärteil *m*, *n* [*Akustik*]

~ **point,** mathematical ~ · ideeller Punkt *m*, gedachter ~, imaginärer ~

~ **(pre)stressing,** fictitious ~, ~ stretching, ~ tensioning · fiktive Vorspannung *f*

~ **quantity,** ~ number · imaginäre Zahl *f*

~ **stressing** → ~ pre~

~ **stretching** → ~ (pre)stressing

~ **tensioning** → ~ (pre)stressing

imbrex · Imbrex *m*, Regenziegel *m* [*In der griechisch-römischen Baukunst ein konvex liegender Hohlziegel, der den Stoß zwischen zwei Flachziegeln oder konkav gelegten Hohlziegeln überdeckt*]

imbricated ornament · schuppenförmige Verzierung *f*

~ **plate** · Schuppenblech *n*

~ **roof** · schuppenartig gedecktes Dach *n*

imitation marble, man-made ~, manufactured ~, art(ificial) ~ · Kunstmarmor *m* [*Fehlnamen: künstlicher Marmor, Glanzstein m*]

~ **of style,** stilistic imitation · Stilimitierung *f*, Stilnachahmung

~ **travertine,** man-made ~, manufactured ~, artificial ~ · Kunsttravertin *m*

immersion compression test · Wasserbad-Druckprüfverfahren *n*, Wasserlagerungs-Druckfestigkeitsprüfung *f*, Tauchdruckversuch *m* [*Bestimmung der Verformbarkeit bituminöser Gemische*]

~ **gilding** · nasse Vergoldung *f*

~ **heater** → ~ water ~

immersion heating — imperial dome 510

~ **heating**, ~ water ~, ~ hot water ~ · Tauch-Wassererwärmung f

~ ~ **appliance** → ~ (water) heater

~ ~ **element** · Einsteckvorwärmer m

~ **hot water heater** → ~ (water) ~

~ ~ ~ **heating**, ~ (water) ~ · Tauch-Wassererwärmung f

~ ~ ~ ~ **appliance** → ~ (water) heater

~ **in water**, water immersion · Wasserlagerung f

~ **test** · Wasserlagerungsprüfung f, Wasserlagerungsversuch m, Wasserlagerungsprobe f

~ **thermostat**, insertion ~ · Tauchthermostat m

~**(-type) rotary (water) meter** · Naßläufer m

~ **(water) heater**, ~ (~) heating appliance, ~ hot water heater, ~ hot water heating appliance · Tauch(wasser)heizer m

~ **(~) heating**, ~ hot ~ ~ · Tauch-Wassererwärmung f

immiscible · unvermischbar

immovability, fixity · Unverschieblichkeit f

immov(e)able, fixed · fest, unverschieblich

(~) end fixity, (~) ~ restraint, (fixed-)end ~ · feste Einspannung f, unverschiebliche ~, Endeinspannung

~ **restraint**, ~ fixity, (fixed-)end ~ · feste Einspannung f, unverschiebliche ~, Endeinspannung

immunizing, passivating · passivierend

~, passivating · Passivieren n

~ **coat**, passivating ~ · Passivierungsanstrich m, Passivierungsaufstrich f

impact · Stoß m

~ · Schlag m

~ **allowance**, ~ factor, allowance for impact, factor for impact · Stoßzuschlag m, Stoßfaktor m

~ **bending strength** · Schlagbiegefestigkeit f

~ ~ **test** · Schlagbiegeprobe f, Schlagbiegeversuch m, Schlagbiegeprüfung f

~ **damage** · Stoßschaden m

~ **factor**, ~ allowance, allowance for impact, factor for impact · Stoßzuschlag m, Stoßfaktor m

~ **hardness** · Schlaghärte f

~ **insulation** → ~ sound ~

~ **load**, impulsive ~ [*An imposed load whose effect is increased due to its sudden application*] · Stoßlast f

~ **loading**, impulsive ~ · Stoßbelastung f

~ **resistance**, resistance to impact, toughness · Schlagfestigkeit f, Stoßwiderstand m, (Schlag)Zähigkeit f [*Widerstand eines Gesteins gegen Bruch unter Einwirkung von Stößen*]

~ ~ **test**, toughness ~ · Schlagfestigkeitsprüfung f, Schlagfestigkeitsprobe f, Schlagfestigkeitsversuch m, Zähigkeitsprüfung, Zähigkeitsprobe, Zähigkeitsversuch

~ **-resistant**, impact-resisting, tough · schlagfest, (schlag)zäh

impact-resisting, impact-resistant, tough · schlagfest, (schlag)zäh

impact sound, structure-borne ~, 'contact noise' · Körperschall m [*Schall, der sich in festen Stoffen fortpflanzt (Erschütterungen ergeben Körperschall)*]

~ **(~) insulation**, structure-borne ~, structural sound ~, sound-insulation against structure-borne sounds, insulation of impact sounds [*Means taken to reduce the transmission of impact sound*] · Körperschall(ab)dämmung f, Körperschallschutz m

~ ~ ~ **material**, structure-borne ~ ~ ~ · Körperschall(ab)dämmstoff m

~ ~ ~ **tile**, structure-borne ~ ~ ~ · Körperschalldämmplatte f

~ ~ **intensity**, structure-borne ~ ~ · Körperschallstärke f

~ ~ **transmission**, structure-borne ~ ~ · Körperschallübertragung f

~ ~ ~ **level**, structure-borne ~ ~ ~ [*In a given octave band, between two rooms. The average octave band pressure level, throughout one room, produced by impacts delivered to the structure of the other room by a standard tapping machine*] · Körperschallpegel m

~ **strength** · Stoßfestigkeit f

~ **stress** · Schlagbeanspruchung f

~ **test** · Schlagprobe f, Schlagprüfung f, Schlagversuch m

impedance · Impedanz f [*Akustik. Impedanzen heißen – in Analogie zur Elektrotechnik – die komplexen Quotienten aus dem Zeiger einer dynamischen Feldgröße und dem Zeiger einer kinematischen Feldgröße, deren Produkt eine Leistung oder Intensität ergibt*]

impenetrable by water → impervious to ~

imperfect amber, impure ~, bastard ~ · Kunstbernstein m

~ **frame** → (statically) indeterminate ~

~ **framing** → (statically) indeterminate frame

Imperial apartments [*Palace of Diocletian at Spalato*] · kaiserliche Gemächer npl

imperial basilica, secular ~, pagan ~, (civic) ~, Roman ~ · römisch-heidnische Basilika f, heidnisch-römische ~, (römische) (Zivil)Basilika

~ **cathedral** · Kaiserdom m

~ **cupola**, bulbous ~, Moorish ~, ~ dome · Zwiebelkuppel f

~ **dome**, Moorish ~, bulbous ~, ~ cupola · Zwiebelkuppel f

imperial palace — impost in the form of a bracket-like ...

~ **palace**, palace of the emperor · Kaiserpalast *m*, Kaiserschloß *n*

Imperial Roman style · Stil *m* der römischen Kaiserzeit

imperial roof · Zwiebeldach *n*, Kaiserdach, Zwiebelhaube *f*, welsche Haube

impermeability, tightness, imperviousness · Dichtheit *f*, Dichtigkeit, Undurchlässigkeit

~ **of concrete**, tightness ~ ~, imperviousness ~ ~ · Betondichtheit *f*, Betondichtigkeit, Betonundurchlässigkeit

~ ~ **joint(s)**, impervousness ~ ~, tightness ~ ~ · Fugenundurchlässigkeit *f*, Fugendichtheit, Fugendichtigkeit

~ **to gas** → imperviousness ~ ~

~ ~ **rain**, imperviousness ~ ~, rain impermeability, rain imperviousness, raintightness · Regendichtheit *f*, Regendichtigkeit, Regenundurchlässigkeit [*Fehlname: Regendichte f*]

~ ~ **sound(s)**, imperviousness ~ ~, sound imperviousness, sound impermeability, soundtightness · Schalldichtheit *f*, Schalldichtigkeit, Schallundurchlässigkeit [*Fehlname: Schalldichte f*]

~ ~ **water** → water impermeability

~ ~ (~) **vapour** → (water) vapour impermeability

impermeable, tight, impervious · dicht, undurchlässig

~ **course** → impervious ~

~ **layer** → impervious course

~ **material** → barrier ~

~ **to chemicals**, impervious ~ ~, tight ~ ~ · chemikalienundurchlässig, chemikaliendicht

~ ~ **gas(olene)** → impervious ~ ~

~ ~ **oil** → impervious ~ ~

~ ~ **petrol** (Brit.) → impervious to gas(olene)

~ ~ **sound(s)**, impervious ~ ~ · schalldicht, schallundurchlässig

~ ~ **surface water** → impervious ~ ~ ~

~ ~ **water** → impervious ~ ~

~ ~ (~) **vapour(s)** (Brit.); ~ ~ (~) vapor(s) (US); impervious ~ (~) ~ · wasserdampfundurchlässig, wasserdampfdicht

impervious, impermeable, tight · dicht, undurchlässig

~ **course**, ~ layer, impermeable ~, barier (membrane) · (Ab)Dicht(ungs)lage *f*, (Ab)Dicht(ungs)schicht *f*, Sperrschicht, Sperrlage, Sperre *f*

~ **layer** → ~ course

~ **material** → barrier ~

~ **to chemicals**, impermeable ~ ~, tight ~ ~ · chemikalienundurchlässig, chemikaliendicht

~ ~ **gas(olene)**, impermeable ~ ~, tight ~ ~, ~ ~ gasoline (US); ~ ~ petrol (Brit.) · benzinundurchlässig, benzindicht

~ ~ **oil**, impermeable ~ ~, tight ~ ~, oil-tight · öldicht, ölundurchlässig

~ ~ **petrol** (Brit.) → ~ ~ gas(olene)

~ ~ **sound(s)**, impermeable ~ ~ · schalldicht, schallundurchlässig

~ ~ **surface water**, impermeable ~ ~ ~, tight ~ ~ ~ · oberflächenwasserdicht, tagwasserdicht

~ ~ **vermin**, vermin-resistant, verminproof · ungezieferfest, ungeziefersicher, ungezieferbeständig

~ ~ **water**, impermeable ~ ~, watertight, impenetrable by water, WT · wasserdicht, wasserundurchlässig

~ ~ (~) **vapour(s)** (Brit.) → impermeable ~ (~) ~

imperviousness, tightness, impermeability · Dichtheit *f*, Dichtigkeit, Undurchlässigkeit

~ **of concrete**, impermeability ~ ~, tightness ~ ~ · Betondichtheit *f*, Betondichtigkeit, Betonundurchlässigkeit

~ ~ **joint(s)**, impermeability ~ ~, tightness ~ ~ · Fugenundurchlässigkeit *f*, Fugendichtheit, Fugendichtigkeit

~ **to gas**, impermeability ~ ~, tightness ~ ~, gas impermeability, gastightness, gas imperviousness · Gasdichtigkeit *f*, Gasdichtheit, Gasdurchlässigkeit [*Fehlname: Gasdichte f*]

~ ~ **rain**, impermeability ~ ~, rain impermeability, rain imperviousness, raintightness · Regendichtheit *f*, Regendichtigkeit, Regenundurchlässigkeit [*Fehlname: Regendichte f*]

~ ~ **sound(s)**, impermeability ~ ~, sound impermeability, sound imperviousness, soundtightness · Schalldichtheit *f*, Schalldichtigkeit, Schallundurchlässigkeit [*Fehlname: Schalldichte f*]

~ ~ **water** → water impermeability

~ ~ (~) **vapour** → (water) vapour impermeability

implement shed [*farm building*] · Geräteschuppen *m*

impluvium [*In Roman houses, a shallow tank under the compluvium, or opening in the roof of an atrium*] · Impluvium *n*, Regenbehälter *m*, Regenbecken *n*

imported style · eingeführter Stil *m*

imposed deformation · Zwang *m*

~ **floor load**, variable ~ ~, floor live ~ · veränderliche Deckenlast *f*, wechselnde ~, bewegliche ~, Decken-Verkehrslast, Verkehrs-Deckenlast

impost, springer, summer, skewback [*The place where the vertical support for an arch terminates and the curve of the arch begins*] · Kämpfer *m*

~ **block**, dosseret, superabacus, supercapital, pulvin(us) · Pulvinus *m*

~ **capital** · Kämpferkapitell *n*, Kämpferkapität

~ **hinge** · Kämpfergelenk *n*

~ **in the form of a bracket-like moulding** (Brit.)/**molding** (US) · Kämpfer(ge)sims *m*, (*n*)

impost joint — in-built

~ **joint** · Kämpferfuge f
~ **level** · Kämpferhöhe f, Kämpferebene f [*Höhe des Kämpfers über dem Boden*]
~ **moulding** (Brit.); ~ **molding** (US) [*A mo(u)lding at the level of an impost*] · Kämpferleiste f
~ **section** · Kämpferschnitt m
impregnability · Tränkbarkeit f, Imprägnierbarkeit
impregnable · tränkbar, imprägnierbar
to impregnate · imprägnieren, tränken
impregnated · getränkt, imprägniert
~ **expanded cork brick** · imprägnierter Exp.-Korkstein m, getränkter ~
~ **paper** · getränktes Papier n, imprägniertes ~
impregnating · Imprägnieren n, Tränken
~ **agent,** ~ **composition** · Imprägnier(ungs)masse f, Imprägnier(ungs)mittel n, Tränkmasse, Tränkmittel
~ **asphalt,** saturating ~, penetrationgrade ~, hot ~ (US); 'penetrationgrade' (asphaltic) bitumen, refinery (asphaltic) bitumen of penetration-grade, hot (asphaltic-)bitumen (Brit.) · Heißbitumen n, Tränkbitumen, Imprägnierbitumen
~ **composition,** ~ **agent** · Imprägnier(ungs)masse f, Imprägnier(ungs)mittel n, Tränkmasse, Tränkmittel
~ **installation,** impregnation ~ · Imprägnier(ungs)anlage f, Tränk(ungs)anlage
~ **mix(ture)** · Imprägnier(ungs)gemisch n, Imprägnier(ungs)mischung f, Tränk(ungs)gemisch, Tränk(ungs)mischung
~ **plant,** impregnation ~, ~ **installation** · Imprägnier(ungs)anlage f, Tränk(ungs)anlage
~ **scumble** · Imprägnier(ungs)lasur f, Tränk(ungs)lasur
~ **temperature** · Imprägnier(ungs)temperatur f, Tränk(ungs)temperatur
~ **test** · Imprägnier(ungs)versuch m, Imprägnier(ungs)prüfung f, Imprägnier(ungs)probe f, Tränk(ungs)versuch, Tränk(ungs)probe, Tränk(ungs)prüfung
impregnation · Imprägnierung f, Tränkung
~ **bath** · Tränk(ungs)bad n, Imprägnier(ungs)bad
~ **degree,** degree of impregnation · Tränk(ungs)grad m, Imprägnier(ungs)grad
~ **installation,** impregnating ~, ~ **plant** · Imprägnier(ungs)anlage f, Tränk(ungs)anlage
~ **of the base of posts** · Einstelltränkung f, Einstellimprägnierung [*Holzpfostenenden*]
~ **period,** ~ **time** · Tränk(ungs)zeit f, Imprägnier(ungs)zeit
~ **plant,** impregnating ~, ~ **installation** · Imprägnier(ungs)anlage f, Tränk(ungs)anlage

~ **speed,** speed of impregnation · Imprägnier(ungs)geschwindigkeit f, Tränk(ungs)geschwindigkeit
~ **time,** ~ **period** · Tränk(ungs)zeit f, Imprägnier(ungs)zeit
~ **with creosote** · Kreosotierung f
to improve, to modify · vergüten
improved, modified · vergütet
~ **land,** developed ~, ~ **area** · erschlossenes Bauland n, baufertiges Land, erschlossene Fläche f, baufertige Fläche
~ **rubber,** modified ~ · vergüteter Gummi m, vergütetes ~ n
~ **solid wood,** modified ~ ~ · vergütetes Vollholz n, ~ Massivholz
improvement, modification · Vergütung f [*Beton; Mörtel*]
~ **of plaster bond** · Verbesserung f der Putzhaftung
improver, modifier, modifying agent · Vergütungsmittel n, Vergüter m
impulse clock · Impulsuhr f
~ **loading** · Impulsbelastung f
impulsive load, impact ~ [*An imposed load whose effect is increased due to its sudden application*] · Stoßlast f
~ **loading,** impact ~ · Stoßbelastung f
~ **testing of concrete beams** · Stoßuntersuchungen fpl an Betonbalken(-trägern)
impure amber, imperfect ~, bastard ~ · Kunstbernstein m
~ **(clay-)shale** · Schieferletten m [*unreiner Schieferton*]
impurity · Verunreinigung f, (schädliche) Beimengung
imputrescible, rotproof, anti-rot · fäulnisbeständig, unfaulbar, fäulnisfest, unverrottbar, fäulniswidrig, verrottungsfest, verrottungswidrig, verrottungsbeständig
in antis temple, templum in antis · Megarontempel m, Tempel mit Anten, Antentempel, Wandtempel
~ **powder form,** powdery, powdered; pulverized (US); pulverised (Brit.) · pulv(e)rig, pulverförmig, gepulvert, pulverartig, pulverisiert
~ **ramp** · Einfahrtrampe f
inaccuracy · Ungenauigkeit f
~ **of erection,** ~ ~ **fitting,** ~ ~ **setting (up)** · Aufbauexzentrizität f, Montageexzentrizität
inactive solvent, diluent · Nichtlöser m, inaktiver Löser [*Ein Lösungsmittel, das im Unterschied zu einem echten Lösungsmittel einen Rohstoff nicht allein zu lösen vermag; es kann aber einer Lösung mit echten Lösungsmitteln vielfach in erheblicher Menge ohne Ausfällung beigegeben werden*]
inarticulation · Silbenverwischung f [*Raumakustik*]
inaugural exhibition, opening ~ · Einweihungsausstellung f
in-built, BLT-IN, built-in · eingebaut

in-built ashtray — indanthrone blue

~ **ashtray**, built-in ~ · Einbauaschenbecher *m*

~ **antisplash**, built-in ~ · Wasserstrahlregler *m* [*Hahn*]

~ **(bath)tub** → built-in ~

~ **furniture** → fitment

~ **garage** *f* built-in ~

~ **kitchen**, built-in ~ · Einbauküche *f*

~ ~ **cabinet**, built-in ~ ~ · Einbauküchenschrank *m*

~ **shower stall**, built-in ~ · Einbau-Duschstand *m*

~ **tub** → built-in (bath)tub

~ **units**, built-in ~, fixtures, trim · Einbauten *f* im Bauwesen, Einbauteile *mpl*, *npl* ~ ~

~ **wardrobe**, built-in ~ · Einbau-Kleiderschrank *m*, Wand-Kleiderschrank

incandescent lamp, glow ~ · Glühlampe *f*

incidence angle → light ~

~ **of light** · Lichteinfall *m*

incident sound · auftreffender Schall *m*

incineration, waste ~, refuse ~; rubbish ~ (US) · (Müll)Verbrennung *f*, Abfall(stoff)verbrennung

~ **plant** (refuse) incinerator ~

incinerator, destructor, waste ~, refuse ~; rubbish ~ (US) · Abfall(stoff)verbrenner *m*, (Müll)Verbrenner

~ **plant** → refuse ~ ~

incipient crack, ~ tear, flaw · Anriß *m* [*Baustahl*]

to incise [*e.g. to incise a decoration in bronze*] · eintreiben

incised [*e.g. an incised decoration in bronze*] · eingetrieben

~ **decoration in bronze** · Treibarbeit *f* in Bronze

inclined arch · fallender Bogen *m*

~ **barrel vault** (Brit.); (skewed) arch barrel, (skewed) barrel arch (US) · schief(liegend)es Tonnengewölbe *n*

~ **clerestory**, ~ clear-story · geneigtes Lichtband *n*, ~ Glasband [*Siehe Anmerkung unter „Lichtband"*]

~ **escalator shaft**, ~ motorstair ~, ~ moving stair(case) ~ · Rolltreppenschrägschacht *m*, Fahrtreppenschrägschacht, Treppenaufzugschrägschacht

~ **glazing**, sloping ~ · Schrägeinglasung *f*, Schrägverglasung

~ **haunch** [*An overstress occurring in nonuniform beams may be eliminated by increasing the cross-section area towards the supports through inclined haunches*] · Schräge *f*, Voute *f*

~ **haunched beam** · Voutenbalken(träger) *m*

~ **motorstair shaft**, ~ escalator ~, ~ moving stair(case) ~ · Rolltreppenschrägschacht *m*, Fahrtreppenschrägschacht, Treppenaufzugschrägschacht

~ **moving stair(case) shaft**, ~ motorstair ~, ~ escalator ~ · Rolltreppenschrägschacht *m*, Fahrtreppenschrägschacht, Treppenaufzugschrägschacht

~ **stirrup** · Schrägbügel *m*

~ **web** · geneigter Steg *m*

inclosure, enclosure · Umschließung *f*

~ **of space**, enclosure ~ ~ · Raumabschluß *m*

~ ~ ~, enclosure ~ ~ · Raumhülle *f*

~ **wall**, enclosure ~ [*An exterior nonbearing wall in skeleton construction, anchored to columns, piers, or floors, but not necessarily built between columns or piers*] · nicht(last)tragende Außenwand *f* [*Skelettbauweise*]

inclusion · Einschluß *m*

incombustibility, noncombustibility · Nichtbrennbarkeit *f*, Unbrennbarkeit [*DIN 4102*]

incombustible, noncombustible · nichtbrennbar, unbrennbar [*DIN 4102*]

incoming solar irradiation → insolation

incompatibility · Unverträglichkeit *f*

incongealable · ungefrierbar

inconstancy of volume · Raumunbeständigkeit *f*

increase, rise · Anstieg *m*, Zunahme *f*

~ **in volume**, expansion · Treiben *n*

~ ~ ~, volume increase · Raumzunahme *f*, Volumenzunahme

~ ~ ~ **of cement** · Zementtreiben *n*

~ **of cross-section** · Querschnittvergrößerung *f*

~ ~ **loading** · Belastungssteigerung *f*, Belastungszunahme *f*

increaser, taper(ed) fitting, tapering fitting · (Rohr)Übergang *m*

increasing strength, rising ~ · ansteigende Festigkeit *f*, zunehmende ~

increment value; excess ~ (US) · Wertsteigerung *f*

~ ~ **tax**, betterment levy; excess value tax · Wertzuwachssteuer *f* [*im Grundstückswesen*]

incremental application of load, ~ load application · etappenweiser Lastangriff *m*, stufenweiser ~

~ **pressure** · Steigdruck *m*

incrustation, incrusting · Krustenbildung *f*, Verkrustung

~, **inlay** · Inkrustation *f* [*Steineinlagen in Stein*]

~ **(in pipe(s))** · Anlagerung *f* (in Rohrleitungen) [*Die infolge einer Reaktion im Wasser, ohne oder durch Mitwirkung des Rohrwerkstoffes, entstandenen und an der Innenwandung der Rohrleitung haftenden Stoffe*]

incrusting, incrustation · Krustenbildung *f*, Verkrustung

indanthrone blue · Indanthrenblau RS *n*, Indanthron *n*

indanthrone vat colour — individual portal frame

~ **vat colour** (Brit.); ~ ~ color (US); ~ (~) dye · Indanthrenküpenfarbstoff *m*

indefinite integral · unbestimmtes Integral *n*

indeformable → undeformable

indene resin · Indenharz *n*

indentation · Tiefung *f*

~ **machine** · Kugelhärteprüfer *m*

indented bar, ~ rod · Nockenstab *m* [*Bewehrung*]

~ **chisel, notched** ~ · Zahneisen *n* [*Steinhauerwerkzeug*]

~ **joint** · Verzahnung *f* [*Holzbau*]

~ **ribbed bar,** ~ ~ rod, ribbed indented ~ · Nockenrippenstab *m*, Nori-Stab

~ ~ **bars,** ~ ~ rods, ~ ~ rounds, ribbed indented ~ · Nockenrippenstahl *m*, Nori-Stahl [*Mit schrägen Rippen; 8 bis 26 mm ⌀*]

~ **wire**, profil(ed) ~, wire of irregular shape · Dessindraht *m*, Formdraht, Profildraht, Fassondraht, profilierter Draht

indenting course, toothing [*The stretchers project $2^{1}/_{4}$ in. at the end of a masonry wall to bond with future work. The bricks project like teeth from alternate courses*] · Zahnschicht *f*, Zahnlage *f*

independent architect, free-lance ~, private ~ · freischaffender Architekt *m*

~ **footing,** isolated ~ · Einzelfundament *n*

~ **foundation,** isolated ~ · Einzelgründung *f*

~ **wire rope core, IWRC** · unabhängige Stahlseele *f*

indeterminacy, statical ~ · (statische) Unbestimmtheit *f*

indeterminate → statically ~

~ **frame** → statically ~ ~

~ **framing** → (statically) indeterminate frame

~ **to the first degree** → statically ~ ~ ~ ~ ~

~ ~ ~ **n-th degree** → statically ~ ~ ~ ~ ~

~ ~ ~ **second degree** → statically ~ ~ ~ ~ ~

~ ~ ~ **third degree** → statically ~ ~ ~ ~ ~

indetermined → (statically) indeterminate

index of acidity, acidity index · Säureindex *m*

~ ~ **activity,** activity index · Aktivitätsindex *m* [*Zement*]

~ ~ **plasticity,** plasticity index · Plastizitätsindex *m*

Indian red pigment · Indischrot(pigment) *n*

indicator · Indikator *m* [*Ein Farbstoff, der anzeigt, ob eine Lösung sauer oder basisch reagiert. Nachweis freier Säuren und Lösungen, z.B. aggressiver Kohlensäure. Die häufigsten Indikatoren sind Lackmus, Phenolphtalein, Methylorange und Methylrot*]

~ **colouring** (Brit.); ~ coloring (US) · Indikatorfärbung *f*

~ **paper** · Indikatorpapier *n*

~ **sign post** · Straßenleitpfosten *m*

indigo [*A deep blue, originally obtained from plants. Now artificially made on a large scale from coal-tar*] · Indigo *n*

indirect action · Zwängungsbeanspruchung *f*

~ **glare** · indirekte Blendung *f*

~ **heating, convection** ~, convective ~ · Konvektionsheizung *f*

~ **illumination, concealed** ~, ~ lighting · indirekte Beleuchtung *f*

~ **light, concealed** ~ · indirektes Licht *n*

~ **lighting, concealed** ~, ~ illumination · indirekte Beleuchtung *f*

~ ~ **component** · indirekter Beleuchtungsanteil *m*

~ ~ **material** [*A material which is not physically incorporated into the work(s)*] · (Bau)Hilfsstoff *m*, Hilfsbaustoff; (Bau)Hilfsmaterial *n*, Hilfsbaumaterial

~ **path of sound transmission** · (akustischer) Nebenweg *m*

~ **stress** · Zwängungsspannung *f*

~ **tensile test, splitting** ~ ~ · Spaltzugversuch *m*, Spaltzugprobe *f*, Spaltzugprüfung *f*

individual asphalt shingle (US) → ~ prepared-roofing ~

~ **(asphaltic-)bitumen shingle** (Brit.) → ~ prepared-roofing ~

~ **cellar** · Einzelkeller *m*

~ **coat** · Anstrichschicht *f*, Aufstrichschicht

~ ~ **of paint,** ~ paint coat · Farb(an-strich)schicht *f*, Farbaufstrichschicht

~ **consumer** · Einzelabnehmer *m*

~ **drinking water supply** · Einzel-Trinkwasserversorgung *f*

~ **fabrication,** ~ manufacture, ~ making · Einzelfertigung *f*, Einzelherstellung

~ **form of art, art of the individual** · Individualistenkunst *f*

~ **heating** · Einzelheizung *f*

~ **line** · Einzelleitung *f*

~ **making,** ~ manufacture, ~ fabrication · Einzelfertigung *f*, Einzelherstellung

~ **manufacture,** ~ fabrication, ~ making · Einzelfertigung *f*, Einzelherstellung

~ **mounting** · Einzelanordnung *f* [*z.B. Leuchte*]

~ **office** · Einzelbüro *n*

~ **paint coat,** ~ coat of paint · Farb(anstrich)schicht *f*, Farbaufstrichschicht

~ **portal frame** [*As opposed to interconnected portal frames*] · Einzel-Portalrahmen *m*

individual prepared-roofing shingle — indoor swimming...

~ **prepared-roofing shingle;** ~ asphalt ~ (US); ~ (asphaltic-)bitumen ~ (Brit.) [*These shingles consist of shingle units cut in a shingle pattern, in distinction to the so-called strip-shingles which are cut in units having a repetition of the pattern so as to simulate two or more industrial shingles joined together*] · Einzel-Pappschindel f, Einzel-Asphaltschindel, Einzel(-Bitumen)-schindel

~ **room** · Einzelzimmer n

~ **sculpture** · Einzelplastik f, Freiplastik, Einzelskulptur f, Freiskulptur

~ **section of pipe**, pipe section, pipe joint · Rohrschuß m, Rohrabschnitt m

~ **supply** · Einzelversorgung f

(~) **system** [*A water or sewerage system serving a single property*] · Grundstücksanlage f, Einzelanlage

~ **tar coat** ~ coat of tar · Teeranstrichschicht f, Teeraufstrichschicht

~ **tile** · Einzelfliese f, Einzel(belag)platte f

~ **warm water preparation** · Einzelwarmwasserbereitung f

~ **water distribution** · Einzel-Wasserzuführung f, Einzel-Wasserzuleitung

~ ~ **supply** · Einzelwasserversorgung f

~ ~ ~ **installation** ~ ~ ~ system · Einzelwasserversorgungsanlage f

indoor air, inside ~, room ~, interior ~, internal ~, inner ~ · Raumluft f, Zimmerluft

~ ~ **cooler** → inside ~ ~

~ **arena** · Hallenstadion n

~ **building board** → interior ~ ~

~ (~) **panel** → interior (~) ~

~ ~ **sheet** → interior building board

~ **chlorinated rubber paint**, inside ~ ~ ~, inner ~ ~ ~, internal ~ ~ ~, interior ~ ~ ~ · Innen-Chlorkautschukfarbe f

~ (**clear**) **varnish** · Innenklarlack m, (farbloser) Innenlack

~ **climate**, interior ~, inside ~, internal ~, room ~, inner ~ · Raumklima n, Innenklima

~ **coating**, internal ~, inside ~ · Innenbeschichtung f, Innenüberzug m [*als Schicht*]

~ **decor**, internal ~, inside ~, interior ~, inner ~ · Innengestaltung f [*Als Ergebnis des Innengestaltens*]

~ **decorating**, interior ~, inside ~, internal ~, inner ~ · Innengestalten n, Innengestaltung f

~ **design temperature** · Bemessungsraumtemperatur f

~ **emulsion paint**, inside ~ ~, inner ~ ~, internal ~ ~, interior ~ ~ · Innen-Emulsionsfarbe f

~ **finish(ing) paint** → interior ~ ~

~ **fixture** → ~ luminaire (~)

~ **fountain** → illuminated ~ ~

~ **glass door**, internal ~ ~, inside ~ ~, interior ~ ~, inner ~ ~ ~ · Innenglastür f

~ **gloss (clear) varnish** → interior ~ (~) ~

~ **heat** → room ~

~ ~ **gain** → internal ~ ~

~ **humidity** → ~ moisture

~ **ice rink**, covered skating ~, ice palace · Halleneis(lauf)bahn f, Eispalast m, Eisstadion n, Eis(lauf)halle f

~ **illumination** → ~ lighting

~ **installation** · Gebäudeinstallation f, Hausinstallation

~ **lacquer**, ~ pigmented varnish · Innenlackemaille f, Innenlackfarbe f, pigmentierter Innenklarlack m

~ **learner's pool**, ~ teaching ~ · Lehr(schwimm)becken n im Hallenbad, LSB ~ ~

~ **light fitting** (Brit.) → ~ luminaire (fixture)

~ **lighting**, ~ illumination, room ~, interior ~, inside ~, internal ~, inner ~ · Raumbeleuchtung f, Innen(raum)beleuchtung

~ (**light(ing)**) **fixture** → ~ luminaire (~)

~ **luminaire** (**fixture**) (US); ~ light fitting (Brit.); ~ (light(ing)) fixture · Innenleuchte f

~ **marble**, inner ~, inside ~, interior ~ · Innenmarmor m, Marmor für Innenverkleidungen

~ **market**, roofed ~, covered ~, market hall · (Markt)Halle f

~ **masonry** (**dividing**) **wall** → internal ~ (~) ~

~ **moisture**, ~ humidity, interior ~, internal ~, inner ~, inside ~, room ~ · Raumfeuchte f, Raumfeuchtigkeit f, Innenfeuchte, Innenfeuchtigkeit

~ **noise**, interior ~, inside ~, internal ~, inner ~ · Innenlärm m, Hauslärm Gebäudelärm

~ **-outdoor carpet**, anywhere ~ · Allzweck-Teppichboden m, Allzweck-Textilboden(belag) m

indoor panel → interior (building) ~

~ **pigmented varnish**, ~ lacquer · Innenlackemaille f, Innenlackfarbe f, pigmentierter Innenklarlack m

~ **piping**, interior ~, internal ~, inner ~, inside ~ · Innenrohrleitung f

~ **plant** · Raumpflanze f

~ **relative humidity** → internal relative moisture

~ ~ **moisture** → internal ~ ~

~ **slatted blind**, inside ~ ~, inner ~ ~, interior ~ ~, internal ~ ~ · Innenjalousie f

~ **swimming bath(s)** → covered ~ ~

~ ~ **pool** → covered swimming bath(s)

indoor swimming pool with artificial waves — industrial heat

~ ~ ~ **with artificial waves** · Wellenbad *n*

~ **teaching pool,** ~ learner's ~ · Lehr-(schwimm)becken *n* im Hallenbad, LSB ~ ~

~ **temperature control,** internal ~ ~, interior ~ ~, inner ~ ~, room ~ ~, inside ~ ~ · Raumtemperatursteuerung *f,* Innentemperatursteuerung

~ **tile,** inside ~, inner ~, internal ~, interior ~ · Innen(belag)platte *f,* Innenfliese *f*

~ **track** · Hallenbahn *f* [*Leichtathletik*]

~ **varnish,** ~ clear ~ · Innenklarlack *m,* (farbloser) Innenlack

~ **window cill** (Brit.) → interior window sill

~ ~ **sill** → interior ~ ~

induced draught (Brit.); ~ draft (US) · Saugzug *m*

~ ~ **fan** (Brit.); ~ draft ~ (US); exhaust(ing) ~, extract ~ · Saugzugventilator *m*

~ ~ **water cooler** (Brit.); ~ draft ~ ~ (US) · Saugzugwasserkühler *m*

induction hardening · Induktionshärtung *f*

~ **heating** · induktive Erwärmung *f*

~ **unit** · (Hochdruck-)Induktionsgerät *n*

inductive effect [*screen*] · induktive Beeinflussung *f* [*Sieb*]

indurated talc · Schiefertalk *m*

industrial acid · Industriesäure *f*

~ **adhesive,** ~ glue · Industrieleim *m*

~ **architect** · Industriearchitekt *m*

~ **architecture** · Industriearchitektur *f,* Industriebaukunst *f*

~ **art** · Kunstindustrie *f*

~ **asphalt(ic) tile** · Asphalt(belag)platte *f* für Industrie(fuß)böden, Asphaltfliese *f* ~ ~

~ **atmosphere;** ~ vapours (Brit.); ~ vapors (US) · Industrieatmosphäre *f,* Industrieluft *f*

~ **block** → ~ (frame(d)) ~

~ ~, ~ building, factory ~ · Industriegebäude *n,* Werkgebäude, Fabrikgebäude

~ **building** → ~ (frame(d)) block

~ ~, ~ block, factory ~ · Industriegebäude *n,* Werkgebäude, Fabrikgebäude

~ ~, prefab(ricated) ~ · Elementhochbau *m,* Montagehochbau, Fertig(teil)-hochbau, Hochbau mit Fertigteilen

~ **buildings and structures** · Industriebauten *f*

~ **burning appliance,** ~ fire, ~ furnace · technische Feuerung *f,* ~ Feuerstätte *f*

~ **centralization** · Industrieballung *f*

~ **chemical** · Industriechemikalie *f*

~ **chimney,** ~ stack, factory ~, (chimney) stack, chimney stalk, chimney fun, big chimney · (Fabrik)Esse *f,* (Fabrik-)Schlot *m,* (Fabrik)Kamin *m,* Fabrikschornstein *m,* Industrieschornstein, freistehender Schornstein

~ **construction** · Industriebau *m*

~ ~ **project** · Industriebauvorhaben *n,* Industriebauprojekt *n*

~ ~ **site** · Industriebaustelle *f*

~ **curtain wall** → industrial-type ~ ~

~ **decentralization** · Industrieentballung *f*

~ **design** · industrielle Form(geb)ung *f*

~ **dust** · Industriestaub *m,* technischer Staub

~ **exhaust system** · Industrieabluftanlage *f*

~ **extract ventilation unit,** ~ extraction ~, ~ extractor, ~ fan · Industrie(ent)lüfter *m*

~ **extraction unit,** ~ extract ventilation ~, ~ extractor, ~ fan · Industrie(ent)lüfter *m*

~ **extractor,** ~ extract ventilation unit, ~ extraction unit, ~ fan · Industrie(ent)lüfter *m*

~ **fan,** ~ extractor, ~ extract ventilation unit, ~ extraction unit · Industrie(ent)lüfter *m*

~ **finish** · Industrielackierung *f*

~ **fire,** ~ furnace, ~ burning appliance · technische Feuerung *f,* ~ Feuerstätte *f*

~ **fixture** → ~ luminaire (~)

~ **floor** · Industrie(stockwerk)decke *f,* Industrietrenndecke, Industrieetagendecke, Industriegebäudedecke, Industriegeschoßdecke

~ **floor(ing) (finish),** ~ floor cover(-ing) · Industrie(fuß)boden(belag) *m,* Betriebs(fuß)boden(belag), Werk(fuß)boden(belag), Fabrik(fuß)boden(-belag)

~ ~ **tile** · Betriebs(fuß)bodenfliese *f,* Industrie(fuß)bodenfliese, Industrie-(fuß)bodenplatte, *f* Betriebs(fuß)bodenplatte, Werk(fuß)bodenplatte, Werk(fuß)bodenfliese, Fabrik(fuß)bodenplatte, Fabrik(fuß)bodenfliese

~ **(frame(d)) block,** factory (~) ~, ~ (~) building, ~ hangar · Rahmenhalle *f,* Werk~, Werkhalle, Industrie-(rahmen)halle, (Fabrikrahmen)Halle, Fabrikhalle

~ **furnace,** ~ fire, ~ burning appliance · technische Feuerung *f,* ~ Feuerstätte *f*

~ **garage** · Industriegarage *f*

~ **glass** · Industrieglas *n*

~ **glazing** · Industrieverglasung *f,* Industrieeinglasung

~ **glue,** ~ adhesive · Industrieleim *m*

~ **grade benzene** · Lösungsbenzol *n*

~ ~ **block,** ~ parquet(ry) ~ · Parkettstab *m* für gewerbliche Räume [*DIN 280*]

~ **ground** · Industriegelände *n,* Werkgelände, Fabrikgelände

~ **heat** · Industriewärme *f*

517 industrial heating — industrialized housing (construction)

~ heating · Industrieheizung f
~ ~ facility, ~ ~ system ~ ~ installation · Industrieheiz(ungs)anlage f, Industrieheiz(ungs)einrichtung f
~ hygiene, factory ~ · Arbeitshygiene f, Industriehygiene
~ kitchen · Werkküche f
~ laminate(d) board, ~ ~ sheet · technische Schichtpreßstoffplatte f
~ light fitting (Brit.) → ~ luminaire (fixture)
~ (light(ing)) fixture → ~ luminaire (~)
~ lime · Industriekalk m
~ luminaire (fixture) (US); ~ light fitting (Brit.); ~ (light(ing)) fixture · Fabrikbeleuchtungskörper m, Fabrikleuchte f
~ mastic floor(ing) (or floor finish, or floor cover(ing)) containing (asphaltic) bitumen (Brit.) (or asphalt (US)) emulsion [It is laid cold and provides a tough and durable surface capable of resisting extremely severe impact as well as heavy point loads and continuous traffic wear] · Bitumenemulsions-Industrie(fuß)boden(belag) m, Kaltbitumen-Industrie(fuß)boden(belag)
~ meter · Industriezähler m
~ noise · Industrielärm m
~ paint · Industrie(anstrich)farbe f
~ parquet(ry) block, ~ grade ~ · Parkettstab m für gewerbliche Räume [DIN 280]
~ partition (wall) · Industrietrennwand f
~ pipe · Industrierohr n
~ plant · Industrieanlage f
~ premises, ~ property · bebautes Industriegrundstück n
~ property, ~ premises · bebautes Industriegrundstück n
~ quarter, manufacturing town, cité industrielle [Planned by Tony Garnier] · Industriestadt f
~ roof · Industriedach n
~ sewage · Industrieabwasser n, Industrieabwässer npl, industrielles Abwasser, industrielle Abwässer
~ shutter door · Industrietor n
~ site · Industriestandort m
~ space-heating · Industrieraumheizung f
~ stack → ~ chimney
~ stair(case) · Industrietreppe f
~ storied block, ~ ~ building · Industriegeschoßgebäude n
~ ~ building, ~ ~ block · Industriegeschoßgebäude n
~ structure · Industriebauwerk n
~ tile · Industrie(belag)platte f, Industriefliese f

~ (-type) curtain wall · Industrie-Vorhangwand f
~ vapours (Brit.); ~ vapors (US); ~ atmosphere · Industrieatmosphäre f, Industrieluft f
~ varnish · Industrielack m
~ wall tile · Industrie-Wand(belag)platte f, Industrie-Wandfliese f [Glasierte keramische Wandfliese, deren Scherben weiß oder elfenbeinfarbig bis gelb getönt sein kann und meist etwas gemahlene Schamotte enthält]
~ window · Industriefenster n

industrialization emigration (US); industrialisation ~ (Brit.) · Landflucht f

~ of building and civil engineering, ~ ~ construction industry (US) [British spelling is 'industrialisation'] · Industrialisierung f des Bauwesens
~ ~ construction industry → ~ ~ ~ building and civil engineering

industrialized (US); industrialised (Brit.) · industrialisiert
~ apartment building (US) → industrially-built block (of flats) (Brit.)
~ building (US); industrialised ~ (Brit.); ~ construction, prefab(ricated) ~, system ~ · Bauen n mit Fertigteilen, ~ Montageteilen, Fertig(teil)bau m, Montage(teil)bau [Fehlname: Elementbau]
~ (~) construction (US) → system (~) ~
~ concrete construction (US) → (pre)cast (concrete) ~
~ ~ house building factory (US); industrialised ~ ~ ~, ~ (Brit.) · Betonwerk n für Fertighäuser
~ ~ system construction (US) → (pre)cast (concrete) ~
~ construction (US) → ~ building
~ ~ method (US); system ~ ~, prefab(ricated) ~ ~ [British spelling is, "industrialised"] · Fertig(teil)bauweise f, Montagebauweise Fertig(teil)bauverfahren n, Montagebauverfahren [Fehlnamen: Elementbauweise, Elementbauverfahren]
~ domestic construction, ~ housing (~) (US); prefab(ricated) ~ (~) [British spelling is "industrialised"] · industrialisierter Wohn(ungs)bau m, ~ Wohnhausbau, ~ WBau, Fertig(teil)wohn(ungs)bau, Montage(wohn(ungs))bau
~ façade (US); system-built ~, prefab(ricated) ~ [British spelling is 'industrialised"] · Fertigfassade f, Montagefassade; Elementfassade [Fehlname]
~ garage (US); system-built ~, prefab(ricated) ~ [British spelling is "industrialised"] · Fertig(bau)garage f; Elementgarage [Fehlname]
~ housing (construction), ~ domestic ~ (US); prefab(ricated) ~ (~) [British spelling is "industrialised"] industrialisierter Wohn(ungs)bau m,

industrialized housing ... — infill(ing) concrete

~ Wohnhausbau, ~ WBau, Fertig-(teil)woh(nungs)bau, Montage-wohn(ungs)bau

~ **prestressed concrete (system) construction** (US) → (pre)cast prestressed (concrete) ~

~ **R.C. construction** (US) → (pre-)cast reinforced (concrete) ~

~ ~ ~ **system construction** (US) → (pre)cast reinforced (concrete) ~

~ **reinforced concrete (system) construction** (US) → (pre)cast reinforced (concrete) ~

~ **structure** (US); prefab(ricated) ~, system-built ~ [*British spelling is "industrialised"*] · Fertig(teil)bau(werk) *m*, (*n*) Montagebau(werk) Systembau(werk); Elementbau(werk) [*Fehlnamen*]

~ **wall** (US); system-built ~, prefab(-ricated) ~ [*British spelling is "industrialised"*] · Fertigwand *f*, Montagewand; Elementwand [*Fehlname*]

industrially-built block (of flats), industrialised ~ (~ ~), ~ flats (Brit.); industrialized apartment building (US) · (Beton-)Fertig(teil)-Mehrfamilienhaus *n*

industrially manufactured house, factory-built ~ · industriell gefertigtes Haus *n*

inelastic, plastic, nonelastic · nichtelastisch, unelastisch, plastisch

~ **behaviour,** plastic ~, nonelastic ~ (Brit.); ~ behavior (US) [*Deformation that does not disappear on removal of the force that produced it*] · plastisches Verhalten *n*, unelastisches ~, nichtelastisches ~

~ **deflection** → ~ deflexion

~ **deflexion,** ~ deflection, creep ~, nonelastic ~, plastic ~ · Kriechdurchbiegung *f*, Kriechdurchsenkung, plastische Durchbiegung, plastische Durchsenkung

~ **deformation,** creep ~, nonelastic ~, plastic ~ · plastische Verformung *f*, ~ Formänderung, Kriechverformung, Kriechformänderung

~ **problem,** nonconservative ~ · nichtkonservative Aufgabe *f*, nichtkonservatives Problem *n*

~ **range,** nonelastic ~, plastic ~ · unelastischer Bereich *m*, nichtelastischer ~, unelastisches ~ *n*, nichtelastisches ~, plastischer ~ *m*, plastisches ~ *n*

~ **strain,** plastic ~, nonelastic ~, creep ~ · (positive) Kriechdehnung *f*, plastische Dehnung

~ **system,** nonconservative ~ · nichtkonservatives System *n*

(inert) filler, (~) filling material [*An adulterant or base used in paint to regulate weight and cost: barytes, calcium carbonate, charcoal, gypsum, etc.*] · Füllstoff *m*, Füller *m*

(~) **filling material,** (~) filler [*An adulterant or base used in paint to regulate weight and cost: barytes, calcium carbonate, charcoal, gypsum, etc.*] · Füllstoff *m*, Füller *m*

~ **gas** · Edelgas *n*

~ ~ **luminous tube light** · Edelgas-Leuchtröhre *f*

~ **pigment** → (paint) extender

inertia · Beharrungsvermögen *n*, Trägheit(svermögen) *f*, (*n*)

~ **force** · Trägheitskraft *f*

~ **modulus,** modulus of inertia · Trägheitsmodul *m*

~ **resistance** · Trägheitswiderstand *m*

infant's bath, children's ~ · Kinderbad *n*

~ **(bath)tub,** children's ~, ~ bath · Kinder(bade)wanne *f*

inferential meter · Turbinenzähler *m*

infestation, attack [*The presence, within or contiguous to, a structure or premises of insects, rodents, vermin or other pests*] · Befall *m*

~ (US); insect outbreak, insect attack · Insektenbefall *m*

~ **by termites** · Termitenbefall *m*

infill block → (in)filler ~

~ **brick** → infill(ing) ~

~ **panel** → (in)filler ~

~ **slab** → (in)filler

~ **tile** → (in)filler block

~ **wall** → (in)filler ~

~ ~, panel ~, cladding · Aufachung *f*, Ausfüllung [*Süddeutschland: Ausriegelung*]

(in)filler block, infill(ing) ~, ~ tile [*See remark under 'Block'*] · Ausfachungsblock *m*, (Aus)Füll(ungs)block, (Aus)Füll(ungs)(block)stein *m*, Aufachungs(block)stein

~ **brick** → infill(ing) ~

~ **concrete panel,** infill(ing) ~ ~ · Ausfachungsbetonafel *f*, (Aus)Füll(ungs)betontafel

~ **masonry (work)** → infill(ing) ~ (~)

~ **material** → infill(ing) ~

~ **panel,** infill(ing) ~ · (Aus)Füll(ungs)-tafel *f*, Ausfachungstafel

~ **slab,** infill(ing) ~ · Ausfachungsplatte *f*, (Aus)Füll(ungs)platte

~ **tile** → ~ block

~ **wall,** infill(ing) ~, panel ~ · Ausfachung *f*, Ausfüllung [*Süddeutschland: Ausriegelung*]

infilling · Ausfüllen *n*; Ausriegeln [*Süddeutschland*]

infill(ing) block → (in)filler ~

~ **brick,** (in)filler ~ · Ausfachungsziegel *m*, (Aus)Füll(ungs)ziegel

~ **concrete** · Ausfachungsbeton *m*, (Aus)Füll(ungs)beton

infill(ing) concrete panel — infusible

~ ~ panel, (in)filler ~ ~ · Ausfachungsbetontafel *f*, (Aus)Füll(ungs)betontafel

~ masonry (work), (in)filler ~ (~) · Ausfachungsmauerwerk *n*, Mauerwerkausfachung *f*, Mauerwerkausfüllung, (Aus)Füll(ungs)mauerwerk, (Fachwerk)Ausmauerung

~ material, (in)filler ~ · Ausfachungs(bau)stoff *m*, (Aus)Füll(ungs)(bau)stoff [*Süddeutschland*: *Ausriegelungs(bau)stoff*]

~ panel, (in)filler ~ · (Aus)Füll(ungs)tafel *f*, Ausfachungstafel

(infilling) panel [*A panel is formed by the structural columns and beams of a framed building*] · Fach *n*

infill(ing) slab → (in)filler ~

~ tile → (in)filler block

~ wall, (in)filler ~, panel ~ · Ausfachung *f*, Ausfüllung [*Süddeutschland: Ausriegelung*]

infinite number · unendliche Anzahl *f*

~ plate, ~ slab · unendliche Platte *f*

~ series · unendliche Reihe *f*

~ slab, ~ plate · unendliche Platte *f*

~ strip · unendlicher Streifen *m*

infinitely · unendlich

~ small resultant · unendlich kleine Mittelkraft *f*

infinitesimal deformation · infinitesimale Formänderung *f*

~ displacement · unendliche Verrückung *f*

infinity plug · Dosenstecker *m*

(in)firmary · Infirmeria *f*, Krankenhaus *n* [*Teil eines Klosters*]

~ for lay brethren · Laienkrankenhaus *n*, Laienfirmaria *f*

(in)flammability · Entzündbarkeit *f*, Entflammbarkeit

(in)flammable [*The term 'flammable' is sometimes preferred to 'inflammable' because of the possibility of confusion over the prefix in-, which in most words is a negative, meaning not, non, or un-*] · entflammbar, entzündlich

inflatable · aufblasbar

~ building, air-inflated ~, air-supported ~, ~ structure, pneumatic ~ · Pneusystem *n*, luftgetragene Halle *f*, luftgestützte Halle, Traglufthalle, luftgestütztes System *n*, Pneusystem

~ rubber tube → deflatable ~ ~

~ structure → ~ building

inflection (US); inflexion (Brit.); contraflexure · Wendekrümmung *f*

inflexion (Brit.); inflection (US); contraflexure · Wendekrümmung *f*

inflow of water · Wasserzufluß *m*

influence · Einfluß *m*

~ area, ~ surface, ~ field · Einflußfeld *n*, Einflußfläche *f*

~ chart · Einflußtafel *f*, Einflußtabelle *f*

~ coefficient · Einflußbeiwert *m*, Einflußfunktion *f*, Einflußzahl *f*

~ diagram · Einflußdiagramm *n*

~ field, ~ surface, ~ area · Einflußfeld *n*, Einflußfläche *f*

~ line, line of influence · Einflußlinie *f*, Greensche Funktion *f*

~ ~ analysis · Einflußlinienverfahren *n*

~ ~ for an arch · Bogeneinflußlinie *f*

~ ~ of reactions, A-line · Einflußlinie *f* der Auflagerkraft, A-Linie

~ of heat, heat influence · Wärmeeinfluß *m*

~ ordinate · Einflußordinate *f*

~ surface, ~ field, ~ area · Einflußfeld *n*, Einflußfläche *f*

~ ~ point · Aufpunkt *m*

~ value · Einflußgröße *f*, Einflußwert *m*

~ zone · Einflußbereich *m*, *n*, Einflußzone *f*

information counter · Informationsstand *m*

~ sheet · Übersichtstabelle *f*

~ show · Beispielschau *f*

infrared drying, ~ stoving, radiant heat ~ [*A stoving treatment in which heat is transferred to the paint surface mainly by radiation from a hot surface, e.g. electric lamps or gas heated panels*] · Infrarottrocknung *f*

~ ~ by electric lamps, ~ stoving ~ ~ ~, radiant heat ~ ~ ~ ~ ~ · Trocknung *f* durch Hellstrahler

~ ~ ~ gas heated panels, ~ stoving ~ ~ ~ ~, radiant heat ~ ~ ~ ~ ~ · Trocknung *f* durch Gasglühstrahler, ~ ~ Hochtemperaturstrahler

~ fire → ~ heating appliance

~ heater → ~ heating appliance

~ heating *f* · Höchsttemperatur-Strahlungsheizung *f*, Infrarotheizung

~ ~ appliance, ~ ~ unit, ~ ~ device, ~ warming ~, ~ heater, ~ fire, ~ warmer · Höchsttemperatur-Strahlungsheizer *m*, Infrarotheizer

~ radiation · Infrarotstrahlung *f*

~ spectroscopy [*Use of spectrophotometer for determination of infrared absorption spectra (2.5 to 18 micron wave lengths) of materials. Used for detection, determination, and identification of organic materials and the reaction between organic admixture and concrete components*] · Infrarot-Spektroskopie *f*

~ stoving → ~ drying

~ ~ by electric lamps → ~ drying ~ ~ ~

~ warmer → ~ heating appliance

~ warming appliance → ~ heating ~

infrasonics · Infraschall *m*

infusible · nichtschmelzbar, unschmelzbar

infusorial earth — initial set(ting) test

infusorial earth · Infusorienerde f

ingle [*A medieval Scotch word for a fire upon a hearth against a wall*]; hearth fire · Kaminfeuer n

~-nook [*Scotland*]; chimney-corner · Kamin(sitz)ecke f

ingoing, jamb · Gewändepfosten m, Gewändesäule f, Gewändeständer m

ingoings, jambs · Gewände n

ingot gold · Stangengold n

ingrain lining paper, engrain ~ ~ · Rauhfasermakulatur f

~ wallpaper, engrain ~ · Rauhfaser(tapete) f

~ ~ coat, engrain ~ ~ · Rauhfaseranstrich m, Rauhfaseraufstrich

ingredient · Inhaltsstoff m;

~ → mix(ture) component

ingress of dirt · Schmutzeintritt m

~ ~ liquid(s) · Flüssigkeitseintritt m

inherent concrete heat, natural ~ ~ · Betoneigenwärme f

~ heat, natural ~ · Eigenwärme f

~ moisture, natural ~, water of composition · Eigenfeuchte f, Eigenfeuchtigkeit f

~ ~ of aggregate(s), water contained in ~ · Eigenfeuchtigkeit f der (Beton-)Zuschläge, ~ ~ (Beton)Zuschlagstoffe

~ oscillation, ~ vibration, natural ~ · Eigenschwingung f

~ rigidity. ~ stiffness, natural ~ · Eigensteifigkeit f, Eigenstarrheit [*Statik*]

~ settlement [*The sinking of a foundation caused by the loads it superimposes on the soil below it, rather than by the loads on any adjacent foundation*] · Eigensetzung f

~ stiffness, ~ ridigity, natural ~ · Eigensteifigkeit f, Eigenstarrheit [*Statik*]

~ strength, natural ~ · Eigenfestigkeit f

~ stress, natural ~ · Eigenspannung f

~ vibration, ~ oscillation, natural ~ · Eigenschwingung f

inherently safe · eigensicher

inhibiting pigment, corrosion ~ ~ · korrosionshemmendes Pigment n

inhibitor · Hemmstoff m

initial acceptance · vorläufige Abnahme f

~ bending · Anfangsbiegung f

~ boiling point · Anfangssiedepunkt m

~ bond · Anfangsverbund m, Frühverbund, anfänglicher Verbund [*Spannbeton*]

~ ~ · Anfangshaftung f, Anfangsverbund m

~ buckling · Knickbeginn m

~ compressive strength, ~ crushing ~ · Anfangsdruckfestigkeit f

~ condition · Anfangsbedingung f

~ crushing strength, ~ compressive ~ · Anfangsdruckfestigkeit f

~ dehydration, water-smoking · Durchwärmung f, Vorwärmung, Schmauchen n [*Ziegelbrennen*]

~ displacement · Anfangsverrückung f

~ drying shrinkage, ~ water-loss ~ · Anfangsschrumpfen n [*als Vorgang*]

~ ~ ~, ~ water-loss ~ [*The difference between the length of a specimen — mo(u)lded and cured under stated conditions - its length when first dried to constant length, expressed as a percentage of the moist length*] · Anfangsschrumpfung f

~ equation · Ausgangsgleichung f

~ hardening, early ~ · Anziehen n [*Anfängliches Steifwerden des Betons oder Mörtels durch Aufquellen des Zements*]

~ ~ · Anfangserhärtung f

~ loading, early ~ · Erstbelastung f, Anfangsbelastung, Frühbelastung

~ (pre)stress [*The (pre)stress occurring in prestressed concrete members before any losses occur*] · Anfangs(vor)spannung f

~ set(ting) · Erstarren n, Erstarrung f [*Übergang aus dem plastischen in den festen Zustand. Siehe Anmerkung unter "Abbinden"*]

~ ~ capacity → power of initial set(ting)

~ ~ curve, curve of initial set(ting) · Erstarrungskurve f [*Siehe Anmerkung unter "Abbinden"*]

~ ~ energy, energy of initial set(ting) · Erstarrungsenergie f [*Beton; Mörtel*]

~ ~ heat, heat of initial set(ting) · Erstarrungswärme f [*Beton; Mörtel*]

~ ~ of cement · Zementerstarrung f

~ ~ period → time of initial set(ting)

~ ~ power → power of initial set(ting)

~ ~ process, process of initial set(ting) · Erstarrungsvorgang m, Erstarrungsverlauf m, Erstarrungsprozeß m, Erstarrungsablauf

~ ~ property → power of initial set(ting)

~ ~ quality → power of initial set(ting)

~ ~ rate, rate of initial set(ting) · Erstarrungsgeschwindigkeit f [*Beton; Mörtel*]

~ ~ reaction, reaction of initial set(ting) · Erstarrungsreaktion f [*Beton; Mörtel*]

~ ~ shrinkage · Erstarrungsschwindung f

~ ~ test · Erstarrungsprobe f, Erstarrungsprüfung f, Erstarrungsversuch m [*Beton; Mörtel*]

~ ~ time → time of initial set(ting)

~ stage · Anfangsstadium *n*

~ state · Anfangszustand *m*

~ ~ of stress · Anfangsspannungszustand *m*

~ strain · Anfangsdehnung *f*

~ strength, green ~ · Anfangsfestigkeit *f*

~ stress → **~ pre~**

~ temperature · Anfangstemperatur *f*

~ water-loss shrinkage → **~ drying ~**

initially slow-setting · langsamerstarrend [*hydraulisches Bindemittel*]

injection agent → grouting ~

~ aid → grouting agent

~ cement → grouting ~

~ gun, grouting ~ · Injektions(spritz)-pistole *f*, Einpreß(spritz)pistole, Injektionsspritze, Einpreßspritze *f*, Auspreß(spritz)pistole, Verpreß(spritz)pistole, Auspreßspritze, Verpreßspritze, Injizier(spritz)pistole, Injiziersspritze

~ material · Auspreßgut *n*, Einpreßgut, Verpreßgut, Injektionsgut, Injiziergut

~ method · Auspreßverfahren *n*, Verpreßverfahren, Einpreßverfahren, Injektionsverfahren, Injizierverfahren

~ mortar → intrusion ~

~ moulding (Brit.); **~** molding (US) · Spritzgießen *n*

~ ~ (Brit.); **~** molding (US) · Spritzguß *m*

~ resin, grouting ~ · Injektionsharz *n*, Einpreßharz, Auspreßharz, Verpreßharz, Injizierharz [*Zum monolithischen Verbund von Rissen in Beton, Betonfertigteilen und Zementestrichen*]

inlaid lino(leum) [*The pattern is produced by pigments in the composition and does not wear off. It was introduced in 1880*] · Inlaidlinoleum *n*

inlaid-strip floor cover(ing) → (wood-)strip flooring

inlaid vinyl goods, ~ ~ products [*Such as floor coverings*] · Einrakelware *f*

inlay, marquetry, marqueterie [*Inlay is a method of enrichment by the insertion, or inlaying, of one material into another in order to provide a decorative contrast*] · Einlegearbeit *f*, Marketerie *f*, eingelegte Arbeit

~, incrustation · Inkrustation *f* [*Steineinlagen in Stein*]

~, mosaic woodwork, (in)tarsia · Intarsia *f*, Holzeinlegearbeit *f*

~ work of coloured marble (Brit.); **~ ~ ~** colored **~** (US) · Einlegearbeit *f* aus buntem Marmor

inlet, gull(e)y · (Regen)Wasserablauf *m*, Regen(wasser)einlauf, Sinkkasten *m*, Gully *m* [*DIN 4052*]

~, junction, branch, pipe ~ · (Rohr)Abzweig *m*, (Rohr)Zulauf *m*

~ air block → **~ ~** tile

~ ~ tile, ~ ~ block [*See remark under 'Block'*] · Belüftungsblock(stein) *m*, Belüftungsstein

~ compartment · Einlaufkammer *f*

~ grate, gull(e)y ~, drain(age) ~, draining ~, discharge ~, ~ grid, ~ grating · Ablaufrost *m*, Einlaufrost, Gullyrost, Sinkkastenrost, Abflußrost, Entwässerungsrost

~ grating → **~** grate

~ grid → **~** grate

~ grille, supply (air) ~ · Zuluftgitter *n*

~ opening, gull(e)y ~ · Einlauföffnung *f*, Ablauföffnung

~ pipe · Zulaufrohr *n*

~ surround, gull(e)y ~ · Einlaufeinfassung *f*, Ablaufeinfassung

inmost shadow · Kernschatten *m*

inn, hostel(ry) · Herberge *f*

inner air, interior ~, room ~, internal ~, inside ~, indoor ~ · Zimmerluft *f*, Raumluft

~ ~ cooler → inside ~ ~

~ aisle, ~ side ~, ~ nave ~ · inneres (Seiten)Schiff *n*, innere Abseite *f* [*Kirche*]

~ arch, inside ~, interior ~, internal ~ · Innenbogen *m*

~ bending moment → internal ~ ~

~ (building) board → interior ~ ~

~ (~) panel → interior (~) ~

~ (~) sheet → interior building board

~ chlorinated rubber paint, indoor ~ ~ ~, inside ~ ~ ~, internal ~ ~ ~, interior ~ ~ ~ · Innen-Chlorkautschukfarbe *f*

~ climate → inside ~

~ coat, inside ~, internal ~, interior ~ · Innenanstrich *m*, Innenaufstrich

~ ~ of paint → interior paint coat

~ column, internal ~, inside ~, interior ~ · Innensäule *f*

~ core, internal ~, inside ~, interior ~ · Innenkern *m*

~ corner, inside ~, internal ~, interior ~ · Innenecke *f*

~ corridor, inside ~, internal ~, interior ~ · Innenkorridor *m*

~ court, inside ~, interior ~, internal ~, central ~ [*An open, outdoor space enclosed on all sides by exterior walls of a building or by exterior walls and property lines on which walls are allowable*] · Innenhof *m*

inner curtain (wall) — inner wall surface

~ **curtain (wall)**, ~ enceinte (~) · Innenkurtine f; Innenmittelwall m; Innenmittelmauer f [mittelalterlicher Festungsbau]

~ **decor**, internal ~, indoor ~, inside ~, interior ~ · Innengestaltung f [Als Ergebnis des Innengestaltens]

~ **decorating**, interior ~, inside ~, internal ~, indoor ~ · Innengestalten n,

~ **dimension** → clear ~

~ **door**, interior ~, inside ~, internal ~ · Innentür f

~ **emulsion paint**, inside ~ ~, indoor ~ ~, internal ~ ~, interior ~ ~ · Innen-Emulsionsfarbe f

~ **enceinte (wall)**, ~ curtain (~) · Innenkurtine f; Innenmittelwall m; Innenmittelmauer f [mittelalterlicher Festungsbau]

~ **facing** → ~ lining

~ **fibreboard finish** (Brit.) → interior fiberboard ~

~ **finish(ing) paint** → interior ~ ~

~ **fixtures**, internal ~, inside ~, interior ~ · Innenausbau(ten) m, (f), innerer Ausbau [Als Ergebnis der (Innen-)Ausbauarbeiten]

~ **gallery**, interior ~, inside ~, internal ~ · Innen-Laubengang m

~ ~ **apartment building**, inside ~ ~ ~, interior ~ ~ ~, internal ~ ~ ~ · Innen-(Lauben)ganghaus n

~ **garden**, interior ~, internal ~ · Innengarten m

~ **glass door**, internal ~ ~, inside ~ ~, interior ~ ~, indoor ~ ~ ~ · Innenglastür f

~ **glazing** → internal ~

~ **gloss (clear) varnish** → interior ~ (~)

~ **handrail** → internal ~

~ **hardboard finish**, inside ~ ~, internal ~ ~, interior ~ ~ · Innen-Hart(faser)plattenbelag m, Innen-(Holz)Faserhartplattenbelag

~ **heat** → room ~

~ ~ **gain** → internal ~ ~

~ **humidity** → indoor moisture

~ **illumination** → indoor lighting

~ **insulation**, inside ~, internal ~, interior ~ · Innenisolierung f

~ ~, internal ~, inside ~, interior ~ · Innendämmung f

~ **joinery**, inside ~, internal ~, interior ~ · Innen-Holzeinbauten f

~ **layout** → internal ~

~ **lighting** → indoor ~

~ **lining**, ~ (sur)facing, internal ~, interior ~, inside ~ · Innenauskleidung f, Innenverkleidung, Innenbekleidung

~ **marble**, interior ~, inside ~, indoor ~, internal ~ · Innenmarmor m, Marmor für Innenverkleidungen

~ **masonry (dividing) wall** → internal ~ (~) ~

~ **moisture** → indoor ~

~ **nave aisle**, ~ (side) ~ · inneres (Seiten)Schiff n, innere Abseite f [Kirche]

~ **noise**, inside ~, indoor ~, internal ~, interior ~ · Innenlärm m, Hauslärm, Gebäudelärm

~ ~, internal ~, inside ~, interior ~ · Innengeräusch n, Gebäudegeräusch, Hausgeräusch

~ **paint**, inside ~, internal ~ · Innen(anstrich)farbe f

~ ~ **coat** → interior ~ ~

~ **panel** → interior (building) ~

~ **partitioning** → (interior) ~

~ **piping**, interior ~, indoor ~, internal ~, inside ~ · Innenrohrleitung f

~ **primer**, inside ~, internal ~, interior ~ · Innen-Grundanstrichmittel n, Innen-Grundanstrichstoff m, Innen-Grundiermittel, Innen-Grundierstoff, Innen-Grund(ierung) m, (f)

~ **product, scalar** ~ · skalares Produkt n, inneres ~, Skalarprodukt

~ **redecoration**, inside ~, internal ~, interior ~, indoor ~ · Innenrenovierung f

~ **relative moisture**, ~ ~ humidity, interior ~ ~, inner ~ ~, indoor ~ ~, room ~ ~ · Raumluftfeuchte f, Raumluftfeuchtigkeit f

~ **reveal**, inside ~, internal ~, interior ~ · Innenleibung f, Innenlaibung

~ **seal(ing)**, internal ~, inside ~, interior ~ · Innen(ab)dichtung f

~ **(side) aisle**, ~ nave ~ · inneres (Seiten)Schiff n, innere Abseite f [Kirche]

~ **skin**, inside ~, internal ~, interior ~ · Innenhaut f

~ **slatted blind**, interior ~ ~, inside ~ ~, indoor ~ ~, internal ~ ~ · Innenjalousie f

~ **stairrail** → internal handrail

~ **stud**, interior ~, inside ~, internal ~ · Innenpfosten m [Fachwerkwand]

~ **surface of arch** → (arch) intrados

~ ~ ~ **vault(ing)**, soffit ~ ~, underside ~ ~, (vault(ing)) intrados [The inner line or surface of the concave side of a vaulting] · innere Wölbungsfläche f, ~ Gewölbefläche

~ **(sur)facing** → ~ lining

~ **temperature control**, indoor ~ ~, internal ~ ~, interior ~ ~, room ~ ~, inside ~ ~ · Raumtemperatursteuerung f, Innentemperatursteuerung

~ **tile**, indoor ~, inside ~, internal ~, interior ~ · Innen(belag)platte f, Innenfliese f

~ **tracery** → internal ~

~ **wall surface** → interior ~ ~

inner window — inside decor

~ **window,** interior ~, inside ~, internal ~ · Innenfenster n [*Bei einem Doppelfenster*]

~ ~ **cill** (Brit.) → interior window sill

~ ~ **frame,** inside ~ ~, interior ~ ~, internal ~ ~, indoor ~ ~ · Innenfensterrahmen m

~ ~ **sill** → interior ~ ~

~ **work** → finishings and services

innermost part, sanctuary · Sanktuarium n, Allerheiligste n [*Der Platz des Altars in altchristlichen Kirchen*]

inodorous; odor(-)free (US); odour(-)free (Brit.) · geruchlos, geruchfrei

inorganic · anorganisch

~ **acid** . anorganische Säure f

~ **aggregate** → ~ concrete ~

~ ~ → ~ construction ~

~ **building material** → ~ constructional ~

~ **(concrete) aggregate** · (Beton)Zuschlag(stoff) m ohne ausglühbare Bestandteile, (Beton)Zuschlagmaterial n ~ ~ ~, anorganisches (Beton)Zuschlagmaterial, anorganischer (Beton-)Zuschlag(stoff)

~ **(construction) aggregate** · Zuschlag(stoff) m ohne ausglühbare Bestandteile, Zuschlagmaterial n ~ ~ ~

~ **constructional material,** ~ building ~, ~ structural ~ · anorganischer Baustoff m; anorganisches Baumaterial n [*Schweiz*]

~ **fibre board** (Brit.); ~ fiber ~ (US) · anorganische Faserplatte f

~ **heat insulating material,** ~ ~ insulation(-grade) ~, ~ ~ insulator, ~ ~ insulant · anorganischer Wärmedämmstoff m, anorganisches Wärmedämmaterial n

~ **insulation(-grade) material,** ~ insulating ~, ~ insulator, ~ insulant · anorganischer Dämmstoff m, anorganisches Dämmaterial n

~ **pigment** · anorganisches Pigment n [*Fehlnamen: anorganischer Farbkörper m, anorganische Körperfarbe f*]

~ **structural material** → ~ constructional ~

~ **synthetic dye(stuff)** · künstlicher organischer Farbstoff m

in-place construction, insitu ~, in(-)situ ~ · Ortbau m

~ ~ **method,** in(-)situ ~ ~, insitu ~ ~ · Ortbauverfahren n

inquiry desk, enquiry ~ · Auskunftsschalter m

inrush of water, water inrush · Wasserandrang m, Wassereinbruch m

inscription, lettering · Beschriftung f, Inschrift f

insect attack, ~ outbreak; infestation (US) · Insektenbefall m

~ **cloth,** ~ screening ~ · Fliegengaze f, Fliegennetz n

~ **outbreak,** ~ attack; infestation (US) · Insektenbefall m

~ **proof** · insektenbeständig, insektenfest

~ **screen,** window ~ · Fenstergaze f

~ **screening** [*of doors and windows*] · Fliegengazeschutz m, Fliegennetzschutz

~ **(~) cloth** · Fliegengaze f, Fliegennetz n

insecticide for timber, ~ ~ wood · insektenwidriges Holzschutzmittel n

insert, insertion · Einlage f, Träger(stoff) m

inserting, insertion · Einfügen n

insertion, inserting · Einfügung

insert(ion) · Einlage f, Träger(stoff) m

insertion thermostat, immersion ~ · Tauchthermostat m

in-service carbonation · Karbonatisierung f in eingebautem Zustand

inset balcony · zurückgesetzter Balkon m

~ **grate** · Einsatz m [*Eine geschlossene Feuerstätte*]

inside air, indoor ~, room ~, interior ~, internal ~, inner ~ · Zimmerluft f, Raumluft

~ ~ **cooler,** indoor ~ ~, room ~ ~, interior ~ ~, internal ~ ~, inner ~ ~ · Raumluftkühler m, Innenluftkühler

~ **arch,** inner ~, internal ~, interior ~ · Innenbogen m

~ **bath(room)** [*A bath(room) placed on the inside of a building*] · innenliegendes Bad(ezimmer) n

~ **board** → interior (building) ~

~ **building board** → interior ~ ~

~ **(~) panel** → interior (~) ~

~ **(~) sheet** → interior building board

~ **cellar wall** · Kellerinnenwand f

~ **chlorinated rubber paint,** indoor ~ ~ ~, inner ~ ~ ~, internal ~ ~ ~, interior ~ ~ ~ ~ · Innen-Chlorkautschukfarbe f

~ **climate,** indoor ~, internal ~, interior ~, room ~, inner ~ · Raumklima n, Innenklima

~ **coat,** inner ~, interior ~, internal ~ · Innenanstrich m, Innenaufstrich

~ ~ **of paint** → interior paint coat

~ **coating,** interior ~, internal ~ · Innenbeschichtung f, Innenüberzug m [*als Schicht*]

~ **column,** interior ~, inner ~, internal ~ · Innensäule f

~ **core,** inner ~, internal ~, interior ~ · Innenkern m

~ **corner,** inner ~, internal ~, interior ~ · Innenecke f

~ **corridor,** inner ~, internal ~, interior ~ · Innenkorridor m

~ **corrosion** → internal ~

~ **court** → inner ~

~ **decor,** interior ~, indoor ~, internal ~, inner ~ · Innengestaltung f [*Als Ergebnis des Innengestaltens*]

inside decorating — in(-)situ(-)cast aerated concrete

~ **decorating**, internal ~, indoor ~, interior ~, inner ~ · Innengestalten *n*
~ **dimension** → clear ~
~ **door**, interior ~, inner ~, internal ~ · Innentür *f*
~**-door lock**, room-door ~ · Zimmertürschloß *n*, Raumtürschloß, Stubentürschloß
inside emulsion paint, indoor ~ ~, inner ~ ~, internal ~ ~, interior ~ ~ · Innen-Emulsionsfarbe *f*
~ **facing** → inner lining
~ **fibreboard finish** (Brit.) → interior fiberboard ~
~ **finish(ing) paint** → interior ~ ~
~ **fixtures**, internal ~, inner ~, interior ~ · Innenausbau(ten) *m*, (*f*), innerer Ausbau [*Als Ergebnis der (Innen)Ausbauarbeiten*]
~ **gallery**, interior ~, inner ~, internal ~ · Innen-Laubengang *m*
~ ~ **apartment building** interior ~ ~ ~, internal ~ ~ ~, inner ~ ~ ~ · Innen(-Lauben)ganghaus *n*
~ **glass door**, interior ~ ~, indoor ~ ~, internal ~ ~, inner ~ ~ · Innenglastür *f*
~ **glazing** [*External glazing in which the glass is inserted from inside the building*] · Außenverglasung *f* von innen her, Außeneinglasung ~ ~ ~
~ ~ → internal ~
~ **gloss (clear) varnish** → interior ~ (~)
~ **handle** [*door*] · Innengriff *m*
~ **handrail** → internal ~
~ **hardboard finish**, inner ~ ~, internal ~ ~, interior ~ ~ · Innen-Hart(faser)plattenbelag *m*, Innen-(Holz)Faserhartplattenbelag
~ **heat** → room ~
~ ~ **gain** → internal ~ ~
~ **humidity** → indoor moisture
~ **illumination** → indoor lighting
~ **insulation**, inner ~, internal ~, interior ~ · Innenisolierung *f*
~ ~, internal ~, interior ~, inner ~ · Innendämmung *f*
~ **joinery**, inner ~, internal ~, interior ~ · Innen-Holzeinbauten *f*
~ **kitchen** · innenliegende Küche *f*
~ **layout** → internal ~
~ **lighting** → indoor ~
~ **lining** → inner ~
~ **marble**, interior ~, indoor ~, inner ~ · Innenmarmor *m*, Marmor für Innenverkleidungen
~ **masonry (dividing) wall** → internal ~ (~) ~
~ **moisture** → indoor ~
~ **noise**, internal ~, indoor ~, interior ~, inner ~ · Innenlärm *m*, Hauslärm, Gebäudelärm
~ ~, internal ~, inner ~, interior ~ · Innengeräusch *n*, Gebäudegeräusch, Hausgeräusch
~ **paint**, inner ~, interior ~, internal ~ · Innen(anstrich)farbe *f*
~ ~ **coat** → interior ~ ~
~ **panel** → interior (building) ~
~ **partitioning** → (interior) ~
~ **piping**, internal ~, indoor ~, interior ~, inner ~ · Innenrohrleitung *f*
~ **pressure pneumatic system reinforced by cables** · seilverstärktes Innendruckpneusystem *n*
~ ~ ~ ~ ~ ~ **membrane ribs** · rippenverstärktes Innendruckpneusystem *n*
~ ~ ~ ~ **with interior anchor points** · Innendruckpneusystem *n* mit innen gelegenen Abspannpunkten
~ **primer**, inner ~, internal ~, interior ~ · Innen-Grundanstrichmittel *n*, Innen-Grundanstrichstoff *m*, Innen-Grundiermittel, Innen-Grundierstoff Innen-Grund(ierung) *m*, (*f*)
~ **redecoration**, inner ~, internal ~, interior ~ · Innenrenovierung *f*
~ **reveal**, interior ~, inner ~, internal ~ · Innenleibung *f*, Innenlaibung
~ **seal(ing)**, internal ~, inner ~, interior ~ · Innen(ab)dichtung *f*
~ **sheet** → interior (building) board
~ **skin**, internal ~, interior ~, inner ~ · Innenhaut *f*
~ **slatted blind**, inner ~ ~, indoor ~ ~, interior ~ ~, internal ~ ~ · Innenjalousie *f*
~ **stairrail** → internal handrail
~ **stud**, internal ~, inner ~, interior ~ · Innnenpfosten *m* [*Fachwerkwand*]
~ **(sur)facing** → inner lining
~ **temperature control** → inner ~ ~
~ **tile**, inner ~, indoor ~, internal ~, interior ~ · Innen(belag)platte *f*, Innenfliese *f*
~ **tracery** → internal ~
~ **wall surface** → interior ~ ~
~ **window**, interior ~, inner ~, internal ~ · Innenfenster *n* [*Bei einem Doppelfenster*]
~ ~ **cill** (Brit.) → interior window sill
~ ~ **frame**, interior ~ ~, inner ~, internal ~ ~ · Innenfensterrahmen *m*
~ ~ **sill** → interior ~ ~
~ **work** → finishings and services ~
in(-)situ aerated concrete → cast(-)in(-)situ ~ ~
~ **architectural concrete** → cast-in-place ~ ~
~ **brickwork** [*As opposed to brick panels*] · Ort-Ziegelmauerwerk *n*
in(-)situ(-)cast, poured(-)in(-)place, cast(-)in(-)place, cast(-)in(-)situ · ortbetoniert, Ortbeton......
~ **aerated concrete** → cast(-)in(-)situ ~ ~

~ (~) architectural concrete → cast-in-place ~

~ (~) concrete, cast(-)in(-)situ ~, cast-in-place ~, site-placed ~, poured(-in-place) ~, field ~ ~ · Ortbeton m [DIN 1045]

~ (~) (~) balcony, cast(-)in(-)situ (~) ~, cast-in-place (~) ~, site-placed (~) ~, field ~ ~, poured(-in-place) (~) ~ · Ortbetonbalkon m

~ (~) (~) cable duct, cast(-)in(-)situ (~) ~ ~, cast-in-place (~) ~ ~, site-placed (~) ~ ~, field ~ ~ ~, poured(-in-place) (~) ~ ~ · Ortbetonkanal m

~ (~) (~) eave(s) unit cast(-)in(-)situ (~) ~ ~, (cast-)insitu (~) ~ ~, cast-in-place (~) ~ ~, site-placed (~) ~ ~, field ~ ~ ~, poured(-in-place) (~) ~ ~ · Ortbeton-Traufenteil m, n

~ (~) (~) filling cast(-)in(-)situ (~) ~, cast-in-place (~) ~, site-placed (~) ~, field ~ ~, poured(-in-place) (~) ~ · Ortbetonfüllung f

~ (~) (~) floor cast(-)in(-)situ (~) ~, cast-in-place (~) ~, site-placed (~) ~, field ~ ~, poured(-in-place) (~) ~ · Ortbetondecke f

~ (~) (~) frame, ~ (~) (~) framing, cast(-)in(-)situ (~) ~, cast-in-place (~) ~, site-placed (~) ~, field ~ ~, poured(-in-place) (~) ~ · Ortbetonrahmen m

~ (~) (~) rib(bed) floor, cast(-)in(-)situ (~) ~ ~, cast-in-place (~) ~ ~, site-placed (~) ~ ~, field ~ ~ ~, poured(-in-place) (~) ~ ~ · Ortbeton-Rippendecke f

~ (~) (~) shell, cast(-)in(-)situ (~) ~, cast-in-place (~) ~, site-placed (~) ~, field ~ ~, poured(-in-place) (~) ~ · Ortbetonschale f

~ (~) (~) stair(case), cast(-)in(-)situ (~) ~, cast-in-place (~) ~, site-placed (~) ~, field ~ ~, poured(-in-place) (~) ~ · Ortbetontreppe f

~ (~) (~) structure, cast(-)in(-)situ (~) ~, cast-in-place (~) ~, site-placed (~) ~, field ~ ~, poured(-in-place) (~) ~ · Ortbetonbauwerk n

~ (~) light(weight) concrete, cast(-)in(-)situ ~ ~, cast-in-place ~ ~, site-placed ~ ~, field ~ ~, poured(-in-place) ~ ~ · Ortleichtbeton m, Leicht-Ortbeton

~ (~) mortar, cast(-)in(-)situ ~, cast-in-place ~, site-placed ~, field ~, poured(-in-place) ~ · Ortmörtel m

~ (~) reinforced concrete, ~ (~) R. C., cast(-)in(-)situ ~ ~, cast-in-place ~ ~, site-placed ~ ~, field ~ ~, poured(-in-place) ~ ~ · Ort-Stahlbeton m, Stahlortbeton m

~ (~) (~) floor, ~ (~) R. C. ~, cast(-)in(-)situ ~ ~ ~, cast-in-place ~ ~ ~, site-placed ~ ~ ~, field ~ ~ ~, poured(-in-place) ~ ~ ~ · Ort-stahlbetondecke f, Stahlortbetondecke

~ concrete → cast ~ ~

~ ~ structural topping, structural in situ ~, structural concrete ~ · Konstruktions-Aufbeton m [Decke]

~ construction, insitu ~, in-place ~ · Ortbau m

~ construction method, insitu ~ ~, in-place ~ ~ · Ortbauverfahren n

~ floor cover(ing) → jointless floor(ing)

~ foam · Ortschaum m

~ foaming · An-Ort-Schäumen n, An-Ort-Schäumung f

~ light(weight) concrete · Ortleichtbeton m, Leichtortbeton

~ mortar · Ortmörtel m

~ prestressed concrete pile · Ort-Spannbetonpfahl m

~ R. C. lintel, ~ reinforced concrete ~, reinforced in-situ concrete ~ [deprecated: lintol] · Ort-Stahlbeton-Oberschwelle f, Ort-Stahlbetonsturz m

(~) structural topping (concrete) → topping (slab)

(~) ~ ~ (mortar), (structural mortar), topping (slab) · (Mörtel)Druckplatte f, (Mörtel)Druckschicht f

~ topping → topping (slab)

insolation, sun(light) penetration, incoming solar irradiation, entry of direct sunshine · Besonnung f, Sonneneinfall m, einfallende Sonnenstrahlung, Wärmeeinstrahlung

insoluble · unlöslich

~ in benzene → extrinsic insolubles

~ ~ carbon disulfide (US); ~ ~ ~ disulphide (Brit.) · unlöslich in SC_2

~ ~ water, water insoluble · wasserunlöslich

~ matter [misnomer: free carbon] · Unlösliche n [Fehlname: freier Kohlenstoff m]

~ organic dyestuff · unlöslicher organischer Farbstoff m

~ pigment · unlösliches Pigment n

~ residue · unaufgeschlossener Rückstand m

~ ~ [The material remaining after cement is treated successively with hydrochloric acid and sodium hydroxide solutions of specific concentrations for designated periods of time] · unlöslicher Rückstand m

inspection, visual ~ · Augenscheinnahme f

~ · Begehung f

~ → quality audit

~ chamber → cleaning ~

~ chart → (quality) control ~

~ cover, ~ plate, cleanout ~, cleaning ~, access ~, rodding ~ · Putzdeckel m, Reinigungsdeckel

~ directorate · Zentralprüfamt n

inspection eye — insulating board

~ eye, ~ opening, cleanout ~, cleaning ~, access ~, rodding ~ · Putzöffnung f, Reinigungsöffnung

~ fitting, cleanout ~, rodding ~, cleaning ~, access ~ · Putzformstück n, Reinigungsformstück

~ opening, ~ eye, cleanout ~, cleaning ~, access ~, rodding ~ · Putzöffnung f, Reinigungsöffnung

~ pipe, cleanout ~, cleaning ~, access ~, rodding ~ · Rohr n mit Putzöffnung

~ pit → cleaning chamber

~ plate, ~ cover, cleanout ~, cleaning ~, access ~, rodding ~ · Reinigungsdeckel m, Putzdeckel

~ plug, ~ screw, rodding ~, access ~, cleanout ~, cleaning ~ · Putzstopfen m, Reinigungsstopfen, Putzschraube f, Reinigungsschraube

~ screw, ~ plug, rodding ~, access ~, cleanout ~, cleaning ~ · Putzstopfen m, Reinigungsstopfen, Putzschraube f, Reinigungsschraube

~ staff → quality-control ~

~ tube, cleanout ~, rodding ~, cleaning ~, access ~ · Reinigungsrohr n, Putzrohr, Reinigungsstutzen m, Putzstutzen [*Formstück in Abflußleitungen zur Reinigung derselben. DIN 1986*]

instability, lability · Labilität f, Instabilität

~ coefficient → lability ~

~ due to sliding, lability ~ ~ ~ · Labilität f durch Gleiten, Instabilität ~ ~

~ ~ ~ uneven settlement, lability ~ ~ ~ ~ [*e.g. Leaning Tower of Pisa*] · Labilität f durch schiefe Setzung, Instabilität ~ ~

~ effect, lability ~ · Labilitätswirkung f, Instabilitätswirkung

~ number → lability coefficient

instable, unstable [*A description of a structure which is liable to fail as a whole, generally, by overturning or sliding*] · nichtstandsicher, beweglich, mobil, labil, instabil

~ frame, unstable ~ · labiles Netz n, bewegliches ~, instabiles ~ [*ebenes Fachwerk*]

installation → service(s) (and technical equipment)

~ · Einbau m

~, internal ~, gas ~ (Brit.) [*The gas pipes and appliances on the consumer's side of the control cock at the board's gas meter*] · Gasinstallation f

~ dimensions · Anschlußmaße npl

~ drawing · Einbauzeichnung f

~ for centrifugally cast concrete, ~ ~ spun ~ · Betonschleuderanlage f, Schleuderbetonanlage

~ ~ manufacturing prepared roofing, ~ ~ ~ ~ ready ~, ~ ~ ~ ~ composition ~, ~ ~ ~ roof(ing) felt · Dachpappenanlage f

~ ~ spun concrete, ~ ~ centrifugally cast ~ · Schleuderbetonanlage f, Betonschleuderanlage

~ pipe [*This term refers to any pipe between the primary meter and gas appliances*] · Installationsrohr n

~ work, internal ~ ~ (Brit.); gas ~ ~ · Gasinstallationsarbeiten fpl

~ ~, work for installing the building equipment · Installationsarbeiten fpl

installation(s) → service(s) (and technical equipment)

installer, fitter · Installateur m, Monteur

~ for heating installations, fitter ~ ~ ~ · Heizungsmonteur m, Heizungsinstallateur

instant bathroom (unit) · anschlußfertige Badezimmereinheit f

instantaneous gas water heater, non-storage ~ ~ ~, flow-type ~ ~ ~, ~ ~ ~ heating appliance · (Durchlauf-) Gaswasserheizer m, Geyser [*DIN 3368, 3369*]

~ loading, sudden ~, shock ~, impact ~, impulsive ~ · Stoßbelastung f

~ strain · Sofortdehnung f

~ warm water · Durchlaufwarmwasser n

~ water heater, non-storage ~ ~, flow-type ~ ~, ~ ~ heating appliance · Durchlauf-Wasserheizer m

instruction · Anleitung f, Anweisung

~ for erection (work) · Montageanweisung f

~ in draughtmanship; ~ ~ draftsmanship (US) · Zeichenunterricht m

instructional (work)shop, training ~ · Lehrwerkstatt f

instrument of expression · Ausdrucksmittel n

~ plumbing, optical ~ · optisches Loten n, optische Lotung f

insulant → insulating material

to insulate · (ab)dämmen

insulated heater wire · isolierter Heizleiter m aus Widerstandsdraht [*Elektro(fuß)bodenheizung*]

~ roof member assembly, IRMA [*Manufactured by Dow Chemical*] · IRMA-Dachaufbau m, wärmegedämmte Feuchtigkeits(ab)dichtung f

(~) steam curing cloche, (~) ~ ~ cover · Dampfhaube f [*Warmbehandlung von Beton*]

insulating · (Ab)Dämmen n [*als Tätigkeit*]

~, insulation · Isolieren n [*allgemein*]

~ aggregate for loose fill · Dämmschüttstoff m, Dämmschüttmaterial n

~ article → insulation(-grade) product

~ base · Isoliergrund m

~ block, insulation(-grade) ~, ~ tile [*See remark under 'Block'*] · Dämmblock(stein) m, Dämmstein

~ board, ~ slab, ~ sheet, insulation (-grade) ~ · Dämm(aterial)platte f, Dämmstoffplatte [*gegen Wärme, Kälte oder Schall*]

insulating board — insulating peat

~ ~, ~ sheet, ~ slab, insulation(-grade) ~ · Isolierplatte f

~ **brick**, insulation(-grade) ~ · Dämmziegel m, Dämmstein m

~ ~, insulation(-grade) ~ · Isolierziegel m, Isolierstein m

~ **building material** → ~ construction(al) ~

~ **capacity**, ~ quality, ~ property, ~ power · Dämmfähigkeit f, Dämmvermögen n

~ **ceiling**, insulation(-grade) ~ · Isolierdecke f

~ ~ **board**, insulation(-grade) ~ ~ · Isolierdeckenplatte f, Deckenisolierplatte

~ **coating** → insulation(-grade) ~

~ **compound**, insulation(-grade) ~ · Isolierkleb(e)masse f [*Kleb(e)masse zur Herstellung von Dichtungen mit Isolierbahnen*]

~ ~, insulation(-grade) ~ · Dämmasse f

~ ~, insulation(-grade) ~ · Isoliermasse f

~ **concrete**, insulation(-grade) ~ · Isolierbeton m

~ ~, insulation(-grade) ~ [*Concrete having low thermal conductivity, used as thermal insulation*] · Dämmbeton m

~ **construction(al) material**, insulation(-grade) ~ ~, ~ building ~, ~ structural ~ · Bauisolierstoff m, Isolierbaustoff; Isolierbaumaterial n, Bauisoliermaterial [*Schweiz*]

~ **core**, insulation(-grade) ~ · Dämmkern m

~ **cork**, insulation(-grade) ~ · Dämmkork m

~ **corkboard**, insulation(-grade) ~ · Dämmkorkplatte f, Korkdämmplatte

~ **cork sheet(ing)**, insulation(-grade) ~ ~ · Dämmkorkbahn f, Korkdämmbahn

~ **corrugated cardboard**, insulation (-grade) ~ ~ · Wellpapierplatte f [*organischer Dämmstoff*]

~ **course** → ~ layer

~ **door**, insulation ~ · Dämmtür f

~ **efficiency**, insulation ~ · Dämmwirkung f

~ **facing** → ~ lining

~ **felt**, insulation(-grade) ~ · Dämmfilz m

~ **fibre board** (Brit.); ~ fiber ~ (US) · Isolierfaserplatte f

~ **figure**, insulation ~, ~ value · Dämmwert m

~ ~, ~ value, insulation ~ · Isolierwert m

~ **floor** · Dämmdecke f

~ **flue brick** · Zugdämmziegel m

~ **foam**, insulation(-grade) ~ · Dämmschaum(stoff) m, Schaumdämmstoff

~ ~ **board**, ~ ~ sheet, insulation (-grade) ~ ~ · Dämmschaum(stoff)platte f, Schaumdämm(stoff)platte

~ ~ **sheet**, ~ ~ board, insulation (-grade) ~ ~ · Schaumdämm(stoff)platte f, Dämmschaum(stoff)platte

~ **foil**, insulation(-grade) ~ · Dämmfolie f

~ ~, insulation(-grade) ~ · Isolierfolie f

~ **glass**, insulation(-grade) ~, double ~ · Dämmglas n, Doppelglas, Isolierglas

~ **glaze**, insulation(-grade) ~ · Isolierglasur f

~ **glazing** · Dämmverglasung f, Dämmeinglasung, Doppelscheibenverglasung, Doppelscheibeneinglasung

~ ~ **unit**, heat-~ ~ ~ · Glas-Isoliereinheit f, Isolier-Glaseinheit

~ **gypsum**, insulation(-grade) ~ · Isoliergips m

~ ~ **board** → ~ (~) plasterboard

~ (~) **plasterboard**, ~ ~ board; ~ plate [*Scotland*] [*A gypsum plasterboard (except perforated type) with a bright metal veneer of low emissivity on one or both sides*] · Dämm-Gipskartonplatte f, Gipskarton-Dämmplatte

~ **insert(ion)**, insulation(-grade) ~ · Dämmeinlage f

~ ~, insulation(-grade) ~ · Isoliereinlage f

~ **jacket**, insulation(-grade) ~ · (Dämm-) Binde f

~ ~, insulation(-grade) ~ · (Isolier-) Binde f

~ **layer**, insulation(-grade) ~, ~ course · Dämmlage f, Dämmschicht f

~ **lead felt**, insulation(-grade) ~ ~ · Bleidämmpappe f

~ **lining**, ~ (sur)facing, insulation (-grade) ~ · Dämmauskleidung f, Dämmbekleidung, Dämmverkleidung

~ **masonry (work)** · Dämm-Mauerwerk n

~ **material**, insulation(-grade) ~, insulator, insulant · Dämmstoff m, Dämmmaterial n

~ ~, insulation(-grade) ~ · Isolierstoff m

~ **(mixed) plaster**, insulation(-grade) (~) ~ · Dämm(innen)(ver)putz m

~ (~) ~, insulation(-grade) (~) · Isolier(innen)(ver)putz m

~ **mortar**, insulation(-grade) ~ · Isoliermörtel m

~ ~, insulation(-grade) ~ · Dämmörtel m

~ **oil**, electrical ~ · Isolieröl n

~ **panel**, insulation(-grade) ~ · Dämmtafel f

~ ~, insulation(-grade) ~ · Isoliertafel f

~ **paper**, insulation(-grade) ~ [*See remark under 'Pappe'*] · Dämmpapier n

~ ~, insulation(-grade) ~ [*See remark under 'Pappe'*] · Dämmpappe f

~ **partition (wall)** · Dämmtrennwand f

~ **peat**, insulation(-grade) ~ · Dämmtorf m

insulating plank — insulation coating 528

~ **plank**, insulation(-grade) ~ · Dämmdiele *f*

~ **plaster** → ~ mixed ~

~ **plasterboard** → ~ gypsum ~

~ **plate** [*Scotland*] → ~ (gypsum) plasterboard

~ **powder**, insulation(-grade) ~ · Isolierpulver *n*

~ **power**, ~ capacity, ~ quality, ~ property · Dämmfähigkeit *f*, Dämmvermögen *n*

~ **product** → insulation(-grade) ~

~ **profile** → ~ section

~ **property**, ~ quality, ~ power, ~ capacity · Dämmfähigkeit *f*, Dämmvermögen *n*

~ **pumice**, insulation(-grade) ~ · Dämmbims *m*

~ ~ **gravel**, insulation(-grade) ~ ~ · Dämmbimskies *m* [*Gewaschener oder von Feinkorn befreiter Naturbimskies, aus dem Isolierschichten aus Bimsbeton hergestellt werden. Möglich ist auch die Verwendung als wärmedämmende Füllung*]

~ **quality**, ~ power, ~ capacity, ~ property · Dämmfähigkeit *f*, Dämmvermögen *n*

~ **refractory**, insulation(-grade) ~ [*A good grade of refractory fireclay brick with a large percentage of open pore space. This open pore space may be about 70–75 percent as compared to approximately 20 percent for high-duty fireclay brick*] · Isolierstein *m*

~ **roof fill**, insulation(-grade) ~ ~ · Dachdämmschüttung *f*

~ **roof(ing) material**, insulation (-grade) ~ ~ · Dachdämmstoff *m*

~ ~ **tile**, insulation(-grade) ~ ~ · Dachdämmstein *m*

~ **screed**, insulation(-grade) ~ · Isolierestrich *m* [*Schicht*]

~ ~, insulation(-grade) ~ · Dämmestrich *m* [*Schicht*]

~ ~ **material**, insulation(-grade) ~ ~ · Dämmestrich *m* [*Baustoff*]

~ ~ ~, insulation(-grade) ~ ~ · Isolierestrich *m* [*Baustoff*]

~ **section**, insulation(-grade) ~, pipe ~ ~ · (Rohr)Dämmschale *f*

~ ~, ~ shape, ~ unit, ~ trim, ~ profile, insulation(-grade) ~ · Dämmprofil *n*

~ **shape** → ~ section

~ **sheet**, ~ board, ~ slab, insulation (-grade) ~ · Isolierplatte *f*

~ **sheet(ing)**, insulation(-grade) ~ · Dämmbahn *f*

~ ~, insulation(-grade) ~ · Isolierbahn *f*

~ **skin**, insulation(-grade) ~ · Isolierhaut *f*

~ **slab**, ~ sheet, ~ board, insulation (-grade) ~ · Isolierplatte *f*

~ **straw board**, insulation(-grade) ~ ~ · Strohdämmplatte *f*

~ **strip**, insulation(-grade) ~ · Isolierstreifen *m*

~ ~, insulation(-grade) ~ · Dämmstreifen *m*

~ **structural material** → ~ construction(al) ~

~ ~ **panel**, insulation(-grade) ~ ~ · Isolier-Konstruktionstafel *f*

~ **(sur)facing** → ~ lining

~ **system** · Dämmkonstruktion *f*

~ **tile** → ~ block

~ **trim** → ~ section

~ **tube** · (elektrisches) Isolationsrohr *n*, (~) Isolierrohr

~ **unit** → ~ section

~ ~, insulation(-grade) ~ · Isolierelement *n*

~ ~, insulation(-grade) ~ · Dämmelement *n*

~ **value**, ~ figure, insulation ~ · Isolierwert *m*

~ ~, insulation ~, ~ figure · Dämmwert *m*

~ **varnish** [*A varnish specifically designed for insulation of electrical appliances formulated to have a high resistance to electrical passage*] · Isolierlack *m*

~ **wall** · Dämmwand *f*

~ **wallboard**, insulation(-grade) ~ · Dämmwandplatte *f*

~ **wallpaper**, insulation(-grade) ~ · Isoliertapete *f*

~ **window** · Dämmfenster *n*

~ **wool**, insulation(-grade) ~ · Dämmwolle *f*

insulation · (Ab)Dämmung *f* [*als Ergebnis der Tätigkeit*]

~, insulating · Isolieren *n* [*allgemein*]

~ · Isolierung *f* [*gegen Feuchtigkeit*]

~ **against oscillation**, ~ ~ vibration, vibration insulation, oscillation insulation · Schwingungsisolierung *f*, Erschütterungsisolierung

~ ~ **vibration**, ~ ~ oscillation, vibration insulation, oscillation insulation · Schwingungsisolierung *f*, Erschütterungsisolierung

~ **article** → insulation(-grade) product

~ **block** → insulating ~

~ **board** → insulating ~

~ **brick**, insulation-grade ~, insulating ~ · Isolierziegel *m*, Isolierstein *m*

~ **building material** → insulating construction(al) ~

~ **by aerated concrete**, aerated concrete insulation · Porenbetondämmung *f*

~ **ceiling**, insulation-grade ~, insulating ~ · Isolierdecke *f*

~ ~ **board**, insulation-grade ~ ~, insulating ~ ~ · Isolierdeckenplatte *f*, Deckenisolierplatte

~ **coating** → insulation(-grade) ~

insulation compound — insulation section

~ **compound**, insulation-grade ~, insulating ~ · Dämmasse *f*

~ ~, insulation-grade ~, insulating ~ · Isoliermasse *f*

~ ~, insulation-grade ~, insulating ~ · Isolierkleb(e)masse *f* [*Kleb(e)masse zur Herstellung von Dichtungen mit Isolierbahnen*]

~ **concrete** → insulating ~

~ **construction(al) material** → insulating ~ ~

~ **core** → insulating ~

~ **cork** → insulating ~

~ ~ **sheet(ing)** → insulating ~ ~

~ **corkboard** → insulating ~

~ **course** → insulating layer

~ **door**, insulating ~ · Dämmtür *f*

~ **efficiency**, insulating ~ · Dämmwirkung *f*

~ **facing** → insulating lining

~ **felt** → insulating ~

~ **figure**, ~ value, insulating ~ · Isolierwert *m*

~ ~, insulating ~, ~ value · Dämmwert *m*

~ **foam** → insulating ~

~ ~ **board** → insulating ~ ~

~ ~ **sheet** → insulating ~ ~

~ **foil** → insulating ~

~ **glass** → insulating ~

~ **glaze**, insulation-grade ~, insulating ~ · Isolierglasur *f*

insulation(-grade) article → ~ product

~ **asbestos-cement board**, ~ ~ sheet, insulating ~ ~; ~ cement asbestos ~ (US) · Asbestzement-Dämmplatte *f*, Dämm-Asbestzementplatte

~ **block** → insulating ~

~ **board**, ~ slab, ~ sheet, insulating ~ · Isolierplatte *f*

~ **brick**, insulating ~ · Dämmstein *m*, Dämmziegel *m*

~ ~, insulating ~ · Isolierziegel *m*, Isolierstein *m*

~ **building material** → insulating construction(al) ~

~ **ceiling**, insulating ~ · Isolierdecke *f*

~ ~ **board**, insulating ~ ~ · Isolierdeckenplatte *f*, Deckenisolierplatte

~ **cement asbestos board**, ~ ~ ~ sheet, insulating ~ ~ ~ (US); ~ asbestos-cement ~ · Asbestzement-Dämmplatte *f*, Dämm-Asbestzementplatte

~ **coating**, insulating ~ · Dämmbeschichtung *f*

~ **compound**, insulating ~ · Isolierkleb(e)masse *f* [*Kleb(e)masse zur Herstellung von Dichtungen mit Isolierbahnen*]

~ ~, insulating ~ · Dämmasse *f*

~ ~, insulating ~ · Isoliermasse *f*

~ **concrete** → insulating ~

~ **construction(al) material** → insulating ~ ~

~ **core** → insulating ~

~ **cork** → insulating ~

~ **corkboard** → insulating ~

~ **cork sheet(ing)** → insulating ~ ~

~ **corrugated cardboard**, insulating ~ ~ · Wellpapierplatte *f* [*organischer Dämmstoff*]

~ **course** → insulating layer

~ **facing** → insulating lining

~ **felt** → insulating ~

~ **foam**, insulating ~ · Schaumdämmstoff *m*, Dämmschaum(stoff) *m*

~ ~ **board** → insulating ~ ~

~ ~ **sheet**, ~ ~ board, insulating ~ ~ · Schaumdämm(stoff)platte *f*, Dämmschaum(stoff)platte

~ **foil** → insulating ~

~ **glass** → insulating ~

~ **glaze**, insulating ~ · Isolierglasur *f*

~ **gypsum**, insulating ~ · Isoliergips *m*

~ **insert(ion)**, insulating ~ · Isoliereinlage *f*

~ ~, insulating ~ · Dämmeinlage *f*

~ **jacket**, insulating ~ · (Dämm)Binde *f*

~ ~, insulating ~ · (Isolier)Binde *f*

~ **layer** → insulating ~

~ **lead felt**, insulating ~ ~ · Bleidämmpappe *f*

~ **lining** → insulating ~

~ **material** → insulating ~

~ **(mixed) plaster** → insulating (~) ~

~ **mortar** → insulating ~

~ **panel** → insulating ~

~ **paper**, insulating ~ [*See remark under 'Pappe'*] · Dämmpappe *f*

~ ~, insulating ~ [*See remark under 'Pappe'*] · Dämmpapier *n*

~ **peat**, insulating ~ · Dämmtorf *m*

~ **plank** → insulating ~

~ **plaster** → insulating (mixed) ~

~ **powder**, insulating ~ · Isolierpulver *n*

~ **product**, insulating ~, ~ article · Dämmartikel *m*, Dämmgegenstand *m*, Dämmerzeugnis *n*

~ **profile** → insulating section

~ **pumice** → insulating ~

~ ~ **gravel** → insulating ~ ~

~ **refractory** → insulating ~

~ **roof fill** → insulating ~ ~

~ **roof(ing) material** → insulating ~ ~

~ ~ **tile** → insulating ~ ~

~ **screed** → insulating ~

~ ~ **material** → insulating ~ ~

~ **section**, insulating ~, pipe ~ ~ · (Rohr)Dämmschale *f*

~ ~ → insulating ~

insulation shape — integral hardener

~ **shape** → insulating section
~ **sheet**, ~ slab, ~ board, insulating ~ · Isolierplatte *f*
~ **sheet(ing)** → insulating ~
~ **skin**, insulating ~ · Isolierhaut *f*
~ **slab**, ~ sheet, ~ board, insulating ~ · Isolierplatte *f*
~ **strawboard**, insulating ~ · Strohdämmplatte *f*
~ **strip**, insulating ~ · Isolierstreifen *m*
~ **structural material** → insulating construction(al) ~
~ ~ **panel**, insulating ~ ~ · Isolier-Konstruktionstafel *f*
~ **(sur)facing** → insulating lining
~ **tile** → insulating block
~ **trim** → insulating section
~ **unit** → insulating section
~ ~ → insulating ~
~ **wallboard** → insulating ~
~ **wallpaper**, insulating ~ · Isoliertapete *f*
~ **wool** → insulating ~
insulation gypsum, insulation-grade ~, insulating ~ · Isoliergips *m*
~ **in bags** · Sackdämmung *f*
~ **insert(ion)**, insulation-grade ~, insulating ~ · Isoliereinlage *f*
~ ~, insulation-grade ~, insulating ~ · Dämmeinlage *f*
~ **installation**, ~ work · Dämmarbeiten *fpl*
~ **jacket** · Dämmantel *m*
~ **layer** → insulating ~
~ **lead felt**, insulation-grade ~ ~, insulating ~ ~ · Bleidämmpappe *f*
~ **lining** → insulating ~
~ **material** → insulating ~
~ **(mixed) plaster** → insulating (~) ~
~ **mortar** → insulating ~
~ **of impact sounds** → impact (sound) insulation
~ **panel** → insulating ~
~ **paper**, insulation-grade ~, insulating ~ [*See remark under 'Pappe'*] · Dämmpappe *f*
~ ~, insulation-grade ~, insulating ~ [*See remark under 'Pappe'*] · Dämmpapier *n*
~ **peat**, insulation-grade ~, insulating ~ · Dämmtorf *m*
~ **plank** → insulating ~
~ **plaster** → insulating (mixed) ~
~ **product** → insulation(-grade) ~
~ **profile** → insulating section
~ **pumice** → insulating ~
~ ~ **gravel** → insulating ~ ~
~ **refractory** → insulating ~
~ **screed** → insulating ~
~ ~ **material** → insulating ~ ~
~ **section** → insulating ~
~ **shape** → insulating section
~ **sheet** → insulating ~
~ **sheet(ing)** → insulating ~
~ **skin**, insulation-grade ~, insulating ~ · Isolierhaut *f*
~ **slab** → insulating board
~ **strawboard**, insulation-grade ~, insulating ~ · Strohdämmplatte *f*
~ **strip**, insulation-grade ~, insulating ~ · Isolierstreifen *m*
~ **structural material** → insulating construction(al) ~
~ ~ **panel**, insulation-grade ~ ~, insulating ~ ~ · Isolier-Konstruktionstafel *f*
~ **(sur)facing** → insulating lining
~ **tile** → insulating block
~ **trim** → insulating section
~ **unit** → insulating section
~ ~ → insulating ~
~ **value**, insulating ~, ~ figure · Dämmwert *m*
~ ~, ~ figure, insulating ~ · Isolierwert *m*
~ **wallboard** → insulating ~
~ **wallpaper**, insulation-grade ~, insulating ~ · Isoliertapete *f*
~ **wool** → insulating ~
~ **work**, ~ installation · Dämmarbeiten *fpl*
insulator → insulating material
insusceptibility · Unempfindlichkeit *f*
insusceptible to moisture, ~ ~ humidity · feuchtigkeitsunempfindlich, feuchteunempfindlich
in-swinging, inward-swinging, in-opening · nach innen schlagend, ~ ~ öffnend [*Fenster*]
~ **window**, inward-swinging ~, in-opening ~ · Einwärtsfenster *n*
intaglio [*A form of decoration in which the depth of cutting is intermediate between deep cutting and engraving*] · Flachschliff *m* [*Glas*]
~ · Intaglio *n*, Gemme *f* mit vertieften Figuren, Schnitzwerk *n*
(in)tarsia, inlay, mosaic woodwork · Intarsia *f*, Holzeinlegearbeit *f*
(integral and monolithic concrete) encasement · volle Betonummantelung *f* [*Rohr*]
~ **colouring anodising (process)** (Brit.); ~ coloring anodizing (~) (US) · Anodisieren *n* mit direkt im Salzbad erzeugten lichtbeständigen Farbtönen
~ **hardener**, ~ hardening agent · Zusatz-Härtemittel *n*, Zusatz-Härtungsmittel, Zusatz-Härtungsstoff *m*, Zusatz-Härter *m*

integral hardening agent — inter-floor stair(case)

~ **hardening agent,** ~ hardener · Zusatz-Härtemittel n, Zusatz-Härtungsmittel, Zusatz-Härtungsstoff m, Zusatz-Härter m

~ **lath(ing)** → sheet metal ~ ~

~ **multiple** · ganzzähliges Vielfaches n

~ **process** · Wirkstoffbeigabe f zum Beton

~ **proofer,** ~ protective agent, ~ protection agent [*e.g. for oil-proofing, waterproofing, anti-fungus growth, chemical resistance, concreting during frost, etc.*] · Zusatz-Schutzmittel n

~ **proofing liquid** → liquid integral waterproofing agent

~ **protection agent,** ~ protective ~, ~ proofer [*e.g. for oil-proofing, waterproofing, anti-fungus growth, chemical resistance, concreting during frost, etc.*] · Zusatz-Schutzmittel n

~ **protective agent,** ~ protection ~, ~ proofer [*e.g. for oil-proofing, waterproofing, anti-fungus growth, chemical resistance, concreting during frost, etc.*] · Zusatz-Schutzmittel n

(~) **waterproofer** → (~) waterproof(ing) agent

~ **waterproofing** · Sperrung f [*Durch die Sperrung wird ein Baustoff oder Bauteil durch einen geeigneten Stoff im Inneren undurchlässig gemacht*]

(~) **waterproof(ing) agent,** (~) waterproofer, (~) waterrepeller, (~) water-repellent admix(ture), (~) water repelling agent, densifying agent, densifying admix(ture), densifier, permeability reducing agent [*Water repellent substance introduced into the body of such materials as concrete at the mixing stage, as distinct from surface waterproofers, which are applied as a film to the face of the finished concrete*] ·(Ab)Dicht(ungs)mittel n, (Ab)Dicht(ungs)stoff m, Dichter m, DM, sperrendes Zusatzmittel, sperrender Zusatz(stoff) m, Sperrzusatz(stoff), Sperr(zusatz)mittel [*für Mörtel oder Beton*]

~ ~ **liquid** → liquid integral waterproofing agent

(~) **water-repellent ad(mixture)** → (~) waterproof(ing) agent

(~) **waterrepeller** → (~) waterproof(ing) agent

(~) **water repelling agent** → (~) waterproof(ing) ~

integrally-cast [*Elements cast in one piece*] · einteilig betoniert

integrally coloured (Brit.); ~ colored (US); pigmented · pigmentiert, eingefärbt, durchgefärbt, pigmenthaltig

integrated building plaster mill and plaster board plant · Baugips- und Gipsplattenwerk n

integration constant, constant of integration · Integrationskonstante f

intensity of load, load intensity · Laststärke f

~ ~ **loading,** loading intensity · Belastungsintensität f

~ ~ **oscillation,** ~ ~ vibration · Schwingungsstärke f, Erschütterungsstärke

interacting arches [*A series of arches springing from alternate columns so that they cross each other*] · verschränkte Bögen mpl

intercepted matter · abgeschiedener Stoff m, Abscheidungsstoff

intercepting chamber [*A manhole with interceptor*] · Fangschacht m, Fängerschacht, (Ab)Scheiderschacht

~ **conduit-type sewer** · Sammelkanal m

interceptor, separator [*A device designed and installed so as to separate and retain deleterious, hazardous, or undesirable matter from normal wastes while permitting normal sewage or liquid wastes to discharge into the drainage system by gravity*] · (Ab-)Scheider m, Fang m, Fänger

interchangeable anti-siphonage device · Aufsatz-Rohrbelüfter m

intercolumnal screen · Brüstungsmauer f zwischen Säulen

(inter)columniation · Intercolumnium n, Interkolumnium, Säulenabstand m [*Der in Säulendurchmessern angegebene Säulenabstand von Achse zu Achse. Vitruvius hat für diesen Abstand fünf Maße festgelegt: 1. pyknostylos = engsäulig mit 1 1/2 Säulendurchmessern; 2. systylos = gedehnt mit 2 Durchmessern; 3. eustylos = schönsäulig mit 2 1/4 Durchmessern; 4. diastylos = weitsäulig mit 3 Durchmessern und 5. aräostylos = lichtsäulig mit 3 1/2 bis 4 Durchmessern; von diesen ist der Eustylos am gebräuchlichsten*]

inter-communicating (tele)phone, internal ~ · 1.) Heimfernsprecher m; 2.) Hausfernsprecher

~ ~ **system,** internal ~ ~ · 1.) Heimfernsprechanlage f; 2.) Hausfernsprechanlage

intercom(munication system), front door telephone [*The installation in houses to facilitate answering the door*] · (Haus)Türtelefon n, (Haus)Türsprechanlage f

intercrystalline attack → intergranular ~

~ **corrosion** → intergranular attack

~ **crack** · interkristalliner Riß m, Korngrenzriß [*Sich entlang einer Korngrenze auslösender Spannungsriß, der durch das Schweißgut verläuft*]

interface · Grenzfläche f

~ **strength** → adhesion (property)

interfacial activity · Grenzflächenwirkung f

~ **tension** · Grenzflächenspannung f

inter-floor stair(case) · Etagentreppe f, Geschoßtreppe, Stockwerktreppe

interfloor traffic — interior garden

~ traffic · Etagenverkehr *m*, Geschoßverkehr, Stockwerkverkehr
intergranular attack, ~ corrosion, intercrystalline ~, transcrystalline ~ · interkristalline Korrosion *f*, transkristalline ~, Kornzerfall *m*, Korngrenzenkorrosion
~ corrosion → ~ attack
~ martensite · interkristalliner Martensit *m*
to intergrind · vermahlen, zumahlen
intergrinding · Vermahlung *f*, Zumahlung
~ · Vermahlen *n*, Zumahlen
~ of bentonite · Bentonitvermahlung *f*, Bentonitzumahlung
to interground · vermahlen, zumahlen
~ · vermahlen, zugemahlen
interior adhesive → ~ bonding agent
~ air, internal ~, room ~, inside ~, indoor ~, inner ~ · Zimmerluft *f*, Raumluft
~ ~ cooler → inside ~ ~
~ arch, internal ~, inner ~, inside ~ · Innenbogen *m*
~ bending moment → internal ~ ~
~ bonding agent, ~ ~ medium, ~ (~) adhesive, ~ cement(ing agent) · Kleber *m* für Innenverwendung, Kleb(e)mittel *n* ~ ~, Kleb(e)stoff *m* ~ ~
~ (building) board, ~ (~) sheet, internal (~) ~, inner (~) ~, inside (~) ~, indoor (~) ~ · Innen(bau)platte *f*
~ (~) panel, internal (~) ~, inner (~) ~, inside (~) ~, indoor (~) ~ · Innen(bau)tafel *f*
~ cement(ing agent) → ~ bonding ~
~ chlorinated rubber paint, internal ~ ~ ~, inside ~ ~ ~, indoor ~ ~ ~, inner ~ ~ ~ · Innen-Chlorkautschukfarbe *f*
~ climate, internal ~, indoor ~, inside ~, room ~, inner ~ · Raumklima *n*, Innenklima
~ coat, internal ~, inner ~, inside ~ · Innenanstrich *m*, Innenaufstrich
~ ~ of paint → ~ paint coat
~ column, inside ~, internal ~, inner ~ · Innensäule *f*
~ concrete column · Innenbetonstütze *f*
~ core, internal ~, inside ~, inner ~ · Innenkern *m*
~ corner, internal ~, inner ~, inside ~ · Innenecke *f*
~ corridor, inner ~, internal ~, inside ~ · Innenkorridor *m*
interior-corrdidor type block with multi-stor(e)y flats, ~ ~ building ~ ~ ~ ~ ~ ~ ~ apartments, ~ ~ ~ ~ ~ apartment units; ~ ~ ~ ~ ~ living units (US) · Innenganghaus *n* mit mehrgeschossigen Wohnungen [*Der gemeinsame Innengang ist nur in jedem zweiten oder dritten Geschoß. Er erschließt an beiden Gangseiten Wohnungen, die jeweils mit einer internen Treppe in das darüberliegende oder das darunterliegende Geschoß übergreifen, in einem dieser Geschosse meist die ganze Haustiefe einnehmend*]

~ ~ ~ ~ single-stor(e)y flats, ~ ~ ~ building ~ ~ ~, ~ ~ ~ ~ ~ apartments, ~ ~ ~ ~ ~ apartment units; ~ ~ ~ ~ ~ living units (US) · Innenganghaus *n* mit eingeschossigen Wohnungen [*Ein Innengang in jedem Geschoß erschließt den Zugang zu an ihm beiderseits aufgereihten Wohnungen*]
~ ~ building, ~ ~ block · Innenganghaus *n*
interior corrosion, internal ~ · Innenkorrosion *f*
~ court → inner ~
~ decor, inside ~, internal ~, indoor ~, inner ~ · Innengestaltung *f* [*Als Ergebnis des Innengestaltens*]
~ decorating, inside ~, internal ~, indoor ~, inner ~ · Innengestalten *n*, Innengestaltung *f*
~ decoration, ~ design · Innenarchitektur *f*, Raumgestaltung *f*
~ decorator → house ~
~ design, ~ decoration · Innenarchitektur *f*, Raumgestaltung *f*
~ designer → house decorator
~ dimension → clear ~
~ door, inner ~, internal ~, inside ~ · Innentür *f*
(~) doorjamb, recess [*The surrounding case into which, and out of which, a door closes and opens. It consists of two upright pieces, called jambs, and a head, fitted together and rabbeted*] · (Tür)Gewände *f*
(~) ~ block, (~) ~ tile · Türgewändeblock(stein) *m*, Türgewändestein
(~) ~ tile, (~) ~ block · Türgewändeblock(stein) *m*, Türgewändestein
~ emulsion paint, internal ~ ~, inside ~ ~, indoor ~ ~, inner ~ ~ · Innen-Emulsionsfarbe *f*
~ face · Kleb(e)seite *f* [*Dachkonstruktion*]
~ facing → inner lining
~ fiberboard finish, inner ~ ~, inside ~ ~, internal ~ ~ (US); ~ fireboard ~ (Brit.) · Innen-(Holz-)Faserplattenbelag *m*
~ finish(ing) paint, internal ~ ~, inside ~ ~, indoor ~ ~, inner ~ ~ · Innendeck(anstrich)farbe *f*
~ fixtures, internal ~, inside ~, inner ~ · Innenausbau(ten) *m*, (*f*), innerer Ausbau [*Als Ergebnis der (Innen)Ausbauarbeiten*]
~ gallery, inside ~, internal ~, inner ~ · Innen-Laubengang *m*
~ ~ apartment building, internal ~ ~ ~, inside ~ ~ ~, inner ~ ~ ~ · Innen(-Lauben)ganghaus *n*
~ garden → inner ~

interior glass door — interlocking clay roof(ing) tile

~ **glass door,** inner ~ ~, internal ~ ~, inside ~ ~, indoor ~ ~ · Innenglastür *f*

~ **glazing** → internal ~

~ **gloss (clear) varnish,** internal ~ (~) ~, inside ~ (~) ~, indoor ~ (~) ~, inner ~ (~) ~ · Innen-Glanz(klar)lack *m*

~ **handrail** → internal ~

~ **hardboard finish,** internal ~ ~, inside ~ ~, inner ~ ~ · Innen-Hart(faser)- plattenbelag *m*, Innen-(Holz)Faser- hartplattenbelag

~ **heat** → room ~

~ ~ **gain** → internal ~ ~

~ **humidity** → indoor moisture

~ **illumination** → indoor lighting

~ **insulation,** inner ~, internal ~, inside ~ · Innendämmung *f*

~ ~, internal ~, inner ~, inside ~ · Innenisolierung *f*

~ **joinery,** internal ~, inside ~, inner ~ · Innen-Holzeinbauten *f*

~ **layout,** internal ~ · Innenraumaufteilung *f*, Innenraumeinteilung

~ **lighting** → indoor ~

~ **lining** → inner ~

~ **marble,** inside ~, indoor ~, inner ~ · Innenmarmor *m*, Marmor für Innenverkleidungen

~ **masonry (dividing) wall** → internal ~ (~) ~

~ **moisture** → indoor ~

~ **noise,** indoor ~, internal ~, inside ~, inner ~ · Innenlärm *m*, Hauslärm, Gebäudelärm

~ ~, inner ~, internal ~, inside ~ · Innengeräusch *n*, Gebäudegeräusch, Hausgeräusch

~ **paint,** internal ~, inner ~, inside ~ · Innen(anstrich)farbe *f*

~ ~ **coat,** inner ~ ~, internal ~ ~, inside ~ ~, ~ coat of paint · Innenfarbanstrich *m*, Innenfarbaufstrich

~ **panel** → ~ building ~

(~) **partitioning,** indoor ~, inside ~, internal ~, inner ~ · Abtrennung *f* durch Trennwände, Einteilung ~ ~, Einteilung von Räumen, Raumeinteilung

~ **piping,** indoor ~, internal ~, inside ~, inner ~ · Innenrohrleitung *f*

~ **primer,** internal ~, inner ~, inside ~ · Innen-Grundanstrichmittel *n*, Innen-Grundanstrichstoff *m*, Innen-Grundiermittel, Innen-Grundierstoff, Innen-Grund(ierung) *m*, (*f*)

~ **redecoration,** internal ~, inside ~, inner ~, indoor ~ · Innenrenovierung *f*

~ **relative humidity** → internal relative moisture

~ ~ **moisture** → internal ~ ~

~ **reveal,** internal ~, inside ~, inner ~ · Innenleibung *f*, Innenlaibung

~ **seal(ing),** internal ~, inside ~, inner ~ · Innen(ab)dichtung *f*

~ **sheet** → ~ (building) board

~ **skin,** internal ~, inside ~, inner ~ · Innenhaut *f*

~ **slatted blind,** inner ~ ~, internal ~ ~, inside ~ ~, indoor ~ ~ · Innenjalousie *f*

~ **span,** internal ~ · Innenfeld *n*, Zwischenfeld

~ **stain** → ~ wood ~

~ **stairrail** → internal handrail

~ **stud,** internal ~, inside ~, inner ~ · Innenpfosten *m* [*Fachwerkwand*]

~ **support, intermediate** ~ · Zwischenauflager(ung) *n*, (*f*)

~ **sur(facing)** → inner lining

~ **temperature control,** internal ~ ~, indoor ~ ~, inner ~ ~, room ~ ~, inside ~ ~ · Raumtemperatursteuerung *f*, Innentemperatursteuerung

~ **tile,** internal ~, indoor ~, inside ~, inner ~ · Innen(belag)platte *f*, Innenfliese *f*

~ **tracery** → internal ~

~ **view** · Innenansicht *f*

~ **wall surface,** internal ~ ~, inner ~ ~, inside ~ ~ · Wandinnenseite *f*

~ **window,** inner ~, internal ~, inside ~ · Innenfenster *n* [*Bei einem Doppelfenster*]

~ ~ **cill** (Brit.) → ~ ~ sill

~ ~ **frame,** inner ~ ~, internal ~ ~, inside ~ ~, indoor ~ ~ · Innenfensterrahmen *m*

~ ~ **sill;** ~ ~ cill (Brit); internal ~ ~, inner ~ ~, inside ~ ~, indoor ~ ~ · Innen(fenster)sohlbank *f*, Innen-Fensterbank

~ **(wood) stain** · (Holz)Beize *f* für Innenverwendung

~ **work** → finishings and services ~

interjoist [*The space between two joists*] · Unterzugfeld *n*

interlaboratory study, ~ test · Ringanalyse *f*

~ ~ **data,** ~ test ~ · Ringanalysendaten *f*

interlayer · (Verbund-)Zwischenschicht *f* [*Verbund-Sicherheitsglas*]

~ **(of spun glass),** sandwich ~ ~ ~ · Glasfaserschicht *f* [*Thermolux*]

interlocked socket with switch · abschaltbare verriegelte Steckdose *f*

interlocking · Ineinandergreifen *n*, Verspannung *f* [*Schüttsteine; Zuschläge; Mineralmasse*]

~ **board,** ~ sheet · Falzplatte *f*

~ **(building) insulating board,** ~ (~) ~ slab, ~ (~) ~ sheet, ~ (~) insulation(-grade) ~ · Falz(bau)dämmplatte *f* [*gegen Wärme, Kälte oder Schall*]

~ (~) **panel** · Falz(bau)tafel *f*

~ **clay roof(ing) tile,** ~ roof(ing) clay ~ · (Dach)Falzziegel *m*, Muldenfalzziegel, Falzdachziegel [*Auf Stempelpres-*

interlocking clay roof(ing) tile — internal (building) sheet

se hergestellter Dachziegel mit Kopf- und Seitenverfalzung; Ausführung mit einfacher oder doppelter Verfalzung. Auf der Oberfläche sind zwei Längsmulden und eine Mittelrippe. Bei ihrer Deckung entsteht an der Seitenverfalzung eine nach oben gerichtete Deckfuge]

~ **concrete pipe**, concrete interlocking ~ · Betonrohr n mit Falzverbindung, Zementrohr ~ ~, Betonfalzrohr, Falzbetonrohr, Zementfalzrohr, Falzzementrohr

(inter)locking cone · Spannkegel m, Spannkonus m [Spannbeton]

interlocking insulating board → ~ building ~ ~

~ ~ **sheet** → ~ (building) insulating board

~ ~ **slab** → ~ (building) insulating board

~ **insulation board** → ~ (building) insulating ~

~ ~ **sheet** → ~ (building) insulating board

~ ~ **slab** → ~ (building) insulating board

~ **insulation(-grade) board** → ~ (building) insulating ~

~ ~ **sheet** → ~ (building) insulating board

~ ~ **slab** → ~ (building) insulating board

~ **joint** · Verfalzung f, Falzverbindung

~ **panel**, ~ building ~ · Falz(bau)tafel f

~ **pipe** · Falzrohr n

~ **roof(ing) clay tile** → ~ clay roof(ing) ~

~ (~) **tile** · Falzdachstein m, (Dach)Falzstein

~ **sheet**, ~ board · Falzplatte f

~ **tile** → ~ roof(ing) ~

~ ~ **with snow rib** · Schneefangziegel m

intermediate arch · Querrippe f im sechsteiligen Gewölbe parallel zu den Gurten

~ **breaking** → ~ crushing

~ **cap** · Mittelkaschierung f [Lichtleiste]

~ **column** · Zwischenstütze f

~ **controlling dimension** [The intermediate controlling dimensions are subdivisions of the main framework of controlling dimensions, e.g. sill head heights] · Einzelmaß n [Ein Maß für Einzelheiten des Rohbaues oder Ausbaues]

~ **course**, sandwich ~, ~ layer · Zwischenlage f, Zwischenschicht f

~ **crushing**, ~ breaking [discharge at sizes 1/2 or 3/8 inch] · Mittelbrechen n, Zwischenbrechen

~ **(door) rail** · (Tür)Zwischenriegel m

~ **fill** · Zwischenfüllung f

(~) **floor** · (Gebäude)Decke f, Trenndecke, Hochbaudecke, Etagendecke, Stockwerkdecke, Geschoßdecke

(~) (~) **joist**, ceiling ~ · Deckenunterzug m, Trenn~, Etagen~, Stockwerk~, Geschoß~

~ ~ **slab**, suspended ~ ~ [A slab forming the continuous loadbearing structure of a floor and spanning between supports] · Trenndeckenplatte f

~ **foam layer**, sandwich ~ ~ · Schaumzwischenlage f, Schaumzwischenschicht f

~ **frame** · Zwischenrahmen m

~ **igneous rock** · Erstarrungsgestein n mit 55 bis 66% Kieselsäure

~ **jack rafter** · Mittelschifter m

~ **joist** → ~ floor ~

~ **layer**, sandwich ~, ~ course · Zwischenlage f, Zwischenschicht f

~ **pier** · Zwischenpfeiler m

~ **rafter**, common ~, spar · Leersparren m, Zwischensparren

~ **rafters**, common ~, spars · Leergebinde n, Leergespärre n, Leersparren mpl, Zwischensparren

~ **rail**, ~ door ~ · (Tür)Zwischenriegel m

~ **rib**, tierceron · Zwischenrippe f

~ **sealing glass**, solder ~ · Einschmelzglas n, Zwischenglas, Lötglas, Glaslot n

~ **section** · Zwischenschnitt m

~ **stair(case)** · Zwischentreppe f

~ **stiffener** · Zwischensteife f [Blechträger]

~ **strength** · Zwischenfestigkeit f

~ **support**, interior ~ · Zwischenauflager(ung) n, (f)

~ **temperature setting glue**, ~ ~ ~ adhesive, warm-setting ~, cooked glue, hot glue · Warmleim ~

~ **tubular column**, tubular intermediate ~ · Rohrzwischenstütze f

~ **value** · Zwischenwert m

intermetallic · intermetallisch

intermittent line · gestrichelte Linie f

~ **operation** [heating system] · Sperrzeitenbetrieb m

to intermix, to blend · vermischen

intermixable, blendable · vermischbar

intermixing, blending · Vermischen n [als Tätigkeit]

~, blending · Vermischung f [als Ergebnis der Tätigkeit]

~ · Zumischung f

internal air, room ~, inner ~, interior ~, inside ~, indoor ~ · Zimmerluft f, Raumluft

~ ~ **cooler** → inside ~ ~

~ **arch**, interior ~, inner ~, inside ~ · Innenbogen m

~ **bending moment**, interior ~, inner ~ ~, inside ~ · inneres Biegemoment n, ~ Biegungsmoment

~ **(building) board** → interior (~) ~

~ (~) **panel** → interior (~) ~

~ (~) **sheet** → interior (building) board

internal cable method — internal noise

~ **cable method** · Verfahren *n* mit Innenkabeln [*Spannbetonbehälterbau*]

~ **chlorinated rubber paint,** interior ~ ~ ~, inside ~ ~ ~, indoor ~ ~ ~, inner ~ ~ ~ · Innen-Chlorkautschukfarbe *f*

~ **climate,** interior ~, indoor ~, inside ~, inner ~, room ~ · Innenklima *n*, Raumklima

~ **coat,** interior ~, inner ~, inside ~ · Innenanstrich *m*, Innenaufstrich

~ ~ **of paint** → interior paint coat

~ **coating,** inside ~, interior ~ · Innenbeschichtung *f*, Innenüberzug *m* [*als Schicht*]

~ **column** inside ~, interior ~, inner ~ · Innensäule *f*

~ **core,** interior ~, inside ~, inner ~ · Innenkern *m*

~ **corner,** interior ~, inner ~, inside ~ · Innenecke *f*

~ **corridor,** interior ~, inside ~, inner ~, indoor ~ · Innenkorridor *m*

~ **corrosion,** interior ~, inside ~ · Innenkorrosion *f*

~ **court** → inner ~

~ **decor,** indoor ~, interior ~, inside ~, inner ~ · Innengestaltung *f* [*Als Ergebnis des Innengestaltens*]

~ **decorating,** indoor ~, interior ~, inside ~, inner ~ · Innengestalten *n*, Innengestaltung *f*

~ **decorator** → house ~

~ **designer** → house decorator

~ **diameter, ID** · lichter Durchmesser *m*, Innendurchmesser

~ ~ **(of pipe)** · (Rohr)Lichtweite *f*

~ **dimension** → clear ~

~ **door,** inner ~, interior ~, inside ~ · Innentür *f*

~ **elevation** · Innenaufriß *m*

~ **emulsion paint,** interior ~ ~, inside ~ ~, indoor ~ ~, inner ~ ~ · Innen-Emulsionsfarbe *f*

~ **facing** → inner lining

~ **fibreboard finish** (Brit.) → interior fiberboard ~

~ **finish(ing) paint** → interior ~ ~

~ **(fire) hazard** · gebäudebedingte Brandgefahr *f*, ~ Feuergefahr, Eigengefahr

~ **fire-extinguishing system,** indoor ~ ~ · 1.) Gebäudefeuerlöschanlage *f*; 2.) Hausfeuerlöschanlage

~ **fixtures,** interior ~, inside ~, inner ~, indoor ~ · Innenausbau(ten) *m*, (*f*), innerer Ausbau [*Als Ergebnis der (Innen)Ausbauarbeiten*]

~ **force** · Schnittkraft *f* [*Biegemomente, Längs- und Querkräfte eines Tragsystems*]

~ ~ **distribution** · Schnittkraftverlauf *m*

~ **gallery,** inner ~, interior ~, inside ~ · Innen-Laubengang *m*

~ ~ **apartment building,** interior ~ ~ ~, inside ~ ~ ~, inner ~ ~ ~ · Innen(-Lauben)ganghaus *n*

~ **glass door,** indoor ~ ~, interior ~ ~, inside ~ ~, inner ~ ~ · Innenglastür *f*

~ **glazing,** indoor ~, interior ~, inside ~, inner ~ [*Glazing, neither side of which is exposed outside the building*] · Innenverglasung *f*, Inneneinglasung

~ **gloss (clear) varnish** → interior ~ (~) ~

~ **handrail,** inside ~, interior ~, inner ~, ~ stairrail · Innenhandlauf *m*, Innenhandleiste *f* [*Treppe*]

~ **hardboard finish,** interior ~ ~, inside ~ ~, inner ~ ~ · Innen-Hart(faser)-plattenbelag *m*, Innen-(Holz)Faserhartplattenbelag

~ **hazard** → ~ fire ~

~ **heat** → room ~

~ ~ **gain,** inner ~ ~, interior ~ ~, inside ~ ~, indoor ~ ~, room ~ ~ · Innenwärmegewinn *m*, Raumwärmegewinn

~ **humidity** → indoor moisture

~ **illumination** → indoor lighting

(~) **installation,** gas ~ (Brit.) [*The gas pipes and appliances on the consumer's side of the control cock at the board's gas meter*] · Gasinstallation *f*

(~) ~ **work** (Brit.); gas ~ ~ · Gasinstallationsarbeiten *fpl*

~ **insulation,** interior ~, inner ~, inside ~ · Innenisolierung *f*

~ ~, inside ~, interior ~, inner ~ · Innendämmung *f*

~ **joinery,** interior ~, inside ~, inner ~ · Innen-Holzeinbauten *f*

~ **layout,** interior ~, indoor ~, inside ~, inner ~ · Innenraumaufteilung *f*, Innenraumeinteilung

~ **leaf,** ~ wythe, ~ withe, ~ skin, ~ tier, ~ shell, ~ layer, interior ~, inner ~, inside ~ · Innenschale *f* [*Hohlwand; Hohlmauer*]

~ **lighting** → indoor ~

~ **lining** → inner ~

~ **marble** → inner ~

~ **masonry (dividing) wall,** interior ~ (~) ~, inner ~ (~), inside ~ (~) ~, indoor ~ (~) ~ · Innenmauer *f*, Zwischenmauer; Gebäude~; Haus~

~ ~ **wall separating two occupancies** · Scheid(e)mauer *f*, Trennmauer

~ **moisture** → indoor ~

~ **moment** · Innenmoment *n*

~ ~ **beyond the elastic limit** · Innenmoment *n* jenseits der Elastizitätsgrenze

~ **noise,** inside ~, interior ~, inner ~ · Innengeräusch *n*; Gebäudegeräusch; Hausgeräusch

~ ~, inside ~, interior ~, indoor ~, inner ~ · Innenlärm *m*; Hauslärm; Gebäudelärm

internal paint — interpolation

~ **paint,** interior ~, inside ~, inner ~ · Innen(anstrich)farbe *f*

~ ~ **coat** → interior ~ ~

~ **panel** → interior (building) ~

~ **part of a building,** ~ ~ ~ ~ block · Innenbauteil *m, n* eines Gebäudes

~ **partitioning** → (interior) ~

~ **pedestrian traffic** · Gebäudefußgängerverkehr *m*

~ **piping,** inside ~, interior ~, indoor ~, inner ~ · Innenrohrleitung *f*

(~) plastering [*The range of operations involved in the application of plaster to internal surfaces*] · (Innen)Putzarbeit *f*, (Innen)(Ver)Putzen *n*

~ **plumbing,** (sanitary) plumbing (system), sanitation system, system of sanitation · sanitäre (Gebäude)Installation *f*, ~ Hausinstallation, ~ Einrichtung(en) *f(pl)*, ~ Anlagen *fpl,* Sanitärinstallation, Sanitäreinrichtung(en), Sanitäranlage(n)

~ **porosity of the aggregate particles** · Haufwerk(s)porigkeit *f*

~ **pressure** · Innendruck *m* [*Rohrleitung*]

~ **prestress** · interne Vorspannung *f*

~ **primer,** interior ~, inner ~, inside ~ · Innen-Grundanstrichmittel *n*, Innen-Grundanstrichstoff *m*, Innen-Grundiermittel, Innen-Grundierstoff, Innen-Grund(ierung) *m*, (*f*)

~ **redecoration,** interior ~, inside ~, inner ~, indoor ~ · Innenrenovierung *f*

~ **relative moisture,** ~ ~ humidity, interior ~ ~, inner ~ ~, indoor ~ ~, room ~ ~ · Raumluftfeuchte *f*, Raumluftfeuchtigkeit *f*

~ **resilience,** elastic deformation energy · elastische Verformungsenergie *f*, Formänderungsenergie, federnde ~

~ **reveal,** interior ~, inside ~, inner ~ · Innenleibung *f*, Innenlaibung

~ **seal(ing),** interior ~, inside ~, inner ~ · Innen(ab)dichtung *f*

~ **shaft** [*chimney*] · Innenschaft *m* [*Schornstein*]

~ **skin,** interior ~, inside ~, inner ~ · Innenhaut *f*

~ **slatted blind,** interior ~ ~, inside ~ ~, indoor ~ ~, inner ~ ~ · Innenjalousie *f*

~ **span** → interior ~

~ **stairrail** → ~ handrail

~ **stud,** interior ~, inside ~, inner ~ · Innenpfosten *m* [*Fachwerkwand*]

~ **surface** · Innenfläche *f* [*Rohr*]

~ **(sur)facing** → inner lining

~ **(tele)phone,** inter-communicating ~ · 1.) Heimfernsprecher *m*; 2.) Hausfernsprecher

~ **(~) system,** inter-communicating ~ · 1.) Heimfernsprechanlage *f*; 2.) Hausfernsprechanlage

~ **temperature control,** interior ~ ~, indoor ~ ~, inner ~ ~, room ~ ~, inside ~ ~ · Raumtemperatursteuerung *f*, Innentemperatursteuerung

~ **tile,** interior ~, indoor ~, inside ~, inner ~ · Innen(belag)platte *f*, Innenfliese *f*

~ **tracery,** inside ~, inner ~, interior ~ · Innenmaßwerk *n*

~ **wall surface** → interior ~ ~

~ **window,** inside ~, interior ~, inner ~ · Innenfenster *n* [*Bei einem Doppelfenster*]

~ ~ **cill** (Brit.) → interior window sill

~ ~ **frame,** inner ~ ~, interior ~ ~, inside ~ ~ · Innenfensterrahmen *m*

~ ~ **sill** → interior ~ ~

~ **work** → finishings and services ~

International Association for Bridge and Structural Engineering, IABSE · Internationale Vereinigung *f* für Brücken- und Hochbau

(international) de luxe type hotel, luxury ~ · Luxushotel *n*

International House · "Haus *n* der Nationen" [*Tokio*]

~ **Modern** · Internationaler Stil *m* [*Ein in Amerika durch das 1932 in New York erschienene Buch 'The International Style, Architecture since 1922' von Henry-Russel Hitchcock und Philip Johnson geprägter Begriff, der den neuen Architekturstil des 2. Viertels des 20. Jhs. bezeichnet*]

international (passenger) terminal building · Abfertigungsgebäude *n* für Auslandsverkehr, Empfangsgebäude ~

~ **terminal building,** ~ passenger ~ ~ · Abfertigungsgebäude *n* für Auslandsverkehr, Empfangsgebäude ~ ~

International Union of Building Societies and Savings and Loan Associations · Internationaler Bausparkassenverband *m*

international waiting room · Auslandswarteraum *m* [*Flughafen*]

interoffice traffic · Verkehr *m* von Büro zu Büro [*Bürogebäude*]

(inter)penetration · Durchdringung *f*

~ **of folded cylindrical surfaces** · Durchdringung *f* gefalteter Zylinderflächen

~ ~ **internal and external space** · Durchdringung *f* von Innen- und Außenraum

~ ~ **spaces** · Raumdurchdringung *f*

~ ~ **two parallel barrel vaults** · Durchdringung *f* zweier parallel laufender Tonnen

inter-plant bridge · Werkbrücke *f*

interplay · Wechselspiel *n*, Beziehungsspiel

(inter)play of forces · Kräftespiel *n*

~ ~ **light and shade** · Spiel *n* von Licht und Schatten

interpolation · Einschaltung *f*, Interpolation *f*

interpolation formula — inverted throat

~ **formula** · Interpolationsformel f

interposed vault · eingeschobenes Gewölbe n

to interpret geometrically, ~ explain ~ · geometrisch deuten

interrupted (lighting) row · aufgelockertes Lichtband n

~ **production** · Produktionsausfall m

~ **row,** ~ **lighting** ~ · aufgelockertes Lichtband n

to intersect · schneiden

intersecting, intersection, groining · Verschneidung f [*von zwei Gewölben*]

~ **barrel** · Kreuzkappe f [*Kappe eines Kreuzgewölbes*]

~ **roof, intersection** ~**, roof with valley, valley roof** [*A pitched roof with a V-shaped cross-section*] · Dach n mit Wiederkehr, Wiederkehrdach, Kehlendach

~ **surfaces** · einander durchschneidende Flächen fpl

~ **vault, cross** ~ · Kreuz(kappen)gewölbe n [*Es setzt sich aus vier Tonnenkappen zusammen, das heißt, zwei Tonnengewölbe gleichen Querschnitts schneiden sich rechtwinklig. Die Schnittstellen heißen Grate*]

~ **vaulting, cross** ~ · Kreuz(kappen)wölbung f

intersection · Überschneidung f

~ · Verschneidung f

~ **line, line of intersection** · Schnittlinie f

~ **point of diagonals** · Diagonalenschnittpunkt m

~ **roof** → **intersecting** ~

interstice, pore, void [*The space in a material occupied by air or water, or both air and water*] · Pore f, Hohlraum m

intertie, cross timber [*framed partition*] · Sturzriegel m

interval · Zwischenweite f

~ **of columns** → **column spacing**

~ ~ **supports** → **column spacing**

~ ~ **time, time interval** · Zeitabstand m

interwoven · verschlungen

(in-)town station, urban ~**, municipal** ~ · Stadtbahnhof m

intrados → **arch** ~

~ → **inner surface of vault(ing)**

~ **width, soffit** ~ · Bogentiefe f [*Die Tiefe der Bogenleibung*]

intricate (cross) section, complicated (~) ~ · komplizierter Querschnitt m

~ **section,** ~ **cross** ~**, complicated (cross)** ~ · komplizierter Querschnitt m

intrusion mortar, grouting ~**, injection** ~**, grout(ing fluid)** [*A fluid mix(ture) of cement, sand, and water*] · Einpreßmörtel m, Auspreßmörtel, Verpreßmörtel, Injektionsmörtel, Eindringmörtel, Injiziermörtel

intrusive rock, (igneous) plutonic ~**, abyssal** ~**, abysmal** ~ · abyssisches Gestein n, subkrustales ~, plutonisches ~, Tiefengestein, Plutonit m, älteres Eruptivgestein, Intrusivgestein

invar (metal) · Invarstahl m [*Nickelstahl mit 36% Nickel. Die Bezeichnung Invarstahl kommt von invariabilis = unveränderlich*]

inventiveness · Erfindungskraft f

to inventory · inventarisieren

inverse relationship · spiegelbildliches Verhältnis n

inversion · schnelle Umwandlung f [*Schnelle und reversible Kristallumwandlung durch Temperaturänderung*]

~ **point** · Umwandlungstemperatur f [*Temperatur, bei der eine schnelle Umwandlung erfolgt*]

invert, bottom [*e.g. of a sewer*] · Sohle f

~ **level, bottom** ~ [*e.g. of a sewer*] · Sohlenhöhe f

inverted arch, reversed ~ · Grundbogen m, Gegenbogen, Konterbogen, umgekehrter Bogen, Erdbogen

~ **catenary** · umgekehrte Kettenlinie f

~ **cavetto,** ~ **throat** · Anlauf m [*Konkav kurvierte Vermittlung zwischen einem vorspringenden unteren und einem zurücktretenden oberen Bauglied*]

~ **cone** · zugekehrter Kegel m

~ **curb** → **curb below ground**

~ **kerb** → **curb below ground**

~ **king (post) truss, single-strut trussed beam, trussed beam** [*It is used for short spans in connection with wood construction*] · umgekehrter einfacher Hängebock m, ~ einsäuliger ~, umgekehrtes einfaches Hängewerk n, umgekehrtes einsäuliges Hängewerk

~ ~ (~) ~**, trussed beam, belly-rod truss** · umgekehrter Hängebock m, umgekehrtes Hängewerk n

~ ~ **truss,** ~ ~ **post** ~**, trussed beam** [*Is used for short spans in connection with wood construction*] · umgekehrtes einsäuliges Hängewerk n, ~ einfaches ~, umgekehrter einfacher Hängebock m, umgekehrter einsäuliger Hängebock

~ ~ ~**,** ~ ~ **post** ~**, belly-rod** ~**, trussed beam** · umgekehrter Hängebock m, umgekehrtes Hängewerk n

~ **parabola** · umgekehrte Parabel f

~ **pyramid** · umgekehrte Pyramide f

~ **queen (post) truss, trussed beam** [*Is used for short spans in connection with wood construction*] · umgekehrter doppelter Hängebock m, umgekehrtes doppeltes Hängewerk n

~ **s** · verkehrt steigender Karnies m, ~ ~ Karnies, tragender ~, Kehlstoß m

~ **T(ee) section,** ~ **tee** ~ · umgekehrter T-Querschnitt m, ~ ⊥-Querschnitt

~ **throat** → ~ **cavetto**

inverted vault — iron (blastfurnace) slag sand

~ **vault,** reversed ~ · umgekehrtes Gewölbe *n*, verkehrtes ~, überdecktes ~, Kontergewölbe, Erdgewölbe, Gegengewölbe, Grundgewölbe, Sohlengewölbe

investigation into buckling · Beuluntersuchung *f*

invisible frame · Blindrahmen *m* [*Ein unsichtbarer Rahmen, z.B. bei einer Sperrholztür, einem Ölbild oder einer Wandbespannung*]

~ **radiation** · unsichtbare Strahlung *f*

involute · Evolvente *f*

in(ward)-swinging, in-opening · nach innen schlagend, ~ ~ öffnend [*Fenster*]

~ **window,** in-opening ~ · Einwärtsfenster *n*

iodine scale · Jodfarbskala *f*

~ **value** · Jod(farb)zahl *f*, JFZ

ion exchange · Ionenaustausch *m*

~ **exchanger** · Ionenaustauscher *m*

Ionic architectural order, ~ order (of architecture) · ionische (Säulen)Ordnung *f*, I.O.

~ **architecture** · ionische Architektur *f*, ~ Baukunst *f*

~ **base,** ~ column ~ · ionischer (Säulen-)Fuß *m*, ionische Basis *f*

~ **colonnade** · ionische Kolonnade *f*

~ **column** · ionische Säule *f*

~ **(~) base** · ionischer (Säulen)Fuß *m*, ionische Basis *f*

~ **cyma(tium),** cyma(tium) reversa; egg and tongue moulding, egg and dart moulding (Brit.); egg and tongue molding, egg and dart molding (US) · ionisches Kyma(tion) *n*, Eierstab *m*

~ **entablature** · ionisches Gebälk *n*

~ **order (of architecture),** ~ architectural order · ionische (Säulen)Ordnung *f*, I.O.

~ ~ ~ **the Asia Minor type** · kleinasiatisch-ionische (Säulen)Ordnung *f*

~ **pilaster** · ionischer Pilaster *m*

~ **portico** · ionischer Portikus *m*

~ **style** · ionischer Stil *m*

~ **temple** · ionischer Tempel *m*

~ **volute** · ionische Volute *f*, Schneckenlinie *f*, Spirale *f*, Schneckenverzierung *f*

iridescence · Iris(glanz) *f*, (*m*)

iridizing · Irisierung *f*, Irisieren *n*

Irish architecture · irische Architektur *f*, ~ Baukunst *f*

~ **moss,** carragheen [*A seaweed of the Atlantic found on the coasts of Ireland and America. It varies from purple to green in colour, is used as a food and a jelly and by painters to make size*] · irländisches Moos *n*, Perlmoos, Knorpeltang *m*

IRMA, insulated roof member assembly [*Manufactured by Dow Chemical*] · IRMA-Dachaufbau *m*, wärmegedämmte Feuchtigkeits(ab)dichtung *f*

iron (air) trap → ferrous (~) ~

iron-alumina ratio $\dfrac{Fe_2O_3}{Al_2O_3}$ [*It varies from plant to plant, depending on raw materials and type of cement being produced. At some plants the reciprocal is used for control*] · Tonerdemodul *m* [*früher: Eisenmodul*]

iron angle → steel ~

~ **arch(ed girder)** · Eisenbogen(träger) *m*

~ **architecture** · Eisenarchitektur *f*, Eisenbaukunst *f*

~ **article,** ~ product, ferrous ~ · Eisenartikel *m*, Eisengegenstand *m*, Eisenerzeugnis *n*

~-**based material** · eisenhaltiger (Werk-)Stoff *m*

iron beam · Eisenbalken(träger) *m*

~ **black (pigment)** → black (iron) oxid(e) (~)

(~) (blastfurnace) slag (Brit.); cinder (US) [*The US term embodies both a slag, especially that produced from making pig iron in blast furnaces (Hochofenschlacke), and ordinarily the residue of burnt coal, being the impurities thereof fused together to form lumps (Feuerungsschlacke)*] · (Hochofen)Schlacke *f*, HOS

(~) (~) ~ aggregate (Brit.); cinder ~ (US) · (Hochofen)Schlackenzuschlag(-stoff) *m*, (Hochofen)Schlackenzuschlagmaterial *n*

(~) (~) ~ built-up roof(ing) (Brit.); cinder ~ ~ · (Schlacken)Kleb(e)-dach(belag) *n*, (*m*)

(~) (~) ~ chip(ping)s (Brit.); cinder ~ (US) · (Hochofen)Schlackensplitt *m*

(~) (~) ~ coarse aggregate (Brit.); cinder ~ ~ (US) [*B.S. 1047*] · (Hochofen)Schlacken-Grobzuschlag(stoff) *m*, (Hochofen)Schlacken-Grobzuschlagmaterial *n*

(~) (~) ~ concrete (Brit.); cinder ~ (US) · (Hochofen)Schlackenbeton *m*

(~) (~) ~ dust, (~) (~) ~ filler (Brit.); cinder ~ (US) · (Hochofen)Schlackenfüller *m*, (Hochofen)Schlackenfüllstoff *m*

(~) (~) ~ fibre (Brit.); cinder fiber (US) · (Hochofen)Schlackenfaser *f*

(~) (~) ~ filler, (~) (~) ~ dust (Brit.); cinder ~ (US) · (Hochofen-)Schlackenfüller *m*, (Hochofen)Schlackenfüllstoff *m*

(~) (~) ~ fill(ing) (Brit.); cinder ~ (US) · (Hochofen)Schlacken(auf)füllung *f*, (Hochofen)Schlackenschüttung

(~) (~) ~ (paving) sett (Brit.); cinder (~) ~ (US) · (Hochofen)Schlackenpflasterstein *m*

(~) (~) ~ sand, granulated (~) ~ ~ (Brit.); (granulated) cinder ~ (US) · gekörnte Hochofenschlacke *f*, granulierte ~, Hochofenschlackensand *m*, (künstlicher) Schlackensand, Hüttensand

(~) (~) ~ ~ **concrete,** granulated (blast-furnace) slag ~ (Brit.); cinder sand ~, granulated cinder ~ (US) · (Hochofen)Schlackensandbeton *m*, Hüttensandbeton

~ **blue,** ferrocyanid(e) ~ · Zyaneisenblau *n*, Zyaneisenfarbe *f*, Eisencyan(-pigment) *n*

~ **brick,** blue ~ · Schlackenstein *m*, Eisenklinker *m*, (künstlicher) Baustein, gebundener Baustein, Eisen-Schmelz-Verblender [*Aus kalkarmen, eisenhaltigen Tonen hergesteller Ziegel mit völlig dichtem Scherben*]

~ ~ **paving,** blue ~ ~ · Eisenklinkerpflaster *n*, Schlackensteinpflaster, Fps

~ **brown (pigment)** → brown (iron) oxid(e) (~)

~**-carbon diagram** · Eisen-Kohlenstoff-Schaubild *n*

iron carrying frame(work) construction → ~ (structural) ~ ~

~ ~ **framing construction** → ~ (structural) frame(work) ~

~ **cement** → iron-rust ~

~ **channel,** channel (iron) · U-Eisen *n*

~ **chimney connector** → ~ smoke pipe

~**-chromium binary diagram** · Zweistoffdiagramm *n* Eisen/Chrom

~ **connector** → timber ~

~ **disconnecting (air) trap** → ferrous (~) ~

~ **dog** · Eisenklammer *f*, Eisenkrempe *f*

~ **dowel** · Eisendollen *m*, Eisendübel *m*

~ **dust** · Eisenmehl *n*

~ **elimination,** ~ removal, deferrization · (Wasser)Enteisenung *f*

~ **fighter** → (reinforcing) iron worker

~ **filings,** ~ turnings · Eisen(feil)späne *mpl*

(~) **firedog,** andiron [*It is used for supporting logs an the hearth of an open fire-place*] · Kaminbock *m*, Feuerbock

~ **fluosilicate** · Eisenfluat *n*

~ **forms,** ~ formwork, ~ shuttering · Eisenschalung *f*

~ **formwork,** ~ forms, ~ shuttering · Eisenschalung *f*

~ **frame(work) construction** → ~ structural ~ ~

~ **framing construction** → ~ (structural) frame(work) ~

~ **gate** · Eisentor *n*

~ **girder** · Eisenträger *m*

~ **glazing bar,** ~ sash ~; ~ muntin (US) · Sprosseneisen *n*

ironing room · Bügelraum *m*, Bügelzimmer *n*, Plätteraum, Plättezimmer

iron intercepting (air) trap → ferrous (~) ~

~ **interceptor** → ferrous (air) trap

~ **lath(ing)** · eiserner Putzträger *m*

~ **lintel;** ~ lintol [*deprecated*] · Eisenoberschwelle *f*, Eisensturz *m*

~ **(load)bearing frame(work) construction** → ~ (structural) ~ ~

~ ~ **framing construction** → ~ (structural) frame(work) ~

~ **mica** → micaceous iron oxide

~ ~ **paint** → micaceous iron oxid(e) ~

ironmongery · Eisenwaren *fpl*

iron muntim (US); iron glazing bar, iron sash bar · Sprosseneisen *n*

~ **ocher** (US); ~ ochre (Brit.) · Berggelb *n*, Eisenocker *m*

~ **oleate** · Eisenölseife *f*

iron-ore aggregate, ~ concrete ~ · (Eisen)Erz(beton)zuschlag(stoff) *m*

~ **cement,** Ferrari ~ · (Eisen)Erzzement *m*, Ferrarizement

~ **(concrete) aggregate** · (Eisen)Erz(beton)zuschlag(stoff) *m*

iron oxide (Brit.); ~ oxid(e) (US) · Eisenoxid *n*, Ferrioxid [*Es kommt als Eisenglanz oder Roteisenstein vor*]

~ **(oxid(e)) black (pigment)** → black (iron) oxid(e) (~)

~ **(oxide) brown (pigment)** → brown (iron) oxid(e) (~)

~ **oxid(e) (pigment)** (US); ~ oxide (~) (Brit.) [*B.S. 851*] · (Eisen)Oxidfarbe *f*, (Eisen)Oxidpigment *n*, Eisenoxid(pigment)

~ **(oxid(e)) red (pigment)** → red (iron) oxid(e) (~)

~ **(oxid(e)) yellow (pigment)** → yellow (iron) oxid(e) (~)

~ **paving** → cast-~ ~

~ **pipe,** ferrous ~ · Eisenrohr *n*

~ **pipeline** · Eisenrohrleitung *f*

~ **powder,** powder(ed) iron · Eisenpulver *n*

~ **product,** ~ article, ferrous ~ · Eisenartikel *m*, Eisengegenstand *m*, Eisenerzeugnis *n*

(~) **pyrite(s),** yellow ~, fool's gold, mundic · Schwefeleisen *n*, Schwefelkies *m*, Eisenkies

~ **red (pigment)** → red (iron) oxid(e) (~)

~ **removal,** ~ elimination, deferrization · (Wasser)Enteisenung *f*

~ **ridging,** steel ~ · Stahlfirsthaube *f*, Stahlfirstkappe *f*

~ **roof cladding** → steel (sheet) roof cover(ing)

~ ~ **cover(ing)** → steel (sheet) ~ ~

~ ~ **sheathing** → steel (sheet) roof cover(ing)

~ **roofing** → steel (sheet) roof cover(ing)

~**(-rust) cement** · Graphitzement *m*, Metallzement, Metallkitt *m*, Eisenkitt [*Kleb(e)- und Vergußmasse aus leicht*

iron(-rust) cement — ISO fit

schmelzenden Metallverbindungen mit Schwefel und Graphit. Also kein Zement]

iron salt · Eisensalz *n*

~ **sash bar**, ~ glazing ~; ~ muntin (US) · Sprosseneisen *n*

~ **section**, section iron · Eisenprofil *n*, Formeisen *n*, Fassoneisen, Profileisen

~ **sheet**, steel ~, sheet steel, sheet iron · Stahl(fein)blech *n* [*DIN 1541*]

~ (~) **roof cladding** → steel (sheet) roof cover(ing)

~ (~) ~ **cover(ing)** → steel (~) ~ ~

~ (~) ~ **sheathing** → steel (sheet) roof cover(ing)

~ (~) **roofing** → steel (sheet) roof cover(ing)

~ **sheetpile** · Eisen(spund)bohle *f*

~ **shot** · Eisenschrot *m*

~ ~ **concrete** [*It is particularly used for (biological) radiation shielding*] · Eisenschrotbeton *m*

~ **shuttering**, ~ formwork, ~ forms · Eisenschalung *f*

~ **skeleton framing construction** → ~ (structural) frame(work) ~

(~) **slag** → (~) blastfurnace ~

(~) ~ **aggregate** → (~) (blastfurnace) ~ ~

(~) ~ **built-up roof(ing)** → (~) (blastfurnace) ~ ~ ~

(~) ~ **chip(ping)s** → (~) blastfurnace ~ ~

(~) ~ **coarse aggregate** → (~) (blastfurnace) ~ ~ ~

(~) ~ **concrete**, (~) blastfurnace ~ ~ (Brit.); cinder ~ (US) · (Hochofen-)Schlackenbeton *m*

(~) ~ **dust** → (~) (blastfurnace) slag filler

(~) ~ **fibre** → (~) (blastfurnace) ~ ~

(~) ~ **filler** → (~) blastfurnace ~ ~

(~) ~ **fill(ing)** → (~) (blastfurnace) ~ ~

(~) ~ **(paving) sett** → (~) (blastfurnace) ~ (~) ~

(~) ~ **sand** · (~) (blastfurnace) ~ ~

(~) ~ **sett** → (~) (blastfurnace) slag (paving) ~

~ **smoke, pipe**, ~ ~ tube, ~ stove ~, ~ chimney connector · Eisen-Rauchrohr *n*, Eisen-Ofenrohr [*DIN 1298*]

~ ~ **tube** → ~ ~ ~ pipe

~ **soap** · Eisenseife *f*

~ **spot** · Eisenfleck *m* [*Feuerfestindustrie. Eisenhaltige Ausschmelzung in einem gebrannten Erzeugnis*]

~ **stair(case)** · Eisentreppe *f*

~ **stove** · Kanonenofen *m*, Eisenofen, eiserner Ofen

~ ~ **pipe** → ~ smoke ~

~ ~ **tube** → ~ smoke pipe

~ **(structural) frame(work) construction**, ~ (~) framing ~, ~ loadbearing ~ ~, ~ (weight-)carrying ~, ~ skeleton ~ · Eisen(trag)gerippebau *m*, Eisen(trag)skelettbau, Eisen(trag)rahmenbau

~ (~) **framing construction** → ~ (~) frame(work) ~

~ **(timber) connector**, ferrous (~) ~ (Brit.); ~ (~) connecter (US) · Eisendübel *m* [*Holzverbinder*]

~ **tower** · Eisenturm *m*

~ **trap** → ferrous (air) ~.

~ **turnings**, ~ filings · Eisen(feil)späne *mpl*

~ **(weight-)carrying frame(work) construction** → ~ (structural) ~ ~

~ ~ **framing construction** → ~ (structural) frame(work) ~

~ **window** · Eisenfenster *n*

~ ~ **bar** · Fensterstange *f*, Windeisen *n*

~ **wire**, ferrous ~ · Eisendraht *m*

~ ~, annealed ~, lashing ~, binding ~, tying ~ [*Soft steel wire used for binding reinforcement*] · Rödeldraht *m*, Bindedraht

ironwork [*Wrought or cast iron, usually decorative*] · Eisenarbeit *f*

iron worker → reinforcing ~ ~

~ **yellow (pigment)** (Brit.) → yellow (iron) oxid(e) (~)

irradiated plastic (material) · bestrahlter Kunststoff *m*

irregular, uneven · uneben, unregelmäßig [*Oberfläche*]

~ **(paving) sett** · Schroppenpflasterstein *m*, Wildpflasterstein

~ **sett** → ~ paving ~

irregularity · Unebenheit *f*

irreversible creep · nichtumkehrbares Kriechen *n*

irrigation pipe · Bewässerungsrohr *n*

irrotational wave · Dehnwelle *f* [*Eine Longitudinalwelle in einem festen Körper. Sie tritt nur in stabförmigen Gebilden auf, wo sie keine großflächige Oberflächenbewegung verursachen kann, die für eine Schallabstrahlung eine Notwendigkeit ist*]

isinglass, fish glue · Fischleim *m* [*Aus Fischabfällen gewonnener saurer Leim. Er wird als Klebstoff für Papier und Gewebe und als Kitt für Porzellan und Glas benutzt*]

Islamic architecture → Muslim ~

island platform, ~ station ~ · Inselbahnsteig *m*

~ ~ **roof**, ~ station ~ ~ · Inselbahnsteigdach *n*

~ **site** · Wohnblock *m*

~ **station** · Inselbahnhof *m*

~ (~) **platform** · Inselbahnsteig *m*

~ ~ (~) **roof** · Inselbahnsteigdach *n*

ISO fit · ISO-Passung *f*

isocyanate — iterative process

isocyanate · Isocyanat *n*

isodomum of granite blocks, opus ~ ~ ~ ~ · Granitquadermauerwerk *n*, Granitquaderverband *m*

isolated, detached, free-standing [*Said of a structure which is completely surrounded by permanent open spaces*] · freistehend

~ **(bath)tub**, free-standing ~, ~ bath, detached ~ · freistehende (Bade-)Wanne *f*, Freisteh(bade)wanne [*DIN 4470 bis 4477*]

~ **bell-tower**, detached ~, free-standing ~, campanile, belfry · freistehender Glockenturm *m*, Campanile *m*, Kampanile

~ **block** → free-standing house

~ **building**, detached ~, free-standing ~ · freistehendes Gebäude *n*, Einzelgebäude

~ **chapel**, freestanding ~, detached ~ · freistehende Kapelle *f*

~ **column**, free-standing ~, detached ~ · freistehende Säule *f*, eingestellte ~, Vollsäule, Freisäule

~ **footing**, independent ~ · Einzelfundament *n*

~ **foundation**, independent ~ · Einzelgründung *f*

~ **house**, detached ~, free-standing ~ · freistehendes Haus *n*, Einzelhaus

~ **masonry wall**, detached ~ ~, free-standing ~ ~ · freistehende Mauer *f*, Einzelmauer

~ **motif** · Einzelmotiv *n*

~ **support**, free-standing ~, detached ~ · freistehende Stütze *f*, eingestellte ~, Freistütze, Vollstütze

~ **tub**, ~ bath(tub), free-standing ~ · freistehende (Bade)Wanne *f*, Freisteh(bade)wanne [*DIN 4470 bis 4477*]

isolating test coating [*Is a paint coating to which certain outdoor conditions by a nearby chemical plant, or blast furnace(s), or cement factory etc. are admitted under observation, so that the effect of destroying the pigments (also by atomic fall-out) may be studied*] · Versuchs-Isolieranstrich *m*, Versuchs-Isolieraufstrich

~ **valve**, isolation ~ [*Any valve fixed for the purpose of shutting off part of a pipe system from the remainder in the case of a pipe burst*] · Rohrbruchsicherung *f*, Selbstschlußventil *n*, Rohrbruchwächter *m*, Rohrbruchventil

isolation of noise · Geräuschdämmung *f*

~ **reed mat** · Rohrgewebe *n*, Schilf~, (Schilf)Rohrmatte *f*, (Isolier)Rohrung *f* [*Fehlname: Rohrgeflecht n. Die Rohrstengel sind durch die Drähte verwebt, nicht verflochten*]

~ **valve**, isolating ~ [*Any valve fixed for the purpose of shutting off part of a pipe system from the remainder in the case of a pipe burst*] · Rohrbruchsicherung *f*, Selbstschlußventil *n*, Rohrbruchwächter *m*, Rohrbruchventil

isolator, vibration ~, oscillation ~ · Schwingungsdämpfer *m*, Erschütterungsdämpfer

isomerization (process) · Isomerisieren *n*

isomerized linsed oil, linseed oil isomer · isomerisiertes Leinöl *n*

~ **rubber** · Cyclokautschuk *m*, cyclisierter Kautschuk, isomerisierter Kautschuk

isometric projection · isometrische Projektion *f*, isometrischer Riß *m*

isostatic, perfect, statically determined, statically determinate · (statisch) bestimmt

~ **frame**, perfect ~ · perfekter Rahmen *m*

~ **line** → line of principal stress

~ **structure**, statically determinate ~ · statisch bestimmtes Bauwerk *n*

isotope room · Isotopenraum *m*

isotropic [*Having the same physical properties in all directions*] · isotrop

~ **body** · isotroper Körper *m*

~ **continuous skew(ed) plate**, ~ ~ ~ slab · schiefwink(e)lige isotrope Durchlaufplatte *f*

~ **cylindrical shell roof** · isotropes kreiszylindrisches Schalendach *n*

~ **hardening** · isotrope Stoffverfestigung *f*, ~ (Werkstoff)Verfestigung

~ **material** · isotroper (Werk)Stoff *m*

~ **plate**, ~ slab · isotrope Platte *f*

~ **skew(ed) plate**, ~ ~ slab · schiefwinkelige isotrope Platte *f*

~ **slab**, ~ plate · isotrope Platte *f*

Italian architecture · italienische Architektur *f*, ~ Baukunst *f*

~ **Art Nouveau**, ~ Modern Style · italienischer Jugendstil *m*

~ **asbestos**, tremolite (~) · Tremolit *m* (Min.)

~ **Gothic** · italienische Gotik *f*

~ **Modern Style**, ~ Art Nouveau · italienischer Jugendstil *m*

~ **ochre** (Brit.); ~ ocher (US) · römischer Ocker *m*

~ **Renaissance** · italienische Renaissance *f*

~ **Romanesque** · italienische Romanik *f*, ~ romanische Architektur *f*, ~ romanische Baukunst *f*

item · Position *f*

iteration method, iterative ~ · Iterationsverfahren *n*

~ **process**, iterative ~ · Iterationsvorschrift *f*

~ **sequence**, iterative ~ · Iterationsfolge *f*

~ **solution**, iterative ~ · Iterationslösung *f*

iterative method, iteration ~ · Iterationsverfahren *n*

~ **process**, iteration ~ · Iterationsvorschrift *f*

iterative sequence — jaspe lino(leum)

~ **sequence**, iteration ~ · Iterationsfolge f

~ **solution**, iteration ~ · Iterationslösung f

ivory black (pigment) · Elfenbeinschwarz(pigment) n

~ **chip** · Elfenbeinspan m

~-**coloured** (Brit.); ivory-colored (US) · elfenbeinfarbig

~ **glazed coat(ing)**, ~ glazing, ~ glaze(d finish) · Elfenbeinglasur f, Elfenbeinbeglasung f

~ **glaze(d finish)**, ~ glazing, ~ glazed coat(ing) · Elfenbeinglasur f, Elfenbeinbeglasung f

~ **glazing**, ~ glazed coat(ing), ~ glaze(d finish) · Elfenbeinglasur f, Elfenbeinbeglasung f

~ **sculpture**, sculpture in ivory · Elfenbeinplastik f, Elfenbeinskulptur f

~ **work** · Elfenbeinbildwerk n

ivy-leaf · Efeublatt n

IWRC, independent wire rope core · unabhängige Stahlseele f

J

jack → ~ rafter

~, jacking device [*A device for raising slipforms*] · Presse f, Heber m

~ **arch**, flat ~, segmental ~ [*An arch with low rise-to-span ratio*] · flacher Bogen m, platter ~, Stichbogen, Segmentbogen, Flachbogen [*veraltet: Kreisteilbogen, Teilzirkelbogen*]

~ **arch (lintel)** → straight ~ (~)

~ **for prestressed concrete** → jacking device ~ ~ ~

~ **(rafter)**, creeping ~, cripple ~ [*A short rafter between hip rafter and eave(s) or between valley and ridge*] · Gratstichbalken m, Schiftsparren m, Schifter m

~ **rib** · Kurzrippe f

~ **rod** [*Plain rod, usually $^7/_8$ or 1 in. in diameter, with square cut or threaded ends to support sliding forms in connection with a jack. In some cases, these jack rods are also used as a portion of the vertical reinforcement required*] · Gleitstange f

~ ~ **sleeve** [*Piece of pipe which joins two jack rods for end-to-end butt splicing*] · Gleitstangenmuffe f

~ **vault**, straight ~, flat ~; floor ~ (US) · scheitrechtes Gewölbe n, g(e)rades ~, flaches ~, Geradgewölbe, Sturzgewölbe, Horizontalgewölbe, Flachgewölbe

jacket · Mantel m

jacking anchorage · (Vor)Spann(ungs)verankerung f

jack(ing) device) [*A device for raising slipforms*] · Presse f, Heber m

jack(ing) device) for prestressed concrete, tensioning jack, stretching jack, (pre)stressing jack · Spann(beton)presse f

jacking end of a bed · Spannende n eines Spannbettes

~ **force** [*Temporary force exerted by the device which introduces tension into (pre)stressing tendons*] · Spann(beton)pressenkraft f

~ ~ [*The force exerted by a device for raising slipforms*] · Pressenkraft f, Heberkraft

~ **stress** [*The maximum stress occurring in a prestressed tendon during stressing*] · (Spann)Pressenspannung f

Jacobean style, Good King Jame's Gothic · Stil m der Zeit Jakobs I

jagged · (aus)gezackt

jail cell · Gefängniszelle f

Jain architecture · jainistische Architektur f, ~ Baukunst f

~ **temple** · jainistischer Tempel m

jalousie, louvres, louvers, slatted blind [*A screen of spaced parallel slats*] ·Jalousie f

~ **door**, slatted blind ~ · Jalousietür f

~ **window**, slatted blind ~, louvre ~, louver ~ · Jalousiefenster n

jamb, ingoing · Gewändepfosten m, Gewändesäule f, Gewändeständer m

jamb wall · Drempel m, Kniestock m [*Er entsteht durch Anheben des Dachfußes um 0,80 bis 1,50 m über die Geschoßdecke beim Kehlbalken- oder Pfettendach. Der Drempel ergibt mehr und besser nutzbaren Dachraum. Seine Konstruktion ist jedoch umständlich, teuer und unwirtschaftlich, seine Ausführung technisch unlogisch, so daß ohne wesentlich größeren Kostenaufwand ein Vollgeschoß ausgeführt werden kann*]

~ ~ **roof** · Drempeldach n, Kniestockdach

jambs, ingoings · Gewände n

jami (masjid) → Friday mosque

Japanese architecture · japanische Architektur f, ~ Baukunst f

(~) **lacquer** [*A glossy lacquer obtained by tapping the sap from the Japanese varnish tree or sumach*] · japanischer Lack m

jaspe lino(leum) · Jaspé(linoleum) n [*Eine Art von Waltonlinoleum mit fein geäderter Musterung*]

Jasper ware · Jasperware f

Jena planetarium [*The first thin-shell concrete dome designed as a membrane structure by F. Dischinger in 1922. It is a hemisphere with a span of 82 ft. (24.9 m)*] · Planetarium n in Jena

jerry builder [*A builder who builds with poor materials and workmanship*] · „Bruchbudenbauer" m

~ **building** · Schwindelbau m

Jesuit church · Jesuitenkirche f

jet and fuel resisting joint sealing compound, JFR ~ · düsentreibstoffeste Fugenvergußmasse f

~ **regulator** · Strahlregler m

~ **shower** · Strahldusche f [*Das Wasser wird in geschlossenem Strahl gegen den Körper geleitet*]

jetty → jutty

jeweller's shop · Juwelierladen m

Jew's pitch, bitumen judaicum, Dead Sea asphalt · Judenpech n

Jewish bema · Bema n [*Die erhöhte Kanzel in einer Synagoge zur Verlesung des Pentateuch*]

JFR compound, jet and fuel resisting joint sealing ~ · düsentreibstoffeste Fugenvergußmasse f

jib door, gib ~, secret ~, concealed ~ [*A door whose face is flush with the wall and decorated so as to be as little seen as possible*] · Geheimtür f, Tapetentür

to jigger · (über)drehen [*Steinzeugindustrie*]

jiggering · (Über)Drehen n [*Steinzeugindustrie*]

jobber, builder's handyman [*A semi-skilled man who can do any sort of repair to small houses*] · Reparaturhochbauarbeiter m

jobbing sheet, medium ~, light plate, medium plate · Mittelblech n

job-mix(ed) concrete, field ~ · Baustellenbeton m

~ **plaster** [*As opposed to ready-mix(ed) plaster*] · Baustellen(ver)putz m

job report · Baubericht m

job-site prestressing → (on-)site ~

~ **stretching** → (on-)site prestressing

~ **tensioning** → (on-)site prestressing

jog (US) [*An offset or change in the direction of a line or a surface*] · Unregelmäßigkeit f

to joggle, to offset · (ab)kröpfen [*Einen Profil- oder Stabstahl aus seiner ursprünglichen Ebene in eine innerhalb der Konstruktion dazu versetzten Ebene örtlich biegen*]

joggle · Verklammerung f

~-**joint** · verklammerter Stoß m

joggle jointing · Verklammern n

~-**piece** · verklammertes Stück n

joggle post (US) → king ~

joggled lintel · Hakensturz m, Hakenoberschwelle f

to join, to connect [*bar; girder*] · verbinden, anschließen [*Stab; Träger*]

~ ~ · verbinden

~ ~ · abbinden [*Bauholz*]

~ ~ **by prestressing,** to stress together, to tension together · zusammenspannen [*Fertigteile durch Vorspannung miteinander verbinden*]

joined · abgebunden [*Bauholz*]

joiner's adhesive, ~ glue · Tischlerleim m

~ **glue,** ~ adhesive · Tischlerleim m

joinery [*Timber made into fittings and finishings or its preparation, assembly and fixing as distinct from carpentry*] · Tischlereiwesen n

~ **component** → ~ unit

~ **member** → ~ unit

~ **timber,** ~ wood · Tischlerholz n

~ **unit,** ~ component, ~ member [*A window, a door etc.*] · Bautischlerelement n, Bautischlerteil m, n

~ **wood,** ~ timber · Tischlerholz n

~ **work** · (Bau)Schreinerarbeiten fpl, (Bau)Tischlerarbeiten [*DIN 18355*]

joining, trimming · Abbund m, Abbindung f, Abbinden n [*Anreißen, Zuschneiden, Ablängen und sonstiges Bearbeiten von Bauhölzern an Hand zeichnerischer Unterlagen*]

~ · Verbinden n

~ **shop,** ~ work~, trimming ~ · Abbundhalle f [*Zimmereibetrieb*]

~ **(work)shop,** trimming ~ · Abbundhalle f [*Zimmereibetrieb*]

~ **yard,** trimming ~ · Abbindeplatz m, Abbundplatz f [*Zimmerei*]

to joint · nacharbeiten [*von Mörtelfugen*]

joint, node point · Knoten(punkt) m

~, connection · Verbindung f, Anschluß m [*bei Fachwerkstäben*]

~ · Fuge f

~ · Stoß m [*Verbindungsstelle zweier Konstruktionselemente*]

~ **allowance** · Fugentoleranz f

~ **angle,** connecting ~ · Beiwinkel m, Anschlußwinkel

~ **architect** · Miterbauer m

~ **assembly** → coupling of pipes

~ **bridging** · Fugenüberbrückung f

joint cement — joint velocity 544

joint cement, sewer joint(ing) compound, pipe joint(ing) compound · Füllmasse *f*, Vergußmasse [*Zur Vermuffung von Rohren*]

~ **centre** (Brit.); ~ center (US) · Fugenmittenabstand *m*

~ **compound** → jointing ~

~ **cover(ing)** · Fugenüberdeckung *f*

~ **cross** · Fugenkreuz *n*

~ **depth** · Fugentiefe *f*

~ **design** · Fugendimensionierung *f*

~ ~ · Fugenausbildung *f*

~ **displacement,** node point ~ · Knoten(punkt)verrückung *f*

~ **dowel** · Fugendübel *m*

~ **equation** · Knoten(punkt)gleichung *f*

~ **equilibrium,** node point ~ · Knoten(punkt)gleichgewicht *n*

~ **fastener,** corrugated ~, wiggle nail dog; mitre brad (Brit.); miter brad (US) · Wellennagel *m*, gewellter Nagel

(~) **filler** → (~) sealing strip

~ ~ **strip** · Fugenfüllstreifen *m*

(~) **filling** · (Fugen)(Ab)Dichten *n*, Fugenverfüllen [*Das Ausfüllen einer Fuge*]

(~) ~, jointing · (Fugen)(Ab)Dichtung *f*, Ausfugung, (Fugen)(Aus)Füllung, Verfugung, (Fugen)Verfüllung

(~) ~ **compound,** (~) seal(ing) ~, (~) sealant · (Fugen)(Ver)Füllmasse *f*, Fugenmasse, (Fugen)(Ver)Füller *m*, Fugen(ab)dicht(ungs)masse

~ **fixing** · Fugenbefestigung *f*

~ **floor(ing) (finish),** ~ floor cover(-ing) · fugenzeigender (Fuß)Boden(belag) *m*

~ **for allowance** · Überdeckungsstoß *m*

(~) **gap** · (Fugen)Spalt *m*

~ **grid** · Fugennetz *n*, Fugenwerk *n*

~ **holding moment,** node point ~ ~ · Knoten(punkt)festhaltemoment *n*

~ **load,** node point ~ · Knoten(punkt)last *f*

~ **loading,** node point ~ · Knoten(punkt)belastung *f*

(~) **masking tape** · Fugen(ab)deckband *n*, (Ab)Deckband

~ **measurement** · gemeinsames Aufmaß *n*

~ **mechanism,** node point ~ · Knoten(punkt)mechanismus *m*

~ **mobility,** node point ~ · Knoten(punkt)verschieblichkeit *f*

~ **moment,** node point ~ · Knoten(punkt)moment *n*

~ **mortar** → jointing ~

~ **movement** · Fugenbewegung *f*

~ ~, node point ~ · Knoten(punkt)bewegung *f*

~ **of rupture** · Bruchfuge *f*

~ **permeability,** ~ perviousness · Fugendurchlässigkeit *f*

~ **plate,** gusset ~, fish ~, corner ~, binding ~, connecting ~, connection ~, knee bracket ~, node point ~ · Knoten(punkt)verbindung *f*

(~) **pouring** · (Fugen)Verguß *m*, (Fugen)Ausguß

(~) ~ **compound** · (Fugen)Gießmasse *f*, (Fugen)Ausgußmasse, Fugen(verguß)masse, Vergußmasse

(~) ~ ~ **for (natural) stone sett paving** · (Natur)Steinpflasterausgußmasse *f*, (Natur)Steinpflastervergußmasse

~ **ring** [*Metal ring used to strengthen structural timber joints*] · Ringdübel *m*

~ **rotation,** node point ~ · Knoten(punkt)drehung *f*

~ ~ **angle,** node point ~ · Knoten(punkt)drehwinkel *m*

~ **rule,** pointing template · Lagerfugenschablone *f*

~ **runner,** pouring rope · Strick *m* [*Strick-Blei-Dichtung*]

~ **seal** → ~ sealing

~ ~ **compound** → ~ sealing ~

~ ~ **strip** → ~ sealing ~

(~) **sealant** → (~) filling compound

~ **sealed by cover strip** → (preformed) gasket joint

~ **seal(ing)** · Fugen(ab)dichtung *f*

(~) **sealing** · (Fugen)Versiegeln *n*, (Fugen)Absiegeln [*Abschließen einer Fuge nach außen zur Verhinderung des Eindringens von Wasser oder Feuchtigkeit*]

(~) **seal(ing) compound** → (~) filling ~

(~) **sealing filler** → (~) ~ strip

~ **seal(ing) strip** · Fugen(ab)dicht(ungs)streifen *m*

(~) **sealing strip,** (expansion) (joint) sealing filler, (expansion) joint(ing) strip, premo(u)lded (strip) joint filler, strip of pre-formed filling material, (pre-formed) (joint) filler [*Material used to fill a joint to prevent the infiltration of debris*] · Fugeneinlage *f*, (feste) Einlage, Fugenstreifen *m*

~ **section** · Rollenlappen *m*, Teilung *f* [*Scharnier*]

~ **set in cement mortar,** pipe ~ ~ ~ ~ ~ · (Rohr)Stoßdichtung *f* mit Zementmörtel

~ **strength** · Fugenfestigkeit *f*

~ ~, node point ~ · Knoten(punkt)festigkeit *f*

~ **strip** → (crack-control) (metal) ~ ~

~ ~ → (~) sealing ~

joint-tight · fugendicht

joint trajectory, node point ~ · Knoten(punkt)weg *m*

~ **translation,** node point ~ · Knoten(punkt)verschiebung *f*

~ **velocity,** node point ~ · Knoten(punkt)geschwindigkeit *f*

joint venture work — junction piece without saddle

~ **venture work** · Gemeinschaftsarbeit *f*

~ **which does not allow expansion** · Preßfuge *f*

~ **width** · Fugenbreite *f*

~ **with butt strap, butt joint with cover** · Überlaschung *f*, Stoß *f* mit Lasche

~ **zone** · Fugenbereich *m, n*

jointing [*Finishing brickwork or masonry joints with richer mortar than that used for bedding the bricks or stones*] · (Fugen)Verstreichen *n*, (Fugen)Ausstreichen, (Ver)Fugen, Ausfugen

~, **(joint) filling** · (Fugen)(Aus)Füllung *f*, Ausfugung, (Fugen)(Ab)Dichtung, Verfugung, (Fugen)Verfüllung

~ · Fugung *f*

~ **cast units by prestressing** → stressing together of (pre)cast units

joint(ing) compound · Ausfugmasse *f*, Verfugemasse

jointing material · Fugenstoff *m*, Fugenmaterial *n*

~ **method**, ~ **system, method of jointing, system of jointing** · Verbindungssystem *n*, Verbindungsverfahren *n*

joint(ing) mortar, masonry ~ · Ausfugmörtel *m*, Vermauerungsmörtel, Mauermörtel, Fug(ungs)mörtel, Mauerspeise *f*, Fugenmörtel, Verfugemörtel; Speis *m* [*Süddeutschland*]

~ **piece, connecting** ~, **connection** ~· Anschlußstück *n*, Verbindungsstück

~ **precast units by prestressing, stressing together of precast units, tensioning together of precast units** · Zusammenspannen *n* von (Beton)Fertigteilen, Verbinden durch Vorspannung

~ **refractory cement** · feuerfester Fugenmörtel *m*, ff. ~ [*Feingemahlenes, meist angefeuchtetes feuerfestes Erzeugnis zum Ausfüllen von Fugen beim Zusammensetzen von Steinen. Der feuerfeste Mörtel muß in seiner Zusammensetzung den Steinen angepaßt sein*]

~ **rivet, connecting** ~, **connection** ~ · Anschlußniet *m*, Verbindungsniet

joint(ing) strip → (joint) sealing ~

jointing system, ~ **method, method of jointing, system of jointing** · Verbindungssystem *n*, Verbindungsverfahren *n*

jointless · fugenfrei, fugenlos

~ **floor(ing), seamless** ~, **composition** ~, **in-situ** ~, ~ **floor finish**, ~ **floor cover(ing), COMPF** [*In spite of the name, many jointless floors are best laid with joints at about 8 ft. apart, particularly those containing cement, to allow for shrinkage*] · fugenloser (Fuß)Boden(belag) *m*, (Fuß)Boden-Verbundbelag

joist [*One of a series of parallel beams, especially when forming part of a floor, ceiling or roof*] · Unterzug *m*

~, **(intermediate) floor** ~, **ceiling** ~, **intermediate** ~ · Deckenunterzug *m*, Trennß, Etagen~, Stockwerk~, Geschoß~

~ **floor, joisted** ~, **beam** ~, **single** ~ · Balken(träger)decke *f*, Unterzugdecke

~ **grillage** · Unterzugrost *m*

joist(ed) floor, single ~, **beam** ~ · Balken(träger)decke *f*, Unterzugdecke

joisted sub-floor, ~ **underfloor** · Unterboden *m* auf Unterzügen

~ **timber sub-floor**, ~ **wood(en)** ~ · Holzunterboden *m* mit Unterzügen

~ **underfloor**, ~ **sub-floor** · Unterboden *m* auf Unterzügen

~ **wood(en) sub-floor**, ~ **timber** ~ · Holzunterboden *m* mit Unterzügen

to jolt · schocken

jolt moulding (Brit.); ~ **molding (US)** · schockende Rüttelverformung *f* [*Formgebung, bei der die Form mit der Masse einer Reihe von Stößen ausgesetzt wird, wobei von oben ein zusätzlicher Druck ausgeübt werden kann*]

jolting · Schocken *n*, schockende (Ein-)Rütt(e)lung *f*

~ **table** · Schocktisch *m*

Jómon style [*A traditional Japanese style of architecture*] · Jómon-Stil *m*

journeyman, tradesman, craftsman · Geselle *m*

~ **painter** [*One who has had at least three years' experiance and schooling as an apprentice*] · Anstreichergeselle *m*, Malergeselle

jubé, jube · Lettner *m*

~, **rood loft, jube** [*A loft or gallery over the rood screen in a church*] · Lettnerempore *f*

jubilee exhibition, anniversary ~ · Jubiläumsausstellung *f*

judas, (door) viewer · (Tür)Gucker *m*, (Tür)Spion *m*

Julian basilica · Basilika *f* Julia

jumbo brick [*A generic term indicating a brick larger in size than the standard. Some producers use this term to describe oversize brick of specific dimensions manufactured by them*] · Großziegel *m*

jump [*A step in a brick or masonry course or in a foundation*] · Sprung *m*

jumping vault [*This constructional form is a regional speciality of the Silesians and represents another decisive break with the High Gothic principle of regularity*] · Springgewölbe *n*

junction, inlet, branch, pipe ~ · (Rohr-)Abzweig *m*, (Rohr)Zulauf *m*

~ **box** → conduit ~

~ **of masonry walls, masonry wall junction** · Maueranschluß *m*

~ ~ **walls, wall junction** · Wandanschluß *m*

~ **piece without saddle** · Einlaß *m* ohne Flansch [*Kanalisationssteinzeug*]

junior department store · Kleinwarenhaus n

junk pipe, sub-standard ~ · nichtnormengerechtes Rohr n

Jurassic limestone · Jurakalk(stein) m

~ sandstone · Jurasandstein m

jute backing · Juteunterlage f

~ board, ~ sheet · Gewebebauplatte f [Aus mehreren imprägnierten Jutelagen unter hydraulischem Druck gepreßte Platte]

~ burlap (US); ~ **hessian** (canvas) (Brit.) · Hessian n, Juteleinen n

~ ~ mat (US); ~ **hessian** (canvas) ~ (Brit.) · Juteleinenbahn f, Hessianbahn

(~) canvas, CANV, can · Baumwolljute f

~ factory, ~ mill, ~ works, ~ plant · Jutefabrik f, Jutewerk n

~ (fiber) (US); ~ (fibre) (Brit.) · Jute(faser) f [Jute ist die Bastfaser der in Ostindien wachsenden Pflanzen Corchorus capsularis und Corchorus oliotorius. Die gegen Feuchtigkeit widerstandsfähigen Fasern, die infolge ihrer Verholzung brüchig und nur mäßig zerreißfest sind, werden zu Geweben für Linoleum, Bitumengewebebahnen, Fugendeckstreifen und Bespannstoffen (Juteleinen, Hessian, Rupfen) für Wände verarbeitet]

~ hessian (canvas) (Brit.); ~ **burlap** (US) · Hessian n, Juteleinen n

~ ~ (~) mat (Brit.); ~ **burlap** ~ (US) · Juteleinenbahn f, Hessianbahn

~ insert(ion) · Juteeinlage f

~ lamination · Jutekaschierung f

~ mill, ~ works, ~ plant, ~ factory · Jutefabrik f, Jutewerk n

~ plant, ~ mill, ~ works, ~ factory · Jutefabrik f, Jutewerk n

~ sacking · Jutegrobgewebe n

~ sheet → ~ board

~ twine · Juteschnur f

~ waste · Juteabfall m

~ webbing · Jutegewebe n

~ works, ~ plant, ~ mill, ~ factory · Jutefabrik f, Jutewerk n

~ wrap(ping) · Jutebandage f, Juteumwick(e)lung f

jutty, jetty, projection, fore part [A projecting or overhanging part of a building] · Vorsprung m

K

K factor · Wärmedurchgangszahl f, K-Wert m, K-Zahl f

Kaiser dome · Kaiserkuppel f

~ floor · Kaiserdecke f [Eine Geschoßdecke der Kaiser-Decken G.m.b.H. & Co.]

~ wall · Kaiserwand f [Eine Wand der Kaiser-Decken G.m.b.H. & Co.]

Kaiserworth at Goslar · Kaiserpfalz f zu Goslar

kalasa [A finial of vase or 'melon' form] · Kalasa m [Vasenförmiger Aufsatz in der indischen Architektur]

Kani('s) method · Kani-Verfahren n

kaolin, china clay, porcelain clay, porcelain earth · Kaolin m, Porzellanerde f, Weißerde, Porzellanton m, weißer Ton, Weißton [Wenig plastischer, weißbrennender, aus verhältnismäßig grobkristallinem Kaolinit bestehender Ton aus primären oder sekundären Lagerstätten. Man unterscheidet den Rohkaolin, der noch Reste des Muttergesteins enthält, und den Reinkaolin (aus sekundärer Lagerstätte oder abgewaschener Rohkaolin)]

~ powder, powder(ed) kaolin · Kaolinpulver n

~ sand · Kaolinsand m

kaolinisation · Kaolinisierung f

kaolinite, $Al_2Si_2O_5(OH)_4$ · Kaolinit m [Tonmineral der Kaolinitgruppe; Hauptbestandteil des Kaolins]

~ group · Kaolinit-Gruppe f

kaolinitic clay · kaolinitischer Ton m, Kaolinton

Kauri copal · Kaurikopal m

~ resin · Kauriharz n

KB → kneebrace

K. Ct. → Keene's cement

keel arch · persischer Bogen m, zwiebelförmiger ~, Kielbogen, Wellenbogen

Keene's cement, flooring ~, K. Ct.; class D (gypsum-)plaster, (gypsum-)plaster of Class D (Brit.) [B.S. 1191] · Hartalabaster m, Marmorgips m [Fehlname: Marmorzement m. Doppelt gebrannter und zwischen den beiden Brennvorgängen in geeigneter Weise entweder mit Borax oder Alaun getränkter Gips. DIN 1168]

keep, donjon, dungeon · Donjon m, Bergfried m, Belfried, Berchfrit m

~ and bailey castle · Bergfriedburg f, Belfriedburg

keeper (plate), strike (~), striking ~; (lock) forend (Brit.); lock front, lock faceplate, lock strike (US) · Schließblech n [DIN 18251]

keeping dry · Trockenhalten n

~-room (US); sitting-room, living-room (Brit.) · Wohnzimmer n

keep-like tower · donjonähnlicher Turm m

Keramzite concrete [A type of expanded clay-aggregate concrete in the USSR] · Keramsitbeton m

keratophyre · Keratophyr m

kerb (Brit.); curb · Bordstein m [DIN 483 Betonbordsteine; DIN 482 Naturbordsteine]

~ below ground → curb ~ ~

~ mould, concrete ~ ~ (Brit.); (concrete) curb mold (US) · (Beton)Bordsteinform f

kerbed footway (Brit.); curbed ~ · Fußweg m mit Bordstein

kern · (Querschnitt)Kern m, Kernfläche f [Bereich eines Stabquerschnittes innerhalb dessen eine Normalkraft, z.B. eine Druckkraft, angreifen kann, ohne daß irgendwo Biegezugspannungen entstehen]

~ **concrete** · Kernbeton m [umschnürte Säule]

~ **cross-section, core** ~ · Kernquerschnitt m [umschnürte Stahlbetonstütze]

~ **limit** · Kerngrenze f

~ **line** · Kernlinie f [Querschnitt]

~ **point** · Kernpunkt n [Grenzpunkt der Kernfläche in einer Hauptachse des Querschnittes]

~ ~ **moment** · Kern(punkt)moment m [Biegemoment, bezogen auf die Kernpunkte eines Querschnittes]

~ **strength, core** ~ · Kernfestigkeit f [umschnürte Betonstütze]

kerosine (US); **paraffin oil** (Brit.) · Paraffinöl n aus Erdöl hergestellt, paraffinum liquidum

~**-fluxed** · kerosingefluxt

kerosine number · Kerosinzahl f

ketone · Keton n [DIN 53247]

~ **resin** · Ketonharz n

kettle, gypsum ~ · (Gips)Kammerofen m

~ **boiled linseed oil, pale bodied** ~ ~ [Linseed oil in which enough lead, manganese or cobalt salts have been incorporated to make the oil harden more rapidly when spread in thin coatings. B.S. 259] · gekochtes Leinöl n, (Leinöl)Firnis m

key [That property of a surface, inherent or introduced, that facilitates the bonding of another material to it] · Hafteigenschaft f [einer Oberfläche]

~ · Haftgrund m

~ ~ → ~ **frieze**

~ [A slotted joint in concrete, such as tongue and groove] · Schlitzfuge f

~, (coding) **legend** · Legende f, Zeichenerklärung f, Zeichenschlüssel m

~ → **mechanical** ~

~, **top, crown, vertex, apex** · Scheitel(-punkt) m

(~) **bit** · (Schlüssel)Bart m

~ **block, top** ~, **apex** ~, **crown** ~, **vertex** ~, **closer** · (Bogen)Schlußstein m, (Bogen)Scheitelstein [veraltet: König m, Kolophon m]

~ **course, keystone layer** [A course of stones instead of a keystone at the crown of a vault or wider arch] · Schlußsteinlage f, Schlußsteinschicht f

~ **keyed, hacked** · aufgerauht, rauh [zum Verputzen]

~, **grooved** · gerillt, (lang)genutet

~ **beam, compound** ~, **built-up** ~ · zusammengesetzter Holzbalken(träger) m

~ **dowel, grooved** ~ · gerillter (Stab-)Dübel m, (lang)genuteter ~

~ **girder, built-up** ~, **compound** ~ · zusammengesetzter Holzträger m

~ **joint, open** ~ · Hohlfuge f, offene Fuge [Unausgefüllter Zwischenraum zweier zusammenstoßender fester Bauteile oder Baustoffe, z.B. bei Trockenmauerwerk]

~ **soffit, hacked** ~ [for plaster finish] · aufgerauhte Untersicht f, rauhe ~

key function · Schlüsselfunktion f

~ **groove** → **mechanical** ~ ~

~ **head** · Schlüsselkopf m

~ **hinge, top** ~, **crown** ~, **apex** ~, **vertex** ~ · Scheitelgelenk n

~ **hog, top** ~, **apex** ~, **crown** ~, **vertex** ~ · Scheitelüberhöhung f

keyhole · Schlüsselloch n

keyholed back plate · Anschraubplatte f mit Schlüsselloch, Unterplatte ~ ~

keying, hacking · Aufrauhen n [zum Verputzen]

key-in knob (door) lock → **knob** (~) ~

key joint, crown ~, **top** ~, **vertex** ~, **apex** ~ · Scheitelfuge f, Schlußfuge [Fuge am höchsten Gewölbepunkt oder Bogenpunkt, wenn kein Scheitelstein vorhanden ist]

keyless lock · schlüsselloser Verschluß m

key-operated lock · Schlüsselverschluß m

key pattern, Greek ~ ~, **Grecian fret, (Greek) fret** · rechtwink(e)lig gebrochener Mäander m, ~ gebrochenes Mäanderornament n, à la greque-Ornament

~ **plate,** ~ (e)**scutcheon** · Schild n, Schlüssel~, Schlüssellochdeckel m

~ **rack** · Schlüsselbrett n

~ **sag, top** ~, **crown** ~, **apex** ~, **vertex** ~ · Scheitelsenkung f

keystone, top stone, crown stone, apex stone, vertex stone [The central stone of an arch or a vault; sometimes carved] · Scheitelstein m aus Naturstein, Schlußstein ~ ~

~ **layer, key course** [A course of stones instead of a keystone at the crown of a vault or wide arch] · Schlußsteinlage f, Schlußsteinschicht f

to key up · spannen [Bogen; Gewölbe]

khān, caravanserai, caravansary · Karawanserei f, Konak m, (C)Han m, karawan serail m

kick(ing) plate [A metal plate placed along the lower edge of a door to prevent the marring of the finish by shoe marks] · Trittplatte f, Stoßplatte, Sockelblech n, Stoßblech, Sockelplatte

~ **strip** [A metal strip placed along the lower edge of a door to prevent the marring of the finish by shoe marks] · Trittleiste f, Stoßleiste

kieselguhr, Tripoli-powder, diatomaceous earth [It is sometimes erroneously called 'infusorial earth'] · Kieselgur f, m, Diatomeenerde f [Kieselige Rückstände aus der organischen Natur. Sie bestehen entweder aus den Skeletten einfacher Pflanzen, der Diatomeen, oder

kieselguhr — kitchen system

sie sind tierischen Ursprungs und aus den Schalen von Radiolarien aufgebaut]

~ **brick**, Tripoli-powder ~, diatomaceous earth ~ · Kieselgurziegel *m* [*Fehlname: Kieselgurstein m. Er wird aus Kieselgur, Ton und Ausbrennstoff durch Brennen hergestellt*]

~ **concrete**, Tripoli-powder ~ · Kieselgurbeton *m*

~ **covering cord**, Tripoli-powder ~ ~ · Kieselgurschnur *f* [*für Dämm- und Isolierzwecke*]

~ **slab**, Tripoli-powder ~ · Kieselgurplatte *f*

killed alloy, fully ~ ~, stabilized ~, dead ~, quiet ~ · stabilisierte Legierung *f*, beruhigte ~

~ **spirits** · wässerige Zinkchloridlösung *f*, wäßrige ~, Lötwasser *n*, $ZnCl_2$

~ **steel** → fully ~ ~

killing substance, destroying ~ · Vernichtungsmittel *n* [*z.B. gegen Schimmel, Bakterien, Insekten, Algen usw.*]

kiln, burning ~ · (Brenn)Ofen *m* [*Keramische Industrie und Zementindustrie*]

~ **brick**, ~ refractory ~ · Ofenstein *m*

~ **building** · Ofenhalle *f*

(kiln-)burned, (kiln-)burnt, (kiln-)fired · (ofen)gebrannt

kiln cart · Ofenwagen *m*

~ **discharge** · Ofenaustrag *m*

(kiln-)fired, (kiln-)burnt, (kiln-)burned · (ofen)gebrannt

kiln-fresh brick · ofenfrischer Ziegel *m*

kiln insulation · Ofenisolierung *f*

~ **(refractory) brick** · Ofenstein *m*

~ **scum** · Abbrandanflug *m*, Aschenanflug [*Auf den Ofensteinen*]

~ **size** · Ofengröße *f*

~ **waste heat** · Ofenabhitze *f*

kilometre post · Kilometerstein *m*

kilowatt-hour meter [*B.S. 37*] · Kilowattstundenzähler *m*

kinematic chain · kinematische Kette *f*

~ **indeterminacy** · kinematische Unbestimmtheit *f*

~ **similarity**, ~ similitude · kinematische Ähnlichkeit *f*

~ **solution**, upper bound ~ · kinematische Lösung *f*

~ **theorem**, upper bound ~ · kinematischer Satz *m*

~ **theory of framework** · kinematische Theorie *f* des Fachwerks, ~ Fachwerktheorie

~ **viscosity**, KV [*The ratio of viscosity to density*] · kinematische Viskosität *f*

kinematically determinate · kinematisch bestimmt

~ **indeterminate** · kinematisch unbestimmt

~ ~ **structure** · kinematisch unbestimmtes Bauwerk *n*

~ **rigid** · kinematisch starr

kinetic energy · kinetische Energie *f*, Energie der Bewegung, Bewegungsenergie

king-and-queen (roof) truss → queen post (~) ~

~ **post** · einfach stehender (Dach)Stuhl *m*

~ ~ · Firstpfosten *m*, Firstsäule *f*

~ ~, broach ~, crown ~; joggle ~ (US) [*Of a king-post roof truss*] · Hängesäule *f*

~ ~ **and wind filling** · einfach stehender (Dach)Stuhl *m* und Versenkung

king-post roof truss · einfaches Hängewerk *n*, einsäuliges ~, einsäuliger Hängebock *m*, einfacher Hängebock

king's chamber · Königskammer *f*

~ **master mason** · Hofbaumeister *m*, königlicher Baumeister, kgl. Baumeister

~ **tomb**, royal ~ · Königsgrab *n*

Kirchhoff('s) theory · Kirchhoffsche Theorie *f*

kitchen building block module, unitized kitchen unit · Küchen(installations)block *m*, Küchenraumblock, Küchenraumzelle

~ **burning appliance**, ~ fire, ~ furnace · Küchenfeuerstätte *f*, Küchenfeuerung *f*

~ **central heating** · Küchenzentralheizung *f*

~ **closet** · Küchen-Einbauschrank *m*, Küchen-Wandschrank

~ **court**, ~ yard · Küchenhof *m*

kitchen/dining room, dining kitchen, dwelling kitchen · Wohnküche *f*, Eßküche

kitchen fire, ~ furnace, ~ burning appliance · Küchenfeuerstätte *f*, Küchenfeuerung *f*

~ **fitments**, ~ fittings · Küchenausstattung *f*

~ **fittings**, ~ fitments · Küchenausstattung *f*

~ **floor;** ~ story (US); ~ storey (Brit.) · Küchenetage *f*, Küchenstockwerk *n*, Küchengeschoß *n*

~ **for large-scale catering** · Großküche *f*

~ **furnace**, ~ fire, ~ burning appliance · Küchenfeuerstätte *f*, Küchenfeuerung *f*

~ **garden** · Küchengarten *m*

~ **installation**, ~ system · Küchenanlage *f*, Kücheninstallation *f*, Kücheneinrichtung *f*

~ **of works canteen** · Betriebsküche *f*

(~) **range**, kitchener · (Küchen)Herd *m*

(~) **sink**, KS · Spüle *f*

~ **storey** (Brit.) → ~ floor

~ **system**, ~ installation · Küchenkeinrichtung *f*, Kücheninstallation *f*, Küchenanlage *f*

kitchen tower — kraft paper foil

~ **tower** · Küchenturm *m*

~ **waste** · Küchenmüll *m*

~ ~ → slop water

~ ~ **disposal pipe** · Küchenfallrohr *n* [*Aus Steinzeugrohren hergestellt*]

~ ~ ~ **shaft** · Küchenfallschacht *m* [*Aus Formsteinen hergestellt*]

~ **yard,** ~ **court** · Küchenhof *m*

kitchener, (kitchen) range · (Küchen-) Herd *m*

kitchenet(te) · Kleinstküche *f*, Kochnische *f*

Kleine (hollow) floor [*It is made up of hollow clay blocks in rows, but not cemented together, spaces being left between them. Into these spaces the reinforcement is introduced, and then the entire assembly is enclosed in a fine quality of concrete, so producing a uniform slab*] · Kleinedecke *f*, Kleinesche (Steineisen)Decke

~ (~) ~ **(clay) brick,** ~ ((~) ~ (~)) **block** · Kleinescher (Decken)Ziegel *m*; ~ (Decken)Stein *m* [*Fehlname*]

Kleinlogel metal(lic) aggregate, ~ ~ **abrasive (material)** · Stahlbeton *m* Kleinlogel [*Markenbezeichnung für einen Hart(beton)stoff zur Herstellung von Stahlbetonbelägen*]

Klemm glue · Klemmleim *m*, WHK-Leim [*Nach dem Erfinder Klemm benannter Kaltleim*]

kneebrace, KB · Strebe *f* [*Ein diagonales Konstruktionsglied von einer Wand oder Mauer zu einem Dachbinder zur Aussteifung gegen Windlasten*]

knee bracket plate, connection ~, **connecting** ~, **corner** ~, **fish** ~, **joint** ~, **gusset** ~, **binding** ~ · Knoten-(punkt)verbindung *f*

kneeling figure · Beterstandbild *n*

knife application · Auftrag(en) *m*, (*n*) mit Messer, Messerauftrag

knife-blade test, knife-scratch ~ · Spanprüfung *f* von Anstrichen [*DIN 53155*]

knife cut, flat-cut, sliced · gemessert, vermessert [*Furnier*]

knife-cut veneer, sliced ~, flat-cut ~ · Messerfurnier *n* [*DIN 68330*]

knife edge load, strip ~, line ~, (col-) linear ~ [*Forces on a long narrow member, e.g. a beam*] · Schneidenlast *f*, Linienlast, Streckenlast

~ ~ **loading** → line ~

knife-scratch test, knife-blade ~ · Spanprüfung *f* von Anstrichen [*DIN 53155*]

knifing filler, ~ **stopper,** ~ **stopping;** ~ **Swedish putty,** ~ **spactling compound (US)** [*A filling composition suitable for application with a filling knife as distinct from one made for brush application*] · Ziehspachtel(-masse) *m*, (*f*), Messerspachtel(masse)

knitting layer [*A layer of cement grout or fine concrete between old and new concrete*] · Verbundschicht *f*, Verbundlage *f*

knob, top · Knopf *m* [*Dachverzierung*]

~, **door** ~ · (Tür)Knopf *m*

~ **(door) fitting,** ~ (~) **furniture (door) knob** ~ · Knopf(tür)beschlag *m*, Türknopfbeschlag

~ (~) **fittings** → (door) knob ~

~ (~) **furniture** → ~ (~) **fitting**

~ (~) **hardware** → (door) knob fittings

~ (~) **lock, key-in** ~ (~) ~ · Knopf-(zylinder)schloß *n*, Knopftürschloß

~ **fitting** → ~ door ~

~ **fittings** → door ~ ~

~ **furniture** → ~ (door) fitting

~ **hardware** → (door) knob fittings

~ **lock** → ~ door ~

knobb(l)ing, skiffling [*Dressing stones roughly in the quarry by removing protruding humps*] · Rohbearbeitung *f*

knobboss, pendant (boss) · (Zapfen-) Knauf *m*

knocked down [*Description of building components or machinery, delivered to a site in unassembled state*] · zerlegt

knocker, door ~ · (Tür)Klopfer *m*

knock-out · ausbrechbare Vorpressung *f* [*Isolierpreßstoffleuchte*]

knot · kleiner (Gewölbe)Schlußstein *m*

~ [*A localized glassy inclusion in glass*] · Tropfen(schliere) *m*, (*f*)

knuckle · Sicke *f*

~ **length** · Gewerbelänge *f*, Länge der Scharnierrolle, Rollenlänge

Koenen floor · Koenen-Decke *f*, Koenensche Plandecke, Plandecke von Koenen

~ **plate** · Rippendecken-Schalblech *n*, Koenenblech

Kommerell bead bend test · Aufschweißbiegeprüfung *f* nach Kommerell, Aufschweißbiegeprobe *f* ~ ~, Aufschweißbiegeversuch *m* ~ ~, Kommerellversuch, Kommerellprobe, Kommerellprüfung [*Baustahl. DIN 17100 und Ö Norm M 3052*]

Kraemer-Sarnow softening point · Erweichungspunkt *m* Krämer-Sarnow, Erweichungstemperatur *f* ~, KS-Erweichungspunkt, KS-Erweichungstemperatur [*Ist in °C die Temperatur, bei der eine 5 g schwere Quecksilbersäule durch eine in ein Glasröhrchen eingeschmolzene, 5 mm hohe Kohlenteerpechsäule oder ähnlichem mit 7 mm Durchmesser bei Erwärmung von 1 grd/Minute hindurchtritt*]

kraft paper [*A strong brown paper, made from wood pulp and sulphate*] · Kraftpapier *n*

~ ~ **foil** · Kraftpapierfolie *f*

Kremnitz white · Kremserweiß n [Bleiweißsorte feinster Art, nur als Malfarbe gebräuchlich]

KS, (kitchen) sink · Spüle f

Kubelka-Munk theory [The theoretical principles of colo(u)r mixing laid down by Kubelka and Munk] · Zweikonstantentheorie f, Kubelka-Munk-Theorie

Kufic inscription, ~ **lettering** · kufische Inschrift f

Kühl cement · Bauxitlandzement m, Kühl-Zement

kukkersite · estnischer Ölschiefer m

KV → kinematic viscosity

k-value · Wärmedurchgangszahl (k) f, k-Wert m [kcal/m/h°C. Wärmemenge, die in 1 Stunde durch 1 m² einer Wand von der Dicke d (in m) hindurchgeht, wenn der Temperaturunterschied $t_i - t_a$ zwischen der beiderseits angrenzenden Luft 1°C beträgt]

kyanite · Cyanit m, Disthen m, Zyanit [Eines der drei Minerale die die gleiche Formel $Al_2O_3 \cdot SiO_2$ haben, jedoch in ihrer Struktur verschieden sind. In Erweiterung dient dieser Ausdruck auch zur Bezeichnung des Gesteins (Rohstoffs)]

L

L threshold, angle ~ · Winkel(tür)schwelle f

LA, lightning arrester · (Blitz)Ableiter m

label → hood-mould(ing)

~, scroll, banderol(e), streamer · Spruchband n, Schriftband, Banderole f

labile, quick-breaking, rapid-setting · schnellzerfallend, labil, unstabil [Bitumenemulsion]

lability, instability · Labilität f, Instabilität

~ coefficient, instability ~, ~ **number** · Labilitätszahl, Instabilitätszahl

~ due to sliding, instability ~ ~ ~ · Labilität f durch Gleiten, Instabilität ~ ~

~ ~ ~ uneven settlement, instability ~ ~ ~ ~ ~ [e.g. Leaning Tower of Pisa] · Labilität f durch schiefe Setzung, Instabilität ~ ~ ~

~ effect, instability ~ · Labilitätswirkung f, Instabilitätswirkung

~ number → ~ coefficient

lab(oratory) bench tile · Labor(atoriums)tischfliese f [DIN 12912]

~ tile · Labor(atoriums)fliese f

laboratory tower · Labor(atoriums)turm m

labyrinth · Labyrinth n, Jerusalemsweg m [Eine musivische Fußbodenverzierung]

~ of Crete · Palast m des Minotaurus auf Kreta

~ waterstop, ~ **waterbar** · Labyrinthfugenband n

lac · Schellack m

~ without sticks, seedlack · Körner(schel)lack m

lace, braid · Litze f

laced valley · eingebundene Kehle f

lace-like spire, openwork ~ · durchbrochenes Zeltdach n, durchbrochener Turmhelm m [Fehlname: durchbrochene Pyramide f]

lacework · Netzwerk n

lacing [The distribution of steel of a reinforced-concrete slab] · Armierungsverteilung f, Bewehrungsverteilung

~ of flat bars → flat (rolled) iron lacing

lack of style, absence ~ ~ · Stillosigkeit f

laconicum, sudatorium, caldarium, (dry) sweating room, hot room [The (dry) sweating room in a Roman bath building] · römischer Schwitzraum m, Sudatorium n, Schwitzraum einer römischen Therme, römisches Schwitzbad n, Caldarium n, Sudatio n, Assun n

lacquer · Lackfarbe f

~ curtain coating (method) · Lackgießen n, Lackgießverfahren, Gießlackierung f, Gießlackieren

~ film · Lackfarbenfilm m

~ for building construction purposes · Bautenlackfarbe f [Fehlname: Malerlackfarbe]

~-grade resin, varnish ~ · Lackharz n

lacquer solution · Lackfarbenlösung f

~ thinner · Lackfarben-Verdünnungsmittel n

lacquered hardboard · lackierte Hartplatte f, ~ harte Holzfaserplatte, Lackplatte

lactic acid · Milchsäure f

lacunar, laquear · Lakunarie f, vertieftes Feld n

ladder access · Leiter(auf)gang m

~ frame · Leiterrahmen m

~ hook · Leiterhaken m

(~) rung, stave, tread, rundle, LR · (Leiter)Sprosse f

~ scaffold(ing) · Leitergerüst n [DIN 4411]

~ web · Leiterkordel f [Jalousie]

ladies' changing room, women's ~ ~, **female** ~ ~ · Damenumkleide(raum) f, (m), Frauenumkleide(raum)

~ (drawing) room, women's (~) ~, **female (~)** ~ [See remark under 'drawing room'] · Damenzimmer n, Damenraum m

~ hairdressing shop, women's ~ ~, **female** ~ ~ · Damen(friseur)salon m

~ room → ~ drawing ~

~ toilet, women's ~, **female** ~, **ladies' room** · Damentoilette f

ladle · Gießlöffel m [Maurerwerkzeug]

ladle clay — laminated lattice girder

~ **clay,** foundry ~ · Gießton *m*

Lady Chapel [*A chapel dedicated to the Virgin, usually built east of the chancel and forming a projection from the main building, in the U.K. it is normally rectangular in plan*] · Marienkapelle *f*, Scheitelkapelle, Muttergotteskapelle

lagging section (Brit.); (pipe) ~, preformed (pipe insulation) ~ · Schale *f* [*Für Isolier- und Dämmzwecke*]

~ ~ **for cold protection** → preformed (pipe insulation) ~ ~ ~ ~

~ ~ ~ **heat protection** (Brit.) → preformed (pipe insulation) ~ ~ ~ ~

Lagrange's multiplier · Lagrangescher Multiplikator *m*

laid contrary to the stratum · andersgelegt [*Natursteinblock*]

laid-on thread, applied ~ · Fadenauflage *f* [*Plastische Verzierung der Oberfläche von Hohlgläsern*]

lake → ~ pigment

~ **asphalt,** ~ pitch [*In this type of naturally occurring asphalt the mineral matter is finely divided and dispersed through the (asphaltic) bitumen (Brit.)/ asphalt (US) which is the major component*] · Seeasphalt *m*

~ **colour** (Brit.) → ~ (pigment)

~ **(pigment),** ~ colour (Brit.); dyestuff lake [*A special class of pigments consisting of organic colouring matter, chemically or physically adsorbed on an inorganic base or carrier. A typical base is alumina. Lake colours are characterized by bright colour and pronounced translucency when made into paint*] · Farblack *m*

~ **pitch,** ~ asphalt [*In this type of naturally occurring asphalt the mineral matter is finely divided and dispersed through the (asphaltic) bitumen (Brit.)/ asphalt (US) which is the major component*] · Seeasphalt *m*

~-**village** · Pfahldorf *n*

'**Lambda' system** · ,,Lambda"-System *n* [*Dieses System mit ,,T" und ,,L"-förmigen Stützen und in den Momentennullpunkten gelenkig angeschlossenem Riegel wird bei geneigtem Dach und bei kurzen, steifen Stielen ausgeführt*]

lamb's(-)wool cylinder · Lammfellrolle *f*, Lammfellwalze *f*, Lammfellroller *m* [*Farbrollgerät*]

~ **roller** · Lammfell-Farbrollgerät *n*

~ **tool** · Lammfellwerkzeug *n*

lamella cupola, ~ dome, lattice(d) ~ · Lamellenkuppel *f*

~ **dome,** ~ cupola, lattice(d) ~ · Lamellenkuppel *f*

~ **mat** · Lamell-Matte *f* [*Rockwool-Erzeugnis; patentrechtlich geschützt*]

~ **roof** · Lamellendach *n*

~ **system,** lattice(d) ~ · Lamellensystem *n* [*Kuppel*]

laminate, paper ~, all-paper ~ · (Kunst-) Schichtstoffplatte *f*

~ **insulating board** → laminated ~

laminated · kaschiert

~, multi(ple)-layer(ed) · viellagig, mehrlagig, vielschichtig, mehrschichtig

~ **arch(ed girder)** → (glue(d)) laminated (timber) ~ (~)

~ **article,** ~ product · Schichtstoffartikel *m*, Schichtstoffgegenstand *m*, Schichtstofferzeugnis *n*

~ **basalt** · Plattenbasalt *m*

~ **beam** → (glue(d)) laminated (timber) ~

laminate(d) board, ~ sheet · Schichtplatte *f*, Mehrschichtenplatte, mehrschichtige Platte

laminated board; laminboard (Brit.) · Tischlerplatte *f* mit Stäbchenmittellage, Stäbchenplatte

~ **cover(ing)** · Mehrschichtenbelag *m*

~ **curved beam** · gebogener Schichtholzbalken(träger) *m*

~ **edge beam** → (glue(d)) laminated (timber) ~ ~

~ **fabric** → ~ roofing ~

~ **fiber wallboard** (US); ~ fibre ~ (Brit.) · Schichtfaserwandplatte *f*, Schichtwandfaserplatte

~ **form(work) board,** ~ forms ~, ~ shuttering ~, ~ ~ sheet · Mehrschichten-Schal(ungs)platte *f*

~ **frame** → (glue(d)) laminated (timber) ~

~ **girder** → (glue(d)) laminated (timber) ~

~ **insulating board,** ~ ~ sheet, ~ ~ slab, ~ insulation(-grade) ~, laminate ~ ~ · Mehrschichten-Isolierplatte *f*

~ ~ **glass,** ~ insulation(-grade) ~ Mehrscheibenisolierglas *n*

~ ~ **glazing,** ~ insulation(-grade) ~ · Mehrscheiben-Isolierverglasung *f*, Mehrscheiben-Isoliereinglasung

~ ~ **sheet,** ~ ~ board, ~ ~ slab, ~ insulation(-grade) ~ · Mehrschichten-Isolierplatte *f*

~ ~ **slab,** ~ ~ sheet, ~ ~ board, ~ insulation(-grade) ~ · Mehrschichten-Isolierplatte *f*

~ **insulation(-grade) board,** ~ ~ sheet, ~ ~ slab, ~ insulating ~ Mehrschichten-Isolierplatte *f*

~ ~ **glass,** ~ insulating ~ · Mehrscheibenisolierglas *n*

~ ~ **glazing,** ~ insulating ~ · Mehrscheiben-Isolierverglasung *f*

~ ~ **sheet,** ~ ~ board, ~ ~ slab, ~ insulating ~ · Mehrschichten-Isolierplatte *f*

~ ~ **slab,** ~ ~ sheet, ~ ~ board, ~ insulating ~ · Mehrschichten-Isolierplatte *f*

~ **lattice girder** → (glue(d)) laminated (timber) ~ ~

laminated light(weight) building slab — lamination

~ **light(weight) building slab** · Mehrschichtenleichtbauplatte f

~ **limestone,** platy ~, slabby ~ · Kalkschiefer m, Plattenkalk(stein) m

~ **material,** ~ plastic, glued laminate · Schichtstoff m

~ **melamine resin board** · Melaminharz-Schichtstoffplatte f

~ **overlay,** ~ topping · Mehrschichtenüberzug m

~ **paper** [See remark under 'Pappe'] · Schichtpappe f

~ ~, duplex ~ · Hartpapier n, HP, kaschiertes Papier, Mehrschichtenpapier

~ **plastic,** ~ material, glued laminate · Schichtstoff m

~ ~ **board** · Schichtstoffplatte f

~ ~ **panel** · Schichtstofftafel f

~ ~ ~ **with decorative surface,** ~ ~ ~ ~ ornamental ~ · dekorative Schicht(preß)stofftafel f

~ ~ ~ ~ **ornamental surface,** ~ ~ ~ ~ decorative ~ · dekorative Schicht(preß)stofftafel f

~ **polyvinyl chloride cover(ing),** ~ PVC ~ · Polyvinylchlorid-Mehrschichtenbelag m, Mehrschichten-Polyvinylchloridbelag, Mehrschichten-PVC-Belag, PVC-Mehrschichtenbelag

~ **portal frame** → (glue(d)) laminated (timber) ~ ~

~ **product,** ~ article · Schichtstoffartikel m, Schichtstoffgegenstand m, Schichtstofferzeugnis n

~ **PVC cover(ing),** ~ polyvinyl chloride ~ · Polyvinylchlorid-Mehrschichtenbelag m, Mehrschichten-Polyvinylchloridbelag, Mehrschichten-PVC-Belag, PVC-Mehrschichtenbelag

~ **rafter** → (glue(d)) laminated (timber) ~

~ **(raking) strut** → (glue(d)) laminated (timber) (~) ~

~ **(roofing) fabric,** multiple-layer(ed) (~) ~, ~ fabric for roofing · Mehrlagen-Roh(dach)pappe f, Mehrschichten-Roh(dach)pappe

~ **safety glass** · Mehrscheiben(sicherheits)glas n, Mehrschichten(sicherheits)glas, Mehrfachglas, Verbund(sicherheits)glas, laminiertes Sicherheitsglas [Es trägt auf der Scheibe eine Kollodiumschicht von so großer Adhäsionskraft, daß das eventuell zersprungene Glas an ihr haften bleibt, also nicht zerfällt]

laminate(d) sheet, ~ board · Schichtplatte f, Mehr~, mehrschichtige Platte

laminated shell roof → (glue(d)) laminated (timber) ~ ~

~ **shuttering board** → ~ form(work) ~

~ **strut** → (glue(d)) laminated (timber) (raking) ~

~ **system,** multilayer(ed) ~ · mehrlagige Konstruktion f, mehrschichtige ~, viellagige ~, vielschichtige ~

~ **timber** (Brit.) → glulam (wood)

~ **(~) arch(ed girder)** → (glue(d)) laminated wood ~ (~)

~ **(~) beam** → (glue(d)) ~ (~) ~

~ **(~) edge beam** → (glue(d)) ~ (~) ~ ~

~ **(~) frame** → (glue(d)) ~ (~) ~

~ **(~) girder** → (glue(d)) ~ (~) ~

~ **(~) lattice girder** → (glue(d)) ~ (~) ~ ~

~ **(~) portal frame** → (glue(d)) ~ (~) ~ ~

~ **(~) rafter** → (glue(d)) ~ (~) ~

~ **(~) (raking) strut** → (glue(d)) ~ (~) (~) ~

~ **(~) shell roof** → (glue(d)) ~ (~) ~ ~

~ **(~) strut** → (glue(d)) laminated (timber) (raking) ~

~ **(~) truss** → (glue(d)) ~ (~) truss(ed girder)

~ **topping,** ~ overlay · Mehrschichtenüberzug m

~ **truss(ed girder)** → (glue(d)) ~ (timber) ~ (girder)

~ **wall component,** ~ ~ member, ~ ~ unit · Mehrschichtenwandelement n

~ ~ **member,** ~ ~ unit, ~ ~ component · Mehrschichtenwandelement n

~ ~ **unit,** ~ ~ member, ~ ~ component · Mehrschichtenwandelement n

~ **wire(d) glass,** wire(d) laminated ~ · Drahtverbund(sicherheits)glas n, Stahlfadenverbundglas, Drahtsicherheitsglas

~ **wood** (Brit.) → glulam

~ ~ **arch(ed girder)** → glue(d) ~ ~ ~ (~)

laminating · Kaschieren n

~ [Peeling away in thin flakes, as in defective tiles] · Abschälen n

~ [The process of bonding laminations, or thin plates, together with adhesives] · Schichtverleimen n

~ **composition** · Kaschiermasse f

~ **film,** ~ sheeting · Schichtfolie f [Kunststoff]

~ **sheeting,** ~ film · Schichtfolie f [Kunststoff]

lamination · Texturfehler m [Feuerfestindustrie. 1) S-förmige Textur. S-Textur: Gerichtete Texturfehler, die zumeist beim Strangpressen entstehen. 2) Lagenbildung: Lagenförmige Textur, die manchmal beim Trockenpressen oder beim Nachpressen von Rohlingen (Batzen) auftritt]

~ · Schicht(en)bildung f, Blättrigkeit f [Keramikindustrie]

~ [Separation into two or more layers due to some discontinuity in the iron, usually a layer of nonmetallic inclusions] · Dopp(e)lung f

lamination — lantern roof

~ · Kaschierung f
laminboard (Brit.); laminated board · Tischlerplatte f mit Stäbchenmittellage, Stäbchenplatte
lamp · Lampe f
lampblack (pigment), vegetable black (~) · Lampenruß(pigment) m, (n), Lampenschwarz n
lamp compartment · Lampenraum m
~ **cord** (US); flex, flexible cable · (Geräte)Anschlußschnur f, Verbindungsschnur
(~) dimmer · Lichtregler m
~ **holder**, ~ socket · Lampenfassung f
~ **post** · Laternenpfahl m
lancet arch, acute ~ · überhöhter Spitzbogen m, lanzet(t)förmiger ~, Lanzet(t)bogen [*veraltete Benennung: überspitzter Bogen*]
~ **(window)** [*A narrow, sharply pointed window without tracery, set in a lancet arch*] · Lanzet(t)(bogen)fenster n
land, ground · Gelände n
~ **acquisition**, ~ purchase, acquisition of land, purchase of land · Grunderwerb m, Baulandbeschaffung f; Grundeinlösung [*Österreich*]
~ **asphalt** ~ pitch, shore asphalt · Landasphalt m [*Trinidad*]
~ **for housing construction** · Wohnbauland n
landing, floor, stair(case) ~ · (Treppen-)Absatz m, (Treppen)Podest n
~ **beam** → (stair(case)) ~ ~
~ **bearer** → (stair(case)) ~ ~
~ **binder** → (stair(case)) landing bearer
~ **(binding) joist** → (stair(case)) landing bearer
~ **ceiling joist** → (stair(case)) landing bearer
~ **door** · Wohnungstür f [*einer Etagenwohnung*]
~ **entrance** → ~ opening
~ **girder** → (stair(case)) landing beam
~ **header** → (stair(case)) ~ ~
~ **joist** → (stair(case)) landing beam
~ **length** → (stair(case)) ~ ~
~ **level** → (stair(case)) ~ ~
~ **opening**, ~ entrance · Aufzugöffnung f [*Durch eine Tür verschlossen*]
~ **post** → (stair(case)) ~ ~
~ **slab** → (stair(case)) ~ ~
~ **width** → (stair(case)) ~ ~
land pitch → ~ asphalt
~ **planning** · Baulandplanung f
~ **purchase**, ~ acquisition, purchase of land, acquisition of land · Grunderwerb m, Baulandbeschaffung f; Grundeinlösung [*Österreich*]
~ **-register** (Brit.) → plat
~ **speculation** · Bodenspekulation f

~ **tile** [*A porous clay pipe with open (butt) joints*] · perforiertes Tondränagerohr n
~ **use act** · Baunutzungsordnung f
to landscape · ländlich gestalten
landscape · Landschaft f
~ **architect** · Landschaftsarchitekt m
~ **design**, ~ treatment, ~ development, landscaping · Land(schafts)gestaltung f
~ **development** → ~ design
~ **gardener** · Landschaftsgärtner m
~ **park** · Landschaftspark m
~ **planning** · Landschaftsplanung f
~ **preservation** · Landschaftspflege f
~ **protection** · Landschaftsschutz m
~ ~ **area** · Landschaftsschutzgebiet n
~ **treatment** → ~ design
~ **work**, landscaping ~ · landschaftsgärtnerische Arbeiten fpl [*DIN 18320*]
landscaped interior · Wohnlandschaft f
~ **office room** · Bürogroßraum m
~ **terrace** · Grünterrasse f
landscaping → landscape design
~ **work**, landscape ~ · landschaftsgärtnerische Arbeiten fpl [*DIN 18320*]
lane, aisle, traffic ~ · Fahrgasse f [*Parkhaus; Tiefgarage*]
Langer beam · Langerscher Balken m
language lab(oratory) · Sprachlabor(atorium) n
lantern · Laterne f [*Beleuchtungskörper*]
~ → lantern(-light)
~ [*The room containing the lamp at the top of a lighthouse*] · Laterne f
~, light fitting (Brit.); (street lighting) luminaire (fixture) (US); light(ing) fixture [*A complete lighting device consisting of a light source, together with its direct appurtenances, such as globe, reflector, refractor, housing, and such support as is integral with the housing. The mast or bracket is not considered a part of the luminaire*] · Straßenleuchte f
(~) column of tapered sheet construction · Steckmast m aus Stahlblech, Stahlblech-Steckmast [*Ein Lichtmast, bei dem die konischen Schüsse von 1,50 m Länge ineinander gesteckt werden*]
(~) ~ ~ welded sheet construction · Schweiß-Beleuchtungsmast m, Schweiß(-Licht)mast
~ **girder** · Laternenträger m
~ **(-light)** lantern(-type) roof light [*A glazed construction, standing above the surface of a flat roof, designed to admit light to the space below*] · (Dach-)Laterne f, Aufdach n, Überdach, Dachkappe f, Dachreiter m, Dachhaube f, Aufreiter, Dachaufsatzfenster n, stehendes (Dach)Oberlicht n
~ **(light) roof** · Laternendach n
~ **ring** · Laternenring m
~ **roof**, ~ light ~ · Laternendach n

~ ~ light → lantern(-light)
~ tower, cimborio · Cimborio *m*, Laterne *f*
lantern(-type) roof light → lantern(-light)
to lap · überlappen
~ ~, over~ · überdecken [*Dachziegel*]
lap, over~ · Überdeckung *f* [*Dachziegel*]
~, lapping, over~ · Überdeckung *f*, Überlappung
~ [*The distance by which successive tiers of glazing lap one over the other*] · Überdeckung *f* [*kittlose Verglasung*]
~ → ~ width
~ joint, overlap(ping) ~ · Überlapp(ungs)stoß *m*, Übergreifungsstoß
~ ~ · Nahtüberdeckung *f*
~ length, over~ ~ · Überlappungslänge *f*
(~) siding (US) → weatherboarding
~ (width) · Überdeckung(sbreite) *f* [*Dachfalzstein*]
lap(ping), over~ · Überdeckung *f*, Überlappung
laquear, lacunar · Lakunarie *f*. vertieftes Feld *n*
larch shingle · Lärchenschindel *f*
larder · Speisekammer *f*
large-area specular reflector luminaire (US); ~ ~ ~ light fitting (Brit.) · Großflächen-Spiegelleuchte *f*
large block → ~ building ~
~ brickblock → large-sized clay ~
~ (building) block, ~ (~) tile [*See remark under 'Block'*] · Großblock *m*, Groß(block)stein *m*
~ (~) slab · Groß(bau)platte *f*
~ (~) tile, ~ (~) block [*See remark under 'Block'*] · Großblock *m*, Groß(block)stein *m*
large-capacity air raid shelter · Großluftschutzbunker *m*
~ boiler · Groß(heiz)kessel *m*
large cast (concrete) panel → ~ pre~ (~) ~
~ clay brickblock → large-sized ~ ~
~ flat head nail · Breitkopfnagel *m*
~ format · Großformat *n*
~ ~ board, ~ ~ sheet · Großformatplatte *f*, großformatige Platte
~ ~ sheet, ~ ~ board · Großformatplatte *f*, großformatige Platte
~ housing estate · Großsied(e)lung *f*
~ panel; storey-height ~ (Brit.); story-height ~ ~ (US) · Großtafel *f*
~ ~ construction; storey-height ~ ~ (Brit.); story-height ~ ~ (US) · Großtafelbau *m*
~ ~ shuttering, ~ ~ form(work); storey-height ~ ~ (Brit.); story-height ~ ~ (US) · Großtafelschalung *f*

~ ~ wall; storey-height ~ ~ (Brit.); story-height ~ ~ (US) · Großtafelwand *f*
~ ~ ~ block → ~ ~ ~ building
~ ~ ~ building, ~ ~ ~ structure, ~ ~ ~ block; storey-height ~ ~ ~ (Brit.); story-height ~ ~ ~ (US) · Großtafelgebäude *n*
~ ~ ~ structure → ~ ~ ~ building
~ ~ ~ system; storey-height ~ ~ ~ (Brit.); story-height ~ ~ ~ (US) · Großtafelbauweise *f*, Großtafelbausystem *n*
~ panelled structure · Großtafelbau(werk) *m*, (*n*)
~ (paving) sett, large-sized (~) ~ · Großpflasterstein *m* [*DIN 4300*]
~ praying chamber · Gebetshalle *f*
~ (pre)cast (concrete) panel, ~ prefab(ricated) ~ ~ · Groß-Betontafel *f*
~ prefab(ricated) concrete panel, ~ (pre)cast (~) ~ · Groß-Betontafel *f*
~ project → large-scale ~
~ rolling shutterdoor, ~ ~ shutter door · Großrolltor *n*
~ roof → ~-scale ~
large(-scale) project · Großprojekt *n*
~ roof · Großraumdach *n*
~ test · Großversuch *m*, Großprobe *f*, Großprüfung *f*
large sett → large(-sized) (paving) ~
~ shutterdoor, ~ shutter door · Großtor *n*
large(-sized) (clay) brickblock · Ziegelgroßblock *m*
~ (paving) sett · Großpflasterstein *m* [*DIN 4300*]
~ sett, ~ paving ~ · Großpflasterstein *m* [*DIN 4300*]
large slab, ~ building ~ · Groß(bau)platte *f*
large-span beam, long-span ~, wide-span ~ · Weitspannbalken(träger) *m*
~ floor slab, long-span ~, wide-span ~ ~ · Weitspanndeckenplatte *f*
~ frame, long-span ~, wide-span ~ · Weitspannrahmen *m*
~ lattice beam → long-span trussed girder
~ ~ girder → long-span trussed ~
~ (load)bearing system, wide-span ~ ~, long-span ~ ~ · Weitspann-Tragwerk *n*
~ (pre)cast beam → ~ ~ (concrete) ~
~ ~ (concrete) beam, long-span ~ (~) ~, wide-span ~ (~) ~ · Weitspann-(Beton)Fertigbalken(träger) *m*
~ prestressed (concrete) (building) unit → long-span ~ (~) (~) ~
~ rib, long-span ~, wide-span ~ · Weitspannrippe *f*

large-span roof — lateral reinforcement

~ **roof, long-span ~, wide-span ~** · Weitspanndach *n*

~ **shell, long-span ~, wide-span ~** · Weitspannschale *f*

~ ~ **vault, wide-span ~ ~, long-span ~ ~** · Weitspann-Schalengewölbe *n*

~ **truss(ed) girder** → **long-span ~ ~**

~ ~ **roof** · Weitspann-Fachwerkbinderdach *n*

large test → **~-scale ~**

~ **tile** → **~ building ~**

~**-town citizen** · Großstädter *m*

larger than life size · überlebensgroß

Lascar closet [*deprecated*] → squatting W.C. pan

~ **W.C. pan** → sqatting ~ ~ ~

lashing wire, binding ~, annealed ~, iron ~, tying ~ [*Soft steel wire used for binding reinforcement*] · Rödeldraht *m*, Bindedraht

last step, top ~ · Austritt(stufe) *m*, (*f*), Podeststufe, Durchgänger *m*

latch · (Schloß)Falle *f*

~ **bolt** (US); spring latch (Brit.) · Federfalle *f*, federnde Falle

~ **head** · Fallenkopf *m*

~ **lock** · Fallenschloß *n*

~ **spring** · Fallenfeder *f*

late Art Nouveau, ~ Modern Style · später Jugendstil *m*

~ **Baroque** · Spätbarock *m*

~ ~ **architect** · Spätbarockarchitekt *m*

late-Frankish architecture · spätfränkische Architektur *f*, ~ Baukunst *f*

late geometrical [*English tracery*] · spätgeometrisch [*englisches Maßwerk*]

Late Gothic, late Gothic style · Spätgotik *f*, spätgotischer dekorativer Stil *m*, Verfallstil [*1429–1500*]

~ ~ **hall-church** · spätgotische Hallenkirche *f* [*z.B. Sandkirche in Breslau*]

~ ~ **Royal Chapel** · spätgotische Königskapelle *f*

~ ~ **structure** · spätgotisches Bauwerk *n*

late Gothic style, Late Gothic · Spätgotik *f*

Late Gothic tracery · spätgotisches Maßwerk *n*

~ ~ **vault** · spätgotisches Gewölbe *n*

late(-)mediaeval · spätmittelalterlich

~ **architecture, ~ Baukunst** · spätmittelalterliche Architektur *f*, ~ Baukunst *f*

Late Modern Style, ~ Art Noveau · später Jugendstil *m*

late opus, ~ work · Spätwerk *n*

Late Pointed Style, Rectilinear ~, Perpendicular ~, Perpendicular Gothic, Perpendicular architecture · Perpendicularstil *m*, Spätphase *f* der englischen Gotik [*Die letzte Phase der gotischen Architektur in England von 1360–1550. Vertikalzug, besonders in der Fenster- und Wandgliederung*]

~ **Renaissance architecture, baroque ~** · Spätrenaissancearchitektur *f*, Spätrenaissancebaukunst *f*, Barockarchitektur, Barockbaukunst

~ **Roman** · spätrömisch

~ **Romanesque church** · spätromanische Kirche *f*

~ ~ **(style)** · Spätromanik *f*

late strength · Spätfestigkeit *f*

~ **work, ~ opus** · Spätwerk *n*

latent heat · latente Wärme *f*, verborgene ~, gebundene ~

~ **hydraulic substance** · latent hydraulischer Stoff *m*

~ **solvent** [*This solvent is active in the blend*] · latentes Lösungsmittel *n*

late(r) style · Spätstil *m*

Later Temple of Artemis at Ephesus · Artemision *n* zu Ephesus

lateral arch, side ~ · Seitenbogen *m*

~ **buckling of girders** · Kippung *f* von Trägern

~ **chapel, side ~** · Seitenkapelle *f*, Einsatzkapelle

~ **colonnade** · Seitenkolonnade *f*

~ **deformation** · seitliche Formänderung *f*, ~ Verformung

~ **diagonal** · Querschräge *f*

~ **dimension** · Querabmessung *f*, Quermaß *n* [*z.B. einer Stütze*]

~ ~ · Seitenabmessung *f*, Seitenmaß *n*

~ **elevation, side ~** · Seiten(auf)riß *m* [*Seitenansicht eines Bauwerkes in Normalprojektion*]

~ **entrance** · Seiteneingang *m*

~ **escape** [*The squeezing out of soft soils from under the foundations of heavy structures, which is prevented by sheet piling*] · Verdrückung *f*

~ **façade** · Seitenfassade *f*

~ **load** · Seitenlast *f*

~ **loading, transverse ~** · Querbelastung *f*

~ **masonry wall, side ~ ~, flank ~ ~, end ~ ~** · Seitenmauer *f*, Stirnmauer [*Fehlname: Giebelmauer*]

(~) penetration of rain, (~) rain penetration · Durchfeuchtung *f*

(~) ~ ~ through wall, (~) rain penetration ~ ~ · Wanddurchfeuchtung *f*

~ **pressure** · Seitendruck *m*

(~) rain penetration, (~) penetration of rain · Durchfeuchtung *f*

(~) ~ ~ through wall, (~) penetration of rain ~ ~ · Wanddurchfeuchtung *f*

~ **reinforcement, hoop ~, hoops, binders, tie, hooping** [*Binders in the form of rings (other than helical) round the main reinforcement in columns or piles*] · Ringarmierung *f*, Ringbewehrung, Ring(stahl)einlagen *fpl*

lateral reinforcement — lattice(d) steel girder

~ ~, helical ~, transverse ~, helical binding, helix; spiral reinforcement [*misnomer*] · Querbewehrung *f* nach der Schraubenlinie, Spiralbewehrung, Spiralarmierung, Spiral(stahl)einlagen *fpl*, Umschnürung

~ **restraint** · seitliche Einspannung *f*, Seiteneinspannung

~ **rigidity** → ~ stiffness

~ **stability** · Seitenstabilität *f*, Seitenstandfestigkeit *f*, Seitenstandsicherheit

~ **stiffness**, ~ rigidity · Seitensteifigkeit *f*, Seitenstarrheit

~ **strain**, transverse ~ · Querdehnung *f*

~ **strength**, transverse ~, flexural ~, modulus of rupture [*The strength of a specimen tested in transverse bending; normally synonymous with 'modulus of rupture' but also used to refer to breaking load (see B.S. 340, 368, 550 and 2028)*] · Querbiegefestigkeit *f*

~ **support** · Seitenabstützung *f*

~ **thrust**, side ~, axial ~, outward ~, overturning ~, vault ~ · (Seiten)Schub *m*, Axialschub, achsrechter Schub, Wölbungsschub, Horizontalschub, Gewölbeschub [*Die waag(e)rechte Resultierende einer Gewölbekraft*]

~ **wall**, side ~, end ~, flank ~ · Stirnwand *f*, Seitenwand [*Fehlname: Giebelwand*]

~ **wind** · Seitenwind *m*

~ ~ **pressure** · Seitenwinddruck *m*

laterally loaded, transversely ~ · querbelastet

~ ~ · seitenbelastet, seitlich belastet

laterite chip(ping)s, lateritic ~ · Lateritsplitt *m*

~ **gravel**, lateritic ~ · Lateritkies *m*

lateritic chip(ping)s, laterite ~ · Lateritsplitt *m*

~ **gravel**, laterite ~ · Lateritkies *m*

latex · Latex *m*

~, rubber ~ · Kautschukmilch *f*, (Kautschuk)Latex *m*

~ **adhesive**, ~ glue · Latexleim *m*

~ **base** · Latexbasis *f*, Latexgrundlage *f*

~-**bound** · latexgebunden

latex-cement-aggregate mix(ture), rubber ~ ~ · Vergußmasse *f* aus Kautschukmilch, Zement und Zuschlägen

latex-cement sealing compound, rubber ~ ~ ~ · Kautschukmilch-Zement-Vergußmasse *f*, (Kautschuk)Latex-Zement-Vergußmasse

latex floor(ing) (finish), ~ floor cover(ing) · Latex(fuß)boden(belag) *m*

~ ~ (~) **paint**, ~ floor cover(ing) ~ · Latex(fuß)boden(anstrich)farbe *f*

~ **foam**, foam(ed) latex · Schaumlatex *m*, Latexschaum *m*

~ **glue**, ~ adhesive · Latexleim *m*

~ **mastic compound**, ~ ~ composition · Latexmastix *m*

~ **paint** · Latexfarbe *f*

~ **wall paint** · Latexwand(anstrich)farbe *f*

lath, slat, curtain ~, shutter ~ · (Abschluß)Lamelle *f*

~ [*A board used as a base for plaster*] · Bautafel *f* [*Putzträger*]

~ · Latte *f*

~, stambha [*A monumental pillar, standing free without any structural foundation. Inscriptions were carved on the shaft. The capital, which was usually persepolitan in form, was crowned with animal supporters bearing 'chakra' or 'wheel of the law'. The emblem of the Republic of India is the capital of the stambha at Sarnath*] · Stambha *m*

~ → plaster lath(ing)

~-**and-plaster** → one-coat-work

lath ceiling → lath(ing) ~

~ **hammer** · Gipserbeil *n*

~ **insulating mat** → lath(ing) ~ ~

~ **mesh**, lathing ~ · Putz(träger)-Maschenmatte *f*, Maschenmatte als Putzträger

~ **nail** → lath(ing) ~

~ **shutter**, slat ~ · Lamellenabschluß *m*

lathe-check · Schälriß *m* [*Furnier*]

lathe-checking · Schälrißbildung *f* [*Furnier*]

lather → (reinforcing) iron worker

lath(ing) → plaster ~

~ **ceiling** · Putzträgerdecke *f*

~ **insulating mat**, ~ insulation(-grade) ~ · Putzträgerdämmatte *f*

~ **mesh** · Putz(träger)-Maschenmatte *f*, Maschenmatte als Putzträger

~ **nail**, gypsum-~-~ · Gipsdielenstift *m*

laths → (plaster) lath(ing)

Latin cross · Passionskreuz *n*, crux imissa, lateinisches Kreuz, hohes Kreuz

lattice [*A framework of crossed and spaced wood strips with a standard dimension of 5/16" thick and 1¹⁄₈" to 2¹⁄₄" wide. Used mainly to support vines or to obstruct clear sight, as around or under porches, summer houses, and such*] · Spalier *n*

lattice(d) column · Gitterstütze *f*

~ **cupola**, ~ dome, lamella · Lamellenkuppel *f*

~ **door** · Gittertür *f*

~ **fence** · Spalierzaun *m*, Ästelzaun

~ **girder** · Gitterträger *m*

~ **mast** · Gittermast *m*

~ **purlin(e)** · Gitterpfette *f*

~ **shell** · Gitterschale *f*

~ **steel column**, lattice-form ~ ~, steel lattice(d) ~ · Stahlgitterstütze *f*

~ ~ **girder**, lattice-form ~ ~, steel lattice(d) ~ · Stahlgitterträger *m*

~ ~ mast, lattice-form ~ ~, steel lattice(d) ~ · Stahlgittermast *m*

~ ~ window, steel lattice(d) ~, lattice-form steel ~ · Stahlgitterfenster *n*

~ steeple · Pyramidenflechtwerk *n*

~ web · Gittersteg *m*

~ ~ girder · Gitterstegträger *m*

lattice-form steel column, lattice(d) ~ ~, steel lattice(d) ~ · Stahlgitterstütze *f*

~ ~ girder, lattice(d) ~ ~, steel lattice(d) ~ · Stahlgitterträger *m*

~ ~ mast, lattice(d) ~ ~, steel lattice(d) ~ · Stahlgittermast *m*

lattice plate, space frame(work), grid structure, grid frame(work), three-dimensional frame(work), spatial frame(work) [*Grid structures, apart from single layer flat grids, are three-dimensional structures. Unlike shells or folded slabs, however, they are constructed not with solid membranes but with lattice or grid frameworks. In some systems, however, the grid is formed by the edge junctions of bent or folded sheet panels of suitable material in which the skin strength of the sheet element forms a very large proportion of the total strength of the structure*] · Raumfachwerk *n*, räumliches Fachwerk, dreidimensionales Fachwerk

~ structure, lattice(work) · Gitter(werk) *n*, Gitterkonstruktion *f* [*Das Netzwerk von Tragwerken aus Stahl, Holz, Leichtmetall, Stahlbeton usw., z.B. für Binder, Brücken, Maste, Türme, Kuppeln und dgl.*]

~ tower → latticework ~

~ window, lead(ed) light · Butzenscheibenfenster *n*

lattice(work), lattice structure · Gitter(werk) *n*, Gitterkonstruktion *f* [*Das Netzwerk von Tragwerken aus Stahl, Holz, Leichtmetall, Stahlbeton usw., z.B. für Binder, Brücken, Maste, Türme, Kuppeln und dgl.*]

~ tower · Gitter(werk)turm *m*

laundry · Wäscherei *f*

~ chute, clothes ~, (soiled) linen ~ · (Schmutz)Wäscheabwurfanlage *f*, (Schmutz)Wäscherutsche *f*

~ club, common laundry, communal laundry · Gemeinschaftswäscherei *f*

~ drying ground → (clothes-)drying ~

~ room · Wäschereiraum *m*

~ wastes · Wäschereiabwasser *n*

laurel leaf, bay ~ · Lorbeerblatt *n*

laurel-leaf swag, ~ festoon, ~ encarpa, ~ garland, bay-leaf ~ · Lorbeerblattgehänge *n*, Lorbeerblattgewinde *n*, Lorbeerblattgirlande *f*, Lorbeerblattfeston *n*, Lorbeerblätterstrang *m*

lauric acid · Laurinsäure *f*

lavatory, wash room, WR [*A room equipped with basin(s) for washing hands and/or face*] · Waschraum *m*

~ (basin), washbowl, wash basin, washhandbasin [*The term 'lavatory' has now come to mean the room containing the wash basin (Waschraum) and by extension the room containing a WC (Spülklosettraum)*] · (Hand)Waschbecken *n*, Waschtisch *m*

(~ ~) range, basins in range · Reihenwaschanlage *f*, Waschreihe *f*

~ bowl → bowl

~ equipment, wash room ~, WR ~ · Waschraumausrüstung *f*

~ fan, closet ~, toilet ~ · Abortventilator *m*, Klosettventilator, Toilettenventilator

(~) flush(ing), toilet ~, closet ~ · Spülung *f*, Abort~, Klosett~, Toiletten~

(~) ~ pipe, toilet ~ ~, closet ~ ~ [*B.S. 1125*] · Spülrohr *n*. Klosett~, Abort~, Toiletten~

(~) ~ water, toilet ~ ~, closet ~ ~ · Spülwasser *n*, Abort~, Klosett~, Toiletten~

~ pan → bowl

(~) seat, toilet ~, closet ~, W.C. ~ [*B.S. 1254*] · (Abort)Sitz *m*, Klosettsitz, Toilettensitz

~ ~ lid, closet ~ ~, (toilet) ~ ~ · (Abort)Deckel *m*, Toilettendeckel, Klosettdeckel

~ tray, wash room ~, WR ~ · Waschraumaschenbecher *m*

lavishly decorated → profusely enriched

~ enriched → profusely ~

~ gilt, profusely ~ · überreich vergoldet

~ ornamented → profusely enriched

law of compatibility, compatibility law · Verträglichkeitsgesetz *n* [*Jedes Bauwerk wird durch die Einwirkung der äußeren Kräfte verformt. Die Verformung wächst solange an, bis der hierdurch hervorgerufene Widerstand der inneren Kräfte mit den äußeren Kräften im Gleichgewicht ist. Das Verträglichkeitsgesetz besagt, daß die Verformungen der Einzelelemente eines Bauwerkes zueinander passen müssen, sich also miteinander vertragen*]

~ ~ conservation of energy · Energieerhaltungsgesetz *n*

~ ~ elasticity, Hooke's law · Elastizitätsgesetz *n*, Hookesches Gesetz

~ ~ frontality · Frontalgesetz *n*

~ ~ minimum potential energy, principle ~ ~ ~ ~, theorem ~ ~ ~ ~ · Prinzip *n* vom Minimum der potentiellen Energie

~ ~ particle size distribution according to R.R.S. · Exponentialgesetz *n* der Kornverteilung nach Rosin-Rammler-Sperling, Kornverteilungsgesetz

~ ~ proportionality, proportional(ity) law · Proportionalitätsgesetz *n*, P-Gesetz

~ ~ superposition, principle ~ ~, theorem ~ ~, superposition law, superposition theorem · Überlagerungsgesetz *n* Superpositionsgesetz

law of virtual displacements — lead (base) (priming) paint 558

~ ~ virtual displacements, principle ~ ~ ~, theorem ~ ~ ~, virtual-displacement theorem, virtual-displacement principle, virtual-displacement law · Prinzip *n* der virtuellen Verrückungen

~ ~ ~ work, theorem ~ ~ ~, principle ~ ~ ~, virtual-work theory, virtual-work law, virtual-work principle · Prinzip *n* der virtuellen Arbeit

laws of space and colo(u)r · Gesetze *npl* von Raum und Farbe

to lay · verlegen

lay architect · Laienbruderarchitekt *m*

to lay edgewise · hochkant(ig) verlegen

layer, coat · Lage *f*, Schicht *f*

~ → felt ~

~, leaf, wythe, withe, tier, shell skin [*cavity wall*] · Schale *f*, Wand~ [*Hohlwand*]

~-cake form of elevation, horizontal division · Horizontalgliederung *f*

~-corrosion · Schichtkorrosion *f*

layer of foam, foam layer · Schaumlage *f*, Schaumschicht *f*

~ ~ wire, wire layer, wire insert(ion) · Drahteinlage *f*

~ silicate → clay mineral

~ thickness, coat ~ · Lagendicke *f*, Schichtdicke

lay-in ceiling · Einlegedecke *f*

~ connecter, ~ connector, ~ timber ~, ~ wood ~ · Einlaßdübel *m* [*Holzverbinder*]

laying, ~ work · Verlegung *f*, Verlegen *n*, Verlegearbeiten *fpl*

~ blocks, ~ tiles, block laying, tile laying [*See remark under 'Block'*] · Vermauern *n* [*Blocksteine*]

~ (clay) bricks, (clay) bricklaying, bricking · Ziegelmauern *n*, Mauern mit Ziegeln, Vermauern von Ziegeln

~ drawing · Verlegeplan *m*, Verlegezeichnung *f*

~ length, effective ~ · Baulänge *f* [*Rohr*]

~ ~ · Verlegelänge *f*

~ material · Verlegematerial *n*

~ of cables, placing ~ ~, cable laying, cable placing · Kabeleinbau *m*, Kabelverlegung *f*

~ on · Reliefauftragung *f* auf Porzellan

~ pattern · Verband *m*, Verlegemuster *n* [*Plattenverlegung*]

~ tiles, ~ blocks, block laying, tile laying [*See remark under 'Block'*] · Vermauern *n* [*Blocksteine*]

~ (work) · Verlegen *n*, Verlegung *f*, Verlegearbeiten *fpl*

~ (~), setting (~) [*The placing of building stone in position in a structure*] · Versetzen *n*, Versetzarbeiten *fpl*, Verlegen, Verlegung *f*, Versetzung, Verlegearbeiten

lay-in panel · Einlegetafel *f*

~ profile → ~ shape

~ section → ~ shape

~ shape, ~ section, ~ trim, ~ unit, ~ profile · Einlaßprofil *n*

~ timber connecter, ~ wood ~, ~ ~ connector, ~ connector, ~ connecter · Einlaßdübel *m* [*Holzverbinder*]

~ trim → ~ shape

~ unit → ~ shape

~ wood connecter, ~ timber ~, ~ ~ connector, ~ connecter, ~ connector · Einlaßdübel *m* [*Holzverbinder*]

lay light, ceiling ~ [*A glazed opening in a ceiling, designed to admit light to the space below*] · Deckenoberlicht *n*

lay-off in winter · Winterpause *f* [*bei Bauarbeiten*]

to lay on, to apply [*plaster*] · antragen [*Putz*]

layout → ~ plan

~, arrangement · Anordnung *f*

~ grid · Verlegeraster *m* [*Fliesenverlegen*]

~ ~ · Rohbauraster *m*

~ of reinforcement, reinforcement layout · Armierungsführung *f*, Bewehrungsführung

~ office · Arbeitsvorbereitungsbüro *n*

~ (plan) · Gesamtübersicht *f*, Übersichtsplan *m*, Übersichtszeichnung *f*, Grundrißanordnung

LC → lead-covered

lcd, least common denominator · kleinster gemeinsamer Nenner *m*

lcm, least common multiple · kleinstes gemeinschaftliches Vielfaches *n*

L.C.V., lower calorific value · (unterer) Heizwert *m*, H_u [*in kcal/Nm³*]

LD steel-making bay · LD-Stahlwerkhalle *f*

leaching (out) · Auslaugen *n*

~ pit, ~ well [*It has porous walls which permit the contents to seep into the ground*] · Sickergrube *f*

lead · Blei *n*, Pb [*DIN 1719*]

~ acetate, acetate of lead · Bleizetat *n*

~ alloy, ~ base ~, lead-based ~ · Bleilegierung *f* [*DIN 1728*]

lead-alloy (cable) sheath [*B.S. 810*] · Bleilegierungs(kabel)mantel *f*

~ pipe · Bleilegierungsrohr *n*

~ sheath, ~ cable ~ [*B.S. 810*] · Bleilegierungs(kabel)mantel *m*

~ tube · Bleilegierungsröhre *f*

lead antimoniate, antimoniate of lead · Bleiantimoniat *n*, antimonsaures Blei *n*

~ apron [*For flashing the front of a chimney*] · Blei(front)schürze *f*, vordere Bleischürze

~ azide, azide of lead · Bleiazid *n*

~ (base) alloy, lead-based ~ · Bleilegierung *f* [*DIN 1728*]

~ (~) (priming) paint, ~ (~) primer [*B.S. 2521, 2523*] · Bleigrundierfarbe *f*

lead bell type flush(ing) tank — lead glazing

~ **bell type flush(ing) tank,** ~ ~ ~ ~ cistern, ~ ~ ~ water waste preventer · Bleiglocke f, Spülkastenglocke aus Blei

~ **biological shield,** ~ radiation ~, ~ shield, LS · Bleischirm m [*Strahlenschutz*]

~ (~) **shielding wall,** ~ radiation ~ ~ · Blei-Abschirmwand f

~ **block** · Bleibaustein m, Bleiziegel m [*DIN 25407. Für Abschirmwände gegen ionisierende Strahlungen*]

~ **box rainwater gutter,** ~ ~ (roof) ~, ~ ~ R.W. ~ · Blei-Kasten(dach)rinne f

~ **bronze** → lead(ed) ~

~ **cable** → lead-covered ~

~ (~) **sheath** [*B.S. 810*] · Blei(kabel)-mantel m

~ **came** · Bleirute f [*Verglasung*]

~ **capping,** ~ **coping** · Bleiabdeckung f, Bleiabwässerung

~ **carbonate,** carbonate of lead · Bleikarbonat n, PbCO$_3$

~ **ca(u)lked** · bleiverstemmt, blei(ab)gedichtet

~ **ca(u)lking** · Blei(ab)dichtung f, Bleiverstemmung

~ **chrom(at)e,** chrom(at)e of lead · Bleichromat n

~ ~ **pigment** · Bleichromatpigment n

~ **closet flush(ing) pipe** → ~ (lavatory) ~ ~

~ ~ **waste water pipe,** ~ toilet ~ ~ ~, ~ soil ~ (Brit.) [*A lead pipe collecting from W.C.s and urinals*] · Bleiabortrohr n, Bleiklosett(abwasser)rohr, Bleitoiletten(abwasser)rohr, Bleiabortfallrohr, Bleifallrohr für Aborte

~-**coated copper flashing (piece)** [*It is used adjacent to light-colo(u)red stone or white painted wood which might be stained by the weathering of bare copper*] · bleiüberzogener Kupfer-(blech)anschluß(streifen) m

lead coating, ~ plating · Verbleiung f

~ **compound** · Bleiverbindung f

~ **coping,** ~ capping · Bleiabdeckung f, Bleiabwässerung

~ **core** · Bleikern m

~-**covered** · blei(ab)gedeckt

~, lead-sheathed, LC · mit Bleimantel (versehen)

lead(-covered) cable, lead-sheathed ~ [*B.S. 480*] · Blei(mantel)kabel n

~ **cupola,** ~ dome · Bleikuppel f

~ **dome,** ~ cupola · Bleikuppel f

lead crystal (glass), full ~ ~ (~) · englisches Kristallglas n, Bleikristall(glas) n [*unter Zusatz von Bleioxid hergestellt*]

~ **cupola** → lead(-covered) ~

~ **dampcourse,** ~ dampproof(ing) course, ~ dpc, ~ d.p.c., ~ DPC · Bleifeuchtigkeitssperrschicht f, Bleifeuchtesperrschicht

~ **discharge pipe** → ~ draining ~

~ **dome** → lead(-covered) ~

~ **dowel** · Bleidübel m

~ **dpc** → ~ dampcourse

~ **draining pipe,** ~ drain(age) ~, ~ discharge ~, ~ waste (~) · Bleiabflußrohr n, Bleiablaufrohr, Bleientwässerungsrohr, Bleidränrohr [*Fehlnamen: Bleiabfluß m, Bleiablauf*]

~ **drier,** ~ dryer · Bleisikkativ n

~ **dust** · Bleistaub m

leaded · gebleit

~ · verbleit

lead(ed) bronze · Bleibronze f [*DIN 1716*]

~ **light,** lattice window · Butzenscheibenfenster n

~ **zinc oxide(e)** (US); ~ ~ oxide (Brit.) [*B.S. 1481*] · gebleites Zinkoxid n

lead elbow, ~ pipe ~ · Blei(rohr)bogen m [*DIN 1263*]

leader → downpipe

~ **head,** conductor ~; cistern ~ (US); rainwater ~, R. W. ~ [*The enlarged entrance at the head of a downpipe. It collects the water from the gutters*] · (Dach)Rinnenkasten m, (Dach)Rinnenkessel m, Regenrinnenkasten, Regenrinnenkessel, Wasserfangkasten, Abflußrinnenkasten, Abflußrinnenkessel

lead facing, ~ sur~, ~ lining · Bleiauskleidung f, Bleiverkleidung, Bleibekleidung, Bleibelag m

~ **filler,** ~ insert(ion) · Bleieinlage f, Bleizwischenlage

~ **flashing (piece),** ~ soaker [*See remark under 'Anschluß'*] · Bleianschluß-(streifen) m

~ **flat (roof),** ~ roof · Bleiflachdach n, Flachbleidach

~ **fluosilicate,** fluosilicate of lead · Bleifluat n, Bleisilicofluorid n

~ **flush(ing) pipe** → ~ lavatory ~ ~

~ **foil** · Bleifolie f

~ **foil sheet(ing)** · Bleifolienbahn f

~ **font** · Blei-Taufbecken n

~-**free,** leadless · bleifrei

lead glance, blue lead, galena · Galenit m, PbS, Bleiglanz m

~ ~ **pulp,** blue lead ~, galena ~ · Bleiglanztrübe f, Galenittrübe, PbS-Trübe

~ **glass** · Bleiglas n

~ **glaze(d finish),** ~ glazing, ~ glazed coat(ing) · Bleiglasur f, Bleibeglasung f

~ **glazing** [*Lead cames of various widths and shapes are used in either free or geometrical patterns to frame in windows made up of small pieces of glass, made weatherproof by being set in a special cement. Steel-cored cames or iron saddle-bars are required to stiffen all but the smallest panes as the soft nature of the metal and the small*

lead glazing — lead-sheathed

pieces of glass have little resistance to wind or other lateral pressure] · Bleiverglasung f, Bleieinglasung

~ ~, ~ glazed coat(ing), ~ glaze(d finish) · Bleiglasur f, Bleibeglasung f

~ gutter, ~ roof ~, ~ rainwater ~, ~ R.W. ~ · Bleiregenrinne f, Blei(dach)rinne

~ hinge · Bleigelenk n

~ hip · Bleigrat m

~ insert(ion), ~ filler · Bleieinlage f, Bleizwischenlage

~ insulation · Bleiisolierung f

~ joint · Bleimuffe f

~-lag circuit with separate units [*It is obtained by connecting two luminaires, one with p.f. uncorrected and the other with leading p.f., in parallel*] · Duoschaltung f mit getrennten Einheiten [*Leuchten unkompensiert und kapazitiv zusammengeschaltet*]

lead (lavatory) flush(ing) pipe, ~ toilet ~ ~, ~ closet ~ ~ · Bleispülrohr n

leadless, lead-free · bleifrei

lead light → lead(ed) ~

~ line, ~ plumb [*A line with a lead weight attached*] · Blei(schnur)lot n, Bleisenkel m, Senkblei n, Bleisenklot

lead-lined cistern · bleiverkleidete Zisterne f, bleiausgekleidete ~, bleibekleidete ~

~ pipe · bleiverkleidetes Rohr n, bleiausgekleidetes ~, bleibekleidetes ~

lead lining, ~ (sur)facing · Bleiauskleidung f, Bleiverkleidung, Bleibekleidung, Bleibelag m

~ linoleate, linoleate of lead · Bleilinoleat n

~ manganese drier, ~ ~ dryer · Bleimangantrockenstoff m

~ (mon)oxid(e) (US); ~ (mon)oxide (Brit.) [*chemical name*], litharge [*substance*] · Bleioxid n, Bleiglätte f, PbO [*veraltete Benennung: Königsgelb n*]

~ naphthenate, naphthenate of lead · Bleinaphthenat n

~ ore · Bleierz n

~ oxid(e) (US); ~ oxide (Brit.) · Bleioxid n

~ paint → ~ (base) (priming) ~

~ patenting [*In the wire industry, both the metallic-hardening process (Badpatentieren) and the double-lead process (Tauchpatentieren) are generally referred to as 'lead patenting'*] · Bleipatentieren n

~ paving · Bleipflaster n

~ pencil scratch test · Bleistiftprobe f, Bleistiftversuch m, Bleistiftprüfung f

~ pigment · Bleipigment n

~ pipe [*B.S. 602, 1085*] · Bleirohr n [*DIN 1263. Abflußrohr für Entwässerungsanlagen*]

~ (~) elbow · Blei(rohr)bogen m [*DIN 1263*]

~ ~ soldering · Bleirohrlötung f

~ ~ work · Bleirohrarbeiten fpl

~ plate · Bleiplatte f [*Verwendung als Gelenke von Brücken und Tragwerken*]

~ plating, ~ coating, leading · Verbleiung f

~ plug, ~ seal · Bleiplombe f

~ ~ casting machine, ~ seal ~ ~ · Bleiplombengießmaschine f

~ plumb [*A line with a lead weight attached*] · Blei(schnur)lot n, Bleisenkel m, Senkblei n, Bleisenklot

~ poisoning · Bleivergiftung f

~ powder, powder(ed) lead · Bleipulver n, Bleimehl n

~ pressure pipe · Bleidruckrohr n [*DIN 1262*]

~ primer → ~ (base) (priming) paint

~ (priming) paint → ~ base (~) ~

~ profile press → ~ section ~

~ radiation shield, ~ biological ~, ~ shield, LS · Bleischirm m [*Strahlenschutz*]

~ ~ shielding wall, ~ (biological) ~ ~ · Blei-Abschirmwand f

~ rainwater gutter, ~ (roof) ~, ~ R.W. ~ · Bleiregenrinne f, Blei(dach)rinne

~ regulus, reguline of lead · Bleistein m, englisches Bleiweiß n

~ resinate, resinate of lead · Bleiresinat n

~ ridge · Bleifirst m

~ roof, ~ flat (roof) · Bleiflachdach n, Flachbleidach

~ ~ cladding, ~ ~ cover(ing), ~ ~ sheathing, ~ roofing · Bleibedachung f, Blei(dach)(ein)deckung

~ ~ gutter, ~ ~ trough, (eaves) lead ~, rainwater lead ~, roof lead ~, R. W. lead ~ · (Dach)Bleirinne f, Bleidachrinne

~ rope · Bleistrick m

~ R.W. gutter, ~ rainwater ~, ~ (roof) ~ · Bleiregenrinne f, Blei(dach)rinne

~ salt, salt of lead · Bleisalz n

~ seal, ~ plug · Bleiplombe f

~ ~ → ~ seal(ing)

~ ~ casting machine, ~ plug ~ ~ · Bleiplombengießmaschine f

~-sealed · blei(ab)gedichtet, bleivergossen

lead seal(ing) · Bleiverguß m, Blei(ab)dichtung f

~ section press, ~ shape ~, ~ unit ~, ~ trim ~, ~ profile ~ · Bleiprofilpresse f

~ sheath, ~ cable ~ [*B.S. 810*] · Blei(kabel)mantel m

lead-sheathed, lead-covered, LC · mit Bleimantel (versehen)

lead-sheathed cable — League of Nations Building

~ **cable,** lead(-covered) ~ [*B. S. 480*] · Blei(mantel)kabel *n*

lead sheet, sheet lead, milled lead [*Lead rolled into sheets from cast slabs*] · Blei(fein)blech *n*, Walzblei *n*, Tafelblei [*DIN 59610*]

~ **shield,** ~ biological ~, ~ radiation ~, LS · Bleischirm *m* [*Strahlenschutz*]

~ **shielding wall,** ~ biological ~ ~, ~ radiation ~ ~ · Blei-Abschirmwand *f* [*Strahlenschutz*]

~ **shot** · Bleischrot *n, m*

~ **slag** · Blei(hochofen)schlacke *f* [*Beim Erschmelzen von Bleisilbererz in feuerflüssigem Zustand entstehendes Nebenerzeugnis, das im wesentlichen aus Kalk-Eisenoxydul-Silikaten und Aluminaten mit wechselndem Gehalt an Begleitstoffen, wie Magnesia, Manganoxydul, Zinkoxid, Bleioxid usw. und geringen Mengen Sulfidschwefel besteht*]

~ **soaker,** ~ flashing (piece) [*See remark under 'Anschluß'*] · Bleianschluß(streifen) *m*

~ ~ · Bleigebindewinkel *m*, Gebindebleiwinkel, winkelförmiger Bleilappen *m*

~ **soap** · Bleiseife *f*

~ **soil pipe** (Brit.); ~ closet waste water ~, ~ toilet waste water ~ [*A lead pipe collecting from W.C.s and urinals*] · Bleiabortrohr *n*, Bleiklosett(abwasser)rohr, Bleitoiletten(abwasser)rohr, Bleiabortfallrohr, Bleifallrohr für Aborte

~ **spar** · Bleibary t *m*

~ **splash lap** · Bleispritzschutz *m* [*Schornsteindichtung*]

~ **strip** · Bleiband *n*

~ **sulfate,** sulfate of lead (US); lead sulphate, sulphate of lead (Brit.) · Bleisulfat *n*, PbSO₄

~ **(sur)facing,** ~ lining · Bleiauskleidung *f*, Bleiverkleidung, Bleibekleidung, Bleibelag *m*

~ **tack** · Bleihafter *m*

~ **toilet flush(ing) pipe** → ~ (lavatory) ~ ~

~ ~ **waste water pipe,** ~ closet ~ ~ ~, ~ soil ~ ~ [*A lead pipe collecting from W.C.s and urinals*] · Bleiabortrohr *n*, Bleiklosett(abwasser)rohr, Bleitoiletten(abwasser)rohr, Bleiabortfallrohr, Bleifallrohr für Aborte

~ **trap** · Blei-(Wasser)(Geruch)Verschluß *m* [*DIN 1260. Fehlnamen: Bleisiphon m, Bleisyphon, Bleitraps m*]

~ **tray** · Bleieinfassung *f* [*Schornstein; Lüftungsrohr*]

~ **trim press** → ~ section ~

~ **trough,** ~ gutter, ~ roof ~, eaves lead ~, roof lead ~ · (Dach)Bleirinne *f*, Bleidachrinne

~ **tube** · Bleiröhre *f*

~ **unit press** → ~ section ~

~ **valley (gutter)** · Bleikehl(rinn)e *f*

~ **washer** · Bleiplättchen *n*, Bleiunterlegscheibe *f*

~ **waste (pipe)** → ~ draining ~

~ **weathering** · Bleifeuchtigkeits(ab)dichtung *f*, Bleifeuchte(ab)dichtung [*Erzeugnis*]

~ **wedge** · Bleikeil *m*

~ **wire** · Bleidraht *m*

~ **wool,** spun lead [*Lead prepared in long filaments twisted together like yarn and used for cold caulking*] · Bleiwolle *f*

leadwork · Bleiarbeiten *fpl*

lead zinc oxid(e) (US) → lead(ed) ~ ~

leaf, door ~ · (Tür)Blatt *n*, (Tür)Flügel *m* [*Beweglicher Verschluß der Öffnung einer Tür*]

~, layer, wythe, withe, tier, shell, skin [*cavity wall*] · Schale *f*, Wand~ [*Hohlwand*]

~ **and dart moulding** (Brit.); ~ ~ ~ molding (US) · griechischer Eierstab *m*

~ **crown** · Blattkrone *f*

~ **door** · Flügeltür *f*

leafed aluminium powder, flake(d) ~ ~ (Brit.); ~ aluminum ~ (US) · blättchenförmiges Alu(minium)pulver *n*

~ **iron oxide,** flake(d) ~ ~ (Brit.); ~ ~ oxid(e) (US) · blättchenförmiges Eisenoxid *n*, Schuppeneisenoxid

~ **pigment,** flake(d) ~ · Schuppenpigment *n*, blättchenförmiges Pigment

~ **powder,** flake(d) ~ · Blättchenpulver *n*, blättchenförmiges Pulver

leaf-gilding · Blattvergoldung *f*

leaf-like decoration, foliation · Blattverzierung *f*, Blattschmuck *m*, Blattdekor(ation) *m, (f)*

leaf of blocks block leaf · Block(stein)schale *f*, Steinschale [*Hohlwand*]

~ **pattern** · Blattmuster *n*

leaf-shaped curve · Blatt *n* [*gotisches Maßwerk*]

leaf work [*See remark under 'Gehänge'*] · Blattgehänge *n*, Blattgirlande *f*, Blattgewinde *n*, Blattfeston *n*

leafy frieze, foliage ~, foliated ~ · Blatt(werk)fries *m*, Laub(werk)fries, Blätterfries

League of Nations Building, ~ ~ ~ Palace · Völkerbundpalast *m* [*in Genf*]

leak(age) current — leaves

leak(age) current, stray ~, current from irregular source(s) · Streustrom *m*, vagabundierender (Erd)Strom, Irrstrom Erdstrom, Schleichstrom

leakage water outlet · Leckwasserablauf *m*

leakless, leakproof · lecksicher

leak plugging · Leckstellen(ab)dichtung *f*

leakproof, leakless · lecksicher

lean · gemagert, mager

~ clay · magerer Ton *m*, sandiger ~, Magerton

~ concrete, lean-mixed ~ · Füllbeton *m*, Magerbeton, Sparbeton, zementarmer Beton, magerer Beton

~ ~ (test) cube, lean-mixed ~ (~) ~ · Magerbeton(probe)würfel *m*, Magerbetonprüfwürfel

~ ~ (~) cylinder, lean-mixed ~ (~) ~ · Magerbetonprobezylinder *m*, Magerbeton(prüf)zylinder

~ fresh(ly-mixed) concrete · magerer Frischbeton *m*, zementarmer ~, Magerfrischbeton, Frischmagerbeton, Magerfüllbeton, Füllmagerbeton, Sparmagerbeton, Magersparbeton

leaning · angelehnt, angebaut [*Ein kleineres an ein größeres Gebäude*]

~ place, arm-rest · Armstütze *f*, Armlehne *f*

~ tower · schiefer Turm *m*, hängender ~

Leaning Tower of Pisa · Schiefer Turm *m* von Pisa, Pisanerturm

lean lime, poor ~, magnesian ~, dolomitic ~ · Magerkalk *m*, Graukalk, Dolomitkalk [*90% Kalksubstanz und mehr als 5% Magnesiumoxid*]

~(-mixed) concrete · Füllbeton *m*, Magerbeton, Sparbeton, zementarmer Beton, magerer Beton

~ mortar · Sparmörtel *m*, Füllmörtel, Magermörtel, magerer Mörtel

~ rolled concrete, dry ~ ~ · Magerwalzbeton *m*, Walzmagerbeton

lean mix(ture) [*A mix(ture) with a high proportion of aggregate*] · Spargemisch *n*, Sparmischung *f*, Magergemisch, Magermischung

lean-to · Pultanbau *m*

~ mansard (roof) · Mansard(en)dach *n* in Pultform, Pult-Mansard(en)dach

~ ring roof · Ringpultdach *n* [*Es liegt ringförmig um einen höheren, zentralen Baukörper, z.B. einem Chor*]

~ roof, single pitch ~, monopitch ~, half-span ~ [*A roof pitched in one plane only*] · freitragendes Pultdach *n*

~ ~ purlin(e) · Bockpfette *f*

~ ~ strut · Bocksäule *f* [*Dach*]

~ trussed strut · Bockstütze *f*

lear → lehr

learner's pool, teaching ~ · Lehr-(schwimm)becken *n*, Nichtschwimmerbecken, LSB

least common denominator, lcd · kleinster gemeinsamer Nenner *m*

~ ~ multiple, lcm · kleinstes gemeinschaftliches Vielfaches *n*

~ cross-section → minimum ~

~ dimension, minimum ~ · Kleinstabmessung *f*, Mindestabmessung, Kleinstmaß *n*, Mindestmaß

~ ~ on plan, minimum ~ ~ ~ · kleinste Grundrißabmessung *f*

~ distance, minimum ~ · Kleinstabstand *m*, Mindestabstand

~ grain size, minimum ~ ~ · Kleinstkorn *n*, Mindestkorn

~ load, minimum ~ · Kleinstlast *f*, Mindestlast

~ moment, minimum ~ · Kleinstmoment *n*, Mindestmoment, Minimalmoment

~ radius of gyration, minimum ~ ~ ~ · kleinster Trägheitshalbmesser *m*

~-work principle, ~ theorem · Satz *m* vom Minimum der Formänderungsarbeit

least-work theorem, ~ principle · Satz *m* vom Minimum der Formänderungsarbeit

leather adhesive → ~ glue

~ cement → ~ glue

~ cloth → coated cloth

~ diaphragm · Ledermembran(e) *f*

~ door · Ledertür *f*

~ dubbing · Lederfett *n*

~ fabric [*misnomer*] → coated cloth

~ glue, ~ cement, ~ adhesive · L, Lederleim *m*

leather-hanging, Spanish leather · Ledertapete *f*

leather|-hard · lederhart [*Zustand eines nicht vollständig getrockneten Tonerzeugnisses*]

~-hardness · Lederhärte *f* [*Steinzeugindustrie*]

leather-like · lederähnlich

leather packing ring → ~ seal(ing) ~

~ ~ strip, ~ seal(ing) ~ · Leder(ab)dicht(ungs)streifen *m*

~ powder, powder(ed) leather · Ledermehl *n*

~ seal(ing) ring, ~ packing ~, ~ washer · Leder(ab)dicht(ungs)ring *m*, Lederunterlegscheibe *f*

~ ~ strip, ~ packing ~ · Leder(ab)dicht(ungs)streifen *m*

~ tar · Lederteer *m*

~ varnish · Lederlack *m*

~ washer → ~ seal(ing) ring

leaves, foliage (scrolls) · Laub(werk) *n*, Blattwerk

Leca block, ~ tile [*Leca = light(weight) expanded clay aggregate. See remark under 'Block'*] · Leca-Block(stein) *m*, Leca-Stein

lectern · Chorpult *n*

~ · Rednerpult *n*

lecture hall, ~ theatre, aula, auditorium · Auditorium *n*, Aula *f*, Vortragssaal *m*, Hörsaal, Vorlesungssaal

~ **room** · Vorlesungsraum *m*, Vortragsraum

~ **theatre,** ~ hall, aula, auditorium · Auditorium *n*, Aula *f*, Vortragssaal *m*, Hörsaal, Vorlesungssaal

~ **tour** · Vortragsreise *f*

ledge, door ~ · Querleiste *f*, Tür~ [*Brettertür*]

ledged-and-braced door [*Developed from the ledged door, this type is stiffened and prevented from dropping by diagonal braces cut into the ledges. The door is hung on the side to which the braces thrust down*] · Brettertür *f* mit Bug

ledged door, batten ~, barred ~ [*A door faced with vertical boards fixed on to two or more horizontal ledges at the back, which are often clench-nailed to the facing and sometimes diagonally braced. It has no frame round the edge*] · Brettertür *f*

ledger · Längsstange *f*, Streichstange [*Holzgerüst*]

leer → lehr

left-hand designation · Linksbezeichnung *f*

~ **door** · linksaufschlagende Tür *f*, Linkstür

~ **hinge** · Linksband *n* [*Beschlag für Fenster und Türen*]

~ **lock** · linkes Schloß *n*, Schloß DIN links [*DIN 107*]

left-luggage office, cloakroom; checkroom (US) · Handgepäckaufbewahrung *f*

left stair(case) · Linkstreppe *f*

leftward skew slab · linksschiefe Platte *f*

leg · Schenkel *m* [*Winkelstahl*]

~ → frame column

~ · Zunge *f* [*Hubdeckenverfahren*]

~, post wood(en) pillar, timber pillar · Pfosten *m*, Stiel *m*, Ständer *m*, (Stand-) Säule *f* [*Senkrechtes Holz beim Fachwerk-, Stab-, Ständer- und Dachstuhlbau*]

legend, coding ~, key · Legende *f*, Zeichenerklärung *f*, Zeichenschlüssel *m*

~ **plate,** key ~ · Legendeschild *n*, Zeichenerklärungsschild, Zeichenschlüsselschild

legibility · Lesbarkeit *f*

~ **distance** · Lesbarkeitsweite *f*

lehr, leer, lier, lear · Kanalkühlofen *m*, Tunnelkühlofen, Kühlbahn *f* [*Glasherstellung*]

leiocome → starch gum

~ **glue** → starch gum ~

leisure centre, recreation(al) ~ (Brit.); ~ center (US) · Freizeitzentrum *n*, Erholungszentrum

lemon (chrome) yellow · Zitronengelb *n*

~ **shellac** · Lemonschellack *m*

lending library · Leihbücherei *f*, Leihbibliothek *f*

~ **section** · Ausleihe *f* [*Bücherei*]

length change, change in length · Längenänderung *f*

~ **dimension** · Längenabmessung *f*, Längenmaß *n*

~ **measurement** · Längenmessung *f*

~ **of each bar** · Länge *f* der Position [*Stahlliste*]

~ ~ **jaspe sheet** · Jaspébahn *f*

~ ~ **roll,** roll length · Rollenlänge *f*

~ ~ **step,** step length · Stufenlänge *f*

~ ~ **the corrugation(s)** · Wellenlänge *f* [*Wellplatte; Welltafel*]

~ ~ **time,** period ~ ~, time period, time interval · Zeitdauer *f*, Zeitraum *m*, Zeitspanne *f*

~ **unit** · Längenmaß(einheit) *n*, (*f*)

lengthening · Längerwerden *n*

Leonidaion · Gästehaus *n* des Leonidas von Naxos, Leonidaion [*in Olympia*]

lepers hospital · Leprosenhaus *n*

Lesbian cyma(tium) · (griechisch-)lesbisches Kyma(tion) *n*

~ **leaf** · Herzblatt *n*

lesene, pilaster-strip [*A pilaster without a base and capital*] · Lisene *f*, Lesene

let-in flap · Einstemmlappen *m*, Fitschenlappen, Fi(t)schbandlappen

lettable, rentable · vermietbar

to letter · beschriften

letter box blue · Briefkastenblau *n*

~ **decoration,** ~ ornament, ~ enrichment, ~ decorative fixture · Buchstabenornament *n*, Buchstabenschmuck *m*, Buchstabenverzierung *f*

~ **enrichment,** ~ ornament, ~ decoration, ~ decorative fixture · Buchstabenornament *n*, Buchstabenschmuck *m*, Buchstabenverzierung *f*

~ **ornament,** ~ decoration, ~ enrichment, ~ decorative fixture · Buchstabenornament *n*, Buchstabenschmuck *m*, Buchstabenverzierung *f*

~ **plate,** letter-box ~, letter-drop ~ [*A front-door fitting to receive letters, consisting of a slotted plate fixed to the outside of the door. B. S. 2911*] · Briefeinwurf *m*

~ ~ **with bell-push and card-holder** · Briefeinwurf *m* mit Klingelknopf und Namenschildausschnitt

~(-type) **combination lock,** ~ dial ~ · Buchstabenschloß *n*

lettering, inscription · Inschrift *f*, Beschriftung *f*

letting-in flush (on both meeting faces) — life-size

letting-in flush (on both meeting faces), flush fixing · Einstemmen *n* [*Einstemmband*]

letting of the contract, ~ ~ ~ order, contract letting, order letting · Auftragerteilung *f*, Vergabe *f*

leucite · Leuzit *m*

~-basalt · Leuzitbasalt *m*

leucite basanite · Leuzitbasanit *m*

~ tephrite · Leuzittephrit *m*

leucitic tuff · Leuzittuff *m*

to level · (aus)ebnen, einebnen, egalisieren, nivellieren, ausgleichen

level · Pegel *m*

~ → ~ to

~, non-sloping, flat, planar, plane · gefälleos, eben

~, spirit **~**, mechanic's **~**, water **~**, plumb · Wasserwaage *f*

~ · Höhenstufe *f*

~ difference → equivalent sound pressure ~ ~

~ ~ · Pegelunterschied *m*

~ gutter → flat (roof) ~

~ light · Streiflicht *n*

~ of background noises · Störpegel *m*

~ ~ floor(ing) (finish), ~ ~ floor cover(ing) · OKF *f*, Oberkante *f* (Fuß-)Boden(belag)

~ ~ ground, ground level, grade · Geländehöhe *f*, Niveau *n*

~ ~ stress, stress level · Spannungshöhe *f*

to level off · abgleichen

level R.W. gutter → flat (roof) ~

~ rainwater gutter → flat (roof) ~

~ (roof) gutter → flat (~) ~

~ switch · Niveauschalter *m*

~ (to), flush (with), flush to, dead level · bündig (mit), niveaueben

levelling (Brit.); leveling (US) · (Aus-)Ebnen *n*, Egalisieren, Einebnen, Nivellieren, Ausgleichen

levelling composition, ~ compound, ~ mass, ~ material (Brit.); leveling ~ (US) · Ausebnungsmasse *f*, Ausgleichmasse, Nivellierspachtel(masse) *m*, *(f)*, Ausgleichspachtel(masse), Ausgleichmittel *n*, Ausebnungsmittel, Nivelliermittel, Nivelliermasse, Egalisierspachtel(masse), Egalisiermittel, Egalisiermasse [*Zum Ebnen unregelmäßiger Fußbodenflächen*]

~ compound → ~ composition

~ course, ~ layer (Brit.); leveling ~ (US) · Ausgleichlage *f*, Ausgleichschicht *f*, Nivellierlage, Nivellierschicht

~ layer → ~ course

~ mass → ~ composition

~ material → ~ composition

~ mortar (Brit.); leveling ~ (US) · Ausebnungsmörtel *m*, Egalisiermörtel, Ausgleichmörtel, Nivelliermörtel

~ off (Brit.); leveling ~ (US); flushing · (Aus)Ebnen *n*, Egalisieren, Einebnen, Nivellieren, Ausgleichen, Abgleichen

~ ring (Brit.); leveling ~ (US) · Ausgleichring *m* [*Straßenablauf*]

~ screed (material) (Brit.); leveling ~ (~) (US) · Ausgleichestrich *m*, Nivellierstrich [*als Baustoff*]

~ ~ (topping) (Brit.); leveling ~ (~) (US) · Ausgleichestrich *m*, Ausebnungsestrich, Egalisierestrich, Nivellierestrich [*als verlegter Baustoff*]

~ work (Brit.); leveling ~ (US) · Ausgleicharbeiten *fpl*, Nivellierarbeiten

lever → ~ tumbler

~ → ~ handle

~ arm, moment ~ · Hebelarm *m*

~ handle · Hebelgriff *m*

~ (~), door ~ · (Tür)Drücker *m*, (Tür-)Klinke *f* [*DIN 18255*]

~ (~) fittings → door ~ ~

~ (~) hardware → door handle fittings

(~) handle-plate · Stützringschild *m* [*Türdrücker*]

~ lock → ~-tumbler ~

~ mechanism · Hebelmechanismus *m*

~ principle · Hebelprinzip *n*

~-test · Hebelprobe *f*, Hebelprüfung *f*, Hebelversuch *m* [*Korrosionsprüfung*]

lever (tumbler), tumbler · Zuhaltung *f* [*Schloß*]

~(-tumbler) lock, tumbler ~ · Zuhaltungsschloß *n*

Lewis acid · Lewissäure *f*, Friedel-Craffts-Katalysator *m*

liability to efflorescence · Ausblühungsneigung *f*

liable to be washed off (readily) · nichtwasserfest [*Leimfarbe*]

~ ~ subsidence · setzungsempfindlich

Lias(sic) clay · Liaston *m*

~ limestone · Liaskalk(stein) *m*

~ sandstone · Liassandstein *m*

Library of Pantainos · Bibliothek *f* des Pantainos [*Agora von Athen*]

Libyan suburb [*of Thebes*] · Stadt *f* der Toten, Totenstadt

lich gate → lych ~

lid, cover · Deckel *m*

lier → lehr

lierne (rib) [*A rib which does not originate either from a main springer or a central boss, and is employed as a decorative link between the main ribs and tiercerons*] · Lierne *f*

~ vault [*A ribbed vault to which liernes, which do not spring from the wal supports, are added to link the main ribs and tiercerons*] · Liernengewölbe *n*

life expectancy · Lebenserwartung *f*

~-size · lebensgroß

lift — lifting construction technique

lift [*B.S. 2655*]; elevator (US) [*An enclosed platform for carrying goods or passengers from one stor(e)y to another in a tall building*] · Aufzug *m*

~, passenger ~ (Brit.); (passenger) elevator (US) · Fahrstuhl *m*, (Personen)Aufzug *m* [*DIN 15301 und DIN 15302*]

~, concrete ~ [*The concrete placed between two consecutive horizontal construction joints; usually contains several layers or courses*] · Betonierlage *f*, Betonierschicht *f*, Betoneinbaulage, Betoneinbauschicht

~ apartment block (Brit.) → elevator residential building

~ ~ building (Brit.) → elevator residential ~

~ ~ house (Brit.) → elevator residential building

~ attendant (Brit.); elevator ~ (US) · Aufzugführer *m*

~ away shutter door · Hubtor *n*

~ block, ~ building (Brit.); elevator ~ (US) · 1.) Fahrstuhlgebäude *n*; 2.) Fahrstuhlhaus *n*

(~) car (Brit.); (elevator) cage (US) · (Aufzug)Korb *m*, (Aufzug)Kabine *f*, Fahrkorb, Fahrkabine

~ control (Brit.); elevator ~ (US) · Aufzugsteuerung *f*

~ door, passenger ~ ~ (Brit.); (passenger) elevator ~ ~ (US) · (Personen-)Aufzugtür *f*, Fahrstuhltür

~ dwelling block (Brit.) → elevator residential building

~ ~ building (Brit.) → elevator residential ~

~ ~ house (Brit.) → elevator residential building

~ entrance (Brit.); elevator ~ (US) · Aufzugeingang *m*

~ ~ → (passenger) lift (landing) ~

~ guide rail (Brit.); elevator ~ ~ (US) · Aufzugführungsschiene *f*

~ hall (Brit.); elevator ~ ~ (US) · Aufzughalle *f*

~ installation → passenger ~ ~

~ landing (Brit.); elevator ~ (US) · Aufzug(treppen)podest *n*, Aufzug(treppen)absatz *m*

~ (~) entrance → passenger ~ (~) ~

~ latch (US) → thumb ~

~ machine room (Brit.); elevator ~ ~ (US) · Aufzug(maschinen)raum *m*

~ maker (Brit.); elevator ~ (US) · Aufzughersteller *m*

~ multiple dwelling (Brit.) → elevator residential building

~-plate floor, lift-slab ~ · Hubplattendecke *f*

lift residence block (Brit.) → elevator residential building

~ ~ building (Brit.) → elevator residential ~

~ ~ house (Brit.) → elevator residential building

~ residential block (Brit.) → elevator residential building

~ ~ building (Brit.) → elevator ~ ~

~ ~ house (Brit.) → elevator residential building

lift-slab · Hub(decken)platte *f*

(lift-)slab collar, steel lifting ~, shear ~ · Deckenkragen *m*, (Stahl)Kragen [*Hubdeckenverfahren*]

lift-slab column · Hubdeckenstütze *f*

~ concrete floor · Hub(-Beton)decke *f*

~ construction · Hubdeckenbau *m*

~ floor, lift-plate ~· Hubplattendecke *f*

~ method (of construction), ~ construction [*This method of construction is associated with flat slab design. It consists of casting the upper floors and roof of a building around the columns at ground level, using the ground floor slab as the initial soffit form and subsequently lifting them by means of hydraulic jacks to their correct positions, where they are permanently connected to the columns. A separating medium is incorporated between each slab*] · Hubdeckenverfahren *n*, Hubplattenverfahren, Hubplattenbau(weise) *m*, (*f*), Hubdeckenbau(weise)

~ roof · Hubdach *n*

~ span · Hub(decken)plattenweite *f*

~ structure · Hubdeckenbauwerk *n*

lift/stair(case) core, stair(case)/lift ~, well (Brit.); elevator/stair(case) ~, stair(case)/elevator ~ (US) · Aufzug-Treppen-Schacht *m*, Treppen-Aufzug-Schacht

to lift the bed by wedging, to wedge · abkeilen [*Gestein*]

lift-type car park (Brit.); elevator-type ~ ~ (US) · Aufzuggarage *f*

lift well (Brit.); (elevator) hoistway, (elevator) shaft(way) (US) · Aufzugschacht *m*, Aufzugkern *m*, Fahrschacht, Fahrkern

~ ~ door (Brit.); (elevator) shaft(way) ~, (elevator) hoistway ~ (US) · Aufzugkerntür *f*, Aufzugschachttür, Fahrkerntür, Fahrschachttür

lift with automatic push-button control (Brit.); elevator ~ ~ ~ ~ (US) · Selbstfahrer(aufzug) *m*

lifting · Abheben *n*

~ and operating key · Aushebe- und Bedienungsschlüssel *m* [*Schachtdeckel*]

~ appliance · Hebevorrichtung *f*

~ construction technique, ~ ~ technic · Hubtechnik *f* [*Hubdeckenverfahren*]

lifting door — (light-)diffusing ceiling

~ **door** [*It is moved by a lifting appliance*] Hebetür *f*
~ ~ **fitting**, ~ ~ furniture · Hebetürbeschlag *m*
~ ~ **fittings**, ~ ~ hardware · Hebetürbeschläge *mpl*
~ ~ **furniture**, ~ ~ fitting · Hebetürbeschlag *m*
~ ~ **hardware**, ~ ~ fittings · Hebetürbeschläge *mpl*
~ **eye**, ~ lug · Huböse *f*
~ **from the bearings** · Abheben *n* von den Lagern [*DIN 1050, DIN 4112*]
~ **insert** [*of a panel*] · Hubeinlage *f*
~ **key** · Aushebeschlüssel *m* [*Schachtdeckel*]
~ **lug**, ~ eye · Huböse *f*
~ **mechanism** · Hebemechanismus *m*
~ **sliding door**, sliding lifting ~ · Schiebehebetür *f*, Hebeschiebetür
~ **sliding door fitting**, ~ ~ ~ furniture, sliding lifting ~ ~ · Hebeschiebetürbeschlag *m*, Schiebehebetürbeschlag
~ ~ ~ **fittings**, ~ ~ ~ hardware, sliding lifting ~ ~ · Hebeschiebetürbeschläge *mpl*, Schiebehebetürbeschläge
~ ~ ~ **furniture**, ~ ~ ~ fitting, sliding lifting ~ ~ · Hebeschiebetürbeschlag *m*, Schiebehebetürbeschlag
~ ~ ~ **hardware**, ~ ~ ~ fittings, sliding lifting ~ ~ · Hebeschiebetürbeschläge *mpl*, Schiebehebetürbeschläge
~ ~ **window**, sliding lifting ~ · Schiebehebefenster *n*, Hebeschiebefenster
~ **window** · Hebefenster *n* [*Ein Schiebefenster, dessen beweglicher Flügel gegen einen meist feststehenden oberen Teil gehoben und festgestellt wird*]
~ ~ **fitting**, ~ ~ furniture · Hebefensterbeschlag *m*
~ ~ **fittings**, ~ ~ hardware · Hebefensterbeschläge *mpl*
~ ~ **furniture**, ~ ~ fitting · Hebefensterbeschlag *m*
~ ~ **hardware**, ~ ~ fittings · Hebefensterbeschläge *mpl*
light, bright · hell
~, window · Fenster *n*
~, day, (window) aperture, (window) opening · Fensteröffnung *f*, Fensterlicht *n*, Fensterloch *n*
light-admitting, light-passing · lichteinlassend, lichtdurchlässig
~ **board**, ~ sheet, light-passing ~ · Lichtplatte *f*
~ **grill(e)**, light-passing ~ · Lichtgitter *n*
~ **plastic (material)**, light-passing ~ (~) · organisches Glas *n*, Kunststoffglas [*Die Bezeichnung „Glas" ist nicht ganz zutreffend, weil unter „Glas" Silikatglas verstanden wird. Die Verwendung dieses Wortes ist auf die lichtdurchlässige Plattenform zurückzuführen*].

~ ~ **sheet(ing)**, ~ sheet(ing) plastic, light-passing ~ ~ · (Kunststoff)Lichtbahn *f*
~ **sheet**, ~ board, light-passing ~ · Lichtplatte *f*
~ **sheet(ing) plastic**, ~ plastic sheet(ing), light-passing ~ ~ · (Kunststoff-)Lichtbahn *f*
light adobe brick → light(weight) ~ ~
~ **aggregate** → light(weight) (concrete) ~
~ **alloy** · Leichtlegierung *f*
~ **angle**, incidence ~, angle of light, angle of incidence · Lichteinfallwinkel *m*
~ **basis weight plate** · Feinstblech *n*
~ **beam** · Lichtstrahl *m*
~ **brick** → light(weight) (clay) ~
~ **building block** → light(weight) (structural) (concrete) ~ ~
~ ~ **board** → light(weight) building sheet
~ ~ **material** → light(weight) ~ ~
~ ~ **sheet** → light(weight) ~ ~
~ (~) **unit** → light(weight) (~) ~
~ **cast member** → light(weight) precast (concrete) ~
~ **chamotte brick** → light(weight) ~ ~
~ **cinder aggregate** → light(weight) ~
~ (**clay**) **brick** → light(weight) (~) ~
~ **coarse aggregate** → light(weight) coarse(-grain(ed)) (concrete) ~
light-coloured (Brit.); light-colored (US) · hellfarbig
light component → light(weight) (building) unit
~ **concrete** → light(weight) ~
~ (~) **aggregate** → light(weight) (~) ~
~ ~ **beam** → light(weight) ~ ~
~ ~ **building** → light(weight) ~ ~
~ (~) ~ **block** → light(weight) (structural) (~) ~ ~
~ ~ **chimney** → light(weight) ~ ~
~ ~ ~ **pot** → light(weight) ~ ~ ~
~ ~ **column** → light(weight) ~ ~
light conditioning · Lichtsteuerung *f*, Helligkeitsreg(e)lung
~ **conditions** · Lichtverhältnisse *f*
~ **construction method**, lightweight ~ · Leichtbauweise *f*
~ **core** → light(weight) ~
light-cupola, domed roof-light, dome-(light), saucer dome · (Dach)Lichtkuppel *f*, Oberlichtkuppel
light demolition work, ~ wrecking ~ · leichte Abbrucharbeit(en) *f(pl)*, Abreißarbeit(en) [*DIN 4420*]
(**light-)diffusing ceiling**, luminous ~, illuminated ~, luminescent ~ · Leuchtdecke *f*, Lichtdecke

light-diffusing ceiling system — light-metal (builders') ...

~ ~ **system**, luminous ~ ~, illuminated ~ ~, · Leuchtdeckenkonstruktion *f*, Lichtdeckenkonstruktion

~ **glass**, lighting ~ · Lichtsteuerglas *n*, lichtstreuendes Glas

~ **panel**, lighting ~ · Lichtstreutafel *f*, lichtstreuende Tafel

~ **unit**, lighting diffuser · Lichtstreuelement *n*, lichtstreuendes Element

~ **wall**, illuminated ~, luminous ~, luminescent ~ · Lichtwand *f*, Leuchtwand

light diffusion · Lichtstreuung *f*

light-directing · lichtlenkend, lichtrichtend

light ditch, air ~ · Lichtgraben *m*

~ **duty flexible (swing) door** · leichte flexible Pendeltür *f*

lightening · Aufhellung *f* [*Anstrichtechnik*]

lightfast, fast to light, lightproof, proof to light, light resistant, resistant to light · lichtbeständig, lichtecht

lightfastness, lightproofness, fastness to light, proofness to light, light resistance, stability to light · Lichtechtheit *f*, Lichtbeständigkeit *f*

light filler block → light(weight) (concrete) (floor) ~ ~

~ **filtration** · Lichtfiltration *f*

(~) **fitting** (Brit.) → luminaire (fixture)

~ ~ **with integral mounting rail** (Brit.); luminaire (fixture) ~ ~ ~ ~ (US); (light(ing)) fixture ~ ~ ~ ~ · Schienenbeleuchtungskörper *m*, Schienenleuchte *f*

~ ~ ~ **transistorized inverter control gear** (Brit.); luminaire (fixture) ~ ~ ~ ~ ~ (US) · Transistor-Wechselrichter-Leuchte *f*

~ **fixture** → luminaire (~)

~ **fuel oil** [*200 seconds*] · Heizöl L *n*, leicht(flüssig)es Heizöl [*DIN 51603*]

light-gauge copper tube [*B.S. 659*] · Leichtkupferrohr *n*

~ **structure** · Blechkonstruktion *f*

lighting, illumination · Beleuchtung *f*

~ **by roof-light(s)** · (Dach)Oberlichtbeleuchtung *f*

~ **cable**, illumination ~ · Lichtstromkabel *n*

~ **calculation**, illumination ~ · Beleuchtungsberechnung *f*

~ **circuit**, illumination ~ · Lichtstromkreis *m*

(~) **column** (Brit.); mast (US) · Beleuchtungsmast *m*, (Licht)Mast, (Straßen-)Leuchtenmast

(~) ~ **with bracket** (Brit.); (~) mast with arm (US) · Auslegerbeleuchtungsmast *m*, Ausleger(licht)mast, Auslegerleuchtenmast

(~) ~ ~ **two brackets** (Brit.); mast with two arms (US) · Doppelausleger-(Licht)Mast *m*

~ **component**, illumination ~ · Beleuchtungsanteil *m*

~ **current**, illumination ~ · Lichtstrom *m*

~ **device**, illuminating ~ · Beleuchtungsgerät *n*

~ **diffuser**, (light-)diffusing unit · Lichtstreuelement *n*, lichtstreuendes Element

~ **engineer**, illumination ~ · Beleuchtungsingenieur *m*

~ **engineering**, illumination ~ · Beleuchtungstechnik *f*

(**light(ing)) fixture** → luminaire (~)

(~) ~ **with integral mounting rail**; luminaire (fixture) ~ ~ ~ ~ (US); light fitting ~ ~ ~ ~ ~ (Brit.) · Schienenbeleuchtungskörper *m*, Schienenleuchte *f*

~ **installation**, illumination ~ · Beleuchtungsanlage *f*

~ **line** · Lichtleitung *f* [*im Haus*]

~ **load**, illumination ~, light ~ · Beleuchtungslast *f*, Lichtlast

~ **mast** · Beleuchtungsmast *m*, Leuchtenmast, Lichtmast [*DIN 49778 und DIN 49779*]

(~) ~ **with arm** (US); (~) column with bracket (US) · Auslegerbeleuchtungsmast *m*, Auslegerleuchtenmast, Ausleger(licht)mast

~ **panel**, (light-)diffusing ~ · Lichtstreutafel *f*, lichtstreuende Tafel

~ ~ · Lichtschalttafel *f*

~ **row** → strip-line (light(ing)) fixtures

~ **system**, illumination ~ · Lichtinstallation *f*, Lichtsystem *n*, · Beleuchtungsinstallation, Beleuchtungssystem

~ **tariff**, illumination ~ · Lichttarif *m*

light installation, ~ plant, ~ system · Lichtanlage *f*

~ **lime-sand brick** → light(weight) calcium silicate ~

~ **load**, lightweight ~ · Leichtlast *f*

~ ~, illumination ~, lighting ~ · Lichtlast *f*, Beleuchtungslast

~ **loss** · Lichtverlust *m*

lightly loaded · leichtbelastet

~ **rusted** · angerostet

light-metal alloy, lightweight metal ~ · Leichtmetallegierung *f*, Leichtlegierung

~ **(blind) slat**, lightweight metal (~) ~ · Leichtmetallamelle *f*, Leichtmetallstäbchen *n* [*Jalousie*]

~ **(builders') furniture**, ~ (~) fitting, lightweight metal (~) ~ · Leichtmetall-(bau)beschlag *m*

~ **(~) hardware**, ~ (~) fittings, lightweight metal (~) ~ · Leichtmetall-(bau)beschläge *mpl*

light-metal construction — light-passing sheet

~ **construction**, lightweight metal ~ · Leichtmetallbau *m*

~ ~ **section**, ~ ~ shape, ~ ~ unit, ~ ~ trim, ~ ~ profile, lightweight metal ~ ~ · Leichtmetall-Bauprofil *n*

~ **door**, lightweight metal ~ · Leichtmetalltür *f*

~ ~ **closer** → lightweight metal ~ ~

~ **façade**, lightweight metal ~ · Leichtmetallfassade *f*

~ **fitting** → ~ (builders') furniture

~ **fittings** → ~ (builders') hardware

~ **frame**, lightweight metal ~ · Leichtmetallrahmen *m*

~ **furniture** → ~ builders' ~

~ **glazing**, lightweight metal ~ · Leichtmetallverglasung *f*, Leichtmetalleinglasung [*Die Leichtmetalleisten und -sprossen sind mit einer Eloxalschicht überzogen*]

~ **hardware** → ~ builders' ~

~ **jalousie** → ~ slatted blind

~ **lattice(d) girder**, lightweight metal ~ ~ · Leichtmetallgitterträger *m*

~ **lever handle**, lightweight metal ~ ~ · Leichtmetall-Türdrücker *m*

~ **louvers** → ~ slatted blind

~ **partition (wall)**, lightweight metal ~ (~) · Leichtmetalltrennwand *f*

~ **plain web(bed) beam**, ~ solid ~ ~, lightweight metal ~ ~ ~ · Leichtmetall-Vollwandbalken(träger) *m*

~ ~ ~ **girder**, ~ solid ~ ~ ~, lightweight metal ~ ~ ~ ~ · Leichtmetall-Vollwandträger *m*

~ **profile** → light(weight) metal section

~ **roof cladding**, ~ ~ cover(ing), ~ ~ sheathing, lightweight metal ~ ~, light(weight) metal roofing · Leichtmetalldach(belag) *n*, (*m*), Leichtmetall-(dach)(ein)deckung *f*, Leichtmetallbedachung

~ ~ **truss**, ~ ~ lattice ~, light(weight) metal roof (lattice) ~ · Leichtmetall-Fachwerk(dach)binder *m*

~ **section** → light(weight) metal ~

~ **shape** → light(weight) metal section

~ **shutter door**, lightweight metal ~ ~ · Leichtmetalltor *n*, Metalleichttor

~ **slatted blind**, ~ louvers, ~ jalousie, ~ louvres, light(weight) metal jalousie, lightweight metal slatted blind, lightweight metal louvers, lightweight metal louvres · Leichtmetalljalousie *f*

~ ~ **roller blind**, lightweight metal ~ ~ ~ · Leichtmetallrolljalousie *f*, Leichtmetallrolladen *m*

~ **solid web(bed) beam** → ~ plain ~ ~

~ ~ ~ **girder** → ~ plain ~ ~

~ **space (load)bearing structure**, ~ three-dimensional ~ ~, ~ spatial ~ ~, ~ ~ (weight-carrying) ~, lightweight metal ~ (~) ~ · Leichtmetall-Raumtragwerk *n*

~ **structural engineering**, lightweight metal ~ ~ · Leichtmetallbau(technik) *m*, (*f*)

~ **three-dimensional (load)bearing structure** → ~ space ~ ~

~ **trim** → light(weight) metal section

~ **truss(ed girder)**, lightweight metal ~ (~) · Leichtmetall-Fachwerk(träger) *n*, (*m*)

~ **tube**, lightweight metal ~ · Leichtmetallrohr *n* für Schalungsträger

~ **tubular scaffold(ing)**, lightweight metal ~ ~ · Leichtmetallrohrgerüst *n*, Leichtmetallrohrrüstung *f*

~ **unit** → light(weight) metal section

~ **window**, lightweight metal ~ · Leichtmetallfenster *n*

~ ~ **sill**; ~ ~ cill (Brit.); lightweight metal ~ ~ · Leichtmetall-(Fenster)Sohlbank *f*, Leichtmetall-Fensterbank

~ **work**, lightweight metal ~ · Leichtmetallarbeiten *fpl*

light mineral aggregate → lightweight ~ ~

~ **mud brick** → light(weight) adobe ~

lightning arrester, LA · (Blitz)Ableiter *m*

(~) conductor, ~ rod · (Blitz)Ableiterstange *f*, (Blitz)Ableiterstab *m*

~ **damage** · Blitzschaden *m*

~ **protection** · Blitzschutz *m*

~ ~ **system**, ~ protective ~ · Blitzschutzanlage *f* [*DIN 18384*]

~ **rod**, (~) conductor · (Blitz)Ableiterstange *f*, (Blitz)Ableiterstab *m*

~-**safe** · blitz(schlag)sicher

light opening · Lichtöffnung *f*

~ **output** · Lichtleistung *f*

light-painted · hellgestrichen

light panel → light(weight) ~

~ **partition wall** → light(weight) ~ ~

light-passing, light-admitting · lichteinlassend, lichtdurchlässig

~ **board**, ~ sheet, light-admitting ~ · Lichtplatte *f*

~ **grill(e)**, light-admitting ~ · Lichtgitter *n*

~ **plastic (material)**, light-admitting ~ (~) · organisches Glas *n*, Kunststoffglas [*Die Bezeichnung „Glas" ist nicht ganz zutreffend, weil unter „Glas" Silikatglas verstanden wird. Die Verwendung dieses Wortes ist auf die lichtdurchlässige Plattenform zurückzuführen*]

~ ~ **sheet(ing)**, ~ sheet(ing) plastic, light-admitting ~ ~ · (Kunststoff) Lichtbahn *f*

~ **sheet**, ~ board, light-admitting ~ · Lichtplatte *f*

~ **sheet(ing) plastic**, ~ plastic sheet-(ing), light-admitting ~ ~ · (Kunststoff)Lichtbahn *f*

light penetration · Lichteintritt *m*

~ **permeability**, ~ transmittance · Lichtdurchlässigkeit *f*

~ **plant**, ~ installation, ~ system · Lichtanlage *f*

~ **plate**, medium ~, jobbing sheet, medium sheet · Mittelblech *n*

~ **point** · Lichtstelle *f*

~ **prefabrication** · leichte Vorfertigung *f*

lightproof, proof to light, lightfast, fast to light, light resistant, resistant to light, ltprf · lichtbeständig, lichtecht

lightproofness, lightfastness, fastness to light, proofness to light, light resistance, stability to light · Lichtechtheit *f*, Lichtbeständigkeit *f*

light-red silver ore, proustite · Proustit *m*, Arsensilberblende *f*, lichtes Rotgültigerz *n*

light reflection value · Lichtreflektionswert *m*

~ **resistance**, stability to light, fastness to light, proofness to light, lightfastness, lightproofness · Lichtechtheit *f*, Lichtbeständigkeit *f*

~ **resistant**, resistant to light, lightproof, proof to light, lightfast, fast to light · lichtbeständig, lichtecht

~ **roof** → light(weight) ~

~ **sand-lime brick** → light(weight) calcium silicate ~

~ **scaffold(ing)** → light(weight) ~

light-scattering photometer · Streulichtphotometer *n*

light screed → light(weight) ~

~ **section** → light(weight) ~

~ **section(al) steel** → light(weight) ~ ~

light-sensitive device · Lichtfühler *m*

light shape → light(weight) ~

~ **slag** → light(weight) ~

~ ~ **aggregate** → light(weight) ~ ~

~ ~ **concrete** → light(weight) ~ ~

~ ~ **powder** → light(weight) ~ ~

~ **solid block** → light(weight) concrete ~ ~

~ ~ **tile** → light(weight) (concrete) solid block

~ **steel construction** → light(weight) ~ ~

~ ~ **girder** → light(weight) ~ ~

~ ~ **structure** → light(weight) ~ ~

~ ~ **unit** → light(weight) ~ ~

~ **stopper** → light(weight) ~

~ **structural concrete** → light(weight) ~ ~

~ **stucco** → light(weight) ~

~ **switch** · Lichtschalter *m*

~ **system**, ~ plant, ~ installation · Lichtanlage *f*

~ **tar oil** · leichtes Teeröl *n*

light-tight · lichtundurchlässig

~ **blind**, black(out) ~, dark ~ · (Verdunkelungs)Rollo *n*, Verdunkelung(sblende) *f*

~ **door**, dark ~, blackout ~, BOD · Verdunkelungstür *f*

~ **installation** → blackout ~

~ **jalousie**, dark ~, blackout ~, ~ louvres, ~ louvers, ~ slatted blind · Verdunkelungsjalousie *f*

~ **louvres**, dark ~, blackout ~, ~ louvers, ~ jalousie, ~ slatted blind · Verdunkelungsjalousie *f*

~ **slatted blind**, dark ~ ~, blackout ~ ~, ~ jalousie, ~ louvres, ~ louvers · Verdunkelungsjalousie *f*

~ **system** → blackout installation

~ **window**, blackout ~, dark ~, BOW · Verdunkelungsfenster *n*

light tile → light(weight) ~

~ **transmittance**, ~ permeability · Lichtdurchlässigkeit *f*

~ **trim** → light(weight) ~

~ **unit** → light(weight) building ~

~ ~ ~ → light(weight) trim

~ **wall** → light(weight) ~

light(weight) adobe brick, ~ mud ~, ~ sun-dried ~ · Leichtlehmstein *m* [*Raumgewicht 600 bis 1400 kg/m³*]

~ **aggregate** → ~ (concrete) ~

~ ~ **concrete** · Leichtzuschlag(stoff)beton *m*, Leichtstoffbeton, Leichtzuschlagmaterialbeton

~ ~ **(~) (building) block**, ~ ~ (~) (~) tile · Leichtzuschlag(stoff)-Betonblock *m*, Leichtzuschlag(stoff)-Beton(block)stein *m*

~ **base (system)** → ~ deck(ing) (~)

~ **beam** · Leichtbalken(träger) *m*

~ **block**, ~ tile [*See remark under 'Block'*] · Leichtstein *m*, Leichtblock(stein) *m*

~ ~ **masonry (work)**, ~ tile ~ (~) [*See remark under 'Block'*] · Leichtblock(stein)mauerwerk *n*, Leichtsteinmauerwerk

~ ~ **partition (wall)**, ~ tile ~ (~) [*See remark under 'Block'*] · Leichtblock(stein)wand *f*, Leichtsteinwand [*Leichte Trennwand. DIN 4103*]

~ **brick**, ~ clay ~ · Leichtziegel *m* [*Fehlname: Leichtstein m. DIN 18505*]

~ **building block** → ~ (structural) (concrete) ~ ~

~ ~ **board**, ~ ~ sheet · Leicht(bau)platte *f*

~ **(~) component** → ~ (~) unit

~ ~ **felt** · Leicht-Baufilz *m*

~ ~ **insulation(-grade) board**, ~ ~ ~ sheet, ~ ~ insulating ~ · Leichtisolierbauplatte *f*, Isolierleichtbauplatte

light(weight) building material — light(weight) (concrete)...570

~ ~ **material,** ~ construction(al) ~ · Leichtbaustoff *m*; Leichtbaumaterial *n* [*Schweiz*]

~ (~) **member** → ~ (~) unit

~ ~ **sheet,** ~ ~ board · Leicht(bau)platte *f*

~ (~) **unit,** ~ (~) member, ~ (~) component [*See remark under '(Bau-) Element'*] · Leicht(bau)element *n*, Leicht(bau)körper *m* [*Fehlname: Leichtbaueinheit f*]

~ **calcium silicate brick,** ~ lime-sand ~, ~ sand-lime ~ · Kalksandleichtstein *m*, Leichtkalksandstein

~ **cast component** → ~ (pre)cast (concrete) member

~ ~ **(concrete) component** → ~ (pre)cast (concrete) member

~ ~ (~) **compound unit** → ~ (pre-)cast (~) ~ ~

~ ~ (~) **member** → ~ pre~ (~) ~

~ ~ (~) **unit** → ~ (pre)cast (concrete) member

~ ~ (~) **ware** → mass-produced light(weight) (pre)cast (~) ~

~ ~ **member** → ~ (pre)cast (concrete) ~

~ ~ **unit** → ~ (pre)cast (concrete) member

~ ~ **wall slab** → ~ concrete ~ ~

~ **cast(ing)** → ~ (pre)cast (concrete) member

~ **cavity block** → ~ (concrete) hollow ~

~ ~ **tile** → ~ (concrete) hollow block

(~) **cellular(-expanded) concrete screed** · Zellenbetonestrich *m*

~ **chamotte brick** · Schamotteleichtstein *m*, Schamotteleichtziegel *m*, Leichtschamottestein, Leichtschamotteziegel

~ **cinder aggregate,** expanded ~ ~ (US); ~ slag ~; foamed (iron) (blastfurnace) slag ~ [*B.S. 877*] · (Hochofen)Schaumschlackenzuschlag(stoff) *m*, (Hochofen)Schaumschlackenzuschlagmaterial *n*

~ **(clay) brick** · Leichtziegel *m* [*Fehlname: Leichtstein m. DIN 18505*]

~ **coarse(-grain(ed)) (concrete) aggregate** [*B.S. 3797*] · grob(körnig)er Leicht(beton)zuschlag(stoff) *m*, grob(körnig)es Leicht(beton)zuschlagmaterial *n*

~ **component** → ~ (building) unit

~ **composite floor of prefabricated steel lattice girders and hollow fillers** · Stahlleichtträgerdecke *f* mit Hohlkörpern

~ **concrete,** LWC · Leichtbeton *m* [*Beton mit einem Trockenraumgewicht von weniger als 1800 kg/m³*]

~ (~) **aggregate** [*B.S. 3797*] · (Beton)Leichtzuschlag(stoff) *m*, Leichtbetonzuschlag(stoff), (Beton)Leichtzuschlagmaterial *n*, Leichtbetonzuschlagmaterial

~ (~) ~ **works,** ~ (~) ~ plant · Leicht(beton)zuschlag(stoff)werk *n*, Leicht(beton)zuschlagmaterialwerk

~ ~ **beam** · Leichtbetonbalken(träger) *m*

~ ~ **bearing frame** → ~ ~ (structural) ~

~ ~ **building** · Leichtbetongebäude *n*

~ (~) ~ **block** → ~ structural (~) ~ ~

~ ~ (~) **component** → ~ ~ (~) unit

~ ~ ~ **(construction) element** · Leichtbeton-Hochbauelement *n*

~ ~ (~) **member** → ~ ~ ~ (~) unit

~ (~) **cast(ing)** → ~ (pre)cast (concrete) member

~ (~) **cavity block** → ~ (~) hollow ~

~ (~) ~ **tile** → ~ (~) hollow block

~ ~ **chimney** · Leichtbeton-Schornstein *m*

~ ~ ~ **pot** · Schornstein-Leichtbetonformstück *n*

~ ~ **column** · Leichtbetonstütze *f*

~ ~ **construction engineering element** · Leichtbeton-Tiefbauelement *n*

~ ~ **core** · Leichtbetonkern *m*

~ ~ **façade** · Leichtbetonfassade *f*

~ (~) **filler tile** → ~ (~) (floor) filler block

~ ~ **floor** · Leichtbetondecke *f*

~ (~) (~) **filler** · Leicht(beton)-Zwischenbauteil *m, n* [*Rippendecke*]

~ (~) (~) ~ **block,** ~ (~) (~) ~ tile · Leicht(beton)-(Decken)Füllkörper *m*, Leicht(beton)-(Decken)Füllstein *m*, Leicht(beton)-(Decken)Füllblock(stein) *m* [*DIN 4158. Ein Leicht(beton)-Zwischenbauteil, der sich über die volle Höhe der Rohdecke erstreckt*]

~ (~) ~ **slab** · Leicht(beton)deckenplatte *f*

~ ~ **frame** → ~ ~ structural ~

~ ~ **garage** · Leichtbetongarage *f*

~ ~ **girder** · Leichtbetonträger *m*

~ (~) **hollow block,** ~ (~) cavity ~, ~ (~) ~ tile, ~ (~) pot [*See remark under 'Block'*] · Hohlblockleichtbetonstein *m*, Leicht(beton)-Hohlblock(stein) *m*, Leicht(beton)-Hohlstein, Hbl [*DIN 18151*]

~ (~) ~ **(floor) filler** · Leicht(beton)-(Decken)Hohlkörper *m* [*DIN 4158*]

~ (~) ~ **tile** → ~ (~) ~ block

~ ~ **(in)filler slab,** ~ ~ infill(ing) ~ · Leichtbeton-Ausfachungsplatte *f*, Leichtbeton-Ausfüllungsplatte

~ ~ **lintel;** ~ ~ lintol [*deprecated*] [*A light(weight) concrete beam spanning an opening*] · Leichtbetonoberschwelle *f*, Leichtbetonsturz *m*

~ ~ **(load)bearing frame** → ~ ~ (structural) ~

~ ~ **panel** · Leichtbetontafel *f*

~ (~) **plank** · Leicht(beton)diele *f*

571 light(weight) (concrete) pot — light(weight) insulation ...

~ (~) pot → ~ (~) hollow block

~ ~ product → ~ (pre)cast (~) ~

~ ~ roof(ing) slab · Leichtbeton-Dachplatte f, Leichtbeton-Bedachungselement n, Leichtbeton-Bedachungsplatte, Leichtbeton-Dachelement, Leichtbeton-Dach(ein)deck(ungs)element

~ ~ screed (material) · Leichtbeton-estrich m [als Baustoff]

~ ~ ~ (topping) · Leichtbetonestrich m [als verlegter Baustoff]

~ ~ slab · (Beton)Leicht(bau)platte f, Leichtbetonplatte [DIN 18162]

~ (~) solid block, ~ (~) ~ tile [See remark under 'Block'] · Leicht(beton)-vollblock(stein) m, Leicht(beton)vollstein [DIN 18152]

~ ~ ~ floor · Leichtbetonvolldecke f

~ ~ (structural) frame, ~ ~ (load-)bearing ~, ~ ~ weight-carrying ~, ~ ~ supporting ~ · Leichtbeton-(Trag)rahmen m

~ ~ supporting frame → ~ ~ (structural) ~

~ ~ topping (slab) [The light(weight) concrete laid to form the compression flange of the T-beams which it makes with the ribs. It is usually about 2 in. thick] · Leichtbetondruckplatte f, Leichtbetondruckschicht f

~ ~ wall · Leichtbetonwand f

~ (~) ~ slab, ~ ~ (pre)cast ~ ~ ~ · Leichtbetonwand(bau)platte f, Wand(bau)-platte aus Leichtbeton [DIN 18162]

~ ~ wall(ing) (building) unit, ~ ~ ~ (~) member, ~ ~ ~ (~) component · Leichtbeton-Wand(bau)element n, Leichtbeton-Wand(bau)körper m [Fehlname: Leichtbeton-Wandbaueinheit f]

~ ~ weight-carrying frame → ~ ~ (structural) ~

~ construction · Leichtbau m

~ ~ method · Leichtbauweise f

~ construction(al) material, ~ building ~ · Leichtbaustoff m. Leichtbaumaterial n [Schweiz]

~ core · Leichtkern(schicht) m, (f)

~ cored-out floor · Leicht-Kassetten-Decke f, LKD

~ ~ ~ unit · LKD-Körper m, Leicht-Kassetten-Deckenkörper

~ ~ ~ plastic floor unit · Leicht-Kassetten-Kunststoff-Deckenkörper m, LKD-K-Körper

~ deck(ing) (system), ~ substructure (~), ~ base (~), ~ substrate (~) · Leicht-(Dach)Unterlage f [zur Aufnahme der Dachhaut]

~ expanded clay aggregate · Leca n

~ ~ (concrete) aggregate · geblähter Leichtbetonzuschlag(stoff) m

~ ~ plastic → ~ foamed ~

~ exposed concrete → fair-faced light(weight) ~

~ ~ ~ block → fair-faced light(weight) ~ ~

~ ~ ~ tile → fair-faced light(weight) concrete block

~ exterior plaster → ~ (external) rendering

~ external plaster → ~ (~) rendering

~ (~) rendering (Brit.); ~ stucco (US); ~ exterior plaster, ~ external plaster [See remark under 'Putz'] · Leicht-(außen)(ver)putz m, Leichtaußenwandverputz

~ extrusion · Leichtstrangpreßteil m, n

~ façade · Leichtfassade f

~ fair-faced concrete → fair-faced light(weight) ~

~ ~ ~ block → fair-faced light(weight) ~ ~

~ ~ ~ tile → fair-faced light(weight) concrete block

~ filler, ~ filling material · Leichtfüllstoff m, Leichtfüller m

~ ~ → ~ (concrete) (floor) ~

~ ~ block → ~ (concrete) (floor) ~ ~

~ ~ slab · Leicht(-Füll)Deckenplatte f, Leicht-(Decken)Füllplatte, (Decken-)Leichtplatte

~ fines · leichte Feinstoffe mpl [Zuschlag(stoff)]

~ floor · Leichtdecke f

~ (~) filler slab · Leicht-(Decken)Füllplatte f, (Decken)Leichtplatte, Leichtdeckenplatte, Leicht-Füll-Deckenplatte

~ (~) ~ tile → ~ (concrete) (floor) filler block

~ ~ girder · Decken-Leichtträger m

~ ~ slab, ~ concrete ~ ~ · Leicht(beton)deckenplatte f

~ foamed plastic, ~ expanded ~, ~ foam ~, ~ plastic foam · Leicht-(Kunst-)Schaum(stoff) m, Leicht-Kunststoffschaum(stoff), Leicht-Schaumkunststoff

~ girder · Leicht(bau)träger m [Breit- und parallelflanschiger Doppel-T-Stahl mit dünnem Steg, der mit Höhen von 100, 120, 140, 150 und 160 mm gewalzt und als LB I bis V bezeichnet wird]

~ gypsum (building) plaster → ~ mixed (~) (~) ~

~ ~ partition tile · Gipsleicht(bau)stein m, Gipsleicht(bau)block(stein) m

~ hollow block → ~ concrete ~ ~

~ ~ filler → ~ concrete hollow floor ~

~ insulating concrete, ~ insulation(-grade) ~, LWIC · Leichtdämmbeton m

~ insulating screed, ~ insulation(-grade) ~ · Leicht-Dämmestrich m [Schicht]

~ ~ ~ material, ~ insulation(-grade) ~ ~ · Leicht-Dämmestrich m [Baustoff]

~ insulation(-grade) board, ~ ~ sheet, ~ insulating ~ · Leichtisolierplatte f

~ **lime concrete,** lime-bound aerated ~ · Kalkleichtbeton m, Leichtkalkbeton [*Dampfgehärteter, kalkgebundener Porenbeton*]

~ ~ ~ **block,** ~ ~ ~ tile, lime-bound aerated ~ ~ · Leichtkalkbetonblock(stein) m, Leichtkalkbetonstein, Kalkleichtbetonblock(stein), Kalkleichtbetonstein

~ ~ ~ **tile** → lime-bound aerated concrete block

~ **lime-sand brick,** ~ sand-lime ~, ~ calcium silicate ~ · Kalksandleichtstein m, Leichtkalksandstein

~ **load** · Leichtlast f

~ **loading** · Leichtbelastung f

~ **loam** · Leichtleim m

~ ~ **slab** · Leichtlehmplatte f

~ ~ **wall** · Leichtlehmwand f

~ **masonry (work)** · Leichtmauerwerk n

~ **member** → ~ (building) unit

~ **metal** · Leichtmetall n

~ ~ **alloy** · Leichtmetallegierung f, Leichtlegierung

~ ~ **(blind) slat** · Leichtmetallamelle f, Leichtmetallstäbchen n [*Jalousie*]

~ ~ **(builders') furniture,** ~ ~ (~) fitting · Leichtmetall(bau)beschlag m

~ ~ **(~) hardware,** ~ ~ (~) fittings · Leichtmetall(bau)beschläge mpl

~ ~ **construction** · Leichtmetallbau m

~ ~ ~ **profile** → light-metal construction section

~ ~ ~ **section** → light-metal ~ ~

~ ~ ~ **shape** → light-metal construction section

~ ~ ~ **trim** → light-metal construction section

~ ~ ~ **unit** → light-metal construction section

~ ~ **door** · Leichtmetalltür f

~ ~ ~ **closer,** ~ ~ ~ closing device, ~ ~ ~ closing mechanism · Leichtmetall-Türschließer m, Leichtmetall-Türschließvorrichtung f

~ ~ **façade** · Leichtmetallfassade f

~ ~ **fitting** → light-metal (builders') furniture

~ ~ **fittings** → ~ ~ (builders') hardware

~ ~ **frame** → light-metal ~

~ ~ **furniture** → light-metal (builders') ~

~ ~ **glazing** · Leichtmetallverglasung f, Leichtmetalleinglasung [*Die Leichtmetalleisten und -sprossen sind mit einer Eloxalschicht überzogen*]

~ ~ **hardware** → ~ ~ builders' ~

~ ~ **jalousie,** ~ ~ louvers, ~ ~ slatted blind, ~ ~ louvers, light-metal slatted blind, light-metal jalousie, light-metal louvers, light-metal louvres · Leichtmetalljalousie f

~ ~ **lattice(d) girder** · Leichtmetallgitterträger m

~ ~ **lever handle** · Leichtmetall-Türdrücker m

~ ~ **louvers** → light-metal slatted blind

~ ~ **partition (wall)** · Leichtmetalltrennwand f

~ ~ **plain web(bed) beam** ~ ~ solid ~ ~ · Leichtmetall-Vollwandbalken(träger) m, Vollwand-Leichtmetallbalken(träger)

~ ~ ~ **girder,** ~ ~ solid ~ ~ · Leichtmetall-Vollwandträger m, Vollwand-Leichtmetallträger

~ ~ **plank** · Leichtmetalldiele f

~ ~ **profile** → ~ ~ section

~ ~ **roll-up overhead door,** ~ ~ ~ up-and-over ~, ~ ~ overhead door of the roll-up type, ~ ~ up-and-over door of the roll-up type · Leichtmetallrolltor n

~ ~ **roof cladding** → light-metal roof cladding

~ ~ ~ **covering** → light-metal roof cladding

~ ~ ~ **(lattice) truss** · Leichtmetall-Fachwerk(dach)binder m

~ ~ ~ **sheathing** → light-metal roof cladding

~ **roof(ing)** → light-metal roof cladding

~ ~ **section,** ~ ~ unit, ~ ~ shape, ~ ~ trim, ~ ~ profile · Leichtmetallprofil n

~ ~ **shape** → ~ ~ section

~ ~ **shutter door** · Leichtmetalltor n

~ ~ **slatted blind** → ~ ~ ~ jalousie

~ ~ ~ **roller blind** · Leichtmetallrolljalousie f, Leichtmetallrolladen m

~ ~ **solid web beam** → ~ ~ ~ plain ~ ~

~ ~ ~ ~ **girder** → ~ ~ ~ plain ~ ~

~ ~ **space (load)bearing structure** → light-metal ~ ~

~ ~ **spatial (load)bearing structure** → light-metal space ~ ~

~ ~ **structural engineering** · Leichtmetallbau(technik) m, (f)

~ ~ **three-dimensional (load)bearing structure** → light-metal space ~ ~

~ ~ **trim** → ~ ~ section

~ ~ **truss(ed girder)** · Leichtmetall-Fachwerk(träger) n, (m)

~ ~ **tube** · Leichtmetallrohr n für Schalungsträger

~ ~ **tubular scaffold(ing)** · Leichtmetallrohrgerüst n, Leichtmetallrohrrüstung f

~ ~ **unit** → ~ ~ section

~ ~ **window** · Leichtmetallfenster n

~ ~ ~ **sill;** ~ ~ cill (Brit.) · Leichtmetall-(Fenster)Sohlbank f, Leichtmetall-Fensterbank

~ **mineral aggregate** · mineralischer Leichtzuschlag(stoff) m, mineralisches Leichtzuschlagmaterial n

~ **(mixed) (calcined) gypsum plaster** (US) → ~ (~) gypsum (building) ~

~ (~) gypsum (building) plaster (Brit); ~ (~) (calcined) gypsum ~ (US); ~ gypsum based ~ · Leichtgipsputz *m*

~ mud brick → ~ adobe ~

~ normal cast-iron adapter (US); ~ ~ ~ adaptor, ~ ~ ~ reducing fitting · LNA-Paßstück *n*, LNA-Übergangsstück

~ ~ ~ drain(age) pipe, ~ ~ ~ draining ~, ~ ~ ~ discharge ~, ~ ~ ~ C.I. ~ ~ ~ · leichtes Normalabflußrohr *n*, LNA-Rohr [*DIN 1172 bis 1178*]

~ ~ ~ offset, ~ ~ ~ swanneck · LNA-Etagenbogen *m*, LNA-S-Stück *n*, LNA-Schwanenhals *m*, LKN-Sprungrohr *n*

~ panel · Leichttafel *f*

~ partition (wall), non(load)bearing ~ (~), non-weight-carrying ~ (~) · leichte Trennwand *f*, nicht (last)tragende ~ [*DIN 4103*]

~ pe(a)rlite curtain wall · Leichtperlit-Vorhangwand *f*

~ pipe · Leichtrohr *n*

~ plank, ~ concrete ~ · Leicht(beton)diele *f*

~ plastic foam → ~ foamed plastic

~ pot → ~ (concrete) hollow block

~ (pre)cast component → ~ ~ (concrete) member

~ ~ (concrete) component → ~ ~ (~) member

~ ~ (~) compound unit, ~ prefab(ricated) ~ ~ ~ · Leicht(beton)fertig(bau)teil *m*, *n*, Leichtfertig(beton)bauteil, Leicht(beton)montage(bau)teil, Leichtmontage(beton)bauteil [*Fehlname: Leichtbetonbauteil*]

~ ~ (~) member, ~ ~ (~) unit, ~ (~) component, ~ cast-concrete ~, ~ (concrete) cast(ing) · Leicht(beton)(bau)element *n*, Leichtbeton(bau)körper *m*, Leichtbetonmontageelement, Leichtbetonmontagekörper, Leichtbetonfertig(bau)körper, Leichtbetonfertig(bau)element [*Fehlnamen: Leichtbeton(bau)einheit f, Leichtbetonmontageeinheit*]

~ ~ (~) product, ~ concrete ~, ~ (pre)cast concrete [*Light(weight) concrete which is cast in separate units before being placed in position in a structure*] · Leichtbetonerzeugnis *n*, Leichtbetonstein *m* [*Siehe Anmerkung unter "Betonstein"*]

~ ~ (~) unit → ~ ~ (~) member

~ ~ (~) ware → mass-produced ~ ~ (~) ~

~ ~ member → ~ ~ concrete ~

~ ~ unit → ~ ~ (concrete) member

~ ~ wall slab → ~ (concrete) ~ ~

~ prefab(ricated) brick panel (unit) · Leichtziegelplatte *f* [*DIN 18505. Fehlname: Leichtsteinplatte*]

~ ~ concrete compound unit → ~ (pre)cast (~) ~ ~

~ prestressed concrete, prestressed light(weight) ~ · Leichtspannbeton *m*, vorgespannter Leichtbeton

~ ~ ~ component, prestressed light(weight) ~ ~, ~ ~ ~ ~ member, ~ ~ ~ unit · Leichtspannbetonelement *n*, Spannbetonleichtelement

~ ~ ~ member, prestressed light(weight) ~ ~, ~ ~ ~ ~ unit, ~ ~ ~ component · Leichtspannbetonelement *n*, Spannbetonleichtelement

~ ~ ~ unit, prestressed light(weight) ~ ~, ~ ~ ~ ~ component, ~ ~ ~ member · Leichtspannbetonelement *n*, Spannbetonleichtelement

~ profile → ~ section

~ refractory brick · feuerfester Leichtstein *m*, ff. ~

~ ~ material → ~ ~ (product)

~ ~ (product), ~ ~ material [*A refractory material with low bulk density*] · feuerfestes Leichterzeugnis *n*, ff. ~

~ reinforced concrete, ~ R.C., reinforced light(weight) concrete · Leichtstahlbeton *m*, Stahlleichtbeton

~ rendering → ~ external ~

~ roof · Leicht(bau)dach *n*

~ roof(ing) tile · Leichtdachstein *m*

~ sand · Leichtsand *m*

~ sand-lime brick, ~ lime-sand ~, ~ calcium silicate ~ · Kalksandleichtstein *m*, Leichtkalksandstein

~ scaffold(ing) · Leichtgerüst *n*, Leichtrüstung *f*

~ screed · Leichtestrich *m*

~ section, ~ trim, ~ unit, ~ shape, ~ profile · Leichtprofil *n*

~ section(al) steel, ~ steel section · Stahlleichtprofil *n*, Leichtprofilstahl *m*, Leichtfassonstahl, Fassonleichtstahl, Leichtformstahl, Formleichtstahl, Leichtstahlprofil, Profilleichtstahl

~ shape → ~ section

~ slag, expanded ~; expanded cinder (US); foam(ed) (iron) (blastfurnace) slag [*B.S. 877*] · schaumige Hochofenschlacke *f*, geschäumte ~, aufgeblähte ~, (Hochofen)Schaumschlacke [*Die gebrochene, geschäumte Hochofenschlacke wird "Hüttenbims" oder "Kunstbims" genannt*]

~ ~ block → foamed (blastfurnace) slag (concrete) (building) ~

~ ~ (building) block → foamed (blastfurnace) slag (concrete) (~) ~

~ ~ (~) tile → foamed (blastfurnace) slag (concrete) (building) block

~ ~ concrete, expanded ~ ~; expanded cinder ~ (US); foam(ed) (iron) (blastfurnace) slag ~ (Brit.) · (Hochofen)Schaumschlackenbeton *m*, (Kunst)Bimsbeton, Hüttenbimsbeton

~ ~ (~) block → foamed (blastfurnace) slag (concrete) (building) ~

light(weight) slag (concrete) tile — lime agitator

~ ~ (~) tile → foamed (blastfurnace) slag (concrete) (building) block

~ ~ powder, expanded ~ ~; expanded cinder ~, foamed (iron) (blastfurnace) slag ~ (Brit.) · Hüttenbimsmehl n, (Kunst)Bimsmehl

~ ~ tile → foamed (blastfurnace) slag (concrete) (building) block

~ sloping roof, sloping light(weight) ~ · Gefälle-Leichtdach n

~ solid block → ~ concrete ~ ~

~ ~ tile → ~ (concrete) solid block

~ steel beam · Stahlleichtbalken(träger) m, Leichtstahlbalken(träger)

~ ~ component → steel light(weight) member

~ ~ construction · Stahlleichtbau m [DIN 4115]

~ ~ floor · Stahlleichtdecke f

~ ~ frame, ~ ~ framing · Leichtstahlrahmen m, Stahlleichtrahmen

~ ~ girder, steel light(weight) ~ · Stahlleicht(bau)träger m, Leichtstahl(bau)träger

~ ~ ~ floor · Stahlleichtträgerdecke f, Leichtstahlträgerdecke

~ ~ member → steel light(weight) ~

~ ~ sanitary building block module, ~ ~ ~ unitized unit · Leichtstahl-Sanitär(raum)zelle f, Leichtstahl-Sanitär(raum)block m, Leichtstahl-Sanitärinstallationszelle, Leichtstahl-Sanitärinstallationsblock

~ ~ section, ~ section(al) steel · Stahlleichtprofil n, Leichtprofilstahl m, Leichtfassonstahl, Fassonleichtstahl, Leichtformstahl, Formleichtstahl, Leichtstah.-profil, Profilleichtstahl

~ ~ structures, steel light(weight) ~ · Stahlleichtbauten f

~ ~ unit → steel light(weight) member

~ stopper, ~ stopping · Leicht-Spachtel(masse) m, (f) [Anstrichtechnik]

~ structural clay product · keramisches Leichtbauerzeugnis n, keramischer Leichtbauartikel m, keramischer-Leicht-baugegenstand m

~ ~ concrete, structural light(weight) ~, L. S. C. · Konstruktionsleichtbeton m, konstruktiver Leichtbeton

~ (~) (~) building block, ~ (~) (~) ~ tile [B.S. 2028] [See remark under 'Block'] · Leicht(beton)block(stein) m, Leicht(beton)stein [DIN 18152 für Leicht(beton)vollsteine und DIN 18151 für Leicht(beton)hohlsteine]

~ stucco (US) → ~ (external) rendering

~ substrate (system) → ~ deck(ing) (~)

~ substructure (system) → ~ deck(ing) (~)

~ sun-dried brick → ~ adobe ~

~ tile, ~ block [See remark under 'Block'] · Leichtstein m, Leichtblock(stein) m

~ ~ masonry (work), ~ block ~ (~) [See remark under 'Block'] · Leichtblock(stein)mauerwerk n, Leichtsteinmauerwerk

~ ~ partition (wall), ~ block ~ (~) [See remark under 'Block'] · Leichtblock(stein)wand f, Leichtsteinwand [Leichte Trennwand. DIN 4103]

~ trim, ~ section, ~ unit, ~ shape, ~ profile · Leichtprofil n

~ truss(ed) girder · Leicht(bau)-Fachwerk(träger) n, (m)

~ unit → ~ building ~

~ vault · Leichtgewölbe n

~ vertical coring (clay) brick · Leichthochlochziegel m [DIN 18505]

~ wall · Leichtwand f

~ ~ slab → ~ concrete ~ ~

~ ~ ~ ~ · Leichtwandplatte f

light well, air shaft · Lichtschacht m

~ wrecking work → ~ ~ demolition ~

lignin · Lignin n

~ adhesive; sulphite lye ~ (Brit.); sulfite lye ~ (US) · Sulfit(ab)laugekleber m

~ paste · Ligninpaste f

~ sulphonate (Brit.); ~ sulfonate (US) · Ligninsulfonat n

lignite · Lignit n

~ tar · Lignitteer m

~-tar pitch · Lignitteerpech n

like-grained, uniform, single-sized, equigranular, even-grained · einkörnig, gleichkörnig

~ aerated concrete, uniform ~ ~, single-sized ~ ~, short range aggregate ~ ~, equigranular ~ ~, even-grained ~ ~ · einkörniger Porenbeton m, gleichkörniger ~, Einkorn-Porenbeton

~ concrete, uniform ~, single-sized ~, short range aggregate ~, equigranular ~, even-grained ~ · Einkornbeton m, einkörniger Beton, gleichkörniger Beton [DIN 4163]

~ gravel, even-grained ~, uniform ~, single-sized ~, equigranular ~, short range ~ · einkörniger Kies m, gleichkörniger ~, monodisperser ~, Einkornkies

~ mortar, uniform ~, single-sized ~, short range aggregate ~, even-grained ~, equigranular ~ · einkörniger Mörtel m, gleichkörniger ~, Einkornmörtel

lily-flower, fleur-de-lis · (Bourbonische) Lilie f, Wappenlilie

limb, wing · Seitengebäude n, Nebengebäude, Gebäudeflügel m, Abseite f, (Erweiterungs)Flügel, Hausflügel, Seitenhaus n, Nebenhaus

~ of cross, cross limb · Kreuzarm m

lime [B.S. 890] · Kalk m

~ addition, addition of lime, adding of lime · Kalkbeigabe f, Kalkzugabe, Kalkzusatz m, Kalkbeigeben n, Kalkzusetzen, Kalkzugeben

~ agitator · Kalkrührwerk n

lime base — lime fel(d)spar

~ **base** · Kalkbasis f, Kalkgrundlage f [z.B. Mauermörtel auf Kalkbasis]

~ ~ **grease,** calcium ~ · Kalkfett n, Kalkseifenfett, kalkverseiftes Fett

~ **basecoat** [Lime basecoats are mixed using lime putty, sand, and water. Gaging plaster, which may be gypsum, gaging plaster, Keene's cement, or portland cement, is often added to produce early strength and counteract possible shrinkage in setting] · Kalkunterschicht f

~ **based** · kalkhaltig [Ein Stoff ist kalkhaltig, wenn ihm Kalk in irgendeiner Form künstlich beigegeben wurde. Gegensatz: Kalk(halt)ig, wenn ein Stoff von Natur aus Kalk enthält]

~ **blue** · Kalkblau n [Aus basischem Teerfarbstoff durch Verlackung auf Grünerde hergestellte Pigmentfarbe]

lime-bound · kalkgebunden

~ **aerated concrete,** light(weight) lime ~ · Leichtkalkbeton m, Kalkleichtbeton [Dampfgehärteter, kalkgebundener Porenbeton]

~ ~ ~ **block,** ~ ~ ~ **tile,** light(weight) lime ~ ~ [See remark under 'Block-(stein)'] · Kalkleichtbetonblock(stein) m, Kalkleichtbetonstein, Leichtkalkbetonblock(stein), Leichtkalkbetonstein

~ **(building) component** → ~ (~) unit

~ **(~) member** → ~ (~) unit

~ **(~) unit,** ~ (~) member, ~ (~) component · Kalkgebundener (Bau-) Körper m, kalkgebundenes (Bau)Element n [Fehlname: kalkgebundene Baueinheit f]

~ **component** → ~ (building) unit

~ **gas concrete** · kalkgebundener Gasbeton m

~ **member** → ~ (building) unit

~ **unit** → ~ (building) ~

lime burning · Kalkbrennen n

~ ~ **plant** · Kalkbrennerei f, Kalkwerk n, Kalkfabrik f

(~) **caving** · (Kalk)Nachlöschen n

(~) ~ **bin** · (Kalk)Nachlöschbunker m

~ **cement** · Kalkzement m

lime-cement exterior plaster, ~ external ~; ~ stucco (US); ~ (external) rendering (Brit.) · Kalkzementaußenputz m

~ **finish,** ~ (mixed) plaster · Kalkzementverputz m

~ **(mixed) plaster,** ~ finish · Kalkzementverputz m

~ **(~) ~** · Kalkzementputz m

~ **stucco** (US); ~ (external) rendering (Brit.); ~ external plaster, ~ exterior plaster · Kalkzementaußenputz m

lime(-cemented) sandstone, calcareous ~ · kalk(halt)iger Sandstein m, Kalksandstein

lime clay, calcareous ~ · Kalkton m

~ **compatibility** · Kalkverträglichkeit f

~ **concrete** · Kalkbeton m [Beton aus herkömmlichen Zuschlägen mit hochhydraulischem Kalk als Bindemittel. Seit der Herstellung der Zemente ist der Kalkbeton technisch und wirtschaftlich überholt]

~ **content** · Kalkanteil m, Kalkgehalt m

~ **desintegration** · Kalkzerfall m

~ **encrusted** · verkalkt

limed rosin · Kalkharz n

lime emulsion · Kalkemulsion f

~ **exterior plaster** → ~ (external) rendering

~ ~ ~ **mix(ture)** → ~ (external) rendering stuff

~ ~ ~ **stuff** → ~ (external) rendering ~

~ **external plaster** → ~ (~) rendering

~ ~ ~ **mix(ture)** → ~ (~) rendering stuff

~ ~ ~ **stuff** → ~ (~) rendering ~

~ **(~) rendering** (Brit.); ~ stucco (US); ~ exterior plaster, ~ external plaster · Kalk(außen)(ver)putz m

~ **(~) ~ mix(ture)** → ~ (~) ~ stuff

~ **(~) ~ stuff,** ~ (~) ~ mix(ture) (Brit.); ~ stucco ~ (US); ~ exterior plaster ~, ~ external plaster ~ · Kalkaußenputzmörtel m, Kalkaußenputzmasse f

~ **factor** · Kalkfaktor m

limefast, fast to lime · kalkecht [Kalkecht, d.h. gegen Basen widerstandsfähig sind nur Farben, die sich, in Kalkmilch oder Kalkwasser erhitzt, nicht verändern]

~ **cement colour** → ~ ~ ~ pigment

~ ~ **pigment;** ~ ~ colour, ~ colour for incorporating in cement, ~ pigment for colouring cement · Kalkfarbe f [Kalkechte lichtbeständige Zementfarbe]

~ **colour for incorporating in cement** → ~ ~ cement pigment

~ **pigment** · kalkechte Farbe f [Solche Farben müssen beständig gegen gelöschten Kalk und Zement sein und dürfen ihre Nuance nicht verlieren. Hierzu gehören gebrannter Ocker, Grünerde, Oxide, Ultramarin und Kobalt]

~ ~ **for colouring cement** → ~ cement pigment

lime fastness, ~ resistance, resistance to lime, fastness to lime · Kalkbeständigkeit f, Kalkechtheit, Kalkwiderstand m, Kalkfestigkeit

~ **fel(d)spar,** anorthite · $CaAl_2Si_2O_8$, Kalkfeldspat m, Anorthit m

lime finish — lime silo

~ finish, ~ plaster · Kalkverputz *m*

~ ~ coat [*Lime finish coats are made from the same ingredients as lime basecoats except that finer sand is used as aggregate*] · Kalkoberschicht *f*

~ glass · Kalkglas *n*

~ grain, ~ particle · Kalkkorn *n*, Kalkteilchen *n*

~ green · Kalkgrün *n* [*Aus basischem Teerfarbstoff durch Verlackung auf Grünerde hergestellte Pigmentfarbe*]

lime-gypsum mortar · Kalkgipsmörtel *m* [*Der Kalkanteil ist größer als der Gipsanteil. Sonst Gipskalkmörtel*]

lime hydrating machine, (~) slaking ~, hydrator · (Kalk)Löschmaschine *f*

lime-incrustation remover · Entkalkungsmittel *n*, Entkalker *m*

lime industry, limestone ~ · Kalk(stein)industrie *f*

~ insulating plaster ~ insulation(-grade) ~ · Kalkisolierputz *m*, Isolierkalkputz

~ kiln · Kalk(brenn)ofen *m*

~ lump · Kalkstück *n*

~ marl, calcareous ~ · Kalkmergel *m* [*In Deutschland 75%–90% $CaCO_3$*]

~ modulus, modulus of lime · Kalkmodul *m*

~ mortar, L.M. · Kalkmörtel *m*

~ ~ flooring, L.M. ~ · Kalkestrich *m*, russischer Mörtelestrich

~ mud rock, calcilutyte · Kalktonstein *m*

~ nitrate, nitrate of lime · Kalksalpeter *m*, Kalziumnitrat *n*, salpetersaurer Kalk *m*, salpetersaures Kalzium *n*, $Ca(NO_3)_2$

~ particle, ~ grain · Kalkkorn *n*, Kalkteilchen *n*

~ paste, ~ putty, plasterer's putty [*A stiff paste resulting from slaking quicklime or soaking hydrated lime in water*] · Kalkbrei *m*, Kalkteig *m*, Breikalk *m*, Schlämpe *f*, Schlempe [*Fehlname: Fettkalk*]

~ pat, circular-domed pat of lime · Kalkkuchen *m*, Probekuchen aus Kalk

~ pit · Sumpfgrube *f*

~ plaster, ~ finish · Kalkverputz *m*

~ ~ · Kalkputz *m*

~ pocket · Kalkeinschluß *m*

lime-portland cement mix(ture) · Kalk-Portlandzement-Gemisch *n*, Kalk-Portlandzement-Mischung *f*

lime product · Kalkerzeugnis *n*

lime(-)proof, lime(-)resisting, lime(-)resistant · kalkbeständig, kalkfest, kalkunempfindlich

lime putty → ~ paste

~ raker, ~ stirrer · Kalkkrücke *f*, Kalkrührer *m*

~ red · Kalkrot *n* [*Aus basischem Teerfarbstoff durch Verlackung auf Grünerde hergestellte Pigmentfarbe*]

~ removal · Entkalkung *f*, Entkalken *n*

~ rendering → ~ external ~

~ ~ mix(ture) → ~ (external) rendering stuff

~ ~ stuff → ~ external ~ ~

~ resistance, ~ fastness, resistance to lime, fastness to lime · Kalkbeständigkeit *f*, Kalkechtheit, Kalkwiderstand *m*, Kalkfestigkeit

lime(-)resistant, lime(-)resisting, lime(-)proof · kalkbeständig, kalkfest, kalkunempfindlich

lime(-)resisting, lime(-)resistant, lime(-)proof · kalkbeständig, kalkfest, kalkunempfindlich

lime-rich · kalkreich

lime sand, calcareous ~ · Kalksand *m*

lime-sand brick → sand-lime ~

~ ~ lintel → sand-lime ~ ~

~ ~ machine, sand-lime ~ ~ · Kalksandsteinmaschine *f*

~ ~ 1:8, sand-lime ~ ~ · Piséstein *m* [*Kalkmörtelstein aus Branntkalk und Sand (1:8) gestampft*]

~ facing brick, sand-lime ~ ~, calcium-silicate ~ ~ · Kalksandverblender *m*, Kalksandverblendstein *m*

~ (mixed) plaster [*1. A mix based on lime and sand, which is applied while plastic to internal building surfaces and which hardens after application. 2. This material in its hardened form*] · Kalksand(innen)(ver)putz *m*

~ mix(ture) · Kalk-Sand-Gemisch *n*, Kalk-Sand-Mischung *f*

~ mortar, lime:sand ~, coarse stuff · Kalksandmörtel *m*

~ plaster → ~ mixed ~

~ ratio · Kalk-Sand-Verhältnis *n*

lime sandstone, lime-cemented ~, calcareous ~ · kalk(halt)iger Sandstein *m*, Kalksandstein

lime-saturated · kalkgesättigt

lime saturation · Kalksättigung *f*

~ ~ degree, degree of lime saturation · Kalksättigungsgrad *m*

~ ~ factor, LSF · Kalksättigungsfaktor *m*

~ silicate, calcium ~ · Kalksilikat *n*, Kalziumsilikat, KS, $CaSiO_3$

~ silo · Kalksilo *m*

(lime) slaking — limit-load approach

(~) slaking, running to putty, hydrating · (Ab)Löschen n, Naßlöschen [*Kalk*]

(~) ~ box · (Kalk)Löschkasten m, (Kalk-)Löschpfanne f

(~) ~ drum · (Kalk)Löschtrommel f, (Kalk)Trommel-Löscher m

(~) ~ machine, ~ hydrating ~, hydrator · (Kalk)Löschmaschine f

(~) ~ pit · Kalkgrube f, (Kalk)Löschgrube

(~) ~ process · (Kalk)Löschvorgang m

(~) ~ trough · (Kalk)Löschbank f

(~) ~ vessel · (Kalk)Löschgefäß n

lime-soda glass · Kalknatronglas n, französisches Glas

lime stirrer, ~ raker · Kalkkrücke f, Kalkrührer m

limestone; cauk, cawk [*Scotland*]; LS · $CaCO_3$, Kalkstein m [*Sedimentationsgestein mit dem Hauptbestandteil Kalziumkarbonat in dicht und körnig kristalliner Form*]

~ aggregate, ~ concrete ~ · Kalkstein-(beton)zuschlag(stoff) m

~ block · Kalksteinblock m

~ chip(ping)s · Kalksteinsplitt m

~ column · Kalksteinsäule f

~ concrete · Kalksteinbeton m

~ (~) aggregate · Kalkstein(beton)-zuschlag(stoff) m

~ dust → powder(ed) limestone

~ filler · Kalk(mehl)füller m, Kalksteinfüller

~ gravel · Kalksteinkies m

~ impregnated with asphaltic bitumen (Brit); ~ ~ ~ ~ asphalt (US) · Naturasphaltkalkstein m

lime(stone) industry · Kalk(stein)industrie f

~ lime → high-calcium ~

limestone marble, calcitic ~, crystalline limestone · Kalkmarmor m, kristalliner Kalkstein m

~ masonry wall · Kalksteinmauer f

~ ~ (work) · Kalksteinmauerwerk n

~ mastic · Kalkkitt m, Kalksteinmastix m

~ monument, monument of limestone · Kalksteinmonument n

~ panel · Kalksteintafel f

~ phyllite · Kalkphyllit m

~ powder → powder(ed) limestone

~ quarry · Kalksteinbruch m

~ red earth · Kalksteinroterde f

~ rubble · Kalkstein-Bruchstein m

~ slab floor cover(ing), ~ ~ floor(ing) (finish) · Fbka m, Kalksteinplatten-(fuß)boden(belag) m

~ slate, calcareous ~ · Kalktonschiefer m

~ tarmacadam · Kalksteinteermakadam m

~ washer, ~ washing machine · Kalksteinwaschmaschine f, Kalksteinwäsche f

lime stucco (US) → ~ (external) rendering

~ ~ mix(ture) (US) → ~ (external) rendering stuff

~ ~ stuff (US) → ~ (external) rendering ~

~ sulfate (US) → calcium sulphate

~ sulphate → calcium ~

~ suspension, suspension of lime · Kalksuspension f

lime-trass mortar · Kalktraßmörtel m

lime type, type of lime · Kalkart f

~ uranite, autunite · Autunit n, Kalkuranglimmer m

to limewash, to limewhite, to whiten, to whitewash · kalken, tünchen, schlämmen, weißen

limewash → whitewash

~ coat → whitewash ~

limewashing, limewhiting, whitening, whitewashing · Kalken n, Tünchen, Weißen, Schlämmen

lime water [*1. A saturated solution of lime in water. 2. Water in which slaked lime has been dissolved*] · kalk(halt)iges Wasser n, Kalkwasser

to limewhite, to whitewash, to whiten, to limewash · kalken, tünchen, schlämmen, weißen

limewhiting, whitewashing, whitening, limewashing · Kalken n, Tünchen, Weißen, Schlämmen

liming-up · Verkalken n

limit angle, limiting ~ · Grenzwinkel m

~ bending moment → limit(ing) ~ ~

~ curve → limit(ing) grading ~

~ deformation · Grenzformänderung f, Grenzverformung, Grenzgestaltänderung

~ design · Traglastverfahren n [*Ein Verfahren, mit dem die Traglasten unter Berücksichtigung der nichtelastischen Vorgänge, die zu inneren oder äußeren Kräfteumlagerungen führen, ermittelt werden*]

~ load, plastic ~ · Traglast f

~-load approach, plastic-load ~ · Ansatz m nach dem Traglastverfahren

limit loading — line of curvature

limit loading, ultimate ~, rupture ~, breaking ~ · Bruchbelastung *f*, Grenzbelastung
~ method, plastic ~ · Traglastverfahren *n* [*Ein Verfahren, mit dem die Traglasten unter Berücksichtigung der nichtelastischen Vorgänge, die zu inneren oder äußeren Kräfteumlagerungen führen, ermittelt werden*]
~ of endurance, ~ ~ fatigue, fatigue limit, endurance limit · Ermüdungsgrenze *f*
~ ~ fatigue in tension · Zugermüdungsgrenze *f*
~ ~ fineness, fineness limit · Feinheitsgrenze *f*
~ ~ proportionality, proportional(ity)-limit · P-Grenze *f*, Proportionalitätsgrenze
~ ~ slenderness, slenderness limit · Schlankheitsgrenze *f*
~ ~ space, space limit · Raumgrenze *f*
~ ~ stability, stability limit · Stabilitätsgrenze *f*, Standfestigkeitsgrenze, Standsicherheitsgrenze
~ ~ stress, stress limit · Spannungsgrenze *f*
~ ~ the ultimate strength, failure limit · Bruchgrenze *f* [*Druckspannung im Beton bzw. Zugspannung im Stahl die den Bruch verursachen*]
~ ~ tolerance, tolerance limit · Abmaßgrenze *f*
~ screen size · Grenzkorn(größe) *n*, (*f*), Siebgrenzgröße [*Das Korn, das annähernd die Größe der Maschenweite besitzt und sich daher am schwierigsten sieben läßt*]
~ state [*The state of a structure, or a member thereof, in which a requirement for the fulfilment of its purpose is just exactly satisfied and ceases to be satisfied if the action-effects are increased or the structure is weakened. This definition also covers the conventional limit states, e.g. the limit state of decompression*] · Grenzzustand *m*
~ ~ of cracking, cracking limit state · Rißbildungs-Grenzzustand *m*
~ ~ ~ deformation, deformation limit state · Verformungs-Grenzzustand *m*
~ ~ ~ serviceability, serviceability limit state · Gebrauchsfähigkeits-Grenzzustand *m*
~ strength, limiting ~, strength ceiling · Grenzfestigkeit *f*
~ theorem, plastic ~ · Traglastsatz *m*
limitation of space · Raumbegrenzung *f*
~ ~ ~ · Raumbeschränkung *f*
~ ~ types, reduction ~ ~ · Typeneinschränkung *f*
limit(ing) angle · Grenzwinkel *m*
~ bending moment · Grenzbiegemoment *n*, Grenzbiegungsmoment
~ curve → **~ grading** ~
~ dimension · Grenzabmessung *f*, Grenzmaß *n*
~ equation · Grenzgleichung *f*
~ (grading) curve, particle (distribution) limit, gradation limit, grading limit · Grenzsieblinie *f*, Siebgrenze *f*
~ height · Grenzhöhe *f*
~ layer · Grenzschicht *f*
~ manostat · Begrenzer-Manostat *m*
~ pressure · Grenzdruck *m*, kritischer Druck
~ screen aperture · Korngrenzenöffnung *f*
~ size · Grenzgröße *f*
~ slenderness · Grenzschlankheit *f*
~ state · Grenzzustand *m*
~ strength, strength ceiling · Grenzfestigkeit *f*
~ value, ultimate ~ · Grenzwert *m*
Limpet asbestos, sprayed ~, sprayable ~ [*The trade name of a composition of asbestos and a bonding agent applied by gun spraying for fire-protection, thermal insulation, and the prevention of condensation. It is produced by Turner's Asbestos Cement Co. Ltd. Manchester and Limpet Spritzasbest GmbH, Frankfurt (M)*] · Spritzasbest *m*
limy, calcareous [*Of, like, or containing calcium carbonate, calcium, or lime*] · kalk(halt)ig
~ gravel, calcareous ~ · Kalkkies *m*
linchpin · Pflöckchen *n*
to line · ausfüttern, ausfuttern
~ ~, to (sur)face · auskleiden, bekleiden, verkleiden
line, piano lines, drawing lines · Kämmung *f* [*Flachglasfehler*]
~ [*A cord used for setting out building work*] · Schnur *f*
~, run · Leitung *f*
~ drawing · Strichzeichnung *f*
~ installed in plaster · Unterputzleitung *f*
~ ~ on insulators · Leitung *f* auf Isolatoren
~ ~ ~ plaster · Leitung *f* auf Putz
~ installer, pipe~ ~ · Rohr(fern)leitungsbauer *m*
~ integral · Linienintegral *n* [*Vektor*]
~ load, strip ~, knife edge ~, (col-)linear ~ [*Forces on a long narrow member, e.g. a beam*] · Schneidenlast *f*, Linienlast, Streckenlast
~ loading, strip ~, knife edge ~, (col-)linear ~ · Linienbelastung *f*, Streckenbelastung
~ of action · Wirkungslinie *f*
~ ~ arch, outline ~ ~, arch (out)line · Bogenprofil *n*, Bogenlinie *f*, Wölbung *f*
~ ~ columns, row ~ ~, ~ ~ supports · Stützenreihe *f*
~ ~ curvature, curvature line · Krümmungslinie *f*

line of force — linen tape

~ ~ **force** · Kraftlinie *f*
~ ~ **holes** · Lochreihe *f*
~ ~ **horizontal stress** · Einflußlinie *f* des Bogenschubs, H-Linie
~ ~ **influence,** influence line · Einflußlinie *f*, Greensche Funktion *f*
~ ~ **intersection,** intersection line · Schnittlinie *f*
~ ~ **least pressure,** ~ ~ minimum ~ · Mindestdrucklinie *f*
~ ~ **loading,** loading line · Belastungslinie *f*
~ ~ **main curvature** → ~ ~ principal ~
~ ~ ~ **stress** → ~ ~ ~ principal ~
~ ~ **maximum pressure,** maximum pressure line · Größtdrucklinie *f*, Höchstdrucklinie, Maximaldrucklinie
~ ~ **principal curvature,** ~ ~ main ~, principal curvature line, main curvature line · Hauptkrümmungslinie *f*
~ ~ ~ **stress,** trajectory ~ ~ ~, ~ ~ main ~, principal stress line, main stress line, isostatic line · Hauptspannungslinie *f*, Hauptspannungstrajektorie *f*
~ ~ **space** · Raumgerade *f*
~ ~ **supports,** row ~ ~, ~ ~ columns · Stützenreihe *f*
~ ~ **thrust,** thrust line, (funicular) pressure line · Stützlinie *f*, Mittelkraftlinie, Drucklinie [*Die „natürliche" Kräftelinie des formaktiven Drucksystems*]
~ ~ **vault** → vault (out)line
~ **ornament** · Linienornament *n*
~ **pin** · Schnurstift *m*
~ **pipe,** conduit ~ · Leitungsrohr *n*
~ **protection breaker** · Leitungsschutzschalter *m*
~ **supported** · liniengelagert
lineal foot → foot run
linear air distribution · lineare Luftverteilung *f*
~ **arch,** funicular ~ [*An arch which is purely in compression under a series of point loads. It is the reverse of a string carrying the same load system as a suspension cable*] · Stützbogen *m*
~ **bearing system** → ~ structure ~
~ **bending theory** · lineare Biegetheorie *f*
~ **building** · Zeilenbau *m*
~ **displacement** · lineare Verrückung *f*
~ **distribution** · lineare Verteilung *f*
~ **elasticity** · linearisierte Elastizität *f*, klassische ~
~ **expansion** · lineare Ausdehnung *f*
~ **function** · lineare Funktion *f*
~ **interpolation** · gerad(linig)e Interpolierung *f*
~ **load** → line ~

~ **(load)bearing system** → ~ structure ~
~ **load-carrying system** → ~ structure ~
~ **loaded system** → ~ structure ~
~ **loading** → line ~
~ **moment** · lineares Moment *n*
~ **pattern** · Linienmuster *n*
~ **plastic theory,** simple ~ ~, first-order ~ · (Spannungs)Theorie *f* 1. Ordnung, einfache plastische Theorie, lineare plastische Theorie
~ **(pre)stressing,** ~ tensioning, ~ stretching [*(Pre)Stressing as applied to linear members, such as beams, columns, etc.*] · lineare Vorspannung *f*
~ **progression of stresses** · linearer Verlauf *m* der Kräfte
~ **relation** · lineare Beziehung *f*
~ **shell theory** · lineare Schalentheorie *f*
~ **shrinkage** · lineare Schwindung *f*
~ **space truss** · lineares Raumfachwerk *n*
~ **state of stress,** one-dimensional ~ ~ ~, ~ stress state · einachsiger Spannungszustand *m*, linearer ~
~ **stress distribution** · lineare Spannungsverteilung *f*
~ ~ **state,** one-dimensional ~ ~, ~ state of stress · einachsiger Spannungszustand *m*, linearer ~
~ **stressing** → ~ pre~
~ **stretching** → ~ (pre)stressing
~ **structure system,** ~ (load)bearing ~, ~ weight-carrying ~, ~ supporting ~, ~ load-carrying ~, ~ loaded ~ · lineares Tragsystem *n*, ~ (last)tragendes System
~ **style of ornamentation** · lineare Ornamentik *f*
~ **supporting system** → ~ structure ~
~ **tensioning** → ~ (pre)stressing
~ **town** · Bandstadt *f*, lineare Stadt [*Das Rückgrat dieser Stadtform ist ein Verkehrsband an das sich hintereinander gestaffelt die Zonen der menschlichen Betätigung reihen. Die Theorie stammt von dem Spanier Soria y Mala aus dem Jahre 1882*]
~ **translation** · lineare Verschiebung *f*
~ **weight-carrying system** → ~ structure ~
linearity · Linearität *f*
linearly elastic · linear elastisch
~ **varying strain** · linear veränderliche Dehnung *f*
linen chute → soiled ~ ~
~ **closet** · Wäsche-Einbauschrank *m*, Wäsche-Wandschrank
~ **cupboard** · Wäscheschrank *m*
~ **room** · Wäschekammer *f*, Wäscheraum *m* [*Hotel*]
~ **tape** · Leinenbandmaß *n*

liner — linseed oil for paints

liner → lining material

~, lining · Futter *n*

~ · Abklebung *f* [*Preßstrohplatte*]

~fold panelling (Brit.); **~ paneling** (US) · Faltwerkfüllung *f*

lining, cladding, skin · (Außenwand-)Versteifung *f*

~, liner · Futter *n*

~, (sur)facing · Auskleidung *f*, Bekleidung, Verkleidung, Belag *m*

~ → soffit board

~ board, ~ sheet, (sur)facing ~ · Auskleidungsplatte *f*, Verkleidungsplatte, Bekleidungsplatte

~ brick · Futterziegel *m*

~ component → ~ unit

~ concrete · Auskleidungsbeton *m*, Verkleidungsbeton, Bekleidungsbeton

~ ~ slab, (sur)facing ~ ~ · Auskleidungsplatte *f* aus Beton, Verkleidungsplatte ~ ~, Bekleidungsplatte ~ ~, Beton-Auskleidungsplatte, Beton-Verkleidungsplatte, Beton-Bekleidungsplatte

~ foil, (sur)facing ~ · Auskleidungsfolie *f*, Verkleidungsfolie, Bekleidungsfolie

~ material, (sur)facing ~, covering ~, liner · Auskleidungsstoff *m*, Verkleidungsstoff, Belagstoff, Bekleidungsstoff [*Baustoff, der zur Erhöhung der Lebensdauer oder zur Verschönerung eines Bauwerkes dient*]

~ member → ~ unit

~ out (by chalk line) · Schnurschlag *m*

~ panel, cladding ~ · (Außenwand-)Versteifungstafel *f*

~ ~, (sur)facing ~ · Bekleidungstafel *f*, Auskleidungstafel, Verkleidungstafel

~ paper · Makulatur *f*

~ profile → ~ section

~ section, ~ shape, ~ trim, ~ unit, ~ profile · Auskleidungsprofil *n*, Verkleidungsprofil, Bekleidungsprofil

~ shape → ~ section

~ sheet → ~ board

~ slab, cladding ~ · (Außenwand)Versteifungsplatte *f*

~ (stone)ware, (sur)facing ~ · Auskleidungssteinzeug *n*, Verkleidungssteinzeug, Bekleidungssteinzeug

~ trim → ~ section

~ turf · Plaggenrasen *m*, Sodenrasen

~ unit, (sur)facing ~, ~ member, ~ component · Auskleidungselement *n*, Verkleidungselement, Bekleidungselement

~ ~ → ~ section

~ ware, ~ stone~, (sur)facing ~ · Auskleidungssteinzeug *n*, Verkleidungssteinzeug, Bekleidungssteinzeug

link, binder · Bügel *m* [*Bewehrung*]

~ curve → funicular polygon

~ polygon → funicular ~

~ unit · Verbindungstrakt *m*

linked → hinged

~ arch(ed girder) → pin(ned) ~ (~)

~ bar → hinge(d) ~

~ connection → hinge(d) joint

~ frame → hinge(d) ~

~ joint → hinge(d) ~

~ purlin(e) → hinge(d) ~

~ system → articulated ~

links → binders

linkway, enterclose, connecting corridor, connection corridor · Verbindungsgang *m*

linoleate · Linoleat *n*

~ of lead, lead linoleate · Bleilinoleat *n*

~ ~ manganese, manganese linoleate · Manganlinoleat *n*

lino(leum) · Linoleum *n* [*DIN 18171*]

~ adhesive → ~ bonding ~

~ (bonding) adhesive, ~ cement(ing agent), ~ bonding agent, ~ bonding medium ~ · Linoleumkleber *m*, Linoleumkleb(e)stoff *m*, Linoleumkleb(e)mittel *n* [*Fehlname: Linoleumkitt m*]

~ calendered on to a bitumen impregnated paper felt, felt-backed lino(leum) [*B.S. 1863*] · Linoleum *n* auf Filzhinterlegung, ~ ~ Filzunterlage, ~ Filzrücklage, ~ ~ Filzträger(schicht)

~ cement(ing agent) → ~ (bonding) adhesive

~ cover · Linoleumbelag *m*

~ floor cover(ing), ~ floor(ing) (finish) · Fbl *m*, Linoleum(fuß)boden(belag) *m*

~ gauge (Brit.); **~ gage** (US) · Linoleumdicke *f*

~-laying · Linoleumverlegung *f*

~ mass, plastic ~ · Linoleumgrundmasse

~ tar · Linoleumteer *m*

~ tile [*B.S. 810*] · Linoleumfliese *f*, Linoleum(belag)platte *f*

~ tiles [*B.S. 810*] · Fliesenlinoleum *n*, Linoleumfliesen *fpl*, (Belag)Plattenlinoleum Linoleum(belag)platten

~ work · Linoleumarbeiten *fpl*

linseed, flax-seed · Flachssamen *m*, Leinsaat *f*

~ cake, oil ~ · Ölkuchen *m*, Leinkuchen

~ oil · Leinöl *n*

~ ~ acid · Leinölsäure

~ ~ alkyd · Leinölalkyd *n*

~ ~ base · Leinölbasis *f*, Leinölgrundlage

~ oil-bearing · leinölhaltig

~ oil drying · Leinöltrocknung *f*

~ ~ emulsion · Leinölemulsion *f*

~ ~ for paints [*B.S. 242*] · Leinöl *n* für (Anstrich)Farben

linseed oil isomer — liquid integral waterproofing agent

~ ~ **isomer,** isomerized linseed oil · isomerisiertes Leinöl *n*

~ ~ **paint** · Leinöl(anstrich)farbe *f*

~ ~ **priming agent,** ~ ~ primer · Leinöl-Grundier(ungs)mittel *n*

~ ~ **putty** · Leinölkitt *m*

~ ~ **stand oil** · Leinölstandöl *n*

~ ~ **substitute** · Leinölersatz *m*

~ ~ **without foots** · entschleimtes Leinöl *n*

~ ~ **wood oil stand oil** · Leinöl-Holzöl-Standöl *n*

lintel, header; lintol *[deprecated]* [*The horizontal framing member over window or door openings*] · Oberschwelle *f,* Sturz(balken) *m*

~ **brick;** lintol ~ *[deprecated]* · Sturzformziegel *m*

~-**falseblock;** lintol-falseblock *[deprecated]* · Sturz-Schalungsblock *m*

~ **in prestressed clay** → Stahlton (prestressed) lintel

~ ~ **Stahlton** → Stahlton (prestressed) lintel

~ **reinforcement;** lintol ~ *[deprecated]* · Sturzarmierung *f,* Sturzbewehrung, Sturz(stahl)einlagen *fpl*

linter [*The short fibrous hair that grows on the cotton seed*] · Linter *m*

Linville (roof) truss; Pratt (~) ~ (US); N-truss · Pratt(-Dach)binder *m*

lion frieze · Löwenfries *m*

Lion Gate, Gate of Lions [*Mycenae*] · Löwentor *n*

lion mask · Löwenmaske *f*

Lion Tomb at Cnidos · Löwengrab *n* zu Knidos

lip · Leiste *f [Deckenziegel]*

~, **lipping** · Umleimer *m*

~ · Lippe *f*

~ **seal(ing) ring** · Lippen(ab)dicht(ungs)ring *m*

lipped floor (clay) brick, ~ ~ (~) block · Deckenstein *m* mit Leisten, Deckenziegel *m* ~ ~

lip(ping) · Umleimer *m*

liquation → eliquation

liquefaction of air · Luftverflüssigung *f*

liquefied resin, liquid ~ · Flüssigharz *n*

liquefying, deliquescence · Zerfließen *n,* Flüssigwerden

liquid adhesive · Kleb(e)flüssigkeit *f*

~ **admix(ture),** ~ agent, ~ concrete ~ · flüssiger (Beton)Wirkstoff *m,* ~ (Beton)Zusatz(stoff) *m,* flüssiges (Beton-)Zusatzmittel *n*

~ **agent,** ~ admix(ture), ~ concrete ~ · flüssiger (Beton)Wirkstoff *m,* ~ (Beton)Zusatz(stoff) *m,* flüssiges (Beton)Zusatzmittel *n*

~ **air-entraining agent** · Mischöl *n*

~ **asphalts,** ~ asphalt(ic) (road) materials (US) [*Products so soft that their consistency cannot be measured by the normal penetration test (such as road oils or asphaltic cutbacks)*] · Verschnittbitumen *n* und Straßenöle *npl*

~ **coating (material),** ~ ~ composition, ~ ~ medium, surface ~ (~) · Anstrich(stoff) *m,* Anstrichmittel *n,* Aufstrichmittel, Aufstrich(stoff), flüssiger Beschichtungsstoff, Anstrichmaterial *n,* Aufstrichmaterial

~ ~ (~) **for concrete,** ~ ~ composition ~ ~, ~ ~ medium ~ ~, surface ~ (~) ~ ~ · Betonanstrich(mittel) *m,* (*n*), Betonanstrichstoff *m,* Betonaufstrich(stoff), Betonaufstrichmittel, flüssiger Betonbeschichtungsstoff, Betonanstrichmaterial *n,* Betonaufstrichmaterial

~ ~ (~) ~ **the preservation of structures** · Bautenschutz-Anstrich(stoff) *m,* Bautenschutz-Anstrichmittel

~ **(concrete) admix(ture),** ~ (~) agent · flüssiger (Beton)Wirkstoff *m,* ~ (Beton)Zusatz(stoff) *m,* flüssiges (Beton)Zusatzmittel *n*

~ **(~) agent,** ~ (~) admix(ture) · flüssiger (Beton)Wirkstoff *m,* ~ (Beton)Zusatz(stoff) *m,* flüssiges (Beton)Zusatzmittel *n*

~ ~ **floor hardener,** ~ ~ ~ hardening agent · Betonhärteflüssigkeit *f,* Betonhärtungsflüssigkeit, flüssiges Betonhärtungsmittel *n,* flüssiger Betonhärtungsstoff *m,* flüssiger Betonhärter *m*

~ **damp-proofing and permeability reducing agent** · Sperröl *n*

~ **densifier** → ~ integral waterproofing agent

~ **densifying admix(ture)** → ~ integral waterproofing agent

~ ~ **agent** → ~ integral waterproofing ~

~ **drier,** soluble ~ (US); ~ dryer (Brit.); siccative · Sikkativ *n,* Trockenstoff *m* in gelöster Form [*DIN 55901*]

~ **fuel** · flüssiger Brennstoff *m*

~ ~ **burning appliance,** ~ ~ fire, ~ fuel(-fired) furnace · Feuerung *f* für flüssigen Brennstoff, Feuerstätte *f* ~ ~ ~

~ **grease** · flüssiges Fett *n,* Flüssigfett

~ **hardener,** ~ hardening agent · flüssiges Härtemittel *n,* ~ Härtungsmittel, flüssiger Härtungsstoff *m,* flüssiger Härter *m,* flüssiger Härtestoff

~ **heating fuel** · flüssiger Heiz(ungs)stoff *m*

~ **integral waterproofing agent,** ~ ~ waterproofer, ~ ~ waterrepeller, ~ ~ water repelling agent, ~ densifying agent, ~ densifying admix(ture), ~ densifier, ~ water repellent admix(ture), integral (water)proofing liquid · flüssiges Zusatz(ab)dicht(ungs)mittel *n,* ~

liquid integral waterproofing ... — liturgical watervessels 582

Sperrzusatzmittel, flüssiger Zusatz(ab)-dicht(ungs)stoff *m*, flüssiger Sperrzusatz(stoff) *m*, sperrende Zusatzflüssigkeit *f*, Sperrzusatzflüssigkeit

~ **magnesium** · flüssiges Magnesium *n*

~ ~ **chloride**, magnesium chloride solution (Brit.); liquid magnesium chlorid(e), magnesium chlorid(e) solution (US) · Magnesiumchloridlösung *f*, MgCl$_2$-Lösung; (Chlormagnesium)Lauge *f*, Magnesiumchloridlauge [*Fehlnamen*]

~ **manure gutter** · Jaucherinne *f*

~ ~ **pit** · Jauchegrube *f*

(~) **membrane (concrete) curing** · (Beton)Nachbehandlung *f* mit (Ab-)Dicht(ungs)mittel

(~) ~ (~) ~ **agent** → (concrete) curing compound

~ **mortar densifier**, ~ ~ **waterproofing agent**, ~ ~ **waterproofer**, ~ ~ **waterrepeller**, ~ ~ **water repellent admix(ture)**, ~ ~ **densifying agent** · MF *m*, flüssiger MD *m*, flüssiger Mörteldichter *m*, flüssiger Mörtelsperrmittel *n*, flüssiges Mörtel(ab)dicht(ungs)mittel, flüssiges DM *n*

~ **petrolatum** · flüssige Vaseline *f*, Flüssigvaseline

~ **phase sintering** · Sintern *n* mit flüssiger Phase, Schmelzsintern

~ **plasticizing aid** (US); ~ **plasticising** ~ (Brit.); ~ **workability** ~, ~ ~ **agent** · flüssige Verarbeitungshilfe *f* [*Für Beton oder Mörtel*]

~ **polishing agent** · Polierflüssigkeit *f*

~ **polymer** · Flüssigpolymer *n*, flüssiges Polymer

~ **resin, liquefied** ~ · Flüssigharz *n*, flüssiges Harz

~ **rosin** [*misnomer*]; tall oil · Tallöl *n*

~ **siccative** · Handelssikkativ *n*

~ **soap dispenser** · Seifencremespender *m*

~ **surface waterproofing agent**, ~ ~ **waterproofer**, ~ ~ **waterrepeller**, ~ ~ **water repelling agent, surface (water-)proofing liquid** · flüssiges Oberflächen-Sperrmittel *n*, flüssiger Oberflächen-Sperrstoff *m*, Oberflächen-Sperrflüssigkeit *f*, sperrende Oberflächen-Flüssigkeit, flüssiges Oberflächen-(Ab)Dicht(ungs)mittel, flüssiger Oberflächen-(Ab)Dicht(ungs)stoff *m*, flüssiges Oberflächen-DM, Oberflächen-DM-Flüssigkeit

~-**tight** · flüssigkeitsdicht

(~) **waste, domestic** ~ [*Used water from baths, lavatory basins, sinks and similar appliances, which does not contain human or animal excreta*] · Haushaltsschmutzwasser *n* ohne Abortspülwasser, häusliches Abwasser ~ ~

~ **waterproof(ing) agent**, ~ **waterproofer**, ~ **waterrepeller**, ~ **water repelling agent, (water)proofing liquid, (water) repellent liquid, waterproof(ing) liquid** · flüssiges Sperrmittel *n*, flüssiger Sperrzusatz *m*, Sperrflüssigkeit *f*, sperrende Flüssigkeit, flüssiges (Ab)Dicht(ungs)mittel, flüssiger (Ab)Dicht(ungs)stoff, flüssiges DM, DM-Flüssigkeit *f*

~ **water repellent admix(ture)** → ~ integral waterproofing agent

~ **waterrepeller** → ~ waterproofing agent

~ **water repelling agent** → ~ waterproofing ~

~ **wax** · flüssiges Wachs *n*, Flüssigwachs

~ **workability agent** → ~ plasticizing aid

liquidus line [*The line separating the liquid from the liquid-solid phase*] · Liquiduslinie *f*

~ **temperature** [*The maximum temperature at which a solid is in equilibrium with its melt*] · Liquidustemperatur *f*

liquor · Lauge *f* [*Ein Lösungsgemisch, das viele Bestandteile haben kann, z.B. Sulfitablauge*]

~ **store** · Spirituosenlager *n*

list of architects · Architektenliste *f*, Architektenverzeichnis *n*

~ ~ **constructions**, ~ ~ **structures** · Bauwerkverzeichnis *n*, Bauwerkliste *f*

~ ~ **monuments** · Denkmalliste *f*, Denkmalverzeichnis *n*

~ ~ **standard spec(ification)s** · Normenverzeichnis *n*, Normenliste *f*

~ ~ **structures**, ~ ~ **constructions** · Bauwerkverzeichnis *n*, Bauwerkliste *f*

listel, fillet · Band *n*, Riemen *m*, Plättchen *n* [*antike Säule*]

~, **fillet** · Steg *m* [*Zwischen zwei Einkehlungen einer kannelierten Säule*]

litharge [*substance*]; **lead (mon)oxide** (Brit.); **lead (mon)oxid(e)** (US) [*chemical names*] · Bleioxid *n*, Bleiglätte *f*, PbO [*veraltete Benennung: Königsgelb n*]

lithograph stone · Lithographiekalk(stein) *m*, Lithographenkalk(stein), Lithographenstein, Lithographiestein

lithol red [*An aniline pigment used in printing inks as well as paints*] · Litholrot *n*

~ **yellow** · Litholgelb *n*

lithopone [*B.S. 296*] [*It is a fairly modern pigment, discovered by a Scottish chemist, John B. Orr, in the 1860s, and sometimes called Orr's zinc white after him*] · Lithopone *f*, BaSO$_4$ZnS [*Fehlname: Deckweiß n*]

litmus · Lackmus *m, n*

~ **paper** · Lackmuspapier *n*

little figure · kleine Statue *f*

~ **jamb** · Versenkungssäule *f* für die Versenkungswand, ~ ~ ~ Kniestockwand [*Dach*]

liturgical watervessels · doppelte Waschbecken *npl*

live load — (load)bearing partition (wall)

live load [*The load caused by people*] · Verkehrslast *f*
~ ~ **moment** · Verkehrslastmoment *n*
~ **steam** · Frischdampf *m*
~ **wire** · stromdurchflossene Leitung *f*
lived in · bewohnt, bezogen
lively design · lebendiger Entwurf *m*
livering · Stocken *n* [*Anstrichtechnik*]
living area, housing ~, populated ~, residential (building) ~ · Wohn(bau)gebiet *n*, Wohn(bau)zone *f*, Wohnungsbaugebiet, Wohnungsbauzone
~ **conditions**, housing ~ · Wohnbedingungen *fpl*
~ **hut** · Wohnbaracke *f*
~ **level** · Wohnebene *f*
~ **requirements**, housing needs · Wohnbedürfnisse *npl*
~ **room** [*This term does not include 'working rooms' (Arbeitsräume) as the German term does. It is thus not a true synonym for the German term*] · Aufenthaltsraum *m* [*Ein Raum, der zum längeren, nicht nur vorübergehenden Aufenthalt von Menschen dient oder nach seiner Lage und Größe jederzeit dazu benutzt werden kann. Dies sind z.B. Wohn- und Arbeitsräume*]
living-room, sitting-room (Brit.); keeping-room (US) · Wohnzimmer *n*
~ **closet** · Wohnzimmer-Einbauschrank *m*, Wohnzimmer-Wandschrank
living room-entrance hall · Wohndiele *f*
(~) **(stage) theatre** · (Bühnen)Theater *n*
~ **terrace** · Wohnterrasse *f*
~ **unit** · Wohnzelle *f*
~ ~ (US); flat, apartment (unit) [*A self-contained dwelling on one stor(e)y in a multi-stor(e)y building*] · Stockwerkwohnung *f*, Etagenwohnung, (Geschoß)Wohnung
~ ~ **entrance** (US); apartment (~) ~, flat ~ · (Geschoß)Wohnungseingang *m*, Etagenwohnungseingang, Stockwerkwohnungseingang
~ ~ ~ **door** (US) → apartment (~) ~ ~
~ ~ **floor space** (US); apartment (~) ~ ~, flat ~ ~ · Etagenwohn(ungs)fläche *f*, Stockwerkwohn(ungs)fläche, (Geschoß)Wohn(ungs)fläche
~ ~ **kitchen** (US); apartment (~) ~, flat ~ ~ · (Geschoß)Wohnungsküche *f*, Stockwerkwohnungsküche, Etagenwohnungsküche
~ **zone** · Wohnzone *f* [*in einem Einfamilienhaus*]
~ ~ · Wohnbereich *m, n*
L. M., lime mortar · Kalkmörtel *m*
to load · belasten
load · Last *f*
~, shipment · Ladung *f* [*Waggonladung; LKW-Ladung usw.*]
~ **action** · Lasteinwirkung *f*

~ **application**, application of load, loading · Belasten *n*, Lastaufbringung *f*, Lastangriff *m*, Belastung
~ **axis** · Lastachse *f*
(load)bearing, weight-carrying, load-carrying, supporting, loaded · belastet, (last)tragend
~ **brick**, weight-carrying ~, load-carrying ~, supporting ~ · (last)tragender Ziegel *m*, statisch mitwirkender ~
~ ~ **cross-wall** → ~ clay ~ ~
~ **capability** → load-carrying capacity
~ **capacity** → load-carrying ~
~ ~ **of beam(s) without cast-in-situ concrete**, supporting ~ ~ ~ ~ ~ ~, weight-carrying ~ ~ ~ ~ ~ ~, load-carrying ~ ~ ~ ~ ~ ~, structural ~ ~ ~ ~ ~ ~ · Montagetragfähigkeit *f*
~ **(clay) brick cross-wall**, supporting (~) ~ ~ ~, weight-carrying (~) ~ ~, load-carrying (~) ~ ~, loaded (~) ~ ~ · Ziegelschottenwand *f*
~ **construction**, supporting ~, weight-carrying ~, load-carrying ~, structural ~ · Bau *m* von (last)tragenden Teilen, ~ ~ Tragteilen, ~ ~ Konstruktionsteilen
~ **diaphragm** · lastnehmende Scheibe *f*
~ **face work** → ~ facing masonry (~)
~ **facing** → ~ ~ masonry (work)
~ ~ **masonry (work)**, weight-carrying ~ ~ (~), ~ face ~, ~ facing · tragendes (Ver)Blendmauerwerk *n*, ~ Vorsatzmauerwerk, tragende Verblendung *f*
~ **floor (clay) brick**, ~ ~ (~) block, weight-carrying ~ (~) ~, load-carrying ~ (~) ~, supporting ~ (~) ~ · (last)tragender Deckenziegel *m*, ~ Deckenstein *m*, statisch mitwirkender ~ [*DIN 4159*]
~ **frame**, supporting ~, (structural) ~, weight-carrying ~, load-carrying ~, loaded ~ · (Trag)Rahmen *m*
~ **in longitudinal direction**, weight-carrying ~ ~ ~, load-carrying ~ ~ ~, supporting ~ ~ ~, loaded ~ ~ ~ · längstragend, längsbelastet
~ ~ **transverse direction**, weight-carrying ~ ~ ~, load-carrying ~ ~ ~, supporting ~ ~ ~, loaded ~ ~ ~ · quertragend, querbelastet
~ **masonry (work)**, weight-carrying ~ (~), load-carrying ~ (~), structural ~ (~), supporting ~ (~), loaded ~ (~) · (last)tragendes Mauerwerk *n*, Auflagermauerwerk, Tragmauerwerk, Konstruktionsmauerwerk, belastetes Mauerwerk
~ **mechanism**, weight-carrying ~, load-carrying ~, supporting ~, loaded ~ · Tragmechanismus *m*
~ **partition (wall)**, weight-carrying ~ (~), load-carrying ~ (~), supporting ~ (~), loaded ~ (~) · (last)tragende Trennwand *f*, belastete ~

(load)bearing plane — load-deformation curve

~ **plane,** weight-carrying ~, load-carrying ~, supporting ~, loaded ~ · Tragebene f

~ **power** → load-carrying capacity

~ **property** → load-carrying capacity

~ **quality** → load-carrying capacity

~ **rib,** structural ~, weight-carrying ~, supporting ~, load-carrying ~, loaded ~ · Tragrippe f, Konstruktionsrippe, (last)tragende Rippe, Auflagerrippe

~ **skeleton,** weight-carrying ~, (structural) ~, loaded ~ · (Trag)Skelett n, (Trag)Gerippe n

~ ~ **construction** → (structural) ~ ~

~ ~ **member** → (structural) ~ ~

~ ~ **structure** → (structural) ~ ~

~ **structure,** (weight-carrying) ~, loaded ~, supporting ~, load-carrying ~ · Tragwerk n [Ein materielles System von Bauelementen bzw. Trägern]

~ ~ ~ **of plain web girders,** ~ ~ ~ solid ~ ~, (weight-carrying) ~ ~ ~ ~ ~, supporting ~ ~ ~ ~ ~ ~ ~ · Vollwandtragwerk n [Ein Tragwerk, dessen tragende Elemente Vollwandträger sind]

~ **system,** structure ~, weight-carrying ~, supporting ~, load-carrying ~ · (last)tragendes System n, Tragsystem [Das aus einer Konstruktion bzw. aus einem Tragwerk abstrahierte gedankliche Gebilde, das man mit den Methoden der Baustatik untersuchen kann]

~ **wall,** supporting ~, weight-carrying ~, structural ~, load-carrying ~ · (last)tragende Wand f, Tragwand, Auflagerwand, Konstruktionswand

~ ~ **construction** → ~ ~ structure

~ ~ **structure,** ~ ~ construction, weight-carrying ~ ~, supporting ~ ~, structural ~ ~, load-carrying ~ ~ · Bauwerk n mit (last)tragenden Wänden, ~ ~ Tragwänden, ~ ~ Auflagerwänden, ~ ~ Konstruktionswänden

load boom, ~ flange, ~ chord · Lastgurt m

~ **capability** · Lastaufnahmevermögen n

load-carrying, weight-carrying, (load-)bearing, supporting, loaded · belastet, (last)tragend

~ **brick,** weight-carrying ~, (load)bearing ~, supporting ~, loaded ~ · statisch mitwirkender Ziegel m, (last)tragender ~

~ **capability** → ~ capacity

~ **capacity,** ~ power, ~ property, ~ quality, ~ capability, (load)bearing ~, weight-carrying ~, structural strength · Tragfähigkeit f, Tragvermögen n

~ ~ **of beam(s) without cast-in-situ concrete** → (load)bearing ~ ~ ~ ~ ~ ~

~ **(clay) brick cross-wall** → (load-)bearing (~) ~ ~

~ **construction** → (load)bearing ~

~ **floor block** → (load)bearing floor (clay) brick

~ ~ **brick** → (load)bearing floor (clay) ~

~ ~ **(clay) block** → (load)bearing floor (clay) brick

~ ~ **(~) brick** → (load)bearing ~ (~) ~

~ **frame,** supporting ~, weight carrying ~, (load)bearing ~, (structural) ~ · (Trag)Rahmen m

~ **in longitudinal direction,** supporting ~ ~ ~, weight carrying ~ ~ ~, (load-)bearing ~ ~ ~ · längstragend

~ ~ **transverse direction,** supporting ~ ~ ~, weight carrying ~ ~ ~, (load-)bearing ~ ~ ~ · quertragend

~ **masonry (wall)** → (load)bearing ~ (~)

~ **mechanism,** weight-carrying ~, (load)bearing ~, supporting ~, loaded ~ · Tragmechanismus m

~ **partition (wall)** → (load)bearing ~ (~)

~ **plane,** loaded ~, weight-carrying ~, supporting ~, (load)bearing ~ · Tragebene f

~ **power** → ~ capacity

~ **property** → ~ capacity

~ **quality** → ~ capacity

~ **rib,** weight-carrying ~, (load)bearing ~, supporting ~, structural ~ · Tragrippe f, Konstruktionsrippe, (last)tragende Rippe, Auflagerrippe

~ **skeleton** → weight-carrying ~

~ **structure** → (load)bearing ~

~ **system** → (load)bearing ~

~ **wall,** structural ~, weight-carrying ~, supporting ~, (load)bearing ~ · (last-)tragende Wand f, Tragwand, Auflagerwand, Konstruktionswand

~ ~ **construction** → (load)bearing wall structure

~ ~ **structure** → (load)bearing ~ ~

load case, loading ~ · Belastungsfall m, Lastfall

~ **coefficient** · Lastbeiwert m, Lastzahl f

~ **chord,** ~ boom, ~ flange · Lastgurt m

~ **collection** · Lastenbündelung f

~ **combination** · Lastkombination f

~ **compensation** · Lastenausgleich m

~ **compilation** · Lastzusammenstellung f

~ **component** · Lastkomponente f

~ **condition** · Lastbedingung f

~ **curve** · Lastkurve f

~ **cycle,** loading ~, cycle of load(ing), repeated loading · Lastspiel n, Belastungsspiel

(~) cycles to failure, loading ~ ~ ~, repeated loadings ~ ~ · Lastspiele npl bis zum Bruch, Belastungsspiele ~ ~

load-deflection diagram, load-deflexion ~ · Last-Durchbiegungs-Diagramm n, Last-Durchsenkungs-Diagramm

load-deformation curve · Lastformänderungskurve f, Lastverformungskurve

load-deformation diagram — load(ing) state

~ **diagram** · Last-Verformungs-Diagramm *n*, Last-Formänderungs-Diagramm

~ **relation** · Last-Formänderungs-Beziehung *f*, Last-Verformungs-Beziehung

load determination · Lastermitt(e)lung *f*

~ **diagram** · Lastdiagramm *n*

load-distributing, load-spreading · lastverteilend

~ **ability**, load-spreading ~, load distribution ~ · Lastverteilungsvermögen *n*

~ **curve**, load-spreading ~, load distribution ~ · Lastverteilungskurve *f*

load distribution, distribution of load, spreading of load · Lastverteilung *f*

~ ~ **ability**, load-distributing ~, load-spreading ~ · Lastverteilungsvermögen *n*

~ ~ **curve**, load-distributing ~, load-spreading ~ · Lastverteilungskurve *f*

~ **drop** · Lastabfall *m*

~ **due to wind pressure** · Winddrucklast *f*

loaded, supporting, weight-carrying, (load)bearing, load-carrying · belastet, (last)tragend

~ **area**, area of loading, field of load · Lastfeld *n*, Lastfläche *f*, belastetes Feld, belastete Fläche

~ **brick** → weight-carrying ~

~ **(clay) brick cross-wall** → (load-) bearing (~) ~ ~

~ **frame** → (load)bearing ~

~ **in longitudinal direction** → (load-) bearing ~ ~ ~

~ ~ **transverse direction** → (load-) bearing ~ ~ ~

~ **masonry (work)** → (load)bearing ~ (~)

~ **mechanism**, supporting ~, weight-carrying ~, load-carrying ~, (load-) bearing ~ · Tragmechanismus *m*

~ **partition (wall)** → (load)bearing ~ (~)

~ **plane**, (load)bearing ~, supporting ~, load-carrying ~, weight-carrying ~ · Tragebene *f*

~ **rib** → (load)bearing ~

~ **skeleton** → (load)bearing ~

~ **space structure** → space (load)bearing ~

~ **spatial structure** → space (load-) bearing ~

~ **structure** → (load)bearing ~

~ **three-dimensional structure** → space (load)bearing ~

~ **wall** → weight-carrying ~

load equivalent · Lastäquivalent *n*, Lastgleichwert *m*

~ **factor** · Lastfaktor *m*

~-**factor design (method)**, ultimate design (~), ultimate strength ~ (~) [*It is based on the ultimate strength of the section*] · *n*-freie Berechnungsweise *f*, *n*-freies Verfahren *n*, *n*-freie Bemessung *f*, Bruchtheorie *f*, Bruchsicherheitsnachweis *m*

~ **stress** · Tragspannung *f*

load flange, ~ **chord**, ~ **boom** · Lastgurt *m*

~ **increase** · Lastzunahme *f*, Laststeigerung *f*, Lastzuwachs *m*

~ **increment**, ~ **stage** · Laststufe *f*

loading · Belastung *f*

~ **and unloading ramp** · (Ver)Laderampe *f*

~ **area** · Belastungsfläche *f*

~ **arrangement** · Belastungsanordung *f*

~ **calculation**, calculation of loading · Belastungsberechnung *f*

load(ing) case · Belastungsfall *m*, Lastfall

loading condition · Belastungsbedingung *f*

~ **conditions** · Belastungsverhältnisse *npl*

~ **curve** · Belastungskurve *f*

load(ing) cycle, cycle of load(ing), repeated loading · Belastungsspiel *n*, Lastspiel

loading cycles to failure, (load) ~ ~ ~, repeated loadings ~ ~ · Lastspiele *npl* bis zum Bruch, Belastungsspiele ~ ~ ~

~ **data** · Belastungsangaben *fpl*

~ **degree**, degree of loading · Belastungsgrad *m*

~ **density**, density of loading · Belastungsdichte *f*

~ **diagram** · Lastenschema *n*, Lastenanordnung *f*

~ **distribution**, distribution of loading · Belastungsverteilung *f*

~ **equation** · Belastungsgleichung *f*

~ **function** · Belastungsfunktion *f*

~ **intensity**, intensity of loading · Belastungsintensität *f*

~ **line**, line of loading · Belastungslinie *f*

~ **moment**, moment of loading · Belastungsmoment *n*

~ **on part of area** · (Platten)Teilbelastung *f*

~ **over the entire area** · (Platten)Vollbelastung *f*

~ **pattern**, pattern of loading · Belastungsschema *n*

~ **period**, ~ **time**, period of loading, time of loading · Belastungszeit *f*, Belastungsdauer *f*

~ **plane**, plane of loading · Belastungsebene *f*

~ **ramp** · Verladerampe *f*

~ **rate** · Belastungsgeschwindigkeit *f*

load(ing) shock · Belastungsstoß *m*, Laststoß

~ **state** · Belastungszustand *m*, Lastzustand

loading system — local color 586

loading system · Belastungssystem *n*
load(ing) term · Belastungsglied *n*, Lastglied
~ **test** · Belastungsprobe *f*, Belastungsprüfung *f*, Belastungsversuch *m*
loading time, ~ **period, time of loading, period of loading** · Belastungszeit *f*, Belastungsdauer *f*
~ **type, type of loading** · Belastungsart *f*
~ **weight** · Belastungsgewicht *n*
load intensity, intensity of load · Laststärke *f*
~ ~ **diagram** · Laststärkediagramm *n*
~ **limit** · Lastgrenze *f*
~ **line** [*In graphic statics, the line of a force polygon on which the loads are laid off*] · Lastlinie *f*
~ **loss** · Lastverlust *m*
~ **magnitude** · Lastgröße *f*
~ **moment** · Lastmoment *n*
~ **over the entire area** · (Platten)Volllast *f*
~ **position, position of load** · Laststellung *f*
~ **range** · Lastbereich *m, n*
~**-reducing influence** · lastmindernder Einfluß *m*
load reduction · Lastminderung *f*
~ **removal, removal of load** · Lastwegnahme *f*
~ **separation point** · Lastscheide *f*
~**-settlement curve** · Lastsetzungskurve *f*, Lastsetzungslinie *f*
~ **diagram** · Lastsetzungsdiagramm *n*
load shock, loading ~ · Belastungsstoß *m*, Laststoß
load/span factor · Spannweite/Last-Faktor *m*
load-spreading, load-distributing · lastverteilend
~ **ability,** load-distributing ~, load distribution ~ · Lastverteilungsvermögen *n*
~ **curve,** load-distributing ~, load distribution ~ · Lastverteilungskurve *f*
load stage, ~ **increment** · Laststufe *f*
~**-strain curve** · Last-Dehnungskurve *f*
load stress · Lastspannung *f*
~ ~ · Lastbeanspruchung *f*
~ **strip** · Laststreifen *m*
~ **system, system of loads** · Lastsystem *n*
~ **table** · Lasttabelle *f*, Lasttafel *f*
~ **term, loading** ~ · Lastglied *n*, Belastungsglied
~ **test, loading** ~ · Belastungsprobe *f*, Belastungsversuch *m*, Belastungsprüfung *f*
to load to failure · bis zum Bruch belasten
(load) transfer, (~**) transmission** · Ableitung *f*, Abtragung, Übertragung, Last~
~ **triangle** · Lastdreieck *n*

~ **variation** · Lastschwankung *f*
~ **vector** · Lastvektor *m*
~ **zone** · Lastzone *f*
loam · Lehm *m* [*DIN 1169. Er besteht aus Ton, Feinsand und stark verwitterten steinigen Bestandteilen*]
~ **concrete** · Lehmboden *m* [*Aus handweichem Lehm und Zement*]
~ **construction** · Lehmbau *m* [*DIN 18951*]
~ **fill(ing)** · Lehm(auf)füllung *f*
~ **for construction purposes** · Baulehm *m*
~ **mortar** · Lehmmörtel *m* [*ohne Sandzusatz, mit Häckseln und Tierhaaren. Nicht wetterbeständig*]
~ **screed,** dirt ~ · Lehmestrich *m*
~ **shingle** · Lehmschindel *f*
~ ~ **roof cover(ing),** ~ ~ ~ **sheathing,** ~ ~ ~ **cladding,** ~ ~ **roofing** · Lehmschindel(dach)(ein)deckung *f*, Lehmschindelbedachung
~ **structures** · Lehmbauten *f* [*DIN 18951*]
~ **wall** · Lehmwand *f*
loamy gravel · Lehmkies *m*
~ **marl** · Lehmmergel *m*
lobby, entrance foyer [*A circulation space into which one or more rooms open. A small vestibule*] · Diele *f*
~ · Eingangsraum *m*
lobe, foil [*Foils are small arches inside Gothic (window) tracery and intersecting as cusps*] · Paß *m*, Nasenschwung *m*, Zirkelschlag *m* [*gotisches Maßwerk*]
local architecture → town ~
~ **authority** · Ortsbehörde *f*
~ ~ **apartment (unit)** → publicly-assisted ~ (~)
~ ~ **dwelling** → publicly-assisted dwelling unit
~**-authority engineer** · Ortsbehördeningenieur *m*
~ **authority estate** → ~ ~ housing ~
~ ~ **house-building,** ~ ~ **housing, public authority** ~, **publicly-assisted** ~, **low-rent** ~, **subsidized** ~, **low-cost (municipal)** ~, **social** ~ [*Provision of flats or houses for low-in-come groups, partly financed with the aid of public funds. Financing includes certain tax and interest concession*] · öffentlich geförderter Wohnungsbau *m*, Sozialwohnungsbau, sozialer Wohn(ungs)bau, sozialer WBau
~ ~ **(housing) estate** · Sozial-Sied(e)lung, Sozial-Wohnsied(e)lung
~ **buckling** · örtliches Knicken *n*
~ **cell** · Lokalelement *n* [*elektrochemische Korrosion*]
~ **climate** · Kleinklima *n*
~ **color (US);** ~ **colour (Brit.)** · Lokalfarbe *f*

local failure — log hut

~ **failure** · örtlicher Bruch *m*
~ **gas network** · Gasortsnetz *n*
~ **material,** near-by ~ · örtliches Material *n*
~ **stress** · örtliche Spannung *f*
~ **style,** native ~ · Heimatstil *m*
location of the sun, position ~ ~ ~ · Sonnenstand *m*, Stand der Sonne
~ **plan** · Lageplan *m*
Locher two-piece ring · Locherdübel *m* [*Holzverbinder*]
lock, door ~ · (Tür)Schloß *n* [*DIN 18251*]
lockable, closable, lockfast, lock fitted · verschließbar
(lock) case · (Schloß)Kasten *m*
(~) ~ front, (~) fore-end · (Schloß-)Stulp(e) *m*, (f) [*Die Vorderseite des Schloßkastens aus der Riegel und Falle austreten*]
~ **(door) rail** · mittlerer Querfries *m*, mittleres Querrahmenstück *n*, mittlerer (Tür)Riegel *m*
locked position · verriegelte Stellung *f*
locker, cloak-room ~ · Garderobenschrank *m*, Spind *m*
~ **room** · Spindraum *m*
lockfast, lockable, closable, lock fitted · verschließbar
lock fitted, lockfast, lockable, closable · verschließbar
(~) forend (Brit.); ~ faceplate, ~ strike, ~ front (US); keeper (plate), strike (plate), striking plate · Schließblech *n* [*DIN 18251*]
~ **function** · Schloßfunktion *f*
locking · Verriegelung *f*
~ · Verriegeln *n*
~ · Verschließen *n*
~ **cone** → inter~ ~
~ **device,** ~ mechanism · (Ab)Schließvorrichtung *f*, Verschluß *m* [*Tür; Tor*]
~ **mechanism,** ~ device · (Ab)Schließvorrichtung *f*, Verschluß *m* [*Tür; Tor*]
~ **plate,** sandwich ~ · Sandwich-Platte *f* [*Spannbeton*]
~ ~ · Ankerplatte *f*, Verankerungsplatte
~ ~ · Sicherungsblech *n* [*Nach dem Festziehen der Verbindung formschlüssige Schraubensicherung. Sichert Schraube und Mutter gegen Lösen, insbesondere bei nicht erschütterungsfreier Belastung*]
~ **system** · Verriegelung(ssystem) *f*, (*n*)
~ **the wire in place** · Nietwalzen *n* [*Scharnier*]
lockmaking, lock manufacture · Schloßbau *m*, Schloßherstellung *f*
lock manufacture, lockmaking · Schloßbau *m*, Schloßherstellung *f*
~ **pin** · Zuhaltungsstift *m*

~ **rail** · mittleres Querrahmenstück *n*, mittlerer (Tür)Riegel *m* [*Holzfüllungstür*]
~ **seam,** (welted) ~, welt · Falz *m* [*Metallbedachung*]
lockset · Schloßgarnitur *f*
(lock) soldered seam · Falz *m* mit (Löt)Hafter [*Metallbedachung*]
lock-up · Lückenbau *m* [*Ein Gebäude, welches in einer Baulücke gebaut wird*]
loco(motive) clinker (Brit.); ~ cinder (US) · Lokomotivschlacke *f*
locutory, parlatory, speak-house, (convent) parlour · Sprechsaal *m*, Parlatorium *n*
lodge-book · Bauhüttenbuch *n*
lodging house, boarding ~, tourist ~, rooming ~ [*A building arranged or used for the lodging with or without meals, for compensation, of more than live and not more than twenty individuals*] · Pension *f*, Logierhaus *n*
loess · Löß *m*
loft (US); attic (storey) (Brit.) [*The space within the sloping roof of a building or the upper storey of a building if less high than the other*] · Dachstockwerk *n*, Dachetage *f*, Dachgeschoß *n*, (Dach)Boden *m*, DG
~ [*A storage space entirely within the roof space of a building*] · Rumpelkammer *f*
~ · Hängeboden *m*
~ **insulation by loose fill** · Dachbodenschüttdämmung *f*
~ **ladder,** ~ stair, folding ~, disappearing ~ · Schiebetreppe *f*, Einschiebtreppe, hochschiebbare Treppe; Aufzugtreppe [*Schweiz*]
~ **room** (US) → attic ~
~ **stair,** ~ ladder, folding ~, disappearing ~ · Schiebetreppe *f*, Einschiebtreppe, hochschiebbare Treppe; Aufzugtreppe [*Schweiz*]
lofty · hoch [*Kuppel; Gewölbe*]
log cab(in), ~ house, ~ hut · Blockhaus *n*, Blockhütte *f*
log-diagram, log grading curve · logarithmische Siebliniendarstellung *f*, Siebliniendarstellung im logarithmischen Maßstab [*Die Lochdurchmesser der Siebe sind auf der Waag(e)rechten im logarithmischen Maßstab aufgetragen*]
log grading curve, log-diagram · Siebliniendarstellung *f* im logarithmischen Maßstab, logarithmische Siebliniendarstellung [*Die Lochdurchmesser der Siebe sind auf der Waag(e)rechten im logarithmischen Maßstab aufgetragen*]
~ **house,** ~ cab(in), ~ hut · Blockhaus *n*, Blockhütte *f*
~ **hut,** ~ cab(in), ~ house · Blockhaus *n*, Blockhütte *f*

log scale — long-span trussed girder

~ scale, logarithmic ~ · (einfach) logarithmischer Maßstab m, (~) logarithmische Darstellung f

~(-walled) sauna hut · Blockhaussauna f, Sauna-Blockhaus n

logarithmic scale → log ~

logeion, speaking-place · Logeion n [griechische Theaterbaukunst]

loggia · Loggia f, Hauslaube f

~ parapet · Loggiabrüstung f

LOI → loss on ignition

Lombardic architecture · lombardische Architektur f, ~ Baukunst f

long-and-short (angle-)quoin · Eckquader m bei Lang- und Kurzwerk

~ technique, ~ technic, ~ work, ~ quoining · Lang- und Kurzwerk n [In der englischen Baukunst die Eckquader des Mauerwerkes eines Turms, die abwechselnd mit der längeren bzw. kürzeren Seite einbinden]

long church, church built on the axial principle · Longitudinalhauskirche f, Langhauskirche [Kirchenbaukunst. Gegensatz „Zentralbaukirche"]

long-continued load, long-time ~, long-term ~ · langfristige Last f, Langzeitlast

~ loading, long-term ~, long-time ~ · langfristige Belastung f, Langzeitbelastung

~ strength, long-term ~, long-time ~ · Langzeitfestigkeit f, langfristige Festigkeit

long cross garnet, ~ tee hinge · Langband n, Haspenband n [Es ist länger als ⅓ der Türflügelbreite]

~ diamond mesh · Spitzmasche f [Siebtechnik]

long-distance heat · Fernwärme f

~ ~ intake · Übergabestation f für Fernwärme

~ ~ supply · Fernwärmeversorgung f

~ ~ ~ pipeline · Fernwärme(rohr)leitung f

~ train station · Fernbahnhof m

~ water supply · Fernwasserversorgung f

~ ~ ~ pipeline · Fernwasserversorgungs(rohr)leitung f

long face, stretcher ~ · Längsseite f eines Läufer(stein)s

~ fibred (Brit.); ~ fibered (US) · langfas(e)rig

~ glass, slow-setting ~ · langes Glas n

~ ~ fibres (Brit.); ~ ~ fibers (US); (glass) silk, spun glass, glass filaments · gesponnenes Glas n, Langfasern fpl, Glasgespinst n, Glasseide f

long-handle float, ~ spreader · Stielglätter m [Putztechnik]

~ spreader, ~ float · Stielglätter m [Putztechnik]

long-jump pit · Weitsprunggrube f

long-lasting · langlebig

longlobed pointed trefoil · Dreipaß m aus schmalen spitzen Blättern

long oil [A high ratio of oil to resin in a medium] · fett [Anstrichfarbe]

long-oil alkyd resin · fettes Alkydharz n, langöliges ~ [Ölgehalt 60%–70%]

long oil varnish, ~ oleo-resinous ~ · fetter Öllack m

~ shell · lange Schale f

~ side · Längsseite f [Block(stein); Stein; Ziegel; Platte; usw.]

long-span arch, large-span ~, wide-span ~ · Weitspannbogen m

~ beam, large-span ~, wide-span ~ · Weitspannbalken(träger) m

~ concrete shell roof, large-span ~ ~, wide-span ~ ~ ~ · Weitspann-Betonschalendach n

~ construction, wide-span ~, large-span ~ · Weitspannkonstruktion f

~ cupola, ~ dome, wide-span ~, large-span ~ · Weitspannkuppel f

~ floor slab, wide-span ~ ~, large-span ~ ~ · Weitspanndeckenplatte f

~ frame, wide-span ~, large-span ~ · Weitspannrahmen m

~ lattice beam → ~ trussed girder

~ ~ girder → ~ trussed ~

~ (load)bearing system, wide-span ~ ~, large-span ~ ~, ~ load-carrying ~, ~ weight-carrying ~ · Weitspann-Tragwerk n, Weitspann-Tragsystem n

~ (pre)cast beam → large-span (pre)cast (concrete) ~

~ ~ (concrete) beam → large-span ~ (~)

~ prestressed (concrete) (building) unit, ~ ~ (~) (~) member, ~ (~) (~) component, large-span ~ (~) (~) ~, ~ (~) (~) ~ · Weitspann-Spannbeton(bau)element n, Weitspann-Spannbeton(bau)körper m [Fehlnamen: Weitspann-Spannbeton(bau)einheit f]

~ ~ (~) slab, prestressed (concrete) long-span ~ · Spannbeton-Weitspannplatte f, Weitspannbetonplatte

~ rib, large-span ~, wide-span ~ · Weitspannrippe f

~ roof, large-span ~, wide-span ~ · Weitspanndach n

~ (~) structure · Weitspann(dach)bauwerk n

~ shell, large-span ~, wide-span ~ · Weitspannschale f

~ ~ vault, wide-span ~, large-span ~ ~ · Weitspann-Schalengewölbe n

~ structure, ~ roof ~ · Weitspann-(dach)bauwerk n

~ trussed beam → ~ ~ girder

~ ~ girder, wide-span ~ ~, large-span ~ ~, ~ lattice ~, ~ ~ beam · Weitspann-Fachwerkträger m

long-span tube floor — lookout gallery

~ **tube floor** · Weitspann-Hohlbalkendecke *f* mit kreisförmigen Aussparungen

long structure, structure built on the axial principle · Langbau(werk) *m*, (*n*), Longitudinalbau(werk) [*Bei einem Langbau dominiert die Längsachse*]

~ **tee hinge,** ~ **cross garnet** · Langband *n*, Haspenband [*Es ist länger als ⅓ der Türflügelbreite*]

long-term load, long-continued ~, long-time ~ · langfristige Last *f*, Langzeitlast

~ **loading,** long-time ~, long-continued ~ · langfristige Belastung *f*, Langzeitbelastung

~ **strength,** long-time ~, long-continued ~ · Langzeitfestigkeit *f*, langfristige Festigkeit

long thread · Langgewinde *n*

long-time load, long-term ~, long-continued ~ · langfristige Last *f*, Langzeitlast

~ **loading,** long-term ~, long-continued ~ · langfristige Belastung *f*, Langzeitbelastung

~ **service testing** · langfristige Versuche *mpl* über Betriebsverhalten

~ **strength,** long-term ~, long-continued ~ · Langzeitfestigkeit *f*, langfristige Festigkeit

longer side · Langseite *f*.

longitudinal action · Längswirkung *f*

~ **arch** [*In a basilican structure, a longitudinal arch runs the length of a nave, defining the length of a bay*] · Längsbogen *m*

~ **axis;** ~ **centre line** (Brit.); ~ **center line** (US) · Längsachse *f*, Längsmittellinie *f*

~ **bar,** ~ **rod** [*Any reinforcing bar placed in the long direction of the member*] · Längseisen *n*, Längsstab *m*

~ **bending** · Längsbiegung *f*

~ ~ **moment** · Längsbiegemoment *n*

~ ~ **strength** · Längsbiegefestigkeit *f*

~ ~ **stress** · Längsbiegespannung *f*

~ **bracing** · Längsverband *m* [*Windverband eines Sparrendaches*]

~ ~ → ~ **stiffening**

~ **cavity** · Längshohlraum *m*

~ ~ · Hohlraum *m* [*Tonhohlplatte*]

~ **centre joint** (Brit.); ~ **center** ~ (US) · Längsmittelfuge *f*, Mittellängsfuge

~ ~ **line** (Brit.); ~ **center** ~ (US); ~ **axis** · Längsachse *f*, Längsmittellinie *f*

~ **church** · Längsbau(werk) *m*, (*n*)

~ **construction joint** · Längsarbeitsfuge *f*

~ **deformation** · Längsverformung *f*, Längsformänderung

~ **direction** · Längsrichtung *f*

~ **edge** · Längsrand *m*

~ ~ **section** · Randlängsschnitt *m*

~ **fold** · Längsfalte *f*

~ **force** · Längskraft *f*

~ **frame** · Längsrahmen *m*

~ **girder** · Längsträger *m*

~ **interval,** ~ **spacing** · Längsabstand *m*

~ **jack rafter** · Langseitenschifter *m*

~ **load** · Längslast *f*

~ **membrane action** · Membran(e)-Längswirkung *f*

~ **moment** · Längsmoment *n*

~ **overlap(ping)** · Längsüberdeckung *f*, Längsüberlappung

~ **prestress(ing)** · Längsvorspannung *f*

~ ~ **force,** ~ **stretching** ~, ~ **tensioning** ~ · Längs(vor)spannkraft *f*

~ **reinforcement** · Längsarmierung *f*, Längsbewehrung, Längs(stahl)einlagen *fpl*

~ **reinforcing** → ~ **stiffening**

~ **rib** · Längsrippe *f*

~ **ridge** [*vault*] · Längsscheitel *m* [*Gewölbe*]

~ ~ **rib** · Längsscheitelrippe *f*

~ **rigidity,** ~ **stiffness** · Längssteifigkeit *f*, Längsstarrheit

~ **rod,** ~ **bar** [*Any reinforcing bar placed in the long direction of the member*] · Längseisen *n*, Längsstab *m*

~ **running girder** · Längslaufträger *m*

~ **seal(ing)** · Längs(ab)dichtung *f*

~ **section** · Längsschnitt *m*

~ **spacing,** ~ **interval** · Längsabstand *m*

~ **stiffener** · Längssteife *f*

~ **stiffening,** ~ **bracing,** ~ **reinforcing** · Längsabsteifung *f*, Längsaussteifung, Längsversteifung, Längsverstärkung

~ **stiffness,** ~ **rigidity** · Längssteifigkeit *f*

~ **stress** · Längsspannung *f*

~ **stretching force** → ~ **prestress(ing)** ~

~ **tension stress,** ~ **tensile** ~ · Längszugspannung *f*

~ **tensioning force** → ~ **prestress(ing)** ~

~ **wall** · Längswand *f*

~ ~ **construction** · Längswandbau *m*

~ **wave** · Längswelle *f*, Longitudinalwelle

longitudinally corrugated · längsgewellt

~ **-planned church** · Längskirche *f*, sakraler Längsbau *m*

longitudinally stiffened, ~ **braced,** ~ **reinforced** · längsabgesteift, längsversteift, längsverstärkt, längsausgesteift

Lonja de la Seda at Valencia, silk exchange ~ ~ · Seidenbörse *f* zu Valencia

lookout deck → **viewing** ~

~ **floor** → **viewing** ~

~ **gallery,** **viewing** ~ · Aussichtsgang *m* [*Besucherturm*]

lookout gondola — Louis-seize (style)

~ gondola, viewing ~ · Aussichtskabine f [*Besucherturm*]

~ platform → viewing deck

~ room, viewing ~ · Aussichtsraum m

~ story (US) → viewing floor

~ tower, viewing ~, standing ~ · Aussichtsturm m, (Aussichts)Warte f

~ ~, standing ~, belvedere, gazebo [*A turret or lantern on a house to afford a view*] · Belvedere n, Aussichtsturm m

loop · Schlaufe f

~ · Lappen m [*Ösenteil eines Scharniers*]

~ anchorage · Schlaufenverankerung f

~ joint · Schlaufenstoß m

~ plane · Schlaufenebene f

~-test bar · Schlaufenprobe f, Schlaufenprüfung f, Schlaufenversuch m [*Korrosionsprüfung*]

loop (window), loopwhole [*A vertical slot in wall for air and light*] · Sehschlitz m [*in einer Mauer*]

looped (pipe)line · Doppel(rohr)leitung f

loophole, arrow loop, slit window · Mauerschlitz m, Schießscharte f, Schlitzfenster n [*Burg*]

~, loop (window) [*A vertical slot in a wall for air and light*] · Sehschlitz m [*in einer Mauer*]

loopholed gallery · Sehschlitzgang m

loose core [*Coarse aggregate which has become separated from a concrete mix by incorrect handling during mixing and placing*] · entmischter (Beton)Grobzuschlag(stoff) m

~ fill · Trockenschüttung f [*Dämmstoff*]

(~) ~ · Beschüttung f [*Sandschüttung in Holzbalkendecke oder Lagerung für Weichholzfußböden*]

(loose-)fill insulation · Schütt(ab)dämmung f [*Wärme- und Schallschutz*]

loose-housing shed · Freilaufstall m

loose main diagonal, ~ principal ~ · schlaffe Hauptschräge f, ~ Hauptdiagonale

~ material · loses Material n

~ pe(a)rlite · Schüttperlit m

~ powder sintering, pressureless ~ · Sintern n von losem Pulver, Schüttsintern

~ principal diagonal, ~ main ~ · schlaffe Hauptschräge f, ~ Hauptdiagonale

~ vegetable fibers, uncompressed ~ ~ (US); ~ ~ fibres (Brit.) · pflanzliche Fasern fpl, lose ~

~ wool · lose Wolle f

lopsided arch → rampant ~

Lorraine cross · lothringisches Kreuz n, Lothringer ~

lorry terminal (Brit.); truck(ing) ~ (US) · Fernlaster-Bahnhof m, LKW-Bahnhof

loss due to creep · Kriechverlust m

~ in weight, ~ of ~, weight loss · Gewichtsverlust m

~ of adhesion, adhesion loss · Haft(ungs)verlust m

~ ~ gloss, dulling · Glanzverlust m, Blindwerden n, Mattwerden [*Anstrichtechnik*]

~ ~ hardness, hardness loss · Härteverlust m

~ ~ heat, heat loss · Wärmeverlust m

~ ~ rigidity, ~ ~ stiffness, stiffness loss, rigidity loss · Steifigkeitsverlust m, Starrheitsverlust

~ ~ stiffness, ~ ~ rigidity, stiffness loss, rigidity loss · Steifigkeitsverlust m, Starrheitsverlust

~ ~ weight, ~ in ~, weight loss · Gewichtsverlust m

~ on ignition, ignition loss, LOI · Glühverlust m

lost head nail · gestauchter Nagel m

lot [*A parcel of land that is described by reference to a recorded plat or by metes and bounds*] · (Kataster)Parzelle f

~ line [*A line bounding the lot as described in the title to the property*] · (Kataster)Parzellengrenze f

~ planning · (Kataster)Parzellenplanung f

lotos blossom capital, lotus ~ ~ · Lotosblütenkapitell n, Lotosblütenkapitäl

~ bud, lotus ~ · Lotosknospe f, Lotosknolle f

~ ~ capital, lotus ~ ~ · Lotosknospenkapitell n, Lotosknospenkapitäl, Lotosknollenkapitell, Lotosknollenkapitäl

~ column, lotus ~ · Lotossäule f

~ flower, lotus ~ · Lotosblume f

~ leaf, lotus ~ · Lotosblatt n

~ ornament, lotus ~ · Lotosornament n

loudness [*An observer's auditory impression of the strength of a sound*] · Schallempfindung f, Lautheit f, Lautstärke f [*Maß für die Stärke der Wahrnehmung, bei welchem eine Verdopelung des Zahlenwertes einer Verdopplung der Stärke der Wahrnehmung entspricht. Zum Unterschied von dem in phon angegebenen Lautstärkepegel wird hinter den Zahlenwert der Lautheit „sone" gesetzt (siehe DIN 45630 Blatt 1). Anmerkung: Die Beziehung zwischen der Lautheit und dem Lautstärkepegel ist so festgelegt, daß ein Schall mit dem Lautstärkepegel 40 phon die Lautheit 1 sone hat und daß eine Verdopplung der Lautheit im Bereich von 20 bis 120 phon eine Zunahme des Lautstärkepegels um 10 phon ergibt (siehe DIN 45630 Blatt 1 und ISO-Empfehlung R 131)*]

~ level · Lautstärkepegel m

loud speaker system → public-address ~ ~ ~

Louis-seize (style) · Zopfstil m

lounge — low-odour

lounge · Aufenthaltshalle f [*Hotel*]

louver, louvre, lvr · (Be- und Ent)Lüftungsklappe f [*zum Einbau in Fenster*]

~, louvre · Großraster m [*Leuchte*]

~ boards, louvre ~, luffer ~ · Schallblatt n, Schalldach n, Schirmbretter [*Glockenturm*]

~ window, louvre ~, jalousie ~, slatted blind ~ · Jalousiefenster n

~ with specular enamel finish, louvre ~ ~ ~ ~ · Großraster m mit Spiegeleffektlackierung [*Leuchte*]

louvers, louvres, jalousie, slatted blind [*A screen of spaced parallel slats*] · Jalousie f

low-alkali cement · alkaliarmer Zement m

low-alloy steel · niedriglegierter Stahl m

low-angle sunlight · flach einfallendes Sonnenlicht n

low-bake finish · 80°-Lack m

low block, ~ building, flat ~ · Flachgebäude n [*Fehlnamen: Flachbau(-werk) m, (n). Im Gegensatz zum Hochhaus*]

~ boiler · Niedrigsieder m, niedrigsiedendes Lösungsmittel n [*Lacktechnik. Siedepunkt bis 100°C*]

~ brass · Hellrottombak m, MS 80 n, Ms 80, Messing 80

~ building, ~ block, flat ~ · Flachgebäude n [*Fehlnamen: Flachbau(-werk) m, (n). Im Gegensatz zum Hochhaus*]

low-carbon wire · Draht m mit geringem Kohlenstoffgehalt

low-cost (municipal) house-building, ~ (~) housing, local authority ~, public authority ~, publicly-assisted ~, low-rent ~, social ~ ,subsidized ~ [*Provision of flats or houses for low-income groups, partly financed with the aid of public funds. Financing includes certain tax and interest concession*] · öffentlich geförderter Wohnungsbau m, Sozialwohnungsbau, sozialer Wohn(ungs)bau, sozialer WBau

low cycle fatigue · Ermüdung f bei geringer Lastspielanzahl

~ down closet, ~ ~ suite · Niederspülabort m

low-frequency sound insulation, ~ ~ protection · Niederfrequenz-Schallschutz m

low friction operation · reibungsarmer Betrieb m

low-grade · minderwertig

~ lime · Bastardkalk m [*Bezeichnung für minderwertigen Brannt- und Löschkalk*]

~ silicate cotton → ~ slag wool

~ slag wool, ~ silicate cotton · Bauwolle f [*Eine geringere Sorte Hüttenwolle mit dickeren und kürzeren Fäden. Sie wird direkt am Hochofen gewonnen und ist hellbraun bis graubraun*]

low hall · Flachhalle f

~ heat of hydration (US); ~ ~ ~ ~ setting (Brit.); ~ ~ generated while taking initial set · niedrige (Ab)Bindewärme f

~ ~ (~ ~) cement, slow hardening ~; Portland cement Type IV, type IV cement (US) · Portlandzement m mit sehr geringer Abbindewärme, Massenbauzement

low-income block, ~ building, low-rent ~ · Sozialwohngebäude n

~ building, ~ block, low-rent ~ · Sozialwohngebäude n

~ housing → ~ residential ~

~ project, ~ housing ~, low-rent (housing) ~ · Sozialwohn(ungs)bauprojekt n

~ residences, ~ (residential) housing · Sozialwohnbauten f

~ (residential) housing, ~ residences · Sozialwohnbauten f

low-lead · bleiarm

low(-)level flush toilet, ~ water closet, ~ type of W.C. [*A room in which one or more low-level water closet pans are installed*] · Spülabort m mit Tiefspülkasten, Wasserabort ~, Spülklosett ~ ~, Wasserklosett ~ ~

~ flushing cistern, ~ ~ tank, ~ water waste preventer · Tiefspülkasten m [*(Spül)Abort*]

~ suite · Tiefspülkastenaborteinrichtung f, Tiefspülkastenklosetteinrichtung

~ type of W.C., ~ water closet, ~ flush toilet [*A room in which one or more low-level water closet pans are installed*] · Spülabort m mit Tiefspülkasten, Wasserabort ~ ~, Spülklosett n ~ ~, Wasserklosett ~ ~

~ (W.C.) flushing tank, ~ (~ ~) (~) cistern, ~ (~ ~) water waste preventer · tiefhängender Spülkasten m

~ water closet, ~ flush toilet, ~ type of W.C. [*A room in which one or more low-level water closet pans are installed*] · Spülabort m mit Tiefspülkasten, Wasserabort ~ ~, Spülklosett n ~ ~, Wasserklosett ~ ~

~ ~ tank · Tiefbehälter m [*Ein Wasserbehälter ohne Einfluß auf den Versorgungsdruck*]

~ ~ waste preventer, ~ flushing tank, ~ flushing cistern · Tiefspülkasten m [*(Spül)Abort*]

low-mass panel · Tafel f mit geringem Massenwiderstand [*Dieser Widerstand setzt sich der Erregung durch den Schalldruck entgegen*]

low-odour, (Brit.); low-odor (US) · geruchmild

low-pitch gable roof — lower boom

low-pitch gable roof, low pitched ~ ~, slightly pitched ~ ~ · niedriges Giebeldach *n*

~ glazing, low pitched ~, slightly pitched ~ · flach geneigte Verglasung *f*, ~ ~ Einglasung

~ roof, low pitched ~, slightly pitched ~ · flachgeneigtes (Giebel)Dach *n*, niedriges ~

low pitched glazing, slightly ~ ~, low-pitch ~ · flach geneigte Verglasung *f*, ~ ~ Einglasung

~ ~ roof, slightly ~ ~, low-pitch ~ · flachgeneigtes (Giebel)Dach *n*, niedriges ~

~ point of the slope · tiefster Gefällepunkt *m* [*Dachrinne*]

low-pressure air conditioning system, ~ ~ ~ plant · Niederdruck-Klimaanlage *f*

~ boiler, ~ steam ~, atmospheric-pressure (steam) ~ · Niederdruck-(dampf)kessel *m*

~ equipment, atmospheric-pressure ~ · Niederdruckgerät *n*

~ fan · Niederdruckventilator *m*

~ gas, atmospheric-pressure ~ · Niederdruckgas *n*

~ ~ system, atmospheric-pressure ~ ~ · Niederdruckgasanlage *f*

~ piping · Niederdruck(rohr)leitung *f*

~ saturated steam, ~ wet ~, atmospheric-pressure ~ ~ · niedergespannter Naßdampf *m*

~ spraying, atmospheric-pressure ~ · Niederdruckspritzen *n*

~ (steam) boiler, atmospheric-pressure (~) ~ · Niederdruck(dampf)kessel *m*

~ steam-cured, atmospheric-pressure ~, cured by atmospheric-pressure steam, cured by low-pressure steam · dampfbehandelt, wärmebehandelt [*Beton*]

~ steam curing → atmospheric pressure ~ ~

~ ~ ~ of concrete, atmospheric-pressure ~ ~ ~ ~ · Niederdruckdampfbehandlung *f* von Beton

~ ~ heating, atmospheric-pressure ~ · Niederdruck-Dampfheizung *f*

~ ~ pipe, atmospheric-pressure ~ ~ · Niederdruckdampfrohr *n*

~ system, installation, atmospheric-pressure ~ · Niederdruckanlage *f* [*Heizung*]

~ wet steam, ~ saturated ~, atmospheric-pressure ~ ~ · niedergespannter Naßdampf *m*

low relief, bas-relief [*It is very shallow, like the relief of a coin*] · Flachrelief *n*

~ ~ frieze, bas-relief ~ · Flachrelieffries *m*

low-rent apartment (unit) → publicly-assisted ~ (~)

~ block, ~ building, low-income ~ · Sozialwohngebäude *n*

~ building, ~ block, low-income ~ · Sozialwohngebäude *n*

~ dwelling (Brit.) → publicly-assisted dwelling unit

~ house-building, ~ housing, subsidized ~, local authority ~, public authority ~, publicly-assisted ~, low-cost (municipal) ~, social ~ [*Provision of flats or houses for low-in-come groups, partly financed with the aid of public funds. Financing includes certain tax and interest concession*] · öffentlich geförderter Wohnungsbau *m*, Sozialwohnungsbau, sozialer Wohn(-ungs)bau, sozialer WBau

~ (housing) project, low income (~) ~ · Sozialwohn(ungs)bauprojekt *n*

~ project, ~ housing ~, low-income (housing) ~ · Sozialwohn(ungs)bauprojekt *n*

low-rise building, ~ block · niedriges Gebäude *n*

~ residential blocks, ~ ~ buildings · niedrige Wohnbauten *f*

~ shell, shallow ~, flat ~ · krumme Platte *f*, ~ Schale *f*, schwach gekrümmte ~, Flachschale, flache Schale

~ spherical shell, shallow ~ ~, flat ~ ~ · flache Kugelschale *f*, schwach gekrümmte ~

low-suction backing · schwachsaugender Untergrund *m*

~ surface · nicht stark saugende Fläche *f*

low-temperature brown-coal tar, ~ lignite ~ · Braunkohlen-Schwelteer *m*

~ calcination of (raw) gypsum · Gipskochen *n* [*Erhitzen des Gipssteines bei verhältnismäßig niedrigen Temperaturen. Bei diesem Erhitzen unterhalb der Gluthöhe entweicht das Wasser mit zischendem Geräusch, was sich wie das Sieden von Wasser anhört*]

~ chimney · Kaltschornstein *m* [*Schornstein mit Abgasen bis 100° C*]

~ coal-tar · Schwelteer *m*, Steinkohlen-~, Tieftemperaturteer, Urteer

~ construction · Kühl- und Gefrierraumbau *m*

~ lignite tar, ~ brown-coal ~ · Braunkohlen-Schwelteer *m*

~ peat tar · Torfurteer *m*

low-tension main distribution station · Niederspannungs-Hauptverteilung *f*

low-water alarm · Wassermangelsicherung *f*

lower basement, sub-basement [*The second storey below the ground, the storey below the basement*] · zweites Kellergeschoß *n*, Tiefkellergeschoß

~ bed, bottom ~ · untere Lagerfläche *f*, harte ~, unteres Lager *n*, hartes Lager [*Werkstein*]

~ bond theorem, static ~ · statischer Satz *m*

~ boom, ~ flange, ~ chord, bottom ~ · Untergurt(ung) *m*, (*f*)

~ ~ bar → ~ chord ~

~ ~ junction plate → bottom ~ ~ ~

~ ~ longitudinal bar → ~ chord ~ ~

~ ~ plate, ~ chord ~, ~ flange ~, bottom ~ ~ · Untergurtlamelle *f*

~ calorific value, L.C.V. · (unterer) Heizwert *m*, H_u [*in kcal//Nm³*]

~ chapel · Unterkapelle *f*

~ chord, ~ boom, ~ flange, bottom ~ · Untergurt(ung) *m*, (*f*)

~ ~ bar, ~ boom ~, ~ flange ~, bottom ~ ~ · Untergurtstab *m*

~ ~ junction plate → bottom boom ~ ~

~ ~ longitudinal bar, ~ boom ~ ~, ~ flange ~ ~, bottom ~ ~ ~ · Untergurtlängsstab *m*

~ ~ plate → ~ boom ~

~ church · Unterkirche *f*

~ citadel · Unterburg *f* [*Tiryns*]

~ (door) rail, bottom (~) ~ · unterer Querfries *m*, unteres Querrahmenstück *n*, unterer (Tür)Riegel *m* [*Holzfüllungstür*]

~ flange, ~ chord, ~ boom, bottom ~, · Untergurt(ung) *m*, (*f*)

~ ~ bar → ~ chord ~

~ ~ junction plate → bottom boom ~ ~

~ ~ longitudinal bar → ~ chord ~ ~

~ ~ plate → ~ boom ~

~ guide, bottom ~ · untere Führung *f*

~ ~ track, bottom ~ ~ · untere Führungsschiene *f* [*Tor*]

~ layer · Unterlage *f*, Unterschicht *f* [*(Fuß)Boden*]

~ part · Unterteil *m*, *n*

~ rail, bottom ~ · unteres Querrahmenstück *n*, unterer (Tür)Riegel *m*, unterer Querfries *m* [*Holzfüllungstür*]

Lower Triassic sandstone, bunter ~, mottled ~; variegated ~ (Brit.) · Buntsandstein *m*

lowering, decrease, drop, decline, fall · Rückgang *m*, Abnahme *f*, Abfall *m*

~ of (the) freezing point · Gefrierpunkterniedrigung *f*

~ ~ viscosity, fall ~ ~, drop ~ ~ · Viskositätsrückgang *m*, Zähigkeitsrückgang, Viskositätsabfall *m*, Zähigkeitsabfall

lozenge, diamond (shape) · Raute *f*

~ cloth, diamond ~, ~ woven fabric; ~ fabric [*misnomer*] [*See remark under 'Gewebe'*] · Rauten(maschen)gewebe *n*

~ expanded metal, diamond ~ ~ · Rautenstreckmetall *n*

~ fabric [*misnomer*] → ~ cloth

~ frieze, diamond ~ · Rautenfries *m*

~ glass, lozenge-patterned ~ (US); diamond-patterned ~ · gerautetes Glas *n*, Rautenglas, rautenförmig gemustertes Glas

~ mesh, diamond ~ · Rautenmasche *f*

~ motif, diamond(-shaped) ~ · Rautenmotiv *n*

~ net(work) · Rautennetz(werk) *n*

~ pattern, diamond ~ · Rautenmuster *n*

~-patterned, diamond-patterned, with diamond pattern, with lozenge pattern · gerautet

lozenge(-patterned) glass (US); diamond-patterned ~ · gerautetes Glas *n*, Rautenglas, rautenförmig gemustertes Glas

lozenge plate, diamond ~ · Rauten-(grob)blech *n*

lozenge-shaped, diamond-shaped · rautenförmig

~ core, diamond(-shaped) ~ · rautenförmiger Kern *m*

~ (ground(-))plan, diamond(-shaped) ~ · rautenförmiger Grundriß *m*

lozenge woven fabric → ~ cloth

LP → lime putty

LR, tread, rundle, (ladder) rung, stave · (Leiter)Sprosse *f*

LS → lead shield

~ → limestone

L.S.C. → light(weight) structural concrete

L-section, angle (section), angle bar · Winkel(profil) *m*, (*n*)

LSF, lime saturation factor · Kalksättigungsfaktor *m*

L-shaped block, ~ tile [*See remark under 'Block'*] · L-Block(stein) *m*, L-Stein [*Plattenförmiger Block(stein) aus Leicht- oder Schwerbeton in L-Form*]

~ frame · L-Rahmen *m*

~ step · L-Stufe *f*

~ tile → ~ block

ltprf → lightproof

lucarne · Lukarne *f* [*Dacherker bzw. Zwerchhaus, meist mit reicher Fensterrahmung und Giebelkontur*]

Lüders strain · Lüdersdehnung *f*

Ludowici tile, French ~, Marseilles pattern ~ · Ludowici-Falzziegel *m*, Muldenfalzziegel, Doppelfalzziegel

luffer boards, louvre ~, louver ~ · Schirmbretter *npl*, Schallblatt *n*, Schalldach *n* [*Glockenturm*]

luggage store · Kofferraum *m* [*in einer Wohnung*]

lumber (US); milled products [*Australia*] mill run, sawn wood, sawn timbeı, sawed timber, converted timber [*All the timber produced in a mill without reference to grade. The term 'lumber' is sometimes reserved in the USA for the German terms 'Bretter and Bohlen'*

lumber — lump sum

and the German terms 'Kantholz and Balken' are then called 'timbers'. Thus 'Schnittholz' may also be called in the USA 'lumber and timbers'] · Schnittholz n, Schnittware f [*Erzeugnisse, die durch Aufschneiden des Rundholzes entstehen. Hierzu gehören Bretter, Bohlen, Kantholz, Balken, Latten usw.*]

lumen per watt · Lumen n je Watt lm/W

lumen-hour · Lumenstunde f lmh

luminaire efficiency · Leuchtenwirkungsgrad m [*Das Verhältnis des aus der Leuchte austretenden Lichtstroms zu dem von den Lampen (oder der Lampe) in der Leuchte erzeugten Lichtstrom*]

~ **(fixture)** (US); (light(ing)) fitting (Brit.); (light(ing)) fixture, lighting unit · Beleuchtungskörper m, Leuchte f

~ **(~) with integral mounting rail** (US); light fitting ~ ~ ~ ~ ~ (Brit.); (light(ing)) fixture ~ ~ ~ ~ ~ · Schienenbeleuchtungskörper m, Schienenleuchte f

~ **(~) ~ transistorized inverter control gear** (US); light fitting ~ ~ ~ ~ ~ (Brit.) · Transistor-Wechselrichter-Leuchte f

~ **grid suspension ceiling** · Lichtrasterdecke f

~ ~ ~ **(~) system** · Lichtrasterdeckensystem n

luminance · Leuchtdichte B f

~ **factor** · Leuchtdichtefaktor m

~ **meter, brightness ~** · Leuchtdichtemesser m

luminescent, luminous · lumineszierend, leuchtend

~ **ceiling, luminous ~, illuminated ~,** (light-)diffusing ~ · Leuchtdecke f, Lichtdecke

~ ~ **system** → (light-)diffusing ~ ~

~ **composition, luminous ~, ~ compound** · Leuchtmasse f

~ **compound, luminous ~, ~ composition** · Leuchtmasse f

~ **foil, luminous ~** · Leuchtfolie f

~ **glass, luminous ~** · leuchtendes Glas n, Leuchtglas

~ **momentary-contact push button, luminous ~ ~ ~** · Leuchttastschalter m

~ **paint, luminous ~** · Leucht(anstrich)farbe f, Lumineszenzfarbe

~ **pigment, luminous ~** · Leuchtpigment n

~ **wall, illuminated ~, luminous ~,** (light-)diffusing ~ · Lichtwand f, Leuchtwand

luminosity · Lichtausbeute f

luminous, luminescent · lumineszierend, leuchtend

~ **ceiling, illuminated ~, luminescent ~,** (light-)diffusing ~ · Leuchtdecke f, Lichtdecke

~ ~ **system** → (light-)diffusing ~ ~

~ **composition, luminescent ~, ~ compound** · Leuchtmasse f

~ **compound, luminescent ~, ~ composition** · Leuchtmasse f

~ **energy** · Lichtmenge f Q, Lichtarbeit f Q

~ **flux (F)** · Lichtstrom m

~ **foil, luminescent ~** · Leuchtfolie f

~ **glass, luminescent ~** · leuchtendes Glas n, Leuchtglas

luminous intensity · Lichtstärke f I [cd]

~ ~ **distribution** · Licht(stärke)verteilung f

~ ~ ~ **curve** · Licht(stärke)verleitungskurve f

~ **momentary-contact push button, luminescent ~ ~ ~** · Leuchttastschalter m

~ **paint, luminescent ~** · Leucht(anstrich)farbe f, Lumineszenzfarbe

~ **pigment, luminescent ~** · Leuchtpigment n

~ **system, illuminated ~** · Licht(bau)system n

~ **wall, illuminated ~, luminescent ~,** (light-)diffusing ~ · Lichtwand f, Leuchtwand

lump cinder (US); blastfurnace lump slag (Brit.) [*See remark under '(Hochofen)Schlacke'*] · Hochofenstück(en)schlacke f

~ **formation, formation of lump** · Klumpenbildung f [*Zement*]

lump(-)free · klumpenfrei, klumpenlos, knollenfrei, knollenlos

lump gypsum · Stück(en)gips m

~ **lac** · Kuchenlack m, Klumpenlack, Lackkuchen m

~ **(quick)lime** [*The product resulting from the calcination of limestone in a shaft kiln. It ranges in size from approximately 4 to 12 in. in diameter*] · Stück(en)kalk m, (ungelöschter) stückiger (Brannt)Kalk [*DIN 1060*]

~ **slag** · Klotzschlacke f; Stück(en)schlacke [*Stück(en)- und Klotzschlacke sind in der Verwendungsart gleich. Die Stück(en)schlacke wird durch Aufbaggern und Brechen der in Beeten erkalteten Hochofenschlacke gewonnen, während die Klotzschlacke in der Schlackenpfanne erkaltet, gekippt, gebrochen und klassiert wird*]

~ **sum** · Pauschalsumme f, Pauschalpreis m

lump-sum contract · Pauschalpreisvertrag *m*
~ tender, ~ offer (Brit.); ~ proposal, ~ bid (US) · Pauschalpreisangebot *n*
lumps of marble · Marmorbruch *m*
lunar caustic · salpetersaures Silberoxid *n*, Silbernitrat *n*, Höllenstein *m*, AgNO$_3$
lunette [*Semicircular or crescent-shaped space where a vault intersects a wall or another vault, often occupied by a window*] · Lichtraum *m*, Ohr *n*
~ · Lunette *f*, Lünette [*Bogenfeld über einer Tür oder einem Fenster, das oft dekoriert ist und hauptsächlich in der Barockbaukunst vorkommt*]
~ · Lünette *f*, Lunette [*Beim Spiegelgewölbe das unter einer Stichkappe liegende, halbkreisförmige Wandfeld*]
~ vault · Ohrengewölbe *n*, Lichtraumgewölbe
luster (finish) (US); lustre (~) (Brit.); satin ~ · Lüster *m*, Luster *m* [*Oberflächenwirkung eines Anstriches oder Druckes: metallisch, bronzeartig, irisierend oder ähnlich schimmernd*]
lux, lx · Lux *n*, lx [*Einheit der Beleuchtungsstärke, 1 lx ist vorhanden, wenn der Lichtstrom 1 lm auf die Fläche von 1m^2 gestrahlt wird*]
luxury apartment (unit) → ~ flat
~ (bath)tub, ~ bath · Luxus(bade)wanne *f* [*in Feuerton oder Marmor*]
~ flat, ~ apartment (unit); ~ living unit (US) [*A self-contained luxury dwelling on one stor(e)y in a larger building*] · Luxus(-Geschoß)wohnung *f*, Luxus-Etagenwohnung, Luxus-Stockwerkwohnung
~ floor(ing) (finish), ~ floor cover(ing) · Luxusboden(belag) *m*, Luxusfußboden(belag)
~ hotel, (international) de luxe type ~ · Luxushotel *n*
~ living unit (US) → ~ flat
~ partition (wall) · Luxustrennwand *f*
lvr → louver
LWC → light(weight) concrete
LWIC → light(weight) insulating concrete
lych gate, lich ~, corpse ~ · überdachtes Friedhofstor *n*
lyctus-suspectible wood · splintholzkäferanfälliges Holz *n*
lye · Lauge *f* [*Die wäßrige Lösung einer Base, z.B. Kalilauge*]
lyophile colloid · lyophiles Kolloid *n*
~ protective colloid · lyophyles Schutzkolloid *n*
lyophobe colloid · lyophobes Kolloid *n*

M

m, modular ratio (~) [*The ratio of the modulus of elasticity of steel to that of concrete = E_s/E_c*] · Beiwert *n m*, *n*-Wert

MA → magnesium aluminate
***m*-design**, *m*-method, modular ratio ~ · *n*-Verfahren *n*
***m*-method**, *m*-design, modular ratio ~ · *n*-Verfahren *n*
***m*-problem**, modular ratio ~ · *n*-Frage *f*
***m*-times** · *n*-fach
mac(adam) · Makadam *m*
~ aggregate type road mix surfacing, ~ ~ ~ ~ ~ pavement · Baumischbelag *m* nach Art des Makadam, offener Baumischbelag
machicolation [*An opening between the corbels which support a projecting parapet, or in the floor of a gallery or the roof of a portal, through which combustibles, molten lead, stones, etc., were dropped upon assailants. Also, a projecting structure containing such openings*] · Pechnase *f*, Gußerker *m*, Maschikuli *m*
machicolations · Maschikulis *mpl*, Gußerkerkranz *m*, Pechnasenkranz, Fallschirme *mpl* [*Ausgußöffnungen für heißes Pech und Öl im Boden der an Burgmauern und -türmen auf Konsolen vorkragenden Wehrgänge; als erkerartiger Ausguß, meist über dem Burgtor*]
'machine(-age)' aesthetic(ism) [*Appreciation of machine forms such as cylinders, cones, cubes, etc.*] · Maschinenästhetik *f*, technische Ästhetik
machine applied (mixed) plaster, spray (~) ~ · maschinell aufgetragener Putz *m*, Spritzputz, Maschinenputz
~-banded pipe, continuous stave-pipe, wood-stave pipe [*A pipe made of wooden staves. The assembly is held together in a machine and tightly wrapped with wire. The pipe is made in definite lengths and joined in the field by couplings. Such pipe is rarely made larger than 24 in. in diameter*] · Holzdaubenrohr *n*
machine-brocken metal (Brit.); ~ stone (US) · Maschinenschotter *m*
machine casting · maschineller Einbau *m* von Gußasphalt
~-cut peat · Maschinentorf *m*
(machine-)extruded terra-cotta · Strangpreßterrakotta *f*
machine for letting in mounts, hardware mounting machine · Beschlag-Einlaßmaschine *f*
'machine for living in' [*Term coined by Le Corbusier*] · „Wohnmaschine" *f*
machine-made · maschinell gefertigt, maschinengefertigt
~ brick · Maschinenziegel *m*
~ mortar, machine-mixed ~ · maschinell gemischter Mörtel *m*, Mischermörtel
~ plaster, machine-mixed ~ · maschinell gemischter Putz *m*
machine-mixed concrete, machine-made ~ · maschinell gemischter Beton *m*, Mischerbeton
~ mortar, machine-made ~ · maschinell gemischter Mörtel *m*, Mischermörtel

~ plaster, machine-made ~ · maschinell gemischter Putz *m*
machine-printed (wall)paper · Maschinendruck(papier)tapete *f*
machine room → machinery ~
~ station → machine(ry) ~
machinery base, ~ foundation · Maschinengründung *f*
~ block → ~ building
~ building, ~ block [*Sometimes erroneously called 'machine(ry) hall'*] · Maschinengebäude *n*, Maschinenhaus *n*, Maschinenhalle *f*
~ foundation, ~ base · Maschinengründung *f*
~ noise · Maschinenlärm *m*
machine(ry) room, mechanical ~, (mechanical) equipment ~, plant ~ · Maschinenraum *m*
~ station, mechanical ~, (mechanical) equipment ~, plant ~ · Maschinenzentrale *f*
machinery vibration, ~ oscillation · Maschinenerschütterung *f* [*Erschütterungsschutz*]
machining allowance · Bearbeitungstoleranz *f*
~ shop · Bearbeitungsraum *m*
maculose rock, fleckschiefer, mottled schist, spotted schist · Fleck(en)schiefer *m*
madder lake · Krapplack *m*, Krapprot *n*, Alizarinrot, Rötelack
~ plant · Färberröte *f*, Krapp *m*
made ground → made-up ~
made(-up) ground, man-made ~ [*Ground built up with excavated material or refuse as distinct from the natural, undisturbed soil*] · aufgefülltes Gelände *n*, aufgeschüttetes ~
madrasah, collegiate mosque, medressa · Medersa *f*, Medres(s)e *f*, Moscheehochschule *f*, Madrasa, Medressa, Tempelschule [*Um einen Hof gruppierte Sonderform einer Moschee, die als Schule dient*]
Magnel anchoring system, ~ anchorage ~ · Magnel-Verankerung *f* [*Spannbeton*]
magnesia; magnesium oxide (Brit.); magnesium oxid(e) (US) · Magnesia *f*, Magnesiumoxid *n*, MgO
~ brick, magnesite ~, ~ refractory · Magnesiaziegel *m*, Magnesitstein *m*
~ cement · hydraulische Magnesia *f*, Magnesiazement *m*
~ ~; magnesium oxide ~ (Brit.); magnesium oxid(e) ~ (US) · Magnesiumoxidzement *m*
~ ~ concrete; magnesium oxide ~ ~ (Brit.); magnesium oxid(e) ~ ~ (US) · MO-Beton *m* [*Beton mit Magnesiumoxidzement*]
~ hardness · Magnesiahärte *f*
~ refractory → ~ brick

magnesian lime, dolomitic ~, lean ~, poor ~ · Magerkalk *m*, Graukalk, Dolomitkalk
~ ~ paste → ~ ~ putty
~ ~ putty, ~ ~ paste, dolomitic ~ ~ · Dolomitkalkteig *m* [*DIN 1060*]
~ marble, dolomitic ~ · Dolomitmarmor *m* mit zwischen 5–40% Magnesiumkarbonat
~ quicklime · Dolomitstückkalk *m* [*DIN 1060*]
~ semi-hydraulic lime · dolomitischer Wasserkalk *m* mit mehr als 5 Gew-% MgO [*Fehlnamen: Magnesiawasserkalk, Magnesitwasserkalk*]
magnesite, bitter spar · Bitterspat *m*, Magnesit *m*, $MgCO_3$ (Min.)
~ board, ~ sheet, ~ building ~ · Magnesit-Bauplatte *f* [*DIN 1101*]
~-bound · magnesitgebunden
magnesite brick, magnesia ~, ~ refractory · Magnesiaziegel *m*, Magnesitstein *m*
~ (building) board, ~ (~) sheet · Magnesit-Bauplatte *f* [*DIN 1101*]
~ cement → magnesium oxychloride (composition)
~-chrome refractory (product), ~ ~ material [*A refractory material made from a mix(ture) of dead-burned magnesite and chrome ore, the magnesite preponderating*]· Magnesit-Chrom-Erzeugnis *n*
magnesite-chrom(it)e refractory (product) · Magnesia-Chrom(it)-Erzeugnis *n*
magnesite floor(ing); magnesium oxychloride ~ (Brit.); magnesium oxychlorid(e) ~ (US)· Steinholzestrich *m*, Fes *m*, Steinholz(fuß)boden(belag) *m*
~ ~ tile; magnesium oxychloride ~ ~ (Brit.); magnesium oxychlorid(e) ~ ~ (US) · Steinholzplatte *f*
~ refractory → ~ brick
~ ~ (product), ~ ~ material · Magnesiterzeugnis *n* [*Vorwiegend aus Magnesia bestehendes feuerfestes Erzeugnis*]
~ rock · Magnesitgestein *n*
~ sheet, ~ board, ~ building ~ · Magnesite-Bauplatte *f* [*DIN 1101*]
~ subfloor; magnesium oxychloride ~ (Brit.); magnesium oxychlorid(e) ~ (US) · Steinholzunterboden *m*, Steinholz-Unterlage *f*
magnesium · Mg *n*, Magnesium *n* [*DIN 17800*]
~ alloy · Magnesiumlegierung *f*
~ aluminate, MA · Magnesiumaluminat *n*
~ carbonate · Magnesiumkarbonat *n*, $MgCO_3$
~ casting alloy · Magnesiumgußlegierung *f*
~ chloride (Brit.); ~ chlorid(e) (US) · Chlormagnesium *n*, Magnesiumchlorid *n*, $MgCl_2$ [*DIN 273 Bl. 2*]

magnesium chloride solution — main alloying constituent

~ ~ **solution,** liquid magnesium chloride (Brit.); liquid magnesium chlorid(e), magnesium chlorid(e) solution (US) · Magnesiumchloridlösung f, MgCl$_2$-Lösung; (Chlormagnesium)Lauge f, Magnesiumchloridlauge [Fehlnamen]

~ **compound** · Magnesiumverbindung f

~ **fluosilicate** · Magnesiumfluat n, Mg-Fluat, Kieselfluormagnesium n

~ **hydroxid(e)** (US); ~ hydroxide (Brit.) [The product of slaking magnesium oxid(e)] · Magnesiumhydroxid n

~ **limestone** → dolomite rock

~ **oxide** (Brit.); ~ oxid(e) (US); magnesia · Magnesia f, Magnesiumoxid n, MgO

~ ~ **cement** (Brit.); ~ oxid(e) ~ (US); magnesia ~ · Magnesiumoxidzement m

~ ~ ~ **concrete** (Brit.); ~ oxid(e) ~ ~ (US); magnesia ~ ~ · MO-Beton m [Beton mit Magnesiumoxidzement]

(~) **oxychlorid(e) cement,** ~ oxychlorid(e) (US); (~) oxychloride cement, ~ oxychloride (Brit.); Sorel('s) cement · Magnesiabinder m [DIN 273. Fehlnamen: Sorelzement, Sorelscher Zement]

~ ~ **composition** (Brit.); ~ oxychlorid(e) ~ (US) [It is made from a mixture of magnesia, magnesium chlorid(e) solution, fillers and pigments] · Steinholzestrich m, Magnesiumestrich, Magnesiaestrich, Estrich aus Magnesiamörtel, magnesiagebundener Estrich, Steinholz n [als Baustoff]

~ ~ (~) (Brit.); ~ oxychlorid(e) (~), oxychloric cement (US); Sorel's cement, magnesite cement · Magnesiamörtel m, Sorelzement m, Sorelmörtel, Magnesitbinder m [Fehlnamen: Magnesiazement, Magnesitzement]

~ ~ **floor(ing)** (Brit.); ~ oxychlorid(e) ~ (US); magnesite ~ · Steinholzestrich m, Fes m, Steinholz(fuß)boden(-belag) m

~ ~ ~ **tile** (Brit.); ~ oxychlorid(e) ~ ~ (US); magnesite ~ ~ · Steinholzplatte f

~ ~ **(industrial) floor(ing)** (Brit.); ~ oxychlorid(e) (~) ~ (US) · magnesiagebundener Belag m, ~ Boden(-belag), ~ Industriefußboden(belag)

~ ~ **screed (topping),** ~ ~ jointless floor(ing) (US); ~ oxychloride ~ (~) (Brit.) · magnesiagebundener Estrich m, Estrich aus Magnesiamörtel, Magnesiaestrich, Steinholzestrich, Magnesitestrich [als verlegter Baustoff. DIN 273]

~ ~ **subfloor** (Brit); ~ oxychlorid(e) ~ (US); magnesite ~ · Steinholzunterboden m, Steinholz-Unterlage f

~ ~ **tile floor cover(ing),** ~ ~ ~ floor(ing) (finish) (Brit); ~ oxychlorid(e) ~ ~ (~) (US) · Fbsh, Steinholzplatten(fuß)boden(belag) m

~ ~ ~ **floor(ing) (finish),** ~ ~ ~ floor cover(ing) (Brit); ~ oxychlorid(e) ~ ~ (~) (US) · Steinholzplatten-(fuß)boden(belag) m, Fbsh m

~ **salt** · Magnesiumsalz n

~ **silicate,** silicate of magnesium 3 SiO$_3$Mg·SH$_2$O, Magnesiumsilikat n

~ ~ **pigment** · Magnesiumsilikatpigment n

~ **solution** · Magnesiumlösung f

~ **stearate** · Magnesiumstearat n

~ **sulphate** (Brit.); ~ sulfate (US) Magnesiumsulfat n

magnetic iron ore, magnetite · Magneteisenstein m, Hammerschlag m, Magneteisenerz n, Magnetit m, Fe$_3$O$_4$

~ ~ ~ **concrete,** magnetite ~ · Beton m mit Magneteisenerzzuschlag(stoff), Magnetitbeton

~ **seal(ing)** · Magnet(ab)dichtung f

~ **test** · Magnetprobe f, Magnetprüfung f, Magnetversuch m [zerstörungsfreie Werkstoffprüfung]

magnetite, magnetic iron ore · Magneteisenerz n, Hammerschlag m, Magneteisenstein m, Magnetit m, Fe$_3$O$_4$

~ **concrete,** magnetic iron ore ~ · Beton m mit Magneteisenerzzuschlag (stoff), Magnetitbeton

~ (~) **aggregate** · Magnetit(beton)-zuschlag(stoff) m, Magnetit(beton)-zuschlagmaterial n

magnification factor · Stoßzahl f [Eine Verkehrslast ist mit einer Stoßzahl zu vervielfachen, wenn sie Stöße oder Schwingungen verursacht]

magnitude of creep · Kriechgröße f, Kriechmaß n

~ ~ **stress** · Spannungsgröße f

~ ~ **the bending stress,** ~ ~ ~ flexural ~ · Biegespannungsgröße f

mahogany brown · Mahagonibraun n

mahogany-faced, mahogany-lined · mahogonibekleidet, mahagoniausgekleidet, mahagoniverkleidet

mahogany-lined, mahogany-faced · mahogonibekleidet, mahagoniausgekleidet, mahagoniverkleidet

Mahometan architecture → Muslim ~

maid's changing room · Umkleide(-raum) f, (m) für (Haus)Mädchen [Hotel]

~ **room** · (Haus)Mädchenzimmer n

mail sorting room · Briefverteilerraum m

mailing facilities, ~ facility · Poststelle f [In einem großen Bürogebäude]

main [The principal pipe artery to which branches may be connected] · Haupt(rohr)strang m, Haupt(rohr)leitung f

~ [The supply authority's pipe or cable] · Hauptleitung f

~ **alloying constituent,** principal ~ ~ · Hauptlegierungsbestandteil m

main altar — main loading case

~ **altar,** principal ~ · Hauptaltar *m*

(~) **archway** · Durchgang *m*, Durchfahrt *f* [*Stadttor*]

~ **assembly hall** · Plenarsaal *m*

~ **axis,** principal ~ · Hauptachse *f*

~ ~ **of inertia,** principal ~ ~ ~ · Haupttrageheitsachse *f*

~ **bar,** ~ round ~, principal (round) ~ · Haupt(rund)stab *m*, Längs(rund)stab [*Betonstahlmatte*]

~ **beam,** principal ~, primary ~ · Hauptbalken(träger) *m*

~ ~, **footing** ~, **tie** ~, principal ~ · Hauptbalken *m*, Zugbalken, Spannbalken, Trambalken [*einsäuliges Hängewerk*]

~ ~, principal ~ [*A beam supporting the ends of secondary beams, which may in turn support the ends of tertiary beams*] · Hauptbalken(träger) *m*

~ **bearing structure** → ~ loadbearing ~

~ **block,** principal ~, ~ building · Hauptgebäude *n*

~ **building,** principal ~, ~ block · Hauptgebäude *n*

~ ~, principal ~, aisled hall · Langhaus *n* [*Teil einer Kirche zwischen Fassade und Querhaus bzw. Chor*]

~ ~ **bay,** principal ~ ~, aisled hall ~ · Langhausjoch *n*

~ ~ **vault,** principal ~ ~, aisled hall ~ · Langhausgewölbe *n*

~ **cable,** principal ~ · Hauptkabel *n*

~ **case of loading** → ~ loading case

~ **center** (US); ~ centre (Brit.); principal ~ · Hauptzentrum *n*

~ ~ **line of inertia** (Brit.) → principal axis ~ ~

~ **centre** (Brit.); ~ center (US); principal ~ · Hauptzentrum *n*

~ **chapel,** principal ~ · Hauptkapelle *f*

~ **choir,** principal ~, ~ quire · Hauptchor *m*

~ **cock,** principal ~ · Haupthahn *m*

~ **collector** → ~ sewer

~ **column,** principal ~ · Hauptstütze *f*

~ ~ **foundation,** principal-column ~ · Hauptstützenfundament *n*

~ **compression stress,** principal ~ ~, ~ compressive ~ · Hauptdruckspannung *f*

~ **compressive stress,** principal ~ ~, ~ compression ~ · Hauptdruckspannung *f*

~ **constituent,** principal ~ · Hauptbestandteil *m*

~ **controlling dimension,** principal ~ ~ [*A dimension between key reference planes, e.g. floor-to-floor height or stor(e)y height*] · Ausbaumaß *n*

~ **cupola,** ~ dome, principal ~ · Hauptkuppel *f*

~ **curvature,** principal ~ · Hauptkrümmung *f*

~ ~ **line** → line of principal curvature

~ **data,** principal ~ · Hauptdaten *f*

~ **diagonal,** principal ~ · Hauptdiagonale *f*, Hauptschräge *f*

~ ~ **rib,** principal ~ ~ · Hauptdiagonalrippe *f*

~ **dimension,** principal ~ · Hauptabmessung *f*, Hauptmaß *n*

~ **direction,** principal ~ · Hauptrichtung *f*

~ ~ **of curvature,** principal ~ ~ ~ · Hauptkrümmungsrichtung *f*

~ **distribution line,** principal ~ ~ · Hauptverteilungsleitung *f*

~ ~ **panel,** principal ~ ~ · Hauptverteilungstafel *f*

~ **dome,** ~ cupola, principal ~ · Hauptkuppel *f*

~ **entrance,** principal ~ · Haupteingang *m*

~ ~ **hall,** principal ~ ~ · Haupteingangshalle *f*

~ **façade,** principal ~, frontispiece · Hauptfassade *f*

~ **floor,** principal ~; ~ storey (Brit.); ~ story (US) · Hauptgeschoß *n*, Hauptstockwerk *n*, Hauptetage *f* [*Geschoß in Wohnhäusern und öffentlichen Gebäuden mit den Haupträumen des Hauses, früher oft durch größere Geschoßhöhe gekennzeichnet*]

~ ~ **beam,** principal ~ ~ · Hauptdeckenbalken(träger) *m*

~ **flue,** up-take, breeching (US); flue connection to stack, flue connection to chimney · (Schornstein)Fuchs(kanal) *m* [*Waag(e)rechter oder mit leichter Steigung von der Heizanlage zum Schornstein führender Rauchkanal*]

~ **frame,** principal ~ · Hauptrahmen *m*

~ **fuse,** principal ~, company's ~ · Hauptsicherung *f*

~ **girder,** principal ~ · Hauptträger *m*

~ **grid,** principal ~ · Hauptraster *m*

~ **hall,** principal ~ · Haupthalle *f*

~ **inspection chamber,** principal ~ ~ [*See remark under 'Revisionsschacht'*] · Hauptrevisionsschacht *m*

~ **kitchen,** principal ~ · Hauptküche *f*

~ **living area,** principal ~ ~ · Hauptwohnzone *f*

~ **load,** principal ~ · Hauptlast *f*

~ **(load)bearing structure,** principal ~ ~, ~ (weight-carrying) ~, ~ loaded ~, ~ supporting ~, ~ load-carrying ~ · Haupttragwerk *n*

~ **load-carrying structure** → ~ (load-)bearing ~

~ **loaded structure** → ~ (load)bearing ~

~ **loading case,** principal ~ ~, ~ case of loading · Hauptlastfall *m*

main longitudinal force — maintenance-free

~ **longitudinal force**, principal ~ ~ · Hauptlängskraft *f*

~ **mall**, principal ~ · Hauptkorso *m*

~ **masonry wall**, principal ~ ~ · Hauptmauer *f*

~ **moment**, principal ~ · Hauptmoment *n*

~ ~ **of inertia**, principal ~ ~ ~ · Hauptträgheitsmoment *n*

~ **motif**, principal ~ · Leitmotiv *n*

~ **normal**, principal ~ · Hauptnormale *f*

~ **office**, principal ~ · Hauptbüro *n*

~ **pedestrian zone**, principal ~ ~ · Hauptfußgängerbereich *m, n*

~ **pipe**, principal ~ · Hauptrohr *n*

~ **plane**, principal ~ · Hauptebene *f* [*Baustatik*]

~ **portal**, principal ~ · Hauptportal *n*

~ **post** → principal ~

~ **quire**, principal ~, ~ choir · Hauptchor *m*

~ **radius of inertia**, principal ~ ~ ~ · Hauptträgheitshalbmesser *m*

~ **rafter**, principal (~), blade · Hauptsparren *m*, Bundsparren, Bindersparren

~ **rafters**, principal ~, blades, principals [*The main rafters are those in the roof truss which carry the purlin(e)s on which the common rafters are laid*] · Bindersparren *mpl*, Hauptsparren, Bundsparren, Bundgespärre *n*, Bindergespärre

~ **(railroad) station** → central (railway) ~

~ **(railway) station** → central (~) ~

~ **reinforcement**, principal ~ · Hauptarmierung *f*, Hauptbewehrung, Haupt(stahl)einlagen *fpl*

~ **restaurant**, principal ~ · Hauptspeisesaal *m* [*Hotel*]

~ **rib**, principal ~ · Hauptrippe *f*

~ **riser**, principal ~, rising main · Hauptsteig(e)leitung *f*

~ **(round) bar**, principal (~) ~ · Haupt(rund)stab *n*, Längs(rund)stab [*Betonstahlmatte*]

~ **services centre**, principal ~ ~ (Brit.); ~ ~ center (US) · technische Hauptzentrale *f* [*Eines Hochhauses oder eines Gebäudekomplexes*]

~ **sewer**, principal ~, public ~, ~ collector [*A common sewer directly controlled by public authority*] · Hauptsammler *m*, Hauptabwasserleitung *f*, öffentlicher Sammler, öffentliche Abwasserleitung

~ **shear(ing) stress**, principal ~ ~ · Hauptschubspannung *f*

~ **stage**, principal ~ · Hauptbühne *f*

~ **stair(case)**, principal ~ · Haupttreppe *f*

~ **station** → central (railway) ~

~ **steel beam**, principal ~ ~ · Hauptstahlbalken(träger) *m*

~ ~ **girder**, principal ~ ~ · Stahlhauptträger *m*

~ **storey** (Brit.) → ~ floor

~ **strain**, principal ~ · Hauptdehnung *f*

~ **stress**, principal ~ · Hauptspannung *f*

~ ~ **line** → line of principal stress

~ **structure** → ~ (load)bearing ~

~ ~, principal ~ · Hauptbau(werk) *m*, (*n*)

~ **stud** → principal post

~ **stupa(-mound)**, principal ~, major ~, ~ tope(-mound) · Hauptstupa *m*

~ **supporting structure** → ~ (load-)bearing ~

~ **switch board**, principal ~ ~ · Hauptschalttafel *f*

~ **switchroom**, principal ~ · Hauptschaltraum *m*

~ **symbol**, principal ~ · Hauptzeichen *n* [*Baustatik*]

~ **temple**, principal ~ · Haupttempel *m*

~ **tensile reinforcement**, principal ~ ~ · Hauptzugarmierung *f*, Hauptzugbewehrung, Hauptzug(stahl)einlagen *fpl*

~ ~ **stress**, principal ~ ~ · Hauptzugspannung *f*

~ ~ ~ **limit**, principal ~ ~ ~ · Hauptzugspannungsgrenze *f*

~ **terminal building**, principal ~ ~ · zentrales Abfertigungsgebäude *n* [*Flughafen*]

~ **tope(-mound)** → ~ stupa(-mound)

~ **transept**, principal ~ · Hauptquerschiff *n*, Hauptquerhaus *n*

~ **valley**, principal ~ · Hauptkehle *f* [*Dach*]

~ **value**, principal ~ · Hauptwert *m*

~ **vault**, principal ~ · Hauptgewölbe *n*

~ **vertical** → principal post

~ **walk**, principal ~ · Hauptgehweg *m*

~ **(weight-carrying) structure** → ~ (load)bearing ~

~ **wind direction**, principal ~ ~ · Hauptwindrichtung *f*

~ **wire feeder**, principal ~ ~ · Einfädelvorrichtung *f* [*Herstellung von Baustahlmatten*]

mains subway, service duct, duct for services · Betriebskanal *m*, Leitungskanal

~ **water**, tap ~ · Leitungswasser *n*

maintenance, upkeep · Instandhaltung *f*, Unterhaltung, Wartung

~ **clause** · Unterhaltungsklausel *f*, Wartungsklausel, Instandhaltungsklausel

~ **cost(s)**, upkeep ~ · Instandhaltungskosten *f*, Unterhaltungskosten, Wartungskosten

~ **facility** · Unterhaltungsanlage *f*

~**-free** · wartungsfrei

maintenance hangar, technical (aircraft) ~ · (Flugzeug)Wartungshalle, (Flugzeug)Werfthalle

~ **obligation**, upkeep ~ · Instandhaltungspflicht *f*, Unterhaltungspflicht, Wartungspflicht

~ **painting (work)** · Unterhaltungsanstreicherarbeiten *fpl*, Unterhaltungsanstricharbeiten, Unterhaltungsmalerarbeiten [*DIN 18363*]

~ **period**, retention ~ · Garantiezeit *f*

~ **personnel**, ~ staff · Unterhaltungspersonal *m*, Wartungspersonal

~ **requirement** · Unterhaltungsaufwand *m*, Wartungsaufwand, Instandhaltungsaufwand

~ **shop**, ~ work~ · Unterhaltungswerkstatt *f*, Wartungswerkstatt

~ **staff**, ~ personnel · Unterhaltungspersonal *n*, Wartungspersonal

~ **undertaking**, upkeep ~ · Instandhaltungsbetrieb *m*, Unterhaltungsbetrieb, Wartungsbetrieb

~ **work** · Unterhaltungsarbeit *f*, Wartungsarbeit, Instandhaltungsarbeit

(**work**)**shop** · Unterhaltungswerkstatt *f*, Wartungswerkstatt

maisonette · Außenganghaus *n*, Maisonnette *f* [*1. Jeder Außengang bedient die Wohnungen mehrerer (2 oder 3) Vollgeschosse. Außengang also nur in jedem zweiten oder dritten Vollgeschoß. 2. Jeder Außengang bedient Wohnungen, die in sich mehrgeschossig sind. Außengang in jedem 2. Vollgeschoß*]

~, duplex apartment · zweistöckige Wohnung *f*, doppelstöckige ~

majolica, maiolica · Majolika *f*, spanisch-maurische Fayence *f*

~ **glazed coat(ing)**, ~ glaze(d finish), maiolica ~ ~, ~ glazing · Majolikaglasur *f*, Majolikabeglasung *f*

~ **mosaic**, maiolica ~ · Majolikamosaik *n*

~ ~ **wall tile**, maiolica ~ ~ ~ · Majolikamosaik-Wand(belag)platte *f*, Majolikamosaik-Wandfliese

~ **wall tile**, maiolica ~ ~ · Majolika-Wand-(belag)platte *f*, Majolika-Wandfliese

major fire, serious ~ · Großbrand *m*, Großfeuer *n* [*Ein Brand, zu dessen Bekämpfung mehr als drei C-Rohre eingesetzt werden (1 B-Rohr = 2 C-Rohre)*]

~ **load transfer** · Hauptlastabtragung *f*

~ **stupa(-mound)** → main ~

~ **(swimming) pool** · Haupt(schwimm)-becken *n*

~ **tope(-mound)** → main stupa(-mound)

make · Fabrikat *n*

to make, to manufacture, to fabricate · fertigen, herstellen

~ ~ **a paste**, to form ~ ~, to form into ~ ~ · anpasten

~ ~ **good**, to repair · reparieren, instandsetzen, ausbessern

~ ~ **lean by adding sand** · magern

make-believe Tudor imitations · Pseudo-Tudor *m*

'make' contact · Schließkontakt *m*

maker, manufacturer, fabricator, producer · Erzeuger *m*, Hersteller, Fabrikant *m*

maker's certificate, manufacturer's ~ · Herstellerzeugnis *n*

~ **instructions**, manufacturer's ~ · Herstelleranweisungen *fpl*

~ **mark**, manufacturer's ~ · Herstellerzeichen *n*

~ **test**, fabricators' ~, manufacturers' ~ · Werkprobe *f*, Werkprüfung *f*, Werkversuch *m*

makeup air [*Outside air required to replace air being exhausted*] · Nachholluft *f*

making, fabrication, manufacturing, fabricating · Fertigen *n*, Herstellen

~ **cost(s)**, manufacturing ~, fabrication ~ · Fertigungskosten *f*, Herstellungskosten, Fabricationskosten

~ **cycle**, manufacturing ~, fabrication ~ · Fertigungszyklus *m*, Herstellungszyklus, Fabrikationszyklus

~ **fullest use of available space** · Raumaufteilen *n*

~ **good**, repairing · Reparieren *n*, Instandsetzen, Ausbessern

~ ~, repair · Reparatur *f*, Ausbesserung *f*, Instandsetzung

~ **lean by adding sand** · Magern *n* [*Von Mörteln und Tonen durch Beigabe von Sand*]

malachite green · Malachitgrün *n*

male caryatid → atlante

~ **toilet**, men's ~ · Herrentoilette *f*, Männertoilette

maleic acid · Maleinsäure *f*

~ **ester resin** · maleinsäuremodifiziertes Esterharz *n*

maleinized oil · Maleinatöl *n*

malleable cast iron, MCI · Temperguß *m*, Te [*Fehlnamen: Halbstahl m, Temperstahlguß*]

Maltese cross · Johanniterkreuz *n*, Malteserkreuz

maltha, mineral tar, pissasphalt(um) · Bergteer *m*

Mammisi temple → Birth House

management · Betriebsführung *f*

mandapam, mantapam [*An open pavilion or porch in front of an Indian temple*] · Mandapa *m*

mandarah · Mandara *m* [*Empfangshalle des Hausherrn im arabischen Wohnhaus, hauptsächlich in Ägypten*]

mandorla, aureole, vesica piscis · Heiligenschein *m*, Mandorla *f*, Mandelglorie *f*

(**mandrel**) **bend(ing) test** · Dornbiegeprobe *f*, Dornbiegeprüfung *f*, Dornbiegeversuch *m* [*DIN 53152*]

~ pressure roll · Gegendruckrolle *f* [*Dachpappenanlage*]

manganese → manganese(i)um

~, black ~ [*A black mineral, now recognized as an oxide of a metal, used in glass-making and other processes*] · Mangan *n*

~ black (pigment) · Manganschwarz-(pigment) *n*

~ blue (pigment) · Manganblau(pigment) *n*

~ bronze [*It has 58% copper content*] · Messing 58 *n*, Standardmessing für Bohr- und Drehqualität, Ms 58, MS 58

~ ~ [*deprecated*]; high tensile brass · Manganbronze *f*

~ cement · Manganzement *m*

~ drier, ~ dryer · Mangantrockenstoff *m*

~ elimination, ~ removal, demanganization · (Wasser)Entmanganung *f*

~ linoleate, linoleate of manganese · Manganlinoleat *n*

~ naphthenate · Mangannaphthenat *n*

~ pigment · Manganpigment *n*

~ removal, ~ elimination, demanganization · (Wasser)Entmanganung *f*

~ resinate, resinate of manganese · Manganresinat *n*

~ salt · Mangansalz *n*

~ soap · Manganseife *f*

~ steel · Manganstahl *m*

~ violet (pigment) · Manganviolett-(pigment) *n*

manganes(i)um, manganese [*The metallic element of which 'black manganese' is the oxide*] · Mangan *n*, Mn [*in der Chemie*]

manganocalcite · Kalkmanganspat *m*

mangling [*Flattening of plates, hot or cold, by passing through a multi-roll straightening machine*] · Richten *n*

man-headed winged bull · Flügelstier *m* mit Menschenhaupt

manhole, manway, mh [*A chamber with or without access shaft, constructed over a sewer or principal drain to permit inspection and access for cleaning and maintenance*] · Einsteigschacht *m*, Manneinsteigloch *n*, Mannloch, (Einstieg)Schacht, Manneinstieg(loch) *m*, (*n*)

~ cover, manway **~,** manlid · Mannlochdeckel *m*, Schachtdeckel

~ covering, manway **~** · Schachtabdeckung *f*, Mannlochabdeckung [*DIN 1229*]

~ frame, manway **~** · Mannlochrahmen *m*, Schachtrahmen

~ grid, ~ grill(ag)e [*Sometimes spelled 'grill'*] · Schachtrost *m*, Mannlochrost

~ grill(ag)e, ~ grid [*Sometimes spelled 'grill'*] · Schachtrost *m*, Mannlochrost

~ grille, ~ grillage, ~ grid [*Sometimes spelled 'grill'*] · Schachtrost *m*, Mannlochrost

~ head, manway **~** [*The cast-iron fixture surmounting a manhole. It is made up of two parts: a frame, which rests on the masonry of the shaft, and a removable cover. Frames are either fixed or adjustable in height. Covers are 'tight', 'ventilated', or 'anti-rattling'*] · Schachtdeckel *m* und -rahmen *m*

~ junction box, manway **~ ~** · Schachtkabelkasten *m*

~ masonry (work), manway **~ (~)** · Mannlochmauerwerk *n*, Schachtmauerwerk

~ ring, manway **~** · Schachtring *m*; Zwischenring [*Fehlname*] [*DIN 4034*]

~ sewer brick, manway **~ ~** · Kanalschachtklinker *m*

~ step iron [*B.S. 1247*] · Mannloch-Steigeisen *n*

~ ventilating cover for carriageways with through traffic, manway **~ ~ ~ ~ ~ ~ ~** · Schachtdeckel *m* mit Lüftungsöffnungen für Straßen mit Durchgangsverkehr [*DIN 4292*]

~ ~ ~ ~ ~ without through traffic, manway **~ ~ ~ ~ ~ ~ ~** · Schachtdeckel *m* mit Lüftungsöffnungen für Gehbahnen öffentlicher Verkehrswege [*DIN 1229*]

~ ~ ~ ~ ~ public footways accessible to wheeled and tracked vehicles, manway **~ ~ ~ ~ ~ ~ ~ ~** · Schachtdeckel *m* mit Lüftungsöffnungen für befahrbare Gehbahnen öffentlicher Verkehrswege [*DIN 4273*]

~ ~ ~ ~ ~ ~ inaccessible to wheeled and tracked vehicles, manway **~ ~ ~ ~ ~ ~ ~ ~ ~** · Schachtdeckel *m* mit Lüftungsöffnungen für Gehbahnen öffentlicher Verkehrswege [*DIN 1229*]

Manil(l)a copal · Manil(l)akopal *m*

~ fibre (Brit.); **~ fiber** (US) · Manil(la)faser *f*

~ hawser, ~ rope; grass rope (US) [*B.S. 2052*] · Manil(l)a-Hanfseil *n*, Manil(l)aseil

~ hemp, abacá · Abakahanf *m*, Musahanf, Bananenhanf, Manil(l)ahanf

manipulation · Handhabung *f*

manison, country **~,** manor house, manor-castle · Landsitz *m*

manlid, manhole cover, manway cover · Mannlochdeckel *m*, Schachtdeckel

man-made adhesive → synthetic (resin(-based)) (bonding) **~**

~ aggregate → **~** concrete **~**

~ asbestos, artificial **~** · künstlicher Asbest *m*

~ (bonding) adhesive → synthetic (resin(-based)) (**~**) **~**

~ ~ agent → synthetic (resin(-based)) (bonding) adhesive

~ ~ medium → synthetic (resin(-based)) (bonding) adhesive

~ **building material,** ~ construction ~, ~ structural ~ · Industriebaustoff *m*, Kunstbaustoff; Industriebaumaterial *n*, Kunstbaumaterial [*Schweiz*]

~ ~ **product** → manufactured construction(al) ~

~ **cement(ing agent)** → synthetic (resin(-based)) (bonding) adhesive

~ **coarse (concrete) aggregate,** artificial ~ (~) ~ · künstlicher (Beton-)Grobzuschlag(stoff) *m*, künstliches (Beton)Grobzuschlagmaterial *n*

~ **(concrete) aggregate,** artificial (~) ~ · künstlicher (Beton)Zuschlag(stoff) *m*, künstliches (Beton)Zuschlagmaterial *n*

~ **construction material,** ~ building ~, ~ structural ~ · Industriebaustoff *m*, Kunstbaustoff; Industriebaumaterial *n*, Kunstbaumaterial [*Schweiz*]

~ **construction(al) product** → manufactured ~ ~

~ **fibre** (Brit.); ~ fiber (US); synthetic ~ · Kunstfaser *f*, Chemiefaser

~ ~ **fabric** (Brit.); ~ fiber ~ (US); synthetic ~ ~ · Kunstfasergewebe *n*

~ ~ **material** (Brit.); ~ fiber ~ (US); synthetic ~ ~ · Kunstfaserstoff *m*

~ **fine (concrete) aggregate,** artificial ~ (~) ~ · künstlicher Feinzuschlag(-stoff) *m*, ~ Beton~

~ **glue** → synthetic (resin(-based)) (bonding) adhesive

~ **ground** → made(-up) ~

~ **marble,** manufactured ~, art(ificial) ~, imitation ~, marezzo · Kunstmarmor *m* [*Fehlnamen: künstlicher Marmor, Glanzstein m*]

~ **masonry unit** → artificial ~ ~

~ **plastic (material)** → synthetic ~ (~)

~ **pozzolan(ic material)** → artificial ~ (~)

~ **pozz(u)olana** → artificial pozzolan(ic material)

~ **resin,** artificial ~, manufactured ~, synthetic ~ · Kunstharz *n*, synthetisches Harz

~ **(resin(-based)) adhesive** → synthetic (resin(-based)) (bonding) ~

~ **rubber,** manufactured ~, synthetic ~ · Kunstgummi *m*, *n*, Synthesegummi, synthetischer Gummi *m*, synthetisches Gummi *n*

~ **structural material,** ~ building ~, ~ construction ~ · Industriebaustoff *m*, Kunstbaustoff; Industriebaumaterial *n*, Kunstbaumaterial [*Schweiz*]

~ ~ **product** → manufactured construction(al) ~

~ **travertine,** manufactured ~, artificial ~, imitation ~ · Kunsttravertin *m*

mannered · manieriert

Mannerism, Mannerist architecture · Manierismus *m*

Mannerist device · manieristisches Element *n*

~ **trait** · manieristischer Zug *m*

manor-castle, (country) manison, manor house · Landsitz *m*

mansard · halbschräger Dachraum *m*, Mansarde *f* [*Dachraum bei einem Mansard(en)dach*]

~ → ~ roof

~ **cornice moulding** (Brit.); ~ ~ molding (US) · Mansard(en)(ge)sims *m*, (*n*)

~ **dormer window** · Mansard(en)dachfenster *n* [*Bei einem halbschrägen Dachraum*]

~ **flat roof** (Brit.); deck ~ (US) [*It slopes in four directions, but has a deck at the top*] · Mansard(en)flachdach *n*

~ **(roof),** French ~; gambrel ~, gambril ~ (US) [*A roof with two pitches on each side of the ridge, the steeper commencing at the eaves and intersecting with a flatter pitch finishing at the ridge*] · Mansard(en)dach *n* [*Nach dem französischen Baumeister Jules Hardouin Mansart (1648–1708) benannt. Geknicktes Dach mit steiler Neigung im unteren Teil. Es ermöglicht halbschräge Dachräume = Mansarden*]

~ **(roof) truss** · Mansard(en)(dach)binder *m*

~ **(~) with braced king post resting on collar** · Mansard(en)dach *n* mit mit abgesprengter Firstsäule

~ **(~) ~ king post resting on tie beam** · Mansard(en)dach *n* mit durchgehender Firstsäule

~ **(~) ~ post and parapet** · Mansard(en)dach *n* mit stehendem Stuhl und Versenkung

~ **(~) ~ slanted struts and wind filling** · Mansard(en)dach *n* mit liegendem Stuhl und Versenkung

~ **truss,** ~ roof ~ · Mansard(en)(dach)-binder *m*

mantapam → mandapam

mantel(piece), mantle [*An ornamental frame of wood, metal, or stone around and above a fireplace, often having an 'overmantel' above it*] · Kaminrahmen *m*

mantel (shelf), overmantel [*The shelf above the mantelpiece*] · Kamin(ge)sims *m*, (*n*)

manual blending mixer → ~ (water) mixing valve

~ **fire alarm,** manually operated ~ ~ · Handfeuermelder *m*

~ **gas shut-off valve** · Hand-Gasabsperrschieber *m*

~ **mixer (valve)** → ~ (water) mixing ~

~ **mixing valve** → ~ water ~ ~

~ **operation,** hand ~ · Handbedienung *f*, Handbetätigung, Handbetrieb *m*

~ **plastering,** hand ~ · Hand(ver)putzen *n* [*Innenputz*]

~ **power,** hand ~ · Handkraft *f*

~ **rendering,** hand ~ · Hand(ver)putzen *n* [*Außenputz*]

manual riveting — manufacturing dimension

~ **riveting,** hand ~, riveting by hand · Handnieten *n* [*Von Hand geschlagene Nietung mit Handdöpper und Hammer*]

~ ~ **machine,** hand ~ ~ · Handnietmaschine *f*

~ **showermixer** → ~ (water) mixing valve

~ **switchroom** · Handamtsraum *m* [*Fernsprechzentrale*]

~ **(water) blending mixer** → ~ (~) mixing valve

~ **(~) mixer (valve)** → ~ (~) mixing ~

~ **(~) mixing valve,** non-thermostatic (~) ~ ~, ~ (~) mixer (~), ~ (~) showermixer, ~ (~) blending mixer [*B.S. 1415. Such a valve is used to mix cold water with hot water*] · Hand-Badebatterie *f*

~ **(~) showermixer** → ~ (~) mixing valve

manual(ly operated) fire alarm · Handfeuermelder *m*

manual(ly operated) furnace · handbediente Feuerung *f* [*Feuerbett wird von Hand geschürt und entschlackt*]

manually reset time switch · Handzeitschalter *m*

Manueline style, ~ architecture · (e)manueli(ni)scher Stil *m*, Emanuelstil [*Baustil zur Regierungszeit König Emanuels des Glücklichen (1495–1521) in Portugal*]

to manufacture, to make, to fabricate · fertigen, herstellen

manufacture, fabrication, making · Fertigung *f*, Herstellung, Fabrikation *f*

~ **of acetyline gas** · Acetylengewinnung *f*

~ ~ **bricks,** brickmaking · Ziegelherstellung *f*

~ ~ **lacquers** · Lackfarbenherstellung *f*

manufactured adhesive → synthetic (resin(-based)) (bonding) ~

~ **brick chip(ping)s** → ~ clay ~ ~

~ ~ **sand** → ~ clay ~ ~

~ **building product** → ~ construction(al) ~

~ **cement(ing agent)** → synthetic (resin(-based)) (bonding) adhesive

~ **(clay) brick chip(ping)s** · Trümmersplitt *m*, Ziegelsplitt

~ **(~) ~ sand** · Ziegelsand *m* [*DIN 4163*]

~ **coarse sand,** coarse manufactured ~ · Brechgrobsand *m*, Grobbrechsand

~ **construction(al) product,** ~ building ~, ~ structural ~, synthetic ~ ~, man-made ~ ~ [*e.g. concrete, brick, tile, steel, panel, alumin(i)um, block, plaster, mortar, etc.*] · synthetischer Baustoff *m*; synthetisches Baumaterial *n* [*Schweiz*]

~ **fine sand,** fine manufactured ~ · Brechfeinsand *m*, Feinbrechsand

~ **gas** · technisch hergestelltes Gas *n*

~ **glue** → synthetic (resin(-based)) (bonding) adhesive

~ **marble,** art(ificial) ~, man-made ~, imitation ~, marezzo · Kunstmarmor *m* [*Fehlnamen: künstlicher Marmor, Glanzstein m*]

~ **plastic (material)** → synthetic ~ (~)

~ **resin,** man-made ~, artificial ~, synthetic ~ · Kunstharz *n*, synthetisches Harz

~ **(resin(-based)) adhesive** → synthetic (resin(-based)) (bonding) ~

~ **(~) (bonding) adhesive** → synthetic (~) (~) ~

~ **(~) ~ agent** → synthetic (resin(-based)) (bonding) adhesive

~ **(~) ~ medium** → synthetic (resin(-based)) (bonding) adhesive

~ **(~) cement(ing agent)** → synthetic (resin(-based)) (bonding) adhesive

~ **(~) glue** → synthetic (resin(-based)) (bonding) adhesive

~ **rubber,** man-made ~, synthetic ~ · Kunstgummi *m, n*, Synthesegummi, synthetischer Gummi *m*, synthetisches Gummi *n*

~ **sand,** artificial ~, stone ~, crushed stone ~, (stone) screening(s), crusher screening(s) · Steinsand *m*, Brechsand [*Er umfaßt in den USA den Kornstufenbereich 0–4,76 mm*]

~ **structural product** → ~ construction(al) ~

~ **travertine.** man-made ~, artificial ~, imitation ~ · Kunsttravertin *m*

manufacturer, fabricator, producer, maker · Erzeuger *m*, Hersteller. Fabrikant *m*

manufacturer's certificate, maker's ~ · Herstellerzeugnis *n*

~ **instructions,** maker's ~ · Herstelleranweisungen *fpl*

~ **mark,** maker's ~ · Herstellerzeichen *n*

~ **test,** fabricators' ~, maker's ~ · Werkprobe *f*, Werkprüfung *f*, Werkversuch *m*

manufacturing, fabricating, making, fabrication · Fertigen *n*, Herstellen

~ **bay,** fabrication ~, fabricating ~ · Fabrikationsabteilung *f*, Herstellungsabteilung, Produktionsabteilung, Fertigungsabteilung

~ **cost(s),** fabrication ~, fabricating ~ · Herstellungskosten *f*, Fabrikationskosten, Produktionskosten, Fertigungskosten

~ **cycle,** fabrication ~, fabricating ~ · Herstellungszyklus *m*, Fabrikationszyklus, Produktionszyklus, Fertigungszyklus

~ **defect,** fabricating ~, fabrication ~ · Fabrikationsfehler *m*, Herstellungsfehler, Produktionsfehler, Fertigungsfehler

~ **dimension,** fabrication ~, fabricating ~ · Fertigungsabmessung *f*, Fertigungsmaß *n*, Herstellungabmessung, Herstellungsmaß, Fabrikationsabmessung, Fabrikationsmaß, Produktionsabmessung, Produktionsmaß

manufacturing drawing — marble grain mix(ture) 604

~ **drawing**, fabrication ~, fabricating ~ · Herstellungszeichnung f, Fabrikationszeichnung, Produktionszeichnung, Fertigungszeichnung

~ **hangar**, production ~ · Fertigungshalle f, Produktionshalle, Fabrikationshalle, Herstellungshalle

~ **method**, fabrication ~, fabricating ~ · Herstellungsverfahren n, Fabrikationsverfahren, Produktionsverfahren, Fertigungsverfahren

~ **plant**, fabrication ~, fabricating ~ · Herstellungsbetrieb m, Fabrikationsbetrieb, Produktionsbetrieb, Fertigungsbetrieb, Herstellerwerk n, Fertigungswerk, Produktionswerk

~ **process**, fabricating ~, fabrication ~ · Fertigungsprozeß m, Herstellungsprozeß, Fertigungsvorgang m, Herstellungsvorgang, Herstellungsverlauf m, Fertigungsverlauf, Fabrikationsprozeß, Fabrikationsvorgang, Fabrikationsverlauf, Produktionsprozeß, Produktionsverlauf, Produktionsvorgang

~ **program** (US); ~ programme (Brit.); fabrication ~, fabricating ~ · Fabrikationsprogramm n, Herstellungsprogramm, Fertigungsprogramm, Produktionsprogramm

~ **regulations** · Herstellungsbestimmungen fpl

~ **technique**, ~ technic, fabrication ~, fabricating ~ · Fertigungstechnik f, Herstellungstechnik, Fabrikationstechnik, Produktionstechnik

~ **technology**, fabrication ~, fabricating ~ · Herstellungstechnologie f, Fabrikationstechnologie, Produktionstechnologie, Fertigungstechnologie

~ **town**, industrial quarter, cité industrielle [Planned by Tony Garnier] · Industriestadt f

manway, manhole [A chamber with or without access shaft, constructed over a sewer or principal drain to permit inspection and access for cleaning and maintenance] · Schacht m, Einstieg(~) m, Mannloch n, Einsteigschacht, Manneinsteigloch, Manneinstieg(loch) m, (n)

~ **cover**, manhole ~, manlid · Mannlochdeckel m, Schachtdeckel

~ **covering**, manhole ~ · Schachtabdeckung f, Mannlochabdeckung [DIN 1229]

~ **frame**, manhole ~ · Mannlochrahmen m, Schachtrahmen

~ **head**, manhole ~ [The cast-iron fixture surmounting a manhole. It is made up of two parts: a frame which rests on the masonry of the shaft, and a removable cover. Frames are either fixed or adjustable in height. Covers are 'tight', 'ventilated', or 'anti-rattling'] · Schachtdeckel m und -rahmen m

~ **junction box**, manhole ~ ~ · Schachtkabelkasten m

~ **masonry (work)**, manhole ~ (~) · Mannlochmauerwerk n, Schachtmauerwerk

~ **ring**, manhole ~ · Zwischenring m [Fehlname]; Schachtring [DIN 4034]

~ **sewer brick**, manhole ~ ~ · Kanalschachtklinker m

~ **ventilating cover for public footways accessible to wheeled and tracked vehicles**, manhole ~ ~ ~ ~ ~ ~ ~ ~ ~ ~ ~ · Schachtdeckel m mit Lüftungsöffnungen für befahrbare Gehbahnen öffentlicher Verkehrswege [DIN 4273]

many-columned, polystyle · mehrsäulig, vielsäulig, säulenreich

many-gabled style · Vielgiebelstil m, Mehrgiebelstil ·

map of sewers · Kanalisationskarte f

maqsurah, enclosed space · Fürstenloge f, Maqsura f [Moschee]

to marble · marmorieren

marble · Marmorfigur f

~, mbl · Marmor m

~ **aggregate** · Marmorzuschlag(stoff) m, Marmorzuschlagmaterial n

~ **balda(c)chino** · Marmorbaldachin m

~ **beam** · Marmorbalken(träger) m

~ **bench** · Marmorbank f

~ **building** · Marmorgebäude n

~ **candelabrum** · Marmorkandelaber m

~ **chip(ping)s** · Marmorkörnungen fpl, Terrazzo-Körnungen aus Marmorvorkommen, Marmorsplitt m

~ **column** · Marmorsäule f

~ **Corinthian column** · korinthische Marmorsäule f

~ **cross** · Marmorkreuz n

~ **crypt** · Marmorkrypta f, Marmorgruft

~ **cutter** · Marmorhauer m

~ **decorative finish**, ~ ~ feature, ~ ornamental ~, ~ decoration, ~ enrichment · Marmorschmuck m, Marmorverzierung f

~ **door** · Marmortür f

~ **dressing** · Marmorbearbeitung f

~ **dust** → ~ flour

~ **effect** → marble(ize)d ~

~ **enrichment** → ~ decorative finish

~ **façade** · Marmorfassade f

~ **facing** → ~ lining

~ **filter gravel** · Marmor-Filterkies m

~ **fireplace** · Marmorkamin m

~ **floor(ing) (finish)**, ~ floor cover(ing), ~ pavement · Marmor(platten)-(fuß)boden(belag) m, Fbm

~ **flour**, ~ dust, ~ powder, powder(ed) marble · Marmormehl n, Marmorstaub m, Marmorpulver n

~ **frieze** · Marmorfries m

~ **grain mix(ture)**, mixed marble grains, mix(ture) of marble grains · Marmorkörnergemisch n, Marmorkorngemisch, Marmorkörnung f

marble gravel — marine paint

~ **gravel** · Marmorkies *m*

~ **grille** [*sometimes spelled 'grill'*] · Marmorgitter *n*

~ **inlay** · Marmoreinlegearbeit

~ ~ · Marmoreinlage *f*

~ **lining,** ~ (sur)facing; ~ panelling (Brit.); ~ paneling (US) · Marmorverkleidung *f*, Marmorauskleidung, Marmorbekleidung, Marmorbelag *m*

~ **masonry (work)** · Marmormauerwerk *n*

~ **mosaic** · Marmormosaik *n*

~ **ornament** · Marmorornament *n*

~ **ornamental finish** → ~ decorative ~

Marble Palace at Leningrad · Marmorpalast *m* in Leningrad

marble panel · Marmortafel *f*

~ **panelling** (Brit.) → ~ lining

~ **pattern** → marble(ize)d ~

~ **pavement** · Marmorplattenpflaster *n*

~ ~ → ~ floor(ing) (finish)

~ **plaster,** mixed ~ ~ · Marmorputz *m*

~ **plate,** ~ slab · Marmorplatte *f*

~ **polishing machine** · Marmorpoliermaschine *f*

~ ~ **material** · Marmorpoliermittel *n*

~ **powder** → ~ flour

~ **pulpit** · Marmorkanzel *f*

~ **quadriga** · Marmorviergespann *n*

~ **quarry** · Marmorbruch *m*

~ **relief** · Marmorrelief *n*

~ **roof** · Marmordach *n*

~ **roof(ing) slab** · Marmordachplatte *f*

~ (~) **tile** · Marmor(dach)stein *m*

~ **sarcophagus** · Marmorsarkophag *m*

~ **sawing plant** · Marmorsägewerk *n*, Marmorsägerei *f*

~ **setter** · Marmor(ver)leger *m*

~ **shaft** · Marmordienst *m*

~ ~ · Marmorschaft *m*

~ **slab,** ~ plate · Marmorplatte *f*

~ ~ **(stair) tread** · Marmortritt(stufe) *m*, (*f*)

~ **sphinx** · Marmorsphinx *f*

~ **(statue)** · Marmorstatue *f*

~ **structure** · Marmorbauwerk *n*

~ **stucco,** stuccolustro · Marmorstuck(putz) *m*, Stuccolustro *m*, Stuckmarmor *m* [*Flächenstuck, der polierten Marmor nachahmt. Er besteht aus Weißkalk, Marmorstaub, Alabaster und Gips*]

~ **sunblind,** ~ sunbreaker · Marmor-Sonnen(schutz)blende *f*

~ **(sur)facing** → ~ lining

~ **tabernacle** · Marmortabernakel *n*

~ **texture** → marble(ize)d ~

~ **throne** · Marmorthron *m*

~ **tile** · Marmor(belag)platte *f*, Marmorfliese

~ ~, ~ roof(ing) ~ · Marmor(dach)stein *m*

~ **wall** · Marmorwand *f*

~ **window sill;** ~ ~ cill (Brit.) · Marmorfensterbank *f*, Marmorsohlbank

~ **work** · Marmorarbeiten *fpl*

marbled effect → marble(ize)d ~

~ **pattern** → marble(ize)d ~

~ **texture** → marble(ize)d ~

marble(ize)d · jaspiert

~ · marmoriert

~ **effect,** ~ pattern, ~ texture, marble ~ · Marmorierung *f*, Marmormusterung

~ **lino(leum)** · Marmorlinoleum *n*

~ **pattern,** ~ texture, ~ effect, marble ~ · Marmorierung *f*, Marmormusterung

~ **texture,** ~ pattern, ~ effect, marble ~ · Marmorierung *f*, Marmormusterung

marbling [*Imitating with finishing materials the figure and texture of polished marble or other decorative stones*] · Marmorieren *n*

marcasite, white iron pyrites · Kammkies *m*, Sperrkies, Markasit *m*, FeS$_2$

marezzo, imitation marble, manufactured marble, art(ificial) marble, man-made marble · Kunstmarmor *m* [*Fehlnamen: künstlicher Marmor, Glanzstein m*]

margin, deviation, off-size · Abmaß *n*, Maßabweichung *f*, Genauigkeitsgrad *m* [*DIN 18201. Der Unterschied zwischen Grenz- und Nennmaß*]

~ **of safety** · Sicherheitsspanne *f*

marginal (clay) tile (for gables) · Bordziegel *m*, Saumziegel, Kanten(dach)ziegel

~ **condition,** fringe ~, edge ~, boundary ~ · Randbedingung *f*

~ **tile (for gables)** · Bordstein *m*, Saumstein, Kanten(dach)stein

~ **torque moment,** ~ torsion(al) ~, ~ twist(ing) ~, fringe ~ ~, edge ~ ~, boundary ~ ~ · Randdrillmoment *n*, Randtorsionsmoment, Randverdrehungsmoment, Randverwindungsmoment

~ **torsion(al) moment,** ~ twist(ing) ~, ~ torque ~, fringe ~ ~, edge ~ ~, boundary ~ ~ · Randdrillmoment *n*, Randtorsionsmoment, Randverdrehungsmoment, Randverwindungsmoment

~ **twist(ing) moment,** ~ torsion(al) ~, ~ torque ~, fringe ~ ~, edge ~ ~, boundary ~ ~ · Randdrillmoment *n*, Randtorsionsmoment, Randverdrehungsmoment, Randverwindungsmoment

marine atmosphere · Meer(es)atmosphäre *f*

~ **clay** · Meer(es)ton *m*

~ **concrete** · Seebaubeton *m*

~ **glue** · Marineleim *m*

~ **gravel** · Meer(es)kies *m*

~ **paint** · Schiffsfarbe *f*

marine terminus building — masonry

~ **terminus building** · Schiffahrtsgebäude *n*

~ **timber** · Seebauholz *n*

mark · Kennzeichen *n* [*Baustoff*]

~ → (registered) trade~

~ → signboard

to mark · kennzeichnen

~ ~ **by chalk line** · abkreiden, abschnüren

market building · Marktgebäude *n*

~ **church** · Marktkirche *f*

~ **cross** · Markt(platz)kreuz *n*

market-garden · Marktgemüsegarten *m*, Gärtnerei *f*

market hall, covered market, roofed market, indoor market · (Markt)Halle *f*

Market of Caesar and Augustus · Bazar *m* [*Agora von Athen*]

market place, agora, town square · Agora *f*, Markt(platz) *m* [*Platz einer griechischen Stadt im Altertum, auf dem Versammlungen und Märkte abgehalten wurden*]

market-place, market-stead, square · Marktplatz *m*

market-stead, market-place, square · Marktplatz *m*

market town · Marktstadt *f*

marking · Kennzeichnung *f*

~ · Musterung *f* [*Linoleum*]

~ **chalk** · Signierkreide *f*

~ **composition** → (road) marking compound

~ **compound** → road ~ ~

~ **material** · Markierungsstoff *m*

~ **out**, scribing · Anreißen *n*, (Zu)Reißen, Anzeichnen, Anriß *m* [*Werkstücke*]

~ ~ **dimension**, scribing ~ · Anreißmaß *n*, Anrißmaß, (Zu)Reißmaß, Anzeichnungsmaß [*Werkstücke*]

~ **paint**, road ~ ~, road-line ~ · (Straßen)Markierungsfarbe *f*

marl · Mergel *m*

marly clay · Mergelton *m* [*4–10% CaCO₃*]

~ **limestone** · merg(e)liger Kalkstein *m*, Mergelkalk(stein) *m* [*90–96% CaCO₃*]

~ **sandstone** · Mergelsandstein *m*

marque, proprietary product · Markenartikel *m*, Markenerzeugnis *n*, Markenfabrikat *n*

marquee · Zeltbau *m*

marqueterie → inlay

marquetry → inlay

marquise, outside awning blind · Markise *f*

marriage-gate → bride-door

married quarters · Familienunterkünfte *fpl*

Marseilles pattern tile → Ludowici ~

Marshall (cylindrical) test-head · Marshall-Prüfpresse *f*

~ **flow value** · Fließwert *m* nach Marshall, Marshall-Fließwert

Marshall stability · Marshall-Stabilität *f*

Marshall test · Marshall-Prüfung *f*, Marshall-Probe *f*, Marshall-Versuch *m*

~ ~ **specimen** · Marshall-Probekörper *m*

martempering · gestuftes Härten *n*, Warmbadhärten, Thermalhärten

martensitic component, ~ constituent · martensitischer Bestandteil *m*

~ **stainless steel** · martensitischer (rostfreier) Edelstahl *m*

~ **steel** · martensitischer Stahl *m*

~ **structure** · martensitische Struktur *f*, martensitischer Aufbau *m*, martensitisches Gefüge *n*

martyrium, commemorative church, memorial church · Coemetrialkirche *f*, Martyria *f*, Memoria(lkirche) *f*, Denkmalkirche, Gedächtniskirche, Memorienkirche [*Kirche auf oder in einem Coemeterium, meist nahe oder über einem Märtyrergrab*]

~ → commemorative basilica

Masjid-i-Juma → Friday mosque

to mask · unsichtbar machen [*Fuge*]

mask of beaten gold · Goldmaske *f*

masking · (Ab)Decken *n* [*Schutzabdeckung bei Anstricharbeiten*]

~ **film**, ~ sheeting · (Ab)Deckfolie *f* [*Anstrichtechnik*]

~ **frame** · Manschette *f* [*für Aufputz-Verteilungsschrank*]

~ **material** · Abdeckmittel *n* [*zur Schutzabdeckung bei Anstricharbeiten*]

~ **paper** · (Ab)Deckpapier *n* [*Als Bauhilfsstoff werden (Ab)Deckpapiere am häufigsten von Putzern, Anstreichern und Tapezierern verwendet, um (Fuß)Böden usw. bei nachträglichen Arbeiten an Decken und Wänden vor dem Verschmutzen zu bewahren. Mitunter „Schrenzpappe" oder „Schrenzpapier" genannt*]

~ **sheeting**, ~ film · (Ab)Deckfolie *f* [*Anstrichtechnik*]

~ **tape**, joint ~ ~ · Fugen(ab)deckband *n*, (Ab)Deckband

~ ~, adhesive ~ ~ · (Ab)Deckband *n* [*Anstrichtechnik*]

mason, brick ~ (US); bricklayer · Maurer *m*

mason-architect, master-mason · Baumeister *m* im Mittelalter

masoned cast stone, ~ reconstructed ~, ~ patent ~; ~ artificial ~ [*deprecated*] [*Cast stone, after reaching a mature state, treated by hand or by machine to produce surfaces commonly used for natural stone – e.g. boasted, bush-hammered, sparrow pecked, tooled and rubbed*] · Betonwerkstein *m* mit bearbeiteter Sichtfläche

Masonite board · Masonit-Platte *f*

masonry, ~ work · Mauerwerk *n* [*DIN 1053*]

(masonry) anchor — masonry painting

(~) anchor → ~ wall ~

~ anchorage · Mauerwerkverankerung f

~ apartment tower (US) → ~ (work) residence ~

~ arch, ~ work ~ · gemauerter Bogen m, Mauerwerkbogen

~ back-up, backing (masonry), back-up (masonry) · Hintermauerung f, Hintermauerwerk n

~ block → ~ (building) tile

~ ~ → ~ (work) building

(~) bond · (Mauerwerk)Gefüge n, (Mauerwerk)Verband m, Mauerverband, Mauergefüge

(~) ~ principles · Verbandsregeln fpl

(~) ~ type, type of (masonry) bond · (Mauer)Verbandsart f

(~) bracket → (~) corbel

(~) brick · (gebrannter) Mauer(werk)stein m, Mauer(werk)ziegel m [DIN 105. „Backstein" ist eine historische und volkstümliche Bezeichnung]

(~) ~ for chimney shafts, (~) ~ ~ free-standing ~ · (gebrannter) Mauer(werk)stein m für freistehende Schornsteine, Mauer(werk)ziegel m ~ ~ ~

~ bridge, ~ work ~ · gemauerte Feuerbrücke f, Mauerwerkfeuerbrücke [Teil einer Feuerung]

~ building → ~ work ~

~ (~) block → ~ (~) tile

~ (~) component → (structural) masonry (building) unit

~ (~) member → (structural) masonry (building) unit

~ (~) tile, ~ (~) block [See remark under 'Block'] · (gebundener) Mauer(werk)block(stein) m, (~) Mauer(werk)stein

~ (~) unit → structural ~ (~) ~

(~) cavity tie, (~) (wall) ~, (~) (wall) anchor · (Mauer)Anker m, Mauer(werk)haken m, Mauerwerkanker

~ cement, mortar ~, cementing material for masonry · Fugenmörtelzement m, Mauerwerkbinder m, Mauermörtelzement, Mauerwerkzement, PM-Binder, (Putz- und) Mauer(werk)binder

~ chimney, ~ work ~ · gemauerter Schornstein m, Mauerwerkschornstein

~ cleaning → ~ work ~

~ clean(s)er, clean(s)er for masonry · Mauerwerkreinigungsmittel n, Mauerwerkreiniger m, Mauerwerkreinigungsstoff m

~ component → (structural) masonry (building) unit

~ conduit-type sewer · gemauerter Abwasserkanal m, Mauerwerk-Abwasserkanal

~ construction, ~ work ~ · Mauerwerkbau m

~ ~ → ~ (structural) system

(~) corbel, (~) bracket, (~) shoulder [A cantilevered bracket generally formed by one or more courses of masonry projecting to form a bearing for supporting a load] · (Mauerwerk)Konsole f

(~) course, ~ work ~ [A horizontal layer of masonry units such as brick, tile, stone, or other materials, as they are laid in a masonry wall] · (Mauerwerk)Schar f, (Mauerwerk)Schicht f, (Mauerwerk)Lage f

~ cupola → ~ (work) dome

~ diaphragm, ~ work ~ · gemauerte Scheibe f, Mauerwerkscheibe

~ dome → ~ work ~

~ donjon → ~ work ~

~ dowel · Mauerwerkdübel m, Steindübel

~ drill · Mauerwerkbohrer m

~ duct → ~ work ~

~ dungeon → ~ work ~

~ dwelling tower → ~ work residence ~

~ facing material, ~ lining ~ · Mauerwerkverblendmaterial n

~ failure test → ~ work ~ ~

~ fastener, ~ fixing · Mauerwerk-Befestigungsmittel n

~-filled · ausgefacht mit Mauerwerk, ausgemauert

masonry fireplace · Mauerwerkkamin m

~ fixing, ~ fastener · Mauerwerk-Befestigungsmittel n

~ footing wall, footing masonry ~ · Fundamentmauer f

~ foundation wall, foundation masonry ~ · Grundmauer f, Gründungsmauer

~ high flats → ~ (work) residence tower

~ joint, ~ work ~ · Mauer(werk)fuge f

~ joints of different colo(u)rs · abgesetzte Fugen fpl [Verschieden gefärbte Stoß- und Lagerfugen]

~ keep → ~ work ~

~ layer → ~ work ~

~ leaf → ~ (work) layer

~ lining → ~ work ~

~ ~ material, ~ facing ~ · Mauerwerkverblendmaterial n

~ mass, mass of masonry · Mauerwerkmasse f

~ material · Mauerwerkstoff m

~ member → (structural) masonry (building) unit

~ moisture seal(ing agent), ~ work ~ ~, (~) · Mauerwerk-Imprägnier(ungs)mittel n

~ mortar → ~ joint(ing) ~

~ nail · Mauernagel m

~ opening, ~ work ~ · Mauerwerköffnung f

~ paint · Mauerwerk(anstrich)farbe f

~ painting · Anstreichen n von Mauerwerk

~ **panel** · Mauerwerktafel f
~ **partition (wall)** · Steinwand f [*Leichte Trennwand. DIN 4103. Aus Ziegeln oder Leichtsteinen gemauert*]
~ **pier**, ~ work ~ · gemauerter Pfeiler m, Mauerwerkpfeiler
(~) **platform**, (~) podium · hoher Unterbau m, Podium n [*antike Baukunst*]
(~) ~ **temple**, (~) podium ~ · Podientempel m, Podiumtempel [*Frontseitig ausgerichteter Tempel auf hohem Unterbau*]
(~) **podium**, (~) platform · hoher Unterbau m, Podium n [*antike Baukunst*]
(~) ~ **temple**, (~) platform ~ · Podientempel m, Podiumtempel [*Frontseitig ausgerichteter Tempel auf hohem Unterbau*]
~ **principle** · Mauerregel f
~ **reinforcement** → ~ work ~
~ **residence tower** → ~ work ~ ~
~ **residential tower** → ~ work residence ~
~ **sand** · Mau(r)ersand m
~ **screen**, ~ work ~ · gemauerte Sichtblende f, Mauerwerk-Sichtblende
~ **seepage pit** · Mauerwerksickergrube f
~ **shell** → ~ (work) layer
(~) **shoulder** → (~) corbel
~ **silo**, ~ work ~ · gemauerter Silo m, gemauertes ~ n, Mauerwerksilo
~ **skin** → ~ (work) layer
~ **stone** · (natürlicher) Mauer(werk)stein m, Natur-Mauer(werk)stein
~ **strength**, ~ work ~ · Mauerwerkfestigkeit f
~ **(structural) system**, ~ construction · Mauerwerkkonstruktion(ssystem) f, (n)
~ **structure**, ~ work ~ · gemauertes Bauwerk n, Mauerwerkbauwerk
~ **structures**, ~ work ~ · gemauerte Bauten f, Mauerwerkbauten
~ **style**, ~ work ~ · Mauerwerkstil m
~ **system** → ~ structural ~
~ **tall block (of flats)** → ~ (work) residence tower
~ ~ **flats** → ~ (work) residence tower
~ **technique** → ~ work ~
~ **tie** → ~ wall ~
~ **tier** → ~ (work) layer
~ **tile** → ~ building ~
~ **tomb**, ~ work ~ · gemauertes Grab n, Mauerwerkgrab
~ **treatment**, ~ work ~ · Mauerwerkbehandlung f
~ **type**, type of masonry · Mauerwerkart f
~ **unit** → (structural) masonry (building) ~
~ **wall** · Mauer f [*Fehlname: gemauerte Wand f*]

(~) (~) **anchor**, (~) ~ **tie**, (~) cavity tie ~ · (Mauer)Anker m, Mauer(werk)haken m, Mauerwerkanker
~ ~ **base** · Mauerfuß m
~ ~ **beam** · Mauerbalken m
(~) ~ **block** → (~) ~ building ~
~ ~ **breakthrough** · Mauerdurchbruch m
(~) (~) **brick** · Mauerziegel m
(~) ~ **(building) block**, (~) ~ (~) tile [*See remark under 'Block'*] · Mauer(bau)stein m, Mauer(bau)block(-stein) m, Wand(bau)stein m, Wand(bau)block(stein) [*Fehlnamen*]
~ ~ **capping**, ~ ~ coping · Mauerabwässerung f, Mauerabdeckung
~ ~ ~ **brick**, ~ ~ coping ~ · Mauer(ab)deckziegel m
~ ~ ~ **slab**, ~ ~ coping ~ · Mauer(ab)deckplatte f [*DIN 455*]
~ ~ **center line** (US); ~ ~ centre ~ (Brit.) · Mauerachse f
~ ~ **construction** · Mauerbau m
~ ~ **coping**, ~ ~ capping [*A construction designed to protect the top of a masonry wall, usually overhanging the surface below*] · Mauerabdeckung f, Mauerabwässerung
~ ~ ~ **brick**, ~ ~ capping ~ · Mauer(ab)deckziegel m
~ ~ ~ **slab**, ~ ~ capping ~ · Mauer(ab)deckplatte f [*DIN 455*]
~ ~ **core** · Mauerkern m
~ ~ **course** · Mauerlage f, Mauerschicht
~ ~ **crack** · Mauerriß m
~ ~ **crossing**, crossing of masonry walls · Mauerkreuzung f
~ ~ **crown**, ~ ~ top · Mauerkrone f
~ ~ **dissolution**, dissolution of the masonry wall · Mauerauflösung f, Auflösung der Mauer
~ ~ **element** · Mauerelement n
~ ~ **enclosure** · Ummauerung f
~ ~ **flashing** [*See remark under 'Anschluß'*] · Maueranschluß m
~ ~ ~ **(piece)** · Maueranschluß(streifen) m
~ ~ **footing** · Mauerfundament n
~ ~ **head** · Mauerkopf m, Mauerhaupt n
~ ~ **hollow**, ~ ~ recess · Mauervertiefung f
~ ~ **insulation** · Mauerisolierung f
~ ~ **junction**, junction of masonry walls · Maueranschluß m
~ ~ ~ **brick** · Maueranschlußziegel m
~ ~ **length** · Mauerlänge f
~ ~ **line** · Mauerflucht f
~ ~ **lining** · Mauerbekleidung f, Mauerauskleidung, Mauerverkleidung
~ ~ **material** · Mauerbaumaterial n [*Schweiz*]; Mauerbaustoff m
~ ~ **niche** · Mauernische f

masonry wall opening — masonry (work) shell

~ ~ opening · Maueröffnung f

~ wall-pointing machine · Mauerfuggerät n

~ wall recess, ~ ~ hollow · Mauervertiefung f

~ ~ skin · Mauerdichtung f [Unterkellerung]

~ ~ slot · Mauerschlitz m

~ ~ stability · Mauerstabilität f

~ ~ strength · Mauerfestigkeit f

~ ~ system · Mauerkonstruktion f

~ ~ thickness · Mauerdicke f [Fehlname: Mauerstärke f]

(~) (~) tie, (~) cavity ~, (~) (~) anchor · (Mauer)Anker m, Mauer(werk)haken m, Mauerwerkanker

(~) ~ tile → (~) ~ (building) block

~ ~ top, ~ ~ crown · Mauerkrone f

~ ~ tower · Mauerturm m

~ ~ wing · Mauerflügel m

~ water tower, ~ work ~ ~ · gemauerter Wasserturm m, Mauerwerk-Wasserturm

~ withe → ~ (work) layer

~ work · Maurerarbeiten fpl [DIN 18330]

~ (~) · Mauerwerk n [DIN 1053]

~ (~) (angle) bead, (angle) ~ · (Mauer)Kantenschützer m, (Mauer-)Kantenschoner, (Mauer)Kantenschutzwinkel m

~ (~) apartment tower (US) → ~ (~) residence ~

~ (~) arch · gemauerter Bogen m, Mauerwerkbogen

~ (~) bead, ~ (~) angle ~, (angle) ~ · (Mauer)Kantenschützer m, (Mauer-)Kantenschoner, (Mauer)Kantenschutzwinkel m

~ (~) bridge · gemauerte Feuerbrücke f, Mauerwerkfeuerbrücke [Teil einer Feuerung]

~ (~) building, ~ (~) block · Mauerwerkgebäude n

~ (~) chimney · gemauerter Schornstein m, Mauerwerkschornstein

~ (~) cleaning · Mauerwerkreinigung f

~ (~) construction · Mauerwerkbau m

~ (~) ~ type, ~ (~) type of construction · Mauerwerkbauart f

~ (~) course → (~) course

~ (~) cupola → ~ (~) dome

~ (~) diaphragm · gemauerte Scheibe f, Mauerwerkscheibe

~ (~) dome, ~ (~) cupola · gemauerte Kuppel f, Mauerwerkkuppel

~ (~) donjon, ~ (~) keep, ~ (~) dungeon · Mauerwerkdonjon m, Mauerwerkbergfried m, Mauerwerkbelfried, Mauerwerkberchfrit m

~ (~) duct · Mauerwerkkanal m [Luftanlage; Klimaanlage]

~ (~) dungeon, ~ (~) keep, ~ (~) donjon · Mauerwerkdonjon m, Mauerwerkbergfried m, Mauerwerkbelfried, Mauerwerkberchfrit m

~ (~) dwelling tower → ~ (~) residence ~

~ (~) facing → ~ (~) lining

~ (~) failure test · Mauerwerkbruchprobe f, Mauerwerkbruchprüfung f, Mauerwerkbruchversuch m

~ (~) haunching · Ummauerung f [Abdichten von Rohrstößen im Erdreich]

~ (~) high (rise) block (of flats) → ~ (~) residence tower

~ (~) ~ (~) flats → ~ (~) residence tower

~ (~) joint · Mauer(werk)fuge f

~ (~) keep, ~ (~) donjon, ~ (~) dungeon · Mauerwerkdonjon m, Mauerwerkbergfried m, Mauerwerkbelfried, Mauerwerkberchfrit m

~ (~) layer, ~ (~) leaf, ~ (~) wythe, ~ (~) withe, ~ (~) tier, ~ (~) shell, ~ (~) skin [Each continuous vertical section of a masonry wall one masonry unit in thickness] · Mauer(werk)schale f

~ (~) leaf → ~ (~) layer

~ (~) lining, ~ (~) (sur)facing · Mauerwerkauskleidung f, Mauerwerkverkleidung, Mauerwerkbekleidung

~ (~) metal (angle) bead, metal (~) ~ · (Mauer)Kantenschützer m aus Metall, Mauerwerkkantenschutzwinkel m ~, (Mauer)Kantenschoner ~

~ (~) ~ bead → ~ (~) ~ angle ~

~ (~) moisture seal(ing agent) · Mauerwerk-Imprägnier(ungs)mittel n

~ (~) of parallelepipedal cut stones · Quader(stein)mauerwerk n [Die Steine werden nach Plan aus großen Blöcken herausgeschnitten, nach Plan bearbeitet und mit Mörtel verlegt]

~ (~) ~ vertical coring (clay) bricks · Hochlochziegel-Mauerwerk n

~ (~) opening · Mauerwerköffnung f

~ (~) pier · gemauerter Pfeiler m, Mauerwerkpfeiler

~ (~) reinforcement, ~ (~) reinforcing · Mauerwerkarmierung f, Mauerwerkbewehrung, Mauerwerk(stahl)-einlagen fpl

~ (~) residence tower, ~ (~) residential ~, ~ (~) dwelling ~; ~ (~) high (rise) block (of flats), ~ (~) high (rise) flats, ~ (~) tall block (of flats), ~ (~) tall flats (Brit.); ~ (~) apartment tower (US) · Mauerwerk-Wohnhochhaus n, gemauertes Wohnhochhaus, Mauerwerk-Hochwohnhaus, gemauertes Hochwohnhaus, Mauerwerk-Wohnturm m, gemauerter Wohnturm

~ (~) screen · gemauerte Sichtblende f, Mauerwerk-Sichtblende

~ (~) shell → ~ (~) layer

masonry (work) silo — Master of the work

~ (~) silo · gemauerter Silo m, gemauertes ~ n, Mauerwerksilo

~ (~) skin → ~ (~) layer

~ (~) strength · Mauerwerkfestigkeit f

~ (~) structure · gemauertes Bauwerk n, Mauerwerkbauwerk

~ (~) structures · gemauerte Bauten f, Mauerwerkbauten

~ (~) style · Mauerwerkstil m

~ (~) (sur)facing → ~ (~) lining

~ (~) tall block (of flats) → ~ (~) residence tower

~ (~) technique, ~ (~) technic · Mauerwerktechnik f

~ (~) tier → ~ (~) layer

~ (~) tomb · gemauertes Grab n, Mauerwerkgrab

~ (~) treatment · Mauerwerkbehandlung f

~ (~) type, type of masonry (work) · Mauerwerkart f

~ (~) ~ of construction, ~ (~) construction type · Mauerwerkbauart f

~ (~) water tower · gemauerter Wasserturm m, Mauerwerk-Wasserturm

~ (~) withe → ~ (~) layer

~ (~) wythe → ~ (~) layer

mason's guild · Freimaurerbrüderschaft f

~ lodge, stone ~ ~ · Bauhütte f

~ mark, stone ~ ~ · Steinmetzzeichen n

mass, material, composition, compound · Masse f [*Erzeugnis*]

~ concrete → massive ~

~ ~ structure → massive ~ ~

~ element, ~ point · Massenpunkt m

~ fabrication → ~ production

~ element, ~ point · Massenpunkt m

~ fabrication → ~ production

~ housing · Volkswohnungen fpl

~ law · Massengesetz n

~ of air [*The frequency of resonance is determined by the mass of air in the neck resonating in conjunction with the compliance of the air in the cavity*)] · Luftpfropfen m [*Resonator*]

~ ~ masonry, masonry mass · Mauerwerkmasse f

~ point, ~ element · Massenpunkt m

(mass-produced) asbestos-cement ware; (~) cement asbestos ~ (US) · Asbestzementware(n) f(pl)

(~) light(weight) (pre)cast (concrete) ware · Leichtbetonware(n) f, Leichtbetonzeug n

(~) (pre)cast (concrete) ware, (~) ~ (~) goods, (~) ~ (~) articles, (~) ~ (~) products, concrete ware, concrete goods, concrete articles, concrete products · Betonartikel mpl, Betonware(n) f, Betongegenstände mpl, Betonerzeugnisse npl; Zementware(n) [*Schweiz*]

(~) sintered ware · Sinterware(n) f, Sinterzeug n [*Durch Brennvorgang erzeugte Tonware(n) gebrannt bis zur Sinterung*]

mass production, ~ fabrication, day-to-day ~ · laufende Fertigung f, ~ Herstellung, ~ Fabrikation, Massenherstellung, Massenfertigung, Massenproduktion

massage room · Massageraum m

massicot [*Yellow lead oxid(e)*] · Bleigelb n

massing, volume, building mass, structural mass · Baumasse f

~ · Baukörper m, Raumkörper

mass(ive) concrete, bulk ~, concrete-in-mass · Massenbeton m

~ ~ structure, bulk ~ ~, concrete-in-mass ~ · Massenbetonbauwerk n

(~) gypsum, natural ~, raw ~; gypsum rock, plaster rock, plaster stone, potter's stone (Brit.) · Rohgips m, Naturgips m, Gipsstein m, Gipsgestein n. CaSO$_4$·2H$_2$O

~ masonry wall · wuchtige Mauer f

~ pier · ungegliederter Pfeiler m

~ wall · wuchtige Wand f

massively grouped · massiv gruppiert

mast · Mast m

~ (US) → (lighting) column (Brit.)

~ arm (US); column bracket (Brit.) · Mastausleger m

~ extension · Mastverlängerung f

Mast (impact-)driven concrete pile · Betonrammpfahl m System Mast, Mast-Betonrammpfahl

mast mold (US); ~ mould (Brit.) · Mast(en)form f

~ section · Mastschuß m

~ with arm → lighting ~ ~ ~

~ ~ two arms (US); (lighting) column with two brackets (Brit.) · Doppelausleger-(Licht)Mast m

mastaba(h) (tomb), ~ mound · Mastaba f

master bedroom · Hauptschlafzimmer n

~ carpenter · Zimmermeister m

~ clock · Hauptuhr f, Zentraluhr

master-designer · Formmeister m

master key, MK · Hauptschlüssel m

master-keyed lock · Hauptschlüsselschloß n

~ series, series of master-keyed locks · Hauptschlüsselanlage f

master-mason, mason-architect · Baumeister m im Mittelalter

master mould, upper ~ (Brit.); ~ mold (US) · Mutterform f [*Ziegelindustrie*]

Master of the Kings' Masons to Windsor Castle · Meister m der kgl. Bauhütte von Schloß Windsor

~ ~ ~ work · Werkbaumeister m [*im mittelalterlichen Kathedralenbau*]

master-piece — matched (floor) boarding

master-piece · Meisterwerk n, Hauptwerk

master plan · Generalplan m

~ **radio antenna,** central receiving radio aerial · Gemeinschaftsrundfunkantenne f

~ **suite,** adult ~ [*These rooms are separated from the children's bedrooms and the family rooms*] · Erwachsenenräume mpl

~ **television antenna,** central receiving T.V. aerial · Gemeinschaftsfernsehantenne f

~ **traffic plan** · Generalverkehrsplan m

mastic → ~ joint sealer

~ · Mastix(harz) m, (n)

~ **asphalt** [*B. S. 1446*]; asphalt(ic) mastic (US) · Bitumenmastix m, (Asphalt)Mastix

~ ~ **for jointless floor(s),** ~ ~ ~ ~ flooring(s) · Gußasphaltestrich m [*als Baustoff*]

~ ~ **jointless floor(ing)** · Gußasphaltestrich m [*als verlegter Baustoff*]

(~) ~ roof(ing), (~) ~ roof cover(ing) · Mastixdach(belag) n, (m)

~ **block** · Asphaltbrot n, Naturasphalt-Mastixbrot, (Asphalt)Mastixbrot

~ **cement** · Mastixzement m

~ **composition** → ~ system

~ **filler** · Mastixvergußmasse f

~ **in drops** · auserlesenes Mastixharz n, auserlesener Mastix m

~ **joint** · Mastixfuge f

~ ~ **sealer,** (building) mastic · plastische Fugen(ab)dicht(ungs)masse f, ~ Fugenmasse, ~ (Fugen)(Ver)Füllmasse, plastischer (Fugen)(Ver)Füller m, Fugen(ab)dicht(ungs)kitt m, (Ver-)Füllkitt, (Fugen)Kitt, (Fugen)Mastix, (Ab)Dicht(ungs)mastix

~ **jointing** → ~ pointing

~ **membrane** · Mastixhaut f

~ **pointing,** ~ jointing · Mastixausfugung f, Mastixverfugung Mastixfugenausfüllung

~ **seal(ing)** · Mastixabsieg(e)lung f, Mastixversieg(e)lung

~ **system,** ~ composition [*A finishing system for piping, comprising a primer, asphalt paint, mineral filler and whitewash*] · Aufbau m, System n

mat [*A grid of reinforcing bars*] · Stabmatte f

~ → reinforcing ~

~, **building** ~ [*It has a low density*] · (Bau)Matte f, Dämmatte

~ [*A glass fibre product having the texture of felt*] · Glasvlies n [*DIN 52141*]; Glasvließ [*Österreich*]

~, **pad** · Matte f [*allgemein*]

~, **flat** [*The description of a painted surface which scatters or absorbs the light falling on it, so as to be substantially free from gloss or sheen*] · matt

~ **cutting** · Mattschliff m [*Hohlglas*]

~ **enamel,** flat ~ · Mattemaillelack m

mat-etching paste · Streichmatt n [*Glasbehandlung*]

~ **salt** [*Usually ammonium fluoride*] · Mattsalz n [*Glasbehandlung*]

mat finish, flat ~ [*A term applied to surfaces free from gloss or polish*] · mattes Aussehen n

~ ~ **paint,** flat ~ ~ · Mattglanzdeckschicht(anstrich)farbe f

mat-glazed, flat-glazed · mattglasiert, mattbeglast

mat glazed coat(ing) → flat(-surface) ~ ~

~ **glaze(d finish)** → flat(-surface) glazed coat(ing)

~ **glazing** → flat(-surface) glazed coat(ing)

mat gloss, flat ~ [*Practically free from sheen even when viewed from oblique angles*] · Mattglanz m

~ ~ **oil paint,** flat ~ ~ ~ · Mattglanzölfarbe f

~ **paint,** flat ~ · Matt(anstrich)farbe f

mat-pattern, mat-work · Flechtwerk n, Flechte f [*romanische Verzierung*]

mat porcelain enamel, ~ vitreous ~, flat ~ ~ · Mattschmelzemail(le) n, (f), Schmelzmattemail(le)

~ **sheet(ing)** · Glasvliesbahn f; Glasvließbahn [*Österreich*]

mat(-surface) glazed coat(ing) · flat(-surface) ~ ~ ~

~ **glaze(d finish)** → flat(-surface) glazed coat(ing)

~ **glazing** → flat(-surface) glazed coat(ing)

mat varnish, flat ~ · Mattlack m

~ **vitreous enamel,** ~ porcelain ~, flat ~ ~ · Mattschmelzemail(le) n, (f), Schmelzmattemail(le)

~ **wall paint,** flat ~ ~ · Mattwand(anstrich)farbe f

mat-work, mat-pattern · Flechtwerk n, Flechte f [*romanische Verzierung*]

to match · angleichen

matchboard · Profilbrett n, (Nut- und) Spundbrett

match(board)ing · Nuten n und Spunden

matchboarding · Profilbretter npl, (Nut- und) Spundbretter

matched, tongued and grooved (together), T&G · (genutet und) gespundet, mit Nut und Feder

~ **aggregate** → (dry-)batched ~

~ **ceiling,** tongued-and-grooved ~, T&G ~ · Spunddecke f, gespundete Decke

~ **(floor) boarding,** tongued-and-grooved (~), T&G (~) ~ · gespundeter (Fuß)Boden(belag) m, Spund(-Fuß)boden(belag)

matched lumber — matting process

~ lumber, ~ timber, ~ wood · genutetes und gespundetes Holz *n*

~ materials → (dry-)batched aggregate

~ shingle, tongued-and-grooved ~, T&G ~ · Nutschindel *f*

~ sub-floor, tongued-and-grooved ~, T&G ~ · gespundeter Unterboden *m*, Spundunterboden

~ timber, ~ wood, ~ lumber · genutetes und gespundetes Holz *n*

~ veneer · Furnierbild *n*

~ wood, ~ lumber, ~ timber · genutetes und gespundetes Holz *n*

matching, matchboarding · Nuten *n* und Spunden

~, colour ~ (Brit.); (color) ~ (US) · (Farb)Angleichung *f*

mate · Gehilfe *m*

material · Material *n*, (Werk)Stoff *m*

~, mass, composition, compound · Masse *f* [*Erzeugnis*]

~, particles, grains · Korn *n*, Körner *npl*, Gekörn *n*

~ aggressive to concrete, substance ~ ~ ~ · Betonschädling *m*

~ behaviour (Brit.); **~ behavior** (US) · Materialverhalten *n*, (Werk)Stoffverhalten

~ constant · Materialkennwert *m*, (Werk)Stoffkennwert

~ defect, ~ flaw · Materialfehler *m*, (Werk)Stoffehler

~ designation · Materialbezeichnung *f*, (Werk)Stoffbezeichnung

~ flaw, ~ defect · Stoffehler *m*, Werk~, Materialfehler

~ for electrical systems, ~ ~ ~ ~ installations · (Elektro)Installationsmaterial *n*

~ ~ interior work · Ausbaumaterial *n* [*Schweiz*]; Ausbaustoff *m* [*Im Gegensatz zum Rohbaustoff*]

~ ~ scratch work, sgraffito material · Sgraffito(putz)material *n*, Kratzgrundmaterial, Kratzputzmaterial

~ ~ services · Installationsmaterial *n* [*für Wasser- und Gasleitungen*]

~ list, ML, bill of material(s) [*A list of the various portions of material for a construction, either proposed or completed, giving dimension and weights or other quantitative measurements*] · Stoffliste *f*, Materialliste

~ of sculpture · Plastik(werk)stoff *m*, Plastikmaterial *n*, Skulptur(werk)stoff, Skulpturmaterial

~ point · materieller Punkt *m*

~ quantity, quantity of material · Stoffmenge *f*

~ thickness · Materialdicke *f*, (Werk-)Stoffdicke

~ to be screened, (screen) head, (screen) feed · Siebgut *n*, Einlaufgut Haufwerk *n*, Aufgabegut [*Siebtechnik*]

~ unit price, ~ ~ rate · Materialeinheitspreis *m*, (Werk)Stoffeinheitspreis

~ ~ rate, ~ ~ price · Stoffeinheitspreis *m*, Werk~, Materialeinheitspreis

material(s) consumption · Materialverbrauch *m*

(materials) dressing, (~) processing, (~) preparation · Stoffaufbereitung *f*, Werk~, (Material)Aufbereitung

~ engineering · Materialtechnik *f*, (Werk)Stofftechnik

~ fluctuation clause, ~ variation ~ · Materialpreisgleitklausel *f*, (Werk-)Stoffpreisgleitklausel

(~) preparation, (~) dressing, (~) processing · Stoffaufbereitung *f*, Werk~, (Material)Aufbereitung

(~) processing, (~) dressing, (~) preparation · (Material)Aufbereitung *f*, (Werk)Stoffaufbereitung

material(s) quantity · Materialmenge *f*

~ requirement · Materialbedarf *m*, (Werk)Stoffbedarf

~ shortage · Materialknappheit *f*, Materialverknappung *f*, (Werk)Stoffknappheit, (Werk)Stoffverknappung

(material(s)) strength · (Material-)Festigkeit *f*, (Werk)Stoffestigkeit

materials testing institute · (Material-)Prüf(ungs)anstalt *f*, MPA

~ ~ lab(oratory) · (Material-)Prüf(ungs)stelle *f*

material(s) testing machine · Materialprüfmaschine *f*, (Werk)Stoffprüfmaschine

materials variation clause, ~ fluctuation ~ · Stoffpreisgleitklausel *f*, Werk~, Materialpreisgleitklausel

maternity unit · Entbindungsstation *f*, Entbindungsabteilung *f*

mathematical point, imaginary ~ · ideeller Punkt *m*, gedachter ~, imaginärer ~

~ theory of elasticity · mathematische Elastizitätstheorie *f*

matrix → cementing material

~, ground mass · Grundmasse *f*, Matrix *f* [*Substanz, in die Körner oder Kristalle eingebettet sind*]

~ · Matrix *f*

~ algebra · Matrizenrechnung *f*

~ (material) → cementing ~

~ method · Matrizenmethode *f*, Matrizenverfahren *n*

matter, substance, agent · Mittel *n*, Stoff *m*, Substanz *f* [*z.B. für Sperranstriche*]

matting · Mattenbelag *m*

~ agent, flatting ~, gloss reducer [*A material incorporated in a paint, varnish or other coating material to reduce the gloss of the dried film*] · Matt(ierungs)mittel *n*, Matt(ierungs)stoff *m*

~ operation → flatting down

~ process, flatting ~ · Mattierungsverfahren *n*

mattness — mean compression strength

mattness, dullness · Vermattung f
mattock man, topman, demolisher, wrecker · (Gebäude)Abbrucharbeiter m, Hausabbrucharbeiter
mattress [*A concrete slab at ground level used as a base for a machine*] · Betongrundplatte f
~ · Bewehrungsmatte f, Armierungsmatte
mature · reif
~ · gar gebrannt
maturing · Garbrand m
~ [*The process by which clarity, brightness, working properties, etc., are improved by storing the varnish in tanks*] · Reifen n, Lack~
~ · Reifen n
~ **temperature** · Garbrandtemperatur f
Mausoleum at Halicarnassos, Halicarnassos Mausoleum · Mausoleum n zu Halikarnass
~ **of Augustus** · Augustus-Mausoleum n
~ ~ **Theoderic at Ravenna** · Mausoleum n Theoderichs zu Ravenna
maximal crack width · Größtrißbreite f, Höchstrißbreite
to maximize · maximieren
maximum bending moment · Höchstbiegemoment n, Größtbiegemoment, Maximalbiegemoment, Maximalbiegungsmoment, Größtbiegungsmoment, Höchstbiegungsmoment
~ ~ **stress** · Höchstbiegespannung f, Größtbiegespannung, Maximalbiegespannung
~ **clearance** · Größtspiel n, Höchstspiel, Maximalspiel
~ **demand** · Höchstbedarf m, Größtbedarf, Maximalbedarf
~ ~ **meter** [*B.S. 37*] · Zähler m mit Höchstverbrauchsangabe, ~ ~ Größtverbrauchsangabe, ~ ~ Maximalverbrauchsangabe
~ **density** · Höchstdichte f, Größtdichte, Maximaldichte
~ **dimension** · Größtmaß n, Höchstmaß, Maximalmaß, Größtabmessung f, Höchstabmessung, Maximalabmessung
~ **distance**, ~ spacing · Höchstabstand m, Größtabstand, Maximalabstand
~ **eccentricity** · Höchstausmittigkeit f, Größtausmittigkeit
~ **grain (size)** · Größtkorn n
~ **load**, peak ~ · Höchstlast f, Spitzenlast, Maximallast
~ **moment** · Größtmoment n, Höchstmoment, Maximalmoment
~ ~ **region** · Maximalmomentenbereich m, n, Höchstmomentenbereich, Größtmomentenbereich
~ **permissible stress** · zulässige Höchstspannung f, ~ Größtspannung

~ **positive bending moment** · positives Größtbiegemoment n, ~ Höchstbiegemoment, ~ Maximalbiegemoment, ~ Größtbiegungsmoment, ~ Höchstbiegungsmoment, ~ Maximalbiegungsmoment
~ ~ **moment** · positives Höchstmoment n, ~ Größtmoment, ~ Maximalmoment
~ **pressure line**, line of maximum pressure · Größtdrucklinie f, Höchstdrucklinie, Maximaldrucklinie
~ **principle** · Maximumprinzip n
~ **rafter distance**, ~ ~ spacing · Höchst(dach)sparrenabstand m, Größt(dach)sparrenabstand, Maximal(dach)sparrenabstand
~ **spacing**, ~ distance · Höchstabstand m, Größtabstand, Maximalabstand
~ **strain** · Höchstdehnung f, Größtdehnung, Maximaldehnung
~ **strength** · Höchstfestigkeit f, Größtfestigkeit, Maximalfestigkeit
~ **stress** · Größtspannung f, Höchstspannung, Maximalspannung
~ **temperature** · Größttemperatur f, Höchsttemperatur, Maximaltemperatur
~ **thickness** · Höchstdicke f, Größtdicke, Maximaldicke [*Fehlnamen: Höchststärke f, Größtstärke, Maximalstärke*]
~ **value** · Größtwert m, Höchstwert, Maximalwert
~ **width** · Höchstbreite f, Größtbreite, Maximalbreite
~ **wind velocity** · Höchstwindgeschwindigkeit f, Windhöchstgeschwindigkeit, Maximalwindgeschwindigkeit
Maxwell('s) diagram, ~ polygon of forces · Maxwellscher Kräfteplan m
~ **liquid** · Maxwellsche Flüssigkeit f
~ **polygon of forces**, ~ diagram · Maxwellscher Kräfteplan m
~ **theorem** · Satz m von Maxwell, Maxwellscher Satz [*Spezialfall des allgemeinen Bettischen Satzes und die Grundlage zur Ermittlung der Einflußlinien*]
Mayan architecture · Mayaarchitektur f, Mayabaukunst f
mbl → marble
M.B.V. process, modified Bauer-Vogel ~ · MBV(-Behandlung) n, (f), modifiziertes Bauer-Vogel-Verfahren n
MC → medium curing cutback
MCI → malleable cast iron
mean [*Intermediate as to position occupied; half-way between extremes; equidistant from given limits*] · mittlere; mittleres; Mittel.....
~, average · durchschnittlich
~, average · Mittel n
~ **compression strength**, ~ compressive ~, average ~ ~ · mittlere Druckfestigkeit f, durchschnittliche ~

mean compressive strength — mechanical impedance

~ **compressive strength,** ~ compression ~, average ~ ~ · mittlere Druckfestigkeit f, durchschnittliche ~

~ **grain diameter,** average ~ ~, ~ particle ~ · mittlerer Korndurchmesser m, durchschnittlicher ~

~ **particle diameter,** average ~ ~, ~ grain ~ · mittlerer Korndurchmesser m, durchschnittlicher ~

~ **reflectance,** average ~ · mittlerer Rückstrahlungsgrad m, durchschnittlicher ~ [*Tageslichtberechnung*]

~ **strength,** average ~ · mittlere Festigkeit f, durchschnittliche ~

~ **temperature,** average ~ · Mitteltemperatur f

~ **tensile strength,** average ~ ~ · mittlere Zugfestigkeit f, durchschnittliche ~

~ **thickness,** average ~ · mittlere Dicke f, durchschnittliche ~ [*Fehlnamen: mittlere Stärke, durchschnittliche Stärke*]

~ **volume of grain,** average ~ ~ ~, ~ ~ ~ particle · mittleres Kornvolumen n, durchschnittliches ~

~ ~ ~ **particle,** average ~ ~ ~, ~ ~ ~ grain · mittleres Kornvolumen n, durchschnittliches ~

means of erection · Montagemittel n

~ ~ **escape,** provision for escape of occupants · Fluchtmöglichkeit f

measurable · meßbar

to measure · aufmessen [*Bauarbeiten*]

~ ~, to proportion, to batch; to gauge; to gage (US) · abmessen, zumessen, zuteilen, dosieren

~ ~ **flat overall** · flach übermessen

~ ~ **overall** · übermessen

measurement, measuring · Maßnehmen n

~ **and payment** · Aufmaß n und Abrechnung f

~ **condition,** measuring ~ · Meßbedingung f

~ **data** · Meßdaten f

~ **item** · Aufmaßposition f

~ **length** · Meßlänge f

~ **of consistency** · Steifemessung f, Konsistenzmessung

~ ~ **daylight** · Tageslichtmessung f

~ **(~ finished work)** · Aufmessen n

~ **range** · Meßbereich m, n

measurement(s) of heat (capacities), calorimetry, calorimetric measurement(s) · Kalorimetrie f, Wärmemengenmessung(en) f(pl)

measuring, measurement · Maßnehmen n

~ **condition,** measurement ~ · Meßbedingung f

~ **of colours** (Brit.); ~ ~ **colors** (US); colorimetry; colour measurement (Brit.); color measurement (US) · Farbmessung f, Farbmetrik f [*DIN 5033*]

~ ~ **hardness** · Härtemessung f

~ ~ **viscosity** · Viskositätsmessung f

Meat Market at Haarlem · Fleischhalle f in Haarlem

meccano-like system of unit construction · Baukastensystem n

mechanic of continua, continuum mechanics · Kontinuumsmechanik f

mechanical analysis, combined sieve and sedimentation test · kombinierte Sieb- und Schlämmanalyse f

~ **application of mortar,** spray ~ ~ ~ · maschineller Mörtelauftrag m, Spritzmörtelauftrag

~ **bond** → (~) **key**

~ **classification** · mechanische Korntrennung f

~ **compaction** · mechanische Verdichtung f

~ **concept of order** · mechanisches Ordnungsprinzip n

~ **core,** utility ~, service ~, building ~, (reinforced) concrete ~, R.C. ~ · (Hoch)Hauskern m, (Stahl)Betonkern, Betriebskern, (Gebäude)Kern

~ **corrosion** · mechanische Korrosion f

~ **draft** (US); ~ **draught** (Brit.) · Gebläsezug m

~ ~ **burner** (US); ~ **draught** ~ (Brit.) · Gebläsebrenner m

~ **draught gas(-fired) burner** (Brit.); ~ **draft** ~ ~ (US) · Gas-Gebläsebrenner m

~ **drawing** · Reißbrettzeichnung f

~ **equipment** · Betriebseinrichtungen f pl, technische Einrichtungen [*Hochhaus*]

~ ~ **(of a building);** building services (US) [*Lifts, escalators or similar mechanical equipment*] · (Haus)Betriebsanlagen f pl, (Gebäude)Betriebsanlagen, (Haus)Betriebseinrichtungen f pl, Gebäudebetriebseinrichtungen, technische Anlagen, technische Einrichtungen

(~) ~ **room** → machine(ry) ~

(~) ~ **station** → machine(ry) ~

~ **exterior plastering** → spray (external) rendering

~ ~ **rendering** → spray (external) ~

~ **external plastering** → spray (external) rendering

~ (~) **rendering** → spray (~) ~

~ **extractor,** ~ extraction unit, ~ ventilator, ~ extract ventilation unit [*It has a fan for positive air flow*] · mechanischer (Ent)Lüfter m

~ **fastener** · mechanisches Befestigungsmittel f

(~) **garbage grinder** → (~) **rubbish** ~

~ **impedance** · mechanische Impedanz f

(~) key, ~ bond grip(ping) · mechanische Haftung f, mechanischer Verbund m, mechanisches Haften n [Haftung ohne Bindemittel oder Kleb(e)stoff]

(~) ~ groove, grip(ping) ~ [e.g. on the back of an architectural panel] · Haftrille f, Verbundrille

~ keying · mechanisches Aufrauhen n für den (Ver)Putz

~ manipulation · mechanische Handhabung f

~ mixing · maschinelles Mischen n, maschinelle Mischung f

~ painting (work) · maschineller Anstrich m, maschinelles Anstreichen n

~ plastering, spray ~, ~ rendering · maschinelles (Ver)Putzen n, Spritz(ver)putzen

~ polishing · mechanisches Polieren n [Fehlname: zerspanende Bearbeitung]

~ property · mechanische Eigenschaft f

~ reaming · maschinelles Aufreiben n

**(~) refuse grinder, (~) waste ~;
(~) rubbish ~** (US) · Müllwolf m, Müllkleinerer m, Abfall(stoff)vernichter, Abfall(stoff)zerkleinerer [Er zerkleinert die Haus- und Küchenabfälle unter Wasserzufluß und spült sie über einen Geruchverschluß in die Kanalisation]

~ resistance · mechanischer Widerstand m

~ roof extractor, ~ ~ extraction unit, ~ ~ ventilator, ~ ~ extract ventilation unit [It has a fan for positive air flow] · mechanischer Dach(ent)lüfter m

~ room → machine(ry) ~

(~) rubbish grinder (US) → (~) refuse ~

~ service room · Technikraum m

~ station → machine(ry) ~

~ strength · mechanische Festigkeit f

~ tower → service ~

~ trade [e.g. plumbing trade] · technisches Gewerk n

~ treatment · maschinelle Behandlung f [Betonsichtfläche]

~ ventilation · mechanische Be- und Entlüftung f

(~) waste grinder → (~) refuse ~

mechanically blown · mechanisch geblasen [Glas]

~ deposited (sedimentary) rock → clastic (~) ~

mechanic's level, water ~, (spirit) ~, plumb · Wasserwaage f

mechanism · Mechanismus m

~ for closing, device ~ ~, closing device, closing mechanism, closer · (Ver-)Schließvorrichtung f, Schließer m, Verschluß m

~ of creep, creep mechanism · Kriechmechanismus m

~ ~ hardening · Härtungsmechanismus m, Er~

~ ~ set(ting), set(ting) mechanism · (Ab)Bindemechanismus m, Verfestigungsmechanismus

mechano-chemical reaction · mechanochemische Reaktion f

medallion [A circular or oval frame having within it an ornamental motif] · Medaillon n

medi(a)eval · ma., mittelalterlich

~ city wall · mittelalterliche Stadtmauer f

meditation chapel · Gebetskapelle f

Mediterranean architecture · Baukunst f des Mittelmeerraumes, Architektur f ~ ~

medium, vehicle [The liquid portion of paint, in which the pigment is dispersed; it is composed of the binder and the thinner, if any] · Bindemittellösung f [Anstrichfarbe]

~ → (paint) binding ~

~ baked brick · Mittelbrandziegel m

~ base → vehicle ~

~ boiler · Mittelsieder m, mittelsiedendes Lösungsmittel n [Lacktechnik. Siedepunkt 100–150°C]

medium-breaking → normal-setting

medium chip(ping)s → medium-size(d) ~

~ coarse sand · Mittelgrobsand m

~ curing cutback, MC [An asphalt cement cut back with kerosene. MC-0 to MC-5] · mittelschnellabbindendes Verschnittbitumen n

~ dimension · Mittelabmessung f, Mittelmaß n

~ dispersion, binding ~ ~, binder ~ · (Farben)Bindemitteldispersion f, Anstrichdispersion

~ duty flexible (swing) door · mittelschwere flexible Pendeltür f

~ emulsion, binding ~ ~, binder ~ · (Farben)Bindemittelemulsion f, Anstrichemulsion

~ format → medium(-size(d)) ~

~-frequency sound insulation, ~ ~ protection · Mittelfrequenz-Schallschutz m

medium fuel oil → heavy ~ ~

medium-grained, middle-sized · mittelkörnig

~ grains, ~ material, ~ particles, middle-sized ~ · Mittelkörner npl, Mittelkorn n

~ gravel, middle-sized ~ · Mittelkies m [6–20 mm]

~ material, ~ particles, ~ grains, middle-sized ~ · Mittelkörner npl, Mittelkorn n

~ particles, ~ material, ~ grains, middle-sized ~ · Mittelkörner npl, Mittelkorn n

~ sand, middle-sized ~ · Mittelsand m [0,2–0,6 mm]

~ sandstone, middle-sized ~ · mittelkörniger Sandstein m

~ sandy gravel, ~ gravelly sand, middle-sized ~ ~ · Mittelkiessand m [<30 mm]

medium-grained silt — melting viscosity

~ **silt**, middle-sized ~ · Mittelschluff *m* [0,006–0,02 mm]

medium-hard, semi-hard · halbhart, mittelhart

medium hardboard, semi-hardboard · halbharte (Holz)Faserplatte *f*, Halbhartplatte, HFH1/2 [*Rohwichte 480 bis 850 kg/m³*]

medium-hard coal-tar pitch, semi-hard ~ ~ · Mittelhartpech *n*, mittelhartes Steinkohlenteerpech

medium-high partition · halbhohe Trennwand *f*

medium mosaic → medium(-size(d)) ~

~ ~ **panel** → medium(-size(d)) ~ ~

~ ~ **tile** → medium(-size(d)) ~ ~

~ **oil** · Mittelöl *n* [*Ein zwischen 170° und 230° siedendes Öl, das bei der Destillation von Steinkohlenteer erhalten wird*]

medium-oil · halbfett, mittelfett, mittelölig, halbölig

~ **alkyd resin** · mittelöliges Alkydharz *n*, mittelfettes ~

medium (paving) sett → medium(-size(d)) (~) ~

~ **plate**, light ~, medium sheet, jobbing sheet · Mittelblech *n*

medium-rise block, ~ building · mittelhohes Gebäude *n*

~ **building**, ~ block · mittelhohes Gebäude *n*

medium sett → medium(-size(d)) (paving) ~

medium-setting → normal-setting

~ · mittelschnellabbindend

medium sheet, jobbing ~, light plate, medium plate · Mittelblech *n*

medium(-size(d)) chip(ping)s · Mittelsplitt *m*

~ **format** · Mittelformat *n*

~ **mosaic** · Mittelmosaik *n*

~ ~ **panel** · Mittelmosaiktafel *f*

~ ~ **tile** · Mittelmosaik(belag)platte *f*, Mittelmosaikfliese *f*

~ **(paving) sett** · Mittelpflasterstein *m*

medium-slaking · mittelschnell(ab)löschend [*Kalk*]

medium-span roof · Mittelspanndach *n*

medium suspension, binding ~ ~, binder ~ · (Farben)Bindemittelsuspension *f*, Dispersionsbinder *m*

medium-temperature chimney · Warmschornstein *m* [*Schornstein mit Abgasen von 100 °C bis 300 °C*]

medium-weight load · Mittellast *f*

medressa → madrasah

meerschaum, sepiolite, agaric chalk · Meerschaum *m*, Steinmark *n*, mineralischer Lerchenschwamm *m*

meeting hall, assembly ~ · Versammlungshalle *f*, Versammlungssaal *m*

~ **place** · Versammlungsplatz *m*

~ ~, assembly ~ · Versammlungsstätte *f*

~ **rail** · Querfries *m* [*Senkrecht-Schiebe-(flügel)fenster*]

~ **room**, assembly ~ · Versammlungsraum *m*

megalith [*A large hewn or unhewn stone such as is found in cyclopean masonry*] · Großstein *m*, Riesenstein, Megalith *m*

megalithic burial chamber, ~ tomb ~, ~ sepulchral ~, ~ (chamber) tomb [*Megalithic (chamber) tombs are often colloquially called 'giants' graves', 'fairies houses' or 'hunsbeds'*] · Großsteingrab *n*, Riesensteingrab, Megalithgrab [*Volkstümliche Benennungen sind „Hünengrab", „Hünenbett" n und „Opfertisch" m*]

~ **masonry (work)** [*Masonry (work) in very large stones so exactly hewn that a knife blade cannot be inserted in the joints*] · Megalithmauerwerk *n*

~ **monument** · Megalithbauwerk *n*

megaron · Herrenhaus *n*, Megaron *n* [*Haupthalle mit Herd im griechischen Wohnhaus, davor meist eine Vorhalle zwischen Anten. Das Megaronhaus kommt schon in Troja und Tiryns vor und ist die Vorstufe des griechischen Antentempels*]

melamine-formaldehyde (resin), MF · Melaminformaldehyd(harz) *n*, MF

melamine impregnated · melaminharzgetränkt, melaminharzimprägniert

~ **resin** · Melaminharz *n*

~ ~ **adhesive**, ~ ~ glue · Melaminharzleim *m*

~ ~ **decorative plastic film**, ~ ~ ~ ~ sheeting, ~ ~ ornamental ~ ~ · Melaminharz-Dekor(ations)folie *f*, Melaminharz-Zierfolie, Melaminharz-Ornamentfolie

~ ~ **glue**, ~ ~ adhesive · Melaminharzleim *m*

~ ~ **ornamental plastic film** → ~ ~ decorative ~ ~

~ ~ **plastic** · Melaminharzkunststoff *m*

~ ~ **varnish** · Melaminharzlack *m*

melamine(-sur)faced, melamine-coated · melaminharzbeschichtet

melamine varnish resin · Melamin-Lackharz *n*

melanterite, green vitriol, copperas · Melanterit *m*

melaphyre, black porphyry · Melaphyr *m*, schwarzer Porphyr [*DIN 52100*]

melilite · Honigstein *m*, Melilith *n*

melt · Schmelze *f*

~ **point range** · Schmelzbereich *m*, *n*

melting heat, heat of fusion · Schmelzwärme *f*

~ **point of rock asphalt (US)**; ~ ~ ~ ~ (natural) ~ (Brit.) · Asphaltschmelzpunkt *m*

~ **(until seed-free)** · Blankschmelze *f* [*Glasschmelze*]

~ **viscosity** · Schmelzviskosität *f*

~ water · Schmelzwasser *n*
Melvoon · Melvoion *n* [*Agora von Athen*]
member → (prefab(ricated)) (building) unit
~, bar, rod, element · Füll(ungs)stab *m*, Gitterstab, Glied *n*, (Träger)Stab
~ **buckling**, bar ~, rod ~, element ~ · Stabknickung *f*, Stabknicken *n*, Gliedknickung, Gliedknicken
~ **centre line** (Brit.); ~ center ~ (US); element ~ ~, bar ~ ~, rod ~ ~ · Stabmittellinie *f*, Stabachse *f*, Gliedmittellinie, Gliedachse
~ **connection**, element ~, bar ~, rod ~ · Stabanschluß *m*, Gliedanschluß [*Stabwerkkonstruktion*]
~ **cross-section**, bar ~, element ~, rod ~ · Stabquerschnitt *m*, Gliedquerschnitt [*Stabwerkkonstruktion*]
~ **field**, bar ~, rod ~, element ~ · Stabfeld *n*, Gliedfeld [*Stabwerkkonstruktion*]
~ **force**, bar ~, rod ~, element ~ · Stabkraft *f*, Gliedkraft [*Stabwerkkonstruktion*]
~ **length**, element ~, rod ~, bar ~ · Stablänge *f*, Gliedlänge
~ **loading**, bar ~, rod ~, element ~ · Gliedbelastung *f*, Stabbelastung
~ **moment**, bar ~, rod ~, element ~ · Stabmoment *n*, Gliedmoment
~ **shape**, element ~, rod ~, bar ~ · Gliedform *f*, Stabform
~ **size**, bar ~, rod ~, element ~ · Stabgröße *f*, Gliedgröße [*Stabwerkkonstruktion*]
~ **slope**, bar ~, rod ~, element ~ · Gliedablenkung *f*, Stabablenkung [*Rahmenträger*]
~ **stress**, rod ~, bar ~, element ~ · Stabspannung *f*, Gliedspannung [*Stabwerkkonstruktion*]
~ **subject to buckling**, rod ~ ~ ~, bar ~ ~ ~ · Knickstab *m*
~ **system**, rod ~, bar ~ · Stabsystem *n*, Stabwerk *n*
~ **transformation**, ~ transposition, bar ~, rod ~, element ~ · Stabvertauschung *f*, Gliedvertauschung [*Stabwerkkonstruktion*]
~ **transposition**, ~ transformation, bar ~, rod ~, element ~ · Stabvertauschung *f*, Gliedvertauschung [*Stabwerkkonstruktion*]
membrane, skin, film · Film *m*, Membran(e) *f*, Haut *f*, Häutchen *n*
~ [*A membrane is a sheet of material so thin that, to all practical purposes, it cannot resist compression, bending, or shear, but only tension*] · Membran(e) *f*
~, soap bubble · Seifenhaut *f*
~ **action** · Membran(e)wirkung *f*
~ **analogy**, soap bubble ~ · Seifenhautgleichnis *n*, Membran(e)gleichnis, Seifenhautanalogie *f*, Membran(e)analogie

~ **analysis** · Membran(e)berechnung *f*
~ **(concrete) curing**, liquid ~ (~) ~ · (Beton)Nachbehandlung *f* mit (Ab-)Dicht(ungs)mittel
~ **(~) ~ agent** → (concrete) curing compound
~ **(~) ~ compound** → (concrete) ~ ~
~ **curing**, ~ concrete ~, liquid membrane concrete ~ · (Beton)Nachbehandlung *f* mit (Ab)Dicht(ungs)mittel
~ ~ **agent** → (concrete) curing compound
~ ~ **compound** → (concrete) ~ ~
~ **displacement** · Membran(e)verrückung *f*
~ **flashing** → cloth ~
~ ~ **(piece)** · cloth ~ (~)
~ **force** · Membran(e)kraft *f*
~ **rib** · Membran(e)rippe *f*
~ **rotation** · Membran(e)drehung *f*
~ **shear(ing) force** · Membran(e)schubkraft *f*
~ **shell** → thin ~
~ **state of stress** · Membran(e)spannungszustand *m*
~ **stress** · Membran(e)spannung *f*
~ **surface** · Membran(e)fläche *f*
~ **theory** · Membran(e)theorie *f*
~ **thrust** · Membran(e)schub *m*
~ **translation** · Membran(e)verschiebung *f*
memorial · Gedächtnismal *n*, Mahnmal
~ · Denkmal *n*
~ **arch**, commemorative ~ · Ehrenbogen *m*, Gedächtnisbogen, Gedenkbogen, Memorialbogen
~ **basilica** → commemorative ~
~ **chapel**, commemorative ~ · Gedächtniskapelle *f*, Totenkapelle · Memoirenkapelle, Memorialkapelle
~ **church**, commemorative ~, martyrium · Coemetrialkirche *f*, Martyria *f*, Memoria(lkirche) *f*, Denkmalkirche, Gedächtniskirche, Memorienkirche [*Kirche auf oder in einem Coemeterium, meist nahe oder über einem Märtyrergrab*]
~ **column**, commemorative ~ · Ehrensäule *f*, Gedenksäule, Gedächtnissäule, Memorialsäule
~ **cross**, commemorative ~ · Gedenkkreuz *n*, Gedächtniskreuz, Memorialkreuz, Ehrenkreuz
~ **figure**, commemorative ~ · Gedenkfigur *f*
~ **hall**, commemorative ~ · Memorienhalle *f*, Gedächtnishalle, Memorialhalle, Totenhalle
~ **monument**, commemorative ~ · Gedenkmonument *n*, Memorialmonument, Ehrenmonument, Gedächtnismonument
~ **stone**, commemorative ~ · Gedenkstein *m*, Gedächtnisstein, Ehrenstein, Memorialstein

memorial structure — metal-and-paper flashing (piece)

~ **structure, commemorative** ~ · Memorialbau *m*, Gedächtnisbau, Gedenkbau, Ehrenbau

~ **tablet, commemorative** ~, **plaque** · Gedenktafel *f*, Gedächtnistafel, Ehrentafel, Memorialtafel

Memorial to the Third International in Moscow 1920 · Denkmal *n* der Dritten Internationale in Moskau 1920

mender · Blech *n* zweiter Wahl

mendicant order church · Bettelordenskirche *f* [*Bettelordenskirchen sind die Kirchen der Franziskaner (Minoriten, Barfüßer) und Dominikaner (Prediger)*]

menhaden oil · Menhadenöl *n*

menhir, monolith · Menhir *m* [*Vorgeschichtliches Totenmal in Form eines großen aufrechtstehenden Steines*]

men's changing room · Herrenumkleide(raum) *f*, (*m*), Männerumkleide(raum)

~ **toilet, male** ~, **men's room** · Herrentoilette *f*, Männertoilette

mensa, super-altar, altar-table, altar-slab [*The slab forming the top of an altar*] · Altarplatte *f*, Mensa *f*

mental hospital · Krankenhaus *n* für Nerven- und Gemütsleiden; Spital *n* ~ ~ ~ ~ [*Schweiz*]

~ **image** · Gedankenbild *n*

~ **institution** · Heil- und Pflegeanstalt *f*

mercantile centre (Brit.); ~ **center** (US) · Handelszentrum *n*

Mercator's projection · Merkatorprojektion *f*

merchant bar, bar-steel, rod-steel · Stabeisen *n* [*Fehlname*]; Stabstahl *m* [*DIN 59051*]

~ **bar(s), black** ~, **commercial grade steel** · Handelsstahl *m*

(merchant's) mark → signboard

mercuric chloride (Brit.); ~ **chlorid(e)** (US); **corrosive sublimate** [*It is a white crystalline solid, sparingly soluble in cold, more easily in hot, water*] · Quecksilberchlorid *n*, Hg Cl$_2$

mercurous salt · Quecksilberoxydulsalz *n*

mercury discharge lamp; ~ **vapour** ~ (Brit.); ~ **vapor** ~ (US) · Quecksilberdampflampe *f*

~ **gilding** · Feuervergoldung *f*

~ **iodine lamp** · Quecksilber-Jod-Lampe *f*

~ **pigment** · Quecksilberpigment *n*

~ **vapour lamp** (Brit.); ~ **vapor** ~ (US); ~ **discharge** ~ · Quecksilberdampflampe *f*

merging · Verschleifung *f*

~ **of interior and exterior** · Ineinanderfließen *n* von Innenraum und Außenraum

meridian rib · Meridianrippe *f*

~ **stress, meridional** ~ · Meridianspannung *f*

meridional bending · Meridianbiegung *f*

~ **cable** · Meridianseil *n*

~ **direction** · Meridianrichtung *f*

~ **force** · Meridiankraft *f*

~ **stress, meridian** ~ · Meridianspannung *f*

~ ~ **resultant** · Meridionalspannungsresultante *f*, Meridionalspannungsresultierende *f*

~ **tangent** · Meridiantangente *f*

merlon, cop · Zinne *f*, Mauerzacke *f*, Windberg *m*, Zinnenzahn *m* [*Zur Deckung der Verteidiger schildartige Erhöhung der Brustwehr am Wehrgang und an der Wehrplatte eines Turmes*]

merry-go-round [*A machine for running the wires round a tank for prestressed concrete*] · Behälterwickelmaschine *f*

~ **for baggage,** ~ ~ **luggage** · Gepäckkarussell *n*

mesh [*Mesh is made by three methods; by weaving or twisting metal wires; by welding metal wires; and by piercing sheet metal and then stretching or expanding it*] · Maschenmatte *f*

~ **gage** (US) ~ **scale, screen scale, screen series** · Siebfolge *f*, Siebreihe *f*, Siebskala *f*

~ **number, sieve** ~ · (Sieb)Gewebenummer *f*

~**-reinforced** · netzarmiert, netzbewehrt, mattenarmiert, mattenbewehrt

mesh reinforcement → fabric (~)

~ **scale, screen** ~, **screen series; mesh gage** (US) · Siebfolge *f*, Siebreihe *f*, Siebskala *f*

~ **wire** · Maschendraht *m*

meshes [*net vault*] · Rippenwerk *n* [*Netzgewölbe*]

messenger calling system · Botenrufanlage *f*

metacenter (US); **metacentre** (Brit.) · Metazentrum *n*

metal (Brit) → road-~

~ **abrasive (material)** → metall(ic) aggregate

~ **additive** → gas-forming agent

~ **adhesive** [*A synthetic resin adhesive which is capable of bonding metals*] · Metallkleber *m*, Metallkleb(e)stoff *m*, Metallkleb(e)mittel *m*

~ **aggregate** → metal(lic) ~

metal-aggregate mortar cover(ing) → metal(lic)-aggregate ~ ~

metal (air) duct · Metall(uft)kanal *m*

~ **anchor,** ~ **tie** [*B.S. 1243*] · Metallanker *m*

~ **anchorage,** ~ **tying** · Verankerung *f* mit Metallanker

metal-and-paper flashing [*See remark under 'Anschluß'*] · Metall-Papier-Anschluß *m*

~ ~ **(piece)** · Metall-Papier-Anschluß(streifen) *m*

metal angle — metal duct

metal angle · Metallwinkel *m*

~ (~) bead, masonry (work) ~ (~) ~ · (Mauer)Kantenschützer *m* aus Metall, (Mauer)Kantenschutzwinkel *m* ~ ~, (Mauer)Kantenschoner ~ ~

~ astragal → ~ glazing bar

~ bar, ~ rod · Metallstab *m*

~ base flashing · unterer Metallanschluß *m* [Siehe Anmerkung unter „Anschluß"]

~ base plate [*Scotland*] → ~ skirting

~ bas-relief, ~ low relief · Metallflachrelief *n*

~ batten · Metall-Fugendeckleiste *f*

~ bead → ~ angle ~

~ bearing system → ~ load~ ~

~ binding plate → ~ corner ~

~ block, ~ building · Metallgebäude *n*

~ bonding, bonding of metal(s) · Metall(ver)kleben *n*, Metall(ver)klebung *f*

~-bound brush · blechgefaßter Pinsel *m*

metal bronze → metal(lic) flakes

~ (builders') fitting, ~ (~) furniture · Metall(bau)beschlag *m*

~ (~) fittings, ~ (~) hardware · Metall(bau)beschläge *mpl*

~ (~) furniture, ~ (~) fitting · Metall(bau)beschlag *m*

~ (~) hardware, ~ (~) fittings · Metall(bau)beschläge *mpl*

~ building, ~ 'block · Metallgebäude *n*

~ ~ entrance door · Metall-Gebäudetür *f*, Metall-Haustür

~ ~ material, ~ structural ~, ~ construction(al) ~, metallic ~ ~ · Metallbaustoff *m;* Metallbaumaterial *n* [*Schweiz*]

~ (~) panel · Metall(bau)tafel *f*

~ caisson → ~ pan(el)

~ ~ (type) ceiling → ~ waffle (~) ~

~ cap flashing, ~ counter) ~ · oberer Metallanschluß *m* [Siehe Anmerkung unter „Anschluß"]

metal-cased brick, ferro-clad ~ · blechummantelter Stein *m*

~ refractory (product), ferro-clad ~ (~) · blechummanteltes feuerfestes Erzeugnis *n*, ~ ff. ~

metal casement · Metall-Dreh(fenster)flügel *m*

~ cassette → ~ pan(el)

~ ~ type ceiling → ~ waffle ~ ~

~ ceiling · Metalldecke *f*

~ ~ panel · Metalldeckentafel *f*

~ channel, U-shaped ~ ~ · Metall-U-Profil *n*

~ chimney, plate ~ · Metallschornstein *m*, Blechschornstein

metal-clad door → metal-covered ~

~ window → metal-covered ~

metal cladding · Metall-(Außen)Versteifungswand *f*

~ ~ → ~ lining

~ ~ sheet · Metall-(Außenwand)Versteifungsplatte *f*

~ cleaning · Metallreinigung *f*

(~) cleat · Hafter *m*

(~) ~ locked into the seam · Falzhafter *m* [*Metallbedachung*]

metal-coated paper [*See remark under 'Pappe'*] · metallbeschichtete Pappe *f*

metal coat(ing), ~ finish · Metallbeschichtung *f*, Metallüberzug *m* [*als Schicht*]

~ ~ → anti-rust ~ ~

~ coating · Metallbeschichten *n*, Metallüberziehen, Metallbeschichtung *f*, Metallüberzug *m* [*als Tätigkeit*]

~ coffer → ~ pan(el)

~ ~ type ceiling → ~ waffle ~ ~

~ column · Metallstütze *f*

~ connecting plate → ~ corner ~

~ connection plate → ~ corner ~

~ connector, timber ~ · Metalldübel *m* [*Holzverbinder*]

~ constituent → metal(lic) ~

~ construction · Metallbau *m*

~ construction(al) material → ~ building ~

~ core · Metalleinlage *f*, Metallkern *m*, Metallseele *f* [*Drahtseil*]

~ corner plate, ~ connecting ~, ~ connection ~, ~ binding ~, ~ joint ~, ~ fish ~, ~ knee bracket ~, ~ gusset ~ · Eckblech *n*, Anschlußblech, Knotenblech

~ cornice flashing (piece), flexible ~ ~ ~ (~), sheet metal ~ ~ (~) · (Ge)Simsabdeckung *f* aus Blech, (Ge-)Simsblech *n*

~ counter ceiling · Metallunterdecke *f*

~ ~ flashing, ~ cap ~ · oberer Metallanschluß *m* [*Siehe Anmerkung unter „Anschluß"*]

~ cover strip · Metalldeckleiste *f*

metal-covered door, metal-(sur)faced ~, metal-clad ~ · metallausgekleidete Tür *f*, metallverkleidete ~, metallbekleidete ~

~ window, metal-(sur)faced ~, metal-clad ~ · metallausgekleidetes Fenster *n*, metallverkleidetes ~, metallbekleidetes ~

metal cupola, ~ dome · Metallkuppel *f*

~ curtain wall · Metallvorhangwand *f*

~ ~ ~ panel · Metall-Vorhangwandtafel *f*

~ dome, ~ cupola · Metallkuppel *f*

~ door · Metalltür *f*

~ ~ factory · Metalltürenfabrik *f*, Metalltürenwerk *n*

~ ~ frame [*B.S. 1245*] · Metall-Tür(blend)rahmen *m*, Metall-Türfutter(rahmen) *n*, (*m*)

~ duct, ~ air ~ · Metall(uft)kanal *m*

metal eave(s) gutter — metal mould

~ **eave(s) gutter,** ~ ~ trough · Metalltraufrinne *f*

~ **edge sealed glazing unit** [*The two sheets of glass, which enclose an air space, are hermetically sealed at their edges with a permanent metal-to-glass bond*] · Metallverbundrand-Verglasungseinheit *f*

~ **endurance,** ~ fatigue · Metallermüdung *f*

~ **façade** · Metallfassade *f*

metal-faced, metallüberzogen

~ **board** → metal-surfaced ~

~ **door** → ~ metal-covered ~

~ **rubber** · Metallgummi *m, n*

~ **window** → metal-covered ~

metal facing → ~ lining

~ **fatigue,** ~ endurance · Metallermüdung *f*

~ **(fence) picket** → ~ (~) stake

~ **(~) post** → ~ (~) stake

~ **(~) stake,** ~ (~) picket, ~ (~) post, ~ fencing ~ · Metall(zaun)pfahl *m*, Metall(zaun)pfosten *m*

~ **fencing stake** → ~ (fence) ~

~ **finish,** ~ coat(ing) · Metallbeschichtung *f*, Metallüberzug *m* [*als Schicht*]

~ ~ → (anti-rust) metal coat(ing)

~ ~, metallic ~ · Metalleffektlackierung *f*

~ **firring** → ~ furring

~ **fish plate** → ~ corner ~

~ **fitting** → ~ builders' ~

~ ~ → ~ pipe ~

~ **fittings** → ~ builders' ~

~ **flagpole** · Metallflaggenmast *m*, Metallfahnenmast

~ **flakes** → metallic ~

~ **flashing** · Metallanschluß *m* [*Siehe Anmerkung unter ,,Anschluß''*]

~ ~ **(piece), flexible** ~ ~ (~), sheet metal ~ (~), [*See remark under 'Anschluß'*] · Anschlußblech(streifen) *n, (m)*, Blechanschluß(streifen) *m*

~ **floor(ing) (finish),** ~ floor cover(ing) · Metall(fuß)boden(belag) *m*

~ **foil** · Blechfolie *f*, Metallfolie

~ ~ **flashing** [*See remark under 'Anschluß'*] · Metallfolienanschluß *m*, Blechfolienanschluß

~ ~ ~ **(piece)** · Blechfolienanschluß(streifen) *m*, Metallfolienanschluß(streifen)

~ ~ ~ **insert(ion)** · Blechfolieneinlage *f*, Metallfolieneinlage

~ ~ **layer** · Blechfolienlage *f*, Blechfolienschicht *f*, Metallfolienlage, Metallfolienschicht

~ **folding door** · Metallfalttür *f*

~ **for hammering** · hämmerbares Metall *n*

~ **forms,** ~ shuttering, ~ form(work) · Metall(-Beton)schalung *f*

~ **frame,** ~ framing · Metallrahmen *m*

~ ~ · Metall(blend)rahmen *m*, Metallfutter(rahmen) *n, (m)* [*Tür; Fenster*]

~ **framed partition (wall)** · Metall-Fachwerk(trenn)wand *f*, Metall-Riegel-(trenn)wand

~ **frame(d) window** · Metallrahmenfenster *n*

~ **frieze** · Metallfries *m*

~ **furniture** → ~ builders' ~

~ **furring,** ~ firring · Metall-Unterkonstruktion *f* [*Putztechnik*]

~ **glazing bar,** ~ sash ~, ~ astragal · Metallfenstersprosse *f*

~ **grid floor(ing) (finish),** ~ ~ floor cover(ing) · Metallrost(fuß)boden(belag) *m*

~ **grill(e)** · Metallgitter *n*

~ **grit** → metal(lic) ~

~ **gusset plate** → ~ corner ~

~ **handle** · Metallgriff *m*

~ **hanger** · Metallhänger *m*

~ **hardener** → metal(lic) grit

~ **hardening process,** metallic-~ · Badpatentieren *n*

~ **hardware** → ~ builders' ~

~ **hinge** · Metallband *n* [*Baubeschlag*]

~ **hose** → ~ reinforced ~

~ **insert(ion)** · Metalleinlage *f*

~ **jacket,** metallic ~ · Blechmantel *m*

~ **joint plate** → ~ corner ~

(~) ~ **strip** → crack-control (~) ~ ~

~ **knee bracket plate** → ~ corner ~

~ **lath(ing) (for plastering),** metallic ~ (~ ~) [*B.S. 1369*] · Metallnetz als Putzträger, Metallgewebe *n* ~ ~, Metallputzträger *m*

~ **leaf** · Blattmetall *n*

~ **lining,** ~ (sur)facing, ~ cladding · Metallauskleidung *f*, Metallverkleidung, Metallbekleidung, Metallbelag *m*

~ **lintel;** ~ lintol [*deprecated*] [*A metal beam spanning an opening*] · Metalloberschwelle *f*, Metallsturz *m*

~ **(load)bearing system,** ~ weight-carrying ~, ~ load-carrying ~ · Metalltragwerk *n*, Metalltragsystem *n*

~ **louver,** ~ louvre · Metallraster *m* [*Leuchte*]

~ **low relief,** ~ bas-relief · Metallflachrelief *n*

~ **masonry wall flashing (piece),** flexible ~ ~ ~ ~ (~), sheet ~ ~ ~ ~ (~) [*See remark under 'Anschluß'*] · Mauerabdeckung *f* aus Blech, Mauerblech *n*

~ ~ ~ **tie** [*B.S. 1243*] · Metallmaueranker *m*

~ **mesh** · Metallmaschenmatte *f*

~ **mould** (Brit.); ~ **mold** (US) · Metallform *f*

metal nailing plug — metal sheet roof cover(ing)

~ **nailing plug,** ~ wall ~ · Metall-Mauerdübel *m*
~ **newel(-post)** · Metall(treppen)spindel *f*
~ **paint** → bronze ~
~ **painting** [*Painting with bronzing fluid as a vehicle*] · Bronzieren *n*
~ **panel,** ~ building ~ · Metall(bau)tafel *f*
~ **pan(el),** ~ coffer, ~ waffle, ~ cassette, ~ caisson · Metall(decken)kassette *f*
~ **panel ceiling** · Metalltafeldecke *f*
~ **pan(el) type ceiling** → ~ waffle ~
~ **partition (wall)** · Metalltrennwand *f*
~ **picket** → ~ (fence) stake
~ **pickling** · Metallbeizen *n*
~ **pigment** → metal(lic) flakes
~ **pipe,** metallic ~ · Metallrohr *n*
~ **(~) fitting,** metallic (~) ~ · Metall(rohr)fitting *m*, Metall(rohr)formstück *n*
~ **plate,** metallic ~ · Blechplatte *f*, Metallplatte
(~) ~, heavy ~ ~ · (Grob)Blech *n*
(~) ~ **cover(ing)** → heavy (~) ~ ~
~ ~ **curved in two planes** · bombiertes Blech *n*, gewölbtes ~
(~) ~ **girder** → heavy (~) ~ ~
(~) ~ **lining** → heavy (~) ~ ~
(~) ~ **rigidity** → · (heavy) (metal) plate stiffness
(~) ~ **stiffness** → heavy (~) ~ ~
(~) ~ **(sur)facing** → (heavy) (metal) plate lining
(~) ~ **suspension roof(ing)** → heavy (~) ~ ~ ~
~ **post** → ~ (fence) stake
~ **powder** → metal(lic) ~
~ ~ **method** → powder spray(ing) ~
~ ~ **system** → powder spray(ing) method
~ **pretreatment** · Metallvorbehandlung *f*
~ **primer** · Metallgrundier(ungs)mittel *n*
~ **priming** · Metallgrundierung *f*
~ **principal post** → ~ stud
~ **profile** → ~ section
~ **protection** · Metallschutz *m*
~ **rail** · Metallschiene *f*
~ ~ · Metallriegel *m*
~ **railing** · Metallgeländer *n*
metal-reinforced composition roofing, ~ prepared ~, ~ ready ~ · blechverstärkte Dachpappe *f*
metal (reinforced) hose, flexible (metallic) tube · Metallschlauch *m*, Panzerschlauch
metal-reinforced prepared roofing, ~ ready ~, ~ composition ~ · blechverstärkte Dachpappe *f*
~ **ready roofing,** ~ composition ~, ~ prepared ~ · blechverstärkte Dachpappe *f*

metal revolving door · Metall-Drehtür *f*
~ **rib lath(ing)** → rib(bed) (expanded) (metal) mesh ~
~ **rod,** ~ bar · Metallstab *m*
~ **rolling grill(e),** ~ roller ~ [*See remark under 'Gitter'*] · Metall-Rollgitter *n*
~ **roof** → (sheet-)metal roof cladding
~ ~ **cladding** → sheet-~ ~ ~
~ ~ **cover(ing)** → (sheet-)metal roof cladding
~ **roof-light** · Metall(dach)oberlicht *n*
~ **roof sheathing** → (sheet-)metal roof cladding
~ **roof(ing)** → (sheet-)metal roof cladding
~ ~ **sheet(ing)** · Metall-Dachbahn *f*
~ **rung** · Metallsprosse *f*
~ **salt,** metallic ~ · Metallsalz *n*
~ **sandwich wall** [*It may consist, for example, of a steel backup, a glass-fibre insulation and aluminium*] · Metalldreilagenwand *f*, Metalldreischichtenwand
~ **sanitary cove** (US) → ~ skirting
~ **sash,** ~ window ~ · Metall(fenster)flügel *m*
~ ~ **bar** → ~ glazing ~
~ ~ **putty** · Metallfensterkitt *m* [*Kitt für Metallfensterverglasung*]
~ **scaffold(ing)** [*B.S. 1139*] · Metallgerüst *n*, Metallrüstung *f*
~ **seal(ing),** metallic ~ · Metall(ab)dichtung *f*
~ **section,** ~ shape, ~ unit, ~ trim, ~ profile · Metall(bau)profil *n*
~ **shape** → ~ section
~ **sheathed cable** · Metallmantelkabel *n*
~ **sheath(ing),** sheet-~ ~ [*prestressed concrete*] · Blechgleitkanal *m*, Blechspannkanal, Blechhüllrohr *n*, Blechhülle *f*, Blechröhre *f*
(~) **sheet,** sheet metal · (Fein)Blech *n*
(~) ~ **caisson,** (~) ~ cassette, (~) ~ coffer, (~) ~ waffle, (~) ~ pan(el) · (Fein)Blech(decken)kassette *f*
(~) ~ **cassette,** (~) ~ caisson, (~) ~ coffer, (~) ~ waffle, (~) ~ pan(el) · (Fein)Blech(decken)kassette *f*
(~) ~ **coffer,** (~) ~ waffle, (~) ~ pan(el), (~) ~ cassette, (~) ~ caisson · (Fein)Blech(decken)kassette *f*
(~) ~ **cover(ing),** sheet metal ~ · (Fein)Blechabdeckung *f*
(~) ~ **pan(el),** (~) ~ coffer, (~) ~ waffle, (~) ~ cassette, (~) ~ caisson, · (Fein)Blech(decken)kassette *f*
(~) ~ **panel,** sheet metal ~ · (Fein-)Blechtafel *f*
~ ~ **roof cladding** → (sheet-)metal ~ ~
~ ~ ~ **cover(ing)** → (sheet-)metal roof cladding

metal sheet roof sheathing — metal(lic) abrasive (material) 622

~ ~ ~ **sheathing** → (sheet-)metal roof cladding

~ ~ **roof(ing)** → (sheet-)metal roof cladding

(~) ~ **waffle,** (~) ~ coffer, (~) ~ pan(el), (~) ~ cassette, (~) ~ caisson · (Fein)Blech(decken)kassette *f*

~ **shingle** · Metallschindel *f*

~ **shower stall,** metallic ~ ~ · Metallduschstand *m*

~ **shutter** → ~ window ~

~ **shuttering,** ~ form(work), ~ forms · Metallschalung *f*, Metall-Betonschalung

~ **siding** · Metallverschalung *f*, Metallwandbeschlag *m*, Metallwandschirm *m*, Metallwetterschirm [*Wetterschutz für Außenmauern*]

~ **silo** · Metallsilo *m*

~ **sink** [*B.S. 1244*] · Metallausguß(bekken) *m*, (*n*)

~ **skirting** [*B.S. 1246*]; ~ sanitary cove (US); ~ base plate [*Scotland*] · Metallscheuerleiste *f*, Metallfußleiste, Metallsockelleiste

~ **skylight** · Metall(-Dach)raupe *f*

~ **soap,** metallic ~ · Metallseife *f*

~ ~ **formation** · Metallseifenbildung *f*

metal-sprayed · metallgespritzt

~ **coat(ing),** metallic sprayed ~ · (auf-)gespritzte Metallschicht *f*, (auf)gespritzter Metallüberzug *m*

metal spraying, metallic ~ · Spritzmetallisierung *f*, Metallüberzugspritzen *n*

(~) ~ **gun** · Pistole *f*, Spritz~, Metallisierungs-Spritz~

~ ~ **system** · Spritzmetallisierungsverfahren *n*

~ **stair(case)** · Metalltreppe

~ **stake** → ~ fence ~

~ **strap** · Metallasche *f*

~ **strip** · Metallstreifen *m*

~ ~ **stiffener** [*e.g. in a wall*] · Metallstreifenverstärker *m*

~ **structural material** → ~ building ~

~ **stud,** ~ principal post · Metall-Bundstiel *m*, Metall-Bundsäule *f*, Metall-Bundständer *m*, Metall-Bundpfosten *m*

~ ~ **partition (wall)** · Metallgerippewand *f*, Metallskelettwand [*DIN 4103*]

~ **studs** · Metallgerippe *n*, Metallskelett *n* [*Leichte Trennwand, DIN 4103*]

metal-(sur)faced board · Panzerplatte *f* [*Furnier- oder Tischlerplatte mit Decklagen aus Metallfolien oder dünnen Blechen*]

~ **door** → ~ metal-covered ~

~ **window** → metal-covered ~

metal (sur)facing → ~ lining

~ **surround** · Metalleinfassung *f*

~ **tie,** ~ anchor [*B.S. 1243*] · Metallanker *m*

~ **tile** · Metall(belag)platte *f*, Metallfliese *f*

~ **(timber) connector;** ~ (~) connecter (US) · Metalldübel *m* [*Holzverbinder*]

metal-to-glass bond · Metall/Glas-Verbindung *f*

metal-to-metal seal(ing) · Metall-(auf-)Metall-Dichtung *f*

metal trim → ~ section

~ **tying,** ~ anchorage · Verankerung *f* mit Metallanker

~ **unit** → ~ section

~ **valley** [*A valley gutter lined with lead, zinc, copper, or alumin(i)um*] · Metall(-Dach)kehle *f*

~ **vapour lamp** (Brit.); ~ vapor ~ (US) · Metalldampflampe *f*

~ **waffle** → ~ pan(el)

~ ~ **(type) ceiling,** ~ coffer (~) ~, ~ cassette (~) ~, pan(el) (~) ~, ~ caisson (~) ~ · Metallkassetten-Akustikdecke *f*, Metallkassetten-Schallschluckdecke

~ **wall** · Metallwand *f*

~ ~ **panel** · Metallwandtafel *f*

~ ~ **plug,** ~ nailing ~ · Metall-Mauerdübel *m*

~ ~ **tie** [*B.S. 1243*] · Metallwandanker *m*

~ **waterstop,** ~ waterbar · Metallfugenband *n*

~ **welding** · Metallschweißen *n*

~ **window** · Metallfenster *n*

~ ~ **for domestic buildings** [*B.S. 990*] · Metallfenster *n* für Wohnungsbau

~ ~ **frame** · Metall-Fenster(blend)rahmen *m*, Metall-Fensterfutter(rahmen) *n*, (*m*)

~ (~) **sash** · Metall(fenster)flügel *m*

~ (~) **shutter** · Metall(fenster)laden *m*

~ ~ **sill;** ~ ~ cill (Brit.) · Metallfensterbank *f*, Metall(fenster)sohlbank

(~) **wire** · (Metall)Draht *m*

~ ~ **method,** ~ ~ system · Drahtspritzverfahren *n*, Spritzmetallisierung *f* [*Der Draht wird in einer Spritzpistole mittels einer preßluftgetriebenen Turbine oder eines Elektromotors durch eine Düse geschoben und vor der Düse durch eine Gas-Sauerstoff-Flamme oder einen Lichtbogen geschmolzen. Das geschmolzene Metall wird durch Preßluft zerstäubt und auf die Oberfläche des zu bespritzenden Gegenstandes geschleudert*]

~ **wool** · Metallwolle *f*

~ **work** · Metallbauarbeiten *fpl* [*DIN 18360*]

~**(working) shop** · Metallwerkraum *m* [*Schule*]

~ **zinc** → metal(lic) ~

~ ~ **pigment** → (metal(lic)) ~ ~

metal(lic) abrasive · metallisches Strahlmittel *n*

~ ~ **(material)** → ~ aggregate

metal(lic) additive — method of calculating lighting

~ **additive** → gas-forming agent

~ **aggregate,** ~ abrasive (material) · Stahlbeton-Härtemittel n, Stahlbeton-Hartstoff m [Fehlname: Stahlbeton-Härtematerial n. Ein metallischer Hart(beton)stoff m, der meist einem Mörtel aus Quarzsand und Portlandzement beigemischt wird (Stahlbetonmörtel) zur Herstellung von Stahlbetonbelägen]

~ ~ · Metallzuschlag(stoff) m

metal(lic)-aggregate mortar → mortar with metal(lic) aggregate

~ ~ **cover(ing)** · Stahlbetonbelag m [Fehlname: Stahl(beton)estrich m. Ein solcher Belag wird hergestellt, indem der Hartbetonstoff Gruppe B nach DIN 1100, aus metallischem Material bestehend, mit Portlandzement zu Mörtel verarbeitet und als Hartbetonbelag aufgetragen wird]

metal(lic) bronze · (Métall)Bronze f [Metalleffektpigment]

~ **building material** → ~ construction

~ **constituent** · metallischer Bestandteil m [Hartbetonbelag]

~ **construction(al) material,** ~ building ~ · metallischer Baustoff m; metallisches Baumaterial n [Schweiz]

~ **finish** · Metalleffektlackierung f

~ **fitting** → metal (pipe) ~

~ **flakes,** ~ powder, ~ pigment · Metalleffektpigment n, Metallpulver n [nicht verwechseln mit Metallpigment]

~ **grit,** ~ hardener [Dressing for a cement-based floor] · Metall-Hart(beton)stoff m

~ **hardener** → ~ grit

metal(lic)-hardening process · Badpatentieren n

metal(lic) jacket · Blechmantel m

~ **lath(ing) (for plastering)** [B.S. 1369] · Metallnetz n als Putzträger, Metallgewebe n ~ ~, Metallputzträger m

~ **paint** → bronze ~

~ **pigment,** ~ powder, ~ flakes · Metalleffektpigment n, Metallpulver n [nicht verwechseln mit Metallpigment]

metal(lic) pipe · Metallrohr n

~ (~) **fitting** → metal (~) ~

~ **plate** · Blechplatte f, Metallplatte

~ **powder, powder(ed) metal** · Metallpulver n

~ **powder,** ~ pigment, ~ flakes · Metalleffektpigment n, Metallpulver n [nicht verwechseln mit Metallpigment]

~ **salt** · Metallsalz n

~ **seal(ing)** · Metall(ab)dichtung f

~ **shower stall** · Metallduschstand m

~ **soap** · Metallseife f

~ ~ **formation** · Metallseifenbildung f

~ **sprayed coat(ing)** · (auf)gespritzte Metallschicht f, (auf)gespritzter Metallüberzug m

~ **spraying** · Metallüberzugspritzen n, Spritzmetallisierung f

~ **zinc,** zinc metal · metallisches Zink n

(~) ~ **pigment** · Zinkfarbe f, Zinkpigment n

metalloid · Halbmetall n

metallurgical cement · Hüttenzement m [Fehlname: Schlacken-Portland(-zement). Ein Gemisch aus Portlandzement und Hochofenschlacke bestimmter Zusammensetzung]

~ ~ **rendering** · Hüttenzementputz m

~ **coke** · Hüttenkoks m

metamorphic rock, transformed ~, metamorphosed ~ · metamorphes Gestein n, Umwandlungsgestein, Umprägungsgestein

~ **schist,** metamorphosed ~, transformed ~ · metamorpher Schiefer m

metamorphosed rock → metamorphic ~

~ **schist,** metamorphic ~, transformed ~ · metamorpher Schiefer m

meter · Zähler m, Zählvorrichtung f, Messer, Zählapparat m, Zählgerät n, Zählwerk n

~ → (concrete) (air) (entrainment) ~

~ **arrangement** · Zähleranordnung f

~ **board** · Zählerblech n, Zählerbrett n, Zählertafel f [Grundplatte für Zähleranbringung. DIN 43853]

~ **box** · Zählerkasten m

~ **compartment,** ~ room · Zähler(ablese)raum m

~ **cupboard** · Zählerschrank m

~ **enclosure,** ~ niche · Zähler(ablese)nische f [DIN 18013]

~ **for liquids** · Flüssigkeitszähler m

~ **niche,** ~ enclosure · Zähler(ablese)nische f [DIN 18013]

~ **pit,** water ~ ~ [A chamber for housing a meter, constructed in the ground and surrounded by a surface box or manhole cover] · (Wasser)Zählerschacht m

~ **room,** ~ compartment · Zähler(ablese)raum m

~ **station** · Zählerstation f

methanol, methyl alcohol, wood alcohol [B.S. 506] · Methanol n, Methylalkohol m, Holzgeist m, CH_3OH

method, system · Verfahren n

~ **of anchoring,** system ~ ~, anchoring method, anchoring system · Verankerungssystem n, Verankerungsverfahren n

~ ~ **application,** application method · Auftragverfahren n [Anstrichtechnik]

~ ~ **calculating lighting,** ~ ~ ~ illumination · Beleuchtungsberechnungsverfahren n

method of calculation — mica of commerce

~ ~ **calculation**, calculation method, calculating method · Rechenverfahren *n*, Berechnungsverfahren, rechnerisches Verfahren

~ ~ **combination** · Zusammensetzverfahren *n* [*Berechnung von Faltwerken*]

~ ~ **design**, design method · Entwurfsverfahren *n*

~ ~ ~, design method · Bemessungsverfahren *n*

~ ~ **differences**, constant segment method, analysis by finite differences · Differenzenmethode *f*, Differenzenverfahren *n*

~ ~ **erection**, assembling method · Montageweise *f*, Montageverfahren *n*, Montagemethode *f*, Zusammenbauweise, Zusammenbauverfahren, Zusammenbaumethode

~ ~ **expansion into series** · Reihenentwick(e)lungsverfahren *n*

~ ~ **fabrication**, ~ ~ manufacture, manufacturing method, fabrication method · Fertigungsverfahren *n*, Herstellungsverfahren

~ ~ **facing** → facing system

~ ~ **finite differences** · Differenzenverfahren *n*

~ ~ **fixed points** · Methode *f* der Festpunkte

~ ~ **flashing** [*See remark under 'Anschluß'*] · Anschlußverfahren *n*

~ ~ **jointing**, system ~ ~, jointing method, jointing system · Verbindungssystem *n*, Verbindungsverfahren *n*

~ ~ **joints** · Knoten(punkt)verfahren *n*

~ ~ **laying** · Verlegeweise *f*

~ ~ **manufacture**, ~ ~ fabrication, manufacturing method, fabrication method · Fertigungsverfahren *n*, Herstellungsverfahren

~ ~ **measurement (of building works)** · Aufmaßverfahren *n*

~ ~ **presentation** · Darstellungsmethode *f*

~ ~ **sculpture** · Plastikverfahren *n*, Plastikmethode *f*, Skulpturverfahren, Skulpturmethode

~ ~ **sections** · Schnittkraftverfahren *n*

~ ~ **taking samples**, sampling method · Probenahmeverfahren *n*

~ ~ **virtual work** · Verfahren *n* der virtuellen Arbeit

methyl alcohol, wood ~, methanol [*B.S. 506*] · Methanol *n*, Methylalkohol *m*, Holzgeist *m*, CH$_3$OH

~ **cellulose** · Methylzellulose *f*

~ ~ **glue** · Methylzelluloseleim *m*

~ **derivative** · Methylabkömmling *m*, Methylderivat *n*

~ **orange** · Methylorange *f*

~ **red** · Methylrot *n*

methylene removal of stress, ~ stress relieving · autogenes Entspannen *n*, mechanisches Entspannen durch Wärmedehnung [*Baustahl*]

~ **stress relieving** → removal of stress

methylmethacrylate · Methylmethacrylat *n*

metope [*The square space between two triglyphs in the frieze of a Doric order; it may be carved or left plain*] · Zwischenfeld *n*, Metope *f*

metre module · Metermodul *n*

metric nut · metrische Mutter *f*

~ **screw** · metrische Schraube *f*

~ **series** · metrische Reihe *f*

~ **system** · metrisches (Maß)System *n*

~ **thread** · metrisches Gewinde *n*

metrication · metrische Umrechnung *f*

metropolis · Riesenstadt *f*

metropolitan area · Stadtregion *f*, Städteregion

~ **railroad** (US); ~ **railway** (Brit.); urban rapid transit system · S-Bahn *f*, Stadt(schnell)bahn

~ ~ **station** (US); ~ railway ~ (Brit.) · Stadt(schnell)bahnstation *f*, S-Bahnstation

~ ~ **track** (US); ~ railway ~ (Brit.) · Stadtbahngleis *n*, S-Bahngleis

metroum · Metronom *n* [*Olympia*]

mews · Marstall *m* [*in London*]

Mexican onyx, onyx marble, (calcareous) alabaster [*A carbonate of lime*] · Kalkalabaster *m*, Kalkonyx *m*, Onyx(marmor) *m*

Mexico asphalt (US); ~ (asphaltic-) bitumen (Brit.) · Mexiko(-Asphalt)-bitumen *n*

mezzanine, entresol · Zwischengeschoß *n*, Mezzanin *n*, Halbstockwerk *n*, Halbetage *f*, Halbgeschoß, Beigeschoß, Zwischenetage, Zwischenstockwerk

~ **floor**, entresol ~ · Zwischengeschoßdecke *f*, Beigeschoßdecke, Mezzanindecke, Halbgeschoßdecke, Halbstockwerkdecke, Halbetagendecke

MF → melamine-formaldehyde (resin)

mh → manhole

mica · Glimmer *m*

~ **cleavage** · Glimmerspaltung *f*

~ **dust** → ~ flour

~ **flake** · Glimmerblättchen *n*, Glimmerschüppchen Glimmerplättchen, Glimmerschuppe *f*

mica-flap valve [*A sheet of mica at a fresh air inlet, hinged to allow air to flow inwards only*] · Glimmer-Verschlußkappe *f*

mica flour, ~ dust, ~ powder, powder(-ed) mica · Glimmermehl *n*, Glimmerstaub *m*, Glimmerpulver *n*, Glimmerpuder *n*

~ **in sheets**, sheet mica, book mica · Spaltglimmer *m*, Plattenglimmer [*Er wird aus Blockglimmer durch Spalten in dünne Lagen hergestellt*]

~ **of commerce** · Handelsglimmer *m*

mica paper — mild steel plate

~ **paper** [*See remark under 'Pappe'*] · Glimmerpappe *f*

~ **pigment** · Glimmerpigment *n*

~ **powder** → ~ flour

micaceous · glimmerführend, glimmer(halt)ig

~ **iron oxide** (Brit.); ~ ~ oxid(e) (US); MIO, iron mica · Eisenglimmer *m* [*Eisenoxid von blätt(e)rig-glimmerartiger Struktur*]

~ ~ **oxid(e) paint** (US); ~ ~ oxide ~ (Brit.); MIO ~ · Rostschutzfarbe *f* aus Eisenglimmer [*Fehlname: Glimmerfarbe*]

~ **porphyry** · Glimmerporphyr *m*

~ **sand** · Glimmersand *m*

~ **sandstone** · Glimmersandstein *m*

~ **schist** · Glimmerschiefer *m*

micanite, reconstructed mica · Marienglas *n*, Mikanit *m*

Michaelis' salt · Zementbazillus *m*, Ettringit *m*

microbore · Kleinstrohrweite *f*

micro-concrete [*Concrete for use in small-scale structural models. Its aggregate has been scaled down*] · Mikrobeton *m*

microcrack · Mikroriß *m*

microcracking · Mikrorißbildung *f*, Mikrorissebildung

microgranite · Mikrogranit *m*

microhardness · Mikrohärte *f*

~ **tester** · Mikrohärteprüfer *m*

micropegmatite · Mikropegmatit *m*

micro(scopic) examination · mikroskopische Untersuchung *f*

~ **void**, ~ pore · Mikropore *f*, Feinpore

microtensile strength · Mikrozugfestigkeit *f*

midden, refuse heap, waste heap · Abfall(stoff)haufen *m*, Müllhaufen

Middle Gothic Style → Curvilinear ~

middle layer, core · Einlage *f* [*Sandwichplatte*]

~ **plane**, neutral ~ ~ · Mittelebene *f* [*Platte*]

Middle Pointed Style → Curvilinear ~

middle purlin(e), central ~, centre ~ (Brit.); center ~ (US) · Zwischenpfette *f*, Mittelpfette

~ ~ **connection**, central ~ ~; centre ~ ~ (Brit.); center ~ ~ (US) · Zwischenpfettenanschluß *m*, Mittelpfettenanschluß

~ **relief** · halberhabenes Relief *n*

middle-sized, medium-grained · mittelkörnig

~ **grains**, ~ particles, ~ material, medium-grained ~ · Mittelkörner *npl*, Mittelkorn *n*

~ **gravel**, medium-grained ~ · Mittelkies *m* [*6–20 mm*]

~ **material**, ~ grains, ~ particles, medium-grained ~ · Mittelkörner *npl*, Mittelkorn *n*

~ **particles**, ~ material, ~ grains, medium-grained ~ · Mittelkörner *npl*, Mittelkorn *n*

~ **sand**, medium-grained ~ · Mittelsand *m* [*0,2–0,6 mm*]

~ **sandstone**, medium-grained ~ · mittelkörniger Sandstein *m*

~ **sandy gravel** → medium-grained ~

~ **silt**, medium-grained ~ · Mittelschluff *m* [*0,006–0,02 mm*]

Middle stoa · Mittelhalle *f* [*Agora von Athen*]

middle strip, central ~; center ~ (US); centre ~ (Brit.) · Mittelstreifen *m*

~ **surface** · Mittelfläche *f* [*Platte*]

~ **vessel**, (church) nave · Hauptschiff *n*, Mittelschiff, Lang(haus)schiff, Mittelhaus *n* [*Kirche*]

~ ~ **arcade**, (church) nave ~ · Mittelschiffarkade *f*, Hauptschiffarkade, Lang(haus)schiffarkade, Mittelhausarkade

~ ~ **bay** → (church) nave (vault) ~

~ ~ **ceiling**, (church) nave ~ · Mittelschiffdecke *f*, Hauptschiffdecke, Lang(haus)schiffdecke, Mittelhausdecke

~ ~ **pier**, (church) nave ~ · Hauptschiffpfeiler *m*, Mittelschiffpfeiler, Lang(haus)schiffpfeiler, Mittelhauspfeiler

~ ~ **range of columns** → (church nave ~ ~ ~

~ ~ **row of columns** → (church) nave range ~ ~

~ ~ **vault**, (church) nave ~ · Hauptschiffgewölbe *n*, Mittelschiffgewölbe, Lang(haus)schiffgewölbe, Mittelhausgewölbe

~ ~ **(~) bay** → (church) nave (~) ~

~ ~ **window**, (church) nave ~ · Hauptschiffenster *n*, Mittelschiffenster, Lang(haus)schiffenster, Mittelhausfenster

mid-feather, withe · Schornsteinzunge *f* [*Trenn(ungs)mauer der Rauchkanäle*]

mid-span · Feldmitte *f*

migration · Wandern *n*

mihrab, praying niche, prayer niche · Gebetsnische *f* [*Moschee*]

mild steel, m.s. · Flußstahl *m* [*früher: Gußstahl. Früher wurde dieser im flüssigen Zustand gewonnene Stahl im Gegensatz zum teigigen Schweißstahl auch „Gußstahl" genannt. Nur in der Drahtindustrie und bei Werkzeugstahl wird noch häufig von Gußstahl gesprochen. Gußstahl ist nicht zu verwechseln mit Stahlguß*]

~ ~ **angle**, m.s. ~ · Flußstahlwinkel *m*

~ ~ **flat**, m.s. ~ · Flußstahlflachprofil *n*

~ ~ **hollow section**, m.s. ~ ~ · Flußstahlhohlprofil *n*

~ ~ **pipe**, m.s. ~ · Flußstahlrohr *n*

~ ~ **plate**, m.s. ~ · Flußstahlplatte *f*

mild steel reinforcement of... — mineral aggregate

~~ reinforcement of prestressed concrete elements, un-tensioned ~ ~~~~~~ · schlaffe Bewehrung f von Spannbetonbauteilen, ~ Armierung ~ ~

~ ~ (reinforcing), ordinary ~ (~), un-tensioned ~ ~, ~ ~ (reinforcement) · schlaffe Armierung f, ~ Bewehrung, ~ (Stahl)Einlagen fpl

~~ (~) bar, ~ ~ (~) rod, m.s. (~) ~ · Flußstahlarmierungsstab m, Flußstahl(bewehrungs)stab

~~ structural tube, ~ ~ ~ pipe, m.s. ~ ~ · Flußstahl-Konstruktionsrohr n

~~ window, m.s. ~ · Flußstahlfenster n

~~ wire, m s. ~ · Flußstahldraht m, Gußstahldraht [Siehe Anmerkung unter „Flußstahl"]

military architecture · Wehrbau m, Kriegsbaukunst f, Kriegsarchitektur f

~ brick architecture · Backstein-Wehrbau m, Backstein-Kriegsarchitektur f, Backstein-Kriegsbaukunst f

~ building · Militärgebäude n

~~ construction · Militärhochbauwesen n

~ camp · Standlager n [im Altertum]

~ construction · Militärbau m

~ hospital · Lazarett n

~ stronghold → fortification

~ tower · Festungsturm m

milk-bar · Milchbar f

milk casein · Milchkasein n

~ glass · Milchglas n, Knochenglas, Beinglas, Mondscheinglas [Ein in der Masse oder in der Überfangschicht durchgefärbtes Glas, das am Tage in der Ansicht porzellanweiß erscheint, bei Beleuchtung aber noch 20% bis 30% Licht durchläßt]

milkiness · Weißanlaufen n, milchiges Aussehen von Anstrichfilmen

milk of lime → whitewash

~~~ coat → whitewash ~

~ parlour (Brit.); ~ parlor (US) · Milchraum m [Bestandteil einer Kuhstall-Anlage]

milk-processing plant · Milchverarbeitungsbetrieb m

to mill, to shape, to dress, to hew · (steinmetzmäßig) bearbeiten, (~) behauen, (~) zurichten

~~ coarsely → ~ dress ~

~~ roughly → ~ dress coarsely

mill board, news ~, grey ~, gray ~ · Graupappe f

mill-painted, factory-painted, shop-painted · werkgestrichen

mill-primed, shop-primed, factory-primed · werkgrundiert

mill primer → factory ~

~ priming → factory ~

~ run, sawn wood, sawn timber, sawed timber, converted timber; milled products [Australia]; lumber (US) [All the timber produced in a mill without reference to grade. The term 'lumber' is sometimes reserved in the USA for the German terms 'Bretter and Bohlen' and the German terms 'Kantholz and Balken' are then called 'timbers'. Thus 'Schnittholz' may also be called in the USA 'lumber and timbers']

mill-run mortar, plant-mix(ed) ~ · maschinengemischter Mörtel m

(mill) scale [Scale produced in the finishing mill] · Abbrand m, Walzhaut f, (Walz)Zunder m

~ weld · Werknaht f

~ work, wood ~ ~, wood fixtures, wood trim, wood in-built units, wood built-in units · Bautischlereinbauten f, Holzeinbauten, Holzeinbauteile mpl, npl

milled, shaped, dressed, hewn · (steinmetzmäßig) bearbeitet, (~) behauen, (~) zugerichtet

~ fair face → (natural) stone finish

~ joint [of a steel structure] · Werkstoß m

~ lead, sheet ~, lead sheet [Lead rolled into sheets from cast slabs] · Blei(fein)blech n, Walzblei n, Tafelblei [DIN 59610]

~ (natural) stone → dressed (~) ~

~ products [Australia] → mill run

~ stone → dressed (natural) ~

~ stonework, (dressed) ~, shaped ~, hewn ~ · zugerichtete Werksteine mpl, bearbeitete ~, behauene ~

millefiore glass, thousand-flower ~ · Millefioriglas n

millefleurs garden tapestry · Millefleursteppich m

millerite, capillary pyrite · Haarkies m, Millerit m, NiS (Min.)

milling, shaping, dressing, hewing · (Natur)Steinbearbeitung f, Bearbeitung, Behauen n, Zurichten

millstone · Mühlenkalkstein m

Milori blue (pigment) · Miloriblau(pigment) n

~ green (pigment) · Milorigrün(pigment) n

mimbar, minbar, pulpit · Mimbar m, Minbar [Kanzel für die Freitagspredigt in einer großen Moschee]

minaret, prayer-tower · Gebetsturm m, Minarett n

minaret-like · gebetsturmähnlich, minarettähnlich

minbar, mimbar, pulpit · Mimbar m, Minbar [Kanzel für die Freitagspredigt in einer großen Moschee]

mineral acid · Mineralsäure f

~ aggregate, ~ construction ~, stone (construction) ~ · mineralischer Zuschlag(stoff) m, Zuschlag(stoff) aus Gestein, mineralisches Zuschlagmaterial n, Zuschlagmaterial aus Gestein

mineral aggreagate filling — mineral substrate

~ ~ **filling** · mineralischer strukturgebender Füllstoff m [*Putz*]

~ **binder** · mineralischer Binder m, mineralisches Bindemittel n

~ **black** · Mineralschwarz n

~ **board** → ~ fibre ~

~ **bound** · mineralisch gebunden

~ **building material** → ~ construction(al) ~

~ **caoutchouc**, elaterite, elastic bitumen [*Old name: elastic mineral pitch. Variety of bitumen which, when fresh, is elastic, but which on exposure becomes hard and brittle. First described under the name 'Fungus subterraneus' by M. Lister*] · Elaterit n, elastisches Erdharz n

~ **charcoal**, mother of coal, fusain, motherham · mineralische Holzkohle f

~ **colloid** · Mineralkolloid n

~ **concrete aggregate**, stone ~ ~ · Betonzuschlag(stoff) m aus Gestein, mineralischer Betonzuschlag(stoff)

~ **(construction) aggregate**, stone (~) ~ · mineralischer Zuschlag(stoff) m, Zuschlag(stoff) aus Gestein, mineralisches Zuschlagmaterial n, Zuschlagmaterial aus Gestein

~ **construction(al) material**, ~ building ~, ~ structural ~ · mineralischer Baustoff m, mineralisches Baumaterial n [*Schweiz*]

~ **content** · Mineralgehalt m [*z.B. beim Naturasphalt*]

~ **cord** → ~ fibre ~

~ **dust** → (~) filler

mineral-faced, mineral-surfaced · mineralabgestreut, mineralbestreut [*Dachpappe*]

mineral facing → ~ sur~

~ **fiber acoustic(al) tile** (US); ~ fibre ~ ~ (Brit.); ~ ~ sound-control ~, ~ ~ (sound) absorbent ~, ~ ~ (sound) absorbing ~ · Mineralfaser-Akustikplatte f, Mineralfaser-Schallschluckplatte, Mineralfaser-Schallschluckfliese, Mineralfaser-Akustikplatte

~ ~ **pipe section** (US) → preformed mineral fibre (pipe insulating) ~ (Brit.)

~ **fibre** (Brit.); ~ fiber (US) · Mineralfaser f, mineralische Faser, Gesteinsfaser [*Aus Schmelzen von Sedimentärgesteinen hergestellte Faser. DIN 60001*]

~ (~) **board** (Brit.); ~ (fiber) ~ (US) · Mineralfaserplatte f

~ (~) ~ **acoustic(al) ceiling** (Brit.); ~ (fiber) ~ ~ ~ (US); ~ ~ ~ sound-control ~, ~ ~ ~ (sound) absorbent ~, ~ ~ ~ (sound) absorbing ~, ~ ~ ~ (sound) absorptive ~, ~ ~ ~ acoustic tiled ~ · Mineralfaser(-platten)-Schallschluckdecke f, Mineralfaser(platten)-Akustikdecke

~ (~) ~ **ceiling** (Brit.); ~ (fiber) ~ ~ (US); ~ ~ ~ sheet ~ · Mineralfaser(platten)decke f, MF-Decke

~ (~) **cord** (Brit.); ~ (fiber) ~ (US) · Mineralfaserschnur f

~ (~) **insulating material**, ~ ~ insulation(-grade) ~ (Brit.); ~ (fiber) insulation(-grade) ~ (US); ~ ~ fiber insulating material (US); ~ ~ ~ insulation · mineralischer Faserdämmstoff m

~ (~) **mat** (Brit.); ~ (fiber) ~ (US) · Mineralfasermatte f

~ (~) **pipe section** (Brit.) → preformed mineral (fibre) (pipe insulating) ~

~ ~ **slab** (Brit.); ~ fiber ~ (US) · Mineralfaserplatte f

~ ~ **tile** (Brit.); ~ fiber ~ (US) · Mineralfaser(belag)platte f, Mineralfaserfliese f

(~) **filler**, ~ dust, granular ~ · (Mineral-)Füller m (Mineral)Füllstoff m, mineralischer Füller, mineralischer Füllstoff

~ **flax** · Faserasbest m

~ **grain** · Mineralkorn n, Gesteinskorn

~ **grains** · Steingekörn n

~ **granules**, ~ (sur)facing, granular (sur)facing, dusting finish · Mineralabstreuung f, Mineralbestreuung, (mineralische) Bestreuung, (mineralische) Abstreuung, Streuschicht f [*Dachpappe und Spachteldachbelag*]

~ **green**, green basic copper carbonate · Berggrün n [*Malachit*]

~ **ground** (Brit.) → ~ substrate

~ **insulation** → ~ fibre ~

~ **mat** → ~ fibre ~

~ **matter** · Mineralstoff m

~ **matter** · mineralische Stoffe mpl [*im Abwasser*]

~ **oil** · Mineralöl n

~ ~ **concentrate** · Mineralölkonzentrat n

~ **pigment** → natural ~

~ **pipe section** → ~ fibre ~ ~

~ **powder**, powder(ed) mineral · Mineralmehl n, Mineralpulver n

~ **raw material** · mineralischer Rohstoff m

~ **rubber** · mineralischer Gummi m, mineralisches ~ m

~ **skeleton** · Steingerüst n, Mineralgerüst

~ **solvent for paints**, white spirit; turpentine substitute [*deprecated*]; mineral turpentine [*Australia*] [*The most commonly used thinner for paints and varnishes*] · Testbenzin n, Lackbenzin, künstliches Terpentinöl n, Kristallöl [*Fehlname: Terpentin(öl)ersatz m*]

~ **stability number** · Mineralbeständigkeitszahl f [*Bitumenemulsion*]

~ **structural material** → ~ construction(al) ~

~ **substance** · mineralischer Stoff m

~ **substrate**; ~ ground (Brit.) · mineralischer Anstrich(unter)grund m, ~ Aufstrich(unter)grund, mineralische Aufstrichfläche f, mineralische Anstrichfläche

mineral-(sur)faced — minimum loading

mineral-(sur)faced · mineralabgestreut, mineralbestreut [*Dachpappe*]

mineral (sur)facing, ~ granules, granular (sur)facing, dusting finish · Mineralabstreuung *f*, Mineralbestreuung, (mineralische) Bestreuung, (mineralische) Abstreuung, Streuschicht *f* [*Dachpappe und Spachteldachbelag*]

~ **tallow** → ozokerit(e)

~ **tar,** pissasphalt(um), maltha · Bergteer *m*

~ **turpentine** [*Australia*]; turpentine substitute [*deprecated*] [*The most commonly used thinner for paints and varnishes*] · Testbenzin *n*, Lackbenzin, künstliches Terpentinöl *n*, Kristallöl [*Fehlname: Terpentin(öl)ersatz m*]

~ **wax** → ozokerit(e)

~ **wool** · Mineralwolle *f*

~~ **board,** ~~ sheet · Mineralwolleplatte *f*

~~ **felt** · Mineralwollefilz *m*

~~ **insulating material,** ~~ insulation(-grade) ~ · Mineralwolleisolierstoff *m*

~~ **insulation** · Mineralwolle(ab)dämmung *f*

~~~ · Mineralwolleisolierung *f*

~~ **insulation(-grade) mat,** ~~ insulating ~, ~~~ blanket, ~~ (~) quilt; ~~ (~) bat(t) (US) · Mineralwolle(däm)matte *f*

~~~ **material,** ~~ insulating ~ · Mineralwolleisolierstoff *m*

~~ **panel** · Mineralwolletafel *f*

~~ **(pipe insulation) section,** preformed ~~ (~ ~) ~ · Mineralwolleschale *f*

~~ **sheet,** ~~ board · Mineralwolleplatte *f*

~~ **strip** · Mineralwollestreifen *m*

mineralizer · Mineralisator *m*, Mineralbildner *m*

mineralogical composition · mineralogische Zusammensetzung *f*

minerals industry → nonmetallic ~~

miner's housing construction · Bergarbeiterwohnungsbau *m*

~~ **estate** · Bergarbeitersied(e)lung *f*

miniature lancet (window) · Klein-Lanzettfenster *n*

minibore central heating · Sammelheizung *f* mit Kleinstrohrweiten [*Fehlname*]; Zentralheizung ~ ~

to minimize, to absorb · abbauen [*Last; Kraft; Spannung*]

minimizing principle of Castigliano → Castigliano's theorem

minimum area · Mindestfläche *f*

~ **average value,** ~ mean ~ · Mindestmittelwert *m*

~ **bearing capacity** → ~ load-carrying ~

~~ **power** → ~ load-carrying capacity

~~ **property** → ~ load-carrying capacity

~~ **quality** → ~ load-carrying capacity

~ **bending tension strength,** ~ ~ tensile ~ · Mindestbiegezugfestigkeit *f*

~ **cement content** · Mindestzementmenge *f*, Mindestzementgehalt *m*

~ **compressive strength** · Mindestdruckfestigkeit *f*

~ **(concrete) cover** · Mindest(beton)-deckung *f*

~ **content** · Mindestgehalt *m*

~ **cover,** ~ concrete ~ · Mindest(beton)deckung *f*

~ **cross-section,** least ~ · Kleinstquerschnitt *m*, Mindestquerschnitt [*Der aus Gründen der Einhaltung zulässiger Spannungen, aus Stabilitätsgründen, aus Korrosionsgründen und aus fertigungstechnischen Gründen mindestens erforderliche Querschnitt eines Bauteiles bzw. der Anschlußquerschnitt einer Verbindung*]

~ **cube strength** · Mindestwürfel-(druck)festigkeit *f*

~ **(design) load factor** · Mindesttraglast *f*

~ **dimension,** least ~ · Kleinstabmessung *f*, Mindestabmessung, Kleinstmaß *n*, Mindestmaß

~ **on plan,** least ~ ~ ~ · kleinste Grundrißabmessung *f*

~ **distance,** least ~ · Kleinstabstand *m*, Mindestabstand

~ **eccentricity** · Mindestausmittigkeit *f*

~ **energy principle** · Prinzip *n* der minimalen Gesamtpotentialenergie, Minimalenergieprinzip

~ **failure strength** · Mindestbruchfestigkeit *f*

~ **grain size,** least ~ · Kleinstkorn *n*, Mindestkorn

~ **heat insulation** [*See remark under 'Wärmeschutz'*] · Mindestwärmeschutz *m* [*DIN 4108*]

~~~ [*See remark under 'Wärmedämmung'*] · Mindestwärme(ab)dämmung *f*

~~~ **value** · Mindestwärmedämmwert *m*

~ **length** · Mindestlänge *f*

~ **live load,** ~ variable ~ · Mindestverkehrslast *f*

~ **load,** least ~ · Kleinstlast *f*, Mindestlast

~ **load-carrying capacity,** ~ ~ power, ~ ~ property, ~ ~ quality, ~ bearing ~, ~ structural strength · Kleinsttragfähigkeit *f*, Mindesttragfähigkeit

~~ **power** → ~ ~ capacity

~~ **property** → ~ ~ capacity

~~ **quality** → ~ ~ capacity

~ **load factor,** ~ design ~ ~ · Mindesttraglast *f*

~ **loading** · Mindestbelastung *f*

~ longitudinal (pre)stressing, ~ ~ stretching, ~ ~ tensioning · Mindestlängsvorspannung f

~ ~ stressing, ~ ~ pre~, ~ ~ stretching, ~ ~ tensioning · Mindestlängsvorspannung f

~ ~ stretching, ~ ~ tensioning, ~ ~ (pre)stressing · Mindestlängsvorspannung f

~ ~ tensioning, ~ ~ stretching, ~ ~ (pre)stressing · Mindestlängsvorspannung f

~ moment, least ~ · Kleinstmoment n, Mindestmoment, Minimalmoment

~ (pre)stressing, ~ stretching, ~ tensioning · Mindestvorspannung f

~ radius of gyration, least ~ ~ ~ · kleinster Trägheitshalbmesser m

~ ~ ~ inertia · Mindestträgheitshalbmesser m

~ rafter spacing · Mindest(dach)sparrenabstand m

~ reinforcement · Mindestarmierung f, Mindestbewehrung, Mindest(stahl)einlagen fpl

~ rib width · Mindestrippenbreite f

~ roof slope, ~ ~ pitch · Mindestdachneigung f

~ room height · Mindestraumhöhe f, Raummindesthöhe

minimum-sized apartment (unit) → ~ flat

~ bathroom · Kleinstbadezimmer n

~ flat, ~ apartment (unit) [*A minimum-sized self-contained dwelling on one stor(e)y in a larger building*] · Kleinst(-Geschoß)wohnung f, Kleinst-Etagenwohnung, Kleinst-Stockwerkwohnung

minimum sound insulation · Mindestschallschutz m [*DIN 4109*]

~ strength · Mindestfestigkeit f

~ stressing → ~ stretching

~ stretching, ~ tensioning, ~ (pre-)stressing · Mindestvorspannung f

~ structural strength → ~ load-carrying capacity

~ tensile strength, ~ tension ~ · Mindestzugfestigkeit f

~ tension strength, ~ tensile ~ · Mindestzugfestigkeit f

~ tensioning, ~ stretching, ~ (pre-)stressing · Mindestvorspannung f

~ thickness · Mindestdicke f

~ transverse (pre)stressing, ~ ~ stretching, ~ ~ tensioning · Mindestquervorspannung f

~ ~ stressing, ~ ~ pre~, ~ ~ stretching, ~ ~ tensioning · Mindestquervorspannung f

~ ~ stretching, ~ ~ tensioning, ~ ~ (pre)stressing · Mindestquervorspannung f

~ ~ tensioning, ~ ~ stretching, ~ ~ (pre)stressing · Mindestquervorspannung f

~ variable load, ~ live ~ · Mindestverkehrslast f

~ wall thickness · Mindestwanddicke f, Wandmindestdicke [*Fehlnamen: Wandmindeststärke f, Mindestwandstärke*]

~ water requirement · Mindestwasserbedarf m

~ width · Mindestbreite f

~ window size · Mindestfenstergröße f

~ yield point · Mindeststreckgrenze f

mining damage · Berg(senkungs)schaden m

Ministry of Housing · Wohn(ungs)bauministerium n

~ ~ ~ and Public Works · Ministerium n für Wohnungsbau und öffentliche Arbeiten

~ ~ Labour and Social Welfare · Ministerium n für Arbeit und Sozialfürsorge

minium, red lead [*substance*], red lead oxid(e) [*chemical name*] · (Blei-)Mennige f, Pb_3O_4 [*DIN 55916*]

minium-based (building) mastic → red lead-based (~) ~

Minoan architecture · minoische Architektur f, ~ Baukunst f

minor hypothesis · Minorannahme f

minor-operating theatre · kleiner Operationssaal m

minor pool, ~ swimming ~ · Neben(schwimm)becken n

~ (swimming) pool · Neben(schwimm)becken n

minster → dome

MIO → micaceous iron oxide

~ paint → micaceous iron oxid(e) ~

miraculous image · Gnadenbild n, Mirakelbild

mirror dehumidifier · Spiegelentfeuchter m

~ finished · hochglanzpoliert

miscibility · Mischbarkeit f

~ with water; mixability ~ ~, mixibility ~ ~ (US) · Wasser(ver)mischbarkeit f

~ ~ ~ test · Mischbarkeitsprobe f mit Wasser, Mischbarkeitsversuch m ~ ~ ~, Mischbarkeitsprüfung f ~ ~

miscible · mischbar

misericord · Miserikordie f [*Konsolartiger Unterbau am Klappsitz eines Chorgestühls, der den stehenden Mönchen als Gesäßstütze dient*]

misplaced material · Fehlgut n [*Ist der Fehlaustrag bei der Sortierung*]

~ size, outsize · Fehlkorn n [*Über- und/oder Unterkorn*]

~ ~ determination, outsize ~ · Fehlkornbestimmung f [*Der prozentuale Gehalt an Fehlkorn wird durch Prüfsiebung bestimmt*]

misplacement — mixed product

misplacement · Fehlverlegung *f*

~ of the reinforcing, ~ ~ ~ reinforcement · Verdrücken *n* der Bewehrung, ~ ~ Armierung, ~ ~ (Stahl)Einlagen

mission tile (US); convex ~, over-tile · Deckziegel *m*, Mönch(ziegel) *m*, Preiße *m*

~ ~ (US); concave ~, undertile · Haken *m*, Nonne(nziegel) *f*, (*m*), Rinnenziegel

~ tiling (US); over-tile and under-tile roof(ing) (Brit.) · Mönch-Nonne-Ziegel-(dach)(ein)deckung *f*, Mönch-Nonnen-Dach(ein)deckung, Mönch-Nonnen-Dach *n*, Priependach

mist sprayer, fogger · Sprühgerät *n*

mist-spraying, fog spray(ing), atomization, atomizing, diffusion, diffusing · Zerstäubung *f*, Zerstäuben *n*, (Ver-)Sprühen, Versprühung

miter (US); mitre (Brit.) · Gehrung *f*

~ brad (US); mitre ~ (Brit.); corrugated fastener, joint fastener, wiggle nail, dog · Wellennagel *m*, gewellter Nagel

~ joint (US); mitre ~ (Brit.) · Gehrungsfuge *f*

mitre (Brit.); miter (US) · Gehrung *f*

~ brad (Brit.); miter ~ (US); corrugated fastener, joint fastener, wiggle nail, dog · Wellennagel *m*, gewellter Nagel

~ joint (Brit.); miter ~ (US) · Gehrungsfuge *f*

to mix · anmachen, mischen

mix → (glass) batch

~ → mixture

~, mixture, combined materials · Mischung *f*, Gemisch *n*

~ component → mixture ~

~ composition → mixture ~

~ ~, mixture ~ · Rezept(ur) *n*, (*f*), Versatzformel *f* [*Steinzeugindustrie*]

(~) ingredient → mix(ture) component

~ of barite grains → barite grain mix(ture)

~ ~ barytes grains (Brit.) → barite grain mix(ture)

~ ~ grains → mixed grains

~ ~ hydrocarbons of high molecular weight, mixture ~ ~ ~ ~ ~ ~ · hochmolekulare Kohlenwasserstoffverbindung *f*

~ ~ styles, mixture ~ ~ · Stilmischung *f*

~ proportioning → mixture ~

~ proportions, ~ ratio · Misch(ungs)verhältnis *n*

~ ~ by volume, ~ ratio ~ ~ · Misch(ungs)verhältnis *n* nach Raumteilen

~ ~ ~ weight, ~ ratio ~ ~ · Misch(ungs)verhältnis *n* nach Gewichtsteilen

~ ratio, ~ proportions · Misch(ungs)verhältnis *n*

~ ~ by volume, ~ proportions ~ ~ · Misch(ungs)verhältnis *n* nach Raumteilen

~ ~ ~ weight, ~ proportions ~ ~ · Misch(ungs)verhältnis *n* nach Gewichtsteilen

~ water → mix(ing) ~

mixability with water, mixibility ~ ~ (US); miscibility ~ ~ · Wasser(ver)mischbarkeit *f*

mixed anilin point · Mischanilinpunkt *m* [*Kohlenwasserstoff-Lösungsmittel*]

~ barytes grains (Brit.) → barite grain mix(ture)

~ bituminous macadam · bituminöser Mischmakadam *m*

~ development → ~ housing

~ ~ area, ~ ~ zone · Mischgebiet *n*

~ fused resin, ~ ~ rosin, ~ ~ colophony · Mischharzharz *n*

~ glue → ready-~ ~

mixed-grained · gemischtkörnig

mixed grains, mix(ture) of grains, grain mix(ture), aggregate mix(ture) · Kornmasse *f*, Körnungsgemisch *n*, Korngemisch, Körnergemisch, Körnung *f*, Körnungsmischung, Körnermischung, Körnungsgemenge *n*, Körnergemenge, Kornmischung

~ (housing) development · gemischte Bebauung *f*, Mischbebauung, Mischbauweise *f*, gemischte Bauweise

mixed-in-place construction (road) tar · (Straßen)Teer *m* für Kaltmischverfahren auf der Straße

mixed load · gemischte Last *f* [*Eine gemischte Last kann bestehen aus gleichmäßig verteilter Last + Einzellast, gleichmäßig verteilter Last + Streckenlast, Streckenlast + Einzellast und gleichmäßig verteilter Last + Streckenlast + Einzellast*]

~ loading · gemischte Belastung *f* [*Eine Belastung durch verschiedenartige Lasten*]

~ marble grains → marble grain mix(ture)

(~) ~ plaster · Marmor(ver)putz *m*

~ material · Mischgut *n*

~ pigment, composite ~ · Mischpigment *n*

(~) plaster [*1. A paste-like material, usually a mix(ture) of portland cement, lime, or gypsum with water and sand; fiber or hair may be added as a binder; applied to surfaces such as walls or ceilings in the plastic state; later it sets to form a hard surface. 2. This material in its hardened form = finish = Verputz*] · Putz *m*

(~) ~, finish · Verputz *m*

(~) ~ cupola, (~) ~ dome · Putzkuppel *f*

(~) ~ on wire lath(ing) · Draht(ver)putz *m*

~ product · Fertiggut *n* [*Beton; bituminöses Gemisch usw.*]

mixed sedimentary rock — modified alkyd resin

~ **sedimentary rock** · gemischtes Sedimentgestein n, gemischt mechanisch-chemisches ~

~ **stand oil** · Mischstandöl n

~ **tar** · Mischteer m

mixer protecting agent · Mischerschutz m

~ **(valve), mixing** ~, showermixer, blending mixer, blender [B.S. 1415] · Badbatterie f

mixibility with water, mixability ~ ~ (US); miscibility ~ ~ · Wasser(ver)mischbarkeit f

mixing · Anmachen n, Mischen, Mischung f

~ **aid** · Mischhilfe f

~ **cock for cold and hot water with one connection** · Ein-Loch-Batterie f

~ **of primary pigment colours** (Brit.); ~ ~ ~ ~ colors (US) · Farbenmischen n

~ **operation** · Mischvorgang m

~ **sequence** · Mischfolge f

~ **spec(ification)s** · Mischungsvorschrift f

~ **stage** · Mischstadium n

~ **time** · Mischdauer f

~ **valve,** mixer (~), showermixer, blending mixer, blender [B.S. 1415] · Badbatterie f

~ **varnish** [A varnish designed to add luster or hardness to paints] · (Farben-)Mischlack m

mix(ing) water; gauging ~ [B.S. 3148]; gaging ~ (US) · Anmach(e)wasser n, Anmengwasser, Anmach(e)flüssigkeit f, Mischwasser, Mischflüssigkeit, Betonwasser

mix(ture) → (glass) batch

~, **combined materials** · Mischung f, Gemisch n

~, **stuff, plaster** · Putzmasse f, Putzmörtel m

~ **component,** (~) ingredient · (Gemisch)Bestandteil m, Mischungsbestandteil, (Mischungs)Komponente f, Gemischkomponente

~ **composition** · Gemischaufbau m, Mischungsaufbau, Gemischzusammensetzung f, Mischungszusammensetzung

~ ~ · Rezept(ur) n, (f), Versatzformel f [Steinzeugindustrie]

(~) ingredient → ~ component

~ **of barite grains** → barite grain mix(-ture)

~ ~ **barytes grains** (Brit.) → barite grain mix(ture)

~ ~ **glass fibres and cement and some additives** (Brit.); ~ ~ ~ fibers ~ ~ ~ ~ (US) · Glasfaserzement m

~ ~ **grains** → mixed grains

~ ~ **hard (or granular) abrasive materials (or abrasives) for grano(lithic) (concrete) toppings (or overlays)** · Hart(beton)stoff-Gemisch n, Hart(beton)stoff-Mischung f [DIN 1100]

~ ~ **hydrocarbons of high molecular weight** · hochmolekulare Kohlenwasserstoffverbindung f

~ ~ **marble grains** → marble grain mix(ture)

~ ~ **styles** · Stilmischung f

~ **proportioning** · Gemischdosierung f, Mischungsdosierung

MK → master key

ML, bill of material(s), material list [A list of the various portions of material for a construction, either proposed or completed, giving dimensions and weights or other quantitative measurements] · Stoffliste f, Materialliste

moat, foss(e), fortress castle-ditch · Burggraben m, Halsgraben, Befestigungsgraben

mobile home · bewegliche Raumzelle f [Siehe Anmerkung unter "Bauen mit Raumzellen"]

mobility tester · Rohrgerät n nach Nycander [Prüfung von Frischbeton]

mock arcade · Scheinarkade f

~ **architecture** · Scheinarchitektur f, Scheinbaukunst f [Durch Malerei vorgetäuschte Architekturteile an Wänden oder Decken, die den Innenraum illusionistisch erweitern]

model concrete shell · Betonmodellschale f, Modellbetonschale

~ **photo** · Modellaufnahme f

~ **(structural) analysis** · Modellstatik f

~ **structure** · Modellbauwerk n

~ **test** · Modellprobe f, Modellversuch m, Modellprüfung f

~ **top view** · Modellaufsicht f

moderate heat of hydration cement, ~ sulphate resisting ~; Portland cement Type II (US) · mäßiger Gipsschlackenzement m, ~ Sulfathüttenzement

~ **sulphate resisting cement,** ~ heat of hydration ~; Portland cement Type II (US) · mäßiger Gipsschlackenzement m, ~ Sulfathüttenzement

moderately stiff fresh(ly-mixed) concrete · mäßig steifer Frischbeton m

modern connecter (US) → (timber) connector

Modern Style, Art Nouveau · Jugendstil m

~ ~ **faience,** Art Nouveau ~ · Jugendstilfayence f

modernism · Modernismus m

modernity, modernness · Modernität f

modernness, modernity · Modernität f

modification, improvement · Vergütung f [Beton; Mörtel]

modified, improved · vergütet

~ **alkyd resin** · modifiziertes Alkydharz n

modified Bauer-Vogel process — modulus of rigidity 632

~ **Bauer-Vogel process**, M.B.V. ~ · MBV(-Behandlung) n, (f), modifiziertes Bauer-Vogel-Verfahren n, MBV-Verfahren

~ **oil** · modifiziertes Öl n

~ **rubber**, improved ~ · vergüteter Gummi m, vergütetes ~ n

~ **solid wood**, improved ~ ~ · vergütetes Vollholz n, ~ Massivholz

modifier, improver, modifying agent · Vergütungsmittel n, Vergüter m

to modify, to improve · vergüten

modifying agent, modifier, improver · Vergütungsmittel n, Vergüter m

modular brick, ~ clay ~ · Modul(ton)ziegel m

~ **(building) unit**, ~ (~) member, ~ (~) component [*A component that has coordinating dimensions (i.e. the dimensions that affect the size of adjoining components) in whole multiples of the 4" basic module*] · Modul(bau)-element n, Modul(bau)körper m [*Fehlname: Modulbaueinheit f*]

~ **(clay) brick** · Modul(ton)ziegel m

~ **component** → ~ (building) unit

~ **construction** · Modulbau m

~ ~ **(method)** · Modulbauweise f

~ **co-ordination** [*Dimensional co-ordinating using the international basic module, multimodules, sub-modules and a modular reference system*] · Modulordnung f

~ **curtain wall** · Modulvorhangwand f

~ **deviation** [*The difference between actual size and modular size*] · Modulabweichung f

~ **dimension** [*A dimension that is a full multiple of the basic module*] · Modulabmessung f, Modulmaß n

~ **drafting** (US); ~ draughting (Brit.) · Maßordnungszeichen n

~ **format** · Modulformat n

~ **grid**, ~ reference ~ · Modulraster m

~ **housing** (US); unitized unit method, (building block) module method · (Raum)Zellenbauweise f, Installationszellenbauweise, Installationsblockbauweise, Bauen n mit Raumzellen [*Die Bauten sind mit dem Grundstück dauerhaft verbunden. Gegensatz: bewegliche Raumzellen = mobile homes*]

~ **length** · Maßordnungslänge f, Modullänge

~ **line** [*A line of a modular reference system*] · Modullinie f

~ **(measure) system**, dimensional framework · Maßsystem n (gegenseitig zusammenhängender Maße)

~ **member** → ~ (building) unit

~ **plane** [*A plane of a modular reference system*] · Modulebene f

~ **point** [*A point of a modular reference system*] · Modulpunkt m

~ **ratio** (m) [*The ratio of the modulus of elasticity of steel to that of concrete $=E_s/E_c.=15$ is usually used*] · (Beiwert) n, n-Wert m, Verhältnis n der E-Module

(~ ~) **m-design**, (modular ratio) m-method · n-Verfahren n

(~ ~) **m-method**, (~ ~) m-design · n-Verfahren n

(~ ~) **m-problem** · n-Frage f

~ **(reference) grid** · Modulraster m

~ ~ **system** [*A reference system in which the distance between adjacent parallel planes or lines is the international basic module or a multiple thereof*] · Modulsystem n

~ **size** · Modulgröße f

~ **space** [*A space bounded by modular planes*] · Modulraum m

~ **tile** · Modul(belag)platte f, Modulfliese

~ **unit** → ~ building ~

~ **width** · Modulbreite f, Maßordnungsbreite

~ **zone** [*A zone between modular planes*] · Modulzone f, Modulbereich m, n

module · Modul m [*Eine am Bau abgeleitete Maßeinheit, die als Grundlage für die Abmessungen aller Bauteile dient*]

module-built block, ~ building · Modulgebäude n

module method → building block ~ ~

modulus of creep, creep modulus · Kriechmodul m [*Baustoffkonstante, die zur Berechnung der Kriechverformung von Beton dient*]

~ ~ **deformation**, deformation modulus · Deformationsmodul m, Verformungsmodul, Formänderungsmodul, Gestaltänderungsmodul

~ ~ **elasticity**, elastic modulus, Young's modulus (of elasticity), stiffness · Elastizitätsmodul m, E-Modul, E-Wert m, E-Maß n, Elastizitätsmaß, Elastizitätswert m, E-Zahl f, Elastizitätszahl

~ ~ ~ **in compression** · Druck-E-Modul m, Druck-Elastizitätsmodul

~ ~ ~ ~ **shear** → ~ ~ rigidity

~ ~ **elongation** · Dehn(ungs)maß n, Dehn(ungs)ziffer f [*Reziprokwert des Elastizitätsmoduls. Bei Stahl bis zur Proportionalitätsgrenze keine Konstante, bei Beton eine mit der Spannung veränderliche Zahl*]

~ ~ **fineness** → fineness modulus

~ ~ **inertia**, inertia modulus · Trägheitsmodul m

~ ~ **lime**, lime modulus · Kalkmodul m

~ ~ **rigidity**, shear modulus (of elasticity), modulus of elasticity in shear [*The ratio of unit shearing stress to the corresponding unit shearing strain; referred to as 'shear modulus' and 'modulus of elasticity in shear'; denoted by the symbol G*] · Schubelastizitätsmodul m, Schub-E-Modul

modulus of rupture — molasse

~ ~ **rupture,** lateral strength, flexural strength, transverse strength [*The strength of a specimen tested in transverse bending; normally synonymous with 'modulus of rupture' but also used to refer to breaking load (see B.S. 340, 368, 550 and 2028)*] · Querbiegefestigkeit *f*

~ ~ **torsion,** torsion(al) modulus, twist(ing) modulus · Torsionsmodul *m*, Drill(ungs)modul

Moghrebin architecture · nordafrikanisch-maurische Architektur *f*, ~ Baukunst *f*

~ **minaret** · nordafrikanisch-maurisches Minarett *n*, nordafrikanisch-maurischer Gebetsturm *m*

Mogul architecture, Mughal ~ [*Muslim architecture in India during Mughal rule, usually reckoned from the invasion of Babur, A.D. 1526, to the death of Aurungzeb, A.D. 1707*] · Mogularchitektur *f*, Mogulbaukunst *f*

Mohammedan architecture → Muslim ~

Mohr's bending curve · Mohrsche Biegelinie *f*

~ **circle of stress** · Mohrscher Spannungskreis *m*

~ **correction method** · Mohrsches Verfahren *n*, Seileckverfahren

Mohs' hardness · Mohs-Härte *f*, Mohs'sche Härte

~ **scale of hardness** · Mohs-Härtereihe *f*, Mohs-Härteskala *f*, Mohs'sche Härteskala, Mohs'sche Härtereihe
[1 Talk   6 Orthoklas
 2 Steinsalz oder Gips   7 Quarz
 3 Kalkspat   8 Topas
 4 Flußspat   9 Korund
 5 Apatit   10 Diamant]

moil · Heftglas *n*, Nabelscherben *m*

moiré (lino(leum)), moire (~) · Moiré-linoleum *n*

moist, damp, humid · feucht

to moist-cure · nachbehandeln mit Feuchtigkeit [*Beton*]

to moisten, to humidify, to damp · anfeuchten, befeuchten

moistening, humidifying, humidification · Anfeuchten *n*, Befeuchten

~ **agent,** humidifying ~, humidification ~ · Anfeuchtungsstoff *m*, Befeuchtungsstoff

moist room, wet ~ · Naßraum *m*

~ ~ **dampproofing,** wet ~ ~ · Naßraum(ab)dichtung *f*

~ ~ **luminaire (fixture),** wet ~ ~ (~) (US); ~ ~ light fitting (Brit.); ~ ~ (light(ing)) fixture · Naßraumleuchte *f*

~ ~ **partition (wall),** wet ~ ~ (~) · Naßraumtrennwand *f*

~ ~ **service(s),** wet ~ ~ · Naßrauminstallation(en) *f(pl)*

moisture, humidity, dampness · Feuchtigkeit *f*, Feuchte *f*

~, humidity · nichtdrückendes Wasser *n*

~ **absorption,** humidity ~ · Feuchtigkeitsaufnahme *f*, Feuchteaufnahme

~ **barrier,** ~ seal, ~ stop, humidity ~ · Feuchtesperre *f*, Feuchtigkeitssperre, Feuchtigkeitssperrschicht *f*, Feuchtesperrschicht

~ **content,** humidity ~ · Feuchteanteil *m*, Wasseranteil, Feuchtigkeitsanteil, Feuchtegehalt *m*, Feuchtigkeitsgehalt, Wassergehalt

~ **control,** humidity ~ · Feuchteregelung *f*, Feuchtigkeitsregelung

moisture(-)controlling, humidity(-)controlling · feuchtigkeitsregulierend, feuchteregulierend

moisture cover, humidity ~ · Feuchtigkeitsbelag *m*, Feuchtebelag

~ **entry,** humidity ~ · Feuchteeintritt *m*, Feuchtigkeitseintritt

~ **equilibrium,** humidity ~ · Feuchtegleichgewicht *n*, Feuchtigkeitsgleichgewicht

moisture-free, humidity-free · feuchtefrei

moisture increase, humidity ~ · Feuchtezuwachs *m*, Feuchtigkeitszuwachs

moisture-laden air, humid ~ · Feuchtluft *f*

moisture limit, humidity ~ · Feuchtigkeitsgrenze *f*, Feuchtegrenze

~ **migration** → humidity ~

~ **movement** → humidity migration

~ **passage,** humidity ~ · Feuchtigkeitsdurchgang *m*, Feuchtedurchgang

~ **penetration,** humidity ~ · Feuchtigkeitseindringung *f*, Feuchteeindringung

~ **permeability,** humidity ~ · Feuchtigkeitsdurchlässigkeit *f*, Feuchtedurchlässigkeit

~-**proof** → resistant to moisture

moisture proof roof(ing) material · Dach(ab)dicht(ungs)stoff *m*

~ ~ ~ **sheet(ing),** humidity ~ ~ ~ · Dach(ab)dicht(ungs)bahn *f*

~ **quantity,** humidity ~ · Feuchtigkeitsmenge *f*, Feuchtemenge

~ **removal from roof(s),** humidity ~ ~ ~ · Dachentfeuchtung *f*

~ **resistance,** humidity ~ · Feuchtigkeitsfestigkeit *f*, Feuchtefestigkeit

~ **seal,** ~ stop, ~ barrier, humidity ~ · Feuchtesperre *f*, Feuchtigkeitssperre, Feuchtigkeitssperrschicht *f*, Feuchtesperrschicht

~ **stop,** ~ seal, ~ barrier, humidity ~ · Feuchtesperre *f*, Feuchtigkeitssperre, Feuchtigkeitssperrschicht *f*, Feuchtesperrschicht

molasse · Molasse(sandstein) *f*, *(m)*

mold — moment diagram

mold (US); mould (Brit.) · Form f
~ (US) → mould(ing)
~ (US); mould (Brit.); slump cone, conical shell · Setzbecher m, Trichter m [*Zur Ermittlung des Setzmaßes von Beton*]
~ construction (US); mould ~ (Brit.) Formenbau m
~ for (pre)cast work (US); mould ~ ~ ~ (Brit.) · Fertigteilform f [*Betonsteinindustrie*]
~ oil (US) → (concrete) mould (release) ~
~ opening (US); mould ~ (Brit.) · Formöffnung f
~ release agent (US); mould ~ ~ (Brit.) · Form(en)entschalungsmittel n
~ (~) oil (US) → (concrete) mould (~)

molded (US); moulded (Brit.) · gewunden [*Bogen*]
~ base (US) → moulded ~
~ plastic (US); moulded ~ (Brit.) · Kunstpreßstoff m
~ ~ luminaire (fixture) (US); moulded plastic light fitting (Brit.); ~ ~ (light(ing)) fixture · Isolierpreßstoff-Beleuchtungskörper m, Isolierpreßstoffleuchte f

mold(ing) (US) → mould(ing)
~ compound (US) → moulding ~
~ plaster (US); moulding ~ (Brit.) · Modellgips m, keramischer Gips
~ pressure (US) → moulding ~
~ sand (US); moulding ~ (Brit.) · (Gießerei-)Formsand m

molecular attraction · molekulare Anziehung f
~ heat · Molekularwärme f
~ structure · Molekularstruktur f
~ weight · Molekulargewicht (M) n

moler · Molererde f
~ brick · Molerstein m
~ cement · Molerzement m
~ chip(ping)s · Molersplitt m

moline cross [*It is shaped like a 'milliron'*] · Ankerkreuz n

molten (blastfurnace) slag · (Hochofen)Schmelzschlacke f
~ dust, ~ filler · geschmolzener Füller m, ~ Füllstoff m [*z.B. Glaspuder*]
~ filler, ~ dust · geschmolzener Füller m, ~ Füllstoff m [*z.B. Glaspuder*]
~ slag, ~ blastfurnace ~ · (Hochofen-)Schmelzschlacke f
~ solder · geschmolzenes Lot n

molybdate orange (pigment) · Molybdatorange(pigment) f, (n)
~ red (pigment) · Molybdatrot(pigment) n

molybdenite · Molybdänglanz m, Molybdänit m, MoS_2

molybdenum bearing austenite steel · molybdänhaltiger Austenitstahl m
~ solder glass, ~ (intermediate) sealing ~ · Molybdän-Einschmelzglas n, Molybdän-Lötglas, Molybdän-Glaslot n, Molybdän-Zwischenglas

moment [*The product of a force multiplied by the distance through which it acts*] · Moment n
~ allowance · Momentendeckung f
~ ~ curve · Momentendeckungslinie f [*Die Linie der zulässigen Momente aus der Bewehrung eines Trägers. Sie soll außerhalb der tatsächlichen Momentenlinie liegen*]
~ area · Momentenfläche f

moment-area method [*It is used for solving the beam equation*] · Momentenflächenverfahren n

moment arm, lever ~ · Hebelarm m
~ ~ of the internal forces · Hebelarm m der inneren Kräfte
~ at base, ~ ~ foot, foot moment, base moment · Fußmoment n
~ ~ column, ~ ~ support · Stützenmoment n [*Das Biegemoment über der Unterstützung eines Durchlaufträgers*]
~ ~ fixed end → (fixed-)end moment
~ ~ foot, ~ ~ base, foot moment, base moment · Fußmoment n
~ ~ head, head moment · Kopfmoment n
~ ~ point of fixation → (fixed-)end moment
~ ~ support, ~ ~ column · Stützenmoment n [*Das Biegemoment über der Unterstützung eines Durchlaufträgers*]
~ axis; ~ center line (US); ~ centre line (Brit.) · Drehachse f, Momentenmittellinie f, Momentennullinie, Momentenachse

moment-balance method → Cross (moment distribution) ~

moment balancing · Momentenausgleich m
~ buckling · Momentenknickung f
~ capacity · Momentenvermögen n
~ center line (US); ~ centre ~ (Brit.); ~ axis · Drehachse f, Momentenmittellinie f, Momentennullinie, Momentenachse
~ check(ing) · Momentennachweis m
~ coefficient · Momentenbeiwert m
~ condition · Momentenbedingung f
~ connection · Momentenanschluß m
~ curvature, shape of the moment diagram · Momentenverlauf m

moment-curvature law · Beziehungen fpl zwischen Moment und Krümmung

moment curve · Momentenkurve f, Momentenlinie f
~ determination · Momentenermitt(e)lung f
~ diagram · Momentendiagramm n, Momentenschaubild n

moment differential — mono-functional

~ **differential** · Momentengefälle n
~ **distribution** · Momentenverteilung f
~ ~ **by successive approximations** · stufenweiser Momentenausgleich m
~ ~ **method** → Cross (moment distribution) ~
~ ~ **without successive approximations**, direct moment distribution · direkter Momentenausgleich m
~ **equation**, equation of moments · Momentengleichung f
~ **equilibrium** · Momentengleichgewicht n

moment-free → momentless

moment in end span, ~ ~ extreme ~ · Endfeldmoment n
~ ~ **extreme span**, ~ ~ end ~ · Endfeldmoment n
~ **influence** · Momenteneinfluß m
~ ~ **line** · Momenteneinflußlinie f
~ ~ **ordinate** · Momenteneinflußordinate f
~ **method** · Momentenmethode f, Momentenverfahren n [*Müller-Breslau*]
~ **of a force** · Kräftemoment n
~ ~ ~ **higher order** · höheres Moment n
~ ~ **an area**, area moment · Flächenmoment n
~ ~ **deformation** · Verformungsmoment n
~ ~ **flow** · Fließmoment n
~ ~ **inertia**, second moment (of area) [*of a section*] · Trägheitsmoment n
~ ~ **loading**, loading moment · Belastungsmoment n
~ ~ **resistance**, resisting moment · Moment n der inneren Kräfte
~ ~ **span** · Feldmoment n [*Biegemoment eines Tragwerkes innerhalb einer Spannweite oder eines Plattenfeldes*]
~ ~ **torsion** → torsion(al) moment
~ **ordinate** · Momentenordinate f
~ **percentage** · Momentenanteil m
~ **pole**; centre of rotation (Brit.); center of rotation (US) [*Point about which a moment is taken*] · Drehpunkt m, Momentenpunkt, Momentenpol m
~ **redistribution**, redistribution of moment(s) · Momentenumlagerung f
~ **reversal**, reversal of moment(s) · Momentenumkehr f
~ **table**, table of moments · Momententabelle f
~ **triangle**, triangle of moments · Momentendreieck n

momental vector · freier Vektor m, Momentenvektor

momentary-contact push button · Tastschalter m

momentless, moment-free, having zero moment · momentenfrei, momentenlos

monastery · Mönchskloster n

~ **cemetery**, paradise · Mönchsklosterfriedhof m
~ **garden**, paradise · Mönchsklostergarten m

monastic architecture · Klosterarchitektur f, Klosterbaukunst f, monastische Architektur, monastische Baukunst
~ **building**, coventual ~ · Klostergebäude n
(~) **cell**, clauster · Klausur f, Klause f, (Mönchs)Zelle f
~ **cemetery** · Klosterfriedhof m
~ **choir**, monk's ~, ~ quire · Mönchschor m
~ **church**, conventual ~, conventional ~ · Klosterkirche f, Konventualkirche
~ **community**, conventual ~ · Wohngemeinschaft f eines Klosters
~ **hall**, refectory, frater [*The communal dining-hall in a convent*] · Klosterspeisesaal m, Refektorium n, Speisesaal im Kloster
~ **house** · Klosterhaus n
~ **kitchen**, conventual ~ · Klosterküche f
~ **library** · Klosterbibliothek f, Klosterbücherei f
~ **quire**, monk's ~, ~ choir · Mönchschor m
~ **recreation room** · Recreatorium n, Klostererholungsraum m, Erholungsraum im Kloster

Monel flashing (piece) · Monel-Anschluß(streifen) m [*See remark under 'Anschluß'*]
~ **metal** · Monelmetall n

monial, munnion, mullion · Fensterpfosten m

monitor (US); ~ roof (Brit) [*A portion of a roof raised above the adjoining roof and having a continuous vertical or near vertical section of glazing on the perimeter*] · Firstlaterne f
~ **roof** (Brit.); monitor (US) [*A portion of a roof raised above the adjoining roof and having a continuous vertical or near vertical section of glazing on the perimeter*] · Firstlaterne f

monk's choir, monastic ~, ~ quire · Mönchschor m

monochromatic, monochrome · einfarbig
~ **painting** → monochrome ~

monochrome, monochromatic · einfarbig
~ **painting**, monochromatic ~, dominant harmony [*A colo(u)r scheme built up from the tints and shades of any one colo(u)r, e.g., pale and deep tones of green*] · einfarbiger Aufbau m

monocord control · Ein-Schnur-Zug m [*Jalousie*]
~ **venetian blind** · Ein-Schnur-Raffjalousie f, Ein-Schnur-Zugjalousie

mono-functional · monofunktional

monolith — monument of liberty

monolith, menhir · Menhir *m* [*Vorgeschichtliches Totenmal in Form eines großen aufrechtstehenden Steines*]

~ [*A single block of stone fashioned into a pillar or an obelisk*] · Monolith *m*

monolithic, one-leaf, single-leaf [*wall*] · einschalig [*Wand*]

~ · monolithisch, ungegliedert

~ · monolithisches Futter *n* [*Gestampfte oder gegossene fugenlose Auskleidung*]

~ **arch** · monolithischer Bogen *m*

~ **arch(ed girder) without voussoirs** · monolithischer Bogen(träger) *m*

~ **beam** · monolithischer Balken(träger) *m*

~ **column** · monolithische Säule *f*

~ ~ **shaft** · monolithischer Säulenschaft *m*

~ **concrete** · Monolithbeton *m*

(~) ~ **floor screed (material)** → (~) (fine) ~ ~ ~ (~)

~ ~ **masonry wall** · monolithische Betonmauer *f*

~ ~ **panel wall** · monolithische Betontafelwand *f*

(~) ~ **screed (material)** → (~) (fine) ~ ~ (~)

~ **constructing,** ~ construction · Monolithbau *m*, monolithisches Bauen *n*

~ **construction** [*When a screed is laid on an in situ concrete base before it has set, complete bonding is obtained*] · monolithische Bauweise *f* [*Estrichverlegung*]

~ ~, ~ **constructing** · Monolithbau *m*, monolithisches Bauen *n*

~ ~, ~ **(structural) system** · monolithisches Bausystem *n*, ~ (Konstruktions-)System, monolithische Konstruktion *f*

~ ~ **(method)** · monolithische Bauweise *f*

(~) **(fine) concrete floor screed (material)** · (Fein)Beton(fuß)bodenestrich *m* [*als Baustoff*]

(~) (~) ~ ~ ~ **(topping)** · (Fein)Beton(fuß)bodenestrich *m* [*als verlegter Baustoff*]

(~) (~) ~ **screed (material)** · (Fein-)Betonestrich *m* [*als Baustoff*]

(~) (~) ~ ~ **(topping)** · (Fein)Betonestrich *m* [*als verlegter Baustoff*]

~ **fireproof floor** → ~ nonmetallic ~ ~

~ **floor** · monolithische Decke *f*, Monolithdecke

~ **footing** · monolithisches Fundament *n*

~ **foundation** · monolithische Gründung *f*

~ **joint,** gap filled ~ [*It is made with in-situ concrete, grout or synthetic resin*] · harte Fuge *f*, Hartfuge

~ **masonry wall** · einschalige Mauer *f*, monolithische ~

~ **material** · monolithischer Werkstoff *m*

~ **multi(ple)-layer(ed) wall,** multi(ple)-layer(ed) monolithic ~ · mehrschichtige einschalige Mauer *f*, ~ monolithische ~

~ **noncombustibe floor** → ~ (nonmetallic) fireproof ~

~ **(nonmetallic) fireproof floor,** ~ noncombustible ~ · monolithische Massivdecke *f*

~ **one-layer(ed) masonry wall** → ~ single-layer(ed) ~ ~

~ **pillar,** obelisk · Gedenkpfeiler *m*, Ehrenpfeiler, Obelisk *m*, Gedächtnispfeiler

(~) **prestressed (concrete) wall,** prestressed monolithic (~) ~ · Spannbetonwand *f*

(~) **R.C. wall** → (~) reinforced (concrete) ~

~ **reinforced concrete,** ~ R.C. · monolithischer Stahlbeton *m*

(~) ~ (~) **wall,** (~) R.C. ~ · Stahlbetonwand *f*

~ **roof** · Massivdach *n*

~ **single-layer(ed) masonry wall,** ~ one-layer(ed) ~, single-layer(ed) monolithic ~ ~, one-layer(ed) monolithic ~ ~ · einschichtig einschalige Mauer *f*, monolithisch ~, einschalig einschichtige ~, einschalig monolithische ~

~ **slab** · monolithische Platte *f*, Monolithplatte

~ **solid roof** · monolithisches Massivdach *n*

~ **(structural) system,** ~ construction · monolithisches Bausystem *n*, ~ (Konstruktions)System, monolithische Konstruktion *f*

~ **system,** ~ structural ~, ~ construction · monolithisches Bausystem *n*, ~ (Konstruktions)System, monolithische Konstruktion *f*

~ **terrazzo** · Fet *m*, Terrazzoestrich *m*

monolithically assembled floor panels · geschlossene Deckenscheibe *f*

monomer [*The unit molecule from which a polymer is built up*] · Monomer *n*

monopitch roof, single pitch ~, lean-to ~, half-span ~ [*A roof pitched in one plane only*] · freitragendes Pultdach *n*

monopteral temple, monopteron · Monopteros *m*, runder offener Tempel *m* [*Ein griechischer oder römischer Rundtempel mit Säulenkranz, jedoch ohne Cella. Im Barock und Klassizismus als Gartentempel verwendet*]

monotony · Einförmigkeit *f*

montan pitch · Montanpech *n*

montmorillonitic clay · montmorillonitischer Ton *m*

monument · (Bau)Denkmal *n*, Monument *n*

~ **of liberty,** freedom memorial · Freiheitsdenkmal *n*

monument of limestone — mortar admix(ture)

~ ~ **limestone,** limestone monument · Kalksteinmonument *n*

~ ~ **Lysikrates at Athens** [*334 B.C.*] · Monument *n* des Lysikrates in Athen

monumental arch · Ehrenbogen *m*, Ehrenpforte *f*, Gedenkpforte, Gedenkbogen

~ **architecture** · Monumentalbaukunst *f*, Monumentalarchitektur *f*

~ **brass** · Grabplatte *f* [*Die englischen „monumental brasses" sind Steinplatten, in denen die aus Messingtafeln geschnittenen Darstellungen eingelassen sind*]

~ **building** · Monumentalgebäude *n*

~ **chapel** · Monumentalkapelle *f*

~ **church** · Monumentalkirche *f*

~ **column** · Monumentalsäule *f*

~ **courtyard** · Monumentalhof *m*

~ **effect** · monumentale Wirkung *f*

~ **entrance** · Monumentaleingang *m*

~ **façade** · Monumentalfassade *f*

~ **gateway,** propyl(ai)on, propylaeum · Propyl(ai)on *n*, Eingangshalle *f*, Torbau *m*

~ **height** · monumentale Höhe *f*

~ **material** · Baumaterial *n* für Monumentalbauten [*Schweiz*]; Baustoff *m* ~ ~

~ **portal** · Monumentalportal *n*

~ **ruin** · Großruine *f*

~ **sculpture** · monumentale Skulptur *f*, ~ Plastik *f*, Monumentalskulptur, Monumentalplastik

~ **stairway** · Monumentaltreppe *f*

~ **style** · Monumentalstil *m*

~ **tomb** [*Monumental tombs are the most typical Roman class, descended from the Etruscan tumuli, with their embracing ring of stones or rock. They consisted of large cylindrical blocks, often on a quadrangular podium, topped with a conical crown of earth or stone*] · (römisches) Tumulusgrab *n*

monumentality, monumentalism · Monumentalität *f*

moon-chalk · Mondmilch *f*, Lerchenschwamm *m*

moonstone, adularia [*A colourless and translucent variety of orthoclase usually in pseudo-orthorhombic crystals*] · Adular *m*

Moorish arabesque → moresque

~ **arch,** ~ horseshoe ~, pointed horseshoe ~ · Hufeisenspitzbogen *m*, maurischer Hufeisenbogen

~ **architecture** [*The Muslim architecture of Spain and North Africa*] · maurische Architektur *f*, ~ Baukunst *f*

~ **capital** · maurisches Kapitell *n*, ~ Kapitäl

~ **cupola,** imperial ~, bulbous ~, ~ dome · Zwiebelkuppel *f*

~ **dome,** imperial ~, bulbous ~, ~ cupola · Zwiebelkuppel *f*

~ **(horseshoe) arch,** pointed ~ ~ · Hufeisenspitzbogen *m*, maurischer Hufeisenbogen

~ **multifoil(ed) arch** · maurischer Vielpaßbogen *m*, ~ Mehrpaßbogen

~ **palace** · maurischer Palast *m*

mopboard → sanitary cove

~ **component** → base (board) unit

~ **heater,** scrub board ~, base (board) ~, washboard ~, sanitary cove ~ (US); skirting (board) ~ (Brit.); base plate ~ [*Scotland*] · Scheuerleistenheizer *m*, Fußleistenheizer, Sockelleistenheizer

~ **heating,** washboard ~, scrub board ~, base (board) ~, sanitary cove ~ (US); skirting (board) ~ (Brit.); base plate ~ [*Scotland*] · Scheuerleistenheizung *f*, Fußleistenheizung, Sockelleistenheizung

~ **member** → base (board) unit

~ **radiator,** washboard ~, scrub board ~, base (board) ~, sanitary cove ~ (US); skirting (board) ~ (Brit.); base plate ~ [*Scotland*] · Scheuerleisten-Radiator *m*, Sockelleisten-Radiator, Fußleisten-Radiator

~ **unit** → base (board) ~

mopping (method) · Gieß- und Einwalzverfahren *n* [*Abdichtung gegen Grundwasser und/oder Feuchtigkeit*]

~ **of hot asphalt** (US); ~ ~ ~ asphalt(ic) bitumen (Brit.) · Bitumenheißaufstrich *m*, Bitumenheißanstrich, Heißbitumenlage *f*, Bitumenheißlage, Heißbitumenaufstrich, Heißbitumenanstrich, Heißbitumenschicht *f*, Heißbitumen(ab)dicht(ungs)lage, Heißbitumen(ab)dicht(ungs)schicht

morainal chip(ping)s · Moräne(n)splitt *m*

~ **gravel** · Moräne(n)kies *m*

~ **sand** · Moräne(n)sand *m*

more-centered arch (US); more-centred ~ (Brit.); compound ~, basket(-handle) ~, semielliptical ~, anse de panier [*An arch whose curve resembles that of the handle of a basket. It is formed by a segment of a large circle continued left and right by two segments of much smaller circles*] · Korb(henkel)bogen *m*, Ratebogen

moresque, Moorish arabesque [*This form of arabesque is the true Mohammadan form and is based solely on vegetable and abstract shapes and must be distinguished from the Italian form of arabesque which is the version based by Raphael on Greco-Roman work and which includes quasi-human and animal forms*] · Mureske *f*, arabisches Rankenwerk *n*

mortar · Mörtel *m* [*DIN 1053*]

~ **admix(ture),** ~ agent · Mörtelwirkstoff *m*, Mörtelzusatz(stoff) *m*, Mörtelzusatzmittel *n* [*DIN 18550*]

~ **aerated with foam,** foam(ed) mortar · Schaummörtel *m*

~ **agent** → ~ admix(ture)

~ **aggregate** · Mörtelzuschlag(stoff) *m*, Mörtelzuschlagmaterial *n*

~ **aid** · Mörtelhilfe *f*, Mörtelhilfsmittel *n*, Mörtelhilfsstoff *m*

~ **base (course),** underbed [*The base mortar usually horizontal*] · Mörtelbett *n*, Mörtelunterlage *f*

mortar-bed method, conventional ~ ~, thick-bed ~ · Dickbettverfahren *n* [*Ansetzen von Fliesen*]

mortar bond · Mörtelhaftung *f*

mortar-bound · angemörtelt [*z.B. die Bekleidung an einer Wand*]

mortar cement, masonry ~, cementing material for masonry · PM-Binder *m*, (Putz- und) Mauer(werk)binder, Fugenmörtelzement *m*, Mauerwerkbinder, Mauermörtelzement, Mauerwerkzement

~ **composition** · Mörtelzusammensetzung *f*

~ **consistency,** ~ consistence · Mörtelkonsistenz *f*, Mörtelsteife *f*

~ **content** → ~ fraction

~ **course,** ~ layer · Mörtellage *f*, Mörtelschicht *f*

~ **cover** · Mörteldeckung *f*

~ **creep,** creep of mortar · Mörtelkriechen *n*

~ **cube** · Mörtelwürfel *m*

~ **cylinder** · Mörtelzylinder *m*

(~) **dab** · (Mörtel)Punkt *m*

~ **densifier** → ~ densifying agent

~ **densifying agent,** ~ ~ admix(ture), ~ densifier, ~ integral waterproofer, ~ integral waterproof(ing) agent, ~ integral waterrepeller, ~ integral water repellent admix(ture), ~ integral water repelling agent · MD *m*, Mörtel-DM *n*, Mörteldichter *m*, Mörtel(ab)dicht(ungs)mittel *n*, Mörtel(ab)dicht(ungs)stoff *m*

~ **dropping,** ~ splashing · Mörtelrest *m*, Mörtelspritzer *m*

~ **droppings** · Mörtelkruste *f*

~ **fabrication,** ~ preparation · Mörtel(auf)bereitung *f*, Mörtelherstellung, Mörtelerzeugung

~ **factory** → ~ plant

~ **fill(ing)** · Mörtelverguß *m*, Mörtelfüllung *f*

~ **for (clay) brickwork,** (clay) brick(work) mortar · Ziegel(mauerwerk)mörtel *m*

~ ~ **(natural) stone block work,** ~ ~ (~) ~ masonry (work), ~ ~ stone block masonry (work) · Steinblockmauerwerkmörtel *m*, (Natur)Steinmauerwerkmörtel

~ ~ (~) ~ **masonry (work),** ~ ~ stone block ~ (~), ~ ~ (natural) stone block work · (Natur)Steinmauerwerkmörtel *m*, Steinblockmauerwerkmörtel

~ **fraction,** ~ content, ~ percentage · Mörtelanteil *m*, Mörtelprozentsatz *m*, Mörtelgehalt *m*

~ **gauging water** (Brit.) → ~ mix(ing) ~

to mortar in, to fill with mortar · ausmörteln, vermörteln, bemörteln [*Mauerwerkfuge*]

mortar ingredient, ~ material · Mörtelbestandteil *m*, Mörtelkomponente *f*

~ **integral waterproofer** → ~ densifying agent

~ ~ **waterproof(ing) agent** → ~ densifying ~

~ ~ **waterrepellent admix(ture)** → ~ densifying agent

~ ~ **waterrepeller** → ~ densifying agent

~ ~ **water repelling agent** → ~ densifying ~

~ **joint,** abreuvoir [*In masonry, the joint to be filled with mortar*] · Mörtelfuge *f*

~ ~ **pipe** · Mörtelfugenrohr *n*

~ ~ **reinforcement** · Mörtelfugenbewehrung *f*, Mörtelfugenarmierung, Mörtelfugen(stahl)einlagen *fpl*

~ **layer,** ~ course · Mörtellage *f*, Mörtelschicht *f*

mortarless, dry · mörtelfrei, mörtellos, trocken

mortar lump · Mörtelklumpen *m*

~ **masonry (work)** · Mörtelmauerwerk *n*

~ **material** → ~ ingredient

~ **mix proportions,** ~ ~ ratio · Mörtelmisch(ungs)verhältnis *n*

~ ~ **ratio,** ~ ~ proportions · Mörtelmisch(ungs)verhältnis *n*

~ **mixing aid** · Mörtelmischhilfe *f*

~ ~ **water;** ~ gauging ~ (Brit.); ~ gaging ~ (US) · Mörtelanmengwasser *n*, Mörtelmischwasser, Mörtelanmach(e)wasser, Mörtelanmach(e)flüssigkeit *f*, Mörtelmischflüssigkeit

~ **mix(ture)** · Mörtelgemisch *n*, Mörtelmischung *f*

~ **percentage** → ~ fraction

~ **plant,** ~ works, ~ factory · Mörtelwerk *n*, Mörtelbetrieb *m*

~ **plasticizing agent** → ~ workability ~

~ **plug** · Mörtelpfropfen *m*

~ **preparation** → ~ fabrication

~ **prism** · Mörtelprisma *n*

~ **reducing** · mörtelsparend

~ **sand,** sand for mortar [*B.S. 1200*] · Mörtelsand *m*

~ **screed (for plastering)** · Putzleiste *f* aus Mörtel, Mörtelputzleiste [*Ein schmales Mörtelband an Decken und Wänden, nach der Sollage der Putzoberfläche vor dem Verputzen als Richtfläche hergestellt*]

~ **seal(ing)** · Mörtel(ab)dichtung *f*

mortar skin — mosaic terrazzo

~ **skin,** skin of mortar · Mörtelhaut *f*
~ **specimen** · Mörtelprobe(körper) *f*, (*m*)
~ **splashing,** ~ dropping · Mörtelrest *m*, Mörtelspritzer *m*
~ **stain** · Mörtelfleck *m*
~ **strength** · Mörtelfestigkeit *f*
~ **strip** · Querschlag *m*, Mörtelstrich *m* [*Doppeldach*]
~ ~ · Mörtelstreifen *m*
~ **waterproofer,** ~ waterproofing powder [*It is incorporated in the dry mix*] · Mörteldichter *m*, Mörtelsperrpulver *n*
~ **water-reducing agent** → ~ workability ~
~ **wetting agent** (Brit.) → ~ workability ~
~ **with metal(lic) aggregate,** metal(lic)-aggregate mortar · Stahlbetonmörtel *m* [*Er wird nach verschiedenen Verfahren hergestellt. Grundlegend ist die Verwendung von zerkleinertem Metall und Portlandzement. Außer zerkleinertem Metall können auch andere Hartbetonstoffe, z.B. Quarz, dem Mörtel zugesetzt werden*]
~ ~ **synthetic resin dispersion** · Plastmörtel *m*, kunststofflegierter Mörtel, Kunstharzmörtel [*Dem Anmachewasser wird eine wäßrige Kunststoffdispersion zugesetzt*]
~ **workability agent,** ~ plasticizing ~, ~ water-reducing ~, ~ workability aid, ~ plasticizer; ~ wetting agent (Brit.) · Mörtelplastifizierungsmittel *n*, Mörtelverflüssiger *m*, Mörtelweichmacher, Mörtelverarbeitungshilfe *f*
~ ~ **aid** → ~ ~ agent
~ **works** → ~ plant
mortared · ausgemörtelt [*Fuge*]
mortice (Brit.); mortise (US); tenon hole · Zapfenloch *n* [*nicht durchgehend*]
~ **gauge** (Brit.); mortise ga(u)ge (US); counter ~ · Zapfenlochlehre *f*
~ **latch,** ~ lock (Brit.); mortise ~ (US) · Einsteckschloß *n*
morticing (Brit.); mortising (US) · Einstemmen *n*
mortise and tenon joint (US); mortice ~ ~ ~ (Brit.); tenon jointing · (Ver-)Zapfung *f*, Zapfenverbindung, Zapfenfuge *f* [*Holzverbindung*]
mortuary basilica → cemetery ~
~ **(block),** dead-house · Totenhaus *n*, Leichenhaus
~ **chapel,** funeral ~, cemetery ~, graveyard ~ · Friedhofskapelle *f*, Totenkapelle
~ **church,** funeral ~, cemetery ~, graveyard ~ · Friedhofskirche *f*
~ **cult** · Totenkult *m*
~ **temple,** funerary ~ · Gedächtnistempel *m*, Memnonium *n*, Totentempel, Memorie *f*, Memorialbau *m*

mosaic · Mosaik *n*
~ **artist** · Mosaikkünstler *m*
~ **church** · Mosaikkirche *f*
mosaic-clad → mosaic-(sur)faced
mosaic clay tile, ceramic mosaic ~ · Keramikmosaik(belag)platte *f*, Keramikmosaikfliese *f*, keramische Mosaik(belag)platte, keramische Mosaikfliese
~ **cover(ing)** · Mosaikbelag *m*
~ **cupola,** ~ dome · Mosaikkuppel *f*
~ **decoration** → ~ decorative finish
~ **decorative finish,** ~ ~ feature, ~ ornamental ~, ~ decoration, ~ enrichment · Mosaikschmuck *m*, Mosaikverzierung *f*
~ **dome,** ~ cupola · Mosaikkuppel *f*
~ **enrichment** → ~ decorative finish
~ **exterior finish** → external mosaic ~
~ **external finish** → external mosaic ~
~ **façade** · Mosaikfassade *f*
mosaic-faced → mosaic-surfaced
(mosaic) fingers, mosaic parquet(ry) · Sparparkett *n*, Lamellenparkett, Kleinparkett, Mosaikparkett, Dünnparkett
~ **floor(ing) (finish),** ~ floor cover(ing) · Mosaik(fuß)boden(belag) *m*
mosaic-lined → mosaic-(sur)faced
mosaic masonry (work) → polygonal (random rubble) ~ (~)
~ **of leaded glass** · Bleiglasmosaik *n*
~ **ornamental feature** → ~ decorative finish
~ **outdoor finish** → external mosaic ~
~ **outer finish** → external mosaic ~
~ **panel** · Mosaiktafel *f*
~ **parquet(ry),** (~) fingers · Sparparkett *n*, Lamellenparkett, Kleinparkett, Mosaikparkett, Dünnparkett
~ ~ **sheet** · Sparparkettplatte *f*, Lamellenparkettplatte, Kleinparkettplatte, Mosaikparkettplatte, Dünnparkettplatte
~ **pattern** · Mosaikbild *n*, Mosaikmuster *n*
~ **paving** → ~ sett ~
~ **(~) sett** · Mosaik(pflaster)stein *m* [*Schweiz: Bogenpflasterstein*]
~ **piece,** (~) tessera [*A small cube of stone, glass, or marble, used in making mosaics*] · (Mosaik)Steinchen *n*, Tessera *f*, (Mosaik)Würfel *m*
~ **(random rubble) masonry (work)** → polygonal (~ ~) ~ (~)
~ **sett,** ~ paving ~ · Mosaik(pflaster)stein *m* [*Schweiz: Bogenpflasterstein*]
~ **(~) paving** · Mosaikpflaster(decke) *n*, (*f*)
~ **stair(case)** · Mosaiktreppe *f*
mosaic-(sur)faced, mosaic-lined, mosaic-clad · mosaikausgekleidet, mosaikbekleidet, mosaikverkleidet
mosaic terrazzo · Mosaikterrazzo *m*

(mosaic) tessera — moulded plastic

(~) tessera, ~ piece [*A small cube of stone, glass, or marble, used in making mosaics*] · (Mosaik)Steinchen *n*, Tessera *f*, (Mosaik)Würfel *m*
~ tile · Mosaik(belag)platte *f*, Mosaikfliese
~ vault · Mosaikgewölbe *n*
~ wall tile · Mosaikwandfliese *f*, Mosaikwand(belag)platte
~ window · Mosaikfenster *n*
~ woodwork, inlay, (in)tarsia · Intarsia *f*, Holzeinlegearbeit *f*
~ work · Mosaikarbeiten *fpl*
Moslem architecture → Muslim ~
mosque · Moschee *f*
Mosque and Mausoleum of Sultan Hasan at Cairo · Grabmoschee-Medresse *f* des Sultans Hassan in Kairo [*1356–63*]
mosque arch → (round) horseshoe ~
~ architecture · Moscheenarchitektur *f*, Moscheenbaukunst *f*
Mosque of al-Aqsà at Jerusalem · Moschee *f* el Aksa zu Jerusalem
~ ~ Ibn Tūlūn at Cairo · Moschee *f* Ibn Tūlūn zu Kairo
moss-covered · bemoost
motel · Rasthof *m*, Raststätte *f* mit Übernachtung
mother and baby unit · Wöchnerinstation *f*
~ of coal, mineral charcoal, fusain, motherham · mineralische Holzkohle *f*
motherham, fusain, mineral charcoal, mother of coal · mineralische Holzkohle *f*
to mothproof · mottensicher machen
mothproof · mottenecht, mottensicher
mothproofness · Mottenbeständigkeit *f*, Mottenfestigkeit
Motī Masjid, Pearl Mosque at Agra · Perlenmoschee *f* in der Feste Agra
motif [*In architecture, the dominant or distinctive feature or element of design*] · Motiv *n*
motion picture screen · Kinoleinwand *f*
~ ~ theatre, cinema · Kino *n*, Lichtspielhaus *n*, Lichtspieltheater *n*
~ study · Bewegungsanalyse *f*
motor car lacquer · Autolackfarbe *f*
~ chamber · Motorenraum *m* [*Aufzug*]
(~) garage · (Auto)Garage *f*
motorized door · motorbetätigte Tür *f*
motorstair, moving stair(case), escalator, moving stairway [*B.S. 2655*] · Fahrtreppe *f*, Treppenaufzug *m*, Rolltreppe
~ shutter, escalator ~, moving stair(case) ~ · Fahrtreppenabdeckung *f*, Rolltreppenabdeckung, Treppenaufzugabdeckung
(motor vehicle) repair shop · (Kfz.-)Reparaturwerkstatt *f*
motorway restaurant · Rasthaus *n*

motte · Motte *f* [*Ein künstlich angelegter kegelförmiger Hügel, meist aus dem Grabenaushub aufgeschüttet und an seinem Fuß von Palisaden umgeben. Eine spätere Form ist die Hochmotte*]
~ castle, mound ~ · Motte(nburg) *f*, Erdkegelburg
~ ditch · Mottegraben *m*
motte-top · Hochmotte *f*
~ castle · Hochmotte(nburg) *f*
mottled glazed coat(ing), ~ glaze(d finish), ~ glazing · Buntglasur *f*, Buntbeglasung *f* ·
~ osseous amber · buntknochiger Bernstein *m*
~ pig iron · halbiertes Roheisen *n*, meliertes ~
~ sandstone, bunter ~, Lower Triassic ~; variegated ~ (Brit.) · Buntsandstein *m*
~ schist, spotted ~, fleckschiefer *m*, maculose rock · Fleck(en)schiefer *m*
mottling, sheariness, spotting · Fleckenbildung *f* [*Anstrichmittel*]
mould (Brit.); mold (US) · Form *f*
~ (Brit.); mold (US); slump cone, conical shell · Setzbecher *m*, Trichter [*Zur Ermittlung des Setzmaßes von Beton*]
~ construction (Brit.); mold ~ (US) · Formenbau *m*
~ for (pre)cast work (Brit.); mold ~ ~ ~ (US) · Fertigteilform *f* [*Betonsteinindustrie*]
~ formation (Brit.); mold ~ (US) · Schimmelbildung *f*
~ oil (Brit.) → (concrete) mould (release) ~
~ opening (Brit.); mold ~ (US) · Formöffnung *f*
~ release agent (Brit.); mold ~ ~ (US) · Form(en)entschalungsmittel *n*
~ (~) oil (Brit.) → concrete ~ (~) ~
mo(u)ldable refractory (material) · plastische feuerfeste Masse *f*, ~ ff. ~, plastischer feuerfester Stoff *m*, plastischer ff. Stoff [*Verarbeitungsfertige, plastische Masse, die umgeformt oder vorgeformt geliefert wird; sie kann chemische Stoffe enthalten, die die Erhärtung bei niedrigen Temperaturen bewirken. Ihre Verarbeitung erfolgt durch Verformung von Hand oder mit einem geeigneten Stampfgerät*]
moulded (Brit.); molded (US) · gewunden [*Bogen*]
~ base (Brit.); molded ~ (US); Attic ~ · attischer Säulenfuß *m*, attische Basis *f* [*Ein Säulenfuß aus zwei Wülsten, die durch eine Hohlkehle getrennt sind*]
~ chamfer (Brit.); molded ~ (US) · profilierte Fase *f* mit 45°, ~ Schmiege ~ ~ ~
~ masonry (work) (Brit.); molded ~ (~) (US) · profiliertes Mauerwerk *n*
~ plastic (Brit.); molded ~ (US) · Kunstpreßstoff *m*

moulded plastic light fitting — Muhammadan architecture

~~ light fitting (Brit.) → molded plastic luminaire (fixture)

~~ (light(ing)) fixture (Brit.) → molded plastic luminaire (~)

mould(ing) (Brit.); mold(ing) (US) · Dekor(ations)profil *n*, Zierprofil, Ornamentprofil, Schmuckprofil

~ (Brit.); mold(ing) (US) · Dekor(ations)leiste *f*, Zierleiste, (Ornament)Leiste

~ (Brit.); mold(ing) (US) · Form(geb)ung *f* in Formen

~ (Brit.); molding (US) · Stab *m* [*Ein stabförmiges Zierglied oder Teile desselben*]

~ compound (Brit.); molding ~ (US) · Preßmasse *f*, Preßstoff *m*

~ plaster (Brit.); molding ~ (US) · Modellgips *m*, keramischer Gips

~ pressure (Brit.); molding ~ (US) · Formdruck *m*, Form(geb)ungsdruck [*Beim Formen in einer Form*]

~ sand (Brit.); molding ~ (US) · (Gießerei-)Formsand *m*

mo(u)lding(s) · (Ge)Simswerk *n*

mound castle, motte ~ · Motte(nburg) *f*, Erdkegelburg

~ of earth, earthen mound · Erdhügel *m*

mountain green · Steingrün *n*, Berggrün, Schiefergrün, Erdgrün, grüne Asche *f*

~ leather · Bergleder *n*

~ lime → high-calcium ~

~ wood · Holzasbest *m* [*Eine faserige und nicht brennbare Hornblendeart. Er wird für feuerbeständige Konstruktionen verwendet*]

mounting bracket · Halterung *f* [*z.B. für einen Feuerlöscher*]

~ channel · Montageschiene *f* [*Deckenleuchte*]

~ flush with the ceiling · deckenbündiger Einbau *m* [*Leuchte*]

mouseproof · mäusesicher

movability of the point of intersection · Verschieblichkeit *f* des Knotenpunktes, ~ ~ Knotens

mov(e)able · verschiebbar, verschieblich [*Knoten(punkt)*]

~ connection · beweglicher Anschluß *m*, mobiler ~

~ glass wall · mobile Glaswand *f*, bewegliche ~

~ shower, hand ~ · Schlauchdusche *f*, Handdusche

~ spray, hand ~ · Schlauchbrause *f*, Handbrause

movement · Stilrichtung *f*

movie palace · Filmpalast *m*

moving load, rolling ~ · bewegliche Last *f*, veränderliche ~, Wanderlast

~ loading, rolling ~ · veränderliche Belastung *f*, bewegliche ~, Wanderbelastung

~ pavement → pedestrian conveyor

~ single load · wandernde Einzellast *f*

~ stair(case), ~ stairway, motorstair, escalator [*B.S. 2655*] · Fahrtreppe *f*, Treppenaufzug *m*, Rolltreppe

~ ~ shutter, escalator ~, motorstair ~ · Fahrtreppenabdeckung *f*, Rolltreppenabdeckung, Treppenaufzugabdeckung

m.s. → mild steel

m.s. angle, mild steel ~ · Flußstahlwinkel *m*

m.s. flat, mild steel ~ · Flußstahlflachprofil *n*

m.s. hollow section, mild steel ~ · Flußstahlhohlprofil *n*

m.s. pipe, mild steel ~ · Flußstahlrohr *n*

m.s. plate, mild steel ~ · Flußstahlplatte *f*

m.s. (reinforcing) bar → mild steel (~) ~

m.s. structural pipe, ~ ~ ~ tube, mild steel ~ ~ · Flußstahl-Konstruktionsrohr *n*

m.s. window, mild steel ~ · Flußstahlfenster *n*

m.s. wire, mild steel ~ · Flußstahldraht *m*, Gußstahldraht [*Siehe Anmerkung unter „Flußstahl"*]

much-weathered · stark verwittert

muck · Puddelstahl *m*

~ bar [*A semi-finished bar produced in the forge*] · Puddelluppe *f*, Rohschiene *f*

mud · Lehmschlamm *m*

~ · (Naß)Schlamm *m* [*Straßenentwässerung*]

~ box, grit ~, silt ~, ~ bucket [*A loose iron box fitted in the bottom of a gulley for collecting deposited silt. It can be removed periodically for emptying and flushing*] · (Naß)Schlammfang *m*, Schmutzfang, (Naß)Schlammfänger *m*, Schmutzfänger, (Naß)Schlamm(fang)eimer *m*, Schmutzfangeimer

~ brick, sun-dried ~, sun-baked ~, air-dried ~ · Schlamm(bau)stein *m*, Schlammbatzen *m*, Schlammpatzen, Lehm(bau)stein, Lehmpatzen, Lehmbatzen, Grünling *m* [*Fehlnamen: Luftstein, Luftziegel m, Schlammziegel, Lehmziegel*]

~ bucket → ~ box

~ removal · Abschlämmen *n* [*Beseitigung von Schlamm in Dampfkesseln durch kurzzeitiges Betätigen von Abschlämmventilen*]

~ trap, grit ~, gull(e)y (~) · Schlammfang *m* [*Ein Straßen- oder Hofablauf mit Rostabdeckung und aushebbarem Schlammeimer*]

Mudéjar architecture · Mudéjararchitektur *f*, Mudéjarbaukunst *f* [*Vermischung maurischer mit gotischen Stilelementen bzw. Renaissanceformen in Spanien*]

Mughal architecture → Mogul ~

Muhammadan architecture → Muslim ~

mulching paper · Bodenpappe *f* [*für die Landwirtschaft*]

Müller-Breslau principle [*An unknown internal force can be expressed in terms of a known external force. This gives the Müller-Breslau principle for finding influence lines in linearly elastic redundant structures*] · Prinzip *n* von Müller-Breslau

mullion, munnion, monial · Fensterpfosten *m*

~ [*An intermediate vertical member of a frame to an opening. If placed in the center it is called 'Mittelpfosten' in German*] · Zwischenpfosten *m*

mullion(ed) window, cross ~ [*A window with one mullion and one transom*] · Kreuzfenster *n*, Pfostenfenster

mullions · Stabwerk *n* [*Senkrechte Stäbe zur Unterteilung der Glasfläche unter dem Maßwerk gotischer Fenster*]

~ radiating from the centre, radiating tracery · speichenartige Unterteilung *f* [*Radfenster*]

multi-aisle → multi(ple)-aisle

multiangular · vielwinkelig, mehrwinkelig

~, polygonal · vieleckig, mehreckig, polygonal

~ bar, polygonal ~, ~ rod · Polygonalstab *m*, Vieleckstab, Mehreckstab

~ block, ~ building, polygonal ~ · Polygonalgebäude *n*, Vieleckgebäude, Mehreckgebäude

~ bond → ~ masonry ~

~ building, ~ block, polygonal ~ · Polygonalgebäude *n*, Vieleckgebäude, Mehreckgebäude

~ cavity block → polygonal hollow ~

~ ~ tile → polygonal hollow block

~ choir, polygonal ~, ~ quire · Polygonalchor *m*, Vieleckchor, Mehreckchor [*Chor mit vieleckigem Schluß, meist in der Gotik*]

~ church, polygonal ~ · Polygonalkirche *f*, Vieleckkirche, Mehreckkirche

~ column, polygonal ~ · Polygonalstütze *f*, Vieleckstütze, Mehreckstütze

~ cupola → ~ dome

~ diminutive tower, polygonal ~ ~, ~ small ~, ~ turret · kleiner Polygonalturm *m*, ~ Vieleckturm, Polygonaltürmchen *n*, Vielecktürmchen, Mehrecktürmchen

~ dome, polygonal ~, ~ cupola, dome of polygonal plan, dome of multiangular plan, cupola of polygonal plan, cupola of multiangular plyn · Polygonalkuppel *f*, Vieleckkuppel, Mehreckkuppel

~ donjon → polygonal keep

~ drum, polygonal ~ · polygonaler Kuppelunterbau *m*, vieleckiger ~, mehreckiger ~, Polygonaltrommel *f*, Vielecktrommel, Mehrecktrommel, polygonale Trommel, vieleckige Trommel, mehreckige Trommel

~ dungeon → polygonal keep

~ exposed concrete column, ~ fair-faced ~ ~, polygonal ~ ~ ~ · Polygonalsichtbetonstütze *f*, Vielecksichtbetonstütze, Mehrecksichtbetonstütze

~ fair-faced concrete column, ~ exposed ~ ~, polygonal ~ ~ ~ · Polygonalsichtbetonstütze *f*, Vielecksichtbetonstütze, Mehrecksichtbetonstütze

~ frame, polygonal ~ · Polygonalrahmen *m*, Vieleckrahmen, Mehreckrahmen

~ (ground(-))plan, polygonal ~ vieleckiger Grundriß *m*, mehreckiger ~, polygonaler ~, Vieleckgrundriß, Mehreckgrundriß, Polygonalgrundriß

~ hall-choir, ~ hall-quire, polygonal ~ · Polygonalhallenchor *m*, Vieleckhallenchor, Mehreckhallenchor

~ hall-quire, ~ hall-choir, polygonal ~ · Polygonalhallenchor *m*, Vieleckhallenchor, Mehreckhallenchor

~ hollow block → polygonal ~ ~

~ keep → polygonal ~

~ (masonry) bond, polygonal (~) ~ · Polygonal(mauerwerk)verband *m*, Vieleck(mauerwerk)verband, Mehreck(mauerwerk)verband

~ ornament, polygonal ~ · Polygonalornament *n*, Vieleckornament, Mehreckornament [*Ornament aus vieleckigen Platten*]

~ plan → ~ ground(-)~

~ plate, polygonal ~, ~ slab · Polygonalplatte *f*, Vieleckplatte, Mehreckplatte

~ pot → polygonal hollow block

~ quire, polygonal ~, ~ choir · Polygonalchor *m*, Vieleckchor, Mehreckchor [*Chor mit vieleckigem Schluß, meist in der Gotik*]

~ rod, polygonal ~, ~ bar · Polygonalstab *m*, Vieleckstab, Mehreckstab

~ roof, polygonal ~, pavilion ~ · Polygon(al)dach *n*

~ slab, polygonal ~, ~ plate · Polygonalplatte *f*, Vieleckplatte, Mehreckplatte

~ small tower, polygonal ~ ~, ~ diminutive ~, ~ turret · kleiner Polygonalturm *m*, ~ Vieleckturm, Polygonaltürmchen *n*, Vielecktürmchen, Mehrecktürmchen

~ termination, polygonal ~ · Vieleck(ab)schluß *m*, Mehreck(ab)schluß, Polygonal(ab)schluß, polygonaler (Ab-)Schluß, vieleckiger (Ab)Schluß, mehreckiger (Ab)Schluß

multiangular tower — multi-gas burner

~ **tower,** polygonal ~ · Mehreckturm m, Vieleckturm, Polygonalturm

~ **truss,** polygonal ~ · Polygonalsprengwerk n, Vielecksprengwerk, Mehrecksprengwerk

~ **turret,** polygonal ~, ~ small tower, ~ diminutive tower · kleiner Polygonalturm m, ~ Vielecktürmchen, Polygonaltürmchen n, Vielecktürmchen, Mehrecktürmchen

~ **vault,** polygonal ~ · Polygonalgewölbe n, Vieleckgewölbe, Mehreckgewölbe

multiarched · mehrbogig, vielbogig

multiarticulated · mehrgelenkig, vielgelenkig

multibarrel system · Mehrfachtonnenkonstruktion f

multi-bay frame · Mehrfeldrahmen m

multi-building development, ~ project, ~ scheme, housing ~ · Wohn(ungs)(bau)projekt n, Wohn(ungs)-(bau)vorhaben n

~ **project,** ~ scheme, ~ development, housing ~ · Wohn(ungs)(bau)projekt n, Wohn(ungs)(bau)vorhaben n

~ **scheme,** ~ project, ~ development, housing ~ · Wohn(ungs)(bau)projekt n, Wohn(ungs)(bau)vorhaben n

(multi)cellular glass, foam(ed) ~ · poriges Glas n, Schaumglas, Vielzellenglas [*Es besteht aus meist hermetisch geschlossenen Mikroglaszellen und hat deshalb keine kapillare Wirkung*]

~ ~ **block,** foam(ed) ~ ~, ~ ~ tile [*See remark under 'Block'*] · Schaumglasblock(stein) m, Vielzellenglasblock(stein), Schaumglasstein, Vielzellenglasstein

~ ~ **tile,** foam(ed) ~ ~, ~ ~ block [*See remark under 'Block'*] · Schaumglasblock(stein) m, Vielzellenglasblock(stein), Schaumglasstein, Vielzellenglasstein

multicolour effect (Brit.); multicolor ~ (US) [*e.g. of a mosaic wall*] · Mehrfarbenwirkung f, Vielfarbenwirkung

multi-coloured system (Brit.); multicolored ~ (US) [*e.g. of a mosaic walling*] · Mehrfarbensystem n, Vielfarbensystem

multi-component lacquer · Mehrkomponentenlackfarbe f

~ **product** · Mehrkomponentenerzeugnis n

~ **varnish** · Mehrkomponentenlack m

multi-compound bronze · Mehrstoffbronze f

multi-degree-of-freedom system · System n mit mehreren Freiheitsgraden, ~ mehrerer Freiheitsgrade

multidimensional · mehrdimensional, vieldimensional

multi-family block (US) → block (of flats)

~ **building** (US) → block (of flats)

~ **dwelling** (US) → block (of flats)

~ **habitation** · Mehrfamilienbehausung f

~ **house** (US) → block (of flats)

~ **housing,** apartment ~ · Mehrfamilien-(wohn)bauten f

multiflight stair(case) · mehrläufige Treppe f, mehrarmige ~, vielläufige ~, vielarmige ~

multi-floor building, ~ block; multi-storey ~ (Brit.); multi-story ~ (US) · Geschoßgebäude n, Etagengebäude, Stockwerkgebäude, Geschoßbau m, Etagenbau, Stockwerkbau

~ **car park;** multi-story ~ ~ (US); multi-storey ~ ~ (Brit.); ~ garage · Stockwerkgarage f, Hochgarage, Geschoßgarage, Etagengarage

~ **factory block** → multi-storey factory building

~ ~ **building** → multi-storey ~ ~

~ **garage;** multi-story ~ (US); multi-storey ~ (Brit.); ~ car park · Stockwerkgarage f, Hochgarage, Geschoßgarage, Etagengarage

~ **hotel;** multi-storey ~ (Brit.); multi-story ~ (US) · Hotelhochhaus n, Hochhaushotel n

~ **library;** multi-storey ~ (Brit.); multi-story ~ (US); book tower · Bücherturm m

~ **parking building;** multi-story ~ ~ (US); multi-storey ~ ~ (Brit.); ~ facility · mehrgeschossiges Parkgebäude n, mehrstöckiges ~, mehretagiges ~, vielgeschossiges ~, vielstöckiges ~, vieletagiges ~, ~ Parkhaus n

~ **system composed of three-hinge(d) frames** → multi-storey ~ ~ ~ ~

multi-flue · mehrzügig [*Schornstein*]

multifoil · Mehrblatt n, Vielblatt

multifoil(ed) arch [*An arch whose intrados has many scallops or cusps, usually more than five. This type is common in the Islamic architecture of Asia Minor and India*] · Vielpaßbogen m, Mehrpaßbogen

multiform abacus, ~ raised table, ~ padstone · gegliederte Kapitellplatte f, ~ (Säulen)Deckplatte, gegliederter Abakus m

~ **padstone,** ~ abacus, ~ raised table · gegliederte Kapitellplatte f, ~ (Säulen-)Deckplatte, gegliederter Abakus m

~ **raised table,** ~ padstone, ~ abacus · gegliederte Kapitellplatte f, ~ (Säulen-)Deckplatte, gegliederter Abakus m

multiformity · (Viel)Glied(e)rigkeit f

multi-functional concept, multi-functionality · Mehrfachfunktionalität f

~ **room** · Gemeinschaftsraum m [*Hotel*]

multi-functionality, multi-functional concept · Mehrfachfunktionalität f

multi-gas burner · Allgasbrenner m, Mehrgasbrenner

multilayer(ed) system — multiple rib pillar

multilayer(ed) system, laminated ~ · mehrlagige Konstruktion f, mehrschichtige ~, viellagige ~, vielschichtige ~
multi-leaf door · Mehrblattür f, Vielblattür
~ up and over door · Mehrblatt-Kipptor n, Mehrblatt-Schwingtor, Vielblatt-Schwingtor, Vielblatt-Kipptor
multi-legged portal frame · durchlaufender Portalrahmen m, mehrstieliger ~, Durchlaufportalrahmen
multi-level road system · Straßenführung f in mehreren Ebenen
~ town → multi-storey ~
multi-lobe tracery · Vielpaß m, Mehrpaß
multi-nave → multi(ple)-nave
multipartite · mehrteilig, vielteilig
~ door · mehrteilige Tür f, vielteilige ~
~ vault · mehrteiliges Gewölbe n, vielteiliges ~
multiple · Mehrfache n
multi(ple)-aisle, multi(ple)-nave · mehrschiffig, vielschiffig [*Kirche*]
multi(ple)-bay, multi(ple)-span · mehrschiffig, vielschiffig [*Halle*]
~ frame, cellular ~, multiple ~ · Mehrfeldrahmen m
~ ~ as spandrel beam, multiple ~ ~ ~ ~ · Mehrfeldrahmen-Abfangträger m
~ portal frame, multiple ~ ~ · Mehrfeldportalrahmen m, Mehrfachportalrahmen
~ prismoid(al) (slab) roof · Mehrfach-Prismoiddach n
multiple coat application · Anstrichaufbau m [*Das Übereinanderstreichen von Anstrichen*]
~ ~ scheme, ~ ~ system, paint ~ · (Anstrich)System n [*Der fertig aufgebaute Anstrich*]
~ ~ system, ~ ~ scheme, paint ~ · (Anstrich)System n [*Der fertig aufgebaute Anstrich*]
multiple dwelling building (Brit.) → block (of flats)
~ ~ type (US); residential building ~, domestic building ~, residence building ~, residential block ~, domestic block ~, residence block ~ · Wohngebäudeart f, Wohnhausart, Wohngebäudetyp m, Wohnhaustyp
~ ~ (unit building) (US) → block (of flats)
multi(ple-floor warehouse (building) → multi(ple)-storey ~ (~)
multiple frame, cellular ~, multi(ple)-bay ~ · Mehrfeldrahmen m
~ ~ as spandrel beam, multi(ple-)bay ~ ~ ~ ~ · Mehrfeldrahmen-Abfangträger m
~ glazing [*A form of glazing based on the same principle as double glazing, but incorporating three or more panes of glass*] · Mehrfachverglasung f, Vielfachverglasung, Mehrfacheinglasung, Vielfacheinglasung
~ ~ unit, ~ pane ~ · Mehrfach(glas)scheibe f
~ joint, tie-bar ~ · Knoten(punkt)gelenk n
multi(ple)-layer(ed) · mehrschalig [*Decke*]
~, laminated · viellagig, mehrlagig, vielschichtig, mehrschichtig
~ composition roofing → ~ ready ~
~ fabric for roofing → ~ (roofing) fabric
~ insulation, laminated ~ · Mehrlagenisolierung f, Viellagenisolierung, Mehrschichtenisolierung, Vielschichtenisolierung
~ monolithic wall, monolithic multi(ple)-layer(ed) ~ · mehrschichtige einschalige Mauer f, ~ monolithische ~
~ panel, laminated ~ · mehrlagige Tafel f, mehrschichtige ~, viellagige ~, vielschichtige ~
~ (prepared) roofing → ~ ready ~
~ ready roofing, ~ (prepared) ~, ~ composition ~, laminated ~ · Mehrlagendachpappe f, Viellagendachpappe, Mehrschichtendachpappe, Vielschichtendachpappe
~ roofing → ~ ready ~
~ (~) fabric, laminated (~) ~, ~ fabric for roofing · Mehrlagen-Roh(dach)pappe f, Mehrschichten-Roh(dach)pappe
~ seal(ing), laminated ~ · Mehrlagen-(ab)dichtung f, Viellagen(ab)dichtung, Mehrschichten(ab)dichtung, Vielschichten(ab)dichtung
~ tile · Mehrschichten(belag)platte f, Mehrschichtenfliese
~ wall · Mehrschichtenwand f
~ waterproofing · Mehrlagen(ab)dichtung f, Viellagen(ab)dichtung, Mehrlagensperrung, Viellagensperrung
multi(ple)-leaf, multi(ple)-wythe, multi(ple)-withe (Brit.); multi(ple)-tier (US) · mehrschalig [*Wand; Mauer*]
multi(ple)-lobe tracery · Vielpaß m, Mehrpaß [*gotisches Maßwerk*]
multiple masonry wall · Mehrfachmauer f
multi(ple)-nave · multi(ple)-aisle · mehrschiffig, vielschiffig [*Kirche*]
multiple pane unit, ~ glazing ~ · Mehrfach(glas)scheibe f
multiple-panel door, framed and ~ ~ · Mehrfüllungstür f
multiple portal frame, multi(ple-)bay ~ ~ · Mehrfeldportalrahmen m, Mehrfachportalrahmen
~ reduction (wire-)drawing machine · Mehrfach-(Draht)Ziehbank f
~ rib pillar → clustered ~

multiple ribless shell — multi-reflected sound

~ **ribless shell** · rippenlose Zylinderschale f, mehrfeld(e)rige Zylinderschale mit flachen und breiten Querrippenbändern

multi(ple)-room building, ~ block · Mehrraumgebäude n

~ **dwelling unit** (US); ~ dwelling (Brit.) · Mehrraumwohnung f, Vielraumwohnung

~ **heating** · Mehrzimmerheizung f

multiple-sash window (US) · mehrflügeliges Fenster n, Mehrflügelfenster [*Siehe Anmerkung unter „Flügel"*]

~ **shingle-strip**, strip shingle · Schindelplatte f, Schindelreihe f, Schindelstreifen m [*aus Pappschindeln*]

multiple-sided dowel pin · kantiger Verbandstift m [*DIN 1156*]

multiple socket · Mehrfach-Steckdose f

multi(ple)-span, multi(ple)-bay · mehrschiffig, vielschiffig [*Halle*]

~ **gabled frame** · mehrfeld(e)riger Giebelrahmen m

multiple spans · mehrere Schiffe npl [*Halle*]

multi(ple)-storey warehouse (building) (Brit.); multi(ple)-story ~ (~) (US); multi(ple)-floor ~ (~) · mehrstöckiges Lagergebäude n, mehretagiges ~, mehrgeschossiges ~, Speicher m

multi(ple)-tier (US) → multi(ple)-leaf

multi(ple-)use, multi-purpose use · Mehrzweckverwendung f, Vielzweckverwendung

~ **(bonding) adhesive** → multi-purpose ~

~ **building**, multi-purpose ~, ~ block · Mehrzweckgebäude n, Vielzweckgebäude

~ **(~) block** → multi-purpose (~) ~

~ **cement(ing agent)** → multi-purpose adhesive

~ **door**, multi-purpose ~ · Mehrzwecktür f, Vielzwecktür

~ **hall**, multi-purpose ~ · Mehrzweckhalle f, Vielzweckhalle

~ **high rise building**, multi-purpose ~ ~ ~, ~ ~ block · Mehrzweckhochhaus n, Vielzweckhochhaus

~ **liquid coating (material)** → multi-purpose ~ ~ (~)

~ **lock**, multi-purpose ~ · Mehrzweckschloß n, Vielzweckschloß

~ **(mixed) plaster**, multi-purpose ~ (~) [*It is designated for application to all backgrounds*] · Mehrzweck(innen)(ver)putz m, Vielzweck(innen)(ver)putz

~ **stadium**, multi-purpose ~ · Mehrzweckstadion n, Vielzweckstadion

~ **stage**, multi-purpose ~ · Mehrzweckbühne f, Vielzweckbühne

~ **steel door**, multi-purpose ~ ~ · Stahl-Mehrzwecktür f, Stahl-Vielzwecktür

~ **tile** → multi-purpose (building) block

multiple wall · Mehrfachwand f, Vielfachwand

multi(ple)-way cable duct, ~ ~ conduit, ~ ~ subway, ~ CD; ~ conduit tile (US) · mehrzügiger Kabel(kanal)formstein m, mehrzügiges Kabelformstück n [*DIN 457*]

~ **cock** · Vielwegehahn m

multi(ple)-wing door · mehrflügelige Tür f, vielflügelige ~

multi(ple)-withe → multi(ple)-leaf

multi(ple)-wythe → multi(ple)-leaf

multiplicity of images · Vielbildigkeit f

multi-purpose adhesive, multi(ple-)use ~, ~ cement(ing agent), ~ bonding agent, ~ bonding medium, ~ bonding adhesive · Mehrzweckkleb(e)stoff m, Mehrzweckkleber m, Mehrzweckkleb(e)mittel n, Vielzweckkleb(e)stoff, Vielzweckkleber, Vielzweckkleb(e)mittel

~ **block** → ~ building →

~ **building**, multi(ple-)use ~, ~ block · Mehrzweckgebäude n, Vielzweckgebäude

~ **(~) block**, ~ (~) tile, multi(ple-)use (~) ~ [*See remark under 'Block'*] · Mehrzweckstein m, Vielzweckstein, Mehrzweckblock(stein) m, Vielzweckblock(stein)

~ **cement(ing agent)** → ~ adhesive

~ **door**, multi(ple-) use ~ · Mehrzwecktür f, Vielzwecktür

~ **hall**, multi(ple-)use ~ · Mehrzweckhalle f, Vielzweckhalle

~ **high rise building**, multi(ple-)use ~ ~ ~ · Mehrzweckhochhaus n, Vielzweckhochhaus

~ **liquid coating (material)** multi(ple-)use ~ (~) ~ · Mehrzweckanstrich(stoff) m, Mehrzweckanstrichmittel n, Mehrzweckaufstrich(stoff), Mehrzweckaufstrichmittel, flüssiger Mehrzweckbeschichtungsstoff, Vielzweckanstrich(stoff), Vielzweckanstrichmittel, Vielzweckaufstrich(stoff), Vielzweckaufstrichmittel, Vielzweckaufstrich(stoff), flüssiger Vielzweckbeschichtungsstoff

~ **lock** multi(ple-)use ~ · Mehrzweckschloß n, Vielzweckschloß

~ **(mixed) plaster**, multi(ple-)use (~) ~ [*It is designated for application to all backgrounds*] · Mehrzweck(innen)(ver)putz m, Vielzweck(innen)(ver)putz

~ **stadium**, multi(ple-)use ~ · Mehrzweckstadion n, Vielzweckstadion

~ **stage**, multi(ple-)use ~ · Mehrzweckbühne f, Vielzweckbühne

~ **steel door**, multi(ple-)use ~ ~ · Stahl-Mehrzwecktür f, Stahl-Vielzwecktür

~ **tile** → ~ (building) block

~ **use**, multi(ple-)use ~ · Mehrzweckverwendung f, Vielzweckverwendung

multi-reflected sound, reverberant ~ · Nachhallschall m

multi-ribbed floor — municipal palace

multi-ribbed floor · Vielrippendecke *f*, Mehrrippendecke

multi-span girder · Mehrfeldträger *m*, Vielfeldträger

~ rigid frame · Mehfeldsteifrahmen *m*, Mehrfeldstarrahmen

multi-storey building, ~ block (Brit.); multi-story ~ (US); multi-floor ~ · Geschoßgebäude *n*, Etagengebäude, Stockwerkgebäude, Geschoßbau *m*, Etagenbau, Stockwerkbau

~ car park (Brit.); multi-story ~ ~ (US); multi-floor ~ ~, ~ garage · Stockwerkgarage *f*, Hochgarage, Geschoßgarage, Etagengarage

~ factory building, ~ ~ block (Brit.); multi-story ~ ~ (US); multi-floor ~ ~ · Fabrikgeschoßbau *m*, Fabrikgeschoßgebäude *n*, Fabrikstockwerkbau, Fabrikstockwerkgebäude, Fabriketagenbau, Fabriketagengebäude

~ frame (Brit.); multi-story ~ (US) · mehrstöckiger Rahmen *m*, mehrgeschossiger ~, mehretagiger ~, vielstöckiger ~, vielgeschossiger ~, vieletagiger ~

~ garage (Brit.); multi-story ~ (US); multi-floor ~, ~ car park · Stockwerkgarage *f*, Hochgarage, Geschoßgarage, Etagengarage

~ hotel (Brit.); multi-story ~ (US); multi-floor ~ · Hotelhochhaus *n*, Hochhaushotel *n*

~ library (Brit.); multi-story ~ (US); multi-floor ~; book tower · Bücherturm *m*

~ parking building → multi-floor ~ ~

~ steel car park (Brit) → steel-frame(d) multi-storey ~

~ system composed of three-hinge(d) frames (Brit.); multi-story ~ ~ ~ ~ ~ (US); multi-floor ~ ~ ~ ~ ~ · Mehretagensystem *n* aus Dreigelenkrahmen, Mehrgeschoßsystem ~ ~, Mehrstockwerksystem ~ ~

~ town (Brit.); multi-story ~ (US); multi-level ~ · Stadt *f* in mehreren Ebenen

~ villa (Brit.); multi-story ~ (US) · Villen-Hochhaus *n*

multistoried; multistoreyed (Brit.) · mehretagig, vielstöckig, vielgeschossig, vieletagig, mehrgeschossig, mehrstöckig

multi-strand steel (pre)stressing cable · zusammengefaßtes (Vor)Spannkabel *n*

multi-terraced site · terrassiertes Grundstück *n*

multi-tone etching, French embossing · Tonätzung *f* [*Säurebehandlung von Glas*]

multitubular slab for cable → (multiple way) cable duct

multi-use → multiple-use

multi-web(bed) T-beam · Plattenrippenwerk *n*, mehrstegiger Plattenbalken(träger) *m*

multi-wire connection · Mehrleiteranschluß *m* [*Elektrotechnik*]

multi-zone air-conditioning · Mehrzonenklimatisierung *f*

mummy chamber · Mumienkammer *f*

mundic, fool's gold, (iron) pyrite(s), yellow pyrite(s) · Eisenkies *m*, Schwefelkies, Schwefeleisen *n*

municipal architecture → town ~

~ area, town ~, urban ~ · Stadtgebiet *n*

~ block, urban ~, town ~ [*A division of a city bounded by four streets*] · Stadtviertel *n*

~ building (construction) department · Stadthochbauamt *n*, (städtisches) Hochbauamt

~ centre (Brit.); ~ center (US); town ~, urban ~ · Stadtmitte *f*

~ chapel, urban ~, town ~ · Stadtkapelle *f*

~ church, town ~, urban ~ [*A church in a town*] · Stadtkirche *f*

~ civil engineering · städtischer Tiefbau *m*

~ configuration, town ~, urban ~ · Stadtfigur *f*

~ destructor, ~ incineration plant · städtische Abfall(stoff)verbrennungsanlage *f*, ~ Müllverbrennungsanlage

~ development, urban ~, town ~ · Städtebau *m*

~ ~, town ~, urban ~ · Stadtentwick(e)lung *f*

~ ~ committee, urban ~ ~, town ~ ~ · Städtebauausschuß *m*

~ engineering, town ~, urban ~ · Stadtbautechnik *f*, Städtebautechnik

~ expressway, urban ~, town ~ · Stadtschnellstraße *f*

~ extension, town ~, urban ~ · Stadterweiterung *f*

~ forest, urban ~, town ~ · Stadtwald *m*

~ garden, urban ~, town ~ · Stadtgarten *m*

~ hall, urban ~ · Stadthalle *f*

~ heating, urban ~, town ~ · Stadtheizung *f*

~ hotel, urban ~, town ~ · Stadthotel *n*

~ incineration plant, ~ destructor · städtische Abfall(stoff)verbrennungsanlage *f*, ~ Müllverbrennungsanlage

~ library, urban ~, town ~ · Stadtbibliothek *f*, Stadtbücherei *f*

~ living-space, town ~, urban ~ · städtischer Lebensraum *m*

~ market, wholesale ~ · Großmarkt(halle) *m*, (*f*)

~ museum, urban ~, town ~ · Stadtmuseum *n*

~ orphanage, urban ~, town ~ · städtisches Waisenhaus *n*

~ palace, urban ~, town ~ · Stadtpalast *m*

municipal park — to nail

~ **park**, urban ~, town ~ · Stadtpark *m*
~ **planner**, urban ~, town ~ · Städtebauer *m*, Stadtbauer, Städteplaner, Stadtplaner
~ **planning**, urban ~, town ~ · städtebauliche Planung *f*, Stadtplanung, Städteplanung
~ ~ **institute**, urban ~ ~, town ~ ~ · Städtebauinstitut *n*
~ ~ **studies**, town ~ ~, urban ~ ~, Stadtbaulehre *f*, städtebauliche Lehre
~ ~ **system**, town ~ ~, urban ~ ~ · Stadtbausystem *n*
~ ~ **theory**, urban ~ ~, town ~ ~ · Städtebautheorie *f*
~ **pool**, town ~, urban ~, ~ swimming bath · Stadtbad *n*
~ **refuse**, ~ waste, town ~; ~ rubbish (US) · Stadtabfall(stoff) *m*, Stadtmüll *m*
~ **road** → urban ~
~ **rubbish**, town ~ (US); ~ refuse, ~ waste · Stadtabfall(stoff) *m*, Stadtmüll *m*
~ **sauna bath**, town ~ ~, urban ~ ~ · Stadt-Sauna(bad) *f*, (*n*)
~ **station**, urban ~, (in-)town ~ · Stadtbahnhof *m*
~ **swimming bath**, town ~ ~, urban ~ ~, ~ ~ pool · Stadtbad *n*
~ **theatre**, urban ~, town ~, ~ theater · Stadttheater *n*
~ **wall**, urban ~, town ~ · Stadtmauer *f*
~ **waste**, ~ refuse, town ~; ~ rubbish (US) · Stadtabfall(stoff) *m*, Stadtmüll *m*
~ **water supply** · städtische Wasserversorgung *f*

munnion, mullion, monial · Fensterpfosten *m*

muntin (US) → (window) glazing bar
~ [*In a panelled wooden door, the vertical member between any two panels*] · Höhenfries *m* innen [*Holzfüllungstür*]
~ **window** (US); astragal ~, sash bar ~, glazing bar ~, division bar ~ · Sprossenfenster *n*

Muntz metal, yellow ~, malleable brass [*It contains 60 per cent copper and 40 per cent zinc*] · MS 60 *n*, Ms 60, Muntzmetall *n*

mural · Wandbild *n*
~ **decoration** → wall enrichment
~ **enrichment** → wall ~
~ **hanging**, wall ~ · Wandbehang *m*
~ **mosaic**, wall ~ · Wandmosaik *n*
~ **ornamentation** → wall enrichment
~ **painting**, wall ~ · Wandmalerei *f*
~ **tomb**, wall ~ · Wandgrab *n*, Mauergrab

muriatic acid · Salzsäure *f*, HCl

muscovite → muscovy glass
muscovy glass, muscovite, common mica, potash mica · heller Glimmer *m*, Kaliglimmer
museum architect · Museumsarchitekt *m*
~ **design and planning** · Museumsgestaltung *f*
~ **library** · Museumsbücherei *f*, Museumsbibliothek *f*
Museum of Folk Art · Volkskunstmuseum *n*
~ ~ **Modern Art** · Museum *n* für Moderne Kunst
~ ~ **Visual Arts** · Museum *n* für bildende Künste
mushroom column → ~ head ~
~ **construction**, flat-slab ~ · Pilzdeckenbau *m*
~ **floor**, flat-slab ~ · Pilzdecke *f*
~ ~ **slab** · Pilzdeckenplatte *f*
~ **head**, flared ~, flaring ~, support ~, column ~, flared haunch [*In flat slab construction. An enlargement at the top of a column supporting a flat slab, designed and constructed to act monolithically with the column and with the flat slab*] · Pilzkopf *m*, Stützenkopf
~ (~) **column**, flared ~ ~, flaring ~ ~ · Pilz(decken)stütze *f* [*Fehlnamen: Tragsäule f, Pilzsäule*]

music (class)room · Musikzimmer *n*
(~) **conservatory** · Konservatorium *n*
~ **hall**, concert ~ · Konzerthalle *f*, Konzerthaus *n*, Tonhalle
~ **library** · Musikbücherei *f*, Musikbibliothek *f*
~ **room** · Musikzimmer *n*, Musikraum *m*
musical scale · Tonskala *f*
~ **sound** · Klang *m*
~ **water-works**, ~ waters · Musikwasserspiele *npl*, Musikspringbrunnen *m*
Muslim architecture, Arab(ian) ~, Mohammadan ~, Mohammedan ~, Mahometan ~, Moslem ~, Islamic ~, Saracenic ~, Muslem ~ · islamische Architektur *f*, mohammedanische ~, ~ Baukunst
muslin scrim · Oxidiernessel *f* [*Linoleumherstellung*]
mutual benefit building society · gemeinnütziges Wohnungsunternehmen *n*
mutule [*The projecting square block above the triglyph and on the soffit of a Doric cornice*] · Mutulus *m*, Dielenkopf *m*, Via *f*, Hängeplatte *f*, Tropfenplatte
Mycenaean architecture · mykenische Baukunst *f*, ~ Architektur

N

N.A., neutral axis, zero line · neutrale Achse *f*, ~ Linie *f*, Nullachse, Nulllinie
to nail · nageln

nailability · Nagelbarkeit f, Nagelfestigkeit

nailable · nagelfest, nagelbar

~ base, fixing ~ · nagelbare Unterlage f, nagelfeste ~

~ brick, ~ block, fixing ~, nailing ~, wood ~; anchor ~ (US) · nagelbarer Stein m, nagelfester ~, ~ Block m, Dübelstein, Dübelblock

~ concrete, fixing ~ · nagelfester Beton m, nagelbarer ~

nailed beam · genagelter Balken(träger) m

~ connection, ~ joint · Nagelverbindung f

~ construction, ~ (structural) system · Nagelbausystem n, Nagelkonstruktion f, Nagel(konstruktions)system

~ ~ method · Nagelbauweise f

~ girder · genagelter Träger m

~ joint, ~ connection · Nagelverbindung f

~ roof truss · Nagel(dach)binder m

~ (structural) system, ~ construction · Nagelbausystem n, Nagelkonstruktion f, Nagel(konstruktions)system

~ structure · genageltes Bauwerk n

~ system → ~ structural ~

nailer → fixing (fillet)

nail for reed · (Schilf)Rohrnagel m

(nail-)glued (roof) truss · Leim(dach)binder m

nail-head (moulding) (Brit.); ~ molding (US); ~ ornament · Nagelkopf(verzierung), Nagelkopfornament n, Nagelkopfstab m

nail hole · Nagelloch n

nailing · Nagelung f

~ · Nageln n

~ base · nagelbare Unterlage f

~ batten · Nagelleiste f

~ block → nailable brick

~ brick → nailable ~

~ pattern · Nagelungsmuster n

~ plug, wall ~ · Mauerdübel m

~ strip → fixing (fillet)

nail material · Nagelwerkstoff m

~ plate [A metal gusset plate containing holes through which nails are driven into two or more pieces of timber] · Nagel-Knotenblech n, Nagel-Anschlußblech, Nagel-Eckblech

name-plate · Bezeichnungschild n

naos, statue chamber · Naos m

naphtha · Naphtha n, f

naphthalene, naphthalin(e) · Naphthalin n

naphthenate of lead, lead naphthenate · Bleinaphthenat n

naphthol dyestuff · Naphtholfarbstoff m

~ lake colour (Brit.); ~ ~ color (US); ~ ~ (pigment) · Naphtholfarblack m

Naples yellow, antimony ~ · Neapelgelb n, (Blei)Antimongelb

narrow-flanged · schmalflanschig

narrow side, short end · Schmalseite f

~ street · Gasse f

narthex, galilee [In an early-Christian basilica, the antechamber to the nave, from which it is separated, by columns, rails, or a wall. Not to be confused with the porch, which opens on to the street] · Narthex m, Galilaea f, Galiläa

'national' architecture [Term usually used to indicate a style of building approved by the State] · Staatsarchitektur f

~ monument · Nationaldenkmal n

National Romantic style [Finnish version of Art Nouveau] · Nationalromantik f, romantisch-nationale Formensprache f, romantisch-nationaler Stil m

native minium; ~ red oxide of lead (Brit.); ~ red oxid(e) of lead (US) · rotes Bleioxid n, natürliche (Blei)Mennige f

~ paraffin → ozokerit(e)

~ red oxide of lead → ~ minium

~ style, local ~ · Heimatstil m

natural, rough-shuttered, board-marked · schalungsrauh

~ abradant, ~ abrasive · natürliches Schleifmittel n

~ abrasive, ~ abradant · natürliches Schleifmittel n

~ acanthus leaf · unstilisiertes Akanthusblatt n, ~ Bärenklaublatt

~ adhesive → ~ bonding ~

~ aggregate → ~ concrete ~

~ ~, ~ construction ~ · Naturzuschlag(-stoff) m, natürlicher Zuschlag(stoff), Naturzuschlagmaterial n, natürliches Zuschlagmaterial

~ ~ concrete, ~ rock ~, stone-aggregate ~ · Beton m mit natürlichen Zuschlägen, ~ ~ ~ Zuschlagstoffen

~ ~ light(weight) concrete · Leichtbeton m mit natürlichen Zuschlägen, ~ ~ ~ Zuschlagstoffen

~ anhydrite · Naturanhydrit m, n, natürliches Anhydrit n, natürlicher Anhydrit m

(~) asphalt (Brit.); rock ~ (US) · (Natur)Asphalt m, natürliches Bitumen-Mineralgemisch n, natürliches Bitumen-Mineralmischung f [Das natürlich vorkommende Bitumen mit seinem Begleitgestein]

~ ~ tile (US); ~ (asphaltic-)bitumen ~ (Brit.) · Naturasphalt(belag)platte f, Naturasphaltfliese f

natural bar — natural gravel-sand mix(ture)

~ **bar** → billet ~

~ **barium sulfate**, barite (US); natural barium sulphate, barytes (Brit.) [*A mineral used in pure or impure form as concrete aggregate primarily for the construction of high-density radiation shielding concrete*] · Schwerspat *m*, Baryt *m*, BaO

(~) **bd.**, (~) board · Brett *n*

~ **bed** · Bruchlager *n*, natürliches Lager [*(Natur)Stein*]

(~) **board**, (~) bd. · Brett *n*

~ **(bonding) adhesive**, ~ ~ agent, ~ ~ medium, ~ cement(ing agent), ~ glue [*Natural adhesives are animal glues, blood albumen glues, casein glues, starch derivative adhesives and vegetable derivative adhesives*] · natürlicher Kleb(e)stoff *m*, ~ Kleber *m*, natürliches Kleb(e)mittel *n*

~ **building sand**, ~ construction(al) ~, building sand from natural sources, construction(al) sand from natural sources [*B.S. 1198–1200*] · Natur-Bausand *m*

~ **cement** · Naturzement *m*

~ **cement(ing agent)** → ~ (bonding) adhesive

~ **chalk** · Rohkreide *f*

~ **clay** · Naturton *m*

~ **cleft**, ~ split · spaltrauh, bruchrauh [*Schiefer*]

~ **coarse sand** · Naturgrobsand *m*

~ **colour** (Brit.); ~ color (US) · Naturfarbe *f*

~ **coloured** (Brit.); natural-colored (US) · naturfarbig

~ **(concrete) aggregate**, concrete aggregate from natural sources [*B.S. 882; B.S. 1201*] · natürliches (Beton-)Zuschlagmaterial *n*, natürlicher (Beton-)Zuschlag(stoff) *m*, (Natur)Steinzuschlag(stoff), (Natur)Steinzuschlagmaterial [*DIN 4226*]

~ ~ **heat**, inherent ~ ~ · Betoneigenwärme *f*

~ **(concreting) sand**, ~ concrete ~, ~ fine aggregate [*This term refers to an aggregate mainly passing a 3/16 in. B.S. test sieve*] · Betonsand *m*, natürlicher Feinzuschlag(stoff) *m*, natürliches Feinzuschlagmaterial *n* [*Durchgang durch das Rundlochsieb 7 nach DIN 1170*]

~ **(construction) aggregate** · Naturzuschlag(stoff) *m*, natürlicher Zuschlag(stoff), Naturzuschlagmaterial *n*, natürliches Zuschlagmaterial

~ **construction(al) sand**, ~ building ~, building sand from natural sources, construction(al) sand from natural sources [*B.S. 1198–1200*] · Natur-Bausand *m*

~ **copal** · natürlicher Kopal *m*, Naturkopal

~ **cork** [*As opposed to composition cork*] · Naturkork *m*

~ ~ **insulating board**, ~ ~ ~ slab, ~ ~ ~ sheet, ~ ~ insulation(-grade) ~ · Naturkork-Dämmplatte *f*

~ **draught** (Brit.); ~ draft (US) · natürlicher Zug *m*

~ ~ **chimney** (Brit.); ~ draft ~ (US) Naturzugschornstein *m*

~ ~ **ventilation unit** (Brit.); ~ draft ~ (US) · Naturzugentlüftungsanlage *f*

~ **dyestuff** · natürlicher Farbstoff *m*

~ **earth**, ~ pigment, earth colour, mineral pigment, earth pigment [*B.S. 2015*] Many of the colo(u)r pigments are natural earths consisting of earthy substances such as sand and clay mixed with such materials as the oxides of iron and manganese which provide the colo(u)r] · Erdpigment *n*, natürliches (anorganisches) Pigment [*Fehlbezeichnung: Erdfarbe f*]

~ **emulsion** · natürliche Emulsion *f*

(~) **face stone** · Sicht(natur)stein *m* [*(Natur)Steinmauerwerk*]

~ **fine aggregate** → ~ (concreting) sand

~ ~ **grain** · Naturfeinkorn *n*

~ ~ **sand** · Naturfeinsand *m*

~ **finish** → ~ (clear) varnish

~ ~ [*Natural finishes are various types of coatings, some nearly colo(u)rless, which are used on attractively-grained or figured-wood finishing lumber. Very few of the finishes change the colo(u)r of the wood, and properly used they may make the grain even more attractive. All clear varnishes are often called natural finishes, such as the natural dammars, some lacquers, and many synthetics such as cellulose nitrates which are truly colo(u)rless*] · Naturton *m*

~ **flag(stone)**, ~ paving ~ · (Natur-)Stein-Pflasterplatte *f*

~ **foliage** · natürlich dargestelltes Blattwerk *n*, ~ ~ Laubwerk

(~) **footpath flagstone** (Brit.) → (~) stone sidewalk (paving) flag

~ **foundation(s)** [*Earth requiring no preparation to sustain a structure*] · tragfähiger Baugrund *m*

~ **frequency** [*The frequency of a free vibration*] · Eigenfrequenz *f*

~ **fresh air** · Außenfrischluft *f*

(~) **(fresh-)air inlet stack**, (~) ~ intake, ~ · (Frisch)Luft(ansaug)schornstein *m*

(~) ~ **intake**, outside-air ~, FAI · (Außen)Frischlufteinlaß *m*

~ **garden** · Naturgarten *m*

~ **glue** → ~ bonding adhesive

~ **grade** [*The elevation of the original or undisturbed natural surface of the ground*] · natürliche Geländehöhe *f*

~ **gravel** · Naturkies *m*

~ **gravel-sand mix(ture)** · Naturkiessand *m*

natural gray — natural split

~ **gray**, ~ grey · naturgrau

~ **gypsum**, raw ~, (massive) ~; gypsum rock, plaster rock, plaster stone, potter's stone (Brit.) · Rohgips *m*, Naturgips, Gipsstein *m*, Gipsgestein *n*, $CaSO_4 \cdot 2H_2O$

~ **hard aggregate concrete tile** · Hart(ge)stein-Beton(belag)platte *f*, Hart(ge)stein-Betonfliese *f* [*Hartgestein als Zuschlag(stoff)*]

'**natural hardness**' · Naturhärte *f* [*z.B. bei Betonstahl. Sie wird im Gegensatz zur Härtung durch Kaltverfestigen (Ziehen, Verwinden) durch Zugabe von Legierungsbestandteilen bei der Stahlherstellung erreicht*]

natural heat, inherent ~ · Eigenwärme *f*

~ **heating** · natürliche Heizung *f*

~ **history museum** · Naturkundemuseum *n*

~ **light**, daylight · Tageslicht *n* [*DIN 5034*]

~ **lighting**, daylight illumination, daylighting · Innen(raum)beleuchtung *f* mit Tageslicht, Tages(licht)beleuchtung [*Fehlnamen: (Tages)Belichtung*] [*DIN 5034*]

~ **light(weight) (concrete) aggregate** · natürlicher (Beton)Leichtzuschlag(stoff) *m*, natürliches (Beton-)Leichtzuschlagmaterial *n*

~ **marble** · Naturmarmor *m*

~ **material** · natürlicher Stoff *m*

~ **medium sand** · Naturmittelsand *m*

~ **moisture**, inherent ~, water of composition · Eigenfeuchte *f*, Eigenfeuchtigkeit *f*

~ **monument** · Naturdenkmal *n*

~ **oil** · Naturöl *n*

~ **organic dye** · natürlicher organischer Farbstoff *m*

~ ~ **pigment** · natürliches organisches Pigment *n*; natürliche organische Farbe *f* [*Fehlname*]

~ **oscillation**, ~ vibration, inherent ~ · Eigenschwingung *f*

~ **(outdoor) weathering test** · natürliche Verwitterungsprobe *f*, ~ Verwitterungsprüfung *f*, natürlicher Verwitterungsversuch *m*

~ **oxid(e) of iron** (US); ~ oxide ~ ~ (Brit.) · natürliches Eisenoxid *n*

~ **(paving) flag(stone)** · (Natur)Stein-Pflasterplatte *f*

~ **(~) sett**, (~) stone (~) ~ · (Natur)Steinpflasterstein *m*, Naturpflasterstein [*DIN 18502*]

~ **pigment** · natürliches Pigment *n*

~ **plastic (material)** · Kunststoff *m* auf natürlicher Basis, natürlicher Kunststoff

~ **pozz(u)olana**, ~ pozzolan(ic material) [*See remark under 'Puzzolane'*] · natürliche Puzzolane *f*, natürlicher hydraulischer Zuschlag *m*, Naturpuzzolane

~ **product** · Naturerzeugnis *n*

~ **resin**, plant ~ · (Natur)Harz *n* [*Aus Pflanzensäften stammend; Kohlenstoffverbindungen; erhärten durch Polymerisation; Grundstoff für Lacke und Firnisse*]

~ ~ **adhesive**, ~ ~ glue · Naturkleb(e)harz *n*, Naturharzkleber *m*

~ **resin-base(d) (concrete) curing agent**, plant ~ (~) ~ ~, ~ ~ (~) ~ compound, ~ ~ (liquid) membrane (~) ~ ~ · (Beton)Nachbehandlungsmittel *n* auf Naturharzbasis

~ ~ **mastic**, plant ~ ~ · Naturharzkitt *m*

~ **resin glue**, ~ ~ adhesive · Naturkleb(e)harz *n*, Naturharzkleber *m*

~ ~ **varnish** · Naturharzlack *m*

~ **rigidity**, ~ stiffness, inherent ~ · Eigensteifigkeit *f*, Eigenstarrheit [*Statik*]

~ **rock aggregate** · Natursteingranulat *n* [*Buntsteinputz*]

~ ~ **concrete** → ~ aggregate ~

~ **rod** → billet bar

~ **rubber**, raw ~, caoutchouc · (Natur-)Kautschuk *m* [*Fehlnamen: Naturgummi m, n, Rohgummi*]

~ ~ **emulsion**, raw ~ ~, caoutchouc ~ · (Natur)Kautschukemulsion *f*

~ ~ ~ **paint**, raw ~ ~ ~, caoutchouc ~ ~ · (Natur)Kautschukemulsionsfarbe *f*

~ ~ **powder**, raw ~ ~, caoutchouc ~, powder(ed) natural rubber, powder(ed) raw rubber, powder(ed) caoutchouc · (Natur)Kautschukpulver *n*

~ **sand**, ~ concreting ~, ~ concrete ~, ~ fine aggregate [*This term refers to an aggregate mainly passing a 3/16 in. B.S. test sieve*] · Betonsand *m*, natürlicher Feinzuschlag(stoff) *m*, natürliches Feinzuschlagmaterial *n* [*Durchgang durch das Rundlochsieb 7 nach DIN 1170*]

~ ~ · Natursand *m*

~ ~ **aggregate** · Natursandzuschlag(-stoff) *m*, Natursandzuschlagmaterial *n*

natural-sand fine aggregate · Natursandfeinzuschlag(stoff) *m*, Natursandfeinzuschlagmaterial *n*

natural scale · Maßstab 1:1 *m*

~ **sett** → (~) (paving) ~

(~) sidewalk flagstone (US) → (~) stone sidewalk (paving) flag

~ **sienna**, raw ~ [*B.S. 312*] · Terra *f* di) Siena *f* natur, ungebrannte (Terra di) Siena

~ **size** · Naturgröße *f*

~ **split**, ~ cleft · spaltrauh, bruchrauh [*Schiefer*]

natural stiffness — (natural) stone finish

~ stiffness, ~ rigidity, inherent ~ · Eigensteifigkeit f, Eigenstarrheit [*Statik*]

(~) stone [*B.S. 1232*] · (Natur)Stein m, natürlicher Stein [*DIN 52100 bis 52112*]

(~) ~ altar · (Natur)Steinaltar m

(~) ~ ~ screen, (~) ~ ~ piece, (~) ~ ~ retable, (~) ~ ~ reredos · (Natur)Stein(altar)retabel n, (Natur)Steinaltaraufsatz m [*Siehe Anmerkung unter ,,Altaraufsatz"*]

(~) ~ (angle-)quoin · Eckquader m, Winkelquader

(~) ~ arcade · (Natur)Steinarkade f

(~) ~ arch · (Natur)Steinbogen m

(~) ~ balcony · (Natur)Steinbalkon m

(~) ~ baluster, (~) ~ ban(n)ister · (Natur)Steinbaluster m

(~) ~ ban(n)ister, (~) ~ baluster · (Natur)Steinbaluster m

(~) ~ barrel vault, (~) ~ tunnel ~, (~) ~ wagon ~ · Steintonne(ngewölbe) f, (n), Natur~

(~) ~ beam · (Natur)Steinbalken(träger) m

(~) ~ bench · (Natur)Steinbank f

(~) stone-block paving · (Natur)Steinplattenpflaster n

(~) stone blockwork, (~) ~ masonry (work), stone block masonry (work) · Steinblockmauerwerk n, (Natur)Steinmauerwerk [*DIN 1053*]

(~) ~ bond · (Natur)Steinverband m

(~) ~ boundary wall · (Natur)Stein-Grundstückmauer f

(~) ~ bracket, (~) ~ corbel, (~) ~ shoulder, console, corbel [*A small supporting piece of stone, often formed of scrolls or volutes, to carry a projecting weight*] · Kragstein m, Konsole f, steinerner Konsolträger m, Tragstein, (Natur)Steinkonsole, Kraftstein, Notstein, Balkenstein

(~) ~ building, (~) stone-built ~ · (Natur)Steingebäude n

(~) ~ ~ material, (~) ~ construction(al) ~ · (Natur)Steinbaustoff m; (Natur)Steinbaumaterial n [*Schweiz*]

(~) stone-built building, (~) stone ~ · (Natur)Steingebäude n

(~) stone capping, (~) ~ coping · Stein-Mauerabdeckung f, Natur~

(~) ~ ~ slab, (~) ~ coping ~ · (Ab-)Deckplatte f aus Naturstein, (Natur)Stein(ab)deckplatte

(~) ~ castle · (Natur)Steinburg f

(~) ~ chip(ping)s; (~) ~ screening(s) [*deprecated*] · (Naturstein)Splitt m, Steinsplitt

(~) ~ ~ · (Natur)Steinkörnungen fpl

(~) ~ church · (Natur)Steinkirche f

(~) ~ column · (Natur)Steinsäule f

(~) ~ construction method · (Natur-)Steinbau(weise) m, (f)

(~) ~ construction(al) material, (~) ~ building ~ · (Natur)Steinbaustoff m; (Natur)Steinbaumaterial n [*Schweiz*]

(~) ~ coping, (~) ~ capping · (Natur-)Stein-Mauerabdeckung f

(~) ~ ~ slab, (~) ~ capping ~ · (Ab-)Deckplatte f aus Naturstein, (Natur)Stein(ab)deckplatte

(~) ~ corbel, (~) ~ bracket, (~) ~ shoulder, console, corbel [*A small supporting piece of stone, often formed of scrolls or volutes, to carry a projecting weight*] · Kragstein m, Konsole f, steinerner Konsolträger m, (Natur)Steinkonsole, Kraftstein, Notstein, Balkenstein

(~) ~ course, (~) ~ layer · (Natur)Steinlage f, (Natur)Steinschicht f

(~) ~ cradle vault, (~) ~ cylindrical ~ · walzenförmiges (Natur)Steingewölbe n, zylindrisches ~

(~) ~ cross · (Natur)Steinkreuz n

(~) ~ curb; (~) ~ kerb (Brit.) · Steinbordstein m, Natur~ [*DIN 482*]

(~) ~ curtain (wall) · (Natur)Steinkurtine f

(~) ~ curving, curved work · nichtgerad(linig)e (Natur)Steinbearbeitung f

(~) ~ cutting, straight-line work · gerad(linig)e (Natur)Steinbearbeitung f

(~) ~ cylindrical vault, (~) ~ cradle ~ · walzenförmiges (Natur)Steingewölbe n, zylindrisches ~

(~) ~ discharge gutter, (~) ~ draining ~, (~) ~ drain(age) ~ · Steinabflußrinne f, Natur~, (Natur)Steinentwässerungsrinne, (Natur)Steinablaufrinne

(~) ~ (door) threshold · (Natur)Stein(tür)schwelle f

(~) ~ drain(age) gutter, (~) ~ draining ~, (~) ~ discharge ~ · (Natur-)Steinabflußrinne f, (Natur)Steinentwässerungsrinne, (Natur)Steinablaufrinne

(~) ~ dressed ready for building · baugerechter (Natur)Stein m

(~) ~ dressing plant · (Natur)Steinbearbeitungswerk n

(~) ~ dust, (~) ~ filler · Steinfüller m, Steinfüllstoff m, Natur~

(~) ~ façade · (Natur)Steinfassade f

(~) ~ female figure · weibliche (Natur-)Steinfigur f

(~) ~ figure · (Natur)Steinfigur f

(~) ~ filler, (~) ~ dust · (Natur-)Steinfüller m, (Natur)Steinfüllstoff m

(~) ~ finish, surface ~, dressed fair face, milled fair face · bearbeitete (Natur)Stein(sicht)fläche f

(natural) stone finishing — (natural) stone threshold 652

(~) ~ **finishing** · (Natur)Steinnachbearbeitung f

(~) ~ **floor cover(ing)**, (~) ~ slab floor(ing) (finish) · (Naturstein)Platten(fuß)boden(belag) m, Stein(fuß)boden(belag)

(~) ~ **font** [*A bowl of (natural) stone to hold the water used in baptismal services*] · Taufstein m [*Norddeutschland: Fünte f*]

(~) ~ **footing** · (Natur)Steinfundament n

(~) ~ **footpath (paving) flag** (Brit.) → (~) ~ sidewalk (~) ~

(~) ~ **foundation** · (Natur)Steingründung f

(~) ~ **frieze** · (Natur)Steinfries m

(~) ~ **grille** · (Natur)Steingitter n

(~) ~ **hinge** · (Natur)Steingelenk n

(~) ~ **keep** · (Natur)Steinbelfried m, (Natur)Steinbergfried

(~) ~ **kerb** (Brit.); (~) ~ curb · Steinbordstein m, Natur~ [*DIN 482*]

(~) ~ **layer**, (~) ~ course · Steinlage f, Steinschicht f, Natur~

(~) **stone-like** · (natur)steinähnlich

(~) **stone lintel**; (~) ~ lintol [*deprecated*] [*B.S. 1240*] · Steinoberschwelle f, Steinsturz m ,Natur~

(~) ~ **male figure** · männliche (Natur-)Steinfigur f

(~) ~ **masonry (work)**, stone block ~ (~), (natural) stone blockwork · (Natur)Steinmauerwerk n, Steinblockmauerwerk [*DIN 1053*]

(~) ~ **matting** · (Natur)Steinmatte f

(~) ~ **mosaic** · (Natur)Steinmosaik n

(~) ~ **mullion(ed) window** · (Natur-)Steinpfostenfenster n, (Natur)Steinkreuzfenster

(~) ~ **of one-quarter brick size** · (Natur)Steinriemchen n

(~) ~ **Order** · (Natur)Steinsäulenordnung f

(~) ~ **(ornamental) string (course)** · (Natur)Steingurt(ge)sims m, (n)

(~) ~ **paving** → (~) ~ sett ~

(~) ~ **(~) sett**, natural (~) ~ · (Natur)Steinpflasterstein m, Naturpflasterstein [*DIN 18502*]

(~) ~ **pier** · (Natur)Steinpfeiler m

(~) ~ **pillar** · (Natur)Steinfreipfeiler m

(~) ~ **portal** · (Natur)Steinportal n

(~) ~ **preservative**, (~) ~ preserving agent · (Natur)Steinerhaltungsmittel n, (Natur)Steinschutzmittel, (Natur-)Steinschutz(stoff) m

(~) ~ **pulpit** · Steinkanzel f, Natur~

(~) ~ **railing** · (Natur)Steingeländer n

(~) ~ **rib(bed) cupola**, (~) ~ ~ dome · Steinrippenkuppel f, Natur~

(~) ~ ~ **vault** · Steinrippengewölbe n, Natur~

(~) ~ **roof**, roof of (natural) stone · (Natur)Steindach n

(~) ~ ~ **cover(ing)** → (~) ~ slab roofing

(~) ~ ~ **spire** · (Natur)Stein-Dachreiter m

(~) ~ **(roof(ing)) tile** · Natursteindachstein m

(~) ~ **screening(s)** [*deprecated*] → (~) ~ chip(ping)s

(~) ~ **sculpture**, sculpture in (natural) stone · (Natur)Steinplastik f, (Natur-)Steinskulptur f

(~) ~ **sett** → (~) ~ (paving) ~

(~) ~ **(~) paving** · (Natur)Steinpflaster n

(~) ~ **shoulder**, (~) ~ corbel, (~) ~ bracket, console, corbel [*A small supporting piece of stone, often formed of scrolls or volutes, to carry a projecting weight*] · Kragstein m, Konsole f, steinerner Konsolträger m, Tragstein, (Natur)Steinkonsole, Kraftstein, Notstein, Balkenstein

(~) ~ **sidewalk (paving) flag** (US); (~) ~ footpath (~) ~ (Brit.); (~) sidewalk flagstone, (~) footpath flagstone · (Natur)Stein-Bürgersteigplatte f, (Natur)Stein-Gehbahnplatte, (Natur)Stein-Gehwegplatte, (Natur)Stein-Fußsteigplatte, (Natur)Stein-Fußwegplatte, (Natur)Stein-Gehsteigplatte [*DIN 484*]

(~) ~ **slab** · (Natur)Steinplatte f

(~) ~ ~ **floor(ing) (finish)**, (~) ~ floor cover(ing) · (Naturstein)Platten(fuß)boden(belag) m, Stein(fuß)boden(belag)

(~) ~ ~ **roofing**, (~) ~ roof cover(ing) · (Natur)Stein(platten)(dach)-(ein)deckung f

(~) ~ **(~) (sur)facing**, (~) ~ (~) lining, (~) ~ (~) cladding · (Natur-)Stein(platten)auskleidung f, (Natur-)Stein(platten)verkleidung, (Natur-)Stein(platten)bekleidung, (Natur-)Stein(platten)verblendung

(~) ~ **stair(case)** · (Natur)Steintreppe f

(~) ~ **step**, stepstone · (Natur)Steinstufe f

(~) ~ **strength** · (Natur)Steinfestigkeit f

~ ~ **string** → ~ ~ ornamental string course

(~) ~ **structure** · (Natur)Steinbau(werk) m, (n)

(~) ~ **(sur)facing**, (~) ~ lining · (Natur)Steinauskleidung f, (Natur-)Steinverkleidung, (Natur)Steinbekleidung

~ ~ **table altar** · (Natur)Stein(platten)altar m

(~) ~ **temple** · (Natur)Steintempel m

(~) ~ **threshold** · (Natur)Steinschwelle f

(~) ~ **throne** · (Natur)Steinthron m

(~) ~ **tile** · (Natur)Stein(belag)platte f, (Natur)Steinfliese f

(~) ~ **tunnel vault**, (~) ~ barrel ~, (~) ~ wagon ~ · Steintonne(ngewölbe) f, (n), Natur~

(~) ~ **two-sided city gateway**, (~) ~ ~ town ~ · (Natur)Steinstadttor n

(~) ~ **vault** · (Natur)Steingewölbe n

(~) **stone-vaulted ceiling** · (Natur-)Steingewölbedecke f

(~) ~ **roof** · (Natur)Steingewölbedach n

(~) **stone vaulting** · (Natur)Stein-(über)wölbung f, (Natur)Steineinwölbung

(~) ~ **veneer** · Verblendung f aus dünnen (Natur)Steinplatten

(~) ~ **wagon vault**, (~) ~ tunnel ~, (~) ~ barrel ~ · Steintonne(ngewölbe) f, (n), Natur~

(~) ~ **wall** · (Natur)Steinmauer f, Steinblockmauer

(~) ~ ~ **tile** · (Natur)Steinwand(belag)-platte f, (Natur)Steinwandfliese f

(~) ~ **window sill**; (~) ~ ~ cill (Brit.) [*B.S. 1230*] · (Natur)Stein-(fenster)sohlbank f, (Natur)Steinfensterbank

~ **strength**, inherent ~ · Eigenfestigkeit f

~ **stress**, inherent ~ · Eigenspannung f

~ **ultramarine** · natürliches Ultramarin n

~ **varnish resin** · Lacknaturharz n, Naturlackharz, natürliches Lackharz

~ **ventilation**, ~ venting · natürliche Be- und Entlüftung f, ~ Lüftung

~ **vibration**, ~ oscillation, inherent ~ · Eigenschwingung f

(~) **walling stone** · (Natur)Wandbaustein m

~ **wax** · Naturwachs n

~ **weathering** · natürliche Bewitterung f

~ ~ **test** → ~ outdoor ~ ~

naturalistic form · naturnahe Form f

'**naturally hard' steel** [*Its high strength is due, first, to a comparatively high carbon content, and second, to certain alloying elements*] · naturharter Stahl m

naturally lighted, daylighted · tagesbelichtet [*Fehlname: belichtet*]

~ ~ **from one side**, daylighted ~ ~ ~ · einseitig tagesbelichtet [*Fehlname: einseitig belichtet*]

(~ **occurring**) **siliceous volcanic rock**, volcanic glass(-like material), vulkanisches Glas n, Naturglas, glasartig erstarrtes vulkanisches Gestein n

nature · Zustand m, Beschaffenheit f

~ **reserve** · Natur(schutz)park m

naumachy · Naumachie f [*Mit Wasser gefüllte Kampfbahn der Römer, in der Bootskämpfe und Seeschlachten stattfanden*]

nave, church ~, middle vessel · Hauptschiff n, Mittelschiff, Lang(haus)schiff, Mittelhaus n [*Kirche*]

~ **aisle**, (side) ~, ele, eling [*A lateral division parallel with the nave in a basilica or church*] · (Seiten)Schiff n, Abseite f

~ ~ **bay**, (side) ~ ~ · (Seiten)Schiffjoch(feld) n, Abseitenjoch(feld), (Seiten)Schiffeld, Abseitenfeld

~ ~ **gallery**, (side) ~ ~ · Abseitenempore f, (Seiten)Schiffempore

~ **aisleless**, (side) ~ · abseitenlos, (seiten)schifflos

~ **aisle passage**, (side) ~ ~ · Abseitengang m, (Seiten)Schiffgang

~ ~ **pier**, (side) ~ ~ · (Seiten)Schiffpfeiler m, Abseitenpfeiler

~ ~ **roof**, (side) ~ ~ · Abseitendach n, (Seiten)Schiffdach

~ **aisle-vault**, (side) ~ · (Seiten)Schiffgewölbe n, Abseitengewölbe

~ **aisle wall**, (side) ~ ~ · Schiffwand f, Seiten~, Abseitenwand

~ ~ (~) **window** → (side) ~ (~) ~

~ **arcade**, church ~ ~, middle vessel ~ · Mittelschiffarkade f, Hauptschiffarkade, Lang(haus)schiffarkade, Mittelhausarkade

~ **bay** → (church) nave (vault) ~

~ **ceiling**, church ~ ~, middle vessel ~ · Mittelschiffdecke f, Hauptschiffdecke Lang(haus)schiffdecke, Mittelhausdecke

~ **pier**, church ~ ~, middle vessel ~ · Hauptschiffpfeiler m, Mittelschiffpfeiler, Lang(haus)schiffpfeiler, Mittelhauspfeiler

~ **range of columns** → church ~ ~ ~ ~

~ **row of columns** → (church) nave range ~ ~

~ **vault**, church ~ ~, middle vessel ~ · Hauptschiffgewölbe n, Mittelschiffgewölbe, Lang(haus)schiffgewölbe, Mittelhausgewölbe

~ (~) **bay** → church ~ (~) ~

~ **window**, church ~ ~, middle vessel ~ · Hauptschiffenster n, Mittelschiffenster, Lang(haus)schiffenster, Mittelhausfenster

Navier's hypothesis · Naviersche Theorie f

NDT, nondestructive testing · zerstörungsfreies Prüfen n

near-by material, local ~ · örtliches Material n

near vision · Nahsicht f

neat cement grout [*1. A fluid mix(ture) of hydraulic cement and water, with or without admix(ture); 2. The hardened equivalent of such mix(ture)*] · (reine) Zementschlämme f

nebulé moulding — neoprene paint

nebulé moulding (Brit.); ~ molding (US); curled clouds · Wolkenverzierung *f*, rundliches Zickzack *n*

necessary work auxiliary to the accomplishment of the contract · Nebenleistungen *fpl*

neck → necking

~ moulding (Brit.); ~ molding (US); neck(ing), necking band, col(l)ar(ino) [*The upper part of the shaft of a column, just below the capital, when differentiated from the rest by the omission of fluting or by the presence of grooves or of a convex mo(u)lding as a lower limit. Often adorned with carved ornament*] · (Säulen)Hals *m*

necking down, reduction in area, (con-)striction · Einschnürung *f*

necking-groove · (Säulen)Halsring *m*

necropolis · Totenstadt *f*, Nekropole *f*, Gräberstadt, Stadt der Toten [*Friedhof mit architektonisch gestalteten Gräbern oder mit Grabbauten, die oft noch gruppiert oder um größere Grabbauten regelmäßig angeordnet sind*]

needle scaffold [*A scaffold supported by cantilevers thrown out from the face of a building*] · Kraggerüst *n*, Kragrüstung *f*

negative area of influence · negative Einflußfläche *f*

~ bending · negative Biegung *f*, negatives Biegen *n*

~ ~ moment · negatives Biegemoment *n*

~ elongation, shortening · Verkürzung *f*, negative Dehnung

~ moment, hog(ging) ~, support ~ [*A bending moment which tends to cause hog such as occurs at the supports of a beam*] · Aufwölbungsmoment *n*, negatives Moment

~ reinforcement [*Reinforcement placed in concrete to resist negative bending moments*] · Armierung *f* gegen negative Biegemomente, Bewehrung ~ ~ ~, (Stahl)Einlagen *fpl* ~ ~ ~

~ rigidity, ~ stiffness · negative Steifigkeit *f*

~ stiffness, ~ rigidity · negative Steifigkeit *f*

~ transparency, transparent positive original · Mutterpause *f*

negligible · vernachlässigbar

negotiated contract · freihändige Vergabe *f*

neighboring blocks, ~ buildings (US); neighbouring ~ (Brit.); adjacent ~, adjoining ~ · Nachbarbebauung *f*

neighbourhood unit (Brit.); neighborhood ~ (US) · Nachbarschaft *f*, Wohneinheit *f* [*Ein Ortsteil, der alle für ein nachbarliches Zusammenleben seiner Bewohner nötigen Gemeinschafts- und Versorgungseinrichtungen enthält. Nach Le Corbusier*]

neighbouring opening, ~ span (Brit.); neighboring ~ (US); adjacent ~, adjoining ~ · Nachbarfeld *n*, Nachbaröffnung *f*

~ owner (Brit.); neighboring ~ (US); adjoining ~, adjacing ~ · Angrenzer *m*

~ premises (Brit.) → ~ property

~ property (Brit.); neighboring ~ (US); adjacent ~, adjoining ~, ~ premises · Nachbargrundstück *n*

~ room (Brit.); neighboring ~ (US); adjacent ~, adjoining ~ · Nachbarraum *m*

~ span, ~ opening (Brit.); neighboring ~ (US); adjacent ~, adjoining ~ · Nachbarfeld *n*, Nachbaröffnung *f*

~ wall (Brit.); neighboring ~ (US); adjacent ~, adjoining ~ · Nachbarwand *f*

neo-Academic formalism · neo-akademischer Formalismus *m*

neo-Baroque · Neobarock *m*, Neubarock

neoclassic architecture · neoklassizistische Architektur *f*, ~ Baukunst *f*

neo-classical · neoklassisch

neo-Gothic · neo-gotisch, neu-gotisch

Neo-Gothic, revived Gothic style, Gothic Revival · posthume Gotik *f*, Neugotik, Neogotik

neo-Liberty [*Reversion of postwar Italian architects to Art Neouveau forms*] · Neoliberty-Stil *m*

neo-medi(a)eval · neo-mittelalterlich, neo-ma.

neon argon luminous tube light · Neon-Argon-Leuchtröhre *f*

~ lamp · Neonlampe *f*

~ tube (light) · Neon(-Leucht)röhre *f*

neo-objectivity, new objectivity · Neue Sachlichkeit *f*

neoprene adhesive, ~ rubber ~, ~ (rubber) glue · Neoprenkleber *m*, Neoprenleim *m*

~ base · Neoprenbasis *f*, Neoprengrundlage *f*

~ bearing · Neoprenlager *n*

~ (~) pad · Neoprenlagerkissen *n*

~ channel · Neopren-U-Profil *n*

~ foam, expanded neoprene, foamed neoprene · Neoprenschaum(stoff) *m*

~ gasket → ~ preformed ~

~ glazing · Neoprenverglasung *f*, Neopreneinglasung

~ glue, ~ rubber ~, ~ (rubber) adhesive · Neoprenkleber *m*, Neoprenleim *m*

~ hanger · Neopren(ab)hänger *m*, Neoprenhängeglied *n* [*Drahtputzdecke*]

~ insert(ion) · Neopreneinlage *f*

~ pad, ~ bearing ~ · Neoprenlagerkissen *n*

~ paint · Neoprenfarbe *f*

neoprene pot bearing — newly-placed concrete

~ **pot bearing** · Neoprentopflager n

~ **(preformed) gasket,** ~ sealing ~, ~ structural ~, preformed neoprene ~ · Neopren(ab)dicht(ungs)profil n, Neoprenselbstdichtung f

~ **rubber,** ~ (synthetic rubber) · Neopren n

~ **(~) adhesive,** ~ (~) glue · Neoprenkleber m, Neoprenleim m

~ **(~) glue,** ~ (~) adhesive · Neoprenkleber m, Neoprenleim m

~ **sealing gasket** → ~ (preformed) ~

~ **seal(ing) ring** · Neopren(ab)dicht(ungs)ring m

~ **section expansion joint** · Neopren-Dehnprofil(-Übergangs)konstruktion f

~ **sheet expansion joint** · Neoprenplatten(-Übergangs)konstruktion f

~ **structural gasket** → ~ (preformed) ~

~ **(synthetic rubber),** ~ rubber · Neopren n

~ **washer** · Neopren(unterleg)scheibe f

~ **waterstop,** ~ waterbar · Neopren(fugen)band n

neo-Renaissance · Neurenaissance f

nepheline basalt · Nephelinbasalt m

Nereid Monument · Nereiden-Denkmal n [zu Xanthos]

nervure [The side rib of vaulted roofs, to distinguish from diagonal ribs] · Seitenrippe f

nest of smoke pipes, ~ ~ ~ tubes · Rauchrohrbündel n

nesting, cottage community (US); (housing) estate, housing colony · Wohnkolonie f, (Wohn)Sied(e)lung f

~ **unit,** cottage community ~ (US); (housing) estate ~, (housing) colony ~ · Sied(e)lungshaus n

net floor area · Nettogeschoßfläche f, Nettostockwerkfläche, Nettoetagenfläche

net vault · Netz(rippen)gewölbe n, Rautengewölbe

~ ~ **meshes** · Rippenwerk n [Netzgewölbe]

netting · Geflecht n

~ **lath(ing)** · Putz(träger)geflecht n

network · Netz(werk) n

~ **cupola,** ~ dome · Netzwerkkuppel f

~ **dome,** ~ cupola · Netzwerkkuppel f

~ **former** · Netzwerkbildner m [Glasherstellung]

~ **modifier** · Netzwerkwandler m [Glasherstellung]

~ **of piping,** pipe network · Rohr(leitungs)netz n

~ ~ **system lines** · Netzplan m der Systemlinien

~ ~, zero line, N.A. · neutrale Achse f, ~ Linie f, Nullachse, Nullinie

~ **conductor** · Nulleiter m

~ **fat** · Neutralfett n

~ **fibre** (Brit.); ~ fiber (US) · spannungslose Faser f, neutrale ~

~ **glass** [A glass of high chemical durability] · Neutralglas n

(~) middle plane · Mittelebene f [Platte]

~ **point** · Nullpunkt m

~ **refractory (product),** ~ ~ material · neutrales feuerfestes Erzeugnis n, ~ ff. ~, ~ Feuerfesterzeugnis

~ **solution** · neutrale Lösung f

~ **tinted glass,** ~ grey ~ · graues Glas n, Grauglas

Neuwied green · Neuwiedergrün n

new block, ~ building · Neubau m, neues Gebäude n

New Brutalism · Neuer Brutalismus m

new building, ~ block · Neubau m, neues Gebäude n

~ **construction** · Neubau m

New Empiricism [Scandinavian style of the 1940s] · Neuer Empirismus m

~ **Formalism** [Term used to describe the rediscovery of classical traditions in architecture] · Neuer Formalismus m

~ **Guard House at Berlin** · Neue Wache f in Berlin

new objectivity, neo-objectivity · Neue Sachlichkeit f

new town [Township designed to relieve pressure on major cities. In contrast to the satellite town, it is also intended to attract various types of industry away from the cities] · Neustadt f

new white (pigment) · Neuweiß(pigment) n

~ **yellow (pigment)** · Neugelb(pigment) n

newel → ~ post

~ **cap** · (Treppen)Spindelkappe f

~ **pipe,** ~ tube · Mittelrohr n, Spindelrohr [Wendeltreppe]

~ **(post)** [A solid central post in which the narrow ends of the steps of a circular stair(case) are supported] · (geschlossene) (Treppen)Spindel f, massive ~ [Wendeltreppe]

~ **tube,** ~ pipe · Mittelohr n, Spindelohr [Wendeltreppe]

newly-made panel, green ~, fresh(ly-made) ~ · Tafelformling m, Tafelgrünling, Tafelfrischling, frischgeformte Tafel f

~ **product** → green ~

~ **slab,** fresh(ly-made) ~, green ~ · frischgeformte Platte f, Plattenformling m, Plattengrünling, Plattenfrischling

newly-placed concrete · frisch eingebauter Beton m

news board — noble antique (style)

news board, mill ~, grey ~, gray ~ · Graupappe f
~ cinema · Aktualitätenkino n
~ kiosk, newspaper ~, ~ stand · Zeitungskiosk m, Zeitungsstand m
news(paper) kiosk, ~ stand · Zeitungskiosk m, Zeitungsstand m
~ office, press building · Zeitungsgebäude n
~ stand, ~ kiosk · Zeitungskiosk m, Zeitungsstand m
Newton's alloy · Newton-Metall n
nib, cog · (Aufhänge)Nase f [*Dachziegel*]
niche, blocked doorway [*A small recess in a wall, not extending to the floor*] · Nische f
~ baldaquin, ~ baldachin, ~ canopy · Nischenbaldachin m
~ canopy, ~ baldachin, ~ baldaquin · Nischenbaldachin m
~ containing the cult statue, blocked doorway ~ ~ ~ ~ · Kultnische f
~ pediment · Nischendreieckgiebel m, Dreiecknischengiebel
nickel · Nickel n
~ bronze, silver ~; nickel silver (US) [*Not to be confused with nickel silver = Neusilber*] · Nickelbronze f
~ leaded bronze · Nickel-Bleibronze f
~ plating · Vernickeln n
~ silver, German ~ [*Not to be confused with nickel silver (US) = Nickelbronze*] · Neusilber n
~ ~ (US); nickel bronze, silver bronze [*Not to be confused with nickel silver = Neusilber*] · Nickelbronze f
~ steel, structural ~ ~ · Nickel(bau)stahl m
~ titanate yellow (pigment) · Nickeltitangelb n
nigger head, cobble (stone) · Katzenkopf m, Kopfstein m [*Pflasterstein*]
night bolt, ~ latch · Nachtriegel m
~ charging, off peak ~ · Nachtaufheizzeit f
~ ~ with supplementary day heating, off peak ~ ~ ~ ~ ~ · Nachtaufheizzeit f mit Tagesnachheizzeit
~ illumination, ~ lighting · Nachtbeleuchtung f
~ latch, ~ bolt · Nachtriegel m
~ lighting, ~ illumination · Nachtbeleuchtung f
night-only tariff, off-peak ~ · Nachtstromtarif m
night safe · Nachttresor m
~ storage heater → (electric) (block) ~ ~
~ ~ (hot) water heater, ~ ~ (~) ~ heating appliance, off-peak (hot water heating appliance, off-peak (hot) water heater · Nachtstrom-Wassererhitzer m, Nachtstrom-Wasserheizer, Nachtstrom-Wasserheizgerät n, Nachtstrom-Wassererwärmer

Ni-Hard martensitic white cast iron · Sondergußeisen n, Ni-Hard mit martensitisch-weißem Gefüge
Nile mud brick · Nilschlammziegel m
90° (pipe) bend (one-)quarter (~) ~ · 90°-Rohr)Krümmer m
~ ~ junction (piece); flanged nozzle (US); flanged socket · Rohransatz m, (Rohr)Stutzen m
niobium stabilized · Nb-stabilisiert [*rostfreier Stahl*]
nipping · Vorknicken n [*Scharnierherstellung*]
nipple · Nippel m
niter, saltpeter, potassium nitrate · Kalisalpeter m, Kaliumnitrat n, KNO$_3$
nitrate of lime, lime nitrate · Kalksalpeter m, Kalziumnitrat n, salpetersaurer Kalk m, salpetersaures Kalzium n, Ca(NO$_3$)$_2$
nitration · Nitrierung f
nitric acid · Salpetersäure f, Stickstoffsäure, HNO$_3$
nitride · Nitrid n
~ bond containing silicon oxynitride · Siliziumoxynitridbindung f
~ refractory material, ~ ~ (product) Nitriterzeugnis n
~ ~ (product), ~ ~ material · Nitriterzeugnis n
nitrided · nitriert
~ surface · nitrierte Oberfläche f
nitriding (process) · Nitrieren n, Nitrierhärtung f, Stickstoffhärtung
~ steel, nitrided ~ · Nitrierstahl m
~ temperature · Nitriertemperatur f
nitrile rubber · Nitrilkautschuk m; Perbunan n [*Handelsbezeichnung der Farbenfabriken Bayer*]
~ (~) glue, ~ (~) adhesive, Buna N · Nitrilkleber m, Nitrilkleb(e)stoff m
nitrobenzene nitrobenzol(e) · Nitrobenzol n, Mirbanöl n, C$_6$H$_5$NO$_2$
nitrobenzol(e), nitrobenzene · Nitrobenzol n, Mirbanöl n, C$_6$N$_5$NO$_2$
nitrocellulose → cellulose nitrate
~ lacquer, cellulose (nitrate) ~, pyroxylin(e) ~, cellulose enamel · Celluloselack m, (Nitro)Zelluloselack, Nitro(cellulose)lack
~ paint, cellulose nitrate ~, pyroxylin ~ · Nitrofarbe f
~ stopper cellulose nitrate ~, pyroxylin ~ · Nitro(cellulose)spachtel(masse) m (f), Nitrozellulosespachtel(masse)
~ varnish · Nitrocellulose(klar)lack m, farbloser Nitrocelluloselack
nitro dyestuff · Nitrofarbstoff m
nitrogen content · Stickstoffgehalt m
nitrous acid · salpetrige Säure f
no air · Entgasungsmittel n [*Anstrichtechnik*]
noble antique (style), distinguished ~ (~) · repräsentative Antike f

no-bond (pre)stressing, ~ stretching, ~ tensioning · (Vor)Spannen *n* ohne Verbund

node → panel point

~ (point), joint · Knoten(punkt) *m*

~ (~) displacement, joint ~ · Knoten(punkt)verrückung *f*

~ (~) equilibrium, joint ~ · Knoten(punkt)gleichgewicht *n*

~ (~) holding moment, joint ~ ~ · Knoten(punkt)festhaltemoment *n*

~ (~) load, joint ~ · Knoten(punkt)last *f*

~ (~) loading, joint ~ · Knoten(punkt)belastung *f*

~ (~) mechanism, joint ~ · Knoten(punkt)mechanismus *m*

~ (~) mobility, joint ~ · Knoten(punkt)verschieblichkeit *f*

~ (~) moment, joint ~ · Knoten(punkt)moment *n*

~ (~) movement, joint ~ · Knoten(punkt)bewegung *f*

~ (~) plate → joint ~

~ (~) rotation, joint ~ · Knoten(punkt)drehung *f*

~ (~) ~ angle, joint ~ ~ · Knoten(punkt)drehwinkel *m*

~ (~) strength, joint ~ · Knoten(punkt)festigkeit *f*

~ (~) trajectory, joint ~ · Knoten(punkt)weg *m*

~ (~) translation, joint ~ · Knoten(punkt)verschiebung *f*

~ (~) velocity, joint ~ · Knoten(punkt)geschwindigkeit *f*

nodular band · knollenartiger Streifen *m*

~ graphite · Kugelgraphit *m*

~ (~) cast iron, spheroidal (~) ~ ~, ductile ~ ~ · Gußeisen *n* mit Kugelgraphit, Sphäroguß *m*, sphärolitisches Gußeisen [*Kurzbezeichnung GGG = gegossen – Gußeisen – globular. DIN 1963. Ein Eisen-Kohlenstoff-Gußwerkstoff, dessen als Graphit vorhandener Kohlenstoffanteil nahezu vollständig in weitgehend kugeliger Form vorliegt*]

nodule · Knollen *m*

no-fines concrete, even-grained ~, single-sized ~, like-grained ~, uniform ~, equigranular ~, short range aggregate ~ · gleichkörniger Beton *m*, einkörniger ~, Einkornbeton [*DIN 4163*]

~ (light(-weight)) concrete wall · geschüttete (Leicht)(Beton)Wand *f*, (Leicht)Schüttbetonwand [*DIN 4232*]

nogging (piece), nog [*A horizontal short timber which stiffens a stud of a stud partition (wall)*] · (Holz)Riegel *m*

no-heat adhesive → cold bonding agent

no-hinged, hingeless, fixed, encastré, with fixed ends, without articulations, rigid, encastered, built-in · eingespannt, gelenklos [*Bogen; Träger; Stütze; Balken(träger); Rahmen(tragwerk)*]

~ arch → fixed ~

~ beam → fixed ~

~ column → fixed support

~ girder → built-in ~

~ support → fixed ~

noise · Lärm *m*

~ abatement, ~ reduction · Lärmdämpfung *f*, Lärmminderung

~ ~ device · Lärmdämpfer *m*

~ absorption · Lärmschluckung *f*

~ barrier · Lärmschranke *f*, Lärmsperre *f*

~ control, ~ suppression · Lärmabwehr *f*, Lärmbekämpfung *f*

~ development · Lärmentwick(e)lung *f*

~ insulation · Lärmschutz *m*

~ level · Lärmpegel *m*

~ measurement · Lärmmessung *f*

~ nuisance · Lärmbelästigung *f*, Lärmstörung

~ physics · Lärmphysik *f*

~ range, range of noises · Lärmbereich *m, n*

noise-reduced · lärmarm

noise reduction, ~ abatement · Lärmdämpfung *f*, Lärmminderung

~ research · Lärmforschung *f*

~ source · Lärmquelle *f*

~ ~ · Geräuschquelle *f*

~ suppression, ~ control · Lärmbekämpfung *f*, Lärmabwehr *f*

~ transmission · Lärmübertragung *f*

noisy · lärmreich

nominal cross section · Nennquerschnitt *m*

~ curve, ~ line · Sollkurve *f*

~ depth · Solltiefe *f*

~ dimension, theoretical ~ · Sollabmessung *f*, Sollmaß *n*, Nennabmessung, Nennmaß [*DIN 18201*]

~ ~ range · Nennabmessungsbereich *m, n*, Nennmaßbereich, Sollabmessungsbereich, Sollmaßbereich

~ grading curve, ideal ~ ~ · Idealkurve *f*, Idealsieblinie *f*, Sollkurve, Sollsieblinie [*Sieblinie des gewünschten Endproduktes*]

~ grain size, ~ particle ~, ideal ~ ~ · Sollkorngröße *f*, Idealkorngröße, nominelle Korngröße [*Korngröße des gewünschten Endproduktes*]

~ heating output · Nennheizleistung *f*

~ height, theoretical ~ · Nennhöhe *f*, Sollhöhe

~ line, ~ curve · Sollkurve *f*

~ particle size, ~ grain ~, ideal ~ ~ · Sollkorngröße *f*, Idealkorngröße, nominelle Korngröße [*Korngröße des gewünschten Endproduktes*]

~ rigidity, ~ stiffnes · Nennsteifigkeit *f*

~ stiffness, ~ rigidity · Nennsteifigkeit *f*

~ strength · Nennfestigkeit *f*

nominal thickness — non-deductible opening

~ thickness · Nenndicke *f*
~ value · Sollwert *m*, Nennwert
nomogram → nomograph
nomograph, nomogram; alignment chart (Brit.); alinement chart (US) · Nomogramm *n*, Rechentafel *f*
nomography · geometrische Darstellung *f*, Nomographie *f*
nonabsorbent surface, nonabsorbing ~ · nichtsaugende Fläche *f*
nonabsorbing surface, nonabsorbent ~ · nichtsaugende Fläche *f*
nonacceptance, rejection · Nichtabnahme *f*, Abnahmeverweigerung *f*
nonadhesive · nichtklebend
non-air-entrained concrete · Nicht-Luftporenbeton *m*
non-air entraining · nichtlufteinführend, nichtluftporenbildend
non-attendant service · Selbstfahrbetrieb *m* [*Aufzug*]
nonbearing, nonloadbearing, nonsupporting, non-weight-carrying · nicht-(last)tragend, statisch nicht mitwirkend
~ brick → non(load)bearing ~
~ facade → non(load)bearing ~
~ floor block → non(load)bearing floor (clay) brick
~ ~ brick → non(load)bearing floor (clay) ~
~ ~ (clay) block → non(load)bearing floor (clay) brick
~ ~ (~) brick → non(load)bearing ~ (~) ~
~ partition wall → non(load)bearing ~ ~
non-bent-up reinforcing bar, ~ ~ rod, ~ reinforcement ~ · Tragstab *m* [*Tragstäbe liegen in der Zugzone. Sie haben Endhaken und werden als „gerade" Einlagen angeordnet, wenn die Zugkräfte nur unten (vollständig frei aufliegend) oder nur oben (auskragend) auftreten*]
non-bonded joint, dry ~ · Knirschfuge *f*, Trockenfuge
nonbreakable bond, unbreakable ~ · unzerstörbare Haftung *f*
~ glass, unbreakable ~ · unzerbrechliches Glas *n*
nonbreathing · nichtatmend
non-bronze blue (pigment) · nichtbronzierendes Blau(pigment) *n*
non-built up area · nichtbebautes Gebiet *n*
non-carbonate hardness, permanent ~ · Mineralsäurehärte *f*, Nichtkarbonathärte [*Der Unterschied zwischen Gesamthärte und Karbonathärte*]
non-carved waterspout · Abtraufe *f*, Ansetztraufe [*Schmuckloser Wasserspeier in Form einer Röhre oder Ablaufrinne*]
non-ceramic tile · nichtkeramische (Belag)Platte *f*, ~ Fliese *f*

non-chalking · nicht(ab)kreidend, nichtauskreidend [*Farbanstrich*]
nonchromatic, plain [*As opposed to 'colo(u)red'*] · unbunt, ungefärbt
nonclassical shell problem · Schalenproblem *n* über die klassische Theorie hinaus, Schalenaufgabe *f* ~ ~ ~ ~ ~, nichtklassische Schalenaufgabe, nichtklassisches Schalenproblem
non-clay block · ungebrannter Baustein *m*
noncombustibility, incombustibility · Nichtbrennbarkeit *f*, Unbrennbarkeit [*DIN 4102*]
noncombustible, incombustible · nichtbrennbar, unbrennbar [*DIN 4102*]
~ construction, (nonmetallic) fireproof ~ · Massivbau *m*
~ construction(al) material → (nonmetallic) fireproof ~ ~
~ floor, (nonmetallic) fireproof ~ · Massivdecke *f*
~ ~ with suspenced ceiling → (nonmetallic) fireproof ~ ~ ~ ~
~ (intermediate) floor → (nonmetallic) fireproof (~) ~
~ material · unbrennbarer Stoff *m*
~ prefab(ricated) (building) element → (nonmetallic) fireproof ~ (~) ~
~ roof floor, (nonmetallic) fireproof ~ ~ · Massiv-Dachdecke *f*
~ slab floor, (nonmetallic) fireproof ~ ~ · Massivplattendecke *f*
~ stair(case), (nonmetallic) fireproof ~ · Massivtreppe *f*
~ uncovered floor, (nonmetallic) fireproof ~ ~ · massive Rohdecke *f*, Massivrohdecke [*DIN 4237. Achs(en)maße*]
non-compliance · Nichteinhaltung *f* [*Norm; Bestimmung; Vorschrift usw.*]
noncompressed asbestos-cement panel; ~ cement-asbestos ~ (US) · ungepreßte Asbestzementtafel *f* [*DIN 274*]
~ cement-asbestos panel (US); ~ asbestos-cement ~ · ungepreßte Asbestzementtafel *f* [*DIN 274*]
nonconcordant tendon · nichtzwängungsfreies Spannglied *n*
non-conductor · Nichtleiter *m*
nonconservative problem, inelastic ~ · nichtkonservative Aufgabe *f*, nichtkonservatives Problem *n*
~ system, inelastic ~ · nichtkonservatives System *n*
noncontinuous sense of direction of forces in a stress diagram · unstetiger Umfahrungssinn *m* eines Kraftecks
noncritical wind velocity · nichtkritische Windgeschwindigkeit *f*
non-deducted opening · übermessene Öffnung *f*
non-deductible opening · übermeßbare Öffnung *f*

non-deformable → undeformable

nondestructive · zerstörungsfrei [*Werkstoffprüfung*]

~ testing, NDT · zerstörungsfreies Prüfen *n*

nondevelopable · nichtabwickelbar

nondirectional, devoid of directionality · richtungslos

nondomestic block, ~ building, nonresidential ~, nonhousing ~ · Nichtwohngebäude *n*

~ building, ~ block, nonresidential ~, nonhousing ~ · Nichtwohngebäude *n*

~ construction, nonresidential ~, nonhousing ~ · Nichtwohn(ungs)bau *m*

~ development, nonhousing ~, nonresidential ~ · industrielle Bebauung *f*

~ sector, nonhousing ~, nonresidential ~ · Nichtwohn(ungs)bausektor *m*

non-draining compound · Haftmasse *f* [*Zur Imprägnierung der Papierisolation von Hochspannungskabeln*]

non-drip paint · tropffreie (Anstrich-) Farbe *f*

nondrying · nichttrocknend

~ oil · nichttrocknendes Öl *n*

non-dusting · nicht(ab)staubend

non-ecclesiastical architecture, secular ~, civic ~, profane ~ · weltliche Architektur *f*, ~ Baukunst *f*, Profanarchitektur, Profanbaukunst

~ building, ~ structure, secular ~, profane ~, civic ~ · Profanbau(werk) *m*, (*n*), Profangebäude *n*

~ Gothic (style), civic ~ (~), profane ~ (~), secular ~ (~) · Profangotik *f*, weltliche Gotik

~ monument, profane ~, secular ~, civic ~ · Profanmonument *n*

~ structure, ~ building, civic structure, secular ~, profane ~ · Profanbau(werk) *m*, (*n*), Profangebäude *n*

~ structures, secular ~, profane ~, civic ~ · Profanbauten *f*, Profangebäude *npl*

nonefflorescence · Nicht-Ausblühen *n*

nonelastic, inelastic, plastic · nichtelastisch, unelastisch, plastisch

~ behaviour (Brit.) → inelastic ~

~ deflection → inelastic deflexion

~ deflexion → inelastic ~

~ deformation, creep ~, inelastic ~, plastic ~ · plastische Verformung *f*, ~ Formänderung, Kriechverformung, Kriechformänderung

~ range, inelastic ~, plastic ~ · unelastischer Bereich *m*, nichtelastischer ~, unelastisches ~ *n*, nichtelastisches ~, plastischer ~, plastisches ~

~ strain, creep ~, inelastic ~, plastic ~ · (positive) Kriechdehnung *f*, plastische Dehnung

nonfading · nichtverblassend

nonferrous metal · NE-Metall *n*, Nichteisenmetall

nonfibered (US) → nonfibrated

nonfibrated, unfibrated; nonfibre, unfibred (Brit.); nonfibered, unfibered (US) · ohne Faserzusatz, ~ Fasern, ungefasert, faserfrei, faserlos, nichtgefasert, nichtfaserarmiert, nichtfaserverstärkt

nonfibred (Brit.) → nonfibrated

non-frost-active, frost(-)resistant, frost(-)resisting, frostproof · frostbeständig, frostsicher, frostunempfindlich

~ (clay) brick → frost(-)resistant (~) ~

non-frost proof · nichtfrostbeständig

nonfunctional, abstract · zweckfrei

non-glare (US); anti-dazzle, dazzle-free, glare-free, glare-reducing · abblendend, blend(ungs)frei

~ glass (US); anti-dazzle ~, dazzle-free ~, glare-free ~, glare-reducing ~ · abblendendes Glas *n*, Blendschutzglas

nonhardened, unhardened · nichtgehärtet, ungehärtet

nonhardening, permanently ~, permanently plastic · nichthärtend, dauerplastisch

non-heat-treatable · nicht warm aushärtbar [*Alu(minium)legierung*]

non-heat-treated · nicht warm ausgehärtet [*Alu(minium)legierung*]

nonhomogeneous plastic body · inhomogener plastischer Körper *m*

~ state of stress, ~ stress state · nichthomogener Spannungszustand *m*

~ stress state, ~ state of stress · nichthomogener Spannungszustand *m*

nonhousing block, ~ building, nondomestic ~, nonresidential ~ · Nichtwohngebäude *n*

~ building, ~ block, nondomestic ~, nonresidential ~ · Nichtwohngebäude *n*

~ construction, nondomestic ~, nonresidential ~ · Nichtwohn(ungs)bau *m*

~ development, nondomestic ~, nonresidential ~ · industrielle Bebauung *f*

~ sector, nondomestic ~, nonresidential ~ · Nichtwohn(ungs)bausektor *m*

non-hydraulic · unhydraulisch, nichthydraulisch [*z.B. Luftkalk*]

~ lime, air-slaked ~ · Luftkalk *m*

~ mortar, air-setting ~ · Luftmörtel *m*

~ ~ cementing agent, air-setting ~ ~ ~ · mechanischer Mörtelstoff *m*

non-hygroscopic · nichthygroskopisch

non-ionic · nichtionogen [*Netzmittel*]

non-lagged electric (thermal) storage (water) heater, ~ ~ (~) ~ (~) heating appliance · Boiler *m*

non-limefast mix(ture) of coal tar dyes with mineral powder · Kalkfarbe *f* [*Nicht kalkechtes Gemisch von Teerfarbstoff mit Mineralmehl*]

nonlinear distribution · nichtlineare Verteilung *f*

nonlinear elasticity — nonreverberant room

~ **elasticity** · nichtlineare Elastizität *f*

~ **equation** · nichtlineare Gleichung

~ **plastic theory,** exact ~ ~ · genaue plastische Theorie *f*, nichtlineare ~ ~ [*Bestimmen der Grenzlast eines Tragwerkes nach der Theorie 2. Ordnung bzw. Verhalten im überkritischen Bereich, d.h. unter Berücksichtigung des Einflusses endlicher Verformungen*]

~ **problem** · nichtlineare Aufgabe *f*

~ **structure** · nichtlineares Bauwerk *n*

~ **theory** · nichtlineare Theorie *f*

~ ~ **of elasticity** · nichtlineare Elastizitätstheorie *f*

non-linearity · Nichtlinearität *f*

nonlinearly elastic · nichtlinear elastisch

~ ~ **structure** · nichtlineares elastisches Bauwerk *n*

non(load)bearing, nonsupporting, non-weight-carrying · nicht(last)tragend, statisch nicht mitwirkend

~ **brick** · nicht(last)tragender Ziegel *m*

~ **facade** · nicht(last)tragende Fassade *f*

~ **floor block** → ~ ~ (clay) brick

~ ~ **brick** → ~ ~ clay ~

~ ~ **(clay) block** → ~ ~ ~ (~) brick

~ ~ **(~) brick,** ~ ~ (~) block, non-weight-carrying ~ (~) ~, nonsupporting ~ (~) ~ · nicht(last)tragender Deckenstein *m*, ~ Deckenziegel *m*, statisch nicht mitwirkender ~ [*DIN 4160*]

~ **panel,** non-weight-carrying ~ · nicht(last)tragende Tafel *f*

~ **partition (wall),** light(weight) ~ (~), non-weight-carrying ~ (~) · leichte Trennwand *f*, nicht(last)tragende ~ [*DIN 4103*]

non-matting · nichtmattierend

nonmetal · Nichtmetall *n*

nonmetallic element · nichtmetallisches Element *n*

(~) **fireproof building material** → (~) ~ **construction(al)** ~

(~) ~ **construction,** noncombustible ~ · Massivbau *m*

(~) ~ **construction(al) material,** (~) ~ building ~, (~) ~ structural ~, noncombustible ~ ~ · Massivbaustoff *m*; Massivbaumaterial *n* [*Schweiz*] [*Massivbaustoffe sind die Baustoffe auf der Grundlage der Steine und Erden*]

(~) ~ **floor,** noncombustible ~ · Massivdecke *f*

(~) ~ ~ **with suspended ceiling,** (~) ~ ~ ~ hung ~, noncombustible ~ ~ ~ ~ · Massivdecke *f* mit untergehängter Decke, zweischalige Massivdecke

(~) ~ **(intermediate) floor,** noncombustible (~) ~ · Massivtrenndecke *f*, Massiv-Etagendecke, Massiv-Stockwerkdecke, Massiv-Geschoßdecke

(~) ~ **prefab(ricated) (building) element,** (~) ~ ~ (~) member, ~ ~ (~) unit, noncombustible ~ (~) ~ · Massiv-Fertig(bau)teil *m, n*

(~) ~ **roof floor,** noncombustible ~ ~ · Massiv-Dachdecke *f*

(~) ~ **slab floor,** noncombustible ~ ~ · Massivplattendecke *f*

(~) ~ **stair(case),** noncombustible ~ · Massivtreppe *f*

(~) ~ **uncovered floor,** noncombustible ~ ~ · massive Rohdecke *f*, Massivrohdecke [*DIN 4237. Achs(en)maße*]

~ **mineral** · nichtmetallisches Mineral *n*

(~) **minerals industry,** pit and quarry ~ · Steine- und Erdenindustrie *f*

~ **pipe** · Nichtmetallrohr *n*

nonmilitary architecture · Zivilarchitektur *f*, Zivilbaukunst *f*

non-moving stair(case) · stationäre Treppe *f*, ortsfeste ~ [*Im Gegensatz zur Rolltreppe*]

non-nailable · nichtnagelbar, unnagelbar

non-oily · nichtölig

nonperforated, unperforated · ungelocht, glatt

non-pigmented, unpigmented · nichtpigmentiert, unpigmentiert

nonplastic material · Mager(ungs)mittel *n* [*Die gekörnten, nicht plastischen Bestandteile einer ff. Mischung*]

nonporous · porenfrei, porenlos, nichtporös, unporig

non(pre)stressed, untensioned · schlaff (bewehrt), ~ armiert, mit schlaffen (Stahl)Einlagen

non-prismatic member · nichtprismatischer Stab *m*

nonreactive, unreactive · reaktionsfrei, reaktionslos

non-reflecting glass, non-reflective ~ · reflexfreies Glas *n*

nonrental area, nonrentable ~, ~ space · Nichtmietfläche *f*

nonresidential block, ~ building, non-domestic ~, nonhousing ~ · Nichtwohngebäude *n*

~ **building,** ~ block, nondomestic ~, nonhousing ~ · Nichtwohngebäude *n*

~ **construction,** nonhousing ~, non-domestic ~ · Nichtwohn(ungs)bau *m*

~ **development,** nonhousing ~, non-domestic ~ · industrielle Bebauung *f*

~ **sector,** nondomestic ~, nonhousing ~ · Nichtwohn(ungs)bausektor *m*

nonreverberant, anechoic · nachhallfrei, echowidrig

~ **chamber** → anechoic room

~ **room** → anechoic ~

non-revivalist, historicising · historisierend

nonrevolving · nichtdrehend

nonrigid, flexible · biegeweich, nichtstarr, schmiegsam, unsteif

~ **floor**, flexible ~ [*A timber floor may be regarded as a flexible floor in comparison with a reinforced concrete floor which is stiffer*] · biegeweiche Decke *f*

~ **steel arch**, flexible ~ ~ · biegeweicher Stahlbogen *m*

non-rising · nichtsteigend

non-safety lock · gewöhnliches Schloß *n*

non-saponifiable · nichtverseifbar

non-scrubbable, non-washable · nichtwaschfest; nichtabwaschbar [*Fehlbezeichnung*]

non-setting minium, ~ red lead · nichtabsetzende (Blei)Mennige *f*, disperse ~; nichtabsetzendes Minium *n*, disperses Minium [*Österreich*]

~ **red lead**, ~ minium · nichtabsetzende (Blei)Mennige *f*, disperse ~; nichtabsetzendes Minium *n*, disperses Minium [*Österreich*]

nonshrink · schwindfrei

~ **grout(ing compound)** · (Ab)Dicht(ungs)schlämme *f*

nonshrinkage · Schwindfreiheit *f*

nonsilvered · unbelegt, unversilbert, unverspiegelt [*Glas*]

nonskid → anti-skid

~ **paint**, skid-proof ~, anti-skid ~, anti-slip ~, non-slippery ~, non-slip(ping) ~ · rutschfeste (Anstrich)Farbe *f*, trittsichere ~, gleitsichere ~, Gleitschutz-(anstrich)farbe

~ **rib(bed) tile** → (anti-slip) ~ ~

non-slip, anti-slip, slip-resistant · gehsicher

~ **aggregate**, anti-slip ~, slip-resistant ~ · gehsicherer Zuschlag(stoff) *m*

non-slippery → anti-skid

~ **paint**, non-slip(ping) ~, nonskid ~, skidproof ~, anti-skid ~, anti-slip ~ · rutschfeste (Anstrich)Farbe *f*, trittsichere ~, gleitsichere ~ · Gleitschutz(anstrich)-farbe

~ **rib(bed) tile** → (anti-slip) ~ ~

non-slip(ping) → anti-skid

~ **paint**, non-slippery ~, nonskid ~, skidproof ~, anti-skid ~, anti-slip ~ · rutschfeste (Anstrich)Farbe *f*, trittsichere ~, gleitsichere~, Gleitschutz(anstrich)-farbe

~ **rib(bed) tile** → (anti-slip) ~ ~

non-sloping, level, flat, planar, plane · gefällelos, eben

non-sparking, sparkproof, spark resistant [*e.g. a hardened concrete floor*] · funkenfrei, funkensicher

non-spring loaded · nichtfederbelastet

non-standard clay roof(ing) tile, ~ roof(ing) clay ~ · Zubehör(dach)ziegel *m*, Zubehör-Tondachstein *m* [*Ein besonders ausgebildeter Dachziegel, z.B. Firstanschlußziegel usw. Dieser Dachziegel ist nicht genormt. Seine Ausbildung bleibt dem Hersteller überlassen. Dieser Dachziegel muß allerdings so sein, daß er zusammen mit den genormten Dachziegeln (DIN 456) einwandfrei gedeckt werden kann*]

~ **profile**, ~ shape, ~ section, ~ unit, ~ trim · nichtgenormtes Profil *n*

~ **roof(ing) clay tile**, ~ clay roof(ing) ~ · Zubehör(dach)ziegel *m*, Zubehör-Tondachstein *m* [*Ein besonders ausgebildeter Dachziegel, z.B. Firstanschlußziegel usw. Dieser Dachziegel ist nicht genormt. Seine Ausbildung bleibt dem Hersteller überlassen. Dieser Dachziegel muß allerdings so sein, daß er zusammen mit den genormten Dachziegeln (DIN 456) einwandfrei gedeckt werden kann*]

~ **section** → rolled ~ ~

~ **unit** → (rolled) non-standard section

non-stickiness, non-tackiness · Kleb(e)-freiheit *f*

non-storage calorifier, flow-type ~ · Durchflußerhitzer *m*, Durchlauferhitzer

~ **gas water heater**, flow-type ~ ~ ~, instantaneous ~ ~ ~, ~ ~ ~ heating appliance · (Durchlauf-)Gaswasserheizer *m*, Geyser [*DIN 3368, 3369*]

~ **water heater** → instantaneous ~ ~

nonstressed → untensioned

nonstretched → untensioned

non-stripping agent → activator

nonstructural (bonding) adhesive, ~ ~ medium, ~ ~ agent, ~ cement(ing agent) · Nicht-Konstruktionskleber *m*, Nicht-Konstruktionskleb(e)mittel *n*, Nicht-Konstruktionskleb(e)stoff *m*

~ **connection by tack welding** · Schweißheftung *f*

~ **top screed** · Überbeton *m* [*Nicht am Tragvermögen einer Decke beteiligt*]

nonsupporting, non(load)bearing, non-weight-carrying · statisch nicht mitwirkend, nicht(last)tragend

nonsymmetrical loading · unsymmetrische Belastung *f*

non-tackiness, non-stickiness · Kleb(e)-freiheit *f*

nontensioned → untensioned

non-thermostatic blending mixer → manual (water) mixing valve

~ **mixer (valve)** → manual (water) mixing ~

~ **mixing valve** → manual (water) ~ ~

~ **showermixer** → manual (water) mixing valve

~ **(water) blending mixer** → manual (water) mixing valve

~ **(~) mixer (valve)** → manual (water) mixing ~

non-thermostatic (water) mixing valve — normal concrete 662

~ (~) mixing valve → manual (~) ~ ~

~ (~) showermixer → manual (water) mixing valve

nontoxic · ungiftig, giftfrei

non-trussed purlin(e) roof · strebenloses Pfettendach n

non-twisted · unverwunden

non-uniform bearing structure, ~ load~ ~, ~ (weight-carrying) ~, ~ supporting ~ · Tragwerk n mit veränderlichen Trägheitsmomenten

~ load, non-uniformly distributed ~ · ungleichmäßig verteilte Last f, ungleichmäßige ~

~ (load)bearing structure, ~ (weight-carrying) ~, ~ supporting ~ · Tragwerk n mit veränderlichen Trägheitsmomenten

~ sand · ungleichförmiger Sand m

~ structure, ~ weight-carrying ~, ~ (load)(bearing ~, ~ supporting ~ · Tragwerk n mit veränderlichen Trägheitsmomenten

~ supporting structure, ~ (load)bearing ~, ~ (weight-carrying) ~ · Tragwerk n mit veränderlichen Trägheitsmomenten

~ (weight-carrying) structure, ~ (load)bearing ~, ~ supporting ~ · Tragwerk n mit veränderlichen Trägheitsmomenten

non-uniformity · Ungleichmäßigkeit f

non-uniform(ly distributed) load · ungleichmäßig verteilte Last f, ungleichmäßige ~

non-ventilated flat roof · einschaliges Flachdach n, Warmdach, nichtdurchlüftetes Flachdach [Bei diesem Dach bildet die Dachdecke die oberste Geschoßdecke. Sie hat auf der Oberseite einen trittfesten Wärmedämmbelag von ausreichendem Wärmedurchlaßwiderstand]

nonvolatile component · nichtflüchtiger Bestandteil m [Anstrichstoff]

~ portion, ~ content · nichtflüchtiger Anteil m, ~ Gehalt

non-walking-way (rainwater) gutter, ~ roof ~, ~ R.W. ~ · nichtbegehbare (Dach)Rinne f, ~ Regenrinne

non-washable, non-scrubbable · nichtwaschfest; nichtabwaschbar [Fehlbezeichnung]

non-weight-carrying, nonsupporting, non(load)bearing · nicht(last)tragend, statisch nicht mitwirkend

~ floor block → non(load)bearing floor (clay) brick

~ ~ brick → non(load)bearing floor (clay) ~

~ ~ (clay) block → non(load)bearing floor (clay) brick

~ ~ (~) brick → non(load)bearing ~ (~) ~

~ panel, nonloadbearing ~ · nicht(last)tragende Tafel f

~ partition (wall), non(load)bearing ~ (~), light(weight) ~ (~) · leichte Trennwand f, nicht(last)tragende ~ [DIN 4103]

non-wet room · Normalraum m [im Gegensatz zum Naßraum]

non-woven fabric · Textilverbundstoff m

non-yellowing · (ver)gilbungsfrei, nicht-(ver)gilbend

noodle style [French term for Art Nouveau] · Nudelstil m

nook [A small recess or secluded spot, as, for instance, a bed nook] · Nische f

noraghe, nurag(h)e [One of a class of prehistoric stone structures numerous in Sardinia] · Nurag(h)e f, (mediterranes rundes) Steinhaus n

Norfolk latch → thumb ~

normal · Mittelwert m

~ aggregate → normal(-weight) (concrete) ~

~ atmosphere · normale Atmosphäre f

~ bend test, face ~ ~ · Faltversuch m, Biegeprobe f, Normalversuch mit der Raupe im Zug [Die Raupe liegt im Zug. „R.i.Z."]

~ block, ~ tile [See remark under 'Block'] · Normalblock(stein) m, Normalstein

~ bond → ~ masonry ~

~-breaking → normal-setting

normal cast → normal(-weight) concrete (pre)cast component

~ ~ block → normal(-weight) (pre)cast (concrete) ~

~ ~ concrete → normal(-weight) (pre-)cast (concrete) product

~ ~ tile → normal(-weight) (pre)cast (concrete) ~

~ ~ (concrete) block → normal (-weight) (pre)cast (~) ~

~ ~ (~) tile → normal(-weight) (pre-)cast (~) ~

~ ~ (~) ware → normal(-weight) (pre)cast (~) ~

~ cast-iron drain(age) pipe, ~ ~ draining ~, ~ ~ discharge ~, ~ ~ waste (~), ~ C.I. ~ ~, ~ C.I. waste · NA-Rohr n, Normal-Abflußrohr [DIN 364]

~ cast product → normal(-weight) (pre)cast (concrete) ~

~ cement, ordinary ~ · Normalzement m [Zement von der Güteklasse Z 225. Gegensatz: Hoch- und höherwertiger Zement]

~ C.I. waste (pipe) → ~ cast-iron drain(age) ~

~ climate · Normalklima n

~ component · Normalkomponente f

~ compressive stress, direct ~ ~ · Normaldruckspannung f

~ concrete → ~-weight ~

~ (~) aggregate → normal(-weight) (~) ~

~ ~ building element → normal(-weight) concrete building (construction) ~

~ ~ cast component → normal(-weight) concrete (pre)cast ~

~ ~ ~ member → normal(-weight) concrete (pre)cast ~

~ (~) cast(ing) → normal-(weight) concrete (pre)cast component

~ ~ construction engineering element → ~-weight ~ ~ ~ ~

~ ~ floor → ~-weight ~ ~

~ (~) hollow block → normal(-weight) (precast) (concrete) ~ ~

~ (~) ~ tile → normal(-weight) (precast) (concrete) ~ ~

~ ~ lintel → normal(-weight) ~ ~

~ ~ pile → ~-weight ~ ~

~ ~ pipe → ~-weight ~ ~

~ ~ (pre)cast component → normal (-weight) ~ ~ ~

~ ~ product → normal(-weight) ~ ~

~ ~ slab → ~-weight ~ ~

~ ~ wall → ~-weight ~ ~

~ cube → ~ test ~

~ dimension · Normalabmessung *f*, Normalmaß *n*

~ factory production · Serienbau *m*, Serienfertigung *f*, Serienherstellung

~ force · Normalkraft *f*

~ format · NF *n*, Normalformat *n*

normal-hardening cement · Normalerhärter(zement) *m*

normal hollow block → normal(-weight) (precast) (concrete) ~ ~

~ ~ concrete tile → normal(-weight) (precast) (concrete) hollow block

~ ~ tile → normal(-weight) (precast) (concrete) ~ ~

~ humidity, ~ moisture · Normalfeuchtigkeit *f*, Normalfeuchte *f*

~ load · Normallast *f*

~ (masonry) bond, typical (~) ~ · Regelverband *m*

~ mode [*A characteristic distribution of the amplitudes of free vibration of a common frequency in a mechanical system or sound field subject to elastic restoring forces. In a mechanical system, there exist as many independent uncoupled characteristic distributions, and hence normal modes, as there are degrees of freedom; in a continuum, infinite sets of such distributions are determined by the boundary conditions. Any vibration in a conservative system may be considered as a linear combination of normal modes taking place simultaneously with independent values of amplitude and relative phase*] · Eigenfunktion *f*

~ moisture, ~ humidity · Normalfeuchtigkeit *f*, Normalfeuchte *f*

~ mortar · Normalmörtel *m*

~ portland cement, ordinary ~ ~, Portland cement for general use, OPC; Portland cement type I (US) · normaler Portlandzement *m*, gewöhnlicher ~ [*in Deutschland Z 225*]

~ (pre)cast concrete → normal(-weight) (pre)cast (concrete) product

~ ~ (~) block → normal(-weight) (~) ~

~ (~) (~) hollow block → normal(-weight) (~) (~) ~ ~

~ (~) (~) ~ tile → normal(-weight) (~) (~) ~ ~

~ ~ (~) product → normal(-weight) ~ (~) ~

~ ~ (~) tile → normal(-weight) ~ (~) ~

~ ~ (~) ware → normal(-weight) ~ (~) ~

~ (~) hollow block → normal(-weight) (precast) (concrete) ~ ~

~ (~) ~ (concrete) tile → normal(-weight) (precast) (concrete) hollow block

~ ~ ware → normal(-weight) (pre-)cast (concrete) ~

~ R.C. → ~-weight ~ ~

~ reinforced concrete → ~(-weight) reinforced ~

~ sand · Normalsand *m*

~ section · Normalprofil *n* [*Formstahl; Walzträger*]

normal-setting, medium-setting, semi-stable, medium-breaking, normal-breaking · halbstabil, mittelschnellbrechend [*Bitumenemulsion*[

~ · normal(ab)bindend [*hydraulisches Bindemittel*]

~ cement · Normalbinder(zement) *m*

normal stress, direct ~ [*A stress which is entirely tensile or entirely compressive, without any bending or shear*] · Normalspannung *f*

~ tensile stress, direct ~ ~ · Normalzugspannung *f*

~ (test) cube, typical (~) ~ · Regelwürfel *m*, Normalwürfel *m*

~ tile → ~ block

normal(-weight) aggregate, ~ concrete ~ · Normalbetonzuschlag(stoff) *m*, Schwerbetonzuschlag(stoff)

~ cast block → ~ (pre)cast (concrete) ~

~ ~ building construction component → ~ (pre)cast (concrete) building construction unit

~ ~ ~ member → ~ (pre)cast (concrete) building construction unit

~ ~ ~ ~ unit → ~ (pre)cast (concrete) ~ ~ ~

~ ~ compound unit → ~ (pre)cast (concrete) ~ ~

~ ~ concrete → ~ (pre)cast (concrete) product

normal(-weight) cast... — normal(-weight) (pre)cast...

~ ~ (~) block → ~ (pre)cast (~) ~

~ ~ (~) building construction component → ~ (pre)cast (concrete) building construction unit

~ ~ (~) ~ ~ member → ~ (pre)cast (concrete) building construction unit

~ ~ (~) ~ ~ unit → ~ pre~ (~) ~ ~ ~

~ ~ (~) compound unit → ~ (pre-)cast (~) ~ ~

~ ~ (~) member → ~ concrete (pre-)cast ~

~ ~ (~) tile → ~ (pre)cast (~) ~

~ ~ (~) ware → ~ pre~ (~) ~

~ ~ product → ~ (pre)cast (concrete) ~

~ ~ tile → ~ (pre)cast (concrete) ~

~ cast(ing) → (pre)cast normal(-weight) (concrete) (building) unit

~ concrete · Schwerbeton *m*, Normalbeton, gewöhnlicher Beton [*Rohdichten von 1,9 bis 2,5 kg/dm³*]

~ (~) aggregate · Normalbetonzuschlag(stoff) *m*, Schwerbetonzuschlag-(stoff), Normalbetonzuschlagmaterial *n*, Schwerbetonzuschlagmaterial

~ ~ building (construction) element · Schwerbeton-Hochbauelement *n*, Normalbeton-Hochbauelement

~ ~ cast component → ~ ~ (pre)cast ~

~ ~ ~ member → ~ ~ ~ (pre)cast ~

~ (~) cast(ing) → (pre)cast normal(-weight) (concrete) (building) unit

~ ~ construction engineering element · Schwerbeton-Tiefbauelement *n*, Normalbeton-Tiefbauelement

~ ~ floor · Schwerbetondecke *f*, Normalbetondecke

~ (~) hollow block → ~ (precast) (concrete) ~ ~

~ (~) ~ tile → ~ (precast) (concrete) ~ ~

~ ~ layer, ~ ~ leaf, ~ ~ wythe, ~ ~ withe, ~ ~ tier, ~ ~ shell, ~ ~ skin · Normalbeton-Schale *f*, Schwerbeton-Schale [*Hohlwand*]

~ ~ leaf → ~ ~ layer

~ ~ lintel; ~ ~ lintol [*deprecated*] [*A normal(-weight) concrete beam spanning an opening*] · Schwerbetonoberschwelle *f*, Schwerbetonsturz *m*, Normalbetonsturz, Normalbetonoberschwelle

~ ~ pile · Normalbetonpfahl *m*, Schwerbetonpfahl

~ ~ pipe · Schwerbetonrohr *n*, Normalbetonrohr

~ ~ (pre)cast component, ~ ~ ~ member, ~ cast-concrete component, ~ (concrete) cast(ing) · Schwerbetonfertigteil *m, n*, Schwerbetonmontageteil, Normalbetonfertigteil, Normalbetonmontageteil

~ ~ ~ member, ~ ~ ~ component, ~ cast-concrete ~, ~ (concrete) cast(ing) · Schwerbetonfertigteil *m, n*, Schwerbetonmontageteil, Normalbetonfertigteil, Normalbetonmontageteil

~ ~ product, ~ (pre)cast (concrete) ~, ~ (pre)cast concrete [*Normal(-weight) concrete which is cast in separate units before being placed in position in a structure*] · Schwerbetonerzeugnis *n*, Schwerbetonstein *m*, Normalbetonerzeugnis, Normalbetonstein [*Siehe Anmerkung unter „Betonstein"*]

~ ~ shell → ~ ~ ~ layer

~ ~ skin → ~ ~ ~ layer

~ ~ slab · Schwerbetonplatte *f*, Normalbetonplatte

~ ~ solid slab · Normalbeton-Vollplatte *f*, Schwerbeton-Vollplatte

~ ~ tier → ~ ~ ~ layer

~ ~ wall · Schwerbetonwand *f*, Normalbetonwand *f*

~ ~ ~ slab · Normalbeton-Wandplatte *f*, Schwerbeton-Wandplatte

~ ~ withe → ~ ~ ~ layer

~ ~ wythe → ~ ~ ~ layer

~ fine(-grained) concrete · Schwerfeinbeton *m*, Normalfeinbeton

~ hollow concrete tile → ~ (precast) (concrete) hollow block

~ ~ filler block, ~ ~ ~ ~ tile [*See remark under 'Block'*] · Normalbeton-(decken)hohlkörper *m*, Schwerbeton-(decken)hohlkörper, Normalbeton-Hohl-(Decken)Füllstein *m*, Schwerbeton-Hohl-(Decken)Füllstein, Normalbeton-Hohl-(Decken)Füllblock(stein)*m*, Schwerbeton-Hohl-(Decken) Füllblock-(stein), Normalbeton-Hohldeckenblock-(stein), Schwerbeton-Hohldeckenblock(stein), Normalbeton-Hohldeckenstein, Schwerbeton-Hohldeckenstein, Normalbeton-Deckenhohl(block)-stein, Normalbeton-Deckenhohlblock, Schwerbeton-Deckenhohlblock, Normalbeton-Hohldeckenblock, Schwerbeton-Hohldeckenblock

~ (pre)cast block → ~ ~ ~ (concrete) ~

~ ~ building construction component → ~ ~ ~ (concrete) building construction unit

~ ~ ~ ~ member → ~ ~ ~ (concrete) building construction unit

~ ~ ~ ~ unit → ~ ~ ~ concrete ~ ~ ~

~ ~ compound unit → ~ ~ ~ concrete ~ ~

~ ~ concrete, ~ ~ (~) product, ~ concrete product [*Normal(-weight) concrete which is cast in separate units before being placed in position in a structure*] · Schwerbetonerzeugnis *n*, Schwerbetonstein *m*, Normalbetonerzeugnis, Normalbetonstein [*Siehe Anmerkung unter „Betonstein"*]

~ ~ (~) block, ~ ~ (~) tile · Schwerbetonblock(stein) *m*, Normalbetonblock-(stein), Schwerbetonstein, Normalbetonstein [*Fehlname: Klinker m*]

~~ (~) building construction unit, ~~ (~) ~~ member, ~~ (~) ~~ component, ~ prefab(ricated) ~ ~ ~ ~ · Normalbeton-Hochbau(montage)-element *n*, Schwerbeton-Hochbau(montage)element, Normalbeton-Hochbau(montage)körper *m*, Schwerbeton-Hochbau(montage)körper, Normalbeton-Hochbaufertigelement, Schwerbeton-Hochbaufertigelement, Normalbeton-Hochbaufertigkörper, Schwerbeton-Hochbaufertigkörper [*Fehlnamen: Normalbeton-Hochbau(montage)einheit f*]

~~ (~) **compound unit**, prefab(ricated) ~ ~ ~ · Schwerbetonfertig(bau)teil *m, n*, Schwerbetonmontage(bau)teil, Normalbetonfertig(bau)teil, Normalbetonmontage(bau)teil [*Fehlnamen: Schwerbetonbauteil; Normalbetonbauteil*]

~ (~) (~) **hollow block**, ~ (~) (~) ~ tile, ~ (~) hollow concrete ~ · Schwerbetonhohlblock(stein) *m*, Normalbetonhohlblock(stein), Normalbetonhohlstein, Schwerbetonhohlstein

~ (~) (~) ~ **tile**, ~ (~) (~) ~ block, ~ (~) hollow concrete ~ · Schwerbetonhohlblock(stein) *m*, Normalbetonhohlblock(stein), Normalbetonhohlstein, Schwerbetonhohlstein

~~ (~) **product**, ~ concrete ~, ~ (pre)cast concrete [*Normal(-weight) concrete which is cast in separate units before being placed in position in a structure*] · Schwerbetonerzeugnis *n*, Schwerbetonstein *m*, Normalbetonstein, Normalbetonerzeugnis [*Siehe Anmerkung unter „Betonstein"*]

~~ (~) **tile**, ~~ (~) block · Schwerblock(stein) *m*, Normalbetonblock(stein), Schwerbetonstein, Normalbetonstein [*Fehlname: Klinker m*]

~~ (~) **ware** · Schwerbetonware(n) *f*, Normalbetonware(n)

~ **prefab(ricated) concrete building construction component** → ~ (pre-)cast (concrete) building construction unit

~ ~ ~ **compound unit** → ~ (pre)cast (~) ~ ~

~ **R.C.**, ~ reinforced concrete · Schwer-Stahlbeton *m*, Normal-Stahlbeton, gewöhnlicher Stahlbeton, Stahlschwerbeton

~ **reinforced concrete**, ~ R.C. · gewöhnlicher Stahlbeton *m*, Normal-Stahlbeton, Schwer-Stahlbeton, Stahlschwerbeton

normalized footstep sound transmission level (US); normalised ~ ~ ~ ~ (Brit.) · Normtrittschallpegel *m*

~ **impact sound transmission level** (US); normalised ~ ~ ~ ~ (Brit.) · Normkörperschallpegel *m*

~ **level difference** (US); normalised ~ ~ (Brit.) · Normschallpegeldifferenz *f*

normalizing (US); normalising (Brit.) · Normalglühen *n*, Normalisieren [*Baustahl*]

Norman · normannisch

~ **architecture** · normannische Baukunst *f*, ~ Architektur *f*

~ **crypt** · normannische Krypta *f*, ~ Gruft *f*

~ **Gothic style** · normannische Gotik *f*

~ **style** · normannischer Stil *m*

~ **vault** · normannisches Gewölbe *n*

~ **window** · normannisches Fenster *n*

North Italian Quattrocento, vestigially period · Quattrocento *m*

northern foot, Drusian ~ [*13.12 in., 333.25 mm*] · drusianischer Fuß *m*

north(-facing) façade · Nordfassade *f*

~ **wall** · Nordwand *f*

~ **window** · Nordfenster *n*

north-light · Sägedachfenster *n*, Sägezahndachfenster, Shed(dach)fenster

north(-light) barrel shell roof, saw-tooth ~ ~ ~, ~ cylinder segment ~ · Tonnen(schalen)-Sheddach *n*

~ **cupola** → ~ (saucer) dome

~ **cylinder segment roof**, saw-tooth ~ ~ ~, ~ barrel shell ~ · Tonnen(schalen)-Sheddach *n*

~ **cylindrical shell**, saw-tooth ~ ~ · Säge(zahn)dachzylinderschale *f*, Zylindersäge(zahn)dachschale, Shed(dach)zylinderschale, Zylindershed(dach)schale

~ **dome(d rooflight)** → ~ (saucer) dome

~ **hypar shell frame(d) block**, ~ ~ ~ ~ building, saw-tooth ~ ~ ~ ~ ~ · HP-Shed(rahmen)halle *f*

~ **prestressed (concrete) shell** · Spannbetonshedschale *f*

~ **rainwater gutter**, ~ roof ~, saw-tooth ~ ~, ~ R.W. ~ · Säge(zahn)dach(regen)rinne *f*, Shed(dach)(regen)rinne

~ **R.C. shell** → ~ reinforced (concrete) ~

~ **reinforced (concrete) shell**, ~ R.C. ~, reinforced (concrete) northlight ~ · Stahlbetonshedschale *f*

~ **roof**, saw-tooth ~ · Säge(zahn)dach *n*, Sheddach

~ ~ **bay**, ~ ~ span, saw-tooth ~ ~ · Säge(zahn)dachschiff *n*, Shed(dach)schiff

~ ~ **building**, saw-tooth ~ ~ · Shed(dach)bau *m*, Shed(dach)gebäude *n*

~ ~ **frame**, saw-tooth ~ ~ · Säge(zahn)dachrahmen *m*, Shed(dach)rahmen

~ ~ **frame(d) block**, ~ ~ ~ building, saw-tooth ~ ~ ~ · Säge(zahn)dach(rahmen)halle *f*, Shed(dach)(rahmen)halle

~ ~ **glazing**, saw-tooth ~ ~ · Säge(zahn)dachverglasung *f*, Shed(dach)verglasung

~ ~ **gutter**, ~ rainwater ~, saw-tooth ~ ~, ~ R.W. ~ · Säge(zahn)dach(regen)rinne *f*, Shed(dach)(regen)rinne

~ ~ rib, saw-tooth ~ ~ · Säge(zahn)-dachrippe f, Shed(dach)rippe

~ ~ roof-light, saw-tooth ~ ~ · Säge(zahn)dachoberlicht n, Shed(dach)oberlicht

~ ~ span, ~ ~ bay, saw-tooth ~ ~ · Säge(zahn)dachschiff n, Shed(dach)schiff

~ ~ truss, saw-tooth ~ ~ · Sägedachbinder m, Shed(dach)binder

~ (saucer) dome, ~ (~) cupola, ~ domed rooflight, ~ domelight · Nordlichtkuppel f [*Sie hat den Lichteffekt eines Sheddaches*]

~ shell, saw-tooth ~ · Shed(dach)schale f

~ ~ roof, saw-tooth ~ ~ · Säge(zahn)-schalendach n, Shedschalendach

north lighting · Nordbelichtung f

~ **orientation** · Nordorientierung f

~ **roof building** → ~-light ~ ~

~ **shell**, ~-light ~, saw-tooth ~ · Shed(dach)schale f

~ **tower** · Nordturm m

~ **transept** · Nordquerhaus n

~ **wall**, north-facing ~ · Nordwand f

~ **window**, north-facing ~ · Nordfenster n

Norwegian architecture · norwegische Architektur f, ~ Baukunst f

~ **stave church** [*See remark under 'Stabkirche'*] · norwegische Mastenkirche f, ~ Stabkirche, Reiswerkkirche

nose section · Nasenprofil n

no-slump concrete → earth-moist ~

not built upon · unbebaut

no-tension rigidity, ~ stiffness · Steifigkeit f ohne Zugbeanspruchung

not fit to live in, ~ habitable, uninhabitable, unfit for human habitation · unbewohnbar

~ **habitable**, ~ fit to live in, uninhabitable, unfit for human habitation · unbewohnbar

~ **soundproof** · hellhörig

~ **up to Standard** · nichtnorm(en)gerecht

notch effect · Kerbwirkung f

~ **sensitive** · kerbempfindlich

~ **sensitivity** · Kerbempfindlichkeit f

~ **strength** · Kerbfestigkeit f

~ **stress** · Kerbspannung f

notched area · Kerbbereich m, n

~ **chisel**, indented ~ · Zahneisen n [*Steinhauerwerkzeug*]

notching · Überschneidung f [*Holzbau*]

note of authorization · Zulassungsbescheid m

notion of style, concept ~ ~, idea ~ ~ · Stilbegriff m, Stilkonzeption f

novolac resin · Novolak n [*Nicht selbsthärtendes Phenolharz, das dauernd löslich und schmelzbar ist*]

no weathering exposure, NW · wettergeschützt

nozzleman [*e.g. in spray plastering*] · Spritzenbediener m

N-S curve, Wöhler ~ · Wöhler-Linie f, Zeitfestigkeitskurve f

N-truss, Linville (roof) truss; Pratt (roof) truss (US) · Pratt(-Dach)binder m

nucleus → business area

~, central city · Kernstadt f

number · Anzahl f

~ **designation** · Zahlenbezeichnung f

~ **in each** · Anzahl f der Positionen [*Stahlliste*]

~ **of air changes** · Luftwechsel(an)zahl f

~ ~ **bar** → bar number

~ ~ **bars**, ~ ~ members, ~ ~ rods, ~ ~ elements · Gliedzahl f, Stabzahl

~ ~ **elements**, ~ ~ rods, ~ ~ members, ~ ~ bars · Gliedzahl f, Stabzahl

~ ~ **house properties** · Hausbestand m

~ ~ **members**, ~ ~ bars, ~ ~ elements, ~ ~ rods · Gliedzahl f, Stabzahl

~ ~ ~ · Bauteil-Anzahl f [*Stahlliste*]

~ ~ **rod** → bar number

~ ~ **rods**, ~ ~ elements, ~ ~ bars, ~ ~ members · Gliedzahl f, Stabzahl

numeral(-type) dial lock, ~ combination ~ · Ziffernschloß n, Zahlenschloß

numerical calculation · numerische Berechnung f

~ **example** · Zahlenbeispiel n

~ **integration** · numerische Integration f

~ **method** · numerische Methode f, numerisches Verfahren n

~ **theory** · numerische Theorie f

~ **value** · Zahlenwert m

nunnery · Nonnenkloster n

~ **church** · Nonnenkirche f

nun's choir, ~ quire · Nonnenchor m, Nonnenempore f

nurag(h)e, noraghe [*One of a class of prehistoric stone structures numerous in Sardinia*] · Nurag(h)e f, (mediterranes rundes) Steinhaus n

nursery · Baumschule f

~ · Kinderzimmer n

~ **for passengers with small children** · Raum m für Mutter und Kind [*Flughafen*]

nurses' hostel · Schwestern(wohn)heim n

~ **teaching block**, ~ ~ unit, ~ ~ accommodation · Schwesternlehrtrakt m

nursing unit, ward ~ · Station f [*Krankenhaus*]

nut oil · Nußöl n

NW, no weathering exposure · wettergeschützt

nylon cloth, ~ woven fabric; ~ fabric [*misnomer*] · Nylongewebe *n*
~ **coating** · Nylonüberzug *m*
~ **fabric** [*misnomer*]; ~ cloth, ~ woven fabric · Nylongewebe *n*
~ **grille** [*See remark under 'Gitter'*] · Nylongitter *n*
~ **woven fabric,** ~ cloth; ~ fabric [*misnomer*] · Nylongewebe *n*

nymphaeum [*Literally 'a temple of the Nymphs', but applied rather vaguely to Roman pleasure-houses, especially when containing flowers, fountains, and statues*] · Nymphäum *n*

O

oak (fence) post, ~ (~) picket · Eichen(zaun)pfosten *m*, Eichen(zaun)pfahl *m*
~ **floor cover(ing),** ~ ~ finish, ~ floor(ing) · Eichen(fuß)boden(belag) *m*
~ **parquet(ry)** · Eichenparkett *n*, Fhep
~ **picket** → ~ (fence) post
~ **post** → ~ fence ~
~ **shingle** · Eichenschindel *f*
~ **slat fence,** ~ stake ~ · Eichenlattenzaun *m*, Eichenstaket *n*
~ **stake fence,** ~ slat ~ · Eichenlattenzaun *m*, Eichenstaket *n*
~ **strip floor cover(ing),** ~ ~ floor(ing) (finish) · Eichenriemen(fuß)boden(belag) *m*, Fhe
~ **threshold** · Eichenschwelle *f*

oakum · Werg *n*

obelisk, monolithic pillar · Gedenkpfeiler *m*, Obelisk *m*, Ehrenpfeiler, Gedächtnispfeiler

objectivization · Objektivierung *f*

oblique-angled (pipe) junction, side (~) ~, ~ (~) inlet, ~ (~) branch · einfach schräger (Rohr)Zulauf *m*, ~ ~ (Rohr)Abzweig *m*, (Rohr)Seitenzulauf, (Rohr)Seitenabzweig
~ **axes** → ~ system of ~
~ **bond** → diagonal (masonry) ~
~ **cocking** → bevelled ~
~ **cracking** · Schrägrissebildung *f*, Auftreten *n* von Schrägrissen
~ **end cocking** → bevelled end cogging
~ ~ **cogging** → bevelled ~ ~
~ ~ **corking** → bevelled end cogging
~ **halved joint with butt ends** · Schrägblatt *n*, schräges Blatt [*Holzverbindung*]
~ **joint;** beveled ~ (US); bevelled ~ (Brit.) · schräger Stoß *m* [*Holzverbindung*]
~ **(masonry) bond** → diagonal (~) ~
~ **(~) pattern** (US) → diagonal (masonry) bond
~ **projection** · schiefe Projektion *f*, schiefer Riß *m*, Schrägriß, Schrägprojektion

~ **rib** · Schrägrippe *f*
~ **saddle junction piece** · Einlaß *m* mit schrägem Flansch [*Kanalisationszeug*]
~ **scarf (joint),** French ~ (~) · französisches Blatt *n*, schräges Hakenblatt [*Holzverbindung*]
~ ~ **(~) with wedge,** French ~ (~) ~ ~ · schräges Hakenblatt *n* mit Keil [*Holzverbindung*]
~ **strength** · Schrägfestigkeit *f*
~ **(system of) axes** · schiefwinkeliges Achsenkreuz *n*

obliterating power → hiding ~

oblong · ungleichmäßig viereckig

obscure · durchblickverhindernd, durchsichtverhindernd [*Glas*]

obscure(d) glass, vision-proof ~ · Trübglas *n* [*Sammelbezeichnung für alle durch bestimmte Gemengezuschläge und mit oder ohne Zusatz von Farbstoffen absichtlich getrübten, d.h. undurchsichtig gemachten Gläser*]

obscuring · Mattieren *n* [*Glas*]
~ · Mattierung *f* [*Glas*]

observation deck, ~ platform · Beobachtungsplattform *f*
~ **error** · Beobachtungsfehler *m*
~ **floor;** ~ storey (Brit.); ~ story (US) · Beobachtungsetage *f*, Beobachtungsstockwerk *n*, Beobachtungsgeschoß *n*
~ **gallery** · Beobachtungsgang *m*
~ **of settlement(s)** · Setzungsbeobachtung *f*
~ **platform,** ~ deck · Beobachtungsplattform *f*
~ **room** · Beobachtungsraum *m*
~ **storey** (Brit.) → ~ floor
~ **tower** · Beobachtungsturm *m*
~ ~, **watch** ~ · (Burg)Warte *f*, Wachtturm *m*, Wartturm, Pfefferbüchse *f* [*Im Mittelalter ein Turm mit Plattform, von dem aus herannahende Feinde frühzeitig erkannt werden konnten*]

(observer's) field of view · Blickfeld *n* [*Tageslichtberechnung*]

obsolescence · funktionelle Veralterung *f*

obstruction of vision · Sichtbehinderung *f*

obtuse arch, blunt ~ · gedrückter Bogen *m*
~ **quoin (of (masonry) wall),** birdsmouth ~ (~ (~) ~) · stumpfwinkelige Mauerecke *f*

occupancy, occupation, human ~ · Belegung *f* [*Haus*]
~ **load,** use ~, superimposed ~ [*The load of machinery, equipment, furniture and people on floors, corridors, balconies, stairs, etc.*] · Gebrauchslast *f*, Nutzlast

occupant → room ~

occupation · Beziehen *n*, Belegen [*Gebäude*]

occupation — odour-tight

~, occupancy, human ~ · Belegung f [Haus]

occupiable · bezugsfertig [Raum]

occupied · bezogen, belegt [Gebäude]

ochre (Brit.); ocher (US) [B..S. 337] · Ocker m

ocrated concrete, concrete treated with SiF_4 · Ocratbeton m, Okratbeton

ocrating · Okratieren n, Ocratieren [Es dient zur Erhöhung der Festigkeit und chemischen Widerstandsfähigkeit von Beton. Er wird in Druckkammern mit Siliziumtetrafluoridgas (SiF_4) behandelt, die Umwandlung erfolgt nach der Gleichung: $2Ca(OH_2) + SiF_4 \rightarrow 2CaF_2 + SiO_2 \cdot 2H_2O$. Durch Zeit- und Druckveränderungen können beliebige Eindringtiefen des Gases in den Beton erreicht werden. Das Verfahren wird nur in der Betonfertigteilindustrie angewendet]

octagon, octagonal figure, eight-sided figure · Achteck n, Oktogon n

~ · Achtort n [In der gotischen Baukunst das regelmäßige Achteck, das für die Grundrißbildung gotischer Türme, Pfeiler usw. oft grundlegend ist. ,,Ort" = der alte Steinmetzausdruck für Ecke, Spitze]

octagonal aisle, eight-sided ~ · Achteckschiff n, Achtkantschiff

~ **bar,** ~ rod, eight-sided ~ · Achteckstab m, Achtkantstab

~ **block,** ~ building, eight-sided ~ · Achteckgebäude n, Achtkantgebäude

~ **building,** ~ block, eight-sided ~ · Achteckgebäude n, Achtkantgebäude

~ **chamber,** eight-sided ~ · Achteckraum m, Achtkantraum [Nebenraum im Sakralbau]

~ **chapter-house,** eight-sided ~ · achteckiges Kapitelhaus n, achteitiges ~

~ **chimney,** eight-sided ~ · Achteckschornstein m, Achtkantschornstein

~ **column,** eight-sided ~ · Achteckstütze f, Achtkantstütze

~ **cupola,** eight-sided ~, ~ dome · Achteckkuppel f, Achtkantkuppel

~ **dome,** eight-sided ~, ~ cupola · Achteckkuppel f, Achtkantkuppel

~ **donjon** → ~ keep

~ **dungeon** → ~ keep

octagon(al figure), eight-sided ~ · Achteck n, Oktogon n

octagonal footing, eight-sided ~ · Achteckfundament n, Achtkantfundament

~ **girder four columns space frame,** eight-sided ~ ~ ~ ~ ~ · räumlicher Vier-Säulen-Rahmen m als Achteckträger

~ **(ground)(-)plan,** eight-sided ~ · Achteck-Grundriß m, Achtkant-Grundriß

~ **keep,** ~ donjon, ~ dungeon, eight-sided ~ · Achteck-Donjon m, Achtkant-Donjon, Achteck-Bergfried m, Achtkant-Bergfried, Achteck-Belfried m, Achtkant-Belfried, Achteck-Berchfrit m, Achtkant-Berchfrit

~ **lantern,** eight-sided ~ · Achtecklaterne f, Achteck-Dachkappe f, Achtkantlaterne, Achtkant-Dachkappe

~ **mosaic tile,** eight-sided ~ ~ · Achteckmosaikfliese f, Achteckmosaik(belag)platte f, Achtkantmosaik(belag)platte, Achtkantmosaikfliese

~ **plan** → ~ ground(-)~

~ **pyramid,** eight-sided ~ · achtseitige Pyramide f, achteckige ~

~ **rod,** ~ bar, eight-sided ~ · Achteckstab m, Achtkantstab

~ **spire,** eight-sided ~ · Achteck(turm)- helm m, Achtkant(turm)helm

~ **steel,** eight-sided ~ · Achteckstahl m, Achtkantstahl

~ **tile,** eight-sided ~ · Achteckfliese f, Achteck(belag)platte f, Achtkantfliese, Achtkant(belag)platte

~ **tower,** eight-sided ~ · Achteckturm m, Achtkantturm

~ **turret,** eight-sided ~ · Achtecktürmchen n, Achtkanttürmchen

~ **vault,** eight-sided ~ · Achteckgewölbe n, Achtkantgewölbe

~ **wire,** eight-sided ~ · Achteckdraht m, Achtkantdraht

octastyle, eight columned · achtsäulig

~ [A portico having a row of eight front(-ed) columns] · Oktastylos m

~ **peripteral temple with seventeen columns on the flanks,** peripteral octastyle ~ ~ ~ ~ ~ ~ ~ · Peripterostempel m von 8:17 Säulen

~ **temple** · Oktastylostempel m [Griechischer Tempel mit acht Säulen an der Giebelseite]

octofoil, eight-lobe tracery · Achtpaß m [gotisches Maßwerk]

octopartite vault · achtteiliges Gewölbe n

octyl phenol · Octylphenol n

oculus (window), bull's-eye (~), oxeye (~) [A round or oval window, usually with glazing bars radiating from a circular centre] · Ochsenauge n

ode(i)on, odeum [In Greek and Roman architecture, a building for musical performances] · Odeion n, Odeum

odour barrier (Brit.); odor ~ (US) · Geruchsperre f

~ **control** (Brit.); odor ~ (US) · Geruchsbekämpfung f

~(-)**free** (Brit.) → inodorous

odour nuisance (Brit.); odor ~ (US) · Geruchbelästigung f

~-**tight** (Brit.); odor-tight (US) · geruchdicht

oecus [*1. Hellenic house. 2. Principal apartment in a Hellenic house. 3. Principal living-room in a Roman house*] · Oecus *m*

of accurate shape · form(en)genau

~ **high viscosity** · hochviskos, zähflüssig, dickflüssig

~ **large format** · großformatig

~ **long reverberation time** · hallig, mit langer Nachhallzeit

~ **low cement content** · zementarm

~ ~ **solvent content** · lösungsmittelarm

~ ~ **viscosity** · dünnflüssig, niedrigviskos

~ **medium viscosity** · mittelviskos

~ **natural asphalt colour** (Brit.); ~ ~ ~ **color** (US) · naturfarbig [*Hochdruck-Asphaltplatte*]

~ **small format, small-sized** · kleinformatig

~ **standard particle size distribution** → correct(ly sized)

~ **storey height** (Brit.); ~ **story** ~ (US) · geschoßhoch, etagenhoch, stockwerkhoch

~ **welding quality, weldable** · schweißbar

off-center (US); **off-centre** (Brit.); eccentric · ausmittig, exzentrisch

~ **application of force** (US); off-centre ~ ~ ~ (Brit.); eccentric ~ ~ ~ · ausmittiger Kraftangriff *m*, exzentrischer ~

~ **load** (US); off-centre ~ (Brit.); eccentric ~ · ausmittige Last *f*, exzentrische ~

~ **loading** (US); off-centre ~ (Brit.); eccentric ~ · ausmittige Belastung *f*, exzentrische ~

off-centre (Brit.); **off-center** (US); eccentric · ausmittig, exzentrisch

~ **application of force** (Brit.); off-center ~ ~ ~ (US); eccentric ~ ~ ~ · ausmittiger Kraftangriff *m*, exzentrischer ~

~ **load** (Brit.); off-center ~ (US); eccentric ~ · ausmittige Last *f*, exzentrische ~

~ **loading** (Brit.); off-center ~ (US); eccentric ~ · ausmittige Belastung *f*, exzentrische ~

offcut · Verschnitt *m*

offcuts, ends, trim [*Short pieces trimmed from round or rough-sawn timber when cutting them to length*] · Sparrholz *n*, Ablängreste *mpl*, kleines Bauholz

offensive fill(ing) of ground · gesundheitsschädliche (Gelände)Auffüllung *f*

offering-chapel · Opferkapelle *f*

offering-table · Opfertisch *m*

offertory-box, poor's pyx · Opferstock *m*

off-formwork concrete, off-shuttering ~, off-forms ~ · Beton *m* ohne Oberflächenbehandlung

office · Dienstraum *m*, Dienstzimmer *n* [*Büroraum in einem Behördengebäude*]

office-and-flat block, ~ building, flats-and-offices ~ · Büro- und Wohnhaus *n*, Wohn- und Bürohaus

office and residential tower · Büro- und Wohnhochhaus *n*

~ **area** · Bürofläche *f*

~ **block,** ~ building · Bürogebäude *n*, Bürohaus *n*

~ **building,** ~ block · Bürogebäude *n*, Bürohaus *n*

~ **dumbwaiter** · Aktenaufzug *m*

~ **entrance** · Büroeingang *m*

~ **floor** · Büro(trenn)decke *f*, Bürogeschoßdecke, Büroetagendecke, Bürostockwerkdecke

~ **for the preservation of monuments** · Bau(denkmal)pflegeamt *n*

~ **furniture factory** · Büromöbelwerk *n*, Büromöbelfabrik *f*

~ **hut** · Bürobaracke *f*

~ **illumination,** ~ **lighting** · Bürobeleuchtung *f*

~ **landscape,** open plan office, open landscaped office space · Bürolandschaft *f*, Großraumbüro *n*

~ **landscaping** · Bürolandschaftsgestaltung *f*

~ **lighting,** ~ illumination · Bürobeleuchtung *f*

~ **partition (wall)** · Bürotrennwand *f*

~ **portion** · Bürotrakt *m*

~ **quieting** · Büroschalldämmung *f*

~ **skyscraper** · Bürowolkenkratzer *m*

~ **storey** (Brit.); ~ **story** ~ (US) · Büroetage *f*, Bürostockwerk *n*, Bürogeschoß *n*

~ **story** (US); ~ **storey** (Brit.) · Büroetage *f*, Bürostockwerk *n*, Bürogeschoß *n*

~ **tower** · Bürohochhaus *n*

~ **window** · Bürofenster *n*

~ **wing** · Bürotrakt *m*

~ **work for the execution of the construction operations** · Ausführungsbearbeitung *f*

official materials testing institute · Prüfamt *n*, Materialprüf(ungs)amt, MPA

to off-load, to unload · abladen

off-loading ramp, unloading ~ · Entladerampe *f*, Ausladerampe

off peak charging, night ~ · Nachtaufheizzeit *f*

~ ~ ~ **with supplementary day heating,** night ~ ~ ~ ~ ~ · Nachtaufheizzeit *f* mit Tagesnachheizzeit

off-peak electric current, ~ electricity · Nachtenergie *f*, Nachtstrom *m*

~ ~ ~ **heating,** ~ electricity ~ · Nachtstromspeicherheizung *f*, Nachtenergiespeicherheizung

~ ~ **supply** · Nachtstrom *m*

off-peak electricity heating — oil content

~ **electricity heating,** ~ electric current ~ · Nachtstromspeicherheizung f, Nachtenergiespeicherheizung

~ **(hot) water heater,** ~ (~) ~ heating appliance, night storage (hot) water heater, night storage (hot) water heating appliance · Nachtstrom-Wassererhitzer m, Nachtstrom-Wasserheizer, Nachtstrom-Wasserheizgerät n, Nachtstrom-Wassererwärmer

~ **storage water heating** · Nachtstrom-Speicherwassererhitzung f, Nachtstrom-Speicherwassererwärmung

~ **tariff,** night-only ~ · Nachtstromtarif m

to offset, to joggle · (ab)kröpfen [*Einen Profil- oder Stabstahl aus seiner ursprünglichen Ebene in eine innerhalb der Konstruktion dazu versetzte Ebene örtlich biegen*]

offset, swan-neck, swan's neck, gooseneck [*A pipe fitting used to connect two pipes whose axes are parallel but not in line*] · Schwanenhals m, S-Stück n, Etagenbogen m, Sprungrohr n, Springrohr [*DIN 19506*]

~ · Sprungmaß n

~ · (Ab)kröpfung f [*Profil- oder Stabstahl*]

~ · Abknickung f [*einer Fassade*]

~ · Mauerabsatz m

~ **conduit nipple** · Sprungnippel m

~ **unit** · Sprungstück n

offsetting, cranking · Verkröpfen n, Verkröpfung f

off-shuttering concrete → off-formwork ~

off-site fabrication · Herstellung f im Werk [*Im Gegensatz zur Herstellung auf der Baustelle*]

off-size, margin, deviation · Abmaß n, Maßabweichung f, Genauigkeitsgrad m [*DIN 18201. Der Unterschied zwischen Grenz- und Nennmaß*]

(off-street) parking facility · Parkanlage f

O.G. arch → saddle(-shaped) ~

O.G. (roof) gutter → ogee (~) ~

OGA, open-grain(ed) (mineral) aggregate · offen abgestuftes Mineralgemisch n

ogee arch → saddle(-shaped) ~

~ **(moulding)** (Brit.) → cyma(tium)

~ **(roof) gutter,** ~ rainwater ~, ~ R.W. ~, O.G. (roof) ~, O.G. rainwater ~, O.G. R.W. ~ [*An eaves gutter with cyma-recta contour on the face*] · Sima(dach)rinne f, Simaregenrinne

ogival arch · Diagonalbogen m, Kreuzbogen, Kreuzgurt m, Gratbogen des Kreuz(grat)gewölbes [*Im Kreuz(grat)gewölbe diagonal verlaufender Bogen; zu unterscheiden vom Kreuzungsbogen*]

oil absorption · Ölaufnahme f

~ ~ **test** · Bestimmung f der Ölzahl, Spatelverfahren n [*DIN 53199*]

~ ~ **value** · Ölzahl f [*DIN 53199*]

~ **addition** · Ölbeigabe f, Ölzusatz m

~ **alkyd,** oil-modified ~ · Ölalkyd n

~ ~ **paint** · Ölalkydharzlackfarbe f

~ ~ **(resin),** oil-modified ~ (~) · Mischester m, ölmodifiziertes Alkydharz n, Ölalkyd n

~ **appliance** → oil-burning ~

~ **base** · Ölgrundlage f, Ölbasis f [*Bindemittellösung einer Anstrichfarbe*]

oil-base(d) (building) mastic, oil-type (~) ~, ~ mastic joint sealer · Öl(fugen)mastix m, Öl(fugen)kitt m, Öl(ver)füllkitt, Ölfugen(ab)dicht(ungs)kitt, plastische Öl-Fugen(ab)dicht(ungs)masse f, plastische Öl-Fugenmasse, plastische Öl-(Fugen)(Ver)Füllmasse, plastischer Öl-(Fugen)(Ver)Füller m

~ **mastic joint sealer** → ~ (building) mastic

oil(-base(d)) medium → ~ vehicle

~ **paint,** oil-type ~ · Öl(anstrich)farbe f

~ ~ **coat,** oil-type ~ ~ · Ölfarb(en)anstrich m, Ölfarb(en)aufstrich

~ **scumble glaze,** oil-type ~ ~ · Öllasur(farbe) f

~ **stain,** oil-type ~ [*A transparent solution of a dye powder soluble in aromatic hydrocarbons. B.S. 1215*] · Ölbeize f

~ **vehicle,** ~ medium, oil-type ~ · Bindemittellösung f auf Ölbasis, ~ ~ Ölgrundlage [*Anstrichfarbe*]

oil bodying, thermal polymerization of oil · Öleindicken n

~ **boiler house,** oil-fired ~ ~, oil-burning ~ ~ · Kesselhaus n mit Ölfeuerung

oil burner, oil-fired ~, oil-burning ~ · Ölbrenner m

oil-burning, oil-fired · ölgefeuert

~ **appliance,** ~ fire, ~ furnace, oil(-fired) ~ · Ölfeuerstätte f, Ölfeuerung f

~ **boiler,** oil(-fired) ~ · Öl(feuerungs)kessel m, ölgefeuerter (Heiz)Kessel

~ ~ **house,** oil(-fired) ~ ~ · Kesselhaus n mit Ölfeuerung

~ **burner,** oil(-fired) ~ · Ölbrenner m

~ **fire,** ~ appliance, ~ furnace, oil(-fired) ~ · Ölfeuerstätte f, Ölfeuerung f

~ **furnace,** ~ fire, ~ appliance, oil(-fired) ~ · Ölfeuerstätte f, Ölfeuerung f

~ **heating,** oil(-fired) ~ · Öl(be)heizung f

~ ~ **system,** oil(-fired) ~ ~ · Ölheizung(sanlage) f

~ **warm air heater,** oil((-fired) ~ ~ ~ · Öl-(Warm)Lufterhitzer m, Öl-(Warm-)Luftheizgerät n

oil cake, linseed ~ · Leinkuchen m, Ölkuchen

oilcloth · Öltuch n

oil compatibility · Ölverträglichkeit f

~ **content** · Ölanteil m, Ölgehalt m

(~) distillate fraction, tar-oil ~, tar distillation ~ · Ölfraktion *f* [*Herstellung präparierten Teeres*]

oil-fast, oil-resisting, oil-resistant · ölbeständig, ölfest, ölwiderstandsfähig

oil fastness, ~ resistance · Ölfestigkeit *f*, Ölbeständigkeit

oil-filled radiator → electric ~ ~

oil fire → oil-burning appliance

oil-fired, oil-burning · ölgefeuert

oil(-fired) appliance, ~ fire, ~ furnace, oil-burning ~ · Ölfeuerstätte *f*, Ölfeuerung *f*

~ boiler, oil-burning ~ · Öl(feuerungs)kessel *m*, ölgefeuerter (Heiz)Kessel

~ ~ house, oil-burning ~ ~ · Kesselhaus *n* mit Ölfeuerung

~ burner, oil-burning ~ · Ölbrenner *m*

~ central heating, fuel ~ ~ ~, heating fuel ~ ~ ~ · (Heiz)Öl-Zentralheizung *f*

~ fire, ~ appliance, ~ furnace, oil-burning ~ · Ölfeuerstätte *f*, Ölfeuerung *f*

~ furnace, ~ fire, ~ appliance, oil-burning ~ · Ölfeuerstätte *f*, Ölfeuerung *f*

~ heating, oil-burning ~ · Öl(be)heizung *f*

~ ~ system, oil-burning ~ ~ · Ölheizung(sanlage) *f*

~ warm air heater, oil-burning ~ ~ · Öl-(Warm)Lufterhitzer *m*, Öl-(Warm)Luftheizgerät *n*

oil-free, oilless · ölfrei, öllos

oil furnace → oil-burning appliance

oil-gas tar, Ölgasteer *m*, Fettgasteer

oil-gas-tar pitch · Ölgasteerpech *n*, Fettgasteerpech

oil gloss · Ölglanz *m*

~ ~ paint · Ölglanz(anstrich)farbe *f*

~ heating, oil-fired ~, oil-burning ~ · Öl(be)heizung *f*

~ ~ chimney · Ölheizungsschornstein *m*

~ ~ system, oil-fired ~ ~, oil-burning ~ ~ · Ölheizung(sanlage) *f*

oil-impregnated paper · Ölpapier *n*

~ wood · Ölholz *n*

oiliness · Filmbildungsfähigkeit *f* [*Siliconöl*]

oil interceptor → fuel ~ ~

oil-in-water emulsion · O/W-Emulsion *f*, Öl-in-Wasser-Emulsion

oil length, oil/resin ratio · Öl/Harz-Verhältnis *n*, Öllänge *f*

oilless, oil-free · ölfrei, öllos

oil-like · ölähnlich, ölartig

oil medium → oil(-base(d)) vehicle

~ meter · Ölzähler *m*

oil-modified · ölmodifiziert

oil(-modified) alkyd (resin) · Mischester *m*, ölmodifiziertes Alkydharz *n*, Ölalkyd *n*

oil of turpentine, wood ~ [*It is obtained by the distillation of scrap wood such as sawdust and tree stumps containing resin instead of the balsam from the living trees*] · Holzterpentinöl *n*, Wurzelterpentinöl

~ paint, oil-base(d) ~ · Öl(anstrich)farbe *f*

~ ~ coat → oil(-base(d)) ~ ~

~ pipe, fuel ~ ~, heating ~ ~ · (Heiz-)Ölrohr *n*

~ pitch, petroleum ~ · Petroleumpech *n*

oil(-)polluted · verölt

oilproof, oil-resistant, fuel ~ · (heiz)ölfest, (heiz)ölbeständig

~ rendering · Ölwannenbeschichtung *f* [*als Material*]

oil reactivity · Ölreaktivität *f*

~ removal · Entölung *f*

~ requirement · Ölbedarf *m*

~ residue · Ölrückstand *m*

oil/resin ratio, oil length · Öl/Harz-Verhältnis *n*, Öllänge *f*

oil resistance, ~ fastness · Ölfestigkeit *f*, Ölbeständigkeit

oil-resistant, oilproof, fuel ~ · (heiz)ölfest, (heiz)ölbeständig

oil-resisting, oil-resistant, oil-fast · ölbeständig, ölfest, ölwiderstandsfähig

oil-saturated hemp rope · Ölstrick *m* [*Ölgetränkter Hanfstrick als Rohrmuffendichtung*]

oil scumble glaze → oil(-base(d)) ~ ~

~ shale [*It yields oil when heated in a retort*] · Ölschiefer *m*

~ ~ cement · Ölschieferzement *m* [*Er besteht aus mindestens 70% Portlandzementklinkern und höchstens 30% in besonderen Ofenanlagen getemperten Ölschiefermineralien*]

~ ~ slag · Ölschieferschlacke *f*

~ ~ tar · Ölschieferteer *m*

~ solubility · Öllöslichkeit *f*

oil-soluble · öllöslich

~ dye · öllöslicher Küpenfarbstoff *m*

oil stain · Ölfleck *m*

~ ~, oil-base(d) ~, oil-type ~ [*A transparent solution of a dye powder soluble in aromatic hydrocarbons. B.S. 1215*] · Ölbeize *f*

~ storage, fuel ~ ~, heating ~ ~ · (Heiz)Öllagerung *f*

~ ~ cellar · Ölkeller *m*

~ (~) tank → fuel ~ (~) ~

~ store → heating ~ ~

~ sump · Ölauffangwanne *f*

oil-susceptible · ölempfindlich

oil tank → (fuel) oil (storage) ~

oil-tempered hardboard · ölgehärtete Hartplatte *f*

oil-tight, fuel ~, heating ~ · (heiz-)öldicht, (heiz)ölundurchlässig

oil-type (building) mastic — Omnia (concrete) floor 672

oil-type (building) mastic, oil-base(d) (~) ~, oil-type mastic joint sealer · Öl(fugen)mastix *m*, Öl(fugen)kitt *m*, Öl(ver)füllkitt, Ölfugen(ab)dicht(ungs)-kitt, plastische Öl-Fugen(ab)dicht(ungs)masse *f*, plastische Öl-Fugen-masse, plastische Öl-(Fugen)(Ver-)Füllmasse, plastischer Öl-(Fugen)(Ver-)Füller *m*

~ **mastic joint sealer** → oil-base(d) (building) mastic

~ **paint,** oil(-base(d)) ~ · Öl(anstrich)farbe *f*

~ ~ **coat,** oil(-base(d)) ~ ~ · Ölfarb(en)anstrich *m*, Ölfarb(en)aufstrich

~ **scumble glaze,** oil(-base(d)) ~ ~ · Öllasur(farbe) *f*

~ **stain,** oil(-base(d)) ~ [*A transparent solution of a dye powder soluble in aromatic hydrocarbons. B.S. 1215*] · Ölbeize *f*

oil varnish, oleoresinous ~ · Öllack *m*

~ **vehicle** → oil(-base(d)) ~

oil warm air heater, oil fired ~ ~ ~, oil-burning ~ ~ ~ · Öl-(Warm)Lufterhitzer *m*, Öl-(Warm)Luftheizgerät *n*

oil-well cement [*Hydraulic cement suitable for use under high pressure and temperature in sealing water and gas pockets and setting casing during the drilling and repair of oil wells; often contains retarders to meet the requirements of use*] · Erdölzement *m*, Ölbohrzement, Tiefbohrzement

oil-wetted sharpening stone · Ölabziehstein *m*

oiling · (Ein)Ölen *n*

oily · ölig

oily-looking dim amber · flohmiger Bernstein *m*

oily waste · Ölschmutzwasser *n*

oiticica oil · Oiticicaöl *n*

old apartment (unit), ~ flat ; ~ living unit (US) · Alt(bau)-Etagenwohnung *f*, Alt(bau)-Geschoßwohnung, Alt(bau)-Stockwerkwohnung

~ **area** · Altfläche *f*

~ **concrete** · Altbeton *m*

~ **Dutch process** · holländisches Verfahren *n* [*Bleiweißherstellung*]

~ **dwelling unit** (US); ~ dwelling (Brit.) · Alt(bau)wohnung *f*

~ **flat** ~ apartment (unit); ~ living unit (US) · Alt(bau)-Etagenwohnung *f*, Alt(bau)-Geschoßwohnung, Alt(bau)-Stockwerkwohnung

~ **living unit** (US); ~ apartment (~), ~ flat · Alt(bau)-Etagenwohnung *f*, Alt(bau)-Geschoßwohnung, Alt(bau)-Stockwerkwohnung

~ **peoples' apartment (unit)** → aged persons' ~ (~)

~ ~ **community centre** (Brit.); ~ ~ center (US); aged ~ ~ ~, ~ persons' ~ ~ · Altenstätte *f*

~ ~ **dwelling** → aged persons' ~

~ ~ **flat** → aged persons' apartment (unit)

~ ~ **home** → ~ persons' ~

~ **persons' apartment (unit)** → aged ~ ~ (~)

~ ~ **community centre** (Brit.); ~ ~ center (US); aged ~ ~ ~, ~ peoples' ~ ~ · Altenstätte *f*

~ ~ **dwelling** → aged ~ ~

~ ~ ~ **unit** → aged ~ ~ ~

~ ~ **flat** → aged persons' apartment (unit)

~ ~ **home,** aged ~ ~, ~ peoples' ~ · Altenheim *n*, Altersheim [*Ein Heim zur wohnlichen Unterbringung bejahrter Menschen, die nicht mehr willens oder in der Lage sind, sich selbst zu versorgen uhd die deshalb keine selbständige Haushaltführung haben*]

old process patenting, O.P. ~, air · Luftpatentieren *n*

~ **quarters** · Altstadt *f*

oleic acid · Ölsäure *f*

oleo-alkyd resin · Ölalkyd(harz) *n*

oleoresin from conifers · Nadelholzbalsam *m*

oleoresinous mix(ture) · Öl-Harz-Gemisch *n*, Öl-Harz-Mischung *f*

~ **paint,** varnish ~ · Öllackfarbe *f*

~ **varnish,** oil ~ · Öllack *m*

olive green (pigment) · Olivgrün(pigment) *n*

olivine · Olivin *m*

~ **basalt** · Olivinbasalt *m*

~ **brick** · Olivinstein *m*

~ **refractory material** ~ ~ (product) [*A forsterite refractory material made from olivine*] · Olivinerzeugnis *n*

~ ~ **(product),** ~ ~ material [*A forsterite refractory material made from olivine*] · Olivinerzeugnis *n*

olivine-rock, dunite · Olivinfels *m*, Olivinstein *m*, Dunit *m*

Olympieion, Temple of Zeus Olympius at Athens · Zeustempel *m* zu Athen

omitted-size fraction · Sperrkörnung *f*, Ausfallkörnung, Auslaßkörnung

~ **grain,** ~ particle · Sperrkorn *n*, Ausfallkorn, Auslaßkorn

~ **particle,** ~ grain · Ausfallkorn *n*, Auslaßkorn, Sperrkorn

~ **(type) grain concrete,** ~ (~) particle ~ · Sperrkornbeton *m*, Auslaßkornbeton, Ausfallkornbeton

~ **(~) particle concrete,** ~ (~) grain ~ · Ausfallkornbeton *m*, Auslaßkornbeton, Sperrkornbeton

Omnia (concrete) floor [*It is a composite floor consisting of lightweight precast planks with reinforcement accurately located in the planks under factory conditions, mass produced hollow concrete blocks, and in-situ concrete*] · Omnia(beton)decke *f*, Verbundgitterträgerdecke

673 Omnia (concrete) plank — one-floor warehouse (building)

~ (~) plank · (schmale) Omnia-Vollbetonplatte f

~ (floor) slab · Omnia-Deckenplatte f

~ lattice · Omnia-Gitterträger m

~ rib(bed) floor · Omnia-Rippendecke f [Mit Leichtbetonhohlkörpern. Druckplatte mindestens 5 cm; ein- und zweischalig]

~ roof · Omniadach n

~ trimmer (concrete) plank, ~ trimming (~) ~ [These planks incorporate precast upstands of structural floor depth and provide permanent shuttering for openings such as stairwells, chimneys, skylights, etc.] · (schmale) Omnia-Wechselvollbetonplatte f

~ wide slab · Großflächenplatte f für die Omnia-Vollbetondecke, Omnia-Großflächenplatte

on grade [At ground level or supported directly on the ground] · ebenerdig

one and a half level (building operational) system · Eineinhalbebenensystem n [Passagier- und Gepäckabfertigung auf Flughäfen]

one-bath method, single-bath ~ · Einbadverfahren n [Dachpappenherstellung]

one-bay, one-span, single-span, single-bay · einschiffig [Rahmenhalle]

~ beam → single-span ~

~ frame → simple ~

~ girder → single-span ~

~ slab → single-span ~

~ two-hinged frame → single-span ~ ~

one-bed, single-bed · einbettig

~ (guest) room, single (guest) bedroom · Ein-Bett-Raum m, Ein-Bett-Zimmer n, Einzel(bett)zimmer, Einzel(schlaf)raum [Hotel]

one-bedroom(ed) apartment (unit), ~ flat; ~ living unit (US) · Ein-Schlafzimmer-Etagenwohnung f, Ein-Schlafzimmer-Geschoßwohnung, Ein-Schlafzimmer-Stockwerkwohnung

~ dwelling unit (US); ~ dwelling (Brit.) · Ein-Schlafzimmer-Wohnung f

~ flat, ~ apartment (unit); ~ living unit (US) · Ein-Schlafzimmer-Etagenwohnung f, Ein-Schlafzimmer-Geschoßwohnung, Ein-Schlafzimmer-Stockwerkwohnung

~ living unit (US); ~ apartment ~, ~ flat · Ein-Schlafzimmer-Etagenwohnung f, Ein-Schlafzimmer-Geschoßwohnung, Ein-Schlafzimmer-Stockwerkwohnung

one-brick (masonry) wall · ein-Steinstarke Mauer f

one-centered arch (US); one-centred ~ (Brit.) · Ein-Zentrum-Bogen m

one-coat → single-coat

~ plaster(ed) ceiling → single-coat ~ ~

one-coat-work, lath-and-plaster [A coat of coarse stuff, 1/4 in. to 3/8 in. thick laid on the lathing and smoothed off with the trowel] · einlagiger Putz m auf Putzträgergewebe

one-component → one-part

~ adhesive → ~ bonding ~

~ (bonding) adhesive, single-component (~) ~, one-part (~) ~, one-pack (~) ~, singke-part (~) ~, single-pack (~) ~, ~ ~ agent, ~ ~ medium, ~ cement(ing agent) · Einkomponenten-Kleb(e)stoff m, Einkomponenten-Kleb(e)mittel n, Einkomponenten-Kleber m

~ cement → single-component ~

~ cement(ing agent) → ~ (bonding) adhesive

~ coating → one-part ~

~ etching primer, single-component ~ ~, one-part ~ ~, single-part ~ ~, one-pack ~ ~, single-pack ~ ~, wash ~, ~ pretreatment ~, ~ self etch ~ · Einkomponenten-Aktivgrund m, Einkomponenten-Haftgrund(ierung) m, (f), Einkomponenten-Haftgrund(ier)mittel n

~ plastic, single-component ~, one-part ~, single-part ~, one-pack ~, single-pack ~ · Einkomponenten-Kunststoff m

~ pretreatment primer → ~ etching ~

~ primer, one-part ~, single-component ~, one-pack ~, single-part ~, single-pack ~ · Einkomponenten-Grund(ierung) m, (f), Einkomponenten-Grundanstrichstoff m, Einkomponenten-Grundanstrichmittel n, Einkomponenten-Grundierstoff, Einkomponenten-Grundiermittel

~ self etch primer → ~ etching ~

~ system, one-part ~, single-component ~, single-part ~, single-pack ~, one-pack ~, one-pot ~, single-pot ~ · Einkomponentensystem n

~ wash primer → ~ etching ~

one-course → single-coat

one-dimensional · eindimensional

~ load transfer · einachsige Lastabtragung f

~ stress state, linear ~ ~, ~ state of stress · einachsiger Spannungszustand m, linearer ~

(one-)eighth (pipe) bend, 45° (~) ~ · (Rohr)Krümmer m 45°, 45°-(Rohr-)Krümmer, Achtel(rohr)krümmer

one-family dwelling → house

(~) home → house

~ unit → house

one-floor finger sytem → one-storey ~ ~ (Brit.)

~ house → single-story ~

~ warehouse (building) → single-story ~ (~)

one-hand block — one-piece plastic cable clip

one-hand block, ~ tile [*See remark under 'Block'*] · Einhandblock m, Einhand(block)stein m, Einhänder m

~ cavity block → ~ hollow ~

~ ~ tile → ~ hollow block

~ (clay) brick · E.H.Z. m, Einhandziegel m; Einhandstein m [*Fehlname*] [*Ein Mauerziegel, der beim Vermauern mit nur einer Hand gehandhabt werden kann*]

~ hollow block, ~ cavity ~, ~ ~ tile, ~ pot [*See remark under 'Block'*] · Einhandhohlblock(stein) m, Einhandhohlstein

~ ~ (clay) brick · Einhandhohlziegel m

~ ~ tile → ~ ~ block

~ pot → ~ hollow block

~ tile, ~ block [*See remark under 'Block'*] · Einhandblock m, Einhand(block)stein m, Einhänder m

one-hinge(d) arch(ed girder), one-pin(ned) ~ (~), single-hinged ~ (~), single-pin(ned) ~ (~) · Eingelenkbogen(träger) m, gekrümmter Eingelenkträger

~ frame, one-pin(ned) ~, single-hinged ~, single-pin(ned) ~ · Eingelenkrahmen m

~ parabolic arch(ed girder), one-pin(ned) ~ ~ (~), single-hinged ~ ~ (~), single-pin(ned) ~ ~ (~) · Eingelenkparabelbogen(träger) m, gekrümmter Eingelenkparabelträger

100 % relative humidity, dew point, saturation point, condensation temperature · Kondensationstemperatur f, Taupunkt m

one-layer(ed) → single-coat

~ monolithic masonry wall → monolithic single-layer(ed) ~ ~

one-leaf, single-leaf, monolithic [*wall*] · einschalig [*Wand*]

~ door, single-leaf ~ · einflügelige Tür f, Einflügeltür

~ room door, single-leaf ~ ~ · einflügelige Zimmertür f, Einflügel-Zimmertür

~ shutterdoor, single-leaf ~, ~ shutter door · einflügeliges Tor n

~ sliding shutter door, single-leaf ~ ~ ~, ~ ~ shutterdoor · einflügeliges Schiebetor n

~ wall, single leaf ~, one-wythe ~, single-wythe ~, one-withe ~, single-withe ~ (Brit.); one-tier ~, single-tier ~ (US) · Einfachwand f, einschalige Wand

one-level (building operational) system · Einebenensystem n [*Passagier- und Gepäckabfertigung auf Flughäfen*]

~ garage, single-level ~ · Flachgarage f

~ operation · Einebenenbetrieb m [*Flughafen*]

one-light steel window · einscheibiges Stahlfenster n

one-off design [*This term is used with reference to architectural designs for special purposes. For example, a design for a prestige building such as the British Petroleum Building in Moorfield, London. Other examples of one-off designs are concert halls, theatres, and so on, in fact any building built with specific purposes, to an original design which is not used for any other building*] · Sonderentwurf m, Spezialentwurf

one-pack → one-part

~ (bonding) adhesive → one-component (~) ~

~ cement → single-component ~

~ cement(ing agent) → one-component (bonding) adhesive

~ coating → one-part ~

~ etching primer → one-component ~ ~

~ plastic → one-component ~

~ pretreatment primer → one-component etching ~

~ primer → one-component ~

~ self etch primer → one-component etching ~

~ system → one-component ~

~ wash primer → one-component etching ~

one-part, one-component, one-pack, single-part, single-component, single-pack · einkomponentig, 1-komponentig

~ (bonding) adhesive → one-component (~) ~

~ cement → single-component ~

~ cement(ing agent) → one-component (bonding) adhesive

~ coating, one-component ~, single-part ~, single-component ~, single-pack ~, one-pack ~ · Einkomponenten-Flüssigkunststoff m

~ etching primer → one-component ~ ~

~ plastic → one-component ~

~ pretreatment primer → one-component etching ~

~ primer → one-component ~

~ self etch primer → one-component etching ~

~ system → one-component ~

~ up and over door · Schwingtor n mit einteiligem Torblatt, Kipptor ~ ~ ~, einteiliges Schwingtor, einteiliges Kipptor

~ wash primer → one-component etching ~

one-piece, single-piece · einteilig

~ aerated concrete panel, single-piece ~ ~ ~ · einteilige Porenbetontafel f

~ casting, single-piece ~ · einteiliges Gußstück n

~ panel, single-piece ~ · einteilige Tafel f

~ plastic cable clip, single-piece ~ ~ ~ · einteilige Kunststoffkabelschelle f

one-pin(ned) arch(ed girder) → one-hinge(d) ~ (~)

~ frame, one-hinge(d) ~, single-hinged ~, single-pin(ned) ~ · Eingelenkrahmen *m*

~ parabolic arch(ed girder) → one-hinge(d) ~ ~ (~)

one-pipe · Einrohr *n* [*Zentralheizung*]

~ drop system [*The hot water is taken up in one riser and distributed at high level to a number of drops, each serving a series of radiators*] · Einrohrheizung *f* mit senkrechten Fallrohrsträngen, Einrohrsystem *n* mit oberer Verteilung

~ forced heating, forced one-pipe ~ · Einrohr-Pumpenheizung *f*, Pumpen-Einrohrheizung

~ gravity(-type) heating, gravity(-type) one-pipe ~ · Einrohr-Schwerkraftheizung *f*, Schwerkraft-Einrohrheizung

~ (heating) system, single pipe (~) ~ · Einrohrheizung *f*, Einrohrsystem *n*, Niederdruck Warmwasserheizung(ssy - stem), Ein-Rohr-Heiz(ungs)system

~ hot water heating · Einrohr-Heißwasserheizung *f*

~ meter, single pipe ~ · Einrohrzähler *m*

~ plumbing, single stack ~ · Einrohrgrundstücksentwässerung *f*

~ ring system · Einrohr-Ringsystem *n*, waag(e)rechte Einrohrheizung *f* [*Ein Heizsystem mit getrennt in Fußbodennähe in jedem Stockwerk verlegtem waag(e)rechten Verteilrohr, das gleichzeitig auch Rücklaufrohr ist*]

~ system → ~ heating ~

~ ~ [*This term is somewhat misleading in that this system has two pipes. All soil and waste discharges into one common pipe and all branch ventilating pipes into one main ventilating pipe*] · Zwei-Rohr-Sanitäranlage *f*

one-pot system → one component ~

one-quarter brick (masonry) bond · Viertelziegelverband *m*, (Ein)Quartierverband, Riemchenverband, Quartierstückverband, Vierstelstückverband [*Fehlname: Viertelsteinverband*]

~ circle, quarter-circle, quadrant · Viertelkreis *m*

~ (clay) brick · Viertelziegel *m*, (Ein-)Quartier *m*, Riemchen *n*, Quartierstück *n*, Viertelstück; Viertelstein *m* [*Fehlname*]

(one-)quarter (pipe) bend, 90° (~) ~ · 90°-(Rohr)Krümmer *m*

one-room dwelling unit (US); ~ dwelling (Brit.) · Ein-Raum-Wohnung *f*, Ein-Zimmer-Wohnung

one-room(ed) apartment (unit), ~ flat, flatlet · Ein-Raum-Etagenwohnung *f*, Ein-Raum-Geschoßwohnung, Ein-Raum-Stockwerkwohnung, Ein-Zimmer-Stockwerkwohnung, Ein-Zimmer-Geschoßwohnung, Ein-Zimmer-Etagenwohnung

~ dwelling unit (US); ~ dwelling (Brit.) · Ein-Raum-Wohnung *f*, Ein-Zimmer-Wohnung

~ flat, single-room(ed) ~, ~ apartment (unit), flatlet · Ein-Raum-Etagenwohnung *f*, Ein-Raum-Geschoßwohnung, Ein-Raum-Stockwerkwohnung, Ein-Zimmer-Stockwerkwohnung, Ein-Zimmer-Geschoßwohnung, Ein-Zimmer-Etagenwohnung

one-row brick-on-edge arch, single-row ~ ~ · Einzelbogen *m*, Rollbogen [*Ziegelbogen*]

one-sash(ed) window, single-sash(ed) ~ [*See remark under 'Flügel'*] · einflügeliges Fenster *n*, Einflügelfenster

one-side formwork, ~ shuttering, ~ forms · einhäuptige Schalung *f* [*Das stehende Erdreich ersetzt eine Seitenschalung der Wand*]

one-sided core, side ~ · seitlicher Kern *m*

one-sixteenth bend · 22½-(Rohr)Krümmer *m*

one-span, one-bay, single-span, single-bay · einschiffig [*Rahmenhalle*]

~ beam → single-span ~

~ frame → simple ~

~ girder, single-span ~, single-bay ~, one-bay ~, girder of one bay, girder of one span · Einfeldträger *m*

~ slab → single-span ~

~ two-hinged frame → single-span ~ ~

one spray coat application, single ~ ~ ~ · Einschicht-Spritzauftrag *m*

one-stack plumbing single-stack ~ · Ein-Rohr-Grundstücksentwässerung *f*

one-storey finger system, single-storey ~ ~ (Brit.); one-story ~ ~, single-story ~ ~ (US); one-floor ~ ~ · Ein-ebenenfingersystem *n* [*Flughafen*]

~ warehouse (building) (Brit.) → single-story ~ (~)

one-story house (US) → single-story ~

one-third (masonry) bond [*The vertical joints occur at the third points of the units above and below*] · schleppender Mauerverband *m*, ~ (Mauerwerk)Verband, schleppendes Mauergefüge *n*, schleppendes (Mauerwerk)Gefüge [*DIN 18151. Die Stoßfugen sind um ⅓ Steinlänge gegeneinander versetzt*]

one-tier wall (US) → one-leaf ~

one-way arch · Eintoranlage *f*, eintoriger (Straßen)Bogen *m*

~ cable duct, single-way ~ ~, ~ conduit, ~ ~ subway, ~ CD; ~ conduit tile (US) · einzügiger Kabel(kanal)formstein *m*, einzügiges Kabel(kanal)formstück *n*

~ floor(ing) (structural) system, ~ ~ construction, ~ ~ ~ system · Deckenkonstruktion(ssytem) *f*, (*n*) mit einfacher Armierung, ~ ~ ~ Bewehrung, ~ ~ einfachen (Stahl)Einlagen

~ **reinforced** · einfach armiert, ~ bewehrt, einachsig ~, mit einfachen (Stahl)Einlagen [*Gegenteil: kreuzbewehrt*]

~ ~ **plate,** ~ ~ slab · einachsig bewehrte Platte f, ~ armierte ~, einfach ~ ~, Platte mit einfachen (Stahl)Einlagen

~ **solid slab floor** · Plattendecke f mit Hauptbewehrung in (nur) einer Richtung, Voll(beton)decke ~ ~ ~ (~) ~ ~, ~ ~ Hauptarmierung ~ (~) ~ ~, ~ ~ Haupt(stahl)einlagen ~ (~) ~ ~

one-window one-piece panel, single-window ~ ~, ~ single-piece ~ · einteilige Ein-Fenstertafel f

~ **panel,** single-window ~ · Ein-Fenstertafel f

one-wing(ed) block → single-wing(ed) building

~ **building** → single-wing(ed) ~

one-withe wall → one-leaf ~

one-wythe wall → one-leaf ~

onion helm [*See remark under 'Turmhelm'*] · Zwiebelhelm m

~ **tower** · Zwiebelturm m [*Turm mit Zwiebeldach*]

onset of foaming · Schäumungsbeginn m

(on-)site handling · Transport m auf der Baustelle, ~ vor Ort

~ **prefabrication** [*Fabrication on the site, before incorporation into a structure*] · Vorfertigung f auf der Baustelle, Baustellen-Vorfertigung

~ **(pre)stressing,** job-site ~, ~ stretching, ~ tensioning · An-Ort-Vorspannen n, Vorspannen auf der Baustelle

~ **tiling** · Verfliesen n auf der Baustelle, An-Ort-Verfliesen

on-stream desludging of cooling systems · Reinigung f von Kühlanlagen während des Betriebs

on-the-job mixing, site ~ · Mischen n auf der Baustelle

onyx marble, Mexican onyx, (calcareous) alabaster [*A carbonate of lime*] · Kalkalabaster m, Kalkonyx m, Onyx(marmor) m

oolite (US) → oolitic limestone

oolith [*An ellipsoidal or spherical body, commonly less than 1 mm in diameter, and composed of concentric layers of calcite, aragonite or iron carbonate; typical of oolithic limestone*] · Kügelchen n

oolitic limestone, roestone; oolite (US) · Rogen(kalk)stein m, Bernburger Grauwacke f, oolitischer Kalk(stein) m, Oolith-(en)kalk(stein). Eisteinkalk, Kalkoolith m [*Aus Kalkspatkügelchen zusammengesetzt, die durch kalkiges Bindemittel verkittet sind. Farbe weiß, gelblich, grau, rötlich. Durch Herauswittern der Kügelchen aus dem Verband entsteht der Schaumkalk*]

~ **sand** · Oolith(en)sand m

O.P. patenting, old process ~, air ~ · Luftpatentieren n

opacifier [*A mineral or chemical compound used in the batch to produce opal glass*] · Trübungsmittel n

opacity → hiding power

opaion, eye · Opäum n, (Kuppel)Auge n, Nabel m, Opaion, Opaeum, Rauchloch n, Laternenöffnung f, Scheitelöffnung [*Kreisrunde Lichtöffnung im Scheite einer Kuppel*]

opal [*An amorphous form of hydrated silica*] · Opal m

~ **glass** [*Glass which is white or colo(u)red and varies from translucent to completely opaque. If it is completely opaque it is called 'Opakglas' in German*] · Opalglas n

opalescence · Opaleszenz f, Opalschiller m

opalescent glass · Opaleszenzglas n [*Gegossenes oder geblasenes Zierglas, nicht klar durchsichtig und mit einer etwas unebenen Oberfläche, ähnlich wie Kathedralglas*]

opaline glass · Opalinglas n

opaque · opak, nur durchschimmernd, undurchsichtig

~ **coat** · Deckanstrich m, Deckaufstrich, deckender Anstrich, deckender Aufstrich

~ **colour** (Brit.); ~ color (US) · deckende Farbe f, Deckfarbe

~ **glass** · opakes Glas n, Opakglas

~ **glaze,** enamel (~), ~ glazing, ~ glazed coat(ing) · Email-(glasur) n, (f), Emaille f, opake Glasur, Emailbeglasung f, opake Beglasung

~ ~ **made with oxid(e) of tin** · Zinnglasur f

~ **glazed coat(ing)** → ~ glaze

~ ~ **finish** → ~ glaze

~ **glazing** → ~ glaze

~ **paint** · Deck(anstrich)farbe f

OPC, ordinary portland cement, normal portland cement, Portland cement for general use; Portland cement type I (US) · normaler Portlandzement m, gewöhnlicher ~ [*in Deutschland Z 225*]

O.P.D., out-patients' department · Ambulanz f [*Krankenhaus*]

open, unroofed, uncovered · offen, nicht überdacht

openable burning appliance, ~ fire, ~ furnace · geschlossene Feuerstätte f, ~ Feuerung f [*Siehe Anmerkung unter „Feuerstätte"*]

~ **fire,** ~ furnace, ~ burning appliance · geschlossene Feuerstätte f, ~ Feuerung f [*Siehe Anmerkung unter „Feuerstätte"*]

~ **furnace,** ~ fire, ~ burning appliance · geschlossene Feuerstätte f, ~ Feuerung f [*Siehe Anmerkung unter „Feuerstätte"*]

open-air basilica → ~ type ~

~ **bath,** outdoor ~ · Freibad n

~ **cinema,** outdoor ~ · Freilichtkino n

open-air clinker stor(age) area — open layout

~ **clinker stor(age) area, outdoor** ~ ~ ~ · Klinkerfreilager *n*

~ **corridors,** permanent hack, drying shed · Freiluftschuppen *m* [*Ziegelindustrie*]

~ **facility** → outdoor ~

~ **hydrant** dutdoor ~ · Außenhydrant *m*

~ **installation** → outdoor facility

~ **museum, outdoor** ~ · Freilichtmuseum *n*, Freiluftmuseum

~ **pool, outdoor** ~ · Freiluft(-Schwimm)- becken *n*

~ **school, outdoor** ~ · Freiluftschule *f*

~ **space, outdoor** ~ · Außenraum *m* [*Der Raum um Gebäude oder ein Gebäude herum*]

~ **sports facility, outdoor** ~ ~ · Freiluftsportanlage *f*, Außensportanlage

~ **stage, outdoor** ~ · Freilichtbühne *f*

~ **storage, outdoor** ~ · Außenlagerung *f*, Freilagerung

~ ~ **area, outdoor** ~ ~ · Freilagerfläche *f*, Außenlagerfläche

~ ~ **yard, outdoor** ~ ~ · Freilagerplatz *m*, Außenlagerplatz

~ **structure** · Freiluftbauwerk *n*

~ **swimming pool, outdoor** ~ ~ · Außenschwimmbecken *n*

~ ~ ~, **outdoor** ~ ~ · Freischwimmbad *n*

~ **terrace, outdoor** ~ · Freiterrasse *f*

~ **theatre, outdoor** ~ · Freilichttheater *n*, Freilichtbühne *f*

~ **track, outdoor** ~ · Freiluftbahn *f* [*Leichtathletik*]

~ **(type) basilica,** Hellenistic ~ · hellenistische Basilika *f*

~ **weathering, outdoor** ~ · Freibewitterung *f*

open apron system · System *n* des offenen Vorfeldes [*Flughafen*]

~ **(arch) spandrel** · offener (Bogen-)Zwickel *m*

~ **(architectural) form** · offene Form *f*

~ **area** · Freifläche *f* [*Eine Fläche, die von Verkehr und Bebauung frei bleibt, sie kann begrünt oder befestigt werden*]

~ **building block module with longitudinal subdivisions** · längsaufgeteilte offene Raumzelle *f*, längsoffene ~

~ ~ ~ ~ ~ **transverse subdivisions** · queraufgeteilte offene Raumzelle *f*, queroffene ~

~ **channel** · Halbschale *f* [*zur Entwässerung*]

~ **column** · offene Stütze *f*

~ **court of a quadrangle,** paradise, garth [*A square yard enclosed by principal monastic buildings*] · Ambitushof *m*, Rechteckhof, Kreuzganghof

~ **cusp,** soffit ~ · Schlußring *m*, Steinkranz *m* [*Gewölbe*]

open-deck car park, ~ garage, open-sided multi-store()y car park, open-sided multi-stor(e)y garage · offenes Parkgebäude *n*, ~ Parkhaus

~ **garage,** ~ car park, open-sided multi-stor(e)y car park, open-sided multi-stor(e)y garage · offenes Parkgebäude *n*, ~ Parkhaus *n*

open development · offene Bebauung *f*

open-end(ed) hangar, ~ shed · Durchgangshalle *f*, Halle in Durchgangsform

~ **shed,** ~ hangar · Durchgangshalle *f*, Halle in Durchgangsform

open fire, ~ (burning) appliance, ~ furnace · offene Feuerstätte *f*, ~ Feuerung *f*

~ **floor** [*A floor, in which the joists are exposed beneath, since it is not ceiled*] · Decke *f* mit sichtbaren Unterzügen

~ ~ ; ~ **story (US)** ; ~ **storey (Brit.)** · Freietage *f*, Freigeschoß *n*, Freistockwerk *n*

~ **form** → ~ architectural ~

open-frame girder, ~ truss, Vierendeel ~, open-web ~ [*It does not satisfy the definition of a truss but is given that designation*] · Vierendeelträger *m*

open-fronted tomb · Felsenfassade [*Von Beni-Hassan in Mittelägypten*]

open furnace, ~ fire, ~ (burning) appliance · offene Feuerstätte *f*, ~ Feuerung *f*

~ **gradation** · offene Kornabstufung *f*, ~ Granulometrie *f*

open-graded · offen (abgestuft)

~ **(mineral) aggregate,** OGA · offen abgestuftes Mineralgemisch *n*

open(-)grained steel, coarse(-grained) ~ · Grobkornstahl *m*

open-hearth steel · Siemens-Martin-stahl *m*

opening [*abbreviated: opg.*] · Öffnung *f*

~, **aperture, window** ~, **day, light** · Fensteröffnung *f*, Fensterlicht *n*, Fensterloch *n*

~ **exhibition, inaugural** ~ · Einweihungsausstellung *f*

~ **height** · Öffnungshöhe *f* [*Tor*]

~ **movement** · Öffnungsbewegung *f*

~ **position** · Öffnungsstellung *f*

~ **temperature, releasing** ~ · Auslösetemperatur *f* [*Sprinkler*]

~ **width** · Öffnungsbreite *f*

open joint, keyed ~ · Hohlfuge *f*, offene Fuge [*Unausgefüllter Zwischenraum zweier zusammenstoßender fester Bauteile oder Baustoffe, z.B. bei Trockenmauerwerk*]

~ **landscaped office space,** ~ plan office, office landscape · Bürolandschaft *f*, Großraumbüro *n*

~ **layout** · lockere Anlage *f*

open light — optimum solution

~ **light**, ~ window [*A window which can be opened and closed, as opposed to a 'dead light'*] · bewegliches Fenster *n*

open-newel (post) · offene (Treppen-) Spindel *f*

(open) peristyle court, garden ~ · Peristylhof *m* [*Von einem Peristyl umgebener Hof*]

~ **plan office**, ~ landscaped office space, office landscape · Bürolandschaft *f*, Großraumbüro *n*

open-pored · offenporig

open position · Offenstellung *f*

~ **roof** [*A roof in which the principals are on view. No ceiling*] · offenes Dach *n*

~ **shed** · offener Schuppen *m*

open-sided block → ~ building

~ **building**, ~ block, ~ house · Gebäude *n* ohne Umfassungswände, Haus *n* ~ ~

~ **house** → ~ building

~ **multi-stor(e)y car park**, ~ ~ garage, open-deck car park, open-deck garage · offenes Parkgebäude *n*, ~ Parkhaus *n*

~ ~ **garage**, ~ ~ car park, open-deck car park, open-deck garage · offenes Parkgebäude *n*, ~ Parkhaus

open soffit [*As opposed to the flush soffit*] · unterbrochene Untersicht *f*

~ **space** · Freiraum *m*

~ **spandrel**, ~ arch ~ · offener (Bogen-) Zwickel *m*

~ **stalk**, ~ web · offener (Träger)Steg *m*, durchbrochener ~

~ **steel floor(ing)** · Stahlrost(fuß)boden *m*

~ **storey** (Brit.) → ~ floor

~ **string**, cut ~, stepped ~; ~ stringer (US) [*An outer string which is cut to the profile of the steps*] · Sattelwange *f*

open(-string) stair(case), cut-string ~, bridge board ~; open-stringer ~, cut-stringer ~ (US) · aufgesattelte Treppe *f*, aufgesetzte ~

open stringer, cut ~ (US); ~ string (Brit.) [*An outer string(er) which is cut to the profile of the steps*] · Sattelwange *f*

open-topped vessel · deckelloses Gefäß *n*, Gefäß ohne Deckel

(open) trellis bond, pierced ~, honeycomb(ed) ~, pigeon-hole(d) ~ · Kästelverband *m*

(~) ~ **(masonry) wall** → honeycomb(ed) (~) ~

(~) ~ ~ **(work)**, pierced ~ (~), honeycomb(ed) ~ (~), pigeon-hole(d) ~ (~) · durchbrochenes Mauerwerk *n*, Kästelmauerwerk

(~) ~ **wall** → honeycomb(ed) (masonry) ~

~ **valley** · offene Kehle *f*

~ **web**, ~ stalk · offener (Träger)Steg *m*, durchbrochener ~

open-web girder, open-frame ~, Vierendeel ~, ~ truss [*It does not satisfy the definition of a truss but is given that designation*] · Vierendeelträger *m*

open window → ~ light

~ **wiring** [*Electrical wiring held on porcelain insulators away from the wall*] · Überputzverdrahtung *f*

~ **wood shed** · Holzschopf *m* [*Schuppen ohne Umfassungswände*]

openwork · Durchbruch *m*

~ **gable** · durchbrochener Giebel *m*

~ **gablet** · Wimperg *m*, Wimberg [*Giebelartiger offener Überbau von gotischen Portalen und Fenstern, oft mit Maßwerk geschmückt*]

~ **rosette** · durchbrochene Rosette *f*

~ **spire**, lace-like ~ · durchbrochenes Zeltdach *n*, durchbrochener Turmhelm *m* [*Fehlname: durchbrochene Pyramide f*]

~ **tracery** · durchbrochenes Maßwerk *n*

operable window · bedienbares Fenster *n* [*Es läßt sich öffnen und schließen im Gegensatz zum festen Fenster*]

operating lever · Bedienungshebel *m*

~ **pressure** · Betriebsdruck *m*

~ **scheme** · Betriebsschema *n*

~ **theatre** operation ~ · Operationssaal *m* [*Krankenhaus*]

operation theatre, operating ~ · Operationssaal *m* [*Krankenhaus*]

operational research program(me) · Betriebsforschungsprogramm *n*

operations research · Unternehmensforschung *f*

operator [*Any person who has charge, care or control of a structure or premises which are let or offered for occupancy*] · Vermieter *m*

~ · Betreiber *m*

~ · Antrieb(vorrichtung) *m*, (*f*)

~ , analyst · Versuchslaborant *m*

operatorless · bedienerlos

opg. [*abbreviated*]; **opening** · Öffnung *f*

opisthodomos, rear portico [*The enclosed section of the rear of a Greek temple, sometimes used as a treasury*] · Opisthodomos *m*, Hinterraum *m*, Rückhalle *f*

opposite folding · gegenläufige Faltung *f*

~ **side** · Gegenseite *f*

~ **sign** · umgekehrtes Vorzeichen *n*

optical plumbing, instrument ~ · optisches Loten *n*, optische Lotung *f*

~ **plummet** · optisches Lot *n*

~ **pyrometer** · Teilstrahlungspyrometer *m*

optimizing method · Optimierungsverfahren *n*

optimum solution · Bestlösung *f*

optimum strength — organ-shaped façade

~ **strength** · optimale Festigkeit f

opulent Renaissance · reiche Renaissance f

opus · Opus n [*Sammelbezeichnung für die Arbeitstechniken der römischen Antike auf den Gebieten Mauerwerk, Mauerverband, Verputz, Verkleidung und (Fuß)Boden(belag)*]

~ **alexandrinum**, Alexandrinum work · Opus n Alexandrinum [*Ornamentales Fußbodenmosaik aus farbigen zu geometrischen Mustern geordneten Marmorsteinen, besonders in Verbindung von Mosaik und Opus sectile*]

~ **antiquum** → ~ incertum

~ **emplectum** · Füllmauerwerk n [*römische Antike*]

~ **figuratum** · figurierter Verband m

~ **incertum**, ~ antiquum, incertum opus · Bruchsteinbau m [*Römisches Mauerwerk aus unregelmäßigen Bruchsteinen mit Mörtelguß*]

~ **isodomum of granite blocks**, isodomus ~ ~ ~ · Granitquadermauerwerk n

~ **mixtum** · Opus n listatum, ~ mixtum [*Römisches Mauerwerk, bei welchem Schichten kleiner Natursteinblöcke mit Ziegelsteinen wechseln*]

~ **quadratum** · Opus n quadratum [*Römisches Quadermauerwerk*]

~ **reticulatum**, reticulated (masonry) work, reticulated masonry · Netz(mauer)werk n

~ **rusticum** → rustic(ated) ashlar

~ **sectile**, Roman mosaic · Plattenmosaik n

~ **spicatum** · Ähren(mauer)werk n, Fischgräten(mauer)werk [*Mauerwerk, bei dem die Steine ein Ähren- oder Fischgrätmuster bilden*]

~ **tesselatum**, tesselated pavement, Roman mosaic · (Fußboden)Würfelmosaik n

oracle sanctuary, oracular ~ · Orakelheiligtum n, Orakelstätte f

~ **temple**, oracular ~ · Orakeltempel m

oracular sanctuary, oracle ~ · Orakelheiligtum n, Orakelstätte f

~ **temple**, oracle ~ · Orakeltempel m

oral cupola, ~ dome · Oralkuppel f

~ **dome**, ~ cupola · Oralkuppel f

orange alizarin(e) lake · Alizarinorange f

~ **chrome yellow** · Chromorange(pigment) f, (n)

~ **lead** [*This has the same formula, Pb_3O_4, as red lead, but is normally freer from load monoxide*] · orangegefärbte Bleimennige f

~ **peel(ing)**, ~ peel effect, pebbling, pock-marking [*The pock-marked appearance, in particular of a sprayed film, resembling the skin of an orange due to the failure of the film to flow out to a level surface*] · Orangenschaleneffekt m, Apfelsinenschaleneffekt

orange-red sienna, burned ~, burnt ~ gebrannte (Terra f di) Siena, (Terra di) Siena gebrannt

orange shellac · Orangeschellack m

orangery [*A building having large windows on the south side, used in northern climates for growing oranges*] · Orangerie f

oratory · Betkapelle f

~ · Oratorium n [*Loge für hochgestellte Persönlichkeiten in einer mittelalterlichen Kirche*]

~ · Betchor m

Oratory of Gallerus · Betkammer f des hl. Gallarus auf der Halbinsel Dingle

orchestra · Orchestra f [*Der kreisförmige Tanzplatz im Zentrum eines griechischen Theaters*]

~ **floor** · Orchesterstand m

~ **pit** · Orchestergraben m

order → ~ of architecture

~ **drawing** · Bestellzeichnung f

~ **letting**, contract ~, letting of the contract, letting of the order · Auftragerteilung f, Vergabe f

~ **(of architecture)**, architectural order [*A column together with its entablature, which is the beam and other horizontal members resting upon it*] · (Säulen)Ordnung f, Bauordnung f

~ ~ **knighthood** · Ritterorden m

orderly effect of symmetry · ordnende Wirkung f der Symmetrie

ordinary cement, normal ~ · Normalzement m [*Zement von der Güteklasse Z 225. Gegensatz: Hoch- und höherwertiger Zement*]

~ **forms**, fixed ~, ~ form(work), ~ shuttering · Standschalung f

~ **form(work)**, fixed ~, ~ forms, ~ shuttering · Standschalung f

~ **portland cement**, normal ~ ~, Portland cement for general use, OPC; Portland cement type I (US) · normaler Portlandzement m, gewöhnlicher ~ [*in Deutschland Z 225*]

~ **rubble masonry**, rough ~ ~ [*Masonry composed of unsquared or field stones laid without regularity of coursing*] · Feldsteinmauerwerk n

~ **shuttering**, fixed ~, ~ form(work), ~ forms · Standschalung f

~ **steel (reinforcing)**, mild ~ (~), untensioned ~ ~, ~ ~ (reinforcement) · schlaffe Armierung f, ~ Bewehrung, ~ (Stahl)Einlagen fpl

ordinary-strength steel · Normalstahl m

organ front · Orgelprospekt m, Orgelschauseite f

~ **gallery**, ~ loft · Orgelbühne f, Orgelempore f, Orgelchor m

~ **loft**, ~ gallery · Orgelbühne f, Orgelempore f, Orgelchor m

organ-shaped façade · orgelförmige Fassade f

organic acid — ornamental architecture

organic acid · organische Säure f

~ **adhesive** [*An adhesive for fixing of ceramic tiles in which the principal bonding component is an organic material. The term includes only those organic adhesives capable of application by the thin-bed fixing technique, and is limited to materials supplied ready for use and not requiring the addition of water or any other substance*] · organischer Kleber m

~ ~ **method** · Dünnbettverfahren n mit organischem Kleber, Kleb(e)verfahren ~ ~ ~ [*Ansetzen von Fliesen*]

~ **aggregate**, ~ concrete ~ · pflanzlicher (Leichtbeton)Zuschlag(stoff) m, organischer ~ [*z.B. Holzspäne*]

~ **architecture** [*It is based on the theory that architecture should, in its appearance, have a character similar to a natural organism and give the same impression of unity*] · organische Architektur f, ~ Baukunst f

~ **building** [*Based on the principle that the shape or form of a building should be derived form its function*] · organhaftes Bauen n

~ **chemical** · organische Chemikalie

~ **chemistry** · organische Chemie f

~ **compound**, ~ system · organische Verbindung f

~ **(concrete) aggregate** · pflanzlicher (Leichtbeton)Zuschlag(stoff) m, organischer ~ [*z.B. Holzspäne*]

~ **dust** · organischer Staub m

~ **dyestuff** · organischer Farbstoff m

~ **fiber** (US); ~ **fibre** (Brit.) · organische Faser f

~ **filler** · organischer Füllstoff m, ~ Füller m

~ **form of nature** · organische Naturform f

~ **heat insulating material**, ~ ~ insulation(-grade) ~, ~ ~ insulator, ~ ~ insulant · organischer Wärmedämmstoff m, organisches Wärmedämmaterial n

~ **impurity** · organische Verunreinigung f

~ ~, ~ matter, ~ substance · organische Beimengung f, ausglühbarer Bestandteil m [*(Beton)Zuschlag(stoff)*]

~ **insulation(-grade) material** ~ insulating ~, ~ insulator, ~ insulant · organischer Dämmstoff m, organisches Dämmaterial n

~ **matter**, ~ impurity, ~ substance · organische Beimengung f, ausglühbarer Bestandteil m [*(Beton)Zuschlag(stoff)*]

~ **oil** · organisches Öl n

~ **pigment** [*B.S. 3599*] · organisches Pigment n [*Fehlnamen: organischer Farbkörper m, organische Körperfarbe*]

~ **solvent** · organisches Lösungsmittel n

~ **substance**, ~ matter, ~ impurity · organische Beimengung f, ausglühbarer Bestandteil m [*(Beton)Zuschlag(stoff)*]

~ **synthetic pigment**, synthetic organic ~ · künstliches organisches Pigment n, organisches künstliches ~

~ **system**, ~ compound · organische Verbindung f

~ **test for fine aggregate** → Abrams' test

~ **theory of architecture** · organische Architekturtheorie f

organosol [*A dispersion of finely divided resin particles in an organic liquid which may be wholly or partly volatile. After application the coating is heated and the resin particles with any non-volatile portions of the carrier are fused to a continuous film*] · Organosol n

organzine, thrown-silk · Organsin n

oriel · (Obergeschoß)Erker m [*Früher: Ausgebäude n. Vor die Fassade vorspringender Ausbau in den Obergeschossen als Erweiterung des anschließenden Raumes*]

~ **window** [*A bay window or bow window not rising from the ground, and generally supported on brackets*] · (Obergeschoß)Erkerfenster n

~ **with window** · (Obergeschoß)Fenstererker m

oriental cupola, ~ dome · orientalische Kuppel f

~ **dome**, ~ cupola · orientalische Kuppel f

orientation · Himmelslage f, Orientierung f [*Bauwerk*]

~ · Orientierung f, Ostung [*Ausrichtung der Bauachse einer Kirche nach Osten*]

original bedding · ursprüngliche Schichtung f [*Tonschiefer*]

~ **sample weight** · Einwaage f

~ **strength** · Ursprungsfestigkeit f

O-ring, rubber ~ · Vollgummiring m [*Rohrverbindung*]

ormolu · Malergold n

ornament → pattern

~, decorative fixture, enrichment · Ornament n, Zierelement n, Zierglied n, Dekor(ations)element, Dekor(ations)glied, Schmuckglied, Schmuckelement, Verzierung f

ornamental acoustical gypsum waffle slab, ~ ~ ~ pan(el) n, ~ ~ ~ ~ cassette ~, ~ ~ ~ caisson ~, ~ ~ ~ ~ coffer(ed) ~, decorative ~ ~ ~ ~ · Dekor-Akustik-Gipskassettenplatte f

~ **aggregate**, decorative ~ · Dekor(ations)zuschlag(stoff) m, Zierzuschlag(stoff)

~ **aluminium**, decorative ~ (Brit.); ~ aluminum (US) · Dekor(ations)aluminium n, Ornamentaluminium, Zieraluminium, Schmuckaluminium

~ **arch**, decorative ~ · Dekor(ations)bogen m, Zierbogen, Ornamentbogen, Schmuckbogen

~ **architecture**, florid ~, decorative ~ · Dekor(ations)architektur f, Ornament-

ornamental architecture — ornamental glass block

architektur, Zierarchitektur, Schmuckarchitektur, Dekor(ations)baukunst f, Ornamentbaukunst, Zierbaukunst, Schmuckbaukunst

~ **archivolt**, decorative ~, decorated ~ · ornamentierte Archivolte f, dekorierte ~

~ **area**, decorative ~, decorated ~ · Ornamentfläche f, Schmuckfläche, Zierfläche, Dekor(ations)fläche

~ **art**, decoration ~, decorating ~, decorative ~ · Ornamentik f, Zierkunst f, Ornamentkunst, dekorative Kunst

~ **artificial stone** → decorative reconstructed ~

~ **band** → band crnament(al feature)

~ **barrel vault**, ~ tunnel ~, ~ wagon ~ · dekorative Tonne f, dekoratives Tonnengewölbe n

~ **board**, decorative ~, ~ sheet · Ornamentplatte f, Zierplatte, Dekor(ations)platte, (dekorative) Sichtplatte, Schmuckplatte

~ **bond** → ~ masonry ~

~ **bracket** → ~ wall ~

~ **brick**, decorative ~ · Dekor(ations)ziegel m, Zierziegel, Ornamentziegel, Schmuckziegel

~ ~ **masonry (work)** (US) → decorative (pattern) brickwork

~ **brickwork** → decorative (pattern) ~

~ **bronze** · Dekor(ations)bronze f, Zierbronze, Ornamentbronze, Schmuckbronze

~ **(building) unit**, decorative (~) ~ · Dekor(ations)(bau)element n, Dekor(ations)(bau)körper m

~ **capacity** → decorative property

~ **cast block** → decorative (pre)cast (concrete) ~

~ ~ **(concrete) block** → decorative (pre)cast (~) ~

~ ~ **(~) product** → decorative (pre-)cast (~) ~

~ ~ **(~) tile** → decorative (pre)cast (concrete) block

~ ~ **product** → decorative (pre)cast (concrete) ~

~ ~ **stone** → decorative reconstructed ~

~ ~ **tile** → decorative (pre)cast (concrete) block

~ **ceiling**, decorative ~, decorating ~ · Dekor(ations)decke f, Zierdecke, Ornamentdecke, Schmuckdecke

~ ~ **board**, ~ ~ sheet, decorative ~ ~ · Ornamentdeckenplatte f, Zierdeckenplatte, Deckenzierplatte, Dekor(ations)deckenplatte, Dekorativdeckenplatte, Schmuckdeckenplatte

~ **coat(ing)**, decorative ~, ~ finish · Ornamentbeschichtung f, Ornamentüberzug m, Dekor(ations)beschichtung, Dekor(ations)überzug, Zierbeschichtung, Zierüberzug, Schmucküberzug [als Schicht]

~ **(cold-)water paint**, ~ water-carried ~, decorative ~ ~ · Schmuck-Binderfarbe f, Schmuck-Dispersionsfarbe

~ **column**, decorative ~ · Dekor(ations)stütze f, Zierstütze, Ornamentstütze, Schmuckstütze

~ **concrete**, decorative ~ · Dekor(ations)beton m, Zierbeton, Ornamentbeton, Schmuckbeton

~ ~ **product** → decorative (pre)cast (~) ~

~ ~ **tile**, decorative ~ ~ · Zier-Beton(belag)platte f, Zier-Betonfliese f, Dekor(ations)beton(belag)platte, Dekor(ations)betonfliese, Ornament-Beton(belag)platte, Ornament-Betonfliese, Schmuck-Beton(belag)platte, Schmuck-Betonfliese

~ **door**, decorative ~, decorated ~ · Dekor(ations)tür f, Ziertür, Ornamenttür, Schmucktür

~ **element**, decorative ~ · (architektonisches) Glied n, Ornamentglied, Schmuckglied, Dekor(ations)glied, Zierglied [Fries, Stab, Karnies usw.]

~ **embossment**, decorative ~ · Ornamentprägung f, Dekor(ations)prägung, Zierprägung, Schmuckprägung

ornament(al feature) → pattern

~ **(~)**, decorative ~ · Ornamentelement n, Zierelement, Dekor(ations)element, Schmuckelement

~ **felt(ed fabric)**, decorative ~ (~) · Dekor(ations)filz m, Zierfilz, Ornamentfilz, Schmuckfilz

~ **finish**, decorative ~ · Effekt(ver)putz m, Ornament(ver)putz, Dekor(ations)-(ver)putz, Zier(ver)putz, Schmuck(ver)putz [Oberbegriff für Innen- und Außen(ver)putz]

~ ~ → ~ coat(ing)

(~) ~ → pattern

~ **fittings** → ~ hardware

~ **fixture** → decorative luminaire (~)

~ **floor cover(ing)** → ~ floor(ing)

~ ~ **finish** → ~ floor(ing)

~ **floor(ing)**, decorative ~, ~ floor cover(ing), ~ floor finish · Dekor(ations)(fuß)boden(belag) m, Zier(fuß)boden(belag), Schmuck(fuß)boden(belag), Ornament(fuß)boden(belag)

~ **foil**, decorative ~ · Dekor(ations)folie f, Zierfolie, Ornamentfolie, Schmuckfolie

~ **form**, decorative ~ · Ornamentform f, Schmuckform, Zierform, Dekor(ations)form, Verzierungsform

~ **gable**, decorative ~ · Dekor(ations)giebel m, Ornamentgiebel, Schmuckgiebel, Ziergiebel

~ **glass** → pattern(ed) ~

~ ~ **block**, ~ ~ **brick**, decorative ~ ~ · Dekor(ations)-Glas(bau)stein m, Schmuck-Glas(bau)stein, Zier-Glas(bau)stein, Ornament-Glas(bau)stein

ornamental glass brick — ornamental reconstituted stone 682

~ ~ **brick,** decorative ~ ~, ~ ~ block · Ornament-Glas(bau)stein *m*, Dekor(ations)-Glas(bau)stein, Zier-Glas(bau)stein, Schmuck-Glas(bau)stein

~ **grille,** decorative ~ ~ [*A decorative openwork screen within an opening. Sometimes spelled 'grill'*] · Dekor(ations)gitter *n*, Ziergitter, Ornamentgitter, Gitter, Schmuckgitter

~ **hardware,** decorative ~, ~ fittings · Ornamentbeschläge *mpl*, Zierbeschläge, Dekor(ations)beschläge, Schmuckbeschläge

~ **heavy ceramics,** ~ structural ~, decorative ~ ~ · dekorative Baukeramik *f*

~ **hung ceiling** → decorative suspended ~

~ **iron,** decorative ~ · Dekor(ations)eisen *n*, Ziereisen, Ornamenteisen, Schmuckeisen

~ **ironwork,** decorative ~ · Kunstschmiedearbeit(en) *f(pl)*

~ ~ **technique,** ~ ~ technic, decorative ~ ~ · Kunstschmiedetechnik *f*

~ **joint,** decorative ~ · Dekor(ations)fuge *f*, Zierfuge, Ornamentfuge, Schmuckfuge

~ **lake** · Ziersee *m*

~ **laminate(d) board,** ~ ~ sheet, decorative ~ ~ · Ornament-Schichtpreßstoffplatte *f*, Dekor(ations)-Schichtpreßstoffplatte, Zier-Schichtpreßstoffplatte, Schmuck-Schichtpreßstoffplatte

~ **light fitting** (Brit.) → ~ luminaire (fixture)

~ **link,** decorative ~ · Dekor(ations)zwischenglied *n*, Ornamentzwischenglied, Schmuckzwischenglied, Zierzwischenglied

~ **lock,** decorative ~ · Dekor(ations)schloß *n*, Zierschloß, Ornamentschloß, Schmuckschloß

~ **luminaire (fixture),** decorative ~ (~) (US); ~ light fitting (Brit.); ~ (light(ing)) fixture · Ornamentleuchte *f*, Zierleuchte, Dekor(ations)leuchte, Schmuckleuchte

~ **(masonry) bond,** decorative (~) ~ · Dekor(ations)verband *m*, Zierverband, Ornamentverband, Schmuckverband [*Mauerwerk*]

~ **metal,** decorative ~ · Dekor(ations)metall *n*, Ziermetall, Ornamentmetall, Schmuckmetall

~ **modelled coat** (Brit.); ~ modeled ~ (US); decorative ~ ~ · plastischer Anstrich *m*, ~ Aufstrich, Plastikanstrich, Plastikaufstrich [*Eine reliefartig modellierte Anstrichschicht, die eine Flächenbelebung darstellt und bei mehrfarbiger Ausführung (mit Zwischenschleifen) dekorative Effekte bietet*]

~ ~ **stuccowork** (Brit.); ~ modeled ~ (US); decorative ~ ~ · (plastische) Stuckverzierung *f*, Stukkatur *f*, Stuckplastik *f*

~ **motif,** decorative ~ · Dekor(ations)motiv *n*, Ziermotiv, Ornamentmotiv, Schmuckmotiv

~ ~ **taken from nature,** decorative ~ ~ ~ · Ornamentmotiv *n* aus der Natur, Schmuckmotiv ~ ~ ~, Ziermotiv ~ ~ ~, Dekor(ations)motiv ~ ~ ~

~ **nail,** decorative ~ · Schmucknagel *m*, Ziernagel, Ornamentnagel, Dekor(ations)nagel

~ **niche,** decorative ~ · Ziernische *f*, Schmucknische, Dekor(ations)nische, Ornamentnische

~ **paint,** decorative ~ · Schmuck(anstrich)farbe *f*

~ **painting,** decorative ~ · Schmuckmalerei *f*, Verzierungsmalerei

~ **panel,** decorative ~ · Dekor(ations)tafel *f*, Ziertafel, Ornamenttafel, Schmucktafel

~ **patent stone** → decorative reconstructed ~

~ **pattern,** decorative ~ · Dekor(ations)muster *n*, Ziermuster, Ornamentmuster, Schmuckmuster

(~) ~ → pattern

(~) ~ brick masonry (work) (US) → decorative (pattern) brickwork

(~) ~ brickwork → decorative (~) ~

~ **pavilion,** decorative ~, casino · Zierpavillon *m*, Schmuckpavillon

~ **paving** → ~ sett ~

~ **perforation,** decorative ~ · Dekor(ations)lochung *f*, Zierlochung, Ornamentlochung, Schmucklochung

~ **plastic board,** decorative ~ ~, ~ ~ sheet · (dekorative) Kunststoffsichtplatte *f*, Kunststoffdekor(ations)platte, Kunststoffzierplatte, Kunststoffornamentplatte

~ ~ **film** → ~ ~ sheeting

~ ~ **sheet** → ~ ~ board

~ ~ **sheeting,** decorative ~ ~, ~ ~ film · Ornamentfolie *f* aus Kunststoff, Zierfolie ~ ~, Dekor(ations)folie ~ ~, Schmuckfolie ~ ~

~ **pool,** decorative ~ · Dekor(ations)becken *n*, Zierbecken, Ornamentbecken, Schmuckbecken

~ **portal,** decorative ~ · Schmuckportal *n*, Zierportal

~ **power** → decorative property

~ **(pre)cast (concrete) block** → decorative ~ (~) ~

~ ~ **(~) product** → decorative ~ (~) ~

~ ~ **(~) tile** → decorative (pre)cast (concrete) block

~ **property** → decorative ~

~ **quality** → decorative property

~ **railing,** decorative ~ · Dekor(ations)geländer *n*, Ziergeländer, Ornamentgeländer, Schmuckgeländer

~ **reconstituted stone** → decorative reconstructed ~

ornamental reconstructed stone — oscillation energy

~ **reconstructed stone** → decorative ~ ~

~ **rib**, decorative ~ · Gurtrippe f [Bei einem Kragstein oder einer Konsole]

~ **~**, decorative ~ · Dekor(ations)rippe f, Zierrippe, Schmuckrippe, Ornamentrippe

~ **ro(w)lock paving**, decorative ~ ~ · zierendes Rollschichtpflaster n, ~ Rollscharpflaster, dekoratives ~

~ **SC** → decorative suspended ceiling

~ **screen**, decorative ~ · Schauwand f [z.B. ein Retabel]

~ **(sett) paving**, decorative (~) ~ · Dekor(ations)pflaster(decke) n, (f), Ornamentpflaster(decke), Zierpflaster(-decke), Schmuckpflaster(decke)

~ **sheet** → ~ board

~ **sintered glass**, decorative ~ ~ · Glaspaste f

~ **steel**, decorative ~ · Dekor(ations)stahl m, Zierstahl, Ornamentstahl, Schmuckstahl

~ **structural ceramics**, ~ heavy ~, decorative ~ ~ · dekorative Baukeramik f

~ **structure**, decorative ~ · Zierbau(-werk) m, (n)

~ **style**, decorative ~, style of ornamentation · Ornamentstil m, Schmuckstil, Dekor(ations)stil, Zierstil

~ **surface**, decorative ~ · Dekor(ations)oberfläche f, Zieroberfläche, Ornamentoberfläche, Schmuckoberfläche

~ **suspended ceiling** → decorative ~ ~

~ **tablet**, decorative ~, plaque · Schmucktafel f, Ziertafel, Ornamenttafel, Dekor(ations)tafel

~ **tile** → decorative ~

~ **touch**, decorative ~ · dekorativer Anklang m

~ **tower**, decorative ~ · Zierturm m, Schmuckturm

~ **town gateway**, decorative ~ ~ · Schmucktor n, Ziertor [z.B. das Hadrianstor in Athen]

~ **trim**, decorative ~ · Ziereinfassung f, Schmuckeinfassung, Dekor(ations)einfassung, Ornamenteinfassung, Simswerk n

~ **tunnel vault**, ~ barrel ~, ~ wagon ~, decorative ~ ~ · dekorative Tonne f, dekoratives Tonnengewölbe n

~ **turret**, (decorative) ~, diminutive tower, small tower · kleiner (Zier)Turm m, (Zier)Türmchen n

~ **unit** → ~ building ~

~ **vault**, decorative ~ · dekoratives Gewölbe n, Ziergewölbe, Schmuckgewölbe, Ornamentgewölbe, Dekor(ations)gewölbe

~ **wagon vault**, ~ tunnel ~, ~ barrel ~, decorative ~ ~ · dekorative Tonne f, dekoratives Tonnengewölbe n

~ **wall**, decorative ~ · Dekor(ations)wand f, Ornamentwand, Zierwand, Schmuckwand

~ **(~) bracket**, decorative (~) ~ · Dekor(ations)(wand)konsole f, Schmuck(wand)konsole, Zier(wand)konsole, Ornament(wand)konsole

~ **water-carried paint**, ~ (cold-)water ~, decorative ~ ~ · Schmuck-Binderfarbe f, Schmuck-Dispersionsfarbe

~ **water paint**, ~ cold-~ ~, ~ water-carried ~, decorative ~ ~ · Schmuck-Binderfarbe f, Schmuck-Anstrichfarbe

~ **window**, decorative ~ · Dekor(ations)fenster n, Zierfenster, Schmuckfenster, Ornamentfenster

~ **wire(d) glass** → figure(d) ~ ~

~ **work**, decorative ~ · Schmuckarbeit f, Ornamentarbeit, Zierarbeit, Dekor(ations)arbeit

ornamentation, decoration · Dekor(ation) n, (f) [Die Gesamtheit der „Ausschmückung" von Bauwerken, besonders von Innenräumen, im Gegensatz zum Ornament, das als einzelnes Schmuckmotiv nur ein Teil der Dekoration ist]

ornamented, adorned, decorated, enriched · geziert, verziert, geschmückt

orphan home, orphanage · Waisenhaus n

orphanage, orphan home · Waisenhaus n

orpiment · Auripigment n, Rauschgelb n, As_2S_3

orthoclase · Orthoklas m

orthodox construction method, · conventional ~ ~, classic ~ ~ · herkömmliche Bauweise f

orthogonal anisotropic plate, ~ ~ slab · orthogonal anisotrope Platte f

~ **geometry** · orthogonale Geometrie f

~ **reinforcement** · Orthogonalarmierung f, Orthogonalbewehrung, Orthogonal-(stahl)einlagen fpl

~ **rib** · Orthogonalrippe f

orthosilicic acid · Orthokieselsäure f, H_4SiO_4

orthotropic skew(ed) plate, ~ ~ slab · schiefwink(e)lige orthotrope Platte f

Orton cone [The standard pyrometric cone used in the United States of America] · Ortonkegel m

oscillation, vibration · Schwingung f, Erschütterung

~ **check (calculation)**, vibration ~ (~) · Schwingungsnachweis m, Erschütterungsnachweis

~ **damping**, vibration ~ · Schwingungsdämpfung f, Erschütterungsdämpfung

~ ~ **material**, vibration ~ ~ · Schwingungsdämmstoff m

~ **energy**, vibration ~ · Schwingungsenergie f, Erschütterungsenergie

oscillation flanking transmission — outdoor space

~ flanking transmission, vibration ~ ~ · Erschütterungs-Flankenübertragung *f*, Schwingungs-Flankenübertragung

~ insulation, vibration ~, insulation against vibration, insulation against oscillation · Schwingungsisolierung *f*, Erschütterungsisolierung

~ isolator, (vibration) ~ · Schwingungsdämpfer *m*, Erschütterungsdämpfer

oscillation-less, vibration-less · schwingungsfrei, erschütterungsfrei, vibrationsfrei

oscillation of a foundation, vibration ~ ~ ~ · Fundamentschwingung *f*

~ source, vibration ~, source of oscillation, source of vibration · Erschütterungsquelle *f*, Schwingungsquelle

~ test, vibration ~ · Schwingungsprobe *f*, Schwingungsprüfung *f*, Schwingungsversuch *m*, Erschütterungsprobe, Erschütterungsprüfung, Erschütterungsversuch

~ transmission, vibration ~ · Schwingungsübertragung *f*, Erschütterungsübertragung, Vibrationsübertragung

oscillator load [*A load which increases and decreases in time periodically*] · Schwellast *f*

~ loading · Schwellbelastung *f*

osculatory, pax(board) · Kußtäfelchen *n*, Pax, Pacem, Pacifiale *f*

Osiris pillar · Osirispfeiler *m*

osmotic method · Osmoseverfahren *n*, Osmosemethode *f*

~ pressure · osmotischer Druck *m*

Ostwald double cone, ~ system · Ostwaldscher Farbenkegel *m*, Farbenkegel nach Ostwald

~ system, ~ double-cone · Farbenkegel *m* nach Ostwald, Ostwaldscher Farbenkegel

Ottoman architecture · osmanische Architektur *f*, ~ Baukunst *f*

Ottonian architecture · ottonische Architektur *f*, ~ Baukunst *f*

~ church · ottonische Kirche *f*

~ ecclesiastical architecture · ottonische Kirchenarchitektur *f*

~ Renaissance · ottonische Renaissance *f*

oubliette [*A cellar with trap-door entrance*] · Kellerverlies *n*

outbreak of fire, fire outbreak · Brandausbruch *m*, Feuerausbruch

out-building [*A detached building, subordinate and accessory to a main building*] · Außengebäude *n*

outdoor aerial · Außenantenne *f*

~ air, atmospheric ~, external ~, exterior ~ · Außenluft *f*

~ (~) temperature · Außen(luft)temperatur *f*

~ (~) ~ sensing device · Außen(luft)temperaturfühler *m*

~ architecture, external ~, exterior ~ · Außenarchitektur *f*, Außenbaukunst *f*

~ bath, open-air ~ · Freibad *n*

~ cinema, open-air ~ · Freilichtkino *n*

~ clinker storage area, open-air ~ ~ ~ · Klinkerfreilager *n*

~ closet, ~ toilet [*The term 'outdoor lavatory' is also used as euphemism, for 'outdoor toilet' or 'outdoor closet'*] · Außenklosett *n*, Außenabtritt *m*, Außenabort *m*, Außentoilette *f*

~ corridor, outside ~, exterior ~, external ~, access gallery, access balcony [*A balcony intended to give access to a number of seperate dwellings above the first story*] · offener Gang *m*, Laubengang

~ facility, ~ installation, open-air ~ · Außenanlage *f* [*Zu den Außenanlagen gehören Entwässerungs- und Versorgungsanlagen vom Hausanschluß bis an das öffentliche Netz oder an nicht öffentliche Anlagen, die Daueranlagen sind, außerdem alle anderen Entwässerungs- und Versorgungsanlagen außerhalb der Gebäude, kleine Kläranlagen, Sammelgruben, Brunnen, Zapfstellen usw., sowie Höfe, Wege, Einfriedungen, nicht öffentliche Spielplätze usw., Gartenanlagen und Pflanzungen, die nicht gärtnerisch genutzt werden, nicht mit einem Gebäude verbundene Freitreppen, Stützmauern, fest eingebaute Flaggenmaste, Teppichklopfstangen, Wäschepfähle usw. Zu den Außenanlagen gehören auch in besonderen Gebäuden untergebrachte Gemeinschaftsanlagen, wie Sammelwasch- oder -badeanlagen*]

(~) grass play area, grass playground (for children) · Spielwiese *f*, Kinder~

~ heating · Außenheizung *f* [*Für Terrassen, Tribünen usw. mit Infrarotstrahlern*]

~ home decoration → exterior ~

~ hydrant, open-air ~ · Außenhydrant *m*

~ illumination, external ~, outside ~, exterior ~, ~ lighting · Außenbeleuchtung *f*

~ installation → ~ facility

~ learner's pool, ~ teaching ~ Lehr(schwimm)becken *n* im Freien, LSB ~ ~

~ lighting → ~ illumination

~ mosaic finish → external ~ ~

~ museum, open-air ~ · Freilichtmuseum *n*, Freiluftmuseum

~ opening [*A door, window, louver or skylight openable to the outside atmosphere*] · Öffnung *f* mit nach außen gehendem Abschluß

~ pool, open-air ~ · Freiluft(-Schwimm)-becken *n*

~ school, open-air ~ · Freiluftschule *f*

~ space, open-air ~ · Außenraum *m* [*Der Raum um Gebäude oder ein Gebäude herum*]

~ **sports facility,** open-air ~ ~ · Freiluftsportanlage f, Außensportanlage
~ **stage,** open-air ~ · Freilichtbühne f
~ **storage,** open-air ~ · Außenlagerung f, Freilagerung
~ ~ **area,** open-air ~ ~ · Freilagerfläche f
~ ~ **yard,** open-air ~ ~ · Freilagerplatz m
~ **swimming pool,** open-air ~ · Außenschwimmbecken n
~ ~ ~, open-air ~ ~ · Freischwimmbad n
~ **teaching pool,** ~ learner's ~ · Lehr(schwimm)becken n im Freien, LSB ~ ~
~ **temperature,** ~ air ~ · Außen(luft)temperatur f
~ ~ **sensing device,** ~ air ~ ~ ~ · Außen(luft)temperaturfühler m
~ **terrace,** open-air ~ · Freiterrasse f
~ **theatre,** open-air ~ · Freilichttheater n, Freilichtbühne f
~ **toilet** → ~ closet
~ **track,** open-air ~ · Freiluftbahn f [*Leichtathletik*]
~ **weathering,** open-air ~ · Freibewitterung f
~ **work** → external ~
outer aisle, ~ side ~, ~ nave ~ · äußeres (Seiten)Schiff n, äußere Abseite f [*Kirche*]
~ **application** → exterior ~
~ **bending moment,** outside ~ ~, external ~ ~, exterior ~ ~ · äußeres Biegemoment n, ~ Biegungsmoment
~ **blind** → outside ~
~ **brick,** outside ~, exterior ~, external ~ · Außenziegel m
~ **(building) panel** → external (~) ~
~ **chlorinated rubber paint** → external ~ ~ ~
~ **coat,** outside ~, exterior ~, external ~ · Außenanstrich m, Außenaufstrich
~ ~ **of paint** → external paint coat
~ **coating,** external ~, outside ~, exterior ~ · Außenbeschichtung f, Außenüberzug m [*als Schicht*]
~ **column** → perimeter ~
~ ~, perimeter ~, outside ~, edge ~, external ~, exterior ~ ~ · Randsäule f, Perimetersäule, Außensäule
~ **core,** outside ~, external ~, exterior ~ · Außenkern m
~ **corner** → outside ~
~ **court** · Außenhof m
~ **cross wall** · Außenschott n
~ **cupola** → ~ dome
~ **defense** (US); ~ defence (Brit.); outwork, fortalice, fortilage · Vorwerk n, Außenwerk, Veste f
~ **ditch** · Außengraben m

~ **dome,** external ~, exterior ~, ~ cupola · Schutzkuppel f
~ **door,** outside ~, exterior ~, external ~ · Außentür f
~ **fibre** → external ~
~ **floor slab** → external ~ ~
~ **force** → outside ~
~ **gallery,** outside ~, external ~, exterior ~ · Außen-Laubengang m
~ **gloss paint** → exterior ~ ~
~ **handrail** → exterior ~
~ **insulation,** exterior ~, outside ~, external ~ · Außen(ab)dämmung f
~ **layer** → exterior leaf
~ **leaf** → exterior ~
~ **loading** → external ~
~ **marble** → outside ~
~ **masonry** → exterior ~
~ ~ **wall** → exterior ~ ~
~ ~ ~ **column** → exterior ~ ~ ~
~ ~ ~ **facing** → exterior masonry wall lining
~ ~ ~ **lining** → exterior ~ ~ ~
~ ~ ~ **(sur)facing** → exterior masonry wall lining
~ ~ **(work)** → exterior ~ (~)
~ **mosaic finish** → external ~ ~
~ **nave aisle,** ~ (side) ~ · äußeres (Seiten)Schiff n, äußere Abseite f [*Kirche*]
~ **oil paint,** exterior ~ ~, outside ~ ~, external ~ ~ · Außen(ölanstrich)farbe f
~ **paint,** outside ~, external ~, exterior ~ · Außen(anstrich)farbe f
~ ~ **coat** → external ~ ~
~ **painting (work)** → external ~ (~)
outer-pane · Außenscheibe f [*Glas*]
outer panel → external (building) ~
~ **precast block** → exterior ~ ~
~ ~ **brick** → exterior precast block
~ **primer** → external ~
~ **product,** cross ~, vector ~ · äußeres Produkt n, Vektorprodukt
~ **pulpit,** outside ~, exterior ~, external ~ · Außenkanzel f
~ **reveal,** outside ~, external ~, exterior ~ · Außenleibung f
~ **sealing,** outside ~, external ~, exterior ~ · Außen(ab)dichtung f
~ **shaft** → external ~
~ **sheet,** outside ~, external ~, exterior ~ · Außenplatte f [*einer Sandwichplatte*]
~ **shell** → exterior leaf
~ ~**component** → ~ ~ ~ unit
~ ~ **member** → ~ ~ ~ unit
~ ~ **unit,** exterior ~ ~, external ~ ~, outside ~ ~, ~ ~ member, ~ ~ component · Außenschalen-Fertigteil m, n [*Fertigteil-Betonschornstein*]

outer (side) aisle — outside coating

~ **(side) aisle**, ~ nave ~ · äußeres (Seiten)Schiff *n*, äußere Abseite *f* [*Kirche*]

~ **skin** → exterior leaf

~ **slatted blind** → exterior ~ ~

~ **stairrail** → exterior ~

~ **string** (Brit.); ~ stringer (US) · Freiwange *f*, Spindelwange, Öffnungswange, Lichtwange, Treppenlochwange

~ **(structural) system** → external wall construction

~ **stud**, outside ~, exterior ~, external ~ · Außenpfosten *m* [*Fachwerkwand*]

~ **system** → external wall construction

~ **tier** → exterior leaf

~ **tile** → exterior ~

~ **torque** → external twist(ing) moment

~ **torsion(al) moment** → external twist(ing) ~

~ **twist(ing) moment** → external ~ ~

~ **undercoat(er)**, outside ~, external ~, exterior ~, undercoat(er) for external use · Außenvorlack *m*

~ **use** → exterior application

~ **varnishing**, outside ~, external ~, exterior ~ · Außenlackierung *f*

~ **veneer** → face ~

~ **vinyl paint** → exterior ~ ~

~ **wall** → exterior ~

~ ~ **block** → external ~ ~

~ ~ **(building) component** → external wall (building) unit

~ ~ **(~) member** → external wall (building) unit

~ ~ **(~) unit** → external ~ (~) ~

~ ~ **component** → external wall (building) unit

~ ~ **construction** → external ~ ~

~ ~ **facing** → exterior wall lining

~ ~ **finish** → exterior ~ ~

~ ~ **lining** → exterior ~ ~

~ ~ **member** → external wall (building) unit

~ ~ **panel** → external ~ ~

~ ~ **slab** → external ~ ~

~ ~ **(sur)facing** → exterior wall lining

~ ~ **tile** → external wall block

~ ~ **unit** → external wall (building) ~

~ **ward** · Zwinger *m* [*Der Bereich zwischen Vor- und Hauptmauer einer Burg oder einer Stadtbefestigung*]

~ **window** → exterior ~

~ ~ **blind** · Sommerladen *m*

~ ~ **check** [*Scotland*] → external window rabbet

~ ~ **frame** → storm ~ ~

~ ~ **rabbet** → external ~ ~

~ ~ **sill** → external ~ ~

~ **work** → external ~

~ **wythe** → exterior leaf

outgoing air, exit ~ · Fortluft *f*

~ ~ **station**, exit ~ ~ · Fortluftstation *f*

outhouse · Außenhaus *n*

~ [*A detached outdoor toilet*] · Außentoilette *f*

outlet · Auslaß *m* [*allgemein*]

~, trap ~, overflow connection · Ablaufstutzen *m*, Auslauf *m* [*Geruchverschluß*]

~ · Auslaufventil *n*

~ **compartment** · Ablaufkammer *f*

~ **vent** · Dunstrohr *n*

outline · Umrißlinie *f*

(out)line of arch, arch (out)line · Bogenlinie *f*, Bogenprofil *n*, Wölbung *f*

~ ~ **vault**, vault (out)line · Gewölbelinie *f*, Gewölbeprofil *n*

outlining terrazzo patterns · Aufteilen *n* von Terrazzoflächen, Aufteilung *f* ~ ~

out-opening, out(ward)-swinging · nach außen schlagend, ~ ~ öffnend [*Fenster*]

out-patients' department, O.P.D. · Ambulanz *f* [*Krankenhaus*]

out ramp, exit ~ · Ausfahrtrampe *f*, Abfahrtrampe

outrigger (US); cantilever(ed) beam, cantilevering beam · Freibalken(träger) *m*, Krag(arm)balken(träger), vorkragender Balken(träger), Auslegerbalken(träger), auskragender Balken(träger)

~ **(wall-mounted) flagpole**, ~ wall set ~ · Schräg-Fahnenmast *m*, Schräg-Flaggenmast

~ **wall set flagpole**, ~ (wall-mounted) ~ · Schräg-Fahnenmast *m*, Schräg-Flaggenmast

outside application → exterior ~

~ **awning blind**, marquise · Markise *f*

~ ~ ~ **with expanding arms** · Scherenarm-Markise *f*

~ **bath(room)** · außenliegendes Bad(ezimmer) *n*

~ **bending moment**, outer ~ ~, external ~ ~, exterior ~ ~ · äußeres Biegemoment *n*, ~ Biegungsmoment

~ **blind**, external ~, exterior ~, outer ~ · Außenblende *f* [*An einem Fenster gegen Sonneneinstrahlung, gegen Einblick, zur Verdunkelung und/oder als Einbruchsicherung*]

~ **brick**, outer ~, exterior ~, external ~ · Außenziegel *m*

~ **(building) panel** → external (~) ~

~ **chlorinated rubber paint** → external ~ ~ ~

~ **coat**, outer ~, exterior ~, external ~ · Aulenanstrich *m*, Außenaufstrich

~ ~ **of paint** → external paint coat

~ **coating**, external ~, exterior ~, outer ~ · Außenbeschichtung *f*, Außenüberzug *m* [*als Schicht*]

outside column — outside work

~ **column** → perimeter ~

~ ~, outer ~, perimeter ~, edge ~, external ~, exterior ~ · Randsäule f, Perimetersäule, Außensäule

~ **core**, external ~, exterior ~, outer ~ · Außenkern m

~ **corner**, external ~, exterior ~, outer ~ · Außenecke f

~ **corridor**, outdoor ~, external ~, exterior ~, access gallery, access balcony [*A balcony intended to give access to a number of separate dwellings above the first story*] · offener Gang m, Laubengang

~ **door**, outer ~, exterior ~, external ~ · Außentür f

~ **film coefficient** [*BTU/h sqft. F*] · äußere Wärmeübergangszahl f

~ **floor slab** → external ~ ~

~ **force**, outer ~, external ~, exterior ~ · Außenkraft f, äußere Kraft

~ **gallery**, outer ~, external ~, exterior ~ · Außen-Laubengang m

~ **glazing** [*External glazing in which the glass is inserted from outside the building*] · Außenverglasung f von außen her, Außeneinglasung ~ ~ ~

~ **gloss paint** → exterior ~ ~

~ **handrail** → exterior ~

~ **illumination** → outdoor ~

~ **insulation**, external ~, exterior ~, outer ~ · Außen(ab)dämmung f

~ **kitchen** · außenliegende Küche f

~ **layer** → exterior leaf

~ **leaf** → exterior ~

~ **lighting** → outdoor illumination

~ **loading** → external ~

~ **marble**, outer ~, external ~, exterior ~ · Außenmarmor m, Marmor für Außenverkleidungen

~ **masonry** → exterior ~

~ ~ **wall** → exterior ~ ~

~ ~ ~ **column** → exterior ~ ~ ~

~ ~ ~ **facing** → exterior masonry wall lining

~ ~ ~ **lining** → exterior ~ ~ ~

~ ~ ~ **(sur)facing** → exterior masonry wall lining

~ ~ **(work)** → exterior ~ (~)

~ **oil paint**, outer ~ ~, exterior ~ ~, external ~ ~ · Außenöl(anstrich)farbe f

~ **paint**, outer ~, exterior ~, external ~ · Außen(anstrich)farbe f

~ ~ **coat** → external ~ ~

~ **painting (work)** → external ~ (~)

~ **panel** → external (building) ~

~ **precast block** → exterior ~ ~

~ ~ **brick** → exterior precast block

~ **primer** → external ~

~ **pulpit**, exterior ~, external ~, outer ~ · Außenkanzel f

~ **reveal**, outer ~, external ~, exterior ~ · Außenleibung f

~ **sealing**, outer ~, external ~, exterior ~ · Außen(ab)dichtung f

~ **shaft** → external ~

~ **sheet**, outer ~, external ~, exterior ~ · Außenplatte f [*einer Sandwichplatte*]

~ **shell** → exterior leaf

~ ~ **component** → outer shell unit

~ ~ **member** → outer shell unit

~ ~ **unit** → outer ~ ~

~ **skin** → exterior leaf

~ **slatted blind** → exterior ~ ~

~ **stairrail** → exterior handrail

~ **string** → outer ~

~ **(structural) system** → external wall construction

~ **stud** → outer ~

~ **system** → external wall construction

~ **tier** → exterior leaf

~ **tile** → exterior ~

~ **torque** → external twist(ing) moment

~ **torsion(al) moment** → external twist(ing) ~

~ **twist(ing) moment** → external ~ ~

~ **undercoat(er)**, outer ~, external ~, exterior ~, undercoat(er) for external use · Außenvorlack m

~ **use** → exterior application

~ **varnishing**, outer ~, external ~, exterior ~ · Außenlackierung f

~ **veneer** → face ~

~ **vinyl paint** → exterior ~ ~

~ **wall** → exterior ~

~ ~ **block** → external ~ ~

~ ~ **(building) component** → external wall (building) unit

~ ~ **(~) member** → external wall (building) unit

~ ~ **(~) unit** → external ~ (~) ~

~ ~ **component** → external wall (building) unit

~ ~ **construction** → external ~ ~

~ ~ **facing** → exterior wall lining

~ ~ **finish** → exterior ~ ~

~ ~ **lining** → exterior ~ ~

~ ~ **member** → external wall (building) unit

~ ~ **panel** → external ~ ~

~ ~ **slab** → external ~ ~

~ ~ **(sur)facing** → exterior wall lining

~ ~ **tile** → external wall block

~ ~ **unit** → external wall (building) ~

~ **window** → exterior ~

~ ~ **sill** → external ~ ~

~ ~ **frame** → storm ~ ~

~ **withe** → exterior leaf

~ **work** → external ~

outside wythe — overflow seating

~ wythe → exterior leaf

outsize, misplaced size · Fehlkorn *n* [*Über- und/oder Unterkorn*]

~ **determination,** misplaced size ~ · Fehlkornbestimmung *f* [*Der prozentuale Gehalt an Fehlkorn wird durch Prüfsiebung bestimmt*]

outskirt · Stadtrand *m*

outstanding flange, ~ leg, projecting ~ · abstehender Schenkel *m* [*Winkelstahl*]

~ **leg,** ~ flange, projecting ~ · abstehender Schenkel *m* [*Winkelstahl*]

out(ward)-swinging, out-opening · nach außen schlagend, ~ ~ öffnend [*Fenster*]

~ **side hung (window) casement,** out-opening ~ ~ (~) ~ · Auswärts-Dreh-(fenster)flügel *m*

~ **window,** out-opening ~ · Auswärtsfenster *n*

outward thrust, side ~, axial ~, lateral ~, overturning ~, vault ~ · Gewölbeschub, Wölbungsschub *m*, Horizontalschub, (Seiten)Schub, Axialschub, achsrechter Schub [*Die waag(e)rechte Resultierende einer Gewölbekraft*]

outwork, fortilage, fortalice; outer defence (Brit.); outer defense (US) · Vorwerk *n*, Außenwerk, Veste *f*

oval column · Ovalstütze *f*

~ **(door) knob** · Ovalknopf *m*, Ovaltürknopf

~ **knob door furniture,** ~ ~ ~ set [*B.S. 1331*] · Ovalknopfgarnitur *f*, Ovaltürknopfgarnitur

~ **luthern** · Schwalbenschwanzfenster *n*, Fledermausluke *f*

~ **plate,** ~ slab · Ovalplatte *f*

~ **ribbed wire** · ovalgerippter Draht *m*

~ **slab,** ~ plate · Ovalplatte *f*

~ **wire** · Ovaldraht *m*

oven-dry · ofentrocken

~ **weight** · ofentrockenes Gewicht *n*

oven drying test, ~ ~ method · Auswiegen *n* [*Verfahren zur Bestimmung des Feuchtigkeitsgehaltes von Parkettstäben*]

ovenproof glass, flame-resistant ~, flameproof ~, ovenware [*Glass which does not crack easily when exposed to heat or flames*] · flammwidriges Glas *n*

oven soldering · Ofenlöten *n* [*Löten im Topf- oder Muffelofen, vorwiegend jedoch im Durchlaufofen unter Schutzgas, wobei ein endloses Band die Werkstücke durch die Erwärm-, die Löt- und die Abkühlzone des Ofens führt*]

ovenware → ovenproof glass

overall average, total ~ · Gesamtdurchschnitt *m*

~ **collapse** · Gesamtzusammenbruch *m*

~ **cost,** total ~, aggregate ~ · Gesamtkosten *f*

~ **depth** [*beam*] · Gesamthöhe *f* [*Balken(träger)*]

~ ~, total ~, aggregate ~ [*beam*] · Gesamthöhe *f* [*Balken(träger)*]

~ **dimension,** total ~, aggregate ~ · Gesamtabmessung *f*, Gesamtmaß *n*

~ **erection time** · Montagegesamtzeit *f*

~ **floor depth,** total ~ ~, aggregate ~ ~ · Gesamtdeckendicke *f*

~ **form** · Gesamtform *f*

~ **height,** total ~, aggregate ~ · Gesamthöhe *f*, Höhe über alles

~ **length,** total ~, aggregate ~ · Länge *f* über alles, Gesamtlänge

~ **number,** aggregate ~, total ~ · Gesamtanzahl *f*

~ **plan** · Gesamtplan *m*

~ **planning** · Gesamtplanung *f*

~ ~ **(scheme)** · übergeordnete Planung *f*

~ **reinforcement area** → total steel ~

~ **reinforcing area** → total steel ~

~ **rigidity,** ~ stiffness · Gesamtsteifigkeit *f*, Gesamtstarrheit

~ **stability** · Gesamtstabilität *f*

~ **steel area** → total ~ ~

~ **stiffness,** ~ rigidity · Gesamtsteifigkeit *f*, Gesamtstarrheit

~ **strength,** total ~ · Gesamtfestigkeit *f*

~ **thickness,** total ~, aggregate ~ · Gesamtdicke *f*

~ **volume of construction,** total ~ ~, aggregate ~ ~ ~ · Gesamtbauvolumen *n*

~ **width,** aggregate ~, total ~ · Gesamtbreite *f*, Breite über alles

overcrowding · Überbelegung *f* [*Wohnung*]

overcurrent protection, excess-current ~ · Überstromschutz *m*

~ **protective breaker,** excess-current ~ ~ · Überstrom-Schutzschalter *m*

over-decorated, over-ornamented · überladen [*mit Verzierungen*]

overdoor, soprapoŗta, hyperthyrum · Supraporte *f*, Soprapoŗte, Portalbekrönung *f*, Türbekrönung [*Ein Wandfeld (mit Relief oder Gemälde) über einer Tür oder einem Portal, besonders beim Rokoko*]

over-firing · Überbrand *m* [*zu hoher Brand*]

overflow connection · Überlaufanschluß *m*

~ ~, (trap) outlet · Ablaufstutzen *m*, Auslauf *m* [*Geruchverschluß*]

~ **hole** · Überlaufloch *n* [*Waschbecken; Badewanne*]

~ **line** · Überlaufleitung *f*

~ **pipe** · Überlaufrohr *n*

~ **seating** · Reservebestuhlung *f*

overflow valve — to overspray

~ valve · Überlaufventil *n*

~ water heater · Überlaufspeicher *m*

overhang · Überhang *m*

~, horizontal ~ · Überstand *m* [*Sonnenschutz*]

overhanging angle(-type) step · Winkelstufe *f* mit unterschnittenem Profil

~ rafter · Krag(dach)sparren *m*

~ wall · überhängende Wand *f*, Überhangwand

overhead device for closing → ~ door closer

~ door closer, ~ ~ closing device, ~ ~ closing mechanism, ~ device for closing · Oben(-Tür)schließer *m*, Oben(-Tür)schließvorrichtung *f*

~ ~ of the roll-up type, up-and-over ~ ~ ~ ~ ~, roll-up overhead door, roll-up up-and-over door · Rolltor *n*

~ ~ ~ ~ swing-up type, up-and-over ~ ~ ~ ~ ~, swing-up overhead door, swing-up up-and-over-door · Kipptor *n*, Schwingtor

~ glazing · Obenverglasung *f*, Obeneinglasung

~ GPO line (Brit.); ~ post office ~, ~ telecommunication ~ · Fernmelde-Freileitung *f*

~ illumination → ~ lighting

~ joint · Überkopffuge *f*

~ lighting, ~ illumination, top ~ · Obenbeleuchtung *f*

~ line · Freileitung *f* [*im Gegensatz zur erdverlegten Leitung*]

~ live cable · Freileitungskabel *n*

~ post office line, ~ telecommunication ~; ~ GPO ~ (Brit.) · Fernmelde-Freileitung *f*

~ service entry · Freileitungseinführung *f* [*elektrische Hausanlage*]

~ shower · Überkopfdusche *f*, Hochdusche

~ spray · Überkopfbrause *f*, Hochbrause

~ track · Deckenschiene *f* [*Türanlage*]

~ ~, (trolley) ~ · Laufschiene *f* [*Tor*]

over-heating · Überheizung *f*

overhouse aerial, roof ~ · Dachantenne *f*

to (over)lap · überdecken [*Dachziegel*]

~ ~ [*force polygons*] · sich überdecken, ~ überschlagen [*Kraftecke*]

(over)lap → (over)lapping

~ · Überdeckung *f* [*Dachziegel*]

~ length · Überlappungslänge *f*

(over)lap(ping) · Überdeckung *f*, Überlappung

~ joint · Überlapp(ungs)stoß *m*, Übergreifungsstoß

overlap-welded steel pipe · überlapptgeschweißtes Stahlrohr *n*, wassergas-~

over-large, oversize · übergroß, übermäßig groß

overlay, topping · Überzug(schicht) *m*, (*f*)

~ paper, (concrete-)curing ~ · Abdeckungspapier *n*, (Beton)Nachbehandlungspapier

overlength · Zugabe *f* [*Beim Bewehrungsstumpfschweißen erforderliche Überlänge des Stahls, die beim Schweißen verloren geht*]

overload condition · Überlastbedingung *f*

overloading · Überbelastung *f*

over-long · überlang

overmantel, mantel(shelf) [*The shelf above the mantelpiece*] · Kamin(ge)sims *m*, (*n*)

over-ornamented, over-decorated · überladen [*mit Verzierungen*]

to overpaint, to topcoat [*A primer with a paint*] · überstreichen

over-pigmentation, excess pigment dispersion · Überpigmentierung *f*

to over(pre)stress, to overstretch · über(vor)spannen [*Spannbeton*]

over(pre)stressed, overstretched · über(vor)gespannt [*Spannbeton*]

over(pre)stressing, overstretching · Über(vor)spannen *n* [*Spannbeton*]

overreinforced · überarmiert, überbewehrt

over-rigid · überstarr, übersteif

oversailing conoid, cantilevering ~, cantilever(ed) ~ · Kragkonoid *n*, Auslegerkonoid

~ course → cantilever(ing) ~

~ floor, cantilever(ed) ~, cantilevering ~ · Auslegerdecke *f*, Kragdecke, auskragende Decke, vorkragende Decke

oversintered · übersintert

oversize, over-large · übergroß, übermäßig groß

~, screen residue · Rückstand *m*, Überkorn *n*, Überlauf *m*, Sieb~ [*Betriebssieb*]

~, sieve residue · Rückstand *m*, Überlauf *m*, Überkorn *n*, Sieb~ [*Prüfsieb*]

~ in the undersize · Fehlüberkorn *n*

~ percentage, sieve residue ~ · Überkornanteil *m*, Überlaufanteil

overspill [*This term describes the number of persons in any specific area who are surplus to an ideal density of population in that area*] · Bevölkerungsüberschuß *m*

~ area [*This term refers to population in a given area*] · Überschußgebiet *n*

~ in industrial centres · Bevölkerungsüberschuß *m* in Industriegebieten

to overspray · überspritzen

over-story — ozokerit(e)

over-story, clearstory, clerestory · Ober-(licht)gaden *m*, Fenstergaden, (Licht-)Gaden [*Der über der Bogenstellung des Mittelschiffs einer Basilika sich erhebende Wandabschnitt mit den Hochschiff-Fenstern*]

~ **window**, clearstor(e)y ~, clerestor(e)y ~, high-light ~ · Ober(gaden)fenster *n*, (Licht)Gadenfenster, Hochschiffenster

to overstress, to overprestress, to overstretch · über(vor)spannen [*Spannbeton*]

~ ~ **(and overstrain)** · überbeanspruchen

overstressed, overprestressed, overstretched · über(vor)gespannt [*Spannbeton*]

overstressing, overprestressing, overstretching · Über(vor)spannen *n* [*Spannbeton*]

overstress(ing) (and overstraining) · Überbeanspruchung *f*

to overstretch, to over(pre)stress · über(vor)spannen [*Spannbeton*]

overstretched, over(pre)stressed · über(vor)gespannt [*Spannbeton*]

overstretching, over(pre)stressing · Über(vor)spannen *n* [*Spannbeton*]

to over-thin · übermäßig verdünnen

overthrown · gestürzt [*Kapitäl*]

over-tile, convex tile; mission tile (US) · Deckziegel *m*, Mönch(ziegel) *m*, Preiße *m*

~ **and under-tile roofing** (Brit.) → mission tiling

overturning · (Um)Kippen *n* [*Bauwerk*]

~ **effect** [*Of wind pressure or wind section*] · Kippwirkung *f*

~ **force** · Kippkraft *f* [*Kippen eines Bauwerkes*]

~ **moment** · Kippmoment *n*, Umsturzmoment [*Baustatik*]

~ **thrust**, vault ~, axial ~, outward ~, side ~, lateral ~ · Gewölbeschub *m*, Wölbungsschub, Horizontalschub, achsrechter Schub, Axialschub, (Seiten-)Schub [*Die waag(e)rechte Resultierende einer Gewölbekraft*]

over-vulcanization · Heißvulkanisation *f*

ovolo (moulding) (Brit.); ~ **(molding)** (US) [*A convex mo(u)lding used in all periods of classical architecture. The Greek ovolo or echinus is elliptical in section; the Roman is a quarter-circle*] · konvexer Stab *m* [*Architektur*]

own load → dead weight

~ **weight**, self ~, dead ~ · Eigengewicht *n*, EG, Totgewicht

~ ~ **moment**, dead ~ ~, self ~ ~ · Eigengewichtsmoment *n*, EG-Moment, Totgewichtsmoment

owner-occupied house, home · Eigenheim *n*

oxalic acid · Kleesäure *f*, Oxalsäure [*Die einzige Säure welche Beton nicht angreift, sondern festigt*]

oxeye (window), bull's-eye (~), oculus (~) [*A round or oval window, usually with glazing bars radiating form a circular centre*] · Ochsenauge *n*

ox-head → bucrane

oxidation, oxidizing · Oxidation *f*

~ · Frischen *n* [*Stahlerzeugung*]

~ **agent**, oxidizing ~ · Oxidationsmittel *n*

oxide of non-metal (Brit.); oxid(e) ~ (US) · Nichtmetalloxid *n*

~ **paint** (Brit.); oxid(e) ~ (US) · Oxid-(anstrich)farbe *f*

oxidizable · oxidierbar

oxidized (asphaltic) bitumen, air-rectified (~) ~, air-blown (~) ~ (Brit.); ~ asphalt (US) · oxidiertes Bitumen *n*, geblasenes ~, Industriebitumen [*Geblasene Bitumen sind die durch Einblasen von Luft in geschmolzene, weiche Bitumen hergestellten hochschmelzenden Bitumen mit ausgeprägten plastischen und elastischen Eigenschaften*]

~ **linseed oil** · oxidiertes Leinöl *n*

oxidizing, oxidation · Oxidation *f*

~, air-rectification, (air-)blowing · Blasen *n* [*(Erdöl)Bitumen*]

~ **agent**, oxidation ~ · Oxidationsmittel *n*

~ **installation** → blowing ~

ox-skull → bucrane

oxy-acetylene welding of mild steel [*B.S. 693*] · Sauerstoff-Azetylen-Schweißen *n* von Flußstahl

oxy-acid, oxyacid · Oxysäure *f*

oxychloric cement (US) → magnesium oxychloride (composition)

oxychlorid(e) cement (US) → magnesium ~ ~

oxy-gas flame, ~ cone · Sauerstoff-Gas-Flamme *f*

oxygen absorption, ~ uptake · Sauerstoffaufnahme *f*

~ **free high conductivity copper** · OFHC-Kupfer *n*

~ **uptake**, ~ absorption · Sauerstoffaufnahme *f*

oyster-shell · Muschelschale *f*

~ **concrete**; tabby (US) · Muschel(schalen)beton *m*, Schillbeton

~ **lime** → shell(y) limestone

oyster shells · Schill *m*

ozocerite pitch (US); ozokerit(e) ~ (Brit.) · Ozokeritpech *m*

ozokerit(e) (Brit.); ozocerite, native paraffin, mineral tallow, mineral wax · Ozokerit *m*, Erdwachs *n*, Neftgil *n*, Bergtalg *m*, Bergwachs, Montanwachs

P

P SL →; (pipe) sleeve
pack · Paket *n*
~ of (clay) bricks, pre-packed (clay) bricks, (clay) brick pack · Ziegelpaket *n*

~ stability · Lagerfähigkeit *f* [*Anstrichmittel*]
package(d) boiler · Paketkessel *m*
packed bricks · paketierte Ziegel *mpl*
packing piece · Futter *n* [*Fachwerkwand*]
pad, mat · Matte *f* [*allgemein*]
~ → fixing (fillet)
padded door · Polstertür *f*
paddling pool, children's ~, wading ~ · Planschbecken *n*, Kinderbecken
padlock, portable lock, PL(K) · Vorhängeschloß *n* [*DIN 7465*]
padstone, raised table, abacus [*The slab between the lintel and the supporting column, designed to concentrate the load. In the Greek Doric order the abacus is a simple square block; in the Roman orders it is thinner and moulded*] · (Säulen)Deckplatte *f*, Abakus *m*, Kapitellplatte
pagan basilica, secular ~, imperial ~, (civic) ~, Roman ~ · (römische) (Zivil)Basilika *f*, römisch-heidnische Basilika, heidnisch-römische Basilika
~ temple · Heidentempel *m*
pageant arena · Volksfestarena *f*
paging system · (drahtlose) (Personen-)Suchanlage *f*
pagod(a) · Pagode *f*
painfully loud sound · physiologische Schmerzschwelle *f* [*Lautstärke*]
to paint, to coat · (an)streichen [*Fehlname: malen*]
paint, PNT [*A mix(ture) of pigment with vehicle, intended to be spread in thin coats for decoration, or protection or both*] · Anstrichfarbe *f* [*Der Ausdruck „Farbe" ist nicht mehr zu verwenden. Ein pigmenthaltiger Anstrichstoff*]

(~) air brush → (~) spray gun
(~) binder → (~) (binding) medium
(~) (binding) medium, (~) binder [*The nonvolatile portion of the vehicle of a paint; it binds or cements the pigment particles together, and the paint film as a whole to the material to which it is applied*] · (Farben)Bindemittel *n*
~ brush · Mal(er)pinsel *m*
~ burning, burning off (paint) [*The removal of paint by a process in which the paint is softened by heat, e.g. from a flame, and then scraped off while still soft*] · Abbrennen *n*, Flammstrahlreinigen
~ chemist · (Anstrich)Farbenchemiker *m*
~ clay · Farbton *m*

~ coat, coat of paint · Farbanstrich *m*, Farbaufstrich
~ ~ failure, ~ ~ fault · Farbanstrichschaden *m*, Farbaufstrichschaden
~ consistency, ~ consistence · Farbkonsistenz *f*, Farbsteife *f*
~-destroying agency · Farbenschadstoff *m*
(paint) extender, inertpigment, filler [*An inorganic material in powder form which has a low refractive index and consequently little obliterating power, but is used as a constituent of paints to adjust the properties of the paint, notably its working and film forming properties and to avoid settlement on storage*] · Streckmittel *n*, Streckzusatz *m*, Verschnittmittel für Pigmente, Streckungsmittel

~ film, ~ membrane, ~ skin · (Anstrich-)Farbfilm *m*, (Anstrich)Farbhaut *f*, (Anstrich)Farbmembran(e) *f*
~ filter · Farbstaubfilter *m*, *n*
~ for (building) construction purposes · Bauten(anstrich)farbe *f*
~ ~ preservation of structures · Bautenschutz(anstrich)farbe *f*
~ ~ the building and construction industry · Bauten(anstrich)farbe *f*
~ formulation · (Anstrich)System *n* [*Das Rezept für einen Anstrichaufbau*]
~ hose · Farbschlauch *m*
~ industry → ~ manufacturing ~
~ kettle [*A cylindrical pail used by painters for holding paint and dipping the brush into*] · Malereimer *m*
~ manufacturer · (Anstrich)Farbenhersteller *m*
~ (manufacturing) industry · (Anstrich)Farbenindustrie *f*
~ membrane → ~ film
~ mill · Farbwerk *n*
~ mist · Farbnebel *m*
~ oil, drying ~, fixed ~ · trocknendes Öl *n*
~ particle · Farbteilchen *n*
~ prepared for use, P.F.U. paint, ready mixed paint, prepared paint · anstrichfertige Farbe *f*, gebrauchsfertige ~, verarbeitungsfertige ~
~ pump, ~ spray ~ · Farbspritzpumpe *f*
(~) remover, (~) stripper [*B.S. 3761*] · Abbeizer *m*, (Ab)Beizmittel *n*, Farbenlöser, Farbenentferner, Lacklöser, Lackbeize *f*, Ablaugemittel *n* [*Vom Anstreicher kurz „Lauge" genannt*]
(~) ~ in paste form, ~ stripper ~ ~ ~, paste(-)type paint remover, paste(-)type paint stripper · (Ab)Beizpaste *f*, pastenartiges (Ab)Beizmittel *n*
(~) ~ ~ powder form, ~ stripper ~ ~ ~, powder(ed) paint remover, powder(-ed) paint stripper · pulv(e)riges (Ab-)Beizmittel *n*, Ablaugpulver *n*, (Ab)Beizpulver

paint residue — Palace of Persepolis

~ **residue** · Farbrest *m*, Farbrückstand *m*

~ **scheme**, ~ system, multiple coat ~ · (Anstrich)System *n* [*Der fertig aufgebaute Anstrich*]

~ **scraper** · Farb(ab)kratzer *m*

~ **shop**, ~ work~ · Anstreicherwerkstatt *f*, Malerwerkstatt

~ **skin** → ~ film

(~) **spray gun**, (~) air brush, (~) spraying pistol, aerograph · Farbspritzpistole *f*, Farbspritzgerät *n*

~ (~) **pump** · Farbspritzpumpe *f*

~ ~ **room** · Farbspritzkabine *f*

~ **spraying** · Farbspritzen *n*

~ ~ **machine** · Farbzerstäubungsmaschine *f*

(~) ~ **pistol** → (~) spray gun

~ **store** · Anstreicherlager *n*, Malerlager

(~) **stripper**, (~) remover [*B.S. 3761*] · Abbeizer *m*, (Ab)Beizmittel *n*, Farbenlöser, Farbenentferner, Lacklöser, Lackbeize *f*, Ablaugemittel *n* [*Vom Anstreicher kurz "Lauge" genannt*]

~ ~ **in paste form**, (~) remover ~ ~ ~, paste-type paint stripper, paste-type paint remover · pastenartiges (Ab)Beizmittel *n*, (Ab)Beizpaste *f*

~ ~ ~ **powder form**, (~) remover ~ ~ ~, powder(ed) paint remover, powder(-ed) paint stripper · pulv(e)riges (Ab-)Beizmittel *n*, Ablaugpulver *n*, (Ab)Beizpulver

(~) **stripping** · Abbeizen *n* von Farbanstrichen, ~ ~ Farbaufstrichen

~ **system**, ~ scheme, multiple coat ~ · (Anstrich)System *n* [*Der fertig aufgebaute Anstrich*]

~ **tank** · Farbbehälter *m*

~ **technician** · (Anstrich)Farbentechniker *m*

~ **technology** · (Anstrich)Farbentechnologie *f*

~ **(work)shop** · Anstreicherwerkstatt *f*, Malerwerkstatt

paintability · Farbhaftung *f* [*Untergrund*]

paintable · anstreichbar

painted decoration → ~ decorative finish

~ **decorative finish**, ~ ~ feature, ~ ornamental ~, ~ enrichment, ~ decoration · gemalte Verzierung *f*, gemalter Schmuck *m*

~ **enamel** · Malerschmelz *m*

~ **enrichment** → ~ decorative finish

~ **motif** · gemaltes Motiv *n*

~ **ornamental finish** → ~ decorative ~

painter, house ~ · Anstreicher *m*

painter's putty · Malerkitt *m*

~ **tool**, house ~ ~ · Malerwerkzeug *n*, Anstreicherwerkzeug

~ **torch** · Maler-Abbrennlampe *f*

~ **trade** · Malergewerbe *n*, Anstreichergewerbe

painting → ~ work

~ **contractor** · Malerfirma *f*

~ **defect** · Aufstrichschaden *m*, Anstrichschaden

~ **device** · Anstrichgerät *n*

~ **practice**, coating ~ · Anstrichtechnik *f*, Anstrichwesen *n*

~ **scheme** → ~ system

~ **system**, ~ scheme · (Anstrich)Farbenaufbau *m*, (Anstrich)Farbensystem *n*

~ **(work)** · Anstreicherarbeiten *fpl*, Anstricharbeiten, Malerarbeiten [*DIN 18363*]

pair of columns, paired ~, twin ~ · Säulenpaar *n*

~ ~ **diminutive towers**, ~ ~ small ~, ~ ~ turrets · Türmchenpaar *n*

~ ~ **gateways**, ~ ~ pylons · Pylonenpaar *n*

~ ~ **minarets** · Gebetsturmpaar *n*, Minarettpaar

~ ~ **piers** · Pfeilerpaar *n*

~ ~ **pylons**, ~ ~ gateways · Pylonenpaar *n*

~ ~ **rafters** · Gebinde *n* [*Sparrenpaar einer Dachkonstruktion*]

~ ~ **ribs** · Rippenpaar *n*

~ ~ **small towers**, ~ ~ diminutive ~, ~ ~ turrets · Türmchenpaar *n*

~ ~ **towers** · Turmpaar *n*

~ ~ **turrets**, ~ ~ diminutive towers, ~ ~ small towers · Türmchenpaar *n*

paired columns, twin ~, pair of ~ · Säulenpaar *n*

palace architecture · Palastarchitektur *f*, Palastbaukunst *f*

Palace at Ctesiphon, Sassanian ~ ~ ~ · Palast *m* zu Ktesiphon

~ ~ **Feruz-Abad** · Palast *m* von Firuz-Abad

palace building, ~ construction · Palastbau *m*

~ ~ · Palastgebäude *n*

~ **complex** · Palastanlage *f*, Palastkomplex *m*

~ **construction**, ~ building · Palastbau *m*

Palace of Cyrus the Great at Pasargadae · Königsburg *f* des Kyros zu Pasargadae

palace of delights [*e.g. La Zisa, Palermo*] · Lustschloß *n*, Lusthaus *n*, Gartenschloß

Palace of Diocletian at Split → Diocletian's palace at ~

~ ~ **King Minos at Knossos** · Palast *m* von Knossos

~ ~ **Nations** [*Brasilia*] · Palast *m* der Nationen

~ ~ **Persepolis** [*It was begun in 518 B.C. by Darius I, was mostly executed by Xerxes I (486–465 B.C.) and finished by Artaxerxes I about 460 B.C.*] · Palast *m* von Persepolis

Palace of Sargon — panel

~ ~ **Sargon** · Palast(anlage) m, (f) von Khorsabad, Palastkomplex m ~ ~, Sargonsburg f

~ ~ **Sarvistan** · Palast m zu Sarbistan

~ ~ **Shapur I at Bishapur** · Palast m von Bischapur [*in den Bergen des Südiran*]

~ ~ **States** [*Brasilia*] · Palast m der Staaten

~ ~ **the Arts** [*Brasilia*] · Palast m der Künste

~ ~ ~ **Dawn** [*Presidential palace in Brasilia*] · Palast m der Morgenröte

palace of the emperor, imperial palace · Kaiserpalast m, Kaiserschloß n, Herrscherpalast

Palace of the Popes at Avignon · Papstpalast m in Avignon, Papstschloß n ~ ~

~ ~ **Whitehall** · Palast m von Whitehall

palace terrace · Palastterrasse f

~ **wing** · Palastflügel m

Palaces of the Emperors at Rome · Kaiserpaläste mpl zu Rom

palaestra · Palästra f [*Ringerschule im antiken Griechenland*]

palatial house · Palais n

~ **style** · Palaistil m

pale, round stake · Rundling m [*Zaun*]

~ **fence** · Rundlingszaun m

palisade fence [*B.S. 1722. A neat fencing allowing a view through at the same time as acting as an efficient barrier. It is particularly attractive when painted white, as is the usual tradition*] · Palisadenzaun m

Palladian · palladianisch

~ **architecture** → Palladianism

~ **Classicism** · palladianischer Klassizismus m

~ **motif (window)** → Venetian ~

~ **revival** · Wiederbelebung f des Palladianismus

Palladianism, Palladian architecture · Palladianismus m [*Auf den it. Baumeister Andrea Palladio (1508–1580) zurückgehende Sonderform der Spätrenaissance und des Barock. Schließt sich besonders eng an die römische Antike an, reduziert darum die Fassadendekoration und sucht klare, strenge Proportionen. Seine Besonderheit ist die Kolossalordnung. Der Palladianismus beherrscht seit etwa 1600 die englische Baukunst völlig, hat seit etwa 1650 starke Einflüsse auf Frankreich und das übrige Europa*]

pallet → fixing (fillet)

palm capital [*misnomers: proto-Ionic capital, Aeolic capital*] · Palmenblattkapitell n, Palmenblattkapitäl

~ **kernel oil** · Palmenkernöl n

~ **leaf ornament** · Palmenblattornament n

~ **shaft column** · Palmensäule f [*Säule der ägyptischen Baukunst mit einem Palm(en)blattkapitell*]

~ **vault** · Palmengewölbe n, Strahlengewölbe

palmette, honeysuckle, anthemion (ornament), spray [*A fan-shaped ornament composed of narrow divisions like a palm leaf*] · Palmette f

palmitate · Palmitat n

palmitic acid · Palmitinsäure f, $C_{15}H_{31}CO_2H$

pan, coffer, waffle, cassette, caisson, panel [*A recessed panel in a concrete, metal or timber soffit*] · (Decken)Kassette f, Deckenfeld n, Deckenfach n

~ → bowl

~, gypsum ~ · (Gips)Kessel m

pan-calcined gypsum · Pfannengips m

pan ceiling, waffle ~, caisson ~, rectangular grid ~, cored ~, cassette ~, coffer(ed) ~, panel ~ · Kassettendecke f, kassettierte Decke

~ **design** → waffle pattern

~ **floor** → waffle (slab) ~

~ **(~) panel** → rectangular grid (floor) slab

~ **(~) plate** → rectangular grid (floor) slab

~ **(~) slab** → rectangular grid (~) ~

~ **grid** → waffle pattern

~ **joist floor** · Kassetten-Unterzugdecke f

~ **panel** → rectangular grid (floor) slab

~ **(~) floor** → waffle (slab) ~

~ **pattern** → waffle ~

~ **plate** → rectangular grid (floor) slab

~ **(~) floor** → waffle (slab) ~

~ **slab** → rectangular grid (floor) ~

~ **(~) floor** → waffle (~) ~

~ **soffit**, rectangular grid ~, cassette ~, coffer(ed) ~, caisson ~, waffle ~, cored ~, panel ~ · Kassettenuntersicht f, kassettierte Untersicht

panache · Zwickelfeld n

Panathenaic frieze · Fries m des Parthenon, Parthenonfries

~ **way** · Panathenaiastraße f [*Agora von Athen*]

pane → window ~

~ → ~ of glass

~ **of a roof**, roof pane · Dachfläche f, Dachseite f, Dachschräge f [*Österreich: Dachresche f. Beim geneigten Dach*]

~ **(of glass)**, glass pane, square [*A piece of glass cut to size and shape ready for glazing*] · (Glas)Scheibe f

~ **separation**, window ~ ~ · (Fenster-)Scheibentrennung f

to panel · vertäfeln

panel, ((pre)cast) (concrete) ~, prefab(ricated) concrete ~ · Betontafel f

panel — pantile

~, infilling ~ [*A panel is formed by the structural columns and beams of a framed building*] · Fach *n*

~, door ~ · (Tür)Füllung *f*

~ [*A distinct portion of a floor, roof slab or wall supported by a frame*] · (Bau-)Tafel *f*

~ → pan

~ area · Tafelfläche *f*

~ arrangement, door ~ ~ · (Tür)Füllungsausbildung *f*

pan(el) ceiling → pan ~

panel ceiling heating → (radiant) ~ ~

~ construction → panelized ~

~ ~ method · Tafelbauweise *f*

~ ~ system, ~ (structural) ~ · Tafel(bau)system *n*, Tafelkonstruktion(ssystem) *f*, (*n*)

pan(el) design → waffle pattern

panel door → panel(led) ~

~ edge · Tafelrand *m*

~ erection · Tafelmontage *f*

~ façade · Tafelfassade *f*

~ fence, ((pre)cast) concrete ~ ~, prefab(ricated) concrete ~ ~ · Betontafelzaun *m*

~ forms, ~ formwork, ~ shuttering · Tafelschalung *f*

~ formwork, ~ forms, ~ shuttering · Tafelschalung *f*

~ frame, ~ framing · Tafelrahmen *m*

~ framing → panel(led) ~

pan(el) grid → waffle pattern

panel heating · Flächenheizung *f*, Niedertemperatur-Strahlungsheizung [*Erwärmung des Raumes durch Wärmeabgabe beheizter Flächen, wie Decken, Wände und Fußböden. Heiz(ungs)mittel meistens Warmwasser*]

~ ~ unit, radiant ~ ~ · Flächenheizkörper *m*

~ interchangeability · Tafelaustauschbarkeit *f*

~ joint · Tafelfuge *f*

~ masonry wall [*A masonry wall faced with (stone) facing slabs*] · Plattenverblendmauer *f*

~ of judges, adjudicating panel · Preisgericht *n*

~-painting · Tafelmalerei *f*

pan(el) pattern → waffle ~

panel pin · gestauchter Stift *m*

~ point, truss(ed girder) ~ ~, panel point of a truss(ed girder), node · Fachwerk(träger)-Knoten(punkt) *m*

~ ~ of a truss(ed girder), (truss(ed girder)) panel point · Fachwerk(träger)-Knoten(punkt) *m*

~ radiator · Plattenheizkörper *m*

~ roof · Tafeldach *n*

~ shell · Tafelschale *f* [*Kerntafel*]

~ shuttering, ~ forms, ~ formwork · Tafelschalung *f*

~ siding · Tafel-Wandbeschlag *m*, Tafel-Wetterschirm *m*, Tafel-Wandschirm [*Wetterschutz für Außenwände*]

~ strength · Tafelfestigkeit *f*

~ (structural) system, ~ construction ~ · Tafel(bau)system *n*, Tafelkonstruktion(ssystem) *f*, (*n*)

~ system, ~ structural ~, ~ construction ~ · Tafel(bau)system *n*, Tafelkonstruktion(ssystem) *f*, (*n*)

~ tracery → rectilinear ~

~-type of resonator · Tafelresonator *m* [*Schallabsorption*]

panel wall · ((pre)cast) (concrete) ~ ~

~ ~, curtain ~, filler ~ [*It is a non-bearing wall in skeleton construction, built between columns, posts or piers and wholly supported at each stor(e)y*] · Tafelwand *f*

~ ~, (in)filler ~ infill(ing) ~ · Ausfachung *f*, Ausfüllung [*Süddeutschland: Ausriegelung*]

panel-wall block, ~ building, curtain-wall ~ · Vorhangwandgebäude *n*

~ building, ~ block, curtain-wall ~ · Vorhangwandgebäude *n*

panel with window opening, ((pre-)cast) concrete ~ ~ ~ ~, prefab(ricated) concrete ~ ~ ~ ~ ~ · Betontafel *f* mit Fensteröffnung

panel(ized) construction, paneling (US); panel(lised) construction, panelling (Brit.) · Tafelbau *m*

panel(led) door (Brit.); paneled ~ (US) [*A door built of a framed surround with the spaces between the framing members filled with panels of thinner material*] · Rahmen-Füllungstür *f*

~ ~, framed and ~ ~ (Brit.); (framed and) panel(ed) ~ (US) · Füllungstür *f*

~ framing (Brit.); paneled ~ (US) [*Framing consisting of stiles (vertical) with rails (horizontal) tenoned into them and, in wide frames, muntins (vertical) tenoned into the rails. The frames contain panels*] · Füllungsrahmen *m* [*Tür*]

panelled in oak (Brit.); paneled ~ ~ (US) · eichenvertäfelt

panoramic view, scenic ~ · Panoramaansicht *f*

~ (wall)paper · (Papier)Tapete *f* mit Darstellung von Landschaften, Wand~ ~ ~ ~ ~

~ window, picture ~ · Panoramafenster *n*

Pantheon at Rome · Pantheon *n* in Rom

~ dome, ~ cupola [*A shallow dome similar to that of the Pantheon in Rome, though not necessarily open in the centre*] · Pantheonkuppel *f*

pantile [*A single-lap tile shaped like an S laid horizontally – thus ω. Each tile overlaps its neighbour on the right (looking at the roof from the ground in front of the house) and is overlapped by its neighbour on the left*] · Dachpfanne *f*, Hohlpfanne, (S-)Pfanne, holländische Pfanne

pantile lath — paper tube

~ lath · Pfannenlatte *f*

pantiling · (Dach)Eindecken mit Pfannen, Dach(ein)deckung ~ ~, Pfannendach(ein)deckung

pantry · Anrichte *f*

papal cross, triple ~ · päpstliches Kreuz *n*, dreifaches ~

paper · Papier *n*

~ [*The word 'paper' also covers the German word 'Papier', since paper is defined as being available in sheets, rolls and boards in a wide diversity of types ranging from facial tissues to thick, spongy insulating boards and from fine, thin printing papers to high-density building boards. Paper may be smooth or creped single or laminated, cored, corrugated, uncoated or finished and sized in wide variety of surfaces and textures*] · Pappe *f*

~, wall~ [*Formerly known as 'paperhangings' and 'paper tapistry'*] · Tapete *f*, (Wand)Papier~

~ adhesive → wall~ ~

~ back, felt ~ · Papp(en)unterlage *f* [*(Fuß)Boden(belag)*]

paper-base(d) laminated board, ~ ~ sheet · Schichtstoffplatte *f* mit Papierbahn(en)

~ ~ sheet, ~ ~ board · Schichtstoffplatte *f* mit Papierbahn(en)

paper board, ~ sheet, sheet of paper, board of paper · Pappenplatte *f*

~ chute → ~ disposal shaft

~ cover moulding, wall~ ~ ~ (Brit.); ~ ~ molding (US) · Tapetenleiste *f*, (Wand)Papier~

paper-covered · papierbeschichtet

~ veneer · papierkaschiertes Furnier *n*

paper (disposal) chute, ~ (~) shaft, ~ disposer · Papierabwurfanlage *f*, Papier(abwurf)schacht *m*, Papierschlucker *m*, Abwurfschacht für Papier, Abwurfanlage für Papier

~ (~) shaft, ~ (~) chute, ~ disposer · Abwurfanlage *f* für Papier, Abwurfschacht *m* ~ ~, Papierschlucker *m*, Papier(abwurf)schacht, Papierabwurfanlage

~ disposer, ~ (disposal) shaft, ~ (disposal) chute · Papierabwurfanlage *f*, Papier(abwurf)schacht *m*, Papierschlucker *m*, Abwurfschacht für Papier, Abwurfanlage für Papier

papered, wall~ · tapeziert mit (Wand-)Papiertapete

~ wall · tapezierte Wand *f*

paperfaced · papierabgedeckt [*Baumatte*]

paper factory, wall~ ~ · Tapetenfabrik *f*, (Wand)Papier~

~ for Häusler (type) roof(ing) · Holzzementpapier *n*

paperhanger, wall~, (paper)hanger · Tapezierer *m*

paperhanging, papering, wall~ · Tapezieren *n* mit (Wand)Papiertapete, Tapezierung *f* ~ ~

~ · Papiertapete *f*

paper(hanging) adhesive → (wall)paper(hanging) (bonding) ~

~ agent → (wall)paper(hanging) (bonding) adhesive

~ (bonding) adhesive → wall~ (~) ~

~ cement(ing agent) → (wall)paper(hanging) (bonding) adhesive

~ medium → (wall)paper(hanging) (bonding) adhesive

~ paste, wallpaper hanging ~, paste for (paper)hanging, paste for wallpaperhanging [*B.S. 3046*] · (Wand)Papiertapetenkleister *m*, Tapezierkleister, Tapetenkleister

paper incinerator · Papierverbrenner *m*

papering, paperhanging, wall~ · Tapezieren *n* mit (Wand)Papiertapete, Tapezierung *f* ~ ~

~ work, wall~ ~ · Tapezierarbeiten *fpl* mit (Wand)Papiertapete

paper insert(ion) · Papiereinlage *f*

paper-insulated cable [*B.S. 480*] papierisoliertes Kabel *n*, Papierkabel

~ enamelled wire (Brit.); ~ enameled ~ (US) · Lackpapierdraht *m* [*für feste Verlegung von Leitungen für Schwachstromanlagen*]

~ lead-covered cable · Papierbleikabel *n*

(paper) laminate, all-paper ~ · (Kunst-) Schichtstoffplatte *f*

~ layer · Papierlage *f*, Papierschicht *f*

~ liner · Papierverkleidung *f* [*Strohplatte*]

~ meal · Papiermehl *n*

~ mill waste · Papierfabrikabwasser *n*

~ model · Papiermodell *n*

~ refuse, ~ waste · Papiermüll *m*

~ roll, wall~ ~ · Tapetenrolle *f*, (Wand-)Papier~

~ ~ · Pappenrolle *f*

~ shaft → ~ disposal

~ sheet, ~ board, sheet of paper, board of paper · Pappenplatte *f*

~ sheet(ing), wall~ ~ · Tapetenbahn *f*, (Wand)Papier~

~ ~ · Papierbahn *f*

~ ~ → wall~ ~

~ strength · Papierfestigkeit *f*

~ tape · Papierband *n*

~ towel dispenser · Papierhandtuchspender *m*

~ trimmer, wall~ ~ · Tapetenschneider *m*, (Wand)Papier~

~ tube [*Used as cores to form holes in concrete for the accommodation of bolts, etc.*] · Kartonröhre *f*, Pappröhre, Kartonrohr *n*, Papprohr

paper tube — parapet brick

~ ~ · Papierrohr *n*

~ **waste,** ~ **refuse** · Papiermüll *m*

papyrus-bud capital · Papyrusknospenkapitell *n*, Papyrusknospenkapitäl

papyrus capital · Papyruskapitell *n*, Papyruskapitäl

~ **column** · Papyrussäule *f* [*Die nach einem Vorbild der Papyruspflanze ausgebildete ägyptische Säule. Ihr Schaft ist unten eingezogen und wächst aus Kelchblättern heraus*]

~ **half-column** · Papyrus-Halbsäule *f*

parabola equation · Parabelgleichung *f*

parabolic arch · Parabelbogen *m*

~ **arched girder** · Parabelbogenträger *m*, parabolischer Bogenträger

~ **conoid** · parabolisches Konoid *n*, Parabel-Konoid

~ ~ **shell** · parabolische Konoidschale *f*, Parabel-Konoidschale

~ **cupola,** ~ **dome** · Parabelkuppel *f*, parabolische Kuppel

~ **dome,** ~ **cupola** · Parabelkuppel *f*, parabolische Kuppel

~ **form** · Parabelform *f*

~ **girder** · Parabelträger *m*, parabolischer Träger

~ **load** · parabolische Last *f*

~ **loading** · Parabelbelastung *f*

~ ~ **diminishing from left to right** · rechts abfallende Parabelbelastung *f*

~ ~ **increasing from left to right** · rechts ansteigende Parabelbelastung *f*

~ **rib** · parabolische Rippe *f*, Parabelrippe

~ **(roof) truss** · Parabel(dach)binder *m*

~ **shell** · parabolische Schale *f*, Parabelschale

~ **truss,** ~ **roof** ~ · Parabel(dach)binder *m*

~ **vault** · Parabelgewölbe *n*, parabolisches Gewölbe

paraboloid · Paraboloid *n*

paraboloid(al) roof · Paraboloiddach *n*

~ **shell** · Paraboloidschale *f*

~ ~ **of revolution (subjected to loads of rotational symmetry),** ~ ~ ~ rotational symmetry · Drehparaboloidschale *f*, Rotationsparaboloidschale, drehsymmetrische Paraboloidschale

~ ~ ~ **rotational symmetry,** ~ ~ ~ revolution (subjected to loads of rotational symmetry) · Drehparaboloidschale *f*, Rotationsparaboloidschale, drehsymmetrische Paraboloidschale

~ **umbrella roof of folded shell,** ~ ~ shell roof · Paraboloid-Regenschirmschalendach *n*

~ ~ **shell roof,** ~ ~ roof of folded shell · Paraboloid-Regenschirmschalendach *n*

parachute vault, umbrella ~ · Schirmgewölbe *n*

paradise, cloister cemetery · Ambitusfriedhof *m*, Kreuzgangfriedhof

~, open court of a quadrangle [*A square yard enclosed by principal monastic buildings*] · Ambitushof *m*, Rechteckhof, Kreuzganghof

~ → ceremonial forecourt

~, monastery cemetery · Mönchsklosterfriedhof *m*

~, monastery garden · Mönchsklostergarten *m*

paraffin · Paraffin *n* [*Gemisch fester Kohlenwasserstoffe*]

~ **(biological) shielding wall,** ~ radiation ~ ~ · Paraffin-Abschirmwand *f*

~ **oil** · (dunkles) Paraffinöl *n*

~ ~ (Brit.); kerosine (US) · Paraffinöl *n* aus Erdöl hergestellt, parraffinum liquidum

~ **radiation shielding wall,** '~ (biological) ~ ~ · Paraffin-Abschirmwand *f*

~ **shielding wall** → ~ **radiation** ~ ~

~ **solution** · Paraffinlösung *f*

paraffin(e) base (concrete) curing compound, ~ ~ (~) ~ agent, ~ ~ (liquid) membrane (~) ~ ~ · (Beton-) Nachbehandlungsmittel *n* auf Paraffinbasis

paraffinic-base crude, ~ (crude) petroleum · paraffinbasisches (Erd)Öl *n*

parallel-boom truss, parallel-chord ~, parallel-flange ~ · Parallel(gurt)träger *m*

parallel-chord truss, parallel-flange ~, parallel-boom ~ · Parallel(gurt)träger *m*

parallel-flange truss, parallel-boom ~, parallel-chord ~ · Parallel(gurt)träger *m*

parallel lattice cupola, ~ ~ dome · Parallelgitterkuppel *f*

~ ~ **dome,** ~ ~ cupola · Parallelgitterkuppel *f*

~ ~ **girder** · Parallelgitterträger *m*

~ **projection,** axonometric ~ · Parallelriß *m*, Parallelprojektion *f*, Parallelperspektive *f*, parallele Projektion, Militärperspektive, parallele Perspektive

~ **system of forces** · parallele Kräftegruppe *f*

~ **trace of lines** · Parallelenzug *m*

parallel-wire cable · Spannkabel *n* mit parallel angeordneten Drähten

parallelepiped of forces · Kräfterechtkant *m*, Kräfteparallelepiped *n*

parallelepipedal cut stone · Quader(stein) *m*, Parallelepiped *n*

parallelism · Parallelität *f*

parallelogram of forces, force parallelogram · Parallelogramm *n* der Kräfte, Kräfteparallelogramm

~ **plate,** ~ slab · Parallelogrammplatte *f*

~ **slab,** ~ plate · Parallelogrammplatte *f*

parapet · Brüstung *f*

~ → (under-)window spandrel

~ **brick,** ~ wall clay ~ · Brüstungsziegel *m*

~ **(building) component** → spandrel (building) unit

~ **(~) member** → spandrel (building) unit

~ **(~) unit** → spandrel (~) ~

~ **clay brick** → ~ wall ~ ~

~ **component** → spandrel (building) unit

~ **facing** → spandrel (wall) (sur)facing

~ **grille** · Brüstungsgitter *n*

~ **lining** → spandrel (wall) (sur)facing

~ **masonry wall** [*A low masonry wall protecting the edge of a roof, bridge, terrace or quay*] · Brüstung(smauer) *f*, Brustmauer

~ **member** → spandrel (building) unit

~ **panel** → (under-)window spandrel ~

~ **slab** · Brüstungsplatte *f*

~ **(sur)facing** → spandrel (wall) ~

~ **unit** → spandrel (building) ~

~ **wall** [*A low wall protecting the edge of a roof, bridge, terrace or quay*] · Brüstung(swand) *f*

~ ~ **brick** → ~ ~ clay ~

~ **(~) (clay) brick** · Brüstungsziegel *m*

parasitic infestation, pest ~ · Schädlingsbefall *m*

paraskenion [*In an ancient Greek treatre, one of the wings of the scena projecting into the orchestra*] · Paraskenion *n*, vorspringender Flügel *m*

parcel, batch · Bündel *n* [*Z.B. aus Parkettstäben*]

~ **of land** · Grundstück *n*

parclose · Scheid(e)wand *f* [*Chorgestühl*]

~ **screen** [*In medieval architecture, a screen dividing a chantry chapel or a tomb from the body of a church*] · Schranken *fpl*, Gitter *n*

parent glass, base ~ · Grundglas *n*, Stammglas, Mutterglas

parent's bath · Elternbad *n*

~ **bedroom** · Elternschlafraum *m*, Elternschlafzimmer *n*

~ **room** · Elternzimmer *n*

parget(ing), parging, pargetting, pargework, perget [*Exterior plastering of a timber-framed building, usually modelled in designs, e.g., vine pattern, foliage and figures*] · gemusterter Außen(ver)putz *m*

Parian marble · parischer Marmor *m*

~ **plaster,** ~ **cement** · Boraxgips, *m*, Parianalabaster *m*, Parianzement *m*

parianite, Trinidad refined asphalt, Trinidad épuré · gereinigter Trinidad-Asphalt *m*, Trinidad-Epuré *n*

Paris black (pigment) · Pariserschwarz *n*

~ **blue (pigment)** · Pariserblau *n*

~ **white, whiting** · Schlämmkreide *f* [*Kreide ist eine natürliche Mineralfarbe. Sie besteht im wesentlichen aus kohlensaurem Kalk (= Kalziumkarbonat* $CaCO_3$*). Nach dem Schlämmverfahren wird sie Schlämmkreide genannt. Benennungen nach den Fundorten: Rügener Kreide, Champagnerkreide, schwedische Kreide, Bologneser Kreide*]

~ **yellow (pigment)** · Parisergelb *n*

parish centre (Brit.); ~ **center** (US) · (Pfarr)Gemeindezentrum *n*, Kirchenzentrum

~ **church** · Pfarrkirche *f*, Parochialkirche, Hauptkirche

~ **hall,** ~ **room, church hall** · (kirchlicher) Gemeinderaum *m*

~ **house, parochial** ~ · Gemeindehaus *n*, kirchliches ~

~ **room,** ~ **hall, church hall** · (kirchlicher) Gemeinderaum *m*

parison, blank [*A preliminary shape or blank from which a glass article is to be formed*] · Külbel *m*

park · Park *m*

~ **architecture** · Parkarchitektur *f*, Parkbaukunst *f*

~ **bench** · Parkbank *f*

~ **path** · Parkweg *m*

~ **road** · Parkstraße *f*

Parkerizing · Parkern *n*, Parker-Rostschutzverfahren *n*

Parker's cement, Roman ~ · Romankalk *m* [*DIN 1060. Aus Tonmergel unterhalb der Sintergrenze gebrannt. Fehlnamen: Romanzement, römischer Zement, Parkerzement, schwarzer Zement*]

parking area · Parkfläche *f*, Parkplatz *m*

~ **building** · Parkbau *m*, Parkhaus *n*, Parkgebäude *n*, Parkgarage *f* [*Ein ein- oder mehrgeschossiges ober- oder unterirdisches Gebäude, das dem Parken dient*]

~ ~ **with staggered main floors and intermediate levels** · Parkhaus *n* mit versetzten Haupt- und Podestgeschossen, Parkgebäude *n* ~ ~ ~ ~ ~, Parkbau *m* ~ ~ ~ ~ ~ ~, Parkgarage *f* ~ ~ ~ ~ ~

~ **capacity** · Parkfassungsvermögen *n*, Parkleistungsfähigkeit *f*

~ **compound** [*Of a rental row-house development*] · Sammelparkplatz *m*

~ **deck** · Parkplatte *f*, Parkdeck *n*

~ **facility** → off-street ~ ~

~ **floor;** ~ **story** (US); ~ **storey** (Brit.) · Parketage *f*, Parkstockwerk *n*, Parkgeschoß *n*

~ **garage, car park** · Großgarage *f*

~ **lane** · Parkspur *f*, Parkstreifen *m*

~ **level** · Parkebene *f*

~ **ramp** · Parkrampe *f*

~ **roof,** car ~ ~ · Parkdach *n*

~ **shed** · Parkhalle *f*

~ **space (per car)** · Parkraum *m* (pro PKW)

parking storey — partial system (of sewerage)

~ storey (Brit.); **~ story** (US); **~ floor** · Parketage f, Parkstockwerk n, Parkgeschoß m

~ street · Parkstraße f [Ausschließlich dem parkenden Verkehr vorbehaltene Stadtstraße]

~ structure · Parkbauwerk n

~ terrace · Parkterrasse f

~ time · Parkdauer f

~ tower, autostacker, pidgeonhole (parking structure) · Autosilo m, Parkturm m

parlatory, (convent) parlour, locutory, speak-house · Sprechsaal m, Parlatorium n

parliament block, ~ building · Parlamentsgebäude n

parlour, convent ~, locutory, speakhouse, parlatory · Parlatorium n, Sprechsaal m

parochial house, parish ~ · Gemeindehaus n, kirchliches ~

parquet(ry) · Parkett n

~ block · Parkettstab m [DIN 280]

~ composite · Fertigparkett n

~ floor cover(ing), **~ floor(ing) (finish)** · Parkett(fuß)boden(belag) m

~ sealing · Parkettversiegelung f

~ timber, **~ wood** · Parkettholz n

~ wood, **~ timber** · Parkettholz n

~ work · Parkettarbeiten fpl [DIN 18356]

parsonage · Pfarrwohnung f

~ (building), rectory, priest's house [In the Roman Catholic Church called presbytery'] · Pfarre f, Pfarrhaus n

part of a building, building part · Gebäudeteil m, n, [Räumlich und/oder funktionell abgegrenzter Teil eines Gebäudes. Beispiele: Treppenhaus; Aufzugschacht; Geschoß usw.]

~ ~ ~ medium · Mediumteil m, n [Akustik]

~ ~ ~ site not covered by a building · unbebaute Fläche f eines Baugrundstückes

~ ~ ~ structure · Bauwerkteil m, n [z.B. Hochhauskern; Raumzelle; Dachstuhl usw.]

parterre · Gartenparterre n [Eine ebene Gartenfläche, die im französischen Garten unmittelbar an das Haus oder Schloß anschließt und sich auf seine Architektur bezieht, mit symmetrisch ornamental gestalteten Beeten]

Parthenon · Parthenon m [Tempel auf der Akropolis von Athen]

~ pediment · Parthenongiebel m

Parthian architecture · Partherarchitektur f, Partherbaukunst f

partial · Teilton m [A pure tone component of a complex tone]

~ air conditioning · Teilklimatisierung f

~ casing → ~ (concrete) encasement

~ collapse · Teileinsturz m

~ (concrete) casing → ~ (~) encasement

~ (~) encasement, ~ (~) encasure, ~ (~) haunching ~ (~) sheath coat, ~ (~) casing · Teilumhüllung f aus Beton, Teilummantelung ~ ~

~ (~) encasure → ~ (~) encasement

~ (~) haunching → ~ (~) encasement

~ (~) sheat coat → ~ (~) encasement

~ drawing · Teilzeichnung f

~ encasement → ~ concrete ~

~ encasure → ~ (concrete) encasement

~ fixity, **~ restraint** · Teileinspannung f

~ haunching → ~ (concrete) encasement

~ hip, half ~ · halber Walm m, Krüppelwalm, Schopfwalm, Kielende n, Kühlende

~ integration · partielle Integration f, teilweise ~

~ load · Teillast f

~ loading · Teilbelastung f

~ prefabrication · Teilvorfertigung f

~ pressure · Teildruck m

~ (pre)stressing, ~ tensioning, ~ stretching · beschränkte Vorspannung f, teilweise ~, Teilvorspannung

~ purification · Teilreinigung f [Abwasser]

~ reaction, **~ reactive force** · Teilstützkraft f, Teil-Auflagerwiderstand m, Teil-Auflagerreaktion f, Teilstützreaktion, Teil-Auflagerkraft, Teilstützdruck m, Teilgegendruck, Teilstützwiderstand, Teil-Auflagerdruck

~ reactive force, **~ reaction** · Teilstützkraft f, Teil-Auflagerwiderstand m, Teil-Auflagerreaktion f, Teilstützreaktion, Teil-Auflagerkraft, Teilstützdruck m, Teilgegendruck, Teilstützwiderstand, Teil-Auflagerdruck

~ restraint, **~ fixity** · Teileinspannung f

~ saturation · Teilsättigung f

~ sewerage (system) → ~ system (of sewerage)

~ shear crack · Teilschubriß m

~ sheath coat → ~ (concrete) encasement

~ solution · Teillösung f

~ stressing, ~ pre~, ~ tensioning, ~ stretching · beschränkte Vorspannung f, teilweise ~, Teilvorspannung

~ stretching, ~ tensioning, ~ (pre-)stressing · beschränkte Vorspannung f, teilweise ~, Teilvorspannung

~ system (of sewerage), ~ ~ ~ sewers, ~ sewerage (system) · Teilkanalisation f, Teilsystem n [Sie führt nur Brauchwasser und feste und flüssige Fäkalien, vereinzelt auch Gewerbeabwasser ab, nicht aber Niederschlags-

partial system (of sewerage) — partition penetration

wasser, welches von Hof- und Straßenflächen durch Rinnen abgeleitet wird und an geeigneter Stelle versinkt]

~ **tensioning**, ~ stretching, ~ (pre-)stressing · beschränkte Vorspannung f, teilweise ~, Teilvorspannung

~ **venting** · Teilentlüftung f [*Grundstücksentwässerung*]

~ **vitrification** · Klinkerung f, Teilverglasung [*Entsteht durch thermische Behandlung eines Stoffes oder einer Mischung, wobei sich eine gewisse Menge an Schmelz- oder Glasphase bildet, die einen niedrigen Anteil offener Poren ergibt*]

partially air-conditioned · teilklimatisiert

~ **dry steam** → wet ~

~ **fixed** · teilweise eingespannt

~ ~ **joint**, semi-flexible ~, semi-rigid ~ · halbstarre Verbindung f

~ **(pre)stressed**, ~ stretched, ~ tensioned · beschränkt vorgespannt, teilweise ~

~ **stretched**, ~ (pre)stressed, ~ tensioned · beschränkt vorgespannt, teilweise ~

~ **tensioned**, ~ stretched, ~ (pre-)stressed · teilweise vorgespannt, beschränkt ~

~ **transparent** → translucent

~-**vacuumed cavity** · Teilvakuumhohlraum m

partially vented · teilentlüftet

particle · Teilchen n

~, **grain** · Korn n

~ **diameter**, grain ~ · Korndurchmesser m

~ ~ · Teilchendurchmesser m

~ **(distribution) limit**, limiting (grading) curve, gradation limit, grading limit · Siebgrenze f, Grenzsieblinie f

~ **fineness**, grain ~ · Kornfeinheit f

~ **limit** → ~ distribution ~

~ **porosity**, grain ~, porosity of grains, porosity of particles · Korneigenporigkeit f

~ **shape** · Teilchenform f

~ ~, grain ~ · Kornform f, Korngestalt f

~ ~ **factor**, grain ~ ~ · Kornformfaktor m, Korngestaltfaktor

~ ~ **test**, grain ~ ~ · Kornformprobe f, Kornformversuch m, Kornformprüfung f

~ **size** · Teilchengröße f

~ ~, grain ~ · Korngröße f [*Größenbezeichnung für ein Korn in mm oder µm. Das Meßverfahren ist anzugeben. Ist kein Meßverfahren angeführt, dann gilt die Loch- bzw. Maschenweite nach DIN 1170 bzw. 4188*]

particle-size analysis, grain-size ~, grading ~, test for grading [*The process of determining the proportions of different particle sizes in a granular material by sieving, sedimentation, elutriation or other means*] · Korn(größen)analyse f

~ **determination**, grain-size ~ · Korngrößenbestimmung f

~ **distribution**, grain-size ~, grading, texture, granulometric composition · Kornaufbau m, Kornzusammensetzung f, Korn(größen)verteilung

~ ~ **curve**, grain-size ~ ~, (aggregate) grading ~, sieve ~ · Siebkurve f, Sieblinie f, Körnungskurve, Körnungslinie, Kornverteilungskurve, Kornverteilungslinie

~ **limit**, grain-size ~ · Korngrenze f

particle strength, grain ~ · Kornfestigkeit f

~ **surface**, grain ~ · Kornoberfläche f

~ **velocity** [*At a point in a sound field. The alternating component of the total velocity of movement of the medium at the point i.e. the total velocity minus the velocity (if any) which is not due to sound. Symbol u. The unit is the metre per second. Note. The term 'particle velocity' may be qualified by the terms 'instantaneous', 'maximum', 'r.m.s.'. etc. The unqualified term 'particle velocity' is frequently taken to imply r.m.s. value*] · Schallschnelle f [*Wechselgeschwindigkeit eines schwingenden Teilchens. Anmerkung: In der Akustik wird die Wechselgeschwindigkeit als „Schnelle" bezeichnet, um Verwechslungen mit der Ausbreitungsgeschwindigkeit zu vermeiden*]

particles, grains, material · Gekörn n, Körner npl, Korn n

particular integral · Partikularintegral n

particularistic Gothic, German Late Gothic (style) · (deutsche) Sondergotik f

parting agent, ~ medium, ~ compound · Antikleb(e)mittel n, Trennmittel, Antikleb(e)stoff m, Antikleber m

~ **compound**, ~ medium, ~ agent · Antikleb(e)mittel n, Trennmittel, Antikleb(e)stoff m, Antikleber m

~ **medium**, ~ compound, ~ agent · Antikleb(e)mittel n, Trennmittel, Antikleb(e)stoff m, Antikleber m

partition [*walls and floors*] · Trennkonstruktion f [*Wände und Decken*]

~ → ~ wall

~ **block** → ~ wall ~

~ **blockwork** → ~ wall ~

~ **brick** → ~ wall ~

~ **(building) component** → ~ (wall) (building) unit

~ (~) **member** → ~ (wall) (building) unit

~ (~) **unit** → ~ wall (~) ~

~ **component** → ~ (wall) (building) unit

~ **member** → ~ (wall) (building) unit

~ **panel**, ~ wall ~ · Trennwandtafel f

~ **penetration**, ~ wall ~ · Trennwanddurchgang m

partition pot — passenger(-handling) facility 700

~ **pot** → hollow partition (wall) block
~ **profile** → ~ (wall) unit
~ **ratio** · (Ver)Teilungszahl f [*Siebtechnik*]
~ **section** → ~ wall ~
~ **shape** → ~ wall ~
~ **slab** → ~ wall ~
~ **system** → partitioning ~
~ **tile** → ~ wall ~
~ **trim** → ~ wall ~
~ **unit** → ~ wall ~
~ **(wall), PTN** · Trennwand f
~ **(~) block,** ~ (~) tile [*See remark under 'Block'*] · Trennwandblock(stein) m, Trennwandstein
~ **(~) blockwork** · Trennwand-Blockmauerwerk n, Trennwand-(Block)Steinmauerwerk
~ **(~) brick** · Trennwandziegel m
~ **(~) (building) unit,** ~ (~) (~) member, ~ (~) (~) component · Trennwand(bau)element n, Trennwand(bau)körper m [*Fehlname: Trennwandbaueinheit f*]
~ **(~) component** → ~ (~) (building) unit
~ **(~) member** → ~ (~) (building) unit
~ **(~) panel** · Trennwandtafel f
~ **(~) penetration** · Trennwanddurchgang m
~ **(~) pot** → hollow partition (wall) block
~ **(~) profile** → ~ (~) unit
~ **(~) section,** ~ (~) trim, ~ (~) shape, ~ (~) profile · Trennwandprofil n
~ **(~) shape,** ~ (~) section, ~ (~) unit, ~ (~) trim, ~ (~) profile · Trennwandprofil n
~ **(~) slab** · Trennwandplatte f
~ ~ **system,** partition(ing) ~ · Trennwandsystem n
~ **(~) tile,** ~ (~) block [*See remark under 'Block'*] · Trennwandblock(stein) m, Trennwandstein
~ **(~) ~** · Trennwand(belag)platte f, Trennwandfliese f
~ **(~) trim,** ~ (~) unit, ~ (~) shape, ~ (~) section, ~ (~) profile · Trennwandprofil n
~ **(~) unit** → ~ (~) building ~
~ **(~) ~,** ~ (~) section, ~ (~) shape, ~ (~) trim, ~ (~) profile · Trennwandprofil n
~ **(~) which can be lowered** · Versenkwand f
partitioning, interior ~ · Abtrennung f durch Trennwände, Einteilung ~ ~, Einteilung von Räumen, Raumeinteilung
partition(ing) glazing · Trennwandeinglasung f, Trennwandverglasung

~ **system,** partition wall ~ · Trennwandsystem n
party corbel [*A corbel projecting from the face of a building at the end of the party wall for decoration or to check the spread of fire*] · Brandmauerkonsole f, Kommunmauerkonsole, Feuermauerkonsole
~ **(masonry) wall** → fire division (~) ~
parvis(e) → ceremonial forecourt
pass window · Durchreichfenster n, Durchgabefenster
passage [*A narrow thoroughfare within or alongside a building*] · Durchfahrt f
~, **fauces** · Gang m [*in einem römischen Privathaus*]
~ **of air** · Luftdurchgang m
passage(way); areaway (US) · Durchgang m, Passage f
passenger and luggage handling level · Abfertigungsebene f, Empfangsebene, Empfangsfläche, Abfertigungsfläche [*Waag(e)rechte Teilfläche im Abfertigungsgebäude eines Flughafens mit organisatorischer und funktioneller Aufteilung der Verkehrswege und Abfertigungsvorgänge für Fluggäste und Gepäck*]
~ **block** → passenger(-handling) building
~ **building** → ~-handling ~
~-**carrying capacity** · Tragfähigkeit f [*Fahrstuhl*]
passenger counter, ~-handling ~ · Fahrgastschalter m, Passagierschalter
(~) elevator (US); (~) lift (Brit.) · Fahrstuhl m, (Personen)Aufzug m [*DIN 15301 und DIN 15302*]
(~) ~ door (US); (~) lift ~ (Brit.). · (Personen)Aufzugtür f, Fahrstuhltür
(~) ~ entrance (US) → (~) lift (landing) ~
(~) elevator hoistway, ~ ~ shaft(way) (US); ~ **lift well (Brit.)** · Personenaufzugschacht m, Personenaufzugkern m, Fahrstuhlschacht, Fahrstuhlkern
(~) ~ installation (US) → (~) lift ~
(~) ~ (landing) entrance (US) → (~) lift (~) ~
~ **facility** → ~-handling ~
passenger(-handling) block, ~ building · Passagier(abfertigungs)gebäude n, Fahrgast(abfertigungs)gebäude
~ **building,** ~ block · Fahrgast(abfertigungs)gebäude n, Passagier(abfertigungs)gebäude
~ **counter** · Passagierschalter m, Fahrgastschalter
~ **facility,** ~ **installation** · Fahrgast(abfertigungs)anlage f, Passagier(abfertigungs)anlage

passenger(-handling) installation — patch mortar

~ **installation**, ~ facility · Passagier(abfertigungs)anlage f, Fahrgast(abfertigungs)anlage

~ **point** · Abfertigungsstelle f [Flugsteigkopf]

passenger installation → passenger-(-handling) facility

(~) **lift** (Brit.); (~) elevator (US) · Fahrstuhl m, (Personen)Aufzug m [DIN 15301 und DIN 15302]

(~) ~ **car** (Brit.); (~) elevator ~ (US) · Fahrstuhlkorb m, Fahrstuhlkabine f

(~) ~ **door** (Brit.); (~) elevator ~ (US) · (Personen)Aufzugtür f, Fahrstuhltür

(~) ~ **entrance** → (~) ~ landing ~

(~) ~ **installation** (Brit.); (~) elevator ~ (US) · (Personen)Aufzuganlage, Fahrstuhlanlage

(~) ~ **(landing) entrance**; (~) elevator (~) ~ (US) · Fahrstuhleingang m

(~) ~ **well** (Brit.); ~ elevator shaft(way), ~ elevator hoistway (US) · Personenaufzugschacht m, Personenaufzugkern m, Fahrstuhlschacht, Fahrstuhlkern

~ **loading apron**, ramp · Abfertigungsgebäuderampe f, Empfangsgebäuderampe

~ **platform** · Personenbahnsteig m

~ **point**, ~-handling ~ · Abfertigungsstelle f [Flugsteigkopf]

~ **railroad station** (US); ~ railway ~ (Brit.) · Personenbahnhof m

~ **railway station** (Brit.); ~ railroad ~ (US) · Personenbahnhof m

~ **room** · Fluggastraum m

(~) **terminal** · Abfertigungsanlage f, Empfangsanlage [Flughafen]

(~) ~ **block**, (~) ~ building · Abfertigungsgebäude n, Empfangsgebäude [Teil einer Abfertigungsanlage eines Flughafens]

(~) ~ **building**, (~) ~ block · Abfertigungsgebäude n, Empfangsgebäude [Teil einer Abfertigungsanlage eines Flughafens]

~ **walkway** · Fluggastbrücke f

to passify · passivieren

passing a pipe through a wall · Rohrdurchführung f

passivating, immunizing · Passivieren n

~, immunizing · passivierend

~ **coat**, immunizing ~ · Passivierungsanstrich m, Passivierungsaufstrich

passivation · Passivierung f

passive fire defense; ~ ~ defence (Brit.) · baulich bedingter Brandschutz m, ~ ~ Feuerschutz

pastas, prostas(is) · Prostas(is) m, Pastas m [Vorhalle des griechischen Wohnhauses]

to paste · kleistern, mit Kleister bestreichen

paste · Paste f

~ · Kleister m

~ **drier**, patent ~, ~ dryer [Driers made by grinding suitable compounds of lead and manganese with a small amount of water, linseed oil and Paris white, with or without other mineral extenders, to form a stiff paste. They are still sometimes used by painters when mixing their own linseed oil paints, but are now largely superseded by soluble and liquid driers] · Trockenstoff m in fester Form [DIN 55901]

~ **filler** · Füllpaste f

~ **flux**, flux paste · Flußmittel n [für Lötpaste]

~ **for hanging** → (paper)hanging paste

~ ~ **(paper)hanging** → (paper)hanging paste

~ ~ **wallpaperhanging** → (paper-)hanging paste

paste-in-oil basic lead carbonate, ~ (white lead) · Ölpaste f [Bleiweiß mit 10% bis 12% Leinöl]

~ **(white lead)**, ~ basic lead carbonate · Ölpaste f [Bleiweiß mit 10% bis 12% Leinöl]

paste-like, pasty · pastenförmig, pastös

paste matrix, hardened cement paste · erhärteter Zementleim m, ~ Zementbrei m, erhärtete Zementpaste f, Zementstein m

~ **paint** · Farbpaste f

~ **polish** · Polierpaste f

~ **residue** · Kleisterrest m, Kleisterrückstand m

~ **resin** · Pastenharz n

~ **spot** · Kleisterdurchschlag m

paste-type paint remover, ~ ~ stripper, paint remover in paste form, paint stripper in paste form · pastenartiges (Ab)Beizmittel n, (Ab)Beizpaste f

paste white lead, white lead paste · Bleiweißpaste f, Pastenbleiweiß n

pastel colour (Brit.); ~ color (US) · Pastellfarbe f

~ **painting** · Pastellmalerei f

~ **shade** · Pastellton m

pasting · Bestreichen n mit Kleister, Kleistern

~ **and applying to wall** · Aufkleben n mit Kleister [(Papier)Tapete]

pasty, paste-like · pastenförmig, pastös

pat of cement-water paste, cement pat, circular-domed pat of cement, soundness test pat · (Probe)Kuchen m (aus Zement), Zementkuchen

~ **test** · Kuchenprobe f [Zement]

patch mortar, patching ~, repair ~ · Ausbesserungsmörtel m, Flickmörtel

patch of sky — pattern

~ of sky · Himmelsausschnitt m [Tageslichtberechnung]

~ ~ visible sky · sichtbarer Himmelsausschnitt m [Tageslichtberechnung]

patching, repairing · (Aus)Flicken n, Ausbessern

patch(ing) composition, ~ compound, repair ~ · Flickmasse f, Ausbesserungsmasse

~ compound, ~ composition, repair ~ · Flickmasse f, Ausbesserungsmasse

~ concrete, repair ~ · Flickbeton m, Ausbesserungsbeton

~ emulsion, repair ~ · Flickemulsion f, Ausbesserungsemulsion

~ mortar, repair ~ · Ausbesserungsmörtel m, Flickmörtel

~ plaster, repair ~ [*A special plaster made for repairing plaster walls*] · Ausbesserungsputz m, Flickputz

~ work, repair ~ · Flickarbeiten fpl, Ausbesserungsarbeiten

patchy · fleckig [*Putzfläche*]

patent drier → paste ~

~ glass → (polished) plate ~

~ glazing, puttyless ~, dry ~ · kittlose Verglasung f, ~ Einglasung, kittloses Verglasen n, kittloses Einglasen

~ ~ bar, puttyless ~ ~ [*A glazing bar of special type and profile designed for dry glazing, i.e. without the use of putty, mastic or like substances*] · Sprosse f [*Für kittlose Oberlichter und Glasdächer*]

~ ~ roof, puttyless ~ ~, dry ~ ~ · kittloses Glasdach n

~ roof glazing, puttyless ~ ~, dry ~ ~ · kittlose Dachverglasung f

~ stone → cast ~

~ ~ floor cover(ing) → cast stone floor(ing) (finish)

~ ~ floor(ing) (finish) → cast ~ ~ (~)

~ ~ shop → reconstituted ~ ~

~ ~ skin → cast ~ ~

~ ~ stair(case) → cast ~ ~

~ ~ tile → reconstituted ~ ~

~ ~ ~ floor cover(ing) → cast stone tile floor(ing) (finish)

~ ~ waterproofer → cast ~ ~

~ ~ work → cast ~ ~

patented floor · Patentdecke f

~ wire · patentierter Draht m

patenting [*Patenting is a heat treatment applied to rods and wire having a carbon content of 0.40 per cent and higher, the term being peculiar to the wire industry. The object of patenting is to obtain a structure which combines high tensile strength with the high ductility and thus impart to the wire the ability to withstand heavy drafting to produce the desired finished sizes possessing a combination of high tensile strength and good toughness*] · Patentieren n [*Draht*]

~ by electrical resistance heating · Widerstandspatentieren n

~ furnace · Durchlaufofen m [*Patentieren*]

patera [*A small, flat, circular or oval ornament in classical architecture, often decorated with acanthus leaves or rose petals*] · Opferschale f, Patera f

paternoster (lift) [*B.S. 2655*] · Paternoster(-Aufzug) m, Elevator m, Umlaufaufzug

path gravel, binding ~; hoggin (Brit.) [*Well graded gravel having enough natural clay binder to make it suitable, with consolidation, for forming light-duty roads or paths*] · Fußwegkies m

~ of (pre)stressing force, ~ ~ stretching ~, ~ ~ tensioning ~ · Spannweg m

~ ~ stressing force, ~ ~ pre~ ~, ~ ~ tensioning ~, ~ ~ stretching ~ · Spannweg m

~ ~ stretching force, ~ ~ tensioning ~, ~ ~ (pre)stressing ~ · Spannweg m

~ ~ tensioning force, ~ ~ stretching ~, ~ ~ (pre)stressing ~ · Spannweg m

~ surround · Wegeinfassung f

~ tile · Wege(belag)platte f, Wegefliese f

patient division · Bettenabteilung f [*Krankenhaus*]

patient's bathroom · Patientenbadezimmer n

~ garden · Patienten-Garten m

patina, greenish ~ [*The thin, stable film of oxide or other metallic compounds which forms on metal surfaces on exposure to air*] · Edelrost m, Patina f

patio, terrace [*An unroofed, paved area immediately adjacent to a house and overlooking a lawn or garden. Abbreviated: ter*] · Terrasse f

~ [*In Spanish and Spanish American architecture, an inner courtyard open to the sky*] · Lichthof m, Patio m

~ door, terrace ~ · Terrassentür f

~ ~ fitting, terrace ~ ~, ~ ~ hardware item · Terrassentürbeschlag m

~ ~ fittings, terrace ~ ~, ~ ~ furniture, ~ ~ hardware · Terrassentürbeschläge mpl

~ ~ furniture, terrace ~ ~, ~ ~ fittings, ~ ~ hardware · Terrassentürbeschläge mpl

~ ~ hardware, terrace ~ ~, ~ ~ fittings, ~ ~ furniture · Terrassentürbeschläge mpl

~ ~ ~ item, terrace ~ ~ ~, ~ ~ ~ fitting · Terrassentürbeschlag m

~ masonry wall · Lichthofmauer f

patriarchal cross, double ~ · Patriarchenkreuz n, Patriarchalkreuz, Kardinalskreuz, Doppelkreuz

to pattern, to give a decorative finish · ornamentieren, mustern

pattern · Bildmuster n, Schema n

~, finish, decorative ~, ornamental ~,

decoration, decorative feature, ornament(al feature), enrichment · Dekor(ation) m, (f), Ornament(ierung) n, (f), Schmuck m, Verzierung, Muster(ung) n, (f)

~ **bond** · Musterverband m

~ **brick masonry (work)** (US) → decorative (pattern) brickwork

~ **brickwork** → decorative (~) ~

~ **floor(ing) (finish) tile** → patterned ~ (~) ~

~ **for diffusion** · Lichtdiffusionsmuster n [Glas]

~ **glass** → patterned ~

~ **-glazed** · dekorativ-glasiert

pattern of deformation · Form(geb)ung f [Bewehrungsstab]

~ ~ **light and shade** · Licht- und Schattenmuster n

~ ~ **loading**, loading pattern · Belastungsschema n

pattern(ed) floor cover(ing) tile, ~ floor(ing) (finish) ~ · profilierte (Fuß-) Boden(belag)platte f, ~ (Fuß)Bodenfliese f [Die Oberfläche einer solchen Fliese ist zwecks Gleitsicherheit genarbt, gekörnt, geriffelt, gerippt oder mit scharfkantigen Nocken versehen]

~ **floor(ing) (finish) tile,** ~ floor cover(ing) ~ · profilierte (Fuß)Boden(belag)platte f, ~ (Fuß)Bodenfliese f [Die Oberfläche einer solchen Fliese ist zwecks Gleitsicherheit genarbt, gekörnt, geriffelt, gerippt oder mit scharfkantigen Nocken versehen]

~ **glass,** ornamental ~, decorative ~, (figur(ed)) rolled ~ · Ornamentglas n, Zierglas, Dekor(ations)glas, ornamentiertes Glas, Schmuckglas

patterned veneer, fancy ~, rare ~, figured ~ · Maserfurnier n

pattern(ed) wallpaper · gemusterte Tapete f

~ **wire(d) glass** → figure(d) ~ ~

paved area · befestigte Fläche f

~ **footway,** ~ walk · befestigter Fußweg m, ~ Gehweg

~ **play area** · befestigte Spielfläche f

~ **walk,** ~ footway · befestigter Gehweg m, ~ Fußweg

pavement cement; paving ~ (US) · Deckenzement m [Sonderzement für Betonstraßen, Er bindet langsam ab, ist hochzugfest, genügend druckfest und wenig schwindend]

~ **concrete** · Belagbeton m

~ **entrance** · Zugang m zu einem U-Bahnhof von der Straße aus

~ **light** [A means of admitting air or light to premises under or abutting on the street] · Kellerlichtschacht m

~ ~, **vault** ~ [A light formed of solid glass blocks cast into concrete or set in a cast-iron frame over a basement so as to let in daylight] · Kelleroberlicht n

~ **prism** [A glass block fitted in a pavement light] · Kelleroberlicht-Glasbaustein m

pavilion · Pavillon m

~ **-like** · pavillonähnlich

pavilion roof, multi-angular ~, polygonal ~ · Polygon(al)dach n

~ ~, pyramidal hipped ~ · (ab)gewalmtes Pyramidendach n

~ **school** · Pavillonschule f

pavilion(-type) classroom · Pavillonklasse f

~ **structure** · Pavillon-Bauwerk n

pavimentum [A classical pavement formed by pieces of tile, marble, stone, flints, or other material set in cement and consolidated by beating down with a rammer] · Pavimentum n

paving · Pflaster(decke) n, (f), Steinpflaster, Pflasterung f, Fp [Schweiz: Pflästerung]

~ **asphalt** → ~ grade ~

~ ~ **with road tar addition,** A.C. ~ ~ ~ ~, asphalt cement ~ ~ ~ ~ (US); (asphaltic-)bitumen for road purposes ~ ~ ~ ~ (Brit.) · Teerbitumen n, TB [Straßenbaubitumen mit einem anzugebenden Zusatz von Straßenteer]

~ **brick** → ~ clinker ~

~ **cement** (US) → pavement ~

~ **(clinker) brick,** paving clinker · Pflasterziegel m, Pflasterklinker m, Straßen(bau)klinker, Straßen(bau)ziegel

~ **(grade) asphalt,** A.C., asphalt cement (US); (asphaltic-)bitumen for road purposes (Brit.) [B.S. 3690] · Straßenbaubitumen n [DIN 1995]

~ **in rows,** coursed paving · Großpflaster(decke) n, (f) in Reihenform, Reihen(stein)pflaster(decke)

~ **of engineering bricks,** engineering brick paving · Klinkerpflaster(decke) n, (f)

(~) **sett,** pavior · Pflasterstein m

~ **tile** · Pflasterfliese f

~ **wood** · Pflasterholz n

pavior · Pflasterer m, Steinsetzer

~, (paving) sett · Pflasterstein m

pax(board), osculatory · Kußtäfelchen n, Pax, Pacem, Pacifiale f

Paxton gutter [Structural member designed by Joseph Paxton for collecting both internal and external moisture in conservatories and greenhouses] · Paxton-Rinne f

pay day · Lohntag m, Zahltag

~ **station** → public (tele)phone coin box

P. B. S. → prefab(ricated) bituminous surfacing

PC → portland cement

P. C. C., Portland cement concrete, portland cement concrete · Portlandzementbeton m

PCRV, prestressed (concrete) reactor vessel · Spannbeton-Druckbehälter *m*

PE → polyethylene

P. E. Sabine absorption coefficient · Sabinescher Absorptionsgrad *m*, ~ Schluckgrad [*Die auf 1 m² bezogene äquivalente Schallschluckfläche*]

P. E. Sabine formula · Sabinesche Formel *f*

pea gravel · Erbskies *m*, Perlkies

peak current · Spitzenenergie *f*, Spitzenstrom *m*

~ **demand heating plant** · Spitzenheizwerk *n*

~ **load,** maximum ~ · Höchstlast *f*, Spitzenlast, Maximallast

~ **moment** · Spitzenmoment *n*

~ **period** · Spitzenperiode *f*, Spitzenzeit *f*

~ **quantity** · Spitzenmenge *f*

~ **stress,** stress raiser · Spannungsspitze *f*

~ **supply** · Abgabespitze *f*

pearl glue → Scotch glue in pearl form

Pearl Mosque at Agra, Motī Masjid · Perlenmoschee *f* in der Feste Agra

pe(a)rlite · Perlit *m* [*Gefügebestandteil des langsam abgekühlten Kohlenstoffstahls*]

~ [*a volcanic glass*] · Perlit *m* [*ein vulkanisches Glas*]

~ **absorbent ceiling** → ~ acoustic(al) ~

~ **acoustic(al) ceiling,** ~ sound-control ~, ~ (sound) absorbent ~, ~ (sound) absorbing ~, ~ (sound) absorptive ~, ~ acoustic tiled ~ · Perlit-Schallschluckdecke *f*, Perlit-Akustikdecke, Perlit-Schallabsorptionsdecke

~ **aggregate** · Perlitzuschlag(stoff) *m*

pe(a)rlite/asphalt concrete (US); pe(a)rlite/(asphaltic-)bitumen ~ (Brit.) [*A monolithic insulating fill made with perlite aggregate and asphalt (US)/(asphaltic-)bitumen (Brit.) to form an insulating roofing material*] · Perlit-Bitumen-Dämmschicht *f* [*Markenname in Deutschland: Thermoperl*]

pe(a)rlite concrete → ~ light(weight) ~

~ ~, ~ insulating ~ · Perlit(dämm)beton *m*

~ ~ **roof** · Perlitbetondach *n*

~ ~ ~ **slab,** ~ insulating ~ ~ ~ · Perlit(dämm)betondachplatte *f*

~ ~ **slab** · Perlitbetonplatte *f*

~ **expansion plant** · Expansionsanlage *f* für Perlitkies

~ **gravel** · Perlitkies *m*

~ **(insulating) concrete** · Perlit(dämm)beton *m*

~ **(~) ~ roof slab** · Perlit(dämm)betondachplatte *f*

~ **insulation** · Perlit(ab)dämmung *f*

~ **(light(weight)) concrete** · Perlit(leicht)beton *m*

~ **loose fill** · Perlitschüttung *f*

~ ~ ~ **insulation** · Perlitschütt(ab)-dämmung *f*

~ **ore,** (crude) pe(a)rlite (rock) [*The petrographic terms for a naturally ocurring siliceous volcanic rock*] · (Roh)Perlit *m*

~ **plaster** · Perlitputz *m*

~ **popping** · Leichtperlit-Aufbereitung *f*

~ **(rock),** crude ~ (~), pe(a)rlite ore [*The petrographic terms for a naturally occurring siliceous volcanic rock*] · (Roh)Perlit *m*

~ **(sound) absorbent ceiling** → ~ acoustic(al) ~

pearlite steel · perlitischer Stahl *m*

pe(a)rlite wall · Perlitwand *f*

pear-shaped moulding (Brit.); ~ molding (US) · Birn(en)stab *m*

~ **profile** · Birnenprofil *n*

~ **shaft** · Birn(en)stabdienst *m* [*Pfeiler*]

peat · Torf *m* [*DIN 4047*]

~ **brick** · Torfstein *m*

~ **brown** · torfbraun

~ **cinder** (US); ~ clinker (Brit.) · Torfschlacke *f*

~ **clinker** (Brit.); ~ cinder (US) · Torfschlacke *f*

~ **concrete** · Torfbeton *m*

~ **cord covering** · Torfschnur *f* [*für Dämm- und Isolierzwecke*]

~ **dust,** ~ meal, ~ powder · Torfmehl *n*, Torfmull *m*

~ **fibre** (Brit.); ~ fiber (US) · Torffaser *f*

~ ~ **cord** (Brit.); ~ fiber ~ (US) · Torffaserschnur *f*

~ **filler,** ~ floor ~ · Torf-Zwischenbauteil *m*, *n* [*Rippendecke*]

~ **(floor) filler** · Torf-Zwischenbauteil *m*, *n* [*Rippendecke*]

~ **insulating board,** ~ insulation(-grade) ~, ~ ~ sheet · Dämm-Torf-(faser)platte *f*, Torf(faser)(dämm)platte

~ **meal,** ~ dust, ~ powder · Torfmehl *n*, Torfmull *m*

~ **powder,** ~ dust, ~ meal · Torfmehl *n*, Torfmull *m*

~ **tar** · Torfteer *m*

peat-tar pitch · Torfteerpech *n*

pebble [*A roundish rock fragment between 4 and 64 mm in diameter*] · Kiesel(stein) *m*

pebble-dash → rough cast

pebbling, orange peel(ing), pock-marking, orange peel effect [*The pockmarked appearance, in particular of a sprayed film, resembling the skin of an orange due to the failure of the film to flow out to a level surface*] · Orangenschaleneffekt *m*, Apfelsinenschaleneffekt

pedestal · Abortmuschel *f* ohne Brille, Toilettenmuschel ~ ~, (Klosett-) Muschel ~ ~

pedestal — pendant luminaire (fixture)

~, foot stall [*A support for a column, statue, urn, etc. When detailed according to the orders, it consists of a plinth (or base), a die (or dado), and a cap (or cornice)*] · Sockel *m*, Postament *n*, Unterbau *m*, Piedestal *n*

~ **ashtray** · Standaschenbecher *m*

~ **bearing** · Stehlager *n*

~ **frieze** · Sockelfries *m*

pedestal-type drinking fountain, floor-mounted ~ ~ · Säulenbrunnen *m*

pedestal urinal · Beckenurinal *n*

pedestrian barrier · Fußgängerabsperrung *f*

~ **conveyor;** ~ conveyer (US); moving pavement [*A continuous horizontal belt set in a pavement*] · rollender Bürgersteig *m*, ~ Gehsteig, Rollsteig

~ **deck** · Fußgängerdeck *n*, Fußgängerebene *f*

(~) **entrance** [*A confined passageway immediately adjacent to the door through which people enter a building*] · Eingang *m*

~ **metal guard rail** [*B.S. 3049*] · Fußgängerplanke *f* aus Metall

~ **network** · Fuß(gänger)wegnetz *n*

~ **precinct,** ~ zone · Fußgängerbezirk *m*, Fußgängerbereich *m*, *n*, Fußgängerzone *f*

~ **ramp** · Fußgängerrampe *f*

~ **stair(case)** · Fußgängertreppe *f*, Massenverkehrstreppe

~ **street** → ~ walk

~ **traffic** · Fußgängerverkehr *m*

~ ~ **door** · Fußgängertür *f*

~ ~ **zone** · Verkehrszone *f* [*Gebäude*]

~ **tunnel,** ~ underpass · Fußgängertunnel *m*, Gehwegtunnel

~ **underpass,** ~ tunnel · Fußgängertunnel *m*, Gehwegtunnel

pedestrian/vehicle separation · Trennung *f* des Fußgängerverkehrs vom Fahrzeugverkehr

pedestrian walk, ~ street · Gehstraße *f*, Fußgängerstraße

~ **zone,** ~ precinct · Fußgängerbezirk *m*, Fußgängerbereich *m*, *n*, Fußgängerzone *f*

pediment [*A classic equivalent of the gable. It is triangular in Greek or Roman temples but likely to be curved, arched or broken in baroque buildings*] · Ziergiebel *m*

~ · Verdachung *f* [*bei einer Flügeltür*]

~ **apex** · Giebelfirst *m* [*griechischer Tempel*]

~ **foot** · Giebelecke *f* [*griechischer Tempel*]

pedimented door frame · Türrahmen *m* mit Giebel, Türstock *m* ~ ~

~ **window** · Fenster *n* mit Giebel

peel(-tower), pele [*One of the massive towers built in the border counties of England and Scotland, especially during the sixteenth century, as a defence against border raids*] · Wehrturm *m*, fester Turm

peeled veneer, rotary(-cut) ~ [*Usually called 'commercial veneer'*] · (rund-)geschältes Furnier *n*, (Rund)Schälfurnier

peeling, shelling · Abblättern *n*, Abblätterung *f* [*Feuerfestindustrie*]

~ [*The dislodgement of plaster from its backing*] · Ablösen *n*

~ [*The dislodgement of paint from its backing*] · Abschälen *n*, Losschälen [*Anstrich*]

to peen · kalthämmern

peening · Kalthämmern *n*

peg → pin (US)

to peg out, to stake · abwinkeln, auswinkeln, abstecken, ausstecken, abtragen [*Bauwerk auf einer Baustelle*]

peg stay · Stiftfeststeller *m*, Stiftsperre *f* [*Fensterfeststeller*]

pegmatite · Pegmatit *m*, grob(körnig)er Granit *m*

pele, peel(-tower) [*One of the massive towers built in the border counties of England and Scotland, especially during the sixteenth century, as a defence against border raids*] · Wehrturm *m*, fester Turm

pellet ornament, bezant; disc frieze (Brit.); disk frieze (US) · Scheibenfries *m*

pellet(ed) pitch · Perlpech *n*, Kugelpech

pelletizing shaft furnace · Pelletier-Schachtofen *m*

pelting rain, wind-driven ~, driving ~ · Schlagregen *m* [*Mit Regen verbundener Wind von mindestens Beaufortstärke 5*]

~ ~ **humidity,** ~ ~ moisture · Schlagregenfeuchtigkeit *f*, Schlagregenfeuchte *f*

pen roof → pent(house) ~

pencil hardness · Bleistifthärte *f*

pencilling [*Painting mortar joints of brickwork with white paint to bring out the contrast between the joints and the brickwork*] · weißer Fugenanstrich *m*, ~ Fugenaufstrich

pendant (boss), knobboss · (Zapfen-)Knauf *m*

~ **light fitting** (Brit.); ~ luminaire (fixture) (US); ~ (light(ing)) fixture · Pendelbeleuchtungskörper *m*, Pendelleuchte *f*

~ **(light(ing)) fixture,** ~ light fitting (Brit.); ~ luminaire (fixture) (US) · Pendelbeleuchtungskörper *m*, Pendelleuchte *f*

~ **luminaire (fixture)** (US); ~ light fitting (Brit.); ~ (light(ing)) fixture · Pendelleuchte *f*, Pendelbeleuchtungskörper *m*

pendant mounting channel — pentice

~ mounting channel · Pendel-Montageschiene f [*Deckenleuchte*]

pendentive · Pendentif n, Gewölbezwickel m, Hängebogen m [*Das Pendentif ist formal ein sphärisches Dreieck wie der Hängezwickel, konstruktiv ein selbständiger Eckzwickel. Fehlnamen: (Eck)Zwickel, Hängezwickel*]

pendulum bearing, tumbler ~ · Pendellager n

~ leaf, ~ plate · Gelenkblatt n, Pendelblech n [*Pendelgelenk*]

~ plate, ~ leaf · Gelenkblatt n, Pendelblech n [*Pendelgelenk*]

penetrameter, radiographic image quality indicator · Bildgüteprüfsteg m

~ sensitivity (US); **wire ~** (Brit.); **radiographic ~** · Drahterkennbarkeit f, DE [*bei einem Drahtsteg*]

penetrating aid → waterproof(ing) compound

(~) floor(ing) seal(er) [*This is a type of varnish that penetrates the wood instead of remaining as a film on the surface*] · (Fuß)Bodensiegel n, (Fuß-)Bodenversieg(e)lungsmittel n, (Fuß-)Bodenabsieg(e)lungsmittel [*Fehlname: (Fuß)Bodenüberzug m*]

~ sealer → waterproofing (compound)

~ stain, spirit ~ · Spiritusbeize f, Spritbeize

penetration · Eindringung f, Penetration f

~, inter~ · Durchdringung f

~ depth, depth of penetration · Eindring(ungs)tiefe f

penetration-grade asphalt, hot ~, saturating ~, impregnating ~ (US); 'penetration-grade' (asphaltic) bitumen, refinery (asphaltic) bitumen of penetration-grade, hot (asphaltic-)bitumen (Brit.) · Heißbitumen n, Tränkbitumen, Imprägnierbitumen

'penetration-grade' (asphaltic) bitumen, refinery (asphaltic) bitumen of penetration-grade, hot (asphaltic-)bitumen (Brit.); penetration-grade asphalt, hot asphalt, saturating asphalt, impregnating asphalt (US) · Heißbitumen n, Tränkbitumen, Imprägnierbitumen

penetration macadam · Tränkmakadam m

~ of folded cylindrical surfaces, inter~ ~ ~ ~ ~ · Durchdringung f gefalteter Zylinderflächen

~ ~ internal and external space, inter~ ~ ~ ~ ~ ~ · Durchdringung f von Innen- und Außenraum

~ ~ rain, lateral ~ ~ ~, (lateral) rain penetration · Durchfeuchtung f

~ ~ spaces, inter~ ~ ~ · Raumdurchdringung f

~ ~ two parallel barrel vaults, inter~ ~ ~ ~ ~ ~ · Durchdringung f zweier parallel laufender Tonnen(gewölbe)

~ test · Eindring(ungs)probe f, Eindrin(gungs)prüfung f, Eindring(ungs)versuch m

penpit · vorgeschichtliche Höhlenwohnung f in Großbritannien

pent roof → penthouse ~

pentacle (of Salomon) · Alpenkreuz n, Drudenfuß m, Fünfstern m, Pentagramm n, Albfuß

pentaerythritol · Pentaerythrit m

pentagon · Fünfeck n

pentagonal bastion · Fünfeckbastei f, Fünfeckbastion f, Fünfkantbastei, Fünfkantbastion

~ (ground(-))plan · Fünfeck-Grundriß m

~ plan, ~ ground(-)plan · Fünfeck-Grundriß m

~ tile · Fünfeckfliese f, Fünfkantfliese, Fünfeck(belag)platte f, Fünfkant(belag)platte

~ tower · Fünfeckturm m, fünfeckiger Turm

pentagram, pentacle (of Salomon) · Drudenfuß m, Pentagramm n, Fünfstern m, Alpenkreuz n, Albfluß m, Pentalpha n

pentane [*A hydrocarbon occurring in petroleum*] · Pentan n

pentastyle [*Having five columns in front*] · pentastyl, fünfsäulig

~ [*A portico or colonnade having five columns in a row*] · Pentastylos m

~ temple · Pentastylostempel m, Tempel mit fünfsäuliger Giebelfront

Pentelic marble [*A fine-grained white marble in which it was possible to carve the delicate precise details which the Greeks admired. The Parthenon is of Pentelic marble*] · pentelischer Marmor m

penthouse, pentice · Dachaufbau m

~ apartment (unit), ~ (flat), pentice; penthouse living unit (US) [*An apartment (unit) on the flat roof of a building*] · Flachdachwohnung f

~ (flat), ~ apartment (unit), pentice; penthouse living unit (US) [*An apartment (unit) on the flat roof of a building*] · Flachdachwohnung f

~ living unit (US); **~ apartment (~), ~ (flat), pentice** [*An apartment (unit) on the flat roof of a building*] · Flachdachwohnung f

~ machine room · Dachaufbaumaschinenraum m

pent(house) roof, shed ~, pen ~ [*A roof with a slope on one side only. It differs from a lean-to-roof (freitragendes Pultdach) in that it covers the higher wall*] · Pultdach n, Flugdach, Halb(sattel)dach, Schleppdach, einhängiges Dach, halbes Satteldach, Taschendach

pentice, penthouse · Dachaufbau m

pentice — perforated concrete brick

~, penthouse apartment (unit), penthouse (flat); penthouse living unit (US) [*An apartment (unit) on the flat roof of a building*] · Flachdachwohnung *f*

peperino · Pfefferstein *m*, Albanerstein, Peperin(o) *m*, albanischer Stein

peptizing · Peptisation *f* [*Feste Verunreinigungen, z.B. Staub, werden in einer Flüssigkeit verteilt*]

~ **agent** · Peptisierungsmittel *n*

perambulator/passenger lift car (Brit.); ~ **elevator cage** (US) · Tiefkabine *f* [*Aufzug*]

perambulator storage room, pram ~ ~ · Kinderwagenraum *m*

percent by volume · Raumteil *m*, *n*, Rtl.

~ ~ **weight** · Gewichtsteil *m*, *n*, Gwtl., GT

percentage, content, fraction · Gehalt *m*, Prozentsatz *m*, Anteil *m*

~ **by volume** · Raumteile *mpl*, *npl*, Rtl.

~ ~ **weight** · Gewichtsprozente *mpl*, Gewichtsprozentsatz *m*, Gewichtsteile *mpl*, *npl*

~ **of carbon,** carbon content · Kohlenstoffanteil *m*, Kohlenstoffgehalt *m*

~ ~ **dust** · Staubanteil *m*, Staubgehalt *m*

~ ~ **fines,** fines content · Feinkornanteil *m*, Feinkorngehalt *m*

~ ~ **humidity,** ~ ~ moisture · Feuchteprozentsatz *m*, Feuchtigkeitsprozentsatz *m*, Feuchtegehalt *m*, Feuchteanteil *m*, Feuchtigkeitsgehalt, Feuchtigkeitsanteil

~ ~ **moisture** → ~ ~ humidity

~ ~ **reinforcement** · Armierungsgehalt *m*, Bewehrungsgehalt, Armierungsprozentsatz *m*, Bewehrungsprozentsatz

~ ~ **voids** → porosity

~ **residue,** % ~ · Rückstand *m* in %, Sieb~ ~ ~

~ **weight of grading fraction** · (Korn-)Fraktionsgewicht *n*, Korngruppengewicht, Kornklassengewicht, Körnungsgewicht

perchlorethylene, tetrachlorethylene · Tetrachloräthylen *n*

perfect, isostatic, statically determined, statically determinate · (statisch) bestimmt

~ **form** · Form(en)ideal *n*

~ **frame,** isostatic ~ · perfekter Rahmen *m*

~ **(pre)stressing,** ~ stretching, ~ tensioning · vollkommene Vorspannung *f*

~ **restraint** · perfekte Einspannung *f*

~ **stressing,** ~ pre~, ~ stretching, ~ tensioning · vollkommene Vorspannung *f*

~ **stretching,** ~ tensioning, ~ (pre-)stressing · vollkommene Vorspannung *f*

~ **tensioning,** ~ stretching, ~ (pre-)stressing · vollkommene Vorspannung *f*

perfectly plastic mechanism, ideal ~ ~ · ideal-plastischer Mechanismus *m*

~ ~ **theory,** ideal ~ ~ · ideal-plastische Theorie *f*

perforated · durchlocht, gelocht

~ **asbestos-cement pipe;** ~ **cement asbestos** ~ (US) · Asbestzementsikkerrohr *n*, Sicker-Asbestzementrohr, Asbestzementlochrohr, Loch-Asbestzementrohr

~ **backing** → ~ base

~ **base,** ~ backing, ~ underlay, ~ substrate · gelochter Träger *m*, durchlochter ~, gelochte Trägerschicht *f*, durchlochte Trägerschicht, gelochte Hinterlegung *f*, durchlochte Hinterlegung, gelochte Unterlage *f*, durchlochte Unterlage, gelochte Rücklage, durchlochte Rücklage

~ ~ **sheet(ing)** → ~ roof(ing) ~ ~

~ **baseboard** → ~ gypsum ~

~ **block** [*Holes passing through the block exceed 25 per cent of its volume, but the holes are small. For the purpose of this definition, a small hole is a hole less than 3/4 in. wide or less than 0.8 in² in area. Up to three larger holes, not exceeding 5 in² each, may be incorporated as aids to handling, within the total of 25 per cent. B.S. 3921*] · Lochgroßblockziegel *m* mit kleinen Hohlräumen

~ **board,** ~ sheet · durchlochte Platte *f*, gelochte ~, Lochplatte

~ **brick,** cored ~ · Lochziegel *m* [*DIN 105*]

~ ~, ~ clay ~ · Viellochziegel *m*; Viellochstein *m* [*Fehlname*] [*Hochlochziegel A nach DIN 105 mit mindestens 13 Löchern auf 100 cm²*]

~ ~ **masonry (work),** cored ~ ~ (~) · Lochziegelmauerwerk *n* [*Fehlname: Lochsteinmauerwerk*]

~ **calcium silicate brick,** ~ sandlime ~, ~ lime-sand ~ · KSL *m*, Kalksandlochstein *m*, Lochkalksandstein [*DIN 106*]

~ **ceiling board,** ~ ~ sheet · Deckenlochplatte *f* [*für Deckenuntersichten*]

~ ~ **sheet,** ~ ~ board · Deckenlochplatte *f* [*für Deckenuntersichten*]

~ ~ **tile** · Deckenlochfliese *f*, Deckenlochplatte *f* [*für Deckenuntersichten*]

~ **cement asbestos pipe** (US); ~ asbestos-cement ~ · Sicker-Asbestzementrohr *n*, Asbestzementsickerrohr, Asbestzementlochrohr, Loch-Asbestzementrohr

~ **(clay) brick** · Viellochziegel *m*; Viellochstein *m* [*Fehlname*] [*Hochlochziegel A nach DIN 105 mit mindestens 13 Löchern auf 100 cm²*]

~ **concrete block,** ~ ~ brick, ~ ~ tile [*See remark under 'Block'*] · Viellochstein *m* [*aus Beton*]

~ ~ **brick,** ~ ~ tile, ~ ~ block [*See remark under 'Block'*] · Viellochstein *m* [*aus Beton*]

perforated concrete pipe — perforation

~ ~ **pipe** · Beton-Lochrohr n, Loch-Betonrohr

~ ~ **tile**, ~ ~ block, ~ ~ brick [See remark under 'Block'] · Viellochstein m [aus Beton]

~ **corrugated aluminium** (Brit.); ~ ~ aluminum (US) · Loch-Wellalu(minium) n, Well-Lochalu(minium)

~ ~ **metal pipe** · durchlochtes Wellblechrohr n, gelochtes ~, Wellblechlochrohr

~ **deck(ing)** → ~ (roof(ing)) base sheeting

~ **fibre hardboard** (Brit.); ~ fiber ~ (US) · durchlochte Hartfaserplatte f, gelochte ~, Hartfaserlochplatte

~ **fibrous plaster sheet** · durchlochte Gipsfaserplatte f, gelochte ~, Loch-Gipsfaserplatte, Gipsfaser-Lochplatte

~ **(floor) panel**, air supply ~ · Lochtafel f [Doppel(fuß)boden]

~ **glass block**, ~ ~ brick · Lochglasbaustein m

~ ~ **brick**, ~ ~ block · Lochglasbaustein m

~ **(gypsum) baseboard**, ~ ~ board; ~ plate [Scotland] [A gypsum baseboard or lath having equally spaced circular large perforations designed to provide a mechanical key for plaster] · (Gipskarton-)Stuckplatte f mit Lochung, gelochte (Gipskarton-)Stuckplatte

~ ~ **(building) board**, ~ ~ (~) sheet · Loch-Gips(bau)platte f, Loch-Baugipsplatte, gelochte Gips(bau)platte, gelochte Baugipsplatte, durchlochte Gips(bau)platte, durchlochte Baugipsplatte, Lüftungsplatte aus Gips, Gips-Lüftungsplatte

~ ~ **ceiling board** · durchlochte Gipsdeckenplatte f, gelochte ~, Loch-Gipsdeckenplatte

~ ~ **lath**, ~ sheet of gypsum plasterboard · Loch-Gipsbautafel f [als Putzträger]

~ **(~) plasterboard (sheet)**, ~ ~ board; ~ plate ~ [Scotland] · gelochte Gipskartonplatte f, durchlochte ~, Loch-Gipskartonplatte

~ ~ **sheet** → ~ ~ (building) board

~ **lath(ing)** · durchlochter Putzträger m, gelochter ~, Loch-Putzträger

~ **lime-sand brick**, ~ sand-lime ~, ~ calcium silicate ~ · KSL m, Kalksandlochstein m, Lochkalksandstein [DIN 106]

~ **marble slab** → pierced ~ ~

~ **mat sheet(ing)** · Glasvlieslochbahn f; Glasvließlochbahn [Österreich]

~ **metal** · Lochmetall n

~ ~ **strip** · Lochmetallstreifen m

~ ~ **tile**, pierced ~ ~ ~ · Lochmetall(belag)platte f, Lochmetallfliese f

~ **panel**, ~ floor ~, air supply ~ · Lochtafel f [Doppel(fuß)boden]

~ ~, pierced ~ · durchlochte Tafel f, gelochte ~, Lochtafel

~ **paper**, cored ~ [See remark under 'Pappe'] · durchlochte Pappe f, gelochte ~, Lochpappe

~ **pipe** · durchlochtes Rohr n, gelochtes ~, Lochrohr

~ **plasterboard (sheet)** → ~ gypsum ~ (~)

~ **plate** · durchlochtes Blech n, gelochtes ~, Lochblech

~ ~ [Scotland] → ~ (gypsum) baseboard

~ ~ **board** [Scotland] → ~ (gypsum) plasterboard (sheet)

~ ~ **for test sieves** · durchlochtes Blech n für Prüfsiebe, gelochtes ~ ~ ~, Lochblech ~ ~

~ ~ **sheet** [Scotland] → ~ (gypsum) plasterboard (~)

~ **protector** · Schutzsieb n

~ **(roof(ing)) base sheeting**, ~ (~) deck(ing), ~ (~) substructure, ~ (~) substrate · durchlochte (Dach-)Unterlagsbahn f, gelochte ~, Loch-(Dach)Unterlagsbahn

~ **(~) deck(ing)** → ~ (~) base sheeting

~ **(~) substrate** → ~ (~) base sheeting

~ **(~) substructure** → ~ (~) base sheeting

~ **sand-lime brick**, ~ lime-sand ~, ~ calcium silicate ~ · KSL m, Kalksandlochstein m, Lochkalksandstein [DIN 106]

~ **screen**, hole ~ · Loch(blech)sieb n

~ **sheet**, ~ board · durchlochte Platte f, gelochte ~, Lochplatte

~ ~ **metal lath(ing)** · Putz-Lochblech n, Loch-Putzblech, gelochtes Putzblech, durchlochtes Putzblech

~ ~ **of gypsum plasterboard**, ~ gypsum lath · Loch-Gipsbautafel f [als Putzträger]

~ **sheet(ing)** · Lochbahn f

~ **slab of marble** → pierced ~ ~ ~

~ **substrate** → ~ base

~ ~ → ~ (roof(ing)) base sheeting

~ **substructure** → ~ (roof(ing)) base sheeting

~ **underlay** → ~ base

~ **visible soffit**, ~ ~ under-face, ~ ~ underside · durchlochte Untersicht f, geloch.e ~, Loch-Untersicht

~ ~ **under-face**, ~ ~ underside, ~ ~ soffit · durchlochte Untersicht f, gelochte ~, Loch-Untersicht

~ ~ **underside**, ~ ~ under-face, ~ ~ soffit · durchlochte Untersicht f, gelochte ~, Loch-Untersicht

perforation · kleines Loch n [Ziegel]

~ · Lochung f

perforation of screen — peripteral

~ **of screen**, punching ~ ~, hole pattern · Sieblochung *f*

~ **pattern** · Lochbild *n*

performance characteristic · Verhaltensmerkmal *n*

~ **test** · Leistungsprüfung *f*, Leistungsversuch *m*, Leistungsprobe *f*

perfume box · Rauchbecken *n*

Pergamum frieze · Pergamonfries *m*

pergola · Pergola *f* [*Laubengang in einer Gartenanlage. Die Unterzüge liegen auf Stützen und tragen ein von Pflanzen umranktes Gebälk*]

periapsidial aisle · Umgang *m*

peribolos, sacred precinct, temenos, peribolus · geweihter (Tempel)Bezirk *m*, heiliger ~, Altis *f*, Peribolos *m*, Temenos *n*

~, peribolus [*The enclosing wall or colonnade surrounding a temenos or sacred enclosure, and hence sometimes applied to the enclosure itself*] · Peribolos *m*

periclase · Periklas *m* [*kristallisiertes Magnesiumoxid*]

~ **brick** · Magnesitstein *m* mit 96% MgO

perilla oil [*B.S. 654*] · Perillaöl *n*

perimeter bonding technique, ~ ~ technic · Randverklebetechnik *f*

~ **bracket** · Ringkonsole *f*

~ **column**, edge ~, external ~, exterior ~, outside ~, outer ~ · Perimeterstütze *f*, Randstütze, Außenstütze

~ **frame** · Außenrahmen *m* [*Gebäude*]

~ **masonry wall** → exterior ~ ~

~ ~ ~ **column** → exterior ~ ~ ~

~ ~ ~ **facing** → exterior masonry wall lining

~ ~ ~ **lining** → exterior ~ ~ ~

~ ~ ~ **(sur)facing** → exterior masonry wall lining

~ ~ **(work)** → exterior ~ (~)

~ **(pre)stressed (concrete) column**, external ~ (~) ~, exterior ~ (~) ~, ~ stretched (~) ~, ~ tensioned (~) ~ · Spannbeton-Außenstütze *f*

~ **R.C. column** → exterior reinforced (concrete) ~

~ **reinforced column** → exterior reinforced (concrete) ~

~ ~ **(concrete) column** → exterior ~ (~) ~

~ **stretched (concrete) column** → ~ (pre)stressed (~) ~

~ **(structural) system** → external wall construction

~ **system** → external wall construction

~ **tensioned (concrete) column** → ~ (pre)stressed (~) ~

~ **wall** → exterior ~

~ ~ **(building) component** → external wall (building) unit

~ ~ **(~) member** → external wall (building) unit

~ ~ **(~) unit** → external ~ (~) ~

~ ~ **component** → external wall (building) unit

~ ~ **construction** → external ~ ~

~ ~ **facing** → exterior wall lining

~ ~ **finish** → exterior ~ ~

~ ~ **lining** → exterior ~ ~

~ ~ **member** → external wall (building) unit

~ ~ **(sur)facing** → exterior wall lining

~ ~ **unit** → external wall (building) ~

period of architecture · Architekturepoche *f*

~ ~ **curing**, time ~ ~, curing period, curing time · (Ab)Bindedauer *f*, (Ab-)Bindezeit *f*, (Ab)Bindefrist *f* [*Verschnittbitumen*]

~ ~ **hardening** → hardening time

~ ~ **initial set(ting)** → time ~ ~ ~

~ ~ **loading**, time ~ ~, loading period, loading time · Belastungsdauer *f*, Belastungszeit *f*

~ ~ **maximum temperature** · Halten *n* der Höchsttemperatur [*Dampfbehandlung von Beton*]

~ ~ **oscillation**, ~ ~ vibration · Schwingungsdauer *f*, Schwingungszeit *f*, Erschütterungsdauer, Erschütterungszeit

~ ~ **test(ing)** → test(ing) time

~ ~ **time**, length ~ ~, time period, time interval · Zeitdauer *f*, Zeitraum *m*, Zeitspanne *f*

~ ~ **transition**, phase ~ ~, transitional phase, transitional period · Übergangsperiode *f*, Übergangszeit *f*, Übergangsphase *f* [*von einem Stil zum anderen*]

~ ~ **treatment** · Behandlungsdauer *f*, Behandlungszeit *f*

~ ~ **vibration**, ~ ~ oscillation · Schwingungsdauer *f*, Schwingungszeit *f*, Erschütterungsdauer, Erschütterungszeit

~ ~ **warming**, time ~ ~, warming period, warming time · Anwärmungsdauer *f*, Anwärmungszeit *f*, Erwärmungsdauer, Erwärmungszeit

~ **style** · historischer Stil *m*

periodical room · Zeitschriftenraum *m*

peripheral core · Peripheriekern *m*

~ **tie beam** · Ringanker *m* [*Die Hohlkörper bei Hohlkörperdecken werden nur soweit gelegt, wie die Schalung reicht, also bis vor die tragenden Wände. Die Bewehrung dagegen ragt mit ihren zu Haken umgebogenen Enden bis über die tragenden Wände hin und wird dort vom Beton aufgenommen. Nach dem Erhärten bildet dann dieser Beton den Ring, in dem die Bewehrung verankert ist*]

peripteral [*Having a single peristyle or row of pillars surrounding it, as a Greek temple*] · peripteral

peripteral building — permissible

~ building · Peripteralgebäude n, Peripteros m

~ colonnade → peristyle

~ hexastyle temple with fourteen columns on the flanks, hexastyle peripteral ~ ~ ~ ~ ~ ~ ~ · Peripterostempel m von 6:14 Säulen

~ octastyle temple with seventeen columns on the flanks, octastyle peripteral ~ ~ ~ ~ ~ ~ ~ · Peripterostempel m von 8:17 Säulen

~ temple · einlaubiger Tempel, Periptertaltempel m, Peripteros(tempel) m [Tempel mit von einem Pteron umgebener Cella]

to perish · zerfallen [Zerstörung eines festen Körpers durch Einwirkung der Atmosphäre, wie z.B. bei gebranntem Dolomit]

peristyle, peripteral colonnade [In both ancient and modern writers usually confined to a colonnade round the inside of a court or room, or to a court or room so adorned, but occasionally used of an external 'peripteral' colonnade] · Peristyl n, Peripteralkolonnade f

~, garden court · Peristylhof m

~ building · Peristylhaus n

~ ceiling · Peristyldecke f

~ column · Peristylsäule f

~ columns · Säulenkranz m

~ court, open ~ ~, garden ~ · Peristylhof m [Von einem Peristyl umgebener Hof]

~ house · Peristylhaus n

permanent blue (pigment) · Permanentblau n

~ cast light(weight) concrete form(s) → (pre)cast permanent light(weight) concrete formwork

~ deflection, ~ deflexion · plastische Durchbiegung f

~ deflexion, ~ deflection · plastische Durchbiegung f

~ forms → ~ shuttering

~ ~ of reinforced concrete slabs → ~ shuttering ~ ~ ~ ~

~ ~ ~ R.C. slabs → ~ shuttering of reinforced concrete ~

~ form(work) → ~ shuttering

~ ~ of R.C. slabs → ~ shuttering of reinforced concrete ~

~ ~ ~ reinforced concrete slabs → ~ shuttering ~ ~ ~ ~

~ green (pigment) · Permanentgrün n

~ hack, drying shed, open air corridors · Freiluftschuppen m [Ziegelindustrie]

~ hardness, non-carbonate ~ · Mineralsäurehärte, Nichtkarbonathärte f [Der Unterschied zwischen Gesamthärte und Karbonathärte]

~ heating, continuous ~ · Dauerheizung f

~ humidity, ~ moisture · Dauerfeuchte f, Dauerfeuchtigkeit f

~ load · ruhende Last f, ständige ~, dauernde ~, Dauerlast [Die Summe der unveränderlichen Lasten, also das Gewicht der tragenden oder stützenden Bauteile und der unveränderlichen, von den tragenden Bauteilen dauernd aufzunehmenden Lasten, z.B. (Fuß)Bodenbeläge, (Auf)Füllungen, Putz usw.]

~ loading · stetige Belastung f, bleibende ~, Dauerbelastung

~ moisture, ~ humidity · Dauerfeuchte f, Dauerfeuchtigkeit f

~ partition (wall) [Any permanent wall in the interior of a building] · unbewegliche Trennwand f

~ (pre)cast light(weight) concrete form(s) → (pre)cast permanent light(weight) concrete formwork

~ (pre)stressing, ~ stretching, ~ tensioning · Dauervorspannung f

~ red (pigment) · Permanentrot n

~ shuttering, ~ form(work), ~ forms · Dauerschalung f, verlorene Schalung

~ ~ of R.C. slabs → ~ ~ ~ reinforced (concrete) ~

~ ~ ~ reinforced concrete slabs, ~ formwork ~ ~ ~ ~, ~ forms ~ ~ ~ ~, ~ ~ ~ R.C. ~ · Stahlbetonplattenschalung f [Als verlorene Schalung bei Massivbeton]

~ strain · bleibende Dehnung f, stetige ~, Dauerdehnung

~ stressing → ~ pre~

~ stretching → ~ (pre)stressing

~ tensioning → ~ (pre)stressing

~ ventilation · Dauerlüftung f

~ white → precipitated barium sulphate

~ yellow (pigment) [barium yellow] · Permanentgelb n

permanently elastic · dauerelastisch

(~) nonhardening, ~ plastic · nichthärtend, dauerplastisch

~ plastic, (~) nonhardening · nichthärtend, dauerplastisch

permeability, perviousness · Durchlässigkeit f, Undichtigkeit, Undichtheit

~ of concrete, perviousness ~ ~ · Betondurchlässigkeit f, Betonundichtheit, Betonundichtigkeit

~ reducing agent → (integral) waterproof(ing) ~

~ to air, perviousness ~ ~ · Luftdurchlässigkeit f

~ ~ diffusion, perviousness ~ ~ · Diffusionsdurchlässigkeit f

~ ~ (water) vapour (Brit.); ~ ~ (~) vapor (US) · Dampfdurchlässigkeit f

permeable to air, pervious ~ ~ · luftdurchlässig

Permian limestone · Zechsteinkalk m

permissible, admissible, allowable, safe · zulässig

permissible deviation of constructional .. — petrographic ..

~ **deviation of constructional elements** · Bautoleranz f

~ **load,** admissible ~, allowable ~, working ~, safe ~ · zulässige Last f

~ **stress,** admissible ~, allowable ~, safe ~, working ~, design ~ · zulässige Spannung f, Bemessungsspannung

permissible-stress design, ~ method, elastic ~, working load ~ [*It is based on service loads and on permissible stresses in concrete and steel*] · Verfahren n zur Ermitt(e)lung der Schnittgrößen nach der Elastizitätstheorie

~ **method,** ~ design, working load ~, elastic ~ [*It is based on service loads and on permissible stresses in concrete and steel*] · Verfahren n zur Ermitt(e)lung der Schnittgrößen nach der Elastizitätstheorie

peroxide; peroxid(e) (US) · Peroxid n Superoxid

perpend (stone), perpent [*A (natural) stone header extending through a wall so that one end appears on each side of it*] · Natureckstein m, Naturwinkelstein

Perpendicular architecture, ~ Gothic, ~ Style, Rectilinear Style, Late Pointed Style · Perpendikularstil m, Spätphase f der englischen Architektur [*Die letzte Phase der gotischen Architektur in England von 1360–1550. Vertikalzug, besonders in der Fenster- und Wandgliederung*]

~ **cathedral** · Perpendikular-Kathedrale f

perpendicular cut (of jack rafter) · Lotschmiege f

Perpendicular Gothic, ~ architecture, ~ Style, Rectilinear Style, Late Pointed Style · Perpendikularstil m, Spätphase f der englischen Gotik [*Die letzte Phase der gotischen Architektur in England von 1360–1550. Vertikalzug, besonders in der Fenster- und Wandgliederung*]

perpendicular joint, vertical ~, side ~; cross ~ (Brit.); (head) ~, build (US) · Stoßfuge f

Perpendicular Style, Rectilinear ~, Late Pointed ~, Perpendicular Gothic, Perpendicular architecture · Perpendikularstil m, Spätphase f der englischen Gotik [*Die letzte Phase der gotischen Architektur in England von 1360–1550. Vertikalzug, besonders in der Fenster- und Wandgliederung*]

~ **tower** · Turm m im Baustil der Spätphase der englischen Gotik

perpendicular tracery → rectilinear ~

perpetual lamp · ewige Lampe f

perron, flight of front steps [*An outside stair(case), usually extending up the slope of a terrace, as to the front entrance of a building*] · Hauseingangstreppe f, Freitreppe, Gebäudeeingangstreppe

~ **landing** · Freitreppenpodest n, Gebäudeeingangstreppenpodest, Hauseingangstreppenpodest

Persian → atlante

~ **architecture** · persische Architektur f, ~ Baukunst f

~ **column** · persische Säule f

person proposing to build, applicant ~ ~ ~ · Bauantragsteller m

personnel accommodation portion → staff ~ ~

~ **aisle,** staff ~ · Personalgang m

~ **block** → staff building

~ **building** → staff ~

~ **canteen,** staff ~ · Personalkantine f

~ **changing room,** staff ~ ~ · Personalumkleide(raum) f, (m)

~ **dining room,** staff ~ ~ · Personalspeiseraum m, Personaleßraum

~ **entrance,** staff ~ · Personaleingang m

~ **house** → staff building

~ **lock,** staff ~ · Personenschleuse f

~ **room,** staff ~ · Sozialraum m, Personalraum

~ **toilet,** staff ~ · Personaltoilette f

~ **traffic,** staff ~ · Personalverkehr m

~ **training,** staff ~ · Unterweisung f des Bedienungspersonals

perspective construction · perspektivische Konstruktion f, Perspektivkonstruktion

~ **drawing** · perspektivische Zeichnung f, Perspektivzeichnung

~ **view** · Perspektivansicht f, perspektivische Ansicht

perspex (Brit.); plexiglass (US) · Plexiglas n [*Warenzeichen für glasartig durchsichtigen Kunststoff aus Polymethacrylsäureestern. Zugfestigkeit etwa 700 kg/cm²*]

pervious to air, permeable ~ ~ · luftdurchlässig

~ ~ **moisture,** ~ ~ humidity · feuchtigkeitsdurchlässig

~ ~ **water** · wasserdurchlässig, wasserundicht

perviousness, permeability · Durchlässigkeit f, Undichtigkeit, Undichtheit

~ **of concrete** → permeability ~ ~

~ **to air,** permeability ~ ~ · Luftdurchlässigkeit f

~ ~ **diffusion,** permeability ~ ~ · Diffusionsdurchlässigkeit f

pest control · Schädlingsbekämpfung f

~ **infestation,** parasitic ~ · Schädlingsbefall m

peterlineum → carbolineum

petrification, petrifaction · Versteinerung f

~ **agent,** petrifaction ~ · Verstein(er)ungsmittel n

petrifying liquid · Steinfarbe f [*Sie dient zum Schutz von Natursteinen gegen Witterungseinflüsse. Sie ist also ein Sperranstrichmittel*]

petrographic characteristic · petrographisches Merkmal n [*Zuschlag(stoff)*]

petrol-proof (Brit.); gas(oline)-proof, gasolene-proof (US) · benzinfest

petroleum, crude oil · Erdöl n, Roh(erd)öl, (Roh)Petroleum n, Öl [*Man nennt die hellen Öle ,,Naphtha", die gelblichen ,,Petroleum" und die bräunlichen, zähen ,,Bergteere"*]

~ **asphalt** (US); ~ (asphaltıc-)bitumen (Brit.) · Erdölbitumen n

~ **(asphaltic-)bitumen** (Brit.) → ~ asphalt

~ **bitumen** (Brit.) → ~ asphalt

~ **distillation residue** · Erdöl(destillations)rückstand m

~ **pitch,** oil ~ · Petrolpech n

pew · Kirchenbank f

p.f. cor., ~ ~ corrected · kompensiert [*Leuchtstofflampe*]

PFA, fly ash; pulverized fuel ash (US); pulverised fuel ash (Brit.) · Filterasche f, Flugasche [*DIN E 4209*]

PFA aggregate → fly ash ~
PFA cement → (sintered) fly ash ~
PFA collector → fly ash ~
PFA-lime block → fly ash-lime ~
~ **tile** → fly ash-lime block

P.F.U. paint, prepared ~, ready-mixed ~, paint prepared for use · anstrichfertige Farbe f, gebrauchsfertige ~, verarbeitungsfertige ~, Fertig(anstrich)farbe

p.f. uncor., ~ uncorrected · unkompensiert [*Leuchtstofflampe*]

PH BRZ → phosphor-bronze

phantastic architecture · phantastische Architektur f, ~ Baukunst f, Phantasiearchitektur, Phantasiebaukunst

Pharos lighthouse at Alexandria · Leuchtturm m zu Alexandria

phase-change coefficient, phase constant, wavelength coefficient, wavelength constant [*The imaginary part of the propagation coefficient. The phase-change coefficient β is $2\pi/\lambda$*] · Phasenkonstante f, Phasenkoeffizient m, Kreiswellenzahl f [*Phasenmaß dividiert durch den Abstand der in Richtung der Schallausbreitung hintereinanderliegenden Punkte*]

phase constant, phase-change coefficient, wave-length coefficient, wavelength constant [*The imaginary part of the propagation coefficient. The phase-change coefficient β is $2\pi/\lambda$*] · Phasenkonstante f, Phasenkoeffizient m, Kreiswellenzahl f [*Phasenmaß dividiert durch den Abstand der in Richtung der Schallausbreitung hintereinanderliegenden Punkte*]

~ **diagram** · Phasendiagramm n

phase-equilibrium diagram · Phasen-Gleichgewichts-Diagramm n

phase of transition, period ~ ~, transitional phase, transitional period · Übergangsperiode f, Übergangszeit f, Übergangsphase f [*von einem Stil zum anderen*]

phased development · etappenweise Entwick(e)lung f

phenol, carbolic acid, coal tar creosote [*B. S. 144*] · C_6H_5OH, Steinkohlenteerkreosot n, Phenol n, Phenylalkohol m, Karbolsäure f

~ **formaldehyde resin,** phenol(ic) ~ · Phenol(-Formaldehyd)harz n, Phenoplast n, PF n

~ **resin bonding,** phenolic ~ ~ · Phenolharz(ver)leimen n, Phenolharz(ver)leimung f

phenol(ic) adhesive → ~ resin (bonding) ~

~ **aniline resin** · Phenol-Anilinharz n

~ **(bonding) adhesive** → ~ resin (~) ~

~ ~ **agent** → ~ resin ~ ~
~ ~ **medium** → ~ resin ~ ~
~ **cement(ing agent)** → ~ resin ~ (~)
~ **foam** → ~ resin ~

phenolic laminated board, ~ ~ sheet [*B.S. 2572*] · Phenolharz-Schichtstoffplatte f

~ ~ **sheet,** ~ ~ board [*B.S. 2572*] · Phenolharz-Schichtstoffplatte f

phenol(ic) medium → ~ resin ~

~ **plastic** → ~ resin ~

~ **resin,** phenol formaldehyde ~ · Phenol(-Formaldehyd)harz n, Phenolplast n, PF n

~ ~ **bonded** · phenolharzverleimt

~ ~ **bonding** · Phenolharz(ver)leimen n, Phenolharz(ver)leimung f

~ (~) (~) **adhesive,** ~ (~) ~ agent, ~ (~) ~ medium, ~ (~) cement(ing agent), ~ (~) glue · Phenolharzkleber m, Phenolharzkleb(e)mittel n, Phenolharzkleb(e)stoff m [*Fehlname: Phenolharzleim m*]

~ (~) **foam** · Phenolharzschaum(stoff) m

~ (~) **glue** → ~ (~) (bonding) adhesive

~ (~) **medium,** ~ (~) vehicle · Phenolharz-Bindemittellösung f [*Anstrichfarbe*]

~ (~) **plastic** · Phenolharzkunststoff m

~ (~) **varnish** · Phenolharzlack m

~ (~) **vehicle,** ~ (~) medium · Phenolharz-Bindemittellösung f [*Anstrichfarbe*]

phenolic synthetic resin cement, ~ ~ ~ putty · Phenol-Kunstharzkitt m

~ ~ ~ **putty,** ~ ~ ~ cement · Phenol-Kunstharzkitt m

phenol(ic) varnish → ~ resin ~

~ **varnish resin** · Phenol-Lackharz n

~ **vehicle** → ~ resin ~

phenolphthalein [*A whitish or yellowish-white crystalline compound,$C_{20}H_{14}O_4$, obtained by treating phenol with phthalic anhydride. Because its brilliant red alkaline solutions are readily decolorized by acid, it is valuable as an indicator in acid-base titrations*] · Phenolphthalein n

phenomena of ineffable space [*Le Corbusier*] · Erscheinungen *fpl* des unsäglichen Raums

phenoxy resin · Phenoxyharz *n*

phenyl phenol · Phenylphenol *n*

philharmonic hall · Philharmonie *f*

philippeum · Philippeion *n* [*Olympia*]

philosophy of (architectural) design · Architekturphilosophie *f*

phone booth, tele~ ~ · Fernsprechzelle *f*

~ duct, tele~ ~ · Fernsprechkabelkanal *m*

~ exchange, tele~ ~ · Fernsprechzentrale *f*

~ installation, tele~ ~ · Fernsprecherinstallation *f*

~ line, tele~ ~ · Fernsprechleitung *f*

~ meter, tele~ ~ · (Fernsprech)Gebührenzähler *m*

~ point, tele~ ~ [*e.g. in a wall or floor*] · Fernsprechanschluß *m*

~ socket, tele~ ~ · Fernsprech(steck)dose *f*

phonolite, clinkstone · Phonolith *m*, Klingstein *m* [*Fehlname: Porphyrschiefer m*]

phosphate(-base(d)) solution · Phosphatlösung *f*

phosphate/chromate etch primer · passivierender und phosphatierender Haftgrund *m*

phosphate coating · Phosphatbeschichtung *f*

phosphating · Phosphatbehandlung *f*, Phosphatieren *n* [*Behandeln von Eisen- und Stahloberflächen mit speziellen Phosphorsalzlösungen in der Wärme oder in der Kälte, um dünne Rostschutzschichten zu erzielen. DIN 50942*]

~ agent · Phosphatierungsmittel *n*

phosphor-bronze, PH BRZ · Phosphorbronze *f* [*Fehlname*]; (Guß-)Zinnbronze [*Legierung aus Kupfer und Zinn. DIN 1705*]

phosphorescent [*Able to emit visible light for some time after the activating radiation has ceased*] · phosphoreszierend, nachleuchtend

~ paint · phosphoreszierende Leuchtfarbe *f*, nachleuchtende ~

phosphoric acid · Phosphorsäure *f*, Knochensäure *f*, H_3PO_4

~ acid-based flux · Flußmittel *n* auf Phosphorsäurebasis

phosphor-solder · Phosphorlot *n* [*Hartlot nach DIN 1733*]

photocell, electric eye · elektrisches Auge *n*, Photozelle *f*

(photo)copy machine · (Photo)Kopiergerät *n*

photoelastic · spannungsoptisch

~ investigation · spannungsoptische Untersuchung *f*

photoelasticity · Spannungsoptik *f*

(photographic) dark room · Dunkelarbeitsraum *m*, Dunkelkammer *f*

photometry · Lichtmessung *f*, Lichtstärkemessung

photosensitive glass · lichtempfindliches Glas *n*

photostat printing · Photokopieren *n*

phthalic acid [*One of three aromatic crystalline compounds, $C_8H_6O_4$, derived variously, as by oxidation of naphthalene: formerly called alizaric acid, naphthalic acid*] · Phthalsäure *f*

~ anhydride · Phthalsäureanhydrid *n*

phthalocyanine blue · Phthalocyaninblau *n*

~ dyestuff [*Any of a group of organic dyestuffs related to phorphyrin and yielding blue and green pigments*] · Phthalocyaninfarbstoff *m*

~ green · Phthalocyaningrün *n*

pH-value · pH-Wert *m*, pH-Zahl *f*, Wasserstoffzahl H

phyllite [*A dark-grey or greenish metamorphic rock derived from clayey deposits; usually foliated with a glossy sheen on surfaces of splitting. The rock is easily cleared into a weak form of slate; used locally for roofing purpose*] · Phyllit *m*

physical behaviour (Brit.); ~ **behavior** (US) · physikalisches Verhalten *n*

~ check · Stückzählung *f* [*Lagerbestand*]

~ constant · physikalische Konstante *f*

~ deterioration · Überalterung *f* von Material

~ property · physikalische Eigenschaft *f*

~ structure [*e.g. of concrete*] · Aufbau *m* [*z.B. von Beton*]

~ waterproofing · physikalische (Ab-)Dichtung *f*, ~ Sperrung, mechanische ~

physics block, ~ **building** · Physikgebäude *n*

~ of cement, cement physics · Zementphysik *f*

~ relating to building (construction) · Hochbauphysik *f*

~ ~ ~ construction · Bauphysik *f*

physiopsychological-sympathy · Einfühlung *f*

Pl → plasticity index

~ ~ → point of intersection

piano hinge · Klavierband *n*

~ lines, drawing ~, line · Kämmung *f* [*Flachglasfehler*]

~ nobile [*The first floor of an Italian palazzo, containing the principal rooms*] · Beletage *f*, Piano Nobile *n*

~ wire [*It is made of electric-furnace steel and used, among other purposes, in prestressed concrete*] · Stahlsaite *f*

to pick · öffnen mit Dietrich

picking [*Opening of a lock with a device other than a key*] · Öffnen *n* mit einem Dietrich

picking pistol — pig iron for steel making purposes

~ **pistol** · Aufsperrpistole f für verschlossene YALE-Schlösser

pickled wire · gebeizter Draht m

pickling [*A treatment for the removal of rust and mill scale from steel by immersion in an acid solution containing an inhibitor. Pickling should be followed by thorough washing and drying before painting*] · (chemisches) Beizen n

~ **bath containing an inhibitor** [*hydrogen-evolution type of corrosion*] · Sparbeize f [*Korrosion unter Wasserstoffentwicklung*]

~ **inhibitor** [*hydrogen-evolution type of corrosion*] · Sparbeizzusatz m [*Korrosion unter Wasserstoffentwicklung*]

picrolite · Bastardasbest m, Pikrolith m

pictorial composition · Bildkomposition f

~ **projection** · Projizieren n auf eine Bildebene

pictorialness · Bildmäßigkeit f

picture-frame stage · Guckkastenbühne f

picture (framing) glass · Bilderglas n

~ **gallery** · Gemäldegalerie f, Bildergalerie

~ **glass,** ~ **framing** ~ · Bilderglas n

~ **hook** · Bilderhaken m

~ **rail** · Bilderleiste f

~ **tile** · Bild(belag)platte f, Bildfliese f

~ **window, panoramic** ~ · Panoramafenster n

picturesque · malerisch

~ **Romantic style** · malerische Romantik f

pidgeonhole (parking structure), parking tower, autostacker · Autosilo m, Parkturm m

piece work; gyppo (US) · Akkordarbeit f

piend [*Scotland*] → hip

pier [*1. The mass between doors, windows, and other openings in buildings; 2. A support as distinct from a column; 3. A name often given to Romanesque and Gothic pillars varying from a square to a composite section*] · Pfeiler m [*Er kann Basis und Kapitell haben*]

~ [*A mass of masonry, as distinct from a column, from which an arch springs, in an arcade or bridge*] · Bogenpfeiler m

~**, Gothic pillar** · gotischer (freistehender) Pfeiler m

~**, bearing-shaft** · Steinpfosten m [*gotisches Portal*]

~ **arcade** · Pfeilerarkade f

~ ~ **arch** · Pfeilerarkade f; Pfeilerarkadenbogen m [*Fehlname*]

~ **arcading** · Pfeilerarkatur f, Pfeilerbogenlaube f, Pfeilerbogengang m, Pfeilerbogenreihe f

~ **base (plate)** · Pfeilerbasis f, Pfeilerfuß m

~ **basilica** → ~**-type** ~

~ **bond** → ~ **masonry** ~

~ **capital** · Pfeilerkapitell n, Pfeilerkapital f

~ **core** · Pfeilerkern m

~ **guard, column** ~ · Kantenschutz m [*für Betonstützen und Betonpfeiler*]

~ **impost** · Pfeilerkämpfer m

~ **(masonry) bond** · Pfeilerverband m [*Ein Mauerwerkverband bei welchem unter Beibehaltung eines quadratischen Grundrisses jede zweite Schicht um 90 Grad versetzt ist*]

~ ~ **(work)** · Pfeilermauerwerk n

~ **of brickwork, brick(work) pier** · Ziegelpfeiler m

~ **shaft** · Pfeilerschaft m

~**(-type) basilica** · Pfeilerbasilika f

~ **with concave side** · Pfeiler m mit im Grundriß konkav gekrümmter Fläche

to pierce · durchbrechen, kästeln

pierced · durchbrochen, gekästelt

~**, perforated** · durchlocht, gelocht

~ **arcade** · durchbrochene Arkade f

~ **bond, (open) trellis** ~**, honeycomb(ed)** ~**, pigeon-hole(d)** ~ · Kästelverband m

~ **concrete block screen wall,** screen wall of pierced concrete blocks · durchbrochene Sichtschutzwand f aus Betonformsteinen, ~ Betonformsteinwand [*Zur Gliederung von Gartenräumen oder zur Abschirmung geschützter Sitzplätze in Gärten*]

~ **floor finish,** ~ ~ **cover(ing),** ~ **floor(ing)** · durchbrochener (Fuß)Boden(belag) m

~ **marble slab, perforated** ~ ~**, pierced slab of marble, perforated slab of marble** · Lochmarmorplatte f, Marmorlochplatte

~ **(masonry) wall** → honeycomb(ed) (~) ~

~ ~ **(work), (open) trellis** ~ **(~), honeycomb(ed)** ~ **(~), pigeon-hole(d)** ~ **(~)** · durchbrochenes Mauerwerk n, Kästelmauerwerk

~ **metal tile, perforated** ~ ~ · Lochmetall(belag)platte f, Lochmetallfliese f

~ **panel, perforated** ~ · Lochtafel f, gelochte Tafel, durchlochte Tafel

~ ~ **(wall)** · durchlochte Sichtschutzwand f, gelochte ~, Loch-Sichtschutzwand

~ **slab of marble,** ~ **marble slab, perforated slab of marble, perforated marble slab** · Lochmarmorplatte f, Marmorlochplatte

~ **steel plank(ing), P.S.P.** · gelochtes Startbahnblech n, Rollfeldbelagplatte f

~ **wall** → honeycomb(ed) (masonry) ~

pig iron · Roheisen n

~ ~ **for steel making purposes,** stahl-eisen · Stahl(roh)eisen n [*Im Hochofen erschmolzenes Roheisen für die Weiterverarbeitung nach dem Siemens-Martin- oder LD-Verfahren*]

pig lead — pillar

~ **lead** · Hüttenweichblei *n*
pigeon-cote → columbarium
pigeonhole, gap · Kästel *n*, Durchbruch *m* [*Mauer*]
pigeonhole(d) bond, honeycomb(ed) ~, pierced ~, (open) trellis ~ · Kästelverband *m*
~ **(masonry) wall** → honeycomb(ed) (~) ~
~ ~ **(work),** (open) trellis ~ (~), honeycomb(ed) ~ (~), pierced ~ (~) · durchbrochenes Mauerwerk *n*, Kästelmauerwerk
pigeon-house → columbarium
pigment [*The insoluble dispersed particles in a paint which give the dried film its characteristic properties of colour and opacity. In modern usage, the term is often used to include 'extenders' as well as the white or coloured pigments*] · Pigment *n* [*Fehlnamen: Farbkörper m, Körperfarbe f*]
~ **absorption** · Pigmentaufnahme *f*
pigment/binder ratio, pigment/binder ~ [*The ratio of total pigment (white and/or coloured pigment plus extender) to binder in a paint, preferably expressed as a ratio by volume*] · Pigment/Bindemittel-Verhältnis *n*
pigment-binder system · Pigment-Bindemittel-System *n*
pigment blend · Pigmentmischung *f*
~ **compatibility** · Pigmentverträglichkeit *f*
~ **concentration,** concentration of pigment-vehicle system · Pigmentvolumenkonzentration *f*, PVK
~ **content** · Pigmentgehalt *m*, Pigmentanteil *m*
~ **dispersion,** pigmentation · Pigmentierung *f*, Einfärbung, Durchfärbung
~ **dyestuff** → pigmentary ~
~ **fineness** · Pigmentfeinheit *f*
(~) **flushing process,** (~) ~ (method) · Pigmentdispergierungsverfahren *n* durch Phasenwechsel
~ **for colouring cement** → cement pigment
~ ~ ~ **concrete** [*B.S. 1014*]; ~ ~ coloring ~ (US) · Betonpigment *n*, Farbzusatz *m*
~ ~ **protective coats on façades** · Fassadenfarbe *f*
~ **grain,** ~ particle · Pigmentteilchen *n*
~ **miscibility** · Pigmentmischbarkeit *f*
~ **particle,** ~ grain · Pigmentteilchen *n*
~ **paste** · Pigmentpaste *f*
~ **powder** · Pigmentpulver *n*
~ **settlement** · Pigmentabsetzen *n*
~ **stain** · Farbbeize *f*
~ **volume,** PV · Pigmentvolumen *n*
pigment(ary) dyestuff · Pigmentfarbstoff *m* [*Durch Synthese direkt erzeugtes organisches Pigment*]

pigmentary size · Pigmentteilchengröße *f*
pigmentation, pigment dispersion · Pigmentierung *f*, Einfärbung, Durchfärbung
pigmented; integrally coloured (Brit.); integrally colored (US) · eingefärbt, pigmentiert, durchgefärbt, pigmenthaltig
~ **cement;** coloured ~ (Brit.); colored ~ (US) · Farbzement *m*, Buntzement
~ **concrete;** coloured ~ (Brit.); colored ~ (US) · Buntbeton *m*, farbiger Beton, Farbbeton
~ **flatting varnish,** ~ rubbing ~ · pigmentierter Vorlack *m*, halbfetter Schleiflack
~ **floor(ing) varnish,** floor(ing) lacquer (Fuß)Bodenlackemaille *f*, (Fuß)Bodenlackfarbe *f*
~ **garden tile;** coloured ~ ~ (Brit.); colored ~ ~ (US) · farbige Gartenplatte *f*, Gartenbuntplatte
~ **mastic asphalt;** coloured ~ ~ (Brit.); colored ~ ~ (US) · Buntgußasphalt *m*, Farbgußasphalt, farbiger Gußasphalt
~ **mortar;** coloured ~ (Brit.); colored ~ (US) · Buntmörtel *m*, farbiger Mörtel, Farbmörtel
~ **paint** · pigmentierte (Anstrich)Farbe *f*
~ **rubbing varnish,** ~ flatting ~ · pigmentierter Vorlack *m*, halbfetter Schleiflack
~ **tile;** coloured ~ (Brit.); colored ~ (US) · Bunt(belag)platte *f*, Buntfliese *f*, Farb(belag)platte, Farbfliese
pilaster → engaged pier
~ **capital** → engaged pier ~
~ **-strip,** lesene [*A pilaster without base and capital*] · Lisene *f*, Lesene
pilastered façade · Halbpfeilerfassade *f*, Wandpfeilerfassade, Pilasterfassade
pilchard oil · Pilchardöl *n*
pile → stock ~
(pile and sheetpile) driving work · Rammarbeiten *fpl* [*DIN 18304*]
pile for driving · Rammpfahl *m*
~ **foundation** · Pfahlgründung *f*
~ **loading** · Pfahlbelastung *f*
pilgrimage altar · Gnadenaltar *m*, Pilgeraltar, Wallfahrtsaltar
~ **chapel** · Gnadenkapelle *f*, Pilgerkapelle, Wallfahrtskapelle
~ **church** · Wallfahrtskirche *f*, Gnadenkirche, Prozessionskirche, Pilgerkirche [*Die Kapellen sind durch einen Umgang mit dem Hauptraum verbunden*]
~ **house** · Pilgerhaus *n*
~ **road** · Pilgerstraße *f*
~ **stair(case)** · Wallfahrtstreppe *f*, Bußtreppe, Bittstiege *f*, Prozessionstreppe
pillar, PLR [*A free-standing upright member which, unlike a column, need not be cylindrical or conform with any of the orders*] · freistehender Pfeiler *m*, eingestellter ~, Freipfeiler

pillar hydrant — pipe circulating system

~ **hydrant**, surface ~, above-grade ~, above-ground ~ · Überflurhydrant m, Oberflächenhydrant, oberirdischer Hydrant m, oberedriger Hydrant

~ **of victory**, victory pillar, column of triumph, triumphal column · Siegessäule f, gekuppelte Säule, Doppelsäule, Triumphsäule

~ **tap** · Standhahn m

pillared hall · Pfeilerhalle f

pilot (light), continuous pilot [*A small gas flame which on some gas water heaters is left always burning so as to ignite the main gas burners immediately the tap is opened*] · Sparflamme f

~ ~, indicator ~, signal ~, indicator lamp, signal lamp · Kontrollampe f

pilotis · Pilotis f [*Pfeiler oder Stützen, die ein Bauwerk tragen, das dadurch erst in Höhe des ersten Stockes beginnt, wobei das Erdgeschoß offen bleibt. Hauptvertreter einer solchen Bauweise war Le Corbusier*]

~ **building**, ~ block [*A building, often of many stor(e)ys, which stands upon rows of widely spaced reinforced concrete columns, thus leaving the whole of the ground-floor space available for car-parking and other purposes*] · Pilotisgebäude n

pin · Hespe f, Angel f, Kloben m, Haspe f [*Drehzapfen an Fenster- oder Türbändern*]

~ · Dorn m [*Einstemmband*]

~ · Stift m

~ **(US)**; stake, peg, surveyor ~ · Absteckpfahl m, Absteckpflock m

~ **arch(ed girder)** → pinned ~ (~)

~ **bar** → hinge(d) ~

~**-based column**, pin-ended ~ · Gelenkstütze f

pin-connected joint → hinge(d) ~

pin connection → hinge(d) joint

~**-ended column**, pin-based ~ · Gelenkstütze f

pin frame → hinge(d) ~

~ **hinge** · Bolzengelenk n

~ **joint** → hinge(d) ~

pin(-)jointed → hinged

~ **arch(ed girder)** → pin(ned) ~ (~)

~ **bar** → hinge(d) ~

~ **frame** → hinge(d) ~

~ **purlin(e)** → hinge(d) ~

~ **system** → articulated ~

pin of a hinge, pintle, hinge(d) pin · Scharnierstift m

~ **plate** · Gelenkstoßblech n

~ **purlin(e)** → hinge(d) ~

~ **system** → articulated ~

pinacotheca [*A building to contain painted pictures*] · Pinakothek f

pine cone · Pinienzapfen m

~ **oil** · Kiefernholzöl n

~ **shingle** · Kiefernschindel f

~ **tar** · Nadelholzteer m

pine-tar pitch · Nadelholzteerpech n

pink glass · Rosalinglas n

pinnacle · (Strebe)Pfeilertürmchen n, Fiale f, Spitzsäule f, Spitztürmchen [*Spitzpfeiler, dessen Schaft (auch Leib genannt) mit Maßwerk besetzt ist und über einem Satteldach oder Giebel einen mit Krabben besetzten Helm trägt*]

~ **terminating in conic(al) form** · kegelförmige Fiale f

~ ~ ~ **pyramidal form** · pyramidenförmige Fiale f

pinnacled canopy · Fialbaldachin m

pinned → hinged

pin(ned) arch(ed girder), linked ~ (~), hinged ~ (~), articulated ~ (~), pin-jointed ~ (~) · Gelenkbogen(träger) m, gekrümmter Gelenkträger

~ **bar** → hinged ~

~ **connection** → hinge(d) joint

~ **frame** → hinged ~

~ **joint** → hinge(d) ~

~ **purlin(e)** → hinged ~

~ **system** → articulated ~

pintle, pin of a hinge, hinge(d) pin · Scharnierstift m

pinwheel (ground)plan · hakenkreuzförmiger Grundriß m

pioneering architect · Architekturpionier m

to pipe · berohren, verrohren

pipe · Rohr n

~ **back**, ~ bore side · Rohrinnenseite f

(~) **barrel** [*That portion of a pipe throughout which the internal diameter and thickness of wall remain uniform*] · (Rohr)Schaft m, Durchgangsrohr n

(~) **base** · (Rohr)Fuß m

(~) **bend** · (Rohr)Krümmer m

~ **(bonding) adhesive**, ~ ~ agent, ~ ~ medium, ~ cement(ing agent), ~ glue · Rohrkleber m, Rohrkleb(e)mittel n, Rohrkleb(e)stoff m

~ **bore side**, ~ back · Rohrinnenseite f

(~) **branch**, (~) inlet, (~) junction · Zulauf m, Abzweig m, Rohr~

~ **branching** · Rohrverzweigung f

~ **bridge** · Rohr(leitungs)brücke f

~ **burst** · Rohrbruch m

(~) **cap** · (Rohr)Deckel m, (Rohr)Kappe f

~ **casting** · Rohrguß m

~ **cement** · Rohrkitt m

~ **cement(ing agent)** → ~ (bonding) adhesive

~ **circulating system**, ~ circulation ~, circulation pipework · Umlaufrohrnetz n, Umwälzrohrnetz

(pipe) circulation line — pipe pier

(~) circulation line · Umlauf(rohr)leitung f, Umwälz(rohr)leitung

~ ~ system, ~ circulating ~, circulation pipework · Umlaufrohrnetz n, Umwälzrohrnetz

~ clean(s)ing agent · Rohrreinigungsmittel n

~ column, tubular ~ · Rohrstütze f

~ concrete · Rohrbeton m

~ connection · Rohrverbindung f [*Rohrverbindungsarten sind: Schweißverbindung, Lötverbindung, Muffenverbindung, Flanschverbindung, Verschraubung und Klammerverbindung*]

~ connector, ~ nipple · Rohrnippel m

~ core, core pipe · Rohrkern m, Kernrohr n [*Teil eines Betonrohres*]

(~) coupling [*A (pipe) fitting used for connecting together pipes or fittings*] · Rohrkupplung f

~ ~, (~) joint assembly, coupling of pites · Rohrkuppeln n, Kuppeln von Rohren

(~) covering tape · (Rohr)Isolierband n

(~) cross · (Rohr)Kreuz(stück) n

~ cross-section · Rohrquerschnitt m

~ cutter · Rohr(ab)schneider m

~ diameter · Rohrdurchmesser m

~ duct · Rohrkanal m

~ earthing · Rohrerdung f [*Blitzschutz*]

~ end, end of a pipe · Rohrstirnfläche f, Stirnfläche eines Rohres

~ fitting [*Anything fitted to a pipe for jointing, connecting or changing the direction or bore of a pipe*] · (Rohr)Fitting m, (Rohr)Formstück n

~ fixing · Rohrbefestigung f

~ flange, pipeline ~ · Rohrflansch m, Rohrleitungsflansch

~ frame, tubular ~, barrel ~, tubing ~, tube ~ · Rohrrahmen m

~ gasket · Rohrselbstdichtung f

~ glue → ~ (bonding) adhesive

~ grid · Rohrregister n [*Strahlungsheizung*]

~ handrail, tube ~, tubing ~, tubular ~, barrel ~ · Rohrhandlauf m

(~) hanger · (Rohr)Schelle f, (Rohr)Bügel m

(~) heating tape, electrically heated ~ [*Such tapes with a low wattage loading are used for wrapping pipework in chemical and oil plants to maintain suitable viscosity in external pipework in cold weather*] · (Elektro)Heizband(age) n, (f)

~ incrustation · Rohrverkrustung f

(~) inlet, (~) junction, (~) branch · (Rohr)Abzweig m, (Rohr)Zulauf m

~ installation · Rohrinstallation f

(~) insulating section, (~) insulation(-grade) ~ · (Rohr)Dämmschale f

~ insulation; ~ lagging (Brit.) · Rohrdämmung f

~ ~; ~ lagging (Brit.) · Rohrisolierung f

(~) insulation(-grade) section, (~) insulating ~ · (Rohr)Dämmschale f

~ ~ loose fill; ~ lagging ~ ~ (Brit.) · Rohrschüttdämmung f

~ joint, ~ section, individual section of pipe · Rohrschuß m, Rohrabschnitt m

(~) ~ assembly, ~ coupling, coupling of pipes · Rohrkuppeln n, Kuppeln von Rohren

~ ~ seal(ing) compound · Rohrvergußmasse f

(~) ~ set in cement mortar · (Rohr-)Stoßdichtung f mit Zementmörtel

~ joint(ing) compound, sewer ~ ~, joint cement · Füllmasse f, Vergußmasse f [*Zur Vermuffung von Rohren*]

(~) junction, (~) inlet, (~) branch · (Rohr)Abzweig m, (Rohr)Zulauf m

~ lagging (Brit.); ~ insulation · Rohrdämmung f

~ ~ (Brit.); ~ insulation · Rohrisolierung f

~ ~ loose fill (Brit.); ~ insulation ~ ~ · Rohrschüttdämmung f

(~) ~ section (Brit.) → preformed (pipe insulation) ~

pipe(line) flange · Rohrflansch m, Rohrleitungsflansch

~ installer · Rohr(fern)leitungsbauer m

~ noise · Rohrgeräusch n, Rohrleitungsgeräusch

pipeline parts, piping ~, pipe network ~ · Rohr(leitungs)teile mpl, npl

pipemaking · Rohrfertigung f, Rohrherstellung

pipe mandril · Rohrdorn m

~ marking; colour ~ (Brit.); color ~ (US) · Farbkennzeichnung f von Rohrleitungen, Rohrkennzeichnung [*DIN 2403*]

~ mast, tubular ~, tube ~, barrel ~, tubing ~ · Rohrmast m

~ material · Rohrmaterial n, Rohrwerkstoff m

~ mould → concrete ~ ~

~ network, network of piping · Rohr(leitungs)netz n

~ ~ parts, piping ~, pipeline ~ · Rohr(leitungs)teile mpl, npl

~ newel, tubular ~, tube ~, tubing ~, barrel ~ · (Treppen)Rohrspindel f

~ nipple, ~ connector · Rohrnippel m

~ noise, pipeline ~ · Rohrgeräusch n, Rohrleitungsgeräusch

~ O.D., pipe outside diameter · Rohraußendurchmesser m

~ outside diameter, ~ O. D. · Rohraußendurchmesser m

~ penetration · Rohrdurchgang m

~ pier, ~ support, thrust block · (Rohr-)Festpunkt m

pipe pile — pitch

~ **pile** · Rohrpfahl *m*

~ **plant** · Rohrfertigungsanlage *f*

~ **plastic** · Rohrkunststoff *m*

(~) **plug,** (~) stopper, seal(ing) ~ · Pfropfen *m*, Stopfen *m*, Verschluß *m*, Rohr~

~ **profile,** ~ section · Rohrprofil *n*, Rohrschnitt *m*

~ **protection against corrosion** · Rohrschutz *m* [*Schutz von Rohren gegen Korrosion*]

~ **purlin(e),** barrel ~, tube ~, tubing ~, tubular ~ · (Dach)Rohrpfette *f*

~ **railing,** tube ~, tubing ~, barrel ~ · Rohrgeländer *n*

~ ~ **fitting,** barrel ~ ~, tubing ~ ~, tubular ~ ~ · (Rohr)Geländerfitting *m*, (Rohr)Geländerformstück *n*

(~) **reducer** → diminishing piece

(~) **return bend** · (Rohr)Doppelkrümmer *m*

piperun [*The general layout of the pipes in a building*] · Rohrführung *f*

pipe section, ~ profile · Rohrprofil *n*, Rohrschnitt *m*

~ ~, ~ joint, individual section of pipe · Rohrschuß *m*, Rohrabschnitt *m*

(~) ~; (~) lagging ~ (Brit.); preformed (pipe insulation) ~ · Schale *f* [*Für Isolier- und Dämmzwecke*]

~ **separator** [*for steel beams*] · Rohr-Stegverbindungsstück *n*

~ **sewer (line)** · Abwasserrohrleitung *f*, Kanal(isations)rohrleitung

~ **shaft** · Rohrschacht *m*

~ **shape** · Rohrform *f*, Rohrgestalt *f*

~ **sizing** · Rohrbemessung *f*

~ **skeleton,** tubular ~, tube ~, barrel ~, tubing ~ · Rohrskelett *n*, Rohrgerippe *n*

(~) **sleeve,** P SL · (Rohr)Muffe *f*

~ **spigot,** spigot (end) · (Rohr)Einsteckende *n*, (Rohr)Spitzende, Falz *m*

~ **steel reinforcement** [*Hoops, either hooked, butt or lap welded, or a continuous helix or fabric suitably welded, longitudinals or some other method being adopted to control spacing and shape, and to permit safe handling*] · Rohrarmierung *f*, Rohrbewehrung, Rohr(stahl)einlagen *fpl*

~ **still** · Röhrendestillationsanlage *f*

(~) **stopper,** (~) plug, seal(ing) ~ · Pfropfen *m*, Stopfen *m*, Verschluß *m*, Rohr~

~ **stress analysis** · Rohrspannungsuntersuchung *f*

~ **support,** ~ pier, thrust block · (Rohr-)Festpunkt *m*

~ **suspension** · Rohraufhängung *f*

~ **system,** pipework · Rohr(leitungs)system *n*

(~) **tape covering** · (Rohr)Bandisolierung *f*

~ **thread** [*B.S. 21*] · Rohrgewinde *n*

~ **top** · Rohrscheitel *m*

~ **trench** · Rohrgraben *m*

(~) **wall** · (Rohr)Wand(ung) *f*

pipework, pipe system · Rohr(leitungs)system *n*

~ **basement** · Rohrkellergeschoß *n*, Rohrleitungskellergeschoß

~ **cellar** · Rohrkeller *m*, Rohrleitungskeller

~ **system** · (Rohr)Leitungssystem *n*

pipe works · Rohrwerk *n*

piping · Verrohrung *f*

~ · Rohrleitung *f*

~ **parts,** pipeline ~, pipe network ~ · Rohr(leitungs)teile *mpl, npl*

piscina [*In Christian churches, a perforated stone basin for disposal of the water after the priest had washed his hands and the sacred vessels*] · Wasserablauf *m* am Altar

pisé construction, ~ de terre ~, rammed-earth ~, rammed-loam ~, cob ~ · Lehmstampfbau *m*, Piseebau, Kastenwerk *n*

~ **(de terre), cob** [*A mix(ture) of stiff clay and chopped straw, well kneaded, used for building the walls of cottages, etc.*] · Pisee *m*

~ (~ ~) **construction,** rammed-loam ~, rammed-earth ~, cob ~ · Lehmstampfbau *m*, Piseebau, Kastenwerk *n*

pisolite, pisolitic limestone · Erbsenstein *m*, Pisolith *m*

pisolitic limestone, pisolite · Pisolith *m*, Erbsenstein *m*

pissasphalt(um), maltha, mineral tar · Bergteer *m*

pistol range · Pistolenschießstand *m*

pit, dig · Grübchen *n* [*Fehler im optischen Glas*]

~, well, shaft · Schacht *m* [*Ein senkrechter Hohlraum von meist geringem Querschnitt, z.B. Luftschacht*]

~ **and quarry industry,** (nonmetallic) minerals ~ · Steine- und Erdenindustrie *f*

~ **cover** · Grubendeckel *m*

~ **covering** · Grubenabdeckung *f*

~ **gravel,** pit-run ~ [*Untreated gravel from a pit*] · ungesiebter Grubenkies *m*, ~ Wandkies

~ **head bath** · (Wasch)Kaue *f*

~ **lime** · eingesumpfter Kalk *m*, Grubenkalk, Sumpfkalk

~ **material** · Grubenmaterial *n*

pit(-run) gravel [*Untreated gravel from a pit*] · ungesiebter Grubenkies *m*, ~ Wandkies

~ **sand** [*Untreated sand from a pit*] · Grubensand *m*

pit slag · Grubenschlacke *f*

pitch · Pech *n*, Säureharzasphalt *m*

~ [*The angle of slope to the horizontal*] · Neigungswinkel *m* zur Horizontalen

pitch — plain floor cover(ing) tile

~ [*That attribute of auditory sensation in terms of which sound may be ordered on a scale related primarily to frequency*] · Tonhöhe f [*Zuordnung eines Tones oder Tongemisches zu einer bestimmten Skala zwischen tiefen und hohen Tönen. Anmerkung: Das Wort Tonhöhe entstammt der Musik. Allgemein ist die Tonhöhe ein psychologisches Merkmal des Hörereignisses. In der physikalischen Akustik wird die Tonhöhe durch die Frequenz gekennzeichnet*]

~ **between 100 and 3,200 cycles** · Normaltonhöhe f [*Sie liegt zwischen 100 und 3.200 Hz*]

~ **coke** · Pechkoks m

~ **line, walking** ~ · Ganglinie f, Gehlinie, Teilungslinie, Lauflinie [*Treppe; DIN 18064*]

~ **of roof** → roof pitch

~ **(~ the corrugation(s)), depth** (~ ~ ~) · Wellenhöhe f [*Wellplatte; Welltafel*]

~ **peat** · fetter Torf m, Pechtorf

~ **resin** · Pechharz n

~ **varnish** · Teerlack m, Teerlösung f

pitched roof [*A roof the pitch of which is greater than 10° to the horizontal*] · geneigtes Dach n

~ ~ **area, sloped** ~ ~ · geneigte Dachfläche f

pitcher, granite (paving) sett [*B.S. 435*] · Granitpflasterstein m [*DIN 18502*]

~, **blockstone, hand-placed stone, hand-packed stone, hand-pitched stone, pitching stone** · Setzpacklagestein m, Vorlagestein, Stückstein

pitching stone, hand-packed ~, **hand-placed,** ~, **hand-pitched** ~, **picher, blockstone** · Setzpacklagestein m, Vorlagestein, Stückstein

pitting · Grübchenbildung f

~ **resistance** · Grübchenbildungswiderstand m

pivot hinge · Drehachse f [*Schwing(flügel)fenster*]

~ **pin** · Drehzapfen m

pivoted · drehzapfengelagert

~ **window** · Drehzapfenfenster n [*1. Schwing(flügel)fenster; 2. Wende(flügel)fenster*]

to place · einbauen, einbringen, verarbeiten [*Baustoff*]

~ ~ · einleiten [*z.B. Zug in eine Stütze*]

~ ~ **head to head** · affrontieren

place brick, salmon ~, **chuff** (~) · Ausschußziegel m

~ **of outstanding architectural merit, architecturally beautiful square** · Architekturalplatz m

~ ~ **worship, worshipping place; centre of cult (Brit.); center of cult (US)** · Kultstätte f, Anbetungsstätte, Gotteshaus n, Verehrungsstätte, Andachtsstätte

placeability · Betonierbarkeit f

placement number · Positionsnummer f [*zum Einbau von großformatigen Fertigteilen*]

placer → (reinforcing) iron worker

placing · Einbauen n, Einbringen, Verarbeiten [*Baustoff*]

~ **drawing** [*A detailed drawing which gives the size of the bars, location, spacing and all other information required by the iron worker*] · Verlegezeichnung f [*Bewehrung*]

~ **head to head** · Affrontieren n

~ **of cables, laying** ~ ~, **cable laying, cable placing** · Kabeleinbau m, Kabelverlegung f

~ ~ **concrete** → pouring

~ ~ **dry-mix shotcrete** · Torkretieren n

~ ~ **shotcrete** → shooting

(~ the) roofing; healing, helying (Brit.) · (Dach)Eindecken n, Bedachung f, Dach(ein)deckung, (Be)Dachen

plain [*wall(ing) surface*] · geschlossen [*Wandfläche*]

~, **nonchromatic** [*As opposed to 'colo(u)red'*] · unbunt, ungefärbt

~ · schlicht [*im Gegensatz zu profiliert*]

~, **unfaced** · nichtabgedeckt [*Baumatte*]

~, **unreinforced** · nichtarmiert, nichtbewehrt, unbewehrt, unarmiert

~ **artificial stone** [*deprecated*]; ~ **reconstructed** ~, ~ **patent** ~, ~ **cast** ~ · unbearbeiteter Betonwerkstein m

~ **(back)ground** · glatter Fond m [*(Papier)Tapete*]

~ **bar** → ~ **steel** ~

~ **board** → ~ **run** ~

~ **cast stone,** ~ **reconstructed** ~, ~ **patent** ~; ~ **artificial** ~ [*deprecated*] · unbearbeiteter Betonwerkstein m

~ **cement (roof(ing)) tile** → ~ **concrete** (~) ~

~ ~ **tile** → ~ **concrete (roof(ing))** ~

~ **chromium steel, chromium stainless** ~ · Chromstahl m

~ **concrete** · unbewehrter Beton m

~ ~ **(roof(ing)) tile,** flat ~ (~) ~, plane ~ (~) ~, cement (~) ~, concrete plain (~) ~, concrete plane (~) ~, cement plain (~) ~, cement plane (~) ~, concrete flat (~) ~, cement flat (~) ~ [*B.S. 473*] · Beton-Dachblatt n, Beton-Ochsenzunge f, Beton-Dachtasche f, Beton-Dachplatte f, Beton-Flachwerk n, Beton-Flachstein m, Beton-Zungenstein, Betonbiber(-schwanz)(stein) m [*DIN 1116*]

~ **cube** · reiner Kubus m

~ **floor cover(ing) tile,** ~ **floor(ing) (finish)** ~ · (Fuß)Boden(belag)platte f mit ebener Oberfläche, (Fuß)Bodenfliese ~ ~ ~

plain floor(ing) (finish) tile — planar frame element 720

~ **floor(ing) (finish) tile,** ~ floor cover(ing) ~ · (Fuß)Boden(belag)platte f mit ebener Oberfläche, (Fuß)Bodenfliese f ~ ~ ~

~ ~ **tile,** ~ ~ finish ~, ~ floor cover(-ing) ~ · (Fuß)Boden(belag)platte f mit ebener Oberfläche, (Fuß)Bodenfliese f ~ ~ ~

~ **glass roof(ing) tile,** plane ~ ~ ~ · Glasbiber(schwanz) m

~ **glazed coat(ing),** → ~ glaze(d finish)

~ **glaze(d finish),** ~ glazing, ~ glazed coat(ing) [*See remark under 'Glasur'*] · unbunte Beglasung f, ungefärbte ~, ~ Glasur f

~ **glazing** → ~ glaze(d finish)

~ **ground** → ~ back~

~ **gypsum lath,** ~ sheet of gypsum plasterboard · ungelochte Gipsbautafel f [*als Putzträger*]

~ **hinge** · Gleitgelenk n

~ **lino(leum),** Walton's ~ · einfarbiges Linoleum n, Unilinoleum, Waltonlinoleum

~ ~ **cement,** Walton's ~ ~ · Waltonzement m

~ **loop for ceilings,** ~ stirrup ~ ~ · einfacher Deckenbügel m

~ **panel,** ~ run ~ [*A panel devoid of ornamentation*] · glatte Tafel f

~ **paper** → ~ wall →

~ **patent stone,** ~ cast ~, ~ reconstructed ~; ~ artificial ~ [*deprecated*] · unbearbeiteter Betonwerkstein m

~ **reconstructed stone,** ~ patent ~, ~ cast ~; ~ artificial ~ [*deprecated*] · unbearbeiteter Betonwerkstein m

~ **reinforcement bar** → ~ (steel) ~

~ ~ **rod** → ~ (steel) bar

~ **reinforcing bar** → ~ (steel) ~

~ ~ **rod** → ~ (steel) bar

~ **rod** → ~ (steel) bar

~ **rolled glass,** horticultural ~ · Gartenrohrglas n

~ **(roof(ing)) tile,** plane (~) ~, double lap ~ · Biber(schwanz) m [*Diese Benennung umfaßt Biber-(schwanz)ziegel und Biber(schwanz)-stein*]

~ **round bar,** ~ ~ rod · glatter Rundstab m, querschnittgleicher ~

~ ~ **bars,** ~ ~ rods · glatter Rundstahl m, querschnittgleicher ~

~ ~ **rod,** ~ ~ bar · glatter Rundstab m, querschnittgleicher ~

~ ~ **rods,** ~ ~ bars · glatter Rundstahl m, querschnittgleicher ~

~ **(run) board,** ~ (~) sheet [*A board or sheet devoid of ornamentation*] · glatte Platte f

~ **(~) panel** [*A panel devoid of ornamentation*] · glatte Tafel f

~ **(~) sheet,** ~ (~) board [*A board or sheet devoid of ornamentation*] · glatte Platte f

~ **sheet** → ~ run ~

~ ~ **of gypsum plasterboard,** ~ gypsum lath · ungelochte Gipsbautafel f [*als Putzträger*]

~ **(steel) bar,** ~ (~) rod, ~ reinforcing ~, ~ reinforcement ~ · glatter Bewehrungsstab m, ~ Armierungsstab, querschnittgleicher ~

~ **(~) rod** → ~ (~) bar

~ **stirrup for ceilings,** ~ loop ~ ~ · einfacher Deckenbügel m

~ **tail** · Schwanzende n [*Rohr*]

~ ~ **pipe** · Schwanzendenrohr n

~ **tile** → ~ (roof(ing)) ~

~ ~ **roof cladding,** plane ~ ~ ~, ~ ~ ~ cover(ing), ~ ~ ~ sheathing, ~ ~ roofing · Biber(schwanz)dach-(ein)deckung f, Biber(schwanz)bedachung

~ **tube economiser** · Glattrohreko(no-miser) m, Glattrohr-Rauchgas-Wasservorwärmer m

~ **(wall)paper** · Eintontapete f, Uni-Tapete [*Diese Tapete hat keine Musterung, sondern nur eine Grundfarbe*]

~ **web,** solid ~, ~ stalk · Vollsteg m

plain-web(bed) arched girder, solid-web(bed) ~ ~ · Vollwandbogenträger m, Vollwandträger in Bogenform

~ **beam,** solid-web(bed) ~ · Vollwandbalken(träger) m, vollwandiger Balken-(träger)

~ **three-hinge(d) arched girder,** solid-web(bed) ~ ~ ~ · Vollwand-Dreigelenkbogen(träger), m, Vollwand-Dreigelenkträger in Bogenform

plain wire · Glattdraht m, querschnittgleicher Draht

~ **zed** · nichtabgekantetes Z-Profil n

plaining, (re)fining · Läutern n, Läuterung f [*Glasherstellung*]

~ **agent,** (re)fining ~ · Läuterungsmittel n [*Glasherstellung*]

plait-band → guilloche

to plan · planen

~ ~ **and design** · projektieren

plan → ground(-)~

~ **area** → ground(-)~ ~

~ **dimension** → ground(-)~ ~

~ **form** → (ground(-))plan shape

~ **geometry** → ground(-)~ ~

~ **shape** → ground(-)~ ~

~ **type** → ground(-)~ ~

planar, plane, flat, level, non-sloping · eben, gefälleloses

~ **bearing structure** → plane (load-)bearing ~

~ **frame,** plane ~, flat ~ · ebener Rahmen m

~ ~ **element,** flat ~ ~, plane ~ ~ · ebenes Rahmenelement n

planar frame structure — planetarium

~ ~ **structure, plane** ~ ~, **flat** ~ ~ · ebenes Rahmentragwerk *n*
~ **(load)bearing structure** → plane ~ ~
~ **parallel system, plane** ~ ~, **flat** ~ ~ · ebenes Parallelsystem *n* [*Seilsystem*]
~ **rotational system** → plane ~
~ **state of stress, plane** ~ ~ ~, **two-dimensional** ~ ~ ~, **flat** ~ ~ ~ ~, **state of plane** ~ · zweidimensionaler Spannungszustand *m*, ebener ~
~ **stress problem, plane** ~ ~, **flat** ~ ~ · ebene Spannungsaufgabe *f*, ebenes Spannungsproblem *n*
~ **structure** → plane (load)bearing ~
~ **supporting structure** → plane (load)bearing ~
~ **theory of elasticity, plane** ~ ~ ~ · ebene Elastizitätstheorie *f*
~ **(weight-carrying) structure** → plane (load)bearing ~

plance(e)r piece → soffit board

plane, planar, flat, level, non-sloping · eben, gefällelos
~ · Ebene *f* [*Baustatik*]
~ **area-covering structural element** · ebenes Flächentragwerk *n*
~ **bearing structure** → ~ load~ ~
~ **cement (roof(ing)) tile** → plain concrete (~) ~
~ ~ **tile** → plain concrete (roof(ing)) ~
~ **concrete (roof(ing)) tile** → plain ~ (~) ~
~ ~ **tile** → plain concrete (roof(ing)) ~
~ **deformation** · ebene Verformung *f*, ~ Formänderung
~ ~ **state, state of plane deformation** · ebener Formänderungszustand *m*, ~ Verformungszustand
~ **diffuser** · glatte Wanne *f* [*Leuchte*]
~ **distortion state, state of plane distortion** · ebener Verzerrungszustand *m*
~ **elasticity** · ebene Elastizität *f*
~ **force(s) system,** ~ **system of forces** · ebenes Kraftsystem *n*, ~ Kräftesystem
~ **frame, planar** ~, **flat** ~ ~ · ebener Rahmen *m*
~ ~ **element, planar** ~ ~, **flat** ~ ~ · ebenes Rahmenelement *n*
~ ~ **structure, planar** ~ ~, **flat** ~ ~ · ebenes Rahmentragwerk *n*
~ **framework** · ebenes Fachwerk *n*
~ **geometry** · Flächenlehre *f*, Planimetrie *f*, Geometrie der Ebene, ebene Geometrie
~ **glass roof(ing) tile, plain** ~ ~ ~ · Glasbiber(schwanz) *m*
~ **(load)bearing structure, planar** ~ ~, **flat** ~ ~, ~ **(weight-carrying)** ~, ~ **supporting** ~ · ebenes Tragwerk *n* [*Ein Tragwerk mit zwei Tragrichtungen. Die am meisten verwendeten ebenen Tragwerke sind kreuzweise bewehrte Platten, Scheiben und Pilzdecken*]
~ **of a structure, structure plane** · Bauwerkebene *f*
~ ~ **bars,** ~ ~ **rods,** ~ ~ **members,** ~ ~ **elements** · Gliedebene *f*, Stabebene
~ ~ **elements,** ~ ~ **members,** ~ ~ **rods,** ~ ~ **bars** · Gliedebene *f*, Stabebene
~ ~ **loading, loading plane** · Belastungsebene *f*
~ ~ **members,** ~ ~ **elements,** ~ ~ **bars,** ~ ~ **rods** · Gliedebene *f*, Stabebene
~ ~ **projection, projection plane** · Bildebene *f*, Bildtafel *f*, Rißtafel, Rißebene, Projektionstafel, Projektionsebene
~ ~ **rods,** ~ ~ **bars,** ~ ~ **members,** ~ ~ **elements** · Gliedebene *f*, Stabebene
~ ~ **symmetry** · Symmetrieebene *f*
~ ~ **transposition** · Verschiebungsplan *m* [*Zeichnerische Bestimmung der Verschiebung von Knotenpunkten kinematischer Ketten mit Hilfe der um 90° gedrehten Geschwindigkeiten*]
~ **parallel system, planar** ~ ~, **flat** ~ ~ · ebenes Parallelsystem *n* [*Seilsystem*]
~ **problem of the theory of elasticity** · Elastizitätslehre *f* ebener Tragwerke
~ **projecting diffuser** · glatte überstehende Wanne *f* [*Leuchte*]
~ **(roof(ing)) tile** → plain (~) ~
~ **rotational system, flat** ~ ~, **planar** ~ ~ · ebenes Rotationssystem *n* [*Seilsystem*]
~ **state of stress, planar** ~ ~ ~, **two-dimensional** ~ ~ ~, **flat** ~ ~ ~ ~, **state of plane** ~ · zweidimensionaler Spannungszustand *m*, ebener ~
~ **strain** · ebene Dehnung *f*
~ **stress** · ebene Spannung *f*
~ ~ **problem, planar** ~ ~, **flat** ~ ~ · ebene Spannungsaufgabe *f*, ebenes Spannungsproblem *n*
~ **structure** → ~ (load)bearing ~
~ **supporting structure** → ~ (load-)bearing ~
~ **system of forces,** ~ **force(s) system** · ebenes Kraftsystem *n*, ~ Kräftesystem
~ **theory of elasticity, planar** ~ ~ ~ · ebene Elastizitätstheorie *f*
~ **tile** → plain (roof(ing)) ~
~ ~ **roof cladding** → plain ~ ~ ~
~ **wave** [*A wave in which successive wave fronts are parallel planes*] · ebene Welle *f* [*Schallausbreitung. Welle, bei der alle Feldgrößen in Ebenen senkrecht zur Ausbreitungsrichtung konstant sind*]
~ **(weight-carrying) structure** → ~ (load)bearing ~

planetarium · Planetarium *n*

plank — plant-mix(ed) mortar

plank → ((pre)cast) concrete ~

~, plk, PLK [*A general term for a long piece of square-edged timber, usually 2–4 in. thick and 6 in. or more wide*] · (Holz)Bohle f, Belagbohle

~ · Diele f

~ floor · Bohlendecke f

~ ~, ~ unit ~ · Dielendecke f

~ ~ cover(ing), ~ floor(ing) · Bohlen(fuß)boden(belag) *m*, Bohlenbelag, (Bohlen)Dielung f

~ floor(ing), ~ floor cover(ing) · Bohlen(fuß)boden(belag) *m*, Bohlenbelag, (Bohlen)Dielung f

~ in prestressed clay, ~ ~ Stahlton, Stahlton (prestressed) plank, prestressed clay plank · Spanntonbrett *n*, Stahltonbrett, vorgespanntes Ziegelbrett, Tonelementbalken *m*

~ lath(ing) · Putz(träger)diele f

~ (roof) truss · Bohlen(dach)binder *m*

~ (unit) · Diele f

~ (~) floor · Dielendecke f

planned maintenance · laufende Unterhaltung f, Routineunterhaltung

planner · Planer *m*

planning · Planung f

~ and design office · Projektierungsbüro *n*

~ board · Planungsverband *m*

~ competition · Planungswettbewerb *m*

~ documents · Planungsunterlagen *fpl*

~ engineer · Planungsingenieur *m*

~ flexibility · Planungsanpassungsfähigkeit f

(~) grid, structural ~ [*Not to be confused with a grid plan = Rasterplan*] · Raster *m*, Entwurfs~, Zeichen~, Konstruktions~, Ausbau~, Planungs~ [*Beim architektonischen Entwerfen legt ein Raster ein im Grundriß oder Aufriß stets wiederkehrendes Grundmaß, z.B. die Knotenpunkte einer Skelettkonstruktion, fest*]

~ group, ~ team · Planungsgruppe f, Planungsgemeinschaft f

~ legislation · Planungsgesetzgebung f

~ of buildings, ~ ~ blocks, ~ ~ a building, ~ ~ a block · Gebäudeplanung f

~ ~ project finance · Projektfinanzierungsplanung f

~ office · Planungsbüro *n*

~ restriction · Planungsbeschränkung f

~ team, ~ group · Planungsgruppe f, Planungsgemeinschaft f

~ to (anticipated) requirements · Bedarfsplanung f

~ work · Planungsarbeit f, Planungstätigkeit f

plant bowl · Pflanzenschale f

~ column · Pflanzensäule f

~ decoration, ~ decorative finish, **~** ornamental finish, **~** decorative feature, **~** ornament(al feature), **~** enrichment, **~** pattern · Pflanzenmuster(ung) *n*, (f), Pflanzenschmuck *m*, Pflanzenverzierung, Pflanzenornament(ierung) *n*, (f), Pflanzendekor(ation) *n*, (f)

~ decorative feature → **~** decoration

~ enrichment → **~** decoration

~ form · Pflanzenform f

~ mixing, mechanical ~ · Maschinenmischen *n*

~ mix(ture) · Maschinengemisch *n*, Maschinenmischung f

~ motif · Pflanzenmotiv *n*

~ ornament(al feature) → **~** decoration

~ ornamental finish → **~** decoration

~ pattern → **~** decoration

~ resin → natural **~**

~ resin-base(d) (concrete) curing agent, natural ~ (~) ~ ~, ~ ~ (~) ~ compound, **~ ~** (liquid) membrane (~) **~ ~** · (Beton) Nachbehandlungsmittel auf Naturharzbasis

~ ~ (~) ~ compound, natural **~ (~) ~ ~, ~ ~ (~) ~** agent, **~ ~** (liquid) membrane (~) **~ ~ ~** · (Beton-) Nachbehandlungsmittel auf Naturharzbasis

~ ~ mastic, natural ~ ~ · Naturharzkitt *m*

~ room → machine(ry) **~**

~ scroll · Pflanzenranke f

~ station → machine(ry) **~**

~ trough · Pflanzentrog *m*

~ tub · Pflanzenkübel *m*

plantation house · Plantagenhaus *n*

planting · Bepflanzung f

~ sod(s), (turfing by) sodding · Rasensodenandeckung f, Ansoden *n*

plant-mix(ed) · maschinengemischt

~ asphaltic macadam (US); ~ (asphaltic-)bitumen **~** (Brit.) · Asphaltmischmakadam *m*, Bitumenmischmakadam

~ (asphaltic-)bitumen macadam (Brit.); **~** asphaltic **~** (US) · Asphaltmischmakadam *m*, Bitumenmischmakadam

~ bitumen macadam, ~ asphaltic-**~ ~** (Brit.); **~** asphaltic **~** (US) · Asphaltmischmakadam *m*, Bitumenmischmakadam

~ bituminous mix(ture) · maschinengemischtes bituminöses Gemisch *n*, maschinengemischte bituminöse Mischung f

~ gravelly sand (concrete) aggregate, ~ sandy-gravel (~) **~** · werkgemischter Betonkiessand *m*

~ macadam · Mischmakadam *m*

~ mortar, mill-run ~ · maschinengemischter Mörtel *m*

723 plant-mix(ed) sandy-gravel (concrete) ... — plasterboard

~ **sandy-gravel (concrete) aggregate,** ~ gravelly sand (~) ~ · werkgemischter Betonkiessand *m*

~ **tarmacadam** · Teermischmakadam *m*

plaque, ornamental tablet · Schmucktafel *f*, Ziertafel, Ornamenttafel, Dekor(ations)tafel

~ · Platten-Luftverteiler *m*

~, commemorative tablet, memorial tablet · Gedenktafel *f*, Gedächtnistafel, Ehrentafel, Memorialtafel

to plaster, to render · (ver)putzen

plaster → gypsum stuff

~ → mixed ~

~, plastering mix(ture), mortar for plastering · Putzmasse *f*, Putzmörtel *m*

~, mixed ~ [*1. A paste-like material, usually a mix(ture) of portland cement, lime, or gypsum with water and sand; fiber or hair may be added as a binder; applied to surfaces such as walls or ceilings in the plastic state; later it sets to form a hard surface. 2. This material in its hardened form = finish = Verputz*] · Putz *m*

~, mixed ~, finish · Verputz *m*

~ **area** · Putzfläche *f*

~ **base** · Putz(unter)grund *m*

~ **baseboard,** baseboard for plaster · Putzträgerplatte *f*

~ **bond** · Putzhaftung *f*

~ **ceiling** · Putzdecke *f*

~ **coat** → plastering ~

~ **corner** · Putzecke *f*

~ **crack** · Putzriß *m*

~ **cupola,** ~ dome, mixed ~ ~ · Putzkuppel *f*

(~) **dot,** (~) dab · Lehrkopf *m*, Gipspunkt *m* [*Putz- und Rabitzarbeiten*]

to plaster externally, ~ render (~) (Brit.); to stucco (US) · (außen)(ver-)putzen

plaster for X-ray rooms, X-ray protective plaster, X-ray shielding plaster [*A plaster containing barium sulphate as the aggregate*] · Röntgen(strahlen)-schutzputz *m*

~ **frieze** · Putzfries *m*

~ **ingredient** · Putzbestandteil *m*, Putzkomponente *f*

~ **jointless floor(ing),** ~ ~ floor cover(ing) · Feg, Gips(fuß)bodenestrich *m*

~ **lath(ing)** [*deprecated*] → gypsum (board) ~

(~) ~, plaster's ~, (~) laths [*Lath(-ing) is a base for plaster. The oldest type still in use is spaced wood slats, standardized sizes 3/8" x 11/2" x 32" or 48" long. It is largely superseded as a plaster base in modern homes by gypsum board (rock lath) which may be either perforated or plain. Fiberboard heat-insulating lath is also used. Where there is a fire hazard, various types of perforated, formed, or expanded metal lath are used*] · Putz(mörtel)träger *m*

(~) **laths** → (~) lath(ing)

~ **manufacturer** · Putzhersteller *m*

~ **(mix(ture))** → gypsum stuff

~ ~ → ~ stuff

~ ~ **based on lime** → plastering ~ ~ ~ ~

~ **mould** (Brit.); ~ mold (US) · Gipsform *f*

~ **of Class A** (Brit.) → ~ of Paris

~ ~ ~ **B** (Brit.) · retarded hemihydrate (gypsum-)plaster

~ ~ ~ **C** (Brit.) → anhydrous (gypsum-) plaster

~ ~ ~ **D** (Brit.) → Keene's cement

~ ~ **Paris,** unretarted hemihydrate (gypsum-)plaster, class A plaster, (gypsum-)plaster of Class A (Brit.); stucco [*Scotland*] [*B.S. 1191*] · Stuckgips *m* [*DIN 1168*]

~ ~ ~ **finish** · Stuckputz *m*, Stuck(verputz) *m*

~ ~ ~ **mortar** · Stuckgipsmörtel *m*

~ **on metal (lath(ing))** · Putz *m* auf Metallputzträger

~ ~ **plasterboards** · Putz *m* auf Gipsdielen

~ ~ **reed lath(ing)** · Rohrputz *m* [*Putz auf Rohrgewebe*]

~ ~ **wire lath(ing),** mixed ~ ~ ~ ~ · Draht(ver)putz *m*

~ ~ **wood(en) lath(ing)** · Putz *m* auf Holzstabgewebe

~ **rock,** ~ stone, gypsum rock, potter's stone (Brit.); (massive) gypsum, natural gypsum, raw gypsum · Rohgips *m*, Naturgips, Gipsstein *m*, Gipsgestein *n*, $CaSO_4 \cdot 2H_2O$

~ **room** · Gipserraum *m* [*Krankenhaus*]

~ **scheme,** ~ system · Putzaufbau *m*, Putzsystem *n*

~ **screed** [*A band of plaster carefully laid to the correct surface as a guide for the rule when plastering. The band is level with the final surface*] · Gipsleiste *f*

~ **soffit** · Putzuntersicht *f*

~ **stain** · Putzfleck *m*

~ **stone,** ~ rock, gypsum rock, potter's stone (Brit.); (massive) gypsum, natural gypsum, raw gypsum · Rohgips *m*, Naturgips, Gipsstein *m*, Gipsgestein *n*, $CaSO_4 \cdot 2H_2O$

~ **store** · Gipslager *n* [*Krankenhaus*]

~ **stuff,** ~ mix(ture) · Deckputzmasse *f*, Deckputzmörtel *m*, Oberputzmasse, Oberputzmörtel, Feinputzmasse, Feinputzmörtel

~ **system,** ~ scheme · Putzaufbau *m*, Putzsystem *n*

~ **wall** → plastered ~

plasterboard → (gypsum) plasterboard (sheet)

plasterboard ceiling — plastic (building) unit

~ ceiling → dry ~

~ panel → gypsum ~ ~

~ ~ partition (wall) → gypsum ~ ~ ~ (~)

~ partition (wall) → (gypsum) plasterboard (sheet) ~ (~)

~ (sheet) → gypsum ~ (~)

~ (~) ceiling → dry ~

~ (~) partition (wall) → gypsum ~ (~) ~ (~)

~ (~) wall → gypsum ~ (~) ~

~ wall → (gypsum) plasterboard (sheet) ~

plastered · (innen)verputzt

~ both sides · beidseitig verputzt

plaster(ed) ceiling · Putzdecke *f*

plastered counter ceiling · Putzunterdecke *f*

~ (on) both sides · beidseitig geputzt, ~ verputzt

plaster(ed) wall [*The opposite of a dry wall*] · Putzwand *f*

plasterer · Putzer *m*

plasterer's darby · Putzabziehlatte *f*

~ float · Reib(e)brett *n* [*Brett mit Handgriff zum Verreiben des Putzes*]

~ hair · Putzhaar *n*

~ lath(ing) → (plaster) ~

~ laths → (plaster) lath(ing)

~ putty, lime ~, lime paste [*A stiff paste resulting from slaking quicklime or soaking hydrated lime in water*] · Kalkbrei *m*, Kalkteig *m*, Breikalk *m*, Schlämpe *f*, Schlempe [*Fehlname: Fettkalk*]

~ scaffold(ing) · Putzergerüst *n*, Putzerrüstung *f*, Ver~

plastering, rendering, ~ work · (Ver-)Putzarbeiten *fpl*, (Ver)Putzen *n* [*DIN 18550*]

plaster(ing) coat · Putzhaut *f*, Putzüberzug *m*, Putzschicht *f*, Putzlage *f*

plastering material · Putz(bau)stoff *m*

~ method · Putzweise *f*, Putzverfahren *n*

~ mix(ture), plaster, mortar for plastering · Putzmasse *f*, Putzmörtel *m*

~ sand · Putzsand *m*

~ work, rendering (~) · (Ver)Putzarbeiten *fpl*, (Ver)Putzen *n* [*DIN 18550*]

plastic, ~ compound, ~ composition, ~ mass, ~ material · Kunststoff *m*, ~masse *f*

~, nonelastic, inelastic · nichtelastisch, unelastisch, plastisch

~ addition, addition of plastic, adding of plastic · Kunststoffbeigabe *f*, Kunststoffzusatz *m*, Kunststoffzugabe, Kunststoffbeigeben *n*, Kunststoffzusetzen, Kunststoffzugeben

~ adhesive → ~ bonding →

~ admix(ture), ~ agent · Kunststoffwirkstoff *m*, Kunststoffzusatz(mittel) *m*, (*n*) [*Zur Herstellung von elastischem Beton, Vorsatzbeton, Haftschichten, Ausgleichestrichen, Nivellierschichten, Spachtelmassen und Fugenmörtel*]

~ analysis, ~ calculation, limit ~ · plastische Berechnung *f*, Berechnung nach dem Traglastverfahren

~ article → ~ product

~ bar → ~ element

~ barrier material · Sperrmittel *n* aus Kunststoff, Sperrstoff *m* ~ ~ [*Eine thermoplastische Folie oder Bahn aus Kunststoff*]

~ base · Kunststoffbasis *f*, Kunststoffgrundlage *f*

~ based · kunststoffhaltig

plastic(-based) floor(ing) (finish) material, ~ floor cover(ing) ~ · Kunststoff(uß)bodenmaterial *n*

plastic bathroom (inlet) gull(e)y → ~ ~ outlet

~ ~ outlet, ~ ~ (inlet) gull(e)y · Kunststoff-Badablauf *m*

~ (bath)tub, ~ bath · Kunststoff(bade)wanne *f*

~ beam bending · plastische Balkenbiegung *f*, ~ Balkenträgerbiegung

~ bearing structure → ~ load~ ~

~ behaviour (Brit.) → inelastic ~

~ bending · plastisches Biegen *n*

~ ~ · plastische Biegung *f*

~ ~ moment · plastisches Biegemoment *n*, ~ Biegungsmoment

~ ~ strength · plastische Biegefestigkeit *f*

~ binder · plastisches Bindemittel *n*, plastischer Binder *m*

~ (biological) shielding wall, ~ radiation ~ ~ · Kunststoff-Abschirmwand *f*

~ board, ~ sheet · Kunststoffplatte *f*

~ body · plastischer Körper *m*

~ (bonding) adhesive, ~ ~ agent, ~ ~ medium, ~ ~ cement(ing agent) · Kunststoffkleb(e)stoff *m*, Kunststoffkleb(e)mittel *n*, Kunststoffkleber *m*

~ ~ emulsion · Kunststoff-Haftemulsion *f*, Kunststoff-Verbundemulsion

~ bound · kunststoffgebunden

~ buckling · plastische Knickung *f*

~ ~ · plastisches Knicken *n*

~ (building) component → ~ (~) unit

~ ~ material, ~ construction ~, construction plastic, building plastic · Bau-Kunststoff *m*

~ (~) member → ~ (~) unit

~ (~) unit, ~ (~) member, ~ (~) compound [*A plastic building material which is formed as a single article complete in itself but which is intended to be part of a compound unit or build-*

plastic (building) unit — plastic dynamism

ing or structure. Examples are tile, section gutter, dome(light)] · Kunststoff-(bau)element *n*, Kunststoff(bau)körper *m* [*Fehlname: Kunststoffbaueinheit f*]

~ **cable** · Kunststoffkabel *n*

~ ~ **clip** · Kunststoffkabelschelle *f*

~ **calculation,** ~ **analysis, limit** ~ · plastische Berechnung *f*, Berechnung nach dem Traglastverharen

~ **ceiling dome(light),** ~ ~ **saucer dome,** ~ ~ **light cupola** · Kunststoff-Deckenlichtkuppel *f*

~ ~ **light cupola** → ~ ~ dome(light)

~ ~ **plaster** · Kunststoff-Deckenputz *m*

~ ~ **saucer dome** → ~ ~ dome(light)

~ **cement,** ~ **putty** · plastischer Kitt *m*

plastic-cement cold glaze, cement-plastic ~ ~, ~ vitreous surfacing · Kaltglasur *f* aus Zement und Kunststoff, Kaltkeramik *f* ~ ~ ~ ~

~ **vitreous surfacing,** cement-plastic ~ ~, ~ cold glaze · Kaltglasur *f* aus Zement und Kunststoff, Kaltkeramik *f* ~ ~ ~ ~

plastic cement(ing agent) → ~ (bonding) adhesive

~ **channel (section)** · Kunststoff-U-Profil *n*

~ **cistern** · Kunststoffzisterne *f*

~ **clay, ball** ~**, potter's** ~ · hochplastischer Ton *m*, Letten *m*, Ballton, Töpferton

~ **clip** · Kunststoffschelle *f*

~ **coat** · Kunststoffanstrich *m*, Kunststoffaufstrich

~ ~ · Kunststoffbeschichtung *f*, Kunststoffüberzug *m* [*als Schicht*]

plastic-coated, plastic-(sur)faced kunststoffbeschichtet, kunststoffüberzogen

~ **hardboard** → ~ laminated ~

plastic coating · Kunststoffbeschichtung *f*

~ **cold bonding agent,** ~ ~ ~ medium, ~ ~ (~) adhesive, ~ ~ cement(ing agent) · Kunststoffkaltkleber *m*, Kunststoffkaltkleb(e)mittel *n*, Kunstsotffkaltkleb(e)stoff *m*

~ **(cold-)water paint,** ~ distemper ~ · Kunststoffbinderfarbe *f*, Kunststoffdispersionsbinder *m*, Kunststoffdispersionsfarbe

~ **component** → ~ (building) unit

~ **composition,** ~ (compound), ~ mass, ~ material · Kunststoff *m*, ~masse *f*

~ **(compound),** ~ composition, ~ mass, ~ material · Kunststoff *m*, ~masse *f*

~ **(concrete) reinforcement distance piece,** ~ (~) ~ spacer · (Stahl)Betonabstandhalter *m* aus Kunststoff, Kunststoff-(Stahl)Betonabstandhalter

~ **(~)** ~ **spacer,** ~ (~) ~ distance piece · (Stahl)Betonabstandhalter *m* aus Kunststoff, Kunststoff-(Stahl)Betonabstandhalter

~ **cone** · Kunststoffkegel *m*, Kunststoffkonus *m*

~ **construction,** ~ (structural) system · Kunststoffbausystem *n*, Kunststoff-(konstruktions)system, Kunststoffkonstruktion *f*

~ ~ **material,** ~ building ~, construction plastic, building plastic · Bau-Kunststoff *m*

~ **core** · Kunststoffkern *m*

~ **corrugated board,** ~ ~ sheet, corrugated plastic ~ · gewellte Kunststoffplatte *f*, Kunststoffwellplatte, Well-Kunststoffplatte

~ ~ **film,** ~ ~ sheeting, corrugated plastic ~ · Kunststoffwellfolie *f*

~ ~ **sheet,** ~ ~ board, corrugated plastic ~ · gewellte Kunststoffplatte *f*, Kunststoffwellplatte, Well-Kunststoffplatte

~ ~ **sheeting,** corrugated plastic ~ · Kunststoffwellbahn *f*, Well-Kunststoffbahn, gewellte Kunststoffbahn

~ **cupola,** ~ dome · Kunststoffkuppel *f*

~ **deflection** → inelastic deflexion

~ **deflexion** → inelastic ~

~ **deformation,** inelastic ~, non-elastic ~, creep ~ · plastische Verformung *f*, ~ Formänderung, Kriechverformung, Kriechformänderung

~ ~ **zone** · plastischer Verformungsbereich *m*, ~ Formänderungsbereich, ~ Gestaltänderungsbereich, plastisches Formänderungsbereich, plastisches Verformungsbereich, plastisches Gestaltänderungsbereich

~ **design,** limit-load ~, ultimate-strength ~ · Traglastverfahren *n*

~ **dispersion** · Kunststoffdispersion *f*

~ **distemper paint** → ~ (cold-)water ~

~ **divider strip** · Kunststoff-Terrazzostreifen *m*, Kunststoff-Terrazzo(trenn)-schiene *f*

~ **dome,** ~ cupola · Kunststoffkuppel *f*

~ **domed roof-light,** ~ saucer dome, ~ dome(light), ~ light cupola · Kunststoff-(Dach)Lichtkuppel *f*, Kunststoff-Oberlichtkuppel

~ **dome(light),** ~ saucer dome, ~ light cupola, ~ domed roof-light · Kunststoff-(Dach)Lichtkuppel *f*, Kunststoff-Oberlichtkuppel

~ **door** · Kunststofftür *f*

~ ~ **leaf** · Kunststofftürblatt *n*

~ **(~) pull (handle)** · Kunststoff(tür)-griff *m*

~ **drainage pipe** · Kunststoffdrän(age)-rohr *n*

~ **dressing paint** · Kunststoff-Dachfarbe *f*

~ **dynamism** [*The basis of Futurism signifying a breakaway from traditional architecture*] · plastischer Dynamismus *m*, plastische Dynamik *f*

plastic element — plastic insulation(-grade) tube 726

~ **element,** ~ member, ~ bar, ~ rod · Kunststoffglied *n*, Kunststoffstab *m* [*Teil einer Stabwerkkonstruktion*]

~ **emulsion** · Kunststoffemulsion *f*

~ **equilibrium** · plastisches Gleichgewicht *n*

~ **façade** · Kunststoffassade *f*

~**-faced,** plastic-surfaced, plastic-coated · kunststoffbeschichtet, kunststoffüberzogen

plastic faced hardboard → ~ laminated ~

~ **facing** → ~ lining

~ **factory** · Kunststoffwerk *n*

~ **fan** · Kunststoffventilator *m*

~ **fence** · Kunststoffzaun *m*

~ **filler** → ~ stopper

~ **film,** ~ sheeting · Kunststoffolie *f*

~ ~ **for roofing,** ~ sheeting ~ ~ · Kunststoff-Dachfolie *f*

~ **finger plate** · Kunststoffschonschild *n* [*Baubeschlag*]

~ **finish,** synthetic resin dispersion ~, plastic plaster · Kunststoff(ver)putz *m*, Kunstharzdispersions(ver)putz [*Kunststoff(ver)putze sind mit Kunststoffgranulaten verschiedener Färbung oder farbigen mineralischen Splittern gefüllte Dispersionen für dickschichtige Anstriche auf Mauerwerk*]

~ **fitting** · Kunststoffitting *n*, Kunststoffformstück *n*

~ **fixture** → ~ (light(ing)) ~

~ **flake** · Kunststoffschuppe *f*

~ **flashing (piece)** [*See remark under 'Anschluß'*] · Kunststoffanschluß(streifen) *m*

~ **floor(ing) (finish),** ~ floor cover(ing) · Kunststoff(uß)boden(belag) *m*

~ **flow,** ~ loss, creep · Kriechen *n* plastischer Fluß *m*

~ **foam,** foam(ed) (plastic), expanded plastic · Schaum(kunst)stoff *m*, Schaum-(stoff), Kunststoffschaum *m*, Kunstschaum(stoff) [*Genau genommen ist „Schaum(kunst)stoff" der technisch richtige Ausdruck, denn Schäume, z.B. Seifenschaum, sind nicht beständig und vergehen, während Schaumstoffe beständig sind. Die Kurzform „Schaum-" für „Schaum(kunst)stoff" ist allerdings üblich. Das gleiche gilt für den englischen Begriff*]

~ ~ **board** → foam(ed) (plastic) ~

~ ~ **concrete** → foam(ed) (plastic) (light(weight)) ~

~ ~ **cupola,** ~ ~ dome, foam(ed) plastic ~, expanded plastic ~ · Schaum(stoff)-kuppel *f*, Schaumkunststoffkuppel, Kunststoffschaumkuppel

~ ~ **dome** → ~ ~ cupola

~ ~ **insulant,** ~ ~ insulator, ~ ~ insulation(-grade) material, ~ ~ insulating material · Schaum(stoff)dämmstoff *m*, Schaumkunststoffdämmstoff, Kunststoffschaumdämmstoff

~ ~ **insulation,** foam(ed) (plastic) ~, expanded plastic ~ · Schaumdämmung *f*, Schaumstoffdämmung, Kunstschaum-(stoff)dämmung, Kunststoffschaumdämmung, Schaumkunststoffdämmung

~ ~ **insulation(-grade) material,** ~ ~ insulating ~, ~ ~ insulant, ~ ~ insulator · Schaum(stoff)dämmstoff *m*, Schaumkunststoffdämmstoff, Kunststoffschaumdämmstoff

~ ~ **insulator,** ~ ~ insulant, ~ ~ insulation(-grade) material, ~ ~ insulating material · Schaum(stoff)dämmstoff *m*, Schaumkunststoffdämmstoff, Kunststoffschaumdämmstoff

~ ~ **(light(weight)) concrete** → foam(ed) (plastic (~) ~

~ ~ **plaster baseboard,** foam(ed) plastic ~ ~, expanded plastic ~ ~ · Putzträgerplatte *f* aus Kunststoffschaum, Kunststoffschaum-Putzträgerplatte, Schaum(kunst)stoff-Putzträgerplatte

~ ~ **seal(ing),** expanded plastic ~, foam(ed) (plastic) ~ · Schaum(kunst)-stoff(ab)dichtung *f*, Kunststoffschaum-(ab)dichtung, Schaum(ab)dichtung, Kunstschaum(stoff)(ab)dichtung

~ ~ **sheet** → foam(ed) (plastic) board

~ **form(work),** ~ forms, ~ shuttering · Kunststoffschalung *f*

~ **fountain basin** · Kunststoff-(Spring) Brunnenbecken *n*

~ **gasket** → ~ preformed ~

~ ~ **joint** → ~ preformed ~ ~

~ **grass** · Kunststoffgras *n*

~ **guard rail** → ~ handrail

~ **gutter** → ~ roof ~

~ **handrail,** ~ guard rail, ~ stairrail · Kunststoff(-Treppen)handlauf *m*, Kunststoff(-Treppen)handleiste *f*

~ **hinge** · plastisches Gelenk *n*, Fließgelenk

~**-hinge method** · Fließgelenkmethode *f*, Fließgelenkverfahren *n*, plastisches Gelenkverfahren, plastische Gelenkmethode

plastic hollow (floor) filler · Kunststoff-Hohlkörper *m* für Decken, Kunststoff-Deckenhohlkörper

~ **hose** · Kunststoffschlauch *m*

~**-impregnated** · kunststoffgetränkt, kunststoffimprägniert

plastic insulating material → ~ insulation (~)

~ ~ **tube,** ~ insulation(-grade) ~ · Kunststoffisolierröhre *f*

~ **insulation(-grade) material** → ~ insulation (~)

~ ~ **tube,** ~ insulating ~ · Kunststoffisolierröhre *f*

plastic insulation (material) — plastic range of stress

~ **insulation (material)**, ~ insulating ~, ~ insulation-grade ~, ~ insulator · Dämmkunststoff *m*

~ **insulator** → ~ insulation (material)

~ **laminate heat shields** · Schichtkunststoffe *mpl* als Wärmeschutz

~ **(~) (sur)faced hardboard** → ~ laminated ~

~ **laminated hardboard**, ~ (laminate) (sur)faced ~, ~ coated ~ · (kunststoff)kaschierte Hartplatte *f*, einfache Verbundplatte, einfache VBP

~ ~ **plywood** · kunststoffkaschiertes Sperrholz *n*

~ **laminating of steel** · Kunststoffkaschierung *f* von Stahl

~ **latch** · Kunststoffalle *f*, Kunststoff-Schloßfalle

~ **lay-in panel** · Kunststoff-Einlegetafel *f*

~ **letter** · Kunststoffbuchstabe *f*

~ **light cupola**, ~ dome(light), ~ saucer dome, ~ domed roof-light · Kunststoff-(Dach)Lichtkuppel *f*, Kunststoff-Oberlichtkuppel

~ ~ **fitting** (Brit.) → ~ (light(ing)) fixture

~ **(light(ing)) fixture**; ~ luminaire (~) (US); ~ light fitting (Brit.) · Kunststoffleuchte *f*

~ **limit load** · plastische Grenzlast *f*

~ **lining**, ~ (sur)facing · Kunststoffauskleidung *f*, Kunststoffverkleidung, Kunststoffbekleidung

~ **lip(ping)** · Kunststoffumleimer *m*

~ **load**, limit ~ · Traglast *f*

~ **-load approach**, limit-load ~ · Ansatz *m* nach dem Traglastverfahren

plastic (load)bearing structure, ~ (weight-carrying) ~, ~ loaded ~, ~ supporting ~, ~ load-carrying ~ · Kunststofftragwerk *n* [*Ein materielles System von Kunststoffbauelementen*]

~ **load-carrying structure**→ ~ (load-)bearing ~

~ **loaded structure** → ~ (load)bearing ~

~ **loss**, ~ flow, creep · Kriechen *n*, plastischer Fluß *m*

~ **luminaire (fixture)** (US) → ~ (light(ing)) ~

~ **making** · plastische Verformung *f* [*Formgebung einer Masse, die ausreichende Mengen plastischer Bestandteile und genügend Wasser enthält, so daß ein Strang vorgezogen werden kann. Die Masse ist dementsprechend verschieden steif.*]

~ **mass**, lino(leum) ~ · Linoleumgrundmasse *f*

~ ~, ~ material, ~ composition, ~ (compound) · Kunststoff *m*, ~masse *f*

~ **material**, ~ (compound), ~ composition, ~ mass · Kunststoff *m*, ~masse *f*

~ **member** → ~ (building) unit

~ ~ → ~ element

~ **membrane** · Kunststoffmembran(e) *f*

~ **method** → limit ~

~ **methods of structural analysis** · Plastizitätstheorie *f* in der Baustatik

~ **-modified** · kunststoffvergütet

plastic molding (US); ~ moulding (Brit.) · Kunststoffdekor(ations)leiste *f*, Kunststoffornamentleiste, Kunststoff-(zier)leiste

~ **moment** · plastisches Moment *n*

~ **mortar** · Weichmörtel *m*

~ **mould for concrete** (Brit.); ~ mold ~ ~ (US) · Kunststoffform *f* für Beton

~ **moulding** (Brit.); ~ molding (US) · Kunststoffzierleiste *f*, Kunststoffdekor(ations)leiste, Kunststoff(ornament)-leiste

~ **mounting channel** · Kunststoff-Montageschiene *f* [*für Lichtbandanordnung*]

~ **numeral** · Kunststoffziffer *f*

~ **pail** · Kunststoffeimer *m*

~ **paint** [*A vague term for a paint whose medium is a plastic, e.g. a synthetic resin*] · Kunstharz(anstrich)farbe *f*

~ **panel** · Kunststofftafel *f*

~ **partition (wall)** · Kunststofftrennwand *f*

~ **pipe** · Kunststoffrohr *n*

~ ~ **cap** · Kunststoffrohrkappe *f*

~ **plaster** → ~ finish

~ **(preformed) gasket**, ~ sealing ~ Kunststoff(ab)dicht(ungs)profil *n*, Kunststoffselbstdichtung *f*

~ **(~) ~ joint**, ~ sealing ~ ~, ~ structural ~ ~ · Kunststoffabdeckfuge *f*

~ **process** [*Manufacture of flooring tile and wall tile*] · Strangpressenformung *f* mit Nachpressung in halbtrockenem Zustand

~ **product**, ~ article · Kunststoffartikel *m*, Kunststoffgegenstand *m*, Kunststofferzeugnis *n*

~ **profile** → (construction(al)) plastic shape

~ **pull (handle)**, ~ door ~ (~) · Kunststoff(tür)griff *m*

~ **putty**, ~ cement · plastischer Kitt *m*

~ **pyramid** · Kunststoffpyramide *f*, Kunststoffspitzsäule *f*

~ **radiation shielding wall**, ~ (biological) ~ ~ · Kunststoff-Abschirmwand *f*

~ **rail** · Kunststoffschiene *f*

~ **rainwater articles** → ~ ~ goods

~ ~ **goods**, ~ ~ products, ~ ~ articles, ~ R.W. ~ · Kunststoff-Dachzubehör *n*

~ ~ **gutter** → ~ (roof) ~

~ ~ **products** → ~ ~ goods

~ **range**, inelastic ~, nonelastic ~ · nichtelastischer Bereich *m*, nichtelastisches ~ *n*, unelastischer ~, unelastisches ~, plastischer ~, plastisches ~

~ ~ **of stress**, ~ stress range · plastischer Spannungsbereich *m*, plastisches ~ *n*

plastic refractories — plastic theorem

~ **refractories**, castable ~ · feuerfeste Stampf-, Flick- und Spritzmassen *fpl* auf der Basis von Schamotte (fireclay), Sillimanit, Korund, Magnesit, Chrommagnesit, Chromerz und Siliziumkarbid

~ **reinforcement distance piece** → ~ concrete ~ ~ ~

~ ~ **spacer** → ~ concrete ~ ~

~ **resin(-based) jointless cover(ing)** · Kunststoffestrich *m*

~ **rod** → ~ element

~ **roller shutter**, ~ rolling ~ · Kunststoff-Rollabschluß *m*

~ **rolling shutter**, ~ roller ~ · Kunststoff-Rollabschluß *m*

~ **(roof) gutter**, ~ rainwater ~, ~ R.W. ~ · Kunststoff(dach)rinne *f*, Kunststoffregenrinne

~ **roof-light** [*A plastic lantern-light or skylight*] · Kunststoff(dach)oberlicht *n*

~ **rose** · Kunststoffrosette *f*

~ **rotation** · plastische Drehung *f*

~ **R.W. articles** → ~ rainwater goods

~ **R.W. goods** → ~ rainwater ~

~ **R.W. gutter** → ~ (roof) ~

~ **R.W. products** → ~ rainwater goods

~ **sandwich system** · Kunststoff-Dreilagenkonstruktion *f*, Kunststoff-Dreischichtenkonstruktion

~ **saucer dome**, ~ dome(light), ~ light cupola, ~ domed roof-light · Kunststoff·(Dach)Lichtkuppel *f*, Kunststoff-Oberlichtkupel

~ **seal** · Kunststoff-(Ab)Dichtung *f* [*Erzeignis*]

~ **sealant** → ~ seal(ing) material

~ **sealer** → ~ seal(ing) material

~ **seal(ing)** · Kunststoffabsieg(e)lung *f*, Kunststoffversieg(e)lung

~ ~ · Kunststoff-(Ab)Dichtung *f*

~ **sealing gasket** → ~ (preformed) ~

~ ~ ~ **joint** → ~ (preformed) ~ ~

~ **seal(ing) material**, ~ sealer, ~ sealant · Kunststoff(ab)dicht(ungs)mittel *n*, Kunststoff(ab)dicht(ungs)stoff *m*

~ ~ **sheet(ing)** · Kunststoff-(Ab)Dicht(ungs)bahn *f*

~ **section** → ~ (construction(al)) plastic shape

~ ~ · plastifizierter Querschnitt *m*, plastischer ~

~ **shape** → ~ construction(al) ~ ~

~ **sheath(ing)** [*prestressed concrete*] · Kunststoffgleitkanal *m*, Kunststoffspannkanal, Kunststoffhüllrohr *n*, Kunststoffhülle *f*, Kunststoffröhre *f*

~ **sheet**, ~ board · Kunststoffplatte *f*

~ **sheeting**, ~ film · Kunststoffolie *f*

~ **sheet(ing)**, sheet(ing) plastic · Kunststoffbahn *f*

~ **sheeting for roofing** → ~ film ~ ~

~ **shell** · plastische Schale *f*

~ ~ · Kunststoffschale *f*

~ **shielding wall**, ~ biological ~ ~, ~ radiation ~ ~ · Kunststoff-Abschirmwand *f*

~ **shrinkage** · plastisches Schwinden *n*

~ **shutter** · Kunststoffabschluß *m*

~ **shuttering**, ~ forms, ~ form(work) · Kunststoffschalung *f*

~ **siding** · Kunststoffverschalung *f*, Kunststoffwandbeschlag *m*, Kunststoffwandschirm *m*, Kunststoffwetterschirm [*Wetterschutz für Außenmauern*]

~ **skylight** · Kunststoff(-Dach)raupe *f*

~ **slatted roller blind** · Kunststoffrolladen *m*, Kunststoffrolljalousie *f*

~ **solution** · Kunststofflösung *f*

~ **stability theory** · plastische Stabilitätstheorie *f*

~ **stairrail** → ~ handrail

~ **state** · bildsamer Zustand *m*, plastischer ~, Plastizitätszustand, Bildsamkeitszustand

~ **stopper**, ~ stopping, ~ filler · Kunststoffausfüller *m*, Kunststoffspachtel(-masse) *m*, (*f*) [*Siehe Anmerkung unter „Ausfüller"*]

~ **stopping** → ~ stopper

~ **strain**, inelastic ~, creep ~, nonelastic ~ · (positive) Kriechdehnung *f*, plastische Dehnung

~ **stress distribution** · plastische Spannungsverteilung *f*

~ ~ **range** → ~ range of stress

~ ~ **redistribution** · plastische Spannungsumlagerung *f*

~ ~-**strain relation** · plastisches Spannungs-Dehnungsverhältnis *n*

~ **structural gasket joint** → ~ (preformed) ~ ~

~ **(~) system** → ~ construction

~ **structure** · plastisches Bauwerk *n*

~ ~ ~ → ~ (load)bearing ~

~ **supporting structure** → ~ (load-)bearing ~

plastic-(sur)faced, plastic-coated · kunststoffbeschichtet, kunststoffüberzogen

plastic (sur)faced hardboard → ~ laminated ~

~ **(sur)facing** → ~ lining

~ **suspension** · Kunststoffsuspension *f*

~ **swimming pool** · Kunststoffschwimmbecken *n*

~ **system** → ~ construction

~ **tape** · Kunststoff(-Aufzug)band *n* [*Raffjalousie*]

~ ~ · Kunststoffband *n*

~ **testing machine** · Kunststoffprüfmaschine *f*

~ **theorem**, limit ~ · Traglastsatz *m*

plastic theory — plastisol

~ theory, theory of plasticity · Bildsamkeitstheorie f, Plastizitätstheorie, plastische Theorie

~ tile · Kunststofffliese f, Kunststoff(belag)platte f

~ trim → (construction(al)) plastic shape

~ unit → (construction(al)) plastic shape

~ ~ → ~ building ~

~ unity · plastische Einheit f

~ up-and-over door of the roll-up type, ~ overhead ~ ~ ~ ~ ~, ~ roll-up overhead door, ~ roll-up up-and-over door · Kunststoffrolltor n

~ veneer · Kunststoffurnier n

~ viscosity · plastische Viskosität f

~ wall cover(ing) · Kunststoffwandbelag m

~ ~ plaster · Kunststoff-Wandputz m

~ waterbar → ~ waterstop

~ water paint → ~ cold-~ ~

~ ~ pipe · Kunststoff-Wasser(leitungs)-rohr n

~ waterstop, ~ waterbar · Kunststoff(ugen)band n

~ (weight-carrying) structure → ~ (load)bearing ~

~ window · Kunststoffenster n

~ ~ frame · Kunststoffensterrahmen m

~ ~ gasket · Kunststoffenster(ab)dichtung f, Kunststoffenster(ab)dicht(ungs)-profil n

~ ~ section, ~ ~ unit, ~ ~ shape, ~ ~ trim, ~ ~ profile · Kunststoffensterprofil n

~ wood → crack filler

~ yield → (~) flow

plastically conceived · plastisch konzipiert

plasticimeter · Plastizitätsmesser m

plasticisation, plasticising (Brit.); plasticization, plasticizing (US) · Plastifizierung f

to plasticise (Brit.); to plasticize (US) · plastifizieren

plasticised (Brit.); plasticized (US) · plastifiziert

plastic(ised) concrete (Brit.); plastic(ized) ~ (US); high-slump ~, buttery ~ · Weichbeton m, weicher Beton [Fehlname: plastischer Beton]

~ mortar (Brit.); plastic(ized) ~ (US) · plastifizierter Mörtel m

plasticiser, plasticising resin (Brit.); plasticizer, plasticizing resin (US) · Weichmacher m, Weichmachungsmittel n

plasticising, plasticisation (Brit.); plasticizing, plasticization (US) · Plastifizierung f

~ action (Brit.); plasticizing ~ (US) plastifizierende Wirkung f

~ agent (Brit.); plasticizing ~ (US) · Plastifizierungsmittel n

~ ~ (Brit.) → (concrete) workability ~

~ frost protection agent (Brit.); plasticizing ~ ~ ~ (US) · plastifizierendes Frostschutzmittel n

~ of concrete (Brit.); plasticizing ~ ~ (US) · Betonverflüssigung f

~ resin, plasticiser (Brit.); plasticizing resin, plasticizer (US) · Weichmacher m, Weichmachungsmittel n

~ ~ (Brit.); plasticizing ~ (US) · Weichharz n

plasticity · Bildsamkeit f, Plastizität f

~ condition, condition of plasticity · Plastizitätsbedingung f

~ index, index of plasticity, PI · Plastizitätsindex m

~ law · Plastizitätsgesetz n

~ range · Plastizitätsbereich m, n, Bildsamkeitsbereich, Plastizitätszone f, Bildsamkeitszone, plastischer Bereich, bildsamer Bereich, plastische Zone, bildsame Zone, plastisches Bereich n, bildsames Bereich n

plasticization, plasticizing (US); plasticising, plasticisation (Brit.) · Plastifizierung f

to plasticize (US); to plasticise (Brit.) · plastifizieren

plasticized (US); plasticised (Brit.) plastifiziert

plastic(ized) concrete (US); plastic(ised) ~ (Brit.); high-slump ~, buttery ~ · Weichbeton m, weicher Beton [Fehlname: plastischer Beton]

~ mortar (US); plastic(ised) ~ (Brit.) · plastifizierter Mörtel m

plasticizer, plasticizing resin (US); plasticiser, plasticising resin (Brit.) · Weichmacher m, Weichmachungsmittel n

plasticizing, plasticization (US); plasticising, plasticisation (Brit.) · Plastifizierung f

~ action (US); plasticising ~ (Brit.) · plastifizierende Wirkung f

~ agent (US) → (concrete) workability ~

~ frost protection agent (US); plasticising ~ ~ ~ (Brit.) · plastifizierendes Frostschutzmittel n

~ of concrete (US); plasticising ~ ~ (Brit.) · Betonverflüssigung f

~ resin, plasticizer (US); plasticising resin, plasticiser (Brit.) · Weichmacher m, Weichmachungsmittel n

~ resin (US); plasticising ~ (Brit.) · Weichharz n

plastisol [*Dispersions of finely divided resin particles (often polyvinyl chloride or copolymer) in a plasticizer or mixture of plasticizers. After application, the coating is heated and the plasticizer diffuses into and softens the resin particles which fuse to a continuous film without significant loss of volatile matter*] · Plastisol n

plastoelastic — plate R. W. gutter 730

plastoelastic · plastisch-elastisch
- ~ **composition**, ~ compound, ~ mass, ~ material · plastoelastische Masse f

plat (US); land-register, register of real estates (Brit.) [*A map, plan or chart of a city, town, section or subdivision indicating the location and boundaries of individual properties*] · Kataster *m, n*, Grundbuch *n* [*Register, bestehend aus einem Katasterkartenwerk und den Katasterbüchern, in denen alle Grundstücke und grundstücksgleichen Rechte nachgewiesen sind*]

to plate · plattieren

plate, (heavy) metal ~ · (Grob)Blech *n*
- ~ [*Scotland*]; gypsum (base)board · (Gipskarton-)Stuckplatte f
- ~ → polished plate glass
- ~, slab ~ · Platte f [*Ebenes Flächentragwerk. Es ist durch normal zur Mittelebene wirkende Belastung belastet und dadurch auf Biegung und Drillung beansprucht*]
- ~, footing piece, solepiece · Unterschiebling *m* [*Dach*]
- ~, girt [*A rail or intermediate beam in wooden-framed buildings, often carrying floor joists*] · Saumschwelle f, Brustschwelle, Sattelschwelle, Setzschwelle
- ~, pole ~ · Schwelle f [*Dach*]
- ~ **action**, slab ~ · Plattenwirkung f
- ~ **analysis**, slab ~ · Plattenstatik f
- ~ ~, slab ~, ~ calculation · Plattenberechnung f
- ~**-and-angle separator** [*for steel beams*] · Stegverbindungsstück *n* aus Blech und Winkeln

plate and knob · Knopf-Stützringschild *n* [*Türbeschlag*]
- ~ **arch(ed girder)** · Blechbogen(träger) *m*
- ~ **bearing structure** → ~ load~ ~
- ~ **bending**, slab ~ · Plattenbiegen *n*
- ~ **bending**, slab ~ · Plattenbiegung f
- ~ **calculation**, slab ~, ~ analysis · Plattenberechnung f
- ~ **ceiling** [*Scotland*] → dry ~
- ~ **chimney**, metal ~ · Metallschornstein *m*, Blechschornstein
- ~ **circumference**, slab ~ · Plattenumfang *m*
- ~ **construction type**, ~ type of construction · Scheibenbauart f [*In der Regel ist es technisch und wirtschaftlich vorteilhafter die waag(e)rechten Lasten, z.B. Windlasten, durch waag(e)rechte Scheiben in der Regel durch die Decken auf lotrechte Scheiben und diese in den Baugrund zu übertragen. Die Stützen werden dann als Pendelstützen ohne biegefeste Verbindung mit der Deckenträgern gerechnet. Die lotrechten Scheiben müssen ebenfalls in etwa rechtwinklig zueinanderstehenden Ebenen angeordnet werden. Sie können ebenso wie die waag(e)rechten Scheiben vollwandig, z.B. aus Stahlbeton oder als Dreieckfachwerk z.B. bei Stahlgerippebauten ausgebildet werden*]
- ~**-covered step** · Belagblechstufe f

plate cover(ing) → (heavy) metal ~ ~
- ~ **depth**, slab ~ · Plattendicke f [*Fehlname: Plattenstärke*]
- ~ **displacement**, slab ~ · Plattenverrückung f
- ~ **duct** · Blechkanal *m*
- ~ **edge**, slab ~ · Plattenrand *m*
- ~ **end**, slab ~ · Plattenende *n*
- ~ **facing** → (heavy) plate lining
- ~ **failure**, slab ~ · Plattenversagen *n*
- ~ **for standing seams**, standing seam plate · Stehfalzblech *n* [*Blech zur Herstellung von Stehfalzbedachungen*]
- ~ ~ **walls** [*Scotland*] → gypsum wallboard
- ~ **girder** → (heavy) (metal) ~ ~
- ~ ~ **stalk** → ~ ~ web
- ~ ~ **web**, ~ ~ stalk · Blechträgersteg *m*
- ~ **(glass)** → polished ~ (~)
- ~ ~ ~ → float ~
- ~ **gutter**, ~ roof ~, ~ rainwater ~, ~ R.W. ~ · Blech(dach)rinne f
- ~ **lining** → (heavy) metal ~ ~
- ~ **(linseed) oil** · argentinisches Leinöl *n*
- ~ **load**, slab ~ · Plattenlast f
- ~ **(load)bearing structure**, slab ~ ~, ~ (weight-carrying) ~, ~ supporting ~ · Plattentragwerk *n*
- ~ **loaded in its own plane**, slab ~ ~ ~ ~ ~ · Platte f in ihrer Ebene belastet
- ~ **moment**, slab ~ · Plattenmoment *n*
- ~ **of constant depth**, slab ~ ~ ~ ~ · planparallele Platte f
- ~ **oil**, ~ linseed ~ · argentinisches Leinöl *n*
- ~ **panel** [*Scotland*] → (gypsum) plasterboard ~
- ~ ~ **partition (wall)** [*Scotland*] → (gypsum) plasterboard ~ ~ (~)
- ~ **partition (wall)** [*Scotland*] → (gypsum) plasterboard (sheet) ~ (~)
- ~ **pipe** · Blechrohr *n*
- ~ **pipeline** · Blechrohrleitung f
- ~ **problem**, slab ~ · Plattenaufgabe f, Plattenproblem *n*
- ~ **rainwater gutter**, ~ (roof) ~, ~ R.W. ~ · Blech(dach)rinne f
- ~ **rigidity** → (heavy) (metal) plate stiffness
- ~ ~, slab ~, ~ stiffness · Plattenstarrheit f, Plattensteifigkeit
- ~ **(roof) gutter**, ~ rainwater ~, ~ R.W. ~ · Blech(dach)rinne f
- ~ **roofing** · Dachverblechung f, Blech(dach)(ein)deckung
- ~ **rotation**, slab ~ · Plattendrehung f
- ~ **R.W. gutter** → ~ (roof) ~

plate scrap — pliability

~ scrap · Blechschrott *m*

~ span, slab ~ · Plattenfeld *n*

~-stalk girder, plate-web ~ · Blechstegträger *m*

~ stiffness → (heavy) metal ~ ~

~ ~, slab ~, ~ rigidity · Plattenstarrheit *f*, Plattensteifigkeit

~ strength, slab ~ · Plattenfestigkeit *f*

~ structure → ~ (load)bearing ~

~ supported on three sides, slab ~ ~ ~ ~ · dreiseitig gelagerte Platte *f*

~ supporting structure → ~ (load-)bearing ~

~ (sur)facing → (heavy) (metal) plate lining

~ suspension roof(ing) → (heavy) metal ~ ~ ~

~ testing machine · Blechprüfmaschine *f*

~ theory, slab ~ · Plattentheorie *f*

~ thickening, slab ~ · Plattenverstärkung *f*

~ tracery [*A rudimentary or embryonic form of Gothic tracery, in which geometrical shapes were pierced through a solid slab or 'plate' of stone, as opposed to later tracery formed of mo(u)lded stone bars*] · negatives Maßwerk *n*

~ translation, slab ~ · Plattenverschiebung *f*

~ type of construction → ~ construction type

~ wall [*Scotland*] → (gypsum) plasterboard (sheet) ~

~-web girder, plate-stalk ~ · Blechstegträger *m*

~ weight-carrying structure, slab ~ ~, ~ (load)bearing ~ · Plattentragwerk *n*

~ width, slab ~ · Plattenbreite *f*

~ with edge beam, slab ~ ~ ~ · Platte *f* mit Randbalken, randausgesteifte Platte, randverstärkte Platte

platen · Druckplatte *f* [*Druckprüfmaschine*]

~-pressed chipboard, ~ particle board · [*Particle board made by pressing between platens. The process may be batch or continuous. The particles lie mainly with their larger dimensions parallel with the plane of the board*] · plattengepreßte Spanplatte *f*

Plateresque style, ~ architecture · Platereskenstil *m*, Platerostil [*Ein im 16. Jahrhundert in Spanien beliebter überladener Baustil*]

platform, station ~ · Bahnsteig *m*

~ · Bühne *f*, Plattform *f*

~, podium, masonry ~ · hoher Unterbau *m*, Podium *n* [*antike Baukunst*]

~ loudspeaker system, station ~ ~ ~ · Bahnsteig-Lautsprecheranlage *f*

~ roof, station ~ ~ · Bahnsteigdach *n*

~ ~, truncated ~ · abgestumpftes Dach *n*

~ ~ [*Scotland*] → flat ~

~ stair(case), dog-leg(ged) ~ · g(e)rade zweiläufige Treppe *f* mit Richtungswechsel, ~ doppelläufige ~ ~ ~, gegenläufige Treppe

~ temple → masonry ~ ~

~ tunnel, station ~ ~ · Bahnsteigtunnel *m*

plating · elektrolytisches Plattieren *n*, Plattieren durch Elektrolyse

platinum wire · Platindraht *m*

platy limestone, slabby ~, laminated ~ · Kalkschiefer *m*, Plattenkalk(stein) *m*

Plauen limestone · Pläner Kalk *m*

play area, children's ~ ~ · Spielfläche *f*

~ ~ with structural and mechanical equipment, playground ~ ~ ~ ~ ~, toy-lot · Spielgeräteplatz *m*

~ equipment item → childrens' playground ~ ~

playfield · Spielfeld *n*

playful use of space, 'space game' · Raumspiel *n*

playground · Tummelplatz *m*

~ equipment item → childrens' ~ ~ ~

~ with structural and mechanical equipment, play area ~ ~ ~ ~ ~, toy-lot · Spielgeräteplatz *m*

playhouse · Schauspielhaus *n*

play of forces, inter~ ~ ~ · Kräftespiel *n*

~ ~ light and shade, inter~ ~ ~ ~ ~ · Spiel *n* von Licht und Schatten

playroom · (Kinder)Spielzimmer *n*

play street · Spielstraße *f*

plaza, square · Platz(anlage) *m*, (*f*) [*Nichtbebaute Grundfläche in einer Stadt, deren Umbauung architektonisch gestaltet ist oder die eine besondere Aufgabe zu erfüllen hat*]

pleasure garden · Lustgarten *m*

pleasurehouse, summerhouse [*In a garden*] · Gartenpavillon *m*

plenum chamber [*An air chamber kept at a pressure slightly above atmospheric*] · Überdruckkammer *f*

~ heater → air ~

~ heating, air ~ · Luft(be)heizung *f* [*Warmluft wird mit oder ohne Ventilator in die zu beheizenden Räume geführt*]

~ ~ system → (warm) air ~ ~

~ ~ unit → air heater

Plewa vent(ing) duct · Plewarohr *n* [*Ein Ton-Entlüftungsrohr aus scharf gebranntem, unglasierten Ziegelton oder aus Schamotte*]

plexiglass (US); **perspex** (Brit.) · Plexiglas *n* [*Warenzeichen für glasartig durchsichtigen Kunststoff aus Polymethacrylsäureestern. Zugfestigkeit etwa 700 kg/cm^2*]

pliability → bending capacity

plinth — plywood and door factory

plinth, ground course, base course, earth table, ground-table, grass-table, foot stall [*A distinct feature forming the lowest part of a masonry column or wall. It usually projects from the surface above and may be of a more durable material. Definition from British Standard 3589*] · Plinthe f, Sockel m, Plinthus m

~ **brick** · Plintheziegel m, Sockelziegel

~ **course** [*The top course of a brick plinth*] · oberste Plintheziegelschicht f

~ **masonry wall** · Plinthemauer f, Sockelmauer

~ ~ **(work)** · Plinthemauerwerk n, Sockelmauerwerk

~ **tile** · Plinthe(belag)platte f, Plinthefliese f, Sockel(belag)platte, Sockelfliese

plk → plank

PLK → plank

PL(K) → padlock

plot [*A parcel of land consisting of one or more lots or portions thereof, which is described by reference to a recorded plat or by metes and bounds*] · liegender Grund m

~ → graphic representation

~ **line,** property ~ [*A recorded boundary of a plot*] · Grundstücksgrenze f

~ **planning** · Grundstücksplanung f

ploughshare vault, sexpartite ~ [*The intermediate vault cones are constricted to a shape resembling ploughshares*] · sechsteiliges Gewölbe n

PLR → pillar

plug, tapered ~, tapering ~ · drehbarer Kegel m, (Hahn)Küken n

~ · Dorn m, Scharnierstift m [*Schloß*]

~ → pipe ~

~ · Reiber m

~-**in point,** aerial ~ ~ · Antennenanschluß m [*In einer Wohnung an eine Gemeinschaftsantenne*]

plug-on connection · Steckeranschluß m

plug rolling · Stopfenwalzen n [*von Rohren*]

(~) socket for cleaners, power point ~ ~; socket outlet ~ ~ (Brit.); receptacle outlet ~ ~ (US) · Staubsaugersteckdose f

~ **with earthing contact** · Schutzkontaktstecker m

plugging [*Drilling holes in masonry which are to be filled with plugs of wood or fibre or metal as fittings for nails, drive screws, wood screws, etc.*] · Dübelbohren n

plum, displacer · Zyklopenbeton-Stein m, Stein beim Prepaktbeton

to plumb · bleien, senkeln, loten, ab~

plumb, vertical · lotrecht, senkrecht, vertikal

~, water level, (spirit) level, mechanic's level · Wasserwaage f

~ [*A line with a weight attached*] · (Schnur)Lot n, Senkel m, Senklot

~ **bob** [*A weight, often tapering to a point, suitable for use on a plumb line*] · (Schnur)Lotgewicht n, Senkelgewicht, Senklotgewicht

~ **line deviation** · Abweichung f von der Lotrechten, ~ ~ ~ Senkrechten

plumbago · Plumbago m, Rohgraphit m [*natürlicher unreiner Graphit*]

~ **refractory (product),** ~ ~ material · Graphit-Ton-Erzeugnis n

plumber · Blechner m, Klempner, Flaschner, Spengler

plumbers' shop, ~ workshop, plumbery · Klempnerei f, Klempnerwerkstatt f

~ **solder** [*A soft solder containing roughly two parts of lead to one part of tin and used for making wiped soldered joints and seams*] · Weichlot n mit rund 2 Teilen Blei und 1 Teil Zinn

~ **work,** plumbing (~) · Klempnerarbeiten fpl, Spenglerarbeiten, Flaschnerarbeiten, Blechnerarbeiten, Klempner- und Installationsarbeiten [*DIN 18339*]

~ **(work)shop,** plumbery · Klempnerei f, Klempnerwerkstatt f

plumbery, plumbers' (work)shop · Klempnerei f, Klempnerwerkstatt f

plumbing → ~ work

~ **line,** ~ run · Sanitärleitung f

~ **pipe** · Sanitärrohr n

~ **piping** · Sanitärleitungen fpl

~ **run,** ~ line · Sanitärleitung f

~ **(system)** → internal plumbing

~ **(work),** plumber's ~ · Klempnerarbeiten fpl, Spengerlarbeiten, Flaschnerarbeiten, Blechnerarbeiten, Klempner- und Installationsarbeiten [*DIN 18339*]

plutonic rock → intrusive ~

ply → (felt) layer

~ [*A single thickness, usually thin, of any material used in a lamination, such as in plywood or built-up roof covers*] · Lage f

~ **glass** [*Glassware having a layer of opal glass covered on one or both sides with coloured or colourless transparent glass, normally used for illuminated globes and lighting shades*] · Opalüberfang(hohl)glas n

Plyglass · Thermolux n [*Ein Mehrscheibenisolierglas, das aus zwei Glasscheiben mit dazwischenliegender 1—3 mm dicker Glasfaserschicht besteht, die durch einen Verbundrand eingeschlossen wird*]

plymetal, metal-clad plywood; armoured plywood, armourply (Brit.); armored plywood, armorply (US) · Panzersperrholz n, Metall(schicht)sperrholz

plywood and door factory · Sperrholz- und Türenfabrik f, Sperrholz- und Türenwerk n

plywood binding plate — point of application of a force

~ **binding plate** → ~ corner ~
~ **box beam** · Sperrholzkastenbalken(-träger) m
~ **connecting plate** → ~ corner ~
~ **connection plate** → ~ corner ~
~ **core** · Sperrholzkern m
~ **corner plate,** ~ binding ~, ~ connection ~, ~ connecting ~, ~ joint ~, ~ fish ~, ~ knee bracket ~, ~ gusset ~ · Sperrholz-Knoten(punkt)-verbindung f
~ **door** · Sperrholztür f
~ **(~) panel** · Sperrholzfüllung f, Sperrholztürfüllung
~ **exterior sheathing** · Sperrholz-Außenverkleidung f
~ **factory,** ~ plant · Sperrholzwerk n
~ **fish plate** → ~ corner ~
~ **flush door** · abgesperrte Sperrholztür f, Sperrholz-Flächentür, Sperrholz-Sperrtür
~ **forms,** ~ form(work), ~ shuttering · Sperrholzschalung f
~ ~ **coating,** ~ form(work) ~, ~ shuttering ~ · Sperrholzschalungsbeschichtung f
~ **form(work),** ~ forms, ~ shuttering · Sperrholzschalung f
~ ~ **coating,** ~ shuttering ~, ~ forms ~ · Sperrholzschalungsbeschichtung f
~ **girder** · Sperrholzträger m
~ **gusset plate** → ~ corner ~
~ **joint plate** → ~ corner ~
~ **knee bracket plate** → ~ corner ~
~ **panel** → ~ door ~
~ ~ · Sperrholztafel f
~ **(~) board for construction purposes,** ~ (~) ~ ~ building · Bau-Furnierplatte f [DIN 68705]
~ **plant,** ~ factory · Sperrholzwerk n
~ **portal frame** · Sperrholz-Portalrahmen m
~ **roof sheathing** · Sperrholzdach(ver)-schalung f, Sperrholzdachschale f
~ **sheathing** · Sperrholzverschalung f
~ **shuttering,** ~ form(work), ~ forms · Sperrholzschalung f
~ ~ **coating,** ~ form(work) ~, ~ forms ~ · Sperrholzschalungsbeschichtung f
~ **siding** · Sperrholzverschalung f, Sperrholzwandbeschlag m, Sperrholzwandschirm m, Sperrholzwetterschirm [Wetterschutz für Außenmauern]
~ **wall sheathing** · Sperrholzwandverschalung f
~ **web** · Sperrholzsteg m
~ **with boilproof glue line(s)** · kochfest verleimtes Sperrholz n

pneumatic gun, (compressed-)air ~ · Druckluft(spritz)pistole f, Preßluft-(spritz)pistole. Druckluftspritze f, Preßluftspritze

~ **mortar, gun-applied** ~ · pneumatisch aufgetragener Mörtel m
~ **sliding door drive,** (compressed-)air ~ ~ ~ · pneumatischer Schiebetürantrieb m, Druckluft-Schiebetürantrieb, Preßluft-Schiebetürantrieb
~ **test** · Luftdruckprobe f [Abdrücken einer Rohrleitung]
~ **tube installation,** ~ ~ system, ~ tubes, (carrier) air tube system, (carrier) air tube installation, (carrier) air tubes, pneumatic-tube message system · Rohrpost(anlage) f [DIN 6651]
~ **applied concrete** → sprayed(-on) ~
~ ~ **mortar,** sprayed mortar, air-blown mortar, shotcrete [Mortar conveyed through a hose and projected at high velocity onto a surface] · Spritzmörtel m, Gebläsemörtel
~ **placed concrete,** air-placed ~ · druckluftgeförderter Beton m, preßluftgeförderter ~

PNT → paint

pock-marking, pebbling, orange peel(-ing), orange peel effect [The pockmarked appearance, in particular of a sprayed film, resembling the skin of an orange due to the failure of the film to flow out to a level surface] · Orangenschaleneffekt m, Apfelsinenschaleneffekt

pocket, cavity, blockout, recess, embrasure · Aussparung f

~ → beam box

~ **setting,** boxing-in · Einbauen n, Einschachteln [Feuerfestindustrie. Das Anordnen von Schutzsteinen, um Verdrückungen zu vermeiden]

pock-marking → orange peel(ing)

podium, platform, masonry ~ · hoher Unterbau m, Podium n [antike Baukunst]

~ **temple** → masonry ~ ~

poetic architecture, ~ style of ~ · poetische Architektur f, ~ Baukunst f

~ **(style of) architecture** · poetische Architektur f, ~ Baukunst f

to point · auskratzen und ausfugen, ~ verfugen [Mörtelfuge]

point block, ~ building · Punktgebäude n, Punkthaus n

~ **building,** ~ block · Punktgebäude n, Punkthaus n

~ **force,** concentrated ~ · Punktkraft f

~ **load,** concentrated ~ · Punktlast f

~ ~ **at the crown,** concentrated ~ ~ ~ · Kronenpunktlast f

point-load stress, concentrated-load ~ · Punktlastspannung f

~ **system,** concentrated-load ~ · Punktlastsystem n

point loading, concentrated ~ · Punktbelastung f

~ **of application of a force** · Angriffspunkt m, Angriffsstelle f, Kraft~

point of bending up — polished asbestos-cement board

~ ~ **bending up,** portion ~ ~ ~, bent(-up) point, bent(-up) portion · Abbiegestelle f [*Bewehrungsstab*]

~ ~ **consumption,** ~ ~ demand, consumption point, demand point · Abnehmer m, Verbrauchsstelle f [*Wasser; Strom; Gas; Dampf; Druckluft*]

~ ~ **demand,** ~ ~ consumption, consumption point, demand point · Abnehmer m, Verbrauchsstelle f [*Wasser; Strom: Gas; Dampf; Druckluft*]

~ ~ **emission** · Emissionsstelle f [*Rauch; Schadgas*]

~ ~ **entry** · Eintrittsstelle f

~ ~ **fabrication,** ~ ~ manufacture · Fertigungsort m, Herstellungsort

~ ~ **hot water consumption** · Warmwasserabnehmer m, Warmwasserverbrauchsstelle f, WW-Abnehmer, WW-Verbrauchsstelle

~ ~ **intersection,** Pl · Schnittpunkt m, Kreuzungsstelle f

~ ~ **load application** · Lastangriffspunkt m

~ ~ ~ **collection** · Bündelungspunkt m

~ ~ **manufacture,** ~ ~ fabrication · Fertigungsort m, Herstellungsort

~ ~ **origin** · Anfallstelle f [*Abwasser*]

~ ~ **shipment delivery** · Versandort m

(~ ~) **support** · Auflagerpunkt m, Auflager(stelle) n, (f)

~ ~ ~ · Verbindungsstelle f [*Zur biegefesten Verbindung von (Außen)Versteifungswand mit der Skelettkonstruktion*]

~ ~ **water inrush** · Wasserandrangstelle f, Wassereinbruchstelle

~ ~ **zero moment,** zero point of moments · Momentennullpunkt m

pointed · gespitzt [*Werksteinbearbeitungsart*]

~ **arch,** Gothic ~, peak ~ · Spitzbogen m, gotischer Bogen [*Aus zwei konvexen Schenkeln gebildeter, spitzer Bogen; im engeren Sinne ein gleichseitiger Spitzbogen, im weiten Sinne jeder spitz zulaufende Bogen, wie z.B. Eselsrücken und Giebelbogen*]

~ ~ ~ **of brickwork,** brick(work) pointed arch · Ziegelspitzbogen m

~ **arched corbel-table** · Spitzbogenfries m

~ **architecture,** Gothic ~, ~ (building) style, ~ architectural style · gotische Architektur f, ~ Baukunst f, Spitzbogenstil m, Spitzbogenarchitektur, Gotik f, Spitzbogenbaukunst, germanischer Baustil, gotischer (Bau)Stil

~ **barrel vault,** ~ tunnel ~, ~ wagon-(head) ~ · Spitztonnengewölbe n, Spitztonne f

~ **dome,** ~ cupola · Spitzkuppel f [*Eine Kuppel mit spitzbogigem Querschnitt*]

~ **horseshoe arch,** Moorish (~) ~ · Hufeisenspitzbogen m, maurischer Hufeisenbogen

~ **transverse barrel vault,** ~ ~ tunnel ~, ~ ~ wagon(head) ~ · Spitzquertonne(ngewölbe) f, (n)

~ ~ **tunnel vault,** ~ ~ barrel ~, ~ ~ wagon(head) ~ · Spitzquertonne(ngewölbe) f, (n)

~ ~ **wagon(head) vault,** ~ ~ tunnel ~, ~ ~ barrel ~ · Spitzquertonne(ngewölbe) f, (n)

~ **trowel** · Spitzkelle f [*DIN 6441*]

~ **tunnel vault,** ~ barrel ~, ~ wagon-(head) ~ · Spitztonnengewölbe n, Spitztonne f

~ **wagon(head) vault,** ~ barrel ~, ~ tunnel ~ · Spitztonnengewölbe n, Spitztonne f

~ **wire-rod** · angespitzter Walzdraht f

pointing template, joint rule · Lagerfugenschablone f

pointwise connection · punktweiser Anschluß m

poison cupboard, dangerous drug ~ · Giftschrank m

polar diagram, funicular ~ · Seildiagramm n

~ **force** · Polarkraft f

~ **line,** funicular ~ · Seillinie f, Seilstrahl m, Pollinie, Polstrahl, Seilkurve f

~ **moment of inertia,** ~ second moment (of area) [*of a section*] · polares Trägheitsmoment n

~ **second moment (of area),** ~ moment of inertia [*of a section*] · polares Trägheitsmoment n

polarized glass screen (US); polarised ~ ~ (Brit) · Sonnenschutzscheibe f

pole, post · Pfahl m, Pfosten m

(~) **plate** · Schwelle f [*Dach*]

~ ~ **system** · Schwellenkranz m [*Dachkonstruktion*]

police building · Polizeigebäude n

~ **hostel** · Polizeiheim m

~ **station** · Polizeiwache f, Polizeistation f

polish · Politur f [*Beschaffenheit einer Oberfläche*]

~ · Polierwasser n

~ · Politur f, polierte Fläche f

~, polishing agent · (Glanz)Poliermittel n, Politur f

~ **emulsion,** emulsion polish · Wachsemulsion f

~ **layer** · Polierschicht f

polishable · polierbar, polierfähig

polished → poliert

~ **asbestos-cement board,** ~ ~ sheet; ~ cement asbestos ~, ~ CEM AB (US) · Glanzasbestplatte f [*Eine polierte Asbestzementplatte*]

~ ~ sheet, ~ ~ board; ~ cement asbestos ~, ~ CEM AB (US) · Glanzasbestplatte f [Eine polierte Asbestzementplatte]

~ CEM AB, ~ cement asbestos board, ~ cement asbestos sheet (US); ~ asbestos-cement board, ~ asbestos-cement sheet · Glanzasbestplatte f [Eine polierte Asbestzementplatte]

~ cement asbestos board, ~ ~ ~ sheet, ~ CEM AB ~ (US); ~ asbestos-cement ~ · Glanzasbestplatte f [Eine polierte Asbestzementplatte]

~ ~ ~ sheet, ~ ~ ~ board, ~ CEM AB (US); ~ asbestos-cement ~ · Glanzasbestplatte f [Eine polierte Asbestzementplatte]

(~) plate (glass), PPGL, patent glass [Transparent glass, the two surfaces of which have been ground and polished to make them flat and parallel, so as to provide clear, undistorted through-vision and reflection] · (Kristall)Spiegelglas n [Die Bezeichnung „Spiegelglas" stammt von der Herstellung der Spiegel. Heute ist sie eine übliche Kurzbezeichnung für „Kristallspiegelglas"]

~ wire(d) glass → (flat) wire(d) (clear) (polished) plate (~)

~ ~ plate, (flat) wire(d) (clear) (polished) plate (glass) · Spiegeldrahtglas n, Drahtspiegelglas

polishing · Polieren n

~ agent, polish · (Glanz)Poliermittel n, Politur f

~ compound · Poliermasse f

~ fluosilicate · Polierfluat n

~ paper · Polierpapier n

~(-type) wax · Polierwachs n

polishing varnish, rubbing ~, flatting ~ · Polierlack m [Es gibt Polierlacke aus Schellack, spritlöslichen Kunstharzen oder Nitrozellulose-Harz-Kombinationen]

polluted water · verunreinigtes Wasser n, verseuchtes ~

pollution · Verschmutzung f, Verseuchung, Verunreinigung

polyacrylate · Polyacrylat n

polyalcohol, polyhydric alcohol · vielwertiger Alkohol m, mehrwertiger ~

polyamide (resin) · Polyamid(harz) n, PA

polycarbonate · Polycarbonat n, PC

polychloroprene · Polychloropren n

polychromatic finish [Apart from its literal meaning, this term is specifically applied to a finish which has a metallic lustre and gives an iridescent scintillating effect when viewed from different angles. The effect is produced by the application of special lacquers or enamels which contain metallic powders in flake form, in addition to transparent colouring matter] · schillernder (Oberflächen)Abschluß m

~ opulence · Farbenschwelgerei f, polychrome Schwelgerei

polychrome · mehrfarbig, vielfarbig

~ brick · Vielfarbenziegel m, Mehrfarbenziegel

~ glazed-brick decoration [at Susa] · Flachrelief n aus vielfarbigen glasierten Ziegeln, ~ ~ mehrfarbigen ~ ~, Backsteintafel f [in Susa]

polychromy · Mehrfarbigkeit f, Vielfarbigkeit, Polychromie f

polycondensation · Polykondensation f

~ reaction · Polyreaktion f

~ resin · Polykondensationsharz n

polyester · Polyester m

~ adhesive → ~ (resin) bonding agent

~ board → ~ resin ~

~ (bonding) adhesive → ~ (resin) bonding agent

~ ~ agent → ~ resin ~ ~

~ ~ medium → ~ (resin) bonding agent

~ cast(ing) resin · Polyestergießharz n, Polyesterschmelzharz

~ cement(ing agent) → ~ (resin) bonding agent

~ coat(ing) → ~ resin ~

~ compound, ~ resin ~ · Polyester(harz)verbindung f

~ 'concrete', ~ resin ~ [It comprises a binder or matrix of portland cement chemically crosslinked, in the presence of water, with polyester resin] · Polyester(harz)beton m, Polybeton

~ ~ panel, ~ resin ~ · Polyester(harz)betontafel f

~ corrugated sheet(ing) → ~ resin ~ ~

~ fibre → ~ resin ~

~ film → ~ resin ~

~ finish → ~ resin ~

~ floor cover(ing) → ~ (resin) floor(ing)

~ floor(ing) → ~ resin ~

~ mortar → ~ resin ~

~ resin · Polyesterharz n [Polyesterharze sind Lösungen von ungesättigtem Polyester in Styrol oder anderen Monomeren. Sie härten durch Polymerisation unter Zusatz von Katalysatoren und Beschleunigern]

~ (~) adhesive → ~ (~) bonding agent

~ (~) board, ~ (~) sheet · Polyester(harz)platte f

~ (~) (bonding) adhesive → ~ (~) ~ agent

~ (~) ~ agent, ~ (~) ~ medium, ~ (~) (~) adhesive, ~ (~) cement(ing agent) · Polyester(harz)kleber m, Polyester(harz)kleb(e)stoff m, Polyester(harz)kleb(e)mittel n

polyester (resin) bonding medium — polygonal centrally-... 736

~ (~) ~ medium → ~ (~) ~ agent

~ (~) cement(ing agent) → ~ (~) bonding agent

~ ~ coated, ~ resin-(sur)faced · polyester(harz)beschichtet

~ (~) coat(ing), ~ (~) finish · Polyester(harz)beschichtung f, Polyester(harz)überzug m [als Schicht]

~ (~) compound · Polyester(harz)verbindung f

~ (~) 'concrete' [It comprises a binder or matrix of portland cement chemically crosslinked, in the presence of water, with polyester resin] · Polyester(harz)beton m, Polybeton

~ (~) ~ panel · Polyester(harz)betontafel f

~ (~) corrugated light-admitting board, ~ (~) ~ ~ sheet · Polyester(harz)-Lichtwellplatte f

~ (~) ~ sheet(ing), currugated polyester (resin) ~ · Polyester(harz)-Wellbahn f

~ resin-faced → ~ resin-coated

~ (resin) fibre (Brit.); ~ (~) fiber (US) · Polyester(harz)faser f

~ (~) film, ~ (~) sheeting · Polyester(harz)folie f

~ (~) finish, ~ (~) coat(ing) · Polyester(harz)beschichtung f, Polyester(harz)überzug m [als Schicht]

~ (~) floor cover(ing) → ~ (~) floor(ing)

~ (~) floor(ing), ~ (~) floor cover(ing) · Polyester(harz)(fuß)boden(belag) m

~ (~) light-admitting board, ~ (~) ~ sheet · Polyester(harz)-Lichtplatte f

~ (~) mortar · Polyester(harz)mörtel m

~ (~) sheet, ~ (~) board · Polyester(harz)platte f

~ (~) sheeting, ~ (~) film · Polyester(harz)folie f

~ ~-(sur)faced, ~ resin-coated · polyester(harz)beschichtet

~ (resin) window · Polyester(harz)fenster n

~ sheet → ~ resin ~

~ sheeting → ~ resin ~

~ window → ~ resin ~

polyethylene, polythene, PE · PE n, Polyäthylen n

~ bathroom gull(e)y → polythene bathroom outlet

~ ~ inlet → polythene bathroom outlet

~ ~ outlet → polythene ~ ~

~ film → polythene (protective) ~

~ pipe, polythene ~ [B.S. 3796] · Polyäthylenrohr n, PE-Rohr [Es gibt Polyäthylenweichrohre (DIN 8072 und 8073) und Polyäthylenhartrohre (DIN 8074 und 8075)]

~ protection film → polythene (protective) ~

~ ~ sheeting → polythene (protective) film

~ (protective) film → polythene (~) ~

~ (~) sheeting → polythene (protective) film

~ rod, polythene ~ · PE-Stab m, Polyäthylenstab

~ sheeting → polythene (protective) film

~ sheet(ing) dampproof(ing) course, polythene ~ ~ ~, ~ ~ dampcourse, ~ ~ d.p.c., ~ ~ dpc, ~ ~ DPC · PE-Bahn-Feuchtigkeitssperrschicht f, Polyäthylenbahn-Feuchtigkeitssperrschicht

polygon, polygonal figure · Polygon n, Vieleck n, Mehreck

~ of forces, ~ ~ force vectors, force polygon [A polygonal figure illustrating a theorem relating to a number of forces acting at one point, each of which is represented in magnitude and direction by one of the sides of the figure] · Kraftecк m, Kräftevieleck, Kräftezug m, Kräftepolygon n

~ ~ choir, ~ ~ quire · Chorpolygon n

polygonal, multiangular · vieleckig, mehreckig, polygonal

~ arch · geknickter Bogen m, gebrochener ~, polygonaler ~, Knickbogen, Polygon(al)bogen

~ bar, multiangular ~, ~ rod · Polygon(al)stab m, Vieleckstab, Mehreckstab

~ bay window · Polygon(al)-Auslucht f

~ block, ~ building, multiangular ~ · Polygon(al)gebäude n, Vieleckgebäude, Mehreckgebäude

~ bond → ~ masonry ~

~ bowstring girder, segmental ~ ~ · Bogensehnenträger m, Segmentträger

~ building, ~ block, multiangular ~ · Polygon(al)gebäude n, Vieleckgebäude, Mehreckgebäude

~ cavity block → ~ hollow ~

~ ~ tile → ~ hollow block

~ centralized church, ~ centrally-planned, ~ church with central space · polygonale zentrale Anlage f, vieleckige ~ ~, mehreckige ~ ~, polygonaler Zentralbau m, vieleckiger Zentralbau, mehreckiger Zentralbau

~ centrally-planned church, ~ centralized ~, ~ church with central space · polygonale zentrale Anlage f, vieleckige ~ ~, mehreckige ~ ~, polygonaler Zentralbau m, vieleckiger Zentralbau, mehreckiger Zentralbau

polygonal choir — polygonal (random rubble) masonry ...

~ **choir,** multiangular ~, ~ quire · Polygon(al)chor *m*, Vieleckchor, Mehreckchor [*Chor mit vieleckigem Schluß, meist in der Gotik*]

~ **church,** multiangular ~ · Polygon(al)- kirche *f*, Vieleckkirche, Mehreckkirche

~ ~ **with central space,** ~ centralized church, ~ centrally-planned church · polygonale zentrale Anlage *f*, vieleckige ~ ~, mehreckige ~ ~, polygonaler Zentralbau *m*, vieleckiger Zentralbau, mehreckiger Zentralbau

~ **cloister vault** (US); ~ domical ~ (Brit.) · Klostergewölbe *n*, Walmkuppel *f*, Haubengewölbe [*Gewölbeform, die nur aus Wangen zusammengesetzt ist, die auf den Umfassungsmauern polygonaler Bauten ruhen, und im Gegensatz zur formal verwandten Kuppel eine gebrochene Laibung hat*]

~ **column,** multiangular ~ · Mehreckstütze *f*, Vieleckstütze, Polygon(al)- stütze

~ ~, multiangular ~ · Polygon(al)säule *f*, Vielecksäule, Mehrecksäule

~ **cupola** → multiangular dome

~ **diminutive tower,** multiangular ~ ~, ~ small, ~ turret · kleiner Polygonalturm *m*, ~ Vieleckturm, Polygon(al)- türmchen *n*, Vieleckturmchen, Mehreckturmchen

~ **dome** → multiangular ~

~ **domical vault** (Brit.); ~ cloister ~ (US) · Klostergewölbe *n*, Walmkuppel *f*, Haubengewölbe [*Gewölbeform, die nur aus Wangen zusammengesetzt ist, die auf den Umfassungsmauern polygonaler Bauten ruhen, und im Gegensatz zur formal verwandten Kuppel eine gebrochene Leibung hat*]

~ **donjon** → ~ keep

~ **drum,** multiangular ~ · polygonaler Kuppelunterbau *m*, vieleckiger ~, mehreckiger ~, Polygon(al)trommel *f*, Vielecktrommel, Mehrecktrommel, polygonale Trommel, vieleckige Trommel, mehreckige Trommel

~ **dungeon** → ~ keep

~ **exposed concrete column,** ~ fairfaced ~ ~, multiangular ~ ~ · Polygon(al)sichtbetonstütze *f*, Vielecksichtbetonstütze, Mehrecksichtbetonstütze

~ **fair-faced concrete column,** ~ exposed ~ ~, multiangular ~ ~ ~ · Polygon(al)sichtbetonstütze *f*, Vielecksichtbetonstütze, Mehrecksichtbetonstütze

polygon(al figure) · Polygon *n*, Vieleck *n*, Mehreck

polygonal folded plate roof, ~ ~ slab ~, ~ prismatic shell ~ ~; ~ hipped-plate ~, ~ tilted-slab ~ (US) · Polygon(al)faltwerk)dach *n*, Polygon(al)- dachfaltwerk *n*, Vieleckfalt(werk)dach, Vieleckdachfaltwerk

~ ~ **slab roof,** ~ ~ plate ~, ~ prismatic shell ~; ~ hipped-plate ~, ~ tilted-slab ~ (US) · Polygon(al)falt(werk)- dach *n*, Polygon(al)dachfaltwerk *n*, Vieleckfalt(werk)dach, Vieleckdachfaltwerk

~ **frame,** multiangular ~ · Polygon(al)- rahmen *m*, Vieleckrahmen, Mehreckrahmen

~ **(ground(-))plan,** multiangular ~ · vieleckiger Grundriß *m*, mehreckiger ~, polygonaler ~, Vieleckgrundriß, Mehreckgrundriß, Polygon(al)grundriß

~ **hall-choir,** ~ hall-quire, multiangular ~ · Polygon(al)hallenchor *m*, Vieleckhallenchor, Mehreckhallenchor

~ **hall-quire,** ~ hall-choir, multiangular ~ · Polygon(al)hallenchor *m*, Vieleckhallenchor, Mehreckhallenchor

~ **hipped-plate roof,** ~ tilted-slab ~ (US); ~ folded slab ~, ~ folded plate ~, ~ prismatic shell ~ · Polygon(al)- falt(werk)dach *n*, Polygon(al)dachfaltwerk *n*, Vieleckfalt(werk)dach, Vieleckdachfaltwerk, Mehreckfalt(werk)- dach, Mehreckdachfaltwerk

~ **hollow block,** multiangular ~ ~, ~ ~ tile, ~ cavity ~, ~ pot [*See remark under 'Block'*] · Polygon(al)hohlblock(-stein) *m*, Vieleckhohlblock(stein), Polygon(al)hohlstein, Vieleckhohlstein, Mehreckhohlblock(stein), Mehreckhohlstein

~ **keep,** multiangular ~, ~ donjon, ~ dungeon · polygonaler Bergfried *m*, ~ Berchfrit, ~ Belfried, ~ Donjon, vieleckiger ~, mehreckiger ~

~ **(masonry) bond,** multiangular (~) ~ · Polygon(al)(mauerwerk)verband *m*, Vieleck(mauerwerk)verband, Mehreck(mauerwerk)verband

~ ~ **(work)** → ~ random rubble ~ (~)

~ **ornament,** multiangular ~ · Polygon(al)ornament *n*, Vieleckornament, Mehreckornament [*Ornament aus vieleckigen Platten*]

~ **pier** · Polygon(al)pfeiler *m*, Vieleckpfeiler, Mehreckpfeiler

~ **plan** → ~ ground(-)~

~ **plate,** multiangular ~, ~ slab · Polygon(al)platte *f*, Vieleckplatte, Mehreckplatte

~ **pot** → ~ hollow block

~ **prismatic shell roof** → ~ folded slab ~

~ **quire,** multiangular ~, ~ choir · Polygon(al)chor *m*, Vieleckchor, Mehreckchor [*Chor mit vieleckigem Schluß, meist in der Gotik*]

~ **(random rubble) masonry (work),** mosaic (~ ~) ~ (~), cobweb (~ ~) ~ (~) [*The stones are irregular in shape without parallel edges and are shaped to fit the spaces they are to occupy, the joints being more or less uniform in thickness*] · Vieleckmauerwerk *n*, Polygon(al)mauerwerk, Zyklopenmauerwerk mit netzartigen Fugen, zyklopisches Mauerwerk mit netzartigen Fugen

polygonal rod — polystyrene foam tile 738

~ **rod**, multiangular ~, ~ bar · Polygon(al)stab m, Vieleckstab, Mehreckstab

~ **roof**, multiangular ~ · Polygon(al)dach n,

~ **sett paving** · Polygon(al)pflaster(-decke) n, (f)

~ **slab**, multiangular ~, ~ plate · Polygon(al)platte f, Vieleckplatte, Mehreckplatte

~ **small tower**, multiangular ~ ~, ~ diminutive ~, ~ turret · kleiner Polygon(al)turm m, ~ Vieleckturm, Polygon(al)türmchen n, Vieleckturmchen, Mehreckturmchen

~ **spire** · Dachhelm m, Turmhelm, Helm(-dach) m, (n), Zeltdach über vieleckigem Grundriß, Zeltdach über polygonalem Grundriß, Zeltdach über mehreckigem Grundriß

~ **termination**, multiangular ~ · Vieleck(ab)schluß m, Mehreck(ab)schluß, Polygon(al)(ab)schluß, polygonaler (Ab)Schluß, vieleckiger (Ab)Schluß, mehreckiger (Ab)Schluß

~ **tilted-slab roof**, ~ hipped-plate ~ (US); ~ prismatic shell ~, ~ folded slab ~, ~ folded plate ~ · Polygon(al)falt(werk)dach n, Polygon(al)dachfaltwerk n, Vieleckfalt(werk)dach, Vieleckdachfaltwerk, Mehreckfalt(werk)dach, Mehreckdachfaltwerk

~ **tower**, multiangular ~ · Mehreckturm m, Vieleckturm, Polygon(al)turm

~ **truss**, multiangular ~ · Polygon(al)-sprengwerk n, Vielecksprengwerk, Mehrecksprengwerk

~ **turret**, multiangular ~, ~ small tower, ~ diminutive tower · kleiner Polygon(al)turm m, ~ Vieleckturm, Polygon(al)türmchen n, Vieleckturmchen, Mehreckturmchen

~ **vault**, multiangular ~ · Polygon(al)gewölbe n, Vieleckgewölbe, Mehreckgewölbe

polyhydric alcohol, polyalcohol · mehrwertiger Alkohol m, vielwertiger ~

polyisobutylene · PIB n, Polyisobutylen n

~ **film**, ~ sheeting · PIB-Folie f, Polyisobutylenfolie

~ **sheeting**, ~ film · PIB-Folie f, Polyisobutylenfolie

polymer [A substance, the molecules of which consist of one or more structural units repeated any number of times; vinyl resins are examples of true polymers. The name is also frequently applied to large molecules produced by any chemical process, e.g. condensation in which water or other products are produced; alkyd resins are examples of these. Homo-polymer. Polymer of which the molecules consist of one kind of structural unit repeated any number of times; polyvinyl chloride and polyvinyl acetate are examples.
Copolymer. Polymer of which the molecules consist of more than one kind of structural unit derived from more than one monomer; polyvinyl chloride-acetate, or polyvinyl acetate-acrylic copolymers are examples] · Polymer(isat) n

~ **emulsion** · Polymeremulsion f

~ **modified oil** · Polymeröl n

polymeric · polymer

~ **viscosity modifier** · polymerer Viskositätsindex-Verbesserer m

polymerisable (Brit.); polymerizable · polymerisierbar

polymerisation (Brit.); polymerization · Polymerisation f

~ (Brit.); polymerization, setting · Aushärtung f [Betonkleber]

~ **resin** (Brit.); polymerization ~ · Polymerisat(ions)harz n

~ **time** (Brit.); polymerization ~, setting ~ · Aushärtezeit f [Betonkleber]

polymerised (Brit.); polymerized · polymerisiert

polymerizable; polymerisable (Brit.) · polymerisierbar

polymerization, setting; polymerisation (Brit.) · Aushärtung f [Betonkleber]

~, polymerizing; polymerisation, polymerising (Brit.) · Polymerisation f

~ **resin**; polymerisation ~ (Brit.) · Polymerisat(ions)harz n

~ **time**, setting ~; polymerisation ~ (Brit.) · Aushärtezeit f [Betonkleber]

polymerizing, polymerization; polymerising, polymerisation (Brit.) · Polymerisation f

polypropylene, PP · Polypropylen n, PP n

~ **film**, ~ sheeting · Polypropylenfolie f, PP-Folie

~ **pipe** · Polypropylenrohr n, PP-Rohr [DIN 8077 Maße und DIN 8078 Allgemeine Güteanforderungen und Prüfung]

~ **sheeting**, ~ film · Polypropylenfolie f, PP-Folie

polystyle, many-columned · mehrsäulig, vielsäulig, säulenreich

polystyrene, PS · Polystyrol n, PS n

~ **ceiling tile** [B. S. 2552] · Polystyroldecken(belag)platte f, Polystyroldeckenfliese f, PS-Decken(belag)platte, PS-Deckenfliese

~ **film**, ~ sheeting · Polystyrolfolie f, PS-Folie

~ **foam**, foam(ed) polystyrene, expanded polystyrene · Polystyrolschaum(stoff) m, Schaum(stoff)polystyrol n, PS-Schaum(stoff)

~ ~ **board for thermal insulation purposes**, expanded polystyrene ~ ~ ~ ~, foam(ed) polystyrene ~ ~ ~ ~ ~ [B.S. 3837] · Polystyrolschaum(stoff)wärmedämmplatte f

~ ~ **tile**, foam(ed) polystyrene ~, expanded polystyrene ~ · Polystyrolschaum(stoff)(belag)platte f, Polystyrolschaum(stoff)fliese f

polystyrene insulant — polyurethane (floor(ing)) seal(er)

~ **insulant** → ~ insulation(-grade) material

~ **insulating material** → ~ insulation(-grade) ~

~ **insulation(-grade) material,** ~ insulating ~, ~ insulator, ~ insulant · Polystyroldämmstoff *m*, PS-Dämmstoff, Polystyroldämmaterial *n*, PS-Dämmmaterial

~ **insulator** → ~ insulation(-grade) material

~ **profile,** ~ section, ~ shape, ~ unit, ~ trim [*B.S. 3932*] · Polystyrolprofil *n*, PS-Profil

~ **rod** · Polystyrolstab *m*, PS-Stab

~ **section,** ~ shape, ~ profile, ~ unit, ~ trim [*B.S. 3932*] · Polystyrolprofil *n*, PS-Profil

~ **shape,** ~ section, ~ profile, ~ unit, ~ trim [*B.S. 3932*] · Polystyrolprofil *n*, PS-Profil

~ **sheeting,** ~ film · Polystyrolfolie *f*, PS-Folie

~ **tile** · Polystyrol(belag)platte *f*, Polystyrolfliese *f*, PS-(Belag)Platte, PS-Fliese

~ ~ **adhesive** · Polystyrol(belag)plattenkleber *m*, Polystyrolfliesenkleber, PS-(Belag)Plattenkleber, PS-Fliesenkleber

~ **trim,** ~ unit, ~ shape, ~ section, ~ profile [*B.S. 3932*] · Polystyrolprofil *n*, PS-Profil

~ **unit,** ~ trim, ~ section, ~ shape, ~ profile [*B.S. 3932*] · Polystyrolprofil *n*, PS-Profil

~ **wall tile** [*B.S. 2552*] · Polystyrolwand(belag)platte *f*, Polystyrolwandfliese *f*, PS-Wand(belag)platte, PS-Wandfliese

polysulfide polymer (US); polysulphide ~ (Brit.) · Polysulfidpolymer *n*

polysulphide(-based) composition, ~ compound, ~ mass, ~ material (Brit.); polysulfide(-based) ~ (US) · Polysulfidmasse *f*

~ **rubber** (Brit.); polisulfide(-based) ~ (US) · Polysulfidkautschuk *m*

~ ~ **(building) mastic** (Brit.); polisulfide(-based) ~ (~) ~ (US) · Polisulfidkautschukkitt *m*

polytetrafluorethylene, PTFE · Polytetrafluoräthylen *n*, PTFE *n*

polythene, polyethylene, PE · PE *n*, Polyäthylen *n*

~ **bathroom gull(e)y** → ~ ~ outlet

~ ~ **inlet** → ~ ~ outlet

~ ~ **outlet,** polyethylene ~ ~, ~ ~ inlet, ~ ~ gull(e)y · PE-Badablauf *m*, PE-Badeinlauf, Polyäthylen-Badablauf, Polyäthylen-Badeinlauf

~ **film** → ~ protective ~

~ **pipe,** polyethylene ~ [*B.S. 3796*] · Polyäthylenrohr *n*, PE-Rohr [*Es gibt Polyäthylenweichrohre (DIN 8072 und 8073) und Polyäthylenhartrohre (DIN 8074 und 8075)*]

~ **protection film** → ~ (protective) ~

~ ~ **sheeting** → ~ (protective) film

~ **(protective) film,** polyethylene (~) ~, ~ (~) sheeting, ~ protection ~ · PE-(Schutz)folie *f*, Polyäthylen(-Schutz)folie

~ (~) **sheeting** → ~ (~) film

~ **rod,** polyethylene ~ · PE-Stab *m*, Polyäthylenstab

~ **sheeting** → ~ (protective) film

polytrifluoro chloro ethylene · Polytrifluorchloräthylen *n*, PTFCE *n*

polyurethane · Polyurethan *n*, PUR *n*

~ **base** · Polyurethanbasis *f*, Polyurethangrundlage *f*, PUR-Basis, PUR-Grundlage

~ **(bonding) adhesive,** ~ ~ agent, ~ ~ medium, ~ cement(ing agent) · Polyurethan-Kleb(e)stoff *m*, Polyurethan-Kleber, PUR-Kleber *m*, Polyurethan-Kleb(e)mittel *n*, PUR-Kleb(e)stoff, PUR-Kleb(e)mittel

~ ~ **agent,** ~ ~ medium, ~ (~) adhesive, ~ cement(ing agent) · Polyurethan-Kleb(e)stoff *m*, Polyurethan-Kleber *m*, PUR-Kleber, Polyurethan-Kleb(e)mittel *n*, PUR-Kleb(e)stoff, PUR-Kleb(e)mittel

~ ~ **medium,** ~ ~ agent, ~ (~) adhesive, ~ cement(ing agent) · Polyurethan-Kleb(e)stoff *m*, Polyurethan-Kleber *m*, PUR-Kleber, Pollyurethan-Keb(e)mittel *n*, PUR-Kleb(e)stoff, PUR-Kleb(e)mittel

~ **cement,** ~ putty · Polyurethankitt *m*

~ **cement(ing agent),** ~ (bonding) adhesive, ~ bonding agent, ~ bonding medium · Polyurethan-Kleb(e)stoff *m*, Polyurethan-Kleber *m*, PUR-Kleber, Polyurethan-Kleb(e)mittel *n*, PUR-Kleb(e)stoff, PUR-Kleb(e)mittel

~ **clearcolle** · Polyurethan-Decklack *m*, PUR-Decklack

(poly)urethane coating, ~ surface ~, ~ lacquer · Polyurethanlack *m*

polyurethane composition, ~ compound, ~ material, ~ mass · Polyurethanmasse *f*, PUR-Masse

~ **compound,** ~ composition, ~ material, ~ mass · Polyurethanmasse *f*, PUR-Masse

~ **floor cover(ing)** → ~ floor(ing)

~ **floor(ing),** ~ floor cover(ing) · Polyurethan(fuß)boden(belag) *m*

~ **(floor(ing)) sealant,** ~ (~) seal(er), ~ (~) seal(ing) material · Polyurethan-Bodensiegel *m*, Polyurethan-Fußbodensiegel, Polyurethansiegel, PUR-(Fuß-)Bodensiegel, PUR-Siegel

~ (~) **seal(er),** ~ (~) sealant, ~ (~) seal(ing) material · Polyurethan-Bodensiegel *m*, Polyurethan-Fußbodensiegel, Polyurethansiegel, PUR-(Fuß)Bodensiegel, PUR-Siegel

polyurethane (floor(ing)) ... — polyvinyl chlorid(e) ... 740

~ (~) seal(ing) material, ~ (~) sealant, ~ (~) seal(er) · Polyurethan-Bodensiegel m, Polyurethan-Fußbodensiegel, Polyurethansiegel, PUR-(Fuß)Bodensiegel, PUR-Siegel

~ foam, foamed polyurethane, expanded polyurethane · Polyurethanschaum(stoff) m, PUR-Schaum(stoff)

~ ~ board, expanded polyurethane ~, ~ ~ sheet · Polyurethanschaumplatte f, PUR-Schaumplatte

~ ~ sheet → ~ ~ board

~ ~ strip, foamed polyurethane ~, expanded polyurethane ~ · Polyurethanschaum(fugen)band n, PUR-Schaum(fugen)band

~ insulant, ~ insulator, ~ insulating material, ~ insulation(-grade) material · Polyurethandämmstoff m, PUR-Dämmstoff

~ insulating core · Polyurethan-Isolierkern m

~ ~ material, ~ insulator, ~ insulant, ~ insulation(-grade) material · Polyurethandämmstoff m, PUR-Dämmstoff

~ insulator, ~ insulant, ~ insulating material, ~ insualtion(-grade) material · Polyurethandämmstoff m, PUR-Dämmstoff

(poly)urethane lacquer, ~ (surface) coating · Polyurethanlack m

polyurethane mass, ~ material, ~ compound, ~ composition · Polyurethanmasse f, PUR-Masse

~ material, ~ mass, ~ compound, ~ composition · Polyurethanmasse f, PUR-Masse

~ paint · Polyurethan(anstrich)farbe f, PUR-(Anstrich)Farbe

~ putty, ~ cement · Polyurethankitt m

~ resin · Polyurethanharz n [*Polyurethanharze werden durch Polyaddition von Polyisocyanaten und Polyhydroxilverbindungen hergestellt*]

~ rigid foam, rigid polyurethane ~, expanded rigid polyurethane · Polyurethanhartschaum(stoff) m, Hartpolyurethanschaum(stoff), PUR-Hartschaum(stoff)

~ ~ ~ (building) board, ~ ~ ~ (~) sheet · Polyurethan-Hartschaum(bau)platte f, PUR-Hartschaum(bau)platte

~ ~ ~ (~) sheet, ~ ~ ~ (~) board · Polyurethan-Hartschaum(bau)platte f, PUR-Hartschaum(bau)platte

~ ~ ~ laminated (building) board, ~ ~ ~ ~ (~) sheet · Polyurethan-Hartschaumschichtstoff(bau)platte f, PUR-Hartschaumschichtstoff(bau)platte

~ sealant → ~ floor(ing) ~

~ seal(er) → ~ floor(ing) ~

~ seal(ing) material → ~ floor(ing) ~

~ strip · Polyurethanband n

(poly)urethane (surface) coating, ~ lacquer · Polyurethanlack m

polyurethane two-part (bonding) adhesive · Polyurethan-Zweikomponentenkleber m

polyvinyl acetal · Polyvinylazetal n

~ acetate, pva, PVA, p.v.a. · Polyvinylazetat n, PVA(C) n

~ ~ adhesive → ~ ~ glue

~ ~ emulsion, PVA ~, pva ~, p.v.a. ~ · Polyvinylazetatemulsion f, PVA(C)-Emulsion

~ ~ ~ paint, PVA ~ ~, pva ~ ~, p.v.a. ~ ~ · Polyvinylazetatemulsionsfarbe f, PVA(C)-Emulsionsfarbe

~ ~ floor cover(ing) → ~ ~ floor(ing)

~ ~ floor(ing), ~ ~ floor cover(ing), PVA floor(ing), PVA floor cover(ing) · Polyvinylazetat(fuß)boden(belag) m, PVA(C)-(Fuß)Boden(belag)

~ ~ glue, ~ ~ adhesive, PVA ~, pva ~, p.v.a. ~ · Polyvinylazetatleim m, PVA(C)-Leim

~ bonding medium, ~ ~ agent, ~ (~) adhesive, ~ cement(ing agent), ~ glue [*A synthetic adhesive made from polyvinyl resins*] · Polyvinylkleber m, Polyvinylkleb(e)stoff m, Polyvinylkleb(e)mittel n

~ butyral · Polyvinylbutyral n

~ cement(ing agent), ~ (bonding) adhesive, ~ bonding agent, ~ bonding medium [*A synthetic adhesive made from polyvinyl resins*] · Polyvinylkleber m, Polyvinylkleb(e)stoff m, Polyvinylkleb(e)mittel n

~ chlorid(e) (US); ~ chloride (Brit.); PVC · Polyvinylchlorid n, PVC

~ ~ acetate (US); ~ chloride ~ (Brit.) · Polyvinylchloridacetat n

~ ~ base, PVC ~ · Polyvinylchlorid-Basis f, Polyvinylchlorid-Grundlage f, PVC-Basis, PVC-Grundlage

~ ~ based, PVC ~ · polyvinylchloridgebunden, pvc-gebunden

~ ~ building board → PVC building slab

~ ~ ~ sheet → PVC building slab

~ ~ ~ slab → PVC ~ ~

~ ~ ceiling, PVC ~ · Polyvinylchloriddecke f, PVC-Decke

~ ~ ~ profile → PVC ceiling shape

~ ~ ~ section → PVC ceiling shape

~ ~ ~ shape → PVC ~ ~

~ ~ ~ trim → PVC ceiling shape

~ ~ ~ unit → PVC ceiling shape

~ ~ coating, PVC ~ · Polyvinylchloridbeschichtung f, PVC-Beschichtung

~ ~ construction profile → PVC construction unit

~ ~ ~ section → PVC construction unit

~ ~ ~ shape → PVC construction unit

~ ~ ~ trim → PVC construction unit

~ ~ ~ unit → PVC ~ ~

polyvinyl chlorid(e) corrugated board — poor(s)house

~ ~ **corrugated board**, ~ ~ ~ sheet, PVC ~ ~ · Polyvinylchlorid-Wellplatte f, PVC-Wellplatte

~ ~ ~ **sheet(ing)**, PVC ~ ~ · Polyvinylchlorid-Wellbahn f, PVC-Wellbahn

~ ~ **cover(ing)**, PVC ~ ~ · Polyvinylchloridbelag f, PVC-Belag

~ ~ **film**, ~ ~ sheeting, PVC ~ · Polyvinylchloridfolie f, PVC-Folie

~ ~ **floor finish** → PVC ~ ~

~ ~ **floor(ing)** → PVC floor finish

~ ~ **flower box**, PVC ~ ~ · Polyvinylchlorid-Blumenkasten m, PVC-Blumenkasten

~ ~ ~ **trough**, PVC ~ ~ · Polyvinylchlorid-Blumentrog m, PVC-Blumentrog

~ ~ **foam** → PVC ~

~ ~ **hollow profile** → PVC hollow shape

~ ~ ~ **section** → PVC hollow shape

~ ~ ~ **shape** → PVC ~ ~

~ ~ ~ **trim** → PVC hollow shape

~ ~ ~ **unit** → PVC hollow shape

~ ~ **insulating film** → PVC ~ ~

~ ~ ~ **sheeting** → PVC insulating film

~ ~ **insulation(-grade) film** → PVC insulating ~

~ ~ **sheeting** → PVC insulating film

~ ~ **pipe**, PVC ~ · Polyvinylchloridrohr n, PVC-Rohr

~ ~ **pressure pipe**, PVC ~ ~ · Polyvinylchlorid-Druckrohr n, PVC-Druckrohr

~ ~ **profile** → PVC section

~ ~ **rainwater articles** → ~ ~ ~ goods

~ ~ ~ **goods**, ~ ~ ~ products, ~ ~ ~ articles, PVC ~ ~ · Polyvinylchlorid-Dachzubehör(teile) m, (mpl, npl), PVC-Dachzubehör(teile)

~ ~ ~ **products** → ~ ~ ~ goods

~ ~ ~ **system**, PVC ~ ~ · Polyvinylchlorid-Regenablaufkonstruktion f, PVC-Regenablaufkonstruktion [PVC-Regenrinne + PVC-Regenfallrohr + PVC-Zubehör]

~ ~ **(resin)**, PVC (~) · Polyvinylchlorid n, PVC

~ ~ **roof tile**, PVC ~ ~ · Polyvinylchlorid-Dachplatte f, PVC-Dachplatte

~ ~ **seal(ing)** → PVC ~ ~

~ ~ ~ **sheeting**, ~ ~ ~ film, PVC ~ ~ · Polyvinylchlorid-(Ab)Dicht(ungs)folie f, PVC-(Ab)Dicht(ungs)-folie

~ ~ **section** → PVC ~

~ ~ **shape** → PVC section

~ ~ **sheathed cable**, PVC ~ ~ · PVC-Mantel-Kabel n, Polyvinylchloridmantelkabel

~ ~ **sheeting**, ~ ~ film, PVC ~ · Polyvinylchloridfolie f, PVC-Folie

~ ~ **sheet(ing)**, PVC ~ · Polyvinylchlorid-Bahn f, PVC-Bahn

~ ~ ~ **board** → PVC building slab

~ ~ ~ **structural profile** → PVC construction unit

~ ~ ~ **shape** → PVC construction unit

~ ~ ~ **unit** → PVC construction ~

~ **chloride-tar (mix(ture))**, PVC-tar (~) · Polyvinylchlorid-Teer-Gemisch n, Polyvinylchlorid-Teer(-Mischung) m, (f), PVC-Teer(-Gemisch), PVC-Teer-Mischung

~ **chloride thermal insulation**, PVC ~ ~ · PVC-Wärmedämmung f, Polyvinylchlorid-Wärmedämmung

~ ~ **tile**, PVC ~ · Polyvinylchlorid(belag)platte f, Polyvinylchloridfliese f, PVC-(Belag)Platte, PVC-Fliese

~ ~ **trim** → PVC section

~ ~ **unit** → PVC section

~ ~ **wall board**, ~ ~ ~ sheet, PVC ~ ~ · Polyvinylchloridwandplatte f, PVC-Wandplatte

~ ~ ~ **sheet** → ~ ~ ~ ~ board

~ ~ **waterbar** → ~ ~ waterstop

~ ~ **waterstop**, ~ ~ waterbar, PVC ~ · Polyvinylchlorid-Fugenband n, PVC-Fugenband

~ ~ **window profile** → PVC window section

~ ~ ~ **section** → PVC ~ ~

~ ~ ~ **shape** → PVC window section

~ ~ ~ **trim** → PVC window section

~ ~ ~ **unit** → PVC window section

~ **glue** → ~ bonding medium

~ **resin** [General name given to a series of resins formed by the polymerization of monomers containing the vinyl group $(CH_2 : CH-)$] · Polyvinylharz n

~ **waterbar**, ~ waterstop · Polyvinylfugenband n

~ **waterstop**, ~ waterbar · Polyvinylfugenband n

polyvinylidene chloride; ~ **chlorid(e)** (US) · Polyvinylidenchlorid n, PVDC n

Pompeian architecture · pompejanische Baukunst f, ~ Architektur

ponceau · Ponceau m [scharlachroter Naphthalin-Azofarbstoff]

ponding [The formation of shallow pools of water on a surface] · (Wasser-)Lachenbildung f, Wasseransammlung

pool hall → swimming-pool ~

~ **of water**, water pool · Wasserbecken n [Als Verzierung eines Platzes]

poor adhesion · schlechtes Haften n

~ **lime**, lean ~, magnesian ~, dolomitic ~ · Magerkalk m, Graukalk, Dolomitkalk [90 % Kalksubstanz und mehr als 5 % Magnesiumoxid]

poor's pyx, offertory-box · Opferstock m

poor(s)house, almshouse [A house built and endowed for the poor and aged] · Armenhaus n

popcorn concrete — porous absorbent system

popcorn concrete (US); no-fines ~ (Brit.) [*A concrete mix(ture) containing little or no fine aggregate*] · Schüttbeton *m*, entfeinter Beton [*DIN 4232*]

~ (~) terrace(d) house (US); no-fines (~) ~ ~ (Brit.) · Terrassenhaus *n* aus entfeintem Beton

poppyseed oil · Mohn(samen)öl *n*

popular sink unit, economy ~ ~ · Volksspültisch *m*, Sied(e)lungsspültisch, Volksabwaschtisch, Sied(e)lungsabwaschtisch

~ taste · Massengeschmack *m*, Massengeist *m*

populated area, housing ~, residential (building) ~, living ~ · Wohn(bau)gebiet *n*, Wohn(bau)zone *f*, Wohnungsbaugebiet, Wohnungsbauzone

population census · Volkszählung *f*

~ served, contributary population · angeschlossene Bevölkerung *f*

porcelain bath, ~ (bath)tub · Porzellan(bade)wanne *f*

~ clay → kaolin

~ discharge pipe, ~ draining ~, ~ drain(age) ~, ~ waste (~) · Porzellanabflußrohr *n*, Porzellanablaufrohr, Porzellandränrohr, Porzellanentwässerungsrohr [*Fehlnamen: Porzellanablauf m, Porzellanabfluß*]

~ drain(age) pipe, ~ draining ~, ~ discharge ~, ~ waste (~) · Porzellanabflußrohr *n*, Porzellanablaufrohr, Porzellandränrohr, Porzellanentwässerungsrohr [*Fehlnamen: Porzellanablauf m, Porzellanabfluß*]

~ draining pipe, ~ drain(age) ~, ~ discharge ~, ~ waste (~) · Porzellanabflußrohr *n*, Porzellanablaufrohr, Porzellandränrohr, Porzellanentwässerungsrohr [*Fehlnamen: Porzellanablauf m, Porzellanabfluß*]

~ earth → kaolin

~ enamel, vitreous ~ · Schmelzemail(le) *n*, (f)

~ ~ finish, vitreous ~ ~ · Schmelzemailleüberzug *m*

~ enameled building panel; vitreous ~ ~ ~ (US); ~ enamelled ~ ~ (Brit.) · schmelzemaillierte(Bau)Tafel *f*, Schmelzemaille(bau)tafel

~ fixture → ~ luminaire (~)

~ light fitting (Brit.) → ~ luminaire (fixture)

~ (light(ing)) fixture → ~ luminaire (~)

~ luminaire (fixture) (US); ~ lightfitting (Brit.); ~ (light(ing)) fixture · Porzellanleuchte *f*

~ mortar · Reibschale *f*, Mörser *m* [*DIN 12906*]

~ (roof) tile · Porzellandachstein *m*

~ tile · Porzellan(belag)platte *f*, Porzelanfliese *f*

~ ~ → ~ roof ~

~ tower [*A famous tower at Nankin(g) in China, covered with porcelain tiles*] · Porzellanturm *m*

~ tub → ~ bath

~ ware · Sanitärporzellan(ware) *n*, (f)

~ waste (pipe), ~ drain(age) ~, ~ draining ~, ~ discharge ~ · Porzellanabflußrohr *n*, Porzellanablaufrohr, Porzellandränrohr, Porzellanentwässerungsrohr [*Fehlnamen: Porzellanablauf m, Porzellanabfluß*]

porch, church ~ · (Kirchen)Vorhalle *f*

~ enamel, deck ~, deck paint [*It is used for boat decks, porch floors, and such*] · Überwasser(anstrich)farbe *f*

pore, void, interstice [*The space in a material occupied by air or water, or both air and water*] · Hohlraum *m*, Pore *f*

~ characteristic · Porenmerkmal *n*

~ content · Porenanteil *m*, Porengehalt *m*, Porigkeit *f*

~ diameter · Porendurchmesser *m*

~ distribution, distribution of pores · Porenverteilung *f*

~ filling · Porenfüllung *f*, Porenverschluß *m*

pore-filling · porenfüllend, porenschließend

pore form, ~ shape · Porengestalt *f*, Porenform *f*

~ formation · Porenbildung *f*

~ ratio, void ~ · Hohlraumverhältnis *n*, Porenziffer *f* [*Das Verhältnis des im Korngemisch enthaltenen Hohlraumes H zum Festraum aller im Gemisch enthaltenen Körner S:h*]

~ seal(ing) · Poren(ab)dichtung *f*

~ ~ preparation · Poren(ab)dichtungspräparat *n*

~ shape, ~ form · Porengestalt *f*, Porenform *f*

~ type · Porenart *f*

~ volume · Porenvolumen *n*

porosity, percentage of voids, content of voids, voids content [*The ratio, usually expressed as a percentage, of the volume of voids in a material to the total volume of the material, including the voids*] · Hohlraumanteil *m*, Hohlraumprozentsatz *m*, Hohlraumgehalt *m*, Porigkeit *f*, Porosität *f* [*Das Verhältnis zwischen dem Hohlraum und dem aus Festraum + Hohlraum bestehenden Gesamtraum in einem Korngemisch*]

~ of grains, ~ ~ particles, grain porosity, particle porosity · Korneigenporigkeit *f*

~ ~ particles ~ ~ grains, grain porosity, particle porosity · Korneigenporigkeit *f*

porous absorbent material, ~ ~ system, ~ absorber · poröser (Schall)Absorber *m*, ~ Schallschlucker

~ ~ system, ~ ~ material, ~ absorber · poröser (Schall)Absorber *m*, ~ Schallschlucker

porous absorber — portico

~ **absorber,** ~ absorbent material, ~ absorbent system · poröser (Schall)Absorber m, ~ Schallschlucker

~ **body** → ~ (clay) ~

~ **brick** · Poren(mauer)ziegel m, PMz m [DIN 105. *Mauerziegel mit vielen kleinen Poren, hervorgerufen durch Einmischen von Luft, Holzspänen oder Kohleteilchen in den Ton vor dem Brennen*]

~ **building material,** ~ construction(al) ~ · Porenbaustoff m, porosierter Baustoff; Porenbaumaterial n, porosiertes Baumaterial [*Schweiz*]

~ **(clay) body,** ~ stone · poröser Scherben m [*Keramik*]

~ **concrete** · Filterbeton m

~ ~ **pipe,** concrete porous ~ [*B.S. 1194*] · wasserdurchlässiges Betonrohr n, Sikkerbetonrohr, Betonsickerrohr

~ **construction(al) material,** ~ building ~ · Porenbaustoff m, porosierter Baustoff; Porenbaumaterial n, porosiertes Baumaterial [*Schweiz*]

~ **earthware pipe** · wasserdurchlässiges Irdengutrohr n, ~ Steingutrohr, Irdengutsickerrohr, Steingutsickerrohr

~ **(natural) stone** · poröser (Natur-)Stein m

~ **pipe** · Sickerrohr n, wasserdurchlässiges Rohr

~ **stone,** ~ (clay) body · poröser Scherben m [*Keramik*]

~ ~ → ~ natural ~

porphyric filler · Orthophyrfüller m, Porphyrfüller

~ **melaphyre** · Melaphyrporphyr m

~ **(paving) sett** · Orthophyrpflasterstein m, Porphyrpflasterstein

~ **sand** · Orthophyrsand m, Porphyrsand

~ **sett,** porphyric (paving) ~ · Porphyrpflasterstein m, Orthophyrpflasterstein

~ **tuff** · Orthophyrtuff m, Porphyrtuff

porphyrite · Porphyrit m

porphyritic texture · porphyrisches Gefüge n

porphyroid granite, granite-porphyry · Granitporphyr m

porphyry · Orthophyr m, Porphyr [*DIN 52100. Die Bezeichnung Orthophyr (= Orthoklasporphyr) ist sprachlich besser, da die Bezeichnung „Porphyr" für die Struktur gilt*]

~ **(asphaltic-)bitumen concrete** (Brit.); ~ asphalt(ic) ~ (US) · Porphyr-Asphaltbeton m, Orthophyr-Asphaltbeton

~ **column** · Porphyrsäule f

port, air hole, air vent · Zugloch n, Luftloch

PORT CEM → portland cement

portable altar · Tragaltar m

~ **fire extinguisher** · Handfeuerlöscher m [*DIN 14406*]

~ **lock,** padlock · Vorhängeschloß n [*DIN 7465*]

portal · Portal n, Prunktor n

~ **arch** · Portalbogen m, Prunktorbogen

~ **architecture** · Portalarchitektur f, Portalbaukunst f, Prunktorarchitektur, Prunktorbaukunst

~ **effect** · Portalwirkung f

~ **(frame)** [*A frame consisting of two verticals and member which may be horizontal, sloping, or arched*] · Portalrahmen m

~ **(~) beam** · Portalrahmenbalken(träger) m

~ **(~) block,** ~ (~) building · Portalrahmenhalle f

~ **(~) building,** ~ (~) block · Portalrahmenhalle f

~ **(~) compound unit** · Portalrahmenfertigteil m, n

~ **(~) span** · Portalrahmenschiff n

~ **(~) with lean-to** · Portalrahmen m mit Pultanbau

~ **girder** · Portalträger m

~ **leg** · Portalpfosten m, Portalstiel m

~ **method** · Portal-Methode f [*Baustatik*]

~ **openwork gablet** · Portalwimperg m

portcullis, herse [*A heavy iron or wooden grating, constructed to slide vertically in grooves cut at the sides of the gateway of a medieval castle, as a defence against assault*] · Fallgatter n, Falltor n, Schutzgatter

porte-cochère, carriage-entrance [*A gateway for carriages, leading into a courtyard*] · Wageneinfahrt f

porter, gatekeeper, doorkeeper · Pförtner m

porter, caretaker · Hausmeister m, Hauswart m

~ **system** [*With such a system in the hall, tenants can speak to callers, order from tradesmen, deal with casual callers, etc.*] · Hausfernsprecheranlage f im Hausflur

porter's apartment (unit) → caretaker's flat

~ **dwelling,** doorkeeper's ~, gatekeeper's ~ (Brit.); ~ unit (US) · Pförtnerwohnung f

~ **flat** → carataker's ~

~ **house** → ~ lodge

~ **lodge,** ~ house, gatekeeper's ~, doorkeeper's ~, guardhouse · Wache f, Pförtnerhaus n

~ **room,** doorkeeper's ~, gatekeeper's ~ · Pförtnerraum m

~ **unit** (US) → ~ dwelling

port-hole · Schießöffnung f [*in einer Mauer*]

portico · Portikus m [*Eine von Säulen, seltener von Pfeilern getragene Vorhalle vor der Hauptfront eines Gebäudes die besonders häufig in der klassizistischen Architektur vorkommt. Portikus ist auch eine Säulenhalle mit geschlossener Rückwand, ähnlich einer Stoa*]

~ of columns · Säulen(um)gang m, Säulenportikus m

portion, accommodation, block, unit · (Bau)Trakt m, Gebäudetrakt

~ of bending up, point ~ ~ ~, bent(-up) point, bent(-up) portion · Abbiegestelle f [Bewehrungsstab]

portland blastfurnace cement [B.S. 146] · Eisenportlandzement m, EPZ [Fehlname: Steinscher Zement. Max. 30% Schlacke. DIN 1164]

(~) (~) slag cement · Hochofenschlackenzement m, HOZ; Montanzement [Süddeutschland] [DIN 1164]

~ cement, Portland ~, PC, PORT CEM [B.S. 12] · Portlandzement m, PZ [DIN 1164]

(~) ~ artificial marble, (~) ~ imitation ~, (~) ~ man-made ~, (~) ~ manufactured ~ · Portlandzement-Betonmarmor m, Portlandzement-Marmorbeton m

~ ~ clinker · Portlandzementklinker m, PZ-Klinker

~ ~ concrete, P.C.C. · Portlandzementbeton m

~-cement exterior plaster, ~ external plaster; ~ (external) rendering (Brit.); ~ (mortar) stucco (US); [See remark under '(Außen)(Ver)Putz'] · Portlandzement(außen)(ver)putz m

Portland cement for general use, OPC, ordinary portland cement, normal portland cement; Portland cement type I (US) · normaler Portlandzement m, gewöhnlicher ~ [in Deutschland Z 225]

portland cement glazed coat(ing), ~ ~ glazing, ~ ~ glaze(d finish) · Portlandzementglasur f, Portlandzementbeglasung f

~ ~ grout(ing compound), ~ ~ slurry · Portlandzementschlämme f

(~) ~ imitation marble, (~) ~ man-made ~, (~) ~ artificial ~, (~) ~ manufactured ~ · Portlandzement-Betonmarmor m, Portlandzement-Marmorbeton m

(~) ~ man-made marble, (~) ~ imitation ~, (~) ~ artificial ~, (~) ~ manufactured ~ · Portlandzement-Betonmarmor m, Portlandzement-Marmorbeton m

(~) ~ manufactured marble, (~) ~ artificial ~, (~) ~ imitation ~, (~) ~ man-made ~ · Portlandzement-Betonmarmor m, Portlandzement-Marmorbeton m

~ ~ mortar · Portlandzementmörtel m

~-cement (mortar) stucco (US); ~ (external) rendering (Brit.); ~ exterior plaster, ~ external plaster [See remark under 'Außen)(Ver)Putz'] · Portlandzement(außen)(ver)putz m

portland cement panel · Portlandzement(beton)tafel f

~ ~-sand grout · Ausgußmörtel m

~ cement slurry → ~ ~ grout(ing) (compound)

Portland cement type I (US); OPC, normal portland cement, ordinary portland cement, Portland cement for general use · normaler Portlandzement m, gewöhnlicher ~ [in Deutschland Z 225]

~ ~ ~ II (US); moderate sulphate resisting cement, moderate heat of hydration cement · mäßiger Gipsschlackenzement m, ~ Sulfathüttenzement

~ ~ ~ IV (US); low heat (of hydration) cement, slow hardening cement · Portlandzement m mit sehr geringer Abbindewärme, Massenbauzement

~ pozzolanic cement, Portland-pozzolan ~ [It is made of a mix(ture) of portland cement clinker and pozzolan, a siliceous material which will react with lime in the presence of water. The pozzolan may be a natural material or artificial product such as blast furnace slag] · Puzzolanportlandzement m

~ stone [oolitic freestone] · Portlandstein m

~ trass cement · Traßzement m, TrZ; Traßportlandzement [Fehlname] [DIN 1164 und 1167]

Portuguese architecture · portugiesische Architektur f, ~ Baukunst f

position energy, potential ~, energy of position, geodetic head [It is the energy possessed by a body in virtue of its position relative to some zero position] · Potential n, Energie f der Lage, potentielle Energie, latente Energie

~ function · Ortsfunktion f

~ of load, load position · Laststellung f

~ ~ the sun, location ~ ~ ~ · Sonnenstand m, Stand der Sonne

positional welding, tack ~ · Heftschweißen n, Heftschweißung f

positive area of influence, ~ influence area · positive Einflußfläche f

~ bending [It occurs at a section when the deflected form of the beam is concave upwards at the section. Under such bending, tension occurs in the lower fibres of the beam] · positive Biegung f, positives Biegen n

~ ~ moment · positives Biegemoment n, ~ Biegungsmoment

~ moment · positives Moment n

~ reinforcement [Reinforcement placed in concrete to resist positive bending moments] · Armierung f gegen positive Biegemomente, Bewehrung ~ ~ ~, (Stahl)Einlagen fpl ~ ~ ~

~ rigidity, ~ stiffness · positive Starrheit f, ~ Steifigkeit

~ rotation · positive Drehung f

~ shear(ing) · positiver Schub m

~ stiffness, ~ rigidity · positive Starrheit f, ~ Steifigkeit

~ total-flow gas meter · Balgengaszähler m

post · (Dach)Stuhlsäule f

~, pole · Pfahl m, Pfosten m

post — potash glass

~, leg, wood(en) pillar, timber pillar · Pfosten m, Stiel m, Ständer m, (Stand-) Säule f [Senkrechtes Holz beim Fachwerk-, Stab-, Ständer- und Dachstuhlbau]

~ → frame ~

~ **and beam construction**: storey post and beams (Brit.); story post and beams (US) · Ständerbau m

~ ~ ~ **house** · Pfostenhaus n, Ständerhaus

postal knocker [A letter plate which includes a door knocker] · Briefeinwurf m mit (Tür)Klopfer

post-buckling · überkritisches Knicken n

~ **behaviour** (Brit.); ~ behavior (US) · Nachknickverhalten n

post-chlorinated polyvinyl chlorid(e) (US); ~ ~ chloride (Brit.); ~ PVC · C-PVC n, nachchloriertes PVC

~ **PVC**; ~ polyvinyl chlorid(e) (US); ~ polyvinyl chloride (Brit.) · C-PVC n, nachchloriertes PVC

postcooling · Nachkühlen n

postern [A small secondary entrance, usually at the rear of a building] · Hintereingang m

poster panel · Plakattafel f

post-fabrication · Nachverarbeitung f

post-hole · Pfostenloch n

posticum [The Latin term for the rear porch of a temple] · Posticum n

Post-Impressionism · Nachimpressionismus m

post-medi(a)eval · nachmittelalterlich

post-Norman · nachnormannisch

post office cable, telecommunication ~; GPO ~ (Brit.) · Fernmeldekabel n

~ ~ **line**, telecommunication ~; GPO ~ (Brit.) · Fernmeldeleitung f

~ ~ **tower**, telecommunication ~; GPO ~ (Brit.) · Fernmeldeturm m

posts · Ständer(fach)werk n [Die Stiele eines Fachwerkbaues]

post-shrinkage · Nachschwinden n, NS

post-stressing [obsolete] → post-tensioning

post-tensioned brickwork · vorgespanntes Ziegelmauerwerk n mit nachträglichem Verbund

post-tensioning; post-stressing [obsolete] [The tendons are tensioned after the concrete has hardened] · (Vor-)Spannen n im erhärteten Beton

post-top luminaire (US); ~ light fitting (Brit.); ~ (light(ing)) fixture · (Mast-)Aufsatzleuchte f

post-war architecture · Nachkriegsarchitektur f, Nachkriegsbaukunst f

~ **block**, ~ building · Nachkriegsgebäude n

~ **building**, ~ block · Nachkriegsgebäude n

~ **housing** · Nachkriegswohnungsbau m

post-welded heat treatment · Wärmebehandlung f nach dem Schweißen

POT → potable water

pot → hollow block

~ **bearing** · Topflager n

~ **clay** · Hafenton m [Ton, der zur Herstellung von Glashäfen und Schmelztiegeln für die Stahlindustrie dient. Anmerkung: In Großbritannien bezeichnet man mit dem Ausdruck "pot clay" auch eine aus Hafenton und Schamottezusatz bestehende Masse, die zur Herstellung von Glashäfen und Schmelztiegeln für die Stahlindustrie dient]

~ **floor** → hollow block ~

~ **for walls** → hollow block ~ ~

~ **furnace** · Hafenofen m [Glasherstellung]

~ **-lead**, graphite, black lead [An allotropic crystalline form of carbon] · Graphit m

pot life [The period after mixing the two packs of a two-pack paint during which the paint remains usable] · Topfzeit f, Verarbeitungszeit

~ **making machine** → hollow-block ~ ~

~ **masonry wall** → hollow block ~ ~

~ ~ **(work)** → hollow block ~ (~)

~ **mould** → hollow-block ~

~ **-opal glass** · hafenfertiges getrübtes Opalglas n

pot roof → hollow tile ~

~ **ruby** · hafenfertiges Rubinglas n

~ **step**, hollow block ~, cavity block ~ · Block-Hohlstufe f

~ **wall** → hollow block ~

potable water, drinking ~, POT W · Trinkwasser n, Gebrauchswasser

~ ~ **network**, drinking ~ ~ · Trinkwassernetz n

~ ~ **pipework for buildings** · Trinkwasserleitungsanlagen fpl in Grundstücken [DIN 1988]

~ ~ **pressure pipe**, drinking ~ ~ ~ · Trinkwasser-Druckrohr n

~ ~ **reservoir**, drinking ~ ~, ~ ~ tank · Trinkwasserbehälter m

~ ~ **steel pipe line** · Trinkwasser-Stahlrohrleitung f [DIN 4279]

~ ~ **supply**, drinking ~ ~ · Trinkwasserversorgung f

~ ~ ~ **area**, ~ ~ ~ zone, drinking ~ ~ ~ · Trinkwasserversorgungsgebiet n

~ ~ ~ **pipe**, drinking ~ ~ ~ · Trinkwasserrohr n

~ ~ ~ **piping**, drinking ~ ~ ~ · Trinkwasserrohrleitung f

~ ~ **tank**, drinking ~ ~, ~ ~ reservoir · Trinkwasserbehälter m

potash → potassium carbonate

~ **glass**, potassium carbonate ~ · Kaliglas n

potash-lead crystal glass — poured(-)in(-)place ... 746

~-**lead crystal glass,** potassium oxide-lead ~ ~, (full) lead ~ (~) · englisches Kristallglas n, Kalibleiglas, Bleikristall-(glas) [*Unter Zusatz von Bleioxid hergestellt*]

potash-lime glass, potassium carbonate-lime ~, Bohemian crystal (~) · Kalikalkglas n, böhmisches Kristallglas [*mit Kalk erschmolzen*]

potash mica, common ~, muscovy glass, muscovite · heller Glimmer m, Kaliglimmer, Muskovit m

~ **soap** · Kaliseife f, Schmierseife

potassium bromide · Kaliumbromid n, Bromkali n, KBr

~ **carbonate,** (carbonate of) potash · Kaliumkarbonat n, Pottasche f, kohlensaures Kalium n, K_2CO_3

~ ~ **glass,** potash ~ · Kaliglas n

~ ~-**lime glass,** potash-lime ~, Bohemian crystal (~) · Kalikalkglas n, böhmisches Kristallglas [*mit Kalk erschmolzen*]

~ **chlorate** · Kaliumchlorat n, $KClO_3$

~ **chloride** (Brit.); ~ **chlorid(e)** (US) · Kaliumchlorid n

~ **cyanide** · Kaliumzyanid n, Zyankali n, KCN

~ **fluosilicate** · Kaliumfluat n

~ **hydrate** → caustic potash

~ **hydroxide** (Brit.) → caustic potash

~ **nitrate,** niter, saltpeter · Kalisalpeter m, Kaliumnitrat n, KNO_3

~ **oxide-lead crystal glass,** potash-lead ~ ~, (full) lead ~ (~) · englisches Kristallglas n, Kalibleiglas, Bleikristall-(glas) n [*Unter Zusatz von Bleioxid hergestellt*]

~ **permanganate** · Kaliumpermanganat n, $KMnO_4$

~ **silicate** · Kaliumsilikat n, Kaliwasserglas n, K_2SiO_3

~ **sulfate,** sulfate of potash (US); potassium sulphate, sulphate of potash (Brit.) · Kaliumsulfat n

potatoe cellar · Kartoffelkeller m

~ **meal** · Kartoffelmehl n

~ **peeler (machine)** · Kartoffelschälmaschine f

~ **starch** · Kartoffelstärke f

~ ~ **paste** · Kartoffelstärkekleister m

potent cross · Henkelkreuz n

potential energy, position ~, energy of position, geodetic head [*It is the energy possessed by a body in virtue of its position relative to some zero position*] · Energie f der Lage, Potential n, latente Energie, potentielle Energie

~ **equation** · Potentialgleichung f

potter's clay, plastic ~, ball ~ · hochplastischer Ton m, Letten m, Ballton, Töpferton

~ **stone** → plaster rock

pottery · Gefäßkeramik f, Feinkeramik

~ **industry** · feinkeramische Industrie f, Feinkeramikindustrie, Gefäßkeramikindustrie

~ **mosaic** · Tonmosaik n

poultry hall · Geflügelhalle f

~ **netting** · Hühnerdrahtgeflecht n

pounce · Feinbimsmehl n, Bimsfeinmehl

to pour, to concrete, to cast · betonieren

~ ~ **in a hot state** · heiß vergießen [*Rohrmuffe*]

pour consistency → pourable ~

pourable · (ver)gießbar, gießfähig

pour(able) consistency, ~ consistence · Gießkonsistenz f, Gießsteife f

poured aerated concrete → cast(-)in(-)situ ~ ~

~ **architectural concrete** → cast-in-place ~ ~

~-**concrete foundation wall** · Ortbeton-Gründungswand f

poured(-)in(-)place, cast(-)in(-)place, (cast(-))in(-)situ, in(-)situ(-)cast, site-placed · ortbetoniert, Ortbeton........

~ **aerated concrete** → cast(-)in(-)situ ~ ~

~ **architectural concrete** → cast-in-place ~ ~

~ **concrete,** in(-)situ(-)(cast) ~, cast(-) in(-)situ ~, cast(-)in(-)place ~, site-placed ~, field ~ · Ortbeton m [*DIN 1045*]

~ (~) **balcony,** in(-)situ (cast) (~) ~, cast(-)in(-)place (~) ~, cast-in-place (~) ~, site-placed (~) ~, field ~ ~ · Ortbetonbalkon m

~ (~) **cable duct,** site-placed (~) ~, cast-in-place (~) ~ ~, field ~ ~ ~, cast(-)in(-)situ (~) ~, in(-)situ (cast) (~) ~ ~ · Ortbetonkanal m

~ (~) **eave(s) unit,** site-placed (~) ~, cast-in-place (~) ~, (cast-)in-situ (~) ~ ~, in(-)situ (cast) (~) ~ ~, field ~ ~ ~ · Ortbeton-Traufenteil m,

~ (~) **filling,** cast-in-place (~) ~, site-placed (~) ~, field ~ ~, cast(-)in(-)situ (~) ~, in(-)situ (cast) (~) ~ · Ortbetonfüllung f

~ (~) **floor,** cast-in-place (~) ~, site-placed (~) ~, field ~ ~, cast(-)in(-)situ (~) ~, in(-)situ (cast) (~) ~ · Ortbetondecke f

~ (~) **frame,** ~ (~) framing, cast-in-place (~) ~, site-placed (~) ~, field ~ ~, cast(-)in(-)situ (~) ~, in(-)situ (cast) (~) ~ · Ortbetonrahmen m

~ (~) **rib(bed) floor,** cast-in-place (~) ~ ~, cast(-)in(-)situ (~) ~ ~, in(-)situ (cast) (~) ~ ~, site-placed (~) ~ ~, field ~ ~ ~ · Ortbeton-Rippendecke f

~ (~) **shell,** site-placed (~) ~, cast-in-place (~) ~, field ~ ~, cast(-)in(-)situ (~) ~, in(-)situ (cast) (~) ~ · Ortbetonschale f

~ **(~) stair(case)**, field ~ ~, site-placed (~) ~, cast-in-place (~) ~, cast(-)in(-)situ (~) ~, in(-)situ (cast) (~) ~ · Ortbetontreppe f

~ **(~) structure**, cast-in-place (~) ~, site-placed (~) ~, field ~ ~, cast(-)in(-)situ (~) ~, in(-)situ (cast) (~) ~ · Ortbetonbauwerk n

~ **light(weight) concrete**, cast(-)in(-)situ ~ ~, in(-)situ (cast) ~ ~, cast-in-place ~ ~, site-placed ~ ~, field ~ ~ · Ortleichtbeton m, Leicht-Ortbeton

~ **mortar**, cast(-)in(-)situ ~, in(-)situ (cast) ~, cast-in-place ~, site-placed ~, field ~ · Ortmörtel m

~ **reinforced concrete**, ~ (~) R.C., site-placed ~ ~, field ~ ~, cast-in-place ~ ~, cast(-)in(-)situ ~ ~, in(-)situ (cast) ~ ~ · Ort-Stahlbeton m, Stahlortbeton

~ ~ ~ **floor**, ~ R.C. ~, cast(-)in(-)situ ~ ~, in(-)situ (cast) ~ ~ ~, cast-in-place ~ ~ ~, site-placed ~ ~ ~, field ~ ~ ~ · Ortstahlbetondecke f, Stahlortbetondecke

poured joint · Vergußfuge f

pouring, concreting, placing of concrete, concrete placing · Betoneinbringung f, Betonieren n, Betoneinbau m, Betonier(ungs)arbeiten fpl, Betonverarbeitung, Einbringen des Betons

~, **joint** ~ · (Fugen)Verguß m, (Fugen)Ausguß

~ **compound** → joint ~ ~

~ ~ **for stone sett paving** → (joint) pouring compound for (natural) ~ ~ ~

~ **rope**, joint runner · Strick m [Strick-Blei-Dichtung]

~**-type granular insulation material**, ~ ~ insulation(-grade) ~ · Schüttdämmaterial n

pouring wool · (Dämm)Schüttwolle f

powder additive for mortar · Mörtelwirkstoffpulver n, Mörtelzusatzpulver

~ **casein** → powdered ~

~ **cleaner** → clean(s)ing powder

~ **clean(s)ing agent** → clean(s)ing powder

~ **coal** → powdered ~

~ **coating** · Pulverbeschichten n

~ ~ · Pulverlack m

~ **cork**, powdered ~, ground ~, cork powder, cork flour · Korkmehl n

~ **corundum**, powdered ~, corundum powder · Korundmehl n

~ **gold**, powdered ~, gold powder · Pudergold n, Staubgold, Goldpuder n, Goldstaub m

~ **gun** · Pistole f für das Pulverspritzverfahren, Spritz~ ~ ~ ~ [Spritzmetallisierung]

~ **insulation** · Pulverisolierung f

~ **lead** → powdered ~

~ **limestone** → powdered ~

~ **metallurgy** · Pulvermetallurgie f

~ **room** · Kosmetikraum m [Hotel]

~ **rubber** → powdered ~

~ **solder**, powdered ~; pulverized ~ (US); pulverised ~ (Brit.) · pulverisiertes Lötzinn n, ~ Lot n

~ **spray(ing) method**, ~ ~ system, metal powder ~ · Pulverspritzverfahren n [Spritzmetallisierung. Durch Injektorwirkung wird Pulver aus einem Behälter abgesaugt und durch den Preßstrom aufgespritzt]

powdered, powdery, in powder form; pulverized (US); pulverised (Brit.) · pulv(e)rig, pulverförmig, gepulvert, pulverartig, pulverisiert

powder(ed) additive [A powder added in small quantities to the **binder** to produce some desired modifications to the properties of the mix(ture) or of the hardened product] · Wirkstoffpulver n, Zusatzpulver

~ ~ **for concrete**, concrete additive powder · Betonwirkstoffpulver n, Betonzusatzpulver

~ **adhesive**, ~ glue, glue powder, adhesive powder · Leimpulver n, Trockenleim m, Pulverleim [Leim in Pulverform, meist Pflanzenleim oder Zelluloseleim]

~ **admix(ture)** [A powder added in small quantities to the **mix(ture)** to produce some desired modifications to the properties of the mix(ture) or of the hardened product] · Wirkstoffpulver n, Zusatzpulver

~ **asbestos**, asbestos powder, asbestos flour · Asbestmehl n, Asbestpulver n

~ **asphalt** → ~ natural rock ~

~ **basalt**, basalt(ic) meal, basalt(ic) powder · Basaltmehl n

~ **bronze**, bronze powder, bronze pigment, bronze flakes · Bronzepulver n [Metalleffektpigment]

~ **calcium carbide**, calcium carbide powder · Kalziumkarbidpulver n

~ **caoutchouc** → natural rubber powder

~ **casein**, casein powder · Kaseinpulver n

~ **clay**, clay powder, finely ground fire clay · Tonmehl n, Tonpulver n

~ **cleaner** → clean(s)ing powder

~ **clean(s)ing agent** → clean(s)ing powder

~ **coal**, coal powder; pulverised coal (Brit.); pulverized coal · Kohle(n)staub m, Kohle(n)pulver n

~ ~ **fuel**, coal powder ~; pulverized coal ~ (US); pulverised coal ~ (Brit.) Kohle(n)staub m als Brenstoff, Kohle(n)pulver n ~ ~

~ **colouring agent**, ~ ~ substance, ~ ~ matter (Brit.); ~ coloring ~ (US) · färbendes Pulver n

~ ~ **matter** → ~ ~ agent

~ ~ **substance** → ~ ~ agent

~ **concrete hardener**, ~ ~ hardening agent · pulv(e)riges Betonhärtungsmittel n, ~ Betonhärtemittel, pulv(e)riger

powder(ed) concrete hardener — power failure

Betonhärtungsstoff m, pulv(e)riger Betonhärter m, Betonhärtepulver n, Betonhärtungspulver

~ **cork**, ground ~, cork powder, cork flour · Korkmehl n

~ **corundum**, corundum powder · Korundmehl n, Korundpulver n

~ **densifying admix(ture)** ~ densifying agent, ~ densifier, ~ integral waterproofer, ~ ~ waterproofing agent, ~ ~ waterrepeller, ~ ~ water repelling agent, ~ ~ water repellent admix(ture) · pulv(e)riges (Ab)Dicht(ungs)mittel n, ~ Sperrzusatzmittel, ~ DM, DM-Pulver n, Sperrpulver, sperrendes Pulver, puv(e)riger (Ab)Dicht(ungs)stoff m, pulv(e)riger Sperrzusatz(stoff)

~ **glass** → glass powder

~ **glue,** ~ adhesive, glue powder, adhesive powder · Leimpulver n, Trockenleim m, Pulverleim [*Leim in Pulverform, meist Pflanzenleim oder Zelluloseleim*]

~ **gold,** gold powder · Pudergold n, Staubgold, Goldpuder n, Goldstaub m

~ ~ **bronze,** gold bronze powder · Goldbronzepulver n

~ **granite,** granite flour, granite dust, granite powder · Granitmehl n, Granitpulver n, Granitstaub m, Granitpuder n

~ **gypsum,** ground ~, gypsum powder · gemahlener Gips m, Gipsmehl n, Gipspulver n

~ **hardener,** ~ hardening agent · Härtepulver n, Härtungspulver, pulv(e)riges Härtungsmittel n, pulv(e)riges Härtemittel, pulv(e)riger Härtungsstoff m, pulv(er)riger Härter m

~ **hibiscus root,** hibiscus root powder · gepulverte Eibischwurzel f

~ **integral waterrepeller,** ~ ~ water repellent admix(ture), ~ ~ water repelling agent, ~ ~ waterproofing agent, ~ ~ waterproofer, ~ densifying agent, ~ densifying admix(ture), ~ densifier · pulv(e)riges (Ab)Dicht(ungs)mittel n ~ Sperrzusatzmittel, ~ DM, DM-Pulver n, Sperrpulver, pulv(e)riger Sperrzusatz(stoff) m, sperrendes Pulver, pulv(e)riger (Ab)Dicht(ungs)stoff m

~ **iron,** iron powder · Eisenpulver n

~ **kaolin,** kaolin powder · Kaolinpulver n

~ **lead,** lead powder · Bleipulver n, Bleimehl n

~ **leather,** leather powder · Ledermehl n

~ **limestone,** ground ~, pulverized ~, limestone dust, limestone powder, flour limestone · Kalksteinpulver n, Kalk(stein)mehl n

~ **marble** → marble flour

~ **metal,** metal(lic) powder · Metallpulver n

~ **mica** → mica flour

~ **mineral,** mineral powder · Mineralmehl n, Mineralpulver n

~ **(natural rock) asphalt** · (Natur-)Asphalt(roh)mehl n [*Gemahlener Naturasphalt mit mindestens 4 Gewichts-% natürlichem Bitumen und mindestens 40 Gewichts-%Füller – Körnung unter 0,09 mm – bezogen auf das bitumenfreie Mehl*]

~ **(~ ~)** ~ **mastic** · Naturasphaltmastix m

~ ~ **rubber** → natural rubber powder

~ **paint remover,** ~ ~ stripper, paint remover in powder form, paint stripper in powder form · (Ab)Beizpulver n, Ablaugpulver, pulv(e)riges (Ab)Beizmittel

~ ~ **stripper** → ~ ~ remover

~ **pumice (stone),** pumice meal, pumice dust, pumice powder · (Natur)Bims(stein)mehl n

~ **raw rubber** → natural rubber powder

~ **retarder** · Pulververzögerer m

~ **rubber,** rubber powder · Gummipulver n, Gummimehl n

~ **sandstone,** sandstone powder · Sandsteinmehl n

~ **silver,** silver powder · Pulversilber n, Silberpulver n

~ **soap,** soap powder · Seifenpulver n

~ **solder;** pulverized ~ (US); pulverised ~ (Brit.) · pulverisiertes Lötzinn n, ~ Lot n

~ **spar,** spar dust, spar flour, spar powder · Spatmehl n, Spatstaub m, Spatpulver n

~ **sulfur,** sulfur powder (US); powder(ed) sulphur, sulphur powder (Brit.) · Schwefelpulver n

~ **sulphur,** sulphur powder (Brit.); powder(ed) sulfur, sulfur powder (US) · Schwefelpulver n

~ **talc** → fine ~

~ ~ **surfacing** → talcum (powder) ~

~ **trass,** trass powder · Traßmehl n

~ **white pigment,** white pigment powder · Weißpigmentpulver n

~ **zinc,** zinc powder, zinc dust [*It is used as the pigment in zinc-rich paint. The zinc powder acts not only as a pigment but as a corrosion inhibitor*] · Zinkpulver n, Zinkstaub m

powdery, powdered, in powder form; pulverized (US); pulverised (Brit.) · pulv(e)rig, pulverförmig, gepulvert, pulverartig, pulverisiert

powel, ball · Turmknopf m

power, capability, property, capacity, quality · Eigenschaft f, Vermögen n, Fähigkeit f

~ **circut** · Stromkreis m

~ **consumer,** electrical ~ ~, electric current ~, electricity ~ · Stromabnehmer m

~ **-driven stud** · eingeschossener Stiftbolzen m

power failure, electrical ~ ~, electric current ~, (electricity) supply ~ · Stromausfall m

powerful gravity · wuchtige Schwere f
power of expression, expressiveness · Ausdruckskraft f, Aussagekraft

~ ~ **hardening** · Härtungsvermögen n, Er~

~ ~ **initial set(ting),** property ~ ~ ~, capacity ~ ~ ~, quality ~ ~ ~, initial set(ting) power, initial set(-ting) property, initial set(ting) quality, initial set(ting) capacity · Erstarrungsfähigkeit f, Erstarrungsvermögen n, Erstarrungseigenschaft f [Beton; Mörtel]

~ ~ **set(ting)** → set(ting) power

~ **plant** · E-Werk n, Elektrizitätswerk, Kraftwerk

~ **plug** · Netzstecker m

~ **point for cleaners,** (plug) socket ~, socket outlet ~ ~ · Staubsauger-(steck)dose f

~ **requirement,** electric ~ ~ · Kraftbedarf m, Strombedarf, Elektrizitätsbedarf

~ **socket,** receptacle · Kraftsteckdose f, Starkstrom-Steckdose

~ **supply,** electric ~ ~, electricity ~, electric current ~ · Stromversorgung f, Elektrizitätsversorgung, Energieversorgung

~ **tariff,** electrical ~ ~, electric current ~, electricity ~ · Stromtarif m

pozzolan(a) → pozzolan(ic material)

pozzolanic aggregate · Puzzolanzuschlag(stoff) m

~ **cement** [Not to be confused with Portland pozzolanic cement] · Puzzolanzement m

~ ~ ~ **of artificial pozzolan(ic material)** · Puzzolanzement m aus künstlicher Puzzolane

~ ~ ~ **natural pozzolan(ic material)** · Puzzolanzement m aus natürlicher Puzzolane

pozzolan(ic material), pozz(u)olana, pozzolan [A siliceous or siliceous and aluminous material, which in itself possesses little or no cementitious value but will in finely divided form and in the presence of moisture, chemically react with calcium hydroxide at ordinary temperatures to form compounds possessing cementitious properties] · hydraulischer Zuschlag m, Puzzolane f, [Plural: die Puzzolanen]

pozzolanic mortar · Puzzolanmörtel m

pozz(u)olana, pozzolan(ic material), pozzolan [A siliceous or siliceous and aluminous material, which in itself possesses little or no cementitious value but will, in finely divided form and in the presence of moisture, chemically react with calcium hydroxide at ordinary temperatures to form compounds possessing cementitious properties] · Puzzolane f, hydraulischer Zuschlag m [Plural: die Puzzolanen]

PP → polypropylene
PPGL → (polished) plate (glass)
p-phenyl phenol · p-Phenylphenol n
(practically) absolute demineralization · Vollentsalzung f [Wasser]

practice, technique, technic · Technik f [Als Anwendung, nicht als Wissenschaft]

~ **hall** · Trainingshalle f, Übungshalle

prairie house [Frank Lloyd Wright's earliest major contribution to modern architecture. Characterised by X, L and T-shaped plans] · Präriehaus n

Prairie style [Evolved by Frank Lloyd Wright] · Präriestil m

pram storage room, perambulator ~ ~ · Kinderwagenraum m

Pratt (roof) truss (US); Linville (~) ~, N-truss · Pratt(-Dach)binder m

prayer niche, praying ~, mihrab, mehrab · Gebetsnische f [Moschee]

~-**tower,** minaret · Gebetsturm m, Minarett n

praying niche, prayer ~, mihrab, mehrab · Gebetsnische f [Moschee]

pre-assembled [Fixed together on or off the site before incorporation into a building or structure] · vorzusammengebaut

~ · vormontiert

prebending · Vorbiegen n [als Tätigkeit]

~ · Vorbiegung f [als Ergebnis der Tätigkeit]

preboring · Vorbohren n

pre-carbonation (treatment) · Vorkarbonatisieren n

(pre)cast · vorgefertigt [aus Beton]

~ **aerated concrete,** prefab(ricated) ~ ~ · Fertigteil-Porenbeton m, Poren-Fertigteilbeton

(~) ~ ~ wall panel, prefab(ricated) ~ ~ ~ · Porenbetonwand(bau)tafel f

(~) ~ ~ ~ slab, prefab(ricated) ~ ~ ~ · Porenbetonwand(bau)platte f

(~) ~ ~ works, prefab(ricated) ~ ~ ~ · Porenbetonwerk n

(pre)cast air-raid sheltering bunker → ~ (concrete) ~ ~ ~

~ **apartment tower** (US) → ~ residence ~

((pre)cast) architectural concrete · Architektur-Betonerzeugnis n, Architektur-Betonstein m

~ ~ **(~) compound unit,** prefabricated ~ ~ ~ ~ · architektonischer (Beton)Fertigteil m, ~ Fertigbetonteil, ~ (Beton)Montageteil, ~ Montagebetonteil, ~ (Beton)Fertigbauteil, architektonisches (Beton)Fertigteil n, architektonisches Fertigbetonteil, architektonisches (Beton)Montageteil, architektonisches Montagebetonteil, architektonisches (Beton)Fertigbauteil

(pre)cast architectural (concrete)..—(pre)cast (concrete).. 750

~ ~ (~) product, architectural concrete ~, architectural (pre)cast concrete ~ · Architektur-Betonerzeugnis n, Architektur-Betonstein m

~ articles → (mass-produced) (pre)cast (concrete) ware

(pre)cast beam, ~ concrete ~, prefab(ricated) concrete ~ · Montage(-Beton)balken(träger) m, Fertig(teil)-Betonbalken(träger), (Beton-)Fertig(teil)-balken(träger)

(~) ~ and filler floor, cast ~ ~ ~ ~ · Balkendecke f mit Zwischenbauteilen [DIN 4225. Decke mit Stahlbeton-Fertigbalken im Mittenabstand von höchstens 1,25 m mit Zwischenbauteilen, deren Mitwirkung beim Nachweis der Tragfähigkeit der Decke nicht in Rechnung gestellt wird, wohl aber unter Umständen Ortbeton zur Verstärkung der Druckzone des Balkens]

((pre)cast) block flue → ~ (concrete) ~ ~

(pre)cast bomb shelter → ~ (concrete) ~ ~

((pre)cast) (building) component → ~ (concrete) building) unit

~ (~) member → ~ (concrete) (building) unit

~ (~) unit → ~ concrete (~) ~

~ cladding panel → ~ (concrete) (in)filler ~

~ ~ slab → ~ (concrete) (in)filller ~

(pre)cast column → ~ concrete ~

~ ~ ~ → ~ (concrete) (lighting) ~

((pre)cast) component → ~ (concrete) (building) unit

~ compound unit → ~ concrete ~ ~

~ ~ ~ for building construction → ~ concrete ~ ~ ~ ~ ~

(pre)cast concrete → ~ (~) product

~ ~, prefab(ricated) ~ [Concrete cast elsewhere than its final position in the structure] · Fertigteilbeton m

~ ~ admix(ture), ~ ~ agent · Betonstein-Wirkstoff m, Betonstein-Zusatz(-mittel) m, (n)

~ (~) air-raid sheltering bunker, ~ (~) bomb shelter, prefab(ricated) concrete air-raid sheltering bunker, prefab(ricated) concrete bomb shelter · Bombenschutzbunker m aus Betonfertigteilen, (Luft)Schutzbunker ~ ~

((pre)cast) (~) articles → (mass-produced) (pre)cast (concrete) ware

(pre)cast (concrete) balcony, prefab(ricated) ~ ~ · (Beton-)Fertigbalkon m

~ (~) beam, prefab(ricated) ~ ~ · Montage(-Beton)balken(träger) m, Fertig(teil)-Betonbalken(träger), (Beton-)Fertig(teil)balken(träger)

~ (~) ~ floor, prefab(ricated) ~ ~ ~ ~ · (Beton-)Fertig(teil)balkendecke f, Montage(-Beton)balkendecke, Fertig(teil)-Betonbalkendecke

(~) (~) (~) lintel block, (~) (~) (~) ~ tile; (~) (~) (~) lintol ~ [deprecated] [See remark under 'Block'] · (Beton)Sturzblock(stein) m, (Beton-)Sturzstein

(pre)cast concrete block → ~ ~ (building) ~

~ (~) ~ flue, ~ (~) tile ~, prefab(ricated) ~ ~ ~ · Betonblock(stein)zug m, Betonsteinzug

(pre)cast (concrete) bomb shelter, ~ (~) airraid sheltering bunker, prefab(ricated) concrete air-raid sheltering bunker, prefab(ricated) concrete bomb shelter · Schutzbunker m aus Betonfertigteilen, Luft~ ~ ~, Bomben ~ ~ ~

(~) (~) bond beam block, (~) (~) ~ ~ tile, prefabri(cated) ~ ~ ~ ~ [See remark under 'Block'] · Balkenblock(stein) m, Balkenstein, Beton~

~ (~) boundary beam → ~ (~) edge ~

~ (~) building, ~ (~) block, prefab(ricated) ~ ~ · (Beton-)Fertig(teil)-gebäude n, Fertig(teil)-Betongebäude

(pre)cast concrete (building) block, (~) ~ (~) tile, prefab(ricated) ~ (~) ~, CONC B, conc blk [A walling unit (other than a unit used for bonding, e.g. half block) exceeding in length, width or height the dimensjon specified for a brick in BS 3921. The height of the block shall not exceed either its length or six times its thickness to avoid confusion with slabs or panels. Definition from B.S. 2028, 1364. See also remark under 'Block'] · Betonblock(stein) m, Betonstein

~ (~) (~) component → ~ (~) (~) unit

~ (~) (~) member → ~ (~) (~) unit

~ (~) (~) unit, ~ (~) (~) member, ~ (~) (~) component, prefab(ricated) ~ (~) ~, (concrete) cast(ing) ~ · Betonmontageelement n, Beton(bau)element, Betonmontagekörper m, Beton(bau)körper, Betonfertig(bau)körper, Betonfertig(bau)element [Fehlnamen: Beton(bau)einheit f, Betonmontageeinheit]

(pre)cast (concrete) chimney, shell-cast (~) ~, prefab(ricated) ~ ~ [The outer shell is a precast structure of high-density concrete; the inner shell is of insulating concrete] · (Beton-)Fertig(teil)schornstein m, Fertig(teil)-Betonschornstein

~ ~ cill (Brit.) → ~ ~ sill

((pre)cast) (concrete) cladding, prefab(ricated) ~ ~ · Beton-(Außen)Versteifungswand f

~ (~) ~ panel → ~ (~) (in)filler ~

~ (~) ~ slab → ~ (~) (in)filler ~

(pre)cast (concrete) column, ~ (~) support, prefab(ricated) ~ ~ · (Beton-)Fertigstütze f, Fertig-Betonstütze

~ (~) ~ ~ → ~ (~) (lighting) ~

(pre)cast (concrete) component → ~ (~) (building) unit

(pre)cast (concrete) ... — (pre)cast (concrete) gutter

~ (~) **compound unit,** prefab(ricated) ~ ~ ~ ~ · (Beton)Fertig(bau)teil *m, n,* (Beton)Montage(bau)teil, Fertigbeton(bau)teil, Monatagebeton(bau)teil, [*Fehlname: Betonbauteil*]

~ (~) ~ ~ **for building construction,** prefab(ricated) ~ ~ ~ ~ ~ ~ · Hochbau(-Beton)Fertig(bau)teil *m, n,* Hochbau(-Beton)Montage(bau)teil, Hochbau-Fertigbeton(bau)teil, Hochbau-Montagebeton(bau)teil

(pre)cast (concrete) construction, prefab(ricated) ~ ~, industrialized ~ ~, ~ (~) system ~ · Bauen *n* mit Betonfertigteilen, ~ ~ Betonmontageteilen, (Beton)Fertig(teil)bau *m,* (Beton)Montage-(teil)bau, Fertigbetonbau [*Fehlname: Betonelementbau*]

~ (~) ~ **division,** prefab(ricated) ~ ~ ~ · (Beton-)Fertig(teil)bauabteilung *f* [*einer Firma*]

~ (~) ~ **method,** ~ (~) system building ~, prefab(ricated) (concrete) construction ~, prefab(ricated) (concrete) system building ~, industrialized construction ~, system building ~ · (Beton-)Montagebauweise *f,* (Beton-)Fertig(teil)bauweise, (Beton-)Elementbauweise

~ (~) **cupola** → ~ (~) dome

~ (~) **curb of white granite aggregate;** ~ (~) kerb ~ ~ ~ ~ (Brit.); prefab(ricated) ~ ~ ~ ~ ~ ~ · Kunstgranitbordstein *m* mit weißem Quarzitkorn

~ (~) **dome,** ~ (~) cupola, prefab(ricated) ~ ~ · (Beton-)Fertig(teil)kuppel *f,* Fertig(teil)-Betonkuppel

~ (~) **door frame,** prefab(ricated) ~ ~ ~ · (Beton-)Fertigtürrahmen *m,* Fertig-Betontürrahmen

((pre)cast) (concrete) **eave(s) gutter,** ~ (~) ~ trough, ~ (~) ~ trow, prefab(ricated) ~ ~ ~ [*B.S. 2908*] · (Beton-)Fertig(teil)traufrinne *f*

(pre)cast (concrete) **edge beam,** ~ (~) boundary ~, prefab(ricated) ~ ~ ~ · (Beton-)Fertigrandbalken(träger) *m*

((pre)cast) (concrete) **end-block,** prefab(ricated) ~ ~ · (Beton-)Fertig-Endblock *m,* Fertig-Betonendblock

~ (~) **exposed aggregate panel,** prefab(ricated) ~ ~ ~ ~ · (Beton-)Fertigtafel *f* mit bloßgelegten Zuschlägen, ~ ~ freigelegten ~, Fertig-Betontafel ~ ~ ~

~ (~) ~ ~ **slab,** prefab(ricated) ~ ~ ~ ~ · (Beton-)Fertig(teil)platte *f* mit freigelegten Zuschlägen, Fertig(teil)-Betonplatte ~ ~ ~ ~, ~ ~ bloßgelegten ~

(pre)cast (concrete) **façade,** prefab(ricated) ~ ~ ~ · (Beton-)Fertig(teil)fassade *f,* (Beton-)Montagefassade, (Beton-)Elementfassade, Fertig(teil)betonfassade, Montagebetonfassade

((pre)cast) **concrete factory,** ~ ~ plant, (concrete) (pre)casting ~, ((pre)cast) concrete ware ~ · (Beton(stein)-werk *n,* (Beton)Fertigteilwerk, Betonwarenwerk; Zementwarenwerk [*Schweiz*]

~ (~) **filler (block),** ~ (~) ~ tile, concrete ~ (~), prefab(ricated) concrete filler (block), prefab(ricated) concrete filler tile [*See remark under 'Block-(stein)'*] · Betondeckenblock(stein) *m,* Betondeckenstein, Beton(decken)füllblock(stein), Beton(decken)füllstein, Betondecken(füll)körper *m,* Füllkörper [*Statisch nicht tragender (Beton)Formstein zur Herstellung von Rippendecken*]

~ (~) ~ **panel** → ~ (~) infiller ~

~ (~) ~ **slab** → ~ (~) (in)filler ~

~ (~) ~ **tile** → ~ (~) ~ (block)

~ (~) **flag** [*B.S. 368*] → sidewalk concrete flag(stone)

(pre)cast (concrete) **flight (of stairs),** prefab(ricated) ~ ~ (~ ~), stair unit · (Beton-)Fertigtreppenlauf *m,* Fertig-Betontreppenlauf

~ (~) **floor,** prefab(ricated) ~ ~ · (Beton-)Elementdecke *f,* (Beton-)Montagedecke, (Beton-)Fertig(teil)decke

((pre)cast) (concrete) **floor member,** (concrete) floor cast(ing) · Beton-Deckenfertigteil *m, n,* Beton-Deckenmontageteil, Decken-Betonfertigteil, Decken-Betonmontageteil

~ (~) ~ **rib,** prefab(ricated) ~ ~ ~ · (Beton-)Fertigdeckenrippe *f*

~ (~) ~ **slab,** prefab(ricated) ~ ~ ~ · (Beton-)Fertig(teil)deckenplatte *f,* Fertig(teil)-Betondeckenplatte

(pre)cast (concrete) **floor(ing) construction** → ~ (~) ~ system

~ (~) ~ **system,** ~ (~) ~ construction, prefab(ricated) ~ ~ ~ ~ · (Beton-)Fertig(teil)decken(bau)system *n,* (Beton-)Fertig(teil)deckenkonstruktion(ssystem) *f, (n)*

((pre)cast) (concrete) **flue,** prefab-(ricated) ~ ~ · Fertigzug *m* aus Beton

(~) ~ ~ **block,** (pre)cast ~ ~ · Beton-Rauch(gas)kanalstein *m,* Rauch(gas)-kanalbetonstein

~ (~) **gable,** prefab(ricated) ~ ~ · (Beton)Fertig(teil)giebel *m*

~ (~) ~ **beam,** prefab(ricated) ~ ~ ~ · (Beton-)Fertiggiebelbalken(träger) *m*

~ (~) **garage,** prefab(ricated) ~ ~ ~ · (Beton-)Fertig(teil)garage *f,* Fertig(teil)-Betongarage

((pre)cast) (concrete) **garden (building) unit,** prefab(ricated) ~ ~ (~) ~ · Beton-Garten(-Bau)element *n,* Beton-Garten(-Bau)körper *m*

(pre)cast (concrete) **girder,** prefab(ricated) ~ ~ · (Beton-)Fertigträger *m,* Fertig-Betonträger

(pre)cast (concrete) **goods** → (mass-produced) (pre)cast (concrete) ware

(pre)cast (concrete) **grandstand,** prefab(ricated) ~ ~ · (Beton)Fertig(teil)tribüne *f*

(pre)cast (concrete) **green block,** ~ (~) ~ tile, prefab(ricated) ~ ~ ~ [*See remark under 'Block'*] · Betonblockfrischling *m,* Beton(block)steinfrischling

~ (~) **gutter,** prefab(ricated) ~ ~ (Beton-)Fertigsohlschale *f*

((pre)cast) (concrete) ... — (pre)cast (concrete) product 752

(~) (~) **hollow block,** (~) (~) **cavity** ~, (~) (~) ~, (~) (~) **pot,** (~) **hollow (concrete) tile (or block)** [*A block shall be demeed to be hollow if it has one or more large holes or cavities which pass through the block and the solid material is between 50% and 75% of the total volume of the block calculated from the overall dimensions. Definition from BS 2028, 1364: 1968. See also remark under 'Block'*] · (Beton)Hohlblock(stein) *m*, (Beton)Hohlstein

(pre)cast (concrete) **home,** prefab(ricated) ~~~ · (Beton-)Fertig(teil)(wohn)haus *n*, Fertig-Beton(wohn)haus, (Beton-)Montage(wohn)haus, (Beton-)Element(wohn)haus, Fertig(teil)beton(wohn)haus, Montagebetonwohnhaus

~ (~) ~ **construction,** prefab(ricated) ~ ~ ~ · (Beton-)Fertighausbau *m*

~ (~) **housing (construction),** prefab(ricated) ~ ~ (~) · (Beton-)Fertig(teil)wohn(ungs)bau *m*, Fertig(teil)-Betonwohn(ungs)bau, Beton-Montagewohn(ungs)bau

~ (~) **industry** · Betonsteinindustrie *f*

((pre)cast) (concrete) **(in)filler panel,** ~ (~) **infill(ing)** ~, ~ (~) **cladding** ~, prefab(ricated) ~ ~ ~ ~ · Beton-Ausfachungstafel *f*, Beton-(Aus)Füll(ungs)tafel

~ (~) ~ **slab,** ~ (~) **infill(ing)** ~, ~ (~) **cladding** ~ · Beton-(Aus)Füll(ungs)platte *f*, Beton-Ausfachungsplatte

~ (~) **infill(ing) slab** → ~ (~) **(in-)filler** ~

(pre)cast (concrete) **inspection chamber,** prefab(ricated) ~ ~ ~ · (Beton-)Fertigrevisionsschacht *m*

~ (~) **kerb of white granite aggregate** (Brit.) → ~ (~) **curb** ~ ~ ~ ~

~ (~) **landing,** prefab(ricated) ~ ~ · (Beton-)Fertig(teil)podest *n*, Fertig(teil)-Betonpodest

~ (~) **(lighting) column** (Brit.); ~ (~) (~) **mast** (US); prefab(ricated) ~ (~) ~ · Fertigteil-Beleuchtungsmast *m*, Fertigteil(Straßen)Leuchtmast, Fertigteil(-Licht)mast

~ (~) **lintel;** ~ (~) **lintol** [*deprecated*]; prefab(ricated) ~ ~ [*B.S. 1239*] · (Beton-)Fertigsturz *m*, Fertig-Betonsturz, Fertig-Betonoberschwelle, (Beton-)Fertigoberschwelle

~ (~) **(load)bearing skeleton** → ~ (~) **(structural)** ~

~ (~) **manhole,** ~ (~) **manway,** prefab(ricated) ~ ~ · (Beton-)Fertigeinsteigschacht *m*, (Beton-)Fertig(einstieg)schacht, (Beton-)Fertigmannloch *n*

~ ~ **manufacturer** → ~ (~) **product** ~

((pre)cast) (concrete) **member** → ~ (~) **(building) unit**

(pre)cast (concrete) **non-housing construction,** prefab(ricated) ~ ~ ~ · (Beton-)Fertignichtwohn(ungs)bau *m*, Fertig-Betonnichtwohn(ungs)bau

~ (~) **nonresidential building,** ~ (~) ~ **block,** prefab(ricated) ~ ~ ~ · (Beton-)Fertig(teil)-Nichtwohngebäude *n*

((pre)cast) (concrete) **panel** → prefab(ricated) ~ ~

(~) (~) ~ **fence,** prefab(ricated) ~ ~ ~ · Betontafelzaun *m*

(~) (~) ~ **wall,** prefab(ricated) ~ ~ ~ · Betontafelwand *f*

(~) (~) ~ **with window opening,** prefab(ricated) ~ ~ ~ ~ ~ · Betontafel *f* mit Fensteröffnung

(pre)cast (concrete) **parachute,** ~ (~) **umbrella** · vorgefertigter Betonschirm *m*

~ (~) **parapet,** prefab(ricated) ~ ~ · (Beton-)Fertig(teil)brüstungsmauer *f*

~ (~) **partition (wall) block,** ~ (~) ~ (~) (~) **tile,** ~ **partition (wall) (concrete)** ~ [*See remark under 'Block'*] · Beton-Trennwandblock(stein) *m*, Beton-Trennwandstein

~ (~) **perimeter frame,** prefab(ricated) ~ ~ ~ · (Beton-)Fertig(teil)außenrahmen *m*

~ (~) **pilaster block,** ~ (~) ~ **tile,** prefab(ricated) ~ ~ ~ [*See remark under 'Block'*] · Pilaster(beton)block(stein) *m*, Wandpfeiler(beton)block(stein), Pilaster(beton)stein, Wandpfeiler(beton)stein, Halbpfeiler(beton)block(stein), Halbpfeiler(beton)stein

~ (~) ~ **tile** → ~ (~) ~ **block**

~ (~) **pipe,** prefab(ricated) ~ ~ ~ · (Beton-)Fertigrohr *n*, Fertig-Betonrohr

((pre)cast) (concrete) **plank,** prefab(ricated) ~ ~ ~ · (Beton) Streifenplatte *f* [*Omniavollbetondecke*]

(pre)cast (concrete) **pointed arch,** prefab(ricated) ~ ~ ~ ~ · (Beton-)Fertigspitzbogen *m*, Fertig-Betonspitzbogen

~ (~) **portal (frame),** prefab(ricated) ~ ~ (~) · (Beton-)Fertig(teil)-Portalrahmen *m*, Fertig(teil)-Betonportalrahmen

~ ~ **producer** → ~ (~) **product manufacturer**

(~) (concrete) **product,** concrete ~, (pre)cast concrete [*Concrete which is cast in separate units before being placed in position in a structure*] · Betonerzeugnis *n*, Betonstein *m* [*Alle werksmäßig hergestellten Erzeugnisse aus Beton. Es werden unterschieden: Betonware(n), die eine Massenfertigung bedingen, z.B. Gehplatten, Betonrohre, Betonfenster, Hochblocksteine usw.; Betonfertig(bau)teile, die in Serie hergestellt werden, z.B. Binder, Masten, Stürze, Stützen, Träger, usw.; Betonwerksteine, die sich von den Betonwa-*]

ren und Fertig(bau)teilen dadurch unterscheiden, daß ihre Sichtflächen bearbeitet sind]

~ (~) ~ **maker** → ~ (~) ~ manufacturer

~ (~) ~ **manufacturer**, ~ (~) ~ maker, ~ (~) ~ producer, concrete ~ ~, (pre)cast concrete ~ · Betonsteinhersteller *m*

~ (~) ~ **producer** → ~ (~) ~ manufacturer

~ (~) **products** → (mass-produced) (pre)cast (concrete) ware

~ (~) ~ **for roads and streets** · Straßenbaubetonware(n) *f(pl)*

~ (~) **profile(d) panel**, profile(d) (pre-)cast (concrete) · Profilbetontafel *f*

~ (~) **purlin(e)**, prefab(ricated) ~ ~ · (Beton-)Fertig(teil)pfette *f*, Fertig(teil)-Betonpfette

~ (~) **(raking) strut**, prefab(ricated) ~ (~) ~ · (Beton-)Fertigstrebe *f*, Fertig-Betonstrebe

~ (~) **rib**, prefab(ricated) ~ ~ · (Beton-)Fertig(teil)rippe *f*, Fertig(teil)-Betonrippe

~ (~) ~ **slab**, prefab(ricated) ~ ~ ~ · (Beton-)Fertig(teil)rippenplatte *f*

~ (~) **rib(bed) floor**, prefab(ricated) ~ ~ ~ · (Beton-)Fertig(teil)rippendecke *f*, Rippendecke aus (Beton)Fertig(bau)teilen

~ **(concrete) roof**, prefab(ricated) ~ ~ · (Beton-)Fertig(teil)dach *n*, Fertig(teil)-Betondach

~ (~) **septic tank** · vorgefertigte Beton-Hauskläranlage *f*, ~ Beton-Grundstückskläranlage, ~ Beton-Kleinkläranlage

~ (~) **shell**, prefab(ricated) ~ ~ · (Beton-)Fertig(teil)schale *f*, Fertig(teil)-Betonschale

~ (~) **shop** · Betonsteinbetrieb *m*, Betonsteinwerkstätte *f* [*Eine Erzeugungsstätte für Betonstein jeder Art kleinen, also handwerklichem, Umfangs*]

~ (~) **sill**, ~ (~) **threshold**; ~ (~) **cill** (Brit.) [*B.S. 1237*] · Fertig-Beton(tür)-schwelle *f*

~ (~) **silo**, prefab(ricated) ~ ~ · (Beton-)Fertig(teil)silo *m*, Fertig(teil)-Betonsilo

~ (~) **skeleton** → ~ (~) structural ~

~ (~) **slab**, prefab(ricated) ~ ~ · (Beton-)Fertig(teil)platte *f*, Fertig(teil)-Betonplatte, (Beton)Plattenelement *n*

~ (~) ~ **floor**, prefab(ricated) ~ ~ ~ · (Beton-)Fertig(teil)plattendecke *f*, Fertig(teil)-Betonplattendecke

(~) **(concrete) solid block**, (~) (~) ~ **tile**, prefab(ricated) ~ ~ [*A block shall be deemed to be solid if the solid material is not less than 75% of the total volume of the block calculated from the overall dimensions. Definition from B.S. 2028, 1364: 1968. See also remark under 'Block'*] · Betonvollstein *m*, Betonvollblock(stein) *m*

(~) (~) ~ **tile** → (~) (~) ~ block

(pre)cast (concrete) stair(case), prefab(ricated) ~ ~ · (Beton-)Fertigtreppe *f*, Fertig-Betontreppe, Montage-Betontreppe, Beton-Montagetreppe

~ (~) ~ **flight**, prefab(ricated) ~ ~ ~ · Fertig(teil)(treppen)lauf *m*

~ (~) **stave**, prefab(ricated) ~ ~ [*B.S. 2810*] · Betondaube *f*, plattenförmiger Silofertigteil *m*, plattenförmiges Silofertigteil *n*

~ (~) ~ **silo**, prefab(ricated) ~ ~ ~ [*B.S. 2810*] · (Beton-)Fertig(teil)-Daubensilo *m*, Fertig(teil)-Betondaubensilo

~ (~) **step**, prefab(ricated) ~ ~ · (Beton-)Fertig(teil)stufe *f*

~ (~) **storey height wall panel** (Brit.); ~ (~) **story** ~ ~ ~ (US); prefab(ricated) ~ ~ ~ ~ · Großwand(beton)-tafel *f*

~ (~) **string** (Brit.); ~ (~) **stringer** (US); prefab(ricated) ~ ~ · (Beton-)Fertig(teil)wange *f*, (Beton-)Montagewange, (Beton-)Elementwange, Fertig(teil)betonwange, Montagebetonwange

~ (~) **(structural) skeleton**, prefab(ricated) (~) (~) ~, ~ (~) (load)bearing ~, ~ (~) weight-carrying ~ · (Beton-)Fertig(teil)(trag)skelett *n*, (Beton-)Fertig(teil)(trag)gerippe *n*

~ (~) (~) **system**, ~ (~) construction, prefab(ricated) concrete (structural) system, prefab(ricated) concrete construction · (Beton-)Fertig(teil) konstruktion(ssystem) *f, (n)*, (Beton-)Montagekonstruktion(ssystem)

~ (~) (~) **wall**, prefab(ricated) ~ (~) ~ · (Beton-)Fertig(teil)wand *f*, (Beton-)Montagewand, (Beton-)Elementwand, Fertig(teil)betonwand, Montagebetonwand

~ (~) **structure**, system-built (~) ~, prefab(ricated) ~ ~ · (Beton-)Fertigbauwerk *n*, (Beton)Montagebauwerk, Fertig(teil)(-Beton)bauwerk

~ (~) **support** → ~ (~) column

~ ~ **symposium**, congress on (pre)cast concrete · Betonsteinkongreß *m*

~ (~) **system building** → ~ (~) construction

~ (~) **threshold** → ~ ~ sill

~ (~) **tile flue** → ~ (~) block ~

~ (~) **tower block**, ~ (~) ~ building, prefab(ricated) ~ ~ ~ · (Beton-)Fertig(teil)hochhaus *n*, Fertig(teil-)Betonhochhaus

~ (~) **tread**, prefab(ricated) ~ ~ · (Beton-)Fertigtritt(stufe) *m*, (*f*), Fertig-Betontritt(stufe)

~ (~) **umbrella**, ~ (~) parachute · vorgefertigter Betonschirm *m*

~ (~) unit → ~ (~) building ~

~ (~) valley beam, ~ (~) ~ girder, prefab(ricated) ~ ~ ~ · (Beton-)Fertigrinnenträger m, (Beton-)Fertigrinnenbalken(träger) m [Shedrahmen]

~ (~) ~ gutter, prefab(ricated) ~ ~ ~ · (Beton-)Fertigkehlrinne f

~ (~) vault, prefab(ricated) ~ ~ · (Beton-)Fertig(teil)gewölbe n, Fertig(teil-)Betongewölbe

~ (~) vent(ilation) duct, ~ (~) ventilating ~, prefab(ricated) ~ ~ ~ · (Beton-)Fertiglüftungskanal m, Fertig-Betonlüftungskanal

~ (~) wall → ~ (~) structural ~

((pre)cast) (concrete) wall panel, prefab(ricated) ~ ~ ~ · (Beton)Wand(bau)tafel f

(~) (~) ~ slab, prefab(ricated) ~ ~ ~ · (Beton)Wand(bau)platte f

~ (~) ~ with preinstalled services · nasse Wand f mit einbetonierten Leitungen, Installationswand ~ ~ ~ [Mit kürzesten Leitungen können an ihr alle erforderlichen sanitären Objekte installiert werden]

(pre)cast (concrete) ware → mass-produced ~ (~) ~

~ (~) weight-carrying skeleton → ~ (~) (structural) ~

~ (~) window frame, prefab(ricated) ~ ~ ~ · (Beton-)Fertigfensterrahmen m, Fertig-Betonfensterrahmen

~ ~ worker · Betonsteinarbeiter m

~ dwelling tower → ~ residence ~

~ expanded concrete (building) component → ~ gas concrete (building) unit

~ factory manufacture · fabrikmäßige Vorfertigung f

~ floor with in-situ structural topping of concrete, prefab(ricated) concrete ~ ~ ~ ~ ~ ~ ~ · Teilmontagedecke f [Die Decke erhält erst mit einer Ortbeton-Druckplatte das volle Tragvermögen]

~ ~ without in-situ structural topping of concrete [An on-structural top screed may be provided] · Vollmontagedecke f [Alle Deckenbauteile sind ohne Ortbeton-Druckplatte voll tragfähig]

~ gable, ~ concrete ~, prefab(ricated, concrete ~ · (Beton)Fertig(teil)giebel m

~ gas concrete (building) unit, ~ expanded ~ (~) ~, ~ ~ ~ (~) member, ~ ~ ~ (~) component, prefab(ricated) ~ ~ (~) ~, gas concrete cast(ing), expanded concrete cast(ing) · Gasbeton(bau)element n, Blähbeton(bau)element, Gasbeton(bau)körper m Blähbeton(bau)körper, Gasbetonmontageelement, Blähbetonmontageelement, Gasbetonmontagekörper, Blähbetonmontagekörper, Gasbetonfertig(bau)element, Blähbetonfertig(bau)element, Gasbetonfertig(bau)Körper Blähbetonfertig(bau)körper [Fehlnamen: Gasbeton(bau)einheit f, Blähbeton(bau)einheit, Gasbetonmontageeinheit, Bläh-betonmontageeinheit]

~ ~ ~ compound unit, prefab(ricated) ~ ~ ~ ~ · Gasbetonfertig(bau)teil m, n, Blähbetonfertig(bau)teil, Gasbetonmontage(bau)teil, Blähbetonmontage(bau)teil [Fehlnamen: Gasbetonbauteil; Blähbetonbauteil]

~ goods → (mass-produced) (pre)cast (concrete) ware

~ gypsum product, prefab(ricated) ~ ~, gypsum (pre)cast building unit, gypsum prefab(ricated) building unit · Gipsformstück n

~ high (rise) block (of flats) (Brit.) → ~ residence tower

~ ~ (~) floor, prefab(ricated) ~ (~) ~ · Hohl(beton)fertigdecke f, Betonhohlfertigdecke

~ light(weight) concrete box-type of construction, ~ ~ ~ ~ box construction type · Kastenbauart f mit Leichtbetonfertigteilen

~ ~ (~) (building) unit, ~ ~ (~) (~) member, ~ ~ (~) (~) component, prefab(ricated) ~ ~ (~) ~, light(weight) (concrete) cast(ing) · Leichtbeton(bau)element n, Leichtbeton(bau)körper, Leichtbetonmontageelement, Leichtbetonmontagekörper m, Leichtbetonfertig(bau)element, Leichtbetonfertig(bau)körper [Fehlnamen: Leichtbeton(bau)einheit f Leichtbetonmontageeinheit]

~ ~ ~ factory, prefab(ricated) ~ ~ ~ · Leichtbeton(stein)werk n

~ marble tile [Precast marble tiles differ from reconstituted marble tiles. In this process marble pieces of suitable thickness are placed in a tile-size form, together with a white portland cement and chippings mortar, coloured to match the natural marble with mineral pigments. The whole is then compressed and vibrated. When cured the tiles are grouted and rubbed to a honed or polished finish] · vorgefertigte Marmorfliese f, ~ Marmor(belag)platte f

~ normal(-weight) (concrete) (building) unit, ~ ~ (~) (~) member, ~ ~ (~) (~) component, prefab(ricated) ~ ~ (~)~, normal(-weight) (concrete) cast(ing) · Normalbetonmontageelement n, Normalbeton(bau)element, Normalbetonmontagekörper m, Normalbeton(bau)körper, Normalbetonfertig(bau)körper, Normalbetonfertig(bau)element, Schwerbetonmontageelement, Schwerbeton(bau)element, Schwerbetonmontagekörper, Schwerbeton(bau)körper, Schwerbetonfertig(bau)körper, Schwerbetonfertig(bau)element [Fehlnamen: Schwerbeton(bau)einheit f, Schwerbetonmontageeinheit, Normalbeton(bau)einheit, Normalbetonmontageeinheit]

~ ~ (~) compound unit, prefab(ricated) ~ ~ ~ ~ · Normalbetonfertig(bau)teil m, n, Normalbetonmontage-

(bau)teil, Schwerbetonfertig(bau)teil, Schwerbetonmontage(bau)teil [*Fehlnamen: Normalbetonbauteil, Schwerbetonbauteil*]

(~) panel → prefab(ricated) concrete ~

(~) ~ wall, ~ concrete ~ ~, prefab(ricated) concrete ~ ~ · Betontafelwand *f*

~ parachute, ~ concrete ~, ~ (concrete) umbrella · vorgefertigter Betonschirm

~ permanent light(weight) concrete formwork, permanent (pre)cast ~ ~ ~, ~ ~ ~ ~ ~ shuttering, ~ ~ ~ ~ ~ form(s) · vorgefertigte verlorene Leichtbetonschalung *f*, verlorene vorgefertigte ~

~ prestressed (concrete) beam, prestressed (pre)cast (~) ~ · Spannbetonfertigträger *m*

~ ~ (~) (building) unit, ~ ~ (~) (~) member, ~ ~ (~) (~) component, prefab(ricated) ~ ~ (~) ~, prestressed cast-concrete (~) ~, prestressed (concrete) cast(ing) · Spannbeton(bau)element *n*, Spannbeton(bau)körper *m*, Spannbetonmontageelement, Spannbetonmontagekörper, Spannbetonfertig(bau)element, Spannbetonfertig(bau)körper [*Fehlnamen: Spannbeton(bau)einheit f, Spannbetonmontageeinheit*]

~ ~ (~) construction, prefab(ricated) ~ ~ ~, industrialized ~ ~ ~, ~ ~ (~) system ~ · Bauen *n* mit Spannbetonfertigteilen, ~ ~ Spannbetonmontageteilen, Spannbetonfertig(teil)bau *m*, Spannbetonmontage(teil)bau [*Fehlname: Spannbetonelementbau*]

~ ~ (~) ~, ~ ~ (~) (structural) system · Spannbeton-Fertig(teil)konstruktion(ssystem)*f*, (*n*), Spannbeton-Montage-konstruktion(ssystem)

~ ~ (~) floor, prestressed (pre)cast (~) ~, prefab(ricated) prestressed ~ ~, prestressed prefab(ricated) ~ ~ · Montage-Spannbetondecke *f*, Spannbeton-Montagedecke, Spannbeton-Fertig(teil)decke, Fertig(teil)-Spannbetondecke

~ ~ (~) ~ component → ~ ~ (~) ~ unit

~ ~ (~) ~ member → ~ ~ ~ (~) ~ unit

~ ~ (~) ~ unit, ~ ~ (~) ~ member, ~ ~ (~) ~ component · Spannbetondecken(bau)element *n*, Spannbetondecken(bau)körper *m*, Spannbetondeckenmontageelement

~ ~ (~) lintel, prestressed (pre)cast (~) ~; ~ ~ (~) (~) lintol [*deprecated*] · Spannbeton-Fertigoberschwelle *f*, Spannbeton-Fertigteiloberschwelle, vorgefertigte Spannbetonoberschwelle, vorgefertigter Spannbetonsturz *m*, Spannbeton-Fertig(teil)sturz

~ ~ (~) panel, prestressed (pre)cast (~) ~ · Spannbetonfertigtafel *f*

~ ~ (concrete) slab, prestressed (pre-)cast (~) ~ · Spannbeton-Fertigplatte *f*

~ ~ (~) string, prestressed (pre)cast (~) ~ (Brit.); ~ ~ (~) stringer (US) · Spannbeton-Fertig(teil)wange *f*

~ ~ (~) (structural) system, ~ ~ (~) construction · Spannbeton-Fertigkonstruktion(ssystem) *f*, (*n*), Spannbeton-Fertigteilkonstruktion(ssystem), Spannbeton - Montagekonstruktion(ssystem)

~ ~ (~) tee-section, prestressed (pre)cast (~) ~ · Spannbeton-Fertig-T-Profil *n*

~ ~ (~) wall, prestressed (pre)cast (~) ~, prefab(ricated) prestressed ~ ~, prestressed prefab(ricated) ~ ~ · Montagespannbetonwand *f*, Spannbeton-Montagewand, Spannbeton-Fertig(teil)wand, Fertig(teil)-Spannbetonwand

~ ~ (~) ~ slab, prestressed (pre)cast (~) ~ ~ · Spannbeton-Wand(bau)platte *f* [*vorgefertigt*]

~ ~ floor component → ~ ~ (concrete) floor unit

~ ~ ~ member → ~ ~ (concrete) floor unit

~ ~ ~ unit → ~ ~ (concrete) ~ ~

~ ~ light(weight) aggregate concrete, prefab(ricated) ~ ~ ~ ~ ~ · Fertigteil-Leichtzuschlag(stoff)-Spannbeton *m*

~ products → (mass-produced) (pre-)cast (concrete) ware

~ pumice concrete, prefab(ricated) ~ ~ [*Pumice concrete cast elsewhere than its final position in the structure*] · Fertigteil-(Natur)Bimsbeton *m*

~ ~ (~) (building) member, ~ ~ (~) (~) unit, ~ ~ (~) (~) component, pumice (concrete) cast(ing) · (Natur-)Bims(beton)(bau)element *n*, (Natur-)Bims(beton)(bau)körper *m*, (Natur-)Bims(beton)montageelement, (Natur-)Bims(beton)montagekörper, (Natur-)Bims(beton)fertig(bau)element, (Natur)Bims(beton)fertig(bau)körper [*Fehlnamen: (Natur)Bims(beton)(bau)einheit f, (Natur)Bims(beton)montageeinheit*]

~ R.C. beam → ~ reinforced (concrete) ~

~ R.C. beam floor → ~ reinforced (concrete) ~ ~

~ R.C. (building) component → ~ reinforced (concrete) (building) unit

~ R.C. (building) member → ~ reinforced (concrete) (building) unit

~ R.C. (building) unit → ~ reinforced (concrete) (~) ~

~ R.C. component → ~ reinforced (concrete) (building) unit

~ R.C. compound unit → ~ reinforced (concrete) ~ ~

~ R.C. construction → ~ reinforced (concrete) ~

~ R.C. floor → reinforced (concrete) (pre)cast ~

(pre)cast R.C. frame — (pre)cast stone

~ R.C. frame, ~ reinforced (concrete) ~, R.C. (pre)cast ~, reinforced (concrete) (pre)cast ~ · Stahlbeton-Fertigrahmen *m*

~ R.C. girder → reinforced (pre)cast (concrete) ~

~ R.C. member → ~ reinforced (concrete) (building) unit

~ R.C. panel → ~ reinforced (concrete) ~

~ R.C. pile → prefab(ricated) reinforced (concrete) ~

~ R.C. rib → ~ reinforced (concrete) ~

~ R.C. slab, ~ reinforced (concrete) ~ · Stahlbeton-Fertigplatte *f*

~ R.C. system construction → ~ reinforced (concrete) ~

~ R.C. unit → ~ reinforced (concrete) (building) ~

~ R.C. wall → prefab(ricated) reinforced (concrete) ~

~ R.C. wall slab → ~ reinforced (concrete) ~ ~

~ reinforced beam → ~ ~ concrete ~

~ ~ ~ floor → ~ reinforced (concrete) ~ ~

~ ~ (building) component → ~ ~ (concrete) (building) unit

~ ~ (~) member → ~ ~ ~ (concrete) (building) unit

~ ~ (~) unit → ~ ~ concrete (~) ~

~ ~ component → ~ ~ (concrete) (building) unit

~ ~ compound unit → ~ ~ concrete ~ ~

~ ~ (concrete) beam, ~ R.C. ~ · Stahlbetonfertigbalken(träger) *m*

~ ~ (~) beam floor, ~ R.C. ~ ~ · Stahlbetonfertigbalken(träger)decke *f* [DIN 4233]

~ ~ (~) (building) unit, ~ ~ ~ (~) (~) member, ~ ~ (~) (~) component, prefab(ricated) ~ ~ (~) ~, reinforced cast-concrete (~) ~, (pre)cast R.C. (~) ~, reinforced (concrete) cast(ing) · Stahlbeton(bau)element *n*, Stahlbeton(bau)körper *m*, Stahlbetonmontageelement, Stahlbetonmontagekörper, Stahlbetonfertig(bau)element, Stahlbetonfertig(bau)körper [*Fehlnamen: Stahlbeton(bau)einheit f, Stahlbetonmontageeinheit*]

~ ~ (~) compound unit, ~ R.C. ~ ~, prefab(ricated) ~ ~ ~ ~ · Stahlbetonfertig(bau)teil *m, n*, Stahlbetonmontage(bau)teil [*Fehlname: Stahlbetonbauteil*] [DIN 4225]

~ ~ (~) construction, prefab(ricated) ~ ~ ~, industrialized ~ ~ ~, ~ ~ (~) system ~, ~ ~ R.C. ~, ~ ~ R.C. system ~ · Bauen *n* mit Stahlbetonfertigteilen, ~ ~ Stahlbetonmontageteilen, Stahlbetonmontage(teil)bau [*Fehlname: Stahlbetonelementbau*]

~ ~ (~) floor → reinforced (concrete) (pre)cast ~

~ ~ (~) frame → ~ R.C. ~

~ ~ ~ manufacturing yard, ~ R.C. ~ ~ · bewegliches Montagestahlbetonwerk *n*, Stahlbeton-Vorfertigungsstelle *f*

~ ~ (~) member → ~ ~ ~(~) (building) unit

~ ~ (~) panel, ~ R.C. ~ · Stahlbetonfertigtafel *f*

~ ~ (~) pile, prefab(ricated) ~ (~) ~, ~ R.C. ~ · Stahlbeton-Fertigpfahl *m*

~ ~ (~) rib, ~ R.C. ~ · Stahlbetonfertigrippe *f*

~ ~ (~) slab, ~ R.C. ~ · Stahlbeton-Fertigplatte *f*

~ ~ (~) step · Stahlbetonfertigstufe *f*

~ ~ (~) system construction → ~ ~ (~) construction

~ ~ (~) wall → prefab(ricated) ~ (~) ~

~ ~ (~) ~ slab, ~ R.C. ~ ~ · Stahlbeton-Wand(bau)platte *f* [*vorgefertigt*]

~ ~ fair-faced concrete compound unit, prefab(ricated) ~ ~ ~ ~ ~ · Stahlbetonsicht-Fertig(bau)teil *m, n*, Sichtstahlbeton-Fertig(bau)teil, Stahlsichtbeton-Montagebauteil, Sichtstahlbeton-Montagebauteil [*Fehlnamen: Stahlsichtbetonbauteil', Sichtstahlbetonbauteil*]

~ ~ floor → reinforced (concrete) (pre-)cast ~

~ ~ frame → ~ R.C. ~

~ ~ member → ~ ~ (concrete) (building) unit

~ ~ panel → ~ ~ concrete ~

~ ~ rib → ~ ~ concrete ~

~ ~ slab, ~ ~ (concrete) ~, ~ R.C. ~ · Stahlbeton-Fertigplatte *f*

~ ~ step → ~ ~ ~ concrete ~

~ ~ wall → prefab(ricated) reinforced (concrete) ~

~ residence tower, ~ residential ~, ~ dwelling ~; ~ high (rise) block (of flats), ~ high (rise) flats, ~ tall block (of flats), ~ tall flats, high industrialized block (of flats), tall industrialized block (of flats), high industrialized flats, tall industrialized flats (Brit.); (pre)cast apartment tower (US); prefab(ricated) concrete residence tower · (Beton-)Fertig(teil)-Hochwohnhaus *n*, (Beton-)Fertig(teil)-Wohnhochhaus, (Beton-)Fertig(teil)-Wohnturm

(~) rib and filler (block) floor, (~) ~ ~ ~ tile ~ · Rippendecke *f* mit Füllkörpern, Füllkörperdecke [DIN 4225. *Eine Decke mit Stahlbeton-Fertigbalken im Mittenabstand von höchstens 1,25 m und Zwischenbauteilen, deren Mitwirkung für die Tragfähigkeit der Balkenrippen in Rechnung gestellt wird*]

~ stone → cast ~

(pre)cast structural concrete — prefab(ricated) aerated ...

~ **structural concrete,** prefab(ricated) ~ ~ · Fertigteil-Konstruktionsbeton *m*

~ ~ (~) **compound unit,** prefab(ricated) ~ (~) ~ ~ · konstruktiver (Beton-)Fertig(bau)teil *m*, konstruktives ~ *n*, ~ (Beton)Montage(bau)teil, ~ Fertigbeton(baut)eil, ~ Montagebeton(bau)teil [*Fehlname:* ~ *Beton(-bau)teil*)]

~ ~ (~) **panel** · Konstruktionsbetontafel, Betonmontagetafel, Montagebetontafel

~ **system** → ~ (concrete) (structural) ~

~ ~ **construction** → ~ (concrete) ~

~ **tall block (of flats)** (Brit.) → ~ residence tower

~ ~ **flats** (Brit.) → ~ residence tower

~ **terrazzo,** terrazzo tile [*B.S. 4131*] · Terrazzo(belag)platte *f*, Terrazzofliese *f*

~ ~, prefab(ricated) ~ · Fertig(teil)terrazzo *m*

~ ~ **wall tile,** (concrete) ~ ~ ~ · Terrazzowand(belag)platte *f*, Terrazzowandfliese *f*

~ **umbrella,** ~ concrete ~, ~ (concrete) parachute · vorgefertigter Betonschirm *m*

~ **ware** → (mass-produced) (pre)cast (concrete) ~

~ **weight-carrying skeleton** → ~ (concrete) (structural) ~

~ **window frame** → ~ (concrete) ~ ~

~ **wood concrete block,** (~) ~ ~ tile [*See remark under 'Block(stein)'*] · Holzbetonblock(stein) *m*, Holzbetonstein

~ ~ ~ **tile,** (~) ~ ~ block [*See remark under 'Block(stein)'*] · Holzbetonblock(stein) *m*, Holzbetonstein

(pre)caster · (Beton-)Fertigteilhersteller *m*

(pre)casting · Vorfertigung *f* aus Beton

~ **concrete ware** · Betonwarenfertigung *f*

~ **factory,** ~ plant · (Beton)Fertigteilwerk *n*, Betonwerk

~ **plant,** ~ factory · (Beton)Fertigteilwerk *n*, Betonwerk

~ **system,** concrete prefab(ricated) ~ · (Beton)Fertigteilsystem *n*, (Beton-)Fertigteilverfahren *n*, (Beton)Fertigteil(bau)weise *f*

~ **yard** · (Beton-)Fertigteilplatz *m*

precaution against fire · Brandschutzmaßnahme *f*, Feuerschutzmaßnahme

prechlorinating, prechlorination · Vorchlorierung *f*

prechlorination, prechlorinating · Vorchlorierung *f*

pre-Christian building style, ~ architectural ~ · vorchristlicher Baustil *m*

precious metal · Edelmetal *n*

precipitated · (aus)gefällt

~ **barium sulphate** (Brit.); ~ ~ sulfate (US); blanc fixe, permanent white (pigment) [*B.S. 1795*] · Blanc fixe *n*, Permanentweiß *n*, Barytweiß, künstlicher Schwerspat *m*

~ **pigment** · (aus)gefälltes Pigment *n*

~ **white lead** [*Lead is dissolved in acetic acid in the presence of air producing basic lead acetate, and the basic carbonate is precipitated from the acetate solution by carbon dioxide*] · Fällungsbleiweiß *n*

precipitating · Niederschlagen *n*

precipitation · Niederschlag *m*

~ **moisture** · Niederschlagsfeuchtigkeit *f*, Niederschlagsfeuchte *f*

~ **water** · Niederschlagswasser *n*

precision, austerity, severity (of style) · Strenge *f* [*Stil*]

precoat · Voranstrich *m*, Voraufstrich

precoating agent, prewetting ~ · Vorbenetzungsmittel *n*

~ **compound,** ~ material, ~ composition, ~ mass, undercoating (material) · Voranstrichmasse *f*, Voraufstrichmasse, Voranstrichmittel *n*, Voraufstrichmittel

~ **material,** ~ composition, ~ compound, ~ mass, undercoating (material) · Voranstrichmasse *f*, Voraufstrichmasse, Voranstrichmittel *n*, Voraufstrichmittel

~ **composition,** ~ mass, ~ compound, ~ material, undercoating (material) · Voranstrichmasse *f*, Voraufstrichmasse, Voranstrichmittel *n*, Voraufstrichmittel

~ **mass,** ~ composition, ~ material, ~ compound, undercoating (material) · Voranstrichmasse *f*, Voraufstrichmasse, Voranstrichmittel *n*, Voraufstrichmittel

precompressed compression zone · vorgedrückte Druckzone *f*

~ **tensile zone,** ~ tension ~ · vorgedrückte Zugzone *f*

~ **tension zone,** ~ tensile ~ · vorgedrückte Zugzone *f*

~ **zone** [*The area of a flexural member which is compressed by the prestressing tendons*] · vorgedrückter Bereich *m*, vorgedrücktes ~ *n*

pre-condensation · Präkondensation *f*

pre-cooling · Vorkühlen *n*, Vorkühlung *f*

~ **coil** · Vorkühlschlange *f*

predella · (Altar)Staffel *f*, Predella *f*

~ **panel** · Altarblatt *n*

to pre-draw · entnehmen [*Kaltwasser für Warmwasserversorgung*]

predrying · Vortrocknung *f*

pre-expanded, pre-foamed [*See remark under 'geschäumt'*] · vorgeschäumt [*Kunststoff*]

prefab(ricated) · vorgefertigt

~ **aerated concrete,** (pre)cast ~ ~ · Fertigteil-Porenbeton *m*, Poren-Fertigteilbeton

prefab(ricated) aerated ... — prefab(ricated) concrete ... 758

~ ~ ~ **wall panel**, (pre)cast ~ ~ ~ ~ · Porenbetonwand(bau)tafel *f*

~ ~ ~ ~ **slab**, (pre)cast ~ ~ ~ ~ · Porenbetonwand(bau)platte *f*

~ ~ ~ **works**, (pre)cast ~ ~ ~ ~ · Porenbetonwerk *n*

~ **architectural concrete component** → (pre)cast architectural (concrete) member

~ ~ ~ **member** → (pre)cast ~ (~) ~

~ **asphalt sheet(ing)** → ~ (asphaltic-) bitumen ~

~ **(asphaltic-)bitumen sheet(ing)** (Brit.); ~ asphalt ~ (US) · Bitumenfertigbahn *f*, Bitumengewebebahn, Asphaltgewebebahn, Asphaltfertigbahn

~ **bathroom unit**, bathroom building block module, (unitized) bathroom (and lavatory) unit · Sanitär(raum)zelle *f*, Sanitärelement *n*, Sanitäreinheit *f*, Naß-(raum)zelle, Naßeinheit, Naßelement, Naß((installations)zelle, Naß(installations)block *m*, Hygiene(raum)zelle, Hygieneeinheit, Hygieneelement, Installations(raum)zelle, Installationselement, Installationseinheit, Bade(raum)zelle, Badezimmerzelle, Bade(zimmer)block, Badeinheit, Bedeelement, Fertigbad *n*

~ **bitumen sheet(ing)** → ~ asphaltic-~ ~

~ **bituminous joint** · bituminöse Fugenarmatur *f*

~ **block** → factory-made building

~ **brick floor** → ~ clay ~ ~

~ ~ **lintel**; ~ ~ lintol [*deprecated*] · vorgefertigte Ziegeloberschwelle *f*, vorgefertigter Ziegelsturz *m*

~ ~ ~ **with untensioned reinforcement**; ~ ~ lintol ~ ~ ~ [*deprecated*]; ~ reinforced brick lintel; ~ reinforced brick lintol [*deprecated*] · vorgefertigter Ziegelsturz *m* mit schlaffer Bewehrung, ~ ~ ~ ~ Armierung, ~ ~ ~ schlaffen (Stahl)Einlagen, vorgefertigte Ziegeloberschwelle *f* ~ ~ ~

~ ~ **panel (unit)** → prefabricated clay brick panel (unit)

~ **brickwork** · vorgefertigte Bauteile *mpl*, *npl* aus Ziegeln

~ ~ **construction** → ~ clay ~ ~

~ ~ **element** → ~ clay ~ ~

~ ~ **member** → ~ (clay) brick(work) element

~ ~ **unit** → ~ (clay) brick(work) element

~ **building** → factory-made ~

~ ~ → industrialized ~

(~) (~) **component** → (~) (~) unit

~ (~) **construction** → system (~) ~

(~) (~) ~ **unit**, (~) ~ ~ ~ member, (~) ~ ~ ~ ~ component · Hochbau-(montage)element *n*, Hochbau(montage)körper *m*, Hochbaufertigelement, Hochbaufertigkörper [*Fehlnamen: Hochbau(montage)einheit f*]

~ ~ **material** → ~ structural ~

(~) (~) **member** → (~) (~) unit

~ ~ **sheet**, ~ ~ board · Fertigbauplatte *f*

(~) (~) **unit**, (~) (~) member, (~) (~) component [*Building material which is formed as a single article complete in itself but which is intended to be part of a compound unit or structure. Examples are brick, block, tile, lintel*] · (Bau)Element *n*, (Bau-)Körper *m*, Montageelement, Montagekörper, Fertig(bau)element, Fertig(bau-)körper [*Fehlnamen: (Bau)Einheit f, Montageeinheit*]

~ **ceramic tiling**, ceramic tile panel · Keramik(belag)plattentafel *f*, Keramikfliesentafel, Tafel aus keramischen Fliesen, Tafel aus keramischen (Belag-)Platten, Tafel aus Keramikfliesen, Tafel aus Keramik(belag)platten [*Zu einer Verlegeeinheit zusammengefaßte Keramikfliesen*]

~ **chimney**, factory-built ~ · Fertigschornstein *m*

~ **circular stair(case)** · Montage-Rundtreppe *f*, Fertig-Rundtreppe

~ **(clay) brick ceiling panel (unit)** · Ziegeldeckenplatte *f*

~ (~) ~ **floor** · Ziegelmontagedecke *f*

~ (~) ~ **panel (unit)** · Ziegelplatte *f*

~ (~) **brickwork construction**, (clay) brick(work) system building · Bauen *n* mit Ziegelfertigteilen, ~ ~ Ziegelmontageteilen, Ziegelmontage(teil)bau *m*, Ziegelfertig(teil)bau [*Fehlname: Ziegelelementbau*]

~ (~) **brick(work) element**, ~ (~) ~ member, ~ (~) ~ unit · Ziegelfertig(bau)teil *m*, *n*

~ **column**, ~ **support** · Fertigstütze *f*

~ ~ ~ → (pre)cast (concrete) ~

~ **compound unit** · Fertig(bau)teil *m*, *n*, Montage(bau)teil [*Fehlname: Bauteil*]

~ **concrete** → cast ~

~ ~ **air-raid sheltering bunker**, ~ ~ bomb shelter, (pre)cast (concrete) air-raid sheltering bunker, (pre)cast (concrete) bomb shelter · Schutzbunker *m* aus Betonfertigteilen, Luft~ ~ ~, Bomben~ ~ ~

~ ~ **balcony** → (pre)cast (~) ~

~ ~ **beam**, (pre)cast (~) ~ · Montage-(Beton)balken(träger) *m*, Fertig(teil)-Betonbalken(träger), (Beton-)Fertig-(teil)balken(träger)

~ ~ ~ **floor**, (pre)cast (~) ~ ~ · (Beton-)Fertig(teil)balkendecke *f*, Montage(-Beton)balkendecke, Fertig(teil)-Betonbalkendecke

~ ~ **block** → ((pre)cast) concrete (building) ~

~ ~ ~ → ~ ~ building

~ ~ ~ **flue** → (pre)cast (~) ~ ~

~ ~ **bomb shelter**, ~ ~ air-raid sheltering bunker, (pre)cast (concrete) air-raid sheltering bunker, (pre)cast

759 prefab(ricated) concrete ... — prefab(ricated) concrete ...

(concrete) bomb shelter · Schutzbunker *m* aus Betonfertigteilen, Luft~ ~ ~, Bomben~ ~ ~

~ ~ **bond beam block** → ((pre)cast) (~) ~ ~ ~

~ ~ **boundary beam** → (pre)cast (concrete) edge ~

~ ~ **building,** ~ ~ block, (pre)cast (~) ~ · (Beton-)Fertig(teil)gebäude *n*, Fertig(teil)-Betongebäude

~ ~ (~) **block** → ((pre)cast) ~ (~) ~

~ ~ ~ **component** → (pre)cast (concrete) (building) unit

~ ~ ~ **member** → (pre)cast (concrete) (building) unit

~ ~ (~) **tile** → ((pre)cast) concrete (building) block

~ ~ ~ **unit** → pre(cast) (~) (~) ~

~ ~ **chimney** → (pre)cast (~) ~

~ ~ **cladding,** ((pre)cast (~) ~ · Beton-(Außen)Versteifungswand *f*

~ ~ ~ **panel** → (pre)cast (concrete) (in)filler ~

~ ~ **column** → (pre)cast (concrete) (lighting) ~

~ ~ ~, ~ ~ **support,** (pre)cast (~) ~ · (Beton-)Fertigstütze *f*, Fertig-Betonstütze

~ ~ **component** → (pre)cast (concrete) member

~ ~ ~ **for building construction** → (pre)cast (concrete) member ~ ~ ~

~ ~ **compound unit** → (pre)cast (~) ~ ~

~ ~ ~ ~ **for building construction** → (pre)cast (~) ~ ~ ~ ~ ~

~ ~ **construction** → (pre)cast (~) ~

~ ~ ~ **division,** (pre)cast (~) ~ ~ · (Beton-)Fertig(teil)bauabteilung *f* [*einer Firma*]

~ (~) ~ **method** → (pre)cast (~) ~ ~

~ ~ **cupola** → ~ ~ **dome**

~ ~ **curb of white granite aggregate** → (pre)cast (~) ~ ~ ~ ~ ~

~ ~ **dome,** ~ ~ cupola, (pre)cast (~) ~ · (Beton-)Fertig(teil)kuppel *f*, Fertig(teil)-Betonkuppel

~ ~ **door frame,** (pre)cast (~) ~ ~ · (Beton-)Fertigtürrahmen *m*, Fertig-Betontürrahmen

~ ~ **eave(s) gutter** → (pre)cast (~) ~ ~

~ ~ ~ **trough** → (pre)cast (concrete) eave(s) gutter

~ ~ **edge beam** → (pre)cast (~) ~ ~

~ ~ **end-block** → (pre)cast (~) ~

~ ~ **exposed aggregate panel,** (pre)cast (~) ~ ~ ~ · (Beton-)Fertigtafel *f* mit bloßgelegten Zuschlägen, ~ ~ freigelegten ~, Fertig-Betontafel ~ ~ ~

~ ~ ~ ~ **slab,** (pre)cast (~) ~ ~ ~ · (Beton-)Fertig(teil)platte *f* mit freigelegten Zuschlägen, Fertig(teil)-Betonplatte ~ ~ ~, ~ ~ bloßgelegten ~

~ ~ **façade** → (pre)cast (~) ~

~ ~ **filler (block)** → (pre)cast (~) ~ (~)

~ ~ ~ **panel** → (pre)cast (concrete) (in)filler ~

~ ~ ~ **tile** → (pre)cast (concrete) filler (block)

~ ~ **flight (of stairs)** → (pre)cast (~) ~ (~ ~)

~ ~ **floor** → (pre)cast (~) ~

~ ~ ~ **rib** → (pre)cast (~) ~ ~

~ ~ ~ **slab** → (pre)cast (~) ~ ~

~ ~ ~ **with in-situ structural topping of concrete,** (pre)cast ~ ~ ~ ~ ~ ~ ~ · Teilmontagedecke *f* [*Die Decke erhält erst mit einer Ortbeton-Druckplatte das volle Tragvermögen*]

~ ~ **floor(ing) construction** → (pre-)cast (concrete) floor(ing) system

~ ~ ~ **system** → (pre)cast (~) ~ ~

~ ~ **flue** → (pre)cast (~) ~

~ ~ **gable,** (pre)cast (~) ~ · (Beton-)Fertig(teil)giebel *m*

~ ~ ~ **beam** → (pre)cast (~) ~ ~

~ ~ **garage,** (pre)cast (~) ~ · (Beton-)Fertig(teil)garage *f*, Fertig(teil)-Betongarage

~ ~ **garden (building) unit,** (pre)cast (~) ~ (~) ~ · Beton-Garten(-Bau)-element *n*, Beton-Garten(-Bau)körper *m*

~ ~ **girder,** (pre)cast (~) ~ · (Beton-)Fertigträger *m*, Fertig-Betonträger

~ ~ **grandstand** → (pre)cast (~) ~

~ ~ **green block** → (pre)cast (~) ~ ~

~ ~ ~ **tile** → (pre)cast (concrete) green block

~ ~ **gutter,** (pre)cast (~) ~ · (Beton-)Fertigsohlschale *f*

~ ~ **home** → (pre)cast (~) ~

~ ~ ~ **construction** → (pre)cast (~) ~ ~

~ ~ **housing (construction)** → (pre-)cast (~) ~ (~) ~

~ ~ **industry,** (pre)cast (~) ~ · (Beton-)Fertigteilindustrie *f*

~ ~ **(in)filler panel** → (pre)cast (~) ~ ~

~ ~ **inspection chamber** → (pre)cast (~) ~ ~

~ ~ **kerb of white granite aggregate** → (pre)cast (concrete) curb ~ ~ ~ ~

~ ~ **landing,** (pre)cast (~) ~ · (Beton-)Fertig(teil)podest *n*, Fertig(teil)-Betonpodest

~ ~ **(lighting) column** → (pre)cast (~) (~) ~

~ ~ (~) **mast** (US) → (pre)cast (concrete) (lighting) column (Brit.)

~ ~ **lintel** → (pre)cast (~) ~

~ (~) **(load)bearing skeleton** → (pre)cast (concrete) (structural) ~

~ ~ **manhole** → (pre)cast (~) ~

prefab(ricated) concrete ... — prefab(ricated) concrete ... 760

~ ~ **manway** → (pre)cast (concrete) manhole

~ ~ **mast** (US) → (pre)cast (concrete) (lighting) column (Brit.)

~ ~ **member** → (pre)cast (~) ~

~ ~ ~ **for building construction** → (pre)cast (~) ~ ~ ~ ~

~ ~ **nonhousing construction** → (pre)cast (~) ~ ~ ~

~ ~ **nonresidential building**, ~ ~ ~ block, (pre)cast (~) ~ ~ · (Beton-)Fertig(teil)-Nichtwohngebäude *n*

~ ~ **panel**, ((pre)cast) (~)~ · (Beton-)Fertig(teil)tafel *f*, Fertig(teil)-Betontafel, Betontafel

~ ~ ~ **fence** → ((pre)cast) (~) ~ ~

~ ~ ~ **wall**, ((pre)cast) (~) ~ ~ · Betontafelwand *f*

~ ~ ~ **with window opening**, ((pre)cast) (~) ~ ~ ~ ~ · Betontafel *f* mit Fensteröffnung

~ ~ **perimeter frame**, (pre)cast (~) ~ ~ (Beton-)Fertig(teil)außenrahmen *m*

~ ~ **pilaster block** → (pre)cast (~) ~ ~

~ ~ ~ **tile** → (pre)cast (concrete) pilaster block

~ ~ **pile**, (pre)cast (~) ~ [*A reinforced concrete pile manufactured in a casting plant or at the site but not in its final position*] · (Beton-)Fertigpfahl *m*, Fertig-Betonpfahl

~ ~ **pipe**, (pre)cast (~) ~ · (Beton-)Fertigrohr *n*, Fertig-Betonrohr

~ ~ **plank** → ((pre)cast) (~) ~

~ ~ **pointed arch**, (pre)cast (~) ~ ~ (Beton-)Fertigspitzbogen *m*, Fertig-Betonspitzbogen

~ ~ **portal (frame)**, (pre)cast (~) ~ (~) · (Beton-)Fertig(teil)-Portalrahmen *m*, Fertig(teil)-Betonportalrahmen

~ ~ **purlin(e)**, (pre)cast (~) ~ · (Beton-)Fertig(teil)pfette *f*, Fertig(teil)-Betonpfette

~ ~ **(raking) strut**, (pre)cast (~) (~) ~ · (Beton-)Fertigstrebe *f*, Fertig-Betonstrebe

~ ~ **residence tower** → (pre)cast ~ ~

~ ~ **rib** → (pre)cast (~) ~

~ ~ ~ **slab**, (pre)cast (~) ~ · (Beton-)Fertig(teil)rippendecke *f*

~ ~ **rib(bed) floor** → (pre)cast (~) ~ ~

~ ~ **roof**, (pre)cast (~) ~ · (Beton-)Fertig(teil)dach *n*, Fertig(teil)-Betondach

~ ~ **shell**, (pre)cast (~) ~ · (Beton-)Fertig(teil)schale *f*, Fertig(teil)-Betonschale

~ ~ **sill** → ~ ~ threshold

~ ~ **silo**, (pre)cast (~) ~ · (Beton-)Fertig(teil)silo *m*, Fertig(teil)-Betonsilo

~ (~) **skeleton** → (pre)cast (concrete) (structural) ~

~ ~ **slab**, (pre)cast (~) ~ · (Beton-)Fertig(teil)platte *f*, Fertig(teil)-Betonplatte, (Beton)Plattenelement *n*

~ ~ ~ **floor**, (pre)cast (~) ~ ~ · (Beton-)Fertig(teil)plattendecke *f*, Fertig(teil)-Betonplattendecke

~ ~ **solid block** → ((pre)cast) (~) ~ ~

~ ~ ~ **tile** → ((pre)cast) (concrete) solid block

~ ~ **stair(case)**, (pre)cast (concrete) ~ · (Beton-)Fertigtreppe *f*, Fertig-Betontreppe, Montage-Betontreppe, Beton-Montagetreppe

~ ~ ~ **flight** → (pre)cast (~) ~ ~

~ ~ **stave** → (pre)cast (~) ~

~ ~ ~ **silo**, (pre)cast (~) ~ ~ [*B.S. 2810*] · (Beton-)Fertig(teil)-Daubensilo *m*, Fertig(teil)-Betondaubensilo

~ ~ **step**, pre(cast) (~) ~ · (Beton-)Fertig(teil)stufe *f*

~ ~ **storey height wall panel** → (pre-)cast (~) ~ ~ ~ ~

~ ~ **string** → (pre)cast (~) ~

~ ~ **(structural) frame(work)** → (pre)cast (~) (~) ~

~ (~) (~) **skeleton** → (pre)cast (~) (~) ~

~ ~ (~) **system** → (pre)cast (concrete) (~) ~

~ ~ (~) **wall** → (pre)cast (~) (~) ~

~ ~ **structure** → (pre)cast (~) ~

~ ~ **strut** → ~ ~ (raking) ~

~ ~ **support** → ~ ~ column

~ ~ **system** → (pre)cast (concrete) (structural) ~

~ (~) ~ **building method** → (pre)cast (concrete) construction ~

~ ~ ~ **construction** → (pre)cast (concrete) ~

~ ~ **threshold**, ~ ~ sill, (pre)cast (~) ~ [*B.S. 1237*] · (Beton-)Fertig(teil)(tür)schwelle *f*, Fertig(teil)-Beton(tür)schwelle

~ ~ **tile** → ((pre)cast) concrete (building) block

~ ~ ~ **flue** → (pre)cast (concrete) block ~

~ ~ **tower block**, ~ ~ ~ building, (pre)cast (concrete) ~ ~ · (Beton-)Fertig(teil)hochhaus *n*, Fertig(teil)-Betonhochhaus

~ ~ **tread**, (pre)cast (~) ~ · (Beton-)Fertigtritt(stufe) *m*, (*f*), Fertig-Betontritt(stufe)

~ ~ **valley beam** → (pre)cast (~) ~ ~

~ ~ ~ **girder** → (pre)cast (concrete) valley beam

~ ~ ~ **gutter** → (pre)cast (~) ~ ~

~ ~ **vault**, (pre)cast (~) ~ · (Beton-)Fertig(teil)gewölbe *n*, Fertig(teil)-Betongewölbe

~ ~ **vent(ilation) duct** → (pre)cast (concrete) ~ ~

~ ~ **wall** → (pre)cast (concrete) (structural) ~

~ ~ ~ **panel** → ((pre)cast) (~) ~ ~

~ ~ ~ **slab** → ((pre)cast) (~) ~ ~

~ ~ **window frame** → (pre)cast (~) ~ ~

~ **construction** → industrialized building

~ ~ → ~ (structural) system

~ ~ **method,** system ~ ~; industrialized ~ ~ (US) [*British spelling is 'industrialised'*] · Fertig(teil)bauweise f, Fertig(teil)bauverfahren n, Montagebauweise, Montagebauverfahren [*Fehlnamen: Elementbauweise, Elementbauverfahren*]

~ **construction(al) material** → ~ structural ~

~ **domestic construction,** ~ housing (~), industrialized ~ (~) · industrialisierter Wohn(ungs)bau m, ~ Wohnhausbau, ~ WBau, Fertig(teil)wohn(ungs)bau, Montagewohn(ungs)bau

~ **door** → stock (machine-made) ~

~ ~ **element,** factory-built ~ ~, stock (machine-made) ~ ~ · Fertigtürelement n

~ **expanded concrete (building) component** → (pre)cast gas concrete (building) unit

~ ~ ~ (~) **member** → (pre)cast gas concrete (building) unit

~ ~ ~ (~) **unit** → (pre)cast gas concrete (building) ~

~ ~ ~ **component** → (pre)cast gas concrete (building) unit

~ ~ ~ **member** → (pre)cast gas concrete (building) unit

~ ~ ~ **unit** → (pre)cast gas concrete (building) ~

~ **façade,** system-built ~; industrialized ~ (US) [*British spelling is 'industrialised'*] · Fertigfassade f, Montagefassade; Elementfassade [*Fehlname*]

~ **facing** → ~ lining

~ **fireplace,** factory-built ~ · Fertigkamin m

~ **fireproof floor,** ~ non-metallic ~, ~ non-combustible ~ · Fertig(teil)- Massivdecke f, Montage-Massivdecke, Massiv-Montagedecke, Massiv-Fertig(teil)decke

~ **floor** · Fertig(teil)decke f, Montagedecke

~ **garage,** system-built ~; industrialized ~ (US) [*British spelling is 'industrialised'*] · Fertig(bau)garage f; Elementgarage [*Fehlname*]

~ **gas concrete (building) component** → (pre)cast gas concrete (building) unit

~ ~ ~ (~) **member** → (pre)cast gas concrete (building) unit

~ ~ ~ (~) **unit** → (pre)cast ~ ~ (~) ~

~ ~ ~ **component** → (pre)cast gas concrete (building) unit

~ ~ ~ **compound unit** → (pre)cast ~ ~ ~ ~

~ ~ **concrete member** → (pre)cast gas concrete (building) unit

~ ~ ~ **unit** → (pre)cast gas concrete (building) ~

~ **girder,** factory-built ~ · Fertigträger m, Montageträger

~ **gypsum product,** (pre)cast ~ ~, gypsum (pre)cast building unit, gypsum prefab(ricated) building unit · Gipsformstück n

~ **hollow (concrete) floor,** (pre)cast ~ (~) ~ · Hohl(beton)fertigdecke f, Betonhohlfertigdecke

~ ~ **floor** → ~ ~ (concrete) ~

~ **home construction** · Fertighausbau m

~ **house** → factory-made ~

~ **housing (construction),** ~ domestic ~, industrialized ~ ~, industrialized housing · industrialisierter Wohn(ungs)bau m, ~ Wohnhausbau, ~ WBau, Fertig(teil)wohn(ung)sbau, Montagewohn(ungs)bau

~ **joint** · Fugenarmatur f

~ **light(weight) concrete (building) component** → (pre)cast light(weight) (concrete) (building) unit

~ ~ ~ (~) **member** → (pre)cast light(weight) (concrete) (building) unit

~ ~ ~ (~) **unit** → (pre)cast ~ (~) (~) ~

~ ~ ~ **component** → (pre)cast light (weight) (concrete) (building) unit

~ ~ ~ **factory,** (pre)cast ~ ~ ~ · Leichtbeton(stein)werk n

~ ~ ~ **member** → (pre)cast light-(weight) (concrete) (building) unit

~ ~ ~ **unit** → (pre)cast light(weight) (concrete) (building) ~

~ **lining,** ~ (sur)facing · Fertig(teil)-Auskleidung f, Fertig(teil)-Verkleidung, Fertig(teil)-Bekleidung

~ **(load)bearing skeleton** → (pre)cast (concrete) (structural) ~

~ **materials industry** · Fertigteilindustrie f

~ **noncombustible floor,** ~ nonmetallic ~, ~ fireproof ~ · Fertig(teil)-Massivdecke f, Montage-Massivdecke, Massiv-Montagedecke, Massiv-Fertig(teil)decke

~ **nonmetallic floor,** ~ noncombustible ~, ~ fireproof ~ · Fertig(teil)-Massivdecke f, Montage-Massivdecke, Massiv-Montagedecke, Massiv-Fertig(teil)-decke

~ **normal(-weight) concrete building component** → (pre)cast normal-(weight) (concrete) (building) unit

prefab(ricated) normal(-weight) .. — prefab(ricated) shell 762

~ ~ ~ (~) **member** → (pre)cast normal(-weight) (concrete) (building) unit

~ ~ ~ (~) **unit** → (pre)cast ~ (~) (~) ~

~ ~ ~ **component** → (pre)cast normal(-weight) (concrete) (building) unit

~ ~ ~ **compound unit** → (pre)cast ~ (~) ~ ~

~ ~ ~ **member** → (pre)cast normal-(weight) (concrete) (building) unit

~ ~ ~ **unit** → (pre)cast normal(-weight) (concrete) (building) ~

~ **office** · Fertig(teil)büro *n*, Montagebüro

~ **panel** · Fertigtafel *f*

~ **partition (wall)**, factory-built ~ (~) · Trennmontagewand *f*, Fertigtrennwand, Montagetrennwand, Trennfertigwand, vorgefertigte Trennwand

~ **pavilion** · Montagepavillon *m*, Fertig(teil)pavillon

~ **pile** · Fertigpfahl *m* [*Pfähle aus Holz, Stahl oder Beton, die eingerammt, eingespült, eingedrückt, eingebohrt oder eingeschraubt werden*]

~ **pipe** · Fertigrohr *n*, vorgefertigtes Rohr

~ **prestressed brick lintel**; ~ ~ ~ lintol [*deprecated*] · vorgefertigter Ziegelsturz *m* mit vorgespannter Bewehrung, ~ ~ ~ Armierung, ~ ~ ~ vorgespannten (Stahl)Einlagen, vorgefertigte Ziegeloberschwelle *f* ~ ~ ~, Ziegelspannsturz

~ ~ **compound unit** → ~ ~ concrete ~ ~

~ ~ **concrete (building) component** → (pre)cast prestressed (concrete) (building) unit

~ ~ (~) **member** → (pre)cast prestressed (concrete) (building) unit

~ ~ ~ (~) **unit** → (pre)cast ~ (~) (~) ~

~ ~ ~ **component** → (pre)cast prestressed (concrete) (building) unit

~ ~ (~) **compound unit**, (pre)cast ~ (~) ~ ~ · Spannbetonfertig(bau)teil *m, n*, Spannbetonmontage(bau)teil [*Fehlname: Spannbetonbauteil*]

~ ~ ~ ~ **floor** → (pre)cast ~ (~) ~

~ ~ ~ **member** → (pre)cast prestressed (concrete) (building) unit

~ ~ ~ **construction** → (pre)cast ~ (~) ~

~ ~ ~ **system construction** → (pre-)cast prestressed (concrete) ~

~ ~ ~ **unit** → (pre)cast prestressed (concrete) (building) ~

~ ~ ~ **wall** → (pre)cast ~ (~) ~

~ ~ **light(weight) aggregate concrete**, (pre)cast ~ ~ ~ ~ · Fertigteil-Leichtzuschlag(stoff)-Spannbeton *m*

~ **pumice concrete**, (pre)cast ~ ~ ~ [*Pumice concrete cast elsewhere than its final position in the structure*] · Fertigteil-(Natur)Bimsbeton *m*

~ **R.C. compound unit** → (pre)cast reinforced (concrete) ~ ~

~ **R.C. construction** → (pre)cast reinforced (concrete) ~

~ **R.C. pile**, (pre)cast ~ ~ ~, ~ reinforced (concrete) ~ · Stahlbeton-Fertigpfahl *m*

~ **R.C. system construction** → (pre-)cast reinforced (concrete) ~

~ **R.C. wall** → ~ reinforced (concrete) ~

~ **reinforced brick lintel** → ~ brick lintel with untensioned reinforcement

~ ~ **concrete (building) component** → (pre)cast reinforced (concrete) (building) unit

~ ~ ~ (~) **member** → (pre)cast reinforced (concrete) (building) unit

~ ~ ~ (~) **unit** → (pre)cast ~ (~) (~) ~

~ ~ ~ **component** → (pre)cast reinforced (concrete) (building) unit

~ ~ ~ **compound unit** → (pre)cast ~ (~) ~ ~

~ ~ ~ **construction** → (pre)cast ~ (~) ~

~ ~ (~) **floor** → reinforced (concrete) (pre)cast ~

~ ~ ~ **member** → (pre)cast reinforced (concrete) (building) unit

~ ~ (~) **pile**, (pre)cast ~ (~) ~, R.C. ~ · Stahlbeton-Fertigpfahl *m*

~ ~ ~ **system construction** → (pre-)cast reinforced (concrete) ~

~ ~ ~ **unit** → (pre)cast reinforced (concrete) (building) ~

~ ~ (~) **wall**, (pre)cast ~ (~) ~, ~ R.C. ~, reinforced (concrete) (pre)cast ~, R.C. (pre)cast ~, reinforced prefab(ricated) (concrete) ~ · Montagestahlbetonwand *f*, Stahlbetonmontagewand, Stahlbetonfertig(teil)wand, Fertig(teil)-Stahlbetonwand

~ ~ **fair-faced concrete compound unit** → (pre)cast ~ ~ ~ ~ ~

~ ~ **floor** → reinforced (concrete) (pre)cast ~

~ ~ **pile** → ~ ~ ~ (concrete) ~

~ ~ **wall** → ~ ~ ~ concrete ~

~ **reinforcement** · Fertigarmierung *f*, Fertigbewehrung, Fertig(stahl)einlagen *fpl*

~ **rib vault** · Rippenmontagegewölbe *n*

~ **(roof) truss** (US) [*There is no all-embracing term for '(Dach)Binder' in the United Kingdom, since '(roof) truss' is defined there as a double-pitched triangulated structure as opposed to a roof frame which is a structure with continuity between vertical and spanning members*] · Fertig(teil)-(Dach)Binder *m*, Montage-(Dach)Binder

~ **shell** · Fertig(teil)schale *f*, Montageschale, vorgefertigte Schale

763 (prefab(ricated)) (single) .. — preformed (pipe insulation) ..

(~) (single) T(ee) (building) unit, (~) (~) ~ (~) member, (~) (~) ~ (~) component · T-(Bau)Element n, T-(Bau)Körper m, T-Montageelement, T-Montagekörper, T-Fertig(bau)element, T-Fertig(bau)körper [Fehlnamen: T-(Bau)Einheit f, T-Montageeinheit]

~ skeleton → (pre)cast (concrete) (structural) ~

~ stair(case), factory-built ~ · Montagetreppe f, Fertig(teil)treppe

~ step · Fertigstufe f

~ string stair(case) (Brit.); ~ stringer ~ (US) · Montage-Wangentreppe f

~ structural concrete, (pre)cast ~ ~ · Fertigteil-Konstruktionsbeton m

~ ~ (~) compound unit → (pre)cast ~ (~) ~ ~ ~

~ ~ material, ~ construction(al) ~, ~ building ~ · vorgefertigter Baustoff m; vorgefertigtes Baumaterial n [Schweiz]

~ (~) skeleton → (pre)cast (concrete) (~) ~

~ (~) system, ~ construction · Montagekonstruktion(ssystem) f, (n), Fertig(teil)konstruktion(ssystem)

~ structure, system-built ~; industrialized ~ (US) [British spelling is 'industrialised'] · Fertig(teil)bau(werk) m, (n), Montagebau(werk), Systembau(werk); Elementbau(werk) [Fehlnamen]

~ support → (pre)cast (concrete) column

~ ~, ~ column · Fertigstütze f

~ (sur)facing → ~ lining

~ system → ~ structural ~

~ ~ building method → (pre)cast (concrete) construction ~

(~) T(ee) (building) component → ~ (single) T(ee) (building) unit

~ ~ (~) member → ~ (single) T(ee) (building) unit

(~) ~ (~) unit → ~ single ~ (~) ~

~ terrazzo, (pre)cast ~ · Fertig(teil)-terrazzo m

~ tile partition (wall) · vorgefertigte (Belag)Plattentrennwand f, ~ Fliesentrennwand

~ tiling, tile panel · Plattentafel f, Belag~, Fliesentafel [Zu einer Verlegeeinheit zusammengefaßte Fliesen]

~ ~ cubicle for clothes · vorgefertigter Fliesen-Garderobenschrank m

~ timber house, ~ wood(en) ~ · Holz-Fertighaus n, Holz-Montagehaus, Fertig-Holzhaus, Montage-Holzhaus

~ truss → ~ roof ~

~ wall, system-built ~; industrialized ~ (US) [British spelling is 'industrialised'] · Fertigwand f, Montagewand; Elementwand [Fehlname]

~ window · Montagefenster n, Fensterelement n

~ wood(en) house, ~ timber ~ · Holz-Fertighaus n, Holz-Montagehaus, Fertig-Holzhaus, Montage-Holzhaus

prefabrication · Vorfertigung f

~ content, factory ~, ~ percentage, ~ fraction · Prozentsatz m der Vorfertigung, Anteil m ~ ~, Gehalt m ~ ~

~ on site · örtliche Vorfertigung f

prefab(rication) site · Vorfertigungsstelle f

~ yard · Vorfertigungsplatz m [auf einer Baustelle]

prefabricator · Fertigteilhersteller m

preferred angle · Vorzugswinkel m

~ dimension · Vorzugsabmessung f, Vorzugsmaß n

~ section · Vorzugsprofil n

~ size [A size chosen in advance of others for specific purposes] · Vorzugsgröße f

~ thickness · Vorzugsdicke f [Fehlname: Vorzugsstärke f]

Preflex beam · Preflexträger m, Preflex-Verbundträger, Preflexbalken(träger) m, vorgebogener Balken(träger)

pre-foamed, pre-expanded [See remark under 'geschäumt'] · vorgeschäumt [Kunststoff]

preformed cork (pipe insulating) section, cork pipe ~ · Korkschale f

~ duct insulation · Rohrleitungs-Isoliersystem n

(~) filler → (joint) sealing strip

~ flashing (piece) · vorgefertigter Anschluß(streifen) m

~ foam · Sonderschaum m, Spezialschaum [Leichtbetonherstellung]

(~) gasket, sealing ~, structural ~ [A gasket, unlike a wet seal, does not rely on adhesion but on the compressive forces acting on it to ensure the joint is sealed and the gasket is not released by subsequent movements] · Selbst(ab)dichtung f, (Fugen)(Ab)Dicht(ungs)profil n, Dicht(ungs)manschette f, Flach(ab)dichtung

(~) ~ joint, sealing ~ ~, structural ~, joint sealed by cover strip · Abdeckfuge f

(~) (joint) filler → (joint) sealing strip

~ kieselguhr (pipe insulation) section, ~ ~ pipe ~, ~ Tripoli-powder (~ ~) ~ · Kieselgurschale f

~ mineral fibre (pipe insulating) section, mineral fibre pipe ~ (Brit.); preformed mineral fiber (pipe insulating) ~, mineral fiber pipe ~ (US) · Mineralfaserschale f

~ ~ ~ section (Brit.) → ~ ~ ~ pipe insulating ~

(~) ~ wool (pipe insulation) section · Mineralwolleschale f

(~) neoprene gasket → neoprene (preformed) ~

~ (pipe insulation) section, (pipe) ~; (pipe) lagging ~ (Brit.) · Dämmschale f, Rohrschale

preformed (pipe insulation) section — preparation 764

~ (~ ~) ~, (pipe) ~; (pipe) lagging ~ (Brit.) · Isolierschale f, Rohrschale

~ (~ ~) ~ for cold protection, ~ (pipe) ~ ~ ~ ~; lagging section ~ ~ ~ (Brit.) · Korkschale f für Kältekorkschutz, Kältekorkschale

~ (~ ~) ~ ~ heat protection, ~ (pipe) ~ ~ ~ ~; lagging section ~ ~ ~ (Brit.) · Korkschale f für Wärmeschutz, Wärmekorkschale

~ section → ~ pipe insulation ~

~ Tripoli-powder (pipe insulation) section → ~ kieselguhr (~ ~) ~

pre-functionalist building · präfunktionalistisches Gebäude n

pre-Gothic · vorgotisch

to preheat · vorerhitzen, vorwärmen

preheated air · vorgewärmte Luft f

preheater · Vorwärmapparat m, Vorwärmer m

preheaters · Vorimprägnierung f [Dachpappenmaschine]

pre-heating · Vorerhitzung f, Vorwärmung

~ of oil · Ölvorwärmung f

pre-Hellenic architecture · vorhellenische Baukunst f, ~ Architektur f

prehistoric · vorgeschichtlich

~ architecture · urgeschichtliche Architektur f, vorgeschichtliche ~, ~ Baukunst f

pre-impregnated · vorgetränkt, vorimprägniert

pre-impregnating · Vorimprägnieren n, Vortränken

pre-impregnation · Vorimprägnierung f, Vortränkung

pre-islamic architecture · vorislamische Architektur f, ~ Baukunst f

preliminary design, schematic ~ · Vorentwurf m

~ ~ drawing, schematic ~ ~ · Vorentwurfszeichnung f

~ ~ phase, schematic ~ ~ · Vorentwurfsstadium n

~ project, ~ scheme · Vorprojekt n

~ scheme, ~ project · Vorprojekt n

~ screeding · Vorspachtelung f

~ test · Eignungsprobe f, Eignungsversuch m, Eignungsprüfung f

~ treatment, preparatory ~, pre-treatment, preparation · Vorbehandlung f

~ work · Vorarbeit(en) f(pl)

to preload · vorbelasten

preload · Vorlast f

~ machine, wire-winding ~ · Wickelmaschine f [Herstellung von Spannbetonbehältern]

~ tank · Wickelbehälter m [aus Spannbeton]

preloading · Vorbelastung f

~ [Preflex beam] · Vorbiegen n

~ [Preflex beam. This preloading induces stresses in the steel of not less than those calculated to occur under full working load] · Vorbiegung f

premature stiffening → false set(ting)

premises, property [A lot, plot or parcel of land including the buildings or structures and inprovements thereon] · bebautes Grundstück n

to pre-mix · vormischen

premix(ed) coloured exterior plaster → ready-mix(ed) coloured (external) rendering

~ ~ external plaster → ready-mix(ed) coloured (external) rendering

~ ~ rendering → ready-mix(ed) coloured (external) ~

~ ~ stucco (US) → ready-mix(ed) coloured (external) rendering

~ gypsum stuff → gypsum ready-mix(ed) plaster

~ light(weight) gypsum plaster → gypsum ready-mix(ed) ~

~ material · lagerfähiges Mischgut n [Straßenbau]

~ plaster → ready-mix(ed) stuff

~ stuff → ready-mix(ed) ~

~ wet paste, ready-mix(ed) ~ ~ · Putzfüller m, Kunstharz-Feinputz m

pre-mixing · Vormischen n

premo(u)lded filler → (joint) sealing strip

~ (strip joint) filler → (joint) sealing strip

pre-packaged mix(ture) [Cement and aggregates, all pre-measured and thoroughly dried and mixed, usually requiring no further preparations except the addition of water. Excellent for small jobs and repairs] · Fertig-Trocken-Mischung f, Fertig-Trocken-Gemisch n, Trocken-Fertig-Gemisch, Trocken-Fertig-Mischung

prepacked(-aggregate) concrete, pre-placed-aggregate ~ [Concrete produced by placing coarse aggregate in a form and later injecting a portland cement-sand grout, usually with admix(tur)es, to fill the voids] · Ausgußbeton m, Prepaktbeton, vorgepackter Beton, Skelettbeton, Schlämmbeton

pre-packed (clay) bricks, (clay) brick pack, pack of (clay) bricks · Ziegelpaket n

~ coarse aggregate · Grobzuschlag-(stoff)packung f, Grobzuschlagmaterialpackung

to pre-paint · vor(an)streichen [Fehlname: vormalen]

pre-painting · Vor(an)streichen n; Vormalen [Fehlname]

preparation, fabrication [sometimes incorrectly called 'mixing'] · Aufbereitung f, Herstellung, Erzeugung [Beton; Mörtel; Schwarz(decken)mischgut]

~ · Präparat n

~ → (materials) processing

~, pre-treatment, preparatory treatment, preliminary treatment · Vorbehandlung f

preparatory treatment, preliminary ~, pre-treatment, preparation · Vorbehandlung f

to prepare, to fabricate [*sometimes incorrectly called 'to mix'*] · aufbereiten, herstellen, erzeugen [*Beton; Mörtel; Schwarz(decken)mischgut*]

prepared gypsum plaster → gypsum ready-mix(ed) ~

~ ~ **stuff** → gypsum ready-mix(ed) plaster

~ **paint,** ready-mixed ~, P.F.U. ~, paint prepared for use · gebrauchsfertige Farbe f, anstrichfertige ~, verarbeitungsfertige ~

~ **roofing** → asphalt ready ~

~ ~ **manufacture** → ready ~ ~

prepared-roofing shingle → asphalt ~

prepared sheet roofing (paper) → ready ~ ~ (~)

to pre-patinate · patinieren

pre-patinated clay roof(ing) tile, ~ roof(ing) clay ~ · Patina(dach)ziegel m, Patina-Tondachstein [*Dachziege l mit künstlich erzeugter Patina*]

~ **concrete roof(ing) tile** · Patina-Betondachstein m [*Betondachstein mit künstlich erzeugter Patina*]

~ **roof(ing) clay tile,** ~ clay roof(ing) ~ · Patina(dach)ziegel m, Patina-Tondachstein [*Dachziegel mit künstlich erzeugter Patina*]

pre-patinating · Patinieren n [*Künstliche Erzeugung von Patina*]

~ **agent** · Patiniermittel n

~ **paint** · Patinierfarbe f

prepayment gas meter · Münzgaszähler m

~ **meter** [*B.S. 37*] · Münzzähler m

preplaced-aggregate concrete → prepacked(-aggregate) ~

Pre-Raphaelite Brotherhood [*Creation of W. Holman Hunt, D.G. Rossetti and others. Its aim was a reaction against current art traditions and a return to the earnest spirit of art found in Raphael's precursors*] · präraphaelitischer Kreis m

pre-Romanesque sculpture · vorromanische Plastik f

presaturator · Vortränkpfanne f, Vortränker m [*Dachpappenanlage*]

presbytery → sanctuary

pre-school children's playground · Kleinkinderspielplatz m

prescreening · Vorabsiebung f

preservation · Haltbarmachung f, Konservierung

~ **coat** · Konservierungsanstrich m, Konservierungsaufstrich

~ **of monuments,** historic preservation · Denkmalpflege f

~ ~ **structures** · Bautenschutz m

~ **plastic film** → protective ~ ~

~ ~ **sheeting,** protection ~ ~, protecting ~ ~, protective ~ ~, ~ ~ film · Schutzfolie f, Bauten~

preservative, preserver, protective agent, protecting agent · Konservierungsmittel n, Schutzmittel, Konservierungsstoff m, Schutzstoff

~ → wood ~

~ **against blue stain** · Bläueschutzmittel n

~ **chemical** · Schutzchemikal n

~ **for structures and buildings** · Bautenschutzmittel n, Bautenschutzstoff m

~ **salt** → wood ~ ~

~ **solution,** preserver ~ · Schutzmittellösung f

~ **treatment** · Schutzbehandlung f

preserver → (wood) preservative

~, preservative, protective agent, protecting agent · Konservierungsmittel n, Schutzmittel, Konservierungsstoff m, Schutzstoff

~ **solution,** preservative ~ · Schutzmittellösung f

preserving action against blue stain · Bläueschutzwirkung f

pre-setting of water temperature · Vorwahl f der Wassertemperatur

president's palace · Präsidentenpalast m

press · Presse f [*Maschine zur Verformung von Werkstoffen*]

press-and-blow process · Preß-Blasverfahren n [*Glasherstellung*]

press box · Pressekabine f

~ **brake** (US); folding press, folding machine (Brit.) · Abkantpresse f, Abkantmaschine f

~ **building,** newspaper offices · Zeitungsgebäude n

press-button, pushbutton · Druckknopf m

~ **control,** pushbutton ~ · Druckknopfsteuerung ,

~ **station,** pushbutton ~ · Druckknopftaster m

~ **switch,** pushbutton ~ · Druckknopfschalter m

press roll → pressure ~

pressed (clay) brick [*The process of manufacture for pressed bricks depends upon the consistency of clay which is used. Stiff, plastic or semi-dry pressed bricks have a characteristic frog on one or both sides. They are produced by mechanical process, the clay being confined in steel moulds*] · Preßziegel m, gebrannter Preßstein m; Preßstein [*Fehlname*]

pressed clay roof(ing) tile — pressure-gun type exterior ... 766

~ ~ roof(ing) tile, ~ roof(ing) clay ~ · Preßdachziegel *m* [*Ein auf einer Stempelpresse – Revolver- oder Handpresse – hergestellter Dachziegel. DIN 456*]

~ distillate, blue oil · blaues Öl *n*

~ felt → ready roofing

~ ~ manufacture → ready roofing ~

~ glass, ~ ware; pressware (US) [*These terms embrace pavement lights, decorative mo(u)lded panels, certain types of glass tile, etc.*] · Preßglas *n*

~ metal · Preßmetall *n*

~ nail · gepreßter Nagel *m*

~ panel · Preßtafel *f*

~ profile, ~ section, ~ shape, ~ unit, ~ trim · Preßprofil *n*, gepreßtes Profil

~ raw (clay) brick · gepreßter (Ziegel-) Rohling *m*

~ roof(ing) clay tile, ~ clay roof(ing) ~ · Preßdachziegel *m* [*Ein auf einer Stempelpresse – Revolver- oder Handpresse – hergestellter Dachziegel. DIN 456*]

~ section, ~ unit, ~ trim, ~ shape, ~ profile · gepreßtes Profil *n*, Preßprofil

~ shape, ~ section, ~ unit, ~ trim, ~ profile · Preßprofil *n*, gepreßtes Profil

~ (sheet) steel · Preßblech *n*

~ steel · Preßstahl *m*

~ ~ door frame · Preßstahltürrahmen *m*

~ ~ duct · Preßstahlkanal *m*

~ ~ eave(s) gutter, ~ ~ ~ trough · Preßstahltraufrinne *f*

~ ~ ~ trough, ~ ~ ~ gutter · Preßstahltraufrinne *f*

~ ~ flange(d) shear plate · runde Flansch(en)scheibe *f* aus Preßstahl [*Holzverbinder*]

~ ~ lintel; ~ ~ lintol [*deprecated*] · Preßstahlsturz *m*, Preßstahloberschwelle *f*

~ ~ manhole cover, ~ ~ manway ~ · Preßstahlmannlochdeckel *m*, Preßstahlschachtdeckel

~ ~ manway cover, ~ ~ manhole ~ · Preßstahlmannlochdeckel *m*, Preßstahlschachtdeckel

~ ~ panel · Preßstahltafel *f*

~ ~ partition (wall) · Preßstahltrennwand *f*

~ ~ pipe [*B.S. 1091*] · Preßstahlrohr *n*

~ ~ profile → ~ ~ trim

~ ~ rainwater pipe · Preßstahl-Regen(wasser)rohr *n*

~ ~ section → ~ ~ trim

~ ~ sectional tank [*B.S. 1564*] · Preßstahl-Gliederbehälter *m*

~ ~ shape → ~ ~ trim

~ ~ stair(case) · Preßstahltreppe *f*

~ ~ string (Brit.); ~ ~ stringer (US) · Preßstahl(treppen)wange *f*

~ ~ trim, ~ ~ shape, ~ ~ profile, ~ ~ section, ~ ~ unit · Preßstahlprofil *n*

~ ~ unit → ~ ~ trim

~ ~ valley gutter · Preßstahlkehlrinne *f*

~ tile · Preß(belag)platte *f*, Preßfliese *f*

~ trim, ~ unit, ~ shape, ~ section, ~ profile · Preßprofil *n*, gepreßtes Profil

~ unit, ~ trim, ~ shape, ~ section, ~ profile · Preßprofil *n*, gepreßtes Profil

~ ware, ~ glass; pressware (US) [*These terms embrace pavement lights, decorative moulded panels, certain types of glass tile, etc.*] · Preßglas *n*

~ wood · Preßholz *n*

pressing · Pressen *n*

~ · Prägen *n*

pressure at rest · Ruhedruck *m*

~ build-up, build-up of pressure · Druckaufbau *m*

~ coefficient, wind ~ ~ · (Wind-)Druckbeiwert *m*

~ decline, ~ decrease, ~ drop, decline in pressure, drop in pressure, decrease in pressure · Druckrückgang *m*, Druckabfall *m*, Druckabnahme *f*

~ decrease, ~ decline, ~ drop, decline in pressure, drop in pressure, decrease in pressure · Druckrückgang *m*, Druckabfall *m*, Druckabnahme *f*

~ die casting · Druckgußstück *n*

~ distribution, distribution of pressure · Druckverteilung *f*

~ drop, ~ decrease, ~ decline, decline in pressure, drop in pressure, decrease in pressure · Druckrückgang *m*, Druckabnahme *f*, Druckabfall *m*

~ effect · Druckwirkung *f*

~ equalizing layer, de-aerating ~, relieving ~ · (Druck)Ausgleichsschicht *f*, Dampf~, Entlüftungsschicht, Entspannungsschicht

~ fluctuation · Druckschwankung *f*

~ force · Druckkraft *f*

pressure-glued · druckverleimt

pressure-gun type asphalt, gunned ~, gun-grade ~, sprayed(-on) ~, spray(ing) · Spritzasphalt *m*

~ ~ cement → gun(-grade) ~

~ ~ (clear) varnish, sprayed(-on) (~) ~, spray(ing) (~) ~, gun-grade (~) ~, gunned (~) ~ · Spritz(klar)lack *m*

~ ~ composition, ~ ~ compound, ~ ~ mass, ~ ~ material, sprayed(-on) ~, spray(ing) ~, gun-grade ~, gunned ~ · Spritzmasse *f*

~ ~ compound, ~ ~ material, ~ ~ mass, ~ ~ composition, sprayed(-on) ~, spray(ing) ~, gun-grade ~, gunned ~ · Spritzmasse *f*

~ ~ cork, sprayed(-on) ~, spray(ing) ~, gun-grade ~, gunned ~ · Spritzkork *m*

~ ~ exterior plaster(ing) → gun(-grade) (external) rendering

~ ~ ~ rendering → gun(-grade) (external) ~

767 pressure-gun type (external) ... — (pre)stressed clay roof

~ ~ (external) plaster(ing) → gun(-grade) (external) rendering

~ ~ (~) rendering → gun(-grade) (~) ~

~ ~ foam, sprayed(-on) ~, spray(ing) ~, gun-grade ~, gunned ~ · Spritzschaum m

~ ~ mass, ~ ~ material, ~ ~ compound, ~ ~ composition, sprayed(-on) ~, gun-grade ~, spray(ing) ~, gunned ~ · Spritzmasse f

~ ~ mastic, sprayed(-on) ~, spray(ing) ~, gun-grade ~, gunned ~ · Spritzmastix m

~ ~ material, ~ ~ compound, ~ ~ mass, ~ ~ composition, sprayed(-on) ~, spray(ing) ~, gun-grade ~, gunned ~ · Spritzmasse f

~ ~ plaster(ing) → gun(-grade) (external) rendering

~ ~ plastic, sprayed(-on) ~, spray(ing) ~, gun-grade ~, gunned ~ · Spritzkunststoff m

~ ~ putty → gunned ~

~ ~ ~ → gun(-grade) cement

~ ~ rendering → gun(-grade) (external) ~

~ ~ vermiculite, sprayed(-on) ~, spray(ing) ~, gun-grade ~, gunned ~ · Spritzvermiculite m

pressure head, head of pressure · Druckhöhe f

~ **jet (oil) burner** · Druckzerstäubungs(öl)brenner m

pressureless sintering, loose powder ~ · Sintern n von losem Pulver, Schüttsintern

pressure line, funicular ~ ~, thrust ~, line of thrust · Drucklinie f, Stützlinie, Mittelkraftlinie [Die „natürliche" Kräftelinie des formaktiven Drucksystems]

~ ~ **arch** → funicular ~ ~ ~

~ ~ **method** → funicular ~ ~ ~

~ ~ **vault** → funicular ~ ~ ~

~ **of saturation,** saturation pressure · Sättigungsdruck m

~ **on forms,** ~ ~ formwork, ~ ~ shuttering · Schal(ungs)druck m

~ ~ **formwork,** ~ ~ shuttering, ~ ~ forms · Schal(ungs)druck m

~ ~ **impost(s)** · Kämpferdruck m [Druck eines Bogens oder Gewölbes auf die Kämpfer]

~ ~ **shuttering,** ~ ~ formwork, ~ ~ forms · Schal(ungs)druck m

~ **pipe,** ~ water · Druck(wasser)rohr n

~ **pipeline** · Druckrohrleitung f

~ **(pipe)line** → ~ water ~

~ **reflection coefficient** → sound ~ ~ ~

~ **rising curve** · Druckanstiegkurve f

press(ure) roll · Preßwalze f [Dachpappenanlage]

pressure type (storage) cylinder · Druck(innen)kessel m [Heißwasserspeicher]

~ ~ **water heater,** ~ ~ ~ heating appliance · Druckspeicher m [Ein Heißwasserspeicher, der unter dem Druck der Wasserleitung arbeitet, wobei das Wasser durch Ventile im Ausflußrohr entnommen wird]

~ **vessel,** autoclave · Autoklav m, (Druck)Härtekessel m, Druckkessel, (Dampf)Härtekessel, Dampfdruckerhitzer m

~ ~ · Druckbehälter m

~ **(water) pipe** · Druck(wasser)rohr n

~ **(~) (pipe)line** · Druck(wasser)rohrleitung f

pressware (US); pressed glass, pressed ware [These terms embrace pavement lights, decorative moulded panels, certain types of glass tile, etc.] · Preßglas n

presteaming period, holding ~, delay ~ [In the manufacture of concrete products, the time between mo(u)lding of a concrete product and start of the temperature-rise period] · Vorlageerungsdauer f, Vorlager(ungs)zeit f

prestige building · Repräsentationsgebäude n

prestress eccentricity · Vorspannausmittigkeit f

~ **fabricator** · Hersteller m von Spannbetonerzeugnissen

(pre)stressed aerated concrete, aerated prestressed ~ · Porenspannbeton m

prestressed cable system with suspension and stabilization in one direction · vorgespanntes Seilsystem n mit gleichgerichteter Stabilisierung

~ ~ ~ ~ **transverse stabilization** · vorgespanntes Seilsystem n mit querlaufender Stabilisierung

(pre)stressed centrifugally cast pipe → ~ (concrete) spun ~

~ **clay,** Stahlton · Stahlton m, Spannton

~ ~ **beam** → Stahlton ((pre)stressed) ~

~ ~ **door lintel** → Stahlton ((pre-)stressed) ~ ~

~ ~ **factory,** ~ **plant,** Stahlton ~ · Spanntonwerk n, Stahltonwerk

~ ~ **floor,** Stahlton ((pre)stressed) ~, floor in (pre)stressed clay · Spanntondecke f, Stahltondecke, vorgespannte Ziegeldecke

~ ~ **lintel** → Stahlton ((pre)stressed) ~

~ ~ **plank,** Stahlton ((pre)stressed) ~, plank in (pre)stressed clay · Spanntonbrett n, Stahltonbrett, vorgespanntes Ziegelbrett

~ ~ **plant,** ~ **factory,** Stahlton ~ · Spanntonwerk n, Stahltonwerk

~ ~ **roof,** Stahlton (prestressed) ~, roof in prestressed clay · Spanntondach n, Stahltondach, vorgespanntes Ziegeldach

(pre)stressed clay roof slab — (pre)stressed (concrete) ... 768

~ ~ ~ **slab**, Stahlton (prestressed) ~ ~, roof slab in prestressed clay · Spanntondachplatte *f*, Stahltondachplatte, vorgespannte Ziegeldachplatte

~ ~ **wall panel** → wall unit in (pre-)stressed clay

~ ~ **window lintel** → Stahlton (prestressed) ~ ~

~ **concrete**, P. S. [*Prestressing combines and enhances the inherent characteristics of two of the foremost construction materials – the compressive strength of concrete with the high tensile strength of stress-relieved cold drawn steel wire and strand*] · Spannbeton *m* [*DIN 4227*]

~ (~) **arch** · Spannbetonbogen *m*

~ (~) **arch(ed girder)**, ~ (~) arch ~ · gekrümmter Spannbetonträger *m*, Spannbetonbogenträger

~ (~) **barrel vault**, ~ (~) tunnel ~, ~ (~) wagon ~ · Spannbeton-Tonne(ngewölbe) *f*, (*n*)

~ (~) **barrel-vault shell**, ~ (~) tunnel-vault ~, ~ (~) wagon-vault ~ · Spannbeton-Tonnenschale *f*

~ (~) **beam** · Spannbetonbalken(träger) *m*

~ (~) ~ **floor** · Spannbetonbalkendecke *f*, Spannbetonbalkenträgerdecke

~ (~) **bearer**, ~ (~) (binding) joist, ~ (~) ceiling joist, ~ (~) binder joist · Spannbeton(decken)unterzug *m*

~ (~) **bearing skeleton** → ~ ~ load~ ~

~ (~) **binder joist**, ~ (~) ceiling ~, ~ (~) (binding) ~, ~ (~) bearer · Spannbeton(decken)unterzug *m*

~ (~) **(binding) joist**, ~ (~) ceiling ~, ~ (~) binder ~, ~ (~) bearer · Spannbeton(decken)unterzug *m*

~ (~) **block**, ~ (~) building · Spannbetongebäude *n*

~ (~) **block-beam** · Spannbeton-Hohlblockträger *m*, Spannbeton-Hohlsteinträger

~ (~) **bowstring**, ~ (~) tie-rod, ~ (~) (horizontal) tie(back) · Spannbetonzugband *m*

~ (~) **box girder** · Spannbetonkasten(-träger) *m*

~ (~) **bracket** · Spannbetonkonsole *f*

~ (~) **building**, ~ (~) block · Spannbetongebäude *n*

~ (~) (~) **unit**, ~ (~) (~) member, ~ (~) (~) component, (pre)cast prestressed (~) ~, prestressed cast-concrete (~) ~, prestressed (concrete) cast(ing) · Spannbeton(bau)element *n*, Spannbeton(bau)körper *m* [*Fehlnamen: Spannbeton(bau)einheit f*]

~ (~) **cassette plate**, ~ (~) pan(el) ~, ~ (~) waffle ~, ~ (~) coffer ~, ~ (~) ~ slab, ~ (~) rectangular grid ~ · Spannbetonkassetten(decken)platte *f*

~ (~) **cast(ing)** → (pre)cast prestressed (concrete) (building) unit

~ (~) **ceiling joist**, ~ (~) binder ~, ~ (~) (binding) ~, ~ (~) bearer · Spannbeton(decken)unterzug *m*

~ (~) **centrifugally cast pipe**, ~ (~) spun ~ · Betonschleudervorspannrohr *n*, Schleuderbetonvorspannrohr

~ (~) **coffer plate**, ~ (~) waffle ~, ~ (~) pan(el) ~, ~ (~) cassette ~, ~ (~) ~ slab, ~ (~) rectangular grid ~ · Spannbetonkassetten(decken)-platte *f*

~ (~) **column**, ~ (~) support · Spannbetonstütze *f*

~ (~) **compound unit** · Spannbetonbauteil *m*, *n* [*z. B. Spannbetonstütze; Spannbetonbinder usw.*]

~ (~) **construction** · Spannbetonbau *m*

~ (~) ~ **type**, ~ (~) type of construction · Spannbetonbauart *f*

~ (~) **continuous beam**, continuous prestressed (concrete) ~ · Spannbeton-Durchlaufbalken(träger) *m*, Durchlauf-Spannbetonbalken(träger) durchlaufender Spannbetonbalken(träger)

~ (~) ~ **frame**, continuous prestressed (concrete) ~ · durchlaufender Spannbetonrahmen *m*, Durchlauf-Spannbetonrahmen, Spannbeton-Durchlaufrahmen

~ (~) **cross-wall** · Spannbetonquerwand *f*

~ (~) **cupola**, ~ (~) dome · Spannbetonkuppel *f*

~ (~) **cylindrical shell**, cylindrical prestressed (~) · Spannbetonzylinderschale *f*

~ (~) **design and construction**, ~ (~) engineering · Spannbetontechnik *f*, Vorspanntechnik

~ (~) **dome**, ~ (~) cupola · Spannbetonkuppel *f*

~ (~) **door lintel**; ~ (~) ~ lintol [*deprecated*] · Spannbetontürsturz *m*

~ (~) **engineering**, ~ (~) design and construction · Spannbetontechnik *f*, Vorspanntechnik

~ (~) **fence** · Spannbetonzaun *m*

~ (~) **flexure test beam** · Spannbetonbiegebalken *m*, Spannbetonprobebalken

~ (~) **floor** → ~ (~) suspended ~

~ (~) ~ **beam** · Spannbeton-Deckenbalken(träger) *m*

~ (~) ~ **slab**, ~ (~) ~ plate · Spannbetondeckenplatte *f*

~ (~) **floor-slab member**, ~ (~) ~ unit, ~ (~) floor-plate ~ · Spannbeton-Deckenplattenelement *n*

~ (~) **floor(ing) construction**, ~ (~) ~ (structural) system · Spannbetondecken(bau)system *n*, Spannbetondeckenkonstruktion(ssystem *f*,(*n*)

~ (~) **folded plate (structure)**, ~ (~) ~ slab (~), ~ (~) prismatic shell (~); ~ (~) hipped-plate (~), ~ (~) filled-slab (~) (US) · Spannbeton-Faltwerk *n*, Spannbeton-Plattenfaltwerk

prestressed (concrete)... — prestressed (concrete)...

~ (~) ~ **slab roof**, ~ (~) ~ plate ~, ~ (~) prismatic shell ~; ~ (~) hipped-plate ~, ~ (~) tilted-slab ~ (US) · Spannbetondachfaltwerk *n*, Spannbetonfalt(werk)dach *n*

~ (~) **for buildings** · Hochbau-Spannbeton *m*

~ (~) **foul water pipe**, ~ (~) refuse water ~, ~ (~) sewage ~, ~ (~) sewer ~ · Spannbeton-Abwasserrohr *n*, Spannbeton-Kanal(isations)rohr

~ (~) **frame** · Spannbetonrahmen *m*

~ (~) **girder** · Spannbetonträger *m*

~ (~) ~ **floor** · Spannbetonträgerdecke *f*

~ (~) **header** · Spannbetonwechsel(-balken) *m*

~ (~) **high-pressure pipe** · Spannbeton-Hochdruckrohr *n*

~ (~) **hipped-plate roof**, ~ (~) tilted-slab ~ (US); ~ (~) folded slab ~, ~ (~) folded plate ~, ~ (~) prismatic shell ~ · Spannbetondachfaltwerk *n*, Spannbetonfalt(werk)dach *n*

~ (~) ~ **(structure)** (US) → ~ (~) folded plate (~)

~ (~) **hollow beam floor**, hollow prestressed (concrete) ~ · ~ · Spannbeton-Hohlbalkendecke *f*

~ (~) **hollow(-core) plank** · Spannbetonhohldiele *f*, Spannbetonstegdiele

~ (~) ~ ~ **floor** · Spannbetonhohldielendecke *f*, Spannbetonstegdielendecke

~ (~) ~ **pile** · Spannbeton-Hohlpfahl *m*

~ (~) ~ **slab floor**, hollow prestressed (concrete) ~ ~ · Spannbetonhohl(platten)decke *f*

~ (~) **(horizontal) tie(back)**, ~ (~) bowstring, ~ (~) tie-rod · Spannbetonzugband *n*

~ (~) **I-beam** · Spannbeton-Doppel-T-Träger *m*, Spannbeton-I-Träger

~ (~) **insert(ion)** [*Is a small prestressed concrete element of octagonal, rectangular, square or any other cross section*] · vorgespannte Betoneinlage *f*

~ (~) **intermediate floor** → ~ (~) (suspended) ~

~ (~) **joist** → ~ ~ ~ binding ~

~ (~) **lattice girder** · Spannbetongitterträger *m*

~ (~) **lift-slab** · Spannbeton-Hub(decken)platte *f*

~ (~) ~ **construction** · Spannbeton-Hub(decken)bau *m*

~ (~) ~ ~ **method** · Spannbeton-Hubplattenbauweise *f*, Spannbeton-Hubplattenverfahren *n*

~ (~) ~ **structure** · Spannbeton-Hub(decken)bau(werk) *m*, (*n*)

~ (~) **lighting mast** · Spannbeton-Beleuchtungsmast *m*, Spannbeton-Lichtmast, Spannbeton-Leuchtmast

~ (~) **(load)bearing skeleton**, ~ (~) (structural) ~, ~ (~) weight-carrying ~, ~ (~) supporting ~, ~ (~) loaded ~, ~ (~) load-carrying ~ · Spannbetongerippe *n*, Spannbetontraggerippe, Spannbeton(trag)skelett *n*

~ (~) **long-span slab**, long-span prestressed (concrete) ~ · Spannbeton-Weitspannplatte *f*, Weitspannbetonplatte

~ (~) **mast** · Spannbetonmast *m* [*DIN 4228*]

~ (~) **panel** · Spannbetontafel *f*

~ (~) **pan(el) slab**, ~ (~) waffle ~, ~ (~) ~ (~) coffer ~, ~ (~) cassette ~, ~ (~) ~ plate, ~ (~) rectangular grid ~ · Spannbetonkassetten(decken)platte *f*

~ (~) **parachute**, ~ (~) umbrella · Spannbetonschirm *m*

~ (~) **parallel truss** · Spannbeton-Parallelfachwerkträger *m*

~ (~) **parking deck** · Spannbetonparkplatte *f*

~ (~) ~ **structure** · Spannbeton-Parkbauwerk *n*

~ (~) **pile** · Spannbetonpfahl *m*

~ (~) **pipe** · Spannbetonrohr *n*

~ (~) **pipeline** · Spannbetonrohrleitung *f*

~ (~) **plain web(bed) beam**, ~ (~) solid ~ ~ · Spannbeton-Vollwandbalken(träger) *m*

~ (~) ~ **girder**, ~ (~) solid ~ ~ · Spannbeton-Vollwandträger *m*

~ (~) **plank (unit)** · Spannbetondiele *f*, vorgespannte Diele

~ (~) ~ **(unit) floor** · Spannbetondielendecke *f*, vorgespannte Dielendecke

~ (~) **plate**, ~ (~) slab · Spannbetonplatte *f* [*Ein Flächentragwerk aus Spannbeton bei dem die Kräfte quer zur Mittelebene angreifen*]

~ (~) ~ **base** → ~ (~) slab ~

~ (~) ~ **foundation** → ~ (~) slab ~

~ (~) **portal frame** · Spannbetonportalrahmen *m*

~ (~) **power mast**, ~ (~) ~ pole · Spannbeton-Leitungsmast *m*

~ (~) **pressure pipe** · Spannbetondruckrohr *n*

~ (~) ~ **vessel** · Spannbetondruckgefäß *n*

~ (~) **prismatic shell roof**, ~ (~) folded slab ~, ~ (~) folded plate ~; ~ (~) hipped-plate ~, ~ (~) tilted-slab ~ (US) · Spannbetondachfaltwerk *n*, Spannbetonfalt(werk)dach *n*

~ (~) **problem** · Spannbetonaufgabe *f*

~ (~) **purlin(e)** · Spannbetonpfette *f*

~ (~) **railroad tie** (US); ~ (~) railway sleeper (Brit.) · Spannbeton(gleis)schwelle *f*, Spannbetonschienenschwelle

prestressed (concrete)... — prestressed (concrete)...

~ (~) **railway sleeper** (Brit.); ~ (~) railroad tie (US) · Spannbeton(gleis)schwelle f, Spannbetonschienenschwelle

~ (~) **reactor vessel,** PCRV · Spannbeton-Druckbehälter m

~ (~) **rectangular grid slab** → ~ ~ pan(el) plate

~ (~) **refuse water pipe,** ~ (~) foul water ~, ~ (~) sewage ~, ~ (~) sewer ~ · Spannbeton-Abwasserrohr n, Spannbeton-Kanal(isations)rohr

~ (~) **reservoir,** ~ (~) tank · Spannbetonbehälter m

~ (~) **reservoir** · Spannbetonbecken n

~ (~) **rib** · Spannbetonrippe f

~ (~) **rib(bed) floor** · Spannbetonrippendecke f

~ (~) ~ **slab** · Spannbetonrippenplatte f

~ (~) **rigid frame,** rigid prestressed (concrete) ~ · Spannbeton-Steifrahmen m

~ (~) **ring beam** · Spannbetonringbalken(träger) m

~ (~) **roof beam** · Spannbetondachbalken(träger) m

~ (~) ~ **cladding,** ~ (~) ~ covering, ~ (~) ~ sheathing, ~ (~) roof(ing) · Spannbetondach(belag) n, (m), Spannbeton(dach)(ein)deckung f, Spannbetonbedachung

~ (~) ~ **covering,** ~ (~) ~ cladding, ~ (~) ~ sheathing, ~ (~) roof(ing) · Spannbetondach(belag) n, (m), Spannbeton(dach)(ein)deckung f, Spannbetonbedachung

~ (~) ~ **sheathing,** ~ (~) ~ covering, ~ (~) ~ cladding, ~ (~) roof(ing) · Spannbetondach(belag) n, (m), Spannbeton(dach)(ein)deckung f, Spannbetonbedachung

~ (~) **roof(ing),** ~ (~) roof cladding, ~ (~) roof covering, ~ (~) roof sheathing · Spannbetondach(belag) n (m), Spannbeton(dach)(ein)deckung f, Spannbetonbedachung

~ (~) ~ **slab** · Spannbeton-Bedachungselement n, Spannbeton-Dachelement, Spannbeton-Bedachungsplatte f, Spannbeton-Dachplatte

~ (~) **seating slab** · Spannbetonsitzplatte f [*Stadionbau*]

~ (~) **section** · Spannbetonquerschnitt m

~ (~) **sewage pipe,** ~ (~) sewer ~, ~ (~) foul water ~, ~ (~) refuse water ~ · Spannbeton-Abwasserrohr n, Spannbeton-Kanal(isations)rohr

~ (~) **shell** · Spannbetonschale f

~ (~) ~ **construction** · Spannbetonschalenbau m

~ (~) ~ **roof** · Spannbetonschalendach n

~ (~) **silo** · Spannbetonsilo m

~ (~) **skeleton** → ~ (~) structural ~

~ (~) **slab,** ~ (~) plate · Spannbetonplatte f [*Ein Flächentragwerk aus Spannbeton bei dem die Kräfte quer zur Mittelebene angreifen*]

~ (~) ~ **base,** ~ (~) ~ foundation, ~ (~) plate ~ · Spannbeton-Plattenfundament n

~ (~) ~ **floor,** ~ (~) plate ~ · Spannbetonplattendecke f

~ (~) ~ **foundation,** ~ (~) ~ base, ~ (~) plate ~ · Spannbeton-Plattenfundament n

~ (~) **slab-and-beam,** ~ (~) T(ee)-beam, ~ (~) tee-beam · Spannbeton-Plattenbalken m

~ (~) ~ **floor,** ~ (~) T(ee)-beam ~, ~ (~) tee-beam ~ · Spannbeton-Plattenbalkendecke f

~ (~) **solid plank** · Spannbetonvolldiele f

~ (~) ~ **slab,** ~ (~) ~ plate · Spannbetonvollplatte f

~ (~) ~ **web(bed) beam,** ~ (~) plain ~ ~ · Spannbeton-Vollwandbalken(träger) m

~ (~) ~ **girder,** ~ (~) plain ~ ~ · Spannbeton-Vollwandträger m

~ (~) **space (load)bearing structure,** ~ (~) three-dimensional ~, ~ (~) spatial ~ ~, ~ (~) ~ (weightcarrying) ~, ~ (~) ~ supporting ~, ~ (~) ~ loaded ~ · Spannbeton-Raumtragwerk n

~ (~) **spun pipe,** ~ (~) centrifugally cast ~ · Betonschleudervorspannrohr n, Schleuderbetonvorspannrohr

~ (~) **stair(case)** · Spannbetontreppe f

~ (~) **storage tank** · Spannbetonlagertank m, Spannbetonlagerbehälter m

~ (~) **stringer** (US); ~ (~) string (Brit.) · Spannbeton(treppen)wange f

~ (~) **(structural) skeleton,** ~ (~) (load)bearing ~, ~ (~) weightcarrying ~ · Spannbeton(trag)skelett n, Spannbeton(trag)gerippe n

~ (~) **structure** · Spannbetonbau(werk) m, (n), Spannbetonkonstruktion f

~ (~) **system** · Spannbeton-Tragsystem n

~ (~) **support,** ~ (~) column · Spannbetonstütze f

~ (~) **supporting skeleton** → ~ (~) (load)bearing ~

~ (~) **(suspended) floor,** ~ (~) intermediate ~, ~ (~) suspension ~ · (Gebäude-)Spannbetondecke f, Spannbeton-Trenndecke, Spannbeton-Etagendecke, Spannbeton-Geschoßdecke, Spannbeton-Stockwerkdecke, Hochbau-Spannbetondecke, Geschoß-Spannbetondecke, Stockwerk-Spannbetondecke, Etagen-Spannbetondecke, Spannbetondecke im Hochbau

~ (~) ~ **roof,** ~ (~) suspension ~ · Hänge-Spannbetondach n, Spannbeton-Hängedach

prestressed (concrete)... — prestressed (pre)cast...

~ (~) suspension floor → ~ (~) (suspended) ~

~ (~) ~ roof, ~ (~) suspended ~ · Spannbeton-Hängedach n, Hänge-Spannbetondach

~ (~) tank, ~ (~) reservoir · Spannbetonbehälter m

~ (~) T(ee)-beam, ~ (~) slab-and-beam, ~ (~) tee-beam · Spannbeton-Plattenbalken m

~ (~) ~ floor, ~ (~) slab-and-beam ~, ~ (~) tee-beam ~ · Spannbeton-Plattenbalkendecke f

~ (~) three-dimensional (weight-carrying) structure → ~ (~) space (load)bearing ~

~ (~) tie-rod, ~ (~) bowstring, ~ (~) (horizontal) tie(back) · Spannbetonzugband n

~ (~) tilted-slab roof, ~ (~) hipped-plate ~ (US); ~ (~) folded slab ~, ~ (~) folded plate ~, ~ (~) prismatic shell ~ · Spannbetondachfaltwerk n, Spannbetonfalt(werk)dach n

~ (~) triangular truss · Spannbeton-Dreieckfachwerkträger m

~ (~) trimmer plank (unit) · Spannbetonstreichdiele f [*Auswechs(e)lung*]

~ ~ truss → ~ ~ lattice ~

~ (~) truss(ed girder) · Spannbetonfachwerk(träger) n, (m)

~ (~) tunnel vault, ~ (~) barrel ~, ~ (~) wagon ~ · Spannbeton-Tonne(ngewölbe) f, (n)

~ (~) type of construction, ~ (~) construction type · Spannbetonbauart f

~ (~) umbrella, ~ (~) parachute · Spannbetonschirm m

~ (~) vault · Spannbetongewölbe n

~ (~) Vierendeel girder, ~ (~) ~ truss [*It does not satisfy the definition of a truss but is given that designation*] · Spannbeton-Vierendeelträger m, Vierendeel-Spannbetonträger

~ (~) waffle slab, ~ (~) pan(el) ~, ~ (~) coffer ~, ~ (~) cassette ~, ~ (~) plate ~, ~ (~) rectangular grid ~ · Spannbetonkassetten(decken)-platte f

~ (~) wagon vault, ~ (~) barrel ~, ~ (~) tunnel ~ · Spannbeton-Tonne(ngewölbe) f, (n)

~ ~ wall → monolithic ~ ~ ~

~ (~) ~ panel · Spannbetonwandtafel f

~ (~) water tower · Spannbeton-Wasserturm m

~ (~) weight-carrying skeleton, ~ (~) (structural) ~, ~ (~) (load)bearing ~, ~ (~) supporting ~, ~ (~) load-carrying ~, ~ (~) loaded ~ · Spannbetongerippe n, Spannbetontraggerippe, Spannbeton(trag)skelett n

~ (~) window lintel; ~ (~) ~ lintol [*deprecated*] · Spannbetonfensteroberschwelle f, Spannbetonfenstersturz m

~ ~ with thin wires, Hoyer method · Saitenbeton m, Stahl~, Bauweise f Hoyer

~ (~) work · Spannbetonarbeit(en) f(pl)

~ connection, stretched ~, tensioned ~ · (Vor)Spannverbindung f

~ in pairs, stretched ~, tensioned ~ ~ · paarweise vorgespannt [*Spanndrähte*]

~ light(weight) aggregate concrete · Leichtzuschlag(stoff)-Spannbeton m

~ ~ concrete, light(weight) prestressed ~ · Leichtspannbeton m, vorgespannter Leichtbeton

~ ~ ~ member, light(weight) prestressed ~ ~, ~ ~ ~ unit, ~ ~ ~ component · Leichtspannbetonelement n, Spannbetonleichtelement, Leichtspannbetonkörper m, Spannbetonleichtkörper [*Fehlname: Leichtspannbetoneinheit f*]

~ ~ ~ roof(ing) slab · Leichtspannbeton-Dachplatte f

~ masonry tank, ~ ~ · reservoir · vorgespannter gemauerter Behälter m, ~ Mauerwerkbehälter

~ monolithic (concrete) wall, (monolithic) prestressed (~) ~ · Spannbetonwand f

~ mortar · Spannmörtel m

~ (pre)cast (concrete) beam, (pre-)cast prestressed (~) ~ · Spannbetonfertigträger m

~ ~ (~) construction, (pre)cast prestressed (~) ~, ~ ~ (~) system building · Spannbeton-Fertigteilbau m, Spannbeton-Montagebau, Bauen n mit Spannbetonfertigteilen

~ ~ (~) floor, (pre)cast prestressed (~) ~ · Spannbeton-Fertigdecke f, Spannbeton-Fertigteildecke, Spannbeton-Montagedecke, Montage-Spannbetondecke

~ ~ (~) lintel, (pre)cast prestressed (~) ~; ~ ~ ~ (~) lintol [*deprecated*] · Spannbeton-Fertigoberschwelle f, Spannbeton-Fertigteiloberschwelle, vorgefertigte Spannbetonoberschwelle vorgefertigter Spannbetonsturz m, Spannbeton-Fertig(teil)sturz

~ ~ (~) panel, (pre)cast prestressed (~) ~ · Spannbetonfertigtafel f

~ ~ (~) slab, (pre)cast prestressed (~) ~, ~ ~ (~) plate · Spannbeton-Fertigplatte f

~ ~ (~) string, (pre)cast prestressed (~) ~ (Brit.); ~ ~ ~ (~) stringer (US) · Spannbeton-Fertig(teil)wange f

~ ~ (~) system building, (pre)cast prestressed (~) ~ ~, ~ ~ (~) construction · Spannbeton-Fertigteilbau m, Spannbeton-Montagebau, Bauen n mit Spannbetonfertigteilen

~ ~ (~) tee-section, (pre)cast prestressed (~) ~ · Spannbeton-Fertig-T-Profil n

~ ~ (~) wall, (pre)cast prestressed (~) ~ · Spannbeton-Fertig(teil)wand f, Montagespannbetonwand, Spannbeton-Montagewand

~ ~ (~) ~ slab, (pre)cast prestressed (~) ~ · Spannbeton-Wand(bau)platte f [vorgefertigt]

~ ~ floor → (pre)cast prestressed (concrete) ~

~ prefab(ricated) concrete floor → (pre)cast prestressed (~) ~

~ ~ ~ wall → (pre)cast prestressed (~) ~

~ structure, ~ concrete ~ · Spannbetonbau(werk) m, (n), Spannbetonkonstruktion f

~ system composed of straight-edged cable nets with opposite curvatures · vorgespanntes System n zusammengesetzt aus gradlinig begrenzten Seilnetzen mit gegensinniger Krümmung

~ wall → monolithic prestressed concrete ~

(pre)stressing, stretching, tensioning · (Vor)Spannen n [Spannbeton]

~, stretching, tensioning · Vorspannung f

~ area, tensioning ~, stretching ~, ~ zone · Spnan(ungs)zone f, Vor~

~ bar, tensioning ~, stretching ~, ~ rod · Spannstab m, Vor~

~ bed, ~ table, ~ line; ~ mold (US); ~ mould (Brit.) · Spannbahn f, Spannbett n

~ block, tensioning ~, stretching ~ · Spannblock m [Spannbeton]

~ element, tensioning ~, stretching ~ · Spannelement n

~ factory → ~ plant

~ force → ~ stress

~ jack, tensioning ~, stretching ~, jack(ing device) for prestressed concrete · Spann(beton)presse f

~ lesene, ~ pilaster-strip · Spannlisene f

~ line, ~ bed, ~ table; ~ mold (US); ~ mould (Brit.) · Spannbahn f, Spannbett n

~ loss, tensioning ~, stretching ~ [*The reduction of the (pre)stressing force which results from the combined effects of creep in the steel and creep and shrinkage of the concrete. This term does not normally include friction losses but may include the effect of elastic deformation of the concrete*] · (Vor-)Spann(ungs)verlust m

~ method, ~ system, tensioning ~, stretching ~ · Spannbetonverfahren n, (Vor)Spann(ungs)verfahren

~ mold (US); ~ mould (Brit.); ~ line, ~ bed, ~ table · Spannbahn f, Spannbett n

~ moment · (Vor)Spannmoment n

~ order, tensioning ~, stretching ~ · (Vor)Spannfolge f

~ pilaster-strip, ~ lesene · Spannlisene f

~ plant, ~ yard, ~ factory, tensioning ~, stretching ~ · Vorspannwerk n, Spannbetonwerk

~ process, process of (pre)stressing · Aufbringen n der Vorspannung

~ reinforcement, tensioning ~, stretching ~, ~ steel [*B.S. 2691*] · (Vor)Spann(stahl)einlagen fpl, (Vor)Spannbewehrung f, (Vor)Spannarmierung, (Vor-)Spann(beton)stahl m

~ rod, tensioning ~, stretching ~, ~ bar · Spannstab m, Vor~

~ steel → ~ reinforcement

(~) strand, tensioning ~, stretching ~ [*A prestressing tendon composed of a number of wires most of which are twisted about a center wire or core*] · (Vor)Spannlitze f, (Draht)(Seil)Litze

~ stress, ~ force, stretching ~, tensioning ~ · (Vor)Spannkraft f

~ system, ~ method, tensioning ~, stretching ~ · Spannbetonverfahren n, (Vor)Spann(ungs)verfahren

~ table, ~ bed, ~ line; ~ mold (US); ~ mould (Brit.) · Spannbahn f, Spannbett n

(~) tendon, stretching ~, tensioning ~ [*A stretched element used in a concrete member or structure to impart prestress to the concrete*] · (Vor)Spannglied n

~ value, tensioning ~, stretching ~ · (Vor)Spann(ungs)wert m

~ wedge, tensioning ~, stretching ~ · Spannkeil m [Spannbeton]

~ wire, steel wire for prestressed concrete [*B.S. 2691*] · (Vorspann)Bündeldraht m, Spann(beton)(kabel)draht

~ wires in pairs, tensioning ~ ~ ~, stretching ~ ~ ~ · paarweise Vorspannung f [Spanndrähte]

~ yard → ~ plant

~ zone, tensioning ~, stretching ~, ~ area · Spann(ungs)zone f, Vor~

to pretension · (vor)spannen der Spannelemente vor dem Betonieren

pretensioned (prestressed) (concrete) beam · Spannbetonbalken(träger) m in Vorspannung mit sofortigem Verbund

~ ~ (~) girder · Spannbetonträger m mit sofortigem Verbund

~ tendon · (Vor)Spannglied n mit sofortigem Verbund

pretensioning [*In pretensioning, the tendons are first tensioned against abutments. Concrete is placed around them, and when it hardens the tendons are*

pretensioning — priming (coat)

released – (pre)stressing the concrete] · Vorspannung f mit sofortigem Verbund, ~ vor dem Betoneinbau

~ **bed** · Spannbett n für Vorspannung mit sofortigem Verbund

~ **tendon** · (Vor)Spannglied n für sofortigen Verbund

to pre-treat · vorbehandeln

pre-treatment, preparation, preparatory treatment, preliminary treatment · Vorbehandlung f

~ **agent** · Vorbehandlungsmittel n

~ **fluosilicate** · Vorfluat n, Avantfluat

~ **primer** → etching ~

prevailing weather · Wetterrichtung f

preven(ta)tive remedy · Vorbeugungsmaßnahme f, Pflegemaßnahme

prevention · Verhütung f

~ **of damage** · Schadensverhütung f

~ ~ **skin formation** · Hautverhinderung f, Hautverhütung [*Anstrichtechnik*]

preventive maintenance · vorbeugende Instandhaltung f, Pflege f

~ **remedy, preventative** ~ · Vorbeugungsmaßnahme f, Pflegemaßnahme

~ **wood protection** · vorbeugender Holzschutz m, pflegender ~

previous church · Vorgängerkirche f

pre-war Expressionismus · Vorkriegsexpressionismus m

~ **housing** · Vorkriegswohnungsbau m

pre-weld heat treatment · Wärmebehandlung f vor dem Schweißen

pre-wetting · Vornässen n

~ **agent, precoating** ~ · Vorbenetzungsmittel n

price group · Preisklasse f

priced bill (of quantities) · ausgefülltes Leistungsverzeichnis n, ~ LV

pricing, costing · (Kosten)Kalkulation f

~ **department, costing** ~ · Kalkulationsbüro n, Kalkulationsabteilung f

pricking-up coat [*The first undercoat of three-coat work on lath(ing)*] · Unterputzschicht f auf Putzträger, Unterputzlage f ~ ~, Grobputzschicht ~ ~, Grobputzlage ~ ~, Rauhwerk n ~ ~

prick-through type lampholder Schnellanzapfstecker m für Lampen

priests' choir, ~ **quire** · Priesterchor m

priest's house, parsonage (building), rectory [*In the Roman Catholic Church called 'presbytery'*] · Pfarre f, Pfarrhaus n

prillion, tin extracted from slag · Schlakkenzinn n

primary air [*Any air which is mixed with the fuel at or in the burner or fuel bed, for the purpose of promoting combustion of the fuel or combustible materials*] · Erstluft f, Primärluft f

~ **beam, principal** ~**, main** ~ · Hauptbalken(träger) m

primary bending stress · Hauptbiegespannung f, Hauptbiegungsspannung

~ **circulator,** ~ **gas (water)** ~ · Haupt-Umlauf-Gaswasserheizer m, Haupt-(Gas)Heiztherme f

~ **clay** · Urton m

~ **deformation** · primäre Verformung f, ~ Formänderung

~ **gas (water) circulator,** ~ circulator · Haupt-Umlauf-Gaswasserheizer m, Haupt-(Gas)Heiztherme f

~ **particle** · Primärteilchen n, Einzelteilchen [*Pigment*]

~ **product** · Vorprodukt n

~ **return** · Erstrücklauf m, Hauptrücklauf

~ **rock, igneous** ~ · Magmagestein n, Glutflußgestein, Erstarrungsgestein, Massengestein, Magmatit m, massiges Gestein; älteres Eruptivgestein [*im weiteren Sinne*]

~ **school, elementary** ~ · Grundschule f

prime, best quality [*The standard of first-quality ware*] · erste Wahl f

to prime (coat) · grundieren

prime coat, priming (~), primer · Grund(ier)anstrich m, Grund(ier)aufstrich, Grund(ierung) m, (f) [*Ein Grund(ier) anstrich besteht aus einer Anstrichschicht oder mehreren Anstrichschichten, die geeignet ist oder sind, als Verbindungsglied zwischen dem Untergrund und den auf den Grundanstrich aufgebrachten Anstrichschichten zu dienen. Er kann auch noch besondere Aufgaben, wie Korrosionsschutz usw., erfüllen. Im heutigen Sprachgebrauch wird der Begriff ,,Grundierung" auch noch für den Anstrichstoff zum Grundieren verwendet*]

~ **coating, priming** · Vor(an)streichen n, Grundieren

~ ~ **(road) tar** · Erstbehandlungs(straßen)teer m

~ ~ **with linseed oil, priming** ~ ~ ~ · Leinölgrundieren n, Leinölgrundierung f

~ **cost, flat** ~ · Gestehungskosten f

primed · grundiert

primer · Grundanstrichstoff m, Grundanstrichmittel n, Grundierstoff, Grundiermittel, Grund(ierung) m, (f)

~ → prime coat

primer-filler, primer-sealer, primer-surfacer · Füllgrund m, Grundierfüller m, Einheitsmaterial n [*Anstrichtechnik*]

primer paint, priming ~ · Grundier(anstrich)farbe f, Grundfarbe

primer-sealer, primer-surfacer, primer-filler · Füllgrund m, Grundierfüller m, Einheitsmaterial n [*Anstrichtechnik*]

primer-surfacer, primer-filler, primer-sealer · Füllgrund m, Grundierfüller m, Einheitsmaterial n [*Anstrichtechnik*]

priming, prime coating · Vor(an)streichen n, Grundieren

~ **(coat)** → prime ~

priming emulsion — principal pedestrian zone

~ emulsion · Grundieremulsion *f*
~ paint, primer ~ · Grundier(anstrich)farbe *f*, Grundfarbe
~ solution · Grundierlösung *f*
~ with linseed oil, prime coating ~ ~ ~ · Leinölgrundieren *n*, Leinölgrundierung *f*
primus stove (Brit.) · Brennspirituskocher *m*
principal → ~ rafter
~ alloying constituent, main ~ ~ · Hauptlegierungsbestandteil *m*
~ altar, main ~ · Hauptaltar *m*
~ axis, main ~ · Hauptachse *f*
~ ~ of inertia, main ~ ~ ~ · Hauptträgheitsachse *f*, Trägheitshauptachse
~ bar, ~ round ~, main (round) ~ · Haupt(rund)stab *m*, Längs(rund)stab [*Betonstahlmatte*]
~ beam, primary ~, main ~ · Hauptbalken(träger) *m*
~ ~, main ~ · Hauptbalken *m* [*doppeltes Hängewerk*]
~ ~, footing ~, tie ~, main ~ · Hauptbalken *m*, Zugbalken, Spannbalken, Trambaken [*einsäuliges Hängewerk*]
~ bearing structure → main (load) bearing ~
~ block, main ~, ~ building · Hauptgebäude *n*
~ building, main ~, ~ block · Hauptgebäude *n*
~ ~, main ~, aisled hall · Langhaus *n* [*Teil einer Kirche zwischen Fassade und Querhaus bzw. Chor*]
~ ~ bay, main ~ ~, aisled hall ~ · Langhausjoch *n*
~ ~ vault, main ~ ~, aisled hall ~ · Langhausgewölbe *n*
~ cable, main ~ · Hauptkabel *n*
~ case of loading → main loading case
~ centre (Brit.); ~ center (US); main ~ · Hauptzentrum *n*
~ chapel, main ~ · Hauptkapelle *f*
~ choir, main ~, ~ quire · Hauptchor *m*
~ cock, main ~ · Haupthahn *m*
~ collector → main sewer
~ column, main ~ · Hauptstütze *f*
principal-column foundation, maincolumn ~ · Hauptstützenfundament *n*
principal compressive stress, main ~ ~, ~ compression ~ · Hauptdruckspannung *f*
~ constituent, main ~ · Hauptbestandteil *m*
~ controlling dimension, main ~ ~ [*A dimension between key reference planes, e.g. floor-to-floor height or stor(e)y height*] · Ausbaumaß *n*

~ cupola, ~ dome, main ~ · Hauptkuppel *f*
~ curvature, main ~ · Hauptkrümmung *f*
~ ~ line → line of principal curvature
~ data, main ~ · Hauptdaten *f*
~ diagonal, main ~ · Hauptdiagonale *f*, Hauptschräge *f*
~ ~ rib, main ~ ~ · Hauptdiagonalrippe *f*
~ dimension, main ~ · Hauptabmessung *f*, Hauptmaß *n*
~ direction, main ~ · Hauptrichtung *f*
~ ~ of curvature, main ~ ~ ~ · Hauptkrümmungsrichtung *f*
~ distribution line, main ~ ~ · Hauptverteilungsleitung *f*
~ ~ panel, main ~ ~ · Hauptverteilungstafel *f*
~ dome, ~ cupola, main ~ · Hauptkuppel *f*
~ entrance, main ~ · Haupteingang *m*
~ ~ hall, main ~ ~ · Haupteingangshalle *f*
~ façade, main ~ · Hauptfassade *f*
~ floor → main ~
~ ~ beam, main ~ ~ · Hauptdeckenbalken(träger) *m*
~ frame, main ~ · Hauptrahmen *m*
~ fuse, main ~, company's ~ · Hauptsicherung *f*
~ girder, main ~ · Hauptträger *m*
~ grid, main ~ · Hauptraster *m*
~ hall, main ~ · Haupthalle *f*
~ inspection chamber, main ~ ~ [*See remark under 'Revisionsschacht'*] · Hauptrevisionsschacht *m*
~ kitchen, main ~ · Hauptküche *f*
~ living area, main ~ ~ · Hauptwohnzone *f*
~ load, main ~ · Hauptlast *f*
~ (load)bearing structure → main ~
~ load-carrying structure → main (load)bearing ~
~ loaded structure → main (load) bearing ~
~ loading case → main ~ ~
~ longitudinal force, main ~ ~ · Hauptlängskraft *f*
~ mall, main ~ · Hauptkorso *m*
~ masonry wall, main ~ ~ · Hauptmauer *f*
~ moment, main ~ · Hauptmoment *n*
~ ~ of inertia, main ~ ~ ~ · Hauptträgheitsmoment *n*
~ motif, main ~ · Leitmotiv *n*
~ mo(u)lding → ~ cornice
~ normal, main ~ · Hauptnormale *f*
~ office, main ~ · Hauptbüro *n*
~ pedestrian zone, main ~ ~ · Hauptfußgängerbereich *m, n*

principal pipe — principle of virtual forces

~ **pipe**, main ~ · Hauptrohr *n*
~ **plane**, main ~ · Hauptebene *f* [*Baustatik*]
~ **portal**, main ~ · Hauptportal *n*
~ **post**, ~ stud, main ~, door ~, door check · Türpfosten *m*, Türständer *m*, Türsäule *f* [*Fach(werk)wand*]
~ ~, ~ vertical, main ~, corner ~, angle ~, corner stud · Eckpfosten *m*, Eckständer *m*, Eckstiel *m*, Ecksäule *f* [*Fachwerkbau*]
~ **quire**, main ~, ~ choir · Hauptchor *m*
~ **radius of inertia**, main ~ ~ ~ · Hauptträgheitshalbmesser *m*
~ **(rafter)**, main ~, blade · Hauptsparren *m*, Bundsparren, Bindersparren
~ **rafters**, main ~, principals, blades [*The main rafters, those in the roof truss which carry the purlin(e)s on which the common rafters are laid*] · Bindersparren *mpl*, Hauptsparren, Bundsparren, Bundgespärre *n*, Bindergespärre
~ **(railroad) station** → central (railway) ~
~ **(railway) station** → central (~) ~
~ **reinforcement**, main ~ · Hauptarmierung *f*, Hauptbewehrung Haupt-(stahl)einlagen *fpl*
~ **restaurant**, main ~ · Hauptspeisesaal *m* [*Hotel*]
~ **rib**, main ~ · Haupttrippe *f*
~ **riser**, main ~, rising main · Hauptsteig(e)leitung *f*
~ **(round) bar**, main (~) ~ · Haupt-(rund)stab *m*, Längs(rund)stab [*Betonstahlmatte*]
~ **services centre**, main ~ ~ (Brit.); ~ ~ center (US) · technische Hauptzentrale *f* [*Eines Hochhauses oder eines Gebäudekomplexes*]
~ **sewer** → main ~
~ **shear(ing) stress**, main ~ ~ · Hauptschubspannung *f*
~ **stage**, main ~ · Hauptbühne *f*
~ **stair(case)**, main ~ · Haupttreppe *f*
~ **station** → central (railway) ~
~ **steel beam**, main ~ ~ · Hauptstahlbalken(träger) *m*
~ ~ **girder**, main ~ ~ · Stahlhauptträger *m*
~ **storey** (Brit.) → main floor
~ **strain**, main ~ · Hauptdehnung *f*
~ **stress**, main ~ · Hauptspannung *f*
~ ~ **line** → line of principal stress
~ **structure**, main ~ · Hauptbau(werk) *m*, (*n*)
~ ~ ~ → main (load)bearing ~
~ **stud**, ~ post, door ~, door check · Türpfosten *m*, Türständer *m*, Türsäule *f* [*Fach(werk)wand*]
~ **stupa(-mound)** → main ~
~ **supporting structure** → main (load)bearing ~

~ **switch board**, main ~ ~ · Hauptschalttafel *f*
~ **switchroom**, main ~ · Hauptschaltraum *m*
~ **symbol**, main ~ · Hauptzeichen *n* [*Baustatik*]
~ **temple**, main ~ · Haupttempel *m*
~ **tensile reinforcement**, main ~ ~ · Hauptzugarmierung *f*, Hauptzugbewehrung, Hauptzug(stahl)einlagen *fpl*
~ ~ **stress**, main ~ ~ · Hauptzugspannung *f*
~ ~ ~ **limit**, main ~ ~ ~ · Hauptzugspannungsgrenze *f*
~ **terminal building** → main ~ ~
~ **tope(-mound)** → main stupa (-mound)
~ **transept** → main ~
~ **valley**, main ~ · Hauptkehle *f* [*Dach*]
~ **value**, main ~ · Hauptwert *m*
~ **vault**, main ~ · Hauptgewölbe *n*
~ **vertical**, ~ post, corner ~, main ~, angle ~, corner stud · Ecksäule *f*, Eckpfosten *m*, Eckstiel *m*, Eckständer *m* [*Fachwerkbau*]
~ **walk**, main ~ · Hauptgehweg *m*
~ **(weight-carrying) structure** → main (load)bearing ~
~ **wind direction**, main ~ ~ · Hauptwindrichtung *f*
~ **wire feeder** → main ~ ~
principals → principal rafters
principle of complementary virtual work, ~ ~ virtual forces [*It states that the increment of complementary strain energy is equal to the increment of the complementary work done by the virtual forces acting through the real displacement*] · Prinzip *n* der virtuellen Kräfte
~ ~ **equilibrium** · Gleichgewichtsprinzip *n*
~ ~ **least work (of deformation)** · Prinzip *n* vom Minimum der Formänderungsarbeit
~ ~ **minimum potential energy**, theorem ~ ~ ~ ~, law ~ ~ ~ ~ · Prinzip *n* vom Minimum der potentiellen Energie
~ ~ **style** · Stilgesetz *n*
~ ~ **superposition**, theorem ~ ~, law ~ ~, superposition law, superposition theorem, superposition principle · Überlagerungsgesetz *n*, Superpositionsgesetz
~ ~ **virtual displacements**, theorem ~ ~ ~, law ~ ~ ~, virtual-displacement theorem, virtual-displacement principle, virtual-displacement law · Prinzip *n* der virtuellen Verrückungen
~ ~ ~ **forces**, ~ ~ complementary virtual work [*It states that the increment of complementary strain energy is equal to the increment of the complementary work done by the virtual forces acting through the real displacements*] · Prinzip *n* der virtuellen Kräfte

principle of virtual work — process of adaptation

~ ~ ~ **work,** theorem ~ ~ ~, law ~ ~ ~, virtual-work theory, virtual-work law, virtual-work principle · Prinzip *n* der virtuellen Arbeit

print, tracing · (Licht)Pause *f*

printed design, ~ pattern · Druckmuster *n*

~ **lino(leum),** stamped ~ [*This lino-(leum) has a pattern printed on the surface with oil paint*] · Drucklinoleum *n*

~ **pattern,** ~ design · Druckmuster *n*

~ **picture tile** · bedruckte Bildfliese *f*, ~ Bild(belag)platte *f*

~ **(wall)paper** · Druck(papier)tapete *f*, gedruckte (Papier)Tapete

printing block, ~ building · Druckereigebäude *n*

~ **building,** ~ block · Druckereigebäude *n*

~ **room** · Druckerei *f* [*als Teil eines Bürogebäudes*]

priory, charterhouse · Kartäuserhaus *n*

~ · Propstei *f*

prismatic · prismenförmig

~ **beam,** rectangular (cross-section(al)) ~ · Balken(träger) *m* mit gleichbleibendem Querschnitt, Rechteckbalken(träger), prismatischer Balken(träger)

~ ~ **bending test** · Prismen-Biegeprobe *f*, Prismen-Biegeprüfung *f*, Prismen-Biegeversuch *m*

~ ~ **crushing strength** · Prismendruckfestigkeit *f*

~ **bearing structure** → ~ supporting ~

~ **cupola,** ~ dome · Prismenkuppel *f*

~ **diffuser** · Prismenwanne *f* [*Leuchte*]

~ **dome,** ~ cupola · Prismenkuppel *f*

~ **glass** [*Glass with sawtooth section on one side to refract the light*] · prismatisches Glas *n*, Prismenglas

~ **lead spar,** red ~ ~ · hemiprismatisches Bleibaryt *n*

~ **(load)bearing structure,** ~ (weight-carrying) ~, ~ supporting ~ · Prismentragwerk *n*

~ **(pitched-slab) structure** · prismatisches Faltwerk *n*

~ **roof** · prismatisches Dach *n*

~ **shell cupola** → folded plate dome

~ ~ **dome** → folded plate ~

~ ~ **roof** → folded plate ~

~ ~ **segment** → folded plate ~

~ ~ **(structure)** → folded plate (~)

~ **space truss** · prismatisches Raumfachwerk *n*

~ **structure** → ~ supporting ~

~ ~, ~ pitch-slab ~ · prismatisches Faltwerk *n*

~ **supporting structure,** ~ (load)bearing ~, ~ (weight-carrying) ~ · Prismentragwerk *n*

~ **(weight-carrying) structure,** ~ (load)bearing ~, ~ supporting ~ · Prismentragwerk *n*

prismoid(al) (slab) roof · Prismoiddach *n*

prison building, ~ construction · Strafanstaltbau *m*

~ **construction,** ~ building · Strafanstaltbau *m*

privacy · Abgeschlossenheit *f*

private access; drive (Brit.); driveway (US) · Privatzufahrt *f*

~ **architect,** free-lance ~, independent ~ · freischaffender Architekt *m*

~ **balcony** · Einzelbalkon *m* [*Im Gegensatz zum Laubengang*]

~ **bathroom** · Zimmerbad *n* [*Hotel*]

~ **building,** ~ house · Privathaus *n*, Privatgebäude *n*

~ **chapel,** domestic ~ · Hauskapelle *f*, Privatkapelle, private Kapelle

~ **conduit-type sewer** · privater Abwasserkanal *m*

~ **corridor** · Privatflur *m*, Privatgang *m*, Privatkorridor *m* [*Im Gegensatz zum öffentlichen Flur*]

~ **development** · private Bebauung *f*

~ **dining-room** · Privatspeiseraum *m* [*Hotel*]

~ **dwelling house** · Privatwohnhaus *n*

~ **garage** · Privatgarage *f*

~ **ground** · Privatgelände *n*

~ **house,** ~ building · Privathaus *n*, Privatgebäude *n*

~ **housing** · privater Wohn(ungs)bau *m*

~ **letter-box** · Hausbriefkasten *m*

~ **open area** · private Freifläche *f*

~ **path** · Privatweg *m*

~ **provision of water** → ~ water supply

~ **sewer** · private Abwasserleitung *f*

~ **water supply,** ~ WS, ~ provision of water · Eigenwasserversorgung *f*

~ **well** · Privatbrunnen *m*

privy pit, f(a)eces ~ · Fäkaliengrube *f*, Abortgrube, Latrinengrube, Abtrittgrube

prize for architecture, architectural award · Architekturpreis *m*

prize-winning, award-winning · preisgekrönt

probabilistic design method, ~ method of design [*A design method in which the safety conditions are expressed by specifying a priori the probability that a structure will preserve its functional capacity over a given period of time*] · Wahrscheinlichkeits-Bemessungsverfahren *n*

problem · Aufgabe *f*

process · Ablauf *m*, Vorgang *m*, Verlauf *m*, Prozeß *m*

~ **of adaptation,** ~ ~ adjustment · Anpassungsprozeß *m*

process of curing — profile(d) pipe

~ ~ **curing,** curing process · (Ab)Bindeprozeß m, (Ab)Bindevorgang m, (Ab-)Bindeverlauf m [*Verschnittbitumen*]

~ ~ **hardening,** hardening process · (Er-)Härtungsvorgang m, (Er)Härtungsprozeß m, (Er)Härtungsverlauf m, (Er)Härtungsablauf, Härtevorgang, Härteverlauf, Härteprozeß, Härteablauf

~ ~ **hydration,** hydration process [*The process of formation of a compound by the combining of water with some other substance; in concrete, the chemical reaction between cement and water*] · Hydra(ta)tionsvorgang m, Hydra(ta)tionsprozeß m, Hydra(ta)tionsablauf m, Hydra(ta)tionsverlauf

~ ~ **initial set(ting),** initial set(ting) process · Erstarrungsvorgang m, Erstarrungsverlauf m, Erstarrungsprozeß m, Erstarrungsablauf

~ ~ **(pre)stressing,** ~ ~ tensioning, ~ ~ stretching, (pre)stressing process, tensioning process, stretching process · Aufbringen n der Vorspannung

~ ~ **set(ting),** set(ting) process · (Ab-)Bindeprozeß m, (Ab)Bindeablauf m, (Ab)Bindevorgang m, (Ab)Bindeverlauf [*hydraulisches Bindemittel*]

~ ~ **stressing** → ~ ~ pre~

~ ~ **stretching** → ~ ~ (pre)stressing

~ ~ **tensioning** → ~ ~ (pre)stressing

processing → materials ~

~ **addition** [*A material that is interground or blended in limited amounts into a hydraulic cement during manufacture to aid in manufacturing and handling the cement*] · Aufbereitungshilfe f [*Zement*]

~ **of passengers,** handling ~ ~ · Fahrgastabfertigung f, Passagierabfertigung

~ ~ **swimming pool water** · Aufbereitung f von Schwimmbeckenwasser

processional circuit · Prozessionsweg m [*Tempel*]

~ **path** · Ringpfad m [*Stupa*]

~ **temple,** cult ~ · Kulttempel m, Göttertempel

~ **walk** · Prozessionsgang m

~ **way of sphinxes,** avenue ~ ~ · Spinxallee f

producer, maker, manufacturer, fabricator · Erzeuger m, Hersteller, Fabrikant m

producer-gas brown-coal tar, ~ lignite ~ · Braunkohlen-Generatorteer m

~ **coal tar,** gas-producer ~ ~ · Steinkohlengeneratorteer m, Steinkohlenheizgeneratorteer m

~ **lignite tar,** ~ brown-coal ~ · Braunkohlen-Generatorteer m

~ **tar** · Generatorteer m

~ ~ **pitch** · Generatorteerpech n

product, article · Artikel m, Gegenstand m, Erzeugnis n

~ **maker** → (pre)cast (concrete) product manufacturer

~ **manufacturer** → (pre)cast concrete ~ ~

~ **of combustion** · Verbrennungserzeugnis n

~ ~ **inertia** · Trägheitsprodukt n

~ **performance evaluation** → quality audit

~ **producer** → (pre)cast (concrete) product manufacturer

production hangar, manufacturing ~ · Fertigungshalle f, Produktionshalle, Fabrikationshalle, Herstellungshalle

products, articles, ware, goods · Artikel mpl, Ware(n) f, Erzeugnisse npl, Gegenstände mpl

profane architecture, secular ~, civic ~, non-ecclesiastical ~ · weltliche Architektur f, ~ Baukunst f, Profanarchitektur, Profanbaukunst

~ **Gothic (style),** secular ~ (~), civic ~ (~), non-ecclesiastical ~ (~) · Profangotik f, weltliche Gotik

~ **monument,** secular ~, civic ~, non-ecclesiastical ~ · Profanmonument n

~ **structure,** secular ~, civic ~, non-ecclesiastical ~ · Profanbau(werk) m, (n)

~ **structures,** secular ~, civic ~, non-ecclesiastical ~ · Profanbauten f

professional image · Berufsbild n

profile, section · Profil n, Schnitt m [*Umrißlinie eines durchschnittenen Körpers*]

~, shape, section, unit, trim · Profil n

~ → construction(al) shape

~ **fabricator** → shape maker

~ **for interior work,** shape ~ ~ ~, trim ~ ~ ~, section ~ ~ ~, unit ~ ~ ~ · Ausbauprofil n [*Verglasungsleiste, Türdichtung, Fensterdichtung, Einbau-Vorhangschiene, Badewannen-Wanddichtung usw.*]

~ **maker** → shape ~

~ **of rib,** rib-profile · Rippenprofil n

~ **view** · Profilansicht f

profile(d) aluminium panel, aluminium profile(d) ~ (Brit.); profile(d) aluminum ~, aluminum profile(d) ~ (US) · Alu(minium)-Profiltafel f

~ ~ **roof(ing) sheet** (Brit.); ~ aluminum ~ ~ (US) · Alu(minium)-Profilplatte f für Dacheindeckungen

~ **board,** ~ sheet · Profilplatte f

~ **cast (concrete) panel** → ~ pre~ (~) ~

~ **coping,** ~ capping, ~ cope · Abdeckprofil n [*Flachdach*]

~ **curb;** ~ kerb (Brit.) · Profilbordstein m

~ **element** · Profilelement n

~ **kerb** (Brit.); ~ curb · Profilbordstein m

~ **panel** · Profiltafel f

~ **pipe** · profiliertes Rohr n [*Rohr von nicht kreisförmigem Querschnitt*]

profile(d) plate — proof to swelling

~ **plate**, formed ~ · profiliertes Grobblech *n*, Profilgrobblech

~ **(pre)cast (concrete) panel**, (pre-)cast (concrete) profile(d) ~ · Profilbetontafel *f*

~ **rib** · Profilrippe *f*

~ **sheet**, formed ~ · Profilblech *n*

~ ~, ~ **board** · Profilplatte *f*

~ **sheet(ing)** · Profilbahn *f*

~ **strip** · Profilleiste *f*

~ **surface** · profilierte Oberfläche *f* [*Im Gegensatz zu einer ebenen Oberfläche*]

~ **wire**, indented ~, wire of irregular shape · Profildraht *m*, Formdraht, Dessindraht, Fassondraht, profilierter Draht

profiling · Profilierung *f* [*Durchgestaltung der Umrißlinie*]

profusely enriched, lavishly ~, ~ decorated, ~ ornamented · überreich geschmückt, ~ verziert, ~ geziert

~ **gilt**, lavishly ~ · überreich vergoldet

progress chart · (Bau)Fristenplan *m*

~ **report** · Bauwochenbericht *m*

progressive plane wave · fortschreitende ebene Welle *f*, ebene fortschreitende ~ [*Schalltechnik*]

project, scheme · Projekt *n*

~ **representative** · Bauleiter *m*

projected window, PW · Lüftungsflügelfenster *n*

projecting, salient · vorspringend, ausspringend, vorstehend

~ · Ausladung *f*

~ **angle**, salient ~ · ausspringender Winkel *m*, vorspringender ~

~ **bar** → starter ~

~ **corner**, salient ~ · vorspringende Ecke *f*, ausspringende ~

~ **cover** · Verdachung *f* [*Ein vorspringendes Bauglied über einer Maueröffnung*]

~ **curvature**, curved projection · Verwölbung *f*

~ **diffuser** · überstehende Wanne *f* [*Leuchte*]

~ **flange**, ~ leg, outstanding ~ · abstehender Schenkel *m* [*Winkelstahl*]

~ **leg**, ~ flange, outstanding ~ · abstehender Schenkel *m* [*Winkelstahl*]

projection → jutty

~ · Projektion *f*, Riß *m*

~, attachment · Vorlage *f* [*Ein einer Wand oder Mauer vorgelegtes Bauglied wie Dienst, Lisene oder Pilaster*]

~, attachment · Vorlage *f*, Risalit *m*

~ · Überkragung *f* [*Gewölbe*]

~, forebuilding · Vorbau *m*, vorspringender Bau

~ **both** · Bildwerferraum *m*, Vorführraum [*Kino*]

~ **chamber** · Projektionsraum *m*

~ **cupola**, ~ dome [*e.g. in a planetarium*] · Projektionskuppel *f*

~ **dome**, ~ cupola [*e.g. in a planetarium*] · Projektionskuppel *f*

~ **from a masonry wall**, ~ of ~ ~ ~, attachment to ~ ~ ~ ~ · Mauervorlage *f*, Mauervorsprung *m* [*Ein einer Mauer vorgelegtes Bauglied wie Dienst, Lisene oder Pilaster*]

~ ~ ~ **wall**, attachment to ~ ~ · Wandvorlage *f* [*Ein einer Wand vorgelegtes Bauglied wie Dienst, Lisene oder Pilaster*]

~ **into a street** · Vorsprung *m* in eine Stadtstraße

~ **method** · Projektionsverfahren *n*, Rißverfahren

~ **of a masonry wall** → ~ from ~ ~ ~

~ **plane**, plane of projection · Bildebene *f*, Bildtafel *f*, Rißtafel, Rißebene, Projektionstafel, Projektionsebene

prolate cycloid, ~ trochoid · verschlungene Zykloide *f*

promenade roof(ing) [*Where flat roofs are to be used a promenades it is necessary to surface them in a material that will withstand foot traffic*] · begehbare (Dach)(Ein)Deckung *f*, begehbares Dach *n* [*DIN 4122*]

~ **slab roof(ing)** · begehbares Plattendach *n*, begehbare Platten(dach)(ein)deckung *f*

promoter, accelerator, catalyst [*Strictly speaking a substance which increases the rate of a chemical reaction, but which remains itself chemically unchanged at the end of the reaction*] · Katalysator *m*, (Reaktions)Beschleuniger

promotion of binder adhesion, doping of binders · Haft(fähigkeits)verbesserung *f*, Haftanregung [*Von plastischen Bindemitteln am Gestein*]

promotional lounge · Empfangsraum *m* [*Messestand*]

pronaos · Pronaos *m*, Pronaon *n*, Vorhalle *f* des Antentempels

proof, resistant, resisting, fast · beständig, fest, echt gegen, sicher, widerstandsfähig

~ **to light**, lightproof, fast to light, lightfast, resistant to light, light resistant · lichtbeständig, lichtecht

~ ~ **swelling**, fast ~ ~, resistant ~ ~ · quellfest, quellsicher, quellbeständig, quellwiderstandsfähig

proofing liquid — protection against frost

proofing liquid → liquid waterproofing agent

proofness to light, fastness to light, lightfastness, lightproofness, light resistance, stability to light · Lichtechtheit f, Lichtbeständigkeit f

propagation → sound ~

~ coefficient, ~ constant · Ausbreitungskoeffizient m, Ausbreitungskonstante f [*Akustik. Komplexe Summe von Dämpfungskoeffizient (Realteil) und Phasenkoeffizient (Imaginärteil)*]

property, capacity, quality, power, capability · Eigenschaft f, Vermögen n, Fähigkeit f

~, characteristic quality · Güteeigenschaft f

~, premises [*A lot, plot or parcel of land including the buildings or structures and improvements thereon*] · bebautes Grundstück n

~ line, plot ~ [*A recorded boundary of a plot*] · Grundstücksgrenze f

~ of initial set(ting) → power ~ ~ ~

~ ~ set(ting) → set(ting) power

~ room · Kulissenraum m

~ speculator · Bodenspekulant m

~ well · Hausbrunnen m, Grundstücksbrunnen

to proportion, to measure, to batch, to gauge; to gage (US) · abmessen, zumessen, zuteilen, dosieren

proportion, ratio · Maßverhältnis n, Proportion f

proportionality · Proportionalität f

proportional(ity) law, law of proportionality · Proportionalitätsgesetz n, P-Gesetz ·

~ limit, limit of proportionality · P-Grenze f, Proportionalitätsgrenze

proportionality of stress to strain · Spannungs-Dehnung-Proportionalität f

propped cantilever (beam) (US); beam simply supported at one end and fixed at the other · einseitig eingespannter und einseitig freiauffliegender Balken(träger) m

~ ~ (girder) (US); girder simply supported at one end and fixed at the other · einseitig eingespannter und einseitig freiauffliegender Träger m

propping · Deckenstützensystem n

~ (of floor(s)) · Deckenabstützung f

proprietary door · Markentür f

~ hospital · Privatkrankenhaus n

~ name, brand ~ · Markenname m, Markenbezeichnung f

~ product, marque · Markenartikel m, Markenerzeugnis n, Markenfabrikat n

propylaeum, propyl(ai)on, monumental gateway · Eingangshalle f, Torbau m, Propyl(ai)on n

propyl(ai)on, propylaeum, monumental gateway · Propyl(ai)on n, Eingangshalle f, Torbau m

propylene glycol · Propylenglykol n

proscenium [*1. In an ancient theatre, the space between the scena and the orchestra; hence, the stage. 2. In a modern theatre, the architectural frontispiece of the stage, facing the auditorium*] · Proszenium n, Proskenion n

prospect · Prospekt m [*Die naturgetreue Wiedergabe eines Bauwerks, einer Baugruppe oder Stadtansicht in Kupferstichtechnik oder Malerei*]

prostas(is), pastas · Prostas(is) m, Pastas m [*Vorhalle des griechischen Wohnhauses*]

prostyle [*Literally 'having columns in front'*] · frontsäulig

~ column, front(ed) ~, frontal ~ · Giebelseitensäule f, Frontsäule

~ temple · Prostylos(tempel) m [*Ein Tempel mit einer den Pronaos umschließenden Säulenvorhalle an der Frontseite*]

protected metal sheeting · Stahlwellblech n dessen beide Oberflächen durch Schichten von Asphalt, Asbestgeweben und Farbanstrichen geschützt sind

protecting agent, protective ~, preservative, preserver · Konservierungsmittel n, Schutzmittel, Konservierungsstoff m, Schutzstoff

~ circuit, protective ~ · Schutzschaltung f

~ fluosilicate, protective ~ · Schutzfluat n, Schutzfluorsilikat n [*Gegen schädliche Einflüsse auf Beton, Putz und Mörtel*]

~ foil, cover(ing) ~ · (Ab)Deckfolie f

~ layer, protective ~ · Schutzlage f, Schutzschicht f

~ masonry wall, protective ~ ~ · Schutzmauer f

~ measure, protective ~ · Schutzmaßnahme f

~ plastic film → protective ~ ~

~ ~ sheeting → protective plastic film

~ primer, protective ~ · Schutzgrund(ierung) m, (f)

~ railing, protective ~, safety ~ · Schutzgeländer n

~ salt → wood-~ ~

~ scaffold(ing), protective ~, safety ~ · Schutzgerüst n, Schutzrüstung f

~ screed, protective ~ · Schutzestrich m

~ skin, protective ~ · Schutzhaut f

~ varnish, protective ~ · Schutzlack m

protection against acids, acid protection · Säureschutz m

~ ~ condensation · Kondensatschutz m, Tauwasserschutz, Kondenswasserschutz, Schwitzwasserschutz

~ ~ fire, fire protection · Brandschutz m, Feuerschutz

~ ~ frost · Frostschutz m

protection against moisture — protein glue

~~ **moisture**, ~ ~ humidity · Feuchtigkeitsschutz m, Feuchteschutz

~ ~ **oscillation(s)**, ~ ~ vibration(s) · Erschütterungsschutz m, Schwingungsschutz [DIN 4150. Richtlinien für Bemessung und Ausführung von Bauten in deutschen Erdbebengebieten DIN 4149]

~ ~ **rain** · Regenschutz m

~ ~ **vibration(s)**, ~ ~ oscillation(s) · Schwingungsschutz m, Erschütterungsschutz [DIN 4150. Richtlinien für Bemessung und Ausführung von Bauten in deutschen Erdbebengebieten DIN 4149]

~ **during construction** · Bauschutz m

~ **of monuments** · Denkmalschutz m

~ **painting (work)** · Schutzanstrich m [Aufbringen von Schutzanstrichen]

~ **pigment**, protective ~ · Schutzpigment n

~ **plastic film** → protective ~ ~

~ ~ **sheeting**, protecting ~ ~, perservation ~ ~, protective ~ ~, ~ ~ film · Schutzfolie f, Bauten~

~ **wall**, protective ~ · Schutzwand f

protective action, ~ effect · Schutzwirkung f

~ **agent**, protecting ~, preservative, preserver · Konservierungsmittel n, Schutzmittel, Konservierungsstoff m, Schutzstoff

~ **arch** · Schutzbogen m

~ **circuit**, protecting ~ · Schutzschaltung f

~ **coat** · Schutzanstrich m, Schutzaufstrich

~ ~ **on asbestos cement;** ~ ~ ~ cement asbestos (US) · Asbestzementanstrich m, Asbestzementaufstrich

~ ~ ~ **concrete** · Beton(schutz)anstrich m, Beton(schutz)aufstrich

~ ~ ~ **façade** · Fassadenanstrich m, Fassadenaufstrich

(~) ~ ~ **metal** · Metall(schutz)anstrich m, Metall(schutz)aufstrich

~ ~ ~ **timber**, ~ ~ ~ wood · Holzanstrich m, Holzaufstrich

~ ~ ~ **window** · Fensteranstrich m, Fensteraufstrich

~ ~ ~ **wood**, ~ ~ ~ timber · Holzanstrich m, Holzaufstrich

~ **coating**, ~ (sur)facing · Schutzbeschichten n, Schutzbeschichtung f, Schutzüberzug m, Schutzüberziehen [als Tätigkeit]

~ **coat(ing)**, ~ finish · Schutzbeschichtung f, Schutzüberzug m [als Schicht]

~ **coating (material)** · Schutzanstrichmittel n, Schutzanstrich(stoff) m, Schutzaufstrich(stoff), Schutzaufstrichmittel

~ ~ ~, ~ ~ composition, ~ ~ compound, ~ ~ mass, ~ ~ finish ~, (sur-)facing ~ · Schutzbeschichtungsmasse f, Schutzbeschichtungsstoff m, Schutzüberzugmasse, Schutzüberzugsstoff

~ **colloid** → emulsifying agent

~ **cover on a coat** · Aufstrich-Schutzbelag m, Anstrich-Schutzbelag [Überzug von mineralischen Stoffen auf Anstrichen. Hierdurch wird die Haltbarkeit dieser Anstriche bedeutend verlängert]

~ **earth wall**, rampart [A defensive bank of earth, with or without a stone parapet] · Erdwall m, (Festungs)Wall, Umwallung f

~ **effect**, ~ action · Schutzwirkung f

~ **facing** → ~ coating

~ **finish**, ~ coat(ing) · Schutzbeschichtung f, Schutzüberzug m [als Schicht]

~ ~ **mass**, ~ (sur)facing ~, ~ coating ~, ~ ~ material, ~ ~ compound, ~ ~ composition · Schutzbeschichtungsmasse f, Schutzbeschichtungsstoff m, Schutzüberzugmasse, Schutzüberzugsstoff

~ **fluosilicate**, protecting ~ · Schutzfluat n, Schutzfluorsilikat [Gegen schädliche Einflüsse auf Beton, Putz und Mörtel]

~ **layer**, protecting ~ · Schutzlage f, Schutzschicht f

~ ~ **of fine-grained concrete** · Feinbetonschutzschicht f

~ **masonry wall**, protecting ~ ~ · Schutzmauer f

~ **measure**, protecting ~ · Schutzmaßnahme f

~ **multiple earthing** · Nullung f

~ **packing** · Schutzverpackung f

~ **paint** · Schutz(anstrich)farbe f

~ **pigment**, protection ~ · Schutzpigment n

~ **plastic film**, ~ ~ sheeting, protection ~ ~, preservation ~ ~, protecting ~ ~ · (Bauten)Schutzfolie f

~ **primer**, protecting ~ · Schutzgrund(ierung) m, (f)

~ **railing**, protecting ~, safety ~ · Schutzgeländer n

~ **scaffold(ing)**, protecting ~, safety ~ · Schutzgerüst n, Schutzrüstung f

~ **screed**, protecting ~ · Schutzestrich m

~ **skin**, protecting ~ · Schutzhaut f

~ **stone wall**, rampart · (Natur)Steinmauer f zur Befestigung

~ **(sur)facing**, ~ coating · Schutzbeschichten n, Schutzbeschichtung f, Schutzüberzug m, Schutzüberziehen [als Tätigkeit]

~ ~ **mass**, ~ finish ~, ~ coating ~, ~ ~ material, ~ ~ compound, ~ ~ composition · Schutzbeschichtungsmasse f, Schutzbeschichtungsstoff m, Schutzüberzugmasse, Schutzüberzugsstoff

~ **varnish**, protecting ~ · Schutzlack m

~ **wall**, protection ~ · Schutzwand f

protein glue · Proteinleim m

prothesis · Prothesis f [*Nebenraum byzantinischer und frühchristlicher Kirchenbauten zur Vorbereitung des Meßopfers. Die Prothesis lag symmetrisch zum Diakonikon neben der Apsis. Beide sind die Pastophorien*]

Proto-Baroque architecture · Vorbarock(architektur) n, (f), Vorbarockbaukunst f, Protobarock(architektur), Protobarockbaukunst

Proto-Doric column · protodorische Säule f

protogene gneiss, protogenic ~, protogin(e ~) · Alpengneis m

proto-Ionic capital [*misnomer*] → palm ~

Proto-Renaissance architecture · Vorrenaissancearchitektur f, Vorrenaissancebaukunst f, Protorenaissancearchitektur, Protorenaissancebaukunst

protractor, circular ~ · Winkelmesser m für Linienwinkel

proustite, light-red silver ore · Proustit m, Arsensilberblende f, lichtes Rotgültigerz n, Ag₃AsS₃

to provide the necessary facilities · einrichten

provided by the Owner, supplied ~ ~ ~ · bauseits geliefert

provincial administration building · Provinzialverwaltungsgebäude n

~ exhibition, regional ~ · Landesausstellung f

proving ground, testing ~, test ~ · Versuchsfeld n, Versuchsgelände n, Prüffeld, Prüfgelände

provision for escape of occupants, means of escape, · Fluchtmöglichkeit f

~ of facilities · Einrichten n

~ ~ heat, heat supply · Wärmeversorgung f

~ ~ water, water supply, WS · Wasserversorgung f

Prussian blue (pigment), royal ~ (~) [*Apart from being a generic term, Prussian blue usually refers to the same type as a pure bronze blue, i.e. both are strong, deep shades with a reddish or violet-blue undertone. B.S. 283*] · Preußischblau n

~ (cap) vault · flachbogiges Kappengewölbe n, preußisches ~, preußische Kappe f

Prüß reinforced (masonry) block partition (wall) · Prüß-Wand f [*Eine kreuzweise bewehrte Steinmauer*]

prytaneion, prytaneum [*The public hall of a Greek state or city, in which the sacred fire was kept burning; especially in ancient Athens, the hall in which distinguished citizens, foreign ambassadors, and the successive presidents of the senats were entertained at the public charge*] · Prytaneion n, Prytaneum n

PS → polystyrene

P.S., prestressed concrete [*Prestressing combines and enhances the inherent characteristics of two of the foremost construction materials – the compressive strength of concrete with the high tensile strength of stress-relieved cold drawn steel wire and strand*] · Spannbeton m [*DIN 4227*]

psammite, arenaceous deposit · Psammit m

pseudo acceleration · Pseudobeschleunigung f

~-basilica (church) · Pseudobasilika f, Staffelhalle f [*Mehrschiffiger Raum mit erhöhtem Mittelschiff, jedoch ohne Fenster im Obergaden*]

pseudo-classical · pseudo-antik, pseudo-klassisch

pseudo-cruciform · pseudo-kreuzförmig

pseudodipteral [*Literally 'with false double wings'*] · pseudodipteral

~ temple, false double-winged ~ Pseudodipteros(tempel) m, falscher Dipteros(tempel) [*1. Tempel mit Wandsäulen und umgebendem Säulenkranz. 2. Tempel mit doppelt breitem Pteron, jedoch ohne die innere Stützenreihe eines Dipteros*]

pseudoperipteral, false peripteral pseudoperipteral

~ temple → false(ly) peripteral ~

pseudo|peripteros (temple) → false(ly) peripteral ~

~prostyle temple, false(ly) prostyle ~ · Pseudoprostylos(tempel) m, falscher Prostylos(tempel) [*Ein griechischer Tempel mit Wandsäulen anstelle der Säulen an den Stirnseiten*]

pseudo-scroll, pseudo-volute · pseudoschnecke f, Pseudovolute f

~sexpartite · pseudosechsteilig

~ vault · pseudosechsteiliges Gewölbe n

pseudo-style · Pseudostil m

pseudo velocity · Pseudogeschwindigkeit f

pseudo-volute, pseudo-scroll · Pseudoschnecke f, Pseudovolute f

psilomelane, black iron ore · · Psilomelan m, schwarzer Glaskopf m, Hartmanganerz n

P.S.P., pierced steel plank(ing) · gelochtes Startbahnblech n, Rollfeldbelagplatte f

psychrometer [*A thermometer-like instrument for measuring wet bulb and dry bulb temperatures simultaneously*] · Psychrometer m, Luftfeuchtigkeitsmesser m

pteroma, pteron [*The space between the lateral walls of the naos of a temple and the peristyle columns*] · Pteron n, Pteroma n [*Fläche zwischen Cella und Säulenkranz des griechischen Tempels*]

p-tertiary butyl phenol · p-tert.-Butyphenol n

~ octyl phenol · p-tert.-Octylphenol n

PTFE → polytetrafluorethylene
PTN → partition (wall)
Ptolemaic temple · Ptolemäertempel *m*
(public-address) loud speaker system, ~ system · Lautsprecheranlage *f*
public (air-raid) shelter, ~ bomb ~ · öffentlicher (Luft)Schutzraum *m*
public-assisted dwelling unit, low-rent ~ ~, local authority ~ ~, public authority ~ ~ (US); publicly-assisted dwelling, low-rent dwelling, subsidized dwelling, local authority dwelling, public authority dwelling (Brit.) · öffentlich geförderte Wohnung *f*, Wohnung des sozialen Wohnungsbaues, Sozialwohnung

~ **authority housing,** ~ ~ house-building local authority ~, publicly-assisted ~, low-rent ~, subsidized ~, low-cost (municipal) ~, social ~ [*Provision of flats or houses for low-income groups, partly financed with the aid of public funds. Financing includes certain tax and interest consession*] · öffentlich geförderter Wohnungsbau *m*, Sozialwohnungsbau, sozialer Wohn(ungs)bau, sozialer WBau
~ **baths** · Badeanstalt *f*, Bad *n*
~ **block,** ~ building · öffentliches Gebäude *n*, Behördengebäude
~ **boarding school** · Volkspensionsanstalt *f*
~ **bomb shelter,** ~ (air-raid) ~ · öffentlicher (Luft)Schutzraum *m*
~ **building,** ~ block · Behördengebäude *n*, öffentliches Gebäude
~ **collector** → main sewer
~ **conduit-type sewer** · öffentlicher Abwasserkanal *m*
~ **convenience,** ~ sanitary ~, ~ toilet · (öffentliche) Bedürfnisanstalt *f*
~ **corridor** · öffentlicher Flur *m*, ~ Gang *m*, ~ Korridor *m* [*im Gegensatz zum Privatflur*]
~ **dwelling construction,** ~ housing (~) · öffentlicher Wohn(ungs)bau *m*, ~ WBau
~ **(electric current) grid** · öffentliches (Strom)Netz *n*
~ **funds** · öffentliche Mittel *npl*
~ **garden** · öffentlicher Garten *m*
~ **green area,** ~ ~ zone · (öffentliches) Grün *n*, öffentliche Grünanlagen *fpl*
~ **grid** → ~ electric current ~
~ **health authority** · Gesundheitsbehörde *f*
~ ~ **engineering,** sanitation, sanitary engineering in the wider sense · Sanitärtechnik *f*
~ **housing (construction),** ~ dwelling ~ · öffentlicher Wohn(ungs)bau *m*, ~ WBau
~ **library** · öffentliche Bücherei *f*, ~ Bibliothek *f*
~ **open area** · öffentliche Freifläche *f*

~ **park** · öffentlicher Park *m*
~ **phone** → ~ tele~
~ **room** · öffentlicher Raum *m*, Publikumsraum [*Hotel*]
~ **(sanitary) convenience,** ~ toilet · (öffentliche) Bedürfnisanstalt *f*
~ **sewer** → main ~
~ **shelter** → ~ air-raid ~
~ **structures** · Bauten *fpl* der öffentlichen Hand
~ **(tele)phone** · öffentlicher Fernsprecher *m*
~ ~ **coin box,** pay station, call box, coin-box (tele)phone · Münzfernsprecher *m*
~ **toilet,** ~ (sanitary) convenience · (öffentliche) Bedürfnisanstalt *f*
~ **traffic** · öffentlicher Verkehr *m*
~ **transport** · öffentlicher Massenverkehr *m*, Beförderung *f* von Menschenmassen
(~) utilities · Stadtversorgung *f*
~ **utility,** supply undertaking, utility undertaking · (öffentlicher) Versorgungsbetrieb *m*
~ **water consumption** · öffentlicher Wasserverbrauch *m*, allgemeiner ~
~ ~ **supply,** ~ WS, ~ provision of water · allgemeine Wasserversorgung *f*, öffentliche ~

publicly assisted · öffentlich gefördert [*Wohn(ungs)bau*]
publicly-assisted house-building, ~ housing, local authority ~, public authority ~, low-rent ~, subsidized ~, low-cost (municipal) ~, social ~ [*Provision of flats or houses for low-income groups, partly financed with the aid of public funds. Financing includes certain tax and interest concession*] · öffentlich geförderter Wohnungsbau *m*, Sozialwohnungsbau, sozialer Wohn(ungs)bau, sozialer WBau
puddingstone · Flintkonglomerat *n*, Puddingstein *m*, Nagelfluh *f*
puddle, puddling, clay ~ · Lehmschlag *m*, Tonschlag, Puddle *m*
puddling, swording; rodding (US); punning (Brit.) · Stochern *n*, Stocherverdichtung *f* [*Beton*]
puff pipe, backsiphonage preventer, anti-siphoning device, anti-siphoning pipe, anti-siphonage device, anti-siphonage pipe · Rohrbelüfter *m* [*Fehlname: Rohrunterbrecher. DIN 3266*]
pugging · (Aus)Füllung *f* [*Holzdecke*]
~ **board** [*wood-joist floor*] · Brett *n* zur Aufnahme der Füllung [*Holzbalkendecke*]
pull, tensile force, tension force · Zugkraft *f* [*beanspruchend*]
~ · Zug *m* [*Spannbeton*]
pull-chord · Zugschnur *f*
pull(-chord) (type) switch · Zugschnurschalter *m*

pull (handle), door ~ (~) · (Tür)Griff *m*

~ (~) · Ziehgriff *m*

~ rod · Hubstange *f*, Zugstange [*Hubdeckenverfahren*]

pull-rod spacing · Hubstangenabstand *m*, Zugstangenabstand [*Hubdeckenverfahren*]

pull switch · Zugschalter *m*

pulling · Ziehen *n* [*Spannbeton*]

pulpit · Kanzel *f*

~, mimbar, minbar · Mimbar *m*, Minbar [*Kanzel für die Freitagspredigt in einer großen Moschee*]

~ baldachin, ~ baldaquin, ~ canopy · Kanzelbaldachin *m*

~ canopy, ~ baldachin, ~ baldaquin · Kanzelbaldachin *m*

~ capital · Kanzelkapitäl *n*, Kanzelkapitell

~ over sarcophagus · Sarkophagkanzel *f*

~ stair(case) · Kanzeltreppe *f*

pulpitum · Pulpitum *n* [*1. Rednertribüne. 2. Mittelteil des Proszeniums des antiken Theaters*]

~ [*A screen, usually of stone, supporting a gallery between the nave and ritual choir of a cathedral or greater church. It might support the rood and frequently the organ for singers. The west face would form a reredos for the parochial altar in the nave*] · Pulpitum *n*

pulsating compressive loading · Druckschwellbelastung *f*

pulverised (Brit.); pulverized (US); powdered, powdery, in powder form · pulv(e)rig, pulverförmig, gepulvert, pulverartig, pulvérisiert

~ coal fuel (Brit.); pulverized ~ ~ (US); powder(ed) ~ ~, coal powder ~ ~ · Kohle(n)staub *m* als Brennstoff, Kohlenpulver *n* ~ ~

~ dolomitic lime, ~ magnesian ~ (Brit.); pulverized ~ ~ (US) · Dolomitfeinkalk *m* [*DIN 1060*]

~ fuel ash (Brit.); pulverized ~ ~ (US); fly ~, PFA · Filterasche *f*, Flugasche [*DIN E 4209*]

~ lime (Brit.) → pulverized (quick-) lime

~ magnesian lime, ~ dolomitic ~ (Brit.); pulverized ~ ~ (US) · Dolomitfeinkalk *m* [*DIN 1060*]

~ (quick)lime (Brit.) → pulverized ~

~ solder (Brit.); pulverized ~ (US); powder(ed) ~ · pulverisiertes Lötzinn *n*, ~ Lot

pulverized (US); pulverised (Brit.); powdered, powdery, in powder form · pulv(e)rig, pulverförmig, gepulvert, pulverartig, pulverisiert

~ ash collector (US) → fly ~ ~

~ coal (US) → powder(ed) ~

~ ~ fuel (US); pulverised ~ ~ (Brit.); powder(ed) ~ ~, coal powder ~ ~ · Kohle(n)staub *m* als Brennstoff, Kohlenpulver *n* ~ ~

~ dolomitic lime, ~ magnesian ~ (US); pulverised ~ ~ (Brit.) · Dolomitfeinkalk *m* [*DIN 1060*]

~ fuel ash (US); pulverised ~ ~ (Brit.); fly ~, PFA · Filterasche *f*, Flugasche [*DIN E 4209*]

~ ~ ~ aggregate (US) → fly ~ ~

~ ~ ~ cement (US) → (sintered) fly ~ ~

~ ~ ash-lime block (US) → fly ~ ~

~ ~ ~ tile (US) → fly ash-lime block

~ lime (US) → ~ quick~

~ limestone (US) → powder(ed) ~

~ magnesian lime, ~ dolomitic ~ (US); pulverised ~ ~ (Brit.) · Dolomitfeinkalk *m* [*DIN 1060*]

~ (quick)lime (US); pulverised ~ (Brit.); air-slaked ~ · Staubkalk *m*, luftgelöschter Kalk, Pulverkalk

~ solder (US); pulverised ~ (Brit.); powder(ed) ~ · pulverisiertes Lötzinn *n*, ~ Lot *n*

pulvin(us), superabacus, dosseret, supercapital, impost block · Pulvinus *m*

pulvinated frieze, swell(ed) ~, cushioned ~ [*A frieze with a convex face*] · Pulvinusfries *m*, konvexer Fries

to pumice [*To clean, polish, etc. with pumice*] · abbimsen

pumice → ~ stone

~ aggregate → ~ (concrete) ~

~ block → ~ (concrete) (building) ~

~ building block → ~ (concrete) ~ ~

~ ~ material, ~ construction(al) ~, ~ structural ~ · (Natur)Bimsbaumaterial *n* [*Schweiz*]; (Natur)Bimsbaustoff *m*

~ ~ materials factory, ~ construction(al) ~ ~, ~ structural ~ ~, ~ ~ ~ plant · (Natur)Bimsbaustoffwerk *n*

~ ~ tile → ~ (concrete) building block

~ cast(ing) → (pre)cast pumice (concrete) (building) member

~ chip(ping)s · (Natur)Bimssplitt *m*

~ concrete · (Natur)Bimsbeton *m*

~ (~) aggregate · (Natur)Bims(beton)-zuschlag(stoff) *m*

~ (~) (building) block, ~ (~) (~) tile [*See remark under 'Betonblock(-stein)'*] · Bimsbaustein *m*, (Natur-)Bims(beton)block(stein) *m*, (Natur-)Bims(beton)stein [*Fehlnamen: Schwemmstein (aus (Natur)Bimsbeton)*]

pumice (concrete) building unit — pumice (stone)

~ (~) ~ unit · Schwemmstein m (aus (Natur)Bimsbeton) [Fehlname]; (Natur)Bims(beton(stein), (Natur)Bims(beton)block(stein) m, Bimsbaustein [Siehe Anmerkung unter „Betonblock(stein)"]

~ (~) cast(ing) → (pre)cast pumice (concrete) (building) member

~ (~) cavity block, ~ (~) ~ tile, ~ (~) hollow ~, ~ (~) pot [See remark under 'Block'] · (Natur)Bims(beton)hohl(block)stein m, (Natur)Bims(beton)hohlblock m [DIN 18151]

~ (~) floor · (Natur)Bims(beton)decke f

~ (~) ~ block, ~ (~) ~ tile [See remark under 'Block'] · (Natur)Bims(beton)deckenblock(stein) m, (Natur)Bims(beton)deckenstein

~ (~) ~ (building) unit · Bims(beton)decken(bau)körper m, Bims(beton)decken(bau)element n, Natur~

~ (~) (~) filler block, ~ ~ (~) ~ tile (Natur)Bims(beton)(decken)füllkörper m, (Natur)Bims(beton)(decken)füllstein m [Ein Bims(beton)zwischenbauteil, der sich über die volle Höhe der Rohdecke erstreckt]

~ (~) ~ slab · (Natur)Bims(beton)deckenplatte f [DIN 4028]

~ (~) girder floor · (Natur)Bims(beton)trägerdecke f

~ (~) hollow beam, reinforced ~ (~) ~ ~ · (Natur)Bims(beton)hohlbalken(träger) m

~ (~) ~ block, ~ (~) ~ tile, ~ (~) cavity ~, ~ (~) pot [See remark under 'Block'] · (Natur)Bims(beton)hohlblock m, (Natur)Bims(beton)hohl(block)stein m [DIN 18151]

~ (~) ~ ~ masonry (work), ~ (~) ~ tile ~ (~), ~ (~) cavity ~ ~ (~), ~ (~) pot ~ (~) · (Natur)Bims(beton)hohlblockmauerwerk n, (Natur)Bims(beton)hohl(block)steinmauerwerk

~ (~) ~ (building) unit · (Natur)Bims(beton)hohl(bau)körper m, (Natur)Bims(beton)hohl(bau)element n

~ (~) hollow(-core) plank → reinforced ~ (~) ~ ~

~ (~) ~ roof(ing) plank → reinforced ~ (~) ~ ~ ~

~ (~) hollow filler (block), ~ ~ ~ ~ tile [See remark under 'Block'] · (Natur)Bims(beton)(decken)hohlkörper m, (Natur)Bims(beton)-Hohl-(Decken-)Füllstein, (Natur)Bims(beton)-Hohl-(Decken)Füllblock(stein) m [DIN 4158]

~ (~) ~ slab · (Natur)Bims(beton)hohlplatte f

~ (~) ~ tile, ~ (~) ~ block, ~ (~) cavity ~, ~ (~) pot [See remark under 'Block'] · (Natur)Bims(beton)hohl(block)stein m, (Natur)Bims(beton)hohlblock m [DIN 18151]

~ (~) lintel; ~ ~ lintol [deprecated] · (Natur)Bims(beton)oberschwelle f, (Natur)Bims(beton)sturz m

~ (~) plank · (Natur)Bimszementdiele f [Eine unarmierte Bimsbetonplatte aus Bimskies und Zement. Die Dielen sind der Länge nach meist mit Nut und Feder versehen]

~ (~) ~, reinforced ~ (~) ~ · (Natur)Bims(beton)diele f [DIN 18162]

~ (~) pot, ~ (~) hollow tile, ~ (~) hollow block, ~ (~) cavity block, ~ (~) cavity tile [See remark under 'Block'] · (Natur)Bims(beton)hohl(block)stein m, (Natur)Bims(beton)hohlblock m [DIN 18151]

~ (~) roller box · (Natur)Bims(beton)rolladenkasten m, (Natur)Bims(beton)rolljalousiekasten

~ (~) roof(ing) slab · (Natur)Bims(beton)dachplatte f

~ (~) slab → (reinforced) ~ (~) ~

~ (~) solid block, ~ (~) ~ tile [See remark under 'Block(stein)'] · (Natur)Bims(beton)vollblock(stein) m, (Natur)Bims(beton)vollstein [DIN 18152]

~ (~) ~ slab · (Natur)Bims(beton)vollplatte f

~ (~) wall slab · (Natur)Bims(beton)-Wand(bau)platte f

~ construction(al) material → ~ building ~

~ ~ materials factory → ~ building ~ ~

~ dust, ~ meal, ~ powder, powdered pumice (stone) · (Natur)Bims(stein)mehl n

~ expanded concrete, ~ gas ~, gas pumice ~, expanded pumice ~ · (Natur)Bims-Gasbeton m, (Natur)Bims-Blähbeton

~ gas concrete, ~ expanded ~, gas pumice ~, expanded pumice ~ · (Natur)Bims-Gasbeton m, (Natur)Bims-Blähbeton

~ grain, ~ particle · (Natur)Bimskorn n

~ gravel, pumiceous ~ · (Natur)Bimskies m [Bims mit mehr als 7 mm Korndurchmesser]

~ ~ fill(ing) · (Natur)Bimskiesschüttung f

~ hollow(-core) plank → reinforced pumice (concrete) ~ ~

~ industry, ~ stone ~ · (Natur)Bims(stein)industrie f

~ meal, ~ dust, ~ powder, powdered pumice (stone) · (Natur)Bims(stein)mehl n

~ particle, ~ grain · Bimskorn n, Natur~

~ powder, ~ dust, ~ meal, powdered pumice (stone) · (Natur)Bims(stein)mehl n

~ sand, pumiceous ~ · (Natur)Bimssand m [Bims mit 0–7 mm Korndurchmesser]

~ slab → (reinforced) pumice (concrete) ~

~ (stone) · Bimsstein m, (Natur)Bims m [Schaumig aufgeblähte vulkanische Lava]

~ (~) industry · (Natur)Bims(stein)industrie f
~ (~) tuff, pumiceous ~ · Bimssteintuff m
~ structural material → ~ building ~
~ ~ materials factory → ~ building ~ ~
~ tile → ~ (concrete) (building) block
~ tuff, ~ stone ~, pumiceous ~ · Bimssteintuff m
pumiceous tuff, pumice (stone) ~ · Bimssteintuff m
pumicing · Abbimsen n
pump room · Pumpenraum m
pump-room [spa] · Trinkhalle f [Heilbad]
pumpability · Pumpfähigkeit f
pumped concrete · Pumpbeton m
pumping aid · Pumphilfe f [Pumpbeton]
~ of concrete, concrete pumping · Betonverpumpen n, Pumpbetoneinbringung f
to pun [To ram wet concrete or earth with a punner so as to consolidate it by driving the air out] · stochern
punch · (Loch)Stempel m, Stanze f, Punze [Zum Einschlagen von Löchern in Schieferdachplatten]
punched work, broached ~ · punzierte Arbeit f, gepunzte ~
punching · (Löcher)Einschlagen n mit Stempel, Stanzen
~ of screen, hole pattern, perforation of screen · Sieblochung f
punctuated façade [A façade with units pierced for openings] · Lochfassade f
punctuation [It is achieved in a façade by ranges of windows] · Lochung f [Fassade]
puncturing [e.g. in the sentence 'Material should be strong enough to withstand puncturing during pouring of concrete'] · Durchschlagen n
pungent · stechend [Geruch]
punning (Brit.); rodding (US); puddling, sworChording · Stochern n, Stocherverdichtung f [Beton]
puntying, grinding of base · Bodenschleifen n [Hohlglas]
pupil capacity · Schülerfassungsvermögen n [Schule]
Purbeck marble · Purbeckmarmor m
purchase of land, acquisition ~ ~, land purchase, land acquisition · Grunderwerb m, Baulandbeschaffung f; Grundeinlösung [Österreich]
purchased design · Ankauf m
pure · rein
~ agglomerated cork, ~ baked ~, ~ rock ~ [Agglomerated cork made by using the resin from the cork itself] · Backkork m mit korkeigenem Harz gebunden

~ baked cork → ~ agglomerated ~
~ bending · reine Biegung f
~ cast iron, ~ C.I. · Spiegeleisen n
~ cement clinker · reiner Zementklinker m
~ clay · reiner Ton m, Edelton
~ coal, vitrain · Vitrit m, Glanzkohle f
~ compression, direct ~ · reiner Druck m
~ flexure, ~ bending, direct ~ · reine Biegung f
~ lime → high-calcium ~
~ ~ mortar, white ~ ~, rich ~ ~, high-calcium ~ ~ · Weißkalkmörtel m
~ ~ paste → high-calcium lime putty
~ ~ putty → high-calcium ~ ~
~ load, direct ~ · reine Last f
~ lump lime, white ~ ~, rich ~ ~, high-calcium ~ ~ · Weißstück(en)kalk m [DIN 1060]
~ marble, white ~ · weißer Marmor m, Weißmarmor
~ metal · Reinmetall n
~ nickel · Reinnickel n
~ quicklime, white ~, rich ~, high-calcium ~ · Weißbranntkalk m
~ rock cork → ~ agglomerated ~
~ style · purifizierter Stil m
~ tension, direct ~ · reiner Zug m
~ tone, fundamental (~) [A sound in which the sound pressure varies sinusoidally with time. The waveform may be represented by sin] · (einfacher) Ton m, reiner ~, Grundton [Sinusförmige Schallschwingung im Hörbereich. Anmerkung: Die in der Musik übliche Bestimmung des Begriffes Ton weicht im allgemeinen von der in der Akustik üblichen ab. Der Musiker nennt das Schallergebnis, das einer einzelnen Note entspricht, Ton, während es sich nach der Terminologie der Akustik in den meisten Fällen – wegen der Obertöne – um einen Klang handelt]

purely plastic state · rein plastischer Zustand m
purified air, clean ~ · Gutluft f, Reinluft
~ clay · Feinkeramikton m
~ style, stripped-down ~ · gereinigter Stil m
purifying (with air), converting (~ ~), air blowing, air refining · Windfrischen n [Stahlerzeugung]
Purism [Form of art invented by Ozenfant and Le Corbusier. It was to be unsullied by decoration, fantasy or individuality, and inspired by the machine] · Purismus m
purist house [e.g. the Steiner House in Vienna] · puritanisches Haus n [z.B. das Haus Steiner in Wien]
purity · Reinheit f
~ of style, stylistic purity · stilistische Reinheit f

purlin(e) — purpose-made material

purlin(e), binding rafter · (Stuhl)Pfette *f*, Dach(stuhl)pfette

~ anchoring · (Dach)Pfettenverankerung *f*

~ arrangement · (Dach)Pfettenanordnung *f*

~ connection · (Dach)Pfettenanschluß *m*

~ head · (Dach)Pfettenkopf *m*

~ hinge · (Dach)Pfettengelenk *n*

~ joint · (Dach)Pfettenstoß *m*

~ layout · (Dach)Pfettenplan *m*

~ level · (Dach)Pfettenebene *f*

~ load · (Dach)Pfettenlast *f*

~ nail · (Dach)Pfettennagel *m*

~ projection · (Dach)Pfettenüberstand *m*

~ spacing · (Dach)Pfettenabstand *m*

purple · Purpur *m* [*Aus Purpurschnecken gewonnene natürliche Farbe*]

~ pigment · Purpurpigment *n*

purpose-made block, ~ tile, special (purpose) ~ [*See remark under 'Block'*] · Sonderblock(stein) *m*, Sonderstein, Profilblock(stein), Profilstein, Spezialblock(stein) Spezialstein, Formblock(-stein), Formstein

~ (bonding) adhesive, ~ ~ medium, **~ ~** agent, **~** cement(ing agent), special (purpose) (~) ~ · Sonderkleb(e)stoff *m*, Sonderkleber *m*, Spezialkleb(e)stoff, Spezialkleber, Sonderkleb(e)mittel *n*, Spezialkleb(e)mittel

~ box (roof) gutter, ~ ~ rainwater ~, special (purpose) ~ (~) ~ · Sonder-Kasten(dach)rinne *f*, Spezial-Kasten(dach)rinne

~ brick, special (purpose) ~ · gebrannter Formstein *m*, ~ Profilstein, Profil(ton)ziegel *m*, Form(ton)ziegel

~ (builders') fitting, ~ (~) furniture, special (purpose) (~) ~ · Sonder(bau)beschlag *m*, Spezial(bau)beschlag

~ (~) fittings, ~ (~) hardware, special (purpose) (~) ~ · Sonder(bau)beschläge *mpl*, Spezial(bau)beschläge

~ (~) furniture, ~ (~) fitting, special (purpose) (~) ~ · Sonder(bau)beschlag *m*, Spezial(bau)beschlag

~ (~) hardware, ~ (~) fittings, special (purpose) (~) ~ · Sonder(bau)beschläge *mpl*, Spezial(bau)beschläge

~ building material, ~ structural ~, ~ construction(al) ~, special (purpose) ~ ~ · Sonder-Baumaterial *n*, Spezial-Baumaterial [*Schweiz*]; Sonderbaustoff, *m*, Spezialbaustoff

~ (burnt) (clay) brick, ~ burned (~) ~, ~ fired (~) ~, special (duty) (~) (~) ~, special purpose (~) (~) ~ · gebrannter Sonderstein *m*, ~ Spezialstein, Sonder(ton)ziegel *m*, Spezial(ton)-ziegel

~ cement, special (purpose) ~ · Sonderzement *m*, Spezialzement

~ cement(ing agent), ~ (bonding) adhesive, **~** bonding medium, **~** bonding agent, special (purpose) (~) ~ · Sonderkleb(e)stoff *m*, Sonderkleber *m*, Spezialkleb(e)stoff, Spezialkleber, Sonderkleb(e)mittel *n*, Spezialkleb(e)mittel

~ composition, ~ compound, **~** material, **~** mass, special (purpose) ~ · Sondermasse *f*, Spezialmasse

~ compound, ~ composition, **~** material, **~** mass, special (purpose) ~ · Sondermasse *f*, Spezialmasse

~ concrete, special (purpose) ~ · Sonderbeton *m*, Spezialbeton

~ ~ product, special (purpose) ~ ~ · (Beton)Formstück *n*

~ construction(al) material, ~ building ~, **~** structural ~, special (purpose) ~ ~ · Sonder-Baumaterial *n*, Spezial-Baumaterial [*Schweiz*]; Spezial-Baustoff *m*, Sonderbaustoff

~ ~ profile, ~ ~ section, **~ ~** shape, **~ ~** unit, **~ ~** trim, **~** structural ~, special (purpose) ~ ~ · Sonder-Bauprofil *n*, Spezial-Bauprofil

~ cover(ing) foil, ~ protecting ~, special (purpose) ~ ~ · Sonder(-Ab)deckfolie *f*, Sonderschutzfolie, Spezial(-Ab)deckfolie, Spezialschutzfolie

~ decorative block, ~ ~ tile, special ornamental ~, special decorative ~ [*See remark under 'Block'*] · Ornament(-Form)block(stein) *m*, Ornament(-Form)stein, Ornament-Profilstein, Dekor(ations)(-Form)stein, Dekor(ations)(-Form)block(stein), Dekor(ations)-Profilblock(stein), Dekor(ations)-Profilstein, Ornament-Profilblock(stein)

~ door, special (purpose) ~ · Sondertür *f*, Spezialtür

~ duct, special (purpose) ~ · Sonderkanal *m*, Spezialkanal

~ fitting, ~ furniture, **~** builders' ~, special (purpose) (builders') fitting, special (purpose) (builders') furniture · Sonder(bau)beschlag *m*, Spezial(bau)beschlag

~ gate, special (purpose) ~ · Sondertor *n*, Spezialtor

~ grout, ~ slurry, special (purpose) ~ · Sonderschlämme *f*, Spezialschlämme

~ hardware → **~** builders' ~

~ lock, special (purpose) ~ · Sonderschloß *n*, Spezialschloß

~ mass, ~ material, **~** compound, **~** composition, special (purpose) ~ · Sondermasse *f*, Spezialmasse

~ material, ~ compound, **~** composition, **~** mass, special (purpose) ~ · Sondermasse *f*, Spezialmasse

~ **mortar**, special (purpose) ~ · Sondermörtel *m*, Spezialmörtel

~ **ornamental block**, ~ decorative ~, ~ ~ tile, special (purpose) ~ ~, special (purpose) decorative ~ [*See remark under 'Block'*] · Dekor(ations)(-Form)block(stein) *m*, Dekor(ations)(-Form)stein, Ornament(-Form)stein, Ornament(-Form)block(stein), Ornament-Profilstein, Ornament-Profilblock(stein), Dekor(ations)-Profilblock(stein), Dekor(atins)-Profilblock(stein)

~ **paper**, special (purpose) ~ [*See remark under 'Pappe'*] · Sonderpappe *f*, Spezialpappe

~ **pitch**, special (purpose) ~ · Sonderpech *n*, Spezialpech

~ **plaster**, special (purpose) ~ · Sonderputz *m*, Spezialputz

~ **profile**, ~ section, ~ shape, ~ unit, ~ trim, special (purpose) ~ · Sonderprofil *n*, Spezialprofil

~ **protecting foil**, ~ cover(ing) ~, special (purpose) ~ ~ · Sonder(-Ab)deckfolie *f*, Sonderschutzfolie, Spezial(-Ab)deckfolie, Spezialschutzfolie

~ **reinforcement**, special (purpose) ~ · Sonderarmierung *f*, Sonderbewehrung, Spezialarmierung, Spezialbewehrung, Sonder(stahl)einlagen *fpl* Spezial(stahl)einlagen

~ ~ **steel**, special (purpose) ~ · Sonderbetonstahl *m*, Spezialbetonstahl

~ **rolled profile**, ~ ~ section, ~ ~ shape, ~ ~ unit, ~ ~ trim, special (purpose) ~ ~ · Sonderwalzprofil *n*, Spezialwalzprofil

~ **section**, ~ profile, ~ shape, ~ unit, ~ trim, special (purpose) ~ · Sonderprofil *n*, Spezialprofil

~ **shape**, ~ section, ~ profile, ~ unit, ~ trim, special (purpose) ~ · Sonderprofil *n*, Spezialprofil

~ **slurry**, ~ grout, special (purpose) ~ · Sonderschlämme *f*, Spezialschlämme

~ **steel window**, special (purpose) ~ ~ · Sonder-Stahlfenster *n*, Spezial-Stahlfenster

~ **step**, special (purpose) ~ · Profilstufe *f*

~ **structural material**, ~ building ~, ~ construction(al) ~, special (purpose) ~ ~ · Sonder-Baumaterial *n*, Spezial-Baumaterial [*Schweiz*]; Sonderbaustoff *m*, Spezialbaustoff

~ ~ **profile**, ~ ~ section, ~ ~ shape, ~ ~ unit, ~ ~ trim, ~ construction(al) ~, special (purpose) ~ ~ · Sonder-Bauprofil *n*, Spezial-Bauprofil

~ **tile**, ~ block, special (purpose) ~ [*See remark under 'Block'*] · Sonderblock(stein) *m*, Sonderstein, Profilblock(stein), Profilstein, Spezialblock(stein), Spezialstein, Formblock(stein), Formstein

~ **timber window**, ~ wood(en) ~ · Sonder-Holzfenster *n*, Spezial-Holzfenster

~ **trim**, ~ unit, ~ shape, ~ section, ~ profile, special (purpose) ~ · Sonderprofil *n*, Spezialprofil

~ **unit**, ~ trim, ~ shape, ~ section, ~ profile, special (purpose) ~ · Sonderprofil *n*, Spezialprofil

~ **valley gutter**, special (purpose) ~ ~ · Sonderkehlrinne *f*, Spezialkehlrinne

~ **window**, special (purpose) ~ · Sonderfenster *n*, Spezialfenster

~ **wire**, special ~ · Sonderdraht *m*, Spezialdraht

~ **wood(en) window**, ~ timber ~ · Sonder-Holzfenster *n*, Spezial-Holzfenster

pushbutton, press-button · Druckknopf *m*

~ **control**, press-button ~ · Druckknopfsteuerung *f*

~ **station**, press-button ~ · Druckknopftaster *m*

~ **switch**, press-button ~ · Druckknopfschalter *m*

push handle → swing door ~ ~

push-through tie · Durchsteckanker *m*

push-up door · (Auf)Stoßtür *f*

~ **leaf** · (Auf)Stoßflügel *m*

putlog · Rüstbalken *m*

~-**hole** · (Ge)Rüstloch *n*

putrescible [*Liable to undergo putrefaction*] · faulbar, fäulnisfähig

putto [*Small angel or cherub in the form of a plump, chubby-faced, curlyheaded child, often winged, and always of symbolic significance*] · Putte *f*

putty, cement · Kitt *m*

~ **for laminated glass** · Verbundglaskitt *m* [*Spezialkitt für Verbundglas*]

~ **glazing** · Kittverglasung *f*, Kitteinglasung

~ **knife**, spattle · Kittmesser *n*

puttyless aluminium glazing bar → aluminium glazing ~ ~

~ **glazing**, patent ~, dry ~ · kittlose Verglasung *f*, ~ Einglasung; kittloses Verglasen *n*, kittloses Einglasen

~ ~ **bar**, patent ~ ~ [*A glazing bar of special type and profile designed for dry glazing, i.e. without the use of putty, mastic or like substances*] · Sprosse *f* [*Für kittlose Oberlichter und Glasdächer*]

~ ~ **roof**, patent ~ ~, dry ~ ~ · kittloses Glasdach *n*

~ **roof glazing**, patent ~ ~, dry ~ ~ · kittlose Dachverglasung *f*, ~ Dacheinglasung

puttyless steel bar — PVC rainwater system

~ steel bar · Stahlsprosse f [*kittlose Verglasung*]

putty removal, removal of putty · Entkitten n [*Verglasung*]

puzzle lock, combination ~, dial ~ · Kombi(nations)schloß n, Vexierschloß, Ringschloß, Buchstabenschloß

puzzolanic capability, ~ capacity, ~ power, ~ property, ~ quality · puzzolanische Fähigkeit f, ~ Eigenschaft, puzzolanisches Vermögen n

PV → pigment volume

pva, PVA, p.v.a., polyvinyl acetate · Polyvinylazetat n, PVA(C) n

PVA adhesive → polyvinyl acetate glue

PVA emulsion, pva ~, p.v.a. ~, polyvinyl acetate ~ · Polyvinylazetatemulsion f, PVA(C)-Emulsion

PVA emulsion paint, pva ~ ~, p.v.a. ~ ~, polyvinyl acetate ~ ~ · Polyvinylazetatemulsionsfarbe f, PVA(C)-Emulsionsfarbe

PVA floor cover(ing) → polyvinyl acetate floor(ing)

PVA floor(ing) → polyvinyl acetate ~

PVA glue → polyvinyl acetate ~

PVC, pigment volume concentration · Pigmentvolumenkonzentration f, PVK

PVC; polyvinyl chlorid(e) (US); polyvinyl chloride (Brit.) · Polyvinylchlorid n, PVC n

PVC asbestos floor(ing) tile, asbestos-pvc ~ ~ [*A flooring tile composed of asbestos bonded with polyvinyl chloride. B.S. 3260*] · Asbest-PVC-(Fuß)Bodenplatte f

PVC base, polyvinyl chlorid(e) ~ · Polyvinylchlorid-Basis f, Polyvinylchlorid-Grundlage f, PVC-Basis PVC-Grundlage

PVC based, polyvinylchlorid(e) ~ · polyvinylchloridgebunden, pvc-gebunden

PVC building board, ~ ~ sheet, ~ ~ slab, ~ sheeting board, polyvinyl chlorid(e) ~ ~ · Polyvinylchlorid-Bauplatte f, PVC-Bauplatte

PVC ceiling, polyvinyl chlorid(e) ~ · Polyvinylchloriddecke f, PVC-Decke

PVC ceiling shape, ~ ~ profile, ~ ~ section, ~ ~ unit, ~ ~ trim, polyvinyl chlorid(e) ~ ~ · Polyvinylchlorid-Deckenprofil n

PVC coating, polyvinyl chlorid(e) ~ · Polyvinylchloridbeschichtung f, PVC-Beschichtung

PVC construction profile, ~ ~ trim, ~ ~ shape, ~ ~ section, ~ ~ unit, ~ structural ~, polyvinyl chlorid(e) ~ · Polyvinylchlorid-Bauprofil n, PVC-Bauprofil

PVC corrugated board → ~ ~ sheet

PVC corrugated film, ~ ~ sheeting, polivinyl chlorid(e) ~ · Polyvinylchlorid-Wellfolie f, PVC-Wellfolie

PVC corrugated sheet, ~ ~ board, polyvinyl chlorid(e) ~ ~ · Polyvinylchlorid-Wellplatte f, PVC-Wellplatte

PVC corrugated sheeting, ~ ~ film, polyvinyl chlorid(e) ~ · Polyvinylchlorid-Wellfolie f, PVC-Wellfolie

PVC corrugated sheet(ing), polyvinyl chlorid(e) ~ ~ · Polyvinylchlorid-Wellbahn f, PVC-Wellbahn

PVC cover(ing), polyvinyl chlorid(e) ~ · Polyvinylchloridbelag m, PVC-Belag

PVC film, ~ sheeting, polyvinyl chlorid(e) ~ · Polyvinylchloridfolie f, PVC-Folie

PVC floor cover(ing), ~ ~ finish, polyvinyl chloride ~ ~, PVC floor(ing), polyvinyl chlorid(e) floor(ing) · Polyvinylchlorid-Boden(belag) m, Polyvinylchlorid-Fußboden(belag), PVC-(Fuß)Boden(belag)

PVC floor finish, ~ ~ cover(ing), polyvinyl chlorid(e) ~ ~, PVC floor(ing), polyvinyl chlorid(e) floor(ing) · Polyvinylchlorid-Boden(belag) m, Polyvinylchlorid-Fußboden(belag), PVC-(Fuß)Boden(belag)

PVC flower box, polyvinyl chlorid(e) ~ ~ · Polyvinylchlorid-Blumenkasten m, PVC-Blumenkasten

PVC flower trough, polyvinyl chlorid(e) ~ ~ · Polyvinylchlorid-Blumentrog m, PVC-Blumentrog

PVC foam, polyvinyl chlorid(e) ~, foam(ed) PVC, foam(ed) polyvinyl chlorid(e), expanded PVC, expanded polyvinyl chlorid(e) · Polyvinylchloridschaum-(stoff) m, PVC-Schaum(stoff)

PVC hollow profile, ~ ~ section, ~ ~ shape, ~ ~ unit, ~ ~ trim, polyvinyl chlorid(e) ~ ~ · Polyvinylchlorid-Hohlprofil m, PVC-Hohlprofil

PVC homogeneous floor cover(ing), ~ ~ ~ finish, ~ ~ floor(ing) · Polyvinylchlorid-Einschicht-Boden(belag) m, Polyvinylchlorid-Einschicht-Fußboden(belag), PVC-Einschicht-(Fuß)Boden(belag)

PVC insulating film, ~ ~ sheeting, ~ insulation(-grade) ~, polyvinyl chlorid(e) ~ ~ · Polyvinylchloridisolierfolie f, PVC-Isolierfolie

PVC insulating sheeting, ~ ~ film, ~ insulation(-grade) ~, polyvinyl chlorid(e) ~ ~ · Polyvinylchloridisolierfolie f, PVC-Isolierfolie

PVC pipe, polyvinyl chlorid(e) ~ · Polyvinylchloridrohr n, PVC-Rohr

PVC pressure pipe, polyvinyl chlorid(e) ~ ~ · Polyvinylchlorid-Druckrohr n, PVC-Druckrohr

PVC profile → ~ section

PVC rainwater articles → polyvinyl chlorid(e) rainwater goods

PVC rainwater system, polyvinyl chlorid(e) ~ ~ · Polyvinylchlorid-Regenablaufkonstruktion f, PVC-Regenablaufkonstruktion [*PVC-Regenrinne + PVC-Regenfallrohr + PVC-Zubehör*]

PVC (resin) — pyrite(s)

PVC (resin), polyvinyl chlorid(e) ~ · PVC *n*, Polyvinylchlorid *n*

PVC roof tile, polyvinyl chlorid(e) ~ ~ · Polyvinylchlorid-Dachplatte *f*, PVC-Dachplatte

PVC seal(ing), polyvinyl chlorid(e) ~ · Polyvinylchlorid-(Ab)Dichtung *f*, PVC-(Ab)Dichtung

PVC seal(ing) film, ~ ~ sheeting, polyvinyl chlorid(e) ~ ~ · Polyvinylchlorid-(Ab)Dicht(ungs)folie *f* PVC-(Ab)Dicht(ungs)folie

PVC seal(ing) sheeting, ~ ~ film, polyvinyl chlorid(e) ~ ~ · Polyvinylchlorid-(Ab)Dicht(ungs)folie *f*, PVC-(Ab)Dicht(ungs)folie

PVC section, ~ profile, ~ trim, ~ shape, ~ unit, polyvinyl chlorid(e) ~ · Polyvinylchloridprofil *n*, PVC-Profil

PVC shape → ~ section

PVC sheathed cable, polyvinyl chlorid(e) ~ ~ · PVC-Mantel-Kabel *n*, Polyvinylchloridmantelkabel

PVC sheet(ing), polyvinyl chlorid(e) ~ · Polyvinylchlorid-Bahn *f*, PVC-Bahn

PVC sheeting, ~ film, polyvinyl chlorid(e) ~ · Polyvinylchloridfolie *f*, PVC-Folie

PVC sheeting board → ~ building slab

PVC structural profile → ~ construction unit

PVC structural section → ~ construction unit

PVC structural shape → ~ construction unit

PVC structural unit → ~ construction ~

PVC-tar (mix(ture)), polyvinyl chlorid(e)-tar (~) · Polyvinylchlorid-Teer-Gemisch *n*, Polyvinylchlorid-Teer(-Mischung) *m*, (*f*), PVC-Teer(-Gemisch), PVC-Teer-Mischung

PVC thermal insulation, polyvinyl chlorid(e) ~ ~ · PVC-Wärmedämmung *f*, Polyvinylchlorid-Wärmedämmung

PVC tile, polyvinyl chlorid(e) ~ · Polyvinylchlorid(belag)platte *f*, Polyvinylchloridfliese *f*, PVC-(Belag)Platte, PVC-Fliese

PVC tiling · Polyvinylchloridplattenbelag *m*, PVC-Plattenbelag

PVC trim → ~ section

PVC unit → ~ section

PVC wall board, ~ ~ sheet, polyvinyl chlorid(e) ~ ~ · Polyvinylchloridwandplatte *f*, PVC-Wandplatte

PVC wall sheet, ~ ~ board, polyvinyl chlorid(e) ~ ~ · Polyvinylchloridwandplatte *f*, PVC-Wandplatte

PVC waterbar, ~ waterstop, polyvinyl chlorid(e) ~ · Polyvinylchlorid-Fugenband *n*, PVC-Fugenband

PVC waterstop, ~ waterbar, polyvinyl chlorid(e) ~ · Polyvinylchlorid-Fugenband *n*, PVC-Fugenband

PVC window section, ~ ~ profile, ~ ~ shape, ~ ~ unit, ~ ~ trim, polyvinyl chlorid(e) ~ ~ · Polyvinylchlorid-Fensterprofil *n*, PVC-Fensterprofil

PW → projected window

pycastyle, pycnostyle [*A term given when the space between two columns is 1½ bottom diameters*] · engsäulig, pyknostylos

pycnometer, fruit jar ~, weighing bottle, density bottle · (Flaschen)Pyknometer *n*

pycnostyle, pycastyle [*A term given when the space between two columns is 1½ bottom diameters*] · engsäulig, pyknostylos

pylon, gateway [*The mass of masonry with central opening, forming a monumental entrance to Egyptian temples*] · Pylon(e) *m*, (*f*)

pyramid · Pyramide *f*, Spitzsäule *f* [*Ein Körper, der von einem Vieleck als Grundfläche und von einer nach der Zahl der Ecken sich richtenden Anzahl von Dreiecken als Seitenflächen, die alle eine gemeinsame Spitze haben, begrenzt wird*]

~ **builder** · Pyramidenbauer *m*

~ **building**, ~ construction · Pyramidenbau *m*

~ **complex** · Pyramidenanlage *f*

~ **construction**, ~ building · Pyramidenbau *m*

~ **glass** · Ornamentglas *n* Nr. 552, Pyramidal-mittel *n*

Pyramid of the Moon · Mondpyramide *f* [*in Teotihuacan*]

~ ~ ~ **Sun** · Sonnenpyramide *f* [*in Teotihuacan*]

pyramid tower → ziggurat

pyramidal crown of stone slabs · pyramidenförmige Krone *f* aus (Natur-) Steinplatten

~ **folded plate** · pyramidal gefaltete Platte *f*

~ ~ **structure system** · pyramidales Faltwerksystem *n*, pyramidenförmiges ~

~ **form** → ~ shape

~ **roof** · Pyramidendach *n*, Dachpyramide *f*, Zeltdach über quadratischem Grundriß

~ **shape**, ~ form · Pyramidenform *f*, Pyramidengestalt *f*

~ **space truss** · pyramidales Raumfachwerk *n*, pyramidenförmiges ~

~ **tomb** · Pyramidengrab *n*

pyramidion · Riese(n) *m*, (pyramidenförmiger) Helm *m*, Ryse *m*, Haupt *n* [*Pyramidenförmiger, krabbenbesetzter und in einer Kreuzblume endigender Helm einer Fiale*]

Pyrex glass [*tradename*] · Pyrexglas *n*

pyridine-insoluble matter, ~ substance · Pyridin-Unlösliche *n*

pyrite · Pyrit *m*

pyrite(s), iron ~, yellow ~, fool's gold, mundic · Eisenkies *m*, Schwefelkies, Schwefeleisen *n*

pyrobitumen · Bitumen *n* größtenteils unlöslich in CS_2 und größtenteils unverseifbar [*Beispiele: Elaterit, Torf, Braunkohle, Ölschiefer*]

pyrobituminous shale → asphaltic ~ ~

pyrogallic acid · Pyrogallussäure *f*

pyrolusite · Braunstein *m*, Glasmacherseife *f*, Pyrolusit *m*

(pyrometric) cone · (Brenn)Kegel *m* [*Pyrometer aus Tonerdesilikaten zur Bestimmung der Wärmegrade in keramischen Brennöfen*]

(~) ~ equivalent · Feuerfestigkeit *f*, (Brenn)Kegelfallpunkt *m* [*Bestimmung des Wärmegrades in einem keramischen Brennofen*]

(~) Seger cone equivalent · Segerkegelfallpunkt *m*, SK-Fallpunkt

pyrophyllite · Pyrophyllit *m* [*Hydratisiertes Alumosilikat. In Erweiterung dient dieser Ausdruck auch zur Bezeichnung des Gesteins (Rohstoffs)*]

pyroxylin → cellulose nitrate

~ lacquer, nitrocellulose ~, cellulose (nitrate) ~, cellulose enamel · Celluloselack *m*, (Nitro-)Zelluloselack, Nitro(cellulose)lack

~ paint → nitrocellulose ~

~ stopper → nitrocellulose ~

Q

QC → quality audit

Q-floor unit, cellular steel ~ ~, cellular section · Zellenprofil *n*, Profiltafel *f* [*Robertson-Stahlzellendecke*]

quadrangle [*A square or rectangular court enclosed on all sides by buildings; or, occasionally, with one side left open*] · viereckiger Hof *m*

quadrant, ¼ circle, quarter-circle · Viertelkreis *m*

quadratura · Quadratur *f*

~ painter · Quadraturmaler *m*

quadriga, four-horse(d) chariot [*A sculpture, often surmounting a monument*] · Quadriga *f*, Viergespann *n*

quadrille paper, coordinate ~ · Koordinatenpapier *n*

quadripartite · vierteilig

~ cross-rib(bed) vault, four-part ~ ~ · vierteiliges Kreuzrippengewölbe *n*

~ narrow multi-storey block, ~ ~ ~ building (Brit.); ~ ~ ~ multi-story ~ (US); four-part ~ ~ ~ ~ · Vierscheibenhaus *n*, Vierscheibengebäude *n*

~ rib vault · vierteiliges Rippengewölbe *n*

~ shutter, four-part ~ · vierteiliger (Raum)Abschluß *m*

~ tracery, four-part ~ · vierteiliges Maßwerk *n*

~ vault, four-part ~ · vierteiliges Gewölbe *n*

quake-proof → (earth)quake-resistant

quality · Qualität *f*, Güte *f*

~, power, capability, property, capacity · Eigenschaft *f*, Vermögen *n*, Fähigkeit *f*

~ audit, (~) control, product performance evaluation, inspection, QC · Gütesicherung *f*, Güteüberwachung *f*

~ characteristic · Qualitätsmerkmal *n*, Gütemerkmal

~ check(ing) · Gütenachweis *m*, Nachweis der Güte

~ clause · Güteklausel *f*

~ control → ~ audit

(~) ~ chart, ~ audit ~, inspection ~ · Güteüberwachungstabelle *f*

quality-control staff, quality-audit ~, inspection ~ · Güteüberwachungspersonal *n*

quality description · Qualitätsbeschreibung *f*, Gütebeschreibung

(~) grade · Güteklasse *f*

(~) ~ description · Güteklassebeschreibung *f*

(~) ~ of concrete, concrete (quality) grade · Betongüteklasse *f*

~ of concrete, concrete quality · Betongüte *f*, Betonqualität *f*

~ ~ initial set(ting) → power ~ ~ ~

~ ~ material(s) · Materialgüte *f*

~ ~ set(ting) → set(ting) power ~

~ regulations · Gütebestimmungen *fpl*

~ requirement · Güteanforderung *f*

~ spec(ification)s · Gütebedingungen *fpl*

~ standard · Gütenorm *f*

~ test · Güteprobe *f*, Güteprüfung *f*, Güteversuch *m*

quantities placed · eingebaute Mengen *fpl*

quantity change, ~ variation · Mengenänderung *f*

~ of material, material quantity · Stoffmenge *f*

~ ~ mortar required, required quantity of mortar · Mörtelbedarf *m*

~ ~ shipment · Liefermenge *f*

quantity-produced sink unit, series-produced ~ · Serien-Spültisch *m*, Serien-Abwaschtisch

quantity surveying · Massenberechnung *f*

~ unit · Mengeneinheit *f*

~ variation, ~ change · Mengenänderung *f*

quarrel, quarry [*A small pane of glass, square or diamond-shaped, but usually the latter*] · (Fenster)Scheibenfach *n*

quarry → ceramic flooring tile

~ → ~ tile

~, quarrel [*A small pane of glass, square or diamond-shaped, but usually the latter*] · (Fenster)Scheibenfach *n*

~ **face** [*It is a face which is on a stone when it comes from the quarry. It may be formed by the quarrying operations, or may be due to a natural seam and is then called a seam face*] · bruchrauhe Fläche *f* [*(Natur)Stein*]

~ **for animal shelters** → (flooring) quarry (tile) ~ ~ ~

(~) **sap**, ~ water [*The moisture in freshly quarried stone*] · Bergfeuchtigkeit *f*, Bergfeuchte *f*

~ **(tile)** → ceramic flooring ~

~ **(~), clay** ~, clay block [*Burnt clay, flooring or wall-facing tiles of black, buff, or red colour. They are from 9 × 9 to 4 × 4 in. in size, unglazed, but not porous*] · gebrannter Block(stein) *m*, ~ Stein

~ **(~) for animal shelters** → flooring ~ (~) ~ ~ ~

~ **waste**; grout (US) · Abfallsteine *mpl*, Steinbruchabfall *m*

~ **water,** (~) sap [*The moisture in freshly quarried stone*] · Bergfeuchtigkeit *f*, Bergfeuchte *f*

quarter-circle, ¼ circle, quadrant · Viertelkreis *m*

quarter closure, ~ closer, (queen) ~ [*A brick cut in half along its length to keep the bond correct at the corner of a brick wall*] · Schlußziegel *m*

quarter-column · Viertelsäule *f*

quarter joint · Viertelfuge *f*

~ **(pipe) bend**, one-~ (~) ~, 90° (~) ~ · 90°-(Rohr)Krümmer *m*

~ **point** · Viertelpunkt *m*

~ ~ **moment** · Viertelpunktmoment *n*

quarter-round (moulding) (Brit.); Roman ovolo (~), ¼ RD · Viertelstab *m*

quarter small column · Viertelsäulchen *n*, Vierteldienst *m*

quarter (s)pace (landing) · Viertelpodest *n*, Viertel(treppen)absatz *m*

quarter-turn stair(case) with winders · (ein)viertelgewendete Treppe *f*

~ **(with winders)** · (Ein)Viertel(s)-wendung *f* [*Treppe*]

quartering · Vierteilung *f*

quartz · Quarz *m* [*allotrope Modifikation der Kieselsäure*]

~ **aggregate,** ~ concrete ~ · Quarz(beton)zuschlag(stoff) *m*, Quarz(beton)zuschlagmaterial *n*

~ **cement** · Quarzzement *m*

~ **chip(ping)s** · Quarzsplitt *m*

~ **(concrete) aggregate** · Quarz(beton)zuschlag(stoff) *m*, Quarz(beton)-zuschlagmaterial *n*

quartz-diorite · Quarzdiorit *m*

quartz-free diorite, true ~ · quarzfreier Diorit *m*

~ **porphyry**, true ~ · quarzfreier Porphyr *m*

quartz glass, silica ~, fused silica, vitreous silica, fused quartz [*A vitreous material consisting almost entirely of silica, made in translucent and transparent forms. The former has minute gas bubbles disseminated in it*] · Quarzglas *n* [*Fehlname*]; Kiesel(säure)glas

~ **keratophyre** · Quarzkeratophyr *m*

~ **pebbles** · Quarzkies *m*

quartz-porphyry · Quarzporphyr *m* [*DIN 52100*]

quartz-schist, firestone · Quarzschiefer *m* [*Kieselsäurehaltiges Gestein, das nur gesägt wird und ohne weitere Verarbeitung zur Auskleidung von Öfen dient*]

quartz-syenite · Quarzsyenit *m*

quartz-trachyte · Quarztrachyt *m*

quartz wool · Quarzwolle *f*

quartzite · Quarzit *m*

quartzite-schist · Quarzitschiefer *m*

quartzite slab · Quarzitplatte *f*

quatrefoil, four-leaved tracery, tracery with four leaf-shaped curves · Vierblatt *n* [*gotisches Maßwerk*]

~ **oculus window** · Vierblattokulusfenster *n*

~ **tracery** · Vierpaßmaßwerk *n*

Queen Anna's summer house, Belvedere at Prague · Belvedere *n* zu Prag

queen closer, soap (brick), furring (brick) · Meisterquartier *m*, Riemen(stein) *m*, Riem(en)stück *n*, Riemchen *n*, Längsquartier

(~) ~, (~) **closure**, quarter ~ [*A brick cut in half along its length to keep the bond correct at the corner of a brick wall*] · Schlußziegel *m*

~ **post** · doppelt stehender (Dach)Stuhl *m*

~ ~ [*Of a queen post truss*] · Hängesäule *f*

~ ~ **and wind filling** · doppelt stehender (Dach)Stuhl *m* und Versenkung *f*

~ ~ **purlin(e)** · Säulenpfette *f*

~ ~ **(roof) truss**, double hanging (~) ~, king-and-queen (~) ~ [*A form of timber truss in which two vertical queen posts are framed at their heads into the principal rafters, and at their feet into the tie-beam. This truss is statically determinate, but unstable without counterbracing under unsymmetrical loadings*] · doppelter Hängebock *m*, doppeltes Hängewerk *n*

queen's chamber · Königin(nen)kammer *f*

Queen's megaron · Gemach *n* der Königin [*Palast zu Knossos*]

queen's suite — rabbet ledge

queen's suite · Königingemächer *npl*
to quench · härten [*Stahl*]
quenched and subsequently tempered steel, heat-treatable ~ · Vergütungsstahl *m*
~ cullet, dragladled ~ (Brit.); shrended ~ (US) · abgeschrecktes und in Brocken zerfallenes Glas *n*
quenching · Härten *n* [*Abkühlen von Stahl von Temperaturen oberhalb Umwandlungstemperaturen — z.B. 900° bei gewöhnlichem Stahl — mit solcher Geschwindigkeit, daß eine beträchtliche Steigerung der Härte eintritt. Abschrecken mit Wasser, Öl oder Luft*]
quick-acting folding shutter door, rapid-acting ~ ~ ~ · Schnellfalttor *n*
quick-assembly method, rapid-assembly ~, rapid-erection ~, quick-erection ~ · Schnell(montage)bauweise *f*, Schnell(montage)verfahren *n*
quick-breaking, rapid-setting, labile · labil, unstabil, schnellzerfallend [*Bitumenemulsion*]
~ emulsion, labile ~, rapid-setting ~ · U-Emulsion *f*
quick coupling · Schnellkupplung *f* [*Rohr*]
quick-drying, rapid-drying · schnelltrocknend
quick-erection method, rapid-erection ~, rapid-assembly ~, quick-assembly ~ · Schnell(montage)bauweise *f*, Schnell(montage)verfahren *n*
quick fixing, rapid ~ · Schnellbefestigung *f*
~ freezer (space) · Schnellgefrierraum *m*
~ hardener → hardening accelerator
(quick)lime [*substance*] → calcium oxid(e)
quicklime for structural purposes, ~ ~ building ~, construction quicklime, building quicklime · Baubranntkalk *m*, Baubrennkalk
quick set(ting) → false ~
quick-setting glass, short ~, fast-setting ~ · kurzes Glas *n*
quiet alloy, (fully) killed ~, dead ~, stabilized ~ · stabilisierte Legierung *f*, beruhigte ~
~ room · ruhiger Raum *m*
~ steel → (fully) killed ~
quilt, building ~ [*It has a high density*] · (Bau)Matte *f*, Isoliermatte
quinquepartite · fünfteilig
quint-point arch · Fünftelsbogen *m*
quire, choir [*The part of a church where divine service is sung*] · Chor *m*
~ aisle, choir ~, ~ side ~ · Chorseitenschiff *n*
~ arcade, choir ~ · Chorarkade *f*
~ arch, choir ~ · Chorbogen *m* [*Bogen, der einen Chor vom Langhaus bzw. der Vierung trennt*]
~ architecture, choir ~ · Chorbaukunst *f*, Chorarchitektur *f*
~ bay, choir ~ · Chorjoch(feld) *n*, Chorfeld
~ ~ wall, choir ~ ~ · Chorjochwand *f*, Chorfeldwand
~ buttress, choir ~ · Chorstrebepfeiler *m*
~ chapel, choir ~, apsidal ~ · Chorkapelle *f*, Apsidialkapelle, Absidenkapelle, Apsidenkapelle, Apsiskapelle, Abseitenkapelle
~ fresco, choir ~ · Chorfreske *f*
~ gallery, ~ loft, choir ~ · Sängerempore *f*, Sängergalerie *f*, Chorempore, Chorgalerie, Sängerbühne *f*, Chorbühne
~ grille, choir ~, ~ (lattice(d)) screen · Chorgitter *n*
~ (lattice(d)) screen, choir (~) ~, ~ grille · Chorgitter *n*
~ limb, choir ~ · Chorflügel *m*
~ loft, ~ gallery, choir ~ · Sängerempore *f*, Sängergalerie *f*, Chorempore, Chorgalerie, Sängerbühne *f*, Chorbühne
~ pier, choir ~ · Chorpfeiler *m*
~ school, choir ~ · Chorschule *f*
~ screen, choir ~, ~ lattice(d) ~, ~ grille · Chorgitter *n*
~ (side) aisle, choir (~) ~ · Chorseitenschiff *n*
~ stall, choir ~ · Chorgestühl *n*, Chorstühle *mpl*
~ termination, choir ~ · Chor(ab)schluß *m*
~ tower, choir ~ · Chorturm *m*
~ vault, choir ~ · Chorgewölbe *n*
~ wall, choir ~ · Chorwand *f*
quirk [*A narrow sinking, or groove, forming part of a mo(u)lding*] · spitze Kehlung *f*, Spitzkehlung
quoin · (Faltwerk)Kante *f*
~ → angle-~
~ bonder → ~ header
~ bondstone → ~ header
~ brick, corner ~ [*A brick set in a salient corner of a wall*] · Eckziegel *m*
~ header, corner ~, ~ bonder, ~ bondstone [*A corner header in the face wall which is a stretcher in the side wall*] · Eck-Binder(stein) *m*

R

rabbet → (window) rebate
~, rebate; check [*Scotland*] · Falz *m*, Anschlag *m*
~ ledge, rebate ~ · Schlagleiste *f* [*Beim zweiflügeligen Fenster bzw. bei der zweiflügeligen Tür*]

rabbetted siding, rebated ∼, shiplap ∼ · gefalzter Wandbeschlag *m*, ∼ Wandschirm *m*, ∼ Wetterschirm, gefalzte Verschalung *f*

∼ (wood(en)) siding, rebated (∼) ∼, shiplap (∼) ∼, shiplap (boards) · gefälzte (waag(e)rechte) (Bretter)Schalung *f* [*Wetterschutz für Außenwände*]

rabbit-ear faucet (US) · Löffelhahn *m* [*In Toiletten, anstelle der Zugkette für die Wasserspülung*]

Rabitz ceiling plaster, ∼ type ∼ ∼ · Rabitzdeckenputz *m*, Drahtgewebedeckenputz

∼ finish · Rabitz(ver)putz *m*

∼ strip(-type) (wire) cloth lath(ing), ∼ ∼ woven (wire) fabric ∼; ∼ ∼ (wire) fabric ∼ [*misnomer*] · Rabitzstreifengewebe *n* [*12, 16, 20, 24, 30, 40 und 50 cm breit*]

∼ type · Rabitzbauart *f* [*Ein- oder doppelseitiger Kalk-, Gips- oder Zementmörtelbewurf auf Drahtgeflecht aus verzinktem Stahldraht von 2 cm Maschenweite und etwa 1 mm Dicke*]

∼ (∼) board, ∼ (∼) sheet · Rabitzplatte *f*

∼ (∼) box · Rabitzkasten *m*

∼ (∼) casing · Rabitzmantel *m* [*Umkleidung von Stahlstützen, Trägern, Rohrkanalwänden und Luftkanalwänden aus Gipsmörtel, mit Rabitzgewebe armiert*]

∼ (∼) ceiling plaster · Rabitzdeckenputz *m*, Drahtgewebedeckenputz

∼ (∼) cement wall · Zementrabitzwand *f*

∼ (∼) clay (pellet) lath(ing) · Ziegelrabitz *n*, Sterndelrabitz

∼ (∼) cornice · Rabitz(ge)sims *m*, (*n*)

∼ (∼) counter ceiling · Rabitz(unter)decke *f*, Drahtgewebe(unter)decke

∼ (∼) ∼ ∼ plaster · Rabitz(unter)deckenputz *m*, Drahtgewebe(unter)deckenputz

∼ (∼) duct · Rabitzkanal *m* [*Luftanlage; Klimaanlage*]

∼ (∼) gypsum · Rabitzgips *m*

∼ (∼) lining, ∼ (∼) (sur)facing · Rabitzauskleidung *f*, Rabitzverkleidung, Rabitzbekleidung

∼ (∼) mortar · Rabitzmörtel *m* [*Er besteht meistens aus 1 Bauteil Stuckgips, 1 Raumteil Weißkalk, 3 Raumteilen Sand sowie Tierhaaren und Leimbrei*]

∼ (∼) plaster wall · Gipsrabitzwand *f*

∼ (∼) sheet, ∼ (∼) board · Rabitzplatte *f*

∼ (∼) (sur)facing, ∼ (∼) lining · Rabitzauskleidung *f*, Rabitzverkleidung, Rabitzbekleidung

∼ (∼) vault · Rabitzgewölbe *n*

∼ (∼) wall · Rabitzwand *f*, Mörtelwand

∼ (∼) wire fabric lath(ing) welded on to reinforcing mats, ∼ (∼) woven wire (mesh) ∼ ∼ ∼ ∼ ∼ · Baustahl-Rabitzmatte *f* 1,00 × 5,00 m [*Das Rabitzgewebe ist auf Beton-Bewehrungsmatten aufgeschweißt. Längsstäbe im Abstand von 75 mm, Querstäbe von 200 mm. Für Verkleidungen, Hängedecken und Trennwände*]

∼ (∼) ∼ lath(ing) · Rabitzdraht *m* [*Gewebter oder geschweißter Putzträger*]

∼ (∼) work · Rabitzarbeit(en) *f*(*pl*)

∼ vault, ∼ type ∼ · Rabitzgewölbe *n*

racecourse (grand)stand, racetrack ∼, turf ∼ · Pferderennbahntribüne *f*, Rennplatztribüne

rack for curing concrete blocks, curing rack · Hordengestell *n* [*Betonsteinherherstellung*]

radial acceleration · Radialbeschleunigung *f*

radial-arch-roof · Radialbogendach *n*

radial beam · Radialbalken(träger) *m*

∼ bending moment · Radialbiegemoment *n*, Radialbiegungsmoment

∼ ∼ stress · Radialbiegespannung *f* Radialbiegungsspannung

∼ block → ∼ tile

∼ (bonding) header, radiating (∼) ∼, compass (∼) ∼, ∼ bonder, ∼ bondstone · Radialstrecker *m*, Radialbinder(-stein) *m*

∼ brick, radiating ∼, compass ∼ [*A brick the two end faces of which are parts of concentric cylinders*] · Ringziegel *m*, Radialziegel, Schachtziegel, Brunnenziegel, Rz

∼ ∼ industrial chimney, ∼ ∼ ∼ stack, big brick ∼ · freistehender Ziegelschornstein *m*, Industrie-Ziegelschornstein, Ziegel-Industrieschornstein, Ziegelesse *f*, Ziegelschlot *m*

∼ component of load · Radiallastkomponente *f*

∼ crack · Radialriß *m*

∼ cracking · Radialrißbildung *f*

∼ direction · Radialrichtung *f*, radiale Richtung

∼ engineering brick, radiating ∼ ∼, compass ∼ ∼ [*It tapers in at least one direction*] · R 350 *m*, Radialklinker *m*, Ringklinker

∼ force · radiale Kraft *f*, Radialkraft

radial format — radiating engineering brick

~ **format,** radiating ~, compass ~ · Radialformat *n*

~ **girder** · Radialträger *m*

~ **hard brick** → ~ well-burnt ~

~ **header** → ~ bonding ~

~ **line** · Radiallinie *f*

~ **load** · Radiallast *f*

~ **pressure** · Radialdruck *m*

~ **rib** · Radialrippe *f*

radial-rib cupola, ~ dome · Radialrippenkuppel *f*

radial roof fan · Radial-Dachlüfter *m*

~ **section shingle,** ~ surface ~; edge grain ~ *[deprecated]* · Spiegelschnittschindel *f*, Radialschnittschindel, Spaltschnittschindel

~ **sewer network** · Verästelungsnetz *n* *[Stadtentwässerung. Fehlnamen: Radialnetz, Radialsystem n, Fächernetz]*

~ **shear** · Radialschub *m*

~ **solid block,** compass ~ ~, radiating ~ ~, ~ ~ tile *[See remark under 'Block']* · Radialvollblock(stein) *m*, Radialvollstein, Ringvollblock(stein), Ringvollstein, Rs 150

~ ~ **brick,** radiating ~ ~, compass ~ ~ · Radialmauerziegel *m*, Ringmauerziegel, Radialvollziegel, Rz 150

~ ~ **tile** → ~ ~ ~ block

~ **strain** · Radialdehnung *f*

~ **stress** · Radialspannung *f*

~ **stretcher,** radiating ~, compass ~ · Radialläufer *m*

~ **strut** · Radialstrebe *f*

~ **surface shingle,** ~ section ~; edge grain ~ *[deprecated]* · Spiegelschnittschindel *f*, Radialschnittschindel, Spaltschnittschindel

~ **system** · Radialanlage *f* *[Städtebau]*

~ **tile,** radiating ~, compass ~ ~, ~ ~ tile *[See remark under 'Block']* · Radialstein *m*, Radialblock(stein) *m*, Ringstein, Ringblock(stein) *[DIN 1057]*

~ **well-burnt brick,** radiating ~ ~, compass ~ ~, ~ well-burned ~, ~ hard ~ · Radialhart(brand)ziegel *m*, Ringhart(brand)ziegel, Rz 250 *[DIN 1057]*

radian, ~ unit · Bogeneinheit *f*, Radiant *m*, Einheit im Bogenmaß

~ **measure** · Bogenmaß *n*

~ **unit,** radian · Bogeneinheit *f*, Radiant *m*, Einheit im Bogenmaß

(radiant) ceiling heating, panel ~ ~, electric(al) ~ ~, electric(al) ceiling panel ~ · (Elektro)Decken(strahlungs)-heizung *f*, (Elektro)Strahlungs-Deckenheizung

(~) ~ (panel) heating, (~) ~ coil ~ · Decken(-Hochtemperatur)-Strahlungsheizung

~ **chapel** · Radialkapelle *f*

~ **electric heater,** electric radiant ~ · Elektrostrahler *m*

~ ~ **heating,** electric radiant ~ · Elektrostrahlungsheizung *f*

~ **element** · Strahlungselement *n*

~ **energy** · Strahlungsenergie *f*

~ **floor** · Strahlungsdecke *f*

~ ~ **cover(ing),** ~ ~ finish, ~ floor(-ing) · Heiz(ungs)(fuß)boden(belag) *m*

~ **gas heater** → gas radiant ~

~ **heat,** ~ warmth · Strahlungswärme *f* *[Raumheizung]*.

~ ~ **drying** → infrared ~

~ ~ ~ **by electric lamps** → infrared ~ ~ ~ ~

~ ~ ~ ~ **gas heated panels** → infrared ~ ~ ~ ~ ~

~ ~ **stoving** → infrared drying

~ ~ ~ **by electric lamps** → infrared drying ~ ~ ~

radiant-heated · strahlungsbeheizt

radiant heater · Strahlungsheizer *m*

~ **heating** · Strahlungsheizung *f*

radiant-heating glass panel, glass heating ~, electrically heated glass ~ · strahlungsgeheizte Glastafel *f*

radiant heating installation, ~ ~ system, ~ ~ plant · Strahlungsheizung(s-anlage) *f*

~ ~ **panel,** ceiling ~ ~ · Deckenheiz(ungs)platte *f*

~ ~ **plant,** ~ ~ system, ~ ~ installation · Strahlungsheizung(sanlage) *f*

~ ~ **system,** ~ ~ plant, ~ ~ installation · Strahlungsheizung(sanlage) *f*

~ ~ **unit,** panel ~ ~ · Flächenheizkörper *m*

~ **panel** · Strahl(ungs)platte *f* *[Flachheizkörper]*

~ ~ **heating** · Strahl(ungs)plattenheizung *f*, Hochtemperatur-Strahlungsheizung

~ **warmth,** ~ heat · Strahlungswärme *f* *[Raumheizung]*

radiating block → ~ tile

~ **bonder** → ~ (bonding) header

~ **(bonding) header,** radial (~) ~, compass (~) ~, ~ bonder, ~ bondstone · Radialstrecker *m*, Radialbinder(stein) *m*

~ **bondstone** → ~ (bonding) header

~ **brick,** radial ~, compass ~ *[A brick the two end faces of which are parts of concentric cylinders]* · Ringziegel *m*, Radialziegel, Schachtziegel, Brunnenziegel, Rz

~ **chapels** · radiante Kapellen *fpl*, radiale ~, ausstrahlende ~ *[Kapellenkranz eines Chors]*

~ **engineering brick,** radial ~ ~, compass ~ ~ *[It tapers in at least one direction]* · R 350 *m*, Radialklinker *m*, Ringklinker

radiating format — radiographic sensitivity

~ format, radial ~, compass ~ · Radialformat n

~ hard brick → ~ well-burnt ~

~ header → ~ bonding ~

~ solid block, radial ~ ~, compass ~ ~, ~ ~ tile [*See remark under 'Block'*] · Radialvollblock(stein) m, Radialvollstein, Ringvollblock(stein), Ringvollstein, Rs 150

~ ~ brick, radial ~ ~, compass ~ ~ · Radialmauerziegel m, Ringmauerziegel, Radialvollziegel, Rz 150

~ ~ tile, ~ ~ block, radial ~ ~, compass ~ ~ [*See remark under 'Block'*] · Radialvollblock(stein) m, Radialvollstein, Ringvollblock(stein), Ringvollstein, Rs 150

~ stretcher, radial ~, compass ~ · Radialläufer m

~ tile, radial ~, compass ~, ~ block [*See remark under 'Block'*] · Radialstein m, Radialblock(stein) m, Ringstein, Ringblock(stein) [*DIN 1057*]

~ tracery, mullions radiating from the centre · speichenartige Unterteilung f [*Radfenster*]

~ well-burnt brick, radial ~ ~, compass ~ ~, ~ well-burned ~, ~ hard ~ · Radialhart(brand)ziegel m, Ringhart(brand)ziegel, Rz 250 [*DIN 1057*]

radiation loss · Strahlungsverlust m

~ pressure (of a sound wave) [*The unidirectional thrust per unit area exerted by the sound wave at a point on an obstacle. Forces due to streaming are excluded*] · Schall-Strahlungsdruck m [*Gleichdruck auf einer Trennfläche durch die Schallwelle infolge nichtlinearer Effekte*]

(~) shielding → biological ~

~ ~ block, ~ ~ tile, (biological) ~ ~ [*See remark under 'Block'*] · Abschirm(ungs)stein m, Strahlenschutzstein, Abschirm(ungs)block(stein) m, Strahlenschutzblock(stein)

(~) ~ concrete, biological ~ ~ · Abschirm(ungs)beton m, Strahlenschutzbeton [*Zur Abschirmung von Gamma- und Neutronenstrahlen*]

~ ~ design, (biological) ~ ~ · Abschirm(ungs)berechnung f [*Strahlenschutz*]

(~) ~ door, biological ~ ~ · Strahlenschutztür f, Abschirm(ungs)tür

~ ~ glass, (biological) ~ ~ · Strahlenschutzglas n, Abschirm(ungs)glas

(~) ~ material, biological ~ ~ · Abschirm(ungs)(bau)stoff m, Strahlenschutz(bau)stoff; Abschirm(ungs)-(bau)material n, Strahlenschutz(bau)material [*Schweiz*]

~ ~ tile, ~ ~ block, (biological) ~ ~ [*See remark under 'Block'*] · Abschirm(ungs)stein m, Strahlenschutzstein, Abschirm(ungs)block(stein) m, Strahlenschutzblock(stein)

~ ~ wall, (biological) ~ ~ · Abschirm(ungs)wand f [*Zur Abschirmung von Gamma- und Neutronenstrahlen werden Wände aus Beton, Gußeisen, Stahl, Blei, Kunststoff oder Paraffin errichtet*]

~ temperature · Strahlungstemperatur f

radiative heat transfer · Strahlungswärmeübergang m

radiator [*The heating industry has accepted the definition of the term 'radiator' as a heating unit exposed to view within a room or space heated, although such units transfer heat by convection as well as radiation*] · Radiator m, (Glieder)Heizkörper m

~ coat · (Glieder)Heizkörperanstrich m, (Glieder)Heizkörperaufstrich, Radiatoranstrich, Radiatoraufstrich

~ control valve · (Glieder)Heizkörper-Regelventil n, (Glieder)Heizkörper-Regulierventil, Radiator-Regelventil, Radiator-Regulierventil

~ grill(e) · (Glieder)Heizkörpergitter n, Radiatorgitter

~ guard · (Glieder)Heizkörperverkleidung f, Radiatorverkleidung

~ heating · Radiatorenheizung f, (Glieder)Heizkörperheizung

~ niche · (Glieder)Heizkörpernische f, Radiatornische

~ paint · (Glieder)Heizkörper(anstrich)-farbe f, Radiator(anstrich)farbe

~ priming paint · Heizkörper-Grund(ier)(anstrich)farbe f, Glieder~, Radiator-Grund(ier)(anstrich)farbe

~ section · Radiatorglied n, Heizkörperglied

~ (shutoff) valve · Radiator(-Absperr)-ventil n, (Glieder)Heizkörper(-Absperr)-ventil

radio line · Rundfunkleitung f

~ mast · Funkmast m

~ paging system · Funkpersonensuchanlage f

~ suppression · Funkentstörung f

~ teleprinter · Funkfernschreiber m

~ tower · Funkturm m

radioactive paint, self-luminous ~, radioluminous ~ · radioaktive Leuchtfarbe f, selbstleuchtende ~ [*DIN 5043*]

~ pigment, self-luminous ~, radioluminous ~ · radioaktives Leuchtpigment n, selbstleuchtendes ~ [*DIN 5043*]

radiographic examination, ~ inspection, ~ testing · Durchstrahlen n, Durchstrahlung f

~ image quality indicator, penetrameter · Bildgüteprüfsteg m

~ inspection, ~ examination, ~ testing · Durchstrahlen n, Durchstrahlung f

~ quality index · Bildgütezahl f

~ sensitivity, penetrameter ~ (US); wire ~ (Brit.) · Drahterkennbarkeit f, DE [*bei einem Drahtsteg*]

radiographic testing — rainfall intensity

~ **testing**, ~ examination, ~ inspection · Durchstrahlen *n*, Durchstrahlung *f*

radioluminous paint, radioactive ~, self-luminous ~ · radioaktive Leuchtfarbe *f*, selbstleuchtende ~ [*DIN 5043*]

~ **pigment**, radioactive ~, self-luminous ~ · radioaktives Leuchtpigment *n*, selbstleuchtendes ~ [*DIN 5043*]

radius of curvature · Krümmungshalbmesser *m*

~ ~ ~ **of tendon** · (Vor)Spanngliedkrümmungshalbmesser *m*

~ ~ **inertia** · Trägheitshalbmesser *m*

~ ~ **rotation** · Drehhalbmesser *m*

radome · Radialkuppel *f*

raft → ~ **foundation**

(~) **batten** · Lagerholz *n* [*schwimmender Holz(fuß)boden(belag)*]

(~) **battens in the fill(ing)** · Lagerhölzer *npl* in der Auffüllung

(~) ~ **on resilient (quilt) strips and beams** · Lagerhölzer *npl* auf Dämmstreifen(unterlagen) und Balken

~ **(foundation)**, mat ~, spread ~ · Plattengründung *f*, Flächengründung

rafter, rftr. [*A sloping structural member extending from the eave(s) to the ridge of a roof. It may be a common rafter or a principal rafter*] · (Dach)Sparren *m*

~ **cleat**, ~ clench · (Dach)Sparrenhalter *m*

~ **clench**, ~ cleat · (Dach)Sparrenhalter *m*

~ **connection** · (Dach)Sparrenstoß *m*, (Dach)Sparrenverbindung *f*

~ **cross-section** · (Dach)Sparrenquerschnitt *m*

~ **end**, ~ head · (Dach)Sparrenkopf *m*

~ **head**, ~ end · (Dach)Sparrenkopf *m*

~ **interval**, ~ spacing, distance between rafters · Sparrenabstand *m*, Dach~

~ **nail** · (Dach)Sparrennagel *m*

~ **slope** · (Dach)Sparrenneigung *f*

~ **spacing**, ~ interval, distance between rafters · (Dach)Sparrenabstand *m*

~ **span** · (Dach)Sparrenweite *f*

rafter-supporting purlin(e) · (Dach-)Sparrenpfette *f*

rafter system, system of rafters · (Dach-)Sparrenlage *f*

rafters · Gespärre *n*, Sparrenwerk *n* [*Alle Sparren eines Daches*]

rag · Wollumpen *m*

~ **bolt**, stone ~ · Steinschraube *f*, Klauenschraube

~ **felt**, wool ~ [*The term 'wool felt' is somewhat of a misnomer, since no roofing felt is composed entirely of wool fibres*] · Wollfilz(dach)pappe *f*

rag-felt floor cover(ing), ~ floor(ing) (finish), wool-felt ~ (~) · Wollfilzpappenbelag *m*, Wollfilzpappen(fuß)bodenbelag

~ **floor(ing) (finish)**, ~ floor cover(ing), wool-felt ~ (~) · Wollfilzpappenbelag *m*, Wollfilzpappen(fuß)bodenbelag

rag fiber (US); ~ fibre (Brit.) · Lumpenfaser *f*

rags · Lumpen *mpl*

ragstone, gritstone, coarse(-grain(ed)) sandstone · grob(körnig)er Sandstein *m*, Kristallsandstein

~ · bröckeliger Bruchstein *m*

rail, track · (Führungs)Schiene *f* [*Türanlage*]

~, **window** ~, sash ~ [*The horizontal member in a window sash*] · (Fenster-)Riegel *m*

~, **cross member**, horizontal member [*A horizontal bar of wood or metal extending from one post or support to another as a guard or barrier in a fence, balustrade, staircase, etc.*] · Querstück *n*, Riegel *m*

~, **door** ~ · Querrahmenstück *n*, (Tür-)Riegel *m* [*Holzfüllungstür*]

railing · Geländer *n*

~ **barrel**, ~ tubing, ~ tube · Geländerrohr *n* [*DIN 989*]

~ **height** · Geländerhöhe *f*

~ **material** · Geländerbaustoff *m*

~ **tube**, ~ barrel, ~ tubing · Geländerrohr *n* [*DIN 989*]

railroad architecture (US); railway ~ (Brit.) · Eisenbahnarchitektur *f*, Eisenbahnbaukunst *f*

(~) **ballast** (US); (railway) ~ (Brit.) · (Eisen)Bahnschotter *m*, Gleisschotter, Schienenschotter

rain barrier → ~ **water** ~

(~) **conductor** → **downpipe**

~ **impermeability**, rain imperviousness, raintightness, imperviousness to rain, impermeability to rain · Regendichtheit *f*, Regendichtigkeit, Regenundurchlässigkeit [*Fehlname: Regendichte f*]

~ **imperviousness**, rain impermeability, raintightness, imperviousness to rain, impermeability to rain · Regendichtheit *f*, Regendichtigkeit, Regenundurchlässigkeit [*Fehlname: Regendichte f*]

(~) **leader** → **downpipe**

~ **penetration**, lateral ~ ~, (lateral) penetration of rain · Durchfeuchtung *f*

~ ~ ~ · Regendurchschlag *m*

rain resistance · Regenwiderstand *m*

~ **spotting** [*The particular case of 'water spotting' caused by rain*] · Regenfleckigkeit *f*

rainfall intensity · Regendichte *f*, Regenintensität *f*, Regenhöhe *f* in der Minute

rainfall map — ram-headed sphinx

~ **map** · Regenkarte f [*Karte mit Verbindungslinien von Orten gleicher Regenmenge*]

raining machine, rain water ~ · Regenmaschine f [*Zur Durchführung künstlicher Bewitterungsversuche*]

rainproof, raintight, RT · regensicher, regenfest, regendicht, regenundurchlässig

~ **masonry wall** · Regenschutzmauer f [*Fehlname: Regenschutzwand f. In Gegenden mit starkem Schlagregen wird oft eine ½-Stein dicke Mauerschale als Regenschutzmauer vor eine bereits genügend wärmedichte Außenmauer im Abstand vorgesetzt*]

rain-repelling, rain-repellent · regenabweisend

raintight, RT, rainproof · regendicht, regenundurchlässig, regensicher, regenfest

raintightness, rain impermeability, rain imperviousness, imperviousness to rain, impermeability to rain · Regendichtheit f, Regendichtigkeit, Regenundurchlässigkeit [*Fehlname: Regendichte f*]

rainwater, storm water, R.W. [*Excess water during rainfall or continuously following and resulting therefrom*] · Regenwasser n

~ **articles** → ~ goods

rain(water) barrier, R.W. ~ · Regen(wasser)sperre f

rainwater cistern, R.W. ~ · Regen(wasser)zisterne f

~ **goods,** ~ products, ~ articles · Dachzubehör(teile) n, (*mpl, npl*)

~ **gutter,** (roof) ~, R.W. ~ · (Dach-)Rinne f, Regenrinne, Abflußrinne [*DIN 18460*]

~ ~ **board** → (roof) ~ ~

~ ~ **heating** → (roof) ~ ~

~ ~ **hook** → (roof) ~ ~

~ ~ **sheet** → (roof) ~ ~

~ **head;** cistern ~ (US); leader ~, conductor ~, R.W. ~ [*The enlarged entrance at the head of a downpipe. It collects the water from the gutters*] · Regenrinnenkasten m, Regenrinnenkessel m, (Dach)Rinnenkasten, (Dach)Rinnenkessel, Abflußrinnenkasten, Abflußrinnenkessel, Wasserfangkasten

~ **hopper** [*A hopper-shaped rainwater head, sometimes also used in the middle of a long downpipe*] · Trichter m

~ **machine,** raining ~ · Regenmaschine f [*Zur Durchführung künstlicher Bewitterungsversuche*]

~ **outlet,** R.W. ~ · Regen(wasser)ablauf m [*am Dach*]

~ **pipe** → downpipe

~ ~, R.W. ~ · Regenrohr n, Regenwasserrohr

~ ~ **hanger,** R.W. ~ ~ · Regen(wasser)rohrschelle f

~ **products** → ~ goods

~ **removal,** removal of rainwater · Regen(wasser)abführung f

~ **system,** R.W. ~ · Regenablaufkonstruktion f [*Regenrinne + Regenfallrohr + Zubehör*]

~ **tank,** R.W. ~ · Regen(wasser)behälter m

~ ~, R.W. ~ · Regen(wasser)(auffang)becken n

to raise, to bend up, to drape, to deflect · ablenken, anheben [*Litze in der Spannbetontechnik*]

raised arch · überhöhter Bogen m

~ **block,** ~ building, heightened ~ · aufgestocktes Gebäude n

~ **building,** ~ block, heightened ~ · aufgestocktes Gebäude n

raised-cable technique → deflected-strand ~

raised choir, upper ~, ~ quire, coro alto · Oberchor m, Hochchor

~ **field,** ~ panel ~ · überhobene Füllung f

~ **grain** · aufgerauhte Faser f [*Holz*]

~ **panel,** fielded ~ · Tafel f mit überhobener Füllung

~ (~) **field** · überhobene Füllung f

~ **quire,** upper ~, ~ choir, coro alto · Oberchor m, Hochchor

raised-strand technique → deflected-strand ~

raised table, abacus, padstone [*The slab between the lintel and the supporting column, designed to concentrate the load. In the Greek Doric order the abacus is a simple square block; in the Roman orders it is thimmer and mo(u)lded*] · Abakus m, Kapitellplatte f, (Säulen)Deckplatte

raising cord · Aufzugkordel f [*Jalousie*]

~ **of steam** → steam generation

~ ~ **strands,** deflecting ~ ~, bending up cables · Anheben n der Litzen, Ablenken ~ ~, Litzenanheben, Litzenablenken [*Spannbeton*]

to rake out · auskratzen

raker [*An inclined beam*] · Schrägbalken(-träger) m

raking bond → diagonal (masonry) ~

~ ~ → herringbone (masonry) ~

~ **flashing** [*See remark under 'Anschluß'*] · Schräganschluß m

~ ~ (**piece**) · Schräganschluß(streifen) m

~ **support,** ~ shore, inclined ~ · Schrägstütze f

Rames(s)eum · Memnonium n Ramses' II., Rames(s)eum n

ram-headed sphinx · Widdersphinx f

rammed-earth construction — rape seed oil 798

rammed-earth construction, rammed-loam ~, pisé (de terre) ~, cob ~ · Lehmstampfbau *m*, Piseebau, Kastenwerk *n*
rammed lime · Kalkpisee *m*
rammed-loam construction, rammed-earth ~, pisé (de terre) ~, cob ~ · Lehmstampfbau *m*, Piseebau, Kastenwerk *n*
ramp · Rampe *f*
~, passenger loading apron · Abfertigungsgebäuderampe *f*, Empfangsgebäuderampe
~ **between floors,** ~ ~ **stories** · Geschoßrampe *f*
~ **incline** · Rampenschräge *f*
~ **tower,** heliciine, spiral ramp, circular ramp, helic(oid)al ramp · Schraubenrampe *f*, Wendelrampe, Spiralrampe
ramp-type garage, ~ parking structure · Rampen-Parkhaus *n*, Rampen(-Park)garage *f*, Rampen-Parkbau *m*
rampant arch, rising ~, lopsided ~ · (an)steigender Bogen *m*, abschüssiger ~, abfallender ~, einhüftiger ~, geschobener, einschenkliger ~, Schwanenhalsbogen, Hornbogen [*veraltet: Bogentreppe f, geschwungener Bogen, Spannbogen*]
~ **barrel vault,** ~ tunnel ~, ~ wagon ~, rising ~ ~ · einhüftiges (Tonnen)Gewölbe *n*, (an)steigendes ~, einhüftige Tonne *f*, (an)steigende Tonne [*Tonnengewölbe mit ungleichhohen Fußlinien*]
~ **tunnel vault** → ~ barrel ~
~ **vault,** rising ~ · einhüftiges Gewölbe *n*, (an)steigendes ~, fallendes ~, geschobenes ~, abschüssiges ~
~ **wagon vault** → ~ barrel ~
rampart, protective stone wall · Steinmauer *f* zur Befestigung, Natur~ ~ ~
~, protective earth wall [*A defensive bank of earth, with or without a stone parapet*] · Erdwall *m*, (Festungs)Wall, Umwallung *f*
ramparts · Stadtumwallung *f*
random bond → ~ masonry ~
~ **check,** spot ~ · Stichprobe *f*
~ **crack** · wilder Riß *m*
~ **cracking** · wilde Rißbildung *f*
~ **eccentricity** · zufällige Ausmittigkeit *f*
~ **(masonry) bond** · wilder Verband *m* [*Möglichst viele Läufer ergeben ein unregelmäßiges Bild. Die zur Durchbindung erforderlichen Köpfe sind so verteilt, daß sie in einem jeweils übersehbaren Abschnitt möglichst nicht übereinander liegen. Läufer und Abtreppungen von ¼-Steinen sollten sich nicht mehr als fünfmal wiederholen*]
~ ~ **(work)** → ~ range ~ (~)
~ **perforated,** ~ pierced · unregelmäßig gelocht, ~ durchlocht

~ **(range) masonry (work)** [*In random (range) masonry (work) no attempt is made to form courses*] · ungeschichtetes Mauerwerk *n*, unregelmäßiges ~
~ **rubble masonry (work)** → uncoursed ~ ~ (~)
~ **sample** · Stichprobe *f*
~ **sampling** · Stichprobenahme *f*
range · Bereich *m, n*
~, kitchen ~, kitchener · (Küchen)Herd *m*
~ · Schießstand *m*
~ → basins in ~
~ [*The difference between the highest and the lowest value*] · (Wert)Bereich *m, n*
~ **hood, (cooker)** ~ · Dunstabzug(-haube) *m, (f)*, Dunsthaube [*Über einem Küchenherd*]
~ **(lavatory) basin** · Reihenstück *n* [*Waschreihe*]
~ (~) ~ · Reihenwaschtisch *m*
~ **masonry (work)** [*The stones are laid in courses, each course being uniform in thickness throughout its length. All courses, however, need not to be of the same thickness*] · regelmäßiges Schicht(en)mauerwerk *n*, geschichtetes Mauerwerk
~ **of audibility,** audible range, audibility range · Hör(barkeits)bereich *m, n*, Hörsamkeitsbereich
~ ~ **colours** (Brit.); ~ ~ **colors** (US) · Farbbereich *m, n*
~ ~ **columns,** row ~ ~ · Säulenstellung *f*, Säulenreihe *f*
~ ~ **compression strength** → compression strength range
~ ~ **compressive strength** → compression strength range
~ ~ **crushing strength** → compression strength range
~ ~ **grading** → size range
~ ~ **hardness,** hardness range · Härte(n)bereich *m, n*
~ ~ **noises,** noise range · Lärmbereich *m, n*
(~ ~) **scatter** · Streubereich *m, n* [*Versuchsergebnisse*]
~ ~ **screening** → size range
~ **of steel stress** · Schwingbreite *f* [*Stahlspannung*]
~ ~ **strength,** strength range · Festigkeitsbereich *m, n*
~ ~ **urinal stalls** · Pißstandreihe *f*, Urinalstandreihe
~ ~ **viscosity,** viscosity range · Viskositätsbereich *m, n*
~ **socket** · Herdsteckdose *f*
Rape of the Sabines · Raub *m* der Sabinerinnen [*von Giovanne da Bologna, Marmor, 1583*]
rape seed oil · Raps(samen)öl *n*, Rüböl

**rapid-acting folding shutter door, **
quick-acting ~ ~ ~ · Schnellfalttor *n*

rapid-assembly method, quick-assembly ~, quick-erection ~, rapid-erection ~ · Schnell(montage)bauweise *f*, Schnell(montage)verfahren *n*

rapid cleaning agent, ~ cleaner · Schnellreiniger *m*

~ core drill anchor, self drilling ~, self-drill ~ · Selbstbohrdübel *m*

rapid-curing cutback, RC [*An asphalt cement cut back with gasoline or naphtha. RC–0 to RC–5*] · schnell-(ab)bindendes Verschnittbitumen *n*

rapid-drying, quick-drying · schnelltrocknend

rapid-erection method, quick-erection ~, quick-assembly ~, rapid-assembly ~ · Schnell(montage)bauweise *f*, Schnell(montage)verfahren *n*

rapid fixing, quick ~ · Schnellbefestigung *f*

~ hardener, accelerator for hardening, hardening accelerator, hardening acceleration promotor, hardening accelerating agent · Schnell(er)härter *m*, (Er)Härtungs(zeit)beschleuniger

rapid hardening · Schnell(er)härten *n*

~ ~ · Schnell(er)härtung *f*

rapid-hardening · schnell(er)härtend

~ cement, RHC · schnell(er)härtender Zement *m*, Schnell(er)härterzement

~ (Portland) cement type III (US) → high early (or initial) strength (Portland) cement

rapid-setting, quick-breaking, labile · labil, unstabil, schnellzerfallend [*Bitumenemulsion*]

~ · schnell(ab)bindend [*hydraulisches Bindemittel*]

~ cement, cement of rapid initial set(-ting) · Schnellbinder *m* [*Fehlname*]; Schnellerstarrer [*Zement. DIN 1164*]

~ emulsion, labile ~, quick-breaking ~ · U-Emulsion *f*

~ moulding plaster (Brit.); ~ molding ~ (US) · Geschwindgips *m* [*Ein besonders schnell abbindender Modellgips*]

rapid transit · Schnellverkehr *m* [*öffentlicher Massenverkehr*]

rare books library · Bücherei *f* für seltene Bücher, Bibliothek *f* ~ ~ ~

rare earth, RE · seltene Erde *f*

rare-earth oxid(e) (US); ~ oxide (Brit.) · Seltene-Erden-Oxid *n*

rare veneer, figured ~, fancy ~, patterned ~ · Maserfurnier *n*

rat barrier · Rattensperrvorrichtung *f* [*Zur Bekämpfung der Rattenplage in Grundstücksentwässerungsanlagen*]

rate-and-price indicator · Börsenkursanzeiger *m*

rate of action · Beanspruchungsgeschwindigkeit *f*

~ ~ adding, ~ ~ addition, adding rate, addition rate · Zusatzdosis *f*, Beigabedosis

~ ~ addition, ~ ~ adding, adding rate, addition rate · Zusatzdosis *f*, Beigabedosis

~ ~ adsorption, adsorption rate · Adsorptionsgeschwindigkeit *f*

~ ~ assembling → assembling speed

~ ~ assembly → assembling speed

~ ~ burning → burning rate

~ ~ combustion, combustion rate · Brenngeschwindigkeit *f* [*Baustoff*]

~ ~ creep, creep rate [*The slope of the creep-time curve at a given time*] · Kriechgeschwindigkeit *f*

~ ~ curing, curing rate · (Ab)Bindegeschwindigkeit *f* [*Verschnittbitumen*]

~ ~ drying, drying rate · Trocknungsgeschwindigkeit *f*

~ ~ erection → assembling speed

~ ~ evaporation, evaporation rate · Verdunstungsgeschwindigkeit *f*

~ ~ firing → burning rate

~ ~ hardening, hardening rate · (Er-)Härtungsgeschwindigkeit *f*

~ ~ heat leak to the environment · Wärmeabgabegeschwindigkeit *f* an die Umgebung

~ ~ hydration, hydration rate · Hydra-(ta)tionsgeschwindigkeit *f*

~ ~ initial set(ting), initial set(ting) rate · Erstarrungsgeschwindigkeit *f* [*Beton; Mörtel*]

~ ~ oscillation, ~ ~ vibration · Schwingungsgeschwindigkeit *f*, Erschütterungsgeschwindigkeit

~ ~ reaction, reaction rate · Reaktionsgeschwindigkeit *f*

~ ~ set(ting), set(ting) rate · (Ab)Bindegeschwindigkeit *f* [*hydraulisches Bindemittel*]

~ ~ slide (operation), speed ~ ~ (~) · Ziehgeschwindigkeit *f*, Gleitgeschwindigkeit [*Gleitschalung*]

~ ~ strain, strain rate · Dehn(ungs)-geschwindigkeit *f*

~ ~ strength gain · Festigkeitszunahmegeschwindigkeit *f*

~ ~ vibration, ~ ~ oscillation · Schwingungsgeschwindigkeit *f*, Erschütterungsgeschwindigkeit

~ ~ warming, warming rate · Anwärmungsgeschwindigkeit *f*, Erwärmungsgeschwindigkeit

~ sensitive · geschwindigkeitsabhängig [*(Werk)Stoffverhalten*]

rating test · Nennprobe *f*, Nennprüfung *f*, Nennversuch *m*

ratio, proportion · Maßverhältnis *n*, Proportion *f*

~ · Quotient *m*
~ **of longitudinal reinforcement** · Längsarmierungsanteil *m*, Längsbewehrungsanteil, Längs(stahl)einlagenanteil
~ ~ **reinforcement for tension,** ~ ~ tensile reinforcement, ~ ~ tension reinforcement · Zugarmierungsanteil *m*, Zugbewehrungsanteil, Zug(stahl)einlagenanteil
~ ~ **plate edge lengths,** ~ ~ slab ~ ~ · Plattenseitenverhältnis *n*
~ ~ **slab edge lengths,** ~ ~ plate ~ ~ · Plattenseitenverhältnis *n*
~ ~ **steel stress to concrete stress** · Verhältnis *n* Stahlspannung/Betonspannung
~ ~ **tensile reinforcement,** ~ ~ tension ~, ~ ~ reinforcement for tension · Zugarmierungsanteil *m*, Zugbewehrungsanteil, Zug(stahl)einlagenanteil
~ ~ **tension reinforcement,** ~ ~ tensile ~, ~ ~ reinforcement for tension · Zugarmierungsanteil *m*, Zugbewehrungsanteil, Zug(stahl)einlagenanteil

ratiometer, concrete mix electric testing apparatus · Gerät *n* zur Bestimmung des W/Z-Faktors

rationalist architecture · rationale Architektur *f*, ~ Baukunst *f*
~ **period** · rationalistische Epoche *f*

Ratisbon Cathedral · Regensburger Dom *m*

rat-proof · rattensicher

rattle free, ~ proof · klapperfrei, klappersicher

ravelin [*In military architecture, an outwork formed of two faces of a salient angle and constructed beyond the main ditch and in front of the curtain wall*] · Ravelin *m*

raw asbestos · Rohasbest *m*
~ **castor oil** · Ricinusrohöl *n*
(~) **(China) wood oil,** (~) tung ~ [*B.S. 391*] · (rohes) Holzöl *n*, (~) Tungöl [*Das Produkt, das durch Auspressen oder Extrahieren von Samen des Tungbaumes gewonnen wird; es muß frei von Beimischungen anderer Öle oder Fette sein. DIN 55936*]
(~) **clay** · (Roh)Ton *m* [< 0,002 mm]
~ **copal** · Rohkopal *m*
~ **cord** · Rohkord *m*
~ **cork** [*Cork having undergone no treatment whatsoever after stripping*] · Rohkork *n*
~ **gravel** · Rohkies *m*
~ **gypsum,** natural ~, (massive) ~; gypsum rock, plaster rock, plaster stone, potter's stone (Brit.) · Rohgips *m*, Naturgips, Gipsstein *m*, Gipsgestein, CaSO$_4$ · 2 H$_2$O
~ **linseed oil** [*It is the oil obtained from the seed of the flax plant, the most important sources are India (Calcutta oil), Argentina (Plate oil) and the Baltic provinces of the Soviet Union (Baltic oil). B.S. 243 and 632*] · Rohleinöl *n*, rohes Leinöl
~ **material** · Rohmaterial *n*, Rohstoff *m*
~ ~ **deposit** · Rohmaterialvorkommen *n*, Rohstoffvorkommen [*Stein- und Erden-Industrie*]
~ ~ **for ready roofing,** ~ ~ ~ composition ~, ~ ~ ~ prepared ~, ~ ~ ~ roof(ing) felt, ~ ~ ~ roofing paper · Dachpappenrohstoff *m*
~ ~ **grinding** · Rohmaterialmahlung *f* [*Zementerzeugung*]
~ **materials storage** · Rohmateriallagerung *f*, Rohstofflagerung
~ **meal** · Rohmehl *n* [*Zementherstellung*]
~ ~ **mixing plant** · Rohmehlmischanlage *f* [*Zementwerk*]
~ ~ **silo** · Rohmehlsilo *m*
~ **mill** · Rohmehlmahlanlage *f* [*Zementherstellung*]
~ **mix(ture)** · Rohgemisch *n*, Rohmischung *f* [*Zementerzeugung*]
~ **rubber,** natural ~, caoutchouc · (Natur)Kautschuk *m* [*Fehlnamen: Naturgummi m, n, Rohgummi*]
~ ~ **emulsion,** natural ~ ~, caoutchouc ~ · (Natur)Kautschukemulsion *f*
~ ~ ~ **paint,** natural ~ ~ ~, caoutchouc ~ ~ · (Natur)Kautschukemulsionsfarbe *f*
~ ~ **powder** → natural ~ ~
~ **sand** · Rohsand *m*
~ **sienna,** natural ~ [*B.S. 312*] · (Terra *f* di) Siena *f* natur, ungebrannte (Terra di) Siena
~ **slag** · Rohschlacke *f*
~ **slurry** · Rohschlamm *m* [*Zementherstellung*]
~ ~ **mixer** · Rohschlammischer *m* [*Zementherstellung*]
~ **stone** [*lime industry*] · Rohgestein *n*
(~) **tung oil** → (~) (China) wood ~
~ **umber** [*B.S. 313*] · Rohumbra *f*, ungebrannte Umbra, Umbra natur
(~) **vermiculite,** ripidolite · Glimmer *m* als Ausgangsstoff für Vermiculite
~ **water,** RW · Rohwasser *n*
~ **wood oil** · rohes Holzöl *n*

razor socket · (Elektro)Rasierersteckdose *f*

RB, Rockwell hardness B-scale · Rockwellhärte-B-Skala *f*

RC, Rockwell hardness C-scale · Rockwellhärte-C-Skala *f*

RC, rapid-curing cutback [*An asphalt cement cut back with gasoline or naphtha. RC-0 to RC-5*] · schnell(ab)bindendes Verschnittbitumen *n*

R.C., reinforced concrete · Stahlbeton *m*

R.C. apron → reinforced (concrete) spandrel (wall)

R.C. apron wall (US) → reinforced (concrete) spandrel (~)

R.C. arch, reinforced (concrete) ~ · Stahlbetonbogen *m*
R.C. barrel vault → reinforced (concrete) ~ ~
R.C. barrel-vault shell, reinforced (concrete) ~ ~ · Stahlbeton-Tonnenschale *f*
R.C. beam, reinforced (concrete) ~ · Stahlbetonbalken(träger) *m*
R.C. beam and slab → reinforced (concrete) ~ ~ ~
R.C. beam floor, reinforced (concrete) ~ ~ · Stahlbetonbalken(träger)decke *f*
R.C. bearer → reinforced (concrete) binding joist
R.C. binder → reinforced (concrete) binding joist
R.C. binding joist → reinforced (concrete) ~ ~
R.C. block → reinforced (concrete) building
R.C. box girder, reinforced concrete ~ · Stahlbetonkasten(träger) *m*
R.C. bracket, reinforced concrete ~ · Stahlbetonkonsole *f*
R.C. breast → reinforced (concrete) spandrel (wall)
R.C. building → reinforced (concrete) ~
R.C. bunker, reinforced (concrete) ~ · Stahlbetonbunker *m*
R.C. cast floor → reinforced (concrete) (pre)cast ~
R.C. cast frame → (pre)cast R. C. ~
R.C. cast wall → prefab(ricated) reinforced (concrete) ~
R.C. ceiling joist → reinforced (concrete) binding ~
R.C. cellar window, reinforced (concrete) ~ ~ · Stahlbeton-Kellerfenster *n*
R.C. chimney, reinforced (concrete) ~ · Stahlbetonschornstein *m*
R.C. chimney shaft, reinforced (concrete) ~ ~ · Stahlbetonschornsteinschaft *m*
R.C. church, reinforced (concrete) ~ · Stahlbetonkirche *f*
R.C. column, reinforced (concrete) ~ · Stahlbetonstütze *f*
R.C. column, reinforced (concrete) ~ · Stahlbetonsäule *f*
R.C. combined footing, reinforced. concrete ~ ~ · zusammengefaßtes Stahlbetonfundament *n*
R.C. compound unit, reinforced concrete ~ ~ · Stahlbetonbauteil *m, n* [z.B. Stütze; Wand; Binder usw.]
R.C. compression ring, reinforced (concrete) ~ ~ · Stahlbeton-Druckring *m*
R.C. construction, reinforced (concrete) ~ · Stahlbetonbau *m* [*DIN 1045*]
R.C. construction type, reinforced concrete ~ ~, reinforced concrete type of construction, R. C. type of construction · Stahlbetonbauart *f*

R.C. continuous frame → reinforced (concrete) ~ ~
R.C. core, (reinforced) concrete ~, service ~, utility ~, building ~, mechanical ~ · (Hoch)Hauskern *m*, (Stahl-) Betonkern, Betriebskern, (Gebäude-) Kern
R.C. cross member → reinforced (concrete) rail
R.C. cross wall → reinforced (concrete) shear ~
R.C. cross-wall, reinforced (concrete) ~ · Stahlbetonquerwand *f*
R.C. cupola → reinforced (concrete) dome
R.C. cylindrical shell → reinforced (concrete) ~ ~
R.C. design and construction → reinforced (concrete) ~ ~ ~
R.C. dome → reinforced (concrete) ~
R.C. door lintel → reinforced (concrete) ~ ~
R/C duct floor, reinforced concrete ~ ~ · Stahlbetonkanaldecke *f*
R.C. engineering → reinforced (concrete) design and construction
R.C. facing → reinforced (concrete) lining
R.C. flat roof, reinforced concrete ~ ~ · Stahlbetonflachdach *n*
R.C. flat slab, reinforced (concrete) ~ ~ · Stahlbeton-Pilzdeckenplatte *f*
R.C. flexible foundation beam → reinforced (concrete) ~ ~ ~
R.C. floor → reinforced (concrete) (intermediate) ~
R.C. floor beam → reinforced (concrete) joist
R.C. floor slab, reinforced (concrete) ~ ~ · Stahlbetondeckenplatte *f*
R.C. floor-slab member → reinforced (concrete) floor-slab unit
R.C. floor-slab unit → reinforced (concrete) ~ ~
R.C. floor(ing) construction → reinforcing (concrete) floor(ing) (structural) system
R.C. floor(ing) (structural) system → reinforced (concrete) ~ (~) ~
R.C. floor(ing) system → reinforced (concrete) floor(ing) (structural) ~
R.C. folded plate roof → reinforced (concrete) ~ ~ ~
R.C. folded slab roof → reinforced (concrete) folded plate ~
R.C. footing, reinforced concrete ~ · Stahlbetonfundament *n*
R.C. foul water pipe → reinforced (concrete) sewer ~
R.C. foundation, reinforced (concrete) ~ · Stahlbetongründung *f*
R.C. frame, reinforced (concrete) ~ · Stahlbetonrahmen *m*

R.C. garage — R.C. rib(bed) floor 802

R. C. garage, reinforced (concrete) ~ · Stahlbetongarage *f*

R. C. girder, reinforced (concrete) ~ · Stahlbetonträger *m*

R. C. girder floor, reinforced (concrete) ~ ~ · Stahlbetonträgerdecke *f*

R. C. girder wall, reinforced concrete ~ ~ · Stahlbetonträgerwand *f*

R. C. header, reinforced (concrete) ~ · Stahlbetonwechsel(balken) *m*

R. C. high-pressure pipe, reinforced (concrete) ~ ~ · Stahlbeton-Hochdruckrohr *n*

R. C. hinge, reinforced (concrete) ~ · Stahlbetongelenk *n*

R. C. hipped-plate roof (US) → reinforced (concrete) folded plate ~

R. C. hollow beam, reinforced (concrete) ~ ~ · Stahlbeton-Hohlbalken(träger) *m*

R. C. hollow beam floor, reinforced (concrete) ~ ~ ~ · Stahlbeton-Hohlbalkendecke *f*

R. C. hollow(-core) plank, (reinforced) concrete ~ ~ · Stahlbeton(hohl)diele *f*, Steg(zement)diele *[DIN 4028]*

R. C. hollow pile, reinforced (concrete) ~ ~ · Stahlbeton-Hohlpfahl *m*

R. C. hollow plank → (reinforced) concrete hollow(-core) ~

R. C. hollow slab, (reinforced concrete) ~ ~ · (Stahlbeton-)Hohlplatte *f*

R. C. hollow slab floor → (reinforced (concrete)) ~ ~ ~

R. C. hollow slab floor(ing) construction → (reinforced (concrete)) hollow slab floor(ing) system

R. C. hollow slab floor(ing) system → (reinforced (concrete)) ~ ~ ~ ~

R. C. horizontal member → reinforced (concrete) rail

R. C. (intermediate) floor → reinforced (concrete) (~) ~

R. C. joist → reinforced (concrete) ~

R. C. lattice girder, reinforced (concrete) ~ ~ · Stahlbetongitterträger *m*

R. C. lift-slab, reinforced (concrete) ~ · Stahlbeton-Hub(decken)platte *f*, Hub-Stahlbeton(decken)platte

R. C. lift-slab construction, reinforced (concrete) ~ ~ · Stahlbeton-Hub(decken)bau *m*

R. C. lift-slab structure, reinforced concrete ~ ~ · Stahlbeton-Hub(decken)bauwerk *n*

R. C. lighting mast, reinforced (concrete) ~ ~ · Stahlbeton-Beleuchtungsmast *m*, Stahlbeton-Leuchtenmast, Stahlbeton-Lichtmast

R. C. lightweight aggregate, reinforced-concrete ~ ~ · Stahlleicht(beton)zuschlag(stoff) *m*

R. C. lining → reinforced (concrete) ~

R. C. mast, reinforced (concrete) ~ · Stahlbetonmast *m [DIN 4234]*

R. C. mosque, reinforced (concrete) ~ · Stahlbetonmoschee *f*

R. C. panel, reinforced (concrete) ~ · Stahlbetontafel *f*

R. C. panel wall, reinforced (concrete) ~ ~ · Stahlbetontafelwand *f*

R. C. parachute → reinforced (concrete) umbrella

R. C. parallel truss, reinforced (concrete) ~ ~ · Stahlbeton-Parallelfachwerkträger *m*

R. C. parapet → reinforced (concrete) spandrel (wall)

R. C. parking deck, reinforced (concrete) ~ ~ · Stahlbetonparkplatte *f*

R. C. parking structure, reinforced (concrete) ~ ~ · Stahlbeton-Parkbauwerk *n*

R. C. partition (wall), reinforced (concrete) ~ (~) · Stahlbetonwand *f [Leichte Trennwand. DIN 4103]*

R. C. patent glazing bar → reinforced (concrete) ~ ~ ~

R. C. pile, reinforced (concrete) ~ · Stahlbetonpfahl *m*

R. C. pipe, reinforced (concrete) ~ · Stahlbetonrohr *n [DIN 4035]*

R. C. pipeline, reinforced (concrete) ~ · Stahlbetonrohrleitung *f*

R. C. plain web beam → reinforced (concrete) ~ ~ ~

R. C. plain web girder → reinforced (concrete) ~ ~ ~

R. C. plate, ~ slab, reinforced (concrete) ~ · armierte (Beton)Platte *f*, bewehrte ~, (Beton)Platte mit (Stahl-)Einlagen, Stahlbetonplatte

R. C. plate floor → reinforced (concrete) slab ~

R. C. portal frame, reinforced (concrete) ~ ~ · Stahlbetonportalrahmen *m*

R. C. (pre)cast floor → reinforced (concrete) ~ ~

R. C. (pre)cast frame → (pre)cast R. C. ~

R. C. (pre)cast wall → prefab(ricated) reinforced (concrete) ~

R. C. pressure pipe → reinforced (concrete) ~ ~

R. C. problem, reinforced (concrete) ~ · Stahlbetonaufgabe *f*

R. C. purlin(e), reinforced (concrete) ~ · Stahlbeton(dach)pfette *f*

R. C. puttyless glazing bar → reinforced (concrete) patent ~ ~

R. C. rafter, reinforced (concrete) ~ · Stahlbetonsparren *m*

R. C. rail → reinforced (concrete) ~

R. C. refuse water pipe → reinforced (concrete) sewer ~

R. C. rib, reinforced (concrete) ~ · Stahlbetonrippe *f*

R. C. rib(bed) floor, reinforced (concrete) ~ ~ · Stahlbetonrippendecke *f [DIN 1045]*

R. C. rib(bed) slab, reinforced (concrete) ~ ~ · Stahlbetonrippenplatte f

R. C. rigid frame, reinforced (concrete) ~ ~ · Stahlbeton-Steifrahmen m

R. C. roof, reinforced (concrete) ~ · Stahlbetondach n

R. C. roof beam, reinforced (concrete) ~ ~ · Stahlbetondachbalken(träger) m

R. C. roof cladding → reinforced (concrete) ~ ~

R. C. roof covering → reinforced (concrete) roof cladding

R. C. roof sheathing → reinforced (concrete) roof cladding

R. C. (roof) truss → reinforced (concrete) (~) ~

R. C. roof(ing) → reinforced (concrete) roof cladding

R. C. roof(ing) slab, reinforced (concrete) ~ ~ · Stahlbeton-Dachplatte f, Stahlbeton-Bedachungselement n, Stahlbeton-Dachelement, Stahlbeton-Bedachungsplatte

R. C. sandwich slab, reinforced (concrete) ~ ~ · Stahlbeton-Dreilagenplatte f, Stahlbeton-Sandwichplatte

R. C. screed, reinforced (concrete) ~ · Stahlbetonestrich m

R. C. section, reinforced (concrete) ~ · Stahlbetonquerschnitt m

R. C. sewage pipe → reinforced (concrete) sewer ~

R. C. sewer pipe → reinforced (concrete) ~ ~

R. C. shear wall → reinforced (concrete) ~ ~

R. C. shell, reinforced (concrete) ~ · Stahlbetonschale f

R. C. shell construction, reinforced (concrete) ~ ~ · Stahlbetonschalenbau m

R. C. shell roof, reinforced (concrete) ~ ~ · Stahlbetonschalendach n

R. C. silo, reinforced (concrete) ~ · Stahlbetonsilo m

R. C. skyscraper, reinforced (concrete) ~ · Stahlbeton-Wolkenkratzer m

R. C. slab, ~ plate, reinforced (concrete) ~ · armierte (Beton)Platte f, bewehrte ~, (Beton)Platte mit (Stahl)Einlagen, Stahlbetonplatte

R. C. slab base → reinforced (concrete) ~ ~

R. C. slab floor → reinforced (concrete) ~ ~

R. C. slab foundation → reinforced (concrete) slab base

R. C. solid floor, reinforced (concrete) ~ ~ · Stahlbetonvolldecke f

R. C. solid plank (unit), reinforced (concrete) ~ ~ (~) · Stahlbetonvolldiele f

R. C. solid slab, reinforced (concrete) ~ ~ · Stahlbetonvollplatte f

R. C. solid web beam → reinforced (concrete) plain ~ ~

R. C. solid web girder → reinforced (concrete) plain ~ ~

R. C. space bearing structure → reinforced (concrete) space (load)bearing ~

R. C. space (load)bearing structure → reinforced (concrete) ~ ~ ~

R. C. space structure → reinforced (concrete) space (load)bearing ~

R. C. space (weight-carrying) structure → reinforced (concrete) space (load)bearing ~

R. C. spandrel (wall) → reinforced (concrete) ~ (~)

R. C. spatial bearing structure → reinforced (concrete) space (load)bearing ~

R. C. spatial (load)bearing structure → reinforced (concrete) space ~ ~

R. C. spatial structure → reinforced (concrete) space (load)bearing ~

R. C. spatial (weight-carrying) structure → reinforced (concrete) space (load)bearing ~

R. C. spun pipe, reinforced (concrete) ~ ~ · Schleuderstahlbetonrohr n, Stahlbetonschleuderrohr

R. C. stair(case), reinforced (concrete) ~ · Stahlbetontreppe f

R. C. step, reinforced (concrete) ~ · Stahlbetonstufe f

R. C. storage tank, reinforced (concrete) ~ ~ · Stahlbeton-Lagerbehälter m

R. C. string → reinforced (concrete) ~

R. C. structure, reinforced (concrete) ~ · Stahlbetonbauwerk n [DIN 1045]

R. C. structure, ~ ~ system, reinforced (concrete) ~ · Stahlbetontragsystem n, Stahlbetontragwerk n

R. C. sun breaker → reinforced (concrete) sun shade

R. C. sun screen → reinforced (concrete) sun shade

R. C. sun shade → reinforced (concrete) ~ ~

R. C. (sur)facing → reinforced (concrete) lining

R. C. T-beam → reinforced (concrete) beam and slab

R. C. T-beam floor → reinforced (concrete) T(ee)-beam ~

R. C. T(ee)-beam → reinforced (concrete) beam and slab

R. C. T(ee)-beam floor → reinforced (concrete) ~ ~

R. C. tension member, reinforced (concrete) ~ ~ · Stahlbetonzugglied n

R. C. three-dimensional (weight-carrying) structure → reinforced (concrete) space (load)bearing ~

R. C. topping, reinforced (concrete) ~ · Stahlbeton-Druckschicht f, Stahlbeton-Druckplatte f

R. C. tower — ready-mix(ed) mortar

R. C. tower → service ~
R. C. trimmer plank (unit), reinforced (concrete) ~ ~ (~) · Stahlbetonstreichdiele f [*Auswechs(e)lung*]
R. C. truss → reinforced (concrete) (roof) ~
R. C. truss(ed girder), reinforced (concrete) ~ (~) · Stahlbetonfachwerk(träger) n, (m)
R. C. tunnel vault → reinforced (concrete) barrel ~
R. C. two-hinge(d) arch → reinforced (concrete) ~ ~
R. C. two-pin(ned) arch → reinforced (concrete) two-hinge(d) ~
R. C. type of construction, reinforced concrete ~ ~ ~, reinforced concrete construction type, R. C. construction type · Stahlbetonbauart f
R. C. umbrella → reinforced (concrete) ~
R. C. vault, reinforced (concrete) ~ · Stahlbetongewölbe n
R. C. wagon vault → reinforced (concrete) barrel ~
R. C. wall, reinforced (concrete) ~ · Stahlbetonmauer f
R. C. wall panel, reinforced (concrete) ~ ~ · Stahlbetonwandtafel f
R. C. window lintel → reinforced (concrete) ~ ~
R. C. work, reinforced (concrete) ~ · Stahlbetonarbeiten fpl [*DIN 18331*]
RCCP, reinforced (concrete) culvert pipe · Stahlbetondurchlaßrohr n
RCP, rust-converting primer · Rostumwandler m
~ → reinforced (concrete) pipe
RE, rare earth · seltene Erde f
reactance · Reaktanz f [*Akustik. Der Imaginärteil der Impedanz*]
reaction · Reaktion f
~, reactive force [*The upward resistance of a support such as a column or wall against the downward pressure of a loaded member such as a girder*] · Auflagerdruck m, Stützkraft f, Auflagerwiderstand m, Auflagerreaktion f, Stützreaktion, Auflagerkraft, Stützwiderstand, Stützdruck, Gegendruck, Reaktionskraft
~ **capacity**, ~ property, ~ quality, ~ power · Reaktionseigenschaft f, Reaktionsvermögen n, Reaktionsfähigkeit f
~ **heat**, heat of reaction · Reaktionswärme f
~ **of hardening** · Härtungsreaktion f, Er~
~ ~ **imposts** · Kämpferreaktion f
~ ~ **initial set(ting)**, initial set(ting) reaction · Erstarrungsreaktion f [*Beton; Mörtel*]
~ ~ **set(ting)**, set(ting) reaction · (Ab-)Bindereaktion f [*hydraulisches Bindemittel*]

~ **power**, ~ capacity, ~ property, ~ quality · Reaktionseigenschaft f, Reaktionsvermögen n, Reaktionsfähigkeit f
~ **property**, ~ quality, ~ power, ~ capacity · Reaktionseigenschaft f, Reaktionsvermögen n, Reaktionsfähigkeit f
~ **quality**, ~ property, ~ capacity, ~ power · Reaktionseigenschaft f, Reaktionsvermögen n, Reaktionsfähigkeit f
~ **rate**, rate of reaction · Reaktionsgeschwindigkeit f
~ **temperature**, temperature of reaction · Reaktionstemperatur f
reactive · reagierend
~ **aggregate** → (alkali) reactive material in concrete
~ **force** → reaction
~ **material in concrete** → alkali ~ ~ ~ ~
reactivity · Reaktivität f
reactor block, ~ building · Reaktorgebäude n
~ **building**, ~ block · Reaktorgebäude n
~ **cupola**, ~ dome · Reaktorkuppel f
~ **dome**, ~ cupola · Reaktorkuppel f
~ **shielding** · Reaktorabschirmung f
~ ~ **concrete** · Reaktorbeton m
reading desk · Lesepult n
~ **hall** · Lesesaal m
~ **room** · Leseraum m
readout · Ablesen n
~ **unit** · Ablesevorrichtung f
ready for mixing, ready-to-mix · mischfertig
~ ~ **occupation** · nutzungsbereit, beziehbar [*Gebäude*]
ready-made tiled partition [*It eliminates on-site tiling*] · Fertig-Fliesentrennwand f
ready-mix(ed) coloured (external) rendering, premix(ed) ~ (~) ~ (Brit); ~ ~ stucco (US); ~ ~ external plaster, ~ ~ exterior plaster · Edel(ver)putz m
~ **concrete** · Fertigbeton m, Transportbeton, Lieferbeton
~ ~ **fabricator**, ~ ~ supplier, ~ ~ plant operator · Transportbetonhersteller m
(ready-)mixed glue [*Synthetic resin glue with an accelerator mixed with it in the pot*] · Fertigleim m, gebrauchsfertiger Leim
ready-mix(ed) gypsum plaster → gypsum ready-mix(ed) ~
~ ~ **stuff** → gypsum ready-mix(ed) plaster
~ **lean concrete** · Fertig-Magerbeton m, Liefer-Magerbeton, Transport-Magerbeton
~ **light(weight) gypsum plaster** → gypsum ready-mix(ed) ~
~ **mortar** [*Mortar, usually lime and sand, mixed before delivery to the site*] · Transportmörtel m

~ **oil-base(d) paint** · streichfertige Ölfarbe f

~ **paint**, prepared ~, P.F.U. ~, paint prepared for use · anstrichfertige Farbe f, gebrauchsfertige ~, verarbeitungsfertige ~, Fertig(anstrich)farbe

~ **plaster** → ~ stuff

~ **stuff**, premix(ed) ~, ~ plaster · Trocken(putz)mörtel, Fertig(putz)mörtel, Trockenputzmasse f, Fertigputzmasse

~ **wet paste**, premix(ed) ~ ~ · Kunstharz-Feinputz m, Putzfüller m

ready roofing, composition ~, prepared ~, roof(ing) felt, roof(ing) paper, (com-)pressed felt [*B.S. 747*] · Dachpappe f [*DIN 52121*]

~ ~ **manufacture**, composition ~ ~, prepared ~ ~, roof(ing) felt ~, roof(ing) paper ~, (com)pressed felt ~ · Dachpappenherstellung f

ready-roofing shingle → asphalt ~

ready sheet roofing (paper), composition ~ ~ (~), prepared ~ ~ (~) (US); sheet roof(ing) felt [*Prepared roofing supplied in flat sheets*] · Bahnendachpappe f, Dachpappe in Bahnenform

ready-to-assemble · zusammenbaufertig

ready to be walked on · begehbereit [*(Fuß)Boden(belag)*]

ready-to-erect · aufbaufertig, montagefertig

ready-to-mix, ready for mixing · mischfertig

ready-to-paint · anstreichfertig

ready-to-place · einbaufertig

ready-to-spray · spritzfertig

ready-to-use · gebrauchsfertig, verarbeitungsfertig

~ **material** · Fertigfabrikat n

~ **paste** · Fertigpaste f

ready wired for connection · anschlußfertig verdrahtet

real allowance, actual ~ · Istabmaß n, tatsächliches Abmaß

~ **clay** · natürlicher Ton m

~ **construction time**, actual ~ ~ · Istbauzeit f, tatsächliche Bauzeit

~ **cross-section**, actual ~ · Istquerschnitt m, tatsächlicher Querschnitt

~ **(design) load factor** · tatsächliche Traglast f, Ist-Traglast

~ **dimension**, actual ~ · Istabmessung f, Istmaß n, tatsächliche Abmessung, tatsächliches Maß

~ **displacement** · wirkliche Verrückung f

~ **estate agent** (US); house ~ (US) · Grundstücksmakler m, Häusermakler

~ **load factor**, ~ design ~ ~ · tatsächliche Traglast f, Ist-Traglast

~ **part** · Realteil m, n [*Akustik*]

~ **personnel**, actual ~, ~ staff · Istpersonalbestand m, tatsächlicher Personalbestand

~ **size**, actual ~ · Istgröße f, tatsächliche Größe

~ **staff**, actual ~, ~ personnel · Istpersonalbestand m, tatsächlicher Personalbestand

~ **time**, actual ~ · Istzeit f, tatsächliche Zeit

realgar · Rotrauschgelb n, Realgar m, Rauschrot n (Min.)

ream · Schliere f [*Flachglasfehler*]

reaming · Aufreiben n

re-analysis, re-calculation, structural ~ · statische Nachrechnung f

to re-analyze · statisch nachberechnen

rear access · Hinterzugang m, rückwärtiger Zugang

~ **arch** → rere-arch

~ **balcony** · Hofbalkon m

~ **masonry wall of a niche** · Schildmauer f [*Die verbleibende durchgehende Mauer einer Mauernische*]

~ ~ ~ ~ ~ **slot** · Schildmauer f [*Die verbleibende durchgehende Mauer eines Mauerschlitzes*]

~ **plot line**, ~ property ~ · hintere Grundstücksgrenze f

~ **portico**, opisthodomos [*The enclosed section of the rear of a Greek temple, sometimes used as a treasury*] · Opisthodomos m, Hinterraum m, Rückhalle f

~ **property line**, ~ plot ~ · hintere Grundstücksgrenze f

~ **view** · Hinteransicht f, Rückansicht

~ **wall**, back ~ · Rückwand f, rückwärtige Wand

~ **yard**, backyard [*The yard across the full width of the plot opposite the front yard, extending from rear line of building to rear property line. The rear yard of a corner lot is the yard opposite the selected front yard*] · Hinterhof m

rearrangement of (interior) partitioning · Neueinteilung f von Räumen

reasonable price · angemessener Preis m

rebate → window ~

~ → rabbet

~ **for putty** · Glasfalz m, Kittfalz

~ **ledge**, rabbet ~ · Schlagleiste f [*Beim zweiflügeligen Fenster bzw. bei der zweiflügeligen Tür*]

rebated boarding → ~ floor ~

~ **floor** · gefalzter Dielen(fuß)boden m, halbgespundeter ~, halbgespundete Dielung f, gefalzte Dielung

~ (~) **boarding**, ~ floor(ing) (finish), ~ floor cover(ing) · gefalzte Dielung f, halb gespundete ~

~ **siding**, rabbetted ~, shiplap ~ · gefalzter Wandbeschlag m, ~ Wandschirm m, ~ Wetterschirm, gefalzte Verschalung f

to rebend — reconstructed granite paving slab

to rebend · rückbiegen
rebending · Rückbiegen *n*
~ test · Rückbiegeprobe *f*, Rückbiegeprüfung *f*, Rückbiegeversuch *m*
reboil bubble · Spätblase *f*, Spätgispe *f* [*Glas*]
rebound · Rückprall *m*
~ deflection, elastic ~, ~ deflexion · elastische Durchbiegung *f*, ~ Durchsenkung
~ height · Rücksprunghöhe *f*
~ tester, concrete test hammer, scleroscope [*A tester indexing the compressive strength of concrete by the height of elastic rebound*] · Rückprallhammer *m*, Betonprüfhammer, Betonschlaghammer, Rückprall-Härteprüfer
to rebuff · nachbohnern
to rebuild · wiederaufbauen
rebuilding · Wiederaufbau *m*
re-calculation, re-analysis, structural ~ · statische Nachrechnung *f*
receiver vessel, receiving ~ · Aufnahmebehälter *m*
receiving pipe · Einsatzrohr *n* [*Das Rohr, auf welches ein (Ab)Dicht(ungs)ring aufgezogen wird*]
~ room · Empfangsraum *m* [*Bei der Bestimmung der Schallpegeldifferenz D*]
~ vessel, receiver ~ · Aufnahmebehälter *m*
receptacle, power socket · Kraftsteckdose *f*, Starkstrom-Steckdose
reception desk · Empfangsschalter *m* [*Hotel*]
~ hall → (entrance) ~
~ lounge · Hotelhalle *f*
~ office · Empfangsbüro *n*
~ stall · Einfahrtstand *m* [*Parkhaus*]
recess, blockout, embrasure, cavity, pocket · Aussparung *f*
~ → (interior) doorjamb
~ for concealed lighting, ~ ~ indirect ~, ~ ~ ~ ~ illumination · Beleuchtungsblende *f*
recessed · zurückweichend
~ (bath)tub, ~ bath · Nischen(bade)-wanne *f*
~ ceiling(-mounted) luminaire (fixture) (US); ~ ~ light fitting (Brit.); ~ ~ (light(ing)) fixture · Einbau-Deckenleuchte *f*
~ joint · vertiefte Fuge *f*
~ margin · Kantenschlag *m*, Randschlag [*Die zugerichtete Kante eines Quadersteins*]
~ order of an arch · Bogenrundung *f*
~ soap holder, ~ ~ tray · Einbauseifenschale *f*, eingebaute Seifenschale
~ waste fitting, waste (fitting) · Kelchplatte *f*
~ wide-ledge (bath)tub, ~ ~ bath · Nischen(bade)wanne *f* mit breitem Rand, Breitrand-Nischen(bade)wanne

reciprocal displacements, reciprocity of ~ · Gegenseitigkeit *f* der Verrückungen
~ force polygon, Bow's ~ · reziproker Kräfteplan *m*, Bowscher ~ [*ebenes Fachwerk*]
~ relation, reciprocity · Gegenseitigkeit *f*
~ theorem · Gegenseitigkeitssatz *m*, Reziprozitätssatz [*Baustatik*]
~ (value) · Kehrwert *m*, reziproker Wert
reciprocity of displacements, reciprocal ~ · Gegenseitigkeit *f* der Verrückungen
recirculated air · Umluft *f* [*Abluft, die nach Filterung und meistens nach Mischen mit Außenluft den zu belüftenden Räumen wieder zugeführt wird*]
~ ~ operation · Umluftbetrieb *m*
recirculation duct · Umluftkanal *m*
reclaim(ed) filler · Eigenfüller *m*
reclaimed ground, ~ land · Neuland *n*
~ land, ~ ground · Neuland *n*
reclaim(ed) rubber · regenerierter Gummi *m*, aufgearbeiteter ~, regeneriertes ~ *n*, aufgearbeitetes ~ *n*, Altgummi
~ ~ solution · Altgummilösung *f*
reclaiming, reclamation · Aufarbeitung *f*, Aufarbeiten *n* [*z.B. von Altstahl*]
reclamation, reclaiming · Aufarbeitung *f*, Aufarbeiten *n* [*z.B. von Altstahl*]
recoatability · Überlackierbarkeit *f*
re-coating · Anstricherneuerung *f*
recombined aggregate → (dry-)batched ~
~ materials → (dry-)batched aggregate
reconstituted marble [*Lumps of marble, unsuitable for cutting into slabs, are stacked in large moulds, the interstices filled with chippings and the whole resin-bonded under pressure. After curing the resultant block of reconstituted marble can be treated similarly to natural marble, and sawn into slabs or tiles which are usually available in either bonded or polished finish, at much lower prices than natural marble*] · gepreßter Marmorbruch *m*
~ ~ tile · Fliese *f* aus gepreßtem Marmorbruch, (Belag)Platte *f* ~ ~ ~ ~
~ stone → cast ~
~ ~ shop, cast ~ ~, reconstructed ~ ~, patent ~ ~; artificial ~ ~ [*deprecated*] · Betonwerksteinbetrieb *m*, Betonwerksteinwerkstätte *f* [*Fehlnamen: Kunststeinbetrieb, Kunststeinwerkstätte. Eine Erzeugungsstätte für Betonwerkstein jeder Art kleinen, also handwerklichem, Umfangs*]
~ ~ tile, cast ~ ~, reconstructed ~ ~, patent ~ ~; artificial ~ ~ [*deprecated*] · Betonwerksteinplatte *f* [*Fehlname: Kunststeinplatte*]
~ ~ work → cast ~ ~
reconstructed granite paving slab · Granitoid-Gehwegplatte *f* [*Betonhartsteinplatte mit Granitkörnung in der Gehschicht. DIN 485*]

reconstructed mica — rectangular pattern

~ **mica,** micanite · Marienglas *n,* Mikanit *m*
~ **stone** → cast ~
~ ~ **floor cover(ing)** → cast stone floor(ing) (finish)
~ ~ **shop** → reconstituted ~ ~
~ ~ **skin** → cast ~ ~
~ ~ **stair(case)** → cast ~ ~
~ ~ **tile** → reconstituted ~ ~
~ ~ ~ **floor cover(ing)** → cast stone tile floor(ing) (finish)
~ ~ **waterproofer** → cast ~ ~
~ ~ **work** → cast ~ ~
recoverable heat · rückgewinnbare Wärme *f,* wiedergewinnbare ~
recreation(al) area, ~ ground · Erholungsbereich *m, n,* Erholungsfläche *f,* Erholungsgebiet *n*
~ **centre,** leisure ~ (Brit.); ~ center (US) · Freizeitzentrum *n,* Erholungszentrum
~ **facility** · Erholungsanlage *f*
~ **ground,** ~ area · Erholungsbereich *m, n,* Erholungsfläche *f,* Erholungsgebiet *n*
~ **room** · Erholungsraum *m*
recrushing · Nachbrechen *n*
rectangle · Rechteck *n*
rectangular · rechteckig
~ **apse,** ~ apsis · Rechteckabside *f,* Rechteckapside, Rechteckapsis *f*
~ **area** · Rechteckfläche *f*
~ ~ **grating** · Rechteckgitterrost *m*
~ **axes,** ~ system of ~ · rechtwinkeliges Achsenkreuz *n*
~ **bar,** ~ rod · Rechteckstab *m,* rechteckiger Stab
~ **bay,** ~ vault ~ · Rechteck(gewölbe)-joch *n*
~ ~ **window** · Rechteck-Auslucht *f*
~ **beam** → ~ cross-section(al) ~
~ **brass** · Rechteckmessing *n,* rechteckiges Messing
~ **brick** → ~ clay ~
~ **building** · Rechteckgebäude *n*
~ **cantilever(ed) step,** ~ cantilevering ~ · Auslegerblockstufe *f,* Kragblockstufe, auskragende Blockstufe, vorkragende Blockstufe
~ **chamber** · Rechteckraum *m* [*Nebenraum im Sakralbau*]
~ **chapel** · Rechteckkapelle *f*
~ **choir,** ~ quire · Rechteckchor *m*
~ **(clay) brick** · Rechteckstein *m* [*Fehlname*]; Rechteckziegel *m*
~ **column** · Rechteckstütze *f,* rechteckige Stütze
~ **copper** · Rechteckkupfer *n,* rechteckiges Kupfer
~ **cross section** · Rechteckquerschnitt *m*
~ **(cross-section(al)) beam,** prismatic ~ · Balken(träger) *m* mit gleichbleibendem Querschnitt, Rechteckbalken-(träger), prismatischer Balken(träger)

~ **crossing of masonry walls,** ~ masonry wall crossing · rechtwinkelige Mauerkreuzung *f*
~ **design** → waffle pattern
~ **dowel** · eckiger Dollen *m,* ~ (Stab-)Dübel *m,* Rechteckdollen, Rechteck-(stab)dübel
~ **forecourt** · Rechteckvorhof *m*
~ **frame,** ~ framing · Rechteckrahmen *m*
~ ~ **with three hinges,** three-hinge(d) rectangular frame, three-pin(ned) rectangular frame · Dreigelenkrechteckrahmen *m*
~ **grid** · Rechteckraster *m*
~ ~ ~ → waffle pattern
~ ~ **ceiling,** cored ~, waffle ~, caisson ~, pan(el) ~, cassette ~, coffer(ed) ~ · Kassettendecke *f,* kassettierte Decke
~ ~ **design** → waffle pattern
~ ~ **floor** → waffle (slab) ~
~ ~ **(~) slab,** ~ ~ (~) panel, ~ ~ (~) plate, cassette (~) ~, caisson (~) ~, waffle (~) ~, pan (~) ~, coffer(ed) (~) ~, cored (~) ~ · Kassetten(decken)platte *f,* kassettierte (Decken)Platte
~ ~ (~) **floor** → waffle (slab) ~
~ ~ **pattern** → waffle ~
~ ~ **plate** → ~ ~ (floor) slab
~ ~ (~) **floor** → waffle (slab) ~
~ ~ **slab** → ~ ~ (floor) ~
~ ~ (~) **floor** → waffle (~) ~
~ ~ **soffit,** pan(el) ~, cassette ~, coffer(ed) ~, caisson ~, waffle ~ · Kassettenuntersicht *f,* kassettierte Untersicht
~ **gutter** → box(ed) (roof) ~
rectangular-headed loophole, square-headed ~, ~ loop (window) · oben rechteckiger Sehschlitz *m*
rectangular hyperbolic paraboloid · rechteckig hyperbolisches Paraboloid *n*
~ **junction of masonry walls,** ~ masonry wall junction · rechtwinkeliger Maueranschluß *m,* (~) Mauerstoß *m*
~ **manhole,** ~ manway · Rechteck(einstieg)schacht *m,* Rechteckeinstiegschacht, Rechteckmannloch *m*
~ **manway,** ~ manhole · Rechteck(einstieg)schacht *m,* Rechteckeinstiegschacht, Rechteckmannloch *n*
~ **masonry corner** · rechtwinkelige Mauerecke *f*
~ ~ **wall crossing,** ~ crossing of masonry walls · rechtwinkelige Mauerkreuzung *f*
~ ~ ~ **junction,** ~ junction of masonry walls · rechtwinkeliger Maueranschluß *m* (~) Mauerstoß *m*
~ **membrane** · Rechteckmembran(e) *f*
~ **panel** · Rechtecktafel *f,* rechteckige Tafel
~ **pattern** → waffle ~

rectangular pier — to redecorate

~ **pier** · Rechteckpfeiler *m*, rechteckiger Pfeiler

~ **pipe,** box-shaped ~ · Flachrohr *n*, Viereckrohr, Vierkantrohr, Rechteckrohr, viereckiges Rohr, flaches Rohr, rechteckiges Rohr

~ **plate,** ~ slab · Rechteckplatte *f*, rechteckige Platte

~ **profile,** ~ section · Rechteckprofil *n*, Rechteckschnitt *m* [*Rechteckige Umrißlinie eines durchschnittenen Körpers*]

~ **pyramid** · Rechteckpyramide *f*, Rechteckspitzsäule *f*

~ **quire,** ~ choir · Rechteckchor *m*

~ **rainwater gutter**→ box(ed) (roof) ~

~ **refractory brick** · feuerfester Rechteckstein *m*, ff. ~ [*DIN 1081*]

~ **rib** · Rechteckrippe *f*

~ **rod,** ~ bar · Rechteckstab *m*, rechteckiger Stab

~ **(roof) gutter** → box(ed) (~) ~

~ **roof-light** · Rechteck(decken)oberlicht *n*

~ **R. W. gutter** → box(ed) (roof) ~

~ **section,** ~ profile · Rechteckprofil *n*, Rechteckschnitt *m* [*Rechteckige Umrißlinie eines durchschnittenen Körpers*]

~ **slab,** ~ plate · Rechteckplatte *f*, rechteckige Platte

~ **steel** · Rechteckstahl *m*, rechteckiger Stahl

~ **step,** flyer · Blockstufe *f*, Klotzstufe [*Massive Stufe mit rechteckigem Querschnitt*]

~ **stress distribution** · rechtwinkelige Spannungsverteilung *f*

~ **structure** · Rechteckbau(werk) *m*, (*n*)

~ **(system of) axes** · rechtwinkeliges Achsenkreuz *n*

~ **temple** · Rechtecktempel *m*

~ **tile** · Rechteck(belag)platte *f*, Rechteckfliese *f*

~ **(vault) bay** · Rechteck(gewölbe)joch *n*

~ **window** · Rechteckfenster *n*, rechteckiges Fenster *f*

~ **wire** · Rechteckdraht *m*, rechteckiger Draht

~ ~ **mesh** · Rechteck-Drahtmaschenmatte *f*

~ ~ **rod** · Rechteckwalzdraht *m*, rechteckiger Walzdraht

rectification · Mängelbehebung *f*

Rectilinear Style, Perpendicular ~, Late Pointed ~, Perpendicular Gothic, Perpendicular architecture · Perpendikularstil *m*, Spätphase *f* der englischen Gotik [*Die letzte Phase der gotischen Architektur in England von 1360–1550. Vertikalzug, besonders in der Fenster- und Wandgliederung*]

rectilinear tracery, panel ~, perpendicular ~ · [*It was introduced in the fifteenth century. The mullions pass uninterrupted to the head of the arch. The tracery consists of upright, straight-sided panels above the window lights*] · rechtwink(e)liges Maßwerk *n*

rectory, priest's house, parsonage (building) [*In the Roman Catholic Church called 'presbytery'*] · Pfarre *f*, Pfarrhaus *n*

recumbent effigy · Liegefigur *f*

red alizarin(e) lake · Alizarinrot *n*, Krapprot

~ **brass** · Rotguß *m*, Rg [*DIN 1705. Eine Kupfer-Zinn-Zink-Bleilegierung mit Gehalten von 4–10% Sn, 2–7% Zn, 1–4% Pb, Rest Cu. Goldgelb bis rötlich. Gut gießbar, polierfähig, hart lötbar*]

~ **chalk** · Braunröte *f*, englisches Braunrot *n*, Rotstein *m*

~ **chrome (pigment),** chrome red (~) · Chromrot(pigment) *n*

red-figure style · rotfiguriger Stil *m* [*Vasenmalerei*]

~ **vase** · rotfigurige Vase *f*

red fir strip floor(ing) (finish), ~ ~ ~ floor cover(ing), Scots ~ ~ ~ (~) · Fhk *m*, Kiefernriemen(fuß)boden(belag) *m*

~ **(iron) oxid(e) (pigment),** ~ oxid(e) of iron (~), iron (oxid(e)) red (~) (US); red (iron) oxide (~), red oxide of iron (~), iron (oxide) red (~) (Brit.) · (Eisen)Oxidrot(pigment) *n*, Eisenrot(pigment)

~ **lead,** minium [*substance*], red lead oxid(e) [*chemical name*] · [*B.S.* 217] · (Blei)Mennige *f*, Pb₃O₄ [*DIN 55916. Österreich: Minium n*]

~ **lead-based (building) mastic,** minium-based (~) ~ · (Blei)Mennigekitt *m* [*Bleimennige + Leinöl oder (Leinöl)Firnis*]

~ ~ **oxid(e)** [*chemical name*], red lead, minium [*substance*] [*B. S.* 217] · (Blei)Mennige *f*, Pb₃O₄ [*DIN 55916. Österreich: Minium n*]

~ ~ **paint** · Bleimennigefarbe *f*

~ ~ **spar,** hemiprismatic ~ ~ · hemiprismatisches Bleibaryt *n*

~ **litmus paper** · rotes Lackmuspapier *n*

~ **ocher** (US); ~ ochre · roter Ocker *m*

~ **organic pigment** · rotes organisches Pigment *n*, organisches Rot(pigment)

~ **oxide of iron (pigment)** (Brit.) → ~ (iron) oxid(e) (~)

~ **oxid(e) (pigment)** → ~ iron ~ (~)

~ **pigment** [*B.S.* 333] · Rotpigment *n*

~ **sandstone** · Rotsandstein *m*

~ **seal** · Rotsiegel *n* [*pulverförmiges Mörteldichtungsmittel*]

~ ~ · Rotsiegel *n* [*30% ZnS*]

~ **ultramarine** · Ultramarinrot *n*, rotes Ultramarin *n*

redan · Redan *m* [*kleiner Ravelin*]

reddish-brown · rötlich-braun

to redecorate, to renovate, to embellish · renovieren, verschönern

redecoration, embellishment · Verschönerung f
~ work, embellishment ~ · Verschönerungsarbeiten fpl
to re-design · umkonstruieren
redeveloped area, ~ zone, ~ site · erneuertes (Stadt)Gebiet n
redeveloping area → (urban) renewal ~
redevelopment, rehabilitation · Wiederherstellung f
~ → urban ~
~ area → (urban) renewal ~
~ work, rehabilitation ~ · Wiederherstellungsarbeiten fpl
redirection of forces · Kraftumlenkung f
~ ~ traffic sources · Verlagerung f von Verkehrsquellen
to redistribute · umlagern [Spannung]
redistributed moment, secondary (bending) ~ · negatives Zusatzmoment n, Umlagerungsmoment, umgelagertes Moment
redistribution · Umlagerung f [Baustatik]
~ of forces · Umlagerung f der Kräfte
~ ~ moments, moment redistribution · Momentenumlagerung f
~ ~ stress(es), stress redistribution · Spannungsumlagerung f
redoubt · Redoute f
to reduce, to comminute · zerkleinern
~ ~ [to unit basis] · umrechnen [auf Einheitswerte beziehen]
~ ~ full-strength colo(u)rs to a tint [with white, etc.] · ausmischen
reduced line of loading, ~ loading line · reduzierte Belastungslinie f
~ loading line, ~ line of loading · reduzierte Belastungslinie f
~ main stress, principal ~ · reduzierte Hauptspannung f
~ moment · reduziertes Moment n
~ principal stress, ~ main ~ · reduzierte Hauptspannung f
reducer → thinner
~ → diminishing piece
reducibility · Reduzierbarkeit f
reducing agent · Reduktionsmittel n
~ cross [A double branch in the form of a reducing fitting] · Reduktionskreuzstück n, Reduzierkreuzstück
(~) die, (wire-)drawing ~ · Zieheisen n, Ziehstein m, Draht~
~ firing, second ~ · Schwarzbrennen n [Glas]
~ fitting → diminishing piece
~ piece → diminishing ~
~ (pressure) valve, pressure reducing ~, reducer · Druckminderventil n, Reduzierventil, Reduktionsventil

~ process · Reduktion(sverfahren) f, (n)
~ tee, ~ T(ee) · Reduzier-T-Stück n, Reduktions-T-Stück
reduction · Minderung f, Herabsetzung
~ coefficient, coefficient of reduction · Herabsetzungsbeiwert m, Herabsetzungszahl f, Minderungsbeiwert, Minderungszahl
~ Gothic (style) · Reduktionsgotik f
~ in area, (con)striction, necking down · Einschnürung f
~ ~ cross-section, ~ ~ area · Querschnittschwächung f, Querschnitt(ver)minderung
~ ~ moments · Momentenabminderung f
~ ~ rigidity, ~ ~ stiffness · Steifigkeitsabnahme f, Starrheitsabnahme
~ ~ stiffness, ~ ~ rigidity · Steifigkeitsabnahme f, Starrheitsabnahme
~ ~ (the) moment of support · Abminderung f des Stützenmomentes, Stützenmomentabminderung
~ ~ types, limitation ~ ~ · Typeneinschränkung f
~ theorem, theorem of reduction · Reduktionssatz m
redundancy · überzählige Größe f
~ · Überzähligkeit f
redundant · überflüssig, überzählig [Baustatik]
~ · Überzählige f
~ bar, ~ rod, ~ member · überzähliger Stab m [Fachwerk]
~ force · überzählige Kraft f
~ frame → (statically) indeterminate ~
~ framing → (statically) indeterminate frame
~ member, ~ bar, ~ rod · überzähliger Stab m [Fachwerk]
~ moment · überzähliges Moment n
~ rod, ~ bar, ~ member · überzähliger Stab m [Fachwerk]
~ to the second degree · überflüssig zweiten Grades, überzählig ~ ~
reed · Pfeife f, Falte f
~ · Ried n, Ret(h) n, (Schilf)Rohr n
~ board, ~ sheet · Rohrplatte f, Schilf~
~ lath(ing) · (Putzträger-)Rohrgewebe n, (Schilf)Rohrgewebe-Putzträger m
~ ~ plaster, ~ ~ finish · Rohrgewebeverputz m
~ mat factory · Rohrmattenwerk n, Schilf~
(~) roof(ing), ~ thatch(ing) · Rohr(dach)(ein)deckung f, Rohrdach n, Schilf(rohr)(dach)(ein)deckung, Schilf(rohr)dach [Norddeutschland: Ried(dach)(ein)deckung, Ret(h)(dach)(ein)deckung, Rieddach, Ret(h)dach]
~ sheet, ~ board · Rohrplatte f, Schilf~
~ thatch · Ret(h) n für Dach(ein)deckungszwecke, Ried n ~ ~ [Norddeutschland]; (Schilf)Rohr n ~ ~

(~) thatch(ing), ~ roof(ing), fleaking · Rohr(dach)(ein)deckung f, Rohrdach n, Schilf(rohr)(dach)(ein)deckung, Schilf(rohr)dach [*Norddeutschland: Ried(dach)(ein)deckung, Ret(h)-(dach)(ein)deckung, Rieddach, Ret(h)dach*]

reeding, reeds [*A series of convex mo(u)ldings of equal width, side by side: the inverse of fluting. The fluting of the lower third of column shafts was sometimes infilled with reeds to strengthen them against damage*] · Pfeifen *fpl*, Falten *fpl*

reeds → reeding

reel · Scheibe f [*Astragal*]

~ and bead (enrichment) → bead and reel (~)

re-entrant angle, re-entering ~, internal ~ · einspringender Winkel *m*

~ corner · einspringende Ecke f

refectory, frater, monastic hall [*The communal dining-hall in a convent*] · Klosterspeisesaal *m*, Refektorium *n*, Speisesaal im Kloster

~ [*The communal dining-hall in a college*] · Speisesaal *m*, Gemeinschaftsspeiseraum *m*

~ · Rem(p)ter *m* [*Das Refektorium in Burgen geistlicher Ritterorden*]

~ for lay brethren → frater ~ ~ ~

reference beam · Ersatzbalken(träger) *m*

~ direction · Bezugsrichtung f

~ grid, grid plan [*A plan in which setting-out lines called grid lines coincide with the most important wall and other building components. Prefabricated buildings are usually designed to fit a grid plan. A grid plan is not a planning grid = Raster*] · Rasternetz *n*

~ library · Nachschlagebücherei f, Nachschlagebibliothek f

~ line, datum-line · Bezugslinie f

~ material · Bezugswerkstoff *m*

~ plane, datum(-plane) [*An assumed horizontal plane used as a basis for computing elevations*] · Bezugshöhe f, Bezugsebene f, Leitebene

~ point · Meßpunkt *m* [*Tageslichtbeleuchtung*]

~ ~, datum · Bezugspunkt *m*, Meßpunkt

~ sound · Bezugsschall *m*

~ ~ pressure · Bezugsschalldruck *m*

~ stress · Bezugsspannung f

~ system, dimensional ~ ~ [*A system of points, lines and planes to which sizes and positions of a building component or assembly may be related*] · (Maß)Bezugssystem *n*

~ tone · Bezugston *m*

~ value · Richtwert *m*, Richtzahl f, Bezugswert, Bezugszahl, Bezugsgröße f, Richtgröße

refiltration · Nachfiltern *n*

~ · Nachfilterung f

refined antimony, regulus (of antimony) · Antimon regulus *n*

~ copper · Raffinadekupfer *n*

~ linseed oil · Lackleinöl *n*

~ soybean oil, varnish ~ ~ (US); ~ soya bean ~ (Brit.) · raffiniertes Soja(bohnen)öl *n*, Lacksojaöl

~ tall oil · destilliertes Tallöl *n*

refinement · Verfeinerung f

refinery (asphaltic) bitumen of penetration-grade, 'penetration-grade' (asphaltic) bitumen, hot (asphaltic-) bitumen (Brit.); penetration-grade asphalt, hot asphalt, saturating asphalt, impregnating asphalt (US) · Heißbitumen *n*, Tränkbitumen, Imprägnierbitumen

(re)fining, plaining · Läutern *n*, Läuterung f [*Glasherstellung*]

~ agent, plaining ~ · Läuterungsmittel *n* [*Glasherstellung*]

to reflect sun rays · zurückwerfen von Sonnenstrahlen

reflected component · Rückstrahlanteil *m*

~ glare · Rückstrahlblendung f

reflecting bead → reflective (glass) ~

~ (glass) bead → reflective (~) ~

~ paint, reflective ~ · reflektierende (Anstrich)Farbe f, Reflex(ions)(anstrich)farbe

~ type water level indicator · Reflexions-Wasserstandanzeiger *m*

reflection factor · Rückstrahlgrad *m*

reflective bead → ~ glass ~

~ (glass) bead, reflecting (~) ~ · reflektierende (Glas)Perle f, Reflex(glas)perle, Glasperle, Reflexionsperle [*für Fahrbahnmarkierungen*]

~ paint, reflect(oriz)ing ~ · reflektierende (Anstrich)Farbe f, Reflex(ions)-(anstrich)farbe

~ traffic paint, reflect(oriz)ing ~ ~ · reflektierende Markierungsfarbe f, ~ Verkehrsfarbe, Reflexfarbe

reflector light fitting (Brit.); ~ luminaire (fixture) (US); ~ (light(ing)) fixture · Schirmbeleuchtungskörper *m*, Schirmleuchte f

reflect(oriz)ing road stud, ~ traffic ~, ~ street marker · Verkehrs-Leucht-Nagel *m*, Markierungs-Leuchtnagel, Straßen-Leucht-Nagel, Markierungs-Leuchtknopf *m*

~ street marker, ~ traffic stud, ~ road stud · Verkehrs-Leucht-Nagel *m*, Markierungs-Leuchtnagel, Straßen-Leucht-Nagel, Markierungs-Leucht-Knopf *m*

~ traffic paint, reflective ~ ~ · reflektierende Markierungsfarbe f, ~ Verkehrsfarbe, Reflexfarbe

~ ~ stud, ~ street marker, ~ road stud · Verkehrs-Leucht-Nagel *m*, Markierungs-Leuchtnagel, Straßen-Leucht-Nagel, Markierungs-Leuchtknopf *m*

reflector-layer lamp — refractory structural material

reflector-layer lamp · Reflexschichtlampe *f*

reflux process, solvent ~ · Kreislaufverfahren *n*, Umlaufverfahren [*Alkydharzherstellung*]

refractive index · (Licht)Brechungsindex *m*

~ **power,** ~ quality, ~ property · (Licht-)Brechungsvermögen *n*

~ **property,** ~ quality, ~ power · (Licht)Brechungsvermögen *n*

~ **quality,** ~ power, ~ property · (Licht)Brechungsvermögen *n*

refractoriness · Feuerfestigkeit *f* [*Charakteristische Eigenschaft eines ff. Erzeugnisses hohen Temperaturen standzuhalten*]

refractory · feuerfest, ff. [*Keramische Rohstoffe, Massen und Werkstoffe werden als ,,feuerfest" bezeichnet wenn ihr Segerkegelfallpunkt, bestimmt nach DIN 51063, mindestens dem des kleinen Segerkegels 18/150°/h (mittlerer Fallpunkt 1520°C) entspricht. Begriffsbestimmung gemäß DIN 51060 Blatt 1*]

~ → ~ product

~ → ~ material

~ **aggregate,** ~ concrete ~ · feuerfester (Beton)Zuschlag(stoff) *m*, feuerfestes (Beton)Zuschlagmaterial *n*, ff. ~

~ **brick,** fireclay ~, firebrick, fireclay refractory material [*A refractory material that in the fired state consists essentially of aluminosilicates and silica, and contains less than 78 per cent of silica and less than 38 per cent of alumina*] · teuerfester Stein *m*, ff. ~

~ **building material,** ~ structural ~, ~ construction(al) ~ · feuerfester Baustoff *m*, ff. ~ [*DIN 1061 Prüfverfahren; DIN 1081 Abmessungen*]; feuerfestes Baumaterial *n*, ff. Baumaterial [*Schweiz*]

~ **cement,** fire ~, ~ mortar · feuerfester Mörtel *m*, ff. ~, ~ Zement *m*, Feuerzement [*Zum Einsetzen feuerfester Steine in Feuerungsanlagen u.ä.*]

~ **coat** · feuerfester Anstrich *m*, ~ Aufstrich, ff. ~ [*Anstrich aus einem unbrennbaren Anstrichstoff, z.B. Silikatfarben oder Speziallacken*]

~ **coatings,** ~ wash, ~ gunning materials · Spritz- und Anstrichmassen [*Feuerfestindustrie. Feuerfester Versatz dessen Eigenschaften denen des feuerfesten Mörtels entspricht und dessen Kornaufbau die Verwendung als Anstrich oder Oberflächenschutz ermöglicht*]

~ **composition** · feuerfeste (keramische) Masse *f*, ff. (~) ~

~ **compound** · Baumasse *f* für den Feuerungsbau

~ **(concrete) aggregate** · feuerfester (Beton)Zuschlag(stoff) *m*, feuerfestes (Beton)Zuschlagmaterial *n*, ff. ~

~ **construction(al) material,** ~ structural ~, ~ building ~ · feuerfester Baustoff *m*, ff. ~ [*DIN 1061 Prüfverfahren; DIN 1081 Abmessungen*]; feuerfestes Baumaterial *n*, ff. Baumaterial [*Schweiz*]

~ **gunning materials,** ~ wash, ~ coatings · Spritz- und Anstrichmassen *fpl*, Anstrich- und Spritzmassen [*Feuerfestindustrie. Feuerfester Versatz, dessen Eigenschaften denen des feuerfesten Mörtels entspricht und dessen Kornaufbau die Verwendung als Anstrich oder Oberflächenschutz ermöglicht*]

~ **industry,** ~ material ~ · Feuerfestindustrie *f*

~ **insulating concrete** [*Refractory concrete having low thermal conductivity*] · feuerfester Dämmbeton *m*, ff. ~

~ **lining** · feuerfeste Auskleidung *f*, ff. ~, Feuerschutzfutter *n*

~ **(material)** [*A non-metallic material (but not excluding those containing a proportion of metal) having a pyrometric cone equivalent corresponding to not less than 1,500°C*] · feuerfester (keramischer) Werkstoff *m*, tf. (~) ~

~ **(~) industry** · Feuerfestindustrie *f*

~ **materials for monolithic construction,** ~ products ~ ~ ~ · Reparatur- und Baumassen *fpl*, Bau- und Reparaturmassen [*Feuerfestindustrie. Mit diesen Erzeugnissen kann man monolithische Teile oder Auskleidungen in der notwendigen Schichtdicke herstellen. Die feuerfeste Masse hat einen der Verwendung angepaßten Körnungsaufbau; sie kann gestampft oder gespritzt werden*]

~ **mortar** → ~ cement

~ **(product)** [*A nonmetallic product (but not excluding those containing a proportion of metal) having a pyrometric cone equivalent corresponding to not less than 1,500°C*] · feuerfestes (keramisches) Erzeugnis *n*, ff. (~) ~

~ **products for monolithic construction,** ~ materials ~ ~ ~ · Bau- und Reparaturmassen *fpl*, Reparatur- und Baumassen [*Feuerfestindustrie. Mit diesen Erzeugnissen kann man monolithische Teile oder Auskleidungen in der notwendigen Schichtdicke herstellen. Die feuerfeste Masse hat einen der Verwendung angepaßten Körnungsaufbau; sie kann gestampft oder gespritzt werden*]

~ **ramming material** · Stampfmasse *f* [*Feuerfestindustrie. Körnige, feuerfeste Masse, die unter Einwirkung von Hitze durch keramische Bindung erhärtet. Die Masse wird durch Stampfen verarbeitet, nachdem sie gegebenenfalls mit einer geeigneten Flüssigkeit versetzt worden ist*]

~ **raw material** · feuerfester (keramischer) Rohstoff *m*, ff. (~) ~

~ **structural material,** ~ construction(-al) ~, ~ building ~ · feuerfester Baustoff *m*, ff. ~ [*DIN 1061 Prüfverfahren; DIN 1081 Abmessungen*]; feuerfestes Baumaterial *n*, ff. Baumaterial [*Schweiz*]

~ technology · Technologie *f* der Feuerfeststoffe

~ wash, ~ coatings ~ gunning materials · Spritz- und Anstrichmassen *fpl*, Anstrich- und Spritzmassen [*Feuerfestindustrie. Feuerfester Versatz, dessen Eigenschaften denen des feuerfesten Mörtels entspricht und dessen Kornaufbau die Verwendung als Anstrich oder Oberflächenschutz ermöglicht*]

refreshment room · Erfrischungsraum *m*

~ ~ · Trinkhalle *f*

refrigerant · Kälteflüssigkeit *f*, Kälteträger *m*, Kältemittel *n* [*DIN 8962*]

~ system · Gefrieranlage *f*, Kälteanlage

refrigeration compressor · Kompressions-Kältemaschine *f*

~ cycle · Kälte(mittel)kreislauf *m*

~ unit · Gefriermaschine *f*, Kältemaschine

refuse, waste; rubbish (US) [*Combustible and non-combustible waste materials, except garbage, and the term shall include the residue from the burning of wood, coal, coke, and other combustible materials, paper, rags, cartons, boxes, wood, excelsior, rubber, leather, tree branches, yard trimmings, tin cans, metals, mineral matter, glass, crockery and dust and other similar materials*] · Müll *m*, Abfall(stoff) *m*

~, solid waste · fester Abfall(stoff) *m*

~ box, waste ~; rubbish ~ (US) · Abfall(stoff)kasten *m*, Müllkasten

~ cartage, ~ collection, waste ~; rubbish ~ (US) · Abfall(stoff)abfuhr *f*, Müllabfuhr

~ chute → dispose-all

~ clinker, ~ furnace ~ (Brit.); rubbish (furnace) cinder (US) · Müllschlacke *f* [*Sie wird durch Verbrennen von Müll in Verbrennungsöfen gewonnen*]

~ ~ block → ~ furnace ~ ~

~ ~ tile → ~ (furnace) clinker block

(~) collecting chamber, (~) storage ~, waste ~ ~; rubbish ~ ~ (US) · Abfall(stoff)sammelraum *m*, (Müll-)Sammelraum

~ collection, ~ cartage, waste ~; rubbish ~ (US) · Abfall(stoff)abfuhr *f*, Müllabfuhr

~ container → waste ~

~ destructor, ~ incinerator, waste ~; rubbish ~ (US); incinerator, destructor · Abfall(stoff)verbrenner *m*, (Müll-)Verbrenner

~ disposal, waste ~, disposal of refuse, disposal of waste(s), rubbish disposal, disposal of rubbish (US) · Abfall(stoff)beseitigung *f*, Müllbeseitigung

~ (furnace) clinker (Brit.); rubbish (furnace) cinder (US) · Müllschlacke *f* [*Sie wird durch Verbrennen von Müll in Verbrennungsöfen gewonnen*]

~ (~) ~ block, ~ ~ ~ tile (Brit.); rubbish (furnace) cinder ~ (US) · Müllschlackenblock(stein) *m*, Müllschlackenstein

~ grinder → mechanical ~ ~

~ heap, waste ~, midden; rubbish heap (US) · Abfall(stoff)haufen *m*, Müllhaufen

~ incineration, (waste) ~; rubbish ~ (US) · Abfall(stoff)verbrennung *f*, (Müll)Verbrennung

~ incinerator, ~ destructor, waste ~; rubbish ~ (US); incinerator, destructor · Abfall(stoff)verbrenner *m*, (Müll-)Verbrenner

(~) ~ plant, (~) incineration ~, (~) ~ installation, waste ~ ~; rubbish ~ ~ (US) · Abfall(stoff)verbrennungsanlage *f*, (Müll)Verbrennungsanlage

~ pit, waste ~; rubbish ~ (US) · Abfall(stoff)grube *f*, Müllgrube

~ shaft → dispose-all

(~) storage chamber → (~) collecting ~

~ tip, waste ~; rubbish ~ (US) · Müllkippe *f*, Müllhalde *f*, Müllablagerungsplatz *m*, Abfallkippe, Abfallhalde, Abfallablagerungsplatz, Müllabladeplatz, Abfall(stoff)abladeplatz

~ utilization, waste ~; rubbish ~ (US) · Müllverwertung *f*, Abfall(stoff)verwertung

~ water, foul ~, sewage [*Any water contaminated by soil, waste or trade effluent. This definition excludes 'rain water' which is, however, included in the German term 'Abwasser'. Sometimes loosely called 'discharge'*] · Abwasser *n*

~ ~ disposal facility, foul ~ ~ ~, sewage ~ ~ · Abwasserbeseitigungsanlage *f*

~ ~ gallery, ~ ~ tunnel, foul ~ ~, sewage ~, sewer ~ · Abwasserstollen *m*, Kanal(isations)stollen

~ ~ pipe → sewer ~

~ ~ (~) trench → sewer (~) ~

~ ~ purification, foul ~ ~, sewage ~ · Abwasserreinigung *f*

~ ~ trench → sewer (pipe) ~

~ ~ tunnel, ~ ~ gallery, foul ~ ~, sewer ~, sewage ~ · Abwasserstollen *m*, Kanal(isations)stollen

regatta course · Regattastrecke *f*

Régence ornament, foliate and strapwork · Laub- und Bandelwerk *n*

regenerated fibre (Brit.); ~ fiber (US) [*'Regenerated' means made into better form. Such fibres include acetate, casein, glass, soybean and viscous rayon*] · regenerierte Faser *f*

regina purple, aniline violett · Anilinviolett *n*

regional exhibition, provincial ~ · Landesausstellung *f*

register of real estates (Brit.) → plat

(registered) certification, ~ (trade) mark, (trade)mark · Güteschutzzeichen *n*, Güteschutzmarke *f*, eingetragenes Warenzeichen

(~) ~ (trade)mark scheme · Güteschutz *m*

(~) (trade)mark, (~) certification · Güteschutzzeichen *n*, Güteschutzmarke *f*, (eingetragenes) Warenzeichen [*Fehlnamen: (Schutz)Marke*]

to reglaze · nachverglasen, nacheinglasen

reglazing · Nachverglasung *f*, Nacheinglasung

regression analysis · Regressionsberechnung *f*

regrinding · Nachmahlen *n*
~ · Nachschleifen *n*

reground · nachgeschliffen

regula, regulus [*The short band, under the triglyphs, beneath the t(a)enia of the Doric entablature, and to which the guttae are attached*] · (Tropfen)Regulus *m*, (Tropfen)Regula *f*, (Tropfen)Riemchen *n*, (Tropfen)Plättchen *n*

regular classroom · Normalklassenzimmer *n*

~ octagon(al figure) · Achtort *n* [*In der gotischen Architektur das regelmäßige Achteck. "Ort" ist ein Steinmetzausdruck für Ecke, Spitze*]

regularly perforated, ~ pierced · regelmäßig gelocht, ~ durchlocht

reguline of lead, lead regulus · Bleistein *m*, englisches Bleiweiß *n*

regulus → regula

~ (of antimony), refined antimony · Antimon regulus *n*

rehabilitation, redevelopment · Wiederherstellung *f*

~ work, redevelopment ~ · Wiederherstellungsarbeiten *fpl*

rehardening · Nach(er)härtung *f*

reheater, RH(T)R · Nachwärmer *m*

reheating, warming-in · Anwärmen *n* [*Glasherstellung*]
~ · Nachwärmen *n*
~ · Nachwärmung *f*

rehydration · Nachhydra(ta)tion *f*

re-impregnating, re-saturating · Nachimprägnieren *n*, Nachtränken

rein, springing wall · unteres Drittel *n* der Bogenachse, ~ ~ des Bogenschenkels

to reinforce, to steel-~ · mit (Stahl)Einlagen versehen, armieren, bewehren
~ ~ · verstärken

reinforced · verstärkt
~, steel-~ · armiert, bewehrt, mit (Stahl-)Einlagen (versehen)

~ aerated concrete, aerated reinforced ~, aerated R.C. · Porenstahlbeton *m*, Stahlporenbeton

~ apron → ~ (concrete) spandrel (wall)

~ ~ wall (US) → ~ (concrete) spandrel (~)

~ arch, ~ concrete ~, R.C. ~ · Stahlbetonbogen *m*

~ arch(ed girder) → ~ concrete ~ (~)

~ barrel vault → ~ concrete ~ ~

~ barrel-vault shell, ~ concrete ~ ~, R.C. ~ ~ · Stahlbeton-Tonnenschale *f*

~ beam, ~ concrete ~, R.C. ~ · Stahlbetonbalken(träger) *m*

~ ~ and slab → ~ concrete ~ ~ ~

~ ~ floor, ~ concrete ~ ~, R.C. ~ ~ · Stahlbetonbalken(träger)decke *f*

~ bearer → ~ (concrete) binding joist

~ binder → ~ (concrete) binding joist

~ binding joist → ~ concrete ~ ~

~ block → ~ (concrete) building

~ ~ beam · Massivbalken *m*, Stein-(eisen)balken, Stahlsteinbalken [*Herstellung von Steineisendecken*]

~ ~ floor · Stahlsteindecke *f*, Steineisendecke [*DIN 1046. Mit Stahl bewehrte Steindecke bei der die Steine zur Spannungsaufnahme herangezogen werden. Dazu müssen die Steine so untereinander verbunden sein, daß eine einwandfreie Übernahme der Kräfte gewährleistet ist*]

~ ~ partition (wall) → ~ masonry ~ ~ (~)

~ ~ roof floor · Stahlstein-Dachdecke *f*, Steineisen-Dachdecke

~ box girder, ~ concrete ~ ~, R.C. ~ ~ · Stahlbetonkasten(träger) *m*

~ bracket, ~ concrete ~, R.C. ~ · Stahlbetonkonsole *f*

~ breast → ~ (concrete) spandrel (wall)

~ brickwork · bewehrtes Ziegelmauerwerk *n*, armiertes ~, Ziegelmauerwerk mit (Stahl)Einlagen

~ brick(work) lintel; ~ ~ lintol [*deprecated*] · armierter Ziegelsturz *m*, bewehrter ~, armierte Ziegeloberschwelle *f*, bewehrte Ziegeloberschwelle

~ ~ pier · bewehrter Ziegelmauerwerkpfeiler *m*, armierter ~, Ziegelmauerwerkpfeiler mit (Stahl)Einlagen

~ building → ~ concrete ~

~ bunker, ~ concrete ~, R.C. ~ · Stahlbetonbunker *m*

~ cast → (pre)cast reinforced (concrete) (building) unit

~ cast-concrete (building) component → (pre)cast reinforced (concrete) (building) unit

~ ~ (~) member → (pre)cast reinforced (concrete) (building) unit

~ ~ (~) unit → (pre)cast reinforced (concrete) (~) ~

~ ~ component → (pre)cast reinforced (concrete) (building) unit

~ ~ member → (pre)cast reinforced (concrete) (building) unit

~ ~ unit → (pre)cast reinforced (concrete) (building) ~

~ cast floor → ~ (concrete) pre~ ~

reinforced cast frame — reinforced (concrete) design

~ ~ **frame** → (pre)cast R.C. ~
~ ~ **girder** → ~ (pre)cast (concrete) ~
~ ~ **wall** → prefab(ricated) reinforced (concrete) ~
~ **cast(ing)** → (pre)cast reinforced (concrete) (building) unit
~ **ceiling joist** → ~ (concrete) binding ~
~ **cellar window**, ~ concrete ~ ~, R.C. ~ ~ · Stahlbeton-Kellerfenster *n*
~ **cellular concrete** · Stahl-Zellenbeton *m*
~ **(cement) mortar** [*developed by Prof. P. L. Nervi in Italy*] · Stahlmörtel *m*
~ **chimney**, ~ concrete ~, R.C. ~ · Stahlbetonschornstein *m*
~ ~ **shaft**, ~ concrete ~ ~, R.C. ~ ~ · Stahlbetonschornsteinschaft *m*
~ **church**, ~ concrete ~, R.C. ~ · Stahlbetonkirche *f*
~ **coat** · armierter Anstrich *m*, ~ Aufstrich
~ **column**, ~ concrete ~, R.C. ~ · Stahlbetonstütze *f*
~ ~, ~ concrete ~, R.C. ~ · Stahlbetonsäule *f*
~ ~ **with bracket** → ~ (concrete) (lighting) ~ ~ ~
~ **compression ring**, ~ concrete ~ ~, R.C. ~ ~ · Stahlbeton-Druckring *m*
~ **concrete**, R.C. · Stahlbeton *m*
~ ~ **aerated with foam**, ~ foam(ed) concrete · Schaumstahlbeton *m*, Stahlschaumbeton
~ **(~) apron** → ~ (~) spandrel (wall)
~ **(~) ~ wall** (US) → ~ (~) spandrel (~)
~ **(~) arch**, R.C. ~ · Stahlbetonbogen *m*
~ **(~) arch(ed girder)**, ~ (~) arch ~, R.C. ~ (~) · gekrümmter Stahlbetonträger, Stahlbetonbogenträger
~ **(~) barrel vault**, ~ (~) tunnel ~, ~ (~) wagon ~, R.C. ~ ~ · Stahlbeton-Tonnengewölbe *n*
~ **(~) barrel-vault shell**, R.C. ~ ~ · Stahlbeton-Tonnenschale *f*
~ **(~) beam**, R.C. ~ · Stahlbetonbalken(träger) *m*
~ **(~) ~ and slab**, ~ (~) T(ee)-beam, R.C. beam and slab, R.C. T(ee)-beam · Stahlbeton-Plattenbalken *m*
~ **(~) ~ floor**, R.C. ~ ~ · Stahlbetonbalken(träger)decke *f*
~ **(~) bearer** → ~ (~) binding joist
~ **(~) binder** → ~ (~) binding joist
~ **(~) binding joist**, ~ (~) ceiling ~, R.C. ~ ~, reinforced (concrete) binder, reinforced (concrete) bearer, R.C. binder, R.C. bearer · Stahlbetonunterzug *m*
~ **(~) block** → ~ (~) building
~ **(~) box girder**, R.C. ~ ~ · Stahlbetonkasten(träger) *m*
~ **(~) bracket**, R.C. ~ · Stahlbetonkonsole *f*

~ **(~) breast** → ~ (~) spandrel (wall)
~ **(~) building**, ~ (~) block, R.C. ~ · Stahlbetongebäude *n*
~ **(~) bunker**, R.C. ~ · Stahlbetonbunker *m*
~ **(~) cast** → (pre)cast reinforced (concrete) (building) unit
~ **(~) ~ floor** → ~ (~) pre~ ~
~ **(~) ~ frame** → (pre)cast R.C. ~
~ **(~) ~ wall** → prefab(ricated) reinforced (concrete) ~
~ **(~) cast(ing)** → (pre)cast reinforced (concrete) (building) unit
~ **(~) ceiling joist** → ~ (~) binding ~
~ **(~) cellar window**, R.C. ~ ~ · Stahlbeton-Kellerfenster *n*
~ **(~) chimney**, R.C. ~ · Stahlbetonschornstein *m*
~ **(~) ~ shaft**, R.C. ~ ~ · Stahlbetonschornsteinschaft *m*
~ **(~) church**, R.C. ~ · Stahlbetonkirche *f*
~ **(~) column**, R.C. ~ · Stahlbetonstütze *f*
~ **(~) ~**, R.C. ~ · Stahlbetonsäule *f*
~ **(~) ~ with bracket** → ~ (~) (lighting) ~ ~ ~
~ **(~) combined footing**, R.C. ~ ~ · zusammengefaßtes Stahlbetonfundament *n*
~ **(~) compound unit**, R.C. ~ ~ · Stahlbetonbauteil *m*, *n* [*z.B. Stütze; Wand; Binder usw.*]
~ **(~) compression ring**, R.C. ~ ~ · Stahlbeton-Druckring *m*
~ **(~) construction**, R.C. ~ · Stahlbetonbau *m* [*DIN 1045*]
~ **(~) ~ type**, R.C. ~ ~, reinforced concrete type of construction, R.C. type of construction · Stahlbetonbauart *f*
~ **(~) continuous frame**, R.C. ~ ~ · Durchlauf-Stahlbetonrahmen *m*, Stahlbeton-Durchlaufrahmen, durchlaufender Stahlbetonrahmen, durchgehender Stahlbetonrahmen
~ **(~) core**, R.C. ~, service ~, utility ~, building ~, mechanical ~ · (Hoch-) Hauskern *m*, (Stahl)Betonkern, Betriebskern, (Gebäude)Kern
~ **(~) cross member** → ~ (~) rail
~ **(~) cross-wall**, R.C. ~ · Stahlbetonquerwand *f*
~ **(~) cross wall** → ~ (~) shear ~
~ **(~) culvert pipe**, RCCP · Stahlbetondurchlaßrohr *n*
~ **(~) cupola** → ~ (~) dome
~ **(~) cylindrical shell**, R.C. ~ ~, cylindrical reinforced (concrete) ~, cylindrical R.C. ~ · Stahlbetonzylinderschale *f*
~ **(~) design**, R.C. ~, design in reinforced concrete · Bemessung *f* im Stahlbetonbau, Stahlbetonbemessung

815 reinforced (concrete) design... — reinforced (concrete) mast

~ (~) ~ **and construction**, R.C. ~ ~ ~, reinforced (concrete) engineering, R.C. engineering · Stahlbetontechnik *f*

~ (~) **dome**, ~ (~) cupola, R.C. ~ ~ · Stahlbetonkuppel *f*

~ (~) **door lintel**; ~ (~) ~ lintol [*deprecated*]; R.C. ~ ~ · Stahlbetontürsturz *m*

~ ~ **duct floor**, R/C ~ ~ · Stahlbetonkanaldecke *f*

~ (~) **engineering** → ~ (~) design and construction

~ (~) **facing** → ~ (~) lining

~ (~) **flat roof**, R.C. ~ ~ · Stahlbetonflachdach *n*

~ (~) ~ **slab**, R.C. ~ ~ · Stahlbeton-Pilzdeckenplatte *f*

~ (~) **flexible foundation beam**, R.C. ~ ~ ~, flexible reinforced (concrete) ~ ~, flexible R.C. ~ ~ · Stahlbetonzerrbalken *m*, Zerrstahlbetonbalken

~ (~) **floor** → ~ (~) intermediate ~

~ (~) ~ **beam** → ~ (~) joist

~ (~) ~ **slab**, R.C. ~ ~ · Stahlbetondeckenplatte *f*

~ (~) **floor-slab member** → ~ (~) ~ unit

~ (~) ~ **unit**, ~ (~) ~ member, R.C. ~ ~ · Stahlbeton-Deckenplattenelement *n*

~ (~) **floor(ing) (structural) system** R.C. ~ (~) ~, R.C. floo(ring) construction · Stahlbetondecken(bau)system *n*, Stahlbetondeckenkonstruktion(ssystem) *f*, (*n*)

~ (~) ~ **system** → ~ ~ ~ (structural) ~

~ (~) **folded plate roof**, ~ (~) ~ slab ~, R.C. ~ ~ ~ (Brit.); reinforced (concrete) hipped-plate ~, R.C. hipped-plate ~ (US) · Stahlbeton-Dachfaltwerk *n*, Stahlbeton-Falt(werk)dach

~ (~) ~ **slab roof** → ~ (~) ~ plate ~

~ (~) **footing**, R.C. ~ · Stahlbetonfundament *n*

~ (~) **foul water pipe** → ~ (~) sewer ~

~ (~) **foundation**, R.C. ~ · Stahlbetongründung *f*

~ (~) **frame**, R.C. ~ · Stahlbetonrahmen *m*

~ (~) **garage**, R.C. ~ · Stahlbetongarage *f*

~ (~) **girder**, R.C. ~ · Stahlbetonträger *m*

~ (~) ~ **floor**, R.C. ~ ~ · Stahlbetonträgerdecke *f*

~ (~) ~ **wall**, R.C. ~ ~ · Stahlbetonträgerwand *f*

~ (~) **header**, R.C. ~ · Stahlbetonwechsel(balken) *m*

~ (~) **high-pressure pipe**, R.C. ~ ~ · Stahlbeton-Hochdruckrohr *n*

~ (~) **hinge**, R.C. ~ · Stahlbetongelenk *n*

~ (~) **hipped-plate roof** (US) → ~ (~) folded plate ~

~ (~) **hollow beam**, R.C. ~ ~ · Stahlbeton-Hohlbalken(träger) *m*

~ (~) ~ ~ **floor**, R.C. ~ ~ ~ · Stahlbeton-Hohlbalkendecke *f*

~ (~) **hollow(-core) plank**, R.C. ~ ~ · Stahlbeton(hohl)diele *f*, Steg(zement)diele [*DIN 4028*]

~ (~) **hollow pile**, R.C. ~ ~ · Stahlbeton-Hohlpfahl *m*

~ (~) ~ **plank** → ~ (~) hollow-core ~

~ (~) ~ **slab**, R.C. ~ ~ · (Stahlbeton-)Hohlplatte *f*

~ (~) ~ ~ **floor**, R.C. ~ ~ ~ · (Stahlbeton-)Hohlplattendecke *f*

~ (~) ~ ~ **floor(ing) construction** → (~ ~) ~ ~ ~ system

~ (~) ~ ~ ~ **system**, (~ ~) ~ ~ ~ construction, R.C. ~ ~ ~ ~ · (Stahlbeton-)Hohlplattendecken(konstruktions)system *n*, (Stahlbeton-)Hohlplattendeckenkonstruktion *f*

~ (~) **horizontal member** → ~ (~) rail

~ (~) **I-beam** · Stahlbeton-Doppel-T-Träger *m*, Stahlbeton-I-Träger

~ (~) **(intermediate) floor**, R.C. (~) ~ · Stahlbetondecke *f*, Stahlbeton-Gebäudedecke, Stahlbeton-Trenndecke, Stahlbeton-Etagendecke, Stahlbeton-Geschoßdecke, Stahlbeton-Stockwerkdecke, Stahlbeton-Hochbaudecke

~ (~) **joist**, ~ (~) floor beam, R.C. joist, R.C. floor beam · Stahlbetondeckenbalken(träger) *m*

~ (~) **lattice girder**, R.C. ~ ~ · Stahlbetongitterträger *m*

~ (~) **lift-slab**, R.C. ~ · Stahlbeton-Hub(decken)platte *f*, Hub-Stahlbeton-(decken)platte

~ (~) ~ **construction**, R.C. ~ ~ · Stahlbeton-Hub(decken)bau *m*

~ (~) ~ **structure**, R.C. ~ ~ · Stahlbeton-Hub(decken)bauwerk *n*

~ (~) **(lighting) column with bracket** (Brit.); ~ (~) (~) mast with arm (US) · Stahlbeton-Ausleger(licht)mast *m*, Stahlbeton-Auslegerbeleuchtungsmast, Stahlbeton-Auslegerleuchtenmast

~ (~) ~ **mast**, R.C. ~ ~ · Stahlbeton-Beleuchtungsmast *m*, Stahlbeton-Leuchtenmast, Stahlbeton-Lichtmast

~ (~) (~) ~ **with arm** · Stahlbeton-Ausleger(licht)mast *m*, Stahlbeton-Auslegerbeleuchtungsmast, Stahlbeton-Auslegerleuchtenmast

~ (~) **lightweight aggregate**, R.C. ~ ~ · Stahlleicht(beton)zuschlag(stoff) *m*

~ (~) **lining**, ~ (~) (sur)facing, R.C. ~ · Stahlbetonauskleidung *f*, Stahlbetonverkleidung, Stahlbetonbekleidung

~ (~) **mast**, R.C. ~ · Stahlbetonmast *m* [*DIN 4234*]

reinforced (concrete) mast with arm — reinforced... 816

~ (~) ~ with arm → ~ (~) (lighting)
~ ~ ~

~ (~) mosque, R.C. ~ · Stahlbetonmoschee f

~ (~) northlight shell → northlight reinforced (concrete) ~

~ (~) panel, R.C. ~ · Stahlbetontafel f

~ (~) ~ wall, R.C. ~ ~ · Stahlbetontafelwand f

~ (~) parachute → ~ (~) umbrella

~ (~) parallel truss, R.C. ~ ~ · Stahlbeton-Parallelfachwerkträger m

~ (~) parapet → ~ (~) spandrel (wall)

~ (~) parking deck, R.C. ~ ~ · Stahlbetonparkplatte f

~ (~) ~structure, R.C. ~ ~ · Stahlbeton-Parkbauwerk n

~ (~) partition (wall), R.C. ~ (~) · Stahlbetonwand f [*Leichte Trennwand. DIN 4103*]

~ (~) patent glazing bar, ~ (~) puttyless ~ ~, R.C. ~ ~ ~ · Stahlbetonsprosse f [*kittlose Verglasung*]

~ (~) pile, R.C. ~ · Stahlbetonpfahl m

~ (~) pipe, R.C. ~, RCP · Stahlbetonrohr n [*DIN 4035*]

~ (~) pipeline, R.C. ~ · Stahlbetonrohrleitung f

~ (~) plain web beam, ~ (~) solid ~ ~, R.C. ~ ~ ~ · Stahlbeton-Vollwandbalken(träger) m

~ (~) ~ ~ girder, ~ (~) solid ~ ~, R.C. ~ ~ ~ ~ · Stahlbeton-Vollwandträger m

~ (~) plate, ~ (~) slab, R.C. ~ · armierte (Beton)Platte f, bewehrte ~, (Beton)Platte mit (Stahl)Einlagen, Stahlbetonplatte

~ (~) ~ floor → ~ (~) slab ~

~ (~) portal frame, R.C. ~ ~ · Stahlbetonportalrahmen m

~ (~) (pre)cast floor, R.C. ~ ~, (pre)cast R.C. ~, (pre)cast reinforced (concrete) ~, prefab(ricated) reinforced (concrete) ~, reinforced prefab(ricated) (concrete) ~ · Montage-Stahlbetondecke f, Stahlbeton-Montagedecke, Stahlbeton-Fertig(teil)decke, Fertig(teil)-Stahlbetondecke

~ (~) ~ frame → (pre)cast R.C. ~

~ (~) ~ wall → prefab(ricated) reinforced (concrete) ~

~ (~) pressure pipe, R.C. ~ ~ · Stahlbetondruckrohr n [*DIN 4036 Bedingungen für die Lieferung und Prüfung von Stahlbetondruckrohren und DIN 4037 Richtlinien für die Abnahme von Stahlbetondruckrohrleitungen*]

~ (~) problem, R.C. ~ · Stahlbetonaufgabe f

~ (~) purlin(e), R.C. ~ · Stahlbeton(dach)pfette f

~ (~) puttyless glazing bar → ~ (~) patent ~ ~

~ (~) rafter, R.C. ~ · Stahlbetonsparren m

~ (~) rail, ~ (~) cross member, ~ (~) horizontal member, R.C. rail, R.C. cross member, R.C. horizontal member · Stahlbetonriegel m

~ (~) railroad tie (US); ~ (~) railway sleeper (Brit.) · Stahlbeton(gleis)schwelle f, Stahlbetonschienenschwelle

~ (~) railway sleeper (Brit.); ~ (~) railroad tie (US) · Stahlbeton(gleis)schwelle f, Stahlbetonschienenschwelle

~ (~) refuse water pipe → ~ (~) sewer ~

~ (~) rib, R.C. ~ · Stahlbetonrippe f

~ (~) rib(bed) floor, R.C. ~ ~ · Stahlbetonrippendecke f [*DIN 1045*]

~ (~) ~ slab, R.C. ~ ~ · Stahlbetonrippenplatte f

~ (~) rigid frame, R.C. ~ ~ · Stahlbeton-Steifrahmen m

~ (~) roof, R.C. ~ · Stahlbetondach n

~ (~) ~ beam, R.C. ~ ~ · Stahlbetondachbalken(träger) m

~ (~) ~ cladding, ~ (~) ~ covering, ~ (~) ~ sheathing, R.C. ~ ~, reinforced (concrete) roof(ing), R.C. roof(ing) · Stahlbetondachbedachung f, Stahlbetondach(belag) n, (m), Stahlbeton(dach)(ein)deckung

~ (~) ~ covering → ~ (~) ~ cladding

~ (~) ~ sheathing → ~ (~) ~ cladding

~ (~) (~) truss, R.C. (~) ~ (US) [*There is no all-embracing term for '(Dach)Binder' in the United Kingdom, since '(roof) truss' is defined there as a double-pitched triangulated structure as opposed to a roof frame which is a structure with continuity between vertical and spanning members*] · Stahlbeton(dach)binder m

~ (~) roof(ing) → ~ (~) roof cladding

~ (~) ~ slab, R.C. ~ ~ · Stahlbeton-Dachplatte f, Stahlbeton-Bedachungselement n, Stahlbeton-Dachelement, Stahlbeton-Bedachungsplatte

~ (~) sandwich slab, R.C. ~ ~ · Stahlbeton-Dreilagenplatte f, Stahlbeton-Sandwichplatte

~ (~) screed, R.C. ~ · Stahlbetonestrich m

~ (~) section, R.C. ~ · Stahlbetonquerschnitt m

~ (~) sewage pipe → ~ (~) sewer ~

~ (~) sewer pipe, ~ (~) sewage ~, ~ (~) foul water ~, ~ (~) refuse water ~, R.C. sewer ~, R.C. sewage ~, R.C. foul water ~, R.C. refuse water ~ · Stahlbeton-Abwasserrohr n, Stahlbeton-Kanal(isations)rohr

~ (~) shear wall, ~ (~) cross ~, R.C. ~ ~ [*See remark under '(Wand-) Scheibe'*] · Stahlbeton(wand)scheibe f

~ (~) shell, R.C. ~ · Stahlbetonschale f

~ (~) ~ construction, R.C. ~ ~ · Stahlbetonschalenbau m

reinforced concrete shell roof — reinforced (concrete) ...

~ (~) ~ roof, R.C. ~ ~ · Stahlbeton-schalendach *n*

~ (~) ~ silo, R.C. ~ · Stahlbetonsilo *m*

~ (~) ~ skyscraper, R.C. ~ · Stahlbeton-Wolkenkratzer *m*

~ (~) ~ slab, ~ (~) plate, R.C. ~ · armierte (Beton)Platte *f*, bewehrte ~, (Beton)Platte mit (Stahl)Einlagen, Stahlbetonplatte

~ (~) ~ → ~ (~) flat ~

~ (~) ~ base, ~ (~) ~ foundation, R.C. ~ ~ · Stahlbeton-Plattenfundament *n*

~ (~) ~ floor, ~ (~) plate ~, R.C. ~ ~ · Stahlbeton-Plattendecke *f*

~ (~) ~ foundation → ~ (~) ~ base

~ (~) ~ solid floor, R.C. ~ ~ · Stahlbetonvolldecke *f*

~ (~) ~ plank (unit), R.C. ~ ~ (~) · Stahlbetonvolldiele *f*

~ (~) ~ slab, R.C. ~ ~ · Stahlbetonvollplatte *f*

~ (~) ~ web beam → ~ (~) plain ~ ~

~ (~) ~ ~ girder → ~ (~) plain ~ ~

~ (~) space bearing structure → ~ (~) space (load)bearing ~

~ (~) ~ (load)bearing structure, ~ (~) three-dimensional ~ ~, ~ (~) spatial ~ ~, ~ (~) ~ (weight-carrying) ~, R.C. ~ (~) ~ · Stahlbeton-Raumtragwerk *n*

~ (~) ~ structure → ~ (~) ~ (load-)bearing ~

~ (~) ~ (weight-carrying) structure → ~ (~) ~ (load)bearing ~

~ (~) spandrel (wall), R.C. ~ (~), ~ (~) breast, ~ (~) apron, ~ (~) parapet; ~ (~) apron wall (US) [*The rectangular R.C. infilling in a multistor(e)y building between a window sill and the window head below*] · Stahlbeton-(Fenster)Brüstung *f*

~ (~) spatial (load)bearing structure → ~ (~) space ~ ~

~ (~) ~ structure → ~ (~) space (load)bearing ~

~ (~) ~ (weight-carrying) structure → ~ (~) space (load)bearing ~

~ (~) spun pipe, R.C. ~ ~ · Schleuderstahlbetonrohr *n*, Stahlbetonschleuderrohr

~ (~) stair(case), R.C. ~ · Stahlbetontreppe *f*

~ (~) step, R.C. ~ · Stahlbetonstufe *f*

~ (~) storage tank, R.C. ~ ~ · Stahlbeton-Lagerbehälter *m*

~ (~) string (Brit.); ~ (~) stringer (US); R.C. ~ · Stahlbeton(treppen)wange *f*

~ (~) structural topping · armierter Konstruktions-Aufbeton *m*, bewehrter ~, Konstruktions-Aufbeton mit (Stahl)Einlagen

~ (~) structure, R.C. ~ · Stahlbetonbauwerk *n* [*DIN 1045*]

~ (~) ~, ~ (~) system, R.C. ~ · Stahlbetontragsystem *n*, Stahlbetontragwerk *n*

~ (~) sun breaker → ~ (~) ~ shade

~ (~) ~ screen → ~ (~) ~ shade

~ (~) ~ shade, ~ (~) ~ screen, ~ (~) ~ breaker, R.C. ~ ~ · Stahlbetonsonnenblende *f*

~ (~) (sur)facing → ~ (~) lining

~ (~) suspended roof, ~ (~) suspension ~, R.C. ~ ~, suspended reinforced (concrete) ~ · Hänge-Stahlbetondach *n*, Stahlbeton-Hängedach

~ (~) system, ~ (~) structure, R.C. ~ · Stahlbetontragsystem *n*, Stahlbetontragwerk *n*

~ (~) T(ee)-beam → ~ (~) beam and slab

~ (~) ~ floor, R.C. ~ ~ · Stahlbetonplattenbalkendecke *f*

~ (~) tension member, R.C.~ ~ · Stahlbetonzugglied *n*

~ (~) three-dimensional (load)bearing structure → ~ (~) space ~ ~

~ (~) topping, R.C. ~ · Stahlbeton-Druckschicht *f*, Stahlbeton-Druckplatte *f*

~ (~) tower → service ~

~ (~) trimmer plank (unit), R.C. ~ ~ (~) · Stahlbetonstreichdiele *f* [*Auswechs(e)lung*]

~ (~) truss → ~ (~) roof ~

~ (~) truss(ed girder), R.C. ~ (~) · Stahlbetonfachwerk(träger) *n*, (*m*)

~ (~) tunnel vault → ~ (~) barrel ~

~ (~) two-hinge(d) arch, ~ (~) two-pin(ned) ~, R.C. ~ ~, two-hinge(d) reinforced (concrete) ~, two-pin(ned) reinforced (concrete) ~, two-hinge(d) R.C. ~, two-pin(ned) R.C. ~ · Stahlbeton-Zweigelenkbogen *m*, Zweigelenk-Stahlbetonbogen

~ (~) two-pin(ned) arch → ~ (~) two-hinge(d) ~

~ (~) type of construction, R.C. ~ ~, reinforced concrete construction type, R.C. construction type · Stahlbetonbauart *f*

~ (~) umbrella, ~ (~) parachute, R.C. ~ · Stahlbetonschirm *m*

~ (~) vault, R.C. ~ · Stahlbetongewölbe *n*

~ (~) wagon vault → ~ (~) barrel ~

~ (~) wall, R.C. ~ · Stahlbetonmauer *f*

~ (~) ~ panel, R.C. ~ ~ · Stahlbetonwandtafel *f*

~ (~) window, R.C. ~ · (Stahl)Betonfenster *n* [*Fenster mit Stahlbetonrahmen*]

~ (~) ~ frame, R.C. ~ ~ · (Stahl)Betonfensterrahmen *m*

~ (~) ~ **lintel**; ~ (~) ~ lintol [*deprecated*]; R.C. ~ ~ · Stahlbetonfensteroberschwelle f, Stahlbetonfenstersturz m

~ (~) **work**, R.C. ~ · Stahlbetonarbeiten fpl [*DIN 18331*]

~ **construction**, ~ concrete ~, R.C. ~ · Stahlbetonbau m [*DIN 1045*]

~ ~ **type** → ~ concrete ~ ~

~ **continuous frame** → ~ concrete ~ ~

~ **core** → ~ (concrete) tower

~ **cored block floor**, ~ perforated ~ ~ · Stahlsteindecke f mit Lochsteinen, Steineisendecke ~ ~ [*DIN 1046*]

~ ~ **brick floor**, ~ perforated ~ ~ · Stahlsteindecke f mit Lochziegeln, Steineisendecke ~ ~ [*DIN 1046*]

~ **cross member** → ~ (concrete) rail

~ **cross-wall**, ~ concrete ~, R.C. ~ · Stahlbetonquerwand f

~ **cross wall** → ~ (concrete) shear ~

~ **culvert pipe**, ~ concrete ~ ~, RCCP · Stahlbetondurchlaßrohr n

~ **cupola** → ~ (concrete) dome

~ **cylindrical shell** → ~ concrete ~ ~

~ **design and construction** → ~ concrete ~ ~ ~

~ **dome** → ~ concrete ~

~ **door lintel** → ~ concrete ~ ~

~ **engineering** → ~ (concrete) design and construction

~ **expanded concrete**, ~ gas ~ · Stahl-Gasbeton m, Gasstahlbeton, Stahl-Blähbeton, Blähstahlbeton

~ **exposed concrete**, ~ fair-faced ~, fair-faced R.C., exposed R.C., fair-faced reinforced concrete, exposed reinforced concrete · Sichtstahlbeton m, Stahlsichtbeton

~ **facing** → ~ (concrete) lining

~ **fair-faced concrete**, ~ exposed ~, fair-faced R.C., exposed R.C., fair-faced reinforced concrete, exposed reinforced concrete · Sichtstahlbeton m, Stahlsichtbeton

~ ~ **slab** ~ concrete ~ ~, R.C. ~ ~ · Stahlbeton-Pilzdeckenplatte f

~ **flexible foundation beam** → ~ concrete ~ ~ ~

~ **floor** → ~ (concrete) (intermediate) ~

~ ~ **beam** → ~ (concrete) joist

~ ~ **slab**, ~ concrete ~ ~, R.C. ~ ~ · Stahlbetondeckenplatte f

~ **floor-slab member** → ~ (concrete) floor-slab unit

~ ~ **unit** → ~ concrete ~ ~

~ **floor(ing) (structural) system** → ~ (concrete) ~ (~) ~

~ **foam(ed) concrete**, ~ concrete aerated with foam · Schaumstahlbeton m, Stahlschaumbeton

~ ~ ~ **floor slab**, ~ ~ ~ structural ~, ~ ~ ~ ~ panel · armierte Schaumbetondeckenplatte f, bewehrte ~, Schaumbetondeckenplatte mit (Stahl)Einlagen [*DIN 4223*]

~ ~ ~ **roof(ing) slab** · armierte Schaumbetondachplatte f, bewehrte ~, Schaumbetondachplatte mit (Stahl)Einlagen [*DIN 4223*]

~ ~ ~ **structural panel**, ~ ~ ~ ~ slab, ~ ~ ~ floor ~ · Schaumbetondeckenplatte f mit (Stahl)Einlagen, bewehrte Schaumbetondeckenplatte, armierte Schaumbetondeckenplatte, [*DIN 4223*]

~ ~ ~ ~ **slab**, ~ ~ ~ floor ~, ~ ~ ~ ~ panel · Schaumbetondeckenplatte f mit (Stahl)Einlagen, bewehrte Schaumbetondeckenplatte, armierte Schaumbetondeckenplatte [*DIN 4223*]

~ **folded plate roof** → ~ concrete ~ ~ ~

~ ~ **slab roof** → ~ (concrete) folded plate ~

~ **for compression** · druckarmiert, druckbewehrt

~ ~ **handling** · transportarmiert, transportbewehrt

~ **foul water pipe** → ~ (concrete) sewer ~

~ **foundation**, ~ concrete ~, R.C. ~ · Stahlbetongründung f

~ **frame**, ~ concrete ~, R.C. ~ · Stahlbetonrahmen m

~ **garage**, ~ concrete ~, R.C. ~ · Stahlbetongarage f

~ **gas concrete**, ~ expanded ~ · Stahl-Gasbeton m, Gasstahlbeton, Stahl-Blähbeton, Blähstahlbeton

~ ~ ~ **floor panel** → ~ ~ ~ ~ ~ slab

~ ~ ~ ~ **slab**, ~ ~ ~ ~ structural ~, ~ ~ ~ ~ panel · armierte Gasbetondeckenplatte f, bewehrte ~, ~ Blähbetondeckenplatte, Gasbetondeckenplatte mit (Stahl)Einlagen, Blähbetondeckenplatte mit (Stahl)Einlagen [*DIN 4223*]

~ ~ ~ **roof(ing) slab** · armierte Gasbetondachplatte f, bewehrte ~, ~ Blähbetondachplatte, Gasbetondachplatte mit (Stahl)Einlagen, Blähbetondachplatte mit (Stahl)Einlagen [*DIN 4223*]

~ ~ ~ **structural panel** → ~ ~ ~ ~ floor slab

~ ~ ~ ~ **slab** → ~ ~ ~ ~ floor ~

~ **girder**, ~ concrete ~, R.C. ~ · Stahlbetonträger m

~ ~ **floor**, ~ concrete ~ ~, R.C. ~ ~ · Stahlbetonträgerdecke f

(~) glass concrete · Glasstahlbeton m [*DIN 4229*]

(~) ~ ~ construction · Glasstahlbetonbau m

(~) ~ ~ ~ → (~) ~ ~ (structural) system

(~) ~ ~ floor · Glasstahlbetondecke f

(~) ~ ~ (load)bearing structure, (~) ~ ~ (weight-carrying) ~, (~) ~ ~ supporting ~ · Glasstahlbeton-Tragwerk n [*DIN 4229*]

819 (reinforced) glass concrete plank — reinforced perforated..

(~) ~ ~ **plank** · Glasstahlbetondiele *f*

(~) ~ ~ **rooflight** · Glasstahlbeton(-Dach)oberlicht *n*

(~) ~ ~ **(structural) system,** (~) ~ ~ construction · Glasstahlbetonkonstruktion *f*, Glasstahlbetonbausystem *n*, Glasstahlbeton(konstruktions)system

(~) ~ **fibre mould** (Brit.); (~) ~ **fiber mold** (US) · Glasfaserform *f*

~ **grouted masonry** · armiertes verpreßtes Mauerwerk *n*, bewehrtes ~ ~, ~ ausgepreßtes ~, ~ eingepreßtes ~, ~ injiziertes ~

~ **header,** ~ concrete ~, R. C. ~ ~ · Stahlbetonwechsel(balken) *m*

~ **high-pressure pipe,** ~ concrete ~, R. C. ~ ~ · Stahlbeton-Hochdruckrohr *n*

~ **hinge,** ~ concrete ~, R. C. ~ ~ · Stahlbetongelenk *n*

~ **hipped-plate roof** (US) → ~ (concrete) folded plate ~

~ **hollow beam,** ~ concrete ~ ~, R. C. ~ ~ · Stahlbeton-Hohlbalken(träger) *m*

~ ~ ~ **floor,** ~ concrete ~ ~ ~, R. C. ~ ~ ~ · Stahlbeton-Hohlbalkendecke *f*

~ ~ **pile,** ~ concrete ~ ~, R. C. ~ ~ ~ · Stahlbeton-Hohlpfahl *m*

~ ~ **plank** → ~ (concrete) hollow-core ~

~ ~ **slab** → ~ (concrete) ~ ~

~ ~ ~ **floor** → ~ (concrete) ~ ~ ~

~ **horizontal member** → ~ (concrete) rail

~ **I-beam,** ~ concrete ~ · Stahlbeton-Doppel-T-Träger *m*, Stahlbeton-I-Träger

~ **in-situ concrete lintel,** in-situ reinforced ~ ~, concrete ~ R. C. ~ [*deprecated: lintol*] · Ort-Stahlbeton-Oberschwelle *f*, Ort-Stahlbetonsturz *m*

~ **(intermediate) floor** → ~ concrete (~) ~

~ **joist** → ~ concrete ~

~ **lattice girder,** ~ concrete ~ ~, R. C. ~ ~ · Stahlbetongitterträger *m*

~ **lift-slab,** ~ concrete ~, R. C. ~ · Stahlbeton-Hub(decken)platte *f*, Hub-Stahlbeton(decken)platte

~ ~ **construction,** ~ concrete ~ ~, R. C. ~ ~ · Stahlbeton-Hub(decken)bau *m*

~ ~ **structure,** ~ concrete ~ ~, R. C. ~ ~ · Stahlbeton-Hub(decken)bauwerk *n*

~ **(lighting) column with bracket** → ~ concrete (~) ~ ~ ~

~ ~ **mast,** ~ concrete ~ ~, R. C. ~ ~ · Stahlbeton-Beleuchtungsmast *m*, Stahlbeton-Leuchtenmast, Stahlbeton-Lichtmast

~ (~) ~ **with arm** → ~ (concrete) (~) ~ ~ ~

~ **light(weight) concrete,** light(weight) R. C. · Leichtstahlbeton *m*, Stahlleichtbeton

~ **lining** → ~ concrete ~

~ **masonry** · bewehrtes Mauerwerk *n*, armiertes ~

~ (~) **block partition (wall)** · Stahlsteinmauer *f*, Steineisenmauer [*Fehlnamen: Stahlsteinwand f, Steineisenwand*]

~ ~ **lintel;** ~ ~ lintol [*deprecated*] · armierte Mauerwerkoberschwelle *f*, bewehrte ~, bewehrter Mauerwerksturz *m*, armierter Mauerwerksturz

~ ~ **wall** · bewehrte Mauerwerkwand *f*, armierte ~, Mauerwerkwand mit (Stahl-)Einlagen

~ ~ **(work)** · bewehrtes Mauerwerk *n*, armiertes ~, Mauerwerk mit (Stahl-)Einlagen

~ **mast,** ~ concrete ~ ~, R. C. ~ ~ · Stahlbetonmast *m* [*DIN 4234*]

~ ~ **with arm** → ~ (concrete) (lighting) ~ ~ ~

~ **mortar,** ~ cement ~ [*developed by Prof. P. L. Nervi in Italy*] · Stahlmörtel *m*

~ **mosque,** ~ concrete ~, R. C. ~ · Stahlbetonmoschee *f*

~ **northlight shell** → northlight reinforced (concrete) ~

~ **panel,** ~ concrete ~, R. C. ~ · Stahlbetontafel *f*

~ ~ **wall,** ~ concrete ~ ~, R. C. ~ ~ · Stahlbetontafelwand *f*

~ **parachute** → ~ (concrete) umbrella

~ **parallel truss,** ~ concrete ~ ~, R. C. ~ ~ · Stahlbeton-Parallelfachwerkträger *m*

~ **parapet** → ~ (concrete) spandrel (wall)

~ **parking deck,** ~ concrete ~ ~, R. C. ~ ~ · Stahlbetonparkplatte *f*

~ ~ **structure,** ~ concrete ~ ~, R. C. ~ ~ · Stahlbeton-Parkbauwerk *n*

~ **partition (wall),** ~ concrete ~ (~), R. C. ~ (~) · Stahlbetonwand *f* [*Leichte Trennwand. DIN 4103*]

~ **patent glazing bar** → ~ concrete ~ ~ ~

~ **perforated block floor,** ~ cored ~ ~ · Stahlsteindecke *f* mit Lochsteinen, Steineisendecke ~ ~ [*DIN 1046*]

~ ~ **brick floor,** ~ cored ~ ~ · Stahlsteindecke *f* mit Lochziegeln, Steineisendecke [*DIN 1046*]

reinforced pier — reinforced space (load)bearing structure

~ **pier** · gruppierter Pfeiler *m*

~ **pile,** ~ concrete ~, R.C. ~ · Stahlbetonpfahl *m*

~ **pipe,** ~ concrete ~, R.C. ~ · Stahlbetonrohr *n* [*DIN 4035*]

~ **pipeline,** ~ concrete ~, R.C. ~ · Stahlbetonrohrleitung *f*

~ **plain web beam** → ~ concrete ~ ~ ~

~ ~ ~ **girder** → ~ (concrete) ~ ~ ~

~ **plastic** · verstärkter Kunststoff *m*

~ **plate,** ~ concrete ~, ~ (concrete) slab, R.C. ~ · armierte (Beton)Platte *f*, bewehrte ~, (Beton)Platte mit (Stahl-) Einlagen, Stahlbetonplatte

~ ~ **floor** → ~ (concrete) slab ~

~ **portal frame,** ~ concrete ~ ~, R.C. ~ ~ · Stahlbetonportalrahmen *m*

~ **(pre)cast (concrete) girder,** (pre-)cast R.C. ~ · Stahlbetonfertigträger *m* [*DIN 4225*]

~ ~ **floor** → ~ concrete ~ ~

~ ~ **frame** → (pre)cast R.C. ~

~ ~ **girder** → ~ concrete ~

~ ~ **wall** → prefab(ricated) reinforced (concrete) ~

~ **prefab(ricated) (concrete) floor** → ~ (concrete) (pre)cast ~

~ ~ **(~) wall** → prefab(ricated) reinforced (~) ~

~ ~ **floor** → ~ (concrete) (pre)cast ~

~ ~ **wall** → prefab(ricated) reinforced (concrete) ~

~ **pressure pipe** → ~ concrete ~ ~

~ **problem,** ~ concrete ~, R.C. ~ · Stahlbetonaufgabe *f*

(~) **pumice (concrete) hollow beam** · (Natur)Bims(beton)hohlbalken(träger) *m*

(~) ~ (~) **hollow(-core) plank** · (Natur)Bims(beton)hohldiele *f*, (Natur-)Bims(beton)stegdiele [*DIN 4028*]

(~) ~ (~) **plank** · (Natur)Bims(beton)-diele *f* [*DIN 18162*]

(~) ~ (~) **slab** · (Natur)Bims(beton)-(bau)platte *f* [*Fehlnamen: Schwemmstein-Bauplatte (aus (Natur)Bimsbeton)*]

~ **purlin(e),** ~ concrete ~, R.C. ~ · Stahlbeton(dach)pfette *f*

~ **puttyless glazing bar** → ~ (concrete) patent ~ ~

~ **rafter,** ~ concrete ~, R.C. ~ · Stahlbetonsparren *m*

~ **rail** → ~ concrete ~

~ **railroad tie** → ~ concrete ~ ~

~ **railway sleeper** → ~ concrete ~ ~

~ **refuse water pipe** → ~ (concrete) sewer ~

~ **rib,** ~ concrete ~, R.C. ~ · Stahlbetonrippe *f*

~ **rib(bed) floor,** ~ concrete ~ ~, R.C. ~ ~ · Stahlbetonrippendecke *f* [*DIN 1045*]

~ ~ **slab,** ~ concrete ~ ~, R.C. ~ ~ · Stahlbetonrippenplatte *f*

~ **rigid frame,** ~ concrete ~ ~, R.C. ~ ~ · Stahlbeton-Steifrahmen *m*

~ **roof,** ~ concrete ~, R.C. ~ · Stahlbetondach *n*

~ ~ **beam,** ~ concrete ~ ~, R.C. ~ ~ · Stahlbetondachbalken(träger) *m*

~ ~ **cladding** → ~ concrete ~ ~

~ ~ **covering** → ~ (concrete) roof cladding

~ ~ **sheathing** → ~ (concrete) roof cladding

~ (~) **truss** → ~ concrete (~) ~

~ **roof(ing)** → ~ (concrete) roof cladding

~ ~ **slab,** ~ concrete ~ ~, R.C. ~ ~ · Stahlbeton-Dachplatte *f*, Stahlbeton-Bedachungselement *n*, Stahlbeton-Dachelement, Stahlbeton-Bedachungsplatte

~ **sandwich slab,** ~ concrete ~ ~, R.C. ~ ~ · Stahlbeton-Dreilagenplatte Stahlbeton-Sandwichplatte, *f*

~ **section,** ~ concrete ~, R.C. ~ · Stahlbetonquerschnitt *m*

~ **sewage pipe** → ~ (concrete) sewer ~

~ **sewer pipe** → ~ concrete ~ ~

~ **shear wall** → ~ concrete~ ~

~ **shell,** ~ concrete ~, R.C. ~ · Stahlbetonschale *f*

~ ~ **construction,** ~ concrete ~ ~, R.C. ~ ~ · Stahlbetonschalenbau *m*

~ ~ **roof,** ~ concrete ~ ~, R.C. ~ ~ · Stahlbetonschalendach *n*

~ **silo,** ~ concrete ~, R.C. ~ · Stahlbetonsilo *m*

~ **skyscraper,** ~ concrete ~, R.C. ~ · Stahlbeton-Wolkenkratzer *m*

~ **slab,** ~ concrete ~, ~ (concrete) plate, R.C. ~ · armierte (Beton)Platte *f*, bewehrte ~, (Beton)Platte mit (Stahl-) Einlagen, Stahlbetonplatte

~ ~ → ~ (concrete) (flat) ~

~ ~ **base** → ~ concrete ~ ~

~ ~ **floor** → ~ concrete ~ ~

~ ~ **foundation** → ~ (concrete) slab base

~ **solid block floor** · Stahlsteindecke *f* mit Vollsteinen, Steineisendecke ~ ~ [*DIN 1046*]

~ ~ **floor,** ~ concrete ~ ~, R.C. ~ ~ · Stahlbetonvolldecke *f*

~ ~ **plank (unit),** ~ concrete ~ ~ (~), R.C. ~ ~ (~) · Stahlbetonvolldiele *f*

~ ~ **slab,** ~ concrete ~ ~, R.C. ~ ~ · Stahlbetonvollplatte *f*

~ ~ **web beam** → ~ (concrete) plain ~ ~

~ ~ ~ **girder** → ~ (concrete) plain ~ ~ ~

~ **space (load)bearing structure** → ~ concrete ~ ~ ~

~ ~ structure → ~ (concrete) space (load)bearing ~

~ ~ (weight -carrying) structure → ~ (concrete) space (load)bearing ~

~ spandrel (wall) → ~ concrete ~ (~)

~ spatial (load)bearing structure → ~ (concrete) space ~ ~

~ ~ structure → ~ (concrete) space (load)bearing ~

~ ~ (weight-carrying) structure → ~ (concrete) space (load)bearing ~

~ spun pipe → ~ concrete ~ ~

~ stair(case), ~ concrete ~, R.C. ~ · Stahlbetontreppe f

~ step, ~ concrete ~, R.C. ~ · Stahlbetonstufe f

~ storage tank, ~ concrete ~ ~, R.C. ~ ~ · Stahlbeton-Lagerbehälter m

~ string → ~ concrete ~

~ structural topping → ~ concrete ~

~ structure, ~ concrete ~, R.C. ~ · Stahlbetonbauwerk n [DIN 1045]

~ ~, ~ system, ~ concrete ~, R.C. ~ · Stahlbetontragsystem n, Stahlbetontragwerk n

~ sun breaker → ~ (concrete) sun shade

~ ~ screen → ~ (concrete) sun shade

~ ~ shade → ~ concrete ~ ~

~ (sur)facing → ~ (concrete) lining

~ system, ~ structure, ~ concrete ~, R.C. ~ · Stahlbetontragsystem n, Stahlbetontragwerk n

~ T(ee)-beam → ~ (concrete) beam and slab

~ ~ floor → ~ concrete ~ ~

~ tension member, ~ concrete ~ ~, R.C. ~ ~ · Stahlbetonzugglied n

~ three-dimensional (load)bearing structure → ~ (concrete) space ~ ~

~ ~ structure → ~ (concrete) space (load)bearing ~

~ ~ (weight-carrying) structure → ~ (concrete) space (load)bearing ~

~ topping, ~ concrete ~, R.C. ~ · Stahlbeton-Druckschicht f, Stahlbeton-Druckplatte f

~ tower → (~) concrete ~

~ trimmer plank (unit), ~ concrete ~ ~ (~), R.C. ~ ~ (~) · Stahlbetonstreichdiele f [Auswechs(e)lung]

~ truss → ~ (concrete) (roof) ~

~ truss(ed girder), ~ concrete ~ (~), R.C. ~ (~) · Stahlbetonfachwerk(träger) n, (m)

~ tunnel vault → ~ (concrete) barrel ~

~ two-hinge(d) arch → ~ concrete ~ ~

~ two-pin(ned) arch → ~ (concrete) two-hinge(d) ~

~ type of construction → ~ concrete ~ ~ ~

~ umbrella → ~ concrete ~

~ vault, ~ concrete ~, R.C. ~ · Stahlbetongewölbe n

~ wagon vault → ~ (concrete) barrel ~

~ wall, ~ concrete ~, R.C. ~ · Stahlbetonmauer f

~ ~ panel, ~ concrete ~ ~, R.C. ~ ~ · Stahlbetonwandtafel f

~ window → ~ concrete ~

~ ~ lintel → ~ concrete ~ ~

~ with fibre (Brit.); ~ ~ fiber (US) · faserverstärkt

~ work, ~ concrete ~, R.C. ~ · Stahlbetonarbeiten fpl [DIN 18331]

reinforcement, concrete ~, concrete steel, reinforcing steel · (Beton)Bewehrung f, (Beton)Armierung, (Beton)Stahleinlagen fpl

~ · Verstärkung f

~ against tensile splitting · Spaltzugarmierung f, Spaltzugbewehrung, Spaltzug(stahl)einlagen fpl

~ bar → (rolled) (steel) ~

~ bending yard, steel ~ ~ · Stahlbiegeplatz m, Bewehrungsbiegeplatz, Armierungsbiegeplatz

~ binding, ~ tying, binding (reinforcement), tying (reinforcement) · Rödeln n (von Bewehrung(en)), Rödelung f (~ ~), Flechten (~ ~), Bewehrungsflechten

(~) cutting and bending, steel ~ ~ ~ · Betonstahlbearbeitung f

(~) ~ ~ ~ (work)shop, steel ~ ~ ~ ~ · Bewehrungswerkstatt f, Armierungswerkstatt

~ cylinder · Bewehrungszylinder m, Armierungszylinder

~ displacement · Armierungsverrückung f, Bewehrungsverrückung

~ distance piece → concrete ~ ~ ~

~ for compression → compression reinforcement

~ ~ stresses in erection → erection reinforcement

~ ~ tension, tension reinforcement, tensile reinforcement · Zugarmierung f, Zugbewehrung, Zug(stahl)einlagen fpl

~ in compression, compression reinforcement, compressed reinforcement · gedrückte Armierung f, ~ Bewehrung, ~ (Stahl)Einlagen fpl

~ ~ ribs, steel ~ ~ ~ · Rippenarmierung f, Rippenbewehrung, Rippen-(stahl)einlagen fpl

~ joint · Bewehrungsstoß m, Armierungsstoß

reinforcement layout — reinforcing steel bars

~ **layout**, layout of reinforcement · Armierungsführung f, Bewehrungsführung

~ **level**, steel ~ · Höhe f der Armierung, ~ ~ Bewehrung, ~ ~ (Stahl)Einlagen

~ **loop**, concrete ~ ~ · (Beton)Stahlschlaufe f

~ **mat** → (reinforcing) ~

~ **of twin-twisted round bars** · Istegbewehrung f, Istegarmierung, Isteg(stahl)einlagen fpl [*Sie besteht aus zwei nebeneinanderliegenden und mit ortsfesten Enden verbundenen Rundeisen*]

~ **ring** · Armierungsring m, Bewehrungsring

~ **rod** → (rolled) (steel) bar

~ **sheet** → (reinforcing) mat

~ **shop** · Biegerei f [*Betonsteinwerk*]

~ **spacer** → concrete ~ ~

~ **steel**, reinforcing ~ · Beton(ierungs)stahl m, Bewehrungsstahl, Armierungsstahl, Bewehrungseisen n, Armierungseisen, Beton(ierungs)eisen [*früher: Moniereisen*]

~ ~ **bars**, ~ ~ rods, reinforcing ~ ~ · Betonstabstahl m

~ ~ **rods**, ~ ~ bars, reinforcing ~ ~ · Betonstabstahl m

~ **storage yard**, steel ~ ~ · Armierungsstahllager n, Bewehrungsstahllager, Betonstahllager

~ **store**, steel ~ · Stahllager n, Bewehrungslager, Armierungslager

~ **system** · Armierungsanordnung f, Bewehrungsanordnung, Anordnung der (Stahl)Einlagen

~ **tying**, ~ binding, binding (reinforcement), tying (reinforcement) · Rödeln n (von Bewehrung(en)), Rödelung f (~ ~), Flechten (~ ~), Bewehrungsflechten

~ **work** · Armierungsarbeiten fpl, Bewehrungsarbeiten

~ **yard** · Armierungsstahlverarbeitungsanlage f, Bewehrungsstahlverarbeitungsanlage, Betonstahlverarbeitungsanlage, zentraler Betonstahlverarbeitungsplatz

reinforcing, stiffening, bracing [*The act of inserting braces into a structure*] · Absteifen n, Aussteifen, Versteifen, Verstärken

~, stiffening, bracing [*The result of the act of inserting braces into a structure or gap site*] · Absteifung f, Aussteifung, Verstärkung, Versteifung

~ **against buckling**, stiffening ~, bracing ~ ~ · Knickaussteifung f, Knickversteifung, Knickverstärkung

~ **angle**, bracing ~, stiffening ~, stiffener ~ · Aussteif(ungs)winkel m, Versteifungswinkel, Verstärkungswinkel

~ **bar** → (rolled) (steel) ~

~ **beam**, stiffening ~, bracing ~, · Aussteif(ungs)balken(träger) m Versteifungsbalken(träger), Verstärkungsbalken(träger)

~ **by diagonals** → stiffening ~ ~

(~) **cage** · Bewehrungskorb m, Armierungskorb

~ **coat** · Armierungsanstrich m, Armierungsaufstrich

~ **diaphragm**, stiffening ~, bracing ~ · Aussteif(ungs)scheibe f, Versteifungsscheibe, Verstärkungsscheibe

~ **fabric** → fabric (reinforcement)

~ **for compression** → compression reinforcement

~ **girder**, stiffening ~, bracing ~ · Aussteif(ungs)träger m, Versteifungsträger, Verstärkungsträger

~ **frame** → stiffening ~

~ **iron** → stiffening ~

(~) ~ **worker**, steel fixer, rod-setter, bar-setter, (bar) placer, iron fighter; rod buster (US. colloquial) [*A workman who handles and places steel and ornamental iron, including all types of reinforcing steel and bar supports. Also, in the Metropolitan Area of New York City, depending upon local union jurisdiction, such a workman is called 'lather'*] · Eisenflechter m, Eisenleger, Betoneisenarbeiter

~ **limit** · Bewehrungsgrenze f

(~) **mat**, reinforcement ~, (~) sheet · Baustahlgewebe n [*Markenname*]; Baustahlmatte f, Armierungsmatte, Bewehrungsmatte, Betonstahlmatte [*Mit unverschieblichen Knotenpunkten aus kaltgezogenem Sonderbetonstahl IV nach DIN 1045 hergestellt*]

~ **material** · Verstärkungswerkstoff m [*z.B. Glasfasern*]

~ ~ · Armierungsgut n [*z.B. Fasern in Putz oder Anstrich*]

~ **mesh** · Baugewebe n [*als Bewehrung*]

~ **plate** → stiffening ~

~ ~ · Beilage(platte) f, Zuwachsfläche f

~ **purlin(e)** → bracing ~

~ **rib**, stiffening ~, bracing ~ · Aussteif(ungs)rippe f, Versteifungsrippe, Verstärkungsrippe

~ **ring**, stiffening ~, bracing ~ · Aussteif(ungs)ring m, Versteifungsring, Verstärkungsring

~ **rod** → (rolled) (steel) bar

~ ~ **distance piece** → ~ ~ ~ spacer

~ ~ **separator** → ~ ~ spacer

~ ~ **spacer**, ~ ~ separator, ~ ~ distance piece, bar spacer, bar separator, bar distance piece · (Betonstahl)Abstandhalter m

(~) **sheet** → (~) mat

~ **spiral** · Armierungsspirale f, Bewehrungsspirale

~ **steel**, reinforcement ~, RST · Beton(ierungs)stahl m, Bewehrungsstahl, Armierungsstahl, Bewehrungseisen n, Armierungseisen, Beton(ierungs)eisen [*früher: Moniereisen*]

~ ~ **bars**, ~ ~ rods, reinforcement ~ ~ · Betonstabstahl m

reinforcing steel rods — to remove

~ ~ **rods**, ~ ~ bars, reinforcement ~ ~ · Betonstabstahl *m*

~ ~ **hook** · Betonstahlhaken *m*

~ **wall** → stiffening ~

~ **wire** · Armierungsdraht *m*, Bewehrungsdraht *m* [*Mauerwerkbewehrung*]

rejection, nonacceptance · Nichtabnahme *f*, Abnahmeverweigerung *f*

~ **of plans** · Ablehnung *f* von Plänen

relamping · Lampenwechsel *m*

to relate to each other · aufeinander beziehen

relative brightness · relative Helligkeit *f*

~ **humidity**, RH · relative (Luft)Feuchtigkeit *f*, ~ (Luft)Feuchte *f*, Feuchtigkeitsgrad *m*, Feuchtegrad [*Das Verhältnis der absoluten Feuchtigkeit zur größtmöglichen, d.h. zum gesättigten Zustand; es wird in Prozenten angegeben, 100% sind der gesättigte Zustand*]

~ **movement** · Relativbewegung *f*

~ **permeability**, ~ perviousness · relative Durchlässigkeit *f*

~ **perviousness**, ~ permeability · relative Durchlässigkeit *f*

~ **resistance to water vapour conductance** (Brit.); ~ ~ ~ ~ vapor ~ (US) · relativer Wasserdampfleitwiderstand *m*

~ **velocity** · Relativgeschwindigkeit *f*

relaxation · Relaxation *f*, Spannungsabfall *m* bei gleichbleibender Spannung [*Spannbeton*]

~ **method** · Relaxationsverfahren *n*

~ **table** · Relaxationstabelle *f*

release, stripping, forms removal, form(work) removal, shuttering removal · Ausschalung *f*, Entschalung

~ **agent**, form(work) ~, forms ~, shuttering ~, form(work) sealer, forms sealer, shuttering sealer · (Ent)Schal(ungs)mittel *n*, (Ent)Schal(ungs)hilfe *f*, Ausschal(ungs)mittel, Ausschal(ungs)hilfe

~ ~ **for fair face concrete** · Sichtbeton-(Ent)Schal(ungs)mittel *n*

~ **lube**, ~ oil, shuttering ~, forms ~, form(work) ~ · (Ent)Schal(ungs)öl *n*, Ausschal(ungs)öl

~ **of humidity**, ~ ~ moisture · Feuchtigkeitsabgabe *f*, Feuchteabgabe

~ **oil** → ~ lube

~ **paste**, form(work) ~, forms ~, shuttering ~ · (Ent)Schal(ungs)paste *f*

~ **wax**, form(work) ~, forms ~, shuttering ~ · (Ent)Schal(ungs)wachs *n*

releasing the pull · Nachlassen *n* [*Spannbeton*]

~ **temperature**, opening ~ · Auslösetemperatur *f* [*Sprinkler*]

reliable trench sheeting and bracing · Verbau *m* der Rohrgräben in unfallsicherer Ausführung

relief · Relief *n*

~ · Entlastung *f*

~ **bronze door** · Reliefbronzetür *f*

~ **frieze** · Relieffries *m*

~ **sewer** · Entlastungs-Abwasserleitung *f*

~ **style** · Reliefstil *m*

relieved · entlastet

~ · aufgelöst [*Wand(ober)fläche*]

relieving arch, discharging ~, safety ~, rough ~ · Entlastungsbogen *m*, Ablastebogen, Überfangbogen, Verstärkungsbogen, Versteifungsbogen

~ **layer** → pressure equalizing ~

~ **vault**, discharging ~ · Entlastungsgewölbe *n*, Ablastegewölbe, Überfanggewölbe, Verstärkungsgewölbe, Versteifungsgewölbe

religion institute · Religionsinstitut *n*

religious architecture, church ~, ecclesiastical ~ · kirchliche Architectur *f*, ~ Baukunst *f*, Kirchenbaukunst, Kirchenarchitektur, Sakralbaukunst, Sakralarchitektur

~ **building**, ecclesiastical ~ · Sakralgebäude *n*

~ **Gothic (style)**, ecclesiastical ~ (~) · Sakralbaugotik *f*

~ **house** → convent

~ **monument**, ecclesiastical ~ · Sakraldenkmal *n*, Sakralmonument *n*

~ **painting** · Andachtsmalerei *f*

~ **structure**, ecclesiastical ~ · Sakralbau(werk) *m*, (*n*)

reliquary [*A light portable receptacle for sacred relics*] · Reliquiar *n*

to reload · nachbelasten

reloading · Nachbelastung *f*

remains · Baureste *mpl*

remelt zinc · Umschmelzzink *n*

remote readout · Fernablesen *n*

~ **window control equipment** · Fensterfernbedienungsgeräte *npl*

removable ceiling · abnehmbare Decke *f*, Einlegedecke

removable grate, ~ grating · Einlegerost *m*

removal · Beseitigung *f*, Entfernung

~ **of coat(s)** · Anstrichentfernung *f*, Aufstrichentfernung, Anstrichbeseitigung, Aufstrichbeseitigung

~ ~ **putty**, putty removal · Entkitten *n* [*Verglasung*]

~ ~ **rainwater**, rainwater removal · Regen(wasser)abführung *f*

~ ~ **refuse water by conduit-type sewer(s)**, ~ ~ foul ~ ~ ~ ~, ~ ~ sewage ~ ~ ~ · Abwasserableitung *f* durch Kanäle

~ ~ **scale** → descaling

~ ~ **stress**, stress removal. stress relieving · Spannungsfreimachen *n*, Entspannen [*Baustahl*]

to remove · beseitigen, wegräumen [*(Abbruch)Schutt*]

to remove a paint or varnish film with... — rental housing 824

~ ~ a paint or varnish film with paint remover [*The paint remover softens a paint or varnish film, so that it can be easily scraped or brushed off*] · (ab-)beizen [*Anstrich von seinem Untergrund*]

~ ~ blemishes by polishing · beipolieren

~ ~ by hammering · abschlagen [*Putz*]

~ ~ foul air, ~ extract ~ ~ · entlüften

~ ~ scale, to descale · abzundern, entzundern

~ ~ with caustics · abätzen

remover, stripper, paint ~ · Abbeizer *m*, (Ab)Beizmittel *n*, Farbenlöser, Farbenentferner, Lacklöser, Lackbeize *f*, Ablaugemittel *n* [*Vom Anstreicher kurz „Lauge" genannt*]

removing old paint coats with soda-based paint remover · Ablaugen *n* alter Anstrichschichten

Remy floor · Remydecke *f* [*Warenzeichen. Stahlbetonrippendecke unter Verwendung von (Natur)Bimsbetonhohlkörpern*]

Renaissance · Renaissance *f* [*Wiederaufleben antiker Formen am Ende des Mittelalters. Als Stil vom Barock abgelöst*]

~ acanthus leaf · Renaissance-Akanthusblatt *n*, Renaissance-Bärenklaublatt

~ arcade · Renaissancearkade *f*

~ architect · Renaissancearchitekt *m*

~ architecture · Renaissancearchitektur *f*, Renaissancebaukunst *f*

~ bridge · Renaissancebrücke *f*

~ building · Renaissancegebäude *n*

~ church · Renaissancekirche *f*

~ dome · Renaissancedom *m*

~ form · Renaissanceform *f*

~ ornament · Renaissanceornament *n*

~ palace · Renaissancepalast *m*

render coat → rendering ~

to render, ~ plaster · (ver)putzen

rendered building, ~ block · Putzgebäude *n* [*Gebäude mit verputzten Außenflächen im Gegensatz zu unverputzten Gebäuden*]

~ façade · Putzfassade *f*

~ structure · Putzbau(werk) *m*, (*n*) [*Bauwerk mit verputzten Außenflächen im Gegensatz zu unverputzten Bauwerken*]

rendering, plastering, ~ work · (Ver-)Putzen *n*, (Ver)Putzarbeiten *fpl* [*DIN 18550*]

~ (US); application of mortar · Mörtelauftrag *m*

~ aggregate → external ~ ~

~ and plastering work (Brit.); stucco and plaster ~ (US) · Putzarbeiten *fpl* [*DIN 18550*]

~ base, external ~ ~, exterior ~ ~ (Brit.); external plaster(ing) ~, exterior plaster(ing) ~ [*This product is used as a base for the application of stucco on the outer walls of buildings*] · (Außen)(Ver)Putzträgerplatte *f*

~ ~, external ~ ~, exterior ~ ~ (Brit.); external plaster(ing) ~, exterior plaster(ing) ~ · (Außen)Putz(unter)grund *m*

render(ing) coat, scratch ~ [*It consists of mortar of lime, sand and considerable hair*] · Unterputzschicht *f*, Unterputzlage *f*, Grobputzschicht, Grobputzlage, (Außen)Rauhwerk *n*

rendering (coat), plaster(ing) ~, internal ~ ~ [*A first coat of plaster internally*] · Innenunterputzschicht *f*, Innenunterputzlage *f*

~ ~, external ~ ~, exterior ~ ~ (Brit.); external plaster(ing) ~, exterior plaster(ing) ~, exterior plaster(ing) ~ · (Außen)Putzüberzug *m*, (Außen)Putzschicht *f*, (Außen)Putzhaut *f*, (Außen-)Putzlage *f*

~ mix(ture) → (external) rendering stuff

~ practice → external ~ ~

~ resisting pelting rain · Nässeputz *m* gegen Schlagregen

~ scheme → external ~ ~

~ stuff → external ~ ~

~ system → (external) rendering scheme

~ technique → (external) rendering practice

~ (work), plastering (~) · (Ver)Putzarbeiten *fpl*, (Ver)Putzen *n* [*DIN 18550*]

renewal · Erneuerung *f*

~ → (urban) redevelopment

~ area → urban ~ ~

~ work · Erneuerungsarbeiten *fpl*

to renovate, to redecorate, to embellish · renovieren, verschönern

renovation · Renovierung *f*, bauliche Neugestaltung

~ work · Renovierungsarbeiten *fpl*

rentable, lettable · vermietbar

~ area → rental ~

~ space → rental area

rental apartment (unit), ~ flat; ~ living unit (US) · Miet-Stockwerkwohnung *f*, Miet-Etagenwohnung, Miet(-Geschoß)wohnung

~ area, rentable ~, ~ space · Mietfläche *f*

~ flat, ~ apartment (unit), ~ living unit (US) · Miet-Stockwerkwohnung *f*, Miet-Etagenwohnung, Miet(-Geschoß)wohnung

~ housing, ~ residential ~ · Mietwohnbauten *f*

rental living unit — repelling property

~ living unit (US); ~ apartment (~), ~ flat · Miet-Stockwerkwohnung f, Miet-Etagenwohnung, Miet(-Geschoß)wohnung

~ (residential) housing · Mietwohnbauten f

~ row house, ~ town ~ · Mietreihenhaus n

~ space → ~ area

~ town house, ~ row ~ · Mietreihenhaus n

rent-free · mietfrei

repaintable · nachstreichbar

repainting · Nach(an)streichen n

~, weather-coating renewal · Pflegeanstrich m, Pflegeaufstrich [*Dachpappe*]

~ coat · Nachanstrich m, Nachaufstrich

to repair, to make good, reparieren, instandsetzen, ausbessern

repair, making good · Reparatur f, Ausbesserung f, Instandsetzung

~ composition, ~ compound, patch(ing) ~ · Flickmasse f, Ausbesserungsmasse

~ compound, patch(ing) ~, ~ composition · Flickmasse, Ausbesserungsmasse

~ concrete, patch(ing) ~ · Flickbeton m, Ausbesserungsbeton

~ emulsion, patch(ing) ~ · Flickemulsion f, Ausbesserungsemulsion

~ glazing · Reparaturverglasung f, Reparatureinglasung

~ mortar, patch(ing) ~ · Ausbesserungsmörtel m, Flickmörtel

~ plaster, patch(ing) ~ [*A special plaster made for repairing plaster walls*] · Ausbesserungsputz m, Flickputz

~ shop, ~ (work)shop · Reparaturwerkstatt f

~ ~, motor vehicle ~ ~ · (Kfz.-)Reparaturwerkstatt f

~ work, patch(ing) ~ · Flickarbeiten fpl, Ausbesserungsarbeiten

~ ~ · Ausbesserungsarbeiten fpl, Instandsetzungsarbeiten, Reparaturarbeiten

~ (work)shop · Reparaturwerkstatt f

repairing, making good · Reparieren n, Instandsetzen, Ausbessern

~, patching · (Aus)Flicken n, Ausbessern

to repaper · nachtapezieren

repeat design · Rapport m, Wiederkehr f des Musters [*(Papier)Tapete*]

~ ~ · Rapport m, Wiederkehr f der Form [*Dekoration, z.B. Fries*]

~ test · Wiederholungsprobe f, Wiederholungsprüfung f, Wiederholungsversuch m

repeatability range · Wiederhol-Streubereich m, n [*Ein Beobachter (englisch: analyst, operator) an einem Meßgerät*]

repeated loading, load(ing) cycle, cycle of load(ing) · Lastspiel n, Belastungsspiel

~ loadings, cyclic loading · Lastspiele npl

~ ~ to failure, loading cycles ~ ~, (load) cycles ~ ~ · Lastspiele npl bis zum Bruch, Belastungsspiele ~ ~ ~

repellent · Abweismittel n

~, repelling, water-~, waterproofing, waterrejecting · wasser(ab)dichtend, sperrend

~ building paper → waterproof(ing) ~ ~

~ capacity → (water-)repelling ~

~ cement → water-~ ~

~ coat → waterproof(ing) ~

~ concrete → water-~ ~

~ emulsion → water-~ ~

~ finish → waterproof(ing) plaster

~ grout(ing compound) → water-~ ~ (~)

~ liquid → liquid waterproofing agent

~ material → water-~ ~

~ membrane → water-~ ~

~ mixed plaster → waterproof(ing) ~

~ mortar → water- ~ ~

~ paper → waterproof(ing) ~

~ plaster → waterproof(ing) ~

~ power → (water-)repelling capacity

~ property → (water-)repelling capacity

~ quality → (water-)repelling capacity

~ screed → water-~ ~

~ solution, repelling ~, water-~ ~, waterproof(ing) ~ · Imprägnier(ungs)-lösung f

repelling · abweisend

~, repellent, water-~, waterproofing, waterrejecting · wasser(ab)dichtend, sperrend

~ agent → water-~ ~

~ building paper → waterproof(ing) ~ ~

~ capacity → water-~ ~

~ cement → water-~ ~

~ coat → waterproof(ing) ~

~ concrete → water-~ ~

~ emulsion → water-~ ~

~ finish → waterproof(ing) plaster

~ grout(ing compound) → water-~ ~ (~)

~ membrane → water-~ ~

~ mixed plaster → waterproof(ing) ~ ~

~ mortar → water-~ ~

~ paper → waterproof(ing) ~

~ plaster → waterproof(ing) ~

~ power → (water-)repelling capacity

~ property → (water-)repelling capacity

repelling quality — residential (building) area 826

~ **quality** → (water-)repelling capacity

~ **screed** → water-~ ~

~ **solution**, repellent ~, water-~ ~, waterproof(ing) ~ · Imprägnier(ungs)lösung f

repetition method → ~ work ~

~ **work**, repetitive operations · Taktarbeit f

~ **(~) method** · Taktverfahren n [*Planmäßige Aufteilung eines Produktionsverfahrens in einzelne Arbeitsabschnitte, die zeitlich so aufeinander abgestimmt sind, daß von den gleichen Arbeitskräften jeweils die gleichen oder ähnlichen Arbeiten in entsprechend zugeordneten Zeitmaßen ausgeführt werden*]

repetitive operations, repetition work · Taktarbeit f

replanning · Umplanung f

replastering · Nach(ver)putzen n

replica · Nachbildung f

re-pointing · Nachausfugung f, Nachverfugung [*Mauerwerk*]

repolishing · Nachpolieren n

reporting room · Anmelderaum m, Anmeldezimmer n

repose · Ruhepunkt m

repressed brick · nachgepreßter Ziegel m

re-pressing · Nachpressen n

reproducibility · Reproduzierbarkeit f

~ **range** · Vergleichs-Streubereich m, n [*Verschiedene Beobachter (englisch: analysts) an verschiedenen Meßgeräten*]

required amount of water · Wasseranspruch m, Wasserbedarf m

requirement · Forderung f [*Baustatik*]

rere-arch, rear arch, scuncheon arch, scoinson arch [*The inner arch over a door or window when such an arch differs from the outer one*] · innerer Bogen m

reredos, retable, altar piece, altar screen · Retabel n, Altar~, Altaraufsatz m, Altarstock m [*Im Deutschen oft nur „Altar" genannt. Eine entweder auf die Mensa des katholischen Altars aufgesetzte, auf einem Zwischenstück (Predella) oder hinter diesem auf einem Unterbau stehende Schauwand, die im Mittelalter aufkam*]

re-roofing · Nach(dach)eindeckung f

~ · Wiederbedachen n, Nachbedachen

resaturated · nachgesättigt

re-saturating, re-impregnating · Nachimprägnieren n, Nachtränken

re-screening · Nachsieben n

resealing · Nach(ab)dichten n

research institute · Forschungsanstalt f

~ **lab(oratory)** · Forschungslabor(atorium) n

reserve of strength, strength reserve · Festigkeitsreserve f

residence accommodation, residential ~ · Wohnunterkunft f

~ **block** → residential building

~ ~ **type**, domestic ~ ~, residential ~ ~, ~ building ~; multiple dwelling ~ (US) · Wohngebäudeart f, Wohnhausart, Wohngebäudetyp m, Wohnhaustyp

~ **brick block** → residential clay ~ ~

~ ~ **building** → ~ clay ~ ~

~ **building** → residential ~

~ ~ **type**, domestic ~ ~, residential ~ ~, ~ block ~; multiple dwelling ~ (US) · Wohngebäudeart f, Wohnhausart, Wohngebäudetyp m, Wohnhaustyp

~ **(clay) brick block**, domestic (~) ~ ~, residential (~) ~ ~, ~ (~) ~ building; (clay) brick dwelling (US) · Ziegel-Wohnhaus n, Ziegel-Wohngebäude n

~ **(~) ~ building**, domestic (~) ~ ~, residential (~) ~ ~, ~ (~) ~ block; (clay) brick dwelling (US) · Ziegel-Wohnhaus n, Ziegel-Wohngebäude n

~ **tower**, residential ~, dwelling ~ housing ~, high ~, high (rise) block (of flats), high (rise) flats, tall block (of flats), tall flats (Brit.); apartment tower (US) · Wohnhochhaus n, Hochwohnhaus, Wohnturm m

residences, (residential) housing [*A collective term used to designate human shelter*] · Wohnbauten f

resident, (apartment) dweller, (room) occupant, user · Raumbenutzer m, Wohnungs)Benutzer, (Raum)Insasse m, Wohnungsinsasse, Bewohner

~ **engineer**, Engineer · Bauleitung f (der Bauherrschaft)

residential accommodation, residence ~ · Wohnunterkunft f

~ ~ → ~ **portion**

~ **air-conditioning** · Hausklimatisierung f

~ **architecture** · Wohngebäudearchitektur f, Wohngebäudebaukunst f

~ **area**, ~ building ~, populated ~, building ~, living ~ · Wohn(bau)gebiet n, Wohn(bau)zone, Wohnungsbaugebiet, Wohnungsbauzone

~ **balcony** · Wohnbalkon m

~ **block** → ~ building

~ ~ → ~ **portion**

~ ~ **type**, domestic ~ ~, residence ~ ~, ~ building ~; multiple dwelling ~ (US) · Wohngebäudeart f, Wohnhausart, Wohngebäudetyp m, Wohnhaustyp

~ **brick block** → ~ clay ~ ~

~ ~ **building** → ~ clay ~ ~

~ **building**, domestic ~, residence ~, ~ block; dwelling (US) [*A building designed or used as the living quarters for one or more families*] · Wohngebäude n, Wohnhaus n

~ **(~) area**, populated ~, housing ~, living ~ · Wohn(bau)gebiet n, Wohn(bau)zone f, Wohnungsbaugebiet, Wohnungsbauzone

residential building type — resilient quilt

~ ~ type, domestic ~ ~, residence ~ ~, ~ block ~; multiple dwelling ~ (US) · Wohngebäudeart f, Wohnhausart, Wohngebäudetyp m, Wohnhaustyp

~ camp · Wohnlager n

~ (clay) brick building, domestic (~) ~ ~, residence (~) ~ ~, ~ (~) ~ block; (clay) brick dwelling (US) · Ziegel-Wohnhaus n, Ziegel-Wohngebäude n

~ community · Wohnortschaft f [*Sie hat wenig oder gar keine Industrie*]

~ density · Belegungsziffer f, Wohndichte f

~ developer · Wohnungsbauträger m

~ flat window on pitched roof Dachwohn(raum)fenster n, Wohn-(raum)dachfenster

~ floor, apartment ~; ~ storey (Brit.); ~ story (US) · Wohnetage f, Wohnstockwerk n, Wohngeschoß n

~ garage, domestic ~ · Hausgarage f, Einzelgarage

~ gas (burning) appliance, domestic ~ (~) ~ · Haushalt-Gasgerät n

~ ground floor · Wohnerdgeschoß n

~ heating, domestic ~ · Wohnungs(be)-heizung f

~ ~ installation, domestic ~ ~, ~ ~ system · Wohnungsheiz(ungs)anlage f, Wohnungs(be)heizungsanlage

~ ~ plant → domestic heating installation

~ ~ system, domestic ~ ~, ~ ~ installation · Wohnungsbeheiz(ungs)-anlage f, Wohnungs(be)heizungsanlage

~ home → hostel

(~) housing, residences [*A collective term used to designate human shelter*] · Wohnbauten f

~ illumination, ~ lighting · Hausbeleuchtung f

~ kindergarten · Internatskindergarten m

~ lighting, ~ illumination · Hausbeleuchtung f

~ location · Wohnlage f

~ park · Wohnpark m

~ plot · Wohngrundstück n

~ portion, ~ accomodation, ~ block, ~ unit · Wohntrakt m

~ quarter, domestic ~ · Wohnvierte l n

~ school · Internatsschule f

~ sliding door · Wohnungsschiebetür f

~ ~ window · Wohnungsschiebefenster n

~ storey, apartment ~ (Brit.); ~ story (US) · ~ floor · Wohnetage f, Wohnstockwerk n, Wohngeschoß n

~ street · Wohnstraße f

~ swimming pool [*Any constructed pool which is used, or intended to be used, as a swimming pool in connection with a single family residence*] · Hausschwimmbecken n

~ tower → residence ~

~ town · Wohnstadt f

~ type hotel, apartment ~ ~ · Hotel garni n

~ unit → ~ portion

~ window, domestic ~ · Wohn(gebäude)fenster n, Wohnhausfenster, Wohnungsfenster

~ wiring · Hausverdrahtung f

residual error · Restfehler m

~ hardness · Resthärte f [*Die nach der Enthärtung im Wasser noch vorhandene Härte*]

~ humidity, ~ moisture · Restfeuchtigkeit f, Restfeuchte f

~ lime · Restkalk m

~ moisture, ~ humidity · Restfeuchtigkeit f, Restfeuchte f

~ moment capacity · Restmomentvermögen n

~ oxygen · Restsauerstoff m

~ pebble · Restkiesel m

~ (pre)stressing force, ~ stretching ~, ~ tensioning ~, ~ ~ stress · Restvorspannkraft f

~ product · Rückstandserzeugnis n

~ rust · Restrost m

~ strain · Restdehnung f

~ strength · Restfestigkeit f

~ stress · Restspannung f

~ stressing force → ~ stretching ~

~ stretching force, ~ tensioning ~, ~ (pre)stressing ~, ~ ~ stress · Restvorspannkraft f

~ tensioning force, ~ stretching ~, ~ (pre)stressing ~, ~ ~ stress · Restvorspannkraft f

~ thickness · Restdicke f [*Fehlname: Reststärke f*]

~ water vapour (Brit.); ~ ~ vapor (US) · Restwasserdampf m

residue by distillation, distillation residue · Destillationsrückstand m

residue-on-sieving test · Lagerbeständigkeitsprüfung f durch Siebung, Lagerbeständigkeitsprobe f ~ ~, Lagerbeständigkeitsversuch m ~ ~ [*Emulsion*]

resilience, elasticity · Elastizität f

resilient, elastic · geschmeidig, elastisch

~ board, ~ sheet · elastische Platte f

~ floor cover(ing), ~ floor (finish), ~ flooring · elastischer (Fuß)Boden(belag) m, federnder ~

~ layer · Dämmlage f, Dämmschicht f [*schwimmender (Fuß)Boden(belag); Stabparkett*]

~ mounting · schwingungsisolierte Aufstellung f, ~ Lagerung, erschütterungsisolierte ~, vibrationsfreie ~

~ quilt · Faserdämmstofflage f, Faserdämmstoffschicht f [*schwimmender (Fuß)Boden(belag); Stabparkett*]

resilient (quilt) strip — resistance to alkali(s)

~ (~) strip · Dämmstreifen(unterlage) m, (f) [schwimmender Holz(fuß)boden-(belag)]

~ sheet, ~ board · elastische Platte f

~ strip, ~ quilt ~ · Dämmstreifen(unterlage) m, (f) [schwimmender Holz(fuß)-boden(belag)]

~ tile · elastische (Belag)Platte f, ~ Fliese f

resin, rosin, colophony, Colophonian (resin) · Kolophonium n, Spiegelharz n, griechisches Pech n, Geigenharz [DIN 55935]

~ · Harz n

~ **adhesive**, ~ glue · Harzkleber m, Klebeharz n

~ **alcohol** · Harzalkohol m

~ **base** · Harzbasis f, Harzgrundlage f

~ ~ **(concrete) curing agent**, ~ ~ (~) ~ compound, ~ ~ (liquid) membrane (~) ~ ~ · (Beton)Nachbehandlungsmittel n auf Harzbasis

~ ~ (~) ~ **compound**, ~ ~ ~ (~) ~ agent, ~ ~ (liquid) membrane (~) ~ ~ · (Beton)Nachbehandlungsmittel n auf Harzbasis

~ ~ **(liquid) membrane (concrete) curing agent**, ~ ~ (~) ~ (~) ~ compound, ~ ~ ~ (concrete) curing compound, ~ ~ (concrete) curing agent · (Beton)Nachbehandlungsmittel n auf Harzbasis

~ **based** · harzhaltig

resin-base(d) cement → resin(ous) ~

~ **putty** → resin(ous) cement

resin bonded [Glued with synthetic resin, therefore usually moisture-resistant] · harzgeleimt

resin-bound, bound with resinous material · harzgebunden

resin cement → resinous ~

~ **(clear) varnish**, synthetic ~ (~) ~ · Kunstharzlack m [Ein Lack mit Kunstharz als Bindemittel]

~ **coat** · Harzanstrich m, Harzaufstrich

~ **component**, ~ constituent · Harzbestandteil m

~ **constituent**, ~ component · Harzbestandteil m

resin-cored solder wire [B.S. 441] · Röhrenlötzinn n mit Kolophonium gefüllt, ~ ~ Geigenharz n

resin emulsion · Harzemulsion f

~ ~ **paint** · Harzemulsionsfarbe f

~ **ester** · Harzester m [Durch Umsetzung von Kolophonium mit Glycerin veredeltes Naturharz, wobei sich aus Harzsäure und Glycerin Ester bildet]

~-**forming alcohol** · harzbildender Alkohol m

resin glue, ~ adhesive · Harzkleber m, Klebeharz n

~ **grout** · Harzmörtel m

~ **impregnated**, ~ saturated · harzgetränkt

~ **industry** · Kunstharzindustrie f

~ **panel** · Kunstharztafel f

~ **particle** · Harzteilchen n

~ **powder** · Harzpulver n

~ **putty** → resin(ous) cement

~ **saturated**, ~ impregnated · harzgetränkt

~ **soap** · Harzseife f

~ **solution** · Harzlösung f

~ **suspension** · Harzsuspension f

~ **system** · Harzsystem n

~ **varnish** · Tränkharz n [Schichtstoff]

~ ~, (synthetic) resin (clear) ~ · Kunstharzlack m [Ein Lack mit Kunstharz als Bindemittel]

~ ~ · Harzlack m

resinate · Resinat n

~ **of cobalt**, cobalt resinate · Kobaltresinat n

~ ~ **lead**, lead resinate · Bleiresinat n

~ ~ **manganese**, manganese resinate · Manganresinat n

resinification · Verharzung f

to resinify · verharzen

resinous · harzig

resin(ous) cement, ~ putty, resin-base(d) ~ · Harzkitt m

to resist · standhalten, widerstehen

resistance, fastness [Ability to resist attacks] · Beständigkeit f, Festigkeit, Widerstand m, Echtheit

~ **against damage**, fastness ~ ~, damage resistance, damage fastness · Beständigkeit f gegen Beschädigungen, Festigkeit ~ ~, Widerstand m ~ ~

~ ~ **pelting rain** · Schlagregensicherheit f, Schlagregenwiderstand m, Schlagregenbeständigkeit

~ ~ **rust**, rust resistance · Rostsicherheit f, Rostbeständigkeit, Rostwiderstand m

~ **brazing**, ~ hard soldering · (elektrisches) Widerstandshartlöten n, (elektrische) Widerstandshartlötung f

~ **degree**, fastness ~, degree of resistance, degree of fastness · Widerstandsgrad m, Festigkeitsgrad, Beständigkeitsgrad

~ **flash welding** · Abbrennstumpfschweißung f [DIN 4100]

~ **hard soldering**, ~ brazing · (elektrisches) Widerstandshartlöten n, (elektrische) Widerstandshartlötung f

~ **of tearing**, tearing strength · Zerreißfestigkeit f

~ **property**, fastness ~ · Beständigkeitseigenschaft f, Echtheitseigenschaft

~ **soldering** · elektrische Widerstandslötung f

~ **to alkali(s)**, fastness ~ ~, alkali resistance, alkali fastness · Alkali(en)-festigkeit f, Alkali(en)widerstand m, Alkali(en)beständigkeit, Alkali(en)echtheit

resistance to abrasion — resistant to light

~ ~ **abrasion** → abrasion resistance

~ ~ **aggressive influences** · Aggressivbeständigkeit f

~ ~ **alcohol,** fastness ~ ~, alcohol resistance, alcohol fastness · Alkoholbeständigkeit f, Alkoholfestigkeit, Alkoholechtheit, Alkoholwiderstand m

~ ~ **alkali(s),** fastness ~ ~, alkali fastness, alkali resistance · Alkalibeständigkeit f, Alkaliwiderstand m, Alkalifestigkeit, Alkaliechtheit

~ ~ **attrition** → abrasion resistance

~ ~ **bending** → bending resistance

~ ~ **bleeding,** fastness ~ ~ · Ausblutechtheit f [*Pigment*]

~ ~ **cold,** fastness ~ ~ · Kältebeständigkeit f, Kältewiderstand m, Kälteechtheit, Kältefestigkeit

~ ~ **compression** → compression resistance

~ ~ **cracking,** extensibility, cracking strength · Rißfestigkeit f

~ ~ ~ **deformation** · Verformungswiderstand m

~ ~ **efflorescence,** efflorescence resistance · Ausblühungsbeständigkeit f, Aussalzungsbeständigkeit, Ausschlagbeständigkeit, Auswitterungsbeständigkeit, Auskristallisationsbeständigkeit

~ ~ **frost attack,** ~ ~ freezing, freezing resistance, frost resistance, frostresisting property · Frostbeständigkeit f, Frostwiderstand m, Frostsicherheit f, Frostunempfindlichkeit

~ ~ **hair cracking,** hair cracking resistance · Haarrißfestigkeit f

~ ~ **heat,** fastness ~ ~, stability ~ ~, heat resistance, heat fastness, heat stability, thermal stability · Hitzebeständigkeit f, Hitzeechtheit, Hitzefestigkeit, Hitzewiderstand m

~ ~ ~ **transmission** · Wärmedurchlaßwiderstand m

~ ~ ~ ~ · Hitzedurchlaßwiderstand m

~ ~ **impact,** toughness, impact resistance · Schlagfestigkeit f, Stoßwiderstand m, (Schlag)Zähigkeit f [*Widerstand eines Gesteins gegen Bruch unter Einwirkung von Stößen*]

~ ~ **lime,** fastness ~ ~, lime resistance, lime fastness · Kalkbeständigkeit f, Kalkechtheit, Kalkwiderstand m, Kalkfestigkeit

~ ~ **moisture,** ~ ~ humidity · Feuchtebeständigkeit f, Feuchtigkeitsbeständigkeit

~ ~ **oil** → oil fastness

~ ~ **oscillation(s),** ~ ~ vibration(s) · Schwingungsfestigkeit f

~ ~ **scrubbing** · Scheuerfestigkeit f

~ ~ **soluble glass,** ~ ~ water ~ fastness ~ ~ ~ · Wasserglasechtheit f

~ ~ **spirit** → spirit resistance

~ ~ **swelling,** fastness ~ ~, swelling resistance, swelling fastness · Quellfestigkeit f, Quellbeständigkeit

~ ~ **temperature changes** · Temperaturwechselbeständigkeit f

~ ~ **termite attack** · Termitenbeständigkeit f, Termitenfestigkeit, Termitenwiderstand m

~ ~ **(the action of) weather,** weather proofness, weathering quality, weather resistance · Wetterbeständigkeit f, Wetterfestigkeit, Witterungsbeständigkeit, Witterungsfestigkeit

~ ~ **vibration(s),** ~ ~ oscillation(s) · Schwingungsfestigkeit f

~ ~ **washing,** fastness ~ ~ · (Ab-)Waschfestigkeit f, (Ab)Waschwiderstand m, (Ab)Waschbeständigkeit

~ ~ **water,** fastness ~ ~, water resistance, water fastness · Wasserbeständigkeit f, Wasserfestigkeit, Wasserwiderstand m

~ ~ ~ **glass,** ~ ~ soluble ~, fastness ~ ~ ~ · Wasserglasechtheit f

~ ~ **(~) vapour diffusion** (Brit.); ~ ~ (~) vapor ~ (US); ~ ~ damp ~ · Wasserdampfdiffusionswiderstand m

~ ~ **(~) ~ transmission** (Brit.); ~ ~ (~) vapor ~ (US) · Wasserdampfdurchgangswiderstand m

~ ~ **wear(ing),** wear(ing) resistance · Abnutz(ungs)widerstand m, Abnutz(ungs)beständigkeit f, Abnutz(ungs)festigkeit, Verschleißwiderstand m, Verschleißbeständigkeit, Verschleißfestigkeit

~ ~ **weather,** ~ ~ the action of ~, weather proofness, weathering quality, weather resistance · Wetterbeständigkeit f, Wetterfestigkeit, Witterungsbeständigkeit, Witterungsfestigkeit

resistant, proof, resisting, fast · beständig, fest, echt gegen, sicher, widerstandsfähig

~ **to alkali(s),** alkali resistant · alkali(en)beständig, alkali(en)fest, alkali(en)widerstandsfähig, alkali(en)echt, alkali(en)sicher

~ ~ **bending** → flexurally rigid

~ ~ **cold,** cold-resistant, cold-resisting, coldproof · kältebeständig, kältesicher, kältefest, kältewiderstandsfähig

~ ~ **heat,** heat-resistant, heat-resisting, heatproof · hitzebeständig, hitzefest, hitzewiderstandsfähig, hitzesicher

~ ~ **humidity** → ~ ~ moisture

~ ~ **hydrostatic pressure,** waterresisting · wasserdruckhaltend

~ ~ **light,** light resistant, proof to light, lightproof, fast to light, lightfast · lichtbeständig, lichtecht, lichtsicher, lichtwiderstandsfähig

~~ **moisture**, ~~ humidity, moisture-proof, humidity-proof · feuchtigkeitsbeständig, feuchtebeständig, feuchtigkeitsfest, feuchtefest, feuchtigkeitssicher, feuchtesicher, feuchtigkeitswiderstandsfähig, feuchtewiderstandsfähig

~~ **pelting rain**, · schlagregensicher, schlagregenbeständig, schlagregenwiderstandsfähig

~~ **saponification**, fast ~~, proof ~~ · verseifungswiderstandsfähig, verseifungsbeständig, verseifungsfest, verseifungssicher

~~ **sunlight**, fast ~~, proof ~~, sunlightfast, sunlightproof, sunlight resistant · sonnenlichtfest, sonnenlichtsicher, sonnenlichtbeständig, sonnenlichtwiderstandsfähig

~~ **swelling**, fast ~~, proof ~~ · quellfest, quellsicher, quellbeständig, quellwiderstandsfähig

~~ **the penetration by cellulose solvents** · nitrofest, nitrobeständig, nitrosicher, nitrowiderstandsfähig

~~ **wheel-chairs**, fast ~~, proof ~~ [*floor(ing)*] · rollstuhlwiderstandsfähig, rollstuhlfest, rollstuhlbeständig, rollstuhlsicher

resisting, resistant, proof, fast · beständig, fest, echt gegen, sicher, widerstandsfähig

~ **moment**, moment of resistance · Moment *n* der inneren Kräfte

resol · Resol *n* [*eigenhärtendes Phenolharz*]

to resolve [*force*] · zerlegen [*Kraft*]

resolving of a force · Kraftzerlegung *f*

resonance action · Resonanzwirkung *f*

~ **frequency**, frequency of resonance · Resonanzfrequenz *f*

resonant absorbent material, ~~ system, ~ absorber [*An absorber operating by virtue of the physical resonance of some part of this structure or the air associated with it. The commonest form consists of a panel or a flexible membrane which vibrates and absorbs sound*] · Resonanz-(Schall)Absorber, *m*, Resonanz-Schallschlucker

~ **load** · Resonanzlast *f*

~ **oscillation**, ~ vibration · Resonanzschwingung *f*

resonator · Resonator *m* [*Schallabsorption*]

~ **wall** · Resonatorwand *f*

resorcinol formaldehyde adhesive, ~~ glue · Resorcin-Formaldehyd-(harz)leim *m*

~~ **resin** · Resorcin-Formaldehydharz *n*

~ **resin** · Resorcinharz *n*

respond · Blendarkaturpilaster *m*

rest bench · Ruhebank *f*

~ **room** · Ruheraum *m*

restaurant floor, ~ level; ~ storey (Brit.); ~ story (US) · Restaurantgeschoß *n*, Restaurantstockwerk *n*, Restaurantetage *f*

~~ **drive system** · Restaurant-Drehantrieb *m*

~ **for domestic passengers** · Restaurant *n* für Inlandsfluggäste

~~ **international passengers** · Restaurant *n* für Auslandsfluggäste

~ **kitchen** · Restaurationsküche *f*

~ **level**, ~ floor; ~ storey (Brit.); ~ story (US) · Restaurantgeschoß *n*, Restaurantstockwerk *n*, Restaurantetage *f*

resting place [*e.g. a stair(case) landing*] · Ruheplatz *m*

restoration · Restauration *f*, Restaurierung *f*

~ **work** · Restaurationsarbeiten *fpl*, Restaurierungsarbeiten

restorer · Restaurator *m*

to restrain, to fix · (gelenklos) einspannen

restrained · gedämpft [*Stil*]

~ **from rotating** · drehungsfrei [*Enden eines eingespannten Balken(träger)s*]

restraining system for parallel suspension cable · Rückhaltesystem *n* für Parallel-Tragseil

restraint, fixity, (immov(e)able) end ~, fixed-end ~ · unverschiebliche Einspannung *f*, feste ~, Endeinspannung

restricted height, height restriction · Höhenbeschränkung *f*

resultant (force) · Mittelkraft *f*, Resultierende *f*, Resultante *f*, Ersatzkraft

~ **load** · resultierende Last *f*

~ **pressure** · resultierender Druck *m*

retable, reredos, altar piece, altar screen · Retabel *n*, Altar~, Altaraufsatz *m*, Altarstock *m* [*Im Deutschen oft nur ,,Altar" genannt. Eine entweder auf die Mensa des katholischen Altars aufgesetzte, auf einem Zwischenstück (Predella) oder hinter diesem auf einem Unterbau stehende Schauwand, die im Mittelalter aufkam*]

(retail) shopping complex, (~) business ~, shops · (Ein)Kaufkomplex *m*, Ladenkomplex, Geschäftekomplex

(~) ~ **street**, (~) ~ parade, (~) business ~, shops street, shops parade · (Ein)Kaufstraße *f*, Ladenstraße, Geschäftsstraße

retained heat, stored ~ · gespeicherte Wärme *f*

retainer, fastener · Halter(ung) *m*, (*f*)

retaining bolt, fixing screw · Befestigungsschraube *f* [*Sie dient zur festen, aber lösbaren Verbindung von Teilen*]

to retard · verzögern [*Das Abbinden bzw. das Erhärten eines Gemisches mit einem hydraulischen Binder*]

retardation · Verzögerung *f*

~ **of set(ting)** · (Ab)Binde(zeit)verzögerung *f* [*hydraulisches Bindemittel*]

retardation time — reversely curved cable net

~ time, ~ period · Verzögerungsdauer *f*

retarded hemihydrate (gypsum-)plaster; Class B ~, (gypsum-)plaster of Class B (Brit.) [*B.S. 1191*] · verzögertes Halbhydrat *n*, verzögerter Halbhydratputzgips *m*

~ plasticized plaster (US); ~ plasticised ~ (Brit.) · Mörtelgips *m*

retarder (of set(ting)) → (set(ting)) retarder

retarding agent → (set(ting)) retarder

re-tarring · Nachteeren *n*

~ · Nachteerung *f*

retempering [*Restoring the plasticity of partially hardened concrete or mortar by adding water and remixing*] · Wiederaufbereitung *f* [*Beton; Mörtel*]

retention period, maintenance ~, ~ time · Garantiezeit *f*

to re-test · nachprüfen [*Einen Nachversuch durchführen*]

re-test · Nachprobe *f*, Nachprüfung *f*, Nachversuch *m*

reticulated masonry, ~ (~) work, opus reticulatum · Netz(mauer)werk *n*

~ tracery, reticular ~ · Netzmaßwerk *n*

retort lignite · Retortenlignit *m*

~ process · Retortenverfahren *n*

retractable roof · einziehbares Dach *n*

retro-choir, retro-quire [*The part of a major church which lies beyond the presbytery, i.e. east of the high altar (but not inlcuding the Lady Chapel)*] · Retrochor *m*

return · Rücklauf *m* [*in einer Leitung*]

~, setting back [*The side or part which falls away, usually at right angles, from the front or direct line of a structure*] · (Rück)Sprung *m*

~ air · Rückluft *f*

~ ~ duct · Rückluftkanal *m*

~ ~ grille [*sometimes spelled 'grill'*] · Rück(führ)luftgitter *n*, Rück(führ)luftrost *m*

~ ~ system · Rückluftanlage *f*

~ bend, pipe ~ ~ (Rohr)Doppelkrümmer *m*

~ cullet · Kehrbrocken *m*, Kehrscherben *m* [*Glasgemenge*]

~ duct · Rücklaufkanal *m*

~ end → ~ wall

~ line · Rücklaufleitung *f*

~ pipe · Rücklaufrohr *n*

~ side [*heat exchanger*] · Rücklaufseite *f*

~ temperature · Rücklauftemperatur *f*

~ wall, ~ end, returned corner, wing wall [*A short length of wall perpendicular to an end of a longer wall*] · Flügelwand *f*

~ water · Rücklaufwasser *n*

returned corner → return wall

re-use · Wiederverwendung *f*

reveal [*The vertical face revealed in the thickness of an opening or the depth of a recess*] · Leibung *f*

reverberant · nachhallig

~ · nachhallend

~ level, average ~, reverberation ~, ~ sound ~ · Nachhall(schall)pegel *m*

~ room, reverberation ~, ~ chamber · Nachhallraum *m*

~ sound, multi-reflected ~, reverberation ~ · Nachhallschall *m*

~ (~) absorption coefficient · Nachhall-Schluckbeiwert *m*

~ (~) field · Nachhallfeld *n*

~ (~) level, reverberation (~) ~, average (~) ~ · Nachhall(schall)pegel *m*

reverberation, water hammer, concussion [*A hammering sound caused by violent surges of pressure in water pipes*] · Wasserstoß *m*, Wasserschlag *m*, Druckstoß

~ · Nachhall *m*

~ chamber → ~ room

~ characteristic · Nachhallmerkmal *n*

~ control · Nachhallregelung *f*

~ damping · Nachhalldämpfung *f*

~ level, average ~, reverberant ~, ~ sound ~ · Nachhall(schall)pegel *m*

~ room, reverberant ~, ~ chamber · Nachhallraum *m*

~ (sound) level, reverberant (~) ~, average (~) ~ · Nachhall(schall)pegel *m*

~ (~) time · Nachhallzeit T *f*, Nachhalldauer T *f*

reversal of moment(s), moment reversal · Momentenumkehr *f*

~ ~ stress, stress reversal · Spannungsumkehr *f*

~ form · Umkehrform *f* [*Zweigelenkrahmen*]

~ ogee (moulding) (Brit.); ~ ~ (molding) (US) [*A double-curved mo(u)lding, convex above and concave below*] · steigendes Karnies *n*; steigende Karniese *f*, ~ Karnische *f* [*Österreich*]

~ rotation, counterrotation · Gegendrehung *f*

~ side, back · Rückseite *f*

reversed arch, inverted ~ · Grundbogen *m*, Gegenbogen, Konterbogen, umgekehrter Bogen, verkehrter Bogen, Erdbogen

~ system · Umkehrsystem *n*

~ vault, inverted ~ · umgekehrtes Gewölbe *n*, verkehrtes ~, überdecktes ~, Kontergewölbe, Erdgewölbe, Gegengewölbe, Grundgewölbe, Sohlengewölbe

reversely curved cable net, cable net with opposite curvature · gegensinnig gekrümmtes Seilnetz *n*

reversible fan · verstellbarer Ventilator *m*
revert scrap, home ~ · Rücklaufschrott *m*, Umlaufschrott
revibration · Nachrüttlung *f*
to revitalize; to revitalise (Brit.) · regenerieren
revived Gothic style, Gothic Revival, Neo-Gothic · posthume Gotik *f*, Neugotik, Neogotik
revolving (air)plane hangar, rotary ~ ~, rotating ~ ~ · Dreh-Flugzeughalle *f*
~ apartment tower, rotating ~ ~, rotary ~ ~ (US); ~ residence ~, ~ residential ~, ~ dwelling ~, ~ housing ~ · Dreh-Wohnhochhaus *n*, Dreh-Hochwohnhaus, Dreh-Wohnturm *m*
~ door, rotating ~, rotary ~ · Drehtür *f* [*Eine Tür, bei der sich 3 oder 4 Flügel um eine gemeinsame Achse in einem Windfanggehäuse drehen*]
~ dwelling tower → ~ apartment ~
~ floor, rotating ~, rotary ~ · Dreh(fuß)boden *m*
revolving(-floor) restaurant, rotary(-floor) ~, rotating(-floor) ~ · Drehrestaurant *n*
revolving house, rotating ~, rotary ~ · Drehhaus *n*
~ housing tower → ~ apartment ~
~ leaf, rotary ~, rotating ~ · Drehtürflügel *m*
~ platform, rotary ~, rotating ~ · Drehplattform *f*
~ position, rotary ~, rotating ~ · Drehstellung *f*
~ residence tower → ~ apartment ~
~ residential tower → ~ apartment ~
~ restaurant, rotary ~, rotating ~, ~-floor ~ · Drehrestaurant *n*
~ stage, rotating ~, rotary ~ · Drehbühne *f* [*Theater*]
to reweigh · nachwiegen
re-wettable · nachbenetzbar
rework · Nacharbeit *f*
re-zoning plan · Zonen-Neuordnungsplan *m*
rftr, rafter [*A sloping structural member extending from the eave(s) to the ridge of a roof. It may be a common rafter or a principal rafter*] · (Dach)Sparren *m*
Rh, Rockwell hardness · Rockwellhärte *f*
RH → relative humidity
RHC, rapid-hardening cement · schnell(er)härtender Zement *m*, Schnell(er)härterzement
Rheims Cathedral · Kathedrale *f* von Reims
Rhenish architecture · rheinische Architektur *f*, ~ Baukunst *f*
(~) trass, (~) terras· Traß *m*, feingemahlener (vulkanischer) Tuffstein *m*, gemahlener massiger Bimsstein [*DIN 51043 für Begriff, Eigenschaften, Prüfung und DIN 51044*

für chemische Untersuchung. Mundartliche Bezeichnungen: Duckstein; D(a)uchstein]
rheological property · rheologische Eigenschaft *f*
rheology · Rheologie *f*, Fließlehre *f*
rheopexy [*The property because of which certain materials exhibit dilatancy under small shearing stress followed by thixotropy under greater stress*] · Rheopexie *f*
rhodium plating · Rhodiumüberzug *m*
rhomb porphyry · rautenförmiger Purpurstein *m*, Rhombenporphyr *m*
rhombic dodecahedron · Rhombendodekaeder *n*
rhombicuboctahedron · entecktes und entkantetes Hexaeder *n*
rhomboidal lead spar · rhomboedrischer Bleibaryt *m*
RH(T)R, reheater · Nachwärmer *m*
rhyolite [*A volcanic rock of acid composition generally having crystals of quartz and orthoclase set in a glassy or fine-grained felsitic groundmass*] · Rhyolit *m*
rhyolitic tuff · Rhyolittuff *m*
rib · französische Leiste *f* [*Metallbedachung*]
~ · Rippe *f*
~ and block floor → hollow filler ~ ~
~ ~ ~ floor(ing) system → ~ ~ tile ~ ~
~ ~ filler (block) floor → ((pre)cast) ~ ~ ~ (~) ~
~ ~ ~ tile floor → ((pre)cast) rib and filler (block) ~
~ ~ panel vault [*A framework of ribs supports thin stone panels*] · Rippenplattengewölbe *n*
~ ~ tile floor → hollow filler block ~
~ ~ ~ floor(ing) system, ~ ~ block ~ ~, hollow filler block ~, hollow filler (tile) ~ [*See remark under 'Block'*] · Hohl(körper)decken(bau)system *n*, Hohl(körper)deckenkonstruktion(ssystem) *f*, (*n*)
~ cross section · Rippenquerschnitt *m*
~ depth · Rippenhöhe *f*
~ footing, arch ~ ~ · (Bogen)Rippenfundament *n*
~ forms → rib(bed) ~
~ form(work) → rib(bed) ~
~ heater → strip ~
~ heating pipe → fin(ned) ~ ~
rib-intersection · Rippenschnittpunkt *m*
rib interval, ~ spacing, distance between ribs · Rippenabstand *m*
ribless · rippenfrei, rippenlos
rib loading · Rippenbelastung *f*
~ of column, column rib · Säulenrippe *f*
~ oval wire, ribbed ~ ~ · gerippter Ovaldraht *m*, Ovalrippendraht

rib pipe — ribbed rag felt

~ **pipe** → fin(ned) ~
rib-profile, profile of rib · Rippenprofil *n*
rib profile → rib(bed) ~
~ **roof,** ribbed ~ · französisches Leistendach *n*
~ **section** → rib(bed) ~
~ **shape** → rib(bed) ~
~ **shuttering** → rib(bed) ~
~ **slope** · Rippenneigung *f*
~ **spacing,** ~ interval, distance between ribs · Rippenabstand *m*
rib-span forms, ~ shuttering, ~ formwork · Rippendeckenschalung *f*
rib-strengthened · rippenversteift
rib system · Rippennetz *n*, Rippensystem *n*, Rippenwerk *n*
~ **tile** → (anti-slip) rib(bed) ~
~ **trim** → rib(bed) ~
~ **unit** → rib(bed) ~
~ **valley** · Rippenkehle *f*
rib-vaulted c(h)ancel → cross-~ ~
~ **church** · Rippengewölbekirche *f*
~ **construction** · Rippengewölbebau *m*
~ **edifice** · Rippengewölbebau(werk) *m*, (*n*)
ribbed · gerippt
rib(bed) arch · Rippenbogen *m*
~ **bar,** ~ re-~, ~ rod · Rippenstab *m* [*Bewehrung*]
~ **bars** → ~ (re-)bars
~ **beam** · Rippenbalken(träger) *m*
~ ~ **floor** · Balken(träger)-Rippendecke *f*
~ **(clay) brick floor** · Ziegelrippendecke *f*
~ **(~) ~ panel** · Rippentafel *f* [*Ziegelmontagebau*]
~ **cupola,** ~ dome · Rippenkuppel *f*
~ **dome,** ~ cupola · Rippenkuppel *f*
~ **duplex tube,** fin(ned) ~ ~, g(r)illed ~ ~ · Duplex-Rippenrohr *n*, Duplex-Lamellenrohr, beripptes Duplexrohr
~ **EM,** ~ XPM, ~, expanded metal, ~ (expanded (metal) mesh · Rippenstreckmetall *n*
~ ~ **ceiling,** ~ XPM ~, ~ expanded metal ~, ~ expanded (metal) mesh ~ · Rippenstreckmetalldecke *f*
~ **(expanded) (metal) mesh lath(ing),** ~ XPM ~, ~ EM ~, metal rib ~ · Rippen(streckmetall)putzträger *m*
~ ~ **(~) ~ reinforcement,** ~ XPM ~, ~ EM ~ · Rippenstreckmetallarmierung *f*, Rippenstreckmetallbewehrung, Rippenstreckmetalleinlagen *fpl*
~ **extrusion,** extruded rib shape, extruded rib section, extruded rib trim, extruded rib unit · stranggepreßtes Rippenprofil *n*, Strangpreß-Rippenprofil

~ **floor** · Rippendecke *f* [*In Rippen aufgelöstes System einer Betondecke; die Rippen werden an der Oberseite durch eine Druckplatte miteinander verbunden*]
~ ~ **slab** · Rippendeckenplatte *f*
~ ~ **with in(-)situ (cast) ribs** · Rippendecke *f* mit Ortbetonrippen [*DIN 4225. Eine Decke, deren Rippen im Mittenabstand von höchstens 1,25 m am Ort betoniert sind, während die Druckplatte aus Zwischenbauteilen besteht*]
~ ~ ~ ~ (~) **structural topping** · Rippendecke *f* mit Ortbeton(druck)platte [*DIN 4225. Decke aus Stahlbeton-Fertigbalken im Mittenabstand von höchstens 1,25 m, deren Druckplatte am Ort auf Schalung oder Zwischenbauteilen betoniert wird*]
~ ~ ~ ~ **slabs** [*The slabs fill the spaces between the ribs*] · Rippendecke *f* mit plattenförmigen Zwischenbauteilen, ~ Füllplatten [*DIN 4225*]
~ **forms,** ~ shuttering, ~ form(work) · Rippenschalung *f*
~ **form(work),** ~ forms, ~ shuttering · Rippenschalung *f*
~ **girder** · Rippenträger *m*
~ **glass** · Rippenglas *n*, geripptes Glas, gestreiftes Glas
~ **half cupola,** ~ ~ dome · Rippenhalbkuppel *f*
~ ~ **dome,** ~ ~ cupola · Rippenhalbkuppel *f*
~ **heater,** g(r)illed ~, (fin(ned)) strip ~ · Rippenheizkörper *m*, berippter Heizkörper, Lamellenheizkörper
~ **heating tube,** g(r)illed ~ ~, (fin(ned)) strip ~ ~ · Rippenheizrohr *n*, beripptes Heizrohr, Lamellenheizrohr
~ **(heavy) plate** · Rippen(grob)blech *n*
~ **indented bar,** indented ribbed ~ · Nockenrippenstab *m*, Nori-Stab
~ ~ **bars** → indented ribbed ~
~ **joint** · französische Leistenverbindung *f* [*Metallbedachung*]
~ **(metal) lath(ing)** → ~ expanded (~) ~
~ ~ **wall** · Rippenmetallwand *f*
~ **oval wire** · gerippter Ovaldraht *m*, Ovalrippendraht
~ **perforated metal,** ~ pierced ~ · Rippelochmetall *n*
~ **pipe,** (fin)ned)) strip ~, g(r)illed ~ · Rippenrohr *n*, beripptes Rohr, Lamellenrohr
~ ~ **heater,** (fin(ned)) strip ~ ~, g(r)illed ~ ~ · Rippenrohrheizkörper *m*
~ **plate,** ~ slab, T(ee)-beam ~, concrete joist construction · Rippenplatte *f*
~ ~, ~ heavy ~ · Rippen(grob)blech *n*
~ **profile,** ~ trim, ~ shape, ~ section, ~ unit · Rippenprofil *n* [*Erzeugnis*]
~ **rag felt,** ~ wool ~ · Rippen(wollfilz)pappe *f*

ribbed (re-)bar — ridge board

~ **(re-)bar**, ~ rod · Rippenstab *m* [*Bewehrung*]

~ **(re-)bars**, ~ (steel reinforcing) bars, ~ steel (reinforcing) rods · quergerippter Betonformstahl *m*, Queri *m*, (Beton)Rippenstahl, Querrippenstahl [*Die gleichmäßig auf die ganze Stablänge verteilten Querrippen stehen rechtwink(e)lig zur Stabachse und erstrecken sich über den ganzen Stabumfang*]

~ **rod**, ~ (re-)bar · Rippenstab *m* [*Bewehrung*]

~ **roof** · französisches Leistendach *n*

~ ~ **cladding** → batten (seam) roof(ing)

~ **rubber flooring** · Rippen-Gummi-(fuß)boden(belag) *m*

~ **seam**, batten ~ · Leistenfalz *m* [*Metallbedachung*]

~ **(~) roof cladding** → batten (seam) roof(ing)

~ **(~) ~ covering** → batten (seam) roof(ing)

~ **(~) ~ sheathing** → batten (seam) roof(ing)

~ **(~) roof(ing)** → · batten (~) ~

~ **section**, ~ trim, ~ unit, ~ shape, ~ profile · Rippenprofil *n* [*Erzeugnis*]

~ **shape**, ~ profile, ~ trim, ~ section, ~ unit · Rippenprofil *n* [*Erzeugnis*]

~ **shuttering**, ~ form(work), ~ forms · Rippenschalung *f*

~ **slab**, T(ee)-beam ~, ~ plate, concrete joist construction · Rippenplatte *f*

~ **steel** · Rippenstahl *m*

~ ~ **pantile** · Rippen-Stahldachpfanne *f*

~ ~ **(reinforcing) rods**, ~ (~ ~) bars, ~ (re-)bars · quergerippter Betonformstahl *m*, Queri *m*, (Beton)Rippenstahl, Querrippenstahl [*Die gleichmäßig auf die ganze Stablänge verteilten Querrippen stehen rechtwink(e)lig zur Stabachse und erstrecken sich über den ganzen Stabumfang*]

~ **surface** · gerippte Oberfläche *f*, Rippenoberfläche

~ **tile** → anti-slip ~ ~

~ **timber cupola**, ~ ~ dome, ~ wood(en) ~ · Holz-Rippenkuppel *f*

~ ~ **dome**, ~ ~ cupola, ~ wood(en) ~ · Holz-Rippenkuppel *f*

~ **trim**, ~ unit, ~ shape, ~ profile, ~ section · Rippenprofil *n* [*Erzeugnis*]

~ **tube**, (fin(ned)) strip ~, g(r)illed ~ · berippte Röhre *f*, Rippenröhre, Lamellenröhre

~ ~ **economiser** · Rippenrohreko(nomiser) *m*, Rippenrohr-Rauchgas-Wasservorwärmer *m*

~ ~ **heater** → fin(ned) ~ ~

~ ~ **radiator** → fin(ned) tube heater

~ **unit**, ~ shape, ~ profile, ~ section, ~ trim · Rippenprofil *n* [*Erzeugnis*]

~ **vault** · Rippengewölbe *n*

~ **wood(en) cupola**, ~ ~ dome, ~ timber ~ · Holz-Rippenkuppel *f*

~ ~ **dome**, ~ ~ cupola, ~ timber ~ · Holz-Rippenkuppel *f*

~ **wool felt**, ~ rag ~ · Rippen(wollfilz)-pappe *f*

~ **XPM**, ~ EM, ~ expanded metal, ~ expanded (metal) mesh · Rippenstreckmetall *n*

~ **XPM ceiling**, ~ EM ~, ~ expanded metal ~, ~ expanded (metal) mesh ~ · Rippenstreckmetalldecke *f*

ribbing · Rippenkonstruktion *f*

~ · Rippung *f*

ribbon [*A narrow strip of wood or other material used in formwork*] · Schal(ungs)leiste *f*

~, **flake** · Filmspan *m* [*DIN 53155*]

~ **and round-tower housing estate** · Bandwurm- und Rundturmsied(e)lung *f*

~ **building**, ~ development · Bandbebauung *f*

~ **clip** · Bandschelle *f*

~ **development**, ~ building · Bandbebauung *f*

~ **gneiss**, banded ~ · Lagengneis *m*, Bändergneis

rice husk [*Rice husks are used as a lightweight aggregate*] · Reisschale *f*

~ **starch** · Reisstärke *f*

~ ~ **paste** · Reisstärkekleister *m*

rich concrete, cement-~ ~, fat ~ · fetter Beton *m*, zementreicher ~

~ **lime** → high-calcium ~

~ ~ **mortar**, pure ~ ~, white ~ ~, high-calcium ~ ~ · Weißkalkmörtel *m*

~ ~ **paste** → high-calium lime putty

~ ~ **putty** → high-calcium ~ ~

~ **lump lime**, white ~ ~, pure ~ ~, high-calcium ~ ~ · Weißstück(en)kalk *m* [*DIN 1060*]

~ **mix(ture)**, fat ~ [*A mix(ture) with a high proportion of binder*] · fette Mischung *f*, fettes Gemisch *n*

~ **mortar**, fat ~ · fetter Mörtel *m*, Fettmörtel

~ **quicklime**, pure ~, white ~, high-calcium ~ · Weißbranntkalk *m*

richly adorned with sculptures, lavishly sculptured, profusely sculptured · skulpturenreich

~ **decorated**, ~ ornamented, highly ~ · reich geziert, ~ geschmückt, ~ verziert

~ **ornamented**, highly ~, ~ decorated · reich geziert, ~ geschmückt, ~ verziert

richness of detail · Detailreichtum *m*

ridge, ~ line [*The horizontal line formed by the junction of two sloping areas of a roof*] · (Dach)First(linie) *m*, (*f*), (Dach-)Förste *f*

~ **beam**, ~ piece · Firstbalken(träger) *m*

~ **board**, ~ piece [*The piece of timber along the line of the ridge, against which rest the upper ends of the sloping rafters*] · Firststück *n*, Firstbrett *n*

ridge capping — rigid expanded polyester

~ **capping**, ~ covering · Firstabdeckung f

~ ~ **tile**, ~ cover(ing) ~, ridging ~ · Firstkappe f, Firsthaube f, Firstrundziegel m

~ **channel** · Firstwinkel m [*Stahldach*]

~ **corner tile** · Firstdecke f

~ **cover tile** → ~ capping ~

~ **covering**, ~ capping · Firstabdeckung f

~ **cover(ing) tile** → ~ capping ~

~ **crest(ing)**, (roof) ~ [*A line of ornament on the ridge of a roof*] · (Dach-)Firstbekrönung f, (Dach)Firstkrone f, (Dach)Firstverzierung, Dachkamm m

~ **extract ventilation** · First(ent)lüftung f

~ ~ ~ **unit** → ~ ventilator

~ **extraction unit** → ~ ventilator

~ **extractor** → ~ ventilator

~ **folding** · Firstfaltung f

~ **form** · Firstausbildung f, Firstgestaltung, Firstform f

~ **girder** · Firstträger m

~ **gusset plate** · Lasche f [*Dach*]

~ **height** · Firsthöhe f

~ **(line)** [*The horizontal line formed by the junction of two sloping areas of a roof*] · (Dach)First(linie) m, (f), (Dach)Förste f

~ **piece**, ~ board [*The piece of timber along the line of the ridge, against which rest the upper ends of the sloping rafters*] · Firststück n, Firstbrett n

~ ~, ~ **beam** · Firstbalken(träger) m

~ **point** · Firstpunkt m

~ **purlin(e)** · Firstpfette f, Scheitelpfette, Firstbaum m

~ ~ **support** · Firstpfettenauflager n, Scheitelpfettenauflager, Firstbaumauflager

~ **rib**, axial ~ · Scheitelrippe f [*Sie verläuft entlang der Scheitellinie eines Gewölbes. Die Scheitelrippe kommt meistens beim Fächergewölbe, Strahlengewölbe und Palmengewölbe der englischen Baukunst vor*]

~ **shingle** · Firstschindel f

~ **starting tile**, starting ridge ~ · Firstanfänger m, Walmanfänger f [*Der Ausdruck ,,Walmanfänger'' wird auch für den Gratanfänger verwendet*]

~ **tile** · Dachkenner m, Walmstein m, Firststein, Kammstein m [*Der Ausdruck ,,Walmstein'' wird auch für den Gratstein verwendet*]

ridge-to-ridge folding · First-zu-First-Faltung f

ridge-to-valley folding · First-zu-Kehle-Faltung f

ridge-type rooflight · Firstoberlicht n

~ **skylight** · Firstraupe f

ridge ventilator, ~ extractor, ~ extraction unit, ~ extract ventilation unit · First(ent)lüfter m

ridging · First(ein)decken n, First(ein)deckung f

~ **tile** → ridge capping ~

Rieppel girder · dreiwandiger Träger m, Rieppelträger

riffler [*A rasp bent for abrading concave surfaces*] · Raspel f für konkave Flächen

rifle range · Gewehrschießstand m

rigger [*A man who erects and maintains lifting tackle, hand-operated derricks, ropes, slings, cradles and other scaffoldings*] · Monteur m

~ [*A man who erects tubular or other metal scaffolding*] · Metallgerüstbauer m

rigger's scaffold(ing) · Monteurgerüst n, Monteurrüstung f

right-angled valve, angle (shut-off) ~ · Eck(absperr)ventil n [*Ventil, bei dem die Ablaufrichtung um 90° gegen die Zulaufrichtung gedreht ist*]

right-hand designation · Rechtsbezeichnung f

~ **door** · Rechtstür f, rechts aufschlagende Tür

~ **handrail** · Rechtsgeländer n

~ **hinge** · Rechtsband n [*Beschlag für Fenster und Türen*]

~ **lock** · rechtes Schloß n, Schloß DIN rechts

right stair(case), ~ stairway, right-hand ~ · Rechtstreppe f

rightward skew slab · rechtsschiefe Platte f

rigid, no-hinged, hingeless, fixed, encastré, with fixed ends, without articulations, encastered · eingespannt, gelenklos [*Bogen; Träger; Stütze; Balken(träger); Rahmen(tragwerk)*]

~ → flexurally ~

~ **arch** [*A continuous arch which is fully fixed throughout*] · (voll)eingespannter Bogen m

~ **bearing**, ~ support · starre Auflagerung f, steife ~, starres Auflagern n, steifes Auflagern

~ **concrete frame** · Betonsteifrahmen m, Betonstarrahmen

~ **connection** → ~ joint

~ **construction(al) system**, ~ (structural) ~, ~ construction · starres Bausystem n, steifes ~, ~ (Konstruktions-) System, starre Konstruktion f, steife Konstruktion

~ **core**, stiff ~ · steifer Kern m, starrer ~

~ **(end-)restraint** · starre Einspannung f, steife ~

~ **expanded phenol(ic) resin**, ~ foam ~ ~, ~ phenol(ic) resin foam · Phenolharzhartschaum(stoff) m, starrer Phenolharzschaum(stoff)

~ ~ **polyester**, ~ foam ~, ~ polyester foam · Polyesterhartschaum(stoff) m, starrer Polyesterschaum(stoff)

rigid expanded polyvinyl chloride — rigid foam plastic... 836

~ ~ **polyvinyl chloride** → expanded rigid PVC

~ ~ **PVC** → expanded rigid ~

~ ~ **foam** → ~ ~ plastic

~ ~ **adhesive** → ~ ~ bonding ~

~ ~ **block**, ~ ~ tile, [*See remark under 'Block'*] · Hartschaum(stoff)block(stein) *m*, Hartschaum(stoff)stein

~ ~ **board** → ~ foam plastic sheet

~ ~ **(bonding) adhesive**, ~ ~ ~ agent, ~ ~ ~ medium, ~ ~ cement(ing agent) · Hartschaumkleb(e)stoff *m*, Hartschaumkleb(e)mittel *n*, Hartschaumkleber *m*

~ ~ **(building) component** → ~ ~ (~) unit

~ ~ **(~) insulating board** → ~ ~ plastic ~ ~

~ ~ **(~) ~ sheet** → ~ ~ plastic insulating board

~ ~ **(~) ~ slab** → ~ ~ plastic insulating board

~ ~ **(~) member** → ~ ~ (~) unit

~ ~ **(~) unit**, ~ ~ (~) component, ~ ~ (~) member · Hartschaum(stoff)-(bau)element *n*, Hartschaum(stoff)-(bau)körper *m* [*Fehlnamen: Hartschaum(stoff)(bau)einheit f*]

~ ~ **ceiling board** → ~ ~ plastic ~ ~

~ ~ ~ **sheet** → ~ ~ plastic ceiling board

~ ~ **cement(ing agent)** → ~ ~ (bonding) adhesive

~ ~ **component** → ~ ~ (building) unit

~ ~ **core** → ~ ~ plastic ~

~ ~ **core(d) wall panel** · Hartschaumkernwandtafel *f*

~ ~ **decorative board** → ~ ~ plastic ~ ~

~ ~ ~ **sheet** → ~ ~ plastic decorative board

~ ~ **fill(ing)** · Hartschaum-Füllung *f*, Hartschaumstoffüllung

~ ~ **insulant** → ~ ~ plastic insulating material

~ ~ **insulating board** → ~ ~ plastic ~ ~

~ ~ ~ **material** → ~ ~ ~ plastic ~ ~

~ ~ **(~) roof(ing) board**, ~ ~ (insulation(-grade)) ~, ~ ~ (~) ~ sheet · Hartschaum(stoff)-Dach(isolier)platte *f*

~ ~ ~ **sheet** → ~ ~ plastic insulating board

~ ~ ~ **slab** → ~ ~ plastic insulating board

~ ~ **insulator** → ~ ~ plastic insulating material

~ ~ **laminate(d) board**, ~ ~ ~ sheet · Hartschaum-Schichtplatte *f*, Hartschaum(stoff)-Schichtplatte

~ ~ **member** → ~ ~ (building) unit

~ ~ **ornamental board** → ~ ~ plastic decorative ~

~ ~ ~ **sheet** → ~ ~ plastic decorative board

~ ~ **phenol(ic) resin**, ~ expanded ~ ~, ~ phenol(ic) resin foam · Phenolharzhartschaum(stoff) *m*, starrer Phenolharzschaum(stoff)

~ ~ **plastic**, ~ expanded ~, ~ (plastic) foam · Hartkunstharzschaum(stoff) *m*, Hartschaum(kunst)stoff, (Kunststoff-) Hartschaum *m*, Hartkunst(stoff)schaum (stoff), starrer Schaum

~ ~ ~ **board** → ~ ~ ~ ~ sheet

~ ~ ~ **ceiling board**, ~ ~ ~ ~ sheet, ~ expanded ~ ~ ~, ~ (plastic) foam ~ ~ · Hartkunstharzschaum(stoff)-Deckenplatte *f*, Hartschaum(kunst)stoff-Deckenplatte, (Kunststoff)Hartschaum-Deckenplatte, Hartkunst(stoff)schaum(stoff)-Deckenplatte

~ ~ ~ **core**, ~ expanded ~ ~, ~ (plastic) foam ~ · Hartschaum(kunst)-stoffkern *m*, (Kunststoff)Hartschaumkern, Hartkunst(stoff)schaum(stoff)-kern, Hartkunstharzschaum(stoff)kern

~ ~ ~ **decorative board**, ~ expanded ~ ~, ~ ~ ~ ~ sheet, ~ ~ ~ ornamental ~, ~ (plastic) foam ~ ~ · Hartschaum(kunst)stoff-Sichtplatte *f*, (Kunststoff)Hartschaum-Sichtplatte, Hartkunst(stoff)schaum(stoff)-Sichtplatte, Hartkunstharzschaum(stoff)-Sichtplatte, Hartschaum(kunst)stoff-Ornamentplatte, Hartschaum(kunst)stoff-Dekor(ations)platte, (Kunststoff-)Hartschaum-Ornamentplatte, (Kunststoff)-Hartschaum-Dekor(ations)platte, Hartkunst(stoff)schaum(stoff)-Zierplatte, Hartkunst(stoff)schaum(stoff)-Ornamentplatte, Hartkunst(stoff)-schaum(stoff)-Dekor(ations)platte, Hartkunstharzschaum(stoff)-Zierplatte, Hartkunstharzschaum(stoff)-Ornamentplatte, Hartkunstharzschaum(stoff)-Dekor(ations)platte

~ ~ ~ **insulant** → ~ ~ ~ ~ insulating material

~ ~ ~ **insulating board**, ~ ~ ~ insulation(-grade) ~, ~ ~ ~ ~ sheet, ~ ~ ~ ~ slab, ~ expanded ~ ~ ~, ~ foam (building) ~ ~, ~ (plastic) foam ~ ~ · Hartkunst(stoff)schaum(stoff)-Isolierplatte *f*, Kunstharzschaum(stoff)-Isolierplatte, Hartschaum(stoff)-Isolier(bau)platte, (Kunststoff)Hartschaum-Isolierplatte

~ ~ ~ **material**, ~ ~ ~ insulation(-grade) ~, ~ expanded ~ ~ ~, ~ ~ ~ insulator, ~ ~ ~ insulant, ~ (plastic) foam insulating material, ~ (plastic) foam insulation(-grade) material, ~ (plastic) foam insulator, ~ (plastic) foam insulant · Hartschaum(kunst)-stoff-Dämmstoff *m*, (Kunststoff-)Hartschaum-Dämmstoff, Hartkunst(stoff)schaum-Dämmstoff, Hartkunstharzschaum(stoff)-Dämmstoff, Hartschaum(stoff)-Dämmaterial *n*, Hartschaum(stoff)-Dämmstoff

~ ~ ~ **ornamental board** → ~ ~ ~ decorative ~

~ ~ ~ ~ **sheet** → ~ ~ ~ decorative board

~ ~ ~ **sheet,** ~ ~ ~ board, ~ expanded ~ ~, ~ (plastic) foam ~ · Hartschaum-(kunst)stoffplatte f, (Kunststoff)Hartschaumplatte, Hartkunst(stoff)schaum-(stoff)platte, Hartkunstharzschaum-(stoff)platte

~ ~ **polyester,** ~ expanded ~, ~ polyester foam · Polyesterhartschaum(stoff) m, starrer Polyesterschaum(stoff)

~ ~ **polystyrene,** ~ polystyrene foam · Polystyrol-Hartschaum(stoff) m, starrer Polystyrolschaum(stoff)

~ ~ **roof(ing) board** → ~ ~ ~ insulating ~ ~

~ ~ **sheet** → ~ ~ ~ plastic ~

~ ~ **tile,** ~ ~ ~ block [See remark under 'Block'] · Hartschaum(stoff)block(stein) m, Hartschaum(stoff)stein

~ ~ **unit** → ~ ~ ~ building ~

~ ~ **wallboard** · Hartschaum(stoff)-Wand(bau)platte f

~ **foamed polyvinyl chloride** → expanded rigid PVC

~ ~ **PVC** → expanded rigid ~

~ **foundation** · starre Gründung f, steife ~

~ **frame, stiff(-jointed)** ~ · starrer Rahmen m, Steifrahmen

~ ~ **formula** · Steifrahmenformel f

~ ~ **foundation,** Vierendeel truss ~ · Vierendeelträgergründung f

~ ~ **slab, stiff(-jointed)** ~ ~ · Steifrahmenplatte f

~ **insulating foam,** ~ insulation (-grade) ~ · Dämmhartschaum(stoff) m, Hartdämmschaum(stoff)

~ **insulation,** board ~, ~ thermal ~ · (Hart)Platten(wärme)dämmung f

~ **insulation(-grade) material,** ~ insulating ~, ~ insulator, ~ insulant · Hartdämmaterial n, Hartdämmstoff m

~ **joint, stiff** ~, ~ connection · (biege-) steifer Knoten(punkt) m, ~ Anschluß m, (biege)steife Verbindung f, Steifknoten(punkt) [Die (biege)steife Verbindung eines Stabes an einen zweiten oder an mehreren Stäben]

rigid-jointed, stiff-jointed · steif(knotig), starr

~ **flat frame,** ~ plane ~, ~ planar ~, stiff-jointed ~ ~ · steifknotiger ebener Rahmen m, ebener steifknotiger ~, ebener Rahmen mit starren Ecken

(rigid) nodal point, (~) node ~, joint · (Skelett)Knoten(punkt) m, Gerippeknoten(punkt), Rahmenknoten(punkt), starrer Knoten(punkt), starre Knotenverbindung f

~ **phenol(ic) resin foam,** ~ foam phenol(ic) resin, ~ expanded phenol(ic) resin · Phenolharzhartschaum(stoff) m, starrer Phenolharzschaum(stoff)

~ **plastic** · Hartkunststoff m, starrer Kunststoff

~ (~) **foam** → ~ foam plastic

~ (~) ~ **board** → ~ foam plastic sheet

~ (~) ~ **ceiling board** → ~ foam plastic ~ ~

~ (~) ~ **core** → ~ foam plastic ~

~ (~) ~ **decorative board** → ~ foam plastic ~ ~

~ (~) ~ **insulant** → ~ foam plastic insulation material

~ (~) ~ **insulating board** → ~ foam plastic ~ ~

~ (~) ~ ~ **material** → ~ foam plastic ~ ~

~ (~) ~ ~ **sheet** → ~ foam plastic insulating board

~ (~) ~ ~ **slab** → ~ foam plastic insulating board

~ (~) ~ **insulator** → ~ foam plastic insulating material

~ (~) ~ **ornamental board** → ~ foam plastic decorative ~

~ (~) ~ **sheet** → ~ foam plastic ~

~ ~ **sandwich panel** · Hartkunststoff-Dreilagenplatte f, Hartkunststoff-Dreischichtenplatte

~ ~ **tube** · Hartkunststoffröhre f

~ **polyester foam,** ~ expanded polyester, ~ foam polyester · Polyesterhartschaum(stoff) m, starrer Polyesterschaum(stoff)

~ **polyethylene,** ~ polythene · Hartpolyäthylen n

~ ~ **pipe,** ~ polythene ~ · Hartpolyäthylenrohr n, Hart-PE-Rohr [DIN 8074 Maße; DIN 8075 Technische Lieferbedingungen]

~ **polystyrene foam,** ~ foam polystyrene · Polystyrol-Hartschaum(stoff) m, starrer Polystyrolschaum(stoff)

~ **polythene,** ~ polyethylene · Hartpolyäthylen n

~ ~ **pipe,** ~ polyethylene ~ · Hartpolyäthylenrohr n, Hart-PE-Rohr [DIN 8074 Maße; DIN 8075 Technische Lieferbedingungen]

~ **polyurethane foam,** polyurethane rigid ~, eypanded rigid polyurethane · Polyurethanhartschaum(stoff) m, Hartpolyurethanschaum(stoff), PUR-Hartschaum(stoff), starrer Polyurethanschaum(stoff)

~ **poly(vinyl),** ~ PVC, ~ vinyl · Hart-PVC n, Hart-Polyvinylchlorid n

~ ~ **chloride foam** → expanded rigid PVC

~ ~ **corrugated sheet(ing),** ~ vinyl ~ ~, ~ PVC ~ ~ · Hart-PVC-Wellbahn f

~ ~ **drain(age) pipe,** ~ PVC ~ ~, ~ vinyl ~ ~, ~ ~ draining ~, ~ ~ discharge ~, ~ ~ waste (~) · Hart-PVC-Abflußrohr n, Hart-PVC-Ablaufrohr, Hart-PVC-Entwässerungsrohr, Hart-PVC-Dränrohr [Fehlnamen: Hart-PVC-Ablauf m, Hart-PVC-Abfluß]

rigid poly(vinyl) extrusion — rigid vinyl pressure pipe 838

~ ~ **extrusion,** ~ PVC ~, ~ vinyl ~ · Hart-PVC-Strangprofil n

~ ~ **fitting** → ~ ~ pipe ~

~ ~ **jamb liner,** ~ vinyl ~ ~, ~ PVC ~ ~ · Hart-PVC-Gewändeauskleidung f

~ ~ **light-admitting board** → ~ vinyl ~ ~

~ ~ **pipe** → ~ vinyl ~

~ ~ **(~) fitting,** ~ PVC (~) ~, ~ vinyl (~) ~ · Hart-PVC-Fitting m, Hart-PVC-Rohrverbindungsstück n, Hart-PVC-(Rohr)Formstück [*DIN 19531*]

~ ~ **pressure pipe,** ~ PVC ~ ~, ~ vinyl ~ ~ · Hart-PVC-Druckrohr n

~ ~ **strip for outlining patterns,** ~ PVC ~ ~ ~ ~, ~ vinyl ~ ~ ~ ~ · Hart-PVC-Terrazzostreifen m, Hart-PVC-Terrazzoschiene f

~ ~ **tile,** ~ vinyl ~, ~ PVC ~ · Hart-PVC-Fliese f, Hart-PVC-Platte f

~ ~ **wall lining** → ~ vinyl ~ ~

~ ~ **waste (pipe)** → ~ ~ drain(age) ~

~ ~ **window,** ~ PVC ~, ~ vinyl ~ · Hart-PVC-Fenster n

~ ~ ~ **fitting** → ~ vinyl window furniture

~ ~ ~ **fittings** → ~ vinyl window hardware

~ ~ ~ **furniture** → ~ vinyl ~ ~

~ ~ ~ **hardware** → ~ vinyl ~ ~

~ **portal (frame)** · Steifportalrahmen, starrer Portalrahmen

~ **prestressed (concrete) frame,** prestressed (concrete) rigid ~ · Spannbeton-Steifrahmen m, starrer Spannbetonrahmen

~ **PVC,** ~ vinyl, ~ poly(vinyl) · Hart-PVC n, Hart-Polyvinylchlorid n

~ ~ **corrugated sheet(ing),** ~ vinyl ~ ~, ~ poly ~ ~ · Hart-PVC-Wellbahn f

~ ~ **discharge pipe** → ~ poly drain(age) ~

~ ~ **drain(age) pipe** → ~ poly ~ ~

~ ~ **extrusion,** ~ poly ~, ~ vinyl ~ · Hart-PVC-Strangprofil n

~ ~ **fitting** → ~ poly (pipe) ~

~ ~ **foam** → expanded rigid PVC

~ ~ **jamb liner,** ~ poly ~, ~ vinyl ~ ~ · Hart-PVC-Gewändeauskleidung f

~ ~ **light-admitting board** → ~ vinyl ~ ~

~ ~ **pipe** → ~ vinyl ~

~ ~ **(~) fitting** → ~ poly (~) ~

~ ~ **pressure pipe,** ~ vinyl ~ ~, ~ poly ~ ~ · Hart-PVC-Druckrohr n

~ ~ **strip for outlining patterns,** ~ poly ~ ~ ~ ~, ~ vinyl ~ ~ ~ ~ · Hart-PVC-Terrazzostreifen m, Hart-PVC-Terrazzoschiene f

~ ~ **tile,** ~ poly ~, ~ vinyl ~ · Hart-PVC-Fliese f, Hart-PVC-Platte f

~ ~ **wall lining** → ~ vinyl ~ ~

~ ~ **waste (pipe)** → ~ ~ poly drain(age) ~

~ ~ **window,** ~ poly ~, ~ vinyl ~ · Hart-PVC-Fenster n

~ ~ ~ **fitting** → ~ vinyl window furniture

~ ~ ~ **fittings** → ~ vinyl window hardware

~ ~ ~ **furniture** → ~ vinyl ~ ~

~ ~ ~ **hardware** → ~ vinyl ~ ~

~ **restraint** → ~ end-restraint

~ **shell** · starre Schale f, steife ~

~ **solution** · strenge (Auf)Lösung f

~ **(structural) system,** ~ construction(al), ~ construction · starres Bausystem n, steifes ~, ~ (Konstruktions-) System, starre Konstruktion f, steife Konstruktion

~ **structure,** stiff ~ · starres Bauwerk n, steifes ~

~ **support,** ~ bearing · starre Auflagerung f, steife ~, starres Auflagern n, steifes Auflagern

~ **system,** ~ structural ~, ~ construction(al) ~, ~ construction · starres Bausystem n, steifes ~, ~ (Konstruktions)System, starre Konstruktion f, steife Konstruktion

~ **theory** · strenge Theorie f

~ **vinyl,** ~ poly(vinyl), ~ PVC · Hart-PVC n, Hart-Polyvinylchlorid n

~ ~ **corrugated sheet(ing),** ~ poly(-vinyl) ~ ~, ~ PVC ~ ~ · Hart-PVC-Wellbahn f

~ ~ **discharge pipe** → ~ poly(vinyl) drain(age) ~

~ ~ **drain(age) pipe** → ~ poly(vinyl) ~ ~

~ ~ **draining pipe** → ~ poly(vinyl) drain(age) ~

~ ~ **extrusion,** ~ poly(vinyl) ~, ~ PVC ~ · Hart-PVC-Strangprofil n

~ ~ **fitting** → ~ poly(vinyl) (pipe) ~

~ ~ **jamb liner,** ~ poly(vinyl) ~ ~, ~ PVC ~ ~ · Hart-PVC-Gewändeauskleidung f

~ ~ **light-admitting board,** ~ ~ ~ sheet, ~ poly(vinyl) ~ ~, ~ PVC ~ ~ · Hart-PVC-Lichtplatte f

~ ~ ~ **sheet** → ~ ~ board

~ ~ **pipe,** ~ poly(vinyl) ~, ~ PVC ~ · Hart-PVC-Rohr n [*DIN 19531 für Abwasserleitungen innerhalb von Gebäuden; DIN 19532 für Trinkwasserversorgung; DIN 1187 für Dränrohre; DIN 6660 für Rohrpostanlagen; DIN 8061 Allgemeine Güteanforderungen und Prüfung; DIN 8062 Maße und DIN 16929 Chemische Beständigkeit*]

~ ~ **(~) fitting** → ~ poly(vinyl) (~) ~

~ ~ **pressure pipe,** ~ poly(vinyl) ~ ~, ~ PVC ~ ~ · Hart-PVC-Druckrohr n

839 rigid vinyl strip for outlining patterns — rise-to-span ratio

~ ~ **strip for outlining patterns**, ~ poly(vinyl) ~ ~ ~, ~ PVC ~ ~ ~ ~ · Hart-PVC-Terrazzostreifen m, Hart-PVC-Terrazzoschiene f

~ ~ **tile**, ~ poly(vinyl) ~, ~ PVC ~ · Hart-PVC-Fliese f, Hart-PVC-Platte

~ ~ **wall lining**, ~ poly(vinyl) ~ ~, ~ PVC ~ ~, ~ ~ ~ (sur)facing · Hart-PVC-Wandauskleidung f, Hart-PVC-Wandverkleidung, Hart-PVC-Wandbekleidung

~ ~ ~ **(sur)facing** → ~ ~ ~ lining

~ ~ **waste (pipe)** → ~ poly(vinyl) drain(age) ~

~ ~ **window**, ~ poly(vinyl) ~, ~ PVC ~ · Hart-PVC-Fenster n

~ ~ ~ **fitting** → ~ ~ ~ furniture

~ ~ ~ **fittings** → ~ ~ ~ hardware

~ ~ ~ **furniture**, ~ poly(vinyl) ~ ~, ~ PVC ~ ~, ~ ~ ~ fitting · Hart-PVC-Fensterbeschlag m

~ ~ ~ **hardware**, ~ poly(vinyl) ~ ~, ~ PVC ~ ~, ~ ~ ~ fittings · Hart-PVC-Fensterbeschläge mpl

rigidity, stiffness · Starrheit f, Steifigkeit [Statik]

~ **condition**, stiffness ~, condition of stiffness, condition of rigidity · Starrheitsbedingung f, Steifigkeitsbedingung [Statik]

~ **development** → development of rigidity

~ **factor**, stiffness ~ · Steifigkeitsfaktor m, Starrheitsfaktor

~ **in torsion** → torsion(al) strength

~ **loss**, stiffness ~, loss of rigidity, loss of stiffness · Steifigkeitsverlust m, Starrheitsverlust

~ **matrix**, stiffness ~ · Steifigkeitsmatrix f, Starrheitsmatrix

~ **of form** · Form(en)starrheit f, Form(en)steifheit

rigidly jointed cupola, ~ ~ dome · starre Kuppel f, steife ~

~ **restrained** · starr eingespannt, steif ~

rigorous · streng [Baustatik]

rim lock · aufliegendes Schloß n, Kasten(riegel)schloß, Aufsatzschloß

Ring and Ball softening point · Erweichungspunkt m Ring und Kugel, Erweichungstemperatur f ~ ~ ~ ~ [Ist in °C die Temperatur, bei der in einen genormten Metallring, 6,4 mm hoch, 15,9 mm Durchmesser, eingestrichenes, aufgeschmolzenes Bitumen durch eine aufgelegte genormte Stahlkugel, 3,5 g, 9,5 mm Durchmesser, belastet wird und bei Erwärmung von 5 grd/Minute eine solche Fließfähigkeit erreicht, daß die Stahlkugel durchfällt]

ring bar, ~ member · Ringstab m [Raumfachwerk]

~ **beam**, ring-shaped ~, circular ~ · Ringbalken(träger) m

~ **cable** · Ringseil n

~ **compression theory** · Ringdruckverfahren n [Bemessung biegbarer stählerner Tunnelauskleidungen und dünnwandiger Rohre aus Stahlblech]

~ **footing** · Ringfundament n

~ **foundation** · Ringgründung f

~ **girder**, ring-shaped ~, circular ~ · Ringträger m

ringing-loft, bell-gable, gable wall belfry · Glockengiebel m

ringing wire · Klingeldraht m

ring joint · Ringfuge f

~ **main system** · Ringnetz n [Elektrotechnik]

~ **member**, ~ bar · Ringstab m [Raumfachwerk]

~ **of chapels** → surrounding chapels

~ ~ **columns** · Säulenring m

~ ~ **statues** · Statuenkranz m

~ **plate**, ~ slab · Ringplatte f

ring(-shaped) beam, circular ~ · Ringbalken(träger) m

~ **girder**, circular ~ · Ringträger m

ring slab, ~ plate · Ringplatte f

ring-stiffened · ringversteift

ring stiffening · Ringaussteifung f

~ **stress**, hoop ~ · Ringspannung f

~ **tension**, hoop ~ · Ringzug m

~ **water main** · Ringwasserleitung f

ring-work · Ringmauer f, Bering m, Mauerring, Zingel m [Mit Verteidigungseinrichtungen ausgerüstete starke Mauer rings um eine mittelalterliche Burg]

~ **castle** · Ringmauerburg f

to rinse, to wash down · abwaschen

rinsed, washed down · abgewaschen

rinsing, washing down · Abwaschen n

riotous welter of ornament · Ornamentgewoge n

ripidolite, (raw) vermiculite · Glimmer m als Ausgangsstoff für Vermiculite

ripple metal sheet · Rippen(fein)blech n

rip-rap stone · Rigolstein m [Naturbruchstein für Entwässerung von Dämmen u.a.; als Packung eingebracht]

rise · Pfeil(höhe) m, (f), Stich(höhe) m, (f)

~, increase · Anstieg m, Zunahme f

~ · (Treppen)Steigung f [Lotrechtes Maß von der Trittfläche einer Stufe bis zur Trittfläche der folgenden Stufe. DIN 4174]

~ → arch ~

rise/run ratio · (Treppen)Steigungsverhältnis n, [Verhältnis von (Treppen-) Steigung zu Auftrittbreite]

rise-span ratio · Pfeil(höhen)verhältnis n, Stich(höhen)verhältnis

rise table · (Treppen)Steigungstabelle f

rise-to-span ratio · Stich-Spannweiten-Verhältnis n

riser — riveting gang

riser, stair ~ [*The member forming the vertical face of a step*] · Setzstufe f, Stoßtritt m, Stoßfläche f, Futterstufe [*wenn aus Holz = Futterbrett*]

~, rising line, vertical (utility) run, vertical utility line, rising run, vertical service run · Steig(e)leitung f, Standleitung [*Ein Hauptrohrstrang einer Verbrauchsleitung innerhalb eines Gebäudes*]

~less · setzstufenlos, futterstufenlos

rising · Ansteigen n

~ arch → rampant ~

~ barrel vault, ~ tunnel ~, ~ wagon ~, rampant ~ ~ · einhüftiges (Tonnen-)Gewölbe n, (an)steigendes ~, einhüftige Tonne f, (an)steigende Tonne [*Tonnengewölbe mit ungleich hohen Fußlinien*]

~ butt (hinge) · steigendes Einstemmband n, ~ Fi(t)schband, steigende Fitsche f

~ connector · Mehrleiter-Verteilerschacht m [*Robertson-Stahlzellendecke*]

~ duct, duct riser [*A duct which extends vertically one full stor(e)y or more*] · Steig(e)kanal m

~ electrical main [*An electrical power supply cable which passes up through one or more storeys of a building*] · Steig(e)-Elektroleitung f

~ humidity, ~ moisture · aufsteigende Feuchtigkeit f, ~ Feuchte f

~ line → ~ pipe~

~ ~ → riser

~ main [*A main gas pipe or water supply pipe which passes up through one or more storeys of a building*] · Hauptsteigrohr n, Hauptstandrohr

~ ~, main riser, principal riser · Hauptsteig(e)leitung f

~ moisture, ~ humidity · aufsteigende Feuchtigkeit f, ~ Feuchte f

~ (pipe)line, vertical ~ · Falleitung f [*Eine senkrechte Entwässerungsleitung für Schmutzwasser in einem Gebäude*]

~ piping · steigende Rohrleitung f, Steigrohrleitung

~ run → riser

~ service pipe, vertical ~ ~ · Versorgungssteigrohr n

~ steel structure · Stahlhochbau(werk) m, (n) [*DIN 1000*]

~ ~ structures · Stahlhochbauten f [*DIN 1000*]

~ strength, increasing ~ · zunehmende Festigkeit f, ansteigende ~

~ structure · Hochbau m [*als Baukonstruktion*]

~ structures · Hochbauten f [*als Baukonstruktion*]

~ tunnel vault → ~ barrel ~

~ vault, rampant ~ · einhüftiges Gewölbe n, (an)steigendes ~, fallendes ~, geschobenes ~, abschüssiges ~

~ wagon vault → ~ barrel ~

~ warded mechanism · steigendes Riegelgesperre n [*Buntbartschloß*]

risk of buckling, buckling risk · Knickgefahr f

~ ~ damage · Beschädigungsgefahr f

~ ~ rusting · Rostgefahr f

~ ~ segregation · Entmischungsgefahr f

Ritter's dissection · Ritterscher Schnitt m

~ equation of moments · Rittersche Momentengleichung f

~ method of dissection · Rittersches Schnittverfahren n, Rittersche Schnittmethode f [*Der von Ritter angegebene Weg zur Ermitt(e)lung der Stabkräfte eines innerlich statisch bestimmten Fachwerkträgers*]

rivelling → crinkling

riven (wood) siding shingle → hand cleft (~) ~ ~

river gravel · Stromkies m

to rivet · (ab)nieten

rivet · Niet m

~ calculation · Nietberechnung f

~ cross-section · Nietquerschnitt m

~ hole · Nietloch n

~ interval, distance between rivets · Nietabstand m

~ material · Nietwerkstoff m

~ pattern · Nietanordnung f, Nietbild n

~ pitch · Nietteilung f [*Abstände der Nieten voneinander und vom Profilrand*]

~ steel · Nietstahl m

~ symbol · Nietzeichen n

~ wire · Nietdraht m

riveted chimney, ~ stack · genieteter Schornstein m, Nietschornstein

~ connection · Nietverbindung f

~ flange · Nietflansch m [*DIN 2600–2613*]

~ frame · Nietrahmen m

~ girder, ~ plate ~ · genieteter Träger m, Nietträger

~ m.s. pipe → ~ mild steel ~

~ mild steel pipe, ~ m.s. ~ · genietetes Flußstahlrohr n

~ (plate) girder · genieteter Träger m, Nietträger

~ stack → ~ chimney

~ steel pipe · genietetes Stahlrohr n

~ tank · Nietbehälter m, genieteter Behälter

riveting by hand, hand riveting, manual riveting · Handnieten n, Handnietung f [*Von Hand geschlagene Nietung mit Handdöpper und Hammer*]

~ gang, ~ crew, ~ team, ~ party · Nietkolonne f, Niettrupp m, Nietmannschaft f

road binder — rock(-cut) seated colossal statue

road binder, highway ~ · (Straßenbau-) Bindemittel *n*, (Straßenbau)Binder *m*, Straßenbauhilfsstoff *m*

~ **chip(ping)s,** highway ~, ~ chipping, ~ stone chips · Straßenbausplitt *m*

~ **concrete,** highway ~ · Straßenbeton *m*

~ ~ **sand,** highway ~ ~ · Straßenbetonsand *m*

~ **emulsion,** highway ~, emulsion for highway construction, emulsion for road construction · Straßenbauemulsion *f*

~ **fabric,** ~ mesh, ~ steel ~ · Straßenarmierungsmatte *f*, Straßenbewehrungsmatte

~ **furniture,** highway ~ · Straßenware(n) *f(pl)*

~ **gravel,** highway ~ · Straßenbaukies *m*

~ **gull(e)y,** ~ inlet, street ~ · Rinnenschacht *m*, Straßen~, Straßenablauf *m*, Straßeneinlauf, Straßengully *m*, Straßensinkkasten *m* [*DIN 4052*]

~ **inlet,** ~ gull(e)y, street ~ · Rinnenschacht *m*, Straßen~ Straßenablauf *m*, Straßeneinlauf, Straßengully *m*, Straßensinkkasten *m* [*DIN 4052*]

~ **lighting mast,** highway ~ ~ · Straßen-Beleuchtungsmast *m*, Straßen-Lichtmast, Straßen-Leuchtenmast

road-line paint, (road) marking ~ · (Straßen)Markierungsfarbe *f*

road lining (paper), sub-soil ~, underlay ~, concreting ~, concrete subgrade ~ · Papierunterlage *f*, (Autobahn-)Unterlagspapier *n*, Straßenbaupapier

(~) marking composition, (~) ~ compound · (Straßen) Markierungsmasse *f*; weißer (Guß)Asphalt *m* [*Fehlname*]

(~) ~ compound, (~) ~ composition · (Straßen) Markierungsmasse *f*; weißer (Guß)Asphalt *m* [*Fehlname*]

(~) ~ paint, road-line ~ · (Straßen-) Markierungsfarbe *f*

~ **material,** highway ~ · Straßenbaustoff *m*

~ **mesh,** ~ fabric, ~ steel ~ · Straßenarmierungsmatte *f*, Straßenbewehrungsmatte

(road-)metal (Brit.); broken stone, broken rock, crushed rock · Schotter *m*, Brech~, Steinschlag *m*, Straßen(bau)-schotter

road oil, dust-laying ~ · Straßenöl *n* [*Ein hochsiedendes Steinkohlenteeröl zur Wiederbelebung alter bituminöser Straßendecken als Behelfsmaßnahme*]

roadside restaurant · Raststätte *f*

road steel fabric, road mesh, road fabric, road steel mesh · Straßenarmierungsmatte *f*, Straßenbewehrungsmatte

~ **stone chips,** highway ~ ~, ~ chipping, ~ chip(ping)s · Straßenbausplitt *m*

(~) tar, tar for road purposes [*B.S. 76*] · (Straßen)Teer *m*, T [*DIN 1995*]

~ ~**-asphalt mix(ture)** (US); ~ tar-(asphaltic-)bitumen ~ (Brit.) · Straßenteer-Asphaltbitumen-Mischung *f*, Straßenteer-Asphaltbitumen-Gemisch *n*

~ **tar emulsion,** emulsion of road tar · Straßenteeremulsion *f*

~ ~ **type penetration macadam,** tar ~ ~, tar-grouted stone (Brit.) · Teertränkmakadam *m*

~ ~ **visco(si)meter** · Straßenteerviskosimeter *n*

~ **with engineering brick paving,** ~ ~ paving of engineering bricks · Klinkerstraße *f*

roasted zinc · Hüttenzink *n* [*DIN 1706. Durch Reduktion und Destillation, gegebenenfalls mit anschließender Seigerraffination, hergestellt*]

robe hook, cloak ~, coat ~ · Kleiderhaken *m*

rocaille, scroll work, shell work [*A graceful design of delicate scroll and counter-scroll outline, varying in form yet maintaining everywhere its characteristic asymmetrical harmony*] · Rocaille *n, f*, Muschelwerk *n*

rock · (Natur)Gestein *n*

~ **architecture** → rock-cut ~

~ **asphalt** (US); (natural) ~ (Brit.) · (Natur)Asphalt *m*, natürliches Bitumen-Mineralgemisch *n*, natürliche Bitumen-Mineralmischung *f* [*Das natürlich vorkommende Bitumen mit seinem Begleitgestein*]

~ **assembly hall** → (rock(-cut)) chaitya ~

~ **chamber,** rock-cut ~, rock-hewn ~, cave in rock · Felsenkammer *f*

~ **cork** → agglomerated ~

~ ~ **brick,** agglomerated ~ ~, baked ~ ~ · Backkorkstein *m*

rock(-cut) architecture, rock-hewn ~, cave ~ · Felsarchitektur *f*, Felsbaukunst *f*, Höhlenarchitektur, Höhlenbaukunst, Grottenarchitektur, Grottenbaukunst

~ **assembly hall** → (~) chaitya ~

(~) chaitya hall, ~ assembly ~, cave ~ ~, rock-hewn ~ ~ [*See remark under 'Tschaitya'*] · (Felsen)Tschaitya-Halle *f*, (Felsen)Gebetshalle, Höhlen-Tschaitya-Halle, Höhlen-Gebetshalle [*Indisches Höhlenheiligtum mit tonnengewölbtem Mittelschiff zwischen halbtonnengewölbten Seitenschiffen, die als Umgang eine halbrunde Apsis umschließen, in der eine Stupa steht*]

~ **chamber,** rock-hewn ~, cave in rock · Felsenkammer *f*

~ **church,** rock-hewn ~, cave ~ · Felsenkirche *f*, Höhlenkirche [*In den anstehenden Fels gehauene Kirche aus frühchristlicher Zeit*]

~ **ditch,** rock-hewn ~ · Felsgraben *m*

~ **hall,** rock-hewn ~, cave ~ · Felsenhalle *f*

~ **monastery** → cave ~

~ **sanctuary** → cave ~

~ **seated colossal statue,** rock-hewn ~ ~ ~ · riesiges sitzendes Steinbild *n* [*z.B. beim Felsentempel Abu-Simbel*]

rock(-cut) seated statue — rock wool insulation(-grade) ... 842

~ ~ **statue**, rock-hewn ~ ~ · sitzendes Steinbild *n*

~ **sepulchre** → rock-hewn ~

~ **statue**, rock-hewn ~ · Steinbild *n*

~ **temple** → rock-hewn ~

~ **tomb**, rock-hewn ~, cave ~ · Felsen(kammer)grab *n*, Felsengrab

rock dust, stone ~, ~ flour, powder(ed) mineral, mineral powder · Staub *m*, Gesteins~, Blume *f*, (Stein)Mehl *n*, Gesteinsmehl, Steinstaub, Mineralmehl, Mineralstaub, Mineralpulver *n*

rocked pipe, cold pilgered ~ · kaltgepilgertes Rohr *n*

rocker bar → ~ member

~ **column**, socketed ~ · Pendelstütze *f*

~ **element** → ~ member

~ **member**, hinge(d) ~, socketed ~, pin(ned) ~, pin-jointed ~, articulated ~, linked ~, ~ element, ~ bar, ~ rod · Pendelstab, Gelenkstab, gelenkig angeschlossener Stab [*Der an seinem Ende gelenkig gelagerte Stab eines Tragwerks, der nur von Normalkräften (Zug und Druck) beansprucht wird*]

~ **rod** → ~ member

rockery, rock-garden · Steingarten *m*, Fels(en)garten

rock-faced (masonry) work, cyclopean (~) ~, ~ rustication, ~ masonry [*Rusticated masonry (work) in squared blocks, popularised by the Renaissance in the fifteenth century, which either have the rough hewn texture resulting from quarrying, or an artful imitation thereof*] · Rustika(mauer)werk *n*, Bossage *f*, Bossen(stein)(mauer)werk, Rustika *f*

rock fibre (Brit.); ~ **fiber** (US) · Steinfaser *f*, Gesteinsfaser

~ **flour** → ~ dust

rock-forming · gesteinsbildend

rock-garden, rockery · Steingarten *m*, Fels(en)garten

rock hall → ~-cut ~

rock-hewn architecture → rock(-cut) ~

~ **chamber**, rock(-cut) ~, cave in rock · Felsenkammer *f*

~ **ditch**, rock(-cut) ~ · Felsgraben *m*

~ **hall**, rock(-cut) ~, cave ~ · Felsenhalle *f*

~ **monastery** → cave ~

~ **sanctuary** → cave ~

~ **seated colossal statue**, rock(-cut) ~ ~ ~ · riesiges sitzendes Steinbild *n* [*z.B. beim Felsentempel Abu-Simbel*]

~ **seated statue**, rock(-cut) ~ ~ · sitzendes Steinbild *n*

~ **sepulchre**, rock(-cut) ~, cave ~ [*e.g. the Tomb of Darius at Naksh-i-Rustam*] · Felsen-Grabkammer *f*, Felsen-Grablege *f*, Grablege in einen Felsen hineingetrieben, Grabkammer in einen Felsen hineingetrieben

~ **statue**, rock(-cut) ~ · Steinbild *n*

~ **temple**, rock(-cut) ~, cave ~ · Felsentempel *m*, Grottentempel, Höhlentempel [*Tempel, der entweder als Höhlung in den Felsen hineingetrieben ist (Ägypten) oder aus einem Felsblock herausgehauen ist (Indien)*]

~ **tomb**, rock(-cut) ~, cave ~ · Felsen(kammer)grab *n*

rocking frame [*An oscillating frame on which mo(u)lds are set during the placing of concrete in order to compact it*] · Rüttelbock *m*

rock lath(ing) → gypsum (board) ~

~ **monastery** → cave ~

~ **salt**, common ~, halite · Salzgestein *n*, Steinsalz *n*

~ **sanctuary** → cave ~

~ **seated colossal statue** → rock(-cut) ~ ~ ~

~ **sepulchre** → rock-hewn ~

(~) **spall** · (Aus)Zwicker *m*, (Aus)Zwickstein *m* [*Ein kleiner Stein zum Auszwicken der Hohlräume bei Bruchsteinmauerwerk und im Straßenbau bei Packe*]

~ **statue**, rock-cut ~, rock-hewn ~ · Steinbild *n*

~ **temple** → rock-hewn ~

~ **test**, aggregate ~ · Gesteinsprobe *f*, Gesteinsprüfung *f*, Gesteinsversuch *m*

~ **type**, type of rock · Gesteinsart *f*

~ **wool** · Gesteinswolle *f*, Steinwolle [*Ein steiniger Faserstoff, der vorwiegend aus geschmolzenem Kalkstein und Mergel gewonnen wird. Er wird sowohl in Platten als auch Matten weiterverarbeitet*]

~ ~ **(building) board**, ~ ~ (~) slab, ~ ~ (~) sheet, ~ ~ sheeting board · Steinwolle(bau)platte *f*, Gesteinswolle(bau)platte

~ ~ (~) **mat** [*It has a low density*] · Gesteinswolledämmatte *f*, Steinwolledämmatte, Gesteinswolle(bau)matte, Steinwolle(bau)matte

~ ~ (~) **quilt** [*It has a high density*] · Gesteinswolle(bau)matte *f*, Steinwolle(bau)matte, Gesteinswolleisoliermatte, Steinwolleisoliermatte

~ ~ (~) **sheet**, ~ ~ (~) board, ~ ~ (~) slab, ~ ~ sheeting board · Steinwolle(bau)platte *f*, Gesteinswolle(bau)platte

~ ~ (~) **slab**, ~ ~ (~) board, ~ ~ (~) sheet, ~ ~ sheeting board · Steinwolle(bau)platte *f*, Gesteinswolle(bau)platte

~ ~ **cord covering** · Gesteinswolleschnur *f*, Steinwolleschnur

~ ~ **felt** · Gesteinswollefilz *m*, Steinwollefilz

~ ~ **fibre** (Brit.); ~ ~ **fiber** (US) · Gesteinswollefaser *f*, Steinwollefaser

~ ~ **insulation(-grade) material**, ~ ~ insulating ~, ~ ~ insulator, ~ ~

rock wool insulation(-grade) material — rod subject ...

insulant · Gesteinswolledämmaterial n, Steinwolledämmmaterial, Gesteinswolledämmstoff m, Steinwolledämmstoff

~ ~ ~ slab, ~ ~ insulating ~ · Gesteinswolledämmplatte f, Steinwolledämmplatte

~ ~ insulator, ~ ~ insulant, ~ ~ insulation(-grade) material, ~ ~ insulating material · Steinwolledämmmaterial n, Gesteinswolledämmaterial, Steinwolledämmstoff m, Gesteinswolledämmstoff

~ ~ lagging section (Brit.); ~ ~ preformed (pipe insulation) ~, ~ ~ (pipe) ~ · Steinwolleschale f, Gesteinswolleschale [für Dämmzwecke]

~ ~ mat → ~ ~ building ~

~ ~ (pipe) section, ~ ~ (pipe insulation) ~; ~ ~ lagging ~ (Brit.) · Steinwolleschale f, Gesteinswolleschale [für Dämmzwecke]

~ ~ preformed (pipe insulation) section, ~ ~ (pipe) ~, ~ ~ lagging ~ (Brit.) · Gesteinswolleschale f, Steinwolleschale [für Dämmzwecke]

~ ~ quilt → ~ ~ building ~

~ ~ section → ~ ~ preformed (pipe insulation) ~

~ ~ sheet → ~ ~ building ~

~ ~ sheeting board, ~ ~ (building) board, ~ ~ (building) sheet, ~ ~ (building) slab · Steinwolle(bau)platte f, Gesteinswolle(bau)platte

~ ~ slab → ~ ~ building ~

Rockwell hardness, Rh · Rockwellhärte f

~ ~ B-scale, RB · Rockwellhärte-B-Skala f

~ ~ C-scale, RC · Rockwellhärte-C-Skala f

~ ~ number · Rockwellhärtezahl f

~ ~ scale · Rockwellhärteskala f

~ ~ test · Rockwellhärteprüfung f, Rockwellhärteprobe f, Rockwellhärteversuch m, Rockwellverfahren n

Rococo architecture [*The Rococo is not a style in its own right, like the Baroque, but the last phase of the Baroque*] · Rokokoarchitektur f, Rokokobaukunst f

rod, bar, element, member · Füll(ungs)stab m, Gitterstab, Glied n, (Träger-)Stab

~ → (rolled) (steel) bar

~ **bender**, steel ~, bar ~ [*colloquially: iron fighter*] · Eisenbieger m

~ ~, ~ bending machine [*A powered device, with movable rollers and clamps, used to bend steel reinforcing rods to shapes required in reinforced concrete*] · Eisenbiegemaschine f

~ **buckling**, bar ~, member ~, element ~ · Stabknickung f, Stabknicken n, Gliedknickung f, Gliedknicken

~ **buster** (US. Colloquial) → (reinforcing) iron worker

~ **centre line** (Brit.); ~ center ~ (US); bar ~ ~, member ~ ~, element ~ ~ · Stabachse f, Stabmittellinie f, Gliedachse, Gliedmittellinie

~ **connection**, bar ~, element ~, member ~ · Stabanschluß m, Gliedanschluß [*Stabwerkkonstruktion*]

~ **cross-section**, member ~, bar ~, element ~ · Stabquerschnitt m, Gliedquerschnitt [*Stabwerkkonstruktion*]

~ **cut-off**, bar ~ · Bewehrungsabstufung f, Armierungsabstufung, (Stahl-)Einlagenabstufung

~ **diameter**, bar ~, diameter of rod, diameter of bar · Stabdurchmesser m, Stahldurchmesser, Eisendurchmesser [*Bewehrung*]

~ **field**, member ~, bar ~, element ~ · Stabfeld n, Gliedfeld [*Stabwerkkonstruktion*]

~ **force**, bar ~, member ~, element ~ · Stabkraft f, Gliedkraft [*Stabwerkkonstruktion*]

~ **length**, bar ~ · Stablänge f [*Bewehrung*]

~ ~, bar ~, member ~, element ~ · Stablänge f, Gliedlänge

~ **list** → bar schedule

~ **loading**, bar ~, member ~, element ~ · Gliedbelastung f, Stabbelastung

~ **moment**, bar ~, member ~, element ~ · Stabmoment n, Gliedmoment

~ **number** → bar ~

~ **schedule** → bar ~

rod-setter → (reinforcing) iron worker

rod shape, bar ~; member ~, element ~ · Gliedform f, Stabform

~ ~, bar ~ · Armierungsform f, Bewehrungsform, Eisenform Stahl(einlagen)form

~ ~ **code** → ~ (bar) ~

~ **size**, bar ~, member ~, element ~ · Stabgröße f, Gliedgröße [*Stabwerkkonstruktion*]

~ ~ → bar diameter

~ **slope**, bar ~, member ~, element ~ · Stabablenkung f, Gliedablenkung [*Rahmenträger*]

~ **spacing**, bar ~ [*Distance between parallel reinforcing bars measured from centre-to-centre of the bars perpendicular to their longitudinal axes*] · Eisenabstand m, Stababstand, Stahlabstand [*Bewehrung*]

~ **steel**, bar-steel, merchant steel · Stabeisen n [*Fehlname*]; Stabstahl m [*DIN 59051*]

~ **stress**, element ~, bar ~, member ~ · Stabspannung f, Gliedspannung [*Stabwerkkonstruktion*]

~ **subject to buckling**, bar ~ ~ ~, member ~ ~ ~ · Knickstab m

rod system— rolled section in stainless steel

~ **system,** bar ~, member ~ · Stabsystem *n*, Stabwerk *n*

~ **transformation,** ~ transposition, bar ~, member ~, element ~ · Stabvertauschung *f*, Gliedvertauschung [*Stabwerkkonstruktion*]

~ **transposition,** ~ transformation, bar ~, member ~, element ~ · Stabvertauschung *f*, Gliedvertauschung [*Stabwerkkonstruktion*]

roddability [*The susceptibility of fresh concrete or mortar to compaction by means of a tamping rod*] · Stocherbarkeit *f*

rodding (US); punning (Brit.); puddling, sworing · Stochern *n*, Stocherverdichtung *f* [*Beton*]

~ · Stocherreinigung *f*

~ **chamber** → cleaning ~

~ **cover,** ~ plate, cleanout ~, cleaning ~, access ~, inspection ~ · Reinigungsdeckel *m*, Putzdeckel

~ **eye,** ~ opening, cleanout ~, cleaning ~, access ~, inspection ~ · Putzöffnung *f*, Reinigungsöffnung

~ **fitting,** cleaning ~, cleanout ~, access ~, inspection ~ · Putzformstück *n*, Reinigungsformstück

~ **opening,** ~ eye, cleanout ~, cleaning ~, access ~, inspection ~ · Putzöffnung *f*, Reinigungsöffnung

~ **pipe,** cleanout ~, cleaning ~, access ~, inspection ~ · Rohr *n* mit Putzöffnung

~ **pit** → cleaning chamber

~ **plate,** ~ cover, cleanout ~, cleaning ~, access ~, inspection ~ · Reinigungsdeckel *m*, Putzdeckel

~ **plug,** ~ screw, cleanout ~, cleaning ~, access ~, inspection ~ · Putzstopfen *m*, Reinigungsstopfen, Putzschraube *f*, Reinigungsschraube

~ **screw,** ~ plug, cleanout ~, cleaning ~, access ~, inspection ~ · Putzstopfen *m*, Reinigungsstopfen, Putzschraube *f*, Reinigungsschraube

~ **tube** → inspection ~

rodent barrier · Nagetiersperre *f*

rodent-proof · nagetierfest

roestone → oolitic limestone

roll · Rolle *f* [*z.B. Dachpappenrolle*]

~ · Ballen *m*, Rolle *f* [*Rohfilzpappe*]

(~) **billet (frieze)** [*It consists of several bands of raised short cylinders placed at regular intervals*] · Rollenfries *m*

rolled · gewalzt

~ **angle bar** → ~ ~ (section)

~ ~ **(section),** ~ ~ bar, ~ L-section · gewalzter Winkel *m*, gewalztes Winkelprofil *n*, Walz-Winkel(profil) *m*, (*n*)

~ **article,** ~ product · Walzartikel *m*, Walzgegenstand *m*, Walzerzeugnis *n*

~ **asphalt** · Walzasphalt *m*

(~) **bar** · (~) (steel) ~

~ **beam** → (rolled-)steel joist

~ ~, ~ section, ~ girder · Walzträger *m*

~ **channel (section),** ~ U-shaped ~ · gewalztes U-Profil *n*, Walz-U-Profil

~ **concrete** · Walzbeton *m*

~ ~ **pipe** · Walzbetonrohr *n*

~ **copper strip** [*B.S. 899*] · Walzkupferband *n*

~ **flange** · Walzflansch *m* [*DIN 2575–2593*]

~ **girder** → (rolled-)steel joist

~ ~, ~ beam, ~ section · Walzträger *m*

~ **glass** [*A.S.T.M. C 162–56*] · gewalztes Glas *n*

~ ~ [*B.S. 3447 and ASTM C 162–56*], cast ~ [*Flat glass, one surface of which bears a pattern or texture made by rolling either on a table or between rollers*] · gegossenes (Flach)Glas *n*, Gußglas

~ ~ → pattern(ed) ~

~ ~ **balcony parapet,** cast ~ ~ ~ · Gußglasbalkonbrüstung *f*

~ ~ **canopy,** cast ~ ~, ~ ~ roof overhang · Gußglasvordach *n*, Gußglasabdach, Gußglaswetter(schutz)dach

~ ~ **door,** cast ~ ~ · Gußglastür *f*, Tür aus gegossenem (Flach)Glas

~ ~ **partition (wall),** cast ~ ~ (~) · Gußglastrennwand *f*

~ ~ **roof overhang,** cast ~ ~ ~, ~ ~ canopy · Gußglasvordach *n*, Gußglasabdach, Gußglaswetter(schutz)dach

~ **joist** → (rolled-)steel ~

~ **L-section** → ~ angle (section)

~ **m.s. section,** ~ mild steel ~ · Flußstahlwalzprofil *n*

~ **mild steel section,** ~ m.s. ~ · Flußstahlwalzprofil *n*

(~) **non-standard section,** (~) ~ unit, "Universal" ~, universal (mill) plate · Breitflachstahl *m* [*Fehlnamen: Breitflacheisen n, Universaleisen. DIN 1612*]

(~) ~ **unit** → (~) ~ section

~ **product,** ~ article · Walzartikel *m*, Walzgegenstand *m*, Walzerzeugnis *n*

(~) **rod** → (~) (steel) bar

~ **round bars** · gewalzter (Beton)Rundstahl *m* [*DIN 488*]

~ **section** → (roll-formed) ~

~ ~, ~ girder, ~ beam · Walzträger *m*

~ ~ → (rolled-)steel joist

~ ~ **in stainless steel** · Edelstahlwalzprofil *n*

rolled shape — rolling mill product

~ **shape** → (roll-formed) section

~ **sheet glass,** ~ window ~, cast ~ ~ · Fenstergußglas *n*, Gußfensterglas

~ **steel** · Walzstahl *m*

rolled-steel angle · Walzstahlwinkel *m*

(rolled) (steel) bar, (~) (~) rod, reinforcing ~, reinforcement ~ [*B.S. 785*] · (Bewehrungs)Stab *m*, Armierungsstab, Betoneisenstab, Betonstahlstab

(rolled-)steel joist, RSJ, r.s.j., rolled joist, I-beam (section) [*An I-beam made of one piece of steel passed through a hot-rolling mill*] · Doppel-T-Stahl *m*, Doppel-T-Träger *m*, Doppel-T-Profil *n*, I-Träger, I-Stahl, I-Profil

~ ~ **(beam),** r.s.j. (~) · Walzträgerunterzug *m*

(rolled) (steel) rod → (~) (~) bar

rolled-steel section · Stahlwalzprofil *n*, Walzstahlprofil

~ **slab** · Walzstahlplatte *f*

roll(ed-strip) roof(ing) felt, ~ roofing (paper) [*Prepared roofing wound up in rolls*] · Rollendachpappe *f*, Dachpappe in Rollenform

~ ~ **(paper),** ~ roof(ing) felt [*Prepared roofing wound up in rolls*] · Dachpappe *f* in Rollenform, Rollendachpappe

rolled unit → (roll-formed) section

~ **U-shaped section,** ~ channel (~) · gewalztes U-Profil *n*, Walz-U-Profil

~ **window glass,** ~ sheet ~, cast ~ ~ · Fenstergußglas *n*, Gußfensterglas

~ **wire(d) glass** · Drahtgußglas *n*, Gußdrahtglas

~ **zinc** · Walzzink *n*

~ ~ **article,** ~ ~ product · Zinkwalzerzeugnis *n*, Walzzinkerzeugnis [*Blech und Band*]

~ ~ **product,** ~ ~ article · Zinkwalzerzeugnis *n*, Walzzinkerzeugnis [*Blech und Band*]

~ **formed from** · gewalzt aus

(roll-formed) section, (~) shape, (~) unit, rolled ~ [*Any rolled beam or bar used in a structure*] · (Walz)Profil *n*

(~) shape → (~) section

(~) unit → (~) section

roll length, length of roll · Rollenlänge *f*

~ **moulding,** torus (~) (Brit.); ~ (molding) (US) · Wulst *m, f*, Torus *m* [*Band mit vorwiegend halbkreisförmigem Querschnitt*]

~ **roof(ing) felt** → roll(ed-strip) roofing (paper)

~ ~ **(paper)** → roll(ed-strip) ~ (~)

~ ~ **winding mandrel** · Wickelvorrichtung *f* [*Dachpappenanlage*]

roller [*A cylinder covered with lambswool, felt, foamed plastic or other materials, used for applying paint*] · Farbrollgerät *n*

~, **paint** · (Farb)Rollgerät *n*

~ · Welle *f* [*Rolladen*]

~ **application** · Rollen *n* [*Anstrichtechnik*]

~ **coating** [*A process by which a film is applied mechanically to sheet material; the sheet is passed between horizontal rollers, one of which is kept coated with a film of liquid varnish, enamel or lacquer*] · Walzenlackierverfahren *n*

roller-coating enamel · aufgerollter Emaillelack *m*

~ **machine** · Farbrollmaschine *f*

roller curtain (type) filter, continuous roll (~) ~ · Rollbandfilter *m, n* [*Lüftungszentrale*]

~ **grille,** rolling ~ [*See remark under 'Gitter'*] · Rollgitter *n*

~ **jalousie,** slatted roller blind · Rolladen *m*, Rolljalousie *f* [*Er besteht aus schmalen Stäbchen, die durch Gurtbänder, Metallketten usw. gelenkig miteinander verbunden sind und auf einer Welle hinter dem Fenstersturz mit Hilfe eines Gurtes aufgerollt werden*]

~ ~ **gate,** slatted roller blind ~ · Rolladentor *n*

~ ~ **housing,** slatted roller blind ~ · Rolladenkasten *m*, Rolljalousiekasten

~ ~ **lintel** → slatted roller blind ~

~ ~ **section** → slatted roller blind trim

~ ~ **shape** → slatter roller blind trim

~ ~ **trim** → slatter roller blind ~

~ ~ **unit** → slatter roller blind trim

~ ~ **work,** slatted roller blind ~ · Rolladenarbeiten *fpl* [*DIN 18358*]

~ **partition** · Rollwand *f*

roller-printed (wall)paper · Rotationsdrucktapete *f*

roller shutter, rolling ~ · Rollabdeckung *f* [*z.B. für Schwimmbäder*]

~ ~, rolling ~ · Rollabschluß *m*

~ **support** · Lager-Auflager *n*

rolling friction · Rollreibung *f*

~ **gasket,** ~ O-ring ~ · Rollring *m*

~ **greenhouse** · Roll(gewächs)haus *n*

~ **grille,** roller ~ [*See remark under 'Gitter'*] · Rollgitter *n*

~ **load,** moving ~ · bewegliche Last *f*, veränderliche ~, Wanderlast

~ **loading,** moving ~ · veränderliche Belastung *f*, bewegliche ~, Wanderbelastung

~ **mill product** · Walzwerkzeugnis *n*

rolling (O-ring) gasket — Romanesque school 846

~ **(O-ring) gasket** · Rollring *m*

~ ~ **joint** · Rolldichtung *f*, Rollverbindung

~ **partition (wall)** · Rolltrennwand *f*

~ **process** [*A process for making flat glass in which it is formed between rollers*] · Walzverfahren *n*

~ **roof** · Rolldach *n*

~ **rubber** · Rollgummi *m*, *n* [*Rohrverbindung*]

~ ~ **O-ring joint,** ~ ~ ~ **seal(ing),** ~ ~ ~ **gasket** · Rollgummiverbindung *f*, Gummirollverbindung, Gummirolldichtung, Rollgummidichtung

~ **scaffold(ing)** · Rollgerüst *n*, Rollrüstung *f*

~ **shutter, roller** ~ · Rollabschluß *m*

~ ~, **roller** ~ · Rollabdeckung *f* [*z.B. für Schwimmbäder*]

~ **the wire rod, wire rod rolling** · Drahtwalzen *n*

rolo(c)k, rowlock, rollock [*A brick-on-edge course*] · Rollschar *f*, Rollschicht *f*

~, **rowlock, rollock, (clay) brick-on-edge course** · Ziegelrollschar *f*, Ziegelrollschicht *f*

~ **arch, rowlock** ~, **rollock** [*A brick relieving arch of two concentric courses of headers set on edge*] · Bogen *m* aus zwei (Ziegel)Rollschichten

~ **paving, rowlock** ~, **rollock** ~ · (Ziegel) Rollscharfpflaster *n*, (Ziegel)Rollschichtpflaster

Roman acanthus leaf · römisches Akanthusblatt *n*, ~ Bärenklaublatt

~ **amphitheatre** · römisches Amphitheater *n*

~ **architectural style,** ~ **building** ~ · römischer Baustil *m*

~ **architecture** · römische Architektur *f*, ~ Baukunst *f*

~ **basilica, pagan** ~, **secular** ~, **imperial** ~, **(civic)** ~ · (römische) (Zivil)Basilika *f*, römisch-heidnische Basilika, heidnisch-römische Basilika

~ **bath building** · römisches Hallenbad *n*

~ **bath(s)** · römische Thermenanlage *f*

~ **brick** · römischer Ziegel *m*, Verblender *m*, Verblendstein *m*

~ **building style,** ~ **architectural** ~ · römischer Baustil *m*

~ **cement, Parker's** ~ · Romankalk *m* [*DIN 1060. Aus Tonmergel unterhalb der Sintergrenze gebrannt. Fehlnamen: Romanzement, römischer Zement, Parkerzement, schwarzer Zement*]

~ **city wall** · römische Stadtmauer *f*

~ **column** · römische Säule *f*

~ **Corinthian capital** · römisch-korinthisches Kapitell *n*, ~ Kapitäl

~ ~ **order (of architecture)** · römisch-korinthische (Säulen)Ordnung *f*

~ **cross-vault** · römisches Kreuzgewölbe *n*

~ **Doric capital** · römisch-dorisches Kapitell *n*, ~ Kapitell

~ ~ **order (of architecture)** · römisch-dorische (Säulen)Ordnung *f*

~ ~ **temple** · römisch-dorischer Tempel *m*

~ **foot** · römischer Fuß *m* [*296 mm; 11.65 inch*]

~ **fort** · römische Festung *f*

~ **gentlemen's house** · römisches Herrenhaus *n*

~ **hall of justice** · Gerichtsbasilika *f*

~ **High Renaissance** · römische Hochrenaissance *f*

~ **Ionic capital** · römisch-ionisches Kapitell *n*, ~ Kapitäl

~ ~ **order (of architecture)** · römisch-ionische (Säulen)Ordnung *f*

~ **mosaic, opus tesselatum, tesselated pavement** · (Fußboden)Würfelmosaik *n*

~ ~, **opus sectile** · Plattenmosaik *n*

~ **order (of architecture)** · römische (Säulen)Ordnung *f*

~ **ornament** · römisches Ornament *n*

~ **ovolo (moulding)** (Brit); ~ ~ (molding) (US); **quarter-round** (~) · Viertelstab *m*

~ **palazzo style** · römischer Palastbaustil *m*

~ **structure** · Römer(bau)werk *n*

~ **thermae** [*The palatial public baths of Imperial Rome*] · Kaiserthermen *fpl*

~ **triumphal arch** · römischer Triumphbogen *m*

Romanesque architectural style, ~ **building** ~ · romanischer Baustil *m*, Rundbogenstil

~ **architecture** [*The name given to the style of architecture, founded on Roman architecture, and prevalent in Western Europe from the nineth to the twelfth century*] · romanische Architektur *f*, ~ Baukunst *f*

~ **base,** ~ **column** ~ · romanischer (Säulen)Fuß *m*, romanische Basis *f*

~ **basilica** · romanische Basilika *f*

~ ~ **of St. George on the Hradcany Hill at Prague** · St. Georg auf dem Hradschin zu Prag

~ **building style,** ~ **architectural** ~ · romanischer Baustil *m*, Rundbogenstil

~ **church** · romanische Kirche *f*

~ **(column) base** · romanischer (Säulen-) Fuß *m*, romanische Basis *f*

~ **foliage,** ~ **leaves** · romanisches Laubwerk *n*, ~ Blattwerk

~ **leaves,** ~ **foliage** · romanisches Laubwerk *n*, ~ Blattwerk

~ **school** · romanische Bauschule *f*

847 Romanesque sculpture — roof cladding with prepared...

~ sculpture · romanische Plastik *f*
~ (style) · Romanik *f*, romanischer Stil *m*
~ transept · romanisches Querhaus *n*
~ vault(ing) system · romanisches Gewölbesystem *n*
Romantic classicism · früher Klassizismus *m*
Romanticism · Romantizismus *m*
rood, crucifix · Kruzifix *n*
~, cross · Kreuz *n* [*Kirche*]
~ arch · Lettnermittelbogen *m* [*Mittelbogen in einem Lettner, auf dem das Kreuz angebracht ist*]
~ beam · Lettnerbalken *m* [*Das Kreuz tragender Balken über dem Chor einer Kirche*]
~ loft, jubé, jube [*A loft or gallery over the rood screen in a church*] · Lettnerempore *f*
rood-screen, jubé, jube · Lettner *m*
to roof, to cover · bedachen, abdecken, (ein)decken
roof, building ~, block ~ · (Gebäude-)Dach *n*
~ → ~ cladding
~ accessories → roof(ing) ~
~ aerial, overhouse ~ · Dachantenne *f*
~ aluminium (Brit.) → roof(ing) ~
~ anchorage · Dachverankerung *f*
~ area · Dachfläche *f*
~ asphalt (US) → roof(ing) ~
~ (asphaltic-)bitumen (Brit.) → roof(ing) ~
~ base sheeting → roofing ~ ~
(~) batten · Ziegellatte *f*, (Dach)Latte
(~) battens, ~ lathing · Ziegellattung *f*, (Dach)Lattung
~ beam grillage · Dachbalken(träger)rost *m*
~ bitumen (Brit.) → roof(ing) (asphaltic-)bitumen
~ boarding → ~ boards
~ boards, ~ boarding, ~ sheathing [*Boards laid touching each other, usually with tongued and grooved joints, nailed to the common rafters as a base for flexible-metal roofing or roofing felt under slates or tiles*] · Dach(ver)schalung *f*, Dachschale *f*, Holzschalung, Holzschale
~ boiler room, ~-top ~ ~ · Dach-Kesselraum *m*
~ boss → boss
~ bracing · Dachversteifung *f*, Dachaussteifung
~ cantilever · Dachkragarm *m*
~ car park → ~-top ~ ~
~ chimney [*That part of a chimney that is external to a building*] · Dachschornstein *m*
~ chip(ping)s, roofing ~ · Dachsplitt *m*

~ cladding, ~ covering, ~ sheathing, roof(ing) · Bedachung *f*, Dach(belag) *n*, (*m*), (Ein)Deckung, Dach(ein)deckung
~ ~ metal sheet, ~ covering ~ ~, ~ sheathing ~ ~, ~ ~ sheet-metal, roof(ing) metal sheet, roof(ing) sheet-metal · Bedachungsblech *n*, Dach(ein)deck(ungs)blech, Dachblech
~ ~ sheet-metal → ~ ~ metal sheet
~ ~ with asphalt composition roofing → ~ cover(ing) with asphalt ready ~
~ ~ ~ ~ prepared roofing → ~ cover(ing) with asphalt ready ~
~ ~ ~ ~ ready roofing → ~ cover(ing) ~ ~ ~ ~
~ ~ ~ ~ roof(ing) felt → ~ cover(ing) with asphalt ready roofing
~ ~ (asphaltic-)bitumen composition roofing (Brit.) → ~ cover(ing) with asphalt ready ~
~ ~ ~ ~ prepared roofing (Brit.) → ~ cover(ing) with asphalt ready ~
~ ~ ~ ~ ready roofing (Brit.) → ~ cover(ing) with asphalt ~ ~
~ ~ ~ ~ roof(ing) felt (Brit.) → ~ cover(ing) with asphalt ready roofing
~ ~ ~ bitumen composition roofing (Brit.) → ~ cover(ing) with asphalt ready ~
~ ~ ~ ~ prepared roofing (Brit.) → ~ cover(ing) with asphalt ready ~
~ ~ ~ ~ ready roofing (Brit.) → ~ cover(ing) with asphalt ~ ~
~ ~ ~ ~ roof(ing) felt (Brit.) → ~ cover(ing) with asphalt ready roofing
~ ~ ~ composition roofing, ~ ~ ~ prepared ~, ~ ~ ~ rolled-strip ~, ~ ~ ~ ready ~, ~ ~ ~ roll ~, ~ covering ~ ~ ~, ~ sheathing ~ ~ ~ · Pappdach(belag) *n*, (*m*), Papp(dach)eindeckung *f*, Pappbedachung
~ ~ ~ fluxed pitch composition roofing (Brit.) → ~ cover(ing) with tar(red) ready ~
~ ~ ~ ~ prepared roofing (Brit.) → ~ cover(ing) with tar(red) ready ~
~ ~ ~ ~ ready roofing (Brit.) → ~ cover(ing) with tar(red) ~ ~
~ ~ ~ interlocking clay (roof(ing)) tiles, ~ ~ ~ ~ ~ (roof(ing)) clay ~, ~ covering ~ ~ ~ (~) ~, ~ sheathing ~ ~ ~ (~) ~, roof(ing) ~ ~ ~ (~) ~ · Falzziegel(dach)(ein)deckung *f*, Falzziegeldach(belag) *n*, (*m*), Falzziegelbedachung
~ ~ ~ ~ (roof(ing)) tiles, ~ cover(ing) ~ ~ (~) ~, ~ sheathing ~ ~ (~) ~, roof(ing) ~ ~ (~) ~ · Falzstein(dach)(ein)deckung *f*, Falzsteindach(belag) *n*, (*m*), Falzsteinbedachung
~ ~ ~ prepared roofing, ~ ~ ~ ~ composition ~, ~ ~ ~ ~ rolled-strip ~, ~ ~ ~ ~ ready ~, ~ ~ ~ ~ roll ~, ~ covering ~ ~ ~, ~ sheathing ~ ~ ~ · Pappdach(belag) *n*, (*m*), Papp(dach)eindeckung *f*, Pappbedachung

roof cladding with ready roofing — roof flashing

~ ~ ~ **ready roofing,** ~ ~ ~ roll ~, ~ ~ ~ composition ~, ~ ~ ~ prepared ~, ~ ~ ~ ~ rolled-strip ~, ~ covering ~ ~ ~, ~ sheathing ~ ~ ~ · Pappdach(belag) n, (m), Papp(dach)-eindeckung f, Pappbedachung

~ ~ ~ **roll roofing,** ~ ~ ~ ~ ready ~, ~ ~ ~ composition ~, ~ ~ ~ ~ prepared ~, ~ ~ ~ ~ rolled-strip ~, ~ covering ~ ~ ~, ~ sheathing ~ ~ ~ · Pappdach(belag) n, (m), Papp(dach)-eindeckung f, Pappbedachung

~ ~ ~ **rolled-strip roofing,** ~ ~ ~ composition ~, ~ ~ ~ ~ prepared ~, ~ ~ ~ ready ~, ~ ~ ~ ~ roll ~, ~ covering ~ ~ ~, ~ sheathing ~ ~ ~ · Pappdach(belag) n, (m), Papp(dach)-eindeckung f, Pappbedachung

~ ~ ~ **tar(red) composition roofing** → ~ cover(ing) with tar(red) ready ~

~ ~ ~ ~ **prepared roofing** → ~ cover(ing) with tar(red) ready ~

~ ~ ~ ~ **ready roofing** → ~ cover(ing) ~ ~ ~ ~

~ ~ ~ ~ **roof(ing) felt** (US) → ~ cover(ing) with tar(red) ready roofing

~ **clay tile,** roofing ~ ~, clay (roof(ing)) ~ · Tondachstein m, Dachziegel m [DIN 456]

~ ~ ~ **factory** → roofing ~ ~ ~

~ **coating** · Dachbeschichtung f

~ **column** · Dachstütze f

~ **component,** ~ unit, ~ member · Dachbauteil m, n, Dachelement n

~ **concreting,** ~ pour(ing) · Dachbetonieren n

~ **construction** · Dachbau m

~ **continuous over three spans** · Dreifelddach n

~ **cork,** roofing ~ · Dachkork m

~ **course** · Dachgebinde n, Dachgespärre n

~ **covering,** ~ sheathing, ~ cladding, roofing · Dachbelag m, (Ein)Deckung f, Dach(ein)deckung, Bedachung

~ ~ **metal sheet** → ~ cladding ~ ~

~ ~ **sheet-metal** → ~ cladding metal sheet

~ **cover(ing) with asphalt ready roofing,** ~ cladding ~ ~ ~ ~, ~ sheathing ~ ~ ~ ~, ~ ~ ~ ~, ~ ~ ~ composition ~, ~ ~ ~ ~ prepared ~, ~ ~ ~ ~ ~ roof(ing) felt (US); ~ ~ ~ (asphaltic-)bitumen ~ ~ (Brit.) · Bitumen-Pappdach(belag) n, (m), Bitumen-Papp(ein)deckung f, Bitumen-Pappdach(ein)deckung, Bitumen-Pappbedachung

~ ~ ~ **fluxed pitch ready roofing** (Brit.)' → ~ ~ ~ ~ tar(red) ~ ~ ~

~ ~ ~ **roll roofing,** ~ sheathing ~ ~ ~, ~ cladding ~ ~ ~ ~, ~ ~ ~ ~ ready ~, ~ ~ ~ composition ~, ~ ~ ~ prepared ~, ~ ~ ~ ~ rolled-strip ~ · Pappdach(belag) n, (m), Papp(dach)eindeckung f, Pappbedachung

~ ~ ~ **tar(red) ready roofing,** ~ cladding ~ ~ ~ ~ ~, ~ sheathing ~ ~ ~ ~, ~ ~ ~ composition ~, ~ ~ ~ ~ prepared ~, ~ ~ ~ ~ ~ roof(ing) felt (US); ~ ~ ~ fluxed pitch ~ ~ (Brit.) · Teer-Pappdach(belag) n, (m), Teer-Papp(ein)deckung f, Teer-Pappdach(ein)deckung, Teer-Pappbedachung

~ **cradle,** wall lift. (window) cradle machine, (window) cleaning cradle [*Motorized carriage running vertically on rails let into the window frames*] · (Fenster)Putzwagen m, (Fenster)Reinigungswagen

(~) **crest(ing),** ridge ~ [*A line of ornament on the ridge of a roof*] · (Dach-)Firstbekrönung f, (Dach)Firstkrone f, (Dach)Firstverzierung

~ **cross(-)section** · Dachquerschnitt m

(~) **curb** · Dachbruch m, (Dach)Knick m [*Jene Linie des Daches, an der die steilere Neigung der Hauptdachfläche in weichem Übergang in die sanfter geneigte Dachfläche an der Traufe durch den Aufschiebling übergeleitet wird*]

(~) ~ **clay tile** · Dachbruchziegel m

(~) ~ **tile** · Dachbruchstein m

~ **deck(ing) sheeting** → (roof(ing)) base ~

~ **decoration** → ~ decorative finish

~ **decorative feature** → ~ ~ ~ finish

~ ~ **finish,** ~ ~ feature, ~ ornamental ~, ~ decoration, ~ enrichment · Dachschmuck m, Dachverzierung f

~ **design** · Dachausmitt(e)lung f, Dachentwurf m, Dachzerfallung Dachzerlegung [*Die waag(e)rechte Projektion der Dachformen, wie sie sich durch das Festlegen der Begrenzungslinien für die Dachflächen ergibt*]

~ **dome,** ~ cupola · Dachkuppel f

(~) **dormer** [*The structure containing a dormer window*] · (Dach)Gaube f, (Dach)Gaupe

(~) ~ **cheek** · (Dach)Gaubenwange f, (Dach)Gaupenwange, senkrechte (Dach)Gaubenfläche f, senkrechte (Dach)Gaupenfläche

(~) ~ **covering** · (Dach)Gaubendeckung f, (Dach) Gaupendeckung

(~) ~ **(window),** luthern · (Dach)Gaubenfenster n, (Dach)Gaupenfenster

(~) ~ ~ ~ → **hip(ped)** (~) ~ (~)

~ **drainage** · Ableitung f des Dachwassers, Dachentwässerung

~ **edge** · Dachkante f

~ **enrichment** → ~ decorative finish

~ **fall** → ~ pitch

~ **felt** → asphalt ready roofing

~ ~ **manufacture** → ready roofing ~

~ **flashing** · Dachanschluß m [*Siehe Anmerkung unter „Anschluß"*]

~ ~, ~ ~ piece, ~ ~ strip [*See remark under 'Anschluß'*] · Dachanschluß(streifen) *m*

~ ~ block · Dachanschlußstein *m*

~ ~ method · Dachanschlußverfahren *n*

~ ~ (piece), ~ ~ strip [*See remark under 'Anschluß'*] · Dachanschluß(streifen) *m*

~ ~ strip, ~ ~ (piece) [*See remark under 'Anschluß'*] · Dachanschluß(streifen) *m*

~ floor · Dachdecke *f*, Abschlußdecke gegen die Außenluft

~ ~ cross-section · Dachdeckenquerschnitt *m*

~ foil → roofing ~

~ form, ~ shape · Dachform *f*, Dachgestalt *f*

~ ~ cross-section, ~ shape ~ · Dachformquerschnitt *m*, Dachgestaltquerschnitt

~ frame, ~ framing · (Dach)Binder *m*

~ framing, ~ frame · (Dach)Binder *m*

~ garden, ~-top terrace ~ · Dachgarten *m*

~ ~ bar · Dachgartenbar *f*

~ ~ planting · Dachgarten-Bepflanzung *f*

~ ~ restaurant · Dachgartenrestaurant *n*

roof-gardening · Dachgartengestaltung *f*

roof girder · Dachträger *m*, Rahmenriegel *m*

~ glazing · Dachverglasen *n*, Dacheinglasen

~ ~ · Dachverglasung *f*, Dacheinglasung

~ gravel, roofing ~ · Bedachungskies *m*, Dachkies

(~) gutter, rainwater ~, R.W. ~ · (Dach)Rinne *f*, Regenrinne, Abflußrinne [*DIN 18460*]

(~) ~ board, rainwater ~ ~, R.W. ~ ~ · (Dach)Rinnenbrett *n*, Regenrinnenbrett

(~) ~ heating, rainwater ~ ~, R.W. ~ ~ · Regenrinnenbeheizung *f*, (Dach-)Rinnenbeheizung

(~) ~ hook, rainwater ~ ~, R.W. ~ ~ · (Dach)Rinnenhaken *m*, Regenrinnenhaken

(~) ~ sheet, rainwater ~ ~, R.W. ~ ~ · (Dach)Rinnenblech *n*, Regenrinnenblech

~ hatch · Dachluke *f*

~ heat · Dachwärme *f*

~ ~ insulation · Dachwärme(ab)dämmung *f*

~ helicopter airport → roof-top ~ ~

~ heliport → roof(-top) helicopter airport

~ hook · Ausbesserungshaken *m*, Dachknappe *m*, Reparaturhaken, Dachhaken [*DIN 18480*]

~-hung ductwork · dachabgehängte Kanäle *mpl*

~ load · Dachhängelast *f*

roof in prestressed clay, Stahlton (prestressed) roof, prestressed clay roof · Spanntondach *n*, Stahltondach, vorgespanntes Ziegeldach

~ ~ Stahlton → Stahlton (prestressed) roof

~ insulating material, ~ insulation(-grade) · Dachisoliermaterial *n*, Isolierdachmaterial

~ insulating plank → roof(ing) insulation(-grade) ~

~ ~ slab, ~ insulation(-grade) ~ · Dachisolierplatte *f*, Isolierdachplatte

~ ~ ~, ~ insulation(-grade) ~ · Dämmdachplatte *f*, Dachdämmplatte

~ ~ unit → roof(ing) insulation(-grade) ~

~ insulation · Dachdämmung *f*

~ ~ · Dachisolierung *f*

~ insulation(-grade) material, ~ insulating ~ · Dachisoliermaterial *n*, Isolierdachmaterial

~ ~ slab, ~ insulating ~ · Dachdämmplatte *f*, Dämmdachplatte

~ insulation plank → roof(ing) insulation(-grade) ~

~ ~ slab → ~ insulating ~

~ joint · Dachfuge *f*

~ joist · Flachdachrofen *m* [*Schweiz*]; Flachdachsparren

~ ~, binder, binding beam, binding joist · Bundbalken *m*, Binderbalken

~ lacquer → roofing ~

~ ladder, cat ~, duck board · Dachleiter *f*

~ ~ hook · Dachleiterhaken *m* [*Zum Einhängen von Dachleitern bei Dachreparaturen*]

~ lathing, (~) battens · Ziegellattung *f*, (Dach)Lattung

roofless · dachlos

roof level · Dachhöhe *f*

roof-light [*A lantern-light or skylight*] · (Dach)Oberlicht *n*

~ fitting, ~ furniture · (Dach)Oberlichtbeschlag *m*

~ opener · (Dach)Oberlichtöffner *m*

~ opening · (Dach)Oberlichtöffnung *f*

~ sheet [*An asbestos-cement roofing sheet with an opening, generally an upstand, in the middle for glazing*] · (Dach)Oberlichtbahn *f*

~ system · (Dach)Oberlichtkonstruktion *f*, (Dach)Oberlichtsystem *n*

roof-lighting · Dach-Tages(licht)beleuchtung *f* [*Fehlnamen: Dach(-Tages)-belichtung*]

~ system · Dach-Tages(licht)beleuchtungssystem *n* [*Fehlnamen: Dach(-Tages)belichtungssystem*]

roof line · Dachsilhouette *f*

~ load · Dachlast *f*

~ loading · Dachbelastung *f*

roof mast — roof sheathing with interlocking (roof(ing))... 850

~ mast · Dachmast *m*

~ material → roofing ~

~ member, ~ component, ~ unit · Dachbauteil *m, n*, Dachelement *n*

~ metal, roofing ~ · Dachmetall *n*, Bedachungsmetall, Dach(ein)deck(ungs)-metall

~ ~ sheet → ~ cladding ~ ~

roof-mounted flagpole, roof set ~ · Dach-Fahnenmast *m*, Dach-Flaggenmast

roof nail → roofing ~

~ of (natural) stone, (natural) stone roof · (Natur)Steindach *n*

~ ~ prefab(ricated) elements · Dach *n* aus vorgefertigten Teilen

~ ornament · Dachverzierung *f*

~ ornamental feature → ~ decorative finish

~ ~ finish → ~ decorative ~

~ outlet, flat ~ ~ · (Flach)Dachablauf *m*

to roof (over) · überdachen

roof overhang · Dachüberstand *m*

~ ~ · Abdach *n*, Vordach, Windfangdach, Wetter(schutz)dach

~ pane, pane of a roof · Dachfläche *f*, Dachseite, Dachschräge *f* [*Österreich*: *Dachresche f. Beim geneigten Dach*]

~ panel → roofing ~

~ paper → ready roofing

~ parapet slab, ~ ~ wall ~ · Attikaplatte *f*, Dachbrüstungsplatte

~ ~ (wall) · Dachbrüstung *f*, Attika *f*

~ ~ (~) slab · Attikaplatte *f*, Dachbrüstungsplatte

~ parking area → ~-top ~ ~

~ ~ deck → ~-top ~ ~

~ paste, roofing ~ · Dachpaste *f*

~ pergola · Dachpergola *f*

~ pitch, ~ slope, pitch of roof, slope of roof, roof fall, fall of roof · Dachgefälle *n*, Dachneigung *f* [*Österreich: Dachresche f*]

~ plan · Dachgrundriß *m*

~ plane · Dachebene *f*

~ plank → roofing ~

~ playground, ~-top ~ · Dachspielplatz *m*

~ plumbing [*Roof plumbing consists of making watertight all joints between the roof covering and the roof abutments, such as parapet walls, chimneys, vents, etc., and in providing and fixing the means of carrying away the rain water that has fallen on the roof area*] · Dachklempnerarbeiten *fpl*

~ pour(ing), ~ concreting · Dachbetonieren *n*

~ preservation coat · Dachkonservierungsanstrich *m*, Dachkonservierungsaufstrich

~ preservative, ~ preserver, roofing ~ · Dachschutzmittel *n*, Dachpflegemittel

~ preserver, ~ preservative, roofing ~ · Dachschutzmittel *n*, Dachpflegemittel

~ promenade, roof-top ~ · Dachpromenade *f*

~ railing · Dachgeländer *n*

~ repair · Dachausbesserung *f*

~ restaurant, ~-top ~ · Dachrestaurant *n*

~ rib · Dachrippe *f*

roofscape · Dachlandschaft *f*

roof screed (material) · Dachestrich *m* [*als Baustoff*]

~ ~ (topping) · Dachestrich *m* [*als verlegter Baustoff*]

~ seal(ing) · Dach(ab)dichtung *f*

~ set flagpole, roof-mounted ~ · Dach-Fahnenmast *m*, Dach-Flaggenmast

~ shake → (wood(en)) ~ ~

~ shape, ~ form · Dachform *f*, Dachgestalt *f*

~ ~ cross-section, ~ form ~ · Dachformquerschnitt *m*, Dachgestaltquerschnitt

~ sheathing · Dach(ver)schalung *f*, Dachschale *f*

~ ~ → ~ boards

~ ~, ~ covering, ~ cladding, roof(ing) · Dach *n*, Dachbelag *m*, (Ein)Deckung *f*, Dach(ein)deckung, Bedachung

~ ~ → ~ boards

~ ~ metal sheet → ~ cladding ~ ~

~ ~ paper [*Sheathing paper under roofing. See remark under 'Pappe'*] · Unterkonstruktionspappe *f* [*Dach(ein)deckung*]

~ ~ sheet-metal → ~ cladding metal sheet

~ ~ with asphalt composition roofing → ~ cover(ing) with asphalt ready ~

~ ~ ~ ~ prepared roofing → ~ cover(ing) with asphalt ready ~

~ ~ ~ ~ ready roofing → ~ cover(ing) ~ ~ ~ ~

~ ~ ~ ~ roof(ing) felt → ~ cover(ing) with asphalt ready roofing

~ ~ ~ (asphaltic-)bitumen composition roofing (Brit.) → ~ cover(ing) with asphalt ready ~

~ ~ ~ ~ prepared roofing (Brit.) → ~ cover(ing) with asphalt ready ~

~ ~ ~ ~ ready roofing (Brit.) → ~ cover(ing) with asphalt ~ ~

~ ~ ~ ~ roof(ing) felt (Brit.) → ~ cover(ing) with asphalt ready roofing

~ ~ ~ fluxed pitch composition roofing (Brit.) → ~ cover(ing) with tar(red) ready ~

~ ~ ~ interlocking clay (roof(ing)) tiles → ~ cladding ~ ~ ~ (~)

~ ~ ~ ~ (roof(ing)) tiles → ~ cladding ~ ~ (~) ~

~ ~ ~ **roll roofing**, ~ covering ~ ~ ~, ~ **cladding** ~ ~ ~, ~ ~ ~ ~ **ready** ~, ~ ~ ~ ~ **composition** ~, ~ ~ ~ ~ **prepared** ~, ~ ~ ~ **rolled-strip** ~ · Pappdach(belag) *n*, (*m*), Papp(dach)eindeckung *f*, Pappbedachung

~ ~ ~ **tar(red) composition roofing** → ~ cover(ing) with tar(red) ready ~

~ **sheet(ing)**, roofing ~ · Bedachungsbahn *f*, Dachbahn, Dach(ein)deck(ungs)bahn

~ ~, ~ **sheets**, roofing ~ · Dachplatten *fpl*

~ **sheet-metal** → ~ cladding metal sheet

~ **shell** · Dachschale *f*

~ **shingle**, roofing ~ · (Dach)Schindel *f*

~ **shop**, ~-top ~ · Dachladen *m*

~ **skin**, roofing ~ · Dachhaut *f*

~ **slab** → roofing ~

~ ~ **in prestressed clay**, Stahlton (prestressed) roof slab, prestressed clay roof slab · Spanntondachplatte *f*, Stahltondachplatte, vorgespannte Ziegeldachplatte

~ ~ ~ **Stahlton** → Stahlton (prestressed) roof slab

~ **slag**, roofing ~ · Bedachungsschlacke *f*, Dachschlacke

~ **slate** → roof(ing) ~

~ **slope** → ~ pitch

~ **soffit** (Brit.); soffit (US) · Unterseite *f* des Dachüberhanges

~ **space**, ~ **void**, attic [*Accessible space between top of uppermost ceiling and underside of roof. Inaccessible spaces are considered structural cavities*] · Dachraum *m*, Dachboden *m* [*volkstümlich „Bühne" f genannt*]

~ **spire** [*A tall pyramidal, polygonal, or conical structure rising from a roof, usually of a church, and terminating in a point*] · Dachreiter *m*, Aufreiter

~ **stair(case)** · Dachtreppe *f*

~ **stilted upon suspension cable** · Dach *n* auf Tragseil gestützt

~ **stone** → roof(ing) ~

~ **structure**, ~ system · Dachkonstruktion *f*

~ **substrate sheeting** → (roof(ing)) base ~

~ **substructure sheeting** → (roof(ing)) base ~

~ **support** · Dachauflager *n* [*Für Dachstühle die Holzbalkendecke über dem letzten Vollgeschoß; bei Massivdecken bilden fest mit ihnen verbundene Schwellen, Pfetten oder Sattelhölzer das Auflager*]

~ **surround** · Dacheinfassung *f*

~ **system**, ~ structure · Dachkonstruktion *f*

~ **tank** · Dachbehälter *m*

~ **terrace**, ~-top ~ · Dachterrasse *f*

~ **tile** → roof(ing) ~

~ ~ **factory**, roofing ~ ~ · Dachsteinwerk *n*, Dachsteinfabrik *f*

~ **tiler**, (building) roofer · Dachdecker *m*

roof(-top) boiler room · Dach-Kesselraum *m*

~ **car park**, ~ parking deck, ~ parking area · Dachparkplatz *m*

~ **helicopter airport**, elevated ~ ~, ~ heliport · Hubschrauber-Dachflugplatz *m*

~ **parking area**, ~ ~ deck, ~ car park · Dachparkplatz *m*

~ ~ **deck**, ~ ~ area, ~ car park · Dachparkplatz *m*

~ **playground** · Dachspielplatz *m*

~ **promenade** · Dachpromenade *f*

~ **restaurant** · Dachrestaurant *n*

~ **shop** · Dachladen *m*

~ **terrace** · Dachterrasse *f*

~ ~ **garden** · Dachgarten *m*

roof trackway · Dachgleis *n*

(~) **truss** · (Dach)Binder *m*

~ **type**, type of roof · Dachart *f*

~ **unit**, ~ component, ~ member · Dachbauteil *m*, *n*, Dachelement *n*

(~) **valley**; flank [*local term*] · (Dach-)Kehle *f*, (Dach)Kehlung *f*, Einkehle; Ichsen *m* [*Schweiz*]

(~) ~ **clay tile**, valley clay roof(ing) ~, ~ roof(ing clay) ~ · (Rinnen)Kehlziegel *m*, Schwenkziegel

(~) ~ **post** · (Dach)Kehlenstütze *f* [*mehrschiffige Halle*]

(~) ~ **tile**, valley roof(ing) ~ · Kehlstein *m*

~ **vault** · Dachgewölbe *n*

~ **vent block** → ~ ventilating ~

~ ~ **tile** → ~ venti(lating) block

~ **vent(ilating) block**, attic ~ ~, ~ tile, ~ ventilator (~) [*An opening in a gable or ventilator in the roof. See remark under 'Block'*] · Dachlüfter *m*, Dachlüftungsstein *m*, Dachlüftungsblock(stein) *m*, Dachsiebblock(stein), Dachsiebstein

~ ~ **tile** → ~ ~ ~ block

~ **ventilation** · Dachlüftung *f*

~ **ventilator**, attic ~ [*A mechanical device to force ventilation by the use of a power-driven fan*] · Dachlüfter *n*

~ ~ **(block)** → ~ vent(ilating) ~

~ ~ **tile** → ~ vent(ilating) block

~ **void**, ~ space, attic [*Accessible space between top of uppermost ceiling and underside of roof. Inaccessible spaces are considered structural cavities*] · Dachraum *m*, Dachboden *m* [*volkstümlich „Bühne" genannt*]

~ **walkway** · Dachlaufsteg *m*

~ **water** [*This water is sometimes collected an used for drinking purposes*] · Dachwasser *n*

roof waterbar — roof(ing) membrane

~ **waterbar** → roof(ing) ~
~ **waterstop** → roof(ing) ~
~ **window** · Dachfenster *n*
~ **with air circulation** → flat ~ ~ ~ ~
~ ~ **45° pitch** · Winkeldach *n*
~ ~ **pitch of 1 : 5** · Fünfteldach *n*
~ ~ ~ ~ **1 : 4** · Vierteldach *n*
~ ~ ~ ~ **1 : 3** · Drittedach *n*
~ ~ **valley** → intersecting roof
~ **work** · Dacharbeiten *fpl*
~ **worker** · Dacharbeiter *m*
~ **zone** [*The zone provided for the component or components which make up the roof construction*] · Dachbereich *m, n*
roofed, covered · bedacht
~ **in wood** · holzgedeckt
~ **market,** covered ~, indoor ~, market hall · (Markt)Halle *f*
~ ~ **(place),** covered ~ (~) · überdachter Markt(platz) *m*, gedeckter ~
~ **passage,** covered ~, ~ way, ~ walk · überdachter Gang *m*, gedeckter ~
~ **railroad station** (US); ~ railway (Brit.); covered ~ ~ · Hallenbahnhof *m*
~ **railway station** (Brit.); ~ railroad (US); covered ~ ~ · Hallenbahnhof *m*
~ **shrine,** covered ~ · überdachtes Heiligtum *n*, gedecktes ~
~ **spectator's stand,** covered ~ · Dachtribüne *f*
~ **swimming bath(s)** → covered ~ ~
~ ~ **pool** → covered swimming bath(s)
~ **walk,** covered ~ · Laube *f* [*Offener, meist gewölbter Bogengang als Teil des Erdgeschosses, besonders von Wohn- und Rathäusern der deutschen Renaissance, auch dem Erdgeschoß vorgelagert*]
~ **walk,** covered ~, ~ way, ~ passage · überdachter Gang *m*, gedeckter ~
~ **way,** covered ~, ~ walk, ~ passage · überdachter Gang *m*, gedeckter ~
~ **timber bridge,** ~ wood(en) ~, covered ~ ~ · Dachbrücke *f*
~ **wood(en) bridge,** ~ timber ~, covered ~ ~ · Dachbrücke *f*
roofer, building ~, roof tiler · Dachdecker *m*
roofer's mortar · Dachdeckermörtel *m*
~ **nail** · Dachdeckernagel *m*
~ **work,** roofing ~ · Dachdeckerarbeiten *fpl*, Dach(ein)deck(ungs)arbeiten [*DIN 18338*]
roofing → placing the ~
roof(ing), roof cladding, roof covering, roof sheathing · Dach *n*, Dachbelag *m*, (Ein)Deckung *f*, Dach(ein)deckung, Bedachung
~ **accessories** · Bedachungszubehör *n*, (Dach)Eindeckungszubehör
~ **aluminium** (Brit.); ~ aluminum (US) · Dachaluminium *n*

~ **asphalt** (US); ~ (asphaltic-)bitumen (Brit.) · Dachbitumen *n*
~ **(asphaltic-)bitumen** (Brit.); ~ asphalt (US) · Dachbitumen *n*
(~) base sheeting, (~) deck(ing) ~, (~) substructure ~, (~) substrate ~ · (Dach)Unterlagsbahn *f*
(~) ~ (system) → (~) substructure (~)
~ **bitumen,** ~ asphaltic-~ (Brit.); ~ asphalt (US) · Dachbitumen *n*
~ **chip(ping)s** · Dachsplitt *m*
~ **clay tile,** clay (roof(ing)) ~ · Tondachstein *m*, Dachziegel *m* [*DIN 456*]
~ ~ ~ **factory,** clay roof(ing) ~ ~ · Dachziegelei *f*, Dachziegelfabrik *f*, Dachziegelwerk *n*
~ **contractor** · Dachdeckerunternehmer *m*
~ **copper** · Dachkupfer *n*
~ **cork** · Dachkork *m*
(~) deck(ing) sheeting → (~) base ~
(~) ~ (system) → (~) substructure (~)
(~) fabric, fabric for roofing · Roh(dach)pappe *f*
(~) ~ fiber (US); (~) ~ fibre (Brit.) · Roh(dach)pappenfaser *f*
~ **fastener,** ~ fastening, ~ fixing (accessory) · Dach(ein)deck(ungs)befestigungsmittel *n*
~ **fastening,** ~ fastener, ~ fixing (accessory) · Dach(ein)deck(ungs)befestigungsmittel *n*
~ **felt** → asphalt ready roofing
~ ~ **manufacture** → ready roofing ~
~ **fixing (accessory),** ~ fastener, ~ fastening · Dach(ein)deck(ungs)befestigungsmittel *n*
~ **foil** · Dach(belag)folie *f*
~ **granules** → granular cover material
~ **gravel** · Bedachungskies *m*, Dachkies
~ **insulation(-grade) plank,** ~ insulating ~ · Bedachungsdämmdiele *f*, Dachdämmdiele, Dacheindeck(ungs)dämmdiele, Dachdeck(ungs)dämmdiele
~ ~ **unit,** ~ insulating ~ · Dachdämmelement *n*
~ **lacquer** · Dachteer *m* [*Fehlname: Dachlack m. Zum pflegenden Nachteeren von Dächern*]
~ **lead sheet,** hard ~ ~, antimonial ~ ~ · Dachdeckerblei *n*, Hartbleiblech *n*, Antimonbleiblech
~ **material** · Bedachungsmaterial *n*, Dach(eindeckungs)material, Dachdeck-(ungs)material, Bedachungsstoff *m*, Dach(eindeckungs)stoff, Dachdeck(ungs)stoff, Dachbaustoff
~ **membrane** [*Roof(ing) membranes are applied to a substrate as sprayed or brushed finish or as sheet(ing)*] · Kunststoffdach(ein)deckung *f*, Kunststoff-(ein)deckung, Kunststoffbedachung, Kunststoffdach(belag) *n*, (*m*)

roof(ing) membrane sheet(ing) — room enclosing area

~ ~ **sheet(ing)** · Kunststoffdach(belag)bahn f

~ **metal** · Dachmetall n, Bedachungsmetall, Dach(ein)deck(ungs)metall, (Ein)Deckungsmetall

~ ~ **sheet** → roof cladding ~ ~

~ **panel** · Dachtafel f

~ **nail** · Dachnagel m

~ **(over)** · Überdachen n

~ **(~)** · Überdachung f

~ **paper** → ready roofing ~

~ ~ **manufacture** → ready roofing ~

~ **paste** · Dachpaste f

~ **pitch** · Teer(dach)spachtelmasse f, Teerdeckaufstrichmittel n, Teerdeckmasse, Teerdeckanstrichmittel

~ **plank** · Bedachungsdiele f, Dachdiele, Dacheindeck(ungs)diele, Dachdeck(ungs)diele

~ **preservative**, ~ preserver · Dachschutzmittel n, Dachpflegemittel

~ **preserver**, ~ preservative · Dachschutzmittel n, Dachpflegemittel

roofing product · (Dach)(Ein)Deckungserzeugnis n

~ **rags** · Dachpappenlumpen mpl

~ **shaft** · Halbsäule f in einer Blendarkatur

roof(ing) sheeting, ~ sheets · Dachplatten fpl

~ ~ · Bedachungsbahn f, Dachbahn, Dach(ein)deck(ungs)bahn

~ **sheet-metal** → roof cladding metal sheet

~ **sheets**, ~ sheeting · Dachplatten fpl

~ **shingle** · (Dach)Schindel f

~ **skin** · Dachhaut f

~ **slab** · Bedachungselement n, Dachplatte f, Bedachungsplatte, Dachelement, Dach(ein)deck(ungs)element

~ ~ [A slab forming the continuous load-bearing structure of a roof and spanning between supports] · Dachplatte f

~ **slag** · Bedachungsschlacke f, Dachschlacke

(~) **slate** [B.S. 680] · Schiefer m, Dach~ [Die bautechnische und geologische Bezeichnung für sich als Dachdeckungsstoff eignenden Tonschiefer] [DIN 52201–52206]

~ **stone** [The pre-eminent stone for roofing purposes is slate, and less often phyllite. Locally exposed thinly bedded sandy limestones and flagstones are also used] · Dachdeck(ungs)stein m, Dachstein, Dacheindeck(ungs)stein

(~) **substrate sheeting** → (~) base ~

(~) ~ **(system)** → (~) substructure (~)

(~) **substructure sheeting** → (~) base ~

(~) ~ **(system)**, (~) deck(ing) (~), (~) base (~), (~) substrate (~) · Dachhautträger m, (Dach)Unterlage f [zur Aufnahme der Dachhaut]

~ **terracotta** · Dachterrakotta f

~ **tile** · Dachstein m, Dach(ein)deck(ungs)stein

~ ~ **factory** · Dachsteinwerk n, Dachsteinfabrik f

roofing trade · Dachdeckerhandwerk n

roof(ing) waterbar, ~ waterstop · Dachfugenband n [Fugenband für Flachdachabdichtungen]

~ **waterstop**, ~ waterbar · Dachfugenband n [Fugenband für Flachdachabdichtungen]

~ **with interlocking clay (roof(ing)) tiles** → roof cladding ~ ~ ~ (~) ~

~ ~ ~ **(roof(ing)) tiles** → roof cladding ~ ~ (~) ~

~ **work**, roofer's ~ · Dachdeckerarbeiten fpl, Dach(ein)deck(ungs)arbeiten [DIN 18338]

room, chamber · Zimmer n, Raum m

~ · Raum m

~ · Wohneinheit f

~ **acoustics** · Raumakustik f

~ **air**, indoor ~, inside ~, interior ~, internal ~, inner ~ · Zimmerluft f, Raumluft

(~) ~ **conditioner** → (air) conditioning unit

~ **conditioning system** · Raumklimaanlage f

~ ~ **cooler** → inside ~ ~

~ ~ **heating burning appliance**, ~ ~ ~ furnace, ~ ~ ~ fire · Luftheizofen m

~ ~ ~ **fire**, ~ ~ ~ furnace, ~ ~ ~ burning appliance · Luftheizofen m

~ ~ ~ **furnace**, ~ ~ ~ fire, ~ ~ ~ burning appliance · Luftheizofen m

~ **area**, [The net floor area of a room] · Raumfläche f

~ **brightness** · Raumhelligkeit f

room-by-room · raumweise

room climate, indoor ~, inside ~, interior ~, internal ~, inner ~ · Raumklima n, Innenklima

~ **containing the source** · Senderaum m [Bei der Bestimmung der Schallpegeldifferenz D]

~ **cooling**, space ~ · Raumkühlung f

room-cooling unit · Raumkühlgerät n

(room) divide, division element · Raumteiler m, Raumteilungselement n [z.B. eine versetzbare (Montage)Trennwand]

room-dividing · raumtrennend

room door · Flurabschlußtür f, Gangabschlußtür, Korridorabschlußtür

~ ~, chamber ~ · Zimmertür f, Raumtür

room-door lock, chamber-door ~ · Zimmertürschloß n, Raumtürschloß

room efficiency · Wirkungsgrad m [Heizung]

~ **enclosing area** · Raumbegrenzungsfläche f

room facing a yard — rope(-suspended) cantilever(ed) roof 854

~ **facing a yard** · Hofraum *m*, Hofzimmer *n*

~ ~ **the garden** · Gartenzimmer *n*, Gartenraum *m*

~ **for arts and crafts** · Raum *m* für musische Tätigkeiten

~ ~ **branches to a house,** ~ ~ ~ ~ ~ **building** · Hausanschlußraum *m*, Gebäudeanschlußraum [*DIN 18012*]

~ ~ **drunks** · Ausnüchterungsraum *m*, Ausnüchterungszimmer *n* [*Krankenhaus*]

~ **heat,** interior ~, indoor ~, inside ~, internal ~, inner ~ · Raumwärme *f*, Innenwärme, Zimmerwärme

~ ~ **gain** → internal ~ ~

~ **heater,** ~ warmer, ~ heating appliance, ~ warming appliance · Raumheizer *m*, Raumheizgerät *n*

~ **heating,** ~ warming, space ~ · Raumerwärmung *f*, Raumheizung

~ ~ **appliance,** ~ warming ~, ~ heater, ~ warmer · Raumheizgerät *n*, Raumheizer *m*

(~) ~ **strip** · (Raum)Heizleiste *f*

~ **height** · Raumhöhe *f*

room-high · raumhoch

~ **panel** · Raumhoch-Tafel *f*

~ **window,** full-height ~, floor-to-ceiling ~ · raumhohes Fenster *n*

room humidity → indoor moisture

~ **illumination** → indoor lighting

~ **lighting** → indoor ~

~ **moisture** → indoor ~

~ **noise** · (Wohn)Geräusch *n*

(~) **occupant,** user, resident, (apartment) dweller · Raumbenutzer *m*, (Wohnungs)Benutzer, (Raum)Insasse *m*, Wohnungsinsasse, Bewohner

~ **relative humidity** → internal relative moisture

~ ~ **moisture** → internal ~ ~

~ **size** · Raumgröße *f*

~(-size) **unit,** unitized ~, building block module · (Raum)Zelle *f*, Installationszelle, Installationsblock *m*

room-sized · raumgroß

room sound · Raumschall *m*

~ ~ **attenuation** · Raumschalldämpfung *f*

~ ~ **insulation** · Raumschall(ab)dämmung *f*

~ **steam-curing** · Kammerbedampfung *f* [*Betonwaren*]

~ **temperature** · Raumtemperatur *f*, Zimmertemperatur

~ ~ **comfort curve** · Raumtemperatur-Behaglichkeitskurve *f*, Zimmertemperatur-Behaglichkeitskurve

~ ~ **control,** inner ~ ~, indoor ~ ~, internal ~ ~, interior ~ ~ · Raumtemperatursteuerung *f*, Innentemperatursteuerung

~ **thermostat** [*B.S. 3955*] · Raumtemperaturfühler *m*, Raumtemperaturregler, Raumthermostat *m*

~ **(unit) air conditioner** · Raumklimagerät *n*

~ **ventilation,** ~ venting · Raumbe- und -entlüftung *f*, Raumlüftung

~ **wall** · Raumwand *f*

(room-)wall sized · (raum)wandgroß

room warmer, ~ heater, ~ heating appliance, ~ warming appliance · Raumheizer *m*, Raumheizgerät *n*

~ **warming,** ~ heating, space ~ · Raumerwärmung *f*, Raumheizung

~ ~ **appliance,** ~ heating ~, ~ heater, ~ warmer · Raumheizgerät *n*, Raumheizer *m*

~ **width** · Raumbreite *f*

~ **window** · Raumfenster *n*, Zimmerfenster

rooming house, boarding ~, tourist ~, lodging ~ [*A building arranged or used for the lodging with or without meals, for compensation, of more than five and not more than twenty individuals*] · Pension *f*, Logierhaus *n*

roomy → spacious

root diagram, ~ grading curve · Siebliniendarstellung *f* im Wurzelmaßstab [*Auf der Waag(e)rechten sind nicht die Korngrößen bzw. Sieblochdurchmesser aufgetragen, sondern die Wurzeln dieser Sieblochdurchmesser*]

~ **grading curve,** ~ diagram · Siebliniendarstellung *f* im Wurzelmaßstab [*Auf der Waag(e)rechten sind nicht die Korngrößen bzw. Sieblochdurchmesser aufgetragen, sondern die Wurzeln dieser Sieblochdurchmesser*]

rootproof · wurzelabweisend

rope · Strick *m*

~ **action,** cable ~ · Kabelwirkung *f*, Seilwirkung

~ **cantilevering roof** → ~-suspended ~ ~

~ **elliptic(al) roof** → ~-suspended ~ ~

~ **family,** cable ~, family of ropes, family of cables · Seilschar *f*

~ **fibre** (Brit.); ~ fiber (US) · Strickfaser *f*

~ **flat roof** → ~-suspended ~ ~

~ **moulding** (Brit.); ~ molding (US); cable ~ · Taustab *m*, Schiffstauverzierung *f* [*Tauartig gedrehter Stab als Schmuckglied der normannischen Baukunst*]

~ **roof** → ~-suspended ~

~ **sag,** cable ~, sag of rope, sag of cable · Kabeldurchhang *m*, Seildurchhang

~ **sealing,** sealing by rope · Strick(ab)dichtung *f*

rope(-suspended) cantilever(ed) roof, ~ cantilevering ~, cable(-suspended) ~ ~ · Kabelkragdach *n*, Kabelauslegerdach, Seilkragdach, Seilauslegerdach

~ **elliptic(al) roof**, cable(-suspended) ~ ~ · elliptisches Kabelhängedach n, ~ Seilhängedach, Ellipsen-Kabelhängedach, Ellipsen-Seilhängedach

~ **flat roof**, cable(-suspended) ~ ~ · Kabelhängeflachdach n, Seilhängeflachdach

~ **roof, cable(-suspended)** ~, suspended ~, suspension ~ · Seil(hänge)dach n, Kabel(hänge)dach, Hängedach

rope system, cable ~ · Seilsystem n, Kabelsystem

~ **wire**, cable ~ · Kabeldraht m, Seildraht

rose · (Tür)Drückerrosette f, (Stützring-) Rosette [*DIN 18258*]

~, wind~ · Windrose f

rose-arbour · Rosenlaube f

rose pattern · Rosenmuster n

rose-patterned glass · Rosenmusterglas n

rose window, traceried ~ ~ · Maßwerkrose(nfenster) f, (n), (Fenster-) Rose, Rosenfenster [*Mit Maßwerk geschmücktes gotisches Rundfenster*]

Röseler reinforced block floor · Röseler-Decke f

Rose's alloy · Rose-Metall n

rosette [*Any conventional ornament carved or modelled to resemble a rose*] · Rosette f

~, **resin, colophony,** Colophonian (resin) · Kolophonium n, Spiegelharz n, griechisches Pech n, Geigenharz [*DIN 55935*]

~ **ester**, ester gum, esterified natural resin · Esterharz n

~ ~ **varnish**, ester gum ~, esterified natural resin ~ · Esterharz(klar)lack m

rosin-modified maleic resin · Maleinatharz n

~ ~ **varnish resin** · Maleinat-Lackharz n

~ **phenolic resin**, synthetic copal · Kunstkopal m, (harzsäure)modifiziertes Phenolharz n

rostral column, columna rostrata [*A monumental Roman column erected to commemorate a naval victory and decorated with the figure-heads of captured vessels*] · Gedenksäule f für einen Seesieg, Schiffssäule

rostrum [*This term denotes the raised tribune in the Forum Romanum, from which orators adressed the people, and was so called because decorated with the prows of ships taken in war as were rostral columns*] · Rostrum n

rotary airplane hangar, rotating ~ ~, revolving ~ ~ · Dreh-Flugzeughalle f

~ **apartment tower**, rotating ~ ~, revolving ~ ~ (US); ~ residence ~, ~ residential ~, ~ dwelling ~, ~ housing ~ · Dreh-Wohnhochhaus n, Dreh-Hochwohnhaus, Dreh-Wohnturm m

~ **bolt** · Drehriegel m [*Schloß*]

~ **branch switch**, turn ~ ~ · Drehschalter m

~**(-cut) veneer**, peeled ~ [*Usually called 'commercial veneer'*] · (rund-) geschältes Furnier n, (Rund)Schälfurnier

rotary door → revolving ~

~ **dwelling tower** → ~ apartment ~

~ **floor**, revolving ~, rotating ~ · Dreh(fuß)boden m

~**(-floor) restaurant**, revolving(-floor) ~ · Drehrestaurant n

rotary house, rotating ~, revolving ~ · Drehhaus n

~ **housing tower** → ~ apartment ~

~ **kiln cement** · Rotierofenzement m, Drehofenzement

~ ~ **method** · Drehofenverfahren n, Rotierofenverfahren

~ ~ **(produced) expanded shale (clay)**; ~ ~ (~) bloating ~ (~), ~ (~) bloated ~ (~) (Brit.) · Drehofen-Blähschieferton m, Rotierofen-Blähschieferton

~ **kiln-type plaster of Paris** · Drehofengips m, Rotierofengips [*Im Drehofen hergestellter Stuckgips*]

~ **leaf**, rotating ~, revolving ~ · Drehtürflügel m

~ **lime kiln** · Kalkdrehofen m, Kalkrotierofen

~ **meter** → ~ water ~

~ **motion**, rotation [*Turning around on an axis or centre*] · Drehung f, Drehen n

~ **platform**, revolving ~, rotating ~ · Drehplattform f

~ **residence tower** → ~ apartment ~

~ **residential tower** → ~ apartment ~

~ **restaurant**, revolving ~, ~-floor ~ · Drehrestaurant n .

~ **sintering kiln**, rotating ~ ~ · Sintertrommelofen m, Trommelsinterofen

~ **stage**, rotating ~, revolving ~ · Drehbühne f [*Theater*]

~ **veneer** → rotary-cut ~

~ **warded mechanism** · drehendes Riegelgesperre n [*Buntbartschloß*]

~ **(water) meter**, rotating (~) ~ [*This type of meter is used to measure the amount of water supplied to bulk consumers. The flow through the meter rotates a vane or propeller which drives the mechanism and registers on a dial*] · Flügelrad(wasser)messer m

rotatably supported · drehbar (auf-) gelagert

rotating (air)plane hangar, rotary ~ ~, revolving ~ ~ · Dreh-Flugzeughalle f

~ **apartment tower**, rotary ~ ~, revolving ~ ~ (US); ~ residence ~, ~ residential ~, ~ dwelling ~, ~ housing ~ · Dreh-Wohnhochhaus n, Dreh-Hochwohnhaus, Dreh-Wohnturm m

rotating door — rough-shuttered

~ **door** → revolving ~

~ **dwelling tower** → ~ apartment ~

~ **floor**, revolving ~, rotary ~ · Dreh(fuß)boden *m*

~**(-floor) restaurant** → revolving(-floor) ~

rotating house, rotary ~, revolving ~ · Drehhaus *n*

~ **housing tower** → ~ apartment ~

~ **leaf**, rotary ~, revolving ~ · Drehtürflügel *m*

~ **residence tower** → ~ apartment ~

~ **residential tower** → ~ apartment ~

~ **sintering kiln**, rotary ~ ~ · Sintertrommelofen *m*, Trommelsinterofen

~ **stage**, rotary ~, revolving ~ · Drehbühne *f* [*Theater*]

~ **templet**, rotary ~ · Leier *f* [*zum Einwölben*]

rotation, rotary motion [*Turning around on an aixs or centre*] · Drehung *f*, Drehen *n*

~ **due to torsion** · Torsionsdrehung *f*, Verwindungsdrehung, Drill(ungs)drehung

~ **factor** · Drehungsfaktor *m*

~ **of a girder**, ~ ~ girders · Trägerdrehung *f*

~ ~ **girders**, ~ ~ a girder · Trägerdrehung *f*

~ **surface**, surface of revolution · Drehfläche *f*

rotation(al) angle of bar, ~ ~ ~ rod, ~ ~ ~ member, ~ ~ ~ element · Stabdrehwinkel *m*, Glieddrehwinkel, Stabverschwenkungswinkel, Gliedverschwenkungswinkel

rotational deformation · Drehverformung *f*

~ **paraboloid** · Drehparaboloid *n*, Rotationsparaboloid

~ **rigidity**, ~ stiffness · Drehsteifigkeit *f*, Drehstarrheit

~ **shell**, shell of rotational symmetry, shell of revolution (subjected to loads of rotational symmetry) · Drehschale *f*, Rotationsschale, drehsymmetrische Schale

~ **stiffness**, ~ rigidity · Drehsteifigkeit *f*, Drehstarrheit

~ **visco(si)meter** · Rotationsviskosimeter *n*

~ **wave**, transverse ~, shear ~ · Transversalwelle *f*, Querwelle [*Im Gegensatz zu Gasen und Flüssigkeiten können in festen Körpern jedoch auch Schubkräfte übertragen werden, so daß Körperschall hauptsächlich in Form von Transveralwellen auftritt, bei denen die Teilchen quer zur Ausbreitungsrichtung schwingen*]

rotationally symmetric, axi-symmetric rotationssymmetrisch, drehsymmetrisch

rotonda, rotunda [*A building circular outside and inside and usually domed*] · Rotunde *f*

~ **arch**, rotunda ~ · Rotundebogen *m*

rotproof, anti-rot, imputrescible · fäulnisbeständig, unfaulbar, fäulnisfest, unverrottbar, fäulniswidrig, verrottungsfest, verrottungswidrig, verrottungsbeständig

rottenstone · englischer Tripel *m*

rotunda → rotonda

~ **arch**, rotonda ~ · Rotundenbogen *m*

rough arch, safety ~, discharging ~, relieving ~ · Entlastungsbogen *m*, Ablastebogen, Überfangbogen, Verstärkungsbogen, Versteifungsbogen

~ **(builder's) fittings**, ~ (~) hardware · rohe (Bau)Beschläge *mpl*

~ **(~) hardware**, ~ (~) fittings · rohe (Bau)Beschläge *mpl*

to rough-cast · berappen

rough cast, pebble-dash; harl(e). harling [*Scotland*] · Rauhputz *m*, Berapp *m*, Anwurf *m* [*Bei diesem groben Außenputz wird die Fläche zweimal mit Mörtel und Sand beworfen, denen beim zweiten Bewurf Kiesel oder zerquetschte Steine zugemischt sind*]

~ ~ **glass** [*Rolled translucent glass, one surface of which has a definite texture, made by rolling molten glass either on a table or between rollers. B.S. 3447*] · gewalztes Glas *n*

~ ~ **plate (glass)**; ~ plate (glass) (US) · Rohspiegelglas *n*, Spiegelrohglas

~ **concrete** · Rauhbeton *m*

~ **fittings**, ~ hardware, ~ builders' ~ · rohe (Bau)Beschläge *mpl*

~ **float** · Rauhscheibe *f* [*Putzerwerkzeug*]

~ **floor** (US); counter ~, dead ~, wood(-en) sub-floor, timber sub-floor · Blendboden *m*, Blindboden, Holzunterboden [*Bretterlage über der Deckenkonstruktion als Unterlage für Riemen- oder Parkett(fuß)böden*]

~ **forms**, ~ shuttering, ~ form(work) · Rauhschalung *f*

~ **form(work)**, ~ shuttering, ~ forms · Rauhschalung *f*

~ **hardware**, ~ fittings, ~ builders' ~ · rohe (Bau)Beschläge *mpl*

to rough-hew · bossieren, bosseln [*Einen Werkstoff oder Quader(stein) an seiner Vorderseite grob zuhauen, so daß eine erhabene Fläche, die Bosse, stehenbleibt*]

rough-hewing · Bossieren *n*, Bosseln *n*

rough-hewn · bossiert, gebosselt

rough plate (glass) (US); ~ cast plate (~) · Rohspiegelglas *n*, Spiegelrohglas

~ **rolled glass** · Rohgußglas *n*, Gußrohglas

~ **rubble masonry** → ordinary ~ ~

rough-shuttered, board-marked, natural · schalungsrauh

rough shuttering, ~ forms, ~ form(-work) · Rauhschalung *f*

~ stone, rubble (~) · Bruchstein *m* [*Er wird vom Maurer zurechtgerichtet wenn für Mauerwerk verwendet*]

~ ~masonry wall, rubble(-stone) (~) ~ · Bruchsteinmauer *f*

~ ~ ~ (work), rubble(~) ~ (~), rubblework · Bruchsteinmauerwerk *n*

~ T and G boarding, ~ tongued and grooved ~, ~ T&G ~ · Rauhspund(-bretter) *m*, (*npl*)

~ texture · Grobstruktur *f* [*Putz*]

~ work [*Brickwork, which will eventually be hidden by plaster, facing bricks, joinery etc.*] · Grobziegelmauerwerk *n*

roughing-in [*Doing the first rough work of any trade such as plumbing, plastering etc. In plumbing, installing all pipes as far as the points where they must be joined to their fixtures*] · Grobarbeiten *fpl*

roughing out · erste Behauung *f*, Abschrotung

roughening · Aufrauhen *n*

roughly dressed, coarsely ~, ~ shaped · grob zugerichtet [*(Natur)Stein*]

roughness · Rauhigkeit *f*

round · fett [*Anstrichuntergrund*]

~ · Rund(leiter)sprosse *f*

~ · Rundprofil *n*

~, ~ bar · Rundstab *m*

~ aggregate → ~ concrete ~

~ (air) diffusor, ~ (~) diffuser · (Luft)Runddiffusor *m*

~ apse, ~ apsis, ~ exedra · Rundapsis *f*, Rundapside *f*, Rundabseite *f*, Rundexedra *f*, Rundabside *f* [*Halbrunder Abschluß einer romanischen Basilika. Im weiteren Sinne jeder runde Chorschluß einer Kirche. Manchmal auch „Rundabseite" genannt*]

~ arch, half-~, semicircular ~; full-centred ~ (Brit.); full-centered ~ (US) · Rundbogen *m*, Halbkreisbogen, römischer Bogen [*veraltet: Vollbogen, voller Bogen*]

round-arched · rundbogig

~ arcade · Rundbogenarkade *f*, Halbkreisbogenarkade, rundbogige Arkade

~ barrel vault, ~ tunnel ~, ~ wagon ~ · rundbogiges Tonnengewölbe *n*, rundbogige Tonne *f*

~ corbel-table, round-headed ~ · Rundbogenfries *m*, Halbkreisbogenfries, rundbogiger Fries

~ merlon · Rundbogenzinne *f*, Halbkreisbogenzinne, rundbogige Zinne

~ opening · rundbogige Öffnung *f*

~ tunnel vault, ~ barrel ~, ~ wagon ~ · rundbogiges Tonnengewölbe *n*, rundbogige Tonne *f*

~ wagon vault, ~ tunnel ~, ~ barrel ~ · rundbogiges Tonnengewölbe *n*, rundbogige Tonne *f*

~ window · Rundbogenfenster *n*, Halbkreisbogenfenster, rundbogiges Fenster

round bar → ~ reinforcing ~

~ (~) · Rundstab *m*

~ ~ reinforcement, ~ ~ steel · Rundstahlbewehrung *f*, Rundstahlarmierung, Rund(stahl)einlagen *fpl*

~ ~ steel, ~ ~ reinforcement · Rundstahlbewehrung *f*, Rundstahlarmierung, Rund(stahl)einlagen *fpl*

~ ~ web, ~ rod ~, circular ~ ~, cylindrical ~ ~ · Rundstabsteg *m*

~ bars, ~ reinforcing ~, ~ reinforcement ~, rounds · (Beton)Rundstäbe *mpl*, (Beton)Rund(stab)stahl *m* [*Fehlnamen: (Beton)Rundeisen n*]

~ bastion, squat round tower · Rundbastion *f* [*rundes Verteidigungsbauwerk aus (ursprünglich) befestigtem Erdreich; später mit starker Mauer ummantelt*]

~ beam · Rundbalken(träger) *m*

~ block, ~ building · Rundgebäude *n*

~ brick window → ~ clay ~ ~

~ building, ~ block · Rundgebäude *n*

~ campanile, circular ~, cylindrical ~ · runder freistehender Glockenturm *m*, freistehender runder ~

~ capital, circular ~ · Rundkapitell *n*, Rundkapitäl

~ cella, circular ~ · Rundcella *f*

~ chapel, circular ~, chapel-in-the-round · Rundkapelle *f*

~ chimney, circular ~, cylindrical ~ · Rundschornstein *m*

~ church, circular ~, church-in-the-round · Rundkirche *f*

~ (clay) brick window, circular (~) ~ ~ · Ziegelrundfenster *n*, Ziegelkreisfenster

~ column, circular ~, cylindrical ~ · Rundsäule *f*

~ ~, circular ~, cylindrical ~ · Rundstütze *f*

~ (concrete) aggregate, rounded (~) ~ [*An aggregate the particles of which are fully water-worn or completely shaped by attrition*] · rolliger (Beton-)Zuschlag(stoff) *m*, rund(lich)er ~, rolliges (Beton)Zuschlagmaterial *n*, rund(lich)es (Beton)Zuschlagmaterial

~ ~ column, cylindrical ~ ~, circular ~ ~ · Betonrundstütze *f*

~ ~ flue block → chimney ~

~ (construction timber) → timber in the round (for construction purposes)

~ core, circular ~, cylindrical ~ · Rundkern *m* [*Hochhaus*]

~ cross-section, circular ~, cylindrical ~ · Rundquerschnitt *m*, Kreisquerschnitt

~ diffuser → ~ air ~

~ diminutive tower, cylindrical ~ ~, circular ~ ~, small ~, ~ turret · Rundtürmchen *n*, kleiner Rundturm *m*

~ donjon → ~ keep

round (door) knob — round reinforcement bars

~ **(door) knob** · Rund(tür)knopf m
~ **dowel** · Runddollen m, Runddübel m, runder (Stab)Dübel, runder Dollen
~ ~ **pin** · runder Verbandstift m [*DIN 1156*]
~ **dungeon** → ~ keep
rounded (concrete) aggregate, round (~), ~ [*An aggregate the particles of which are fully water-worn or completely shaped by attrition*] · rolliger (Beton)Zuschlag(stoff) m, rund(lich)er ~
rounded-edge tile · Rundkant(belag)platte f, Rundkantfliese
round edge tile fitting · Rundungs(belag)platte f, Rundungsfliese
round-edged · rundkantig
round(ed) moulding, roll ~, convex ~, circular ~ (Brit.); ~ molding (US); bead (~), bowtel(l), boltel, edge roll · Rundstab m
roundel · rundes Flachbild n
round end of a choir, ~ ~ ~ ~ quire · (Chor)Rundhaupt n
~ **exedra,** ~ apsis, ~ apse · Rundapsis f, Rundapside f, Rundabseite f, Rundexedra f, Rundabside f [*Halbrunder Abschluß einer romanischen Basilika. Im weiteren Sinne jeder runde Chorabschluß einer Kirche. Manchmal auch "Rundabseite" genannt*]
~ **façade** · Rundfassade f
~ **fence picket,** ~ ~ post, ~ ~ stake, ~ fencing ~ · Rundzaunpfahl m, Rundzaunpfosten m
~ **floor,** circular ~; ~ story (US); ~ storey (Brit.) · Rundetage f, Kreisetage f, Rundstockwerk n, Kreisstockwerk, Rundgeschoß n, Kreisgeschoß
~ ~ **folded plate roof** → circular ~ ~ ~
~ ~ **slab roof** → circular folded plate ~
~ ~ **footing,** circular ~ · Kreisfundament n, Rundfundament
~ **foundation,** circular ~ · Kreisgründung f, Rundgründung
~ **girder** · Rundträger m
~ **glass tower,** cylindrical ~ ~, circular ~ ~ · Rundglasturm m, Glasrundturm
~ **grain,** ~ particle · abgerundetes Korn n, rolliges ~, kugeliges ~, rund(lich)es ~, Rundkorn
~ **(ground(-))plan,** circular ~ · runder Grundriß m, kreisförmiger ~
~ **guard rail profile** → ~ handrail section
~ ~ **section,** ~ ~ profile, ~ ~ shape, ~ ~ unit, ~ ~ trim, ~ guard rail ~ · Rundprofilhandlauf m
~ **hanger** · Rundhänger m, Rundhängeeisen n [*Hängedecke*]
round-headed corbel-table, round-arched ~ · Rundbogenfries m, Halbkreisbogenfries, rundbogiger Fries

~ **loophole,** arch(ed) ~, ~ loop (window) · Rundbogensehschlitz m
~ **window,** arch(ed) ~ · (Rund)Bogenfenster n
round hipped-plate roof (US) → circular folded plate ~
~ **hole,** circular ~ · Rundloch n, Kreisloch
(~) **horseshoe arch,** Saracenic ~, mosque ~, Arabic ~ · (arabischer) Hufeisen(rund)bogen m, Dreiviertelkreisbogen, Überhalbkreisbogen, maurischer Bogen [*Dieser Bogen ist unten eingezogen, da ihm der Dreiviertelkreis zugrunde liegt. Er kommt auch in spitzer Form vor*]
roundhouse · Ringschuppen m [*Lok(omotiv)schuppen*]
round house, circular ~ · Rundhaus n
~ **interlocking pipe,** cylindrical ~ ~, circular ~ ~ · rundes Falzrohr n
~ **keep,** circular ~, ~ donjon, ~ dungeon, cylindrical ~ · Rundbergfried m, Rundbelfried, Rundberchfrit, Runddonjon m
~ **knob,** ~ door ~ · Rund(tür)knopf m
~ ~ **door furniture,** ~ ~ ~ set [*B.S. 1331*] · Rund(tür)knopfgarnitur f
~ **ladder,** stave ~, rung ~, rundle ~, tread ~ · Sprossenleiter f
round-log construction · Blockhausbau m
round manhole, cylindrical ~, circular ~, ~ manway · Kreisschacht m, Rundschacht
~ **manway,** cylindrical ~, circular ~, ~ manhole · Kreisschacht m, Rundschacht
~ **mesh** · Rundloch n [*Sieb*]
~ ~ **screen** · Rundloch-Grobsieb n
~ ~ **sieve** · Rundloch-Feinsieb n
~ ~ **test sieve** · Rundloch(-Prüf)sieb n
~ **office block,** ~ ~ building, circular ~ ~, cylindrical ~ ~ · Rund-Bürogebäude n, Büro-Rundgebäude
~ **particle,** ~ grain · abgerundetes Korn n, rolliges ~, kugeliges ~, rund(lich)es ~, Rundkorn
~ **peripteral temple,** circular ~ ~ · Ringhallentempel m, Peripteralrundtempel
~ **pier,** cylinder · Rundpfeiler m, Kreispfeiler [*Er hat kreisrunden Grundriß, jedoch keine Verjüngung und keine Entasis wie die Säule*]
~ **plan,** ~ ground(-)~, circular ~ · runder Grundriß m, kreisförmiger ~
~ **plate,** circular ~, ~ slab · kreisförmige Platte f, ~ Scheibe, runde ~, Kreisplatte, Kreisscheibe, Rundplatte, Rundscheibe
~ **reinforcement bar** → ~ (reinforcing) ~
~ ~ **bars,** ~ (reinforcing) ~, rounds · (Beton)Rundstäbe mpl, (Beton)Rund(stab)stahl m [*Fehlnamen: (Beton-)Rundeisen n*]

858

round reinforcement rod — row of posts

~ ~ rod → ~ (reinforcing) bar

~ **(reinforcing) bar,** ~ reinforcement ~, ~ ~ rod, circular (~) ~, cylindrical (~) ~ · (Beton)Rund(stahl)stab *m*; (Beton)Rundeisenstab [*Fehlnamen*]

~ **(~) bars,** ~ reinforcement ~, rounds · (Beton)Rundstäbe *mpl*, (Beton)Rund(stab)stahl *m* [*Fehlnamen: (Beton)Rundeisen n*]

~ **(~) rod** → ~ (~) bar

~ **rod** → ~ (reinforcing) bar

~ ~ **web** → ~ bar ~

~ **roof,** circular ~ · Kreisdach *n*, Runddach

~ **roof-light,** circular ~ · Rund(decken)-oberlicht *n*, Kreis(decken)oberlicht

rounds, round (reinforcing) bars, round reinforcement bars · (Beton)Rundstäbe *mpl*, (Beton)Rund(stab)stah! *m* [*Fehlnamen: (Beton)Rundeisen n*]

round sand · Rundsand *m*

~ **shaft,** circular ~ · Rundschaft *m*, Kreisschaft

~ **shed,** circular ~ · Rundschuppen *m*, Kreisschuppen

~ **silo,** cylindrical ~, circular ~ · Rundsilo *m*, Kreissilo

~ **slab,** circular ~, ~ plate · kreisförmige Platte *f*, ~ Scheibe, runde ~, Kreisplatte, Kreisscheibe, Rundplatte, Rundscheibe

~ **small tower,** circular ~ ~, cylindrical ~ ~, ~ diminutive ~, ~ turret · Rundtürmchen *n*, kleiner Rundturm *m*

~ **stair(case),** circular ~, cylindrical ~ · Rundtreppe *f*, kreisrunde Wendeltreppe

~ **(~) well,** circular (~) ~, cylindrical (~) ~ · (Treppen)Auge *n*, Schneckenauge, Lichtspindel *f*, Hohlspindel [*Wendeltreppe*]

~ **steel column,** circular ~ ~, cylindrical ~ ~ · Rundstahlstütze *f*, Stahlrundstütze

~ **story** (US); ~ storey (Brit.); ~ floor, circular ~ · Rundetage *f*, Kreisetage, Rundstockwerk *n*, Kreisstockwerk, Rundgeschoß *n*, Kreisgeschoß

~ **temple,** circular ~ · Rundtempel *m*

~ **tilted-slab roof** (US) → circular folded plate ~

~ **timber,** roundwood, timber in the round [*logs and bolts*] · Rundholz *n*

~ **toothed plate** · Zahnringdübel *m*, runder Zahndübel [*Holzdübel*]

~ **tower,** circular ~, cylindrical ~ · Rundturm *m*

~ **traceried window,** circular ~ ~ · Rundmaßwerkfenster *n*

~ **tube,** circular ~, cylindrical ~ · Rundröhre *f*, Kresröhre, runde Röhre, kreisförmige Röhre, Zylinderröhre

~ **turret,** circular ~, cylindrical ~, ~ diminutive tower, ~ small tower · Rundtürmchen *n*, kleiner Rundturm *m*

~ **well** → ~ (stair(case)) ~

~ **wire,** cylindrical ~, circular ~ · Runddraht *m*

~ ~ **rod,** cylindrical ~ ~, circular ~ ~ · Rundwalzdraht *m*

rounds-type truss(ed girder) · R-Träger *m*, Rundstahl(fachwerk)träger [*Ober- und Untergurt bestehen aus ⊥-Stählen, die Füllstäbe aus einer eingeschweißten Rundstahlschlange*]

roundwood → timber in the round (for construction purposes)

rove, roving · Grobgespinst *n*, Grobgarn *n*

roving, rove · Grobgespinst *n*, Grobgarn *n*

roving(s) · Glasseidenstrang *m*, Glasseidenfäden *mpl*

row · Zeile *f* [*Häuser; Gebäude; Läden*]

~ **construction (method)** · Reihenbau(weise) *m*, (*f*) [*Die Hausreihen laufen mit den Straßen gleich. Die Vorderfronten liegen in einer Flucht oder sind gleichmäßig gestaffelt*]

~ **home** · Reihenfamilienhaus *n*, eingebautes Familienhaus

~ **house** · eingebautes Haus *n*, Reihenhaus

row-house development · Reihenhausbebauung *f*

row-house-type dwelling unit (US); ~ dwelling (Brit.) · Reihenhauswohnung *f*

row installation · Reihenanlage *f*

rowlock, rollock, rolo(c)k, (clay) brick on edge course · (Ziegel)Rollschar *f*, (Ziegel)Rollschicht *f*

~ **paving,** rollock ~, rolo(c)k ~ · (Ziegel)Rollscharpflaster *n*, (Ziegel)Rollschichtpflaster

row of Apostles · Apostelreihe *f*

~ ~ **arches** · Bogenreihe *f*

~ ~ **bars,** ~ ~ rods, ~ ~ members, ~ ~ elements · Gliedreihe *f*, Stabreihe

~ ~ **billets** · Schindelfries *m*

~ ~ **blocks,** ~ ~ buildings · Gebäudezeile *f*

~ ~ **buildings,** ~ ~ blocks · Gebäudezeile *f*

~ ~ **chairs** · Stuhlreihe *f*

~ ~ **columns,** line ~ ~, ~ ~ supports · Stützenreihe *f*

~ ~ ~, range ~ ~ · Säulenstellung *f*, Säulenreihe *f*

~ ~ **coring,** coring row · Lochreihe *f* [*Mauerziegel*]

~ ~ **elements,** ~ ~ members, ~ ~ bars, ~ ~ rods · Stabreihe *f*, Gliedreihe

~ ~ **houses** · Wohnzeile *f*, Häuserzeile, Hauszeile

~ ~ ~ **'linked' together** · Kettenhäuser *npl*

~ ~ **members,** ~ ~ elements, ~ ~ rods, ~ ~ bars · Gliedreihe *f*, Stabreihe

~ ~ **piers** · Pfeilerreihe *f*

~ ~ **posts** · Pfostenreihe *f*

~~ **rods,** ~~ **bars,** ~~ **members,** ~~ **elements** · Gliederreihe f, Stabreihe

~~ **seats, tier** ~ ~ · Sitzreihe f

~~ **stores** · Ladenzeile f

~~ **supports, line** ~ ~, ~ ~ **columns** · Stützenreihe f

rowlock arch [A brick relieving arch of two concentric courses of headers set on edge] · Bogen m aus zwei (Ziegel-)Rollschichten, ~ ~ ~ (Ziegel)Rollscharen

royal blue (pigment), Prussian ~ (~) [Apart from being a generic term, Prussian blue usually refers to the same type as a pure bronze blue, i.e. both are strong, deep shades with a reddish or violet-blue undertone. B.S. 283] · Preußischblau n

~ **castle,** king's ~ · königliches Schloß n, Königsschloß

~ **chapel,** king's ~ · Königskapelle f

~ **garden** · königlicher Garten m, Hofgarten

~ **gardener** · königlicher Gartenbaumeister m, kgl. ~, Hofbaumeister

~ **mastaba(h) tomb** · Königsmastaba f, Herrschermastaba [altägyptische Grabform]

~ **palace,** king's ~ · Königspalast m

~ **pyramid,** king's ~ · Königspyramide f

'**Royal Square**', Maidan-i-Shān [Isfahan] · Meidan-Platz m

royal suite, king's ~ · Königssuite f, Königsgemächer npl

~ **tomb,** king's ~ · Königsgrab n

RSJ → (rolled-)steel joist

r.s.j. → (rolled-)steel joist

RST → reinforcing steel

RT, raintight, rainproof · regendicht, regenundurchlässig, regensicher, regenfest

to rub down · mattieren

~~ **over with a wash-leather** [After wet flatting, for example] · abledern

rubbed · abgerieben

~ **finish** [A finish obtained by using an abrasive to remove surface irregularities from concrete] · abgeriebene Betonfläche f

rubber, vulcanized ~ · Gummi m, n [vulkanisiert]

rubber-asphalt composition → ~ mass

~ **compound** → ~ mass

rubber/asphalt emulsion (US); rubber/(asphaltic-)bitumen (Brit.) · Gummi-Bitumenemulsion f

rubber-asphalt mass, ~ composition, ~ material, ~ compound (US); rubber-(asphaltic-)bitumen ~ (Brit.) · Gummi-Bitumen-Masse f

~ **material** → ~ mass

rubber/asphalt strip (US); rubber/(asphaltic-)bitumen ~ (Brit.) · Gummi-Bitumen-Streifen m

rubber-(asphaltic-)bitumen composition (Brit.) → rubber-asphalt mass

~ **compound** (Brit.) → rubber-asphalt mass

rubber/(asphaltic-)bitumen emulsion (Brit.) → rubber/asphalt ~

rubber-(asphaltic-)bitumen mass (Brit.) → rubber-asphalt ~

~ **material** (Brit.) → rubber-asphalt mass

rubber/(asphaltic-)bitumen strip (Brit.); rubber/asphalt ~ (US) · Gummi-Bitumen-Streifen m

rubber-base(d) sealant, ~ sealer, ~ seal(ing) medium, ~ seal(ing) material · Gummi-(Ab)Dicht(ungs)material n, Gummi-(Ab)Dicht(ungs)stoff m, Gummi-(Ab)Dicht(ungs)mittel n

rubber-bitumen composition (Brit.) → rubber-asphalt mass

~ **compound** (Brit.) → rubber-asphalt mass

rubber/bitumen emulsion (Brit.) → rubber/asphalt ~

rubber-bitumen mass (Brit.) → rubber-asphalt ~

~ **material** (Brit.) → rubber-asphalt mass

rubber/bitumen strip, rubber/asphaltic-bitumen ~ (Brit.); rubber/asphalt ~ (US) · Gummi-Bitumen-Streifen m

rubber buffer · Gummipuffer m

~ **(building) mastic** · Kautschukkitt m

rubber-coated, rubber-(sur)faced · gummibeschichtet

rubber-compatible · gummiverträglich

rubber conduit · Gummirohr n [Hartgummirohr (in Stangen) oder Weichgummirohr (in Rollen) zur Verlegung von Leitungen unter Putz]

~ **cone** · Gummikegel m

~ **cord** · Gummischnur f

rubber-coupled · gummigekuppelt [Rohrleitung]

rubber coupling, ~ pipe ~ · Gummi-(Rohr)kupplung f

~ **distance piece,** ~ spacer · Gummiabstandhalter m

~ **door** · Gummitür f

~~ **leaf** · Gummitürblatt n

rubber-faced, rubber-surfaced, rubber-coated · gummibeschichtet

rubber felt · Gummifilz m

~ **filler,** cell rubber (joint) ~ · Gummi-(fugen)einlage f

~ **floor cover(ing),** ~ floor(ing) (finish) · Fbg m, Gummi(fuß)boden(belag) m

~ **foil** · Gummifolie f

~ **gasket** → ~ preformed ~

~~ **joint** · Gummiabdeckfuge f

~ **glazing channel** · Gummiprofil n zur Verglasung, ~ ~ Einglasung, Verglasungs-Gummiprofil, Einglasungs-Gummiprofil

~ **glue** · Gummileim m

rubber hand grip — rubbish box

~ **hand grip** · Gummihandgriff *m*
~ **hose**, ~ **tube** · Gummischlauch *m*
~ **insert(ion)** · Gummieinlage *f*, Gummiträger *m*
rubber-insulated · gummiisoliert
~ **cable** [*B.S.* 7] · Gummikabel *n*, GK
rubber insulating board, ~ insulation(-grade) ~, ~ ~ sheet · Gummidämmplatte *f*
~ ~ **sheet** → ~ ~ **board**
~ **(joint) filler, cell** ~ (~) ~ · Gummi-(fugen)einlage *f*
(~) **latex** · Kautschukmilch *f*, (Kautschuk)Latex *m*
(~) **latex-cement-aggregate mix(ture)** · Verguẞmasse *f* aus Kautschukmilch, Zement und Zuschlägen
(~) **latex-cement sealing compound** · Kautschukmilch-Zement-Verguẞmasse, (Kautschuk)Latex-Zement-Verguẞmasse
rubber-like, rubbery · gummiähnlich
rubber mastic, ~ **building** ~ · Kautschukkitt *m*
~ **mat** · Gummimatte *f*
rubber-metal product · Gummi-Metall-Element *n*
(rubber) O-ring · Vollgummiring *m* [*Rohrverbindung*]
~ **packing ring**, ~ **seal(ing)** ~, ~ **washer** · Gummi(ab)dicht(ungs)ring *m*
~ **panel** · Gummitafel *f*
~ **(pipe) coupling** · Gummi(-Rohr)-kupplung *f*
~ **powder**, powder(ed) rubber · Gummimehl *n*, Gummipulver *n*
~ **(preformed) gasket,** ~ **sealing** ~, ~ **structural** ~ [*See remark under 'Selbstdichtung'*] · Gummiselbstdicht(ungs)profil *n*, Gummiselbstdichtung *f*
~ **profile**, ~ unit, ~ trim, ~ shape, ~ section · Gummiprofil *n*
~ **ring** · Gummiring *m*
~ **seal**, ~ stop · Gummi(ab)dichtung *f*
~ **sealed flexible joint** · Gummidichtung *f*, Gummiverbindung [*Rohrverbindung*]
~ **seal(ing) gasket** → ~ **(preformed)** ~
~ ~ **ring**, ~ packing ~, ~ washer · Gummi(ab)dicht(ungs)ring *m*
~ ~ **strip** · Gummi(ab)dichtungsleiste *f*
~ **section**, ~ profile ~ unit, ~ trim, ~ shape · Gummiprofil *n*
~ **set(ting)** → false ~
~ **shape**, ~ trim, ~ section, ~ profile, ~ unit · Gummiprofil *n*
~ **sheathed cable** · Gummimantelkabel *n*
~ **sheet(ing)** · Gummibahn *f*
~ **shock absorber** · Gummistoẞdämpfer *m*
~ **sleeve** · Gummi-Überschiebmuffe *f*

~ ~ · Gummi-Schalhülse *f* [*Leoba-Spannglied*]
~ **solution** · Gummilösung *f*
~ **spacer**, ~ distance piece · Gummiabstandhalter *m*
~ **squeegee** · Gummischieber *m*, Gummischwabber
~ **stop** · Gummianschlag *m*
~ ~, ~ seal · Gummi(ab)dichtung *f*
~ **strip** · Gummistreifen *m*
~ **structural gasket** → ~ (preformed) ~
rubber-(sur)faced, rubber-coated · gummibeschichtet
rubber-synthetic resin mix(ture) · Gummi-Kunstharz-Gemisch *n*, Gummi-Kunstharz-Mischung *f*
rubber tape [*An adhesive elastic tape made from a rubber compound; used extensively in electrical work for insulating purposes*] · Isolierband *n*
rubber/tar composition, ~ compound, ~ material, ~ mass · Gummi-Teer-Masse *f*
rubber tile · Gummifliese *f*, Gummi(belag)platte *f*
~ **tiling** · Gummifliesenbelag *m*, Gummiplattenbelag
~ **trim**, ~ shape, ~ unit, ~ section, ~ profile · Gummiprofil *n*
~ **tube**, ~ hose · Gummischlauch *m*
~ **underlay** · Gummiunterlage *f*
~ **unit**, ~ trim, ~ shape, ~ section, ~ profile · Gummiprofil *n*
~ **washer**, ~ seal(ing) ring, ~ packing ring · Gummi(ab)dicht(ungs)ring *m*
~ **waterbar**, ~ waterstop · Gummi(fugen)band *n*
~ **waterstop**, ~ waterbar · Gummi(fugen)band *n*
rubberized coal tar pitch emulsion · Gummi-Steinkohlenteerpech-Emulsion *f*
~ **paint** · Kautschukfarbe *f*
~ **tar** · Gummiteer *m*
rubbery, rubber-like · gummiähnlich
rubbing (US) · Schleifen *n* von Werksteinen
~ → flatting down
~ **varnish**, flatting ~ [*A hard-drying varnish which may be rubbed with an abrasive and water or oil to a uniform level(l)ed surface*] · Schleiflack *m*, Präparationslack, Vorlack, Hartmattlack
~ ~ **work** · Lackschliffarbeiten *fpl*
rubbish · Bauschutt *m* [*Der nach Beendigung der Bauarbeiten wegzuräumende Schutt*]
~ (US) → refuse
~ (US); rubble (Brit.) · Trümmer *f*, Schutt *m*
~ **box** (US); refuse ~, waste ~ · Abfall(stoff)kasten *m*, Müllkasten

rubbish cartage — rule

~ **cartage** (US) → refuse ~
~ **chute** → dispose-all
~ **cinder**, ~ furnace ~ (US); refuse (furnace) clinker (Brit.) · Müllschlacke *f* [*Sie wird durch Verbrennen von Müll in Verbrennungsöfen gewonnen*]
~ ~ **block** → refuse (furnace) clinker ~
~ ~ **tile** (US) → refuse (furnace) clinker block
~ **collecting chamber** (US) → (refuse ~ ~
~ **collection** (US) → refuse cartage
~ **container** (US) → refuse ~
~ **destructor**, ~ incinerator (US); waste ~, refuse ~, incinerator, destructor · Abfall(stoff)verbrenner *m*, (Müll)Verbrenner
~ **disposal**, disposal of rubbish (US); disposal of refuse, disposal of waste(s), refuse disposal, waste disposal · Abfall(stoff)beseitigung *f*, Müllbeseitigung
~ **(furnace) cinder** (US); refuse (furnace) clinker (Brit.) · Müllschlacke *f* [*Sie wird durch Verbrennen von Müll in Verbrennungsöfen gewonnen*]
~ **(~)** ~ **block** → refuse (furnace) clinker ~
~ **(~)** ~ **tile** (US) → refuse (furnace) clinker block
~ **grinder** (US) → (mechanical) refuse ~
~ **heap** (US) → refuse ~
~ **incineration** (US) → refuse ~
~ **incinerator**, ~ destructor (US); waste ~, refuse ~, destructor, incinerator · Abfall(stoff)verbrenner *m*, (Müll)Verbrenner
~ ~ **plant** (US) → (refuse) ~ ~
~ **load** (US); rubble ~ (Brit.) · Trümmerlast *f*, Schuttlast
~ ~ **of a wall** (US); rubble ~ ~ ~ ~ (Brit.) · Trümmerlast *f* einer Wand, Schuttlast ~ ~, Wandtrümmerlast, Wandschuttlast
~ **pit** (US) → refuse ~
~ **removal** (US); rubble ~ (Brit.) · Trümmerbeseitigung *f*, Enttrümmerung, Trümmer(auf)räumung, Schuttbeseitigung, Schutt(auf)räumung
~ **shoot** · Bauschuttrutsche *f*
~ **storage chamber** (US) → (refuse) collecting ~
~ **tip** (US); refuse ~, waste ~ · Müllkippe *f*, Müllhalde *f*, Müllablagerungsplatz *m*, Abfallkippe, Abfallhalde, Abfallablagerungsplatz, Müllabladeplatz, Abfall(stoff)abladeplatz
~ **utilization** (US) → refuse ~
rubble → ~ stone
~ (Brit.); rubbish (US) · Trümmer *f*, Schutt *m*
~ **ashlar masonry (work)**, ~ ashler ~ (~); ~ hewn stone ~ (~) (US) [*An ashlar-faced wall, backed with rubble*]

· Hausteinmauerwerk *n* mit Bruchsteinhinterfüllung, (Natur)Werksteinmauerwerk ~ ~
~ **concrete** [*Concrete similar to cyclopean concrete except that small stones (such as a man can handle) are used*] · Bruchsteinbeton *m* mit kleinen Steinen
~ ~ [*Concrete made with rubble from demolished or destroyed structures*] · Schuttbeton *m*
~ **fireplace** (Brit.); fieldstone ~ (US) · Kamin *m* aus Feldsteinen, Feldsteinkamin
~ **hewn stone masonry (work)** (US) → ~ ashlar ~ (~)
~ **load** (Brit.); rubbish ~ (US) · Trümmerlast *f*, Schuttlast
~ ~ **of a wall** (Brit.); rubbish ~ ~ ~ ~ (US) · Trümmerlast *f* einer Wand, Schuttlast ~ ~, Wandtrümmerlast, Wandschuttlast
~ **masonry (work)** · Bruchsteinmauerwerk *n* [*Aus natürlichen, lagerhaften Steinen mit Mörtel hergestellt*]
~ **removal** (Brit.); rubbish ~ (US) · Trümmerbeseitigung *f*, Enttrümmerung, Trümmer(auf)räumung, Schuttbeseitigung, Schutt(auf)räumung
~ **(stone), rough** ~ · Bruchstein *m* [*Er wird vom Maurer zurechtgerichtet wenn für Mauerwerk verwendet*]
~ ~ ; field ~ (US) · Feldstein *m*, Findling *m*
rubble (stone) (masonry) wall, rough stone (~) ~ · Bruchsteinmauer *f*
~ **(~) (work)**, rough ~ ~ (~), rubblework · Bruchsteinmauerwerk *n* [*Aus natürlichen, lagerhaften Steinen mit Mörtel hergestellt*]
rubble vault · Bruchsteingewölbe *n*
~ **wall**, ~ masonry ~ · Bruchsteinmauer *f*
Ruberoid roofing · Ruberoid(dach)-(ein)deckung *f*
~ ~ **felt** · Ruberoid-Dachpappe *f*
~ **slate** · Ruberoid-Schindel *f*
ruby glass [*Glass coloured red by colloidal suspensions of elemental gold, copper or selenium*] · Rubinglas *n*
ruin, ruined structure · Ruine *f*
ruined, destroyed · zerstört
~ **by fire**, (fire-)gutted, burnt down, burned down, destroyed by fire · abgebrannt, ausgebrannt, niedergebrannt
~ **church** · Kirchenruine *f*
~ **palace** · Palastruine *f*
~ **portal** · Portalruine *f*
ruin(ed structure) · Ruine *f*
ruined temple · Tempelruine *f*
ruins hill · Ruinenhügel *m*
ruin-sown · ruinenbesät
rule [*A straightedge for working plaster or dots to a plane surface*] · Abziehlineal *n*
~ · Regel *f*

~ · Lineal n

~ of addition · Zusammenzählregel f, Additionsregel, Additionsgesetz n

ruled surface · Regelfläche f

rumbling, tumbling [A process by which paint is applied to small articles such as hairpins, children's building bricks, etc., which are unsuitable for coating by any of the normal methods. The articles are placed in a drum together with a little more paint than will be sufficient to cover the total surface of all the articles and the drum is rotated until the paint is evenly distributed. The articles are then emptied from the drum, generally on to wire trays, and the coating air-dried or stoved] · Trommellackierung f, Rommeln n

to run [To pass plaster or lime putty through a sieve] · sieben [Putz; Kalkteig]

~ ~ a hydraulic test, ~ ~ ~ cold water ~ · abdrücken [Leitungen und Druckgefäße mit kaltem Wasser]

~ ~ to putty → to slake

run [The general layout of the pipes or cables in a building] · Führung f

~, sag, curtain [An irregularity of a surface due to uneven flow, frequently due to application of a coat that is too heavy, and not brushed out well] · Läufer m, Gardine f, Nase f [Fehler beim Verarbeiten von Lack oder Lackfarbe]

~, line · Leitung f

~, barrow ~ · Schubkarrensteg m

~, going · (Auf)Trittbreite f, Auftrittmaß n [Die Breite der Stufe, auf der Ganglinie waagerecht gemessen von Vorderkante Setzstufe zur Vorderkante Setzstufe der nächsthöheren Stufe (senkrecht projiziert)]

~ copal, fused ~ · ausgeschmolzener Kopal m

rundle, (ladder) rung, stave, tread, LR · (Leiter)Sprosse f

~ ladder, tread ~, rung ~, stave ~ · Sprossenleiter f

rung, ladder ~, stave, rundle, tread, LR · (Leiter)Sprosse f

~ ladder, stave ~, rundle ~, tread ~ · Sprossenleiter f

runic character · Rune f

Runic cross, Celtic ~ · keltisches Kreuz n

runner · Trageisen n [Hängedecke]

running, fusing · Ausschmelzen n [Kopal]

~, sagging, curtaining · Nasenbildung f, Läuferbildung, Gardinenbildung [Fehler beim Verarbeiten von Lack oder Lackfarbe]

~ bond → (conventional) running (masonry) ~

~ cost · Betriebskosten f

~ dog → (Vitruvian) wave scroll

~ down · Ablaufen n [Farbe; Kleber usw.]

~ economy · Betriebswirtschaftlichkeit f

~ girder · Laufträger m

~ (masonry) bond → conventional ~ (~) ~

~ ornament · laufende Verzierung f

~ rail · Laufschiene f

~ to putty, hydrating, (lime) slaking · (Ab)Löschen n, Naßlöschen [Kalk]

~ track · Laufbahn f

run-of-kiln lime · unsortierter Branntkalk m

run plank, runway ~, walk ~ · Laufbohle f, Karrbohle

~ to putty, slaked, hydrated · (ab)gelöscht, naßgelöscht [Kalk]

run-up track · Anlaufbahn f

runway, (walk)way · (Lauf)Steg m

~ bracket, (walk)way ~ · Laufstegkonsole f

run(way) plank, walk ~ · Karrbohle f, Laufbohle

rupture, breaking, failure · Bruch m

~ bending angle, ultimate ~ ~, breaking ~ ~ · Bruchbiegewinkel m, Bruchbiegungswinkel

~ ~ moment, ultimate ~ ~, breaking ~ ~ · Bruchbiegemoment n, Bruchbiegungsmoment

~ compressive load, breaking ~ ~, ultimate ~ ~ · Bruchdrucklast f

~ ~ strength, ultimate ~ ~, breaking ~ ~ · Bruchdruckfestigkeit f

~ condition, ultimate ~, breaking ~ · Bruchbedingung f

~ cross-section, failure ~, breaking ~ · Bruchquerschnitt n

~ in buckling → failure ~ ~

~ line [The line along which rupture occurs or would occur if the piece were tested to destruction] · Bruchlinie f

~ load, breaking ~, ultimate ~ · Bruchlast f

~ loading, breaking ~, limit ~, ultimate ~ · Bruchbelastung f, Grenzbelastung

~ moment, ultimate ~, breaking ~ · Bruchmoment n

~ ~ capacity, breaking ~ ~, ultimate ~ ~ · Burchmomentenvermögen n

rupture-proof, fracture-proof, breakproof · bruchsicher

rupture shear(ing) strength, ultimate ~ ~, breaking ~ ~ · Bruch-Schubfestigkeit f, Bruch-Schubwiderstand m

~ ~ stress, ultimate ~ ~, breaking ~ ~ · Bruch-Schubspannung f

~ strength, ultimate ~, final ~, breaking ~ · Endfestigkeit f, Endwiderstand m, Bruchfestigkeit, Bruchwiderstand

~ stress, breaking ~, ultimate ~ · Bruchspannung f

~ ~ condition, breaking ~ ~, ultimate ~ ~ · Bruchspannungsbedingung f

rupture tensile stress — rust preventing hard gloss paint 864

~ **tensile stress**, ultimate ~ ~, breaking ~ ~ · Bruchzugspannung *f*

~ **test**, breaking ~, failure ~ · Bruchprüfung *f*, Bruchversuch *m*, Bruchprobe *f*

~ **zone**, failure ~, breaking ~ · Bruchzone *f*

rupturing elongation → breaking ~

rural aggregate · dörfliche Agglomeration *f*

~ **architecture** · ländliche Architektur *f*, ~ Baukunst *f*

~ **church**, village ~, country ~ · Dorfkirche *f*, Landkirche

~ **community** · Landgemeinde *f*

~ **hospital** · Landkrankenhaus *n*

rush-hour station · Spitzenzeitbahnhof *m*

rush mat · Binsenmatte *f*

Russian chimney pipe · russische Röhre *f*

~ **(oil of) turpentine**, ~ spirit ~ ~ · russisches Terpentinöl *n*

rust · Rost *m* [*Durch Korrosion von Eisen und Stahl entstehende Oxydschicht*]

rust-converting primer, RCP · Rostumwandler *m*

rust creep · Unterrosten *n*

~ **film** · Rostfilm *m*

~ **formation**, formation of rust, rusting · Rostbildung *f*, Rosten *n*

rust-forming · rostbildend

rust from external sources · Fremdrost *m*

rustic (angle-)quoin · Rustikaeckstein *m*, Rustikawinkelstein

~ **brick** [*A brick with a surface which has been roughened by covering it with sand, by impressing it with a pattern, or by other means*] · Rustikaziegel *m*

~ **cabin** [*A term coined by Marc-Antoine Laugier (1713–1769)*] · rustikale Hütte *f*

~ **joint** [*A joint sunk back from the surface of stone, seen in rusticated ashlar*] · Rustikafuge *f*

~ **(masonry) work** → rustic(ated) ashlar

~ **quoin**, ~ angle-~ · Rustikaeckstein *m*, Rustikawinkelstein

rustic(ated) ashlar, ~ ashler, ~ masonry (work), ~ (masonry) work, drafted masonry (work), rustication, opus rusticum [*Ashlar on which the face is left rough and stands out from the joints, the stones being cut back at the edges by bevelling or rebating. In other types of rustication (e.g. rustic quoins), alternate stones project about one inch beyond the others. It is an ancient practice being found in masonry of the time of Cyrus (500 B.C.), in the castles of the Crusaders and in masonry done during the Renaissance*]

· Rustika(mauerwerk) *f*, (*n*), Bossen(mauer)werk, Buckelquader(mauer)werk

~ **basement** · Sockelgeschoß *n* mit Bossenwerk

~ **column**, ringed ~, banded ~ · Ringsäule *f*, Bundsäule [*Säule mit durch ringförmige Zwischenglieder unterteiltem Schaft*]

~ **(masonry) work** → ~ ashlar

rustication → rustic(ated) ashlar

rusticity · Rustizierung *f*

rustiness, rusty quality · Rostneigung *f*

~, rusty state · Verrostung *f*

rusting, rust formation, formation of rust · Rostbildung *f*, Rosten *n*

~ **degree**, degree of rusting · Rostgrad *m*

rust(ing)-inhibiting, rust(ing)-preventing · rosthemmend, rost(ver)hindernd

rust(ing)-preventing, rust(ing)-inhibiting · rosthemmend, rost(ver)hindernd

rusting process · Rostungsverlauf *m*

rust inhibition, ~ prevention · Rost(ver)hinderung *f*, Rosthemmung

rust-inhibitive, rust-preventing · rostverhindernd

rust inhibitive action → ~ preventive ~

~ ~ **enamel** → ~ preventive ~

~ ~ **grease** → ~ preventing ~

~ ~ **hard gloss paint** → ~ preventive enamel

~ ~ **oil** → ~ preventing ~

~ ~ **paint** → ~ preventive ~

~ ~ **pigment** → ~ preventive ~

~ ~ **solution** → ~ preventive ~

~ ~ **treatment** → ~ preventive ~

~ **joint** [*A joint between cast-iron pipes, eaves gutters, etc., made with iron cement*] · Graphitzementfuge *f*, Metallzementfuge, Metallkittfuge, Eisenkittfuge

~ **layer** · Rostschicht *f*

rustless, stainless · rostfrei

~ **iron**, stainless ~ · rostfreies Eisen *n*

rust-preventing, rust-inhibitive · rostverhindernd

rust preventing action → ~ preventive ~

~ ~ **agent** → ~ preventive ~

~ ~ **coat** → ~ preventive ~

~ ~ **compound**, ~ preventive ~, ~ protection ~, ~ inhibitive ~, ~ proofing ~, anti-rust ~ · Rostschutzverbindung *f*

~ ~ **enamel** → ~ preventive ~

~ ~ **grease**, ~ preventive ~, ~ protection ~, ~ inhibitive ~, ~ proofing ~, anti-rust ~ · Rostschutzfett *n*

~ ~ **hard gloss paint** → ~ preventive enamel

~ ~ **oil,** ~ preventive ~, ~ inhibitive ~, ~ protection ~, ~ proofing ~, anti-rust ~ · Rostschutzöl *n*

~ ~ **paint** → ~ preventive ~

~ ~ **pigment** → ~ preventive ~

~ ~ **solution** → ~ preventive ~

~ ~ **treatment** → ~ preventive ~

~ **prevention,** ~ inhibition · Rost(ver)-hinderung *f*, Rosthemmung

~ ~, ~ proofing, ~ protection · Rostschutz(behandlung) *m*, (*f*) [*DIN 50942*]

~ **preventive action,** ~ preventing ~, ~ inhibitive ~, ~ protection ~, ~ proofing ~, anti-rust ~ · Rostschutzwirkung *f*

~ ~ **agent,** ~ preventing ~, ~ inhibitive ~, ~ protection ~, ~ proofing ~, anti-rust ~ · Rostschutzmittel *n*, Rostschutzstoff *m*

~ ~ **coat,** ~ preventing ~, ~ protection ~, ~ proofing ~, ~ inhibitive ~, anti-rust ~ · Rostschutzanstrich *m*, Rostschutzaufstrich

~ ~ **compound** → ~ preventing ~

~ ~ **enamel,** ~ preventing ~, ~ inhibitive ~, ~ protection ~, ~ proofing ~, ~ ~ hard gloss paint, anti-rust enamel, anti-rust hard gloss paint · Rostschutzlackfarbe *f* [*Fehlname: Rostschutzlack m*]

~ ~ **grease** → ~ preventing ~

~ ~ **hard gloss paint** → ~ ~ enamel

~ ~ **oil** → ~ preventing ~

~ ~ **paint,** ~ preventing ~, ~ inhibitive ~, ~ protection ~, ~ proofing ~, anti-rust ~ · Rostschutzfarbe *f*

~ ~ **pigment,** ~ preventing ~, ~ inhibitive ~, ~ protection ~, ~ proofing ~, anti-rust ~ · Rostschutzpigment *n*

~ ~ **solution,** ~ preventing ~, ~ inhibitive ~, ~ protection ~, ~ proofing ~, anti-rust ~ · Rostschutzlösung *f*

~ ~ **treatment,** ~ preventing ~, ~ inhibitive ~, ~ protection ~, ~ proofing ~, anti-rust ~ · Rostschutzbehandlung *f*

rustproof, rust-resistant · rostbeständig, rostsicher

rust proofing, ~ prevention, ~ protection · Rostschutz(behandlung) *m*, (*f*) [*DIN 50942*]

~ ~ **action** → ~ preventive ~

~ ~ **agent** → ~ preventive ~

~ ~ **coat** → ~ preventive ~

~ ~ **compound** → ~ preventing ~

~ ~ **enamel** → ~ preventive ~

~ ~ **grease** → ~ preventing ~

~ ~ **hard gloss paint** → ~ preventive enamel

~ ~ **oil** → ~ preventing ~

~ ~ **paint** → ~ preventive ~

~ ~ **pigment** → ~ preventive ~

~ ~ **solution** → ~ preventive ~

~ ~ **treatment** → ~ preventive ~

~ **protection,** ~ prevention, ~ proofing · Rostschutz(behandlung) *m*, (*f*) [*DIN 50942*]

~ ~ **action** → ~ preventive ~

~ ~ **agent** → ~ preventive ~

~ ~ **coat** → ~ preventive ~

~ ~ **compound** → ~ preventing ~

~ ~ **enamel** → ~ preventive ~

~ ~ **grease** → ~ preventing ~

~ ~ **hard gloss paint** → ~ preventive enamel

~ ~ **oil** → ~ preventing ~

~ ~ **paint** → ~ preventive ~

~ ~ **pigment** → ~ preventive ~

~ ~ **solution** → ~ preventive ~

~ ~ **treatment** → ~ preventive ~

~ **removal** · Entrostung *f* [*technisches Verfahren*]

~ ~ · Entrosten *n*, Abrosten, Rostentfernen [*technischer Vorgang*]

~ **remover,** derusting agent · Rostentfernungsmittel *n*, Entrostungsmittel, Abrostungsmittel, Rostbeseitigungsmittel

~ **removing brush** · Abrostbürste *f*, Entrostbürste

rust-removing procedure · Entrostungsverfahren *n*, Abrostungsverfahren, Rostentfernungsverfahren

rust resistance, resistance against rust · Rostsicherheit *f*, Rostbeständigkeit

~ ~ **test** · Rostbeständigkeitsprüfung *f*, Rostbeständigkeitsprobe *f*, Rostbeständigkeitsversuch *m*, Rostsicherheitsprüfung, Rostsicherheitsprobe, Rostsicherheitsversuch

rust-resistant, rustproof · rostbeständig, rostsicher

rust spot · Roststelle *f*

~ **stain** · Rostfleck *m*

~ **staining** · Rostfleckigkeit *f*, Rostflecken *mpl*

to rust through · durchrosten

~ ~ **up** · einrosten

rusty quality, rustiness · Rostneigung *f*

~ **state,** rustiness · Verrostung *f*

rutile · Rutil *m*, TiO$_2$

~ **pigment** · Rutilpigment *n*

~ **titanium dioxid(e)** (US); ~ ~ dioxide (Brit.) · Rutil-Titandioxid *n*

RW, raw water · Rohwasser *n*

R.W., rainwater, storm water [*Excess water during rainfall or continuously following and resulting therefrom*] · Regenwasser *n*

R.W. barrier, rain (water) ~ · Regensperre *f*, Regenwassersperre

R.W. cistern, rainwater ~ · Regen(wasser)zisterne *f*

R.W. gutter, rainwater ~, (roof) ~ · (Dach)Rinne f, Regenrinne, Abflußrinne [*DIN 18460*]
R.W. gutter board → (roof) ~ ~
R.W. gutter heating → (roof) ~ ~
R.W. gutter hook → (roof) ~ ~
R.W. gutter sheet → (roof) ~ ~
R.W. gutter steel bearer → (roof) ~ ~ ~
R.W. gutter steel hanger → (roof) ~ ~ ~
R.W. outlet, rainwater ~ · Regen(wasser)ablauf m [*am Dach*]
R.W. pipe, rainwater ~ · Regenrohr n, Regenwasserrohr
R.W. pipe hanger, rainwater ~ ~ · Regenrohrschelle f, Regenwasserrohrschelle
R.W. system, rainwater ~ · Regenablaufkonstruktion f [*Regenrinne + Regenfallrohr + Zubehör*]
R.W. tank, rainwater ~ · Regen(wasser)behälter m
R.W. tank, rainwater ~ · Regen(wasser)(auffang)becken n
rye paste · Roggenmehlkleister m
~ starch · Roggenstärke f
~ straw · Roggenstroh n

S

S. Antonio at Padua · Franziskanerkirche f in Padua
S. Demetrius (basilican church) at Salonica · Demetriusbasilika f in Thessalonich
S.F., shear(ing) force [*The shear(ing) force at any section of a beam is the algebraic sum of all the normal external forces acting to one side of that section*] · Schubkraft f
S.F.D., shear force diagram · Schubkraftdiagramm n
S.F. transmission, shear(ing) force ~ · Schubkraftübertragung f
S. Nicholas at Prague · St. Nikolaus auf der Kleinseite in Prag
S. Nicholas' church · Nikolaikirche f
SS. Sergius and Bacchus church at Constantinople · Sergius-und-Bacchus-Kirche f in Konstantinopel
S. Stephen's Cathedral at Vienna · Stephansdom m zu Wien
'S' trap · S-förmiger (Geruch)Verschluß m, ~ Wassergeruchsverschluß, Syphon(geruch)verschluß, Syphonwassergeruchverschluß, Knie(geruch)verschluß, Knie-Wassergeruchverschluß, Schwanenhals(geruch)verschluß, Schwanenhalswassergeruchverschluß
sacked cement, bagged ~ · (ab)gesackter Zement m, eingesackter ~, Sackzement

sacking · (Sack)Grobgewebe n
sacrament chapel · Sakramentskapelle f
sacred grove at Olympia · Heiliger Hain m von Olympia
~ ~ of trees · heiliger Hain m
~ precinct, temenos, peribolos · geweihter (Tempel)Bezirk m, heiliger ~, Altis f, Peribolos m, Temenos n
Sacred Rock · Heiliger Fels m [*Jerusalem*]
sacred street · Prozessionsweg m [*zu Altar und Tempel in Delphi*]
sacrificial pit · Opfergrube f
sacristy, vestry · Sakristei f [*Der Priesterraum und meistens auch der Aufbewahrungsort für den Schatz der Kirche*]
~ of la Cartuja at Granada, Charterhouse ~ ~ · Kartause f von Granada
saddle, head tree, crown plate, bolster, corbel piece [*A short timber cap over a post to increase the bearing area under a beam*] · Sattelholz n
~, cricket · Schornsteinsattel m
~ (US); threshold, sill [*A horizontal timber at the foot of an outside door*] · (Holz)(Tür)Schwelle f
~ arch → saddle-shaped ~
saddle(back) roof [*This is a normal pitched roof. The term is most usual for roofs of towers*] · Satteldach n
~ ~ tower · Sattelturm m [*Turm mit einem Satteldach*]
saddle cap flashing, cricket ~ ~, ~ counter ~ [*See remark under 'Anschluß'*] · sattelförmiger Kappenschluß m, ~ Überhanganschluß
~ ~ ~ (piece), cricket ~ ~ (~), ~ counter ~ (~) [*See remark under 'Anschluß'*] · sattelförmige Kappleiste f, ~ Überhangleiste, sattelförmiger Kappstreifen m, sattelförmiger Überhangstreifen
~ counter flashing → ~ cap ~
~ ~ ~ (piece) → ~ cap ~ (~)
~ roof → saddle(back) ~
saddle(-shaped) arch, ogee ~, O.G. ~ · Eselsrücken(bogen) m, Sattelbogen [*Ein Spitzbogen mit geschweiften Schenkeln, die aus zwei Kurven derart zusammengesetzt sind, daß ihr unterer Teil konvex und ihr oberer Teil konkav ist*]
~ form · Sattelform f
~ segment · Sattelsegment n
~ shell · Sattelschale f
saddle shell, saddle-shaped ~ · Sattelschale f
~ stone, apex ~ [*The top stone in a gable end*] · Giebelschlußstein m
~ surface · Sattelfläche f
saddle-type lantern-light · Sattellaterne f
~ monitor (US); ~ ~ roof (Brit.) · Firstsattellaterne f

saddle-type monitor roof — sales office

~ ~ roof (Brit.); ~ monitor (US) · Firstsattellaterne *f*

~ **skylight** · Sattelraupe *f*

safe · Safe *n*

~, allowable, admissible, permissible · zulässig

~ **against buckling** · knicksicher

~ ~ **overturning** · kippsicher

~ **deposit** · Wertstelle *f*

~ **distance** · Sicherheitsabstand *m*

~ **load,** permissible ~, admissible ~, allowable ~, working ~ · zulässige Last *f*

~ ~ **table** · Belastungstabelle *f*

~ **stress,** allowable ~, working ~, design ~, admissible ~, permissible ~ · zulässige Spannung *f*, Bemessungsspannung

safety against buckling · Beulsicherheit *f*

~ ~ **cracking** · Rißsicherheit *f*

~ ~ **overturning** · Kippsicherheit *f*

~ ~ **rupture** · Bruchsicherheit *f*

~ **allowance,** ~ margin, margin of safety · Sicherheitsaufschlag *m*, Sicherheitszuschlag, Sicherheitsspanne *f*

~ **arch,** rough ~, discharging ~, relieving ~ · Entlastungsbogen *m*, Ablastebogen, Überfangbogen, Verstärkungsbogen, Versteifungsbogen

~ **(builders') fitting,** ~ (~) furniture · Sicherheits(bau)beschlag *m*

~ **(~) fittings,** ~ (~), hardware · Sicherheits(bau)beschläge *fpl*

~ **(~) furniture,** ~ (~) fitting · Sicherheits(bau)beschlag *m*

~ **(~) hardware,** ~ (~) fittings · Sicherheits(bau)beschläge *mpl*

~ **cage** → enclosing ~ ~

~ **check** · Sicherheitsnachweis *m*

~ **conditions** · Sicherheitsbedingungen *fpl*

~ **curb;** ~ kerb (Brit.) · Sicherheitsbordstein *m*

safety(-cylinder) lock, security(-cylinder) ~ · Sicherheitsschloß *n*

safety device · Sicherheitsvorrichtung *f*

~ **factor,** factor of safety [*Many authorities prefer to use the term 'reduction factor' as being more realistic than the term 'safety factor'*] · Sicherheitsbeiwert *m*, Sicherheitsgrad *m*, Sicherheitszahl *f*, Sicherheitsfaktor *m* [*Baustoff*]

~ **fence** · Sicherheitszaun *m*

~ **fitting** → ~ builders' ~

~ **fittings** → ~ builders' ~

~ **flow** · Sicherheitsvorlauf *m*

~ **furniture** → ~ builders' ~

~ **glass,** shatterproof ~ · Sicherheitsglas *n*

~ ~ **domelight,** shatterproof ~ ~, ~ ~ light cupola, ~ ~ saucer dome · Sicherheitsglas(licht)kuppel *f*

~ ~ **door,** shatterproof ~ ~ · Sicherheitsglastür *f*

~ **hardware** → ~ builders' ~

~ **illumination,** ~ lighting · Sicherheitsbeleuchtung *f*

~ **in service** · Betriebssicherheit *f*

~ **kerb** (Brit.); ~ curb · Sicherheitsbordstein *m*

~ **lighting,** ~ illumination · Sicherheitsbeleuchtung *f*

~ **line** · Sicherheitsleitung *f*

~ **lintel;** ~ lintol [*deprecated*] [*A lintel, which carries load, to protect another more decorative lintel*] · Entlastungssturz *m*

~ **lock** → ~-cylinder ~

~ **margin,** ~ allowance, margin of safety · Sicherheitsaufschlag *m*, Sicherheitszuschlag, Sicherheitsspanne *f*

~ **measure against buoyancy,** ~ ~ ~ uplift · Auftriebssicherung *f*

~ **net** · Sicherheitsnetz *n*

~ **plate glass,** shatterproof ~ ~ · Sicherheitsspiegelglas *n*

~ **railing,** protective ~, protecting ~ · Schutzgeländer *n*

~ **regulations for high-rise structures** · Hochhausrichtlinien *fpl*

~ **return line** · Sicherheitsrücklaufleitung *f*

~ **rules** · Sicherheitsregeln *fpl*

~ **scaffold(ing),** protective ~, protecting ~ · Schutzgerüst *n*, Schutzrüstung *f*

~ **sheet glass,** ~ window ~, shatterproof ~ ~ · Sicherheitsfensterglas *n*

~ **thermostat** · Sicherheitsthermostat *m*

~ **window glass,** ~ sheet ~, shatterproof ~ ~ · Sicherheitsfensterglas *n*

safflower oil · Saf(f)loröl *n*

sag · Durchhang *m*

~ → run

~ **of cable,** ~ ~ rope, rope sag, cable sag · Kabeldurchhang *m*, Seildurchhang

~ ~ **rope,** ~ ~ cable, rope sag, cable sag · Kabeldurchhang *m*, Seildurchhang

sagging, curtaining · Schleierbildung *f* [*Anstrichschaden*]

~ **of support(s)** → settlement ~ ~

sail · Hängezwickel *m*

~**(-shaped) roof** · segelförmiges Dach *n*

sail vault · Hängekuppel *f*

Saint Venant(s') principle (of elasticity) → de ~ ~ ~ (~ ~)

~ ~ **torsion** → de ~ ~ ~

saint's church · Heiligenkirche *f*

~ **tomb** · Heiligengrab *n*

sala · Sala *m* [*Versammlungshalle buddhistischer Klöster*]

sales depot · Verkaufslager *n*

~ **office** · Verkaufsbüro *n*

sales room — sand asphalt

~ room · Verkaufsraum *m*

salient, projecting · vorspringend, ausspringend

~ **angle, projecting** ~ · ausspringender Winkel *m*, vorspringender ~

~ **corner, projecting** ~ · vorspringende Ecke *f*, ausspringende ~

sally-port [*A postern gate or passage underground from the inner to the outer works of a fortification*] · Ausfallgang *m*

salon [*Post-medi(a)eval successor of a great hall*] · Salon *m*

salt air → ~-laden ~

~ **atmosphere** → ~-laden ~

~ **bath** · Salzbad *n*

saltcake; sodium sulphate (Brit.); sodium sulfate (US) · schwefelsaures Natrium *n*, Natriumsulfat *n*, Glaubersalz *n*, $Na_2SO_4 \cdot 10 H_2O$

salt causing unsightly efflorescence, soluble salt · ausblühfähiges Salz *n*, ausschlagfähiges ~, auswitterungsfähiges ~

salt-containing · salzhaltig

salt content · Salzgehalt *m*

~ **crystal** · Salzkristall *n*

~ **dust** · Salzstaub *m*

(~) efflorescence, efflorescence of salt, flower of salt · (Salz)Ausblühen *n*, (Salz)Ausschlagen, Auswittern, Aussalzen, Auskristallisation *f* (von Salzen) [*Äußerlich sichtbares Ausscheiden von Salzen auf Mauerwerk*]

~ **formation** · Salzbildung *f*

salt-free · salzfrei, salzlos

salt glaze · Salzglasur *f* [*Sie entsteht durch Zusatz von Kochsalz zum Brande: NaCl wird durch die Hitze aufgespalten; Cl entweicht gasförmig, Na bildet mit dem Al-Silikat des Tones an der Oberfläche einen glasartigen Schmelzfluß*]

salt-glazed earthenware pipe · salzglasiertes Irdengutrohr *n*, ~ Steingutrohr

salt glaze(d finish) · Salzbeglasung *f*, Salzglasur *f*

~-**glazed (ware) pipe** [*B.S. 1143*] · salzglasiertes Rohr *n*

salt glazing, glazing by salting · Beglasen *n* durch Salzen, Glasieren ~ ~, Salzglasieren, Salzbeglasen

Saltire cross, St. Andrew's ~, diagonal struts · Andreaskreuz *n*, Kreuzgebälk *n*, Kreuzstreben *fpl*, Abkreuzung *f*, Kreuzverband *m*

~ ~, St. Andrew's ~, crux decussata · Andreaskreuz *n*, Schrägkreuz, burgundisches Kreuz

salt(-laden) air, ~ atmosphere · Salzluft *f*

~ **atmosphere,** ~ air · Salzluft *f*

salt of lead, lead salt · Bleisalz *n*

saltpeter, niter, potassium nitrate · Kalisalpeter *m*, Kaliumnitrat *n*, KNO_3

salt resistance · Salzbeständigkeit *f*

~ **solution** · Salzlösung *f*

~ **store** · Salzlagerhalle *f*

salt-type (wood) preservative, (wood) preservative salt, (wood-)protecting salt · Schutzsalz *n*, Holz ~

salt water-resistant · salzwasserbeständig, meer(es)wasserbeständig

salvage, arisings · Altmaterial *n*

~ **value** · Altmaterialwert *m*

Salvation Army hostel · Nachtasyl *n* der Heilsarmee

to sample, ~ **take samples** · nehmen von Proben

sample → test ~

~ **community** · Demonstrativbauvorhaben *n*, Demonstrativprojekt *n*, Demonstrativsied(e)lung *f*, Demonstrationssied(e)lung, Demonstrationsbauvorhaben, Demonstrationsprojekt

~ **holder** · Probenhalter *m*

~ **mould** → test ~ ~

~ **specification** [*A description of the sampling procedure, such as location, size, time, and how the sample must be handled and preserved*] · Probenahmevorschrift *f*

sampling · Probe(ent)nahme *f*

~ **and testing of light-weight aggregates for concrete** [*B.S. 3681*] · Probenahme *f* und Prüfung *f* von Leichtzuschlägen, ~ ~ ~ ~ Leichtzuschlagstoffen, Probeentnahme ~ ~ ~ ~

~ **date,** date of sampling · Probenahmetermin *m*, Probenahmedatum *n*

~ **method,** method of taking samples · Probenahmeverfahren *n*

~ **tube** · Probenahmerohr *n*

sanctuary, presbytery [*The part of the east end of a church in which the main altar is placed; reserved for clery and choir*] · Altarbereich *m, n*, Altarraum *m*, Altarium *n*, Priesterraum Presbyterium *n*

~, innermost part · Sanktuarium *n*, Allerheiligste *n* [*Der Platz des Altars in altchristlichen Kirchen*]

~ [*A holy place; building or place set aside for worship of a god or gods or God*] · Heiligtum *n*

~ **of Apollo** · Apollo(n)heiligtum *n*

~ ~ **Asclepius** · Tempel *m* von Epidaurus

~ ~ **Zeus** · Zeusheiligtum *n*

sand addition, addition of sand, adding of sand · Sandbeigabe *f*, Sandzusatz *m*, Sandzugabe, Sandbeigeben *n*, Sandzugeben, Sandzusetzen

~ **aggregate** · Sandzuschlag(stoff) *m*

sandarac(h) · Sandarak *n* [*rezentes Lackharz*]

sand asphalt (US); bituminous sandstone, asphaltic sand(stone) · Asphaltsand(stein) *m*, bituminöser Sandstein

~ ~ · Sandasphalt *m*

sand-bentonite slurry · Sand-Betonit-Schlämme f

to sandblast · sandstrahlen, mit Sandstrahl überblasen

(sand)blast · (Sand)Strahl m

sand blast, sandblasting · Sandeln n, Abblasen, Sandstrahlen, Abstrahlen mit Sandstrahlgebläse, Sandstrahlung f, Überblasen mit Sandstrahl

sandblast decorative finish · Sandstrahlmattierung f [Glas]

(sand) blast sand · Gebläsesand m

sandblasted · sandgestrahlt, mit Sandstrahl bearbeitet

~ · sandgestrahlt, sandstrahlmattiert, mit Sandstrahl bearbeitet [Glas]

~ **to sound metal** · metallisch blank sandgestrahlt

sandblasting, sand blast · Sandeln n, Abblasen, Sandstrahlen, Abstrahlen mit Sandstrahlgebläse, Sandstrahlung f, Überblasen mit Sandstrahl

~ **test** · Sandstrahlprobe f, Sandstrahlprüfung f, Sandstrahlversuch m

sand-cast pipe, static-cast ~ · Sandguß(eisen)rohr n

sand casting · Sandguß m [Von Gußeisen oder Stahlguß]

sand-cement grout, cement-sand ~ · Sand-Zement-Schlämme f, Sand-Zement-Schlämpe f, Sand-Zement-Schlempe

sand:coarse aggregate ratio, fine: coarse ~ ~ [Ratio of fine to coarse aggregate in a batch of concrete, by weight or volume] · (Beton)Feinzuschlag(stoff)-Grobzuschlag(stoff)-Verhältnis n

sand-coloured (Brit.); **sand-colored** (US) · sandfarben

sand content · Sandanteil m, Sandgehalt m

~ **dry, surface** ~ [When the paint is dry on the surface but is soft and tacky underneath] · oberflächentrocken

sand(ed) grout · Zement-Sand-Schlämme f

sand-faced (clay) brick [A facing brick coated with sand to give it an attractive rough surface] · Fassadenziegel m mit Sandschicht, Verblendziegel ~ ~, Ziegelverblender m ~ ~, Sand(torm)ziegel, Sandstrichziegel

sand fill(ing) · Sandauffüllung f, Sand(auf)schüttung

sand for (external) rendering, ~ ~ **exterior** ~ [B.S. 1199]; ~ ~ ~ **plaster(ing)** · (Außen)Putzsand m

~ ~ **mortar,** mortar sand [B.S. 1200] · Mörtelsand m

~ ~ **sett paving(s)** · Pflastersand m

~ **gauging box** (Brit.); ~ **gaging** ~ (US); ~ **measuring** ~, ~ **proportioning** ~ · Sandzumeßkasten m

~ **grain** · Sandkorn n, Sandkörnchen n, Sandteilchen

sand-gravel concrete · Sand-Kies-Beton m

sand grinder · Sandmühle f [Mahlen in der Lackindustrie]

sand-gypsum plaster, gypsum-sand ~, patent ~, sanded ~ · Gipssandputz m

sanding sealer · Schnellschliffgrund m

sand-lime brick, lime-sand ~, calcium silicate ~ [B.S. 187] · (künstlicher) Kalksandstein m, (~) Baustein, gebundener Baustein, weißer Mauerstein, KS, gebundener Kalksandstein [DIN 106]

~ ~ **lintel;** ~ ~ lintol [deprecated]; lime-sand ~ ~, calcium silicate ~ ~ · Kalksandsteinoberschwelle f, Kalksandsteinsturz m, Kasa-Oberschwelle, Kasa-Sturz

~ ~ **machine,** lime-sand ~ ~ · Kalksandsteinmaschine f

~ ~ **1:8,** lime-sand ~ ~ · Pisésteinm [Kalkmörtelstein aus Branntkalk und Sand (1:8) gestampft]

~ **facing brick,** lime-sand ~ ~, calcium-silicate ~ ~ · Kalksandverblender m, Kalksandverblendstein m

~ **mix(ture)** · Sand-Kalk-Gemisch n, Sand-Kalk-Mischung f

sand-limestone concrete · Sand-Kalkstein-Beton m

sand-lined mould (Brit.); ~ mold (US) · Sandform f

sand measuring box, ~ proportioning ~, ~ gauging ~ (Brit.); ~ gaging ~ (US) · Sandzumeßkasten m

~ **mortar** · Sandmörtel m

~ **mould** (Brit.); ~ mold (US) · Sandgußform f

to sandpaper irregular surfaces · abschleifen von Unebenheiten

~ ~ **smooth** · glatt schleifen

sand-pit · Sandkasten m, Sandspielkasten

sand proportioning box, ~ measuring ~, ~ gauging ~ (Brit.); ~ gaging ~ (US) · Sandzumeßkasten m

~ **replacement** · Sandersatz m

~ **slurry** · Sandschlämme f

~ **spreading,** spreading of sand · Aufstreuen n von Sand, Sandaufstreuen

sandstone · Sandstein m

~ **ashlar,** ~ ashler; hewn sandstone (US) · Sandstein-Haustein m, Sandstein-Werkstein

~ **ashler,** ~ ashlar; hewn sandstone (US) · Sandstein-Haustein m, Sandstein-Bruchstein

~ **concrete** · Sandsteinbeton m

~ **cube** · Sandsteinwürfel m

~ **curb;** ~ kerb [B.S. 706] · Sandsteinbordstein m

~ **curtain (wall),** ~ rubble ~ (~), ~ (rubble) enceinte · Sandsteinkurtine f [historischer Festungsbau]

sandstone enceinte — sanitary cove

~ enceinte, ~ rubble ~, ~ (rubble) curtain (wall) · Sandsteinkurtine *f* [*historischer Festungsbau*]

~ impregnated with asphaltic bitumen (Brit.); ~ ~ ~ asphalt (US) · Natursphaltsandstein *m*

~ kerb; ~ curb [*B.S. 706*] · Sandsteinbordstein *m*

~ (paving) sett [*B.S. 706*] · Sandsteinpflasterstein *m*

~ portal · Sandsteinportal *n*

~ powder, powder(ed) sandstone · Sandsteinmehl *n*

~ rubble · Sandstein-Bruchstein *m*

~ (~) curtain (wall), ~ (~) enceinte · Sandsteinkurtine *f* [*historischer Festungsbau*]

~ (~) enceinte, ~ (~) curtain (wall) · Sandsteinkurtine *f* [*historischer Festungsbau*]

~ sett → ~ paving ~ [*B.S. 706*]

~ slab · Sandsteinplatte *f*

~ ~ floor cover(ing), ~ ~ floor(ing) (finish) · Sandsteinplatten(fuß)boden(belag) *m*, Fbsa *m*

~ ~ floor(ing) (finish), ~ ~ floor cover(ing) · Sandsteinplatten(fuß)boden(belag) *m*, Fbsa *m*

~ stair(case) · Sandsteintreppe *f*

sand-surfaced · besandet, sandbestreut

~ (on) both sides · beidseitig besandet

sand surfacing · Besandung *f*

~ test · Sandprobe *f*, Sandversuch *m*, Sandprüfung *f*

sandtight · sanddicht

sand-vent · verwitterte Kruste *f* [*Naturstein*]

sandwich [*A waterproof layer interposed between two layers of concrete*] · Sperre *f*

~ beam, flitch(ed) ~ · Sandwich-Balken(träger) *m*

~ course, intermediate ~, ~ layer · Zwischenlage *f*, Zwischenschicht *f*

~ element, ~ unit, ~ member · Sandwicheinheit *f*, Sandwichelement *n*

~ foam layer, intermediate ~ ~ · Schaumzwischenlage *f*, Schaumzwischenschicht *f*

~ layer, intermediate ~, ~ course · Zwischenlage *f*, Zwischenschicht *f*

~ member, ~ unit, ~ element · Sandwicheinheit *f*, Sandwichelement *n*

~ of spun glass, interlayer (~ ~ ~) · Glasserschicht *f* [*Thermolux*]

~ panel, three(-)layer(ed) ~ · Sandwichtafel *f*, Dreilagentafel, Dreischichtentafel [*Fehlname: Sandwichplatte. Bautafel für Außen- und Innenverkleidung bei Rahmenkonstruktionen; kreuzweise bewehrt, dazwischen Glaswolleschicht von etwa 5 cm*]

~ ~ façade, three(-)layer(ed) ~ ~ · Dreilagentafelfassade *f*, Dreischichtentafelfassade

~ plate · Keilplatte *f* [*Spannverfahren Magnel*]

~ ~, locking ~ · Sandwich-Platte *f* [*Spannbeton*]

~ ~, ~ slab, three(-)layer(ed) ~ · Dreilagenplatte *f*, Dreischichtenplatte

sandwich-plate method, Belgian (sandwich cable) method · Spannbetonverfahren *m* Magnel, (Vor)Spann(ungs)verfahren ~

sandwich roof(ing) slab, three(-)layer(ed) ~, ~ ~ ~ · Dreilagendachplatte *f*, Dreischichtendachplatte

~ shell, three(-)layer(ed) ~ · Dreilagenschale *f*, Dreischichtenschale

~ slab, ~ plate, three(-)layer(ed) ~ · Dreilagenplatte *f*, Dreischichtenplatte

~ unit, ~ member, ~ element · Sandwicheinheit *f*, Sandwichelement *n*

~ wall · Dreilagenwand *f*, Dreischichtenwand

~ ~ panel, three(-)layer(ed) ~ ~ · Dreilagenwandtafel *f*, Dreischichtenwandtafel

sandy, arenaceous · sand(halt)ig

~ gravel → gravelly sand

~ ~ aggregate → ~ ~ ~ concrete ~

~ ~ (concrete) aggregate, gravelly sand (~) ~ · Betonkiessand *m*, Monierkies *m* [< 70 mm]

sanidine [*A glassy grey and very fresh variety of orthoclase*] · Sanidin *m*

~ fel(d)spar · Sanidinfeldspat *m*

sanidine-trachyte [*A trachyte containing porphyritic crystals of sanidine. A glassy and very fresh variety of orthoclase*] · Sanidintrachyt *m*

sanitary articles, ~ products, ~ ware, ~ goods · Sanitärartikel *mpl*, Sanitärgegenstände *mpl*, Sanitärware(n) *f*, Sanitärerzeugnisse *npl*

~ building block module, ~ unitized unit · Sanitärinstallationsblock *m*, Sanitärinstallationszelle *f*, Sanitär(raum)block, Sanitär(raum)zelle, sanitärtechnischer Block, sanitärtechnische Zelle

~ castable refractory concrete · Sanitärfeuerbeton *m*

~ cast(ing)s · Sanitärguß *m*

~ conduit-type sewer · Schmutzwasserkanal *m*

~ convenience · Bedürfniseinrichtung *f*, Bedürfnisanlage *f*

~ corner cast(ing) · Scheuerleistenwinkel *m*, Sockelleistenwinkel, Fußleistenwinkel

~ cove, mopboard, washboard, base molding, scrub board, base (board) (US); skirting (board) (Brit.) · base plate [*Scotland*] [*Originally a wooden board set on edge round the foot of a wall to protect it from kicks. It may now be built of metal trim, asphalt, terrazzo, wall tiles, or other material which is more durable than wood*] · Fußleiste *f*, Scheuerleiste, Sockelleiste

~~ **component** (US) → base (board) unit

~~ **heater,** base (board) ~, scrub board ~, mopboard ~, washboard ~ (US); skirting (board) ~ (Brit.); base plate ~ [*Scotland*] · Scheuerleistenheizer *m*, Fußleistenheizer, Sockelleistenheizer

~~ **heating,** base (board) ~, scrub board ~, mopboard ~, washboard ~, skirting (board) ~ (Brit.); base plate ~ [*Scotland*] · Scheuerleistenheizung *f*, Fußleistenheizung, Sockelleistenheizung

~~ **member** (US) → base (board) unit

~~ **radiator,** base (board) ~, scrub board ~, mopboard ~, washboard ~ (US); skirting (board) ~ (Brit.); base plate ~ [*Scotland*] · Scheuerleisten-Radiator *m*, Sockelleisten-Radiator, Fußleisten-Radiator

~~ **unit** → base (board) ~

~ **earthenware** · Sanitärirdengut *n*, Sanitärsteingut

~ **engineering in the wider sense,** sanitation, public health engineering · Sanitärtechnik *f*

~ **equipment** · sanitäre Ausrüstung *f*

~ **fireclay** · Sanitärfeuerton *m*

~ **fitting** · Sanitärarmatur *f*

~ **goods,** ~ ware, ~ articles, ~ products · Sanitärartikel *mpl*, Sanitärgegenstände *mpl*, Sanitärware(n) *f*, Sanitärerzeugnisse *mpl*

~ **incinerator** · Sanitärverbrenner *m*

~ **pipe** → ~ sewage ~

~ **plumbing** → internal ~

~ **products,** ~ articles, ~ ware, ~ goods · Sanitärartikel *mpl*, Sanitärgegenstände *mpl*, Sanitärware(n) *f*, Sanitärerzeugnisse *npl*

~ **science as applied to buildings,** architectural hygiene · Bauhygiene *f*

~ **sewage** → house(hold) ~

~~ [*Sometimes loosely called 'discharge'*] · Schmutzwasser *n*

~ **(~) pipe** · Schmutzwasserrohr *n*

~ **sewer** [*A sewer which carries sewage and excludes storm, surface and ground water*] · Schmutzwasserleitung *f*

~~ **network** · Schmutzwassernetz *n*

~ **shoe** (US); congé [*A small concave mo(u)lding joining the base of a wall to the floor*] · (Fuß)Bodenkehle *f*

~ **stoneware** · sanitäres Steinzeug *n*, weißes ~, Sanitärsteinzeug [*Durchsichtige Glasur auf fast weißem, dichten, durchgesinterten Scherben*]

~ **unitized unit,** ~ building block module · Sanitärinstallationsblock *m*, Sanitärinstallationszelle *f*, Sanitär(raum)block, Sanitär(raum)zelle, sanitärtechnischer Block, sanitärtechnische Zelle

~ **ware** → china ~ ~

~~, ~ goods, ~ articles, ~ products · Sanitärartikel *mpl*, Sanitärgegenstände *mpl*, Sanitärware(n) *f*, Sanitärerzeugnisse *npl*

sanitation, sanitary engineering in the wider sense, public health engineering · Sanitärtechnik *f*

~ **engineer** · Gesundheitsingenieur *m*

~ **engineering** · Gesundheitstechnik *f*

~ **equipment** · gesundheitstechnische Anlagen *fpl*

~ **of buildings (and premises)** · Haus- und Grundstücksentwässerung *f*

~ **system,** system of sanitation, (sanitary) plumbing (system), internal plumbing · sanitäre (Gebäude)Installation *f*, ~ Hausinstallation ~ Einrichtung(en) *fpl*, ~ Anlagen, Sanitärinstallation, Sanitäreinrichtung(en), Sanitäranlage(n)

santorin earth · Santorinerde *f* [*Schlackenartige Erde vulkanischen Ursprungs, als hydraulischer Zuschlag(stoff) für Luftmörtel verwendet. Nach der griechischen Insel Santorin benannt*]

sap → quarry ~

saponifiable · verseifbar

saponification · Verseifen *n* [*Spaltung der Fette in Glycerin und Seifen durch Kochen in Alkalien*]

~ · Verseifung *f*

~ **number** · Verseifungszahl *f*, VZ

~ **resistance** · Verseifungsbeständigkeit *f*, Verseifungsfestigkeit

~ **risk** · Verseifungsgefahr *f*

saponified · verseift

to saponify · verseifen

saponin · Saponin *n* [*Ein Pflanzenextrakt, dessen wäßrige Lösung stark schäumt. Verwendung für Gas- und Schaumbeton*]

Saracenic arch → (round) horseshoe ~

~ **architecture** → Muslim ~

sarcophagus · Sarkophag *m*

~ **on columns** · Säulensarkophag *m*

sash, window ~ · Fensterrahmen *m*

~ **angle** · Scheinecke *f*, Winkel *m* [*Baubeschlag*]

~ **bar** → (window) glazing ~

~~ **window,** division ~ ~, glazing ~, astragal ~; muntin ~ (US) · Sprossenfenster *n*

~ **(counter) weight** · Gegengewicht *n* [*Senkrechtschiebe(flügel)fenster*]

~ **door,** glazed ~, half-glass ~ [*A door of which the upper half is glazed*] · Glasfüllungstür *f*

sash hardware — saturation point diagram

~ **hardware,** window ~ ~ · Fensterrahmenbeschläge *mpl*

~ **lift knob** · Aufziehknopf *m* [*Fenster*]

~ **putty,** glazier's ~, glazing ~ · Fensterkitt *m*, Verglasungskitt, Glaserkitt [*DIN 1975*]

~ **rail,** (window) ~ [*The horizontal member in a window sash*] · (Fenster-) Riegel *m*

~ **weight** · Gegengewicht *n* [*Senkrechtschiebe(flügel)fenster*]

~ **window,** sliding ~ ~ [*A window contained in a cased frame which slides, as opposed to a casement window*] · Schiebefenster *n*

Sassanian architecture · sassanidische Architektur *f*, ~ Baukunst *f*

(~) **Palace at Ctesiphon** · Palast *m* zu Ktesiphon

satellite centre (Brit.); ~ center (US) · Nebenzentrum *n*

~ **city** · Satellitenstadtkreis *m*, Trabantenstadtkreis

~ **town** · Satellitenstadt *f*, Trabantenstadt

satin finish; lustre ~ (Brit.); luster ~ (US) · Lüster *m* [*Oberflächenwirkung eines Anstriches oder Druckes; metallisch, bronzeartig, irisierend oder ähnlich schimmernd*]

~ ~ · Seidenglanz *m*

~ ~ **glass,** velvet ~ ~ · satiniertes Glas *n*, seidenmattes ~, Atlasglas, Seidentonglas

~ ~ **lacquer** · Seidenglanzlackfarbe *f*

~ ~ **varnish** · Seidenglanzlack *m*

satin-finished, satin-polished · gebürstet [*Leichtmetall*]

satin-polished, satin-finished · gebürstet [*Leichtmetall*]

satin spar, fibrous gypsum · Fraueneis *n*, Marienglas *n*, Frauenglas, Fasergips *m*, spätiger Gips, Alabasterglas [*perlmutterglänzender Gipsspat*]

~ **white** · Satinweiß *n*

saturability · Volltränkbarkeit *f*, Vollimprägnierbarkeit

saturant, impregnating agent, impregnating composition, saturating agent, saturating composition · Imprägnier(ungs)masse *f*, Imprägnier(ungs)mittel *n*, Tränkmasse, Tränkmittel

to saturate · volltränken, vollimprägnieren

saturated · gesättigt

~ · vollgetränkt, vollimprägniert

~ **asphalt rag felt** → uncoated ~ ~ ~

~ **compound** · gesättigte Verbindung *f*

~ **expanded cork brick,** impregnated ~ ~ ~ · imprägnierter Exp.-Korkstein *m*, getränkter ~

~ **fatty acid** · gesättigte Fettsäure *f*

~ **felt** → asphalt ready roofing

~ **paper,** impregnated ~ · imprägniertes Papier *n*, getränktes ~

~ **tar(red) rag felt** → uncoated ~ ~ ~

(~) **(water) vapour pressure** (Brit.); (~) (~) vapor ~ (US) · Wasserdampfdruck *m*

saturating · Volltränken *n*, Vollimprägnieren

~ **agent,** ~ composition, impregnating ~, saturant · Imprägnier(ungs)masse *f*, Imprägnier(ungs)mittel *n*, Tränkmasse, Tränkmittel

~ **asphalt,** impregnating ~, penetration-grade ~, hot ~ (US); 'penetration-grade' (asphaltic) bitumen, refinery (asphaltic) bitumen of penetration-grade, hot (asphaltic-)bitumen (Brit.) · Heißbitumen *n*, Tränkbitumen, Imprägnierbitumen

~ **composition,** ~ agent, impregnating ~, saturant · Imprägnier(ungs)masse *f*, Imprägnier(ungs)mittel *n*, Tränkmasse, Tränkmittel

~ **installation,** impregnation ~, impregnating ~, ~ plant · Imprägnier(ungs)anlage *f*, Tränkanlage

~ **mix(ture),** impregnating ~ · Imprägnier(ungs)gemisch *n*, Imprägnier(ungs)mischung *f*, Tränkgemisch, Tränkmischung

~ **plant,** impregnating ~, impregnation ~, ~ installation · Imprägnier(ungs)anlage *f*, Tränkanlage

~ **temperature,** impregnating ~ · Imprägnier(ungs)temperatur *f*, Tränktemperatur

saturation · Sättigung *f*

~ · Vollimprägnierung *f*, Volltränkung

~ **bath,** impregnation ~ · Tränkbad *n*, Imprägnier(ungs)bad

~ **degree,** degree of saturation · Volltränk(ungs)grad *m*, Vollimprägnier(ungs)grad

~ **of the base of posts,** impregnation ~ ~ ~ ~ ~ · Einstelltränkung *f*, Einstellimprägnierung [*Holzpfostenenden*]

~ **percentage** · Sättigungsgehalt *m*

~ **period,** ~ time · Volltränk(ungs)zeit *f*, Vollimprägnier(ungs)zeit

~ **point,** dew ~, condensation temperature, 100% relative humidity · Kondensationstemperatur *f*, Taupunkt *m*

~ ~ **diagram,** dew ~ ~, condensation temperature ~, diagram of 100% relative humidity · Taupunktdiagramm *n*, Kondensationstemperaturdiagramm

saturation pressure — scaffold tube

~ **pressure,** pressure of saturation · Sättigungsdruck *m*

~ **speed,** impregnation ~, speed of saturation, speed fo impregnation · Imprägnier(ungs)geschwindigkeit *f*, Tränk(ungs)geschwindigkeit

~ **time,** ~ period · Volltränk(ungs)zeit *f*, Vollimprägnier(ungs)zeit

~ **value** · Sättigungswert *m*

~ **water vapour pressure** (Brit.); ~ ~ vapor ~ (US) · Sättigungsdampfdruck *m*

saturator · Tränkpfanne *f* [*Dachpappenmaschine*]

saucer dome, dome(light), light cupola, domed roof-light · Oberlichtkuppel *f*, (Dach)Lichtkuppel

sauna bath, ~ installation · Saunabad *n*, Sauna(anlage) *f*

~ **installation,** ~ bath · Saunabad *n*, Sauna(anlage) *f*

~ **stove** · Saunaofen *m*

saving in weight, weight saving · Gewichtsersparnis *f*, Gewichtseinsparung *f*

savings in steel, steel savings · Stahlersparnis *f*

sawcut veneer, sawed ~, sawn ~ · Sägefurnier *n*

sawdust concrete · Sägespänebeton *m*

sawed, sawn · gesägt [*(Natur)Stein*]

~ **engineered timber,** sawn ~ ~, cut ~ ~, wood in building sizes; construction lumber (US) · Schnittholz *n* für Ingenieurholzbau, Bauschnittholz

~ **shingle** → sawn ~

~ **timber** → sawn wood

~ **veneer,** sawn ~, sawcut ~ · Sägefurnier *n*

sawn, sawed · gesägt [*(Natur)Stein*]

~ **engineered timber,** sawed ~ ~, cut ~ ~, wood in building sizes; construction lumber (US) · Schnittholz *n* für den Ingenieurholzbau, Bauschnittholz

~ **shingle,** sawed ~ · gesägte Schindel *f*, geschnittene ~, Maschinenschindel

~ **timber** → ~ wood

~ **veneer,** sawed ~, sawcut ~ · Sägefurnier *n*

~ **wood,** ~ timber, sawed ~, converted ~, mill run; milled products [*Australia*]; lumber (US) [*All the timber produced in a mill without reference to grade. The term 'lumber' is sometimes reserved in the USA for the German terms 'Bretter and Bohlen' and the German terms 'Kantholz and Balken' are then called 'timbers'. Thus 'Schnittholz may also be called in the USA 'lumber and timbers'*]

saw-tooth barrel shell roof, north(-light) ~ ~ ~, ~ cylinder segment ~ · Tonnen(schalen)-Sheddach *n*

~ **ceiling** · Sägezahndecke *f*

~ **cylinder segment roof,** north(-light) ~ ~ ~, ~ barrel shell ~ · Tonnen(schalen)-Sheddach *n*

~ **cylindrical shell,** north(-light) ~ ~ · Säge(zahn)dachzylinderschale *f*, Zylindersäge(zahn)dachschale ,Shed(dach)zylinderschale, Zylindershed(dach)schale

~ **hypar shell frame(d) building,** ~ ~ ~ ~ block, north-light ~ ~ ~ ~ · HP-Shed(rahmen)halle *f*

~ **rainwater gutter,** north(-light) ~ ~, ~ roof ~, ~ R. W. ~ · Säge(zahn)dach(regen)rinne *f*, Shed(dach)(regen)rinne

~ **roof,** north(-light) ~ · Säge(zahn)dach *n*, Sheddach

~ ~ **bay,** north(-light) ~ ~, ~ ~ span · Säge(zahn)dachschiff *n*, Shed(dach)schiff

~ ~ **building,** north(-light) ~ ~ · Shed(dach)bau *m*, Shed(dach)gebäude *n*

~ ~ **frame,** north(-light) ~ ~ · Säge(zahn)dachrahmen *m*, Shed(dach)rahmen

~ ~ **frame(d) block,** north(-lihgt) ~ ~ ~, ~ ~ ~ building · Säge(zahn)dach(rahmen)halle *f*, Shed(rahmen)halle

~ ~ **glazing,** north(-light) ~ ~ · Säge(zahn)dachverglasung *f*, Shed(dach)verglasung

~ ~ **rib,** north(-light) ~ ~ · Säge(zahn)dachrippe *f*, Shed(dach)rippe

~ ~ **roof-light,** north(-light) ~ ~ · Säge(zahn)dachoberlicht *n*, Shed(dach)oberlicht

~ ~ **truss,** north(-light) ~ ~ · Sägedachbinder *m*, Shed(dach)binder

~ **R. W. gutter** → ~ rainwater ~

~ **shell,** north(-light) ~ ~ · Säge(zahn)dachschale *f*, Shed(dach)schale

~ ~ **roof,** north(-light) ~ ~ · Säge(zahn)schalendach *n*, Shedschalendach

Saxon façade, Anglo-~ ~ · (angel-)sächsische Fassade *f*

~ **masonry (work),** Anglo-~ ~ (~) · (angel)sächsisches Mauerwerk *n*

~ **tower,** Anglo-~ ~ · (angel)sächsischer Turm *m*

SB, soot blower · Rußgebläse *n*

SBR → styrol-butadiene-rubber

SC → suspended ceiling

scabbler, squarer, block chopper, stone dresser, stone cutter · Steinmetz *m* [*Handwerker, der Werksteine zurichtet*]

sc(a)ena → scene-building

scaffold board · Gerüstbrett *n*

~ **erector** → scaffolding ~

~ **for maintenance (work)** · Unterhaltungsgerüst *n*

~ **frame** → scaffolding ~

~ **plank,** scaffolding ~ · Gerüstdiele *f*

~ **tube** → scaffolding ~

scaffolding — schedule of weights

scaffolding · Gerüst *n*, Rüstung *f*, Arbeits~, Bau~

scaffold(ing) erector · Gerüstmonteur *m*

~ frame · Gerüstrahmen *m*

~ plank · Gerüstdiele *f*

~ tube · Gerüstrohr *n*

scagliola (compound), ~ marble · Scagliola *f* [*Eine aus feinem Gips, gepulvertem Gipsspat und Leimwasser, letzteres als Gipshärtemittel, zusammengesetzte Gießmasse für die Herstellung von Gipsornamenten. Nach Polieren sieht das Ornament wie Marmor aus*]

~ marble, ~ **(compound)** · Scagliola *f* [*Eine aus feinem Gips, gepulvertem Gipsspat und Leimwasser, letzteres als Gipshärtemittel, zusammengesetzte Gießmasse für die Herstellung von Gipsornamenten. Nach Polieren sieht das Ornament wie Marmor aus*]

scalar position function · skalare Ortsfunktion *f*

~ product, inner ~ · skalares Produkt *n*, inneres ~, Skalarprodukt

scale, mill ~ [*Scale produced in the finishing mill*] · Abbrand *m*, Walzhaut *f*, (Walz)Zunder *m*

~ · Maßstab *m*

~ drawing, scaled ~ · maßstabgerechte Zeichnung *f*, maßstäbliche ~

~ effect · Maßstabeffekt *m*

~ gutter tile · Schuppenfalzziegel *m*

~ imposed through dividing an elevation into storeys · Stockwerkmaßstab *m* [*in der Fassadengestaltung*]

~ of frequencies · Frequenzskala *f*

~ ~ moments · Momentenmaßstab *m*

~ ~ professional charges, fee system · Architektengebührenordnung *f*, Gebührenordnung für Architekten

~ ~ proportions, ~ ~ ratios [*Laid down by Le Corbusier and his colleagues, this is also known as the Modulor. Le C. describes it as a 'harmonious measure to the human scale, universally applicable to architecture and mechanics'*] · Proportionsskala *f*, Modulor *m*

~ ~ ratios, ~ ~ proportions [*Laid down by Le Corbusier and his colleagues, this is also known as the Modulor. Le C. describes it as a 'harmonious measure to the human scale universally applicable to architecture and mechanics'*] · Proportionsskala *f*, Modulor *m*

~ removal → descaling

scale-work · Schuppenornament *n*

scale(d) drawing · maßstabgerechte Zeichnung *f*, maßstäbliche ~

scaling · Abblättern *n* [*Ablösen dünner Schichten von der Betonoberfläche durch Einwirkung von Frost, Tausalz usw.*]

scalloped arch · geschweifter Bogen *m*

~ capital, indented ~ [*A development of the block or cushion capital in which the single lunette on each face is elaborated into on or more truncated cones*] · Faltenkapitell *n*, Faltenkapitäl, Pfeifenkapitell, Pfeifenkapitäl, gefälteltes Kapitell, gefälteltes Kapitäl

~ leaf · eingerolltes Blatt *n*

Scandinavian plaster, thin-wall ~, Swedish sand putty · Dünnputz *m*

scantlings · zugeschnittenes Bauholz *n*, Bindeholz, Brustholz, Bundholz

scarlet · Scharlach *m*

~ vermilion (pigment) · Scharlachzinnober(pigment) *m*, (*n*)

scatter, range of ~ · Streubereich *m*, *n* [*Versuchsergebnisse*]

~ of routine results · Betriebsstreuung *f* [*Streuung der Druckfestigkeiten von Erzeugnissen der Betriebsproduktion*]

scattering of qualities, dispersion in quality · Gütestreuung *f*

~ ~ strengths, dispersion in strength · Festigkeitsstreuung *f*

~ (~ test(s)) · (Prüf)Streuung *f* [*Versuchergebnis*]

scena → scene-building

scene-building, skene, sc(a)ena · Skene(ngebäude) *f*, (*n*), Bühnengebäude

scenic (design) · bildhafte Darstellung *f* [*(Papier)Tapete*]

~ highway, ~ road · Aussichtsstraße *f*, Panoramastraße [*Straße, die auf der Talseite nicht bebaut werden kann, weil der Hang zu steil ist. Sie bietet Aussicht in das Tal und auf die gegenüberliegenden Hänge*]

~ paper, ~ wall~ · Tapete *f*, mit bildhaften Darstellungen, (Wand)Papier~ ~ ~ ~

~ road, ~ highway · Panoramastraße *f*, Aussichtsstraße [*Straße, die auf der Talseite nicht bebaut werden kann, weil der Hang zu steil ist. Sie bietet Aussicht in das Tal und auf die gegenüberliegenden Hänge*]

~ view, panoramic ~ · Panoramaansicht *f*

~ (wall)paper · Tapete *f* mit bildhaften Darstellungen, (Wand)Papier~ ~ ~ ~

scenographic design · szenisch aufgefaßter Entwurf *m*

scent test → smell ~

Schäfer floor · Schäfer-Decke *f*

schedule of accommodation · Gebäudeaufteilung *f* (und Nutzung), Flächennutzung

~ ~ ~ · Kapazitätenplan *m* [*Hotel; Krankenhaus*]

~ ~ sizes · Maßtabelle *f*

~ ~ weights, table ~ ~, weight table, weight schedule · Gewichtstabelle *f*

schedule of weights ... — scoria(ceous lava)

~ ~ ~ **of building materials** [*B.S. 648*] · Baumaterialgewichtsverzeichnis *n* [*Schweiz*]; Baustoffgewichtsverzeichnis

schematic design, preliminary ~ · Vorentwurf *m*

~ ~ **drawing,** preliminary ~ ~ · Vorentwurfszeichnung *f*

~ ~ **phase,** preliminary ~ ~ · Vorentwurfsstadium *n*

~ **illustration** · Schemazeichnung *f*

~ **representation** · schematische Darstellung *f*

schematism · Schematismus *m*

scheme, project · Projekt *n*

~ **of framework** · Fachwerk-Grundfigur *f*, Fachwerk-Grundgebilde *n*

schillerspar, bastite · Schillerspat *m*, Bastit *m*

schist, crystalline ~ · kristalliner Schiefer *m*

schistous amphibolite, horn(blende)-schist [*A foliated metamorphic rock, consisting of hornblende, with various proportions of feldspar, biotite, etc.*] · Hornblendeschiefer *m*

~ **sandstone,** arenaceous shale, foliated grit(-stone) · Sandschiefer *m*

(Schofer's) compound chimney · Schoferkamin *m*, Verbundkamin, Schoferschornstein *m*, Verbundschornstein

school architecture · Schularchitektur *f*, Schulbaukunst *f*

~ **auditorium** · Schulaula *f*

~ **block,** ~ building · Schulgebäude *n*

~ **building,** ~ construction · Schulbau(wesen) *m*, (*n*)

~ ~, ~ block · Schulgebäude *n*

~ ~ **programme** (Brit.); ~ ~ program (US) · Schulbauprogramm *n*

~ ~ **system** · Schulbausystem *n*

~ **buildings,** ~ structures · Schulbauten *fpl*

~ **complex** · Schulbau *m*, Schulanlage *f* [*Alle Gebäude und Anlagen zusammen*]

~ **construction,** ~ building · Schulbau(wesen) *m*, (*n*)

~ **for feeble minded** · Hilfsschule *f*

~ **gym(nasium)** · Schulturnhalle *f*

~ **of applied art,** college ~ ~ ~ · Kunstgewerbeschule *f*

~ ~ **architecture** · Schule *f* der Baukunst, ~ ~ Architektur

School of Delft [*Dominated post-war Dutch architecture until about 1955*] · Delfter Schule *f*

school plant · Schulkomplex *m*

~ **site** · Schulgrundstück *n*

~ **structures,** ~ buildings · Schulbauten *fpl*

~ **swimming pool** · Schulschwimmbecken *n*

~ **village** · Schuldorf *n*

~ **with honeycomb layout** · Wabenschule *f*

Schumann metal(lic)-aggregate mortar cover(ing) · Stahlbeton *m* Schumann [*Stahlbetonbelag, hergestellt mit metallenen Spezialhärtematerialien in verschiedenen Körnungen, je nach Verwendungszweck und zwar Nr. 1 grob, Nr. 2 mittel, Nr. 3 fein. Mischung 1 kg Zement (Portland-, Hochofen- oder Spezialzement), 1 kg Härtematerial und 1 Liter Quarzsand unter 3 mm Korngröße*]

Schürmann's ceiling, arch(ed) ~ · Gewölbeträgerdecke *f*, Schürmannsche Decke

Schwedler(s') dome, ~ cupola · Schwedlersche Kuppel *f*, Schwedlerkuppel

~ **girder** · Schwedlerscher Träger *m*, Schwedlerträger

Schweinfurt green · Schweinfurtergrün *n*

science block → ~ building

~ **building,** ~ block, ~ house · Gebäude *n* für wissenschaftliche Zwecke, Haus *n*

~ ~ ~

~ **house** → ~ building

~ **museum** · Wissenschaftsmuseum *n*

~ **of architecture** · Architekturwissenschaft *f*

~ **of fortification,** art ~ ~ · Festungsbau(wesen) *m*, (*n*)

scientifically designed · durchkonstruiert

scissor lift · Scherenhubtisch *m*

scleroscope, concrete test hammer, rebound tester [*A tester indexing the compressive strength of concrete by the height of elastic rebound*] · Rückprallhammer *m*, Betonprüfhammer, Betonschlaghammer, Rückprall-Härteprüfer

~ **hardness** · Rückprallhärte *f*

scoinson arch → rere-arch

sconce, wall ~ · Wandzierlampe *f*, Zierwandlampe

scope · Geltungsbereich *m*, *n* [*Norm*]

~ **of application,** ~ ~ use · Anwendungsbereich *m*, *n*

~ ~ **supply** · Lieferumfang *m*

~ ~ **use,** ~ ~ application · Anwendungsbereich *m*, *n*

~ ~ **work,** work content · Leistungsumfang *m*, Arbeitsumfang

scoria(ceous lava), foamed ~ · Schaumlava *f*, vulkanische Schlacke *f*, poröse Lava, Lavaschlacke, Lungstein *m*, Lavakrotze *f*, Basaltlava, Basaltschlacke [*Basaltische feinporige bis blasige vulkanische Auswurfmasse. "Lavalit,, ist ein geschützter Handelsname für gebrochene Lavaschlacke, die in verschiedenen Körnungen aufbereitet ist*]

scoria(ceous) lava concrete — screed admix(ture)

~~ **concrete**, foamed ~ ~ · Lavaschlackenbeton *m*, (Schaum)Lavabeton, Basaltlavabeton, Basaltschlackenbeton, Lavakiesbeton

~~ **(~) wall slab**, foamed ~ (~) ~ ~ · (Schaum)Lava(beton-)Wand(bau)platte *f*

Scotch bond (Brit.) → American ~

~ **glue**, animal ~, animal adhesive [*B.S. 745*] · Glutinleim *m*, tierischer Leim, Tierleim [*DIN 53260*]

~~ **in pearl form**, ~ ~ ~ bead ~, pearl glue, bead glue · Perl(en)leim *m*

scotia, throat(ing), weather groove, (water) drip · (Wasser)Nase *f*, Unterschneidung *f*

~ → trochilus

Scots fir strip floor(ing) (finish), ~ ~ ~ floor cover(ing), red ~ ~ ~ (~) · Fhk *m*, Kiefernriemen(fuß)boden(belag) *m*

scouring powder · Scheuerpulver *n*

scove kiln; clamp (Brit.) · Feld(brand)ofen *m*, Meiler *m* [*Ziegelherstellung*]

~ **kiln-burnt brick** (Brit.); ~ kiln-burned ~ (US) · Feld(brand)ofenziegel *m*, Meilerziegel

scrap celluloid, celluloid scrap · Zelluloidabfall *m*, Zellhornabfall

~ **iron** · Abfalleisen *n*, Alteisen

~ ~ **rails** · Alteisen *n*, Altschienen *fpl*

~ **lead** · Altblei *n*, Abfallblei, Bleiabfall *m*

~ **steel** · Stahlschrott *m*

~ **structural iron** · Alteisen *n*, altes Baueisen [*Das aus zerstörten Bauteilen und Bauwerken geborgene Baueisen*]

~ ~ **steel** · alter Baustahl *m*, Altstahl [*Der aus zerstörten Bauteilen und Bauwerken geborgene Baustahl*]

to scrape (off) · abkratzen

scraped rendering (Brit.); ~ stucco (US) · Schabputz *m*, Stockputz, Kratzputz, gekratzter Putz [*Eine Außenputzart, die durch Abziehen der verriebenen, abgebundenen Putzfläche mit einer Ziehklinge oder einem Kratzbrett entsteht*]

~ **stucco** (US); ~ rendering (Brit.) · Kratzputz *m*, gekratzter Putz, Stockputz, Schabputz [*Eine Außenputzart, die durch Abziehen der verriebenen, abgebundenen Putzfläche mit einer Ziehklinge oder einem Kratzbrett entsteht*]

scraper · (Aus)Kratzer *m*, (Aus)Kratzeisen *n*

scraping (off) · Abkratzen *n*

scratch, graze, cut · Schramme *f*, Kratzer *m* [*Fehler im optischen Glas*]

~ **coat**, render(ing) ~ [*It consists of mortar of lime, sand, and considerable hair*] · Unterputzschicht *f*, Unterputzlage *f*, Grobputzschicht, Grobputzlage, (Außen)Rauhwerk *n*

~~, backing (~), basecoat, undercoat [*A plastering or rendering coat other than the final coat*] · Grobputzlage *f*, Grobputzschicht *f*, Grundputzlage, Grundputzschicht, Unterputzlage, Unterputzschicht, Rauhwerk

~ **hardness** · Ritzhärte *f*, Mineralhärte [*Der Widerstand, den Mineralien der Trennung ihrer kleinsten Teilchen beim Ritzen entgegensetzen. Sie wird nach der Mohs'schen Härteskala bestimmt, die 10 Härtegrade erfaßt. Beginnend mit dem weichsten Mineral 1 umfaßt die Skala folgende Mineralien:*

1 Talk	6 Orthoklas
2 Steinsalz oder Gips	7 Quarz
3 Kalkspat	8 Topas
4 Flußspat	9 Korund
5 Apatit	10 Diamant

Jedes dieser Mineralien ritzt einen Körper von vorausgehendem Härtegrad]

~ **removal** · Kratzerbeseitigung *f*

~ **resistance** · Ritzbeständigkeit *f*, Ritzfestigkeit, Kratzbeständigkeit, Kratzfestigkeit, Ritzwiderstand *m*, Kratzwiderstand

scratch(-)resistant, scratchproof, scratch(-)resisting · ritzfest, ritzbeständig, kratzfest, kratzbeständig

scratch(-)resisting, scratchproof, scratch(-)resistant · ritzfest, ritzbeständig, kratzfest, kratzbeständig

scratch test · Mineralhärteprobe *f*, Mineralhärteversuch *m*, Mineralhärteprüfung *f*, Ritzprobe, Ritzprüfung, Ritzversuch

scratchability · Ritzbarkeit *f*, Kratzbarkeit

scratching · Einritzen *n* [*Putz*]

scratchproof, scratch(-)resistant, scratch(-)resisting · ritzfest, ritzbeständig, kratzfest, kratzbeständig

scratchwork, sgraffito [*A plaster surface decorated by scoring a pattern on it while it is soft, and exposing a lower coat of a different colour. The upper layer is often white, the lower layer black or dark red. More than two colours can be used if required*] · Sgraffito(putz) *m*, Kratzgrund *m*, Kratzputz

to screed [*To level off a concrete surface*] · abziehen

screed [*A strip of wood or metal which is moved over guides or screeds (Richtleisten) to strike off or finish a surface*] · Abziehvorrichtung *f*

~ [*A strip, usually of wood or metal, used as a guide for striking off or finishing a surface*] · Richtleiste *f*

~ → ~ floor cover(ing)

~ → ~ material

~ → ~ for plastering

~ **accelerating agent**, ~ accelerator · Estrichbeschleuniger *m*

~ **admix(ture)**, ~ agent · Estrichwirkstoff *m*, Estrichzusatzstoff, Estrichzusatz(mittel) *m*, (*n*)

screed agent — (screwed) bolt

~ **agent,** ~ admix(ture) · Estrichwirkstoff *m*, Estrichzusatzstoff, Estrichzusatz(mittel) *m* ,(*n*)

~ **base** · Estrichunterlage *f*

~ **bay,** ~ topping ~ · Estrichfeld *n*

~ **cracking** · Reißen *n* von Estrichen

~ **floor cover(ing),** ~ floor(ing) (finish), ~ (topping) · Estrich(fuß)-boden(belag) *m*, Fe

~ **(for plastering)** · Putzleiste *f* [*Ein Hilfsmittel zur Erreichung einer ebenen Wandfläche. Bei Deckenausführungen kann im allgemeinen auf Putzleisten verzichtet werden, Rabitzdecken jedoch sind ohne Putzleisten schlecht zu ebnen. Putzleisten fertigt man entweder aus dem zu verarbeitenden Putzmörtel an, bei besserer Ausführung aus Gips (Pariserleiste) oder aus Holz*]

~ **improver,** ~ modifier, ~ modifying agent, ~ improving agent · Estrichvergüter *m*, Estrichvergütungsmittel *n*

~ **joint,** ~ topping ~ · Estrichfuge *f*

~ **laying in (alternate) bays** · Estrichverlegung *f* in Feldern

~ **(material)** · Estrich *m* [*als Baustoff*]

~ **modifier** → ~ improver

~ **modifying agent** → ~ improver

~ **mortar** · Estrichmörtel *m*

~ **of plaster of Paris** · Pariserleiste *f*, Putzleiste aus Stuckgips

~ **rail** [*A heavy rule used for forming a concrete or mortar surface to the desired shape of level*] · Abziehlineal *n*

~ **seal(ing),** ~ topping ~ · Estrichabsieg(e)lung *f*, Estrichversieg(e)lung

~ **surface,** ~ topping ~ · Estrichoberfläche *f*

~ **(topping),** ~ floor(ing) (finish), ~ floor cover(ing) · Estrich(fuß)boden(belag) *m*, Fe

~ (~) **bay** · Estrichfeld *n*

~ (~) **joint** · Estrichfuge *f*

~ (~) **seal(ing)** · Estrichabsieg(e)lung *f*, Estrichversieg(e)lung

~ (~) **surface** · Estrichoberfläche *f*

~ **work** · Estricharbeiten *fpl* [*DIN 18353*]

screeding, surface ~ · Abziehen *n*

screen → screening

(~) **feed,** (~) head, material to be screened · Siebgut *n*, Einlaufgut, Haufwerk *n*, Aufgabegut [*Siebtechnik*]

~ **fence** → (vision) screen(ing) ~

(~) **head,** (~) feed, material to be screened · Aufgabegut *n*, Haufwerk *n*, Siebgut, Einlaufgut [*Siebtechnik*]

screen-printed wallpaper · Siebdrucktapete *f*

screen residue, oversize · (Sieb)Rückstand *m*, (Sieb)Überlauf *m*, (Sieb)Überkorn *n* [*Betriebssieb*]

~ **scale,** ~ series, mesh scale; mesh gage (US) · Siebfolge *f*, Siebreihe *f*, Siebskala *f*

~ **series,** ~ scale, mesh scale; mesh gage (US) · Siebfolge *f*, Siebreihe *f*, Siebskala *f*

~ **(wall)** · Sichtblende *f*, Sichtschutzwand *f*

~ ~ **of pierced concrete blocks,** pierced concrete block screen wall · durchbrochene Sichtschutzwand *f* aus Betonformsteinen, ~ Betonformsteinwand [*Zur Gliederung von Gartenräumen oder zur Abschirmung geschützter Sitzplätze in Gärten*]

screened, graded · (korn)abgestuft, gesiebt [*Mineralmasse*]

~ **aggregate,** ~ concrete ~, graded (concrete) ~ · (korn)abgestufter (Beton)Zuschlag(stoff) *m*, gesiebter ~

~ **(concrete) aggregate,** graded (~) ~ · (korn)abgestufter (Beton)Zuschlag(stoff) *m*, gesiebter ~

~ **glass powder,** graded ~ ~, ~ powder(ed) glass · gesiebtes Glaspulver *n*, (korn)abgestuftes ~

~ **gravel,** graded ~ · gesiebter Kies *m*, (korn)abgestufter ~, Siebkies

~ **material** · gesiebtes Gut *n*, Siebgut

~ **powder(ed) glass,** graded ~ ~, ~ glass powder · gesiebtes Glaspulver *n*, (korn)abgestuftes ~

~ **sand,** graded ~ · (korn)abgestufter Sand *m*, gesiebter ~, Siebsand

~ **slag** · Siebschlacke *f*

screening, shading, solar ~, sunshading · Sonnenschutz *m*, Abschattung *f*, Besonnungsschutz

screen(ing), vision ~ · (Sicht)Blende *f*, (Sicht)Schutz *m*

~ **fence** → (vision) ~ ~

screening operation, ~ process · Siebvorgang *m*

~ **portion** → size range

~ **process,** ~ operation · Siebvorgang *m*

screening(s) → stone ~

screwcrete · Schraubbeton *m*

screw-down tap [*A draw-off tap closed by means of a disc carrying a renewable nonmetallic washer which shuts against the water pressure on a seating at right angles to the axis of the screwed spindle which operates it*] · Niederschraubhahn *m*

screw-extruder, extruder-screw, extrusion auger, auger-type extrusion unit, auger-type machine · Schneckenpresse *f*, Extruder-Schnecke *f*

screw hole · Schraubenloch *n*

~ **hook** · Schraubhaken *m*

~ **interval,** distance between screws · Schraubenabstand *m*

to screw off, to unscrew · losschrauben, lösen, auseinanderschrauben, abschrauben

(screwed) bolt · (Schrauben)Bolzen *m*, Gewindebolzen

screw(ed) connection, ~ joint · Schraubenverbindung f, Schraubenanschluß m, (Anschluß)Verschraubung

screwed coupling · Schraubmuffe f, Schraubmuffenverbindung f

~ ~ pipe · Schraubenmuffenrohr n

~ flange · Schraubflansch m

screw(ed) joint, ~ connection · Schraubenverbindung f, Schraubenanschluß m, (Anschluß)Verschraubung

screwed-on hinge · Aufschraubband n [z.B. für Türen]

~ lock · Aufschraubschloß n

scribing, marking out · (Zu)Reißen n, Anreißen, Anriß m, Anzeichnen [Werkstücke]

~ dimension, marking out ~ · (Zu)Reißmaß n, Anrißmaß, Anreißmaß, Anzeichnungsmaß [Werkstücke]

scrim · grobgewebter Leichtstoff m

scriptorium [A writing-room especially in a medieval monastery, where manuscripts were copied] · Klosterschreibstube f

scroll → spiral ~

~, foliage ~ · Ranke f

~, banderol(e), streamer, label · Spruchband n, Schriftband, Banderole f

~ and leaf pattern · Blatt- und Rankenwerk n

~ capital → scrolled ~

scrolled, scroll-shaped, voluted · schneckenförmig

scroll(ed) capital, scroll-shaped ~, volute(d) ~ · Schneckenkapitell n, Volutenkapitell, Schneckenkapitäl, Volutenkapitäl, ionisches Kapitell, ionisches Kapitäl

~ gable, volute(d) ~, scroll-shaped ~ · Schneckengiebel m, Volutengiebel [Dieser Giebel ist seitlich von Voluten gerahmt]

scroll-shaped, scrolled, voluted · schneckenförmig

~ capital, scroll(ed) ~, volute(d) ~ · Schneckenkapitell n, Schneckenkapitäl, Volutenkapitell, Volutenkapitäl, ionisches Kapitell, ionisches Kapitäl

~ gable, volute(d) ~, scroll(ed) ~ · Schneckengiebel m, Volutengiebel [Dieser Giebel ist seitlich von Voluten gerahmt]

scrollwork, scrolls · Rankenwerk n

~, shell work, rocaille [A graceful design of delicate scroll and counter-scroll outline, varying in form yet maintaining everywhere its characteristic asymmetrical harmony] · Rocaille n, f, Muschelwerk n

scrub board → sanitary cove

~ ~ component → base (board) unit

~ ~ heater, base (board) ~, mopboard ~, washboard ~, sanitary cove ~ (US); skirting (board) ~ (Brit.); base plate ~ [Scotland] · Scheuerleistenheizer m, Fußleistenheizer, Sockelleistenheizer

~ ~ heating, base (board) ~, mopboard ~, washboard ~, sanitary cove ~ (US); skirting (board) ~ (Brit.); base plate ~ [Scotland] · Scheuerleistenheizung f, Fußleistenheizung, Sockelleistenheizung

~ ~ member → base (board) unit

~ ~ radiator, base (board) ~, mopboard ~, washboard ~, sanitary cove ~ (US); skirting (board) ~ (Brit.); base plate ~ [Scotland] · Scheuerleisten-Radiator m, Sockelleisten-Radiator, Fußleisten-Radiator

~ ~ unit → base (~) ~

scrubbable · scheuerbar [Fehlbezeichnung]; scheuerfest

scrubbed concrete · abgebürsteter Waschbeton m, (Bürsten)Waschbeton

~ ~ brush · Waschbetonbürste f

~ ~ facing · Waschbetonvorsatz m

~ ~ flower trough · Waschbetonblumentrog m

~ ~ slab · Waschbetonplatte f

scrubbing · (Ab)Bürsten n [Waschbeton]

scullery, wash-up [A room adjoining the kitchen, where pots and pans are cleaned and sorted or where the rough dirty kitchen work is done] · Abwaschraum m, Aufwaschraum, (Geschirr)Spülraum, Spülküche f

sculptor · Bildhauer m

sculptural block → ~ type ~

~ decoration · Plastikausschmückung f, Plastikverzierung, Plastikschmuck m, Skulptur(en)ausschmückung, Skulptur(en)verzierung, Skulptur(en)schmuck

~ decorative feature → carved pattern

~ ~ finish → carved pattern

~ detail · plastisches Detail n

~ enrichment → carved pattern

~ ornament(al feature) → carved pattern

~ ~ finish → carved pattern

~ pattern → carved ~

~ style, carved ~ · plastischer Stil m

~ (type) block, ~ (~) tile [See remark under 'Block'] · Ornamentblock(stein) m, Ornamentstein, Zierblock(stein), Zierstein, Schmuckblock(stein), Schmuckstein, Dekor(ations)stein, Dekor(ations)block(stein)

to sculpture, to carve, to cut, to hew [out of stone, in ivory, etc.] · skulpt(ur)ieren

sculpture · Plastik f, Skulptur f

~ in ivory, ivory sculpture · Elfenbeinplastik f, Elfenbeinskulptur f

~ ~ (natural) stone, (natural) stone sculpture · (Natur)Steinplastik f, (Natur)Steinskulptur f

sculpture in stone — seal(ing) coat

~ ~ **stone**, ~ ~ natural ~, (natural) stone sculpture · (Natur)Steinplastik *f*, (Natur)Steinskulptur *f*

~ ~ **wood**, wood sculpture · Holzplastik *f*, Holzskulptur *f*

sculptured foliage, carved ~, hewn ~, cut ~ · skulpt(ur)iertes Blattwerk *n*, ~ Laubwerk, plastisch gestaltete Blätter *npl*

~ **frieze** · Skulpturfries *m*, Plastikfries, skulptierter Fries, skulpturierter Fries

sculpturing, carving, cutting, hewing [*out of stone, in ivory, etc.*] · Skulpt(ur)ieren *n*

to scumble · lasieren

scumble · (Farb)Lasur *f*

~ **for fair-faced concrete** · Betonlasur *f*

~ **glaze** [*A transparent preparation used in the scumbling process*] · Lasuranstrichmittel *n*

~ **stain** [*A semi-transparent stain for application over an opaque groundwork of paint. Brush, stipple or sponge may be used for manipulating the scumble, or it may be combed, so that various effects, i.e. wood graining and other more formal patterns, are possible. In this the nonflowing property of the scumble greatly assists*] · Wasserlasur(farbe) *f*

scumbling (process) · Lasieren *n*

~ **technique**, ~ technic · Lasurtechnik *f*

scuncheon arch → rere-arch

scutcheon → escutcheon

sea-grass [*Zostera marina*] · Seegras *n*

~ **(building) mat** [*It has a low density*] · Seegrasdämmatte *f*, Seegras(bau)matte

~ **insulation(-grade) strip**, ~ insulating ~ · Seegrasdämmstreifen *m*

to seal · (ab)dichten, undurchlässig machen, dicht machen

~ ~ · absiegeln, versiegeln

seal, sealing · (Ab)Dichtung *f*

~, sealer, sealant, seal(ing) material · Absieg(e)lungsmittel *n*, Versieg(e)lungsmittel, Siegel *n*, Überzug *m*

~ · (Ab)Dichtung *f* [*Erzeugnis*]

~, sealing · Absieg(elung) *f*, Versieg(e)lung

~ → water ~

~ **coat** → sealing ~

~ **material**, sealing ~, sealant, seal(er) · Absieg(e)lungsmittel *n*, Versieg(e)lungsmittel, Siegel *n*, Überzug *m*

~ **mortar**, sealing ~ · Abschlußmörtel *m*, Vergußmörtel, Stopfmörtel

~ **plug**, seal(ing) ~

~ **ring** → sealing ~

~ **stopper** → seal(ing) plug

~ **water** · Sperrwasser *n* [*Abort*]

~ **weld** [*Any weld used primarily to obtain tightness*] · Dicht(ungs)schweißnaht *f*

sealable transparent cover · plombierte Sichthaube *f*

sealant, seal(er), seal(ing) material · Absperrmittel *n* [*Anstrichtechnik*]

~, sealer, seal(ing) compound, seal(ing) composition · Versieg(e)lungsmasse *f*, Absieg(e)lungsmasse

~, sealer, seal(ing) medium, seal(ing) material · (Ab)Dicht(ungs)material *n*, (Ab)Dicht(ungs)stoff *m*, (Ab)Dicht(ungs)mittel *n*

~, seal(er), seal(ing) material · Siegel *n*, Absiegelungsmittel, Versiegelungsmittel, Überzug *m*

~ → (joint) filling compound

sealed glazing unit · Verbundrand-Verglasungseinheit *f*

seal(er), seal(ing) material, sealant · Absperrmittel *n* [*Anstrichtechnik*]

sealer · Isolieranstrich *m*, Zwischenanstrich [*Um ein Durchschlagen von Farbe zu verhindern*]

~, sealant, seal(ing) material, seal(ing) medium · (Ab)Dicht(ungs)material *n*, (Ab)Dicht(ungs)mittel *n*, (Ab)Dicht(ungs)stoff *m*

~, seal(ing) coat · Absieg(e)lungsschicht *f*, Versieg(e)lungsschicht

~, seal(ing) coat · (Ab)Dicht(ungs)anstrich *m*, (Ab)Dicht(ungs)aufstrich, Zwischenanstrich, Isolieranstrich [*Um ein Durchschlagen von Farbe zu verhindern*]

~, seal(ing) coat · (Ab)Dicht(ungs)beschichtung *f*, (Ab)Dicht(ungs)überzug *m*, (Ab)Dicht(ungs)schicht *f*

seal(er) · Absperrmittel *n*, Siegel *n* [*Anstrichtechnik*]

~, sealant, seal(ing) material · Siegel *n*, Absiegelungsmittel *n*, Versiegelungsmittel, Überzug *m*

sealer, sealant, seal(ing) compound, seal(ing) composition · Versieg(e)lungsmasse *f*, Absieg(e)lungsmasse

seal(ing) · (Ab)Dichtung *f*

~ · Absieg(e)lung *f*, Versieg(e)lung

sealing · (Ab)Dichten *n*

~ → joint ~

~, surface ~ · Versieg(e)lung *f*, Absieg(e)lung

~, welding, fusing [*Joining a piece of glass to glass or another material by heating and pressing together; also applied to the fire finishing of ends of tubular glasses*] · Schweißen *n*, Verschmelzen [*Glas*]

~ **box**, branch ~ · Hausanschlußkasten *m*, Gebäudeanschlußkasten

~ **by rope**, rope sealing · Strick(ab)dichtung *f*

seal(ing) cement, ~ putty · (Ab)Dicht(ungs)kitt *m*

~ **coat**, sealer · (Ab)Dicht(ungs)anstrich *m*, (Ab)Dicht(ungs)aufstrich, Zwischenanstrich, Isolieranstrich [*Um ein Durchschlagen von Farbe zu verhindern*]

seal(ing) coat — seating capacity

~ ~, sealer · Absieg(e)lungsschicht f, Versieg(e)lungsschicht
~ ~, sealer · (Ab)Dicht(ungs)beschichtung f, (Ab)Dicht(ungs)überzug m, (Ab)Dicht(ungs)schicht f
~ ~ emulsion · Porenschlußemulsion f
~ collar · Dicht(ungs)kragen m
~ compound, ~ mass, ~ composition, ~ material · (Ab)Dicht(ungs)masse f
~ ~ →(joint) filling ~
~ concentrate · (Ab)Dicht(ungs)konzentrat n
~ felt(ed fabric) · (Ab)Dicht(ungs)filz m
sealing filler → (joint) sealing strip
seal(ing) fillet · (Ab)Dicht(ungs)leiste f
~ fin → ~ rib
~ foil · (Ab)Dicht(ungs)folie f
~ gasket → (preformed) ~ ~
~ ~ joint → (preformed) ~ ~
~ jacket · (Ab)Dicht(ungs)binde f
~ joint · (Ab)Dicht(ungs)verbindung f
~ lip · (Ab)Dicht(ungs)lippe f [*(Ab-) Dicht(ungs)ring*]
~ mass, ~ compound, ~ composition, ~ material · (Ab)Dicht(ungs)masse f
~ material, ~ medium, sealer, sealant · (Ab)Dicht(ungs)material n, (Ab)Dicht(ungs)mittel n, (Ab)Dicht(ungs)stoff m
~ ~, ~ compound, ~ composition, ~ mass · (Ab)Dicht(ungs)masse f
~ ~, sealant, seal(er) · Absperrmittel n [*Anstrichtechnik*]
~ ~, sealant, seal(er) · Siegel n, Absiegelungsmittel n, Versiegelungsmittel, Überzug m
~ medium, ~ material, sealer, sealant · (Ab)Dicht(ungs)material n, (Ab)Dicht(ungs)mittel n, (Ab)Dicht(ungs)stoff m
~ mix(ture) · (Ab)Dicht(ungs)gemisch n, (Ab)Dicht(ungs)mischung f
~ mortar · Abschlußmörtel m, Vergußmörtel, Stopfmörtel
sealing nipple · (Ab)Dicht(ungs)nippel m
~ off inrushes of water · Abriegelung f von Wassereinbrüchen, ~ ~ Wasserdurchbrüchen
seal(ing) paste · (Ab)Dicht(ungs)paste f
~ plug, (pipe) ~, (~) stopper · Pfropfen m, Stopfen, Verschluß m, Rohr~
~ putty, ~ cement · (Ab)Dicht(ungs)kitt m
~ rib, ~ fin · (Ab)Dicht(ungs)rippe f [*(Ab)Dicht(ungs)ring*]
~ ring, antileak ~ · (Ab)Dicht(ungs)ring m, (Ab)Dicht(ungs)scheibe f
~ rope, pouring ~, joint runner · (Ab-)Dicht(ungs)strick m
~ rubber · (Ab)Dicht(ungs)gummi m, n
~ sheet(ing) · (Ab)Dicht(ungs)bahn f
~ ~ insert(ion) · (Ab)Dicht(ungs)einlage f, (Ab)Dicht(ungs)träger(stoff) m

~ stopper, (pipe) ~, (~) plug · (Rohr-)Pfropfen m, (Rohr)Stopfen, (Rohr)Verschluß m
~ strip · (Ab)Dicht(ungs)band n
~ ~ · (Ab)Dicht(ungs)streifen m
~ ~ → (joint) ~ ~
~ surface · (Ab)Dicht(ungs)fläche f
sealing work · (Ab)Dicht(ungs)arbeiten fpl
seam, welted ~, lock ~ · Falz m [*Metallbedachung*]
~ bonding · Nahtverkleben n
~ cross-section · Nahtquerschnitt m
~ roof cladding → welted ~ ~ ~
~ ~ cover(ing) → (welted) seam roof cladding
~ ~ sheathing → (welted) seam roof cladding
~ roofing → (welted) seam roof cladding
~ spacing, welted ~ ~ · Falzabstand m [*Metallbedachung*]
seam-type metal (sheet) roof(ing) · Blechdach n mit Falz(ein)deckung
seamen's hostel, hostel for seamen · Seemannsheim n
seamless · nahtlos
~ floor cover(ing) → jointless floor(ing)
~ ~ finish → jointless floor(ing)
~ floor(ing) → jointless ~
~ forming of bowl on sink unit · fugenloses Anformen n des Beckens am Spültisch
~ mild steel pipe, ~ m.s. ~ · nahtloses Flußstahlrohr n
~ pipe, nahtloses Rohr n
~ roof skin · nahtlose Dachhaut f
~ steel pipe · nahtloses Stahlrohr n, Siederohr
sea-sand · Seesand m, Meer(es)sand
seaside resort · Seebad n
seat · Sitz m
~ → toilet ~
~ lid, toilet ~ ~, closet ~ ~, lavatory ~ ~ · (Abort) Deckel m, Toilettendeckel, Klosettdeckel
~ of settlement [*The layer of soil beneath a loaded foundation, within which 75 per cent of any settlement takes place*] · Setzungsherd m
seated colossal statue, ~ colossus · sitzende Kolossalstatue f, ~ Riesenfigur f
~ colossus, ~ colossal statue · sitzende Kolossalstatue f, ~ Riesenfigur f
~ figure · Sitzfigur f
~ statue · Sitzbild n
seating [*The surface of the point of support for a heavy load*] · Auflagerfläche f
~ accommodation · Sitzplätze mpl
~ capacity · Sitzplätzeanzahl f

seating slab — secondhand roof(ing) tile

~ slab · Sitzplatte f [*Stadionbau*]

~ space · Sitzraum m

seawater · Meer(es)wasser n, Seewasser

~ concrete · Meer(es)wasserbeton m, Seewasserbeton

~ magnesia · Seewassermagnesia f [*Aus dem Seewasser gewonnenes Magnesiumoxid*]

~ swimming bath · Seewasserschwimmbad n, Meer(es)wasserschwimmbad

~ wave swimming pool · Meer(es)-wasser-Wellenbad n, Seewasser-Wellenbad

seaworthy packing · seefeste Verpackung f, seemäßige ~

sebaceous salt of copper · fettsaures Kupfersalz n

second coat, brown ~ · Mittelputzschicht f, Zwischenputzschicht [*dreilagiger Putz*]

~ ~ · zweite Lage f, ~ Schicht f

~ ~ → floating ~

~ ~ · zweite Putzlage f, ~ Putzschicht f [*zweilagiger Putz*]

~ ~, brown ~ · zweite Unterputzschicht f, ~ Unterputzlage f, ~ Grobputzschicht, ~ Grobputzlage, zweites Rauhwerk n, Zwischenputzschicht, Mittelputzschicht [*dreilagiger Putz*]

~ ~, brown ~ [*It consists of mortar with less hair then the scratch coat. When three-coat work is used, this is trowel(l)ed directly on to the scratch coat*] · Mittelputzschicht f, Zwischenputzschicht

second-degree parabola · Parabel f zweiten Grades

second firing, reducing ~ · Schwarzbrennen n [*Glas*]

~ level · zweite Ebene f

~ moment (of area), moment of inertia [*of a section*] · Trägheitsmoment n

second-order theory, deformation ~ [*Initial deformations are taken into account*] · linearisierte Verformungstheorie f, (Spannungs)Theorie 2. Ordnung

secondary air [*Any air brought in around the burner or through openings in the combustion chamber for the purpose of completing combustion*] · Zweitluft f, Sekundärluft

~ aluminium (Brit.); ~ aluminum (US) · Umschmelzaluminium n

~ beam · lastbringender Balken(träger) m

~ bearing structure → ~ load~ ~

~ (bending) moment, redistributed ~ · negatives Zusatzmoment n, Umlagerungsmoment, umgelagertes Moment

~ ~ stress · Nebenbiegespannung f

~ circulation · Nebenumlauf m, Zweitumlauf [*z.B. bei einer Warmwasserversorgung*]

~ connection · Nebenanschluß m, Zweitanschluß [*z.B. bei einer Warmwasserversorgungsanlage*]

~ core · Nebenkern m

~ deformation · sekundäre Verformung f, ~ Formänderung, ~ Gestaltänderung

~ dust · Sekundärkanal m

~ flow · Nebenvorlauf m, Zweitvorlauf [*z.B. bei einer Warmwasserversorgung*]

~ ~ pipe · Nebenvorlaufrohr n, Zweitvorlaufrohr [*z.B. bei einer Warmwasserversorgung*]

~ girder · lastbringender Träger m

~ (load)bearing structure, ~ (weight-carrying) ~, ~ supporting ~ · Nebentragwerk n

~ mall [*A shaded secondary walk*] · Nebenkorso m, Nebengang m, Nebenpassage f

~ moment, ~ bending ~, redistributed ~ · negatives Zusatzmoment n, Umlagerungsmoment, umgelagertes Moment

~ pier · Nebenpfeiler m

~ portion · Nebentrakt m

~ reinforcement, ~ steel, additional ~ · Zulage(stahl)einlagen fpl, Zulagebewehrung f, Zulagearmierung, Nebenarmierung, Nebenbewehrung, Neben(stahl)einlagen, Zusatz(stahl)einlagen, Zusatzarmierung, Zusatzbewehrung

~ return · Nebenrücklauf m, Zweitrücklauf

~ ~ pipe · Nebenrücklaufrohr n, Zweitrücklaufrohr

~ rib · Sekundärrippe f, Nebenrippe

~ room · Nebenraum m

~ round bars, additional ~ ~ · Zulagerundstäbe mpl, Zulagerundstähle mpl

~ stair(case) · Nebentreppe f

~ steel, ~ reinforcement, additional ~ · Zulage(stahl)einlagen fpl, Zulagearmierung f, Zulagebewehrung, Nebenbewehrung, Nebenarmierung, Neben(stahl)einlagen, Zusatz(stahl)einlagen, Zusatzarmierung, Zusatzbewehrung

~ stress · Nebenspannung f, Zusatzspannung

~ structure → ~ weight-carrying ~

~ supporting structure, ~ (load)bearing ~, ~ (weight-carrying) ~ · Nebentragwerk n

~ walk · Nebengehweg m

~ (weight-carrying) structure, ~ (load)bearing ~, ~ supporting ~ · Nebentragwerk n

~ work · Nebenarbeiten fpl

secondhand block, ~ tile [*See remark under 'Block'*] · Abbruchblock(stein) m, Altstein, Abbruchstein, Altblock(stein)

~ brick · Abbruchziegel m, Altziegel

~ roof(ing) tile · Altdachziegel m

secondhand tile — security glazing

~ **tile**, ~ block [*See remark under 'Block'*] · Abbruchblock(stein) *m*, Altstein, Abbruchstein, Altblock(stein)

second-order equation · Gleichung *f* zweiten Grades, quadratische Gleichung

second quality · zweite Wahl *f*

second-rate · mittelmäßig

second undercoat · zweite Unterputzschicht *f*, ~ Unterputzlage *f*, ~ Grobputzschicht, ~ Grobputzlage, zweites Rauhwerk *n* [*bei allen Putzarten*]

~ ~ · zweite Unterputzschicht *f*, ~ Unterputzlage *f*, ~ Grobputzschicht, ~ Grobputzlage, zweites Rauhwerk *n* · [*Beim dreilagigen Außenputz ohne Putzträger*]

seconds-quality tile · Fliese *f* zweiter Wahl, (Belag)Platte *f* ~ ~

secret, hidden, concealed · verdeckt(liegend)

~ **cable**, concealed ~, hidden ~ · Unterputzkabel *n*

~ **door**, jib ~, gib ~, concealed ~ [*A door whose face is flush with the wall and decorated so as to be as little seen as possible*] · Geheimtür *f*, Tapetentür

~ **dovetail**, blind ~ · verdeckter Schwalbenschwanz *m*

~ **gutter**, hidden ~, concealed ~ · verdeckte Rinne *f*

~ **installation**, hidden ~, concealed ~, buried tubular conduits · Unterputzinstallation *f*

~ **joggle** · verdeckte Verzahnung *f* [*Mauerwerkbau*]

~ **joggled joint** · verdeckte verzahnte Fuge *f* [*Mauerwerkbau*]

secret-nailed, blind-nailed, concealed-nailed · verdeckt genagelt, ~ vernagelt

secret nailing, blind ~, concealed ~ [*The usual method of nailing tongue-and-grooved flooring is by blind nailing on the tongued edge. Face nailing, where the nail head is set and then the nail holes are puttied is not called blind nailing*] · verdeckte Nagelung *f*

~ **pipe**, concealed ~, hidden ~ · Unterputzrohr *n*

~ **tack**, hidden ~, concealed ~ · verdeckter Hafter *m*

~ **valley**, hidden ~, concealed ~ · verdeckte Kehle *f*

~ **valve**, concealed ~, hidden ~ · Unterputzventil *n*

~ **wiring**, hidden ~, concealed ~ · Unterputzverdrahtung *f*

sectio aurea, Golden Mean, Golden Section · Goldener Schnitt *m*, Goldenes Verhältnis *n*

section → roll-formed ~

~ → preformed (pipe insulation) ~

~, unit, trim, profile, shape · Profil *n*

~, profile · Profil *n*, Schnitt *m* [*Umrißlinie eines durchschnittenen Körpers*]

~ **fabricator** → shape maker

~ **factor**, ~ modulus · Widerstandsmoment *n* [*Es wird ermittelt aus dem Trägheitsmoment durch Teilung mit dem größten Faserabstand von der Spannungsnullinie*]

~ **for interior work** → profile ~ ~ ~

~ **iron**, iron section · Eisenprofil *n*, Formeisen *n*, Fassoneisen, Profileisen

~ **maker** → shape ~

~ **modulus**, ~ factor · Widerstandsmoment *n* [*Es wird ermittelt aus dem Trägheitsmoment durch Teilung mit dem größten Faserabstand von der Spannungsnullinie*]

~ **reinforcement**, ~ steel · Profileinlagen *fpl*, Profilstahleinlagen, Profilstahlbewehrung *f*, Profilstahlarmierung

~ **steel**, ~ reinforcement · Profileinlagen *fpl*, Profilstahleinlagen, Profilstahlbewehrung *f*, Profilstahlarmierung

~ ~ → steel section

sectional aerated concrete panel, two-piece ~ ~ ~ · zweiteilige Porenbetontafel *f*

~ **boiler** · Gliederkessel *m*

~ **drawing** · Schnittzeichnung *f*

~ **glue(-jointe)d aerated concrete panel**, two-piece ~ ~ ~ ~ · verleimte zweiteilige Porenbetontafel *f*, zweiteilige verleimte ~

~ ~ **panel** · glue(-jointe)d sectional ~

~ **panel**, two-piece ~ · zweiteilige Tafel *f*

~ **plan**, horizontal section · Horizontalschnitt *m*

section(al) steel, steel section, structural steel section · Fassonstahl *m*, Profilstahl, Formstahl, Stahlprofil *n*

sectorial plate, ~ slab · Sektorplatte *f*

~ **slab**, ~ plate · Sektorplatte *f*

secular architecture, civic ~, profane ~, nonecclesiastical ~ · weltliche Architektur *f*, Baukunst *f*, Profanarchitektur, Profanbaukunst

~ **basilica**, pagan ~, imperial ~, (civic) ~, Roman ~ · (römische) (Zivil)Basilika *f*, römisch-heidnische Basilika, heidnisch-römische Basilika

~ **Gothic structure**, ~ ~ building · gotisches Profanbauwerk *n*

~ ~ **(style)**, profane ~ (~), civic ~ (~), nonecclesiastical ~ (~) · Profangotik *f*, weltliche Gotik

~ **monument**, profane ~, civic ~, nonecclesiastical ~ · Profanmonument *n*

~ **structure**, profane ~, civic ~, nonecclesiastical ~, ~ building · Profanbau(werk) *m*, (*n*), Profangebäude *n*

~ **structures**, profane ~, civic ~, nonecclesiastical ~ · Profanbauten *f*, Profangebäude *npl*

security(-cylinder) lock, safety(-cylinder) ~ · Sicherheitsschloß *n*

security glazing · Sicherheitsverglasung *f*

~ **grille** [*Sometimes spelled 'grill'*] · Sicherheitsgitter *n*

~ **lock** → ~-cylinder ~

~ **window** [*It prevents forcible entry*] · Sicherheitsfenster *n*

sedilia [*Seats for the clergy, generally three (for priest, deacon, and subdeacon), and of masonry, in the wall on the south side of the chancel*] · Steinsitzreihe *f*, Sedilia *f*

sedimentary rock → bedded ~

sedimentation · Bodensatzbildung *f*, Sedimentation *f*

~ **test** → decantation ~ (US)

seed [*ASTM C 162–56*]; fine ~ · Gispe *f*

seed-free time · Ende *f* der Blankschmelze [*Glasschmelze*]

seediness · Lackausscheidung *f*

seedlac, lac without sticks · Körner(schel)lack *m*

seedy glass · gispiges Glas *n*

see-through building · transparentes Bauen *n*

~ **mirror** · Einwegglas *n*, Spionspiegel *m*

~ **visibility** · Durchsichtigkeit *f*

~ **window**, vision panel · Sichtfenster *n* [*Tor*]

Seger cone · Segerkegel *m*, SK [*Pyrometer aus Tonerdesilikaten zur Bestimmung der Wärmegrade in keramischen Brennöfen*]

~ ~ **chart** · Segerkegeltabelle *f*, SK-Tabelle

~ ~ **equivalent** → pyrometric ~ ~ ~

~ ~ **60 mm high** · Normalkegel *m*

~ ~ **30 mm high**, ~ ~ for lab(oratory) use · kleiner Segerkegel *m*, Labor(atoriums)kegel

segment [*Part of a circle smaller than a semicircle*] · Segment *n*

~ **of cylinder**, barrel shell, cylinder segment · Tonnenschale *f*

segmental arch, flat ~, jack ~ [*An arch with low rise-to-span ratio*] · Segmentbogen *m*, Flachbogen, flacher Bogen, platter Bogen, Stichbogen [*veraltet: Teilzirkelbogen, Kreisteilbogen*]

~ ~ **window** · Segmentfenster *n*

~ **arched girder**, flat ~ ~ · Flachbogenträger *m*, Stichbogenträger, Segmentbogenträger, flacher Bogenträger

~ ~ ~ **roof**, flat ~ ~ ~ · Flachbogenträgerdach *n*, Stichbogenträgerdach, Segmentbogenträgerdach

~ **bowstring girder**, polygonal ~ ~ Segmentträger *m*, Bogensehnenträger

~ **ceiling** · Segmentdecke *f*

~ **cylindrical shell** · Segmentzylinderschale *f*

~ **pediment**, curved ~ · Segmentgiebel *m*

~ **plate**, ~ slab · Segmentplatte *f*

~ **shell** · Segmentschale *f*

~ **slab**, ~ plate · Segmentplatte *f*

to segregate · entmischen

segregated · entmischt

segregating, segregation · Entmischen *n*

segregation · Entmischung *f*

~, segregating · Entmischen *n*

~, (e)liquation · Seigerung *f*

Seibert Stinnes hollow beam floor · Seibert-Stinnes-Hohlbalkendecke *f*

Seidel iteration method, ~ iterative ~ · Seidelsches (Iteration)Verfahren *n*

seismic activity, earthquake ~ · Erdbebentätigkeit *f*

~ **area** → earthquake region

~ ~ **map** → eathquake zone ~

seismic-conscious · erdbebenbewußt

seismic construction, earthquake ~ · erdbebensicheres Bauen *n*

~ **design**, earthquake ~ · Erdbebenbemessung *f*, erdbebensichere Bemessung

~ **engineering**, earthquake ~ · Erdbebentechnik *f*, erdbebensicheres Bauwesen *n*

~ **force**, earthquake ~ · Erdbebenkraft *f*

~ **load**, earthquake ~ · Erdbebenlast *f*

~ **oscillation**, ~ vibration, earthquake ~ · Erdbebenerschütterung *f*

~ **overturning moment** · Erdbebenkippmoment *n*

~ **region** → earthquake ~

~ ~ **map** → earthquake zone ~

~ **resistance** · Erdbeben-Widerstandsfähigkeit *f*

~ **response**, earthquake ~ · Erdbebenreaktion *f* eines Bauwerkes oder Gebäudes

~ **shock**, earthquake ~ · Erdbebenstoß *m*

~ **vibration**, ~ oscillation, earthquake ~ · Erdbebenerschütterung *f*

~ **wave**, earthquake ~ · Erdbebenwelle *f*

~ **zone** → earthquake region

~ ~ **map** → earthquake ~ ~

selection of material(s) · Materialwahl *f*, (Werk)Stoffwahl

~ ~ **mix(ture)**, choice ~ ~ · Gemischwahl *f*, Mischungswahl

selenite (gypsum) [*The transparent variety of gypsum which occurs in distinct crystals, often flattened parallel to the plane of symmetry*] · Selenit *m*

self-adhesive, self-bonding · selbstklebend

~ **film**, self-bonding ~, ~ sheeting · Selbstkleb(e)folie *f*

~ **sheeting** → ~ film

~ **tile** · Selbstkleb(e)(belag)platte *f*, Selbstkleb(e)fliese *f*

self-adjusting level · Nivellier(instrument) *n* mit paralleler Platte

self-anchorage — semicircular iron

self-anchorage · Selbstverankerung f, Haftverankerung [Spannbeton]
self bonding, ~ adhesive · selbstklebend
self-bonding film, ~ sheeting, self-adhesive ~ · Selbstkleb(e)folie f
~ sheeting, ~ film, self-adhesive ~ · Selbstkleb(e)folie f
self-cleaning · selbstreinigend
self-cleansing gradient · erforderliche Mindestgradiente f in (Rohr)Leitungen
self-closing · selbstschließend
~ door, fire ~ [A door made of fire-resisting material, generally metal plated, held open by a fusible link, which melts in a fire permitting the door to close and thus delays or prevents the spread of fire by confining it to one compartment] · selbstschließende Tür f
to self-color (US); to self-colour (Brit.) · selbstfärben
self-condensation · Eigenhärtung f [Phenolharz]
self-containedness, unity · Geschlossenheit f
self-control · Selbstüberdachung f
self-desiccation [The removal of free water by chemical reaction so as to leave insufficient water to cover the solid surfaces and to cause a decrease in the relative humidity of the system; applied to an effect occurring in sealed concretes, mortars, and pastes] · Selbstaustrocknung f
self-drill anchor, self drilling ~, rapid core drill ~ · Selbstbohrdübel m
self drilling anchor, self-drill ~, rapid core drill ~ · Selbstbohrdübel m
~ etch primer → etching ~
self-extinguishing · selbstverlöschend
self-finished · belegt [Bitumenpappe]
self-hardening steel · selbsthärtbarer Stahl m, selbsthärtender ~, Selbsthärter m
self-help house · Selbsthilfehaus n
~ housing programme (Brit.); ~ ~ program (US); ~ scheme · Selbsthilfe-(-Wohn(ungs)(bau)plan m
self-ignition, auto-ignition · Selbst-(ent)zündung f
~ temperature, auto-ignition ~ · Selbst-(ent)zündungstemperatur f
self load → dead weight
self-luminous · selbstleuchtend
~ paint, radioluminous ~, radioactive ~ · radioaktive Leuchtfarbe f, selbstleuchtende ~ [DIN 5043]
~ pigment, radioluminous ~, radioactive ~ · radioaktives Leuchtpigment n, selbstleuchtendes ~ [DIN 5043]
self polishing wax, emulsion ~ · Emulsionswachs n

self-sealing · selbstdichtend
~ strip shingle · Schindel f mit Selbstklebestreifen, ~ ~ Selbstkleber
self-service department(al) store · Selbstbedienungs-Kaufhaus n, Selbstbedienungs-Warenhaus
~ facility, ~ installation · Selbstbedienungsanlage f
~ installation, ~ facility · Selbstbedienungsanlage f
~ shop · Selbstbedienungsladen m
self-stressed prestressed concrete · selbstvorspannender Beton m
self-stressing cement · selbstspannender Quellzement m, ~ Expansivzement, ~ Schwellzement, ~ Dehnzement
~ concrete · selbstspannender Beton m
self-supporting · selbsttragend, freitragend
~ partition (wall) · freitragende leichte Trennwand f [Eine Innenwand, die ihr Eigengewicht als wandartiger Träger zwischen den Auflagern (as a slab spanning between supports) selbst trägt; sie muß waag(e)recht bewehrt sein]
self-tapping screw · gewindeschneidende Schraube f
self-vulcanizing · selbstvulkanisierend
self weight, own ~, dead ~ · Eigengewicht n, EG, Totgewicht
~ ~ moment, own ~ ~, dead ~ ~ · Eigengewichtsmoment n, EG-Moment, Totgewichtsmoment
semi-buried cellar · Hochkeller m
semicircular, half-round · halbrund, halbkreisförmig
~ apse → ~ exedra
~ apsis → ~ exedra
~ arch, (half-)round ~, perfect ~; full-centred ~ (Brit.); full-centered ~ (US) · Rundbogen m, Halbkreisbogen, römischer Bogen, halbzirkelförmiger Bogen [veraltet: Vollbogen, voller Bogen]
~ barrel vault, ~ tunnel ~, ~ wagon ~, half-round ~ ~ · halbkreisförmige Tonne f, halbkreisförmiges Tonnengewölbe n
~ bastion, half-round ~ · Halbrundbastei f, Halbrundbastion f
~ ceiling, half-round ~ · Halbkreisdecke f
~ cross-vault, half-round ~ · halbrundes Kreuzgewölbe n
~ cylindrical roof, half-round ~ ~ · Zylinderdach n
~ exedra, ~ apsis, ~ apse, half-round ~ · Halbkreisapsis f, Halbkreisapside f, Halbkreisabside, Halbkreisexedra f, Halbkreisabseite f
~ gutter → ~ roof ~
~ iron, half-round ~ · Halbrundeisen n

semicircular niche — semi-hydraulic lime mortar

~ **niche,** ~ space, hemicycle · Halbkreisnische f [Basilika]

~ **profile,** ~ section, half-round ~ · Halbkreisprofil n, Halbkreisschnitt m [Halbkreisförmige Umrißlinie eines durchschnittenen Körpers]

~ **rainwater gutter** → ~ (roof) ~

~ **rib,** half-round ~ · Halbkreisrippe f

~ **rivet,** half-round ~ · Halbrundniet m [Der Setzkopf ist ein Halbrundkopf. DIN 123, 124, 660 und 663]

~ **(roof) gutter,** ~ rainwater ~, half-round (~) ~, ~ R.W. ~ · halbrunde (Dach)Rinne f, ~ Regenrinne

~ **section,** ~ profile, half-round ~ Halbkreisprofil n, Halbkreisschnitt m· [Halbkreisförmige Umrißlinie eines durchschnittenen Körpers]

~ **space,** ~ niche, hemicycle · Halbkreisnische f [Basilika]

~ **stair(case)** · Kreisbogentreppe f, halbringförmige Treppe

~ **steel,** half-round ~ · Halbrundstahl m

~ **stretcher,** half-round ~ · Halbrundläufer m

~ **termination,** half-round ~ · halbrunder (Ab)Schluß m

~ **tower,** half-round ~, D-shaped ~ · Schalenturm m, Halb(kreis)turm [Nach außen aus der Mauer vorspringender, nach innen jedoch offener Turm einer mittelalterlichen Burg]

~ **transverse arch,** half-round ~ ~ · Halbrundquerbogen m, Halbkreisquerbogen

~ **tunnel vault,** ~ barrel ~, ~ wagon ~, half-round ~ ~ · halbkreisförmige Tonne f, halbkreisförmiges Tonnengewölbe n

~ **wagon vault,** ~ tunnel ~, ~ barrel ~, half-round ~ ~ · halbkreisförmige Tonne f, halbkreisförmiges Tonnengewölbe n

~ **window,** half-round ~ · Halbrundfenster n, Halbkreisfenster

~ **wire,** half-round ~ · Halbrunddraht m

~ **wood screw,** half-round ~ ~ · Halbrund-Holzschraube f

semi-continuous action · Halbdurchlaufwirkung f

semi-court · halboffener Hof m

semi-crystal (glass), half-crystal (~) · Halbkristall(glas) n [Ein Bleiglas, in dem ein Teil des Bleioxids durch Kalk oder Baryt ersetzt ist]

semi-cupola → semidome

semi-darkness · Halbdunkel n

semidetached dwelling, end-row ~ [A dwelling, one side wall of which is a party or lot-line wall] · einseitig angebautes Wohnhaus n, Doppel(wohn)haus

~ **house,** end-row ~ [A house, one side wall of which is a party or lot-line wall] · einseitig angebautes Einfamilienhaus n, ~ ~ Familienheim n, Doppel-Einfamilienhaus, Doppel-Familienheim [Fehlnamen: Doppel(wohn)haus]

semidome, semi-cupola, half-dome, half-cupola, concha, spherical dome, spherical cupola · Kugelkuppel f, Rundkuppel, Halbkuppel, Konche f, Koncha f [Sie hat viertelkreisförmigen Querschnitt über halbkreisförmigem Grundriß]

(semi-)dry pressing · (halb)trockene Formgebung f, Trockenpressen n [Formgebung einer Masse durch hohen Druck. Die Masse enthält unterschiedliche Mengen an nichtplastischen Bestandteilen und hat einen so geringen Feuchtigkeitsgehalt, daß eine Formgebung in plastischem Zustand nicht möglich ist]

semi-drying oil · halbtrocknendes Öl n

semi-elastomer(ic) · halbelastomer, halbgummiartig

semi-ellipse, half-ellipse · Halbellipse f

semielliptical arch → more-centered ~

semi-enclosed · halbumschlossen

semi-fibrated · halbgefasert

semi-flat, semi-mat(te) · halbmatt

~ **glaze,** semi-mat(te) ~ · Halbmattglasur f

~ **gloss,** semi-mat(te) ~ · Halbmattglanz m

semi-flexible joint, semi-rigid ~, partially fixed ~ · halbstarre Verbindung f

semi-glazed · halbglasiert

semi-gloss · Halbglanz m

~ **enamel** · Halbglanzemaillelack m

~ **film** · Halbglanzfilm m

~ **oil paint** · Halbglanzölfarbe f

~ **paint** · Halbglanz(anstrich)farbe f

semigraphical method · halbgraphisches Verfahren n

semi-hard, medium-hard · halbhart, mittelhart

semi-hardboard, medium-hardboard · halbharte (Holz)Faserplatte f, Halbhartplatte, HFH½ [Rohwichte 480 bis 850 kg/m³]

semi-hollow handrail section, ~ ~ shape, ~ ~ unit, ~ ~ trim, ~ ~ profile, ~ guard rail ~ · Halbhohlprofilhandlauf m

semi-hydraulic lime, grey(stone) ~ [It contains a smaller proportion of silicates and aluminates than eminently hydraulic lime and is intermediate in properties between this and non-hydraulic lime] · gemischter Kalk m, hydraulischer ~ [DIN 1060. Fehlnamen: Zementkalk, Schwarzkalk]

~ ~ **mortar,** grey(stone) ~ ~ · Mörtel m aus hydraulischem Kalk, ~ ~ gemischtem ~

semi-immersion(-type) rotary (water) meter · Trockenläufer *m* [*Bei diesem Wassermesser befindet sich das Zählwerk im Wasser, das darüber liegende Zeigerwerk läuft „trocken"*]

semi-infinite · halbunendlich

~ mass, ~ solid, ~ space, halfspace · Halbraum *m*

~ plate, ~ slab · halbunendliche Platte *f*

~ slab, ~ plate · halbunendliche Platte *f*

~ solid, ~ space, ~ mass, halfspace · Halbraum *m*

~ space, ~ mass, ~ solid, halfspace · Halbraum *m*

semikilled steel, semistabilized ~ [*The evolution of gas is controlled by limited addition of deoxidizing agents such as silicon and alumin(i)um*] · halbstabilisierter Stahl *m*, halbberuhigter ~

semi-liquid · halbflüssig

semilogarithmic scale · semilogarithmisches Netz *n*

semi-loggia · Halbloggia *f*

semi-mat(te), semi-flat · halbmatt

~ glaze, semi-flat ~ · Halbmattglasur *f*

~ gloss, semi-flat ~ · Halbmattglanz *m*

semi-metope, demi-metope · Halbmetope *f*, Halbzwischenfeld *n*

Semionotus sandstone · Semionotussandstein *m*, Semionotensandstein

semi-oval stair(case) · Halbovaltreppe *f*

semi-parabolic girder, hog backed ~ · Halbparabelträger *m*

~ ~ with sloping end posts, hog backed ~ ~ ~ ~ ~ · Halbparabelträger *m* mit abgeschrägten Enden

semi-plane, half-plane · Halbebene *f*

semi-plastic making, stiff-plastic ~ · steifplastische Verformung *f* [*Feuerfestindustrie. Dieses Verfahren wird nur in bestimmten Ländern angewendet. Der Wassergehalt der Massen ist so gering, daß man nur Rohlinge (Batzen) formen kann, die danach die endgültige Form erhalten und gegebenenfalls nachgepreßt werden*]

semi-precious material [*e.g. stainless steel, aluminium, nickel, etc.*] · halbveredelter Werkstoff *m*

semi-prefab(ricated) floor · Halbfertigdecke *f*, Halbmontagedecke

semi-probabilistic design method [*A design method in which the safety conditions are based both on probabilistic and on deterministic concepts and are expressed in deterministic form*] · Halbwahrscheinlichkeits-Bemessungsverfahren *n*

semi-producer type furnace, half-gas fired ~ · Halbgasfeuerung *f*

semi-product · Halbfabrikat *n*, Halbzeug *n*

semirigid frame · halbstarrer Rahmen *m*, halbsteifer ~

~ joint, semi-flexible ~, partially fixed ~ · halbstarre Verbindung *f*

semi-rural estate · halbländliche Sied(e)lung *f*

semi-silica brick · Halbsilikastein *m*

~ refractory brick · Quarzschamottestein *m* [*DIN 1089*]

semi-skilled worker · angelernter Arbeiter *m*

şemi-soft wire · halbweicher Draht *m* [*Stahldraht, der nach Zwischenglühen mit stärkerer Abnahme gezogen wird*]

semi-sprung floor · Halbschwing(fuß)-boden *m*

semistabilized steel, semikilled ~ [*The evolution of gas is controlled by limited addition of deoxidizing agents such as silicon and alumin(i)um*] · halbstabilisierter Stahl *m*, halbberuhigter ~

semistable → normal-setting

~ emulsion, normal-setting ~ · H-Emulsion *f*

~ refractory dolomite brick · teergetränkter Dolomitstein *m* [*Gebranntes feuerfestes Erzeugnis, das vorwiegend aus gebranntem Dolomit ohne Zugabe von stabilisierenden Mineralen besteht, jedoch meist durch eine organische Flüssigkeit (wie z.B. Teer, Öl usw.) vor der Luftfeuchtigkeit geschützt ist*]

semi-steel · Gußeisen *n* mit Stahlschrottzusatz

semi-strip · Halbstreifen *m*

sensation of warmth · Wärmeempfindung *f*

sense of design · Form(en)gefühl *n*

~ ~ movement · Bewegtheit *f* [*Architektur*]

~ ~ proportion · Proportionsgefühl *n*

~ ~ space · Raumgefühl *n*

sensible heat [*Heat which, when added to or removed from a substance, results in a change in its temperature*] · fühlbare Wärme *f*

sensitive to friction · reib(ungs)empfindlich

~ ~ solvent(s), solvent(-)susceptible · lösemittelempfindlich, lösungsmittelempfindlich

sensitiveness, sensitivity · Empfindlichkeit *f*

~ of a balance, sensitivity ~ ~ ~ · Wiegegenauigkeit *f*

sensitivity, sensitiveness · Empfindlichkeit *f*

sensitized mat · Kontaktteppich *m* [*Eine vollautomatische Schiebetür öffnet sich beim Betreten des Kontaktteppiches*]

separate construction [*Once the base has set and hardened, monolithic construction can no longer be used. It may, however, be possible to prepare the base in such a way that a good degree*

separate construction — series production

of bonding can be obtained] · getrennte Bauweise f mit Verbund [*Estrichverlegung*]

~ **drainage** · getrennte Entwässerung f

~ **sewerage (system)** → ~ system (of sewerage)

~ **system (of sewerage)**, ~ ~ ~ sewers, ~ sewerage (system) [*A system of sewers in which sewage and storm water are carried in separate conduits*] · Trennentwässerung f, Trennsystem n, Trennkanalisation f

separating into halves · Aufspalten n [*Ein Estrich kann in zwei Hälften aufspalten, wenn ein zu dichtes oder zu dickes Drahtgewebe als Bewehrung eingelegt oder zweischichtig mit unterschiedlichen Mischungsverhältnissen gearbeitet wurde*]

~ **wall** [*A wall separating different occupancies within the same building*] · Wohnungstrennwand f

separation [*The tendency, as concrete is caused to pass from the unconfined ends of chutes or conveyor belts, or similar arrangements, for coarse aggregate to separate from the concrete and accumulate at one side; the tendency, as processed aggregate leaves the ends of conveyor belts, chutes, or similar devices with confining sides, for the larger aggregate to separate from the mass and accumulate at one side; or the tendency for the solids to separate from the water by gravitational settlement*] · Entmischbarkeit f, Entmischungsneigung f

~ **membrane** · Trennmembran(e) f

~ **of moisture**, ~ ~ humidity · Ausscheiden n von Feuchte, ~ ~ Feuchtigkeit

~ ~ **water** · Wasserausscheidung f

separator, spacer, distance piece · Abstandhalter m

~, interceptor [*A device designed and installed so as to separate and retain deleterious, hazardous, or undesirable matter from normal wastes while permitting normal sewage or liquid wastes to discharge into the drainage system by gravity*] · (Ab)Scheider m, Fang m, Fänger

~ [*for wood beams*] · Verkupp(e)lung f

~ **strip** · Trennstreifen m

sepia [*A dark-brown pigment prepared from the inky fluid secreted by cuttlefish*] · Sepia f, Sepie

sepiolite, meerschaum, agaric chalk · Meerschaum m, Steinmark n, mineralischer Lerchenschwamm m

septenary foil · Siebenpaß m [*Eine mittelalterliche Maßwerkfigur. Aus sieben Kreis- oder Spitzbogen gebildet*]

septfoil · Siebenblatt n

septic tank · Grundstückskläranlage f, Hauskläranlage, Kleinkläranlage [*DIN 4261*]

sepulcher (US); sepulchre (Brit.) · Reliquiengrab n

sepulchral architecture, (structural) tomb ~ · Grabarchitektur f, Grabbaukunst f

~ **chamber,** burial ~, tomb ~, chamber tomb, hypogeum tomb · Grabkammer f, Kammergrab n

~ **cross** · Grabkreuz n

~ **monument,** funerary ~, burial ~, headstone · Grabmonument n, Grabdenkmal n

~ **pit,** burial-chamber hypogeum · unterirdische Grabkammer f

~ **slab,** grave ~, funerary ~, tomb ~ · Grabplatte f

~ **temple** · Grabtempel m

sepulchre (Brit.); sepulcher (US) · Reliquiengrab n

sepulcrum of a mensa, table tomb · Mensagrab n

sequence of columns, ~ ~ supports · Stützenfolge f

~ ~ **construction,** construction sequence · Baufolge f

~ ~ **forces** · Kräftefolge f

~ ~ **grain sizes,** ~ ~ particle ~ · Kornfolge f

~ ~ **operations** · Reihenfolge f der Arbeitsvorgänge

~ ~ **particle sizes,** ~ ~ grain ~ · Kornfolge f

~ ~ **supports,** ~ ~ columns · Stützenfolge f

serapeum · Serapeum n, Serapeion n [*Heiligtum des Gottes Serapis, der später mit dem ägyptischen Apis-Stier gleichgesetzt wurde. Der Kult wurde von den Römern und Griechen übernommen*]

serdab · Serdab m [*Unterirdischer Raum der ägyptischen Mastaba, in dem Statuen des Toten aufbewahrt wurden*]

sericite · Seidenglimmer m, Serizit m

~ **schist,** sericitic ~ · Seidenglimmerschiefer m, Serizitschiefer

series of central master-keyed locks, central master-keyed series · Zentralschloß-Anlage f

~ ~ **fire tests** · Brandprüfreihe f, Brandversuchsreihe

~ ~ **grandmaster-keyed locks,** grandmaster-keyed series · Generalhauptschlüsselanlage f

~ ~ **master-keyed locks,** master-keyed series · Hauptschlüsselanlage f

~ ~ **standards** · Normenreihe f

series-produced sink unit, quantity-produced ~ · Serien-Spültisch m, Serien-Abwaschtisch

series production · Fließ(band)fertigung f [*Zur Herstellung von Betonfertigteilen*]

series production method — service stair(case)

~ ~ **method** · Fließ(band)verfahren *n* [*Zur Herstellung von Betonfertigteilen*]
~ **fire**, major ~ · Großbrand *m*, Großfeuer *n* [*Ein Brand, zu dessen Bekämpfung mehr als drei C-Rohre eingesetzt werden (1 B-Rohr = 2 C-Rohre)*]
Serlian(a) motif (window) → Venetian ~
serpentine · Serpentin *m* [*Mineral*]
~ **asbestos** · Serpentinasbest *m*
~ **(rock)**, serpentinite [*A rock containing a major proportion of the mineral serpentine*] · Serpentinfels *m*, Serpentin(-gestein) *m*, (*n*) [*Fehlname: grüner Marmor m*]
~ **(~) slab**, serpentinite ~ · Serpentinplatte *f*
serpentinite, serpentine (rock) [*A rock containing a major proportion of the mineral serpentine*] · Serpentinfels *m*, Schlangenstein *m*, Serpentin(gestein) *m*, (*n*) [*Fehlname: grüner Marmor m*]
serrated spatula, ~ trowel · Zahnspa(ch)tel *m*, gezahnter Spa(ch)tel
~ **trowel**, ~ spatula · Zahnspa(ch)tel *m*, gezahnter Spa(ch)tel
serum albumin, (blood) ~, (~) albumen · Blutalbumin *n* [*genormtes Kurzzeichen: A*]
~ ~ **glue** → (blood) ~ ~
servant's bath · Dienstenbad *n* [*Schweiz*]
~ **room** · Dienstenzimmer *n* [*Schweiz*]
service · Gebrauchszustand *m*
~ [*A system of pipes and fittings in any individual premises*] · Gebäudeleitung(ssystem) *f*, (*n*), Hausleitung(ssystem)
~ → ~ **line**
~ → ~ **run**
~ → **services**
~ **area**, ~ zone, supply ~ · Versorgungsgebiet *n*, Belieferungsgebiet, Versorgungsraum *m*, Belieferungsraum
~ ~, ~ zone · Abfertigungszone *f*, Abfertigungsvorfeld *n* [*Ein Teil des Vorfeldes einschließlich der Abfertigungsstellen eines Flughafens, im allgemeinen dem Abfertigungsgebäude direkt vorgelagert*]
~ ~ · Betriebsfläche *f* [*Fläche zur Unterbringung einer Betriebsanlage*]
~ **block**, ~ building · Dienstgebäude *n*
~ ~, ~ building · Betriebsgebäude *n*
~ **building**, ~ block · Betriebsgebäude *n*
~ ~, ~ block · Dienstgebäude *n*
~ **cable** · Einführungskabel *n*
~ ~, supply ~ · Versorgungskabel *n*
~ **ceiling** ~ service(d) ~
~ **core**, utility ~, mechanical ~, building ~, (reinforced) concrete ~, R.C. ~ · (Hoch)Hauskern *m*, (Stahl)Betonkern, Betriebskern, (Gebäude)Kern

~ **duct**, mains subway, duct for services · Betriebskanal *m*, Leitungskanal
~ **elevator** (US); ~ lift (Brit.) · Betriebsaufzug *m*
~ **entrance** · Dienstboteneingang *m*, Nebeneingang
~ ~ **door** · Diensteingangstür *f*
~ **entry** · Einführung *f*, Hausanschluß *m* [*elektrische Hausanlage*]
~ **equipment** · technische Ausstattung *f* [*Gebäude*]
(~) **hatch**, serving ~ · Durchreiche *f*, Durchreichöffnung *f*, Durchgabe *f*
~ **island** · Abfertigungsinsel *f* [*Eine abgegrenzte und meistens befestigte Vorfeldfläche auf einem Flughafen in bestimmter Entfernung vom Abfertigungsgebäude*]
~ **lift** (Brit.); ~ elevator (US) · Betriebsaufzug *m*
~ ~ (Brit.); dumbwaiter (US) · Speisenaufzug *m*, Kleinaufzug
~ **(line)** · (öffentliche) Versorgungsleitung *f* [*DIN 1998*]
~ ~ → ~ **(run)**
~ **(~) network** · öffentliches Versorgungsnetz *n*
~ **method** · Abfertigungsverfahren *n* [*Abfertigung von Flugzeugen, Passagieren, Fracht und Luftpost auf Flughäfen*]
~ **network** → ~ line ~
~ **of castle-work** · Burgdienst *m*
~ **penetration** · Leitungsdurchgang *m*
~ **pipe** · (öffentliches) Versorgungsrohr *n*
~ ~ · Installationsrohr *n* [*Für die Hausinstallation von Wasser- und Gasleitungen*]
~ **pipeline** · (öffentliche) Versorgungsrohrleitung *f*
~ **plant**, utility ~ · Versorgungseinrichtung *f*
~ **quarters** · Wirtschaftsgebäude *n* [*in der Palastanlage von Khorsabad*]
~ **raceway** → ~ (run)
~ **riser** [*A gas pipe which rises to supply an upper floor*] · Gasstandrohr *n*
~ **room** · Betriebsraum *m*
~ ~ · Dienstraum *m*
~ ~ **for bedroom service** · Aufwarteraum *m* [*Hotel*]
~ **(run)**, utility (~), ~ line, ~ raceway · Betriebsleitung *f* [*z.B. für Heizung, Wasser usw.*]
~ **shaft**, utility ~ · Betriebsschacht *m* [*Hochhaus*]
~ **space** · Betriebsraum *m* [*Volumen zur Unterbringung einer Betriebsanlage, z.B. eines Entwässerungsrohrleitungssystems in einem Gebäude*]
~ **stair(case)** · Betriebstreppe *f*

service stair(case) — set(ting) accelerator additive

~~ · Nebentreppe, Dienst(boten)treppe, Dienertreppe, Hintertreppe f, Lauftreppe [*Für den Personal- und Dienstverkehr innerhalb eines Gebäudes*]

~ **tower**, utility ~, building ~, mechanical ~, (reinforced) concrete ~, R. C. ~ [*A service core moved completely outside the building*] · Betriebsturm m, (Hoch)Hausturm, (Stahl)Betonturm, (Gebäude)Turm

~ **traffic** · Abfertigungsverkehr m [*Flughafen*]

~ **walk** · Betriebsgehweg m, Dienstgehweg

~ **yard** · Betriebshof m

~ **zone**, ~ area, supply ~ · Versorgungsgebiet n, Belieferungsgebiet, Versorgungsraum m, Belieferungsraum

~ ~, ~ area · Abfertigungszone f, Abfertigungsvorfeld n [*Ein Teil des Vorfeldes einschließlich der Abfertigungsstellen eines Flughafens, im allgemeinen dem Abfertigungsgebäude direkt vorgelagert*]

serviceability · (Betriebs)Brauchbarkeit f

~ **limit state**, limit state of serviceability · Gebrauchsfähigkeits-Grenzzustand m

service(d) ceiling, ceiling incorporating a service, ceiling incorporating services · Decke f mit Leitung(en)

services, building ~ (US); mechanical equipment (of a building) [*Lifts, escalators or similar mechanical equipment*] · (Haus)Betriebsanlagen fpl, Gebäudebetriebsanlagen, (Haus-) Betriebseinrichtungen fpl, Gebäudebetriebseinrichtungen, technische Anlagen, technische Einrichtungen

~ **and facilities provided by the Owner** · bauseitige Leistungen fpl

service(s) (and technical equipment), installation(s) [*Installation(s) for (1) the introduction into and distribution within a building or structure of water, air, gas, liquid fuel, electricity, heat or other source of energy, (2) the disposal of waste from a building or structure or (3) firefighting within a building or structure. The term does not apply to lifts, escalators or similar mechanical equipment*] · Installation(en) f(pl), haustechnische Anlagen fpl, Haustechnikanlagen, (Innen)Ausbaumittel npl

serving hatch, (service) ~ · Durchreiche f, Durchreichöffnung f, Durchgabe f

~ **kitchen** · Essenausgabeküche f

session · Arbeitssitzung f

to set, to cure · abbinden [*Kleber*]

~ ~ · abbinden, verfestigen [*erstarren + erhärten. Mörtel; Beton; Zementpaste; Gips*]

~ ~ · versetzen, ansetzen [*Wandplatten*]

~ ~ **each other off** · gegeneinander absetzen

~ ~ **initially** · erstarren [*Siehe Anmerkung unter „Abbinden"*]

~ ~ **off by** [*The classical motifs of column, entablature and arch are set off by plain wall(ing) surfaces*] · hinterfangen [*Die klassischen Formmotive Säule, Gebälk und Bogen sind von geschlossenen Wandflächen hinterfangen*]

~ ~ **tiles** · verfliesen [*Fliesen legen*]

~ ~ **(up)**, to fit, to erect · aufbauen, aufstellen, montieren

set [*e.g. plaster, concrete, etc.*] · abgebunden, verfestigt

~, **unit** · Garnitur f

~ → setting

set-controlling · (ab)binderegelnd, (ab-)bindesteuernd

set process → setting ~

~ **property** → setting ~

~ **quality** → setting ~

~ **rate** → setting ~

~ **reaction** → setting ~

(~) **retarder** → (set(ting)) ~

(~) **retarding agent** → (set(ting)) retarder

~ **shrinkage** → setting ~

set-square; triangle (US) · Winkel m [*Zeichengerät*]

set test → setting ~

~ **testing apparatus** → setting ~ ~

~ **time** → setting ~

set-up, assembly [*for tests*] · Prüf(ungs)-anordnung f

set value → setting ~

sett, paving ~, pavior · Pflasterstein m

(~) **paving** · (Stein)Pflaster n

~ ~ **(joint) pouring compound** · Pflaster(fugen)vergußmasse f, Pflasterfugenmasse, Pflaster(fugen)ausgußmasse, Pflaster(fugen)gießmasse

~ ~ **mastic (joint sealer)** · Pflaster(fugen)kitt m

setting · Gittern n, Setzen [*Anordnung von Formlingen in einem Brennofen (Setzen, Einsetzen) oder Anordnen von Steinen in Ofenteilen (z.B. Gitterung in Regeneratoren)*]

~, **polymerization**; polymerisation (Brit.) · Aushärtung f [*Betonkleber*]

~ → ~ **work**

set(ting) · Abbinden n, Verfestigen [*Mörtel; Beton; Zementpaste; Gips. Das Abbinden wird unterteilt in die erste Phase des „Erstarrens" (Übergang aus dem plastischen in den festen Zustand) und die zweite Phase des „Erhärtens" bis zur Erreichung der Endfestigkeit*]

~ **accelerator additive**, accelerating additive for set(ting) · (Ab)Binde(zeit)-beschleuniger m für hydraulische Bin-

set(ting) anelerator additive — settlement ...

demittel, Erstarrungs(zeit)beschleuniger ~ ~ ~, Schnellbindemittel n, Schnellbinder

~ ~ **admix(ture)**, accelerating admix(ture) for set(ting) · (Ab)Binde(zeit)beschleuniger m für hydraulische Gemische, ~ ~ ~ Mischungen, Erstarrungs(zeit)beschleuniger ~ ~ ~, Schnellbindemittel n, Schnellbinder

setting agent, curing ~ [*e.g. as part of an epoxy resin adhesive*] · Abbindemittel n [*Kleber*]

set(ting) agent · (Ab)Bindemittel n [*Mörtel; Beton; Zementpaste; Gips*]

setting and hardening control(l)ing agent [*A substance which, when present in small quantities, controls the setting and hardening of a cementitious material*] · (Ab)Binde(zeit)regler m, (Er)Härtungs(zeit)regler, Erstarrungs(zeit)regler [*für hydraulische Mischungen*]

set(ting) at high temperatures · Warm-Abbinden n [*Abbinden bei hohen Temperaturen*]

setting back, return [*The side or part which falls away, usually at right angles, from the front or direct line of a structure*] · (Rück)Sprung m

~ **bricks** → ~ clay ~

set(ting) capacity → ~ power

setting (clay) bricks, laying (~) ~, (clay) brick setting, (clay) brick laying, bricking · Ziegelmauern n, Mauern mit Ziegeln, Vermauern von Ziegeln

~ **coat**, third ~ · dritte Putzlage f, ~ Putzschicht f

~ ~ **(plaster)** → finish(ing) ~ (~)

set(ting) curve, curve of set(ting) · (Ab)Bindekurve f, Verfestigungskurve

~ **disturbance**, disturbance of set(ting) · (Ab)Bindestörung f [*hydraulisches Bindemittel*]

setting drawing · Versetzplan m, Versetzzeichnung f

set(ting) energy, energy of set(ting) · (Ab)Bindeenergie f [*hydraulisches Bindemittel*]

~ **heat**, heat of set(ting) · (Ab)Bindewärme f

~ **mechanism**, mechanism of set(ting) · (Ab)Bindemechanismus m, Verfestigungsmechanismus

setting-out line, grid ~ · Rasterlinie f

set(ting) power, ~ quality, ~ capacity, ~ property, power of set(ting), quality of set(ting), capacity of set(ting), property of set(ting) · (Ab)Bindeeigenschaft f, (Ab)Bindevermögen n, (Ab)Bindefähigkeit f [*hydraulisches Bindemittel*]

setting procedure, ~ up ~, erection ~, fitting ~ · Montagevorgang m, Aufbauvorgang, Aufstell(ungs)vorgang

set(ting) process, process of set(ting) · (Ab)Bindeprozeß m, (Ab)Bindeverlauf m, (Ab)Bindevorgang m, (Ab)Bindeablauf [*hydraulisches Bindemittel*]

~ **property** → ~ power

~ **quality** → ~ power

~ **rate**, rate of set(ting) · (Ab)Bindegeschwindigkeit f [*hydraulisches Bindemittel*]

~ **reaction**, reaction of set(ting) · (Ab-)Bindereaktion f [*hydraulisches Bindemittel*]

(~) **retarder**, (~) retarding agent, retarder of set(ting) [*A substance which, when present in small quantities, delays the initial setting and hardening of a cementitious material in a controllable way*] · (Ab)Binde(zeit)verzögerer m, Erstarrungs(zeit)verzögerer, VZ, Verzögerer, (Er)Härtungs(zeit)verzögerer [*für hydraulische Bindemittel*]

(~) **retarding agent** → (~) retarder

set(ting) shrinkage [*A reduction in volume of concrete prior to the final set of cement, caused by settling of the solids and by the decrease in volume due to the chemical combination of water with cement*] · (Ab)Bindeschwindung f [*hydraulisches Bindemittel*]

~ **test** · (Ab)Bindeprobe f, (Ab)Bindeversuch m, (Ab)Bindeprüfung f [*für hydraulische Bindemittel*]

~ **testing apparatus** · (Ab)Bindeprüfer m, (Ab)Bindeprüfgerät n [*für hydraulische Bindemittel*]

~ **time**, time of set(ting) · (Ab)Bindedauer f, (Ab)Bindezeit f, (Ab)Bindefrist f, Verfestigungszeit, Verfestigungsdauer, Verfestigungsfrist [*Mörtel; Beton; Zementpaste; Gips*]

setting time, polymerization ~; polymerisation ~ (Brit.) · Aushärtezeit f [*Betonkleber*]

~ **(up)**, fitting, erection · Aufbau(en) m, (n), Aufstellen, Aufstellung f, Montieren, Montage f

~ (~) **procedure**, fitting ~, erection ~ · Montagevorgang m, Aufbauvorgang, Aufstell(ungs)vorgang

~ (~) **sequence**, erection ~, fitting ~ · Aufbaufolge f, Montagefolge, Aufstell(ungs)folge

~ (~) **shop** → erecting ~

set(ting) value, value of set(ting) · (Ab)Bindewert m

~ **water**, water of set(ting) · (Ab)Bindewasser n

setting (work) · Versetzen n, Versetzung f, Versetzarbeiten fpl [*Wandplatten*]

settleable solids · abschlämmbare Bestandteile mpl, Abschlämmbare n

settlement crack · Setzriß m, Setzungsriß

~ **joint** · Bewegungsfuge f, Setzungsfuge [*Breite je nach Größe der zu erwartenden Setzungen, mindestens aber 15 mm*]

~ **measurement** · Setzungsmessung f

settlement movement — sewer product

~ movement · Setzungsbewegung f

~ (of aggregate) [*Sinking of solid particles in fresh concrete or mortar after placement and before initial set*] · Absinken n

~ ~ support(s), settling ~ ~, sagging ~ ~ · Stützensenkung f

settling · Absetzen n [*Das Sinken des schweren Bestandteiles einer Emulsion, wodurch sich die emulgierten Stoffe trennen*]

~ cone, ~ glass · Absetzglas n [*Es dient zur Bestimmung der Raummenge der während gewisser Zeit absetzbaren Schwebstoffe in cm³/l*]

~ glass → ~ cone

~ of support(s) → settlement ~ ~

~ the accounts · Abrechnung f

seven-day strength · Sieben-Tage-Festigkeit f

seven-domed pilgrimage church · Siebenkuppel-Wallfahrtskirche f

seven-moment equation · Siebenmomentengleichung f

seven-step(ped) pyramid · siebenstufige Pyramide f

seven-towered · siebentürmig

seven-wire · siebendrähtig [*(Vorspann)Litze*]

Seven Wonders of Antiquity · Sieben Weltwunder npl (des Altertums)

seven wreaths of short turrets · Treppentürmchen n pyramidenförmig in sieben Geschossen übereinander gestaffelt [*Nordturm des Straßburger Münsters*]

severely classical architecture · klassisch kühle Architektur f, ~ ~ Baukunst f

severity of fire · Brandhettigkeit f, Feuerheftigkeit f

~ (~ style), austerity, precision · Strenge f [*Stil*]

severy, compartment, bay, vault ~ · (Gewölbe)Feld n, (Gewölbe)Joch n, Gewölbeabteilung f, Gewölbebeschlag m, Jochfeld, Gitterfeld [*Joche werden in der Längsachse gezählt, Schiffe in der Querachse*]

sewage → refuse water

~ construction · Abwasserbau m

~ digestion, digestion (of sewage) · (Abwasser)Faulung f

(~) ~ tower · (Abwasser)Faulturm m

~ disposal facility, ~ ~ system, foul water ~ ~, refuse water ~ ~ · Abwasserbeseitigungsanlage f

~ gallery, ~ tunnel, sewer ~, refuse water ~, foul water ~ · Abwasserstollen m, Kanal(isations)stollen

~ pipe → sewer ~

~ (~) trench → sewer (~) ~

~ purification, refuse water ~, foul water ~ · Abwasserreinigung f

~ scheme · Abwasser(bau)projekt n

~ treatment · Abwasseraufbereitung f

~ trench → sewer (pipe) ~

~ tunnel, ~ gallery, sewer ~, refuse water ~, foul water ~ · Abwasserstollen m, Kanal(isations)stollen

sewer → ~ line

~ article, ~ product · Kanalisationsartikel m

~ articles, ~ products, ~ goods · Kanalisationsartikel mpl

~ brick · Kanalziegel m [*Fehlname: Kanalstein m*]

~ ~ [*It is a clay or shale brick used for sewerage, industrial waste, and storm water conduits*] · Kanalklinker m [*DIN 4051*]

~ connection, ~ line ~ · Abwasserleitungsanschluß m

~ construction · Abwasserleitungsbau m

~ ~ (work), ~ line ~ (~) · Abwasserleitungsbau m, Abwasserleitungsarbeiten fpl [*DIN 18306*]

~ for combined foul and surface water · Mischkanal m

~ gallery, ~ tunnel, sewage ~, refuse water ~, foul water ~ · Abwasserstollen m, Kanal(isations)stollen

~ goods, ~ products, ~ articles · Kanalisationsartikel mpl

~ joint(ing) compound, pipe ~ ~, joint cement · Füllmasse f, Vergußmasse [*Zur Vermuffung von Rohren*]

~ (line) [*A pipe or conduit, generally closed, but normally not flowing full, for carrying sewage and other waste liquids*] · Abwasserleitung f

~ (~) connection · Abwasserleitungsanschluß m

~ (~) construction (work) · Abwasserleitungsbau m, Abwasserleitungsarbeiten fpl [*DIN 18306*]

~ (~) trench · Abwasser(leitungs)-graben m

~ manhole, ~ manway · Kanalschacht m

~ manway, ~ manhole · Kanalschacht m

~ network · Schwemmkanalisation f, Abwassernetz n, Kanal(isations)netz, Schwemmentwässerung f [*Unterirdische Entwässerungsanlage. Sie leitet die aus den Aborten stammenden Fäkalien mit dem Spülwasser zusammen mit den übrigen Schmutz- und Niederschlagswasser ab*]

~ pipe, sewage ~, foul water ~, refuse water ~ · Abwasserrohr n, Kanal(isations)rohr

~ (~) trench, sewage (~) ~, foul water (~) ~, refuse water (~) ~ · Abwasserrohr(leitungs)graben m, Kanal(isations)graben

~ product, ~ article · Kanalisationsartikel m

sewer products — shallow luminaire (fixture)

~ **products,** ~ **articles,** ~ **goods** · Kanalisationsartikel *mpl*

~ **trench,** ~ **line** ~ · Abwasser(leitungs)graben *m*

~ **tunnel,** ~ **gallery, sewage** ~**, refuse water** ~**, foul water** ~ · Abwasserstollen *m*, Kanal(isations)stollen

sewerage (system), system of sewers, system of sewerage [*A collecting system of sewers and appurtenances*] · Ortsentwässerung *f*, Kanalisation *f*

sewing room · Nähzimmer *n*

sewn (building) mat, stitched (~) ~ · versteppte (Bau)Matte *f*, ~ Dämmatte

~ **(~) quilt, stitched** (~) ~ · versteppte (Bau)Matte *f*, ~ Isoliermatte

sexpartite rib(bed) vault · sechsteiliges Rippengewölbe *n*

~ **vault, ploughshare** ~ [*The intermediate vault cones are constricted to a shape resembling ploughshares*] · sechsteiliges Gewölbe *n*

'Sezession' style [*Term for Art Nouveau used in Austria, derived from the Viennese 'Sezession' group*] · Sezessionsstil *m*

S.F.D., shear(ing) force diagram · Schubkraftdiagramm *n*

sgraffito, scratchwork [*A plaster surface decorated by scoring a pattern on it while it is soft, and exposing a lower coat of a different colour. The upper layer is often white, the lower layer black or dark red. More than two colours can be used if required*] · Sgraffito(putz) *m*, Kratzgrund *m*, Kratzputz

~ **material, material for scratchwork** · Sgraffito(putz)material *n*, Kratzgrundmaterial, Kratzputzmaterial

to shade, to hatch · schraffieren

shade, hatching · Schraffur *f*, Schraffierung *f*

~ · Tönung *f*

shaded area, hatched ~ · schraffierte Fläche *f*

shading, screening, solar ~, sunshading · Sonnenschutz *m*, Abschattung *f*, Besonnungsschutz

~**,** hatching · Schraffieren *n*

~ **device,** sun ~ ~**,** solar ~ ~**,** sunblind, sunbreaker, solar screen(ing) · Sonnen(schutz)blende *f*, Abschattungsvorrichtung *f*, Sonnenschutzkonstruktion *f*, Sonnenschutz(anlage) *m*, (*f*)

shadowiness · Schattigkeit *f*

shaft, pit, well · Schacht *m* [*Ein senkrechter Hohlraum von meist geringem Querschnitt, z.B. Luftschacht*]

~**,** chute, disposal ~**,** disposer · Abwurfanlage *f*, Abwurfschacht *m* [*Es gibt Abwurfanlagen für Müll, Papier und Wäsche*]

~**,** column ~**,** fust · (Säulen)Schaft *m*, (Säulen)Rumpf *m*

~ **for riser(s),** ~ ~ **rising main(s)** · Steig(e)leitungsschacht *m*

~ **grave** · Schachtgrab *n*

~ **kiln,** vertical ~ · Schachtofen *m*

~ ~ **cement,** vertical ~ ~ · Schachtofenzement *m*

~ ~ **clinker,** vertical ~ ~ · Schachtofenklinker *m*

~ ~ **lime,** vertical ~ ~ · Schachtofenkalk *m*

shaft lime kiln, vertical ~ ~ · Kalkschachtofen *m*

~ **masonry (work)** · Schachtmauerwerk *n*

~ **mastaba** · Schachtmastaba *f*

shaft-ring, band · Schaftring *m*, Bund *m*, Wirtel *m* [*Ringförmige Verstärkung am Säulenschaft. Der Schaftring ist technisch gesehen ein Binder = Zungenstein, der Wandsäulen mit dem Mauerwerk verbindet. Es gibt aber auch Schaftringe an freistehenden Säulen*]

~**, annulet, gradetto** [*In the Doric order of architecture one of the fillets beneath the capital*] · Riemchen *n*

shaft stair(case) · Schachttreppe *f*, Schlauchtreppe

~ **wall,** well ~ · Schachtwand *f*

~ **with (installed) services** · Installationsschacht *m*, Leitungsschacht

shake → **hand cleft (wood) shingle**

shake-down · Verformungsinstabilität *f*, Formänderungsinstabilität [*Unter der Wirkung aufeinander folgender Wanderlasten können sich plastische Verformungen wiederholen und durch Speichern bewirken, daß der Träger unbrauchbar wird*]

shale (clay) [*In Scotland, the dialect word 'blaes' is in common use for shale. Shale tipped in waste heaps known in Scotland as 'bing' appears to be regarded in some quarters as spectial material. It must be made clear, however, that the 'bing' brick is merely a variety of shale brick*] · Schieferton *m*

~ **(~) brick,** bing ~, blaes ~, cliff ~ [*B.S. 3921*] · Schiefertonziegel *m*

~ **concrete plank,** expanded ~ ~ ~ · Blähschieferbetondiele *f*

~ **oil,** crude ~ ~ · Schieferöl *n*

~ **tar** · Schieferteer *m*

shale-tar pitch · Schieferteerpech *n*

shallow apse · gebrochene Apside *f*, ~ Abside, ~ Apsis, ~ Abseite

~ **bowl** → ~ **pan**

~ ~ **toilet** → ~ **pan closet**

~ **fixture** → ~ **luminaire** (~)

~ **folding** · flache Faltung *f*

~ **(glass) pattern** · leichte (Glas-)Musterung *f*, ~ (Glas)Ornamentierung

~ **light fitting** (Brit.) → ~ **luminaire** (fixture)

~ **(light(ing)) fixture** → ~ **luminaire** (~)

~ **luminaire (fixture)** (US); ~ **light fitting** (Brit.); ~ **(light(ing)) fixture** · Flachleuchte *f*

shallow pan — shear force transmission

~ **pan,** ~ bowl · Auswaschbecken *n*, Flachspülbecken [*(Spül)Abortbecken*]

~ ~ **closet,** ~ bowl ~, ~ ~ toilet · Auswaschabort *m*, Auswaschtoilette *f*, Auswaschklosett *n*, Flachspülabort, Flachspülklosett, Flachspültoilette [*DIN 1381*]

shallow(-rise) cupola → ~ dome

~ **dome,** ~ cupola, flat ~ · Flachkuppel *f*, Stichkugelgewölbe *n*, Kugelkappe(ngewölbe) *f*, (*n*), gedrückte Kuppel [*Der Pfeil ist geringer als der Halbmesser*]

shallow shell, flat ~, low-rise ~ · krumme Platte *f*, flache Schale *f*, schwach gekrümmte Platte, schwach gekrümmte Schale

shallow-shell theory, theory of shallow shells · Theorie *f* der flachen Schalen, ~ ~ krummen Platten

shallow spherical shell, flat ~ ~, low-rise ~ ~ · flache Kugelschale *f*, schwach gekrümmte ~

sham ruin · Scheinruine *f*

shampoo spray · Kopfwaschbrause *f*

shank · Schaft *m* [*Nagel; Schraube*]

shanty method, hand ~ [*Manufacture of roof(ing) slate*] · Spaltung *f* in Spalthütten

to shape, to dress, to mill, to hew · (steinmetzmäßig) bearbeiten, (~) behauen, (~) zurichten

~ ~ **coarsely** → ~ dress ~

~ ~ **roughly** → ~ dress coarsely

shape · Körperlichkeit *f*

~, section, unit, trim, profile · Profil *n*

~ → (roll-formed) section

~ → construction(al) ~

~ **anisotropy** · Gestaltanisotropie *f*

~ **code,** bar ~ ~ · Armierungsformnummer *f*, Bewehrungsformnummer, Eisenformnummer, Eisenform-Nr., Bewehrungsform-Nr., Armierungsform-Nr. [*Stahlliste*]

~ **coefficient** · Beiwert *m* von der Gestalt des Bauwerkes abhängig, Gestaltbeiwert [*Windlast*]

~ **concept** → concept of form

~ **fabricator** → ~ maker

~ **factor** · Formfaktor *m*

~ **for interior work** → profile ~ ~ ~

~ **maker,** section ~, trim ~, unit ~, profile ~, ~ fabricator · Profilhersteller *m*

~ **of the moment diagram,** moment curvature · Momentenverlauf *m*

~ ~ **window,** window shape · Fensterform *f*

shape-retentive, form-rententive · formbeständig, formtreu

shape-retentiveness, form-retentiveness · Formbeständigkeit *f*, Formtreue *f*

shaped, dressed, hewn, milled · (steinmetzmäßig) bearbeitet, (~) behauen, (~) zugerichtet

~ **gable,** curved ~ · kurvenförmiger Giebel *m*, geschweifter ~, Rundgiebel [*Er ist halbkreisförmig im Umriß*]

~ ~ · profilierter Giebel *m*

~ **(natural) stone** → dressed (~) ~

~ **stone** → dressed (natural) ~

~ **stonework,** (dressed) ~, milled ~, hewn ~ · zugerichtete Werksteine *mpl*, bearbeitete ~, behauene ~

shapelessness · Gestaltlosigkeit *f*

shaping, dressing, milling, hewing · (Natur)Steinbearbeitung *f*, Bearbeitung, Behauen *n*, Zurichten

~ **of plastics** · Verformen *n* von Kunststoffen, Verformung *f* ~ ~

sharpening stone · Abziehstein *m*

shatter point, brittle ~, breaking ~ · Starrpunkt *m*, Brechpunkt [*Temperatur bituminöser Stoffe, bei der die Plastizität verschwindet und die Probe bei Biegebeanspruchung bricht. DIN 1995 – Ü 6*]

shattering · Zertrümmerung *f*

shatterproof glass, safety ~ · Sicherheitsglas *n*

~ ~ **domelight,** safety ~ ~, ~ ~ light cupola, ~ ~ saucer dome · Sicherheitsglas(licht)kuppel *f*

~ ~ **door,** safety ~ ~ · Sicherheitsglastür *f*

~ **plate glass,** safety ~ ~ · Sicherheitsspiegelglas *n*

~ **sheet glass** → ~ window ~

~ **window glass,** safety ~ ~, ~ sheet ~ · Sicherheitsfensterglas *n*

sheaf · Schar *f* [*Baustatik*]

~ **of coordinate axes** · Schar *f* zugeordneter Achsen

shear → shear(ing) (off)

~ **along edge,** edge shear · Randschubkraft *f*

~ **behaviour** → shearing ~

~ **calculation** → shearing ~

~ **center (US)** → shear(ing) ~

~ **check** → shearing ~

~ **collar,** (lift-)slab ~, steel lifting ~ · Deckenkragen *m*, (Stahl)Kragen [*Hubdeckenverfahren*]

~ **compression** → shearing ~

~ **connection** → shearing ~

~ **crack** → shearing ~

~ **curve** → shearing ~

~ **deformation angle** → shearing ~ ~

~ **design** → shearing ~

~ **diagram** → shearing ~

~ **difference** → shearing ~

~ **effect** → shearing ~

~ **elasticity** → shearing ~

~ **failure** → shearing ~

~ **force** → shearing ~

~ ~ **diagram** → shearing ~ ~

~ ~ **transmission** → shearing ~ ~

shear force value — shear(ing) stress

~ ~ value → shearing ~ ~

~ key, steel ~ ~ · Stahlbarren *m*, (Verankerungs)Barren [*Hubdeckenverfahren*]

~ load → shearing ~

~ modulus (of elasticity) → modulus of rigidity

~ off → shearing ~

to shear (off) · (ab)scheren

shear plate [*A round steel plate with a flange at the outer edge, used for timber-to-metal joints, or back to back — like single toothed plates — for timber-to-timber connection*] · runde Flansch(en)- scheibe *f* [*Holzverbinder*]

~ range → shearing ~

~ reinforcement, web ~ [*Reinforcement, usually in the form of stirrups and/or bent-up bars designed to resist shear and diagonal tension; dowels are not considered to be shear reinforcement*] · Schubbewehrung *f*, Schubarmierung, Schub(stahl)einlagen *fpl*

~ resistance → shearing ~

shear-resistant, shear-resisting · schubfest

shear-resisting, shear-resistant · schubfest

shear section → shearing ~

~ strength → shearing ~

~ ~ test → shearing ~ ~

~ stress (US) → shearing ~

~ ~ diagram → shearing ~ ~

~ ~ distribution → shearing ~ ~

~ surface, shearing ~ · (Ab)Scherfläche *f*

~ test → shearing ~

~ tie · Schubanker *m*

~ wall, cross ~ [*A wall which in its own plane carries shear resulting from wind, blast, or earthquake forces. It relieves the floors and columns of the necessity or resisting lateral loads and, in addition, it is useful architecturally*] · Scheibe *f*, Wand~, Wind~

~ wave, transverse ~, rotational ~ · Transversalwelle *f*, Querwelle [*Im Gegensatz zu Gasen und Flüssigkeiten können in festen Körpern jedoch auch Schubkräfte übertragen werden, so daß Körperschall hauptsächlich in Form von Transversalwellen auftritt, bei denen die Teilchen quer zur Ausbreitungsrichtung schwingen*]

sheariness, mottling, spotting · Fleckenbildung *f* [*Anstrichmittel*]

shear(ing) · Schub *m*

~ behaviour (Brit.); ~ behavior (US) · Schubverhalten *n*

~ block · Widerlagerstein *m* [*H(o)urdiplattendecke*]

~ calculation · Schubberechnung *f*

~ center (US); ~ centre (Brit.) · Schubmittelpunkt *m*

~ check · Schubnachweis *m*, Schubsicherung *f* [*Der Nachweis über die Aufnahme der aus den Querkräften entstehenden Zugspannungen im Beton mit Schrägeisen und Bügeln*]

~ compression · Schubdruck *m*

~ connection · Schubverbindung *f*

~ crack · Schubriß *m*

~ curve · Schubkurve *f*

~ deformation · Schubformänderung *f*, Schubverformung

~ ~ angle · Schubverformungswinkel *m*, Schubformänderungswinkel

~ design · Schubbemessung *f*

~ diagram · Schubdiagramm *n*

~ difference · Schubunterschied *m*

~ effect · Schubwirkung *f*

~ elasticity · Schubelastizität *f*

~ failure · Schubbruch *m*

~ force, S.F. [*The shear(ing) force at any section of a beam is the algebraic sum of all the normal external forces acting to one side of that section*] · Schubkraft *f*

~ ~ diagram, S.F.D. · Schubkraftdiagramm *n*

~ ~ transmission, S.F. ~ · Schubkraftübertragung *f*

~ ~ value · Schubkraftwert *m*

~ load · Schublast *f*

~ modulus *G* · Gleitmodul *G m*

~ (off) · (Ab)Scheren *n*

~ range · Schubbereich *m, n*

~ resistance · Schubwiderstand *m* [*Siehe Anmerkung unter „Schubspannung"*]

~ section · Schubquerschnitt *m*

~ strength · Schubfestigkeit *f* [*Spannung in kp/mm², die beim Trennen eines Körpers durch Abscheren senkrecht zur Längsachse zu überwinden ist. Siehe Anmerkung unter „shear(ing) stress"*]

~ ~ · (Ab)Scherfestigkeit *f*

~ ~ test · Schubfestigkeitsprobe *f*, Schubfestigkeitsprüfung *f*, Schubfestigkeitsversuch *m*

~ stress · Schubspannung *f* [*Eine Schubspannung kann man sich am Flächenelement in der Ebene wirkend vorstellen, während die dazugehörige Normalspannung in der Flächennormale zu dieser Ebene wirkt, also senkrecht zur Schubspannung angenommen werden muß. Stellt man sich z.B. einen belasteten Balken an einer Stelle geschnitten vor, so ergibt die Integration der Schubspannungen über alle Flächenelemente an einem Schnittufer die Querkraft, während die Integration der Normalspannungen über alle Flächenelemente an einem Schnittufer das Biegemoment an dieser Stelle ergibt. Ist außer einer Querkraft kein Biegemoment an einer Stelle des Balkens vorhanden, also an einem Balken auf zwei Stützen nur an den Auflagern, so kann man statt von*]

Schubspannungen auch von Scherspannungen sprechen, die an den Flächenelementen dieser Stelle wirken, wobei die entsprechenden Normalspannungen nicht vorhanden sind. Dieser Fall tritt z.B. auch beim Abscheren eines Niets auf oder beim Schneiden eines Bleches unter einer Schere. Die Scherspannungen sind somit ein Sonderfall der Schubspannungen. Deshalb ist in DIN 1053 Abschnitt 8.1.3. das Wort ,,Scherspannungen'' zu streichen. Auch in der Bodenmechanik ist der Begriff ,,Scherfestigkeit'' (siehe Neufassung Oktober 1971 von DIN 4015 Nr. 1.54) genau genommen nicht zutreffend, da eigentlich die ,,Schubfestigkeit'' gemeint ist. Hier liegt der Begriffsbildung der direkte Scherversuch im Rahmenschergerät zu Grunde, bei welchem eine Bodenprobe in zwei übereinander liegende Rahmen eingebaut und durch Festhalten des einen und Wegziehen des anderen Rahmens abgeschert wird. Leider haben sich in Deutschland im Gegensatz zum Ausland zwei Begriffe eingebürgert, die nicht der Klarheit und Logik dienen, sondern beim Übersetzen und Dolmetschen, z. B. bei Normen, unnötige Schwierigkeiten machen. Beim künftigen Überarbeiten der entsprechenden Normen sollten diese Gesichtspunkte berücksichtigt werden. Definitionsmäßig gesehen versteht man unter ,,Schubspannung'' die tangentiale Komponente des Spannungsvektors auf eine Innenschnittfläche eines Körpers und unter ,,Scherspannung'' die spezielle Schubspannung bei Erreichen der Festigkeitsgrenze, die durch eine Trennbruchfläche gekennzeichnet ist. Schubspannung ist der Oberbegriff und sollte in der Regel verwendet werden]

~ ~ · Scherspannung *f*

~ ~ **diagram** · Schubspannungsdiagramm *n*

~ ~ **distribution** · Schubspannungsverteilung *f*

~ **surface** · (Ab)Scherfläche *f*

~ **test** · (Ab)Scherprobe *f*, (Ab)Scherprüfung *f*, (Ab)Scherversuch *m* [*Ein Versuch, der die Probe durch (Ab-) Scheren beansprucht*]

sheath → sheathing

~ **coat** → (concrete) encasement

sheathed wire · bewehrter Draht *m*, Rohrdraht [*Elektrotechnik*]

sheath(ing) [*prestressed concrete*] · Gleitkanal *m*, Hüllrohr *n*, Hülle *f*, Röhre *f*, Spannkanal *m*

sheathing board → (gypsum) sheathing plasterboard

~ **paper** [*It is used to provide moisture protection and to resist moisture and wind infiltration*] · Verschalungspapier *n*

~ ~ [*See remark under 'Pappe'*] · Schutzpappe *f*

~ ~ → waterproof ~ ~

~ **plasterboard** → gypsum ~ ~

~ **plate** [*Scotland*] → (gypsum) sheathing plasterboard

shed · Schuppen *m*

~ **for cement,** cement shed · Zement(lager)schuppen *m*

~ **roof** · Satteldach *n* [*Aneinandergereihte Satteldächer, deren beide Dachseiten gleiche Neigung haben. Gegenteil: Sheddach, dessen beide Dachseiten ungleiche Neigung haben*]

~ ~, pen ~, pent(house) ~ [*A roof with a slope on one side only. It differs from a lean-to-roof (freitragendes Pultdach) in that it covers the higher wall*] · Flugdach *n*, Halb(sattel)dach, Schleppdach, einhängiges Dach, halbes Satteldach, Taschendach

sheet → (reinforcing) mat

~, sheeting · Bahn *f*

~, board · Platte *f*

~, metal ~, sheet metal · (Fein)Blech *n*

~, disc; disk (US) · Scheibe *f*, Scheibentragwerk *n* [*Ein Flächentragwerk, das nur durch Kräfte belastet ist, die in seiner Ebene wirken*]

~ **action**; disc ~; disk ~ (US) · Scheibenwirkung *f*

~ **adhesive** → ~ glue

~ **aluminium core** (Brit.); ~ aluminum ~ (US) · Alu(minium)kern *m*

~ **bar** [*A semi-finished hot rolled iron product of approximately rectangular section, sheared to length and used to produce a hot rolled sheet by cross rolling*] · Platine *f*, Vorblech *n*

~ **(bonding) adhesive,** ~ (~) glue, board (~) ~, ~ ~ agent, ~ ~ medium, ~ cement(ing agent) · Plattenkleber *m*, Plattenkleb(e)stoff *m*, Plattenkleb(e)mittel *n*

~ **caisson** → metal ~ ~

~ **cassette** → metal ~ ~

~ **cement(ing agent)** → ~ (bonding) adhesive

~ **coffer** → metal ~ ~

~ **copper,** copper sheet [*B.S. 1569*] · Kupfer(fein)blech *n*

~ **cover(ing),** metal ~ ~, sheet metal ~ · (Fein)Blechabdeckung *f*

~ ~, sheeting ~ · Bahnenbelag *m*

~ **floor** → sheet(ing) floor(ing) (finish)

~ ~ **cover(ing)** → sheet(ing) floor(ing) (finish)

(~) **gauge (No.),** (~) ~ number; (~) gage ~ (US) · (Blech)Lehrennummer *f*

(~) ~ **system;** (~) gage ~ (US) · (Blech)Lehre *f*

~ **glass** · Tafelglas *n*

~ **glue,** film ~, ~ adhesive, adhesive in film form, glue in film form · Leimfilm *m*, Leimfolie *f*, Filmleim, Kleb(e)film, Kleb(e)folie

~ ~ → ~ (bonding) adhesive

sheet iron — shell analysis

~ **iron**, ~ steel, steel sheet, iron sheet · Stahl(fein)blech n [DIN 1541]

~ **lead**, milled ~, lead sheet [Lead rolled into sheets from cast slabs] · Blei(fein)-blech n, Walzblei n, Tafelblei [DIN 59610]

~ **lino(leum)** [B.S. 810] · Fliesenlinoleum n, Bahnware f

~ **material**, sheet(ing) ~· Bahnware f

~ **metal**, (metal) sheet · (Fein)Blech n

~ ~ **cornice flashing (piece)**, (flexible) ~ ~ ~ (~) · (Ge)Simsabdeckung f aus Blech, (Ge)Simsblech n

~ ~ **cover(ing)**, (metal) sheet ~ · (Fein)Blechabdeckung f

~ ~ **flashing (piece)**, (flexible) ~ ~ (~) [See remark under 'Anschluß'] · Anschlußblech(streifen) n, (m), Blechanschluß(streifen) m

(~ ~) **integral lath(ing)**, ~ ~ lath(ing) · Putzblech n

(~ ~) ~ **masonry wall flashing (piece)**, flexible ~ ~ ~ ~ ~ (~) [See remark under 'Anschluß'] · Mauerabdeckung f aus Blech, Mauerblech n

~ ~ **panel**, (metal) sheet ~ · (Fein-)Blechtafel f

(sheet-)metal roof cladding, ~ ~ covering, ~ ~ sheathing, (flexible) metal sheet ~ ~, (sheet-)metal roofing, (flexible) metal sheet roof(ing) · Blechdachbelag m aus ebenen Blechen, Metallbedachung f ~ ~ ~, Blechbedachung ~ ~ ~, Metalldach n ~ ~ ~, Blechdach ~ ~ ~, Metall(dach)eindeckung ~ ~ ~, Blech(dach)eindeckung ~ ~ ~, Metall(dach)deckung ~ ~ ~, Blech(dach)deckung, Metalldachbelag

~ **sheath(ing)** [prestressed concrete] · Blechgleitkanal m, Blechspannkanal, Blechhüllrohr n, Blechhülle f, Blechröhre f

sheet metal valley gutter · Blechkehlrinne f, Kehlblechrinne

~ **mica**, book ~, mica in sheets · Spaltglimmer m, Plattenglimmer [Er wird aus Blockglimmer durch Spalten in dünne Lagen hergestellt]

~ **of felt(ed fabric)** → felt(ed fabric) board

~ ~ **gypsum plasterboard** → gypsum (board) lath(ing)

~ ~ **paper**, board ~ ~, paper sheet, paper board · Pappenplatte f

~ ~ **water** · Wasserfläche f [Zieranlage]

~ **pan(el)** → metal ~ ~

~ **panel**, metal ~ ~, sheet metal ~ · (Fein)Blechtafel f

~ **plastic** → sheet(ing) ~

~ **roof(ing)** [This term includes metal sheet roofing, compound sheet roofing and thermoplastic sheet roofing] · Plattenbedachung f, Platten(dach)eindeckung, Platten(dach)deckung, Plattendach(belag) n, (m)

~ **felt** → ready sheet roofing (paper)

~ **rubber**, sheeting ~ · Gummibahnware f

~ **steel**, steel sheet · Stahl(fein)blech n [DIN 1541]

~ ~ **facing** → steel sheet lining

~ ~ **lining** → steel sheet ~

~ ~ **(sur)facing** → steel sheet lining

sheet-type (load)bearing system with three areas, disc-type ~ ~ ~ ~ ~; disk-type ~ ~ ~ ~ ~ (US) · dreiflächiges Scheibentragwerk n

sheet waffle → metal ~ ~

~ **zinc**, zinc sheet · Zinkblech n [DIN 9721]

~ ~ **cover**, zinc sheet ~ · Zink(blech)-abdeckung f

(~ ~) **roof cladding**, (~ ~) ~ ~ covering, (~ ~) ~ ~ sheathing, (~ ~) ~ ~ roofing [B.S. 849] · Zinkbedachung f, Zinkdachbelag m, Zink(ein)deckung, Zinkdach(ein)deckung, Zinkdach n

(~ ~) ~ **covering**, (~ ~) ~ ~ cladding, (~ ~) ~ ~ sheathing, (~ ~) ~ ~ roofing [B.S. 849] · Zinkbedachung f, Zinkdachbelag m, Zink(ein)deckung, Zinkdeach(ein)deckung, Zinkdach n

sheet(ing) · Bahn f

sheeting · Bretter npl [Brettertür]

~, sheets, boards · Platten fpl

~ **board facing** → building board lining

~ ~ **lining** → building ~ ~

~ ~ **(sur)facing** → building board lining

sheet(ing) cover(ing) · Bahnenbelag m

~ **floor(ing) (finish)**, ~ floor cover(-ing) · Bahnen(fuß)boden(belag) m

~ **lino(leum)** [B.S. 810] · Bahnware f, Fliesenlinoleum n

~ **material** · Bahnware f

~ **plastic**, plastic sheet(ing) · Kunststoffbahn f

~ **rubber** · Gummibahnware f

sheets, sheeting, boards · Platten fpl

shelf bracket, shelving ~ · Regalkonsole f

~ **life** [The time that a paint will keep in good condition when stored in the original sealed containers under normal storage conditions on the shelves of a shop or stock room] · Lagerzeit f

shell, skin, tier, layer, leaf, wythe, withe [cavity wall] · Schale f, Wand~ [Hohlwand]

~ [Canada]; carcass, fabric; carcase [deprecated] [A building or structure that is structurally complete but otherwise unfinished] · Rohbau m

~ · Schale f

~ **action**, ~ effect · Schalenwirkung f

~ **analogy** · Schalenanalogie f

~ **analysis**, ~ calculation · Schalenberechnung f

shell analysis — shell ring

~ ~ · Schalenstatik f
~ **apex**, ~ crown, ~ top, ~ vertex, ~ key · Schalenscheitel(punkt) m
~ **area** · Schalenfläche f
~ **axis**; ~ centre line (Brit.); ~ center line (US) · Schalenachse f, Schalenmittellinie f
~ **bearing system** → ~ load~ ~
~ **belt**, ~ ring; course (US) · Kesselschuß m, Mantelschuß
~ **bending theory** · Schalenbiegetheorie f
~ **boundary**, ~ edge · Schalenrand m
shell-**boundary stress resultant** · Schalenrandspannungsresultierende f
shell **buckling** · Schalenbeulung f
~ **calculation**, ~ analysis · Schalenberechnung f
shell-**cast (concrete) chimney** → (pre)cast (~) ~
shell **centre line** (Brit.); ~ center ~ (US); ~ axis · Schalenachse f, Schalenmittellinie f
~ **coefficient** · Schalenbeiwert m
~ **concrete** · Schalenbeton m
~ ~ **construction** · Betonschalenbau m
~ ~ **roof**, concrete shell ~ · Betonschalendach n, Schalenbetondach
~ ~ ~ **construction**, concrete shell ~ ~ · Betonschalendachbau m
~ **configuration** · Schalenfigur f
~ **constant** · Schalenkonstante f
~ **construction** · Schalenbau m
~ ~ → ~ (load)bearing ~
~ ~ **method** · Schalenbauweise f
~ **cross section** · Schalenquerschnitt m
~ **crown**, ~ top, ~ vertex, ~ key, ~ apex · Schalenscheitel(punkt) m
~ **cupola**, ~ dome · Schalenkuppel f
~ **curvature** · Schalenkrümmung f
~ **curved in two directions** → ~ of double curvature
~ **dead load**, ~ DL · Schalentotlast f, Schaleneigenlast
~ **deflection**, ~ deflexion · Schalendurchbiegung f
~ **deflexion**, ~ deflection · Schalendurchbiegung f
~ **DL**, ~ dead load · Schalentotlast f, Schaleneigenlast
~ **dome**, ~ cupola · Schalenkuppel f
~ **donjon**, ~ keep, ~ dungeon · ummauerter Donjon m, ~ Bergfried, ~ Belfried, ~ Berchfrit, ~ Wohnturm [mittelalterliche Burg]
~ **dungeon**, ~ keep, ~ donjon · ummauerter Donjon m, ~ Bergfried, ~ Belfried, ~ Berchfrit, ~ Wohnturm [mittelalterliche Burg]
~ **edge**, ~ boundary · Schalenrand m
~ **effect**, ~ action · Schalenwirkung f

~ **equation** · Schalengleichung f
~ **fiber** (US); ~ fibre (Brit.) · Schalenfaser f
~ **force** · Schalenkraft f
~ **form**, ~ shape · Schalenform f, Schalengestalt f
~ **formula** · Schalenformel f
~ **foundation** · Schalengründung f
~ **keep**, ~ donjon, ~ dungeon · ummauerter Donjon m, ~ Bergfried, ~ Belfried, ~ Berchfrit, ~ Wohnturm [mittelalterliche Burg]
~ **key**, ~ apex, ~ crown, ~ top, ~ vertex · Schalenscheitel(punkt) m
~ **load** · Schalenlast f
~ **(load)bearing system**, ~ (weight-carrying) ~, ~ load-carrying) ~, ~ supporting ~, ~ structural ~, ~ loaded ~, ~ construction · Schalensystem n, Schalentragwerk n, Schalenkonstruktion f
~ **loading** · Schalenbelastung f
~ **material** · Schalenbaustoff m; Schalenbaumaterial n [Schweiz]
~ **membrane** · Schalenmembran(e) f
~ **model** · Schalenmodell n
~ **moment** · Schalenmoment n
~ **normal** · Schalennormale f
~ **of double curvature**, ~ curved in two directions, doubly curved shell, double curvature shell · doppelt gekrümmte Schale f
~ ~ **negative curvature** · negativ gekrümmte Schale f, Schale negativer Krümmung
~ ~ **positive curvature** · positiv gekrümmte Schale f, Schale positiver Krümmung
~ ~ **revolution (subjected to loads of rotational symmetry)**, ~ ~ rotational symmetry, rotational shell · Drehschale f, Rotationsschale, drehsymmetrische Schale
~ ~ **rotational symmetry**, ~ ~ revolution (subjected to loads of rotational symmetry), rotational shell · Drehschale f, Rotationsschale, drehsymmetrische Schale
~ ~ **single curvature**, single curvature shell, singly curved shell, simply curved shell · einfach gekrümmte Schale f
~ **oscillation**, ~ vibration · Schalenschwingung f
~ **plate**, curve ~ · Schale f
~ **point** · Schalenpunkt m
~ **problem** · Schalenaufgabe f
~ **radius** · Schalenhalbmesser m
~ **reinforcement** · Schalenbewehrung f, Schalenarmierung, Schalen(stahl)einlagen fpl
~ **research** · Schalenforschung f
~ **ring**, ~ belt; course (US) · Kesselschuß m, Mantelschuß

shell roof — shingle hanging

~ **roof** [*A roof formed of a thin curved structural slab*] · Schalendach *n*

~ **sector** · Schalensektor *m*

~ **segment** · Schalensegment *n*

~ **shape**, ~ form · Schalenform *f*, Schalengestalt *f*

~ **slope** · Schalenneigung *f*

~ **stress pattern** · Schalenspannungsbild *n*

~ **structural system** → ~ (load)bearing ~

~ **structure** · Schalenbauwerk *n*

~ **supporting system** → ~ (load-)bearing ~

~ **system** → ~ (load)bearing ~

~ ~ **composed of several hypar surfaces with curved edges** · Schalensystem *n* zusammengesetzt aus mehreren bogenförmig begrenzten hp-Flächen

~ **theory** · Schalentheorie *f*

~ **top**, ~ vertex, ~ key, ~ apex, ~ crown · Schalenscheitel(punkt) *m*

~ **vault** · Schalengewölbe *n*

~ **vertex**, ~ key, ~ apex, ~ crown, ~ top · Schalenscheitel(punkt) *m*

~ **vibration**, ~ oscillation · Schalenschwingung *f*

~ **(weight-carrying) system** → ~ (load)bearing ~

~ **width** · Schalenbreite *f*

~ **with edge (vertical) beams** · Schale *f* mit Randbalken

~ **work** [*Canada*]; carcassing, carcass work, fabric work [*Constructing the carcass of a building*] · Rohbauarbeiten *fpl*, Gebäude~

~ ~, scroll-work, rocaille [*A graceful design of delicate scroll and counterscroll outline, varying in form yet maintaining everywhere its characteristic asymmetrical harmony*] · Rocaille *n, f*, Muschelwerk *n*

shellac · Röhrenlack *m*

shelling, peeling · Abblättern *n*, Abblätterung *f* [*Feuerfestindustrie*]

shell(y) limestone, coquina, oyster shell lime · Muschelkalkstein *m*, Muschelmarmor *m*

~ **sandstone**, beach rock · Muschelsandstein *m*

sheltered car place · (PKW-)Garageneinstellplatz *m*, (PKW-)Garagenabstellplatz, (PKW-)Garagenstandplatz, (PKW-)Garagenparkstand *m* [*Die zum Aufstellen eines PKWs in einer Garage bestimmte Fläche*]

shelving bracket, shelf ~ · Regalkonsole *f*

sheradising (US); sheradizing (Brit.) [*The article to be galvanized is exposed to powdered zinc near its melting point*] · Sherad(is)ieren *n*

shield, bulk ~ · Abschirm(ungs)wand *f* eines Reaktors, Reaktorabschirm(ungs)wand, (biologischer) Schirm *m*

~ **glass** → biological shielding ~

shielded inert gas metal arc welding · Sigmaschweißung *f*, Sigmaschweißen *n*

shielding → biological ~

~ **block**, ~ tile, biological ~ ~, radiation ~ ~ [*See remark under 'Block'*] · Abschirm(ungs)stein *m*, Strahlenschutzstein, Abschirm(ungs)block(stein) *m*, Strahlenschutzblock(stein)

~ **building** · Abschirm(ungs)gebäude *n* [*gegen Wind*]

~ **concrete**, radiation ~ ~, biological ~ ~ · Abschirm(ungs)beton *m*, Strahlenschutzbeton [*Zur Abschirmung von Gamma- und Neutronenstrahlen*]

~ **design**, biological ~ ~, radiation ~ ~ · Abschirm(ungs)berechnung *f* [*Strahlenschutz*]

~ **door** → radiation ~ ~

~ **effect** · Abschirm(ungs)wirkung *f*

~ **glass** → biological ~ ~

~ **heat** · Strahlenschutzwärme *f*, Abschirm(ungs)wärme

~ **material**, radiation ~ ~, biological ~ ~ · Abschirm(ungs)(bau)stoff *m*, Strahlenschutz(bau)stoff; Abschirm(ungs)(bau)material *n*, Strahlenschutz(bau)material [*Schweiz*]

~ **tile**, ~ block, biological ~ ~, radiation ~ ~ [*See remark under 'Block'*] · Abschirm(ungs)stein *m*, Strahlenschutzstein, Abschirm(ungs)block(stein) *m*, Strahlenschutzblock(stein)

~ **wall**, biological ~ ~, radiation ~ ~ · Abschirm(ungs)wand *f* [*Zur Abschirmung von Gamma- und Neutronenstrahlen werden Wände aus Beton, Gußeisen, Stahl, Blei, Kunststoff oder Paraffin errichtet*]

shimming plate [*A plate used as a shim for increasing the elevation of a bearing*] · Einstellblech *n*

shingle [*Shingles are small, thin pieces of material, usually thinner at one end than the other. The thicker end is called the butt. They are made of various materials and are used to cover roofs and exterior walls by one shingle's overlapping the other*] · Schindel *f*

~, wood ~ [*A short thin rectangular piece of timber, usually tapering in thickness along the grain, used in the same way as tiles for covering the roofs and sides of buildings*] · (Holz)Schindel *f*, Spitzbrett *n*

~ [*Rounded or water-worn stones (as occurring in open beach formation) and subsequently free from sand, now used to describe any water-worn gravel*] · Rundkies *n*

~ **applicator** · Schindelleger *m*

~ **cover(ing)** · Schindelschirm *m*, Verschindelung *f*

~ **cutter**, ~ cutting machine · Schindelschneider *m* [*Dachpappenanlage*]

~ **hanging** · senkrechtes Verschindeln *n*

shingle nail — shopping centre

~ **nail** · Schindelnagel *m*
~ **roof**, wood(en) ~ ~, (wood(en)) shingled ~ · (Holz)Schindeldach *n*
~ ~ **cladding**, shingled ~ ~, ~ ~ covering, ~ ~ sheathing, ~ roof(ing) · Schindel(dach)(ein)deckung *f*, Schindeldach(belag) *n*, (*m*), Schindelbedachung
~ **stain** [*It preserves and colo(u)rs shingles but does not bring out the grain. Shingle stains are usually oil or spirit stains with creosote oil added as a preservative*] · Schindelbeize *f*
~ **style** · Schindelstil *m* [*Amerikanischer Begriff für den Stil der in den 1870er und 1880er Jahren erbauten Landhäuser*]
~ **wall**, shingled ~ · Schindelwand *f*
shining soot · Glanzruß *m* [*Er bildet sich auf den Schornsteininnenwandungen als schwarzglänzende Schicht aus Ruß in Mischung mit Flugasche und teerigen Bestandteilen unter Einwirkung von Feuchtigkeit*]
~ **through** → translucent
Shinto shrine · Schreinhalle *f*, Shintoschrein *m*
ship-bottom composition → anti-fouling paint
~ **paint** → anti-fouling ~
ship pulpit · Schiffskanzel *f*
shiplap (boards) → rebated (wood(en)) siding
~ **siding**, rabbetted ~, rebated ~ · gefalzter Wandbeschlag *m*, ~ Wandschirm *m*, ~ Wetterschirm, gefalzte Verschalung *f*
~ **(wood(en)) siding**, rebated (~) ~, rabbetted (~) ~, shiplap (boards) · gefälzte (waag(e)rechte) (Bretter-) Schalung *f* [*Wetterschutz für Außenwände*]
shipment [*Abbreviated: shpt. Goods shipped or consigned*] · Lieferung *f*
~, **shipping** · Liefern *n*, Lieferung *f*
~ **drawing** · Lieferungszeichnung *f*
shipping · Auslieferung *f*, Versand *m*
~, **shipment** · Liefern *n*, Lieferung *f*
~ **date**, date of shipment · Liefertermin *m*, Lieferdatum *n*
shirting · Schirting *n* [*Ein weißes, leinenartiges Baumwollgewebe, meist glänzend appretiert, das zur Herstellung von Schildern und zum Überkleben von Rissen in Anstrichuntergründen dient*]
shive · Achel *f*, Agel *f*, Anne *f*, Schäbe *f*, Schebe *f*, Schewe *f* [*Holziger, beim Brechen des Flachses oder Hanfs anfallender Stengelteil. Acheln werden zur Herstellung von Bauplatten und als Füllstoffe für Leichtbauplatten und Gipsdielen verwendet*]
shock load, instantaneous ~, sudden ~, impact ~, impulsive ~ [*An imposed load whose effect is increased due to its sudden application*] · Stoßlast *f*
~ **loading**, instantaneous ~, sudden ~, impact ~, impulsive ~ · Stoßbelastung *f*
shockproof · stoßfest

shoe [*A short length at the foot of a downpipe bent to direct the flow away from the wall*] · Abflußbogen *m* [*DIN 1099*]
shooting, gunning, placing of shotcrete, shotcreting, guniting, concrete-spraying, cement gun work · Auftragen *n* von Spritzbeton, Betonspritzverfahren
shop · Betrieb *m*, Werkstätte *f* [*Eine Erzeugungsstätte jeder Art kleinen, also handwerklichen Umfangs, z.B. für Betonstein*]
~ · Einkaufstätte *f*, Laden *m*
~ **block**, ~ building, work~ ~ · Werkstatthalle *f*
~ **building**, ~ block, work~ ~ · Werkstatthalle *f*
shop(-driven) rivet · Werkstattniet *m*
shop drawing, work~ ~ · Werkstattzeichnung *f*
~ **entrance door** · Ladeneingangstür *f*
~ **fabrication**, work~ ~ · Werkstattfertigung *f*
~ **fitting** · Ladenbau *m*
~ **floor** → ~ story
~ **front**, store ~ · Ladenfront *f*, Schaufensterfront
~ ~ **section**, ~ ~ profile, ~ ~ trim, ~ ~ unit, store ~ ~ · Ladenfrontprofil *n*, Schaufensterfrontprofil
~ **mitre** (Brit.); ~ miter (US) · Werkstattgehrung *f*
~**-painted**, mill-painted, factory-painted · werkgestrichen
shop premise · Ladenlokal *n*
~**-primed**, factory-primed, mill-primed werkgrundiert
shop primer, factory ~ · Fertigungs-Grundanstrichmittel *n*, Fertigungsgrundiermittel, Fertigungsgrund(ierung) *m*, (*f*), Werkgrund(ierung), Werkgrundiermittel, Werkgrundanstrichmittel
~ **priming**, factory ~ · Fertigungsgrundieren *n*, Fertigungsgrundierung *f*, Werk(statt)grundierung, Werk(statt)-grundieren
~ **rivet** → ~-driven ~
shop-riveted · werkstattgenietet
shop story (US); ~ storey (Brit.); ~ floor · Ladengeschoß *n*, Ladenetage *f*, Ladenstockwerk *n*
~ **weld** [*A weld made in a workshop*] · Werkstatt-Schweißstelle *f*
~ **window**, show ~, display ~ · Schaufenster *n*, Ladenfenster
~ ~, work~ ~ · Werkstattfenster *n*
shopping and living complex · Einkaufs- und Wohnanlage *f*
~ **arcade** [*A covered walk between ranges of shops, e.g. the Burlington Arcade in London*] · Ladenarkade *f*, Verkaufsarkade
~ **area** · (Ein)Kaufzone *f*, Ladenzone
~ **block**, ~ building · Ladengebäude *n*
~ **building**, ~ block · Ladengebäude *n*
~ **centre** (Brit.); ~ center (US); block of grouped shops · (Ein)Kaufzentrum *n*, Ladenzentrum

shopping complex — shortening

~ complex → retail ~ ~
~ **hall** · Einkaufhalle f
~ **lane** · Ladengasse f
~ **level** · (Ein)Kaufebene f, Ladenebene
~ **passage(way)** · Ladengang m, Ladenpassage f, Verkaufsgang, Verkaufspassage
~ **square** · Ladenplatz m
~ **street**, ~ parade, business ~, retail ~ ~, shops street, shops parade · Geschäftsstraße f, Ladenstraße, (Ein-)kaufstraße

shops → (retail) shopping complex

to shore · einrüsten

shore [*A temporary support, usually sloping (raking shore), but occasionally horizontal (flying shore), or vertical (dead shore)*] · Baustütze f
~ **asphalt**, land ~, land pitch · Landasphalt m [*Trinidad*]
~ **column**, shoring ~ · Einrüststütze f
~ **gravel**, beach ~ · Strandkies m

Shore hardness · Rücksprunghärte f nach Shore, Skleroskophärte, Shorehärte
~ ~ **scale** · Shore-Härteskala f
~ (~) **test** · Fallhärteprobe f nach Shore, Fallhärteprüfung f ~ ~, Fallhärteversuch m ~ ~, Rückprall(härte)prüfung ~ ~, Rückprall(härte)versuch ~ ~, Rückprall(härte)probe ~ ~
~ ~ **testing method** · Shore-Verfahren n

shore sand, beach ~ · Strandsand m

Shore scleroscope · Shore-Rücksprunghärteprüfer m

shoring · Einrüstung f, Abstützung
~ **column**, shore ~ · Einrüststütze f
~ **system** · Abstützkonstruktion f, Einrüstkonstruktion
~ **up** · Abstützen n [*Gebäude*]

short (bath)tub, ~ bath · Kurz(bade)wanne f

short-continued behaviour (Brit.); ~ behavior (US); short-time ~, short-term ~ · Kurzzeitverhalten n
~ **load**, short-term ~, short-time ~ · Kurzzeitlast f
~ **loading** → short-term ~
~ **static load**, short-term ~ ~, short-time ~ ~ · kurzfristige statische Last f, statische kurzfristige ~

short cross garnet, ~ tee hinge · Kurzband n [*Es ist kürzer als ⅓ der Türflügelbreite*]
~ **cut**, ~ method [*In an arithmetical operation*] · Rechenvorteil m
~ **cylindrical shell** · Kurzzylinderschale f
~ **end**, narrow side · Schmalseite f
~ **fibred** (Brit.); ~ fibered (US) · kurzfas(e)rig

~ **glass**, quick-setting ~, fast-setting ~ · kurzes Glas n

short-lived material · kurzlebiger Werkstoff m

short method, ~ cut [*In an arithmetical operation*] · Rechenvorteil m

short-oil [*A low ratio of oil to resin in a medium*] · mager [*Anstrichfarbe*]

short oil alkyd resin · kurzöliges Alkydharz n, mageres ~
~ ~ **linsed oil alkyd** · kurzöliges Leinölalkyd n, mageres ~
~ ~ **varnish**, ~ oleo-resinous ~ · magerer Öllack m, kurzöliger ~
~ **oleo-resinous varnish**, ~ oil ~ · magerer Öllack m, kurzöliger ~
~ **ramp** · Anlauf m [*kurze Rampe*]
~ **range aggregate aerated concrete**, uniform ~ ~, single-sized ~ ~, like-grained ~ ~, equigranular ~ ~, even-grained ~ ~ · einkörniger Porenbeton m, gleichkörniger ~, Einkorn-Porenbeton
~ ~ ~ **concrete**, like-grained ~, uniform ~, single-sized ~, equigranular ~, even-grained ~ · Einkornbeton m, einkörniger Beton, gleichkörniger Beton [*DIN 4163*]
~ ~ ~ **mortar** → like-grained ~

short-span barrel vault, ~ tunnel ~, ~ wagon ~ · Kurzspanntonnengewölbe n
~ **roof** · Kurzspanndach n
~ **structure** · Kurzspannweitenbauwerk n

short splice · Kurzspleiß m
~ **tee hinge**, ~ cross garnet · Kurzband n [*Es ist kürzer als ⅓ der Türflügelbreite*]

short-term behaviour (Brit.); ~ behavior (US); short-time ~, short-continued ~ · Kurzzeitverhalten n
~ **load**, short-time ~, short-continued ~ · Kurzzeitlast f
~ **loading**, short-time ~, short-continued ~ · kurzfristige Belastung f
~ **static load**, short-time ~ ~, short-continued ~ ~ · kurzfristige statische Last f

short-time behaviour (Brit.); ~ behavior (US); short-term ~, short-continued ~ · Kurzzeitverhalten n
~ **load**, short-continued ~, short-term ~ · Kurzzeitlast f
~ **loading** → short-term ~
~ **static load**, short-term ~ ~, short-continued ~ ~ · kurzfristige statische Last f

shortage, deficiency · Mangel m, Fehlbedarf m, Klemme f
~ **of water**, deficiency ~ ~, water shortage, water deficiency · Wassermangel m, Wasserfehlbedarf m, Wasserklemme f

shortening, negative elongation · negative Dehnung f, Verkürzung

'shorting' — shrinkage ratio

'shorting' · akustischer Kurzschluß *m*
shot concrete · Schrotbeton *m*
shotcrete → sprayed(-on) concrete
~, air-blown mortar, pneumatically applied mortar, sprayed mortar [*Mortar conveyed through a hose and projected at high velocity onto a surface*] · Spritzmörtel *m*, Gebläsemörtel
~ facing → ~ sur~
~ hose · Spritzbetonschlauch *m*, Betonspritzschlauch, Gebläsebetonschlauch
~ lining, ~ (sur)facing · Spritzbetonauskleidung *f*, Spritzbetonverkleidung, Spritzbetonbekleidung, Gebläsebetonauskleidung, Gebläsebetonverkleidung, Gebläsebetonbekleidung
~ operation · Spritzbetonbetrieb *m*, Gebläsebetonbetrieb
~ (sur)facing, ~ lining · Spritzbetonauskleidung *f*, Spritzbetonverkleidung, Spritzbetonbekleidung, Gebläsebetonaskleidung, Gebläsebetonverkleidung, Gebläsebetonbekleidung
shotcreting → shooting
shot lead · Schrotblei *n*
shoulder → (masonry) corbel
~ [*An unintentional offset in a formed concrete surface usually caused by bulging or movement of formwork*] · Absatz *m*
~ nipple, barrel ~ · Doppelnippel *m*
~ stud, collar ~ · Rundbolzen *m*
shouldered arch · Schulterbogen *m*, Konsolbogen [*Ein scheitrechter Bogen mit Stelzung über Kreissegmenten am Bogenanfang; zu unterscheiden vom Kragsturzbogen*]
show cabinet, display ~, ~ case, silent salesman · Schaukasten *m*, Vitrine *f*
~ case, display ~, ~ cabinet, silent salesman · Schaukasten *m*, Vitrine *f*
shower · Dusche *f*
~ bath · Duschbad *n*
~ ~ partition (wall) · Duschtrennwand *f*
~ column · Duschsäule *f*
~ control · Duschensteuerung *f*
~ cubicle · Duschkabine *f*
~ ~ · Schrankdusche *f*
~ curtain · Duschvorhang *m*
~ head · Duschkopf *m*
~ hose · Duschschlauch *m*
~ installation · Duschanlage *f*
showermixer, blending mixer, blender, mixer (valve), mixing valve · Badbatterie *f*, Mischbatterie
shower receptor, ~ tray · Duschwanne *f*, Duschtasse *f*, Dusch-Badewanne
~ recess · Duschnische *f*, Duschzelle *f*
~ room · Duschraum *m*
~ ~ without cubicles · Massendusche *f* [*Duschraum ohne Zelleneinteilung*]
~ set, ~ unit · Duschgarnitur *f*
~ stall · Duschstand *m*
~ tray, ~ receptor · Duschwanne *f*, Duschtasse *f*, Dusch-Badewanne
~ unit, ~ set · Duschgarnitur *f*
~ valve · Duschventil *n*
~ wall · Duschwand *f*
show metal sheet → fancy sheet metal
showroom · Ausstellungsraum *m*
show sheet metal → fancy ~ ~
show-through [*Unevenness of the surface of a particle board panel faced with thin veneer, usually associated with irregularities in the surface of the board and particularly visible after polishing. Not to be confused with scratches or accidental damage, or defects in polishing the veneer*] · Durchzeichnung *f*
show window, display ~, shop ~ · Schaufenster *n*, Ladenfenster
shrended cullet (US) → quenched ~ (Brit.)
shrine [*A sacred place or object, e.g. a receptacle for relics*] · Schrein *m*
shrinkage [*Volume decrease caused by drying and chemical changes; a function of time but not of temperature or of stress due to external load*] · Schwinden *n*, Schwindung *f*
~ anchoring · Schwindverankerung *f*
~ bar, ~ rod · Schwindbewehrungsstab *m*, Schwindarmierungsstab
~ behaviour (Brit.); ~ behavior (US) · Schwindverhalten *n*
~ coefficient · Schwindbeiwert *m*
shrinkage-compensating [*A characteristic of grout, mortar, or concrete made using an expansive cement in which volume increase if restrained, induces compressive stresses which are intended to approximately offset the tendency of drying shrinkage to induce tensile stresses*] · schwindausgleichend
~ cement · schwindungsausgleichender Quellzement *m*, schwindungskompensierender ~, ~ Expansivzement, ~ Schnellzement, ~ Dehnzement
shrinkage crack · Schwindriß *m*
~ cracking · Schwindrißbildung *f*, Schwindrissebildung
~ curve, ~ line · Schwindkurve *f*
~ deformation · Schwindformänderung *f*, Schwindverformung
~ difference, differential shrinkage · Schwindunterschied *m*
~ force · Schwindkraft *f*
~ limit, SL · Schwindgrenze *f*
~ line, ~ curve · Schwindkurve *f*
~ loss [*The loss of stress in the (pre-)stressing steel resulting from the shrinkage of the concrete*] · (Vor)Spann(ungs)verlust *m* infolge Schwindens
~ ratio, SR, SI · Schwindindex *m*, Schwindverhältnis *n*

~ **reinforcement** · Schwindarmierung f, Schwindbewehrung Schwind(stahl)einlagen fpl

~ **rod** → ~ bar

~ **shortening** · Schwindverkürzung f

~ **stress** · Schwindspannung f

~ **tendency** · Schwindneigung f

~ **tensile stress** · Schwindzugspannung f

~ **test** · Schwindprobe f, Schwindprüfung f, Schwindversuch m

~ **value** · Schwindmaß n, Schwindzahl f

shrink-mixed concrete [*Ready-mixed concrete mixed partially in a stationary mixer and then mixed in a truckmixer*] · nachgemischter Beton m

shrink-proof · schwindfest

(sh)rivelling → crinkling

SH-10 glass cement · Glaszement SH-10 m [*Markenname*]

shuff · rissiger Ziegel m ohne Klang

shut-off unit · Absperrorgan n, Absperrvorrichtung f

shutter [*e.g. a rolling shutter*] · (Raum-)Abschluß m

~ [*A mov(e)able closure to an opening installed in place of or in addition to a door or window for security purposes to control the admission of heat or light, or to delay the spread of fire or smoke*] · beweglicher Abschluß m

~ **window** ~

~ **curtain** · Panzer m [*Rolltor*]

~ **door**, shutterdoor · Tor n

~ ~ **aperture**, ~ ~ **opening** · lichter Durchgang m, Toröffnung f, Torloch n

~ ~ **guide**, shutterdoor ~ · Torführung f

~ ~ **height**, shutterdoor ~ · Torhöhe f

~ ~ **leaf**, shutterdoor ~ · Torflügel m

~ ~ **lintel**, shutterdoor ~ · Torsturz m

~ ~ **opening**, ~ ~ **aperture** · lichter Durchgang m, Toröffnung f, Torloch n

~ ~ **operation**, shutterdoor ~ · Torbedienung f, Torbetätigung, Torbetrieb m

~ ~ **operator**, shutterdoor ~ · Torantrieb(vorrichtung) m, (f)

shutter doorway, ~ **door aperture**, ~ **door opening** · Toröffnung f, Torloch n, lichter Durchgang m

~ **for large building(s)** [*e.g. for an aircraft hangar*] · Großraumabschluß m

~ **lath** → ~ slat

~ **leaf** · Abschlußblatt n

~ **slat**, ~ **lath**, (curtain) ~ · (Abschluß-)Lamelle f

shuttered floor · eingeschalte Decke f

shuttering → concrete ~

~ **agent**, forms ~, form(work) ~, release ~, form(work) sealer, forms sealer, shuttering sealer · (Ent)Schal(ungs)mittel n, (Ent)Schal(ungs)hilfe f, Ausschal(ungs)mittel, Ausschal(ungs)hilfe

~ **aid**, form(work) ~, forms ~ · Schal(ungs)hilfsmittel n

~ **board**, form(work) ~, forms ~ · Schal(ungs)brett n

~ ~, ~ **sheet**, forms ~, form(work) ~ · Schal(ungs)platte f

~ **lining**, form(work) ~, forms ~, ~ (sur)facing [*The material forming the contact face of forms*] · Schal(ungs)auskleidung f, Schal(ungs)bekleidung, Schal(ungs)verkleidung

~ **lube**, ~ **oil**, form(work) ~, forms ~, release ~ · (Ent)Schal(ungs)öl n, Ausschal(ungs)öl

~ **oil** → ~ lube

~ **paint**, form(work) ~, forms ~ · Schal(ungs)farbe f

~ **panel**, form(work) ~, forms ~ · Schal(ungs)tafel f

~ **paste**, release ~, form(work) ~, forms ~ · Schal(ungs)paste f, Ent~

~ **plate**, form(work) ~, forms ~ · Schal(ungs)blech n

~ **poured-in-situ (solid) floor** · selbstschalende Vollbetondecke f

~ **removal**, form(work) ~, forms ~, stripping, release · Ausschalung f, Entschalung

~ **sealer**, form(work) ~, forms ~, ~ **agent**, release agent · (Ent)Schal(ungs)mittel n, (Ent)Schal(ungs)hilfe f, Ausschal(ungs)mittel, Ausschal(ungs)hilfe

~ **sheet**, ~ **board**, form(work) ~, forms ~ · Schal(ungs)platte f

~ **sheet(ing)**, form(work) ~, forms ~ · Schal(ungs)folie f aus Kunststoff

~ **tie**, forms ~, (form(work)) ~, **tie rod** · Schal(ungs)anker m

~ **wax**, release ~, form(work) ~, forms ~ · Schal(ungs)wachs n, Ent~

shutteringless, formworkless · schalungsfrei, schalungslos

shuttle traffic · Pendelverkehr m, Pendelwanderung f

SI, SR, shrinkage ratio · Schwindindex m, Schwindverhältnis n

siccative; soluble drier, liquid drier (US) · Sikkativ n, Trockenstoff m in gelöster Form [*DIN 55901*]

Sicilian marble, Carrara ~ [*It was called 'marmor lunense' in ancient Rome*] · Carraramarmor m

sickle-shaped, crescent · sichelförmig

~ **oblique rib**, crescent ~ ~ · sichelförmige Schrägrippe f

~ **roof**, crescent ~ · sichelförmiges Dach n

sickroom, ward patient's room · Bettenraum m, Bettenzimmer n, Krankenraum, Krankenzimmer

side [*As opposed to the end*] · Längsseite f

(~) aisle, nave ~, ele, eling [*A lateral division parallel with the nave in a basilica or church*] · (Seiten)Schiff n, Abseite f

(~) ~ **bay**, nave ~ ~ · (Seiten)Schiffjoch(feld), Abseitenjoch(feld), (Seiten)Schiffeld, Abseitenfeld

(~) ~ **gallery**, nave ~ ~ · Abseitenempore f, (Seiten)Schiffempore

(~) ~ **aisleless**, nave ~ · abseitenlos, (seiten)schifflos

(~) ~ **church** · Saalkirche f, einschiffige Kirche [*Eine Kirche ohne Seitenschiff(e)*]

(~) ~ **aisle passage**, nave ~ ~ · Abseitengang m, (Seiten)Schiffgang

(~) ~ **pier**, nave ~ ~ · (Seiten)Schiffpfeiler m, Abseitenpfeiler

(~) ~ **roof**, nave ~ ~ · Abseitendach n, (Seiten)Schiffdach

(~) ~ **aisle-vault**, nave ~ · (Seiten)Schiffgewölbe n, Abseitengewölbe

(~) ~ **aisle wall**, nave ~ ~ · Schiffwand f, Seiten~, Abseitenwand

(~) ~ (~) **window**, nave ~ (~) ~ · (Seiten)Schiffenster n, Abseitenfenster

(~) ~ **window** → (~) ~ wall ~

~ **altar**, subordinate ~ · Seitenaltar m, Nebenaltar [*Altar neben dem Hochaltar, meist zu beiden Seiten des Langhausabschlusses oder am Ostende der Seitenschiffe*]

~ **arch**, lateral ~ · Seitenbogen m

side/bottom hung sash · Drehkipp(fenster)flügel m

~ ~ ~ **window** · Drehkipp(flügel)fenster n

~ **sash fitting** · Drehkippbeschlag m

side branch → ~ pipe ~

~ **chamber** · Seitenraum m

~ **channel** · Seiten-U-Eisen n

~ **chapel**, lateral ~ · Seitenkapelle f, Einsatzkapelle

~ **cleat** → ~ metal ~

~ **column** · Seitenstütze f

side-construction tile [*The cells are placed horizontally*] · Längslochblock(stein) m, Längslochstein

side core, one-sided ~ · seitlicher Kern m

~ **corridor** · Seitenflur m, Seitenkorridor m, Seitengang m

~ **daylight illumination**, ~ natural lighting, ~ (day)lighting, window-lighting · Seitentages(licht)beleuchtung f, Fenster-Tages(licht)beleuchtung [*Fehlnamen: Fenster(-Tages)belichtung, Seitenbelichtung*]

~ **(day)lighting**, ~ natural lighting, ~ daylight illumination, window-lighting · Seitentages(licht)beleuchtung f, Fenster-Tages(licht)beleuchtung [*Fehlnamen: Fenster(-Tages)belichtung, Seitenbelichtung*]

~ **door** · Seitentür f

~ **effect** · Nebenwirkung f

~ **elevation**, lateral ~ · Seiten(auf)riß m [*Seitenansicht eines Bauwerkes in Normalprojektion*]

~ **entrance** · Nebeneingang m

side-entry luminaire (fixture) (US); ~ light fitting (Brit.); ~ (light(ing)) fixture · (Mast)Ansatzleuchte f

side fitting, ~ hardware item · Nur-Drehbeschlag m [*Drehkippfenster*]

(~) **footway** · Seitenpforte f, Fußgängerpforte [*in einem Stadttor*]

~ **gallery** · Seitenempore f, Seitengalerie f

~ **groove** · Seitenfalz m [*(Dach)Falzstein*]

~ **hardware item**, ~ fitting · Nur-Drehbeschlag m [*Drehkippfenster*]

~ **hinge** · Seitenscharnier n

~ **hung opening window** · Drehflügelfenster n

side inlet → ~ pipe ~

~ **joint**, vertical ~, perpendicular ~; cross ~ (Brit.); (head) ~, build (US) · Stoßfuge f [*Mauerwerk*]

~ **junction** → ~ pipe ~

~ **lap** · Seitenüberdeckung f, seitliche Überdeckung

~ ~ **(width)** · Seitenüberdeckung(sbreite) f [*Dachfalzstein*]

~ **light** · Seitenlicht n

~ **masonry wall**, flank ~ ~, lateral ~ ~, end ~ ~ · Seitenmauer f, Stirnmauer [*Fehlname: Giebelmauer*]

~ **(metal) cleat** · Leistenhafter m [*Metallbedachung. Für den seitlichen Halt*]

~ **natural lighting**, ~ daylight illumination, ~ (day)lighting, window-lighting · Seitentages(licht)beleuchtung f, Fenster-Tages(licht)beleuchtung [*Fehlnamen: Fenster(-Tages)belichtung, Seitenbelichtung*]

~ **of force polygon** · Polygonalseite f des Kräftezuges, Vieleckseite ~ ~, Kraftecksseite

~ **opening** · Seitenöffnung f [*Triumphbogen*]

~ **patio**, ~ terrace · Seitenterrasse f

~ **(pipe) branch**, ~ (~) inlet, ~ (~) junction, oblique-angled (pipe) junction · (Rohr)Seitenabzweig m, (Rohr)Seitenzulauf m, einfach schräger (Rohr)Abzweig, einfach schräger (Rohr)Zulauf

~ **(~) inlet**, ~ (~) branch, ~ (~) junction, oblique-angled (pipe) junction · (Rohr)Seitenabzweig m, (Rohr-)Seitenzulauf m, einfach schräger (Rohr-)Abzweig, einfach schräger (Rohr)Zulauf

~ **(pipe) junction**, ~ (~) inlet, ~ (~) branch, oblique-angled (pipe) junction · (Rohr)Seitenabzweig m, (Rohr)Seitenzulauf m, einfach schräger (Rohr-)Abzweig, einfach schräger (Rohr)Zulauf

~ **plot line**, ~ property ~ · seitliche Grundstücksgrenze f

~ **portal** · Seitenportal n

~ **property line**, ~ plot ~ · seitliche Grundstücksgrenze f

~ **ratio** · Seitenverhältnis n

siderite — silcrete

siderite [*iron carbonate, FeCO₃*] · Siderit *m*

side-scroll, side-volute · Giebelschnecke *f*, Giebelvolute *f*

side shift(ing) · Seitenverschiebung *f*

~ steel facing → ~ ~ lining

~ ~ lining, vertical ~ ~, ~ ~ (sur-)facing · Stahl-Außen(wand)auskleidung *f*, Stahl-Außen(wand)verkleidung, Stahl-Außen(wand)bekleidung

~ ~ (sur)facing → ~ ~ lining

~ street · Seitenstraße *f*, Nebenstraße

sidesway, horizontal translation · Horizontalverschiebung *f*, Waag(e)rechtverschiebung

side terrace, ~ patio · Seitenterrasse *f*

~ thrust, lateral ~, outward ~ · (Seiten)Schub *m* [*Waag(e)rechte Resultierende einer Gewölbekraft*]

~ tower · Seitenturm *m*

~ track · Seitenführungsschiene *f*

~ transept(al) portal · Querhausseitenportal *n*

~ view · Seitenansicht *f*

side-volute, side-scroll · Giebelschnecke *f*, Giebelvolute *f*

sidewalk concrete flag(stone), ~ ~ paving flag (US); footpath concrete flag(stone), footpath concrete paving flag (Brit.); ~ (pre)cast concrete flag [*B.S. 368*] · Bürgersteig-Betonplatte *f*, Beton-Bürgersteigplatte, Gehsteig-Betonplatte, Beton-Gehsteigplatte, Gehweg-Betonplatte, Beton-Gehwegplatte, Gehbahn-Betonplatte, Beton-Gehbahnplatte, Beton-Fußwegplatte, Fußweg-Betonplatte

~ ~ paving flag (US) → ~ ~ flag(stone)

~ flag (US) → ~ paving ~

~ ~ of basalt(ic) chip(ping)s concrete (US); footpath ~ ~ ~ ~ ~ (Brit.) · Basaltsplittplatte *f* [*Beton-Bürgersteigplatte aus Basaltsplitt und Portlandzement*]

~ flagstone (US) → (natural) stone sidewalk (paving) flag

~ kiosk · Straßenkiosk *m*

~ (paving) flag (US); footpath (~) ~ (Brit.); ~ flagstone · Bürgersteigplatte *f*, Gehbahnplatte, Gehwegplatte, Fußsteigplatte, Fußwegplatte, Gehsteigplatte

~ teller · Bürgersteigschalter *m* [*Bank*]

side wall, lateral ~, end ~, flank ~ · Stirnwand *f*, Seitenwand [*Fehlname: Giebelwand*]

sideways load · seitlich angreifende Last *f*

side window · Seitenfenster *n*

~ wing · Seitenflügel *m*, Seitentrakt *m*

siding · Wandschirm *m*, Wandbeschlag *m*, Wetterschirm, Verschalung *f* [*Wetterschutz für Außenmauern*]

~ (US) → weatherboarding

~ material · Wandbeschlagbaustoff *m*, Wetterschirmbaustoff, Wandschirmbaustoff

~ shake → hand cleft (wood) siding shingle

~ shingle · Wandschindel *f*

~ (wood) shake → hand cleft (wood) siding shingle

Siegwart floor [*This is made up of hollow (pre)cast reinforced concrete beams, set beside each other and formed into a single slab by grouting. A reinforcement is laid over the tops of the beams and covered with a thin layer of mortar. The sides of the beams have channels cut in them to serve as a key for the bonding mortar*] · Siegwartdecke *f*

sienna · (Terra *f* di) Siena *f*

Sierra Leone copal · Sierra Leone-Kopal *m*

sieve analysis · Siebanalyse *f*, Siebversuch *m*, Siebprobe *f*, Prüfen *n* der Kornzusammensetzung durch Siebversuch

~ curve, grain-size distribution ~, particle-size distribution ~, (aggregate) grading ~ · Siebkurve *f*, Sieblinie *f*, Körnungslinie, Körnungskurve, Kornverteilungskurve, Kornverteilungslinie

~ hole size · Sieblochgröße *f*

~ number, mesh ~ · (Sieb)Gewebenummer *f*

~ residue, oversize · Rückstand *m*, Überlauf *m*, Überkorn *n*, Sieb~ [*Prüfsieb*]

~ ~ percentage, oversize ~ · Überkornanteil *m*, Überlaufanteil

sight, tourist attraction · Sehenswürdigkeit *f*

~ glass [*A glass tube used to indicate the liquid condition and level in pipes, tanks, bearings, and similar equipment*] · Schauglas *n*

sightseeing flight counter · Rundflugschalter *m*

signalling line · Signalleitung *f*

signboard, (merchant's) mark · Hausmarke *f*, Hauszeichen *n* [*Figürliches oder geometrisches Symbol zur Kennzeichnung eines Hauses, früher meist am Schlußstein der Eingangstür angebracht. Nach der Hausmarke wurden früher die Häuser benannt (Hausname z.B. „zum Schwanen"), auch wenn es keine Gasthäuser waren. Die Hausmarke ersetzte die moderne Ordnungsnummer*]

~ · Aushängeschild *n*

sign convention · Vorzeichenannahme *f*

Sika-1 · Sesquisol *n*, Sika 1 *n*

sikhara, spire-shaped · Nagara *m*, Sikhara *m* [*Turm über der Cella eines nordindischen Tempels*]

~ of the Great Temple at Tanjore · Tempelturm *m* von Tanjore

silcrete · Silcret *m* [*Quarzit. Bezeichnet insbesondere ein titanreiches südafrikanisches Vorkommen*]

silent salesman, display cabinet, show cabinet, show case, display case · Schaukasten *m*, Vitrine *f*

Silesian (masonry) bond · schlesischer Verband *m* [*In allen Schichten wechseln je ein Kopf und drei Läufer einander ab. Es sind verschiedene Muster möglich*]

silica brick → gannister ~

~ **cement** · kieselsäurehaltiger Zement *m* [*Bindemittel beim Quarzit*]

~ ~, ~ **mortar** · Silikamörtel *m*, Silikazement *m* [*Ein Feuerzement zum Einsetzen feuerfester Steine in Feuerungsanlagen u.ä.*]

~ **dust**, siliceous ~, silicious ~ · Quarzmehl *n*, Quarzstaub *m*, Quarzpulver *n*

~ **fine sand**, ~ sand fines · Quarzfeinsand *m*

~ **gel** · Kiesel(säure)gel *n*, Silika-Gel, aktive Kieselsäure *f*

~ **glass**, quartz ~, vitreous silica, fused silica, fused quartz [*A vitreous material consisting almost entirely of silica, made in translucent and transparent forms. The former has minute gas bubbles disseminated in it*] · Quarzglas *n* [*Fehlname*]; Kiesel(säure)glas

~ **material** · Silikastoff *m*

~ **mortar**, ~ cement · Silikamörtel *m*, Silikazement *m* [*Ein Feuerzement zum Einsetzen feuerfester Steine in Feuerungsanlagen u.ä.*]

~ **refractory** · Silikaerzeugnis *n*

~ **sand**, siliceous ~, silicious ~ · kieselsäurehaltiger Sand *m*, Quarzsand, Kieselsand

~ ~ **fines**, ~ fine sand · Quarzfeinsand *m*

~ **sandstone** · Quarzsandstein *m*

silicate coat · Silikatanstrich *m*, Silikataufstrich

~ **concrete** · Kalksandbeton *m*, Silikatbeton

~ **cotton**, slag wool · Hüttenwolle *f* [*Fehlname: Schlackenwolle*]

~ ~ **block**, slag wool ~ · Hüttenwollestein *m* [*Fehlname: Schlackenwollestein*]

~ ~ **covering cord**, slag wool ~ ~ · Hüttenwolleschnur *f* [*Fehlname: Schlackenwolleschnur*]

~ ~ **felt**, slag wool ~ · Hüttenwollefilz *m* [*Fehlname: Schlackenwollefilz*]

~ ~ **insulation**, slag wool ~ · Hüttenwolle(ab)dämmung *f* [*Fehlname: Schlackenwolle(ab)dämmung*]

~ **ester** · Silikatester *m*

~ **filler** · Silikatfüller *m*

silicate-forming matter · Hydraulefaktor *m*, Silikatbildner *m*, Wasserbildner

silicate glass · Silikatglas *n*

~ **injection** · Silikatauspressung *f*, Silikatverpressung, Silikateinpressung, Silikatinjektion *f*

~ **melt** · Silikatschmelze *f*

~ **(mineral)** · Silikat *n*

~ **of magnesium**, magnesium silicate · $3\,SiO_3Mg \cdot SH_2O$, Magnesiumsilikat *n*

~ ~ **soda**, sodium silicate, soluble glass, waterglass · Natriumsilikat *n*, Natronwasserglas *n*, Na_2SIO_3

~ **paint**, water glass ~ [*Containing silicate of soda; may be made with aluminous cement, but not with portland cement*] · Silikatfarbe *f*, S.-Farbe, Wasserglasfarbe, Mineralfarbe

~ ~ **coat**, water glass ~ ~ · Wasserglasfarbanstrich *m*, Silikatfarbanstrich, Mineralfarbanstrich, Wasserglasfarbaufstrich, Silikatfarbaufstrich, Mineralfarbaufstrich

~ **slag** · Silikatschlacke *f*

~ **solution** · Silikatlösung *f*

siliceous, silicious ~ · kiesel(halt)ig

~ **aggregate** → ~ concrete ~

~ **(concrete) aggregate**, silicious (~) ~ · kieselsäurehaltiger (Beton)Zuschlag(stoff) *m*

~ **dust**, silicious ~, silica ~ · Quarzmehl *n*, Quarzstaub *m*, Quarzpulver *n*

~ **limestone**, silicious ~ · verkieselter Kalk(stein) *m*, kieseliger ~, Kieselkalk(stein)

~ **melt**, silicious ~ · Quarzschmelze *f*

~ **refractory (product)**, silicious ~ (~) · hochsaures Schamotteerzeugnis *n*

~ **sand**, silicious ~, silica ~ · kieselsäurehaltiger Sand *m*, Quarzsand, Kieselsand

~ **sandstone**, silicious ~ · kiesel(halt)iger Sandstein *m*

(~) **sinter**, silicious ~, geyserite · (Kiesel)Sinter *m*

~ **sponge**, silicious ~ · Kieselschwamm *m*

~ **volcanic rock**, silicious ~ ~, naturally occurring ~ ~ ~, volcanic glass (-like material) · vulkanisches Glas *n*, Naturglas, glasartig erstarrtes vulkanisches Gestein *n*

silicic · kieselsauer

silicid refractory (product) · feuerfestes Silizidzeugnis *n*, ff. ~

silicification [*The process of becoming silicified, conversion into silica*] · Verkieselung *f*

silicified [*Converted into silica*] · verkieselt

to silicify · verkieseln

silicofluoride · Silikofluorid *n*

silicon · Si *n*, Silizium *n*

~ **bronze** · Siliziumbronze *f*

~ **carbide**, carbide of silicon, carbon silicide · SiC *n*, Karborund *n*, Siliziumkarbid *n*, Siliziumkohlenstoff *m* [*Synthetisches Erzeugnis mit der Formel SiC. Das industriell hergestellte Produkt kann Verunreinigungen enthalten*]

silicon carbide brick — sillimanite

~ ~ **brick**, carbon silicide ~, carbide of silicon ~ · Siliziumkarbidstein *m*, Ka-r borundstein, Siliziumkohlenstoffstein, SiC-Stein

~ ~ **mortar**, carbon silicide ~, carbide of silicon ~ · Siliziumkarbidmörtel *m*, Karborundmörtel, Siliziumkohlenstoffmörtel, SiC-Mörtel

~ ~ **refractory (product)**, carbon silicide ~ (~), ~ ~ ~ material · Siliziumkarbiderzeugnis *n*, Karborunderzeugnis, Siliziumkohlenstofferzeugnis, SIC-Erzeugnis

~ ~ **slab**, carbon silicide ~, carbide of silicon ~ · Siliziumkarbidplatte *f*, Karborundplatte, Siliziumkohlenstoffplatte, SiC-Platte

~ **chloride** (Brit.); ~ chlorid(e) (US) · Kieselchlorid *n*

~ **iron** · Ferrosilizium *n*

~ ~ **sheet** · Ferrosiliziumblech *n*

silicone [*Silicones are a group of synthetic, semi-organic polymers (polysiloxanes) composed of silicon, carbon, hydrogen and oxygen*] · Silikon *n*

~ **base** · Silikonbasis *f*, Silikongrundlage *f*

~**(-based) waterproof(ing) coating (material)**, ~ waterproofing (compound), ~ (water-)repellent (admix(-ture)), ~ water-proofer, ~ (water-)repeller, ~ water-proof(ing) agent, ~ (water-)repelling agent · Silikon-Bautenschutz(mittel) *m*, (*n*), Silikon-Wetterschutz(mittel), Silikon(-Fassaden)imprägnier(ungs)mittel, Silikonimprägnierung *f* [*Farbloses Imprägnier(ungs)mittel für Stein- und Zementbauteile*]

~ **coat** · Silikonanstrich *m*, Silikonaufstrich

~ **ester** · Silikonester *m*, Äthylsilikat *n*

~ **fluid** · Silikonöl *n*, öliges Silikon *n*

~ **grease** · Silikonfett *n*

~**-modified** · silikonmodifiziert

silicone paint · Silikon(anstrich)farbe *f*

~ **paste** · Silikonpaste *f*

~ **primer** · Silikongrundanstrichmittel *n*, Silikongrundiermittel, Silikongrund(ierung) *m*, (*f*), Silikongrundanstrichstoff *m*, Silikongrundierstoff

~ **proofer**, ~ protective agent, ~ protection agent · Silikon-Schutzmittel *n*

~ **protection agent**, ~ protective ~, ~ proofer · Silikon-Schutzmittel *n*

~ **protective agent**, ~ protection ~, ~ proofer · Silikon-Schutzmittel *n*

~ **repellent (admix(ture))** → silicone(-based) waterproof(ing) coating (material)

~ **repeller** → silicone(-based) waterproof(ing) coating (material)

~ **repelling agent** → silicone(-based) waterproof(ing) coating (material)

~ **resin** · Silikonharz *n*

~ ~ **emulsion** · Silikonharzemulsion *f*

~ ~ **solution** · Silikonharzlösung *f*

~ **rubber** · Silikonkautschuk *m*, kautschukartiges Silikon *n*

~ ~ **sealant** · Silikonkautschuk(ab)-dicht(ungs)mittel *n*

~ ~ **seal(ing) composition**, ~ ~ ~ compound, ~ ~ ~ ~ material, ~ ~ ~ mass · Silikonkautschuk-(Ab)Dicht-(ungs)masse *f*

~ ~ **seal(ing) compound** → ~ ~ ~ composition

~ ~ ~ **mass** → ~ ~ ~ ~ composition

~ ~ ~ **material** → ~ ~ ~ ~ composition

~ **solution** · Silikonlösung *f*

~ **tape** · Silikonband *n*

~ **waterproofer** → silicone(-based) waterproof(ing) coating (material)

~ **waterproof(ing) agent** → silicone(-based) waterproof(ing) coating (material)

~ **(water)repeller** → silicone(-based) waterproof(ing) coating (material)

~ **(water-)repellent (admix(ture))** → silicone(-based) waterproof(ing) coating (material)

~ **(water)repelling agent** → silicone(-based) waterproof(ing) coating (material)

silk → long glass fibres

~ **exchange at Valencia**, Lonja de la Seda ~ ~ · Seidenbörse *f* zu Valencia

~ **gauze**, fine silk mesh · Seidengaze *f*

silkscreen method, ~ printing, ~ process [*Sometimes also called 'serigraphy'. A decorating process in which a design is printed on glass through a silk mesh or similar screen*] · Siebdruck-(verfahren) *m*, (*n*)

silk shavings · Seidenstaub *m* [*Velourstapete*]

~ **wall cover(ing)** → (glass) silk wall lining

~ ~ **lining** → (glass) ~ ~ ~

~ ~ **(sur)facing** → (glass) silk wall lining

sill → window ~

~, sole plate (Brit.); (a)butment piece (US); cill [*deprecated*] (Brit.) [*The lowest horizontal member of a framed partition, or frame construction*] · Schwelle *f*, Holz~ [*Beim Holzfachwerk der untere waag(e)rechte Balken der Riegelwand*]

~, threshold; saddle (US) [*A horizontal timber at the foot of an outside door*] · (Holz)(Tür)Schwelle *f*

~ **block** → window ~ ~

~ **cover** → window ~ ~

~ **(head) height** → window ~ (~) ~

~ **rail** → window ~ ~ ~

~ **tile** → (window) sill block

sillimanite · Sillimanit *m* [*Eines der drei Minerale, die die gleiche Formel $Al_2O_3 \cdot SiO_2$ haben, jedoch in ihrer Struktur*

sillimanite — simple plate

verschieden sind. In Erweiterung dient dieser Ausdruck auch zur Bezeichnung des Gesteins (Rohstoffs)]

~ **brick** · Sillimanitstein *m*

~ **refractory material,** ~ ~ (product) *[A refractory material made from one of the sillimanite group of minerals]* · Sillimaniterzeugnis *n*

silo · Silo *m, n*

~ **bin,** ~ hopper, ~ compartment · Silotasche *f*, Silozelle *f*, Silotrichter *m*, Speicherzelle

~ **block,** ~ tile *[See remark under 'Block']* · Siloblock(stein) *m*, Silostein

~ **bottom** · Siloboden *m*

~ **coating plastic** · Silokunststoff *m [zur Innenbeschichtung von Silos]*

~ **compartment,** ~ hopper, ~ bin · Silotasche *f*, Silozelle *f*, Silotrichter *m*, Speicherzelle

~ **construction** · Silobau *m*

~ **discharge** · Siloentleerung *f*

~ **drawing channel** · Siloabzugrinne *f*

~ **heating** · Silobeheizung *f*

~ **hopper,** ~ compartment, ~ bin · Silotasche *f*, Silozelle *f*, Silotrichter *m*, Speicherzelle

~ **installation,** ~ plant · Siloanlage *f*

~ **outlet** · Siloauslauf *m*

~ **plant,** ~ installation · Siloanlage *f*

~ **storage** · Silolagerung *f*

~ **tile,** ~ block *[See remark under 'Block']* · Siloblock(stein) *m*, Silostein

~ **wall** · Silowand *f*

silt · feinster Staubsand *m*, Schluft *m*

~ **box,** mud ~, grit ~, ~ bucket *[A loose iron box fitted in the bottom of a gulley for collecting deposited silt. It can be removed periodically for emptying and flushing]* · (Naß)Schlammfang *m*, Schmutzfang, (Naß)Schlammfänger *m*, Schmutzfänger, (Naß)Schlamm-(fang)eimer, Schmutzfangeimer

~ **bucket** → ~ box

~ **collector,** mud ~, grit ~ · Schlammfang *m*, Schmutzfang *[Straßenentwässerung]*

silver bronze, nickel ~; nickel silver (US) *[Not to be confused with nickel silver = Neusilber]* · Nickelbronze *f*

~ **compound** · Silberverbindung *f*

~ **foil** · Silberfolie *f*

~ **gray,** ~ grey · silbergrau

silver-leaf · Blattsilber *n*

silver plating · Versilberung *f*

~ **powder,** powder(ed) silver · Pulversilber *n*, Silberpulver *n*

~ **sarcophagus** · Silbersarkophag *m*

~ **shot** · Silberschrot *n, m*

~ **solder** · Silberlot *n [Kupfer-Zink-Silberlegierung nach DIN 1710]*

~ **steel** · Silberstahl *m*

~ **sulphate** (Brit.); ~ sulfate (US) · Silbervitriol *n*

~ **wire** · Silberdraht *m*

silvering *[The application by chemical or other methods of a film of silver to a glass surface]* · Belegen *n*, Verspiegeln, Versilbern

~ **quality glass,** SQ · Beleg(e)glas *n*

silvery *[Having the appearance of silver; like silver in colo(u)r or luster]* · silberhell

~ *[containing silver]* · silberhaltig

~ *[covered with silver]* · versilbert

silvery-white · silberweiß

sima, cima (US); cyma (Brit.) · Sima *f*, Wasserrinne *f*, Rinnleiste *f [antike Ordnung]*

similarity condition → condition of similitude

similitude condition → condition of similitude

simple *[abacus]* · ungegliedert

~ → simply supported

~ **(arched) corbel-table (frieze)** · einfacher Bogenfries *m*

~ **beam,** simply supported ~ *[A beam without restraint or continuity at its supports]* · einfacher Balken(träger) *m*

~ ~ **equation** · einfache Balken(träger)-gleichung *f*

~ **bearing,** ~ support · einfache (Auf-)Lagerung *f*, einfaches Auflager *n*

~ **bending,** ~ flexure · einfache Biegung *f*

~ **circular arch** · einfacher Kreisbogen *m*

~ **column** · einfache Stütze *f*

~ **corbel-table** → ~ arched corbel-table frieze

~ **fixed frame,** fixed simple ~ · einfach eingespannter Rahmen *m*

~ **flexure,** ~ bending · einfache Biegung *f*

~ **frame,** one-span ~, single-span ~, single(-bay) ~, one-bay ~, frame of one bay, frame of one span · einfacher Rahmen *m*, Einfachrahmen, Einfeldrahmen

~ **framework** · einfaches Fachwerk *n*, Einfach-Fachwerk

simple-handle · Einfach-Handgriff *m*

simple hinged frame · einfacher Gelenkrahmen *m*, Einfach-Gelenkrahmen

~ **parallel cable system** · einfaches Parallelseilsystem *n*

~ ~ ~ **with stabilization through roof weight** · einfaches Parallelseilsystem *n* mit Stabilisierung durch Dachlast

~ **plastic theory,** linear ~ ~, first-order ~ · (Spannungs)Theorie *f* 1. Ordnung, einfache plastische Theorie, lineare plastische Theorie

~ **plate,** ~ slab · einfache Platte *f*

simple roof cover(ing) — single-flue chimney

~ **roof cover(ing)**, ~ ~ sheathing, ~ roof(ing) · einfaches Dach *n* [*Es ist 7 bis 8 Zoll weit gelattet*]

~ **safety** · einfache Sicherheit *f*

~ **slab**, ~ plate · einfache Platte *f*

~ **solution** · einfache Lösung *f*

~ **strutted frame** · einfaches Sprengwerk *n*, Einfach-Sprengwerk

~ **support**, ~ bearing · einfache (Auf-)Lagerung *f*, einfaches Auflager *n*

~ **tension** · einfacher Zug *m*

~ **wood ceiling** · einfache Holzdecke *f*

simplified equation · vereinfachte Gleichung *f*

simplifying assumption, ~ hypothesis · vereinfachende Annahme *f*

simply curved shell, singly ~ ~, single curvature ~, shell of single curvature · einfach gekrümmte Schale *f*

~ **supported**, freely ~, supported at both ends, simple · einfach gelagert, ~ auf~, (frei) drehbar ~, freiaufliegend, freigelagert, einfach aufliegend

~ ~ **beam**, simple ~ ~ [*A beam without restraint or continuity at its supports*] · einfacher Balken(träger) *m*

Simpson (parabolic) rule · Simpsonsche Regel *f*

simultaneous equation · Gleichzeitigkeitsgleichung *f*

sine curve · Sinuskurve *f*, Sinuslinie *f*

single-acting door, single action ~ [*This type of swing door can easily be pushed open in one direction only*] · einseitig aufschlagende Pendeltür *f*

single action door → single-acting ~

single-bath method, one-bath ~ · Einbadverfahren *n* [*Dachpappenherstellung*]

single-bay, single-span, one-bay, one-span · einschiffig [*Rahmenhalle*]

~ **beam** → single-span ~

single(-bay) frame → simple ~

~ **gable(d) frame** · Ein-Joch-Giebelrahmen *m*

single-bay girder → single-span ~

single(-bay) rigid frame, ~ stiff(-jointed) ~ · starrer Einteldrahmen *m*, Einfeld-Steifrahmen

single-bay slab → single-span ~

single(-bay) two-hinged frame → single-span ~ ~

single-bed, one-bed · einbettig

single (bed)room → ~ guest ~

~ ~ **with convertible couch-bed** · Studiozimmer *n* [*Hotel*]

single-cantilever shell · Einfachkragschale *f*

single-coat, one-coat, single-layer(ed), one-layer(ed), single-course, one-course, homogeneous · einlagig, einschichtig [*(Ver)Putz und dergleichen*]

single column, ~ support · Einzelstütze *f*

single-component → one-part

~ **(bonding) adhesive** → one-component (~) ~

~ **cement**, one-component ~, one-part ~, single-part ~, one-pack ~, single-pack ~ · Einkomponentenkitt *m*

~ **cement(ing agent)** → one-component (bonding) adhesive

~ **coating** → one-part ~

~ **etching primer** → one-component ~ ~

~ **plastic** → one-component ~

~ **pretreatment primer** → one-component etching ~

~ **primer** → one-component ~

~ **self etch primer** → one-component etching ~

~ **system** → one-component ~

~ **wash primer** → one-component etching ~

single-course → single-coat

single curvature · einfache Krümmung *f*

~ ~ **shell**, singly curved ~, simply curved ~, shell of single curvature · einfach gekrümmte Schale *f*

~ **curved shell system**, ~ curvature ~ · einfach gekrümmtes Schalensystem *n*

~ ~ **spike grid** · einfach gekrümmter (zweiseitiger) Krallendübel *m*, gekrümmtes Krallenplattenpaar *n*

single-degree-of-freedom system · System *n* mit einzelnem Freiheitsgrad

single-depth rooms · einbündig angeordnete Räume *mpl*

single door · Einfachtür *f*

single-duct system · Ein-Kanal-System *n* [*Luftverteilung*]

single expanding wall → ~-screen ~ ~

single-family home → house

~ **unit** → house

single floor, joist(ed) ~, beam(-and-slab) ~ [*A floor system whose floor slab is supported by beams*] · Balken(träger)decke *f*, Unterzugdecke

single-floor heating system; single-story ~ ~ (US); single-storey ~ ~ (Brit.) · Stockwerkheizung *f*, Etagenheizung, Geschoßheizung

~ **hot water heating system**; single-storey ~ ~ ~ ~ (Brit.); single-story ~ ~ ~ ~ (US) · Stockwerk-Warmwasserheizung *f*, Etagen-Warmwasserheizung, Geschoß-Warmwasserheizung

~ **house** → single-story ~

~ **warehouse (building)** → single-story ~ (~)

single-flue · einzügig [*Schornstein; Kessel*]

~ **boiler** · Einrohrkessel *m*

~ **chimney** · Einzelschornstein *m*, einzügiger Schornstein

single frame — single-pipe system

single frame → simple ~

single-frogged brick · Ziegel *m* mit einer Aushöhlung, ~ ~ ~ Austiefung, ~ ~ ~ Vertiefung, ~ ~ ~ Mulde

single gable(d) frame, single-bay ~ ~ · Ein-Joch-Giebelrahmen *m*

~ **girder** · einfacher Träger *m*

single-glazed unit · einfach verglastes Element *n*, ~ eingeglastes ~

single glazing · Einfachverglasung *f*, Einfacheinglasung

~ **(guest) bedroom**, one-bed (guest) room · Ein-Bett-Raum *m*, Ein-Bett-Zimmer *n*, Einzel(bett)zimmer, Einzel(schlaf)raum [*Hotel*]

single-hinge(d) arch(ed girder) · Ein-Gelenk-Bogen(träger) *m*

~ **frame**, single-pin(ned) ~, one-hinged ~, one-pin(ned) ~ · Eingelenkrahmen *m*

~ **parabolic arch(ed girder)** → one-hinged ~ ~ (~)

single-hole mixer · Einloch-Standbatterie *f*

single-hung sash window · Einfach-Senkrecht-Schiebe(flügel)fenster *n*, Einfach-Vertikal-Schiebe(flügel)fenster

single-lamp luminaire (fixture) (US); ~ light fitting (Brit.); ~ (light(ing)) fixture · Ein-Lampenleuchte *f*

single lantern-light · Einzellaterne *f*

single-lap (roof(ing)) tile · Einfalz-(dach)stein *m*

single-layer(ed) → single-coat

~ **fabric for roofing**, ~ (roofing) fabric · Ein-Lagen-Roh(dach)pappe *f*, Ein-Schicht-Roh(dach)pappe

~ **monolithic masonry wall** → monolithic single-layer(ed) ~ ~

~ **(roll) roofing**, ~ ready ~, ~ composition ~, ~ prepared ~, ~ rolled-strip ~ · einlagige Dachpappe *f*, einschichtige ~, Ein-Lagen-Dachpappe, Ein-Schicht-Dachpappe

~ **(roofing) fabric**, ~ fabric for roofing · Ein-Lagen-Roh(dach)pappe *f*, Ein-Schicht-Roh(dach)pappe

single-leaf, one-leaf, monolithic [*wall*] · einschalig [*Wand*]

~ **door**, one-leaf ~ · einflügelige Tür *f*, Einflügeltür

~ **room door**, one-leaf ~ ~ · einflügelige Zimmertür *f*, Einflügel-Zimmertür

~ **shutterdoor**, one-leaf ~ · einflügeliges Tor *n*

~ **sliding shutter door**, one-leaf ~ ~ ~ · einflügeliges Schiebetor *n*

~ **wall** → one-leaf ~

single-level garage, one-level ~ · Flachgarage *f*

single load · Einzellast *f*

~ **loading** · Einzelbelastung *f*

~ **lock seam**, ~ (welted) ~ · einfacher Falz *m* [*Metallbedachung*]

~ **monumental arch**, ~ triumphal ~ · Triumphbogen *m* mit einer Öffnung, Monumentalbogen ~ ~ ~

~ **nailing** · Einfachnagelung *f*

single-pack → one-part

~ **(bonding) adhesive** → one-component (~) ~

~ **cement(ing agent)** → one-component (bonding) adhesive

~ **coating** → one-part ~

~ **etching primer** → one-component ~ ~

~ **plastic** → one-component ~

~ **pretreatment primer** → one-component etching ~

~ **primer** → one-component ~

~ **self etch primer** → one-component etching ~

~ **system** → one-component ~

~ **wash primer** → one-component etching ~

single-panel(led) door (Brit.); single-panel(ed) ~ (US) · Ein-Füllungstür *f*

single-part → one-part

~ **(bonding) adhesive** → one-component (~) ~

~ **cement(ing agent)** → one-component (bonding) adhesive

~ **coating** → one-part ~

~ **etching primer** → one-component ~ ~

~ **plastic** → one-component ~

~ **pretreatment primer** → one-component etching ~

~ **primer** → one-component ~

~ **self etch primer** → one-component etching ~

~ **system** → one-component ~

~ **wash primer** → one-component etching ~

single-piece, one-piece · einteilig

~ **aerated concrete panel** → one-piece ~ ~ ~

~ **casting**, one-piece ~ · einteiliges Gußstück *n*

~ **panel**, one-piece ~ · einteilige Tafel *f*

~ **plastic cable clip**, one-piece ~ ~ ~ · einteilige Kunststoffkabelschelle *f*

single-pin(ned) arch(ed girder) → one-hinged ~ (~)

~ **frame**, single-hinged ~, one-pin(ned) ~, one-hinged ~ · Eingelenkrahmen *m*

~ **parabolic arch(ed girder)** → one-hinged ~ ~ (~)

single-pipe (heating) system, one-pipe (~) ~ · Einrohrheizung *f*, Einrohrsystem *n*, Niederdruck-Warmwasserheizung(ssystem), Ein-Rohr-Heiz(ungs)system

~ **meter**, one-pipe ~ · Einrohrzähler *m*

~ **system** → ~ heating ~

single-pitch roof — single-storey school building

single-pitch roof, lean-to ~, monopitch ~ [*A roof pitched in one plane only*] · freitragendes Pultdach *n*

~ roof-light · pultförmiges (Dach-)Oberlicht *n*

single plate → single(-sided) (toothed) ~

single-pole intermediate switch · einpoliger Kreuzschalter *m*

~ on-off switch · einpoliger Ausschalter *m*

~ switch · einpoliger Schalter *m*

~ two-circuit double interruption switch · einpoliger Gruppenschalter *m*

~ ~ single-interruption switch · einpoliger Serienschalter *m*

~ two-way switch · einpoliger Wechselschalter *m*

single-pot system → one-component ~

single reduction (wire-)drawing machine · Einfach-(Draht)Ziehbank *f*

~ rigid frame → single-bay ~ ~

~ rod reinforcement · Einzelstabbewehrung *f*, Einzelstabarmierung, Einzelstabeinlage *f*

~-roll mill · Einwalzenwerk *n* [*Mahlen in der Lackindustrie*]

single roof cladding, ~ ~ cover(ing), ~ ~ sheathing, ~ roofing · Einfach-(dach)(ein)deckung *f*, Einfachdach(-belag) *n*, (*m*), Einfachbedachung *f*

~ room with convertible couch-bed → ~ (bed)room ~ ~ ~

single-room(ed) apartment (unit) → one-room(ed) flat

~ flat → one-room(ed) ~

single-row brick-on-edge arch → one-row ~ ~

single-sash(ed) window, one-sash(ed) ~ [*See remark under 'Flügel'*] · einflügeliges Fenster *n*, Einflügelfenster

single(-screen) expanding wall · Einfach-Harmonikatür *f*

single seam, ~ welted ~, ~ lock ~ · einfacher Falz *m* [*Metallbedachung*]

single-shear · einschnittig [*Niet- oder Schraubenverbindung, wenn die Niet- oder Schraubenbolzen in der beanspruchten Verbindung nur in je einem Querschnitt abgeschert werden*]

single shell · Einzelschale *f*

single(-sided) (toothed) plate · Zahndübel *m* mit nach einer Seite aufgebogenen Zähnen

single-sized, uniform, like-grained, equigranular, even-grained ~ · einkörnig, gleichkörnig

~ aerated concrete, like-grained ~, uniform ~ ~, short range aggregate ~ ~, even-grained ~ ~, equigranular ~ ~ · einkörniger Porenbeton *m*, gleichkörniger ~, Einkorn-Porenbeton

~ concrete, uniform ~, like-grained ~, short range aggregate ~, equigranular ~, even-grained ~ · Einkornbeton *m*, einkörniger Beton, gleichkörniger Beton [*DIN 4163*]

~ mortar, uniform ~, like-grained ~, short range aggregate ~, equigranular ~, even-grained ~ · einkörniger Mörtel *m*, gleichkörniger ~, Einkornmörtel

single-skin structure, ~ (load)bearing ~, ~ weight-carrying ~, ~ supporting ~, ~ loaded ~, ~ load-carrying ~ · Einzelhaut-Tragwerk *n*

single skylight · Einzelraupe *f*

~ sliding door · Einfach-Schiebetür *f*, Schiebetür mit einem Flügel, einflügelige Schiebetür

~ socket · Einfach-Steckdose *f*

~ ~ with earthing contact · Einfach-Schutzkontaktsteckdose *f*

single-span, single-bay, one-bay, one-span · einschiffig [*Rahmenhalle*]

~ beam, one-span ~, single-bay ~, one-bay ~, beam of one bay, beam of one span · Einfeldbalken(träger) *m*

~ frame → simple ~

~ girder, one-span ~, single-bay ~, one-bay ~, girder of one bay, girder of one span · Einfeldträger *m*

~ skew slab · schiefe Einfeldplatte *f*

~ slab, one-span ~, single-bay ~, one-bay ~, slab of one bay, slab of one span · Einfeldträger *m*

~ two-hinged frame, one-span ~ ~, single(-bay) ~ ~, one-bay ~ ~, two-hinged frame of one span, two-hinged frame of one bay · Einfeld-Zweigelenkrahmen *m*, Zweigelenk-Einfeldrahmen

single spray coat application, one ~ ~ ~ · Einschicht-Spritzauftrag *m*

single-stack plumbing, one-pipe ~ · Einrohrgrundstücksentwässerung *f*

single-stalk girder, single-web(bed) ~ · einwandiger Träger *m*, einstegiger ~, Träger mit einem Steg

~ standing seam · einfach stehender Falz *m* [*Metallbedachung*]

~ stiff(-jointed) frame → single(-bay) rigid ~

single-storey annexe (Brit.); single-story annex (US) · Flachanbau *m*

~ finger system (Brit.) → one-storey ~ ~

~ heating system (Brit.); single-story ~ ~ (US); single-floor ~ ~ ~ · Etagenheizung *f*, Stockwerkheizung, Geschoßheizung

~ hot water heating system (Brit.); single-story ~ ~ ~ ~ (US); single-floor ~ ~ ~ ~ ~ · Stockwerk-Warmwasserheizung *f*, Etagen-Warmwasserheizung, Geschoß-Warmwasserheizung

~ school building (Brit.); single-story ~ ~ (US) · Pavillonschulgebäude *n*

single-story house, one-story ~ (US); single-storey ~, one-storey ~ (Brit.); single-floor ~, one-floor ~ · ebenerdiges Haus *n*, Eingeschoßhaus

~ warehouse (building), one-story ~ (~) (US); single-storey ~ (~), one-storey ~ (~) (Brit.); single-floor ~ (~), one-floor ~ (~) · eingeschossiges Lagergebäude *n*, einetagiges ~, einstöckiges ~, ebenerdiges ~, ~ Lagerhaus *n*, Eingeschoßlagerhaus, Eingeschoßlagergebäude

single-strut trussed beam, inverted king (post) truss, trussed beam [*It is used for short spans in connection with wood construction*] · umgekehrter einfacher Hängeblock *m*, ~ einsäuliger ~, umgekehrtes einfaches Hängewerk *n*, umgekehrtes einsäuliges Hängewerk

single support, ~ column · Einzelstütze *f*

(~) T(ee) (building) component → (prefab(ricated)) (single) T(ee) (building) unit

(~) ~ (~) member → (prefab(ricated)) (single) T(ee) (building) unit

(~) ~ (~) unit → prefab(ricated) (~) ~ (~) ~

(~) ~ component → (prefab(ricated)) (single) (Tee) (building) unit

(~) ~ (floor slab) · T-Deckenelement *n*, T-Deckenplatte *f*

(~) ~ member → (prefab(ricated)) (single) T(ee) (building) unit

(~) ~ panel, (~) tee ~ · T-Tafel *f*

(~) ~ slab · T-Platte *f*

(~) ~ unit → (prefab(ricated)) (single) T(ee) (building) ~

single-tier wall (US) → one-leaf ~

single timber floor, timber joist ~, wood(en) joist ~ · Holzbalken(träger)-decke *f* [*DIN 104*]

~ ~ roof floor, timber joist ~ ~, wood(-en) joist ~ ~ · Holzbalken(träger)-dachdecke *f*

single-towered façade · Einturmfassade *f*

single triumphal arch, ~ monumental ~ · Triumphbogen *m* mit einer Öffnung, Monumentalbogen ~ ~ ~

~ T-roof(ing) slab, ~ tee-roof(ing) ~ · Bedachungselement *n* in Form von T-Trägern, Dachplatte *f* ~ ~ ~ ~ ~, Dachelement ~ ~ ~ ~, Bedachungsplatte ~ ~ ~ ~

~ turn lock · eintouriges (Tür)Schloß *n*

~ two-hinged frame → single-span ~ ~

single-unit · einlängig, 1-längig [*Schienenleuchte*]

single upper floor, upper joist ~ · Balken(träger)-Obergeschoßdecke *f*

~ ~ timber floor, timber joist upper ~, wood(en) joist upper ~ · Obergeschoß-Holzbalkendecke *f*, OG-Holzbalkendecke

~ way cable duct, ~ ~ ~ conduit, ~ ~ ~ subway, ~ ~ CD; ~ ~ conduit tile (US) · einzügiger Kabel(kanal)-formstein *m*, einzügiges Kabel(kanal)-formstück *n* [*DIN 457*]

single-web(bed) · einstegig [*Träger*]

~ girder, single-stalk ~ · einwandiger Träger *m*, einstegiger ~, Träger mit einem Steg

~ I-shaped girder · einsteiger Doppel-T-Träger *m*

single welt(ed seam), ~ seam · einfach liegender Falz *m* [*Metallbedachung*]

~ (~) ~, ~ lock ~ · einfacher Falz *m* [*Metallbedachung*]

~ window · Einfachfenster *n*

single-window one-piece panel, one-window ~ ~, ~ single-piece ~ · einteilige Ein-Fenstertafel *f*

~ panel, one-window ~ · Ein-Fenstertafel *f*

single-wing(ed) building, ~ block, one-winge(d) ~, block with one wing, building with one wing · Einflügelbau *m*, Einflügelgebäude *n*

single wire · Einzeldraht *m* [*Spannbewehrung*]

single-wire line · Eindrahtleitung *f*, Einfachleitung [*Elektrotechnik*]

single wire stretching, ~ ~ tensioning, ~ ~ (pre)stressing · Einzeldrahtvorspannung *f*

single-withe wall → one-leaf ~

single-wythe wall → one-leaf ~

singly curved plane · einfach gekrümmte Fläche *f*

~ ~ shell, simply ~ ~, single curvature ~, shell of single curvature · einfach gekrümmte Schale *f*

singular point of infinity · Unendlichkeitspunkt *m*

sink, kitchen ~, KS · Spüle *f*

~ · Ausguß(becken) *m*, (*n*) [*DIN 4491*]

(~) bib, bibcock, bib tap (Brit.); bib nozzle (US) [*The water tap at a sink which is fed by a horizontal supply pipe, not, as in the usual washbasin, by a pipe from below*] · Ausgußzapfhahn *m*

~ bowl · Spülbecken *n*

~ mixer · Standbatterie *f*

~ unit [*Combined sink and drainer*] · Spültisch *m*, Abwaschtisch, Abwäsche *f*

~ ~ for the trade · Groß-Spültisch *m*, Gewerbe-Spültisch, Groß-Abwaschtisch, Gewerbe-Abwaschtisch, Groß-Abwäsche *f*, Gewerbe-Abwäsche

~ waste → slop water

~ water → slop ~

sinkage · Nachfall *m* [*Anstrich*]

sinking · Einlassen *n* [*Mit der Oberfläche eines Gegenstandes bündig machen*]

to sinter · sintern

sinter — sisal carpenting

sinter → siliceous ~

~ hearth, continuously moving ~ · Sinterband *n*

sintered · gesintert

~ aerated (concrete) aggregate, aerated sintered (~) ~ · Porensinter *m* [*Aufgeblähter Leichtbetonzuschlag(stoff) über Sintergrenze gewonnen*]

~ aggregate, ~ concrete ~, ~ construction ~ · Sintergranulat *n*, Sinterzuschlag(stoff) *m*, gesinterter (Beton-)Zuschlag(stoff), gesintertes (Beton-)Zuschlagmaterial *n*

~ alumina · Sintertonerde *f*

~ ash · Aschensinter *m*, Sinterasche *f*

~ binder · gesintertes Bindemittel *n*, gesinterter Binder *m*

~ bloating clay (Brit.); ~ expanded ~ · Sinterblähton *m*

~ ~ slag (Brit.); ~ expanded ~ · Sinterblähhochofenschlacke *f*

~ bronze · Sinterbronze *f*

~ carbide, cemented ~ · Sinterkarbid *n*

~ cinder (US); ~ slag (Brit.) · Schlackensinter *m*, Sinterschlacke *f*

~ ~ wall slab (US); ~ clinker ~ ~ (Brit.) · Schlacken(sinter)-Wand(bau)platte *f*, Sinterbims-Wand(bau)platte

~ clay · gesinterter Ton *m*, Tonsinter *m*, Sinterton

~ ~ concrete · Sinterbeton *m*

~ clinker wall slab (Brit.); ~ cinder ~ ~ (US) · Schlacken(sinter)-Wand(bau)platte *f*, Sinterbims-Wand(bau)platte

~ (concrete) aggregate, ~ construction ~ · Sintergranulat *n*, Sinterzuschlag(stoff) *m*, gesinterter (Beton-)Zuschlag(stoff), gesintertes (Beton-)Zuschlagmaterial *n*

~ dolomite · Sinterdolomit *m*

~ expanded clay; ~ bloating ~ (Brit.) · Sinterblähton *m*

~ ~ slag; ~ bloating ~ (Brit.) · Sinterblähhochofenschlacke *f*

~ fly ash, ~ PFA, ~ (pulverized) fuel ash; pulverized fuel ash (Brit.) · Flugaschensinter(granulat) *m*, (*n*), Sinterflugasche *f*

~ glass, fritted ~ [*A porous glass made for filtration and other purposes by heating graded glass powder*] · Sinterglas *n*, gefrittetes Glas

~ gravel · Sinterkies *m*

~ iron · Sintereisen *n*

~ light(weight) concrete · Sinterbimsbeton *m* [*DIN 18151 und 18152*]

~ ~ (~) aggregate · Sinterbims *m*, Sinter-Leicht(beton)zuschlag(stoff) *m*, Sinter-Leicht(beton)zuschlagmaterial *n*

[*Oberbegriff für Aschensinter und Schlackensinter*]

~ magnesite, dead-burned ~, deadburnt ~ · Sintermagnesit *m*, Schmelzmagnesit, geglühter Magnesit [*Hochfeuerfester bis zur beginnenden Schmelzung bei rund 1500° C gebrannter Magnesit*]

~ nylon · gesintertes Nylon *n*

~ PFA → ~ fly ash

(~) PFA cement → (~) fly ash ~

~ product · Sintererzeugnis *n*

~ pulverized fuel ash → ~ fly ash

~ slag (Brit.); ~ cinder (US) · Schlackensinter *m*, Sinterschlacke *f*

~ stoneware tile · gesinterte Steinzeug(belag)platte *f*, ~ Steinzeugfliese *f*

~ ware → mass-produced ~ ~

sintering · Sintern *n*, Sinterung *f* [*Verfestigung pulverförmiger Stoffe durch Reaktion im festen Zustand bei einer Temperatur, die unter der Bildungstemperatur einer flüssigen Phase liegt. In der Praxis wird die Sinter-Temperatur manchmal durch Zusätze herabgesetzt, die eine geringe Menge an Schmelzoder Glasphase ergeben*]

~ furnace · Sinterofen *m*

~ grate · Sinterrost *m*

~ limit · Sintergrenze *f*

~ method · Sinterverfahren *n*

~ mix(ture) · Sintergemisch *n*, Sintermischung *f*

~ operation · Sintervorgang *m*

~ plant · Sinteranlage *f*

~ zone · Sinterzone *f*

sinusoidal arch · Sinusbogen *m*

~ load · Sinusoidenlast *f*

siphon · Syphon *m*, Flüssigkeitsheber *m*, Heberohr *n*, Siphon, Saugheber

siphonage, siphonic action · Heberwirkung *f*

siphonic action, siphonage · Heberwirkung *f*

~ bowl → ~ pan

~ closet, ~ W.C. · Absaugeklosett *n*, Saugspülklosett, Absaugeabort *m*, Saugspülabort

~ pan, ~ bowl [*A suction is induced in the outlet which drains out the contents of the pan, leaving the water to wash the sides and refill the trap*] · Absaug(e)-(Abort)becken *n*, Absaug(e)klosettbecken, Absaug(e)-Toilettenbecken

~ W.C., ~ closet · Absaugeklosett *n*, Saugspülklosett, Absaugeabort *m*, Saugspülabort

Siporex slab · Siporexplatte *f*

~ wall slab · Siporexwand(bau)platte *f*

sisal carpeting · Sisalteppich(fuß)boden(belag) *m*

sisal fibre — site stretching

~ **fibre** (Brit.); ~ fiber (US) · Sisalfaser *f*
~ **hemp** · Sisalhanf *m*
~ **reinforced** · sisalfaserverstärkt
~ **rope** [*B.S. 2052*] · Sisalstrick *m*
Sistine chapel · Sixtinische Kapelle *f*
site, field · Baustelle *f*
~ · Lage *f*, Standort *m*
~ **accommodation** · Baustellenunterkunft *f*, Unterkunft bei Bauten
~ **altitude** · Baustellenhöhe *f* über dem Meeresspiegel
~ **area**, ~ space · Baustellenfläche *f*
~ **assembly**, field ~ [*Assembly of components on the site before incorporation into a building or structure*] · Baustellenzusammenbau *m*
~ **cleared of buildings**, zone ~ ~ ~, area ~ ~ ~, cleared site, cleared zone, cleared area · abgebrochenes (Stadt-)Gebiet *n*, abgerissenes ~
~ **connection**, field ~ · Montageverbindung *f*
(~) **development** · Erschließung *f*, Bodenaufschließung [*Maßnahmen, um aus dem rohen Land „baufertige" Grundstücke (= Bauland) herzustellen*]
(~) ~ **area** · Erschließungsgebiet *n*, Bodenaufschließungsgebiet
~ **facilities**, ~ installations, ~ plant · Bau(stellen)einrichtung *f*
~ ~ **programme** (Brit.); ~ ~ program (US) · (Baustellen)Einrichtungsplan *m*
~ **factory** · Feldfabrik *f*
~ **handling** → on-~ ~
~ **hut** · Bau(stellen)baracke *f*
~ **installations**, ~ facilities, ~ plant · Bau(stellen)einrichtung *f*
~ **manufacture** · Baustellenfertigung *f*, Baustellenherstellung
~ **mixing**, on-the-job ~ · Mischen *n* auf der Baustelle
~ **mud** · Baustellenschlamm *m*
~ **office**, field ~ · Baustellenbüro *n*
site-painted, field-painted · baustellengestrichen
site-placed aerated concrete → cast(-)in(-)situ ~ ~
~ **architectural concrete** → cast-in-place ~ ~
~ **concrete**, in(-)situ (cast) ~, cast(-)in(-)situ ~, cast-in-place ~, poured(-in-place) ~, field ~ ~ · Ortbeton *m* [*DIN 1045*]
~ (~) **balcony**, in(-)situ (cast) (~) ~, cast(-)in(-)situ (~) ~, cast-in-place (~) ~, field ~ ~, poured(-in-place) (~) ~ · Ortbetonbalkon *m*
~ (~) **cable duct**, field ~ ~ ~, cast-in-place (~) ~ ~, cast(-)in(-)situ (~) ~ ~, in(-)situ (cast) (~) ~ ~, poured(-in-place) (~) ~ ~ · Ortbetonkanal *m*

~ (~) **eave(s) unit**, cast(-)in(-)situ (~) ~, in(-)situ (cast) (~) ~, cast-in-place (~) ~ ~, field ~ ~ ~, poured(-in-place) (~) ~ ~ · Ortbeton-Traufenteil *m*, *n*
~ (~) **filling**, cast-in-place (~) ~, field ~ ~, cast(-)in(-)situ (~) ~, in(-)situ (cast) (~) ~, poured(-in-place) (~) ~ · Ortbetonfüllung *f*
~ (~) **floor**, field ~ ~, cast-in-place (~) ~, cast(-)in(-)situ (~) ~, in(-)situ (cast) (~) ~, poured(-in-place) (~) ~ · Ortbetondecke *f*
~ (~) **frame**, ~ (~) framing, cast-in-place (~) ~, field ~ ~, cast(-)in(-)situ (~) ~, in(-)situ (cast) (~) ~, poured(-in-place) (~) ~ · Ortbetonrahmen *m*
~ (~) **rib(bed) floor**, cast-in-place (~) ~ ~, field ~ ~ ~, cast(-)in(-)situ (~) ~ ~, in(-)situ (cast) (~) ~ ~, poured(-in-place) (~) ~ ~ · Ortbeton-Rippendecke *f*
~ (~) **shell**, field ~ ~, cast-in-place (~) ~, cast(-)in(-)situ (~) ~, in(-)situ (cast) (~) ~, poured(-in-place) (~) ~ · Ortbetonschale *f*
~ (~) **stair(case)**, cast-in-place (~) ~, cast(-)in(-)situ (~) ~, in(-)situ (cast) (~) ~, field ~ ~, poured(-in-place) (~) ~ · Ortbetontreppe *f*
~ (~) **structure**, field ~ ~, cast-in-place (~) ~, cast(-)in(-)situ (~) ~, in(-)situ (cast) (~) ~, poured(-in-place) (~) ~ · Ortbetonbauwerk *n*
~ **light(weight) concrete**, cast-in-place ~ ~, cast(-)in(-)situ ~ ~, in(-)situ (cast) ~ ~, field ~ ~, poured(-in-place) ~ ~ · Ortleichtbeton *m*, Leicht-Ortbeton
~ **mortar**, cast-in-place ~, cast(-)in(-)situ ~, in(-)situ (cast) ~, field ~, poured(-in-place) ~ · Ortmörtel *m*
~ **reinforced concrete**, ~ R.C., field ~ ~, cast-in-place ~ ~, cast(-)in(-)situ ~ ~, in(-)situ (cast) ~ ~, poured(-in-place) ~ ~ · Ort-Stahlbeton *m*, Stahlortbeton
~ ~ ~ **floor**, ~ R.C. ~, field ~ ~ ~, cast-in-place ~ ~ ~, cast(-)in(-)situ ~ ~ ~, in(-)situ (cast) ~ ~ ~, poured(-in-place) ~ ~ ~ · Ortstahlbetondecke *f*, Stahlortbetondecke
site planning · städtebauliche Planung *f* [*Bei der Herstellung einer Wohnanlage*]
~ **plant**, ~ facilities, ~ installations · Bau(stellen)einrichtung *f*
~ **prefabrication**, on-~ ~ [*Fabrication on the site, before incorporation into a structure*] · Vorfertigung *f* auf der Baustelle, Baustellenvorfertigung
~ (**pre**)**stressing** → on-~ ~
~ **riveting**, field ~ · Baustellennietung *f*
~ **space**, ~ area · Baustellenfläche *f*
~ **staff**, field ~ · Baustellenpersonal *n*
~ **stoppage** · Baustellenstillegung *f*
~ **stressing** → pre~
~ **stretching** → (on-)site (pre)stressing

site tensioning — skew(ed) plate 914

~ tensioning → (on-)site (pre)stressing

~ tiling, on-~ ~ · Verfliesen *n* auf der Baustelle, An-Ort-Verfliesen

site-welded, field-welded · baustellengeschweißt

site welding, field ~ · Baustellenschweißen *n*

sitting-room, living-room (Brit.); keeping-room (US) · Wohnzimmer *n*

six-bay · sechsjochig

six-leaf sliding folding shutterdoor · sechsflügeliges Faltschiebetor *n*, ~ Schiebefalttor

six-lobe tracery · Sechspaß *m* [*gotisches Maßwerk*]

six-moment equation · Sechsmomentengleichung *f*

six-panel(led) door (Brit.); six-panel(ed) ~ (US) · Sechs-Füllungstür *f*

six-pointed star · sechszackiger Stern *m*

six-vesica piscis tracery · Sechsschneuß *m* [*Eine aus sechs Schneußen zusammengesetzte Form des gotischen Maßwerks*]

six-wire · sechsdrähtig [*(Vorspann)Litze*]

size → grain-~

~ → sizing material

~ [*The magnitude of a dimension in terms of a defined unit*] · (Maß)Größe *f*

~ analysis → particle-~ ~

~ bracket → ~ range

~ determination → grain-~ ~

~ distribution → grain-~ ~

~ ~ curve → grain-~ ~ ~

~ ~ diagram → grain-~ ~ ~

~ ~ factor *n* [*R.R.B. diagram*] · Kornverteilungskennzahl *n f* [*R.R.B.*]

(~) fraction → ~ range

~ gradation, granulometry · (Korn)Abstufung *f*, Granulometrie *f*, Korngrößenabstufung *f*

~ limit → grain-~ ~

~ of bar → bar diameter

~ ~ rod → bar diameter

~ range, ~ bracket, (~) fraction, grading ~, screening portion, range of grading, range of screening · Korn(größen)bereich *m, n*, Kornklasse *f*, (Korn)Fraktion *f*, Korngruppe *f*, Kornspanne *f*, Körnung *f* [*DIN 1179*]

~ reduction [*Breaking up large stones by primary crushing or grinding*] · Vorzerkleinerung *f*

sizing · Ableimen *n* [*Anstrichtechnik*]

~ · Größenbemessung *f*

~ material, size [*As used in the paint industry, this term originally referred to an aqueous solution of animal glue, but has subsequently been extended to cover water-soluble cellulose derivatives and starches. It is sometimes also used for any glue*] · wasserlöslicher Kleb(e)stoff *m*, Leim *m*

skate changing room · Anschnallraum *m* für Schlittschuhe

~ hire room · Schlittschuhverleih(raum) *m*

skeleton, structural ~, (load-)bearing ~, weight-carrying ~ · (Trag)Skelett *n*, (Trag)Gerippe *n*

~ building, structural ~ ~, frame(d) ~ · Skelettgebäude *n*, Rahmengebäude, Gerippegebäude

~ construction → structural ~ ~

~ ~ type → ~ type of construction

~ member → structural ~ ~

~ structure → structural ~ ~

~ type of construction, ~ construction type · (Trag)Gerippebauart *f*, (Trag)Skelettbauart [*Bei dieser Bauart werden die senkrechten und waag(e)rechten Lasten von einem Gerippe oder Skelett aus waag(e)rechten und lotrechten Tragteilen – Deckenträger und Stützen oder Säulen – übernommen, die biegefest miteinander verbunden sind. Die Wände werden nicht zum Tragen herangezogen, sie haben nur Aufgaben des Raumabschlusses und soweit erforderlich des Wärme- und Schallschutzes zu erfüllen*]

skene → scene-building

sketch book · (Architektur-)Musterbuch *n*

skew · schiefwinkelig

~ arch [*An arch with its axis oblique with its faces*] · Schrägbogen *m*, schräger Bogen

~ bending, biaxial ~ · schiefe Biegung *f*

~ curve · schiefe Kurve *f*

~ grid · Schrägraster *m*

~ ~ · Schrägrost *m*

~ nailing, slant ~ · Schrägnagelung *f*

~ notch · (einfacher Stirn)Versatz *m*, Versatzung *f* [*Holzkonstruktion*]

~ ~ on masonry wall · Mauerversetzung *f*

~ ~ ~ wall · Wandversetzung *f*

~ penetration of masonry walls · schiefwinkelige Durchdringung *f* von Mauern, ~ Mauerkreuzung

~ three-span slab · schiefe Dreifeldplatte *f*

~ two-span slab · schiefe Zweifeldplatte *f*

(skewed) arch barrel, (~) barrel arch (US); inclined barrel vault (Brit.) · schiefes Tonnengewölbe *n*, schieffliegendes ~

(~) barrel arch, (~) arch barrel (US); inclined barrel vault (Brit.) · schiefes Tonnengewölbe *n*, schieffliegendes ~

skew(ed) frame · schiefer Rahmen *m*

~ junction of masonry walls · schiefwinkeliger Maueranschluß *m*

~ parallelogram plate, ~ ~ slab · schiefwinkelige Parallelogrammplatte *f*

~ plate, ~ slab · schiefe Platte *f*

skew(ed) shell — slab-and-beam floor

~ shell · schiefe Schale *f*
~ slab, ~ plate · schiefe Platte *f*
ski hut · Skihütte *f*
skidproof → anti-skid
~ paint, anti-slip ~, anti-skid ~, non-skid ~, non-slip(ping) ~, non-slippery ~ · rutschfeste (Anstrich)Farbe *f*, trittsichere ~, gleitsichere ~, Gleitschutz-(anstrich)farbe
skiffling, knobb(l)ing [*Dressing stones roughly in the quarry by removing protruding humps*] · Rohbearbeitung *f*
skilled concrete worker · Betonfacharbeiter *m*
~ personnel · Fachkräfte *fpl*, Fachpersonal *n*
~ (pre)cast concrete worker · Betonwerker *m*
skim coat (plaster) → finish(ing) ~ (~)
skimming · Abfehmen *n*, Abfeimen, Abschäumen [*Vorgang zur Förderung der Läuterung und Reinigung einer flüssigen Glasmasse*]
skim(ming) coat (plaster) → finish(ing) ~ (~)
skin, membrane, film · Film *m*, Membran(e) *f*, Haut *f*, Häutchen *n*
~, shell, leaf, layer, tier, wythe, withe [*cavity wall*] · Schale *f*, Wand~ [*Hohlwand*]
~ → curtain wall
~, cladding, lining · (Außenwand)Versteifung *f*
~ adhesive, ~ glue · Hautleim *m* [*genormtes Kurzzeichen: H*]
~ clinic · Hautklinik *f*
skin-forming · hautbildend
skin glue, ~ adhesive · Hautleim *m* [*genormtes Kurzzeichen: H*]
~ irritant · hautreizender Stoff *m*
~ of mortar, mortar skin · Mörtelhaut *f*
~ plate · Blechhaut *f*
skinning [*The formation of a surface skin of paints or varnishes in the container*] · Hautbildung *f*
~ over · (Oberflächen)Abschluß *m* [*Anstrichtechnik*]
skirting (board) (Brit.) → sanitary cove
~ (~) component (Brit.) → base (board) unit
~ (~) heater (Brit.); base plate ~ [*Scotland*]; base (board) ~, scrub board ~, mopboard ~, washboard ~, sanitary cove ~ (US) · Scheuerleistenheizer *m*, Fußleistenheizer, Sockelleistenheizer
~ (~) heating (Brit.); sanitary cove ~, base (board) ~, scrub board ~, mopboard ~, washboard ~ (US); base plate ~ [*Scotland*]; · Scheuerleistenheizung *f*, Fußleistenheizung, Sockelleistenheizung
~ (~) member (Brit.) → base (board) unit

~ (~) radiator (Brit.); base plate ~ [*Scotland*]; base (board) ~, scrub board ~, mopboard ~, washboard ~ sanitary cove ~ (US) · Scheuerleisten-Radiator *m*, Sockelleisten-Radiator, Fußleisten-Radiator
~ (~) unit (Brit.) → base (~) ~
~ component (Brit.) → base (board) unit
~ heater → ~ board ~
~ heating → ~ board ~
~ member (Brit.) → base (board) unit
~ radiator → ~ board ~
~ unit (Brit.) → base (board) ~
skullhouse → carnary
sky component (of the daylight factor) · Himmelslichtanteil *m*
~ factor, window efficiency ratio · Fensterfaktor = f *m*, Senkrechtbeleuchtung *f* im Fenster (E_f), Vertikalbeleuchtung im Fenster (E_f)
sky-glare · Himmelslichtblendung *f*
'Sky House' [*Experimental house designed by Kiyonori Kikutake for himself*] · „Haus *n* des Himmels"
skylight · Raupe *f*, Dach~, liegendes (Dach)Oberlicht *n*
skyline · Silhouette *f*
sky parlor (US) → attic room
to skyscrape · Wokenkratzer bauen
skyscraper · Wolkenkratzer *m*
~ block (of flats), ~ flats (Brit.); apartment skyscraper · Wohn(ungs)-wolkenkratzer *m*
sky-vault · Himmelsgewölbe *n*
SL, snow load · Schneelast *f* [*DIN 1055 Bl. 5*]
SL, shrinkage limit · Schwindgrenze *f*
slab [*A semi-finished rolled product intended for re-rolling or forging. The cross-sectoin is rectangular, usually with a width more than twice the thickness. Slabs may also be produced by forging*] · Bramme *f*
~, plate · Platte *f* [*Ebenes Flächentragwerk. Es ist durch normal zur Mittelebene wirkende Belastung belastet und dadurch auf Biegung und Drillung beansprucht*]
~ action, plate ~ · Plattenwirkung *f*
~ analysis, plate ~, ~ calculation · Plattenberechnung *f*
~ ~, plate ~ · Plattenstatik *f*
slab-and-beam, T-beam, Tee-beam · Plattenbalken(träger) *m*, Balken(träger) mit T-Querschnitt, T-Balkenträger [*Betonkonstruktion, die beim gemeinsamen Betonieren von Balken und Platten entsteht; bei Biegung des Balkens wird ein Teil der Platte als Druckgurt statisch mitverwendet*]
~ floor, T-beam ~, Tee beam ~, teebeam ~ · Plattenbalkendecke *f*

slab- and-beam floor with... — slab supported on three sides 916

~ ~ with nonstructural fillers, T-beam ~ ~ ~ ~, Tee beam ~ ~ ~ ~, tee-beam ~ ~ ~ ~ · Plattendecke f mit nichttragenden Füllkörpern

~ ~ without fillers, T-beam ~ ~ ~, Tee beam ~ ~ ~, tee-beam ~ ~ ~ · Plattendecke f ohne Füllkörper

~ rib, T-beam ~, Tee beam ~, tee-beam ~ · Plattenbalkenrippe f

slab band [*A wide and shallow beam*] · plattenförmiger Balken m

~ ~ floor [*This floor is basically a one-way solid slab system with wide and shallow beams, called slab bands*] · Decke f auf plattenförmigen Balken

~ bearing structure → ~ load~ ~

~ bending, plate ~ · Plattenbiegung f

~ ~, plate ~ · Plattenbiegen n

~ block → ~-type ~

~ building → ~(-type) block

~ calculation, plate ~, ~ analysis · Plattenberechnung f

~ cantilevering in all directions · vierseitig auskragende Platte f

~ cap(ping) · Regenschutzhaube f, Überdachung f [*Schornsteinkopf*]

~ circumference, plate ~ · Plattenumfang m

~ collar, lift-~ ~, steel lifting ~, shear ~ · Deckenkragen m, (Stahl)Kragen [*Hubdeckenverfahren*]

~ compressive strength → concrete ~ ~ ~

~ concreting, ~ pour(ing) · Plattenbetonieren n

~ construction · Plattenbau m

~ core, board ~ · Plattenkern m

~ cross-section · Plattenquerschnitt m

~ crushing strength → (concrete) slab compressive ~

~ depth, plate ~ · Plattendicke f [*Fehlname: Plattenstärke*]

~ displacement, plate ~ · Plattenverrückung f

~ edge, plate ~ · Plattenrand m

~ end, plate ~ · Plattenende n

~ façade · Plattenfassade f

~ facing → ~ sur~

~ ~ · Plattenverblendung f

~ failure, plate ~ · Plattenversagen n

~ floor · Plattendecke f

~ ~ cover(ing), ~ floor(ing) (finish) · Plattenboden(belag) m, Plattenfußboden(belag) f [*Die Bezeichnung ,,Platten(fuß)boden(belag)'' wird auch für einen Fliesen(fuß)boden(belag) verwendet*]

~ ~ floor(ing) (finish), ~ floor cover(ing) · Plattenboden(belag) m, Plattenfußboden(belag) [*Die Bezeichnung ,,Platten(fuß)boden(belag)'' wird auch für einen Fliesen(fuß)boden(belag) verwendet*]

~ footing · Plattenfundament n [*für Mauer, Wand und Stütze*]

~ forming · Platteneinschalung f

~ forms, ~ shuttering, ~ form(work) · Plattenschalung f

~ form(work), ~ shuttering, ~ forms · Plattenschalung f

~ joint · Plattenfuge f, Plattenstoß m

~ lining, ~ (sur)facing · Plattenauskleidung f, Plattenverkleidung, Plattenbekleidung

~ load, plate ~ · Plattenlast f

~ (load)bearing structure, plate ~ ~, ~ weight-carrying ~ · Plattentragwerk n

~ loaded in its own plane, plate ~ ~ ~ ~ ~ · Platte f in ihrer Ebene belastet

~ moment, plate ~ · Plattenmoment n

~ of constant depth, plate ~ ~ ~ planparallele Platte f

~ ~ one bay → single-span slab

~ ~ ~ span → single-span slab

~ ~ small format, small-sized slab · kleinformatige Platte f

slab-on-grade floor · Plattenrostdecke f

slab paper · Verzögerungspapier n, Einlegepapier, (Beton)Plattenpapier [*Betonsteinindustrie*]

~ partition (wall) · Platten(trenn)wand f [*DIN 4103*]

~ paving · Plattenpflasterung f

~ pour(ing), ~ concreting · Plattenbetonieren n

~ problem, plate ~ · Plattenaufgabe f, Plattenproblem n

~ reinforcement · Plattenarmierung f, Plattenbewehrung, Platten(stahl)einlagen fpl

~ rigidity, plate ~, ~ stiffness · Plattenstarrheit f, Plattensteifigkeit

~ roof · Plattendach n

~ rotation, plate ~ · Plattendrehung f

~ shuttering, ~ form(work), ~ forms · Plattenschalung f

~ skew · Plattenschiefe f

~ soffit · Plattenuntersicht f

~ spacer [*Bar support and spacer for slab reinforcement*] · Abstandvorrichtung f für Plattenbewehrung, ~ ~ Plattenarmierung, ~ ~ Platten(stahl)-einlagen

~ span, plate ~ · Plattenfeld n

~ spanning in the longitudinal direction · längsgespannte Platte f

~ ~ ~ ~ transverse direction · quergespannte Platte f

~ step · Plattenstufe f

~ stiffness, plate ~, ~ rigidity · Plattenstarrheit f, Plattensteifigkeit

~ strength, plate ~ · Plattenfestigkeit f

~ supported on three sides, plate ~ ~ ~ ~ · dreiseitig gelagerte Platte f

slab (sur)facing — slat angle

~ **(sur)facing** → ~ lining

~ **theory**, plate ~ · Plattentheorie *f*

~ **thickening**, plate ~ · Plattenverstärkung *f*

~ **translation**, plate ~ · Plattenverschiebung *f*

slab(-type)block, ~ building, straightline ~ · Scheibenhaus *n*

~ **building**, ~ block, straight-line ~ · Scheibenhaus *n*

slab urinal · Standurinal *n*

~ **wall** · Plattenwand *f*

~ **weight-carrying structure**, plate ~ ~, ~ (load)bearing ~ · Plattentragwerk *n*

~ **width**, plate ~ · Plattenbreite *f*

~ **with edge beam**, plate ~ ~ ~ · randausgesteifte Platte *f*, randversteifte ~, Platte mit Randbalken

slabby limestone, laminated ~, platy ~ · Kalkschiefer *m*, Plattenkalk(stein) *m*

slackening · Schlaffwerden *n*

slag · Schlacke *f* [*Nichtmetallische ungeschmolzene Substanz, die sich bei der Verarbeitung oder Reinigung eines Metalles oder beim chemischen Angriff auf ff. Erzeugnisse bildet*]

~ → (iron) (blastfurnace) ~

~ **aggregate** → (iron) (blastfurnace) ~ ~

~ **built-up roof(ing)**, (iron) blastfurnace ~ ~ ~ (Brit.); cinder ~ ~ · (Schlacken)Kleb(e)dach(belag) *n*, (*m*)

~ **cement** [*Finely divided material consisting essentially of an intimate and uniform blend of granulated blastfurnace slag and hydrated lime in which the slag constituent makes up more than a specified minimum percentage*] · Schlackenbinder *m*, Schlackenzement *m* [*Fehlname: schwarzer Zement*]

~ ~, (portland) blastfurnace ~ ~ · Hochofenschlackenzement *m*, HOZ; Montanzement [*Süddeutschland*] [*DIN 1164*]

~ **chip(ping)s** → (iron) (blastfurnace) ~ ~

~ **coarse aggregate** → (iron) (blastfurnace) ~ ~ ~

~ **concrete**, (iron) (blastfurnace) ~ ~ (Brit.); cinder ~ (US) · (Hochofen-)Schlackenbeton *m*

~ **dust** → (iron) (blastfurnace) ~ ~

~ **fibre** → (iron) (blastfurnace) ~ ~

~ **filler** → (iron) (blastfurnace) ~ ~

~ **fill(ing)** → (iron) (blastfurnace) ~ ~

~ **flour**, ground basic slag, Thomas meal · Schlackenmehl *n*, Thomasmehl, Thomasphosphat *n*

~ **from pig iron for steel making purposes**, stahl-eisen slag · Stahl(roh)-eisenschlacke *f*, Stahlschlacke

~ **(paving) sett** → (iron) (blastfurnace) ~ (~) ~

~ **plank** · Schlackendiele *f* [*gips- oder zementgebunden, voll oder hohl*]

~ **pozzolanic cement** · Puzzolanzement *m* aus Hochofenschlacke, Schlackenpuzzolanzement

~ **sand** → (iron) (blastfurnace) ~ ~

~ ~ **block**, ~ ~ tile, granulated slag ~ (Brit.); cinder sand ~, granulated cinder ~ (US) [*See remark under 'Block-(stein)'*] · Hütten(mauer)stein *m*, Zechenstein, HS [*DIN 398. Fehlname: Hochofen-Schlackenstein*]

~ ~ **concrete** → (iron) (blastfurnace) ~ ~ ~

~ ~ **cored block**, granulated slag ~ ~ (Brit.); cinder sand ~ ~, granulated cinder ~ ~ (US) · Hütten-Lochstein *m*, HSL [*DIN 398*]

~ ~ **tile** → ~ ~ block

~ **sett** → (iron) (blastfurnace) slag (paving) ~

~ **wool**, silicate cotton · Hüttenwolle *f* [*Fehlname: Schlackenwolle*]

~ ~ **block**, silicate cotton ~ · Hüttenwollestein *m* [*Fehlname: Schlackenwollestein*]

~ ~ **covering cord**, silicate cotton ~ ~ · Hüttenwolleschnur *f* [*Fehlname: Schlackenwolleschnur*]

~ ~ **felt**, silicate cotton ~ · Hüttenwollefilz *m* [*Fehlname: Schlackenwollefilz*]

~ ~ **insulation**, silicate cotton ~ · Hüttenwolle(ab)dämmung *f* [*Fehlname: Schlackenwolle(ab)dämmung*]

to slake, to run to putty, to hydrate [*To treat quicklime with an excess of water*] · (ab)löschen, naßlöschen [*Kalk*]

slaked, run to putty, hydrated · (ab)gelöscht, naßgelöscht [*Kalk*]

slaking, lime ~, running to putty, hydrating · (Ab)Löschen *n*, Naßlöschen [*Kalk*]

~ **box**, lime ~ ~ · (Kalk)Löschkasten *m*, (Kalk)Löschpfanne *f*

~ **drum**, lime ~ ~ · (Kalk)Löschtrommel *f*, (Kalk-)Trommel-Löscher *m*

~ **machine**, lime ~ ~, lime hydrating ~, hydrator · (Kalk)Löschmaschine *f*

~ **pit**, lime ~ ~ · Kalkgrube *f*, (Kalk-)Löschgrube

~ **process**, lime ~ ~ · (Kalk)Löschvorgang *m*

~ **slag**, desintegrating ~ · Zerfallschlacke *f*

~ **trough**, lime ~ ~ · (Kalk)Löschbank *f*

~ **vessel**, lime ~ ~ · (Kalk)Löschgefäß *n*

slamming · (Zu)Schlagen *n* [*Tür; Fenster*]

slant nailing, skew ~ · Schrägnagelung *f*

slat, lath, curtain ~, shutter ~ · (Abschluß)Lamelle *f*

~, blind ~ · (Jalousie)Lamelle *f*, (Jalousie)Stäbchen *n*

~ **angle** · Lamellenwinkel *m*, Winkelstellung *f* einer Lamelle

slat closure — slender

~ **closure** · Lamellenschluß m, Stäbchenschluß [*Jalousie*]

~ **fence,** stake ~ · Staketenzaun m, Lattenzaun

~ **lift shutter door,** ~ ~ shutterdoor · Lamellen-Hubtor n

~ **rolling shutter,** ~ roller ~ · Lamellen-Rollabschluß m

~ **shutter,** lath ~ · Lamellenabschluß m

slate, roof(ing) ~ [*B.S. 680*] · (Dach-)Schiefer m [*DIN 52201–52206*]

~ · Schieferplatte f [*Dach(ein)deckung*]

~ → clay ~

slate-covered · beschiefert, schiefergedeckt

slate cutter · (Dach)Schieferschneider m

~ **dust,** ~ powder · Schiefermehl n

~ **fixer** · Schieferleger m

slate-fixing nail · Schiefernagel m

slate floor cover(ing), ~ floor(ing) (finish) · Schieferboden(belag) m, Schieferfußboden(belag)

~ **floor(ing) (finish),** ~ floor cover(ing) · Schieferboden(belag) m, Schieferfußboden(belag)

~ **in natural cleft surface** · Rohschiefer m

~ **panel** · Schiefertafel f

~ **powder,** ~ dust · Schiefermehl n

~ **quarry** · (Dach)Schieferbruch m

~ **roof cladding,** ~ ~ cover(ing), ~ ~ sheathing, ~ roofing · Schiefer(dach)(ein)deckung f, Schieferbedachung

~ ~ **cover(ing),** ~ ~ cladding, ~ ~ sheathing, ~ roofing · Schiefer(dach)(ein)deckung f, Schieferbedachung

~ ~ **sheathing,** ~ ~ cladding, ~ ~ cover(ing), ~ roofing · Schiefer(dach)(ein)deckung f, Schieferbedachung

~ **siding** · Schiefer-Wandbeschlag m, Schiefer-Wetterschirm m, Schiefer-Wandschirm

~ **slab** · Schieferplatte f

~ **slag** · Schieferschlacke f [*Aus Schwelöfen oder Destillation von Öl- oder Tonschiefer; schiefrig und mürbe, gelb bis braun; fällt selten an; Gewicht 800 bis 1200 kg/m³; für Leichtbeton tauglich*]

~ **valley** · Schiefer(dach)kehle f

~ **wall panel** · Schieferwandtafel f

slater(-and-tiler) · Schieferdecker m

slating (work) · Schiefer(dach)(ein)decken n, Schiefer(dach)(ein)deckungsarbeiten fpl, Schieferdacharbeiten

slatted blind, jalousie, louvres, louvers [*A screen of spaced parallel slats*] Jalousie f

~ ~ **door,** jalousie ~ · Jalousietür f

~ ~ **window,** jalousie ~, louvre ~, louver ~ · Jalousiefenster n

slat(ted) floor(ing) · Spaltenboden m, Rostboden

slatted roller blind, roller jalousie · Rolladen m, Rolljalousie f [*Er besteht aus schmalen Stäbchen, die durch Gurtbänder, Metallketten usw. gelenkig miteinander verbunden sind und auf einer Welle hinter dem Fenstersturz mit Hilfe eines Gurtes aufgerollt werden*]

~ ~ ~ **gate,** roller jalousie ~ · Rolladentor n

~ ~ ~ **housing,** roller jalousie ~ · Rolladenkasten m, Rolljalousiekasten

~ ~ ~ **lintel;** ~ ~ ~ lintol [*deprecated*]; roller jalousie ~ · Rolladenoberschwelle f, Rolladensturz m, Rolljalousiesturz, Rolljalousieoberschwelle

~ ~ ~ **section,** ~ ~ ~ shape, ~ ~ ~ unit, ~ ~ ~ trim, roller jalousie ~ · Rolladenprofil n, Rolljalousieprofil

~ ~ ~ **shape,** ~ ~ ~ section, ~ ~ ~ unit, ~ ~ ~ trim, roller jalousie ~ · Rolladenprofil n, Rolljalousieprofil

~ ~ ~ **trim,** ~ ~ ~ unit, ~ ~ ~ shape, ~ ~ ~ section, roller jalousie ~ · Rolladenprofil n, Rolljalousieprofil

~ ~ ~ **unit,** ~ ~ ~ shape, ~ ~ ~ section, ~ ~ ~ trim, roller jalousie ~ · Rolladenprofil n, Rolljalousieprofil

~ ~ **work,** roller jalousie ~ · Rolladenarbeiten fpl [*DIN 18358*]

~ **shutterdoor,** ~ shutter door · Rollentor n

slatting · Lamellierung f [*Jalousie*]

slaughter establishment, abattoir, slaughterhouse · Schlachthof m

~ **hall** · Schlachthalle f, Schlachthaus n

slaughterhouse, abattoir, slaughter establishment · Schlachthof m

slave clock · Nebenuhr f

sleek · Haarriß m, Wischer m [*Fehler im optischen Glas*]

sleeper · Wandrute f

~ **wall,** honeycomb(ed) ~, dwarf ~ [*Sleeper walls are foundation walls which are erected at intermediate points between the main outside foundation walls to provide support for the ends of joists or to support partitions above*] · Mauerpfeiler m

sleeping bunk · Schlafkoje f

sleeping-room · Schlafraum m

sleeping-terrace · Schlafterrasse f

sleeve, ferrule, tailpiece · Muffenverbindung f (mit Stemmdichtung)

~ [*For services passing through walls or partitions*] · Hülse f, Manschette f

~, pipe ~ · (Rohr)Muffe f

~ **method of splicing reinforcing bars** · Muffenstoßverfahren n

sleeved pipe, ~ tube · Rohr n mit Überschiebmuffe

~ **tube,** ~ pipe · Rohr n mit Überschiebemuffe

slender · schlank

~ beam [*A beam whose length between lateral restraints exceeds thirty times the breadth of its compression flange*] · schlanker Balken(träger) *m*

~ form · schlanke Form *f*

slenderness · Schlankheit *f*

~ degree, degree of slenderness · Schlankheitsgrad *m*

~ ~ of column · Säulenschlankheitsgrad *m*

~ limit, limit of slenderness · Schlankheitsgrenze *f*

sliced, flat-cut, knife-cut · gemessert, vermessert [*Furnier*]

~ veneer, knife-cut ~, flat-cut ~ · Messerfurnier *n* [*DIN 68330*]

to slide, to slipform · ziehen [*Gleitschalungsbau*]

slide door, sliding ~ · Schiebetür *f*

~ (operation), slipforming, sliding · Ziehen *n* [*Gleitschalungsbau*]

slide-rule · Rechenschieber *m*

~ computational work · Rechenschieberarbeit *f*

sliding, slide (operation), slipforming · Ziehen *n* [*Gleitschalungsbau*]

~ armour door (Brit.); ~ armor ~ (US); ~ fire ~ · Brandschutzschiebetür *f*, Feuerschutzschiebetür

~ bearing · Gleitlager *n*

~ ceiling · Schiebedecke *f*, verschiebliche Decke, verschiebbare Decke

~ door, slide ~ · Schiebetür *f*

~ ~ fitting, ~ ~ furniture · Schiebetürbeschlag *m*

~ ~ fittings, ~ ~ hardware · Schiebetürbeschläge *mpl*

~ ~ furniture, ~ ~ fitting · Schiebetürbeschlag *m*

~ ~ gear, hanger · (Schiebetür)Gehänge *n*, (Schiebetür)Laufwerk *n*

~ ~ hardware, ~ ~ fittings · Schiebetürbeschläge *mpl*

~ ~ lock · Schiebetürschloß *n*

~ ~ track · Schiebetürschiene *f*

~ fire door; ~ armour ~ (US); ~ armour ~ (Brit.) · Brandschutzschiebetür *f*, Feuerschutzschiebetür

~ folding door, folding sliding ~ · Schiebefalttür *f*, Faltschiebetür

~ ~ grille, folding sliding ~ [*See remark under 'Gitter'*] · Schiebefaltgitter *n*, Faltschiebegitter

(~) ~ partition (wall) · Falt(trenn)wand *f*

~ ~ shutter, folding sliding ~ · Schiebefaltabschluß *m*, Faltschiebeabschluß

~ ~ ~ door, folding sliding ~ ~ · Schiebefalttor *n*, Faltschiebetor

~ glass door, glas sliding ~ · Schiebeglastür *f*, Glasschiebetür

~ hatch(way) · Schiebeluke *f*

~ height · Ziehhöhe *f*, Gleithöhe [*Gleitschalungsbau*]

~ joint, slip ~ [*A joint designed to allow relative movement in the plane of the joint between two portions of a structure*] · reib(ungs)behinderte Fuge *f*, Gleitfuge

~ lifting door, lifting sliding ~ · Schiebehebetür *f*, Hebeschiebetür

~ ~ ~ fitting, ~ ~ ~ furniture, lifting sliding ~ ~ · Hebeschiebetürbeschlag *m*, Schiebehebetürbeschlag

~ ~ ~ fittings, ~ ~ ~ hardware, lifting sliding ~ ~ · Hebeschiebetürbeschläge *mpl*, Schiebehebetürbeschläge

~ ~ ~ furniture, ~ ~ ~ fitting, lifting sliding ~ ~ · Hebeschiebetürbeschlag *m*, Schiebehebetürbeschlag

~ ~ ~ hardware, ~ ~ ~ fittings. lifting sliding ~ ~ · Hebeschiebetürbeschläge *mpl*, Schiebehebetürbeschläge

~ ~ window, lifting sliding ~ · Schiebehebefenster *n*, Hebeschiebefenster

~ panel, ~ shutter, slipform ~ · Gleitschalungstafel *f*

~ ~ · Schiebetafel *f*

~ partition (wall), folding ~ (~), concertina ~ (~), accordion ~ (~) · Akkordeontrennwand *f*, (Zieh)Harmonikatrennwand, Falt(trenn)wand

~ patio door, ~ terrace ~ · Terrassen-Schiebetür *f*

~ sash, ~ window ~ · Schiebefensterrahmen *m*

~ shutter · Schiebeladen *m*

~ ~, ~ panel, slipform ~ · Gleitschalungstafel *f*

~ ~ · Schiebe(raum)abschluß *m*

~ ~ door · Schiebetor *n*

~ standard window · Schiebe-Norm-(en)-Fenster *n*

~ steel door · Stahlschiebetür *f*

~ terrace door, ~ patio ~ · Terrassen-Schiebetür *f*

~ window handle · Schiebefenstergriff *m*

~ (~) sash · Schiebefensterrahmen *m*

~ wood patio door, ~ ~ terrace ~ · Terrassen-Holzschiebetür *f*

~ ~ terrace door, ~ ~ patio ~ · Terrassen-Holzschiebetür *f*

slight convex curve · leichte Ausschwingung *f*

slightly inclined ramp · Flachrampe *f*

slightly pitched gable roof — sloped foundation

~ pitched gable roof, low ~ ~ ~, low-pitch ~ ~ · niedriges Giebeldach *n*

~ ~ glazing, low ~ ~, low-pitch ~ · flach geneigte Verglasung *f*, ~ ~ Einglasung

~ ~ roof, low ~ ~, low-pitch ~ · flachgeneigtes (Giebel)Dach *n*, niedriges ~

~ rough · leichtrauh(ig)

~ sloped roof · schwach geneigtes Dach *n*

~ weathered · angewittert

slimline fluorescent lamp · Slimline-Leuchtstofflampe *f*

slimlinelamp fluorescent luminaire (fixture) (US); ~ ~ light fitting (Brit.); ~ ~ (light(ing)) fixture · Slimline-Leuchtstoffbeleuchtungskörper *m*, Slimline-Leuchtstoffleuchte *f*

to slip, to engobe · engobieren

slip · Schlicker *m* [*Im allgemeinen eine stabile Tonsuspension in Wasser, wobei gegebenenfalls Zusätze erfolgen können. Dieser Ausdruck kann auch andere stabile Suspensionen bezeichnen, z.B. Suspensionen von Tonerde*]

~, splinter, sliver · Spließ *m*, Span *m* [*Holzstück, Zinkblechstreifen oder Dachpappenstreifen zur Dichtung der Längsfugen bei einfacher Dachdeckung*]

~ cast · schlickergegossen

~ casting · Schlickergießen *n*, Schlickerguß *m* [*Formgebung durch Gießen eines Schlickers in eine flüssigkeitsabsaugende Form*]

to slipform, to slide · ziehen [*Gleitschalungsbau*]

slipform · Gleitschalung *f*

~ panel, ~ shutter, sliding ~ · Gleitschalungstafel *f*

~ shutter, ~ panel, sliding ~ · Gleitschalungstafel *f*

slipforming, sliding, slide (operation) · Ziehen *n* [*Gleitschalungsbau*]

slip-hazard · Rutschgefahr *f*

slip joint, sliding ~ [*A joint designed to allow relative movement in the plane of the joint between two portions of a structure*] · reib(ungs)behinderte Fuge *f*, Gleitfuge

~ length → slipping ~

slip-resistant, anti-slip, non-slip · gehsicher

~ aggregate, non-slip ~, anti-slip ~ · gehsicherer Zuschlag(stoff) *m*

slip roof, splinter ~ · Spließdach *n*, Spandach [*Dachdeckung, deren senkrechte Fugen mit einem Spließ abgedichtet sind*]

~ test · Abrutschprobe *f*, Abrutschprüfung *f*, Abrutschversuch *m*

~ tile → clay ~ ~

slippage, slip(ping) [*abbreviated: slpg*] · Schlupf *m*

slippery · rutschig

slipping · (Aus)Rutschen *n*

slip(ping), slippage [*abbreviated: slpg*] · Schlupf *m*

slipping, engobing · Engobieren *n*

slip(ping) length · Schlupflänge *f*

slit · Scharte *f* [*Je nach Art der benutzten Waffe schmaler Mauerspalt in verschiedener Form*]

~ window, loophole, arrow loop · Mauerschlitz *m*, Schießscharte *f*, Schlitzfenster *n* [*Burg*]

sliver, slip, splinter · Spließ *m*, Span *m* [*Holzstück, Zinkblechstreifen oder Dachpappenstreifen zur Dichtung der Längsfugen bei einfacher Dachdeckung*]

slop sink, housemaid's ~ [*A low sink, large enough to take a bucket under the tap, often installed in hospitals*] · tiefliegender Ausguß *m*

~ water, sink ~, kitchen waste, sink waste, dishwater [*liquid culinary waste*] · Ausgußwasser *n*, Küchenabwasser, Küchenspülwasser

to slope [*of a surface*] · abfallen

~ ~, to bevel, to cant, to splay · ausschrägen, abschrägen, abkragen, verschrägen

slope, sloping surface, sloping area · abfallende Fläche *f*

~, cant, bevel, splay · Ausschrägung *f*, Abschrägung, Verschrägung, Abkragung, Schräge *f*

~, cant, splay, bevel · Druckschlag *m* [*Gewölbe*]

~ bonder → splay ~

~ bondstone → splay bonder

~ brick → splay ~

~ header → splay bonder

~ moulding → splay ~

~ of a masonry wall → splay ~ ~ ~ ~

~ ~ wall → splay ~ ~ ~

~ ~ roof → roof pitch

~ paving · Böschungspflaster *n*

~ ~ joint sealing compound, ~ ~ ~ ~ composition · Böschungspflaster-Vergußmasse *f*, Böschungspflaster-Ausgußmasse

~ (~) sett · Böschungspflasterstein *m*

~ sett, ~ paving ~ · Böschungspflasterstein *m*

~ stretcher → splay ~

sloped, canted, splayed; bevelled (Brit.); beveled (US) · abgeschrägt, ausgeschrägt, abgekragt

~ coping [*A sloped capping to a wall to throw off water*] · Wasserschräge *f*

~ folding → splayed ~

~ footing, ~ foundation [*A footing having sloping top or side faces*] · geneigtes Fundament *n*

~ foundation, ~ footing [*A footing having sloping top or side faces*] · geneigtes Fundament *n*

sloped roof area — slurry

~ **roof area**, pitched ~ ~ · geneigte Dachfläche f
sloping, canting, splaying; bevelling (Brit.); beveling (US) · Ausschrägen n, Abschrägen, Verschrägen, Abkragen
~ **area**, ~ **surface**, **slope** · abfallende Fläche f
~ **concrete** · Gefällebeton m
~ **course**, ~ **layer** · Gefälleschicht f, Gefällelage f
~ **direction** · Gefällerichtung f
~ **folding** · abgeschrägte Faltung f
~ **glazing**, inclined ~ · Schrägeinglasung f, Schrägverglasung
~ **ground**, ~ **topography** · abfallendes Gelände n
~ **joint** · Gefällefuge f
~ **layer**, ~ **course** · Gefälleschicht f, Gefällelage f
~ **light(weight) roof**, light(weight) sloping ~ · Gefälle-Leichtdach n
~ **masonry wall** · (ab)geböschte Mauer f
~ **member**, diagonal ~ · Strebe f [Fachwerk(träger)]
~ ~ **truss**, diagonal ~ ~ · Strebenfachwerk(träger) n, (m)
~ **parabolic arch** · schräg(liegend)er Parabelbogen m
~ **roof** · Gefälledach n
~ **screed** · Gefälleestrich m
~ **surface**, ~ **area**, **slope** · abfallende Fläche f
~ **topography**, ~ **ground** · abfallendes Gelände n
slot · Schlitz m
~ **(air) diffusor**, ~ (~) **diffuser** · (Luft-)Schlitzdiffusor m
~ **anchor**, ~ **tie** · Schlitzanker m
slot-and-wedge bolt, split-and-wedge (type) ~ · Perfoanker m, Schlitzkeilanker
slot diffuser → ~ **air** ~
~ **pattern** · Schlitzmuster n
~ **tie**, ~ **anchor** · Schlitzanker m
slotted · geschlitzt
~ **angle** [B.S. 4345] · Schlitzwinkel(profil) m, (n) [Geschlitztes Winkeleisen zum Verschrauben]
~ **(gypsum) acoustic(al) plasterboard**, ~ (~) **sound-control** ~, ~ (~) **(sound) absorbent** ~, ~ (~) **(sound) absorbing** ~, ~ (~) **(sound) absorptive** ~ [In Scotland, a (gypsum) plasterboard is called 'plate'] · Gipsakustikfliese f, Gipsakustikplatte f, Gipsschallschluckplatte, Gipsschallschluckfliese, Gipskartonschlitzplatte
~ **pipe** · Schlitzrohr n, geschlitztes Rohr
~ **plate** · Schlitzplatte f
~ **rail** · Schlitzschiene f
~ **steel profile**, ~ ~ **section**, ~ ~ **shape**, ~ ~ **unit**, ~ ~ **trim** · Schlitzstahlprofil n, Stahlschlitzprofil

slow-breaking, slow-setting · langsambrechend, langsamzerfallend [Langsambrechende Emulsionen werden unterteilt in halbstabile (H) bei denen das Brechen durch einen Stabilisator verzögert wird und stabile (S), die hauptsächlich erst bei der Verdunstung des Wassers zerfallen]
slow-combustion stove · Dauerbrandofen m, Dauerbrenner m [DIN 18880]
slow-drying · langsamtrocknend
slow-hardening · langsam(er)härtend
~ **cement**, low heat (of hydration) ~; Portland cement Type IV, type IV cement (US) · Portlandzement m mit sehr geringer Abbindewärme, Massenbauzement
slow-setting · langsam(ab)bindend [hydraulisches Bindemittel]
~ → slow-breaking
~ **cement** · langsam(ab)bindender Zement m, Langsambinder(zement) m
~ **glass**, long ~ · langes Glas n
to slow up · verlangsamen
sludge drain · Schlammdrän m
~ **pit** · Schlammgrube f
~ **removal** · Entschlammung f
slum (area), ~ **zone**, ~ **site** · Elendsviertel n
~ **clearance** · Elendsviertelabbruch m, Elendsviertelabriß m
~ ~ **area**, ~ ~ **zone**, ~ ~ **site**, clearance slum ~ · Abbruchelendsviertel n, Abreißelendsviertel, Abrißelendsviertel
slum-cleared area → cleared slum ~
~ **site** → cleared slum area
~ **zone** → cleared slum area
slum site → ~ (**area**)
~ **zone** → ~ (**area**)
slump · Ausbreit(ungs)maß n, Sackmaß, Fließmaß, Konussenkung f, Setzmaß [Betonprüfung. DIN 1048]
~ **cone**, conical shell; mold (US); mould (Brit.) · Setzbecher m, Trichter m [Zur Ermittlung des Setzmaßes von Beton]
~ **specimen** · Betonkegel m [Zur Ermittlung des Setzmaßes von Beton]
~ **test (for consistency)**, ~ ~ ~ **consistence**, consistency test, consistence test · Ausbreit(ungs)prüfung f, Ausbreit(ungs)versuch m, Ausbreit(ungs)probe f, Setzprobe, Setzversuch, Setzprüfung, Konsistenzprüfung, Konsistenzprobe, Konsistenzversuch, Steifeprüfung, Steifeprobe, Steifeversuch [Betonprüfung. DIN 1048]
slung span continuous beam (Brit.); Gerber girder, hinged girder · Gelenkträger m, Gerberträger
~ ~ **lattice(d) beam** (Brit.); Gerber lattice(d) girder, hinged lattice(d) girder · Gerbergitterträger m, Gelenkgitterträger
slurry · Dickschlamm m [Breiartige, wäßrige Aufschlämmung eines gemahlenen Stoffes]

slurry — smoke-emanating industry

~ · Masse *f* [*Gasbetonherstellung*]

~, grout(ing compound) [*A fluid mix(-ture) of binder, sand and water or of binder and water*] · Schlämme *f*

~ coat · Schlämmeanstrich *m*, Schlämmeaufstrich

~ seal, grout(ing compound) ~ · Schlämmeabsieg(e)lung *f*, Schlämmeversieg(e)lung

slush coat · Haftschicht *f* [*Aus Zement, Wasser und Sperrmittel*]

small appliance, ~ domestic ~ · Klein(haushalt)gerät *n*

~ arch · kleiner Bogen *m*

~ bore heating pipe · Kleinheiz(ungs)rohr *n*

~ ~ pipe · Kleinrohr *n*

~ bronze · Kleinbronze *f*

~ column, colon(n)ette, columella · Säulchen *n*, kleine Säule *f*

~ ~ · Dienst *m*, Gurtträger *m*, Gewölbeträger [*In der gotischen Baukunst das lange, dünne Säulchen oder Halbsäulchen, im Querschnitt auch viertel-, dreiviertelkreis- oder birnenförmig, das Gurte oder Rippen des Kreuzgewölbes oder die Profile der Arkadenbögen aufnimmt*]

~ coring · Kleinlochung *f* [*Ziegel*]

~ (domestic) appliance · Klein(haushalt)gerät *n*

~ dwelling unit → small(-sized) ~ ~

~ format · Kleinformat *n*

~ garage, ~ motor ~ · Kleingarage *f*

~ gateway · mittelgroße Tür *f*, kleines Tor *n*

~ goods elevator (US); ~ ~ lift (Brit.) · Kleingüteraufzug *m*

small-grained · kleinkörnig

small house · Kleinhaus *n*

~ kitchen → small-sized ~

~ mosaic → small-sized ~

~ (motor) garage · Kleingarage *f*

~ panel · Kleintafel *f*

~ ~ construction · Kleintafelbau *m*

~ (paving) sett → small-sized (~) ~

~ ((pre)cast) concrete ware · Beton-Kleinware(n) *f*; Zement-Kleinware(n) [*Schweiz*]

~ pyramid glass · Ornamentglas Nr. 597 *n*, Pyramidal-fein *n*

~ sett → small(-sized) (paving) ~

~ ~ paving, small-sized ~ ~ · Kleinpflaster(decke) *n*, (*f*)

small-sized, of small format · kleinformatig

small(-sized) dwelling unit (US); ~ dwelling (Brit.) · Kleinwohnung *f*

~ hut · Kleinbaracke *f*

~ kitchen · Kleinküche *f*

~ mosaic · Kleinmosaik *n* [*Es besteht aus farbigen keramischen Mosaiksteinchen in verschiedener Ausführung*]

~ (paving) sett · Kleinpflasterstein *m*

~ sett paving · Kleinpflaster(decke) *n*, (*f*)

~ slab, slab of small format · kleinformatige Platte *f*

small-span frame · Kleinspannrahmen *m*

~ triangulated (roof) truss · Dreieck-(dach)binder *m* [*Nicht verwechseln mit (Dach)Binder in Dreieckform, denn der Dreieckbinder vermag ohne Biegungsbeanspruchung des Obergurtes nur eine Fuß- und eine First-Pfette aufzunehmen und ist daher nur für Spannweiten bis zu 6 m brauchbar*]

Small Temple of Abu-Simbel · Hathorgrotte *f*

small tower, diminutive ~, (decorative) turret, ornamental turret · kleiner (Zier-) Turm *m*, (Zier)Türmchen *n*

~ town · Städtchen *n*, Kleinstadt *f*

smalt · Kaiserblau *n*

smell test, scent ~ [*The testing of a drain by pouring a scent with pungent odo(u)r into it, to locate any escape*] · Geruchprobe *f*, Geruchprüfung *f*, Geruchversuch *m*

smith, black-~ · Schmied *m*

Smith (fireproof) floor [*This is primarily designed for resistance to fire, and employs (pre)cast hollow blocks to form the lower surface, so reducing weight. Reinforcement is placed between the blocks, which are laid on a telescopic patent centring, and are therefore so well supported that it is possible for men to walk over them even when carrying materials. After the reinforcement has been placed in position, the entire assembly is grouted with a dense concrete*] · Smith-Decke *f*

smithing · Schmiedehandwerk *n*

smiths' work · Schmiedearbeiten *fpl*

smithy · Schmiede *f*

smog · Stadtdunst *m*, Dunstschicht *f*

smoke · Rauch *m*

~ chimney · Rauchkamin *m*, Rauchschornstein *m* [*Für mit flüssigen oder festen Brennstoffen betriebene Feuerstellen*]

~ detector · Rauchspürer *m*

~ ~, automatic ~ ~ · Rauchmelder *m*, Rauchmeldeautomat *m* [*Brandschutz*]

~ ~ actuated · rauchspürerbetrieben

smoked glass [*ASTM C 162–56*] · rauchiges Glas *n*, graues ~, beschlagenes ~, Rauchglas [*Als farbiges Glas stets Mischfarbe, die durch Zusatz von Nickeloxid, Eisen(III)oxid, Kupfer(II)oxid und Kobaltoxid zu Natronkalkgläsern erhalten wird. Wenig Kali erzeugt schon violetten Stich*]

smoke-emanating industry · rauchabgebende Industrie *f*

smoke extract [*deprecated*]; ~ outlet [*An opening, or a fire-resisting shaft or duct, provided in a building to act as an outlet for smoke and hot gases produced by an outbreak of fire*] · Rauchabzug *m*

~ ~ **duct** [*deprecated*] → ~ outlet ~

~ ~ **shaft** [*deprecated*] → ~ outlet ~

~ **house** · Räucherbetrieb *m*

smoke-laden · rauchgeschwängert

smokeless · rauchfrei, rauchlos

smoke nuisance · Rauchbelästigung *f*

~ **outlet;** ~ **extract** [*deprecated*] [*An opening, or a fire-resisting shaft or duct, provided in a building to act as an outlet for smoke and hot gases produced by an outbreak of fire*] · Rauchabzug *m*

~ ~ **duct;** ~ **extract** ~ [*deprecated*] · Rauchabzugkanal *m*

~ ~ **shaft,** ~ **extract** ~ [*deprecated*] · Rauchabzugschacht *m*

~ **particle** · Rauchteilchen *n*

~ **pipe** · Rauchrohr *n* [*Als Kesselbauteil zur Wärmeübertragung von heißen Rauchgasen durch Wandungen von Stahlrohren an umgebendes Kesselwasser*]

~ ~, ~ **tube, stove** ~, **chimney connector** · Rauchrohr *n*, Ofenrohr [*DIN 1298*]

~ ~ **boiler,** ~ **tube** ~ · Rauchrohrkessel *m*

~ **prevention** · Rauchverhütung *f*

smokeproof tower, fire ~ [*In tall buildings, a stair designed as a fire escape with entries at each floor, protected by fire doors so that smoke cannot enter the stair*] · Feuertreppenschacht *m*, Nottreppenschacht

smoke spread, spread of smoke · Rauchausbreitung *f*

smoke-stop · Rauchabsperrung *f*

~ **door** · Rauchsperrtür *f*

smoke test [*A test for the efficiency of drains carried out with smoke*] · Rauchprobe *f*, Rauchprüfung *f*, Rauchversuch *m*

smoke-tight · rauchdicht

smoke tube, ~ **pipe, stove** ~, **chimney connector** · Rauchrohr *n*, Ofenrohr [*DIN 1298*]

~ ~ **boiler,** ~ **pipe** ~ · Rauchrohrkessel *m*

smoking load [*of a room*] · Rauchlast *f*

smoking-room · Rauchzimmer *n*

smoking withdrawal clinic · Raucher-Entziehungsheim *n*

smoky chimney · rußender Schornstein *m*

to smolder · schwelen

to smooth · glätten

smooth-bore copper tube, ~ ~ **pipe** · Kupferrohr *n* mit glatter Innenwand(ung)

smooth concrete · Glattbeton *m*

~ **finish,** ~ **plaster** · glatter Verputz *m*, geglätteter ~, Glättverputz, Glattverputz [*Er wird nach dem Aufziehen mit dem Reibebrett geglättet und meist noch gefilzt*]

~ ~, ~ **surface** ~ · glatte Oberflächengestaltung *f*

~ **gypsum plaster** · Gipsglattputz *m*, glatter Gipsputz

~ **lime finish,** ~ ~ **plaster** · Kalkglattverputz *m*, glatter Kalkverputz

~ **roll(ed)** · glattgerollt [*Dachpappe*]

~ **soffit,** ~ **visible under-face,** ~ **visible underside** [*It can receive paint or distemper*] · glatte Untersicht *f*

~ **surface** · ebene Oberfläche *f* [*Im Gegensatz zu einer profilierten Oberfläche*]

~ (~) **finish** · glatte Oberflächengestaltung *f*

~ **visible under-face** → ~ **soffit**

~ ~ **underside** → ~ **soffit**

smoothed · geglättet

~ **glass** · savonniertes Glas *n*, feingeschliffenes ~, fertiggeschliffenes ~

smoothing · Savonnieren *n*, Feinschleifen, Fertigschleifen [*Glas*]

~, **flattening** · Strecken *n*, Bügeln [*Tafelglasherstellung*]

~, **surface** ~ · (Ab)Glättung *f*

~ **kiln, flattening** ~ · Streckofen *m* [*Tafelglasherstellung*]

~ **trowel, finishing** ~, **float** · Glättkelle *f*

smoothness · Glätte *f*

smooth-walled · glattwandig

SMT, Square Mesh Tracking [*Trademark*] · Stahlmattenbelag *m*

snack (bar) · (Schnell)Imbißstube *f*, (Schnell)Imbißgaststätte *f*

snap fitted into position · eingeschnappt

~ **header** → **half bat**

~ **hook, spring** ~ · Karabinerhaken *m*

to snap into position · aufziehen [*(Ab)Dicht(ungs)ring auf ein Rohr*]

snow board, ~ **cradling** · Schneefangbrett *n*

~ **conditions** · Schneeverhältnisse *f* [*Winterbau*]

~ **guard** · Schneefang *m*

~ **load, SL** · Schneelast *f* [*DIN 1055 Bl. 5*]

~ ~ **value, value of snow load** · Schneelastwert *m*

~ **loading** · Schneebelastung *f*

snug, cosy, homely · wohnlich

~ · passend, gut sitzend

S.O., supplied only · nur Lieferung

soaked to a putty, run ~ ~ ~ · eingesumpft

soaked weight — sodium hypochlorite solution

~ **weight** · Naßgewicht *n*

soaker [*A small piece of flexible metal cut to shape by the plumber and laid by the slater to interlock with slates or tiles. It makes a watertight joint at a hip or valley or at an abutment between a roof and a wall. It is bent at right-angles for an abutment or at an obtuse angle for a valley*] · Gebindewinkel *m*, winkelförmiger Lappen *m*

soaking, gauging · Einsumpfen *n* [*Kalkteig*]

~ **period** · Abkühl(ungs)dauer *f*, Abkühl(ungs)zeit *f*, Abkühl(ungs)frist *f* [*Dampfbehandlung von Beton*]

~ ~, ~ **time**, gauging ~ · Einsumpfdauer *f*, Einsumpfzeit *f* [*Kalkteig*]

~ **time**, ~ period, gauging ~ · Einsumpfdauer *f*, Einsumpfzeit *f* [*Kalkteig*]

soap-box race track · Seifenkistenrennbahn *f*

soap (brick), furring (~), queen closer · Meisterquartier *m*, Riemen(stein) *m*, Riem(en)stück *n*, Riemchen *n*, Längsquartier

~ **bubble**, membrane · Seifenhaut *f*

~ ~ **analogy**, membrane ~ · Seifenhautgleichnis *n*, Membran(e)analogie *f*, Membran(e)gleichnis, Seifenhautanalogie *f*

~ **dish**, ~ tray · Seifenmulde *f*, Seifenschale *f*

~ ~ **tile**, ~ tray ~ · Seifenmuldenfliese *f*, Seifenschalenfliese

~ **holder** · Seifenhalter *m*

soap-like · seifenartig

soap powder, powder(ed) soap · Seifenpulver *n*

soapproof, fast to soap(s) · seif(en)fest, seifenbeständig, seifenecht

soap solution · Seifenlösung *f*

~ **tray**, ~ dish · Seifenmulde *f*, Seifenschale *f*

~ ~ **tile**, ~ dish ~ · Seifenmuldenfliese *f*, Seifenschalenfliese

soapy water · Seifenwasser *n*

soccer field · Fußballplatz *m*

social building programme; ~ ~ program (US) · soziales Bauprogramm *n*

~ **centre** (Brit.); ~ center (US); civic ~ · Gemeinschaftszentrum *n*

~ **house-building**, ~ housing, low-rent ~, subsidized ~, local authority ~, public authority ~, publicly-assisted ~, low-cost (municipal) ~ [*Provision of flats or houses for low-income groups, partly financed with the aid of public funds. Financing includes certain tax and interest concessions*] · öffentlich geförderter Wohnungsbau *m*, Sozialwohnungsbau, sozialer Wohn(ungs)bau, sozialer W-Bau

socket, coupler (Brit.); bell (US) [*The end of a pipe, or pipe fitting, having an enlarged bore for the reception of the plain or spigot end of another pipe, or pipe fitting, for the formation of a spigot and socket joint*] · (Glocken-) Muffe *f*

~, coupler [*A pipe fitting in the form of a short cylindrical pipe, threaded on its inner surface, used for jointing together two pipes with externally threaded ends*] · Überschiebmuffe *f*, Überwurfverschraubung *f*

~ · Steckdose *f*

~ **outlet for cleaners**, power point ~ ~, (plug) socket ~ ~ · Staubsaugersteckdose *f*

~ **press** (Brit.); bell ~ (US) · Glockenmuffenpresse *f*

~ **spanner** (Brit.); ~ wrench · Aufsatzschlüssel *m*, Steckschlüssel, Hohlschlüssel

socket-type footing · Hülsenfundament *n*

socket with shrouded contacts · Kragensteckdose *f*

~ ~ **switch** · abschaltbare Steckdose *f*

~ **wrench;** ~ spanner (Brit.) · Aufsatzschlüssel *m*, Steckschlüssel, Hohlschlüssel

socketed bar → rocker member

~ **column**, rocker ~ · Pendelstütze *f*

~ **member** → rocker ~

~ **rod** → rocker member

socle [*A base or pedestal*] · Untersatz *m*, Sockel *m*

soda glass · Natronglas *n*

soda-lime glass · Natronkalkglas *n*

sodding, turfing by planting sod(s) · Ansoden *n*, Rasensodenandeckung *f*

sodium · Natrium *n*

~ **alginate** · Natriumalginat *n*

~ **aluminate** · Natriumaluminat *n*, Tonerdenatron *n*

~ **aluminium silicate** (Brit.); ~ aluminum ~ (US) · Natrium-Aluminium-Silikat *n*

~ **benzoate** · Natrium-Benzoesalz *n*

~ **carbonate** · Natriumkarbonat *n*

~ **chloride** (Brit.); ~ chlorid(e) (US); common salt · Kochsalz *n*, Natriumchlorid *n*, Chlornatrium *n*, NaCl

~ **chromate** · Natriumchromat *n*

~ **compound**, ~ system · Natriumverbindung *f*

~ **dichromate** · Natriumbichromat *n*, $Na_2CR_2O_7 \cdot 2H_2O$

~ **hypochlorite solution** · Natriumhypochloritlauge *f*

sodium nitrate — soft paraffin wax

~ **nitrate** · Natriumnitrat *n*, Natronsalpeter *m*, salpetersaures Natrium *n*, NaNO₃

~ **oxalate** · Natriumoxalat *n*, oxalsaures Natrium *n*

~ **phosphate** · Natriumphosphat *n*

~ **silicate**, silicate of soda, soluble glass, waterglass · Natriumsilikat *n*, Natronwasserglas *n*, Na₂SiO₃

~ ~ **bonded sand** · natriumsilikatgebundener Sand *m*, wasserglasgebundener ~

~ **soap** · Natronseife *f*

~ **sulphate** (Brit.); ~ **sulfate** (US); saltcake · Glaubersalz *n*, schwefelsaures Natrium *n*, Natriumsulfat *n*, Na₂SO₄·10H₂O

~ **system**, ~ **compound** · Natriumverbindung *f*

~ **thiosulfate**, **hypo** · Fixiersalz *n*, Natriumthiosulfat *n*, Na₂S₂O₃·5H₂O

~ **vapour lamp** (Brit.); ~ **vapor** ~ (US) · Natrium(dampf)lampe *f*

soffit, visible under-face, visible underside [*abbreviated: soff.*] · Untersicht *f*

~ (US); **roof** ~ (Brit.) · Unterseite *f* des Dachüberhanges

~ **block** → ~ (floor) filler (~)

~ ~ **floor** → ~ filler ~ ~

~ **board**, planceer piece, lining, plancier piece · Verschalungsbrett *n* an einer Unterseite

~ **cusp, open** ~ · Schlußring *m*, Steinkranz *m* [*Gewölbe*]

~ **development**, development of soffit · Abwicklung *f* der Wölbungsleibung

~ **(filler) block floor,** ~ **(~) tile** ~ · Steindecke *f*, Block(stein)decke, Füllblock(stein)decke, Füllsteindecke

~ **(~) tile floor,** ~ **(~) block** ~ · Steindecke *f*, Block(stein)decke, Füllblock(stein)decke, Füllsteindecke

~ **(floor filler) block** → (floor) filler (~)

~ **lined eave(s)** · (Dach)Traufe *f* mit verkleideter Untersicht, Dachfuß *m* ~ ~ ~

~ **of arch** → (arch) intrados

~ ~ **structural slab** → ceiling

~ ~ **vault(ing)** → inner surface ~ ~

~ **tile** → (floor) filler (block)

~ ~ **floor** → ~ (filler) block floor

~ **width**, intrados ~ · Bogentiefe *f* [*Die Tiefe der Bogenleibung*]

soft asphalt (US); ~ **(asphaltic-) bitumen** (Brit.) · Weichbitumen *n* [*Fehlname: Weichasphalt m*]

~ **(asphaltic-)bitumen** (Brit.); ~ **asphalt** (US) · Weichbitumen *n* [*Fehlname: Weichasphalt m*]

~ **base-tar,** ~ **(coal-tar) pitch** · Weich(teer)pech *n*

~ **bitumen,** ~ **asphaltic-**~ (Brit.); ~ **asphalt** (US) · Weichbitumen *n* [*Fehlname: Weichasphalt m*]

softboard · Dämmplatte *f*, ungepreßte (Holz)Faserplatte, (Holz)Faser-Dämmplatte, HFD, porige Holzfaserplatte, Porösplatte, Dämm-Faserplatte, poröse Holzfaserplatte [*Eine Platte, die ohne Pressung im Trockner hergestellt wird. Die häufig anzutreffende Bezeichnung „Weich(faser)platte" ist falsch, weil die Platte nicht notwendigerweise aus Weichholzfasern hergestellt wird. Rohwichte 230–400 kg/m³. Die Dämmplatten gliedern sich in die zum Isolieren (Isolierplatten = insulating softboards) bestimmten und die Akustikplatten. DIN 68750*]

soft brick · Weichziegel *m*

~ **burned,** ~ **burnt** · weichgebrannt

~ **burnt,** ~ **burned** · weichgebrannt

~ **clay** [*A clay which can be dug with a spade and samples easily mo(u)lded in the hand*] · Weichton *m*

~ **(coal-tar) pitch,** ~ **base-tar** · Weich(teer)pech *n*

~ **copal** · Weichkopal(harz) *m*, (*n*)

~ **copper came** · Weichkupferrute *f* [*Verglasung*]

to soften · enthärten [*Wasser*]

~ ~ · erweichen, durchweichen, aufweichen

softener → water ~

softening, water ~ · (Wasser)Enthärtung *f*, (Wasser)Enthärten *n*, Weichmachen

~ **agent** → water ~ ~

~ **method**, water ~ ~ · (Wasser)Enthärtungsverfahren *n*

~ **point** · Erweichungspunkt *m*, E. P.

~ **range** · Erweichungsbereich *m*, *n*

~ **test** · Erweichungsprobe *f*, Erweichungsprüfung *f*, Erweichungsversuch *m*

~ **unit** → water ~ ~

soft expanded natural rubber · Weich-Kautschukschaum(stoff) *m*, Weich-Zellkautschuk *m*

~ **glass** [*Glass with a relatively low softening point*] · weiches Glas *n*, Weichglas

~ **hardwood** · Weichlaubholz *n*

~ **iron wire** · Reineisendraht *m*, Weicheisendraht

~ **lead** · Weichblei *n*

~ ~ **foil** · Weichbleifolie *f*

~ ~ **plate** · Weichblei(grob)blech *n*

~ ~ **pressure pipe** · Weichblei-Druckrohr *n*

~ ~ **sheet** · Weichblei(fein)blech *n*

~ ~ **tube** · Weichbleirohr *n*

~ **paraffin wax** · Weichparaffin *n*

soft phenolic resin — solder(ed) joint

~ **phenolic resin** · Weichphenolharz n, Phenolweichharz

~ **pitch,** ~ coal-tar ~, ~ base-tar · Weich(teer)pech n

~ ~ **concrete tile** · ölfeste Asphaltfeinbeton(belag)platte f, ~ Asphaltfeinbetonfliese [*Diese Platten sind mit Steinkohlenteerweichpech gebunden*]

~ ~ **tile** · Homogen(belag)platte f, Homogenfliese, ölfeste Hochdruck-Asphalt(belag)platte, Steinkohlenteerpechplatte [*DIN 18354*] [*Diese Platten sind mit Steinkohlenteerweichpech gebunden! Die Bezeichnungen "Homogenasphaltplatte" und "Homogenasphaltfliese" sind daher irreführend*]

~ **rags** · Weichlumpen mpl

~ **rubber** · Weichgummi m, n

~ **sand** → building sand from natural sources

~ **solder** [*A solder in which lead and tin are the principal constituents*] · Weichlot n

~ **soldering** · Weichlöten n

~ ~ · Weichlötung f

soft-textured chipped wood concrete · Weichholzspanbeton m, Weichholzspänebeton

~ **wood** · Weichholz n

~ ~ **fibre concrete** (Brit.); ~ ~ fiber ~ (US) · Weichholzfaserbeton m

~ ~ **floor boarding** · Fhw m, Weichholz(fuß)boden(belag) m

soft walked-on finish · weichfedernder Gehbelag m

~ **water** · weiches Wasser n

soil (Brit.); closet waste water, toilet waste water [*The discharge from watercloset and urinals*] · Abort(ab)wasser n, Klosettabwasser, Toilettenabwasser

~ **pipe,** ~ line, closet waste water ~, toilet waste water ~ [*A pipe collecting from W.C.s and urinals*] · Abortrohr n, Klosett(abwasser)rohr, Toiletten(abwasser)rohr

soil-sewage → house(hold) sewage

soil stack · Abortfallrohr n, Abfallrohr für Aborte

soil-waste pipe [*A pipe for conveying both soil and waste water*] · Hausabflußrohr n, Gebäudeabflußrohr, Hausablaufrohr, Gebäudeablaufrohr, Hausdränrohr, Gebäudedränrohr, Hausentwässerungsrohr, Gebäudeentwässerungsrohr

(soiled) linen chute, laundry ~, clothes ~ · (Schmutz)Wäscheabwurfanlage f, (Schmutz)Wäscherutsche f

sol-air temperature · Sonnenlufttemperatur f

solar constant · Solarkonstante f [*Die von der Sonne senkrecht auf die äußere Grenze der Erdatmosphäre gestrahlte Wärmemenge, die sogenannte S., beträgt rund 1 200 kcal/m²h*]

~ **controlled venetian (blind)** [*It is coupled to a light-sensitive device*] · sonnengesteuerte Raffjalousie f, ~ Zugjalousie

~ **gain** → ~ heat ~

~ **glass,** antisun ~ · Sonnenschutzglas n

~ **grating** · Sonnenschutzgitterrost m

~ **grille** [*sometimes spelled 'grill'*] · Sonnenschutz(zier)gitter n

~ **heat** · Sonnenwärme f

~ (~) **gain** · Sonnengewinn m, Sonnenwärmegewinn

~ ~ **load** · Sonnenwärmelast f

~ ~ **radiation** · Sonnenwärmestrahlung f

~ **heating** · Sonnen(be)heizung f

~ **light radiation** · Sonnenlichtstrahlung f

~ **load** · Sonnenstrahlungswärme f

~ **orientation** [*The position of a building in relation to the north or south, with particular reference to the amount of sunshine falling on the walls and windows, and the penetration of the sun through the windows into a building*] · Sonnenlage f

~ **radiation,** sun ~ · Sonnenstrahlung f

~ **screening,** (~) shading, sunshading · Sonnenschutz m, Abschattung f, Besonnungsschutz

~ **screen(ing),** ~ shading device, (sun) shading device, sunbreaker, sunblind · Sonnen(schutz)blende f, Abschattungsvorrichtung f, Sonnenschutz(anlage) m, (f)

(~) **shading,** ~ screening, sunshading · Sonnenschutz m, Abschattung f, Besonnungsschutz

~ ~ **device,** (sun) ~ ~, sunblind, sunbreaker, solar screen(ing) · Sonnen(schutz)blende f, Abschattungsvorrichtung f, Sonnenschutzkonstruktion f, Sonnenschutz(anlage) m, (f)

~ **water heater** · Sonnenenergie-Wassererhitzer m

solarium, sun(-bathing) terrace, sun(-bathing) patio, sun(-bathing) room · Sonnenterrasse f, Solarium n

to solder · löten

solder · Lötmetall n, Lot n

~ **alloy** · Lötlegierung f

~ **glass,** intermediate sealing ~ · Zwischenglas n, Einschmelzglas, Lötglas, Glaslot n

~ **joint** → solder(ed) ~

~ **wire** · Lötdraht m

(soldered) cleat, ~ metal ~ · (Löt-)Hafter m [*Metallbedachung*]

(~) **copper cleat** · Kupfer(löt)hafter m [*Metallbedachung*]

~ **flange** · Lötflansch m [*DIN 2570*]

solder(ed) joint [*A joint in which the parts are united with molten solder*] · Lötverbindung f

soldered (metal) cleat, cleat · (Löt-)Hafter m [Metallbedachung]

~ seam, lock ~ ~ · Falz m mit (Löt-)Hafter [Metallbedachung]

soldering [The term 'soldering' is also used for 'soft soldering' = Weichlötung] · Lötung f

~ [The term 'soldering' is also used for 'soft soldering' = Weichlöten] · Löten n

~ flux · Lötflußmittel n

~ iron, copper(ing) bit · Lötkolben m

~ lamp, blowlamp, blowpipe lamp (Brit.); blowtorch (US) · Lötlampe f [DIN 8502]

~ method · Lötmethode f, Lötverfahren n

~ oven · Lötofen m

~ temperature · Löttemperatur f

~ tongs, brazing ~, soldering-tweezers, hawk-bill (pliers) · Lötzange f

~ torch · Lötrohr n, Lötbrenner m

soldering-tweezers → soldering tongs

soldier course · endkantig gestellte Ziegelschicht f, ~ ~ Ziegellage f

sole plate, sill (Brit.); solepiece, (a)butment piece (US); cill [deprecated] (Brit.) [The lowest horizontal member of a framed partition, or frame construction] · (Holz)Schwelle f [Beim Holzfachwerk der untere waag(e)rechte Balken der Riegelwand]

solemnity (of style) · Feierlichkeit f (des Stils)

solid [As opposed to 'hollow' and 'cellular'] · voll

~, ~ body · Festkörper m

~ · Feststoff m

~ beam · Vollbalken(träger) m

~ block → ((pre)cast) concrete ~ ~

~ ~, ~ tile [See remark under 'Block'] · Vollblock(stein) m, Vollstein

~ (body) · Festkörper m

~ (~) mechanics · Festkörpermechanik f

~ brick, ~ clay ~ · Vollziegel m; Vollstein m [Fehlname] [DIN 105]

~ ~ chimney, ~ clay ~ ~ · Vollziegelschornstein m; Vollsteinschornstein [Fehlname]

~ ~ masonry (work) → ~ clay ~ ~ (~)

~ ~ wall, ~ clay ~ ~ · Vollziegelmauer f; Vollziegelwand f, Vollsteinmauer, Vollsteinwand [Fehlnamen]

~ brickwork → ~ clay ~

~ calcium silicate brick, ~ sand-lime ~, ~ lime-sand ~ · Kalksandvollstein m, KSV [Der Querschnitt darf durch Lochung senkrecht zur Lagerfläche bis zu 25% gemindert sein. DIN 106]

~ character, ~ element · Körperliche n

~ cinder tile (US); ~ clinker ~, ~ ~ block (Brit.) [See remark under 'Block'] · Schlacken(beton)-Vollblock m, Schlakken(beton)-Voll(block)stein m

~ (clay) brick · Vollziegel m; Vollstein m [Fehlname] [DIN 105]

~ (~) ~ chimney · Vollziegelschornstein m; Vollsteinschornstein [Fehlname]

~ (~) ~ masonry (work), ~ (~) brickwork · Vollziegelmauerwerk n; Vollsteinmauerwerk [Fehlname]

~ (~) ~ wall · Vollziegelmauer f; Vollziegelwand f, Vollsteinmauer, Vollsteinwand [Fehlnamen]

~ (~) brickwork, ~ (~) brick masonry (work) · Vollziegelmauerwerk n; Vollsteinmauerwerk [Fehlname]

~ clinker block, ~ ~ tile (Brit.); ~ cinder ~ (US) [See remark under 'Block'] · Schlacken(beton)-Vollblock m, Schlacken(beton)-Voll(block)stein m

~ colloidal substance, colloidal solid ~ · kolloid(al)e Festsubstanz f

~ concrete method · Betonvollbauweise f

~ construction, ~ (structural) system [e.g. a solid (concrete) floor] · Vollbausystem n, Vollkonstruktion f, Voll(konstruktions)system

~ content, solids ~ · Feststoffgehalt m, Feststoffanteil m

~ cross-section · Vollquerschnitt m

~ cross wall, ~ shear ~ · Voll(wand)scheibe f

~ door · Volltür f

~ element, ~ character · Körperliche n

~ expanded cinder concrete block, ~ ~ ~ ~ tile (US); ~ foamed slag ~ ~ (Brit.) [See remark under 'Block(-stein)'] · Hüttenbimsvollblock(stein) m, Hüttenbimsvollstein, Kunstbimsvollblock(stein), Kunstbimsvollstein

~ flat plate floor · Vollflachdecke f

~ foamed slag concrete block, ~ ~ ~ ~ tile (Brit.); ~ expanded cinder ~ ~ (US) [See remark under 'Block(-stein)'] · Hüttenbimsvollblock(stein) m, Hüttenbimsvollstein, Kunstbimsvollblock(stein), Kunstbimsvollstein

~ frame [A door or window frame in which the stiles, etc., are solid, and not built-up, or cased] · Vollrahmen m

~ fuel boiler · Festbrennstoffkessel m

~ ~ (burning) appliance, ~ ~ fire, ~ fuel(-fired) furnace · Feuerung f für festen Brennstoff, Feuerstätte f ~ ~ ~

~ ~ (central heating) system · Festbrennstoffheizung f

~ ~ domestic boiler, domestic solid fuel ~ · Haushalt(heiz)kessel m für feste Brennstoffe

solid fuel(-fired) furnace — to solidify

~ **fuel(-fired) furnace** → ~ fuel (burning) appliance

~ ~ **room heater** → (domestic) stove

~ ~ **stove** · Festbrennstoffofen *m*

~ ~ **water heating** · Wassererwärmung *f* mit festen Brennstoffen

~ **geometry,** descriptive ~, three-dimensional ~ · darstellende Geometrie *f*

~ **gold** · gediegenes Gold *n*

~ **gypsum (building) board,** ~ ~ (~) sheet · Vollgips(bau)platte *f*, Voll-Bau-Gipsplatte, Gips-Vollbauplatte

~ ~ **roof(ing) block,** ~ ~ ~ tile · Gipsdachvollstein *m*, Voll-Gipsdachstein

~ **light(weight) (clay) brick** · Voll-Leichtziegel *m*, Leicht-Vollziegel

~ **lime-sand brick,** ~ sand-lime ~, ~ calcium silicate ~ · Kalksandvollstein *m*, KSV [*Der Querschnitt darf durch Lochung senkrecht zur Lagerfläche bis zu 25% gemindert sein. DIN 106*]

~ **masonry wall** · Vollmauer *f*

~ ~ **(work)** · Vollmauerwerk *n*

~ **mechanics,** ~ body ~ · Festkörpermechanik *f*

~ **melting wax,** hard ~ ~ · Hartparaffin *n*

~ **newel (post)** · Mönch *m* [*Bei Wendeltreppen die innere volle Spindel*]

~ ~ **stair(case)** · Spindeltreppe *f*; Spindelstiege *f* [*Österreich*] [*Monozentrische Wendeltreppe mit voller Spindel*]

~ **of revolution** · Umdrehungskörper *m*

~ **panel** · Volltafel *f*

~ **partition (wall)** [*A partition (wall) without a cavity*] · Volltrennwand *f*

~ **pipe,** high-pressure ~ · Hochdruckrohr *n*, robustes Rohr

~ **rectangular cantilever(ed) step,** ~ ~ cantilevering ~, ~ ~ flyer · Kragblockstufe *f*, Auslegerblockstufe, auskragende Blockstufe, vorkragende Blockstufe, Kragklotzstufe, Auslegerklotzstufe, vorkragende Klotzstufe, auskragende Klotzstufe, Kragmassivstufe, Auslegermassivstufe, auskragende Massivstufe, vorkragende Massivstufe

~ ~ **flyer** → ~ ~ cantilever(ed) step

~ ~ **step,** flyer · Klotzstufe *f*, Blockstufe, Massivstufe [*Stufe mit rechteckigem Querschnitt*]

~ **rubber** · Vollgummi *m, n*

~ **sand-lime brick,** ~ lime-sand ~, ~ calcium silicate ~ · Kalksandvollstein *m*, KSV [*Der Querschnitt darf durch Lochung senkrecht zur Lagerfläche bis zu 25% gemindert sein. DIN 106*]

~ **shear wall,** ~ cross ~ · Voll(wand)scheibe *f*

~ **slab** · Vollplatte *f*

~ ~ **(intermediate) floor** · Vollplattendecke *f*, Vollplatten-Stockwerkdecke, Vollplatten-Etagendecke, Vollplatten-Geschoßdecke, Vollplatten-Gebäudedecke, Vollplatten-Trenndecke, Vollplatten-Hochbaudecke, Plattendecke, Voll(beton)decke [*Sie wird auf geschlossener Schalung mit vollem Querschnitt örtlich betoniert*]

~ **square bar,** ~ ~ rod · quadratischer Vollstab *m*, Quadrat-Vollstab

~ **step,** (natural) stone ~ · (Natur-)Steinstufe *f*

~ **(structural) system,** ~ construction [*e.g. a solid (concrete) floor*] · Vollbausystem *n*, Vollkonstruktion *f*, Voll(konstruktions)system

~ **system,** ~ structural ~, ~ construction [*e.g. a solid (concrete) floor*] · Vollbausystem *n*, Vollkonstruktion *f*, Voll(konstruktions)system

~ **tile** → ((pre)cast) (concrete) solid block

~ ~, ~ block [*See remark under 'Block'*] · Vollblock(stein) *m*, Vollstein

~ **vault** · Vollgewölbe *n*

~ **wall** · Vollwand *f*

~ ~ **construction** · Vollwandkonstruktion *f*

~ ~ ~ **method** · Vollwandbauweise *f*, Vollwandbauart *f*

~ ~ **slab** · Vollwand(bau)platte *f*

~ **waste,** refuse · fester Abfall(stoff) *m*

~ **wax (polish),** wax paste (~) · Wachs(polier)paste *f*

~ **web,** plain ~, ~ stalk · Vollsteg *m*

solid-webbed, plain-webbed · vollwandig, vollstegig

solid-web(bed) arch(ed girder), plain-web(bed) ~ (~) · Vollwandbogen(träger) *m*, Vollwandträger in Bogenform

~ **beam,** plain-web(bed) ~ · Vollwandbalken(träger) *m*

~ **girder,** plain-web(bed) ~ · Vollstegträger *m*, Vollwandträger

~ **joist,** plain-web(bed) ~ · Vollwandunterzug *m*

~ **three-hinge(d) arch(ed girder),** plain-web(bed) ~ (~) · Vollwand-Dreigelenkbogen(träger) *m*, Vollwand-Dreigelenkträger in Bogenform

solidification temperature · Erstarrungspunkt *m* [*Die Temperatur, bei der ein flüssiger Stoff in einen festen Zustand übergeht, z.B. Wasser in Eis*]

to solidify · erstarren [*Vom flüssigen in den festen Zustand übergehen*]

solidly filled — soot door

solidly filled, flat jointed, flush jointed · vollfugig, bündig verfugt

solidness · massive Schwere *f*

solid(s) content · Feststoffgehalt *m*, Feststoffanteil *m*

sol(l)ar · Altan *m*, Söller *m*

solubility · Auflösbarkeit *f*, Löslichkeit

~ **in water,** water solubility · Wasserlöslichkeit *f*

~ **test** · Löslichkeitsprobe *f*, Löslichkeitsversuch *m*, Löslichkeitsprüfung *f*

solubilization [*e.g. of fats and oils*] · Lösen *n*

soluble cobalt drier, cobalt siccative · Kobaltsikkativ *n*, Kobalttrockenstoff *m* in gelöster Form

~ **drier,** liquid ~ (US); ~ dryer (Brit.); siccative · Sikkativ *n*, Trockenstoff *m* in gelöster Form [*DIN 55901*]

~ **dye** · löslicher Küpenfarbstoff *m*

~ **dyestuff** · löslicher Farbstoff *m*

~ **glass,** waterglass, sodium silicate, silicate of soda · Natriumsilicat *n*, Natronwasserglas *n*, Na_2SiO_3

~ ~ **coat,** water ~ ~ · Wasserglasanstrich *m*, Wasserglasaufstrich

~ ~ **mastic,** water ~ ~ · Wasserglaskitt *m* [*Wasserglas + Füllstoffe*]

~ ~ **mix(ture),** water ~ ~ · Doppelwasserglas *n* [*Eine Mischung von Natronwasserglas und Kaliwasserglas*]

~ ~ **solution,** water ~ ~ · Wasserglaslösung *f*

~ **in carbon disulfide** (US); ~ ~ ~ disulphide (Brit.) · löslich in CS_2

~ ~ **water,** water-soluble · wasserlöslich

~ **salt,** salt causing unsightly efflorescence · ausblühfähiges Salz *n*, ausschlagfähiges ~, auswitterungsfähiges ~

~ ~ · lösliches Salz *n*

solution · (Auf)Lösung *f*

(~) **calorimeter** [*The materials are allowed to react in the dissolved state inside an insulated vessel*] · Lösungskalorimeter *n*, Lösungswärmemesser *m*

~ **example,** example of solution · (Auf-)Lösungsbeispiel *n*

~ **of ammonia,** ammonia solution · Ammoniaklösung *f*

~ ~ **dyestuff,** dyestuff solution · Farbstofflösung *f*

~ **polymerisation** (Brit.); ~ polymerization · Lösungspolymerisation *f*

~ **state of matter** · Lösungszustand *m*

solvent, (volatile) thinner · Verdünnungsmittel *n* [*Eine organische Flüssigkeit zur Streichbarmachung von Anstrichfarben*]

~ · Lösemittel *n*, Lösungsmittel, Löser *m*

~ **base** · Lösungsmittelbasis *f*, Lösungsmittelgrundlage *f*

solvent-based · lösemittelhaltig, lösungsmittelhaltig

solvent-base(d) adhesive, ~ glue · Lösungsmittelkleber *m* Lösungsmittelkleb(e)stoff *m*

~ **paint remover,** ~ ~ stripper · flüssiges (Ab)Beizmittel *n*, lösendes ~, neutrales ~, (Ab)Beizfluid *n*, (Ab-)Beizflüssigkeit *f*

solvent blend, ~ mix(ture) · Lösungsmittelmischung *f*, Lösungsmittelgemisch *n*

solvent-carried paint · Lösungsmittelfarbe *f*

solvent coat(ing) · Lösungsmittelanstrich *m*, Lösungsmittelaufstrich

~ **extraction** · Lösungsmittelextraktion *f*, Lösungsmittelauszug *m*

solvent(-)fast → solvent(-)proof

solvent-free, solvent-less · lösungsmittelfrei, lösemittelfrei

solvent-less, solvent-free · lösungsmittelfrei, lösemittelfrei

solvent mix(ture), ~ blend · Lösungsmittelmischung *f*, Lösungsmittelgemisch *n*

~ **naphtha** · Solventnaphtha *n, f*

~ **paint** → bituminous lacquer

~ **process,** reflux ~ · Kreislaufverfahren *n*, Umlaufverfahren [*Alkydharzherstellung*]

solvent(-)proof, solvent(-)fast · lösemittelbeständig, lösemittelfest, lösungsmittelfest, lösungsmittelbeständig, lösemittelecht, lösungsmittelecht

solvent(-)saturated · lösemittelgesättigt, lösungsmittelgesättigt

solvent-soluble · lösungsmittellöslich, lösemittellöslich

~ **dye** · lösungsmittellöslicher Küpenfarbstoff *m*, lösemittellöslicher ~

solvent(-)susceptible, sensitive to solvent(s) · lösemittelempfindlich, lösungsmittelempfindlich

solvent-thinned · lösungsmittelverdünnt, lösemittelverdünnt

solvent vapours (Brit.); ~ vapors (US) · Lösemitteldämpfe *mpl*, Lösungsmitteldämpfe

sommer → summer beam

sonic alarm system · Geräusch-Meldeanlage *f* [*Einbruchschutz*]

soot · Ruß *m* [*Reiner Kohlenstoff, der sich bei der Verfeuerung gasreicher Brennstoffe aus den Verbrennungsgasen ausscheidet, wenn die Verbrennung infolge ungenügender Sauerstoffzufuhr oder infolge zu starker Abkühlung der brennbaren Gase an kalten Flächen unvollständig erfolgt*]

~ **barrier** · Rußabsperrer *m*, Rußsperre *f*

~ **blower,** SB · Rußgebläse *n*

~ **door** [*B.S. 1294*]; ash(pit) ~, cleanout ~, COD (US) · Kamintür *f*, Reinigungstür, Putztür, Schornsteinreinigungsverschluß *m*, Aschentür, Entaschungstür, Rußtür

~ formation · Rußbildung f
~ stain · Rußfleck m
sopraporta, overdoor, hyperthyrum · Supraporte f, Sopraporte, Portalbekrönung f, Türbekrönung [*Ein Wandfeld (mit Relief oder Gemälde) über einer Tür oder einem Portal, besonders beim Rokoko*]
Sorel('s) cement → (magnesium) oxychlorid(e) cement
sort of lime · Kalksorte f
sorting · Sortierung f, Sortieren n
sound · einwandfrei [*in Bezug auf Güte*]
~ · blank [*Metall nach Reinigung*]
~ · nichtverwittert, unverwittert
~ [*Mechanical disturbance, propagated in an elastic medium, of such character as to be capable of exciting the sensation of hearing*] · Hörschall m, Schall im engeren Sinne [*Schall im Frequenzbereich des menschlichen Hörens; Hörbereich etwa 16 Hz bis 16 kHz*]
~ [1. *Mechanical disturbance, propagated in an elastic medium, of such character as to be capable of exciting the sensation of hearing.*
By extension the term 'sound' is sometimes applied to any disturbance, irrespective of frequency, which may be propagated as a wave motion in an elastic medium. Disturbances of frequency too high to be capable of exciting the sensation of hearing are described as 'ultrasonic'. 'Hypersonics' is the name given to ultrasonic disturbances in a medium, whose wavelength is comparable with the intermolecular spacing.
Disturbances of frequency too low to be capable of exciting the sensation of hearing are described as 'intrasonic'.
2. *The sensation of hearing excited by mechanical disturbance*] · Schall m [*Mechanische Schwingung oder Wellenbewegung der Teilchen eines elastischen Mediums*]

(~) absorbent backing, (~) absorbing ~, (~) absorptive ~, sound-control ~, acoustic(al) ~ · Schallschluck-Hinterfüllung f, Akustik-Hinterfüllung, Schallabsorptions-Hinterfüllung [*Gips-Akustikplatte*]

(~) ~ blanket, (~) ~ pad, (~) absorbing ~, (~) absorptive ~, sound-control ~, acoustic(al) ~ · Schallschluckmatte f, Akustikmatte, Schallabsorptionsmatte

(~) ~ board → acoustic(al) ~

(~) ~ brick → (ceramic) acoustic(al) ~

(~) ~ (building) unit, (~) absorbing (~) ~, (~) absorptive (~) ~, sound-control (~) ~, acoustic(al) ~ · Schallschluckelement n, Akustikelement, Schallabsorptionselement, Schallschluckkörper m, Akustikkörper, Schallabsorptionskörper

(~) ~ cassette → (~) ~ pan(el)

(~) ~ ceiling, (~) absorbing ~, (~) absorptive ~, sound-control ~, acoustic(al) ~ · Schallschluckdecke f, Akustikdecke, Schallabsorptionsdecke

(~) ~ ~ paint, (~) absorbing ~ ~, (~) absorptive ~ ~, sound-control ~ ~, acoustic(al) ~ ~ · Schallschluckdecken(anstrich)farbe f, Akustikdecken(anstrich)farbe, Schallabsorptionsdecken(anstrich)farbe

(~) ~ ~ sheet → acoustic(al) ceiling tile

(~) ~ ~ system, (~) absorbing ~ ~, (~) absorptive ~ ~, sound-control ~ ~, acoustic(al) ~ ~, acoustic tiled ~ ~ · Schallschluckdeckensystem n, Akustikdeckensystem, Schallabsorptionsdeckensystem

(~) ~ chamber, (~) absorbing ~, (~) absorptive ~ · Schallschluckkammer f, Schallabsorptionskammer

(~) ~ coffer → (~) ~ pan(el)

(~) ~ construction (method), (~) absorbing ~ (~), (~) absorptive ~ (~), acoustic(al) ~ (~) · Schallschluckbauweise f, Akustikbauweise, Schallabsorptionsbauweise

(~) ~ construction(al) material, (~) absorbing ~ ~, (~) absorptive ~ ~, acoustic(al) ~ ~ · Schallschluckbaustoff m, Akustikbaustoff, Schallabsorptionsbaustoff

(~) ~ cover(ing) → acoustic(al) lining

(~) ~ facing → acoustic(al) lining

(~) ~ felt(ed fabric), (sound) absorbing ~ (~), (sound) absorptive ~ (~), sound-control ~ (~), acoustic(al) ~ (~) · Schallschluckfilz m, Akustikfilz, Schallabsorptionsfilz

(~) ~ ~ ceiling, (sound) absorbing ~ (~) ~, (sound) absorptive ~ (~) ~, sound-control ~ (~) ~, acoustic(al) ~ (~) ~ · Schallschluckfilzdecke f, Schallabsorptionsfilzdecke, Akustikfilzdecke

(~) ~ fibre board → acoustic(al) ~ ~

(~) ~ foil, (~) absorbing ~, (~) absorptive ~, sound-control ~, acoustic(al) ~ · Schallschluckfolie f, Akustikfolie, Schallabsorptionsfolie

(~) ~ glass → sound-control ~

(~) ~ hung ceiling → (~) ~ suspended ~

(~) ~ lining → acoustic(al) ~

(~) ~ masonry wall, (~) absorbing ~ ~, (~) absorptive ~ ~, sound-control ~ ~, acoustic(al) ~ ~ · Schallschluckmauer f, Akustikmauer, Schallabsorptionsmauer

(~) ~ material, (~) absorbing ~, (~) absorptive ~, sound-control ~, acoustic(al) ~ · Schallschluckmaterial n, Akustikmaterial, Schallschluckstoff m, Akustikstoff, Schallabsorptionsmaterial, Schallabsorptionsstoff

(~) ~ metal ceiling, (~) absorbing ~ ~, (~) absorptive ~ ~, sound-control ~ ~, acoustic(al) ~ ~ · Schallschluckmetalldecke f, Metallschallschluckdecke, Akustikmetalldecke, Metallakustikdecke, Schallabsorptionsmetalldecke, Metallschallabsorptionsdecke

(~) ~ **pad** → acoustic(al) blanket

(~) ~ **paint** → acoustic(al) ~

(~) ~ **panel** → sound-control ~

(~) ~ **pan(el)**, (~) ~ coffer, (~) ~ waffle, (~) ~ cassette, (~) absorbing ~, (~) ~ cassette, (~) absorbing ~, acoustic(al) ~ · Schallschluck-Kassette f, Akustikkassette, Schallabsorptionskassette

(~) ~ **plaster**, (~) absorbing ~, (~) absorptive ~, sound-control ~, acoustic(al) ~ · Schallschluckputz m, Akustikputz, Schallabsorptionsputz

(~) ~ ~ **aggregate**, (~) absorbing ~ ~, (~) absorptive ~ ~, sound-control ~ ~, acoustic(al) ~ ~ · Schallschluckputzzuschlag(stoff) m, Akustikputzzuschlag(stoff), Schallabsorptionsputzzuschlag(stoff)

(~) ~ ~ **ceiling**, (~) absorbing ~ ~, (~) absorptive ~ ~, sound-control ~ ~, acoustic(al) ~ ~, APC · Schallschluckputzdecke f, Akustikputzdecke, Schallabsorptionsputzdecke

(~) ~ **sheet** → acoustic(al) board

(~) ~ **sprayed-on plaster** → sound-control ~ ~

(~) ~ **(sur)facing** → acoustic(al) lining

(~) ~ **suspended ceiling**, (~) ~ hung ~, (~) absorptive ~ ~, (~) absorbing ~ ~, acoustic(al) tile ~ ~, suspended acoustic(al) ~, hung acoustic(al) ~ · Hänge-Akustikdecke f, Hänge-Schallschluckdecke, Schallschluck-Hängedecke, Akustik-Hängedecke

(~) ~ **system** → (~) absorptive ~

(~) ~ **tile**, (~) absorbing ~, (~) absorptive ~, sound-control ~, acoustic(al) ~, AT. · Schallschluckfliese f, Akustikfliese, Schallschluckplatte f, Akustikplatte, Schallabsorptionsfliese, Schallabsorptionsplatte

(~) ~ ~ **ceiling**, (~) absorbing ~ ~, (~) absorptive ~ ~, sound-control ~ ~, acoustic(al) ~ ~, ATC · Schallschluckfliesendecke f, Schallschluckplattendecke, Akustikfliesendecke, Akustikplattendecke, Schallabsorptionsfliesendecke, Schallabsorptionsplattendecke

(~) ~ **unit** → (~) absorptive system

(~) ~ **waffle** → (~) ~ pan(el)

(~) ~ **wall** → sound-control ~

(~) ~ ~ **block** → acoustic(al) wall tile

(~) ~ ~ **brick** → sound-control ~ ~

(~) ~ **wallpaper** → sound-control ~

(~) ~ **wall tile** → acoustic(al) ~ ~

(~) ~ ~ ~ → sound-control ~ ~

(~) ~ **wood fibre board** (Brit.) → acoustic(al) ~ ~ ~

~ **absorber** · Schallschluckmittel n, Schallabsorptionsmittel [Tafel; Platte; Folie; Putz; Farbe]

(~) ~ → (~) absorbing system

~ **absorbing**, ~ absorptive, acoustical [*The capability of a material to absorb noise to make a room quieter and more comfortable*] · schallschluckend, schallabsorbierend

(~) ~ **backing**, (~) absorbent ~, (~) absorptive ~, acoustic(al) ~ · Schallschluck-Hinterfüllung f, Akustik-Hinterfüllung, Schallabsorptions-Hinterfüllung [*Gips-Akustikplatte*]

(~) ~ **blanket**, (~) ~ pad, (~) absorbent ~, (~) absorptive ~, sound-control ~, acoustic(al) ~ · Schallschluckmatte f, Akustikmatte, Schallabsorptionsmatte

(~) ~ **board** → acoustic(al) ~

(~) ~ **brick** → (ceramic) acoustic(al) ~

(~) ~ **(building) unit**, (~) absorbent (~) ~, (~) absorptive (~) ~, sound-control (~) ~, acoustic(al) (~) ~ · Schallschluckelement n, Akustikelement, Schallabsorptionselement, Schallschluckkörper m, Akustikkörper, Schallabsorptionskörper

(~) ~ **cassette** → (~) absorbent pan(el)

(~) ~ **ceiling**, (~) absorbent ~, (~) absorptive ~, sound-control ~, acoustic(al) ~, acoustic tiled ~ · Schallschluckdecke f, Akustikdecke, Schallabsorptionsdecke

(~) ~ ~ **board** → acoustic(al) ceiling tile

(~) ~ ~ **paint**, (~) absorbent ~ ~, (~) absorptive ~ ~, sound-control ~ ~, acoustical ~ ~ · Schallschluckdecken(anstrich)farbe f, Akustikdecken-(anstrich)farbe, Schallabsorptionsdecken(anstrich)farbe

(~) ~ ~ **sheet** → acoustic(al) ceiling tile

(~) ~ ~ **system** → (~) absorbent ~ ~

(~) ~ ~ **tile** → acoustic(al) ~ ~

(~) ~ **chamber**, (~) absorbent ~, (~) absorptive ~ · Schallabsorptionskammer f, Schallabsorptionskammer

(~) ~ **coffer** → (~) absorbent pan(el)

(~) ~ **construction (method)**, (~) absorbent ~ (~), (~) absorptive ~ (~), acoustic(al) ~ (~) · Schallschluckbauweise f, Akustikbauweise, Schallabsorptionsbauweise

(sound) absorbing — (sound) absorptive backing

(~) ~ construction(al) material, (~) absorbent ~ ~, (~) absorptive ~ ~, acoustic(al) ~ ~ · Schallschluckbaustoff m, Akustikbaustoff, Schallabsorptionsbaustoff

(~) ~ cover(ing) → acoustic(al) lining

(~) ~ facing → acoustic(al) lining

(~) ~ felt(ed fabric), (sound) absorbent ~ (~), (sound) absorptive ~ (~), sound-control ~ (~), acoustic(al) ~ (~) · Schallschluckfilz m, Akustikfilz, Schallabsorptionsfilz

(~) ~ ~ ~ ceiling, (sound) absorbent ~ (~) ~, (sound) absorptive ~ (~) ~, sound-control ~ (~) ~, acoustic(al) ~ (~) ~ · Schallschluckfilzdecke f, Akustikfilzdecke, Schallabsorptionsfilzdecke

(~) ~ fibre board → acoustic(al) ~ ~

(~) ~ foil, (~) absorbent ~, (~) absorptive ~, sound-control ~, acoustic(al) ~ · Schallschluckfolie f, Akustikfolie, Schallabsorptionsfolie

(~) ~ glass → sound-control ~

(~) ~ hung ceiling → (sound) absorbent suspended ~

(~) ~ lining → acoustic(al) ~

(~) ~ masonry wall, (~) absorbent ~ ~, (~) absorptive ~ ~, sound-control ~ ~, acoustic(al) ~ ~ · Schallschluckmauer f, Akustikmauer, Schallabsorptionsmauer

(~) ~ material, (~) absorbent ~, (~) absorptive ~, sound-control ~, acoustic(al) ~ · Schallschluckmaterial n, Akustikmaterial, Schallschluckstoff m, Akustikstoff, Schallabsorptionsmaterial, Schallabsorptionsstoff

(~) ~ metal ceiling, (~) absorbent ~ ~, (~) absorptive ~ ~, sound-control ~ ~, acoustic(al) ~ ~ · Schallschluckmetalldecke f, Metallschallschluckdecke, Akustikmetalldecke, Metallakustikdecke, Schallabsorptionsmetalldecke, Metallschallabsorptionsdecke

(~) ~ paint → acoustic(al) ~

(~) ~ pan(el) → (~) absorbent ~

(~) ~ panel → sound-control ~

(~) ~ plaster, (~) absorbent ~, (~) absorptive ~, sound-control ~, acoustic(al) ~ · Schallschluckputz m, Akustikputz, Schallabsorptionsputz

(~) ~ ~ aggregate → sound-control ~ ~

(~) ~ ~ ceiling, (~) absorbent ~ ~, (~) absorptive ~ ~, sound-control ~, acoustic(al) ~ ~, APC · Schallschluckputzdecke f, Akustikputzdecke, Schallabsorptionsputzdecke

(~) ~ sheet → acoustic(al) board

(~) ~ sprayed-on plaster → sound-control ~ ~

(~) ~ (sur)facing → acoustic(al) lining

(~) ~ suspended ceiling → (~) absorbent ~ ~

(~) ~ system → (~) absorptive ~

(~) ~ tile, (~) absorbent ~, (~) absorptive ~, sound-control ~, acoustic(al) ~, AT. · Schallschluckfliese f, Akustikfliese, Schallschluckplatte f, Akustikplatte, Schallabsorptionsfliese, Schallabsorptionsplatte

(~) ~ ~ ceiling, (~) absorbent ~ ~, (~) absorptive ~ ~, sound-control ~, acoustic(al) ~ ~, ATC · Schallschluckfliesendecke f, Schallschluckplattendecke, Akustikfliesendecke, Akustikplattendecke, Schallabsorptionsfliesendecke, Schallabsorptionsplattendecke

(~) ~ treatment · Schallschluckbehandlung f, Schallabsorptionsbehandlung

(~) ~ unit → (~) absorbent ~

(~) ~ unit → (~) absorptive system

(~) ~ waffle → (~) absorbent pan(el)

(~) ~ wall → sound-control ~

(~) ~ ~ block → acoustic(al) wall tile

(~) ~ ~ brick → sound-control ~ ~

(~) ~ wallpaper → sound-control ~

(~) ~ wall tile → acoustic(al) ~ ~

(~) ~ ~ ~ ~ → sound-control ~ ~

(~) ~ wood fibre board (Brit.) → acoustic(al) ~ ~ ~

~ **absorption,** absorption of sound · (Schall)Absorption f, (Schall)Schluckung f [*Abschwächung der Luftschallreflexion in geschlossenen Räumen durch schallschluckende Wand- oder Deckenverkleidungen, die in halligen Räumen die Nachhallzeit verkürzen und eine Senkung des Schallpegels bewirken*]

(~) ~ capacity → (~) ~ property

(~) ~ coefficient [*Of a surface or material at a given frequency and under specified conditions. The complement of the sound energy reflection coefficient under those conditions, i.e. is equal to 1 minus the sound energy reflection coefficient of the surface or material*] · (Schall)Absorptionsgrad m, (Schall)Schluckgrad

(~) ~ power → (~) ~ porperty

(~) ~ property, (~) ~ capacity, (~) ~ quality, (~) ~ power [*The property possessed by materials, objects or media of absorbing sound energy*] · (Schall-)Absorptionsfähigkeit f, (Schall)Schluckfähigkeit, (Schall)Absorptionsvermögen n, (Schall)Schluckvermögen

(~) ~ quality → (~) ~ property

~ **absorptive,** ~ absorbing, acoustical [*The capability of a material to absorb noise to make a room quieter and more comfortable*] · schallschluckend, schallabsorbierend

(~) ~ backing, (~) absorbent ~, (~) absorbing ~, sound-control ~, acoustic(al) ~ · Schallschluck-Hinterfüllung f, Akustik-Hinterfüllung, Schallabsorptions-Hinterfüllung [*Gips-Akustikplatte*]

933 (sound) absorptive blanket — (sound) absorptive wallpaper

(~) ~ **blanket**, (~) ~ pad, (~) absorbent ~, (~) absorbing ~, sound-control ~, acoustic(al) ~ · Schallschluckmatte f, Akustikmatte, Schallabsorptionsmatte

(~) ~ **board** → acoustic(al) ~

(~) ~ **brick** → (ceramic) acoustic(al) ~

(~) ~ **(building) unit**, (~) absorbent (~) ~, (~) absorbing (~) ~, sound-control (~) ~, acoustic(al) (~) ~ · Schallschluckelement n, Akustikelement, Schallabsorptionselement, Schallschluckkörper m, Akustikkörper, Schallabsorptionskörper

(~) ~ **cassette** → (~) absorbent pan(el)

(~) ~ **ceiling**, (~) absorbing ~, (~) absorbent ~, sound-control ~, acoustic(al) · Schallschluckdecke f, Akustikdecke, Schallabsorptionsdecke

(~) ~ ~ **board** → acoustic(al) ceiling tile

(~) ~ ~ **paint**, (sound) absorbing ~ ~, (sound) absorbent ~ ~, sound-control ~ ~, acoustic(al) ~ ~ · Schallschluckdecken(anstrich)farbe f, Akustikdecken(anstrich)farbe, Schallabsorptionsdecken(anstrich)farbe

(~) ~ ~ **sheet** → acoustic(al) ceiling tile

(~) ~ ~ **system** → (~) absorbent ~ ~

(~) ~ ~ **tile** → acoustic(al) ~ ~

(~) ~ **chamber**, (~) absorbing ~, (~) absorbent ~ · Schallschluckkammer f, Schallabsorptionskammer

(~) ~ **coffer** → (~) absorbent pan(el)

(~) ~ **construction (method)**, (~) absorbent ~ (~), (~) absorbing ~ (~), acoustic(al) ~ (~) · Schallschluckbauweise f, Akustikbauweise, schallabsorptionsbauweise

(~) ~ **construction(al) material**, (~) absorbent ~ ~, (~) absorbing ~ ~, acoustic(al) ~ ~ · Schallschluckbaustoff m, Akustikbaustoff, Schallabsorptionsbaustoff

(~) ~ **cover(ing)** → acoustic(al) lining

(~) ~ **facing** → accoustic(al) lining

(~) ~ **felt(ed fabric)**, (sound) absorbent ~ (~), (sound) absorbing ~ (~), sound-control ~ (~), acoustic(al) ~ (~), Schallschluckfilz m, Akustikfilz, Schallabsorptionsfilz

(~) ~ ~ ~ **ceiling**, (sound) absorbent ~ (~) ~, (sound) absorbing ~ (~) ~, sound-control ~ (~) ~, acoustic(al) ~ (~) ~ · Schallschluckfilzdecke f, Akustikfilzdecke, Schallabsorptionsfilzdecke

(~) ~ **fibre board** → acoustic(al) ~ ~

(~) ~ **foil**, (~) absorbent ~, (~) absorbing ~, sound-control ~, acoustic(al) ~ · Schallschluckfolie f, Akustikfolie, Schallabsorptionsfolie

(~) ~ **glass** → sound-control ~

(~) ~ **hung ceiling** → (~) absorbent suspended ~

(~) ~ **lining** → acoustic(al) ~

(~) ~ **masonry wall**, (~) absorbent ~ ~, (~) absorbing ~ ~, sound-control ~ ~, acoustic(al) ~ ~ · Schallschluckmauer f, Akustikmauer, Schallabsorptionsmauer

(~) ~ **material**, (~) absorbent ~, (~) absorbing ~, sound-control ~, acoustic(al) ~ · Schallschluckmaterial n, Akustikmaterial, Schallschluckstoff m, Akustikstoff, Schallabsorptionsmaterial, Schallabsorptionsstoff

(~) ~ **metal ceiling**, (~) absorbent ~ ~, (~) absorbing ~ ~, sound-control ~ ~, acoustic(al) ~ ~ · Schallschluckmetalldecke f, Metallschallschluckdecke, Akustikmetalldecke, Metallakustikdecke, Schallabsorptionsmetalldecke, Metallschallabsorptionsdecke

(~) ~ **pad** → acoustic(al) blanket

(~) ~ **paint** → acoustic(al) ~

(~) ~ **panel** → sound-control ~

(~) ~ **pan(el)** → (~) absorbent ~

(~) ~ **plaster**, (~) absorbent ~, (~) absorbing ~, sound-control ~, acoustic(al) ~ · Schallschluckputz m, Akustikputz, Schallabsorptionsputz

(~) ~ ~ **aggregate** → sound-control ~ ~

(~) ~ ~ **ceiling**, (~) absorbent ~ ~, (~) absorbing ~ ~, sound-control ~ ~, acoustic(al) ~ ~, APC · Schallschluckputzdecke f, Akustikputzdecke, Schallabsorptionsputzdecke

(~) ~ **sheet** → acoustic(al) board

(~) ~ **sprayed-on plaster** → sound-control ~ ~

(~) ~ **(sur)facing** → acoustic(al) lining

(~) ~ **suspended ceiling** → (~) absorbent ~ ~

(~) ~ **system**, (~) absorbing ~, (~) absorbent ~, (~) ~ unit, (~) absorber · (Schall)Absorber m, Schallschlucker, Schallschluckkonstruktion f, Schallabsorptionskonstruktion

(~) ~ **tile**, (~) absorbent ~, (~) absorbing ~, sound-control ~, acoustic(al) ~, AT · Schallschluckfliese f, Akustikfliese, Schallschluck(belag)platte f, Akustik(belag)platte, Schallabsorptionsfliese, Schallabsorptions(belag)platte

(~) ~ ~ **ceiling**, (~) absorbent ~ ~, (~) absorbing ~ ~, sound-control ~ ~, acoustic(al) ~ ~, ATC · Schallschluckfliesendecke f, Schallschluck(belag)plattendecke, Akustikfliesendecke, Akustik(belag)plattendecke, Schallabsorptionsfliesendecke, Schallabsorptions(belag)plattendecke

(~) ~ **unit** → (~) ~ system

(~) ~ ~ → (~) ~ building ~

(~) ~ **waffle** → (~) absorbent pan(el)

(~) ~ **wall** → sound-control ~

(~) ~ ~ **block** → acoustic(al) wall tile

(~) ~ ~ **brick** → sound-control ~ ~

(~) ~ **wallpaper** → sound-control ~

(sound) absorptive wall tile — sound-control sheet 934

(~) ~ wall tile → acoustic(al) ~ ~
(~) ~ ~ ~ ~ → sound-control ~ ~
(~) ~ wood fibre board (Brit.) → acoustic(al) ~ ~ ~
~ alarm unit, acoustic(al) ~ ~, audible ~ ~ · akustisches Alarmgerät n
(~) attenuation [*The reduction of the intensity of sounds*] · Schalldämpfung f
(~) ~ duct · Schalldämpfungskanal m
~ barrier · Schallsperre f
~ board · Einschubbrett n, Zwischenbrett [*Bretter(fuß)boden*]
~ boarding [*Horizontal boards fitted closely between joists and resting on them in the thickness of the floor. They carry pugging, which increases the sound and heat insulation of the floor*] · (Decken)Einschub m, Fehlboden m, Streifboden, Einschubdecke f, Einstreifdecke
(~) conduction · Schalleitung f
~ conductor, conductor of sound · Schalleiter m
sound-control backing, acoustic(al) ~, (sound) absorbent ~, (sound) absorbing ~, (sound) absorptive ~ · Schallschluck-Hinterfüllung f, Akustik-Hinterfüllung, Schallabsorptions-Hinterfüllung [*Gips-Akustikplatte*]
~ blanket, ~ pad, acoustic(al) ~, (sound) absorbent ~, (sound) absorbing ~, (sound) absorptive ~ · Schallschluckmatte f, Akustikmatte, Schallabsorptionsmatte
~ board → acoustic(al) ~
~ brick → (ceramic) acoustic(al) ~
~ (building) unit, acoustic(al) (~) ~, (sound) absorbent (~) ~, (sound) absorbing (~) ~, (sound) absorptive (~) ~ · Schallschluckelement n, Akustikelement, Schallabsorptionselement
~ cassette → (sound) absorbent pan(el)
~ ceiling, acoustic(al) ~, (sound) absorbent ~, (sound) absorbing ~, (sound) absorptive ~· Schallschluckdecke f, Akustikdecke, Schallabsorptionsdecke
~ ~ board → acoustic(al) ceiling tile
~ ~ paint, acoustic(al) ~ ~, (sound) absorbent ~ ~, (sound) absorbing ~ ~, (sound) absorptive ~ ~ · Schallschluckdecken(anstrich)farbe f, Akustikdecken(anstrich)farbe, Schallabsorptionsdecken(anstrich)farbe
~ ~ sheet → acoustic(al) ceiling tile
~ ~ system → (sound) absorbent ~ ~
~ ~ tile → acoustic(al) ~ ~
~ coffer → (sound) absorbent pan(el)
~ construction material → acoustic(al) ~ ~
~ ~ (method) → acoustic(al) ~ (~)
~ covering → acoustic(al) lining
~ facing → acoustic(al) lining

~ felt(ed fabric), acoustic(al) ~ (~), (sound) absorbent ~ (~), (sound) absorbing ~ (~), (sound) absorptive ~ (~) · Schallschluckfilz m, Akustikfilz, Schallabsorptionsfilz
~ ~ (~) ceiling, acoustic(al) ~ (~) ~, (sound) absorbent ~ (~) ~, (sound) absorbing ~ (~) ~, (sound) absorptive ~ (~) ~ · Schallschluckfilzdecke f, Akustikfilzdecke, Schallabsorptionsfilzdecke
~ fibre board → accoustic(al) ~ ~
~ foil, acoustic(al) ~, (sound) absorbent ~, (sound) absorbing ~, (sound) absorptive ~ · Schallschluckfolie f, Akustikfolie, Schallabsorptionsfolie
~ glass, acoustic(al) ~ (control) ~, (sound) absorbent ~, (sound) absorbing ~, (sound) absorptive ~ · Schallschluckglas n, Akustikglas, Schallabsorptionsglas
~ lining → acoustic(al) ~
~ masonry wall, acoustic(al) ~ ~, (sound) absorbent ~ ~, (sound) absorbing ~ ~, (sound) absorptive ~ ~ · Schallschluckmauer f, Akustikmauer, Schallabsorptionsmauer
~ material, acoustic(al) ~, (sound) absorbent ~, (sound) absorbing ~, (sound) absorptive ~ · Schallschluckmaterial n, Akustikmaterial, Schallschluckstoff m, Akustikstoff, Schallabsorptionsmaterial, Schallabsorptionsstoff
~ metal ceiling, acoustic(al) ~ ~, (sound) absorbent ~ ~, (sound) absorbing ~ ~, (sound) absorptive ~ ~ · Schallschluckmetalldecke f, Metallschallschluckdecke, Akustikmetalldecke, Metallakustikdecke, Schallabsorptionsmetalldecke, Metallschallabsorptionsdecke
~ pad → acoustic(al) blanket
~ paint → acoustic(al) ~
~ panel, acoustic(al) ~, (sound) absorbent ~, (sound) absorbing ~, (sound) absorptive ~ · Schallschlucktafel f, Akustiktafel, Schallabsorptionstafel
~ pan(el) → (sound) absorbent ~
~ plaster, acoustic(al) ~, (sound) absorbent ~, (sound) absorbing ~, (sound) absorptive ~ · Schallschluckputz m, Akustikputz, Schallabsorptionsputz
~ ~ aggregate, acoustic(al) ~ ~, (sound) absorbent ~ ~, (sound) absorbing ~ ~, (sound) absorptive ~ ~ · Schallschluckputzzuschlag(stoff) m, Akustikputzzuschlag(stoff), Schallabsorptionsputzzuschlag(stoff)
~ ~ ceiling, acoustic(al) ~ ~, (sound) absorbent ~ ~, (sound) absorbing ~ ~, (sound) absorptive ~ ~, APC · Akustikputzdecke f, Schallschluckputzdecke, Schallabsorptionsputzdecke
~ sheet → acoustic(al) board

sound-control sprayed-on plaster — sound impermeability

~ **sprayed-on plaster**, acoustic(al) ~ ~, (sound) absorbent ~ ~, (sound) absorptive ~ ~, (sound) absorbing ~ ~ · Schallschluckspritzputz m, Akustikspritzputz, Schallabsorptionsspritzputz

~ **(sur)facing** → acoustic(al) lining

~ **tile**, acoustic(al) ~, (sound) absorbent ~, (sound) absorbing ~, (sound) absorptive ~, AT. · Schallschluckfliese f, Akustikfliese, Schallschluck(belag)platte f, Akustik(belag)platte, Schallabsorptionsfliese, Schallabsorptions-(belag)platte

~ ~ **ceiling**, acoustic(al) ~ ~, (sound) absorbent ~ ~, (sound) absorbing ~ ~, (sound) absorptive ~ ~, ATC · Schallschluckfliesendecke f, Schallschluck(belag)plattendecke, Akustikfliesendecke, Akustik(belag)plattendecke, Schallabsorptionsfliesendecke, Schallabsorptions(belag)plattendecke

~ **unit** → ~ building ~

~ **waffle** → (sound) absorbent pan(el)

~ **wall**, acoustic(al) ~, (sound) absorbent ~, (sound) absorbing ~, (sound) absorptive ~ · Schallschluckwand f, Akustikwand, Schallabsorptionswand

~ **wall block** → acoustic(al) wall tile

~ ~ **brick**, acoustic(al) ~ ~, (sound) absorbent ~ ~, (sound) absorbing ~ ~, (sound) absorptive ~ ~ · Schallschluckwandziegel m, Akustikwandziegel, Schallabsorptionswandziegel

~ **wallpaper**, acoustic(al) ~, (sound) absorbent ~, (sound) absorbing ~, (sound) absorptive ~ · Schallschlucktapete f, Akustiktapete, Schallabsorptionstapete

~ **wall tile** → acoustic(al) ~ ~

~ ~ ~, acoustic(al) ~ ~, (sound) absorbent ~ ~, (sound) absorbing ~ ~, (sound) absorptive ~ ~ · Schallschluckwandplatte f, Akustikwandplatte, Wandakustikplatte, Wandschallschluckplatte, Schallabsorptionswandplatte, Wandschallabsorptionsplatte, Schallschluckwandfliese f, Akustikwandfliese, Wandakustikfliese, Wandschallabsorptionsfliese, Schallabsorptionswandfliese, Wandschallschluckfliese

~ **wood fibre board** (Brit.) → acoustic(al) ~ ~ ~

sound-deadened · entdröhnt

sound-deadening → ~ treatment

~ **agent**, anti-drumming ~ · Antidröhnmittel n, Entdröhnungsmittel

~ **coat(ing)**, anti-drumming ~ · Antidröhnbelag m, Entdröhnungsbelag

~ **composition**, ~ compound, anti-drumming ~ · Antidröhnmasse f, Entdröhnungsmasse

~ **compound**, ~ composition, anti-drumming ~ · Antidröhnmasse f, Entdröhnungsmasse

~ **(treatment)**, anti-drumming ~ · Entdröhnung f, Entdröhnen n

sound direction, direction of sound · Schallrichtung f

~ **energy** [*Of a part of a medium. The total energy in this part of the medium less the energy that would exist with no sound waves present*] · Schallenergie f, akustische Energie [*In einem Mediumteil. Kinetische und potentielle Energie des Schalles*]

~ ~ **density** [*At a point in a sound field. The sound energy in an infinitesimal part of the medium surrounding the point divided by the volume of that part of the medium. Symbol E. Note: The term 'sound energy density' may be qualified by the terms 'instantaneous', 'maximum', 'peak', 'average', etc. When the term 'average' is used this may refer to time average (at a point) or, by extension, to the space average (at an instant)*] · Schallenergiedichte f, [*Quotient m aus Schallenergie und zugehörigem Volumen. Räumliche Dichte der Schallenergie*]

~ ~ **flux** [*In a specified direction. The average rate of flow of sound energy for one period through a specified area normal to that direction. Symbol P. Note 1. In an isotropic medium of density p for a plane or spherical free progressive wave having a phase velocity c, the sound energy flux through an area S is $(p^2 S/pc) \cos \Theta$, where p is the r.m.s. sound pressure and Θ the angle between the direction of propagation and the normal to S. Note 2. For an individual wave it is customary to define the area S parallel to the wave front.*] · Schallenergiefluß m

~ ~ **reflection coefficient** [*Of a surface or material at a given frequency and under specified conditions. The ratio which the sound energy reflected from the surface or material bears to that incident upon it under those conditions*] · Schallreflexionsgrad m, Schallreflektionsgrad

~ **engineering** · Schalltechnik f [*Die Schalltechnik umfaßt die technischen Probleme der Entstehung und Ausbreitung von Schwingungsvorgängen in gasförmigen, flüssigen oder festen Stoffen oder schwingungsfähigen Systemen (Luft-, Wasser- und Körperschall). Schall und Erschütterungen breiten sich in Form von Längs-, Quer- und Biegewellen aus und gehen aus einem Medium in ein anderes nach ähnlichen Gesetzen wie in der Optik über*]

~ **field** · Schallfeld n

~ **film studio** · Tonfilmstudio n, Klangfilmstudio

(~) **flanking path** · Schallflankenübertragungsweg m

~ **generation** · Schallerzeugung f, Schallentstehung

~ **impermeability**, ~ imperviousness, soundtightness, imperviousness to sound(s), impermeability to sound(s) · Schalldichtheit f, Schalldichtigkeit, Schallundurchlässigkeit [*Fehlname: Schalldichte f*]

sound imperviousness — sound-isolation power

~ imperviousness, ~ impermeability, soundtightness, impermeability to sound(s), imperviousness to sound(s) · Schalldichtheit *f*, Schalldichtigkeit, Schallundurchlässigkeit [*Fehlname: Schalldichte f*]

sounding board, (~) tester [*A board or screen, fixed behind or above a pulpit, in order to reflect the preacher's voice towards the congregation*] · Kanzeldeckel *m*, Schalldeckel, Schalldach *n*, Schallhaube *f*, Kanzelhaube, Kanzelhimmel *m*

(~) tester, ~ board [*A board or screen, fixed behind or above a pulpit, in order to reflect the preacher's voice towards the congregation*] · Kanzeldeckel *m*, Schalldeckel, Schalldach *n*, Schallhaube *f*, Kanzelhaube, Kanzelhimmel *m*

sound insulating; ~ isolating (US) · schall(ab)dämmend

~ ~ board, ~ ~ sheet, ~ insulation(-grade) ~; ~ isolation ~ (US) · Schall(ab)dämmplatte *f*

sound-insulating capability → ~ property

~ capacity → ~ property

sound insulating glass, ~ insulation (-grade) ~; ~ isolation ~ (US) · Schall(ab)dämmglas *n*

~ ~ layer, ~ insulation(-grade) ~; ~ isolation ~ (US) · Schall(ab)dämmlage *f*, Schall(ab)dämmschicht *f*

~ ~ material → ~ insulation(-grade) ~

~ ~ plastered hung ceiling, ~ ~ ~ suspended ~; ~ ~ isolating ~ (US) · Puffdecke *f* [*Unter einer Massivdecke zur Schalldämmung an Leisten aufgehängte geputzte Scheindecke*]

sound-insulating power → ~ property

~ property, ~ power, ~ capacity, ~ capability, ~ quality, sound-insulation ~; ~ sound-isolation ~ (US) · Schalldämmvermögen *n*, Schalldämmfähigkeit *f*, Schalldämmeigenschaft *f*

~ quality → ~ property

sound insulating sheet, ~ ~ board, ~ insulation(-grade) ~; ~ isolation ~ (US) · Schall(ab)dämmplatte *f*

~ ~ window, ~ insulation(-grade) ~; ~ isolation ~ (US) · Schall(ab)dämmfenster *n*

~ insulation; ~ isolation (US) [*Means taken to reduce the transmission of sound, usually by enclosure*] · Schallschutz *m* [*DIN 4109*]

~ ~, acoustic(al) ~, sound-proofing; sound isolation, acoustic(al) isolation (US) [*Of a partition or wall. The property that opposes the transmission of sound from one side to the other*] · Schall(ab)dämmung *f*

~ ~ against structure-borne sounds → impact (sound) insulation

sound-insulation capability → sound-insulating property

~ capacity → sound-insulating property

sound insulation(-grade) board, ~ ~ sheet, ~ insulating ~; ~ isolation ~ (US) · Schall(ab)dämmplatte *f*

~ ~ glass, ~ insulating ~; ~ isolation ~ (US) · Schall(ab)dämmglas *n*

~ ~ layer, ~ insulating ~; ~ isolation ~ (US) · Schall(ab)dämmlage *f*, Schall(ab)dämmschicht *f*

~ ~ material, ~ insulating ~; ~ isolation ~ (US) · Schall(ab)dämmstoff *m*, Schall(ab)dämmaterial *n*

~ ~ sheet, ~ ~ board, ~ insulating ~; ~ isolation ~ (US) · Schall(ab)dämmplatte *f*

~ ~ window, ~ insulating ~; ~ isolation ~ (US) · Schall(ab)dämmfenster *n*

sound insulation material → ~ insulation-grade ~

~ ~ measurement; ~ isolation ~ (US) · Schallschutzmessung *f*

~ ~ of floors; ~ isolation ~ ~ (US) · Decken-Schall(ab)dämmung *f*

~ ~ ~ walls; ~ isolation ~ ~ (US) · Wand-Schall(ab)dämmung *f*

sound-insulation power → sound-insulating property

~ property → sound-insulating ~

~ quality → sound-insulating property

sound intensity [*In a specified direction. The sound energy flux through unit area, normal to that direction. Symbol I. Note. It is customary to define the area parallel to the wave front, in which case $I = p^2/pc$ for a plane or spherical free progressive wave, where p is the density*] · Schallintensität *f* [*Quotient aus Schalleistung und der zur Richtung des Energietransportes senkrechten Fläche. Produkt aus Schalldruck und Schallschnelle*]

~ isolating (US); ~ insulating · schall(ab)dämmend

sound isolation (US) → ~ insulation

~ ~ board, ~ ~ sheet (US); ~ insulating ~, ~ insulation(-grade) ~ · Schall(ab)dämmplatte *f*

sound-isolation capability (US) → sound-insulating property

~ capacity (US) → sound-insulating property

sound isolation glass (US); ~ insulating ~, ~ insulation(-grade) ~ · Schall(ab)dämmglas *n*

~ ~ layer (US); ~ insulating ~, ~ insulation(-grade) ~ · Schall(ab)dämmlage *f*, Schall(ab)dämmschicht *f*

~ ~ material (US) → ~ insulation(-grade) ~

~ ~ measurement (US); ~ insulation ~ · Schallschutzmessung *f*

~ ~ of floors (US); ~ insulation ~ ~ · Decken-Schall(ab)dämmung *f*

~ ~ ~ walls (US); ~ insulation ~ ~ · Wand-Schall(ab)dämmung *f*

sound-isolation power (US) → sound-insulating property

sound-isolation property — sound reduction index

~ **property** (US) → sound-insulating ~

~ **quality** (US) → sound-insulating property

sound isolation sheet, ~ ~ board (US); ~ insulating ~, ~ insulation(-grade) ~ · Schall(ab)dämmplatte *f*

~ ~ **window** (US); ~ insulating ~, ~ insulation(-grade) ~ · Schall(ab)dämmfenster *n*

~ **level** [*A weighted value of the sound pressure level as determined by a sound level meter*] · Schallpegel *m* [*Bei einer Frequenz oder in einem Frequenzbereich: Logarithmiertes Verhältnis einer Schall-Feldgröße oder einer Schall-Energiegröße zu einer gleichartigen Bezugsgröße. Der Wert der Bezugsgröße ist gegebenenfalls anzugeben. Anmerkung: Schallpegel werden im allgemeinen in dB angegeben. Wenn nichts anderes angegeben, sind im Zähler unter der Schall-Feldgröße der Effektivwert dieser Größe und unter der Schall-Energiegröße der zeitlich gemittelte Wert dieser Größe zu verstehen. Der Frequenzbereich ist gegebenenfalls durch Wortzusätze (z.B. Oktavpegel, Terzpegel, Pegel in der Bandbreite 1 Hz) anzugeben*]

~ ~ **difference** · Schallpegelunterschied *m*

~ ~ **meter** [*An instrument designed to measure a frequency-weighted value of the sound pressure level. It consists of a microphone, amplifier and indicating instrument having a declared performance in respect of directivity, frequency response, rectification characteristic and ballistic response*] · Schallpegelmesser *m*, Schallpegelmeßgerät *n*

~ ~ **recorder** · Schallpegelschreiber *m*

~ **measurement** · Schallmessung *f*

~ **of the human singing voice**, tone ~ ~ ~ ~ ~ · Singklang *m*, Sington *m*

soundness · Mängelfreiheit *f*

~ · Raumbeständigkeit *f* [*Zement*]

~ **test** · Raumbeständigkeitsprüfung *f*, Raumbeständigkeitsprobe *f*, Raumbeständigkeitsversuch *m* [*Zement*]

~ ~ **by immersion in boiling water**, boiling test · Kochprobe *f*, Kochprüfung *f*, Kochversuch *m* [*Prüfung von Zement auf Raumbeständigkeit. DIN 1048*]

~ ~ ~ ~ ~ **cold water**, cold water test · Kaltwasserprobe *f*, Kaltwasserprüfung *f*, Kaltwasserversuch *m* [*Prüfung von Zement auf Raumbeständigkeit; DIN 1164*]

~ ~ **pat**, cement pat, pat of cement-water paste, circular-domed pat of cement · (Probe)Kuchen *m* (aus Zement), Zementkuchen

sound oscillation, ~ vibration · Schallschwingung *f*

~ **path** · Schallweg *m*

~ **pressure** [*At a point in a sound field. The alternating component of the pressure at the point. The unit is the newton/square metre. Note. The term 'sound pressure' may be qualified by the terms 'instantaneous', 'peak', 'maximum', 'r.m.s.', etc. The unqualified term 'sound pressuré, symbol p, is frequently taken to imply r.m.s. value*] · Schalldruck *m* [*Durch die Schallschwingung hervorgerufener Wechseldruck*]

~ ~ **level** [*The sound pressure level of a sound, in decibels, is equal to 20 times the logarithm to the base 10 of the ratio of the r.m.s. sound pressure to the reference sound pressure. In case of doubt, the reference sound pressure should be stated. In the absence of any statement to the contrary, the reference sound pressure in air is taken to be 2×10^{-5} N/m^2 and in water 0.1 N/m^2. Note. The use of the micropascal (1×10^{-6} N/m^2) has been suggested as the reference level for sound pressure in underwater work which would have the practical advantage of generally avoiding the use of negative values in expressing sound levels*] · Schalldruckpegel *m*

~ (~) **reflection coefficient**, pressure ~ ~ [*Of a surface or material at a given frequency and under specified conditions. The ratio which the reflected sound pressure from a surface or material bears to the incident sound pressure under those conditions; in general a complex number*] · Schall-Reflexionsfaktor *m*, Schall-Reflektionsfaktor

soundproof door · Anti-Schall-Tür *f*, Schall(ab)dämmtür *f*

sound-proofing → sound insulation

(sound) propagation [*The wave process whereby sound energy is transferred from one part of a medium to another*] · Ausbreitung *f*, Fortpflanzung, Schall~

~ **radiation** · Schallabstrahlung *f*

sound-reduced · schallarm

sound reduction → (equivalent sound pressure) level difference

~ ~ **factor** [*deprecated*]; ~ reduction index (Brit.); ~ transmission loss (US) [*Of a surface, partition or device at a given frequency and under specified conditions. Ten times the logarithm to the base 10 of the reciprocal of the sound transmission coefficient under these conditions. Symbol R. The unit is the decibel (dB). Note 1. Unless otherwise specified, the sound fields on both sides of the surface, partition or device are assumed to be reverberant. Note 2. In American usage, this term is called 'sound transmission loss'*] · Schalldämmaß *n*, Schalldämmzahl *f*, Schallschutzmaß

~ ~ **index** (Brit.); ~ transmission loss (US); ~ reduction factor [*deprecated*] [*Of a surface, partition or device at a given frequency and under specified conditions. Ten times the logarithm to

the base 10 of the reciprocal of the sound transmission coefficient under these conditions. Symbol R. The unit is the decibel (dB).
Note 1. Unless otherwise specified, the sound fields on both sides of the surface, partition or device are assumed to be reverberant.
Note 2. In American usage, this term is called 'sound transmission loss'] · Schalldämmaß n, Schalldämmzahl f, Schallschutzmaß

sound-reflecting · schallhart

sound reflection [Strong sound reflections are generally called 'echoes'] · Schallreflektion f, Schallreflexion

~ ~ **coefficient** → ~ pressure ~ ~

~ **signal**, acoustic(al) ~, audible ~ · Hörsignal n, akustisches Signal, Schallsignal, Akustiksignal

~ **source** · Schallquelle f

~ **spectrum** · Schallspektrum n

~ **tight knot** · gesunder fester Ast m, fester gesunder ~ [Parkettstab]

soundtightness, sound impermeability, sound imperviousness, imperviousness to sound(s), impermeability to sounds · Schalldichtheit f, Schalldichtigkeit, Schallundurchlässigkeit [Fehlname: Schalldichte f]

sound transmission [The transfer of sound energy from one medium to another] · Schallübertragung f

~ ~ **coefficient** [Of a surface, partition or device at a given frequency and under specified conditions. The ratio which the sound energy transmitted through and beyond the surface, partition or device bears to that incident upon it] · Schallübertragungsgrad m

~ ~ **loss** (US); ~ reduction index (Brit.); ~ reduction factor [deprecated] [Of a surface, partition or device at a given frequency and under specified conditions. Ten times the logarithm to the base 10 of the reciprocal of the sound transmission coefficient under these conditions. Symbol R. The unit is the decibel (dB).
Note 1. Unless otherwise specified, the sound fields on both sides of the surface, partition or device are assumed to be reverberant.
Note 2. In American usage, this term is called 'sound transmission loss'] · Schalldämmaß n, Schalldämmzahl f, Schallschutzmaß

~ **type**, type of sound · Schallart f [Man unterscheidet: Körper-, Tritt- und Luftschall]

~ **vibration**, ~ oscillation · Schallschwingung f

~ **warning system** · Schallalarmanlage f

~ **wave** · Schallwelle f

~ ~ **radiation** · Schallstrahlung f

source of oscillation, ~ ~ vibration, vibration source, oscillation source · Schwingungsquelle f, Erschütterungsquelle

~ ~ **vibration**, ~ ~ oscillation, vibration source, oscillation source · Erschütterungsquelle f, Schwingungsquelle

souring, tempering · Einsumpfen n, Mauken [Verbesserung der Plastizität einer Masse durch längeres feuchtes Lagern im Haufen oder in der Sumpfgrube]

~ **house**, tempering ~ · Maukhaus n, Sumpfhaus

~ **plant**, tempering ~ · Sumpfanlage f, Maukanlage

~ **tower**, tempering ~ · Sumpfturm m, Maukturm

South stoa · Süd-Stoa f [Agora von Athen]

south(ern) porch, Caryatid ~ · Karyatidenhalle f vom Erechtheion, Korenhalle ~ ~

~ **portico** · Südhalle f [in Olympia]

~ **transept** · südliches Seitenschiff n, Männerschiff [Es ist gleich hoch mit dem Hauptschiff]

south(-facing) balcony · Südbalkon m

~ **wall** · Südwand f

~ **window** · Südfenster n

South Indian style, Dravidian ~ [A.D. 625–1750] · Dravidastil m

south orientation · Südorientierung f

souvenir shop · Andenkenladen m, Andenkengeschäft n

soya bean adhesive, ~ ~ glue (Brit.); soybean ~, soy(a) bean ~ (US) · Soja(bohnen)leim m

~ ~ **alkyd** (Brit.); soy(a) ~ ~, soybean ~ (US) · Soja(bohnen)alkyd n

~ ~ **fibre** (Brit.); soy(a) bean fiber, soybean fiber (US) · Soja(bohnen)faser f

~ ~ **glue**, ~ adhesive (Brit.); soybean ~, soy(a) bean ~ (US) · Soja(bohnen)leim m

~ ~ **oil** (Brit.); soy(a) ~ ~, soybean ~ (US) [A drying oil, extracted from the soya bean, which has inferior drying properties to linseed oil but may be improved by suitable processing. Paints and varnishes containing soya bean oil are less prone to yellowing than those based on linseed oil] · Soja(bohnen)öl n

~ ~ ~ **fatty acid** (Brit.); soybean ~ ~ ~, soy(a) bean ~ ~ ~ (US) · Soja(bohnen)öl-Fettsäure f

~ ~ ~ **stand oil** (Brit.); soybean ~ ~ ~, soy(a) bean ~ ~ ~ (US) · Soja(bohnen)öl-Standöl n

SP, vertical pipe, standpipe, stack · Senkrechtrohr n, Standrohr, Steigrohr

SP, static pressure · statischer Druck m

spa, health resort · Kurort m

~ **garden,** ~ park, health resort ~ · Kurpark *m*, Kurgarten *m*

~ **hotel,** health resort ~ · Kurhotel *n*

~ **park,** ~ garden, health resort ~ · Kurpark *m*, Kurgarten *m*

~ **promenade,** health resort ~ · Kurpromenade *f*

space · Raum *m*

~ [*Area between things*] · Zwischenraum *m*

~ **bar,** three-dimensional ~, spatial ~, ~ rod · dreidimensionaler Stab *m*, räumlicher ~

~ **bearing structure** → ~ loadbearing ~

~ **between beams** · Balken(träger)feld *n*, Balken(träger)fach *n*, Balken(träger)joch *n* [*Raum zwischen zwei Balken(trägern). Das Maß des Balkenfaches wird im allgemeinen von Bundseite zu Bundseite genommen. Das Lichtmaß heißt Balkenlücke, das an der Mauer gelegene Fach heißt Ortfach*]

~ ~ **girders** · Trägerfeld *n*, Trägerfach *n*, Trägerjoch *n*

'**space cavern**' [*Term applied to the monumental buildings designed by Hans Poelzig, e.g. Berlin's Grand Theatre*] · Raumhöhle *f*

~ **composition,** spatial ~, three-dimensional ~ · Raumkomposition *f*, räumliche Komposition

~ **configuration,** spatial ~, three-dimensional ~ · Raumfigur *f*

~ **construction** → spatial ~

space-consuming · raumfressend

space continuity, spatial ~, three-dimensional ~ · dreidimensionaler Zusammenhang *m*, räumlicher ~

~ **cooling,** room ~ · Raumkühlung *f*

space-creating plane · raumschaffende Fläche *f*

space curve, spatial ~, three-dimensional ~, curve in space · räumliche Kurve *f*, dreidimensionale ~, Raumkurve

~ **deformation** → spatial ~

~ **design,** spatial ~, three-dimensional ~ · dreidimensionaler Entwurf *m*, räumlicher ~

~ ~ → ~ layout

~ **division,** spatial ~ · Raumgliederung *f*

~ **enclosed** → enclosed space

space-enclosing structure · raumumschließendes Bauwerk *n*

~ **wall** · raumabschließende Wand *f*

space enclosure, spatial ~ · Raumumschließung *f*

~ **form** → spatial ~

~ **forms,** ~ formwork, ~ shuttering · Raumschalung *f*

~ **formwork,** ~ shuttering, ~ forms · Raumschalung *f*

~ **frame** · Raumfachwerk *n*

~ ~ **composed of small individual members** · kleinglied(e)rige Raumstruktur *f*

space-frame cupola, ~ dome · Raumfachwerkkuppel *f*

~ **dome,** ~ cupola · Raumfachwerkkuppel *f*

~ **tower** · Raumfachwerkturm *m*

space frame(work), spatial ~, grid structure, grid frame(work), three-dimensional frame(work), lattice plate [*Grid structures, apart from single layer flat grids, are three-dimensional structures. Unlike shells or folded slabs, however, they are constructed not with solid membranes but with lattice or grid frameworks. In some systems, however, the grid is formed by edge junctions of bent or folded sheet panels of suitable material in which the skin strength of the sheet element forms a very large proportion of the total strength of the structure*] · Raumfachwerk *n*, räumliches Fachwerk, dreidimensionales Fachwerk

~ **gain,** gain in space · Raumgewinn *m*

'**space game**', playful use of space · Raumspiel *n*

space heater burning town gas, ~ fire ~ ~ ~, ~ warmer ~ ~ ~ [*B.S. 3561*] · Stadtgas-Raumerhitzer *m*, Stadtgas-Raumheiz(ungs)gerät *n*, Stadtgas-Raumheizer

~ **heating,** ~ warming, room ~ · Raumerwärmung *f*, Raumheizung

~ ~ **plant,** ~ ~ installation · Raumheiz(ungs)anlage *f*

~ **image,** spatial ~, three-dimensional ~, view of space · Raumbild *n*

~ **layout,** spatial ~, three-dimensional ~, ~ design · Raumdisposition *f*

~ **limit,** limit of space · Raumgrenze *f*

~ **(load)bearing structure,** three-dimensional ~ ~, spatial ~ ~, ~ weight-carrying ~, ~ loaded ~, ~ supporting ~, ~ load-carrying ~, loaded space ~, loaded spatial ~, loaded three-dimensional ~, supporting space ~, supporting spatial ~, supporting three-dimensional ~ · dreidimensionales Tragwerk *n*, räumliches ~, Raumtragwerk [*Die bekanntesten Grundformen sind: Faltwerke (sie bestehen aus zu Prismen zusammengesetzten ebenen Scheiben), Schalen (in einer Richtung oder zwei Richtungen gekrümmte Platten) und Kuppeln (aus Schalen zusammengesetzt)*]

~ **load-carrying structure** → ~ (load-)bearing ~

~ **loaded structure** → ~ (load)bearing ~

spacemanship [*The art of making fullest use of available space; overcoming waste of space while enhancing its appearance in commercial, industrial, institutional and residential buildings*] · Raumaufteilungstechnik *f*

space panelling pattern — spandrel

space panelling pattern (Brit.); ~ paneling ~ (US); spatial ~ ~, three-dimensional ~ ~ · dreidimensionales (Ver)Täfelungsmuster *n*, räumliches ~
~ **problem** → three-dimensional ~
~ **purlin(e)**, spatial ~, three-dimensional ~ · dreidimensionale Pfette *f*, räumliche ~
~ **requirement** · Raumbedarf *m*
~ **rod**, three-dimensional ~, spatial ~, ~ bar · dreidimensionaler Stab *m*, räumlicher ~
space-saver door · raumsparende Tür *f*
space saving · Raumeinsparung *f*, Raumersparnis *f*
space-saving, economical of space · raumsparend
space separation · Raumtrennung *f* [*als Brandschutzmaßnahme*]
~ **shape** → spatial form
~ **shuttering**, ~ formwork, ~ forms · Raumschalung *f*
~ **spanning** · Raumüberspannung *f*
~ **(structural) system** → spatial construction
~ **supporting structure** → ~ (load-) bearing ~
~ **structure**, spatial ~, three-dimensional ~ · Raumbau(werk) *m*, (*n*), räumliches Bauwerk, dreidimensionales Bauwerk, räumlicher Bau, dreidimensionaler Bau
~ **system** → spatial construction
~ **unit**, spatial ~, three-dimensional ~ · Raumelement *n*, dreidimensionales Element, räumliches Element
~ ~ · Raumeinheit *f* [*räumliches Fachwerksystem*]
~ **utilization** · Raum(aus)nutzung *f*
~ **warming**, ~ heating, room ~ · Raumerwärmung *f*, Raumheizung
~ **weight-carrying structure** → ~ (load-)bearing ~
spacer, distance piece, separator · Abstandhalter *m*
spacing · Abstand *m* [*räumlich*]
~ **dowel**, dowel spacer · Abstandsdübel *m*
~ **of beams**, arrangement ~ ~ · Balken(träger)anordnung *f*
~ ~ **columns** → column spacing
~ ~ **girders**, arrangement ~ ~ · Trägeranordnung *f*
~ ~ **supports** → column spacing
spacious, roomy · geräumig, weiträumig
spaciousness · Geräumigkeit *f*, Weiträumigkeit
spactling compound bending tester (US) → stopper ~ ~
~ ~ **coat** (US) → stopping ~
~ ~ **for brush application** (US) → filler ~ ~ ~

~ ~ **seal(ing)** (US) → stopper ~
to spall [*To break away the edges of stone*] · abschlagen [*kanten von Steinen*]
~ ~, to chip · abplatzen, zerspringen [*Keramikindustrie*]
spall, rock ~ · (Aus)Zwicker *m*, (Aus-)Zwickstein *m* [*Ein kleiner Stein zum Auszwicken der Hohlräume bei Bruchsteinmauerwerk und im Straßenbau bei Packe*]
spalling, chipping · Abplatzen *n*, Zerspringen [*Keramikindustrie*]
~ · Aufheizrisse *mpl*, Kühlrisse [*Durch verschiedene Ausdehnung hervorgerufene Rißbildung oder Bruch eines ff. Erzeugnisses, die bei einem Temperaturstoß durch ein zu großes Temperaturgefälle oder durch eine kristalline Umwandlung entstehen*]
to span · überspannen
span · Feld *n* [*von Träger(n) überspannt*]
~ [*Length of pipe crossing a gully or depression without additional support and usually carried at the same level as the bottom of the ditch on both banks of the gully*] · freitragendes Rohr *n*
~ · Spannweite *f*
~, bay · (Hallen)Schiff *n* [*Industriebau*]
~ **conditions** · Spannweitenverhältnisse *fpl*
span-depth ratio · Spannweiten-Konstruktionshöhen-Verhältnis *n* [*Platte; Balken(träger); Träger*]
span during erection until hardening of the cast-in-situ concrete · Montagespannweite *f*
~ **limit** · Spannweitenzwangspunkt *m*
~ **line**, ~ pipeline · (Rohr)Freileitung *f*, freitragende (Rohr)Leitung
~ **load** · Feldlast *f*
~ **loading** · Feldbelastung *f*
~ **piece**, collar beam, collar tie · Kehlbalken *m* [*Der beim Kehlbalkendach in die Sparren eingezapfte Balken, auch Querriegel genannt. Darüber hinaus alle oberhalb der Dachgebalks im Dachraum liegenden Balken (= Kehlgebälk) in Quer- und Längsrichtung des Daches*]
~ **(pipe)line** · (Rohr)Freileitung *f*, freitragende (Rohr)Leitung
~ **roof** [*The most common type of roof, having equal pitch on each side*] · gleichseitiges Giebeldach *n*
~ **table** · Spannweitentabelle *f*
~ **width** · Feldbreite *f*, Feldweite
spandrel → (under-)window ~
~, spandril, triangular panel · Spandrille *f*, (Bogen)Zwickel *m*, Dreieckzwickel [*Dreiseitig begrenzte Fläche zwischen einem Bogen und dessen rechtwinkliger Einfassung oder zwischen zwei Bogenspitzen und einem darüberliegenden Gesims; zu unterscheiden von Zwickel = Pendentif*]

~ beam · Brüstungsbalken *m*

~ (building) component → ~ (~) unit

~ (~) member → ~ (~) unit

~ (~) unit, ~ (~) member, ~ (~) component, parapet (~) ~ · Brüstungs(bau)element *n*, Brüstungs(bau)-körper *m* [*Fehlname: Brüstungsbaueinheit f*]

~ cantilever(ed) step, ~ cantilevering ~ · auskragende Dreieckstufe *f*, vorkragende ~, Auslegerdreieckstufe, Kragdreieckstufe

~ component → ~ (building) unit

~ facing → ~ (wall) surfacing

~ lining → ~ (wall) (sur)facing

~ member → ~ (building) unit

~ panel → (under-)window ~ ~

~ step · Dreieckstufe *f*, Keilstufe

~ (sur)facing → ~ wall ~

~ unit → ~ building ~

~ (wall) → (under-)window spandrel

~ (~) facing → ~ (~) surfacing

~ (~) lining → ~ (~) (sur)facing

~ (~) panel → (under-)window spandrel ~

~ (~) (sur)facing, ~ (~) lining, breast ~, apron ~, parapet ~; apron wall ~ (US) · (Fenster)Brüstungsverkleidung *f*, (Fenster)Brüstungsbekleidung, (Fenster)Brüstungsauskleidung

spandril → spandrel

Spanish grass fiber (US) → (h)alfa ~

~ High Gothic (style) · spanische Hochgotik *f*

~ leather, leather-hanging · Ledertapete *f*

~ (oil of) turpentine, ~ spirit ~ ~ · spanisches Terpentinöl *n*

~ spirit of turpentine, ~ (oil of) ~ · spanisches Terpentinöl *n*

~ (type of) Gothic · spanische Gotik *f*

spanning in one direction · einachsig gespannt [*Deckenplatte*]

~ ~ two directions · zweiachsig gespannt [*Deckenplatte*]

spar dust, ~ flour, ~ powder, powder(-ed) spar · Spatmehl *n*, Spatstaub *m*, Spatpulver *n*

~ flour, ~ dust, ~ powder, powder(-ed) spar · Spatmehl *n*, Spatstaub *m*, Spatpulver *n*

~ powder, ~ dust, ~ flour, powder(ed) spar · Spatmehl *n*, Spatstaub *m*, Spatpulver *n*

~ varnish [*A very durable varnish designed for severe service on exterior surfaces. It must be resistant to rain, sunlight and heat. Named from its original use on the spars of ships*] · Außenlack *m*

sparge pipe [*A perforated water pipe for flushing a urinal*] · Urinalspülrohr *n*

spark arrester · Funkenfänger *m*, Funkenschutz *m*

~ formation · Funkenbildung *f*

~ guard [*fireplace*] · Funkenschutz *m*, Funkenfänger *m* [*Kamin*]

sparkproof, spark resistant, non-sparking [*e.g. a hardened concrete floor*] · funkenfrei, funkensicher

spark resistant, non-sparking, sparkproof [*e.g. a hardened concrete floor*] · funkenfrei, funkensicher

spathic iron (ore) · Spateisenstein *m*

spatial, three-dimensional, stereometric, 3-D · dreidimensional, räumlich, stereometrisch

~ bar, three-dimensional ~, space ~, ~ rod · dreidimensionaler Stab *m*, räumlicher ~

~ bearing structure → space (load) bearing ~

~ composition, space ~, three-dimensional ~ · Raumkomposition *f*, räumliche Komposition

~ configuration, space ~, three-dimensional ~ · Raumfigur *f*

~ construction, space ~, three-dimensional ~, ~ (structural) system · Raum(tragwerk)bausystem *n*, Raum(tragwerk)konstruktion *f*, Raum(tragwerk)(konstruktions)system

~ continuity, space ~, three-dimensional ~ · dreidimensionaler Zusammenhang *m*, räumlicher ~

~ curve, space ~, three-dimensional ~, curve in space · räumliche Kurve *f*, dreidimensionale ~, Raumkurve

~ deformation, three-dimensional ~, space ~ · räumliche Formänderung *f*, ~ Verformung, Gestaltänderung, dreidimensionale ~

~ design, space ~, three-dimensional ~ · dreidimensionaler Entwurf *m*, räumlicher ~

~ ~ → ~ layout

~ distribution of forces, three-dimensional ~ ~ ~ · dreidimensionale Kräfteverteilung *f*, räumliche ~

~ division, space ~ · Raumgliederung *f*

~ enclosure, space ~ · Raumumschließung *f*

~ form, ~ shape, space ~ · Raumform *f*, Raumgestalt *f*

~ frame, space ~, three-dimensional ~ · dreidimensionaler Rahmen *m*, räumlicher ~

~ frame(d) supporting structure, ~ ~ (load)bearing ~, ~ ~ (weight-carrying) ~, three-dimensional ~ ~ ~ · räumliches Rahmentragwerk *n*, dreidimensionales ~, Raumrahmentragwerk

spatial frame(work) — special composition

~ **frame(work)** → space ~

~ **image,** space ~, three-dimensional ~, view of space · Raumbild *n*

~ **(inter)penetration,** three-dimensional ~ · dreidimensionale Durchschluchtung *f*, räumliche ~

~ **layout,** space ~, three-dimensional ~, ~ design · Raumdisposition *f*

~ **(load)bearing structure** → space ~ ~

~ **load-carrying structure** → space (load)bearing ~

~ **loaded structure** → space (load-)bearing ~

~ **luxury** · Raumluxus *m*

~ **model** · Raummodell *n*

~ **panelling pattern** (Brit.); ~ **paneling** ~ (US); space ~ ~, three-dimensional ~ ~ · dreidimensionales (Ver)Täfelungsmuster *n*, räumliches ~

~ **parallel system,** three-dimensional ~ ~ · versetztes Parallelsystem *n* [*Seilsystem*]

~ **penetration,** three-dimensional ~, ~ inter~ · dreidimensionale Durchschluchtung *f*, räumliche ~

~ **(pre)stressing** → ~ tensioning

~ **problem** → three-dimensional ~

~ **purlin(e),** space ~, three-dimensional ~ · dreidimensionale Pfette *f*, räumliche ~

~ **rod,** three-dimensional ~, space ~, ~ bar · dreidimensionaler Stab *m*, räumlicher ~

~ **shape** → ~ form

~ **stressing** → ~ tensioning

~ **stretching** → ~ tensioning

~ **(structural) system** → ~ construction

~ **structure** → space (load)bearing ~

~ ~, space ~, three-dimensional ~ · Raumbau(werk) *m*, (*n*), räumliches Bauwerk, dreidimensionales Bauwerk, räumlicher Bau, dreidimensionaler Bau

~ **supporting structure** → space (load)bearing ~

~ **system** → ~ construction

~ **tensioning,** three-dimensional ~, ~ stretching, ~ (pre)stressing · räumliches (Vor)Spannen *n*, dreidimensionales ~

~ **unit,** space ~, three-dimensional ~ · Raumelement *n*, dreidimensionales Element, räumliches Element

~ **weight-carrying structure** → space (load)bearing ~

spatio-dynamic composition · raumdynamische Komposition *f*

spattle · Kittmesser *n*

speaker's platform, dais · Rednertribüne *f*, Rednerpodium *n*

speak-house, locutory, parlatory, (convent) parlour · Sprachsaal *m*, Parlatorium *n*

speaking-place, logeion · Logeion *n* [*griechische Theaterbaukunst*]

special [*Any fabricated metal (pipe) fitting which is not in normal production*] · Sonder(-Rohr)fitting *m*, Spezial(-Rohr)fitting, Sonder(-Rohr-)formstück *n*, Spezial(-Rohr)formstück

~ **adhesive** → ~ purpose bonding ~

~ ~ **composition,** ~ ~ compound, ~ cementing ~ · Sonderkleb(e)masse *f*, Spezialkleb(e)masse

~ ~ **compound,** ~ ~ composition, ~ cementing ~ · Sonderkleb(e)masse *f*, Spezialkleb(e)masse

~ **aggregate** → ~ construction ~

~ **block** → ~ purpose ~

~ **bond** → ~ masonry ~

~ **bonding adhesive** → ~ purpose ~

~ ~ **agent** → ~ purpose ~ ~

~ ~ **medium** → ~ purpose ~ ~

~ **box (rainwater) gutter** → ~ purpose ~ ~ ~

~ ~ **(roof) gutter** → ~ purpose ~ ~

~ **brick** → ~ purpose ~

~ **broken expanded cinder,** ~ crushed ~ (US); ~ ~ foamed (blastfurnace) slag (Brit.) · Sonderhüttenbims *m*, Spezialhüttenbims

~ ~ **foamed (iron) (blastfurnace) slag,** ~ crushed ~ (~) (~) ~ (Brit.); ~ ~ expanded cinder (US) · Sonderhüttenbims *m*, Spezialhüttenbims

~ **builders' fitting** → ~ purpose ~

~ ~ **furniture** → ~ purpose ~ ~

~ ~ **hardware** → ~ purpose ~ ~

~ **building material** → ~ purpose ~

~ ~ **method** · Sonderbauweise *f*, Spezialbauweise

~ **burnt brick** → ~ (duty) (burnt) (clay) ~

~ **casting** [*Any metal pipe casting which is not in normal production and which requires the making of a new pattern*] · Sonder-Rohrguß *m*, Spezial-Rohrguß

~ **cement** → ~ purpose ~

~ **cement(ing agent)** → ~ purpose ~

~ **cementing composition,** ~ ~ compound, ~ adhesive ~ · Sonderkleb(e)masse *f*, Spezialkleb(e)masse

~ ~ **compound,** ~ ~ composition, ~ adhesive ~ · Sonderkleb(e)masse *f*, Spezialkleb(e)masse

~ **(clay) brick** → ~ (duty) (burnt) (~) ~

~ **coal tar pitch,** ~ straight run coal tar · Steinkohlenteersonderpech *n*

~ **coat** · Spezialanstrich *m*, Spezialaufstrich

~ **composition** → ~ purpose ~

special compound — special (purpose) bonding medium

~ compound → ~ purpose ~

~ concrete → ~ purpose ~

~ ~ product, ~ purpose ~ ~, purpose-made ~ ~ · (Beton)Formstück n

~ (construction) aggregate · Sonderzuschlag(stoff) m, Spezialzuschlag(-stoff)

~ ~ profile → ~ purpose ~ ~

~ ~ section → ~ purpose ~ ~

~ ~ shape → ~ purpose ~ ~

~ ~ trim → ~ purpose ~ ~

~ ~ unit → ~ purpose ~ ~

~ construction(al) material → ~ purpose ~ ~

~ covering foil → ~ purpose ~ ~

~ crushed expanded cinder, ~ broken ~ ~ (US), ~ ~ foamed (iron) (blastfurnace) slag (Brit.) · Sonderhüttenbims m, Spezialhüttenbims

~ ~ foamed (iron) (blastfurnace) slag, ~ broken ~ (~) (~) ~ (Brit.); ~ ~ expanded cinder (US) · Sonderhüttenbims m, Spezialhüttenbims

~ decorative block → ~ ~ ~ tile

~ ~ tile, ~ ornamental ~, purpose-made ~ ~, ~ ~ block [See remark under 'Block'] · Ornament(-Form)block(stein) m, Ornament(-Form)stein, Dekor(ations)(-Form)stein, Dekor(ations)(-Form)block(stein), Ornament-Profilstein, Ornament-Profilblock(stein), Dekor(ations)-Profilstein, Dekor(ations)-Profilblock(stein)

~ door → ~ purpose ~

~ duct → ~ purpose ~

~ (duty) (burnt) (clay) brick, ~ (~) burned (~) ~, ~ (~) fired (~) ~, ~ purpose (~) (~) ~, purpose-made (~) (~) ~ · gebrannter Sonderstein m, ~ Spezialstein, Sonder(ton)ziegel m, Spezial(ton)ziegel

~ filler, ~ stopper, ~ stopping; ~ Swedish putty, ~ spactling compound (US) · Sonderspachtel(masse) m, (f), Spezialspachtel(masse)

~ fired (clay) brick → ~ (duty) (burnt) (~) ~

~ fitting → ~ purpose builders' ~

~ fittings → ~ purpose builders' ~

~ fluosilicate · Sonderfluat n, Spezialfluat, Sonderfluorsilikat n, Spezialfluorsilikat

~ fluxed pitch composition roofing (Brit.) → ~ tar(ed) ready ~

~ ~ ~ prepared roofing (Brit.) → ~ tar(red) ready ~

~ ~ ~ ready roofing (Brit.) → ~ tar(red) ready ~

~ form, ~ shape · Sonderform f, Spezialform

~ format · Sonderformat n, Spezialformat

~ furniture → ~ purpose builders' ~

~ glass · Sonderglas n, Spezialglas

~ grout(ing) → ~ purpose ~

~ hardware → ~ purpose builders' ~

~ high-grade zinc · Feinzink n [Es hat mindestens 99,99% Zn und wird durch einmalige oder wiederholte Destillation oder durch Elektrolyse gewonnen. DIN 1706]

~ hospital · Fachkrankenhaus n; Fachspital n [Schweiz]

~ (joint) pouring compound · Sonderfugen(verguß)masse f, Sonder(fugen)ausgußmasse, Sondervergußmasse, Spezialfugen(verguß)masse, Spezial(fugen)ausgußmasse, Spezialvergußmasse

~ lock → ~ purpose ~

~ (masonry) bond · Sonder(mauerwerk)verband m, Spezial(mauerwerk)-verband

~ mass → ~ purpose ~

~ material → ~ purpose ~

~ mortar → ~ purpose ~

~ ornamental block → ~ ~ ~ tile

~ ~ tile, ~ decorative ~, purpose-made ~ ~, ~ ~ block [See remark under 'Block'] · Ornament(-Form)block(stein) m, Ornament(-Form)stein, Dekor(ations)(-Form)stein, Dekor(ations)(-Form)block(stein), Ornament-Profilstein, Ornament-Profilblock(stein), Dekor(ations)-Profilstein, Dekor(ations)-Profilblock(stein)

~ paper → ~ purpose ~

~ pitch → ~ purpose ~

~ plaster → ~ purpose ~

~ pouring compound → ~ joint ~ ~

~ profile → ~ purpose ~

~ protecting foil → ~ purpose ~ ~

~ (purpose) adhesive → ~ ~ ~ bonding ~

~ (~) block, ~ (~) tile, purpose-made ~ [See remark under 'Block'] · Sonderblock(stein) m, Sonderstein, Profilblock(stein), Profilstein, Spezialblock(stein), Spezialstein, Formblock(-stein), Formstein

~ (~) (bonding) adhesive, ~ (~) ~ medium, ~ (~) ~ agent, ~ (~) cement(ing agent), purpose-made (~) ~ · Sonderkleb(e)stoff m, Sonderkleber m, Spezialkleb(e)stoff, Spezialkleber, Sonderkleb(e)mittel n, Spezialkleb(e)mittel

~ (~) ~ agent, ~ (~) ~ medium, ~ (~) (~) adhesive, ~ (~) cement(ing agent), purpose-made (~) ~ · Sonderkleb(e)stoff m, Sonderkleber m, Spezialkleb(e)stoff, Spezialkleber, Sonderkleb(e)mittel n, Spezialkleb(e)mittel

~ (~) ~ medium, ~ (~) ~ agent, ~ (~) (~) adhesive, ~ (~) cement(ing agent), purpose-made (~) ~ · Sonderkleb(e)stoff m, Sonderkleber m, Spezialkleb(e)stoff, Spezialkleber, Sonderkleb(e)mittel n, Spezialkleb(e)mittel

special (purpose)... — special (purpose) protecting foil 944

~ (~) **box rainwater gutter**, ~ (~) ~ (roof) ~, purpose-made ~ (~) ~ · Sonder-Kasten(dach)rinne f, Spezial-Kasten(dach)rinne

~ (~) ~ **(roof) gutter**, ~ (~) ~ rainwater ~, purpose-made ~ (~) ~ · Sonder-Kasten(dach)rinne f, Spezial-Kasten(dach)rinne

~ (~) **brick**, purpose-made ~ · Profil(ton)ziegel m, Form(ton)ziegel, gebrannter Profilstein m, gebrannter Formstein m

~ (~) **(builders') fitting**, ~ (~) (~) furniture, purpose-made (~) ~ · Sonder(bau)beschlag m, Spezial(bau)beschlag

~ (~) (~) **fittings**, ~ (~) (~) hardware, purpose-made (~) ~ · Sonder(bau)beschläge mpl, Spezial(bau)beschläge

~ (~) (~) **furniture**, ~ (~) (~) fitting, purpose-made (~) ~ · Sonder(bau)beschlag m, Spezial(bau)beschlag

~ (~) (~) **hardware**, ~ (~) (~) fittings, purpose-made (~) ~ · Sonder(bau)beschläge mpl, Spezial(bau)beschläge

~ (~) **building material**, ~ (~) structural ~, ~ (~) construction(al) ~, purpose-made ~ ~ · Sonder-Baumaterial n, Spezial-Baumaterial [Schweiz]; Sonderbaustoff m, Spezial-Baustoff

~ ~ **(burnt) (clay) brick** → ~ (duty) (~) (~) ~

~ (~) **cement**, purpose-made ~ · Sonderzement, m Spezialzement

~ (~) **cement(ing agent)**, ~ (~) (bonding) adhesive, ~ (~) bonding medium, ~ (~) bonding agent, purpose-made (~) ~ · Sonderkleb(e)stoff m, Sonderkleber m, Spezialkleb(e)stoff, Spezialkleber, Sonderkleb(e)mittel n, Spezialkleb(e)mittel

~ (~) **composition**, ~ (~) compound, ~ (~) mass, ~ (~) material, purpose-made ~ · Sondermasse f, Spezialmasse

~ (~) **compound**, ~ (~) composition, ~ (~) mass, ~ (~) material, purpose-made ~ · Sondermasse f, Spezialmasse

~ (~) **concrete**, purpose-made ~ · Sonderbeton m, Spezialbeton

~ (~) ~ **product**, purpose-made ~ ~ · (Beton)Formstück n

~ (~) **construction profile**, ~ (~) ~ section, ~ (~) ~ shape, ~ (~) ~ unit, ~ (~) ~ trim, ~ (~) structural ~, purpose-made ~ ~ · Sonder-Bauprofil n, Spezial-Bauprofil

~ (~) ~ **section**, ~ (~) ~ profile, ~ (~) ~ shape, ~ (~) ~ unit, ~ (~) ~ trim, ~ (~) structural ~, purpose-made ~ ~ · Sonder-Bauprofil n, Spezial-Bauprofil

~ (~) ~ **shape**, ~ (~) ~ section, ~ (~) ~ profile, ~ (~) ~ unit, ~ (~) ~ trim, ~ (~) structural ~, purpose-made ~ ~ · Sonder-Bauprofil n, Spezial-Bauprofil

~ (~) ~ **trim**, ~ (~)˙~ unit, ~ (~) ~ shape, ~ (~) ~ section, ~ (~) ~ profile, ~ (~) structural ~, purpose-made ~ ~ · Sonder-Bauprofil n, Spezial-Bauprofil

~ (~) ~ **unit**, ~ (~) ~ trim, ~ (~) ~ shape, ~ (~) ~ section, ~ (~) ~ profile, ~ (~) structural ~, purpose-made ~ ~ · Sonder-Bauprofil n, Spezial-Bauprofil

~ (~) **construction(al) material**, ~ (~) building ~, ~ (~) structural ~, purpose-made ~ ~ Sonder-Baumaterial n, Spezial-Baumaterial [Schweiz]; Sonderbaustoff m, Spezial-Baustoff

~ (~) **cover(ing) foil**, ~ (~) protecting ~, purpose-made ~ ~ · Sonder(-Ab)deckfolie f, Sonderschutzfolie, Spezial(-Ab)deckfolie, Spezialschutzfolie

~ (~) **door**, purpose-made ~, purpose-built ~ · Sondertür f, Spezialtür

~ (~) **duct**, purpose-made ~ · Sonderkanal m, Spezialkanal

~ (~) **(fired) (clay) brick** → ~ (duty) (burnt) (~) ~

~ (~) **fitting** → ~ ~ builders' ~

~ (~) **fittings** → ~ ~ builders' ~

~ (~) **furniture** → ~ ~ builders' ~

~ (~) **grout(ing)**, ~ (~) slurry, purpose-made ~ · Sonderschlämme f, Spezialschlämme

~ (~) **hardware** → ~ ~ builders' ~

~ (~) **lock**, purpose-made ~ · Sonderschloß n, Spezialschloß

~ (~) **mass**, ~ (~) material, ~ (~) composition, ~ (~) compound, purpose-made ~ · Sondermasse f, Spezialmasse

~ (~) **material**, ~ (~) mass, ~ (~) compound, ~ (~) composition, purpose-made ~ · Sondermasse f, Spezialmasse

~ (~) **mortar**, purpose-made ~ · Sondermörtel m, Spezialmörtel

~ (~) **paper**, purpose-made ~ [See remark under 'Pappe'] · Sonderpappe f, Spezialpappe

~ (~) **pitch**, purpose-made ~ · Sonderpech n, Spezialpech

~ (~) **plaster**, purpose-made ~ · Sonderputz m, Spezialputz

~ (~) **profile**, ~ (~) section, ~ (~) shape, ~ (~) unit, ~ (~) trim, purpose-made ~ · Sonderprofil n, Spezialprofil

~ (~) **protecting foil**, ~ (~) cover(-ing) ~, purpose-made ~ ~ · Sonder(-Ab)deckfolie f, Sonderschutzfolie, Spezial(-Ab)deckfolie, Spezialschutzfolie

~ (~) **reinforcement,** purpose-made ~ · Sonderarmierung f, Sonderbewehrung, Spezialarmierung, Spezialbewehrung, Sonder(stahl)einlagen fpl, Spezial(stahl)einlagen

~ (~) ~ **steel,** purpose-made ~ ~ · Sonderbetonstahl m, Spezialbetonstahl

~ (~) **rolled profile,** ~ (~) ~ section, ~ (~) ~ shape, ~ (~) ~ unit, ~ (~) ~ trim, purpose-made ~ ~ · Sonderwalzprofil n, Spezialwalzprofil

~ (~) ~ **section,** ~ (~) ~ trim, ~ (~) ~ unit, ~ (~) ~ shape, ~ (~) ~ profile, purpose-made ~ ~ · Spezialwalzprofil n, Sonderwalzprofil

~ (~) ~ **shape,** ~ (~) ~ section, ~ (~) ~ profile, ~ (~) ~ unit, ~ (~) ~ trim purpose-made ~ ~ · Sonderwalzprofil n, Spezialwalzprofil

~ (~) ~ **trim,** ~ (~) ~ unit, ~ (~) ~ shape, ~ (~) ~ section, ~ (~) ~ profile, purpose-made ~ ~ · Sonderwalzprofil n, Spezialwalzprofil

~ (~) ~ **unit,** ~ (~) ~ trim, ~ (~) ~ shape, ~ (~) ~ protile, purpose-made ~ ~ · Sonderwalzprofil n, Spezialwalzprofil

~ (~) **section,** ~ (~) profile, ~ (~) shape, ~ (~) unit, ~ (~) trim, purpose-made ~ · Sonderprofil n, Spezialprofil

~ (~) **shape,** ~ (~) section, ~ (~) profile, ~ (~) unit, ~ (~) trim, purpose-made ~ · Sonderprofil n, Spezialprofil

~ (~) **slurry,** ~ (~) grout(ing), purpose-made ~, special (purpose) grouting compound, purpose-made grouting compound · Sonderschlämme f, Spezialschlämme

~ (~) **steel window,** purpose-made ~ ~, purpose-built ~ ~ · Sonder-Stahlfenster n, Spezial-Stahlfenster

~ (~) **step,** purpose-made ~ · Profilstufe f

~ (~) **structural material,** ~ (~) construction(al), ~ (~) building ~, purpose-made ~ ~ · Sonder-Baumaterial n, Spezial-Baumaterial [Schweiz]; Sonderbaustoff m, Spezial-Baustoff

~ (~) ~ **profile,** ~ (~) ~ section, ~ (~) ~ shape, ~ (~) ~ unit, ~ (~) ~ trim, ~ (~) ~ construction ~, purpose-made ~ ~ · Sonder-Bauprofil n, Spezial-Bauprofil

~ (~) ~ **section,** ~ (~) ~ profile, ~ (~) ~ shape, ~ (~) ~ unit, ~ (~) ~ trim, ~ (~) ~ construction ~, purpose-made ~ ~ · Sonder-Bauprofil n, Spezial-Bauprofil

~ (~) ~ **shape,** ~ (~) ~ section, ~ (~) ~ profile, ~ (~) ~ unit, ~ (~) ~ trim, ~ (~) ~ construction ~, purpose-made ~ ~ · Sonder-Bauprofil n, Spezial-Bauprofil

~ (~) ~ **trim,** ~ (~) ~ unit, ~ (~) ~ shape, ~ (~) ~ section, ~ (~) ~ profile, ~ (~) construction ~, purpose-made ~ · Sonder-Bauprofil n, Spezial-Bauprofil

~ (~) ~ **unit,** ~ (~) ~ trim, ~ (~) ~ shape, ~ (~) ~ section, ~ (~) ~ profile, ~ (~) construction ~, purpose-made ~ · Sonder-Bauprofil n, Spezial-Bauprofil

~ (~) **tile,** purpose-made ~ · Sonder(belag)platte f, Sonderfliese f, Spezial-(belag)platte, Spezialfliese

~ (~) ~, ~ (~) **block,** purpose-made ~ [See remark under 'Block'] · Sonderblock(stein) m, Sonderstein, Profilblock-(stein), Profilstein, Spezialblock(stein), Spezialstein, Formblock(stein), Formstein

~ (~) **trim,** ~ (~) unit, ~ (~) shape, ~ (~) section, ~ (~) profile, purpose-made ~ · Sonderprofil n, Spezialprofil

~ (~) **unit,** ~ (~) trim, ~ (~) shape, ~ (~) section, ~ (~) profile, purpose-made ~ · Sonderprofil n, Spezialprofil

~ (~) **valley gutter,** purpose-made ~ ~ · Sonderkehlrinne f, Spezialkehlrinne

~ (~) **window,** purpose-built ~, purpose-made ~ · Sonderfenster n, Spezialfenster

~ **reinforcement** → ~ purpose ~

~ ~ **steel** → ~ purpose ~

~ **reinforcing bars grade III** · Sonderbetonstahl III m

~ ~ **steel,** alloy ~ ~ · Legierungsbetonstahl m, legierter Betonstahl

~ **rolled profile** → ~ (purpose) rolled section

~ ~ **section** → ~ purpose ~ ~

~ ~ **shape** → ~ (purpose) rolled section

~ ~ **trim** → ~ (purpose) rolled section

~ ~ **unit** → ~ (purpose) rolled section

~ **sand** · Spezialsand m

~ **section** → ~ purpose ~

~ **shape** → ~ purpose ~

~ ~ · Sonderform f, Sondergestalt f, Spezialform, Spezialgestalt

~ **slurry** → ~ purpose ~

~ **soft iron** · Sonderweicheisen n, Spezialweicheisen

~ **spactling compound,** ~ Swedish putty (US); ~ stopping, ~ stopper, ~ filler · Sonderspachtel(masse) m, (f), Spezialspachtel(masse)

~ **steel,** alloy ~ · legierter Stahl m, Legierungsstahl

~ ~ (Brit.); specialty ~ (US); stainless ~ · Edelstahl m

~ ~ **window** → ~ purpose ~ ~

~ **step** → ~ purpose ~

~ **stopper,** ~ filler, ~ stopping; ~ Swedish putty, ~ spactling compound (US) · Sonderspachtel(masse) m, (f), Spezialspachtel(masse)

~ **stopping,** ~ stopper, ~ filler; ~ Swedish putty, ~ spactling compound (US) · Sonderspachtel(masse) m, (f), Spezialspachtel(masse)

special straight run coal tar pitch — spherical hip(ped end) 946

~ **straight run coal tar pitch,** ~ coal tar pitch · Steinkohlenteersonderpech *n*

~ **structural material** → ~ purpose ~ ~

~ ~ **profile** → ~ purpose ~ ~

~ ~ **section** → ~ purpose ~ ~

~ ~ **shape** → ~ purpose ~ ~

~ ~ **steel,** alloy ~ ~ · legierter Baustahl *m*, Legierungssbaustahl

~ ~ **trim** → ~ purpose ~ ~

~ ~ **unit** → ~ purpose ~ ~

~ **surface treatment** · Sonderoberflächenbehandlung *f*, Spezialoberflächenbehandlung

~ **Swedish putty,** ~ spactling compound (US); ~ stopping, ~ stopper, ~ filler · Sonderspachtel(masse) *m*, (*f*), Spezialspachtel(masse)

~ **tar(red) composition roofing** → ~ ~ ready ~

~ ~ **prepared roofing** → ~ ~ ready ~

~ ~ **ready roofing,** ~ ~ composition ~, ~ ~ prepared ~, ~ ~ roof(ing) felt (US); ~ ~ fluxed pitch ~ ~ (Brit.) · Teer-Sonderdachpappe *f*

~ ~ **roof(ing) felt** (US) → ~ ~ ready roofing

~ **tile** → ~ purpose ~

~ **trim** → ~ purpose ~

~ **unit,** three-dimensional ~ · dreidimensionales Element *n*, räumliches ~

~ ~ → ~ purpose ~

~ **valley gutter** → ~ purpose ~ ~

~ **window** → ~ purpose ~

~ **wire,** purpose-made ~ · Sonderdraht *m*, Spezialdraht

~ **wire(d) glass** · Sonderdrahtglas *n*, Spezialdrahtglas

specialist commission · Fachausschuß *m*

~ **firm,** firm of specialists · Spezialunternehmen *n*, Spezialfirma *f*

specialty steel (US); special ~ (Brit.); stainless ~ · Edelstahl *m*

speckled · gesprenkelt

speculatory, squint, hagioscope [*An oblique opening in a Mediaeval church wall to give a view of the altar*] · Hagioskop *n*

specific acoustic impedance, unit-area ~ · spezifische Schallimpedanz *f*, Feldimpedanz *f* [*Quotient aus Schalldruck und Schallschnelle*]

(~) **adhesion coefficient** · Adhäsionsbeiwert *m*, Adhäsionszahl *f*

(~) ~ **limit** · Adhäsionsgrenze *f*

~ **gravity** → density

~ ~ **factor** · scheinbare (Beton)Zuschlag(stoff)rohdichte *f*

~ **heat** [*The amount of heat required per unit mass to cause a unit rise of temperature oder a small range of temperatures; for ordinary concrete and steel it is approximately 0.22 and 0.12 Btu/1b/deg F (Cal/g/deg C), respectively*] · spezifische Wärme *f*

~ **paper** → ~ wall~

~ **strain** · spezifische Dehnung *f*, bezogene ~

~ **surface** [*The surface area of particles contained in a unit weight or absolute unit volume of a material*] · spezifische Oberfläche *f*

~ **volume** · spezifischer Raum *m*, spezifisches Volum(en) *n*

~ **(wall)paper** · Sonder(papier)tapete *f*, Spezial(papier)tapete

spec(ification) · Leistungsbeschreibung *f*

~ **requirement,** technical ~ · technische Anforderung *f* [*Leistung; Güte*]

spec(ification)s, technical data, engineering data · technische Angaben *fpl*, ~ Daten *f*, ~ Aufzählung *f*

~ **for application** · Verarbeitungsanleitung *f*

~ ~ **laying,** directions ~ ~ · Verlegeanleitung *f*

specified · gefordert [*z.B. Sieblinie*]

(~) **time for completion** · Baufrist *f*

speckled, variegated, dappled [*Marked with spots of a different colo(u)r or shade*] · (bunt)gefleckt

spectator's stand · Tribüne *f*

spectral colour (Brit.); ~ color (US) · körperlose Farbe *f*, Spektralfarbe

~ **density** · spektrale Intensitätsdichte *f*

specular, homologous · spiegelbildlich

~ **enamel finish** · Spiegeleffektlackierung *f*

speed of impregnation, impregnation speed · Imprägnier(ungs)geschwindigkeit *f*, Tränk(ungs)geschwindigkeit

~ ~ **slide** (operation), rate ~ ~ (~) · Ziehgeschwindigkeit *f*, Gleitgeschwindigkeit [*Gleitschalung*]

Spence metal · Eisenthiat *n*, Spencemetall *n*

Sperry process, electrolytic ~ · Fällungsverfahren *n*, Niederschlagsverfahren [*Bleiweißherstellung*]

sphalerite, (zinc)blende, black jack; zinc sulphide (Brit.); zinc sulfide (US) · Zinkblende *f*, Sphalerit *m*, ZnS

sphere impact, ball ~ · Kugelschlag *m*

~ **of function,** zone ~ ~, functional sphere, functional zone · Funktionsbereich *m*, *n*

~ **ring** · Kugelring *m*

(spherical) cap · Kugelhaube *f*, Kugelmütze *f*, (Kugel)Kalotte *f*

~ **cupola** → semi-dome

~ **depolished glass globe** · Kugel-Trübglas *n* [*Leuchte*]

~ **dome** → semi-dome

~ **hip(ped end)** · Kugelwalm *m*

spherical house — spiral-weld(ed) pipe

~ **house**, ball ~ · Kugelhaus n [Haus in Kugelform; der erste Idealentwurf stammt von Claude Nicolas Ledoux für ein Flurwächterhaus aus dem Jahre 1806]

~ **housing**, globe ~ · Kugelgehäuse n

~ **icosahedron** · Kugel-Ikosaeder n

~ **lune** · Kugelzweieck n

~ **plane** · Kugelfläche f

~ **polygon** · sphärisches Polygon n

~ **quadrangle**, ~ quadrilateral · sphärisches Viereck n

~ **quadrilateral**, ~ quadrangle · sphärisches Viereck n

~ **sector** · Kugelsektor m, Kugelausschnitt m

~ **segment** · Kalotte f, Kugelsegment n, Kugelabschnitt m, Kugelhaube f, Kugelhelm m

~ **shell**, circular ~ [A shell with a constant radius of curvature] · Rundschale f, Halbschale, Kugelschale, sphärische Schale, Kreisschale

~ **strip** · Kugelstreifen m

~ **tank** · Kugelbehälter m

~ **tensor** · Kugeltensor m

~ **triangle** . sphärisches Dreieck n

~ **trigonometry** · sphärische Trigonometrie f

~ **vault** · sphärisches Gewölbe n

spheroid, ellipsoid of revolution · Rotationsellipsoid n, Drehellipsoid [Ein durch die Umdrehung einer halben Ellipse und ihre (große oder kleine) Achse entstandener Körper, dessen ebene Schnitte Ellipsen oder Kreise sind]

spheroidal (graphite) cast iron → nodular (~) ~ ~

sphinx gate · Sphinxtorbau m

spigot(-)and(-)socket bend with flange · Flansch(en)muffenkrümmer m

~ **concrete pipe** Brit.) → bell(-)and(-)spigot ~ ~ US)

~ **joint** (Brit.); bell(-)and(-)spigot ~, B&S ~ (US) · Glockenmuffenverbindung f

~ **pipe** (Brit.); bell(-)and(-)spigot ~, B&S ~ (US) · Glockenmuffenrohr n

~ **stoneware pipe**; bell(-)and(-)spigot ~ ~, B&S ~ ~ (US) · Steinzeug-Glockenmuffenrohr n, Glockenmuffen-Steinzeugrohr

spigot (end), pipe spigot · (Rohr)Einsteckende n, (Rohr)Spitzende n, Falz m

spike · Pikeisen n

~ **grid** · (zweiseitiger) Krallendübel m, Krallenplattenpaar n

~ **heel**, stiletto ~ · Pfennigabsatz m

spikes · Schweinsfedern fpl

spill · Becherwerk n [Dachpappenanlage]

spina [The spine wall down the centre of an ancient hippodrome or circus, around which the contestants turned] · Spina f [Trennmauer zwischen den beiden Richtungsbahnen in der Arena eines römischen Zirkus]

spindle oil · Spindelöl n

spindle-shaped · spindelförmig

spine wall · Treppentrennwand f

spinel · Spinell m [Kubische Kristalle der allgemeinen Formel $R''O·R_2'''O_3$, wobei R'' und R''' zwei- und dreiwertige Metalle sind. Dieser Ausdruck bezeichnet insbesondere den Magnesia-Tonerde-Spinell, $MgO·Al_2O_3$]

~ **refractory (product)** · Spinellerzeugnis n [vorwiegend aus Magnesiumaluminat bestehendes feuerfestes Erzeugnis]

spinning, centrifugal action · Schleudern n, Schleuderung f [Herstellung von Rohren, Masten und Pfählen]

~, concrete ~, centrifugal casting of concrete, spinning of concrete · (Beton-)Schleuderung f, (Beton)Schleudern n

~ **method**, concrete ~ ~ · (Beton-)Schleuderverfahren n

~ **of concrete**, centrifugal casting ~ ~, (concrete) spinning · (Beton)Schleuderung f, (Beton)Schleudern n

spiral distortion, twist, wind · Spiralverformung f

spiral-fluted · spiralgerillt

spiral fluting · Spiralkannelierung f, Spiralriefelung

~ **house** · Spiralhaus n

~ **minaret** · spiralförmiger Gebetsturm m, Spiralturm, Spiralminarett n [Ein zylindrischer Turm mit schraubenförmig gewundener Außenrampe, z.B. bei der Malwiyya-Moschee in Samarra]

~ **pier** · spiralig gekehlter Pfeiler m, spiralgekehlter ~, Pfeiler mit Windungen

~ **ramp**, helic(oid)al ~, circular ~, helicline, ramp tower · Schraubenrampe f, Wendelrampe, Spiralrampe

~ ~ **car park** · Wendel-Parkhaus n

~ **reinforcement** [misnomer]; helical ~, transverse ~, lateral ~, helical binding, helix · Querbewehrung f nach der Schraubenlinie, Spiralbewehrung, Spiralarmierung, Spiral(stahl)einlagen fpl, Umschnürung

(~) **scroll**, volute (ornament) · Schneckenschmuck m Schnecke(nverzierung) f, Spiralschmuck, Spiralverzierung, Volutenschmuck, Volute(nverzierung) f, Spirale f

~ **shaft** · Zylinder m [Als Windung bei einem Pfeiler]

~ **stair(case)**, helical ~, circular ~, cockle ~, corkscrew ~, caracole, vis · Wendeltreppe f, Schnecke(ntreppe) f, Schneckenstiege f

~ ~ [misnomer]; helical ~, open well ~, open-newel ~ · gewendelte Treppe f, Hohltreppe [In der Mitte ist ein freier Raum]

spiral-weld(ed) pipe · spiralgeschweißtes Rohr n, geschweißtes Spiralrohr, Spiralschweißrohr, Schweißspiralrohr

spirally bound concrete · spiralumschnürter Beton *m*

spire [*An elongated pyramidal structure erected upon the top of a tower*] · Pyramidenturmdach *n*, Turmdachpyramide *f*, Turmzeltdach über quadratischem Grundriß, (Turm)Helm *m*

~, steeple, broach · Spitz(kirch)turm *m*

spired church tower · Kirchturm *m* mit Zeltdach über quadratischem Grundriß, Pyramidendach-Kirchturm, Dachpyramiden-Kirchturm

spirelet · kleines Pyramidenturmdach *n*, ~ Turmzeltdach über quadratischem Grundriß, kleine Turmdachpyramide *f*

~, bell-turret · Glockentürmchen *n*

(spire-shaped) sikhara · Nagara *m*, Sikhara *m* [*Turm über der Cella eines nordindischen Tempels*]

spirit [*In the paint industry, the term 'spirit' is used somewhat loosely but generally refers to commercial ethyl alcohol normally sold as industrial methylated spirit*] · Spiritus *m*, Sprit *m*, denaturierter Äthylalkohol *m*

~ **fastness** → ~ resistance

~ **flat varnish**, ~ matt(-finish) · Spiritus-Mattlack *m*, Sprit-Mattlack

~ **lacquer** · Spirituslackfarbe *f*

(~) level, mechanic's ~, water ~, plumb ~ · Wasserwaage *f*

~ **matt(-finish)**, ~ flat varnish · Spiritus-Mattlack *m*, Sprit-Mattlack

~ **resistance**, ~ fastness, resistance to spirit, fastness to spirit · Spiritusechtheit *f*, Spritechtheit, Spiritusbeständigkeit, Spritbeständigkeit, Spirituswiderstand *m*, Spritwiderstand, Spiritusfestigkeit, Spritfestigkei;

~ **soluble** · spritlöslich, spirituslöslich

~ **stain**, penetrating ~ · Spiritusbeize *f*, Spritbeize

~ **varnish** · Spiritus(klar)lack *m*, Sprit(klar)lack

splashback [*An independent area of impervious material used to protect the wall surface in the vicinity of a wash basin, sink or bath*] · Rückwand *f*, Spritzwand

splash lap · Spritzschutz *m* [*Schornstein(ab)dichtung*]

~ **proof**, spritzwasserdicht, spritzwassergeschützt

to splay, to cant, to slope, to bevel · ausschrägen, abschrägen, abkragen, verschrägen

splay, slope, cant, bevel · Ausschrägung *f*, Abschrägung, Verschrägung, Abkragung Schräge *f*

~, cant, slope, bevel · Druckschlag *m* [*Gewölbe*]

~ **bonder**, ~ header, ~ bondstone, slope ~, cant ~, bevel ~ [*A spherical brick which is bevelled at about 45° at one end*] · abgeschrägter Binder(stein) *m*, ~ Strecker, ausgeschrägter ~, abgekragter ~

~ **bondstone** → ~ bonder

~ **brick**, slope ~, cant ~, bevel ~ [*A special brick which is bevelled at about 45° at one end (= splay header) or at 45° along one edge (= splay stretcher)*] · abgeschrägter Ziegel *m*, ausgeschrägter ~, abgekragter ~

~ **header** → ~ bonder

~ **moulding** (Brit.); ~ molding (US); cant ~, slope ~, bevel ~ · abgeschrägte Dekor(ations)leiste *f*, ~ Zierleiste, ~ (Ornament)Leiste, ausgeschrägte ~, abgekragte ~

~ **of a masonry wall**, slope ~ ~ ~ ~, cant ~ ~ ~ ~, bevel ~ ~ ~ ~ [*The diagonal surface formed by the cutting away of a masonry wall, as when an opening is wider inside than out or conversely*] · Mauerschräge *f*, Mauerausschrägung *f*, Mauerabschrägung, Mauerabkragung

~ ~ ~ **wall**, slope ~ ~ ~, cant ~ ~ ~, bevel ~ ~ ~ [*The diagonal surface formed by the cutting away of a wall, as when an opening is wider inside than out or conversely*] · Wandschräge *f*, Wandausschrägung *f*, Wandabschrägung, Wandabkragung

~ **stretcher**, slope ~, cant ~, bevel ~ [*A special brick which is bevelled at 45° along one edge*] · abgeschrägter Läufer *m*, ausgeschrägter ~, abgekragter ~

splayed, sloped, canted; bevelled (Brit.); beveled (US) · abgeschrägt, ausgeschrägt, abgekragt

~ **folding**, canted ~, sloped ~; bevelled ~ (Brit.); beveled ~ (US) · abgeschrägte Faltung *f*, ausgeschrägte ~, abgekragte ~

~, canting, sloping; bevelling (Brit.); beveling (US) · Ausschrägen *n*, Abschrägen, Verschrägen, Abkragen

splice [*Connection of one reinforcing bar to another by overlapping, welding, mechanical end connectors, or other means*] · Verbindung *f*

~ **plate** · Stoßblech *n* [*Stahlbau*]

splicing looper (for the dry felt) · Rohpappenausgleichvorrichtung *f* [*Dachpappenanlage*]

to splinter · bestoßen [*Die Kanten eines Steinblocks unbeabsichtigt beschädigen*]

splinter, slip, sliver · Spließ *m*, Span *m* [*Holzstück*, *Zinkblechstreifen oder Dachpappenstreifen zur Dichtung der Längsfugen bei einfacher Dachdeckung*]

~ **roof**, slip ~ · Splieẞdach *n*, Spandach [*Dachdeckung, deren senkrechte Fugen mit einem Spließ abgedichtet sind*]

split · Schlitz *m*, Nut *f* und Feder *f* [*Tuchscherer-Dübel*]

split-and-wedge (type) bolt, slot-and-wedge ~ · Perfoanker *m*, Schlitzkeilanker

split chimney block, half ~ ~ · halber Kamin(form)stein *m*, halbes Schornsteinformstück *n*

split-cube mould (Brit.); ∼ mold (US) · geteilte Würfelform f

split duct, ∼ pipe, channel (stone) · (Rohr)Schale f, (auf)gespaltenes Rohr n, Rinne f

∼ **face** · Spaltfläche f [Natursteinbearbeitung]

split-level house · Halbgeschoßhaus n [z.B. an Berghängen]

split loop, ∼ stirrup · zerlegter Bügel m

∼ **pipe,** ∼ duct, channel (stone) · (Rohr-)Schale f, (auf)gespaltenes Rohr n, Rinne f

∼ **ring (connector)** · geschlitzter Ringdübel m

∼ **sleeve** · zweiteilige (Rohr)Muffe f ohne Gewinde, ∼ Überschiebmuffe

∼ **stirrup,** ∼ loop · zerlegter Bügel m

∼ **T,** ∼ tee · geteiltes T-Stück n

∼ **tee,** ∼ T(ee), ∼ T(ee)-piece · geteiltes T-Stück n

splitting · Spalten n [Naturstein]

∼ **tensile test,** indirect ∼ ∼, diametral compression ∼, Brazilian ∼ · Spaltzugversuch m, Spaltzugprobe f, Spaltzugprüfung f

sponge holder, ∼ tray · Schwammschale f

∼ **rubber,** expansive ∼, swelling ∼, expanded ∼, cellular ∼, foam(ed) (natural) ∼, expanded (natural) ∼ · Gummischaum(stoff) m, Zellgummi m, n, Kautschukschaum(stoff), Quellgummi, Zellkautschuk m, Schaumgummi

∼ **tray,** ∼ holder · Schwammschale f

sponging · Verputzen n mit dem Schwamm [Steinzeugrohrindustrie]

spontaneous evaporation · Selbstverdunstung f

sporadic building, haphazard ∼ · regellose Bebauung f, sporadische ∼, wilde ∼

∼ **development** · planlose Bebauung f

sports area · Sportfläche f

∼ **building** · Sportgebäude n

∼ **centre** (Brit.); ∼ center (US); ∼ forum · Sportzentrum n

∼ **equipment closet** · Sportgeräte-Einbauschrank m, Sportgeräte-Wandschrank

∼ **facility** · Sportanlage f

∼ **field,** ∼ ground · Sportfeld n

∼ **forum;** ∼ centre (Brit.); ∼ center (US) · Sportzentrum n

∼ **ground** · Sportplatz m

∼ ∼, ∼ field · Sportfeld n

∼ ∼ **pavilion** · Sportplatzpavillon m

∼ **hall** · Sporthalle f

∼ **palace** · Sportpalast m

∼ **structures** · Sportbauten f

spot application · punktweises Aufbringen n, ∼ Auftragen [z.B. eines Klebers]

spot-bonded → spot-glued

spot bonding, ∼ gluing, ∼ fixing · Punkt(ver)klebung f

∼ **check,** random ∼ · Stichprobe f

spot-fixed → spot-glued

spot fixing, ∼ bonding, ∼ gluing · Punkt(ver)klebung f

spot-glued, spot-bonded, spot-fixed · punktverklebt, punktgeklebt

spot gluing, ∼ fixing, ∼ bonding · Punkt(ver)klebung f

∼ **heat** · Punktwärme f

to spot weld, ∼ s/w · punktschweißen

spot-welded, s/w · punktgeschweißt

∼ **Rabitz (type) wire fabric lath(ing)** · Stahlnetz-Rabitz(gewebe) n [Das Gewebe ist punktverschweißt]

∼ **round bars,** ∼ ∼ rods · punktverschweißte Rundstähle mpl, punktgeschweißte ∼

spot welding · Punktschweißung f

spot-welding primer · Punktschweißfarbe f

spotted schist, mottled ∼, fleckschiefer, maculose rock · Fleck(en)schiefer m

spotting, sheariness, mottling · Fleckenbildung f [Anstrichmittel]

spout → gargoyle

sprawl, dispersal, suburban ∼ · Zersied(e)lung f

spray → palmette

∼ · Spritzstrahl m

sprayability · Spritzbarkeit f, Spritzfähigkeit

sprayable, gun-grade · spritzbar, spritzfähig

∼ **asbestos,** sprayed(-on) ∼, Limpet ∼ [The trade name of a composition of asbestos and a bonding agent applied by gun spraying for fire-protection, thermal insulation, and the prevention of condensation. It is produced by Turner's Asbestos Cement Co. Ltd., Manchester and Limpet Spritzasbest GmbH, Frankfurt (M)] · Spritzasbest m

spray application → (gun) spraying

∼ ∼ **of mortar,** mechanical ∼ ∼ ∼ · maschineller Mörtelauftrag m, Spritzmörtelauftrag, Gebläsemörtelauftrag

spray-applied — sprayed(-on) mortar

spray-applied · aufgespritzt

spray asphalt → spraying ~

~ booth, ~ cab(in) · Spritzkabine f

~ ~ strippable coating, ~ cab(in) ~ ~, ~ ~ strip-off ~ · aufgespritzter Abziehlack m

to spray by atomizing (US); ~ ~ ~ atomising (Brit.) · aufdüsen, aufsprühen

spray cement → gun(-grade) ~

spray-down, spraying-down · Abspritzen n

sprayed, sprayed-on, gunned, gun-applied · pneumatisch aufgetragen, ~ gespritzt

~ atomized · zerstäubt aufgespritzt, aufgedüst, aufgesprüht

~ cement → gun(-grade) ~

~ concrete → sprayed(-on) ~

~ exterior plastering → sprayed(-on) (external) rendering

~ ~ rendering → sprayed(-on) (external) ~

~ external plastering → sprayed(-on) (external) rendering

~ (~) rendering → sprayed-on (~) ~

sprayed(-on), gunned, gun-applied · pistolengespritzt, pistolenaufgetragen

~, gunned, gun-applied · pneumatisch aufgetragen, ~ gespritzt

~ absorbing ceiling → ~ sound ~ ~

~ acoustic(al) ceiling, ~ sound-control ~, ~ (sound) absorbing ~, ~ (sound) absorbent ~, ~ (sound) absorptive ~ · Spritzakustikdecke f, Spritzschallschluckdecke

~ asbestos, sprayable ~, Limpet ~ [*The trade name of a composition of asbestos and a bonding agent applied by gun spraying for fire-protection, thermal insulation, and the prevention of condensation. It is produced by Turner's Asbestos Cement Co. Ltd.,Manchester and Limpet Spritzasbest GmbH, Frankfurt (M)*] · Spritzasbest m

~ ~ (external) rendering (Brit.); ~ ~ stucco (US); ~ ~ exterior plaster, ~ ~ external plaster · Asbestspritz(außen)(ver)putz m

~ ~ finish · Asbestspritz(ver)putz m

~ ~ insulation [*B.S. 3590*] · Spritzasbestdämmung f

~ ~ plaster · Asbestspritz(innen)(ver)putz m

~ ~ stucco (US) → ~ ~ (external) rendering (Brit.)

~ asphalt, spray(ing) ~, gun-grade ~, gunned ~, pressure-gun type ~ · Spritzasphalt m

~ cement → gun(-grade) ~

~ ~ (external) rendering (Brit.); ~ ~ stucco (US); ~ ~ (exterior) plaster, ~ ~ external plaster, ~ ~ finish · Zementspritz(ver)putz m, Spritzzement(ver)putz

~ (clear) varnish, spray(ing) (~) ~, gun-grade (~) ~, gunned (~) ~, pressure-gun type (~) ~ · Spritz(klar)-lack m

~ coat, spray(ing) ~, gunned ~ · Spritzanstrich m, Spritzaufstrich

~ ~ of paint, spray(ing) ~ ~ ~, gunned ~ ~ ~, ~ paint coat · Spritzfarbanstrich m, Spritzfarbaufstrich

~ coat(ing), spray(ing) ~, gunned ~ · Spritzschicht f

~ composition, ~ compound, ~ mass, ~ material, spray(ing) ~, gun-grade ~, gunned ~, pressure-gun type ~ · Spritzmasse f

~ compound, ~ material, ~ mass, ~ composition, spray(ing) ~, gun-grade ~, gunned ~, pressure-gun type ~ · Spritzmasse f

~ concrete, pneumatically applied ~, shotcrete, gunned concrete [*Concrete conveyed through a hose and projected at high velocity onto a surface*] · Spritzbeton m, Gebläsebeton

~ cork, spray(ing) ~, gun-grade ~, gunned ~, pressure-gun type ~ · Spritzkork m

~ facing → ~ (su r)facing

~ film, spray(ing) ~, gunned ~, ~ membrane · Spritzfilm m, Spritzhaut f

~ fireproofing · Spritz-Brandschutzisolierung f, Spritz-Feuerschutzisolierung

~ foam, spray(ing) ~, gun-grade ~, gunned ~, pressure-gun type ~ · Spritzschaum m

~ insulation, spray-on ~, spray(ing) ~, gunned ~; ~ isolation (US) · Spritzisolierung f

~ lining → ~ (su r)facing

~ mass, ~ material, ~ compound, ~ composition, spray(ing) ~, gun-grade ~, gunned ~, pressure-gun type ~ ~ · Spritzmasse f

~ mastic, spray(ing) ~, gun-grade ~, gunned ~, pressure-gun type ~ · Spritzmastix m

~ material, ~ compound, ~ mass, ~ composition, spray(ing) ~, gun-grade ~, gunned ~, pressure-gun type ~ · Spritzmasse f

~ membrane, spray(ing) ~, gunned ~, ~ film · Spritzfilm m, Spritzhaut f

~ metal, spray(ing) ~, gunned ~ · Spritzmetall n

~ ~ coating, spray(ing) ~ ~, gunned ~ ~ [*B.S. 2569*] · Spritzmetallüberzug m

~ mortar, air-blown ~, shotcrete, pneumatically applied mortar, gunned mortar [*Mortar conveyed through a hose and projected at high velocity onto a surface*] · Spritzmörtel m, Gebläsemörtel

sprayed(-on) paint coat — spray pond

~ **paint coat,** spray(ing) ~ ~, gunned ~ ~, ~ coat of paint · Spritzfarbanstrich *m*, Spritzfarbaufstrich

~ **plastic,** spray(ing) ~, gun-grade ~, gunned ~, pressure-gun type ~ · Spritzkunststoff *m*

~ **putty** → gunned ~

~ ~ → gun(-grade) cement

~ **rendering** → ~ external ~

~ **roof(ing) membrane,** spray(ing) ~, gunned ~ ~ · Spritz-Kunststoffbedachung *f*

~ **seal(ing),** spray(ing) ~, gunned ~ · Spritz(ab)dichtung *f*

~ **(sound) absorbent ceiling,** ~ (~) absorbing ~, ~ (~) absorptive ~, ~ sound-control ~, ~ acoustic(al) ~ · Spritzakustikdecke *f*, Spritzschallschluckdecke

~ **(sur)facing,** ~ lining, spray(ing) ~, gunned ~ · Spritzauskleidung *f*, Spritzverkleidung, Spritzbekleidung

~ **varnish** → ~ clear ~

~ **vermiculite,** spray(ing) ~, gun-grade ~, gunned ~, pressure-gun type ~ · Spritzvermiculite *m*

sprayed putty → gun(-grade) cement

sprayer → (paint) spray gun

spray glazing, ~ glaze(d finish), ~ glazed coat(ing) · Spritzbeglasen *n*, Spritzglasieren

~ **gun** → paint ~ ~

spraying → gun ~

spray(ing) asphalt, sprayed(-on) ~, gun-grade ~, gunned ~, pressure-gun type ~ · Spritzasphalt *m*

~ **cement** → gun(-grade) ~

~ **(clear) varnish,** gun-grade (~) ~, sprayed(-on) (~) ~, gunned (~) ~, pressure-gun type (~) ~ · Spritz(klar)lack *m*

~ **coat,** sprayed(-on) ~, gunned ~ · Spritzanstrich *m*, Spritzaufstrich

~ ~ **of paint,** sprayed(-on) ~ ~ ~, gunned ~ ~ ~, ~ paint coat · Spritzfarbanstrich *m*, Spritzfarbaufstrich

~ **composition,** ~ compound, ~ mass, ~ material, sprayed(-on) ~, gun-grade ~, gunned ~, pressure-gun type ~ · Spritzmasse *f*

~ **cork,** gun-grade ~, gunned ~, sprayed(-on) ~, pressure-gun type ~ · Spritzkork *m*

spray(in)-down · Abspritzen *n*

spray(ing) exterior plastering → sprayed(-on) (external) rendering

~ ~ **rendering** → sprayed(-on) (external) ~

~ **external plastering** → sprayed(-on) (external) rendering

~ **(~) rendering** → sprayed(-on) (~) ~

~ **film,** sprayed(-on) ~, gunned ~, ~ membrane · Spritzfilm *m*, Spritzhaut *f*

~ **foam,** gun-grade ~, gunned ~, sprayed(-on) ~, pressure-gun type ~ · Spritzschaum *m*

spraying glazing, glazing by spraying · Glasieren *n* durch Begießen, Beglasen ~ ~, Gießglasieren, Gießbeglasen

~ **gun** → metal ~ ~

spray(ing) isolation, sprayed(-on) ~, gunned ~, spray-on ~ (US); ~ insulation · Spritzisolierung *f*

~ **mass,** ~ material, ~ compound, ~ composition, gun-grade ~, gunned ~, sprayed(-on) ~, pressure-gun type ~ · Spritzmasse *f*

~ **mastic,** gun-grade ~, gunned ~, sprayed(-on) ~, pressure-gun type ~ · Spritzmastix *m*

~ **material,** ~ compound, ~ mass, ~ composition, gun-grade ~, gunned ~, sprayed(-on) ~, pressure-gun type ~ · Spritzmasse *f*

~ **membrane,** sprayed(-on) ~, gunned ~, ~ fim · Spritzfilm *m*, Spritzhaut *f*

spraying method · Spritzverfahren *n*

spray(ing) paint coat, sprayed(-on) ~ ~, gunned ~ ~, ~ coat of paint · Spritzfarbanstrich *m*, Spritzfarbaufstrich

spraying pistol → (paint) spray gun

spray(ing) plastic, gun-grade ~, gunned ~, sprayed(-on) ~, pressure-gun type ~ · Spritzkunststoff *m*

~ **putty** → gunned ~

~ ~ → gun(-grade) cement

~ **rendering** → sprayed(-on) (external) ~

~ **varnish** → sprayed(-on) (clear) ~

~ **vermiculite,** sprayed(-on) ~, gun-grade ~, gunned ~, pressure-gun type ~ · Spritzvermiculite *m*

spray insulation, spraying ~, spray-on ~, sprayed(-on) ~, gunned ~; ~ isolation (US) · Spritzisolierung *f*

~ **(mixed) plaster,** machine applied (~) ~ · Spritzputz *m*, Maschinenputz, maschinell aufgetragener Putz

to spray on by atomizing · aufdüsen, aufsprühen

spray-painted · gespritzt

spray painting · Spritzauftrag *m* [*Anstrichmittel*]

~ **plastering,** mechanical ~, ~ rendering · Spritz(ver)putzen *n*, maschinelles (Ver)Putzen

~ **plastic finish** · Kunststoffspritzputz *m*, Spritzkunststoffputz

~ **pond,** cooling ~ · Kühlbecken *n*, Kühlteich *m*

spray putty — sprocket (piece)

~ putty → gunned ~

~ ~ → gun(-grade) cement

~ rendering, mechanical ~, ~ plastering · maschinelles (Ver)Putzen *n*, Spritz(ver)putzen

~ shower · Brause *f* [*Das Wasser wird in feiner Verteilung gegen den Körper geleitet. Gegenteil: Strahldusche (jet shower), bei der das Wasser in geschlossenem Strahl gegen den Körper geleitet wird*]

~ shower bath · Brausebad *n*

~ ~ column · Brausesäule *f*

~ ~ control · Brausesteuerung *f*

~ ~ cubicle · Brausekabine *f*

~ ~ curtain · Brausevorhang *m*

~ ~ head · Brausekopf *m*

~ ~ hose · Brauseschlauch *m*

~ ~ installation · Brauseanlage *f*

~ ~ public baths · Brausenbad(eanstalt) *n*, (*f*)

~ ~ receptor · Brause(-Bade)wanne *f*

~ ~ recess · Brausenische *f*, Brausezelle *f*

~ ~ room · Brauseraum *m*

~ ~ rose · Brausetülle *f*, Brauserosette *f*

~ ~ set, ~ ~ unit · Brausegarnitur *f*

~ ~ stall · Brausestand *m*

~ ~ tray · Brausetasse *f*

~ ~ unit, ~ ~ set · Brausegarnitur *f*

~ ~ valve · Brauseventil *n*

~ stucco → spray(ing) ~

~ stuccowork (US); ~ (external) rendering, ~ external plastering (Brit.) · Spritz(außen)(ver)putzen *n*

~ tap · Spritzhahn *m*

spraytight · spritzdicht

to spread, to distribute, to apply · aufbringen, auftragen

~ ~ into [*e.g. an apophyge is the concave curve where the end of a column spreads into its base or capital*] · übergehen

spread footing · Flächenfundament *n*

~ foundation · Flächengründung *f*

~ of fire, ~ ~ flame, fire spread, flame spread · Brandausbreitung *f*, Brandausweitung, Feuerausbreitung, Feuerausweitung, Flammenausbreitung

~ ~ smoke, smoke spread · Rauchausbreitung *f*

spreader, float · Glätter *m* [*Putztechnik*]

~ · (Betonstahl-)Abstandhalter *m* aus Holz

~ bar, yoke [*A stiff beam hanging from a crane hook having several ropes or chains hanging from different points along it. It is used for lifting long objects to prevent them breaking during lifting*] · Traverse *f*, Ausgleichgehänge *n*

spreading, distribution, application · Aufbringen *n*, Auftrag(en) *m*, (*n*)

~ against cable with opposite curvature · Verspannung *f* mit gegensinnig gekrümmtem Seil

~ of load, distribution ~ ~, load distribution · Lastverteilung *f*

~ ~ sand, sand spreading · Aufstreuen *n* von Sand, Sandaufstreuen

~ ~ screed · Ausbreiten *n* des Estrichs

~ rate, body [*This term is now preferred to 'covering power'*] · Ausgiebigkeit *f*, Ergiebigkeit [*Ein Maß für die Fläche, die mit einer Mengeneinheit des Anstrichstoffes und mit einem Anstrich in vereinbarter Arbeitsweise versehen werden kann, wird z.B. in m²/kg oder m²/Liter angegeben*]

~ thickness → distribution ~

spring → springing

~ (bend) [*A pipe fitting being an obtuse bend*] · (Rohr)Knie(stück) *n*

spring-board · Sprungbrett *n* [*Schwimmbad*]

spring constant · Federkennwert *m*

~ contact plug · Bananenstecker *m*

~ hook, snap ~ · Karabinerhaken *m*

~ latch (Brit.); latch bolt (US) · Federfalle *f*, federnde Falle

~ ~ lock · Springhaken(tür)schloß *n*

~ loaded · federbelastet

~ roller(-type) light-tight blind, ~ ~ black(out) ~, ~ ~ dark ~ · Springrollo *n*

~ steel · Federstahl *m*

~ strength · Federstärke *f*

~ water · Quellwasser *n*

springer [*The bottom stone of an arch or vault resting on an impost*] · Anfänger *m*, Anwölber, Anfangstein *m*, Kämpferstein [*Der erste Stein über dem Kämpfer eines Bogens oder Gewölbes*]

~, skewback, summer, impost [*The place where the vertical support for an arch terminates and the curve of the arch begins*] · Kämpfer *m*

springing · Bogenanfang *m*

~, spring · Kämpferfläche *f*, Anfang *m* [*Bogen; Gewölbe*]

~ line · Kämpferlinie *f*

~ wall, rein · unteres Drittel *n* der Bogenachse, ~ ~ des Bogenschenkels

to sprinkle on the surface · aufstreuen

~ ~ with sand · besanden

~ ~ ~ water · schlämmen [*Rohrgraben*]

sprinkler station · Sprinklerzentrale *f*, Sprinklerstation *f* [*Brandbekämpfung*]

~ system, drencher ~, ~ installation, ~ plant · Sprinkleranlage *f* [*Brandbekämpfung*]

sprinkling · Einstreuen *n*

~ · Berieseln *n*, Beries(e)lung *f* [*Brandbekämpfung und Bewässerung*]

sprocket (piece), cocking ~ · Strebeschwarte *f*, Schwibbe *f*, Sturmlatte *f*, Windrispe *f*, Windlatte

spruce shingle — square-edge (floor) boarding

spruce shingle · Fichtenschindel *f*

sprung floor cover(ing), ~ floor(ing) (finish) · Schwing(fuß)boden(belag) *m*

spun, centrifugally cast · geschleudert [*Betonrohr; Betonmast*]

~ **cast-iron pipe**, centrifugal ~ ~, spun-iron ~, spun C.I. ~, centrifugal C.I. ~ · Gußeisenschleuderrohr *n*, gußeisernes Schleuderrohr, Schleudergußrohr

~~ **pressure pipe** → centrifugally cast C.I. ~ ~

~ **C.I. pipe**, centrifugal C.I. ~, spun-iron ~, centrifugal cast-iron ~, spun cast-iron ~ · Gußeisenschleuderrohr *n*, gußeisernes Schleuderrohr, Schleudergußrohr

~ **C.I. pressure pipe** → centrifugally cast ~ ~ ~ ~

~ **column** (Brit.); ~ **mast** (US) · Schleudermast *m*

~ **concrete**, centrifugally cast ~ · Schleuderbeton *m*

~~ **column**, centrifugally cast ~ ~ · Schleuderbetonstütze *f*, Betonschleuderstütze

~~ **drain pipe**, centrifugally cast ~ ~ ~ · Betonschleuderdränrohr *n*, Schleuderbetondränrohr

~~ **mast**, centrifugally cast ~ ~ · Betonschleudermast *m*, Schleuderbetonmast [*DIN 4234*]

~~ **pipe**, centrifugally cast ~ ~ · Betonschleuderrohr *n*, Schleuderbetonrohr

~~ **pressure pipe**, centrifugally cast ~ ~ ~ · Betonschleuderdruckrohr *n*, Schleuderbetondruckrohr

~ **glass** → long glass fibres

~~ **wall cover(ing)** → (glass) silk wall lining

~~~ **lining** → (glass) silk ~ ~

~~~ **(sur)facing** → (glass) silk wall lining

spun-iron pipe, spun C.I. ~, centrifugal C.I. ~, spun cast-iron ~, centrifugal cast-iron ~ · Gußeisenschleuderrohr *n*, gußeisernes Schleuderrohr, Schleudergußrohr

spun lead, lead wool [*Lead prepared in long filaments twisted together like yarn and used for cold caulking*] · Bleiwolle *f*

~ **mast** (US); ~ **column** (Brit.); centrifugally cast ~ · Schleudermast *m*

~ **pipe**, centrifugally cast ~ · Schleuderrohr *n*

~ **reinforced concrete pressure pipe**, ~ R.C. ~ ~, centrifugally cast ~ ~ ~ · Stahlbetonschleuderdruckrohr *n*, Schleuderstahlbetondruckrohr

~ **rivet** · gerollter Niet *m*

spur, griffe [*An ornament, usually of foliage, on the corner of a square plinth surmounted by a circular pier*] · (Teufels)Klaue *f*

~ · Sporn *m*

~ · Ecksporn *m*

~ **(line)**, ~ pipeline · Stich(rohr)leitung *f*

~ **pipeline**, spur (line) · Stich(rohr)leitung *f*

~ **stone** · (Rad)Abweiser *m*, Abweichstein *m*, Prellstein, Radstößer, Radabstoßer, Abweisstein

sputtering, vacuum coating · Metallaufdampfen *n*

SQ, silvering quality glass · Beleg(e)glas *n*

to square · regelmäßig behauen, nach Maß bearbeiten [*Quader(stein)*]

square, plaza · Platz(anlage) *m*, (*f*) [*Nichtbebaute Grundfläche in einer Stadt, deren Umbauung architektonisch gestaltet ist oder die eine bestimmte Aufgabe zu erfüllen hat*]

~ · Quadratprofil *n*

~ · quadratisch

~, pane (of glass), glass pane [*A piece of glass cut to size and shape ready for glazing*] · (Glas)Scheibe *f*

~, market-place, market-stead · Marktplatz *m*

~ **aperture**, ~ **punching** · Quadratlochöffnung *f* [*Siebtechnik*]

~ **ashlar** → squared stone ~

~~ **bond** → squared stone ~

~~ **dressing** → squared stone ~

~~ **masonry (work)** → squared stone ~ (~)

~~ **slab** → squared stone ~

~~ **structure** → squared stone ~

~~ **vault** → squared stone ~

~ **base**, basic square · Grundquadrat *n* [*Kuppel*]

~ **bay** · quadratisches Joch *n*

~ **billet** · Schachbrettverzierung *f*

~ **chamber** · Quadratraum *m* [*Nebenraum im Sakralbau*]

~ **chimney** · Quadratschornstein *m*

~ **column** · quadratische Stütze *f*

~ **corner (bath)tub**, ~ ~ **bath** · Winkel(bade)wanne *f*

~~ **halving** · Ecküberblattung *f* mit geradem Schnitt, gerade Ecküberblattung

~ **cross section** · Quadratquerschnitt *m*

~ **crossing** · quadratische Vierung *f*

square-dressed · stumpf [*Parkettstab*]

square edge · eckige Kante *f*

square-edge (floor) boarding · gesäumter (Fuß)Boden(belag) *m*

square-edge tile — St. Mark's Square

~ tile · Rechteckkantenfliese *f*, Rechteckkanten(belag)platte *f*

square-edged · rechtkantig

square flap → ~ hinge ~

~ (ground(-))plan · Quadratgrundriß *m*

square-headed loophole, rectangular-headed ~, ~ loop (window) · oben rechteckiger Sehschlitz *m*

square (hinge) flap · Quadrat(band)-lappen *m*

~ hole, ~ opening · Quadratöffnung *f*

~ mesh · Quadratloch *n* [*Sieb*]

~ ~ · Quadratmasche *f*

~ ~ screening cloth, ~ opening wire ~ · Quadratmaschengewebe *n*

square-mesh sieve · Quadratlochsieb *n*

Square Mesh Tracking, SMT [*Trademark*] · Stahlmattenbelag *m*

square moment · quadratisches Moment *n*

~ of crossing, crossing square, transept square · Vierungsquadrat *n* [*Es ergibt sich aus der Durchdringung von Langhaus und Querhaus bei gleichen Breiten*]

~ ~ glass [*A piece of glass, of any shape cut to size ready for glazing*] · Verglasungstafel *f*

~ opening, ~ hole · Quadratöffnung *f*

~ ~ wire cloth, ~ mesh screening ~ · Quadratmaschengewebe *n*

~ pier · Quadratpfeiler *m*

~ pipe · Quadratrohr *n*

~ plan, ~ ground(-)~ · Quadratgrundriß *m*

~ planning grid, ~ structural ~ · Quadratraster *m*, Quadratzeichenraster *m*

~ plate, ~ slab · quadratische Platte *f*, Quadratplatte *f*

~ punching, ~ aperture · Quadratlochöffnung *f* [*Siebtechnik*]

~ pyramid · quadratische Pyramide *f*, ~ Spitzsäule *f*

~ recessed (bath)tub, ~ ~ bath · quadratische Nischen(bade)wanne *f*

~ rib-vault · quadratisches Rippengewölbe *n*

~ rod, ~ bar · Quadratstab *m*

~ roof-light · Quadrat(dach)oberlicht *n*

~ saddle junction piece · Einlaß *m* mit geradem Flansch [*Kanalisationssteinzeug*]

~ structural grid, ~ planning ~ · Quadratraster *m*, Quadratzeichenraster *m*

~ toothed plate · quadratischer Zahndübel *m* [*Holzdübel*]

~ tower · Quadratturm *m*, quadratischer Turm

~ tube · Quadratröhre *f*

~ ~, ~ tubing · Quadratrohrprofil *n*

~ tubing, ~ tube · Quadratrohrprofil *n*

~ washer · quadratische Unterlegscheibe *f*

~ wire · Quadratdraht *m*

~ ~ netting · quadratisches Drahtgeflecht *n*

squareness · Rechtwinkeligkeit *f*

~ · Quadrathaltigkeit *f*

squarer, scabbler, block chopper, stone dresser, stone cutter · Steinmetz *m* [*Handwerker, der Werksteine zurichtet*]

squat round tower, round bastion · Rundbastion *f* [*Aus der Mauer vortretendes, rundes Verteidigungsbauwerk aus (ursprünglich) befestigtem Erdreich; später mit starker Mauer ummantelt*]

squatting plate [*A glazed ceramic surround, incorporating raised treads, for a squatting W.C. pan*] · Hockplatte *f* [*Hockabort*]

~ W. C. pan, Eastern ~ ~ ~; Asiatic ~ ~ ~, Lascar ~ ~ ~, Lascar closet [*deprecated*] [*A W.C. pan with an elongated bowl for installing with its top edge at or near floor level so that the user has to adopt a squatting position*] · Hockabort *m*, französischer Abort

squeegee · Schieber *m*, Schwabber

~ gold · Siebdruckgold *n*

squinch (arch) [*A small arch or series of concentric arches built across the angle of a square or polygon to support a superstructure, such as a spire or dome*] · Trompe *f*, Trichtergewölbe *n*, Trichternische *f*, Treppenring *m*, Ecktrichter *m*

squint, hagioscope, speculatory [*An oblique opening in a Mediaeval church wall to give a view of the altar*] · Hagioskop *n*

~ quoin (of (masonry) wall) · spitzwink(e)lige Mauerecke *f*

SR, stress relieved, free of stress · spannungsfrei, entspannt

SR, SI, shrinkage ratio · Schwindindex *m*, Schwindverhältnis *n*

SRA, stress relief annealed [*steel*] · spannungsfreigeglüht

ss → (stair) stringer

st → urban road

St. Andrew's cross, Saltire ~, diagonal struts · Andreaskreuz *n*, Kreuzgebälk *n*, Kreuzstreben *fpl*, Abkreuzung *f*, Kreuzverband *m*

~ ~ ~, Saltire ~ · Andreaskreuz *n*, Schrägkreuz, burgundisches Kreuz [*Lateinisch: crux decussata*]

~ ~ ~ bond, English ~ ~; Dutch ~ [*misnomer*] · holländischer Verband *m*

St. George's cross, Grecian ~, Greek ~ · griechisches Kreuz *n*

St. Kajetan church · Theatinerkirche *f* [*München*]

St. Mark's Square · Markusplatz *m* [*Venedig*]

St. Venant('s) principle (of elasticity)
→ (de) Saint ~ ~ (~ ~)
~ ~ torsion → (de) Saint ~ ~
stability · Beständigkeit f, Stabilität f [*Emulsion*]
~, structural ~ · Stabilität f, Standfestigkeit f, Standsicherheit, räumliche Steifigkeit
~ against oscillation(s), ~ ~ vibration(s) · Erschütterungsstabilität f, Schwingungsstabilität, Erschütterungsstandfestigkeit f, Schwingungsstandfestigkeit, Erschütterungsstandsicherheit, Schwingungsstandsicherheit
~ ~ vibration(s), ~ ~ oscillation(s) · Erschütterungsstabilität f, Schwingungsstabilität, Erschütterungsstandfestigkeit f, Schwingungsstandfestigkeit, Erschütterungsstandsicherheit, Schwingungsstandsicherheit
~ calculation · Stabilitätsberechnung f, Standsicherheitsberechnung, Standfestigkeitsberechnung
~ case, case of stability · Stabilitätsfall m, Standsicherheitsfall, Standfestigkeitsfall
~ condition, condition of stability · Stabilitätsbedingung f, Standfestigkeitsbedingung, Standsicherheitsbedingung
~ degree, degree of stability · Stabilitätsgrad m, Beständigkeitsgrad [*Emulsion*]
~ diagram · Stabilitätsdiagramm n, Standfestigkeitsdiagramm, Standsicherheitsdiagramm
~ drop · Stabilitätsabfall m, Standfestigkeitsabfall, Standsicherheitsabfall
~ equation · Stabilitätsgleichung f, Standfestigkeitsgleichung, Standsicherheitsgleichung
~ formula · Stabilitätsformel f, Standfestigkeitsformel, Standsicherheitsformel
~ function · Stabilitätsfunktion f, Standfestigkeitsfunktion, Standsicherheitsfunktion
~ investigation · Stabilitätsuntersuchung f, Standfestigkeitsuntersuchung, Standsicherheitsuntersuchung
~ limit, limit of stability · Stabilitätsgrenze f, Standfestigkeitsgrenze, Standsicherheitsgrenze
~ of shape, ~ ~ form · Gestaltfestigkeit f, Formfestigkeit
~ ~ volume, constancy ~ ~, volume stability, volume constancy · Raumbeständigkeit f, Raumkonstanz f
~ system · statisches System n
~ theory, theory of stability · Stabilitätstheorie f, Standfestigkeitstheorie, Standsicherheitstheorie
~ to heat, heat resistance, heat-fastness, fastness to heat, resistance to heat, heat stability · Hitzebeständigkeit f, Hitzefestigkeit, Hitzeechtheit, Hitzewiderstand m
~ ~ light, light resistance, fastness to light, proofness to light, lightfastness, lightproofness · Lichtechtheit f, Lichtbeständigkeit f, Lichtfestigkeit
~ under torsion · Torsionsstabilität f
stabilization cable · Stabilisierungsseil n
stabilized alloy, dead ~, (fully) killed ~, quiet ~ · beruhigte Legierung f, stabilisierte ~
~ dolomite refractory (product) · stabilisiertes Dolomit-Erzeugnis n [*Feuerfestes Erzeugnis, das im wesentlichen aus totgebranntem Dolomit und einem stabilisierenden Mineral besteht, das den Kalk abgebunden hat.
Anmerkung: Solche Erzeugnisse können gebrannt oder ungebrannt verwendet werden*]
~ steel → (fully) killed ~
stable · stabil
~ · stabil, standfest, standsicher
~ · stabil, S [*Stabile Emulsionen zerfallen hauptsächlich erst bei Verdunstung des Wassers*]
~ building · Stallgebäude n
~ court · Stallhof m
~ emulsion · S-Emulsion f
stack → industrial chimney
~ · Stapel m
~, vertical pipe, standpipe, SP · Standrohr n, Steigrohr, Senkrechtrohr
~, vertical pipes, standpipes · Standrohre npl, Steigrohre
to stack flat · flach stapeln
stack ladder, chimney ~ · Schornsteinleiter f
stacking · Stapeln n
~ chair · Stapelstuhl m
staddle stone [*A short mushroom-shaped stone post, which supports a stack or granary. Because of its shape, rats cannot climb up it. Now often used as garden ornament*] · Schoberstein m
stadium · Stadion n
~ construction · Stadionbau m
~ facilities · Stadionanlagen fpl
~ grandstand · Stadiontribüne f
staff accommodation portion, personnel ~ ~ · Personalwohntrakt m
~ aisle, personnel ~ · Personalgang m
~ block → ~ building
~ building, personnel ~, ~ house · Personalgebäude n, Sozialgebäude, Belegschaftsgebäude, Personalhaus n, Sozialhaus, Belegschaftshaus
~ canteen, personnel ~ · Personalkantine f
~ changing room · Bedientenraum m [*Hotel*]
~ ~ ~, personnel ~ ~ · Personalumkleide(raum) f, (m)
~ dining room, personnel ~ ~ · Personalspeiseraum m, Personaleßraum
~ entrance, personnel ~ · Personaleingang m

staff house — Stahlton ((pre)stressed) roof slab

~ house → ~ building
~ **location system**, paging ~ · (drahtlose) (Personen)Suchanlage *f*
~ **lock**, personnel ~ · Personenschleuse *f*
~ **rental apartment (unit)**, ~ ~ flat; ~ ~ living unit (US) · Dienst(miet)-Etagenwohnung *f*, Dienst(miet)-Stockwerkwohnung, Dienst(miet)-(Geschoß)Wohnung
~ ~ **dwelling unit** (US); ~ ~ dwelling · Dienst(miet)wohnung *f*
~ ~ **flat**, ~ ~ apartment (unit); ~ ~ living unit · Dienst(miet)-Etagenwohnung *f*, Dienst(miet)-Stockwerkwohnung, Dienst(miet)-(Geschoß)Wohnung
~ ~ **living unit** (US); ~ ~ apartment (~), ~ ~ flat · Dienst(miet)-Etagenwohnung *f*, Dienst(miet)-Stockwerkwohnung, Dienst(miet)-(Geschoß-)Wohnung
~ **room**, personnel ~ · Sozialraum *m*, Personalraum
~ **toilet**, personnel ~ · Personaltoilette *f*
~ **traffic**, personnel ~ · Personalverkehr *m*
~ **training**, personnel ~ · Unterweisung *f* des Bedienungspersonals
stage · Bühne *f* [*Theater*]
~ **and backstage (of a theatre)** · Bühnenhaus *n*
~ **designer** · Bühnengestalter *m*
~ **door** · Bühnentür *f*
~ **equipment** · Bühnenausrüstung *f*
~ **fittings**, ~ hardware · Bühnenbeschläge *mpl*
~ **grouting** · stufenweises Verpressen *n*, ~ Auspressen, ~ Einpressen, ~ Injizieren, stufenweise Injektion *f*
~ **hardware**, ~ fittings · Bühnenbeschläge *mpl*
~ **illumination**, ~ lighting · Bühnenbeleuchtung *f*
~ **lighting**, ~ illumination · Bühnenbeleuchtung *f*
~ **of development** · Entwicklungsstufe *f*
~ ~ **drying** · Trockengrad *m* [*Anstrich*]
~ ~ **strength** · Festigkeitsstadium *n*
~ **space** · Bühnenraum *m*
~ **spotlight** · Bühnenscheinwerfer *m*
(~) **theatre**, living (~) ~ · (Bühnen-)Theater *n*
~ **tower** · Bühnenturm *m*
~ **wall** · Bühnenwand *f*
to stagger · versetzen
staggered · gegeneinander versetzt, verschoben
~ **apses** → apses in echelon
~ **arrangement** · versetzte Anordnung *f*
~ **floors**, ~ stories · versetzte Etagen *fpl*, ~ Geschosse *npl*, ~ Stockwerke *npl*

~ **joints** · versetzte Fugen *fpl*
~ **perspectives** · gegeneinander versetzte Fassadenfluchten *fpl*
~ **stories**, ~ floors · versetzte Etagen *fpl*, ~ Geschosse *npl*, ~ Stockwerke *npl*
staggering of joints · Versetzen *n* der Fugen
stahl-eisen, pig iron for steel making purposes · Stahl(roh)eisen *n* [*Im Hochofen erschmolzenes Roheisen für die Weiterverarbeitung nach dem Siemens-Martin- oder LD-Verfahren*]
~ **slag**, slag from pig iron for steel making purposes · Stahl(roh)eisenschlacke *f*, Stahlschlacke
Stahlton, (pre)stressed clay · Stahlton *m*, Spannton
~ **factory**, ~ plant, (pre)stressed clay ~ · Spanntonwerk *n*, Stahltonwerk
~ **plank**, ~ prestressed ~, prestressed clay ~, plank in prestressed clay, plank in Stahlton · Tonelementbalken *m*, Stahltonbrett *n*, Spanntonbrett, vorgespanntes Ziegelbrett
~ **plant**, ~ factory, (pre)stressed clay ~ · Stahltonwerk *n*, Spanntonwerk
~ **((pre)stressed) beam**, prestressed clay ~, beam in prestressed clay · (vorgespannter) Ziegelbalken(träger) *m*, Spannton(-Fertig)balken(träger), Stahlton(-Fertig)balken(träger), Ziegeltonfertigbalken(träger)
~ (~) **door lintel**; ~ (~) ~ lintol [*deprecated*]; prestressed clay ~ ~, door lintel in prestressed clay, door lintel in Stahlton; door lintol in prestressed clay, door lintol in Stahlton [*deprecated*] · Stahlton-Türsturz *m*, Spannton-Türsturz, vorgespannter Ziegeltürsturz, Stahlton-Türoberschwelle *f*, Spannton-Türoberschwelle, vorgespannte Ziegeltüroberschwelle
~ (~) **floor**, prestressed clay ~, floor in prestressed clay, floor in Stahlton · Stahltondecke *f*, Spanntondecke, vorgespannte Ziegeldecke
~ (~) **lintel**; ~ (~) lintol [*deprecated*]; prestressed clay ~, lintel in prestressed clay, lintel in Stahlton; lintol in prestressed clay, lintol in Stahlton [*deprecated*] · Stahltonsturz *m*, Spanntonsturz, vorgespannter Ziegelsturz, Stahltonoberschwelle *f*, Spanntonoberschwelle, vorgespannte Ziegeloberschwelle
~ (~) **plank**, prestressed clay ~, plank in prestressed clay, plank in Stahlton · Stahltonbrett *n*, Spanntonbrett, vorgespanntes Ziegelbrett, Tonelementbalken *m*
~ (~) **roof**, prestressed clay ~, roof in prestressed clay, roof in Stahlton · Stahltondach *n*, Spanntondach, vorgespanntes Ziegeldach
~ (~) **slab**, prestressed clay ~ ~, roof slab in prestressed clay, roof slab in Stahlton · Stahltondachplatte *f*, Spanntondachplatte, vorgespannte Ziegeldachplatte

Stahlton ((pre)stressed) wall panel — staircase

~ (~) **wall panel** → wall unit in prestressed clay

~ (~) **window lintel**; ~ (~) ~ lintol [*deprecated*]; prestressed clay ~ ~, window lintel in prestressed clay, window lintel in Stahlton; window lintel in prestressed clay window lintel in Stahlton [*deprecated*] · Stahlton-Fenstersturz *m*, Spannton-Fenstersturz, vorgespannter Ziegelfenstersturz, Stahlton-Fensteroberschwelle *f*, Spannton-Fensteroberschwelle, vorgespannte Ziegelfensteroberschwelle

~ **wall panel** → wall unit in (pre)stressed clay

~ ~ **slab** → wall unit in (pre)stressed clay

~ ~ **unit** → wall unit in (pre)stressed clay

to stain · beizen [*Holz*]

stain, wood ~ · (Holz)Beize *f*

~ · Fleck *m*

~ **proof** · fleckensicher

~ **removal** · Fleckenbeseitigung *f*

stained · (ab)gebeizt [*Holz*]

~ **glass**, tinted ~; coloured ~ (Brit.); colored ~ (US) · Farbglas *n*, farbiges Glas, Buntglas, gefärbtes Glas

~ ~ **block** → tinted ~ ~

~ ~ **brick** → tinted glass block

~ ~ **wall**, tinted-glass ~ · Buntglaswand *f*, Farbglaswand

~ ~ **window**, tinted-glass ~ · Buntglasfenster *n*, Farbglasfenster

~ **rough rolled glass**, tinted ~ ~ ~ · gefärbtes Gußrohglas *n*, ~ Rohgußglas

staining · Fleckigwerden *n*

~, wood ~ · (Holz)Beizen *n*

~ **power**, tinting strength [*The degree to which a coloured pigment imparts colour to a white pigment under defined conditions of test. The details of procedure for determining staining power, normally laid down in specifications for pigments, need to be carefully adhered to if consistent results are to be obtained. The corresponding property of a white pigment is 'reducing power'*] · Abtönvermögen *n*, Abtönfähigkeit *f*

stainless, rustless · rostfrei

~ **iron**, rustless ~ · rostfreies Eisen *n*

~ **(metal) sheet**, ~ sheet metal · Edelstahl(fein)blech *n*

~ **sheet**, ~ metal ~, ~ sheet metal · Edelstahl(fein)blech *n*

~ ~ **metal**, ~ (metal) sheet · Edelstahl(fein)blech *n*

~ **steel**; special ~ (Brit.); specially ~ (US) · Edelstahl *m*

~ ~ **beam** · Edelstahlbalken(träger) *m*

~ ~ **bolt** · Edelstahlbolzen *m*

~ ~ **butt (hinge)** · Edelstahl-Einstemmband *n*, Edelstahl-Fi(t)schband, Edelstahl-Fitsche *f*

~ ~ **ceiling** · Edelstahldecke *f*

~ ~ **curtain wall** · Edelstahlvorhangwand *f*

~ ~ **door** · Edelstahltür *f*

~ ~ **electrode** · Edelstahlelektrode *f*

~ ~ **external wall lining**, ~ ~ ~ ~ (sur)facing, ~ ~ exterior ~ ~, ~ ~ outdoor ~ ~, ~ ~ ~ outside ~ ~ · Edelstahl-Außenwand-Verkleidung *f*, Edelstahl-Außwenand-Auskleidung, Edelstahl-Außenwand-Bekleidung

~ ~ **façade** · Edelstahlfassade *f*

~ ~ **facing**, ~ ~ sur~, ~ ~ ~ lining · Edelstahlauskleidung *f*, Edelstahlverkleidung, Edelstahlbekleidung

~ ~ **flashing (piece)** [*See remark under 'Anschluß'*] · Edelstahl(blech)anschluß(-streifen) *m*

~ ~ **heat exchanger** · Edelstahl-Wärme(aus)tauscher *m*

~ ~ **lining**, ~ ~ (sur)facing · Edelstahlauskleidung *f*, Edelstahlverkleidung, Edelstahlbekleidung

~ ~ **mesh**, ~ ~ wire ~ · Edelstahldrahtmaschenmatte *f*

~ ~ **nut** · Edelstahlmutter *f*

~ ~ **outside wall lining** → ~ ~ external ~ ~

~ ~ **outdoor wall (sur)facing** → ~ ~ external wall lining

~ ~ **pin** · Edelstahlstift *m*

~ ~ **pipe**, ~ ~ tube · Edelstahlrohr *n*

~ ~ **rivet** · Edelstahlniet *m*

~ ~ **roof cladding**, ~ ~ ~ cover(ing), ~ ~ ~ sheathing, ~ ~ ~ roofing · Edelstahl(dach)(ein)deckung *f* Edelstahlbedachung

~ ~ **sheet** · Edelstahlfeinblech *n*

~ ~ **sink unit** [*Combined sink and drainer*] · Edelstahl-Abwaschtisch *m*, Edelstahl-Spültisch

~ ~ **(sur)facing** → ~ ~ lining

~ ~ **swing door** · Edelstahl-Pendeltür *f*

~ ~ **tube**, ~ ~ pipe · Edelstahlrohr *n*

~ ~ **wall panel** · Edelstahlwandtafel *f*

~ ~ **window** · Edelstahlfenster *n*

~ ~ **wire** · Edelstahldraht *m*

~ ~ ~ **cable**, ~ ~ ~ rope · Edelstahldrahtseil *n*

~ ~ ~ **cloth**; ~ ~ ~ fabric [*misnomer*] [*See remark under 'Gewebe'*] · Edelstahldrahtgewebe *n*

~ ~ (~) **mesh** · Edelstahldrahtmaschenmatte *f*

~ ~ ~ **rope**, ~ ~ ~ cable · Edelstahldrahtseil *n*

stainlessness, corrosion resistance · Korrosionsbeständigkeit *f*, Korrosionswiderstand *m*, Korrosionsfestigkeit, KF

stair carpet · Treppenteppich *m*, Treppenläufer *m*

staircase, stairwell · Treppenhaus *n*, Treppenraum *m*, Stiegenhaus *n*, Stiegenraum

stair(case), stairway · Treppe f, Aufgang m

~ **access** · Treppenzugang m

staircase-access block (of flats), ~ flats, ~ building with dwelling units (Brit.); ~ apartment building, ~ apartment house, ~ multifamily house, ~ apartment block, ~ multiple dwelling, ~ multi-family building, ~ multi-family block, ~ multi-family dwelling (US) · Mehrfamilien(wohn)haus n mit Wohnungszugängen vom Treppenhaus [*Im Gegensatz zum Laubenganghaus*]

stair(case) builder · Treppenbauer m

~ **construction**, construction of stair(case)s · Treppenbau m

stair(case)/elevator well (US) → lift/stair(case) well (Brit.)

(stair(case)) floor, (~) landing, (~) platform [*Resting space usually arranged at the top of any flight of stairs*] · (Treppen)Absatz m, (Treppen)Podest n

(~) ~ **beam** → (~) landing ~

(~) ~ **bearer** → (~) landing ~

(~) ~ **binder**, (~) landing ~, (~) floor ceiling joist, (~) ~ (binding) joist · Podestunterzug m, Absatzunterzug, Treppen~

(~) ~ **(binding) joist**, (~) ~ ceiling ~, (~) ~ binder, (~) landing ~ · Podestunterzug m, Absatzunterzug, Treppen~

(~) ~ **ceiling joist**, (~) ~ (binding) ~, (~) ~ binder, (~) landing ~ · Podestunterzug m, Absatzunterzug, Treppen~

(~) ~ **girder** → (~) landing beam

(~) ~ **header**, (~) landing ~ · Podestwechsel(balken) m, Absatzwechsel(balken), Treppen~

(~) ~ **joist** → (~) landing beam

(~) ~ **length**, (~) landing ~ · Podestlänge f, Absatzlänge, Treppen~

(~) ~ **level**, (~) landing ~ · Podesthöhe f, Absatzhöhe, Treppen~ [*DIN 18202*]

(~) ~ **post**, (~) landing ~ · Podestpfosten m, Absatzpfosten, Treppen~

(~) ~ **slab**, (~) landing ~ · Podestplatte f, Absatzplatte, Treppen~

(~) ~ **width**, (~) landing ~ · Podestbreite f, Absatzbreite, Treppen~

~ **for building purposes**, ~ ~ construction ~ · Bautreppe f [*Behelfsmäßige Treppe bei Neubauten am Außengerüst oder im Treppenhaus*]

~ ~ **construction purposes**, ~ ~ building ~ · Bautreppe f [*Behelfsmäßige Treppe bei Neubauten am Außengerüst oder im Treppenhaus*]

~ **hall** · Treppenhalle f

(~) **landing**, (~) platform, (~) floor · (Treppen)Podest n, (Treppen)Absatz m

(~) **landing beam**, (~) floor ~, (~) ~ girder, (~) ~ joist · (Treppen)Absatzbalken(träger) m, (Treppen)Absatzträger, (Treppen)Podestbalken(träger), (Treppen)Podestträger

(~) ~ **bearer**, (~) ~ binder, (~) floor ~, (~) ~ ceiling joist, (~) ~ (binding) joist · Absatzunterzug m, Podestunterzug, Treppen~

(~) ~ **binder**, (~) floor ~, (~) ~ ceiling joist, (~) ~ (binding) joist · Podestunterzug m, Absatzunterzug, Treppen~

(~) ~ **(binding) joist** → (~) ~ bearer

(~) ~ **ceiling joist** → (~) ~ bearer

(~) ~ **girder** → (~) ~ beam

(~) ~ **header**, (~) floor ~ · Absatzwechsel(balken) m, Podestwechsel(balken), Treppen~

(~) ~ **joist** → (~) ~ beam

(~) ~ **length**, (~) floor ~ · Absatzlänge f, Podestlänge, Treppen~

(~) ~ **level**, (~) floor ~ · Absatzhöhe f, Podesthöhe, Treppen~ [*DIN 18202*]

(~) ~ **post**, (~) floor ~ · Absatzpfosten m, Podestpfosten, Treppen~

(~) ~ **slab**, (~) floor ~ · Absatzplatte f, Podestplatte, Treppen~

(~) ~ **width**, (~) floor ~ · Absatzbreite f, Podestbreite, Treppen~

~ **layout** · Treppengestaltung f

stair(case)/lift core → lift/stair(case) ~

~ **well** → lift/stair(case) core

stair(case) of hard-textured wood · Hartholztreppe f

~ ~ **solid rectangular steps** · Blocktreppe f [*Treppe aus Blockstufen*]

~ **rail**, stairway ~ · Treppenhandlauf m, Treppenhandleiste f

~ **railing** · Treppengeländer n

~ **shaft** · Treppenschacht m

~ **shape** · Treppenform f

(~) **step unit**, (~) ~ member, (~) ~ component · (Treppen)Stufenelement n

~ **tower** · Treppen(haus)turm m, Außentreppenhaus n, Treppen(haus)vorbau m

~ **turret** · Treppentürmchen n

(~) **well** · Treppenloch n, Treppenöffnung f [*Die Öffnung einer Geschoßdecke oder Balkenlage, durch die eine Treppe führt. Auch die Öffnungen zwischen den Lichtwangen der mehrläufigen Treppe*]

~ ~ **glazing** · Treppenhausverglasung f, Treppenhauseinglasung

(~) ~ **(hole)** · Treppenloch n, Treppenöffnung f [*Die Öffnung einer Geschoßdecke oder Balkenlage, durch die eine Treppe führt. Auch die Öffnungen zwischen den Lichtwangen der mehrläufigen Treppe*]

~ ~ **illumination**, ~ ~ lighting · Treppenhausbeleuchtung f

~ ~ **lighting**, ~ ~ illumination · Treppenhausbeleuchtung f

~ ~ **spandrel** · Treppenhausbrüstung f

~ ~ **switch** · Treppenhausschalter m

~ ~ **wall** · Treppenhauswand f

stair(case) with landing — stalk plate angle

~ **with landing** · Absatztreppe f, Podesttreppe

~ ~ **treads inserted between strings** (Brit.); ~ ~ ~ ~ stringers (US) [*There are no risers*] · eingeschobene Treppe f, eingeschnittene ~, Leitertreppe [*Die Stufen werden in Nuten oder Wangen eingeschoben*]

~ ~ **two cylinders**, double cylinder stair(case) · Doppelspindel(treppe) f, doppelspindlige Treppe [*Eine Wendeltreppe mit zwei Achsen, deren Stufen in ihrer Aufeinanderfolge eine Schleife bilden*]

stair construction, staircase ~, construction of stair(case)s · Treppenbau m

~ **flight**, flight (of stairs) · (Treppen-)Lauf m

~ **floor** → stair(case) ~

~ **illumination**, ~ lighting · Treppenbeleuchtung f

~ **landing** → (stair(case)) floor

~ **lighting**, ~ illumination · Treppenbeleuchtung f

~ **nosing** · Treppenschutzleiste f, Treppenschutzschiene f, Treppen(stoß)kante f [*Profil*]

stairrail, staircase rail, stairway rail · Treppenhandlauf m, Treppenhandleiste f

~ **scroll** · Treppenhandlaufspirale f, Treppenhandleistenspirale

~ **section**, ~ unit, ~ shape, ~ trim, ~ profile · Treppenhandlaufprofil n, Treppenhandleistenprofil

(stair) riser [*The member forming the vertical face of a step*] · Setzstufe f, Stoßtritt m, Stoßtritt f, Futterstufe [*wenn aus Holz = Futterbrett*]

(~) **stringer**, ss (US); (~) string (Brit.) · (Treppen)Wange f

~ **tile** · Treppen(belag)platte f, Treppenfliese f

(~) **tread** [*The member forming the horizontal top surface of a step*] · Auflagestufe f, (Auf)Tritt(stufe) m, (f)

(~) ~ [*The horizontal top surface of a step*] · (Auf)Trittfläche f, Auftritt m

(~) ~ **cover(ing)** · (Tritt)Stufenbelag m, Treppenbelag, Trittbelag

(~) ~ **nosing** · (Tritt)Stufenvorsprung m

~ **trimmer (beam)** · Treppenwechsel(-balken) m

stair-turret · Treppentürmchen n

stair type, type of stair · Treppenart f

stairs, stairway [*From the bottom floor to the top floor*] · Treppenanlage f

stair unit → (pre)cast (concrete) flight (of stairs)

stairway, stair(case) · Aufgang m, Treppe f

~, stairs [*From the bottom floor to the top floor*] · Treppenanlage f

~ **mastaba(h)** · Treppenmastaba f

~ **tomb** · Treppengrab n

stairwell, staircase · Treppenhaus n, Treppenraum m, Stiegenhaus, Stiegenraum

stake → pin (US)

~ **building**, ~ center (US); ~ centre (Brit.) [*It serves as meeting-place for a stake, consisting of The Church of Jesus Christ of Latter-day Saints which are presided over by bishops. It normally consists of a chapel, a cultural hall, class-rooms, offices, wardrobes, a library and a kitchen*] · Pfahlzentrum n, Pfahlgebäude n [*Es dient als Versammlungsgebäude für einen Pfahl, der aus mehreren Gemeinden der Kirche Jesu Christi der Heiligen der Letzten Tage besteht, die Bischöfen unterstellt sind. Normalerweise besteht es aus einem Andachtsraum, einem Unterhaltungssaal, Klassenzimmern, Büros, Garderobenräumen, einer Bücherei und einer Küche*]

~ **fence**, slat ~ · Staketenzaun m, Lattenzaun

to stake, to peg out · abwinkeln, auswinkeln, abstecken, abtragen, ausstecken

stalactite · Stalaktit m, Muqarnas m [*Zellenartiges Schmuckelement der islamischen Baukunst*]

~ **arch** · Tropfsteinbogen m, Stalaktitenbogen

~ **capital** · Tropfsteinkapitell n, Tropfsteinkapitäl, Stalaktitenkapitell, Stalaktitenkapitäl

~ **ceiling** · Tropfsteindecke f, Stalaktitendecke

~ **cupola**, ~ dome · Tropfsteinkuppel f, Stalaktitenkuppel

~ **dome**, ~ cupola · Stalaktitenkuppel f, Tropfsteinkuppel

~ **ornament** · Stalaktitenornament n, Tropfsteinornament

~ **portal** · Tropfsteinportal n, Stalaktitenportal [*Portal der islamischen Baukunst, das von Stalaktiten abgeschlossen wird*]

~ **vault** · Tropfsteingewölbe n, Stalaktitengewölbe

stale atmosphere · abgestandene Luft f

~ **warmed air** · warme abgestandene Luft f

stalk, web · Steg m, Träger~ [*Bei T- und I-förmigen Querschnitten der schmale hohe Teil im Gegensatz zum niedrigen und breiten Flansch oder den niedrigen und breiten Flanschen. Der Steg hat im allgemeinen große Schubkräfte aufzunehmen und wird deshalb mit Bügeln und Schrägeisen bewehrt*]

~ **connection**, web ~ · Steganschluß m

~ **plate**, web ~ [*The vertical plate joining the flanges of a rolled-steel or extruded light alloy joist or of a built-up girder or timber beam*] · Stegblech n, Stehblech

~ ~ **angle**, web ~ ~ · Stegblechwinkel m, Stehblechwinkel

stalk plate connection — standard deviation

~ ~ connection, web ~ ~, ~ ~ joint · Stegblechanschluß m, Stehblechanschluß, Stegblechstoß m, Stehblechstoß

~ ~ depth, web ~ ~ · Stegblechhöhe f, Stehblechhöhe

~ ~ joint, web ~ ~, ~ ~ connection · Stegblechanschluß m, Stehblechanschluß, Stegblechstoß, Stehblechstoß

~ ~ length, web ~ ~ · Stegblechlänge f, Stehblechlänge

~ ~ longitudinal connection, ~ ~ ~ joint, web ~ ~ ~ · Stegblechlängsstoß m, Stehblechlängsstoß, Stegblechlängsanschluß m, Stehblechlängsanschluß

~ ~ moment, web ~ ~ · Stegblechmoment n, Stehblechmoment

~ ~ stay, ~ ~ stiffener, web ~ ~ · Stegblechsteife f, Stehblechsteife

~ ~ stiffener, ~ ~ stay, web ~ ~ · Stegblechsteife f, Stehblechsteife

~ ~ stiffening, web ~ ~ · Stegblechaussteifung f, Stehblechaussteifung

~ ~ stress, web ~ ~ · Stegblechspannung f, Stehblechspannung

~ ~ thickness, web ~ ~ · Stegblechdicke f, Stehblechdicke

~ ~ transverse connection, ~ ~ ~ joint, web ~ ~ ~ · Werkstattstoß m, (Stegblech)Querstoß, Stehblechquerstoß

~ ~ ~ joint, ~ ~ ~ connection, web ~ ~ ~ · Werkstattstoß m, (Stegblech-)Querstoß, Stehblechquerstoß

~ ~ width, web ~ ~ · Stegblechbreite f, Stehblechbreite

~ reinforcement, web ~ · Stegarmierung f, Stegbewehrung, Steg(stahl)-einlagen fpl

~ stay, web ~, ~ stiffener · Stegsteife f

~ stiffener, web ~, ~ stay · Stegsteife f

~ stiffening, web ~ · Stegaussteifung f

stall · Boxe f

~ [*In a church, one of a row of seats separated by arms, and provided for the clergy and choir. The term is applied especially to richly decorated and canopied seats in cathedrals, or monastic or collegiate churches*] · Gestühl n

~ end · Chorstuhlwange f

stallboard riser [*A vertical infilling between the pavement level and the bottom of a shop window*] · Schaufensterbrüstung f

stambha, lath [*A monumental pillar, standing free without any structural foundation. Inscriptions were carved on the shaft. The capital, which was usually persepolitan in form, was crowned with animal supporters bearing 'chakra' or 'wheel of the law'. The emblem of the Republic of India is the capital of the stambha at Sarnath*] · Stambha m

stamp etching, acid ~, stamping · Stempelätzung f [*Glasbehandlung*]

~ gravel · Pochkies m, Quetschkies

~ sand · Quetschsand m, Splittsand, Pochsand

stamped lino(leum), printed ~ [*This lino(leum) has a pattern printed on the surface with oil paint*] · Drucklinoleum n

stamping, stamp etching, acid etching · Stempelätzung f [*Glasbehandlung*]

stancheon, sta(u)nchion (Brit.); steel column, steel support [*In steel-frame construction, a vertical member supporting a girder*] · Stahlstütze f

stand · Stand m

standard artificial stone [*deprecated*] → ~ cast ~

~ asphaltic bitumen (Brit.); ~ asphalt (US) · Norm(en)bitumen n [*DIN 1995*]

~ basalt · Norm(en)basalt m

~ bend, ~ pipe ~ · Normal(rohr)krümmer m

~ block → ~ building ~

~ brick, common ~ · Normalziegel m, Standardziegel

~ briquette · Prisma n [*Zementprüfung*]

~ ~ mould (Brit.); ~ ~ mold (US) · Prismenform f [*Herstellung von Prismen zur Zementprüfung*]

~ ~ strength · Prismenfestigkeit f [*Zementprüfung*]

~ (building) block, ~ (~) tile [*See remark under 'Block'*] · Norm(en)block(-stein) m, Norm(en)stein

~ cast stone, ~ reconstituted ~, ~ patent ~, ~ reconstructed ~; ~ artificial ~ [*deprecated*] · Standardstein m [*Beton(werk)stein*]

~ cement · Norm(en)zement m

~ ~ mortar cube · Norm(en)zementmörtelwürfel m

~ chamotte brick, common ~ ~ · Schamotte-Normalstein m

~ channels · Norm(en)-U-Stahl m

~ compression strength, ~ crushing ~ · Normendruckfestigkeit f

~ construction, ~ (structural) system · Standard(-Bau)system n, Standardkonstruktion(ssystem) f, (n)

~ ~ method · Regelbauweise f, Standardbauweise, Normalbauweise

~ corrugated (rolled) glass · Standardwell(en)glas n

~ crushing strength, ~ compression ~ · Normendruckfestigkeit f

~ curing [*Exposure of concrete test specimens to specified conditions of moisture or humidity or temperature*] · Normennachbehandlung f

~ cut-back (asphaltic) bitumen (Brit.); ~ ~ (asphalt) (US) · Norm(en)verschnittbitumen n

~ cylinder for compression testing · Norm(en)prüfzylinder m

~ deviation · mittlere quadratische Abweichung f, ~ Streuung, mittlerer Fehler m, Standardabweichung

standard dimension — standardized figure for construction

~ **dimension** · Standardabmessung f
~ ~, basic ~ · Grundmaß n, Grundabmessung f, Typenmaß, Typenabmessung
~ **drawing** · Normenzeichnung f
~ **dwelling unit** (US); ~ **dwelling** (Brit.) · Typenwohnung f
~ **emulsion** · Norm(en)emulsion f
~ **factory** · Typenfabrik f
~ **fire** · Normenbrand m
~ ~ **rating curve** · Normenbrandklassenkurve f
~ ~ **test** · Normenbrandprobe f, Normenbrandversuch m, Normenbrandprüfung f
~ **floor**; ~ **story** (US); ~ **storey** (Brit.) · Normaletage f, Normalgeschoß n, Normalstockwerk n
~ ~ · Typendecke f
~ **form**, ~ **shape** · Standardform f [gebogenes Glas]
~ **format** · Standardformat n
~ **frame**, ~ **framing** · Typenrahmen m
~ **frame(d) block**, ~ ~ **building** · Standard(rahmen)halle f
~ ~ **building**, ~ ~ **block** · Typen(rahmen)halle f
~ **hardboard** · Farbtonplatte f
~ **hook** [A hook at the end of a reinforcing bar made in accordance with a standard] · Norm(en)haken m
~ **lamp**, floor standard · Standleuchte f, Stehleuchte
~ **lean-to** · Typenpultanbau m
~ **length** · Standardlänge f
~ **lime** · Norm(en)kalk m
~ **minimum strength** · genormte Mindestfestigkeit f, Normenmindestfestigkeit
~ **module**, basic ~ [It means a module with the dimension of 4 inches] · Grundmodul M m, Modul von 10 cm, Modul von 4 Zoll
~ **mortar** · Norm(en)mörtel m
~ **musical pitch** · Norm-Stimmton m
~ **opening height** · Normalöffnungshöhe f [Tor]
~ **panel** · Standardtafel f
~ **pantile** · Standard(dach)pfanne f
~ **patent stone** → ~ cast ~
~ **pipe** · Normalrohr n
~ ~ · Norm(en)rohr n
~ (~) **bend** · Normal(rohr)krümmer m
~ **portal frame** · Portaltypenrahmen m, Typenportalrahmen
~ **Portland cement**, ~ portland ~ · Norm(en)-Portlandzement m
~ **product** · Normenerzeugnis n
~ **profile** → ~ section
~ **quality** · Normengüte f, Normenqualität f
~ **reconstituted stone** → ~ cast ~

~ **reconstructed stone** → ~ cast ~
~ **road tar** · Norm(en)straßenteer m
~ **rolled section**, ~ ~ **unit**, ~ ~ **shape**, ~ ~ **profile**, ~ ~ **trim** · Norm(en)walzprofil n
~ **sand**, cement testing ~ · Norm(en)sand m [DIN 1164]
~ **section**, ~ **shape**, ~ **unit**, ~ **trim**, ~ **profile** · Norm(en)profil n
~ **shape** → ~ section
~ ~ → ~ form
~ **size** · Regelgröße f, Normalgröße, Typengröße
~ **special (shape)** [A special shape in general use and available from stock] · allgemeine Sonderform f, ~ Spezialform [Ziegel]
~ **specification brick** · Norm(en)ziegel m
~ ~ **format** · Norm(en)format n
~ **stainless steel window**, stock ~ ~ ~ · Standard-Edelstahlfenster n
~ **stock**, ~ **store** · Sollbestand m
~ **store**, ~ **stock** · Sollbestand m
~ **story** (US) → ~ floor
~ **strength** · Normenfestigkeit f
~ **(structural) system**, ~ **construction** · Standard(-Bau)system n, Standardkonstruktion(ssystem) f, (n)
~ **system** → ~ structural ~
~ **test** · Normenprüfung f, Normenprobe f, Normenversuch m
~ ~ **cube** · Norm(en)würfel m
~ ~ **specimen** · Norm(en)körper m, Norm(en)probekörper, Norm(en)probe(stück) f, (n)
~ **thickness** · Standarddicke f
~ ~ · Normdicke f
~ **tile** → ~ (building) block
~ **timber window**, stock ~ ~, ~ **wood(en)** ~ · Standardholzfenster n, Holzstandardfenster
~ **time-temperature curve** · Einheitstemperaturkurve f [Brandverhalten von Bauteilen]
~ **trim** → ~ section
~ **unit** → ~ section
~ **value** · Normenwert m
~ **version** · Standardausführung f
~ **width** · Standardbreite f
~ ~ · Normenbreite f
~ **window** · Norm(en)fenster n
~ **wood(en) window**, stock ~ ~, ~ **timber** ~ · Standardholzfenster n, Holzstandardfenster

standardization · Normung f
standardized · genormt
~ **dimension for construction** · Baunormmaß n, Baunormabmessung f
~ **figure for construction** · Baunormzahl f [Zahl für Baurichtmaße und die daraus abgeleiteten Einzel-, Rohbau- und Ausbaumaße]

standardized test solution — starting a cut

~ test solution · Modellösung f [*Korrosionsprüfungsflüssigkeit*]

stand-by Diesel-produced current · Dieselnotstrom m

standing marble, wall ~ · Wandmarmor m

standing-off period, taking-down ~, cooling-down ~ · Kaltschüren n, Abstehen [*Glasschmelze*]

standing seam → welted ~ ~

~ ~ plate, plate for standing seams · Stehfalzblech n [*Blech zur Herstellung von Stehfalzbedachungen*]

~ ~ roof cladding, ~ ~ cover(ing), **~ ~** sheathing, **~ ~** roofing · Stehfalz(dach)(ein)deckung f, Stehfalzbedachung, Stehfalzsystem n

~ tower → look-out ~

~ traffic · ruhender Verkehr m

~ welt, (welted) standing seam [*The joint formed by turning up the edges of two adjacent sheets perpendicular to the surface and welting them together*] · stehender Falz m, Stehfalz [*Metallbedachung*]

stand oil · Standöl n [*Standöl ist ein ausschließlich durch Erhitzen eingedicktes, trocknendes Öl. Anmerkung: Wird von Leinöl-Standöl, Holzöl-Standöl, Rizinenöl-Standöl, Sojaöl-Standöl und dgl. gesprochen, so darf es nur aus dem genannten Standöl bestehen. Als „Mischstandöle" gelten solche, die aus mehreren Ölarten hergestellt sind, z.B. Leinöl-Holzöl-Standöl 80:20 usw. Der Begriff „trocknendes Öl" ist nicht an ein Mindestwert der Jodzahl gebunden, umfaßt also auch die sog. „halbtrocknenden Öle", soweit sie sich zum Herstellen von Standöl eignen. Die Benennung Dicköl für Standöle im Sinne der obigen Begriffsbestimmung ist nicht zu verwenden*]

~ ~ Chinese white enamel → ~ ~ zinc ~ ~

~ ~ content · Standölgehalt m

~ ~ gloss paint · Standölfarbe f

~ ~ kettle, ~ ~ pot · Standölkochkessel m

~ ~ paint · Standölfarbe f

~ ~ pot, ~ ~ kettle · Standölkochkessel m

~ ~ synthetic resin enamel, synthetic resin enamel ~ · Standöl-Kunstharz-Emaillelack m, Kunstharz-Standöl-Emaillelack

~ ~ (type) varnish · Standöllack m

~ ~ zinc white enamel, ~ ~ Chinese ~ ~, zinc white stand oil ~, Chinese white stand oil ~ · Standöl-Zinkweiß-Emaillelack m, Zinkweiß-Standöl-Emaillelack, Standöl-Schneeweiß-Emaillelack, Schneeweiß-Standöl-Emaillelack

standpipe, vertical pipe, stack, SP · Senkrechtrohr n, Standrohr, Steigrohr

stand sheet → fixed sash

staple, wire ~ · (Draht)Krampe f

~ · Schließkappe f [*Tür*]

~ fibre (Brit.); **~ fiber** (US) [*A glass fibre of relatively short length, generally less than 17 in.*] · Stapelfaser f

stapling · (An)Heften n [*mit Klammern*]

star ornament, astorite · Sternverzierung f, Sternschmuck m, Sterndekor(ation) n, (f), Sternornament n

~ vault, stellar ~ [*Net vaults are not the same thing as star vaults with triradial figures. The terminology used in literature is extremely inexact, and there is no generally recognized definition of the differences. The essential thing in a star vault is that more than three ribs intersect on a common ridge, whereas the essential thing in a net avult is that the ribs (not ridge-ribs) intersect at several points. Net vaults are not a variation of star vaults*] · Stern(rippen)-gewölbe n

starch · Stärke f

~ glue, ~ adhesive · Stärkeleim m

~ gum, British **~,** leiocome, dextrin(e) [*A soluble gummy substance into which starch is converted when subjected to a high temperature, or to the action of dilute alkalis or acids, or of diastase*] · Dextrin n

~ ~ glue, British **~ ~, ~ ~** adhesive, dextrin(e) **~,** leiocome **~** · Dextrinleim m

~ interceptor; ~ intercepter (US) · Stärkeabscheider m

~ laden water · stärkehaltiges Wasser n

~ paste · Stärkekleister m

~ solution [*A solution for starching newly painted walls so that they can be more easily washed*] · Stärkelösung f

starching · Stärken n

star-delta switch · Sterndreieckschalter m

starring · sternförmige Rißbildung f

star-shaped building, ~ block, Y-shaped ~ · Gebäude n mit Y-Grundriß

~ pattern · Sternform f

starter bar, stub-bar, projecting bar, connecting bar, connection bar [*Bar left projecting from concrete in order to locate and provide continuity with other reinforcement*] · Anschluß(bewehrungs)stab m, Anschlußarmierungsstab

~ brick · Anfängerziegel m

~ tile · Anfänger m [*Erster Firstziegel am Giebel oder Walm*]

starting a cut · Aufklopfen n [*Einen Diamant- oder Stahlrädchenschnitt von der dem Schnitt gegenüberliegenden Flächenseite so weit vorsichtig mit dem Hammerkopf des Diamantschneiders beklopfen, daß er sich zu einem die ganze Glasdicke durchdringenden Sprung entwickelt*]

962

starting hip tile — (statically) indeterminate

~ **hip tile** → hip starting ~
~ **newel (post)**, first ~ (~) · Antrittpfosten *m*
~ **ridge tile**, ridge starting ~ · Firstanfänger *m*, Walmanfänger [*Der Ausdruck „Walmanfänger" wird auch für den Gratanfänger verwendet*]
~ **slab**, first ~ · Antrittplatte *f*
~ **step**, first ~ · Antritt(stufe) *m*, (*f*) [*Die erste Stufe eines Treppenlaufes, bei Holztreppen eine Klotz- oder Blockstufe*]
starved joint, hungry ~ · ausgehungerte Fuge *f*
state, condition · Zustand *m*
~ **chamber**, ~ room · Staatsgemach *n*, Prunkzimmer *n*
~ **court** · Vorderhof *m* [*In der Palastanlage von Khorsabad*]
~ **method** [*The safety checks relate to limit states*] · Bemessungsverfahren *n* mit Grenzzuständen
~ **of cracking** · Rißbildungszustand *m*
~ ~ **deformation**, deformation state · Formänderungszustand *m*, Verformungszustand, Gestaltänderungszustand
~ ~ **equilibrium**, equilibrium state, balance · Gleichgewichtszustand *m*
~ ~ **indoor air**, ~ ~ inside ~, ~ ~ room ~ · Raumluftzustand *m*
~ ~ **inertia** · Beharrungszustand *m*, Trägheitszustand
~ ~ **inside air**, ~ ~ indoor ~, ~ ~ room ~ · Raumluftzustand *m*
~ ~ **plane deformation**, plane deformation state · ebener Formänderungszustand *m*, ~ Verformungszustand
~ ~ ~ **distortion**, plane distortion state · ebener Verzerrungszustand *m*
~ ~ ~ **stress**, plane state of ~, planar state of ~, flat state of ~, two-dimensional state of ~ · zweidimensionaler Spannungszustand *m*, ebener ~
~ ~ **pure membrane stress** · reiner Membran(e)spannungszustand *m*
~ ~ **rest** · Ruhezustand *m*
~ ~ **room air**, ~ ~ inside ~, ~ ~ indoor ~ · Raumluftzustand *m*
~ ~ **stress**, stress state · Spannungszustand *m*
~ ~ **surface**, surface state · Oberflächenzustand *m*, Oberflächenbeschaffenheit *f*
~ **room**, ~ chamber · Staatsgemach *n*, Prunkzimmer *n*
stately church · Prachtkirche *f*
~ **gateway**, ~ town ~ · Pracht(straßen)tor *n*
~ **portal** · Prachtportal *n*
~ **stair(case)**, ~ stairway, grand ~ · Prunktreppe *f*, Prachttreppe, Festtreppe, Staatstreppe, Paradetreppe, Kaisertreppe; Kaiserstiege *f* [*Österreich*]
~ **(town) gateway** · Pracht(straßen)tor *n*
static action · statische Beanspruchung *f*
~ **calculation** · statische Berechnung *f*
static-cast pipe, sand-cast ~ · Sandguß(eisen)rohr *n*
static equation · statische Gleichung *f*
~ **equilibrium** · statisches Gleichgewicht *n*
~ ~ **condition**, condition of static equilibrium · statische Gleichgewichtsbedingung *f*
~ ~ **equation**, equation of static equilibrium · statische Gleichgewichtsgleichung *f*
~ ~ **state** · statischer Gleichgewichtszustand *m*
~ **friction** (Brit.); stiction (US) · Ruhereibung *f*, statische Reibung, Haftreibung
~ **load** · ruhende Last *f*, statische ~, Standlast
~ **loading** · ruhende Belastung *f*, statische ~, Standbelastung
~ **moment** · statisches Moment *n*
~ **pressure**, SP · statischer Druck *m*
~ **seal**, gasket ~ · starre (Ab)Dichtung *f*, Flach(ab)dichtung, Manschetten(ab)dichtung
~ **theorem**, lower bond ~ · statischer Satz *m*
statical behaviour (Brit.); ~ behavior (US) · statisches Verhalten *n*
(~) **determinacy**, (~) determinateness · (statische) Bestimmtheit *f*
(~) **determinateness**, (~) determinacy · (statische) Bestimmtheit *f*
~ **failure load**, ~ rupture ~ · statische Bruchlast *f*
(~) **indeterminacy** · (statische) Unbestimmtheit *f*
~ **investigation** · statische Untersuchung *f*
~ **method** · statische Methode *f*, statisches Verfahren *n*
~ **moment of area** · statisches Flächenmoment *n*
~ **rupture load**, ~ failure ~ · statische Bruchlast *f*
statically admissible · statisch zulässig
~ **determinable** · (statisch) bestimmbar
~ **determinate**, ~ determined, isostatic, perfect · (statisch) bestimmt
~ ~ **structure**, isostatic ~ · statisch bestimmtes Bauwerk *n*
~ **determined**, ~ determinate, isostatic, perfect · (statisch) bestimmt
(~) **indeterminate**, (~) indetermined, hyperstatic · (statisch) unbestimmt

(statically) indeterminate frame — steam curing cloche 964

(~) ~ frame, (~) ~ framing, imperfect ~, redundant ~ · (statisch) unbestimmter Rahmen *m*

(~) ~ to the first degree, (~) indetermined ~ ~ ~ ~, hyperstatic ~ ~ ~ ~ ~ · (statisch) unbestimmt ersten Grades

(~) ~ ~ ~ *n*-th degree, (~) indetermined ~ ~ ~ ~ ~, hyperstatic ~ ~ ~ ~ ~ · (statisch) unbestimmt *n*-ten Grades

(~) ~ ~ ~ second degree, (~) indetermined ~ ~ ~ ~ ~, hyperstatic ~ ~ ~ ~ · (statisch) unbestimmt zweiten Grades

(~) ~ ~ ~ third degree, (~) indetermined ~ ~ ~ ~, hyperstatic ~ ~ ~ ~ · (statisch) unbestimmt dritten Grades

(~) indetermined, (~) indeterminate, hyperstatic · (statisch) unbestimmt

~ reinforced concrete · statisch armierter Beton *m*, ~ bewehrter ~

station, central ~ · Zentrale *f*

(~) platform · Bahnsteig *m*

(~) ~ loudspeaker system · Bahnsteig-Lautsprecheranlage *f*

(~) ~ stair(case) · Bahnsteigtreppe *f*

(~) ~ tunnel · Bahnsteigtunnel *m*

~ roof, (~) platform ~ [*A roof with central support only as used on island platforms in railway stations*] · Bahnsteigdach *n*

stationary aggregate(s) plant, ~ concrete ~ ~, commercial (concrete) ~ ~ · (Beton)Zuschlag(stoff)werk *n*

~ continuous brick kiln · Ziegelkammerofen *m*

~ greenhouse · ortsfestes Gewächshaus *n* [*DIN 11535 Bl. 1*]

~ mastic cooking plant · ortsfeste Asphaltkochanlage *f*, stationäre ~, Gußasphaltkocherei *f*

statuary biscuit · Biskuitporzellan *n*, Parian *n*

~ marble · Bildhauermarmor *m*, Statuenmarmor

statue · Statue *f*, Bildnis *n*, Standbild *n*, Bildsäule *f* [*Bei den Steinmetzen plastische Darstellung des Menschen*]

~ chamber, naos · Naos *m*

~ of a deceased · Statue *f* eines Toten

~ ~ an Apostle · Apostelstatue *f*

~ ~ Roland · Rolandsäule *f* [*Vom 14. bis 18. Jahrhundert etwa zwischen Weser und Oder verbreitete Bildsäule aus Holz oder Stein auf den städtischen Hauptplatz. Sie stellt einen Ritter, im Barock einen römischen Krieger mit blankem, aufrecht gehaltenen Schwert dar. Sie ist vermutlich das Symbol der städtischen Gerechtsame*]

~ pedestal · Piedestal *n*, Postament *n*, (Statuen)Sockel *m*, (Statuen)Unterbau *m*

statuette · Statuette *f*, kleines Standbild *n*, kleines Bildnis *n*, kleine Statue *f*, kleine Bildsäule *f*

sta(u)nchion → stancheon

Stauß clay lath(ing) · Staußziegelgewebe *n* [*Markenname für ein quadratisches Drahtgeflecht von 2 cm Maschenweite mit an den Kreuzungspunkten aufgepreßten und gebrannten Tonkreuzchen*]

~ spot-welded round bar mesh · Staußmatte *f*, Stauß-Ziegelgewebeplatte *f* [*1,00 × 2,50 m mit punktverschweißten Rundstählen ø 4,6 mm. Rundstahlabstand längs 20 cm, quer 30 cm*]

stave, tread, rundle, (ladder) rung, LR · (Leiter)Sprosse *f*

~ · Daube *f*

~ church [*A timber-framed and timber-walled church; the walls are of upright planks with corner-post columns*] · Stabkirche *f*, Mastenkirche

~ construction · Stabbau *m* [*Holzbau, dessen runde Eckstäbe zusammen mit den Grundschwellen und den Oberschwellen einen festen Rahmen bilden, in die senkrechte Bohlen eingespundet werden. Die besonders in Skandinavien verbreitete Bauweise erreichte bei den Stabkirchen ihre Vollendung*]

~ ladder, rung ~, rundle ~, tread ~ · Sprossenleiter *f*

stay · Kettelhaken *m*, Sturmhaken

~ → stiffener

~ plate, tie ~, cover ~, brace ~, batten (~) · Schnalle *f*, Bindeblech *n* [*Bei zwei- und mehrteiligen Querschnitten werden die einzelnen Teile durch Bindebleche in ihrem gegenseitigen Abstand gehalten*]

steam boiler · Dampfkessel *m*

to steam-clean · reinigen mit Dampfstrahl

steam coil · Dampfschlange *f*

~ consumption · Dampfverbrauch *m*

to steam cure at high pressure, to autoclave · autoklavi(si)eren, autoklavbehandeln, autoklavhärten, dampfdruckhärten

steam-cured · dampfgehärtet [*Beton*]

~ expanded concrete, ~ gas ~ · Dampfblähbeton *m*, Dampfgasbeton, dampfgehärteter Gasbeton, dampfgehärteter Blähbeton

~ gas concrete, ~ expanded ~ · Dampfblähbeton *m*, Dampfgasbeton, dampfgehärteter Gasbeton, dampfgehärteter Blähbeton

steam curing · Dampfbehandlung *f*, Dampfhärtung, Bedampfung [*Betonwaren*]

~ ~ at atmospheric pressure → atmospheric-pressure steam curing

~ ~ high pressure → autoclaving

~ ~ cloche, ~ ~ cover, insulated ~ ~ · Dampfhaube *f* [*Warmbehandlung von Beton*]

steam curing cycle — steel bell and spigot pipe

~ ~ cycle [*The time interval between the start of the temperature-rise period and the end of the soaking period or the cooling-off period, also a schedule of the time and temperature of periods which make up the cycle*] · Dampfhärtungsspiel *n*, Dampfbehandlungsspiel, Wärmebehandlungsspiel

~ ~ installation · Dampfbehandlungsanlage *f*, Dampfhärtungsanlage

~ ~ room, ~ kiln [*A chamber for steam curing of concrete products at atmospheric pressure*] · Dampfbehandlungsraum *m*, Dampfhärtungsraum *m*, Wärmebehandlungsraum, Behandlungskammer *f*

~ distilled wood turpentine · Holzterpentinöl *n* durch Wasserdampf gewonnen, Wurzelterpentinöl ~ ~ ~

~ distribution · Dampfverteilung *f*

~ flow · Dampfvorlauf *m*

~ generation, ~ generating, ~ raising, raising of steam, generating of steam, generation of steam · Dampferzeugung *f*

~ ~ plant, ~ raising ~ · Dampferzeugungsanlage *f*

~ generator · Dampferzeuger *m*

steam-heated calorifier · dampfbeheizter Gegenstromapparat *m*

steam heating · Dampfheizung *f*

~ ~ system · Dampfheiz(ungs)anlage *f*

steaming · Bedampfung *f*, Dämpfen *n*, Dampfbehandlung

~ · Verdampfen *n* [*(Kalk)Löschen*]

~ installation, ~ plant · Bedampfungsanlage *f*

~ pit · Bedampfungsgrube *f*

~ plant, ~ installation · Bedampfungsanlage *f*

~ tube · Bedampfungsrohr *n*

steam input · Dampfzufuhr *f*

~ installation, ~ system [*A system circulating steam*] · Dampf(umwälz)anlage *f*

~ jacket · Dampf(heiz)mantel *m*

~ kiln, steam-curing room [*A chamber for steam curing of concrete products at atmospheric pressure*] · Dampfbehandlungsraum *m*, Dampfhärtungsraum, Wärmebehandlungsraum, Bedampfungskammer *f*

~ lance · Dampflanze *f*

~ line · Dampfleitung *f*

~ loss · Dampfverlust *m*

~ outlet · Dampfauslaß *m*

~ pipe · Dampfrohr *n*, schweres Gewinderohr [*DIN 2441*]

~ pressure · Dampfdruck *m* [*Fehlname: Dampfspannung f*]

~ ~ curve · Dampfdruckkurve *f*

~ radiator · Dampfheizkörper *m*

~ raising → generation

~ ~ plant, ~ generation ~ · Dampferzeugungsanlage *f*

~ return · Dampfrücklauf *m*

~ riser · Dampf-Steig(e)leitung *f*

~ system, ~ installation [*A system circulating steam*] · Dampf(umwälz)anlage *f*

~ temperature · Dampftemperatur *f*

~ test [*cathodic protection*] · Dampfprobe *f*, Dampfversuch *m*, Dampfprüfung *f*

steam/water mixing valve, ~ mixer (~) · Dampf-Wasser-Mischventil *n*

stearic acid [*misnomer: stearin(e)*] · Stearinsäure *f*

stearin(e)-cored solder wire · Röhrenlötzinn *n* mit Stearin gefüllt

steatite · Steatit *m*

steel anchor plate · Stahlankerplatte *f*

steel-and-concrete floor → composite ~ ~

steel angle, iron ~, angle steel, angle iron · Winkelstahl *m*, Stahlwinkel(profil) *m*, (*n*) [*DIN 1022, DIN 1028, DIN 1029. Fehlnamen: Winkeleisen n, Eisenwinkel(profil)*]

~ ~ lintel; ~ ~ lintol [*deprecated*] · Stahlwinkeloberschwelle *f*, Stahlwinkelsturz *m*

~ ~ stanchion, ~ ~ stancheon (Brit.); ~ ~ column, ~ ~ support · Winkelstahlstütze *f*

~ arch · Stahlbogen *m*

~ arch(ed girder) · Stahlbogen(träger) *m*, Bogenstahlträger

~ architecture · Stahlarchitektur *f*, Stahlbaukunst *f*

~ area grating · Stahlgitterrost *m*

~ article · Stahlartikel *m*, Stahlerzeugnis *n*, Stahlgegenstand *m*

~ ball · Stahlkugel *f*

~ bar, ~ member, ~ rod · Stahlstab *m* [*Fachwerkträger*]

(~) ~ → (rolled) (~) ~

~ barbed wire; ~ bobwire (US) · Stahlstacheldraht *m*

~ base (surface) · Stahluntergrund *m*

~ basement window · Kellergeschoß-Stahlfenster *n*

~ (bath)tub, ~ bath · Stahl(bade)wanne *f*

~ beam · Stahlbalken(träger) *m*

~ ~ grillage · Stahlbalken(träger)rost *m*

~ bearer → ~ (binding) joist

~ bearing · Stahllager *n* [*für Hoch- und Tiefbauten*]

~ ~ skeleton → ~ (structural) ~

~ ~ structure → ~ load~ ~

~ bell and spigot pipe (US); ~ spigot and socket ~ (Brit.) · Stahl-Glockenmuffenrohr *n*

steel bender — steel dome

~ **bender**, rod ~, bar ~ [*colloquially: iron fighter*] · Eisenbieger *m*

~ **bending yard**, reinforcement ~ ~ · Stahlbiegeplatz *m*, Bewehrungsbiegeplatz, Armierungsbiegeplatz

~ **binder** → ~ (binding) joist

~ **binding beam**, ~ ~ joist, ~ binder · Stahlbinderbalken *m*, Stahlbundbalken

~ **(~) joist**, ~ ceiling ~, ~ binder, ~ bearer · Stahlunterzug *m*

~ **(biological) shielding wall**, ~ radiation ~ · Stahl-Abschirmwand *f*

~ **blank** · Zwischenblech *n* [*Zur Abdeckung der Schiene bei aufgelockerter Lichtbandanordnung*]

~ **block**, ~ building · Stahlgebäude *n*

~ **bobwire** (US); ~ barbed wire · Stahlstacheldraht *m*

~ **boiler** · Stahl(heiz)kessel *m*

~ **bowstring**, ~ tie-rod, ~ (horizontal) tie(back) · Stahlzugband *n*

~ **box** · Stahlkasten *m*

~ ~ **girder**, ~ plate ~ ~ · Stahl(blech)-kastenträger *m*

~ **bracket** [*A horizontal steel projection from a vertical or near vertical surface to support a load*] · Stahlkonsole *f*

~ **brad** · Stahlstift *m*

~ **building**, ~ block · Stahlgebäude *n*

~ ~ **block module**, ~ unitized unit · Stahlinstallationsblock *m*, Stahlinstallationszelle *f*, Stahl(raum)zelle

~ ~ **(construction)**, ~ ~ design and ~ · Stahlhochbau *m* [*Bauweise. DIN 1000*]

~ ~ **design and construction**, ~ ~ (construction) · Stahlhochbau *m* [*Bauweise. DIN 1000*]

~ **butt (hinge)** · Stahl-Einstemmband *n*, Stahl-Fi(t)schband, Stahl-Fitsche *f*

~ **cable roof**, ~ rope ~, ~ (Draht)Kabeldach *n*, Stahlseildach, (Stahl)Drahtseildach

~ **caisson** → ~ cassette

~ **casement** · Stahl-Dreh(fenster)flügel *m*

~ **cassette**, ~ waffle, ~ pan, ~ coffer, ~ caisson · Stahl(decken)kassette *f*

~ **cast(ing)** · Stahlguß *m* [*Erzeugnis*]

~ **ceiling joist** → ~ (binding) ~

~ **cellar window** · Stahlkellerfenster *n*

~ **cellular unit**, cellular steel ~ · Abkantprofil *n* [*Stahldecke*]

~ **chamber** · Stahlkammer *f*

~ **channel profile**, ~ ~ (section) · U-Stahl(profil) *m*, (*n*), Stahl-U-Profil [*DIN 1026*]

~ ~ **purlin(e)**, channel iron ~ · U-Eisen-Pfette *f*

~ ~ **(section)**, ~ ~ profile · U-Stahl(-profil) *m*, (*n*), Stahl-U-Profil [*DIN 1026*]

~ **chimney**, ~ stack · Stahl(blech)-schornstein *m*

~ ~ **shaft**, ~ stack ~ · Stahl(blech)-schornsteinschaft *m*

~ **church** · Stahlkirche *f*

~ **cladding**, ~ lining, ~ skin · (Außenwand)Versteifung *f* aus Stahl, Stahl-(außenwand)versteifung

~ **cloth sheet**; ~ fabric ~ [*misnomer*] · Stahlgewebematte *f*

~ **coffer**, ~ cassette, ~ pan, ~ waffle · Stahl(decken)kassette *f*

~ **column** → stancheon

~ ~ → ~ lighting ~

~ **comb** · Stahlkamm *m*

~ **compression ring** · Stahldruckring *m*

~ **compressive stress** · Stahldruckspannung *f*

~ **conduit** · Stahl(panzer)rohr *n*, Staparohr [*Elektroinstallation*]

~ **construction** · Stahlbau *m* [*Stahlbau umfaßt Stahlhochbau, Stahlbrückenbau und Stahlwasserbau*]

~ ~ **engineering**, ~ structural ~ · Stahlbautechnik *f*

~ ~ **firm** · Stahlbaufirma *f*

~ ~ **industry** · Stahlbauindustrie *f*

~ ~ **section**, ~ structural ~ · Stahlbauprofil *n*

~ ~ **type**, ~ type of construction · Stahlbauart *f*

~ **(~) work** · Stahlbauarbeiten *fpl* [*DIN 18335*]

~ **consumption** · Stahlverbrauch *m*

~ **contractor's shop**, ~ workshop · Stahlbauwerkstatt *f*

~ **core** · Stahleinlage *f*, Stahlseele *f*, Stahlkern *m* [*Drahtseil*]

steel-corroding · stahlkorrosiv

steel (counterbalance) weight box · Gegengewichtskasten *m* aus Stahl

~ **creep** · Stahlkriechen *n*

~ **culvert** · Stahlrohr *n* für Durchlässe, ~ ~ Abzugkanäle

~ **cupola**, ~ dome · Stahlkuppel *f*

~ **curtain wall** · Stahl-Vorhangwand *f*

~ **cutting and bending**, (reinforcement) ~ ~ ~ · Betonstahlbearbeitung *f*

~ ~ ~ ~ **(work)shop**, (reinforcement) ~ ~ ~ ~ ~ · Bewehrungswerkstatt *f*, Armierungswerkstatt

~ **(cycle) stand** [*B.S. 1716*] · Stahl-Fahrradstand *m*

~ **deck roof**, ~ roof decking · Stahl-(dach)(ein)deckung *f*, Stahlbedachung

~ ~ **unit** · Stahldachplatte *f*

~ **defect** · Stahlfehler *m*

~ **design** · Bemessung *f* von Stahlbauten, Stahlbemessung

~ **discharge pipe** → ~ draining ~

~ **dome**, ~ cupola · Stahlkuppel *f*

steel door — steel girder

~ **door** · Stahltür f [*DIN 18081, 18082, 18084, 18112, 18240*]
~ ~ **frame** [*B.S. 1245*] · Stahltürrahmen m
~ **dowel** · Stahldollen m, Stab-Stahldübel m, Stahl(stab)dübel
~ **drain pipe** → ~ drainage ~
~ **drain(age) pipe** → ~ ~ draining ~
~ **draining pipe,** ~ drain(age) ~, ~ discharge ~, ~ waste (~) · Stahlablaufrohr n, Stahlablaufrohr, Stahldränrohr, Stahlentwässerungsrohr [*Fehlnamen: Stahlablauf m, Stahlabfluß m*]
~-**engraving** · Stahlstich m
steel erection, erection of steelwork · Stahlbaumontage f
~ **erector,** constructional fitter and erector · Stahlbaumonteur m
~ **erector's labourer** (Brit.); ~ ~ laborer(US); ~ ~ mate · Stahlbauhilfsarbeiter m
~ ~ **mate;** ~ ~ labourer (Brit.); ~ ~ laborer (US) · Stahlbauhilfsarbeiter m
~ **exit gas pipe** · Stahl-Abgasrohr n
~ **expansion dowel** · Stahlspreizdübel m
~ **fabric sheet** [*misnomer*]; ~ cloth ~ Stahlgewebematte f
~ **façade** · Stahlfassade f
~ **fastener,** ~ fastening, ~ fixing (accessory), ~ fixing device, ~ fixing means · Stahlbefestigungsmittel n
~ **fastening,** ~ fastener, ~ fixing (accesory), ~ fixing device, ~ fixing means · Stahlbefestigungsmittel n
~ **fence picket** → ~ ~ post
~ ~ **post,** ~ ~ picket, ~ ~ stake, ~ fencing · Stahl-Zaunpfahl m, Stahl-Zaunpfosten m
~ ~ **stake** → ~ ~ post
~ **fencing picket** → ~ fence post
~ ~ **post** → ~ fence ~
~ ~ **stake** → ~ fence post
~ **fibre concrete** (Brit.); ~ fiber ~ (US) · Stahlfaserbeton m [*Er erhält eine Zugabe von 3 bis 4 cm langen Stahlfasern*]
~ **filings,** ~ turnings · Stahlfeilspäne mpl, Stahlpulver n
~ **filter pipe** · Stahlbrunnenrohr n
~ **fixer** → (reinforcing) iron worker
~ **fixing (accessory),** ~ ~ device, ~ ~ means, ~ fastener, ~ fastening · Stahlbefestigungsmittel n
~ ~ **device,** ~ ~ (accessory), ~ ~ means, ~ fastener, ~ fastening · Stahlbefestigungsmittel n
~ ~ **means,** ~ ~ (accessory), ~ ~ device, ~ fastener, ~ fastening · Stahlbefestigungsmittel n
~ **flagpole** · Stahlfahnenmast m, Stahlflaggenmast
~ **flange** · Stahlflansch m

~ **flat roof truss** (US); ~ roof frame (Brit.) · Stahlfachwerk(dach)binder m, Stahl(dach)binder in Rahmenform, Stahlrahmen(dach)binder, Stahlflachdachbinder
~ (~) **slab** → ~ plate
~ ~ **wire,** flat steel ~ · Flachstahldraht m, Stahlflachdraht
~ **floor** · Stahldecke f
~ ~ **cover(ing),** ~ floor(ing) (finish) · Stahl(fuß)boden(belag) m
~ ~ **element** · Stahldecken(bau)element n
~ ~ **girder** · Stahldeckenträger m
~ **floor(ing) (finish),** ~ floor cover(ing) · Stahl(fuß)boden(belag) m
~ ~ **plate** · (Fuß)Bodenstahlblech n, Stahl(fuß)bodenblech
~ **folded plate roof,** ~ ~ slab ~, ~ prismatic shell ~; ~ hipped-plate ~, ~ tilted slab ~ (US) · Stahldachfaltwerk n, Stahlfalt(werk)dach m
~ ~ **slab roof** → ~ ~ plate ~
~ **for building (construction)** · Hochbaustahl m [*DIN 1050*]
~ **forms,** ~ shuttering, ~ form(work) · Stahl(blech)schalung f, Stahlplattenschalung
~ **form(work),** ~ shuttering, ~ forms · Stahl(blech)schalung f, Stahlplattenschalung
~ **frame,** ~ framing · Stahlrahmen m
steel-frame(d) block → ~ building
~ **building,** ~ block, ~ structure, steel skeleton ~ · Stahlskelettgebäude n, Stahlgerippegebäude, Stahlrahmengebäude, Stahlgerippebauwerk n, Stahlskelettbauwerk
~ **modular construction** · Stahlrahmen-Modulbau m
~ **multi-storey car park** (Brit.); multi-story ~ ~ (US); steel skeleton ~ ~, multi-stor(e)y steel ~ · Stahlskelett-Parkhaus n, Stahlskelett-Parkgebäude n, Stahlgerippe-Parkhaus, Stahlgerippe-Parkgebäude, Stahlrahmen-Parkhaus, Stahlrahmen-Parkgebäude
~ **office building,** ~ ~ block, steel skeleton ~ ~ · Stahlskelettbürogebäude n, Stahlgerippebürogebäude, Stahlrahmenbürogebäude
~ **portal building** · Stahlportalrahmengebäude n
~ **structure** → ~ building
~ **wall** · Stahlfach(werk)wand f, Stahlriegelwand
steel framework · Stahlfachwerk n
~ **framing,** ~ frame · Stahlrahmen m
~ **garage door,** garage steel ~ · Stahl-Garagentor n, Garagen-Stahltor
~ **girder,** (structural) steel section · Stahlprofil n, Trägerstahl m, Profilstahl, Stahlträger m [*Fehlname: Trägereisen, Profileisen. Von den Walzwerken hergestellt-*

steel girder — steel pipe column

ter Formstahl mit I-, IP- und U-Querschnitt, der als Träger für Bauzwecke verwendet wird]

~ ~ **floor** · Stahlträgerdecke f

~ ~ **joint** · Stahlträgerstoß m

steel-glass construction, ~ (structural) system · Stahlglaskonstruktion(ssystem) f, (n)

~ **(structural) system,** ~ construction · Stahlglaskonstruktion(ssystem) f, (n)

~ **system,** ~ structural ~, ~ construction · Stahlglaskonstruktion(ssystem) f, (n)

steel grade · Stahlsorte f

~ **grain** · Stahlkorn n

~ **grid,** ~ grillage · Stahlrost m

~ ~ **footing,** ~ grillage ~ · Stahlrostfundament n

~ **grillage,** ~ grid · Stahlrost m

~ ~ **footing,** ~ grid ~ · Stahlrostfundament n

~ **grille** [See remark under 'Gitter'] · Stahlgitter n

~ **grit,** ~ shot · Stahlschrot m, n

~ ~ **concrete,** ~ shot ~ · Stahlschrotbeton m

~ **hangar shutter door,** ~ ~ shutterdoor · Hallen-Stahltor n, Stahl-Hallentor

~ **helix** · Stahlwendel m [Spannbeton]

~ **hinge** · Stahlscharnier n

~ ~ · Stahlgelenk n

~ ~ · Stahlband n [Baubeschlag]

~ ~ **connection** · Stahlgelenkverbindung f

~ ~ **purlin(e)** · Stahlgelenkpfette f

~ **hipped-plate roof** (US) → ~ folded plate ~

~ **hollow frame section** · Stahlhohlrahmenprofil n

~ **hook** · Stahlhaken m

~ **(horizontal) tie(back),** ~ tie-rod, ~ bowstring · Stahlzugband n

~ **housing,** ~ residential ~, ~ residences · Stahlwohnbauten f

~ **joist** → rolled-~ ~

~ **ladder** · Stahlleiter f

~ **lamella** · Stahllamelle f

~ ~ **cupola,** ~ ~ dome · Stahllamellenkuppel f

~ ~ **dome,** ~ ~ cupola · Stahllamellenkuppel f

~ **landing mat** · Flugplatz-Stahlmatte f

~ **lath,** ~ slat · Stahllamelle f [Rolltor]

~ **lath(ing) (for plastering)** [B.S. 1369] · Metallputzträger m

~ **lattice(d) column,** lattice(d) steel ~, lattice-form steel ~ · Stahlgitterstütze f

~ ~ **girder,** lattice(d) steel ~, lattice-form steel ~ · Stahlgitterträger m

~ ~ **mast,** lattice(d) steel ~, lattice-form steel ~ · Stahlgittermast m

~ **leaf** · Stahlflügel m [Tor]

~ **level,** reinforcement ~ · Höhe f der Armierung, ~ ~ Bewehrung, ~ ~ (Stahl)Einlagen

~ **lifting collar,** (lift-)slab ~, shear ~ · Deckenkragen m, (Stahl)Kragen [Hubdeckenverfahren]

~ **(lighting) column,** ~ (~) mast · Stahl(-Licht)mast m, Stahl-Beleuchtungsmast, Stahl-(Straßen)Leuchtenmast

~ **(~) mast** → ~ (~) column

steel light(weight) girder, light(weight) steel ~ · Stahlleicht(bau)träger m, Leichtstahl(bau)träger

~ ~ **member,** ~ ~ unit, ~ ~ component, light(weight) steel ~ · Stahlleichtbauelement n

~ ~ **structures,** light(weight) steel ~ · Stahlleichtbauten f

~ **lining,** ~ cladding, ~ skin · (Außenwand)Versteifung f aus Stahl, Stahl(außenwand)versteifung

~ **lintel,** structural ~ ~; (structural) steel lintol [deprecated] · Stahloberschwelle f, Stahlsturz m

~ **(load)bearing skeleton** → ~ (structural) ~

~ ~ **structure,** ~ (weight-carrying) ~ · Stahltragwerk n [Ein materielles System von Stahlbauelementen bzw. Stahlträgern]

~ **maker,** ~ producer · Stahlerzeuger m

~ **manhole cover,** ~ ~ lid · Stahlschachtabdeckung f, Stahlschachtdeckel m

~ ~ **frame** · Stahlschachtrahmen m

~ ~ **lid,** ~ ~ cover · Stahlschachtabdeckung f, Stahlschachtdeckel m

~ **mast** · Stahlmast m

~ ~ → ~ (lighting) column

~ **member** · Stahlteil m, n

~ ~, **rod,** ~ bar · Stahlstab m [Fachwerkträger]

steel(-mill) slag · (Eisen)Hüttenschlacke f, Metall(hütten)schlacke

steel nail [B.S. 1202] · Stahlnagel m

~ **netting** · Stahlgeflecht n

~ **pan,** ~ coffer, ~ cassette, ~ waffle · Stahl(decken)kassette f

~ **pantile** [See remark under 'Dachpfanne'] · Stahldachpfanne f, Stahlhohlpfanne, Stahl(-)Pfanne, holländische Stahlpfanne, Pfannenblech n [Verzinktes profiliertes Stahlblech für Dacheindeckungen]

~ **pantiling** · Stahlpfannen(dach)(ein)-deckung f, Stahlpfannenbedachung [Dachdeckung mit verzinkten Stahlpfannen. DIN 59231]

~ **partition (wall)** · Stahltrennwand f

~ **pile** · Stahl(ramm)pfahl m

~ **pipe** · Stahlrohr n

~ ~ **column,** ~ tube ~, tubular steel ~ · Stahlrohrstütze f

steel pipe fitting — steel rung

~ ~ **fitting** · Stahl(rohr)fitting m, Stahl-(rohr)formstück n [DIN 2980/93]

~ ~ **flange** · Stahlrohrflansch m

~ ~ **line** · Stahlrohrleitung f

~ ~ **string, tubular steel** ~ (Brit.); ~ ~ **stringer** (US) · Stahlrohr(treppen)wange f

~ **pivot pin** · Stahldrehzapfen m

~ **plain web beam,** ~ **solid** ~ ~ · Stahl-Vollwandbalken(träger) m

~ ~ ~ **girder,** ~ **solid** ~ ~ · Stahlvollwandträger m

steel-plant boiler house · Stahlwerkkesselhaus n

steel plate, heavy ~ ~ · Stahl(grob)blech n [DIN 1543]

~ ~, ~ (flat) slab [Steel plates constitute the webs of plate-girders and deep beams used in bridges or other large structures] · Stahlplatte f

~ (~) **box girder** · Stahl(blech)kastenträger m

~ ~ **door** · Stahlblechtür f

~ ~ **element,** ~ ~ **unit,** ~ ~ **member** · Stahlblechelement n

~ ~ **garage** · Stahl(blech)garage f

~ ~ **lath(ing)** · Putzträger m aus Stahlblech, Stahlblech-Putzträger

~ ~ **lining** · Stahlfutter n [Schornstein]

~ ~ **member,** ~ ~ **unit,** ~ ~ **element** · Stahlblechelement n

~ ~ **silo** · Stahl(blech)silo m

~ (~) **string** (Brit.); ~ (~) **stringer** (US) · Stahl(treppen)wange f

~ ~ **system** · Stahlblechkonstruktion f

~ ~ **unit,** ~ ~ **member,** ~ ~ **element** · Stahlblechelement n

~ **plates sub-floor** · Stahlplattenunterboden m

~ **platform** · Stahlbühne f, Stahlplattform f

~ **portal frame** · Stahlportalrahmen m

~ **post** · Stahlpfosten m

~ **prismatic shell roof** → ~ **folded plate** ~

~ **producer,** ~ **maker** · Stahlerzeuger m

~ **production,** ~ **working** · Stahlerzeugung f

~ **profile** → (structural) steel section

~ **purlin(e)** · Stahlpfette f

~ **quality** · Stahlgüte f

~ **radiation shielding wall,** ~ (biological) ~ ~ · Stahl-Abschirmwand f

~ **radiator** · Stahl(glieder)heizkörper m, Stahlradiator m [DIN 4722]

~ (~) **section** · Stahl(radiator)glied n

~ **railing** · Stahlgeländer n

to (steel-)reinforce · armieren, bewehren, mit (Stahl)Einlagen versehen

(steel-)reinforced · armiert, bewehrt, mit (Stahl)Einlagen (versehen)

steel reinforcement in ribs, reinforcement ~ ~ · Rippenarmierung f, Rippenbewehrung, Rippen(stahl)einlagen fpl

~ **requirement** · Stahlbedarf m

~ **residences,** ~ (residential) housing · Stahlwohnbauten f

~ **(residential) housing,** ~ **residences** · Stahlwohnbauten f

steel-ribbed cupola, ~ **dome** · Stahlrippenkuppel f

~ **dome,** ~ **cupola** · Stahlrippenkuppel f

steel ridging, iron ~ · Stahlfirsthaube f, Stahlfirstkappe f

~ **rigid foam sandwich element,** ~ ~ ~ **member,** ~ ~ ~ ~ **unit** · Stahl-Hartschaum-Sandwichelement n [Zwei feuerverzinkte, zusätzlich einbrennlackierte oder kunststoffbeschichtete Stahlbänder werden auf einer kontinuierlichen Fertigungsanlage profiliert und gleichzeitig in der gewünschten Wanddicke miteinander verschäumt]

~ ~ **framing,** ~ ~ **frame** · Stahlstarrrahmen m

~ **rivet** · Stahlniet m

~ **roadstud,** ~ **streetmarker,** ~ **traffic stud** · Stahl-Markierungsknopf m, Stahl-Spurnagel m, Stahl-Verkehrsnagel, Stahl-Straßennagel

(~) **rod** → (rolled) (steel) bar

~ ~, ~ **bar,** ~ **member** · Stahlstab m [Fachwerkträger]

~ **roller bearing** · stählernes Rollen(auf)lager n, Stahlrollenlager [für Hoch- und Tiefbauten]

~ ~ **shutter,** ~ **rolling** ~ · Stahlrollabschluß m

~ **rolling grille,** ~ **roller** ~ [See remark under 'Gitter'] · Stahlrollgitter n

~ **roof cladding** → ~ (sheet) roof cover(ing)

~ ~ **cover(ing)** → ~ **sheet** ~ ~

~ ~ **girder** · Dachstahlträger m, Rahmenstahlriegel m

~ ~ **profile** → ~ ~ ~ **shape**

~ ~ **section** → ~ ~ ~ **shape**

~ ~ **shape,** ~ ~ **section,** ~ ~ **unit,** ~ **trim,** ~ ~ **profile** · Stahldachprofil n

~ ~ **sheathing** → ~ ~ (sheet) roof covering

~ ~ **trim** → ~ ~ **shape**

~ ~ **unit** → ~ ~ **shape**

~ **roof(ing)** → ~ (sheet) roof covering

~ **rope roof,** ~ **cable** ~ · (Draht)Kabeldach n, Stahlseildach, (Stahl)Drahtseildach

~ **round** · Halbrund(leiter)sprosse f

~ **rundle,** ~ **rung,** ~ **tread** · Stahl(leiter)sprosse f

~ **rung,** ~ **rundle,** ~ **tread** · Stahl(leiter)sprosse f

steel sash putty — steel storage tank 970

~ **sash putty** · Stahlfensterkitt *m* [*Kitt für Stahlfensterverglasungen*]

~ ~ ~ **of the exterior glazing type** · Stahlfensterkitt *m* für Außenverwendung

~ ~ ~ ~ ~ **interior glazing type** · Stahlfensterkitt *m* für Innenverwendung

~ **savings,** savings in steel · Stahlersparnis *f*

~ **screw** · Stahlschraube *f*

~ ~ **pile** · Stahlschraub(en)pfahl *m*

~ **section** → structural ~ ~

~ ~, ~ **radiator** ~ · Stahl(radiator)glied *n*

~ ~ **string** (Brit.); ~ ~ **stringer** (US) Profilstahlwange *f*

~ **shape** → (structural) steel section

~ **shavings** · Stahlspäne *mpl*

(~) **shear key** · Stahlbarren *m*, (Verankerungs)Barren [*Hubdeckenverfahren*]

~ ~ **wall** · stählerne Windscheibe *f*

steel-sheathed lead pipe · Stahlmantelrohr *n* [*Ein Bleirohr, das zur Erhöhung der Widerstandsfähigkeit gegen Innendruck, Durchbiegung usw. mit einem Stahlmantel versehen ist. Es wird mit Durchmessern von 100 bis 300 mm in Längen bis 4 m mit Flanschenverbindung, nebst Formstücken, hergestellt*]

steel sheet, iron ~, sheet steel, sheet iron · Stahl(fein)blech *n* [*DIN 1541*]

~ ~ **facing** → ~ ~ lining

~ ~ **lining,** sheet steel ~, ~ ~ (sur-)facing · Stahl(fein)blechauskleidung *f*, Stahl(fein)blechverkleidung, Stahl(fein)blechbekleidung

~ (~) **roof cladding** → ~ (~) ~ cover(ing)

~ (~) ~ **cover(ing),** iron (~) ~ ~, ~ (~) ~ sheathing, ~ (~) ~ cladding, ~ (~) ~ roofing · Stahlblech(dach)(ein)deckung *f*, Stahlblechbedachung, Stahl(dach)(ein)deckung

~ (~) ~ **sheathing** → ~ (~) ~ cover(ing)

~ (~) **roofing** → ~ (~) roof cover(ing)

~ ~ **(sur)facing** → ~ ~ ~ lining

~ **sheetpile** · Stahlspundbohle *f*

~ **shelf** · Stahlregal *n*

~ **shell** · Stahlschale *f*

~ **shielding wall,** ~ biological ~ ~, ~ radiation ~ · Stahl-Abschirmwand *f*

~ **shore,** ~ shoring column · Stahl-Einrüststütze *f*

~ **shoring** · Stahleinrüstung *f*

~ ~ **column,** ~ shore · Stahl-Einrüststütze *f*

~ **shot,** ~ grit · Stahlschrot *m, n*

~ ~ **concrete,** ~ grit ~ · Stahlschrotbeton *m*

~ **shutter** · Stahlabschluß *m*

~ ~ **door,** ~ shutterdoor · Stahltor *n* [*DIN 18112*]

~ **shuttering,** ~ form(work), ~ forms · Stahl(blech)schalung *f*, Stahlplattenschalung

~ **skeleton** → ~ structural ~

~ ~ **block** → ~ ~ building

~ ~ **building,** ~ ~ block, ~ ~ structure, steel-frame(d) ~ · Stahlskelettgebäude *n*, Stahlgerippegebäude, Stahlrahmengebäude, Stahlgerippebauwerk *n*, Stahlskelettbauwerk

~ ~ **construction** · Stahlskelettbau *m*, Stahlgerippebau

~ ~ **multi-storey car park** → steel-frame(d) ~ ~ ~

~ ~ **office building,** ~ ~ ~ block, steel-frame(d) ~ ~ · Stahlskelettbürogebäude *n*, Stahlgerippebürogebäude, Stahlrahmenbürogebäude

~ ~ **structure** → ~ ~ building

~ **skin,** ~ cladding, ~ lining · (Außenwand)Versteifung *f* aus Stahl, Stahl(außenwand)versteifung

~ **skyscraper** · Stahlwolkenkratzer *m*

~ **slab** → ~ plate

~ ~ **prop** · Stahldeckenstütze *f*

~ **slag,** ~-mill ~ · (Eisen)Hüttenschlacke *f*, Metall(hütten)schlacke

~ **slat,** ~ lath · Stahllamelle *f* [*Rolltor*]

~ ~ **rolling shutter,** ~ ~ roller ~ · Stahllamellen-Rollabschluß *m*

~ **slatted roller blind** · Stahlrolladen *m*, Stahlrolljalousie *f*

~ **sleeve pipe** · Stahlmuffenrohr *n*

~ **sliding folding shutter door,** ~ ~ ~ shutterdoor · Stahl-Faltschiebetor *n*, Stahl-Schiebefalttor

~ **solid web beam,** ~ plain ~ ~ · Stahl-Vollwandbalken(träger) *m*

~ ~ ~ **girder,** ~ plain ~ ~ · Stahlvollwandträger *m*

~ **space (load)bearing structure,** ~ three-dimensional ~ ~, ~ spatial ~ ~, ~ ~ (weight-carrying) ~ · Stahl-Raumtragwerk *n*

~ **spigot and socket pipe** (Brit.); ~ bell and spigot ~ (US) · Stahl-Glockenmuffenrohr *n*

~ **spring** · Stahlfeder *f*

~ ~ **isolator** · Stahlfederisolator *m*

~ **stabilized with titanium** · titanberuhigter Stahl *m*

~ **stack,** ~ chimney · Stahl(blech)schornstein *m*

~ ~ **shaft,** ~ chimney · Stahl(blech)schornsteinschaft *m*

~ **stair(case)** · Stahltreppe *f*

~ ~ **builder** · Stahltreppenbauer *m*

~ **stanchion,** ~ stancheon; structural-~ (Brit.); (structural-)steel column · Stahlstütze *f*

~ **stand,** ~ cycle ~ [*B.S. 1716*] · Stahl-Fahrradstand *m*

~ **storage tank** · Stahllagerbehälter *m*

steel storage yard — steel wire brush

~ ~ **yard**, reinforcement ~ ~ · Armierungsstahllager *n*, Bewehrungsstahllager, Betonstahllager

~ **store**, reinforcement ~ · Stahllager *n*, Bewehrungslager, Armierungslager

~ **strand** · Stahl(draht)litze *f*

~ **streetmarker**, ~ roadstud, ~ traffic stud · Stahl-Markierungsknopf *m*, Stahl-Spurnagel *m*, Stahl-Verkehrsnagel, Stahl-Straßennagel

~ **stress** · Stahlspannung *f*

~ **string**, ~ plate ~ (Brit.); ~ (plate) stringer (US) · Stahl(treppen)wange *f*

~ ~ **stair(case)** (Brit.); ~ stringer ~ · Stahlwangentreppe *f*

~ **strip** · Stahlband *n*

~ **structural engineering**, ~ construction ~ · Stahlbautechnik *f*

~ ~ **section**, ~ construction ~ · Stahlbauprofil *n*

~ (~) **skeleton**, ~ (load)bearing ~, ~ weight-carrying ~ · (Trag)Stahlgegerippe *n*, (Trag)Stahlskelett *n*

~ **structure** → ~ (load)bearing ~

~ ~ · Stahlbauwerk *n*

~ ~, ~ system, structural steelwork · Stahlkonstruktion *f*

~ **(sub-)floor with an in-built system of underfloor wiring** · Installations-(hohl)boden *m*

~ **sub-purlin(e)** · Stahlunterpfette *f*

~ **support** → stancheon

~ **surround** · Stahleinfassung *f*, Stahlabschluß *m*, Stahlrand *m*

~ **swing door** · Pendeltür *f* aus Stahl, Stahl-Pendeltür

~ **system**, ~ structure, structural steelwork · Stahlkonstruktion *f*

~ **tendon** [*A stretched element of steel used in a concrete member or structure to impart prestress to the concrete*] · Stahlspannglied *n*

~ **tension member** · Stahlzugglied *n*

~ **three-dimensional (load)bearing structure** → ~ space ~ ~

~ **tie-rod**, ~ bowstring, ~ (horizontal) tie(back) · Stahlzugband *n*

~ **tile** · Stahldach(deckungs)element *n*

~ **tilted slab roof** (US) → ~ folded plate ~

~ **tower** · Stahlturm *m*

~ **track** · Stahlschiene *f* [*Türanlage*]

~ **traffic stud**, ~ streetmarker, ~ roadstud · Stahl-Markierungsknopf *m*, Stahl-Spurnagel *m*, Stahl-Verkehrsnagel, Stahl-Straßennagel

~ **transmission pole** · Stahlüberlandmast *m*, Stahl(leitungs)mast

~ **tray** · Stahlzelle *f*, Decken~, Stahlfüllkörper *m* [*Deckenfüllkörper für Stahlbetonrippendecken, Längen 32,5, 65, 75 und 90 cm; Breiten 30, 40, 50, 60 und 75 cm; Höhen 10, 15, 20, 25, 30, 35 cm. Die Füllkörper bestehen aus einem U-förmig gebogenen gerippelten Stahlblech. Sie werden vor dem Einbringen der Bewehrung auf dem Putzträger (z.B. Rippenstreckmetall) befestigt. Die Blech-Füllkörper verbleiben in der Decke. Der Deckenputz läuft auf einheitlichem Putzträger unter den Rippen und Hohlräumen durch*]

~ **tread** · Stahltritt(stufe) *m*, (*f*)

~ ~, ~ rundle, ~ rung · Stahl(leiter)sprosse *f*

~ **trench sheeting** · Stahlkanaldielen *fpl*

~ **trim** → (structural) steel section

~ **trowel** · Stahlkelle *f*

~ **truss frame** · Stahlsprengwerk *n*

~ **trussed arch(ed girder)** · Stahl-Fachwerkbogen(träger) *m*

~ **truss(ed girder)** · Stahlfachwerk(träger) *n*, (*m*)

~ **tub**, ~ bath~, ~ bath · Stahl(bade)wanne *f*

~ **tube** · Stahlröhre *f*

~ ~ **column**, ~ pipe ~, tubular steel ~ · Stahlrohrstütze *f*

~ **tubing lattice tower** · Stahlrohrgitterturm *m* [*Fehlname: Stahlrohrfachwerkturm*]

~ **tubular frame**, tubular steel ~ · Stahlrohrrahmen *m*

~ **turnings**, ~ filings · Stahlfeilspäne *mpl*, Stahlpulver *n*

~ **type of construction**, ~ construction type · Stahlbauart *f*

~ **unit** → (structural) steel section

~ **unitized unit**, ~ building block module · Stahlinstallationsblock *m*, Stahlinstallationszelle *f*, Stahl(raum)zelle

~ **waffle**, ~ pan, ~ coffer, ~ cassette · Stahl(decken)kassette *f*

~ **wall** · Stahlwand *f*

~ **waste (pipe)** → ~ draining ~

~ **water pipe** · Stahlwasserrohr *n*

~ **wedge** · Stahlkeil *m*

~ **weight box**, ~ counterbalance ~ ~ · Gegengewichtkasten *m* aus Stahl

~ **weight-carrying skeleton** → ~ (~) **structure** → ~ (load)bearing ~

~ **wind-bracing wall** · Stahlwindscheibe *f*

~ **window** · Stahlfenster *n*

~ ~ **for agricultural use** [*B.S. 2503*] · Stahlfenster *n* für landwirtschaftliche Gebäude

~ ~ ~ **industrial building** [*B.S. 1787*] · Industrie-Stahlfenster *n*

~ ~ **frame** · Stahlfensterrahmen *m*

~ **wire** · Stahldraht *m* [*Fehlname: Eisendraht. In rundem Querschnitt aus Flußstahl hergestellt*]

~ ~ **brush** · Stahl(draht)bürste *f*

steel wire cloth — step(ped) cap flashing

~ ~ **cloth**, woven steel wire fabric; steel wire fabric [*misnomer*] · Drahtgewebe *n* aus Stahl, Stahl(draht)gewebe

~ ~ **fabric** [*misnomer*] → steel wire cloth

~ ~ **for fences** [*B.S. 4102*] · Zaunstahldraht *m*

~ ~ ~ **(pre)stressed concrete**, prestressing wire [*B.S. 2691*] · (Vorspann-)Bündeldraht *m*, Spann(beton)(kabel)draht

~ ~ **rod** · Stahlwalzdraht *m*

~ **wool** [*It consists of fine shreds of steel matted together for use in the same manner as sandpaper. It is available in several grades of fineness*] · Stahlwolle *f*

~ **work**, ~ construction ~ · Stahlbauarbeiten *fpl* [*DIN 18335*]

(steelwork) erector [*One engaged in erecting steelwork*] · (Stahl)Montagebauarbeiter *m*

steel working, ~ production · Stahlerzeugung *f*

~ **workshop**, ~ contractor's shop · Stahlbauwerkstatt *f*

steening, steining [*The brick, stone, or concrete lining to a well or cesspool*] · Verkleidung *f*, Auskleidung, Bekleidung [*Brunnen; Senkgrube*]

steep arch · Steilbogen *m*

~ **folding** · steile Faltung *f*

~ **gable** · Steilgiebel *m*

~ **parabola** · Steilparabel *f*

~ **parabolic arch(ed girder)** · Steilparabelbogen(träger) *m*

steep-pitched roof, high-peaked ~ · Steildach *n*

steeple, spire, broach · Spitz(kirch)turm *m*

steeplechase course · Hindernisbahn *f* [*Pferderennbahn*]

steeple plain (roof(ing)) tile, ~ plane (~) ~ · Turmbiber(schwanz) *m*

~ **tile** · Schuppenziegel *m*, Turmziegel

~-**window**, belfry-arch ~ · Schalloch *n*, Schallöffnung *f*

steeply-pitched glazing · steil geneigte Verglasung *f*, ~ ~ Einglasung

steining, steening [*The brick, stone, or concrete lining to a well or cesspool*] · Verkleidung *f*, Auskleidung, Bekleidung [*Brunnen; Senkgrube*]

Stelcon armo(u)red concrete flag-(stone) · Stelcon-Panzer-Hartbetonplatte *f*

~ ~ ~ **paving** · Stelcon-Panzerbetonbelag *m*

~ **C.I. plate**, ~ cast iron ~ · Stelcon-Gußeisenplatte *f*

~ **concrete raft** · Stelcon-Großflächenplatte *f*

~ **industrial floor cover(ing)**, ~ ~ floor(ing) (finish) · Stelcon-Industrie(fuß)boden(belag) *m*

~ **(steel) anchor plate** · Stelcon-(Stahl)Ankerplatte *f* [*In Beton verlegte Stahlblechplatte*]

stele [*It consisted of a slab of stone placed upright in the ground, carved in bas-relief and generally terminated with floriated ornament*] · Grabstele *f*, (Relief)Stele, Grabstein *m*

stellar pattern · Sternmuster *n*

~ **vault**, star ~ [*Net vaults are not the same thing as star vaults with triradial figures. The terminology used in literature is extremely inexcat, and there is no generally recognized definition of the differences. The essential thing in a star vault is that more than three ribs intersect on a common ridge, whereas the essential thing in a net vault is that the ribs (not ridge-ribs) intersect at several points. Net vaults are not a variation of star vaults*] · Stern(rippen)gewölbe *n*

(stench) trap → trap

stencil work · Schablonenmalerei *f*, Schablonieren *n*

step, degree · (Treppen)Stufe *f* [*Bauteil zur Überwindung von Höhenunterschieden, der mit einem Schritt begangen werden kann und aus Trittstufe und Setzstufe besteht*]

~ **component** → (stair(case)) step unit

~ **footing**, stepped ~, benched ~ [*A stepped construction to spread the load at the foot of a wall or column*] · abgetrepptes Fundament *n*, treppenförmiges ~

~ **iron**, hand ~, foot ~, access hook · Steigeisen *n*, Klettereisen [*DIN 1211 (kurz), DIN 1212 (lang)*]

stepladder, step (type) ladder · Stufenleiter *f*

step length, length of step · Stufenlänge *f*

step-like · stufenartig

step masonry (work), stepped ~ (~) · Absatz-Mauerwerk *n*

~ **member** → (stair(case)) step unit

~ **profile** · Stufenprofil *n*

~ **pyramid** → terrace(d) mastaba(h)

~ **tile** · Stufen(belag)platte *f*,• Stufenfliese *f*

~ **(type) ladder**, stepladder · Stufenleiter *f*

~ **unit** → stair(case) ~ ~

stepped · abgetreppt

step(ped) artificial hill, temple tower · Stufenberg *m* [*Abgestufter Unterbau eines Hochtempels mit Freitreppen in Mesopotamien (Zikkur(r)at), in Hinterindien (Prang; Prasat) und in Altamerika*]

~ **cap flashing**, ~ counter ~ [*See remark under 'Anschluß'*] · stufenförmiger Kappanschluß *m*, ~ Überhangenschluß

~ ~ ~ **(piece)**, ~ counter ~ (~) [*See remark under 'Anschluß'*] · stufenförmige Kappleiste *f*, ~ Überhangleiste, stufenförmiger Kappstreifen *m*, stufenförmiger Überhangstreifen

~ **counter flashing**, ~ cap ~ [*See remark under 'Anschluß'*] · stufenförmiger Kappanschluß *m*, ~ Überhanganschluß

~ ~ ~ **(piece)** → ~ cap ~ (~)

~ **court** · Stufenhof *m*

~ **flashing** [*A flexible-metal or roofing-felt cover flashing let into the joints of brickwork to make a watertight joint between a wall (often a chimney) and the sloping part of a roof*] · abgetreppter Überhang(streifen) *m*

~ **footing, benched** ~ [*A stepped construction to spread the load at the foot of a wall or column*] · abgetrepptes Fundament *n*, treppenförmiges ~

~ **(funerary) temple** → terrace(d) mortuary ~

~ **masonry (work)** · Absatz-Mauerwerk *n*

~ **mastaba(h)** → terraced ~

~ **merlon** · Stufenzinne *f*

~ **mortuary temple** → terrace(d) ~ ~

~ **pyramid** → terrace(d) mastaba(h)

~ **ramp** · Stufenrampe *f*

~ **roof** · Staffeldach *n* .

~ **soffit** · treppenförmige Untersicht *f* [*Treppe*]

~ **stringer, cut** ~, **open** ~ (US); ~ string [*An outer string which is cut to the profile of the steps*] · Sattelwange *f*

~ **temple** → terrace(d) mortuary ~

~ **terrace** · Stufenterrasse *f*

~ ~ **block**, ~ ~ **building** · Stufenterrassengebäude *n*

stepping, benching · Abtreppen *n* [*Fundament*]

stepping-off · liegende Verzahnung *f*, Abtreppung [*Mauerwerkbau*]

stereobate · Stereobat *m* [*Der zumeist aus Hausteinen hergestellte Kern eines Krepidoma*]

stereometric, three-dimensional, spatial, 3-D · räumlich, dreidimensional, stereometrisch

stereophony [*A process designed to produce the illusion of a spatial distribution of sound sources, by the use of two or more channels of information*] · Stereophonie *f*

stereotomy, stone-cutting · Fugenschnitt *m* [*Diejenige Bearbeitung der Werkstücke durch den Steinmetzen, wodurch sie sich in Mauern und Wölbungen ohne Verbindungsmittel halten*]

sterilization · Entkeimung *f*

~ **with dry heat** · Heißluftverfahren *n* [*Schädlingsbekämpfung*]

sterilizing room · Sterilisierraum *m*

stick-free, tack-free · klebfrei, nichtkleb(e)rig

to stick on · garnieren, zusammensetzen [*Steinzeugrohrindustrie*]

stickiness · Kleb(e)rigkeit *f*

sticking on · Zusammensetzen *n*, Garnieren [*Steinzeugrohrindustrie*]

~ **(together)** · Zusammenkleben *n* [*Die Bestreuung verhindert ein Zusammenkleben von Dachpappe beim Aufrollen*]

sticklac · Stocklack *m* [*Die Harzkruste samt umschlossenem Zweig*]

stick wax · Stangenwachs *n*

sticky, gummy · kleb(e)rig [*Anstrichmittel*]

~ **cement, stockhouse set** ~ [*Finished cement which develops low or zero flowability during or after storage in silos, or after transportation in bulk containers, hopper-bottom cars, etc., may be caused by (a) interlocking of particles; (b) mechanical compaction; (c) electrostatic attraction between particles*] · abgelagerter Zement *m*

stiction (US); **static friction** (Brit.) · Haftreibung *f*, Ruhereibung, statische Reibung

stiff → flexurally rigid

~ **connection** → rigid joint

~ **core, rigid** ~ · steifer Kern *m*

stiffened, braced · ausgesteift, versteift, verstärkt

stiffener, brace, bracing, stiffening member, bracing member, stay · Steife *f*, Versteifungsglied *n*, Verstärkungsglied, Aussteif(ungs)glied, Aussteif(ungs)-element *n*, Verstärkungselement, Versteifungselement

~ **angle, stiffening** ~, **reinforcing** ~, **bracing** ~ · Aussteif(ungs)winkel *m*, Versteifungswinkel, Verstärkungswinkel

stiffening, bracing, reinforcing [*The act of inserting braces into a structure*] · Absteifen *n*, Aussteifen, Versteifen, Verstärken

~, **bracing, reinforcing** [*The result of the act of inserting braces into a structure or gap site*] · Absteifung *f*, Aussteifung, Verstärkung, Versteifung

~ **against buckling, reinforcing** ~ ~, **bracing** ~ ~ · Knickaussteifung *f*, Knickversteifung, Knickverstärkung

~ **angle, reinforcing** ~, **bracing** ~, **stiffener** ~ · Aussteif(ungs)winkel *m*, Versteifungswinkel, Verstärkungswinkel

~ **beam** → reinforcing ~

~ **by diagonals, bracing** ~ ~, **reinforcing** ~ ~, **diagonal stiffening, diagonal bracing, diagonal reinforcing** · Diagonalversteifung *f*, Diagonalaussteifung, Diagonalverstärkung

~ **diaphragm** → reinforcing ~

~ **frame, reinforcing** ~, **bracing** ~ · Aussteif(ungs)rahmen *m*, Versteifungsrahmen, Verstärkungsrahmen

stiffening girder — stock door element

~ girder → reinforcing ~
~ iron, reinforcing ~, bracing ~ · Aussteif(ungs)eisen *n*, Verstärkungseisen, Versteifungseisen
~ member → stiffener
~ plate, reinforcing ~, bracing ~ · Aussteif(ungs)blech *n*, Versteifungsblech, Verstärkungsblech
~ purlin(e) → bracing ~
~ rib → reinforcing ~
~ ring → reinforcing ~
~ wall, reinforcing ~, bracing ~ · Aussteif(ungs)wand *f*, Versteifungswand, Verstärkungswand
stiff frame slab, stiff-jointed ~ ~, rigid ~ ~ · Steifrahmenplatte *f*
~ joint → rigid ~
stiff-jointed, rigid-jointed · steifknotig
stiff(-jointed) flat frame, ~ plane ~, ~ planar ~, rigid(-jointed) ~ ~ · steifknotiger ebener Rahmen *m*, ebener steifknotiger ~, ebener Rahmen mit starren Ecken
~ frame, rigid ~ · starrer Rahmen *m*, Steifrahmen
~ ~ slab, rigid ~ ~ · Steifrahmenplatte *f*
~ planar frame → ~ flat ~
stiff-leaf capital · Blätterkapital *n*, Blätterkapitell, Blattkapital, Blattkapitell
stiff mud process, wire-cut brickmaking · Strangpreßverfahren *n* [*Ziegelherstellung*]
stiffness, rigidity · Starrheit *f*, Steifigkeit [*Statik*]
~ → modulus of elasticity
~ **condition,** rigidity ~, condition of stiffness, condition of rigidity · Starrheitsbedingung *f*, Steifigkeitsbedingung [*Statik*]
~ **factor,** rigidity ~ · Steifigkeitsfaktor *m*, Starrheitsfaktor
~ **in torsion** → torsion(al) strength
~ **loss,** rigidity ~, loss of rigidity, loss of stiffness · Steifigkeitsverlust *m*, Starrheitsverlust
~ **matrix,** rigidity ~ · Steifigkeitsmatrix *f*, Starrheitsmatrix
~ **(~) method,** displacement ~ · Verrückungsverfahren *n*, Steifheitsmatrizenverfahren
stiff-plastic making, semi-plastic ~ · steifplastische Verformung *f* [*Feuerfestindustrie. Dieses Verfahren wird nur in bestimmten Ländern angewendet. Der Wassergehalt der Massen ist so gering, daß man nur Rohlinge (Batzen) formen kann, die danach die endgültige Form erhalten und gegebenenfalls nachgepreßt werden*]
stiff structure, rigid ~ · starres Bauwerk *n*, steifes ~
stile · Höhenfries *m* außen [*Holzfüllungstür*]

stiletto heel, spike ~ · Pfennigabsatz *m*
still air · stehende Luft *f*
stilted, surmounted · gestelzt, getulßt, überhoben, gebürstet [*Bogen oder Gewölbe, dessen Krümmung erst oberhalb einer über dem Kämpfergesims beginnenden Vertikalen aufsteigt*]
~ **arch,** surmounted ~ [*It has its springing line raised by vertical piers above the impost level*] · gestelzter Bogen *m*, gebürsteter ~, byzantinischer ~, gefußter ~, überhobener ~, Stelzbogen
~ **height** · Stelzungshöhe *f*
stilting · Stelzung *f* [*Die kurze Weiterführung der Senkrechten zwischen Kämpfer(gesims) oder Kapitell und Bogen- oder Gewölbekrümmung*]
stink trap → trap
stippled · kleingehämmert [*Kathedralglas*]
~ **pattern** · Tüpfelmuster *n*
stippling · Tüpfeln *n*
to stir · anrühren [*Farbe*]
stirrer, agitator · Rührwerk *n*
stirring, agitation, agitating · Auflockern *n* [*Masse durch Rühren*]
~, agitation, agitating · Nachmischen *n*, Rühren [*Transportbeton*]
~ **period,** ~ **time** · Rührdauer *f*
stirrup · Bügel *m*
to stitch · (ver)steppen
stitch rivet → tack ~
~ **riveting,** tack ~ · Heftnieten *n*
stitched · gesteppt
~ **(building) mat,** sewn (~) · versteppte (Bau)Matte *f*, ~ Dämmatte
~ **(~) quilt,** sewn (~) · ~ versteppte (Bau)Matte *f*, ~ Isoliermatte
stitching · (Ver)Steppung *f*
~ · (Ver)Steppen *n*
~, **tacking** [*Fixing a thing not securely*] · Heften *n*
stoa [*Long colonnaded portico of Hellenic days*] · Stoa *f*
Stoa of Attalos II. on the Agora at Athens · Stoa *f* König Attalos II. zu Athen, Attalos-Stoa
~ ~ **the Hermae** [*unexcavated*] · Stätte *f* der Herma-Halle [*Agora von Athen*]
~ ~ **Zeus Eleutherios** · Zeus- und Königshalle *f* [*Agora von Athen*]
~ **poikile** [*unexcavated*] · Stätte *f* der Stoa Poikile [*Agora von Athen*]
stoa-surrounded court · Säulenhallenhof *m*
stock, store · (Lager)Vorrat *m*, (Lager-) Bestand *m*
~ **control** · Dispositionssystem *n* [*Baustoffe*]
~ **door** → ~ machine-made ~
~ ~ **element,** ~ machine-made ~ ~, factory-built ~ ~, prefab(ricated) ~ ~ · Fertigtürelement *n*

stock heap — stone bolt

~ heap → ~ pile

Stockholm tar, Archangel ~, wood ~ · Holzteer *m*

stockhouse set cement, sticky ~ [*Finished cement which develops low or zero flowability during or after storage in silos, or after transportation in bulk containers, hopper-bottom cars etc., may be caused by (a) interlocking of particles; (b) mechanical compaction; (c) electrostatic attraction between particles*] · abgelagerter Zement *m*

stock-keeping → storage

stock (machine-made) door, factory-built ~, prefab(ricated) ~ · Fertigtür *f*

~ (~) ~ **element**, factory-built ~ ~, prefab(ricated) ~ ~ · Fertigtürelement *n*

~ **pile**, (storage) ~, (~) heap · Materialhalde *f*, (Vorrats)Halde

~ **size** · Lagergröße *f* [*Die Größe eines auf Lager vorrätigen Erzeugnisses*]

~ **stainless steel window**, standard ~ ~ ~ · Standard-Edelstahlfenster *n*

~ **timber window**, standard ~ ~, ~ wood(en) ~ · Standardholzfenster *n*, Holzstandardfenster

~ **type** [*As opposed to a customer-tailored type*] · Serientype *f*

~ **wood(en) window**, standard ~ ~, ~ timber ~ · Standardholzfenster *n*, Holzstandardfenster

stockyard · Viehhof *m*

Stoclet manison at Brussels · Palais *n* Stocklet in Brüssel

Stokes' formula, ~ law · Stokessches Gesetz *n*

stone [*A crystalline inclusion in glass*] · Stein(chen) *m*, (*n*)

~, natural ~ [*B.S. 1232*] · (Natur)Stein *m*, natürlicher Stein [*DIN 52100 bis 52112*]

~, building ~, structural ~ · (Bau)Stein *m*, Baugestein *n*, bautechnisches Gestein, Naturbaustein, natürlicher Baustein

~, (clay) body · (Ton)Scherben *m*, gebrannter Scherben

~ **aggregate**, ~ construction ~, mineral (construction) ~ · mineralischer Zuschlag(stoff) *m*, Zuschlag(stoff) aus Gestein, mineralisches Zuschlagmaterial *n*, Zuschlagmaterial aus Gestein

stone-aggregate concrete, natural aggregate ~, natural rock ~ · Beton *m* mit natürlichen Zuschlägen, ~ ~ natürlichem Zuschlagmaterial

stone altar, natural ~ ~ · (Natur)Steinaltar *m*

~ **altar piece** → (natural) stone altar screen

~ ~ **reredos** → (natural) stone altar screen

~ ~ **retable** → (natural) stone altar screen

~ ~ **screen** → natural ~ ~ ~

~ **(angle-)quoin**, natural ~ ~ · Eckquader *m*, Winkelquader

~ **arcade**, natural ~ ~ · (Natur)Steinarkade *f*

~ **arch**, natural ~ ~ · (Natur)Steinbogen *m*

(~) **ashlar**, (~) ashler; hewn stone, cut stone (US) · Haustein *m*, (Natur-)Werkstein, (natürlicher) Baustein [*Der nach einem Versatzplan mit bestimmtem Fugenschnitt bearbeitete Haustein. Als Parallelepiped „Quader(stein)" genannt*]

(~) ~ **arch**, (~) ashler ~; hewn stone ~, cut stone ~ (US) · Hausteinbogen *m*, (Natur)Werksteinbogen

(~) ~ **bond**, (~) ashler ~; hewn stone ~, cut stone ~ (US) · (Natur)Werksteinverband *m*, Hausteinverband

(~) ~ **bonder**, (~) ~ bondstone, (~) ashler ~, (~) ~ (bonding) header; hewn stone bonder, hewn stone (bonding) header, hewn stone bondstone, cut stone bonder, cut stone (bonding) header, cut stone bondstone (US) · Binderstein *m*, Blockstein [*Großer (Natur)Werkstein, der tief in die Mauer eingreift, um guten Verband zu erzielen*]

(~) ~ **masonry (work)**, (~) ashler ~ (~); hewn stone ~ (~), cut stone ~ (~) (US) · Hausteinmauerwerk *n*, (Natur)Werksteinmauerwerk

(~) ~ **slab**, (~) ashler ~; hewn stone ~, cut stone ~ (US) · (Natur)Werksteinplatte *f*, Hausteinplatte

(~) ~ **structure**, (~) ashler ~; hewn stone ~, cut stone ~ (US) · (Natur-)Werksteinbau(werk) *m*, (*n*), Hausteinbau(werk)

(~) ~ **vault**, (~) ashler ~; hewn stone ~, cut stone ~ (US) · (Natur)Werksteingewölbe *n*, Hausteingewölbe

(~) ~ **window**, (~) ashler ~; hewn stone ~, cut stone ~ (US) · (Natur-)Werksteinfenster *n*, Hausteinfenster

~ **balcony**, natural ~ ~ · (Natur)Steinbalkon *m*

~ **baluster**, ~ ban(n)ister, natural ~ ~ · (Natur)Steinbaluster *m*

~ **bar** · Maßwerkstab *m*

~ **barrel vault** → natural ~ ~ ~

~ **beam**, natural ~ ~ · (Natur)Steinbalken(träger) *m*

~ **bench**, natural ~ ~ · (Natur)Steinbank *f*

~ **block masonry (work)**, (natural) stone ~ (~), (natural) stone blockwork · Steinblockmauerwerk *n*, (Natur-)Steinmauerwerk [*DIN 1053*]

stone-block paving → natural ~ ~ ~

stone blockwork → (natural) stone masonry (work)

~ **bolt**, rag ~ · Klauenschraube *f*, Steinschraube

stone bond — stone flour

~ **bond** → natural ~ ~

~ **boundary wall**, natural ~ ~ ~ · Stein-Grundstückmauer f, Natur~

~ **bracket** → (natural) stone corbel

~ **building**, stone-built ~, natural ~ ~ · (Natur)Steingebäude n

~ ~ **material**, ~ construction(al) ~, natural ~ ~ ~ · (Natur)Steinbaustoff m; (Natur)Steinbaumaterial n [Schweiz]

stone-built building, stone ~, natural ~ ~ · (Natur)Steingebäude n

stone bull · Stierstatue f

~ **capping** → natural ~ ~

~ ~ **slab**, ~ coping ~, natural ~ ~ ~ · (Ab)Deckplatte f aus Naturstein, (Natur)Stein(ab)deckplatte

~ **carving**, natural ~ ~, curved work · nichtgeradlinige (Natur)Steinbearbeitung f

~ **castle**, natural ~ ~ · (Natur)Steinburg f

~ **chip(ping)s**, natural ~ ~ · (Natur-)Steinkörnungen fpl

~ ~, natural ~ ~; (natural) stone screening(s) [deprecated] · (Naturstein-)Splitt m, Steinsplitt

~ **church**, natural ~ ~ · (Natur)Steinkirche f

~ **circle** → cromlech

~ **cladding** → ~ slab ~

~ **column**, natural ~ ~ · (Natur)Steinsäule f

~ **concrete aggregate**, mineral ~ ~ · Betonzuschlag(stoff) m aus Gestein, Betonzuschlagmaterial n ~ ~, mineralischer Betonzuschlag(stoff), mineralisches Betonzuschlagmaterial

~ **(construction) aggregate**, mineral (~) ~ · mineralischer Zuschlag(stoff) m, Zuschlag(stoff) aus Gestein, mineralisches Zuschlagmaterial n, Zuschlagmaterial aus Gestein

~ ~ **method** → natural ~ ~ ~

~ **construction(al) material**, ~ building ~, natural ~ ~ ~ · (Natur)Steinbaustoff m; (Natur)Steinbaumaterial n [Schweiz]

~ **coping** → natural ~ ~

~ ~ **slab**, ~ capping ~, natural ~ ~ ~ · (Ab)Deckplatte f aus Naturstein, (Natur)Stein(ab)deckplatte

~ **corbel** → natural ~ ~

~ **course** → natural ~ ~

~ **cradle vault**, ~ cylindrical ~, natural ~ ~ ~ · walzenförmiges (Natur)Steingewölbe n, zylindrisches ~

~ **cross**, natural ~ ~ · (Natur)Steinkreuz n

~ **crushing strength**, (clay) body ~ · Scherbendruckfestigkeit f

~ **curb** → natural ~ ~

~ **curtain (wall)**, natural ~ ~ (~) · (Natur)Steinkurtine f

~ **curving**, natural ~ ~, curved work · nichtgerad(linig)e (Natur)Steinbearbeitung f

~ **cutter**, ~ dresser, scabbler, squarer, block chopper · Steinmetz m [Handwerker, der Werksteine zurichtet]

~ **cutting**, natural ~ ~, straight-line work · gerad(linig)e (Natur)Steinbearbeitung f

~ ~, stereotomy · Fugenschnitt m [Diejenige Bearbeitung der Werkstücke durch den Steinmetzen, wodurch sie sich in Mauern und Wölbungen ohne Verbindungsmittel halten]

~ **cylindrical vault**, ~ cradle ~, natural ~ ~ ~ · walzenförmiges (Natur)Steingewölbe n, zylindrisches ~

~ **discharge gutter** → (natural) stone drain(age) ~

~ **(door) threshold**, natural ~ (~) ~ · (Natur)Stein(tür)schwelle f

~ **drain(age) gutter** → natural ~ ~ ~

~ **draining gutter** → natural ~ ~ ~

~ **dressed ready for building**, natural ~ ~ ~ ~ ~ · baugerechter (Natur-)Stein m

~ **dresser**, ~ cutter, scabbler, squarer, block chopper · Steinmetz m [Handwerker, der Werksteine zurichtet]

~ **dresser's sign** · Steinmetzzeichen n

~ **dressing plant**, natural ~ ~ · (Natur)Steinbearbeitungswerk n

~ ~ **work**, ~ hewing ~, ~ milling ~, ~ shaping ~ · Steinmetzarbeit(en) f(pl)

~ **dust**, rock ~, ~ flour, powder(ed) mineral, mineral powder · Staub m, Gesteins~, Blume f, Steinmehl n, Gesteinsmehl, Steinstaub, Mineralmehl, Mineralstaub, Mineralpulver n

~ ~ → (natural) stone filler

~ **façade**, natural ~ ~ · (Natur)Steinfassade f

(~) **face slab** (US) → (~) facing ~

stone-faced concrete panel · steinverblendete Betontafel f

~ **rubble masonry** · Kopfmauerwerk n

stone facing → ~ (slab) cladding

(~) ~ **slab** (Brit.); (~) face ~ (US) [Stone facing slabs may be of natural, (pre)cast or artificial stone] · (Ver-)Blendplatte f, Vorsatzplatte, Sichtplatte, Frontplatte

~ **female figure**, natural ~ ~ ~ · weibliche (Natur)Steinfigur f

~ **figure**, natural ~ ~ · (Natur)Steinfigur f

~ **filler** → natural ~ ~

~ **finish** → natural ~ ~

~ **finishing**, natural ~ ~ · Steinnachbearbeitung f, Natur~

~ **floor cover(ing)** → natural ~ ~ ~

~ **floor(ing)** → (natural) stone floor cover(ing)

~ **flour** → ~ dust

stone font — stone spire

~ **font** → natural ~ ~
~ **footing**, natural ~ ~ · (Natur)Steinfundament *n*
~ **footpath (paving) flag** (Brit.) → (natural) stone sidewalk (~) ~
~ **foundation**, natural ~ ~ · (Natur-)Steingründung *f*
~ **frieze**, natural ~ ~ · (Natur)Steinfries *m*
~ **grille**, natural ~ ~ · (Natur)Steingitter *n*
~ **hewing work**, ~ milling ~, ~ shaping ~, ~ dressing ~ · Steinmetzarbeit(en) *f(pl)*
~ **hinge**, natural ~ ~ · (Natur)Steingelenk *n*
~ **house** → (natural) stone building
~ **hut** · Steinhütte *f*
~ **keep**, natural stone keep · Steinbelfried *m*, Steinbergfried, Natur~
~ **kerb** → natural ~ ~
~ **layer** → (natural) stone course
stone-like, natural ~ · (natur)steinähnlich
stone lime → high-calcium ~
~ **lining** → ~ (slab) cladding
~ ~ → (natural) stone (slab) (sur-)facing
~ ~ **of the opaion** · Nabelkranz *m* [*Kuppelauge*]
~ **lintol** → natural ~ ~
~ **male figure**, natural ~ ~ ~ · männliche (Natur)Steinfigur *f*
~ **masonry (work)** → (natural) ~ ~
(stone) mason's lodge · Bauhütte *f*
(~) ~ **mark** · Steinmetzzeichen *n*
stone matting, natural ~ ~ · (Natur-)Steinmatte *f*
~ **milling work**, ~ shaping ~, ~ dressing ~, ~ hewing ~ · Steinmetzarbeit(en) *f(pl)*
~ **mosaic** → natural ~ ~
~ **mullion(ed) window**, natural ~ ~ ~ · (Natur)Steinpfostenfenster *n*, (Natur)Steinkreuzfenster
~ **of one-quarter brick size**, natural ~ ~ ~ ~ ~ · (Natur)Steinriemchen *n*
~ **Order**, natural ~ ~ · (Natur)Steinsäulenordnung *f*
~ **(ornamental) string (course)**, natural ~ (~) ~ (~) · (Natur)Steingurt(ge)sims *m*, (*n*)
~ **paving** → (natural) stone (sett) ~
~ (~) **sett** → (natural) ~ (~) ~
~ **pier**, natural ~ ~ · (Natur)Steinpfeiler *m*
~ **pillar**, natural ~ ~ · (Natur)Steinfreipfeiler *m*
~ **plaster**, stuc · Stein(ver)putz *m*

~ ~ **mix(ture)**, ~ ~ stuff, stuc ~ · Steinputzmasse *f*, Steinputzmörtel *m*
~ ~ **stuff**, ~ ~ mix(ture), stuc ~ · Steinputzmasse *f*, Steinputzmörtel *m*
~ **portal**, natural ~ ~ · (Natur)Steinportal *n*
~ **preservative** → natural ~ ~
~ **preserving agent** → natural ~ ~ ~
~ **pulpit**, natural ~ ~ · (Natur)Steinkanzel *f*, Naturkanzel
~ **quoin**, ~ angle-quoin, natural stone ~ · Eckquader *m*, Winkelquader
~ **railing**, natural ~ ~ · (Natur)Steingeländer *n*
~ **rib** · Maßwerkrippe *f*
~ **rib(bed) cupola** → natural ~ ~ ~
~ ~ **dome** → natural ~ ~ ~
stone-ribbed vault → natural ~ ~
stone roof → natural ~ ~
~ ~ **spire**, natural ~ ~ ~ · (Natur-)Stein-Dachreiter *m*
~ **(roof(ing)) tile**, natural ~ (~) ~ · Natursteindachstein *m*
~ **row; alignment** (Brit.); **alinement** (US) [*A megalithic monument*] · Steinreihe *f*
~ **sand**, crushed stone ~, artificial ~, manufactured ~, (stone) screening(s), crusher screening(s) · Steinsand *m*, Brechsand [*Er umfaßt in den USA den Kornstufenbereich 0–4,76 mm*]
(~) **screening(s)**, crusher ~, artificial sand, manufactured sand, stone sand, crushed stone sand · Steinsand *m*, Brechsand [*Er umfaßt in den USA den Kornstufenbereich 0–4,76 mm*]
~ ~ [*deprecated*] → (natural) stone chip(ping)s
~ **sculpture**, natural ~ ~, sculpture in (natural) stone · (Natur)Steinplastik *f*, (Natur)Steinskulptur *f*
~ **sett** → (natural) stone (paving) ~
~ (~) **paving** → natural ~ (~) ~
~ **shaping work**, ~ milling ~, ~ dressing ~, ~ hewing ~ · Steinmetzarbeit(en) *f(pl)*
~ **shoulder** → (natural) stone corbel
~ **sidewalk (paving) flag** (US) → natural ~ ~ (~) ~
~ **slab**, natural ~ ~ · (Natur)Steinplatte *f*
~ (~) **cladding**, ~ (~) lining, ~ (~) (sur)facing, natural ~ (~) ~ · (Natur-)Stein(platten)auskleidung *f*, (Natur-)Stein(platten)verkleidung, (Natur-)Stein(platten)verblendung, (Natur-)Stein(platten)bekleidung
~ (~) **facing** → ~ (~) cladding
~ ~ **floor(ing) (finish)** → (natural) ~ ~ ~ (~)
~ (~) **lining** → ~ (~) cladding
~ ~ **roof(ing)** → natural ~ ~ ~
~ (~) **(sur)facing** → ~ (~) cladding
~ **spire** · Stein(turm)helm *m*

stone stair(case) — stoneware tank

- ~ **stair(case)** → natural ~ ~
- ~ **step,** natural ~ ~, stepstone · (Natur)Steinstufe *f*
- ~ **strength,** natural ~ ~ · (Natur)Steinfestigkeit *f*
- ~ **string (course),** ~ ornamental ~ (~), natural stone ornamental ~ (~) · (Natur)Steingurt(ge)sims *m*, (*n*)
- ~ **structure,** natural ~ ~ · (Natur-)Steinbauwerk *n*
- ~ **(sur)facing** → ~ (slab) cladding
- ~ **table altar** → natural ~ ~ ~
- ~ **temple,** natural ~ ~ · Steintempel *m*, Natur~
- ~ **threshold,** natural ~ ~ · Steinschwelle *f*, Natur~
- ~ **throne** → natural ~ ~
- ~ **tile,** (natural) stone (roof(ing)) ~ · Natursteindachstein *m*
- ~ **tomb** · Steinkammer *f* [*Eine vorgeschichtliche Grabkammer aus Steinen und darüber aufgeschüttetem Erdhügel*]
- ~ **transom** · Kämpferstein *m* [*steinerne Ausführung eines Fensterkämpfers*]
- ~ **tunnel vault** → natural ~ ~ ~
- ~ **two-sided town gateway,** ~ ~ city ~, natural ~ ~ ~ ~ · (Natur)Steinstadttor *n*
- ~ **vault,** natural ~ ~ · (Natur)Steingewölbe *n*
- **stone-vaulted ceiling,** natural ~ ~ · (Natur)Steingewölbedecke *f*
- ~ **roof,** natural ~ ~ · (Natur)Steingewölbedach *n*
- **stone vaulting,** natural ~ ~ · (Natur-)Steinüberwölbung *f*, (Natur)Steineinwölbung
- ~ **wagon vault** → natural ~ ~ ~
- ~ **wall,** natural ~ ~ · (Natur)Steinmauer *f*, Steinblockmauer
- ~ ~ **plaster** → (natural) ~ ~ ~
- ~ ~ **tile** → natural ~ ~ ~
- ~ **with rough-hewn face** · Bosse(nstein) *f*, (*m*) [*Haustein mit unbearbeiteter Sichtfläche*]
- **stoneware** [*A heavy ceramic ware, commonly used for chemical containers and conduits, consisting of a nonporous vitrified body with or without an impervious glaze which is usually transparent*] · Steinzeug *n*
- ~ **article,** ~ product · Steinzeugartikel *m*, Steinzeugerzeugnis *n*, Steinzeuggegenstand *m*
- ~ **ceiling tile** · Steinzeugdecken(belag)-platte *f*, Steinzeugdeckenfliese *f*
- ~ **discharge gutter,** ~ draining ~, ~ drain(age) ~ · Steinzeugabflußrinne *f*, Steinzeugentwässerungsrinne, Steinzeugablaufrinne
- ~ ~ **pipe,** ~ draining ~, ~ drain(age) ~, ~ waste (~) · Steinzeugabflußrohr *n*, Steinzeugablaufrohr, Steinzeugentwässerungsrohr, Steinzeugdränrohr [*Fehlnamen: Steinzeugabfluß m, Steinzeugablauf m*]
- ~ **drain(age) gutter,** ~ draining ~, ~ discharge ~ · Steinzeugabflußrinne *f*, Steinzeugentwässerungsrinne, Steinzeugablaufrinne
- ~ ~ **pipe,** ~ draining ~, ~ discharge ~, ~ waste (~) · Steinzeugabflußrohr *n*, Steinzeugablaufrohr, Steinzeugentwässerungsrohr, Steinzeugdränrohr, [*Fehlnamen: Steinzeugablauf m, Steinzeugabfluß m*]
- ~ **facing** → ~ sur~
- ~ **factory,** ~ plant · Steinzeugfabrik *f*, Steinzeugwerk *n*
- ~ **filter** · Steinzeugfilter *m*, *n*
- ~ **fitting** → ~ pipe ~
- ~ **floor cover(ing) tile,** ~ floor finish ~, ~ floor(ing) ~ · Steinzeug-(Fuß-)Bodenfliese *f*, Steinzeug-(Fuß)Bodenplatte *f*
- ~ **for sewer pipes** · Abwasserrohrsteinzeug *n*, Kanal(isations)steinzeug
- ~ **goods** · Steinzeugware(n) *f*(*pl*)
- ~ **gutter** → ~ roof ~
- ~ ~ · Steinzeugsohlschale *f* [*DIN 1230*]
- ~ **half-pipe** · Steinzeughalbschale *f*
- ~ **joint(ing) compound** → ~ sewer ~ ~
- ~ **junction** · Steinzeugabzweig(er) *m*, Steinzeugabzweigung *f*
- ~ **lining,** ~ (sur)facing · Steinzeugauskleidung *f*, Steinzeugverkleidung, Steinzeugbekleidung
- ~ **mosaic** · Steinzeugmosaik *n*
- ~ **pipe** · Steinzeugrohr *n* [*DIN 1230*]
- ~ **(~) fitting** [*Anything fitted to a stoneware pipe for jointing, connecting or changing the direction or bore of a stoneware pipe*] · Steinzeug(rohr)fitting *m*, Steinzeug(rohr)formstück *n* [*DIN 1230*]
- ~ ~ **joint cement,** ~ (sewer) joint(ing) compound · Steinzeugrohr-Füllmasse *f*, Steinzeugrohr-Vergußmasse
- ~ **plant,** ~ factory · Steinzeugfabrik *f*, Steinzeugwerk *n*
- ~ **product,** ~ article · Steinzeugartikel *m*, Steinzeugerzeugnis *n*, Steinzeuggegenstand *m*
- ~ **(roof) gutter,** ~ rainwater ~ · Steinzeug(dach)rinne *f*, Steinzeugregenrinne
- ~ **(sewer) joint(ing) compound,** ~ pipe joint cement · Steinzeugrohr-Füllmasse *f*, Steinzeugrohr-Vergußmasse
- ~ **small(-sized) mosaic** · Steinzeug-Kleinmosaik *n*
- ~ **spigot and socket pipe** · Steinzeugmuffenrohr *n* [*DIN 4250*]
- ~ **(sur)facing,** ~ lining · Steinzeugauskleidung *f*, Steinzeugverkleidung, Steinzeugbekleidung
- ~ **tank** · Steinzeugbehälter *m*

stoneware tile — storage warmer

~ **tile** · Steinzeug(belag)platte f, Steinzeugfliese f [DIN 1230]

~ ~ **floor cover(ing)**, ~ ~ floor(ing) (finish) · Steinzeugfliesen(fuß)boden(belag) m, Steinzeugplatten(fuß)boden(belag), Fbsz m

~ **waste (pipe)**, ~ discharge ~, ~ draining ~, ~ drain(age) ~ · Steinzeugabflußrohr n, Steinzeugablaufrohr, Steinzeugentwässerungsrohr, Steinzeugdränrohr [Fehlnamen: Steinzeugablauf m, Steinzeugabfluß m]

stone window sill → natural ~ ~ ~

stonework, dressed ~, milled ~, hewn ~, shaped ~ · zugerichtete Werksteine mpl, behauene ~, bearbeitete ~

~ **decorative finish**, ~ ~ feature, ~ ornamental ~, ~ decoration, ~ enrichment · (Natur)Steinschmuck m, (Natur)Steinverzierung f

~ **enrichment** → ~ decorative finish

~ **ornamental finish** → ~ decorative ~

stony clay, boulder ~ · Geschiebeton m

stop · Anschlag m

~ **chamfer**, stopped ~ · Kehlhalt m [Im Early English und wieder in viktorianischer Zeit gebräuchlicher Abschluß einer Fase, wobei die Ecke des abgefasten Baustückes wieder an den rechten Winkel zurückgeführt wird; auch in der kontinentalen Neugotik gebräuchlich]

stop-end waterbar → construction waterstop

~ **waterstop** → construction ~

stopper, stopping, filler; spactling compound, Swedish putty (US) · Ausfüller m, (Füll)Spachtel(masse) m, (f) [Spachtel ist ein stark pigmentierter und/oder gefüllter Anstrichstoff, vorwiegend zum Ausgleichen von Unebenheiten des Untergrundes. Der Spachtel kann zieh-, streich- oder spritzbar eingestellt werden. Die getrocknete Spachtelschicht muß schleifbar sein. Nach der Zusammensetzung unterscheidet man z.B. Leimspachtel, Dispersionsspachtel, Ölspachtel, Lackspachtel, Nitrocellulosespachtel]

~ ~ → pipe ~

~ **bending tester**, stopping ~ ~, filler ~ ~; spactling compound ~ ~, Swedish putty ~ ~ (US) · (Füll)Spachtel(masse)biegeprüfer m, Ausfüllerbiegeprüfer

~ **coat** → stopping ~

~ **for brush application** → filler ~ ~ ~

~ **gypsum**, stopping ~, filler ~ · Spachtelgips m

~ **powder**, stopping ~, filler ~ · Ausfüllerpulver n, (Füll)Spachtelpulver

~ **seal(ing)**, stopping ~, filler ~; spactling compound ~, Swedish putty ~ (US) · (Füll)Spachtel(masse)(ab)dichtung f, Ausfüller(ab)dichtung

stopping → stopper

~ [Filling cracks and nail holes with putty painting] · Ausspachteln n

~ **bending tester** → stopper ~ ~

~ **coat**, stopper ~, filler ~; spactling compound ~, Swedish putty ~ (US) · (Füll)Spachtel(masse)lage f, (Füll-)Spachtel(masse)schicht f, Ausfüllerlage, Ausfüllerschicht

~ **for brush application** → filler ~ ~ ~

~ **gypsum**, stopper ~, filler ~ · Spachtelgips m

~ **powder**, stopper ~, filler ~ · Spachtelpulver n, Füll~, Ausfüllerpulver

~ **seal(ing)** → stopper ~

storage, stock-keeping · (Ein)Lagern n, (Ein)Lagerung f, (Auf)Speicherung, Bevorratung, Materiallagerung, Lagerhaltung

stor(ag)e area · Lagerfläche f

~ **block**, ~ unit · Lagertrakt m

storage block, ~ element · Speicherblock m [Nachtstromspeicherheizung]

~ **calorifier**, ~ water heater, cylinder · Speicher-Warmwasserbereiter m

stor(ag)e cellar · Lagerkeller m, Vorratskeller

storage chamber → (refuse) collecting ~

stor(ag)e chamber · Magazinraum m

storage cistern [A cistern for storing water] · Zisterne f

(~) **cylinder** · (Innen)Kessel m [Heißwasserspeicher]

~ **element**, ~ block · Speicherblock m [Nachtstromspeicherheizung]

~ **fire** → ~ heater

~ **geyser** → ~-type ~

(~) **heap** → stock pile

~ **heater**, ~ warmer, ~ fire · Speicherheiz(ungs)gerät n, Speicherheizer m, Speichererhitzer

~ ~ → (electric) block ~ ~

~ **heating**, thermal ~ ~ · Speicherheizung f

~ **of samples** · Probenlagerung f

~ ~ **water**, water storage · Wasserbevorratung f, Wasserspeicherung

~ **period** · Lagerdauer f, Lagerzeit f

(~) **pile** → stock ~

~ **principle** · Speicherprinzip n

stor(ag)e room · Lager(raum) n, (m), Vorratsraum

~ **shed** · Lagerschuppen m

~ **space** · Lager(ungs)raum m

~ **tank** · Vorratsbehälter m, Lagerbehälter

storage(-type) geyser · Badspeicher m, Vorratswasserheizer

stor(ag)e unit, ~ block · Lagertrakt m

storage warehouse (building) [As opposed to a wholesale warehouse (building)] · Nur-Lagergebäude n

~ **warmer** → ~ heater

storage water heater — storm window frame

~ **water heater**, ~ calorifier, cylinder · Speicher-Warmwasserbereiter *m*

~ ~ **heating** · Speicherwassererhitzung *f*, Speicherwassererwärmung

~ **yard** · Lagerhof *m*

~ ~ · Lagerplatz *m*

to store · (ein)lagern (auf)speichern, bevorraten

~ ~, **to age** · altern, verwittern, „wettern" [*Steinzeugindustrie*]

store, stock · (Lager)Vorrat *m*, (Lager-)Bestand *m*

~ · Lager *n*, Magazin *n*

~ **area**, storage ~ · Lagerfläche *f*

~ **block**, ~ unit, storage ~ · Lagertrakt *m*

~ **cellar**, storage ~ · Lagerkeller *m*, Vorratskeller

~ **chamber**, storage ~ · Magazinraum *m*

stored heat, retained ~ · gespeicherte Wärme *f*, Speicherwärme

~ **material** · Lagergut *n*

store equipment room, cleaning ~ ~ · Abstellraum *m*, Putzraum, Geräteraum

~ **front**, shop ~ · Schaufensterfront *f*, Ladenfront

~ ~ **profile** → shop front section

~ ~ **section** → shop ~ ~

~ ~ **trim** → shop front section

~ ~ **unit** → shop front section

storekeeper · Lagerhalter *m*, Magazinhalter, Lagerverwalter, Magazinverwalter

store room, storage ~ · Lager(raum) *n*, (*m*), Vorratsraum

~ ~, household ~ ~, (household) cleaning equipment ~ · Abstellraum *m*, Putzraum, (Haus)Geräteraum

~ **shed**, storage ~ · Lagerschuppen *m*

~ **space**, storage ~ · Lager(ungs)raum *m*

~ **tank**, storage ~ · Vorratsbehälter *m*, Lagerbehälter

~ **unit**, ~ block, storage ~ · Lagertrakt *m*

storey (Brit.); story (US); floor · Geschoß *n*, Etage *f*, Stock(werk) *m*, (*n*)

~ **branch** (Brit.); story ~ (US); floor ~ · Stockwerkleitung *f*, Etagenleitung, Geschoßleitung [*Die von einer Steigleitung innerhalb eines Stockwerkes abzweigende Verbrauchsleitung*]

~ **(floor) height** (Brit.); story (~) ~ (US) [*The height between the upper reference floor planes of adjacent zones, i.e. from the top of the floor finish in each case*] · Etagenhöhe *f*, Stockwerkhöhe, Geschoßhöhe [*DIN 4174. Geschoßhöhen im Industriebau DIN 4171*]

~ **frame** (Brit.); story ~ (US) · Stockwerkrahmen *m*, Etagenrahmen, Geschoßrahmen

~ **(ground(-))plan** (Brit.); story ~ (US); floor ~, ~ base · Stockwerkgrundriß *m*, Etagengrundriß, Geschoßgrundriß

~ **height** (Brit.); story ~ (US); floor ~ [*The vertical distance from a finished floor level to the next finished floor level*] · Stockwerkhöhe *f*, Etagenhöhe, Geschoßhöhe

storey-height cladding panel (Brit.); story-height ~ ~ (US); vertical ~ ~ [*It spans vertically between floors from which it obtains support*] · senkrechte (Außenwand)Versteifungstafel *f*

~ **form(work)** (Brit.) → large panel shuttering

~ **panel** (Brit.); story-height ~ (US); large ~ · Großtafel *f*

~ ~ **construction** (Brit.); story-height ~ ~ (US); large ~ ~ · Großtafelbau *m*

~ ~ **wall** (Brit.) → large ~ ~

~ ~ ~ **block** (Brit.) → large panel wall building

~ ~ ~ **building** (Brit.) → large ~ ~ ~

~ ~ ~ **structure** (Brit.) → large panel wall building

~ ~ ~ **system** (Brit.) → large ~ ~ ~

~ **shuttering** (Brit.) → large panel ~

storey landing (Brit.); story ~ (US); floor ~ · Stockwerkpodest *n*, *m*, Etagenpodest, Geschoßpodest, Etagenabsatz *m*, Geschoßabsatz, Stockwerkabsatz [*in Österreich nur n*]

~ **level** (Brit.); story ~ (US); floor ~ · Stockwerkebene *f*, Etagenebene, Geschoßebene

~ **plan** → ~ ground(-)~

~ **post and beams** (Brit.); story post and beams (US); post and beam construction, post-and-lintel construction · Ständerbau *m*

~ **wall** (Brit.); story ~ (US) · Geschoßwand *f*, Etagenwand, Stockwerkwand

storm door, weather ~ [*An additional inner door, used in winter, to insulate a house from hard weather*] · Wintertür *f*

~ **drain** · Regen(wasser)drän *m*

~ ~ **system** · Regen(wasser)entwässerung *f*

~ **lane** · Windgasse *f*

~ **sewage** · Regenabwasser *n*

~ **sewer** · Regenabwasserleitung *f*

~ **water**, rainwater, R.W. [*Excess water during rainfall or continuously following and resulting therefrom*] · Regenwasser *n*

~ **window**, outside ~, external ~, exterior ~, outer ~, ~ sash [*A window with an air space between it and the inner window*] · Außenfenster *n* [*bei einem Doppelfenster*]

~ ~ **frame**, outside ~ ~, exterior ~ ~, external ~ ~, outer ~ ~ · Außenfensterrahmen *m*

story — straight-sided quire

story (US) → storey
~ landing (US) → storey ~
~ wall (US); storey ~ (Brit.) · Geschoßwand f, Etagenwand, Stockwerkwand
storytelling wallpaper · Märchenbildertapete f
stoup, holy water basin [*A vessel to contain holy water, sometimes freestanding, but usually fixed to, or carved out of, a wall placed near the door of a church*] · Weihwasserbecken n
stove → domestic ~
~ and range work · Ofen- und Herdarbeiten fpl [*DIN 18362*]
~ connection, domestic ~ ~ · (Haushalt)Ofenanschluß m, Heizofenanschluß
~ dried · ofengetrocknet
~ drying · Ofentrocknung f
stove-drying · ofentrocknend
stove-enamelled (Brit.); stove-enameled (US) · ofenemailliert
stove heating · Lokalheizung f, örtliche Heizung, Ofenheizung [*Die Erwärmung von Räumen durch Einzelöfen 1. Kamin, 2. Kachelofen, 3. eiserner Ofen*]
~ pipe, smoke ~, ~ tube, chimney connector · Rauchrohr n, Ofenrohr [*DIN 1298*]
~ ~ casing, domestic ~ ~ ~ · Rohrfutter n [*(Haushalt)Ofen*]
~ size, domestic ~ ~ · (Haushalt)Ofengröße f, Heizofengröße
(~) tile · (Ofen)Kachel f [*DIN 409*]
~ tube → ~ pipe
stoved aluminium paint, baked ~ ~ (Brit.); ~ aluminum ~ (US) · Einbrennaluminiumfarbe f
~ resin, baked ~ · Einbrennharz n
stoving, baking [*The process of drying and hardening a paint coating by heating, usually at a temperature above 150°F*] · Einbrennen n, Ofentrocknung f
~ enamel, baking ~, baked ~, ~ industrial ~ · Einbrennemail(le) n, (f), Ofenemail(le), Einbrennschmelz(glas) m, (n), Ofenschmelz(glas)
~ filler, baking ~, ~ filling composition · Einbrennfüller m
~ (industrial) enamel, baking (~) ~, baked (~) ~ · Einbrennemail(le) n, (f), Ofenemail(le), Einbrennschmelz(glas) m, (n), Ofenschmelz(glas)
~ oven, baking ~ · Einbrennofen m
~ paint, baking ~ · Einbrennfarbe f
~ quality, baking ~ · Einbrenngüte f
~ stopper, baking ~ · Einbrennspachtel(masse) m, (f) [*Anstrichtechnik*]
~ temperature, baking ~ · Einbrenntemperatur f
~ varnish, baking ~ · Einbrennlack m, ofentrocknender Lack

straight arch (lintel), flat ~ (~), jack ~ (~), camber (~); floor ~ (~) (US) · scheitrechter Bogen m, gerader ~, Geradbogen, scheitrechter Sturz m, Sturzbogen, Horizontalbogen, Scheitrechtsturz [*Trotz waagerechter Untersicht ein echter Bogen, d.h. die Fugen weisen zu einem angenommenen gemeinsamen Mittelpunkt*]
~ barrel vault, ~ tunnel ~, ~ wagon(-head) ~ · gerade Tonne f, Kufengewölbe n, (gerades) Tonnengewölbe, Zylindergewölbe, Sichelgewölbe, zylindrisches Gewölbe
~ box beam · gerader Kastenbalken(-träger) m
~ cap vault · scheitrechtes Kappengewölbe n
~ (clay) brick lintel; ~ (~) ~ lintol [*deprecated*] · Scheitrechtziegelsturz m, Geradziegelsturz, Scheitrechtziegeloberschwelle f, Geradziegeloberschwelle
~ curb; ~ kerb (Brit.) · gerader Bordstein m
straight-ended choir, ~ quire · gerader geschlossener Chor m
straight(-flight) stair(case), straight flight · gerad(läufig)e Treppe f, geradlinige ~, geradarmige ~, Treppe mit geradem Lauf, Treppe mit geradem Arm
straight generator · gerad(linig)e Erzeugende f
~ kerb (Brit.); ~ curb · gerader Bordstein m
straight-line block, ~ building, slab-type ~ · Scheibenhaus n
~ work, (natural) stone cutting · gerad(linig)e (Natur)Steinbearbeitung f
straight pipe · gerades Rohr n
~ ramp · gerade Rampe f
straight-run asphalt (US); ~ (asphaltic-)bitumen (Brit.) · Destillationsbitumen n, destilliertes Bitumen [*Destillierte Bitumen sind die bei der Destillation gewonnenen weichen bis mittelharten Bitumen*]
straight run coal tar, coal tar pitch [*B.S. 1210*] · Steinkohlenteerpech n [*DIN 55946*]
~ ~ ~ ~ dispersion, coal tar pitch ~ · Steinkohlenteerpechdispersion f
~ ~ ~ ~ emulsion, coal tar pitch ~ · Steinkohlenteerpechemulsion f [*Sie besteht aus feinstverteiltem Steinkohlenteerweichpech und Wasser*]
~ ~ ~ ~ solution, coal tar pitch ~ · Steinkohlenteerpechlösung f
straight-sided choir, ~ quire · Langchor m
~ column [*As opposed to a tapered column*] · parallele Säule f [*im Gegensatz zur konischen Säule*]
~ quire, ~ choir · Langchor m

straight sliding shutter door, ~ ~ shutterdoor · gerades Schiebetor *n* [*im Gegensatz zum Rundlauftor*]

~ stair(case) → ~-flight ~

~ tongueing and grooving · quadratische Spundung *f*

~ tunnel vault → ~ barrel ~

~ vault, flat ~, jack ~; floor ~ (US) · scheitrechtes Gewölbe *n*, gerades ~, Geradgewölbe, Sturzgewölbe, Horizontalgewölbe

~ wagon vault → ~ barrel ~

straightening coat → floating ~

~ of the girder lying flatwise · Flachkantrichten *n* des Trägers

strain [*Change in the dimensions or shape of a body per unit length or angle. A shear strain is a distortion caused by shear stresses. A direct strain is an elongation or shortening caused by tensile or compressive stresses respectively. Strains may be elastic or inelastic*] · Dehnung *f*

~ compatibility · Dehn(ungs)verträglichkeit *f*

~ distribution · Dehnungsverteilung *f*

~ energy · Dehn(ungs)energie *f*

~ ~ method → Castigliano's theorem

~ field · Dehn(ungs)feld *n*

~ hardening · Kaltverfestigung *f* [*Metall*]

~ rate, rate of strain · Dehn(ungs)geschwindigkeit *f*

~ system · Dehnungssystem *n*

strainer · Kieshaube *f*

~ · Sieb *n*

strainhardened, strengthened by cold working · kaltverfestigt

straining beam, ~ piece, strutting piece · Sprengstrebe *f*

Stramit partition (wall) in timber framing · Stramit-Zwischenwand *f*, Stramit-Trennwand [*Zwischenwand aus Halmplankplatten aus gepreßtem Stroh, die allseitig mit Papier verkleidet sind*]

~ (slab) · Stramitplatte *f*

strand → (pre)stressing ~

~ [B.S. 3447 and ASTM C 162-56], continuous ~ [*A plurality of glass filaments in parallel bonded with a size*] · Gespinst *n*, Gesponnene *n*

~ cross-section · Litzenquerschnitt *m*

~ diameter · Litzendurchmesser *m*

~ grip [*A device used to anchor strands*] · Litzengreifer *m*

stranded cable · verdrilltes Kabel *n* [*Spannbeton*]

~ electrode (Brit.); ~ welding wire (US) · verdrillte Elektrode *f*

~ welding wire (US); ~ electrode (Brit.) · verdrillte Elektrode *f*

strap [*For fixing the ends of joists*] · Band *n*

~ bolt, lug ~ · Bügelschraube *f*

~ footing → strip ~

~ hanger [*It is used to secure metal channels to overhead joists in suspended ceiling systems*] · Bandhängeglied *n*, Band(ab)hänger *m*

~ ~ · Rinn(en)eisen *n*

strapping [*Scotland*] → furring

strapwork [*Decoration originating in the Netherlands c. 1540, also common in Elizabethan England, consisting of interlaced bands (Bandverschlingung) and forms similar to fretwork or cut leather; generally used in ceilings, screens, and funerary monuments*] · Band(el)werk *n*, Bandverschlingung *f*, Nestelverzierung

stratification [*The separation of overwet or overvibrated concrete into horizontal layers with increasingly lighter material toward the top; laitance, mortar, and coarse aggregate will tend to occupy successively lower positions in that order; a layered structure in concrete resulting form placing of successive batches that differ in appearance*] · Schichtung *f*

straw · (Getreide)Stroh *n*

~ and loam pugging · Stakung *f* [*Die Ausfüllung von Balkengefachen bei Holzbalkendecken oder Fachwerkwänden mit Stakhölzern, die verflochten und mit Strohlehm umgeben sind*]

strawboard, compressed straw slab · Preßstrohplatte *f* [*Strohplatten werden aus Getreidestroh hergestellt und sind je nach Herstellung entweder Preßstroh-Bauplatten oder Strohfaser-Platten*]

~ partition (wall) · Strohplattentrennwand *f*

straw(-)coloured (Brit.); straw(-)colored (US) · strohfarben

straw fibre board (Brit.); ~ fiber ~ (US) · Strohfaser-Platte *f* [*Dämmplatte aus chemisch aufgeschlossenem Getreidestroh*]

~ meal · Strohmehl *n*

~ roofing, ~ thatch(ing), thatch(-ing) · Stroh(dach)(ein)deckung *f*, Strohbedachung

~ thatch(ing), ~ roofing, thatch(-ing) · Stroh(dach)(ein)deckung *f*, Strohbedachung

stray current, leak(age) ~, current from irregular source(s) · Streustrom *m*, vagabundierender (Erd)Strom, Irrstrom, Erdstrom, Schleichstrom

~ light · Streulicht *n*

streak · Schliere *f*

streaking · Schlierenbildung *f*

stream gravel · Flußkies *m*

streamer, label, scroll, banderol(e) · Spruchband *n*, Schriftband, Banderole *f*

streamline ventilator, continuous ~, ~ extractor, ~ extract ventilation unit, ~ extraction unit · Längs(ent)lüfter *m*

streamlined house · Stromform-Haus *n*

street → urban road

~ bridge · Stadtstraßenbrücke *f*

~ drainage · Stadtstraßenentwässerung *f*

~ façade · Straßenfassade *f*

~ furniture · Stadtstraßenwaren *fpl*, Stadtstraßenzubehör *n*

~ inlet, road ~, road gull(e)y · Rinnenschacht *m*, Straßen~, Straßenablauf *m*, Straßeneinlauf, Straßengully *m*, Straßensinkkasten *m* [*DIN 4052*]

~ (lighting) luminaire (fixture) (US); lantern, light fitting (Brit.); (light(ing) fixture [*A complete lighting device consisting of a light source together with its direct appurtenances, such as globe, reflector, refractor, housing, and such support as is integral with the housing. The mast or bracket is not considered a part of the luminaire*] · Straßenleuchte *f*

~ ~ unit · Mast *m* mit Straßenleuchte

~ name-plate · Straßennamenschild *n*

~ network, ~ system · Stadtstraßennetz *n*

~ noise · Straßenlärm *m*

~ number, building ~ · Gebäudenummer *f*, Hausnummer

Street of the Tombs at Pompeii · Gräberstraße *f* zu Pompeji

~ system, ~ network · Stadtstraßennetz *n*

~ trap · Straßenschlammfang *m*

~ tunnel · Stadtstraßentunnel *m*

strength · Stärke *f* [*Akustik*]

~, (material(s)) ~ · (Werk)Stoffestigkeit *f*, (Material)Festigkeit

~ capability, ~ property, ~ quality, ~ power · Festigkeitseigenschaft *f*, Festigkeitsvermögen *n*, Festigkeitsfähigkeit *f*

~ ceiling, limit(ing) strength · Grenzfestigkeit *f*

~ check(ing) · Festigkeitsnachweis *m*

~ class, ~ grade · Festigkeitsklasse *f*

~ classification of concrete pipes · Festigkeitseinteilung *f* von Betonrohren

~ condition · Festigkeitsbedingung *f*

~ decrease → ~ reduction

strength/density ratio · Festigkeits/Rohdichte-Verhältnis *n*

strength forecast · Festigkeitsvoraussage *f*

~ gain → ~ increase

strength-gaining time, ~ period, strength-increasing ~ · Festigkeitsgewinndauer *f*, Festigkeitserhöhungsdauer, Festigkeitszunahmedauer, Festigkeitszuwachsdauer

strength grade → ~ class

~ group · Festigkeitsgruppe *f*

~ increase, ~ gain · Festigkeitsgewinn *m*, Festigkeitserhöhung *f*, Festigkeitszunahme *f*, Festigkeitszuwachs *m*

strength-increasing · festigkeitssteigernd, festigkeitserhöhend

~ time → strength-gaining ~

strength limit · Festigkeitsgrenze *f*

~ power, ~ quality, ~ capability, ~ property · Festigkeitseigenschaft *f*, Festigkeitsvermögen *n*, Festigkeitsfähigkeit *f*

~ problem · Festigkeitsaufgabe *f*

~ property, ~ capability, ~ power, ~ quality · Festigkeitseigenschaft *f*, Festigkeitsvermögen *n*, Festigkeitsfähigkeit *f*

~ quality → ~ property

~ range, range of strength · Festigkeitsbereich *m*, *n*

~ reduction, ~ decrease, falling off in strength · Festigkeitsabfall *m*, Festigkeitsabnahme *f*, Festigkeitseinbuße *f*, Festigkeitsminderung *f*

~ requirement · Festigkeitsanforderung *f*

~ reserve, reserve of strength · Festigkeitsreserve *f*

~ test · Festigkeitsprobe *f*, Festigkeitsprüfung *f*, Festigkeitsversuch *m*

~ tester · Festigkeitsprüfgerät *n*, Festigkeitsprüfer *m*

~ theory · Festigkeitslehre *f*

~ value · Festigkeitswert *m*

strength/weight ratio · Festigkeits/Gewichtsverhältnis *n*

strength-wise, as regards strength · festigkeitsmäßig

strengthened by cold working, strain-hardened · kaltverfestigt

stress · Spannung *f*

~ analogy · Spannungsanalogie *f*

~ analysis, ~ calculation · Spannungsberechnung *f*, Spannungsanalyse *f*

~ ~, (structural) ~ · (Bau)Statik *f*

~ axis · Spannungsachse *f*

~ behaviour (Brit.); ~ behavior (US) · Spannungsverhalten *n*

~ calculation, ~ analysis · Spannungsberechnung *f*, Spannungsanalyse *f*

~ case · Spannungsfall *m*

~ check (calculation), checking (up) of the stresses · Spannungsnachweis *m*

~ circle · Spannungskreis *m*

~ component · Spannungskomponente *f*, Spannungsteilkraft *f*

~ concentration · Spannungsanhäufung *f*, Spannungskonzentration *f*

~ condition · Spannungsbedingung *f*

~ corrosion · Spannungskorrosion *f*

~ ~ cracking · Spannungsrißkorrosion *f*

~ ~ failure · Spannungskorrosionsbruch *m*

~ crack · Spannungsriß *m*

stress decline — stressing mould

- ~ decline → decrease of stress
- ~ decrease → decrease of stress
- ~ diagram, diagram of stresses [*A skeleton drawing of a truss, upon which are written the stresses in the different members*] · Spannungsdiagramm *n*
- ~ distribution · Spannungsverteilung *f*
- ~ division [*e.g., of axial loads to concrete and steel*] · Spannungs(auf)teilung *f*
- ~ drop → decrease of stress
- ~ effect · Spannungswirkung *f*
- ~ ellipse, ellipse of stress(es) · Spannungsellipse *f*
- ~ ellipsoid, ellipsoid of stresses · Spannungsellipsoid *n*
- ~ equilibrium · Spannungsgleichgewicht *n*
- ~ estimation · Spannungsabschätzung *f*
- ~ field · Spannungsfeld *n*
- ~ flow · Spannungsverlauf *m*
- stress-free annealing · Spannungsfreiglühen *n*
- stress function · Spannungsfunktion *f*
- ~ grade → structural timber ~
- ~ increase · Spannungszunahme *f*
- stress-intensity factor · Spannungsintensitätsfaktor *m*
- stress interval · Spannungsintervall *n*
- stress-less · spannungslos
- stress level, level of stress · Spannungshöhe *f*
- ~ limit, limit of stress · Spannungsgrenze *f*
- ~ loss · Spannungsverlust *m*
- ~ moment · Spannungsmoment *n*
- ~ pattern · Spannungsbild *n*
- ~ point · Spannungsstelle *f*
- ~ problem · Spannungsaufgabe *f*
- ~ raiser, peak stress · Spannungsspitze *f*
- ~ range · Spannungsbereich *m, n*
- ~ ratio · Spannungsverhältnis *n*
- ~ redistribution, redistribution of stress(-es) · Spannungsumlagerung *f*
- ~ reduction factor · Spannungsverminderungsfaktor *m*
- ~ relief annealed, SRA [*steel*] · spannungsfreigeglüht
- ~ relieved, free of stress, SR · spannungsfrei, entspannt
- ~ ~ 7-wire strand for prestressed concrete [*B.S. 3617*] · spannungsfreie 7-drähtige Litze *f*, entspannte ~ ~
- ~ relieving, ~ removal, removal of stress, stress-relief heat treatment · Entspannen *n*, Spannungsfreimachen [*Baustahl*]
- ~ removal, ~ relieving, removal of stress, stress-relief heat treatment · Spannungsfreimachen *n*, Entspannen [*Baustahl*]
- ~ repetition · Spannungsspiel *n*
- ~ resultant · Spannungsresultante *f*, Spannungsresultierende *f*
- ~ reversal, reversal of stress · Spannungsumkehr *f*
- ~ state, state of stress · Spannungszustand *m*
- stress-strain curve · Spannungs-Dehnungs-Linie *f*
- ~ diagram · Spannungs-Dehnungs-Diagramm *n*
- ~ measurement · Spannungs-Dehnungs-Messung *f*
- ~ relation · Spannungs-Dehnungs-Beziehung *f*
- stress system · Spannungssystem *n*
- ~ tensor · Spannungstensor *m*
- ~ theory · Spannungstheorie *f*
- ~ to strength ratio · Spannungs/Festigkeits-Verhältnis *n*
- to stress together, to tension together, to joint by prestressing · zusammenspannen [*Fertigteile durch Vorspannung miteinander verbinden*]
- stress trajectory, trajectory of stress · Spannungstrajektorie *f*, Spannungsweg *m*
- ~ transfer, ~ transmission · Spannungsableitung *f*, Spannungsabtragung, Spannungsübertragung
- ~ transmission, ~ transfer · Spannungsableitung *f*, Spannungsabtragung, Spannungsübertragung
- ~ triangle · Spannungsdreieck *n*
- ~ value · Spannungswert *m*
- ~ variation · Spannungsschwankung *f*
- stressed clay → Stahlton
- ~ connection, pre~ ~, stretched ~, tensioned ~ · (Vor)Spannverbindung *f*
- ~ membrane · gespannte Membran(e) *f*
- stressing, pre~, stretching, tensioning · Vorspannung *f*
- ~, pre~, stretching, tensioning · (Vor-)Spannen *n* [*Spannbeton*]
- ~ area → tensioning zone
- ~ bar → pre~ ~
- ~ bed → pre~ ~
- ~ block → pre~ ~
- ~ cable → pre~ ~
- ~ element → pre~ ~
- ~ factory → (pre)stressing plant
- ~ force → (pre)stressing stress
- ~ jack → pre~ ~
- ~ line → pre~ ~
- ~ loss → pre~ ~
- ~ method, ~ system, pre~ ~ · (Vor-)Spann(beton)verfahren *n*
- ~ mold (US) → pre~ ~
- ~ moment, pre~ ~ · (Vor)Spannmoment *n*
- ~ mould (Brit.) → pre~ ~

stressing order — strike (plate)

~ **order**, pre~ ~, stretching ~, tensioning ~ · (Vor)Spannfolge f

~ **plant** → pre~ ~

~ **process** → process of (pre)stressing

~ **reinforcement** → pre~ ~

~ **rod** → pre~ ~

~ **steel** → (pre)stressing reinforcement

(~) **strand** → pre~ ~

~ **stress** → pre~ ~

~ **system**, ~ method, pre~ ~ · (Vor-)Spann(beton)verfahren n

~ **table** → pre~ ~

(~) **tendon**, pre~ ~, stretching ~, tensioning ~ [*A stretched element used in a concrete member or structure to impart prestress to the concrete*] · (Vor)Spannglied n

~ **together of (pre)cast units**, tensioning ~ ~ ~, jointing (pre)cast units by prestressing · Verbinden n durch Vorspannung, Zusammenspannen von (Beton)Fertigteilen

~ **value**, pre~ ~, tensioning ~, stretching ~ · (Vor)Spann(ungs)wert m

~ **wedge** → pre~ ~

~ **yard** → (pre)stressing plant

~ **zone** → tensioning ~

to stretch, to expand, to draw out · strecken [*Streckmetall*]

stretched connection, tensioned ~, (pre)stressed ~ · (Vor)Spannverbindung f

~ **in pairs**, tensioned ~ ~, prestressed ~ ~ · paarweise vorgespannt [*Spanndrähte*]

stretcher · Läufer m

~ **bond** → (conventional) running (masonry) ~

stretcher-bond type rolock paving, ~ ~ rowlock ~ · Rollscharpflaster n im Läuferverband, Rollschichtpflaster ~

stretcher brick · Läuferziegel m

~ **course**, stretching ~ · Läuferlage f, Läuferschicht f

~ **face**, long ~ · Längsseite f eines Läufer(stein)s

~ **(masonry) bond** → (conventional) running (~) ~

~ **store** · Krankentragenlager n

stretching, tensioning, (pre)stressing · Vorspannung f

~, tensioning, (pre)stressing · (Vor-)Spannen n [*Spanndrähte*]

~ **area**, tensioning ~, (pre)stressing ~, ~ zone · Spann(ungs)zone f, Vor~

~ **bar**, tensioning ~, (pre)stressing ~, ~ rod · Spannstab m, Vor~

~ **block**, tensioning ~, (pre)stressing ~ · Spannblock m [*Spannbeton*]

~ **bond** → (conventional) running (masonry) ~

~ **cable**, tensioning ~, ((pre)stressing) ~, (~) strand [*A prestressing tendon composed of a number of wires most of which are twisted about a center wire or core*] · (Vor)Spannlitze f, (Draht-)Seil n, Litze

~ **course**, stretcher ~ · Läuferschicht f, Läuferlage f

~ **element**, tensioning ~, (pre)stressing ~ · Spannelement n

~ **factory** → (pre)stressing plant

~ **force** → (pre)stressing stress

~ **jack**, (pre)stressing ~, tensioning ~, jack(ing device) for prestressed concrete · Spann(beton)presse f

~ **loss** → (pre)stressing ~

~ **method**, ~ system, tensioning ~, (pre)stressing ~ · Spannbetonverfahren n, (Vor)Spann(ungs)verfahren

~ **order**, tensioning ~, (pre)stressing ~ · (Vor)Spannfolge f

~ **plant** → (pre)stressing ~

~ **process** → process of (pre)stressing

~ **reinforcement** → (pre)stressing ~

~ **rod**, tensioning ~, (pre)stressing ~, ~ bar · Spannstab m, Vor~

~ **steel** → (pre)stressing reinforcement

~ **strand** → ((pre)stressing) ~

~ **stress** → (pre)stressing ~

~ **system**, ~ method, tensioning ~, (pre)stressing ~ · Spannbetonverfahren n, (Vor)Spann(ungs)verfahren

~ **tendon**, tensioning ~, ((pre)stressing) ~ [*A stretched element used in a concrete member of structure to impart prestress to the concrete*] · (Vor)Spannglied n

~ **value**, tensioning ~, (pre)stressing ~ · (Vor)Spann(ungs)wert m

~ **wedge**, tensioning ~, (pre)stressing ~ · Spannkeil m [*Spannbeton*]

~ **wires in pairs**, tensioning ~ ~ ~, prestressing ~ ~ ~ · paarweise Vorspannung f [*Spanndrähte*]

~ **yard** → (pre)stressing plant

~ **zone**, tensioning ~, (pre)stressing ~, ~ area · Spann(ungs)zone f, Vor~

strict rationalism · Rationalismus m strenger Observanz

striction, con~, necking down, reduction in area · Einschnürung f

~ **strain**, con~ ~ · Einschnürungsdehnung f

strictly classical · streng klassisch

to strike off · abziehen

strike (plate), striking plate, keeper, (lock) forend, lock front · Schließblech n [*DIN 18251*]

striking — stripping indicator

striking [*Development of colour or opacity during cooling or reheating*] · Anlaufen *n* [*Handarbeit von Hohlglas*]

string (Brit.) → (stair) stringer

~ (course), belt ~, band ~, strip, cordon · Band(ge)sims *m*, (*n*), Brust(ge)sims, Gurt(ge)sims, Kordon(ge)sims, Stockwerk(ge)sims, Mauerband *n*, Gurtband, (Sims)Band, Gesimsband [*Horizontales, zwei Geschosse im Aufbau trennendes Gesims*]

~ curve → funicular polygon

~ frame (Brit.); stringer ~ (US) · (Treppen)Wangenrahmen *m*

~ masonry wall · (Treppen)Wangenmauer *f*

~ model [*The string represents the structural ribs of the building concerned*] · Bindfadenmodell *n*

~ piece · Streckbalken *m*

~ polygon → funicular ~

~ stair(case) (Brit.); stringer ~ (US) · Wangentreppe *f* [*veraltet: abgebackte Treppe*]

~ wall · (Treppen)Wangenwand *f*

~ wreath · Krümmling *m*, Kropfstück *n*, Kröpfling [*Gewundenes Verbindungsstück zweier Treppenwangen*]

stringer → stair ~

~ · Trag(e)schiene *f* [*Doppel(fuß)boden*]

strip · Band *n* [*z.B. (Ab)Dicht(ungs)band*]

~ · Band *n* [*Walzerzeugnis*]

~ · Paneel *n*

~ · Leiste *f*

~ · Streifen *m*

~, string (course), cordon, belt course · Band(ge)sims *m*, (*n*), Brust(ge)sims, Simsband *n*, (Gesims)Band, Mauerband, Gurt(ge)sims, Kordon(ge)sims, Stockwerk(ge)sims, Gurtband [*Horizontales, zwei Geschosse im Aufbau trennendes Gesims*]

~ bonding · streifenförmiges Verkleben *n*

~ center (US) · Ladenzeile *f* von der Straßenfront zurückverlegt und mit dazwischen liegenden Parkplätzen

~ coating → stripp-off ~

~ copper, copper strip · Kupferband *n*

~ electric heater, fin(ned) ~ ~ ~, electric(al) finned strip ~ · Elektro-Lamellenheizkörper *m*

~ floor cover(ing) → (wood-)strip flooring

~ ~ (finish) → (wood-)strip flooring

~ flooring → wood-~ ~

~ footing, continuous ~, strap ~ · Bankett *n*, Fundamentstreifen *m*, Streifenfundament *n*

~ foundation, continuous ~ · Gründungsstreifen *m*, Streifengründung *f*

~ heater, fin(ned) ~ ~, rib(bed) ~, g(r)illed ~ · Rippenheizkörper *m*, berippter Heizkörper, Lamellenheizkörper

~ heating tube, fin(ned) ~ ~ ~, rib(bed) ~ ~, g(r)illed ~ ~ · Rippenheizrohr *n*, beripptes Heizrohr, Lamellenheizrohr

~ iron, band ~, hoop ~ · Bandeisen *n*

strip-line (light(ing)) fixtures; ~ luminaires (US); ~ light fittings (Brit.); continuous row (light(ing)) fixtures; continuous row luminaires (US); continuous row light fittings (Brit.); lighting row · Leucht(en)band *n*, Lichtband

strip load, line ~, knife edge ~, (col-)linear [*Forces on a long narrow member, e.g. a beam*] · Schneidenlast *f*, Linienlast, Streckenlast

~ loading → line ~

~ metal · Bandmetall *n*

~ mosaic · Streifenmosaik *n*

~ of pre-formed filling material → (joint) sealing strip

strip(-off) coating, strippable ~ · Abzieh(schutz)lack *m*, abziehbarer (Schutz)Lack, (Ab)Decklack, Metallschutzlack [*Durch seine Aufbringung wird ein leicht zu entfernender Schutzfilm erzielt*]

strip-shingle, multiple shingle-strip · Schindelplatte *f*, Schindelreihe *f*, Schindelstreifen *m* [*aus Pappschindeln*]

strip steel · Bandstahl *m* [*Er wird durch Walzen aus Flußstahl hergestellt*]; Bandeisen *n* [*Fehlname*]

~ ~ section, ~ ~ shape, ~ ~ unit, ~ ~ trim, ~ ~ profile · Bandstahlprofil *n* [*Aus warmgewalztem Bandstahl durch Ziehen hergestelltes Profil*]

~ tube, fin(ned) ~ ~, rib(bed) ~, g(r)illed ~ · beripptes Röhre *f*, Rippenröhre, Lamellenröhre

~ ~ heater → (fin(ned)) ~ ~ ~

~ ~ radiator → (fin(ned)) strip tube heater

~ windows, continuous ~ · Bandfenster *n*, Fensterband *n* [*Eine Reihe nebeneinanderliegender Fenster*]

striper · Strichzieher *m* [*Anstrichtechnik*]

strippable coating → strip(-off) ~

stripped-down style, purified ~ · gereinigter Stil *m*

stripper, remover, paint ~ · Abbeizer *m*, (Ab)Beizmittel *n*, Farbenlöser, Farbenentferner, Macklöser, Lackbeize *f*, Ablaugemittel *n* [*Vom Anstreicher kurz „Lauge" genannt*]

stripping, paint ~ · Abbeizen *n* von Farbanstrichen, ~ ~ Farbaufstrichen

~ → detachment

~, release, forms removal, form(work) removal, shuttering removal · Ausschalung *f*, Entschalung

~ → (film) detachment

~ agent → release ~

~ indicator, displacement ~ · Ablösungsanzeiger *m* [*Haftfestigkeit zwischen bit. Bindemittel und Mineralmasse*]

~ **method** · Ablöseverfahren n

~ **(of coat(s))** · Abbeizen n von Aufstrichen, ~ ~ Anstrichen

~ **schedule** · (Aus)Schal(ungs)plan m, Entschal(ungs)plan

~ **strength** · Ausschalungsfestigkeit f, Entschalungsfestigkeit

~ **test (in the presence of water), displacement** ~ (~ ~ ~ ~ ~) · Ablösungsprobe f, Ablösungsversuch m, Ablösungsprüfung f, Wasserlagerungsprüfung, Wasserlagerungsprobe, Wasserlagerungsversuch [Zur Bestimmung der Haftung bituminösen Bindemittels am Gestein]

~ **time** · Entschal(ungs)frist f, (Aus-)Schal(ungs)frist

strip zinc, zinc strip · Zinkband n [DIN 9722]

strong acid · starke Säure f

stronghold → fortification

strongroom, bank ~, strongroom for valuables · Silberkammer f, Tresorraum m

strontium cement · Edelzement m, Strontiumzement

~ **chromate** [B.S. 4313] · Strontiumchromat n

~ **sulphide (pigment)** (Brit.); ~ sulfide (~) (US) · Strontiumsulfid n

~ **white** · Strontiumweiß n

~ **yellow** · Strontiumgelb n

Strouhal number · Strouhalsche Zahl f

struck, tarnished, fogged · angelaufen, beschlagen, blind geworden, erblindet [Glas]

~ **brick** → hand-formed ~

structural · konstruktiv [Aus dem Aufbau und der Anordnung des Ganzen entwickelt, nicht willkürlich oder gekünstelt]

~ **adhesive** → ~ bonding ~

(~) **alteration**, (~) conversion · bauliche Veränderung f, Bauveränderung, Umbau m

(~) ~ **work**, (~) conversion ~ · Umbauarbeiten fpl

~ **aluminium** (Brit.); ~ aluminum (US); construction(al) ~ · Baualu(minium) n

(~) **analysis**, stress ~ · (Bau)Statik f

(~) ~, (~) calculation · (statische) Berechnung f

(~) **arch** m [A series of voussoirs spanning an opening] · Bogen m

(~) ~ **analysis**, arch structural ~ · Bogenstatik f

~ **axis** · Konstruktionsachse f

~ **block partition (wall)**, ~ tile ~ (~) · Konstruktions-Blocktrennwand f

~ **(bonding) adhesive**, ~ ~ medium, ~ ~ agent, ~ cement(ing agent), ~ glue [This adhesive is capable of joining structural elements and maintaining the same resistance to specific stresses as the material itself. The joint thus becomes an integral part of the total structure] · Konstruktionskleb(e)stoff m, Konstruktionskleb(e)mittel n, Konstruktionskleber m, Konstruktionsleim m

~ ~ **agent** → ~ (~) adhesive

~ ~ **medium** → ~ (~) adhesive

(~) **calculation**, (~) analysis · (statische) Berechnung f

~ **capacity of beam(s) without cast-in-situ concrete** → (load)bearing ~ ~ ~ ~ ~ ~ ~

~ **cast-in-place concrete** → ~ in(-)situ cast ~

~ **(cast-)in-situ concrete** → ~ in(-)situ cast ~

~ **cement(ing agent)** → ~ (bonding) adhesive

~ **ceramic (building) unit**, ~ ~ (~) member, ~ ~ (~) component · konstruktiver keramischer (Bau)Körper m, konstruktiver keramischer Bauteil m, konstruktives keramisches Bauteil n, konstruktives keramisches (Bau)Element n [Fehlname: konstruktive keramische Baueinheit f]

~ **ceramics**, heavy ~ · Baukeramik f

~ ~ **articles** → ~ ~ products

~ ~ **goods** → ~ ~ products

~ ~ **products**, heavy ~ ~, ~ ~ articles, ~ ~ goods · baukeramische Erzeugnisse npl

~ **channel** · Konstruktions-U-Profil n, konstruktives U-Profil

~ **characteristic** · Konstruktionsmerkmal n

~ **chimney**, chimney shell, structural shell, chimney shaft [It is protected by the lining] · Schornsteinschaft m

~ **clay article**, heavy ~ ~, ~ ~ product · baukeramischer Artikel m, ~ Gegenstand m, baukeramisches Erzeugnis n

~ ~ **block**, ~ ~ tile · Keramikblock(stein) m, Keramikstein

~ ~ ~ **partition (wall)**, ~ ~ tile ~ (~) · Keramik-Konstruktionstrennwand f

~ ~ **facing block**, ~ ~ ~ tile · (Ver-)Blendkeramikblock(stein) m, (Ver-)Blendkeramikstein m

~ ~ ~ ~ **partition (wall)**, ~ ~ ~ tile ~ (~) · (Ver)Blendkeramik-Konstruktionstrennwand f

~ ~ **flooring tile**, heavy ~ ~ ~ · Baukeramik(fuß)bodenplatte f

~ ~ **industry**, heavy ~ ~ · baukeramische Industrie f

~ ~ **product**, heavy ~ ~, ~ ~ article · baukeramischer Artikel m, ~ Gegenstand m, baukeramisches Erzeugnis n

~ ~ **tile**, ~ ~ block · Keramikstein m, Keramikblock(stein) m

~ ~ ~ **partition (wall)**, ~ ~ block ~ (~) · Keramik-Konstruktionstrennwand f

structural concrete — structural material production

~ **concrete** · Bauwerkbeton *m*, Konstruktionsbeton

~ ~ **core** · konstruktiver Betonkern *m*

~ ~ **panel,** (pre)cast ~ ~ ~ · Konstruktionsbetontafel *f*

~ ~ **plate** → concrete (structural) ~

~ ~ **slab** → concrete (structural)plate

~ ~ **topping,** ~ insitu ~, in situ concrete structural ~ · Konstruktions-Aufbeton *m* [*Decke*]

~ ~ ~ **(slab)** → topping (~)

~ **connection,** ~ joint · Konstruktionsverbindung *f*, konstruktive Verbindung

~ **construction** → (load)bearing ~

(~) **conversion,** (~) alteration · bauliche Veränderung *f*, Bauveränderung, Umbau *m*

(~) ~ **work,** (~) alteration ~ · Umbauarbeiten *fpl*

(~) **design,** DSGN · baulicher Entwurf *m*, (Bau)Entwurf

~ ~ · Durchbildung *f*

(~) ~ **assumption** → design hypothesis

~ ~ **hypothesis** → design ~

(~) **designer** · Statiker *m*

~ **dimension** → ~ size

~ **division** · bauliche Gliederung *f*

~ **dowel** · Baudübel *m*, Konstruktionsdübel

~ **eccentricity** · konstruktive Ausmittigkeit *f*

~ **engineer** · Baukonstruktionsingenieur *m*

~ **enrichment** · konstruktive Verschönerung *f*

~ **extruded product** → ~ ~ section

~ ~ **section,** ~ ~ shape, ~ ~ unit, ~ ~ product, ~ extrusion ~ · Konstruktions-Stangenpreßerzeugnis *n*, Konstruktions-Stangenpreßprofil *n*, konstruktives Stangenpreßprofil, konstruktives Stangenpreßerzeugnis

~ ~ **shape** → ~ ~ ~ section

~ ~ **unit** → ~ ~ ~ section

~ **extrusion product** → ~ extruded section

~ ~ **section** → ~ extruded ~

~ ~ **shape** → ~ extruded section

~ ~ **unit** → ~ extruded section

~ **feasibility** · konstruktive Durchführbarkeit *f*

~ **field concrete** → ~ in(-)situ cast ~

~ **fire precautions,** ~ ~ protection · baulicher Brandschutz *m*, ~ Feuerschutz

~ ~ **protection,** ~ ~ precautions · baulicher Brandschutz *m*, ~ Feuerschutz

~ **form,** ~ design · Konstruktionsform *f*

(~) **frame,** (load)bearing ~, weight carrying ~, load-carrying ~, supporting ~ · (Trag)Rahmen *m*

~ **framework** · Gerüst *n* [*einer Kathedrale*]

~ ~ **system** · Gerüstsystem *n* [*einer Kathedrale*]

~ **gasket** → (preformed) ~ ~

~ ~ **joint** → (preformed) ~ ~

~ **glass** (US); glass blocks, glass bricks · Glas(bau)steine *mpl*

~ ~ **panel** (US); glass block, glass brick · Glas(bau)steintafel *f*

~ **glue** → ~ (bonding) adhesive

~ **gluing** · Konstruktions(ver)leimung *f*

~ **(grade) steel** → construction(al) ~

~ **grid** → (planning) ~

~ **hollow section,** hollow structural ~ · Konstruktionshohlprofil *n*, konstruktives Hohlprofil

~ **in(-)situ cast concrete,** ~ (cast-)in-situ ~, ~ (cast-)insitu ~, ~ cast-in-place ~, ~ site-placed ~, ~ field ~, ~ poured-in-place ~ · Konstruktions-Ortbeton *m*

~ ~ **topping,** ~ concrete ~, in situ concrete structural ~ · Konstruktions-Aufbeton *m* [*Decke*]

~ **iron,** construction ~ · Baueisen *n*

~ **joint,** ~ connection · Konstruktionsverbindung *f*, konstruktive Verbindung

~ **light(weight) aggregate concrete** · Konstruktions-Leichtzuschlag(stoff)beton *m*, Leichtzuschlag(stoff)-Konstruktionsbeton

~ ~ **concrete,** light(weight) structural ~ · Konstruktionsleichtbeton *m*, konstruktiver Leichtbeton

~ **lime,** construction ~, trowel trades ~, building ~ [*B.S. 890*] · Baukalk *m* [*DIN 1060*]

(~) **masonry (building) component** → (~) ~ (~) unit

(~) ~ (~) **member** → (~) ~ (~) unit

(~) ~ (~) **unit,** (~) ~ (~) member, (~) ~ (~) component [*See remark under '(Bau)Element'*] · Mauerwerk(bau)element *n*, Mauerwerk(bau)körper *m* [*Fehlname: Mauerwerkbaueinheit f*]

~ ~ **(wall)** → (load)bearing ~ (~)

~ **mass,** building ~, massing, volume · Baumasse *f*

~ **material,** construction(al) ~, structural ~ · Baustoff *m*; Baumaterial *n* [*Schweiz*]

~ ~ **dealer,** building ~ ~, structural ~ · Baustoffeinzelhändler *m*

~ ~ **engineer** → construction(al) ~ ~

~ ~ **failure,** constructional ~ ~, building ~ ~ · Baustoffschaden *m*

~ ~ **machine** → building ~ ~

~ ~ **manufacturer** → building material producer

~ ~ **producer** → building ~ ~

~ ~ **production** → building ~ ~

988

structural material standard — (structural) steel section

~ ~ **standard** → construction(al) ~ ~

~ **materials delivery,** construction(al) ~ ~, structural ~ ~ · Baustoffanfuhr *f*

~ ~ **deposit,** building ~ ~, construction(al) ~ ~ · Baustoffvorkommen *n*

~ ~ **industry** → construction(al) ~ ~

~ ~ **market** → building ~ ~

~ ~ **practice** → building ~ ~

~ ~ **processing** → building ~ ~

~ ~ **quality** → building ~ ~

~ ~ ~ **control,** construction(al) ~ ~ ~, building ~ ~ ~ · Baustoff(güte)- überwachung *f*

~ ~ **requirement** → building ~ ~

~ ~ **saving** → building ~ ~

~ ~ **scale** → building ~ ~

~ ~ **show** → building ~ ~

~ ~ **storage** → construction(al) ~ ~

~ ~ **store,** construction(al) ~ ~ ~, building ~ ~ · Baustofflager *n*

~ ~ **test** → building ~ ~

~ ~ **testing device,** building ~ ~ ~, construction(al) ~ ~ ~ ~ · Baustoffprüfgerät *n*

~ ~ ~ **institute,** building ~ ~ ~, construction(al) ~ ~ ~ · Baustoffprüf(ungs)anstalt *f*

~ ~ ~ **machine,** construction(al) ~ ~ ~, building ~ ~ ~ · Baustoffprüfmaschine *f*

~ **mechanics** · Baumechanik *f*

~ **member** · Konstruktionsglied *n*

~ **metal** · Konstruktionsmetall *n*

(~ **mortar) topping (slab),** (in-situ) structural topping (mortar) · (Mörtel-)Druckplatte *f*, (Mörtel)Druckschicht *f*

(~) **nickel steel** · Nickel(bau)stahl *m*

~ **panel** · Konstruktionstafel *f*

~ **part** · Konstruktionsteil *m, n*

~ **partition (wall)** · Konstruktionstrennwand *f*

~ **performance** · Bauwerkverhalten *n*

~ **pipe,** ~ **tube** · Konstruktionsrohr *n* [*Ein Rohr, das nicht zum Fortleiten eines Gutes dient, sondern als Konstruktionselement verwendet wird*]

~ **plastic profile** → (construction(al)) plastic shape

~ ~ **section** → (construction(al)) plastic shape

~ ~ **shape** → (construction(al)) ~ ~

~ ~ **trim** → (construction(al)) plastic shape

~ ~ **unit** → (construction(al)) plastic shape

~ **poured-in-place concrete** → ~ in(-)situ cast ~

(~) **profile** → construction(al) shape

~ **property** · bautechnische Eigenschaft *f*

(~) **re-analysis,** (~) re-calculation · statische Nachrechnung *f*

(~) **re-calculation,** (~) re-analysis · statische Nachrechnung *f*

~ **response** · Bauwerkreaktion *f*

~ **rib,** (load)bearing ~, weight-carrying ~, supporting ~, load-carrying ~ · Tragrippe *f*, Konstruktionsrippe, (last-)tragende Rippe, Auflagerrippe

~ **rivet steel** · Konstruktionsnietstahl *m*

~ **rubber profile** → construction(al) rubber shape

~ ~ **section** → construction(al) rubber shape

~ ~ **shape** → construction(al) ~ ~

~ ~ **trim** → construction(al) rubber shape

~ ~ **unit** → construction(al) rubber shape

(~) **section** · Profil *n*

(~) ~ → construction(al) shape

~ **shape** · bauliche Form *f*

(~) ~ → construction(al) ~

~ **shell,** chimney shaft, structural chimney, chimney shell [*It is protected by the lining*] · Schornsteinschaft *m*

~ **site-placed concrete** → ~ in(-)situ cast ~

~ **size,** ~ dimension · Bauholzdimension *f*, Bauholz-Schnittklasse *f*

(~) **skeleton,** (load-)bearing ~, weight-carrying ~ · (Trag)Skelett *n*, (Trag-)Gerippe *n*

(~) ~ **building,** frame(d) ~ · Skelettgebäude *n*, Rahmengebäude, Gerippegebäude

(~) ~ **construction,** (load)bearing ~ ~, weight-carrying ~ ~ · (Trag)Gerippebau *m*, (Trag)Skelettbau

(~) ~ **member,** (load)bearing ~ ~, weight-carrying ~ ~ · Gerippeglied *n*, Skelettglied

(~) ~ **structure,** (load)bearing ~ ~, weight-carrying ~ ~ · (Trag)Gerippebauwerk *n*, (Trag)Skelettbauwerk

~ **slate** · Bauschiefer *m*

~ **solution** · Konstruktionslösung *f*

~ **sound insulation** → impact (~) ~

(~) **stability** · Stabilität *f*, Standfestigkeit *f*, Standsicherheit, räumliche Steifigkeit

~ **steel** → construction(al) ~

~ ~ **core** [*This core is encased in reinforced concrete in the case of columns, beams, etc. constructed as composite sections*] · Baustahlkern *m*

~ ~ **hollow section,** ~ ~ ~ unit, ~ ~ ~ trim, ~ ~ ~ shape, ~ ~ ~ profile · Stahlbau-Hohlprofil *n*, Hohl-Stahlbauprofil

(~) ~ **lintel;** ~ ~ lintol [*deprecated*] · Stahloberschwelle *f*, Stahlsturz *m*

(~) ~ **profile** → (~) ~ unit

(~) ~ **section,** ~ girder · Stahlprofil *n*, Trägerstahl *m*, Profilstahl, Stahlträger *m* [*Fehlnamen: Trägereisen, Profileisen.*

Von den Walzwerken hergestellter Formstahl mit I-, IP- und U-Querschnitt, der als Träger für Bauzwecke verwendet wird]

(~) ~ ~, section(al) steel · Fassonstahl *m*, Profilstahl, Formstahl, Stahlprofil *n*

(~) ~ ~, (~) ~ unit, (~) ~ shape, (~) ~ trim, (~) ~ profile, construction(al) ~ ~ [*B.S. 4*] · Baustahlprofil *n*, Konstruktionsstahlprofil

(~) ~ shape → (~) ~ section

(~) ~ trim → (~) ~ unit

(~) ~ unit → (~) ~ section

~ steelwork, steel system, steel structure · Stahlkonstruktion *f*

~ stone, (building) ~ · (Bau)Stein *m*, Baugestein *n*, bautechnisches Gestein, Naturbaustein, natürlicher Baustein

~ strength → load-carrying capacity

(~) system → construction(al) ~

~ terra-cotta [*It includes such products as hollow clay tile used to construct walls and partitions, where it is serving a structural function*] · Bauterrakotta *f*

~ theory · (Bau)Statiktheorie *f*

~ tile partition (wall), ~ block ~ (~) · Konstruktions-Blocktrennwand *f*

~ timber, building ~, construction(al) ~ · Bauholz *n*

~ ~ grade, building ~ ~, construction(al) ~ ~, stress ~ · (Bauholz)Güteklasse *f*

~ tin, construction(al) ~ · Bauzinn *n*

~ tomb · Grabanlage *f*, Grabbau *m*

(~) ~ architecture, sepulchral ~ · Grabarchitektur *f*, Grabbaukunst *f*

~ topping (concrete) → topping (slab)

~ ~ (mortar), in-situ ~ ~ (~), (structural mortar) topping (slab) · (Mörtel-)Druckplatte *f*, (Mörtel)Druckschicht *f*

(~) trim → construction(al) shape

~ tube, ~ pipe · Konstruktionsrohr *n* [*Ein Rohr, das nicht zum Fortleiten eines Gutes dient, sondern als Konstruktionselement verwendet wird*]

(~) unit → construction(al) shape

~ use of (pre)cast concrete · konstruktionstechnische Verwendung *f* von (Beton)Fertigteilen, bauliche ~ ~ ~

~ wall, load-carrying ~, supporting ~, weight-carrying ~, (load)bearing ~ · (last)tragende Wand *f*, Tragwand, Auflagerwand, Konstruktionswand

~ ~ construction → (load)bearing wall structure

~ ~ structure → (load)bearing ~ ~

~ zinc, construction(al) ~ · Bauzink *n*

structure, construction · Bau(werk) *m*, (*n*), bauliche Anlage *f*

~ · Gefüge *n*, Struktur *f*

~, weight-carrying ~, (load)bearing ~, supporting ~ · Tragwerk *n* [*Ein materielles System von Bauelementen bzw. Trägern*]

structure-borne sound, impact ~, 'contact noise' · Körperschall *m* [*Schall, der sich in festen Stoffen fortpflanzt (Erschütterungen sind Körperschall)*]

~ ~ insulation → impact (~) ~

~ ~ ~ material, impact ~ ~ ~ · Körperschall(ab)dämmstoff *m*

~ ~ ~ tile, impact ~ ~ ~ · Körperschalldämmplatte *f*

~ ~ intensity, impact ~ ~ · Körperschallstärke *f*

~ ~ transmission, impact ~ ~ · Körperschallübertragung *f*

~ ~ ~ level → impact ~ ~ ~

structure built on the axial principle, long structure · Longitudinalbau(werk) *m*, (*n*), Lang(bauwerk) [*Bei einem Langbau dominiert die Längsachse*]

~ indeterminate to the *n*-th degree · *n*-fach statisch unbestimmtes Tragwerk *n*

~ of plain web girders → (load)bearing ~ ~ ~ ~ ~

~ ~ solid web girders → (load)bearing structure of plain ~ ~

~ plane, plane of a structure · Bauwerkebene *f*

~ preservation coat · Bautenschutzanstrich *m*, Bautenschutzaufstrich

~ ~ emulsion · Bautenschutzemulsion *f*

~ system → (load)bearing ~

~ ~ for redirection of wind forces · Umlenkungssystem *n* für Windkräfte

~ ~ in bending · Tragsystem *n* im Biegezustand

~ ~ ~ coordinate tension and compression · Tragsystem *n* im zusammenwirkenden Zug- und Druckzustand

~ ~ ~ single stress condition · Tragsystem *n* im einfachen Spannungszustand

~ ~ ~ surface stress condition · Tragsystem *n* im Flächenspannungszustand

~ ~ through interpenetration of folded surfaces · Tragsystem *n* aus sich durchdringenden Faltflächen

to strut (Brit.); to brace (US) · abstreben

~ · unterstützen [*(Dach)Pfette*]

strut [*A member in compression, especially when short or non-vertical*] · Druckstrebe *f*

~ [*The generic term for a long column of timber or metal*] · lange Stütze *f*

~ · Säule *f*, Stiel *m* [*Pfettendach*]

~ · Strebe *f*

~, wood(en) ~, timber ~ · Stake *f*, Stakholz *n*

~, (angle) brace, angle tie, dragon tie · Bandholz *n*, Kopfband *n*, Kopfstrebe *f*, (Kopf)Bug(holz) *m*, (*n*), Kopfbiege *f*, Strebeband(holz) *n*, Winkelband, Tragband

~ · Fußband *n*, Fußbiege *f* [*Im Zimmerwerk ein schräges Verbandholz vom unteren Teil eines Pfostens bis zu einer Schwelle oder einem Balken*]

strut-framed beam · Sprengwerkbalken(träger) *m*

strutted · unterstützt [*(Dach)Pfette*]

~ **frame** · Sprengwerk *n* [*Ein Tragwerk mit meist waag(e)rechtem Balken, der von unten durch geneigte, gegeneinander abgesteifte Streben unterstützt wird*]

~ **purlin(e) roof** · abgestrebtes Pfettendach *n*

~ **roof** · Sprengwerkdach *n*

strutting · schräge Absteifung *f*, ~ Aussteifung, ~ Verstärkung, ~ Versteifung, Verstrebung

~ · Verspreizung *f*

~ · Unterstützung *f* [*(Dach)Pfette*]

~ **board** · Spannbohle *f* [*Balkenverspreizung*]

stub-bar → starter bar

stub tenon · einfacher Zapfen *m*

stuc, stone plaster · Stein(ver)putz *m*

~ **mix(ture)**, ~ stuff, stone plaster ~ · Steinputzmasse *f*, Steinputzmörtel *m*

~ **stuff**, ~ mix(ture), stone plaster ~ · Steinputzmasse *f*, Steinputzmörtel *m*

stucco, cement ~ (US); smooth external plastering · (Außen)Glatt(ver)putz *m*

~ [*Scotland*] → plaster of Paris

~ [*In strict sense sculptural stucco is dehydrated lime mixed with finely powdered marble dust and glue and sometimes reinforced with hair*] · Stuck *m*

~ **architecture** · Putzarchitektur *f* [*Landschaftlich begrenzte Ausbildung der Oberfläche der Bauwerke in Putz als klimatisch bedingter Schutzüberzug über Backsteinmauerwerk und auch Fachwerk. Die Putzarchitektur variierte oft die Architekturformen des Steinbaues und entwickelte als eigene materialgerechte Schmuckform das plastische und frei modellierte Stuckwerk (Stukkatur) und das flächige und farbige Sgraffito*]

~ **ceiling** · Stuckdecke *f*, Prunkdecke

stucco-encrusted wall · stuckbeladene Wand *f*

stuccoist, stucco worker · Stukkateur *m*

stuccolustro, marble stucco · Marmorstuck(putz) *m* Stuccolustro *m*, Stuckmarmor *m* [*Flächenstuck, der polierten Marmor nachahmt. Er besteht aus Weißkalk, Marmorstaub, Alabaster und Gips*]

~ **rib** · Stuckrippe *f*

stuccowork · Stuck(gips)arbeiten *fpl*

~ · Stuckwerk *n*

stucco worker, stuccoist · Stukkateur *m*

stud · Bundpfosten *m*, Bundstiel *m*, Bundsäule *f*, Bundständer *m* [*Fachwerkbau*]

~ · Jochsäule *f* [*Holzbau*]

~ **behind the face frame** · Klappstiel *m*, Wandstiel *m* [*Fachwerkwand*]

~ **partition (wall)**, ~ wall · Gerippe(trenn)wand *f* [*DIN 4103. Sie besteht aus einem Gerippe, das auf einer oder auf beiden Seiten mit Platten bekleidet ist*]

~ **shooting** · Bolzensetzen *n*

~ **wall**, ~ **partition (wall)** · Gerippe(trenn)wand *f* [*DIN 4103. Sie besteht aus einem Gerippe, das auf einer oder auf beiden Seiten mit Platten bekleidet ist*]

studded tile · Nocken(belag)platte *f*, Nockenfliese *f*

studding [*A series of comparatively slender vertical structural members which, when closely spaced, form the principal supporting elements*] · Gerippe *n* [*DIN 4103*]

students' dwelling unit (US); ~ dwelling (Brit.) · Studentenwohnung *f*

~ **hostel** · Studenten(wohn)heim *n*

~ **quarters** · Studentensied(e)lung *f*

studio · Atelier *n*

~ **house** · Atelierhaus *n*

studs · Gerippe *n* [*Gerippewand; Gerippetrennwand*]

~ **construction type**, ~ type of construction · Gerippebauart *f* [*Trennwandbau. DIN 4103*]

~ **type of construction**, ~ construction type · Gerippebauart *f* [*Trennwandbau. DIN 4103*]

study · Arbeitsraum *m*, Herrenzimmer *n*

study-bedroom · Arbeits-Schlafzimmer *n*

study centre (Brit.); ~ center (US) · Studienzentrum *n*

stuff, mix(ture) · Putzmörtel *m*, Putzmasse *f*

stump · Turmansatz *m*

stupa(-mound) → domic(al) mound

~ **base**, tope (-mound) ~ · Topeunterbau *m*, Stupaunterbau

stupa shrine, tope ~ · Topeschrein *m*, Stupaschrein

stylar façade · Pfeilerfassade *f*

~ ~ · Säulenfassade *f*

style · Formensprache *f*, Stil *m*

~ **character** · Stilcharakter *m*

~ **characteristic**, stylistic feature · Stilmerkmal *n*

~ **detail** → (architectural) feature

~ **device** → (architectural) feature

~ **element** → (architectural) feature

~ **feature** → (architectural) feature

~ **Herrera** · Desornamentadostil *m* [*Richtung der spanischen Renaissance mit Sparsamkeit der Schmuckformen*]

~ **of ornamentation**, decorative style, ornamental style · Ornamentstil *m*, Schmuckstil, Dekor(ations)stil, Zierstil

stylistic apparatus · Stilmittel *n*

~ **conception** · stilistische Konzeption *f*

~ **departure** · Stilabweichung *f*

stylistic development — subsidized apartment (unit)

~ **development**, development of style · Stilentwick(e)lung f

~ **feature**, style characteristic · Stilmerkmal n

~ **forerunner**, ~ predecessor · stilistischer Vorläufer m

~ **form** · Stilform f

~ **formula** · Stilformel f

~ **history** · Stilgeschichte f

~ **idiom** · Formenvokabular n, Formenwortschatz m

~ **imitation**, imitation of style · Stilimitierung f, Stilnachahmung

~ **perfection** · stilistische Vollendung f

~ **phase** · Stilphase f

~ **predecessor**, ~ forerunner · stilistischer Vorläufer m

~ **purity**, purity of style · stilistische Reinheit f

~ **significance** · stilistische Bedeutung f

~ **tendency** · Stiltendenz f

~ **unity** · stilistische Einheit f

stylization · Stilisierung f

to stylize, to conventionalize, to formalize · stilisieren

stylized → divorced from reality

stybolate [*The top step of the crepidoma. The term 'stybolate' is also incorrectly applied to the substructure on which a colonnade stands*] · Stybolat m, Säulenstuhl m, Säulenstand m

styrenated alkyd (resin) · Styrolalkyd(harz) n, styrolisiertes Alkyd(harz)

~ **oil** · Styrolöl n, styrolisiertes Öl

styrene, vinyl benzene · Vinylbenzol n, Styrol n

~ **butadiene copolymer** · Styrol-Butadien-Copolymer n, SB

~ **dispersion** · Styroldispersion f

~ **(resin)** · Styrol(harz) n

styrol-butadien-rubber, SBR · Styrol-Butadien-Kautschuk m; Buna Hüls n [*Bunawerke Hüls*]; Buna S n [*VEB-chemische Werke Buna, Schkopau*]

sub-basement, lower basement [*The second storey below the ground, the storey below the basement*] · zweites Kellergeschoß n, Tiefkellergeschoß

sub-circuit · Hilfsstromkreis m

sub-concrete · Grundbeton m [*Hartbetonplatte. Nicht verwechseln mit „Tragbeton"*]

~ · Unterbeton m

subcontractor · Nachunternehmer m, Nebenunternehmer

to sub-divide · unterteilen

sub-dividing [*e.g. a room with partition walls*] · Unterteilen n, Aufteilen

subdivisible area · unterteilbare Fläche f

sub-environment · Kleinumwelt f

suberic tissue, suber(e)ous ~ · Korkgewebe n

suberin(e) · Korkharz n, Suberin n

suber(e)ous tissue, suberic ~ · Korkgewebe n

subfl., undfl. [*abbreviations*]; underfloor, subfloor · Unterboden m

subfloor, underfloor [*abbreviations: undfl, subfl*] · Unterboden m

~ **filler** → ~ stopper

~ **for lino(leum)** · (Fußboden)Linoleumunterlage f, Linoleumunterboden m, Bodenlinoleumunterlage

~ **stopper**, ~ stopping, ~ filler, underfloor ~ · Unterboden-Ausfüller m, Unterboden-Spachtel(masse) m, (f) [*Zum Vorbehandeln von Unterböden, die mit Bahnen- und Plattenbelägen, Spannteppichen, Parkett usw. belegt werden*]

~ **stopping** → ~ stopper

~ **tile for lino(leum)** · Unterlagsplatte f für Fußbodenlinoleumverlegung

subgrade [*The natural ground below a structure*] · Untergrund m, Baugrund

subject for a motif · Motivobjekt n

~ ~ **decoration** · Zierobjekt n

~ **index** · Sachwortregister n

~ **(wall)paper** · (Papier)Tapete f mit Stilmotiven, Wand~ ~ ~

subjected to compression · druckbeansprucht, auf Druck beansprucht

~ ~ **foot traffic** · begehbar

subjective brightness, apparent ~ · subjektive Helligkeit f

sub-letting · Weitervergabe f, Vergabe an Nachunternehmer

sublimate [*Solid obtained by the direct condensation of vapour without passing through the liquid state. This is possible only for materials whose melting point and boiling point are very close together*] · Sublimat n

sublimation · Sublimieren n

subordinate altar, side ~ · Seitenaltar m, Nebenaltar [*Altar neben dem Hochaltar, meist zu beiden Seiten des Langhausabschlusses oder am Ostende der Seitenschiffe*]

~ **block**, dependent ~, ancillary ~, accessory ~, ~ building · Nebengebäude n

~ **building**, dependent ~, accessory ~, ancillary ~, ~ block · Nebengebäude n

sub-purlin(e) · Unterpfette f

subsequent installation · Nachinstallation f

subsidence damage · Senkungsschaden m

~ **wave** · Senkungswelle f

~ **temple** · Nebentempel m

subsiding ground · nachgiebiger Untergrund m, ~ Baugrund

subsidized apartment (unit) → publicly-assisted ~ (~)

subsidized dwelling — suction type draught regulator

~ **dwelling** (Brit.) → publicly-assisted dwelling unit

~ **house-building**, ~ housing, low-rent ~, local authority ~, public authority ~, publicly-assisted ~, low-cost (municipal) ~, social ~ [*Provision of flats or houses for low-income groups, partly financed with the aid of public funds. Financing includes certain tax and interest concession*] · öffentlich geförderter Wohnungsbau *m*, Sozialwohnungsbau, sozialer Wohn(ungs)bau, sozialer WBau

subsoil [*The weathered soil below the topsoil*] · Erdreich *n*, Untergrund *m*

~ **paper**, road lining (~), underlay ~, concreting ~, concrete subgrade ~ · Papierunterlage *f*, (Autobahn-)Unterlagspapier *n*, Straßenbaupapier

substance, matter, agent · Mittel *n*, Stoff *m*, Substanz *f* [*z.B. für Sperranstriche*]

~ **aggressive to concrete**, material ~ ~ ~ · Betonschädling *m*

substantially insoluble · praktisch unlöslich [*z.B. ein Pigment*]

sub-station · Unterstation *f* [*Stromversorgung*]

substitute frame · Ersatzrahmen *m*

substrate → (roof(ing)) substructure (system)

~, substratum, base, backing, underlay, backup; underlayment (US) · Rücklage *f*, Hinterlegung *f*, Unterlage, Rücken *m*, Träger(schicht) *m*, (*f*)

~ **(system)** → (roof(ing)) substructure (~)

substratum, substrate, base, backing, underlay, back-up; underlayment (US) · Rücklage *f*, Hinterlegung *f*, Unterlage, Träger(schicht) *m*, (*f*), Rücken *m*

~, base (Brit.); ground (US) [*Any surface which is or will be painted*] · Anstrichfläche *f*, Aufstrichfläche, Anstrich(unter)grund *m*, Aufstrich(unter)grund, (Farb)Träger *m*, Substrat *n*, (Farb)Unterlage *f*, Anstrichträger, Aufstrichträger

substructure → (roof(ing)) substructure (system)

~ · Unterbau *m* [*alle Gebäudeteile unter Geländehöhe*]

~ · Teilsystem *n*, Untersystem [*Tragwerkberechnung*]

~ **(system)** → (roof(ing)) ~ (~)

subsurface absorption, ~ disposal · Untergrundberieselung *f*

~ ~ **field**, ~ disposal ~ · Untergrundberieselungsfeld *n*

~ **disposal**, ~ absorption · Untergrundberieselung *f*

~ ~ **field**, ~ absorption ~ · Untergrundberieselungsfeld *n*

subterranean chamber, underground ~, ~ room · unterirdischer Raum *m*

~ **room**, underground ~, ~ chamber · unterirdischer Raum *m*

suburb · Vorstadt *f*

~ · Randbezirk *m*

(suburban) dispersal, (~) sprawl · Zersied(e)lung *f* [*Stadt*]

~ **garden** · Vorortgarten *m*

~ **(housing) estate**; cottage suburb (US) · Vorstadtsied(e)lung *f*, Vorortsied(e)lung

~ **line** · Vorortlinie *f*

~ **populated area** → ~ residential ~

~ **residential area**, ~ populated ~, ~ residences · Außenwohngebiet *n*, Außenwohnviertel *n*, Außenwohnzone *f*

~ **run** · Vorortstrecke *f*

(~) sprawl, (~) dispersal · Zersied(e)lung *f* [*Stadt*]

~ **station**, ~ train ~ · Vorortbahnhof *m*

~ **(train) station** · Vorortbahnhof *m*

~ **villa** · Vorstadtvilla *f*

subwhole · Unterganze *n*

sub-zero temperature · Minustemperatur *f*

succession of arches · Bogenfolge *f*

sucking · saugend

suction, wind ~ · Sog *m*, Wind~

~ **capacity**, ~ power, ~ property, ~ quality · Saugfähigkeit *f*, Saugvermögen *n*, Saugeigenschaft *f*

~ **coefficient**, wind ~ ~ · Sogbeiwert *m*, Wind~

~ **cup** · Abnehmer *m* [*Vorrichtung zum Abnehmen der Wanne bei deckenbündigem Einbau einer Leuchte*]

~ **effect**, wind ~ ~ · Sogwirkung *f*, Wind~

~ **force**, wind ~ ~ · Sogkraft *f*, Wind~

~ **line**, ~ pipe~ · Saugleitung *f*, Saugrohrleitung

~ **pad** · Saugmatte *f*, Vakuum(an)heber *m*, Saugvorrichtung *f* zum Fertigteiltransport

~ **(pipe)line** · Saugleitung *f*, Saugrohrleitung

~ **power**, ~ property, ~ capacity, ~ quality · Saugfähigkeit *f*, Saugvermögen *n*, Saugeigenschaft *f*

~ **property**, ~ quality, ~ capacity, ~ power · Saugfähigkeit *f*, Saugvermögen *n*, Saugeigenschaft *f*

~ **quality**, ~ property, ~ capacity, ~ power · Saugfähigkeit *f*, Saugvermögen *n*, Saugeigenschaft *f*

~ **side**, wind ~ ~ · Sogseite *f*

~ **type draught regulator** (Brit.); ~ ~ draft ~ (US) · (Saug)Zugregler *m*

suction ventilation — sulpho-aluminate cement

~ **ventilation,** ~ venting · Sauglüftung f

~ **venting,** ~ ventilation · Sauglüftung f

~ **zone** · Saugzone f

sudatorium, laconicum, caldarium, (dry) sweating room, hot room [*The (dry) sweating room in a Roman bath building*] · römischer Schwitzraum m, Sudatorium n, Schwitzraum einer römischen Therme, römisches Schwitzbad n, Caldarium n, Sudatio n, Assun n

sudden load, shock ~, impact ~, instantaneous ~, impulsive ~ [*An imposed load whose effect is increased due to its sudden application*] · Stoßlast f

~ **loading,** instantaneous ~, shock ~, impact ~, impulsive ~ · Stoßbelastung f

Suffolk latch → thumb ~

sugar solution · Zuckerlösung f

~ **storage block,** ~ ~ building · Zuckerlagergebäude n

~ ~ **building,** ~ ~ block · Zuckerlagergebäude n

suitability for application with a filling knife · Ziehfähigkeit f [*Ziehspachtel(masse)*]

suitable for being dressed, ~ ~ ~ milled · bearbeitbar [*(Natur)Stein*]

~ ~ ~ **milled,** ~ ~ ~ dressed · bearbeitbar [*(Natur)Stein*]

suite for presidents · Präsidentensuite f

~ **(of rooms),** apartment · Raumflucht f, (Zimmer)Flucht

(sulfate) bloom (US) → (sulphate) ~

~ **of lead,** lead sulfate (US); sulphide of lead, lead sulphate (Brit.) · Bleisulfat n, $PbSO_4$

~ ~ **lime** (US) → calcium sulphate

~ ~ **potash,** potassium sulfate (US); sulphide of potash, potassium sulphate (Brit.) · Kaliumsulfat n

sulfate-resistant, sulfate-resisting (US); sulphate-resistant, sulphate-resisting (Brit.) · sulfatwiderstandsfähig, sulfatbeständig

sulfate-resisting, sulfate-resistant (US); sulphate-resisting, sulphate-resistant (Brit.) · sulfatwiderstandsfähig, sulfatbeständig

sulfite (US); sulphite (Brit.) · Sulfit n

~ **lye** (US) → sulphite ~

~ ~ **adhesive** (US); sulphite ~ ~ (Brit.); lignin ~ · Sulfit(ab)laugekleber m

sulfo-aluminate (US); sulpho-aluminate (Brit.) · Aluminatsulfat n

~ **cement** (US) → sulpho-aluminate ~

sulfur (US); sulphur (Brit.); brimstone, burning stone · Schwefel m

~ **cement** (US) → sulphur ~

~ **powder** (US) → powder(ed) sulphur

~ **trioxide** (US) → sulphur ~

sulfuric acid (US); sulphuric ~ (Brit.) · Schwefelsäure f, H_2SO_4

~ **anhydride** (US) → sulphur trioxide

sulphate attack (Brit.); sulfate (US) ~ [*Deterioration of concrete caused by sulphate salts in solution*] · Sulfatangriff m

sulphate-attacked (Brit.); sulfate-attacked (US) · sulfatbefallen

sulphate-bearing water, sulphate-laden ~ (Brit.); sulfate-laden ~, sulfate-bearing ~ (US) · sulfathaltiges Wasser n

(sulphate) bloom (Brit.); (sulfate) ~ (US) · Feuerweiß n, Hüttenrauch m, Kühlbeschlag m [*Glasherstellung*]

~ **corrosion** (Brit.); sulfate ~ (US) · sulfatische Korrosion f [*Beton*]

~ **efflorescence** (Brit.); sulfate ~ · Sulfatausblühung f

~ **expansion** (Brit.); sulfate ~ (US) · Sulfattreiben n

sulphate-laden water, sulphate-bearing ~ (Brit.); sulfate-laden ~, sulfate-bearing ~ (US) · sulfathaltiges Wasser n

sulphate of lime (Brit.) [*substance*] → calcium sulphate [*chemical name*]

~ **resistance** (Brit.) sulfate ~ · Sulfatbeständigkeit f, Sulfatwiderstand m

sulphate-resistant, sulphate-resisting (Brit.); sulfate-resisting, sulfate-resistant (US) · sulfatwiderstandsfähig, sulfatbeständig

~ **(portland) cement,** ~ Portland ~ [*B.S. 4027. This is a portland cement in which the composition, particularly the tricalcium aluminate content, has been adjusted in order to increase its resistance to attack by sulphate-bearing water*] · sulfatbeständiger Portlandzement m, sulfatwiderstandsfähiger ~, SPZ

sulphate-resisting, sulphate-resistant (Brit.); sulfate-resistant, sulfate-resisting (US) · sulfatwiderstandsfähig, sulfatbeständig

sulphate solution (Brit.); sulfate ~ (US) · Sulfatlösung f

sulphide of cadmium, cadmium sulphide (Brit.); cadmium sulfide, sulfide of cadmium (US) · Kadmiumsulfid n, Schwefelkadmium n

sulphite (Brit.); sulfite (US) · Sulfit n

~ **lye** (Brit.); sulfite ~ (US) [*A waste product of the paper industry sometimes used as a binder for non-plastic and relatively non-plastic material*] · Sulfit(ab)lauge f

~ ~ **adhesive** (Brit.); sulfite ~ ~ (US); lignin ~ · Sulfit(ab)laugekleber m

sulpho-aluminate (Brit.); sulfo-aluminate (US) · Aluminatsulfat n

~ **cement** (Brit.); sulfo-aluminate ~ (US) · Gipstonerdezement m

sulphur cement (Brit.); sulfur ~ (US) · Schwefelzement *m*, Schwefelvergußmasse *f* [*Säurefester Kitt aus Asphalt, Schwefelblüte, Graphit und Eisenoxid*]

sulphur-containing (Brit.); sulfur-containing (US) · schwefelhaltig

sulphur powder → powder(ed) sulphur

~ trioxide (Brit.); sulfur ~, sulfuric anhydride (US); sulphuric anhydride (Brit.) · Schwefeltrioxid *n*, SO_3

sulphuric acid (Brit.); sulfuric ~ (US) · Schwefelsäure *f*, H_2SO_4

~ ~ anodising process (Brit.); sulfuric ~ ~ (US) · Schwefelsäureelektrolytverfahren *n*

~ ~ electrolyte (Brit.); sulfuric ~ ~ (US) · Schwefelsäureelektrolyt *m*

~ anhydride (Brit.) → sulphur trioxide

sum of loads · Lastensumme *f*

~ ~ matrices · Matrizensumme *f*

Sumerian architecture · sumerische Architektur *f*, ~ Baukunst *f*

summation of forces · Addition *f* von Kräften, Zusammenzählung *f* ~ ~

summer air conditioning system · Sommer-Klimaanlage *f*

~ beam, ~ tree, breast-summer, bressumer, sommer [*A long heavy beam, usually timber, carrying a considerable load of brickwork or masonry, often placed over a shop window. It is a large lintel*] · Rähmstück *n*

~ cooling load · Sommerkühllast *f*

~ heat gain · Sommerwärmegewinn *m*

~ house · Sommerhaus *n*

summerhouse, pleasurehouse [*in a garden*] · Gartenpavillon *m*

summer palace · Sommerpalast *m*

~ residence · Sommerresidenz *f*

~ service · Sommerbetrieb *m* [*Heizung*]

~ theatre [*Theatre with a sliding ceiling which allows the night sky to serve as a roof*] · Sommertheater *n*

~ tree → ~ beam

sumptuous · üppig

sun-baked, sun-dried, air-dried, a.d. · luftgetrocknet [*Lehmstein*]

~ brick → mud ~

sun(-bathing) patio, ~ room, ~ terrace, solarium · Sonnenterrasse *f*, Solarium *n*

~ room, ~ terrace, ~ patio, solarium · Sonnenterrasse *f*, Solarium *n*

~ terrace, ~ patio, ~ room, solarium · Sonnenterrasse *f*, Solarium *n*

sunblind, solar screen(ing), sunbreaker, (sun) shading device, solar shading device · Sonnen(schutz)blende *f*, Abschattungsvorrichtung *f*, Sonnenschutzkonstruktion *f*, Sonnenschutz(anlage) *m*, (*f*)

sunbreaker, sunblind, solar screen(ing), (sun) shading device, solar shading device · Sonnen(schutz)blende *f*, Abschattungsvorrichtung *f*, Sonnenschutzkonstruktion *f*, Sonnenschutz(anlage) *m*, (*f*)

sun control device, ~ protection ~ · Sonnenschutzvorrichtung *f*

~ ~ work, ~ protection ~ · Sonnenschutzarbeiten *fpl*

sundial · Sonnenuhr *f*

sun-dried, air-dried, sun-baked, a.d. · luftgetrocknet [*Lehmstein*]

~ brick → mud ~

~ ~ construction, adobe (~) ~, mud-brick ~ · Schlammziegelbau *m*

~ ~ (masonry) wall → adobe ~ (~) ~

sunflower seed oil [*B.S. 1939*] · Sonnenblumensaatöl *n*

sunken garden · Tiefgarten *m*

sunlight · Sonnenlicht *n*

sunlightfast → resistant to sunlight

sunlight glare · Sonnenlichtblendung *f*

sun(light) penetration → insolation

sunlightproof → resistant to sunlight

sunlight resistant → resistant to sunlight

sun parlor (US); glazed veranda(h), glassed-in veranda(h) · Glasveranda *f*

~ path · (Sonnen)Strahlenweg *m*

~ patio, ~ terrace, ~ room, sun-bathing ~, solarium · Sonnenterrasse *f*, Solarium *n*

~ penetration → insolation

sunproof · sonnenfest, sonnenbeständig

sun protection work, ~ control ~ · Sonnenschutzarbeiten *fpl*

~ protective device, ~ control ~ · Sonnenschutzvorrichtung *f*

~ radiation, solar ~ · Sonnenstrahlung *f*

sun-roof · Sonnendach *n*

sun room, ~ patio, ~ terrace, sun-bathing ~, solarium · Sonnenterrasse *f*, Solarium *n*

sunshading, (solar) shading, solar screening · Sonnenschutz *m*, Abschattung *f*, Besonnungsschutz

(sun) shading device, solar ~ ~, sunbreaker, sunblind, solar screen(ing) · Sonnen(schutz)blende *f*, Abschattungsvorrichtung *f*, Sonnenschutzkonstruktion *f*, Sonnenschutz(anlage) *m*, (*f*)

sunstone, aventurine fel(d)spar · Sonnenstein *m*

~ terrace, ~ room ~ patio, sun-bathing ~, solarium · Sonnenterrasse *f*, Solarium *n*

suntime · Sonnenstrahlungszeit *f*

sun visor · Außensonnenblende *f*

superabacus, pulvin(us), dosseret, super-capital, impost block · Pulvinus *m*

super-altar — supply floor

super-altar, altar-slab, altar-table, mensa [*The slab forming the top of an altar*] · Altarplatte *f*, Mensa *f*

superficial content, surface ~, (surface) area · (Ober)Flächeninhalt *m*, Flächenraum *m*

superfine aggregate · Feinstzuschlag(- stoff) *m*

~ **filler** · Feinstfüller *m*, Feinstfüllstoff *m*

~ **flour** · Feinstmehl *n*

~ **powder** · Feinstpulver *n*

~ **powdered marble** · Marmorfeinste *n*

~ **sand**, ultra-fine ~ · Feinstsand *m*

superfinely ground, super-ground · feinstgemahlen

superfines · Feinstteile *mpl* (des (Beton-) Zuschlages), ~ (~ (Beton)Zuschlagstoffes)

super gloss [*The highest grade of gloss*] · Höchstglanz *m*

super-ground, superfinely ground · feinstgemahlen

superheated steam · Heißdampf *m*, überhitzter Dampf

~ **steam current** · Heißdampfstrom *m*

~ ~ **operation** · Heißdampfbetrieb *m*

~ **water** · Heißwasser *n* [*Heiz(ungs)- wasser mit Temperaturen über Siedepunkt*]

~ ~ **heating** · Heißwasserheizung *f*

~ ~ ~ **installation**, ~ ~ ~ system · Heißwasserheiz(ungs)anlage *f*

~ ~ **network** · Heißwassernetz *n*

~ ~ **radiant panel** · Heißwasser-Strahlplatte *f*

superheating · Überhitzung *f*

superimposed dead load [*The load of machinery, equipment, furniture, etc., but excluding live load*] · Gebrauchslast *f* minus Verkehrslast, Nutzlast

~ **load**, occupancy ~, use ~ [*The load of machinery, equipment, furniture and people on floors, corridors, balconies, stairs, etc.*] · Gebrauchslast *f*

superintendent · Oberbauleiter *m*

supermarket · Supermarkt *m*

superposition · Überlagerung *f*

~ **equation** · Superpositionsgleichung *f*, Überlagerungsgleichung

~ **law**, ~ **theorem**, ~ principle, law of superposition, theorem of superposition, principle of superposition · Überlagerungsgesetz *n*, Superpositionsgesetz

~ **of moments** · Momentenüberlagerung *f*

~ **principle**, ~ theorem, ~ law, law of superposition, theorem of superposition, principle of superposition · Überlagerungsgesetz *n*, Superpositionsgesetz

~ **solution** · Überlagerungslösung *f*

~ **theorem**, ~ principle, ~ law, law of superposition, theorem of superposition, principle of superposition · Überlagerungsgesetz *n*, Superpositionsgesetz

superpressed plywood, high density ~, densified ~ · Preßsperrholz *n*, PSP *n*, verdichtetes Sperrholz [*Es entsteht durch Warmpressen dünner Furniere mit dazwischenliegenden härtbaren Kunstharzen*]

~ **wood**, high density ~, densified ~ · Preßvollholz *n*, PVH, verdichtetes Vollholz

~ ~ **door**, high density ~ ~, densified ~ ~ · Preßvollholztür *f*, Vollholzpreßtür, PVH-Tür

super-purity aluminium (Brit.); ~ aluminum (US) · Reinstaluminium *n*

supersaturated · übersättigt

supersaturation · Übersättigung *f*

super-skyscraper, tower [*planned by Le Corbusier*] · Super-Wolkenkratzer *m*

superstructure · aufgehender Bau *m*, Überbau, Oberbau [*alle Gebäudeteile über Geländehöhe*]

supersulphated (slag) cement (Brit.); gypsum slag ~ (US) · Gipsschlackenzement *m*, Sulfathüttenzement, SHZ [*DIN 4210*]

supervision · Überwachung *f*; Überwachen *n*

superwhole · Oberganze *n*

supplied by the Owner, provided ~ ~ ~ · bauseits geliefert

~ **only**, S.O. · nur Lieferung

supplier · Lieferant *m*, Lieferer *m*

suppliers' catalogue · Lieferantenverzeichnis *n*

to supply · versorgen

~ ~ **fresh air to a room**, etc. · belüften

supply · Versorgung *f*

~, **delivery** · (An)Lieferung *f*

~ **air** · Zuluft *f*

supply-air boot · Außenrahmen *m* [*Diffusor*]

supply air equipment · Zuluftgerät *n*

~ ~ **grille**, inlet ~ · Zuluftgitter *n*

~ ~ **hole**, ~ ~ opening · Zuluftöffnung *f*

~ ~ **opening**, ~ ~ hole · Zuluftöffnung *f*

~ **area**, ~ zone, service ~ · Versorgungsgebiet *n*, Belieferungsgebiet, Versorgungsraum *m*, Belieferungsraum

~ **cable**, service ~ · Versorgungskabel *n*

~ **duct** · Versorgungskanal *m* [*in einem Gebäude*]

~ **failure**, electricity ~ ~, (electrical) power ~, electric current ~ · Stromausfall *m*

~ **floor**, delivery ~; ~ story (US); ~ storey (Brit.) · Lieferstockwerk *n*, Lieferetage *f*, Liefergeschoß *n*, Anlieferungsstockwerk, Anlieferungsetage, Anlieferungsgeschoß

~ **installation**, ~ plant · Versorgungsanlage f
~ **level** · Versorgungsebene f
~ **line** · Versorgungsleitung f
~ **network** · Versorgungsnetz n
~ **passage** · Liefergang m
~ **pipe** [*That portion of the service pipe(s) lying within the consumer's premises*] · Grundstücksleitung f, Grundstücksstrang m, Verbrauchsstrang, Verbrauchsleitung
~ **piping** [*The portion lying within the consumer's premises*] · Innenleitung f
~ **plant**, ~ installation · Versorgungsanlage f
~ **point** · Versorgungsstelle f [*Wasser; Strom; Gas; Dampf; Druckluft*]
~ **ramp**, delivery ~ · Liefer(anten)rampe f, (An)Lieferungsrampe
~ **road** · Versorgungsstraße f
~ **shaft** · Versorgungsschacht m
~ **story** (US) → ~ floor
~ **undertaking**, utility ~ · Versorgungsbetrieb m
~ **zone**, ~ area, service ~ · Versorgungsgebiet n, Belieferungsgebiet, Versorgungsraum m, Belieferungsraum

support, point of ~ · Auflagerpunkt m, Auflager(stelle) n, (f)
~, column, floor ~ · (Decken)Stütze f
~ · Stützung f
~, column · Stütze f
~ · (Auf)Lager n
~ **analogy**, column ~ · Stützenanalogie f
~ **anchorage**, column ~ · Stützenverankerung f
~ **bar**, column ~ · Stützenstab m [*Bewehrung*]
~ **base**, ~ foot, column ~ · Stützenfuß m
~ ~, column ~ [*A pad designed to distribute the load from a column*] · Stützenplatte f
~ ~ **(plate)**, (column) ~ (~) · (Stützen)Fuß m, (Stützen)Basis f
~ **bearing**, column ~ · Stützenauflagerung f
~ **bent**, column ~ [*A bent composed of columns and bracing in contradistinction to 'pile bent'*] · Stützen-Querrahmen m
~ **bracket**, column ~ · Stützenkonsole f
~ **cap**, column ~ · Stützenkopfplatte f
~ **casing**, column ~ · Stützenummantelung f (mit Beton)
~ **clamp**, column ~ · Stützenzwinge f
~ **concrete**, column ~ · Stützenbeton m
~ **condition**, column ~ · Stützenbedingung f
~ ~ · Auflagerbedingung f

~ **connection**, column ~ · Stützenanschluß m
~ **core**, column ~ · Stützenkern m
~ **creep**, column ~ · Stützenkriechen n
~ **design**, column ~ · Stützenbemessung f
~ **dimension**, column ~ · Stützenabmessung f, Stützenmaß n
~ **end moment**, column ~ ~ · Stützenendmoment n
~ **facing** → column lining
~ **flange**, column ~ · Stützenflansch m
~ **foot**, ~ base, column ~ · Stützenfuß m
~ **footing**, column ~ · Stützenfundament n
~ **forming**, column ~ · Stützeneinschalen n
~ **forms**, ~ form(work), ~ shuttering, column ~ · Stützenschalung f
~ **formula**, column ~ · Stützenformel f
~ **form(work)**, ~ forms, ~ shuttering, column ~ · Stützenschalung f
~ **foundation**, column ~ · Stützengründung f
support-free, support-less, clear, column-less, column-free · stützenfrei, stützenlos
support grid pattern, column ~ ~ · Stützenraster m [*Anordnung der Stützen im Rastersystem*]
~ **guard**, column ~ · Stützeneckenschutz m, Stützenkantenschutz
~ **head**, column ~, flared ~, flaring ~, mushroom ~, flared haunch [*In flat slab construction. An enlargement at the top a of column supporting a flat slab, designed and constructed to act monolithically with the column and with the flat slab*] · Pilzkopf m, Stützenkopf
~ ~, column ~ · Stützenkopf m
~ **height**, column ~ · Stützenhöhe f
~ **hinge**, column ~ · Stützengelenk n
~ **instability**, column ~ · Stützenlabilität f
~ **interval** → column spacing
~ **layout**, column ~ · Stützenanordnung f
~ **length**, column ~ · Stützenlänge f
support-less, support-free, clear, column-less, column-free · stützenfrei, stützenlos
support lining → column ~
~ **load**, column ~ · Stützenlast f
~ **moment** → negative ~
~ **movement**, column ~ · Stützenbewegung f
~ **opening**, column ~ · Stützenöffnung f
~ **pair**, column ~ · Stützenpaar n
~ **permitting rotation and translation** · drehbare verschiebliche Unterstützung f

support permitting... — supporting structure... 998

~ ~ ~ but no translation · drehbare unverschiebliche Unterstützung f
~ radius, column ~ · Stützenhalbmesser m
~ reaction, column ~ · Stützenreaktion f
~ ~ ordinate · Stützkraftordinate f
~ reinforcement, column ~ · Stützenarmierung f, Stützenbewehrung, Stützen(stahl)einlagen fpl
~ rigidity, ~ stiffness, column ~ · Stützensteifigkeit f
~ ring · Auflagerring m [z.B. Schachtring]
~ section, column ~ · Stützenprofil n, Stützenquerschnitt m
~ shaft, column ~ · Stützenschaft m
~ shuttering, ~ form(work), ~ forms, column ~ · Stützenschalung f
~ side, column ~ · Stützenschalungstafel f
~ size, column ~ · Stützengröße f
~ spacing → column ~
~ stiffness, ~ rigidity, column ~ · Stützensteifigkeit f
~ strength, column ~ · Stützenfestigkeit f
~ stress, column ~ · Stützenspannung f
~ (sur)facing → column lining
support-to-floor connection → column-to-slab ~
support-to-footing connection, column-to-footing ~ · Stützen-Fundament-Verbindung f
support-to-slab connection → column-to-slab ~
support-to-support joint, column-to-column ~ · Stützen-Stützen-Verbindung f
support vector, column ~ · Stützenvektor m
~ web, column ~ · Stützensteg m
~ width, column ~ · Stützenbreite f
~ zone, column ~ · Stützenbereich m, n
supported at both ends → simply supported
~ diaphragm · lastbringende Scheibe f
~ pointwise · punktweise gestützt [Platte]
supporting [vertical (supporting) member] · Stützglied n [z.B. ein Baluster]
~, loaded, load-carrying, weight-carrying, (load)bearing · belastet, (last-)tragend
~ beam · lastabnehmender Balken(träger) m
support(ing) block · Auflagerstein m [H(o)urdiplattendecke]
supporting brick, load-carrying ~, weight-carrying ~, (load)bearing ~ · statisch mitwirkender Ziegel m, (last-)tragender ~
~ capability → load-carrying capacity

~ capacity → load-carrying ~
~ ~ of beam(s) without cast-in-situ concrete → (load)bearing ~ ~ ~ ~ ~ ~
~ channel · Stütz-U-Profil n
~ (clay) brick cross-wall → (load-)bearing (~) ~ ~
~ construction → (load)bearing ~
~ floor block → (load)bearing floor (clay) block
~ ~ brick → (load)bearing floor (clay) ~
~ ~ (clay) block → (load)bearing floor (clay) brick
~ ~ (~) brick → (load)bearing ~ (~)
~ frame, (structural) ~, weight-carrying ~, load-carrying ~, (load)bearing ~ · (Trag)Rahmen m
~ in longitudinal direction, weight-carrying ~ ~ ~, load carrying ~ ~ ~, (load)bearing ~ ~ ~ · längstragend
~ ~ transverse direction, weight-carrying ~ ~ ~, load-carrying ~ ~ ~, (load)bearing ~ ~ ~ · quertragend
~ masonry (wall) · (load)bearing ~ (~)
~ ~ (work) → (load)bearing ~ (~)
~ mechanism, loaded ~, (load)bearing ~, weight-carrying ~, load-carrying ~ · Tragmechanismus m
~ member, vertical (~), (frame) leg, (frame) post, (frame) column, framing post, framing column, framing leg · Pfosten m, Stiel m, Stütze f, Rahmen~
~ partition (wall) → (load)bearing ~ (~)
~ plane, loaded ~, (load)bearing ~, weight-carrying ~, load-carrying ~ · Tragebene f
~ power → load-carrying capacity
~ property → load-carrying capacity
~ quality → load-carrying capacity
~ rib, load-carrying ~, structural ~, weight-carrying ~, (load)bearing ~ · Tragrippe f, Konstruktionsrippe, (last-)tragende Rippe, Auflagerrippe
~ ring · Stützring m
~ scaffold(ing) → Traggerüst n [Arten: Schalungs- oder Lehrgerüst, Montagegerüst, Lagergerüst]
~ section · Stützquerschnitt m
~ skeleton → weight-carrying ~
~ space structure → space (load-)bearing ~
~ spatial structure → space (load-)bearing ~
~ structure → (load)bearing ~
~ ~ of plain web girders → (load)bearing ~ ~ ~ ~ ~ ~
~ ~ ~ solid web girders → (load)bearing structure of plain ~ ~
~ ~ for rotating machine · Stützenkonstruktion f für rotierende Maschine

supporting system — surface hardener

~ system → (load)bearing ~
~ three-dimensional structure → space (load)bearing ~
~ wall, structural ~, (load)bearing ~, load-carrying ~, weight-carrying ~ · (last)tragende Wand f, Tragwand, Auflagerwand, Konstruktionswand
~ ~ construction → (load)bearing wall structure
~ ~ structure → (load)bearing ~ ~
Suprematism [*Term coined by Kasimir Malevich for purely abstract art. He applied the simple elements of form in his painting to abstract architectonic compositions*] · Suprematismus m
suprematist architecture · suprematistische Architektur f, ~ Baukunst f
surbase, chair rail, dado rail, dado capping; dado moulding (Brit.); dado molding (US) [*A mo(u)lding round a room to prevent chairs, when pushed back against the walls, from damaging their surface*] · obere Wandsockelleiste f, Schutzleiste
sure-footed safety · Gehsicherheit f [*(Fuß)Bodenbelag*]
sureness of proportions · Sicherheit f der Proportionen
surface ..., above-ground, above-grade ~ · Überflur ..., Oberflächen ..., obererdig, oberirdisch
to (sur)face, to line · auskleiden, bekleiden, verkleiden
~ ~, to coat · beschichten, überziehen
~ ~ · belegen [*Eine Fläche mit einer Schicht*]
~ ~ with gravel · bekiesen
surface · Oberfläche f
surface-active agent · oberflächenaktiver Stoff m, Tensid n
~ (load)bearing system, ~ weight-carrying ~ · flächenaktives Tragsystem n
~ weight-carrying system, ~ (load-)bearing ~ · flächenaktives Tragsystem n
surface appearance · Oberflächenaussehen n
(~) area, ~ content, superficial content · (Ober)Flächeninhalt m, Flächenraum m
~ bond · Oberflächenhaftung f
~ building, above-ground ~, above-grade ~, ~ block · obererdiges Gebäude n, oberirdisches ~
~ cable · Überputzkabel n
~ capability, ~ capacity, ~ property, ~ power, ~ quality · Oberflächeneigenschaft f, Oberflächenvermögen n, Oberflächenfähigkeit f
~ capacity → ~ capability
surface-coated (wall)paper · Tapete f aus beschichtetem Papier, (Wand-)Papier~ ~ ~ ~
surface coating → liquid coating (material)

(~) coat(ing), cap sheet · Deckschicht f, Decklage f, Aufstrich m, Überzug m [*Dachpappe*]
~ coating composition for concrete → liquid coating (material) ~ ~
~ ~ for concrete → liquid coating (material) ~ ~
surface-coating industry · Beschichtungsindustrie f
surface coating (material) → liquid ~ (~)
~ ~ (~) for concrete → liquid ~ (~) ~ ~
~ ~ medium → liquid coating (material)
~ ~ ~ for concrete → liquid coating (material) ~ ~

(~) condensation, sweating · Schwitzwasserbildung f, Tauwasserbildung, Kondenswasserbildung, Kondensatbildung [*Niederschlag der Luftfeuchtigkeit, z.B. auf Wänden und Decken, an Glasscheiben oder Rohrleitungen, wenn durch die Abkühlung die Feuchtigkeitsaufnahmefähigkeit der Luft sinkt und infolge zu geringer Porigkeit des Untergrundes die Feuchtigkeit nicht aufgesaugt wird*]
~ content, superficial ~, (surface) area · (Ober)Flächeninhalt m, Flächenraum m
~ continuity · flächiger Zusammenhang m
~ crack, check · Kaltsprung m, Riß m, Peture f [*Flachglasfehler*]
~ decoration, ~ decorative finish, ~ ornamental finish, ~ decorative feature, ~ ornament(al feature), ~ enrichment, ~ pattern · (Ober)Flächenmuster(ung) n, (f), (Ober)Flächenschmuck m, (Ober)Flächenverzierung f, (Ober-)Flächenornament(ierung) n, (f), (Ober-)Flächendekor(ation) m, (f)
~ decorative feature → ~ decoration
~ ~ finish → ~ decoration
~ defect · Oberflächenfehler m
~ dry, sand ~ [*When the paint is dry on the surface but is soft and tacky underneath*]
~ drying · Oberflächentrocknung f, oberflächentrocken
~ enrichment → ~ decoration
~ film [*cathodic protection*] · Deckschicht f
(~) finish · (Oberflächen)Anschluß m
~ ~ → (natural) stone ~
surface-fixed hinge · Aufsetzband n, Aufsatzband, Hamburger Band, Fitschband, Fitsche f [*Baubeschlag*]
surface fixing · Aufsetzen n [*Band als Baubeschlag*]
~ force · Oberflächenkraft f
~ hardener, ~ hardening agent · Steinhärtemittel n [*Steinhärtemittel sind solche Sperranstrichmittel, die die Oberfläche von Naturstein, Kunststein und Beton(fuß)boden härten. Es sind meistens Silicofluoride*]

surface hardener — (surface) sealing

~ ~, ~ hardening agent · Oberflächenhärtemittel n, Oberflächenhärter m, Oberflächenhärtungsmittel, Oberflächenhärtungsstoff m

~ **hardening** · Oberflächenhärten n [*Vorgang zum Härten einer Oberfläche*]

~ ~ · Oberflächenhärtung f [*Ergebnis des Oberflächenhärtens*]

~ ~ **agent**, ~ hardener · Oberflächenhärtemittel n, Oberflächenhärter m, Oberflächenhärtungsmittel, Oberflächenhärtungsstoff m

~ ~ ~, ~ hardener · Steinhärtemittel n [*Steinhärtemittel sind solche Sperranstrichmittel, die die Oberfläche von Naturstein, Kunststein und Beton(fuß)boden härten. Es sind meistens Silicofluoride*]

surface-hardening fluosilicate · Härtefluat n, Härtefluorsilikat

surface hardness · Oberflächenhärte f

~ **humidity,** ~ moisture · Oberflächenfeuchtigkeit f, Oberflächenfeuchte f

~ **hydrant,** pillar ~, above-grade ~, above-ground ~ · Überflurhydrant m, Oberflächenhydrant, oberirdischer Hydrant, obererdiger Hydrant

surface-improved · oberflächenvergütet

surface improvement, ~ modification · Oberflächenverbesserung f

~ **in contact with potable water,** ~ ~ ~ ~ drinking ~ · trinkwasserberührte Fläche f

~ **laitance,** cement skin · Zementschleier m

~ **line** → ~ pipe~

~ **masonry wall,** above-ground ~ ~, above-grade ~ ~ · aufgehende Mauer f

~ ~ **(work),** above-grade ~ (~), above-ground ~ (~) · aufgehendes Mauerwerk n

~ **modification,** ~ improvement · Oberflächenverbesserung f

~ **modulation** · Oberflächengestaltung f

~ **moisture,** ~ humidity · Oberflächenfeuchtigkeit f, Oberflächenfeuchte f

surface-mounted conduit · Aufputz-Leitung f, Aufputz-Leerrohr n [*Elektroinstallation*]

~ **distribution board** · Aufputz-Verteiler m, Aufputz-Verteilungsschrank m, Aufputz-Verteilung f

~ **installation,** tubular conduits on the surface · Aufputz-Installation f [*Elektroinstallation*]

surface mounting · Aufputz-Verlegung f, Aufputz-Einbau m [*Elektroinstallation*]

~ **normal** · Flächensenkrechte f

~ **of revolution,** rotation surface · Drehfläche f

1000

~ ~ **rupture** · Bruchfläche f

~ ~ **translation,** translation(al) surface · Translationsfläche f

~ **ornament** → ~ decoration

~ **ornament(al feature)** → ~ decoration

~ ~ **finish** → ~ decoration

~ **parking** · Parken n zu ebener Erde

~ **passivation** · Oberflächenpassivierung f

~ **pattern** → ~ decoration

~ **phenomenon** · Oberflächenerscheinung f

~ **(pipe)line,** above-ground ~, above-grade ~, AG ~ · oberirdische (Rohr-)Leitung f, oberirdische ~,Überflur(rohr)leitung

~ **pore** · Oberflächenpore f

~ **power** → ~ property

~ **proofing liquid** → liquid surface waterproofing agent

~ **property,** ~ quality, ~ capability, ~ capacity, ~ power · Oberflächeneigenschaft f, Oberflächenvermögen n, Oberflächenfähigkeit f

~ **protection** · Oberflächenschutz m

~ ~ **work** · Oberflächenschutzarbeiten fpl

~ **quality,** ~ property, ~ power, ~ capability, ~ capacity · Oberflächeneigenschaft f, Oberflächenvermögen n, Oberflächenfähigkeit f

~ **repellent admix(ture),** ~ water-~ ~, ~ (water-)repelling ~ · Oberflächensperrzusatz(mittel) m, (n), Oberflächensperrzusatzstoff m

~ **repelling admix(ture),** ~ water-~ ~, ~ (water-)repellent ~ · Oberflächensperrzusatz(mittel) m, (n), Oberflächensperrzusatzstoff m

~ ~ **agent** → ~ ~ waterproof(ing) ~

~ **retardant,** concrete ~ ~ [*The retarded surface is usually washed off when the base concrete reaches 1,000–1,500 psi*] · Oberflächenverzögerer m zur Herstellung von Waschbeton, Waschbetonhilfe f, Waschbetonverzögerer

~ ~ **in liquid form,** concrete ~ ~ ~ ~ ~ · Waschbetonflüssigkeit f

~ ~ ~ **paste form,** concrete ~ ~ ~ ~ ~ · Waschbetonpaste f

~ **retarring** · Oberflächennachteerung f

~ **riser,** ~ rising main · Aufputz-Steig(e)leitung f

~ **rising main,** ~ riser · Aufputz-Steig(e)leitung f

(~) **screeding** · Abziehen n

~ **sealer,** ~ sealing agent · Oberflächendichter m, Oberflächenversieg(e)lungsmittel n, Oberflächenabsieg(e)lungsmittel

(~) **sealing** · Oberflächenabsieg(e)lung f, Oberflächenversieg(e)lung

~ ~ **agent**, ~ sealer · Oberflächendichter *m*, Oberflächenversieg(e)lungsmittel *n*, Oberflächenabsieg(e)lungsmittel

~ **shell**, trellis casing · Flechtwerkmantel *m*, Mantelfläche *f* [*Kuppel*]

(~) **smoothing** · (Ab)Glättung *f*

(~) ~ · (Ab)Glätten *n*

~ **smoothness** (US); flatness, evenness accuracy of level(s) · (Plan)Ebenheit *f*, Ebenflächigkeit

~ **socket** · Überputzsteckdose *f*

~ **state**, state of surface · Oberflächenzustand *m*, Oberflächenbeschaffenheit *f*

~ **structures in building** · Bauten *f* mit tragenden Flächen

~ **switch**, ~ type ~ · Aufputzschalter *m*

~ **tarring** · Oberflächenteerung *f*

~ **temperature** · Oberflächentemperatur *f*

~ **tension** · Oberflächenspannung *f*, Koeffizient *m* der ~, Kapillaritätskonstante *f*

~ **thermostat** · Anliegethermostat *m*

~ **treatment** · Oberflächenbehandlung *f*, OB

~ **(type) switch** · Aufputzschalter *m*

~ **wall**, above-ground ~, above-grade ~ · aufgehende Wand *f*

~ **water** · Oberflächenwasser *n*, Tagwasser

~ ~ **drain** · Oberflächenwasserdrän *m*, Tagwasserdrän

~ **waterproofer** → ~ waterproof(ing) agent

~ **waterproof(ing) agent**, ~ (water-)repelling ~, ~ waterrepeller, ~ waterproofer · Sperranstrich(mittel) *m*, (*n*), Sperranstrichstoff *m*, Sperraufstrich(-mittel), Sperraufstrichstoff, Oberflächen(ab)dicht(ungs)mittel, Oberflächen(ab)-dicht(ungs)stoff, Oberflächen-DM *n*

~ ~ **emulsion**, ~ water repelling ~ · Isolieremulsion *f* [*Sperranstrichmittel in Form von Emulsion*]

~ **(water)proofing liquid** → liquid surface waterproofing agent

~ **(water-)repelling admix(ture)**, ~ (water-)repelling ~ · Oberflächensperrzusatz(mittel) *m*, (*n*), Oberflächensperrzusatzstoff *m*

~ **waterrepeller**, ~ waterproofer, ~ waterproof(ing) agent, ~ (water-)repelling agent · Sperranstrich(mittel) *m*, (*n*), Sperranstrichstoff *m*, Sperraufstrich(mittel), Sperraufstrichstoff

~ **(water-)repelling admix(ture)**, ~ (water-)repellent ~ · Oberflächensperrzusatz(mittel) *m*, (*n*), Oberflächensperrzusatzstoff *m*

~ ~ **agent** → ~ waterproof(ing) ~

~ **water repelling emulsion**, ~ waterproofing ~ · Isolieremulsion *f* [*Sperranstrichmittel in Form einer Emulsion*]

(**sur)faced**, coated · beschichtet, überzogen

~ **(on) both sides**, coated (~) ~ ~ · beidseitig beschichtet

~ **with granular cork**, ~ ~ granulated ~ · korkschrotbestreut, korkschrotabgestreut

~ ~ ~ **material** · bestreut, abgestreut [*Dachpappe und (bituminöser) Spachteldachbelag*]

~ ~ **granulated cork** → ~ ~ granular ~

surfacer · Oberflächenmittel *n*

(sur)facing, coating · Beschichten *n*, Beschichtung *f*, Überziehen, Überzug *m* [*als Tätigkeit*]

~, lining · Auskleidung *f*, Bekleidung, Verkleidung, Belag *m*

~ **board** → ~ sheet

~ **component** → ~ unit

~ **composition** → coating material

~ **compound** → coating material

~ **concrete slab** ~ lining ~ ~

~ **foil**, lining ~ · Auskleidungsfolie Verkleidungsfolie, Bekleidungsfolie

~ **mass** → coating material

~ **material** → lining ~

~ ~ → coating ~

~ **member** → ~ unit

~ **panel**, lining ~ · Bekleidungstafel *f*, Auskleidungstafel, Verkleidungstafel

~ **sheet**, ~ board, lining ~ · Auskleidungsplatte *f*, Verkleidungsplatte, Bekleidungsplatte

~ **(stone)ware**, lining ~ · Auskleidungssteinzeug *n*, Verkleidungssteinzeug, Bekleidungssteinzeug

~ **unit**, ~ member, ~ component, lining ~ · Auskleidungselement *n*, Verkleidungselement, Bekleidungselement

~ **ware**, ~ stone~, lining ~ · Auskleidungssteinzeug *n*, Verkleidungssteinzeug, Bekleidungssteinzeug

surfactant → activator

surge arrester · Überspannungsableiter *m*

surgical suite, hospital ~ ~ · chirurgische Abteilung *f*

surmounted, stilted · gestelzt, gefußt, überhoben, gebürstet [*Bogen oder Gewölbe, dessen Krümmung erst oberhalb einer über dem Kämpfergesims beginnenden Vertikalen aufsteigt*]

~ **arch**, stilted ~ [*It has its springing line raised by vertical piers above the impost level*] · gestelzter Bogen *m*, gebürsteter ~, byzantinischer ~, gefußter ~, überhobener ~, Stelzbogen

surround · Abschluß *m*, Einfassung *f*, Rand~, Rand *m*

~ **profile**, ~ section, ~ shape, ~ unit, ~ trim · Randabschlußprofil *n*

~ **section**, ~ shape, ~ unit, ~ trim, ~ profile · Randabschlußprofil *n*

~ **shape**, ~ section, ~ unit, ~ trim, ~ profile · Randabschlußprofil *n*

surround trim — suspension hook

~ trim, ~ unit, ~ shape, ~ section, ~ profile · Randabschlußprofil *n*
~ unit, ~ trim, ~ shape, ~ section, ~ profile · Randabschlußprofil *n*
surrounding chapels, encircling ~, ring of chapels · Kapellenkranz *m*, Kapellenreigen *m* [*Radial auf einen Mittelpunkt bezogene Kapellen, an einem halbrunden oder polygonalen Chor bzw. Chorumgang*]
~ **masonry wall** · Einfassungsmauer *f*
survey · Aufnahme *f*
~ **of a structure** · Bauaufnahme *f* [*Aufzeichnen und Aufmessen eines Bauwerkes und anschließende maßstabgetreue und bauplanmäßige Auftragung*]
surveyor peg → pin
~ **pin** (US) → pin
~ **stake** → pin
susceptibility to frost · Frostempfindlichkeit *f*
~ ~ **heat** · Wärmeempfindlichkeit *f*
susceptible [*When not otherwise qualified, tending to change in consistency with variation in temperature*] · empfindlich
~ **to moisture**, ~ ~ **humidity** · feuchtigkeitsempfindlich, feuchteempfindlich
suspended acoustic(al) ceiling → (sound) absorbent suspended ~
~ **beam** · Hängebalken(träger) *m*
~**-cantilever hangar** · Halle *f* mit Hängekragdach, ~ ~ Kraghängedach
~ **roof** · Hängekragdach *n*, Kraghängedach
suspended ceiling, hung ~, SC [*A ceiling hung at a distance from the floor or roof above and not bearing on the walls*] · Hängedecke *f*, abgehängte Decke, untergehängte Decke
~ ~ **incorporating services**, hung ~ ~ ~, SC ~ ~ · Hängedecke *f* mit Leitungen
~ **concrete base**, ~ ~ (slab) sub-floor · Betonunterboden *m* mit Blindboden [*Fehlname: Betonboden ~ ~*]
~ ~ **floor** · freitragende Betondecke *f*
~ ~ **(slab) sub-floor**, ~ ~ **base** · Betonunterboden *m* mit Blindboden [*Fehlname: Betonboden ~ ~*]
~ ~ **sub-floor**, ~ ~ **slab** ~, ~ ~ **base** · Betonunterboden *m* mit Blindboden [*Fehlname: Betonboden ~ ~*]
~ **counterweight** · Hänge-Gegengewicht *n*
~ **floor** [*A floor that spans between supports*] · freitragende Decke *f*
(~) ~ **beam** · Stockwerkbalken(träger) *m*, Etagenbalken(träger), Geschoßbalken(träger)
~ ~ **slab, intermediate** ~ ~ [*A slab forming the continuous loadbearing structure of a floor and spanning between supports*] · Trenndeckenplatte *f*

~ **forms**, ~ **shuttering**, ~ **formwork** · Hängeschalung *f*
~ **formwork**, ~ **forms**, ~ **shuttering** · Hängeschalung *f*
~ **glazing**, suspension ~, hung ~ · hängende Verglasung *f*, ~ Einglasung, Hängeverglasung, Hängeeinglasung
~ **ground floor** [*Ground floors of cold store and chill rooms are suspended to avoid the effects of low temperature on the subsoil*] · freitragendes Erdgeschoß *n*
~ **guide** · Hängeführung *f*
~ **gutter**, hung ~ · Hängerinne *f*
~ **in water** · aufgeschlemmt in Wasser
~ **metal ceiling**, hung ~ ~ · Hängemetalldecke *f*, Metallhängedecke, abgehängte Metalldecke, untergehängte Metalldecke
~ **partition (wall)**, hung ~ (~) · Hänge(trenn)wand *f*
~ **plaster(ed) ceiling**, hung ~ ~ · Putzhängedecke *f*, Hängeputzdecke, abgehängte Putzdecke, untergehängte Putzdecke
~ **reinforced (concrete) roof** → reinforced (concrete) suspended ~
~ **roof**, suspension ~, rope(-suspended) ~, cable(-suspended) ~ · Seil(hänge)dach *n*, Kabel(hänge)dach, Hängedach
~ **scaffold**, hanging ~, flying ~, hung ~ · Hängegerüst *n*, Hängerüstung *f*
~ **shell**, hung ~ · Hängeschale *f*
~ **shuttering**, ~ **forms**, ~ **formwork** · Hängeschalung *f*
~ **stair(case)** · Hängetreppe *f*
suspender, suspension rod, hanger rod · (Auf)Hängestange *f*
~, suspension post · Hängepfosten *m*
~ **beam** · Überzug *m*
suspending agent, anti-settling ~ · Antiabsetzmittel *n*, Schwebemittel
suspension · Aufschwemmung *f*, Aufschlämmung, Suspension *f*
~ · Aufhängung *f*
~ **building**, ~ **block**, ~**-structure** · Hängegebäude *n*
~ **cable** · Dachkabel *n* [*Hängedach*]
~ ~ · (Auf)Hänge(draht)seil *n*, Trag(draht)seil
~ **construction**, ~ **(structural) system** · Hängebausystem *n*, Hänge(konstruktions)system, Hängekonstruktion *f*
~ **device** · Aufhängevorrichtung *f*
~ **fixture** → ~ **luminaire** (~) (US)
~ **floor** → hanging ~
~ **glazing**, suspended ~, hung ~ · hängende Verglasung *f*, ~ Einglasung, Hängeverglasung, Hängeeinglasung
~ **grid system** · Tragrost *m* [*Hängedecke*]
~ **gypsum slab** · Gipshängeplatte *f*
~ **hook** · Aufhängehaken *m*

suspension light fitting — swell(ed) frieze

~ **light fitting** (Brit.) → ~ luminaire (fixture) (US)

~ **(light(ing)) fixture** → ~ luminaire (~) (US)

~ **luminaire (fixture)** (US); ~ light fitting (Brit.); ~ (light(ing)) fixture · Hängebeleuchtungskörper *m*, Hängeleuchte *f*

~ **of lime**, lime suspension · Kalksuspension *f*

~ **point** · Aufhängepunkt *m*

~ **post**, suspender · Hängepfosten *m*

~ **rod** · Hängeeisen *n*, Hängestange *f*

~ **~**, hanger ~, suspender · (Auf)Hängestange *f*

~ **roof**, suspended ~, rope(-suspended) ~, cable(-suspended) ~ · Seil(hänge)dach *n*, Kabel(hänge)dach, Hängedach

~ **rope** · Aufhängeseil *n*

~ **stage** · Hängebühne *f* [*Theater*]

~ **stay**, ~ strut · Hängestrebe *f*

~ **story** (US) → hanging floor

~ **(structural) system**, ~ construction · Hängebausystem *n*, Hänge(konstruktions)system, Hängekonstruktion *f*

~ **structure** · Hängebauwerk *n*

suspension(-structure) building, ~ block · Hängegebäude *n*

suspension strut, ~ stay · Hängestrebe *f*

~ **switch**, pull ~ · Schnurschalter *m*

~ **system**, (Ab)Hängekonstruktion *f*, (Ab)Hängesystem *n* [*Zwischendecke*]

~ **~** → ~ construction

to sustain, to carry, to accept · aufnehmen [*Last*]

to s/w, ~ spot weld · punktschweißen

s/w, spot-welded · punktgeschweißt

swag, festoon, encarpa, garland [*A carved, modelled or painted garland of flowers, fruit or leaves, suspended in a curve between two points*] · Gehänge *n*, Feston *n*, Gewinde *n*, Girlande *f*

~ **leaf**, festoon ~, garland ~, encarpa ~ · Gehängeblatt *n*, Gewindeblatt, Festonblatt, Girlandenblatt

swallow tail, culvertail, dovetail, DVTL · Schwalbenschwanz *m*

swan-neck, offset, swan's neck, gooseneck [*A pipe fitting used to connect two pipes whose axes are parallel but not in line*] · Schwanenhals *m*, S-Stück *n*, Etagenbogen *m*, Sprungrohr *n* [*DIN 19506*]

sway, hazel(nut) sapling · Haselnuß *f* [*Zum Binden beim Strohdach*]

~, willow sapling · Weide *f* [*zum Binden beim Strohdach*]

~ **brace** · Ecksteife *f* [*Stahlrahmen*]

~ **bracing** · Eckversteifung *f* [*Stahlrahmen*]

swealing → wash heating

sweat-back · Kleben *n* [*Anstrichtechnik*]

sweating, bleeding, water gain [*The separation of water from an unhardened mix(ture)*] · Bluten *n*, Wasserabstoßen, Wasserabsonderung *f*, Abscheiden von Wasser, ungenügende Anmach(e)wasserhaltung, Abscheidung von Wasser

~ · (Aus)Schwitzen *n* [*Das Wandern von Weichmachern oder anderen Bestandteilen des Anstriches auf die Anstrichoberfläche*]

~, (surface) condensation · Schwitzwasserbildung *f*, Tauwasserbildung, Kondenswasserbildung, Kondensatbildung [*Niederschlag der Luftfeuchtigkeit, z.B. auf Wänden und Decken, an Glasscheiben oder Rohrleitungen, wenn durch die Abkühlung die Feuchtigkeitsaufnahmefähigkeit der Luft sinkt und infolge zu geringer Porigkeit des Untergrundes die Feuchtigkeit nicht aufgesaugt wird*]

~ **rate**, bleeding ~, water gain ~ [*The rate at which water is released from an unhardened mix(ture)*] · Wasserabstoßgeschwindigkeit *f*, Wasserabscheidungsgeschwindigkeit, Wasserabsonderungsgeschwindigkeit

~ **room**, dry ~ ~, hot ~, sudatorium, laconicum, caldarium [*The (dry) sweating room in a Roman bath building*] · römischer Schwitzraum *m*, Sudatorium *n*, Schwitzraum einer römischen Therme, römisches Schwitzbad *n*, Caldarium *n*, Sudatio *n*, Assun *n*

~ **tendency**, condensation ~ · Schwitzneigung *f* [*Beeinträchtigung der Atmungs- und Wasserdampfaufnahmefähigkeit*]

Swedish putty, spactling compound (US); filler, stopper, stopping · Spachtel(masse) *m.* (*f*), Füll~, Ausfüller *m* [*Spachtel(masse) ist ein stark pigmentierter und/oder gefüllter Anstrichstoff, vorwiegend zum Ausgleichen von Unebenheiten des Untergrundes. Der Spachtel kann zieh-, streich- oder spritzbar eingestellt werden. Die getrocknete Spachtelschicht muß schleifbar sein. Nach der Zusammensetzung unterscheidet man z.B. Leimspachtel, Dispersionsspachtel, Ölspachtel, Lackspachtel, Nitrocellulosespachtel*]

~ ~ **bending tester** (US) · stopper ~ ~

~ ~ **coat** (US) → stopping ~

~ ~ **for brush application** (US) → filler ~ ~ ~

~ ~ **seal(ing)** (US) → stopper ~

~ **sand putty**, Scandinavian plaster, thin-wall plaster · Dünnputz *m*

sweep long quarter bend · gestreckter 90°-Krümmer *m*

sweeping rib, double-curved ~ · (kurvig) geschwungene Rippe *f*

sweet glass, easily workable ~ · leicht bearbeitbares Glas *n*

swell(ed) frieze, pulvinated ~, cushioned ~ [*A frieze with a convex face*] · Pulvinusfries *m*, konvexer Fries

swelling — symmetrical two-legged multistoried frame 1004

swelling [*e.g. of a filler used in a rubber*] · Aufquellen *n*

~ · Quellen *n*, Quellung *f* [*Vorgang des Quellens*]

~ · Quellung *f* [*Ergebnis des Quellens*]

~ [*A paint fault*] · Quellen *n*, Quellung *f*

~, entasis [*A slight convex curve in the vertical outlines of the shaft of a pilaster or of a column*] · (An)Schwellung *f*, Entase *f*, Entasis *f*

~ **agent**, expanding ~, expansive ~ · Quellwirkstoff *m*, Quellzusatzstoff, Quellzusatz(mittel) *m*, (*n*)

~ **fastness**, ~ resistance, resistance to swelling, fastness to swelling · Quellfestigkeit *f*, Quellbeständigkeit

~ **resistance**, ~ fastness, resistance to swelling, fastness to swelling · Quellfestigkeit *f*, Quellbeständigkeit

~ **rubber**, expanding ~, expansive ~ · Quellgummi *m*

~ **value** · Quellmaß *n* [*Manche Werkstoffe quellen bei Wasseraufnahme. Die Größe des Quellens heißt Quellmaß und wird in mm/m ausgedrückt. Das Quellmaß hängt von Temperatur, Feuchtigkeit der umgebenden Luft und Einwirkungsdauer ab*]

swept valley · Schwenksteinkehle *f* [*Sie wird mit konischen Kehlziegeln eingedeckt*]

swimming and diving pool · Schwimmerbecken *n*

~ **bath** · Schwimmbad *n*

~ **pool** · Schwimmbecken *n*

~ ~ **cover(ing)** · Schwimmbadbelag *m*

~ ~ **filter** · Schwimmbadfilter *m*, *n*

~ ~ **hall** · Schwimm(becken)halle *f*

~ ~ **heating system**, ~ ~ ~ installation · Schwimmbadheiz(ungs)anlage *f*

~ ~ **water** · Schwimmbeckenwasser *n*

swing concertina arm · Scherenspreizer *m* [*In Büros werden manchmal Fernsprecher an der Wand mit Scherenspreizern befestigt*]

~ **door** · Schwingflügeltür *f*, Pendeltür [*Tür mit nach beiden Seiten ausschwingenden Türblättern*]

~ ~ **closer**, ~ ~ closing device, ~ ~ device for closing, ~ ~ closing mechanism · Pendeltürschließer *m*, Pendeltürschließvorrichtung *f*

~ ~ **fitting**, ~ ~ furniture · Pendeltürbeschlag *m*

~ ~ **fittings**, ~ ~ hardware · Pendeltürbeschläge *mpl*

~ ~ **furniture**, ~ ~ fitting · Pendeltürbeschlag *m*

(~ ~) **grip handle**, (~ ~) push ~ · (Pendeltür-)Stoßgriff *m*, Pendeltürgriff

~ ~ **hardware**, ~ ~ fittings · Pendeltürbeschläge *mpl*

(~ ~) **push handle**, (~ ~) grip ~ · (Pendeltür-)Stoßgriff *m*, Pendeltürgriff

(~ ~) **tubular grip handle** · Pendeltürgriff *m* aus Rundrohr, (Pendeltür-) Rohrgriff

swinging post, hanging ~, hinge ~, gatepost [*Timber or metal post to which a gate is hung*] · Torpfosten *m*

Swiss architecture · schweizerische Architektur *f*, ~ Baukunst *f*

~ **cottage**, chalet [*A house built in the Swiss style*] · Schweizerhaus *n*

~ **parallel gutter tile** · Schweizer Parallelfalzziegel *m*

switch clock · Schaltuhr *f*

~ **fuse** · Schalter *m* mit Sicherung

~ **plate**, wall ~ [*A flush plate for an electric switch*] · Wandplatte *f*, Vorlegeplatte

switchroom · Schaltraum *m*

swivel luminaire (fixture) (US); ~ light fitting (Brit.); ~ (light(ing)) fixture · Gelenkleuchte *f*

~ **outlet head** · schwenkbarer Auslauf *m*

swivelling head · Schwenkrosette *f* [*Dusche; Brause*]

swording, puddling; rodding (US); punning (Brit.) · Stochern *n*, Stocherverdichtung *f* [*Beton*]

syenite [*A coarse-grained plutonic rock composed of feldspar (orthoclase and subordinate plagioclase), biotite, hornblende, with little or no quartz. Colour: pink, grey, dark grey; S.G. 2.6–2.8; Cr.St. 21,000–35,000 lb/sq. in. Used in engineering construction and as a decorative stone. In Russia, some of the syenites are associated with valuable ore deposits*] · Syenit *m* [*Fehlname: nordischer Granit m*]

~ **sett paving** · Fpg *n*, Syenitsteinpflaster *n*

symbolic significance · symbolische Bedeutung *f*

symbolism · Symbolismus *m*

~ **of forces** · Kräftesymbolik *f*

~ ~ **form** · Formensymbolismus *m*

symmetrical arch · symmetrischer Bogen *m*

~ ~ **analysis** · symmetrische Bogenstatik *f*

~ **cruciform pier** · regelmäßiger Kreuzpfeiler *m*

~ **load** · symmetrische Last *f*

~ **matrix** · symmetrische Matrix *f*

~ **parabolic loading** · symmetrische Parabelbelastung *f*, spiegelgleiche ~

~ **two-legged multistoried frame** · zweistieliger symmetrischer Stockwerkrahmen *m*, ~ ~ Geschoßrahmen, ~ ~ Etagenrahmen

~ ~ **story frame** (US); ~ ~ storey ~ (Brit.) · symmetrischer zweistieliger Geschoßrahmen m, ~ ~ Etagenrahmen, ~ ~ Stockwerkrahmen

symmetrically-placed · symmetrisch angeordnet

symmetry · Ebenmaß n, Symmetrie f, Spiegelgleichheit f

synchronous clock [*B.S. 472*] · Synchronuhr f

synthetic adhesive → ~ (resin(-based)) (bonding) ~

~ **aggregate light(weight) concrete** · Leichtbeton m mit künstlichen Zuschlägen, ~ ~ ~ Zuschlagstoffen

~ **anhydrite**, chemical ~, by-product ~ · künstlicher Anhydrit m

~ ~ **screed (material)**, chemical ~ ~ (~), by-product ~ ~ (~) · Estrich m aus künstlichem Anhydrit [*als Baustoff*]

~ ~ ~ **(topping)**, chemical ~ ~ (~), by-product ~ ~ (~) · Estrich m aus künstlichem Anhydrit [*als verlegter Baustoff*]

~ **(bonding) adhesive** → ~ (resin (-based)) (~) ~

~ ~ **agent** → ~ (resin(-based)) (bonding) adhesive

~ ~ **medium** → ~ (resin(-based)) (bonding) adhesive

~ **building product** → manufactured construction(al) ~

~ **cement(ing agent)** → ~ (resin (-based)) (bonding) adhesive

~ **concrete curing agent** → ~ (resin (-based)) (concrete) curing compound

~ (~) ~ **compound** → ~ (resin (-based)) (~) ~ ~

~ **construction(al) product** → manufactured ~ ~

~ **copal**, rosin-modified phenolic resin · Kunstkopal m, (harzsäure)modifiziertes Phenolharz n

~ **corundum** [*It is made by fusing bauxite in an electric furnace*] · Elektrokorund m

~ **curing compound** → ~ (resin (-based)) (concrete) ~ ~

~ **dyestuff** · künstlicher Farbstoff m

~ **fibre** (Brit.); ~ fiber (US); man-made ~ · Kunstfaser f, Chemiefaser

~ ~ **fabric** (Brit.); ~ fiber ~ (US); man-made ~ ~ · Kunstfasergewebe n

~ ~ **material** (Brit.); ~ fiber ~ (US); man-made ~ ~ · Kunstfaserstoff m

~ **glue** → ~ (resin(-based)) (bonding) adhesive

~ **indigo** · künstlicher Indigo m

~ **inorganic pigment** · Mineralpigment n, künstliches anorganisches Pigment [*Fehlname: Mineralfarbe f*]

~ **lacquer-grade resin**, ~ varnish ~ · Lackkunstharz n

~ **(liquid) membrane (concrete) curing agent** → ~ (resin(-based)) (concrete) curing compound

~ (~) ~ (~) ~ **compound** → ~ (resin(-based)) (~) ~ ~

~ **oil** · künstliches Öl n

~ **organic pigment**, organic synthetic ~ · künstliches organisches Pigment n, organisches künstliches ~

(~) **plastic coating** · Kunststoffbeschichtung f

~ ~ **(material)**, man-made ~ (~), manufactured ~ (~) · Kunststoff m auf synthetischer Basis, synthetischer Kunststoff

~ **resin**, manufactured ~, man-made ~, artificial ~ [*Strictly speaking, these terms are misnomers, as the substances in question are not natural resins artificially produced, but are different both in composition and properties*] · Kunstharz n, synthetisches Harz

~ ~ **asbestos board**, ~ ~ ~ sheet · Kunstharz-Asbestplatte f [*DIN 16950*]

~ ~ ~ **sheet**, ~ ~ ~ board · Kunstharz-Asbestplatte f [*DIN 16950*]

~ ~ **backing** → ~ ~ base

~ ~ **base**, ~ ~ backing, ~ ~ underlay, ~ ~ substrate, ~ ~ substratum · Kunstharzhinterlegung f, Kunstharzunterlage f, Kunstharzrücken m, Kunstharzrücklage, Kunstharzträger(schicht) m, (f)

~ ~ ~ · Kunstharzbasis f, Kunstharzgrundlage f

~ ~ **based** · kunstharzhaltig

~ **(resin(-based)) (bonding) adhesive**, artificial (~) (~) ~, man-made (~) (~) ~, manufactured (~) (~) ~, ~ (~) ~ medium, ~ (~) ~ agent, ~ (~) cement(ing agent), ~ (~) glue · Kunstharzkleb(e)stoff m, Kunstharzkleb(e)mittel n, Kunstharzkleber m, Kunstharzleim m, synthetischer Leim, synthetischer Kleb(e)stoff, synthetischer Kleber, synthetisches Kleb(e)mittel

~ (~) (~) **curing compound**, ~ (~) ~ ~ agent, ~ (~) liquid membrane (~) ~ ~ ~ · (Beton)Nachbehandlungsmittel n auf Kunstharzbasis

~ (~) **glue** → ~ (~) (bonding) adhesive

~ (~) **(liquid) membrane (concrete) curing compound** → ~ (~) (concrete) curing ~

~ **resin-bonded**, bonded with synthetic resinous material · kunstharzgeleimt

~ (~) **bonding agent** → ~ (~) (~) adhesive

~ **resin-bound**, bound with synthetic resinous material · kunstharzgebunden

~ **resin (building) mastic**, ~ ~ mastic joint sealer · Kunstharz(fugen)mastix m, Kunstharz(fugen)kitt m, Kunstharz-(ver)füllkitt, Kunstharz-Fugen(ab)-dicht(ungs)kitt, plastische Kunstharz-Fugen(ab)dicht(ungs)masse f, plastische Kunstharz-Fugenmasse, plastische Kunstharz-(Fugen)(Ver)Füllmasse, plastischer Kunstharz-(Fugen-)(Ver)Füller m

synthetic resin-cement — synthetic resin waterproofing

~ ~ **cement**, ~ ~ **putty** · Kunstharzkitt *m*

(~) ~ **(clear) varnish** · Kunstharzlack *m* [*Ein Lack mit Kunstharz als Bindemittel*]

~ ~ **coat** · Kunstharzbeschichtung *f*, Kunstharzüberzug *m* [*als Schicht*]

~ ~ ~ · Kunstharzanstrich *m*, Kunstharzaufstrich

~ ~ **coating (material)** → ~ ~ waterproofing (compound)

~ ~ **(cold-)water paint**, ~ ~ water-carried ~ · Kunstharz-Dispersionsfarbe *f*, Kunstharz-Binderfarbe

~ ~ **dispersion** · Kunstharzdispersion *f*, Plastdispersion [*Eine beständige, sahneartige Aufschwemmung von Kunstharzteilchen mit 0,002 bis 0,0002 mm Durchmesser in Wasser, meist mit etwa 50% Feststoffgehalt*]

~ ~ ~ **base** · Kunstharzdispersionsbasis *f*, Kunstharzdispersionsgrundlage *f*

~ ~ ~ **finish**, plastic ~, plastic plaster · Kunststoff(ver)putz *m*, Kunstharzdispersions(ver)putz [*Kunststoff(ver)putze sind mit Kunststoffgranulaten verschiedener Färbung oder farbigen mineralischen Splittern gefüllte Dispersionen für dickschichtige Anstriche auf Mauerwerk*]

~ ~ **emulsion** · Kunstharzemulsion *f*

~ ~ ~ **paint** · Kunstharzemulsions(an)strich)farbe *f*

~ ~ **exterior coat**, ~ ~ external ~, ~ ~ outside ~, ~ ~ outer ~ · Kunstharz-Außenanstrich *m*, Kunstharz-Außenaufstrich

~ ~ **external coat**, ~ ~ exterior ~, ~ ~ outside ~, ~ ~ outer ~ · Kunstharz-Außenanstrich *m*, Kunstharz-Außenaufstrich

~ ~ **flat paint**, ~ ~ matt(-finish) ~ · Kunstharz-Matt(anstrich)farbe *f*

~ ~ **floor cover(ing)**, ~ ~ ~ finish, ~ ~ floor(ing) · Kunstharz(fuß)boden(belag) *m*

~ ~ ~ **finish**, ~ ~ ~ cover(ing), ~ ~ floor(ing) · Kunstharz(fuß)boden(belag) *m*

~ ~ **floor(ing)**, ~ ~ floor finish, ~ ~ floor cover(ing) · Kunstharz(fuß)boden(belag) *m*

~ ~ **impregnated**, ~ ~ saturated · kunstharzgetränkt

~ ~ **impregnating seal(ing) material**, ~ ~ ~ sealant, ~ ~ ~ seal(er) · Kunstharz-Imprägnierabsiegelungsmittel *n*, Kunstharz-Imprägniersiegel *m*, Kunstharz-Imrägnierversiegelungsmittel, Kunstharz-Imprägnierüberzug *m*

~ ~ **joint** · Kunstharzfuge *f*

~ ~ **lacquer** · Kunstharzlackfarbe *f*

~ ~ **mastic** → ~ ~ building ~

~ ~ ~ **joint sealer** → ~ ~ (building) mastic

~ ~ **matt(-finish) paint**, ~ ~ flat · Kunstharz-Matt(anstrich)farbe *f*

~ **resin-modified** · kunstharzvergütet

~ **resin outer coat**, ~ ~ outside ~, ~ ~ external ~, ~ ~ exterior ~ · Kunstharz-Außenanstrich *m*, Kunstharz-Außenaufstrich

~ ~ **outside coat**, ~ ~ outer ~, ~ ~ external ~, ~ ~ exterior ~ · Kunstharz; Außenanstrich *m*, Kunstharz-Außenaufstrich

~ ~ **penetrating aid** → ~ ~ waterproofing (compound)

~ ~ ~ **sealer** → ~ ~ waterproofing (compound)

~ ~ **plaster** · Kunstharzputz *m*

~ ~ **prime coat** · Kunstharzgrundierung *f*, Kunstharzgrund(ier)anstrich *m*, Kunstharzgrund(ier)aufstrich

~ ~ **product**, ~ ~ article · Kunstharzartikel *m*, Kunstharzerzeugnis *n*, Kunstharzgegenstand *m*

~ ~ **putty**, ~ ~ cement · Kunstharzkitt *m*

~ ~ **rigid foam** · Kunstharz-Hartschaum(stoff) *m*

~ ~ **rubber mix(ture)** · Kunstharz-Gummi-Gemisch *n*, Kunstharz-Gummi-Mischung *f*

~ ~ **saturated**, ~ ~ impregnated · kunstharzgetränkt

~ ~ **solution** · Kunstharzlösung *f*

~ ~ **stand oil enamel**, stand oil synthetic resin · Standöl-Kunstharz-Emaillelack *m*, Kunstharz-Standöl-Emaillelack

~ ~ **substrate** → ~ ~ base

~ ~ **surface** · Kunstharzoberfläche *f*

~ ~ ~ **waterproofing agent**, ~ ~ ~ waterproofer, ~ ~ ~ waterrepeller, ~ ~ ~ water repelling agent · Kunstharz-Sperranstrichstoff *m*, Kunstharz-Sperranstrich(mittel) *m*, (*n*), Kunstharz-Sperraufstrich(mittel), Kunstharz-Sperraufstrichstoff

~ ~ ~ **waterrepeller** → ~ ~ ~ waterproofing agent

~ ~ ~ **water repelling agent** → ~ ~ ~ waterproofing ~

~ ~ **underlay** → ~ ~ base

(~) ~ **varnish**, (~) ~ clear ~ · Kunstharzlack *m* [*Ein Lack mit Kunstharz als Bindemittel*]

~ ~ **water-carried paint**, ~ ~ (cold-)water ~ · Kunstharz-Dispersionsfarbe *f*, Kunstharz-Binderfarbe

~ ~ **water paint**, ~ ~ cold-~ ~, ~ ~ water-carried ~ · Kunstharz-Dispersionsfarbe *f*, Kunstharz-Binderfarbe

~ ~ ~ **repellent** → ~ ~ waterproofing (compound)

~ ~ **waterproof coating (material)** → ~ ~ waterproofing (compound)

~ ~ **waterproofing (compound)**, ~ ~ coating (material), ~ ~ penetrating sealer, ~ ~ water repellent, ~ ~ penetrating aid, ~ ~ waterproof coating (material) · Kunstharz-Imprägnierung f, Kunstharz-Wetterschutz m, Kunstharz-Imprägnier(ungs)mittel n, Kunstharz-Imprägnier(ungs)anstrichstoff m, Kunstharz-Imprägnier(ungs)anstrich(mittel) m, (n)

~ **rubber**, man-made ~, manufacture ~ · Kunstgummi m, n, Synthesegummi, synthetischer Gummi n

~ ~ **(based) emulsion** · Kunstkautschukemulsion f

~ ~ **(building) mastic** · Kunstkautschukkitt m

~ ~ **contact (bonding) adhesive,** ~ ~ ~ ~ **medium,** ~ ~ ~ ~ **agent** ~ ~ ~ **cement(ing) agent** · Kunstgummikontaktkleber m, Kunstgummikontaktkleb(e)stoff m, Kunstgummikontaktkleb(e)mittel n

~ ~ ~ **solution** · Kunstharzkautschukkontaktlösung f

~ ~ **dispersion** · Kunstharzkautschukdispersion f

~ ~ **emulsion,** ~ ~ **based** · Kunstkautschukemulsion f

~ ~ **latex** · Kunstkautschuklatex m

~ ~ **mastic,** ~ ~ **building** ~ · Kunstkautschukkitt m

~ **stone** → cast ~

~ **structural product** → manufactured construction(al) ~

~ **ultramarine** · künstliches Ultramarin n

~ **varnish resin,** ~ lacquer-grade ~ · Lackkunstharz n

~ **wax** · Kunstwachs n

Syrian architecture · syrische Architektur f, ~ Baukunst

~ **vault** · syrisches Gewölbe n

system · Aufbau m, System n

~ → construction(al) ~

~, compound, chemical ~ · (chemische) Verbindung f

~ → individual ~

~ **building,** ~ **construction** [*Prefab(ricated) construction method with (non-metallic) fireproof members*] · Montage-Massiv-Bauweise f, MMB

~ ~ → industrialized ~

~ **(~) construction,** prefab(ricated) (~) ~, industrialized (~) ~ · Fertig(teil)-(hoch)bau m, Montage(hoch)bau, Element(hoch)bau, System(hoch)bau

~ ~ **method** → (pre)cast (concrete) construction ~

~ ~ ~, prefab(ricated) construction ~, industrialized construction ~ · Fertig(teil)bauweise f, Elementbauweise, Montagebauweise, Fertig(teil)bauverfahren n, Elementbauverfahren, Montagebauverfahren

system-built (concrete) structure → (pre)cast (~) ~

~ **façade,** prefab(ricated) ~; industrialized ~ (US) [*British spelling is 'industrialised'*] · Fertigfassade f, Montagefassade; Elementfassade [*Fehlname*]

~ **garage,** prefab(ricated) ~; industrialized ~ (US) [*British spelling is 'industrialised'*] · Fertig(bau)garage f; Elementgarage [*Fehlname*]

~ **structure,** prefab(ricated) ~; industrialized ~ (US) [*British spelling is 'industrialised'*] · Fertig(teil)bau(werk) m, (n), Montagebau(werk), Systembau(werk); Elementbau(werk) [*Fehlnamen*]

system-built wall, prefab(ricated) ~; industrialized ~ (US) [*British spelling is 'industrialised'*] · Fertigwand f, Montagewand; Elementwand [*Fehlname*]

system construction → industrialized building

~ ~, ~ building [*Prefab(ricated) construction method with (non-metallic) fireproof members*] · Montage-Massiv-Bauweise f, MMB

~ ~ → ~ building ~

~ ~ **method,** prefab(ricated) ~ ~; industrialized ~ ~ (US) [*British spelling is 'industrialised'*] · Fertig(teil)bauweise f, Fertig(teil)bauverfahren n, Montagebauweise, Montagebauverfahren [*Fehlnamen: Elementbauweise, Elementbauverfahren*]

~ **in which all the walls carry loading** · Allwand-Tragsystem n

~ **line** · Netzlinie f, Systemlinie [*Fachwerkträger; Fachwerk(dach)binder*]

~ **of air voids,** air void system · Luftporensystem n

~ ~ **anchoring,** method ~ ~, anchoring method, anchoring system · Verankerungssystem n, Verankerungsverfahren n

~ ~ **beams and joists in star form** · Sternbalkenlage f, Sterngebälk n

~ ~ **binders and joists** → ~ ~ ~ wood(en) ~ ~ ~

~ ~ ~ ~ **between stories** → ~ ~ wood(en) or timber ~ ~ ~ ~ ~

~ ~ ~ ~ ~ **covering the uppermost story** (US)/**storey** (Brit.) → ~ ~ wood(en) or timber ~ ~ ~ ~ ~ ~ ~

~ ~ ~ ~ ~ **for a tower** → ~ ~ wood(en) ~ ~ ~ ~ ~

~ ~ **bracing,** bracing system · (Aus-)Füll(ungs)system n [*Träger*]

~ ~ **buttresses and flying buttresses,** abutment system · Strebeapparat m, Strebewerk n, Strebesystem n [*Die Gesamtheit von Strebebögen und Strebepfeilern, wie sie vor allem die Gotik ausgebildet hat*]

~ ~ **collar beams,** ~ ~ span pieces · Kehlbalkenlage f, Kehlgebälk n [*Das Kehlgebälk zerlegt den Dachraum in übereinanderliegende Räume*]

~ ~ **coordinates for representation of (grain) size distribution curves R.R.B.,** (grain) size distribution diagram · RRB-Netz n, Körnungsnetz

~~ **dowelled (wood(en)) beams,** ~~~ timber ~ · Dübelbalkenlage f, Dübelbaumlage; Dippelbalkenlage, Dippelbaumlage [Österreich]

~~ **facing** → facing method

~~ **forces** · Kräftegruppe f

~~ **jointing,** method ~ ~, jointing method, jointing system · Verbindungssystem n, Verbindungsverfahren n

~~ **loads,** load system · Lastsystem n

~~ **rafters,** rafter system · (Dach)Sparrenlage f

~~ **sanitation** → sanitation system

~~ **sewerage,** ~ ~ sewers, sewerage (system) [*A collecting system of sewers and appurtenances*] · Kanalisation f, Ortsentwässerung f

~~ **sewers,** ~ ~ sewerage, sewerage (system) [*A collecting system of sewers and appurtenances*] · Ortsentwässerung f, Kanalisation f

~~ **span pieces,** ~ ~ collar beams · Kehlgebälk n, Kehlbalkenanlage f [*Das Kehlgebälk zerlegt den Dachraum in übereinanderliegende Räume*]

(~ ~) **three posts** · dreifach stehender (Dach)Stuhl m

(~ ~) ~ ~ **and wind filling** · dreifach stehender (Dach)Stuhl m und Versenkung f

~~ **timber binders and joists** → ~ ~ (wood(en)) ~ ~ ~

~ ~ ~ ~ ~ **for a tower,** ~ ~ (wood(en)) ~ ~ ~ ~ ~ ~ · Turmbalkenlage f

~~ **tolerances for building (construction)** · Toleranzsystem n (im Hochbau)

~~ **(wood(en)) binders and joists,** ~ ~ timber ~ ~ ~ · (Holz)Balken(träger)lage f, (Holz)Gebälk n [*Der tragende Teil einer hölzernen Decke*]

~~ (~) ~ ~ ~ ~ **for a tower,** ~ ~ timber ~ ~ ~ ~ ~ ~ · Turmbalkenlage f

~~ (~) (**or timber**) **binders and joists between stories** · Zwischengebälk n, Stockgebälk, Zwischenbalkenlage f, Stockbalkenlage [*Das Zwischengebälk trennt die Geschosse voneinander*]

~~ (~) (~ ~) ~ ~ ~ **covering the uppermost story (US)/storey (Brit.)** · Dachgebälk n, Dachbalkenlage f [*Das Dachgebälk deckt das oberste Stockwerk ab und dient zur Aufstellung des Dachgerüstes*]

~ **point** · Systempunkt m

~ **with alternating columns and piers,** alternating rows of pillars ~ ~, alternate system, alternation of supports · (Stützen)Wechsel(system) m, (n) [*Regelmäßige Wechsel von Pfeiler und Säule oder Säulenpaar, in der römischen Basilika durch das gebundene System bedingt*]

~~ **ring-type buildup** · Ringaufbausystem n [*Seilsystem*]

~ ~ ~ ~ **rising toward centre** · Ringaufbausystem n mit zentraler Überhöhung [*Seilsystem*]

~~ **stacked up three-hinged frames** · System n mit übereinandergesetzten Dreigelenkrahmen

~~ **transverse stabilization beams** · System n mit querlaufenden Stabilisierungsbalken

~ ~ ~ ~ **cables** · System n mit querlaufenden Stabilisierungsseilen

systematically laid-out pedestrian street · differenziert gegliederte Fußgängerstraße f

systematization · Systematisierung f

systyle · Systylos m

~ [*An adjective applied to architecture in which the columns are close together, viz. at a distance from each other of twice their thickness*] · systyl, gedehnt

Szerelmey Stonecoat Encaustic, ~ **Stone Liquid** [*A proprietary product*] · Lapidensin n [*Markenname eines Steinschutzmittels*]

T

T, Tee, tee, tee-piece · T-Stück n

T asph, Trinidad asphalt (US); Trinidad (asphaltic-)bitumen (Brit.) · Trinidadbitumen n

T bar, Tee ~, tee ~ · T-Tragschiene f [*Hängedecke*]

~ ~, Tee ~, tee ~, ~ section, ~ steel ~ · (Einfach-)T-Stahl m

T block → tee ~

T cross section, Tee ~ ~ · T-Querschnitt m

T girder, Tee ~, tee ~ · T-Träger m

T hinge → cross garnet (~)

T panel, Tee ~, tee ~, single ~ ~ · T-Tafel f

T section, Tee ~, tee ~, ~ bar, ~ steel ~ · (Einfach-)T-Stahl m

T slab → (single) T(ee) ~

T (steel) bar, Tee (~) ~, tee (~) ~, ~ (~) section · (Einfach-)T-Stahl m

T tile → tee block

tabby (US); oyster-shell concrete · Muschel(schalen)beton m, Schillbeton

tabernacle · Heiligennische *f*

tabernacled statues of the Kings of France, band of ~~~ ~~~ ~, arcade of Kings · Königsgalerie *f* [*Galerie mit Königsstatuen an der Fassade französischer Kathedralen*]

table, tabling [*In medieval architecture, a projecting horizontal string-course*] · Kreuz(ge)sims *m*, (*n*)

~ **altar** · Tischaltar *m*

~ **form** · Form(en)tisch *m* [*Herstellung von Montagebauteilen*]

~ **joint**, tabling · Verschränkung *f*

~ **of moments**, moment table · Momententabelle *f*

~ ~ **standardized figures for construction** · Baunormzahlentafel *f*

~ ~ **weights**, schedule ~ ~, weight table, weight schedule · Gewichtstabelle *f*

~ **stone** → dolmen

~ **tomb**, sepulcrum of a mensa · Mensagrab *n*

~ **top** · Tischplatte *f*

table(d) joint, tabling · Verschränkung *f* [*Holzbau*]

tablet [*A thin sheet of wood, stone, etc., for an inscription*] · Tafel *f*

tabling, table [*In medieval architecture, a projecting horizontal string-course*] · Kreuz(ge)sims *m*, (*n*)

~, table(d) joint · Verschränkung *f* [*Holzbau*]

tablinum [*In Roman architecture, a room with one side open to the atrium or central courtyard*] · Tablinum *n*

tabular data · Tabellenmaterial *n*

to tabulate · tabellenmäßig erfassen

tabulated coefficient · Tabellenbeiwert *m*

tack · Koppe *f*, Zwecke *f*

~ · Hafte *f*

~ **bolt**, ~ screw · Montierschraube *f*, Heftschraube [*Eine zum Zwischenhalten von Stahlkonstruktionsleisten auf der Baustelle vorübergehend eingezogene Schraube. Sie wird später durch einen Niet ersetzt*]

tack-free, stick-free · klebfrei, nichtkleb(e)rig

tack-freedom · Klebfreiheit *f* [*Anstrich*]

tack rivet, stitch ~ [*Rivet introduced merely to hold two or more thicknesses of plate together, as distinct from a load-taking rivet*] · Heftniet *m*

~ **riveting**, stitch ~ · Heftnieten *n*

~ **screw** → ~ bolt

~ **weld** · Heft(schweiß)naht *f*

~ **welding**, positional ~ · Heftschweißen *n*, Heftschweißung *f*

tack(iness) [*Slight stickiness of the surface of a film of paint, varnish or lacquer, apparent when the film is pressed with the finger*] · leichte Kleb(e)rigkeit *f*

tacking, stitching [*Fixing a thing not securely*] · Heften *n*

tacky [*Having a tack*] · leichtkleb(e)rig

t(a)enia, flat raised band [*The small mo(u)lding or fillet along the top of the architrave in the Doric order*] · Stirnband *n*, Tänia *f*, Taenia, flaches Band [*Vorspringende Leiste am Epistyl der dorischen Ordnung*]

tagger · Feinblech *n* [< 3 mm]

tailbeam [*A beam which frames into a header instead of spanning the entire distance between supports*] · Stichbalken *m* [*Auswechs(e)lung*]

tailing [*Fixing the end of a projecting member securely into a wall*] · Einbinden *n*

tailor's shop · Schneiderei *f*

tailpiece, ferrule, sleeve · Muffenverbindung *f* (mit Stemmdichtung)

take-off pipe → branch ~

to take samples, ~ sample · nehmen von Proben

taking-down period, cooling-down ~, standing-off ~ · Kaltschüren *n*, Abstehen [*Glasschmelze*]

talc · Talk(erde) *n*, (*f*), Speckstein *m*

talc-schist [*A soft, greasy metamorphic rock composed of talc together with some mica*] · Talkschiefer *m*

talcum → fine talc

talc(um) powder → fine talc

talcum (powder) surfacing, powder(ed) talc ~, French chalk ~ · Talkumabstreuung *f*, Talkumbestreuung [*Dachpappe*]

talcumed · talkumiert

tall block, ~ building, tower (~), high-rise ~ · Hochhaus *n*, Turmgebäude *n*, Turmhaus

~ ~ **building** → high-rise block construction

~ ~ **construction** → high-rise ~ ~

~ ~ **façade** → tower (~) ~

~ ~ **(of flats)** (Brit.) → residence tower

~ ~ **rising line** → tower (~) ~ ~

~ **building**, ~ block, tower (~), high-rise ~ · Hochhaus *n*, Turmgebäude *n*, Turmhaus

~ ~ **construction** → high-rise block ~

~ ~ **façade** → tower (block) ~

~ ~ **rising line** → tower (block) ~ ~

~ **flats** (Brit.) → residence tower

tall industrialized block (of flats) — taper(ed) junction

~ **industrialized block (of flats)** (Brit.) → (pre)cast residence tower

~~ **flats** (Brit.) → (pre)cast residence tower

~ **oil**; liquid rosin [*misnomer*] · Tallöl *n*

~~ **ester** · Tallölester *m*

~~ **rosin** · Tallharz *n* [*Aus Tallöl gewonnenes Harzsäuregemisch*]

~ **structure**, high-rise ~ · hohes Bauwerk *n*, hochaufgehendes ~

tal(l)us wall, battered ~ · Wand *f* mit einseitigem Anlauf, ~ ~ ~ Anzug, ~ ~ einseitiger Dossierung

tambour, drum, tholobate [*A vertical wall supporting a dome or cupola; it may be circular, square, or polygonal in plan*] · Tambour *m*, Trommel *f*, Kuppelunterbau *m*

~, (circular) vestibule · Drehtürgehäuse *n*

tamped concrete · Stampfbeton *m*

~~ **foundation** · Stampfbetonfundament *n*

~~ **pipe** · Stampfbetonrohr *n*

~~ **spigot and socket pipe** · Stampfbetonglockenmuffenrohr *n*

~~ **wall** · Stampfbetonwand *f*

tamping [*The operation of compacting freshly placed concrete by repeated blows*] · Stampfen *n*, Stampfverdichtung *f*

~ **bar**, ~ **rod** · Stampfstange *f*

~ **rod**, ~ **bar** · Stampfstange *f*

~ **vibration** · Stampfrütt(e)lung *f*

tandem elevator, double-deck ~ (US); ~ lift (Brit.) [*The bottom cab serves odd-numbered floors and the top cab stops at even ones. Inside the entrance, the visitors are directed to a lower level for elevators to odd-numbered floors and to an upper level for those to even ones*] · Tandem-Aufzug *m*

~ **lift** (Brit.) → ~ elevator

T&G, (tongue and groove) matched, tongued and grooved (together) · mit Nut und Feder, (genutet und) gespundet

~ **ceiling**, tongued-and-grooved ~, (tongue and groove) matched ~ · (genutet und) gespundete Decke *f*, Spunddecke

~ **(floor) boarding**, matched (~) ~, tongued-and-grooved ~ · gespundeter (Fuß)Boden(belag) *m*

~ **joint**, tongue(d)-and-groove(d) ~, (tongue and groove) matched ~ · (Nut- und) Spundverbindung *f*

~ **shingle**, tongued-and-grooved ~, matched ~ · Nutschindel *f*

~ **sub-floor**, tongued-and-grooved ~, (tongue and groove) matched ~ · (genuteter und) gespundeter Unterboden *m*, Spundunterboden

tangent plane [*Plane surface which makes contact with a curved surface*] · Tangentenebene *f*

tangential acceleration · Tangentialbeschleunigung *f*

~ **component** · Tangentialkomponente *f*

~ **shear force** · Tangentialschubkraft *f*

~ **shear(ing)** · Tangentialschub *m*

~ **stress** · Tangentialspannung *f*

tank, vat · Küpe *f*, Färberbottich *m*

~ · Tauchbecken *n* [*Elektrotauchlackierung*]

~ **bottom** · Behälterboden *m*

~ **coat(ing)** · Behälteranstrich *m*, Behälteraufstrich

~ **furnace** · Wannenofen *m* [*Glasherstellung*]

~ **jack** · Spannpresse *f* für den Spannbetonbehälterbau

~ **jacket** · Behältermantel *m*

~ **(mixed) plaster** · Behälterputz *m*

~ **tower** · Behälterturm *m*

tanking · Wannen(ab)dichtung *f*, Wannenisolierung, (Ab)Dicht(ungs)trog *m*, Trogisolierung, Isolierwanne *f* [*Sie wird bei hohem Grundwasserstand vorgesehen*]

Tannenberg (masonry) bond · Tannenbergverband *m* [*Je eine Läuferschicht und eine Schicht des gotischen Verbandes wechseln sich ab. Entsprechend dem Ansetzen der Schichten ergeben sich verschiedene Muster*]

tannic acid · Gerbsäure *f*

tantalum · Tantal *n*

to tap · anbohren

tap · Zapfhahn *m*

~ **grease** · Hahnschmiere *f*

~ **hole** · Hahnloch *n*

tape · (Aufzug)Band *n*, (Aufzug)Gurt *m* [*Rolladen*]

~ **covering** · Dämmband *n*

~ ~, pipe ~ ~ · (Rohr)Bandisolierung *f*

~ **mastic** · Kittstreifen *m*

to taper · kegelig machen, verjüngen

taper, taper(ing) · Kegelneigung *f*, Verjüngung, Verjüngungsverhältnis *n* beim Kegel, Kegelverhältnis, Kegelsteigung, Kegeligkeit *f*, Konizität *f*

taper(ed) beam, tapering ~ · konischer Balken(träger) *m*

~ **bend**, tapering ~ · konischer Krümmer *m*, kegeliger ~, Übergangskrümmer

~ **branch** → ~ (pipe) junction

~ **column**, tapering ~ · konische Stütze *f*

~ **corrugated sheet**, corrugated tapered ~ · konische Wellplatte *f*

~ **dowel** · Kegeldübel *m*, Konusdübel

~ **elbow**, tapering ~ · Übergangs(rohr)bogen *m*

~ **fitting**, tapering ~, increaser · (Rohr-)Übergang *m*

~ **foundation**, cone ~, conical ~ · kegelförmige Gründung *f*, konische ~

~ **inlet** → ~ (pipe) junction

~ **junction** → ~ pipe ~

taper(ed) pipe — tar(-coated) sand

~ **pipe**, tapering ~ · konisches Rohr *n* Konusrohr, Übergangsrohr

~ (~) **branch** → ~ (~) junction

~ (~) **inlet** → ~ (~) junction

~ (~) **junction**, ~ (~) inlet, ~ (~) branch, tapering (~) ~ · Übergangs-(rohr)abzweig *m*

~ **plain clay roof(ing) tile**, ~ plane ~ ~ ~ · konischer Biberschwanz *m*, ~ Biber(schwanzziegel) *m*

(~) **plug**, tapering ~ · drehbarer Kegel *m*, (Hahn)Küken *n*

~ **shaft**, tapering ~ · konischer Schaft *m*, kegeliger ~, Kegelschaft

~ **tenon**, tapering ~ · schräger Zapfen *m* [*Holzverbindung*]

~ **thread**, tapering ~ · Kegelgewinde *n*, kegeliges Gewinde, konisches Gewinde

~ **tower**, tapering ~ · konischer Turm *m*

~ **valley clay roof(ing) tile**, ~ ~ roof(ing) clay ~, ~ (roof) valley clay ~ · konischer Kehlziegel *m*

~ **washer** · konische Unterlegscheibe *f*

taper(ing) · Kegelneigung *f*, Verjüngung, Verjüngungsverhältnis *n* beim Kegel, Kegelverhältnis, Kegelsteigung, Kegeligkeit *f*, Konizität *f*

tapering branch → taper(ed) (pipe) junction

~ **inlet** → taper(ed) (pipe) junction

~ **junction** → taper(ed) (pipe) ~

~ **(pipe) branch** → taper(ed) (pipe) junction

~ (~) **inlet** → taper(ed) (pipe) junction

~ (~) **junction** → taper(ed) (~) ~

tapestry · Tapisserie *f*, Wandteppich *m*

tapioca starch · Tapiokastärke *f*

tapped resin · rezentes Harz *n* [*Aus lebenden Pflanzen gewonnenes Harz, z.B. Kolophonium, im Gegensatz zum (rezent)fossilen Harz, z.B. Bernstein*]

tapping · Anbohren *n*

tap(ping) bracket, ~ pipe ~ · Anbohr-(rohr)schelle *f*

~ **(pipe) bracket** · Anbohr(rohr)schelle *f*

~ **valve** · Anbohrschieber *m*

to tar · teeren

tar · Teer *m* [*Nach DIN 55946 durch zersetzende thermische Behandlung organischer Naturstoffe gewonnene flüssige bis halbfeste Erzeugnisse. In der Bautechnik wird unter Teer schlechthin der Steinkohlenteer verstanden*]

~, road ~, tar for road purposes [*B.S. 76*] · (Straßen)Teer *m*, T [*DIN 1995*]

~ **acid** · Teersäure *f*

tar-and-gravel roof cover(ing), ~ ~ cladding, ~ ~ sheathing, ~ roofing · Teer-(Kies)Kleb(e)(ein)deckung *f*, Teer-(Kies)Kleb(e)dach(ein)deckung, Teer-(Kies)Kleb(e)bedachung

tar/asphalt composition roofing → ~ ready ~

~ **mix(ture)** (US); tar/(asphaltic-)bitumen ~ (Brit.) · Teerbitumengemisch *n*, Teerbitumenmischung *f*

~ **prepared roofing** → ~ ready ~

~ **ready roofing**, ~ composition ~, ~ prepared ~, ~ roof(ing) felt (US); fluxed pitch/(asphaltic-)bitumen roof(-ing) felt (Brit.) · Teer-Bitumen-Dachpappe *f* [*Diese Dachpappe ist hauptsächlich eine Teer-, keine Bitumendachpappe; sie unterscheidet sich von der Teer-Sonderdachpappe dadurch, daß der Tränkmasse und/oder der Deckmasse mindestens 25 Gew.-% Bitumen zugemischt sind*]

~ **roof(ing) felt** (US) → ~ ready roofing

tar-(asphaltic-)bitumen mix(ture) (Brit.); tar(-petroleum) asphalt ~ (US) · Teer(-Erdöl)bitumen-Gemisch *n*, Teer(-Erdöl)bitumen-Mischung *f*

tar base · Teerbasis *f*, Teergrundlage *f*

~ ~ **roof preservative**, ~ ~ ~ ~ preserver · Dachschutzmittel *n* auf Teerbasis

~ ~ **(surface)** · Teeruntergrund *m*

~ **based** · teerhaltig

tar(-based) composition, ~ compound · Teermasse *f*

~ **compound**, ~ composition · Teermasse *f*

tar/bitumen mix(ture) → tar/(asphaltic-)bitumen ~

tar (blastfurnace) slag chip(ping)s → tar(-coated) (iron) (~) ~ ~

tar-bonded magnesite · Teermagnesit *m*

tar-bound, tarviated · teergebunden

tar broken rock → tar(-coated) broken stone

~ ~ **stone** → tar-coated ~ ~

~ **coat** · Teeranstrich *m*, Teeraufstrich

tar(-coated) (blastfurnace) slag chip(ping)s → ~ iron (~) ~ ~

~ **broken rock** → ~ ~ stone

~ ~ **stone**, ~ ~ rock, ~ crushed ~; ~ (road-)metal (Brit.) · Teerschotter *m*, teerumhüllter Schotter [*Ein mit Straßenteer umhüllter Schotter*]

~ **chip(ping)s**, tarred ~, chip(ping)s precoated with tar · Teersplitt *m*, teerumhüllter Splitt

~ **cinder chip(ping)s** (US) → ~ (iron) (blastfurnace) slag ~

~ **crushed rock** → ~ broken stone

~ ~ **stone** → ~ broken ~

~ **(iron) (blastfurnace) slag chip(ping)s** (Brit.); ~ ~ ~ (US) · Teerschlacke *f*, teerumhüllte Schlacke [*Ein mit Teer umhüllter Hochofenschlackensplitt*]

~ **limestone**, tarred ~ · Teerkalkstein *m*

~ **(road-)metal** (Brit.) → ~ broken stone

~ **sand** · Teersand *m*, teerumhüllter Sand

tar composition — tar ready sheet roofing (paper) 1012

tar composition → tar-based ~

~ ~ ready sheet roofing (paper) → tar(red) ready ~ ~ (~)

~ compound → tar-based ~

~ concrete · Teerbeton *m*

~ crushed rock → tar(-coated) broken stone

~ ~ stone → tar(-coated) broken ~

~ distillation fraction, tar-oil ~, (oil) distillate ~ · Ölfraktion *f* [*Herstellung präparierten Teeres*]

~ dry penetration surfacing, ~ ~ process penetration macadam · Teerstreudecke *f*, Teerstreumakadam *m*

~ ~ process penetration macadam, ~ ~ penetration surfacing · Teerstreudecke *f*, Teerstreumakadam *m*

~ dyestuff · Teerfarbstoff *m*

~ emulsion · Teeremulsion *f* [*Eine wäßrige Teeraufschlämmung zur Verarbeitung mit feuchten Baustoffen. Nachträgliche Austrocknung ist erforderlich*]

tar-felt roof cladding, ~ ~ covering, ~ ~ sheathing, ~ roofing · Teer-Kleb(e)dach(belag) *n*, (*m*), Teer-Kleb(e)(dach)(ein)deckung *f*, Teer-Kleb(e)bedachung, Teer-Spachteldach(belag), Teer-Spachtel(dach)-(ein)deckung, Teer-Spachtelbedachung

~ roof covering, ~ ~ cladding, ~ ~ sheathing, ~ roofing · Teer-Kleb(e)-dach(belag) *n*, (*m*), Teer-Kleb(e)-(dach)(ein)deckung *f*, Teer-Kleb(e)-bedachung, Teer-Spachteldach(belag), Teer-Spachtel(dach)(ein)deckung, Teer-Spachtelbedachung

~ ~ sheathing, ~ ~ cladding, ~ ~ covering, ~ roofing · Teer-Kleb(e)-dach(belag) *n*, (*m*), Teer-Kleb(e)-(dach)(ein)deckung *f*, Teer-Kleb(e)-bedachung, Teer-Spachteldach(belag), Teer-Spachtel(dach)(ein)deckung, Teer-Spachtelbedachung

~ roofing, ~ roof cladding, ~ roof sheathing, ~ roof covering · Teer-Kleb(e)dach(belag) *n*, (*m*), Teer-Kleb(e)(dach)(ein)deckung *f*, Teer-Kleb(e)bedachung, Teer-Spachteldach(belag), Teer-Spachtel(dach)-(ein)deckung, Teer-Spachtelbedachung

tar for road purposes, (road) tar [*B.S. 76*] · (Straßen)Teer *m*, T [*DIN 1995*]

target date · Frist *f* [*Fertigstellung von Bauarbeiten*]

~ output · Solleistung *f*

tar-grouted stone (Brit.); tar penetration macadam, road tar type penetration macadam · Teertränkmakadam *m*

tariff-rate changeover impulse receiver [*electric storage heating*] · Rundsteuerempfänger *m*

tar-impregnated, coal-~ · teergetränkt, teerimprägniert

tar impregnating, coat-~ · Teerimprägnieren *n*, Teertränken

~ impregnation, coal-~ ~ · Teerimprägnierung *f*, Teertränkung

~ (iron) (blast-furnace) slag chip(ping)s → tar-coated (~) (~) ~ ~

~ (~) slag chip(ping)s → tar(-coated) (iron) (blastfurnace) ~ ~

~ joint runner → tarred ~ ~

tarmacadam [*B.S. 1241–1242*] · Teermakadam *m*

tar mastic · Teermastix *m*

tarnished · angelaufen [*Metall*]

~, fogged, struck · angelaufen, beschlagen, blind geworden, erblindet [*Glas*]

tarnishing, fogging · Erblinden *n*, Anlaufen, Blindwerden, Beschlagen [*Glas*]

~ · Anlaufen *n* [*Metall*]

~ oil · Teeröl *n*

tar-oil fraction, tar distillation ~, (oil) distillate fraction · Ölfraktion *f* [*Herstellung präparierten Teeres*]

tar paint [*B.S. 1070*] · Teeranstrichmittel *n* [*Kalt verarbeitbare Teeranstrichmittel werden durch Auflösen von Steinkohlenteerpech in leicht flüchtigen Lösungsmitteln hergestellt. Sie dienen als Schutzanstrichmittel für Beton, Mauerwerk und Eisen*]

~ paper · Teerpapier *n*

~ ~, tarred ~; fluxed pitch ~ (Brit.) [*See remark under 'Pappe'*] · Teerpappe *f*

~ penetration macadam, road tar type ~ ~; tar-grouted stone (Brit.) · Teertränkmakadam *m*

~ (-petroleum) asphalt mix(ture) (US); tar-(asphaltic-)bitumen ~ (Brit.) · Teer(-Erdöl)bitumen-Gemisch *n*, Teer(-Erdöl)bitumen-Mischung *f*

~ pitch · Teerpech *n* [*Destillationsrückstand des Teeres*]

~ ~ clay pipe sealing compound, ~ ~ CP ~ ~; ~ ~ (drain) tile ~ ~, ~ ~ DT ~ ~ (US) · Teerpech-Tonrohrvergußmasse *f*, Teerpech-Tonrohrausgußmasse

~ pouring rope → tarred ~ ~

~ pre-impregnating, coal-~ ~ · Teervorimprägnieren *n*, Teervortränken

~ pre-impregnation, coal-~ ~ · Teervorimprägnierung *f*, Teervortränkung

~ prepared sheet roofing (paper) → tar(red) ready ~ ~ (~)

~ pre-saturating, ~ pre-impregnating · Teervorimprägnieren *n*, Teervortränken

~ pre-saturation, ~ pre-impregnation · Teervorimprägnierung *f*, Teervortränkung

~ product · Teererzeugnis *n*

~ protective coat(ing) · Teerschutzanstrich *m*, Teerschutzaufstrich *m*

~ ready sheet roofing (paper) → tarred ~ ~ ~ (~)

tarred · geteert
tar(red) chip(ping)s, tar-coated ~, chip(ping)s precoated with tar · Teersplitt *m*, teerumhüllter Splitt
~ coarse chip(ping)s · Teergrobsplitt *m*
~ composition roofing → ~ ready ~
~ ~ sheet roofing (paper) → ~ ready ~ ~ (~)
~ felt(ed fabric) · Teerfilz(pappe) *m*, (*f*)
~ fine chip(ping)s · Teerfeinsplitt *m*
~ joint runner, ~ pouring rope · Teerstrick *m* [*Strick-Blei-Dichtung*]
~ limestone, tar-coated ~ · Teerkalkstein *m*
~ paper; fluxed pitch ~ (Brit.); [*See remark under 'Pappe'*] · Teerpappe *f*
~ pouring rope, ~ joint runner · Teerstrick *m* [*Strick-Blei-Dichtung*]
~ prepared roofing → ~ ready ~
~ ~ sheet roofing (paper) → ~ ready ~ ~ ~ (~)
~ ready roofing, ~ composition ~, ~ prepared ~, ~ roof(ing) felt (US); fluxed pitch roof(ing) felt [*B.S. 981*] · Teerdachpappe *f* [*DIN 52121*]
~ ~ sheet roofing (paper), ~ composition ~ ~ (~), ~ prepared ~ ~ (~), ~ sheet roof(ing) felt (US); fluxed pitch sheet roof(ing) felt [Brit.) · Bahnen-Teerdachpappe *f*, Teerdachpappe in Bahnenform
~ roll(ed-strip) roofing (felt) (US); fluxed pitch ~ ~ (~) (Brit.) · Rollen-Teerdachpappe *f*, Teerdachpappe in Rollenform
~ roof(ing) felt (US) → ~ ready roofing
~ rope · Teerstrick *m* [*DIN 4038*]
~ ~ sealing · Teerstrick(ab)dichtung *f*
~ sheet roof(ing) felt (US) → ~ ready sheet roofing (paper)
tarring, tarspraying · Teeren *n*, Teerung *f*
tar (road-)metal (Brit.) → tar(-coated) broken stone
~ roofing product · Teer(dach)(ein)deckungserzeugnis *n*
tar rope sealing, tarred ~ ~ · Teerstrick(ab)dichtung *f*
tar/rubber material, ~ mass, ~ composition, ~ compound · Teer-Gummi-Masse *f*
tarry smell · Teergeruch *m*
tar sand, tar-coated ~ · Teersand *m*, teerumhüllter Sand
~ saturant · Imprägnier(ungs)teer *m*, Tränkteer
tar-saturated, tar-impregnated, coal-~ · vollteergetränkt, vollteerimprägniert
tar saturating, coal-~ ~ · Teervollimprägnieren *n*, Teervolltränken
~ saturation, coal-~ ~ · Teervollimprägnierung *f*, Teervolltränkung
~ saturator · Teertränkpfanne *f* [*Dachpappenmaschine*]

~ sheet roof(ing) felt → tar(red) ready sheet roofing (paper)
tarsia, in~ · Intarsia *f*, Intarsie *f*, eingelegte Arbeit *f*, Einlegearbeit
~, ~, inlay, mosaic woodwork · Intarsia *f*, Holzeinlegearbeit *f*
tar slurry · Teerschlämme *f*
tarspraying, tarring · Teeren *n*, Teerung *f*
tartar, addle · Weinstein *m*
tartaric acid · Wein(stein)säure *f*
~ tester · Teerprüfgerät *n*
~ tile · Teerplatte *f*
~ tiling · Teerplattenbelag *m*
~ value · Verteerungszahl *f*, VTZ
tarviated, tar-bound · teergebunden
Tau cross, crux commissa · Antoniuskreuz *n*, Taukreuz, ägyptisches Kreuz
Taylor's lino(leum) · Taylorlinoleum *n*
T-beam · Plattenbalken *m*
~ floor, Tee beam ~, slab-and-beam ~, tee-beam ~ · Plattenbalkendecke *f*
~ ~ with nonstructural fillers, Tee beam ~ ~ ~ ~, tee-beam ~ ~ ~ ~, slab-and-beam ~ ~ ~ ~ ~ · Plattendecke *f* mit nichttragenden Füllkörpern
~ ~ without fillers, Tee beam ~ ~ ~, tee-beam ~ ~ ~, slab-and-beam ~ ~ ~ · Plattendecke *f* ohne Füllkörper
~ plate with deep ribs → T(ee)-beam slab ~ ~ ~
~ rib, Tee beam ~, slab-and-beam ~, tee-beam ~ · Plattenbalkenrippe *f*
~ slab with deep ribs · T(ee)-beam ~ ~ ~
TC, td, tin-clad, tinned · verzinnt
TC → terra-cotta
TC, cold tar · Kaltteer *m* [*Steinkohlenteer mit flüchtigen organischen Lösungsmitteln, im allgemeinen Benzol*]
TCC, tendency to corrosion cracking · Korrosionsrißneigung *f*
td, TC, tin-clad, tinned · verzinnt
TE, totally enclosed · ganzgekapselt, vollgekapselt
tea garden · Teegarten *m*
tea-house · Teehaus *n*
tea kitchen, ~ station · Teeküche *f*
~ station, ~ kitchen · Teeküche *f*
teacher room · Lehrerzimmer *n*
Teachers' Training College · Pädagogische Hochschule *f*
teaching block, ~ building · Lehrgebäude *n*
~ ~, ~ unit, ~ portion, ~ accommodation · Lehrtrakt *m*
~ building, ~ block · Lehrgebäude *n*
~ lab(oratory) · Lehrlabor(atorium) *n*
~ pool, learner's ~ · Lehr(schwimm)-becken *n*, Nichtschwimmerbecken, LSB

teaching unit — telamon

~ unit, ~ block, ~ accommodation, ~ portion · Lehrtrakt *m*

teak window · Teakfenster *n*

team(-work) achievement, ~ project · Gemeinschaftsleistung *f*

~ **project,** ~ achievement · Gemeinschaftsleistung *f*

tearing resistance, resistance of tearing · Zerreißfestigkeit *f*

tearing-strength test · Zerreißfestigkeitsprobe *f*, Zerreißfestigkeitsprüfung *f*, Zerreißfestigkeitsversuch *m*

technic, technique, practice · Technik *f* [*Als Anwendung, nicht als Wissenschaft*]

technical (aircraft) hangar, aircraft maintenance ~ · (Flugzeug)Wartungshalle *f*, (Flugzeug)Werfthalle

~ **consultant** · technischer Berater *m*

~ **counsel service,** ~ consultation ~ · technischer Beratungsdienst *m*

~ **data,** engineering ~, spec(ification)s · technische Angaben *fpl*, ~ Daten *f*, ~ Aufzählung *f*

~ **form of expression** · Technizismus *m*

~ **hangar,** ~ aircraft ~, aircraft maintenance ~ · (Flugzeug)Wartungshalle *f*, (Flugzeug)Werfthalle

~ **play equipment** · technische Spielgeräte *npl*

~ **requirement,** specification ~ · technische Anforderung *f* [*Leistung; Güte*]

technique, technic, practice · Technik *f* [*Als Anwendung, nicht als Wissenschaft*]

tectonic · Tektonik *f*

T(ee), tee, tee-piece · T-Stück *n*

tee bar, T(ee) ~, ~ section, ~ steel ~ · (Einfach-)T-Stahl *m*

T(ee) bar, tee ~ · T-Tragschiene *f* [*Hängedecke*]

T(ee)-beam, slab-and-beam, tee beam · Plattenbalken(träger) *m*, Balken(träger) mit T-Querschnitt, T-Balken(träger)

~ **floor,** tee-beam ~, slab-and-beam ~ · Plattenbalkendecke *f*

~ ~ **with nonstructural fillers,** tee-beam ~ ~ ~ ~ ~, slab-and-beam ~ ~ ~ ~ ~ · Plattendecke *f* mit nichttragenden Füllkörpern

~ ~ **without fillers,** tee-beam ~ ~ ~, slab-and-beam ~ ~ ~ · Plattendecke *f* ohne Füllkörper

~ **plate** → ~ slab

~ ~ **with deep ribs,** ~ slab ~ ~ ~, deep-rib(bed) slab, deep-rib(bed) plate, deep concrete joist construction · Rippenplatte *f* mit hohen Rippen

~ **rib,** tee-beam ~, slab-and-beam ~ · Plattenbalkenrippe *f*

~ **slab,** rib(bed) ~, ~ plate, concrete joist construction · Rippenplatte *f*

~ ~ **with deep ribs,** ~ plate ~ ~ ~, deep-rib(bed) slab, deep-rib(bed) plate, deep concrete joist construction · Rippenplatte *f* mit hohen Rippen

tee block, T(ee) ~, ~ tile [*See remark under 'Block'*] · T-Stein *m*, T-Block(-stein) *m*

~ **bolt,** T-head ~ · Hammerschraube *f* [*DIN 261. Rohe Schraube aus Flußstahl mit hammerförmigem Kopf*]

T(ee) (building) component → (prefab(ricated)) (single) T(ee) (building) unit

~ **(~) member** → (prefab(ricated)) (single) T(ee) (building) unit

~ **(~) unit** → (prefab(ricated)) (single) ~ (~) ~

~ **component** → (prefab(ricated)) (single) T(ee) (building) unit

~ **cross section** · T-Querschnitt *m*

~ **(floor slab),** single ~ (~ ~) · T-Deckenelement *n*, T-Deckenplatte *f*

~ **girder,** tee ~ · T-Träger *m*

~ **hinge,** cross garnet [*It is intended for hinging components of ledged construction, such as ledged, braced and battened doors, or where weight must be distributed over a large area*] · Zungenband *n*, gerades Band, Kegelband [*Baubeschlag*]

T(ee)-hinge strap · Kreuzband *n* [*Beschlag*]

~ **junction,** double square ~, t(ee) ~ · Doppelabzweig(er) *m* 90°, T-Stück *n* [*Rohrformstück*]

~ **member** → (prefab(ricated)) (single) T(ee) (building) unit

~ **panel,** tee ~, single ~ ~ · T-Tafel *f*

T(ee)-piece, tee, T(ee) · T-Stück *n*

T(ee) section, tee ~, ~ bar, ~ steel ~ · (Einfach-)T-Stahl *m*

~ **slab,** single ~ ~ ~ · T-Platte *f*

~ **(steel) bar,** tee (~) ~, ~ (~) section · (Einfach-)T-Stahl *m*

T(ee)-steel dowel, tee-steel ~ · (Stab-)Dübel *m* aus T-Stahl, Dolle *f* ~ ~, Dollen *m* ~ ~, Döbel *m* ~ ~; Dippel *m* ~ ~ [*Österreich*]

T(ee) (steel) section, tee (~) ~, ~ (~) bar · (Einfach-)T-Stahl *m*

~ **tile,** tee ~, ~ block [*See remark under 'Block'*] · T-Block(stein) *m*, T-Stein

~ **unit** → (prefab(ricated)) (single) T(ee) (building) ~

TEFC, totally-enclosed fan-cooled · ganzgekapselt und ventilatorgekühlt, vollgekapselt ~ ~

Tego film · Tego(-Leim)film *m* [*genormtes Kurzzeichen: T*]

Tekton cement-bound excelsior building slab (US); ~ ~ wood-wool ~ ~ (Brit.) · Tektonplatte *f* [*zementgebundene Holzwolle-Leichtbauplatte. DIN 1101*]

telamon → atlante

telecommunication cable — temperature regulator

telecommunication cable, post office ~; GPO ~ (Brit.) · Fernmeldekabel *n*
~ line, post office ~; GPO ~ (Brit.) · Fernmeldeleitung *f*
~ station · Funk- und F.M.-Station *f*
~ tower, post office ~; GPO ~ (Brit.) · Fernmeldeturm *m*
telegraph and communications center (US); ~ ~ ~ centre (Brit.) · Fernmeldezentrum *n*, Fernmeldeamt *n*
teleoperation · Fernbedienung *f*
(tele)phone booth · Fernsprechzelle *f*
~ duct · Fernsprechkabelkanal *m*
~ exchange · Fernsprechzentrale *f*
~ installation · Fernsprecherinstallation *f*
~ line · Fernsprechleitung *f*
~ meter · (Fernsprech)Gebührenzähler *m*
~ point [*e.g. in a wall or floor*] · Fernsprechanschluß *m*
~ socket · Fernsprech(steck)dose *f*
teleprinter room, telex ~ · Fernschreibraum *m*
to telescope · teleskopieren, aus(einander)ziehen
telescopic · teleskopartig
~ flagpole · Teleskopfahnenmast *m*, Teleskopflaggenmast
telescoping shore column, ~ shoring ~ · Teleskop-Einrüststütze *f*
~ shoring column, ~ shore ~ · Teleskop-Einrüststütze *f*
~ sliding shutter door, ~ ~ shutter-door · Teleskopschiebetor *n*
Telesterion, Hall of (the) Mysteries at Eleusis · Telesterion *n* zu Eleusis, Weihetempel *m* ~ ~, Mysterienhalle *f* ~ ~, Weihehaus *n* ~ ~
television aerial, T.V. ~ · Fernsehantenne *f*
~ building, T.V. ~ · Fernsehgebäude *n*
~ room, T.V. ~ · Fernsehraum *m*
~ studio, T.V. ~ · Fernsehstudio *n*
~ torch → ~ tower
~ tower, ~ torch, T.V. ~ · Fernsehsendeturm *m*
telex room, teleprinter ~ · Fernschreibraum *m*
teller, counter · (Kunden)Schalter *m*
tellurate · Tellurat *n*
tellurium · Tellur *n*
~ dioxide (Brit.); **~ dioxid(e)** (US) · Tellurdioxid *n*
~ lead · Tellurblei *n*
temenos, peribolos, sacred precinct · geweihter (Tempel)Bezirk *m*, heiliger ~, Altis *f*, Peribolos *m*, Temenos *n*
to temper · anlassen [*Stahl*]
~ ~ · anmachen [*Mörtel*]
temper brittleness · Anlaßsprödigkeit *f* [*Stahl*]

~ hardening · Anlaßhärtung *f*
tempera · Temperamalerei *f*
~ · Temperafarbe *f*
~ colour (Brit.); **~ color** (US) · Temperafarbe *f*
~ painting · Temperamalerei *f*
temperature balance · Temperaturausgleich *m*
~ bars → ~ steel
~ change · Temperaturwechsel *m*
~ control · Temperatursteuerung *f*
temperature-controlled · temperaturgesteuert
temperature controller, ~ regulator, ~ sensor, ~ sensing element, thermostat · Temperaturregler *m*, Wärmeregler, (Temperatur)Fühler, Thermostat *m*, Sicherheitstemperaturbegrenzer
~ curve · Temperaturkurve *f*
~ degree, degree of temperature · Temperaturgrad *m*
~ dependence · Temperaturabhängigkeit *f*
~ difference · Temperaturunterschied *m*
~ distribution · Temperaturverteilung *f*
~ drop · Temperaturrückgang *m*, Temperaturabfall *m*
~ during setting [*e.g. setting of terracotta units*] · Verlegetemperatur *f*
~ effect · Temperatur(aus)wirkung *f*
~ fluctuation · Temperaturschwankung *f*
~ gradient · Temperaturgefälle *n*
temperature-humidity index, THI · Temperatur-Feuchtigkeits-Index *m*, Temperatur-Feuchte-Index
temperature increase → ~ rise
~ influence · Temperatureinfluß *m*
~ insulation · Temperaturdämmung *f*
~ ~ property · Temperaturdämmeigenschaft *f*
~ level · Temperaturpegel *m*
~ measurement · Temperaturmessung *f*
~ of comparison · Vergleichstemperatur *f*
~ ~ hydration, hydration temperature · Hydra(ta)tionstemperatur *f*
~ ~ reaction, reaction temperature · Reaktionstemperatur *f*
temperature-proof, temperature-resistant · temperaturbeständig
temperature radiation, heat ~ · Temperaturstrahlung *f*, Wärmestrahlung, Wärmeübertragung durch Strahlung [*Man bezeichnet als Wärmestrahlung die in einem bestimmten Bereich der Wellenlängen und Temperaturen auftretende Energiestrahlung*]
~ range, ~ span · Temperaturbereich *m*, *n*, Temperaturspanne *f*
~ regulator, ~ sensor, ~ controller, ~ sensing element, thermostat · Temperaturregler *m*, Wärmeregler, (Temperatur)Fühler, Thermostat *m*, Sicherheitstemperaturbegrenzer

temperature reinforcement — Temple of Concorde at Rome

~ **reinforcement** → ~ steel

temperature-resistance · Temperaturbeständigkeit *f*

temperature-resistant, temperature-proof · temperaturbeständig

temperature rise, ~ **increase** [*The increase of temperature caused by absorption of heat or internal generation of heat, as by hydration of cement in concrete*] · Temperaturzunahme *f*, Temperatursteigerung *f*, Temperaturerhöhung, Temperaturanstieg *m*

temperature-rise period [*The time interval during which the temperature of a concrete product rises at a controlled rate to the desired maximum in autoclave or atmospheric pressure steam curing*] · Aufheizdauer *f*, Aufheizzeit *f*

temperature rods → ~ steel

~ **sensing element,** ~ **regulator,** ~ **sensor,** ~ **controller,** ~ **thermostat** · Temperaturregler *m*, Wärmeregler, (Temperatur)Fühler, Thermostat *m*, Sicherheitstemperaturbegrenzer

~ **sensitive** · temperaturabhängig [*(Werk)Stoffverhalten*]

~ **sensor,** ~ **sensing element,** ~ **regulator,** ~ **controller, thermostat** · Temperaturregler *m*, Wärmeregler, (Temperatur)Fühler, Thermostat *m*, Sicherheitstemperaturbegrenzer

~ **span,** ~ **range** · Temperaturbereich *m, n*, Temperaturspanne *f*

~ **steel,** ~ **rods,** ~ **bars,** ~ **reinforcement, distribution** ~ · Verteilerbewehrung *f*, Verteilerarmierung, Verteiler(stahl)einlagen *fpl*, Verteilerstähle *mpl*, Verteilerstäbe *mpl*, Verteilungsstäbe [*Fehlnamen: Verteilereisen npl, Verteilungseisen*]

~ **strain** · Temperaturdehnung *f*

~ **stress** · Temperaturspannung *f*

~ **susceptibility** · Temperaturempfindlichkeit *f*

tempered · angelassen [*Baustahl*]

~ **glass** → toughened (safety) ~

~ **hardboard** · Extrahartplatte *f*, extraharte (Holz)Faserplatte, HFH2 [*Rohwichte über 950 kg/m³*]

~ **plate (glass)** → ~ polished ~ (~)

~ **(polished) plate (glass),** toughened (~) ~ (~), heat-treated (~) ~ (~) [*For instance ARMOURCLAD*] · vorgespanntes (Kristall)Spiegelglas *n*

~ **(safety) glass** → toughened (~) ~

tempering · Anlassen [*Stahl*]

~ · Anmachen *n* [*Mörtel*]

~**, souring** · Einsumpfen *n*, Mauken [*Verbesserung der Plastizität einer Masse durch längeres feuchtes Lagern im Haufen oder in der Sumpfgrube*]

~ · Knetaufbereitung *f*, Kneten *n* [*Mechanische Bearbeitung vom feuchtem Ton (mit oder ohne Magermittel) zur Verbesserung seiner Verarbeitbarkeit*]

~ **hardness** · Anlaßhärte *f* [*Stahl*]

~ **house, souring** ~ · Sumpfhaus *n*, Maukhaus

~ **plant, souring** ~ · Maukanlage *f*, Sumpfanlage

~ **temperature** · Anlaßtemperatur *f* [*Stahl*]

~ **tower, souring** ~ · Maukturm *m*, Sumpfturm

Templars' Church at London, Temple (~) (~ ~) · Templerkirche *f* in London

template · Schlitten *m* [*für Putzprofile*]

~ → templet

temple building, ~ **construction** · Tempelbau *m*

Temple (Church) (at London), Templars' ~ ~ ~ · Templerkirche *f* in London

temple-city · Tempelstadt *f*

temple complex · Tempelanlage *f*, Tempelkomplex *m*

~ **construction,** ~ **building** · Tempelbau *m*

~ **court** · Tempelhof *m*

~ **district,** ~ **enclosure,** ~ **precinct** · Tempelbezirk *m*

~ **enclosure,** ~ **precinct,** ~ **district** · Tempelbezirk *m*

~ **façade** · Tempelfassade *f*

~ **forecourt** · Tempelvorhof *m*

~ **front** · Tempelfront *f*, Tempelvorderseite *f*

~ **gateway** · Tempeltor *n*

~ **(ground(-))plan** · Tempelgrundriß *m*

Temple 'G.T.' at Selenius · Apollo(n)tempel *m* zu Selenius, Tempel G ~ ~

temple nucleus · Tempelkern *m*

Temple of Amon at Karnak, ~ ~ Amen ~ ~ · Amontempel *m* zu Karnak

~ ~ **Aphaia at Aiyina,** ~ ~ ~ ~ Aegina · Tempel *m* der Aphaia in Ägina, Aphaiatempel von Ägina

~ ~ **Aphrodite Ourania** · Tempel *m* der Aphrodite Urania [*Agora von Athen*]

~ ~ **Apollo** · Apollo(n)tempel *m*

~ ~ ~ **Didymaeus** · Tempel *m* des Apollo Didymaeos

~ ~ ~ **Patroos** · Tempel *m* des Apollon Palvoio [*Agora von Athen*]

~ ~ **Ares** · Arestempel *m*

~ ~ **Athena at Syracuse** · Athenatempel *m* der Insel Ortygia zu Syrakus

~ ~ ~ **Polias at Priene** · Athena-Tempel *m* zu Priene

~ ~ **Bacchus** · Bacchustempel *m*

~ ~ **Bel at Palmyra,** ~ ~ Baal ~ ~ · Heiligtum *n* des Baal zu Palmyra, ~ ~ Bel ~ ~

~ ~ **Concorde at Rome** · Konkordientempel *m* zu Rom

~~ **Demeter** · Demetertempel *m*
~~~ **at Paestum** · Demetertempel *m* zu Paestum
~~ **Hera**, heraeum · Hera-Tempel *m*, Heraion *n*
~~~ **Lacinia at Agrigentum** · Tempel *m* der Juno Lacinia zu Agrigent
~~ **Horus** [*at Edfu*] · Horustempel *m*
~~ **Isis** · Isistempel *m*
~~ **Jupiter** · Jupitertempel *m*
~~~ **Heliopolitanus at Baalbek** · Jupitertempel *m* zu Baalbek, Tempel des Jupiter Heliopolitanus von Heliopolis
~~ **King Sethos I** · Sethostempel *m*
~~ **Minerva** · Minervatempel *m*
~~ **Nemesis** · Nemesistempel *m*
~~ **Nikè Apteros at Athens** · Niketempel *m* zu Athen
~~ **Nemesis at Rhamnus** · Tempel *m* der Nemesis zu Rhamnus
~~ **Poseidon** · Poseidontempel *m*
~~~ **at Paestum** · Poseidontempel *m* zu Paestum
~~ **Romulus** · Romulustempel *m*
~~ **Saturn** · Saturntempel *m*
~~ **the Sun** · Sonnentempel *m*
~~ **Venus** · Venustempel *m*
~~~ **and Rome at Rome** · Tempel *m* der Venus und Roma zu Rom
~~ **Vespasian** · Vespasiantempel *m*
~~~ **at Rome** · Vespasiantempel *m* zu Rom
~~ **Vesta at Rome** · Vestatempel *m* zu Rom
~~~~ **Tivoli** · Vesta-Tempel *m* zu Tivoli
temple of wood and brick · Holz-Ziegel-Tempel *m*
Temple of Zeus at Olympia · Zeustempel *m* zu Olympia
~~~ **(Olympius)** · Zeustempel *m*
~~~ **(~) at Athens**, Olympieion · Zeustempel *m* zu Athen
~ **on the Ilissus** · Tempel *m* am Ilissos
temple on top of a ziggurat · Hochtempel *m*, Wohntempel *m* [*Ein auf einem Stufenberg stehender Hochtempel Mesopotamiens, der als Wohnung einer Gottheit galt*]
~ **plan**, ~ **ground(-)~** · Tempelgrundriß *m*
~ **portico** · Tempelportikus *m*
~ **precinct**, ~ **district**, ~ **enclosure** · Tempelbezirk *m*
~ **terrace** · Tempelterrasse *f*
~ **tomb** · Tempelgrab *m*
~ **tower** → stepped artificial hill
~ **tower** · Tempelturm *m*
~ **wall** · Tempelwand *f*
~ **with twin sanctuaries** · Doppeltempel *m*

templet, template, profile [*A thin wood or metal plate, used as a pattern in carrying out some form of detail in construction or decoration*] · Schablone *f*, Profil *n*
templum in antis, in antis temple · Antentempel *m*, Tempel *m* mit Anten, Megarontempel, Wandtempel
Templum vaticanum · Peterskirche *f* in Rom
temporary accommodation · Behelfsunterkunft *f*
~ **block**, ~ building · Behelfsgebäude *n*
~ **building**, ~ block · Behelfsgebäude *n*
~ **column** · Notstütze *f*
~~, erection ~ · Montagestütze *f*
~ **fence** [*B.S. 1722*] · Behelfszaun *m*
~ **hardness**, carbonate ~ · Karbonathärte *f*, vorübergehende Härte, KH
tenacity, ultimate tensile strength · Bruchzugfestigkeit *f*
tenant · Mieter *m*
tenant's meter · Mieterzähler *m*
ten-bay · zehnjochig
tendency to corrosion cracking, TCC · Korrosionsrißneigung *f*
~~ **cracking** · Rißneigung *f*
~~ **flow** · Fließneigung *f*
~~ **shear(ing)** · Schubneigung *f*
tender (Brit.); bid (US) · Angebot *n*
~ **drawing** (Brit.); bid ~ (US) · Angebotszeichnung *f*
tender(ed) price (Brit.); bid sum (US) · Abgabepreis *m*, Angebotspreis
tendering (Brit.); bidding (US) · Ausschreibung *f*
~ **period** (Brit.); bidding ~ (US) · Ausschreibungsdauer *f*
tendon, (pre)stressing ~, tensioning ~, stretching ~ [*A stretched element used in a concrete member of structure to impart prestress to the concrete*] · (Vor-)Spannglied *n*
~ **profile** [*The path or trajectory of the prestressing tendon*] · (Vor)Spanngliedführung *f*, (Vor)Spanngliedverlauf *m*
tenement [*A rented apartment. The term now usually implies one in a building in the poor part of a city, and one which is overcrowded and lacks adequate sanitation*] · Mietwohnung *f*
~ **block** → block (of flats)
~ **building** → block (of flats)
~-**house** · Mietkaserne *f*
tenia → taenia
tenon hole, mortice (Brit.); mortise (US) · Zapfenloch *n* [*nicht durchgehend*]
to tenon into · einzapfen
tenon jointing → mortise (and tenon) joint
tenoned into · eingezapft
ten-point influence line · zehnteilige Einflußlinie *f*

ten-sided — tensioning force

ten-sided, decagonal · zehnseitig, zehneckig

tensile bending stress · Zugbiegespannung f

~ capability, ~ property, ~ capacity, ~ quality, ~ power · Zugeigenschaft f, Zugvermögen n, Zugfähigkeit f

~ capacity, ~ quality, ~ capability, ~ property, ~ power · Zugeigenschaft f, Zugvermögen n, Zugfähigkeit f

~ cracking · Zugrißbildung f

~ force, tension ~, pull · Zugkraft f [*beansprucht*]

~ load · Zuglast f

~ loop joint [*It consists of a pair of horizontal loops in the tension zone, both sides of each loop carrying equal stresses*] · Zugschlaufenstoß m

~ power, ~ capability, ~ property, ~ capacity, ~ quality · Zugeigenschaft f, Zugvermögen n, Zugfähigkeit f

~ property, ~ capability, ~ quality, ~ capacity, ~ power · Zugeigenschaft f, Zugvermögen n, Zugfähigkeit f

~ quality, ~ capacity, ~ property, ~ capability, ~ power · Zugeigenschaft f, Zugvermögen n, Zugfähigkeit f

~ radial stress · Radialzugspannung f

~ reinforcement, tension ~, reinforcement for tension · Zugarmierung f, Zugbewehrung, Zug(stahl)einlagen fpl

~ splitting force · Spaltzugkraft f

~ strain · Zugdehnung f

~ strength, tension ~ [*abbreviated: ts*] · Zugfestigkeit f

~ stress, tension ~ · Zugspannung f

~ system, tension ~ · zugbeanspruchte Konstruktion f

~ test [*A test to determinate the strength and/or elasticity of a material in tension*] · Zugprobe f, Zugprüfung f, Zugversuch m

~ zone, tension(ed) ~ · Zugbereich m, n, Zugzone f

tension [*A stress set up by a pulling force*] · Zug m

~ bar, ~ element, ~ rod, ~ member, tie · Zugglied n, gezogenes Glied, Zugstab m, gezogener Stab

~ boom, ~ chord, ~ flange · Zugflansch m, Zuggurt(ung) m, (f)

~ chord, ~ boom, ~ flange · Zugflansch m, Zuggurt(ung) m, (f)

tension-compression system · Zug-Druck-System n

tension connection, ~ joint · Zugverbindung f

~ diagonal, diagonal in tension, diagonal tie · Zugdiagonale f, Zugschräge f, gezogene Diagonale, gezogene Schräge

~ element, ~ member, ~ bar, ~ rod, tie · Zugglied n, gezogenes Glied, Zugstab m, gezogener Stab

~ flange, ~ boom, ~ chord · Zugflansch m, Zuggurt(ung) m, (f)

~ force, tensile ~, pull · Zugkraft [*beansprucht*]

~ joint, ~ connection · Zugverbindung f

~ member, ~ element, ~ bar, ~ rod, tie · Zugglied n, gezogenes Glied, Zugstab m, gezogener Stab

tension-proof · zugfest

tension reinforcement, tensile ~, reinforcement for tension · Zugarmierung f, Zugbewehrung, Zug(stahl)einlagen fpl

~ resistance · Zugwiderstand m

~ rib · Zugrippe f

~ ring · Zugring m

~ rod, ~ element, ~ bar, ~ member, tie · Zugglied n, gezogenes Glied, Zugstab m, gezogener Stab

~ side · Zugseite f

~ strength, tensile ~ [*abbreviated: ts*] · Zugfestigkeit f

~ stress, tensile ~ · Zugspannung f

~ system, tensile ~ · zugbeanspruchte Konstruktion f

~ tie → ~ element

to tension together, to joint by prestressing, to stress together · zusammenspannen [*Fertigteile durch Vorspannung miteinander verbinden*]

tension zone of the concrete, concrete tensile zone, concrete tension zone · Betonzugzone f

tensional gasket · zugbeanspruchte Selbstdichtung f, zugbeanspruchtes (Ab)Dicht(ungs)profil n

tensioned connection, stretched ~, (pre)stressed ~ · (Vor)Spannverbindung f

~ in pairs, stretched ~ ~, (pre)stressed ~ ~ · paarweise vorgespannt [*Spanndrähte*]

tension(ed) zone, tensile ~ · Zugbereich m, n, Zugzone f

tensioning, stretching, (pre)stressing · (Vor)Spannen n [*Spannbeton*]

~, stretching, (pre)stressing · Vorspannung f

~ area, stretching ~, (pre)stressing ~, ~ zone · Spann(ungs)zone f, Vor~

~ bar, stretching ~, (pre)stressing ~, ~ rod · Spannstab m, Vor~

~ block, stretching ~, (pre)stressing ~ · Spannblock m [*Spannbeton*]

~ cable, stretching ~, ((pre)stressing) ~, ~ strand [*A prestressing tendon composed of a number of wires most of which are twisted about a center wire or core*] · (Vor)Spannlitze f, (Draht)Seil n, Litze

~ element, stretching ~, (pre)stressing ~ · Spannelement n

~ factory → (pre)stressing plant

~ force → (pre)stressing stress

~ **jack,** (pre)stressing ~, stretching ~, jack(ing device) for prestressed concrete · Spann(beton)presse f

~ **loss** → (pre)stresssing ~

~ **method,** ~ system, stretching ~, (pre)stressing ~ · Spannbetonverfahren n, (Vor)Spann(ungs)verfahren

~ **order,** stretching ~, (pre)stressing ~ · (Vor)Spannfolge f

~ **plant** → (pre)stressing ~

~ **process** → process of (pre)stressing

~ **reinforcement** → (pre)stressing ~

~ **rod,** stretching ~, (pre)stressing ~, ~ bar · Spannstab m, Vor~

~ **steel** → (pre)stressing reinforcement

~ **strand** → ((pre)stressing) ~

~ **stress** → (pre)stressing ~

~ **system,** ~ method, stretching ~, (pre)stressing ~ · Spannbetonverfahren n, (Vor)Spann(ungs)verfahren

~ **tendon,** stretching ~, ((pre)stressing) ~ [*A stretched element used in a concrete member of structure to impart prestress to the concrete*] · (Vor)Spannglied n

~ **together of precast units,** stressing ~ ~ ~ ~, jointing precast units by prestressing · Zusammenspannen n von (Beton)Fertigteilen, Verbinden durch Vorspannung

~ **value,** stretching ~, (pre)stressing ~ · (Vor)Spann(ungs)wert m

~ **wedge,** stretching ~, (pre)stressing ~ · Spannkeil m [*Spannbeton*]

~ **wires in pairs,** stretching ~ ~ ~, prestressing ~ ~ ~ · paarweise Vorspannung f [*Spanndrähte*]

~ **yard** → (pre)stressing plant

~ **zone,** stretching ~, (pre)stressing ~, ~ area · (Vor)Spann(ungs)zone f

tensor function · Tensorfunktion f

tent membrane · Zeltmembran(e) f

~ **system** · Zeltsystem n

~ ~ **for construction of high points** · Zeltsystem n zur Konstruktion von Hochpunkten

~ ~ **with exterior support by compression members** · Zeltsystem n mit äußerer Unterstützung durch Druckstäbe

~ ~ ~ **interior arch for high-point construction** · Zeltsystem n mit innerem Stützbogen als Hochpunktkonstruktion

~ ~ ~ ~ **support by compression members** · Zeltsystem n mit innerer Unterstützung durch Druckstäbe

~ ~ ~ **support and anchor points alternating** · Zeltsystem n mit abwechselnden Unterstützungs- und Abspannpunkten

tentative design criteria · vorläufige Bemessungsgrundlagen fpl

~ **standard** · Normenentwurf m, Vornorm f

tentatively modernistic · schüchtern-modernistisch

Tentor reinforcing bars · Tentorstahl m [*Nach dem Walzen durch Zug- und Verdrehkräfte kalt verformt*]

TENV, totally-enclosed nonventilated · ganzgekapselt und unbelüftet, vollgekapselt ~ ~

tepidarium · Tepidarium n [*Der Raum mit einem Bassin mit lauwarmem Wasser in einer römischen Therme*]

term · Glied n [*Gleichung; Matrix*]

terminal, passenger ~ · Abfertigungsanlage f, Empfangsanlage [*Flughafen*]
~ → ~ building

~ **bending moment,** encastré ~ ~, (fixed-)end ~ ~ · Einspann(ungs)-biegemoment n

~ **(block),** ~ building, passenger ~ · Empfangsgebäude n, Abfertigungsgebäude [*Teil einer Abfertigungsanlage eines Flughafens*]

~ **(building),** passenger ~ ~, (passenger) terminal block · Abfertigungsgebäude n, Empfangsgebäude [*Teil einer Abfertigungsanlage eines Flughafens*]

~ **condition** encastré ~, (fixed-)end ~ · Einspann(ungs)bedingung f

~ **degree,** (fixed-)end ~, fixing ~ · Einspann(ungs)grad m

~ **feature,** termination · (Ab)Schluß m, abschließende Raumform f [*Kirchenarchitektur, z.B. eine Apsis*]

~ ~, crowning ~, ~ member · (be-)krönendes Element n

term(inal figure), herm [*A pedestal, pier, pilaster, etc., tapering towards the base and having a sculptured head or upper part of a human figure growing out of it*] · Herme f

terminal member, crowning ~, ~ feature · (be)krönendes Element n

~ **moment** → (fixed-)end ~

~ **pedestal** · Hermenpfeiler m

~ **railroad station** (US); ~ railway ~ (Brit.) · Endbahnhof m

~ **railway station** (Brit.); ~ railroad ~ (US) · Endbahnhof m

~ **sheet** [*A metal sheet of special width used at the extreme end of a roof*] · Endblech n

~ **statue,** term(inal figure), herm, terminus [*A pedestal, pier, pilaster, etc, tapering towards the base and having a sculptured head or upper part of a human figure growing out of it*] · Herme f

terminal unit — terra-cotta tile

~ **unit**, (air) conditioning ~, unit (air) conditioner, (room) air conditioner · Klima(tisierungs)gerät *n*

termination, terminal feature · (Ab-)Schluß *m*, abschließende Raumform *f* [*Kirchenarchitektur, z.B. eine Apsis*]

~ **piece** · Endstück *n* [*Geländer*]

terminus, herm, term(inal figure), terminal statue [*A pedestal, pier, pilaster, etc., tapering towards the base and having a sculptured head or upper part of a human figure growing out of it*]. Herme *f*

termite-proof · termitenbeständig, termitenfest

termite shield · Termitenschutzschild *n*

terneplate · Mattblech *n*

terrace [*A continuous row of houses in a uniform style, e.g. the 'Nash Terraces' round Regent's Park, London*] · Reihenhäuser *npl*

~, patio [*An unroofed, paved area immediately adjacent to a house and overlooking a lawn or garden. Abbreviated: ter*] · Terrasse *f*

~ [*A raised level promenade, paved or covered with turf or gravel, and usually with a balustrade or dwarf on one side*] · Terrasse *f*

~ **access** · Terrassenzugang *m*

~ **(awning) blind** · Terrassenmarkise *f*

~ **blind**, ~ awning ~ · Terrassenmarkise *f*

~ **door**, patio ~ · Terrassentür *f*

~ ~ **fitting**, patio ~ ~, ~ ~ hardware item · Terrassentürbeschlag *m*

~ ~ **fittings**, patio ~ ~, ~ ~ furniture, ~ ~ hardware · Terrassentürbeschläge *mpl*

~ ~ **furniture**, patio ~ ~, ~ ~ fittings, ~ ~ hardware · Terrassentürbeschläge *mpl*

~ ~ **hardware**, patio ~ ~, ~ ~ fittings, ~ ~ furniture · Terrassentürbeschläge *mpl*

~ ~ ~ **item**, patio ~ ~ ~, ~ ~ ~ fitting · Terrassentürbeschlag *m*

~ **dwelling unit** (US); ~ dwelling (Brit.) · Terrassenwohnung *f*

~ **heating** · Terrassenheizung *f*

~ **restaurant** · Terrassenrestaurant *n*

~ **roof**, truncated ~, cut ~, platform ~ [*A pitched roof terminated by a flat roof, thus having no ridge*] · abgestumpftes Dach *n*

terrace-shaped apartment building (US); ~ block (of flats) (Brit.) · Terrassen-Mehrfamilienhaus *n*

~ **block (of flats)** (Brit.); ~ apartment building (US) · Terrassen-Mehrfamilienhaus *n*

terrace-temple · Terrassentempel *m*

terrace tile · Terrassen(belag)platte *f*, Terrassenfliese *f*

~ **with service** · bewirtschaftete Terrasse *f*

terrace(d) dwellings · Terrassenbebauung *f*

~ **(funerary) temple** → ~ mortuary ~

~ **garden** [*e.g. the 'hanging gardens' at Babylon*] · abgetreppter Garten *m*, Terrassengarten [*z.B. die Hängenden Gärten der Semiramis in Babylon*]

~ **mastaba(h)**, ~ pyramid, step(ped) ~ compound mastaba(h) · Stufenmastaba *f*; Stufenpyramide *f* [*Fehlbezeichnung*]

~ **mortuary temple**, ~ (funerary) ~, step(ped) ~ ~ · Terrassen(toten)tempel *m*, Stufen(toten)tempel

~ **pyramid** → ~ mastaba(h)

~ **street** · Terrassenstraße *f*

~ **temple** → ~ mortuary ~

terra-cotta, TC [*Fired but unglazed clay, used mainly for wall covering and ornamentation as it can be fired in mo(u)lds*] · Terrakotta *f*

~ **architecture** · Terrakottaarchitektur *f*, Terrakottabaukunst *f*

~ **block**, ~ tile [*See remark under 'Block'*] · Terrakottablock(stein) *m*, Terrakottastein

~ **decoration** → ~ decorative finish

~ **decorative feature** → ~ ~ finish

~ ~ **finish**, ~ ~ feature, ~ ornamental ~, ~ decoration, ~ enrichment · Terrakottaschmuck *m*, Terrakottaverzierung *f*

~ ~ **fixture**, ~ ornament · Terrakotta-Ornament *n*, Terrakotta-Schmuckelement *n*, Terrakotta-Schmuckglied *n*

~ **enrichment** → ~ decorative finish

~ **facing**, ~ sur~, ~ lining · Terrakottaauskleidung *f*, Terrakottaverkleidung, Terrakottabekleidung

~ **lining**, ~ (sur)facing · Terrakottaauskleidung *f*, Terrakottaverkleidung, Terrakottabekleidung

~ **ornament**, ~ decorative fixture · Terrakotta-Ornament *n*, Terrakotta-Schmuckelement *n*, Terrakotta-Schmuckglied *n*

~ **ornamental feature** → ~ decorative finish

~ ~ **finish** → ~ decorative ~

~ **panel** [*It consists of a terra-cotta facing with a light-weight concrete backing – including setting clips, etc. – and reinforcing*] · Terrakottatafel *f*

~ **partition (wall)** · Terrakottatrennwand *f*

~ **pipe** · Terrakottarohr *n*

~ **roof(ing) tile** · Terrakottadach(eindeckungs)stein *m*, Terrakottastein

~ **statue** · Terrakottastatue *f*

~ **(sur)facing**, ~ lining · Terrakottaauskleidung *f*, Terrakottaverkleidung, Terrakottabekleidung

~ **tile**, ~ block [*See remark under 'Block'*] · Terrakottablock(stein) *m*, Terrakottastein

~ ~, ~ roof(ing) ~ · Terrakotta(dach)stein *m*

terra-cotta wall tile — test run

~ wall tile · Terrakottawand(belag)platte f, Terrakottawandfliese f

terrazzo, concrete ~, terrazzo concrete · Terrazzo m [*Gemisch aus Zement und farbigen schleiffähigen Zuschlägen aus Natursteinen. DIN 1965*]

~ aggregate → concrete ~ ~

~ capping → (concrete) terrazzo (wall) coping

~ chip(ping)s → (concrete) terrazzo aggregate

~ cope → (concrete) terrazzo (wall) coping

~ coping → (concrete) terrazzo (wall) ~

~ cove → concrete ~ ~

~ coving → (concrete) terrazzo cove

~ dado, concrete ~ ~ · Terrazzosockel m

~ floor cover(ing), ~ floor(ing) (finish), concrete ~ ~ (~) · Terrazzo(fuß)boden(belag) m

~ floor(ing) (finish), ~ floor cover(ing), concrete ~ ~ (~) · Terrazzo(fuß)boden(belag) m

~ ~ tile, concrete ~ ~ ~ · Terrazzo(fuß)boden(belag)platte f, Terrazzo(fuß)bodenfliese f

~ grain, concrete ~ ~ · Terrazzokorn n

~ layer · Terrazzoleger m

~ mix(ture), concrete ~ ~ · Terrazzogemisch n, Terrazzomischung f

~ plant, concrete ~ ~ · Terrazzobetrieb m, Terrazzowerk n

~ sink drop, concrete ~ ~ · Terrazzospültisch m

~ skirting, concrete ~ ~ · Terrazzofußleiste f, Terrazzoscheuerleiste

~ slab · Terrazzoplatte f

~ stair tread, concrete ~ ~ ~ · Terrazzotritt(stufe) m, (f)

~ (wall) capping → (concrete) terrazzo (wall) coping

~ (~) cope → (concrete) terrazzo (wall) coping

~ (~) coping → concrete ~ (~) ~

~ ~ tile, concrete ~ ~ ~, (pre)cast ~ ~ ~ · Terrazzowand(belag)platte f, Terrazzowandfliese f

~ ware, concrete ~ ~ · Terrazzoware(n) f

~ window sill, concrete ~ ~ ~; (concrete) terrazzo window cill (Brit.) · Terrazzofensterbank f

~ work, concrete ~ ~ · Terrazzoarbeiten fpl

terre verte (pigment) → green earth (~)

tertiary rib, third ~, tierceron · Tertiärrippe f

terylene ladder web · Terylene-Leiterkordel f [*Jalousie*]

~ tape · Terylene(aufzug)band n [*Raffjalousie*]

tesselated pavement, opus tesselatum, Roman mosaic · Würfelmosaik n

tessera, mosaic ~, mosaic piece [*A small cube of stone, glass, or marble, used in making mosaics*] · (Mosaik-)Steinchen n, Tessera f, (Mosaik)Würfel m

test · Probe f, Prüfung f, Versuch m

~ apparatus · Prüfapparat m

~ application · Probeauftrag m [*Bautenschutzmittel; Farbe*]

~ arrangement · Versuchsaufbau m

~ bed of cement, cement bed · Zementbett n [*Blaine-Gerät*]

~ by bending in opposite directions → alternating bending test

~ certificate · Prüfbescheid m, Prüfzeugnis n, Prüfniederschrift f

(~) cube mould (Brit.); (~) ~ mold (US) · (Probe)Würfelform f, Prüfwürfelform

~ cylinder → concrete (~) ~

~ development, ~ project, ~ scheme · Versuchsbauvorhaben n, Versuchsprojekt n

~ duration → test(ing) time

~ engineer · Prüfungsingenieur m

~ fill(ing), trial ~ · Versuchsschüttung f, Probeschüttung

~ for grading → particle-size analysis

~ ~ organic matter → Abrams' test

~ ~ weight per square metre · Quadratmetergewichtsprüfung f

~ ~ ~ ~ unit area · Flächengewichtsprüfung f

~ ground, proving ~, testing ~ · Versuchsfeld n, Versuchsgelände n, Prüffeld, Prüfgelände

~ lab(oratory) · Prüflabor(atorium) n

~ load · Probelast f, Prüflast, Versuchslast

~ loading · Probebelastung f, Versuchsbelastung, Prüfbelastung

~ method, testing ~ · Versuchsmethode f, Prüfmethode, Versuchsverfahren n, Prüfverfahren

~ operation, ~ run · Versuchsbetrieb m, Probebetrieb

~ period → test(ing) time

~ pressure · Probedruck m, Versuchsdruck, Prüfdruck

~ project, ~ development, ~ scheme · Versuchsbauvorhaben n, Versuchsprojekt n

~ rain · Versuchsregen m

~ ~ temperature · Versuchsregentemperatur f

~ record · Prüfaufzeichnung f

~ report · Prüfbericht m

~ result, experimental ~, ~ finding · Prüfergebnis n, Prüfungsergebnis, Versuchsergebnis

~ room · Prüfraum m

~ run, ~ operation · Versuchsbetrieb m, Probebetrieb

(**~**) **sample** · Probe(körper) f, (m), Prüfkörper, Prüfling m, Probestück, Prüfstück n, Versuchskörper, Versuchsstück

(**~**) **~ mould** (Brit.); (**~**) **~ mold** (US) · Probekörperform f, Prüfkörperform, Versuchskörperform

~ scheme, **~ development**, **~ project** · Versuchsbauvorhaben n, Versuchsprojekt n

~ section, trial **~** · Versuchsabschnitt m, Prüfstrecke f, Probestrecke, Versuchsstrecke, Probeabschnitt, Prüfabschnitt

~ series · Prüfreihe f, Versuchsreihe

~ sieve [B.S. 410] · Prüfsieb n

~ structures · Versuchsbauten f

~ time → testing **~**

~ value · Prüfwert m

~ wall, experimental **~** · Versuchswand f

~ water · Abdrückwasser n, Prüfwasser [Rohrleitungsprüfung]

tester [The canopy over a bed] · Betthimmel m

~ [The canopy over a throne] · Thronhimmel m

~, test(ing) apparatus · Prüfgerät n

~, sounding-board [A board or screen, fixed behind or above a pulpit, in order to reflect the preacher's voice towards the congregation] · Kanzeldeckel m, Schalldeckel, Schalldach n, Schallhaube f, Kanzelhaube, Kanzelhimmel m

testing · Prüfen n, Prüfung f

test(ing) apparatus, tester · Prüfgerät n

~ cab(in) · Prüfkabine f

testing ground, proving **~**, test **~** · Versuchsfeld n, Versuchsgelände n, Prüffeld, Prüfgelände

~ committee · Prüf(ungs)ausschuß m

test(ing) duration → **~** time

testing institute · Versuchsanstalt f

test(ing) method → test **~**

~ ~ standard · Prüf(ungs)norm f

~ mortar · Prüfmörtel m

~ period → **~** time

~ pressure · Prüf(ungs)druck m

~ principle · Prüfgrundsatz m

~ regulations · Prüf(ungs)bestimmungen fpl, Prüf(ungs)vorschriften fpl

~ time, **~ period**, **~ duration**, time of test(ing), period of test(ing), duration of test(ing) · Versuchsdauer f, Versuchszeit f, Prüf(ungs)dauer f, Prüf(ungs)zeit, Probedauer, Probezeit

tetracalcium alumino ferrite · Tetrakalziumaluminatferrit n, $4CaO \cdot Al_2O_3 \cdot Fe_2O_3$, abgekürzt C_4AF

tetrachlorethylene, perchlorethylene · Tetrachloräthylen n

tetrachloromethane, carbon tetrachloride, CCl_4 · Tetra(chlorkohlenstoff) m, Tetrachlormethan

tetrapod [An equiangular figure in the form of a tripod, having a fourth leg, engaging from the intersection of the other three. Solid tetrapods weighing 15 tons, made of concrete, were used successfully to form a breakwater at Casablanca] · Vierfußblock m

tetrapylon [A structure characterized by having four gateways as an architectural feature] · Tetrapylon m

tetrastyle · viersäulig

~ [A portico having a row of four front columns] · Tetrastylos m

~ colonnade · Kolonnade f mit 4 Säulen

~ temple · Tetrastylostempel m [Ein Tempel mit vier Frontsäulen]

TEWC, totally-enclosed watercooled · vollgekapselt und wassergekühlt, ganzgekapselt **~ ~**

textile department store · Textilkaufhaus n

~ dyestuff · Textilfarbstoff m

~ fibre (Brit.); **~** fiber (US) · Textilfaser f

~ wrap(ping) · Textilbandage f, Textilumwick(e)lung f

to texture · profilieren [Glas(bau)stein]

texture, granulometric composition, grading, grain-size distribution, particle-size distribution · Kornaufbau m, Kornzusammensetzung f, Korn(größen)verteilung

~ · Strukturierung f [Fliese; Beton usw.]

textured [Glass blocks are textured with various ribbings and patterns] · profiliert [Glas(bau)stein]

~ · strukturiert, dessiniert

~ board · Strukturplatte f

~ brick slab · Wandscheibe f mit Ziegeltextur

~ (exposed) concrete, **~ fair-faced ~** · strukturierter Sichtbeton m, dessinierter **~**, Strukturbeton

~ fair-faced concrete, **~ (exposed) ~** · strukturierter Sichtbeton m, dessinierter **~**, Strukturbeton

~ finish [A finish having an ornamental patterned or textured surface produced by treatment of the freshly applied final coat with various tools. Ribbed, fan, torn, English cottage, stippled and ashlar are some of these textures] · Struktur f, Oberflächen**~**, Putz**~**

~ metal sheet → fancy sheet metal

~ tile · Struktur(belag)platte f, Strukturfliese f

~ wall(ing) surface · flächige Wandtextur f

TH — theory of sheets

TH, hot tar · Heißteer *m*

thatch → reed thatching

thatched cottage · Strohhütte *f*

thatching → reed ~

thatch(ing), straw ~, straw roofing · Stroh(dach)(ein)deckung *f*, Strohbedachung

thatching → reed ~

thatching reed · Dach(ein)deck(ungs)-schilf(rohr) *n*

~ straw · Dach(ein)deck(ungs)stroh *n*

'The Antique' [*A somewhat vague term used to describe the art of the Greeks and Romans*] · Antike *f*

The Architects Collaborative [*Partnership founded in 1945 between Walter Gropius and seven younger architects*] · Architektengemeinschaft TAC *f*

T-head bolt, tee ~ · Hammerschraube *f* [*Rohe Schraube aus Flußstahl mit hammerförmigem Kopf*]

theatre, (living) (stage) ~ · (Bühnen-)Theater *n*

~ architecture · Theaterarchitektur *f*, Theaterbaukunst *f*

~ auditorium · Theatersaal *m*

~ block → treatment ~

~ building → treatment block

~ dimmer · Theaterlichtregler *m*

~ heating · Theaterheizung *f*

theatre-in-the-round · Rundtheater *n*

Theatre of Marcellus at Rome · Theater *n* des Marcellus zu Rom

theatrical designer · Bühnenzeichner *m*

Thenards' blue (pigment), cobalt ~ (~) [*A blue pigment composed of the oxides of alumin(i)um and cobalt*] · Kobaltblau(pigment) *n*

theorem · Satz *m* [*Baustatik*]

~ of energy · Energiegesetz *n* der Statik

~ ~ five moments · Fünfmomentensatz *m*

~ ~ minimum potential energy, principle ~ ~ ~ ~, law ~ ~ ~ ~ · Prinzip *n* vom Minimum der potentiellen Energie

~ ~ reduction, reduction theorem · Reduktionssatz *m*

~ ~ superposition, principle, ~ ~, law ~ ~, superposition theorem, superposition principle, superposition law · Überlagerungsgesetz *n*, Superpositionsgesetz

~ ~ three moments, Clapeyron's equation, Clapeyron's theorem · Clapeyronsche Gleichung *f*, Dreimomentengleichung

~ ~ virtual displacements, law ~ ~ ~, principle ~ ~ ~, virtual-displacement theorem, virtual-displacement principle, virtual-displacement law · Prinzip *n* der virtuellen Verrückungen

~ ~ ~ work, law ~ ~ ~, principle ~ ~ ~, virtual-work theory, virtual-work law, virtual-work principle · Prinzip *n* der virtuellen Arbeit

theoretical dimension, nominal ~ · Sollabmessung *f*, Sollmaß *n*, Nennabmessung, Nennmaß [*DIN 18201*]

~ elasticity · theoretische Elastizität *f*

~ height, nominal ~ · Nennhöhe *f*, Sollhöhe

~ limit load · theoretische Grenzlast *f*

~ module · Sollmodul *m*

~ shape · Sollform *f*, Sollgestalt *f*

~ size, nominal ~ · Sollgröße *f*, Nenngröße

theory of architecture · Theorie *f* der Architektur, ~ ~ Baukunst

~ ~ barrels, barrel theory · Tonnentheorie *f*

~ ~ buckling · Knicktheorie *f*

~ ~ creep, creep theory · Kriechtheorie *f*

~ ~ deformation, deformation theory · Formänderungstheorie *f*, Verformungstheorie

~ ~ discs, ~ ~ sheets; ~ ~ disks (US) · Scheibentheorie *f* [*Die Lehre von den Scheiben. Scheiben sind Platten, bei denen die äußere Last in der Ebene der Mittelfläche wirkt. Die Scheibentheorie führt zur Airyschen Spannungsfunktion. Oft ist das Beulen wichtiger als die statische Beanspruchung. Ist das nicht der Fall, dann ist die Formänderung eine Verzerrung und von etwaigen kleinen Ausbiegungen der Scheibe senkrecht zur Mittelfläche unabhängig. Freigelagerte Scheiben bilden einen wandartigen Träger*]

~ ~ elastically restrained beams · Theorie *f* der elastisch eingespannten Balken(träger)

~ ~ elasticity, elastic(ity) theory · Elastizitätstheorie *f*

~ ~ empathy [*Formulated by Lipps in 1903*] · Theorie *f* der Einfühlung

~ ~ form and design · Form(en)lehre *f*

~ ~ ideal plasticity · ideale Plastizitätstheorie *f*

~ ~ plastic flow · Theorie *f* des plastischen Fließens

~ ~ plasticity, plastic theory · Bildsamkeitstheorie *f*, Plastizitätstheorie, plastische Theorie

~ ~ probability · Wahrscheinlichkeitstheorie *f*

~ ~ proportions · Proportionstheorie *f*

~ ~ shallow shells, shallow-shell theory · Theorie *f* der flachen Schalen, ~ ~ krummen Platten

~ ~ sheets, ~ ~ discs; ~ ~ disks (US) · Scheibentheorie *f* [*Die Lehre von den Scheiben. Scheiben sind Platten, bei denen die äußere Last in der Ebene der Mittelfläche wirkt. Die Scheibentheorie führt zur Airyschen Spannungsfunktion. Oft ist das Beulen wichtiger als die statische Beanspruchung. Ist das nicht der Fall, dann ist die Formänderung eine Verzerrung und von etwaigen kleinen*

theory of sheets — thermostatic radiator valve

Ausbiegungen der Scheibe senkrecht zur Mittelfläche unabhängig. Freigelagerte Scheiben bilden einen wandartigen Träger]

~ ~ **stability** → stability theory

~ ~ **thin shells** · Theorie f der dünnen Schalen

~ ~ **torsion** · Torsionstheorie f

therm window → thermal ~

therma · Therme f

~ **room** · Thermensaal m

Thermae of Caracalla · Thermen fpl des Caracalla, Caracallathermen

~ ~ **Diocletian,** baths ~ ~ · Diokletiansthermen fpl

~ ~ **Nero,** baths ~ ~ · Nerothermen fpl

~ ~ **Titus,** baths ~ ~ · Titusthermen fpl

~ ~ **Trajan,** baths ~ ~ · Trajansthermen fpl

thermal barrier, ~ break, heat ~ · Thermosperre f, Wärmesperre

~ **break,** ~ barrier, heat ~ · Wärmesperre f, Thermosperre

~ **capacity,** heat ~ [*The capacity for storing heat or cold*] · Temperatur-Speichervermögen n, Temperatur-Speicherfähigkeit f

~ **conductivity** · Wärmedurchgang m

~ **conductor** · Wärmeleiter m

~ **environment** · Temperierung f

~ **insulation,** heat ~ · Wärmedämmung f

~ **output,** heat ~ · thermischer Wirkungsgrad m, Wärmeleistung f

~ **polymerization,** bodying · Eindicken m

~ ~ **of oil,** oil bodying · Öleindicken n

~ **radiation** · Wärmestrahlung f

~ **resistance** · Wärmeübergangswiderstand m

~ · Wärmetrocknung f [*Lackauftrag*]

~ **resistivity** · Wärmeleitwiderstand m

~ **shock** · Temperaturschock m, Temperaturstoß m, Thermoschock, Thermostoß, thermischer Schock, thermischer Stoß [*Plötzliche Temperaturveränderung, die zu einer Rißbildung führen kann*]

~ **storage heating** · Speicherheizung f

~ **transmittance** · Wärmeübergang m

therm(al) window, Diocletian ~ [*A semicircular window divided into three lights by two vertical mullions. It was used in the Thermae of Diocletian, Rome. Its use was revived in the C16 especially by Palladio and is a feature of Palladianism*] · diokletianisches Fenster n, Thermenfenster

thermo-diffusion · Thermodiffusion f

Thermopane glass · Thermopane n [*Ein Mehrscheibenisolierglas, das beim Einfach-Thermopane aus zwei Scheiben und einer Luftschicht und beim Doppel-Thermopane aus drei Scheiben und zwei Luftschichten besteht*]

thermopane-glazed · isolierverglast, isoliereingeglast

Thermopane glazing · Thermopaneverglasung f, Thermopaneeinglasung

~ **pane** · Thermopanescheibe f

~ **unit** · Thermopane-Isoliereinheit f

thermoplastic [*Becoming soft when heated and hard when cooled*] · thermoplastisch

~ **acrylic** · nichthärtbares Acrylat(harz) n

~ **film,** ~ sheeting · thermoplastische Folie f

~ **flooring tile** → ~ tile

~ **(resin)** · Thermoplast m, thermoplastischer Kunststoff m

~ **sheeting,** ~ film · thermoplastische Folie f

~ **tile,** ~ flooring ~, asphalt ~ [*Asphalt tiles were originally so called because they contained mineral asphalt or products from the distillation of oil or coal. They have since come to be known as thermoplastic tiles because of the incorporation of plastic resins to obtain lighter colours than can be obtained with the dark pitch or petroleum bitumen base. B.S. 2592*] · (Asbest-)Hartfliese f, (Fuß)Bodenplatte f auf Kunstharz/Asbestbasis, (Fuß)Bodenfliese auf Kunstharz/Asbestbasis

thermosetting · duroplastisch, (hitze-)härtbar [*Kunststoff*]

~ · Wärmetrocknung f [*Lackauftrag*]

~ **acrylic (resin)** · (hitze)härtbares Acrylat(harz) n

~ **plastic** · Duroplast n, m [*(hitze)härtbarer Kunststoff*]

~ **(synthetic) resin** · härtbares (Kunst-)Harz n, hitze~ ~, Thermoharz

thermostat, temperature regulator, temperature sensor, temperature sensing element, temperature controller · Temperaturregler m, Wärmeregler, (Temperatur)Fühler, Thermostat m, Sicherheitstemperaturbegrenzer

thermostatic · thermostatisch

~ **blending mixer** → ~ (water) (mixing) valve

thermostat(ic) control · Thermostatsteuerung f

thermostatic mixer (valve) → ~ (water) (mixing) ~

~ **radiator valve** · thermostatisches Heizkörperventil n

thermostatic regulator — thinning ratio

~ **regulator** · Regeltemperaturfühler *m*, Regelthermostat *m*

~ **(water) blending mixer** → ~ (~) (mixing) valve

~ **(~) (mixing) valve,** ~ (~) mixer (~), ~ (~) blending mixer [*Such a valve is used to mix cold water with hot water*] · Thermostat-Badebatterie *f*

~ **(~) valve** → ~ (~) mixing ~

thermostatically controlled · thermostatgesteuert

Thersilion at Megalopolis · Thersilion *n* zu Megalopolis

thesaurus, treasure-house, treasury · Schatzhaus *n*, Thesauros *m*, Thesaurus *m* [*Ein kleines Gebäude zur Aufbewahrung von Weihegaben einer Stadt oder eines Landes im Temenos griechischer Kultstätten*]

Theseion, Hephaisteion · Hephästostempel *m* [*Agora von Athen*]

THI, temperature-humidity index · Temperatur-Feuchtigkeits-Index *m*, Temperatur-Feuchte-Index

thick-bed method, (conventional) mortar-bed ~ · Dickbettverfahren *n* [*Ansetzen von Fliesen*]

thick curved bar type of analysis given by Winkler, ~ ~ member ~ ~ ~ ~ ~ ~ · Biegetheorie *f* für gekrümmte Stäbe von W. Winkler, Winklersche (Biege)Theorie

thickened edge plate, ~ ~ slab · randverstärkte Platte *f*

~ ~ **slab,** ~ ~ plate · randverstärkte Platte *f*

~ **portion of the slab,** drop (panel) [*These drop panels are formed at columns to provide increased cross-sectional area and depth to resist negative moments and shears*] · Pilzkopfplatte *f*, Pilzkopfverstärkung *f*, Deckplatte, Verstärkung(splatte) [*zwischen Pilzkopf und Pilzdecke*]

thickener, viscosity adjuster · Verdikkungsmittel *n*

thickening, fattening [*An increase in consistency of paint on storage, not necessarily to such an extent as to make it unusable*] · Nachdicken *n*, Eindicken

thicker shaft · alter Dienst *m* [*Gotik*]

thickness · Dicke *f* [*Fehlname: Stärke f*]

~, **depth** · Dicke *f*, (Konstruktions)Höhe *f*, Bauhöhe; Stärke [*Fehlname*] [*Träger; Decke; Platte*]

~ **measurement** · Dickenmessung *f*

~ **of arch,** depth ~ ~ · Bogendicke *f*, Bogen(konstruktions)höhe, Bogenbauhöhe; Bogenstärke [*Fehlname*] [*Die Höhe der Vorderfläche eines Bogens*]

~ ~ **finish,** ~ ~ plaster · Verputzdicke *f* [*Fehlbezeichnung: Verputzstärke f*]

~ **(~ gauge),** gauge · Dicke *f* [*Linoleum*]

~ ~ **step** · Stufendicke *f*

thick plate (glass), ~ polished ~ (~) · dickes (Kristall)Spiegelglas *n*

~ **(polished) plate (glass)** · dickes (Kristall)Spiegelglas *n*

~ **rough cast plate (glass);** ~ ~ plate ~ (US) · dickes (Kristall)Spiegelrohglas *n*, ~ Rohspiegelglas

~ ~ **plate glass** (US); ~ ~ cast plate (~) · dickes (Kristall)Spiegelrohglas *n*, ~ Rohspiegelglas

~ **sheet glass;** crystal ~ ~, heavy ~ (~) (US) · Dickglas *n*

~ **shell** · dicke Schale *f*

thick-wall(ed), heavy-wall(ed) · dickwandig

thief resistant lock [*B.S. 3621*] · diebesicheres Schloß *n*, diebstahlsicheres ~

to thin · verdünnen

~ ~ [*To a certain viscosity, for example*] · einstellen [*Anstrichtechnik*]

thin-bed adhesive, cement based ~ [*A material in which the principal bonding component is a hydraulic cement, e.g. Portland cement, modified by the inclusion of such other additives as may be necessary in order to achieve satisfactory fixing of ceramic tiles*] · Dünnbettkleber *m*

~ **fixing technique,** ~ method, glue fixing method, (tile) cement fixing method · Dünnbettverfahren *n*, Kleb(e)verfahren [*Ansetzen von Fliesen*]

~ **method,** glue fixing ~, (tile) cement fixing ~, thin-bed fixing technique · Dünnbettverfahren *n*, Kleb(e)verfahren [*Ansetzen von Fliesen*]

thin-cut veneer · Dünnschnittfurnier *n*

thin gauge strip · Dünnblechband *n*

T-hinge → T(ee) ~

thinner, reducer, solvent [*Volatile liquids added to paints and varnishes to facilitate application and to aid penetration by lowering the viscosity. They should be completely miscible with the paint or varnish at ordinary temperatures and should not cause precipitation of the non-volatile portion either in the container or in the film during drying. For some purposes, thinners containing a small proportion of non-volatile material may be used*] · Verdünnungsmittel *n*, Verdünner *m*

~ **shaft,** vaulting ~ · junger Dienst *m* [*Gotik*]

thinness · Dünne *f*

thinning · Verdünnung *f*

~ · Verdünnen *n*

~, **cutting back** · Verschneiden *n*

thinning-out · Auflockerung *f* der Wohnviertel

thinning ratio [*The recommended proportion of thinners to be added to a paint or varnish to render it suitable for a particular method of application*] · Verdünnungsverhältnis *n*

thin sheet glass — three-component hydraulic binder

thin sheet glass · Dünnglas n [*Dicken 0,9; 1,1; 1,3 und 1,6 mm*]

~ **shell, membrane** ~ [*A thin shell is a curved membrane thin enough to develop negligible bending stresses over most of its surface, but thick enough not to buckle under small compressive stresses, as an ideal membrane would*] · Membran(e)schale f, dünne Schale

thin-wall plaster, Scandinavian ~, Swedish sand putty · Dünnputz m

thin-wall(ed) · dünnwandig

~ **hollow brick** · Dünnwandhohlziegel m

~ **pipe,** ~ **tube** · dünnwandiges Rohr n

~ **prefabrication** · dünnwandige Vorfertigung f

~ **section** · dünnwandiger Querschnitt m

~ **tube,** ~ **pipe** · dünnwandiges Rohr n

thiokol [*It is a mistake, in fact, to refer to the two-part rubber-base compounds as thiokols, since this name identifies not a material but the company which supplies the polysulfide liquid polymer used as the base ingredient in their manufacture*] · Thiokol n

thiourea · Thioharnstoff m

third coat, setting ~ · dritte Putzlage f, ~ Putzschicht f

third-degree parabola · Parabel f dritten Grades

third firing · Rotbrennen n [*Glas*]

third-order equation · Gleichung f dritten Grades, kubische Gleichung

~ **theory** · (Spannungs)Theorie f 3. Ordnung

third point · Drittelpunkt m, dritter Punkt

third-point load · Drittelpunktlast f

~ **loading** · Drittelpunktbelastung f

third quality · dritte Wahl f

~ **rib, tertiary** ~, **tierceron** · Tertiärrippe f

thixotropic paint [*The thixotropic paints are sometimes known as one-coat paints because a film of approximately one and a half times the thickness of a normal coat of paint can be achieved in one application. They are not popular for commercial application*] · thixotrope (Anstrich)Farbe f

~ **paste** · thixotrope Paste f

thixotropy · Thixotropie f, Wechselfestigkeit f [*Die Erscheinung, daß eine Suspension durch mechanische Einwirkung (z.B. Schütteln) verflüssigt und nach einer gewissen Zeit wieder ansteift. Dieser Vorgang ist wiederholbar*]

thole → tholus

tholobate → tambour

tholus, circular hut, tholos, thole · Säulenrundbau m, Tholos m [*Tempelform. Runde Cella mit rundem Säulenumgang*]

~ **type of tomb,** beehive ~ [*A subterranean stone-vaulted tomb shaped-like an old-fashioned beehive*] · Tholosgrab n, unterirdisches kuppelförmiges Rundgrab

Thomas iron, basic Bessemer pig ~ · Thomasroheisen n

~ **meal,** slag flour, ground basic slag · Schlackenmehl n, Thomasmehl, Thomasphosphat n

~ **slag,** basic ~ · Thomasschlacke f

~ **steel,** basic converter ~ · Thomasstahl m, T ST [*DIN 17006*]

thoria · Thoriumdioxid n

~ **refractory (product)** · Thoriumdioxiderzeugnis n

thousand-flower glass, millefiore ~ · Millefioriglas n, Mosaikglas

thread · Gewinde n

thread(ed) anchorage · Gewindeverankerung f

~ **bar,** ~ **rod** · Gewindestab m

~ **end** · Gewindeende n

~ **flange** · Gewindeflansch m [*DIN 2563–2569*]

~ **glass globe** · Schraub(gewinde)glas n [*Leuchte*]

~ **hook** · Gewindehaken m

~ **nail** · Gewindenagel m

~ **pipe** · Gewinderohr n

~ **rod,** ~ **bar** · Gewindestab m

threadless · gewindelos

~ **pipe,** TP · gewindeloses Rohr n

three-aisled, three-nave · dreischiffig [*Kirche*]

three-bay, three-span · dreischiffig [*Rahmenhalle*]

~ · dreijochig

three-bed · dreibettig

~ **room** · Dreibettzimmer n

three-bedroom(ed) dwelling unit (US); ~ **dwelling** (Brit.) · Drei-Schlafzimmer-Wohnung f

~ **house** · Dreischlafzimmerhaus n

three-bracket testing · Drei-Klassen-Verteilung f [*in der Güteüberwachung*]

three-centre arch (Brit.); **three-center** ~ (US) · Drei-Zentren-Bogen m

three-centred arch (Brit.); **three-centered** ~ (US) · Drei-Zentren-Bogen m

three(-)coat plaster · Dreilagenputz m, dreilagiger Putz

~ **system, three(-)layer(ed)** ~ · Dreischichtenaufbau m, Dreischichtensystem n, Dreilagenaufbau, Dreilagensystem

three-compartment revolving door · dreiflügelige Drehtür f

three-component epoxy resin, three-part ~ ~, **three-pack** ~ ~ · Dreikomponenten-Epoxidharz n

~ **hydraulic binder, three-part** ~ ~ · Dreistoffbindemittel n, Dreistoffbinder m [*Eine fabrikmäßig hergestellte Mischung aus Traß, Kalk und Zement*]

three-component unit — threefold altarpiece

~ **unit**, three-part ~, three-pack ~ · Dreikomponentenmaterial *n*

three-core brick · Dreikammerziegel *m*

three-degree-of-freedom structure, ~ **construction** · Bauwerk *n* mit drei Freiheitsgraden

three-dimensional, spatial, stereometric, 3-D · räumlich, dreidimensional, stereometrisch

~ **area-covering structural element** · räumliches Flächentragwerk *n*

~ **bar**, space ~, spatial ~, ~ rod · dreidimensionaler Stab *m*, räumlicher ~

~ **bearing structure** → space (load-)bearing ~

~ **composition**, spatial ~, space ~ · Raumkomposition *f*, räumliche Komposition

~ **configuration**, spatial ~, space ~ · Raumfigur *f*

~ **construction** → spatial ~

~ **continuity**, spatial ~, space ~ · dreidimensionaler Zusammenhang *m*, räumlicher ~

~ **curve**, space ~, spatial ~, curve in space · räumliche Kurve *f*, dreidimensionale ~, Raumkurve

~ **deformation**, spatial ~ · räumliche Formänderung *f*, ~ Verformung, ~ Gestaltänderung

~ **design**, spatial ~, space ~ · dreidimensionaler Entwurf *m*, räumlicher ~

~ ~, ~ ~ **layout**, space ~, spatial ~ · Raumdisposition *f*

~ **distribution of forces**, spatial ~ ~, ~ · dreidimensionale Krafteverteilung *f*, räumliche ~

~ **effect** · Raumwirkung *f*

~ **frame**, spatial ~, space ~ · räumlicher Rahmen *m*, dreidimensionaler ~

~ **frame(d) (load)bearing structure** → spatial frame(d) supporting ~

~ **frame(work)** → space ~

~ **geometry**, descriptive ~, solid ~ · darstellende Geometrie *f*

~ **image**, space ~, spatial ~, view of space · Raumbild *n*

~ **(inter)penetration**, spatial ~ · dreidimensionale Durchschluchtung *f*, räumliche ~

~ **layout**, ~ ~ **design**, space ~, spatial ~ · Raumdisposition *f*

~ **(load)bearing structure** → space ~ ~

~ **load-carrying structure** → space (load)bearing ~

~ **loaded structure** → space (load-)bearing ~

~ **modelling** (Brit.); ~ **modeling** (US) · plastische Differenzierung *f*

~ **panelling pattern** (Brit.); ~ **paneling** ~ (US); spatial ~ ~, space ~ ~ · dreidimensionales (Ver)Täfelungsmuster *n*, räumliches ~

~ **parallel system** → spatial ~ ~

~ **penetration**, spatial ~, ~ inter~ · dreidimensionale Durchschluchtung *f*, räumliche ~

~ **photoelasticity** · dreidimensionale Spannungsoptik *f*

~ **(pre)stressing**, ~ stretching, ~ tensioning, spatial ~ · dreidimensionales (Vor)Spannen *n*, räumliches ~

~ **problem**, space ~, spatial ~ · dreidimensionale Aufgabe *f*, räumliche ~

~ **purlin(e)**, spatial ~, space ~ · dreidimensionale Pfette *f*, räumliche ~

~ **rod**, space ~, spatial ~, ~ bar · dreidimensionaler Stab *m*, räumlicher ~

~ **state of stress** · dreiachsiger Spannungszustand *m*, allgemeiner ~, räumlicher ~

~ **stressing** → ~ pre~

~ **stretching**, ~ tensioning, ~ (pre-)stressing, spatial ~ · räumliches (Vor-)Spannen *n*, dreidimensionales ~

~ **(structural) system** → spatial construction

~ **structure**, spatial ~, space ~ · Raumbau(werk) *m*, (*n*), räumliches Bauwerk, dreidimensionales Bauwerk, räumlicher Bau, dreidimensionaler Bau

~ **supporting structure** → space (load)bearing ~

~ **system** → spatial construction

~ ~ **of forces** · räumliche Kräftegruppe *f*

~ **tensioning**, ~ stretching, ~ (pre-)stressing, spatial ~ · räumliches (Vor-)Spannen *n*, dreidimensionales ~

~ **treatment** · plastische Durchbildung *f*

~ **unit**, spatial ~, space ~ · Raumelement *n*, dreidimensionales Element, räumliches Element

~ **wallpaper** [*It has a relief surface*] · Profiltapete *f*, Relief(druck)tapete

~ **weight-carrying structure** → space (load)bearing ~

⅜-inch wide wallpaper cover moulding (Brit.) / **molding** (US) · Dreiachtelstab *m* [*Eine Tapetenleiste von ⅜ Zoll Breite*]

three families house · Dreifamilienhaus *n*

three-flight stair(case), triple-flight ~ · dreiläufige Treppe *f*

three-floored; three-storey (Brit.); **three-story** (US) · dreietagig, dreistöckig, dreigeschossig

three-foil(ed) arcade, trefoil(ed) ~ · Klee(blatt)bogenarkade *f*

~ **arch** → trefoil(-headed) ~

~ **(ground(-))plan**, trefoil(ed) ~ · Klee(blatt)grundriß *m*

~ **plan** → ~ ground(-)~

~ **tracery**, trefoil(ed) ~ · Dreipaßmaßwerk *n*

threefold altarpiece, (folding) triptych · dreiteiliger Klappaltar *m*, Triptychon *n*, Flügelaltarschrein

three-fraction sand · dreistufiger Sand m

three-hinged, three-pinned, triple-hinged, triple-pinned · dreigelenkig

three-hinge(d) arch(ed girder), three-pin(ned) ~ (~), triple-hinge(d) (~), triple-pin(ned) ~ (~) · Dreigelenkbogen(träger) m, gekrümmter Dreigelenkträger

~ **arch-ribbed dome,** ~ ~ cupola, three-pin(ned) ~ ~, triple-hinge(d) ~ ~ · Dreigelenk-Rippenkuppel f

~ **frame,** three-pin(ned) ~, triple-hinge(d) ~, frame with three hinges · Dreigelenkrahmen m

~ **half-frame,** three-pin(ned) ~ triple-hinge(d) ~ · Dreigelenkhalbrahmen m

~ **portal frame,** three-pinned ~ ~, triple-pin(ned) ~ ~, triple-hinge(d) ~ ~ · Dreigelenkportalrahmen m

~ **rectangular frame,** three-pin(ned) ~ ~, triple-hinge(d) ~ ~, rectangular frame with three hinges · Dreigelenkrechteckrahmen m

~ **roof,** three-pin(ned) ~, triple-hinge(d) ~ · Dreigelenkdach n

~ **steel arch,** three-pin(ned) ~ ~, triple-hinge(d) ~ ~ · Stahl-Dreigelenkbogen m

~ **trussed arch(ed girder)** · Dreigelenk-Fachwerkbogen(träger) m

~ **truss(ed) frame,** three-pin(ned) ~, triple-hinge(d) ~ ~ · Dreigelenkfachwerkrahmen m

three-layer(ed) · dreilagig, dreischichtig

~ **chimney** · Mantelschornstein m [Er hat eine dreischichtige Wandung aus Innenrohr, Dämmschicht und Außenmantel]

~ **panel,** sandwich ~ · Sandwichtafel f, Dreilagentafel, Dreischichtentafel [Fehlname: Sandwichplatte. Bauteil für Außen- und Innenverkleidung bei Rahmenkonstruktionen; kreuzweise bewehrt, dazwischen Glaswolleschicht von etwa 5 cm]

~ **façade,** sandwich ~ ~ · Dreilagentafelfassade f, Dreischichtentafelfassade

~ **plate,** ~ slab, sandwich ~ ~ · Dreilagenplatte f, Dreischichtenplatte

~ **roof(ing) slab,** sandwich ~ ~ · Dreilagendachplatte f, Dreischichtendachplatte

~ **shell,** sandwich ~ ~ · Dreilagenschale f, Dreischichtenschale

~ **slab,** ~ plate, sandwich ~ ~ · Dreilagenplatte f, Dreischichtenplatte

~ **system,** three(-)coat ~ · Dreischichtenaufbau m, Dreischichtensystem n, Dreilagenaufbau, Dreilagensystem

~ **wall panel,** sandwich ~ ~ · Dreilagenwandtafel f, Dreischichtenwandtafel

three-leaf folding shutter door, ~ ~ shutterdoor · dreiflügeliges Falttor n

~ **sliding folding shutterdoor,** ~ ~ ~ shutter door · dreiflügeliges Faltschiebetor n, ~ Schiebefalttor

~ **sliding folding shutterdoor,** ~ ~ ~ shutter door · dreiflügeliges Faltschiebetor n, ~ Schiebefalttor

three-level (building operational) system · Dreiebenensystem n [Passagier- und Gepäckabfertigung auf Flughäfen]

~ **operation** · Dreiebenenbetrieb m [Flughafen]

~ **system,** ~ building operational ~ · Dreiebenensystem [Passagier- und Gepäckabfertigung auf Flughäfen]

three-light window → tripartite ~

three-lobe tracery · Dreipaß m [gotisches Maßwerk]

three-moment equation, ~ theorem, equation of three moments, theorem of three moments · Dreimomentengleichung f, Dreimomentensatz m [Zur Ermitt(e)lung der Stützmomente bei durchlaufenden Trägern über drei benachbarte Auflagerpunkte. Die Clapeyronsche Gleichung ist eine Dreimomentengleichung für gleichmäßig verteilte Belastung]

~ **theorem** → ~ equation

three-nave, three-aisle · dreischiffig [Kirche]

three-pack epoxy resin → three-component ~ ~

~ **unit,** three-part ~, three-component ~ · Dreikomponentenmaterial n

three-panel(led) door (Brit.); three-panel(ed) ~ (US) · Dreifüllungstür f

three-part epoxy resin → three-component ~ ~

~ **hydraulic binder,** three-component ~ ~ · Dreistoffbindemittel n, Dreistoffbinder m [Eine fabrikmäßig hergestellte Mischung aus Traß, Kalk und Zement]

~ **unit,** three-pack ~, three-component ~ · Dreikomponentenmaterial n

three-pin plug [B.S. 1778] · Dreifachstecker m, dreipoliger Stecker

three-pinned, three-hinged, triple-pinned, triple-hinged · dreigelenkig

three-pin(ned) arch(ed girder) → three-hinge(d) ~ (~)

~ **arch-ribbed dome,** ~ ~ cupola, three-hinge(d) ~ ~, triple-hinge(d) ~ ~ · Dreigelenk-Rippenkuppel f

~ **frame,** three-hinge(d) ~, triple-hinge(d) ~, frame with three hinges · Dreigelenkrahmen m

~ **half-frame,** three-hinge(d) ~, triple-hinge(d) ~ · Dreigelenkhalbrahmen m

~ **portal frame,** three-hinge(d) ~ ~, triple-hinge(d) ~ ~, triple-pin(ned) ~ ~ · Dreigelenkportalrahmen m

~ **rectangular frame,** three-hinge(d) ~ ~, triple-hinge(d) ~ ~, rectangular frame with three hinges · Dreigelenkrechteckrahmen m

~ **roof,** three-hinge(d) ~, triple-hinge(d) ~ · Dreigelenkdach *n*

~ **steel arch,** three-hinge(d) ~ ~, triple-hinge(d) ~ ~ · Stahl-Dreigelenkbogen *m*

~ **truss(ed) frame,** three-hinge(d) ~ ~, triple-hinge(d) ~ ~ · Dreigelenkfachwerkrahmen *m*

three-ply, 3-ply · dreilagig, dreischichtig [*Kleb(e)dach(belag)*]

~ **built-up roof cladding,** ~ ~ ~ cover(ing), ~ ~ ~ sheathing, ~ ~ roof(ing) · Dreilagen-Kleb(e)dach(belag) *n*, (*m*), Dreilagen-Kleb(e)(dach)-(ein)deckung *f*, Dreilagen-Kleb(e)bedachung, Dreilagen-Spachteldach(belag), Dreilagen-Spachtel(dach)(ein)-deckung, Dreilagen-Spachtelbedachung, Dreischichten-Kleb(e)dach(belag), Dreischichten-Kleb(e)(dach)-(ein)deckung, Dreischichten-Kleb(e)-bedachung, Dreischichten-Spachteldach(belag), Dreischichten-Spachtel-(dach)(ein)deckung, Dreischichten-Spachtelbedachung

three-point support · Dreipunktlagerung *f*

three-portal façade · Drei-Portal-Fassade *f*

three posts, system of ~ ~ · dreifach stehender (Dach)Stuhl *m*

~ ~ **and wind filling,** system of ~ ~ ~ ~ ~ · dreifach stehender (Dach-)Stuhl *m* und Versenkung *f*

three-quarter (attached) column, bowtel, boltel, boultine · Dreiviertelsäule *f* [*Eine Säule, deren Schaft dreiviertel aus der Wand oder einem Pfeilerkern hervortritt*]

~ **block,** ~ tile [*See remark under 'Block'*] · Dreiviertelblock(stein) *m*, Dreiviertelstein

~ **brick,** ~ clay ~ · Dreiquartier *m*, Dreiviertelstein *m*, Dreiviertelziegel *m*

~ **(clay) brick** · Dreiquartier *m*, Dreiviertelstein *m*, Dreiviertelziegel *m*

~ **column** → ~ attached ~

~ **moulding** (Brit.); ~ molding (US) · Dreiviertelstab *m*

~ **niche** · Dreiviertelnische *f*

~ **small column** · Dreiviertelsäulchen *n*, Dreivierteldienst *m*

~ **tile,** ~ block [*See remark under 'Block'*] · Dreiviertelblock(stein) *m*, Dreiviertelstein

three-rate tariff system · Drei-Tarif-System *n*

three-roll mill, triple-roll ~ · Dreiwalzenwerk *n* [*Mahlen in der Lackindustrie*]

three-room(ed) · dreiräumig

~ **apartment (unit),** ~ flat; ~ living unit (US) · Dreizimmer-Geschoßwohnung *f*, Dreizimmer-Etagenwohnung, Dreizimmer-Stockwerkwohnung, Dreiraum-Geschoßwohnung, Dreiraum-Etagenwohnung, Dreiraum-Stockwerkwohnung

~ **dwelling unit** (US); ~ dwelling (Brit.) · Dreiraumwohnung *f*, Dreizimmerwohnung

~ **flat,** ~ apartment (unit); ~ living unit (US) · Dreizimmer-Stockwerkwohnung *f*, Dreizimmer-Etagenwohnung, Dreizimmer-Geschoßwohnung, Dreiraum-Stockwerkwohnung, Dreiraum-Geschoßwohnung, Dreiraum-Etagenwohnung

~ **living unit** (US); ~ apartment (~), ~ flat · Dreizimmer-Geschoßwohnung *f*, Dreizimmer-Etagenwohnung, Dreizimmer-Stockwerkwohnung, Dreiraum-Geschoßwohnung, Dreiraum-Etagenwohnung, Dreiraum-Stockwerkwohnung

three-shift pouring · Betonieren *n* im Drei-Schichtenbetrieb

three-span, three-bay · dreischiffig [*Rahmenhalle*]

~ **beam,** beam of three spans · Dreifeldbalken(träger) *m*

~ **continuous beam** · Dreifeld-Durchlaufbalken(träger) *m*

~ **frame** · Dreifeldrahmen *m*

three-storey (Brit.); **three-story** (US); three-floored · dreigeschossig, dreistöckig, dreietagig

three-story (US); **three-storey** (Brit.); three-floored · dreietagig, dreistöckig, dreigeschossig

three-towered · dreitürmig

three-way arch · Dreitoranlage *f*, dreitoriger (Straßen)Bogen *m*

~ **cable conduit** → ~ ~ duct

~ ~ **duct,** ~ ~ conduit, ~ ~ subway, ~ CD; ~ conduit tile (US) · dreizügiger Kabel(kanal)formstein *m*, dreizügiges Kabelformstück *n*

~ ~ **subway** → ~ ~ duct

~ **CD** → ~ cable duct

~ **conduit tile** (US) → ~ cable duct

~ **tap** · Dreiwegehahn *m*

~ **valve** · Dreiwegeventil *n*

three-webbed · dreistegig [*Träger*]

three-winged · dreiflügelig

three-wire strand · dreidrähtige Litze *f*

threshold · Schwelle *f*

~, door ~ · (Tür)Schwelle *f*

~, sill; saddle (US) [*A horizontal timber at the foot of an outside door*] · (Holz-)(Tür)Schwelle *f*

~ **draft-proofer** (US); ~ draught-proofer (Brit.) · Schwellen-Zug(ab)-dichtung *f*

~ **of audibility** [*deprecated*] → ~ ~ ~ hearing

~ ~ **discomfort** · Reizschwelle *f*, Unbehaglichkeitsschwelle

~ ~ **hearing,** hearing threshold; threshold of audibility [*deprecated*] [*An empirical curve relating the frequency to the lower limit of sound pressure (in decibels) below which persons with normal hearing are unable to perceive sound*] · Hörschwelle *f*

threshold of pain — tie

~ ~ pain · Schmerzschwelle f
~ seal(er), door bottom · untere Türdichtung f
thrice-cut → triglyph
throat → throating
~, cavetto · Ablauf m [Konkave kurvierte Vermittlung zwischen einem vorspringenden oberen und einem zurücktretenden unteren Bauglied]
throat(ing), weather groove, (water) drip, scotia · (Wasser)Nase f, Unterschneidung f
throating · hood-mould(ing)
throne hall, ~ room · Thronzimmer n, Thronraum m, Thronsaal m
~ room, ~ hall · Thronzimmer n, Thronraum m, Thronsaal m
to throttle · (ab)drosseln
throttling · (Ab)Drosseln n
through-crack · durchgehender Riß m
through-dry · durchgetrocknet
to through-dry, to dry through well [The opposite of to skin dry] · durchtrocknen
through-living room · Durchgangswohnzimmer n
through migration · Durchwandern n
through-mortice, through-mortise · Schlitzzapfen m [Holzverbindung]
throughput of water · Wasserdurchsatz m
through section, throughing · Rinnenstahl m, trogförmiger Formstahl
~ station · Durchgangsbahnhof m
through-stone, (wall) tie closer, bond header · Ankerstein m, Durchbinder m
through ventilation · Durchlüftung f [Gebäude]
~ view, cross-vista · Durchblick m
(through-)vision · Durchblick m, Durchsicht f [Glas]
through-wall flashing; thru-wall ~ (US) [See remark under 'Anschluß'] · durchgehender Anschluß m, durchlaufender ~
~ ~ (piece); thru-wall ~ (~) (US) · durchgehender Anschluß(streifen) m, durchlaufender ~
through-wiring · Durchverdrahtung f
throughing, through section · Rinnenstahl m, trogförmiger Formstahl
throw-away-type bag, disposable ~ · Einwegsack m, Wegwerfsack
~ filter, disposable ~ · Wegwerffilter m, n
~ house, disposable ~ · Wegwerfhaus n [Es besteht aus Pappschaumstoff und ist für 35 Jahre Lebensdauer konstruiert]
throwing circle · Wurfkreis m [Leichtathletik]
throwing on · (Putz)Anwerfen n, (Putz-)Anwurf m
~ power · Eindring(ungs)tiefe f, Umgriff m [Elektrotauchverfahren]

thrown-on finish · (Putz)Anwurf m
to throw off, to give ~ [heat] · abgeben [Wärme]
thrown-on plaster partition wall · Anwurfwand f [Leichte Trennwand aus fugenlosem Putz, der auf einer einseitigen Tafelschalung aufgetragen wird]
thrown-silk, organzine · Organsin n
thrust · Schub m
~, side ~, lateral ~ · (Seiten)Schub m [Die waag(e)rechte Resultierende einer Gewölbekraft]
~ action · Beanspruchung f auf Schub, Schubbeanspruchung
~ block, pipe pier, pipe support · (Rohr-)Festpunkt m
~ line, (funicular) pressure ~, line of thrust · Stützlinie f, Mittelkraftlinie, Drucklinie [Die „natürliche" Kräftelinie des formaktiven Drucksystems]
thru-wall flashing (US); through-wall ~ [See remark under 'Anschluß'] · durchgehender Anschluß m, durchlaufender ~
~ ~ (piece) (US); through-wall ~ (~) · durchgehender Anschluß(streifen) m, durchlaufender ~
thumb hole · Daumenloch n
~ latch, Norfolk ~; lift ~ (US); Canadian ~, Suffolk ~, Garden City ~ (Brit.) · (Daumen)Drückerfalle f
~ molding (US) → (Roman) ovolo (moulding)
~ nut, wing ~ · Flügelmutter f
thymele [The altar of Dionysus in the centre of the orchestra in an ancient Greek theatre] · Thymele f
tibari, tibara · Tibara m, Tibari [Säulenhalle des indischen Wohnhauses]
ticket booth · Kasse f [Theater; Kino]
~ hall · (Fahr)Kartenschalterhalle f
ticket-reading gate · Fahrscheinprüfbarriere f [Sie öffnet sich sobald ein Fahrgast einen magnetisch kodierten Fahrschein vorgewiesen hat]
ticket-transfer office · Umbuchungsbüro n, Büro für Umbuchungen [Flughafen]
to tie, to bind · flechten, binden, rödeln [Bewehrung]
tie → ~ rod
~, anchor, wall ~ · (Wand)Anker m
~, brace, angle ~, strut · Kopfband n, (Kopf)Bug m, Kopfstrebe f, Kopfbiege f [Kurze Verstrebung am oberen Ende eines Stiels im Fachwerk]
~, tension element, tension member, tension bar, tension rod · Zugglied n, gezogenes Glied, Zugstab m, gezogener Stab
~, (masonry) wall ~, (masonry) cavity ~, (masonry) (wall) anchor · (Mauer-)Anker m, Mauer(werk)haken m, Mauerwerkanker

tie — tile chimney

~ → lateral reinforcement

tieback → horizontal ~

tie-bar · Betonanker *m*, Verbindungseisen *n*, Ankerstab *m*, Verankerungsstab, Ankerstange *f*, Verankerungsstange, (Zug)Anker, (Anker)Zugstange; Ankereisen [*Schweiz*]

~ joint, multiple ~ · Knoten(punkt)gelenk *n*

tie beam, main ~, footing ~, principal ~ · Hauptbalken *m*, Zugbalken, Spannbalken, Trambalken [*einsäuliges Hängewerk*]

tie-beam, ~ piece · Querriegel *m* [*Dach*]

~, brace · Band(balken) *n*, (*m*)

~ roof [*The tie-beam roof is found in connection both with steeply-pitched and lowpitched roofs. In early use the tiebeam represents a 'baulk-tie' which joined the wall-posts of timber buildings, and in stone buildings was often haphazardly placed to prevent the wall plates from spreading. It came to serve, usually cambered upwards, to carry an ornamental or plain crown-post, which in its turn and with the aid of struts sustained a collar-purlin, linking the collars and giving rigidity to a roof otherwise of the trussed-rafter class*] · Querriegeldach *n*

tie closer, wall ~ ~, through-stone, bond header · Ankerstein *m*, Durchbinder *m*

~ hole, anchor ~ · Ankerloch *n*, Verankerungsloch

~ member → horizontal ~ ~

~ plate, cover ~, brace ~, stay ~, batten (~) · Schnalle *f*, Bindeblech *n* [*Bei zwei- und mehrteiligen Querschnitten werden die einzelnen Teile durch Bindebleche in ihrem gegenseitigen Abstand gehalten*]

~ rod [*A tie, generally a steel rod, often threaded*] · Zuganker *m*

~ ~, TR · Zugstange *f*

~ ~, forms tie, shuttering tie, (form(-work)) tie · Schal(ungs)anker *m*

tied arch(ed girder), bowstring ~, arch(ed girder) with tie · Zugband-Bogen(träger) *m*, Stabbogen(träger), Bogen(träger) mit Zugband, gekrümmter Träger mit Zugband

~ column, ~ support · Stütze *f* mit Bügelbewehrung

~ support, ~ column · Stütze *f* mit Bügelbewehrung

~ to ground, anchored ~ ~ · bodenverankert

~ wall, anchored ~ · verankerte Wand *f*

tier, shell, skin, layer, leaf, wythe, withe [*cavity wall*] · Schale *f*, Wand~ [*Hohlwand*]

~ · Bildstreifen *m*

~ of seats, row ~ ~ · Sitzreihe *f*

tierceron, third rib, tertiary rib · Tertiärrippe *f*

~ vault · Tertiärrippengewölbe *n*

tiered stone 'umbrella' · Chattra *f*, mehrstöckiger schirmartiger Aufbau *m* [*Stupa*]

tiers-point arch · Drittelsbogen *m*

tight, impervious, impermeable · dicht, undurchlässig

~ gum veins · feste Harzbestandteile *mpl* [*Parkettstab*]

~ to chemicals, impermeable ~ ~, impervious ~ ~ · chemikalienundurchlässig, chemikaliendicht

~ ~ gas(olene) → impervious ~ ~

~ ~ oil → impervious ~ ~

~ ~ petrol (Brit.) → impervious to gas(-olene)

~ ~ surface water, impervious ~ ~ ~, impermeable ~ ~ · oberflächenwasserdicht, tagwasserdicht

tightening · Festziehen *n*, Anziehen [*Schraube*]

tightness, impermeability, imperviousness · Dichtheit *f*, Dichtigkeit, Undurchlässigkeit

~ degree, degree of thightness · Dichtigkeitsgrad *m*, Dichtheitsgrad

~ of concrete, impermeability ~ ~, imperviousness ~ ~ · Betondichtheit *f*, Betondichtigkeit, Betonundurchlässigkeit

~ ~ joint(s), impermeability ~ ~, imperviousness ~ ~ · Fugenundurchlässigkeit *f*, Fugendichtheit, Fugendichtigkeit

~ to gas → imperviousness ~ ~

to tile · (ver)fliesen [*mit Fliesen belegen*]

tile, drain ~, DT (US); clay pipe, CP · Tonrohr *n*

~ [*A tile is a relatively small, nonstructural, surfacing unit which is thin in relation to its width and length*] · (Belag)Platte *f*, Fliese *f*

~ → (building) block

~, stove ~ · (Ofen)Kachel *f* [*DIN 409*]

~ adhesive → ~ setting ~

~ arch, block ~ [*See remark under 'Block'*] ~ Block(stein)bogen *m*, Steinbogen

~ beam, block ~ · Block(stein)balken(träger) *m*, Steinbalken(träger)

~ body, ~ clay, ~ stone · (Belag-)Plattenscherben *m*, (Keramik)Fliesenscherben

(~) ~ · Rohfliese *f*

~ ceiling · Fliesendecke *f*, Plattendecke

(~) cement fixing method, thin-bed ~, glue fixing ~, thin-bed fixing technique · Dünnbettverfahren *n*, Kleb(e)verfahren [*Ansetzen von Fliesen*]

~ cement(ing agent) → ~ (setting) adhesive

~ chimney, ~ stack, block ~ · Block(stein)schornstein *m*, Steinschornstein

tile (clay) body — tile setting

~ **(clay) body,** ~ stone · (Belag)Plattenscherben m, (Keramik)Fliesenscherben

~ **cleaning agent** · (Belag)Plattenreiniger m, (Belag)Plattenreinigungsmittel n, Fliesenreiniger, Fliesenreinigungsmittel

~ **construction method,** block ~ ~ [*See remark under 'Block'*] · Steinbau(-weise) m, (f), Block~, Blockbau(weise)

~ **cut across** · Teil(belag)platte f, Teilfliese f

~ **drainage** (US); clay pipe ~ · Tonrohrdränage f

~ **factory** → (building) block plant

~ **finish,** tilework, tiling · Fliesenbelag m, Plattenbelag, Plattierung f

~ **fitting** [*A unit produced in the same way as a tile but having one or more surfaces so glazed that, when used in combination with tiles those surfaces themselves change the plane of the glazed surface of the tiling*] · (Belag-)Plattenformstück n, Fliesenformstück

(~) fixer, (floor-and-wall) tiler · Fliesenleger m, Plattenleger

~ **fixing,** ~ setting, tiling (work) · Plattenarbeiten fpl, Fliesenarbeiten, Fliesen(ver)legen n, Verfliesen, Platten(ver)legen, Plattieren, Plattierungsarbeiten

~ ~ **adhesive** → ~ (setting) ~

~ ~ **agent** → ~ (setting) adhesive

~ ~ **glue** → ~ (setting) adhesive

~ ~ **medium** → ~ (setting) adhesive

~ ~ **work,** floor-and-wall tiling ~ · Fliesen- und Plattenarbeiten fpl [*DIN 18352*]

~ **floor cover(ing),** ~ floor(ing) (finish) · Fliesen(fuß)boden(belag) m, Platten(fuß)boden(belag), Stein(fuß)boden(belag) [*Er besteht aus Kunststeinplatten*]

~ **floor(ing) (finish),** ~ floor cover(-ing) · Fliesen(fuß)boden(belag) m, Platten(fuß)boden(belag), Stein(fuß)boden(belag) [*Er besteht aus Kunststeinplatten*]

~ **format,** block ~ [*See remark under 'Block'*] · Steinformat n, Block~, Blockformat

~ **girder,** block ~ · Block(stein)träger m, Steinträger

~ **glazed coat(ing),** ~ glazing, ~ glaze(d finish) · Fliesenglasur f, Fliesenbeglasung f, (Belag)Plattenbeglasung, (Belag)Plattenglasur

~ **glaze(d finish),** ~ glazing, ~ glazed coat(ing) · Fliesenglasur f, Fliesenbeglasung f, (Belag)Plattenbeglasung, (Belag)Plattenglasur

~ **glazing,** ~ glaze(d finish), ~ glazed coat(ing) · Fliesenglasur f, Fliesenbeglasung f, (Belag)plattenbeglasung, (Belag)Plattenglasur

~ **glue** → ~ (setting) adhesive

~ **hanging,** weather lining · Plattenwandauskleidung f, Plattenwandverkleidung, Plattenwandbekleidung, Wandplattenauskleidung, Wandplattenverkleidung, Wandplattenbekleidung

~ **joint** · (Belag)Plattenfuge f, Fliesenfuge

~ **jointing composition** → ~ ~ compound

~ ~ **compound,** ~ ~ composition, ~ ~ mass, ~ sealing ~, ~ sealant · Fliesenfugenmasse f, (Belag)Plattenfugenmasse

~ ~ **mass** → ~ ~ compound

~ **laying,** block ~, block laying, tile laying [*See remark under 'Block'*] · Vermauern n [*Blocksteine*]

~ **line** → drain ~ ~

~ **lintel** → (building) block ~

~ **making,** block ~, forming of blocks, forming of tiles [*See remark under 'Block'*] · Steinfertigung f, Steinherstellung, Block(stein)herstellung, Block(stein)fertigung

~ **(masonry) wall** → (building) block (~) ~

~ ~ **(work)** → (building) block ~ (~)

~ **panel,** prefab(ricated) tiling · (Belag-)Plattentafel f, Fliesentafel [*Zu einer Verlegeeinheit zusammengefaßte Fliesen*]

~ **partition (wall),** block ~ (~) · Block(stein)trennwand f, Steintrennwand

~ **path** · Plattenweg m

~ **pattern** · (Belag)Plattenbild n, (Belag)Plattenmuster n, Fliesenbild, Fliesenmuster

~ **plant** → (building) block ~

~ **red** · dachziegelrot

~ **roof cladding** → ~ ~ ~ covering

~ ~ **cover(ing),** ~ ~ cladding, ~ ~ sheathing, ~ roofing · Stein-Bedachung f, Stein-(Ein)Deckung, Stein-Dach(ein)deckung, Dachstein(ein)deckung

~ ~ **sheathing** → ~ ~ ~ covering

~ **roofing,** ~ roof cover(ing), ~ roof cladding, ~ roof sheathing · Stein-Bedachung f, Stein-(Ein)Deckung, Stein-Dach(ein)deckung, Dachstein(ein)-deckung

~ **sealant** → ~ jointing compound

~ **sealing composition** → ~ jointing compound

~ ~ **compound** → ~ jointing ~

~ ~ ~, drain ~ ~ ~, DT ~ ~ (US); clay pipe ~ ~, CP · Tonrohrvergußmasse f, Tonrohrausgußmasse

~ ~ **mass** → ~ jointing compound

~ **setting,** ~ fixing, tiling (work) · Plattenarbeiten fpl, Fliesenarbeiten, Fliesen(ver)legen n, Verfliesen, Platten(ver)legen, Plattieren, Plattierungsarbeiten

~ (~) adhesive, ~ (~) glue, ~ fixing, ~, ~ ~ agent, ~ ~ medium, ~ cement(ing agent) · (Belag)Plattenkleber m, (Belag)Plattenkleb(e)stoff m, (Belag)Plattenkleb(e)mittel n, Fliesenkleber, Fliesenkleb(e)stoff, Fliesenkleb(e)mittel

~ ~ agent → ~ (~) adhesive

~ (~) glue → ~ (~) adhesive

~ ~ medium → ~ (~) adhesive

~ stack, ~ chimney, block ~ · Steinschornstein m, Block(stein)schornstein

~ stone, ~ (clay) body · (Belag)Plattenscherben m, (Keramik)Fliesenscherben

~ store · (Belag)Plattenlager n, Fliesenlager

~ strength, block ~ · Block(stein)festigkeit f, Steinfestigkeit

~ valley · Steinkehle f [Dach]

~ wall → (building) block (masonry) ~

tiled · plattiert, gefliest

~ bathroom · Fliesenbad(eraum) n, (m)

~ kitchen · Fliesenküche f

tiled roof · steingedecktes Dach n

~ stair(case) · Fliesentreppe f

~ stove, Dutch ~ · Kachelofen m [DIN 1294]

tiler, floor-and-wall ~, (tile) fixer · Fliesenleger m, Plattenleger

tilework, tiling, tile finish · Fliesenbelag m, Plattenbelag, Plattierung f

tiling, tile finish, tilework · Fliesenbelag m, Plattenbelag, Plattierung f

~ (work), tile setting, tile fixing · Plattenarbeiten fpl, Fliesenarbeiten, Fliesen(ver)legen n, Verfliesen, Platten(ver)legen, Plattieren, Plattierungsarbeiten

tilted-slab cupola (US) → folded plate dome

~ dome (US) → folded plate ~

~ roof (US) → folded plate ~

~ segment (US) → folded plate ~

~ (structure), hipped-plate (~) (US); prismatic shell (~), folded slab (~), folded plate (~) [It is an approximation to the curved shell made by panels] · (Platten)Faltwerk n

tilting fillet → eave(s) board

~ flagpole · Kipp-Fahnenmast m, Kipp-Flaggenmast

~ level · Nivellier(instrument) n mit Kippschraube

~ piece → eave(s) board

~ position · Kippstellung f

tilt-up concrete panel · Aufkippbetontafel f, Richtaufbetontafel

~ construction, ~ method · Aufkippbauweise f, Richtaufbauweise

~ method, ~ construction · Richtaufbauweise f, Aufkippbauweise

~ panel · Aufkipptafel f, Richtauftafel

~ wall · Aufkippwand f, Richtaufwand

timber and brick-clad home, wood ~ ~ ~ · Holz-Ziegel-Haus n

~ arch, wood(en) ~ · Holzbogen m

~ architecture · Holzarchitektur f, Holzbaukunst f

~ baluster, ~ ban(n)ister, wood(en) ~ · Docke f, Togge [Baluster aus Holz]

~ ban(n)ister, ~ baluster, wood(en) ~ · Docke f, Togge [Baluster aus Holz]

~ base, ~ ground, wood(en) ~ · Holz(unter)grund m

~ ~ (board) → wood(en) sanitary cove

~ ~ plate [Scotland] → wood(en) sanitary cove

~ baseplate, wood(en) ~ · Holzgrundplatte f

~ batten, wood(en) ~ [For slating and tiling. B.S. 1318] · Holzleiste f

~ ~, wood(en) ~ · Holz-Fugendeckleiste f

~ ~, wood(en) ~ Holzlatte f

~ beam, wood(en) ~ · Holzbalken(träger) m

~ ~ floor, wood(en) ~ ~, ~ joist ~, single timber ~ · Holzbalken(träger)decke f [DIN 104]

~ bearing structure → wood(en) (load)bearing ~

~ binder → wood(en) binding beam

~ binding beam → wood(en) ~ ~

~ ~ joist → wood(en) binding beam

~ board sheathing, wood(en) ~ ~ · Bretter(ver)schalung f

~ broach → ~ spire

~ building block module, wood(en) ~ ~ ~, ~ unitized unit · Holz(raum)zelle f

~ church, wood(en) ~ · Holzkirche f

~ ciborium, wood(en) ~ · Holzciborium n, Holzziborium Holzbaldachin m

~ cistern, wood(en) ~ · Holzzisterne f

~ column, wood(en) ~; ~ stanchion (Brit.) · Holzstütze f

~ ~, wood(en) ~ · Holzsäule f

~ connection, wood ~, ~ joint · Holzverbindung f

(~) connector, wood ~; modern connecter (US) [These connectors are metal rings, plates, and disks embedded in the contact surfaces of two members. B.S. 1579] · (Holz)Dübel m [Die Kraft wird durch Lochleibungsdruck übertragen]

~ construction → wood(en) (structural) system

~ ~, wood ~ · Holzbau m

~ ~ type, wood(en) ~ ~, ~ type of construction · Holzbauart f

~ counter ceiling, wood(en) ~ ~ · Holzunterdecke f

timber dimension — timber joist floor

~ **dimension** · Holzabmessung f
~ **dome**, wood(en) ~ · Holzkuppel f
~ **door**, wood(en) ~ · Holztür f
~ ~ **frame**, wood(en) ~ ~ [B.S. 1567] · Holz-Tür(blend)rahmen m, Holz-Türfutter(rahmen) n, (m)
~ (~) **threshold**, wood(en) (~) ~ · Holz(tür)schwelle f
~ **dowel**, wood(en) ~ · Holzdollen m, Stab-Holzdübel m, Holz(stab)dübel
~ **eave(s) gutter**, ~ ~ **trow**, ~ ~ **trough**, wood(en) ~ ~ · Holz(-Dach)traufrinne f
~ **facing** → ~ lining
~ **fastener**, wood(en) ~ · (Holz)Verbinder m, (Holz)Verbindungsmittel n [*Dübel, Bolzen, Nägel, Klammern und Schrauben, die die Holzverbindungen dauerhaft und für den jeweilig beabsichtigten Zweck geeignet machen*]
~ **fence**, wood(en) ~ · Holzzaun m
~ (~) **post**, wood(en) (~) ~ · Holzzaunpfahl m, Holz(zaun)pfosten m
~ **fencing**, wood(en) ~ · Holzeinzäunung f, Holzumzäunung
~ **flat roof**, wood(en) ~ ~, flat wood(en) ~, flat timber ~ · Holzflachdach n, Flachholzdach
~ **floating floor cover(ing)** → wood(en) floating floor(ing) (finish)
~ ~ **floor(ing) (finish)**, wood(en) ~ ~ (~), ~ ~ floorcover(ing) · schwimmender Holz(fuß)boden(belag) m, Holz(fuß)boden(belag) auf Lagerhölzern mit Dämmstreifen-Unterlagen
timber floor, wood(en) ~ · Holz(-Gebäude)decke f, Holz-Etagendecke, Holz-Stockwerkdecke, Holz-Geschoßdecke, Holz-Trenndecke, Holz-Hochbaudecke
~ ~ **cover(ing)**, wood(en) ~ ~, ~ floor(ing) (finish) · Holz(fuß)boden(belag) m, Fh
~ ~ **(finish)** → ~ flooring (~)
~ **floor(ing) (finish)**, wood(en) ~ ~, ~ floor cover(ing) · Holz(fuß)boden(belag) m, Fh
~ **folded plate roof** → wood(en) ~ ~ ~
~ ~ **slab roof** → wood(en) folded plate ~
~ **folding door**, wood(en) ~ ~ · Holzfalttür f
~ **forms**, ~ formwork, ~ shuttering, wood(en) ~ · Holzschalung f
~ **formwork**, ~ shuttering, ~ forms, wood(en) ~ · Holzschalung f
~ **frame**, wood(en) ~ · Holzrahmen m
~ ~, wood(en) ~ · Holz(blend)rahmen m, Holzfutter(rahmen) n, (m) [*Tür; Fenster*]
~ ~ **construction**, wood(en) ~ ~ · Holzfachwerkbau m
timber-frame(d) construction, wood-frame(d) ~ · Holzrahmenkonstruktion f

~ **façade**, wood-frame(d) ~ · Holzrahmenfassade f
~ **house**, wood(en) ~ ~ · Holzfachwerkhaus n
~ **mirror**, wood-frame(d) ~ · Holzrahmenspiegel m
~ **structure**, wood-frame(d) ~ · Holzrahmenbauwerk n
~ **wall**, wood(en) ~ ~ · Holzfach(werk)wand f, Holzriegelwand
timber framework, wood(en) ~ · Holzfachwerk n
~ ~ **building**, (wood(en)) ~ ~ · (Holz-)Fachwerkhaus n
~ ~ **wall**, wood(en) ~ ~ · Holzfachwerkwand f, Holzriegelwand
~ **framing** · Fachwerk n [*Holzhausbau*]
~ **gate**, wood(en) ~ · Holztor n
~ **gatehouse**, wood(en) ~ · Holz-Torturm m
~ **girder**, wood(en) ~ · Holzträger m
~ **grid**, ~ grillage, wood(en) ~ · Holzrost m
~ ~ **footing**, wood(en) ~ ~, ~ grillage ~ · Holzrostfundament n
~ **grillage**, ~ grid, wood(en) ~ · Holzrost m
~ ~ **footing**, wood(en) ~ ~, ~ grid ~ · Holzrostfundament n
~ **grille**, wood(en) ~ [*See remark under 'Gitter'*] · Holzgitter n
~ **ground**, ~ base, wood(en) ~ · Holz(unter)grund m
~ ~ **floor**, wood(en) ~ ~ · Holz-Erdgeschoß(fuß)boden m
~ **handrail**, wood(en) ~ · Holzhandlauf m, Holzhandleiste f
~ **header**, wood(en) ~ [*A wood(en) beam which carries the ends of beams which are cut off in framing around an opening*] · Holzwechsel(balken) m, Wechselholz n
~ **hipped-plate roof** (US) → wood(en) folded plate ~
~ **hollow (floor) filler**, wood(en) ~ (~) ~ · Holzhohlkörper m [*Montagedecke*]
~ **hut**, wood(en) ~ · Holzbaracke f
~ **in the round (for construction purposes)**, round (construction timber), (construction) roundwood · (Bau-)Rundholz n
~ **Ionic column**, wood(en) ~ ~ · ionische Holzsäule f
~ **joining method**, wood ~ ~ · Holzverbindungsverfahren n
~ **joint**, wood ~, ~ connection · Holzverbindung f
~ **joist**, wood(en) ~, common ~, boarding ~ [*A wood beam directly supporting a floor*] · Holzdeckenbalken m
~ ~ **floor**, wood(en) ~ ~, ~ beam ~, single timber ~ · Holzbalken(träger)decke f [*DIN 104*]

timber joist roof floor — timber space (load)bearing...

~ ~ **roof floor**, wood(en) ~ ~ ~, single timber ~ ~ · Holzbalken(träger)- dachdecke f

~ ~ **upper floor**, wood(en) joist ~ ~, single upper timber ~ · Obergeschoß-Holzbalkendecke f

~ **ladder**, wood(en) ~ [*B.S. 1129*] · Holzleiter f

~ **lamella cupola** → wood(en) lamella dome

~ ~ **dome** → wood(en) ~ ~

~ **lattice(d) beam**, wood(en) ~ ~ · Holzgitterbalken(träger) m

~ ~ **cupola** → wood(en) lamella dome

~ ~ **dome** → wood(en) lamella ~

~ ~ **girder**, wood(en) ~ ~ · Holzgitterträger m

timber-lined passage, wood-lined ~ · holzverkleideter Gang m

timber lining, wood(en) ~, ~ (sur-)facing · Holzauskleidung f, Holzverkleidung, Holzbekleidung

~ **lintel**, wood(en) ~; ~ lintol [*deprecated*] · Holzoberschwelle f, Holzsturz m

~ **(load)bearing structure** → wood(en) ~ ~

~ **load-carrying structure** → wood(en) (load)bearing ~

~ **loaded structure** → wood(en) (load)bearing ~

~ **mast**, wood(en) ~ · Holzmast m

~ **mold** (US) → ~ mould

~ **mopboard** → wood(en) sanitary cove

~ **mould** (Brit.); ~ mold (US); wood(en) ~ · Holzform f

~ **panel**, wood(en) ~ · Holztafel f

~ **partition (wall)**, wood(en) ~ (~) · Holztrennwand f

~ **patent glazing bar**, ~ puttyless ~ ~, wood(en) ~ ~ ~ · Holzsprosse f [*kittlose Verglasung*]

~ **paving work**, wood(en) ~ ~ · Holzpflasterarbeiten fpl [*DIN 18367*]

~ **pillar**, wood(en) ~, post, leg · Ständer m, Stiel m, Pfosten m ,(Stand-)Säule f [*Senkrechtes Holz beim Fachwerk-, Stab-, Ständer- und Dachstuhlbau*]

~ **plain web(bed) beam**, ~ solid ~ ~, wood(en) ~ ~ ~ · Holz-Vollwandbalken(träger) m

~ ~ ~ **girder**, ~ solid ~ ~, wood(en) ~ ~ ~ · Holz-Vollwandträger m

~ **post**, wood(en) ~ · Holzpfosten m

~ ~, ~ fence ~, wood(en) (fence) ~ · Holz(zaun)pfosten m, Holzzaunpfahl m

~ **prefab(ricated) construction** → wood(en) ~ ~

~ **principal post**, wood(en) ~ ~, ~ stud · Holz-Bundstiel m

~ **prismatic shell roof** → wood(en) folded plate ~

~ **pulpit**, wood(en) ~ · Holzkanzel f

~ **purlin(e)**, wood(en) ~ · Holz(-Dach)-pfette f

~ **puttyless glazing bar**, ~ patent ~ ~, wood(en) ~ ~ ~ · Holzsprosse f [*kittlose Verglasung*]

~ **rafter**, wood(en) ~ · Holz(-Dach)-sparren m [*Schweiz: Holzrofen m*]

~ **rail**, wood(en) ~, framework ~ ~ · (Fachwerk)Holzriegel m

~ **revolving door**, wood(en) ~ · Holzdrehtür f

~ **rigid frame**, wood(en) ~ ~ · Holzsteifrahmen m, starrer Holzrahmen

~ **roller shutter** → ~ rolling ~

~ **rolling shutter**, wood(en) ~ ~, ~ roller ~ · Holzrollabschluß m

~ **roof**, wood(en) ~ · Holzdach n

~ ~ **cladding** → wood(en) ~ ~

~ ~ **cover(ing)** → wood(en) roof cladding

~ ~ **floor**, wood(en) ~ ~ · Holz-Abschlußdecke f gegen die Außenluft, Holz-Dachdecke

~ ~ **sheathing** → wood(en) roof cladding

~ ~ **spire**, wood(en) ~ ~ · Holz-Dachreiter m

~ **(~) truss**, wood(en) (~) ~ · Holz-(dach)binder m

~ **roofing** → wood(en) roof cladding

~ **sanitary cove** (US) → wood(en) ~ ~

~ **screed (for plastering)**, wood(en) ~ (~ ~) · Holzputzleiste f

~ **scrub board** → wood(en) sanitary cove

~ **seat**, wood(en) ~ · Holzsitz m

~ **sheathing**, wood(en) ~ ~ · Holzschale f, Holz(ver)schalung f

~ **shell**, wood(en) ~ · Holzschale f

~ ~ **cupola**, ~ ~ dome, wood(en) ~ ~ · Holzschalenkuppel f

~ ~ **dome**, ~ ~ cupola, wood(en) ~ ~ · Holzschalenkuppel f

~ ~ **roof**, wood(en) ~ ~ · Holzschalendach n

~ **shutter**, ~ window ~, wood(en) (window) ~ · Holz-(Fenster)Laden m

~ ~, wood(en) ~ · Holzabschluß m

~ **shuttering**, ~ forms, ~ formwork, wood(en) ~ · Holzschalung f

~ **skirting (board)** → wood(en) sanitary cove

~ **soffit**, wood(en) ~ · Holzuntersicht f

~ **solid web(bed) beam**, ~ plain ~ ~, wood(en) ~ ~ ~ · Holz-Vollwandbalken(träger) m

~ ~ ~ **girder**, ~ plain ~ ~, wood(en) ~ ~ ~ · Holz-Vollwandträger m

~ **space (load)bearing structure** → wood(en) ~ ~ ~

timber space... — time-deformation curve

~ ~ **weight-carrying structure** → wood(en) space (load)bearing ~

~ **spatial (load)bearing structure** → wood(en) space ~ ~

~ ~ **weight-carrying structure** → wood(en) space (load)bearing ~

~ **spire**, wood(en) ~ · Holz(turm)helm *m*, Holz-Pyramidenturmdach *n*, Holz-Turmdachpyramide *f*, Holz-Turmzeltdach über quadratischem Grundriß

~ ~, ~ **steeple**, ~ **broach**, wood(en) ~ · Holz-Spitz(kirch)turm *m*

~ **stair(case)**, wood(en) ~ [*B.S. 585*] · Holztreppe *f*

~ ~ **builder**, wood(en) ~ ~ · Holztreppenbauer *m*

~ **stanchion**, ~ **stancheon**, wood(en) ~ (Brit.); ~ **column** · Holzstütze *f*

~ **steeple** → ~ spire

~ **step**, wood(en) ~ · Holz(treppen)stufe *f*

~ **strength**, wood(en) ~ · Holzfestigkeit *f*

~ **string** (Brit.); ~ **stringer** (US); wood(en) ~ · Holzwange *f*

~ **(structural) system** → wood(en) (~) ~

~ **structure** → wood(en) (load)bearing ~

(~) strut, wood(en) ~ · Stake *f*, Stakholz *n*

~ **stud**, wood(en) ~, ~ **principal post** · Holz-Bundstiel *m*

timber-stud partition (wall), wood-stud ~ (~) · Holzgerippetrennwand *f* [*DIN 4103*]

~ **wall**, wood-stud ~ · Holzgerippewand *f*

timber studs, wood(en) ~ · Holzgerippe *n* [*Leichte Trennwand. DIN 4103*]

~ **sub-floor**, wood(en) ~, counter floor, dead floor; rough floor (US) · Blendboden *m*, Blindboden, Holzunterboden [*Bretterlage über der Deckenkonstruktion als Unterlage für Riemen- oder Parkett(fuß)böden*]

~ **supporting structure** → wood(en) (load)bearing ~

~ **(sur)facing** → ~ lining

~ **surround**, wood(en) ~ · Holzeinfassung *f*

~ **suspended floor**, wood(en) ~ ~ · freitragende Holzdecke *f*

~ **swing door**, wood(en) ~ ~ · Holz-Pendeltür *f*, Pendeltür aus Holz

~ **system** → wood(en) (structural) ~

~ ~ **construction** → wood(en) prefab(ricated) ~

~ **thickness** · Holzdicke *f* [*Fehlname: Holzstärke f*]

~ **three-dimensional (load)bearing structure** → wood(en) space ~ ~

~ ~ **weight-carrying structure** → wood(en) space (load)bearing ~

~ **threshold**, wood(en) ~ ~ **door** · Holz(tür)schwelle *f*

~ **tilted-slab roof** (US) → wood(en) folded plate ~

timber-to-metal connection, ~ **joint**, wood-to-metal ~ · Holz-Metall-Verbindung *f*

~ **joint**, ~ **connection**, wood-to-metal ~ · Holz-Metall-Verbindung *f*

timber-to-timber connection, ~ **joint**, wood-to-wood ~ · Holz-Holz-Verbindung *f*

~ **joint**, ~ **connection**, wood-to-wood ~ · Holz-Holz-Verbindung *f*

timber tower, wood(en) ~, **brattice** · Holzturm *m* [*historischer Festungsbau*]

~ ~, wood(en) ~ · Holzturm *m*

~ **transom**, wood(en) ~ · Kämpferholz *n*, Losholz [*Querholz zur Unterteilung eines Fensters oder einer Tür*]

~ **tread**, wood(en) ~ · Holztritt(stufe) *m*, (*f*)

~ **truss**, wood(en) ~, ~ **roof** ~ · Holz(dach)binder *m*

~ ~ **frame**, wood(en) ~ ~ · Holzsprengwerk *n*

~ **truss(ed girder)**, wood(en) ~ (~) · Holzfachwerk(träger) *n*, (*m*)

~ **type of construction**, wood(en) ~ ~ ~, ~ **construction type** · Holzbauart *f*

~ **underframe**, wood(en) ~ · Holzrahmen *m*

~ **unitized unit**, wood(en) ~ ~, ~ **building block module** · Holz(raum)zelle *f*

~ **valley gutter**, wood(en) ~ ~ · Holzkehlrinne *f*, Kehlholzrinne

~ **vault**, wood(en) ~ · hölzernes Gewölbe *n*, Holzgewölbe

~ **wall**, wood(en) ~ · Holzwand *f*

~ **washboard** → wood(en) sanitary cove

~ **(weight-carrying) structure** → wood(en) (load)bearing ~

~ **window**, wood(en) ~ [*B.S. 644*] · Holzfenster *n*

~ **(~) shutter**, wood(en) (~) ~ · Holz-(Fenster)Laden *m*

~ **worm** [*A term loosely used for any organism, chiefly insect larvae, that is associated with any excavation in timber*] · Holzwurm *m*

timbre · Klangfarbe *f* [*Musikinstrument*]

time clock of the world's capitals · Welt(zeit)uhr *f*

timed, tmd · zeitlich eingeteilt

time-deformation curve · Zeit-Verformungs-Kurve *f*

time-dependent · zeitabhängig

~ **deformation** [*Combined effects of autogenous volume change, contraction, creep, expansion, shrinkage, and swelling occurring during an appreciable period of time, not synonymous with 'inelastic behaviour' or 'volume change'*] · zeitabhängige Verformung *f*

time for completion, specified ~ ~ ~ · Baufrist *f*

~ ~ **escape** · Fluchtzeit *f* [*im Brandfall*]

~ **interval,** ~ **period, period of time, length of time** · Zeitdauer *f*, Zeitraum *m*, Zeitspanne *f*

~ ~, **interval of time** · Zeitabstand *m*

timekeeper [*Employee on the site of the works responsible for checking and recording the daily arrival and departure of the operatives employed*] · Zeitnehmer *m*

time-lag switch · Verzögerungsschalter *m*

timeless · zeitlos

~ **functional architecture** · zeitlose Zweckarchitektur *f*

timelessness · Zeitlosigkeit *f*

time limit, completion date · Fertigstellungstermin *m*

~ **of curing, period** ~ ~**, curing period, curing time** · (Ab)Bindedauer *f*, (Ab)Bindezeit *f*, (Ab)Bindefrist *f* [*Verschnittbitumen*]

~ ~ **day** · Tageszeit *f*

~ ~ **hardening** → hardening time

~ ~ **initial set(ting), period** ~ ~ ~**, initial set(ting) time, initial set(ting) period** · Erstarrungsdauer *f*, Erstarrungszeit *f*, Erstarrungsfrist *f* [*Beton; Mörtel*]

~ ~ **loading, period** ~ ~**, loading time, loading period** · Belastungszeit *f*, Belastungsdauer *f*

~ ~ **set(ting), set(ting) time** · (Ab-)Bindedauer *f*, (Ab)Bindezeit *f*, (Ab)Bindefrist *f*, Verfestigungszeit, Verfestigungsdauer *f*, Verfestigungsfrist *f* [*Mörtel; Beton; Zementpaste; Gips*]

~ ~ **test(ing)** → test(ing) time

~ ~ **warming** → period ~ ~

~ **period,** ~ **interval, period of time, length of time** · Zeitdauer *f*, Zeitraum *m*, Zeitspanne *f*

~ **relay** · Zeitrelais *n*

~ **schedule** · Zeitplan *m*

~ **switch** · Zeitschalter *m*

~ ~ **for automatic staircase lighting** · Treppenhausautomat *m*

~ **switches** · Rundsteueranlage *f* [*Speicherofenheizung*]

time-temperature curve · Zeit-Temperatur-Kurve *f*

time yield → (plastic) flow

tin · Sn *n*, Zinn *n*

tin-clad, tinned, TC, td · verzinnt

tin-coated steel, tinplate · (feuer)verzinntes Stahlfeinblech *n*, Weißblech [*DIN 1541*]

tin coat(ing) · Zinnüberzug *m*

tin creaking · Zinngeschrei *n*

tin extracted from slag, prillion · Schlackenzinn *n*

tin foil · Zinnfolie *f*, Stanniol *n*

tin-lead solder [*B.S. 219*] · Zinnlot *n* [*Weichlot aus Zinn-Blei-Legierungen zum Löten von Schwermetallen und deren Legierungen und zur Herstellung von Überzügen. DIN 1707*]

tin leaded bronze · Zinn-Bleibronze *f*

tinman's solder [*Tin 62, lead 38 per cent. by weight*] · Lötzinn *n* [*DIN 1707*]

tinned, tin-clad, TC, td · verzinnt

tinning · Verzinnung *f*

tin pipe · Zinnrohr *n* [*Es wird mit einem Bleimantel, der zur Aufnahme der mechanischen Beanspruchungen dient, versehen. Verwendung als Leitungsrohr für sehr weiche, sauerstoff- und kohlensäurereiche Wässer*]

~ ~ **with lead jacket** · (Blei)Mantelrohr *n* [*Zinnrohr mit Außenbleimantel*]

~ **plaque** · Zinnpest *f*

tinplate, tin-coated steel · (feuer)verzinntes Stahlfeinblech *n*, Weißblech [*DIN 1541*]

tin(plate) roof cover(ing), ~ ~ **sheathing,** ~ ~ **cladding,** ~ **roofing** · Zink(dach)(ein)deckung *f*, Zinkbedachung

tin roof · zinkgedecktes Dach *n*

tinstone, black tin, cassiterite · Kassiterit *m*, Zinnstein *m*, SnO_2

to tint [*To adjust the colo(u)r to match a pattern*] · abtönen, nachtönen, nuancieren

tint → tinting shade

tinted · abgetönt [*Anstrichtechnik*]

~ **glass, stained** ~**; coloured** ~ (Brit.); **colored** ~ (US) · Farbglas *n*, farbiges Glas, Buntglas, gefärbtes Glas

~ ~ **block, stained** ~ ~, ~ ~ **brick; coloured** ~ ~ (Brit.); **colored** ~ ~ (US) · Farbglas(bau)stein *m*, Bunt(glas)baustein

~ ~ **brick** → ~ ~ block

~ ~ **wall, stained-glass** ~ · Buntglaswand *f*, Farbglaswand

~ ~ **window, stained-glass** ~ · Buntglasfenster *n*, Farbglasfenster

~ **laminated glass; coloured** ~ ~ (Brit.); **colored** ~ ~ (US) · Farbverbundglas *n*, Verbundfarbglas

~ **rough rolled glass, stained** ~ ~ ~ · gefärbtes Gußrohglas *n*, ~ Rohgußglas

tinter; tinting color (US) [*Coloured pigments ground in media compatible with paint vehicles, added in relatively small proportions to already prepared paints to modify their colour. With the introduction of latex paints of many types, tinters have been developed which* can be used both with organic solvent-thinned paints and with water-thinned paints. Such dual-purpose tinters are known as 'universal tinters'] · Abtönfarbe f, Mischfarbe

~ **paste,** tinting ~ · Abtönpaste f

tinting [*The final adjustment of the colo(u)r of a paint to the exact colo(u)r required*] · Abtönen n, Nachtönen, Nuancieren [*Anstrichtechnik*]

~ **color** (US) → tinter

~ **effect** · Abtönwirkung f

~ **paste,** tinter ~ · Abtönpaste f

tint(ing shade) [*A colour produced by the mixture of white pigment or paint in predominating amount with a coloured pigment or paint, not white. The tint of a colour is, therefore, much lighter and much less saturated than the colour itself*] · Abtönung f

tinting strength → staining power

to be laid touching · knirsch stoßen [*Mauerwerk*]

to tip down(wards), to fold ~, to turn down · umlegen nach unten, abkanten ~ ~

~ ~ **up(wards),** to fold ~ · abkanten nach oben, umlegen ~ ~, aufkanten, hochkanten

tissue paper · Papiergewebe n

~ ~ **for walls** · Wandspann(-Faser)stoff m [*Papiergewebe in Uni-Farben sowie in schablonierten Mustern. Es dient an Stelle von Rupfen zum Bespannen von Treppenhäusern, Dielen und Ausstellungsräumen. Für die Papiergewebe wird z.B. feine Manilahanffaser verwendet*]

titanium · Titan n

~ **carbide-nickel cermet** · Titankarbid-Nickel-Cermet n

~ **dioxid(e) (pigment)** (US); ~ dioxide (~) (Brit.) · Titandioxid(pigment) n

~ **white** · Titanweiß n, TiO_2

~ ~ **coat** · Titanweißanstrich m, Titanweißaufstrich

~ **pigment** [*B.S. 1851*] · Titanpigment n

~ **stabilized** · Ti-stabilisiert [*rostfreier Stahl*]

title block · Schriftfeld n

T-junction, double square junction · Doppelabzweig(er) 90° m, T-Stück n [*Rohrformstück*]

tmd, timed · zeitlich eingeteilt

to-and fro bending test → alternating ~ ~

~ ~ **flexure test** → alternating bending ~

tobacco seed oil · Tabaksamenöl n

~ **warehouse** · Tabakspeicher m

tobermorite [*A mineral found in Northern Ireland and elsewhere, having the approximate formula* $Ca_4(Si_6O_{18}H_2)$ · $Ca \cdot 4H_2O$ *identified approximately with the artificial product tobermorite (G) of Brunauer, a hydrated calcium silicate having* CaO/SiO_2 *ratio in the range 1.39 to 1.75 and forming minute layered crystals that constitute the principal cementing medium in portland cement concrete; a mineral with 5 mols of lime to 6 mols of silica, usually accurring in platelike crystals, which is easily synthesized at steam pressures of about 100 psig and higher, the binder in several properly autoclaved products*] · Tobermorit m

~ **gel** [*The binder of concrete cured moist or in atmospheric-pressure steam, a lime-rich gel-like solid containing 1.5 to 2.0 mols of lime per mol of silica*] · Tobermoritgel n

toed voussoir · Hakenstein m

toe-jointing, birdsmouthed jointing, V-jointing, birdsmouthing, bird's mouth joint, birdsmouth joint; foot cut, seat cut, plate cut (US) [*A cut into the end of a timber to fit it over a cross timber, particularly the cut in a rafter to fit it over a wall plate*] · Klaue f, Verklauung f, Aufklauung, Klauenschiftung, Aufschiftung [*Holzverbindung bei überkreuzten Hölzern*]

toilet, closet [*The term 'lavatory' is also used as a euphemism for 'toilet' or 'closet'*] · Abort m, Toilette f, Klosett n, Abtritt m

toilet-and-shower room · W.C.-Dusch-Raum m

toilet bowl → bowl

~ **cubicle,** closet ~ · Abortkabine f, Toilettenkabine, Klosettkabine, Abtrittkabine, Abortzelle f, Toilettenzelle, Klosettzelle, Abtrittzelle

~ **facility,** closet ~ · Abortanlage f, Toilettenanlage, Klosettanlage

~ **fan,** closet ~, lavatory ~ · Abortventilator m, Klosettventilator, Toilettenventilator

~ **flush(ing),** closet ~, lavatory ~, flush(ing) · Spülung f, Abort~, Klosett~, Toiletten~

~ ~ **pipe,** closet ~ ~, (lavatory) ~ ~ [*B.S. 1125*] · Spülrohr n, Klosett~, Abort~, Toiletten~

~ ~ **water,** closet ~ ~, (lavatory) ~ ~ · Spülwasser n, Abort~, Klosett~, Toiletten~

~ **pan** → bowl

~ **paper dispenser** · Klosettpapierspender m, Toilettenpapierspender

~ ~ **holder,** ~ roll ~ · Klosettpapierhalter m, Toilettenpapierhalter

~ **partition wall** · Toilettentrennwand f

~ **roll holder,** ~ paper ~ · Klosettpapierhalter, Toilettenpapierhalter

~ **room,** closett ~ · Abortraum m, Toilettenraum, Klosettraum, Abtrittraum

toilet seat — to tool with the tooth ax(e)

~ **seat**, closet ~, W. C. ~, (lavatory) ~ [*B.S. 1254*] · Sitz *m*, Abort~, Klosett~, Toiletten~

(~) ~ **lid**, closet ~ ~, lavatory ~ ~ · (Abort)Deckel *m*, Toilettendeckel, Klosettdeckel

~ **stall** · Toilettenstand *m*

~ **waste water**, closet ~ ~; soil (Brit.) [*The discharge from water-closets and urinals*] · Abort(ab)wasser *n*, Klosettabwasser, Toilettenabwasser

~ ~ ~ **pipe**, closet ~ ~ ~; soil ~ (Brit.) [*A pipe collecting from W.C.s and urinals*] · Abortrohr *n*, Klosett(abwasser)rohr, Toiletten(abwasser)rohr, Abortfallrohr, Abfallrohr für Aborte

tolerance · Toleranz *f* [*DIN 7182*]

~ **limit**, limit of tolerance · Abmaßgrenze *f*

~ **number sequence** · Toleranzzahlenfolge *f*

~ **on hardness** · Härtetoleranz *f*

~ **test** · Toleranzprüfung *f*, Toleranzversuch *m*, Toleranzprobe *f*

toll-house · Zollhaus *n* [*für Wegegeld*]

toluidine red [*Is aniline colour, one of the coal-tar derivatives*] · Toluidinrot *n*

toluol [*The name given to the industrial quality of toluene. It is used as a solvent for cellulose ester lacquers*] · Toluol *n*

tomb · Grab *n*

~ **architecture**, structural ~ ~, sepulchral ~ · Grabarchitektur *f*, Grabbaukunst *f*

~ **at Stadthagen** · Mausoleum *n* zu Stadthagen [*von Adrian de Vries, 1617–1620*]

~ **building**, ~ construction · Grabbau *m*

~ **chamber**, sepulchral ~, burial ~, chamber tomb, hypogeum tomb · Grabkammer *f*, Kammergrab *n*

~ ~ **pyramid** · Grabpyramide *f*

~ **chapel**, feretory · Grabkapelle *f*, Coemetrialkapelle

~ **church** · Coemetrialkirche *f*, Grabkirche

~ **ciborium** · Grabbaldachin *m*

~ **construction**, ~ building · Grabbau *m*

tomb-mosque · Grabmoschee *f*

tomb niche, arcosolium [*An arched recess in a catacomb, especially one containing a sarcophagus*] · Arkosol(ium) *n*, Arcosol(ium), Bogengrab *n*, (Wand)Nischengrab, Loculus *m*, Arkosolgrab

Tomb of Agamemnon, Treasury of Atreus (at Mycenae) · Schatzhaus *n* des Atreus, (Kuppel)Grab *n* des Agamemnon in Mykene [*14.–13. Jh. v.Chr.*]

~ ~ **Galla Placidia at Ravenna** · Grab *n* der Galla Placidia in Ravenna

~ ~ **the Julii at S. Rémy** · Julierdenkmal *n* zu S. Remy

~ ~ ~ **Weepers at Sidon** [*It is a sarcophagus in the form of a miniature Ionic temple, with sculptured figures of mourners between the columns*] · Klagefrauensarkophag *m*

tomb slab, funerary ~, grave ~, sepulchral ~ · Grabplatte *f*

~ **tholus** · Grabtholus *m*

~ **tower** · Grabturm *m*

~ **with false (or corbel, or cantilever(-ed), or cantilevering) dome (or cupola) over a rectangular chamber** · Rechteckgrab *n* mit Auslegerkuppel, ~ ~ Kragkuppel

tone of the human singing voice, sound ~ ~ ~ ~ ~ · Singklang *m*, Sington *m*

toned · getont

(tongue and grove) matched, tongued and grooved (together), T & G · mit Nut und Feder, (genutet und) gespundet

(~ ~ ~) ~ ceiling, tongued-and-grooved ~, T&G ~ · (genutete und) gespundete Decke *f*, Spunddecke

(~ ~ ~) ~ joint, tongued-and-grooved ~, T&G ~ · (Nut- und) Spundverbindung *f*

(~ ~ ~) ~ sub-floor, tongued-and-grooved ~, T&G ~ · (genuteter und) gespundete Unterboden *m*, Spundunterboden

tongued-and-grooved, matched, T & G · (genutet und) gespundet

tongue(d)-and-groove(d) boarding, ~ floor ~, matched (floor) ~, T&G (floor) ~ · gespundeter (Fuß)Boden(belag) *m*

~ **ceiling**, T & G ~, (tongue and groove) matched ~ · (genutete und) gespundete Decke *f*, Spunddecke

~ **joint**, T & G ~, (tongue and groove) matched ~ · (Nut- und) Spundverbindung *f*

~ **shingle**, matched ~, T & G ~ · Nutschindel *f*

~ **sub-floor**, (tongue and groove) matched ~, T & G ~ · (genuteter und) gespundeter Unterboden *m*, Spundunterboden

tongued and grooved (together), (tongue and groove) matched, T & G · mit Nut und Feder, (genutet und) gespundet

~ **floor cover(ing)**, ~ floor(ing) · gefederte Dielung *f*, gefederter Dielen(fuß)boden *m*

~ **floor(ing)**, ~ floor cover(ing) · gefederte Dielung *f*, gefederter Dielen(fuß)boden *m*

tool for lead pipe work · Bleirohrwerkzeug *n*

to tool with the tooth ax(e), ~ ~ ~ ~ crandall, ~ ~ ~ ~ roughing hammer

to tool with the patent pick — top joint

~ ~ ~ **patent pick,** ~ ~ ~ ~ patent ax(e) [*The crandall is used to produce roughtextured surfaces somewhat resembling a pointed face where a much finer and more evenly tooled finish is desired that can be secured by pointing. The tooth ax(e) produces a coarser effect than that of the crandall, though similar*] · kröneln

tooled by crandall · gekrönt

~ **finish,** ~ surface · mechanisch bearbeitete Oberfläche *f* [*Betonwerkstein*]

~ **surface** → ~ finish

toothbrush holder (tile) · Zahnbürstenhalterfliese *f*

toothed plate · Zahndübel *m* [*Holzdübel*]

~ **ring connector,** round toothed plate · Zahnringdübel *m*, Alligatordübel, runder Zahndübel

toothing course, indenting [*The stretchers project 2¼ in. at the end of a masonry wall to bond with future work. The bricks project like teeth from alternate courses*] · Zahnschicht *f*, Zahnlage *f*

~ **stone** · Zahnstein *m*

top, crown, key, vertex, apex · Scheitel(-punkt) *m*

~, **knob** · Knopf *m* [*Dachverzierung*]

top beam, ~ timber ~ Ortbalken *m*, Giebelbalken [*Der letzte an einer Giebelwand liegende Balken eines Gebälks*]

~ ~ Katzenbalken *m*, Spitzbalken, kurzer Kehlbalken, Hainbalken, Hahnenbalken [*Im Kehlbalkendach bei großer Sparrenlänge oft noch über dem Kehlgebälk in der Nähe des Firstes waagerecht in die Sparren eingezapfter Querriegel zur Versteifung der Sparrengebinde*]

~ ~ → collar ~

~ ~ **roof** · Hahnenbalkendach *n*, Katzenbalkendach, Spitzbalkendach, Hainbalkendach

~ **bed,** upper ~ · obere Lagerfläche *f*, weiche ~, oberes Lager *n*, weiches Lager [*Werkstein*]

~ **block,** key ~, apex ~, crown ~, vertex ~ · Scheitelstein *m*, Schlußstein

~ **boom,** ~ chord, ~ flange, upper ~ · Oberflansch *m*, Obergurt(ung) *m*, (f)

~ ~ **junction plate,** upper ~ ~ ~, ~ flange ~ ~ ~ chord → ~ Oberflanschknotenblech *n*, Obergurt(ungs)knotenblech

~ ~ **plate,** upper ~ ~, ~ chord ~, ~ flange ~ · Obergurtlamelle *f*

~ **branch** → ~ pipe ~

~ **chord,** ~ boom, ~ flange, upper ~ · Oberflansch *m*, Obergurt(ung) *m*, (f)

~ ~ **plate** → ~ boom ~

to topcoat, to overpaint [*A primer with a paint*] · überstreichen

topcoating · Überstreichen *n*

topcoat(ing) · Über(an)strich *m*, Überaufstrich

top concrete → topping (slab)

~ ~ **layer** → topping (slab)

~ **(course) concrete** → topping (slab)

~ **(door) rail,** upper (~) ~ · oberes Querrahmenstück *n*, oberer (Tür)Riegel *m* [*Holzfüllungstür*]

~ **dressing** · Dachanstrich *m*, Dachaufstrich

~ ~ **compound,** ~ ~ composition · Dachanstrichmasse *f*, Dachaufstrichmasse, Dachanstrichstoff *m*, Dachaufstrichstoff

tope(-mound) → domic(al) mound

~ **base,** stupa(-mound) ~ · Stupaunterbau *m*, Topeunterbau

tope shrine, stupa ~ · Topeschrein *m*, Stupaschrein

~ **flange,** ~ chord ~ boom upper ~ · Oberflansch *m*, Obergurt(ung) *m*, (f)

~ ~ **plate** → ~ boom ~

~ **glazed** · oben verglast, ~ eingeglast

~ **guide** · obere Führung *f*

top-heavy · überlastig, kopflastig, oberlastig

top hinge, key ~, crown ~, apex ~, vertex ~ · Scheitelgelenk *n*

top-hinged casement, top-hung ~, ~ sash, awning (sash), awning casement · Klapp(fenster)flügel *m*

~ **(~) window,** top-hung (~) ~, ~ sash ~, awning (sash) ~, awning casement ~ · Klapp(flügel)fenster *n*

~ **sash,** top-hung ~, ~ casement, awning (sash), awning casement · Klapp(fenster)flügel *m*

top hog, key ~, apex ~, crown ~, vertex ~ · Scheitelüberhöhung *f*

top-hung · oben laufend [*Schiebefalttor*]

~ **casement,** top-hinged ~, ~ sash, awning (sash), awning casement · Klapp(fenster)flügel *m*

~ **(~) window,** top-hinged (~) ~, ~ sash ~, awning (sash) ~, awning casement ~ · Klapp(flügel)fenster *n*

~ **opening outwards window** · Klappflügelfenster *n* nach außen

~ ~ **window** · Klappflügelfenster *n*

~ **sash,** top-hinged ~, ~ casement, awning (sash), awning casement · Klapp(fenster)flügel *m*

~ **(window) casement,** ~ hinge(d) ~, ~ pivoted sash, ~ ventilator, ~ opening sash, ~ opening light · Klapp(fenster)flügel *m*

top illumination, ~ lighting, overhead ~ · Obenbeleuchtung *f*

~ **inlet** → ~ pipe ~

~ **joint,** key ~, crown ~, vertex ~, apex ~ · Scheitelfuge *f* [*Fuge am höchsten Gewölbepunkt oder Bogenpunkt, wenn kein Scheitelstein vorhanden ist*]

top junction — torsion(al) buckling load

~ junction → ~ pipe ~

~ leaf · oberer Flügel m [Tor]

~ lighting, ~ illumination, overhead ~ · Obenbeleuchtung f

~ lined eaves · (Dach)Traufe f mit oberer Verkleidung, Dachfuß m ~ ~ ~

topman, mattock man, demolisher, wrecker · (Gebäude)Abbrucharbeiter m, Hausabbrucharbeiter

top of floor cover(ing), ~ ~ floor(ing) (finish) · Oberfläche f (Fuß)Boden, OFF

topping · Oberdecke f [Alle auf einer Rohdecke aufgebrachten Schichten]

~, overlay · Überzug(schicht) m, (f)
~ → ~ slab

topping-out ceremony, builder's treat · Richtfest n

topping (slab), structural concrete ~ (~) ,(in-situ) structural topping (concrete), top (course) concrete, top concrete layer, concrete topping, in-situ topping [The concrete laid to form the compression flange of the T-beams which it makes with the ribs. It is usually about 2 in. thick] · (Beton)Druckplatte f, (Beton)Druckschicht f, Aufbeton(-schicht) m, (f), Oberbeton(schicht)

~ (~), structural mortar ~ (~), (in-situ) structural topping (mortar) · (Mörtel)Druckplatte f, (Mörtel)Druckschicht f

top (pipe) branch, ~ (~) inlet, ~ (~) junction · (Rohr)Scheitelzulauf m, (Rohr)Scheitelabzweig m, (Rohr-)Scheiteleinlaßstück n

~ (~) inlet, ~ (~) junction, ~ (~) branch · (Rohr)Scheitelzulauf m, (Rohr-)Scheitelabzweig m, (Rohr-)Scheiteleinlaßstück n

~ (~) junction, ~ (~) inlet, ~ (~) branch · (Rohr)Scheitelzulauf m, (Rohr-)Scheitelabzweig m, (Rohr-)Scheiteleinlaßstück n

~-pivoted window · Drehzapfenfenster n mit Obenlagerung

top rail, upper ~, ~ door ~ · oberes Querrahmenstück m, oberer (Tür)Riegel m [Holzfüllungstür]

~ ~ · (Ab)Deckplatte f [Balustrade]

~ reinforcement, upper ~ · Abreißbewehrung f, Abreißarmierung, Abreiß(stahl)einlagen fpl

~ riser · letzte Setzstufe f, oberste ~

~ sag, key ~, crown ~, apex ~, vertex ~ · Scheitelsenkung f

~ sash, upper ~ [It slides on the outside] · oberer Schiebe(fenster)flügel m, Oberflügel

topsoil replacement · Mutterbodenandeckung f

~ stripping · Mutterbodenabtrag m, Mutterbodenabhub m

top speed · Höchstgeschwindigkeit f

~ step, last ~ · Durchgänger m, Austritt(-stufe) m, (f), Podeststufe

~ stone, crown ~, apex ~, vertex ~, keystone [The central stone of an arch or a vault; sometimes carved] · Scheitelstein m aus Naturstein, Schlußstein ~ ~

~ timber, ~ beam · Ortbalken m, Giebelbalken [Der letzte an einer Giebelwand liegende Balken eines Gebälks]

~ track · obere Laufschiene f [Tor]

~ view · Draufsicht f

torch soldering, flame ~ · Flammenlötung f

tore, torus, ~ moulding, roll ~ (Brit.); ~ (molding) (US) · halbkreisförmiges Band n, rundes ~, Wulst m, f, Torus m

torn grain · ausgerissene Faser f [Holz]

toroid shell · Ringschale f

toroidal membrane · Torusmembran(e) f

~ shell · Torusschale f

~ ~ segment · Torusschalensegment n

torque moment, twist(ing) ~, torsion(-al) ~ · Drillmoment n, Torsionsmoment, Verdrehungsmoment, Verwindungsmoment, Drillungsmoment

torsion, twist(ing) · (Ver)Drillung f, Torsion f, Verdrehung, Verwindung

~ bar, ~ rod · Federstab m, Torsionsstab

~ buckling, torsional · Torsionsknickung f

~ degree → degree of torsion

torsion-free, torsion-less, twist-free, twist-less · torsionslos, drillos, verdrehungslos, verwindungslos, torsionsfrei, verdrehungsfrei, drill(ungs)frei, verwindungsfrei, drillungslos

torsion-less → torsion-free

torsion modulus → torsion(al) ~

~ rod, ~ bar · Federstab m, Torsionsstab

~ tester, ~ testing machine · Torsionsprüfmaschine f

~ testing machine, ~ tester · Torsionsprüfmaschine f

~ visco(si)meter · Torsionsviskosimeter n

torsion(al) angle · Drill(ungs)winkel m, Verdrehungswinkel, Verwindungswinkel, Torsionswinkel

~ buckling, twist(ing) ~ · Verdrehungsknicken n, Drillknicken, Torsionsknicken, Verwindungsknicken [Es ist bei geraden Druckstäben mit dünnwandigen, offenen Querschnitten dann vorhanden, wenn der Schubmittelpunkt T und der Schwerpunkt S dieser Querschnitte nicht zusammenfallen. Die in T angreifende innere Schubkraft bildet mit der in S angreifenden äußeren Schubkraft ein Drehmoment]

~ ~ load, twist(ing) ~ ~ · Verdrehungsknicklast f, Torsionsknicklast, Verwindungsknicklast, Drill(ungs)knicklast

torsion(al) constant — total floor space 1042

~ **constant,** twist(ing) ~ · Torsionskonstante f Verdrehungskonstante, Verwindungskonstante, Drill(ungs)konstante

~ **elasticity** · Drill(ungs)elastizität f, Verdrehungselastizität, Verwindungselastizität, Torsionselastizität

~ **failure,** twist(ing) ~ · Torsionsbruch m, Verdrehungsbruch, Verwindungsbruch, Drill(ungs)bruch

~ **instability,** twist(ing) ~ · Drill-Labilität f, Verdrehungslabilität, Verwindungslabilität, Torsionslabilität, Drillungs-Labilität

~ **modulus,** twist(ing) ~, modulus of torsion · Torsionsmodul m, Drill(ungs)-modul

~ **moment,** twist(ing) ~, torque ~, moment of torsion · Torsionsmoment n, Verdrehungsmoment, Verwindungsmoment, Drill(ungs)moment

~ **oscillation,** ~ vibration · Drill(ungs)-schwingung, f, Torsionsschwingung, Verdrehungsschwingung, Verwindungsschwingung

~ **problem** · Torsionsaufgabe f, Drill(ungs)aufgabe, Verdrehungsaufgabe, Verwindungsaufgabe, Torsionsproblem n, Drill(ungs)problem, Verdrehungsproblem, Verwindungsproblem

~ **reinforcement,** ~ steel · Torsionsbewehrung f, Torsionsarmierung, Torsions(stahl)einlagen fpl, Drill(ungs)bewehrung, Drill(ungs)armierung, Drill(ungs)(stahl)einlagen, Verdrehungsbewehrung, Verdrehungsarmierung, Verdrehungs(stahl)einlagen, Verwindungsbewehrung, Verwindungsarmierung, Verwindungs(stahl)einlagen [Zur Aufnahme von Zugkräften an den Aussenflächen von Balken(trägern), die bei Torsion entstehen]

~ **resistance** · Verdrehungswiderstand m, Verwindungswiderstand, Torsionswiderstand, Drill(ungs)widerstand

~ **rigidity** → ~ strength

~ **steel** → ~ reinforcement

~ **stiffness** → ~ strength

~ **strength,** twist(ing) ~, ~ stiffness, ~ rigidity, stiffness in torsion, rigidity in torsion · Torsionsfestigkeit f, Drill(ungs)festigkeit, Verwindungsfestigkeit, Verdreh(ungs)festigkeit, Drill(ungs)steifigkeit, Torsionssteifigkeit, Drill(ungs)steife f, Torsionssteife, Verdreh(ungs)steife, Verdreh(ungs)steifigkeit [Spannung in kp/mm², die senkrecht zur Längsachse eines auf Verdrehung beanspruchten Körpers bis zum Bruch aufzuwenden ist]

~ **stress,** twist(ing) ~ · Torsionsspannung f, Verdrehungsspannung, Verwindungsspannung, Drill(ungs)spannung

~ **test** · Drillprobe f, Drillprüfung f, Drillversuch m, Verdrehungsprobe, Verdrehungsversuch, Verdrehungsprüfung, Verwindeprobe, Verwindeprüfung, Verwindeversuch, Torsionsversuch, Torsionsprüfung, Torsionsprobe

~ **vibration,** ~ oscillation · Drill(ungs)-schwingung f, Torsionsschwingung, Verdrehungsschwingung, Verwindungsschwingung

torsional wave · Torsionswelle f [Schalltechnik]

torsionally rigid → ~ stiff

~ **stiff,** ~ rigid · drillsteif, verdrehungssteif, verwindungssteif, torsionssteif, drillungssteif

Torsteel · Torstahl 42 m, Tor-Rippenstahl, Sonderbetonstahl IIIb [Verwundener Rundstahl mit zwei schraubenförmig verlaufenden Längsrippen]

tortoise shell · Schildpatt n

torus, tore, ~ moulding (Brit.); ~ (molding) (US) · halbkreisförmiges Band n, rundes ~, Wulst m, f, Torus m

total, ~ price, cover price · Gesamtpreis m

~ **absorbing power of the walls and materials in a room** · (Schall)Schluckvermögen n eines Raumes [Es wird als äquivalente Schallschluckfläche (Schallabsorptionsfläche) A angegeben. Es ist dies die Fläche mit vollkommener Schluckung, die den gleichen Anteil an Schallenergie schlucken würde wie die gesamte Oberfläche des Raumes und die in ihm befindlichen Gegenstände und Personen tatsächlich schlucken]

~ **aggregate** → ~ construction ~

~ **air content** · Gesamtluftgehalt m

~ **average,** overall ~ · Gesamtdurchschnitt m

~ **concrete aggregate,** combined ~ ~ · Betonzuschlag(stoff)gemenge n, Betonzuschlag(stoff)gemisch n, Beton-Gesamtzuschlag(stoff) m

~ **(construction) aggregate,** combined (~) ~ · Zuschlag(stoff)gemenge n, Zuschlag(stoff)gemisch n, Gesamtzuschlag(stoff) m

~ **consumption,** cumulative ~ · Gesamtverbrauch m

~ **cost,** aggregate ~, overall ~ · Gesamtkosten f

~ **deformation** · Gesamtformänderung f, Gesamtverformung

~ **depth,** overall ~, aggregate ~ [beam] · Gesamthöhe f [Balken(träger)]

~ **dimension,** aggregate ~, overall ~ · Gesamtabmessung f, Gesamtmaß n

~ **drying time** · Gesamttrocknungszeit f

~ **energy** · Gesamtenergie f

~ **failure** · Gesamtbruch m

~ ~ **strength** · Gesamtbruchfestigkeit f

~ **floor depth,** overall ~ ~, aggregate ~ ~ · Gesamtdeckendicke f

~ ~ **space,** aggregate ~ ~; ~ story ~ (US); ~ storey ~ (Brit.) · Gesamt-Etagenfläche f, Gesamt-Geschoßfläche, Gesamt-Stockwerkfläche

total grain surface — toughened (safety) glass

~ **grain surface** · Oberfläche *f* aller Körner

~ **hardness** · Gesamthärte *f*, GH [*Die Härte eines Wassers, die sich überwiegend aus den Einzelhärten der Erdalkalien Kalzium und Magnesium zusammensetzt. Sie wird manchmal durch Eisen, Mangan und/oder Alu(minium) unwesentlich beeinflußt*]

~ **heat** · Gesamtwärme *f*

~ ~ **requirement** · Gesamtwärmebedarf *m*

~ **heating surface** · Gesamtheizfläche *f*

~ **height,** overall ~, aggregate ~ · Gesamthöhe *f*, Höhe über alles

~ **impurities** · Gesamtbeimengung *f*, Gesamtverunreinigung

~ **length,** overall ~, aggregate ~ · Gesamtlänge *f*, Länge über alles

~ **load** · Gesamtlast *f*

~ **loading** · Gesamtbelastung *f*

~ **mix(ture)** · Gesamtgemisch *n*, Gesamtmischung *f*

~ **moment** · Gesamtmoment *n*

~ **number,** overall ~, aggregate ~ · Gesamtanzahl *f*

~ **plan** · Gesamtplan *m*

~ **porosity,** true ~ · Undichtigkeitsgrad *m*, Undichtheitsgrad, Durchlässigkeitsgrad, wahre Porosität *f*, Gesamtporosität

~ **pressure** · Gesamtdruck *m*

~ **(pre)stressing force,** ~ stretching ~, ~ tensioning ~ · Gesamtvorspannkraft *f*

~ **(price),** cover ~ · Gesamtpreis *m*

~ **reaction,** ~ reactive force · Gesamtstützkraft *f*, Gesamt-Auflagerwiderstand *m*, Gesamt-Auflagerreaktion *f*, Gesamtstützreaktion, Gesamt-Auflagerkraft, Gesamtstützwiderstand, Gesamtstützdruck *m*, Gesamtgegendruck, Gesamt-Auflagerdruck

~ **reactive force,** ~ reaction · Gesamtstützkraft *f*, Gesamt-Auflagerwiderstand *m*, Gesamt-Auflagerreaktion *f*, Gesamtstützreaktion, Gesamt-Auflagerkraft, Gesamtstützwiderstand, Gesamtstützdruck *m*, Gesamtgegendruck, Gesamt-Auflagerdruck

~ **reinforcement area** → ~ **steel** ~

~ **reinforcing area** → ~ **steel** ~

~ **steel area,** ~ reinforcement ~, ~ reinforcing ~, overall ~ ~, aggregate ~ ~ · Gesamtarmierungsfläche *f*, Gesamtbewehrungsfläche, Gesamtstahl-(einlagen)fläche, Gesamteinlagenfläche

~ **story space** (US) → **floor** ~ ~

~ **strain** · (positive) Gesamtdehnung *f*, Gesamtlängung

~ **strength,** overall ~ · Gesamtfestigkeit *f*

~ **stressing force,** ~ pre~ ~, ~ stretching ~, ~ tensioning ~ · Gesamtvorspannkraft *f*

~ **stretching force,** ~ tensioning ~, ~ (pre)stressing ~ · Gesamtvorspannkraft *f*

~ **sulphur** (Brit.); ~ sulfur (US) · Gesamtschwefel *m*

~ ~ **content** (Brit.); ~ sulfur ~ (US) · Gesamtschwefelgehalt *m*

~ **tensioning force,** ~ stretching ~, ~ (pre)stressing ~ · Gesamtvorspannkraft *f*

Total Theatre [*Designed by Walter Gropius in collaboration with Erwin Piscator; it was a theatre capable of being adapted to suit each type of play performed*] · Totaltheater *n*

total thickness, overall ~, aggregate ~ · Gesamtdicke *f*

~ **view** · Gesamtansicht *f*

~ **volume (including the voids)** · Gesamtraum *m* [*Er besteht in einem Korngemisch aus Festraum + Hohlraum*]

~ ~ **of construction,** overall ~ ~ ~, aggregate ~ ~ ~ · Gesamtbauvolumen *n*

~ **wall area** · Gesamtwandfläche *f*

~ ~ **thickness** · Gesamtwanddicke [*Fehlname: Gesamtwandstärke*]

~ **water** · Gesamtwasser *n* [*Beton; Mörtel*]

~ **width,** aggregate ~, overall ~ · Gesamtbreite *f*, Breite über alles

~ **wind force** · Gesamtwindkraft *f*

totally buried · vollüberdeckt

~ **enclosed,** TE · ganzgekapselt, vollgekapselt

totally-encloed fan-cooled, TEFC · ganzgekapselt und ventilatorgekühlt, vollgekapselt ~ ~

~ **nonventilated, TENV** · ganzgekapselt und unbelüftet, vollgekapselt ~ ~

~ **water-cooled, TEWC** · ganzgekapselt und wassergekühlt, vollgekapselt ~ ~

touch-dry, dried to (the) touch · griffest [*Anstrichfarbe*]

to touch up · auffrischen [*Anstrich*]

touching up [*e.g. factory-applied coats on site*] · Nachbessern *n*, (Anstrich-)Auffrischung *f*

~ **warmth,** treading ~ · Fußwärme *f* [*(Fuß)Boden(belag)*]

tough · sprödbruchunempfindlich

~, impact-resistant, impact resisting · schlagfest, (schlag)zäh

toughened glass → ~ **safety** ~

~ **(polished) plate (glass),** tempered (~) ~ (~), heat-treated (~) ~ (~) [*For instance ARMOURCLAD*] · vorgespanntes (Kristall)Spiegelglas *n*

~ **(safety) glass** (Brit.); tempered (~) ~ (US); heat-treated (~) ~, case-hardened (~) ~ [*The term 'hardened glass' is rarely used*] · Einscheiben-Sicherheitsglas *n*, Einschicht-Sicherheitsglas, vorgespanntes (Flach)Glas [*Fehlnamen: gehärtetes Glas „Hartglas*]

toughness — town church

toughness · Sprödbruchunempfindlichkeit f
~, impact resistance, resistance to impact · Schlagfestigkeit f, Stoßwiderstand m, (Schlag)Zähigkeit [*Widerstand eines Gesteins gegen Bruch unter Einwirkung von Stößen*]
~ test, impact resistance ~ · Schlagfestigkeitsprüfung f, Schlagfestigkeitsprobe f, Schlagfestigkeitsversuch m, Zähigkeitsprüfung, Zähigkeitsprobe, Zähigkeitsversuch
tourist attraction, sight · Sehenswürdigkeit f
~ house, rooming ~, lodging ~, boarding ~ [*A building arranged or used for the lodging with or without meals, for compensation, of more than five and not more than twenty individuals*] · Pension f, Logierhaus n
~ terrace · Besucherterrasse f
~ tower · Besucherturm m
tourmaline · Turmalin m
Tournai marble, Belgian black · Tournai-Marmor m
towel bar, ~ rail · Handtuchstange f, Handtuchschiene f
~ ~ fitting → **~ rail ~**
~ cabinet · Handtuchschrank m
~ dispenser · Handtuchspender m
~ holder · Handtuchhalter m
~ hook · Handtuchhaken m
~ rail, ~ bar · Handtuchstange f, Handtuchschiene f
~ ~ fitting, ~ bar ~ [*A pipe fitting – either a tee or an elbow – which is used in the assembly of towel rails to be heated by hot water, and which, for the sake of appearance and ease of cleaning, is made with a bulbous shape*] · Handtuchschienenformstück n, Handtuchstangenformstück, Handtuchschienenfitting m, Handtuchstangenfitting
tower, twr · Turm m
~, super-skyscraper [*Planned by Le Corbusier*] · Super-Wolkenkratzer m
~ arch · Turmbogen m
~ bivane · zweiachsige Windfahne f
~ (block), ~ building, tall ~, high-rise ~ · Hochhaus n, Turmgebäude n, Turmhaus
~ (~) building → high-rise block construction
~ (~) construction → high-rise ~ ~
~ (~) façade, ~ building ~, tall ~ ~, high-rise ~ ~ · Hochhausfassade f
~ (~) rising line, ~ building ~ ~, tall ~ ~, high-rise ~ ~ ~ · Hochhaus-Steigleitung f, Turmhaus-Steigleitung, Turmgebäude-Steigleitung
tower-builder · Turmbauer m
tower building, ~ construction · Turmbau m
~ ~, ~ (block), tall ~, high-rise ~ · Hochhaus n, Turmgebäude n, Turmhaus

~ ~ → high-rise block construction
~ ~ construction → high-rise block ~
~ ~ façade → ~ (block) ~
~ ~ rising line → ~ (block) ~ ~
~ clock · Turmuhr f
~ construction → high-rise block ~
~ ~, ~ building · Turmbau m
~ façade → ~ block ~
~ floor; ~ storey (Brit.); **~ story** (US) · Turmetage f, Turmstockwerk n, Turmgeschoß n
~ gutter tile · Turmfalzziegel m
tower-house · Turmhaus n [*mittelalterlicher Wehrbau*]
tower masonry wall · Turmmauer f
Tower of Babel · Babelturm m (Etemenanki), Turm zu Babel, babylonischer Turm
~ ~ the Winds, [*Horologium of Andronikos Cyrrhestes*] · Horologium n des Andronikos von Kyrrhe, Turm m der Winde [*in Athen*]
tower pier · Turmpfeiler m
~ restaurant · Turmgaststätte f
~ rising line → ~ block ~ ~
~ roof · Turmdach n
~ silo, ~ type ~ · Hochsilo m, Turmsilo [*landwirtschaftlicher Silo*]
~ stair(case) · Turmtreppe f
~ story (US); **~ storey** (Brit.); **~ floor** · Turmetage f, Turmstockwerk n, Turmgeschoß n
~ (type) silo · Hochsilo m, Turmsilo [*landwirtschaftlicher Silo*]
~ with constant batter · Turm m mit gleichmäßigem Anzug
tower(ed) façade · Turmfassade f [*Fassade mit einem Turm oder mehreren Türmen*]
~ fire-temple · Feueraltar m
towing, fettling · Lederhartverputzen n, Verputzen in trockenem Zustand [*Steinzeugrohrindustrie*]
town · Stadt f
Town and Country Planning Association · Vereinigung f für Landesplanung
town architect · Stadtarchitekt m
~ architecture, urban ~, municipal ~; local ~ [*When referring to a specific city*]; civic design [*general term*] · Stadtarchitektur f, Stadtbaukunst f
~ area, urban ~, municipal ~ · Stadtgebiet n
~ block, municipal ~, urban ~ [*A division of a city bounded by four streets*] · Stadtviertel n
~ centre (Brit.); **~ center** (US); urban ~, municipal ~ · Stadtmitte f
~ chapel, urban ~, municipal ~ · Stadtkapelle f
~ church, urban ~, municipal ~ [*A church in a town*] · Stadtkirche f

~ **configeration**, urban ~, municipal ~ · Stadtfigur f
~ **development**, urban ~, municipal ~ · Städtebau m
~ ~, urban ~, municipal ~ · Stadtentwick(e)lung f
~ ~ **committee**, municipal ~ ~, urban ~ ~ · Städtebauausschuß m
~ **district** · Stadtbezirk m
~ **enclosure** · Stadtumschließung f
~ **engineering**, urban ~, municipal ~ · Stadtbautechnik f, Städtebautechnik
~ **expressway**, urban ~, municipal ~ · Stadtschnellstraße f
~ **extension**, urban ~, municipal ~ · Stadterweiterung f
~ **forest**, municipal ~, urban ~ · Stadtwald m
~ **fortification** · Stadtbefestigung f
~ **garden**, municipal ~, urban ~ · Stadtgarten m
~ **gas** · Mischgas n, Stadtgas n, Dowsongas
(~) **gate(way)** · Straßentor n
~ **hall** (Brit.); city ~ (US) · Rathaus m
~ ~ **complex** (Brit.); city ~ ~ (US) · Rathauskomplex m
~ **heating**, urban ~, municipal ~ · Stadtheizung f
~ **hotel**, municipal ~, urban ~ · Stadthotel n
~ **house** · Bürger(wohn)haus n
~ ~ [As opposed to a house in the country] · Stadthaus n
~ **in which housing blocks are separated by parks, etc.** · „Raumstadt" f
~ **library**, municipal ~, urban ~ · Stadtbibliothek f, Stadtbücherei f
~ **living-space**, urban ~, municipal ~ · städtischer Lebensraum m
~ **(master) mason** · Stadtbaumeister m
~ **museum**, municipal ~, urban ~ · Stadtmuseum n
~ **of the future** [Designed by two Milan architects in 1914, it marked the beginning of Futurist architecture] · „Stadt f der Zukunft", Citta f Nuova
'**town on a table mountain**' [Project by Paolo Soleri] · „Stadt f auf einem Tafelberg"
town orphanage, urban ~, municipal ~ · städtisches Waisenhaus n
~ **palace**, urban ~, municipal ~ · Stadtpalast m
~ **park**, urban ~, municipal ~ · Stadtpark m
~ **picture** · Stadtbild n
~ **planner**, municipal ~, urban ~ · Städtebauer m, Stadtbauer, Städteplaner, Stadtplaner
~ **planning**, municipal ~, urban ~ · städtebauliche Planung f, Stadtplanung, Städteplanung

~ ~ **authority**, urban ~ ~ · Stadtplanungsbehörde f
~ ~ **institute**, urban ~ ~, municipal ~ ~ · Städtebauinstitut n
~ ~ **studies**, urban ~ ~, municipal ~ ~ · Städtebaulehre f, städtebauliche Lehre
~ ~ **system**, urban ~ ~, municipal ~ ~ · Stadtbausystem n
~ ~ **theory**, urban ~ ~, municipal ~ ~ · Städtebautheorie f
~ **pool**, municipal ~, urban ~, ~ swimming bath · Stadtbad n
~ **refuse**, ~ waste, municipal ~; ~ rubbish (US) · Stadtabfall(stoff) m, Stadtmüll m
~ **road** → urban ~
~ **rubbish**, municipal ~ (US); ~ waste, ~ refuse · Stadtabfall(stoff) m, Stadtmüll m
~ **sauna bath**, municipal ~ ~, urban ~ ~ · Stadt-Sauna(bad) f, (n)
townscape, urban landscape · Stadtlandschaft f, Städtelandschaft
town square, agora, market place · Agora f, Markt(platz) m [Platz einer griechischen Stadt im Altertum, auf dem Versammlungen und Märkte abgehalten wurden]
~ **station**, in-~ ~, urban ~, municipal ~ · Stadtbahnhof m
~ **swimming bath**, municipal ~ ~, urban ~ ~, ~ ~ pool · Stadtbad n
~ **theatre**, municipal ~, urban ~, ~ theater · Stadttheater n
~ **wall**, urban ~, municipal ~, ~ masonry ~ · Stadtmauer f
~ **waste**, ~ refuse, municipal ~; ~ rubbish (US) · Stadtabfall(stoff) m, Stadtmüll m
toxic hazard · Giftgefahr f
~ **paint** · giftige (Anstrich)Farbe f
toy-lot, playground with structural and mechanical equipment, play area with structural and mechanical equipment · Spielgeräteplatz m
TP, threadless pipe · gewindeloses Rohr n
T-panel (unit) · T-Wandtafel f
TR, tie rod · Zugstange f
trabeated architecture [A style of architecture such as the Greek, in which the beam forms the constructive feature] · Architravarchitektur f, Architravbaukunst f, Gebälkarchitektur, Gebälkbaukunst
~ **building** · Architravgebäude n, Gebälkgebäude
~ **construction**, trabeation [A construction on the post-and-lintel principle, as in Greek architecture, in contrast to an arcuated building] · Architravbau m, Gebälkbau
trace of the plane · Spur f der Ebene
tracer heating · Begleitheizung f

traceried opening · Maßwerkblende f
(~) rose window · Maßwerkrose (nfenster) f, (n), (Fenster)Rose, Rosenfenster [Mit Maßwerk geschmücktes gotisches Rundfenster]
~ window, tracery ~ · Maßwerkfenster n
tracery · Maßwerk n
~ decorating art, ~ decoration ~, ~ ornamental ~ · Maßwerkornamentik f, Maßwerkzierkunst f
~ decoration art, ~ decorating ~, ~ ornamental ~ · Maßwerkornamentik f, Maßwerkzierkunst f
~ filling · Maßwerkfüllung f
~ frieze · Maßwerkfries m
~ motif · Maßwerkmotiv n
~ ornamental art, ~ decorating ~, ~ decoration ~ · Maßwerkornamentik f, Maßwerkzierkunst f
~ pattern · Maßwerkmuster n
~ window, traceried ~ · Maßwerkfenster n
~ with four leaf-shaped curves, quatrefoil, four-leaved tracery · Vierblatt n [gotisches Maßwerk]
~ ~ three leaf-shaped curves · Dreiblatt n [gotisches Maßwerk]
trachyte [A volcanic rock characterized by alkali-feldspar, without quartz but usually with biotite, augite, etc.] · Trachyt m
trachytic tuff · Trachyttuff m
tracing, print · (Licht)Pause f
~, duplicating · Pausen n
~ cloth · Pausleinen n
tracing-house, trasour · Zeichenbüro n eines mittelalterlichen Baumeisters
tracing room, duplicating ~ · Paus(en)raum m
track · Bahn f [Leichtathletik]
~, rail · (Führungs)Schiene f [Türanlage]
~, trolley ~, overhead ~ · Laufschiene f [Tor]
~ lighting · Beleuchtung f mit hängeschienenmontierten Leuchten
traction line · Fahrleitung f [Draht oder Schiene. Sie führen elektrischen Bahnen den Strom vom Bahnnetz an die Fahrzeuge entweder mit an Masten aufgehängter Oberleitung oder mit dritter Schiene zu, die wenig höher als das Gleis und neben den Fahrschienen läuft]
~ pole [B. S. 607] · Fahrleitungsmast m
trade, craft, building ~ · Gewerk n
~ area · Gewerbegebiet n
~ burning appliance → ~ fire
~ crew → ~ gang
~ effluent → ~ waste
~ entrance · Wirtschaftseingang m
~ fire, ~ furnace, ~ burning appliance · gewerbliche Feuerstätte f, ~ Feuerung f [z.B. Backofen, Räucherkammer, Siedekessel in Metzgereien, Großküchenherde usw.]

~ for interior work, ~ ~ finishing ~, ~ ~ inside ~, ~ ~ inner ~, ~ ~ indoor ~ · (Innen)Ausbaugewerbe n
~ ~ mechanical work · Techniker gewerk n
~ furnace → ~ fire
~ gang, ~ crew, ~ team, ~ party, craft ~ · Handwerkerkolonne f
(trade)mark → registered ~
trademark method, ~ system · geschützte Methode f, geschütztes Verfahren n
~ system, ~ method · geschützte Methode f, geschütztes Verfahren n
trade party → ~ gang
~ team → ~ gang
~ waste, ~ effluent [The fluid discharge from any manufacturing process] · gewerbliches Abwasser n
tradesman, journeyman, craftsman · Geselle m
trading town · Handelsstadt f
tradition of building, architectural tradition · Bautradition f
traditional · traditionsgebunden
~ architecture · traditionelle Architektur f, ~ Baukunst f, überlieferte ~, überkommene ~
~ form of building · traditionelle Bauform f, überlieferte ~, überkommene ~
~ style · traditioneller Stil m, überlieferter ~, überkommener ~
(traffic) aisle, (~) lane · Fahrgasse f [Parkhaus; Tiefgarage]
traffic-free precinct · fahrverkehrsfreier Bereich m, fahrverkehrsfreies ~ n
(traffic) lane, (~) aisle · Fahrgasse f [Parkhaus; Tiefgarage]
~ (marking) paint · Verkehrs(markierungs)farbe f
~ noise · Verkehrslärm m
~ paint, ~ marking ~ · Verkehrs(markierungs)farbe f
~ route · Verkehrsweg m [z.B. auf einer Abfertigungsebene eines Flughafen-Abfertigungsgebäudes]
~ tower · Verkehrsturm m
~ vibration · Verkehrserschütterung f [Erschütterungsschutz]
training · Ausbildung f
~ camp · Ausbildungslager n
~ centre (Brit.); ~ center (US) · Ausbildungsstätte f
~ (Brit.)/center (US) for physically and mentally handicapped persons (or people) · Ausbildungsstätte f für körperlich und/oder geistig behinderte Personen
~ kitchen · Lehrküche f
~ school for nurses · Schwesternschule f
~ (work)shop, instructional ~ · Lehrwerkstatt f

Trajan's column, column of Trajan · Trajanssäule *f*

trajectory of main stress → line of principal ~

~ ~ **(pre)stressing force,** ~ ~ tensioning ~, ~ ~ stretching ~ · Spannkraftweg *m*, Vor~

~ ~ **principal stress** → line ~ ~ ~

~ ~ **stress,** stress trajectory · Spannungstrajektorie *f*, Spannungsweg *m*

~ ~ **stretching force,** ~ ~ tensioning ~, ~ ~ (pre)stressing ~ · Spannkraftweg *m*, Vor~

~ ~ **tensioning force,** ~ ~ stretching ~, ~ ~ (pre)stressing ~ · Spannkraftweg *m*, Vor~

transcrystalline attack → intergranular ~

~ **corrosion** → intergranular attack

transducer · Wandler *m* [*Schalltechnik*]

transenna · Transenna *m* [*Verschluß der Fensteröffnung mit durchbrochenen Stein- oder Holzplatten oder dünn geschliffenen Marmorplatten, vor Einführung der Fensterverglasung*]

transept · Querhaus *n*

~ **square,** crossing ~, square of crossing · Vierungsquadrat *n* [*Es ergibt sich aus der Durchdringung von Langhaus und Querhaus bei gleichen Breiten*]

transept(al) apsis, ~ apse · Querhausabseite *f*, Querhausabside *f*, Querhausapside, Querhausapsis

~ **arch** · Querhausbogen *m*

~ **basilica** · Querhausbasilika *f*

~ **ceiling** · Querhausdecke *f*

~ **chapel** · Querhauskapelle *f*

~ **circular window,** circular transept(al) ~ · Querhausrundfenster *n*

~ **façade,** ~ front · Querhausfassade *f*, Querhausfront *f*

~ **gable** · Querhausgiebel *m*

~ **portal** · Querhausportal *n*

~ **tower** · Querhausturm *m*

~ **vault** · Querhausgewölbe *n*

~ **wall** · Querhauswand *f*

~ **window** · Querhausfenster *n*

transept-less · querhauslos, querhausfrei

to transfer, to transmit · ableiten, abtragen, übertragen

transfer, transmission · Ableitung *f*, Abtragung, Übertragung

~, transmission, load ~ · Ableitung *f*, Abtragung, Übertragung, Last~

~, handing over, handover · Übergabe *f*

~ **(decoration)** (Brit.); decal (~) (US) · Übertragungsbild *n*, Abziehbild

~ **length** → transmission ~

~ **matrix** · Übertragungsmatrize *f*

~ **medium** · Träger *m* [*Kälte; Wärme*]

~ **method** → ~ process

~ **of forces** · Kräfteübertragung *f*

~ ~ **moment(s)** · Momentenübertragung *f*

~ ~ **wind load** · Windlastableitung *f*

~ **process,** ~ method (Brit.); decal ~ (US) [*A decorative process in which a design is applied to the glass by means of a transfer*] · Abziehverfahren *n*

~ **strength** [*The concrete strength required before stress is transferrred from the stressing mechanism to the concrete*] · Übertragungsfestigkeit *f*

transference, transferral, heat ~ · (Wärme)Übertragung *f*

transferral, transference, heat ~ · (Wärme)Übertragung *f*

transformation framework · Ersatzfachwerk *n*

~ **matrix** · Übergangsmatrix *f*

~ **member** · Ersatzstab *m*

transformed rock → metamorphic ~

~ **schist,** metamorphosed ~, metamorphic ~ · metamorpher Schiefer *m*

transformer room · Traforaum *m*

transient bending moment · vorübergehendes Biegemoment *n*, ~ Biegungsmoment

~ **hotel** · Reisehotel *n*, Durchgangshotel

~ **moment** · Moment *n* aus Zusatzkräften, Zusatzmoment

transit shed · Transitschuppen *m*

transition arch · Übergangsbogen *m*

~ **from exterior to interior** · Übergang *m* zwischen Außen und Innen

transition-lime, greywacke limestone, graywacke limestone · Grauwackenkalk *m*, Übergangskalk

transitional architecture · Übergangsarchitektur *f*, Übergangsbaukunst *f*

~ ~ **structures,** ~ style ~ · Übergangsbauten *fpl*

~ **period,** ~ phase, period of transition, phase of transition · Übergangsperiode *f*, Übergangszeit *f*, Übergangsphase *f* [*von einem Stil zum anderen*]

~ **phase,** ~ period, period of transition, phase of transition · Übergangsperiode *f*, Übergangszeit *f*, Übergangsphase *f* [*von einem Stil zum anderen*]

~ **style** · Übergangsstil *m*

~ ~ **structures,** ~ architecture ~ · Übergangsbauten *fpl*

translation · Verschiebung *f*

~ **component** · Verschiebungskomponente *f*

~ **factor** · Verschiebungsfaktor *m*

~ **shell of double curvature** · doppelt gekrümmte Translationsschale *f*

~ **state** · Verschiebungszustand *m*

~ **value** · Verschiebungswert *m*

~ **vector** · Verschiebungsvektor *m*

translational rigidity — transverse bending action

translational rigidity, ~ stiffness · Verschiebungssteifigkeit f, Verschiebungsstarrheit

translation(al) shell · Translationsschale f

~ ~ of double curvature, ~ ~ curved in two directions, doubly curved translation(al) shell, double curvature translation(al) shell · doppelt gekrümmte Translationsschale f, zweifach ~ ~

translational stiffness, ~ rigidity · Verschiebungssteifigkeit f, Verschiebungsstarrheit

translation(al) surface, surface of translation · Translationsfläche f

translucent, shining through, partially transparent [*Letting light pass but diffusing it so that objects on the other side cannot be distinguished*] · durchscheinend

~ ceiling · durchscheinende (Raum)- Decke f

~ concrete, glass ~ [*A combination of glass and concrete used together in precast or prestressed panels*] · Glasbeton m

~ ~ floor, glass ~ ~ · Glasbetondecke f

~ ~ window, glass ~ ~ · Glasbetonfenster n

~ diffuser · Kunststoffglaswanne f [*Leuchte*]

~ door [*Such as door is designed to enable persons and objects on the far side to be seen in shaded form. This diminishes all possibility of accidents through collision, and at the same time allows a certain amount of privacy*] · · durchscheinende Tür f

~ enamel · Translucitschmelz m, Reliefschmelz

~ glass [*Glass which transmits light diffusely. Through-vision may vary from almost clear to almost obscured. Diffusiveness is produced by suitable treatment of the surface of clear glass, either by imprinting a pattern or texture, or by sandblasting, acid embossing or other means*] · durchscheinendes Glas n

transmission, transfer · Ableitung f, Abtragung, Übertragung

~, transfer, load ~ · Ableitung f, Abtragung, Übertragung, Last~

~ length, transfer ~, bond ~, grip ~ [*reinforcing bar*] · Einbindelänge f, Verbundlänge, Haftlänge

~ loss · Übertragungsverlust m

~ pole [*B.S. 607*] · Elektroleitungsmast m, Elektro-Überlandmast, Elt-Leistungsmast, Elt-Überlandmast

to transmit, to transfer · ableiten, abtragen, übertragen

transmitted light · Durchlicht n

~ sound · durchgelassener Schall m

transom [*An intermediate horizontal member in a window or door opening*] · Kämpfer(riegel) m [*Waag(e)rechtes feststehendes Zwischenstück eines Fensters oder einer Tür*]

~ light [*A glazed light above a transome bar*] · Kämpfer(riegel)oberlicht n

transparency · Klarsicht f

transparent · durchsichtig, nichtdeckend [*Lasurfarbe*]

~ [*Transmitting light rays so that objects on the other side may be distinctly seen*] · durchsichtig

~, clear; colorless, uncolored (US); colourless uncoloured (Brit.) · farblos

~ flexible (swing) door · Sichtpendeltür f

~ glass, clear ~ · durchsichtiges Glas n, Klarglas

~ hose · Klarsichtschlauch m

~ passage(way) · offener Gang m, durchfensterter ~ [*Kirchenbau*]

~ plastic (building) unit, ~ ~ (~) member, ~ ~ (~) component · Lichtbauelement n auf Kunststoffbasis, ~ Kunststoffgrundlage, Lichtbaukörper m ~ ~ [*Fehlname: Lichtbaueinheit f ~ ~*]

~ ~ roof cover(ing), ~ ~ ~ sheathing, ~ ~ roofing · Lichtdach(belag) n, (m) auf Kunststoffbasis, ~ ~ Kunststoffgrundlage, Licht(dach)(ein)deckung f

~ positive original, negative transparency · Mutterpause f

~ triforium · durchfensteres Triforium n, offenes ~

transplanting semi-mature trees · Umpflanzen n halbreifer Bäume

transportable · transportfähig, transportierbar

transversal rip · Quergurt(bogen) m, Transversalgurt(bogen)

transverse abutment system · Querstrebeapparat m, Querstrebesystem n, Querstrebewerk n

~ arch, arch band · Doppelbogen m, Quergurt(bogen) m, Transversalgurt(bogen), Querbogen, Transversalbogen [*Quer zur Längsachse eines Raumes gespannter Entlastungsbogen*]

~ arm, cross ~ · Kreuzarm m, Kreuzflügel m, Querhausarm, Querhausflügel, Kreuzvorlage f [*Der über das Langhaus vorspringende Teil des Querhauses*]

~ axis; ~ centre line (Brit.); ~ center line (US) · Querachse f, Quermittellinie f

~ bar, ~ rod, ~ round · Quer(rund)- stab m [*Betonstahlmatte*]

~ barrel vault, ~ tunnel ~, ~ wagon ~ · Quertonne(ngewölbe) f, (n) [*Im Gegensatz zur Längstonne verläuft die Scheitellinie der Quertonne quer zur Hauptachse eines Raumes*]

~ beam, cross-beam · Querbalken(träger) m

~ bending · Querbiegen n, Querbiegung f

~ ~ action · Querbiegewirkung f

1048

transverse bending moment — transversely corrugated

~ ~ **moment** · Querbiegemoment *n*, Querbiegungsmoment
~ ~ **rigidity,** ~ ~ **stiffness** · Querbiegesteifigkeit *f*
~ ~ **stiffness,** ~ ~ **rigidity** · Querbiegesteifigkeit *f*
~ ~ **test** · Querbiegeprobe *f*, Querbiegeversuch *m*, Querbiegeprüfung *f*
~ **bracing** · Querversteifung *f* [*von Decken aus Fertigbauteilen*]
~ **centre line** (Brit.); ~ **center** ~ (US); ~ **axis** · Querachse *f*, Quermittellinie *f*
~ **component** · Querkomponente *f*
~ **construction joint** · Querarbeitsfuge *f*
~ **crack** · Querriß *m*
~ **cracking** · Querrißbildung *f*
~ **curvature** · Querkrümmung *f*
~ **deformation** · Querverformung *f*, Querformänderung
~ **diaphragm** · Querscheibe *f*
~ **distribution** · Querverteilung *f*
~ **flexural strength** · Scheiteldruck-Biegefestigkeit *f* [*Rohr*]
~ **force** · Querkraft *f*
~ ~ **determination** · Querkraftermitt(e)lung *f*
~ **frame, bent** [*A structural frame which is self-supporting in two dimensions. It has at least two legs and is generally at right angles to the length of the structure which it supports*] · Querrahmen *m*
~ **hall** · Querhalle *f*, Querraum *m*, Quersaal *m* [*Ein Saal oder Raum dessen längere Achse quer zur Hauptachse verläuft. Beispiele sind die Säulensäle ägyptischer Tempel*]
~ **interval,** ~ **spacing** · Querabstand *m*
~ **joint** · Querfuge *f*
~ ~ **edge** · Querfugenrand *m*
~ **line of influence** · Quereinflußlinie *f*
~ **load** · Querlast *f*
~ **loading**, lateral ~ · Querbelastung *f*
~ **moment** · Quermoment *n*
~ **oval cupola,** ~ ~ **dome** · Querovalkuppel *f*
~ ~ **dome,** ~ ~ **cupola** · Querovalkuppel *f*
~ **plank** → horizontal timber
~ **(pre)stressing,** ~ **stretching,** ~ **tensioning** · Quervorspannung *f*
~ **reinforcement, helical** ~, **lateral** ~, **helical binding, helix; spiral reinforcement** [*misnomer*] · Querbewehrung *f* nach der Schraubenlinie, Spiralbewehrung, Spiralarmierung, Spiral(stahl)-einlagen *fpl*, Umschnürung
~ ~, **cross** ~ [*Reinforcement at right angles to the main reinforcement*] · Querarmierung *f*, Querbewehrung, Quer(stahl)einlagen *fpl*
~ **rib** · Querrippe *f*
~ ~ **slab** · Querrippenplatte *f*

transverse-ribbed · quergerippt
transverse ridge · Querscheitel *m* [*Gewölbe*]
~ **ridge-rib** · Querscheitelrippe *f*
~ **rigidity,** ~ **stiffness** · Quersteifigkeit *f*, Quersteife *f*, Quersteifheit *f*, Seitensteife, Seitensteifheit, Seitensteifigkeit
~ **rod,** ~ **bar,** ~ **round** ~ · Quer(rund)-stab *m* [*Betonstahlmatte*]
~ **roof** · Querdach *n*, Zwerchdach [*Ein Dach mit quer zum First des Hauptdaches verlaufendem First*]
~ **(round) bar,** ~ (~) **rod** · Quer(rund)-stab *m* [*Betonstahlmatte*]
~ (~) **rod,** ~ (~) **bar** · Quer(rund)stab *m* [*Betonstahlmatte*]
~ **shear** · Querschub *m*
~ **spacing,** ~ **interval** · Querabstand *m*
~ **stabilization cable** · querlaufendes Stabilisierungsseil *n*
~ **stiffness,** ~ **rigidity** · Quersteifigkeit *f*, Quersteife *f*, Quersteifheit *f*, Seitensteife, Seitensteifheit, Seitensteifigkeit
~ **strain,** lateral ~ · Querdehnung *f*
~ ~ **moment** · Querdehnungsmoment *n*
~ **strength** · Querfestigkeit *f*
~ ~, **lateral** ~, **flexural** ~, **modulus of rupture** [*The strength of a specimen tested in transverse bending; normally synonymous with "modulus of rupture" but also used to refer to breaking load (see B.S. 340, 368, 550 and 2028)*] · Querbiegefestigkeit *f*
~ **stress** · Querspannung *f*
~ **stressing** → ~ **stretching**
~ **stretching,** ~ **tensioning,** ~ **(pre-)stressing** · Quervorspannung *f*
~ **tendon** · Querspannglied *n*
~ **tensioning,** ~ **stretching,** ~ **(pre)-stressing** · Quervorspannung *f*
~ **tunnel vault,** ~ **wagon** ~, ~ **barrel** ~ · Quertonne(ngewölbe) *f*, (*n*) [*Im Gegensatz zur Längstonne verläuft die Scheitellinie der Quertonne quer zur Hauptachse eines Raumes*]
~ **wagon vault,** ~ **tunnel** ~, ~ **barrel** ~ · Quertonne(ngewölbe) *f*, (*n*) [*Im Gegensatz zur Längstonne verläuft die Scheitellinie der Quertonne quer zur Hauptachse eines Raumes*]
~ **wave, shear** ~, **rotational** ~ · Transversalwelle *f*, Querwelle [*Im Gegensatz zu Gasen und Flüssigkeiten können in festen Körpern jedoch auch Schubkräfte übertragen werden, so daß Körperschall hauptsächlich in Form von Transversalwellen auftritt, bei denen die Teilchen quer zur Ausbreitungsrichtung schwingen*]
~ **web** · Quersteg *m* [*Hohlblock(stein)*]
~ **wire of the cloth, weft wire** · Schußdraht *m*
transversely arranged frame · quergestellter Rahmen *m*
~ **corrugated** · quergewellt

transversely loaded — travelling table mould 1050

~ **loaded**, laterally ~ · querbelastet

trap, stench ~, stink ~ · [*A fitting or part of an appliance or pipe arranged to retain water so as to prevent the passage of foul air*] · (Wasser)(Geruch)Verschluß m [*DIN 1209 und DIN 1210, Fehlnamen: Siphon m, Syphon m, Traps m*]

~ **door** · Klapptür f, Falltür

~ ~ **on roof**, exit opening · Dachausstieg m, Dachausstiegluke f

(~) **outlet**, overflow connection · Ablaufstutzen m, Auslauf m [*Geruchverschluß*]

~ **seal** → (water) ~

~ **with removable lower part** · (Wasser)(Geruch)Verschluß m mit abnehmbarem Unterteil

trapezoid(al) arch · Trapezbogen m, trapezförmiger Bogen

~ **bay**, ~ **vault** ~ · Trapez(gewölbe)joch n, trapezförmiges (Gewölbe)Joch

~ **cross(-)section** · Trapezquerschnitt m

~ **(eave(s)) gutter**, ~ **trough**, ~ **trow** · trapezförmige (Dach)Rinne f, trapezprofilierte ~, Trapez(dach)rinne

~ **footing** · Trapezfundament n

~ **frame** · Trapezrahmen m, trapezförmiger Rahmen

~ **gutter** → ~ eave(s) ~

trapezoidal load · Trapezlast f

~ **loading** · Trapezbelastung f

trapezoid(al) (metal) plate · Trapezgrobblech n, trapezförmiges Grobblech, trapezprofiliertes Grobblech

~ (~) **sheet** · Trapezfeinblech n, trapezförmiges Feinblech, trapezprofiliertes Feinblech

~ **piece** · Trapezkörper m, Trapezstück n, trapezförmiger Nockenkörper, trapezprofilierter Nockenkörper [*Hubdeckenverfahren*]

~ **plate**, ~ metal ~ · Trapezgrobblech n, trapezförmiges Grobblech, trapezprofiliertes Grobblech

~ ~, ~ **slab** · trapezförmige Platte f, trapezprofilierte ~, Trapezplatte

~ **profile** → ~ trim

~ **purlin(e)** · Trapezpfette f, trapezförmige Pfette, trapezprofilierte Pfette

~ **sandwich panel**, ~ **three-layer(ed)** ~ · Trapez-Dreischichtentafel f, Trapez-Dreilagentafel, trapezförmige Dreischichtentafel, trapezförmige Dreilagentafel

~ **section**, ~ shape, ~ unit, ~ trim, ~ profile · Trapezprofil n, trapezförmiges Profil

~ **shape**, ~ section, ~ unit, ~ trim, ~ profile · Trapezprofil n, trapezförmiges Profil

~ **sheet**, ~ metal ~ · Trapezfeinblech n, trapezförmiges Feinblech, trapezprofiliertes Feinblech

~ **slab**, ~ plate · trapezförmige Platte f, trapezprofilierte ~, Trapezplatte

~ **three-layer(ed) panel**, ~ sandwich ~ · Trapez-Dreischichtentafel f, Trapez-Dreilagentafel, trapezförmige Dreischichtentafel, trapezförmige Dreilagentafel

~ **trim**, ~ shape, ~ unit, ~ section, ~ profile · Trapezprofil n, trapezförmiges Profil

~ **truss frame** · Trapezsprengwerk n

~ **unit**, ~ trim ~ shape, ~ section, ~ profile · Trapezprofil n, trapezförmiges Profil

~ **(vault) bay** · Trapez(gewölbe)joch n, trapezförmiges (Gewölbe)Joch

~ **wood lath(ing) (for plastering)** · Trapez(-Holzstab)gewebe n, trapezförmiges Holzstabgewebe, trapezprofiliertes Holzstabgewebe [*Putzträger*]

trapp tuff, basalt(ic) ~ · Trapptuff m, Basalttuff

trapped [*street gully*] · mit Geruchverschluß (versehen)

~ **air** → en~ ~

~ ~ **void** → en~ ~ ~

(~) **bathroom gull(e)y** · Badablauf m, Badeinlauf

~ **humidity** → en~ ~

~ **moisture** → en~ ~

trasour, tracing-house · Zeichenbüro n eines mittelalterlichen Baumeisters

trass → (Rhenish) ~

trass-cement mortar, terras-cement ~ · Traßzementmörtel m [*Ein Mörtel, dessen Bindemittel aus Traß und Zement oder dem fabrikmäßig hergestellten Traßzement besteht*]

trass (or terras) cement with 70 parts by weight of portland cement clinker and 30 parts by weight of trass · Regeltraßzement m

trass lime cement mortar, terras ~ ~ ~ · Traß-Kalk-Zementmörtel m, Traß-Zement-Kalkmörtel, Zement-Kalk-Traßmörtel

~ (~) **mortar**, terras (~) ~ · Traßkalkmörtel m

~ ~ **powder mix(ture)**, terras ~ ~ ~, ~ ~ **putty** · Traßkalk m [*Bindemittel aus Traß und Kalkpulver oder Kalkteig*]

~ **mortar**, ~ lime ~, terras (~) ~ · Traßkalkmörtel m

~ **powder**, terras ~, powder(ed) trass, powder(ed) terras · Traßmehl n

travelling forms, ~ form(work), ~ shuttering (Brit.); traveling ~ (US) · Wanderschalung f

~ **form(work)**, ~ forms, ~ shuttering (Brit.); traveling ~ (US) · Wanderschalung f

~ **lighting gallery** (Brit.); traveling ~ ~ (US) · Beleuchtungsbrücke f

~ **shuttering**, ~ forms, ~ form(work) (Brit.); traveling ~ (US) · Wanderschalung f

~ **table mould** (Brit.); traveling table mold (US) · Wandertischform f

traversable, capable of bearing wheel loads · befahrbar

travertine [*A variety of tufa, often porous, deposited from spring waters*] · Travertin *m*

~ **column** · Travertinsäule *f*

~ **facing,** ~ sur~, ~ lining · Travertinauskleidung *f*, Travertinverkleidung, Travertinbekleidung

~ **lining,** ~ (sur)facing · Travertinauskleidung *f*, Travertinverkleidung, Travertinbekleidung

~ **slab** · Travertinplatte *f*

~ **(sur)facing,** ~ lining · Travertinauskleidung *f*, Travertinverkleidung, Travertinbekleidung

tray · Einfassung *f* [*Schornstein; Lüftungsrohr*]

tread, rundle, (ladder) rung, stave, LR · (Leiter)Sprosse *f*

~, stair ~ [*The member forming the horizontal top surface of a step*] · Auflagestufe *f*, (Auf)Tritt(stufe) *m*, (*f*)

~, stair ~ [*The horizontal top surface of a step*] · (Auf)Trittfläche *f*, Auftritt *m*

~ **cover(ing),** stair ~ ~ · (Tritt)Stufenbelag *m*, Treppenbelag, Trittbelag

~ **ladder,** stave ~, rung ~, rundle ~ · Sprossenleiter *f*

(~) nosing, stair ~ ~ · (Tritt)Stufenvorsprung *m*

~ **plate** · Trittblech *n*

treadplate · Tränenblech *n*

tread tile · (Auf)Trittfliese *f* [*Fliesentreppe*]

treading warmth, touching ~ · Fußwärme *f* [(*Fuß)Boden(belag)*]

treasure-house, treasury, thesaurus · Schatzhaus *n*, Thesauros *m*, Thesaurus *m* [*Ein kleines Gebäude zur Aufbewahrung von Weihegaben einer Stadt oder eines Landes im Temenos griechischer Kultstätten*]

treasury, treasure-house, thesaurus · Schatzhaus *n*, Thesauros *m*, Thesaurus *m* [*Ein kleines Gebäude zur Aufbewahrung von Weihegaben einer Stadt oder eines Landes im Temenos griechischer Kultstätten*]

Treasury of Atreus (at Mycenae), Tomb of Agamemnon · Schatzhaus *n* des Atreus, (Kuppel)Grab *n* des Agamemnon in Mykene [*14.–13.Jh.v.Chr.*]

~ ~ **Sikyon** · Schatzhaus *n* der Sikyonia [*Delphi*]

~ ~ **the Athenians** · Schatzhaus *n* der Athener [*Delphi*]

~ ~ ~ **Siphnians** · Schatzhaus *n* der Siphnier [*Delphi*]

to treat with alum · alaunisieren

treatment · Behandlung *f*

~ **block,** theatre ~, ~ building · Behandlungsgebäude *n*, Behandlungstrakt *m* [*Krankenhaus*]

~ **building** → ~ block

~ **cycle** · Behandlungszyklus *m*

~ **humidity,** ~ moisture · Behandlungsfeuchte *f*, Behandlungsfeuchtigkeit *f*

~ **moisture,** ~ humidity · Behandlungsfeuchte *f*, Behandlungsfeuchtigkeit *f*

~ **pressure** · Behandlungsdruck *m*

~ **room** · Behandlungszimmer *n*

~ **room** · Behandlungsraum *m* [*Krankenhaus*]

~ **technology** · Behandlungstechnologie *f*

~ **temperature** · Behandlungstemperatur *f*

Tree of Jesse · Jessebaum *m*

treeframed view · Blickschneise *f*

tee grill(e) [*for root ventilation*] · Baumrost *m*

tree-lined footpath · baumbestandener Fußweg *m*

tre(e)nail [*Sometimes called a 'drawbore pin', but this term is best reserved for the steel pin which pulls the holes into line before the tre(e)nail is inserted*] · Holznagel *m*

treeplanting · Baumbepflanzung *f*

trefoil · Dreiblatt *n*

trefoilapsis, trefoilapse · kleeblattförmige (Chor)Apsis *f*, ~ (Chor)Apside, ~ (Chor)Abside, ~ (Chor)Abseite, ~ Exedra, ~ Konche, ~ Chornische, kleeblattförmiges Chorhaupt *n*

trefoil arch → trefoil-headed ~

~**(-headed) arch,** trefoil(ed) ~, threefoil(ed) ~ · Klee(blatt)bogen *m*, Dreipaßbogen, dreiblätt(e)riger Bogen [*Fehlname: Nasenbogen mit drei Pässen*]

trefoil-shaped tower (block), ~ ~ building, ~ tall ~, ~ high-rise ~ · Hochhaus *n* in Y-Grundriß, Turmgebäude *n* ~ ~, Turmhaus ~ ~

trefoil(ed) arcade, three-foil(ed) ~ · Klee(blatt)bogenarkade *f*

~ **arch** · Dreipaßbogen *m*, Klee(blatt)bogen, dreiblätt(e)riger Bogen [*Fehlname: Nasenbogen mit drei Pässen*]

~ **(ground(-))plan,** three-foil(ed) ~ · Klee(blatt)grundriß *m*

~ **plan** → ~ ground(-)~

~ **tracery,** three-foil(ed) ~ · Dreipaßmaßwerk *n*

tre(i)llage, trellis [*An ornamental latticework designed to support climbing plants*] · Flechtwerk *n*

trellis → tre(i)llage

~ **bond,** open ~, pierced ~, honeycomb(ed) ~, pigeon-hole(d) ~ · Kästelverband *m*

~ **casing,** surface shell · Flechtwerkmantel *m*, Mantelfläche *f* [*Kuppel*]

~ **cupola,** ~ dome · Flechtwerkkuppel *f*

~ **dome,** ~ cupola · Flechtwerkkuppel *f*

~ ~ **work,** ~ cupola ~ · Kugelflechtwerk *n* [*Kuppel*]

trellis (masonry) wall — triapsidial chevet

~ **(masonry) wall** → honeycomb(ed) (~) ~

~ ~ **(work), open** ~ ~ (~), pierced ~ (~), honey comb(ed) ~ (~), pigeonhole(d) ~ (~) · durchbrochenes Mauerwerk *n*, Kästelmauerwerk

~ **wall** → honeycomb(ed) (masonry) ~

tremie concrete · Kontraktorbeton *m*

tremolite (asbestos), Italian ~ · Tremolit *m* (Min.)

trenched · (quer)genutet

trench-grave, trench-tomb · Bestattungsgrab *n* [*Etrurien. Es hat die Form einer rechteckigen Grube*]

trench-tomb → trench-grave

trenched · (quer)genutet

trial coat · Probeanstrich *m*, Probeaufstrich

~ **design** · Versuchsentwurf *m*

~ **fill(ing)**, test ~ · Versuchsschüttung *f*, Probeschüttung

~ **mix(ture)** · Probemischung *f*, Probegemisch *n*, Prüfmischung, Prüfgemisch, Versuchsmischung, Versuchsgemisch

~ **section**, test ~ · Versuchsabschnitt *m*, Prüfstrecke *f*, Probestrecke, Versuchsstrecke, Probeabschnitt, Prüfabschnitt

~ **solution** · Versuchslösung *f*

triangle (US); set-square · Winkel *m* [*Zeichengerät*]

~ **of force**, force triangle · Krafteck *n*, Kräftedreieck

~ ~ **moments**, moment triangle · Momentendreieck *n*

triangular arch · Giebelbogen *m*, sächsischer Bogen [*Aus Keilsteinen gemauerte, eine Spitze bildende Öffnung mit geraden Schenkeln; zu unterscheiden vom falschen Giebelbogen = Spreizbogen*]

~ **arched corbel-table** · Winkelfries *m*, Zackenfries

~ **bastion** · Dreieckbastion *f*

~ **beam** · Dreieckbalken(träger) *m*

~ **box (section) beam**, ~ hollow(-web) ~ · Dreieckkastenbalken(träger) *m*, Dreieckhohlbalken(träger), Dreieckbalken(träger) mit zwei Stegen

~ **column** · Dreieckstütze *f*

~ ~ · Dreiecksäule *f*

~ **cupola**, ~ dome · Dreieckkuppel *f*

~ **decoration** · Dreieckdekor(ation) *n*, (*f*)

~ **dome**, ~ cupola · Dreieckkuppel *f*

~ **duct** · Dreieckkanal *m*

~ **fillet** · Dreieckleiste *f*, Dreikantleiste

~ **form** → ~ shape

~ **frame**, ~ framing, spandrel ~ · Dreieckrahmen *m*

~ **full loading** · Dreieckvollbelastung *f*

~ **girder** · Dreieckträger *m*

~ **(ground(-))plan** · Dreieckgrundriß *m*

~ **hollow(-web) beam**, ~ box (section) ~ · Dreieckkastenbalken(träger) *m*, Dreieckhohlbalken(träger), Dreieckbalken(träger) mit zwei Stegen

~ **lattice(d) construction**, ~ ~ (structural) system · Dreieckgitterbausystem *n*, Dreieckgitterkonstruktion *f*, Dreieckgitter(konstruktions)system

~ **load** · Dreiecklast *f*

~ **loading** · Dreieckbelastung *f*, dreieck(förm)ige Belastung

~ ~ **on part of area (of plate)** · dreieck(förm)ige (Platten)Teilbelastung *f*

~ **network** · Dreiecknetz *n*

~ **panel** · Dreiecktafel *f*

~ ~ ~ → spandrel

~ **pediment** · Dreieckgiebel *m*, Giebeldreieck *n*

~ **plan**, ~ ground(-)~ · Dreieckgrundriß *m*

~ **plate**, ~ slab · Dreieckplatte *f* [*ebenes Flächentragwerk*]

~ **porch** · dreiseitige Vorhalle *f* [*z.B. bei den Domen zu Erfurt und Regensburg*]

~ **profile** → ~ section

~ **pyramid** · Dreieckpyramide *f*, Dreieckspitzsäule *f*

~ **section**, ~ unit, ~ shape, ~ trim, ~ profile · Dreieckprofil *n*, Dreikantprofil

~ **shape** → ~ section

~ ~, ~ form · Dreieckform *f*, Dreieckgestalt *f*

~ **slab**, ~ plate · Dreieckplatte *f* [*ebenes Flächentragwerk*]

~ **steel post** · Dreieck-Stahlpfosten *m*

~ **stress distribution** · dreieckige Spannungsverteilung *f*

~ **system**, triangulated ~ · Dreieckanordnung *f*, Dreiecksystem *n*

~ **tile** · Dreieckfliese *f*, Dreieck(belag)platte *f*

~ **window** · Dreieckfenster *n*

~ **wire** · Dreieckdraht *m*, Dreikantdraht

~ ~ **mesh** · Dreieck-Drahtmaschenmatte *f*

~ **wood lath(ing) (for plastering)** · Dreikant(-Holzstab)gewebe *n*

~ **trim** → ~ section

~ **unit** → ~ section

triangulated grid framework · dreieckiger Gitterrost *m*

~ **system** → triangular ~

triangulation · Dreieckverband *m* [*Fachwerkträger*]

~ · Triangulatur *f* [*Benutzung des rechtwink(e)ligen oder gleichschenkeligen Dreiecks zur Festlegung von Gliederungspunkten im Bauwerk*]

triapsidial [*Having three apses, usually abreast*] · dreiapsidial

~ **chevet** · Dreiapsidenchor *m* [*Mit parallelen Apsiden im Gegensatz zur Dreikonchenanlage*]

triapsidal church — trimmer plank (unit)

~ **church** · Dreiapsidenkirche f, Dreiapsidenanlage f

triaxial test [*A test in which a specimen is subjected simultaneously to lateral and axial loads*] · Dreiachsenversuch m, Triaxialversuch, Dreiaxialversuch

tribune, gallery [*misnomer: triforium*] · Empore f [*Breiter innerer Laufgang über den Seitenschiffen oder an einer Stirnwand einer Kirche*]

~ [*A gallery in a church*] · Tribüne f

~ [*A raised platform or rostrum*] · Tribüne f

~ [*The apse of a basilica or basilica church*] · Tribuna f

~ · Tribüne f, Empore f

~ **column**, gallery ~ · Emporensäule f

~ **(ground-)plan**, gallery ~ · Emporengrundriß m

~ **niche**, gallery ~ · Emporennische f

~ **plan**, ~ ground-~, gallery ~ · Emporengrundriß m

~ **roof**, gallery ~ · Emporendach n

~ **vault**, gallery ~ · Emporengewölbe n

~ **window**, gallery ~ · Emporenfenster n

tricalcium silicate [*A compound having the composition $3CaO \cdot SiO_2$, abbreviated C_3S, an impure form of which alite is a main constituent of portland cement*] · C_3S, Trikalziumsilikat n

trichlorethylene (solvent) · Tri(chloräthylen) n

triclinium · Triklinium n [1. *Speisezimmer des altrömischen Hauses*; 2. *Speiseraum der Pilger im Kloster*]

triconch · Kleeblattchor m, Trikonchos m, Trichorum n, Dreikonchenchor, Dreimuschelchor

~ **choir**, ~ quire · Trikonchos m, Trichorum n, Dreikonchenchor, Dreimuschelchor

~ **church** · Dreikonchenkirche f, Dreikonchenanlage f [*Kreuzförmige Basilika, deren halbrund geschlossene Querhausarme in Grund- und Aufriß dem Chorteil entsprechen, so daß sich die Gestalt eines regelmäßigen Kleeblattes ergibt, die von der Vierung aus den Eindruck eines Zentralraums erweckt, dem sich nach Westen ein Langhaus anschließt*]

~ **ground(-))plan** · Dreikonchengrundriß m

~ **quire**, ~ choir · Trikonchos m, Trichorum n, Dreikonchenchor, Dreimuschelchor

tricresyl phosphate · Trikresylphosphat n

tridymite · Tridymit m [*Allotrope Modifikation der Kieselsäure*]

trifora [*Of Byzantine origin, it became employed to carry the inner face of the wall of the clearstory of the twelfth-century cathedral, the centre arch being raised to increase the light from the window beyond. It gave its name to the triforium, today wrongly applied to the gallery arcade below*] · Triforium n, Dreibogenöffnung f

~ **arch** · Triforiumbogen m

triforium [*misnomer*] → tribune

~ → ~ gallery

~ **arcade** → ~ (gallery)

~ **arch** · Triforiumbogen m

~ **(gallery)**, ~ arcade · Laufgang m, Dreibogenöffnung f, Triforium n [*Schmale Galerie im Inneren einer Kirche bei gruppenweiser Zusammenfassung der Öffnungen mit Lichtgaden (= offenes Triforium) oder ohne Lichtgaden (= blindes Triforium, Blendtriforium)*]

~ **tracery** · Triforiummaßwerk n

~ **wall with passage; blind-story** ~ ~ ~ (Brit.); **blind-story** ~ ~ ~ (US) · echtes Triforium n [*Zwischen den Arkaden und der Wand befindet sich ein Laufgang*]

~ **window** · Triforiumfenster n

triglyceride · Triglycerid n

~ **fatty acid** · Triglyceridfettsäure f

triglyph, thrice-cut; channelled block (Brit.) [*In architecture, a block applied on the Doric frieze and carved with two full glyphs and two half glyphs. It is the most striking characteristic of the Doric order*] · Triglyph(e) m, (f), Dreischlitz m

~ **frieze**, frieze of the Greek Doric Order · Dreischlitzfries m, Triglyphenfries

trigonometric function, circular ~ · trigonometrische Funktion f

trilithon [*Megalithic feature comprising pair of orthostats supporting lintel*] Dreistein m, Trilith m

to trim, to frame · (aus)wechseln [*Balken(träger)*]

trim → construction(al) shape

~, **offcuts, ends** [*Short pieces trimmed from round or rough-sawn timber when cutting them to length*] · Sparrholz n, Ablängreste fpl, kleines Bauholz

~ [*Accessories fixed to a wall or partition, such as skirtings, dado rails, picture rails, architraves, etc.*] · Wandzubehör n

~, **fixtures, built-in units, in-built units** · Einbauteile mpl, npl im Bauwesen, Einbauten fpl ~ ~

trim-edge Einfassungskante f

trim fabricator → shape maker

~ **for interior work** → profile ~ ~ ~

~ **maker** → shape ~

trimmed hedge · beschnittene Hecke f

trimmer [*A beam at the side of an opening and carrying one end of a header*] · Streichbalken m [*Auswechs(e)lung*]

~ **(beam)** · Wechsel(balken) m, Streichbalken

~ **plank (unit)** · Streichdiele f [*Auswechs(e)lung*]

trimming, joining · Abbinden n, Abbund m, Abbindung f [Abreißen, Zuschneiden, Ablängen und sonstiges Bearbeiten von Bauhölzern an Hand zeichnerischer Unterlagen]

~, framing · (Balken(träger))(Aus-)Wechseln n [DIN 104]

~, framing · Balken(träger)(aus)wechseln n [DIN 104]

~ · Beschneiden n [Zuschneiden von Tapeten, Folien usw.]

~ **shop,** ~ work~, joining ~ · Abbundhalle f [Zimmereibetrieb]

~ **(work)shop,** joining ~ · Abbundhalle f [Zimmereibetrieb]

~ **yard,** joining ~ · Abbindeplatz m, Abbundplatz [Zimmerei]

Trinidad asphalt, T asph (US); Trinidad (asphaltic-)bitumen (Brit.) · Trinidadbitumen n

~ **épuré,** ~ refined asphalt, parianite · gereinigter Trinidad-Asphalt m, Trinidad-Epuré n

~ **Lake asphalt,** crude ~ ~ ~ · Trinidad-(Roh)Asphalt m

~ **refined asphalt,** ~ épuré, parianite · gereinigter Trinidad-Asphalt m, Trinidad-Epuré n

tripartite · dreiteilig

~ **arch,** triple ~ · Drillingsbogen m

~ **presbytery,** triple ~ · dreiteiliges Presbyterium n, Dreizellenraum m

~ **stair(case),** triple ~ · Drillingstreppe f, dreigeteilte Treppe

~ **window,** triple ~, three-light ~, triplet · Drillingsfenster n [Ein durch zwei Mittelsäulen oder -pfeiler unterteiltes Fenster oder drei Fenster, die durch einen übergreifenden Bogen, Blendbogen oder Entlastungsbogen zusammengeschlossen sind]

triple arch, tripartite ~ · Drillingsbogen m

triple-arched · dreibogig

triple corrugated (sheet) iron · Dreifachwellblech n, Tripelwellblech

~ **cross,** Papal ~ · päpstliches Kreuz n, dreifaches ~

triple-flight stair(case), three-flight ~ · dreiläufige Treppe f

triple-glazing · Dreifach(isolier)verglasung f, Dreifach(isolier)einglasung [Ergebnis des Verglasens]

~ · Dreifachverglasen n, Dreifacheinglasen [als Vorgang]

triple-hinged, triple-pinned, three-hinged, three-pinned · dreigelenkig

triple-hinge(d) arch(ed girder) → three-hinge(d) ~ (~)

~ **arch-ribbed dome,** ~ ~ cupola, triple-pin(ned) ~ ~, three-hinge(d) ~ ~, three-pin(ned) ~ ~ · Dreigelenk-Rippenkuppel f

~ **frame,** triple-pin(ned) ~, three-hinge(d) ~, three-pin(ned) ~, frame with three hinges · Dreigelenkrahmen m

~ **half frame,** triple-pin(ned) ~ ~, three-hinge(d) ~ ~, three-pin(ned) ~ ~ · Dreigelenkhalbrahmen m

~ **portal frame,** triple-pin(ned) ~ ~, three-hinge(d) ~ ~, three-pin(ned) ~ ~ · Dreigelenkportalrahmen m

~ **rectangular frame,** triple-pin(ned) ~ ~, three-hinge(d) ~ ~, three-pin(ned) ~ ~, rectangular frame with three hinges · Dreigelenkrechteckrahmen m

~ **roof,** triple-pin(ned) ~, three-hinge(d) ~, three-pin(ned) ~ · Dreigelenkdach n

~ **steel arch,** triple-pin(ned) ~ ~, three-hinge(d) ~ ~, three-pin(ned) ~ ~ · Stahl-Dreigelenkbogen m

~ **trussed arch(ed girder),** triple-pin(ned) ~ ~ (~), three-hinge(d) ~ ~ (~), three-pin(ned) ~ ~ (~) · Dreigelenk-Fachwerkbogen(träger) m

~ **truss(ed) frame,** triple-pin(ned) ~ ~, three-hinge(d) ~ ~, three-pin(ned) ~ ~ · Dreigelenkfachwerkrahmen m

triple-hung sash window · Dreifach-Senkrecht-Schiebe(flügel)fenster n, Dreifach-Vertikal-Schiebe(flügel)fenster

triple lancet (window) · Dreifach-Lanzettfenster n

triple-pinned, triple-hinged, thre-pinned, three-hinged · dreigelenkig

triple-pin(ned) arch(ed girder) → three-hinge(d) ~ (~)

~ **arch-ribbed dome,** ~ ~ cupola, triple-hinge(d) ~ ~, three-pin(ned) ~ ~, three-hinge(d) ~ ~ ~ · Dreigelenk-Rippenkuppel f

~ **frame,** triple-hinge(d) ~, three-hinge(d) ~, three-pin(ned) ~, frame with three hinges · Dreigelenkrahmen m

~ **half frame,** triple-hinge(d) ~ ~, three-hinge(d) ~ ~, three-pin(ned) ~ ~ · Dreigelenkhalbrahmen m

~ **portal frame,** triple-hinge(d) ~ ~, three-hinge(d) ~ ~, three-pin(ned) ~ ~ · Dreigelenkportalrahmen m

~ **rectangular frame,** triple-hinge(d) ~ ~, three-hinge(d) ~ ~, three-pin(ned) ~ ~, rectangular frame with three hinges · Dreigelenkrechteckrahmen m

~ **roof,** triple-hinge(d) ~, three-hinge(d) ~, three-pin(ned) ~ · Dreigelenkdach n

~ **steel arch,** triple-hinge(d) ~ ~, three-hinge(d) ~ ~, three-pin(ned) ~ ~ · Stahl-Dreigelenkbogen m

~ **trussed arch(ed girder),** triple-hinge(d) ~ ~ (~), three-hinge(d) ~ ~ (~), three-pin(ned) ~ ~ (~) · Dreigelenk-Fachwerkbogen(träger) m

~ **truss(ed) frame,** triple-hinge(d) ~ ~, three-hinge(d) ~ ~, three-pin(ned) ~ ~ · Dreigelenkfachwerkrahmen m

triple-pole fuse · dreipolige Sicherung f

~ **on-off switch** · dreipoliger Ausschalter m

triple-roll mill, three-roll ~ · Dreiwalzenwerk n [Mahlen in der Lackindustrie]

triple stair(case), tripartite ~ · Drillingstreppe *f*, dreigeteilte Treppe

triple-unit · dreiläng ig [*Schienenleuchte*]

triple window, tripartite ~ · dreiteiliges Fenster *n*

triplet · Dreieinigkeitsfenster *n*

tripoli · Triepel(erde) *m*, (*f*), Polierschiefer *m*

Tripoli-powder→ kieselguhr

~ brick, kieselguhr ~, diatomaceous earth ~ · Kieselgurziegel *m*; Kieselgurstein *m* [*Fehlname*] [*Er wird aus Kieselgur, Ton und Ausbrennstoff durch Brennen hergestellt*]

~ concrete, kieselguhr ~ · Kieselgurbeton *m*

~ covering cord, kieselguhr ~ ~ · Kieselgurschnur *f* [*für Dämm- und Isolierzwecke*]

~ slab, kieselguhr ~ · Kieselgurplatte *f*

triptych, folding ~, threefold altarpiece · Triptychon *n*, Flügelaltarschrein *m*, dreiteiliger Klappaltar *m*

tristyle · dreisäulig

triumphal arch, monumental ~, arch of triumph · Triumphbogen *m*, Monumentalbogen

~ column, column of triumph, pillar of victory, victory pillar · Triumphsäule *f*, Doppelsäule, Siegessäule, gekuppelte Säule

~ gate(way), gate(way) of triumph · Triumphtor *n*

trochilus, scotia [*The small concave mo(u)lding between the two tori in the base of a column, throwing a deep shadow*] · Skotie *f*, Trochilos *m*, Hohlkehle *f* [*Nicht zu verwechseln mit der Hohlkehle als Bekrönungselement*]

troctolite · Forellenstein *m*

trolley · Laufrolle *f* [*Schiebetor*]

(~) track, overhead ~ · Laufschiene *f* [*Tor*]

trophy case · Trophäenvitrine *f*

tropical hospital · Tropenkrankenhaus *n*

tropicalized packing · tropenfeste Verpackung *f*

trough · Trog *m*

~ plate · Belageisen *n*, Belagstahl *m*, Zoreseisen, Trogplatte *f* [*DIN 1023*]

~ section, troughing · trogförmiger Formstahl *m*, Rinnenstahl

~-shaped · muldenförmig

trough slab → concrete ~ ~

~ vault · Muldengewölbe *n* [*Tonnengewölbe mit durch Wangen geschlossenen Schmalseiten*]

trough(ed) block, ~ tile [*See remark under 'Block'*] · Muldenblock(stein) *m*, Muldenstein

~ profile · Muldenprofil *n*

~ roof cladding, ~ ~ cover(ing), ~ ~ sheathing, ~ roofing · Trapezprofilbedachung *f*, Trapezprofildach(belag) *n*, (*m*), Trapezprofildach(ein)deckung, Trapezprofil(ein)deckung

~ steel roof covering · Stahltrapezblechdach(belag) *n*, (*m*)

~ tile → ~ block

troughing, trough section · trogförmiger Formstahl *m*, Rinnenstahl

trowel application · Verspachteln *n*

trowel-applied (seamless) floor(ing) material, ~ (~) ~ composition, ~ (~) ~ compound · (Fuß)Bodenspachtel(masse) *m*, (*f*)

~ two part (synthetic) resin (based) (seamless) flooring system · Zweikomponenten-(Fuß)Bodenspachtel-(masse) *m*, (*f*)

~ coat · Kellenlage *f*, Kellenschicht *f*

~ finish(ing) · Kellenglattstrich *m*

to trowel off · abreiben mit Kelle

trowel trades hydrated lime · Baukalkhydrat *n*

~ ~ lime, building ~, construction ~, structural ~, mason's ~, finish ~ [*B.S. 890*] · Baukalk *m* [*DIN 1060*]

trowelable (US); trowellable (Brit.) · kellen(ge)recht [*Mörtel oder Putz sind kellen(ge)recht wenn sie ohne zu kleben gut von der Kelle fließen*]

trowelling (Brit.); troweling (US) [*Smoothing with a trowel*] · Kellenglattstreichen *n*

trowel(l)ing consistency · Kellenkonsistenz *f*

truck(ing) terminal (US); lorry ~ (Brit.) · Fernlaster-Bahnhof *m*, LKW-Bahnhof

true annealed sheet, full ~ ~ · Feinblech *n* [*über A_3 hinaus gebeizt*]

~ copal, hard ~, fossil ~ · Hartkopal(harz) *m*, (*n*), fossiler Kopal, fossiles Kopalharz

~ diorite, quartz-free ~ · quarzfreier Diorit *m*

~ porosity, total ~ · Undichtigkeitsgrad *m*, Undichtheitsgrad, Durchlässigkeitsgrad, wahre Porosität *f*, Gesamtporosität

~ porphyry, quartz-free ~ · quarzfreier Porphyr *m*

~ pyramid, geometrically ~ ~ [*As opposed to the step pyramid*] · eigentliche Pyramide *f* [*Im Gegensatz zur Stufenpyramide*]

~ solution · echte Lösung *f*

~ solvent · echtes Lösungsmittel *n*

~ undersize recovery, fines output · Fein(korn)ausbringen *n*, Unterkornausbringen [*Siebdurchgang, Fehlkorn abgerechnet*]

~ vault · echtes Gewölbe *n*

~ vaulting · echte Wölbung *f* [*Die Steine sind zwischen festen Widerlagern eingespannt und das Gewölbe ist vorwiegend druckbeansprucht*]

trueing — tubing frame

trueing · Vorschleifen n [Glas]
trueness · Haltigkeit f
~ of shape, ~ ~ form · Form(en)haltigkeit f
trumeau [A French term designating a vertical stone member or mullion supporting the tympanum of a doorway] · Trumeau m, Pfeilerspiegel m
truncated cone, frustum of a ~ · Kegelstumpf m
~ octahedron · entecktes Oktaeder n
~ pyramid, frustum of a ~ · Pyramidenstumpf m, Spitzsäulenstumpf, abgestumpfte Pyramide f
~ roof, terrace ~, cut ~, platform ~ [A pitched roof terminated by a flat roof, thus having no ridge] · abgestumpftes Dach n
~ tetrahedron · entecktes Tetraeder n
trunk elevator, freight ~, goods ~ (US); ~ lift (Brit.) · Lastenaufzug m, Materialaufzug
~ lift, freight ~, goods ~ (Brit.); ~ elevator (US) · Lastenaufzug m, Materialaufzug
truss, console, ancon(e) [A scrolled bracket] · Konsole f
~· Fachwerk n
~, roof ~ · (Dach)Binder m
~ bar, ~ rod, ~ member · Fachwerkstab m
~ cupola, ~ dome, trussed ~ · Fachwerkkuppel f
~ dome, ~ cupola, trussed ~ · Fachwerkkuppel f
~ joint · Fachwerkknoten(punkt) m
~ member, ~ rod, ~ bar · Fachwerkstab m
~ rod, ~ member, ~ bar · Fachwerkstab m
~ structure, ~ system · Fachwerkkonstruktion f
~ system, ~ structure · Fachwerkkonstruktion f
~ theory · Fachwerktheorie f
~ without diagonal members, ~ ~ sloping ~ [It does not satisfy the definition of a truss but is given that designation] · strebenloser Fachwerkträger m
~ ~ sloping members, ~ ~ diagonal ~ [It does not satisfy the definition of a truss but is given that designation] · strebenloser Fachwerkträger m
trussed arch(ed girder) · Fachwerkbogen(träger) m, gekrümmter Fachwerkträger, gekrümmtes Fachwerk n
~ beam, inverted king (post) truss [Is used for short spans in connection with wood construction] · umgekehrtes einsäuliges Hängewerk n, ~ einfaches ~, umgekehrter einfacher Hängebock m, umgekehrter einsäuliger Hängebock
~ ~ → single-strut ~ ~
~ ~ → inverted queen (post) truss

~ ~ with diagonals and suspenders · Träger m mit Sprengwerk und Hängestäben
truss(ed) column · Fachwerkstütze f
~ cupola, ~ dome · Fachwerkkuppel f
~ dome, ~ cupola · Fachwerkkuppel f
~ frame · Fachwerkrahmen m
truss(ed) girder · Fachwerk(träger) n, (m) [Nach Art des Fachwerkes konstruiertes Tragwerk, bei dem gerade Stäbe im Dreiecksverband verbunden sind]
(truss(ed) joint)) panel point, panel point of a truss(ed girder) · Fachwerk(träger)-Knoten(punkt)m
truss(ed) partition (wall), frame(d) ~ (~) [A partition (wall) built up on its own frame of timber or less commonly of other material such as reinforced concrete or metal] · Riegeltrennwand f, Fachwerktrennwand
~ roof · Binderdach n
T-steel dowel → T(ee)-steel ~
tub → bath~
~ lead trap, bath(tub) ~ ~ · Blei-Badewannen-Geruchverschluß m
tube, tubing · Rohrprofil n
~· Röhre f
~ · kreisförmige Aussparung f [Mehrlochplatte]
~ connector, ~ connecter · Rohrdübel m [Metallrohr-Holzverbinder, der ähnlich wie Schraubenbolzen in die zu verbindenden Hölzer eingebaut wird]
~ floor · Hohlbalkendecke f mit kreisförmigen Aussparungen
~ ~ slab · Hohlbalken-Deckenelement n mit kreisförmigen Aussparungen, Viellochplatte f, Mehrlochplatte
~ frame, pipe ~, tubular ~, barrel ~, tubing ~ · Rohrrahmen m
~ handrail, tubing ~, tubular ~, pipe ~, barrel ~ · Rohrhandlauf m
tube-line tile · Bild(belag)platte f mit Schablonenmalerei, Bildfliese f ~ ~
tube mast, pipe ~, tubular ~, barrel ~, tubing ~ · Rohrmast m
tube-mounted ceiling · rohrmontierte Decke f
tube newel, tubing ~, barrel ~, pipe ~, tubular ~ · (Treppen)Rohrspindel f
~ purlin(e), tubular ~, pipe ~, barrel ~, tubing ~ · (Dach)Rohrpfette f
~ railing, barrel ~, tubing ~, pipe ~ · Rohrgeländer n
~ ~ fitting, barrel ~ ~, tubing ~ ~, pipe ~ ~, tubular ~ ~ · (Rohr)Geländerfitting m, (Rohr)Geländerformstück n
~ skeleton, tubular ~, pipe ~, barrel ~, tubing ~ · Rohrgerippe n, Rohrskelett n
tubing, tube · Rohrprofil n
~ frame, tube ~, barrel ~, tubular ~, pipe ~ · Rohrrahmen m

tubing handrail — Tudor arch

~ **handrail,** tubular ~, tube ~, pipe ~, barrel ~ · Rohrhandlauf *m*

~ **mast,** tubular ~, pipe ~, tube ~, barrel ~ · Rohrmast *m*

~ **newel,** barrel ~, tube ~, tubular ~, pipe ~ · (Treppen)Rohrspindel *f*

~ **purlin(e),** tubular ~, tube ~, pipe ~, barrel ~ · (Dach)Rohrpfette *f*

~ **railing,** tube ~, barrel ~, pipe ~ · Rohrgeländer *n*

~ ~ **fitting,** tube ~ ~, tubular ~ ~, barrel ~ ~, pipe ~ ~ · (Rohr)Geländerfitting *m*, (Rohr)Geländerformstück *n*

~ **skeleton,** tubular ~, barrel ~, pipe ~, tube ~ · Rohrgerippe *n*, Rohrskelett *n*

tub/shower installation, bath~ ~ · (Bade)Wannenfüll- und Duschbatterie *f*

tubular bearing structure → ~ load~

~ **case** → ~ **lock** ~

~ **column,** pipe ~ · Rohrstütze *f*

~ **conduits on the surface,** surface-mounted installation · Aufputz-Installation *f* [*Elektroinstallation*]

~ **construction,** ~ (structure) system · Rohr-Bausystem *n* Rohrkonstruktion(ssystem) *f*, (*n*)

~ **extract ventilation unit,** ~ extraction unit, ~ extractor, ~ ventilator · Rohr(ent)lüfter *m* [*auf einem Dach*]

~ **extraction unit,** ~ extract ventilation unit, ~ extractor, ~ ventilator · Rohr(ent)lüfter *m* [*auf einem Dach*]

~ **extractor,** ~ ventilator, ~ extraction unit, ~ extract ventilation unit · Rohr(ent)lüfter *m* [*auf einem Dach*]

~ **frame,** barrel ~, tube ~, tubing ~, pipe ~ · Rohrrahmen *m*

~ **grip handle,** swing door ~ ~ ~ · Rohrgriff *m*, Pendeltür-~, Pendeltürgriff aus Rundrohr

~ **handrail,** tubing ~, tube ~, pipe ~, barrel ~ · Rohrhandlauf *m*

~ **heater,** electric ~ ~ · (elektrischer) Rohrheizkörper *m*

~ **intermediate column,** intermediate tubular ~ · Rohrzwischenstütze *f*

~ **lamp** [*B.S. 1853*] · Röhrenlampe *f*, Soffittenlampe

~ **lattice(d) mast** · Rohrgittermast *m*

~ **(load)bearing structure,** ~ (weight-carrying) ~ · Rohrtragwerk *n* [*z.B. für Krane und Kranbahnen*]

~ **lock** · Rohrrahmenschloß *n*

~ **(~) case** · Rohr(schloß)kasten *m*

~ **mast,** tube ~, pipe ~, barrel ~, tubing ~ · Rohrmast *m*

~ **metal construction** · Metallrohrkonstruktion *f*

~ **newel,** tube ~, tubing ~, barrel ~, pipe ~ · (Treppen)Rohrspindel *f*

~ **particle board,** ~ chipboard, board with tubular holes [*Particle board, usually extruded, having a series of holes running lengthwise through it*] · Röhren(span)platte *f*

~ ~ **chipboard,** ~ board, board with tubular holes [*Particle board, usually extruded, having a series of holes running lengthwise through it*] · Röhren(span)platte *f*

~ **product** · röhrenförmiger Artikel *m*, röhrenförmiges Erzeugnis *n*

~ **purlin(e),** tube ~, pipe ~, barrel ~, tubing ~ · (Dach)Rohrpfette *f*

~ **railing fitting,** tubing ~ ~, tube ~ ~, pipe ~ ~, barrel ~ ~ · (Rohr)Geländerfitting *m*, (Rohr)Geländerformstück *n*

~ **scaffold(ing)** · (Stahl)Rohrgerüst *n*, (Stahl)Rohrrüstung *f*, Stahlgerüst, Stahlrüstung

tubular-shaped house · Röhrenhaus *n*

tubular skeleton, barrel ~, pipe ~, tube ~, tubing ~ · Rohrgerippe *n*, Rohrskelett *n*

~ **steel column,** steel pipe ~, steel tube ~ · Stahlrohrstütze *f*

~ ~ **construction** · Stahlrohrbau *m* [*DIN 4115*]

~ ~ **frame,** steel tubular ~ · Stahlrohrrahmen *m*

~ ~ **ladder** · Stahlrohrleiter *f*

~ ~ **(lighting) column with bracket** (Brit.); ~ ~ (~) mast with arm (US) · Stahlrohr-Ausleger(licht)mast *m*, Stahlrohr-Auslegerbeleuchtungsmast, Stahlrohr-Auslegerleuchtenmast

~ ~ **(~) mast with arm** (US); ~ ~ (~) column with bracket (Brit.) · Stahlrohr-Ausleger(licht)mast *m*, Stahlrohr-Auslegerbeleuchtungsmast, Stahlrohr-Auslegerleuchtenmast

~ ~ **mast** · Stahlrohrmast *m*

~ ~ **purlin(e)** · Stahlrohrpfette *f*

~ ~ **string,** steel pipe ~ (Brit.); ~ ~ stringer (US) · Stahlrohr(treppen)wange *f*

~ ~ **system** · Stahlrohrkonstruktion *f*

~ ~ **tower** · (Stahl)Gerüstturm *m*

~ ~ **window** · Stahlrohrfenster *n*

~ **structure** → ~ loadbearing ~

~ **(~) system,** ~ construction · Rohr-Bausystem *n*, Rohrkonstruktion(ssystem) *f*, (*n*)

~ **system** → ~ construction

~ **ventilator,** ~ extractor, ~ extraction unit, ~ extract ventilation unit · Rohr(ent)lüfter *m* [*auf einem Dach*]

~ **(weight-carrying) structure,** ~ (load)bearing ~ · Rohrtragwerk *n* [*z.B. für Krane und Kranbahnen*]

Tuchscherer connector, Voss ~ · Tuchscherer-Ringdübel *m*

Tudor arch, four-centred ~ ~ (Brit.); (four-centered) ~ ~ (US) · Tudorbogen *m*, Vier-Zentren-Bogen [*Ein gedrückter Spitzbogen mit geschweiften Schenkeln, aus vier Mittelpunkten konstruiert*]

~ architecture [*It covers the period from 1500 to 1600 in England and thus includes Elizabethan architecture*] · Tudorarchitektur f, Tudorbaukunst f
~ ceiling · Tudordecke f
~ flower → ~ leaf
~ leaf, ~ flower [*A conventional(ized) leaf form, much used as an ornament, especially in rows as a cresting to screens in churches*] · Tudorblatt n, Tudorblume f
~ ornament · Tudorornament n
~ rose [*A conventional(ized) rose much used in Tudor architecture, not to be confused with the Tudor flower*] · Tudorrose f
~ (style) · Tudorstil m [1485–1603]
~ window · Tudorfenster n
tufa → tufaceous limestone
tufaceous limestone, (cal(careous)) tufa, calc tufa [*A porous calcareous deposit sometimes formed near limerich springs*] · Kalktuff m, Tuffkalk m [*Mundartliche Bezeichnungen: Duckstein m, D(a)uchstein*]
tuff, volcanic ~ · (vulkanisches) Tuffgestein n, (vulkanischer) Tuff(stein) m, Feuerbergtuff, Durchbruchsgesteintuff, Duftstein
tufted carpet · Tuftingteppich m
tumbler, lever (~) · Zuhaltung f [*Schloß*]
~ bearing, pendulum ~ · Pendellager n
tumblerholder · (Mund)Becherhalter m
tumbler lock, lever(-tumbler) ~ · Zuhaltungsschloß n
~ switch · Kippschalter m
tumbling → rumbling
tumulus, funerary mound, burial mound · Grabhügel m
tung oil → (raw) (China) wood ~
~ ~ stand oil, (Chian) wood ~ ~ · Holzöl-Standöl n, Tungöl-Standöl
~ ~ varnish, (China) wood ~ ~ · Tungöllack m
~ seed · Tungbaumsamen m
~ stand oil, (China) wood ~ ~ · Holzstandöl n, Tungstandöl
tungsten carbide · Hartmetall n, Wolframkarbid n
~ filament lamp [*B.S. 232*] · Wolframdrahtlampe f
tunnel clinker · Tunnel(bau)klinker m
~ curing kiln · (Beton)Nachbehandlungstunnelofen m
~ kiln · Tunnelofen m
~ ~ plant · Tunnelofenanlage f
~ roof → tunnel-(vault(ed)) ~
~ vault, barrel ~, wagon(head) ~ · Tonne(ngewölbe) f, (n) [*Gewölbeform mit längs einer Achse gleichbleibendem viertelkreis-, halbkreis-, segmentbogen- oder spitzbogenförmigem Querschnitt*]
tunnel-vaulted, barrel-vaulted, wagon-vaulted, wagon-headed · tonnengewölbt

tunnel-(vault(ed)) roof, barrel-(vault(ed)) ~, wagon-(vault(ed)) ~ · Tonnen(gewölbe)dach n
turbidimeter · Trübungsmesser m
turbidity · Trübung f
~ coefficient, coefficient of turbidity · Trübungsbeiwert m
turbine hall · Turbinenhalle f
turf (grand)stand, race-track ~, race-course ~ · Pferderennbahntribüne f, Rennplatztribüne
(turfing by) sodding, planting sod(s) · Ansoden n, Rasenrasendeckung f
Turkey red · Türkischrot n
Turkish architecture · türkische Architektur f, ~ Baukunst f
~ minaret · türkisches Minarett n
~ (type) mosque · türkische Moschee f
to turn · verputzen [*Steinzeugrohrindustrie*]
~ ~ · verschwenken [*Bewehrungseisen*]
~ ~, to balance · verziehen [*Stufe*]
~ ~ down, to tip down(wards), to fold down(wards) · umlegen nach unten, abkanten ~ ~
~ ~ grey, ~ ~ gray · grau werden
turn branch switch, rotary ~ ~ · Drehschalter m
turnbuckle · Spannschloß n
~ · Bandeisenschloß n [*abgehängte Strahlungsheizungsdecke*]
turndown · Abkantung f nach unten
turned bolt, finished ~ · blanke Schraube f
turning mat(t), becoming ~ · Vermatten n [*Anstrich*]
turnings, filings · Feilspäne mpl
turn-key · ausbaufertig, schlüsselfertig [*Der Bauzustand nach Fertigstellung des Ausbaues*]
~ building (construction) · schlüsselfertiges Bauen n, schlüsselfertiger Hochbau m
~ cost(s) estimate · schlüsselfertiger Voranschlag m
~ handover · schlüsselfertige Übergabe f, ausbaufertige ~
~ housing (construction) · schlüsselfertiger Wohnungsbau m, ausbaufertiger ~
~ (type of) contract · Entwurf- und Bauauftrag m
turn-up → upstand
turpentine → pure ~
~ medium, ~ vehicle · Terpentin-Bindemittellösung f [*Anstrichfarbe*]
~ stain · Terpentinbeize f
~ substitute [*deprecated*]; mineral turpentine [*Australia*]; white spirit, mineral solvent for paints [*The most commonly used thinner for paints and varnishes*] · Testbenzin n, Lackbenzin, künstliches Terpentinöl n, Kristallöl [*Fehlname: Terpentin(öl)ersatz m*]

turpentine vehicle — twin-pack etching primer

~ vehicle, ~ medium · Terpentin-Bindemittellösung f [Anstrichfarbe]
turret → decorative ~
turreted tower · Turm m mit Türmchenaufbau
turret-like · türmchenähnlich
Tuscan arch, Florentine ~ · Sichelbogen m; Florentiner Bogen, toskanischer Bogen, Sieneser Bogen [seit der Renaissance]
~ base → ~ column ~
~ capital · toskanisches Kapitell n, ~ Kapitäl
~ column · toskanische Säule f
~ (~) base · toskanischer (Säulen)Fuß m
~ order · toskanische (Säulen)Ordnung f, tusk(an)ische ~
tusk tenon · Brustzapfen m
Tussah (wild) silk · Tussahseide f
T.V. aerial, television ~ · Fernsehantenne f
T.V. building, television ~ · Fernsehgebäude n
TV cheque monitoring system · Telescheckanlage f
T.V. room, television ~ · Fernsehraum m
T.V. studio, television ~ · Fernsehstudio n
T.V. torch → ~ ~ tower
T.V. tower, ~ ~ torch, television ~ · Fernseh(sende)turm m
twelve-bay · zwölfjochig
twelve-wire · zwölfdrähtig [(Vor)Spannlitze]
~ jack · Spannpresse f für 12 Drähte
28 day cube compression strength, ~ ~ (crushing) ~ · 28-Tage-Würfel-(druck)festigkeit f
twenty-sided polygon · zwanzigseitiges Vieleck n
twice crushed and screened chip(ping)s, double broken and double ~ ~ · Edelsplitt m
twice-pressed brick, double pressed ~ · Doppelpreßziegel m
twilled double warp · geschränktes Köpergewebe n
~ herringbone weave · Spitzköper m [Siebtechnik]
~ weave · Köpergewebe n
twin-bedded room · Breitzimmer n, Breitraum m [Hotel. Die Betten liegen durch Nachttische getrennt parallel zueinander]
twin bowls · Doppelbecken n
twin-box girder, double-box ~ · Doppelkastenträger m
twin brick, double-sized ~ · Doppelformatziegel m
~ cable, duplex ~ · doppeladriges Kabel n, paarverseiltes ~

~ cantilever shell, double ~ ~, butterfly ~ ~ · Doppelauslegerschale f, Doppelkragschale
~ chime unit, double ~ ~, dual ~ ~ · Doppel(ton)-Läutewerk n
~ columns, paired ~, pair of ~ · Säulenpaar n
twin-component methacrylate compound → two-component ~ ~
twin cross-section, dual ~, double ~ · zweiteiliger Querschnitt m, doppelter ~
~ dishwashing sink bowls · Doppelspül(ausguß)becken n
~ elbow → ~ pipe ~
~ girder, dual ~, double ~ · Zwillingsträger m
twingrip · Doppel(-Hand)griff m
~ bath(tub), ~ tub · Doppel(-Hand)-griff-Badewanne f
twin ground plate (glass) · Twinglas n
~ house; double ~ [A pair of semi-detached houses] · Doppelhaus n
~ mould (Brit.); ~ mold (US); double ~, dual ~ · Zwillingsform f, Doppelform
~ northlight frame, ~ saw-tooth ~ · Doppelshedrahmen m
~ pack, double ~ · Doppelpaket n
twin-pack adhesive → ~ bonding ~
~ (bonding) adhesive, two-pack (~) ~, two-part (~) ~, two-component (~) ~, ~ ~ agent, ~ ~ medium, ~ cement(ing) agent) · Zweikomponenten-Kleb(e)stoff m, Zweikomponenten-Kleb(e)mittel n, Zweikomponentenkleber m
~ ~ agent, two-pack ~ ~, two-part ~ ~, two-component ~ ~, ~ ~ medium, ~ (~) adhesive, ~ cement(ing) agent) · Zweikomponenten-Kleb(e)stoff m, Zweikomponenten-Kleb(e)mittel n, Zweikomponentenkleber m
~ ~ medium, two-pack ~ ~, two-part ~ ~, two-component ~ ~, ~ ~ agent, ~ (~) adhesive, ~ cement(ing) agent) · Zweikomponenten-Kleb(e)stoff m, Zweikomponenten-Kleb(e)mittel n, Zweikomponentenkleber m
~ cement(ing agent), two-pack ~ (~), two-part ~ (~), two-component ~ (~), ~ bonding agent, ~ bonding medium, ~ (bonding) adhesive · Zweikomponenten-Kleb(e)stoff m, Zweikomponenten-Kleb(e)mittel n, Zweikomponentenkleber m
~ coating composition, ~ ~ compound, two-pack ~ ~, two-part ~ ~, two-component ~ ~ · Zweikomponenten-Beschichtungsmasse f
~ ~ compound, ~ ~ composition, two-pack ~ ~, two-part ~ ~, two-component ~ ~ · Zweikomponenten-Beschichtungsmasse f
~ etching primer, two-pack ~ ~, two-part ~ ~, two-component ~ ~, wash ~, ~ petreatment ~, ~ self etch ~ · Zweikomponenten-Aktivgrund m, Zweikomponenten-Haftgrund(ier)mittel n, Zweikomponenten-Haftgrund(ierung) m, (f)

twin-pack expansion... — twisted-steel sheet 1060

~ **expansion joint mastic (sealer),** two-pack ~ ~ ~ ~ (~), two-part ~ ~ ~ (~), two-component ~ ~ ~ (~) · Zweikomponenten-Dehnungsfugenkitt m, Zweikomponenten-Raumfugenkitt

~ **liquid,** two-pack ~, two-part ~, two-component ~ · Zweikomponenten-Flüssigkeit f

~ **mastic,** two-pack ~, two-part ~, two-component ~ · Zweikomponentenkitt m

~ **methacrylate compound** → two-component ~ ~

~ **paint,** two-pack ~, two-part ~, two-component ~ · Zweikomponenten-(Anstrich)farbe f

~ **polyester adhesive,** two-pack ~ ~, two-part ~ ~, two-component ~ ~, ~ ~ bonding agent ~ ~ bonding medium ~ ~ cement(ing agent) · Zweikomponenten-Polyesterkleb(e)stoff m, Zweikomponenten-Polyesterkleb(e)mittel n, Zweikomponenten-Polyesterkleber m

~ **polysulphide(-based) cement,** ~ ~ composition, two-pack ~ ~, two-part ~ ~, two-component ~ ~ · Zweikomponenten-Polysulfidkitt m

~ **pretreatment primer,** two-pack ~ ~, two-part ~ ~, two-component ~ ~, ~ wash ~, ~ etching ~, ~ self etch ~ · Zweikomponenten-Aktivgrund m, Zweikomponenten-Haftgrund(ier)mittel m, Zweikomponenten-Haftgrund(ierung) m, (f)

~ **protective coat,** two-pack ~ ~, two-part ~ ~, two-component ~ ~ · Zweikomponenten-Schutzanstrich m, Zweikomponenten-Schutzaufstrich

~ **rubber-base compound,** two-pack ~ ~, two-part ~ ~, two-component ~ ~ [Erroneously called 'thiokol'] · Zweikomponenten-Kautschuk-(Ab)-Dicht(ungs)mittel n

~ **seal(ing) composition,** ~ ~ compound, ~ ~ material, ~ ~ mass, two-pack ~ ~, two-part ~ ~, two-component ~ ~ · Zweikomponenten-(Ab)Dicht(ungs)masse f

~ **self etch primer,** two-pack ~ ~ ~, two-part ~ ~ ~, two-component ~ ~ ~, ~ pretreatment ~, ~ etching ~, ~ wash ~ · Zweikomponenten-Aktivgrund m, Zweikomponenten-Haftgrund(ier)mittel n, Zweikomponenten-Haftgrund(ierung) m, (f)

~ **system,** two-pack ~, two-part ~, two-component ~ · Zweikomponenten-Aufbau m, Zweikomponenten-System n

~ **wash primer,** two-pack ~ ~, two-part ~ ~, two-component ~ ~, ~ etching ~, ~ pretreatment ~, ~ self etch ~ · Zweikomponenten-Aktivgrund m, Zweikomponenten-Haftgrund(ier)mittel n, Zweikomponenten-Haftgrund(ierung) m, (f)

twin-part methacrylate compound → two-component ~ ~

twin (pipe) elbow [A symmetrical branch fitting in which two opposite branches are curved through 90° to join a manin pipe] · Doppel(rohr)bogen m

~ **saw-tooth frame,** twin northlight ~ · Doppelshedrahmen m

~ **sliding window** · Doppelschiebefenster n

~ **socket** · Zweifach-Anschlußdose f, Zweifach(-Steck)dose, Doppel(steck)-dose

~ ~ **with earthing contact** · Zweifach-Schutzkontaktsteckdose f

~ **theatre,** ~ theater · Doppeltheater n

~ **timber mast,** ~ wood(en) ~ · Doppelholzmast m

twin-tower façade, double-tower ~, dual-tower ~, two-tower ~ · Doppelturmfassade f, Zweiturmfassade

twin-towered, double towered · doppeltürmig, zweitürmig

~ **gatehouse,** double towered ~ · doppeltürmige Vorburg f, zweitürmige ~

twin towers · Doppeltürme mpl, Zwillingstürme

twin-twisted round bars, ~ ~ rods · Istegstahl m

twin-webbed, two-webbed, double-webbed · zweistegig, doppelstegig

~ **plate girder,** two-webbed ~ ~, double-webbed ~ ~ · Zweistegblechträger m, Doppelstegblechträger

~ **T-beam,** two-webbed ~, double-webbed ~ · zweistegiger Plattenbalken m, doppelstegiger ~

twin wood(en) mast, ~ timber ~ · Doppelholzmast m

twinning → interlace

twist, wind, spiral distortion · Spiralverformung f

twisted · verdreht, verwunden, verdrillt

~ **bars,** ~ rods · Drillwulststahl m, Betonstahl m IIIa

~ **cable ornament** · Verstäbung f

~ **column,** wreathed ~ [A column entwined by a band which presents a twisted or spiral appearance] · gedrehte Säule f, gewundene ~, Schlangensäule

~ **fillet** · Knotenschnur f

~ **fringe,** ~ rope · gedrehtes Tau n

~ **pair** · verdrillte Doppellitze f

~ **rods,** ~ bars · Drillwulststahl m, Betonstahl IIIa

~ **rope,** ~ fringe · gedrehtes Tau n

~ ~ **frieze** · Taufries m

twisted-steel mat, ~ sheet [Factory-made reinforcing mat made from cold-twisted steel bars] · Baustahlmatte f aus Drillstahl, Bewehrungsmatte ~ ~, Armierungsmatte ~ ~, Drillstahlbaustahlmatte, Drillstahlbewehrungsmatte, Drillstahlarmierungsmatte

~ **sheet** → ~ mat

twisted straw · Stroh-Lehm-Strick *m*, Windel(puppe) *f*, Strohlehmwickel *m*

~ ~ **deafening**, ~ ~ deadening · Windel(puppen)boden *m*, Strohlehmwickelboden, Stroh-Lehm-Strickboden [*Einschub von Holzbalkendecken*]

twisted-type (concrete) (reinforcing) bars, high-bond (~) (~) ~, deformed (~) (~) ~, ~ (~) (~) rods · (Beton-)Formstahl *m*

(~) deformed (concrete) (reinforcing) bars grade IIIb · (Beton)Rippenstahl *m* der Betonstahlgruppe IIIb

(~) ~ (~) (~) ~ ~ ~ with oblique sickleshaped ribs · (Beton)Formstahl *m* der Betonstahlgüte IIIb mit schrägen sichelförmigen Rippen

(~) ~ Tor-Steel · Rippen-Torstahl *m*

twist-free → torsion-free

twisting · Drillen *n* [*Bewehrungsstahl*]

~ · Verdrehen *n*, Verwinden, Verdrillen

twist(ing), torsion · (Ver)Drillung *f*, Torsion *f*, Verdrehung, Verwindung

~ **buckling** → torsion(al) ~

~ ~ **load**, torsion(al) ~ ~ · Verdrehungsknicklast *f*, Torsionsknicklast, Verwindungsknicklast, Drill(ungs)knicklast

~ **constant**, torsion(al) ~ · Torsionskonstante *f*, Verdrehungskonstante, Verwindungskonstante, Drill(ungs)konstante

~ **degree** → degree of torsion

~ **failure**, torsion(al) ~ · Torsionsbruch *m*, Verdrehungsbruch, Verwindungsbruch, Drill(ungs)bruch

~ **instability**, torsion(al) ~ · Verdrehungslabilität *f*, Verwindungslabilität, Torsionslabilität, Drill(ungs)-Labilität

~ **modulus**, torsion(al) ~, modulus of torsion · Torsionsmodul *m*, Drill(ungs)-modul

~ **moment**, torsion(al) ~, torque ~ · Torsionsmoment *n*, Verdrehungsmoment, Verwindungsmoment, Drill(ungs)moment

~ **(of) wire**, weaving (~) ~ · Drahtweben *n*

~ **rigidity**, torsion(al) ~ · Verwindungssteifigkeit *f*, Verdrehungssteifigkeit, Drill(ungs)steifigkeit, Torsionssteifigkeit

~ **stiffness** → torsion(al) strength

~ **strength** → torsion(al) ~

~ **stress**, torsion(al) ~ · Torsionsspannung *f*, Verdrehungsspannung, Verwindungsspannung, Drill(ungs)spannung

twisting wire → ~ of ~

twist-less → torsion-free

twist modulus → twist(ing) ~

two-articulated arch(ed) frame, two-pin(ned) ~ ~, two-hinged ~ ~, two-linked ~ ~, double-pin(ned) ~ ~, double-hinge(d) ~ ~, double-linked ~ ~, double-articulated ~ ~ · Zweigelenk-Bogenrahmen *m*

~ **flat arch(ed girder)**, two-pin(ned) ~ ~ (~), two-hinge(d) ~ ~ (~), two-linked ~ ~ (~), double-pin(ned) ~ ~ (~) double-linked ~ ~ (~), double-articulated ~ ~ (~), ~ segmental ~ (~) · Zweigelenk-Flachbogen(träger) *m*, Zweigelenk-Stichbogen(träger), Zweigelenk-Segmentbogen(träger)

~ ~ **parabolic arch(ed girder)**, two-pin(ned) ~ ~ ~ (~), two-hinge(d) ~ ~ ~ (~), two-linked ~ ~ ~ (~), double-pin(ned) ~ ~ ~ (~), double-hinge(d) ~ ~ ~ (~), double-linked ~ ~ ~ (~), double-articulated ~ ~ (~) · Zweigelenkflachparabelbogen-(träger) *m*

~ **frame**, two-pin(ned) ~, two-hinge(d) ~, two-linked ~, double-pin(ned) ~, double-hinge(d) ~, double-articulated ~ · Zweigelenkrahmen *m*

~ **gable(d) frame**, two-pin(ned) ~ ~, two-hinge(d) ~ ~, two-linked ~ ~, double-pin(ned) ~ ~, double-hinge(d) ~ ~, double-linked ~ ~, double-articulated ~ ~ · Zweigelenk-Giebelrahmen *m*

~ **parabolic arch(ed girder)**, two-pin(ned) ~ ~ (~), two-hinge(d) ~ ~ (~), two-linked ~ ~ (~), double-pin(ned) ~ ~ (~), double-hinge(d) ~ ~ (~), double-linked ~ ~ (~), double-articulated ~ ~ (~) · Zweigelenkparabelbogen(träger) *m*

~ **rectangular frame**, two-pin(ned) ~ ~, two-hinge(d) ~ ~, two-linked ~ ~, double-pin(ned) ~ ~, double-hinge(d) ~ ~, double-linked ~ ~, double-articulated ~ ~ · Zweigelenk-Rechteckrahmen *m*

~ **segmental arch(ed girder)**, two-pin(ned) ~ ~ (~), two-hinge(d) ~ ~ (~), two-linked ~ ~ (~), double-pin(ned) ~ ~ (~), double-hinge(d) ~ ~ (~), double-linked ~ ~ (~), double-articulated ~ ~ (~), ~ flat ~ (~) · Zweigelenk-Flachbogen(träger) *m*, Zweigelenk-Stichbogen(träger), Zweigelenk-Segmentbogen(träger)

two-bath method · Zweibadverfahren *n*, kontinuierliches Verfahren [*Dachpappenherstellung*]

two-bay · zweijochig, doppeljochig

~, **two-span** · doppelschiffig, zweischiffig [*Rahmenhalle*]

~ **chapel** · zweijochige Kapelle *f*, doppeljochige ~

~ **frame** · Zweifeldrahmen *m*

~ **gable(d) frame**, gable(d) frame of two bays · Zweifeld-Giebelrahmen *m*

two-bed · zweibettig

~ **sleeping room** · Zweibett(schlaf)zimmer *n*, zweibettiges Schlafzimmer

two-centered arch (US); **two-centred** ~ (Brit.) · Zwei-Zentren-Bogen *m*

two-coat metallic finish · Zweilagen-Metalleffektlackierung *f*, Zweischichten-Metalleffektlackierung two-coat plastering — two-floor garage 1062

~ **plastering**, ~ (plaster)work · zweilagiges (Ver)Putzen n, zweischichtiges ~, doppellagiges ~, doppelschichtiges ~

~ **(plaster)work**, ~ plactering · zweilagiges (Ver)Putzen n, zweischichtiges ~, doppellagiges ~, dcppelschichtiges ~

~ **system** · Zweilagenaufbau m, Zweilagensystem n, Zweischichtenaufbau, Zweischichtensystem

~ **work** → ~ plasterwork

two-compartment septic tank, double compartment ~ ~, dual compartment ~ ~ · Zweikammer-Grundstückskläranlage f, Doppelkammer-Grundstückskläranlage, Zweikammer-Hauskläranlage, Doppelkammer-Hauskläranlage, Zweikammer-Kleinkläranlage, Doppelkammer-Kleinkläranlage [*DIN 4261*]

~ **tank** · Zweikammer-Behälter m

two-component, two-pack, two-part · zweikomponentig

~ **(bonding) adhesive**, two-part (~) ~, two-pack (~) ~, twin-pack (~) ~, ~ ~ agent, ~ ~ medium, ~ cement(ing agent) · Zweikomponenten-Kleb(e)stoff m, Zweikomponenten-Kleb(e)mittel n, Zweikomponentenkleber m

~ **cement(ing agent)**, two-part ~ (~), two-pack ~ (~), twin-pack ~ (~), ~ bonding agent, ~ bonding medium, ~ (bonding) adhesive · Zweikomponenten-Kleb(e)stoff m, Zweikomponenten-Kleb(e)mittel n, Zweikomponentenkleber m

~ **coating composition**, ~ ~ compound, two-part ~ ~, two-pack ~ ~, twin-pack ~ ~ · Zweikomponenten-Beschichtungsmasse f

~ **etching primer**, two-part ~ ~, two-pack ~ ~, twin-pack ~ ~, ~ wash ~, ~ pretreatment ~, ~ self etch ~ · Zweikomponenten-Aktivgrund m, Zweikomponenten-Haftgrund(ier)mittel n, Zweikomponenten-Haftgrund(ierung) m, (f)

~ **expansion joint mastic (sealer)**, two-part ~ ~ ~ (~), two-pack ~ ~ ~ (~), twin-pack ~ ~ ~ (~) · Zweikomponenten-Dehnungsfugenkitt m, Zweikomponenten-Raumfugenkitt

~ **liquid**, two-part ~ ~, two-pack ~ ~, twin-pack ~ ~ · Zweikomponenten-Flüssigkeit f

~ **mastic**, two-part ~, two-pack ~, twin-pack ~ · Zweikomponentenkitt m

~ **methacrylate compound**, ~ ~ composition, ~ ~ mass, ~ ~ material, twin-component ~ ~, twin-pack ~ ~, two-pack ~ ~, twin-part ~ ~, two-part ~ ~ · Methacrylat-Zweikomponentenmasse f

~ **paint**, two-part ~, two-pack ~, twin-pack ~ · Zweikomponenten(anstrich)farbe f

~ **polyester adhesive**, two-part ~ ~, two-pack ~ ~, twin-pack ~ ~, ~ ~ bonding agent, ~ ~ bonding medium, ~ ~ cement(ing agent) · Zweikomponenten-Polyesterkleb(e)stoff m, Zweikomponenten-Polyesterkleb(e)mittel n, Zweikomponenten-Polyesterkleber m

~ **polysulphide(-based) agent**, ~ ~ composition, two-part ~ ~, two-pack ~ ~, twin-pack ~ ~ · Zweikomponenten-Polysulfidkitt m

~ **pretreatment primer**, two-pack ~ ~, two-part ~ ~, twin-pack ~ ~ ~, ~ etching ~, ~ wash ~, ~ self etch ~ · Zweikomponenten-Aktivgrund m, Zweikomponenten-Haftgrund(ier)mittel n, Zweikomponenten-Haftgrund(ierung) m, (f)

~ **protective coat**, two-part ~ ~, two-pack ~ ~, twin-pack ~ ~ · Zweikomponenten-Schutzanstrich m, Zweikomponenten-Schutzaufstrich

~ **rubber-base compound**, two part ~ ~, twin-pack ~ ~, two-pack ~ ~ [*Erroneously called 'thiokol'*] · Zweikomponenten-Kautschuk-(Ab)Dicht(ungs)mittel n

~ **seal(ing) composition**, ~ ~ compound, ~ ~ mass, ~ ~ material, two-part ~ ~, two-pack ~ ~, twin-pack ~ ~ · Zweikomponenten-(Ab)Dicht(ungs)masse f

~ **self etch primer**, two-pack ~ ~ ~, two-part ~ ~ ~, twin-pack ~ ~ ~, ~ etching ~, ~ pretreatment ~, ~ wash ~ · Zweikomponenten-Aktivgrund m, Zweikomponenten-Haftgrund(ier)mittel n, Zweikomponenten-Haftgrund(ierung) m, (f)

~ **system**, two-pack ~, two-part ~, twin-pack ~ · Zweikomponenten-Aufbau m, Zweikomponenten-System n

~ **wash primer**, two-pack ~ ~, two-part ~ ~, twin-pack ~ ~, ~ etching ~, ~ pretreatment ~, ~ self etch ~ · Zweikomponenten-Aktivgrund m, Zweikomponenten-Haftgrund(ier)mittel n, Zweikomponenten-Haftgrund(ierung) m, (f)

two-dimensional · zweidimensional

~ **action** · zweidimensionale Wirkung f

~ **problem** · zweidimensionale Aufgabe f

~ **state of stress**, plane ~ ~ ~, planar ~ ~ ~, flat ~ ~ ~, state of plane ~ · zweidimensionaler Spannungszustand m, ebener ~

two-family house, duplex ~, ~ building; ~ dwelling (US) · Zweifamilien(wohn)haus n

two-flight stair(case), dual-flight ~, double-flight ~ · zweiläufige Treppe f, doppelläufige ~

two-floor; two-story (US); two-storey (Brit.) · zweigeschossig, zweistöckig, zweietagig, zweipelgeschossig, doppelstöckig, doppeletagig [*aus zwei Geschossen bestehend*]

~ **garage** → two-level ~

two-floor height panel — two-linked arch(ed) frame

~ **height panel**; two-story ~ ~ (US); two-storey ~ ~ (Brit.); two-floored ~ · zweigeschossige Tafel f, zweistöckige ~, zweietagige ~, doppelgeschossige ~, doppelstöckige ~, doppeletagige ~

~ **stage** → two-level ~

two-floored · zweigeschossig, zweistöckig, zweietagig, doppelgeschossig, doppelstöckig, doppeletagig [*so hoch wie zwei Geschosse*]

~ **panel**, two-floor height ~; two-story height ~ (US); two-storey height ~ ~ (Brit.) · zweigeschossige Tafel f, zweistöckige ~, zweietagige ~, doppelgeschossige ~, doppelstöckige ~, doppeletagige ~

two-hand block, ~ tile [*See remark under 'Block'*] · Zweihandstein m, Zweihandblock(stein) m

~ **(clay) brick** · Zweihandstein m [*Fehlname*]; Zweihandziegel m [*Ein großformatiger Mauerziegel, der beim Vermauern mit beiden Händen gehandhabt werden muß*]

~ **tile**, ~ block [*See remark under 'Block'*] · Zweihandstein m, Zweihandblock(stein) m

two-hinge(d) arch(ed) frame, two-pin(ned) ~ ~, two-linked ~ ~, two-articulated ~ ~, double-pin(ned) ~ ~, double-hinge(d) ~ ~, double-linked ~ ~, double-articulated ~ ~ · Zweigelenk-Bogenrahmen m

~ **arch(ed girder)**, two-pin(ned) ~ (~) · Zweigelenkbogen(träger) m

~ **flat arch(ed girder)**, two-pin(ned) ~ ~ (~), two-linked ~ ~ (~), two-articulated ~ ~ (~), double-pin(ned) ~ ~ (~), double-hinge(d) ~ ~ (~), double-linked ~ ~ (~), double-articulated ~ ~ (~), ~ segmental ~ (~) · Zweigelenk-Flachbogen(träger) m, Zweigelenk-Stichbogen(träger), Zweigelenk-Segmentbogen(träger)

~ ~ **parabolic arch(ed girder)**, two-pin(ned) ~ ~ ~ (~), two-linked ~ ~ ~, two-articulated ~ ~ ~ (~), double-pin(ned) ~ ~ ~ (~), double-hinge(d) ~ ~ ~ (~), double-linked ~ ~ ~ (~), double-articulated ~ ~ ~ (~) · Zweigelenkflachparabelbogen(träger) m

~ **frame**, two-pin(ned) ~, two-linked ~, two-articulated ~, double-pin(ned) ~, double-hinge(d) ~, double-linked ~, double-articulated ~ · Zweigelenkrahmen m

~ ~ **of one bay** → single-span two-hinged frame

~ ~ ~ ~ **span** → single-span two-hinged frame

~ **gable(d) frame**, two-pin(ned) ~ ~, two-linked ~ ~, two-articulated ~ ~, double-pin(ned) ~ ~, double-hinge(d) ~ ~, double-linked ~ ~, double-articulated ~ ~ · Zweigelenk-Giebelrahmen m

~ **parabolic arch(ed girder)**, two-pin(ned) ~ ~ (~), two-linked ~ ~ (~), two-articulated ~ ~ (~), double-pin(ned) ~ ~ (~), double-hinge(d) ~ ~ (~), double-linked ~ ~ (~), double-articulated ~ ~ (~) · Zweigelenkparabelbogen(träger) m

~ **portal (frame)**, two-pin(ned) ~ (~) · Zweigelenk-Portalrahmen m

~ **R.C. arch** → reinforced (concrete) two-hinge(d) ~

~ **rectangular frame**, two-pin(ned) ~ ~, two-linked ~ ~, two-articulated ~ ~, double-pin(ned) ~ ~, double-hinge(d) ~ ~, double-linked ~ ~, double-articulated ~ ~ · Zweigelenk-Rechteckrahmen m

~ **reinforced (concrete) arch** → reinforced (concrete) two-hinge(d) ~

~ **segmental arch(ed girder)**, two-pin(ned) ~ ~ (~), two-linked ~ ~ (~), two-articulated ~ ~ (~), double-pin(ned) ~ ~ (~), double-hinge(d) ~ ~ (~), double-linked ~ ~ (~), double-articulated ~ ~ (~), ~ flat ~ (~) · Zweigelenk-Flachbogen(träger) m, Zweigelenk-Stichbogen(träger), Zweigelenk-Segmentbogen(träger)

~ **steel arch**, two-pin(ned) ~ ~ · Stahl-Zweigelenkbogen m

two-horse(d) chariot, biga [*A sculpture, often surmounting a monument*] · Biga f, Zweigespann n

2 lamp light fitting (Brit.); ~ ~ (light(ing)) fixture; ~ ~ luminaire (fixture) (US) · Zweilampenleuchte f

two-layer cast stone · zweischichtiger Betonwerkstein m [*DIN 18500*]

two-layer(ed), double-layer(ed) · zweilagig, doppellagig, zweischichtig, doppelschichtig

~ **space frame shell**, double-layer(ed) ~ ~ ~ · zweischaliges Raumfachwerk n, doppelschaliges ~

two layers of wood(en) joists, ~ ~ ~ timber ~ · doppelte Holzbalkenlage f

two-leaf, two-wythe, two-withe (Brit.); two-tier (US) · zweischalig, doppelschalig [*Wand; Mauer*]

~ **door**, double-leaf ~ · zweiflügelige Tür f, Zweiflügeltür

~ **flexible (swing) door** · zweiflügelige flexible Pendeltür f

~ **hinged shutterdoor**, ~ ~ shutter door · zweiflügeliges Drehtor n

~ **sliding shutterdoor**, ~ ~ shutter door · zweiflügeliges Schiebetor n

two-level garage, two-floor ~; two-storey ~ (Brit.); two-story ~ (US) · Doppelgeschoßgarage f, Doppelstockgarage

~ **stage**, two-floor ~; two-story ~ (US); two-storey ~ (Brit.) · Doppelstockbühne f

two-light window, gemel ~ · Zwillingsfenster n, zweiteiliges Fenster

~ ~ · zweischeibiges Fenster n

two-linked arch(ed) frame, two-hinged ~ ~, two-pin(ned) ~ ~, two-articulated ~ ~, double-pin(ned) ~ ~, double-

two-linked arch(ed) frame — two-pack ... 1064

hinge(d) ~ ~, double-linked ~ ~, double-articulated ~ ~ ~ · Zweigelenk-Bogenrahmen *m*

~ **flat arch(ed girder)**, two-pin(ned) ~ ~ (~), two-hinge(d) ~ ~ (~), two-articulated ~ ~ (~), double-pin(ned) ~ ~ (~), double-hinge(d) ~ ~ (~), double-linked ~ ~ (~), double-articulated ~ ~ (~), ~ segmental ~ (~) · Zweigelenk-Flachbogen(träger) *m*, Zweigelenk-Stichbogen(träger), Zweigelenk-Segmentbogen(träger)

~ ~ **parabolic arch(ed girder)**, two-hinge(d) ~ ~ ~ (~), two-pin(ned) ~ ~ ~ (~), two-articulated ~ ~ ~ (~), double-pin(ned) ~ ~ ~ (~), double-hinge(d) ~ ~ ~ (~), double-linked ~ ~ ~ (~), double-articulated ~ ~ ~ (~) · Zweigelenkflachparabelbogen(träger)

~ **frame**, two-hingd(d) ~, two-pin(ned) ~, two-articulated ~, double-pin(ned) ~, double-hinge(d) ~, double-linked ~, double-articulated ~ · Zweigelenkrahmen *m*

~ **gable(d) frame**, two-pin(ned) ~ ~, two-hinge(d) ~ ~, two-articulated ~ ~, double-pin(ned) ~ ~, double-hinge(d) ~ ~, double-linked ~ ~, double-articulated ~ ~ · Zweigelenk-Giebelrahmen *m*

~ **parabolic arch(ed girder)**, two-hinge(d) ~ ~ (~), two-pin(ned) ~ ~ (~), two-articulated ~ ~ (~), double-pin(ned) ~ ~ (~), double-hinge(d) ~ ~ (~), double-linked ~ ~ (~), double-articulated ~ ~ (~) · Zweigelenkparabelbogen(träger) *m*

~ **rectangular frame**, two-pin(ned) ~ ~, two-hing(d) ~ ~, two-articulated ~ ~, double-pin(ned) ~ ~, double-hinge(d) ~ ~, double-linked ~ ~, double-articulated ~ ~ · Zweigelenk-Rechteckrahmen *m*

~ **segmental arch(ed girder)**, two-pin(ned) ~ ~ (~), two-hinge(d) ~ ~ (~), two-articulated ~ ~ (~), double-pin(ned) ~ ~ (~), double-hinge(d) ~ ~ (~), double-linked ~ ~ (~), double-articulated ~ ~ (~), ~ flat ~ (~) · Zweigelenk-Flachbogen(träger) *m*, Zweigelenk-Stichbogen(träger), Zweigelenk-Segmentbogen(träger)

two-pack, two-part ~, two-component · 2-komponentig, zweikomponentig

~ **(bonding) adhesive**, two-part (~) ~, twin-pack (~) ~, two-component (~) ~, ~ ~ agent, ~ ~ medium, ~ ~ cement(ing) agent · Zweikomponenten-Kleb(e)stoff *m*, Zweikomponenten-Kleb(e)mittel *n*, Zweikomponentenkleber *m*

~ **cement(ing) agent**, twin-pack ~ (~), two-part ~ (~), two-component ~ (~), ~ bonding agent, ~ bonding medium, ~ (bonding) adhesive · Zweikomponenten-Kleb(e)stoff *m*, Zweikomponenten-Kleb(e)mittel *n*, Zweikomponentenkleber *m*

~ **coating composition**, ~ ~ compound, two-part ~ ~, twin-pack ~ ~, two-component ~ ~ · Zweikomponenten-Beschichtungsmasse *f*

~ **etching primer**, two-part ~ ~, twin-pack ~ ~, two-component ~ ~, ~ wash ~, ~ pretreatment ~, ~ self etch ~ · Zweikomponenten-Aktivgrund *m*, Zweikomponenten-Haftgrund(ier)mittel *n*, Zweikomponenten-Haftgrund(ierung) *m*, (*f*)

~ **expansion joint mastic (sealer)**, twin-pack ~ ~ ~ (~), two-part ~ ~ ~ (~), two-component ~ ~ ~ (~) · Zweikomponenten-Dehnungsfugenkitt *m*, Zweikomponenten-Raumfugenkitt

~ **liquid**, twin-pack ~, two-part ~, two-component ~ · Zweikomponenten-Flüssigkeit *f*

~ **mastic**, twin-pack ~, two-part ~, two-component ~ · Zweikomponentenkitt *m*

~ **methacrylate compound** → two-component ~ ~

~ **paint**, two-part ~, twin-pack ~, two-component ~ · Zweikomponenten-Anstrichfarbe *f*, Zweikomponenten-Farbe

~ **polyester adhesive**, twin-pack ~ ~, two-part ~, two-component ~ ~, ~ ~ bonding agent, ~ ~ bonding medium, ~ ~ cement(ing agent) · Zweikomponenten-Polyesterkleb(e)stoff *m*, Zweikomponenten-Polyesterkleb(e)mittel *n*, Zweikomponenten-Polyesterkleber *m*

~ ~ **cement(ing agent)**, twin-pack ~ ~ (~), two-part ~ ~ (~), two-component ~ ~ (~), ~ ~ bonding agent, ~ ~ bonding medium, ~ ~ ~ adhesive · Zweikomponenten-Polyesterkleb(e)stoff *m*, Zweikomponenten-Polyesterkleb(e)mittel *n*, Zweikomponenten-Polyesterkleber *m*

~ **polysulphide(-based) cement**, ~ ~ composition, twin-pack ~ ~, two-part ~ ~, two-component ~ ~ · Zweikomponenten-Polysulfidkitt *m*

~ **pretreatment primer**, two-part ~ ~, twin-pack ~ ~, two-component ~ ~, ~ etching ~, ~ wash ~, ~ self etch ~ · Zweikomponenten-Aktivgrund *m*, Zweikomponenten-Haftgrund(ier)mittel *n*, Zweikomponenten-Haftgrund(ierung) *m*, (*f*)

~ **protective coat**, twin-pack ~ ~, two-part ~ ~, two-component ~ ~ · Zweikomponenten-Schutzanstrich *m*, Zweikomponenten-Schutzaufstrich

~ **rubber-base compound**, two-part ~ ~, twin-pack ~ ~, two-component ~ ~ [*Erroneously called 'thiokol'*] · Zweikomponenten-Kautschuk-(Ab-)Dicht(ungs)mittel *n*

~ **seal(ing) composition**, ~ ~ compound, ~ ~ material, ~ ~ mass, two-part ~ ~, twin-pack ~ ~, two-component ~ ~ · Zweikomponenten-(Ab-)Dicht(ungs)masse *f*

~ self etch primer, two-part ~ ~ ~, twin-pack ~ ~ ~, two-component ~ ~ ~, ~ pretreatment ~, ~ etching ~, ~ wash ~ · Zweikomponenten-Aktivgrund *m*, Zweikomponenten-Haftgrund-(ier)mittel *n*, Zweikomponenten-Haftgrund(ierung) *m*, (*f*)

~ system, two-part ~, twin-pack ~, two-component ~ · Zweikomponenten-Aufbau *m*, Zweikomponenten-System *n*

~ wash primer, twin-pack ~ ~, two-part ~ ~, two-component ~ ~, ~ etching ~, ~ pretreatment ~, ~ self etch ~ · Zweikomponenten-Aktivgrundmittel *n*, Zweikomponenten-Haftgrund(ierung) *m*, (*f*)

two-pane sash, double-pane ~, dual-pane ~ · Doppelflügel *m* [*Der doppelt verglaste Flügel eines Verbundfensters*]

two-panel(led) door (Brit.) → two-panel(ed) ~

two-part, two-pack, two-component · zweikomponentig

~ (bonding) adhesive, two-pack (~) ~, twin-pack (~) ~, two-component (~) ~, ~ ~ agent, ~ cement(ing agent) · Zweikomponenten-Kleb(e)stoff *m*, Zweikomponenten-Kleb(e)mittel *n*, Zweikomponentenkleber *m*

~ cement(ing agent), two-pack ~ (~), two-component ~ (~), twin-pack ~ (~), ~ bonding agent, ~ bonding medium, ~ (bonding) adhesive · Zweikomponenten-Kleb(e)stoff *m*, Zweikomponenten-Kleb(e)mittel *n*, Zweikomponentenkleber *m*

~ coating compound, ~ ~ composition, two-component ~ ~, two-pack ~ ~, twin-pack ~ ~ · Zweikomponenten-Beschichtungsmasse *f*

~ etching primer, two-pack ~ ~, twin-pack ~ ~, two-component ~ ~, ~ wash ~, ~ pretreatment ~, ~ self etch ~ · Zweikomponenten-Aktivgrund *m*, Zweikomponenten-Haftgrund(ier)mittel *n*, Zweikomponenten-Haftgrund(ierung) *m*, (*f*)

~ expansion joint mastic (sealer), two-component ~ ~ ~ (~), two-pack ~ ~ ~ (~), twin-pack ~ ~ ~ (~) · Zweikomponenten-Dehnungsfugenkitt *m*, Zweikomponenten-Raumfugenkitt

~ liquid, two-pack ~, twin-pack ~, two-component ~ · Zweikomponenten-Flüssigkeit *f*

~ mastic, two-pack ~, two-component ~, twin-pack ~ · Zweikomponentenkitt *m*

~ methacrylate compound → two-component ~ ~

~ paint, two-pack ~, twin-pack ~, two-component ~ · Zweikomponenten(an-strich)farbe *f*

~ polyester adhesive, two-pack ~ ~, twin-pack ~ ~, two-component ~ ~, ~ ~ bonding agent, ~ ~ bonding medium, ~ ~ cement(ing agent) · Zweikomponenten-Polyesterkleb(e)stoff *m*, Zweikomponenten-Polyesterkleb(e)mittel *n*, Zweikomponenten-Polyesterkleber *m*

~ ~ cement(ing agent), two-pack ~ ~ (~), twin-pack ~ ~ (~), two-component ~ ~ (~), ~ ~ bonding agent, ~ ~ bonding medium, ~ ~ adhesive · Zweikomponenten-Polyesterkleb(e)-stoff *m*, Zweikomponenten-Polyesterkleb(e)mittel *n*, Zweikomponenten-Polyesterkleber *m*

~ polysulphide(-based) cement, ~ ~ composition, two-component ~ ~ ~, two-pack ~ ~ ~, twin-pack ~ ~ ~ · Zweikomponenten-Polysulfidkitt *m*

~ pretreatment primer, two-pack ~ ~, twin-pack ~ ~, two-component ~ ~ ~, ~ wash ~, ~ etching ~, ~ self etch ~ · Zweikomponenten-Aktivgrund *m*, Zweikomponenten-Haftgrund(ier)mittel *n*, Zweikomponenten-Haftgrund(ierung) *m*, (*f*)

~ protective coat, two-pack ~ ~, twin-pack ~ ~, two-component ~ ~ · Zweikomponenten-Schutzanstrich *m*, Zweikomponenten-Schutzaufstrich

~ rubber-base compound, two-pack ~ ~, twin-pack ~ ~, two-component ~ ~ [*Erroneously called 'thiokol'*] · Zweikomponenten-Kautschuk-Dicht-(ungs)mittel *n*, Zweikomponenten-Kautschuk-Abdicht(ungs)mittel

~ seal(ing) composition, ~ ~ compound, ~ ~ material, ~ ~ mass, two-pack ~ ~, twin-pack ~ ~, two-component ~ ~ · Zweikomponenten-(Ab)Dicht(ungs)masse *f*

~ self etch primer, two-pack ~ ~ ~, twin-pack ~ ~ ~, two-component ~ ~ ~, ~ pretreatment ~, ~ etching ~, ~ wash ~ · Zweikomponenten-Aktivgrund *m*, Zweikomponenten-Haftgrund(ier)mittel *n*, Zweikomponenten-Haftgrund(ierung) *m*, (*f*)

~ system, two-pack ~, twin-pack ~, two-component ~ · Zweikomponenten-Aufbau *m*, Zweikomponenten-System *n*

~ up and over door · Schwingtor *n* mit zweiteiligem Torblatt, Kipptor ~ ~ ~, zweiteiliges Schwingtor, zweiteiliges Kipptor

~ wash primer, two-pack ~ ~, twin-pack ~ ~, two-component ~ ~, ~ etching ~, ~ pretreatment ~, ~ self etch ~ · Zweikomponenten-Aktivgrund *m*, Zweikomponenten-Haftgrund(ier)mittel *n*, Zweikomponenten-Haftgrund(ierung) *m*, (*f*)

two-person car · Zweipersonenkabine *f* [*Aufzug*]

two-piece aerated concrete panel, sectional ~ ~ ~ · zweiteilige Porenbetontafel *f*

~ compressed bar, ~ ~ rod, ~ ~ member, ~ ~ element, ~ compression ~ · zweiteiliger Druckstab *m*, gedrückter Stab, zweiteiliges Druckglied *n*, zweiteiliges gedrücktes Glied

two-piece drop system — two-span parabolic arch(ed girder) 1066

~ **drop system** [*central heating*] · Zweirohrsystem *n* mit oberer Verteilung [*Zentralheizung*]

~ **glue(-jointe)d aerated concrete panel,** sectional ~ ~ ~ ~ · verleimte zweiteilige Porenbetontafel *f,* zweiteilige verleimte ~

~ ~ **panel** → glue(-jointe)d sectional ~

~ **laminated insulating glass,** ~ ~ insulation ~ · Zweischeibenisolierglas *n* [*Die beiden Scheiben werden in der Fabrik an den Rändern miteinander verschweißt; die Luft zwischen den Scheiben bleibt vollständig und dauernd von der Außenluft getrennt*]

~ ~ **safety sheet glass** · Zweischeiben-Verbundglas *n,* zweischichtiges Verbundglas

~ **panel,** sectional ~ · zweiteilige Tafel *f*

two pin socket · Zweipol(steck)dose *f*

two-pin(ned) arch(ed) frame, two-hinged ~ ~, two-linked ~ ~, two-articulated ~ ~, double-pin(ned) ~ ~, double-hinge(d) ~ ~, double-linked ~ ~, double-articulated ~ ~ · Zweigelenk-Bogenrahmen *m*

~ **arch(ed girder),** two-hinge(d) ~ (~) · Zweigelenkbogen(träger) *m*

~ **flat arch(ed girder),** two-hinge(d) ~ ~ (~), two-linked ~ ~ (~), two-articulated ~ ~ (~), double-pin(ned) ~ ~ (~), double-hinge(d) ~ ~ (~), double-linked ~ ~ (~), double-articulated ~ ~ (~), ~ segmental ~ (~) · Zweigelenk-Flachbogen(träger) *m,* Zweigelenk-Stichbogen(träger), Zweigelenk-Segmentbogen(träger)

~ ~ **parabolic arch(ed girder),** two-hinge(d) ~ ~ ~ (~), two-linked ~ ~ ~ (~), two-articulated ~ ~ ~ (~), double-pin(ned) ~ ~ ~ (~), double-hinge(d) ~ ~ ~ (~), double-linked ~ ~ ~ (~), double-articulated ~ ~ ~ (~) · Zweigelenkflachparabelbogen(träger) *m*

~ **frame,** two-hinge(d) ~, two-linked ~, two-articulated ~, double-pin(ned) ~, double-hinge(d) ~, double-linked ~, double-articulated ~ · Zweigelenkrahmen *m*

~ **gable(d) frame,** two-hinge(d) ~ ~, two-linked ~ ~, two-articulated ~ ~, double-pin(ned) ~ ~, double-hinge(d) ~ ~, double-linked ~ ~, double-articulated ~ ~ · Zweigelenk-Giebelrahmen *m*

~ **parabolic arch(ed girder),** two-hinge(d) ~ ~ (~), two-linked ~ ~ (~), two articulated ~ ~ (~), double-pin(ned) ~ ~ (~), double-hinge(d) ~ (~) double-linked ~ ~ (~), double-articulated ~ ~ (~) · Zweigelenkparabelbogen(träger) *m*

~ **portal (frame),** two-hinge(d) ~ (~) · Zweigelenk-Portalrahmen *m*

~ **R.C. arch** → reinforced (concrete) two-hinge(d) ~

~ **rectangular frame,** two-hinge(d) ~ ~, two-linked ~ ~, two-articulated ~ ~, double-pin(ned) ~ ~, double-hinge(d) ~ ~, double-linked ~ ~, double-articulated ~ ~ · Zweigelenk-Rechteckrahmen *m*

~ **reinforced (concrete) arch** → reinforced (concrete) two-hinge(d) ~

~ **segmental arch(ed girder),** two-hinge(d) ~ ~ (~), two-linked ~ ~ (~), two-articulated ~ ~ (~), double-pin(ned) ~ ~ (~), double-hinge(d) ~ ~ (~), double-linked ~ ~ (~), double-articulated ~ ~ (~), ~ flat ~ (~) · Zweigelenk-Flachbogen(träger) *m,* Zweigelenk-Stichbogen(träger), Zweigelenk-Segmentbogen(träger)

~ **steel arch,** two-hinged ~ ~ · Stahl-Zweigelenkbogen *m*

two-pipe hot water heating · Zweirohr-Warmwasserheizung *f*

~ **meter,** double-pipe ~ · Zweirohrzähler *m*

~ **plumbing,** two-stack ~ · Zwei-Rohr-Grundstücksentwässerung *f*

~ **rising system** [*central heating*] · Zweirohrsystem *n* mit unterer Verteilung [*Zentralheizung*]

~ **system** [*This term is somewhat misleading in that this system has four pipes. See soil and waste discharges are kept separate and each has its own ventilating pipe. Both pipes eventually combine into one common drain pipe though the main waste pipe is trapped by a gully at the foot before it connects to the drain*] · Vier-Rohr-Sanitäranlage *f*

2-ply tar(red) paper · zweilagiges Teerpapier *n,* zweischichtiges ~, doppellagiges ~, doppelschichtiges ~

two-pole plug [*B.S. 546*] · Zweipolstecker *m*

two-pot system · Zweikomponentensystem *n* [*Lack*]

two quarters → half bat

two-rate meter · Doppeltarifzähler *m*

two-room house · Zweiraumhaus *n*

two-room-size panel · zweiraumgroße Tafel *f*

two-screen expanding wall · Doppel-Harmonikatür *f*

two sheets of heavy paper · Kartonummantelung *f* [*Gipskartonplatte*]

two-sided town gateway, ~ city ~ · Stadttor *n* [*Ein Stadttor ist in einer Mauer eingebunden und hat zwei Seiten, die Stadt- und Feldseite*]

two-span, two-bay · doppelschiffig, zweischiffig [*Rahmenhalle*]

~ **beam,** beam of two spans · Zweifeldbalken(träger) *m*

~ **girder,** girder of two spans · Zweifeldträger *m*

~ **parabolic arch(ed girder),** ~ ~ arch ~ · gekrümmter Zweifeldparabelträger *m,* Zweifeldparabelbogen(träger) *m*

two-span (pre)stressed (concrete) beam — tying point

~ **(pre)stressed (concrete) beam** · Zweifeldspannbetonbalken(träger) *m*

two-stack plumbing, two-pipe · Zwei-Rohr-Grundstücksentwässerung *f*

two-stage comminution, ~ reduction · zweistufige Zerkleinerung *f*

~ **curing** [*A process in which concrete products are cured in low-pressure steam, and then autoclaved*] · zweistufige Warmbehandlung *f*, Zweistufenbehandlung

~ **mixing** · Zwei-Phasen-Mischen *n*

~ **reduction,** ~ comminution · zweistufige Zerkleinerung *f*

two-storey garage (Brit.) → two-level ~

two-storey (height) panel (Brit.); two-story (~) → (US); two-floor (~) ~, two-floored ~ · zweigeschossige Tafel *f*, zweistöckige ~, zweietagige ~, doppelgeschossige ~, doppelstöckige ~, doppeletagige ~

~ **stage** (Brit.) → two-level ~

two-storeyed church · Doppelgeschoßkirche *f*, Zweigeschoßkirche

~ **surrounding aisle** · doppelgeschossiger Umgang *m*, zweigeschossiger ~ [*z.B. Münster zu Aachen*]

two-story (US); two-storey (Brit.); two-floor · zweigeschossig, zweistöckig, zweietagig, doppelgeschossig, doppelstöckig, doppeletagig [*Aus zwei Geschossen bestehend*]

two-tier (US); two-wythe, two-withe, two-leaf (Brit.) · zweischalig, doppelschalig [*Wand; Mauer*]

two-tiered pilastered façade · zweireihige Pilasterfassade *f*, ~ Wandpfeilerfassade, ~ Halbpfeilerfassade, doppelreihige ~

two-tower façade, twin-tower ~, double-tower ~, dual-tower ~,· Doppelturmfassade *f*, Zweiturmfassade

two-walled, double-walled · zweiwandig, doppelwandig

two-way cable conduit, ~ ~ subway, ~ ~ duct, ~ CD; ~ conduit tile (US) · zweizügiger Kabel(kanal)formstein *m*, zweizügiges Kabelformstück *n*

~ ~ **duct,** ~ ~ conduit, ~ ~ subway, ~ CD; ~ conduit tile (US) · zweizügiger Kabel(kanal)formstein *m*, zweizügiges Kabelformstück *n*

~ ~ **subway,** ~ ~ conduit, ~ ~ duct, ~ CD; ~ conduit tile (US) · zweizügiger Kabel(kanal)formstein *m*, zweizügiges Kabelformstück *n*

~ **CD,** ~ cable duct, ~ cable conduit, ~ cable subway; ~ conduit tile (US) · zweizügiger Kabel(kanal)formstein *m*, zweizügiges Kabelformstück *n*

~ **conduit tile** (US); ~ cable duct, ~ cable conduit, ~ cable subway, ~ CD · zweizügiger Kabel(kanal)formstein *m*, zweizügiges Kabelformstück *n*

~ **(pre)stressed (concrete) slab** · kreuzweise vorgespannte Platte *f*

~ ~ **slab,** ~ ~ concrete ~ · kreuzweise vorgespannte Platte *f*

~ **reinforced** · kreuzarmiert, kreuzbewehrt, mit kreuzweisen (Stahl)Einlagen, kreuzweise bewehrt, kreuzweise armiert

~ ~ **slab** · kreuzweise bewehrte Platte *f*, ~ armierte ~

~ **reinforcement** [*Reinforcement arranged in bands of bars at right angles to each other*] · kreuzweise (Stahl)Einlagen *fpl*, ~ Bewehrung *f*, ~ Armierung, Kreuzbewehrung, Kreuzarmierung, Kreuz(stahl)einlagen

~ **slab** [*A slab spanning between beams in two directions*] · kreuzweise gespannte Platte *f*

~ **strap,** forked strap · Gabelband *n*, gegabelte Kopfschiene *f* [*Holzbau*]

~ **valve** · Zweiwegeventil *n*

two-webbed, twin-webbed, double-webbed · zweistegig, doppelstegig

~ **plate girder,** twin-webbed ~ ~, double-webbed ~ ~ · Zweistegblechträger *m*, Doppelstegblechträger

~ **T,beam,** twin-webbed ~, double-webbed ~ · zweistegiger Plattenbalken *m*, doppelstegiger ~

two-window glue(-jointe)d sectional panel, ~ ~ two-piece ~ [*A silicate or resin adhesive is used for glu(e)ing*] · verleimte zweiteilige Zwei-Fenstertafel *f*, zweiteilige verleimte ~

~ ~ **two-piece panel,** ~ ~ sectional ~ · verleimte zweiteilige Zwei-Fenstertafel *f*, zweiteilige verleimte ~

~ **office** · zweifensteriges Büro *n*

~ **one-piece panel** · einteilige Zwei-Fenstertafel *f*

~ **panel** · Zwei-Fenstertafel *f*

~ **welded sectional panel,** ~ ~ two-piece ~ · geschweißte zweiteilige Zwei-Fenstertafel *f*, zweiteilige geschweißte ~

~ ~ **two-piece panel,** ~ ~ sectional ~ · geschweißte zweiteilige Zwei-Fenstertafel *f*, zweiteilige geschweißte ~

two-wing(ed) building, double-wing(ed) ~ · zweiflügeliges Gebäude *n*, doppelflügeliges ~

two-wire jack · Spannpresse *f* für 2 Drähte

two-withe, two-wythe, two-leaf (Brit.); two-tier (US) · zweischalig, doppelschalig [*Wand; Mauer*]

two-wythe, two-withe, two-leaf (Brit.); two-tier (US) · zweischalig, doppelschalig [*Wand; Mauer*]

two-zone air-conditioning system · Zwei-Zonen-Klimaanlage *f*

twr., tower · Turm *m*

tying, anchoring · Verankern *n*

~, anchorage · Verankerung *f* [*Zugfeste Verbindung zweier Bauteile mit Ankern*]

~ **point** · Knüpfpunkt *m*, Knüpfstelle *f* [*Bewehrung*]

tying (reinforcement) — typical floor (ground(-))plan 1068

~ **(reinforcement),** binding (~), reinforcement binding, reinforcement tying · Rödeln *n* (von Bewehrung(en)), Rödelung *f* (~ ~), Flechten (~ ~), Bewehrungsflechten

~ **wire,** iron ~, lashing ~, binding ~, annealed ~ [*Soft steel wire used for binding reinforcement*] · Rödeldraht *m*, Bindedraht

tympanum · Tympanum *n*, Tympanon *n*, Türlünette *f*

~ **enclosed by arch** · (Tür)Bogenfeld *n* [*Das von einem Bogen umfaßte Mauerstück über einer Türöffnung*]

~ ~ ~ **pediment** · Tympanon *n*, Giebelfeld *n* [*Das von einem Giebel umfaßte Mauerstück über einer Türöffnung*]

type I portland cement → ordinary ~

~ **III cement** (US) → high early (or initial) strength (Portland) ~

~ **IV cement,** Portland cement Type IV (US); slow hardening cement, low heat (of hydration) cement · Portlandzement *m* mit sehr geringer Abbindewärme, Massenbauzement

type and size (of reinforcement) · Eisensorte *f* und Durchmesser *m*, Stahlsorte ~ ~ [*Stahlliste*]

type-(ground(-))plan, typical (ground(-))plan · Regelgrundriß *m*

type of anchorage · Verankerungsart *f* [*Spannbeton*]

~ ~ **arch** · Bogenart *f*

~ ~ **bar,** bar type · Eisenart *f*, Stahlart *f*, Stabart [*Bewehrung*]

~ ~ **beam,** beam type · Balken(träger)art *f*

~ ~ **block,** ~ ~ building (structure) · Gebäudetype *f*

~ ~ **board,** ~ ~ sheet · Plattenart *f*

~ ~ **bond,** ~ ~ masonry ~, (masonry) bond type · (Mauer)Verbandsart *f*

~ ~ **brick,** ~ ~ clay ~, (clay) brick type · Ziegelart *f*

~ ~ **building (construction),** building (construction) type · Hochbauart *f*

~ ~ ~ **(structure),** ~ ~ block · Gebäudetype *f*

~ ~ **cement,** cement type · Zementart *f*

~ ~ **(clay) brick,** (clay) brick type · Ziegelart *f*

~ ~ **coating (work)** · Anstrichart *f*, Aufstrichart

~ ~ **concrete,** concrete type · Betonart *f*

~ ~ **construction,** construction type · Bauart *f* [*Die Art in der Baustoffe und Bauteile für sich allein oder gemeinsam zu Bauwerken zusammengefügt werden; nicht zu verwechseln mit Bauweise*]

~ ~ **dome,** ~ ~ cupola · Kuppelart *f*

~ ~ **drawing** · Zeichnungsart

~ ~ **fabrication,** ~ ~ manufacture · Fertigungsart *f*, Herstellungsart

~ ~ **finishing** · Bearbeitungsart *f* [*Betonwerkstein*]

~ ~ **floor** · Deckenart *f*

~ ~ ~ **cover(ing),** ~ ~ floor(ing) (finish) · (Fuß)Boden(belag)art *f*, F

~ ~ **floor(ing) (finish),** ~ ~ floor cover(ing) · (Fuß)Boden(belag)art *f*, F

~ ~ **gypsum** · Gipsart *f*

~ ~ **joint** · Verbindungsart *f* [*Rohr*]

~ ~ **lime,** lime type · Kalkart *f*

~ ~ **line** · Linienart *f*

~ ~ **loading,** loading type · Belastungsart *f*

~ ~ **manufacture,** ~ ~ fabrication · Fertigungsart *f*, Herstellungsart

~ ~ **marble** · Marmorart *f*

~ ~ **(masonry) bond,** (masonry) bond type · (Mauer)Verbandsart *f*

~ ~ ~ **(work),** masonry (work) type · Mauerwerkart *f*

~ ~ **mortar** · Mörtelart *f*

~ ~ **painting (work)** · (Farb)Anstrichart *f*

~ ~ **rock,** rock type · Gesteinsart *f*

~ ~ **roof,** roof type · Dachart *f*

~ ~ **sheet,** ~ ~ board · Plattenart *f*

~ ~ **shell structure** · Schalenbauwerkart *f*

~ ~ **slag** · Schlackenart *f*

~ ~ **sound,** sound type · Schallart *f* [*Man unterscheidet: Körper-, Tritt- und Luftschall*]

~ ~ **stair,** stair type · Treppenart *f*

~ ~ **tar** · Teerart *f*

~ ~ **vault** · Gewölbeart *f*

~ ~ **vaulting** · Wölbungsart *f*

~ ~ **wall,** wall type · Wandart *f*

~ ~ ~ **construction,** wall construction type · Wandbauart *f*

~ ~ **water,** water type · Wasserart *f*

~ ~ **window,** window type · Fensterart *f*

type-plan → type-base

~ **of floor** → typical floor base

type standardization · Typ(isier)ung *f*

typhon [*A simple form or temple in early Egyptian architecture*] · Typhonium *n*

typical bond → ~ masonry ~

~ **column** · Regelstütze *f*

~ **cross-section** · Regelquerschnitt *m*, Normalquerschnitt

~ **cube** → ~ test ~

~ **floor (ground(-))plan,** type-(ground(-))plan of floor · Regel-Geschoßgrundriß *m*, Regel-Etagengrundriß, Regel-Stockwerkgrundriß, Regel-Rohbauplan *m*, Stockwerk-Regelgrundriß, Etagen-Regelgrundriß, Geschoß-Regelgrundriß

typical (ground(-))plan — ultra-smooth finish

~ **(ground(-))plan**, type-(ground(-))plan · Regelgrundriß *m*
~ **length** · Regellänge *f*
~ **load** · Regellast *f*
~ **(masonry) bond**, normal (~) ~ · Regelverband *m*
~ **plan** → ~ ground(-)plan
~ **profile** · Regelprofil *n*
~ **shell** · Regelschale *f*
~ **solution** · Regellösung *f*
~ **(test) cube**, normal (~) ~ · Regelwürfel *m*, Normalwürfel
~ **thickness** · Regeldicke *f*
~ **upper floor plan** · Obergeschoß-Regelrohbauplan *m*
~ **width** · Regelbreite *f*
typists' room, typist's ~ · Schreibmaschinenzimmer *n*
tyraline, anileine, aniline red · Anilinrot *n*

U

U strap · Hängeeisen *n*
UF, urea formaldehyde · Harnstoffformaldehyd *n*
uintaite, gilsonite · Uintait *m*, Gilsonitasphalt *m*
Ulpian basilica · Basilika *f* Ulpia
ultimate bearing capacity → ~ load ~ ~
~ ~ **power** → ~ (load)bearing capacity
~ ~ **property** → ~ (load)bearing capacity
~ ~ **quality** → ~ (load)bearing capacity
~ **bending angle**, breaking ~ ~, rupture ~ ~ · Bruchbiegewinkel *m*, Bruchbiegungswinkel
~ **moment**, breaking ~ ~, rupture ~ · Bruchbiegemoment *n*, Bruchbiegungsmoment
~ **column resistance**, ~ ~ stability, ~ ~ strength, buckling ~ · Knickfestigkeit *f*, Knickwiderstand *m*, Knickstabilität *f*
~ ~ **stability**, ~ ~ resistance, ~ ~ strength, buckling · Knickfestigkeit *f*, Knickwiderstand *m*, Knickstabilität *f*
~ ~ **strength**, ~ ~ resistance, ~ ~ stability, buckling ~ · Knickfestigkeit *f*, Knickwiderstand *m*, Knickstabilität *f*
~ **compressive load**, breaking ~ ~, rupture ~ ~ · Bruchdrucklast *f*
~ ~ **strength**, breaking ~ ~, rupture ~ ~ · Bruchdruckfestigkeit *f*
~ **condition**, breaking ~, rupture ~ · Bruchbedingung *f*
~ **design (method)**, load-factor ~ (~), ultimate strength ~ (~) [*It is based on the ultimate strength of the section*] ·
n-freie Berechnungsweise *f*, *n*-freies Verfahren *n*, *n*-freie Bemessung *f*, Bruchtheorie *f*, Bruchsicherheitsnachweis *m*
~ **limit(ing) state** · Grenzzustand *m* der Tragfähigkeit, Tragfähigkeits-Grenzzustand
~ **load**, rupture ~, breaking ~ · Bruchlast *f*
~ **(load)bearing capacity**, ~ ~ power, ~ ~ quality, ~ ~ property, ~ weight-carrying ~, ~ load-carrying ~ · Grenztragfähigkeit *f*, Bruchtragfähigkeit
~ **loading**, breaking ~, rupture ~, limit ~ · Bruchbelastung *f*, Grenzbelastung
~ **moment**, breaking ~, rupture ~ · Bruchmoment *n*
~ ~ **capacity**, breaking ~ ~, rupture ~ ~ · Bruchmomentenvermögen *n*
~ **shear(ing) strength**, breaking ~ ~, rupture ~ ~ · Bruch-Schubfestigkeit *f*, Bruch-Schubwiderstand *m*
~ ~ **stress**, breaking ~ ~, rupture ~ ~ · Bruch-Schubspannung *f*
~ **strength**, final ~, breaking ~, rupture ~ · Endfestigkeit *f*, Endwiderstand *m*, Bruchfestigkeit, Bruchwiderstand
~ ~ **design (method)**, load-factor ~ (~), ultimate ~ (~) [*It is based on the ultimate strength of the section*] · *n*-freie Berechnungsweise *f*, *n*-freies Verfahren *n*, *n*-freie Bemessung *f*, Bruchtheorie *f*, Bruchsicherheitsnachweis *m*
~ **stress**, breaking ~, rupture ~ · Bruchspannung *f*
~ ~ **condition**, breaking ~ ~, rupture ~ ~ · Bruchspannungsbedingung *f*
~ **tensile strength**, tenacity · Bruchzugfestigkeit *f*
~ **tensile stress**, breaking ~ ~, rupture ~ ~ · Bruchzugspannung *f*
~ **value**, limit(ing) ~ · Grenzwert *m*
~ **weight-carrying capacity** → ~ (load)bearing ~
ultra-fine fraction → ~ ~ particles
ultra fine-grained · feinstkörnig
ultra-fine grains → ~ particles
~ **material** → ~ particles
~ **particles**, ~ grains, ~ material, ~ fraction, finest ~, ultra-fines · Feinste *n*, Feinstgut *n*, Feinstkorn *n*, Aufschlämmbare *n*, aufschlämmbarer Stoff *m*, Feinstmaterial *n*, Feinststoffe *mpl* [< 0,02 mm]
~ **sand**, superfine ~ · Feinstsand *m*
ultra-fines → ultra-fine particles
ultramarine blue, blue ultramarine [*B.S. 314*] · Ultramarinblau *n*, blaues Ultramarin *n*
~ **(pigment)** [*B.S. 314*] · Ultramarin(pigment) *n*, Ultramarinfarbe *f*
ultrared radiation · ultrarote Strahlung *f*
ultra-smooth finish · Superoberflächenschluß *m*

ultrasonic testing of concrete, ~ concrete testing · akustische Betonprüfung f, ~ Betonprobe f, akustischer Betonversuch m

ultraviolet light · ultraviolettes Licht n, UV-Licht

umber [*B.S. 313*] · Umbra f, braunes Erdpigment n, braunes natürliches anorganisches Pigment [*Fehlname: braune Erdfarbe f*]

umbrella form, ~ **shape** [*hyperbolic paraboloid*] · Schirmform f

~ roof (of folded shell), ~ shell roof, station roof · Regenschirmschalendach n

~ shell · Regenschirmschale f

~ stand · Schirmständer m

~ vault, parachute ~ · Schirmgewölbe n

unadorned, undecorated, unenriched, unornamented · schmucklos, zierlos. unverziert, ungeschmückt, nüchtern

unalloyed · einfach, unlegiert

~ steel · unlegierter Stahl m

unaltered direction of arrows · ungestörte Pfeilrichtung f

unattended, unmanned · unbesetzt, unbemannt

unbaked brick · ungebrannter Lehmstein m

unbalanced force · Umlenkkraft f

unbonded member · Spannbetonteil m, n mit gleitbehinderten Spanngliedern

unbodied oil · nichteingedicktes Öl n

unbonded · ohne Verbund

~ construction [*There are many bases with which it is impossible to achieve a bond. These include materials such as mastic asphalt, damp-proof membranes, layers of material for sound and thermal insulation, timber ceramic tiles, metal and concrete that has been impregnated with oil and grease or contains a water repellent admixture. Because there is no bond it is necessary to have a screed at least 50 mm thick*] · verbundlose Bauweise f [*Estrichverlegung*]

~ post-stressing [*obsolete*]; **~ post-tensioning** · (Vor)Spannen n im erhärteten Beton ohne Verbund

unbreakable bond, nonbreakable ~ · unzerstörbare Haftung f

~ glass, nonbreakable ~ · unzerbrechliches Glas n

unbroken, uncrushed · nichtgebrochen, ungebrochen

unburned block, ~ **tile, unburnt ~** [*See remark under 'Block'*] · kaltgebundener Block(stein) m, ~ Stein

~ clay, unburnt ~, unfired ~ · Rohton m, ungebrannter Ton

~ lime, unburnt ~, core · Fehlbrand m, Kalkkern m, (Kalk)Krebs m

~ tile, ~ block, unburnt ~ [*See remark under 'Block'*] · kaltgebundener Block(stein) m, ~ Stein

unburnt block, ~ tile, unburned ~ [*See remark under 'Block'*] · kaltgebundener Block(stein) m, ~ Stein

~ lime, unburned ~, core · Fehlbrand m, Kalkkern m, (Kalk)Krebs m

~ plain roof(ing) tile, ~ plane ~ ~, unburned ~ ~ ~ · Biber(schwanz)stein m

~ tile, ~ block, unburned ~ [*See remark under 'Block'*] · kaltgebundener Block(stein) m, ~ Stein

uncased · nichtbetonumhüllt, nichtbetonummantelt

unclimbable · unübersteigbar

uncoated, dry · roh [*Straßenbaugestein ohne Bindemittelumhüllung*]

~ asphalt rag felt, un(sur)faced ~ ~ ~, saturated ~ ~ ~, ~ ~ wool ~ (US); ~ (asphaltic-)bitumen ~ ~ (Brit.) · nackte Bitumenpappe f [*DIN 52129. Mit Tränkmasse durchtränkte Wollfilzpappe*]

~ chip(ping)s, dry ~ · Rohsplitt m

~ tar(red) rag felt, un(sur)faced ~ ~ ~, saturated ~ ~ ~, ~ ~ wool ~ · nackte Teerpappe f [*DIN 52126*]

uncoloured, colourless (Brit.); **uncolored, colorless** (US); **clear, transparent** · farblos

uncombined carbon, elemental ~ · elementarer Kohlenstoff m

uncompressed vegetable fibres (Brit.); ~ ~ **fibers** (US); **loose ~ ~** · pflanzliche Fasern fpl lose

unconnected shaft · versperrter Schacht m [*Mastaba*]

unconserved (air) conditioning plant, ~ (~) ~ system, ~ (~) ~ installation · Klima(tisierungs)anlage f ohne Wasserrücknahme

unconstrained damping layer, ~ ~ course [*It is placed over the surface of a panel as opposed to a constrained damping layer sandwiched between two non-damping layers*] · Oberflächendämpfungslage f, Oberflächendämpfungsschicht f

uncontrolled ventilation · ungeregelte Lüftung f

uncored brick · ungelochter Ziegel m

uncoursed rubble masonry (work), random ~ ~ (~) [*Masonry composed of roughly shaped stone laid without regularity of coursing, but filled together to form well-defined joints*] · ungeschichtetes Bruchsteinmauerwerk n, unregelmäßiges ~

uncovered, unroofed, open · offen, nicht überdacht

~ floor · Rohdecke f

uncreped · ungekreppt

uncrushed, unbroken · nichtgebrochen, ungebrochen

unctuarium, alipterion, anointing room · Aleipterion n, Salbraum m

undecorated — underlay paper

undecorated, unornamented, unenriched, unadorned · schmucklos, zierlos, unverziert, ungeschmückt, nüchtern

undeformable, non-deformable, indeformable · formtreu, unverformbar

undeformed · formtreu, unverformt

underbed, mortar base (course) [*The base mortar usually horizontal*] · Mörtelunterlage *f*, Mörtelbett *n*

under-burning · Schwachbrand *m* [*Zement*]

~, under-firing · Schwachbrand *m*, Biskuitbrand [*Ziegel*]

undercoat, basecoat, backing (coat), scratch coat [*A plastering or rendering coat other than the final coat*] · Rauhwerk *n*, Unterputzschicht *f*, Unterputzlage *f*, Grobputzschicht, Grobputzlage, Grundputzlage, Grundputzschicht

~ **(mixed) plaster,** basecoat (~) ~, backing (coat) (~) ~ · Grundputz *m*, Unterputz, Grobputz

~ **mix(ture)** → backing (coat) ~

~ **plaster,** basecoat ~, ~ mixed ~, backing (coat) (mixed) ~ · Grundputz *m*, Unterputz, Grobputz

~ ~ → backing (coat) mix(ture)

~ **stuff** → backing (coat) mix(ture)

undercoat(er) for external use, exterior undercoat(er), external undercoat(er), outside undercoat(er), outer undercoat(er) · Außenvorlack *m*

undercoating (material), precoating ~, precoating mass, precoating compound, precoating composition · Voranstrichmasse *f*, Vorau fstrichmasse, Voranstrichmittel *n*, Voraufstrichmittel

under compression, compressed · gedrückt

undercounter refrigerator · Unterbau-Kühlschrank *m*

undercroft · Hallenkrypta *f*

undercutting · Unterbieten *n*

~ · Unterschnitt *m*

to underdesign · unterbemessen, unterdimensionieren

underfelt → felt(ed fabric) base

underfire air [*Any air controlled with respect to quantity and direction, forced or induced, supplied beneath the grate that passes through the fuel bed*] · Unterwind *m*

under-firing, under-burning · Schwachbrand *m*, Biskuitbrand [*Ziegel*]

underfloor, subfloor [*abbreviations: undfl., subfl.*] · Unterboden *m*

~ **filler** → sub-floor stopper

(under)floor heating, ~ warming · FB-Heizung *f*, (Fuß)Boden(strahlungs)-heizung

~ ~ **cable** → (electric(al)) (under)floor warming ~

~ ~ **installation** → (electric) (under-)floor warming ~

~ ~ **system** → (electric) (under)floor warming installation

underfloor socket · Unterflur(steck)dose *f*

~ **stopping** → sub-floor stopper

(under)floor warming, ~ heating · FB-Heizung *f*, (Fuß)Boden(strahlungs)-heizung

~ **stopping** → sub-floor stopper

(under)floor warming, ~ heating · FB-Heizung *f*, (Fuß)Boden(strahlungs)-heizung

~ ~ **cable** → electric(al) ~ ~ ~ ~

~ ~ **installation** → electric ~ ~ ~

~ ~ **system** → (electric) (under)floor warming installation

underfloor wiring · Deckenverdrahtung *f*

underflow · Minderdurchfluß *m*, Minderfließen *n*

underground basilica · unterirdische Basilika *f* [*Lourdes*]

~ **block,** ~ building · unterirdisches Gebäude *n*

~ **building,** ~ block · unterirdisches Gebäude *n*

~ **cable** · unterirdisches Kabel *n*

~ ~ **entry** · Kabeleinführung *f* im Keller [*elektrische Hausanlage*]

~ **car park** · Untergrund-Autospeicher *m*, Tief(groß)garage *f*, Tiefparkanlage *f*, Untergrundgarage, Tief-Autospeicher, Untergrund-Parkanlage

~ **cemetery,** catacomb, hypogeum · Katakombe *f*, unterirdischer Friedhof *m*, Hypogäum *n*

~ **chamber,** subterranean ~, ~ room · unterirdischer Raum *m*

~ **external plaster(work)** (Brit.); ~ stucco (US) · unterirdischer Außen(ver)putz *m*

~ **hydrant** · Unterflurhydrant *m*

~ **pipe entry** · Rohreinführung *f* im Keller

~ **piping** · erdverlegte Rohrleitung *f*

~ **room,** subterranean ~, ~ chamber · unterirdischer Raum *m*

~ **service entry** · Einführung *f* im Keller

~ **stucco** (US); ~ external plaster(work) (Brit.) · unterirdischer Außen(ver)putz *m*

underlay, base, backing, substrate, substratum; underlayment (US) · Rücklage *f*, Hinterlegung *f*, Unterlage, Träger-(schicht) *m*, (*f*), Rücken *m*

~ **paper,** sub-soil ~, road lining (~), concreting ~, concrete subgrade ~ ·

underlay paper — unfired semi-stable... 1072

Papierunterlage f, (Autobahn-)Unterlagspapier n, Straßenbaupapier

~ **sheet(ing)**, base ~, backing ~ · Trägerbahn f

underlayment (US); base, backing, underlay, substrate, substratum, backup · Rücklage f, Hinterlegung f, Unterlage, Träger(schicht) m, (f), Rücken m

to underpin · unterfangen

underpinning [*Underpinning is the provision of permanent support for a structure, or portion of a structure, inserted from below, to prevent subsidence and damage, especially during construction work beneath*] · Unterfangen n

under(pre)stressed, undertensioned, understretched · untervorgespannt

under-purline (insulation) · Unterpfettendämmung f

under-reinforced · unterbewehrt, unterarmiert

under-rusting · Unterrostung f [*Rostbildung unter dem Anstrichfilm*]

undersanded · mit zu wenig Feinzuschlägen

underside · Unterseite f

~ **of arch** → (arch) intrados

~ ~ **vault** → (vault) intrados

undersize · Mindergröße f, Untergröße

~ · Feinkorn n, Unterkorn

understressed → under(pre)stressed

understretched → under(pre)stressed

understructure [*access floor*] · Tragekonstruktion f [*Doppel(fuß)boden*]

undertensioned → under(pre)stressed

under-tile, concave tile; mission tile (US) · Haken m, Nonne(nziegel) f, (m), Rinnenziegel

under-veneer, crossband · Blindfurnier n

underwater coat · Unterwasseranstrich m, Unterwasseraufstrich

~ **coat(ing)** · Unterwasseranstrich(schicht) m, (f), Unterwasseraufstrich(schicht)

~ **parking building** · Unterwasser-Parkhaus n

~ **garage** · Unterwassergarage f

~ **individual coat** · Unterwasseranstrichschicht f, Unterwasseraufstrichschicht

~ **window** [*To assist swimming instruction and television facilities*] · Unterwasserfenster n [*Hallen(schwimm)bad*]

underweight · Fehlgewicht n, Untergewicht

(under-)window spandrel, spandrel (wall), breast, apron, parapet; apron wall (US) [*The rectangular infilling in a multi-stor(e)y building between a window sill and the window head below*] · (Fenster)Brüstung f

~ ~ **panel**, spandrel (wall) ~, breast ~, apron ~, parapet ~; apron wall ~ (US) · (Fenster)Brüstungstafel f

undfl., subfl. [*abbreviations*]; underfloor, subfloor · Unterboden m

(un)dressing cab(in), changing ~, ~ cubicle · Aus- und Ankleidekabine f, Umkleidekabine, Aus- und Ankleidezelle f, Umkleidezelle, Aus- und Anziehkabine, Aus- und Anziehzelle

~ **cubicle** → ~ cab(in)

~ **room**, changing ~ · Aus- und Ankleide(raum) f, (m), Umkleide(raum)

undulated vault · wellenförmiges Gewölbe n

undulating façade · gewellte Fassade f

~ **flow**, flow of curves · Kurvenfluß m

~ **line**, wavy ~ · Wellenlinie f

~ **moulding**, wave ~ (Brit.); (o)undy molding, wave molding (US); swelled chamfer · Wellenmuster n

~ **surface** · Wellenfläche f

unenriched, undecorated, unornamented, unadorned · schmucklos, zierlos, unverziert, ungeschmückt, nüchtern

unequal(-leg) angle iron · ungleichschenk(e)liges Winkeleisen n

~ ~ **(section)**, ~ ~ bar, ~ ~ L-section · ungleichschenk(e)liges Winkelprofil n, ungleichschenk(e)liger Winkel m

~ ~ **steel** · ungleichschenk(e)liger L-Stahl m, ~ Winkelstahl [*DIN 1029*]

~ **bulb-angle** · ungleichschenk(e)liger Wulststahl m

~ **L-section** → ~ angle (section)

unequally distributed · ungleichmäßig verteilt

unequal pointed arch · ungleicher Spitzbogen m

uneven, irregular · uneben, unregelmäßig [*Oberfläche*]

~ **settlement**, differential ~ · Setzungsunterschied m

unexpanded [*vermiculite*] · unaufgebläht

~ **composition cork** [*Composition cork made by a process that does not appreciably alter the suberous tissue*] · nichtexpandierter Backkork m mit nicht korkeigenem Bindemittel, nichtgeblähter ~ ~ ~ ~ ~

~ **pure agglomerated cork**, ~ ~ baked ~ [*Agglomerated cork made by a process that does not appreciably alter the suberous tissue*] · nichtexpandierter Backkork m mit korkeigenem Harz gebunden, nichtgeblähter ~ ~ ~ ~ ~

unfaced, plain · nichtabgedeckt [*Baumatte*]

~ **asphalt rag felt** → uncoated ~ ~ ~

unfibered (US) → nonfibered

unfibrated → nonfibrated

unfibred (Brit.) → nonfibrated

unfired clay, unburned ~, unburnt ~ · Rohton m, ungebrannter Ton

~ **semi-stable dolomite refractory brick** · teergebundener Dolomitstein m, Teer-Dolomit(stein) [*Ungebranntes feuerfestes Erzeugnis, das im wesentlichen aus mit Teer, Öl usw. gebundenen, gebranntem Dolomit besteht. Die Binde-*

mittel dienen als Schutz gegen die Luftfeuchtigkeit (manchmal werden diese feuerfesten Erzeugnisse bei niedrigen Temperaturen (unter 1000° C) teilweise vorgebrannt, um das Bindemittel zu verkracken und zu härten]

unfit for human habitation, not habitable, not fit to live in, uninhabitable · unbewohnbar

unfluted · nichtkanneliert, unkanneliert

unfortified · unbefestigt

un-fused, un-run · nichtausgeschmolzen [*Kopal*]

unglazed · nichtbeglast, unbeglast, nichtglasiert, unglasiert

unhardenable · unhärtbar

unhardened, non-hardened · nichtgehärtet, ungehärtet

unheated · unbeheizt, ungeheizt

~ greenhouse· Kalthaus *n*, unbeheiztes Gewächshaus, ungeheiztes Gewächshaus [*DIN 11535 Bl. 1*]

uniaxial tensile strength · einachsige Zugfestigkeit *f*

uniform, single-sized, like-grained, equigranular, even-grained · einkörnig, gleichkörnig

~ · einheitlich

~ aerated concrete, single-sized ~ ~, like-grained ~ ~, short range aggregate ~ ~, equigranular ~ ~, even-grained ~ ~ · einkörniger Porenbeton *m*, gleichkörniger ~, Einkorn-Porenbeton

~ brightness · gleichmäßige Helligkeit *f*

~ concrete, single-sized ~, like-grained ~, short range aggregate ~, equigranular ~, even-grained ~, no-fines ~ · Einkornbeton *m*, einköniger Beton, gleichkörniger Beton [*DIN 4163*]

~ gravel, like-grained ~, single-sized ~, even-grained ~, equigranular ~, short range ~ · einkörniger Kies *m*, gleichkörniger ~, monodisperser ~, Einkornkies

~ load, uniformly distributed ~ · Gleich(flächen)last *f*, gleichmäßige Last, gleichmäßig verteilte Last

~ mortar, like-grained ~, single-sized ~, short range aggregate ~, equigranular, even-grained ~ · einkörniger Mörtel *m*, gleichkörniger ~, Einkornmörtel

~ sand, like-grained ~, single-sized ~, even-grained ~, equigranular ~, short range ~ · einkörniger Sand *m*, gleichkörniger ~, monodisperser ~, Einkornsand

~ settlement · gleichmäßige Setzung *f*

~ taper(ing) · gleichmäßige Verjüngung *f*

uniformity · Einheitlichkeit *f*

~ of illumination, ~ ~ lighting · Gleichmäßigkeit g_1 und g_2 *f* [*Lichttechnik*]

uniform(ly distributed) load · Gleich(flächen)last *f*, gleichmäßige Last, gleichmäßig verteilte Last

~ (~) loading · Gleichbelastung *f*, gleichförmige Belastung, gleichförmig verteilte Belastung, gleichmäßig verteilte Belastung

~ (~) partial load · Teilgleichlast *f*

~ (~) static load · gleichförmig verteilte statische Last *f*, gleichmäßig ~ ~ ~, gleichförmige ~ ~

uniformly sized grains, grains of equal size · gleichkörniges Gut *n*, monodisperses ~

unilateral illumination, ~ lighting · einseitige Beleuchtung *f*

~ lighting, ~ illumination · einseitige Beleuchtung *f*

~ sunshine · einseitige Besonnung *f*

uninhabitable, unfit for human habitation, not habitable, not fit to live in · unbewohnbar

uninsulated · nichtgedämmt

uninterrupted space · ungeteilter Raum *m*

union (coupling) [*A screwed coupling which facilitates dismantling*] · Schraubmuffe Union *f*

uniqueness theorem (in plasticity) · Einzigkeitssatz *m* [*Er bildet die Grundlage zur Ermittlung der plastischen Grenzlast einer Konstruktion. Zum Ermitteln dient u.a. die Methode der Kombination von Gelenkketten nach Neal und Symonds*]

unisolated · nichtisoliert

unit → construction(al) shape

~ → (prefab(ricated)) (building) ~

~, block, accommodation, portion · (Bau-)Trakt *m*, Gebäudetrakt

~, set · Garnitur *f*

~ → (roll-formed) section

~ (air) conditioner, (room) ~ ~, (air) conditioning unit, terminal unit · Klima(tisierungs)gerät *n*

unit-area impedance, specific acoustic ~ · spezifische Schallimpedanz *f* [*Quotient aus Schalldruck und Schallschnelle*]

unit-built block → factory-made building

~ building → factory-made ~

~ house → factory-made ~

unit conditioner → ~ air ~

~ construction, modular ~ · Modulbau *m*

~ fabricator → shape maker

~ for interior work → profile ~ ~ ~

~ furniture kitchen · Anbauküche *f*

~ heater → air ~

~ load · Belastungseinheit *f*, Einheitslast *f*

~ maker → shape ~

~ masonry (work) · Fugenmauerwerk *n*

~ of area, area unit · Flächeneinheit *f*, Flächenmaß *n*

~ pressure · Einheitsdruck *m*

~ price · Einheitspreis *m*

~ **spacing** · Achs(en)abstand *m*, Achs(en)maß *n* [*Maßordnung*]

~ **volume** · Raumeinheit *f*

United Nations Secretariat Building · UNO-Hauptquartier *n* [*in New-York*]

(unitized) bathroom (and lavatory) unit → prefab(ricated) bathroom ~

~ **kitchen unit,** kitchen building block module · Küchen(installations)block *m*, Küchen(installations)zelle, Küchenraumblock, Küchenraumzelle

~ **unit,** building block module, room(-size) unit · (Raum)Zelle *f*, Installationszelle, Installationsblock *m*

~ ~ **method,** (building block) module ~; modular housing (US) · (Raum-) Zellenbauweise *f*, Installationszellen-bauweise, Installationsblockbauweise, Bauen *n* mit Raumzellen [*Die Bauten sind mit dem Grundstück dauerhaft verbunden. Gegensatz: bewegliche Raumzellen mobile homes*]

unity, self-containedness · Geschlossenheit *f*

~ **of composition,** ~ ~ design · gestalterische Einheit *f*

~ ~ **design,** ~ ~ composition · gestalterische Einheit *f*

univalent radical · einwertiges Radikal *n*

universal adhesive → ~ bonding ~

'Universal' beam (section) · Universal-Walzträger *m*

universal (bonding) adhesive, ~ ~ agent, ~ ~ medium, ~ cement(ing agent) · Universalkleb(e)stoff *m*, Universalkleb(e)mittel *n*, Universalkleber *m*

~ **cement(ing agent)** → ~ (bonding) adhesive

'Universal' column (section) · Universal-Walzstütze *f*

universal compound · Universal-Kleb(e)masse *f*

~ **(mill) plate** → (rolled) nonstandard section

'Universal' section → (rolled) nonstandard ~

universal tinter; ~ tinting color (US) · Universal-Abtönfarbe *f*, Universal-Mischfarbe

~ **tinting color** (US); ~ tinter · Universal-Abtönfarbe *f*, Universal-Mischfarbe

'Universal' unit → (rolled) nonstandard section

University church at Salzburg · Kollegienkirche *f* in Salzburg

university ground, campus · Hochschulgelände *n*

univocal resolving of a force · endgültige Kraftzerlegung *f*

unknown · Unbekannte *f*

~ **quantity** · unbekannte Größe *f*

unleaded · ungebleit

unlighted, unlit [*abbreviated: unltd.*] unbeleuchtet

unlined, exposed · unverkleidet

unlit, unlighted [*abbreviated: unltd.*] · unbeleuchtet

~ **triforium (gallery),** blind ~ (~), ~ ~ arcade · Blendtriforium *n*, nicht durchfenstertes Triforium, blindes Triforium, Blindtriforium

to unload, to off-load · abladen

unloaded · unbelastet

unloading ramp, off-loading ~ · Entladerampe *f*, Ausladerampe

unltd. [*abbreviated*]; unlit, unlighted · unbeleuchtet

unmanned, unattended · unbesetzt, unbemannt

unmannered · unmaniriert

unobstructed access · ungehinderter Zugang *m*

~ **(through-)vision,** clear ~ · ungehinderte Durchsicht *f*, vollständige ~ [*Glas*]

~ **view** · ungehinderte Aussicht *f* [*Fenster*]

~ **vision,** ~ through-~, clear (through-)vision · ungehinderte Durchsicht *f*, vollständige ~ [*Glas*]

unornamented, undecorated unenriched, unadorned · schmucklos, zierlos, unverziert, ungeschmückt, nüchtern

unpainted [*abbreviated: unpntd.*] · roh, ungestrichen

unpaved · unbefestigt [*Straße*]

unpedimented · ohne Giebel(feld)

unperforated, nonperforated · glatt, ungelocht

unpigmented, non-pigmented · nichtpigmentiert, unpigmentiert

~ **(cold-)water paint** → ~ water-carried ~

~ **water-carried paint,** ~ (cold-)water ~ · Binder *m* [*Ein nichtpigmentierter Anstrichstoff auf der Grundlage einer Bindemitteldispersion (Bindemittelemulsion oder Bindemittelsuspension), der mit Wasser verdünnbar ist und nach dem Trocknen einen wasserunlöslichen Anstrich hinterläßt*]

unplastered · roh, unverputzt

~ **ceiling plate** [*Scotland*] → ~ (gypsum) ceiling plasterboard

~ **(gypsum) ceiling plasterboard,** ~ ~ ~ board; ~ ceiling plate [*Scotland*] · Gipskarton-Deckenbauplatte *f*

~ **(~) plasterboard,** ~ ~ board; ~ plate [*Scotland*] · Gipskarton-Bauplatte *f* [*Im Gegensatz zu der Gipskarton-Stuckplatte ist die Gipskarton-Bauplatte unverputzt*]

~ **(~) wall plasterboard,** ~ ~ wallboard; ~ plate for walls [*Scotland*] · Gipskarton-Wandbauplatte *f*

unplastered gypsum wallboard — upper basement

~ ~ wallboard → ~ (~) wall plasterboard

~ plate [*Scotland*] → ~ (gypsum) plasterboard

~ ~ for walls [*Scotland*] → ~ (gypsum) wall plasterboard

~ wall plasterboard → ~ gypsum ~ ~

un(pre)stressed → untensioned

unprimed · nichtgrundiert

unreactive, nonreactive · reaktionsfrei, reaktionslos

unreinforced, plain · nichtbewehrt, nichtarmiert, unbewehrt, unarmiert

unrelievedly cubic general shape · einfache kubische Hauptform *f*

unrestrained · einspannungsfrei, einspannungslos

unretarded hemihydrate (gypsumplaster) → plaster of Paris

unroofed, uncovered, open · offen, nicht überdacht

un-run, un-fused · nichtausgeschmolzen [*Kopal*]

unsaponifiable · unverseifbar

unsaturated [*abbreviated: unsatd.*] · ungesättigt

~ compound · ungesättigte Verbindung *f*

~ fatty acid · ungesättigte Fettsäure *f*

~ hydrocarbon · ungesättigter Kohlenwasserstoff *m*

~ polyester (resin), contact ~ [*misnomers: polyester (resin)*] · ungesättigtes Polyesterharz *n*, UP-Harz, ungesättigter Polyester *m*

unsaturation · Ungesättigtheit *f*, Nichtsättigung *f*

to unscrew, to screw off · lösen, losschrauben, auseinanderschrauben, abschrauben

unserviceability · Unbrauchbarkeit *f*

unserviced hung ceiling, ~ suspended ~ · Hängedecke *f* ohne Leitungen

~ suspended ceiling, ~ hung ~ · Hängedecke *f* ohne Leitungen

unset concrete · unabgebundener Beton *m*

unshaped refractory (product), ~ ~ material · nichtgeformter feuerfester Stoff *m*, ~ ff. ~, nichtgeformtes feuerfestes Erzeugnis *n*, nichtgeformtes ff. Erzeugnis

unsheathed wall · unverschalte Wand *f*

unsintered · nichtgesintert, ungesintert

unslaked · ungelöscht [*Kalk*]

~ and ground quicklime · gemahlener Branntkalk *m*, Mahlkalk, ungelöschter gemahlener Kalk [*Fehlname: treibender Kalk*]

unsound, faulty, defective · fehlerhaft, mangelhaft, schadhaft

unsoundness · Mangelhaftigkeit *f*

unstable, instable [*A description of a structure which is liable to fail as a whole, generally, by overturning or sliding*] · nichtstandsicher, beweglich, mobil, labil, instabil

~ frame, instable ~ · bewegliches Netz *n*, labiles ~, instabiles ~, mobiles ~, nichtstandsicheres ~ [*ebenes Fachwerk*]

unsteamed concrete · unbedampfter Beton *m*

unstiffened · unversteift

unstressed → untensioned

unsupported · trägerlos, füllerlos [*Kunststoffolie*]

~ · nichtunterstützt

un(sur)faced asphalt rag felt → uncoated ~ ~ ~

~ tar(red) rag felt → uncoated ~ ~ ~

unsusceptible · unempfindlich

unsymmetric(al) cruciform pier · unregelmäßiger Kreuzpfeiler *m*

~ roof · unsymmetrisches Dach *n*

untensioned, non(pre)stressed, nonstretched, nontensioned, un(pre)stressed · schlaff (bewehrt), ~ armiert, mit schlaffen (Stahl)Einlagen

~ steel (reinforcement), ~ ~ reinforcing, mild ~ (~), ordinary ~ (~) · schlaffe Armierung *f*, ~ Bewehrung, ~ (Stahl)Einlagen *fpl*

~ ~ ~ of (pre)stressed concrete elements, mild ~ ~ ~ ~ ~ ~ · schlaffe Bewehrung *f* von Spannbetonbauteilen

unthinned · unverdünnt

untrapped [*street gull(e)y*] · ohne Geruchverschluß *m*

untrimmed floor · wechsellose Decke *f*

unvaulted · ungewölbt

unwinder, dry felt jumbo roll · Abwickelbock *m* für Rohfilzpappe, Rohpappenbock [*Dachpappenanlage*]

up-and-over door of the roll-up type, overhead ~ ~ ~ ~ ~, roll-up up-and-over door, roll-up overhead door · Rolltor *n*

~ ~ ~ ~ swing-up type, overhead ~ ~ ~ ~ ~, swing-up overhead door, swing-up up-and-over door · Kipptor *n*, Schwingtor

upholstered seat · Polstersitz *m*

upholstery material · Polstermaterial *n*

upkeep, maintenance · Instandhaltung *f*, Unterhaltung, Wartung

~ cost(s), maintenance ~ · Instandhaltungskosten *f*, Unterhaltungskosten, Wartungskosten

~ obligation, maintenance ~ · Instandhaltungspflicht *f*, Unterhaltungspflicht, Wartungspflicht

~ undertaking, maintenance ~ · Instandhaltungsbetrieb *m*, Unterhaltungsbetrieb, Wartungsbetrieb

uplift, buoyancy · Auftrieb *m*

~ pressure, buoyancy ~ · Auftriebsdruck *m*

upper basement · oberes Kellergeschoß *n*, erstes ~

upper bed — urban centre

~ **bed**, top ~ · obere Lagerfläche f, weiche ~, oberes Lager n, weiches Lager [*Werkstein*]

~ **boom**, top ~, ~ chord, ~ flange · Oberflansch m, Obergurt(ung) m, (f)

~ ~ **junction plate**, top ~ ~, upper flange ~ ~, ~ chord ~ ~ · Oberflanschknotenblech n, Obergurt(ungs)-knotenblech

~ ~ **plate**, top ~ ~, ~ chord ~, ~ flange ~ · Obergurtlamelle f

~ **bound solution**, kinematic ~ · kinematische Lösung f

~ ~ **theorem**, kinematic ~ · kinematischer Satz m

~ **chapel** · Oberkapelle f

~ **choir**, raised ~, ~ quire, coro alto · Oberchor m, Hochchor

~ **chord** → ~ boom

~ ~ **junction plate**, ~ flange ~ ~, ~ boom ~ ~, top ~ ~ ~ · Oberflanschknotenblech n, Obergurt(ungs)-knotenblech

~ ~ **plate** → ~ boom ~

~ **church** · Oberkirche f [*Obergeschoß einer Doppelkirche*]

~ **citadel** · Oberburg f [*Tiryns*]

~ **city**, citadel · Stadtkrone f [*Kernzelle einer Stadt mit den wichtigsten Monumentalbauten und in stark hervortretender Lage, z.B. Akropolis, Kapitol usw.*]

~ **(door) rail**, top (~) ~ · oberes Querrahmenstück n, oberer (Tür)Riegel m [*Holzfüllungstür*]

~ **flange** → ~ boom

~ ~ **junction plate**, ~ chord ~ ~, ~ boom ~ ~, top ~ ~ ~ · Oberflanschknotenblech n, Obergurt(ungs)knotenblech

~ ~ **plate** → ~ boom ~

~ **floor**, ~ story (US); ~ storey (Brit.) · Obergeschoß n, Oberetage f, Oberstockwerk n, Hochgeschoß, Hochetage, Hochstockwerk, OG [*Im Gegensatz zum Kellergeschoß und Erdgeschoß*]

~ ~ **(ground(-))plan**; ~ story ~ (US); ~ storey ~ (Brit.) · Obergeschoßgrundriß m

~ ~ **hearth** · Obergeschoß-Kaminboden m

~ ~ **plan**; ~ story ~ (US); ~ storey ~ (Brit.) · Obergeschoßrohbauplan m

~ ~ ~ → ~ ~ ground(-)~

~ ~ **wall**; ~ story ~ (US); ~ storey ~ (Brit.) · Obergeschoßwand f

~ **joist floor** → single upper ~

~ **mould**, master ~ (Brit.); ~ mold (US) · Mutterform f [*Ziegelindustrie*]

~ **quire**, raised ~, ~ choir, coro alto · Oberchor m, Hochchor

~ **rail**, top ~, ~ door ~ · oberes Querrahmenstück n, oberer (Tür)Riegel m [*Holzfüllungstür*]

~ **reinforcement**, top ~ · Abreißbewehrung f, Abreißarmierung, Abreiß-(stahl)einlagen fpl

~ **residential floor**; ~ ~ story (US); ~ ~ storey (Brit.) · Wohnoberetage f, Wohnoberstockwerk n, Wohnobergeschoß n

~ ~ **storey** (Brit.); ~ ~ story (US); ~ ~ floor · Wohnoberetage f, Wohnoberstockwerk n, Wohnobergeschoß n

~ **sash**, top ~ [*It slides on the outside*] · oberer Schiebe(fenster)flügel m, Oberflügel

~ **storey** (Brit.); ~ story (US); ~ floor · Obergeschoß n, Oberetage f, Oberstockwerk n, Hochgeschoß, Hochetage, Hochstockwerk, OG [*Im Gegensatz zum Kellergeschoß und Erdgeschoß*]

~ ~ **(ground(-))plan** (Brit.) → ~ floor ~

~ ~ **plan** (Brit.); ~ story ~ (US); ~ floor ~ · Obergeschoßrohbauplan m

~ ~ **wall** (Brit.); ~ story ~ (US); ~ floor ~ · Obergeschoßwand f

~ **surface of arch**, back ~ ~, extrados ~ ~, (arch) extrados, (arch) back [*The outer line or surface of the convex side of an arch*] · Rücken m, Bogen~, äußere Bogenfläche f

~ ~ ~ **vault**, back ~ ~, extrados ~ ~, (vault) extrados, (vault) back · Rücken m, Gewölbe~, äußere Gewölbefläche f

upright brick · Rollstein m, Rollstück n [*Auf der Schmalseite stehend vermauerter Ziegel*]

upstand, upturn, turn-up [*That part of a felt or flexible-metal flashing, or roof covering which turns up beside a wall without being turned into it, and is covered usually by a stepped flashing*] · Aufkantung f

up-take, breeching, main flue (US); flue connection to stack, flue connection to chimney · (Schornstein)Fuchs(kanal) m [*Waag(e)rechter oder mit leichter Steigung von der Heizanlage zum Schornstein führender Rauchkanal*]

upturn → upstand

upward camber → (arch) rise

~ **deflexion**, ~ deflection · Aufwölben n

urac [*USA*]; beetle cement [*Great Britain*] · Kauritleim m [*Deutschland*]; Melocol m [*Schweiz*] [*Genormtes Kurzzeichen in Deutschland: K*]

urban aggregate · städtische Agglomeration f

~ **architecture** → town ~

~ **area**, municipal ~, town ~ · Stadtgebiet n

~ **block**, town ~, municipal ~ [*A division of a city bounded by four streets*] · Stadtviertel n

~ **centre** (Brit.); ~ center (US); municipal ~, town ~ · Stadtmitte f

urban chapel — urea-formaldehyde resin

~ **chapel,** municipal ~, town ~ · Stadtkapelle *f*

~ **church,** municipal ~, town ~ [*A church in a town*] · Stadtkirche *f*

~ **configuration,** town ~, municipal ~ · Stadtfigur *f*

~ **construction (work)** · Stadtbauarbeiten *fpl*

~ **development,** town ~, municipal ~ · Städtebau *m*

~ ~, town ~, municipal ~ · Stadtentwickl(e)lung *f*

~ ~ **committee,** municipal ~ ~, town ~ ~ · Städtebauausschuß *m*

~ **engineering,** municipal ~, town ~ · Stadtbautechnik *f*, Städtebautechnik

~ **expressway,** town ~, municipal ~ · Stadtschnellstraße *f*

~ **extension,** municipal ~, town ~ · Stadterweiterung *f*

~ **forest,** municipal ~, town ~ · Stadtwald *m*

~ **fringe** · Stadtsaum *m*

~ **garden,** municipal ~, town ~ · Stadtgarten *m*

~ **hall,** municipal ~ · Stadthalle *f*

~ **heating,** municipal ~, town ~ · Stadtheizung *f*

~ **hotel,** municipal ~, town ~ · Stadthotel *n*

~ **landscape,** townscape · Stadtlandschaft *f*, Städtelandschaft

~ **library,** municipal ~, town ~ · Stadtbibliothek *f*, Stadtbücherei *f*

~ **living-space,** town ~, municipal ~ · städtischer Lebensraum *m*

~ **motorway** · Stadtautobahn *f*

~ **multi-purpose system** · nutzungsneutrales Stadtsystem *n*

~ **museum,** town ~, municipal ~ · Stadtmuseum *n*

~ **network** · Stadtnetz *n*

~ **orphanage,** town ~, municipal ~ · städtisches Waisenhaus *n*

~ **palace,** town ~, municipal ~ · Stadtpalast *m*

~ **park,** municipal ~, town ~ · Stadtpark *m*

~ **planner,** municipal ~, town ~ · Städtebauer *m*, Stadtbauer, Städteplaner, Stadtplaner

~ **planning,** municipal ~, town ~ · städtebauliche Planung *f*, Stadtplanung, Städteplanung

~ ~ **authority,** town ~ ~ · Stadtplanungsbehörde *f*

~ ~ **institute,** town ~ ~, municipal ~ ~ · Städtebauinstitut *n*

~ ~ **studies,** town ~ ~, municipal ~ · Stadtbaulehre *f*, städtebauliche Lehre

~ ~ **system,** town ~ ~, municipal ~ ~ · Stadtbausystem *n*

~ ~ **theory,** town ~ ~, municipal ~ ~ · Städtebautheorie *f*

~ **pool,** municipal ~, town ~, ~ swimming bath · Stadtbad *n*

~ **population** · Stadtbevölkerung *f*

~ **rapid transit system;** metropolitan railway (Brit.); metropolitan railroad (US) · S-Bahn *f*, Stadt(schnell)bahn

(~) **redevelopment,** (~) renewal · Stadterneuerung(smaßnahmen) *f*, (*fpl*), (Stadt)Sanierung [*1. Verbesserung und Neugestaltung von Gebäuden und der Nachbarschaft. 2. Abriß von Gebäuden und/oder Entfernen von Verkehrsanlagen bzw. Freiflächen aller Art um Raum für neue Einrichtungen zu schaffen*]

(~) **renewal area,** (~) ~ zone, (~) ~ site, (~) redevelopment ~, (~) redeveloping ~ · Sanierungsgebiet *n*, (Stadt)Erneuerungsgebiet

~ **road,** town ~, municipal ~, (city) street, urban thoroughfare, city road, st · Stadtstraße *f*

~ **run-off** · Stadtabfluß *m* [*Jener Teil des Niederschlages einer Stadt, der oberirdisch abfließt*]

~ **sauna bath,** municipal ~ ~, town ~ ~ · Stadt-Sauna(bad) *f*, (*n*)

~ **science** · Stadtwissenschaft *f*

~ **station,** municipal ~, (in-)town ~ · Stadtbahnhof *m*

~ **supply network** · Stadtversorgungsnetz *n*

~ **swimming bath,** town ~ ~, municipal ~ ~, ~ ~ pool · Stadtbad *n*

~ **theatre,** municipal ~, town ~, ~ theater · Stadttheater *n*

~ **thoroughfare** → ~ road

~ **traffic** · Stadtverkehr *m*, städtischer Verkehr

~ ~ **planning** · städtische Verkehrsplanung *f*

~ **tramway network** · städtisches Straßenbahnnetz *n*

~ **tunnel** · Stadttunnel *m*

~ **villa** · Stadtvilla *f*

~ **wall,** municipal ~, town ~, ~ masonry ~ · Stadtmauer *f*

urbanity · Urbanität *f*

urbanization · Verstädterung *f*

urbanized area (US); conurbation (Brit.) · verstädterte Zone *f*

urea · Harnstoff *m*, $CO(NH_2)_2$

~ **adhesive** → ~ synthetic resin ~

~ **formaldehyde,** UF · Harnstoffformaldehyd *n*

urea-formaldehyde adhesive, ~ glue · Harnstoffformaldehydleim *m*

~ **foam** → foamed urea-formaldehyde

~ **glue** → urea (synthetic resin) adhesive

~ **resin** · Harnstoff-Formaldehyd(harz) *n*, UF

urea resin · Harnstoffharz n [Durch Kondensation von Harnstoff und Formaldehyd hergestellter Kunststoff. DIN 7735]

~ ~ **foam** · Harnstoffharzschaum(stoff) m

~ ~ **laminate(d) plastic** · Harnstoffharz-Schichtstoff m

~ ~ **moulding compound** (Brit.); ~ ~ **molding** ~ (US) · Harnstoffharz-Preßmasse f

~ ~ **varnish** · Harnstoffharzlack m

~ **(synthetic resin) adhesive,** ~ (~ ~) **glue,** ~ **resin** ~, urea-formaldehyde ~ · Harnstoff-Formaldehyd(harz)leim m, Harnstoffharzleim

~ **varnish resin** · Harnstoff-Lackharz n

urethane coating, (poly)urethane (surface) ~, (poly)urethane lacquer · Polyurethanlack m

~ **foam,** expanded urethane · Urethanschaum(stoff) m

~ **lacquer,** poly~ ~, (poly)urethane (surface) coating · Polyurethanlack m

~ **linseed oil** · Urethan-Leinöl n

~ **paint** · Urethan(anstrich)farbe f

~ **resin** · Carbamidsäureesterharz n, Urethanharz

~ **(surface) coating,** poly~ (~) ~, (poly)urethane lacquer · Polyurethanlack m

urinal · Urinal n

~ **(installation)** · Urinalanlage f

~ **stall** · Pißstand m, Urinalstand

~ **trough** · Pißrinne f, Urinalrinne

urine-repellent, urine-repelling · urinabstoßend

urine-repelling, urine-repellent · urinabstoßend

urine stain · Harnfleck m

urn, cinerary ~, cremation ~ · (Aschen-)Urne f

~ **pit,** cinerary ~ ~, cremation ~ ~ · Brandgrab n, (Aschen)Urnengrab

urological clinic · urologische Klinik f

US Department of Housing and Urban Development · Ministerium n für Wohnungs- und Städtebau der USA

usable floor area · nutzbare Geschoßfläche f, ~ Etagenfläche, ~ Stockwerkfläche

~ **room area** · nutzbare Raumfläche f

use capability → ~ property

~ **capacity** → ~ property

~ **load,** occupancy ~, superimposed ~ [The load of machinery, equipment, furniture and people on floors, corridors, balconies, stairs, etc.] · Gebrauchslast f, Nutzlast

~ **property,** ~ quality, ~ capacity, ~ capability · Anwendungseigenschaft f, Anwendungsfähigkeit f, Anwendungsvermögen n

~ **quality** → ~ property

use-zoning · Zonenbauordnung f

used grease, waste ~ · Altfett n, Abfallfett

~ **oil,** waste ~ · Ab(fall)öl n, Altöl

useful cross-section · nutzbarer Querschnitt m, Nutzquerschnitt

~ **height** · Nutzhöhe f

~ **length** · Nutzlänge f

~ **rock** · Nutzgestein n

~ **width** · Nutzbreite f

user, resident, (apartment) dweller, (room) occupant · Raumbenutzer m, (Wohnungs)Benutzer, (Raum)Insasse m, Wohnungsinsasse, Bewohner

(U-shaped) metal channel · Metall-U-Profil n

~ **patent glazing bar,** ~ puttyless ~ · Rinnensprosse f, U-Sprosse [kittlose Verglasung]

~ **pumice concrete block,** ~ ~ ~ tile [See remark under 'Block(stein)'] [(Natur)Bims(beton)-U-Block(stein) m, (Natur)Bims(beton)-U-Stein

~ **puttyless glazing bar,** ~ patent ~ ~ · Rinnensprosse f, U-Sprosse [kittlose Verglasung]

'Usonian Houses' ['Usonian' was a term coined by Frank Lloyd Wright to describe something ultra-American] · Usonienhäuser npl

utilitarian building, commercial ~, ~ block [A building used principally for business or professional practice] · Geschäftsgebäude n, Geschäftshaus n

~ **classicism** · utilitaristischer Klassizismus m

~ **element** · Nützlichkeitselement n

utilitarianism · Utilitarismus m

utilities, public ~ · Stadtversorgung f

utility, service plant · Versorgungseinrichtung f

~ → service (run)

~ **architecture** · Zweckarchitektur f, Zweckbaukunst f

~ **core,** building ~, service ~, mechanical ~, (reinforced) concrete ~, R.C. ~ · (Hoch)Hauskern m, (Stahl-)Betonkern, Betriebskern, (Gebäude-)Kern

~ **line,** ~ run · Verbrauchsleitung f [innerhalb eines Gebäudes]

~ **raceway** → service (run)

~ **room** · Nutzraum m

~ **run,** ~ line · Verbrauchsleitung f [innerhalb eines Gebäudes]

~ **shaft,** service ~ · Betriebsschacht m [Hochhaus]

~ **tower** → service ~

~ **undertaking,** supply ~, public utility · (öffentlicher) Versorgungsbetrieb m

utilization of refuse water, ~ ~ foul ~, ~ ~ sewage · Abwasserwertung f [Wirtschaftliche Nutzung des Abwassers oder der durch Abwasser-

utilization of refuse water — vapour chimney

reinigung ausgeschiedenen Bestandteile für landwirtschaftliche, gewerbliche oder industrielle Zwecke]

~ ~ ~ **for agricultural purposes,** ~ ~ **foul** ~ ~ ~ ~, ~ ~ **sewage** ~ ~ ~ · *landwirtschaftliche Abwasserverwertung f*

U-tube visco(si)meter · Ostwald-Viskosimeter *n*, U-Rohr-Viskosimeter

U-value, air-to-air heat-transmission coefficient · Wärmeübergangszahl *f*

V

VA, visual aid · Sichthilfe *f*

vacation hostel, holiday ~ · Ferienwohnheim *n*

~ **hotel,** holiday ~ · Ferienhotel *n*

~ **house,** holiday ~ · Ferienhaus *n*

vacuum · Luftleere *f*, Unterdruck *m*, Vakuum *n*

~ **asphalt** (US); ~ (asphaltic-)bitumen (Brit.) · Vakuumbitumen *n*

~ **bottle** → Dewar flask

~ **cleaning,** vacuuming · Absaugen *n* [*(Fuß)Bodenreinigung*]

~ **coating,** sputtering · Metallaufdampfen *n*

~ **concrete** · Saugbeton *m*, Vakuumbeton, Unterdruckbeton

~ ~ **pipe** · Saugbetonrohr *n*, Unterdruckbetonrohr, Vakuumbetonrohr

~ **deep drawing** · Vakuum-Tiefziehen *n*

~ **heating** · Vakuumdampfheizung *f*

~ **lifting** [*Lifting by a crane fitted with a suction pad, employed for such items as precast concrete elements, etc.*] · Vakuumheben *n*

vacuuming, vacuum cleaning · Absaugen *n* [*(Fuß)Bodenreinigung*]

valence, valency · (chemische) Wertigkeit *f*

Valhalla, Hall of Fame · Ruhmeshalle *f*, Walhalla *f* [*bei Regensburg*]

valley, roof ~; flanc [*local term*] · (Dach-) Kehle *f*, (Dach)Kehlung *f*, Einkehle; Ichsen *f* [*Schweiz*]

~ **beam,** ~ girder · Rinnenbalken(träger) *m*, Rinnenträger [*Shedrahmen*]

~ **board** · Kehlbrett *n*

~ **clay roof(ing) tile,** ~ roof(ing) clay ~, (roof) valley clay ~ · (Rinnen-) Kehlziegel *m*, Schwenkziegel

~ **flashing** [*See remark under 'Anschluß'*] · Kehlanschluß *m*

~ ~ **(piece)** · Kehlanschluß(streifen) *m*

~ **girder,** ~ beam · Rinnenbalken(träger) *m*, Rinnenträger [*Shedrahmen*]

~ **gutter** [*A gutter formed at a valley, having sloping sides and exposed to view*] · Kehlrinne *f*

~ **jack (rafter)** · Kehlgratstichbalken *m*

~ ~ **(~)** · Kehlschifter *m*, Wechselsparren *m*

~ **line** · Kehllinie *f*

~ **of corrugation** · Wellental *n*

~ **post,** roof ~ ~ · (Dach)Kehlstütze *f* [*mehrschiffige Halle*]

~ **rafter** · Kehlgratbalken *m*

~ ~ [*A rafter that forms the intersection of an internal roof angle*] · Kehl(grat)sparren *m*

~ **roof** → intersecting ~

~ ~ **tile,** ~ roofing ~, (roof) valley ~ · Kehlstein *m*

~ **roof(ing) clay tile,** ~ clay roof(ing) ~, (roof) valley clay ~ · (Rinnen)Kehlziegel *m*, Schwenkziegel

~ ~ **tile,** (roof) valley ~ · Kehlstein *m*

~ **shingle** · Kehlschindel *f*

~ **slab** · Kehlplatte *f*

~ **slope** · Kehlneigung *f* [*Dach*]

~ **soaker** · Kehlgebindewinkel *m*

~ **soffit** · Kehlrinnenuntersicht *f*

~ **temple** · Taltempel *m*

~ **tile,** roof ~ ~, valley roof(ing) ~ · Kehlstein *m*

value of set(ting), set(ting) value · (Ab)Bindewert *m*

~ ~ **snow load,** snow load value · Schneelastwert *m*

~ ~ **wind load,** wind load value · Windlastwert *m*

vandal-proof, burglat-proof · einbruchsicher

Van Dyck brown · Vandyckbraun *n* [*Erdige Braunkohle, feinste durch Schlämmen gewonnene Sorte des Kasselerbrauns. Nur als Malfarbe verwendet*]

vane, cock, weather ~ · Windfahne *f*, Wetterhahn *m*

vanishing point, accidental ~ · Verschwindungspunkt *m*, Fluchtpunkt, Fl. P.

vapour, water ~ (Brit.); (water) vapor (US) · Wasserdampf *m*

~ **absorption,** water ~ ~ (Brit.); (water) vapor ~ (US) · Wasserdampfaufnahme *f*

~ **barrier foil,** ~ seal ~ (Brit.); vapor ~ ~ (US) · Dampfsperrfolie *f*

~ ~ **(membrane),** ~ seal (~), vapourproof ~ (Brit.); vapor barrier (~), vapor seal (~), vaporproof ~ (US) · Dampfsperre *f*, Dampfsperrschicht *f*, Dampfsperrlage *f*, Dampfdiffusionsbremse *f*

~ ~ **sheet(ing)** (Brit.); vapor ~ ~ (US) · Dampfsperrbahn *f*

~ **barring,** water ~ ~ (Brit.); (water) vapor ~ (US) · (wasser)dampfsperrend

~ **chimney,** water ~ ~ (Brit.); (water) vapor ~ (US) · Wrasenkamin *m*, Wrasenschornstein *m* [*für den Abzug von Wasserdampf*]

vapour condensation — (vat) dye

~ condensation, water ~ ~ (Brit.); (water) vapor ~ (US) · Wasserdampfkondensation *f*

~ content, water ~ ~ (Brit.); (water) vapor ~ (US) · Wasserdampfgehalt *m*

~ diffusion, water ~ ~ (Brit.); (water) vapor ~ (US); damp ~ · Wasserdampfdiffusion *f*

~ impermeability → water ~ ~

~ imperviousness → (water) vapour impermeability

~ lamp (Brit.); vapor ~ (US) · Dampflampe *f*

~ migration, water ~ ~ (Brit.); (water) vapor ~ (US) · Wasserdampfwanderung *f*

~ mist, water ~ ~ (Brit.); (water) vapor ~ (US) · Wasserdampfnebel *m*

~ permeability, water ~ ~ (Brit.); (water) vapor ~ (US) · Wasserdampfdurchlässigkeit *f*

vapour-permeable, water ~ (Brit.); (water) vapor-permeable(US) · wasserdampfdurchlässig

vapour pipe, water ~ ~ (Brit.); (water) vapor ~ (US) · Wrasenrohr *n* [*Lüftungsrohr in Koch-, Wasch- und Futterküchen*]

~ pressure, (saturated) water ~ ~ (Brit.); (saturated) (water) vapor ~ (US) · Wasserdampfdruck *m*

vapourproof membrane → vapour barrier (~)

vapour quantity, water ~ ~ (Brit.); (water) vapor ~ (US) · Wasserdampfmenge *f*

~ release → water ~ ~

~ resistant, water ~ ~ (Brit.); (water) vapor ~ (US) · wasserdampffest

~ seal, water ~ ~ (Brit.); (water) vapor ~ (US) · Wasserdampfbremse *f*

~ ~ foil → ~ barrier ~

~ ~ (membrane) → ~ barrier (~)

vapour-tight (Brit.); vapor-tight (US) · (wasser)dampfdicht

vapour transfer coefficient, water ~ ~ ~ (Brit.); (water) vapor ~ ~ (US) · Wasserdampfübergangszahl *f*

~ transmission, water ~ ~ (Brit.); (water) vapor ~ (US); WVT · Wasserdampfdurchgang *m*

variability · Veränderlichkeit *f*

variable cross-section · veränderlicher Querschnitt *m*

~ depth section frame · Rahmen *m* mit unterschiedlichen Querschnittsgrößen

~ floor load, imposed ~ ~, floor live ~ · veränderliche Deckenlast *f*, wechselnde ~, bewegliche ~, Decken-Verkehrslast, Verkehrs-Deckenlast

~ inertia · veränderliche Trägheit *f*

~ moment of inertia · veränderliches Trägheitsmoment *n*

variation of brightness · Helligkeitsschwankung *f*

~ order · Abänderungsauftrag *m*

variegated, speckled, dappled [*Marked with spots of a different colo(u)r or shade*] · (bunt)gefleckt

~ sandstone (Brit.); mottled ~, bunter ~, Lower Triassic ~ · Buntsandstein *m*

variety store · Kleinpreisgeschäft *n*

varnish → clear ~

~ coat(ing), ~ finish · Lackanstrich *m*, Lackaufstrich, Lacküberzug *m*, Lackbeschichtung *f*

~ film · Lackfilm *m*

~ finish → ~ coat(ing)

~ for building construction purposes, clear ~ ~ ~ ~ ~ · Bautenlack *m* [*Fehlname: Malerlack*]

~ kettle, ~ pot · Lackkessel *m*

~ maker · Lackhersteller *m*

~ manufacture · Lackherstellung *f*

~ medium → clear ~ ~

~ oil, bleached ~ · Lackleinöl *n* [*Helles, entschleimtes Leinöl das für alle Zwecke in der Lackherstellung und zur Anreibung mit Weiß- und Buntpigmenten dient*]

~ paint, oleoresinous ~ · Öllackfarbe *f*

~ pot, ~ kettle · Lackkessel *m*

~ raw material · Lackrohstoff *m*

~ remover, ~ stripper, (paint) ~ [*B.S. 3761*] · Lacklöser *m*, Lackbeize *f*, Abbeizer, Ablaugemittel *n*, (Ab)Beizmittel, Farbenlöser, Farbenentferner [*vom Anstreicher kurz „Lauge" f genannt*]

~ resin, lacquer-grade ~ · Lackharz *n*

~ soybean oil, refined ~ ~ (US); ~ soya bean ~ (Brit.) · raffiniertes Soja(bohnen)öl *n*, Lacksojaöl

~ system, clear ~ ~ · (Klar)Lacksystem *n*

~ vehicle → clear ~ ~

varnishing · Lackieren *n*

~ · Lackierung *f*

~ brush · Lackierpinsel *m*

vase-painting · Vasenmalerei *f*

VAT, vinyl-asbestos tile, asbestos-vinyl tile · Pastellplatte *f*, Flexfliese *f*, Vinylasbestfliese, Flex(belag)platte, Vinylasbest(belag)platte [*DIN 16950*]

vat, tank · Küpe *f*, Färberbottich *m*

~, carbonator · Fällbottich *m* [*Niederschlagsverfahren zur Bleiweißherstellung*]

~, wat · Vat *m* [*buddhistische Klosteranlage*]

~ colour (Brit.) → (~) dye

(~) dye; ~ colour (Brit.); ~ color (US) [*The description 'vat' is derived from the containers (vats or tanks) which hold the dye-liquor while it is undergoing the reducing process, called 'vatting', which converts the dye into its alkali-soluble condition*] · Küpenfarbstoff *m*

vatting · Reduktion(sverfahren) *f*, (*n*) [*Küpenfarbstoff*]

to vault, to concamerate · einwölben, überwölben

vault [*Vault is a structural covering for a space, generally of curved surface and employing the arch principle in construction. Also, the term is used loosely to designate any curved ceiling of a room regardless of construction. The word is also applied to a place especially built for protection of valuables and to a masonry enclosure for a tomb*] · Gewölbe *n*

~ **(a)butment** · Gewölbewiderlager *n*

~ **action** · Gewölbewirkung *f*

~ **apex,** ~ top, ~ vertex,~ key,~ crown · Gewölbescheitel(punkt) *m*

~ ~ **block,** ~ top ~, ~ vertex ~, ~ key ~, ~ crown ~ · Gewölbescheitelstein *m*, Gewölbeschlußstein

~ **arch,** vaulted ~ · Gewölbebogen *m*

~ **axis;** ~ center line (US); ~ centre line (Brit.) · Gewölbeachse *f*, Gewölbemittellinie *f* [*Die gedachte Linie unterhalb des Scheitels in Kämpferhöhe*]

(~) **back,** (~) extrados, upper surface of vault, extrados of vault, back of vault · Rücken *m*, Gewölbe~, äußere Gewölbefläche *f*

~ **basilica,** vaulted ~ · Gewölbebasilika *f*

~ ~ **church** → vault(ed) ~ ~

(~) **bay,** (~) severy, (~) compartment · (Gewölbe)Feld *n*, (Gewölbe)Joch *n*, Jochfeld, Gewölbeschlag *m*, Gewölbeabteilung *f*, Gitterfeld [*Joche werden in Längsachse gezählt, Schiffe in der Querachse*]

~ **block** → ~ wedge(-shaped) ~

~ **bond** · Gewölbeverband *m*

~ **brick**→~ (wedge(-shaped)) (clay) ~

~ **capping,** ~ coping · Abdeckung *f* des Gewölbes, Gewölbe(ab)deckung

~ **centre line** (Brit.); ~ center line (US); ~ axis · Gewölbeachse *f*, Gewölbemittellinie *f* [*Die gedachte Linie unterhalb des Scheitels in Kämpferhöhe*]

~ **Christian basilica** → vault(ed) ~ ~

~ **(clay) brick** → ~ (wedge(-shaped)) (~) ~

(~) **compartment** → (~) bay

~ **construction,** vaulting ~ · Gewölbebau *m*, Wölbungsbau

~ ~ **material** · Gewölbebaustoff *m*, Gewölbebaumaterial *n* [*Schweiz*]

~ **coping,** ~ capping · Abdeckung *f* des Gewölbes, Gewölbe(ab)deckung

~ **corridor** → vaulted ~

vault(-cover)ed, vault-closed · überwölbt, eingewölbt

vault crown, ~ apex, ~ top, ~ vertex, ~ key · Gewölbescheitel(punkt) *m*

~ ~ **block** → ~ apex ~

~ **depth,** ~ thickness · Gewölbedicke *f* [*Fehlname: Gewölbestärke f. Höhe der vorderen Ansichtsfläche eines Gewölbes*]

~ **ecclesiastical basilica** → vault(ed) ~ ~

(~) **extrados,** (~) back, upper surface of vault, extrados of vault, back of vault · Rücken *m*, Gewölbe~, äußere Gewölbefläche *f*

~ **facing,** ~ sur~, ~ lining · Gewölbeauskleidung *f*, Gewölbeverkleidung, Gewölbebekleidung, Gewölbebelag *m*

~ **grid** · Gewölberaster *m*

(~) **groin** [*In vaulting, the line of intersection of two vaults*] · (Gewölbe)Grat *m*, Gierung *f*, Verschneidungslinie *f*

~ **hall** → vaulted ~

~ **haunch** · Gewölbeschenkel *m*

~ **impost** · Gewölbekämpfer *m*

to vault in [*with the rotating templet*] · einwölben [*mit der Leier*]

vault interior, vaulted ~ · Gewölberaum *m*

(~) **intrados** → inner surface of vault(ing)

~ **key,** ~ crown, ~ apex, ~ top, ~ vertex · Gewölbescheitel(punkt) *m*

~ ~ **block** → ~ apex ~

~ **light,** pavement ~ [*A light formed of solid glass blocks cast into concrete or set in a cast-iron frame over a basement so as to let in daylight*] · Kelleroberlicht *n*

~ **line** → ~ out~

~ **lining,** ~ (sur)facing · Gewölbeauskleidung *f*, Gewölbeverkleidung, Gewölbebekleidung, Gewölbebelag *m*

~ **(out)line,** (out)line of vault · Gewölbelinie *f*, Gewölbeprofil *n*

~ **painting** · Gewölbemalerei *f*

~ **pattern** · Gewölbeform *f*

~ **pressure** · Gewölbedruck *m*

~ **rib** · Gewölberippe *f*

~ **rise** · Gewölbepfeil(höhe) *m*, (*f*), Gewölbestich(höhe) *m*, (*f*), Gewölbehöhe [*Höhe eines Gewölbes, gemessen als senkrechter Abstand zwischen Kämpferebene und Schlußstein*]

(~) **severy** → (~) bay

~ **soffit** · Gewölbeuntersicht *f*

~ **span** · Gewölbespannweite *f*

~ **springer** · Gewölbeanfänger *m*, Gewölbeanwölber, Gewölbeanfangsstein *m*, Gewölbekämpferstein

~ **style** · Gewölbestil *m*

~ **(sur)facing,** ~ lining · Gewölbeauskleidung *f*, Gewölbeverkleidung, Gewölbebekleidung, Gewölbebelag *m*

~ **theory** · Gewölbetheorie *f*

~ **thickness** → ~ depth

~ **thrust,** side ~, lateral ~, axial ~, outward ~, overturning ~ · Wölbungsschub *m*, Horizontalschub, (Seiten-)

vault thrust — vegetable filler

Schub, Axialschub, achsrechter Schub, Gewölbeschub [*Die waag(e)rechte Resultierende einer Gewölbekraft*]

~ **top**, ~ vertex, ~ key, ~ crown, ~ apex · Gewölbescheitel(punkt) *m*

~ ~ **block** → ~ **apex** ~

~ **vertex**, ~ key, ~ crown, ~ apex, ~ top · Gewölbescheitel(punkt) *m*

~ ~ **block** → ~ **apex** ~

~ **walk** → **vaulted** ~

~ **(wedge(-shaped)) block** · Gewölbe(keil)stein *m*, Wölbstein, Wölber *m*

~ **(~) (clay) brick** · Gewölbe(keil)ziegel *m*, Wölber *m*, Wölbziegel

~ **which is octagonal externally and square internally** · doppelschaliges Gewölbe *n*, zweischaliges ~ [*z.B. der Moschee Gur Emir in Samarkand*]

~ **with dentated springing lines** · versetztes Gewölbe *n*, Zonengewölbe

vaulted [*constructed as a vault*] · gewölbt

~, vault-closed, vault-covered · überwölbt, eingewölbt

vault(ed) arch · Gewölbebogen *m*

~ **area** · gewölbte Fläche *f*, Wölbfläche

~ **basilica** · Gewölbebasilika *f*

~ ~ **church**, ~ Christian basilica, ~ ecclesiastical basilica · gewölbte christliche Basilika *f*, ~ Basilikakirche *f*, Gewölbebasilikakirche

~ **building** · Gewölbegebäude *n*

~ **ceiling**, concave ~ · Deckengewölbe *n*, Gewölbedecke *f*

~ **chamber** · Gewölbekammer *f*

~ **Christian basilica**, ~ ecclesiastical ~, ~ basilica church · gewölbte christliche Basilika *f*, ~ Basilikakirche *f*, Gewölbebasilikakirche

~ **concrete** · Gewölbebeton *m*

~ **church** · Gewölbekirche *f*

~ **corridor**, ~ walk · Gewölbeflur *m*, Gewölbekorridor *m*, Gewölbegang *m*, überwölbter Flur, überwölbter Gang, überwölbter Korridor

~ **ecclesiastical basilica**, ~ Christian ~, ~ basilica church · gewölbte christliche Basilika *f*, ~ Basilikakirche *f*, Gewölbebasilikakirche

~ **edifice**, ~ structure · Gewölbebau(werk) *m*, (*n*)

~ **hall** · gewölbte Halle *f*, Gewölbehalle

~ **interior** · Gewölberaum *m*

~ **plate**, ~ slab · gewölbte Platte *f*

~ **roof** · gewölbtes Dach *n*, Gewölbedach

~ **slab**, ~ plate · gewölbte Platte *f*

~ **structure**, ~ edifice · Gewölbebau(werk) *m*, (*n*)

~ **walk**, ~ corridor · Gewölbeflur *m*, Gewölbekorridor *m*, Gewölbegang *m*, überwölbter Flur, überwölbter Korridor, überwölbter Gang

vaulted work, vaulting · Gewölbesystem *n*

vaulting · Überwölben *n*

~, vaults · Gewölbe *npl*

~ · Gewölbeausbildung *f*

~ · Einwölbung *f*, (Über)Wölbung

~ · Gewölbeschale *f*, Wölbung *f* [*Die massive Konstruktion in der ganzen Ausdehnung eines Gewölbefeldes*]

~, vaulted work · Gewölbesystem *n*

~ **cone** · Gewölbekegel *m*

vault(ing) construction · Wölbungsbau *m*, Gewölbebau

vaulting engineering · Wölbetechnik *f*

(vault(ing)) intrados → inner surface of vault(ing)

vaulting masonry (work) · Gewölbemauerwerk *n*

~ **shaft**, thinner ~ · junger Dienst *m* [*Gotik*]

~ **surface** · Gewölbefläche *f*, Wölbungsfläche

vaults, vaulting · Gewölbe *npl*

V-column, V-shaped column · V-Stütze *f*, Winkelstütze [*Sie gabelt sich vom Auflager in zwei Äste*]

Vebe apparatus · Vebe-Konsistenzmesser *m*

vector action · Vektorwirkung *f*

vector-active structure system · vektoraktives Tragsystem *n* [*Kennzeichen der vektoraktiven Tragsysteme ist der Dreiecksverband*]

vector addition · Vektoraddition *f*

~ **mechanism** · Vektormechanismus *m*

~ **product**, cross ~, outer ~ · äußeres Produkt *n*, Vektorprodukt

~ **separation** · Vektorspaltung *f*

~ **stress** · Vektorspannung *f*

~ **sum** · Vektorsumme *f*, vektorielle Summe

vegetable adhesive, ~ glue · Pflanzenleim *m*

~ **black (pigment)**, lampblack (~) · Lampenruß(pigment) *m*, (*n*), Lampenschwarz *n*

~ **cellar** · Gemüsekeller *m*

~ **drying oil** · trocknendes Öl *n* pflanzlichen Ursprungs (für Anstrichzwecke)

~ **dust**, ~ filler, ~ filling material · pflanzlicher Füller *m*, ~ Füllstoff [*z.B. Weichholzmehl, Korkmehl*]

~ **fat** · Pflanzenfett *n*

~ **fiber insulation (material)**, ~ ~ insulating ~ (US); ~ fibre ~ ~ (Brit.); ~ ~ insulator · pflanzlicher Faserdämmstoff *m*

~ **fibre** (Brit.); ~ fiber (US) · Pflanzenfaser *f*

~ ~ **material** (Brit.); ~ fiber ~ (US) · Pflanzenfaserstoff *m*

~ **filler**, ~ dust, ~ filling material · pflanzlicher Füller *m*, ~ Füllstoff *m* [*z.B. Weichholzmehl, Korkmehl*]

vegetable filling material — vent cavity

~ **filling material,** ~ dust, ~ filler · pflanzlicher Füller *m*, ~ Füllstoff [*z.B. Weichholzmehl, Korkmehl*]

~ **garden** · Gemüsegarten *m*

~ **glue,** ~ adhesive · Pflanzenleim *m*

~ **oil** · Pflanzenöl *n*, pflanzliches Öl

~ **pigment** · Pigment *n* pflanzlichen Ursprungs

~ **preparation room** · (Gemüse)Putzraum *m*

~ **sink (unit)** [*A vegetable sink (unit) has a compartment for washing and one for rinsing*] · Gemüseabwaschtisch *m*, Gemüsespültisch, Gemüsespülausguß *m*

~ **stor(ag)e** · Gemüselager *n*

~ **wax** · Pflanzenwachs *n*

vehicle, medium, paint base [*The liquid portion of paint, in which the pigment is dispersed; it is composed of the binder and the thinner, if any*] · Bindemittellösung *f* [*Anstrichfarbe*]

~ **base,** medium ~ · Bindemittellösungsbasis *n*, Bindemittellösungsgrundlage *f* [*Anstrichfarbe*]

~ **level** · Fahrebene *f*

~ **traffic** · Fahrverkehr *m*

vehicle-turning area · Fahrzeugwendefläche *f*

(vehicle) wash(down) (yard) · (Auto-)Waschplatz *m*, Wagenwaschplatz

vehicular access, (entrance) drive(way) · (Gebäude)Zufahrt *f*, Hauszufahrt

~ **elevator** (US); ~ lift (Brit.) · Auto-Aufzug *m*

~ **lift** (Brit.); ~ elevator (US) · Auto-Aufzug *m*

~ **stall** · Parkboxe *f*

vein · Ansammlung *f* [*Von festen Harzbestandteilen in einem Parkettstab*]

~ **gypsum** · Adergips *m*

veined · geädert

~ **marble** · Adermarmor *m*

veining · Geäder *n*, Äderung *f* [*Marmor*]

vein-tin · Bergzinn *n*

velocity · Schnelle *f*, Geschwindigkeit *f*

~ **diagram** → diagram of velocities

~ **of falling bodies** · Fallgeschwindigkeit *f*, Fallschnelle *f*

~ **potential** [*Of a sound field in an isotropic fluid medium at rest or in a state of irrotational flow. A scalar potential function, the gradient of which is the negative of the particle velocity at a point in the field.*] · Potential *n* der Schallschnelle, Schnellepotential [*Funktion, deren Gradient die Schallschnelle ist*]

velvet finish glass, satin ~ ~ · satiniertes Glas *n*, seidenmattes ~, Atlasglas, Seidentonglas

(velvety) flock paper · Samttapete *f*, Velourstapete

vending machine · Verkaufsautomat *m*

veneer [*The facing material is attached to a structural backing*] · dünne Verblendung *f*

~ · Furnier *n*

~ [*A masonry facing which is attached to the backup but no so bonded as to act with it under load*] · nicht(last)tragende Mauerverkleidung *f*

~ **(bonding) adhesive,** ~ ~ agent, ~ ~ medium, ~ cement(ing agent) · Furnierkleber *m*, Furnierkle(e)stoff *m*, Furnierkleb(e)mittel *n*

~ **cement(ing agent)** → ~ (bonding) adhesive

veneered door · (über)furnierte Tür *f*, beplankte ~

~ **façade** · (Ver)Blendfassade *f* mit nichttragendem (Ver)Blendmauerwerk

~ **panel** · (über)furnierte Tafel *f*, beplankte ~

~ **plywood** · (über)furniertes Sperrholz *n*, beplanktes ~

~ **wall,** veneer ~ [*The facing is not attached and bonded to the backing to such an extent as to form an integral part of the wall*] · Mauer *f* mit nichttragendem (Ver)Blendmauerwerk

veneering · (Über)Furnieren *n*, Beplanken

~**, wall** ~ · Verblenden *n*

~ **masonry (work),** ~ work · nichttragendes (Ver)Blendmauerwerk *n*

~ **work,** ~ masonry (~) · nichttragendes (Ver)Blendmauerwerk *n*

Venetian arch · venezianischer Bogen *m* [*Von einem Faszienrundbogen überfangener Zwillingsbogen mit Scheitelkreis und Spandrillen*]

~ **(blind),** ~ shutter · Zugjalousie *f*, Raffjalousie

~ **door** [*See remark under 'Venetian window'*] · venezianische Tür *f*

~ **red** [*B.S. 370*] · Venezianischrot *n*

~ **window,** Palladian ~, Serlian(a) ~, Serlian(a) motif (~), Palladian motif (~), Venetian motif (~) [*A tripartite window, the central opening being arched and wider than the side openings, which have flat heads*] · Palladiomotiv *n*, venezianisches Fenster *n*

Veneto-Byzantine style · venezianisch-byzantinischer Stil *m*

vent, ventilator · Entlüfter *m* [*Einrichtung zum Entfernen von Luft aus Rohrleitungen und angeschlossenen Geräten*]

~ **and air-conditioning equipment** → ventilation ~ ~ ~

~ **area,** ventilation ~, vent(ilat)ing ~, air-handling ~ · (Be- und Ent)Lüftungsfläche *f*

~ **bar** → air (distribution) ~

~ **block** → vent(ilat)ing ~

~ **brick** → vent(ilat)ing ~

~ **capping** → vent(ilat)ing ~

~ **cavity,** ventilation ~, vent(ilat)ing ~, air(-handling) ~ · (Be- und Ent)Lüftungsschlitz *m*, Luftschlitz

vent ceiling — vent(ilat)ing ceiling

~ **ceiling** → vent(ilat)ing ~
~ ~ **board** → vent(ilat)ing ~ ~
~ ~ **sheet** → vent(ilat)ing ceiling board
~ ~ **system** → vent(ilat)ing ~ ~
~ **connection,** ventilation ~, vent(ilat)ing ~, air(-handling) ~ · (Be- und Ent)Lüftungsanschluß *m*, Luftanschluß
~ **connector** · Entlüfteranschluß *m*
~ **duct** → ventilation ~
~ **ducting** → ventilation ~
~ **equipment** → ventilation ~
~ **fixture** → air-handling luminaire (~)
~ **flashing** → ~ pipe ~
~ **glass block** → vent(ilat)ing ~ ~
~ ~ **brick** → vent(ilat)ing glass block
~ **grille,** ventilation ~, vent(ilat)ing ~, air-handling ~ [*Sometimes spelled 'grill'*] · (Be- und Ent)Lüftungsgitter *n*
~ **installation** → vent(ilation) system
~ **lay-in ceiling** → vent(ilat)ing ~ ~
~ **light fitting** (Brit.) → air-handling luminaire (fixture)
~ **(light(ing)) fixture** → air-handling luminaire (~)
~ **line,** ventilation ~, vent(ilat)ing ~, air(-handling) ~ · (Be- und Ent)Lüftungsleitung *f*
~ **louvre,** ~ **louver** · Entlüftungskiemen *m*
~ **luminaire (fixture)** → air-handling ~ (~)
~ **opening,** ventilation ~, vent(ilat)ing ~, air-handling ~, ventilator · (Be- und Ent)Lüftungsöffnung *f*, Luftöffnung
~ **panel,** ventilation ~, vent(ilat)ing ~, air(-handling) ~ · (Be- und Ent)Lüftungstafel *f*
~ **piece,** ventilation ~, vent(ilat)ing ~, air(-handling) ~ · (Be- und Ent)Lüftungsstück *n*
~ **pipe,** ventilation ~, vent(ilat)ing ~, air(-handling) ~ · (Be- und Ent)Lüftungsrohr *n*, Luftrohr
~ ~, **exhaust** ~, **expansion** ~ [*A pipe, in a (hot) water heater, for the escape of air and for the safe discharge of any steam generated*] · Expansionsrohr *n*, (Aus)Dehn(ungs)rohr
~ **(~) flashing,** flashing of a vent (pipe) [*See remark under 'Anschluß'*] · Lüftungsrohranschluß *m*
~ **(~) tray** → vent(ilat)ing (~) ~
~ **plant** → vent(ilation) system
~ ~ **room,** ventilation ~ ~, vent(ilat)ing ~ ~, air(-handling) ~ ~ · (Be- und Ent)Lüftungsanlagenraum *m*
~ **position,** ventilation ~, vent(ilat)ing ~, air(-handling) ~ · (Be- und Ent)Lüftungsstellung *f*
~ **ridge,** ventilation ~, vent(ilat)ing ~, air(-handling) ~ · (Be- und Ent)Lüftungsfirst *m*
~ ~ **tile,** ventilation ~ ~, vent(ilat)ing ~ ~ · Firstlüfter *m*

~ **shaft** → ventilating ~
~ **sliding window,** ventilation ~ ~, vent(ilat)ing ~ ~, air(-handling) ~ ~ · (Be- und Ent)Lüftungsschiebefenster *n*
~ **stack** → ventilation ~
~ ~ · Entlüftungsrohr *n*, Abluftrohr [*Grundstücksentwässerung*]
~ **station** → vent(ilat)ing ~
~ **stave,** ventilation ~, vent(ilat)ing ~, air(-handling) ~ · (Be- und Ent)Lüftungsdaube *f*, Luftdaube [*Betonsilo*]
~ **stopper** · Entlüftungsstopfen *m*, Abluftstopfen
~ **system** → ventilation ~
~ **tray** → vent(ilat)ing (pipe) ~
~ **window,** ventilation ~, vent(ilat)ing ~, air(-handling) ~ · (Be- und Ent)Lüftungsfenster *n*

vented cavity · belüfteter Hohlraum *m*
to ventilate [*To circulate fresh air in a room, etc., driving out foul air*] · (be- und ent)lüften
ventilated [*curtain wall*] · hinterlüftet [*Vorhangwand*]
~ **ceiling** → vent(ilat)ing ~
~ **façade,** façade with air circulation · durchlüftete Fassade *f*, zweischalige ~, Kaltfassade
~ **(flat) roof,** (flat) roof with air circulation · zweischaliges Flachdach *n*, durchlüftetes ~, Kaltdach [*Es hat zwischen oberster Geschoßdecke und dem Dach einen durchlüfteten Raum*]
~ **lay-in ceiling** → vent(ilat)ing ~ ~
~ **roof** → ~ flat ~

vent(ilat)ing → ventilation
~ **acoustical ceiling,** vent(ilation) ~, acoustical ventilating ~, acoustical ventilation ~ · Schallschlucklüftungsdecke *f*, Lüftungsschallschluckdecke, Lüftungsakustikdecke, Akustiklüftungsdecke, Schallabsorptionslüftungsdecke, Lüftungsschallabsorptionsdecke
~ **air,** ventilation ~ · Lüftungsluft *f*
~ **and air-conditioning equipment** → vent(ilation) ~ ~ ~
~ **area,** vent(ilation) ~, air-handling ~ · (Be- und Ent)Lüftungsfläche *f*
~ **bar** → air (distribution) ~
~ **block,** vent(ilation) ~, air(-handling) ~ · (Be- und Ent)Lüftungsstein *m*, Luftstein
~ **brick,** vent(ilation) ~, air(-handling) ~ [*A brick which has been cored to provide an air passage for ventilating purposes*] · Luftziegel *m*, Lüftungsziegel
~ **capping,** vent(ilation) ~, air-handling ~, cowl · (Be- und Ent)Lüftungshaube *f*
~ **cavity,** vent(ilation) ~, air(-handling) ~ · (Be- und Ent)Lüftungsschlitz *m*, Luftschlitz
~ **ceiling,** ventilated ~, vent(ilation) ~, air(-handling) ~ · (Raum)(Be- und Ent)Lüftungsdecke *f*

~ ~ **board,** ~ ~ **sheet, vent(ilation)** ~ ~, air(-handling) ~ ~ · (Raum) Lüftungsdeckenplatte f

~ ~ **sheet** → ~ ~ board

~ ~ **system, vent(ilation)** ~ ~, air(-handling) ~ ~ · (Raum) Deckenlüftungssystem n

~ **connection, vent(ilation)** ~, air-handling ~ · (Be- und Ent) Lüftungsanschluß m, Luftanschluß

~ **duct** → vent(ilation) ~

~ **ducting** → vent(ilation) ~

~ **equipment** → vent(ilation) ~

~ **fixture** → air-handling luminaire (~)

~ **glass block,** ~ ~ **brick, vent(ilation)** ~ ~, air(-handling) ~ ~ · (Be- und Ent) Lüftungsglasbaustein m

~ ~ **brick** → ~ ~ ~ block

~ **grille, vent(ilation)** ~, air-handling ~ [*Sometimes spelled 'grill'*] · (Be- und Ent) Lüftungsgitter n

~ **installation** → vent(ilation) system

~ **lay-in ceiling, vent(ilation)** ~ ~, ventilated ~ ~, air(-handling) ~ ~ · (Be- und Ent) Lüftungseinlegedecke f

~ **light fitting** (Brit.) → air-handling luminaire (fixture)

~ **(light(ing)) fixture** → air-handling luminaire (~)

~ **line, vent(ilation)** ~, air(-handling) ~ · (Be- und Ent) Lüftungsleitung f

~ **luminaire (fixture)** → air-handling ~ (~)

~ **opening, vent(ilation)** ~, air-handling ~, ventilator · (Be- und Ent) Lüftungsöffnung f, Luftöffnung

~ **panel, vent(ilation)** ~, air(-handling) ~ · (Be- und Ent) Lüftungstafel f

~ **piece, vent(ilation)** ~, air(-handling) ~ · (Be- und Ent-) Lüftungsstück n

~ **pipe, vent(ilation)** ~, air(-handling) ~ · (Be- und Ent) Lüftungsrohr n, Luftrohr

~ **(~) tray, vent(ilation)** (~) ~, air(-handling) (~) ~ · (Be- und Ent) Lüftungsrohreinfassung f

~ **plant** → vent(ilation) system

~ ~ **room, vent(ilation)** ~ ~, air(-handling) ~ ~ · (Be- und Ent) Lüftungsanlagenraum m

~ **position, vent(ilation)** ~, air(-handling) ~ · (Be- und Ent) Lüftungsstellung f

~ **ridge, vent(ilation)** ~, air(-handling) ~ · (Be- und Ent) Lüftungsfirst m

~ ~ **tile, vent(ilation)** ~ ~ · Firstlüfter m

~ **shaft, ventilation** ~, air(-handling) ~, venting ~ · Luftschacht m, (Be- und Ent) Lüftungsschacht

~ **sliding window, vent(ilation)** ~ ~' air(-handling) ~ ~ · (Be- und Ent-) Lüftungsschiebefenster n

~ **stack** → vent(ilation) ~

~ **station, vent(ilation)** ~, air(-handling) ~ · (Be- und Ent) Lüftungszentrale f, (Be- und Ent) Lüftungsstation f

~ **stave, vent(ilation)** ~, air(-handling) ~ · (Be- und Ent) Lüftungsdaube f, Luftdaube [*Betonsilo*]

~ **system** → vent(ilation) ~

~ **tray** → ~ pipe ~

~ **window, vent(ilation)** ~, air(-handling) ~ · (Be- und Ent-) Lüftungsfenster n

ventilation [*curtain wall*] · Hinterlüftung f [*Vorhangwand*]

~, **vent(ilat)ing, air-handling** · (Be- und Ent) Lüftung f [*DIN 18017 und 18610*]

vent(ilation) acoustical ceiling, vent(ilat)ing ~ ~, acoustical ventilating ~, acoustical ventilation ~ · Schallschlucklüftungsdecke f, Lüftungsschallschluckdecke, Akustiklüftungsdecke, Lüftungsakustikdecke, Schallabsorptionslüftungsdecke, Lüftungsschallabsorptionsdecke

~ **air, vent(ilat)ing** ~ · Lüftungsluft f

~ **and air-conditioning, equipment** vent(ilat)ing ~ ~ ~, air(-handling) ~ ~ ~ · klimatechnische Anlagen fpl, lufttechnische ~

~ **area, vent(ilat)ing** ~, air-handling ~ · (Be- und Ent) Lüftungsfläche f

~ **bar** → air (distribution) ~

~ **block** → vent(ilation) ~

~ **brick** → vent(ilat)ing ~

~ **capping** → vent(ilat)ing ~

~ **cavity, vent(ilat)ing** ~, air-(handling) ~ · (Be- und Ent) Lüftungsschlitz m, Luftschlitz

~ **ceiling** → vent(ilat)ing ~

~ ~ **board** → vent(ilat)ing ~ ~

~ ~ **sheet** → vent(ilat)ing ceiling board

~ ~ **system** → vent(ilat)ing ~ ~

~ **connection, vent(ilat)ing** ~, air(-handling) ~ · (Be- und Ent) Lüftungsanschluß m, Luftanschluß

~ **duct, vent(ilat)ing** ~, air(-handling) ~, airway [*An air passage, usually formed in sheet metal, plastic, etc., for ventilating a building*] · (Be- und Ent-) Lüftungskanal m, Luft(verteilungs)kanal

~ **ducting, vent(ilat)ing** ~, air(-handling) ~, airways · (Be- und Ent) Lüftungskanäle mpl, Luft(verteilungs)kanäle

ventilation engineering · (Be- und Ent) Lüftungstechnik f

vent(ilation) equipment, vent(ilat)ing ~, air(-handling) ~ · (Be- und Ent) Lüftungsgeräte npl

~ ~, **vent(ilat)ing** ~, air(-handling) ~ · lüftungstechnische Anlagen fpl

~ **fixture** → air-handling luminaire (~)

~ **glass block** → vent(ilat)ing ~ ~

~ ~ **brick** → vent(ilat)ing glass block

~ **grille, vent(ilat)ing** ~, air-handling ~ [*Sometimes spelled 'grill'*] · (Be- und Ent) Lüftungsgitter n

vent(ilation) installation — venting position 1086

~ **installation** → ~ system
~ **lay-in ceiling** → vent(ilat)ing ~ ~
~ **light fitting** → (Brit.) · air-handling luminaire (fixture)
~ **(light(ing)) fixture** → air-handling luminaire (~)
~ **line,** vent(ilat)ing ~, air(-handling) ~ · (Be- und Ent)Lüftungsleitung f
~ **luminaire (fixture)** → air-handling ~ (~)
~ **opening,** vent(ilat)ing ~, air-handling ~, ventilator · (Be- und Ent)Lüftungsöffnung f, Luftöffnung
~ **panel,** vent(ilating) ~, air(-handling) ~ · (Be- und Ent)Lüftungstafel f
~ **piece,** vent(ilat)ing ~, air(-handling) ~ · (Be- und Ent)Lüftungsstück n
~ **pipe,** vent(ilat)ing ~, air(-handling) ~ · (Be- und Ent)Lüftungsrohr n, Luftrohr
~ **(~) tray** → vent(ilat)ing (~) ~
~ **plant** → ~ system
~ ~ **room,** vent(ilat)ing ~ ~, air(-handling) ~ ~ · (Be- und Ent)Lüftungsanlagenraum m
~ **position,** vent(ilat)ing ~, air(-handling) ~ · (Be- und Ent)Lüftungsstellung f
~ **ridge,** vent(ilat)ing ~, air(-handling) ~ · (Be- und Ent)Lüftungsfirst m
~ ~ **tile,** vent(ilat)ing ~ ~ · Firstlüfter m
~ **shaft** → vent(ilat)ing ~
~ **sliding window,** vent(ilat)ing ~ ~, air(-handling) ~ ~ · (Be- und Ent-)Lüftungsschiebefenster n
~ **stack,** vent(ilat)ing ~, air(-handling) ~ · (Be- und Ent)Lüftungskamin m, (Be- und Ent)Lüftungsschornstein m, Sammelschacht(anlage) m, (f)
~ **station** → vent(ilat)ing ~
~ **stave,** vent(ilat)ing ~, air(-handling) ~ · (Be- und Ent)Lüftungsdaube f, Luftdaube [*Betonsilo*]
~ **system,** vent(ilat)ing ~, air(-handling) ~, ~ installation, ~ plant · (Be- und Ent)Lüftungsanlage f, (Be- und Ent)Lüftungssystem n, Luftanlage
~ **tray** → vent(ilat)ing (~) ~
~ **window,** vent(ilat)ing ~, air(-handling) ~ · (Be- und Ent)Lüftungsfenster n

vent(ilator) · Entlüfter m [*Einrichtung zum Entfernen von Luft aus Rohrleitungen und angeschlossenen Geräten*]

ventilator, extractor, extract ventilation unit, extraction unit · (Ent)Lüfter m

~, casement ~, opening sash, opening light, pivoted sash, (window) casement, hinged casement · (Fenster)Flügel m

~, vent(ilation) opening, vent(ilat)ing opening, air-handling opening · (Be- und Ent)Lüftungsöffnung f, Luftöffnung

~ **grate,** grille [*sometimes spelled 'grill'*] · Luftrost m, Luftgitter n

venting → ventilation
~ **and air-conditioning equipment** → vent(ilation) ~ ~ ~
~ **area,** ventilating ~, vent(ilation) ~, air-handling ~ · (Be- und Ent)Lüftungsfläche f
~ **bar** → air (distribution) ~
~ **block** → ventilating ~
~ **brick** → ventilating ~
~ **capping** → ventilating ~
~ **cavity,** ventilating ~, vent(ilation) ~, air(-handling) ~ · (Be- und Ent)Lüftungsschlitz m, Luftschlitz
~ **ceiling** → ventilating ~
~ ~ **board** → ventilating ~ ~
~ ~ **sheet** → vent(ilat)ing ceiling board
~ ~ **system** → ventilating ~ ~
~ **connection,** ventilating ~, vent(ilation) ~, air(-handling) ~ · (Be- und Ent)Lüftungsanschluß m, Luftanschluß
~ **duct** → vent(ilation) ~
~ **ducting** → vent(ilation) ~
~ **equipment** → vent(ilation) ~
~ **fixture** → air-handling luminaire (~)
~ **glass block** → ventilating ~ ~
~ ~ **brick** → vent(ilat)ing glass block
~ **grille,** ventilating ~, vent(ilation) ~, air-handling ~ [*sometimes spelled 'grill'*] · (Be- und Ent)Lüftungsgitter n
~ **installation** → vent(ilation) system
~ **lay-in ceiling** → ventilating ~ ~
~ **light fitting** (Brit.) → air-handling luminaire (fixture)
~ **(light(ing)) fixture** → air-handling luminaire (~)
~ **line,** ventilating ~, vent(ilat)ion ~, air(-handling) ~ · (Be- und Ent)Lüftungsleitung f
~ **luminaire (fixture)** → air-handling ~ (~)
~ **opening,** ventilating ~, vent(ilation) ~, air-handling ~, ventilator · (Be- und Ent)Lüftungsöffnung f, Luftöffnung
~ **panel,** ventilating ~, vent(ilation) ~, air(-handling) ~ · (Be- und Ent)Lüftungstafel f
~ **piece,** ventilating ~, vent(ilation) ~, air(-handling) ~ · (Be- und Ent)Lüftungsstück n
~ **pipe,** ventilating ~, vent(ilation) ~, air(-handling) ~ · (Be- und Ent)Lüftungsrohr n, Luftrohr
~ **(~) tray** → ventilating (~) ~
~ **plant** → vent(ilation) system
~ ~ **room,** ventilating ~ ~, vent(ilation) ~ ~, air(-handling) ~ · (Be- und Ent)Lüftungsanlagenraum m
~ **position,** ventilating ~, vent(ilation) ~, air(-handling) ~ · (Be- und Ent-)Lüftungsstellung f

~ **ridge**, ventilating ~, vent(ilation) ~, air(-handling) ~ · (Be- und Ent)Lüftungsfirst *m*
~ ~ **tile**, ventilating ~ ~, vent(ilation) ~ ~ · Firstlüfter *m*
~ **shaft** → vent(ilating) ~
~ **sliding window**, ventilating ~ ~, vent(ilation) ~ ~, air(-handling) ~ ~ · (Be- und Ent)Lüftungsschiebefenster *n*
~ **stack** → vent(ilation) ~
~ **station** → ventilating ~
~ **stave**, ventilating ~, vent(ilation) ~, air(-handling) ~ · (Be- und Ent)Lüftungsdaube *f*, Luftdaube [*Betonsilo*]
~ **system** → vent(ilation) ~
~ **tray** → vent(ilat)ing (pipe) ~
~ **window**, ventilating ~, vent(ilation) ~, air(-handling) ~ · (Be- und Ent-)Lüftungsfenster *n*

veranda(h) · Veranda *f*
~ **(awning) blind** · Verandamarkise *f*

verdigris, basic copper acetate, aerugo [*It is the colo(u)ring ingredient of one type of patina on copper*] · basisches Kupferazetat *n*, ~ Kupferkarbonat *n*, Grünspan *m*, Kupfergrün *n*

verge · Ort(gang) *m* [*Dachabschluß an der Giebelseite eines Sattel-, Shed- oder Pultdaches*]
~ **board** → gable ~
~ **roof(ing) (clay) brick** · Ortziegel *m*, Anziegel
~ ~ **tile** · Ortstein *m*

vermiculite → raw ~
~, exfoliated ~ · (auf)geblähter Glimmer *m*, Vermiculit *m*, Blähglimmer [*Ein Wärme- und Schalldämmstoff aus durch Erhitzen auf ca. 1200° aufgeblähtem Glimmer*]
~ **absorbent plaster** → ~ sound-control ~
~ **absorbing plaster** → ~ sound-control ~
~ **acoustic(al) plaster** → ~ sound-control ~
~ **aggregate**, exfoliated ~ ~ [*A light-(weight) aggregate produced from vermiculite when exfoliated by heat*] · Blähglimmerzuschlag(stoff) *m*, Vermiculitzuschlag(stoff), Blähglimmerzuschlagmaterial *n*, Vermiculitzuschlagmaterial
~ **brick** → (exfoliated) vermiculite (concrete) ~
~ **concrete**, exfoliated ~ ~ · Blähglimmerbeton *m*, Vermiculitbeton
~ **(~) brick** → exfoliated ~ (~) ~
~ ~ **screed**, exfoliated ~ ~ ~ ~ · Blähglimmerestrich *m*, Vermiculitestrich
~ **gypsum plaster**, exfoliated ~ ~ ~ · Blähglimmergipsputz *m*, Vermiculitgipsputz
~ **insulation in bags**, exfoliated ~ ~ ~ ~ · Blähglimmer-Sack(ab)dämmung *f*, Vermiculit-Sack(ab)dämmung
~ **plaster**, exfoliated ~ ~ · Blähglimmer(ver)putz *m*, Vermiculit(ver)putz
~ **slab**, exfoliated ~ ~ · Blähglimmerplatte *f*, Vermiculitplatte
~ **(sound) absorbent plaster** → vermiculite sound-control ~
~ **(~) absorbing plaster** → vermiculite sound-control ~
~ **sound-control plaster**, ~ acoustic(al) ~, exfoliated ~ ~ ~, (exfoliated) vermiculite (sound) absorbent ~, (exfoliated) vermiculite (sound) absorbing ~ · Blähglimmer-Akustikputz *m*, Blähglimmer-Schallschluckputz, Vermiculit-Schallschluckputz, Vermiculit-Akustikputz

vermin · Ungeziefer *n*

vermin-proof, vermin-resistant, impervious to vermin · ungezieferfest, ungeziefersicher, ungezieferbeständig

vermin resistance · Ungezieferbeständigkeit *f*

vermin-resistant, vermin-proof, impervious to vermin · ungezieferfest, ungeziefersicher, ungezieferbeständig

vernacular architecture · einheimische Architektur *f*, ~ Baukunst *f*
~ **construction method** · einheimische Bauweise *f*

Verona brown · Veroneser Braun *n*
~ **green (earth) (pigment)** · Veroneser Grün *n*, ~ Erde *f*
~ **marble** · Veroneser Marmor *m*
~ **yellow** · Veroneser Gelb *n*

versed sine → (arch) rise

vertex, apex, key, top, crown · Scheitel(-punkt) *m*
~ **block**, apex ~, crown ~, top ~, key ~ · Scheitelstein *m*, Schlußstein
~ **hinge**, apex ~, top ~, key ~, crown ~ · Scheitelgelenk *n*
~ **hog**, crown ~, apex ~, key ~, top ~ · Scheitelüberhöhung *f*
~ **joint**, apex ~, key ~, top ~, crown ~ · Scheitelfuge *f* [*Fuge am höchsten Gewölbepunkt oder Bogenpunkt, wenn kein Scheitelstein vorhanden ist*]
~ **sag**, crown ~, apex ~, top ~, key ~ · Scheitelsenkung *f*
~ **stone**, top ~, crown ~, apex ~, keystone [*The central stone of an arch or a vault; sometimes carved*] · Scheitelstein *m* aus Naturstein, Schlußstein ~ ~

vertical, plumb · senkrecht, lotrecht, vertikal
~ · Vertikale *f*
~ → ~ member
~ **assembly**, ~ erection · Senkrechtmontagebau *m*, Senkrechtzusammenbau [*Montagebau*]
~ **axis** · Senkrechtachse *f*
~ ~ **of revolution** · senkrechte Drehachse *f*

vertical bar — vertical service run 1088

~ **bar**, ~ rod, ~ member · Senkrechtstab, m, Vertikalstab [*Träger*]
~ **bending stress** · Senkrechtbiegespannung f, Senkrechtbiegungsspannung
~ **(blind) slat** · Senkrecht(jalousie)lamelle f, Senkrecht(jalousie)stäbchen n
~ **bracing,** ~ reinforcing, ~ stiffening · senkrechte Absteifung f, ~ Aussteifung, ~ Verstärkung, ~ Versteifung
~ **cavity,** ~ core, ~ cell · Hochloch n [*Mauerziegel*]
~ **cell,** ~ cavity, ~ core · Hochloch n [*Mauerziegel*]
~ **centre hung pivot window** (Brit.); ~ center ~ ~ ~ (US) · Wendeflügelfenster n
~ ~ ~ **(window) casement** (Brit.); ~ center ~ (~) (US); ~ ~ ~ hinge(d) ~, ~ ~ ~ ~ pivoted sash, ~ ~ ~ ventilator, ~ ~ ~ opening sash, ~ ~ ~ opening light · Wende(fenster)flügel m
~ **circulation,** ~ transportation, ~ traffic · Senkrechttransport m, Senkrechtverkehr m [*in einem Hochhaus*]
~ **cladding** · senkrechte (Außen)Versteifungswand f
~ ~ **panel;** storey-height ~ ~ (Brit.); story-height ~ ~ (US) [*It spans vertically between floors from which it obtains support*] · senkrechte (Außenwand)Versteifungstafel f
~ **component** · lotrechte Seitenkraft f, senkrechte ~, winkelrechte ~, Vertikalkomponente f
~ ~ **of pressure** · senkrechte Druckkomponente f
~ **core,** ~ cavity, ~ cell · Hochloch n [*Mauerziegel*]
~ **coring** · Hoch(durch)lochung f [*Mauerziegel*]
~ ~ **block,** ~ ~ tile [*See remark under 'Block'*] · Hochlochblock(stein) m, Hochlochstein
~ ~ **brick** → ~ ~ clay ~
~ ~ ~ **panel,** ~ ~ clay ~ ~ · Hochlochtafel f
~ ~ **(clay) brick** · HLz m, Hochlochziegel m [*Mauerziegel nach DIN 105, der senkrecht zur Lagerfläche durchlocht ist*]
~ ~ **(~) ~ panel** · Hochlochtafel f
~ ~ **(~) light(weight) brick** · HLz m, Hochloch-Leichtziegel m [*DIN 18505*]
~ ~ **engineering brick** · Hochlochklinker m, KHLz [*DIN 105*]
~ ~ **light(weight) brick** → ~ ~ ~ clay ~
~ ~ ~ **prefab(ricated) brick panel (unit)** · HLp f, Hochloch-Leichtziegelplatte f [*DIN 18505*]
~ ~ **tile,** ~ ~ block [*See remark under 'Block'*] · Hochlochblock(stein) m, Hochlochstein
~ **cylindrical tank** · stehender Zylinderbehälter m

~ **denticulation** · Stockzahnung f, stehende Verzahnung [*Mauerwerkbau*]
~ **displacement** · vertikale Verrückung f, senkrechte ~, lotrechte ~
~ **drain** · Senkrechtdrän m, Standdrän
~ **erection,** ~ assembly · Senkrechtmontage f, Senkrechtzusammenbau m [*Montagebau*]
~ **extractor with fan,** ~ ventilator ~ ~, ~ extract ventilation unit ~ ~, ~ extraction unit ~ ~ · Rund(ent)lüfter m mit Ventilator
~ **fusion,** ~ scale, verticality, verticalism · Vertikalismus m
~ **glazing** · Stehverglasung f, Steheinglasung
~ **grid** · senkrechter Raster m
~ **jalousie,** ~ louvres, ~ louvers, ~ slatted blind · Senkrechtjalousie f
~ **joint, perpendicular** ~, side ~; cross ~ (Brit.); (head) ~, build (US) · Stoßfuge f, Senkrechtfuge
~ **kiln, shaft** ~ · Schachtofen m
~ ~ **cement, shaft** ~ ~ · Schachtofenzement m
~ ~ **clinker, shaft** ~ ~ · Schachtofenklinker m
~ ~ **lime, shaft** ~ ~ · Schachtofenkalk m
~ **lighting** · Senkrechtbeleuchtung f, Vertikalbeleuchtung
~ **lime kiln, shaft** ~ ~ · Kalkschachtofen m
~ **line** → ~ pipe ~
~ **load** · Senkrechtlast f, Vertikallast
~ **loading** · Senkrechtbelastung f
~ **loop** · Senkrechtschlaufe f
~ **louvres,** ~ louvers, ~ jalousie, ~ slatted blind · Senkrechtjalousie f
~ **member,** ~ rod, ~ bar · Senkrechtstab m, Vertikalstab [*Träger*]
~ **(~)** → frame column
~ **~, ~ supporting** ~, supporting ~ · Stützglied n [*z.B. ein Baluster*]
~ **panel** · Senkrechttafel f, Vertikaltafel
~ **pipe, standpipe, stack,** SP · Senkrechtrohr n, Standrohr, Steigrohr
~ **(pipe)line, rising** ~ · Falleitung f [*Eine senkrechte Entwässerungsleitung für Schmutzwasser in einem Gebäude*]
~ **plane** · Senkrechtebene f, Vertikalebene
~ **reinforcing,** ~ bracing, ~ stiffening · senkrechte Absteifung f, ~ Aussteifung, ~ Verstärkung, ~ Versteifung
~ **rod,** ~ bar, ~ member · Senkrechtstab m, Vertikalstab [*Träger*]
~ **roof bracing** · senkrechte Dachaussteifung f, ~ Dachverstärkung
~ **run** → riser
~ **scale,** ~ fusion, verticality, verticalism · Vertikalismus m
~ **service pipe, rising** ~ ~ · Versorgungssteigrohr n
~ ~ **run** → riser

vertical shaft — vibrated and pressed concrete pipe

~ **shaft** · Mannlochhals *m*, Schachthals

~ **slat** → ~ blind ~

~ **slatted blind**, ~ jalousie, ~ louvres, louvers · Senkrechtjalousie *f*

~ **slide door**, ~ sliding ~ · Senkrechtschiebetür *f*

~ **sliding door**, ~ slide ~ · Senkrechtschiebetür *f*

~ ~ **sash, vertically** ~ ~, ~ ~ window ~ · Senkrecht-Schiebefensterrahmen *m*, Vertikal-Schiebefensterrahmen

~ ~ **shutterdoor, vertically opening** ~, ~ ~ shutter door [*The panels slide vertically and stack above and behind the opening*] · (mehrteiliges) Deckentor *n*

~ ~ **steel shutter door,** ~ ~ ~ shutterdoor · Stahlhubtor *n*

~ ~ **(window) sash, vertically** ~ (~) ~ · Senkrecht-Schiebefensterrahmen *m*, Vertikal-Schiebefensterrahmen

~ **steam boiler** · Standkessel *m*

~ **steel facing** → side steel lining

~ ~ **lining** → side ~ ~

~ ~ **(sur)facing** → side steel lining

~ **stiffener** · Senkrechtsteife *f*

~ **stiffening**, ~ bracing, ~ reinforcing · senkrechte Absteifung *f*, ~ Aussteifung, ~ Verstärkung, ~ Versteifung

~ **stress** · Senkrechtspannung *f*

~ **(strut)** · Pfosten *m* [*Fachwerk(träger)*]

~ ~ **truss** · Pfostenfachwerk(träger) *n*, (*m*) [*Ein Fachwerk(träger), dessen Füllstäbe nur z.T. zu den Gurten geneigt sind, z.T. jedoch senkrecht zu den Gurten verlaufen*]

~ **(supporting) member, supporting** ~ · Stützglied *n* [*z.B. ein Baluster*]

~ **tilework, wall** ~, hung ~, ~ tiling · Wand(fliesen)belag *m*, Wandplattenbelag

~ **tiling, wall** ~, hung ~, ~ tilework · Wand(fliesen)belag *m*, Wandplattenbelag

~ ~, **tile hanging** · Senkrecht-Verfliesung *f*

~ **traffic**, ~ transportation, ~ circulation · Senkrechttransport *m*, Senkrechtverkehr *m* [*in einem Hochhaus*]

~ **translation** · Senkrechtverschiebung *f*, Vertikalverschiebung

~ **transportation**, ~ circulation, ~ traffic · Senkrechttransport *m*, Senkrechtverkehr *m* [*in einem Hochhaus*]

~ ~ **system** · Senkrechttransportsystem *n* [*mehrstöckiges Gebäude*]

~ **truss** · Ständerfachwerk(träger) *n*, (*m*)

~ **utility line** → riser

~ **(~) run** → riser

~ **ventilator with fan**, ~ extractor ~ ~, ~ extract ventilation unit ~ ~, ~ extraction unit ~ ~ · Rund(ent)lüfter *m* mit Ventilator

~ **wall-mounted flagpole**, ~ wall set ~ · Senkrecht-Wandfahnenmast *m*, Senkrecht-Wandflaggenmast

~ **wall set flagpole**, ~ wall-mounted ~ · Senkrecht-Wandfahnenmast *m*, Senkrecht-Wandflaggenmast

~ **wall slab** · senkrechte Wand(bau)platte *f*, vertikale ~

~ **window** · Senkrechtfenster *n*

verticalism, verticality, vertical scale, vertical fusion · Vertikalismus *m*

verticality · Lothaltigkeit *f*

~, verticalism, vertical scale, vertical fusion · Vertikalismus *m*

vertically cast brick panel, ~ ~ brickwork · Mauertafel *f*

~ **opening shutterdoor** → vertical sliding ~

vertical(ly) pivoted door · Wendeflügeltür *f*

~ ~ **shutter** · Wendeflügelladen *m*

~ **sliding sash**, ~ ~ window ~ · Senkrecht-Schiebe(fenster)rahmen *m*, Vertikal-Schiebe(fenster)rahmen

very end of the Late Gothic style · späteste Gotik *f*

~ **long oil**, alkyd ~ · Alkydöl *n*, abgewandeltes Standöl

vesica piscis, aureole, mandorla, glory · Heiligenschein *m*, Mandorla *f*, Mandelglorie *f*, Nimbus *m*, Gloriole *f*, Glorie(nschein)

~ ~, **fish's bladder** [*A pointed oval form like a bladder of a fish*] · Schneuß *m*, Fischblase *f*, Schneuz *m*

vest., vestibule, antechamber, anteroom · Vestibül *n*, Vorraum *m*, Vorzimmer *n*

vestiary, wardrobe, garderobe, cloakroom · Garderobe *f*

vestibule, circular ~, tambour · Drehtürgehäuse *n*

~, vest., antechamber, anteroom · Vestibül *n*, Vorraum *m*, Vorzimmer *n*

vestigially period, North Italian Quattrocentro · Quattrocento *m*

vestry [*A room in a church or church building where prayer meetings, Sunday schools, etc. are held*] · Andachtsraum *m*, Andachtssaal *m*

~, sacristy, revestry · Sakristei *f* [*Der Priesterraum und meistens auch der Aufbewahrungsort für den Schatz der Kirche*]

V-gutter · V-Rinne *f*

Vhn, Vickers hardness number · Vickers-Härtezahl *f*

VI, viscosity index · Viskositätsindex *m*

viability · Lebensfähigkeit *f*

vibrated and pressed concrete pipe Rüttelpreßbetonrohr *n*

vibrated bulk concrete — vineyard pole 1090

~ **bulk concrete,** ~ mass ~ · Rüttelmassenbeton *m,* Massenrüttelbeton

~ **concrete** · Rüttelbeton *m,* Vibrationsbeton

~ ~ **pipe** · Rüttelbetonrohr *n*

~ **mass concrete,** ~ bulk ~ · Massenrüttelbeton *m,* Rüttelmassenbeton

vibration, oscillation · Schwingung *f,* Erschütterung

~ **check (calculation),** oscillation ~ (~) · Schwingungsnachweis *m,* Erschütterungsnachweis

~ **damping,** oscillation ~ · Erschütterungsdämpfung *f,* Schwingungsdämpfung *f*

~ ~ **material,** oscillation ~ ~ · Schwingungsdämmstoff *m*

~ **energy,** oscillation ~ · Erschütterungsenergie *f,* Schwingungsenergie

~ **flanking transmission,** oscillation ~ ~ · Erschütterungs-Flankenübertragung *f,* Schwingungs-Flankenübertragung

~ **insulation,** oscillation ~, insulation against vibration, insulation against oscillation · Schwingungsisolierung *f,* Erschütterungsisolierung

(~) **isolator,** oscillation ~, ~ mount · Schwingungsdämpfer *m,* Erschütterungsdämpfer

vibration-less, oscillation-less · schwingungsfrei, erschütterungsfrei, vibrationsfrei

vibration of a foundation, oscillation ~ ~ ~ · Fundamentschwingung *f*

~ **source,** oscillation ~, source of vibration, source of oscillation · Schwingungsquelle *f,* Erschütterungsquelle

~ **test,** oscillation ~ · Schwingungsprobe *f,* Schwingungsprüfung *f,* Schwingungsversuch *m,* Erschütterungsprobe, Erschütterungsprüfung, Erschütterungsversuch

~ **transmission,** oscillation ~ · Schwingungsübertragung *f,* Erschütterungsübertragung, Vibrationsübertragung

vibratory method of compaction · (Ein) Rüttelverfahren *n [Beton]*

vibro-compaction · Rüttelverdichtung *f*

Vicat apparatus [*A penetration device used in the testing of hydraulic cements and similar materials*] · Vicat-Gerät *n*

~ **needle** [*A weighted needle for determining setting time of hydraulic cements*] · Vicat-Nadel *f*

~ (~) **test** · Vicat-Nadelprüfung *f,* Vicat-Nadelprobe *f,* Vicat-Nadelversuch *m*

vice stair(case), vis(e) ~, vys(e) ~, newel ~, screw ~, winding ~ · Schnekkentreppe *f,* Wendeltreppe, Schnecke(n-stiege) *f*

Vickers' diamond hardness tester · Vickers-Härteprüfer *m*

Vickers hardness · Vickers-Härte *f*

~ ~ **number,** Vhn · Vickers-Härtezahl *f*

Victoria blue · Viktoriablau *n*

~ **green** · Viktoriagrün *n*

Victorian style · viktorianischer Stil *m* [*ca. 1840–1900*]

victory gateway · Siegestor *n*

~ **memorial** · Siegesdenkmal *n*

~ **pillar,** pillar of victory, triumphal column, column of triumph · Siegessäule *f,* gekuppelte Säule, Doppelsäule, Triumphsäule

Vienna Postal Savings Bank · Postsparkassenamt *n* zu Wien

~ **Secession movement** · Wiener Werkstätte *f [1903 von Josef Hoffmann und Kolo Moser gegründet*]

Vierendeel girder, frame ~ · Vierendeelträger *m,* Rahmenträger

view · Ansicht *f*

~ **of space,** spatial image, space image, three-dimensional image · Raumbild *n*

view-endowed site · Aussichtsgrundstück *n*

viewer, door ~, judas · (Tür)Gucker *m,* (Tür)Spion *m*

viewing deck, lookout ~, ~ platform · Aussichtsplattform *f*

~ **floor;** ~ storey (Brit.); ~ story (US); lookout ~ · Aussichtsgeschoß *n,* Aussichtsstockwerk *n,* Aussichtsetage *f*

~ **gallery,** lookout ~ · Aussichtsgang *m [Besucherturm*]

~ **gondola,** lookout ~ · Aussichtskabine *f [Besucherturm*]

~ **platform** → ~ deck

~ **room,** lookout ~ · Aussichtsraum *m*

~ **slot** · Sichtschlitz *m*

~ **storey** (Brit.) → ~ floor

~ **tower,** lookout ~, standing · · Aussichtsturm *m,* (Aussichts)Warte *f*

vihara → cave monastery

villa · Villa *f*

~ **garden** · Villengarten *m*

village church, country ~, rural ~ · Dorfkirche *f,* Landkirche

~ **square** · Dorfplatz *m*

village-type arrangement, ~ grouping · dorfähnliche Gruppierung *f*

~ **grouping,** ~ arrangement · dorfähnliche Gruppierung *f*

vine black (pigment) · Reb(en)schwarz *n* [*Es besteht aus Kohlenstoff und mineralischen Beimengungen. Es wurde früher durch Verkohlen von pflanzlichen Abfällen wie Weinreben, Melasse, Nußschalen und dergleichen, unter Luftabschluß hergestellt. In neuerer Zeit wird vielfach Grudekoks in Naß- und Trockenmühlen fein gemahlen*]

~ **leaf** · Weinblatt *n,* Rebenblatt

Vinsol Resin [*Trademark*] · Kiefernwurzelharz *n* [*Luftporenbildner*]

vineyard pole · Rebpfahl *m*

vinyl — viscosity

vinyl, ~ resin · Vinyl(harz) *n*
~ **acetate** · Vinylazetat *n*
~ **adhesive** → ~ bonding ~
~ **asbestos** · Vinylasbest *m*
vinyl-asbestos composition, ~ compound, ~ mass, ~ material, asbestos-vinyl ~ · Asbest-Vinyl-Masse *f*, Vinyl-Asbest-Masse
~ **compound** → ~ composition
~ **floor cover(ing),** asbestos-vinyl ~ ~, ~ floor(ing) (finish) · Flex-(Fuß-) Boden(belag) *m*, Flexbelag
~ **floor(ing) (finish),** asbestos-vinyl ~ (~), ~ floor cover(ing) · Flex-(Fuß-) Boden(belag) *m*, Flexbelag
~ **mass** → ~ composition
~ **material** → ~ composition
~ **tile,** asbestos-vinyl ~, VAT · Pastellplatte *f*, Flexfliese *f*, Vinylasbestfliese, Flex(belag)platte, Vinylasbest(belag)platte [*DIN 16950*]

vinyl benzene, styrene · Vinylbenzol *n*, Styrol
~ **(bonding) adhesive,** ~ ~ agent, ~ ~ medium, ~ cement(ing agent) · Vinylkleb(e)stoff *m*, Vinylkleber *m*, Vinylkleb(e)mittel *n*
~ **cement(ing agent)** → ~ (bonding) adhesive
~ **chlorid(e)** (US); ~ chloride (Brit.) · Vinylchlorid *n*

vinyl-coated · vinylbeschichtet
vinyl cube · Vinylwürfel *m*
~ **ester** · Vinylester *m*
~ **ether** · Vinyläther *m*
~ **ethylene** · Vinyläthylen *n*
~ **extrusion** → extruded vinyl section
~ **film,** ~ sheeting · Vinylfolie *f*
~ **floor cover(ing),** ~ floor(ing) (finish) · Vinyl(fuß)boden(belag) *m*
~ **floor(ing) (finish),** ~ floor cover(ing) · Vinyl(fuß)boden(belag) *m*
~ **foam** · Vinylschaum(stoff) *m*
~ **insert(ion)** · Vinyleinlage *f*
~ **latex base** · Vinyllatexbasis *f*, Vinyllatexgrundlage *f*
~ **liner** · Vinylabklebung *f* [*(Preß)Stroh-(dämm)platte*]
~ **medium,** ~ resin ~, ~ (resin) vehicle · Vinyl(harz)-Bindemittellösung *f* [*Anstrichfarbe*]
~ **paint** · Vinylfarbe *f*
~ **panel** · Vinyltafel *f*
~ **pipe** · Vinylrohr *n*

vinyl (plastic) tile, VPT · Vinyl(belag)platte *f*, Vinylfliese *f*
~ ~ **floor cover(ing),** ~ ~ floor(ing) (finish), VPT ~ (~) · Vinylfliesen(fuß)boden(belag) *m*, Vinylplatten(fuß)boden(belag)
~ ~ **floor(ing) (finish),** ~ ~ floor cover(ing), VPT ~ (~) · Vinylfliesen-(fuß)boden(belag) *m*, Vinylplatten(fuß)boden(belag)

vinyl (resin) · Vinyl(harz) *n*
~ **(~) medium,** ~ (~) vehicle · Vinyl(harz)-Bindemittellösung *f* [*Anstrichfarbe*]
~ **(~) vehicle,** ~ (~) medium · Vinyl(harz)-Bindemittellösung *f* [*Anstrichfarbe*]
~ **sheeting,** ~ film · Vinylfolie *f*
~ **sheet(ing)** · Vinylbahn *f*
~ **solution** · Vinyllösung *f*
~ **tile** → vinyl (plastic) ~
~ **vehicle,** ~ resin ~, ~ (resin) medium · Vinyl(harz)-Bindemittellösung *f* [*Anstrichfarbe*]
~ **wall facing,** ~ ~ sur~, ~ ~ lining · Vinylwandauskleidung *f*, Vinylwandverkleidung, Vinylwandbekleidung
~ ~ **lining,** ~ ~ (sur)facing · Vinylwandauskleidung *f*, Vinylwandverkleidung, Vinylwandbekleidung
~ ~ **(sur)facing,** ~ ~ lining · Vinylwandauskleidung *f*, Vinylwandverkleidung, Vinylwandbekleidung

violet alizarin(e) lake · Alizarinviolett *n*
~ **pigment** [*B.S. 314*] · Violettpigment *n*, violettes Pigment
~ **ultramarine** · Ultramarinviolett *n*, violettes Ultramarin

VIP reception room · Staatsempfangsraum *m*

virtual deformation · virtuelle Formänderung *f*, ~ Verformung
~ **displacement** · virtuelle Verrückung *f*

virtual-displacement law, ~ principle, ~ theorem, theorem of virtual displacements, principle of virtual displacements, law of virtual displacements · Prinzip *n* der virtuellen Verrückungen
~ **principle,** ~ theorem, ~ law, theorem of virtual displacements, principle of virtual displacements, law of virtual displacements · Prinzip *n* der virtuellen Verrückungen
~ **theorem,** ~ principle, ~ law, theorem of virtual displacements, principle of virtual displacements, law of virtual displacements · Prinzip *n* der virtuellen Verrückungen

virtual force · virtuelle Kraft *f*
~ **loading** · virtuelle Belastung *f*
~ **translation** · virtuelle Verschiebung *f*
~ **work** · gedachte Arbeit *f*, virtuelle ~ [*Einflußlinien*]

virtual-work law → principle of virtual work
~ **principle** → principle of virtual work
~ **theory** → principle of virtual work

visc. [*abbreviated*]; viscous · viskos
visco(si)meter · Viskosimeter *n*
viscosity · Dickigkeit *f*, Viskosität *f*, Zähigkeit

viscosity adjuster — vitreous surfacing

~ **adjuster,** thickener · Verdickungsmittel *n*
~ **index,** VI · Viskositätsindex *m*
~ **modifier** · Viskositätsindex-Verbesserer *m*
~ **range,** range of viscosity · Viskositätsbereich *m, n*
viscous [*abbreviated; visc.*] · viskos
vis(e) stair(case), vys(e) ~, vice ~, newel ~, screw ~, winding ~ · Schnekkentreppe *f*, Wendeltreppe, Schnecke(nstiege) *f*
visible cupola, ~ dome · Sichtkuppel *f*, Innenkuppel [*Im Gegensatz zur Tragkuppel, an der die Sichtkuppel aufgehängt ist*]
~ **dome,** ~ cupola · Sichtkuppel *f*, Innenkuppel [*Im Gegensatz zur Tragkuppel, an der die Sichtkuppel aufgehängt ist*]
~ **face,** ~ side · Sichtseite *f*, Schauseite
~ **side,** ~ face · Sichtseite *f*, Schauseite
~ **under-face,** ~ underside, soffit [*abbreviated: soff.*] · Untersicht *f*
~ **underside,** ~ under-face, soffit [*abbreviated: soff.*] · Untersicht *f*
vision, through-~ · Durchblick *m*, Durchsicht *f* [*Glas*]
~ **panel,** see-through window · Sichtfenster *n* [*Tor*]
vision-proof glass → obscure(d) ~
(vision) screen(ing) · (Sicht)Blende *f*, (Sicht)Schutz *m*
(~) ~ fence · Blendezaun *m*, Sicht~, (Sicht)Schutzzaun
visitor's car · Besucherfahrzeug *n*
~ **drive** · (Auto)Vorfahrt *f* für Besucher
~ **entrance** · Besuchereingang *m*
~ **room** · Besucherraum *m*, Besucherzimmer *n*
~ **traffic** · Besucherverkehr *m*
~ **waiting room** · Besucherwarteraum *m*, Besucherwartezimmer *n*
~ **(walk)way** · Besuchergang *m*
vista · gerichtete Aussicht *f*, Sicht
visual acuity · Sehschärfe *f*
~ **aid,** VA · Sichthilfe *f*
~ **comfort** · Sichtbehaglichkeit *f*
~ **field** · Blickfeld *n*
(~) inspection · Augenscheinnahme *f*
~ **integration,** graphic(al) ~ · zeichnerische Integration *f*, graphische ~, bildliche ~
~ **scale** · optischer Maßstab *m*
vitiated air, foul ~ · Abluft *f*, Schlechtluft [*Ins Freie abströmende Abluft heißt „Fortluft" und ganz oder teilweise nach Filterung wieder der Lüftungszentrale zugeführte Abluft heißt „Umluft"*]
~ ~ **chimney,** foul ~ ~, extract venting ~, extract ventilation ~ · Abluftschornstein *m*, Abluftschlot *m*, Schlechtluftschornstein, Schlechtluftschlot, Entlüftungsschornstein, Entlüftungsschlot

~ ~ **duct,** foul ~ ~, ~ ~ flue, extract venting ~, extract ventilation ~ · Abluftkanal *m*, Entlüftungskanal, Schlechtluftkanal
~ ~ **floor duct,** foul ~ ~ ~, ~ ~ ~ flue, · Abluft-(Fuß)Bodenkanal *m*, Schlechtluft-(Fuß)Bodenkanal
~ ~ ~ **flue,** foul ~ ~ ~, ~ ~ ~ duct · Abluft-(Fuß)Bodenkanal *m*, Schlechtluft-(Fuß)Bodenkanal
~ ~ **flue,** foul ~ ~, ~ ~ duct, extract venting ~, extract ventilation ~ · Abluftkanal *m*, Entlüftungskanal, Schlechtluftkanal
~ ~ **grate,** foul ~ ~ · Schlechtluftrost *m*, Abluftrost
~ ~ **grid** → ~ ~ grating
~ ~ **hole** → foul ~ ~
~ ~ **line,** foul ~ ~, extract ventilation ~, extract venting ~ · Abluftleitung *f*, Entlüftungsleitung, Schlechtluftleitung
~ ~ **opening,** foul ~ ~, ~ ~ hole · Schlechtluftdurchlaß *m*, Schlechtluftöffnung *f*, Abluftöffnung, Abluftdurchlaß; Lufteinlaß [*Fehlname*] [*Eine Öffnung in einer Raumbegrenzungsfläche, durch die Raumluft (Abluft) in den Abluftkanal oder als Fortluft ins Freie abgesaugt oder gedrückt wird*]
~ ~ **pipe,** foul ~ ~, extract ventilation ~, extract venting ~ · Abluftrohr *n*, Entlüftungsrohr, Schlechtluftrohr
~ ~ **shaft,** foul ~ ~, extract ventilation ~, extract venting ~ · Entlüftungsschacht *m*, Abluftschacht, Schlechtluftschacht [*DIN 18017*]
vitrain, pure coal · Vitrit *m*, Glanzkohle *f*
vitreous, vitrified · verglast [*Feuerfestindustrie*]
~ **brick,** vitrified ~ · verglaster Ziegel *m*
~ **china,** vitrified ~ · Diamant-Porzellan *n*, Kristallporzellan
~ **enamel,** vitrified ~, porcelain ~ · Schmelzemail(le) *n, (f)*
~ ~ **finish,** porcelain ~ ~, vitrified ~ ~ · Schmelzemailleüberzug *m*
~ **enamelled building panel** (Brit.); ~ enameled ~ ~ (US); porcelain ~ ~ ~, vitrified ~ ~ ~ · schmelzemaillierte (Bau)Tafel *f*, Schmelzemaille-(bau)tafel
~ ~ **steel** (Brit.); ~ enameled ~ (US); vitrified ~ ~, porcelain ~ ~ · schmelzemaillierter Stahl *m*
~ **rock,** vitrified ~ · glasiges Gestein *n*
~ **silica,** fused ~, vitrified ~, quartz glass, silica glass, fused quartz [*A vitreous material consisting almost entirely of silica, made in translucent and transparent forms. The former has minute gas bubbles disseminated in it*] · Quarzglas *n* [*Fehlname*]; Kiesel-(säure)glas
~ **surfacing,** cold glazing, cold glazed) finish), cold glazed coat(ing), vitrified surfacing · Kaltkeramik *f*, Kaltglasur-(überzug) *f, (m)*, Kaltbeglasung *f*

~ **whiteware body,** vitrified ~ ~ · dichtgebrannte feinkeramische Masse f
vitrification · Verglasung f [*Bildung erheblicher Mengen von Schmelze oder Glas beim Brennen eines ff. Erzeugnisses, wodurch die offene Porosität fast verschwindet*]
vitrified, vitreous · verglast [*Feuerfestindustrie*]
~ **brick,** vitreous ~ · verglaster Ziegel m
~ **china,** vitreous ~ · Diamant-Porzellan n, Kristallporzellan
~ **enamel,** vitreous ~, porcelain ~ · Schmelzemail(le) n, (f)
~ ~ **finish,** vitreous ~ ~, porcelain ~ ~ · Schmelzemailleüberzug m
~ **enamelled building panel** (Brit.); ~ enameled ~ ~ (US); porcelain ~ ~ ~, vitreous ~ ~ ~ · schmelzemaillierte (Bau)Tafel f, Schmelzemaille-(bau)tafel
~ ~ **steel** (Brit.); ~ enameled ~ (US); vitreous ~ ~, porcelain ~ ~ · Schmelzemaillierter Stahl m
~ **fort,** ~ wall · Schlackenwall m, verschlackter Wall [*Ein uralter Steinwall, dessen Zyklopenmauerwerk durch Feuer zu einer festen Masse zusammengeschmolzen ist*]
~ **rock,** vitreous ~ · glasiges Gestein n
~ **silica** ~ vitreous ~
~ **surfacing,** vitreous ~, cold glazing, cold glaze(d finish), cold glazed coat(ing) · Kaltkeramik f, Kaltbeglasung f, Kaltglasur(überzug) f, (m)
~ **wall,** ~ fort · Schlackenwall m, verschlackter Wall [*Ein uralter Steinwall, dessen Zyklopenmauerwerk durch Feuer zu einer festen Masse zusammengeschmolzen ist*]
~ **whiteware body,** vitreous ~ ~ · dichtgebrannte feinkeramische Masse f
to vitrify · verglasen [*Keramikindustrie*]
(Vitruvian) wave scroll, ~ wave, (~) ~ ornament, running dog, Vitruvian scroll · laufender Hund m, Wellenband n
vivianite earth, blue-iron ~ · Blaueisenerz n, Blauerde f, Vivianit m
V-jointing → toe-jointing
vocational (training) college, ~ (~) school · Berufsschule f
void, cavity · Hohlraum m [*z.B. über einer Hängedecke*]
~, **pore, interstice** [*The space in a material occupied by air or water, or both air and water*] · Pore f, Hohlraum m
void-cement ratio [*Volumetric ratio of air plus water to cement*] · Hohlraum-Zement-Verhältnis n
void ratio, pore ~ · Hohlraumverhältnis n, Porenziffer f [*DIN 4015*]
voids content → porosity
vol %, volume percent · Raumprozent n, Volumenprozent

volatile alkali · Salmiakgeist m, NH₄OH
~ **solvent** · flüchtiges Lösemittel n, ~ Lösungsmittel
(~) **thinner,** solvent · Verdünnungsmittel n [*organische Flüssigkeit zur Streichbarmachung von Anstrichfarben*]
volatility · Flüchtigkeit f
volcanic ash · Feuerbergasche f, vulkanische Asche
~ **building material** → ~ construction(al) ~
~ **construction(al) material,** ~ building ~ · vulkanischer Baustoff m; vulkanisches Baumaterial n [*Schweiz*] . [*Bims; Lava; Schaumlava; Tuff; Trachyttuff; Traß; Schlackensand*]
~ **earth from Pozzuoli** · Puzzolan(er)erde f
~ **glass(-like material),** (naturally occurring) siliceous volcanic rock · vulkanisches Glas n, Naturglas, glasartig erstarrtes vulkanisches Gestein n
(~) **tuff** · Durchbruchsgesteintuff m, Feuerbergtuff, (vulkanischer) Tuff(stein) m, (vulkanisches) Tuffgestein n, Duffstein
Völkerschlacht monument · Völkerschlachtdenkmal n [*in Leipzig*]
voltage-operated earth-leakage circuit breaker · Fehlerspannungs-Schutzschalter m
volt-ampere hour meter [*B.S. 37*] · Scheinverbrauchszähler m
volume, massing, structural mass, building mass · Baumasse f
~ · Raum m, Volumen n
~ **change** · Raumänderung f, Volumenänderung
~ **constancy,** ~ stability, stability of volume, constancy of volume · Raumbeständigkeit f, Raumkonstanz f
~ **cost** · Kosten f für den umbauten Raum
~ **decrease,** decrease in volume · Volumenverringerung f, Raumverringerung
~ **increase,** increase in volume · Raumzunahme f, Volumenzunahme
~ **(of construction)** · Baumasse f, Bauvolumen n
~ ~ **grains,** ~ ~ the (solid) particles · Festraum m [*in einem Korngemisch*]
~ ~ **voids** · Hohlraum(volumen) m, (n), Porenraum(volumen), H [*in einem Korngemisch*]
~ **percent,** vol % · Raumprozent n, Volumenprozent
~ **stability,** ~ constancy, constancy of volume, stability of volume · Raumbeständigkeit f, Raumkonstanz f
~ **velocity through a chosen surface** · Schallfluß m [*Produkt aus Schallschnelle und Querschnittsfläche senkrecht zur Schwingungsrichtung*]
~ **weight** → density
volumetrically stable · raumbeständig

volute — wagon vaulted

volute, (spiral) scroll · Schnecke *f*, Volute *f*, Spirale *f*

~ capital → voluted ~

~ helix · Volutenranke *f*

~ ornament, (spiral) scroll · Schneckenschmuck *m*, Schneckenverzierung *f*, Spiralschmuck, Spiralverzierung, Volutenschmuck, Volutenverzierung

voluted, scrolled, scroll-shaped · schneckenförmig

volute(d) capital, scroll(ed) ~, scroll-shaped ~ · Schneckenkapitell *n*, Volutenkapitell, Schneckenkapitäl, Volutenkapitäl, ionisches Kapitell, ionisches Kapitäl

~ gable, scroll(ed) ~, scroll-shaped ~ · Schneckengiebel *m*, Volutengiebel [*Dieser Giebel ist seitlich von Voluten gerahmt*]

vomitory, vomitorium [*In Roman amphitheatres, etc., any of the entrances leading to the tiers of seats*] · Treppenmündung *f*

(von Karman) eddy trail, (~ ~) vortex · (Karmansche) Wirbelstraße *f*

Vorarlberg School, ~ plan, ~ church scheme · Vorarlberger Schema *n*, ~ Schule *f* [*Ein Bauschema, das aus Vorarlberg stammende Meister – Thumb, Beer, Moosbrugger – bei ihren Kirchenbauten oft angewendet haben. Das Schema zeigt ein tonnengewölbtes Langhaus zwischen Kapellennischen und darüberliegenden Emporen. Das Querhaus ladet meist nur wenig aus und ist schmaler als das Mittelschiff des Langhauses. In dem etwas eingezogenen Chor setzt sich das Langhaussystem modifiziert fort*]

vortex trail, eddy ~, von Karman ~ ~ · (Karmansche) Wirbelstraße *f*

Voss connector, Tuchscherer ~ · Tuchscherer-Ringdübel *m*

votive chapel · Weihkapelle *f*

~ stupa(-mound), ~ tope(-mound) · Votivstupa *m*, Votivtope *m*

~ tope(-mound), ~ stupa(-mound) · Votivstupa *m*, Votivtope *m*

voussoir → arch brick

~ [*A wedge-shaped block in an arch*] · Bogen(keil)stein *m*

~ → arch stone

~ (brick) → arch ~

VPT, vinyl-plastic tile · Vinyl(belag)platte *f*, Vinylfliese *f*

VPT tile floor cover(ing) → vinyl-plastic ~ ~ ~

VR, vulcanized rubber · vulkanisierter Gummi *m*

V-shaped column, V-column · V-Stütze *f*, Winkelstütze *f* [*Sie gabelt sich vom Auflager in zwei Äste*]

~ roof · Grabendach *n*

(vulcanized) rubber · Gummi *m* [*vulkanisiert*]

vys(e) stair(case), vis(e) ~, vice ~, newel ~, screw ~, winding ~ · Schneckentreppe *f*, Wendeltreppe, Schnecke(nstiege) *f*

W

wacke [*Residual sand and clay formed by the decay of diabase, basalt, basaltic tuff, and similar rocks*] · Wacke *f*

wad(ding) strip · Wattestreifen *m*

wading pool, paddling ~, children's ~ · Planschbecken *n*, Kinderbecken

waffle → pan

~ ceiling, caisson ~, cassette ~, coffer(ed) ~, pan(el) ~, rectangular grid ~ · Kassettendecke *f*, kassettierte Decke

~ design → ~ pattern

~ floor → ~ slab ~

~ (~) plate → rectangular grid (floor) slab

~ (~) panel → rectangular grid (floor) slab

~ (~) slab → rectangular grid (~) ~

~ grid → ~ pattern

~ (panel) floor → ~ (slab) ~

~ pattern, ~ design, ~ grid, caisson ~, cassette ~, coffer(ed) ~, pan(el) ~, rectangular ~, cored ~ · Kassettenmuster *n*, kassettiertes Muster

~ slab → rectangular grid (floor) ~

~ (~) floor, cassette (~) ~, coffer(ed) (~) ~, pan (~) ~, caisson (~) ~, cored (~) ~, cassette (~) ~, plate ~, panel ~, rectangular grid (~) ~ · Kassettengeschoßdecke *f*, kassettierte Geschoßdecke

~ soffit, caisson ~, cassette ~, coffer(ed) ~, pan(el) ~, rectangular ~, cored ~ · Kassettenuntersicht *f*, kassettierte Untersicht

wages department, ~ office · Lohnabteilung *f*, Lohnbüro *n*

~ office, ~ department · Lohnabteilung *f*, Lohnbüro *n*

wagon(head) vault, tunnel ~, barrel ~ · Tonne(ngewölbe) *f*, (*n*) [*Gewölbeform mit längs einer Achse gleichbleibendem viertelkreis-, halbkreis-, segmentbogen- oder spitzbogenförmigen Querschnitt*]

wagon-headed, wagon-vaulted, tunnel-vaulted, barrel-vaulted · tonnengewölbt

wagon roof → wagon(-vault(ed)) ~

~ vault, wagon-head ~, tunnel ~, barrel ~ · Tonne(ngewölbe) *f*, (*n*) [*Gewölbeform mit längs einer Achse gleichbleibendem viertelkreis-, halbkreis-, segmentbogen- oder spitzbogenförmigen Querschnitt*]

wagon vaulted, tunnel-vaulted, barrel-vaulted, wagon-headed · tonnengewölbt

wagon(-vault(ed)) roof, tunnel(-vault(ed)) ~, barrel(-vault(ed)) ~ · Tonnen(gewölbe)dach *n*

Wailing Wall · Klagemauer *f* [*in Jerusalem*]

wainscot · Lamberie *f*, Lambris *m*, Sokkeltäfelung *f*

~; wood(en) panelling (Brit.); wood(en) paneling (US) [*abbreviated: wnsct*] · Täfelwerk *n*, Täfelung *f*, Getäfel *n*, Tablettenwerk [*Holzverkleidung aus Rahmen und Füllungen, mit Schnitzwerk, Fourniers und eingelegter Arbeit verziert*]

~ · Rückgetäfel *n* [*Chorgestühl*]

waiting bay · Wartebucht *f* [*Krankenhaus*]

~ hall · Wartehalle *f*, Wartesaal *m*

~ room · Warteraum *m*, Wartezimmer *n*

wale (piece) (US) → horizontal timber

waler → horizontal timber

waling → horizontal timber

walk, gallery [*A covered space for walking in, with one side open*] · Galerie *f*, Weg *m*, (Lauf)Gang *m*

~ · Gehweg *m*

walked-on finish · Gehbelag *m*

walk-in closet · begehbarer Einbauschrank *m*, ~ Wandschrank

walking area, ~ surface · Gehfläche *f*

~ distance · Gehentfernung *f*

~ habit · Gehgewohnheit *f*

~ line, pitch ~, line of travel · Ganglinie *f*, Gehlinie, Teilungslinie, Lauflinie [*Treppe: DIN 18064*]

~ surface, ~ area · Gehfläche *f*

~ way · Laufweg *m*

walking-way (rainwater) gutter, ~ roof ~, ~ R.W ~ · begehbare (Dach-)Rinne *f*, ~ Regenrinne

walk plank, run(way) ~ · Laufbohle *f*, Karrbohle

walk-through closet · Doppel-Einbauschrank *m*, Doppel-Wandschrank

walk-up · Treppensteigen *n*

~ apartment house [*An apartment house without elevator(s); generally four storeys or less*] · aufzugloses Haus *n*

~ domestic block, ~ residential ~, ~ residence ~, ~ ~ building; ~ dwelling (US) · Treppenwohngebäude *n*, Treppenwohnhaus *n*

~ ~ building, ~ residence ~, ~ residential ~, ~ ~ block; ~ dwelling (US) · Treppenwohngebäude *n*, Treppenwohnhaus *n*

~ dwelling (US); ~ residence building, ~ residence block, ~ residential building, ~ residential block, ~ domestic building, ~ domestic block · Treppenwohngebäude *n*, Treppenwohnhaus *n*

~ residence block, ~ residential ~, ~ domestic ~, ~ ~ building; ~ dwelling (US) · Treppenwohngebäude *n*, Treppenwohnhaus *n*

~ ~ building, ~ residential ~, ~ domestic ~, ~ ~ block; ~ dwelling (US) · Treppenwohngebäude *n*, Treppenwohnhaus *n*

~ residential block, ~ residence ~, ~ domestic ~, ~ ~ building ~ dwelling (US) · Treppenwohngebäude *n*, Treppenwohnhaus *n*

~ ~ building, ~ residence ~, ~ domestic ~, ~ ~ block; ~ dwelling (US) · Treppenwohngebäude *n*, Treppenwohnhaus *n*

(walk)way, runway · (Lauf)Steg *m*

~ bracket, runway ~ · Laufstegkonsole *f*

wall [*A vertical construction (i) enclosing a building or structure or (ii) dividing the internal space of a building or structure or (iii) serving as a fence when of heavy construction*] · Wand *f*

~, pipe ~ · (Rohr)Wand(ung) *f*

(~) anchor, masonry (~) ~, (masonry) (wall) tie, (masonry) cavity tie · (Mauer)Anker *m*, Mauer(werk)haken *m*, Mauerwerkanker

(~) ~, (~) tie · (Wand)Anker *m*

~ anchorage, ~ tying · Wandverankerung *f*

(~) aperture → beam box

~ arcade, blank ~, dead ~, blind ~, surface ~ [*An arcade applied to a wall face for ornamental purposes*] · Blendarkade *f*, Wandarkade

~ belfry · Glockenwand *f*

~ block → (masonry) wall (building) ~

wallboard, wlbd · Wand(bau)platte *f*

~ factory · Wand(bau)plattenfabrik *f*

wall bonded to piers · Wand *f* zwischen Pfeilern [*Nicht verwechseln mit „Pfeilerwand"*]

~ box → beam ~

~ bracing · Wandaussteifung *f*, Wandversteifung

~ bracket · Wandhalterung *f* [*z.B. für einen Feuerlöscher*]

~ breakthrough · Wanddurchbruch *m*

(~) brick, masonry (~) ~ · Mauerziegel *m*

~ (building) block → masonry ~ (~)

~ (~) component → wall(ing) (building) unit

~ (~) member → wall(ing) (building) unit

~ (~) tile → (masonry) wall (building) block

~ (~) unit → walling (~) ~

~ cavity · Wandhohlraum *m*

~ chase, ~ chasing · Wandnut *f*, Wandrille *f*

~ cladding (bonding) adhesive → ~ tile (~) ~

~ ~ cement(ing) agent) → ~ tile (bonding) adhesive

wall clamp — wall gypsum baseboard

~ **clamp** · Wandklammer f
~ **clock** · Wanduhr f
~ **closet** → wall(-mounted) ~
~ **coat** · Wandanstrich m, Wandaufstrich
~ **column** · Wandstütze f
~ ~ · Wandsäule f [*Einer Wand vorgelagerte Säule. Sie kann mit der Wand auch konstruktiv verbunden sein. Eine Wandsäule von geringem Querschnitt heißt „Dienst"*]
~ ~ **footing** · Wandstützenfundament n
~ **component** → wall(ing) (building) unit
~ **composition** · Wandgliederung f
~ **concrete strength** · Wandbetonfestigkeit f
~ **concreting**, ~ pouring · Wandbetonierung f, Wandbetonieren n
~ **conduit**, ~ wiring ~ · Elektro-Wandleerrohr n, (Elt-)Wandleerrohr
~ **construction** · Wandbau m
~ ~ **method** · Wandbauweise f, Wandbauverfahren n
~ ~ ~ **with heat insulating layer on each side** · Mantelbauweise f [*Wandkonstruktion mit innerer und äußerer Wärmedämmschicht*]
~ ~ **type**, type of wall construction · Wandbauart f
~ **coping** [*See remark under 'built-up roofing with wall coping'*] · Attikakappe f
~ **corner** · Wandecke f, Wandkante f
~ ~ **guard** · Wandeckenschutz m, Wandkantenschutz
~ **cornice** · Wand(ge)sims m, (n)
~ **cover**, ~ covering, ~ finish · Wandbelag m
~ **cover(ing)**, ~ finish · Wandbelag m
~ **crack** · Wandriß m
~ **crossing**, crossing of walls · Wandkreuzung f
~ **cross-section** · Wandquerschnitt m
~ **damp-proof course** · Wandisolierschicht f, Wandisolierlage f
~ **decoration** → ~ enrichment
~ **decorative fixture**, ~ ornament · Wandornament n, Wandschmuckelement, Wandschmuckglied n
~ **deformation** · Wandverformung f
~ **dissolution**, dissolution of the wall · Wandauflösung f, Auflösung der Wand
~ **door catch**, ~ ~ stop · Wandtürpuffer m
~ ~ **stop**, ~ ~ catch · Wandtürpuffer m
~ **drier**, ~ dryer · Wandtrockner m [*Bauaustrocknungsvorrichtung*]
~ **dryer**, ~ drier · Wandtrockner m [*Bauaustrocknungsvorrichtung*]
walled, fortified · befestigt
~ **garden** · ummauerter Garten m
~ **monastery**, fortified ~, fortress-monastery · befestigtes Mönchskloster n
~ **palace**, fortified ~, fortress-palace · befestigter Palast m
~ **passage**, dromos · Dromos m
~ **town**, castle-like ~, fortified ~, fortress-town · befestigte Stadt f
wall enrichment, ~ ornamentation, ~ decoration, mural · Wandschmuck m, Wandverzierung f
~ **erection**, ~ mounting · Wandmontage f
~ **fabric** · Stofftapete f
~ **facing**, ~ sur~, ~ lining · Wandauskleidung f, Wandbekleidung, Wandverkleidung
~ ~ **board**, ~ sur~ ~, ~ lining ~, ~ liner ~ · Wandauskleidungsplatte f, Wandverkleidungsplatte, Wandbekleidungsplatte, Wandbelagplatte
~ ~ **material**, ~ sur~ ~, ~ lining ~, ~ liner ~ · Wandauskleidungsmaterial n, Wandverkleidungsmaterial, Wandbekleidungsmaterial, Wandbelagmaterial
wall(-facing) quarry (tile) · Ziegel-Wandplatte f
~ **tile** · Wand(belag)platte f, Wandfliese f, Wandbekleidungsplatte, Wandverkleidungsplatte, Wandauskleidungsplatte
~ ~ **factory**, ~ Wand(belag)plattenfabrik f, Wandfliesenfabrik
wall fiberboard sheathing (US) → ~ fibreboard ~
~ **fibreboard sheathing** (Brit.); ~ fiberboard ~ (US) · Faserplattenwandverschalung f
~ **filler**, ~ stopper, ~ stopping · Wandausfüller m, Wand(füll)spachtel(masse) m, (f)
~ **finish**, ~ cover(ing) · Wandbelag m
~ **fire warning device** → wall(-mounted) ~ ~ ~
wall-fixed drinking fountain · Wandbrunnen m
wall flagpole → wall(-mounted) ~
~ **foil** · Wandauskleidungsfolie f, Wandverkleidungsfolie, Wand(bekleidungs)-folie
~ **footing** · Wandfundament n
wall-forming · wandbildend
wall forms, ~ form(work), ~ shuttering · Wandschalung f
~ **form(work)**, ~ shuttering, ~ forms · Wandschalung f
~ **frame** → beam box
~ **fresco** · Wandfreske f
~ **gas(-fired) (warm) air (unit) heater** → wall(-mounted) ~ (~) (~) ~
~ **gas geyser**, ~-mounted ~ ~ · Wandgasbadeofen m
~ **glazing** · Wandverglasung f, Wandeinglasung
~ **grab bar** → wall(-mounted) ~ ~
~ **gypsum baseboard**, gypsum wall ~ · (Gipskarton-)Stuckwandplatte f, (Gipskarton-)Wandstuckplatte, (Gips-

karton-)Putzträgerwandplatte, (Gipskarton-)Wandputzträgerplatte

~ ~ **sheathing** · Gipskartonplattenwandverschalung f

~ **(hand)rail** · Wandgeländer n

~ **hanging,** mural ~ · Wandbehang m

wall-hanging · Wandtapete f

~ **(type) tapestry** · (Wand)Bespannung f

wall heating · Wandheizung f

~ ~ **panel,** wall-mounted ~ ~ · Wandheiz(ungs)platte f

~ **hollow,** ~ recess · Wandvertiefung f

~ **hook** · Wandhaken m

~ **hospital luminaire (fixture)** (US) → wall(-mounted) ~ ~ (~)

~ **(hot) water heater** → wall(-mounted) (~) ~ ~

~ **humidity,** ~ moisture · Wandfeuchtigkeit f, Wandfeuchte f

wall-hung closet, ~ toilet, wall-mounted ~ · Wandabort m, Wandabtritt m, Wandklosett n, Wandtoilette f

~ **toilet,** ~ closet, wall-mounted ~ · Wandabort m, Wandabtritt m, Wandklosett n, Wandtoilette f

~ **urinal,** wall-mounted ~ · Pißbecken n, Urinalbęcken, Wandurinal n

wall hydrant · Wandhydrant m

~ **illumination,** ~ lighting · Wandbeleuchtung f

walling [*walls collectively*] · Wände fpl

~ [*Materials for constructing walls*] · Wandbaustoffe mpl; Wandbaumaterialien npl [*Schweiz*]

wall(ing) (building) component → ~ (~) unit

~ (~) **member** → ~ (~) unit

~ (~) **unit,** ~ (~) member, ~ (~) component · Wand(bau)element n, Wand(bau)körper m, Wandmontagekörper, Wandfertig(bau)element, Wandfertig(bau)körper [*Fehlnamen: Wand(bau)einheit f; Wandmontageeinheit*]

~ **component** → ~ (building) unit

~ **member** → ~ (building) unit

walling pattern [*Characteristic walling patterns involve the use of brick, stone and flint in 'chequer work' on medieval buildings*] · Mauermuster n

~ **stone,** natural ~ ~ · (Natur)Wandbaustein m

wall(ing) unit → ~ building ~

wall insulation · Wand(ab)dämmung f [*als Ergebnis der Tätigkeit*]

~ ~ · Wandisolierung f

~ **joint** · Wandfuge f

~ **junction,** junction of walls · Wandanschluß m

~ **key cabinet** · Schlüsselwandschrank m

~ **lavatory (basin)** → wall(-mounted) ~ (~)

wall-less · wandlos

wall lift, roof cradle, (window) cradle machine, (window) cleaning cradle [*Motorized carriage running vertically on rails let into the window frames*] · (Fenster)Putzwagen m, (Fenster)Reinigungswagen

~ **light fitting** → wall(-mounted) luminaire (fixture)

~ **lighting,** ~ illumination · Wandbeleuchtung f

~ **liner board,** ~ lining ~, ~ (sur)facing ~ · Wandauskleidungsplatte f, Wandverkleidungsplatte, Wandbekleidungsplatte, Wandbelagplatte

~ ~ **material,** ~ lining ~, ~ (sur)facing ~ · Wandauskleidungsmaterial n, Wandverkleidungsmaterial, Wandbekleidungsmaterial, Wandbelagmaterial

~ **lining** · Wandfutter n [*Schornstein*]

~ ~, ~ (sur)facing · Wandauskleidung f Wandbekleidung, Wandverkleidung

~ ~ **board,** ~ liner ~, ~ (sur)facing ~ · Wandauskleidungsplatte f, Wandverkleidungsplatte, Wandbekleidungsplatte, Wandbelagplatte

~ ~ **material,** ~ liner ~, ~ (sur)facing ~ · Wandauskleidungsmaterial n, Wandverkleidungsmaterial, Wandbekleidungsmaterial, Wandbelagmaterial

~ **lino(leum)** · Wandlinoleum n

~ **marble,** standing ~ · Wandmarmor m

~ **material** · Wandbaustoff m; Wandbaumaterial n [*Schweiz*]

~ **member** → wall(ing) (building) unit

~ **(mixed) plaster** · Wandputz m [*DIN 18550*]

~ **mix(ture),** ~ plaster, ~ stuff · Wandputzmörtel m, Wandputzmasse f

~ **moisture,** ~ humidity · Wandfeuchtigkeit f, Wandfeuchte f

~ **mosaic,** mural ~ · Wandmosaik n

wall(-)mounted · wandmontiert

wall(-mounted) closet, ~ toilet, wall-hung ~ · Wandabort m, Wandabtritt m, Wandklosett n, Wandtoilette f

~ **fire warning device** · Wandfeuermelder m, Wandbrandmelder, Wandfeuermeldeeinrichtung f, Wandbrandmeldeeinrichtung

~ **flagpole,** wall type ~ · Wand-Fahnenmast m, Wand-Flaggenmast

~ **gas(-fired) (warm) air (unit) heater** · Gas-Wandlufterhitzer m, Gas-Wandluftheizgerät n, Gas-Wandluftheizer

~ **gas geyser** · Wandgasbadeofen m

~ **grab bar** · Wandstange f

~ **heating panel** · Wandheiz(ungs)platte

~ **hospital luminaire** (fixture) (US); ~ ~ **light fitting** (Brit.); ~ ~ **(light(ing)) fixture** · Krankenhaus-Wandleuchte f

wall(-mounted) (hot) water heater — wall pressure 1098

~ **(hot) water heater**, ~ (~) ~ heating appliance · Wand-Wassererhitzer *m*, Wand-Wasserheizgerät *n*, Wand-Wasserheizer, Wand-Wassererwärmer

~ **lavatory (basin)**, ~ washbowl, ~ wash basin, ~ wash-handbasin · Wandwaschbecken *n*

~ **light fitting** → ~ luminaire (fixture)

~ **(light(ing)) fixture** → ~ luminaire (~)

~ **luminaire (fixture)** (US); ~ light fitting (Brit.); ~ (light(ing)) fixture · Wandleuchte *f*

~ **mixing cock for cold and hot water** · Wandbatterie *f*

~ **shower** · Wanddusche *f*

~ **slop bowl**, ~ ~ sink · Wandausguß-(becken) *m*, (*n*)

~ **toilet**, ~ closet, wall-hung ~ · Wandabort *m*, Wandabtritt *m*, Wandklosett *n*, Wandtoilette *f*

~ **urinal**, wall-hung ~ · Pißbecken *n*, Urinalbecken, Wandurinal *n*

~ **warm air heater** · Wandlufterhitzer *m*, Wandluftheizgerät *n*

~ **wash basin**, ~ wash-handbasin, ~ washbowl, ~ lavatory (basin) · Wandwaschbecken *n*

~ **washbowl**, ~ wash basin, ~ washhandbasin, ~ lavatory (basin) · Wandwaschbecken *n*

~ **wash-handbasin**, ~ wash basin, ~ washbowl, ~ lavatory (basin) · Wandwaschbecken *n*

~ **water heater** → ~ hot ~ ~

~ ~ **heating appliance** → ~ (hot) water heater

wall mounting, ~ erection · Wandmontage *f*

~ **niche** · Wandnische *f*

~ **of pier construction** · Pfeilerwand *f* [*Nicht verwechseln mit "Wand zwischen Pfeilern"*]

~ **opening** · Wandöffnung *f*

~ **oriel** · Fassadenerker *m*, Wanderker

~ **ornament**, ~ decorative fixture · Wandornament *n*, Wandschmuckelement, Wandschmuckglied *n*

~ **ornamentation** → ~ enrichment

~ **outlet**, ~ plug, ~ socket · Wandsteckdose *f*

~ **paint** · Wand(anstrich)farbe *f*

~ **painting**, mural ~ · Wandmalerei *f*

~ **panel** · Wand(bau)tafel *f*

~ ~ → ((pre)cast) concrete ~ ~

~ ~ **in (pre)stressed clay** → ~ unit ~ ~ ~

~ ~ ~ **Stahlton** → wall unit in (pre-)stressed clay

wall-panel system · Wandtafelverfahren *n*

(wall)paper [*Formerly known as 'paperhangings' and 'paper tapistry'. B. S. 1248*] · (Wand)Papiertapete *f*, Tapete

~ **cover moulding** (Brit.); ~ ~ molding (US) · Tapetenleiste *f*, (Wand)Papier~

(wall)papered · tapeziert mit (Wand-)Papiertapete

(wall)paper factory · Tapetenfabrik *f*, (Wand)Papier~

(wall)paperhanger, (paper)hanger · Tapezierer *m*

(wall)paperhanging, (wall)papering · Tapezieren *n* mit (Wand)Papiertapete, Tapezierung *f* ~ ~

(wall)paper(hanging) (bonding) adhesive, ~ ~ agent, ~ ~ medium, ~ cement(ing agent) · Tapetenkleb(e)stoff *m*, Tapetenkleb(e)mittel *n*, Tapetenkleb(e)mittel *n*, Tapetenkleber *m*, (Wand)Papier~

~ **paste** → (paper)hanging ~

(wall)papering, (wall)paperhanging · Tapezieren *n* mit (Wand)Papiertapete, Tapezierung *f* ~ ~

~ **work** · Tapezierarbeiten *fpl* mit (Wand-)Papiertapete

(wall)paper roll · (Papier)Tapetenrolle *f*, Wand~

~ **sheet(ing)** · Tapetenbahn *f*, (Wand)-Papier~

~ **trimmer** · Tapetenschneider *m*, (Wand)Papier~

wall-passage [*e.g. in a chapel*] · Laufgang *m* [*z.B. in einer Kapelle*]

~ · Wand(lauf)gang *m*

wall pattern · Wandmuster *n*

~ **pier** → engaged ~

~ ~ **capital** → engaged ~ ~

~ **pillar** [*A buttress taking part of the stress of a ceiling or vault but projecting inwards into a church instead of outwards from the outer wall as in a Gothic church. Wall pillars usually form the walls of side chapels; if deep enough they are found pierced by arches whereby a kind of side aisle is formed*] · Wandpfeiler *m*

~ **plank** · Wanddiele *f*

~ **plaster**, ~ mixed ~ · Wandputz *m* [*DIN 18550*]

~ ~, ~ mix(ture), ~ stuff · Wandputzmörtel *m*, Wandputzmasse *f*

~ **plate** · Streichbalken *m*, Streifbalken, Mauerlatte *f* [*Er liegt an der Mauer oder auf einem Mauerabsatz*]

~ ~, switch ~ [*A flush plate for an electric switch*] · Wandplatte *f*, Vorlegeplatte

~ **plug**, nailing ~ · Mauerdübel *m*

~ ~, ~ socket, ~ outlet · Wandsteckdose *f*

(~) pocket → beam box

~ **pot** → hollow block for walls

~ **pouring**, ~ concreting · Wandbetonierung *f*, Wandbetonieren *n*

~ **pressure** · Wanddruck *m*

wall radiator — wall tomb

~ **radiator** · Wand(glieder)heizkörper m, Wandradiator m

~ **rail,** ~ hand~ · Wandgeländer n

~ **recess,** ~ hollow · Wandvertiefung f

~ **reflection factor** · Wandrückstrahlgrad m

~ **relief** · Wandrelief n

~ **rib** · Mauerbogen m, Wandbogen [*Auf einer Mauer aufliegender Bogen, z.B. (Längs)Schildbogen und Blendbogen*]

~ **rosace** · Mauerrosette f [*Kohlenherd*]

~ **run** [*An opening temporarily left in the wall, especially for the passage of wheel barrows*] · provisorische Wandöffnung f

~ **safe** · Wandsafe n

~ **sample** · Wandprobe f

(~) **scone** · Wandzierlampe f, Zierwandlampe

wall-shaft · Wanddienst m

wall sheathing · Wandverschalung f

~ **shelf** · Wandregal n

~ **shower,** ~-mounted ~ · Wanddusche f

~ **shrine** · Wandschrein m

~ **shuttering,** ~ form(work), ~ forms · Wandschalung f

~ **sized,** room-~ ~ · (raum)wandgroß

~ **skin** · Wandhaut f

~ ~ Wanddichtung f [*Unterkellerung*]

~ **slab** → ((pre)cast) concrete ~ ~

~ ~ **in (pre)stressed clay,** ~ unit ~ ~ ~, ~ panel ~ ~ ~, Stahlton wall unit, Stahlton wall slab, Stahlton wall panel · Stahltonwandtafel f

~ ~ ~ Stahltòn → wall unit in (pre)stressed clay

~ **slate** · Wandschiefer m

~ **slop bowl** → wall(-mounted) ~ ~

~ **slot** · Wandschlitz m

~ **socket,** ~ outlet, ~ plug · Wandsteckdose f

~ **stability** · Wandstandfestigkeit f, Wandstandsicherheit, Wandstabilität f

~ **stopper,** ~ stopping, ~ filler · Wandausfüller m, Wand(füll)spachtel(masse) m, (f)

~ **stopping,** ~ stopper, ~ filler · Wandausfüller m, Wand(füll)spachtel(masse) m, (f)

~ **strength** · Wandfestigkeit f

~ **string** (Brit.); ~ stringer (US) · Wandwange f

~ **stucco** · Wandstuck m

~ **stud** · Kleb(e)pfosten m [*Fehlnamen: Kleb(e)säule f, Wandsäule*]

~ **stuff,** ~ mix(ture), ~ plaster · Wandputzmörtel m, Wandputzmasse f

~ **surface** · Wand(ober)fläche f

~ **(sur)facing,** ~ lining · Wandauskleidung f, Wandbekleidung, Wandverkleidung

~ ~ **board,** ~ lining~, ~ liner ~ · Wandauskleidungsplatte f, Wandverkleidungsplatte, Wandbekleidungsplatte, Wandbelagplatte

~ ~ **material,** ~ lining ~, ~ liner ~ · Wandauskleidungsmaterial n, Wandverkleidungsmaterial, Wandbekleidungsmaterial, Wandbelagmaterial

~ **system** · Wandkonstruktion f

~ **thickness** · Wanddicke f [*Fehlname: Wandstärke f*]

(~) **tie,** cavity ~, masonry (~) ~, (masonry) (wall) anchor · (Mauer)Anker m, Mauer(werk)haken m, Mauerwerkanker

~ ~ ~, ~ anchor · Wandanker m

(~) ~ **closer,** through-stone, bond header · Ankerstein m, Durchbinder m

~ **tile** → (masonry) wall (building) block

~ ~, ~-facing ~ · Wand(belag)platte f, Wandfliese f, Wandbekleidungsplatte, Wandverkleidungsplatte, Wandauskleidungsplatte

~ ~ **adhesive** → ~ ~ bonding ~

~ ~ **body,** ~ ~ clay ~, ~ ~ stone · (Keramik)Wandplattenscherben m, (Keramik)Wandfliesenscherben, Wand(belag)plattenscherben

~ ~ **(bonding) adhesive,** ~ cladding (~) ~ ~ ~ ~ agent, ~ ~ ~ medium, ~ ~ cement(ing agent) · Wandfliesenkleber m, Wandfliesenkleb(e)mittel n, Wandfliesenkleb(e)stoff m, Wand(belag)plattenkleber, Wand(belag)plattenkleb(e)mittel, Wand(belag)plattenkleb(e)stoff

~ ~ **cement(ing agent)** → ~ ~ (bonding) adhesive

~ ~ **(clay) body,** ~ ~ stone · (Keramik-)Wandplattenscherben m, (Keramik-)Wandfliesenscherben, Wand(belag)-plattenscherben

~ ~ **factory,** ~-facing ~ ~ · Wand(belag)plattenfabrik f, Wandfliesenfabrik

~ ~ **fixing by adhesive** · Wandplattenverklebung f, Wandplattenverlegen n im Dünnbettverfahren

~ ~ **glazed on both sides** · Doppelwandplatten f [*Doppelwandplatten werden nicht an Wandflächen angesetzt, sondern bilden die Wand. Sie sind beidseitig glasiert*]

~ ~ **stone,** ~ ~ (clay) body · (Keramik-)Wandplattenscherben m, (Keramik-)Wandfliesenscherben, Wand(belag)-plattenscherben

~ **tilework,** hung ~, vertical ~, ~ tiling · Wand(fliesen)belag m, Wandplattenbelag

~ **tiling,** vertical ~, hung ~, ~ tilework · Wand(fliesen)belag m, Wandplattenbelag

~ **toilet** → wall(-mounted) ~

~ **tomb,** mural ~ · Wandgrab n, Mauergrab

wall-to-wall carpeting, fitted carpet · Teppich(fuß)boden(belag) m, Teppichbelag

wall tracery · Wandmaßwerk n

~ **tying,** ~ **anchorage** · Wandverankerung f

~ **type,** type of wall · Wandart f

~ ~ **flagpole,** wall-mounted ~ · Wand-Fahnenmast m, Wand-Flaggenmast

~ **unit** → wall(ing) (building) ~

~ ~ **in (pre)stressed clay,** ~ panel ~ ~ ~, ~ slab ~ ~ ~, Stahlton wall unit, Stahlton wall slab, Stahlton ((pre)-stressed) wall panel, (pre)stressed clay wall panel, wall unit in Stahlton, wall slab in Stahlton, wall panel in Stahlton · Stahltonwandtafel f, Spanntonwandtafel, vorgespannte Ziegelwandtafel

~ ~ **yielding to blast** · ausblasbares Wandelement n [*Ein Wandelement, das durch eine Explosion weggedrückt wird*]

~ **urinal** → wall(-mounted) ~

~ **vapor barrier** (US); ~ **vapour** ~ (Brit.) · Wanddampfsperre f

(~) veneering · Verblenden n

~ **warm air heater** → wall(-mounted) ~ ~ ~

~ **washbowl** → wall(-mounted) lavatory (basin)

~ **water heater** → wall(-mounted) (hot) ~ ~

~ **weight** · Wandgewicht n

~ **wiring** · Wandverdrahtung f

~ **(~) conduit** · Elektro-Wandleerrohr n, (Elt-)Wandleerrohr

~ **with door(s)** · Türwand f [*Eine Wand mit Tür(en)*]

walnut oil · Walnußöl n

Walton's lino(leum), plain ~ · einfarbiges Linoleum n, Unilinoleum, Waltonlinoleum

~ ~ **cement,** plain ~ ~ · Waltonzement m

~ **process** · Waltonverfahren n [*Linoleumherstellung*]

war memorial · Gefallenendenkmal n, Ehrenmal, Kriegerdenkmal

ward · Riegelsperre f [*Buntbartschloß*]

~, **bailey, ballium** · Burghof m

~ **block,** ~ **building** · Bettengebäude n, Bettenhaus n, Krankenzimmergebäude, Krankenzimmerhaus

~ **building** → ~ block

~ **floor;** ~ **story** (US); ~ **storey** (Brit.) · Krankenzimmeretage f, Krankenzimmerstockwerk n, Krankenzimmergeschoß n

~ **luminaire light fitting** (Brit.); ~ ~ **(fixture)** (US); ~ ~ **(light(ing)) fixture** · Krankenzimmerleuchte f

~ **patient's room, sickroom** · Bettenraum m, Bettenzimmer n, Krankenraum, Krankenzimmer

~ **storey** (Brit.); ~ **story** (US); ~ **floor** · Krankenzimmeretage f, Krankenzimmerstockwerk n, Krankenzimmergeschoß n

~ **unit, nursing** ~ · Station f [*Krankenhaus*]

warded key hole · Buntbartschlüsselloch n

~ **lock** · Buntbartschloß n

~ **(locking) mechanism** · Riegelgesperre f [*Buntbartschloß*]

~ **mortise lock,** ~ **mortice** ~ · Buntbart-Einsteckschloß n

~ **rim lock** · aufliegendes Buntbartschloß n, Buntbart-Aufsatzschloß, Buntbart-Kasten(riegel)schloß

wardrobe, vestiary, garderobe, cloakroom · Garderobe f

~ **closet,** bedroom ~ · Schlafzimmer-Einbauschrank m, Schlafzimmer-Wandschrank

~ ~ **for children,** bedroom ~ ~ ~ · Schlafzimmer-Einbauschrank m für Kinder, Schlafzimmer-Wandschrank ~ ~

~ ~ ~ **men,** bedroom ~ ~ ~ · Schlafzimmer-Einbauschrank m für Männer, Schlafzimmer-Wandschrank ~ ~

~ ~ ~ **women,** bedroom ~ ~ ~ · Schlafzimmer-Einbauschrank m für Frauen, Schlafzimmer-Wandschrank ~ ~

~ **(type) closet bank,** bedroom ~ ~, bank of wardrobe(-type) closets, bank of bedroom closets · Schlafzimmer-Schrankwand f

ware, goods, products, articles · Artikel mpl, Ware(n) f, Erzeugnisse npl, Gegenstände mpl

warehouse (building), WHSE · Lagergebäude n

~ **set(ting)** [*The partial hydration of cement stored for periods of time and exposed to atmospheric moisture*] · Ablagerung f [*Zement*]

warm air · Warmluft f

warm-air blower · Warmluftgebläse n, Warmluftbläser m

(warm-)air (central) heating, fan-assisted ~ (~) ~, warm-air heating system · (Warm)Luft-Zentralheizung f (mit Ventilatoren), (Warm)Luft-Mehrraumheizung (~ ~) [*Die Warmluft wird mit Ventilatoren in die zu beheizenden Räume gedrückt*]

warm-air circulation · Warmluftumwälzung f

~ **circulator** · Warmluftumwälzer m

(warm-)air curtain, ~ **door** ~ · (Warm-)Luftschleier m

~ ~ **(doorway) installation,** ~ ~ (~) **unit, air-curtain door(way)** · (Warm-)Luftschleieranlage f, (Warm)Luftschleiergerät n, (Warm)Lufttür f

warm-air distribution · Warmluftverteilung f

~ ~ **duct** · Warmluft-Verteilungskanal m

(warm-)air (door) curtain, curtain wall of air · (Warm)Luftschleier m

~ duct · Warmluftkanal *m*

~ ~ riser, ~ rising duct · Warmluft-Steig(e)kanal *m*

~ ducting · Warmluftkanalanlage *f*

(warm-)air furnace · (Warm)Luftofen *m*, Luftheizofen

~ heating → **~ central ~**

~ ~ installation, ~ ~ system, ~ ~ plant [*It is a system which circulates warm air for heating*] · (Warm)Luft(be)-heiz(ungs)anlage *f*

~ ~ plant, ~ ~ system, ~ ~ installation [*It is a system which circulates warm air for heating*] · (Warm)Luft(be)-heiz(ungs)anlage *f*

~ ~ system, ~ ~ installation, ~ ~ plant [*It is a system which circulates warm air for heating*] · (Warm)Luft(be)-heiz(ungs)anlage *f*

~ ~ ~, ~ (central) heating, fan-assisted (warm-)air (central) heating · (Warm-)Luft-Zentralheizung *f* (mit Ventilatoren), (Warm)Luft-Mehrraumheizung (~ ~) [*Die Warmluft wird mit Ventilatoren in die zu beheizenden Räume gedrückt*]

~ outlet · Warmluftauslaß *m*

(~) output, heated air ~ · Warmluftleistung *f*

~ register · Warmluftregler *m*

~ rising duct, ~ duct riser · Warmluft-Steig(e)kanal *m* .

warm concrete, heated ~ · Warmbeton *m*

warmed air · erwärmte Luft *f*

~ floor covering, ~ floor(ing) · beheizter (Fuß)Boden(belag) *m*, (Fuß-)Boden(belag) mit Strahlungsheizung

~ floor(ing), ~ floor covering · beheizter (Fuß)Boden(belag) *m*, (Fuß)Boden(belag) mit Strahlungsheizung

warmer → heating appliance

warm glue · Warmleim *m*

warming · Anwärmen *n*, Erwärmen

~ · Erwärmung *f*, Anwärmung

~, heating · (Be)Heizung *f*

~ appliance → heating **~**

~ device → heating appliance

warming-house, calefactory · Calefactorium *n*, Wärmestube *f*

warming-in, reheating · Anwärmen *n* [*Glasherstellung*]

warming period → period of warming

~ rate, rate of warming · Anwärmungsgeschwindigkeit *f*, Erwärmungsgeschwindigkeit

~ time → period of warming

~ unit → heating appliance

~ up · Aufheizen *n* [*Raum*]

~ ~, heating~, firing ~ · (An)Tempern *n*, Auftempern [*Glasherstellung*]

~ ~ period · Aufheizzeit *f* [*Raum*]

warm mortar, heated ~ · Warmmörtel *m*

warm-setting adhesive, ~ glue, intermediate temperature setting ~, hot glue, cooked glue · Warmleim *m*

~ glue, ~ adhesive, intermediate temperature setting ~ · Warmleim *m*

warm spraying · Warmspritzen *n* [*Arbeitstemperaturen von 35 °C bis 40 °C*]

warmth · Wärme *f*

warm to the tread · fußwarm

warning device · (Signal- und) Warngerät *n*, Melder *m*, Warnvorrichtung *f*, Signalvorrichtung

~ light, alarm ~, WL · Warnleuchte *f*, Warnlampe *f*, Warnlicht *n*, optisches Warnsignal *n*

to warp · verziehen, werfen, durchbiegen [*Feuerfestindustrie*]

warpage · Durchbiegung *f*, Verziehen *n*, Werfen [*Die während der Herstellung manchmal entstehende geometrische Abweichung eines ff. Steines von seiner Soll-Form*]

washable, washproof · waschfest, waschbeständig; (ab)waschbar [*Fehlbezeichnungen*]

~ distemper → casein(-bound) **~**

wash basin → lavatory (**~**)

washboard → sanitary cove

~ component → base (board) unit

~ heater, scrub board ~, mopboard ~, base (board) ~, sanitary cove ~ (US); **skirting (board) ~** (Brit.); **base plate ~** [*Scotland*] · Scheuerleistenheizer *m*, Fußleistenheizer, Sockelleistenheizer

~ heating, mopboard ~, base (board) ~, scrub board ~, sanitary cove ~ (US); **skirting (board) ~** (Brit.); **base plate ~** [*Scotland*] · Scheuerleistenheizung *f*, Fußleistenheizung, Sockelleistenheizung

~ member → base (board) unit

~ radiator, mopboard ~, scrub board ~, base (board) ~, sanitary cove ~ (US); **skirting (board) ~** (Brit.); **base plate ~** [*Scotland*] · Scheuerleisten-Radiator *m*, Sockelleisten-Radiator, Fußleisten-Radiator

~ unit → base (board) **~**

wash-boiler · Waschkessel *m*

washbowl → lavatory (basin)

to wash down, to rinse · abwaschen

wash-down bowl, ~ pan · Tiefspülbecken *n*

~ pan, ~ bowl · Tiefspülbecken *n*

~ (type) (water) closet · Tiefspülklosett *n*, Tiefspülabort *m*

~ (yard), vehicle ~ (~) · (Auto)Waschplatz *m*, Wagenwaschplatz

washed concrete · Waschbeton *m*

~ ~ slab paper · Waschbetonpapier *n*

~ down, rinsed · abgewaschen

~ gravel · gewaschener Kies *m*, Waschkies

~ pumice · Waschbims *m*

washed pumice gravel — waste (pipe)

~ ~ **gravel** · Edelbims m [*Bimskies, aus dem durch Waschen der Steinsplitt, die Schülferchen, entfernt ist*]
~ **sand** · gewaschener Sand m, Waschsand
washer, whser · Scheibe f, Unterleg~, Unterlag~
wash fixture · Waschanlage f [*In der Wohnung, meist im Badezimmer, Waschbecken und Badewanne, im Duschraum, Dusche, in Schlafräumen, insbesondere in Hotels, Waschnische, in Fabriken, Sporthallen und ähnlichen Bauten kombinierte Umkleide- und Waschräume mit Waschrinnen oder Waschbrunnen*]
~ **fountain** → ablution ~
wash-handbasin → lavatory (basin)
wash heating, swealing [*Raising the surface temperature of a heated pile bloom, slab or billet, immediately prior to or during rolling, to remove defects by forming a fluid scale*] · Abschweißen n und Entzundern
wash-house · Hauswaschküche f, Waschhaus n, Zentralwaschküche
washing by jet(s) · Strahlwaschen n
~ **down**, rinsing · Abwaschen n
~ **recess** · Waschnische f
~ **trough** · Waschtrog m
washleather · Putzleder n, Waschleder
~ **glazing**, glazing bedded in washleather · Putzlederverglasung f, Waschlederverglasung
wash oil · Waschöl n
~ **prime coat** · haftsichere Grundierung f, haftsicherer Grund(ier)anstrich m, haftsicherer Grund(ier)aufstrich
~ **primer** → etching ~
washproof → washable
wash room, WR, lavatory [*A room equipped with basin(s) for washing hand and/or face*] · Waschraum m
~ ~ **equipment**, lavatory ~, WR ~ · Waschraumausrüstung f
~ ~ **tray**, lavatory ~, WR ~ · Waschraumaschenbecher m
washtub · Waschwanne f
wash-up → scullery
~ **sink (unit)**, dishwashing ~ (~) [*B.S. 1206*] · Geschirrspülausguß m, Geschirrspültisch m, Geschirrabwaschtisch
waste → liquid ~
~ · Abfall(stoff) m
~ → demolition rubbish
~ → refuse
~ → ~ fitting
~ **box**, refuse ~; rubbish ~ (US) · Abfall(stoff)kasten m, Müllkasten
~ **acid tank** · Abfallsäurebehälter m
~ **cartage**, ~ collection, refuse ~ · Abfall(stoff)abfuhr f, Müllabfuhr
~ **collecting chamber**, (refuse) ~ ~, (~) storage ~ · Sammelraum m, Müll~, Abfall(stoff)sammelraum

~ **collection**, ~ cartage, refuse ~ · Abfall(stoff)abfuhr f, Müllabfuhr
~ **connection** · Ablaufverbindung f
~ **container**, refuse ~, container for waste(s), container for refuse; rubbish container, container for rubbish (US) · Abfall(stoff)behälter m, Müllbehälter
~ **destructor**, ~ incinerator, refuse ~; rubbish ~ (US); incinerator, destructor · Abfall(stoff)verbrenner m, (Müll)Verbrenner
~ **disposal**, refuse ~, disposal of refuse, disposal of waste(s); rubbish disposal, disposal of rubbish (US) · Abfall(stoff)beseitigung f, Müllbeseitigung
~ ~ → refuse ~
~ ~ **chute** (Brit.) → dispose-all
~ ~ **shaft** (Brit.) → dispose-all
~ ~ **unit**, ~ food grinder · Küchenabfallzerkleinerer m
~ **disposer** (Brit.) → dispose-all
~ **drainage pipe in basement** · Kellersiel n
~ **elbow**, ~ pipe ~, drain(age) pipe ~, draining pipe ~, discharge pipe ~ · Abflußrohrbogen m, Ablaufrohrbogen, Dränrohrbogen, Entwässerungsrohrbogen, Fallrohrbogen [*DIN 540*]
~ **(fitting)**, recessed waste fitting · Kelchplatte f
~ **food** · Nahrungsmittelabfälle mpl
~ ~ **grinder**, ~ disposal unit · Küchenabfallzerkleinerer m
~ **glass** · Glasabfall m
~ **grease**, used ~ · Abfallfett n, Altfett
~ **grinder** → (mechanical) refuse ~
~ **gypsum** · Abfallgips m
~ **heap**, refuse ~, midden · Abfall(stoff)haufen m, Müllhaufen
~ **heat** · Abwärme f
waste-heat drying, drying by waste heat · Abwärmetrocknung f, Trocknung mit Abwärme
waste heat utilization · Abwärmeausnutzung f
(~) **incineration**, refuse ~; rubbish ~ (US) · Abfall(stoff)verbrennen n, Abfall(stoff)verbrennung f, (Müll-)Verbrennung
~ ~ **installation** → (refuse) incinerator plant
~ **incinerator**, ~ destructor, refuse ~; rubbish ~ (US); incinerator, destructor · Abfall(stoff)verbrenner m, (Müll)Verbrenner
~ ~ **plant** → (refuse) ~ ~
~ **oil**, used ~ · Ab(fall)öl n, Altöl
~ **pipe** [*A pipe collecting from baths basins and sinks*] · Bad- und Küchenabwasserrohr n
~ (~), draining ~, drain(age) ~, discharge ~ · Abflußrohr n, Ablaufrohr, Dränrohr, Entwässerungsrohr [*Fehlnamen: Ablauf m, Abfluß m*]

~ (~) elbow, drain(age) ~ ~, discharge ~ ~, draining ~ ~ · Abflußrohrbogen m, Ablaufrohrbogen, Dränrohrbogen, Entwässerungsrohrbogen, Fallrohrbogen [*DIN 540*]

~ pit, refuse ~; rubbish ~ (US) · Abfall(stoff)grube f, Müllgrube

~ steam · Abdampf m, Ausdampf

~ ~ heat · Abdampfwärme f

~ ~ heating · Abdampfheizung f [*Abdampf einer Dampfkraftanlage wird entweder direkt oder nach Druckminderung als Wärmeträger in Niederdruckdampfheizungen verwendet*]

~ ~ ~ facility, ~ ~ ~ system, ~ ~ ~ installation · Abdampfheiz(ungs)anlage f

~ ~ ~ installation, ~ ~ ~ facility, ~ ~ ~ system · Abdampfheiz(ungs)anlage f

~ ~ ~ system, ~ ~ ~ installation, ~ ~ ~ facility · Abdampfheiz(ungs)anlage f

~ ~ line, ~ ~ pipe~ · Abdampf(rohr)leitung f

~ ~ pipe · Abdampfrohr n, Dampfauslaßrohr

~ ~ (pipe)line · Abdampf(rohr)leitung f

~ storage chamber → (refuse) collecting ~

~ tip, refuse ~; rubbish ~ (US) · Müllkippe f, Müllhalde f, Müllablagerungsplatz m, Abfallkippe, Abfallhalde, Abfallablagerungsplatz, Müllabladeplatz, Abfall(stoff)abladeplatz

~ utilization, refuse ~; rubbish ~ (US) · Müllverwertung f, Abfall(stoff)verwertung

~ well, dry ~, absorbing ~ [*A well used for draining off surface water and conducting it underground, where it is absorbed*] · Sickerbrunnen m

wat, vat · Vat m [*buddhistische Klosteranlage*]

watch (and clock) factory · Uhrenfabrik f

~ factory, ~ and clock ~ · Uhrenfabrik f

~ tower → observation ~

~ turret; bartisan (Brit.); bartizan (US) · Erkertürmchen n

water-absorbing (natural) stone · Nässer m [*Naturstein, der Wasser ansaugt und darum zum Zerfrieren neigt*]

water absorption · Wasseraufnahme f

water-absorptive capacity, absorptive capacity for water · Wasseraufnahmefähigkeit f, Wasseraufnahmevermögen n

water action, action of water · Wasser(ein)wirkung f

~ addition, addition of water, adding of water · Wasserbeigabe f, Wasserzusatz m, Wasserbeigeben n, Wasserzusetzen, Wasserzugabe, Wasserzugeben

water-attracting, water-loving, hydrophile, hydrophibic, hydrophilic · wasserliebend

water bar, weather ~ · Wasserschenkel m, Wetterschenkel

waterbar, waterstop · Fugenband n

~ material, waterstop ~ · Fugenbandwerkstoff m

water barrier → humidity seal

~ base · Wasserbasis f, Wassergrundlage f [*Bindemittellösung einer Anstrichfarbe*]

water-base(d) paint, water-carried ~, (cold-)water ~ · Binderfarbe f, Dispersionsfarbe [*Ein aus Binder und Pigmenten hergestellter Anstrichstoff*]

~ vehicle, ~ medium · Bindemittellösung f auf Wassergrundlage, ~ ~ Wasserbasis [*Anstrichfarbe*]

water bath · Wasserbad n

water/binder ratio · Wasser-Bindemittel-Faktor m

water board · Wasserwirtschaftsamt n

water-borne sound · Wasserschall m

water-carried paint, water-base(d) ~, (cold-)water ~ · Binderfarbe f, Dispersionsfarbe [*Ein aus Binder und Pigmenten hergestellte Anstrichfarbe*]

water-carrier method · Schwemmverfahren n [*Hausmüllbeseitigung*]

water cement, (hydraulic) ~, cement matrix, CEM · Zement m [*hydraulisches Bindemittel*]

water-cement ratio, water/cement ~, w/c ~ · Wasser-Zement-Faktor m, Wasser-Zementwert m, Wasser-Zement-Verhältnis n, WZV, W/Z(-Faktor), W/Z-Wert [*Wassergewicht geteilt durch Zementgewicht einer Betonmischung*]

water channel, condensation ~ · Schwitzwasserrinne f, Kondensatrinne [*Fenster*]

~ charge · Wassergeld n

~ circulation · Wasserumlauf m, Wasserumwälzung f

(~) cistern · (Wasser)Zisterne f

waterclear · wasserhell

water closet, flush toilet, W.C., wc [*A room in which one or more W.C. pans are installed*] · Spülabort m, Wasserabort, Spülklosett n, Wasserklosett

(~) ~ bowl → bowl

(~) ~ pan → bowl

~ colour (Brit.); ~ color (US) · Aquarellfarbe f, lasierende Wasserfarbe

~ consumer, ~ user · Wasserbezieher m, Wasserverbraucher

~ consumption · Wasserverbrauch m

~ contained in aggregate(s), inherent moisture of ~ · Eigenfeuchtigkeit f der (Beton)Zuschläge, ~ ~ (Beton)Zuschlagstoffe

~ cooler, potable ~ ~, drinking ~ ~ [*abbreviated: wcr*] · Trinkwasserkühler m

~ coolers · Kühlpartie f [*Dachpappenmaschine*]

~ cooling coil · Wasserkühlschlange f

water deficiency — water-heated calorifier

~ **deficiency,** ~ shortage, deficiency of water, shortage of water · Wassermangel *m*, Wasserfehlbedarf *m*, Wasserklemme *f*

(~) **demineralization,** (~) desalination, (~) desalting · (Wasser)Entsalzung *f*

(~) **desalination,** (~) desalting, (~) demineralization · (Wasser)Entsalzung *f*

(~) **desalting,** (~) desalination, (~) demineralization · (Wasser)Entsalzung *f*

~ **disinfection;** ~ sterilization (US); ~ sterilisation (Brit.) · Wasserdesinfektion *f*, Wasserentkeimung *f*

~ **dispense point** · Wasserzapfstelle *f*

~ **dispersion** · Wasserdispersion *f*

~ **distribution** · Wasserverteilung *f*

~ ~ **installation** · Wasserverteilungsanlage *f* [DIN 19630]

~ ~ **to buildings,** ~ supply ~ ~ · Hauswasserversorgung *f*

(~) **drip,** throat(ing), weather groove, scotia · (Wasser)Nase *f*, Unterschneidung *f*

waterdrop glass, dewdrop ~ · Regentropfenglas *n*, Tautropfenglas, Ornamentglas Nr. 521

watered silk · Moiréseide *f*

water elutriation · Wasserfiltrationsmethode *f* [Eine Klassifizierungsmethode für Asbest mit dem Apparat nach Bauer-McNett]

~ **examination** · Wasseruntersuchung *f*

~ **fastness,** ~ resistance, resistance to water, fastness to water · Wasserbeständigkeit *f*, Wasserfestigkeit, Wasserwiderstand *m*

water-fearing, water-hating, hydrophobe, water-repellent, hydrophobic, water-repelling, water-rejecting · wasserabstoßend, hydrophob, wasserabweisend, wassermeidend

water-filled radiator, electric ~ ~ · wassergefüllter Radiator *m*

water filtration plant · Wasserfilteranlage *f*, Wasserfiltrieranlage

~ **fitting** [Anything fitted or fixed in connection with the supply, measurement, control, distribution, utilization or disposal of water] · Wasserfitting *m*, Wasserformstück *n*

~ **flow meter** · Wassermesser *m* [Er mißt in der Zeiteinheit die durchfließende Wassermenge (z.B. m³/h oder l/s)]

~ **flushing** · Wasserspülung *f*

~ **foliage,** ~ leaves · Wasserlaub *n*, Wasserblattwerk *n*

~ **for domestic use** · Hauswirtschaftswasser *n*

(~) **fountain** · Brunnen *m* [als Oberflächenbauwerk]

~ **freezing point** · Wassergefrierpunkt *m*

water-front park · Uferpark *m*

water gain, bleeding, sweating [The separation of water from an unhardened mix(ture)] · Bluten *n*, Wasserabstoßen, Wasserabsonderung *f*, Abscheiden von Wasser, ungenügende Anmach(e)wasserhaltung, Abscheidung von Wasser

~ ~ **rate,** sweating ~, bleeding ~ [The rate at which water is released from an unhardened mix(ture)] · Wasserabstoßgeschwindigkeit *f*, Wasserabscheidungsgeschwindigkeit, Wasserabsonderungsgeschwindigkeit

~ **garden** · Wasserbeckengarten *m*

~ **gas,** blue ~ [It is manufactured gas made by passing steam over a bed of incandescent coke, forming a mix(ture) of gases consisting of hydrogen and carbon monoxide] · Blaugas *n*, Wassergas

~ ~ **tar,** blue ~ ~ · Blaugasteer *m*, Wassergasteer

water-gas tar emulsion, emulsion of water-gas tar · Wassergasteeremulsion *f*

water-gas-tar pitch · Wassergasteerpech *n*

water-gate · Wassertor *n*

water glass, soluble ~ [A glassy or stony substance consisting of silicates of sodium or potassium or both, soluble in water, forming a viscous liquid] · Wasserglas *n*, mineralischer Leim *m*

~ ~ **coat,** soluble ~ ~ · Wasserglasanstrich *m*, Wasserglasaufstrich

~ ~ **mastic,** soluble ~ ~ · Wasserglaskitt *m* [Wasserglas + Füllstoffe]

~ ~ **mix(ture),** soluble ~ ~ · Doppelwasserglas *n* [Eine Mischung von Natronwasserglas und Kaliwasserglas]

~ ~ **paint,** silicate ~ ~ [Containing silicate of soda; may be made with aluminous cement, but not with portland cement] · Silikatfarbe *f*, S-Farbe, Wasserglasfarbe, Mineralfarbe

~ ~ ~ **coat,** silicate ~ ~ ~ · Wasserglasfarbanstrich *m*, Silikatfarbanstrich, Mineralfarbanstrich, Wasserglasfarbaufstrich, Silikatfarbaufstrich, Mineralfarbaufstrich

~ ~ **solution,** soluble ~ ~ · Wasserglaslösung *f*

water/(gypsum) plaster ratio · Wasser/Putzgips-Verhältnis *n*

water hammer, concussion, reverberation [A hammering sound caused by violent surges of pressure in water pipes] · Wasserstoß *m*, Wasserschlag *m*, Druckstoß

~ **hardness,** hardness of water · Wasserhärte *f*

water-hating, water-fearing, hydrophobe, water-repellent, hydrophobic, water-repelling, water-rejecting · wasserabstoßend, hydrophob, wasserabweisend, wassermeidend

water-heated calorifier · wasserbeheizter Gegenstromapparat *m*

water heater — water (pressure) load

water heater → hot ~ ~

~ heating · Wassererhitzung f, Wassererwärmung

~ ~ · Wasserheizung f

~ ~ appliance → hot ~ ~ ~

~ ~ coil → hot ~ ~ ~

~ ~ system · Wassererhitzungsanlage f, Wassererwärmungsanlage

~ immersion, immersion in water · Wasserlagerung f

~ impermeability, ~ imperviousness, watertightness, imperviousness to water, impermeability to water · Wasserdichtigkeit f, Wasserundurchlässigkeit, Wasserdichtheit [*Fehlname: Wasserdichte f*]

~ ~ test · Wasserundurchlässigkeitsprobe f, Wasserundurchlässigkeitsprüfung f, Wasserundurchlässigkeitsversuch m

~ imperviousness → ~ impermeability

water-impregnated · wassergetränkt

water-in-oil emulsion · umgekehrte Emulsion f, Wasser-in-Öl-Emulsion

water inrush, inrush of water · Wasserandrang m, Wassereinbruch m

~ insoluble, insoluble in water · wasserunlöslich

water-insoluble matter · Wasser-Unlösliche n

water-leaf · Wasserblatt n

water leakage · Wassereintritt m

~ leaves, ~ foliage · Wasserlaub n, Wasserblattwerk n

~ level, (spirit) ~, mechanic's ~, plumb · Wasserwaage f

~ lime, hydraulic ~ [*Lime containing silicates and aluminates, formed during burning, similar to those present in Portland cement. These constituents give the lime the property of hardening in water, whereas non-hydraulic lime hardens only by combining with carbon dioxide from the air. Semi-hydraulic lime contains a smaller proportion of silicates and aluminates than eminently hydraulic lime and is intermediate in properties between this and non-hydraulic lime*] · Wasserkalk m [*Aus mergeligem Kalkstein durch Brennen unterhalb der Sintergrenze hergestellter Baukalk. DIN 1060*]

~ ~ mortar, hydraulic ~ ~ · Wasserkalkmörtel m

~ line · Wasserleitung f

~ ~ network · Wasserleitungsnetz n

~ load → ~ pressure ~

~ loss · Wasserverlust m

water-loss shrinkage, drying ~ [*Contracting caused by moisture loss*] · Schrumpfen n

~ ~, drying ~ [*Contraction caused by moisture loss*] · Schrumpfung f

~ ~ behaviour (Brit.); ~ ~ behavior (US); drying ~ ~ · Schrumpfverhalten n

~ ~ crack, drying ~ ~ · Schrumpfriß m

~ ~ curve, drying ~ ~ · Schrumpfkurve f, Schrumpflinie f

~ ~ limit, drying ~ ~ · Schrumpfgrenze f

~ ~ stress, drying ~ ~ · Schrumpfspannung f

~ ~ value, drying ~ ~ · Schrumpfmaß n, Schrumpfwert m

water-loving, hydrophile, hydrophibic, hydrophilic, water-attracting · wasserliebend

water main · Hauptwasserleitung f, Wasserhauptleitung

~ mark · Wasserzeichen n

~ meter · Wasserzähler m

~ ~ box · Wasserzählerkasten m

~ ~ for bulk quantities · Großwasserzähler m

(~) ~ pit [*A chamber for housing a meter, constructed in the ground and surmounted by a surface box or manhole cover*] · (Wasser)Zählerschacht m

~ ~ system · Wasserzählanlage f

~ metering · Wassermessung f

~ migration · Wasserwanderung f

~ mixing valve · Wassermischventil n

~ of capillarity → capillary water

~ ~ composition, natural moisture, inherent moisture · Eigenfeuchte f, Eigenfeuchtigkeit f

~ ~ crystallization, combined water · Kristallwasser n [*Wasser, das in Kristallen chemisch gebunden ist*]

~ ~ hydration, hydration water · Hydra(ta)tionswasser n

~ ~ set(ting), set(ting) water · (Ab-)Bindewasser n

water/oil stain · Wasser-Öl-Beize f

water paint, cold-~ ~, water-carried ~, water-base(d) ~ · Binderfarbe f, Dispersionsfarbe [*Ein aus Binder und Pigmenten hergestellter Anstrichstoff*]

~ penetration · Wassereindringung f

~ permeability · Wasserdurchlässigkeit f

~ ~ test · Wasserdurchlässigkeitsversuch m, Wasserdurchlässigkeitsprüfung f, Wasserdurchlässigkeitsprobe f

~ pipe, ~ supply ~ · Wasser(leitungs)rohr n

~ ~ network, ~ supply ~ ~ · Wasserrohrnetz n

~ pocket [*On the surface of concrete*] · Wassernest n

~ pool, pool of water · Wasserbecken n [*Als Verzierung eines Platzes*]

~ ~ · Wasserpfütze f

~ pressure · Wasserdruck m

~ (~) load · Last m aus Wasserdruck, Wasserdrucklast

to water(proof) — waterproof(ing) plaster

to water(proof) · sperren, wasserdicht machen

waterproof, water(-)resistant [*abbreviated: wtrprf*] · wasserfest

~ abrasive paper · Ölschleifpapier *n*

(~) building paper → (~) sheathing ~

waterproofer coat → waterproof(ing) ~

waterproof-glued · wasserfest verleimt

waterproof membrane → waterproofing ~

(~) sheathing paper, (~) building ~, (~) general-use ~ [*See remark under 'Pappe'*] · Baupappe *f*, (Ab)Dicht(ungs)pappe

waterproofer → (integral) waterproof(ing) agent

~, waterrepeller, (water-)repelling agent, waterproof(ing) agent, (water-)repellent (material) · Sperrstoff *m* gegen Feuchtigkeit

~ coat, waterproof(ing) ~, (water-)repellent ~, (water-)repelling ~ · Sperranstrich *m*, Sperraufstrich

waterproofing · (Ab)Dichtung(en) *f(pl)* gegen drückendes Wasser, ~ Grund- und Druckwasser, wasserdruckhaltende (Ab)Dichtung(en), grundwasserhaltende (Ab)Dichtun(gen) [*DIN 18336*]

~ [*The term 'waterproofing' is sometimes restricted to mean 'waterproofing against ground water' whereas the term 'dampproofing' means protection against any moisture. In spite of this, the term 'waterproofing' is generally applied, especially in combined words, as, for instance, 'waterproofing agent' etc.*] · (Ab)Dichtung *f*, Sperrung [*Zur Verhinderung der Durchfeuchtung der Baustoffe und Bauteile werden diese durch geeignete Stoffe entweder selbst wasserundurchlässig gemacht oder mit einem wasser- und unter Umständen auch chemikalienbeständigen Überzug versehen*]

~, water-rejecting, (water-)repelling, (water-)repellent · wasser(ab)dichtend, sperrend

~ → waterproof(ing) compound

~ (against ground water); dampproofing (against (soil) moisture) · Isolieren *n* [*Die Sicherung der Baukonstruktionen gegen das Eindringen von (Boden)Feuchtigkeit und Grundwasser. Der Schutz gegen Wärme- und Schalldurchgang heißt „Dämmung"*]

waterproof(ing) agent → integral ~ ~

~ ~, (water-)repelling ~, (water-)repellent (material), water-repeller, waterproofer · Sperrstoff *m* gegen Feuchtigkeit

waterproofing and dampproofing of masonry (work) · Trockenlegen *n* von Mauerwerk

waterproof(ing) building paper, (water-)repelling ~, (water-)repellent ~ [*See remark under 'Pappe'. B.S. 1521*]

· Bauisolierpapier *n*, Bausperrpapier, Isolierbaupapier, Isoliersperrpapier, wasserfestes Baupapier

waterproofing capacity → (water-)repelling ~

waterproof(ing) cement, waterproof(ed) ~, hydrophobic ~, (water-)repellent ~, (water-)repelling ~ [*A Portland cement having a water-repellent agent added during the process of manufacture, with the intention of resisting the entry of water into the concrete, rendering or mortar*] · Sperrzement *m*, hydrophober Zement

~ coat, (water-)repellent ~, (water-)repelling ~, waterproofer ~ · Imprägnier(ungs)anstrich *m*, Imprägnier(ungs)aufstrich, Wetterschutzanstrich, Wetterschutzaufstrich, Sperranstrich, Sperraufstrich

~ coating (material) → ~ compound

~ compound, ~ coating (material), waterproofing, penetrating sealer, water repellent, penetrating aid, water repelling agent · (Fassaden)Imprägnier(ungs)mittel *n*, (Fassaden)Imprägnier(ungs)anstrich(mittel) *m*, (*n*), (Fassaden)Imprägnier(ungs)anstrichstoff *m*, (Fassaden)Imprägnierung *f*, Wetterschutz *m*

~ concrete, (water-)repellent ~, (water-)repelling ~ · Sperrbeton *m* [*DIN 4117. Gegen Druckwasser und aufsteigende Erdfeuchtigkeit*]

~ course, ~ layer · druckwasserhaltende Isolierung *f*, ~ (Ab)Dichtung

~ emulsion, (water-)repellent ~, (water-)repelling ~ · Sperremulsion *f*

~ felt, ~ paper [*A building material, generally paper or felt, used in wall and roof construction as a protection against the passage of moisture*] · wassersperrende Pappe *f*; wassersperrendes Papier *n*

~ finish → ~ plaster

~ grout(ing compound), (water-)repellent ~ (~), (water-)repelling ~ (~) · Sperrschlämme *f*

~ layer, ~ course · druckwasserhaltende Isolierung *f*, ~ (Ab)Dichtung

~ liquid → liquid waterproof(ing) agent

~ material → (groundwater) waterproofing product

~ membrane, (water-)repelling ~, (water-)repellent ~ · (Ab)Dicht(ungs)haut *f*, Sperrhaut

~ mixed plaster → ~ plaster

~ mortar, (water-)repellent ~, (water-)repelling ~ · Sperrmörtel *m* [*DIN 4117*]

~ paper, (water-)repellent ~, (water-)repelling ~ [*See remark under 'Pappe'*] · Sperrpapier *n*, Isolierpapier

~ ~, (water-)repellent ~, (water-)repelling ~ [*See remark under 'Pappe'*] · Isolierpappe *f*, Sperrpappe

~ plaster, ~ finish, (water-)repellent ~, (water-)repelling ~, ~ mixed plaster · Sperr(ver)putz *m*, Isolierputz, wassersperrender Putz [*DIN 4117*]

waterproofing power → (water-)repelling capacity

waterproof(ing) product → groundwater ~ ~

waterproofing property → (water-)repelling capacity

~ **quality** → (water-)repelling capacity

waterproof(ing) screed, (water-)repellent ~, (water-)repelling ~ · Sperrestrich *m* [*DIN 4117*]

~ **solution,** (water-)repellent ~, (water-)repelling ~ · Imprägnier(ungs)lösung *f*

water purification · Wasserreinigung *f*

~ **ramp, cascade** · Kaskade *f*

~ **rate** · Wassertarif *m*

water-reducing action · wassereinsparende Wirkung *f*

~ **admix(ture)** → (concrete) workability agent

~ **agent** → (concrete) workability ~

water-rejecting, water-repelling, water-repellent, hydrophobic · wasserabweisend, wasserabstoßend, wasserfeindlich, hydrophob

water release · Wasserabgabe *f*

~ **repellency** · hydrophobierende Wirkung *f*, Wasserabweisung

~ **repellent** → waterproof(ing) compound

water-repellent → ~ material

(water-)repellent, water-repelling, water-rejecting, hydrophobic · wasserabweisend, wasserabstoßend, wasserfeindlich, hydrophob

water-repellent admix(ture) → (integral) waterproof(ing) agent

~ **agent,** hydrophobic ~ · Hydrophobierungsmittel *n* [*Pulverförmige Metallseife, die Beton, Mörtel und Putz wasserabweisend macht; in der Praxis zuweilen als Stearat bezeichnet*]

(water-)repellent building paper → waterproof(ing) ~ ~

~ **capacity** → (water-)repelling ~

~ **coat** → waterproof(ing) ~

~ **concrete,** (water-)repelling ~, waterproof(ing) ~ · Sperrbeton *m* [*DIN 4117. Gegen Druckwasser und aufsteigende Erdfeuchtigkeit*]

~ **emulsion,** (water-)repelling ~, waterproof(ing) ~ · Sperremulsion *f*

~ **finish** → waterproof(ing) plaster

~ **grout(ing compound),** (water-)repelling ~ (~), waterproof(ing) ~ (~) · Sperrschlämme *f*

~ **liquid** → liquid waterproofing agent

~ **(material),** (water-)repelling agent, waterproof(ing) agent, water-repeller, waterproofer · Sperrstoff *m* gegen Feuchtigkeit

~ **membrane,** (water-)repelling ~, waterproof(ing) ~ · (Ab)Dicht(ungs)haut *f*, Sperrschicht

~ **mixed plaster** → waterproof(ing) ~

~ **mortar,** (water-)repelling ~, waterproof(ing) ~ · Sperrmörtel *m* [*DIN 4117*]

~ **paper,** (water-)repelling ~, waterproof(ing) ~ [*See remark under 'Pappe'*] · Sperrpappe *f*, Isolierpappe

~ ~, (water-)repelling ~, waterproof(ing) ~ [*See remark under 'Pappe'*] · Sperrpapier *n*, Isolierpapier

~ **plaster** → waterproof(ing) ~

~ **power** → (water-)repelling capacity

~ **property** → (water-)repelling capacity

~ **quality** → (water-)repelling capacity

~ **screed,** (water-)repelling ~, waterproof(ing) ~ · Sperrestrich *m* [*DIN 4117*]

~ **solution,** (water-)repelling ~, waterproof(ing) ~ · Imprägnier(ungs)lösung *f*

~ **treatment of masonry (work),** hydrophobic ~ ~ ~ (~) · Hydrophobierung *f* von Mauerwerk

waterrepeller → (integral) waterproof(ing) agent

~, **waterproofer, waterproof(ing) agent, (water-)repelling agent, (water-)repellent (material)** · Sperrstoff *m* gegen Feuchtigkeit

(water-)repelling, water-repellent, water-rejecting, hydrophobic · wasserabweisend, wasserabstoßend, wasserfeindlich, hydrophob

~ **agent** → (integral) waterproof(ing) ~

~ ~ → waterproof(ing) compound

~ ~, waterproof(ing) ~, (water-)repellent (material), waterrepeller, waterproofer · Sperrstoff *m* gegen Feuchtigkeit

~ **building paper** → waterproof(ing) ~ ~

~ **capacity,** ~ property, ~ quality, ~ power, (water-)repellent ~, waterproofing ~ · Wasserabweisefähigkeit *f*, Wasserabweisevermögen *n*, Sperrfähigkeit, Sperrvermögen

~ **cement,** (water-)repellent ~, waterproof(ing) ~, waterproof(ed) ~, hydrophobic ~ [*A Portland cement having a waterrepellent agent added during the process of manufacture, with the intention of resisting the entry of water into the cement, rendering or mortar*] · Sperrzement *m*, hydrophober Zement

~ **coat** → waterproof(ing) ~

~ **concrete,** (water-)repellent ~, waterproof(ing) ~ · Sperrbeton *m* [*DIN 4117. Gegen Druckwasser und aufsteigende Erdfeuchtigkeit*]

~ **emulsion,** (water-)repellent ~, waterproof(ing) ~ · Sperremulsion *f*

~ **finish** → waterproof(ing) plaster

~ **grout(ing compound),** (water-)repellent ~ (~), waterproof(ing) ~ (~) · Sperrschlämme *f*

(water-)repelling membrane — water supply engineer

~ **membrane**, (water-)repellent ~, waterproof(ing) ~ · (Ab)Dicht(ungs)haut f, Sperrhaut

~ **mixed plaster** → waterproof(ing) ~

~ **mortar**, (water-)repellent ~, waterproof(ing) ~ · Sperrmörtel m [DIN 4117]

~ **paper**, (water-)repellent ~, waterproof(ing) ~ [See remark under 'Pappe'] · Sperrpappe f, Isolierpappe

~ ~ , (water-)repellent ~, waterproof(ing) ~ [See remark under 'Pappe'] · Sperrpapier n, Isolierpapier

~ **plaster** → waterproof(ing) ~

~ **power** → ~ capacity

~ **property** → ~ capacity

~ **quality** → ~ capacity

~ **screed**, (water-)repellent ~, waterproof(ing) ~ · Sperrestrich m [DIN 4117]

~ **solution**, (water-)repellent ~, waterproof(ing) ~ · Imprägnier(ungs)lösung f

water reservoir, ~ tank, WT · Wasserbehälter m

~ **resistance**, ~ fastness, resistance to water, fastness to water · Wasserbeständigkeit f, Wasserfestigkeit, Wasserwiderstand m

water(-)resistant, waterproof [abbreviated: wtrprf] · wasserfest

water-resisting, resistant to hydrostatic pressure · wasserdruckhaltend

water(-)retardant (mixed) plaster, water(-)retarding (~) ~ · wasserhemmender Putz m

water(-)retarding (mixed) plaster, water(-)retardant (~) ~ · wasserhemmender Putz m

water retention, ~ retentivity · Wasserhaltevermögen n, Wasserrückhaltung f

water(-)retentive · wasserhaltend

water retentivity, ~ retention · Wasserhaltevermögen n, Wasserrückhaltung f

water sample · Wasserprobe f

~ **sampler** · Wasserprobenehmer m

water-saturated · wassergesättigt, wassersatt

water saturation · Wassersättigung f

~ ~ **coefficient** · Wassersättigungsbeiwert m

~ ~ **value** · Wassersättigungswert m

~ **seal**, ~ barrier, ~ stop · Wassersperre f

(~) ~, trap ~ [The water in a trap which acts as a barrier to the passage of air through the trap] · Wasserverschluß m

~ **sealing** · Wasser(ab)dichtung f

~ **service pipe** · Wasserinstallationsrohr n

water-shedding moulding (Brit.); ~ molding (US) · Tropfleiste f

water shortage, ~ deficiency, deficiency of water, shortage of water · Wassermangel m, Wasserfehlbedarf m, Wasserklemme f

~ **shutoff** · Wasserabsperren n

water-smoking, initial dehydration · Durchwärmung f, Vorwärmung, Schmauchen n [Ziegelbrennen]

(water) softener, (~) softening agent · Enthärtungsmittel n, Enthärter m, Wasser~

(~) **softening** · (Wasser)Enthärtung f, (Wasser)Enthärten n, Weichmachen

(~) ~ **agent**, (~) softener · Enthärtungsmittel n, Enthärter m, Wasser~

(~) ~ **method** · (Wasser)Enthärtungsverfahren n

(~) ~ **unit** · (Wasser)Enthärter m, (Wasser)Enthärtungsapparat m

~ **solubility**, solubility in water · Wasserlöslichkeit f

water-soluble, soluble in water · wasserlöslich

~ **alkali** · wasserlösliches Alkali n

~ **dye** · wasserlöslicher Küpenfarbstoff m

~ **dyestuff** · wasserlöslicher Farbstoff m

~ **salt** · wasserlösliches Salz n

~ **wood preservative** · wasserlösliches Holzschutzmittel n

water spotting, white spots [The spotty appearance of a paint film which is caused by drops of water on the surface and which remains after the water has evaporated; the effect may or may not be permanent. Water spots usually appear lighter in colour than the surrounding paint] · Wasserfleckigkeit f

waterspout, carved ~, gargoyle [A projecting stone spout, usually carved with a grotesque figure] · (figürlicher) Wasserspeier m

water-spray granulated slag sand · wassergranulierter Schlackensand m

water stain · Ansatz m, Wasserfleck m [im Putz]

~ ~ [Water stains are solutions of dyes of various colours in water, they are generally varnished or wax-polished after application to make them waterproof] · Wasserbeize f

~ **sterilization** (US); ~ sterilisation (Brit.); ~ disinfection · Wasserdesinfektion f, Wasserentkeimung f

~ **stop**, ~ barrier, ~ seal · Wassersperre f

waterstop, waterbar · Fugenband n

~ **material**, waterbar ~ · Fugenbandwerkstoff m

water storage, storage of water · Wasserbevorratung f, Wasserspeicherung

water-struck brick · Wasserstrichziegel m

water supply, provision of water, WS · Wasserversorgung f

~ ~ **area** · Wasserversorgungsgebiet n

~ ~ **engineer** · Wasserversorgungsingenieur m

water supply engineering — waved shell roof

~ ~ **engineering** · Wasserversorgungstechnik f

~ ~ **installation,** ~ ~ **system** ~ ~ **plant,** ~ ~ **scheme** · Wasserversorgungsanlage f, Wasserversorgungssystem n, Wasserversorgungsinstallation f [DIN 1988 und DIN 4279]

~ ~ **law** · Wasserversorgungsrecht n

~ ~ **line** · Wasserversorgungsleitung f

~ ~ **network** · Wasserversorgungs-(rohr)netz n [DIN 2425]

~ (~) **pipe** · Wasserleitungsrohr n

~ (~) ~ **network** · Wasserrohrnetz n

~ ~ **plant,** ~ ~ **system** ~ ~ **installation,** ~ ~ **scheme** · Wasserversorgungsanlage f, Wasserversorgungssystem n, Wasserversorgungsinstallation f [DIN 1988 und DIN 4279]

~ ~ **point,** WSP · Wasserversorgungsstelle f

~ ~ **scheme,** ~ ~ **plant,** ~ ~ **system,** ~ ~ **installation** · Wasserversorgungsanlage f, Wasserversorgungssystem n, Wasserversorgungsinstallation f [DIN 1988 und DIN 4279]

~ ~ **system,** ~ ~ **plant,** ~ ~ **installation,** ~ ~ **scheme** · Wasserversorgungsanlage f, Wasserversorgungssystem n, Wasserversorgungsinstallation f [DIN 1988 und DIN 4279]

~ ~ **to buildings,** ~ distribution ~ ~ · Hauswasserversorgung f

~ **table** → hood-mould(ing)

~ **tank,** ~ reservoir, WT · Wasserbehälter m

water-thinnable · wasserverdünnbar

water(-)thinned · wasserverdünnt

water thinned paint · wasserverdünnte Farbe f

watertight → impervious to water

~ **concrete flat roof** · Sperrbeton-Flachdach n

~ **concrete flat roof** · Sperrbeton-Flachdach n

watertightness → water impermeability

water tower, WT · Wasserturm m

~ **treatment** · Wasseraufbereitung f

water(-treatment) works · Wasserwerk n

water-tube boiler · Wasserrohrkessel m

water type, type of water · Wasserart f

~ **undertaking,** ~ undertaker · Wasserversorgungsunternehmen n

~ **user,** ~ consumer · Wasserbezieher m, Wasserverbraucher

(~) **vapour** (Brit.); (~) vapor (US) · Wasserdampf m

(~) ~ **absorption** (Brit.); (~) vapor ~ (US) · Wasserdampfaufnahme f

(~) ~ **barring** (Brit.); (~) vapor ~ (US) · (wasser)dampfsperrend

(~) ~ **chimney** (Brit.); (~) vapor ~ (US) · Wrasenkamin m, Wrasenschornstein m [für den Abzug von Wasserdampf]

(~) ~ **condensation** (Brit.); (~) vapor ~ (US) · Wasserdampfkondensation f

(~) ~ **content** (Brit.); (~) vapor ~ (US) · Wasserdampfgehalt m

(~) ~ **diffusion** (Brit.); (~) vapor ~ (US); damp ~ · Wasserdampfdiffusion

(~) ~ **impermeability** (Brit.); (~) vapor ~ (US); (~) ~ imperviousness; imperviousness to (water) vapour, impermeability to (water) vapour (Brit.); impermeability to (water) vapor, imperviousness to (water) vapor (US) · Wasserdampfdichtigkeit f

(~) ~ **imperviousness** → (~) ~ impermeability

(~) ~ **migration** (Brit.); (~) vapor ~ (US) · Wasserdampfwanderung f

(~) ~ **mist** (Brit.); (~) vapor~ (US) · Wasserdampfnebel m

(~) ~ **permeability** (Brit.); (~) vapor ~ (US) · Wasserdampfdurchlässigkeit f

(~) **vapour-permeable** (Brit.); (~) vapor-permeable (US) · wasserdampfdurchlässig

(~) **vapour pipe** (Brit.); (~) vapor ~ (US) · Wrasenrohr n [Lüftungsrohr in Koch-, Wasch- und Futterküchen]

(~) ~ **pressure,** saturated (~) ~ ~ (Brit.); (saturated) (water) vapor ~ (US) · Wasserdampfdruck m

(~) ~ ~ **drop** (Brit.); (~) vapor ~ ~ (US) · Wasserdampfdruckgefälle n

(~) ~ ~ **graph** (Brit.); (~) vapor ~ ~ (US) · Wasserdampfdrucklinie f

(~) ~ **quantity** (Brit.); (~) vapor ~ (US) · Wasserdampfmenge f

(~) ~ **release** (Brit.); (~) vapor ~ (US) · (Wasser)Dampfentspannung f

(~) ~ **resistant** (Brit.); (~) vapor ~ (US) · wasserdampffest

(~) ~ **seal** (Brit.); (~) vapor ~ (US) · Wasserdampfbremse f

(~) ~ **transfer coefficient** (Brit.); (~) vapor ~ ~ (US) · Wasserdampfübergangszahl f

(~) ~ **transmission** (Brit.); (~) vapor ~ (US); WVT · Wasserdampfdurchgang m

~ **varnish** · Wasserlack m

~ **vessel** · Gießgefäß n [Dinanderie]

~ **void** [A space in concrete which is occupied or has been formed by surplus water] · Wasserpore f [Beton]

~**-wetted sharpening stone** · Wasserabziehstein m

water white high-grade burning oil · wasserhelles Hydrier-Leuchtöl n

~ **works,** ~-treatment ~ · Wasserwerk n

water(-work)s · Wasserspiele npl [Zierelemente in einem Garten oder Park]

(wattle) hurdle, (fence) ~ · (Zaun-)Hürde f

waved shell roof, corrugated ~ ~ · Well(en)schalendach n

wave-form translation(al) shell — wear(ing) depth 1110

wave-form translation(al) shell · wellenförmige Translationsschale f

wavelength coefficient, wavelength constant, phase-change coefficient, phase change constant [*The imaginary part of the propagation coefficient. The phase change coefficient β is 2 π/λ*] · Phasenkonstante f, Phasenkoeffizient m, Kreiswellenzahl f [*Phasenmaß dividiert durch den Abstand der in Richtung der Schallausbreitung hintereinanderliegenden Punkte*]

~ **constant,** wavelength coefficient, phase-change coefficient, phase-change constant [*The imaginary part of the propagation coefficient. The phase-change coefficient β is 2 π/λ*] · Phasenkonstante f, Phasenkoeffizient m, Kreiswellenzahl f [*Phasenmaß dividiert durch den Abstand der in Richtung der Schallausbreitung hintereinanderliegenden Punkte*]

wave motion · Wellenbewegung f

~ **moulding,** undulating ~ (Brit.); ~ molding, (o)undy molding (US); swelled chamfer · Wellenmuster n

~ **ornament** → ~ scroll

~ **scroll,** ~ ornament, Vitruvian ~ ~, Vitruvian wave, running dog, Vitruvian scroll · laufender Hund m, Wellenband n

wavy cord · Winde f [*Glasschmelzfehler*]

~ **line,** undulating ~ · Wellenlinie f

to wax · (ein)wachsen

wax · Wachs n

~ **agent,** ~ concrete ~, ~ (concrete) curing compound · Wachs-(Beton-)Nachbehandlungsmittel n

~ **coat,** coat of wax · Wachsschicht f

~ **(concrete) agent,** ~ (~) curing compound · Wachs-(Beton)Nachbehandlungsmittel n

~ **(~) curing compound,** ~ (~) agent · Wachs-(Beton)Nachbehandlungsmittel n

~ **curing compound,** ~ concrete ~, ~ (concrete) agent · Wachs-(Beton-)Nachbehandlungsmittel n

~ **paste (polish),** solid wax (~) · Wachs(polier)paste f

~ **polish** · Wachspolitur f

~ **residue** · Wachsrückstand m

~ **solubility** · Wachslöslichkeit f

~ **solution** · Wachslösung f

~ **solvent** · Wachslösungsmittel n, Wachslösemittel

waxed paper · Wachspapier n

~ **rubber wire** · Gummiwachsdraht m [*Für feste Verlegung von Leitungen für Schwachstromanlagen*]

~ **wire** · Wachsdraht m [*Für feste Verlegung von Leitungen für Schwachstromanlagen*]

wax(-)free · wachsfrei

waxing · (Ein)Wachsen n

wax-like · wachsartig

way, walk~, run~ · (Lauf)Steg m

~ **bracket,** walk~ ~, run~ ~ · Laufstegkonsole f

wayside cross · Wegekreuz n

~ **shrine** · Betsäule f, Bildstock m, Votivkreuz n

W.C., water closet, flush toilet, wc [*A room in which one or more W.C. pans are installed*] · Spülabort m, Wasserabort, Spülklosett n, Wasserklosett

WC bowl → bowl

WC installation · WC-Anlage f

WC pan → bowl

w/c ratio → water-cement ~

W.C. seat, toilet ~, closet ~, (lavatory) ~ [*B.S. 1254*] · Sitz m, Abort~, Klosett~, Toiletten~

WD, wind direction · Windrichtung f

weak acid · schwache Säure f

~ ~ **solution** · schwache Säurelösung f

weak-current cable · Schwachstromkabel n

~ **installation** · Schwachstromanlage f

~ **line** · Schwachstromleitung f

~ **paper-insulated lead-covered cable** · Schwachstrom-Papierbleikabel n

~ **relay** · Schwachstromrelais n

weakened · geschwächt

~ **plate** · Platte f mit Störbereich [*z.B. mit Öffnungen*]

weakening · Schwächung f

~ · Schwächen n

wealth of views · Sichtachsenvielfalt f

wealthy villa · Prunkvilla f

wear → wear(ing)

~ **course** → (flooring) wear(ing) surface

~ ~, ~ **layer,** wearing ~ · Verschleißlage f, Verschleißschicht f

~ **layer** → (flooring) wear(ing) surface

~ ~, ~ **course,** wearing ~ · Verschleißlage f, Verschleißschicht f

to wear off · sich abtreten [*(Fuß)Boden(belag)*]

wear surface → (flooring) wear(ing) ~

wear(ing) · Abnutzung f (durch mechanische Einwirkung), Verschleiß m

wearing away, erosion · Erosion f, Abbau m, Abtragung f [*Anstrichfilm*]

~ ~ **by wind-borne particles of grit,** grit erosion · Sanderosion f, Sandabbau m, Sandabtragung f [*Anstrichfilm*]

wear(ing) capacity, ~ quality, ~ property, ~ power · Verschleißeigenschaft f, Abnutz(ungs)eigenschaft

~ **course** → (flooring) wear(ing) surface

~ ~, ~ **layer** · Verschleißlage f, Verschleißschicht f

~ **depth** · Verschleißtiefe f, Abnutz(ungs)tiefe

~ hardness · Abnutz(ungs)härte f, Verschleißhärte

~ inhibitor, ~ inhibiter · Verschleißhemmstoff m

~ layer, ~ course · Verschleißlage f, Verschleißschicht f

~ ~ → (flooring) wear(ing) surface

~ power, ~ capacity, ~ quality, ~ property · Verschleißeigenschaft f, Abnutz(ungs)eigenschaft

~ property, ~ power, ~ capacity, ~ quality · Verschleißeigenschaft f, Abnutz(ungs)eigenschaft

~ quality, ~ property, ~ power, ~ capacity · Verschleißeigenschaft f, Abnutz(ungs)eigenschaft

~ resistance, resistance to wear(ing) · Abnutz(ungs)widerstand m, Abnutz(ungs)beständigkeit f, Abnutz(ungs)festigkeit, Verschleißwiderstand, Verschleißbeständigkeit, Verschleißfestigkeit

~ surface · Verschleißoberfläche f

~ ~ → flooring ~ ~

~ test · Abnutz(ungs)probe f, Abnutz(ungs)versuch m, Abnutz(ungs)prüfung f, Verschleißprobe, Verschleißversuch, Verschleißprüfung

~ thickness · Verschleißdicke f, Abnutz(ungs)dicke [*Fehlnamen: Verschleißstärke f; Abnutz(ungs)stärke*]

to wear-proof · verschleißfest machen, abnutz(ungs)fest ~

to weather away · abwittern

weather bar, water ~ · Wasserschenkel m, Wetterschenkel

weather-board; clapboard (US) · (waag(e)rechtes) Stülpschalungsbrett n

weatherboarding, weather-boards (Brit.); (lap(ped)) siding, bevel siding (US) [*Horizontal boards nailed on edge over the outside of light buildings. The board sgenerally overlap each other, either with or without a rebate at the lower edge of the upper board, which helps to keep out rain and wind*] · (waag(e)rechte) Stülpschalung f [*Wetterschutz für Außenmauern und Außenwände*]

weather boards (Brit.) **→** weatherboarding

weather-coat · Witterungsschutzanstrich m, Witterungsschutzaufstrich

weather-coated · wetterfest beschichtet

weather-coating (material) · Witterungsschutzanstrichmittel n, Witterungsschutzanstrich(stoff) m, Witterungsschutzaufstrichmittel, Witterungsschutzaufstrich(stoff)

~ renewal, repainting · Pflegeanstrich m, Pflegeaufstrich [*Dachpappe*]

weather cock, (~) vane · Windfahne f, Wetterhahn m

~ door, storm ~ [*An additional inner door, used in winter, to insulate a house from hard weather*] · Wintertür f

weathered glass · beschlagenes Glas n

weather face, ~ side · Wetterseite f

weather-fast → weather-resistant

weather groove, throat(ing), (water) drip, scotia · (Wasser)Nase f, Unterschneidung f

weathering [*A sloped upper surface designed to shed rainwater*] · Regenablauffläche f

~ · Aufschluß m durch Freilagern [*Feuerfestindustrie. Eine Veränderung der Rohstoffe durch die Einwirkung der Atmosphäre. Hierbei erfolgt eine Oxydation oder ein Lösen und eine teilweise Entfernung der Verunreinigungen*]

~, wintering · Auswintern n [*Lagern von Rohstoffen über den Winter.* **Anmerkung:** *Der Ausdruck ,,wintering'', der dem Wort ,,Auswintern'' entsprechen würde, wird in Großbritannien nicht gebraucht, sondern nur ,,weathering''*]

~ · Feuchtigkeits(ab)dichtung f [*Erzeugnis*]

~ · Verwitterung f

~ element [*rain; sun; wind; snow; hail; dew; air; ice; frost; heat*] · Witterungselement n

weathering-fastness → weatherproofness

weathering quality, weather resistance, resistance to (the action of) weather, weatherproofness · Wetterbeständigkeit f, Wetterfestigkeit, Witterungsbeständigkeit, Witterungsfestigkeit

~ test · Bewitterungsprüfung f, Bewitterungsprobe f, Bewitterungsversuch m

weather moulding (Brit.) **→** hoodmould(ing)

weatherproof(ed), weather-resistant, weather-resisting, weather-fast · wetterbeständig, (ver)witterungsfest, wetterfest, (ver)witterungsbeständig, wetterecht [*im Falle von Baustahl ,,schwerrostend''*]

weatherproofing · Feuchtigkeits(ab)dichtung f [*von Fenstern und Türen*]

~ compound · Wetterschutzmasse f

weatherproofness, weathering quality, resistance to (the action of) weather, weather resistance, weathering-fastness · Wetterbeständigkeit f, Wetterfestigkeit, (Ver)Witterungsbeständigkeit, (Ver-)Witterungsfestigkeit

weather resistance, weathering quality, resistance to (the action of) weather, weatherproofness, weathering-fastness · Wetterbeständigkeit f, Wetterfestigkeit, (Ver)Witterungsbeständigkeit, (Ver-)Witterungsfestigkeit

weather-resistant, weather-resisting, weatherproof(ed), weather-fast · wetterbeständig, (ver)witterungsfest, wetterfest, (ver)witterungsbeständig, wetterecht [*im Falle von Baustahl ,,schwerrostend''*]

~ tar, weather-resisting ~, weatherproof(ed) ~, weather-fast ~ · alterungsbeständiger Straßenteer m, Wetterteer

weather-resisting, weather-resistant, weatherproof(ed), weather-fast · wetterbeständig, (ver)witterungsfest, wetterfest, (ver)witterungsbeständig, wetterecht [*im Falle von Baustahl „schwerrostend"*]
~ **barrier** [*e.g. in joints in external walls and columns*] · Witterungssperre *f*
weather side, ~ face · Wetterseite *f*
~ **skin** · Wetterhaut *f*
weather-tight · wetterdicht
weather-tightness · Wetterdichtigkeit *f*
weather tiling, tile hanging · Plattenwandauskleidung *f*, Plattenwandverkleidung, Plattenwandbekleidung, Wandplattenauskleidung, Wandplattenverkleidung, Wandplattenbekleidung
weaving (of) wire, twisting (~) ~ · Drahtweben *n*
(~) vane, ~ ceck · Windfahne *f*, Wetterhahn *m*
to web, to frost · eisblumenartig auftrocknen [*Anstrich*]
web, bulb · Steg *m*, Wulst *m, f* [*Fugenband*]
~, stalk · Steg *m*, Träger~ [*Bei T- und L-förmigen Querschnitten der schmale hohe Teil im Gegensatz zum niedrigen und breiten Flansch oder den niedrigen und breiten Flanschen. Der Steg hat im allgemeinen große Schubkräfte aufzunehmen und wird deshalb mit Bügeln und Schrägeisen bewehrt*]
~, **cell** [*One of the compartments of a groin(ed) vault*] · Gewölbekappe *f*, Tonnen(gewölbe)kappe [*Eines der vier Teilstücke des Kreuz(grat)gewölbes, das aus zwei sich rechtwinklig schneidenden Tonnengewölben gleichen Querschnittes entsteht*]
~, **cell** [*One of the compartments of a rib(bed) vault*] · (Rippen)Gewölbekappe *f*
~ **bar** → bent(-up) ~
~ **buckling** · Stegknickung *f*
~ **connection,** stalk ~ · Steganschluß *m*
~ **forms,** ~ shuttering, ~ form(work) · (Träger)Stegschalung *f*
~ **form(work),** ~ shuttering, ~ forms · (Träger)Stegschalung *f*
~ **of dry felt,** dry felt web · Rohfilz(pappen)bahn *f*
~ ~ **fabric,** fabric web · Rohpappenbahn *f*
~ ~ **felt(ed fabric),** felt(ed fabric) web · Filzbahn *f*
~ **panel,** webbed ~ · Stegtafel *f*
~ **plate,** stalk ~ [*The vertical plate joining the flanges of a rolled-steel or extruded lightalloy joist or of a built-up girder or timber beam*] · Stegblech *n*, Stehblech
~ ~ **angle,** stalk ~ ~ · Stegblechwinkel *m*, Stehblechwinkel
~ ~ **connection,** stalk ~ ~, ~ ~ joint · Stegblechanschluß *m*, Stehblechanschluß, Stegblechstoß *m*, Stehblechstoß

~ ~ **depth,** stalk ~ ~ · Stegblechhöhe *f*, Stehblechhöhe
~ ~ **joint,** stalk ~ ~, ~ ~ connection · Stegblechanschluß *m*, Stehblechanschluß, Stegblechstoß *m*, Stehblechstoß
~ ~ **length,** stalk ~ ~ · Stegblechlänge *f*, Stehblechlänge
~ ~ **longitudinal connection,** ~ ~ ~ joint, stalk ~ ~ ~ · Stegblechlängsstoß *m*, Stehblechlängsstoß, Stegblechlängsanschluß, Stehblechlängsanschluß
~ ~ **moment,** stalk ~ ~ · Stegblechmoment *n*, Stehblechmoment
~ ~ **stay,** ~ ~ stiffener, stalk ~ ~ · Stegblechsteife *f*, Stehblechsteife
~ ~ **stiffener,** ~ ~ stay, stalk ~ ~ · Stegblechsteife *f*, Stehblechsteife
~ ~ **stiffening,** stalk ~ ~ · Stegblechaussteifung *f*, Stehblechaussteifung
~ ~ **stress,** stalk ~ ~ · Stegblechspannung *f*, Stehblechspannung
~ ~ **thickness,** stalk ~ ~ · Stegblechdicke *f*, Stehblechdicke
~ ~ **transverse connection,** ~ ~ ~ joint, stalk ~ ~ ~ · Werkstattstoß *m*, (Stegblech)Querstoß, Stehblechquerstoß
~ ~ ~ **joint,** ~ ~ ~ connection, stalk ~ ~ ~ · Werkstattstoß *m*, (Stegblech)-Querstoß, Stehblechquerstoß
~ ~ **width,** stalk ~ ~ · Stegblechbreite *f*, Stehblechbreite
~ **reinforcement,** stalk ~ · Stegarmierung *f*, Stegbewehrung, Steg(stahl)einlagen *fpl*
~ ~, shear ~ [*Reinforcement, usually in the form of stirrups and/or bent-up bars designed to resist shear and diagonal tension; dowels are not considered to be shear reinforcement*] · Schubbewehrung *f*, Schubarmierung, Schub(stahl)einlagen *fpl*
~ **rod** → bent(-up) bar
~ **shuttering,** ~ form(work), ~ forms · (Träger)Stegschalung *f*
~ **stay,** stalk ~, ~ stiffener · Stegsteife *f*
~ **stiffener,** stalk ~, ~ stay · Stegsteife *f*
~ **stiffening,** stalk ~ · Stegaussteifung *f*
webbed dried film, frosted ~ ~ · eisblumenartig aufgetrockneter Film *m*
~ **panel** → web ~
'Wedding Tower' [*Designed by J. M. Olbrich, Darmstadt, 1907*] · „Hochzeitsturm" *m*
to wedge, to lift the bed by wedging · abkeilen [*Gestein*]
wedge · Keil *m*
~ **anchor** · Ankerkeil *m*, Verankerungskeil, Keilanker *m*
~ **anchorage** · Keilverankerung *f* [*Spannbeton*]
~ **sewer brick,** ~-type ~ · Kanalkeilklinker *m*

wedge-shaped, cuneiform · keilförmig
wedge(-shaped) block, ~ tile [*See remark under 'Block'*] · Keilblock(stein) *m*, Keilstein
~ brick → arch ~
~ groove · konische Aussparung *f* als Nut [*Spannverfahren Magnel*]
~ joint, ~ mortar ~ · Keilfuge *f*
~ (mortar) joint · Keilfuge *f*
~ stone → arch ~
~ tile, ~ block [*See remark under 'Block'*] · Keilblock(stein) *m*, Keilstein
wedge(-type) connector, ~ connector · Keildübel *m*
~ sewer brick · Kanalkeilklinker *m*
~ split ring (connector), ~ ~ ~ connecter · geschlitzter Keilringdübel *m*
wedge-wire · Keilprofildraht *m*
~ cloth · Keilprofildrahtgewebe *n*
wedged · verkeilt
~ tenon · Grundzapfen *m*, Keilzapfen
wedging · Verkeilen *n*
weed-covered · unkrautbedeckt
weed killer · Unkrautbekämpfungsmittel *n*
week-day chapel · Werktagskapelle *f*
week-end house · Wochenendhaus *n*
~ ~ zone, ~ ~ area · Wochenendhausgebiet *n*
weep hole, drain ~ · Entwässerungsloch *n*, Sickerloch
weft · Schuß *m* [*Drahtgewebe*]
~ wire, transverse wire of the cloth · Schußdraht *m*
Weigh House at Haarlem · Stadtwaage *f* in Haarlem
weighing · (Ver)Wiegen *n*, Wägung *f*
~ bottle, density ~, (fruit jar) pycnometer · (Flaschen)Pyknometer *n*
~ sensitiveness, ~ sensitivity · Empfindlichkeit *f*, Genauigkeit [*Waage*]
~ sensitivity, ~ sensitiveness · Empfindlichkeit *f*, Genauigkeit [*Waage*]
weight · Gewicht *n*
~ assumption, ~ hypothesis · Gewichtsannahme *f*
~ bearing capability → load carrying capacity
~ ~ capacity → load carrying ~
~ ~ power → load carrying capacity
~ ~ property → load carrying capacity
~ ~ quality → load carrying capacity
weight-carrying, load carrying, (load-)bearing, supporting, loaded · (last)tragend, belastet
~ brick, load-carrying ~, (load)-bearing ~, supporting ~, loaded ~ · (last)tragender Ziegel *m*, statisch mitwirkender ~
~ capability → load-carrying capacity

~ capacity → load-carrying ~
~ ~ of beam(s) without cast-in-situ concrete → (load)bearing ~ ~ ~ ~ ~ ~
~ (clay) brick cross-wall → (load-)bearing (~) ~ ~
~ construction → (load)bearing ~
~ face work → ~ facing masonry (~)
~ facing masonry (work), loadbearing ~ ~ (~), ~ face ~, ~ facing · tragendes (Ver)Blendmauerwerk *n*, ~ Vorsatzmauerwerk, tragende Verblendung *f*
~ floor block → (load)bearing floor (clay) brick
~ ~ brick → (load)bearing floor (clay) ~
~ ~ (clay) block → (load)bearing floor (clay) brick
~ ~ (~) brick → (load)bearing ~ (~) ~
~ frame, ~ framing, load-carrying ~, (load)bearing ~, (structural) ~, supporting ~, loaded ~ · (Trag)Rahmen *m*
~ in longitudinal direction, load-carrying ~ ~ ~, supporting ~ ~ ~, (load)-bearing ~ ~ ~, loaded ~ ~ ~ · längstragend
~ ~ transverse direction, load-carrying ~ ~ ~, supporting ~ ~ ~, (load)-bearing ~ ~ ~, loaded ~ ~ ~ · quertragend
~ masonry (wall) → (load)bearing ~ (~)
~ ~ (work) → (load)bearing ~ (~)
~ mechanism, load-carrying ~, (load-)bearing ~, supporting ~, loaded ~ · Tragmechanismus *m*
~ partition (wall) → (load)bearing ~ (~)
~ plane, load-carrying ~, supported ~, loaded ~, (load)bearing ~ · Tragebene *f*
~ power → load-carrying capacity
~ property → load-carrying capacity
~ quality → load-carrying capacity
~ rib, supporting ~, load-carrying ~, (load)bearing ~, structural ~, loaded ~ · Tragrippe *f*, Konstruktionsrippe, (last)tragende Rippe, Auflagerrippe
~ skeleton, (load)bearing ~, structural ~, load-carrying ~, supporting ~, loaded ~ · (Trag)Skelett *n*, (Trag)Gerippe *n*
~ ~ construction → (structural) ~ ~
~ ~ member → (structural) ~ ~
~ ~ structure → (structural) ~ ~
(~) structure → (load)bearing ~
(~) ~ of plain web girders → (load-)bearing ~ ~ ~ ~ ~
(~) ~ ~ solid web girders → (load-)bearing structure of plain ~ ~
~ system → (load)bearing ~
~ wall, load-carrying ~, (load)bearing ~, supporting ~, structural ~, loaded ~ · (last)tragende Wand *f*, Tragwand, Auflagerwand, Konstruktionswand

weight-carrying wall construction — weldment

~ ~ construction → (load)bearing wall structure
~ ~ structure → (load)bearing ~ ~
weight determination · Gewichtsermitt(e)lung f
weighted silk [*It is weighted with metallic salts*] · schwerer gemachte Seide f
weight hypothesis, ~ assumption · Gewichtsannahme f
~ **loss**, loss in weight, loss of weight · Gewichtsverlust m
weighometer · Gewichtsprüfer m
weight percent, wt% · Gewichtsprozent n
weight-saving · gewicht(s)(ein)sparend
weight schedule, ~ table, schedule of weights, table of weights · Gewichtstabelle f
~ **table**, ~ schedule, schedule of weights, table of weights · Gewichtstabelle f
weights and measures department, ~ ~ ~ office · Eichamt n
weight-to-volume ratio, W/V · Gewichts/Raum-Verhältnis n
weight training room · Konditionsraum m [*Sportanlage*]
weld neck flange · Einschweißflansch m
~ ~ **valve** · Einschweißarmatur f
to weld to · anschweißen
weldability · Schweißbarkeit f
weldable, of welding quality · schweißbar
~ **structural steel**, ~ construction(al) ~ [*B.S. 4360*] · schweißbarer Baustahl m, ~ Konstruktionsstahl
welded arch · Schweißbogen m
~ **area grating** · Schweißgitterrost m, Schweiß(fuß)bodengitter n
~ **article**, ~ product · Schweißartikel m, Schweißgegenstand m, Schweißerzeugnis n, geschweißtes Erzeugnis, geschweißter Artikel, geschweißter Gegenstand
~ **(asphaltic-)bitumen sheet(ing)** (Brit.); ~ asphalt ~ (US) [*It is applied in two layers welded together by blow lamp after adhesion of the first layer to the structure*] · Schweißbahn f, Bitumen-~
~ **column-girder connection** · geschweißter Trägeranschluß m
~ **connection**, ~ joint · geschweißte Verbindung f, geschweißter Stoß m, Schweißstoß, Schweißverbindung, Schweißanschluß m, geschweißter Anschluß
~ **flange** · Schweißflansch m
~ **flat roof** · Schweißflachdach n
~ **heat** · geschweißte Schmelze f, ~ Schmelzung f [*Stahl*]
~ **joint**, ~ connection · geschweißte Verbindung f, geschweißter Stoß m, Schweißstoß, Schweißverbindung, Schweißanschluß m, geschweißter Anschluß

~ **lattice(d) construction** · Schweißgitterkonstruktion f
~ ~ **girder** · Schweißgitterträger m
~ **(metal) mesh**, ~ wire ~ · (geschweißte) Maschenmatte f, (~) Bewehrungsmatte, (~) Armierungsmatte, Baustahlmatte, Schweißmaschenmatte, Maschenschweißmatte, Stahlbeton-Armierungsmatte, Stahlbeton-Bewehrungsmatte [*Baustahlgewebe ist der Markenname für Bewehrungsmatten mit unverschieblichen Knotenpunkten aus kaltgezogenem Sonderbetonstahl IV nach DIN 1045*]
~ **pipe** · geschweißtes Rohr n, Schweißrohr
~ **plate girder** · Schweißträger m
~ **product**, ~ article · Schweißartikel m, Schweißgegenstand m, Schweißerzeugnis n, geschweißtes Erzeugnis, geschweißter Gegenstand, geschweißter Artikel
~ **reinforcement** [*Reinforcement joined together by welding*] · Schweißarmierung f, Schweißbewehrung, Schweiß(stahl)einlagen fpl
~ **rigid frame**, ~ ~ framing · geschweißter starrer Rahmen m, Schweiß-Steifrahmen
~ **rising (steel) structure** · geschweißter Stahlhochbau m, geschweißtes Stahlhochbauwerk n
~ ~ **(~) structures** · geschweißte Stahlhochbauten f [*DIN 4100*]
~ **steel frame** → ~ ~ ~ structural ~
~ ~ **pipe** · geschweißtes Stahlrohr n
~ ~ **(structural) frame**, ~ ~ (~) framing · Schweißstahlrahmen m
~ **tank** · geschweißter Behälter m, Schweißbehälter
welded wire fabric reinforcement, ~ ~ mesh ~, ~ (metal) mesh ~ · punktgeschweißte Mattenarmierung f, ~ Mattenbewehrung
(~) ~ lath(ing) · (geschweißtes) Drahtgewebe n, (~) Rabitzgewebe
welding · Schweißen n
~, fusing, sealing [*Joining a piece of glass to glass or another material by heating and pressing together; also applied to the fine finishing of ends of tubular glasses*] · Schweißen n, Verschmelzen [*Glas*]
~ **glass** · Schweißerschutzglas n
~ **method** · Schweißverfahren n
~ **primer** · Schweißfarbe f
~ **quality** · Schweißgüte f
~ **rod**, ~ wire, filler ~ · Zusatzwerkstoff m, Schweißdraht m [*DIN 1913*]
~ **symbol** · Schweißzeichen n
~ **together** · Zusammenschweißen n
~ **wire**, ~ rod, filler ~ · Zusatzwerkstoff m, Schweißdraht m [*DIN 1913*]
weldment · Schweißkonstruktion f

welfare hospital · Wohlfahrtskrankenhaus *n*

well, shaft, pit · Schacht *m* [*Ein senkrechter Hohlraum von meist geringem Querschnitt, z.B. Luftschacht*]

~ → ~ hole

~ · Brunnen *m* [*Wassergewinnung*]

~ **burned** → well-burnt

well-burned brick → hard(-burned) ~

well-burnt, well-burned, well-fired · gutgebrannt

~ **brick** → hard(-burned) ~

well construction work · Brunnenbauarbeiten *fpl* [*DIN 18302*]

well-fired → hard-fired

~ **brick** → hard(-burned) ~

well-graded aggregate [*Aggregate having a particle size distribution which will produce maximum density, i.e., minimum void space*] · hohlraumarm abgestufter Zuschlag(stoff) *m*

wellhole, drop manhole [*A vertical shaft in which sewage is allowed to fall from one sewer to another at a lower level*] · Absturz(schacht) *m*

well (hole), stair(case) ~ (~) · Treppenloch *n*, Treppenöffnung *f* [*Die Öffnung einer Geschoßdecke oder Balkenlage, durch die eine Treppe führt. Auch die Öffnung zwischen den Lichtwangen der mehrläufigen Treppe*]

well-preserved · guterhalten

well-thinned · gutverdünnt

well-ventilated · gutgelüftet

well wall, shaft ~ · Schachtwand *f* [*Aufzug*]

~ **water supply,** borehole ~ ~ · Brunnenwasserversorgung *f*

welt, (welted) seam, lock seam · Falz *m* [*Metallbedachung*]

(welted) seam, lock ~, welt · Falz *m* [*Metallbedachung*]

(~) ~ **roof cladding,** (~) ~ ~ cover(ing), (~) ~ ~ sheathing, (~) ~ roofing · Falz(dach)(ein)deckung *f*, Falzbedachung, Falzsystem *n*

(~) ~ **spacing** · Falzabstand *m* [*Metallbedachung*]

(~) **standing seam,** standing welt [*The joint formed by turning up the edges of two adjacent sheets perpendicular to the surface and welting them together*] · stehender Falz *m*, Stehfalz [*Metallbedachung*]

Wenko reinforced block floor · Wenko-Decke *f*

West African copal · westafrikanischer Kopal *m*

westblock [*A multistor(e)y gallery at the west end of some German and Netherlandish churches, surmounted by towers or turrets*] · Westblock *m*

west (end) tower, western ~ · Westturm *m*

west(-facing) wall · Westwand *f*

~ **window** · Westfenster *n*

west orientation · Westorientierung *f*

~ **pediment,** western ~ · Westgiebel *m* [*griechischer Tempel*]

~ **tower,** ~ end ~, western ~ · Westturm *m*

~ **transept,** western ~ · westliches Querhaus *n*, Westhaus

~ **wall,** west-facing ~ · Westwand *f*

westwork [*A sanctuary at the west end of the nave either on the ground or first floor of a fortress-like west tower, flanked by turrets and transepts*] · Westwerk *n*, Westbau *m* [*Selbständiger Vorbau im Westen frühmittelalterlicher Basiliken*]

Western architecture · westliche Baukunst *f*, ~ Architektur *f*

west(ern) bay · Westjoch *n*

western Byzantine style · westlicher byzantinischer Stil *m*

west(ern) choir, ~ quire · Westchor *m*

west(ern) façade · Westfassade *f*

~ **gallery** · Westempore *f*

~ **pediment** · Westgiebel *m* [*griechischer Tempel*]

~ **porch** · Westvorhalle *f*

~ **portal** · Westportal *n*

~ **quire,** ~ choir · Westchor *m*

~ **side** · Westseite *f*

~ **tower,** west end ~ · Westturm *m*

~ **transept** · westliches Querhaus *n*, Westhaus

to wet, to coat · umhüllen, benetzen [*mit Bindemittel*]

~ ~ · (an)nässen, benässen

wet · naß

~ **cast pipe** · Betonrohr *n* nach dem Naßverfahren hergestellt, Zementrohr ~ ~ ~ ~

~ ~ **process,** ~ ~ method · Naßverfahren *n* [*Betonrohrherstellung*]

~ **(cement) paste** → cement ~

~ **concrete,** fluid ~, sloppy ~ · flüssiger Beton *m*

~ **construction partition (wall)** · verputzte Trennwand *f*, (Naß)Putztrennwand

~ **cooling** · Naßkühlung *f*

~ **cup method** · Diffusionsmeßverfahren *n* im Feuchtigkeitsbereich 50–100% r.F.

~ **drawing** · Naßziehen *n* [*Draht*]

~ **drawn wire** · naßblank gezogener Draht *m*

~ **film** · Naßfilm *m*

wet glued plywood — whispering cupola

~ **glued plywood** [*Plywood made with natural glues as distinct from resin-bonded plywood employing synthetic adhesives*] · Sperrholz *n* mit Naturleim verleimt

~ **gravel** · Naßkies *m*

to wet-grind · naßmahlen

wet grinding · Naßschleifen *n*

~ **looper** · Feuchtläufer *m*, erste Hänge *f* [*Dachpappenanlage*]

~ **method,** ~ **process** · Naßverfahren *n* [*Zementherstellung; Schlackenaufbereitung*]

~ **mix shotcrete** [*Shotcrete wherein all ingredients, including mixing water, are mixed in the equipment before introduction into the delivery hose; it may be pneumatically conveyed or moved by displacement*] · Naßspritzbeton *m* [*Z.B. Moser-Spritzbeton. Das Gegenteil ist der Torkretbeton, bei dem das naturfeuchte Betongemenge durch Schläuche gefördert und das Wasser kurz vor dem Antragen in der Düse durch einen Wasserschlauch zugesetzt wird*]

~ **mixing** (US) → coating

wet-on-wet coating · Naß-in-Naß-Beschichtung *f*

~ **method** · Naß-in-Naß-Verfahren *n*

wet paint [*Not yet dry paint*] · frische Farbe *f* [*Noch nicht getrocknete Farbe*]

~ **paste** → cement ~

~ **process,** ~ **method** · Naßverfahren *n* [*Zementherstellung; Schlackenaufbereitung*]

~ ~ **kiln** · Naßofen *m*

~ **room,** moist ~ · Naßraum *m*

~ ~ **dampproofing,** moist ~ ~ · Naßraum(ab)dichtung *f*

~ ~ **fixture** → moist room luminaire (~)

~ ~ **light fitting** (Brit.) → moist room luminaire (fixture)

~ ~ **(light(ing)) fixture** → moist room luminaire (~)

~ ~ **luminaire (fixture)** → moist ~ ~ (~)

~ ~ **partition (wall),** moist ~ ~ (~) · Naßraumtrennwand *f*

~ ~ **service(s),** moist ~ ~ · Naßrauminstallation(en) *f(pl)*

~ **sieving** [*Sieving to remove from fresh concrete all aggregate particles larger than a certain size*] · (Ab)Sieben *n* von Frischbeton

~ **steam,** partially dry ~ [*A vapo(u)r consisting of a mix(ture) of water and steam*] · Dampfwassergemisch *n*

~ **storage** · Naßlagerung *f*

~ **strength** · Naßfestigkeit *f*

~ **weather spell** · Feuchtwetterperiode *f*

wetness · Nässe *f*

wettability, coatability · Benetzbarkeit *f*

wettable, coatable · benetzbar

wetting · Benässen *n*, (An)Nässen

~ → coating

~ **action,** coating ~ · Benetzungswirkung *f*

~ **agent,** dope, surfactant, anti-stripping additive, non-stripping agent, adhesion (promoting) agent, anti-stripping agent, activator · Adhäsionsverbesserer *m*, Haftmittel *n*, Haftfestigkeitsverbesserer, Netz(haft)mittel, Haftanreger, adhäsionsfördernder Zusatz(stoff) *m*, adhäsionsförderndes Zusatzmittel, Benetzungsmittel

~ ~ (Brit.) → (concrete) workability ~

~ **angle,** voating ~ · Benetzungswinkel *m*

~ **capacity** → coating power

~ **heat,** coating ~ · Benetzungswärme *f*

~ **mechanism** · Benetzungsmechanismus *m*

~ **power** → coating ~

~ **property** → coating power

~ **quality** → coating power

WF, wind force · Windkraft *f*

WF → wide-flange(d)

WF diagram, wind force ~ · Windkräftediagramm *n*

WH, (hot) water heating appliance, (hot) water heater · Wassererhitzer *m*, Wasserheizer *m*, Wasserheizgerät *n*, Wassererwärmer *m*, Warmwasserheizer, WW-Heizer, WW-Erhitzer, WW-Erwärmer, WW-Heizgerät

w(h)aler → horizontal timber

wheat paste · Weizenmehlkleister *m*

~ **starch** · Weizenstärke *f*

~ **straw** · Weizenstroh *n*

wheat-straw tar · Weizenstrohteer *m*

wheel-chair store · Rollstuhllager *n* [*Krankenhaus*]

wheel step → winder

~ **tracery** · Speichenradmaßwerk *n*

~ **window,** Catherine ~ ~ · Radfenster *n*, Katharinenrad *n* [*Rundfenster mit speichenartiger Unterteilung*]

wheeler → winder

wheel(ing) step → winder

whinstone [*A term loosely used to denote rocks of the basalt type*] · basaltisches Gestein *n*

whiplash style [*Belgian term for Art Nouveau*] · Peitschenschlag-Stil *m*

whispering cupola, ~ gallery, ~ dome · Flüsterkuppel *f*

whispering dome — white pigment

~ **dome,** ~ gallery, ~ cupola · Flüsterkuppel f

~ **gallery,** ~ cupola, ~ dome · Flüsterkuppel f

white aggregate · Weißzuschlag(stoff) m

'white' architecture [*Refers to colour of building materials used*] · „weiße" Architektur f

white asbestos · Weißasbest m

~ **asbestos-cement board,** ~ ~ sheet; ~ cement asbestos ~ (US) · Asbest-Weißzement-Platte f, Weißzement-Asbestplatte

~ **asbestos flour** · Weißasbestmehl n

~ **body,** ~ clay ~, ~ stone · weißer Scherben m [*Keramik*]

~ **cement** · weißer Zement m, Weißzement

~ ~ **asbestos board** (US) → ~ asbestos-cement ~

~ **(chalk) lime** → high-calcium ~

~ **chip(ping)s,** ~ stone ~ · Weißsplitt m

~ **(clay) body,** ~ stone · weißer Scherben m [*Keramik*]

~ **concrete** · Weißbeton m

~ ~ **frame** · Weißbetonrahmen m

~ ~ **panel** · Weißbetontafel f

~ **copal** · Weißkopal m

~ **exposed concrete,** ~ fair-faced ~ · weißer Sichtbeton m [*Architekturbeton*]

~ **fair-faced concrete,** ~ exposed ~ · weißer Sichtbeton m [*Architekturbeton*]

(~) **flint,** flint glass · weißes Hohlglas n, Weißglas

'white' Functionalism · „weißer" Funktionalismus m

white glazed coat(ing), ~ glaze(d finish), ~ glazing · Weißbeglasung f, Weißglasur f

~ **glaze(d finish),** ~ glazing, ~ glazed coat(ing) · Weißbeglasung f, Weißglasur f

~ **glazing** · Weißbeglasen n, Weißglasieren

~ ~, ~ glazed coat(ing), ~ glaze(d finish) · Weißbeglasung f, Weißglasur f

~ **glue** · weißer Leim m, Weißleim

~ **granite chip(ping)s** · Weißgranitsplitt m

~ **hard** · knochentrocken [*Bezeichnung für ein Tonerzeugnis, das so trocken ist, daß die Oberfläche dadurch heller wurde*]

~ **iron pyrites,** marcasite · Kammkies m, Speerkies m, Markasit m, FeS_2

~ **Italian marble,** WIM · weißer italienischer Marmor m

~ **joint mortar,** ~ masonry ~, ~ pointing ~ · Fugenzement m [*Fugenmörtel aus weißem Portlandzement und weißem Steinmehl*]

~ **lac** → ~ shellac

~ **lead** [*It is a body pigment in the form of a white powder but for convenience in use it is mixed with a small percentage of linseed oil by the manufacturers to form a thick paste*] · Bleiweiß n

~ ~ **cement** [*A cement made by mixing paste white lead with a good grade of varnish to heavy brushing or trowel(l)ing consistency*] · Bleiweißkitt m, Bleiweißspachtel m

~ ~ **in oil paste,** ground white lead (in oil) · Ölbleiweiß n

~ ~ **paint** · Bleiweiß(anstrich)farbe f, Bleiweißölfarbe

~ ~ **paste,** paste white lead · Bleiweißpaste f, Pastenbleiweiß n

~ ~ **plant** · Bleiweißanlage f

~ **lime** → high-calcium ~

~ ~ **mortar,** rich ~ ~, pure ~ ~, high-calcium ~ ~ · Weißkalkmörtel m

~ ~ **paste** → high-calcium lime putty

~ ~ **putty** → high-calcium ~ ~

~ **lump lime,** rich ~ ~, pure ~ ~, high-calcium ~ ~ · Weißstück(en)kalk m [*DIN 1060*]

~ **malleable casting** · weißer Temperguß m, Weißguß

~ **marble,** pure ~ · weißer Marmor m, Weißmarmor

~ **masonry mortar,** ~ pointing ~, ~ joint ~ · Fugenmörtel m [*Fugenmörtel aus weißem Portlandzement und weißem Steinmehl*]

~ **mastic** · Weißmastix m

~ **mortar** · Weißmörtel m

to whiten, to limewash, to limewhite, to whitewash · kalken, tünchen, schlämmen, weißen

whiteness · Weiß(e) n, (f)

whitening → whitewash

~, limewashing, limewhiting, whitewashing · Kalken n, Tünchen, Weißen, Schlämmen

~ **coat** → whitewash ~

white noise [*A noise whose spectral density is substantially constant over a significant frequency range. White noise need not neccessarily be random*] · weißes Rauschen n [*Rauschen, dessen spektrale Intensitätsdichte über dem interessierenden Frequenzbereich konstant ist*]

~ **paint** · Weiß(anstrich)farbe f

white-painted · weißgestrichen, weiß angestrichen

white pigment [*B.S. 239*] [*In Great Britain, black pigments are considered to have colo(u)r, whereas white pigments are considered to have none. In Germany, however, white pigments, black pigments and all gray pigments are considered to have no colo(u)r*] · unbuntes Pigment n

~ ~ · Weißpigment n

white pigment powder — wide-span (load)bearing system 1118

~ ~ **powder**, powder(ed) white pigment · Weißpigmentpulver *n*

white(-)pigmented · weißpigmentiert

white pointing mortar, ~ masonry ~, ~ joint ~ · Fugenzement *m* [*Fugenmörtel aus weißem Portlandzement und weißem Steinmehl*]

~ **Portland cement**, ~ portland ~, WPC · weißer Portlandzement *m* [*DIN 1164. Durch Auswahl des Rohmaterials und besondere Brennbedingungen werden die dunkelfarbigen Bestandteile des Portlandzementklinkers zurückgedrängt*]

~ **quicklime**, rich ~, pure ~, high-calcium ~ · Weißbranntkalk *m*

~ **rust** · weißer Rost *m*, Zinkrost

~ **sand** · Weißsand *m*

~ **seal** · Weißsiegel *m* [*Zinkweiß*]

~ **(shel)lac**, bleached ~ · gebleichter Schellack *m*

~ **spirit**, mineral solvent for paints; turpentine substitute [*deprecated*] [*The most commonly used thinner for paints and varnishes*] · Testbenzin *m*, Lackbenzin, künstliches Terpentinöl *n* [*Fehlnamen: Terpentin(öl)ersatz m*]

~ **spots** → water spotting

whitestone · weißer Granulit *m*, Weißstein *m*

white stone, ~ (clay) body · weißer Scherben *m* [*Keramik*]

~ (~) **chip(ping)s** · Weißsplitt *m*

~ **wall tile** · weiße Wandfliese *f*, ~ Wand(belag)platte *f*

white-ware · keramischer Scherben *m*

to whitewash, to whiten, to limewash, to limewhite · kalken, tünchen, schlämmen, weißen

whitewash, limewash, whitening, milk of lime [*A suspension of slaked lime in water resulting from slaking lime with excess water*] · Kalkbrühe *f*, Kalkmilch *f*, Tünche *f*, Weiße *f*

~ **coat**, limewash ~, whitening ~, milk of lime ~ · Kalk(milch)anstrich *m*, Tüncheanstrich, Weißeanstrich, Kalkbrüheanstrich, Kalk(milch)aufstrich, Tüncheaufstrich, Weißeaufstrich, Kalkbrüheaufstrich

whitewashing, whitening, limewashing, limewhiting · Kalken *n*, Tünchen, Weißen, Schlämmen

whiting, Paris white · Schlämmkreide *f* [*Kreide ist eine natürliche Mineralfarbe. Sie besteht im wesentlichen aus kohlensaurem Kalk (= Kalziumkarbonat $CaCO_3$). Nach dem Schlämmverfahren wird sie Schlämmkreide genannt. Benennungen nach den Fundorten: Rügener Kreide, Champagnerkreide, schwedische Kreide, Bologneser Kreide*]

whole beam · Ganzholzbalken(träger) *m*

~ **block**, ~ tile [*See remark under 'Block'*] · ganzer Stein *m*, ~ Block *m*

~ **brick**, ~ clay ~, four quarters · Ganzziegel *m*

~ **(clay) brick**, four quarters · Ganzziegel *m*

~ **hip** · ganzer Walm *m*, Ganzwalm [*Dach*]

wholesale market, municipal ~ · Großmarkt(halle) *m*, (*f*)

~ **warehouse (building)** [*A building designed both for the storage of goods and the transaction of business, other than retail business related to such goods*] · Lagergebäude *n* mit Einrichtungen für Geschäftstätigkeiten

whole size, full ~ · Originalgröße *f*

~ **tile**, ~ block [*See remark under 'Block'*] · ganzer Stein *m*, ~ Block *m*

whser., washer · Scheibe *f*, Unterleg~, Unterlag~

WI, wrought iron · Schmiedeeisen *m*

WI area grating, wrought iron ~ ~ · Schmiedeeisengitterrost *m*

WI strap, wrought-iron [*For fixing the ends of joints*] · schmiedeeisernes Band *n*, Schmiedeeisenband

WI window, wrought-iron ~ · Schmiedeeisenfenster *n*, schmiedeeisernes Fenster

WI window grille, wrought-iron ~ ~ · Schmiedeeisenfenstergitter *n*, schmiedeeisernes Fenstergitter

wicket [*A small gate; or, especially, a small door in a large gate, enabling a person to enter without opening the large gate*] · Schlupftür *f*, Durchgangstür

wide concrete curb; ~ ~ kerb (Brit.) · Betonbordschwelle *f*

~ **curb**; ~ kerb (Brit.) · Bordschwelle *f*

wide-flange(d), broad-flange(d), WF · breitflanschig

~ **beam** (US) → broad-flange(d) ~

~ **girder** (US) → broad-flange(d) beam

wide foil · Breitfolie *f*

~ **kerb** (Brit.); ~ curb · Bordschwelle *f*

wide-ledge (bath)tub, ~ bath · (Bade)Wanne *f* mit breitem Rand

wide (natural) stone curb; ~ (~) ~ kerb (Brit.) · Steinbordschwelle *f*, Natur~

wide-spaced, ar(a)eostyle · lichtsäulig

~ **temple** → ar(a)eostyle ~

wide-span beam, long-span ~, large-span ~ · Weitspannbalken(träger) *m*

~ **compressed component** → long-span prestressed (concrete) (building) unit

~ **floor slab**, long-span ~ ~, large-span ~ ~ · Weitspanndeckenplatte *f*

~ **frame**, large-span ~, long-span ~ · Weitspannrahmen *m*

~ **lattice(d) beam** → long-span trussed girder

~ ~ **girder** → long-span trussed ~

~ **(load)bearing system**, long-span ~ ~, large-span ~ ~, ~ load-carrying ~, ~ weight-carrying ~ · Weitspann-Tragwerk *n*, Weitspann-Tragsystem *n*

~ (pre)cast (concrete) beam → large-span ~ (~) ~
~ (pre)stressed (concrete) (building) unit → long-span ~ (~) (~) ~
~ ~ (~) slab, long-span ~ (~) ~, large-span ~ (~) ~, prestressed (concrete) long-span ~, prestressed (concrete) wide-span ~, prestressed (concrete) large-span ~ · Spannbeton-Weitspannplatte f, Weitspannbetonplatte
~ rib, large-span ~, long-span ~ · Weitspannrippe f
~ roof, large-span ~, long-span ~ · Weitspanndach n
~ shell, large-span ~, long-span ~ · Weitspannschale f
~ ~ vault, long-span ~ ~, large-span ~ ~ · Weitspann-Schalengewölbe n
~ trussed beam → long-span ~ ~
~ ~ girder → long-span ~ ~
~ wall arch · Weitspannmauerbogen m
wide stone curb → ~ (natural) ~ ~
width measurement · Breitenmessung f
~ of step, step width · Stufenbreite f
width-(to-)thickness ratio · Breite-Dicke-Verhältnis n
Wiegmann (roof) truss, Polonceau (~) ~ · Polonceaubinder m, Wiegmannbinder, Polonceauträger
wiggle nail, dog, joint fastener, corrugated fastener; mitre brad (Brit.); miter brad (US) · Wellennagel m, gewellter Nagel
wild man · wilder Mann m [Im 15. und 16. Jahrhundert besonders als Schildhalter im Wappen auftretende nackte, behaarte Männer mit Laubkränzen um Kopf und Hüfte, mit Keulen bewehrt]
~ silk · wilde Seide f
~ woman · wilde Frau f
Williot('s) diagram · Williotscher Verschiebeplan m, Williotplan [Er dient zur graphischen Bestimmung der Verschiebungen der Knotenpunkte eines Fachwerkträgers infolge der elastischen Längenänderungen der Stäbe]
willow sapling, sway · Weide f [Zum Binden beim Strohdach]
WIM, white Italian marble · weißer italienischer Marmor m
wind and dust protection planting · Wind- und Staubschutzpflanzung f
~ area · Windangriffsfläche f
~ beam → collar ~
wind-blown dust · Windstaub m
wind brace · Windstrebe f
~ braced boom, ~ ~ flange, ~ ~ chord · Windstrebenflansch m, Windstrebengurt(ung) m, (f)
wind bracing · Windversteifung f, Windaussteifung, Windverspannung, Windverband m

~ ~ connection · Windverbandanschluß m
~ component · Teilkraft f des Windes, Windkomponente f
~ conditions · Windverhältnisse f
~ direction, WD · Windrichtung f
~ drift · Windverformung f
wind-driven rain, driving ~, pelting ~ · Schlagregen m [Mit Regen verbundener Wind von mindestens Beaufortstärke 5]
wind drumming · Winddröhnung f [Metallbedachung]
~ effect · Windwirkung f
winder, winding machine · Wickelmaschine f [Dachpappenanlage]
~, wheeler, wheel(ing) step, radial step · Wendelstufe f [Eine gleichmäßig auf einen Mittelpunkt hin ausgerichtete Stufe mit keilförmiger Trittfläche, gekrümmtem Hals und gekrümmtem Endstück]
wind excited vibration, ~ ~ oscillation · Windschwingung f
~ force, WF · Windkraft f
wind-force assumption · Windkraftannahme f
~ diagram, WF ~ · Windkräftediagramm n
~ distribution · Windkraftverteilung f
wind girder · Windträger m
windguard; draught fillet (Brit.); draft fillet (US) · (Ab)Dicht(ungs)latte f [kittlose Verglasung]
(wind) gust, gusty wind · böiger Wind m, Böe f
(~) ~ speed, gusty wind ~ · Böengeschwindigkeit f
wind-induced axial force · windeingetragene Achsialkraft f
winding · Wendelung f [Treppe]
~ · Wendeln n [Treppe]
~ handle · Handkurbel f [Raffjalousie]
~ in the length dimension, bowing ~ ~ ~ ~ · Verkrümmung f in der Länge [Tonhohlplatte]
~ reels · Wickelapparatur f [Dachpappenmaschine]
~ stair(case), newel ~, screw ~, vice ~, vis(e) ~, vys(e) ~ · Schneckentreppe f, Wendeltreppe, Schnecke(nstiege) f
windings · Windungen fpl [Pfeiler mit Windungen]
wind load, WL [The force exerted by wind on a structure of part of a structure] · Verkehrslast f aus Wind, Windlast [DIN 1055 Bl. 4]
~ ~ assumption · Windlastannahme f [DIN 1055, Blatt 4]
~ ~ moment · Windlastmoment n
~ ~ regulation · Windlastvorschrift f [DIN 1055]

wind load value — window for animal shelter

~ ~ **value,** value of wind load · Windlastwert *m*

~ **loading** · Windbelastung *f*

~ **moment** · Windmoment *n*

~ ~ **connection** · Windmomentverbindung *f*

~ ~ **equation** · Windmomentengleichung *f*

window, light · Fenster *n*

~ **accessories** · Fensterzubehör *n* [*seltener m*]

~ **(air-conditioning) unit** · Fenster-Klimagerät *n*

(~) **aperture,** (~) opening, day, light · Fensteröffnung *f*, Fensterlicht *n*, Fensterloch *n*

~ **arch** · Fensterbogen *m*

~ **area** · Fensterfläche *f*

~ **awning blind** · Markisolette *f*

~ **band,** ribbon window, continuous light · Bandfenster *n*, Langfenster, Fensterband *n*

~ **bar** → ~ glazing ~

~ **board** [*It is used to provide a finish at sill level on the inside*] · Simsbrett *n*, Deckbrett, Fensterbrett, Lattiebrett

~ **box** · Fensterblumenkasten *m*

(~) **breast rail,** (~) sill ~; (~) cill ~ (Brit.) · Sohlbankriegel *m*, Brustriegel [*Querverbindung unter einer Fensteröffnung im Fachwerk*]

~ **brightness** · Fensterhelligkeit *f*

~ **builder** · Fensterbauer *m*

~ **case,** ~ casing, ~ trim · Fensterzarge *f*

(~) **casement,** hinged ~, pivoted sash, ventilator, opening sash, opening light · (Fenster)Flügel *m*

(~) ~ **frame,** hinged ~ ~, pivoted sash ~, opening sash ~, opening light ~, ventilator ~ · (Fenster)Flügelrahmen *m*

(~) ~ **hardware** · (Fenster)Flügelbeschläge *mpl*

(~) ~ **stay** · (Fenster)Feststeller *m*, (Fenster)Feststellhaken *m*, (Fenster)Sperrhaken, (Fenster)Sperre *f*

(~) **centre light** (Brit); (~) center ~ (US) · (Fenster)Mittelteil *m, n*

~ ~ **line** (Brit.); ~ center ~ (US) · Fensterachse *f*

~ **check** [*Scotland*]; ~ rabbet, ~ rebate · Fensterfalz *m*

(~) **cill** (Brit.); (~) sill · Sohlbank *f*, Fenster~, Fensterbank

(~) ~ **block,** (~) ~ tile (Brit.); (window) sill block, (window) sill tile · Sohlbankblock(stein) *m*, Sohlbankstein, Fenster~, Fensterbankblock(stein), Fensterbankstein

~ ~ **brick** (Brit.); ~ sill ~ · Fensterbankziegel *m*, Fensterbankstein *m*

(~) ~ **cover** (Brit.); (~) sill ~ · Sohlbankabdeckung *f*, Fenster~, Fensterbankabdeckung

(~) ~ **(head) height** (Brit.) → (~) sill (~) ~

(~) ~ **rail** (Brit.); (~) sill ~, (~) breast ~ · Sohlbankriegel *m*, Brustriegel [*Querverbindung unter einer Fensteröffnung im Fachwerk*]

~ ~ **slab** (Brit.); ~ sill ~ · Fensterbankplatte *f*, (Fenster)Sohlbankplatte

(~) ~ **tile,** (~) ~ block (Brit.); (~) sill tile, (~) sill block · Sohlbankblock (stein) *m*, Sohlbankstein, Fenster~, Fensterbankblock(stein), Fensterbankstein

~ **cleaner** · Fensterputzer *m*

(~) **cleaning,** ~ washing · (Fenster-)Putzen *n*, (Fenster)Reinigung *f*

(~) ~ **balcony** · (Fenster)Reinigungsbalkon *m*

(~) ~ **cradle,** (~) cradle machine, wall lift, roof cradle [*Motorized carriage running vertically on rails let into the window frames*] · (Fenster)Putzwagen *m*, (Fenster)Reinigungswagen

(window-)cleaning equipment, window-washing ~ · (Fenster)Reinigungsgerät *n*, (Fenster)Putzgerät

window column · Fenstersäule *f*, Fensterstütze *f*

~ **component,** ~ part · Fensterteil *m, n*

~ **cornice** · Fenster(ge)sims *m*, (*n*)

(~) **cradle machine,** (~) cleaning cradle, wall lift, roof cradle [*Motorized carriage running vertically on rails let into the window frames*] · (Fenster)-Putzwagen *m*, (Fenster)Reinigungswagen

(~) **cross** · Kreuzstock *m*, (Fenster)Kreuz *n*

~ **curtain** · Fenstervorhang *m*

~ **design,** design of window(s) · Fensterform(geb)ung *f*, Fensterdurchformung

~ **dimension** · Fensterabmessung *f*, Fenstermaß *n*

~ **draughtproofing** (Brit.); ~ draftproofing (US) · Fensterzug(ab)dichtung *f*

windowed · befenstert

window(ed) bay, protruded ~ [*misnomer: bay window*] · Auslucht *f*

windowed frieze · Fensterfries *m*

window efficiency ratio, sky factor · Fensterfaktor = f *m*, Senkrechtbeleuchtung *f* im Fenster (E_r), Vertikalbeleuchtung im Fenster (E_r)

~ **engineering** · Fenstertechnik *f*

~ **fan** · Fensterventilator *m*

~ **fitting,** ~ furniture · Fensterbeschlag *m* [*DIN 18270*]

~ **fittings,** ~ hardware · Fensterbeschläge *mpl* [*DIN 18270*]

~ **for animal shelter,** animal shelter window · Stallfenster *n*

~ **frame** [*The fixed, nonoperable frame of a window designed to receive and hold the sash or casement and all necessary hardware*] · (Fenster)Blendrahmen *m*

~ **framing** · Fensterumrahmung *f*

~ **furniture,** ~ fitting · Fensterbeschlag *m* [*DIN 18270*]

~ **gasket,** ~ preformed ~, ~ sealing ~, ~ structural ~ · Fenster-Selbstdichtung *f*, Fenster(Ab)Dicht(ungs)profil *n*

~ **glass** · Fensterglas *n*

(~) ~ **area** · Glasfläche *f*, Lichtfläche, Scheibenfläche [*Fenster*]

~ ~ **pane** → (~) pane

~ **glazing** · Fensterverglasung *f*, Fenstereinglasung

(~) ~ **bar,** sash ~, division ~, window ~, astragal; muntin (US) [*A rebated wood or metal bar which holds the panes of glass in a window. The particular term 'glazing bar' is often kept for roof lights or for patent glazing. Metal windows usually have no glazing bars and thus let in more light*] · (Fenster)Sprosse *f*

~ **grille,** ~ guard, ~ screen [*sometimes spelled 'grill'*] · Fenstergitter *n*

~ **hardware,** ~ fittings · Fensterbeschläge *mpl* [*DIN 18270*]

~ **hinge** · Fensterband *n* [*Teil eines Fensterbeschlages*]

~ **hood** · Fenster-Wetter(schutz)dach *n*

~ **lead** · Fensterblei *n*

windowless · fensterfrei, fensterlos

~ **building,** blackout ~ · fensterloses Gebäude *n*, fensterfreies ~

~ **panel** · fensterlose Tafel *f*, fensterfreie ~

windowlight, (window) pane, window glass pane · (Fenster)Scheibe *f*

window-lighting, side natural lighting, side daylight illumination side (day)-lighting · Seitentages(licht)beleuchtung *f* Fenster-Tages(licht)beleuchtung [*Fehlnamen: Fenster(-Tages)belichtung Seitenbelichtung*]

window lintel; ~ lintol [*deprecated*] · Fensteroberschwelle *f*, Fenstersturz *m*

~ ~ in (pre)stressed clay → Stahlton ((pre)stressed) window lintel

~ ~ ~ Stahlton → Stahlton ((pre)stressed) window lintel

~ ~ **machine;** ~ lintol ~ [*deprecated*] · Fenstersturzmaschine *f*, Fenstersturzfertiger *m*

~ **location** · Fensterlage *f*

~ **manufacture,** ~ making · Fensterfertigung *f*, Fensterherstellung, Fensterbau *m*

~ **masonry wall** · Fenstermauer *f*

~ **material** · Fensterbaustoff *m*; Fensterbaumaterial *n* [*Schweiz*]

~ **module** · Fenstermodul *m*

~ **niche,** ~ recess · Fensternische *f*

~ ~ **arch,** ~ recess ~ · Fensternischenbogen *m*

~ **opener,** ~ opening device · Fensteröffner *m*

(~) **opening,** (~) aperture, day, light · Fensteröffnung *f*, Fensterlicht *n*, Fensterloch *n*

~ ~ **device,** ~ opener · Fensteröffner *m*

~ **openwork gablet** · Fensterwimperg *m*

~ **oscillation,** ~ vibration · Fenstererschütterung *f*, Fensterschwingung

(~) **pane,** ~ glass ~, windowlight · (Fenster)Scheibe *f*

(~) ~ **separation** · (Fenster)Scheibentrennung *f*

~ **panel** · Fenstertafel *f*, Fensterelement *n*

~ **part,** ~ component · Fensterteil *m, n*

~ **pier** · Fensterpfeiler *m*

~ **post** · Setzholz *n*, Fensterpfosten *m*

~ ~, ~ stud · Fenstersäule *f*, Fensterständer *m* [*Fach(werk)wand*]

~ **(preformed) gasket,** ~ sealing ~, ~ structural ~ · Fenster-Selbstdichtung *f*, Fenster(Ab)Dicht(ungs)profil *n*

~ **profile** → ~ section

~ **rabbet,** ~ rebate; ~ check [*Scotland*] · Fensterfalz *m*, Fensteranschlag *m*

(~) **rail,** sash ~ [*The horizontal member in a window sash*] · (Fenster)Riegel *m*

~ **rebate,** ~ rabbet; ~ check [*Scotland*] · Fensterfalz *m*

~ **recess,** ~ niche · Fensternische *f*

~ ~ **arch,** ~ niche ~ · Fensternischenbogen *m*

~ **reveal** · Fensterleibung *f*, Fensterlaibung [*Seitliche Fensterbegrenzung im Innern eines Raumes*]

~ ~ **brick** · Fensteranschlußziegel *m*

(~) **sash** · Fensterrahmen *m*

~ **screen,** insect ~ · Fenstergaze *f*

~ ~, ~ guard, ~ grille [*sometimes spelled "grill"*] · Fenstergitter *n*

~ **seal(ing)** · Fenster(ab)dichtung *f*

~ ~ **fillet** · Fenster(ab)dicht(ungs)leiste *f*

~ ~ **gasket,** ~ structural ~, ~ (preformed) ~ · Fenster-Selbstdichtung *f*, Fenster-(Ab)Dicht(ungs)profil *n*

~ ~ **rope** · Fenster(ab)dichtungsstrick *m*

~ **seat** · Fenstersitz *m*

~ **section,** ~ unit, ~ shape, ~ trim, ~ profile · Fensterprofil *n*

~ shape → ~ section

~ ~, ~ form, shape of window, form of window · Fensterform f

(~) shutter [*A ventilated or louvered panel usually hinged to cover a window. Also used as a decorative unit fastened to the outside wall adjacent to a window*] · (Fenster)Laden m

(~) sill; (~) cill (Brit.) · Sohlbank f, Fenster~, Fensterbank

(~) ~ block, (~) ~ tile; (~) cill ~ (Brit.) · Fensterbankblock(stein) m, Fensterbankstein, (Fenster)Sohlbankblock(stein), (Fenster)Sohlbankstein

~ ~ brick; ~ cill ~ (Brit.) · Fensterbankziegel m, Fensterbankstein m

(~) ~ cover; (~) cill ~ (Brit.) · Fensterbankabdeckung f, (Fenster)Sohlbankabdeckung

(~) ~ (head) height; (~) cill (~) ~ (Brit.) [*This height is the dimension from the top of the floor finish to the top of the sill which forms part of the wall*] · Fensterbankhöhe f

(~) ~ rail, (~) breast ~; (~) cill ~ (Brit.) · Brustriegel m, Sohlbankriegel [*Querverbindung unter einer Fensteröffnung im Fachwerk*]

~ ~ slab; ~ cill ~ (Brit.) · Sohlbankplatte f, Fenster~, Fensterbankplatte

(~) ~ tile, (~) ~ block; (~) cill ~ (Brit.) · Sohlbankblock(stein) m, Sohlbankstein, Fenster~, Fensterbankblock(stein), Fensterbankstein

~ size · Fenstergröße f

~ spandrel → under-~ ~

~ ~ panel → under-~ ~ ~

~ splay · Fensterausschrägung f, Fensterschräge f

~ stay · (Fenster)Kettelhaken m, (Fenster)Sturmhaken

~ structural gasket, ~ seal(ing) ~, ~ (preformed) ~ · Fenster-Selbstdichtung f, Fenster-(Ab)Dicht(ungs)profil n

~ stud, ~ post · Fenstersäule f, Fensterständer m [*Fach(werk)wand*]

~ sunblind · Fenstersonnenblende f, Fenstersonnenschutzkonstruktion f, Fenstersonnenschutz(anlage) m, (f)

~ surround · Fenstereinfassung f

~ template, ~ templet · Fensterlehre f

~ templet → ~ template

~ test chamber · Fensterprüfkammer f

~ tier · Fensterreihe f

~ tracery · Fenstermaßwerk n

~ transom · Fensterkämpfer m

~ trim → ~ section

~ ~, ~ case, ~ casing · Fensterzarge f

~ type, type of window · Fensterart f

~ unit → ~ section

~ ~, ~ air-conditioning ~ · Fenster-(-Klima)gerät n

~ ~ · Fertigfenster n

~ ventilation, ~ venting · Fenster(be- und -ent)lüftung f

~ vibration, ~ oscillation · Fenstererschütterung f, Fensterschwingung

~ wall · Fensterwand f

~ washing, (~) cleaning · (Fenster)-Putzen n, (Fenster)Reinigung f

window-washing cradle, (window-) cleaning ~ (Fenster)Reinigungswagen m, (Fenster)Putzwagen

~ equipment, (window-)cleaning ~ · (Fenster)Reinigungsgerät n, (Fenster)-Putzgerät

wind pressure · Winddruck m

(~) ~ coefficient · (Wind)Druckbeiwert m

~ ~ distribution · Winddruckverteilung f

~ ~ effect · Winddruckwirkung f

~ ~ force · Winddruckkraft f

windproof, windtight · winddicht

(wind)rose · Windrose f

wind screen(ing) · Windschutz m, Windblende f

wind-shear moment · Windschubmoment n

wind speed alarm [*It protects cranes, scaffolds, and workers from accidents caused by high winds*] · Windmelder m

~ stability · Windstandfestigkeit f, Windstandsicherheit, Windstabilität f

~ stress · Windbeanspruchung f

~ study · Winduntersuchung f

(~) suction · Sog m, Wind~

(~) ~ coefficient · Sogbeiwert m, Wind~

(~) ~ effect · Sogwirkung f, Wind~

(~) ~ force · Sogkraft f, Wind~

(~) ~ side · Sogseite f

windtight, windproof · winddicht

wind-tunnel investigation · Windkanaluntersuchung f

wind tunnel model · Windkanalmodell n

~ uplift · Windauftrieb m

~ velocity, WV · Windgeschwindigkeit f

windward side · Windseite f

wing, limb · Seitengebäude n, Nebengebäude, Gebäudeflügel m, Abseite f, (Erweiterungs)Flügel, Hausflügel, Seitenhaus n, Nebenhaus

~ masonry wall · Flügelmauer f

~ pavilion, angle ~ · Eckpavillon m, Winkelpavillon

~ wall → return ~

winged bull · Flügelstier m

~ horse · Flügelroß n

~ lion · geflügelter Löwe m

Winkler's value — wire lath(ing)

Winkler's value · Winklersche Zahl *f* [*Zahlenwert zur Bestimmung der Biegemomente und Querkräfte von Durchlaufträgern*]

winter (air) conditioning system, ~ (~) ~ plant, ~ (~) ~ installation · Winter-Klima(tisierungs)anlage *f*

~ **building (construction)** · Winterhochbau *m*

~ **concreting**, ~ pouring (of concrete) · Betonieren *n* im Winter

~ **conditioning installation** → ~ (air) conditioning system

~ ~ **plant** → ~ (air) conditioning system

~ ~ **system** → ~ air ~ ~

~ **construction**, construction in freezing weather · Winterbau *m*

~ **garden** · Wintergarten *m*

~ **service** · Winterbetrieb *m* [*Heizung*]

~ **shutdown** · Stillegung *f* im Winter

~ **window** · Kastenfenster *n*, Winterfenster [*Ein doppeltes Fenster. Die Fensterflügel haben einen Abstand von 9 cm; das die beiden Blendrahmen verbindende Holz bildet den ,,Kasten"*]

wintering, weathering · Auswintern *n* [*Lagern von Rohstoffen über den Winter. Anmerkung: Der Ausdruck ,,wintering", der dem Wort ,,Auswintern" entsprechen würde, wird in Großbritannien nicht gebraucht, sondern nur ,,weathering"*]

wire, metal ~ · (Metall)Draht *m*

~ **anchor**, ~ tie · Drahtanker *m*

~ **article**, ~ product · Drahtartikel *m*, Drahterzeugnis *n*, Drahtgegenstand *m*

~ **brad** [*A small headless nail made from wire*] · Drahtnagel *m*, Drahtstift *m*

~ **brushing** · (Ab)Bürsten *n* mit Drahtbürste

~ **cable**, ~ rope · (Draht)Kabel *n*, Drahtseil *n*, Stahl(draht)seil

~ ~ **anchorage**, ~ rope ~ · (Draht-)Kabelverankerung *f*, Drahtseilverankerung, Stahl(draht)seilverankerung

~ ~ **clamp**, ~ rope ~ · (Draht)Kabelklemme *f*, Drahtseilklemme, Stahl(draht)seilklemme

~ ~ **construction**, ~ rope ~ · (Draht-)Kabelmachart *f*, Drahtseilmachart, Stahl(draht)seilmachart

~ ~ **grease**, ~ rope ~ · (Draht)Kabelfett *n*, Drahtseilfett, Stahl(draht)seilfett

~ ~ **guard**, ~ rope ~ · (Draht)Kabelschutzverkleidung *f*, Drahtseilschutzverkleidung, Stahl(draht)seilschutzverkleidung

~ ~ **level**, ~ rope ~ · (Draht)Kabelhöhe *f*, Drahtseilhöhe, Stahl(draht)seilhöhe

~ ~ **lubricant**, ~ rope ~ · (Draht)Kabelschmiermittel *n*, Drahtseilschmiermittel, Stahl(draht)seilschmiermittel

~ ~ **spacer** · (Draht)Kabelabstandhalter *m*, Drahtseilabstandhalter, Stahl(draht)seilabstandhalter

~ ~ **wander**, ~ rope ~ · (Draht)Kabelwandern *n*, Drahtseilwandern, Stahl(draht)seilwandern

~ **comb**, ~ scratcher · Drahtkamm *m* [*zum Aufrauhen von Putz*]

wire-cut brick [*A brick shaped by extrusion and then cut to length by wire*] · Strangpreßziegel *m*

~ **brickmaking**, stiff mud process · Strangpreßverfahren *n* [*Ziegelherstellung*]

wire-drawer · Drahtzieher *m*

(wire) drawing, cold work ~ · (Draht)-Ziehen *n*

(wire-)drawing block · (Draht)Ziehtrommel *f*

~ **die**, (reducing) ~ · Zieheisen *n*, Ziehstein *m*, Draht~

~ ~ **orifice**, die ~ · Zieh(eisen)düse *f*, Ziehsteindüse, Draht~

~ **machine** · (Draht)Ziehbank *f*

wire duct [*A tube or conduit used for encasing either moving or stationary wire*] · Drahtkanal *m*

~ **enamel**, ~ lacquer · Drahtlack *m*

~ **fence** · Drahtzaun *m*

~ ~ **picket** → ~ ~ stake

~ ~ **post** → ~ ~ stake

~ ~ **stake**, ~ ~ picket, ~ ~ post, ~ fencing ~ · Drahtzaunpfahl *m*, Drahtzaunpfosten *m*

~ **fencing picket** → ~ fence stake

~ ~ **post** → ~ fence stake

~ ~ **stake** → ~ fence ~

~ **figure(d) glass** → figure(d) wire(d) ~

~ **flat glass** → wire(d) ~ ~

~ **galvanizing** · Drahtverzinkung *f*

~ **gauze**, lawn · Drahtgaze *f*

~ **glass** → wired ~

~ ~ **mesh** → wire(d) mesh

~ **grade** · Drahtsorte *f*

~ **gun** · Pistole *f* für das Drahtspritzverfahren, Spritz~ ~ ~ ~ [*Spritzmetallisierung*]

~ **hanger** [*It is used to secure metal channels to overhead joists in suspended ceiling systems*] · Draht(ab)hänger *m*, Drahthängeglied *n*

~ **hook** · Drahthaken *m*

~ **insert(ion)**, ~ layer, layer of wire · Drahteinlage *f*

~ **lacquer**, ~ enamel · Drahtlack *m*

~ **laminated glass** → wired ~ ~

~ **lath(ing)**, welded ~ ~ · (geschweißtes) Drahtgewebe *n*, (~) Rabitzgewebe

~ **lath(ing)** · Drahtputzträger *m*

wire lath(ing) and . . . — wire(d) glass light cupola 1124

~ ~ **and (cement) rendering partition (wall)** · Zement-Drahtputzwand f

~ ~ ~ **plaster duct** · Drahtputzkanal m

~ ~ ~ ~ **suspended ceiling,** ~ ~ ~ ~ suspension ~ · (hängende) Drahtputzdecke f [*DIN 4121*]

~ ~ ~ ~ **wall** · Drahtputzwand f [*Beiderseits verputzte Wand aus mit Mörtel ausgedrücktem Rabitzgewebe, Ziegeldrahtgewebe oder Streckmetall, das auf einem weitmaschigen Rundstahlgitter aufgespannt ist*]

~ **layer,** layer of wire, wire insert(ion) · Drahteinlage f

~ **loop** · Drahtschlaufe f

~ **mat** → wired ~

~ **mesh** [*Wire mesh is made by two methods; by weaving or twisting metal wires or by welding the metal wires*] · Drahtmaschenmatte f

~ ~ **fence** · Drahtmaschenzaun m

~ ~ **lath(ing)** · Drahtmaschenmatte f als Putzträger

~ **nail,** brad [*A small headless nail. B.S. 1202*] · Drahtnagel m, (Draht-) Stift m

~ **netting** · Drahtgeflecht n

~ ~ **fence** · Drahtgeflechtzaun m

~ ~ **for construction(al) purposes** · Baudrahtgeflecht n

~ ~ **lath(ing)** · Putz(träger)drahtgeflecht n

~ **of irregular shape,** indented wire, profil(ed) wire · Dessindraht m, Formdraht, Profildraht, Fassondraht, profilierter Draht

~ **pattern(ed) glass** → figure(d) wire(d) ~

~ **plate (glass)** → (flat) wire(d) (clear) (polished) ~ (~)

~ **(polished) plate (glass)** → (flat) wire(d) clear (~) ~ (~)

~ **product,** ~ article · Drahtartikel m, Drahterzeugnis n, Drahtgegenstand m

~ **reinforced** · drahtverstärkt

~ **reinforcement** · Drahtverstärkung f

~ **rod** [*While the wire rod represents a finished product of the rolling mills, it constitutes the raw material used in the wire mill and should be considered as the first step in the making of wire*] · Walzdraht m

~ ~ **for screws** · Schrauben(walz)draht m

wire-rod mill · Walzdrahtwerk n

wire rod rolling, rolling the wire rod · Drahtwalzen n

~ **rope,** ~ cable · (Draht)Kabel n, Drahtseil n, Stahl(draht)seil

~ ~ **anchorage,** ~ cable ~ · (Draht)Kabelverankerung f, Drahtseilverankerung, Stahl(draht)seilverankerung

~ ~ **clamp,** ~ cable ~ · (Draht)Kabelklemme f, Drahtseilklemme, Stahl(draht)seilklemme

~ ~ **construction,** ~ cable ~ · (Draht)-Kabelmachart f, Drahtseilmachart, Stahl(draht)seilmachart

~ ~ **grease,** ~ cable ~ · (Draht)Kabelfett n, Drahtseilfett, Stahl(draht)seilfett

~ ~ **guard,** ~ cable ~ · (Draht)Kabelschutzverkleidung f, Drahtseilschutzverkleidung, Stahl(draht)seilschutzverkleidung

~ ~ **level,** ~ cable ~ · (Draht)Kabelhöhe f, Drahtseilhöhe, Stahl(draht)seilhöhe

~ ~ **lubricant,** ~ cable ~ · (Draht)Kabelschmiermittel n, Drahtseilschmiermittel, Stahl(draht)seilschmiermittel

~ ~ **wander,** ~ cable ~ · (Draht)Kabelwandern n, Drahtseilwandern, Stahl(draht)seilwandern

~ **section** · Drahtquerschnitt m

~ **sensitivity** (Brit.); penetrameter ~ (US); radiographic ~ · Drahterkennbarkeit f, DE [*bei einem Drahtsteg*]

~ **slip** · Drahtschlupf m

~ **spacer** · Drahtabstandhalter m

(~) **staple** · (Draht)Krampe f

~ **stirrup** · Drahtbügel m

~ **stress** · Drahtspannung f

~ **thickness** · Drahtdicke f [*Fehlname: Drahtstärke f*]

~ **tie** · Windklammer f [*Dach*]

~ ~, ~ anchor · Drahtanker m

wire-winding machine, preload ~ · Wickelmaschine f [*Herstellung von Spannbetonbehältern*]

wire(d) (clear) plate (glass) → (flat) wire(d) (clear) polished ~ (~)

~ (~) **(polished) plate (glass)** → flat ~ (~) (~) ~ (~)

~ **decorative glass** → figure(d) wire(d) ~

~ **figure(d) glass** → figure(d) wire(d) ~

~ **flat glass,** flat wire(d) ~ · Drahtflachglas n, Flachdrahtlglas

~ **glass** · Drahtglas n [*DIN 4102. Rohglas mit eingewalzter Drahteinlage, wodurch erhöhte Bruchfestigkeit und Belastungsfähigkeit erzielt werden*]

~ ~ **caisson,** ~ ~ waffle, ~ ~ cassette- ~ ~ coffer, ~ ~ pan · Drahtglas-(decken)kassette f

~ ~ **cassette,** ~ ~ caisson, ~ ~ waffle, ~ ~ coffer, ~ ~ pan · Drahtglas(decken)kassette f

~ ~ **coffer,** ~ ~ waffle, ~ ~ cassette, ~ ~ pan, ~ ~ caisson · Drahtglas-(decken)kassette f

~ ~ **domed rooflight** → ~ ~ dome-(light)

~ ~ **dome(light),** ~ ~ light cupola, ~ ~ saucer dome, ~ ~ dome rooflight · Drahtglas(licht)kuppel f

~ ~ **light cupola** → ~ ~ dome(light)

~ ~ **pan,** ~ ~ coffer, ~ ~ waffle, ~ ~ cassette, ~ ~ caisson · Drahtglas(dek, ken)kasssette f

~ ~ **saucer dome** → ~ ~ dome(light)

~ ~ **waffle,** ~ ~ cassette, ~ ~ caisson, ~ ~ coffer, ~ ~ pan · Drahtglas(dek(ken)kassette f

~ **laminated glass,** laminated wire(d) ~ · Drahtverbund(sicherheits)glas n, Stahlfadenverbundglas, Drahtsicherheitsglas

~ **mat** · Platte f auf Drahtgeflecht gesteppt [*aus Mineralwolle*]

~ **opaque white glass,** ~ milk-glass · Milchdrahtglas n

~ **ornamental glass** → figure(d) wire(d) ~

~ **pattern(ed) glass** · figure(d) wire(d) ~

~ **plate (glass)** → (flat) wire(d) (clear) (polished) ~ (~)

~ **(polished) plate (glass)** → (flat) wire(d) clear (~) → (~)

wiring, electric(al) ~ · (Elektro)Verdrahtung f, elektrische Verdrahtung

(~) **conduit,** electrical ~ · Elektroleerrohr n, (Elt)Leerrohr

(~) ~ **line,** electrical ~ ~ · Elektroleerrohrleitung f, (Elt)Leerrohrleitung

(~) ~ **network,** electrical ~ · Elektroleerrohrnetz n, (Elt)Leerrohrnetz

~ **layout** · Verdrahtungsführung f

~ **switch,** branch ~ · Installationsschalter m [*Installationsschalter sind kleine, hauptsächlich für Lichtanlagen verwendete Schalter, je nach Betätigung Dreh-, Kipp-, Druckknopf- und Zugschalter, für Montage auf oder unter Putz, in normaler Ausführung für trockene Räume oder in wasserdichter und stoßfester Ausführung für feuchte Räume*]

with cellar · unterkellert

~ **closed cells** · geschlossenzellig [*Kunststoffmasse*]

~ **diamond pattern,** ~ lozenge ~, diamond-patterned, lozenge-patterned · gerautet

~ **facets** · facettiert

~ **fixed ends,** without articulations, rigid, no-hinged, hingeless, fixed, encastré, encastered · eingespannt, gelenklos [*Bogen; Träger; Stütze; Balken(träger); Rahmen(tragwerk)*]

~ **hammer(tone) finish** · hammerschlaglackiert

~ **hard-stoved enamel finish** · eingebrannt lackiert

~ **interconnecting cells** · offenzellig [*Kunststoffmasse*]

~ **lozenge pattern,** ~ diamond ~, diamond-patterned, lozenge-patterned · gerautet

~ **marbleizing penetrating to full depth of the wear layer** [*Of a floor covering*] · durchjaspiert

~ **merlons** → battlemented

~ **parallel booms,** ~ ~ chords, ~ ~ flanges · parallelgurtig

~ ~ **chords,** ~ ~ booms, ~ ~ flanges · parallelgurtig

~ ~ **flanges,** ~ ~ booms, ~ ~ chords · parallelgurtig

~ **raised portions** → battlemented

~ **red-brown top layer,** ~ ~ ~ course [*This layer is from 8 mm to 10 mm thick*] · (rotbraun) aufgelegt [*Hochdruck-Asphaltplatte*]

withdrawal clinic · Entziehungsheim n

withe, wythe, leaf, layer, tier, shell, skin [*cavity wall*] · Schale f, Wand~ [*Hohlwand*]

~, **mid-feather** · Schornsteinzunge f [*Trenn(ungs)mauer der Rauchkanäle*]

witherite, barium carbonate · Bariumkarbonat n, Bariumcarbonat, BaCO$_3$

without articulations, with fixed ends, rigid, no-hinged, hingeless, fixed, encastré, encastered · eingespannt, gelenklos [*Bogen; Träger; Stütze; Balken(träger); Rahmen(tragwerk)*]

backing, ~ base · trägerlos, trägerfrei [*Bahn*]

~ **base,** ~ backing · trägerfrei, trägerlos [*Bahn*]

~ **filler(s)** · ungefüllert, nichtgefüllert

~ **plasticiser** (Brit.); ~ plasticizer (US) · weichmacherfrei, weichmacherlos

WL, wind load [*The force exerted by wind on a structure of part of a structure*] · Verkehrslast f aus Wind, Windlast [*DIN 1055 Bl. 4*]

WL, warning light, alarm light · Warnleuchte f, Warnlampe f, Warnlicht n, optisches Warnsignal n

wlbd., wallboard · Wand(bau)platte f

wobble coefficient [*A coefficient used in determining the friction loss occurring in post-tensioning, which is assumed to account for the secondary curvature of the tendons*] · Reib(ungs)beiwert m bei Spanngliedern mit gekrümmtem Verlauf

Wöhler curve, N-S ~ · Zeitfestigkeitskurve f, Wöhler-Linie f

wollastonite · Wollastonit m [*natürliches oder synthetisches Kalziummetasilikat*]

women's changing room, ladies' ~ ~, female ~ ~ · Damenumkleide(raum) f, (m), Frauenumkleide(raum)

~ **(drawing) room,** ladies' (~) ~, female (~) ~ [*See remark under 'drawing room'*] · Damenzimmer n, Damenraum m

~ **gallery** · Frauenempore f

~ **hairdressing shop,** ladies' ~ ~, female ~ ~ · Damen(friseur)salon m

~ **quarter,** harim, haram ·hare(e)m Harem m

~ **quarters** · Frauengemächer npl

~ **room** → ~ drawing ~

~ **toilet,** female ~ ladies, ~ · Damentoilette f

wood alcohol, methyl ~, methanol [*B.S. 506*] · Methanol *n*, Methylalkohol *m*, Holzgeist *m*, CH₃OH

~ and brick-clad home, timber ~ ~ ~ · Holz-Ziegel-Haus *n*

~ ash · Holzasche *f*

~ bark tar · Baumrindenteer *m*

~ base → wooden base(board) (US)

wood-based product · holzhaltiges Erzeugnis *n*

wood block · Holzmodel *m* [*für Tapetenhanddruck*]

(~) ~ parquet(ry) (flooring), (~) ~ ~ floor finish (~) ~ ~ floor cover(ing) · Stabparkett *n*

~ boards, ~ siding · Bretterverschalung *f*, Bretterwandschirm *m*, Bretterwandbeschlag *m*, Bretterwetterschirm, Verbretterung [*Wetterschutz für Außenmauern und Außenwände*]

~ built-in units, ~ in-built ~, ~ fixtures, ~ trim, (~) mill work · Holzeinbauten *f*, Holzeinbauteile *mpl*, *npl*, Bautischlereinbauten

wood-carving · Holzschnitzerei *f*

wood chip absorbent ceiling board → ~ particle acoustic(al) ~ ~

~ concrete · Holzbeton *m* [*Holzbetone werden mit Holzspänen, Sägemehl, Holzabfällen oder Holzfasern als Zuschlagstoffe und mit Normenzementen als Bindemittel hergestellt*]

~ ~, chipped ~ ~ · Holzspanbeton *m*, Holzspänebeton

~ ~ block, ~ ~ tile, precast ~ ~ ~ [*See remark under 'Block(stein)'*] · Holzbetonblock(stein) *m*, Holzbetonstein

~ ~ filler → ~ ~ soffit (floor filler) block

~ ~ roof(ing) slab · Holzbetondachplatte *f*

~ ~ slab · Holzbetonplatte *f*

~ ~ soffit (floor filler) block, ~ ~ (~ ~) tile, ~ ~ filler [*See remark under 'Block(stein)'*] · Holzbeton-Deckenstein *m*, Holzbeton-Deckenblock(stein) *m*, Holzbeton-(Decken)Füllblock(stein), Holzbeton(decken)füllstein, Holzbetondeckenbaustein

~ ~ tile, ~ ~ block, precast ~ ~ ~ [*See remark under 'Block(stein)'*] · Holzbetonblock(stein) *m*, Holzbetonstein

~ connection, timber ~, ~ joint · Holzverbindung *f*

~ connector → (timber) ~

~ construction, timber ~ · Holzbau *m*

woodcut · Holzschnitt *m* [*Abdruck eines geschnittenen Holzstockes*]

wood-distilling plant · Holzdestillieranlage *f*

(wood) excelsior (US); ~ wool (Brit.) · Holzwolle *f* [*DIN 4077*]

(~) ~ absorbent board (US) → ~ wool acoustic(al) ~

(~) ~ ~ sheet (US) → ~ wool acoustic(al) board

(~) ~ acoustic(al) board (US) → ~ wool ~ ~

(~) ~ ~ sheet (US) → ~ wool acoustic(al) board

(~) ~ (building) slab (US) → ~ wool (~) ~

(~) ~ concrete (US); ~ wool ~ (Brit.) · Holzwollebeton *m*

(~) ~ ~ slab (US); ~ wool cement ~ [*B.S. 1105*] · Holzwollebetonplatte *f*

(~) ~ covering rope (US); ~ wool ~ ~ (Brit.) · Holzwolleseil [*für Dämm- und Isolierzwecke*]

(~) ~ hollow filler (US); ~ wool ~ ~ (Brit.) · Holzwolle-(Decken)Hohlkörper *m*

(~) ~ insulation (US); ~ wool ~ (Brit.) · Holzwolle(ab)dämmung *f*

(~) ~ slab (US) → ~ wool (building) ~

(~) ~ ~ partition (wall) (US); ~ wool ~ ~ (~) (Brit.) · Holzwolle-Leichtbauplatten-Trennwand *f*

(~) ~ sound-control board (US) → ~ wool acoustic(al) ~

(~) ~ ~ sheet (US) → ~ wool acoustic(al) board

~ fiber concrete (US) → ~ fibre ~

~ ~ plaster baseboard (US); ~ fibre ~ ~ (Brit.) · Putzträgerplatte *f* aus Holzfasern, Holzfaser-Putzträgerplatte

~ ~ silicification (US) → ~ fibre ~

~ fiberboard absorbent ceiling → fibreboard acoustic(al) ~

~ ~ absorbing ceiling (US) → ~ fibreboard acoustic(al) ~

~ ~ absorptive ceiling (US) → ~ fibreboard acoustic(al) ~

~ ~ acoustic tiled ceiling (US) → ~ fibreboard acoustic(al) ~

~ ~ acoustic(al) ceiling (US) → ~ fibreboard ~ ~

~ ~ (sound) absorbent ceiling (US) → ~ fibreboard acoustic(al) ~

~ ~ (~) absorbing ceiling (US) → ~ fibreboard acoustic(al) ~

~ ~ (~) absorptive ceiling (US) → ~ fibreboard acoustic(al) ~

~ ~ sound-control ceiling (US) → ~ fibreboard accoustic(al) ~

wood-fiber(ed) plaster (US) → wood-fibre(d) ~

wood fibre concrete (Brit.); ~ fiber ~ (US) · Holzfaserbeton *m*

~ ~ plaster baseboard (Brit.); ~ fiber ~ ~ (US) · Holzfaser-Putzträgerplatte *f*, Putzträgerplatte aus Holzfasern

~ ~ silicification (Brit.); ~ fiber ~ (US) · Holzfaserverkieselung *f*

(~) fibreboard (Brit.); (~) fiberboard (US) · (Holz)Faserplatte *f* [*DIN 68750*]

1127 (wood) fibreboard acoustic(al) ceiling — (wood) shingle

(∼) ∼ acoustic(al) ceiling (Brit.); ∼ fiberboard ∼ ∼ (US); ∼ ∼ sound-control ∼, ∼ ∼ (sound) absorbent ∼, ∼ ∼ (sound) absorbing ∼, ∼ ∼ (sound) absorptive ∼, ∼ ∼ acoustic tiled ∼ · (Holz)Faser(platten)-Akustikdecke *f*, (Holz)Faser(platten)-Schallschluckdecke

(∼) ∼ ceiling (Brit.); (∼) fiberboard ∼ (US) · (Holz)Faserplattenraumdecke *f*

wood-fibre(d) plaster (Brit.); wood-fiber(ed) ∼ (US) · Holzfaser(innen)-(ver)putz *m*

wood(-finishing) lacquer · Holzlack *m*

wood finishings · Holzinnenausbau *m*

∼ fixtures, ∼ trim, (∼) mill work, ∼ in-built units, ∼ built-in units · Holzeinbauten *f*, Holzeinbauteile *mpl, npl*, Bautischlereinbauten

∼ flour · Holzmehl *n*

wood-frame(d) construction, timber-frame(d) ∼ · Holzrahmenkonstruktion *f*

∼ façade, timber-frame(d) ∼ · Holzrahmenfassade *f*

∼ mirror, timber-frame(d) ∼ · Holzrahmenspiegel *m*

∼ in-built units, ∼ built-in ∼, ∼ fixtures, ∼ trim, (∼) mill work · Holzeinbauten *f*, Holzeinbauteile *mpl, npl*, Bautischlereinbauten

wood in building sizes, sawn engineered timber, sawed engineered timber, cut engineered timber, construction lumber (US) · Schnittholz für Ingenieurholzbau, Bauschnittholz

∼ joint, timber ∼ ∼ connection · Holzverbindung *f*

∼ joining method, timber ∼ ∼ · Holzverbindungsverfahren *n*

∼ lacquer, ∼-finishing ∼ · Holzlack *m*

∼ lath (for plastering) [*B.S. 1317*] · Holzstab *m* [*als Putzträger*]

∼ lath(ing) (for plastering) [*B.S. 1317*] · (Holz)Stabgewebe *n* [*Putzträger*]

∼ laths for plastering [*B.S. 1317*] · Holzlatten-Putzträger *m*

wood-lined passage, timber-lined ∼ · holzverkleideter Gang *m*

wood lintel; ∼ lintol [*deprecated*] · Überlagsholz *n* [*Entlastungsbogen*]

∼ metal window · Holz-Metall-Fenster *n*

(∼) mill work, ∼ trim, ∼ fixtures, ∼ in-built units, ∼ built-in units · Holzeinbauten *f*, Holzeinbauteile *mp, npl*, Bautischlereinbauten

∼ mosaic floor(ing), ∼ ∼ floor finish, ∼ ∼ floor cover(ing) [*B.S. 4050*] · Holzmosaik(fuß)boden(belag) *m*

∼ nailing strip · Holznagelstreifen *m*

∼ oil → (raw) China ∼ ∼

wood-oil reactive resin · holzölreaktives Harz *n*

wood oil stand oil, China ∼ ∼ ∼ ∼ tung ∼ ∼ ∼ · Holzöl-Standöl *n*, Tungöl-Standöl

∼ ∼ varnish, China ∼ ∼ ∼, tung ∼ ∼ · Tungöllack *m*

∼ particle acoustic(al) ceiling board, ∼ chip ∼ ∼ ∼, ∼ ∼ ∼ ∼ tile, ∼ ∼ ∼ ∼ sheet, ∼ ∼ (sound) absorbent ∼ ∼, ∼ ∼ (sound) absorbing ∼ ∼, ∼ ∼ (sound) absorptive ∼ ∼, ∼ ∼ sound-control ∼ ∼ · (Holz)Span-Schallschluckdeckenplatte *f*, (Holz)Span-Akustikdeckenplatte, (Holz)Span-Deckenschallschluckplatte, (Holz)Span-Deckenakustikplatte, (Holz)Spanleichtplatte, (Holz)Leichtspanplatte, leichte (Holz)Spandeckenplatte

∼ ∼ material, chipped wood ∼ · Holzspanwerkstoff *m*, HSW

∼ patio door, ∼ terrace ∼ · Terrassen-Holztür *f*

∼ pavior · Holzpflasterer *m*

∼ pitch · Holzpech *n*

∼ plastic article, ∼ ∼ product · Holz-Kunststoff-Erzeugnis *n*, Holz-Kunststoff-Gegenstand *m*, Holz-Kunststoff-Artikel *m*

∼ ∼ parquet(ry) · Holz-Kunststoff-Parkett *n*

∼ ∼ product, ∼ ∼ article · Holz-Kunststoff-Erzeugnis *n*, Holz-Kunststoff-Gegenstand *m*, Holz-Kunststoff-Artikel *m*

∼ ∼ window · Holz-Kunststoff-Fenster *n*

wood/polymer composite · Polymerholz *n*

wood preservation · Holzkonservierung *f*

(∼) preservative, (∼) preserver [*B.S. 1282*] · (Holz)Konservierungsmittel *n*, (Holz)Schutzmittel, (Holz)Imprägnier(ungs)mittel [*DIN 52163/64. Grundsätzlich unterscheidet man zwei Gruppen von Holzschutzmitteln: 1 Die wasserlöslichen Mittel, 2. Die öligen, ölartigen und öllöslichen Mittel*]

(∼) ∼ salt, (wood-)protecting salt, salt-type (wood) preservative · Schutzsalz *n*, Holz∼

(wood-)protecting salt, salt-type (wood) preservative, (wood) preservative salt · (Holz)Schutzsalz *n*

wood roll · Holzkern *m* [*Durch Drücken der Bleiblechkante über einem Holzkern wird der Holzwulst gebildet*]

wood-roofed basilica, wooden-roofed ∼ · holzgedeckte Basilika *f*

wood rosin · Wurzelharz *n* [*Siehe Anmerkung unter "Kolophonium"*]

∼ sash putty · Holzfensterkitt *m*

∼ screw [*B.S. 1210*] · Holzschraube *f*

∼ sculpture, sculpture in wood · Holzplastik *f*, Holzskulptur *f*

(∼) shake → hand cleft (wood) shingle

∼ shavings tar · Hobelspäneteer *m*

(∼) shingle, wooden ∼ [*A short thin rectangular piece of timber, usually*

(wood) shingle — wood(en) batten

tapering in thickness along the grain, used in the same way as tiles for covering the roofs and sides of buildings] · (Holz)Schindel f, Spitzbrett n

~ **siding**, ~ boards · Bretterverschalung f, Bretterwandschirm m, Bretterwandbeschlag m, Bretterwetterschirm, Verbretterung [*Wetterschutz für Außenmauern und Außenwände*]

~ ~ **shake** → hand cleft (wood) sinding shingle

~ ~ **shingle** · Wand-Holzschindel f, Holz-Wandschindel f

~ **splittings tar** · Holzsplitterteer m

(~) **stain** · (Holz)Beize f

(~) **staining** · (Holz)Beizen n

~ **stand oil**, China ~ ~ ~, tung ~ ~ · Holzstandöl n, Tungstandöl

wood-stave pipe → machine-banded ~

wood strength, timber ~ · Holzfestigkeit f

(**wood-)strip flooring**, inlaid-strip ~, ~ floor (finish), ~ floor cover(ing) · Riemen(fuß)boden m, Wiener Stab(fuß)boden, Schiffs(fuß)boden, Bandparkett n

wood-stud partition (wall), timber-stud ~ (~) · Holzgerippetrennwand f [*DIN 4103*]

~ **wall**, timber-stud ~ · Holzgerippewand f

wood tar, Stockholm ~, Archangel ~ · Holzteer m

wood-tar creosote · Holzteerkreosot n

~ **pitch** · Holzteerpech n

wood terrace door, ~ patio ~ · Terrassen-Holztür f

~ **tin** · Holzzinn n

wood-to-metal connection, ~ joint, timber-to-metal ~ · Holz-Metall-Verbindung f

~ **joint**, ~ connection, timber-to-metal ~ · Holz-Metall-Verbindung f

wood-to-wood connection, ~ joint, timber-to-timber ~ · Holz-Holz-Verbindung f

~ **joint**, ~ connection, timber-to-timber ~ · Holz-Holz-Verbindung f

wood trim, ~ in-built units, ~ fixtures, (~) mill work, ~ built-in units · Holzeinbauten m, Holzeinbauteile mpl, npl, Bautischlereinbauten

~ **turpentine**, oil of turpentine [*It is obtained by the distillation of scrap wood such as sawdust and tree stumps containing resin instead of the balsam from the living trees*] · Holzterpentinöl n, Wurzelterpentinöl

~ **vault** → wooden ~

~ **waste tar** · Holzabfallteer m

~ **wool** (Brit.); (~) excelsior (US) · Holzwolle f [*DIN 4077*]

~ ~ **absorbent board** → ~ ~ ~ accoustic(al) ~

~ ~ ~ **sheet** → ~ ~ ~ acoustic(al) board

~ ~ **acoustic(al) board**, ~ ~ ~ sheet, ~ ~ sound-control ~ (Brit.); (~) excelsior ~ ~, (~) excelsior absorbent board, (~) excelsior absorbent sheet (US); ~ wool absorbent board, ~ wool absorbent sheet (Brit.) · Holzwolle-Akustikplatte f, Holzwolle-Schallschluckplatte

~ ~ ~ **sheet** → ~ ~ ~ ~ board

~ ~ (**building) slab** [*B.S. 1105*] (~) excelsior (~) ~ (US) · Holzwolle-(-Leichtbau)platte f [*DIN 1101 und 1102. Genormtes Kurzzeichen nach DIN 4076: HWP*]

~ ~ **cement slab** [*B.S. 1105*]; (~) excelsior concrete ~ (US) · Holzwollebetonplatte f

~ ~ **concrete** (Brit.); (~) excelsior ~ (US) · Holzwollebeton m

~ ~ **covering rope** (Brit.); (~) excelsior ~ ~ (US) · Holzwolleseil n [*für Dämm- und Isolierzwecke*]

~ ~ **hollow filler** (Brit.); (~) excelsior ~ ~ (US) · Holzwolle-(Decken)Hohlkörper m

~ ~ **insulation** (Brit.); (~) excelsior ~ (US) · Holzwolle(ab)dämmung f

~ ~ **permanent formwork**, ~ ~ ~ shuttering, ~ ~ ~ forms [*B.S. 3809*] · Dauerschalung f aus Holzwolleplatten

~ ~ **slab** → ~ ~ ~ building ~

~ ~ ~ **partition (wall)** (Brit.); (~) excelsior ~ ~ (~) (US) · Holzwolle-Leichtbauplatten-Trennwand f

~ ~ **sound-control board** → ~ ~ acoustic(al) ~

~ ~ ~ **sheet** → ~ ~ ~ acoustic(al) board

wooded site · baumbestandenes Grundstück n

wood(en) arch, timber ~ · Holzbogen m

~ **baluster**, ~ ban(n)ister, timber ~ · Docke f, Togge f

~ **ban(n)ister**, ~ baluster, timber ~ · Docke f, Togge f

~ **base**, ~ ground, timber ~ · Holz-(unter)grund m

~ ~ (**board**), ~ scrub board, ~ sanitary cove, ~ mopboard, ~ washboard (US); ~ skirting (board) (Brit.); ~ base plate [*Scotland*] · Sockelbrett n, Holzfußleiste f, Holzscheuerleiste, Holzsockelleiste [*DIN 68125*]

~ ~ **plate** [*Scotland*]; ~ skirting (board) (Brit.); ~ washboard, ~ mopboard, ~ scrub board, ~ sanitary cove, ~ base (board) (US) · Sockelbrett n, Holzfußleiste f, Holzscheuerleiste, Holzsockelleiste [*DIN 68125*]

~ **baseplate**, timber ~ · Holzgrundplatte f

~ **batten**, timber ~ · Holz-Fugendeckleiste f

~ ~, timber ~ [*For slating and tiling. B.S. 1318*] · Holzleiste f

~ ~, timber ~ · Holzlatte f

wood(en) beam — wood(en) framework wall

~ **beam**, timber ~ · Holzbalken(träger) m

~ ~ **floor**, timber ~ ~, ~ joist ~, single timber ~ · Holzbalken(träger)-decke f [*DIN 104*]

~ **bearing structure** → ~ load~ ~

~ **bevel siding**, weatherboarding · Stülp-(bretter)schalung f aus abgeschrägten Brettern [*Wetterschutz für Außenwände*]

~ **binder** → ~ binding beam

~ **binding beam**, timber ~ ~, ~ ~ joist, ~ binder · Holzbinderbalken m, Holzbundbalken

~ ~ **joist** → ~ ~ beam

~ **block**, ~ paving ~ · (Holz)Pflasterklotz m, Holzstöckel m, (Holz)Pflasterstöckel [*DIN 68701*]

~ ~ **pavement**, ~ ~ paving · Holzpflaster(decke) n, (f), Stöckelpflaster(decke)

~ ~ **paving**, ~ ~ pavement · Holzpflaster(decke) n, (f) Stöckelpflaster(decke)

~ **board lining** · Bretterauskleidung f, Bretterverkleidung, Bretterbekleidung

~ ~ **sheathing**, timber ~ ~ · Bretter-(ver)schalung f

~ **brad** · Hartholzstift m

~ **broach** → ~ spire

~ **building block module**, timber ~ ~ ~, ~ unitized unit · Holz(raum)zelle f

~ **casement window** · Holzflügelfenster n

~ **chipboard**, ~ particle board · Holzspanplatte f, Spanholzplatte [*DIN 68761*]

~ **church**, timber ~ · Holzkirche f

~ **ciborium**, timber ~ · Holzciborium n, Holzziborium, Holzbaldachin m

~ **cistern**, timber ~ · Holzzisterne f

~ **column**, timber ~; ~ stanchion (Brit.) · Holzstütze f

~ ~, timber ~ · Holzsäule f

~ (~) **Order** · Holzsäulenordnung f

~ **comb** · Holzkamm m

~ **construction** → ~ (structural) system

~ ~ **type**, timber ~ ~, ~ type of construction · Holzbauart f

~ **core** · Holzmittellage f

~ **counter ceiling**, timber ~ ~ · Holzunterdecke f

~ **dome**, timber ~ · Holzkuppel f

~ **door**, timber ~ · Holztür f

~ ~ **frame**, timber ~ ~ [*B.S. 1567*] · Holz-Tür(blend)rahmen m, Holz-Türfutter(rahmen) n, (m)

~ (~) **threshold**, timber (~) ~ · Holz(tür)schwelle f

~ **dowel**, timber ~ · Stab-Holzdübel m, Holz(stab)dübel, Holzdollen m

~ **eave(s) gutter**, ~ ~ trow ~ ~ trough, timber ~ ~ · Holz(-Dach)traufrinne f

~ **facing** → timber lining

~ **fastener**, timber ~ · (Holz)Verbinde m, (Holz)Verbindungsmittel n [*Dübel Bolzen, Nägel, Klammern und Schrauben, die die Holzverbindungen dauerhaft und für den jeweilig beabsichtigten Zweck geeignet machen*]

~ **fence**, timber ~ · Holzzaun m

~ (~) **post**, timber (~) ~ · Holzzaunpfahl m, Holz(zaun)pfosten m

~ **fencing**, timber ~ · Holzeinzäunung f, Holzumzäunung

~ **finger plate** · Holzschonschild n [*Baubeschlag*]

~ **firring**, ~ furring · Holz-Unterkonstruktion f [*Putztechnik*]

~ **flat roof**, timber ~ ~, flat wood(en) ~, flat timber ~ · Holzflachdach n, Flachholzdach

~ **floating floor cover(ing)**, timber ~ ~ ~, ~ ~ floor(ing) (finish) · schwimmender Holz(fuß)boden(belag) m, Holz(fuß)boden(belag) auf Lagerhölzern mit Dämmstreifen-Unterlagen

~ ~ **floor(ing) (finish)**, ~ ~ floor cover(ing), timber ~ ~ ~ · Holz(fuß)-boden(belag) m auf Lagerhölzern mit Dämmstreifen-Unterlagen, schwimmender Holz(fuß)boden(belag)

~ **floor**, timber ~ · Holz(-Gebäude)decke f, Holz-Etagendecke, Holz-Stockwerkdecke, Holz-Geschoßdecke, Holz-Trenndecke, Holz-Hochbaudecke

~ ~ **cover(ing)**, timber ~ ~, ~ floor(ing) (finish) · Holz(fuß)boden(belag) m, Fh

~ ~ **(finish)** → ~ flooring (~)

~ **floor(ing) (finish)**, timber ~ ~, ~ floor cover(ing) · Holz(fuß)boden(belag) m, Fh

~ **folded plate roof**, timber ~ ~ ~, ~ ~ slab ~, ~ prismatic shell ~; ~ hipped-plate ~, ~ tilted-slab ~ (US) · Holz-Falt(werk)dach n, Holz-Dachfaltwerk n

~ ~ **slab roof** → ~ ~ ~ plate ~

~ **folding door**, timber ~ ~ · Holzfalttür f

~ **forms**, ~ formwork, ~ shuttering, timber ~ · Holzschalung f

~ **formwork**, ~ shuttering, ~ forms, timber ~ · Holzschalung f

~ **frame**, timber ~ · Holzrahmen m

~ ~ **construction**, timber ~ ~ · Holzfachwerkbau m

~ **frame(d) house**, timber ~ ~ · Holzfachwerkhaus n

~ ~ **wall**, timber ~ ~ · Holzfach(werk)wand f, Holzriegelwand

~ **framework**, timber ~, ~ framing, half-timber construction · Holzfachwerk n

(~) ~ **building**, timber ~ ~ · (Holz-)Fachwerkhaus n

~ ~ **wall**, timber ~ ~ · Holzfachwerkwand f, Holzriegelwand

wood(en) framing — wood(en) principal post

~ **framing**, timber ~, ~ framework, half-timber construction · Holzfachwerk n

~ **furring**, ~ firring · Holz-Unterkonstruktion f [Putztechnik]

~ **gate**, timber ~ · Holztor n

~ **gatehouse**, timber ~ · Holz-Torturm m

~ **girder**, timber ~ · Holzträger m

~ **grid**, ~ grillage, timber ~ · Holzrost m

~ ~ **footing**, timber ~ ~, ~ grillage ~ · Holzrostfundament n

~ **grillage**, ~ grid, timber ~ · Holzrost m

~ ~ **footing**, timber ~ ~, ~ grid ~ · Holzrostfundament n

~ **grill(e)**, timber ~ [See remark under 'Gitter'] · Holzgitter n

~ **ground**, ~ base, timber ~ · Holz(unter)grund m

~ ~ **floor**, timber ~ ~ · Holz-Erdgeschoß(fuß)boden m

~ **gutter** → ~ roof ~

~ **handle** · Holzgriff m

~ **handrail**, timber ~ · Holzhandlauf m, Holzhandleiste f

~ **header**, timber ~ [A wood(en) beam which carries the ends of beams which are cut off in framing around an opening] · Holzwechsel(balken) m, Wechselholz n

~ **hipped-plate roof** (US) → ~ folded plate ~

~ **hollow (floor) filler**, timber ~ (~) ~ · Holzhohlkörper m [Montagedecke]

~ **hut**, timber ~ · Holzbaracke f

~ **Ionic column**, timber ~ ~ · ionische Holzsäule f

~ **joist**, timber ~, boarding ~, common ~ [A wood beam directly supporting a floor] · Holzdeckenbalken m

~ ~ **floor**, timber ~ ~, ~ beam ~, single timber ~ · Holzbalken(träger)decke f [DIN 104]

~ ~ **roof floor**, timber ~ ~ ~, single timber ~ ~ · Holzbalken(träger)dachdecke f

~ ~ **upper floor**, timber ~ ~ ~, single upper timber · Obergeschoß-Holzbalkendecke f

~ **ladder**, timber ~ [B.S. 1129] · Holzleiter f

~ **lamella cupola** → ~ ~ ~ dome

~ ~ **dome**, ~ ~ cupola, ~ lattice(d) ~, timber ~ ~ · Holzlamellenkuppel f

~ **lath(ing) (for plastering)** [B.S. 1317] · Holzputz(mörtel)träger m

~ **lattice(d) beam**, timber ~ ~ · Holzgitterbalken(träger) m

~ ~ **cupola** → ~ ~ lamella dome

~ ~ **dome** → ~ lamella ~

~ ~ **girder**, timber ~ ~ ~ · Holzgitterträger m

~ **lining** → timber ~

~ **lintel**, timber ~; ~ lintol [deprecated] · Holz-Oberschwelle f, Holzsturz m

~ **(load)bearing structure**, timber ~ ~, ~ (weight-carrying) ~, ~ supporting ~, ~ load-carrying ~, ~ loaded ~ · Holztragwerk n [Ein materielles System von Holzbauelementen bzw. Holzträgern]

~ **load-carrying structure** → ~ (load)-bearing ~

~ **loaded structure** → ~ (load)bearing ~

~ **mast**, timber ~ · Holzmast m

~ **mold** (US) → ~ mould

~ **mopboard**, ~ washboard, ~ scrub board, ~ sanitary cove, ~ base (board) (US); ~ skirting (board) (Brit.); ~ base plate [Scotland] · Sockelbrett n, Holzfußleiste f, Holzscheuerleiste, Holzsockelleiste [DIN 68125]

~ **mould** (Brit.); ~ mold (US); timber ~ · Holzform f

~ **nailing plug**, ~ wall ~ · Holz-Mauerdübel m

wooden Order, ~ column ~ · Holzsäulenordnung f

wood(en) palisade fence · Holzpalisadenzaun m

~ **panel**, timber ~ · Holztafel f

~ **panelling** (Brit.); ~ paneling (US); wainscot [abbreviated: wnsct] · Täfelwerk n, Täfelung f, Getäfel n, Tablettenwerk n [Holzverkleidung aus Rahmen und Füllungen, mit Schnitzwerk, Fourniers und eingelegter Arbeit verziert]

~ **particle board**, ~ chipboard · Holzspanplatte f, Spanholzplatte [DIN 68761]

~ **partition (wall)**, timber ~ (~) · Holztrennwand f

~ **patent glazing bar**, ~ puttyless ~ ~, timber ~ ~ · Holzsprosse f [kittlose Verglasung]

~ **paving** · Holzpflaster n, Fph

~ **(~) block** · (Holz)Pflasterklotz m, Holzstöckel m, (Holz)Pflasterstöckel [DIN 68701]

~ ~ **work**, timber ~ ~ · Holzpflasterarbeiten fpl [DIN 18367]

~ **pillar**, timber ~, post, leg · Pfosten m, Stiel m, Ständer m, (Stand)Säule f [Senkrechtes Holz beim Fachwerk-, Stab-, Ständer- und Dachstuhlbau]

~ **plain web(bed) beam**, ~ solid ~, timber ~ ~ · Holz-Vollwandbalken(träger) m

~ ~ **girder**, ~ solid ~ ~, timber ~ ~ ~ · Holz-Vollwandträger m

~ **post**, timber ~ · Holzpfosten m

~ ~, ~ fence ~, timber (fence) ~ · Holzzaunpfahl m, Holz(zaun)pfosten m

~ **prefab(ricated) construction**, timber ~ ~, ~ system ~ · Bauen n mit Holzfertigteilen, ~ Holzmontageteilen, Holzfertig(teil)bau m, Holzmontage(teil)bau [Fehlname: Holzelementbau]

~ **principal post**, timber ~ ~, ~ stud · Holz-Bundstiel m

wood(en) prismatic shell roof — wood(en) string

~ prismatic shell roof → ~ folded plate ~

~ pulpit, timber ~ · Holzkanzel f

~ purlin(e), timber ~ · Holz(-Dach)pfette f

~ puttyless glazing bar, ~ patent ~ ~, timber ~ ~ ~ · Holzsprosse f [kittlose Verglasung]

~ rafter, timber ~ · Holz(-Dach)sparren m [Schweiz: Holzrofen m]

~ rail, timber ~, framework ~ ~ · (Fachwerk)Holzriegel m

~ rainwater gutter → ~ (roof) ~

~ revolving door, timber ~ ~ · Holzdrehtür f

~ rigid frame, timber ~ ~ · starrer Holzrahmen m, Holzsteifrahmen

~ roller shutter → ~ rolling ~

~ rolling shutter, timber ~ ~, ~ roller ~ · Holzrollabschluß m

~ roof, timber ~ · Holzdach n

~ ~ cladding, timber ~ ~, ~ ~ covering, ~ ~ sheathing, ~ roofing · Holzdach(ein)deckung f, Holz(ein)deckung, Holzdachbelag m [aus Holzschindeln]

~ ~ covering → ~ ~ cladding

~ ~ floor, timber ~ ~ · Holz-Abschlußdecke f gegen die Außenluft, Holz-Dachdecke

~ (~) gutter, ~ rainwater ~, ~ R.W. ~ · Holz(-Dach)rinne f, Holz-Regenrinne

(~) ~ shake · gerissene (Holz)Dachschindel f, (hand)gespaltene ~

~ ~ sheathing → ~ ~ cladding

~ ~ spire, timber ~ ~ · Holz-Dachreiter m

~ (~) truss, timber (~) ~ · Holz(dach)binder m

wood(en)-roofed basilica · holzgedeckte Basilika f

wood(en) roofing → ~ roof cladding

~ R.W. gutter → ~ (roof) ~

~ sanitary cove, ~ scrub board, ~ mopboard, ~ washboard, ~ base (board) (US); ~ skirting (board) (Brit.); ~ base plate [Scotland] · Sockelbrett n, Holzfußleiste f, Holzscheuerleiste, Holzsockelleiste [DIN 68125]

~ screed · Abziehbrett n

~ ~ (for plastering), timber ~ (~ ~) · Holzputzleiste f

~ scrub board, ~ mopboard, ~ washboard, ~ sanitary cove, base (board) (US); ~ skirting (board) (Brit.); ~ base plate [Scotland] · Sockelbrett n, Holzfußleiste f, Holzscheuerleiste, Holzsockelleiste [DIN 68125]

~ sculpture · Holzskulptur f

~ seat, timber ~ · Holzsitz m

~ shake → hand cleft (wood) shingle

~ sheathing, timber ~ · Holz(ver)schalung f, Holzschale f

~ shell, timber ~ · Holzschale f

~ ~ cupola, ~ ~ dome, timber ~ ~ · Holzschalenkuppel f

~ ~ dome, ~ ~ cupola, timber ~ ~ · Holzschalenkuppel f

~ ~ roof, timber ~ ~ · Holzschalendach n

~ shingle → (wood) ~

(~) ~ roof · (Holz)Schindeldach n

~ shutter, ~ window ~, timber (window) ~ · Holz-(Fenster)Laden m

~ ~, timber ~ · Holzabschluß m

~ shuttering, ~ forms, ~ formwork, timber ~ · Holzschalung f

~ siding shake → hand cleft (wood) siding shingle

~ ~ shingle · Holz-Wandschindel f, Wand-Holzschindel

~ skirting (board) (Brit.); ~ base plate [Scotland]; ~ washboard, ~ mopboard, ~ scrub board, ~ sanitary cove, ~ base (board) (US) · Sockelbrett n, Holzfußleiste f, Holzscheuerleiste, Holzsockelleiste [DIN 68125]

~ slat · Holzblättchen n, Holzlamelle f [Jalousie]

~ slatted roller blind · Holzrolladen m, Holzjalousie f

~ (~) Venetian (blind) · Holzraffjalousie f, Holzzugjalousie

~ soffit, timber ~ · Holzuntersicht f

~ solid web beam, ~ plain ~ ~, timber ~ ~ ~ ~ · Holz-Vollwandbalken(träger) m

~ ~ ~ girder, ~ plain ~ ~, timber ~ ~ ~ · Holz-Vollwandträger m

~ space bearing structure → ~ ~ load~ ~

~ ~ (load)bearing structure, ~ three-dimensional ~ ~, ~ spatial ~ ~, timber ~ ~ ~, ~ ~ weight-carrying ~ · Holz-Raumtragwerk n

~ ~ weight-carrying structure → ~ ~ (load)bearing ~

~ spatial (load)bearing structure → ~ space ~ ~

~ spire, timber ~ · Holz(turm)helm m, Holz-Pyramidenturmdach n, Holz-Turmdachpyramide f, Holz-Turmzeltdach über quadratischem Grundriß

~ ~, steeple, ~ broach, timber ~ · Holz-Spitz(kirch)turm m

~ stair(case), timber ~ [B.S. 585] · Holztreppe f

~ ~ builder, timber ~ · Holztreppenbauer m

~ stanchion, ~ stancheon, timber ~ (Brit.); ~ column · Holzstütze f

~ steeple → ~ spire

~ step, timber ~ · Holz(treppen)stufe f

~ string (Brit.); ~ stringer (US); timber ~ · Holzwange f

wood(en) stringer — workable raw lead 1132

~ **stringer** (US); ~ string (Brit.); timber ~ · Holzwange f

~ **(structural) system**, timber (~) ~, ~ construction · Holzkonstruktion(ssystem) f, (n)

~ **structure** → ~ (load)bearing ~

~ **strut**, timber ~, strut · Stake f, Stakholz n

~ **stud**, timber ~, ~ principal post · Holz-Bundstiel m

~ ~ **partition (wall)**, timber ~ ~ (~) · Holzgerippewand f [DIH 4103]

~ **studs**, timber ~ · Holzgerippe n [Leichte Trennwand. DIN 4103]

~ **sub-floor**, timber ~, counter floor, dead floor; rough floor (US) · Blendboden m, Blindboden, Holzunterboden [Bretterlage über der Deckenkonstruktion als Unterlage für Riemen- oder Parkett(fuß)böden]

~ **supporting structure** → ~ (load)bearing ~

~ **(sur)facing** → timber lining

~ **surround**, timber ~ · Holzeinfassung f

~ **suspended floor**, timber ~ ~ · freitragende Holzdecke f

~ **swing door**, timber ~ ~ · Holz-Pendeltür f, Pendeltür aus Holz

~ **system** → ~ structural ~

~ ~ **construction** → ~ prefab(ricated) construction

~ **three-dimensional bearing structure** → ~ space (load)bearing ~

~ ~ **(load)bearing structure** → ~ space ~ ~

~ ~ **weight-carrying structure** · ~ space (load)bearing ~

~ **threshold**, ~ door ~, timber (door) ~ · Holz(tür)schwelle f

~ **tilted-slab roof** (US) → ~ folded plate ~

~ **tower**, timber ~, brattice · Holzturm m [historischer Festungsbau]

~ ~, timber ~ · Holzturm m

~ **transom**, timber ~ · Kämpferholz n, Losholz [Querholz zur Unterteilung eines Fensters oder einer Tür]

~ **tread**, timber ~ · Holztritt(stufe) m, (f)

~ **truss**, timber ~, ~ roof ~ · Holz-(dach)binder m

~ ~ **frame**, timber ~ · Holzsprengwerk n

~ **truss(ed girder)**, timber ~ (~) · Holzfachwerk(träger) n, (m)

~ **type of construction**, timber ~ ~ ~ ~, ~ construction type · Holzbauart f

~ **underframe**, timber ~ · Holzrahmen m

~ **unitized unit**, timber ~ ~, ~ building block module · Holz(raum)zelle f

~ **valley gutter**, timber ~ ~ · Holzkehlrinne f, Kehlholzrinne

~ **vault**, timber ~ · hölzernes Gewölbe n, Holzgewölbe

~ **Venetian (blind)**, ~ slatted ~ (~) · Holzraffjalousie f, Holzzugjalousie

~ **wall**, timber ~ · Holzwand f

~ **washboard**, ~ mopboard, ~ scrub board, ~ sanitary cove, ~ base (board) (US); ~ skirting (board) (Brit.); ~ base plate Scotland] · Sockelbrett n, Holzfußleiste f, Holzscheuerleiste, Holzsockelleiste [DIN 68125]

~ **W. C. seat** [B. S. 2089] · Holz-Toilettensitz m, Holz-Klosettsitz, Holz-Abortsitz

~ **wall plug**, ~ nailing ~ · Holz-Mauerdübel m

~ **(weight-carrying) structure** → ~ (load)bearing ~

~ **window**, timber ~ [B.S. 644] · Holzfenster n

~ **(~) shutter**, timber (~) ~ · Holz-(Fenster)Laden m

wool felt, rag-felt [The term 'wool felt' is somewhat of a misnomer, since no roofing felt is composed entirely of wool fibres] · Wollfilz(dach)pappe f

wool-felt floor cover(ing), ~ floor(ing) (finish), rag-felt ~ · Wollfilzpappenbelag m, Wollfilzpappen(fuß)bodenbelag

~ **floor(ing) (finish)**, ~ floor cover(ing), rag-felt ~ (~) · Wollfilzpappenbelag m, Wollfilzpappen(fuß)bodenbelag

wool shavings · Wollstaub m [Velourstapete]

~ **waste** · Wollabfall m

to work · verarbeiten [Beton]

~ ~ · bearbeiten

workability admix(ture) → (concrete) workability agent

~ **agent** → concrete ~ ~

~ **aid** → (concrete) workability agent

~ **(of concrete)**, placeability (~ ~), concrete workability, concrete placeability · (Beton)Verarbeitbarkeit f, (Beton)Verarbeitungsfähigkeit

~ **period**, ~ time · Streichzeit f, Verarbeitungszeit [Die Zeitspanne vom Einstreuen des Gipses in Wasser bis zum Aufhören der Streich- und Glättfähigkeit]

~ **test**, placeability ~, concrete ~ ~ · (Beton)Verarbeitungsprobe f, (Beton-)Verarbeitbarkeitsprüfung f, (Beton)Verarbeitbarkeitsversuch m

~ **time** → ~ period

workable, placeable · verarbeitbar, verarbeitungsfähig [Beton]

~ **in hot state** · heißverarbeitbar

~ **raw lead**, argentiferous ~ · siberhaltiges Blei n, Werkblei [Es wird durch Niederschlagsarbeit, Röstreaktionsarbeit oder Röstreduktionsarbeit gewonnen]

'work as executed' drawing, as-completed ~, as-built ~, as-constructed ~ · (Bau)Bestandsplan *m*, (Bau)Bestandszeichnung *f*

work content, scope of work · Leistungsumfang *m*, Arbeitsumfang

~ **cycle** · Arbeitsspiel *n*

worked example, example of calculation · Rechenbeispiel *n*, Berechnungsbeispiel

work equation, equation of work · Arbeitsgleichung *f*

worker's dwelling (unit) (US); ~ dwelling (Brit.) · Arbeiterwohnung *f*

workers' entrance · Arbeiter-Eingang *m*

~ **(housing) estate** · Arbeitersied(e)lung *f*, Arbeiterwohngemeinde *f*

~ **suburb**, working-class ~ · Arbeitervorstadt *f*, Arbeitervorort *m*

~ **fire brigade** · Werkfeuerwehr *f*, Betriebsfeuerwehr

~ **for buried gas and water pipework** · Gas- und Wasserleitungsarbeiten *fpl* im Erdreich [*DIN 18307*]

~ ~ **installing the building equipment**, installation work · Installationsarbeiten *fpl*

workforce · Arbeitskräfte *fpl*

work-hardened steel [*Steel which has been cold worked, e.g. drawn, twisted or rolled*] · kaltverfestigter Stahl *m*

work index · Arbeitsindex *m* [*Mahlen*]

working · Verarbeitung *f* [*Beton*]

~ **area** · Arbeitsfläche *f*

~ **capacity** → ~ property

~ **-class suburb**, worker's ~ · Arbeitervorort *m*, Arbeitervorstadt *f*

working drawing, final ~ · Ausführungszeichnung *f*, Arbeitszeichnung, Ausführungsplan *m*, Arbeitsplan, Musterriß *m*, Bauriß

~ **kitchen** · Arbeitsküche *f* [*Ein selbständiger Raum mit unmittelbarem Zugang vom Flur. In ihm können alle Küchenarbeiten verrichtet werden*]

~ **life**, pot ~ [*The period after mixing the two packs of a two-pack paint during which the paint remains usable*] · Topfzeit *f*, Verarbeitungszeit

~ **load**, safe ~, admissible ~, permissible ~, allowable ~ · zulässige Last *f*

~ ~ **design**, ~ ~ method, permissible-stress ~, elastic ~ [*It is based on service loads and on permissible stresses in concrete and steel*] · Verfahren *n* zur Ermitt(e)lung der Schnittgrößen nach der Elastizitätstheorie

~ ~ **method**, ~ ~ design, permissible-stress ~, elastic ~ [*It is based on service loads and on permissible stresses in concrete and steel*] · Verfahren *n* zur Ermitt(e)lung der Schnittgrößen der Elastizitätstheorie

~ **niche**, ~ recess · Arbeitsnische *f*

~ **plane** · Arbeitsebene *f*

~ **property**, ~ capacity, ~ quality · Verarbeitungseigenschaft *f* [*Beton; Mörtel; Putz u.ä.*]

~ ~, ~ capacity, ~ quality · Bearbeitungseigenschaft *f*, Bearbeitungsfähigkeit *f*, Bearbeitungsvermögen *n*

~ ~ → ~ property

~ ~ · Bearbeitungsgüte *f*

~ ~ · Verarbeitungsgüte *f* [*Beton; Mörtel; Putz u.ä.*]

~ **recess**, ~ niche · Arbeitsnische *f*

~ **speed** · Rollgeschwindigkeit *f*, Fahrgeschwindigkeit [*Rolltreppe*]

~ **stress**, allowable ~, admissible ~, permissible ~, safe ~ · zulässige Spannung *f*

~ ~ **design** [*A method of proportioning structures or members for prescribed working loads at stresses well below the ultimate, and assuming linear distribution of flexural stresses*] · Gebrauchslastverfahren *n*

~ **temperature** · Betriebstemperatur *f*

~ **voltage** · Arbeitsspannung *f*, Betriebsspannung

workmanship · (Arbeits)Ausführung *f* [*als Gütebegriff*]

work noise · Betriebslärm *m*

~ ~ · Arbeitslärm *m*

~ **of deformation**, deformation work · Formänderungsarbeit *f*, Verformungsarbeit, Gestaltänderungsarbeit

workplace · Arbeitsplatz *m*

~ **illumination**, ~ lighting · Arbeitsplatzbeleuchtung *f*

~ **lighting**, ~ illumination · Arbeitsplatzbeleuchtung *f*

workroom · Arbeitsraum *m*

work sheet, calculation ~ ~ · Kalkulationsvordruck *m*

works canteen · Werkkantine *f*

~ **cube strength** · Werkwürfelfestigkeit *f*

~ **fire brigade** · Betriebsfeuerwehr *f*, Werkfeuerwehr

~ **restaurant** · Werkschänke *f*

~ **traffic** · Werkverkehr *m*

(work)shop block, ~ building · Werkstatthalle *f*

~ **building**, ~ block · Werkstatthalle *f*

~ **drawing** · Werkstattzeichnung *f*

~ **fabrication** · Werkstattfertigung *f*

~ **window** · Werkstattfenster *n*

work top · Arbeitsfläche *f*

world's earthquake belt · Welterdbebengürtel *m*

Wörner reinforced block floor · Wörner-Decke *f*

worshipping place → place of worship

worst possible position of load · ungünstigste Laststellung *f*

woven cotton fabric, cotton cloth; cotton fabric [*misnomer*] · Baumwollgewebe *n*

woven fabric — wythe

~ **fabric** → cloth

~ ~ **lath(ing)**, cloth ~; fabric ~ [*misnomer*] · Putz(träger)gewebe *n*

~ **fabric-reinforced** → cloth-reinforced

~ **steel wire fabric**, steel wire cloth; steel wire fabric [*misnomer*] · Drahtgewebe *n* aus Stahl, Stahl(draht)gewebe

woven-wire fabric reinforcement [*A prefabricated steel reinforcement composed of cold-drawn steel wires mechanically twisted together to form hexagonally shaped openings*] · geknüpfte Armierungsmatte *f*, ~ Bewehrungsmatte

~ ~ **lath(ing)** · verflochtenes Drahtgewebe *n*, ~ Rabitzgewebe

~ ~ **mesh** · verflochtene Drahtmaschenmatte *f*

WPC → white Portland cement

WR, wash room, lavatory [*A room equipped with basin(s) for washing hands and/or face*] · Waschraum *m*

WR equipment, wash room ~, lavatory ~ · Waschraumausrüstung *f*

WR tray, lavatory ~, wash room ~ · Waschraummaschenbecher *m*

wrap-around insulation · Wickelbandage *f*

wrapped (pre)stressed wire reinforcement · aufgewickelte Spannbewehrung *f*

wrap(ping) · Bandage *f*, Umwick(e)lung *f*

wrapping machine · (Um)Wickelmaschine *f*, (Rohr)Bandagiermaschine

wreath (at turn) · Handlaufkrümmling *m*, Handleistenkrümmling

wreathed column, twisted ~ [*A column entwined by a band which presents a twisted or spiral appearance*] · gedrehte Säule *f*, gewundene ~, Schlangensäule

to wreck, to demolish · abbrechen, abreißen, niederreißen, einreißen [*Bauwerk*]

wrecker, demolisher, mattock man, topman · (Gebäude)Abbrucharbeiter *m*, Hausabbrucharbeiter

wrecking, demolition, demolishing, D(E)ML; demolishment [*now rare*] · Abbruch *m*, Abreißen *n*, Abbrechen, Einreißen, Niederreißen [*Bauwerk*]

~ **contract**, demolition ~ · Abbruchvertrag *m*, Abreißvertrag

~ **contractor**, demolition ~ · Abbruchunternehmer *m*

~ **permission**, demolition ~ · Abbruchgenehmigung *f*, Abreißgenehmigung

~ **permit**, demolition ~ · Abbrucherlaubnis *f*, Abbruchschein *m*

~ **project** → demolition ~

~ **scheme** → demolition project

~ **site**, demolition ~ · Abbruchstelle *f*, Abreißstelle

~ **work**, demolition ~ · Abbrucharbeit(en) *f(pl)*, Abreißarbeit(en) [*DIN 4420*]

wrinkling → crinkling

writer on architecture, architectural writer · Architekturschriftsteller *m*

wrot (concrete) shuttering, wrought (~) ~, ~ (~) form(work), ~ (~) forms · gehobelte (Beton)Schalung *f*

wrought alloy · Knetlegierung *f* [*DIN 1725*]

~ **aluminium alloy**, aluminium wrought ~ (Brit.); wrought aluminum ~, aluminum wrought ~ (US) · (Alu(minium)-Knetlegierung *f* [*DIN 1725*]

~ **(concrete) forms** → wrot (concrete) shuttering

~ **(~) form(work)** → wrot (concrete) shuttering

~ **(~) shuttering** → wrot (~) ~

~ **copper alloy**, copper wrought ~ · Kupfer-Knetlegierung *f* [*DIN 17666*]

~ **forms** → wrot (concrete) shuttering

~ **form(work)** → wrot (concrete) shuttering

~ **iron**, WI · Schmiedeeisen *n*

wrought-iron area grating, WI ~ ~ · Schmiedeeisengitterrost *m*

~ **strap**, WI ~ [*For fixing the ends of joints*] · schmiedeeisernes Band Schmiedeeisenband

~ **window**, WI ~ · Schmiedeeisenfenster *n*, schmiedeeisernes Fenster

~ ~ **grille**, WI ~ ~ [*sometimes spelled 'grill'*] · Schmiedeeisenfenstergitter *n*, schmiedeeisernes Fenstergitter

wrought-magnesium alloy · Knetmagnesiumlegierung *f*, Magnesiumknetlegierung

wrought material · Knetwerkstoff *m*

~ **shuttering** → wrot (concrete) ~

~ **zinc** · Knetzink *n*

WS, water supply, provision of water · Wasserversorgung *f*

WSP, water supply point · Wasserversorgungsstelle *f*

WT → impervious to water

WT, water tower · Wasserturm *m*

WT, water tank, water reservoir · Wasserbehälter *m*

wt%, weight percent · Gewichtsprozent *n*

WT/RT radio station · Draht- und Funksprechzentrale *f*

WV, wind velocity · Windgeschwindigkeit *f*

W/V, weight-to-volume ratio · Gewichts/Raum-Verhältnis *n*

WVT, (water) vapour transmission (Brit.); (water) vapor transmission (US) · Wasserdampfdurchgang *m*

wythe, withe, layer, leaf, tier, shell, skin [*cavity wall*] · Schale *f*, Wand ~ [*Hohlwand*]

X

x-fold safety against buckling · x-fache Sicherheit f gegen Knicken

XPM → expanded (metal) mesh

X-ray protection, ~ shielding · Röntgen(strahlen)schutz m

~ **protective concrete,** ~ shielding ~, concrete for X-ray rooms · Röntgen(strahlen)schutzbeton m

~ ~ **glass,** ~ shielding ~, glass for X-ray rooms [*Glass which contains a high percentage of lead and sometimes also barium and which has a high degree of opacity to X-rays. The opacity is usually expressed in terms of the thickness of metallic lead which would give equal absorption of X-rays of stated wavelength*] · Röntgen(strahlen)schutzglas n

~ ~ **plaster,** ~ shielding ~, plaster for X-ray rooms [*A plaster containing barium sulphate as the aggregate*] · Röntgen(strahlen)schutzputz m

~ **room** · Röntgenraum m

~ **shielding,** ~ protection · Röntgen(strahlen)schutz m

~ ~ **concrete,** ~ protective ~, concrete for X-ray rooms · Röntgen(strahlen)schutzbeton m

~ ~ **glass,** ~ protective ~, glass for X-ray rooms [*Glass which contains a high percentage of lead and sometimes also barium and which has a high degree of opacity to X-rays. The opacity is usually expressed in terms of the thickness of metallic lead which would give equal absorption of X-rays of stated wavelength*] · Röntgen(strahlen)schutzglas n

~ ~ **plaster,** ~ protective ~, plaster for X-ray rooms [*A plaster containing barium sulphate as the aggregate*] · Röntgen(strahlen)schutzputz m

x-shaped · x-förmig

xylene · Xylol n

Y

yale lock · Yaleschloß n, Stechschloß

yard, court~ · befestigter Hof m

~ **cellar floor** · Hofkellerdecke f

~ **drainage system** · Hofentwässerungsanlage f

~ **entrance** · Hofeingang m

~ **gull(e)y,** ~ inlet · Hofablauf m, Hofeinlauf, Hofsinkkasten m, Hofgully m [*DIN 1236*]

~ **inlet,** ~ gull(e)y · Hofablauf m, Hofeinlauf, Hofsinkkasten m, Hofgully m [*DIN 1236*]

~ **masonry wall** · Hofmauer f

~ **mosque, court**~ ~ · Hofmoschee f

~ **pavement, court**(~) ~ · Hofbefestigung f

~ **space** · Hofraum m

~ **trap** · Hofschlammfang m

~ **with concrete pavement** · Betonhof m

year of construction · Baujahr n

to yellow · (ver)gilben

yellow brick · gelber Ziegel m

~ **(iron) oxid(e) (pigment),** ~ oxid(e) of iron (~), iron (oxid(e)) yellow (~), (US); yellow (iron) oxide (~), yellow oxide of iron (~), iron (oxide) yellow (~) (Brit.) [*B.S. 851*] · Eisengelb(pigment) n, (Eisen)Oxidgelb(pigment)

~ **ochre** (Brit.); ~ ocher (US) · gelber Ocker m

~ **organic pigment** · gelbes organisches Pigment n

~ **pigment** · Gelbpigment n, gelbes Pigment

~ **pyrite(s),** (iron) ~, fool's gold, mundic · Eisenkies m, Schwefelkies, Schwefeleisen n

yellowing · (ver)gilbend

~ · (Ver)Gilben n

~ **scale** · (Ver)Gilbungsskala f

Yesil Jami, Green Mosque · Grüne Moschee f von Isnik [*Nicaea*]

yield → ductility

~, **flexibility** · Nachgiebigkeit f

~ · (Beton)Ausbeute f [*Das Verhältnis der Betonmenge im Raumteilen zur Summe der einzeln zugegebenen Mengen*]

~ **point** · Streckgrenze f

~ **strength** · Streckfestigkeit f

~ **stress** [*The stress of a material at the yield point*] · Streckspannung f

yielding, flexible · nachgiebig

~ [*If a material is brittle it fractures without yielding*] · Streckung f

yoke → spreader bar

young's modulus (of elasticity) → modulus of elasticity

youth centre (Brit,); ~ center (US) · Jugendstätte f

~ **hostel** · Jugendheim n

Y(-shaped) building, ~ block, star-shaped ~ · Gebäude n mit Y-Grundriß

~ **column,** Y-column · Y-Stütze f

~ **leg,** ~ post, Y-post, Y-leg · Y-Stiel m

~ **post,** ~ leg, Y-post, Y-leg · Y-Stiel m

Z

Zanzibar copal · Sansibarkopal m

Zapon lacquer [*A thin, water-clear cellulose lacquer of low content of film-forming material to protect metal from tarnishing*] · Zaponlack m

Zech floor · Zechdecke f

zed · Z-Profil n

Zeiß-Dywidag dome — zinc gutter

Zeiß-Dywidag dome, ~ cupola · Zeiß-Dywidag-Kuppel f
zeolite · Zeolith m
zero curvature · Nullkrümmung f
~ flowability · Fließunfähigkeit f
~ humidity index, ~ moisture ~ · Nullfeuchtigkeitsindex m
~ line, neutral axis, N.A. · neutrale Achse f, ~ Linie f, Nullachse, Nullinie, Biegeachse
~ matrix, null ~ · Nullmatrix f
~ moisture index, ~ humidity ~ · Nullfeuchtigkeitsindex m, Nullfeuchteindex
~ moment · Nullmoment n
~ point of moments, point of zero moment · Momentennullpunkt m
~ position · Nullage f, Nullstellung f
~ rigidity, ~ stiffness · Nullstarrheit f, Nullsteifigkeit
~ shear(ing) · Nullschub m
~ stiffness, ~ rigidity · Nullsteifigkeit f, Nullstarrheit
~ stress · Nullspannung f
~ value · Nullwert m
ziggurat, ziqqarat, zikkurat, pyramid tower [*A high Mesopotamian staged tower, of which the angles were orientated to the cardinal points, which formed an important element in ancient Mesopotamian temple complexes. An especially sacred ceremony took place annually at the top of the ziggurat in an 'upper temple' having the form of a shrine or bower. The number of stages rose from one to seven in the course of time, and in the Assyrian version the stages were developed into a continuous inclined ramp, circulating the four sides in turn*] · Stufenturm m, Zikku(r)rat m, Rampentempel m
zigzag fluting · Zickzackkannelierung f, Zickzackriefelung
~ frieze · Zickzackfries m
~ moulding → chevron (~)
~ ornament → chevron (moulding)
~ sticks, broken ~ · gebrochene Stäbe mpl [*Verzierung*]
zikkurat → ziggurat
Zimmermann çupola, ~ dome · Zimmermannsche Kuppel f, Zimmermannkuppel [*Sie hat waag(e)rechte Ringe, bei denen die Zahl der Ecken mit steigender Höhe auf die Hälfte abnimmt*]
zinc · Zink n, Zn
~ alloy · Zinklegierung f [*DIN 1724*]
~ batten roof · Zink-Leistendach n
(~) blende, sphalerite, black jack; zinc sulphide (Brit.); zinc sulfide (US) · Zinkblende f, Sphalerit m, ZnS
~ box (roof) gutter, ~ ~ rainwater ~ · Zink-Kasten(dach)rinne f
~ ~ rainwater gutter, ~ ~ (roof) ~ · Zink-Kasten(dach)rinne f

~ carbonate · Zinkkarbonat n, $ZnCO_3$
~ chloride (Brit.); ~ chlorid(e) (US) · Zinkchlorid n, Chlorzink n, $ZnCl_2$
~ chromate · Zinkchromat n, $ZnCrO_4$
~ ~ base · Zinkchromatbasis f, Zinkchromatgrundlage f
~ ~ pigment · Zinkchromatpigment n
~ ~ primer · Zinkchromatgrund(iermittel) m, (n), Zinkchromatgrundierung f, Zinkchromatgrundanstrichmittel, AT-Grundiermittel
to zinc coat, to galvanize; to galvanise (Brit.) · verzinken
zinc coat · Verzinkung f
~ coated, galvanized; galvanised (Brit.) · verzinkt, zinkbeschichtet, zinküberzogen
~ ~ steel tile, galvanized-steel ~; galvanised-steel ~ (Brit.) · verzinktes Stahldach(deckungs)element n
~ ~ wire, galvanized ~; galvanised ~ (Brit.) · verzinkter Draht m
~ coating → galvanizing
~ coat(ing), ~ finish [*B.S. 1706*] · Zinkbeschichtung f, Zinküberzug m [*als Schicht*]
~ coating by spraying · Spritzverzinkung f
~ covered flat roof · Zinkflachdach n
~ die-casting · Zink-Druckguß m
~ divider strip · Zink-Terrazzo(trenn)-schiene f, Zink-Terrazzostreifen m
~ dust, ~ powder, powder(ed) zinc [*It is used as the pigment in zinc-rich paint. The zinc powder acts not only as a pigment but as a corrosion inhibitor*] · Zinkpulver n, Zinkstaub m
~ ~ pigment [*B.S. 3982*] · Zinkstaubpigment n
~ ~ shop primer, zinc-rich primer, zinc-rich paint, cold galvanising paint [*A paint, the pigment of which is zinc powder. It is used as a primer and as a special protection for steel*] · Zinkstaubgrund(ier)farbe f, Kaltzinkfarbe · zinkstaubreiche (Anstrich)Farbe, (Zinkstaub-)Werkstattgrund(ierung) m, (f), Zinkstaubfarbe
~ eave(s) gutter, ~ ~ trough, ~ ~ trow · Zink(-Dach)traufrinne f
~ finish, ~ coat(ing) [*B.S. 1706*] · Zinkbeschichtung f, Zinküberzug m [*als Schicht*]
~ flashing (piece) · Zink(blech)anschluß(streifen) m
~ fluosilicate · Zinkfluat n
~ gauge (No.), ~ ~ number · Zink-(blech)lehrennummer f
~ ~ system · Zink(blech)lehre f
~ green · Zinkgrün n [*Ungiftige Mischfarbe aus Zinkgelb und Eisenblau, wenig kalkecht, meist nur als Ölfarbe gebräuchlich, als solche ziemlich lichtecht*]
~ gutter, ~ roof ~, ~ rainwater ~, ~ R.W. ~ · Zink(dach)rinne f, Zinkregenrinne

zinc metal — Z-steel section

~ **metal**, metallic zinc · metallisches Zink *n*

~ ~ **pigment** · Zinkmetallpigment *n*

~ **nail** · Zinknagel *m*

~ **ore** · zinkhaltiges Erz *n*

~ **oxide** (Brit.); ~ oxid(e) (US) · Zinkoxid *n*, Röstblende *f*

~ **oxid(e) pigment** (US); ~ oxide ~ (Brit.) [*B.S 254 and 273*] · Zinkoxid(pigment) *n*, ZnO [*Pigment. Ein Zinkoxid(pigment), das direkt aus Zinkerzen gewonnen wird und Verunreinigungen — besonders Bleiverbindungen — enthalten kann. Es hat eine schwache Gelb- oder Blaustichigkeit. Man unterscheidet: Zinkoxid(pigment) bleiarm mit mindestens 90% ZnO und Zinkoxid(pigment) bleireich mit mindestens 75% ZnO*]

~ **pigment** → metallic ~ ~

~ **pipe** · Zinkrohr *n*

~ **poor primer** · zinkarme (Anstrich-)Farbe *f*

~ **powder**, ~ dust, powder(ed) zinc [*It is used as the pigment in zinc-rich paint. The zinc powder acts not only as a pigment but as a corrosion inhibitor*] · Zinkpulver *n*, Zinkstaub *m*

~ **R.W. gutter**, ~ rainwater ~, ~ (roof ~ · Zink(dach)rinne *f*, Zinkregenrinne

~ **rainwater gutter**, ~ R.W. ~, ~ (roof) ~ · Zink(dach)rinne *f*, Zinkregenrinne

~ **resinate** · Zinkharz *n*

zinc-rich paint, cold galvanising ~, zinc dust shop primer, zinc-rich primer [*A paint, the pigment of which is zinc powder. It is used as a primer and as a special protection for steel*] · Zinkstaubgrund(ier)farbe *f*, Kaltzinkfarbe, zinkstaubreiche (Anstrich)Farbe, (Zinkstaub)Werkstattgrund(ierung) *m* (*f*), Zinkstaubfarbe

~ **primer** → ~ paint

zinc roof cladding → sheet ~ ~ ~

~ ~ **covering** → sheet ~ ~ ~

~ (~) **gutter**, ~ rainwater ~, ~ R.W. ~ · Zink(dach)rinne *f*, Zinkregenrinne

~ ~ **sheathing** → sheet ~ ~ ~

~ ~ **surround** · Zink-Dacheinfassung *f*

~ **roofing** → sheet ~ ~

~ **salt** · Zinksalz *n*

~ **sheet**, sheet zinc · Zinkblech *n* [*DIN 9721*]

~ ~ **cover**, sheet zinc ~ · Zink(blech)-abdeckung *f*

~ ~ **rainwater gutter**, ~ ~ (roof) ~ · Zink(blech)(dach)rinne *f*

~ ~ **(roof) gutter**, ~ rainwater ~ · Zink(blech)(dach)rinne *f*

~ **shingle** · Zinkschindel *f*

~ **soap** · Zinkseife *f*

~ **strip**, strip zinc · Zinkband *n* [*DIN 9722*]

~ **sulfate** (US); ~ sulphate (Brit.) · Zinksulfat *n*, ZnSO$_4$

~ **sulphide** (Brit.); ~ sulfide (US); (~) blende, sphalerite, black jack · Zinkblende *f*, Sphalerit *m*, ZnS

~ **tetraoxychromate** · Zinktetraoxychromat *n*

~ **tile** · Zinkdach(deckungs)element *n*

~ **valley gutter** · Kehlzinkrinne *f*, Zinkkehlrinne

~ ~ **strip** · Zinkkehlstreifen *m*

~ **white**, Chinese ~ · Zinkweiß *n*, Schneeweiß, ZnO *n* [*Pigment. Ein aus metallischem Zink hergestelltes reinweißes oder ganz schwach gelb- oder blaustichiges technisch reines Zinkoxid (ZnO). Mit absteigendem Feinheitsgrad unterscheidet man die Marken Weißsiegel· Grünsiegel, und Rotsiegel; ZnO-Gehalt mindestens 99%*]

~ ~ **stand oil enamel** → stand oil zinc white ~

~ **wire** · Zinkdraht *m*

~ **yellow** [*A greenish-yellow pigment composed of the double salt of zinc and potassium chromates*] · Zinkgelb(pigment) *n*

ziqqarat → ziggurat

zircon · Zirkon *m*, ZrSiO$_4$

zirconia · Zirkondioxid *n*, ZrO$_2$

~ **refractory (product)** · Zirkondioxiderzeugnis *n*

zirkite · Zirkit *m* [*Rohstoff, der hauptsächlich aus Baddeleyit und Zirkonsilikat besteht*]

zone [*A space between reference planes which is provided for a building component or set of building components which does or do not necessarily fill the space*] · Bereich *m, n*

~ · Zone *f*

zone-by-zone · zonenweise

zone cleared of buildings → site ~ ~ ~

~ **of function**, sphere ~ ~, functional sphere, functional zone · Funktionsbereich *m, n*

~ ~ **transverse force** · Querkraftbereich *m, n*

zoning · Zoneneinteilung *f*

~ **law** · Bebauungsgesetz *n*

~ **plan** · Bebauungsplan *m*, Fluchtlinienplan, Ortsbauplan, Durchführungsplan [*Zeichnerisch dargestellter Gesamtplan und schriftliche Erklärung zur Reg(e)lung der Bebauungsmöglichkeiten und Anlage der Straßen und Plätze*]

~ **regulations** · Bebauungsvorschriften *fpl*

zo(o)phorus · Tierfries *m*

Z-rib pattern · Z-Rippenmuster *n*

Z-steel section · Z-Stahl(profil) *m*, (*n*) [*Z-förmiger Walzstahl nach DIN 1027*]

Appendix
Anhang

Formula / Formel	English / Englisch	German / Deutsch
$2CaO \cdot SiO_2$	belite [A name used by Tornebohm (1897), to identify one form of the constituent of portland cement clinker now known when pure as dicalcium silicate]	Belit *m*
$2CaO \cdot SiO_2$	$\longrightarrow C_2S$	
$2FeO \cdot SiO_2$	fayalite, ferrous orthosilicate	Fayalit *m*, eisenhaltiges Orthosilikat *n*, Eisenglas *n*
$3Al_2O_3 \cdot 2SiO_2$	mullite	Mullit *m* [Aluminiumsilikat mit der theoretischen Formel $3 Al_2O_3 \cdot 2SiO_2$]
$3CaO \cdot Al_2O_3 \cdot 3CaSO_4 \cdot 30–32H_2O$	calcium sulfoaluminate (US); ~ sulphoaluminate (Brit.)	Trikalziumaluminattrisulfathydrat *n*, Kalziumsulfoaluminat *n*, Kalktonerdesulfat
$3CaO \cdot SiO_2$	$\longrightarrow C_3S$	
$3SiO_3Mg \cdot 5H_2O$	magnesium silicate, silicate of magnesium	Magnesiumsilikat *n*
$4CaO \cdot Al_2O_3 \cdot Fe_2O_3$	$\longrightarrow C_4AF$	
Ag_3AsS_3	light-red silver ore, proustite	lichtes Rotgültigerz *n*, Arsensilberblende *f*, Proustit *m*
$AgNO_3$	lunar caustic	Silbernitrat *n*, Höllenstein *m*, salpetersaures Silberoxid *n*
Al	aluminium (Brit.); aluminum (US); alum.	Aluminium *n*
Al_2O_3	corundum, α-alumina [The form of alumina stable at temperatures above about 1,000°C]	Korund *m*, Alpha-Tonerde *f*, α-Tonerde
$Al_2O_3 \cdot 3 H_2O$	hydrargillite, gibbsite [1. A trihydrate of alumina. 2. A rock containing a major proportion of this mineral]	Gibbsit *m*, Hydrargillit *m*
$Al_2O_3 \cdot H_2O$	boehmite [One of the monohydrates of alumina]	Boehmit *m*
$Al_2O_3 \cdot SiO_2$	kyanite, cyanite, disthene	Cyanit *m*, Disthen *m* [Eines der drei Minerale die die gleiche Formel $Al_2O_3 \cdot SiO_2$ haben, jedoch in ihrer Struktur verschieden sind. In Erweiterung dient dieser Ausdruck auch zur Bezeichnung des Gesteins (Rohstoffs)]

Formula / Formel	English / Englisch	German / Deutsch
$Al_2O_3 \cdot SiO_2$	sillimanite	Sillimanit *m* [*Eines der drei Minerale die die gleiche Formel $Al_2O_3 \cdot SiO_2$ haben, jedoch in ihrer Struktur verschieden sind. In Erweiterung dient dieser Ausdruck auch zur Bezeichnung des Gesteins (Rohstoffs)*]
$Al_2SiO_2O_5(OH)_4$	kaolinite	Kaolinit *m* [*Tonmineral der Kaolinitgruppe; Hauptbestandteil des Kaolins*]
Al_2SiO_5	andalusite	Andalusit *m*, Hartspat *m*
$Al_2(SO_4) \cdot 18\ H_2O$	aluminium sulphate (Brit.); aluminum sulfate (US)	Aluminiumsulfat *n*
$AlCl_3$	aluminium chloride (Brit.); aluminum chlorid(e) (US)	Alu(minium)chlorid *n*
$Al(OH)_3$	aluminium hydroxide (Brit.); aluminum hydroxid(e) (US)	Alu(minium)hydroxid *n*, Tonerdehydrat *n*
$Al(OH)_3$	$\longrightarrow Al_2O_3 \cdot 3\ H_2O$	
As	arsen	Arsen *n*
As_2S_3	orpiment	Auripigment *n*, Rauschgelb *n*
Ba	barium	Barium *n*
$BaCl_2$	barium chloride (Brit.); $\sim$ chlorid(e) (US)	Bariumchlorid *n*
$BaCO_3$	barium carbonate, witherite	Bariumkarbonat *n*
$BaCrO_4$	barytes yellow (Brit.); barite $\sim$ (US)	Bariumchromat *n*, Barytgelb *n*
BaO	barytes, barytes natural barium sulphate (Brit.); barite, barite natural barium sulfate (US) [*A mineral used in pure or impure form as concrete aggregate primarily for the construction of high-density radiation shielding concrete*]	Baryt *m*, Schwerspat *m*
$Ba(OH)_2 \cdot 8\ H_2O$	barium hydroxide (Brit.); $\sim$ hydroxid(e) (US)	Ätzbaryt *m*, Bariumhydroxid *n*
$BaSO_4$	barium sulphate (Brit.); $\sim$ sulfate (US)	Bariumsulfat *n*, schwefelsaures Barium *n*
$BaSO_4ZnS$	lithopone	Lithopone *f* [*Fehlname: Deckweiß n*]
Be	beryllium	Beryllium *n*
$Be_3Al_2(SiO_3)_6$	beryl [*The mineral form of beryllium alumino-silicate*]	Beryll *m*
BeO	beryllia, beryllium oxide (Brit.); beryllium oxid(e) (US)	Berylliumoxid *n*
Bi_2O_3	bismite; bismuth ochre (Brit.); bismuth ocher (US)	Bismit *m*, Wismutocker *m*
Bi_2S_3	bismuthinite, bismuth glance	Bismuthin *m*, Wismutglanz *m*
C_2H_2	acetylene	Azetylen(gas) *n* [*Es wurde früher zur Herstellung von Gasbeton verwendet, Wegen seiner Feuergefährlichkeit verwendet man heute andere Blähmittel*]

Formula / Formel	English / Englisch	German / Deutsch
C_2H_3	acetylene	Azetylen *n*
$C_2H_4O_2$	acetic acid	Essigsäure *f*
C_2H_5OH	alcohol	(Äthyl) Alkohol *m*
$C_2S = (2\ CaO \cdot SiO_2)$	dicalcium silicate	Bikalziumsilikat *n*, Dikalziumsilikat
C_3S	alite	Alit *n*
$C_3S = (3\ CaO \cdot SiO_2)$	tricalcium silicate [*A compound having the composition 3 CaO · SiO$_2$, abbreviated C$_3$S, an impure form of which alite is a main constituent of portland cement*]	Trikalziumsilikat *n*
$C_4AF = 4\ CaO \cdot Al_2O_3 \cdot Fe_2O_3)$	tetracalcium aluminoferrite	Tetrakalziumaluminatferrit *n*
C_4H_9OH	butanol, butyl alcohol	Butanol *n*, Butylalkohol *m*
$C_6H_5CH_2$	benzyl	Benzyl *m*
$C_6H_5NH_2$	aniline	Anilin *n*
C_6H_5OH	phenol, carbolic acid, coal tar creosote [*BS 144*]	Steinkohlenteerkreosot *n*, Phenol *n*, Phenylalkohol *m*, Karbolsäure *f*
C_6H_6	benzene, benzole	Benzol *n* [*Klopffester Vergaserbrennstoff; durch Destillation des Steinkohlenteeres oder durch Auswaschen von Kokereigas gewonnen*]
$C_6H_{10}O_5$	cellulose	Cellulose *f*, Zellulose
$C_6H_5NO_2$	nitrobenzene, nitrobenzol(e)	Nitrobenzol *n*, Mirbanöl *n*
C_7H_8O	creosol [*Any of three isomeric, colo(u)rless, oily liquids or solids, prepared by the fractional distillation of coal tar and used in the preparation of disinfectants, fumigating compounds, and dyestuffs*]	Kresol *n*
$C_8H_6O_4$	phthalic acid [*One of three aromatic crystalline compounds, C$_8$H$_6$O$_4$, derived variously, as by oxidation of naphthalene: formerly called alizaric acid, naphthalic acid*]	Phthalsäure *f*
C_8H_{10}	xylene	Xylol *n*
$C_{14}H_8O_4$	alizarin	Alizarin *n.*
$C_{14}H_{10}$	anthracene	Anthrazen *n*, Anthracen
$C_{15}H_{31}CO_2H$	palmitic acid	Palmitinsäure *f*
$C_{17}H_{35}COOC_4H_9$	butyl stearate	Butylstearat *n*
$C_{20}H_{14}O_4$	phenolphthalein [*A whitish or yellowish-white crystalline compound, obtained by treating phenol with phthalic anhydride. Because its brilliant red alkaline solutions are readily decolorized by acid, it is valuable as an indicator in acid-base titrations*]	Phenolphthalein *n*

Formula / Formel	English / Englisch	German / Deutsch
$C_{20}H_{30}O_2$	abietic acid	Tannenharzsäure *f*, Sylvinsäure, Abietinsäure
Ca	calcium	Kalzium *n* [*Erdalkalimetall*]
$CaAl_2Si_2O_8$	anorthide, limefel(d)spar	Anorthit *m*, Kalkfeldspat *m*
CaC_2	calcium carbide, carbide of calcium	Kalziumkarbid *n* [*Durch Zusammenschmelzen von Branntkalk und Kohle gewonnenes Ausgangserzeugnis für Azetylen*]
$CaCl_2$	calcium chloride (Brit.); ~ chlorid(e) (US)	Kalziumchlorid *n*, Chlorkalzium *n* [*Ein Abbinde(zeit)beschleuniger. Die Abbindezeit läßt sich je nach dem Kalziumchloridanteil im Anmach(e)wasser auf Minuten oder sogar Sekunden verkürzen*]
$CaCO_3$	aragonite	Aragonit *m* [*Seltene, rhombische Form des kristallisierten Kalziumkarbonats*]
$CaCO_3$	limestone; caulk, cawk [*Scotland*]	Kalkstein *m* [*Sedimentationsgestein mit dem Hauptbestandteil Kalziumkarbonat in dicht und körnig kristalliner Form*]
$CaCO_3$	calcite, calcspar	Kanonenspat *m*, Kalzit *m*, Kalkspat [*Rhomboedrisch kristallisierte Form des Kalziumkarbonats, gesteinsbildend. Fehlname: Weiß Carrara m*]
$CaCO_3$	calcium carbonate [*chemical name*], carbonate of lime [*substance*]	Kalziumkarbonat *n* [*Hauptbestandteil des Kalksteins und der Kreide*]
CaF_2	calcium fluoride (Brit.); ~ fluorid(e) (US); fluorspar, fluorite	Fluorit *m*, Flußspat *m*, Kalziumfluorid *n*
$Ca(Mg,Fe)(SiO_3)_2 + Al_2O_3$	augite	Augit *m*
$Ca(NO_3)_2$	nitrate of lime, lime nitrate	salpetersaurer Kalk *m*, salpetersaures Kalzium *n*, Kalksalpeter *m*, Kalziumnitrat *n*
CaO	calcium oxid(e)	Kalziumoxid *n*
CaO	calcium oxid(e) [*chemical name*]; common lime, anhydrous lime, (quick) lime, calcined calcium carbonate, burnt lime, burned lime [*substance*]	Branntkalk *m*, gedeihender Kalk, Brennkalk, gebrannter Kalk
$CaOCl_2$	bleaching powder, chloride of lime, chlorinated lime	Bleichpulver *n*, Bleichkalk *m*, Chlorkalk, Kalziumoxychlorid *n*
$Ca(OH)_2$	free lime	freies Kalkhydrat *n*, freier Kalk *m*
$Ca(OH)_2$	calcium hydroxide (Brit.); ~ hydroxid(e) (US)	Kalziumhydroxid *n* [*Molekulargewicht 74,10; es besteht aus 75,7% Kalziumhydroxid und 24,3% Wasser*]
$Ca(OH)_2$	dry hydrate(d lime)	Löschkalk *m*, Kalkhydrat *n*, Feinkalk; (Ver)Putzkalk, Pulverkalk, Mauerkalk, (Bau)Ätzkalk, Sackkalk, (Bau)Sichtkalk, gemahlener Stück(en)kalk [*Fehlnamen*]

Formula / Formel	English / Englisch	German / Deutsch
$CaSiO_3$	calcium silicate, lime ∼	KS, Kalziumsilikat, Kalksilikat
$CaSO_4$	anhydrite [*This occurs as a natural mineral as well as being an industrial by-product. Its chemical name is anhydrous calcium sulphate*]	wasserfreier Gips(stein) *m*, wasserfreies Kalziumsulfat *n*, Anhydrit *m*
$CaSO_4$	anhydrous (gypsum-)plaster, flooring ∼; (anhydrous) calcium sulphate plaster, class C (gypsum-)plaster, (gypsum-)plaster of class C (Brit.); anhydrous calcium sulfate plaster (US)	Estrichgips *m*, Anhydrit I *m, n*, Hochtemperaturanhydrit [*DIN 1060*]
$CaSO_4$	deadburnt gypsum, dead burned ∼	Anhydrit II *m, n*, unlöslicher Anhydrit *m*, unlösliches Anhydrit *n*, Totgebranntes *n*, totgebrannter Gips *m*
$CaSO_4$	calcium sulphate (Brit.); ∼ sulfate (US) [*chemical name*] sulphate of lime, lime sulphate (Brit.); sulfate of lime, lime sulfate (US) [*substance*]	Kalziumsulfat *n*, schwefelsaurer Kalk *m*
$CaSO_4 \cdot 2\,H_2O$	gypsum [*It is a naturally occuring mineral composed of hydrous calcium sulphate with two molecules of combined water and having the chemical formula $CaSO_4 \cdot 2\,H_2O$. It is also formed as a by-product of the manufacture of phosphate rock with sulphuric acid, and gypsum plasters are made from both the natural gypsum and this by-product*]	Gips *m*
$CaSO_4 \cdot 2\,H_2O$	(massive) gypsum, natural ∼, raw ∼; gypsum rock, plaster rock, plaster stone, potter's stone (Brit.)	Rohgips *m*, Naturgips, Gipsstein *m*, Gipsgestein *n*
$CaSO_4 \cdot 2\,H_2O$	alabaster	Alabaster(gips) *m*
$CaU_2P_2O_{12} \cdot 8\,H_2O$	autunite	Autunit *m*, Uranit *m*, Kalkuranglimmer *m*
CCl_4	carbon tetrachloride	Tetrachlorkohlenstoff *m*, Tetrachlormethan *n*
Cd	cadmium	Kadmium *n*
$CH_2{:}CH \cdot CH{:}CH_2$	butadiene	Butadien *n*
$CH_2{:}CH \cdot COOH$	acrylic acid	Acrylsäure *f*
CH_3COCH_3	acetone, dimethyl ketone	Azeton *n*
CH_3OH	methyl alcohol, wood ∼, methanol [*B.S. 506*]	Methylalkohol *m*, Methanol *n*, Holzgeist *m*
C_nH_{n+1}	alkyl	Alkyl *n*
$C_nH_{(2n+2)}$	gasoline	Benzin *n*
Co	cobalt	Kobalt *n*
CO_2	carbon dioxide (Brit.); ∼ dioxid(e) (US)	Kohlendioxid *n* [*Fehlbezeichnung: Kohlensäure f*]

Formula / Formel	English / Englisch	German / Deutsch
$CO(NH_2)_2$	urea	Harnstoff *m*
Cr	chromium	Chrom *n*
CS	casein	Kasein *n*, Käsestoff *m*, Käseeiweiß *n* der Milch
$Cu_2Cl_2 + HCl + aq$	hydrochloric solution of cupreous chloride (Brit.); $\sim \sim \sim \sim$ chlorid(e) (US)	salzsaure Kupferchlorürlösung *f*
$CuSO_4 \cdot 5\, H_2O$	blue vitriol	Kupfervitriol *n*, Kupfer(-II)-Sulfat-Pentahydrat *n*
F	fluorine	Fluor *n*
Fe	iron	Eisen *n*
Fe_2O_3	ferric oxide (Brit.); $\sim$ oxid(e) (US) [*chemical name*]; hematite [*substance*]	Hämatit *m*, Roteisenstein *m*
Fe_3C	cementite	Zementit *m*, Eisenkarbid *n* [*Sehr harte Eisenkohlenstofflegierung*]
Fe_3O_4	magnetite, magnetic iron ore	Magneteisenerz *n*, Hammerschlag *m*, Magneteisenstein *m*, Magnetit *m*
$FeCl_2 + 4\, H_2O$	ferrous chloride (Brit.); $\sim$ chlorid(e) (US)	Eisenchlorür *n*, Ferrochlorid *n*
$FeCO_3$	siderite [*iron carbonate*]	Siderit *m*
$FeO \cdot Al_2O_3$	hercynite, iron spinel	Eisen-Tonerdespinell *m*, Hercynit *m*
$FeO \cdot Cr_2O_3$	chromite [*The ferrous chrome spinel*]	Chromit *m*
$FeO \cdot TiO_2$	ilmenite, ferrous titanate	Eisentitanat *n*, Ilmenit *m*, Titaneisen *n*
FeS_2	marcasite, white iron pyrites	Kammkies *m*, Speerkies, Markasit *m*
H_2CO_2	formic acid	Ameisensäure *f*, Formylsäure
H_2O	water	Wasser *n*
H_2O_2	hydrogen peroxid(e) (US); $\sim$ peroxide (Brit.)	Wasserstoffsuperoxid *n*
H_2SiF_6	fluosilic acid	Flußkieselsäure *f*, Kieselflußsäure, Kiesel(fluor)wasserstoffsäure
H_2SiO_3	silicate	Silikat *n*, Kieselsäuresalz *n*
H_2SO_4	sulphuric acid (Brit.); sulfuric $\sim$ (US)	Schwefelsäure *f*
H_3PO_4	phosphoric acid	Phosphorsäure *f*, Knochensäure
H_4SiO_4	orthosilicic acid	Orthokieselsäure *f*
$HgCl_2$	mercuric chloride (Brit.); $\sim$ chlorid(e) (US); corrosive sublimate [*It is a white crystalline solid, sparingly soluble in cold, more easily in hot, water*]	Quecksilberchlorid *n*, Sublimat *n*
HNO_3	nitric acid	Salpetersäure *f*, Stickstoffsäure

Formula / Formel	English / Englisch	German / Deutsch
K_2CO_3	(carbonate of) potash, potassium carbonate	Kaliumkarbonat *n*, Pottasche *f*, kohlensaures Kalium *n*
$K_2CO_3 1\tfrac{1}{2}H_2O$	hydrated potash	Hydratpottasche *f*
K_2SiO_3	potassium silicate	Kaliumsilikat *n*, Kaliwasserglas *n*
KBr	potassium bromide	Bromkali *n*, Kaliumbromid *n*
$KClO_3$	potassium chlorate	Kaliumchlorat *n*
KCN	potassium cyanide	Kaliumzyanid *n*, Zyankali *n*
KNO_3	potassium nitrate, niter, saltpeter	Kalisalpeter *m*, Kaliumnitrat *n*
$KMnO_4$	potassium permanganate	Kaliumpermanganat *n*
KOH	potassium hydrate, caustic potash; potassium hydroxide (Brit.); potassium hydroxid(e) (US)	Ätzkali *n*, Kaliumhydroxid *n*, Kaliumhydrat *n*
Mg	magnesium	Magnesium *n* [*DIN 17800*]
$MgCl_2$	magnesium chloride (Brit.); $\sim$ chlorid(e) (US)	Magnesiumchlorid *n*, Chlormagnesium *n* [*DIN 273. Bl. 2*]
$MgCO_3$	magnesium carbonate	Magnesiumkarbonat *n*
$MgCO_3$	magnesite, bitter spar	Magnesit *m*, Bitterspat *m* (Min.)
MgO	magnesium oxide (Brit.); $\sim$ oxid(e) (US); magnesia	Magnesia *f*, Magnesiumoxid *n*
$MgSO_4 \cdot H_2O$	kieserite [*Hydrated magnesium sulphate. A white mineral occurring in saline residues*]	Kieserit *m*
Mn	manganese, manganes(i)um	Mangan *n*
MoS_2	molybdenite	Molybdänglanz *m*, Molybdänit *m*
Na	sodium	Natrium *n*
$Na_2B_4O_7$	borax	Borax *m*, borsaures Natron *n*, Natriumborat *n* [*Salz der Tetraborsäure*]
Na_2O	sodium oxide (Brit.); $\sim$ oxid(e) (US); soda	Natriumoxid *n*
Na_2CO_3	sodium carbonate	Natriumkarbonat *n*
$Na_2CR_2O_7 \cdot 2H_2O$	sodium dichromate	Natriumbichromat *n*
Na_2O_3	sodium carbonate	Natriumkarbonat *n*
$Na_2S_2O_3 \cdot 5H_2O$	sodium thiosulfate, hypo	Natriumthiosulfat *n*, Fixiersalz *n*
Na_2SiO_3	sodium silicate, silicate of soda	Natriumsilikat *n*, Natronwasserglas *n*
$Na_2SO_4 \cdot 1 OH_2O$	sodium sulphate (Brit.); $\sim$ sulfate (US); saltcake	Natriumsulfat *n*, Glaubersalz *n*, schwefelsaures Natrium *n*
Na_3AlF_6	fluoride of alumin(i)um and sodium	Natrium-Aluminiumfluorid *n*
$NaCl$	sodium chloride (Brit.); $\sim$ chlorid(e) (US)	Kochsalz *n*, Natriumchlorid *n*, Chlornatrium *n*

Formula Formel	English Englisch	German Deutsch
$NaNO_3$	sodium nitrate	salpetersaures Natrium *n*, Natriumnitrat *n*, Natronsalpeter *m*
NaOH	caustic soda, sodium hydroxid(e)	Natriumhydroxid *n*, Ätznatron *n*, kaustische Soda *f*, kaustisches Soda *n*, Natronhydrat *n*
NH_2NH_2	hydrazin(e)	Hydrazin *n* [*Wasseranziehende alkalische Flüssigkeit; rauchend, giftig, als Treibmittel für Porengips und Porenbeton verwendet*]
NH_3	ammonia	Ammoniak *n*
NH_4	ammonium	Ammonium *n*
NH_4Cl	ammonium chloride (Brit.); $\sim$ chlorid(e) (US)	Ammoniumchlorid *n*, Salmiak *m, n*, Chlorammonium *n*
NH_4OH	volatile alkali	Salmiakgeist *m*
Ni	nickel	Nickel *n*
NiS	millerite, capillary pyrite	Millerit *m*, Haarkies *m* (Min.)
P_2O_5	anhydrous phosphoric acid	Phosphorpentoxid *n*, Phosphorsäureanhydrid *n*, wasserfreie Phosphorsäure *f*
Pb	lead	Blei *n* [*DIN 1719*]
$Pb_3(CO_3)_2OH_2$	basic carbonate white lead	Bleiweiß *n* aus basischem Bleikarbonat, $\sim\sim\sim$ Bleicarbonat [*Im Gegensatz zum Sulfo-Bleiweiß, welches durch Verbrennen von natürlichem Bleierz gewonnen wird*]
Pb_3O_4	orange lead	orangegefärbte Bleimennige *f*
Pb_3O_4	red lead, minium [*substance*], red lead oxid(e) [*chemical name*]	Bleimennige *f* [*DIN 55916. Österreich: Minium n*]
$PbCO_3$	lead carbonate	Bleikarbonat *n*
PbO	lead (mon)oxide (Brit.); $\sim$ (mon)oxid(e) (US) [*chemical names*]; litharge [*substance*]	Bleiglätte *f*, Bleioxid *n* [*veraltete Benennung: Königsgelb n*]
PbS	lead glance, blue lead, galena	Bleiglanz *m*, Galenit *m*
$PbSO_4$	lead sulphate (Brit.); $\sim$ sulfate (US)	Bleisulfat *n*
Sb	antimony	Antimon *n*
Si	silicon	Silizium *n*
SiC	silicon carbide, carbide of silicon, carbon silicide	Karborund *n*, Siliziumkarbid *n*, Siliziumkohlenstoff *m* [*Synthetisches Erzeugnis. Das industriell hergestellte Produkt kann Verunreinigungen enthalten*]
SiO_2	flint [*A chalcedonic variety of quartz, found as noddles and nodular bands in chalk and as residual pebbles*]	Flint(stein) *m*, Feuerstein, Silex *m*

Formula / Formel	English / Englisch	German / Deutsch
Sn	tin	Zinn n
SnO_2	cassiterite, tinstone, black tin	Kassiterit m, Zinnstein m, Zinnerz n
SO_3	sulphur trioxide, sulphuric anhydride (Brit.); sulfuric anhydride, sulfuric trioxide (US)	Schwefeltrioxid n
Te	tellurium	Tellur n
Ti	titanium	Titan n
TiO_2	titanium white	Titanweiß n
TiO_2	rutile	Rutil m
Zn	zinc	Zink n
$ZnCl_2$	zinc chloride (Brit.); ~ chlorid(e) (US)	Zinkchlorid n, Chlorzink n
$ZnCl_2$	killed spirits	wässerige Zinkchloridlösung f wäßrige ~, Lötwasser n
$ZnCO_3$	zinc carbonate	Zinkkarbonat n
$ZnCrO_4$	zinc chromate	Zinkchromat n
ZnO	zinc oxide (Brit.); ~ oxid(e) (US)	Zinkoxid n [*Pigment. Ein Zinkoxid, das direkt aus Zinkerzen gewonnen wird und Verunreinigungen — besonders Bleiverbindungen — enthalten kann. Es hat eine schwache Gelb- oder Baustichigkeit. Man unterscheidet: Zinkoxid bleiarm mit mindestens 90% ZnO und Zinkoxid bleireich mit mindestens 75% ZnO*]
ZnO	zinc white, Chinese ~	Zinkweiß n, Schneeweiß [*Pigment. Ein aus metallischem Zink hergestelltes reinweißes oder ganz schwach gelb- oder blaustichiges technisch reines Zinkoxid (ZnO). Mit absteigendem Feinheitsgrad unterscheidet man die Marken Weißsiegel, Grünsiegel und Rotsiegel; ZnO-Gehalt mindestens 99%*]
ZnS	(zinc) blende, sphalerite, black jack; zinc sulphide (Brit.); zinc sulfide (US)	Sphalerit m, Zinkblende f
$ZnSO_4$	zinc sulphate (Brit.); ~ sulfate (US)	Zinksulfat n
ZrO_2	zirconia	Zirkondioxid n
$ZrSiO_4$	zircon	Zirkon m
β-$CaSO_4$	hard-burnt plaster, hard-burned ~	β-Anhydrit III m, löslicher Anhydrit m, entwässertes Halbhydrat n [*Ofengipsart*]

Wörterbuch für Architektur, Hochbau und Baustoffe

Von H. Bucksch. Format 13,5 x 20,5 cm. Plastik.

Diese Bände beinhalten nicht nur die alphabetische Folge aller Fachbegriffe, sondern darüber hinaus in allen notwendigen Fällen kurze bis ausführliche Erläuterungen zu den Termini. So erhält das Wörterbuch den zusätzlichen Wert eines Baufachlexikons.

Englische Ausgabe:
Dictionary of Architecture, Building Construction and Materials

Band 1: Deutsch-Englisch. 1. Nachdruck 1987 der 2. Auflage 1980. 942 Seiten. Rund 65.000 Stichwörter. DM 240,–
ISBN 3-7625-2576-5 (Best.-Nr.)

Französische Ausgabe:
Dictionnaire pour l'Architecture, le Bâtiment et les Matériaux de Construction

Band 1: Deutsch-Französisch. 1977. 820 Seiten. Rund 52.000 Stichwörter. DM 290,–
ISBN 3-7625-0786-4 (Best.-Nr.)
Band 2: Französisch-Deutsch. 1979. 688 Seiten. Rund 40.000 Stichwörter. DM 290,–
ISBN 3-7625-0787-2 (Best.-Nr.)

Wörterbuch für Bautechnik und Baumaschinen

Von H. Bucksch. Format 12,5 x 17 cm.

Englische Ausgabe:
Dictionary of Civil Engineering and Construction Machinery and Equipment

Band 1: Deutsch-Englisch. 8. Auflage 1982. 1184 Seiten. Rund 68 000 Stichwörter. Plastik DM 180,–
ISBN 3-7625-2032-1 (Best.-Nr.)
Band 2: Englisch-Deutsch. 8. Auflage 1982. 1219 Seiten. Rund 71 000 Stichwörter. Plastik DM 180,–
ISBN 3-7625-2034-8 (Best.-Nr.)

BAUVERLAG GMBH · POSTFACH 1460 · D-6200 WIESBADEN

Wörterbuch für Bautechnik und Baumaschinen

Von H. Bucksch. Format 12,5 x 17 cm.

Französische Ausgabe:
Dictionnaire pour les Travaux publics et l'Equipement des Chantiers de Construction

Band 1: Deutsch-Französisch. 5. Auflage 1982. 875 Seiten. Rund 54 000 Stichwörter. Plastik DM 160,–
ISBN 3-7625-2049-6 (Best.-Nr.)
Band 2: Französisch-Deutsch. 4. Auflage 1978. 911 Seiten. Rund 56.000 Stichwörter. Plastik DM 160,–
ISBN 3-7625-0999-9 (Best.-Nr.)

Zement-Wörterbuch / Dictionary of Cement
Herstellung und Technologie
Manufacture and Technology

Von Dipl.-Ing. C. van Amerongen. Deutsch-Englisch/Englisch-Deutsch. 2., neubearbeitete und erweiterte Auflage 1986. 328 Seiten. Format 13,5 x 20,5 cm. Gebunden DM 130,–
ISBN 3-7625-1341-4 (Best.-Nr.)

Getriebe-Wörterbuch
Dictionary of Mechanisms

Von H. Bucksch. Deutsch-Englisch/Englisch-Deutsch in einem Band. 1976. 286 Seiten mit zahlreichen Zeichnungen. Zusammen rund 16.000 Stichwörter. Format 13,5 x 20,5 cm. Plastik DM 165,–
ISBN 3-7625-0707-4 (Best.-Nr.)

Holz-Wörterbuch
Dictionary of Wood and Woodworking Practice

Von H. Bucksch. Format 13,5 x 17 cm. Gebunden.

Band 1: Deutsch-Englisch. 1. Nachdruck 1986 zur 2. Auflage. 461 Seiten. Rund 20.000 Stichwörter. DM 98,–
ISBN 3-7625-2411-4 (Best.-Nr.)
Band 2: Englisch-Deutsch. 1. Nachdruck 1986 zur 1. Auflage. 536 Seiten. Rund 20.000 Stichwörter. DM 125,–
ISBN 3-7625-2412-2 (Best.-Nr.)

BAUVERLAG GMBH · POSTFACH 1460 · D-6200 WIESBADEN